Bookman's Price Index

CUMULATIVE INDEX TO VOLUMES 62-67

ISSN 0068-0141

Bookman's Price Index

CUMULATIVE INDEX TO VOLUMES 62-67

A Consolidated Index to 90,000 Citations Describing Antiquarian Books Offered For Sale by Leading Dealers

Anne F. McGrath
Managing Editor

Richard Grazide
Editor

GALE GROUP
THOMSON LEARNING

Detroit • New York • San Diego • San Francisco
Boston • New Haven, Conn. • Waterville, Maine
London • Munich

Anne F. McGrath, *Managing Editor*
Richard Grazide, *Editor*

Gale Group, Inc. Staff

Charles B. Montney, *Coordinating Editor*
Teresa Elsey, Dana Ferguson, Nancy Franklin, Prindle LaBarge,
and Heather Price, *Contributing Editors*
Debra M. Kirby, *Managing Editor*

Ronald D. Montgomery, *Manager, Data Capture*
Constance J. Wells, *Data Capture Specialist*
Katrina Coach, Civie Green, Mary Pamula, Elizabeth Pilette,
and Nancy Sheridan, *Data Capture Assistants*

Venus Little, *Manager, Technical Support Services*
Wayne D. Fong, *Programmer/Analyst*

Mary Beth Trimper, *Manager, Composition and Electronic Prepress*
Eveline Abou-el-Seoud, *Assistant Manager, Composition Purchasing and Electronic Prepress*
Dorothy Maki, *Manufacturing Manager*
Lori Kessler, *Manufacturing Supervisor*
Stacy L. Melson, *Buyer*
Michael Logusz, *Graphic Artist*

While every effort has been made to ensure the reliability of the information presented in this publication, Gale Group, Inc. does not guarantee the accuracy of the data contained herein. Gale accepts no payment for listing; and inclusion in the publication of any organization, service, or individual does not imply endorsement of the editors or publisher.

Errors brought to the attention of the publisher and verified to the satisfaction of the publisher will be corrected in future editions.

This publication is a creative work fully protected by all applicable copyright laws, as well as by misappropriation, trade secret, unfair competition, and other applicable laws. The authors and editors of this work have added value to the underlying factual material herein through one or more of the following: unique and original selection, coordination, expression, arrangement, and classification of the information.

All rights to this publication will be vigorously defended.

Copyright © 2002
Gale Group, Inc.
27500 Drake Road
Farmington Hills, MI 48331-3535

All rights reserved including the right of reproduction in whole or in part in any form.

ISBN 0-7876-5308-X
ISSN 0068-0141

Printed in the United States of America
Gale Group and design is a trademark used under license.

10 9 8 7 6 5 4 3 2 1

Contents

Introduction vii

Cumulative Index to *Bookman's Price Index*, Volumes 62-67 1

This work provides speedy access to the 90,000 book titles contained in Volumes 62 through 67 of the *Bookman's Price Index*, which were published between 1999 and 2001. Additional information about these titles is available in the individual volumes.

Introduction

The *Bookman's Price Index* (*BPI*), published since 1964, indicates the availability and price of antiquarian books in the United States, Canada, and the British Isles. Since the *BPI* now numbers close to 70 volumes, searching for specific titles has become a time-consuming task for the user.

This volume is the ninth "cumulative index to the index." It references the entries in Volumes 62 through 67, which were published between 1999 and 2001. This work provides access to approximately 90,000 entries from the original *BPI* volumes.

What Is Included?

Since the primary purpose of this volume is speedy access to tens of thousands of book titles, the complete entry in the original *BPI* volume is not repeated here. Such repetition would necessarily negate the ability to include all this information in one volume, thus defeating its purpose of quick and easy access. This index provides sufficient information for rapid identification of a specific title including the author, date of publication, and place of publication, followed by a list of all the *BPI* volumes in which that book is included.

BPI's regular volumes provide extensive information so that the user can identify a rare book and get some indication of how the particular dealer arrived at its price. This information, taken from rare book dealer catalogs, includes not only the author, title, date and place of publication, publisher, edition, and price, but a thorough description of the book and notes on its condition. The description and condition information includes physical size, illustrations, binding, authors' signatures, general physical condition, specific flaws, and relative scarcity whenever this information has been given by the dealer listing the book.

Arrangement

Entries appear in a single alphabetic sequence, based on the name of the author: in cases of personal authorship, the author's last name; in cases of books produced by corporate bodies such as governments of countries or states, the name of that entity; in cases of anonymous books, the title; and in cases of anonymous classics such as *Arabian Nights*, the customary or well-known title. The editors have tried their best to duplicate the sorting rules of the original volumes, but as these rules have changed over the years that *BPI* has been published, this has been a difficult task. Users are advised to check the listings for possible variants to ensure they find all appropriate entries.

Extensive efforts were made to standardize the names of authors so that all titles belonging to the same author appeared together. However, in compiling the original volumes of *BPI* covered herein, some inconsistencies appeared in the way authors' names were presented between volumes. The editors have brought as much consistency as possible to this index, but in certain cases, changing an author's name for the sake of consistency might have made it impossible for the user to find the entry in the original *BPI* volume. Therefore, some latitude is necessary when searching for a specific author.

Under the author's name, works are arranged in alphabetical sequence according to the first word of the title, excepting initial articles. References to the same title are grouped together unless such grouping would have made it difficult for the user to locate the entry in the original *BPI* volume. Different editions of a single work are arranged according to the date of publication, with the earliest dates first. If the date of publication is the same but the place of publication is different, these entries are then organized alphabetically by the place of publication. Bearing all of this in mind, it would be advisable for users to scan the entire list of an author's works so as not to miss locating information for a specific title.

Sample Entry

The following sample illustrates the components of a typical entry:

> [1] **DE QUINCY, THOMAS**
> [2] *Confessions of an English Opium Eater.* [3] Oxford:
> [4] 1930.   [5] V. 62; 63; 66

1 Author's Name
2 Title
3 Place of publication
4 Date of publication
5 Volumes of the *BPI* in which the complete descriptive entry for copies of this edition can be found.

Acknowledgments

My thanks to Charles Montney, coordinating editor at Gale Group, Inc., and to his associates Nancy Franklin, Prindle LaBarge, and Heather Price and managing editor Debra Kirby for their guiding hands throughout this project, and to Richard Grazide for his assistance in research and editing and his many hours of reviewing and correcting some 90,000 entries in order to bring consistency to the index.

Suggestions and Comments Welcome

Suggestions are always welcome. This index volume is, in part, a result of the suggestions of *BPI* users. The editors invite all comments, especially those that might improve the usefulness of *Bookman's Price Index*. Please contact:

> Editors
> *Bookman's Price Index*
> Gale Group, Inc.
> 27500 Drake Rd.
> Farmington Hills, MI 48331-3535
> Phone: 248-699-GALE
> Toll-Free: 800-347-GALE
> Fax: 248-699-8067

Anne F. McGrath
Managing Editor

A

A B C. London: 1910. V. 65

ABC Book First Steps. New York: 1885. V. 64

THE ABC Both in Latyn and Englyshe.... London: 1889. V. 64

A B C en Six Tableaux. Paris: 1890. V. 63

A B C Fun. Los Angeles: 1920. V. 65

THE A B C Nursery Rhymes. New York: 1903. V. 66

A B C Picture Book With Mother Goose A B C and Animal and Bird Alphabet. 1910. V. 65

A, B, C with Pictures and Verses (Number 2). Greenfield: 1845. V. 64

A., H. E.
The Tribes of My Frontier. Calcutta: 1884. V. 64; 67

AARON, HANK
I Had a Hammer. New York: 1991. V. 63

AARON, SHALE
Virtual Death. Norwalk: 1995. V. 65

ABADDON'S Steam Engine, Calumny, Delineated: Being an Attempt to Stop Its Deleterious Results on Society, the Church, and State.... Philadelphia: 1817. V. 63

ABBADIE, JACQUES
The Deity of Jesus Christ Essential to the Christian Religion: a Treatise on the Divinity of Our Lord Jesus Christ.... Burlington: 1802. V. 66
The Great and Stupendious Mystery of Man's Salvation by Jesus Christ, Asserted and Defended.... London: 1705. V. 64

ABBASI, S. A.
Wetlands of India, Ecology and Threats. New Delhi: 1997. V. 62; 63; 67

ABBATE, E.
Geology and Mineral Resources of Somalia and Surrounding Regions. Firenze: 1993. V. 67

ABBEY, EDWARD
Appalachian Wilderness. New York: 1970. V. 63; 65; 67
Black Sun. New York: 1971. V. 63; 64; 66; 67
The Brave Cowboy. New York: 1956. V. 67
The Brave Cowboy. Salt Lake City: 1993. V. 62; 64; 66
Cactus Country. New York: 1973. V. 67
Confessions of a Barbarian. Santa Barbara: 1986. V. 67
Desert Images an America Landscape. New York: 1979. V. 63
Desert Solitaire. New York: 1968. V. 63
Desert Solitaire. Salt Lake City: 1981. V. 66
Down the River. New York: 1982. V. 67
Fire on the Mountain. New York: 1962. V. 65
The Fool's Progress. New York: 1988. V. 64; 65; 67
Good News. New York: 1980. V. 62, 64, 67
Hayduke Lives. Boston: 1990. V. 65
The Hidden Canyon. New York: 1977. V. 65; 67
In Praise of Mountain Lions. Albuquerque: 1984. V. 62; 64
The Journey Home. New York: 1977. V. 67
The Monkey Wrench Gang. Philadelphia & New York: 1975. V. 63; 65; 66
The Monkey Wrench Gang. Salt Lake City: 1985. V. 65; 66; 67
One Life at a Time, Please. New York: 1988. V. 62; 64; 67
Slickrock, the Canyon Country of. New York: 1971. V. 65
Slumgullion Stew. New York: 1984. V. 62
Sunset Canyon. London: 1972. V. 62; 63; 64; 65; 67
Vox Clamantis in Desierto. Santa Fe: 1989. V. 62; 65; 67

ABBEY, JOHN ROLAND
Catalogue of Valuable Printed Books and Fine Bindings from the Celebrated Collection of Major J. R. Abbey (Parts I to VI). London: 1967-1970. V. 66
The Italian Manuscripts in the Library of Major J. R. Abbey. London: 1969. V. 62; 63; 64; 66
Scenery of Great Britain and Ireland in Aquatint and Lithography 1770-1860. London: 1952. V. 64; 65
Scenery of the British Isles 1775-1860: an Exhibition of Aquatint and Other Colour Plate Books from the Library of J. R. Abbey. London: 1951. V. 62; 64
Travel in Aquatint and Lithography 1770-1860 from the Library of J. R. Abbey. London: 1956. V. 62, 03
Travel in Aquatint and Lithography 1770-1860 from the Library of J. R. Abbey. 1994. V. 64

ABBIATICO, M.
Modern Firearm Engravings. 1980. V. 62; 63

ABBOT, ABIEL
Letters Written in the Interior of Cuba, Between the Mountains of Arcana, to the East and of Cursco to the West. Boston: 1829. V. 63; 66

ABBOT, C.
Flora Bedfordiensis.... 1798. V. 62

ABBOT, GEORGE
The Reasons Which Doctor Hill Hath Brought, for Upholding of Papistry, Which is Falslie Termed the Catholike Religion. Oxford: 1604. V. 66

ABBOT, HENRY L.
Notes on Electricity in Military and Industrial Engineering. 1888. V. 67

ABBOTT, ARTHUR V.
The Electrical Transmission of Energy: a Manual for the Design of Electrical Circuits. New York and London: 1895. V. 63

ABBOTT, BELLE K.
Leah Mordecai. New York: 1875. V. 62

ABBOTT, BENJAMIN
Cone Cut Corners: the Experiences of a Conservative Family in Fanatical Times.... New York: 1855. V. 62

ABBOTT, CARLISLE S.
Recollections of a California Pioneer. New York: 1917. V. 63

ABBOTT, CHARLES
A Treatise of the Law Relative to Merchant Ships and Seamen. London: 1804. V. 63

ABBOTT, E. C.
We Pointed Them North, Recollections of a Cowpuncher. New York: 1939. V. 63; 67

ABBOTT, EDWIN A.
Flatland: a Romance of Many Dimensions. London: 1884. V. 64

ABBOTT, G. F.
Turkey in Transition. London: 1909. V. 64

ABBOTT, HENRY
Report Upon Experiments and Investigations to Develop a System of Submarine Mines for Defending Harbors of the United States. Washington: 1881. V. 62; 64

ABBOTT, HENRY G.
Historical Sketch of the Confectioner Trade of Chicago. Chicago: 1905. V. 65

ABBOTT, MORRIS W.
The Pike's Peak Cog Road. San Marino: 1972. V. 67

ABBOTT, N. J.
Cephalopod Neurobiology, Neuroscience Studies in Squid, Octopus and Cuttlefish. Oxford: 1995. V. 65

ABBOTT, R. T.
American Seashells. Princeton: 1954. V. 67
Indo-Pacific Mollusca, Monographs of the Marine Mollusks of the Tropical Western Pacific and Indian Oceans. Philadelphia and Greenville: 1959-1976. V. 62; 65

ABBOTT, STEPHEN
The First Regiment New Hampshire Volunteers in the Great Rebellion. Keene: 1890. V. 66

ABBOTT, WILBUR C.
Colonel Thomas Blood - Crown-Stealer, 1618-1680. New Haven: 1911. V. 65

ABDULLA BIN ABDULKADAR
Translations from the Hakayit.... London: 1874. V. 64; 65

A'BECKETT, GILBERT ABBOTT
The Comic Blackstone. Part I - Of the Rights of Persons. London: 1844. V. 65
The Comic History of England. London: 1846. V. 62
The Comic History of England. London: 1860. V. 64; 67
The Comic History of England. (with) the Comic History of Rome. London: 1847-1848. V. 62; 63
The Comic History of England. (with) The Comic History of Rome. London: 1864. V. 62; 64
The Comic History of Rome. London: 1860. V. 64
Posthumous Papers of the Wonderful Discovery Club, Formerly of Camden Town.... London: 1838. V. 62

ABEL, ANNIE H.
The History of Events Resulting in Indian Consolidation West of the Mississippi. Washington: 1908. V. 67

ABEL, CLARKE
Narrative of a Journey in the Interior of China; and of a Voyage to and From that Country in the Years 1816 and 1817.... London: 1818. V. 64

ABEL, JOHN JACOB
The Methods of Pharmacology with Experimental Illustrations. Chicago: 1945. V. 62

ABEL, MARY HINMAN
Practical Sanitary and Economic Cooking.... Rochester: 1890. V. 64

ABELARD, PETER
The Letters of Abelard and Heloise. London: 1925. V. 63

ABENDANA, ISAAC
Discourses of the Ecclesiastical and Civil Polity of the Jews. London: 1706. V. 64

ABERCONWAY, CHRISTABEL
A Dictionary of Cat Lovers - XV Century B.C. - XX Century A.D.... London: 1949. V. 63
The Story of Mr. Korah. (with) Mr. Korah and the Monster. London: 1954. V. 62; 63

ABERCROMBIE, JOHN
Abercrombie's Practical Gardener.... 1823. V. 63
The Garden Mushroom, Its Most Effectual General Culture Thoroughly Displayed. London: 1802. V. 65
Inquiries Concerning the Intellectual Powers and the Investigation of Truth. Edinburgh: 1830. V. 65
Pathologische und Praktische Untersuchungen Uber die Krankheiten des Gehirns und Ruckenmarcks.... Bremen: 1829. V. 65
The Philosophy of Moral Feelings. London: 1833. V. 65

ABERCROMBIE, JOHN continued
The Philosophy of Moral Feelings. London: 1834. V. 62

ABERCROMBIE, W. R.
Alaska: 1899 Copper River Exploring Expedition. Washington: 1900. V. 64

ABERCROMBY, JOHN
A Trip through the Eastern Caucasus, with a Chapter on the Languages of the Country. London: 1889. V. 64

ABERIGH-MAC KAY, GEORGE
Twenty-One Days in India, Being the Tour of Sir Ali Baba K.C.B. London: 1896. V. 65

ABERNATHY, JOHN R.
Catch 'Em Alive Jack - The Life and Adventures of an American Pioneer. New York: 1936. V. 64; 67
In Camp with Theodore Roosevelt. Oklahoma City: 1933. V. 63

ABERNETHY, JOHN
Surgical Observations on the Constitutional Origin and Treatment of Local Diseases; and On Aneurisms. London: 1814. V. 65; 66
Surgical Observations on the Constitutional Origin and Treatment of Local Diseases and On Aneurisms. London: 1817. V. 62

ABERT, JAMES WILLIAM
Through the Country of the Comanche Indians in the Fall of the Year 1845. San Francisco: 1970. V. 63; 64; 67
Western America in 1846-1847. San Francisco: 1966. V. 63; 65; 66

ABINGDON, WILLOUGHBY BERTIE, 4TH EARL OF
Dedication to the Collective Body of the People of England, in Which the Source of Our Present Political Distractions are Pointed Out and a Plan Proposed for Their Remedy and Redress. Oxford: 1780. V. 67

ABISH, WALTER
Duel Site. New York: 1970. V. 67

ABLANCOURT, JEAN JACOBE FREMONT D'
Memoirs of the Sieur d'Ablancourt. 1703. V. 65

ABLEMAN, PAUL
I Hear Voices. Paris: 1958. V. 63

ABOUT, EDMOND
Peintures Decoratives Du Grand Foyer de l'Opera. Paris: 1876?. V. 65

ABRAHAM, A.
Introduction to Orchids.... Trivandrum: 1981. V. 67

ABRAHAM, ASHLEY P.
Rock-Climbing in Skye. London: 1908. V. 64; 66

ABRAHAM, GEORGE D.
British Mountain Climbs. London: 1932. V. 63
British Mountain Climbs. London: 1948. V. 64
The Complete Mountaineer. London: 1907. V. 63
Motor Ways at Home and Abroad. London: 1928. V. 64
Mountain Adventures at Home and Abroad. 1910. V. 63; 65
Mountain Adventures at Home and Abroad. London: 1910. V. 63; 64
On Alpine Heights and British Crags. 1919. V. 63; 65
Rock-Climbing in North Wales. 1906. V. 63; 65
Rock Climbing in Skye. 1908. V. 65
Swiss Mountain Climbs. 1911. V. 63; 65
Swiss Mountain Climbs. London: 1911. V. 63; 64

ABRAHAM, JAMES JOHNSTON
Lettsom: His Life, Times, Friends and Descendants. London: 1933. V. 62; 64; 66

ABRAHAMSON, W. G.
Evolutionary Ecology Across Three Trophic Levels, Goldenrods, Gallmakers and Natural Enemies. Princeton: 1997. V. 66

ABRAM, WILLIAM ALEXANDER
Blackburn Characters of a Past Generation. Blackburn: 1894. V. 63
A History of Blackburn, Town and Parish. Blackburn: 1877. V. 62; 65; 66
Members of the Hornby Family Who Have Represented Blackburn in Parliament. London: 1892. V. 62; 65

ABRAMS, L.
Illustrated Flora of the Pacific States: Washington, Oregon and California. Stanford: 1955-1960. V. 65

ABRAMSON, C. I.
Russian Contributions to Invertebrate Behavior. Westport: 1996. V. 67

ABROAD..
London: 1882. V. 62

AN ABSTRACT
of Evidence Delivered Before a Select Committee of the House of Commons in Years 1790 and 1791; on the Part of the Petitioners for the Abolition of the Slave-Trade. London: 1791. V. 64; 66

AN ABSTRACT
of the Several Acts of Parliament, as Relate to the Office and Duties of Surveyors of the Highways and Turnpike Roads in England. Newark: 1829. V. 66

ABU, TALIB IBN MUHAMMAD KHAN
Travels of Mirza Abu Taleb Khan in Asia, Africa and Europe During the Years 1799, 1800, 1801, 1802 and 1803. London: 1810. V. 64

ABU OBEYD
The Celebrated Romance of the Stealing of the Mare. Newtown: 1930. V. 64

ABY, JOE C.
The Tales of Rube Hoffenstein. New York: 1882. V. 66

ACADEMY OF ARTS, NEWCASTLE
150th Anniversary Exhibition of Works and Relics. Academy of Arts, Newcastle-upon-Tyne, September 12th to October 8th, 1903. Newcastle-upon-Tyne: 1903. V. 63

ACADEMY OF NATURAL SCIENCES OF PHILADELPHIA
Proceedings.... Philadelphia: 1875-1958. V. 66
Proceedings.... Philadelphia: 1935. V. 66
Proceedings.... Philadelphia: 1939. V. 66
Proceedings.... Philadelphia: 1941. V. 66
Proceedings.... Philadelphia: 1944. V. 66
Year Books for 1920 through 1931. Philadelphia: 1921-1932. V. 67

ACADEMY OF SCIENCES OF THE U.S.S.R.
Works of the Institute of Higher Nervous Activity. Physiological Series. Volumes 1 and 2. Moscow: 1955-1956. V. 63

ACCADEMIA DEL CIMENTO
Saggi di Naturali Esperienze Fatte nell' Academia del Cimento Sotto la Protezione del Serenissimo Principe Leopoldo di Toscana e Discritte dal Segretario di Essa Accademia. Florence: 1667. V. 63

ACCEPTED
Addresses; or, Praemium Poetarum. To Which are Added Macbeth Travestie, in Three Acts and Miscellanies, by Different Hands. London: 1813. V. 66

ACCOMAZZO, BETTY
Arizona National Ranch Histories. Phoenix: 1980-1990. V. 66

THE ACCOMPLISHED
Officer: a Treatise Containing the Most Essential and Necessary Accomplishments of an Officer Pursuant to the Maxims and Method Establish'd and Observed by the Greatest Generals and Ingeneers in Europe. London: 1708. V. 65

AN ACCOUNT
of Fort Montague, at Knaresborough, in a Letter from a Gentleman at Harrogate, to His Friend in London. Knaresborough: 1815. V. 65

AN ACCOUNT
of the Coal Bank Disaster at Blue Rock, Ohio, In Which Four Men Were Buried Beneath the Hill for Two Weeks.... Malta: 1856. V. 66

AN ACCOUNT
of the Free-School Society of New York. New York: 1814. V. 64

AN ACCOUNT
of the Great Flood in the River Tyne, on Saturday Morning Dec. 30, 1815.... Newcastle: 1816. V. 67

AN ACCOUNT
of the Indisposition of the Late Rev. Mr. John Wesley, and What Passed Between Him and His Friends, Before His Death. Bridlington: 1791. V. 64

AN ACCOUNT
Of the Institution of the Society for the Establishment of a Literary Fund.... London: 1800. V. 62

AN ACCOUNT
of the Proceedings of the Merchants, Manufacturers and Others, Concerned in the Wool and Woolen Trade of Great Britain, in Their Application to Parliament.... London: 1800. V. 63

AN ACCOUNT
of the Restoration and Antiquities of the Church of Saint Mary, Castlegate, York. York: 1873. V. 67

AN ACCOUNT
of the Revenue and National Debt of Ireland. London: 1754. V. 62

AN ACCOUNT
of the Second Commemoration of Shakespeare, Celebrated at Stratford-upon-Avon on Friday the 23rd of April 1830.... Leamington: 1830. V. 62; 65

AN ACCOUNT
of the Society for the Conversion and Religious Instruction and Education of the Negroe (sic) Slaves in the British West India Islands.... London: 1823. V. 63

ACCOUNT
of the Terrific and Fatal Riot at the New York Astor Place Opera House on the Night of May 10th, 1849, with the Quarrels of Forrest and Macready.... New York: 1849. V. 64

ACCUM, FREDERICK
Chemical Amusement.... London: 1818. V. 62
Chemical Amusements, Comprising a Series of Curious and Instructive Experiments in Chemistry.... London: 1819. V. 67
Description of the Process of Manufacturing Coal Gas for the Lighting of Streets, Houses and Public Buildings.... London: 1819. V. 66
A Practical Essay on the Analysis of Minerals, Exemplifying the Best Methods of Analysing Ores, Earths, Stones, Inflammable Fossils.... London: 1804. V. 65
System of Theoretical and Practical Chemistry. Philadelphia: 1808. V. 63
Traite Pratique sur l'Usage et le Mode D'Application des Reactifs Chimiques Fonde sur des Experiences.... Paris: 1819. V. 64

ACERBI, JOSEPH
Travels Through Sweden, Finland and Lapland to the North Cape in the Years 1798 and 1799. London: 1802. V. 65

ACHERLEY, ROBERT
Free Parliaments; or, an Argument on Their Constitution: Proving Some of Their Powers to Be Independent. London: 1731. V. 67

ACHESON, DEAN
Strengthening the Forces of Freedom: Selected Speeches and Statements of the Secretary of State Acheson Feb. 1949-April 1950. (and) Supplement May-June 1950. Washington: 1950. V. 63

ACHILLES TATIUS
Erotikon.... Leiden: 1640. V. 65

ACKER, KATHY
The Adult Life of Toulouse Lautrec. (How Love Can Lead Youngsters to Murder). N.P: 1975. V. 62

The Adult Life of Toulouse Lautrec. (The Life of Johnny Rocco). N.P: 1976. V. 62

ACKERLEY, CHARLES
A Plan for the Better Security of Vessels Navigating the River Thames with Appendices on Nautical Subjects Resulting There From. London: 1834. V. 66

ACKERLEY, J. R.
The Prisoners of War - a Play in Three Acts. London: 1925. V. 62
We Think the World of You. London: 1960. V. 65

ACKERMAN, JACOB FIDELIS
Der Scheintod und das Rettungsverfahren. Frankfurt am Main: 1804. V. 66

ACKERMANN, RUDOLPH
The History of the Abbey Church of St. Peter's Westminster, Its Antiquities and Monuments. London: 1812. V. 66

The History of the Colleges of Winchester, Eton, and Westminister; with the Charter-House, the Schools of St. Paul's, Merchant Taylors, Harrow & Rugby, and the Free School of Christ's Hospital. London: 1816. V. 62; 63; 65; 66; 67

A History of the University of Cambridge, Its Colleges, Halls and Public Buildings. London: 1815. V. 66

A History of the University of Oxford, Its College, Halls and Public Buildings. London: 1814. V. 65; 66

Microcosm of London. London: 1808-1810. V. 63; 64; 65; 67
Microcosm of London. London: 1809. V. 62

The Repository of Arts, Literature, Commerce, Manufactures, Fashions and Politics. London: 1809-1828. V. 66

Swiss Views. London: 1819. V. 64

ACKEY, MARY E.
Crossing the Plains and Early Days in California - Memories of Girlhood Days in California's Golden Age. San Francisco: 1928. V. 64; 67

ACKROYD, PETER
Chatterton. London: 1987. V. 62; 64; 67
Country Life. London: 1978. V. 63
Dressing Up. Transvestism and Drag: the History of an Obsession. London: 1979. V. 62
English Music. Franklin Center: 1992. V. 66
English Music. London: 1992. V. 65
English Music. New York: 1992. V. 67
The Great Fire of London. London: 1982. V. 62
Hawksmoor. London: 1985. V. 62
The Last Testament of Oscar Wilde. London: 1983. V. 62; 65; 66

ACLAND, HENRY W.
The Harveian Oration 1865. London: 1865. V. 65

ACLAND, HUGH DYKE
A Brief Sketch of the History and Present Situation of the Valdenses in Piedmont, Commonly Called Vaudois. London: 1825. V. 65

ACOSTA, GIOSEFFO DI
Historia Naturale, e Morale delle Indie...Novamente Tradotta sell Lingua Spagnuola nell Italiano da Gio Paolo Galucci Salodiano. Venice: 1596. V. 62; 65

ACRELIUS, ISRAEL
A History of New Sweden; or, the Settlements on the River Delaware. Philadelphia: 1876. V. 63; 66

ACTON, ELIZA
Modern Confectionary.... Derby: 1833. V. 64; 66
Modern Cookery for Private Families. London: 1860. V. 63
Modern Cookery, for Private Families. London: 1865. V. 62; 66
Modern Cookery in All Its Branches. Philadelphia: 1863. V. 65

ACTON, HAROLD
Famous Chinese Plays. Peking: 1937. V. 65
Four Cautionary Tales. London: 1947. V. 64
Gamberaia. Florence: 1971. V. 67
The Last Medici. London: 1932. V. 63
The Last Medici. London: 1958. V. 64
The Pazzi Conspiracy: the Plot Against the Medici. London: 1979. V. 67
Tit for Tat and Other Tales. London: 1972. V. 66

ACTON, WILLIAM
Prostitution, Considered in Its Moral, Social and Sanitary Aspects, in London and Other Large Cities. London: 1857. V. 63; 64

ADAIR, F. E.
A Summer in High Asai; Being a Record of Sport and Travel in Balatistan and Ladakh.... London: 1899. V. 64

ADAIR, JAMES
The History of the American Indians. London: 1775. V. 63; 66

ADAIR, JOHN
Hints on the Culture of Ornamental Plants in Ireland. 1878. V. 62

ADAIR FITZGERALD, S. J.
The Wonders of the Secret Cavern and Lands of Flowers and Fancy. London: 1890. V. 65

ADAM, ALEXANDER
Roman Antiquities; or An Account of the Manners and Customs of the Romans.... London: 1836. V. 67

THE ADAM Forepaugh & Sells Brothers Book of Wonders. Buffalo: 1902. V. 65

ADAM Forepaugh's 1882 Annual. Buffalo: 1882. V. 64

ADAM, G. MERCER
The Canadian North-West: Its History and Its Troubles from the Early Days of the Fur Trade to the Era of the Railway.... Toronto: 1885. V. 63; 64; 66

ADAM, MELCHIOR
Dignorum Laude Virorum, Quos Musa Vetatmori, Immortalitas, Seu Vitae Theorlogorum.... Francofurti ad Mdenum: 1705. V. 66

Vitae Germanorum Medicorum: Qui Saeculo Superiori et Qui Excurrit Claruenrunt. Heidelberg: 1620. V. 64; 67

ADAM, ROBERT
Ruins of the Palace of the Emperor Diocletian at Spalatro in Dalmatia. London: 1764. V. 64

ADAM, VICTOR
Nouvel Abecedaire Enigmes. Paris: 1845. V. 66

ADAM, WILLIAM
The Gem of the Peak; or Matlock Bath and Its Vicinity. London: 1843. V. 65
The Gem of the Peak; or Matlock Bath and Its Vicinity. London: 1973. V. 65

ADAMI, J. G.
The Great Omentum. Philadelphia: 1898. V. 67

ADAMIC, LOUIS
My Native Land. New York: 1943. V. 63

ADAMS, A. LEITH
Field and Forest Rambles. 1873. V. 62; 63; 64; 66; 67
Field and Forest Rambles. London: 1873. V. 64; 65

ADAMS, ANDY
The Log of a Cowboy. Boston: 1903. V. 62; 64
The Outlet. Boston and New York: 1905. V. 64; 67
A Texas Matchmaker. Boston and New York: 1904. V. 62

ADAMS, ANSEL
Ansel Adams: Yosemite and the Range of Light. Boston: 1979. V. 63; 65; 67
The Camera. Boston: 1980. V. 63
The Four Seasons in Yosemite National Park. Los Angeles: 1936. V. 64
An Introduction to Hawaii. San Francisco: 1964. V. 63
Making a Photograph: an Introduction to Photography. London and New York: 1935. V. 65
Photographs of the Southwest. Boston: 1976. V. 63; 65
Photographs of the Southwest. New York: 1976. V. 65; 66
Polaroid Land Photography. Boston: 1978. V. 63
Taos Pueblo. Boston: 1977. V. 63

ADAMS, ARCHIBALD
The Western Rajputana States. London: 1899. V. 66

ADAMS, ARTHUR
A Genealogy of the Lake Family of Great Egg Harbor, in Old Gloucester County, in New Jersey, Descended from John Lake of Gravesend, Long Island. N.P: 1915. V. 63; 66
A Manual of Natural History for the Use of Travellers.... 1854. V. 62

ADAMS, BEN Q.
R. C. Gorman: The Graphic Works. Albuquerque: 1987. V. 65

ADAMS, BERNARD
London Illustrated 1604-1851. London: 1983. V. 62

ADAMS, C. C.
The Variations and Ecological Distribution of the Snails of the Genus Io. Washington: 1915. V. 63; 65

ADAMS, C. D.
Flowering Plants of Jamaica. 1972. V. 65

ADAMS, C. WARREN
A Spring in the Canterbury Settlement. London: 1853. V. 64

ADAMS, CHARLES FRANCIS
A Chapter of Erie. Boston: 1869. V. 64; 65

ADAMS, CLARENCE
Three Ranches West. New York: 1972. V. 63

ADAMS, DANIEL
The Medical and Agricultural Register, for the Years 1806 and 1807. Boston: 1806-1807. V. 64

ADAMS, DOUGLAS
The Hitch Hiker's Guide to the Galaxy. London: 1979. V. 62; 64; 65
Last Chance to See. New York: 1991. V. 67
The Restaurant at the End of the Universe. London: 1980. V. 62

ADAMS, E. LEE
The Stripper. N.P: 1954. V. 67

ADAMS, EDWARD C. L.
Congaree Sketches. Scenes from Negro Life in the Swamps of the Congaree and Tales by Tad and Scip of Heaven and Hell with Other Miscellany. Chapel Hill: 1927. V. 64; 66
Potee's Gal. Columbia: 1929. V. 64

ADAMS, EMMA H.
To and Fro in Southern California. Cincinnati: 1887. V. 63

ADAMS, ENA
Deer, Hare and Otter Hunting. London: 1936. V. 67

ADAMS, F. D.
The Birth and Development of the Geological Sciences. London: 1954. V. 67

ADAMS, FRANCIS OTTIWELL
The History of Japan. London: 1875. V. 64

ADAMS, FRANK
The Frog Who Would A-Wooing Go. London: 1918. V. 64
The History of Sam the Sportsman. London. V. 65

ADAMS, FREDERICK B.
Radical Literature in America. Stamford: 1939. V. 62; 63; 64; 66; 67
To Russia with Frost. Boston: 1963. V. 64

ADAMS, GEORGE
An Essay on Electricity; in Which the Theory and Practice of That Useful Science.... London: 1784. V. 63
Essays on the Microscope.... London: 1798. V. 66
Geometrical and Graphical Essays. London: 1791. V. 66
Geometrical and Graphical Essays. London: 1797. V. 62
Lectures on Natural and Experimental Philosophy. London: 1794. V. 62; 65; 67
Lectures on Natural and Experimental Philosophy. Philadelphia: 1807. V. 65
A Treatise Describing the Construction, and Explaining the Use of New Celestial and Terrestial Globes. London: 1782. V. 65

ADAMS, GEORGE W.
Doctors in Blue: the Medical History of the Union Army in the Civil War. New York: 1952. V. 67

ADAMS, H.
The Genera of Recent Mollusca.... 1853-1858. V. 66

ADAMS, H. G.
Cyclopaedia of Female Biography.... Glasgow: 1866. V. 63; 66
Humming Birds Described and Illustrated.... London: 1856. V. 63; 67
Nests and Eggs of Familiar British Birds. London: 1854-1857. V. 67
The Smaller Birds. 1874. V. 62
The Smaller British Birds With Descriptions of Their Nests, Eggs, Habits, Etc. London: 1894. V. 64

ADAMS, H. M.
Catalogue of Books Printed on the Continent of Europe, 1501-1600 in Cambridge Libraries. Mansfield Center: 1999. V. 63

ADAMS, HANNAH
A View of Religions, in Two Parts. Boston: 1801. V. 65

ADAMS, HARRY
Beyond the Barrier with Byrd. New York: 1932. V. 62

ADAMS, HENRY
Democracy: an American Novel. New York: 1880. V. 62
Democracy: an American Novel. London: 1882. V. 62; 63; 64; 66
The Education of Henry Adams. Boston and New York: 1918. V. 65
History of the United States...During the Administration(s) of Thomas Jefferson...James Madison. New York: 1930. V. 63
A Letter to American Teachers of History. Washington: 1910. V. 63
Memoirs of Arli Taimai E Marama of Eimeo, Terilirere of Tooarai. Paris: 1901. V. 62
Mont-Saint Michel & Chartres. Boston & New York: 1905. V. 67

ADAMS, ISAAC
Persia by a Persian. Washington: 1900. V. 64

ADAMS, J.
Ten Thousand Miles through Canada. 1913. V. 67

ADAMS, J. HOWE
History of the Life of D. Hayes Agnew, M.D., LL.D. Philadelphia: 1892. V. 63; 65

ADAMS, J. S.
Florida; Its Climate, Soil and Productions, with a Sketch of Its History, Natural Features and Social Condition.... Jacksonville: 1866. V. 63

ADAMS, JAMES H.
Reports of the Committee to Whom Was Referred the Message of Gov. James H. Adams, Relating to Slavery and the Slave Trade. Columbia: 1857. V. 63

ADAMS, JAMES TRUSLOW
Atlas of American History. New York: 1943. V. 65
Dictionary of American History. New York: 1942. V. 66

ADAMS, JANE
The Greenway. London: 1995. V. 62; 64; 65; 66

ADAMS, JOHN
A Defence of the Constitutions of Government of the United States of America. London: 1787. V. 62; 64
Defense des Constitutions Americaines, ou de la Necessite d'une Balance dans les Pouvoirs d'un Gouvernement Libre.... Paris: 1792. V. 62; 65
Sketches Taken During the Voyages to Africa; Between the Years 1786 and 1800.... London: 1800. V. 64

ADAMS, JOHN COUCH
Lectures on the Lunar Theory. Cambridge: 1900. V. 67
The Scientific Papers of John Couch Adams. Cambridge: 1896-1900. V. 66

ADAMS, JOHN QUINCY
The Duplicate Letters, the Fisheries and the Mississippi. Washington: 1822. V. 66
An Oration Delivered Before the Cincinnati Astronomical Society, on the Occasion of the Laying the Corner Stone of an Astronomical Observatory, on the 10th of November 1843. Cincinnati: 1843. V. 66
Poems of Religion and Society. New York: 1848. V. 62
The Social Compact, Exemplified in the Constitution of the Commonwealth of Massachusetts, with Remarks on the Theories of Divine Right of Hobbes and Filmer, and the Counter Theories of Sidney, Locke, Montesquieu and Rousseau. Providence: 1842. V. 66

ADAMS, JOSEPH H.
Harper's Indoor Book for Boys. New York and London: 1908. V. 65

ADAMS, KATHLEEN
A Book of Enchantment. New York: 1928. V. 66
A Book of Princess Stories. New York: 1927. V. 64; 65

ADAMS, MARCUS
The Rhythm of Children's Features. London: 1935. V. 65

ADAMS, MILDRED
The Story of the Gordon Setter. 1967. V. 67

ADAMS, R.
Die Farben-Harmonie in Ihrer Anwendung auf Die Damentoilette. Leipzig: 1862. V. 64

ADAMS, RAMON F.
The Adams 150 - a Checklist of the 150 Most Important Books on Western Outlaws and Lawmen and Six Score: The 120 Best Books on the Range Cattle Industry. Austin: 1976. V. 67
Burrs Under the Saddle - A Second Look at Books and Histories of the Old West. Norman: 1964. V. 62; 64; 65
Charles M. Russell - The Cowboy Artist and Bibliography. Pasadena: 1948. V. 62; 65; 66
Come an' Get It. The Story of the Old Cowboy Cook. Norman: 1952. V. 66
Cowboy Lingo. Boston: 1936. V. 62; 64; 65
The Cowman and His Code of Ethics. Austin: 1969. V. 63
A Fitting Death for Billy the Kid. Norman: 1960. V. 66
The Old Time Cowhand. Norman: 1961. V. 65
The Rampaging Herd: a Bibliography of Books and Pamphlets on Men and Events.... Norman: 1959. V. 66
Six Guns and Saddle Leather. Norman: 1954. V. 62; 64; 65; 66
Six Guns and Saddle Leather. Norman: 1969. V. 62; 64; 65; 66
Western Words - a Dictionary of the Ranch Cow Camp and Trail. Norman: 1944. V. 66

ADAMS, RANDOLPH G.
The Passports Printed by Benjamin at His Passy Press. Ann Arbor: 1925. V. 62

ADAMS, RICHARD
The Girl in a Swing. London: 1980. V. 62; 64
Plague Dogs. London: 1977. V. 63
Watership Down. London: 1972. V. 63; 66
Watership Down. New York: 1974. V. 63
Watership Down. Hammondsworth: 1976. V. 62

ADAMS, ROBERT
New Topographics: Photographs of a Man-Altered Landscape. Rochester: 1975. V. 63

ADAMS-ROGERS CO.
Bilt Well Mill Work. Indianapolis: Sep. 1920. V. 65

ADAMS, SAMUEL HOPKINS
Average Jones. 1911. V. 62; 63
The Flying Death. 1908. V. 63; 64; 66
The Secret of Lonesome Cove. 1912. V. 63

ADAMS, SPENCER L.
The Long House of the Iroquois. Skaneateles: 1944. V. 67

ADAMS, THOMAS
West Middlesex Regional Planning Scheme. Westminster: 1922-1924. V. 62

ADAMS, THOMPSON & FRY
The Thames from Putney to Staines. Ditchling: 1930. V. 62

ADAMS, W. H. DAVENPORT
Celebrated Women Travellers of the Nineteenth Century. London: 1889. V. 63
The Eastern Archipelago. London: 1880. V. 62
Episodes of Anglo-Indian History. London: 1879. V. 65
The Forest, the Jungle and the Prairie. 1885. V. 67
The Forest, the Jungle and the Prairie. London: 1889. V. 67
The Isle of Wight: Its History, Topography and Antiquities. London: 1884. V. 62

ADAMS, WILLIAM E.
The Slave-Holders War: an Argument for the North and the Negro. Bombay: 1863. V. 64

ADAMSON, A. P.
Brief History of the Thirtieth Georgia Regiment. Griffin: 1912. V. 62; 63

ADAMSON, JOY
The Peoples of Kenya. 1975. V. 66; 67

ADAMSON, W. A.
Lake and Loch Fishing for Salmon and Sea Trout. London: 1961. V. 67

ADCOCK, A. ST. JOHN
Songs of the World-War. London: 1916. V. 64

ADDAMS, JANE
The Spirit of Youth and the City Streets. New York: 1926. V. 66

ADDAMS, JANE continued
Twenty Years at Hull-House. New York: 1910. V. 63

ADDIS, ALFRED
Outlines of a Plan for the Formation of a New State of Society; on the Doctrines and Principles of Christ's Kingdom, As Laid Down by Our Divine Master in the Word of God. London: 1831. V. 66

ADDISON, ALEXANDER
Analysis of the Report of the Committee of the Virginia Assembly, on the Proceedings of Sundry of the Other States in Answer to Their Resolutions. Philadelphia: 1800. V. 63

ADDISON, CHARLES G.
Damascus Palmyra; a Journey to the East, with a Sketch of the State and Prospects of Syria, Under Ibrahim Pasha. London: 1838. V. 64

ADDISON, J.
Remarks on Several Parts of Italy, &c. in the Years 1701, 1702, 1703. London: 1718. V. 67

ADDISON, JOSEPH
The Free-Holder, or Political Essays. London: 1716. V. 62
The Free-Holder; or Political Essays. London: 1758. V. 63
Miscellaneous Works in Verse and Prose. (with) *Remarks on Several Parts of Italy.* London: 1753. V. 66
The Miscellaneous Works in Verse and Prose. London: 1765. V. 65
The Works. Birmingham: 1761. V. 65

ADDISON. MR., PSEUD.
Interesting Anecdotes, Memoirs, Allegories, Essays and Poetical Fragments.... London: 1794. V. 66

ADDISON, MR., PSEUD.
Interesting Anecdotes, Memoirs, Allegories, Essays and Poetical Fragments.... London: 1797. V. 63

ADDISON, THOMAS
On the Constitutional and Local Effects of Disease of the Supra-Renal Capsules. Birmingham: 1980. V. 63

THE ADDRESS of Mr. Everett and the Poem of Dr. O. W. Holmes, at the Dinner Given to H. I. H. Monseigneur The Prince Napoleon September 25th, 1861. Cambridge: 1861. V. 64

ADDRESS of the Minority in the Virginia Legislature to the People of that State: Containing a Vindication of the Constitutionality of the Alien and Sedition Laws. Richmond: 1799. V. 66

THE ADDRESS of the People of South Carolina, Assembled in Convention, to the People of the Slaveholding States of the United States. Charleston: 1860. V. 62; 63

ADDRESS of the Reformers of Fawdon, to Their Brothers the Pitmen, Keelmen and Other Labourers on the Tyne and Wear. Newcastle-upon-Tyne: 1819. V. 63

AN ADDRESS to the Citizens of the United States on the Subject of Slavery. N.P: 1838. V. 64

ADDRESS To the Community, on the Necessity of Legalizing the Study of Anatomy. Boston: 1829. V. 64

AN ADDRESS to the Inhabitants of Pennsylvania, by Those Freemen, of the City of Philadelphia, Who are Now Confined in the Mason's Lodge by Virtue of a General Warrant. Philadelphia: 1777. V. 64

AN ADDRESS to the Labourers, on the Subject of Destroying Machinery. London: 1830. V. 62

AN ADDRESS to the Proprietors of India Stock, Shewing, from the Political State of Indostan, the Necessity of Sending Commissioners to Regulate and Direct Their Affairs Abroad.. London: 1769. V. 65

AN ADDRESS to the Public, in Answer to Two Pamphlets (Intitled, an Appeal to the People of England, and a Letter to a Member of Parliament, Relative to the Case of A(dmira)l B(yng)g) in which is Fully Proved, That Several Parts of the A(dmira)l's Letter,. London: 1756. V. 65

AN ADDRESS to the Right Honourable the First Lord Commissioner of the Admiralty, Upon the Visible Decreasing Spirit, Splendor and Discipline of the Navy. London: 1787. V. 63

ADDRESSES on the Death of Hon. Edward D. Baker Delivered in the Senate and House of Representatives on Wednesday December 11, 1861. Washington: 1862. V. 67

ADDY, SIDNEY OLDALL
Household Tales with Other Traditional Remains Collected in the Counties of York, Lincoln, Derby and Nottingham. London: 1895. V. 63; 64

ADE, GEORGE
People You Know. London: 1903. V. 64

ADELER, MAX
Elbow Room. London: 1883. V. 63

ADELINE, JULES
Le Peinture a l'Eau. Paris: 1890. V. 66; 67

ADELMAN, H. B.
Marcello Malpighi and the Evolution of Embryology. Ithaca: 1966. V. 67

ADEMA, MARCEL
Apollinaire. London: 1954. V. 62

ADER, CLEMENT
L'Aviation Militaire. Paris and Nancy: 1911. V. 66

ADEY, ROBERT
Locked Room Murders and Other Impossible Crimes. London: 1979. V. 65

ADGER, J. B.
Religious Instruction of the Black Population. Charleston: 1847. V. 63

ADJUTANT Stearns. Boston: 1862. V. 62; 63

ADLER, ALFRED
Menschenkenntnis. Leipzig: 1927. V. 65
Praxis und Theorie der Individual-Psychologie: Vortrage zur Einfuhrung in die Psychotherapie fur Arzte Psychologen und Lehrer. Munchen/Wiesbaden: 1920. V. 65
Studie Uber Mindwertigkeit von Organen. (with) *Uber den Nervosen Charakter.* Berlin/Wien: 1907. V. 65
Uber den Nervosen Charakter: Grundzuge einer Vergleichenden Individual-Psychologie und Psychotherapie. Wiesbaden: 1912. V. 65

ADLER, ELMER
An Informal Talk by Elmer Adler at the University of Kansas, April 17, 1953. Lawrence: 1953?. V. 63

ADLER, JANKEL
Jankel Adler. London: 1948. V. 65

ADLER, JEREMY
To Cythera! Four Poems. Marlborough: 1993. V. 62

ADLER, RENATA
Politics. Essays. New York. V. 63

ADNEY, EDWIN TAPPAN
The Bark Canoes and Skin Boats of North America. Washington: 1964. V. 67

ADOLPHUS, JOHN LEYCESTER
Letters to Richard Heber, Esq. Containing Critical Remarks on the Series of Novels Beginning with Waverley, and an Attempt to Ascertain their Author.... London: 1821. V. 62; 65

ADORNO, JUAN
Introduction to the Harmony of the Universe, or, Principles of Physico-Harmonic Geometry. London: 1851. V. 63

ADORNO, THEODOR
Konstruktion des Asthetischen. Tubingen: 1933. V. 67

ADRIAN, E. D.
The Mechanism of Nervous Action. Electrical Studies of the Neurone. London: 1935. V. 64

ADSHEAD, JOSEPH
On Juvenile Criminals, Reformatories and Means of Rendering the Perishing and Dangerous Classes Serviceable to the State. Manchester: 1856. V. 63
Our Present Gaol System Depraving to the Prisoner and a Positive Evil to the Community. Manchester: 1847. V. 63
Prisons and Prisoners. London: 1845. V. 63

ADVANCES in Insect Physiology. London: 1963-1982. V. 67

THE ADVANTAGES of Learning to Read and Write; as Explained in a Conversation Between Tom Jackson and William Smith. Lynn: 1808. V. 64

THE ADVENTURER. London: 1752-1754. V. 66
THE ADVENTURER. Dublin: 1788. V. 66

ADVENTURES Extraordinaires de Monsieur de Krac. Paris: 1910. V. 64

ADVICE from the Shades-Below. Or, A Letter from Thomas Hobbs of Malmsbury, to His Brother.... London: 1710. V. 62

ADVICE to Proprietors on the Care of Valuable Pictures Painted in Oil, with Instructions for Preserving, Cleaning and Restoring Them When Damaged or Decayed. London: 1835. V. 62

ADVICE to the Lord Lieutenants of the Counties Commanding Regiments of Militia. London: 1786. V. 65

AEGIDIUS COLUMNA ROMANUS, BP. OF BOURGES
Regimiento de Los Principes. Seville: 1494. V. 62

AELFRED, KING
A Description of Europe, and the Voyages of Ohthene and Wulfstan.... London: 1853. V. 65
The Will of King Alfred, Reprinted from the Oxford Edition of 1788.... London: 1828. V. 66

AELFRIC GRAMMATICUS
A Saxon Treatise Concerning the Old and New Testament. London: 1623. V. 63

AELIAN
De Historia Animalium Libri XVII. Leyden: 1565. V. 66; 67
De Natura Animalium... 1744. V. 65
Sophistae Varia Historia...Cum Versione Justi Vulteii.... Lugduni in Batavis: 1701. V. 66
Sophistae Variae Historiae. Halae: 1793. V. 65

THE AERO Manual, a Manual Of Mechanically Propelled Human Flight, Covering the History.... London: 1909. V. 64

AESCHYLUS
The Agamemnon. Cambridge: 1969. V. 65
Agamemnon. Oxford: 1978. V. 65
Fragments. Alabama: 1992. V. 64
Oresteia. London: 1904. V. 65
The Oresteian Trilogy. Greenbrae: 1982-1983. V. 65
Prometheus Bound. London: 1947. V. 65

AESOPUS
Aesopi Phyrgis et Aliorum Fabulae, Quorum Nomina Sequens Pagella Indicabit.... Venice: 1757. V. 62
Aesop's Fables. London: 1895. V. 66
Aesop's Fables. Manchester: 1900. V. 62
Aesop's Fables. New York: 1912. V. 62
Aesop's Fables. London: 1924. V. 65
Aesop's Fables. New York: 1933. V. 64
Aesop's Fables. London: 1934. V. 64; 65
Aesop's Fables. New York: 1941. V. 63
Aesop's Fables Retold by Blanche Winder. London: 1924. V. 63
The Fables of Aesop. London: 1793. V. 62
The Fables of Aesop. London: 1909. V. 65; 66
The Fables of Aesop. Waltham St. Lawrence: 1926. V. 67
Fables of Aesop According to Sir Roger L'Estrange. Paris: 1931. V. 67
Fables of Aesop and Other Eminent Mythologists.... London: 1692. V. 62
Fables of Aesop and Other Eminent Mythologists.... 1694. V. 66
The Fables of Aesop and Others. Newcastle-upon-Tyne: 1818. V. 62; 67
The Fables of Aesop and Others. London: 1857. V. 65
The Fables of Aesop and Others. London: 1858. V. 64
The Fables of Aesop, and Others, with Designs On Wood. Newcastle: 1823. V. 67
The Fables of Aesop, Together with the First Three Books of Caxton's Aesop. 1973. V. 65
The Fables...Paraphras'd in Verse, and Adorned with Sculpture by John Ogilby. London: 1651. V. 64
Fabularum Aesopiarum Libri Quinque. Amsterdam: 1667. V. 66
Fabularum Aesopicarum Delectus. Oxoniae: 1698. V. 63
Select Fables of Aesop and Other Fabulists. London: 1809. V. 66
Some of Aesop's Fables with Modern Instances. London: 1883. V. 64

AETIUS OF AMIDA
Contractae ex Veteribus Medicinae Tetrabiblos, Hoc est, Quaternio, Sive Libri Universales Quaturo.... Lugduni: 1549. V. 62; 64

AN AFFECTING History of the Captivity and Sufferings of Mrs. Mary Velnet, an Italian Lady, Who Was Seven Years a Slave in Tripoli.... Boston: 1804?. V. 63; 64

AFLALO, F. G.
A Book of Fishing Stories. 1913. V. 63; 65; 67
A Book of Fishing Stories. London: 1913. V. 67
British Salt-Water Fishes. London: 1904. V. 67
The Encyclopaedia of Sport. London: 1897. V. 64
Half a Century of Sport in Hampshire. London: 1905. V. 67
Regilding the Crescent. London: 1911. V. 64
The Sportsman's Book for India. 1904. V. 64; 67
The Sportsman's Book for India. London: 1904. V. 65

AFRICA and Its Explorers as Told by Its Explorers, Mungo Park, Clapperton, The Landers, Livingstone, Barth, Barkie, Burton, Speke, Schweinfurth.... London: 1900. V. 64; 66

AFRICA Pilot. Washington: 1916. V. 64

AFRICA Redeemed; or the Means of Her Relief Illustrated by the Growth and Prospects of Liberia. London: 1851. V. 63

AFRICAN Arts. 1967-1997. V. 62

AFTER Dinner Speeches at the Lotus Club. New York: 1911. V. 63

AFTON, JEAN
Cheyenne Dog Soliders - a Ledger Book History of Coups and Combat. Niwot: 1997. V. 67

AGAINST Women. Waltham St. Lawrence: 1953. V. 66
AGAINST Women. Waltham St. Lawrence: 1954. V. 62

AGASSIZ, ALEXANDER
Challenger Voyage. Zoology. Part 9. Echinoidea. 1881. V. 66
The Coral Reefs of the Tropical Pacific. Cambridge: 1903. V. 62; 63
The Development of Lepidosteus...Part I (all published). Boston: 1878. V. 67
Echini. The Genus Colobocentrotus. Cambridge: 1908. V. 63; 65
Hawaiian and Other Pacific Echini. Cambridge: 1907-1917. V. 62
Hawaiian and Other Pacific Echini. Cambridge: 1909. V. 64; 65
Letters and Recollections of Alexander Agassiz. Boston: 1913. V. 62
North American Starfishes. Cambridge: 1877. V. 63
On the Young Stages of Bony Fishes. (Part 2 only) Development of the Flounders. Boston: 1878. V. 67
The Panamic Deep Sea Echini. Cambridge: 1904. V. 63
Three Cruises of the Steamer Blake in the Gulf of Mexico, in the Caribbean Sea and Along the Atlantic Coast of the United States from 1877 to 1880. Boston and New York: 1888. V. 62; 66; 67
Three Cruises of the United States Coast and Geodetic Survey Steamer Blake in the Gulf of Mexico, in the Caribbean Sea, and Along the Atlanttic Coast of the United States from 1877 to 1880. Boston: 1888. V. 63; 64

AGASSIZ, LOUIS
Contributions to the Natural History of the United States. Boston: 1857-1962. V. 64
The Development of Osseous Fishes. Part 1-2 (of 3). Cambridge: 1885-1889. V. 67
Geological Sketches. Boston: 1866. V. 64; 65
The Intelligence of Louis Agassiz: A Specimen Book of Scientific Writings. Boston: 1963. V. 64; 67
A Journey in Brazil. Boston: 1868. V. 62; 63; 64; 65
Lake Superior: Its Physical Character Vegetation and Animals. Boston: 1850. V. 66
Methods of Study in Natural History. Boston: 1863. V. 64

Selections from Embryological Monographs. Cambridge: 1882-1884. V. 67
Twelve Lectures on Comparative Embryology, Delivered Before the Lowell Institute in Boston December and January 1848-1849. Boston: 1849. V. 63

AGEE, G. W.
Rube Burrow, King of Outlaws and His Band of Train Robbers. Chicago. V. 62; 65

AGEE, JAMES
Agee on Film: Review and Comments. (with) Agee on Film: Volume II. New York: 1958-1960. V. 66
The Collected Poems of James Agee. Boston: 1968. V. 66
The Collected Short Prose of James Agee. Boston: 1968. V. 66
A Death in the Family. New York: 1957. V. 67
A Death in the Family. London: 1958. V. 63
Four Early Stories. West Branch: 1964. V. 67
The Last Letter of James Agee to Father Flye. Boston: 1969. V. 66
Let Us Now Praise Famous Men. Boston: 1960. V. 65
Letters of James Agee to Father Flye. New York: 1962. V. 63; 67
The Morning Watch. Roma: 1950. V. 67
Permit Me Voyage. New Haven: 1934. V. 62; 65; 67

AGER, WILLIAM
Correspondence, and Other Documents, Concerning the Offers, Which Have Been Repeatedly Made to Enable the United States to Trace, Identify, Seize and Recover, Large Amounts of Money and Other Property.... London: 1867. V. 62

AGG, JOHN
Turning Out: or, St. S---'s In an Uproar: Containing Particulars of the Death and Resurrection of the Heaven-Born Ministers.... London: 1812. V. 67

AGLIONBY, WILLIAM
Painting Illustrated in Three Diallogues, Containing Some Choice Observations Upon the Art, Together With the Lives of the Most Eminent Painters, from Cimabue to the Time of Raphael and Michael Angelo. London: 1685. V. 66; 67

AGNELLI, M.
The Agnelli Gardens of Villar Perosa.... New York: 1998. V. 67

AGNER, DWIGHT
The Books of WAD, a Bibliography of the Books.... Baton Rouge: 1974. V. 62

AGNEW, A. D. Q.
Upland Kenya Wild Flowers. 1974. V. 66

AGNEW, C. MORLAND
Catalogue of the Pictures Forming the Collection of Sir Charles Tennant, Bart. London: 1896. V. 64

AGNEW, S. C.
Garrisons of the Regular U.S. Army in New Mexico 1846-1899. Santa Fe: 1971. V. 67

AGNEW, W. P.
Hemorrhoids and Other Non-Malignant Rectal Diseases. Diagnosis and Treatment. San Francisco: 1902. V. 63

AGOSTINHO DE SANTA MARIA, FATHER
Historia da Fundacao do Real Convento de Santa Monica da Cidade de Goa, Corte do Estado da India & do Imperio Lusitano do Oriente.... Lisbon: 1699. V. 62

LES AGREMENS de la Campagne, ou Remarques Particulieres sur la Construction des Maisons de Campagne plus ou Moins Magnifiques; des Jardins de Plaisance & des Plantages, avec les Ornemens qui en Dependent.... Leiden: 1750. V. 63

AGRICOLA, GEORGIUS
De Re Metallica. New York: 1950. V. 62; 64

AGRICULTURAL State of the Kingdom, in February, March and April, 1816: Being the Substance of the Replies to a Circular Letter Sent by the Board of Agriculture, to Every Part of the Kingdom. London: 1816. V. 66; 67

AGRIPPA VON NETTESHEIM, HEINRICH CORNELIUS
De la Grandeur et de l'Excellence des Femmes, au Dessus des Hommes. Paris: 1713. V. 63
Paradoxe sur l'Incertitude, Vanite & Abus des Sciences. Paris?: 1608. V. 62
Three Books of Occult Philosophy.... London: 1651. V. 64; 66

AGUILAR, GRACE
The Spirit of Judiasm. Philadelphia: 1842. V. 67
The Women of Israel or Characters and Sketches from the Holy Scriptures or Characters and Sketches from the Holy Scriptures and Jewish History. London: 1884. V. 67

AHRONS, E. L.
The British Steam Railway Locomotive 1825-1925. (wth) The British Steam Railway Locomotive 1925-1965. 1963-1966. V. 65

AI
Cruelty. Boston: 1973. V. 67
Vice. New York: 1999. V. 62

AICKMAN, ROBERT
Cold Hand in Mine. London: 1975. V. 66
Night Voices - Strange Stories. London: 1985. V. 65

AIDE, HAMILTON
Mr. and Mrs. Faulconbridge. London: 1864. V. 66

AIKEN, CONRAD
Blue Voyage. New York: 1927. V. 62; 63
Landscape West of Eden. London: 1934. V. 67
Nocturne of Remembered Spring and Other Poems. Boston: 1917. V. 62; 64

AIKEN, CONRAD continued
Selected Poems. New York: 1929. V. 62

AIKIN, A.
A Manual of Mineralogy. 1815. V. 66

AIKIN, JAMES
Journal of James Aikin. Norman: 1919. V. 66

AIKIN, JOHN
England Described.... London: 1818. V. 62
Essays on Song Writing.... London: 1772. V. 65
Essays on Song Writing.... London: 1774. V. 66
Evenings at Home, or, the Juvenile Budget Opened.... London: 1845. V. 63
Evenings at Home, or, the Juvenile Budget Opened.... London: 1870. V. 63
Letters from a Father to a Son on Various Topics, Relative to Literature and the Conduct of Life. London: 1793. V. 64
Letters from a Father to His Son, on Various Topics Relative to Literature and the Conduct of Life. London: 1794. V. 63
Letters to a Young Lady on a Course of English Poetry. London: 1804. V. 65
Letters to a Young Lady on a Course of English Poetry. London: 1807. V. 65
The Woodland Companion; or a Brief Description of British Trees. London: 1802. V. 64; 65

AIKIN, LUCY
The Life of Joseph Addison. London: 1843. V. 62; 65; 66
Memoirs of the Court of Queen Elizabeth. London: 1819. V. 62
Memoirs of the Court of Queen Elizabeth. London: 1879. V. 63

AILESBURY, THOMAS, EARL OF
Memoirs. London: 1890. V. 64

AIME MARTIN, LOUIS
De l'Education des Meres de Famille, ou de la Civilisation du Genre Humain par les Femmes. Paris: 1860. V. 66

AIMES, HUBERT H. S.
A History of Slavery in Cuba, 1511 to 1868. New York and London: 1907. V. 66

AINGER, A. C.
Eton in Prose and Verse, an Anthology. London. V. 67

AINSA, J. Y.
History of the Crabb Expedition Into North Sonora - Decapitation of the State Senator of California, Henry A. Crabb and Massacre of Ninety-Eight of His Friends at Caborca and Sonoita, Sonora, Mexico, 1857. Phoenix: 1951. V. 66

AINSLIE, KATHLEEN
At Great-Aunt Martha's. London: 1904. V. 66
Catharine Susan and Me Goes Abroad. London: 1909. V. 62; 66
Catharine Susan and Me's Coming Out. London: 1910. V. 62
Catharine Susan in Hot Water. London: 1910. V. 62
Catharine Susan's Calendar. London: 1908. V. 62
Dear Dirty Dolly. London: 1909. V. 62
Lady Tabitha and Us. London: 1903. V. 62
Me and Catharine Susan. London: 1903. V. 62
Oh! - Poor Amelia Jane!. London: 1905. V. 62
Sammy Goes A'Hunting. London: 1907. V. 62
Votes for Catharine Susan and Me. London: 1910. V. 62
What I Did. London: 1905. V. 62

AINSWORTH, ED
The Cowboy in Art. New York: 1968. V. 62; 63; 66
Golden Checkerboard. Palm Desert: 1965. V. 62
Painters of the Desert. Palm Desert: 1960. V. 62; 63; 66; 67

AINSWORTH, G. C.
The Fungi, an Advanced Treatise. New York: 1965-1973. V. 64; 66

AINSWORTH, ROBERT
Thesaurus Linguae Latinae Compendarius; or, a Compendious Dictionary of the Latin Tongue.... London: 1752. V. 67

AINSWORTH, WILLIAM FRANCIS
A Personal Narrative of the Euphrates Expedition. London: 1888. V. 64

AINSWORTH, WILLIAM HARRISON
Beatrice Tyldesley. London: 1878. V. 66
Beau Nash; or, Bath in the Eighteenth Century. London: 1879. V. 65
Boscobel; or, the Royal Oak. London: 1872. V. 62; 65
Cardinal Pole; or, the Days of Philip and Mary. London: 1863. V. 63; 65; 66
The Constable de Bourbon. London: 1866. V. 66
Crichton; an Historical Romance. London: 1850. V. 67
The Flitch of Bacon; or, the Custom of Dunmow. London: 1854. V. 65
The Goldsmith's Wife. London: 1875. V. 65
The Good Old Times: The Story of the Manchester Rebels of '45. London: 1873. V. 65
Guy Fawkes; or the Gunpowder Treason. London: 1857. V. 65
Jack Sheppard. London: 1839. V. 65; 66
Jack Sheppard. London: 1840. V. 66
The Lord Mayor of London; or, City Life in the Last Century. London: 1862. V. 66
Merry England; or Nobles and Serfs. London: 1874. V. 66
The Miser's Daughter: a Tale. London: 1843. V. 65
The Miser's Daughter: a Tale. London: 1848. V. 65; 66
The Miser's Daughter: a Tale. London: 1855. V. 64
Old Saint Paul's: A Tale of the Plague and the Fire. London: 1841. V. 62; 65; 66
Old Saint Paul's: A Tale of the Plague and the Fire. London: 1847. V. 66
Old Saint Paul's: A Tale of the Plague and the Fire. London: 1861. V. 67
Ovingdean Grange. London: 1860. V. 65; 66
Rookwood: a Romance. London: 1834. V. 65
Rookwood: a Romance. London: 1836. V. 65
Rookwood: a Romance. London: 1850. V. 67
Rookwood: a Romance. London: 1851. V. 63
The South-Sea Bubble. London: 1902. V. 65
The Spendthrift: a Tale. London: 1857. V. 66
Stanley Brereton. London: 1881. V. 66
The Tower of London. London: 1840. V. 65
Windsor Castle. London: 1843. V. 65
Windsor Castle. London: 1844. V. 65
Windsor Castle. London: 1853?. V. 67
The Works. London: 1850-1851. V. 67

AIRSHIP GUARANTEE COMPANY LTD.
Airship R100. Howden: 1925. V. 64

AIRTH, RENNIE
River of Darkness. London: 1999. V. 65; 66; 67
Snatch!. London: 1969. V. 65; 66; 67

AIRY, GEORGE BIDDELL
Six Lectures on Astronomy, Delivered at the Meetings of the Friends of the Ipswich Museum, at the Temperance Hall, Ipswich, in the Month of March 1848. London: 1849. V. 65
A Treatise on Magnetism for the Use of Students in the University. London: 1870. V. 65

AIRY, OSMUD
Charles II. London: 1901. V. 65

AITCHISON, J.
The Zoology of the Afghan Delimitation Commission. 1889. V. 62

AITKEN, JOHN
On Colour and Colour Sensation. (with) On Harmony of Colour, Part II. Edinburgh: 1873-1874. V. 64

AITKEN, WILLIAM B.
Distinguished Families in America Descended from Wilhelmus Beekman and Jan Thomasse Van Dyke. New York: 1912. V. 63

AITON, W.
Hortus Kewensis; or a Catalogue of the Cultivated in the Royal Botanic Garden at Kew. London: 1810-1813. V. 64

AITZEMA, LION
Notable Revolutions: Being a True Relation of What Hapn'ed in the United Provinces of the Netherlands in the Years MDCL and MDCLI. London: 1653. V. 66

AJISAFE, A. K.
The Laws and Customs of the Yoruba People. London: 1924. V. 64

AKEN, DAVID
Pioneers of the Black Hills or Gordon's Stockade Party of 1874. Milwaukee: 1920. V. 67

AKENSIDE, MARK
An Ode to the Country Gentlemen of England. London: 1758. V. 64
Odes on Several Subjects. London: 1745. V. 63; 64; 65; 66
The Pleasures of Imagination. London: 1744. V. 64; 65; 66
The Pleasures of Imagination. Portland: 1807. V. 63
The Poems. London: 1772. V. 67

AKER, CARL
Carl Aker's Colorado. Fort Collins: 1975. V. 65; 67

AKERMAN, JOHN YONGE
A Descriptive Catalogue of Rare and Unedited Roman Coins. London: 1834. V. 67
Illustrations to Tales of Other Days.... London: 1830. V. 65
Moneys Received and Paid for Secret Services of Charles II and James II (1679-1688). 1851. V. 65
Spring Tide; or, the Angler and His Friends. 1850. V. 62; 63; 65; 67

AKHMATOVA, ANNA
U Samogo Morya. (At the Edge of the Sea). St. Petersburg: 1921. V. 65
Vecher, (Evening). St. Petersburg: 1912. V. 65; 67
Stikhovorenia. Moscow: 1958. V. 65

AKIN, JAMES
Journal of James Akin. Norman: 1919. V. 63

AKIYAMA, AISABURO
Geisha Girl. Tokyo: 1933. V. 67

AKOEV, G. N.
Mechanoreceptors, their Functional Organization. Berlin: 1988. V. 67

AKURGAL, K.
The Art of the Hittites. 1962. V. 65
The Art of the Hittites. New York: 1962. V. 62

AKUTAGAWA, RYUNOSUKE
Rashomon and Other Stories. New York: 1952. V. 63

AL Khamsa Arabians: a Documentation of Al Khamsa Arabians and Their History. Rocford: 1983. V. 64

ALARCON, PEDRO ANTONIO DE
The Infant with the Globe. London: 1955. V. 63

ALASKAN ENGINEERING COMMISSION
Reports of the Alaskan Engineering Commission for the Period from March 12, 1914 to December 31, 1915. Washington: 1916. V. 62

ALASTAIR
Fifty Drawings by Alastair. New York: 1925. V. 62

ALBANESE, E.
Annotazioni Medico-Chirurgiche sulla Cura Della Paralisi Infantile, e Sulla Cura Ortopedica di Talune Deformita Scheletriche. Palermo: 1881. V. 63

ALBAUGH, WILLIAM A.
Confederate Edged Weapons. New York: 1960. V. 63
Confederate Handguns. Concerning the Guns, the Men Who Made Them and the Times of Their Use. Philadelphia: 1963. V. 63
More Confederate Faces. Washington: 1972. V. 62; 63
The Original Confederate Colt - The Story of the Leech and Rigdon and Rigdon Ansley Revolvers. New York: 1953. V. 63; 63
Tyler, Texas, C.S.A. Harrisburg: 1958. V. 63

ALBEE, B. J.
Atlas of the Vascular Plants of Utah. 1988. V. 67

ALBEE, EDWARD
All Over - a Play. New York: 1971. V. 65
The Ballad of the Sad Cafe: Carson McCullers' Novella.... Boston: 1963. V. 63; 67
Box and Quotations from Chairman Mao Tse-Tung. Two Inter-Related Plays. New York: 1969. V. 67
Counting the Ways and Listening. New York: 1977. V. 67
Everything in the Garden. New York: 1968. V. 67
Malcolm. Adapted by Edward Albee. New York: 1966. V. 62
The Sandbox. New York: 1960. V. 64; 67
Who's Afraid of Virginia Woolf?. New York: 1962. V. 66
The Wounding: An Essay on Education. Charleston: 1981. V. 62; 67
Zoo Story. The Death of Bessie Smith. The Sandbox. New York: 1960. V. 64; 67

ALBEE, FRED HOUDLETT
Orthopedic and Reconstruction Surgery, Industrial and Civilian. Philadelphia: 1919. V. 62

ALBEMARLE, GEORGE MONCK, DUKE OF
A Letter from General Monck from Dalkeith 13 October 1659, Directed As Followeth. For the Right Honorable William Lenthal, Esquire, Speaker: to be Communicated to the Parliament of the Common-Wealth of England, at Westminster. London: 1659. V. 64

ALBERGOTTI, AGOSTINO
La Via Della Santita. Lucca: 1845. V. 66

ALBERT Einstein, Philosopher-Scientist. Evanston: 1949. V. 63

ALBERT, NEIL
The February Trouble. New York: 1992. V. 62; 64; 66; 67
The January Corpse. 1991. V. 62; 63; 64; 66
The January Corpse. New York: 1991. V. 62

ALBERT, PRINCE CONSORT
The Principal Speeches and Addresses of His Royal Highness the Prince Consort. London: 1862. V. 64

ALBERTI, GIUSEPPE ANTONIO
I Giuochi Numerici Fatti Arcani Palesati.... Venezia: 1795. V. 64
Instruzioni Pratiche per l'Ingegnero Civile, o sia Perito Agrimensore e Perito d'Acque. Venice: 1748. V. 62
Trattao della Misura delle Fabbriche. Venice: 1757. V. 65

ALBERTI, MICHAEL
Specimen Medicinae Theologicae, Selectiora Quaedam Themata ad Scientiam et Experientiam Medicam Praecipue Pertinentia.... Halae Magdeburgiae: 1726. V. 65

ALBERTI, RAFAEL
A La Pintura, Poema del Color Y La Linea. Buenos Aires. V. 66
Imagen Primera de (1940-1944). Buenos Aires: 1945. V. 62
The Owl's Insomnia. New York: 1973. V. 67
Pleamar (1942-1944). Buenos Aires: 1944. V. 62

ALBERTS, DON
From Brandy Station to Manilla Bay - a Biography of General Wesley Merritt. Austin: 1981. V. 65; 67

ALBERTS, S. S.
A Bibliography of the Works of Robinson Jeffers. Rye: 1966. V. 64

ALBERTSON, A. O.
Nantucket Wild Flowers. New York: 1921. V. 67

ALBERTUS MAGNUS
Albertus Magnus on Animals.... Baltimore: 1999. V. 63
De Secretis Mulierum Libellus, Scholiis Auctus and Amendis Repurgatus.... Argentorati: 1615. V. 63
Sermones de Tempore de Sanctis. Ulm. V. 62

ALBERTZ, JAN
Almanach for the Year 1736. Amsterdam: 1736. V. 67

ALBERY, WILLIAM
A Parliamentary History of the Ancient Borough of Horsham 1295- 1885.... 1927. V. 67

ALBIN, E.
A Natural History of Birds. 1738-1740. V. 63
A Natural History of English Song-Birds. London: 1741. V. 62; 66
A Natural History of English Song-Birds.... London: 1779. V. 65

ALBIN, ELEAZAR
A Natural History of English Insects. London: 1724. V. 64; 66

ALBINUS, BERNHARD SIEGFRIED
Index Supellectilis Anatomicae Quam Academiae Batavae Quae Leidae est Legavit vir Clarissimus Johannes Jacobus Rau.... Leyden: 1725. V. 66
Oratio Inauguralis de Anatome Comparata.... Leyden: 1719. V. 66
Tables of the Skeleton and Muscles of the Human Body. London: 1749. V. 62; 64

ALBION, ROBERT
Naval & Maritime History. An Annotated Bibliography. Mystic: 1972. V. 63

ALBOM, MITCH
Tuesdays with Morrie. New York: 1997. V. 65

ALBRIGHT, T.
Art in the San Francisco Bay Area 1945-1980. Berkeley: 1985. V. 65

THE ALBUM. New York: 1824. V. 62; 64

ALBUM Classico-Romantique. Paris: 1830. V. 66

ALBUM Colette. Paris: 1984. V. 63

ALBUM Comique de Pathologie Pittoresque, Recueil de Vingt Caricatures Medicales Dessinees par Aubry, Chazal, Colin, Bellauge et Pigal. Paris: 1823. V. 66

ALBUM Imperiale d'Haiti. New York: 1852. V. 66

ALBUM Vilmorin, the Vegetable Garden. London: 1986. V. 62

ALCARAZ, RAMON
The Other Side: or Notes for the History of the War Between Mexico and the United States. New York: 1850. V. 62

ALCEDO, DON ANTONIO DE
The Geographical and Historical Dictionary of America and the West Indies. London: 1812-1815. V. 66

ALCEDO Y HERRERA, DIONISIO
Compendio Historico de la Provincia, Partidos, Ciudades Astilleros, Rios, Y Puerto de Guayaquil en las Costas de la Mar del Sur. Madrid: 1741. V. 62

ALCIATI, ANDREA
Diverse Impresse Accomodate a Diuerse Moralita. Lyon: 1564. V. 67
Emblemata. Lvgdvni: 1614. V. 63; 66
Omnia Emblemata, cum Commentariis, Quibus Emblematum Aperta Origine Mens Auctoria Explicatur.... Paris: 1589. V. 65

ALCIPHRON
Alciphron's Epistles; in Which are Described the Domestic Manners, the Courtesans and Parasites of Greece. London: 1791. V. 66

ALCOCK, A. W.
Report on the Natural History Results of the Pamir Boundary Commission.... Calcutta: 1898. V. 62

ALCOCK, CHARLES WILLIAM
Famous Cricketers and Cricket Grounds. London: 1895. V. 66
Famous Cricketers and Cricket Grounds. Ohio: 1917. V. 66

ALCOCK, FREDERICK
Trade and Travel in South America. London: 1907. V. 63

ALCOCK, GEORGE W.
Fifty Years of Railway Trade Unionism. London: 1922. V. 64

ALCOCK, RUTHERFORD
The Capital of the Tycoon; a Narrative of a Three Years' Residence in Japan. London: 1863. V. 64
The Journey of Augustus Raymond Margary, from Shanghae to Ghamo and Back to Manwyne. London: 1876. V. 64

ALCOCK, T.
An Essay on the Use of Chlorurets of Oxide of Sodium and of Lime as Powerful Disinfecting Agents.... London: 1827. V. 62

ALCOCK, WILLIAM CONGREVE
A Report of the Trial of William Congreve Alcock and Henry Derenzy, Esqrs., of an Indictment for the Murder of John Colclough, Esq. at Wexford Assizes 26th March 1808. Dublin: 1808. V. 63

ALCOHOLICS Anonymous, the Story of How Thousands of Men and Women Have Recovered from Alcoholism. New York: 1955. V. 65

ALCORN, GAY DAY
Tough Country - the History of the Saratoga and Encampment Valley 1825-1895. Saratoga: 1984. V. 66

ALCOTT, AMOS BRONSON
Concord Lectures on Philosophy. Cambridge: 1883. V. 62
Observations on the Principles and Methods of Infant Instruction. Boston: 1830. V. 62

ALCOTT, LOUISA MAY
Aunt Jo's Scrap-Bag. London: 1871. V. 65
Aunt Jo's Scrap-Bag. Cupid and Chow-Chow. Boston: 1874. V. 62
Aunt Jo's Scrap-Bag. Shawl Straps. Boston: 1872. V. 62

ALCOTT, LOUISA MAY continued
The Doll's Journey from Minnesota to Maine. Boston: 1902. V. 66
Eight Cousins. Boston: 1875. V. 66
Flower Fables. Boston: 1855. V. 63; 65; 66
Flower Fables. Philadelphia: 1898. V. 65
Good Wives: a Story for Girls. London: 1871?. V. 62
Hospital Sketches. New York: 1963. V. 62
Jack and Jill. Boston: 1880. V. 66
Jo's Boys and How They Turned Out. Boston: 1886. V. 62
Little Button Rose. Boston: 1901. V. 62; 66
Little Men: Life at Plumfield with Jo's Boys. Boston: 1871. V. 63; 64; 66
Little Women. Boston: 1870. V. 66
Little Women, Part Second. Boston: 1869. V. 66
Little Women. (with) Little Women, Part Second. (with) Little Men. Boston: 1868. V. 66
Loring's Tales of the Day. Boston: 1868. V. 66
Louisa May Alcott, Her Life, Letters and Journals. London: 1889. V. 65
An Old Fashioned Girl. Boston: 1870. V. 62; 66
Pansies and Water-Lilies. Boston: 1902. V. 62
Rose in Bloom. Boston: 1876. V. 65
Silver Pitchers. Boston: 1876. V. 66
Work: a Story of Experience. London: 1873. V. 65

ALCOTT, WILLIAM ANDRUS
The Mother's Medical Guide in Children's Diseases. Boston: 1851. V. 67
The Young House-keeper or Thoughts on Food and Cookery. Boston: 1838. V. 62

ALDEN, JOHN ELIOT
Rhode Island Imprints 1727-1800. New York. 1949. V. 65

ALDEN, TIMOTHY
Alden's New Jersey Register and United States' Calendar, for...1811. Newark: 1811. V. 63; 66

ALDERMAN, EDWIN A.
Library of Southern Literature. Atlanta: 1906. V. 67
Library of Southern Literature. Atlanta: 1909. V. 64; 67

ALDERSON, BRIAN
Cakes and Custard. London: 1974. V. 67

ALDERSON, E. A. H.
Pink and Scarlet. 1913. V. 64
With the Mounted Infantry and the Mashonaland Field Force 1896. London: 1898. V. 64

ALDERSON, JAMES
Orthographical Exercises: in a Series of Moral Letters. London: 1815. V. 64

ALDERSON, R.
Lines, Written and Printed at the Request of a Friend, by Whom the Melancholy Story is Related. Newcastle-upon-Tyne: 1825. V. 64; 65; 66

ALDIN, CECIL
An Artist's Models. London: 1930. V. 63
Black Billy. London: 1921. V. 65
Cathedrals of England. London. V. 62
The Children's Sphere: the Children's Christmas Supplement. 1900. V. 66
A Conceited Puppy: Some Incidents in the Life of a Gay Dog. New York: 1905. V. 64
A Dog Day. New York: 1919. V. 67
Dogs of Character. New York: 1927. V. 63
Faithful Friends. London: 1902. V. 64
Field Babies. London: 1910. V. 66
The Great Adventure. London: 1920. V. 62; 64
Hunting Scenes. New York: 1936. V. 62
Just Among Friends. London: 1935. V. 67
Merry and Bright. London: 1911. V. 64
The Mongrel Puppy Book. London: 1912. V. 64
Old Inns. London: 1921. V. 64
Old Inns. London: 1925. V. 65
Old Manor Houses. London: 1921. V. 62
Pale Peter. London: 1921. V. 65
Pickles. London: 1909. V. 66
Ratcatcher to Scarlet. London. V. 62; 67
Ratcatcher to Scarlet. London: 1933. V. 63
Scarlet to M. F. H. 1933. V. 62
Scarlet to M. F. H. New York: 1933. V. 64
A Sporting Garland. London: 1902. V. 67
The Twins. London: 1910. V. 62
The White Puppy Book. New York: 1909. V. 64

ALDINGTON, HENRY
Substance of a Speech...12th February 1799...Relative to Ireland. 1799. V. 67

ALDINGTON, RICHARD
A. E. Housman and W. B. Yeats. Two Lectures. Berkshire: 1955. V. 62; 65; 67
The Berkshire Kennet. Hurst, Reading: 1955. V. 67
The Colonel's Daughter. London: 1931. V. 64
The Dearest Friend - a Selection from the Letters of Richard Aldington to John Cournos. Francestown: 1978. V. 64
Death of a Hero. London: 1929. V. 62
The Eaten Heart. Chapelle-Reanville: 1929. V. 64
Exile and Other Poems. London: 1923. V. 65
Ezra Pound and T. S. Eliot - a Lecture. Hurst, Reading: 1954. V. 65; 67
A Fool I' the Forest: a Phantasmagoria. London: 1925. V. 65
Images. London: 1919. V. 65
Jane Austen. Pasadena: 1948. V. 63
Last Straws. Paris: 1930. V. 62; 66
Lawrence of Arabia. Chicago: 1955. V. 67
Portrait of a Genius, But...The Life of D. H. Lawrence 1885-1930. London: 1950. V. 67
Roads to Glory. London: 1930. V. 62; 66
Stepping Heavenward. Florence: 1931. V. 62; 64; 65; 66; 67

ALDINI, GIOVANNI
Precis des Experiences Galvaniques Faites Recemment a Londres et a Calais.... Paris: 1803. V. 66

ALDINI, TOBIA
Exactissima Descripti Rariorum Quarundam Plantarum, Que Continentur Rome in Horto Farnesiano. Rome: 1625. V. 64; 66; 67

ALDISS, BRIAN W.
The Brightfount Diaries. London: 1955. V. 66
Cracken at Critical and the Magic of the Past. 1987. V. 64
Greybeard. London: 1964. V. 64; 66
Item Eighty-Three - a Bibliography 1954-1972. London: 1972. V. 64
Somewhere East of Life. Norwalk: 1994. V. 65

ALDRICH, HENRY
The Elements of Civil Architecture, According to Vitruvius and Other Ancients, and the Most Approved Practice of Modern Authors.... Oxford: 1824. V. 64; 66

ALDRICH, J. M.
Catalogue of North American Diptera. 1905. V. 63; 66

ALDRICH, JAMES
A Short Sketch of the Lives of James Thomas Aldrich, Esq. and His Wife Mrs. Isabel Coroneus Aldrich. Aiken: 1903. V. 67

ALDRICH, LORENZO D.
A Journal of the Overland Route to California and the Gold Mines. Los Angeles: 1950. V. 63; 64; 65

ALDRICH, THOMAS BAILEY
The Ballad of Babie Bell and Other Poems. New York: 1859. V. 67
The Course of True Love Never Did Run Smooth. New York: 1858. V. 63
Marjorie Daw. Boston and New York: 1908. V. 62
A Sea Turn and Other Matters. Boston and New York: 1902. V. 67
The Shadow of the Flowers. Boston and New York: 1912. V. 66

ALDRIDGE, R.
Ranch Notes in Kansas, Colorado, the Indian Territory and Northern Texas. London: 1885. V. 67

ALDRIN, BUZZ
Men from Earth. New York: 1989. V. 67

ALEANDER, ALEXANDER
A Treatise on the Nature of Vision, Formation of the Eye, and Causes of Imperfect Vision, with Rules for the Application of Artificial Assistance and Observations on the Dangers Arising from the Use of Improper Glasses. London: 1833. V. 62

ALEAUME, JACQUES
La Perspective Speculative et Pratique, ou Sont Demonstrez les Fondemens de Cet Art.... Paris: 1643. V. 64

ALECHINSKY, PIERRE
Pierre Alechinsky. New York: 1977. V. 65

ALECK, and the Mutineers of the Bounty; or, Thrilling Incidents of Life on the Ocean, Being the History of Pitcairn's Island. Boston/Cleveland: 1854. V. 64

ALEGRIA, CIRO
The Golden Serpent. New York: 1943. V. 62

ALEMANNI, NICCOLO
De Lateranensibus Parietinis...Dissertatio Historica.... Rome: 1625. V. 64

ALEMBERT, JEAN LE ROND D'
Traite de l'Equilibre et du Mouvement des Fluides. Paris: 1744. V. 67

ALENCAR, JOSE MARTINIANO DE
As Minas de Prata. Romance. Rio de Janeiro: 1865-1866. V. 62

ALES, STANISLAS
Considerations Cliniques sur les Localisations Cerebrales. Montpellier: 1879. V. 64

ALEXANDER, A. F. O'D.
The Planet Saturn: a History of Observation, Theory and Discovery. London: 1962. V. 67

ALEXANDER, ARCHIBALD
A Discourse Occasioned by the Burning of the Theatre in the City of Richmond, Virginia.... Philadelphia: 1812. V. 63; 66

ALEXANDER, CHARLES BEATTY
Major William Ferguson, member of the American Philosophical Society, Officer in the Army of the United Sates. New York: 1908. V. 66; 67

ALEXANDER, FRANCESCA
The Story of Ida: Epitaph on an Eturia Tomb. Kent: 1885. V. 67

ALEXANDER, H. H.
The Life of Guiteau and the Official History of the Most Exciting Case on Record.... Boston: 1882. V. 67

ALEXANDER, J. A.
The Life of George Chaffey. Melbourne: 1928. V. 64

ALEXANDER, J. J. G.
The Painted Page. Italian Renaissance Book Illumination 1450-1550. Munich: 1994. V. 62

ALEXANDER, JAMES E.
Salmon Fishing in Canada. London: 1860. V. 64

ALEXANDER, JESSE
Looking Back. Santa Barbara: 1982. V. 66

ALEXANDER, JOHN H.
Mosby's Men. New York and Washington: 1907. V. 62; 63; 65

ALEXANDER, KARL
Time After Time. New York: 1979. V. 63; 66

ALEXANDER, LLOYD
Border Hawk: August Bondi. New York: 1958. V. 66
The Fortune Tellers. New York: 1992. V. 65

ALEXANDER, MARY CHARLOTTE
William Patterson Alexander in Kentucky, the Marquesas, Hawaii. Honolulu: 1934. V. 63; 64
William Patterson Alexander in Kentucky, the Marquesas, Hawaii. Honolulu: 1994. V. 62

ALEXANDER, R. D. T.
Some Signposts of Shikar. Calcutta: 1932. V. 64

ALEXANDER, ROBERT
Letter of Sir J. Mackintosh, Explanatory of the Whole Circumstances which Led to the Robbery of the Glasgow Sentinel Office, to the Death of Sir Alexander Boswell, Bart., to the Trial of James Stuart. Glasgow: 1822. V. 63

ALEXANDER, WILLIAM
An Experimental Enquiry Concerning the Causes Which Have Generally Been Said to Produce Putrid Diseases. London: 1771. V. 63
The History of Women, from the Earliest Antiquity, to the Present Time, Giving Some Account of Almost Every Interesting Particular Concerning that Sex.... London: 1782. V. 65
Picturesque Representations of the Dress and Manners of the Chinese.... London: 1814. V. 64
Picturesque Representations of the Dress and Manners of the Russians.... London: 1823. V. 67

ALEXANDER, WILLIAM T.
History of the Colored Race in America. Kansas City: 1887. V. 64

ALEXANDER AB ALEXANDRO
Genialivm Dierum. Parisiis: 1579. V. 63

ALEXANDRA
Queen Alexandra's Christmas Gift Book: Photographs from My Camera. 1908. V. 66

ALEXANDRE, ARSENE
The Modern Poster. New York: 1905. V. 64

ALEXEYEFF, P.
Methodes de Transformation des Combinaisons Organiques. Paris: 1891. V. 64

ALEXIE, SHERMAN
The Business of Fancydancing. New York: 1992. V. 62
First Indian on the Moon. New York: 1993. V. 62; 63; 67
Indian Killer. New York: 1996. V. 64
The Lone Ranger and Tonto Fistfight in Heaven. New York: 1993. V. 66; 67
The Man Who Loves Salmon. Boise: 1998. V. 62; 64
Old Shirts and New Skins. Los Angeles: 1993. V. 62; 63; 64; 66; 67
The Summer of Black Widows. New York: 1996. V. 62

ALFAU, FELIPE
Locos. New York: 1936. V. 67

ALFOLDY, GEZA
Noricum. London: 1974. V. 67

ALFORD, HENRY S. L.
The Egyptian Soudan; Its Loss and Recovery.... London: 1898. V. 64

ALFORD, THOMAS WILDCAT
Civilization. Norman: 1936. V. 63

ALFRED
My Early Years, for Those in Early Life. London: 1828. V. 67

ALFRED A. Knopf: Quarter Century. N.P: 1940. V. 63; 65

ALFRED, GEORGE
The American Student's Guide.... Winchester: 1834. V. 63

ALFRED, HENRY J.
Views on the Thames...Marlow Weir, Near Marlow Bridge, Bisham Abbey, Temple Lock, Hurley, Harleyford. London: 1857. V. 62; 66

ALGAE Abstracts, a Guide to the Literature. New York: 1973-1976. V. 65

ALGAROTTI, COUNT
An Essay on Painting. Bologna: 1762. V. 67
An Essay on Painting. London: 1764. V. 62
The Philosophy of Sir Isaac Newton Explained in Six Dialogues on Light and Colours, Between a Lady and a Gentleman. Glasgow: 1765. V. 66

ALGER, HORATIO
Bertha's Christmas Vision: an Autumn Sheaf. Boston: 1855. V. 64
The Young Circus Rider; or the Mystery of Robert Rudd. Philadelphia: 1883. V. 65

ALGER, R. A.
The Spanish American War. New York: 1901. V. 63

AN ALGONQUIN Sampler. Chapel Hill: 1990. V. 64

ALGREN, NELSON
Chicago: City on the Make. Garden City: 1951. V. 63
Chicago: City on the Make. Oakland: 1968. V. 62; 67
The Man with the Golden Arm. New York: 1949. V. 64; 66
The Man with the Golden Arm. New York: 1951. V. 67
A Walk on the Wild Side. New York: 1956. V. 62; 65; 66

ALI Baba and the Forty Thieves. Boston: 1950. V. 66

ALI, MUHAMMAD
The Greatest: My Own Story. New York: 1975. V. 63

ALI, S.
Birds of Kerala. 1969. V. 63
Birds of Kerala. London: 1969. V. 67
Birds of Kerala. Oxford: 1984. V. 67
The Birds of Kutch. London: 1945. V. 63; 67
The Birds of Sikim. London: 1962. V. 63; 67
The Birds of Travancore and Cochin. London: 1953. V. 63; 67
Handbook of the Birds of India and Pakistan, Together with Those of Nepal, Sikkim, Bhutan and Ceylon. 1968-1974. V. 66; 67
Handbook of the Birds of India and Pakistan, Together with Those of Nepal, Sikkim, Bhutan and Ceylon. London: 1968-1974. V. 63

ALICE Grand Duchess of Hesse, Princess of Great Britain and Ireland. Biographical Sketch and Letters. London: 1884. V. 62

ALICE'S Bridal - A New Alphabet. New York: 1850. V. 64

ALINDER, JAMES
Carleton E. Watkins Photographs of the Columbia River and Oregon. N.P: 1979. V. 67

ALISON, ARCHIBALD
England in 1815 and 1845; or a Sufficient and a Contracted Currency. Edinburgh and London: 1846. V. 63
Essays on the Nature and Principles of Taste. Edinburgh: 1815. V. 66
Essays on the Nature and Principles of Taste. Edinburgh: 1825. V. 63
History of Europe from the Fall of Napoleon in MDCCCXV to the Accession of Louis Napoleon in MDCCCLII. London: 1852-1859. V. 62
Lives of Lord Castlereagh and Sir Charles Stewart, the 2nd and 3rd Marquesses of Londonderry.... Edinburgh: 1861. V. 64

ALKEN, HENRY
The Art and Practice of Etching; with Directions for Other Methods of Light and Entertaining Engravings. London: 1849. V. 67
How to Qualify for a Meltonian Suite of Hand Colored Engravings. London: 1819. V. 67
Hunting, or Six Hours Sport, by Three Real Good Ones, from the East End and Without Seeing a Hound. London: 1823. V. 66
Moments of Fancy and Whim. London: 1822-1823. V. 62; 66
The National Sports of Great Britain. London: 1821. V. 66
The National Sports of Great Britain. London: 1825. V. 64
Qualified Horses and Unqualified Riders, by Ben Taly-Ho. London: 1817. V. 66
Specimens of Riding Near London, Drawn from Life. London: 1823. V. 62

ALL But One Told by the Flowers. London: 1895. V. 64

ALL Saints Church, Richmond, Virginia. From Christmas 1888 to Christmas 1903. Printed for the Congregation. Richmond: 1904. V. 67

ALLA, OGAL
Blue Eye, a Story of the People of the Plains. Portland: 1905. V. 67

ALLAN, JOHN
John Todd and How He Stirred His Own Broth-Pot: A Tale Worth Telling. London: 1864?. V. 64

ALLAN, JOHN STEELE
The Young Angler. Cheltenham: 1949. V. 67

ALLAN Line Royal Mail Steamers to and From Canada and United States 1819-1913. Liverpool: 1913?. V. 67

ALLAN, MAUDE
My Life and Dancing. London: 1908. V. 63

ALLAN, WILLIAM
The Army of Northern Virginia in 1862. Boston and New York: 1892. V. 62
History of the Campaign of Gen. T. J. (Stonewall) Jackson in the Shenandoah Valley of Virginia, from Nov. 4, 1861 to June 17, 1862. Philadelphia: 1880. V. 62; 63; 65

ALLANSON WINN, R. G.
Boxing. London: 1897. V. 67

ALLARD, WILLIAM ABERT
Vanishing Breed. Boston: 1982. V. 63; 66

ALLARDYCE, ALEXANDER
Balmoral; a Romance of the Queen's Country. London: 1893. V. 66

ALLDRIDGE, T. J.
A Transformed Colony: Sierra Leone As It Was and As It Is: Its Progress, Peoples, Native Customs and Undeveloped Wealth. London: 1910. V. 65

ALLDRIDGE, W. J.
The Universal Merchant, in Theory and Practice.... Philadelphia: 1797. V. 63

ALLEGHANY RAILROAD & COAL CO.
Second Report of the Alleghany Railroad and Coal Co. Philadelphia: 1855. V. 67

ALLEN, ALONZO G.
Alonzo and Melissa. Enfield: 1844. V. 64

ALLEN, ARTHUR S.
Under Sail to Greenland - Being an Account of the Voyage of the Cutter Direction, Arthur S. Allen, Jr., Captain, to Greenland in the Summer of 1929. Together with the Log, Letters and Other Memoranda. New York: 1931. V. 62; 63

ALLEN, BRASSEYA JOHNSON
Pastorals, Elegies, Odes, Epistles, and Other Poems. Abingdon: 1806. V. 63; 64

ALLEN, CHARLES DEXTER
American Book-Plates. New York: 1894. V. 62; 66

ALLEN, DAVID O.
India: Ancient and Modern. Boston: 1856. V. 66

ALLEN, DON CAMERON
Four Poets on Poetry. Baltimore: 1959. V. 62

ALLEN, E. J.
Plymouth Marine Invertebrate Fauna. Plymouth: 1904. V. 67

ALLEN, G. L.
The Views and Flowers from Guzerat and Rajpootana. London: 185?. V. 64

ALLEN, G. M.
Bats. Cambridge: 1940. V. 64; 66
The Mammals of China and Mongolia. New York: 1938-1940. V. 62; 65
The Whalebone Whales of New England. Boston: 1916. V. 67

ALLEN, GARDNER W.
The Papers of Francis Gregory Dallas. New York: 1917. V. 63; 66

ALLEN, GARLAND E.
Thomas Hunt Morgan. The Man and His Science. Princeton: 1978. V. 63

ALLEN, GEORGE P.
A History and Genealogical Record of the Alling-Allens of New Haven, Conn., the Descendants of Roger Alling, First and John Alling, Sen., from 1639. New Haven: 1899. V. 63; 66

ALLEN, GRANT
The British Barbarians - a Hill Top Novel. London and New York: 1895. V. 63; 64
Charles Darwin. London: 1888. V. 65; 66
In Memoriam. George Paul MacDonell. London: 1895. V. 64
The Typewriter Girl. London: 1897. V. 63
The Woman Who Did. London and Boston: 1895. V. 63; 64

ALLEN, H.
Monograph of the Bats of North America. Washington: 1864. V. 67
On a Revision of the Ethmoid Bone...with Special Reference to the... Sense of Smelling in the Cheiroptera. Cambridge: 1882. V. 67
On the Embryos of Bats. Philadelphia: 1895. V. 67

ALLEN, HERVEY
Anthony Adverse. New York: 1933. V. 64
New Legends. Poems by.... New York: 1929. V. 62
Wampum and Old Gold. New Haven: 1931. V. 63

ALLEN, I. N.
Diary of a March Through Sinde and Afghanistan, with the Troops Under the Command of Sir William Nott.... London: 1843. V. 64

ALLEN, IRA
A Concise Summary of the Second Volume of the Olive Branch.... Philadelphia: 1806. V. 62
A Concise Summary of the Second Volume of the Olive Branch.... Philadelphia: 1807. V. 63; 66
A Narrative of the Transactions Relative to the Capture of the American Ship Olive Branch. Philadelphia?: 1804. V. 63; 66
The Natural and Political History of the State of Vermont...to Which is Added, an Appendix.... London: 1798. V. 63; 66

ALLEN, J. A.
The American Bisons. Cambridge: 1876. V. 63
History of North American Pinnipeds: a Monograph of the Walruses, Sea-Lions, Sea Bears and Seals of North America. Washington: 1880. V. 64; 66
Primates Collected by the American Museum Congo Expedition. New York: 1925. V. 66

ALLEN, J. FISK
A Practical Treatise on the Culture and Treatment of the Grape Vine.... Boston: 1848. V. 63; 64
A Practical Treatise on the Culture and Treatment of the Grape Vine.... New York: 1858. V. 64

ALLEN, J. TAYLOR
Early Pioneer Days in Texas. Dallas: 1918. V. 64

ALLEN, JAMES LANE
Flute and Violin and Other Kentucky Tales and Romances. New York: 1891. V. 67

ALLEN, JOHN
Modern Judaism; or, a Brief Account of the Opinions, Traditions, Rites and Ceremonies of the Jews in Modern Times. London: 1816. V. 65; 66
An Oration, Upon the Beauties of Liberty, or the Essential Rights of the Americans. Delivered at the Second Baptist Church in Boston, Upon the Last Annual Thanksgiving. Boston: 1773. V. 63
Synopsis Medicinae; or, a Summary View of the Whole Practice of Physic. London: 1749. V. 62

ALLEN, JOHN HOUGHTON
San Juan. San Antonio: 1945. V. 65
Southwest. Philadelphia: 1952. V. 63; 64; 66

ALLEN, JOHN LOGAN
Passage through the Garden - Lewis & Clark, the Image of the American Northwest. Urbana: 1975. V. 67

ALLEN, KENNETH S.
That Bounty Bastard. The True Story of Captain William Bligh. London: 1976. V. 64; 65; 66

ALLEN, LAWRENCE J.
Man's Greatest Adventure. Selah: 1974. V. 67

ALLEN, LEWIS M.
The Allen Press Bibliography. Greenbrae: 1981. V. 63
The Allen Press Bibliography. San Francisco: 1985. V. 64
The Allen Press Bibliography.... Greenbrae: 1985. V. 64; 66
Printing With the Handpress: Herewith a Definitive Manual by Lewis M. Allen.... Kentfield: 1969. V. 62; 63; 64; 66

ALLEN, MARK
Falconry in Arabia. 1980. V. 65

ALLEN, MEA
The Hookers of Kew 1785-1811. 1967. V. 63

ALLEN, NATHAN
The Opium Trade Including a Sketch of Its History, Extent, Effects, Etc.... Lowell: 1853. V. 63; 67

ALLEN, P. H.
The Rain Forests of Golfo Dulce. Gainesville: 1956. V. 65

ALLEN, PETER
Travels in the Cevennes. Risbury: 1998. V. 64

ALLEN, R. M.
The Microscope. London: 1940. V. 67

ALLEN, RICHARD
A Souvenir of Newstead Abbey, Formerly the Home of Lord Byron. Nottingham: 1874. V. 65

ALLEN, SAMUEL A.
My Own Home and Fireside. Philadelphia: 1846. V. 62

ALLEN, STOOKIE
Men of Daring. New York: 1933. V. 63; 66

ALLEN, THOMAS
The Commerce and Navigation of the Valley of the Mississippi.... St. Louis: 1847. V. 63
The History of the County of Lincoln from the Earliest Period to the Present Time. London and Lincoln: 1834. V. 66

ALLEN, W. C.
Centennial of Haywood County and Its County Seat, Waynesville, N.C. Waynesville: 1908. V. 63

ALLEN, WALTER
Governor Chamberlain's Administration of South Carolina. New York and London: 1888. V. 63; 66
King Joe Oliver. Chigwell: 1987. V. 62

ALLEN, WILLIAM
An American Biographical and Historical Dictionary, Containing an Account of the Lives, Characters and Writings of the Most Eminent Persons in North America.... Cambridge: 1809. V. 62
A Narrative of the Expedition Sent by Her Majesty's Government to the River Niger in 1841 Under the Command of Capt. H. D. Trotter.... London: 1848. V. 64
The Works.... London: 1707. V. 63; 65

ALLEN, WILLIAM A.
Adventures with Indians and Games of Twenty Years in the Rockies. Chicago: 1903. V. 66

ALLEN, WILLIAM FRANCIS
Slave Songs of the United States. New York: 1867. V. 63; 66

ALLEN, WOODY
Don't Drink the Water. New York: 1967. V. 67
The Floating Lightbulb. New York: 1982. V. 67
Four Films of Woody Allen. New York: 1980. V. 67
Getting Even. New York: 1971. V. 67
God. New York: 1967. V. 67
Hanna and Her Sisters. New York: 1987. V. 67
Play It Again Sam. New York: 1969. V. 67
Side Effects. New York: 1980. V. 67
Without Feathers. New York: 1975. V. 67
The Woody Allen Reader. New York: 1993. V. 62

ALLEN, Z.
Philosophy of the Mechanics of Nature, and the Source and Modes of Action of Natural Motive Power. New York: 1852. V. 62

ALLENBY, E. H. H.
Brief Record of the Advance of the Egyptian Expeditionary Force July 1917 to October 1918. Cairo: 1919. V. 63

ALLENDE, ISABEL
Civilice a su Troglodita, Los Impertinentes de Isabel Allende. Santiago: 1974. V. 67
Eva Luna. Franklin Center: 1988. V. 62; 67
Casa de los Espiritus. (House of the Spirits). Barcelona: 1982. V. 67
House of the Spirits. London: 1985. V. 67
The House of the Spirits. New York: 1985. V. 62; 64; 66; 67
The Infinite Plan. Franklin Center: 1993. V. 67
Of Love and Shadows. New York: 1987. V. 63
Of Love and Shadows. New York: 1989. V. 67

ALLERTON, JAMES M.
Hawk's Nest, or the Last of the Cahoonshees. Port Jervis: 1892. V. 63; 66

ALLESTREE, RICHARD
Forty Sermons, Whereof Twenty One are Now First Publish'd. Oxford: 1684. V. 67
The Gentleman's Calling. London: 1679. V. 65
The Gentleman's Calling. London: 1696. V. 63
The Ladies Calling. Oxford: 1673. V. 65
The Ladies Calling. Oxford: 1676. V. 64; 66
The Ladies Calling. Oxford: 1705. V. 63
The Ladies Calling in Two Parts. Oxford: 1727. V. 66
The Works of the Learned and Pious Author of the Whole Duty of Man. Oxford: 1684. V. 62

ALLEY & MAC LELLAN LTD.
Vapores e Bateloes Sentinel. Glasgow: 1913. V. 62

ALLEY, FELIX
Random Thoughts and Musings of a Mountaineer. Salisbury: 1941. V. 63

ALLGEMEINE ELEKTRICITATS-GESELLSCHAFT BERLIN
Elektrische Strassenbahnen. Berlin: 1900. V. 65

ALLHANDS, S. L.
Gringo Builders. Joplin: 1931. V. 64; 67

ALLIBONE, S. AUSTIN
A Critical Dictionary of English Literature and British and American Authors, Living and Deceased, from the Earliest Accounts to the Latter Half of the Nineteenth Century.. Philadelphia: 1891. V. 65

THE ALLIES' Fairy Book. London/New York: 1916. V. 63
THE ALLIES' Fairy Book. Philadelphia: 1916. V. 64

ALLINGHAM, HELEN
The Homes of Tennyson. London: 1905. V. 65

ALLINGHAM, MARGERY
All I Did Was This: Chapters of Autobiography.... Nashville: 1982. V. 65
The Gyrth Chalice Mystery. Garden City: 1931. V. 67
The Mind Readers. London: 1965. V. 65
Tether's End. Garden City: 1958. V. 67
Wanted: Someone Innocent. New York: 1946. V. 67

ALLINGHAM, WILLIAM
A Diary. London: 1907. V. 64
An Epitome of Geometry.... London: 1701. V. 65
Evil May-Day, Etc. London: 1883. V. 67
In Fairyland. London: 1870. V. 65
In Fairyland. London: 1875. V. 64
Laurence Bloomfield in Ireland or the New Landlord. 1869. V. 65
The Music Master, a Love Story and Two Series of Day and Night Songs. London: 1855. V. 64
Nightingale Valley. London: 1860. V. 67
Poems of William Allingham. 1912. V. 67
Sixteen Poems. Dundrum: 1905. V. 62

ALLINSON, FRANCESCA
A Childhood. London: 1937. V. 64

ALLIONI, CARLO
Flora Pedemontana Sive Enumeratio methodica Stirpium Indigenarum Pedemontii. Torino: 1785. V. 64; 66

ALLISON, DOROTHY
Bastard Out of Carolina. New York: 1992. V. 62; 64; 66; 67
Two or Three Things I Know For Sure. New York: 1995. V. 62
The Women Who Hate Me. Brooklyn: 1983. V. 62; 63; 64; 67

ALLISON, DRUMMOND
The Collected Poems of Drummond Allison. Bishop's Stortford: 1994. V. 63
The Yellow Night - Poems 1940-1941-1942-1943. London: 1944. V. 62; 66

ALLISON, J.
Allison's Picturesque Pocket Companion and Filey Guide for Visitors. Filey: 1856. V. 64; 65
Allison's Picturesque Pocket Companion Comprising a Succinct Descriptive Sketch of Whitby and Its Neighbourhood.... Whitby: 1850. V. 64

ALLISON, K. J.
A History of the County of York: East Riding, Volume I. The City of Kingston Upon Hull. Oxford: 1969. V. 63

ALLISON, WILLIAM
Memories of Men and Horses. London: 1922. V. 67
My Kingdom For a Horse!. London: 1919. V. 67

ALLIX, PIERRE
Examinations of the Scruples of Those Who Refuse to Take the Oath of Allegiance. London: 1689. V. 62

ALLMAN, G. J.
Challenger Voyage. Zoology. Parts 20 and 70, Hydroida. 1883-1888. V. 66
A Monograph of the Fresh Water Polyzoa.... London: 1856. V. 63; 66
A Monograph of the Gymnoblastic or Tubularian Hydroids. 1871-1872. V. 66
A Monograph of the Gymnoblastic or Tubularian Hydroids. London: 1871-1872. V. 62; 63
Report on the Hydroida Collected During the Exploration of the Gulf Stream. Cambridge: 1877. V. 67

ALLOM, THOMAS
Forty-Six Views of Tyrolese Scenery.... London: 1850. V. 65
France Illustrated. London: 1845. V. 66
The Northern Tourist.... London: 1834. V. 63
Views in the Tyrol, from Drawings by T Allom.... London: 1836. V. 67
Westmorland, Cumberland, Durham and Northumberland Illustrated.... London: 1832. V. 62; 63; 65; 66

ALLRED, B. W.
Flat Top Ranch - The Story of a Grassland Venture. Norman: 1957. V. 67
Great Western Indian Fights. New York: 1886. V. 67

ALLRED, CHARMAY B.
Amazing Mabel: Sketches by Mabel Dodge Luhan. Kansas City: 1996. V. 66

ALLSOPP, FRED W.
Albert Pike - a Biography. Little Rock: 1928. V. 63; 66

ALLSTON, R. F. W.
Essay on Sea Coast Crop, Read Before the Agricultural Association of the Planting States. Charleston: 1854. V. 63

ALLSTON, WASHINGTON
Description of the Grand Historical Picture of Balshazzar's Feast.... Boston: 1844. V. 62

ALLWOERDEN, HENRICUS
Historia. Michaelis. Serveti. Moshemio: 1727. V. 66

ALLYN, DOUG
The Cheerio Killings. New York: 1989. V. 65

ALLYN, JOSEPH PRATT
By Horse, Stage and Pocket - the Far West Letters of Joseph Pratt Allyn. San Francisco: 1988. V. 63; 66

ALMACK, BARUGH
Hints to Landowners. On Tenure, Prices, Rents &c. London: 1846. V. 63

ALMANACH auf Das Jahr 1822. Carlsruhe: 1821. V. 66

ALAMANCH, ou Calendrier Pour l'Annee Mil Sept Cens Quinze. Paris: 1714. V. 66

ALMEIDA, TONY DE
Jaguar Hunting in the Mato Grosso and Bolivia, with Notes on Other Game. 1989. V. 67

ALMIRALL, LEON V.
Canines and Coyotes. Caldwell: 1941. V. 64

ALMON, JOHN
Anecdotes of the Life of the Right Hon. William Pitt, Earl of Chatham. London: 1793. V. 64
Anecdotes of the Life of the Right Hon. William Pitt, Earl of Chatham. London: 1797. V. 66
A Collection of Interesting, Authentic Papers Relative to the Dispute Between Great Britain and America: Shewing the Causes and Progress of that Misunderstanding from 1764 to 1775. London: 1777. V. 64
The New Foundling Hospital for Wit. London: 1786. V. 66

AL-MUBASHSHIR IBN FATIK, ABU AL-WAFA
The Dictes and Sayings of the Philosophers. London: 1877. V. 66
The Dictes and Sayings of the Philosophers. Detroit: 1901. V. 63; 66

ALPATOV, M. V.
Early Russian Icon Painting. Moscow: 1974. V. 62; 65

ALPERT, BARRY
Vort Twenty-First Century Pre-Views: Guy Davenport - Ronald Johnson. Ninth in a Series. Silver Spring: 1976. V. 63

ALPHABET.. Paris: 1920. V. 62

ALPHABET Book. Berkeley: 1997. V. 64

ALPHABET de La Poupee. Paris: 1881. V. 64

ALPHABET du Pere Noel. Paris: 1890. V. 65

THE ALPHABET of Goody Two Shoes.... London: 1860. V. 62

AN ALPHABETICAL Index of All the Towns, Villages, Hamlets &c in the County of York and the County of the City of York. York: 1792. V. 65

ALPHERAKY, SERGIUS
The Geese of Europe and Asia. 1905. V. 66

ALPHERAKY, SERGIUS continued
The Geese of Europe and Asia. London: 1905. V. 67

ALPINE GARDEN SOCIETY
Bulletin. 1930-1999. V. 65

ALPINUS, PROSPERO
De Praesagienda Vita et Morte Aegrotantium Libri Septem.... Venetiis: 1751. V. 67

ALPOIM, JOSE FERNANDES PINTO DE
Exame de Artilheiros Que Comprehende Arithmetica, Geometria, e Artilharia, com Quatro.... Lisbon: 1744. V. 62
Exame de Bombeiros, Que Comprehende des Tratados. Madrid: 1748. V. 62

ALSINET, J.
Nuevas Utilidades de la Quina, Domstradas Confirmadas, y Anadidas. Madrid: 1774. V. 67

ALSOP, RICHARD
The Echo. New York: 1807. V. 62; 64

ALSOP, VINCENT
Melius Inquirendum. Or, a Sober Inquiry into the Reasonings of the Erious Inquiry: Wherein the Inquirers Cavils Against the Principles, His Calumnies Against the Preachings and Practices of the Non-Conformists are Examined and Rebelled. London: 1681. V. 67

ALSTON, E. R.
On Anomalurus (Flying Squirrels). 1875. V. 67

ALSTON, R. C.
A Bibliography of the English Language from the Invention of Printing to the Year 1800. Volume Four: Spelling Books. London: 1967. V. 62

ALSTON, SANDRA
A Bibliography of Canadiana Being Items in the Public Library of Toronto, Canada, Relating to the Early History and Development of Canada. Second Supplement Volume II 1801-1849. Halifax: 1985. V. 67

ALT, ADOLF
Lectures on the Human Eye In Its Normal and Pathological Conditions. London: 1884. V. 65
A Treatise on Ophthalmology.... St. Louis: 1884. V. 65

ALT, CARL FERDINAND RITTER VON
Uber die Verletzungen des Auges. Vienna: 1875. V. 64; 66

ALTER, DINSMORE
Lunar Atlas: Prepared by the Space Sciences Laboratory of the Space Division of North American Aviation, Inc. New York: 1968. V. 67

ALTER, J. CECIL
James Bridger: Trapper, Frontiersman, Scout and Guide. Columbus: 1951. V. 64; 66

ALTHAM, MICHAEL
The Additional Articles in Pope Pius's Creed, no Articles of the Christian Faith, Being an Answer to a Late Pamphlet, Intituled, Pope Pius His Profession of Faith Vindicated from Novelty in Additional Articles and the Prospect of Popery.... London: 1688. V. 67

ALTHAUS, JULIUS
Diseases of the Nervous System. Their Prevalence and Pathology. New York: 1879. V. 64; 66; 67

ALTIERI, FERDINAND
Dizionario Italiano. London: 1749. V. 63
Dizionario Italiano ed Inglese. A Dictionary Italian and English.... Venice: 1751. V. 64

ALTING, MENSONE
Descriptio Secundum Antiquo, Agri Batavi & Frisii.... Amsterdam: 1697-1701. V. 67

ALTMAN, P. L.
Metabolism. Bethesda: 1968. V. 65; 66

ALTROCCHI, JULIA COOLEY
Snow Covered Wagons, a Pioneer Epic: the Donner Party Expedition 1846-1847. New York: 1936. V. 63; 64; 66

ALTSHULER, CONSTANCE W.
Cavalry Yellow and Infantry Blue - Army Officers in Arizona Between 1851-1886. Tucson: 1991. V. 67
Chain of Command, Arizona and the Army 1856-1875. Tucson: 1991. V. 67

ALUNNO, FRANCESCO
Della Fabrica Del Mondo...Libri X.... Venice: 1570. V. 65

ALVAREZ, EMANUEL
An Introduction to the Latin Tongue, or the First Book of Grammar. London: 1689. V. 66

ALVAREZ, JULIA
How the Garcia Girls Lost Their Accent. Chapel Hill: 1991. V. 63; 65; 66; 67
In the Time of the Butterflies. Chapel Hill: 1994. V. 67
My English. Chapel Hill: 1991. V. 67

ALVAREZ Y BAENA, JOSE ANTONIO
Compendio Historico de las Grandezas de la Coronada Villa de Madrid, Corte de la Monarquia Espanola. Madrid: 1786. V. 67

ALVERSON, MARGARET BLAKE
Sixty Years of California Song. Oakland: 1913. V. 65

ALVORD, CLARENCE W.
The First Exploration on the Trans-Allegheny Region by the Virginians 1650-1674. Cleveland: 1912. V. 64; 67
The Mississippi Valley in British Politics.... Cleveland: 1917. V. 65

ALVORD, SAMUEL MORGAN
A Genealogy of the Descendants of Alexander Alvord. Webster: 1908. V. 63

AMADO, JORGE
Gabriela, Clove and Cinnamon. New York: 1962. V. 62
Tent of Miracles. New York: 1971. V. 63; 64; 66

AMALGAMATED ENGINEERING UNION
Rules of the Amalgamated Society of Engineers, Machinists, Millwrights, Smiths, and Pattern Makers.... London: 1874. V. 64

AMANTIUM Irae: Letters of Two Friends 1864-1867. Hammersmith: 1914. V. 62; 67

AMARAL, ANTHONY A.
Comanche: the Horse That Survived the Custer Massacre. Los Angeles: 1961. V. 63; 64; 65; 67
Will James, the Gilt Edged Cowboy. Los Angeles: 1967. V. 64; 67

AMARAL, GERONYMO JOSE DE
A Mulher ou O Anjo Tutelar de Familia. Rio de Janeiro: 1875. V. 66

AMATEUR Work. London: 1880-1890. V. 66

AMBER, JOHN T.
Handloader's Digest. Chicago: 1962. V. 67

AMBLER, CHARLES H.
Francis H. Pierpont: Union War Governor of Virginia and Father of West Virginia. Chapel Hill: 1937. V. 65
A History of Transportation in the Ohio Valley. Glendale: 1932. V. 64

AMBLER, ERIC
The Ability to Kill and Other Pieces. London: 1962. V. 62; 66
The Ability to Kill: True Tales of Bloody Murder. New York: 1987. V. 66
The Army of the Shadows and Other Stories. Helsinki: 1986. V. 63; 65
The Care of Time. New York: 1981. V. 62; 66
A Kind of Anger. London: 1964. V. 67
The Schirmer Inheritance. London: 1953. V. 62

AMBLER, LOUIS
The Old Halls and Manor Houses of Yorkshire. London: 1913. V. 65; 66

AMBROSE, STEPHEN E.
Undaunted Courage - Meriwether Lewis, Thomas Jefferson and the Opening of the American West. New York: 1996. V. 64; 67

AMEDEO, LUIGI
On the Polar Star in the Arctic Sea, with Statements of Commander U. Cagni Upon the Sledge Expedition to 86.34' North and of Dr. A. Cavalli Molinelli Upon His Return to the Bay of Teplitz. New York and London: 1903. V. 65

AMEIL, DENYS
Les Spectacles a Travers Les Ages. Paris: 1931. V. 65

AMELIER, FRANCISCO
Elementos De Geometria Y Fisica Experimental Oara el Uso, e Instruccion de Los Alumos del Real Colegio de Cirujia de Cadiz. Cadiz: 1788. V. 65

AMERICA 1976: a Bicentennial Exhibition Sponsored by the United States Department of the Interior.... N.P: 1976. V. 66

AMERICAN ACADEMY OF ARTS AND SCIENCES
Memoirs of the American Academy of Arts and Sciences; to the end of the Year 1783. Boston: 1785. V. 63; 65

AMERICAN ACADEMY OF FINE ARTS
Catalogue of Paintings of Colonel Trumbull.... New York: 1831. V. 64

THE AMERICAN Bee: a Collection of Entertaining Historics, Selected from Different Authors and Calculated for Amusement and Instruction. Leominster: 1797. V. 63; 66

AMERICAN BOARD OF COMMISSIONERS FOR FOREIGN MISSIONS
Report of the American Board of Commissioners for Foreign Missions, Compiled from Documents Laid Before the Board. Boston: 1827-1831. V. 66

AMERICAN CLASSICAL AND MILITARY LYCEUM
Prospectus of the American Classical and Military Lyceum, at Mount Airy, Near Germantown, Eight Miles from Philadelphia. Philadelphia: 1826. V. 64

AMERICAN Colonization Society, and the Colony at Liberia. Boston: 1832. V. 64

AMERICAN Country Houses of Today. New York: 1913. V. 63

AMERICAN FACE BRICK ASSOCIATION
Brickwork in Italy: a Brief Review from Ancient to Modern Times. Chicago: 1925. V. 62; 65

THE AMERICAN Farmer.... Baltimore: 1821. V. 62

AMERICAN Fern Journal. 1910-1986. V. 65; 66
AMERICAN Fern Journal. London: 1910-1986. V. 63

AMERICAN GEOGRAPHICAL SOCIETY OF NEW YORK
Journal. Volume III. Albany: 1873. V. 64

AMERICAN INSTITUTE
Annual Report of the American Institute of the City of New York for the Year 1867-1868. Albany: 1868. V. 64
Report of a Special Committee of the American Institute, on the Subject of Cash Duties, the Auction System &c. January 12, 1829. New York: 1829. V. 65

THE AMERICAN Journal of Horticulture and Florist's Companion. Boston: 1867-1868. V. 67

AMERICAN Journal of Surgery - Fiftieth Anniversary Edition - January 1941. V. 67

THE AMERICAN Journal of Syphilography and Dermatology. New York: 1871. V. 64

AMERICAN Magazine of Letters and Christianity. Princeton: 1826. V. 63

AMERICAN MEDICAL ASSOCIATION
Code of Ethics...Adopted 1847. Philadelphia: 1848. V. 63
Laws and Regulations...with a Sketch of Detroit, and a Brief History of the University of Michigan and of the Development of the State. Detroit: 1856. V. 63

AMERICAN MEDICO-PSYCHOLOGICAL ASSOCIATION
Proceedings. Volumes 1-27. N.P: 1895-1920. V. 65

AMERICAN MICROSCOPICAL SOCIETY
Proceedings. 1879-1994. V. 65
Transactions. 1966-1976. V. 66

THE AMERICAN Pirate's Own Book. Philadelphia: 1847. V. 67

AMERICAN PSYCHIATRIC ASSOCIATION TASK FORCE
Treatments of Psychiatric Disorders. Washington: 1989. V. 65

AMERICAN RED CROSS
Red Cross Service to Soldiers and Sailors. New York: 1918. V. 66

THE AMERICAN Review. 1845. V. 63

AMERICAN SOCIETY OF LANDSCAPE ARCHITECTS
Colonial Gardens, the Landscape Architecture of George Washington's Time. Washington: 1932. V. 67

AMERICAN SOCIETY OF MAMMALOGIST
Journal of Mammalogy. 1919-1999. V. 65

AMERICAN SOCIETY OF PLANT TAXONOMISTS
Systematic Botany. 1976-2000. V. 67

AMERICAN Statesmen Series. New York: 1917. V. 66

THE AMERICAN Testimonial Banquet to Henry M. Stanley, In Recognition of His Heroic Achievements in the Cause of Humanity, Science and Civilization.... London: 1890. V. 62

AMERICAN Turf Register and Sporting Magazine. Baltimore and New York: 1829. V. 64; 66

THE AMERICAN Yacht List. 1892. New York: 1892. V. 67

THE AMERICAN'S Guide. Trenton: 1813. V. 63; 66

THE AMERICAN'S Text-Book: Being a Series of Letters, Addressed by An American to the Citizens of Tennessee.... Nashville: 1855. V. 66

AMERICAN SOCIETY OF COMPOSERS, AUTHORS & PUBLISHERS
Articles of Association. New York: 1941. V. 63

AMES, AZEL
The May-Flower and Her Log. July 15, 1620-May 6, 1621. Boston and New York: 1901. V. 63; 64; 65

AMES, BLANCHE AMES
Adelbert Ames 1835-1933, General, Senator, Governor: the Story of His Life. North Easton: 1964. V. 62

AMES, GEORGE
Ups and Downs of an Army Officer. Washington: 1900. V. 67

AMES, JAMES
Typographical Antiquities: or an Historical Account of the Origin and Progress of Printing in Great Britain and Ireland. London: 1785-1790. V. 62

AMES, JAMES BARR
Lectures on Legal History and Miscellaneous Legal Essays. Cambridge: 1913. V. 63

AMES, JOSEPH
Typographical Antiquites: Being an Historical Account of Printing in England.... London: 1749. V. 63; 65

AMES, OAKES
An Enumeration of the Orchids of the United States and Canada. Boston: 1924. V. 67
Oakes Ames Jottings of a Harvard Botanist 1874-1950. Cambridge: 1979. V. 67
Orchidaceae, Illustrations and Studies of the Family Orchidaceae.... Boston: 1908. V. 66

AMHURST, NICHOLAS
The Craftsman. London: 1731-1737. V. 66
Terrae-Filius; or, the Secret History of the University of Oxford; in Several Essays. London: 1726. V. 63; 65

AMI, HENRY
Canada and Newfoundland. London: 1915. V. 66

AMICHAI, YEHUDA
Selected Poems. London: 1968. V. 62

AMICIS, EDMONDO DE
Spain and Spaniards. New York: 1885. V. 65

AMIS ET AMILES
Of the Friendship of Amis and Amile.... Hammersmith: 1894. V. 67

AMIS, KINGSLEY
Bright November. 1947. V. 64
A Case of Samples - Poems 1946-1956. London: 1956. V. 62
Collected Short Stories. London: 1980. V. 62
The Crime of the Century. 1989. V. 63
The Crime of the Century. New York: 1989. V. 67
The Darkwater Hall Mystery. Edinburgh: 1978. V. 63; 67
Dear Illusion. London: 1972. V. 63
Difficulties with Girls. London: 1988. V. 65
The Green Man. London: 1969. V. 67
The James Bond Dossier. London: 1965. V. 65; 66; 67
Lucky Jim. London: 1953. V. 65; 66; 67
Lucky Jim. Garden City: 1954. V. 62; 67
The Old Devils. 1986. V. 64
On Drink. London: 1972. V. 65
Socialism and the Intellectuals. London: 1957. V. 62; 65
That Uncertain Feeling. 1955. V. 64
That Uncertain Feeling. London: 1955. V. 62

AMIS, MARTIN
Dead Babies. London: 1975. V. 66
Dead Babies. New York: 1976. V. 62
Le Dossier Rachel. (The Rachel Papers). Paris: 1977. V. 66
Einstein's Monsters. London: 1987. V. 62; 66
The Information. 1995. V. 62; 65
The Information. London: 1995. V. 62; 64; 66
Invasion of the Space Invaders. London: 1982. V. 64
London Fields. London: 1989. V. 62; 64
Money. A Suicide Note. London: 1984. V. 62; 65; 66
The Rachel Papers. London: 1973. V. 66
The Rachel Papers. New York: 1974. V. 62; 65; 66
Success. London: 1978. V. 63; 64; 65; 66
Time's Arrow or the Nature of the Offence. London: 1991. V. 67

AMMONS, A. R.
Expressions of Sea Level. Columbus: 1963. V. 63
Ommateum with Doxology. Philadelphia: 1955. V. 64; 67
The Snow Poems. New York: 1977. V. 63
Tape for the Turn of the Year. Ithaca: 1965. V. 62

AMMONS, NELLE
A Manual of the Liverworts of West Virginia. Notre Dame: 1940. V. 67
Shrubs of West Virginia. Morgantown: 1950. V. 67

AMONG the Pimas, or the Mission to the Pima and Maricopa Indians. Albany: 1893. V. 63; 64

AMOR Librorum. Bibliographic and Other Essays a Tribute to Abraham Horodisch on His Sixtieth Birthday. Zurich: 1958. V. 63

AMORY, THOMAS
The Life of John Buncle, Esq. London: 1825. V. 62; 66

AMOS, ANDREW
The Great Oyer of Poisoning: The Trial of the Earl of Somerset for the Poisoning of Sir Thomas Overbury, in the Tower of London and Various Matters Connected Therewith, from Contemporary Mss. London: 1846. V. 62; 64

AMOS, JAMES E.
Theodore Roosevelt: Hero to His Valet. New York: 1927. V. 66

AMPERE, ANDRE MARIE
Recueil d'Observations Electro-Dynamiques, Contenant Divers Memoires.... Paris: 1822. V. 63

AMSDEN, CHARLES AVERY
Navaho Weaving: Its Technic and History. Santa Ana: 1934. V. 63; 64; 65
Navaho Weaving: Its Technic and History. Albuquerque: 1949. V. 62; 63; 65

AMSINCK, PAUL
Tunbridge Wells and Its Neighbourhood.... London: 1810. V. 62; 66

AMUCHASTEGUI, AXEL
Some Birds and Mammals of South America. 1966. V. 65
Some Birds and Mammals of South America. London: 1966. V. 63

AMUNDSEN, ROALD
Gjennem Luften Til 88 Nord. Oslo: 1925. V. 65
The South Pole. London: 1912. V. 64

THE AMUSING Instructor. London: 1727. V. 62

AMWEL: Past and Prezent. Ringoz: 1910. V. 63

AMY Morgan Price and Her Drawings. London: 1929. V. 62; 64; 66

ANACREON
Anacreon. London: 1800. V. 66
Anacreon Done into English Out of the Original Greek.... London: 1923. V. 64; 67
Anacreon Teius...Opera & Studio Josuae Barnes.... Cantabrigiae: 1705. V. 66
The Extant Fragments. Tuscaloosa: 1991. V. 64
Odaria. Parmae: 1784. V. 64
Odaria. Parmae: 1785. V. 63; 66
Odes D'Anacreon. Paris: 1813. V. 65

THE ANASTATIC Drawing Society for 1858. Ashby-de-la-Zouch: 1859. V. 62; 66

ANBUREY, THOMAS
Travels through the Interior Parts of America. London: 1789. V. 64; 66; 67

ANCELL, SAMUEL
A Journal of the Late and Important Blockade and Siege of Gibraltar, from the Twelfth of September 1779 to the Third Day of February 1783. Edinburgh: 1786. V. 65

ANCIENT and Modern History of Mount's Bay, with Every Civil and Military Transaction in Saint Michael's Mount, Marazion, Penzance, Paul Buryan, Saint Levan.... Penzance: 1831. V. 67

ANCIENT Irish Histories.... 1809. V. 63

ANCIENT Lives of Scottish Saints. Paisley: 1895. V. 62

ANCILLON, CHARLES
Traite des Eunuques, Dans Lequel on Explique Toutes les Differentes Sortes d'Eunuques.... N.P: 1707. V. 64

ANCOURT, ABBE D'
The Lady's Preceptor. London: 1745. V. 65

ANDERDON, J. L.
The Life of Thomas Ken, Bishop of Bath and Wells. London: 1851. V. 62; 66; 67

ANDERSEN, HANS CHRISTIAN
Andersen's Marchen. Leipzig: 1920. V. 66
Ardizzone's Hans Andersen - Fourteen Classic Tales. London: 1978. V. 63
Danish Fairy Legends and Tales. London: 1861. V. 65
The Dream of Little Tuk and Other Tales. Boston and Cambridge: 1848. V. 64; 66
Fairy Tales. London: 1872. V. 66
The Fairy Tales. London: 1899. V. 63
Fairy Tales. London: 1903. V. 65
Fairy Tales. London: 1913. V. 64
Fairy Tales. Toronto: 1913. V. 63
Fairy Tales. New York: 1917. V. 63
Fairy Tales. London and Glasgow: 1924. V. 63; 67
Fairy Tales. New York: 1924. V. 63; 65
Fairy Tales. London: 1930. V. 62; 66
Fairy Tales. London: 1932. V. 64
Fairy Tales. Philadelphia: 1932. V. 62
Fairy Tales. London: 1935. V. 63
Fairy Tales. Copenhagen: 1956. V. 64
The Fir Tree. New York: 1970. V. 66
Het Leelijke Jong Endje. (The Ugly Duckling). Amsterdam: 1893. V. 67
The Little Mermaid. New York: 1939. V. 64; 65
Little Totty. New York: 1870. V. 63
Le Petit Elfe Ferme L'Oeil. (The Little Fairy Sleepy Eyes). Paris: 1924. V. 64
Pictures of Sweden. London: 1851. V. 66
The Red Shoes. Bristol: 1928. V. 67
Sein Oder Nicht Sein. Leipzig: 1857. V. 65
Stories and Fairytales. London and Orpington: 1893. V. 64
Stories from Andersen. London: 1911. V. 62; 64
Stories from Hans Andersen. New York: 1911. V. 64; 65
The Story of the Ungly Duck; versified by G(eorge) N(icholl).... London: 1851. V. 64; 67
Tales by.... New York: 1912. V. 63
Tales from Hans Andersen. London: 1929. V. 63
Twee Hanen. Amsterdam: 1898. V. 66
The Ugly Duckling. New York: 1945. V. 63
Uspavac (The Sandman). Praha (Prague): 1919. V. 64

ANDERSON, A. A.
Experiences and Impressions: the Autobiography of.... New York: 1933. V. 67
Twenty Five Years in a Wagon in the Gold Regions of Africa.... London: 1888. V. 64
Twenty-Five Years in a Waggon. 1974. V. 67

ANDERSON, ABRAHAM C.
Trails of Early Idaho - The Pioneer Life of George W. Goodhart. Caldwell: 1940. V. 65

ANDERSON, ADAM
Historical and Chronological Deduction of the Origin of Commerce. Dublin: 1790. V. 63
Jim Blake's Tour from Cloncave to London. 1867. V. 62

ANDERSON, AENEAS
An Accurate Account of Lord Macartney's Embassy to China.... London: 1795. V. 64

ANDERSON, ALAN
The Tragara Press 1954-1979. A Bibliography. Edinburgh: 1979. V. 67

ANDERSON, ALEX D.
The Silver Country of the Great Southwest. New York: 1877. V. 64; 65

ANDERSON, ALEXANDER
Emblems of Mortality: Representing, by Numerous Engravings, Death Seizing All Ranks and Conditions of People. Charleston & New Haven: 1846. V. 66

ANDERSON, ANNE
The Anne Anderson Fairy Tale Book. New York: 1926. V. 64
The Cuddly-Kitty and the Busy Bunny. London: 1926. V. 65
The Dickie-Birdie Book. London: 1912. V. 65
The Gillyflower (Cloves) Garden Book. London: 1912. V. 62
Humpy and Grumpy. London: 1925. V. 63
The Jacky Horner ABC. London: 1910. V. 64
The Little Busy Bee Book. London: 1912. V. 65
The Mammoth Wonder Book. London: 1935. V. 65

ANDERSON, ARCHER
The Campaign and Battle of Chickamauga. Richmond: 1881. V. 63; 65

ANDERSON, C. H. J.
The Lincoln Pocket Guide: Being Short Account of the Churches and Antiquities of the County, and of the Cathedral of the Blessed Virgin Mary of Lincoln, Commonly Called the Minister. London: 1880. V. 63

ANDERSON, C. M.
Township Plats of King County, Washington, Compiled from Offical Records. Seattle: 1900. V. 63

ANDERSON, CARL
Henry. New York: 1935. V. 65

ANDERSON, CAROLINE D.
The Three Paths; or Truth, Vanity and Profession. London: 1852. V. 65

ANDERSON CARRIAGE CO.
Overland from Detroit to Atlantic City, New Jersey 1060 Miles in a Detroit Electric. Detroit: 1908?. V. 65

ANDERSON, CHARLES C.
Fighting by Southern Federals. New York: 1912. V. 62; 63; 65

ANDERSON, CHARLES HENRY
A Digest of the Principles and Practice of Common Law, Conveyancing, Equity, Bankruptcy and Criminal Law. London: 1867. V. 63

ANDERSON, CHARLES JOHN
Lake Ngami; or, Explorations and Discoveries.... London: 1856. V. 66

ANDERSON, CHRISTOPHER
The Annals of the English Bible. London: 1845. V. 63; 66

ANDERSON, D. M.
Big Middle and Little - the Three Bears - What a Difference!. London: 1948. V. 67

ANDERSON, DAVID
Canada: Or, A View of the Importance of The British American Colonies.... London: 1814. V. 66
The Net in the Bay; or, Journal of a Visit to Moose and Albany. London: 1854. V. 63

ANDERSON, DICE R.
William Branch Giles: a Study in the Politics of Virginia and Nation from 1790 to 1830. Menasha: 1914. V. 63

ANDERSON, E. F.
Peyote, the Divine Cactus. Tucson: 1996. V. 67

ANDERSON, ELLIOTT
The Little Magazine in America; a Modern Documentary History. Yonkers: 1978. V. 65

ANDERSON, EPHRAIM
Memoirs; Historical and Personal.... St. Louis: 1868. V. 63

ANDERSON, F. J.
An Illustrated History of the Herbals. New York: 1977. V. 67

ANDERSON, F. M.
Buttercups and Daisies. London: 1920. V. 64

ANDERSON, G. F. REYNOLDS
The White Book of the Muses. Edinburgh: 1895. V. 64

ANDERSON GALLERIES
The Library of Jerome Kern. New York: 1929. V. 65

ANDERSON, ISABEL
The Great Sea Horse. Boston: 1909. V. 63

ANDERSON, J. CORBET
The Roman City of Uriconium at Wroxeter. London: 1867. V. 64

ANDERSON, J. H.
Notes on the Life of Stonewall Jackson and on His Campaigning in Virginia, 1861-1863. London: 1905. V. 62

ANDERSON, J. P.
Flora of Alaska and Adjacent Parts of Canada. 1959. V. 63

ANDERSON, JAMES
The Bee, or Literary Weekly Intelligencer, Consisting of Original Pieces and Selections from Performances of Merit Foreign and Domestic. Volume Tenth (July 11th-August 29th, 1792). Edinburgh: 1792. V. 67
Collections Relating to the History of Mary Queen of Scotland.... London: 1729. V. 67
The History and Constitutions of the Most Ancient and Honourable Fraternity of Free and Accepted Masons. London: 1746. V. 62; 65
A Practical Treatise on Chimneys. Dublin: 1777. V. 63
Selectus Diplomatum & Numismatum Scotiae Thesaurus. Edinburgi: 1739. V. 63; 66

ANDERSON, JANE
Flying, Submarining and Mine Sweeping. London: 1916. V. 64

ANDERSON, JOHN
Zoology of Egypt: Mammalia. London: 1902. V. 66

ANDERSON, JOHN W.
From the Plains to the Pulpit. Goose Creek: 1907. V. 64; 67

ANDERSON, JOSEPH
Scotland in Early Christan Times. (with) Scotland in Pagan Times. 1879-1886. V. 64; 67

ANDERSON, KENT
Liquor Guns and Ammo. Tucson: 1998. V. 65
Night Dogs. London: 1996. V. 64
Night Dogs. Tucson: 1996. V. 62; 63; 64; 65; 66; 67
Sympathy for the Devil. Garden City: 1987. V. 65; 66; 67

ANDERSON, LIONEL
Tryals and Confessions of Lionel Anderson, Alias Munson, William Russel, alias Napier, Charles Parris, alias Parry, Henry Starkey, James Corker and William Marshall, for High Treason as Romish Priests.... London: 1680. V. 63

ANDERSON, MARIAN
My Lord What a Morning: an Autobiography. New York: 1956. V. 63

ANDERSON, MARTA
Dho Tsu Hwi/Gifts of the Tsetseka Season. Wisconsin: 1974. V. 63

ANDERSON, MARTIN
The Humours of Cynicus. London: 1891. V. 64
The Satires of Cynicus. Cartoons Social and Political. London: 1893. V. 66

ANDERSON, MAXWELL
Anne of a Thousand Days. New York: 1948. V. 66

ANDERSON, NANCY K.
Albert Bierstadt, Art and Enterprise. New York: 1990. V. 62; 65

ANDERSON, PETER
Guide to Culloden Moor and Story of the Battle. Edinburgh: 1874. V. 62

ANDERSON, POUL
Earthman's Burden. 1957. V. 63; 64; 66
Guardians of Time. London: 1961. V. 62; 64; 66
Murder Bound. New York: 1962. V. 65
Murder in Black Letter. New York: 1960. V. 66
Perish the Sword. New York: 1959. V. 65
Three Hearts and Three Lions. Garden City: 1961. V. 63
Three Hearts and Three Lions. New York: 1961. V. 67

ANDERSON, RASMUS B.
The Flatey Book and Recently Discovered Vatican Manuscripts Concerning America as Early as the Tenth Century.... London: 1906. V. 62; 63; 64

ANDERSON, ROBERT
Cumberland Ballads.... Wigton: 1830. V. 64
The Life of Samuel Johnson, LL.D. London: 1795. V. 63

ANDERSON, RUFUS
Memoir of Catherine Brown, a Christian Indian of the Cherokee Nation. London: 1824. V. 63

ANDERSON, SHERWOOD
Dark Laughter. New York: 1925. V. 63
Hello Towns!. New York: 1929. V. 62
Horses and Men. Tales, Long and Short, from Our American Life. New York: 1923. V. 67
Nearer the Grass Roots. San Francisco: 1929. V. 62; 64
A New Testament. New York: 1927. V. 63; 64; 66
Perhaps Women. 1931. V. 62
Sherwood Anderson's Notebook. New York: 1926. V. 63; 64
6 Mid-American Chants. Highlands: 1964. V. 64
Tar: a Midwest Childhood. N.P: 1926. V. 63; 64; 66
Tar. A Midwest Childhood. New York: 1926. V. 62
The Triumph of the Egg. New York: 1921. V. 62
Winesburg, Ohio. New York: 1919. V. 62; 63; 64
Winesburg, Ohio. New York: 1978. V. 62; 63; 64

ANDERSON, T.
Volcanic Studies in Many Lands. 1903. V. 62; 66
Volcanic Studies in Many Lands. London: 1903. V. 67
Volcanic Studies in Many Lands. London: 1930. V. 64

ANDERSON, T. M'CALL
A Treatise on Diseases of the Skin with Special Reference to the Diagnosis and Treatment Including an Analysis of 11,000 Consecutive Cases. Philadelphia: 1887. V. 63; 66

ANDERSON, W.
Cranocerebral Topography. London: 1889. V. 67

ANDERSON, W. H.
The History of the Twenty-Second Cheshire Regiment 1689-1849. London: 1920. V. 63

ANDERSON, WILLIAM
The Pictorial Arts of Japan. London: 1886. V. 62; 66

ANDERSON, WILLIAM MARSHALL
The Rocky Mountain Journals of William Marshall Anderson, the West in 1834. San Marino: 1960. V. 63
The Rocky Mountain Journals of William Marshall Anderson: The West in 1834. San Marino: 1967. V. 64

ANDERSON IMBERT, ENRIQUE
Vigilia. Buenos Aires: 1934. V. 67

ANDERSSON, KARL JOHAN
Lake Ngami: Explorations and Discoveries.... London: 1856. V. 63; 64; 65
Lake Ngami or Explorations and Discoveries.... New York: 1856. V. 63; 64
Lake Ngami or Explorations and Discoveries.... New York: 1857. V. 62; 63; 64
The Okavango River: a Narrative of Travel, Exploration and Adventure. London: 1861. V. 64

ANDERTON, LAWRENCE
The Progenie of Catholicks and Protestants. Roven: 1633. V. 62

ANDRADE, CARLOS DE
Souvenir of the Ancient World. New York: 1976. V. 67

ANDRADE, FRANCISO DE
Cronica do Muyto Alto e Muito Poderoso Rey Destes Reynos de Portugal dom Joao o III deste Nome. Lisbon: 1613. V. 62

ANDRAE, JOHANNES
Super Arboribus Consanguinitatis, Affinitatis, et Cogantionis Spiritualis. Nuremberg: 1476. V. 64

ANDRAL, G.
Clinique Medicale, ou Choix d'Observations Recueillies a l'Hopital de la Charite. Brussels: 1837. V. 65
Essai d'Hematologie Pathologique. Paris: 1843. V. 64
Medical Clinic: Diseases of the Encephalon, with Extracts from Olliver's Work on Diseases of the Spinal Cord and Its Membranes. Philadelphia: 1843. V. 66
Medical Clinic; or, Reports of Medical Cases.... Philadelphia: 1838. V. 67

ANDRE, E. F.
Bromeliaceae Andreanae. Berkeley: 1983. V. 62

ANDRE, EUGENE
A Naturalist in the Guianas. London: 1904. V. 62

ANDRE, JOHN
Major Andre's Journal. Boston: 1903. V. 63

ANDRE, YVES MARIE
Essai sur la Beau. Paris: 1810. V. 67

ANDREAE, JOHANN LUDOVIC
Mathematische und Historische Beschreibung des Gantzen Welt-Gebaudes. Nuremberg: 1718. V. 66; 67

ANDREAE, JOHANN VALENTIN
The Fame and Confession of the Fraternity of R. C.: Commonly, of the Rosie Cross. London: 1652. V. 66

ANDREEV, LEONID
The Dark. 1922. V. 62

ANDRES Brun, Calligrapher of Saragossa. Some Account of His Life and Work by Henry Thomas and Stanley Morison. Verona: 1929. V. 65

ANDREW Marvell 1621-1678. Tercentenary Tributes. London: 1922. V. 62; 65

ANDREW, WILLIAM PATRICK
Our Scientific Frontier. London: 1880. V. 62

ANDREWES, LANCELOT
The Pattern of Catechistical Doctrine at Large; or a Learned and Pious Exposition of the Ten Commandments.... London: 1650. V. 66
Reverendi in Christo Patris, Lanceloti, Episocpi Wintoniensis, Opuscula Quaedam Posthuma. London: 1629. V. 67

ANDREWS, BESSIE AYARS
Reminiscences of Greenwich. Vineland: 1910. V. 66

ANDREWS, C. F.
Mahatma Gandhi: His Own Story. London: 1930. V. 63

ANDREWS, C. W.
Memoir of Mrs. Anne R. Page. Philadelphia: 1844. V. 65
A Monograph of Christmas Island (Indian Ocean), Physical Features and Geology, with Descriptions of the Fauna and Flora by Numerous Contributors. London: 1743. V. 63

ANDREWS, E. C.
Notes on the Limestones and General Geology of the Fiji Islands... Special Reference to the Lau Group. Cambridge: 1900. V. 67

ANDREWS, FRANK D.
A Bibliography of Vineland. Its Authors and Writers. Vineland: 1916. V. 66

ANDREWS, HERBERT C.
The Andrews Family in England and America 1219-1904. Los Angeles: 1904. V. 66

ANDREWS, J.
Flora's Gems; or the Treasures of the Parterre. 1830. V. 65; 66
The Florist, Fruitist and Garden Miscellany. 1860. London: 1860. V. 67
The Parterre; or Beauties of Flora. 1842. V. 65

ANDREWS, JAMES PETTIT
Anecdotes &c., Ancient and Modern, with Observations. Dublin: 1789. V. 63
History of Great Britain, from the Death of Henry VII to the Accession of James VI of Scotland to the Crown of England.... London: 1806. V. 66

ANDREWS, JEAN
Peppers: the Domesticated Capsicums. Austin: 1984. V. 67

ANDREWS, JOHN
Reflections on the Two Prevailing Spirit of Dissipation and Gallantry.... London: 1771. V. 65
Remarks on the French and English Ladies, in a Series of Letters.... London: 1783. V. 65

ANDREWS, JUAN
Sumario Breve d'la Practica de la Arithmetica & Todo el Curso de larte Mercantivol Bien Declardo; el Qual se llama Maestro de Cuento. Valencia: 1515. V. 63

ANDREWS, KENNETH R.
English Privateering Voyages to the West Indies 1588-1595. Cambridge: 1959. V. 63

ANDREWS, MATTHEW PAGE
Virginia: the Old Dominion. Garden City: 1937. V. 66
The Women of the South in War Times. Baltimore: 1923. V. 62; 63

ANDREWS, MILES PETER
Belphegor; or the Wishes. A Comic Opera As It Is Acted at the Theatre-Royal, Smoke-Alley. Dublin: 1788. V. 65

ANDREWS NELSON WHITEHEAD
Imported Handmade Papers from Andrews/Nelson/Whitehead: Yesterday's Craft for Today's Creations. N.P: 1986. V. 63

ANDREWS, R. C.
Ends of the Earth. 1929. V. 62; 63
Monographs of the Pacific Cetacea. New York: 1914-1916. V. 63

ANDREWS, R. W.
Redwood Classic. Seattle: 1952. V. 67

ANDREWS, RICHARD SNOWDEN
Richard Snowden Andrews Lieutenant-Colonel Commanding the First MarylAnd Artillery. Boston: 1887. V. 62
Richard Snowden Andrews Lieutenant-Colonel Commanding the First Maryland Artillery. Baltimore: 1910. V. 63

ANDREWS, STEPHEN PEARL
Discoveries in Chinese or the Symbolism of the Primtive Characters of the Chinese System of Writing, as a Contribution to Philology and Ethnology and a Practical Aid in the Acquisition of the Chinese Language. New York: 1854. V. 62; 64
The Science of Society - No. 1. The Constitution of Government in the Sovereignty of the Individual, as the Final Development of Protestantism, Democracy and Socialism. New York: 1851. V. 66
The Science of Society...No. 1. The Constitution of Government in the Sovereignty of the Individual as the Final Development of Protestantism, Democracy and Socialism. Boston: 1888. V. 66

ANDREWS, VAL
Sherlock Holmes and the Eminent Thespian. Romford, Essex: 1989. V. 67

ANDREWS, WAYNE
Architecture in America. London: 1960. V. 64

ANDREWS, WILLIAM
Bygone Lincolnshire. Hull: 1891. V. 62
Famous Frosts and Frost Fairs in Great Britain. London: 1887. V. 64
Historic Yorkshire. London: 1883. V. 65
North Country Poets, Poems and Biographies of Natives or Residents of Northumberland, Cumberland, Westmorland, Durham, Lancashire and Yorkshire. London: 1888-1889. V. 63

ANDREWS, WILLIAM EUSEBIUS
An Historical Narrative of the Horrid Plot and Conspiracy of Titus Oates, Called the Popish Plot.... London: 1816. V. 66

ANDREWS, WILLIAM LORING
Sextodecimos et Infra. New York: 1899. V. 63

ANDROUET DU CERCEAU, JACQUES
Le Premier (-Second) Volume des Plus Excellents Bastiments de France. Paris: 1576-1579. V. 64

ANDRY DE BOISREGARD, NICOLAS
An Account of the Breeding of Worms in Human Bodies; Their Nature and Several Sorts.... London: 1701. V. 62; 66

ANDUAGA Y GARIMBERTI, JOSE DE
Arto de Escribir por Reglas y sin Muestras, Establecido de Orden Superior en los Reales Sitios de San Ildefonso y Valsain.... Madrid: 1781. V. 65

ANDY Pandy's Nursery Rhymes. Sep. 1950. V. 65

ANECDOTES.. Harrisonburg: 1813. V. 65

ANECDOTES of a Croat; or, the Castle of Serai.... London: 1823. V. 64

ANESAKI, M.
Buddhist Art In Its Relation to Buddhist Ideals with Special Reference to Buddhism in Japan.... Boston: 1923. V. 62; 63; 64

ANGAS, GEORGE FRENCH
A Ramble in Malta and Sicily, in the Autumn of 1841. London: 1842. V. 64
Savage Life and Scenes in Australia and New Zealand. London: 1847. V. 62

ANGEL, MARIE
The Ark. New York: 1973. V. 62

ANGEL, MYRON
History of San Luis Obispo County, California with Illustrations and Biographical Sketches of Its Prominent Men and Pioneers. Berkeley: 1966. V. 64; 67

ANGELICA'S Ladies Library; or Parents and Guardians Present. London: 1794. V. 64

ANGELIS, ALEXANDER DE
In Astrologos Coniectores Libri Quinque. Leyden: 1621. V. 62

ANGELL, NORMAN
The Money Game: How to Play It. London and Toronto: 1928. V. 62

ANGELL, T.
Birds of Prey, on the Pacific Northwest Slope. Seattle: 1972. V. 67

ANGELO, DOMENICO
The School of Fencing, with a General Explanation of the Principle Attitudes and Positions Peculiar to the Art.... London: 1765. V. 63; 64

ANGELO, VALENTI
Valenti Angelo: Author, Illustrator and Printer. 1976. V. 62

ANGELOU, MAYA
All God's Children Need Traveling Shoes. Franklin Center: 1986. V. 62; 63; 65; 67
And Still I Rise. New York: 1978. V. 64; 66
Gather Together in My Name. New York: 1974. V. 62; 64
I Know Why the Caged Bird Sings. New York: 1969. V. 63; 67
Just Give Me a Cool Drink of Water 'Fore I Diiie. New York: 1971. V. 63; 65
Oh Pray My Wings Are Gonna Fit Me Well. New York: 1975. V. 64
On the Pulse of Morning. New York: 1993. V. 63; 65
Shaker, Why Don't You Sing: More Poems. New York: 1983. V. 64; 67
Singin' and Swingin' and Gettin' Merry Like Christmas. New York: 1976. V. 64; 65; 67

ANGIER, BRADFORD
The Best of Colonel Townsend Whelen. Clinton: 1983. V. 65

ANGIOLIERI, CECCO
If I Were Fire. Windhover: 1987. V. 66

L'ANGLETERRE en 1800. Cologne: 1801. V. 66

ANGLUND, JOAN WALSH
Love One Another. San Francisco: 1981. V. 64
Memories of the Heart. New York: 1984. V. 62

ANIMAL A B C. London: 1905. V. 66

AN ANIMAL ABC. New York: 1910. V. 62

ANIMAL Land. Where There are No People. London: 1897. V. 65

THE ANIMAL Picture Book for Kind Little People. London. V. 66; 67
THE ANIMAL Picture Book for Kind Little People. London: Sep. 1890. V. 65

THE ANIMATED Picture Book of Alice in Wonderland. New York: 1945. V. 66

ANKENY, NESMITH
The West As I Knew It. Lewiston: 1953. V. 64; 67

ANKER, J.
Bird Books and Bird Art. Copenhagen: 1938. V. 64

ANLEY, CHARLOTTE
Influence: a Moral Tale for Young People. London: 1822. V. 65

ANN and Her Eleven Sisters. London: 1860. V. 63

ANNABEL, RUSSELL
Alaskan Days, Mexican Nights. Clinton: 1987. V. 65
Tales of a Big Game Guide. New York: 1938. V. 63

ANNALS of Iowa. 1893-1903. V. 62

THE ANNALS of King George, Year the First: Containing Not Only the Affairs of Great Britian, but the General History of Europe During That Time. London: 1716. V. 65

ANNALS of Lloyd's Register Being a Sketch of the Origin, Constitution and Progress of Lloyd's Register of British and Foreign Shipping. London: 1884. V. 66

ANNALS of Medical History. New York: 1917-1942. V. 66

THE ANNALS of the Barber-Surgeons of London, Compiled from their Records and Other Sources by Sidney Young. London: 1890. V. 64

ANNALS of the Propagation of the Faith, a Periodical Collection of Letters from the Bishops and the Missionaries...in the Old and New World. Paris and London: 1838-1847. V. 63

ANNANDALE, N.
Report on the Fishes Taken by the Bengal Fisheries Steamer Golden Crown. Calcutta: 1909. V. 65
Zoological Results of a Tour in the Far East. Calcutta: 1916-1925. V. 63

ANNE of Brittany; an Historical Romance. London: 1810. V. 67

ANNENBERG, MAURICE
Type Foundries of America and Their Catalogs. Delaware: 1994. V. 67

ANNESLEY, GEORGE
Voyages and Travels to India, Ceylon, the Red Sea, Abyssinia and Egypt in the Years 1802, 1803, 1804, 1805 and 1806. London: 1809. V. 64

ANNIE Got Your Gun. London: 1940. V. 65

ANNIGONI, PIETRO
Spanish Sketchbook. London: 1957. V. 65

ANNIN, JIM
They Gazed the Beartooths. Billings: 1964. V. 66

ANONYMIANA; or, Ten Centuries of Observations on Various Authors and Subjects. London: 1809. V. 67

ANOUILH, JEAN
The Lark. New York: 1956. V. 64

ANSA, TINA MC ELROY
Ugly Ways. New York: 1993. V. 67

ANSELL, CHARLES
A Treatise on Friendly Societies, in Which the Doctrine of Interest of Money, and the Doctrine of Probability are Practically Applied to the Affairs of Such Societies.... London: 1835. V. 66

ANSELL, JOHN EVELYN
History of the Name 1086 to about 1600 Showing Descents from a Domesday Tenant-in-Chief. (with) History of the Name. Additional Volume Comprising the Other Counties in Which the Name is Found at an Early Period. London: 1929-1933. V. 62

ANSEN, ALLEN
William Burroughs. Sudbury: 1986. V. 67

ANSON, B. J.
Callander's Surgical Anatomy. Philadelphia: 1952. V. 66; 67

ANSORGE, W. J.
Under the African Sun; a Description of Native Races in Uganda Sporting Adventures and Other Experiences. London: 1899. V. 64

ANSPACH, FREDERICK R.
Sons of the Sires. Philadelphia: 1855. V. 63

ANSTED, D. T.
Geology, Introductory, Descriptive and Practical. 1844. V. 65; 67
The Ionian Islands in the Year 1863. London: 1863. V. 64
The Physical Geography and Geology of the County of Leicester. Westminster: 1866. V. 65
Scenery, Science and Art.... 1854. V. 66
Scenery, Science and Art.... London: 1854. V. 64
A Short Trip in Hungary and Transylvania in the Spring of 1862. London: 1862. V. 64; 65

ANSTER, JOHN
Faustus, a Dramatic Mystery; The Bride of Corinth, The First Wulpurgis Night. London: 1835. V. 67

ANSTEY, CHRISTOPHER
An Election Ball in Poetical Letters from Mr. Incle, at Bath, to His Wife at Glocester.... Bath: 1776. V. 65
The New Bath Guide. London: 1766. V. 66
The New Bath Guide. Bath: 1807. V. 66

ANSTEY, JOHN
The Pleaders Guide.... London: 1796-1802. V. 62

ANSTIE, FRANCIS EDMUND
Neuralgia and the Diseases that Resemble It. London: 1871. V. 65

ANSTIE, JOHN
The Coal Fields of Gloucestershire and Somersetshire and Their Resources. 1873. V. 65
A Letter Addressed to Edward Phelips, Containing General Observations on the Advantages of Manufacturing the Combing Wool of England, Which is Smuggled to France.... London: 1788. V. 65

AN ANSWER to Mr. B----w's Apology, as it Respects His King, His Country, His Conscience and His God. London: 1755. V. 65

ANTARCTICA. The Extraordinary History of Man's Conquest of the Frozen Continent. Sydney: 1998. V. 63

ANTHONY, GENE
The Summer of Love - Haight-Ashbury at Its Highest. Millbrae: 1980. V. 65

ANTHONY, GORDON
Ballerina - Further Studies of Margot Fonteyn. London: 1945. V. 65
Studies of Robert Helpmann. London: 1946. V. 65

ANTHONY, H. E.
The Indigenous Land Mammals of Porto Rico, Living and Extinct. New York: 1918. V. 63

ANTHONY, PIERS
Chthon. 1967. V. 64; 66
Omnivore. London: 1969. V. 63

ANTHONY, SUSAN B.
The History of Woman Suffrage. Volume IV. Rochester: 1902. V. 63

ANTI-ROMAN Pacquet; or, Memoirs of Popes and Popery.... London: 1680. V. 64

ANTIDOTUM Culmerianum; or, Animadversions Upon a Late Pamphlet, Entituled Cathedrall Newes from Canterbury &c. Oxford: 1644. V. 63

THE ANTIQUARIAN Itinerary, Comprising Specimens of Architecture, Monastic, Castelated and Domestic.... London: 1815-1818. V. 63

ANTIQUARIAN SOCIETY OF NEWCASTLE UPON TYNE
First Annual Report (being for the year 1813). Newcastle: 1814. V. 63; 65

ANTIQUITIES Africaines. Paris: 1967-1979. V. 62

ANTON, JOHN
American Precedents of Declarations. Boston: 1802. V. 66

ANTONIL, ANDRE JOAO
Cultura e Opulencia do Brazil, por Suas Drogas e Minas.... Rio de Janeiro: 1837. V. 62

ANTONINUS
(Prima Pars Summa Maioris). Venetiis: 1503. V. 66

ANTONINUS, AUGUSTUS
Antonini Iter Britanniarum Commentariis Illustatum Thomae Gale.... Londoni: 1719. V. 67
Antonini Iter Britanniarum. Commentariis Illustatum Thomae Gale.... London: 1709. V. 66

ANTONINUS, BROTHER
The Blowing of the Seed. New Haven: 1966. V. 62
The Crooked Lines of God: Poems 1949-1954. Detroit: 1959. V. 63
Eastward the Armies: Selected Poems 1935-1942. Torrance: 1980. V. 63; 64; 66
The Engendering Flood: Book One of Dust Shall Be the Serpent's Food (Cantos I-IV). Santa Rosa: 1990. V. 63; 64; 66
The High Embrace. N.P: 1986. V. 63; 64; 66
In Medias Res. Canto One of an Autobiographical Epic.... San Francisco: 1984. V. 62; 64
In the Fictive Wish. Berkeley: 1967. V. 63
The Last Crusade. N.P: 1969. V. 63
The Poet is Dead. A Memorial for Robinson Jeffers. San Francisco: 1964. V. 62
Ravaged with Joy: A Record of the Poetry Reading at the University of California, Davis, on May 16, 1975. Middletown: 1998. V. 66
Renegade Christmas. Northridge: 1984. V. 63; 64; 66
River-Root: a Syzygy for the Bicentennial of These States. Berkeley: 1976. V. 63; 64; 66
Robinson Jeffers: Framents of an Older Fury. Berkeley: 1968. V. 67
The Rose of Solitude. Garden City: 1967. V. 63
San Joaquin. Los Angeles: 1939. V. 64
Single Source. The Early Poems...1934-1940. Berkeley: 1966. V. 64
The Springtide of the Blade. Reno: 1968. V. 63
The Tarantella Rose: Six Poems by .... Santa Cruz: 1995. V. 63; 64; 66
Tendril in the Mesh. Aromas: 19743. V. 63
These Are the Ravens. San Leandro: 1935. V. 64; 67
Triptych for the Living. Oakland: 1951. V. 64; 66
War Elegies. Waldport: 1944. V. 62; 63; 64
Who Is She that Looketh Forth as the Morning. Santa Barbara: 1972. V. 63

ANTONINUS LIBERALIS
Transformationum Congeries. Abrahamus Berkelius Emendavit. Lugduni Batavorum (Leiden): 1674. V. 66

ANTONIUS D'MONELIA
Sursum corda Editu a R. P. F. Antonio d'Monelia.... Bologna: 1522. V. 63

ANTONUCIO, GIOVANNI BAPTISTA
Catechesis, Sev Instrvctio A RR. DD. Examinatoribus Promulgata, & Cunctis ad Confessiones Audiendas, Atq. Placentiae: 1574. V. 63

ANTONY, PAUL
Ian Fleming's Incredible Creation. Chicago: 1965. V. 67

AOYAGI, H.
The Damsel Fishes Found in the Waters of Japan. N.P: 1941. V. 65

APIANUS, PETRUS
La Cosmographia.... Antwerp: 1575. V. 62
Inscriptiones Sacrosanctae Vetustatis non Illae Quidem Romanae.... Ingolstadt: 1534. V. 62
Introductio Geographica...In Doctissimas Verneri Annotationes.... Ingolstadt: 1533. V. 65

APICIUS
Cookery and Dining in Imperial Rome. Chicago: 1936. V. 64

THE APOCRYPHA, According to the Authorized Version. London: 1929. V. 62

APOLLINAIRE, GUILLAUME
Tendre Comme le Souvenir. Paris: 1952. V. 66

APOLLONIO, V.
Marino Marini, Sculptor. Milan: 1953. V. 65

APOLLONIUS OF RHODES
Argonautica (in Greek), with the Scholia of Lucillus, Sophocles and Theon. Florence: 1496. V. 63
Argonauticon. Geneva: 1574. V. 65
Argonauticorum Libri Quatuor. Oxonii: 1777. V. 63; 66
(Greek title, then) Apollonii Rhodii Argonauticorum, Carmine Heroico. Basel: 1572. V. 63; 66

APOLLONIUS OF TYRE
Historia Apollonii Regis Tyri. Waltham St. Lawrence: 1956. V. 62; 63

APOLLONIUS PERGAEUS
Apollonii Pergaei Locorum Planorum Libri II. Glasguae: 1749. V. 65
The Two Books...Concerning Determinate Section as They Have Been Restored.... London: 1772. V. 62; 64

THE APOSTOLICAL Decree at Jerusalem Proved to Be Still in Force, Both from Scripture and Tradition. London: 1734. V. 63

APOSTOOL, CORNELIUS
The Beauties of the Dutch School; Selected from Interesting Pictures of Admired Landscape Painters. London: 1793. V. 64

AN APPEAL from the Protestant Associaton to the People of Great Britain; Concerning the Probable Tendency to the Late Act of Parliament in Favour of the Papists. London: 1779. V. 67

AN APPEAL to the People, Containing, the Genuine and Entire Letter of Admiral Byng to the Sec. of the Ad------y: Observations on Those Parts of Which Were Omitted by the Writers of the Gazette.... London: 1756. V. 65

APPELL, J. W.
The Dream of Poliphilus. 1893. V. 67

APPERLEY, CHARLES JAMES
The Life of a Sportsman. London: 1842. V. 64
The Life of a Sportsman. 1874. V. 62; 63; 64; 66

APPERLEY, CHARLES JAMES continued
The Life of a Sportsman. 1914. V. 62; 63
The Life of John Mytton, Esq. London: 1837. V. 67
Memoirs of the Life of the Late John Mytton. London: 1851. V. 64
Memoirs of the Life of the Late John Mytton. 1900. V. 62; 64
Nimrod's Hunting Tour in Scotland and the North of England. 1857. V. 62; 64
Nimrod's Hunting Tours.... London: 1926. V. 62; 67
Remarks on the Condition of Hunters, the Choice of Horses, and Their Management.... London: 1831. V. 67

APPERLEY, NEWTON WYNNE
North Country Hunting Half a Century Ago. Darlington: 1924. V. 67

APPERSON, G. L.
A Jane Austen Dictionary. 1932. V. 66

APPIANUS, OF ALEXANDRIA
Appiani Alexandrini Romanorum Historiarum (...) Ex Bibliotheca Regia (...) Lutetiae. Paris: 1551. V. 65; 66
De Civilibus Romanorum Bellis Historiarum Libri Quinque.... Paris: 1538. V. 64; 66
De Civilibus Romanorum Bellis Historiarum Libri Quinque.... Lugduni: 1560. V. 65; 66
Historia dele Guerre Esterne de Romani. In Vinetia: 1550. V. 62
Romanarum Historiarum Lib. XII. Nunc Postremo Accessere Eiusdem Appiani Annibalica ex Francisci Beraldi Interpretatione. Lugduni: 1588. V. 66

APPIGNANESI, RICHARD
Italia Perversa. London: 1985-1986. V. 63

APPLAUSI
Poetici Nel Prender l'Abito Religioso nel Venerabil Monastero di San Niccolo di Firenzo l'Illustrissima Signora Anna Maria Ginori col Nome di Donna Anna Fedele.... Florence: 1745. V. 65

APPLE, MAX
The Oranging of America and Other Stories. New York: 1976. V. 63; 64; 66

APPLEGATE, FRANK G.
Native Tales of New Mexico. Philadelphia: 1932. V. 66

APPLEGATE, JESSE
A Day with the Cow Column in 1843. Chicago: 1934. V. 62; 66
A Day with the Cow Column in 1843. Portland: 1952. V. 63; 66

APPLEGATE, JOHN STILLWELL
Early Courts and Lawyers of Monmouth County, Beginning at Its First Settlement, and Down to the Last Half Century. Freehold: 1911. V. 63
Reminiscences and Letters of George Arrowsmith of New Jersey, Late Lieutenant-Colonel...New York State Volunteers. Red Bank: 1893. V. 63; 66

APPLETON, D., & CO.
Appleton's Hand-Book of American Travel. Northern and Eastern Tour. New York: 1876. V. 62
Appleton's Hand-Book of American Travel. Southern Tour. New York: 1876. V. 62

APPLETON, LE ROY H.
Indian Art of the Americas. New York: 1950. V. 64; 67

APPLETON'S Cyclopaedia of Applied Mechanics.... New York: 1881. V. 62

APPLETON'S General Guide to the United States and Canada. Part II Western and Southern States. New York: 1879. V. 62; 65

APPLETON'S General Guide to the United States and Canada Part I and Part II. New York: 1894. V. 64

APPLETON'S Handbook to the United States and Canada, with Railway Maps, Plans of Cities and Illustrations. Edinburgh: 1879. V. 65

APPLIN, ARTHUR
Philandering Angler. London: 1943. V. 67

APPONYI, H.
My Big Game Hunting Diary. 1937. V. 62; 67

APULEIUS
Appuleii Metamorphoseon Libri XI. Leiden: 1786. V. 67
Apuleius Madaurensis Platonicus, Serio Castigatus Ex Museo Pet: Scriveri. (Metamorphoseon). Amsterdam: 1624. V. 62
Cupid and Psyche. London: 1923. V. 62; 64; 65
De Cupidinis et Psyches Amoribus Fabula Ainlis. London and New York: 1901. V. 62; 67
The XI Bookes of the Golden Asse.... 1924. V. 67
The XI Bookes of the Golden Asse.... Chelsea: 1924. V. 63; 64; 65
The Golden Ass. London: 1923. V. 65
The Golden Ass. London: 1924. V. 63
The Golden Ass. 1951. V. 64
L. Apveiii Madavrensis Philosophi Platonici Metamorphoseos, Sive De Asino Aireo. Parisiis: 1536. V. 63
The Most Pleasant and Delectable Tale of the Marriage of Cupid and Psyche. London: 1887. V. 63
The Transformations of Lucius, Otherwise Known as The Golden Ass. Harmondsworth: 1950. V. 62

THE AQUARIUM. 1932-1971. V. 65

ARABIAN NIGHTS
The Adventures of Hunch-Back, and the Stories Connected With It, From the Arabian Nights Entertainment. London: 1814. V. 63
Aladdin and His Wonderful Lamp in Rhyme. London: 1919. V. 64
The Arabian Nights. London: 1811. V. 62
The Arabian Nights. 1838. V. 65
The Arabian Nights. Chicago: 1914. V. 62
The Arabian Nights. London: 1924. V. 65; 67
The Arabian Nights. New York: 1925. V. 62; 67
Arabian Tales. Edinburgh: 1792. V. 63
The Child's Arabian Nights. London: 1904. V. 63
Le Livre Des Mille Nuits et Une Nuit. Paris: 1908-1912. V. 65; 67
The Seven Voyages of Sinbad the Sailor. Park Ridge: 1939. V. 64
Sinbad Le Marin. (Sinbad the Sailor). Paris: 1919. V. 62; 67
Sinbad the Sailor and Other Stories from the Arabian Nights. London: 1914. V. 62; 66
Stories from the Arabian Nights. London: 1907. V. 64
Stories from the Arabian Nights. New York: 1907. V. 62
The Thousand and One Nights, Commonly Called, in England the Arabian Nights' Entertainments. London: 1839-1841. V. 63

ARAGO, DOMINIQUE FRANCOIS JEAN
Historical Eloge of James Watt. London: 1839. V. 65
Popular Astronomy. London: 1855. V. 65

ARAGON, LOUIS
Le Creve-Coeur. 1942. V. 64
Feu de Joie. Paris: 1920. V. 64; 67
Henri Matisse: a Novel. New York: 1971. V. 66

ARAGONA, TULLIA D'
Dialogo Della Infinita di Amore. Vinegia: 1547. V. 66

ARAKI, NOBUYOSHI
Tokyo Lucky Hole. Tokyo: 1990. V. 66

ARAM, EUGENE
Trial of Eugene Aram, for the Murder of Daniel Clark.... London: 1820. V. 64; 65
The Trial of Eugene Aram, for the Murder of Daniel Clark.... 1832. V. 63

ARAMATA, H.
Atlas Anima 2: Fish. Tokyo: 1989. V. 65

ARATUS
Arati Solensis Apparentia. Florentiae: 1765. V. 65
H. Grotii Syntagma Arateorum: Opus Poeticae et Astronomiae Studiosis Utilissimum.... Leiden: 1600. V. 62; 63

ARBECAM, H. PEYTON
The Lowry-Bowyer Telemeter, or Distance Finder: Rules with Illustrations and Examples. Boston: 1896. V. 66

ARBER, AGNES
The Gramineae, a Study of Cereal, Bamboo and Grass. Cambridge: 1934. V. 63
Herbals Their Origin and Evolution. Cambridge: 1912. V. 64; 67
Herbals, Their Origin and Evolution. Cambridge: 1938. V. 62; 63; 66
Herbals. Their Origin and Evolution. Cambridge: 1953. V. 66
Herbals: Their Origin and Evolution, A Chapter in the History of Botany 1470-1670. London, New York, New Rochelle: 1953. V. 64

ARBER, EDWARD
The Term Catalogues 1688-1709 A.D. with a Number for Easter Term, 1711 A.D. London: 1903-1906. V. 62; 63

ARBLAY, FRANCES BURNEY D'
Brief Reflections Relative to the Emigrant French Clergy.... London: 1793. V. 65
Camilla; or, a Picture of Youth. London: 1796. V. 62; 63; 64; 65
Camilla, or a Picture of Youth. London: 1802. V. 63; 66
Cecilia, or Memoirs of an Heiress. London: 1782. V. 63; 64
Cecilia, or Memoirs of an Heiress. London: 1783. V. 64
Cecilia, or Memoirs of an Heiress. London: 1784. V. 63
Cecilia, or Memoirs of an Heiress. London: 1786. V. 64
Cecilia, or, Memoirs of an Heiress. London: 1825. V. 66
Evelina. London: 1779. V. 63
Evelina. London: 1784. V. 65; 66
Evelina. London: 1793. V. 65
Evelina. London: 1794. V. 62
Evelina. New York: 1797. V. 63
Evelina. London: 1825?. V. 66
Evelina. London: 1893. V. 63
Memoirs of an Heiress. London. V. 63
The Wanderer; or, Female Difficulties. London: 1814. V. 65

ARBUTHNOT, JAMES
Natural History of Those Fishes that are Indigenous to, or Occasionally Frequent the Coasts of Buchan.... Aerdeen: 1815. V. 63

ARBUTHNOT, JOHN
An Essay Concerning the Nature of Ailments, and the Choice of Them, According to the Different Constitutions of Human Bodies. London: 1731. V. 64
An Essay Concerning the Nature of Ailments, and the Choice of Them, According to the Different Constitutions of Human Bodies. London: 1735. V. 64
An Essay Concerning the Nature of Ailments and the Choice of Them, According to the Different Constitutions of Human Bodies.... London: 1756. V. 65
An Essay on the Effects of Air on Human Bodies. London: 1751. V. 64
An Inquiry into the Connection Between the Present Price of Provisions and the Size of Farms. London: 1773. V. 67
Tables of Ancient Coins, Weights and Measures. London: 1727. V. 62; 66; 67
Tables of the Grecian, Roman and Jewish Measures, Weights and Coins.... London: 1707?. V. 63

ARCE, MANUEL MAPLES
Poemes Interdits. Bruxelles: 1936. V. 67

ARCH, JOSEPH
Joseph Arch; the Story of His Life.... London: 1898. V. 64

ARCHBOLD, JOHN T.
Archbold's Summary of the Law Relating to Pleading and Evidence in Criminal Cases. New York: 1846. V. 67

ARCHDALE, JOHN
A New Description of that Fertile and Pleasant Province of Carolina...(with) Notices of the Early History of South Carolina. Charleston: 1822. V. 66

ARCHDEACON, PETER
A Sketch of the Passaic Falls of Paterson, N.J. New York: 1845. V. 63

ARCHER, G.
The Birds of British Somaliland and the Gulf of Aden, Their Life Histories, Breeding, Habits and Eggs. London: 1937-1961. V. 67
The Birds of Somaliland and the Gulf of Aden. 1937-1961. V. 65

ARCHER, JAMES
Sermons on Various Moral and Religious Subjects, for all the Sundays and Some of the Principal Festivals of the Year. (with) Sermons on Various Moral and Religious Subjects, for Some of the Principal Festivals of the Year. London: 1785-1789. V. 62

ARCHER, JEAN C.
The Flap-Jack. London: 1904. V. 65

ARCHER, JEFFREY
Not a Penny More, Not a Penny Less. London: 1976. V. 65
Shall We Tell the President. London: 1977. V. 63

ARCHER, JOHN WYKEHAM
Vestiges of Old London. London: 1851. V. 66

ARCHER, M.
Carnivorous Marsupials. Sydney: 1982. V. 63
Vertebrate Zoogeography and Evolution in Australia (Animals in Space and Time). Victoria Park: 1984. V. 66

ARCHER, ROBERT
The Case of the Vanishing Women. New York: 1942. V. 65; 66

ARCHER, THOMAS
Charles Dickens. A Gossip About His Life Works and Characters.... London. V. 64
Charles Dickens: a Gossip About His Life, Works and Characters.... London: 1894?. V. 62
William Ewart Gladstone and His Contemporaries: Fifty Years of Social and Political Progress. London: 1883. V. 64

ARCHER, W. G.
Indian Miniatures. Greenwich: 1960. V. 62; 63; 64

ARCHER, WILLIAM
Play-Making: a Manual of Craftsmanship. London: 1912. V. 66

ARCHEY, G.
The Moa, a Study of the Dinornithiformes. Auckland: 1941. V. 64

ARCHIBALD, W. F. A.
The Metropolitan Police Guide, Being a Compendium of the Civil and Criminal Law Affecting or Relating to the Metropolitan Police. London: 1895. V. 63

ARCHILOCHOS
Carmina Archilochi. Berkeley and Los Angeles: 1964. V. 62; 63

ARCHIMEDES
De iis Quae Vehuntur in Aqua Libri Duo a Federico Commandino in Pristinum Nitorem Restituti, et Commentariis Illustrati. Bologna: 1565. V. 67

THE ARCHITECTURAL Orders. Providence: 1990. V. 62

THE ARCHITECTURAL Work of Graham Anderson Probst and White, Chicago, and Their Predecessors, D. H. Burnham and Co. and Graham Burnham & Co. London: 1933. V. 64

ARCHITECTURE of Allen and Young. Stockton: 1928. V. 65

ARCOS, RENE
Das Gemeinsame. Leipzig: 1927?. V. 64

ARCTIC INSTITUTE OF NORTH AMERICA
Arctic Bibliography. Washington: 1953. V. 65; 66
Arctic Bibliography. Washington: 1954. V. 64
Arctic Bibliography. Volume 5. Washington: 1955. V. 63; 64; 66
Arctic Bibliography. Volume 7. Washington: 1957. V. 63; 64; 66
Arctic Bibliography. Volume 8. Washington: 1959. V. 64; 66

ARDENE, JEAN PAUL DE ROME D'
Traite des Renoucules, Dans Lequel Outre ce Qui Concerne ces Fleurs, on Trouvera.... Paris: 1746. V. 64

ARDIZZONE, EDWARD
Johnny's Bad Day. London: 1970. V. 63
Paul - the Hero of the Fire. London: 1962. V. 63
Peter the Wanderer. London: 1963. V. 62
Tim and Ginger. London: 1965. V. 66
Tim and Lucy Go to Sea. London: 1938. V. 63

ARDIZZONE, NICHOLAS
Edward Ardizzone's World. The Etchings and Lithographs. London: 2000. V. 67

ARDLEY, PATRICIA B.
Mr. and Mrs. Hedgehog. London: 1936. V. 66

ARENAS, REYNALDO
Celestino Antes del Alba. Havana: 1967. V. 67

ARENSBERG, CONRAD M.
Family and Community in Ireland. 1940. V. 64; 67

ARENTZ, FRIEDRICH CHRISTIAN HOLBERG
Beschreibung der Astronomischen Uhr, Welcher von Heern Nicolaus Alexius Johann.... Mainz: 1829. V. 63

ARETINO, PIETRO
Il Sofista Comedia Bellissima del Sig. Lvigi Tansillo. (with) Il Cavallarizzo. Vicenza: 1601. V. 65

AREY, RICHARD FRED
Waterfalls of the Mississippi. Saint Paul: 1998. V. 62

ARGENS, JEAN BAPTISTE DE BOYER, MARQUIS D'
The Jewish Spy; Being a Philsophical, Historical and Critical Correspondence by Letters, which Lately Passed Between Certain Jews.... London: 1766-1765. V. 65
Lettres Juives ou Correspondence Philosophique, Historique, & Critique.... La Haye: 1742. V. 67
Memoirs of the Count du Beauval, Including Some Curious Particulars Relating to the Dukes of Wharton and Ormond, During Their Exiles. London: 1754. V. 66

ARGUEDAS, JOSE MARIA
Agua. Lima: 1935. V. 67

ARGUS, ARABELLA, PSEUD.
The Juvenile Spectator.... London: 1810. V. 67

ARGUS, G. W.
Atlas of the Rare Vascular Plants of Ontario/Atlas des Plantes Vasculaires Rares de l'Ontario. Ottawa: 1982-1987. V. 65; 67

ARGUS, M. K.
Moscow on the Hudson. New York: 1951. V. 67

ARGYLE, HARVEY
As I Saw It. San Francisco: 1902. V. 63; 66

ARGYLL, GEORGE DOUGLAS CAMPBELL, 8TH DUKE OF
The Unseen Foundations of Society; an Examination of the Fallacies and Failures of Economic Science.... London: 1893. V. 64

ARIAS, RON
The Road to Tamazunchale. Reno: 1975. V. 62

ARIETI, SILVANO
American Handbook of Psychiatry.... New York: 1974-1981. V. 65

ARIKHA.. London: 1985. V. 62

ARIOSTO, LODOVICO
Delle Satire e Rime...Libri Due. Londra: 1716. V. 67
Orlando Furioso. Venice: 1548. V. 64
Orlando Furioso. London: 1757. V. 64
Orlando Furioso. Birmingham: 1773. V. 62
Orlando Furioso. London: 1785. V. 66

ARISTOPHANES
Aristophanis Comoediae Undecim, Graece & Latine...Emendationibus... Josephis Scaligeri. Lugduni Batavorum: 1624. V. 65; 66
Aristophanis Comoediae Undecim, Graece et Latine.... Amstelaedami: 1670. V. 65
Aristophanis Comoediae Undecim, Graece et Latine.... Amstelodami: 1710. V. 65
Aristophanis Comoediae Undecim. Graece et Latine.... Lugduni Batavorum: 1760. V. 65
Aristophanis Facetissimi Comoediae Undecim.... 1542. V. 66
Lysistrata. Wien: 1913. V. 64
Lysistrata. London: 1926. V. 67
Lysistrata. New York: 1934. V. 65; 66; 67
The Lysistrata. New York: 1967. V. 64
A Metrical Version of the Acharnians The Knights and The Birds.... London: 1840. V. 62; 63
Women in Parliament. London: 1929. V. 63

ARISTOTELES
Aristotelis De Poetica Liber. Oxonii: 1794. V. 66
Aristotle's Treatise on Poetry. London: 1789. V. 66
Aristotle's Compleat Master Piece, in Three Parts. London: 1749. V. 64; 66; 67
Aristotle's Compleat Master Piece, in Three Parts. London: 1763. V. 66; 67
Compleat Masterpiece in Three Parts...(with) Aristotle's Complete and Experienced Midwife in Two Parts... Aristotle' Book of Problems, With Other Astronomers, Astrologers, Physicians and Philosophers...(with) Aristotle's Last Legacy.... London: 1788. V. 65
De Poetica Liber. Edinburgi: 1731. V. 65
In Hoc Volumine...De Historia Animalium. Libri Ix De Partibus Animalium & Earum Causis. Libri III: De Generatione Animalium. Libri V. De Communi Animalium, Gressu, Liber I. De Communi Animalium Motu Libri I. Parisiis: 1553. V. 62; 63
Meteorologicorum Libri Quatuor. Lyon: 1546. V. 64; 66
Opera, Quae Extant Omnia Brevi Paraphrasi.... Romae: 1668. V. 65
Politics and Poetics. Lunenburg: 1964. V. 65
La Rhetorique d'Aristote en Francois. Lyon: 1691. V. 64
Totius Naturalis Philosophiae. Freiburg: 1540. V. 66
The Works of Aristotle, Complete in Four Parts. London: 1772. V. 64

ARIZONA. GOVERNOR - 1886
Report of the Governor of Arizona. Washington: 1886. V. 63

THE ARK Alphabet. New York: 1880. V. 64

ARKEL and the Princess Sakata. London: 1903. V. 64

ARKELL, W. J.
Jurassic Geology of the World. 1956. V. 63
The Jurassic Geology of the World. Edinburgh: 1956. V. 65; 67
Jurassic System in Great Britain. Oxford: 1970. V. 67
A Monograph of British Corallian Lamellibanchla. 1927-1937. V. 63; 66

ARKWRIGHT, JOHN S.
The Supreme Sacrifice and Other Poems in Time of War. London: 1919. V. 62

ARKWRIGHT, WILLIAM
The Pointer and His Predecessors. An Illustrated History of the Pointing Dog from the Earliest Times. 1902. V. 67
Utinam: a Glimmering of Goddesses. London: 1917. V. 67

ARLEN, MICHAEL
Men Dislike Women - A Romance. London: 1931. V. 64

ARLINGTON, L. C.
The Chinese Drama. Shanghai: 1930. V. 66

ARMAN, MARK
Letterpress Printers' Types and Decorations. Thaxted: 1993. V. 66

ARMENINI, GIOVANNI BATTISTA
De Veri Precetti Della Pittura Libri Tre.... Ravenna: 1587. V. 64

ARMES, ETHEL
Stratford Hall, the Great House of the Lees. Richmond: 1936. V. 64

ARMFIELD, MAXWELL
An Artist in America. London: 1925. V. 62; 65
Homage to Masters. London: 1947. V. 62

ARMISTEAD, J. J.
An Angler's Paradise and How to Obtain It. London: 1895. V. 67

ARMISTEAD, WILSON H.
Trout Waters. London: 1908. V. 67

ARMITAGE, ALBERT B.
Cadet to Commodore. London: 1925. V. 64
Two Years in the Antarctic, Being a Narrative of the British National Antarctic Expedition. London: 1905. V. 63

ARMITAGE, C. M.
A Bibliography of the Works of Louis MacNeice. Edmonton: 1973. V. 63; 67

ARMITAGE, CHARLES H.
Grover Cleveland as Buffalo Knew Him. Buffalo: 1926. V. 67

ARMITAGE, ETHEL
A Country Garden. London: 1936. V. 62

ARMITAGE, EVELYN N.
The Quaker Poets of Great Britain and Ireland. London: 1896. V. 65

ARMITAGE, FLORA
The Desert and the Stars: a Biography of Lawrence of Arabia. New York: 1955. V. 67

ARMITAGE, MERLE
Pagans, Conquistadores, Heroes and Martyrs. Fresno: 1960. V. 66
Rockwell Kent. New York: 1932. V. 64
Warren Newcombe. New York: 1932. V. 63

ARMITAGE, ROBERT
Doctor Johnson: His Religious Life and Death. London: 1850. V. 65

ARMITAGE, THOMAS RHODES
The Education and Employment of the Blind: What It Has Been, Is and Ought to Be. London: 1886. V. 62; 65

ARMITT, MARY L.
Rydal. Kendal: 1916. V. 65
Studies of Lakeland Birds. Second Series. Ambleside: 1901. V. 65

ARMOUR, ALEXANDER WILLIAM
Notables and Autographs. New York: 1939. V. 64

ARMOUR, J. OGDEN
The Packers. The Private Car Line and the People. Philadelphia: 1906. V. 64; 67

ARMS, DOROTHY NOYES
Churches of France. New York: 1929. V. 64; 65
Hill Towns and Cities of Northern Italy. New York: 1932. V. 62; 63; 64

ARMSTRONG, DAVID
Report of the Trial by Jury, David Armstrong, Against George Buchan Vair, and Gideon Alston, for Sending a Challenge to Fight a Duel. Edinburgh: 1823. V. 63

ARMSTRONG, E. S.
The History of the Melanesian Mission. London: 1900. V. 64

ARMSTRONG, HARRY G.
Principles and Practice of Aviation Medicine. Baltimore: 1941. V. 63; 65
Principles and Practice of Aviation Medicine. Baltimore: 1952. V. 63; 65

ARMSTRONG, JAMES
Carolina Light Infantry's Record in the Great War: The Story of a Gallant Company.... Charleston: 1912. V. 65
Notes on Some Birds Collected in the Eastern or Rangoon District of the Irrawaddy Delta. Calcutta: 1880. V. 67

ARMSTRONG, JOHN
The Art of Preserving Health: a Poem. London: 1744. V. 66
The Art of Preserving Health: a Poem. (with) *The Oeconomy of Love.* London: 1754. V. 66
Miscellanies. London: 1770. V. 64
Oeconomy of Love; Art of Preserving Health; Marriage; Benevolence; Taste; Day; Sketches. London: 1766. V. 64
Practical Illustrations of Typhus Fever of the Common Continued Fever and of Inflammatory Diseases. Philadelphia: 1821. V. 67

ARMSTRONG, LE ROY
Pictorial Atlas Illustrating the Spanish American War. New York: 1898. V. 67

ARMSTRONG, LOUIS
Satchmo: My Life in New Orelans. New York: 1954. V. 63
Satchmo: My Life in New Orleans. Englewood Cliffs: 1954. V. 63

ARMSTRONG, MARTIN
Desert: a Legend. New York: 1926. V. 65

ARMSTRONG, N.
After Big Game in the Upper Yukon. 1937. V. 62
After Big Game in the Upper Yukon. 1995. V. 62; 64; 67
Yukon Yesterdays. 1936. V. 62; 64

ARMSTRONG, NELSON
Nuggets of Experience Narratives of the Sixties and Other Days with Graphic Descriptions of Thrilling Personal Adventures. San Bernardino: 1906. V. 65; 67

ARMSTRONG, ROBERT D.
Nevada Printing History, A Bibliography of Imprints and Publications 1858-1880. (with) *A Bibliography of Imprints and Publications 1881-1890.* Reno: 1981-1991. V. 62

ARMSTRONG, W. E.
Saving and Investment. The Theory of Capital in a Developing Community. London: 1936. V. 65

ARMSTRONG, WALTER
Sir Henry Raeburn. London: 1901. V. 62

ARMSTRONG WHITWORTH & CO.
Armstrong Whitworth Ships. Newcastle-upon-Tyne: 1932. V. 62

THE ARMY'S Plea for Their Present Practice: Tendered to the Consideration of All Ingenious and Impartial Men. London: 1659. V. 66

ARMYTAGE, GEORGE J.
Pedigrees Made at the Visitation of Cheshire, 1613.... 1909. V. 63

ARNALL, PHILIP
Portrait of an Airman. London: 1931. V. 64

ARNAULD, ANTOINE
Logic; or, the Art of Thinking; in Which Besides the Common, are Contain'd Many Excellent New Rules.... London: 1685. V. 62, 67
La Logique ou L'Art de Penser.... Amsterdam: 1675. V. 66

ARNAULT DE NOBLEVILLE, LOUIS DANIEL
Les Manuel des Dames De Charite, or Formules de Medicamens Faciles Aprcparcr, Dresses en Faveur Personnes Charitables, qui Distribuent des remedes aux Pauvres dans les villes & dans les Campagnes.... Paris: 1765. V. 64; 65

ARNDT, JOHANN
Des Hocherleuchteten Lehrers...Sechs Bucher Von Wahren Christenthum. Allentown: 1834. V. 64

ARNDT, JOHN STOVER
The Story of the Arndts. The Life Antecedents and Descendants of Bernhard Arndt Who Emigrated to Pennsylvania in the Year 1731. Philadelphia: 1922. V. 63; 66

ARNETT, R. H.
Beetles of the U. S. A Manual for Identification. Washington: 1960. V. 64

ARNIM, IOANNES
Stoicorum Veterum Fragmenta.... Stutgardiae: 1964. V. 65

ARNOLD, A. C. L.
The Living World. Boston: 1868. V. 66; 67

ARNOLD, ARTHUR
Through Persia by Caravan. London: 1877. V. 64

ARNOLD, B. W.
Jamaican Fossil Echini. Cambridge: 1927. V. 63; 64; 66

ARNOLD, C. D.
Official Views of the World's Columbian Exposition Issued by the Deparment of Photography. N.P: 1893. V. 63

ARNOLD, CHANNING
The American Egypt; a Record of Travel in Yucatan. London: 1909. V. 64

ARNOLD, E. C.
Bird Reserves. 1940. V. 67
British Waders. 1924. V. 63; 66

ARNOLD, EDWIN
Japonica. New York: 1892. V. 65
The Light of Asia. Philadelphia: 1932. V. 62; 63
The Light of Asia. Avon: 1976. V. 63; 64

ARNOLD, FRIEDRICH
Icones Nervorum Capitis. Heidelbergae: 1860. V. 65

ARNOLD, GOTTFRIED
A Biographical Sketch of the Life of Taulerus, a Popular Preacher of the Fourteenth Century. Richmond: 1836. V. 62

ARNOLD, H. H.
Global Mission. New York: 1949. V. 67
Winged Warfare. New York: 1941. V. 63

ARNOLD, JAMES N.
The History of the Church Family. Providence: 1887. V. 62

ARNOLD, M. E.
The Painted Window. London: 1856. V. 65

ARNOLD, MATTHEW
Culture and Anarchy: an Essay in Political and Social Criticism. London: 1869. V. 63
A French Eton; or, Middle Class Education and the State. London: 1864. V. 65
The Letters of Matthew Arnold (1866-1878). Chicago: 1998. V. 67
Merope. London: 1858. V. 64; 65
Mixed Essays. London: 1879. V. 67
Notebooks. London: 1902. V. 64
Poems. London: 1857. V. 67
Reports on Elementary Schools 1852-1882. London: 1889. V. 66
The Strayed Reveller and Other Poems. London: 1849. V. 62; 65

ARNOLD, OREN
Hot Irons. Heraldry of the Range. New York: 1940. V. 65

ARNOLD, R. ROSS
Indian Wars of Idaho. Caldwell: 1932. V. 65; 67

ARNOLD, ROBERT
The Dismal Swamp and Lake Drummond, Early Recollections. Norfolk: 1888. V. 66

ARNOLD, ROBERT ARTHUR
The History of the Cotton Famine, from the Fall of Sumter to the Passing of the Public Works Act. London: 1864. V. 63

ARNOLD, SAMUEL BLAND
Defence and Prison Experiences of a Lincoln Conspirator. Hattiesburg: 1943. V. 65

ARNOLD, THOMAS
History of Rome. London: 1838-1843. V. 66
Introductory Lectures on Modern History.... London: 1843. V. 67

ARNOLD, THOMAS JACKSON
Early Life and Letters of Thomas J. Jackson. New York: 1916. V. 62; 63; 65

ARNOLD, WILLIAM DELAFIELD
Oakfield; or Fellowship in the East. London: 1854. V. 65

ARNOLD, WILLIAM HARRIS
Catalogue of the William Harris Arnold Collection of Manuscripts, Books and Autograph Letters. To Be Sold by Order of Gertrude Weld Arnold. New York: 1924. V. 64
First Report of a Book Collector: Comprising: A Brief Answer to the Frequent Question Why First Editions?. Jamaica: 1897-1898. V. 63
A Record of Books and Letters.... Jamaica: 1901. V. 63

ARNOLD, WILLIAM M.
William M. Arnold & Co.'s Patent, Metallic, Indestructible and Air- Exhausted Coffin. New York: 1850. V. 67

ARNOT, WILLIAM
Life of James Hamilton. New York: 1870. V. 67

ARNOTT, SAMUEL
The Column Called the Monument, Described, Erected to Perpetuate the Dreadful Fire of London in the Year 1666. London: 1805. V. 67

ARNOULT, GUILLAUME
Dissertation en Forme de Lettre, sur L'Effet des Topiques dans les Maladies Internes, En Particulier sur Celui de M. Arnoult Contre L'Apolexie.... Paris: 1769. V. 63; 65

ARNY, W. F. M.
Indian Agent in New Mexico: The Journal of Special Agent W. F. M. Arny, 1870. Santa Fe: 1967. V. 64

ARON, PIETRO
Compendiolo di Molti Dvbbi, Segreti et Sentenze Intorno al Canto Fermo, et Figvrato.... Milan: 1545-1550. V. 62

ARP, JEAN
Dreams and Projects. New York: 1952. V. 64
On My Way - Poetry and Essays 1912-1947. New York: 1948. V. 64

ARREDONDO, ANTONIO DE
Arredondo's Historical Proof of Spain's Title to Georgia. Berkeley: 1925. V. 66

ARREOLA, JUAN JOSE
Confabulario. Mexico City: 1952. V. 67

ARROWSMITH, REX
Mines of the Old Southwest: Early Reports on the Mines of New Mexico and Arizona by the Explorers, Abert, Aubry, Browne, Cozzens, Emory, Mowry, Pattie, Whipple, Wislizenus and Others. Santa Fe: 1963. V. 64

ARSENI, EROLE
Walt Disney Magic Moments. Milan: 1973. V. 66

ARSENIEV, V. K.
Dersu, the Trapper. Exploring, Trapping, Hunting in Ussuria. New York: 1941. V. 66

ARSTEIN, HELEN
In Person Lena Horne. New York: 1950. V. 65

ART de Confectionner les Fleurs Artificielles. Paris: 1880. V. 66

ART De La Verrerie. Paris: 1752. V. 63; 66

ART in America: a Survey of American Art With Special Reference to California Painting, Sculpture and Architecture Past and Present Particularly as Those Arts Were Represented at the Panama Pacific International Exposition. Irvine: 1988. V. 62

ART in California: a Survey of American Art with Special Reference to Californian Painting, Sculpture and Architecture Past and Present.... Irvine: 1988. V. 63

ART of Confectionery. Boston: 1866. V. 67

THE ART of Courtship; or, the School of Love. London: 1770?. V. 64

THE ART of Drawing and Painting in Water-Colours. London: 1731. V. 64

THE ART of Drawing in Perspective...and a Mechanical Method of Perspective and Designing.... London: 1809. V. 67

THE ART of Dress; or, Guide to the Toilette: with Directions for Adapting the Various Parts of the Female Costume to the Complexion and Figure: Hints on Cosmetics, etc. London: 1839. V. 62

THE ART of Rigging: 1818. Brighton: 1818. V. 62

L'ART: Revue Hebdomadaire Illustree. Paris: 1879. V. 65

ART Work of Brooklyn, New York. Chicago: 1896. V. 66

ART WORKERS' GUILD
Sketches Made on the Lithograph Night 14th April 1905 by Members of the Art Workers Guild, Clifford's Inn Hall, Published for the Benefit of the Chest. London: 1905. V. 63; 66

ARTARIA, F.
Il Duomo di Milano Ossia Descrizione Storico-Critica di Questo Insigne Tempio e Degli Oggetti d'Arte che lo Adornano.... Milan: 1823. V. 64

ARTAUD, ANTONIN
Tric Trac du Ciel. Paris: 1923. V. 67

THE ARTE of Angling 1577. Princeton: 1958. V. 67

ARTEDI, PETRI
Ichthyologia. Lugduni Batavorum: 1738. V. 65
Ichthyologia. Weineheim: 1962. V. 63

ARTHAUD, C.
Enchanted Visions: Fantastic Houses and Their Treasures. New York: 1972. V. 62; 65
Homes of the Great. Paris: 1967. V. 62; 65

ARTHUR, ELIZABETH
Thunder Bay District. 1821-1892. A Collection of Documents. Toronto: 1973. V. 66

ARTHUR, GEORGE C.
A True History of Bill Wilson, Bushwacker - a Story of Missouri's Most Famous Desperado. Rolla: 1938. V. 62

ARTHUR, GRIFFITH
Michael Collins. Dublin: 1922?. V. 66

ARTHUR H. CLARK CO.
A Catalogue of Rare and Choice Books. Catalogs 1-12. Cleveland: 1906. V. 63

ARTHUR, JOHN PRESTON
Western North Carolina. Asheville: 1914. V. 63

ARTHUR, STANLEY CLISBY
The Story of the West Florida Rebellion. St. Francisville: 1935. V. 66

ARTHUR, TIMOTHY SHAY
Anna Lee. The Maid. The Wife. The Mother. A Tale. London: 1853. V. 67
Six Nights with the Washingtonians: a Series of Original Temperance Tales. Philadelphia: 1842. V. 64
Woman to the Rescue. Philadelphia: 1874. V. 63; 65
The Young Wife's Book.... Philadelphia: 1836. V. 63

ARTHUR, WILLIAM
Italy in Transition: Public Scenes and Private Opinions in the Spring of 1860.... London: 1860. V. 65

ARTIC INSTITUTE OF NORTH AMERICA
Arctic Bibliography. Washington: 1965. V. 63
Arctic Bibliography. Montreal: 1969. V. 63

THE ARTICLES of Settlement of the Benevolent Society, for Granting Annuities to Raise a Stock for Improving the Fisher of Great Britain. London: 1714. V. 63

ARTIST'S Assistant, in the Study and Practice of Mechanical Scienes. London: 1785?. V. 67

THE ARTIST'S Assistant; or, School of Science. Birmingham (and elsewhere): 1801. V. 62
THE ARTIST'S Assistant; or, School of Science. London: 1807. V. 62; 67

ARTMAN, WILLIAM
Beauties and Achievements of the Blind. Rochester: 1879. V. 66

THE ARTS Anthology: Dartmouth Verse 1925. Portland: 1925. V. 63

ARTUS, WILIBALD
Hand Atlas Sammtlicher Medicinisch Pharmaceutischer Gewachse Oder Naturgetreue.... Jena: 1876. V. 63; 66; 67

ARUNDEL, THOMAS HOWARD, 14TH EARL OF
Remembrances of Things Worth Seeing in Italy Given to John Evelyn 25 April 1646. London: 1987. V. 64; 67

AS It Was Yesterday, Brockway County. N.P: 1975. V. 64

ASAKURA, A.
Biological Expedition to the Northern Mariana Islands, Micronesia. Chiba: 1994. V. 66

ASBJORNSEN, PETER CHRISTEN
A L'Est du soleil et a L'Ouest de la Lune. (East of the Sun West of the Moon). Paris: 1919. V. 63

ASCHAM, ROGER
Familiarium Epistolarum Libri Tres. London: 1590. V. 66
The Schoolemaster. London: 1589. V. 65
Schoolmaster; or, a Plain and Perfect Way of Teaching Children to Understand, Write and Speak the Latin Tongue.... London: 1711. V. 64

ASH, JOHN
Grammatical Institutes; or, an Easy Introduction to Dr. Lowth's English Grammar. London: 1779. V. 65
The New and Complete Dictionary of the English Language. London: 1775. V. 64; 67

ASH, LEE
Serial Publications Containing Medical Classics. New Haven: 1961. V. 64; 67

ASHBEE, CHARLES ROBERT
American Sheaves and English Seed Corn: Being a Series of Addresses Delivered in the United States 1900-1901. London: 1901. V. 62
The Building of Thelma. London: 1910. V. 63
Conradin: a Philosophical Ballad. 1908. V. 67
Echoes from the City of the Sun. Campden, Gloucestershire: 1905. V. 62; 67
Grannie. a Victorian Cameo. London: 1939. V. 63; 65
Kingfisher Out of Egypt. London: 1934. V. 63; 65
Lyrics for the Nile by an Anglo Egyptian Civil Servant. London: 1919. V. 63
Lyrics of the Nile. London: 1938. V. 63
The Masque of the Edwards: Being a Coronation Pageant to Celebrate the Crowning of the King. London: 1902. V. 62; 64

ASHBEE, PAUL
The Bronze Age Round Barrow in Britain. London: 1960. V. 62; 66

ASHBERY, JOHN
The Double Dream of Spring. New York: 1970. V. 62
The Grand Eccentrics. New York: 1971. V. 63
Hotel Lautreamont. New York: 1991. V. 62; 63; 64
Locus Solus. France: 1960-1962. V. 62
A Nest of Ninnies. New York: 1969. V. 62; 63; 64
A Nest of Ninnies. Calais: 1975. V. 66
Novel. New York: 1998. V. 62; 64; 65
Selected Poems. London: 1967. V. 62
Selected Poems. New York: 1985. V. 63
Rivers and Mountains. New York: 1966. V. 63
Self-Portrait in a Convex Mirror. New York: 1975. V. 62; 63
Some Trees. New York: 1970. V. 63
Sunrise in Suburbia. Cambridge: 1968. V. 62
Three Madrigals. New York: 1968. V. 62; 63; 66
Three Plays. Calais: 1978. V. 62; 63; 64; 66
Turnadot. New York: 1953. V. 67
A Wave. Poems. New York: 1984. V. 63
Who Knows What Constitutes a Life. Calais: 1999. V. 62; 66; 67

ASHBURN, P. M.
A History of the Medical Department of the United States Army. Boston: 1929. V. 63; 65; 67

ASHBURTON, ALEXANDER BARING, 1ST BARON
The Financial and Commercial Crisis Considered. London: 1847. V. 65

ASHBURTON, ROBERT OFFLEY
Gleanings from Beranger. London: 1889. V. 63

ASHBY, PROFESSOR
Helen Howard, or the Bankrupt and Broker. Boston: 1845. V. 63

ASHBY, THOMAS A.
Life of Turner Ashby. New York: 1914. V. 62; 63; 65
The Valley Campaigns. New York: 1914. V. 62; 63; 65

ASHBY, W. ROSS
Design for a Brain. London: 1952. V. 67

ASHDOWN, EMILY JESSE
British Costume During XIX Centuries (Civil and Ecclesiastical). London: 1929. V. 62

ASHE, GEORGE
A Sermon Preach'd at Christ's Church, January the 30th...Before Their Excellencies the Lords Justices and the House of Lords. Dublin: 1716. V. 65

ASHE, ROBERT P.
Two Kings of Uganda; or, Life by the Shores of Victoria Nyanza. London: 1889. V. 62
Two Kings of Uganda; or, Life by the Shores of Victoria Nyanza. London: 1890. V. 64

ASHE, SAMUEL A'COURT
Rutherford's Expedition Against the Indians. Raleigh: 1904. V. 67
Southern View of the Invasion of the Southern States and the War of 1861-1865. Raleigh: 1938. V. 62

ASHE, THOMAS
The Spirit of The Book, or Memories of Caroline Princess of Hasburgh, a Political and Amatory Romance. London: 1811. V. 63

ASHENDENE PRESS
A Chronological List, with Prices, of the Forty Books Printed at the Ashendene Press MDCCCXCV-MCMXXXV. 1935. V. 62; 67
A Hand-List of the Books Printed at the Ashendene Press MDCCCXCV-MCMXXV. 1925. V. 62; 62; 67

ASHFORD, DAISY
Love and Marriage. London: 1965. V. 65
The Young Visiters, or M. Salteenas Plan. London: 1919. V. 62; 63; 65

ASHLEY, ALFRED
The Art of Etching on Copper. London: 1849. V. 64

ASHLEY, CLIFFORD W.
Whaleships of New Bedford. Boston and New York: 1929. V. 64; 65
The Yankee Whaler. Garden City: 1942. V. 66

ASHLEY, DORIS
Children's Stories from French Fairy Tales. London: 1917. V. 66

ASHLEY, JOHN
Memoirs and Considerations Concerning the Trade and Revenues of the British Colonies in America. London: 1740-1743. V. 63

ASHLEY-COOPER, G.
A Salmon Fisher's Odyssey. 1982. V. 63; 65

ASHLEY COOPER, JOHN
The Great Salmon Rivers of Scotland. London: 1980. V. 67
A Ring of Wessex Waters. London: 1986. V. 67

ASHLEY-MONTAGU, M. F.
The Medio-Frontal Suture and the Problem of Metopism in the Primates. London: 1937. V. 63

ASHMEAD, W. H.
Classification of the Chalcid Flies or the Superfamily Chalcidoidea.... Pittsburgh;: 1904. V. 66
Insects of the Harriman Alaska Expedition. Washington: 1910. V. 66

ASHMEAD-BARTLETT, E.
With the Turks in Thrace. London: 1913. V. 64

ASHMOLE, B.
Architect and Sculptor in Classical Greece. New York: 1972. V. 62; 65

ASHMOLE, ELIAS
The History of the Most Noble Order of the Garter.... London: 1715. V. 63
The Way to Bliss. London: 1658. V. 64

ASHMORE, OWEN
The Industrial Archaeology of Lancashire. Newton Abbot: 1969. V. 65

ASHTON, HERBERT
The Locked Room: a Comedy Mystery in Three Acts. New York: 1934. V. 65

ASHTON, JOHN
Chap-Books of the Eighteenth Century with Facsimile Notes and Introduction. London: 1882. V. 63
Curious Creatures in Zoology. London: 1890. V. 62
English Caricature and Satire on Napoleon I. New York: 1884. V. 62
The Fleet: Its River, Prison and Marriages. London: 1888. V. 62
Humour, Wit and Satire of the Seventeenth Century. London: 1833. V. 64
Humour, Wit and Satire of the Seventeenth Century. London: 1883. V. 63
Modern Street Ballads.... London: 1888. V. 67
Old Times, a Picture of Social Life at the End of the Eighteenth Century.... London: 1885. V. 63

ASHTON, LEIGH
The Art of India and Pakistan. New York. V. 62

ASHTON, THOMAS
An Extract from the Case of the Obligation on the Electors of Eton College to Supply All Vacancies in that Society with Those Who Are or Have Been Fellows of King's College, Cambridge.... London: 1771. V. 62

ASHWAL, STEPHEN
The Founders of Child Neurology. San Francisco;: 1990. V. 66

ASHWORTH, HENRY
Cotton: Its Cultivation, Manufacture and Uses. London: 1858. V. 65
Cotton: Its Cultivation, Manufacture, and Uses. Manchester: 1858. V. 63

ASHWORTH, THOMAS
The Salmon Fisheries of England, 1868.... London: 1868. V. 66

ASIMOV, ISAAC
Casebook of the Black Widowers. Garden City: 1980. V. 66
The End of Eternity. Garden City: 1955. V. 66
Fantastic Voyage II. New York: 1987. V. 62
Of Matters Great and Small. New York: 1975. V. 67
3 by Asimov, Three Science Fiction Tales. New York: 1981. V. 65
A Whiff of Death. New York: 1968. V. 66

ASKEW, ANTHONY
Bibliotheca Askeviana sive Catalogus Librorum Rarissimorum. London: 1775. V. 62

ASKINS, CHARLES
Unrepentant Sinner, the Autobiography of.... San Antonio: 1985. V. 65

ASLANAPA, O.
Turkish Art and Architecture. New York: 1971. V. 62; 65

ASMAR, MARIA THERESA, PRINCESS
Prophecy and Lamentation; or a Voice from the East. London: 1845. V. 65

ASPIN, J.
Cosmorama: a View of the Costumes and Peculiarities of All Nations. London: 1827. V. 63; 65
A Familiar Treatise on Astronomy, Explaining the General Phenomena of the Celestial Bodies.... London: 1834. V. 65; 66

ASPINALL-OGLANDER, CECIL
Admiral's Widow - Being the Life and Letters of the Hon. Mrs. Edward Boscawen from 1761 to 1805. London: 1942. V. 62

ASQUITH, CYNTHIA
The Queen. London: 1937. V. 64
This Mortal Coil. Sauk City: 1947. V. 65; 67

THE ASSASSINATION of Abraham Lincoln...and the Attempted Assassination of William H. Seward...Expressions of Condolence and Sympathy Inspired by These Events. Washington: 1867. V. 65

ASSELINEAU, LEON AUGUSTE
Meubles et Objets Divers du Moyen Age. Paris: 1854?. V. 65

ASSELINEAU, ROGER
The Literary Reputation of Mark Twain from 1910-1950. Paris: 1954. V. 63

ASSHETON, WILLIAM
The Cases of Scandal and Persecution. London: 1674. V. 63

ASSIS IGLESIAS, F. DE
Album Floristico. Rio de Janeiro: 1940. V. 66; 67

ASSOCIATION OF THE NATIONAL ELECTRIC TRAMWAY & LIGHTING CO.
Memorandum of.... Victoria: 1889. V. 66

ASTLE, THOMAS
The Origin and Progress of Writing.... London: 1784. V. 62; 64

ASTLEY, JOHN DUGDALE
Fifty Years of My Life in the World of Sport at Home and Abroad. London: 1894. V. 64; 66; 67
Fifty Years of My Life in the World of Sport at Home and Abroad. London: 1895. V. 67

ASTLEY, PHILIP
Astley's System of Equestria Education, Exhibiting the Beauties of the Horse.... London: 1801. V. 62

ASTON, FRANCIS WILLIAM
Isotopes. London: 1922. V. 63; 67

ASTON, H. I.
Aquatic Plants of Australia. Carlton: 1973. V. 65

ASTOR, JOHN JACOB
A Journey in Other Worlds. 1894. V. 66

ASTOR, WILLIAM WALDORF
Sporza, a Story of Milan. New York: 1889. V. 65

ASTROLABII Quo Primi Mobilis Motus Deprehenduntur Canones. Venice: 1497-1498. V. 63

ASTRUC, JEAN
De Morbis Veneris Libri Sex. Paris: 1736. V. 64
De Morbis Veneris Libri Sex. Parisiis: 1738. V. 64

ASTRUP, ELVIND
With Peary Near the Pole. London: 1898. V. 63

ASTURIAS, MIGUEL ANGEL
Hombres de Maiz. Buenos Aires: 1949. V. 65
Legendes du Guatemala. Marsaille: 1932. V. 67
Los Ojos de Los Enterrados. Buenos Aires: 1960. V. 62
Viento Fuerte. Guatemala: 1954. V. 62

AT a Meeting or Convention of Clergy and Lay-Delegates of the Protestant Episcopal Church of Maryland May 29, 1788. Baltimore: 1788. V. 66

AT the Field's End. Seattle: 1987. V. 62; 64

ATCHESON, NATHANIEL
American Encroachments on British Rights.... London: 1808. V. 65

ATCHLEY, S. C.
Wild Flowers of Attica. Oxford: 1938. V. 62; 63; 65; 66; 67

ATEN, IRA
Six and One-Half Years in the Ranger Service, the Memoirs of Ira Aten, Sergeant Company D. Texas Rangers. Bandera: 1945. V. 65

ATGET, EUGENE
A Vision of Paris. New York: 1963. V. 66
The World of Atget. New York: 1964. V. 66

ATHENAGORAS
Athenagora, Atheniese, Philosopho Chrisitano, Della Risurrettione de' Morti, Tadotto in Lingua Italiana da Girolamo Faleti.... Aluds in Ventia: 1556. V. 66

ATHERTON, FAXON DEAN
The California Diary of...1836-1839. San Francisco: 1964. V. 65

ATHERTON, GERTRUDE
The Conqueror; Being the True and Romantic Story of Alexander Hamilton. New York: 1902. V. 63; 64
Julia France and Her Times. New York: 1912. V. 65
The Splendid Idle Forties. Kentfield: 1960. V. 63
What Dreams May Come. Chicago, N.Y., and S.F: 1888. V. 62; 64; 67

ATHERTON, LEWIS
The Cattle Kings. Bloomington: 1961. V. 67

ATHLONE SOCIETY
Journal of the Old Athlone Society. 1969-1975. V. 67

ATIK, ANNE
Drancy. London: 1989. V. 64

ATKINS, ACE
Crossroad Blues. New York: 1998. V. 65

ATKINS, DAISY
Way Back Yonder - Old West Reminiscences of a Lady On Horseback. El Paso: 1958. V. 66

ATKINS, W. J. L.
Interlude. Poems and Prose. Cork: 1930. V. 67

ATKINSON, CHARLES
The Life and Adventures of an Eccentric Traveller. York: 1818. V. 62

ATKINSON, CHRISTOPHER
A Historical and Statistical Account of New Brunswick, B.N.A. Edinburgh: 1844. V. 67

ATKINSON, D.
Tree Root Systems and Their Mycorrhizas. The Hague: 1983. V. 64

ATKINSON, D. H.
Ralph Thoresby, the Topographer: His Town (Leeds) and Times. Leeds: 1885. V. 62; 63; 64; 65; 66

ATKINSON, FRANK
The Industrial Archaeology of North-East England. London: 1974. V. 62; 65

ATKINSON, GEORGE
The Worthies of Westmorland; or, Notable Persons Born in the County Since the Reformation. London: 1849. V. 62; 63; 65

ATKINSON, GEORGE FRANCKLIN
Curry and Rice on Forty Plates, or the Ingredients of Social Life at Our Station in India. 1860. V. 67

ATKINSON, HAROLD WARING
The Families of Atkinson of Roxby (Lincs) and Thorne and Dearman of Braithwaite and Families Connected With Them Especially Atkinson-Busfeild, Barnes, Beavington, Birchall, Edwards, Miller, Neave, Ransome, Rooke, Sessions, Sinclair, Somerford, Stanley, W. Northwood: 1933. V. 63; 66

ATKINSON, HENRY GEORGE
Letters on the Laws of Man's Nature and Development. London: 1851. V. 62; 65

ATKINSON, HERBERT
Cock-Fighting and Game Fowl from the Note Books of Herbert Atkinson. Bath: 1938. V. 65; 66; 67

ATKINSON, J. C.
British Birds Eggs and Nests Popularly Described. 1862. V. 67
A Glossary of the Cleveland Dialect.... London: 1868. V. 64
A Handbook for Ancient Whitby and Its Abbey. London: 1882. V. 64; 65; 66
Memorials of Old Whitby or Historical Gleanings from Ancient Whitby Records. London: 1894. V. 62; 64; 65

ATKINSON, JASPER
Considerations on the Propriety of the Bank of England Resuming Its Payment in Specie at the Period Prescribed by the Act 37th George III. London: 1802. V. 62; 65

ATKINSON, JOHN AUGUSTUS
Sixteen Scenes Taken from the Miseries of Human Life, by One of the Wretched. London: 1807. V. 62; 66

ATKINSON, JOSEPH
The History of Newark, New Jersey. Newark: 1878. V. 63

ATKINSON, M. E.
The Compass Points North.... London: 1941. V. 65

ATKINSON, M. E. *continued*
Going Gangster. London: 1940. V. 65

ATKINSON, ROBERT
The Passions and Homilies from the Leabhar Breac.... 1887. V. 62

ATKINSON, THOMAS
On the Case of Our National Troubles. A Sermon, Delivered in St. James' Church, Wilmington, N.C. Wilmington: 1861. V. 62

ATKINSON, THOMAS DINHAM
Cambridge Described and Illustrated. London: 1897. V. 66
An Illustrated Catalogue of the Local Collection of Plate, Exhibited in the Fitzwilliam Museum May 1895. Cambridge: 1896. V. 66

ATKINSON, THOMAS WITLAM
Oriental and Western Siberia. London: 1858. V. 66
Travels in Siberia. 1865. V. 62; 63; 64; 66
Travels in the Regions of the Upper and Lower Amoor and Russian Acquisitions on the Confines of India and China. New York: 1860. V. 62; 63; 64; 66

ATKINSON, WILLIAM
Principles of Political Economy, or the Laws of Formation of National Wealth.... London: 1840. V. 62; 64; 65

ATKINSON WILLES, G. L.
Wildfowl in Great Britain. 1963. V. 67

ATKYNS, ARABELLA, PSEUD.
The Family Magazine, in Two Parts. London: 1741. V. 65

AN ATLAS of Gas Poisoning. 19918. V. 63

ATLAS to Accompany Willetts' Easy Grammar of Geography. Poughkeepsie: 1826. V. 64

ATLAS of Bergen County, New Jersey. Reading: 1876. V. 63; 66

ATLAS Of Hunterdon County, New Jersey. Flemington: 1987. V. 63; 66

ATLAS of Monmouth County, New Jersey. From Recent and Actual Surveys and Records Under the Superintendence of F. W. Beers. New York: 1873. V. 63

ATLAS of Oakland Co. Michigan. New York: 1872. V. 67

AN ATLAS of Ripley Co., Indiana. Philadelphia: 1883. V. 63

ATLAS of the City of Plainfield, Union County and Borough of North Plainfield, Somerset County, New Jersey. 1894. Plainfield: 1894. V. 63; 66

ATLAS of the Oranges, Embracing the Cities of Orange and East Orange, Town of West Orange, Village and Township of South Orange, New Jersey. Philadelphia: 1911. V. 63; 66

ATLAS Of the World. Springfield: 1894. V. 63

ATLEE, EDWIN A.
An Inaugural Essay on the Influence of Music in the Cure of Diseases. Philadelphia: 1804. V. 64

ATMORE, CHARLES
The Methodist Memorial.... Bristol: 1801. V. 64

ATOMICS for the Millions. New York: 1947. V. 65

ATTENBOROUGH, DAVID
The Living Planet - a Portrait of the Earth. London: 1984. V. 65
The Trials of Life - a Natural History of Animal Behaviour. London: 1990. V. 63

ATTERBURY, P.
Art Deco Patterns: a Source Book. New York: 1990. V. 62; 65

ATTHILL, WILLIAM
Documents Relating to the Foundation and Antiquities of the Collegiate Church of Middleham in the County of York.... London: 1847. V. 65

THE ATTIC Miscellany.... London: 1791. V. 65

ATTLEE, CLEMENT
As It Happened. London: 1954. V. 65

ATTWATER, DONALD
The Vision of William Concerning Piers the Plowman. London: 1930. V. 67

ATTWELL, MABEL LUCIE
Little People's Painting Book. London: 1907. V. 64
Lucie Attwell's Children's Book. London: 1927. V. 66
Lucie Attwell's Fairy Book. London: 1932. V. 62; 66
Story Book. Racine. V. 66

ATTWOOD, THOMAS
A Second Letter to the Earl of Liverpool, on the Bank Reports, as Occassioning the National Dangers and Distresses. Birmingham: 1819. V. 62

ATWATER, CALEB
Remarks Made on a Tour to Prairie du Chien; Thence to Washington City in 1829. Columbus: 1831. V. 62

ATWATER, FRANCIS
Plymouth Connecticut 1795-1895. Meriden: 1895. V. 67

ATWOOD, A.
The Conquerors - Historical Sketches of the American Settlement of the Oregon Country - Embracing Parts in the Life and Work of Rev. Jason Lee. Tacoma: 1907. V. 64

ATWOOD, MARGARET
The Animals in that Country. Boston: 1968. V. 63
The Blind Assassin. New York: 2000. V. 67
Bluebeard's Egg. Toronto: 1983. V. 67
Cat's Eye. Toronto: 1988. V. 67
Cat's Eye. Bloomsbury: 1989. V. 62
Dancing Girls and Other Stories. Toronto: 1977. V. 63; 65; 67
The Handmaid's Tale. Toronto: 1985. V. 65; 67
Hurricane Hazel and Other Stories. Helsinki: 1988. V. 65
The Journals of Susanna Moodie. Toronto: 1970. V. 63
Lady Oracle. Toronto: 1976. V. 64; 65; 67
Power Politics. New York: 1973. V. 66
The Robber Bride. Franklin Center: 1993. V. 65
Surfacing. Toronto: 1972. V. 62
Wilderness Tips. London: 1991. V. 67

AUBER, DANIEL
Just Starve Us. London: 1839?. V. 65

AUBER, T. C. E. EDOUARD
Hygiene des Femmes Nerveuses ou Conseils Au Femmes Pour les Epoques Critiques de leur Vie. Paris: 1841. V. 65

AUBERT, ROSEMARY
Free Reign. Bridgehampton: 1997. V. 64; 65; 66

AUBERTIN, J. J.
A Fight with Distances. The States the Hawaiian Islands, Canada, British Columbia, Cuba, the Bahamas. London: 1888. V. 64

AUBIGNE, J. H. MERLE D'
History of the Reformation in the Sixteenth Century. Edinburgh: 1853. V. 62
History of the Reformation in the Sixteenth Century. London: 1880. V. 62

AUBIN, NICOLAS
The Cheats and Illusions of Romish Priests and Exorcists. London: 1703. V. 64

AUBREY, JOHN
Brief Lives and Other Selected Writings. London: 1949. V. 65; 66
Letters Written by Eminent Persons in the Seventeenth and Eighteenth Centuries and Lives of Eminent Men. London: 1813. V. 62; 67
Miscellanies Upon the Following Subjects: Day Fatality, Local Fatality, Ostenta, Omens, Dreams, Apparitions.... London: 1721. V. 64

AUBRY, M.
Oxonii Dux Poeticus, Sive Latinis Versibus, Hexametris et Pentametris, Descriptio, Fere Publica Quaeque Oxonii Monumenta Adumbrantur. Oxonii: 1795. V. 66

AUBURY, LEWIS E.
Gold Dredging in California. Sacramento: 1905. V. 63

AUCASSIN ET NICOLETTE
Aucassin and Nicolete. London: 1887. V. 62; 67
Aucassin and Nicolete. London: 1897. V. 67
Aucassin and Nicolete. London: 1911. V. 63
Aucassin and Nicolete in English by Andrew Lang. 1931. V. 65
Aucassin and Nicolete in English by Andrew Lang. Czechoslovakia: 1931. V. 62
Of Aucassion and Nicolette. London: 1925. V. 62; 64
The Song Story of Aucassin and Nicolette. Lexington: 1957. V. 62; 65

AUCHINCLOSS, LOUIS
Civil Wars: Three Tales of Old New York. New York: 1999. V. 66; 67
The Collected Stories. Boston: 1994. V. 63
The Indifferent Children. New York: 1947. V. 67

AUCKLAND INSTITUTE AND MUSEUM
Records of the Auckland Institute and Museum. Auckland: 1964-1988. V. 67

AUCKLAND, WILLIAM EDEN, 1ST BARON
The Substance of a Speech Made in the House of Peers on Thursday, 8th January 1799, on the Third Reading of the Bill for Granting Certain Duties Upon Income. London: 1799. V. 66
Substance of the Speeches of Lord Auckland, in the House of Lords, May 16th and 23rd, 1800, in Support of the Bill for the Punishment and More Effectual Prevention of the Crime of Adultery. London: 1800. V. 62

AUDEN, WYSTAN HUGH
About the House. London: 1966. V. 62; 63
The Age of Anxiety. London: 1948. V. 62; 63; 64; 65
Another Time.... London: 1940. V. 62
The Ascent of F6. London: 1935. V. 65
The Ascent of F6. New York: 1937. V. 63; 64
The Cave of Making. Darmstadt: 1965. V. 62; 66
City Without Walls and Other Poems. New York: 1969. V. 63
Collected Longer Poems. London: 1968. V. 63
Collected Poems. London: 1976. V. 62
The Collected Poetry. New York: 1945. V. 64
Collected Shorter Poems 1927-1957. London: 1966. V. 63
Collected Shorter Poems 1927-1957. New York: 1966. V. 64
The Dance of Death. London: 1933. V. 62; 65; 66
Delia or a Masque of Night. Rome: 1953. V. 65
The Dog Beneath the Skin, or Where is Francis?. London: 1935. V. 65
The Double Man. New York: 1941. V. 63
The Dyer's Hand and Other Essays. New York: 1962. V. 64

AUDEN, WYSTAN HUGH continued
The Enchafed Flood or the Romantic Iconography of the Sea. New York: 1950. V. 65
The Enchafed Flood: or the Romantic Iconography of the Sea. London: 1951. V. 66
The English Auden. Poems, Essays and Dramatic Writings 1927-1939. London: 1977. V. 63
Five Poems. 1983. V. 64
Five Poems. Athens: 1983. V. 65
For the Time Being. New York: 1944. V. 62; 64
For the Time Being. London: 1945. V. 62; 65
Forewords and Afterwords. New York: 1973. V. 63
A Gobble Poem, Snatched from the Notebooks of W. H. Auden, and Now Believed to Be in the Morgan Library. London: 1967. V. 64
Goodbye to the Mezzogiorno.... Milano: 1958. V. 62
Homage to Clio. London: 1960. V. 62; 63
Homage to Clio. New York: 1960. V. 62
The House. New York: 1965. V. 63
Journey to a War. London: 1939. V. 64
Knowing and Judging - an Inaugural Lecture Delivered Before the University of Oxford on 11 June 1956. Oxford: 1956. V. 62
Letters from Iceland. London: 1937. V. 62; 63; 64; 65; 66
Letters from Iceland. New York: 1937. V. 63
Look Stranger! Poems. London: 1936. V. 62; 66
Louis MacNeice: a Memorial Address Delivered at All Souls, Langham Place on 17 October, 1963. London: 1963. V. 66
The Magic Flute. London: 1957. V. 63
Nones. New York: 1950. V. 65
Nones. London: 1952. V. 62; 64; 66; 67
The Old Man's Road. New York: 1956. V. 62
On the Frontier: a Play. London: 1938. V. 62; 64; 66
Oratio Creweiana - MCMLVIII. Oxford: 1958. V. 62
Oratio Creweiana - MDCCCCLX. Oxford: 1960. V. 62
The Orators: An English Study. London: 1932. V. 62; 64; 66
The Orators: An English Study. London: 1934. V. 63; 65
The Orators. An English Study. New York: 1967. V. 63
The Oxford Book of Light Verse. Oxford: 1938. V. 65
The Platonic Blow. Washington: 1970. V. 63
Poem. Bryn Mawr: 1933. V. 62; 64
Poems. London: 1930. V. 62; 63; 66; 67
Poems. London: 1933. V. 63
Poems. New York: 1941. V. 63
Poems 1928 - Reproduced Facsimile for the Ilkley Literature Festival - April 24, 1973. Ilkley: 1973. V. 64
Selections from Poems. 1973. V. 62
Some Poems. London: 1940. V. 63; 66
Sonnet. Paris: 1969. V. 63
Spain. London: 1937. V. 62; 63; 66
The Table Talk of W. H. Auden. New York: 1989. V. 62; 64; 67
Thank You Fog. London: 1974. V. 64
Three Songs for St. Cecillia's Day. New York: 1941. V. 65
Three Unpublished Poems. New York: 1986. V. 62; 64
Two Poems. Bryn Mawr: 1934. V. 62
Two Songs. New York: 1968. V. 64; 67

AUDIBERT, CAMILLO MARIA
Regiae Villae Poetice Descriptae.... Torino: 1711. V. 62

AUDOUIN, FRANCOIS XAVIER
Du Commerce Maritime, de Son Influence sur la Richesse et la Force des Etats, Demontree par l'Historie des Nations Anciennes et Modernes.... Paris: 1800. V. 66

AUDRAN, GERARD
Les Proportions du Corps Humain Measurees sur les Plus Belles Figures d l'Antiquite. Paris: 1683. V. 63
Les Proportions du Corps Humain Mesures sur les Plus Belles Figures d l'Antiquite. Paris: 1801. V. 62; 64

AUDSLEY, GEORGE
The Practical Decorator and Ornamentist: for the Use of Architects, Practical Painters, Decorators and Designers. Glasgow: 1892. V. 62

AUDSLEY, W.
Cottage, Lodge and Villa Architecture. London: 1870. V. 62; 66
Outlines of Ornament in the Leading Styles. London: 1881. V. 62; 67
Polychromatic Decoration as Applied to Buildings in the Mediaeval Styles. London: 1882. V. 63; 65

AUDUBON, JOHN JAMES
Audubon and His Journals. New York: 1897. V. 64
Audubon's America. Cambridge: 1940. V. 64
Audubon's Western Journal 1849-1850. Cleveland: 1906. V. 65
Audubon's Birds of America. New York: 1981. V. 65; 67
The Birds of America. New York: 1967. V. 63; 67
Birds of America. New York: 1985. V. 67
Birds of America. 1997. V. 63
The Birds of America. No. 6. New York and Philadelphia: 1840. V. 63
Delineations of American Scenery and Character. New York: 1926. V. 63; 64; 66
Journal of John James Audubon Made During His Trip to New Orleans in 1820-1821. Boston: 1929. V. 63; 64; 65
Journal of John James Audubon Made While Obtaining Subscriptions to His Birds of America 1840-1843. Boston: 1929. V. 63; 64; 66
Letters of John James Audubon 1826-1840. Boston: 1930. V. 63; 64; 66
The Original Water-Color Paintings by John James Audubon for the Birds of America. New York: 1966. V. 62; 63; 64; 66; 67
Ornithological Biography, or, an Account of the Habits of the Birds of the United States. Edinburgh: 1831-1835. V. 62
Ornithological Biography, or An Account of the Habits of the Birds of the United States. Edinburgh: 1831-1839. V. 64
Ornithological Biography, or, an Account of the Habits of the Birds of the United States. Philadelphia: 1832. V. 64
Scenes de la Nature dans les Etats-Unis et le Nord de l'Amerique Ouvrage Traduit d'Audubon. Paris: 1868. V. 65
Selected Birds of America and Seclected. Kent: 1977. V. 63; 67
A Synopsis of the Birds of North America. Edinburgh: 1939. V. 67
The Viviparous Quadrupeds of North America. Volume I only. London: 1847. V. 62
The Watercolors for The Birds of America. New York: 1991. V. 65
The Watercolors for The Birds of America. New York: 1993. V. 64

AUDUBON, JOHN WOODHOUSE
Audubon's Western Journal: 1849-1850. Cleveland: 1906. V. 64
The Drawings of John Woodhouse Audubon Illustrating His Adventures through Mexico and California, 1849-1850. San Francisco: 1957. V. 62

AUDUBON, L.
The Life of John James Audubon. New York: 1873. V. 64

AUDUBON, M. R.
Audubon and His Journals. New York: 1897. V. 62; 63; 67
Audubon and His Journals. London: 1898. V. 63

AUEL, JEAN
The Clan of the Cave Bear. New York: 1980. V. 64; 65; 67
The Clan of the Cave Bear. The Valley of the Horses. The Mammoth Hunters. The Plains of Passage. New York: 1980-1990. V. 63
The Valley of Horses. New York: 1982. V. 67

AUENBRUGGER, LEOPOLD
Nouvelle Methode Pour Reconnaitre Les Maladies Internes De La Poitrine.... Paris: 1808. V. 66

AUER, ALOIS
Die Entdeckung des Naturselbstrdruckes.... Vienna: 1853. V. 64

AUER, HARRY A.
Camp Fires in the Yukon. Cincinnati: 1916. V. 66
Camp Fires in the Yukon. New York: 1916. V. 64

AUERBACH, HERBERT S.
Father Escalante's Journal 1776-1777. Salt Lake City: 1943. V. 64

AUGER DE MAULEON
Recveil de Divers Memoires, Harangves, Remonstrances, et Lettres Servans a l'Histoire de Nostre Temps. Paris: 1623. V. 62

AUGUSTINUS, AURELIUS, SAINT, BP. OF HIPPO
Confessionum Libri XIII. Lugduni: 1675. V. 63; 66
De La Cita d'Dio. Venice: 1476-1477. V. 66
Opuscula. Venice: 1483. V. 63; 66
Saint Augustine Bishop of Hippo. London: 1908. V. 67
Saint Augustine's Manuell.... London: 1881. V. 66

AUGUSTUS; or, the Ambitious Student. London: 1820. V. 64

AULD, T. M.
The Book of Thoms Rhymer. 1946. V. 66

AULNOY, MARIE CATHERINE LE JUMEL DE BARNEVILLE, COMTESSE D'
D'Aulnoy's Fairy Tales. Philadelphia: 1923. V. 63; 65
Fairy Tales. London: 1894. V. 66
Ingenious and Diverting Letters of a Lady's Travels Into Spain. London: 1717. V. 65
Memoirs of the Court of France. London: 1692. V. 63; 65
Memoirs of the Court of France and City of Paris.... London: 1702. V. 63
Relation du Voyage D'Espagne. La Haye: 1692. V. 67

AULT, NORMAN
The Podgy Book of Tides. London: 1907. V. 62

AUMALE, DUC D'
Inventaire de Tous les Meubles du Cardinal Mazarin. London: 1861. V. 67

AUNGERVILLE, RICHARD
The Philobiblon of Richard de Bury. New York: 1945. V. 62; 63; 64; 67

AUNT Louisa's Coloured Gift Book - Old Nursery Friends. London. V. 66

AUNT Louisa's Fairy Legends. New York: Sep. 1870?. V. 63

AUNT Louisa's Keepsake. London: 1868. V. 66

AUNT Mavor's Nursery Tales. London: 1860. V. 62

AUNT Sally; or the Cross the Way of Freedom. Cincinnati: 1862. V. 65

AUNTY Wonderful's Stories. Boston: 1856. V. 64

THE AUTOMOTOR and Horseless Vehicle Pocket Book of Automotive Formulae and Commercial Intelligence for 1898. London: 1898. V. 62

AURELIANUS, CAELIUS
Caelius Aurelianus on Acute Diseases and on Chronic Diseases. Chicago: 1950. V. 65

AURELIUS ANTONINUS, MARCUS, EMPEROR OF ROME
The Golden Book. London: 1898. V. 67
Marcus Antoninus Imperatoris, De Rebus Suis...Studio Opera.... 1697. V. 65
The Meditations. Oxford: 1944. V. 65
Meditations. New York: 1956. V. 64
The Thoughts. London: 1892. V. 66
The Thoughts. London: 1909. V. 65

AURY, DOMINIQUE
Histoire d'O. Paris: 1954. V. 65

AUSONIUS, DECIMUS MAGNUS
Opera. Amsterdam: 1621. V. 62
Patchwork Quilt. London. V. 65

AUST, SARAH MAESE MURRAY
A Companion and Useful Guide to the Beauties of Scotland, to the Lakes of Westmoreland, Cumberland and Lancashire.... 1799. V. 65

AUSTEN, JANE
Emma. London: 1816. V. 63; 64; 65; 66
Emma. London: 1833. V. 65
Emma. 1850. V. 64
Emma. London: 1851. V. 65; 66
Emma. Boston: 1864. V. 63
Emma. London: 1879. V. 67
Emma. London: 1898. V. 64
Emma. London: 1909. V. 64
Emma. New York: 1964. V. 62; 65
Five Letters to Her Niece Fanny Knight. Oxford: 1924. V. 63; 66
The History of England: from the Reign of Henry the 4th to the Death of Charles the 1st. Market Drayton: 1997. V. 64
Jane Austen's Letters to Her Sister Cassandra and Others. London: 1952. V. 62
Jane Austen's Letters to Her Sister Cassandra and Others. London: 1959. V. 62
Lady Susan. London: 1925. V. 63; 66
Lady Susan. Oxford: 1925. V. 63
Letters to Her Sister Cassandra and Others. London: 1932. V. 63; 66
Letters to Her Sister Cassandra and Others. London: 1952. V. 63
Love and Friendship and Other Early Works. London: 1922. V. 63; 66
Love and Friendship and Other Early Works. New York: 1922. V. 63
Mansfield Park. London: 1814. V. 63; 67
Mansfield Park. London: 1833. V. 64; 65
Mansfield Park. 1851. V. 64
Mansfield Park. Boston: 1864. V. 63
Mansfield Park. Leipzig: 1867. V. 66
Mansfield Park. London: 1875. V. 66
Mansfield Park. Leipzig: 1877. V. 64
Mansfield Park. London: 1880. V. 67
Mansfield Park. London: 1885. V. 65
Northanger Abbey. London: 1880. V. 65
Northanger Abbey. 1971. V. 63; 66
Northanger Abbey; and Persuasion. London: 1818. V. 62; 63; 67
Northanger Abbey and Persuasion. London: 1833. V. 65
Northanger Abbey and Persuasion. 1850. V. 64
Northanger Abbey and Persuasion. London: 1854. V. 64; 66
Northanger Abbey. (and) Persuasion. London: 1880. V. 67
The Northanger Set of Jane Austen Horrid Novels. London: 1968. V. 65
Novels. London: 1872-1877. V. 65
The Novels. London: 1882. V. 66
Novels. London: 1885-1886. V. 65
The Novels. London: 1886-1901. V. 63
The Novels. London: 1894. V. 64
The Novels. Edinburgh: 1911. V. 65
The Novels. Oxford: 1923. V. 64; 65
The Novels. New York: 1925?. V. 63
(Novels). 1948-1979. V. 67
Persuasion. London: 1909. V. 63
Persuasion. London: 1922. V. 63
Persuasion. Paris: 1945. V. 63
Persuasion. 1977. V. 66
Plan of a Novel. Oxford: 1926. V. 66
Pride and Prejudice. London: 1813. V. 63
Pride and Prejudice. London: 1817. V. 63
Pride and Prejudice. London: 1833. V. 64; 65; 66
Pride and Prejudice. London: 1844. V. 63
Pride and Prejudice. London: 1846. V. 65
Pride and Prejudice. London: 1881. V. 67
Pride and Prejudice. London: 1885. V. 65; 66
Pride and Prejudice. London: 1894. V. 64
Pride and Prejudice. London: 1895. V. 65
Pride and Prejudice; and Sense and Sensibility. London: 1851. V. 65
Sense and Sensibility. London: 1811. V. 63
Sense and Sensibility. London: 1813. V. 65
Sense and Sensibility. London: 1833. V. 65
Sense and Sensibility. London: 1837. V. 65
Sense and Sensibility. London: 1879. V. 67
Sense and Sensibility. London: 1886. V. 65; 66
Sense and Sensibility. London: 1899. V. 63
Sense and Sensibility. London: 1986. V. 64
Sense and Sensibility and Persuasion. Boston: 1864. V. 63
Sir Charles Grandison, or the Happy Man. London: 1981. V. 64
Two Chapters of Persuasion, Printed from Jane Austen's Autograph. Oxford: 1926. V. 65
The Watsons. London: 1927. V. 63; 66
The Works. London: 1882. V. 63; 66
The Works. London: 1898. V. 66
Works. London: 1923. V. 67
The Works. London: 1933-1934. V. 66
Works. London: 1957-1964. V. 65

AUSTEN-LEIGH, JAMES EDWARD
A Memoir. London: 1870. V. 65; 66
A Memoir of Jane Austen. London: 1871. V. 65
A Memoir of Jane Austen by Her Nephew.... London: 1879. V. 63; 67
A Memoir of Jane Austen; Lady Susan by Jane Austen. London: 1882. V. 65

AUSTEN-LEIGH, R. A.
The Story of a Printing House. London: 1912. V. 64
William Strahan and His Ledgers. London: 1924. V. 66

AUSTEN-LEIGH, W.
Jane Austen. Her Life and Letters, a Family Record. London: 1913. V. 63; 66

AUSTER, PAUL
The Art of Hunger: Essays, Prefaces, Interviews. Los Angeles: 1992. V. 63; 66; 67
Disappearances: Selected Poems. New York: 1988. V. 62
Facing the Music. Barrytown: 1980. V. 62; 63
Ghosts. Los Angeles: 1986. V. 62; 63; 64
In the Country of Last Things. New York: 1987. V. 66
Leviathan. New York: 1992. V. 65
A Little Anthology of Surrealist Poems. New York: 1972. V. 67
The Locked Room. Los Angeles: 1986. V. 64
Mr. Vertigo. New York: 1994. V. 65
The Music of Chance. New York: 1990. V. 62; 66
The New York Trilogy. London: 1987. V. 66
The New York Trilogy. Los Angeles: 1994. V. 66
Paul Auster's New York. New York: 1997. V. 63; 65
Squeeze Play. New York: 1984. V. 67
Unearth. Weston: 1974. V. 63; 67
Why Write?. Providence: 1996. V. 66

AUSTIN, A. B.
An Angler's Anthology. London: 1930. V. 67

AUSTIN, CYRIL F.
Edward Buttoneye and His Adventures. London: 1908. V. 65

AUSTIN, GABRIEL
Four Oaks Library. Somerville: 1967. V. 63

AUSTIN Hall, or, After Dinner Conversations Between a Father and His Children, on Subjects of Amusement and Instruction. London: 1831. V. 64

AUSTIN, J. P.
The Blue and the Gray. Atlanta: 1899. V. 62; 63; 65

AUSTIN, JOHN
Lectures on Jurisprudence or the Philosophy of Positive Law. London: 1885. V. 64

AUSTIN, MARY
The American Rhythm. New York: 1923. V. 63
Earth Horizon - Autobiography. Boston: 1932. V. 67
The Flock. Boston: 1906. V. 66
The Land of Journey's Ending. New York: 1924. V. 65; 66; 67
The Land of Little Rain. Boston: 1903. V. 62; 63; 65; 67
The Land of Little Rain. Boston: 1950. V. 63; 65; 66
The Land of Little Rain. Cambridge: 1950. V. 65
The Lands of the Sun. Boston: 1927. V. 64; 67
Lost Brothers. New York: 1909. V. 63
One Hundred Miles on Horseback. Los Angeles: 1963. V. 64
Taos Pueblo. Boston: 1974. V. 63

AUSTIN, O. L.
The Birds of Newfoundland Labrador. Cambridge: 1932. V. 62; 67

AUSTIN, PAUL BRITTEN
The Wonderful Life and Adventures of Tom Thumb. Stockholm: 1954-1955. V. 62

AUSTIN, SARAH
The Story Without an End. London: 1872. V. 65

AUSTIN, WILLIAM
A Treatise on the Origin and Component Parts of the Stone.... London: 1791. V. 62

AUSTRALIA; Its Scenery, Natural History and Resources, with a Glance at Its Gold Fields. London: 1854. V. 64

THE AUSTRALIAN Irrigation Colonies on the River Murray, in Victoria and South Australia. London: 1888. V. 67

AUSTRALIAN Handbook and Almanac 1871. London: 1871. V. 64

AUSTYN, C.
Classic Sporting Rifles. 1997. V. 67

AN AUTHENTIC Account of the Conversation and Experience of a Negro. London: 1790. V. 65

AUTHENTIC Copies of the Correspondence of Charles Cotesworth Pinckney, John Marshall and Eldridge Gerry, Esqrs.... London: 1798. V. 65

AUTHENTIC Memoirs, Memorandums and Confessions. London: 1820?. V. 62

AN AUTHENTIC Narrative of the Proceedings of the Expedition Under the Command of Brigadier-Gen. Craufurd, Until Its Arrival at Monte Video; With an Account of the Operations Against Buenos Ayres Under the Command of Lieut.- Gen. Whitelocke. By an Officer. London: 1808. V. 66

AUTOGRAPH Leaves of Our Country's Authors. Baltimore: 1864. V. 65

AUTOGRAPH Poetry in the English Language. London: 1973. V. 65

THE AUTOMOBILE Association and Motor Union Foreign Handbook. London: 1912. V. 65

AUTOMOBILE BLUE BOOKS CORP.
Official Automobile Blue Book 1922. Volume Two. (Middle Atlantic and Southeastern). Chicago: 1922. V. 65

AUTRUM, H.
Handbook of Sensory Physiology. Berlin: 1971-1981. V. 65

AUTRY, GENE
Back in the Saddle Again. Garden City: 1978. V. 66

AUTUMN Songs with Music from Flower Fairies of the Autumn. London: 1927. V. 66

AVALLONE, MICHAEL
Dead Game. 1954. V. 64
The Spitting Image. 1953. V. 64; 66
The Tall Dolores. 1953. V. 64; 66

AVARY, MYRTA LOCKETT
Dixie After the War. New York: 1906. V. 62

AVEBURY, JOHN LUBBOCK, BARON
A Contribution to Our Knowledge of Seedlings. 1892. V. 66

AVEDON, RICHARD
An Auto-Biography Richard Avedon. New York: 1993. V. 65
Avedon: Photographs: 1947-1977. New York: 1978. V. 63
In the American West. New York: 1985. V. 65; 66

AVEIRO, PANTALIAO DE
Itinerario de Terra Sancta, e Todas Suas Particularidades...Agora Novamente Acrecentado.... Lisbon: 1596. V. 62

AVELING, JAMES
Yorkshire. The History of Roche Abbey, From Its Foundation to Its Dissolution. London: 1870. V. 65

AVERILL, ESTHER
Poudre: l'Histoire d'un Poulain, d'une Duchesse et d'un Cirque. Paris: 1933. V. 64
Powder: the Story of a Colt, a Duchess and the Circus. New York: 1933. V. 64

AVERY, PHINEAS O.
History of the Fourth Illinois Cavalry Regiment. Humboldt: 1903. V. 62; 63

AVI
The True Confessions of Charlotte Doyle. New York: 1990. V. 65

AVIATION: Comment L'Oiseau Vole, Comment l'Homme Volera. Paris: 1909. V. 65

AVIRETT, JAMES B.
The Memoirs of General Turner Ashby and His Compeers. Baltimore: 1867. V. 62; 63; 65

AVI-SHAI
Hagenu: Sefer Temunot. (Our Holidays). New York: 1928. V. 64

AVISON, CHARLES
An Essay on Musical Expression. London: 1752. V. 63

AWDLAY, JOHN
Alia Cantalena de Sancta Maria. 1926. V. 62

AWDRY, W.
Belinda Beats the Band. Brockhampton: 1961. V. 66
The Twin Engines. London: 1960. V. 67

AWSITER, J.
Thoughts on Brightelmston Concerning Sea-Bathing and Drinking Sea Water. 1768. V. 62; 63

AXE, J. WORTLEY
The Horse Its Treatment in Health and Disease. London: 1905-1908. V. 66

AXELROD, ALAN
Art of the Golden West. New York: 1990. V. 66

AXELROD, H. R.
The Atlas of Discus of the World. Neptune City: 1991. V. 65
The Most Complete Colored Lexicon of Cichlids, Every Known Cichlid Illustrated in Color. Neptune: 1996. V. 65
Swordtails and Platies. Neptune City: 1991. V. 65

AXELROD, JOSEPH
Around Western Campfires. New York: 1964. V. 63

AXTIUS, JOHANN CONRAD
Tractatus de Arboribus Coniferis et Pice Conficieda. Jena: 1679. V. 64; 66; 67

AYCKBOURN, ALAN
The Norman Conquests. London: 1975. V. 66

AYER, EMMA BURBANK
A Motor Flight through Algeria and Tunisia. Chicago: 1911. V. 62; 63; 64; 66

AYER, JAMES BOURNE
James Ayer: in Memoriam. Boston: 1892. V. 63

AYER, JEAN
Donald Duck and His Friends. Boston: 1939. V. 65

AYER, SARAH CONNELL
Diary. Portland: 1910. V. 67

AYER'S Deutscher Almanack. Lowell: 1875. V. 67

AYERS, E. C.
Hour of the Manatee. New York: 1994. V. 67

AYERS, EDWARD T.
Bowls, Bowling Greens and Bowl Playing. London: 1894. V. 64

AYERS, I. WINSLOW
Life in the Wilds of America and Wonders of the West in and Beyond the Bounds of Civilization. Grand Rapids: 1880. V. 63; 66

AYLIFFE, JOHN
Parergon Juris Canonici Anglicani; or, A Commentary, By Way of Supplement to the Canons and Constitutions of the Church of England. London: 1726. V. 67

AYLOFFE, JOSEPH
Calendars of the Ancient Charters, and of the Welch and Scottish Rolls, Now Remaining in the Tower of London. London: 1774. V. 64

AYME, MARCEL
The Magic Pictures. More About the Wonderful Farm. New York: 1954. V. 63

AYRE, L. R.
The North Lonsdale Magazine and Furness Miscellany. Ulverston: 1894-1902. V. 64; 65

AYRSHIRE and Robert Burns. London. V. 62; 67

AYRTON, MICHAEL
Archilochos. London: 1977. V. 66
Drawings and Sculpture. London: 1962. V. 64
Giovanni Pisano, Sculptor. New York: 1969. V. 62; 65
The Minotaur. London: 1970. V. 66
Tittivulus or the Verbiage Collector. London: 1953. V. 62; 66

AYSCOUGH, SAMUEL
An Index to the Remarkable Passages and Words Made Use of by Shakespeare. 1790. V. 67
An Index to the Remarkable Passages and Words Made Use of by Shakespeare. London: 1790. V. 63

AYTOUN, WILLIAM EDMONSTOUNE
Lays of the Scottish Cavaliers and Other Poems. London: 1881. V. 62

AZAIS, PIERRE H.
Explanation and History of the Artesian Well of Genelle. Boston: 1845. V. 66

AN AZTEC Herbal of 1552. Baltimore: 1940. V. 65

B

B., A.
The Treaty of Seville, and Measures That Have Been Taken for the Four Last Years.... London: 1730. V. 64

B., C.
The Story of a Nursery Rhyme. London: 1883. V. 65

B R Today: a Selection of His Books, with Comments. New York: 1982. V. 62

B., R.
Coral and Steel: a Most Compenius Method of Preserving and Restoring Health. London: 1660?. V. 65

B., W. P.
Messina After the Great Disaster. 1909. V. 62; 66

BAADER, JUAN
The Sailing Yacht. London: 1965. V. 62

BAAS, JOHANN HERMANN
Die Geschichtliche Entwicklung des Aerztlichen Standes und der Medicinischen Wisseshaften. Berlin: 1896. V. 64
Outlines of the History of Medicine and the Medical Profession. New York: 1889. V. 64; 66

BABBAGE, CHARLES
The Ninth Bridgewater Treatise. London: 1837. V. 63
The Ninth Bridgewater Treatise. London: 1838. V. 65
On the Economy of Machinery and Manufactures. London: 1832. V. 62; 64
On the Economy of Machinery and Manufactures. London: 1833. V. 66
On the Economy of Machinery and Manufactures. London: 1835. V. 64
Passages from the Life of a Philosopher. London: 1864. V. 64; 65; 66
Scriptores Optici; or, a Collection of Tracts Relating to Optics. London: 1823. V. 65

BABBITT, BRUCE
Color and Light - the Southwest Canvases of Louis Akin. Flagstaff: 1973. V. 63
Grand Canyon - an Anthology. Flagstaff: 1978. V. 67

BABCOCK, BARBARA A.
The Pueblo Storyteller. Tucson: 1986. V. 67

BABCOCK, BENJAMIN J.
The Merchants Union Express Company's Shipping and Way Billing Directory. New York: 1866. V. 66

BABCOCK, D. S.
The History of Battery D 1st Field Artillery 1792-1934. Fort Sill: 1934. V. 62; 65

BABCOCK, HAVILAH
According to Hoyle: a Glossary of Idiomatic and Colloquial Usage. Columbia: 1928. V. 63
My Health is Better in November. Columbia: 1947. V. 63; 64; 66

BABCOCK, L. L.
The Tarpon, a Description of the Fish Together with Some Hints On Its Capture. N.P: 1936. V. 65

BABCOCK, MALTBIE DAVENPORT
Letters from Egypt and Palestine. New York: 1902. V. 66

BABE Ruth's Baseball Advice. Chicago: 1936. V. 64

BABER, LUCY HARRISON
Behind the Old Brick Wall: a Cemetery Story. Lynchburg. 1900. V. 64

BABER, ZEHIR-ED-DIN MUHAMMED
Memoirs of.... London: 1826. V. 64

THE BABES in the Wood. London: 1890. V. 66

BABINSKI, J.
Reflexes Tendineux and Reflexes Osseux. Paris: 1912. V. 64

BABY.. New York: 1873. V. 64

BABY Bob. London: 1908. V. 67

A BABYLONIAN Anthology. North Hills: 1966. V. 64

BACA, MANUEL C. DE
Vicente Silva and His 40 Bandits. Washington: 1947. V. 64

BACALL, LAUREN
By Myself. London: 1979. V. 65

BACH, ALICE
Moses' Ark: Stories from the Bible. New York: 1989. V. 65

BACHAUS, THEODORE
Private Presses of San Serriffe. N.P: 1980. V. 62

BACHELLER, IRVING
Eben Holden, a Tale of the North Country. Boston: 1900. V. 63

BACHERIUS, PETRUS
Panicvs Tvmvltvs, Rebvs in Belgio Pacatis, ac Mire Tranquillis, Quorundam Improbitate Iniectus. Antwerp: 1568. V. 63

BACHMAN, CHARLES W.
A Manual of Football for High School Coaches. Manhattan: 1923. V. 67

BACHMAN, JOHN
Vindication of Rev. Dr. John Bachman of Charleston, S.C., in Answer to Rev. E. W. Hutter. Charleston: 1868. V. 63; 66

BACHMANN, WALTER
Swiss Gateaux Designs and Decorations. London: 1950. V. 62

BACK, GEORGE
Narrative of the Arctic Land Expedition to the Mouth of the Great Fish River, and Along the Shores of the Arctic Ocean, in the Years 1833, 1834 and 1835. London: 1836. V. 64; 65

BACKEBERG, C.
Cactus Lexicon.... Poole: 1977. V. 67

BACKER, C. A.
The Problem of Krakatoa as Seen by a Botanist. 1929. V. 66

BACKER, LOUIS DE
Le Droit de la Femme Dans l'Antiquite, son Devoir au Moyen Age d'Apres des Manuscrits de la Bibliotheque Nationale. Paris: 1880. V. 63

THE BACKGROUND and Issues of the War. Oxford: 1940. V. 64

BACKHOUSE, JAMES
The Life and Correspondence of William and Alice Ellis of Airton. London: 1849. V. 64; 65
A Narrative of a Visit to the Australian Colonies. London: 1843. V. 64
A Narrative of a Visit to the Mauritius and South Africa. London: 1844. V. 64; 65

BACKUS, ISSAC
A Short Description of the Difference Between the Bond-Woman and the Free, As They are the Two Convenants. Boston;: 1770. V. 66

BACKUS, R. H.
George Bank. Cambridge: 1987. V. 65

BACON, ALBAN F. L.
Enchanted Days with Rod and Gun. London: 1926. V. 67

BACON, ALICE
Japanese Girls and Women. London: 1891. V. 64

BACON, EPHRAIM
Abstract of a Journal Kept by E. Bacon, United States Assistant Agent for the Reception of Recaptured Negroes on the Coast of Africa.... Philadelphia: 1824. V. 64

BACON, FRANCIS, VISCOUNT ST. ALBANS
Baconiana. Or Certain Genuine Remains of Francis Bacon. London: 1679. V. 67
Bacon's Essays and Wisdom of the Ancients. Boston: 1917. V. 67
A Declara(tion) of the Practices and (Treasons) Attempted and Committed by Robe(rt) Late Earle of Essex and His Complices, Against Her Maiestie and Her Kingdoms.... London: 1601. V. 66
De Dignitate & Augmentis Scientiarum, Libri IX. Leyden: 1645. V. 65
The Essayes or Counsels, Civill and Morall.... London: 1625. V. 66; 67
The Essayes or Counsels, Civill and Morall.... London: 1629. V. 64
The Essayes or Covnsels Civill and Morall. London: 1632. V. 63
Essayes, Religious Meditations, Places of Perswasion and Disswasion. 1924. V. 62
Essays and Apothegms of Francis Lord Bacon. London: 1892. V. 62
Essays Moral, Economical and Political. Boston: 1807. V. 66
The Essays of Counsels Civil and Moral and Wisdom of the Ancients of Francis Lord Verulam. London: 1836. V. 62
The Essays of Francis Bacon, Lord Verulam. London: 1910. V. 62
Essays of Lord Bacon. 1894. V. 64
The Essays or Counsels.... London: 1673. V. 64
The Essays or Counsels.... London: 1836. V. 66
The Essays or Counsels.... London: 1845. V. 67
Francisci Baconi de Verulamio Scripta in Naturali et Universali Philosophia. Amsterdam: 1653. V. 66
Historia Naturalis & Experimentalis de Ventis. Amstelodami: 1662. V. 63; 66
The Historie of Life and Death. London: 1638. V. 64
The Historie of the Raigne of King Henry the Seventh. London: 1622. V. 63; 64
The History of the Reigne of King Henry the Seventh. London: 1629. V. 62
The History of the Reigns of Henry the Seventh, Henry the Eighth, Edward the Sixth and Queen Mary.... London: 1686. V. 64
Letters. London: 1702. V. 63; 66
A New Edition of the Works. London: 1825-1834. V. 67
Novum Organum Scientiarum: Containing Rules for Conducting the Understanding in the Search of Truth.... London: 1818. V. 65
Of Gardens. Sweden, Maine: 1991. V. 62
Of Studies by Francis Bacon. San Francisco: 1928. V. 64
Of the Advancement and Proficiencie of Learning of the Partitions of Sciences. Oxford: 1640. V. 63; 65
Of the Advancement and Proficiencie of Learning; or the Partitions of Sciences (in) Nine Books.... London: 1674. V. 66
Of Truth, Beautye and Goodnesse. Chelsea: 1920. V. 62
Resusitatio, or, Bringing Into Publick Light Several Pieces of the Works, Civil, Historical, Philosophical.... London: 1671. V. 66
Sir Francis Bacon His Apologie in Certaine Imputations Concerning the Late Earle of Essex. London: 1642. V. 66
A Speech Delivered by Sir Francis Bacon, in the Lower House of Parliament Quinto Iacobi, Concerning the Article of Naturalization of the Scottish Nation. London: 1641. V. 63
Sylva Sylvarium; or, Naturall History. In Ten Centuries. Whereunto is Newly Added the History Naturall and Experimental of Life and Death. London: 1651. V. 64
Sylva Sylvarum; or a Natural Historie. London: 1628. V. 66
Sylva Sylvarum, or a Natural Historie. London: 1635. V. 63
The Two Bookes of Sr. Francis Bacon Of the Proficience and Advancement of Learning, Divine and Human. (with) The Essayes or Counsels, Civill and Morall.... Oxford: 1633. V. 66
The Two Books....Of the Proficience and Advancement of Learning, Divine and Human. to the King. London: 1825. V. 66
The Twoo Bookes of...The Proficience and Aduancement of Learning, Diuine and Humane. London: 1605. V. 63; 66
The Works. London: 1825. V. 62
The Works. Cambridge: 1863. V. 63
The Works. (with) The Letters and the Life. London: 1883-1892-1861. V. 64

BACON, G. MACKENZIE
On the Writing of the Insane.... London: 1870. V. 64

BACON, JOHN
Liber Regis, vel Thesaurus Rerum Ecclesiasticarum.... London: 1786. V. 63

BACON, JOHN M.
By Land and Sky. London: 1900. V. 64

BACON, NATHANIELL
The Annalls of Ipswche. The Laws, Customes and Government of the Same. London: 1884. V. 62

BACON, NICHOLAS
The Recreations of His Age. Oxford: 1903. V. 66
The Recreations of His Age. Oxford: 1919. V. 66

BACON, RICHARD MACKENZIE
A Memoir of the Life of Edward, Third Baron Suffield. Norwich: 1838. V. 67

BACON, RICHARD NOVERRE
The Report on the Agriculture of Norfolk, to Which the Prize Was Awarded by the Royal Agricultural Society of England. London: 1844. V. 62

BACON, ROGER
Opera Quaedem Hactenus Inedita. London: 1859. V. 63
Opus Majus. London: 1733. V. 63; 67

BACON, THOMAS
First Impressions and Studies from Nature in Hindostan Embracing an Outline of the Voyage to Calcutta and Five Years' Residence in Bengal and the Doab from 1831 to 1836. London: 1837. V. 65

BADCOCK, JOHN
Domestic Amusements or Philosophical Recreations, Containing the Results of Various Experiments in Practical Science and the Useful Arts.... London: 1823. V. 63

BADEAU, ADAM
Conspiracy: a Cuban Romance. New York: 1885. V. 63

BADEN-POWELL, R. S. S.
The Matabele Campaign Being a Narrative of the Campaign in Suppressing the Native Rising in Matabeleland and Mashonaland. London: 1901. V. 63

BADEN-POWELL, ROBERT
Paddle Your Own Canoe or Tips for Boys from the Jungle and Elsewhere. London: 1939. V. 67
Pig Sticking or Hog Hunting, a Complete Account for Sportsmen and Others. 1924. V. 67
Pig-Sticking or Hog Hunting. London: 1924. V. 64; 65

BADESLADE, THOMAS
Chorographia Britanniae. London: 1742. V. 66; 67

BADHAM, C. D.
A Treatise on the Esculent Funguses of England. London: 1847. V. 62
A Treatise on the Esculent Funguses of England. London: 1863. V. 62

BADHAM, CHARLES
The Life of James Deacon Hume, Secretary of the Board of Trade. London: 1859. V. 64

BADHAM, CHARLES DAVID
Prose Halieutics, or Ancient and Modern Fish Tattle. London: 1854. V. 67
The Question Concerning the Sensibility, Intelligence and Instinctive Actions of Insects.... Paris: 1837. V. 67

BADIN, STEPHEN THEODORE
Origine et Progres de la Missiou du Kentucky, (Etats-Unis d'Amerique). Paris: 1821. V. 63; 66

BADINI, CARLO FRANCESCO
Il Disertore: a New Comic Opera. London: 1770. V. 67

BADIUS ASCENSIUS, JODOCUS
Navis Stultifera. Basel: 1506. V. 63; 66
Navis Stultifera. Paris: 1513. V. 64; 66

BADOVICI, JEAN
Grandes Constructions, Beton Arme - Acier - Verre. Paris: 1925. V. 65
Grandes Constructions Realisees par E. Freyssinet et Presentees par Jean Badovici, Architecte. Paris: 1931. V. 65

BAEDEKER, KARL
Austria-Hungary with Excursions to Cetinje, Belgrade and Bucharest. Leipzig: 1911. V. 62
The Dominion of Canada, With Newfoundland and an Excursion to Alaska. Leipsic et al: 1907. V. 65
Egypt and the Sudan. Leipsic: 1908. V. 62
Egypt and the Sudan. Leipzig: 1914. V. 65
Egypt Handbook for Travellers: Part Second: Upper Egypt, with Nubias as Far as the Second Cataract and the Western Oases. Leipsic: 1892. V. 65
Great Britain. Leipzig: 1901. V. 62
Greece Handbook for Travellers. Leipsic: 1894. V. 65
Greece. Handbook for Travellers. Leipsic: 1909. V. 62
Greece. Handbook for Travellers. Leipsic: 1927. V. 64
Italy. Handbook for Travellers. Second Part: Central Italy and Rome. Leipsic: 1875. V. 62
London and Its Environs. Leipsic: 1889. V. 62
Palestine and Syria: Handbook for Travellers. Leipsic & London: 1894. V. 65
The Rhine from Rotterdam to Constance. Handbook for Travellers. Coblenz and Leipsic: 1873. V. 62
The Riviera. South-Eastern France and Corsica, the Italian Lakes and Lake of Geneva. Handbook for Travellers. Leipzig: 1931. V. 62
The Traveller's Manual of Conversation in Four Languages, English, French, German, Italian.... Dulau and Leipsic. V. 62
United States. Leipsic: 1899. V. 62; 66

BAEGERT, JOHANN JAKOB
Observations in Lower California. Berkeley & Los Angeles: 1952. V. 62

BAER, CURTIS O.
Landscape Drawings. New York: 1977. V. 62; 63; 64; 66

BAER, ELIZABETH
Seventeenth Century Maryland, a Bibliography. Baltimore: 1949. V. 63

BAERNREITHER, J. M.
English Associations of Working Men. London: 1889. V. 64
English Associations of Working Men. London: 1893. V. 64

BAEYER, E. VON
Rhetoric and Roses, a History of Canadian Gardening 1900-1930. 1984. V. 67

BAGBY, GEORGE W.
Selections from the Miscellaneous Writings of Dr. George W. Bagby. Richmond: 1884-1885. V. 63

BAGEHOT, WALTER
Biographical Studies. London: 1881. V. 64
The English Constitution. London: 1872. V. 64
Essays on Parliamentary Reform. London: 1883. V. 62
Estimates of Some Englishmen and Scotchmen, a Series of Articles Reprinted by Permission Principally from the National Review. London: 1858. V. 62; 64
Lombard Street: a Description of the Money Market. London: 1873. V. 64

BAGENAL, PHILIP H.
Vicissitudes of an Anglo-Irish Family 1530 to 1800. 1925. V. 65

BAGG, E.
Birds of the Connecticut Valley in Mass. 1937. V. 66

BAGGULEY, WILLIAM H.
Andrew Marvell - 1621-1678 - Tercentenary Tributes.... London: 1922. V. 62; 65

BAGLEY, CLARENCE
The Acquisition and Pioneering of Old Oregon. Seattle: 1924. V. 63

BAGLIONE, GIOVANNI
Le Vite de' Pittori, Scultori, Architetti, ed Intagliation, dal Pontificato di Gregorio XIII del 1572 Fino a' Tempi di Papa Urbano VII nel 1642. Naples: 1733. V. 66

BAGLIVI, GEORGE
Opera Omnia Medico Practica, et Anatomica. Venice: 1738. V. 64

BAGNALL, A. G.
New Zealand National Bibliography to the Year 1960. Wellington: 1980. V. 64

BAGNALL, J. E.
The Flora of Warwickshire. London and Birmingham: 1891. V. 62; 63

BAGNOLD, ENID
National Velvet. London and Toronto: 1935. V. 63
Serena Blandish or the Difficulty of Getting Married, by a Lady of Quality. London: 1924. V. 62

BAGOT, A. G.
Shooting and Yachting in the Mediterranean. London: 1887. V. 65

BAGOT, JOSCELINE
Colonel James Grahme of Levens. Kendal: 1886. V. 64; 65; 66

BAGROW, LEO
History of Cartography. Cambridge: 1964. V. 62
History of Cartography. Chicago: 1985. V. 63

BAGSHAW, WILLIAM
On Man: His Motives, their Rise, Operations, Opposition and Results. London: 1833. V. 63

BAHR, JEROME
All Good Americans. New York: 1937. V. 66

BAHR, LEONARD
Adagio. Harper Woods. V. 63

BAIERLACHER, EDUARD
Die Inductions Elektricitat in Physiologisch Therapeutischer Beziehung. Nurnberg: 1857. V. 65

BAIF, LAZARE DE
Annotationes in Legum II De Captivis and Postlimino Reversis, in Quibus Tractatur de Re Navalis.... Basle: 1541. V. 64

BAIGELL, MATTHEW
The American Scene: American Painting of the 1930's. New York: 1974. V. 63

BAIKOV, N.
Big Game Hunting in Manchuria. 1936. V. 67

BAILEY, A. E.
Cottonseed and Cottonseed Products, Their Chemistry and Chemical Technology. New York: 1948. V. 63

BAILEY, A. M.
Birds of Arctic Alaska. Denver: 1948. V. 64; 67
Birds of Colorado. Denver: 1965. V. 63; 64; 66; 67
Sub-Antarctic Campbell Island. Denver: 1962. V. 64

BAILEY, BENSON
Ilkley, Bolton Abbey, and the Pearls of Craven; or, Sketches of the Prettiest Spots in that Interesting District. Bingley: 1866. V. 67

BAILEY, CAROLYN SHERWIN
Miss Hickory. New York: 1946. V. 64

BAILEY, DAVID
Another Image: Papua New Guinea. London: 1975. V. 63
Goodbye Baby and Amen. A Saraband for the Sixties. London: 1970. V. 66
Imagine. A Book for Band Aid. London: 1985. V. 62; 66
Mixed Moments. London: 1976. V. 66

BAILEY, E. B.
Tertiary and Post Tertiary Geology of Mull, Loch Aline and Oban. 1924. V. 67

BAILEY, FLORENCE MERRIAM
Birds of New Mexico. N.P: 1928. V. 63; 67
Birds of New Mexico. Santa Fe: 1928. V. 67
Birds of New Mexico. Washington: 1928. V. 64

BAILEY, FRANCIS A.
A History of Southport. Southport: 1955. V. 65

BAILEY, H.
Notable Names in Medicine and Surgery. London: 1959. V. 66; 67

BAILEY, H. C.
Dead Man's Effects. London: 1945. V. 66
Mr. Clunk's Text. New York: 1939. V. 66
Shadow on the Wall. London: 1934. V. 66
Slippery Ann. London: 1944. V. 66
The Veron Mystery. London: 1939. V. 66

BAILEY, H. H.
The Birds of Florida.... Baltimore: 1925. V. 64
When New Mexico Was Young. Las Cruces: 1946. V. 64

BAILEY, HAROLD
The Birds of Virginia. Lynchburg: 1913. V. 62

BAILEY, J. D.
Commanders at Kings Mountain. Gaffney: 1926. V. 63; 66; 67
History of Grindal Shoals and Some Early Adjacent Families. Gaffney: 1927. V. 63

BAILEY, J. M.
The Book of Ensilage.... Billerica: 1880. V. 62

BAILEY, J. W.
Biology at the University of Richmond. Richmond: 1939. V. 63

BAILEY, JESSIE B.
Diego De Vardas and the Reconquest of New Mexico. Albuquerque: 1940. V. 65

BAILEY, JOHN
A General View of the Agriculture of the County of Northumberland (Cumberland and Westmoreland).... London: 1805. V. 65

BAILEY, JOHN W.
Pacifying the Plains - General Alfred Terry and the Decline of the Sioux 1866-1890. 1979. V. 67

BAILEY, KENNETH P.
The Ohio Company of Virginia and the Westward Movement 1748-1792: a Chapter in the History of the Colonial Frontier. Glendale: 1939. V. 64; 66

BAILEY, LIBERTY HYDE
The Cultivated Evergreens...in the United States and Canada. 1923. V. 63; 66
Cyclopedia of American Horticulture.... New York: 1900-1903. V. 67
Cyclopedia of American Horticulture.... New York: 1909. V. 67
The Garden of Gourds. New York: 1937. V. 67
The Gardens of Larkspurs. New York: 1939. V. 67
Hortus Third, a Concise Dictionary of Plants Cultivated in the United States and Canada. New York: 1976. V. 64; 67
Manual of Cultivated Plants Most Commonly Grown in the Continental United States and Canada. New York: 1949. V. 67
The Pruning-Book.... New York: 1911. V. 67
The Standard Cyclopedia of Horticulture. New York: 1914-1917. V. 67
The Standard Cyclopedia of Horticulture. New York: 1928. V. 64; 67
The Standard Cyclopedia of Horticulture. New York: 1937. V. 63; 66

BAILEY, NATHAN
The Antiquities of London and Westminster. London: 1722. V. 62; 66
Dictionarium Britannicum.... London: 1730. V. 62

BAILEY, NATHANIEL
The New Universal Etymological English Dictionary. 1776. V. 64
An Universal Etymological Dictionary. London: 1733. V. 64
An Universal Etymological Dictionary. London: 1751. V. 64; 67
An Universal Etymological Dictionary... (with) The Universal Etymological Dictionary...Containing an Additional Collection of Words (Not in the First Volume). London: 1733-1737. V. 62
Universal Etymological English Dictionary. London: 1753. V. 63; 66
An Universal Etymological English Dictionary.... London: 1728. V. 64
An Universal Etymological English Dictionary.... London: 1740. V. 64
An Universal Etymological English Dictionary.... London: 1757. V. 64
An Universal Etymological English Dictionary.... London: 1763. V. 64
An Universal Etymological English Dictionary.... London: 1782. V. 64

BAILEY, PAUL
Great West and Indian Series. Los Angeles: 1953-1968. V. 64

BAILEY, PERCIVAL
A Classification of the Tumors of the Glioma Group on a Histogenetic Basis with a Correlated Study of Prognosis. 1971. V. 67
Further Notes on the Cerebellar Medulloblastomas. The Effect of Roentgen Radiation. 1930. V. 64
Further Remarks Concerning Tumors of the Glioma Group. 1927. V. 64; 67
A Progressive Staining Method for Mitochondria. 1924. V. 67

BAILEY, PHILIP A.
Golden Mirages. Ramona: 1940. V. 66

BAILEY, ROBERT G.
Hell's Canyon: a Story of the Deepest Canyon of the North American Continent, Together with Historical Sketches of Idaho.... Lewiston: 1943. V. 64; 66; 67

BAILEY, ROSALIE FELLOWS
Pre-Revolutionary Dutch Houses and Families in Northern New Jersey and Southern New York. New York: 1936. V. 63; 66

BAILEY, SAMUEL
Discourses on Various Subjects: Read Before Literary and Philosophical Societies. London: 1852. V. 64
Essays on the Formation and Publication of Opinions and Other Subjects. London: 1826. V. 62

BAILEY, T. J.
A Defence of the Holy Orders in the Church of England. Brighton: 1870. V. 62

BAILEY, THOMAS
Handbook to Newstead Abbey. London: 1855. V. 65

BAILEY, V.
Animal Life of Yellowstone National Park. Springfield: 1930. V. 62

BAILEY, VERNON HOWE
Empire State. A Pictorial Record of Its Construction. New York: 1931. V. 64

BAILEY, WASHINGTON
A Trip to California in 1853 - Recollections of a Gold Seeking Trip by Ox Train Across the Plains and Mountains by an Old Illinois Pioneer. Le Roy: 1915. V. 66

BAILLIE, JOANNA
A Collection of Poems.... London: 1823. V. 64
Complete Poetical Works. Philadelphia: 1832. V. 62; 65
Dramas. London: 1836. V. 65
Fugitive Verses. London: 1840. V. 65
A Series of Plays: In Which It Is Attempts to Delineate the Stronger Passions of the Mind.... London: 1806-1812. V. 65

BAILLIE, MATTHEW
A Series of Engravings, Accompanied by Explanations, Which are Intended to Illustrate the Morbid Anatomy of the Most Important Parts of the Human Body. London: 1812. V. 64

BAILLIE, W. W., MRS.
Days and Nights of Shikar. London: 1921. V. 62

BAILLIE-GROHMAN, W. A.
Fifteen Years' Sport and Life in the Hunting Grounds of Western America and British Columbia. London: 1900. V. 64
Sport in the Alps in the Past and Present.... London: 1896. V. 64

BAILLIE-GROHMANN, W. A.
Sport in the Alps in the Past and Present.... New York: 1896. V. 65

BAILLY, JEAN SYLVAIN
Traite de l'Astronomie Indienne et Orientale Ouvrage qui peut Servir de Suite a l'Histoire de l'Astronomie Ancienne. Paris: 1787. V. 62

BAILLY, LOUIS
Sindbad Le Marin. Paris: 1920. V. 65

BAILY, FRANCIS
The Description and Use of a New Chart of History, Exhibiting the Most Material Revolutions that Have Taken Place in the Principal Empires, Kingdoms and States.... London: 1817. V. 65
Tables for the Purchasing and Renewing of Leases, Terms of years Certain and For Lives.... London: 1807. V. 63

BAILY, J. T. HERBERT
Emma, Lady Hamilton. London: 1905. V. 62; 63; 64; 66

BAILY, WILLIAM H.
Figures of Characteristic British Fossils. 1875. V. 65; 67
Figures of Characteristic British Fossils. London: 1875. V. 64

BAILY'S Hunting Directory 1926-1927. London: 1926. V. 67

BAILY'S Hunting Directory 1930-1931. London: 1930. V. 67

BAIN, ALEXANDER
The Emotions and the Will. London: 1859. V. 64
James Mill, A Biography. London: 1882. V. 64

BAIN, F. W.
Christina, Queen of Sweden. London: 1890. V. 62

BAIN, JOSEPH
The Hamilton Papers. Letters and Papers Illustrating the Political Relations of England and Scotland in the 16th Century. 1532-1590. Edinburgh: 1890-1892. V. 66

BAINBRIDGE, BERYL
Another Part of the Wood. London: 1968. V. 63

BAINBRIDGE, GEORGE C.
The Fly Fisher's Guide, Illustrated by Coloured Plates.... Liverpool: 1816. V. 66

BAINBRIDGE, HENRY CHARLES
Peter Carl Faberge. Goldsmith and Jeweller to the Russian Imperial Court. London: 1949. V. 65

BAINBRIDGE, JOHN
The Super-Americans. Garden City: 1961. V. 67

BAINBRIDGE, WILLIAM HENRY
Early Education: Being the Substance of Four Lectures Delivered in the Public Hall of the Collegiate Institution, Liverpool,. London: 1854. V. 64

BAINBRIGGE, PHILIP GILLESPIE
Dialogus Jocundus: Robertus. London: 1926. V. 67

BAINES, EDWARD
A Companion to the Lakes of Cumberland, Westmoreland and Lancashire.... London: 1829. V. 65
History, Directory and Gazetteer of the County of York. Leeds: 1822. V. 66
History, Directory and Gazetteer of the County of York.... Leeds: 1822-1823. V. 63
History, Directory and Gazetteer of the County of York.... Newton Abbot: 1969. V. 63
History of the Cotton Manufacture in Great Britain.... London: 1835. V. 63; 64; 66
The History of the County Palatine and Duchy of Lancaster. London: 1868-1870. V. 63
History of the Wars of the French Revolution, from the Breaking Out of the War in 1792, to the Restoration of a General Peace in 1815.... London: 1818. V. 67
The Life of Edward Baines, Late M.P. for the Borough of Leeds. London: 1851. V. 64

BAINES, F. E.
Records of the Manor, Parish and Borough of Hampstead.... London: 1890. V. 62

BAINES, H.
The Flora of Yorkshire: a Supplement to Baines' Flora. 1840-1854. V. 62

BAINES, MARY ANNE
Domestic Servants As They Are and As They Ought To Be. London: 1859. V. 62

BAINES, T.
Greenhouse and Stove Plants. London: 1894. V. 64; 67

BAINES, THOMAS
The Gold Regions of South Eastern Africa. London: 1877. V. 64

BAINTON, GEORGE
The Art of Authorship. London: 1890. V. 63
The Art of Authorship. New York: 1891. V. 65

BAIRD, ABASLOM
Copies of Authentic Letters and Papers Throwing some Light on the History of Doctor Abaslom Baird of the Army of the Revolution. Pittsburgh: 1909. V. 63

BAIRD, JOSEPH
California's Pictorial Letters Sheets 1849-1869. San Francisco: 1967. V. 65
Times Wondrous Changes: San Francisco Architecture 1776-1915. San Francisco: 1962. V. 62; 63; 65

BAIRD, ROBERT
Impressions and Experiences of the West Indies and North America in 1849. Philadelphia: 1850. V. 66

BAIRD, SPENCER F.
The Birds of North America.... Philadelphia and Salem: 1860-1870. V. 65; 67
Directions for Collecting, Preserving and Transporting Specimens of Natural History. Washington: 1854. V. 63
A History of North American Birds: Land Birds. Boston: 1874. V. 62; 67
A History of North American Birds: Land Birds. Boston: 1905. V. 62; 64; 66; 67
Reports of Explorations...Pacific Railroad Surveys. Washington: 1858-1860. V. 64
Reptiles of the Boundary. Washington: 1859. V. 67
The Water Birds of North America. Boston: 1884. V. 62; 67

BAIRD, W.
The Natural History of the British Entomostraca. London: 1850. V. 62; 63; 66; 67

BAIRD, WILLIAM
Annals of Duddington and Portobello. Edinburgh: 1898. V. 67

BAIRNSFATHER, BRUCE
Fragments from France - Twelve Plates in Colour On Plate Sunk Mounts. London: 1916. V. 64

BAIRNSFATHER, P. R.
Sport and Nature in the Himalayas. 1914. V. 64; 66

BAKAY, LOUIS
The Treatment of Head Injuries in the Thirty Years' War (1618-1648). Springfield: 1971. V. 64

BAKEER, DONALD
Crips: the Story of the L.A. Street Gang from 1971-1985. Los Angeles: 1987. V. 65

BAKELESS, JOHN
Spies of the Confederacy. Philadelphia: 1970. V. 63

BAKER, B. GRANVILLE
Old Cavalry Stations. London: 1934. V. 62

BAKER, C. H. COLLINS
Lely and the Stuart Portrait Painters: a Study of English Portrait Painters Before and After Van Dyck. London: 1912. V. 64

BAKER, CHARLES H.
The Esquire Culinary Companion. New York: 1959. V. 67

BAKER, DAVID
The History of Manned Space Flight. New York: 1982. V. 67

BAKER, DAVID ERSKINE
The Companion to the Play-House.... London: 1764. V. 64; 65

BAKER, DOROTHY
Cassandra at the Wedding. Boston and Cambridge: 1962. V. 63
Young Man with a Horn. Boston: 1938. V. 63
Young Man with a Horn. London: 1938. V. 63

BAKER, E. C. STUART
The Birds of North Cachar, a Catalogue of the Passeriformes, Coraciiformes and the Order Psittacii of the Sub-Class Ciconiiformes. Bombay: 1893. V. 65
The Fauna of British India, Including Ceylon and Burma-Birds. London: 1922-1930. V. 66
The Game Birds of India, Burma and Ceylon. London: 1921-1930. V. 67
Game Birds of India, Burma and Ceylon. London and Bombay: 1921-1935. V. 62
The Indian Ducks and Their Allies. London: 1908. V. 64; 67
Indian Pigeons and Doves. 1913. V. 62
Indian Pigeons and Doves. London: 1913. V. 65; 67

BAKER, ERNEST A.
The Highlands with Rope and Rucksack. London: 1923. V. 62; 63
Moors, Crags and Caves of the High Peak and Neighbourhood. London: 1903. V. 64
Moors, Crags and Caves of the High Peak and the Neighbourhood. Manchester: 1903. V. 64; 65; 66

BAKER, EZEKIEL
Remarks on Rifle Guns: Being the Result of Sixty Years Practice and Observation.... Huntington. V. 67

BAKER, F. C.
The Fresh Water Mollusca of Wisconsin. Madison: 1928. V. 62; 66
The Fresh Water Mollusca of Wisconsin. 1972. V. 66
The Mollusca of the Chicago Area. Chicago: 1898-1902. V. 65

BAKER, FRANK
Before I Go Hence: Fantasia on a Novel. London: 1945. V. 67

BAKER, H.
The Microscope Made Easy; or the Nature, Uses and Magnifying Powers of the Best Kinds of Microscopes. London: 1743. V. 62

BAKER, H. A.
Ericas in Southern Africa. Cape Town: 1967. V. 63

BAKER, H. B.
Zonitid Snails from Pacific Islands. 1938-1941. V. 66

BAKER, HENRY
An Attempt Towards a Natural History of the Polype, in a Letter to Martin Folkes, Esq.... London: 1743. V. 63

BAKER, HENRY H.
Reminiscent Story of the Great Civil War. Second Paper. A Personal Exerpience. New Orleans: 1911. V. 62

BAKER, HERBERT
Architecture and Personalities. London: 1944. V. 67

BAKER, HOZIAL H.
Overland Journey to Carson Valley and California. San Francisco: 1973. V. 63; 66

BAKER, HUMFREY
The Well Spring of Sciences, Which Teacheth the Perfect Worke and Practise of Arithmeticke.... London: 1574. V. 66

BAKER, INEZ
Yesterday in Hall Country. Dallas: 1940. V. 62

BAKER, J. G.
Handbook of the Bromeliaceae. 1889. V. 63
Handbook of the Irideae. 1892. V. 63

BAKER, JAMES
Turkey in Europe. London: 1877. V. 63; 64

BAKER, JOHN R.
Man and Animals in the New Hebrides. 1929. V. 63; 64; 66; 67

BAKER, KARLE WILSON
The Seeker. 1927. V. 62

BAKER, M. L.
Orchid Species Culture. Portland: 1996. V. 67

BAKER, M. N.
The Quest for Pure Water: the History of Water Purification from the Earliest Records to the Twentieth Century. New York: 1949. V. 62

BAKER, NICHOLSON
The Mezzanine. New York: 1988. V. 62; 63; 65; 67
The Mezzanine. New York: 1990. V. 64
Room Temperature. Cambridge: 1990. V. 62
U and I. New York: 1991. V. 62
Vox. New York: 1992. V. 62; 63; 64; 66

BAKER, OLAF
Where the Buffaloes Begin. New York: 1981. V. 65

BAKER, R. H.
The Avifauna of Micronesia, Its Origin, Evolution and Distribution. Lawrence: 1951. V. 67

BAKER, R. T.
A Research on the Pines of Australia. Sydney: 1910. V. 63; 64; 67

BAKER, RICHARD
A Chronicle of the Kings of England, from the Time of the Romans Government Unto the Death of King James.... London: 1665. V. 63
A Chronicle of the Kings of England from the Time of ye Romans. London: 1684. V. 63

BAKER, RICHARD ST. BARBE
Among the Trees. London: 1935. V. 62
Among the Trees. London: 1935-1941. V. 62

BAKER, SAMUEL WHITE
The Albert N'Yanza, Great Basin of the Nile and Explorations of the Nile Sources. 1867. V. 66; 67
The Albert N'Yanza, Great Basin of the Nile and Explorations of the Nile Sources. London: 1867. V. 62; 64
The Albert N'Yanza, Great Basin of the Nile and Explorations of the Nile Sources. 1870. V. 66
Cyprus As I Saw It in 1879. London: 1879. V. 63; 66
Eight Years in Ceylon. 1891. V. 62
Eight Years' Wanderings in Ceylon. Philadelphia: 1874. V. 63
Exploration of the Nile Tributaries of Abyssinia. Hartford: 1868. V. 62
Exploration of the Nile Tributaries of Abyssinia. Hartford: 1869. V. 64
Ismailia. New York: 1875. V. 64
Ismailia. 1890. V. 66
The Nile Tributaries of Abyssinia and the Sword Hunters of the Hamran Arabs. London: 1867. V. 62
The Nile Tributaries of Abyssinia and the Sword Hunters of the Hamran Arabs. 1868. V. 64
The Nile Tributaries of Abyssinia and the Sword Hunters of the Hamran Arabs. London: 1874. V. 64
The Nile Tributaries of Abyssinia and the Sword Hunters of the Hamran Arabs. 1894. V. 66; 67
The Nile Tributaries of Abyssinia and the Sword Hunters of the Hamran Arabs. 1987. V. 66; 67
The Rifle and the Hound in Ceylon. Philadelphia: 1869. V. 63
The Rifle and the Hound in Ceylon. London: 1884. V. 67
Wild Beasts and Their Ways. London: 1890. V. 67
Wild Beasts and Their Ways. 1988. V. 67

BAKER, T. H.
Records of the Seasons, Prices of Agricultural Produce and Phenomena Observed in the British Isles. London: 1883. V. 66

BAKER, THOMAS
Reflections Upon Learning. London: 1700. V. 64
Reflections Upon Learning. London: 1714. V. 64

BAKER, THOMAS BARWICK LLOYD
War With Crime, Being a Selection of Reprinted Papers on Crime, Reformatories, etc. London: 1889. V. 63

BAKER, W. W.
Forty Years - a Pioneer Business Life of Dorsey Syng Baker 1848-1888. Seattle: 1934. V. 62

BAKEWELL, ROBERT
An Introduction to Geology: Intended to Convey a Practical Knowledge of the Science. London: 1833. V. 64; 65; 67
Observations on the Influence of Soil and Climate Upon Wool, from Which is Deduced, a Certain and Easy Method of Improving the Quality of English Clothing Wools.... London: 1808. V. 63; 65
Travels, Comprising Observations Made During a Residence in Tarentaise and Various Parts of the Grecian and Pennine Alps and in Switzerland and Auvergne, in the Years 1820, 1821 and 1822. 1823. V. 65; 66

BAKIS, KIRSTEN
Lives of the Monster Dogs. New York: 1997. V. 67

BAKST, LEON
The Designs of Leon Bakst for the Sleeping Princess. London: 1923. V. 64

BALABAN, JOHN
After Our War. Pittsburgh: 1974. V. 63
Vietnam Poems. Oxford: 1970. V. 63

BALAZS, BELA
Der Sichtbare mensch oder Die Kultur des Films. Vienna & Leipzig: 1924. V. 67

BALBIRNIE, J.
A Treatise on the Organic Diseases of the Womb. London: 1830. V. 62

BALCH, H. E.
The Mendip Caves. Bristol: 1947-1948. V. 64

BALDERSTON, ROBERT R.
Ingleton: Bygone and Present. London: 1888. V. 64; 65; 66
Ingleton: Bygone and Present. London: 1890. V. 62; 63

BALDI, BERNARDINO
Bernardini Baldi Vrbinatis Gvastallae Abbatis in mechanica Aristotellis Problemata Exercitationes.... Mainz: 1621. V. 65
Cronica de Matematici, Ovvero Epitome dell'Istoria delle Vite Loro Opera. Urbino: 1707. V. 66

BALDINGER, ERNEST GOTTFRIED
Catalogus Biblitothecase Medico-Physicae.... Marburg: 1805. V. 66

BALDRIDGE, M.
A Reminiscence of the Parker H. French Expedition through Texas and Mexico to California in the Spring of 1850. Los Angeles: 1959. V. 65

BALDUINUS, BENEDICTUS
De Calceo Antiquo et de Caliga Veterum.... Amsterdam: 1667. V. 66

BALDWIN, ALICE B.
Memoirs of Major General Frank D. Baldwin. Los Angeles: 1929. V. 65; 67

BALDWIN, C. E.
The History and Development of the Port of Blyth. Newcastle-upon-Tyne: 1929. V. 64; 65; 66

BALDWIN, GEORGE C.
Representative Women; from Eve, the Wife of the First, to Mary, the Mother of the Second Adam. New York and Chicago: 1855. V. 63

BALDWIN, H.
The Orchids of New England. New York: 1884. V. 67

BALDWIN, J. D.
Ancient America. New York: 1871. V. 66

BALDWIN, J. H.
The Large and Small Game of Bengal and the North Western Provinces of India. 1877. V. 67
The Large and Small Game of Bengal and the North Western Provinces of India. London: 1877. V. 62

BALDWIN, JAMES
Another Country. New York: 1962. V. 65
Another Country. London: 1963. V. 62
Collected Essays. New York: 1998. V. 65
Early Novels and Stories. New York: 1997. V. 65
Go Tell It On the Mountain. New York: 1953. V. 67
Go Tell It On the Mountain. London: 1954. V. 62
Go Tell It On the Mountain. Franklin Center: 1979. V. 63; 66
Going to Meet the Man. New York: 1965. V. 62; 64; 65; 67
Gypsy and Other Poems. N.P: 1989. V. 64; 66
If Beale Street Could Talk. New York: 1974. V. 66
Just Above My Head. New York: 1979. V. 64
Notes of a Native Son. Boston: 1955. V. 63
The Price of the Ticket. New York: 1985. V. 62
A Rap on Race. New York: 1971. V. 66

BALDWIN, JOSEPH G.
The Flush Times of Alabama and Mississippi. New York: 1853. V. 66

BALDWIN, LELAND D.
Whiskey Rebels. Pittsburgh: 1939. V. 67

THE BALDWIN Locomotive Works. N.P: 1925. V. 65

BALDWIN, ROGER
Liberty Under the Soviets. New York: 1928. V. 63

BALDWIN, SARA MULLIN
Nebraska - Biographical Sketches of Nebraska Men and Women of Achievement Who Have Been Awarded Life Membership in the Nebraska Society. Hebron: 1932. V. 65

BALDWIN, THOMAS
Narrative of the Massacre, by the Savages, of the Wife and Children of Thomas Baldwin, Who, Since the Melancholy Period of the Destruction of His Unfortunate Family.... New York: 1835. V. 66
A New and Complete Gazetteer of the United States.... Philadelphia: 1854. V. 66
Suggestions on the State of Ireland, Chiefly Given in Evidence. 1883. V. 65

BALDWIN, WILLIAM CHARLES
African Hunting and Adventure from Natal to the Zambesi Including Lake Ngami, the Kalahari Desert, etc. from 1852 to 1860. London: 1863. V. 62; 64; 65; 66; 67
African Hunting from Natal to the Zambesi, Including Lake Ngami, the Kalahari Desert, Etc. New York: 1863. V. 64

BALDWIN'S Directory of Belleville and Franklin, Including Soho, Avondale and Nutley. Orange: 1889. V. 63; 66

BALENTINE, F. J. PABLO
Freund and Bro. - Pioneer Gunmakers to the West. Newport Beach: 1997. V. 65

BALESTIER, WOLCOTT
The Average Woman. London: 1892. V. 67

BALFOUR, ALEXANDER
Campbell; or the Scottish Probationer. Edinburgh: 1819. V. 67
Characters, Omitted in Crabbe's Parish Register: with Other Tales. Edinburgh: 1825. V. 66

BALFOUR, EDWARD
The Timber Trees, Timber and Fancy Woods, As Also the Forests of India and of Eastern and Southern Asia. Madras: 1862. V. 63

BALFOUR, F. M.
On the Development of the Skeleton of the Paired Fins of Elasmobranchii. 1881. V. 67
On the Structure and Homologies of the Germinal Layers of the Embryo (& Larva Forms). N.P: 1880. V. 67
Report of a Public Meeting...to Consider a Memorial to Professor Balfour. Cambridge: 1882. V. 67
A Treatise on Comparative Embryology.... London: 1885. V. 62

BALFOUR, ROBERT ARTHUR
Squeeze the Trigger Gentley. 1991. V. 65
Squeeze the Trigger Gentley. Grindleford: 1991. V. 62; 67

BALFOUR KINNEAR, G. P. R.
A Boy Goes Trouting. London: 1959. V. 67
Catching Salmon and Sea Trout. London: 1959. V. 67
Flying Salmon. 1937. V. 63; 65; 67
Flying Salmon. London: 1947. V. 67
Spinning Salmon. London: 1938. V. 67

BALIS, GEORGE U.
The Psychiatric Foundations of Medicine. Boston/London: 1978. V. 65

BALL, BONNIE SAGE
The March of the Sages. N.P: 1967. V. 64

BALL, CHARLES
Slavery in the United States. Pittsburgh: 1854. V. 63

BALL, DOUGLAS
Victorian Publisher's Bindings. London: 1985. V. 65

BALL, F. E.
A History of the County of Dublin. Part IV. Clonsilla, Leixlip. 1906. V. 67

BALL, J. M.
The Sack-'Em-Up Men...the Modern Resurrectionists. Edinburgh: 1928. V. 67

BALL, JOHN
The Central Alps. Part II. London: 1911. V. 63; 64
In the Heat of the Night. New York: 1965. V. 62; 65
John Ball, Member of the Wyeth Expedition to the Pacific Northwest, 1832. Glendale: 1925. V. 62; 65
Peaks, Passes and Glaciers. London: 1859. V. 63; 64
Peaks, Passes and Glaciers. London: 1860. V. 63; 64
Peaks, Passes and Glaciers. London: 1932. V. 63
The Western Alps. London: 1898. V. 63; 64

BALL, NICHOLAS
The Pioneers of '49 - A History of the Excursion of the Society of California Pioneers of New England. Boston: 1891. V. 63; 66

BALL, R.
A Contribution to a Right Knowledge of the Species of Seals (Phociae) Inhabiting the Irish Seas. Dublin: 1838. V. 67

BALL, RICHARD
Hounds Will Meet.... London: 1931. V. 67

BALL, ROBERT
The Story of the Sun. London: 1893. V. 67
The Story of the Sun. London: 1906. V. 63

BALL, ROBERT STAWELL
Experimental Mechanics. A Course of Lectures Delivered at the Royal College of Science for Ireland. London and New York: 1871. V. 63

THE BALLAD of Little Musgrove and Lady Barnet. 1986. V. 66

BALLANCE, CHARLES
Some Points in the Surgery of the Brain and Its Membranes. London: 1907. V. 64; 66

BALLANTA-TAYLOR, NICHOLAS GEORGE JULIUS
Saint Helena Island Spirituals. New York: 1925. V. 63

BALLANTINE, JAMES
The Gaberlunzie's Wallet. London: 1843. V. 66
Sir James Falshaw, Bart.... Edinburgh: 1910. V. 64; 65; 66

BALLANTINE, WILLIAM
A Treatise on the Elder's Office: Shewing the Qualifications of Elders.... Bethany: 1833. V. 66

BALLANTYNE, R. M.
The Lakes of Killarney.... 1859. V. 63
Photographs of Edinburgh, With Descriptive Letterpress. Glasgow: 1870. V. 66
The Red Man's Revenge. London: 1880. V. 63
Ungava: a Tale of Esquimaux-Land. London: 1871. V. 62

BALLARD, COLIN R.
Military Genius of Abrhama Lincoln. Cleveland and New York: 1952. V. 62

BALLARD, G. A.
Rulers of the Indian Ocean. London: 1927. V. 62

BALLARD, GEORGE
Memoirs of British Ladies Who Have Been Celebrated for their Writings or Skill in the Learned Languages Arts and Sciences. London: 1775. V. 65

BALLARD, J. G.
The Atrocity Exhibition. London: 1970. V. 67
The Atrocity Exhibition. San Francisco: 1990. V. 66
Cocaine Nights. Washington: 1998. V. 62
Crash. London: 1973. V. 66; 67
Crash. New York: 1973. V. 62; 63
The Crystal World. 1966. V. 62; 64; 66
The Crystal World. London: 1966. V. 65
The Day of Creation. London: 1987. V. 65; 66
The Disaster Area. London: 1967. V. 65; 66
The Drowned World and the Wind from Nowhere. 1962. V. 66
The Drowned World and the Wind from Nowhere. New York: 1962. V. 62; 64
Empire of the Sun. London: 1984. V. 62; 63; 67
The Impossible Man and Other Stories. New York: 1966. V. 64
The Inner Landscape. London: 1969. V. 64
Low-Flying Aircraft and Other Stories. London: 1976. V. 66
Terminal Beach. New York: 1964. V. 64

BALLARINI, R.
Black Africa's Traditional Arms. Milano: 1992. V. 62

BALLENTINE, GEORGE
Autobiography of an English Solider in the United States Army. New York: 1853. V. 67

BALLER, F. W.
An Analytical Chinese-English Dictionary Compiled for the China Inland Misson. 1900. V. 64

BALLESTER, LUDUVICO
Onomatographia, Sive Descriptio Nominum Varii et Peregrini Idiomatis...(with) Hierologia, sive De Sacro Sermone.... Lugduni: 1617. V. 66

BALLIETT, WHITNEY
Dinosaurs in the Morning. 41 Pieces on Jazz. New York: 1962. V. 63
The Sound of Surprise. New York: 1958. V. 65
The Sound of Surprise. New York: 1959. V. 67

BALLINGALL, JAMES
The Mercantile Navy Improved; or, a Plan for the Greater Safety of Lives and Property in Steam Vessels.... London: 1832. V. 62

BALLIOL College War Memorial Book. 1924. V. 62

BALLOU, ADIN
Autobiography.... Lowell: 1896. V. 64
An Exposition of Views Respecting the Principal Facts, Causes and Peculiarities Involved in Spirit Manifestations. Boston: 1852. V. 64
The True Scriptural Doctrine of the Second Advent.... Hopedale: 1843. V. 62

BALLOU, MATURIN M.
History of Cuba; or, Notes of a Traveller in the Tropics. Boston: 1854. V. 66
The Naval Officer; or the Pirates Cave. Boston: 1845. V. 66

BALLOU, ROBERT
Early Klickitat Valley Days. Goldendale: 1938. V. 66

BALLY, P. R. O.
The Genus Monadenium, a Monographic Study. Berne: 1961. V. 64; 67

BALMONT, KONSTANTIN
Sbornik Stikhotvoreny. Iaroslavl: 1890. V. 67

BALSAM, L. G.
A. G. Warshawsky, Master-Painter and Humanist. 1954. V. 62; 65

BALSTON, JOHN
The Whatmans and Wove Paper. London: 1998. V. 64

BALSTON, THOMAS
The Cambridge University Press Collection of Private Press Styles, Kelmscott, Ashendene, Eragny, Cranach. Cambridge: 1951. V. 62; 67
John Martin, 1789-1854, Illustrator and Pamphleteer. London: 1934. V. 63
Susanna Whatman: Her Housekeeping Book. London: 1945. V. 64
William Balston Paper Maker 1759-1849. London: 1954. V. 62; 63; 65; 67
Wood-Engraving in Modern English Books: the Catalogue of an Exhibition Arranged for the National Book League by Thomas Balston October-November 1949. London: 1949. V. 64

BALTIMORE, FREDERICK CALVERT, BARON
The Trial of Frederick Calvert, Esq.; Baron of Baltimore in the Kingdom of Ireland, for a Rape on the Body of Sarah Woodcock and of Eliz. Griffinburg, and Ann Harvey, Otherwise Darby.... London: 1768. V. 62; 63; 65

BALTIMORE MUSEUM
The History of Bookbinding 525-1950 A.D.: an Exhibition Held at the Baltimore Museum of Art November 12, 1957 to January 12, 1958. Baltimore: 1957. V. 64

BALZAC, HONORE DE
Les Contes Drolatiques. Paris: 1867. V. 62
Oeuvres Completes. Paris: 1855. V. 64
The Physiology of Marriage; or Meditations of an Eclectic Philosopher on Happiness and Unhappiness in Marriage. New York: 1925. V. 67
The Two Young Brides. London: 1903. V. 66
The Works of Honore De Balzac. Philadelphia: 1895. V. 62

BALZAC, JEAN LOUIS GUEZ, SIEUR DE
Le Prince. Paris: 1632. V. 66; 67

BAMBERGER, HEINRICH VON
Lehrbuch der Krankheiten des Herzens. Vienna: 1857. V. 64

BAMFORD, SAMUEL
Dialect of South Lancashire or Tim Bobbin's Tummus and Meary.... Manchester: 1850. V. 64
The Miscellaneous Works of Tim Bobbin, Esq. Manchester: 1775. V. 64
The Miscellaneous Works of Tim Bobbin, Esq. Salford: 1812. V. 64
Passages in the Life of a Radical. London: 1844. V. 66
Passages in the Life of a Radical and Early Days. London: 1893. V. 64

BAMPFEILD, R. W.
An Essay on the Curvatures and Diseases of the Spine, Including All the Forms of Spinal Distoration to Which the Fothergillian Gold Medal Was Awarded by the Medical Society of London. London: 1824. V. 66

BAMPFIELD, FRANCIS
All In One. 1677. V. 62

BANBURY, JEN
Like a Hole in the Head. Boston: 1998. V. 65

BANCROFT, EDWARD
Experimental Researches Concerning the Philosophy of Permanent Colours and the Best Means of Producing Them. London: 1813. V. 66; 67

BANCROFT, FREDERIC
Slave Trading in the Old South. Baltimore: 1931. V. 67

BANCROFT, GEORGE
History of the Colonization of the United States. Boston: 1846. V. 64
History of the United States of America, from the Discovery of the Continent. New York: 1883-1885. V. 63; 64

BANCROFT, HUBERT HOWE
History of Alaska 1730-1885. San Francisco: 1886. V. 65
History of Arizona and New Mexico 1530-1588. Albuquerque: 1962. V. 65
History of British Columbia 1792-1877. San Francisco: 1887. V. 67
History of Central America. San Francisco: 1883-1887. V. 65
History of Mexico. San Francisco: 1883-1887. V. 65
History of Mexico. San Francisco: 1886-1888. V. 64
History of the Northwest Coast. San Francisco: 1884. V. 62
History of the Pacific States of North American - Volume XII. San Francisco: 1888. V. 62; 65
History of Utah 1540-1887. San Francisco: 1890. V. 65
The Native Races. San Francisco: 1886. V. 64; 67
Nevada, Colorado and Wyoming. San Francisco: 1890. V. 63
The Pacific States of North America: Central America. San Francisco: 1883. V. 64
Popular Tribunals. San Francisco: 1871. V. 63; 66
Works: History of the Pacific States. San Francisco: 1882-1891. V. 63; 64
The Works of.... San Francisco: 1883-1887. V. 65
The Works of.... San Francisco: 1886. V. 65
The Works of.... San Francisco: 1887. V. 62; 65
The Works of.... San Francisco: 1888. V. 65
The Works of... Volumes XV and XVI. San Francisco: 1887. V. 62
The Zamorano Index to History of California. Los Angeles: 1985. V. 62

BANCROFT, LAURA
Mr. Woodchuck. Chicago. V. 65

BANDEL, EUGENE
Frontier Life in the Army 1854-1861. Glendale: 1932. V. 64

BANDELIER, ADOLF FRANCIS ALPHONSE
The Delight Makers. New York: 1890. V. 64
Hemenway Southwestern Archaeological Expedtion. Cambridge: 1890. V. 63; 66
Historical Introduction to Studies Among the Sedentary Indians of New Mexico. (and) Report on the Ruins of the Pueblo of Pecos. Boston: 1881. V. 63
A History of the Southwest. The Vatican: 1969. V. 64
A History of the Southwest: a Study of the Civilization and Conversion of the Indians in Southwestern United States and Northwestern Mexico From the Earliest Times to 1700. Rome: 1987. V. 64
Indians of the Rio Grande Valley. N.P: 1937. V. 63
A Scientist on the Trail - Travel Letters of A. F. Bandelier 1800-1881. Berkeley: 1949. V. 63; 66
The Unpublished Letters of.... El Paso: 1942. V. 64

BANDERAS *Sporting Reminiscences of South America 1919-1921.* London: 1922. V. 64

BANDINELLI, RANUCCIO BIANCHI
Hellenistic-Byzantine Miniatures of the Iliad. Olten: 1955. V. 62

BANFIELD, E.J.
The Confessions of a Beachcomber. London: 1908. V. 63

BANFIELD, THOMAS CHARLES
Industry of the Rhine. London: 1846-1848. V. 63

BANGS, JOHN KENDRICK
The Dreamers: a Club. New York: 1899. V. 63; 66
Mr. Munchausen. Boston: 1901. V. 64
A Quest for Song. Boston: 1915. V. 63; 64; 66

BANIM, JOHN
Tales of the O'Hara Family. (and) Second Series. London: 1825-1826. V. 63

BANISTER, JOHN
A Synopsis of Husbandry. London: 1799. V. 65

BANISTER, T. ROGER
The Coastwise Lights of China. Shanghai: 1932. V. 63; 64

BANKES, HENRY
The Civil and Constitutional History of Rome from Its Foundation to the Age of Augustus. London: 1818. V. 67

BANKES, THOMAS EDWARD WARREN BLACKE
A New Royal System of Universal Geography, Antient and Modern. London: 1787. V. 66

BANKHEAD, TALLULAH
Tallulah, My Autobiography. New York: 1952. V. 67

BANKS, CHARLES EDWARD
The Planters of the Commonwealth. Boston: 1930. V. 66
The Winthrop Fleet of 1630. An Account of the Vessels, the Voyage, the Passengers and Their English Homes from Original Authorities. Boston;: 1930. V. 66

BANKS, E.
A Naturalist in Sarawak. 1949. V. 62

BANKS, EDGAR JAMES
Bismya or the Lost City of Adab, a Story of Adventure, of Exploration and of Excavation Among the Ruins of the Oldest of the Buried Cities of Babylonia. New York: 1912. V. 67

BANKS, ELEANOR
Wandersong. Caldwell: 1950. V. 67

BANKS, IAIN
Consider Phlebas. London: 1987. V. 62; 64
Walking on Glass. London: 1985. V. 67
The Wasp Factory. 1984. V. 62
The Wasp Factory. London: 1984. V. 64; 66

BANKS, ISABELLA
Daisies in the Grass: a Collection of Songs and Poems. London: 1865. V. 65

BANKS, JOHN
The History of Francis Eugene, Prince of Savoy.... London: 1742. V. 62
The History of John Duke of Marlborough.... London: 1742. V. 62

BANKS, JONATHAN
The Life of the Right Reverend Father in God, Edw. Rainbow, D.D. London: 1688. V. 62

BANKS, JOSEPH
The Journal of Joseph Banks in the Endeavour. Guildford: 1980. V. 63; 64; 65
The Sheep and Wool Correspondence of Sir Joseph Banks 1781-1820. London: 1979. V. 62
Sir Joseph Banks; the Father of Australia. Sydney: 1909. V. 63

BANKS, LOUIS ALBERT
Immortal Songs of Camp and Field. Cleveland: 1899. V. 63; 65

BANKS, LYNNE REID
Dark Quartet - The Story of the Brontes. New York: 1976. V. 64
The L-Shaped Room. London: 1960. V. 63

BANKS, ROBERT W.
Battle of Franklin, November 30, 1864. The Bloodiest Engagement of the War Between the States. New York and Washington: 1908. V. 62; 63; 65

BANKS, RUSSELL
Affliction. New York: 1989. V. 62; 64
Cloudsplitter. New York: 1998. V. 64; 67
Hamilton Stark. Boston: 1978. V. 62
Rule of the Bone. A Novel. New York: 1995. V. 63
Searching for Survivors. New York: 1975. V. 64; 67
Waiting to Freeze. Northwood Narrows: 1969. V. 62

BANKS, T. C.
Baronia Anglica Concentrata; or a Concentrated Account of all the Baronies Commonly Called Baronies In Fee.... Ripon: 1844. V. 67

BANKS, WILLIAM
The English Master; or, Student's Guide to Reasoning and Composition. London: 1823. V. 64

BANKS, WILLIAM STOTT
A List of Provincial Words in Use at Wakefield in Yorkshire.... London: 1865. V. 64; 65; 66
Walks in Yorkshire: Wakefield an Its Neighbourhood. London: 1871. V. 65

BANKSON, RUSSELL A.
The Klondike Nugget. Caldwell: 1935. V. 65

BANNER, HUBERT S.
Romantic Java: As It Was and Is; a Description of the Diversified Peoples, the Departed Glories and Strange Customs of a Little Known Island.... London: 1927. V. 65

BANNERMAN, DAVID ARMITAGE
Birds of Cyprus. Edinburgh and London: 1958. V. 63; 66
Birds of the Atlantic Islands. 1963-1968. V. 62; 64; 65; 66
Birds of the Atlantic Islands. Edinburgh and London: 1963-1968. V. 63; 64; 67
The Birds of the Balearics. 1983. V. 63
The Birds of the British Isles. 1953. V. 67
The Birds of the British Isles. London: 1953-1956. V. 64
Birds of the British Isles. Edinburgh: 1953-1963. V. 63; 64; 67
The Birds of the British Isles. London: 1953-1963. V. 62
The Birds of the British Isles. London: 1957. V. 64
The Birds of the British Isles. London: 1958. V. 64
The Birds of the British Isles. London: 1959. V. 64
Birds of the Cape Verde Islands. 1968. V. 66
Birds of the Maltese Archipelago. Valletta: 1976. V. 64; 67
The Birds of Tropical West Africa. London: 1930-1951. V. 62; 64; 67
The Birds of West and Equatorial Africa. 1953. V. 63; 64; 65; 67
The Birds of West and Equatorial Africa. Edinburgh: 1953. V. 62; 64
The Birds of West and Equatorial Africa. London: 1953. V. 62; 63; 66
History of the Birds of the Cape Verde Islands. 1968. V. 63
History of the Birds of the Cape Verde Islands. London: 1968. V. 64

BANNERMAN, HELEN
Little Black Sambo. Chicago: 1919. V. 64
Little Black Sambo. Sandusky: 1931. V. 66

BANNERMAN, HELEN continued
Little Black Sambo. Akron: 1932. V. 65
Little Black Sambo. Akron: 1938. V. 65
Little Black Sambo. Akron: 1942. V. 62
Little Black Sambo. New York: 1943. V. 62; 66
Little Black Sambo. New York: 1955. V. 66
Little Black Sambo. The Gingerbread Man. Titty Mouse and Tatty Mouse. Chicago: 1934. V. 65
Pat and the Spider. London: 1904. V. 64
Pat and the Spider: the Biter Bit. London: 1904. V. 66
Pat the Spider; the Biter Bit. New York: 1905. V. 66
Picture Story Book. Chicago: 1943. V. 62
The Story of Little Black Sambo. New York: 1921. V. 66
The Story of Little Black Sambo. Philadelphia: 1946. V. 62
The Story of Little Black Sambo. Berkeley: 1989. V. 67
The Story of the Little Black Quibba. London: 1903. V. 64

BANNET, IVOR
The Amazons. Waltham St. Lawrence: 1948. V. 65; 66

BANNISTER, DOUGLAS
Life of Mr. John Reeve, with Original Anecdotes and Portrait by Wageman. London: 1838. V. 63

BANTA, R. E.
Indiana Authors and Their Books 1816-1916 and 1917-1966. Crawfordsville: 1949-1974. V. 63

BANTA, THEODORE M.
A Frisian Family. The Banta Genealogy. Descandants of Epke Jacobse, Who Cames from Friesland, Netherlands, to New Amsterdam February 1659. New York: 1893. V. 63; 66

BANTOCK, NICK
Griffin & Sabine. San Francisco: 1991. V. 64; 65; 67
Griffin & Sabine. (with) Sabine's Notebook. (with) The Golden Mean. San Francisco: 1991-1993. V. 63; 64; 66

BANVARD, JOHN
Description of Banvard's Panorama of the Mississippi River.... Boston: 1847. V. 62; 66

BANVILLE, JOHN
Birchwood. London: 1973. V. 63; 66
Doctor Copernicus. London: 1976. V. 62; 63
Kepler. London: 1981. V. 63
Long Lankin. London: 1970. V. 63; 66
Mefisto. London: 1986. V. 62; 66
The Newton Letters: an Interlude. London: 1982. V. 62; 63
Nightspawn. London: 1971. V. 63; 66

BANVILLE, THEODORE DE
The Kiss. Edinburgh: 1983. V. 64

BAPTISTA MANTUANUS
De Patientia. Brescia: 1497. V. 64

THE BAPTISTS of Yorkshire. London: 1912. V. 65; 66

BAQUET, CAMILLE
History of the First Brigade, New Jersey Volunteers from 1861 to 1865. Trenton: 1910. V. 63; 66

BARABAS, F.
Menuiserie d'Art Nouveau. Paris: 1900. V. 64

BARABASHOV, N. P.
An Atlas of the Moon's Far Side. New York and London: 1961. V. 63

BARAKA, IMAMU AMIRI
Black Music. New York: 1967. V. 67
Blues People. New York: 1963. V. 62; 64
The Dead Lecturer. Poems. New York: 1964. V. 62

BARANZANO, GIOVANNI ANTONIO
Uranoscopia Seu de Coelo in Qua Universa Coelorum Doctrina Clare.... Geneva: 1617. V. 63

BARBARA'S Flame Fairy. London: 1898. V. 65

BARBARO, FRANCESCO
De Re Uxoria, Libri Duo. Hagenau: 1533. V. 65

BARBATO, JOSEPH
Heart of the Land: Essays on Last Great Places. New York: 1994. V. 64; 66

BARBAULD, ANNA LAETITIA AIKIN
Hymns for Children in Prose. New Haven: 1840. V. 65
Hymns in Prose for Children. London: 1880. V. 67
A Legacy for Young Ladies. Boston: 1826. V. 63
Tales, Poems and Essays. Boston: 1884. V. 63
Works.... Boston: 1826. V. 63; 64

BARBEAU, MARIUS
Haida Myths Illustrated in Argillite Carvings. Ottawa: 1953. V. 63
Indian Days in the Canadian Rockies. Toronto: 1923. V. 63; 64
Totem Poles. Ottawa: 1950. V. 63; 65
Totem Poles of the Gitksan, Upper Skeena River, British Columbia. Ottawa: 1929. V. 64

BARBER, EDWIN A.
Marks of American Potters. Philadelphia: 1904. V. 63

BARBER, HENRY
Furness and Cartmel Notes, or Jottings of Topographical, Ecclesiastical and Popular Antiquities.... Ulverston: 1894. V. 64; 65; 66

BARBER, JOHN
The Life and Character of John Barber, Esq. Late Lord Mayor of London, Deceased. London: 1741. V. 66

BARBER, JOHN WARNER
All the Western States and Territories from the Alleghanies to the Pacific and from the Lakes to the Gulf. Cincinnati: 1867. V. 66
Historical Collections of New Jersey: Past and Present. New Haven: 1868. V. 63; 66
Historical Collections of the State of New Jersey.... New York: 1844. V. 66

BARBER, LYNN
The Heyday of Natural History. 1820-1870. London: 1980. V. 62

BARBER, MARY
The True Narrative of the Five Years' Suffering and Perilous Adventures, Miss Barber, Wife of Squatting Bear. Philadelphia: 1873. V. 64
The True Narrative of the Five Years' Suffering and Perilous Adventures, Miss Barber, Wife of Squatting Bear. Caldwell: 1950. V. 67

BARBER, PHILLIP
Journals of the Late Brevet Major Phillip Norbourne Hopkins Barber Written During the War with Mexico - 1846. New York: 1936. V. 67

BARBER, T. W.
The Port of London and the Thames Barrage. London: 1907. V. 62

BARBER, WILLETTA ANN
Drawn Conclusion. Garden City: 1942. V. 66

BARBERY, W. S.
Story of the Life of Robert Sayers Sheffey. Bluefield: 1948. V. 64

BARBETTE, PAUL
Opera Chirurgico Anatomica, ad Circularem Sanguinis Motum, Aliaque Recentionum Inventa.... Lugd. Batav: 1672. V. 64

BARBEY, W.
Epilobium. Lausanne: 1885. V. 62

BARBEY D'AUREVILLY, JULES
The Anatomy of Dandyism, with Some Observations on Beau Brummell. London: 1928. V. 63
Les Diaboliques. Paris: 1910. V. 64
Les Plus Bel Amour De Don Juan (Les Diaboliques). Paris: 1923. V. 64
Le Rideau Cramoisi (Les Diaboliques). Brussels: 1907. V. 64

BARBEYRAC, CHARLES DE
Medicamentorum Constitutio, seu Formulae. Leyden: 1751. V. 63

BARBIER, CARL PAUL
William Gilpin. Oxford: 1936. V. 66
William Gilpin. Oxford: 1963. V. 67

BARBIER, GEORGE
Vingt-Cinq Costumes Pour Le Theatre. A Paris: 1927. V. 62

BARBIER, J. P.
Islands and Ancestors. Munich: 1988. V. 62

BARBIERI, GIUSEPPE
Cimitero Della Regia Citta di Verona. Verona: 1833. V. 64

BARBOSA RODRIGUES, J.
O Tamakoare Especies Novas da Ordem das Ternstroemiaceas. Manaos: 1887. V. 66

BARBOT, JEAN
Barbot on Guinea. The Writings of Jean Barbot on West Africa. 1678- 1712. London: 1992. V. 64

BARBOUR, AMBROSE
Boz at Idleberg. Lexington: 1951. V. 67

BARBOUR, FLOYD
The Black Power Revolt. Boston: 1968. V. 64; 66

BARBOUR, T.
A Contribution to the Zoogeography of the West Indies, with Especial Reference to Amphibians and Reptiles. 1914. V. 63; 66
Cuban Ornithology. Cambridge: 1943. V. 65; 67

BARBUSSE, HENRI
Pleureuses. Paris: 1895. V. 67

BARCIA CARBALLIDO Y ZUNIGA, ANDRES GONZALES DE
Ensayo Cronologico para la Historia General de la Florida Desde el Ano de 1512...hasta el de 1722. Madrid: 1723. V. 64; 66

BARCLAY, C. N.
The London Scottish in the Second World War 1939-1945. London: 1952. V. 62

BARCLAY, DAVID
An Account of the Emancipation of the Slaves of Unity Valley Pen, in Jamaica. London: 1811. V. 63

BARCLAY, EDGAR
Mountain Life in Algeria. London: 1882. V. 64

BARCLAY, EDGAR *continued*
Stonehenge and It's Earth-Works. London: 1895. V. 62; 66

BARCLAY, JAMES
Barclay's Universal Dictionary. London: 1820?. V. 64

BARCLAY, JOHN
An Apology for the True Christian Divinity, Being an Explanation and Vindication of the Principles and Doctrines of the People Called Quakers. Birmingham: 1765. V. 66
Argenis. Leiden: 1659. V. 64
Argenis. Lugd. Batav. et Roterodi: 1664-1669. V. 63; 66
Diary of Alexander Jaffray, Provost of Aberdeen, One of the Scottish Commissioners to King Charles II, and a Member of Cromwell's Parliament.... London: 1833. V. 65
Euphormio's Satyricon: Euphomionis Satyricon. Waltham St. Lawrence: 1954. V. 62
Satyricon. Lugd. Batav: 1674. V. 62

BARCLAY, ROBERT
An Apology for the True Christian Divinity.... London: 1718. V. 63
An Apology for the True Christian Divinity.... London: 1736. V. 67
An Apology for the True Christian Divinity.... Birmingham: 1765. V. 65
Truth Triumphant through the Spiritual Warfare, Christian Labours and Writings of that Abel and Faithful Servant of Jesus Christ, Robert Barclay. London: 1692. V. 62; 66

BARCROFT, JOSEPH
Features in the Architecture of Physiological Function. Cambridge: 1934. V. 62
The Respiratory Function of the Blood. Part I. Lessons from High Altitudes. (with) The Respiratory Function of the Blood. Part II. Haemoglobin. Cambridge: 1925-1928. V. 62
The Respiratory Function of the Blood. Part II. Haemoglobin. Cambridge: 1928. V. 66; 67

BARD, FLOYD C.
Horse Wrangler. Sixty Years in the Saddle in Wyoming and Montana. Norman: 1960. V. 63; 64

BARD, SAMUEL
A Compendium of the Theory and Practice of Midwifery, Containing Practical Instructions for the Management of Women During Pregnancy, in Labour.... New York: 1807. V. 64; 66
A Compendium of the Theory and Practice of Midwifery, Containing Practical Instructions for the Management of Women, During Pregnancy, in Labour.... New York: 1819. V. 63
Tentamen Medicum Inaugurale, De Viribus Opii. Edinburgh: 1765. V. 66

BARDI, P. M.
The Tropical Gardens of Burle Marx. New York: 1964. V. 64; 67

BARDUZZI, BERNARDINO
A Letter in Praise of Verona (1489). Verona: 1974. V. 62; 65

BARETTI, GIUSEPPE MARCO ANTONIO
A Journey from London to Genoa, through England, Portugal, Spain and France. London: 1770. V. 62; 63; 64

BARFIELD, OWEN
Poetic Diction: a Study in Meaning. London: 1928. V. 67

BARFOOT, J. R.
The Alphabet of Objects, Album Picture Book. London: 1860?. V. 62; 66

BARGER, V.
Classical Mechanics; a Modern Perspective. New York: 1973. V. 67

BARHAM, RICHARD HARRIS
The Garrick Club. Notices of One Hundred and Thirty Five of Its Former Members. New York: 1896. V. 62
The Ingoldsby Legends or Mirth and Marvels. London: 1840-1847. V. 62
The Ingoldsby Legends, or Mirth and Marvels. London: 1855. V. 62; 66
The Ingoldsby Legends; or, Mirth and Marvels. London: 1876. V. 65
The Ingoldsby Legends or, Mirth and Marvels. London: 1907. V. 63; 65
The Jackdaw of Rheims. Philadelphia: 1914. V. 64
The Lay of St. Aloys. London: 1885. V. 63; 66

BARHAM, WILLIAM
Descriptions of Niagara. Gravesend: 1847. V. 66

BARILLET, J.
Les Pensees, Histoire, Culture, Multiplication, Emploi. 1869. V. 62
Les Pensees, Histoire, Culture, Multiplication, Emploi. Paris: 1869. V. 67

BARING, MAURICE
In My End is My Beginning. London: 1931. V. 66
Pastels and Other Rhymes. New Printer, Elon. 1891. V. 00
Per Ardua MCMXIV-MCMXVIII: a Poem. Long Grendon: 1929. V. 62
Poems 1892-1929. London: 1929. V. 63
Poems: 1914-1919. London: 1920. V. 64

BARING GOULD, SABINE
A Book of Ghosts. London: 1904. V. 62
Curious Myths of the Middle Ages. London: 1866. V. 65
The Deserts of Southern France, an Introduction to the Limestone and Chalk Plateaux of Ancient Aquitaine. London: 1894. V. 64
Historic Oddities and Strange Events. London: 1890-1891. V. 62
Iceland: Its Scenes and Sagas. London: 1868. V. 67
In Troubadour-Land, a Ramble in Provence and Languedoc. London: 1891. V. 62
The Land of Teck and Its Neighbourhood. London: 1911. V. 67
Old English Fairy Stories. London: 1896. V. 63
Siegfried. London: 1904. V. 67
Mehalah - a Story of the Salt Marshes. London: 1969. V. 64
The Vicar of Morwenstow. A Life of Robert Stphen Hakwer. London: 1876. V. 66

BARING GOULD, WILLIAM S.
Nero Wolfe of West Thirty-Fifth Street. New York: 1969. V. 67
Sherlock Holmes a Biography. London: 1962. V. 62; 66
Sherlock Holmes of Baker Street. New York: 1962. V. 65; 67

BARJAUD, J. B.
Description de Londres et de ses Edifices. Paris: 1810. V. 63; 66

BARKER, A. L.
A Heavy Feather. London: 1978. V. 66

BARKER, ANSELM HOLCOMB
Anselm Holcomb Barker 1822-1895: Pioneer Builder and EArly Settler of Auraria, His Diary of 1858.... Denver: 1959. V. 64

BARKER, BENJAMIN
Mornilva; or, the Outlaw of the Forest. Boston: 1846. V. 66

BARKER, CHARLES A.
Background of the Revolution in Maryland. New Haven: 1940. V. 66; 67

BARKER, CHARLES H.
Esquire Culinary Companion. New York: 1959. V. 67

BARKER, CICELY MARY
Autumn Songs with Music from Flower Fairies of the Autumn. London: 1927. V. 62
The Book of the Flower Fairies. Poems and Pictures. London: 1927. V. 63
Fairies of the Trees. London: 1940. V. 62; 66
Flower Fairies of the Autumn. London: 1926. V. 64; 65
Flower Fairies of the Spring. London: 1923. V. 64
Flower Fairies of the Summer. London: 1925. V. 64
Flower Fairies of the Wayside. London: 1948. V. 62
A Flower Fairy Alphabet. London: 1934. V. 62; 64; 65; 66
Flowers Songs of the Seasons. London: 1928. V. 65

BARKER, CLIVE
Books of Blood. London: 1984. V. 63; 64; 67
The Books of Blood. New York: 1988. V. 65
Imajica. New York: 1991. V. 67
In the Flesh. New York: 1986. V. 63; 65; 67
The Inhuman Condition. New York: 1986. V. 63
Shadows in Eden. Lancaster: 1991. V. 63
The Thief of Always. New York: 1992. V. 67
Weaveworld. London: 1987. V. 66

BARKER, EDMUND HENRY
A Review of the Arguments for Removing the Lent-Assizes from Thetford to Norwich. Thetford: 1824. V. 63

BARKER, GEORGE
Alanna Autumnal. London: 1933. V. 62
Elegy on Spain. London: 1939. V. 65
Elegy on Spain. Manchester: 1939. V. 62; 65
Thirty Preliminary Poems. London: 1933. V. 64
The True Confession of George Barker. London: 1950. V. 62

BARKER, GEORGE M.
A Tea Planter's Life in Assam. Calcutta: 1884. V. 67

BARKER, JOSEPH
The Abominations of Socialism Exposed in Reply to the Gateshead Observer. Newcastle: 1840. V. 63
The History and Confessions of a Man, as Put Forth by Himself. Wortley: 1846. V. 67

BARKER, LADY
Letters to Guy. London: 1885. V. 64
Station Amusements in New Zealand. London: 1873. V. 64

BARKER, LEWELLYN
The Nervous System and Its Constituent Neurons. New York: 1899. V. 64; 66; 67

BARKER, MATTHEW HENRY
Greenwich Hospital. London: 1826. V. 62; 63; 64; 67
Jem Bunt, by the Old Sailor. London: 1841?. V. 65
Tough Yarns: a Series of Tall Tales and Sketches to Please All Hands. London: 1835. V. 64; 65

BARKER, NICOLAS
Aldus Manutius and the Development of Greek Script and Type in the Fifteenth Century. Sandy Hook: 1985. V. 62
Bibliotheca Lindesiana. London: 1977. V. 63
The Butterfly Books, an Enquiry Into the Nature of Certain Twentieth Century Pamphlets. London: 1987. V. 63
A Potencie of Life, Books in Society. London: 1993. V. 63
The Printer and the Poet. Cambridge: 1970. V. 64; 65

BARKER, NUGENT
Written With My Left Hand. 21 Tales. London: 1951. V. 63

BARKER, PAT
Another World. London: 198. V. 62
The Eye in the Door. London: 1993. V. 66
The Ghost Road. London: 1995. V. 62; 63; 64; 65; 66; 67
Regeneration. New York: 1991. V. 62; 66
Regeneration. (with) The Eye in the Door. (with) The Ghost Road. London: 1991-1995. V. 64

BARKER, SALE, MRS.
Golden Hours. London: 1885. V. 64

BARKER, THOMAS
Forty Lithographic Impressions from Drawings...Selected from His Studies of Rustic Figures After Nature. Bath: 1813. V. 64

BARKER, W. G. M. JONES
Historical and Topographical Account of Wensleydale and the Valley of the Yore in the North of Yorkshire. London: 1856. V. 63; 65
The Three Days of Wensleydale; the Valley of the Yore. London: 1854. V. 65

BARKLEY, HENRY C.
Between the Danube and Black Sea; or, Five Years in Bulgaria. London: 1877. V. 64; 65

BARKLEY, JOHN
Report of the Trial of John Barkley (One of the Shop-Men of Richard Carlile), Prosecuted by the Constitutional Association for Publishing a Seditious and Blasphemous Libel. London: 1822. V. 63

BARKLY, FANNY A.
From the Tropics to the North Sea. 1890. V. 66

BARLACH, ERNST
A Letter from Ernst Barlach. Northampton: 1957. V. 62; 63

BARLETT, I. S.
History of Wyoming. Chicago: 1918. V. 63

BARLOW, ALFRED
The History and Principles of Weaving by Hand and by Power. London: 1878. V. 63

BARLOW, EDWARD
Meterological Essays Concerning the Origin of Springs, Generation of Rain and Production of Wind.... New York: 1972. V. 62

BARLOW, JANE
A Book of Nusery Rhymes. London: 1897. V. 65
The End of Elfintown. London: 1894. V. 62; 64

BARLOW, JOEL
Advice to the Privileged Orders in the Several States of Europe... (with) A Letter to the National Convention of France on the Defects in the Constitution of 1791.... London: 1795. V. 63
The Vision of Columbus: a Poem in Nine Books. Hartford: 1787. V. 62

BARLOW, JOHN
On Man's Power Over Himself to Prevent or Control Insanity. London: 1849. V. 63; 67

BARLOW, NORA
Charles Darwin's Diary of the Voyages of HMS "Beagle". Cambridge: 1933. V. 64

BARLOW, PETER
An Elementary Investigation of the Theory of Numbers, With Its Application to the Indeterminate and Diophantine Analysis, the Analytical and Geometrical Division of the Circle and Several Other Algebraical and Arithemtical Problems. London: 1811. V. 65

BARLOW, ROGER
A Brief Summe of Geographie. London: 1932. V. 63; 64

BARLOW, THOMAS GREAVES
The Journal of Gas Lighting. Volume I. 1849 and 1850. 1850. V. 66

BARLOW, WILLIAM
The Summe and Substance of the Conference, Which It Pleased His Excellent Majestie to Have with the Lords Bishops and Others of His Clergie.... London: 1638. V. 63

BARMAN, CHRISTIAN
The Bridge. A Chapter in the History of Building. London: 1926. V. 67

BARMBY, CUTHBERT
James Cope. New York: 1899. V. 66

BARNABY, HORACE T.
The Long Eared Bat. Akron: 1929. V. 62

BARNARD, CHRISTIAN
The Unwanted. London: 1976. V. 62

BARNARD, E. W.
Fifty Select Poems of Marc Antonio Flaminio, Imitated by.... Chester: 1829. V. 62

BARNARD, EVANS G.
A Rider of the Cherokee Strip. Boston: 1936. V. 64; 67

BARNARD, GEORGE
Drawing from Nature: a Series of Progressive Instructions in Sketching.... London: 1865. V. 63; 66
Handbook of Foliage and Foreground Drawing. 1876. V. 64
The Theory and Practice of Landscape Painting in Water Colours.... London: 1855. V. 64; 66; 67

BARNARD, J. G.
A Report on the Defenses of Washington, to the Chief of Engineers, U. S. Army. Washington: 1871. V. 62

BARNARD, J. H.
Doctor J. H. Barnard's Journal Dec. 1835-June 1836. N.P: 1950. V. 64

BARNARD, J. L.
Gammaridean Amphipoda of Australia. City of Washington: 1974. V. 67

BARNARD, JOHN
A Present for an Apprentice. London: 1740. V. 64; 66
A Present for an Apprentice.... London: 1750. V. 65

BARNARD, K. H.
Descriptive Catalogue of South African Decapod Crustacea (Crabs & Shrimps).... 1950. V. 64; 66

BARNARD, MARJORIE
North of the Yellowstone, South of the Bulls. Billings: 1978. V. 66

BARNARD, ROBERT
At Death's Door. London: 1988. V. 66
Blood Brotherhood. London: 1977. V. 65
Bodies. London: 1986. V. 67
A Corpse in a Gilded Cage. London: 1984. V. 66
Death and the Chaste Apprentice. London: 1989. V. 66; 67
Death and the Princess. London: 1982. V. 65; 66; 67
Death in a Cold Climate. London: 1980. V. 65
Death in Purple Prose. London: 1987. V. 66; 67
Death on the High C's. London: 1977. V. 63; 65; 67
The Disposal of the Living. London: 1985. V. 67
A Little Local Murder. London: 1976. V. 65; 67

BARNARD, THOMAS
An Historical Character Relating to the Holy and Exemplary Life of... Lady Elizabeth Hastings. Leeds: 1742. V. 62

BARNARD, WILLIAM
Serious Thoughts on the Trial of Mr. Barnard. London: 1758?. V. 63

BARNES, CLAUDE
John F. Kennedy. Scrimshaw Collector. Boston: 1969. V. 63; 64

BARNES, DJUNA
The Antiphon - a Play. New York: 1958. V. 65
To the Dogs. N.P: 1982. V. 64; 66
To the Dogs. Rochester: 1982. V. 64

BARNES, GILBERT H.
The Antislavery Impulse 1830-1844. New York & London: 1933. V. 67

BARNES, J. R.
Stream Ecology, Application and Testing of General Ecological Theory. New York: 1983. V. 64; 65

BARNES, JOSEPH K.
Medical and Surgical History of the Rebellion. Washington: 1875-1888. V. 65; 66

BARNES, JULIAN
Before She Met Me. London: 1982. V. 66
Cross Channel. London: 1996. V. 62; 64; 65
Duffy. London: 1980. V. 62; 63; 65; 66
England, England. London: 1998. V. 62
Fiddle City. London: 1981. V. 62; 63; 66
Flaubert's Parrot. London: 1984. V. 62; 65; 66; 67
Flaubert' Parrot. New York: 1985. V. 62; 63; 65; 66; 67
Going to the Dogs. New York: 1987. V. 62
A History of the World in 10 1/2 Chapters. 1989. V. 67
Metroland. 1980. V. 63
Metroland. London: 1980. V. 64; 66; 67
Metroland. New York: 1980. V. 67
Putting the Boot In. London: 1985. V. 62; 63; 66
Talking It Over. London: 1991. V. 62; 65

BARNES, LINDA
Cities of the Dead. New York: 1986. V. 66
Dead Head. New York: 1984. V. 65
A Trouble of Fools. New York: 1987. V. 65; 67

BARNES, RAYMOND P.
History of Roanoke. Radford: 1968. V. 63
History of Roanoke. Roanoke?: 1968. V. 67

BARNES, RUTH A.
Hear America Singing. An Anthology of Folk Poetry. Philadelphia: 1937. V. 62

BARNES, WILL C.
Apaches and Longhorns...The Remiscences of Will C. Barnes. Los Angeles: 1941. V. 64; 67
The Story of the Range. Washington: 1928. V. 64; 67
Tales from the X Bar Horse Camp. The Blue Outlaw and Other Stories. Chicago: 1920. V. 62; 64; 67
Western Grazing Ground and Forest Ranges - a History of the Livestock Industry. Chicago: 1913. V. 62; 66

BARNES, WILLIAM
Early England and the Saxon-English.... London: 1869. V. 66
A Grammar and Glossary of the Dorset Dialect with the History, Outspreading and Bearings of South-Western English. Berlin: 1863. V. 64
Hwomely Rhymes, a Second Collection of Poems in the Dorset Dialect. 1859. V. 65
Hwomely Rhymes. A Second Collection of Poems in the Dorset Dialect. London: 1859. V. 63
Notes on Ancient Britain and the Britons. London: 1858. V. 65
Poems of Rural Life in the Dorset Dialect. First Collection. London: 1866. V. 64

BARNES, WILLIAM continued
Poems of Rural Life in the Dorset Dialect. Third Collection. London: 1869. V. 64
Poems on Rural Life in Common English. London: 1868. V. 65
Poems, Partly of Rural Life. Dorchester: 1846. V. 65
Poems, Partly of Rural Life. London: 1846. V. 66
Select Poems by William Barnes. London: 1908. V. 67
Tiw; or, a View of the Roots and Stems of the English as a Teutonic Tongue. London: 1862. V. 64
Views of Labour and Gold. London: 1859. V. 64

BARNES, WILLIAM HARRISON
The Contemporary American Organ. Glen Rock: 1964. V. 67

BARNETT, E.
The West India Pilot, from Cape North of the Amazons to Cape Sable in Florida with the Outlying Islands. London: 1861. V. 64

BARNETT, JOEL
A Long Trip in a Prairie Schooner. Whittier: 1928. V. 64; 67

BARNEY, LIBEAUS
Letters of the Pike's Peak Gold Rush. San Jose: 1959. V. 63; 64; 65; 66; 67

BARNHART BROS. & SPINDLER
Book of Type: Specimens. Chicago: 1909. V. 67

BARNS, CASS G.
The Sod House Reminiscent Historical and Biographical Sketches Featuring Nebraska Pioneers, 1867-1897. Madison: 1930. V. 63; 64; 65; 67

BARNS, T. ALEXANDER
Across the Great Craterland to the Congo. 1923. V. 62
The Wonderland of the Eastern Congo. London: 1922. V. 62

THE BARNUM & Bailey Greatest Show on Earth Songster. New York: 1893. V. 64

BARNUM, FRANCIS
Life on the Alaska Mission with an Account of the Foundation of the Mission and the Work Performed. Baltimore: 1893. V. 66

BARNUM, PHINEAS TAYLOR
Barnum's Museum. New York and London: 1888. V. 65
The Humbugs of the World. New York: 1866. V. 66
Struggles and Triumphs; or Forty Years' Recollections. Hartford: 1869. V. 64; 65
Struggles and Triumphs; or, Sixty Years' Recollections. Buffalo: 1889. V. 65

BARNUM'S AND LONDON CIRCUS
Barnum and London Circus - Clown and Concert Song and Joke Book. New York: 1885. V. 65
Barnum's Wonders. An Illustrated History of the Hindoo Hairy Family and Other Prodigious and Exclusive Features of the Greatest Show on Earth. New York: 1887. V. 65

BAROJA, PIO
Critica Arbitraria. Madrid: 1924. V. 62

BARON, MICHEL
L'Homme a Bonne Fortune. Paris: 1686. V. 66

BARONIO, GIUSEPPE
On Grafting in Animals - Degli Innesti Animali. Boston: 1985. V. 66; 67

BARR, ALFRED H.
Matisse - His Art and His Public. New York: 1951. V. 65

BARR, JAMES MICHAEL
Confederate War Correspondence of James Michael Barr and Wife Rebecca and Dowling Barr. Taylor: 1963. V. 63

BARR, NEVADA
Bittersweet. New York: 1984. V. 64; 67
Ill Wind. New York: 1995. V. 67
A Superior Death. New York: 1994. V. 64; 65; 66
Track of the Cat. 1993. V. 62; 63; 64; 66
Track of the Cat. New York: 1993. V. 62; 64; 65; 66; 67
Track of the Cat. New York: 1994. V. 62

BARR, ROBERT
N.B. Strange Happenings. London: 1883. V. 67

BARRAS, J.
India and Tiger Hunting. 1883. V. 67
India and Tiger Hunting. Volume I. Series II. 1883-1885. V. 62; 63

BARRATT, STANLEY G. R.
A Short History of Totteridge in the County of Hertford. London: 1934. V. 62

BARRATT, THOMAS J.
The Annals of Hampstead. London: 1912. V. 62; 66

BARRAUD, CHARLES D.
New Zealand: Graphic and Descriptive. London: 1877. V. 64

BARRE, RICHARD
The Innocents. New York: 1995. V. 63; 66; 67

BARRE, WILLIAM VINCENT
History of the French Consulate Under Napoleon Buonaparte. London: 1804. V. 62

BARRERE, ALBERT
Argot and Slang. Paris: 1889. V. 64

BARRESWIL, CHARLES LOUIS
Appendice a Tous les Traites d'Analyse Chimique. Paris: 1843. V. 64
Societe Chimique de Paris. Paris: 1859-1863. V. 64

BARRETT, ANDREA
The Forms of Water. New York: 1993. V. 63; 66
Lucid Stars. New York: 1988. V. 65
Lucid Stars. London: 1989. V. 65
The Middle Kingdom. New York: 1991. V. 64; 66
Ship Fever. New York: 1996. V. 64; 65; 66; 67

BARRETT, BASIL RICHARD
The Life of Cardinal Ximenes. London: 1813. V. 67

BARRETT, C. G.
The Lepidoptera of the British Islands. Volume I (Rhopalocera). 1893. V. 66

BARRETT, CHARLES
Kooborr. London: 1960. V. 65

BARRETT, EATON S.
All the Talents. (with) All the Blocks, or an Antidote to All the Talents. London: 1807. V. 66

BARRETT, ELLEN C.
Baja California 1535-1956. A Bibliography of Historical, Geographical, and Scientific Literature Relating to the Peninsula of Baja California and to the Adjacent Islands in the Gulf of California and the Pacific Ocean. (with) Baja California II 1535-1964. Los Angeles: 1957-1967. V. 62; 64

BARRETT, FRANK
Honest Davie. London: 1883. V. 67

BARRETT, JOHN
An Essay on the Earlier Part of the Life of Swift. London: 1808. V. 66

BARRETT, NEAL
Pink Vodka Blues. New York: 1992. V. 62

BARRETT, P. H.
A Concordance to Darwin's The Descent of Man and Selection in Relation to Sex. Ithaca: 1987. V. 64; 66
A Concordance to Darwin's The Expression of the Emotions in Man and Animals. Ithaca: 1986. V. 64; 66

BARRETT, PETER
Great True Hunts. 1967. V. 62; 63; 64; 66; 67

BARRETT, ROSA M.
Ellice Hopkins: a Memoir. London: 1907. V. 65

BARRETT, THEODOSIA W.
Russell County and Confederate Breadbasket. N.P: 1981. V. 64

BARRETT, TIMOTHY
Japanese Papermaking: Traditions, Tools and Techniques. New York and Tokyo: 1983. V. 62

BARRETT, WILLIAM
The History and Antiquities of the City of Bristol.... Bristol: 1789. V. 66
Irrational Man. London: 1961. V. 67

BARRETT & CO., P.
General and Commercial Directory of Blackburn, Accrington, Darwen, Clitheroe, Great Harwood, Rishton, Church and Oswaldtwistle.... Preston: 1891. V. 63; 65
General and Commercial Directory of Blackburn, Accrington, Darwen, Clitheroe, Great Harwood.... Preston: 1906. V. 63; 65

BARRETTE, B.
Eva Hesse Sculpture: Catalogue Raisonne. New York: 1989. V. 62; 65

BARRETT HAMILTON, G. E. H.
A History of British Mammals. 1910-1921. V. 63; 66

BARRETT-HAMILTON, G. E. H.
A History of British Mammals. London: 1910-1921. V. 62

BARRIE, JAMES MATTHEW
The Admirable Crichton. London: 1914. V. 62; 64
The Admirable Crichton. London: 1916. V. 66
The Admirable Crichton. London: 1918. V. 66
Courage. London: 1922. V. 62
George Meredith. Box Hills - May 22, 1909. Los Angeles: 1911. V. 62
A Kiss for Cinderella. London: 1920. V. 62
The Little Minister. London: 1891. V. 63
The Little White Bird or Adventures in Kensington Gardens. New York: 1902. V. 63
Peter and Wendy. New York: 1902. V. 63
Peter and Wendy. London: 1911. V. 64
Peter and Wendy. New York: 1911. V. 64; 67
Peter Pan - His Pictures, His Career, His Friends. 1909. V. 67
Peter Pan Illustrated with Scenes from the Photoplay - a Paramount Picture. New York: 1911. V. 62
Peter Pan in Kensington Gardens. New York: 1906. V. 64
Peter Pan or the Boy Who Would Not Grow Up. London: 1928. V. 62
The Peter Pan Picture Book. Racine: 1931. V. 62
The Plays of J. M. Barrie. London: 1928. V. 64; 67

BARRIE, JAMES MATTHEW continued
Quality Street. London: 1913. V. 63; 64
Tommy and Grizel. London: 1900. V. 62
What Every Woman Knows, a Comedy. New York: 1920. V. 66

BARRIERE, DOMENICO
Villa Aldobrandini Tusculana. Roma: 1647. V. 64

BARRINGTON, CHARLES GEORGE
Seventy Years' Fishing. London: 1906. V. 62; 67

BARRINGTON, EMILIE ISABEL
Life of Walter Bagehot, by His Sister-in-Law. London: 1914. V. 63; 64
Through Greece and Dalmatia. London: 1912. V. 65

BARRINGTON, GEORGE
A Voyage to New South Wales; with a Description of the Country; the Manners, Customs, Religion &c. of the Natives, in the Vicinity of Botany Bay. London: 1795. V. 63

BARRINGTON, JONAH
Historic Memoirs of Ireland; Comprising Secret Records of the National Convention, the Rebellion and the Union.... London: 1833. V. 67

BARRINGTON, MICHAEL
Grahame of Claverhouse, Viscount Dundee. London: 1911. V. 67

BARRINGTON, SHUTE, BP. OF DURHAM
The Political Life of William Wildman, Viscount Barrinton. London: 1814. V. 62; 66

BARRON, A. L. E.
The Microscope. London: 1948-1965. V. 62

BARRON, EVAN MAC LEOD
Prince Charlie's Pilot. Inverness: 1913. V. 62

BARRON, S. B.
The Lone Star Defenders. New York: 1964. V. 64

BARROS, JOAO DE
Asia de Joam de Barros, dos Fectos Que Os Portugueses Fizeram no Desobrimento & Conquista dos Mares & Terras do Oriente. (with) Segunda Decada da Asia. Lisbon: 1552-1553. V. 62
Da Asia de Joao de Barros e de Diogo do Couto. Lisbon: 1777-1788. V. 62

BARROW, ISAAC
Sermons Selected from the Works...Late Master of Trinity College, Cambridge. Oxford: 1812. V. 62

BARROW, JOHN
An Account of Travels into the Interior of Southern Africa; in the Years 1797 and 1798. London: 1801. V. 64
A Chronological History of Voyage into the Arctic Regions Undertaken Chiefly for the Purpose of Discoverying a North-East, North-West or Polar Passage.... London: 1818. V. 62
Dictionarium Polygraphicum; or, the Whole Body of Arts Regularly Digested. London: 1735. V. 64; 66
The Eventful History of the Mutiny and Piratical Seizure of H.M.S. Bounty: Its Cause and Consequences. London: 1831. V. 62; 67
A New and Universal Dictionary of Arts and Sciences.... London: 1751. V. 64
Sketches of the Royal Society and Royal Society Club. London: 1849. V. 65
Some Account of the Public Life and a Selection from the Unpublished Writings of the Earl of Macartney. London: 1807. V. 63
Travels in China, Containing Descriptions, Observations and Comparisons, Made and Collected in the Course of a Short Residence at the Imperial Palace of Yuen-Min-Yuen.... London: 1804. V. 67
Travels Into the Interior of Southern Africa, in Which are Described the Character and Condition of the Dutch Colonists of the Cape of Good Hope.... London: 1806. V. 64
Voyages of Discovery and Research Within the Arctic Regions, from the Year 1818 to the Present Time. New York: 1846. V. 63

BARROW, WILLIAM
An Essay on Education: In Which are Particularly Considered the Merits and the Defects of the Discipline and Instruction in Our Academies.... London: 1804. V. 64
Twelve Nights in the Hunters' Camp - a Narrative of Real Life. Boston: 1868. V. 67

BARROWS, DAVID P.
A History of the Philippines. Indianapolis: 1905. V. 64

BARROWS, EDWARD M.
The Great Commodore - The Exploits of Matthew Galbraith Perry. New York: 1935. V. 67

BARROWS, JOHN R.
Ubet. Caldwell: 1934. V. 66

BARROWS, MARJORIE
Waggles. Chicago: 1945. V. 63

BARROWS, WILLIAM
The Indian's Side of the Indian Question. Boston: 1887. V. 63; 66
Oregon the Struggle for Possessions. Boston: 1884. V. 63

BARRUS, CLARA
The Life and Letters of John Burroughs. Boston: 1925. V. 67

BARRY, GEORGE
The History of the Orkney Islands. Kirkwall: 1867. V. 62

BARRY, J. W.
A History of the Strollers Club. Toronto: 1927. V. 64

BARRY, JAMES
Lectures on Painting, by the Royal Academicians. London: 1848. V. 66
A Letter to the Dilettanti Society, Respecting the Obtention of Certain Matters Essentially Necessary for the Improvement of Public Taste.... London: 1799. V. 67

BARRY, JOHN BROOKS
The Michaelmas Girls. London: 1974. V. 66

BARRY, JOHN WARREN
Studies in Corsica: Sylvan and Social. London: 1893. V. 62

BARRY, JOSEPH
The Annals of Harper's Ferry, with Sketches of Its Founder. Martinsburg: 1872. V. 64

BARRY, PHILIP
The Philadelphia Story. New York: 1939. V. 66

BARRY, T. A.
Men and Memories of San Francisco, in the Spring of 50. San Francisco: 1873. V. 65
San Francisco in the Spring of '50. San Francisco: 1873. V. 63; 66

BARRY, WILLIAM
Address on the Secrets and Traffic of London, Delivered at the Opening Meeting of...the Society of Arts, on Wednesday, Nov. 16, 1898. London: 1899. V. 66

BARSLEY, MICHAEL
Alice in Wunderground and Other Blits and Pieces. London: 1940. V. 62

BARTELL, E.
Hints for Picturesque Improvements in Ornamental Cottages and Their Scenery; Including Some Observations on the Labourer and His Cottage. London: 1804. V. 64

BARTER, CHARLOTTE
Alone Among the Zulus...The Narrative of a Journey through the Zulu Country. London: 1866. V. 63
Home in South Africa; By a Plain Woman. London: 1867. V. 64

BARTH, HENRY
Travels and Discoveries in North and Central Africa Including Accounts of Timbuktu, Sokoto and the Basins of the Niger and Benuwe. London: 1890. V. 62

BARTH, JOHN
Chimera. New York: 1972. V. 63; 65; 67
The Friday Book: Essays and Other Nonfiction. New York: 1984. V. 63
Giles Goat Boy. Garden City: 1966. V. 62
Letters. New York: 1979. V. 63; 66
L'Opera Flottant. Paris: 1968. V. 62
Lost in the Funhouse. New York: 1968. V. 63; 66
Todd Andrews to the Author: a Letter from Letters. Northridge: 1979. V. 63

BARTHELEMY, JEAN JACQUES
Syphilis. Poem en Deux Chants.... Paris: 1840. V. 67

BARTHELME, DONALD
Come Back, Dr. Caligari. Boston and Toronto: 1964. V. 62; 63; 66; 67
Presents. Dallas: 1980. V. 63
Sixty Stories. New York: 1981. V. 62; 64; 67
Snow White. New York: 1967. V. 63; 65
Snow White. New York: 1976. V. 66

BARTHES, ROLAND
Critique et Verite - Essai. Paris: 1966. V. 64
Degre Zero de Ecriture. Paris: 1953. V. 67
Essais Critiques. Paris: 1964. V. 64
Mythologies. Paris: 1957. V. 63

BARTHEZ, PAUL JOSEPH
Traite des Maladies Goutteuses. Montpellier: 1819. V. 65

BARTHOLINUS, THOMAS
De Lacteis Thoracici, in Homine Brutisque Nuperrime Obseruatis, Historia Anatomica. (with) Vasa Lymphatica, Nuper Hasniae in Animantibus Inuenta... (with) Dubia Anatomica de Lacteis Thoracicis.... Paris: 1653. V. 65
De Unicornu Observationes Novae. Amsterdam: 1678. V. 65; 67

BARTHOLOMAEUS ANGLICUS
De Proprietatibus Rerum. Nurembergi: 1492. V. 66

BARTHOLOMEW, ED
The Biographical Album of Western Gunfighters. Houston: 1958. V. 63; 66; 67
Black Jack Ketchum - Last of the Hold-Up Kings. Houston: 1955. V. 64; 67
Cullen Baker; Premier Texas Gun Fighter. Houston: 1954. V. 67
Jesse Evans, a Texas Hide-Burner. Houston: 1955. V. 67
Kill or Be Killed. Houston: 1953. V. 67
Western Hard Cases. Ruidoso: 1960. V. 67
Wild Bill Longley; a Texas Hard Case. Houston: 1953. V. 67
Wyatt Earp - 1848 to 1880, the Untold Story and 1879 to 1882, the Man the Myth. Toyahvale: 1963-1964. V. 63

BARTHOLOMEW, J. G.
Atlas of Zoogeography. Edinburgh: 1911. V. 62

BARTHOLOMEW, JOHN
Gazetteer of the British Isles Statistical and Topographical.... Edinburgh: 1887. V. 65

BARTHOLOW, ROBERT
Manual of Hypodermic Injections. Philadelphia: 1869. V. 64; 67

BARTLEET, H. W.
Bartleet's Bicycle Book. London: 1931. V. 63; 66

BARTLET, JOHN
The Gentleman's Farriery; or a Practical Treatise on the Diseases of Horses. London: 1785. V. 62; 63; 64; 67
Pharmacopoeia Bartleiana; or, Bartlet's Gentleman Farmer's Respository of Elegant and Approved Remedies for the Diseases of Horses. Eton: 1773. V. 63

BARTLETT, ALFRED DURLING
An Historical and Descriptive Account of Cummor Place, Berks.... London: 1850. V. 62

BARTLETT, D. W.
The Life and Public Services of Hon. Abraham Lincoln. New York: 1860. V. 64
The Life of General Franklin Pierce of New Hampshire. Buffalo: 1852. V. 67
What I Saw in London; or Men and Things in the Great Metropolis. 1853. V. 62

BARTLETT, EDWARD EVERETT
The Typographic Treasures in Europe: and a Study of Contemporaneous Book Production in Great Brtain, France, Italy, Germany, Holland and Belgium.... New York: 1925. V. 62; 63; 64; 66

BARTLETT, H. H.
The Sacred Edifices of the Batak of Sumatra. 1934. V. 62

BARTLETT, HENRIETTA C.
Catalogue of Early English Books Chiefly of the Elizabethan Period. New York: 1926. V. 64

BARTLETT, J. S.
The Physician's Pocket Synopsis.... Boston: 1822. V. 64

BARTLETT, JOHN RUSSELL
Bibliography of Rhode Island. Providence: 1864. V. 62
Dictionary of Americanisms. London: 1860. V. 64
Personal Narrative of Explorations and Incidents in Texas, New Mexico, Calfifornia, Sonora and Chihuahua. London: 1854. V. 66
Personal Narrative of Explorations and Incidents in Texas, New Mexico, California, Sonora and Chihuahua.... New York: 1854. V. 66
The Progress of Ethnology, an Account of Hecent Archaeological, Philogical and Geographical Researches in Various Parts of the Globe.... New York: 1847. V. 64

BARTLETT, JOSEPH
Aphorisms on Man, Manners, Principles and Things. (with) Physiognomy, a Poem. Portsmouth: 1810. V. 66

BARTLETT, NAPIER
A Soldier's Story of the War; Including the Marches and Battles of the Washington Artillery and Of Other Louisianna Troops. New Orleans: 1874. V. 63

BARTLETT, S. W.
My Foot's in the Stirrup. Dallas: 1937. V. 67

BARTLETT, WILLIAM HENRY
Forty Days in the Desert, on the Track of the Israelites; or a Journey from Cairo.... 1860. V. 65
Jerusalem Revisited. London: 1855. V. 64
The Nile Boat; or, Glimpses of the Land of Egypt. New York: 1851. V. 63; 65
The Pilgrim Fathers; or, the Founders of New England in the Reign of James the First. London: 1853. V. 62; 66

BARTLETT, WILLIAM S.
The Frontier Missionary: a Memoir of the Life of the Rev. Jacob Baily, A.M. Missionary at Pownalborough, Maine, Cornwallis and Annapolis, N. S.... New York: 1853. V. 67

BARTOK, BELA
Das Ungarische Volkslied. Berlin: 1925. V. 67

BARTOL, B. H.
A Treatise on the Marine Boilers of the United States. Philadelphia: 1851. V. 63

BARTOLI, DANIELLO
Del Suono de'Tremori Armonici e dell' Udito. Rome: 1679. V. 67

BARTOLI, PIETRO SANTI
Admiranda Romanorum Antiquitatun ac Veteris Sculpturae Vestigia.... Roma: 1693. V. 64
Colonna Trajana Eretta dal Senato, e Poplo Romano all'Imperatore Trajano Augusto ne suo Foro in Roma. Rome: 1673. V. 63; 65; 67

BARTOLINI, C.
Mesozoic Sedimentary and Tectonic History of North Central Mexico. 1999. V. 67

BARTON, BERNARD
Napoleon and Other Poems. London: 1822. V. 65
Poems. London: 1820. V. 63
A Widow's Tale and Other Poems. London: 1827. V. 63

BARTON, CLARA
A Story of the Red Cross. Glimpses of Field Work. New York: 1904. V. 65

BARTON, E. H.
Report to the Louisiana State Medical Society on the Meteorology, Vital Statistics and Hygiene of the State of Lousiana.... New Orleans: 1851. V. 66

BARTON, FRANK T.
The Kennel Encyclopaedia. London. V. 67

BARTON, JOHN
A Lecture on the Geography of Plants. London: 1827. V. 65

BARTON, O. S.
Three Years with Quantrell, a True Story Told by His Scout, John McCorkle. New York: 1966. V. 63; 66

BARTON, PAULE
The Woe Shirt. Lincoln: 1980. V. 64

BARTON, R. T.
Pleading and Practice in the Courts of Chancery. Richmond: 1881. V. 62
Pleading and Practice in the Courts of Chancery. Charlottesville: 1926. V. 66
The Practice in the Courts of Law in Civil Cases. Richmond: 1891. V. 65

BARTON, RICHARD
Some Remarks Towards a Full Description of Upper and Lower Lough Lene, Near Killarney, in the County of Kerry. Dublin: 1751. V. 62

BARTON, RONALD
Jabberwocky Re-Versed and Other Guinness Versions. Dublin: 1935. V. 65

BARTON, ROSE
Familiar London. London: 1904. V. 62; 67

BARTON, W. P. C.
Compendium Florae Philadelphicae.... Philadelphia: 1818. V. 66
A Flora of North America. Philadelphia: 1822. V. 63

BARTON, WILLIAM ELEAZAR
Lieutenant William Barton of Morris County, New Jersey and His Descendants. Oak Park: 1900. V. 63

BARTONE, ELISA
Peepe. The Lamplighter. New York: 1993. V. 65

BARTRAM, JOHN
An Account of East-Florida, with a Journal Kept by John Bartram of Philadelphia. London: 1766. V. 64
The Correspondence of John Bartram 1734-1777. Gainesville: 1992. V. 63; 67

BARTRAM, WILLIAM
Botanical and Zoological Drawings 1756-1788.... Philadelphia: 1968. V. 62; 63; 67
Travels through North and South Carolina, Georgia, East and West Florida. Philadelphia: 1791. V. 62; 63; 67
Travels through North and South Carolina, Georgia, East and West Florida. London: 1792. V. 63; 64
Travels through North and South Carolina, Georgia, East and West Florida. London: 1794. V. 63; 66
Travels through North and South Carolina, Georgia, East and West Florida. Savannah: 1973. V. 66

BARTTELOT, WALTER G.
The Life of Edmund Musgrave Barttelot.... London: 1890. V. 64

BARUCH, BERNARD M.
Baruch: My Own Story. New York: 1957. V. 63

BARUCH, DOROTHY WALTER
Good Times With Our Friends. Chicago: 1941. V. 65
Good Times with Our Friends. Chicago: 1946. V. 64
Pinocchio. Boston: 1940. V. 65

BARWICK, PETRO
Life of the Reverend Dr. John Barwick, D.D. Sometime Fellow of St. John's College in Cambridge.... London: 1724. V. 63
Vita Johannis Barwick, S.T.P. Ecclesiae Christsi & S... Decani, et Collegii Sancti Johannis.... London: 1721. V. 66; 67

BARY, A. DE
Comparative Anatomy of the Vegetative Organs of the Phanerogams and Ferns. Oxford: 1884. V. 63

BARZONI, VITORIO
The Romans in Greece. Boston: 1799. V. 63

BARZUN, JACQUES
A Catalogue of Crime. New York: 1989. V. 65; 66; 67

BASBANES, NICHOLAS A.
A Gentle Madness. 1995. V. 63; 65
A Gentle Madness. New York: 1995. V. 66

BASCHET, ARMAND
Les Femmes Blondes Selon les Peintres de l'Ecole de Venise. Paris: 1865. V. 63

BASCOM, H. B.
The Little Iron Wheel, a Declaration of Christian Rights and Articles, Showing the Despotism of Episcopal Methodism. Nashville: 1857. V. 63

BASDEN, GEORGE THOMAS
Niger Ibos. A Description of the Primitive Life, Customs...of the IboPeople of Nigeria.... London: 1937. V. 62

BASH, B.
Callendar, McAuslan & Troup's Economy Cook Book. Providence: 1883. V. 67

BASHFORD, HERBERT
A Man Unafraid - The Story of John Charles Fremont. San Francisc: 1927. V. 66

BASHKIRTSEFF, MARIE
The Journal of Marie Bashkirtseff. London: 1891. V. 63

BASHO
The Records of a Weather-Exposed Skeleton. London: 1969. V. 63
Traveler, My Name: Haiku of Basho. Norwich: 1984. V. 65; 66

BASIL, SAINT
Omnia D. Basilii Magni Archiepiscopi Caesareae Capadociae, Quae Extant, Opera.... Basiliae: 1540. V. 65

BASILIUS VALENTINUS
...Chymische Schriften alle, so Viel Derer Verhanden, Anitzo Zum Dritten mahl Zusammen Gedruckt, aus Vielen so Wol Geschrieben als Gedruckte Eemplare Vermehret udn Verbessert, und in Zwey Theile Verfasset. Hamburg: 1700. V. 65

BASKERVILLE, PETER
The Bank of Upper Canada. A Collection of Documents. Toronto: 1987. V. 66

BASKET, JAMES
History of the Island of St. Domingo, from Its First Discovery by Columbus to the Present Period. New York: 1824. V. 62

BASKETT, JOHN
The Drawings of Thomas Rowlandson in the Paul Mellon Collection. 1977. V. 65

BASKIN, ESTHER
Creatures of Darknes. Boston: 1962. V. 63; 64; 65; 66

BASKIN, HOSEA
Hosie's Alphabet. New York: 1972. V. 65

BASKIN, LEONARD
Ars Anatomica: a Medical Fantasia. New York: 1972. V. 62; 63
Figures of Dead Men. N.P: 1968. V. 62
Figures of Dead Men. Amherst: 1968. V. 65
Iconologia. New York: 1988. V. 65
Imps, Demons, Hobgoblins, Witches, Fairies and Elves. New York: 1984. V. 64; 65
Leonard Baskin. Brunswick: 1962. V. 65
Sculpture, Reliefs, Drawings, Watercolours, Graphics, First London Exhibition. London: 1981. V. 64; 67
To Color Thought. New Haven: 1967. V. 63

BASLER, ROY
Abraham Lincoln: His Speeches and Writings. New York: 1946. V. 62

BASON, FRED
Fred Bason's Diary. London: 1950. V. 63
Fred Bason's Diary (with 2nd and 3rd Diaries). London: 1950-1952. V. 63
Fred Bason's Second Diary. London: 1952. V. 63

BASS, ALTHEA
Cherokee Messenger. Norman: 1936. V. 66

BASS, MICHAEL T.
Street Music in the Metropolis. London: 1864. V. 62

BASS, RICK
The Book of Yaak. New York: 1996. V. 67
Brown Dog of the Yaak. Minneapolis: 1999. V. 67
The Deer Pasture. College Station: 1985. V. 63; 66
The Lost Grizzlies. Boston: 1995. V. 65; 67
The New Wolves. New York: 1998. V. 67
The Ninemile Wolves. Livingston: 1992. V. 62; 64; 65; 66; 67
Oil Notes. Boston: 1989. V. 63; 67
Oil Notes. London: 1989. V. 67
The Watch. New York: 1989. V. 63; 66; 67
Where the Sea Used to Be. Boston: 1998. V. 67
Wild to the Heart. Harrisburg: 1987. V. 67
Wild to the Heart. New York: 1987. V. 64; 66; 67
Winter. Boston: 1991. V. 64; 67

BASSERMANN JORDAN, ERNST
Montres, Horloges et Pendules. Paris: 1964. V. 62; 67

BASSET, JOSHUA
An Essay Towards a Proposal for Catholick Communion. London: 1704. V. 62

BASSETT, DAVID L.
A Stereoscopic Atlas of the Human Anatomy - the Central Nervous System. Portland: 1952. V. 64; 66

BASSETT, MARNIE
Realms and Islands. The World Voyage of Rose De Freycinet in the Corvette Uranie 1817-1820. London: 1962. V. 63; 64; 65

BASSLER, R. S.
Shelled Invertebrates of the Past and Present. New York: 1931. V. 64; 66

BASSO, HAMILTON
Beauregard the Great Creole. New York: 1933. V. 62; 63; 65

BASTIAT, CLAUDE FREDERIC
Economic Sophisms. Edinburgh: 1873. V. 64
Popular Fallacies Regarding General Interests.... London: 1849. V. 64

BASTIN, BRUCE
Never Sell a Copyright. Joe Davis and His Role in the New York Music Scene. Chigwell: 1990. V. 65

BATAILLE, GEORGES
Death and Sensuality. New York: 1962. V. 67
Histoire de l'Oeil. Seville, 1940: 1947. V. 67

BATCHELLOR, GEORGE CLINTON
Golden Hours from Mother Goose. Philadelphia: 1920. V. 62

BATCHELOR, JOHN
The Ainu of Japan; the Religion, Superstitions and General History of the Hairy Aborigines of Japan. London: 1892. V. 64

BATE, C. S.
Catalogue of Specimens of Amphipodous Crustacea in the British Museum. 1862. V. 66
Catalogue of Specimens of Amphipodous Crustacea in the British Musuem. London: 1862. V. 64
A History of the British Sessile-Eyed Crustacea. 1863-1868. V. 63; 66
A History of the British Sessile-Eyed Crustacea. London: 1863-1868. V. 64

BATE, GEORGE
Elenchus Motuum Nuperorum in Anglia; or, a Short Historical Acocunt of the Rise and Progress of the Late Troublres in England in Two Parts. Motus Compositi; or, the History of the Composing of the Affairs of England by the Restauration of K. Charles the. London: 1685. V. 62; 66

BATE, JULIUS
An Hebrew Grammar: formed on the Usage of the Words by the Inspired Writers. Dublin: 1756. V. 65

BATEMAN, CHARLES SOMERVILLE LATROBE
The First Ascent of the Kasai: Being Some Records of Service Under the Lone Star. New York: 1869. V. 65

BATEMAN, GREGORY C.
The Viarium, Being a Practical Guide to the Construction, Arrangement, and Management of Vivaria.... London: 1897. V. 65

BATEMAN, H. M.
The M. F. H. Who Ran Riot!. London: 1934. V. 62

BATEMAN, J.
The General Turnpike Roads Acts, with Notes and an Index. London: 1836. V. 66

BATEMAN, JAMES
A Monograph of Odontoglossum. London: 1874. V. 63
A Second Century of Orchidaceous Plants.... London: 1867. V. 63; 67

BATEMAN, JOHN FREDERIC LA TROBE
History and Description of the Manchester Waterworks. London: 1884. V. 62; 66
History and Description of the Manchester Waterworks. Manchester: 1884. V. 62

BATEMAN, THOMAS
A Descriptive Catalogue of the Antiquities and Miscellaneous Objects Preserved in the Museum of Thomas Bateman, at Lomberdale House, Derbyshire. Bakewell: 1855. V. 62
A Treatise on Asistment Tithe in Which the Nature, Right, Objects, Mode of Payment and Method of Ascertaining the Value of Each Species of It, are Fully Stated and Explained. London: 1778. V. 63

BATEMAN, WILLIAM O.
The General Commercial Law, as Recognized in the Jurisprudence of the U.S. Philadelphia: 1860. V. 63

BATES, BARNABAS
Peculiarities of the Shakers.... New York: 1832. V. 62

BATES, CADWALLADER JOHN
Thomas Bates and the Kirklevington Shorthorns, a Contribution to the History of Pure Durham Cattle. Newcastle-Upon-Tyne: 1897. V. 63

BATES, CHARLES F.
Custer's Indian Battles. New York: 1936. V. 67

BATES, D. B., MRS.
Incidents on Land and Water, or Four Years on the Pacific Coast. Boston: 1857. V. 63

BATES, E. F.
History and Reminiscences of Denton County. Denton: 1918. V. 65

BATES, ELY
A Cursory View of Civil Government: Chiefly in Relation to Virtue and Happiness. London: 1797. V. 63
Rural Philosophy; or Reflections on Knowledge, Virtue and Happiness.... London: 1803. V. 65; 66

BATES, HERBERT
Book of Drawings. Chicago: 1961. V. 66

BATES, HERBERT ERNEST
Achilles the Donkey. London: 1963. V. 64
The Beauty of the Dead and Other Stories. London: 1940. V. 62; 65
The Black Boxer. London: 1932. V. 63; 64
The Bride Comes to Evensford. London: 1943. V. 63
Catherine Foster. London: 1929. V. 62; 64; 65; 66
Charlotte's Row. London: 1931. V. 63; 64; 66
Colonel Julian and Other Stories. London: 1951. V. 62
The Cruise of the Breadwinner. London: 1946. V. 64
Cut and Come Again - Fourteen Stories. London: 1935. V. 64
Day's End and Other Stories. London: 1928. V. 63
The Death of a Huntsman: Four Short Novels. London: 1957. V. 66
Down the River. London: 1937. V. 63
The Duet. London: 1935. V. 62; 63
Edward Garnett. 1950. V. 62
The Fallow Land. London: 1932. V. 62
Flowers and Faces. Waltham St. Lawrence: 1935. V. 67
The Flying Goat. London: 1939. V. 62
A German Idyll. Waltham St. Lawrence. V. 62; 64; 66
The Hessian Prisoner. London: 1930. V. 64

BATES, HERBERT ERNEST continued
The House with the Apricot and Two Other Tales. Waltham St. Lawrence: 1933. V. 62; 64
How Sleep the Brave and Other Stories by Flying Officer X. London: 1943. V. 62
The Last Bread. 1926. V. 62
The Last Bread. London: 1926. V. 63; 64
A Love of Flowers. London: 1971. V. 65
The Modern Short Story: a Critical Survey. London: 1941. V. 66
Mrs. Esmond's Life. 1931. V. 62
Mrs. Esmond's Life. London: 1931. V. 64
My Uncle Silas. Stories. London: 1939. V. 62
The Nature of Love. London: 1953. V. 65
The Purple Plain. London: 1947. V. 66
The Seekers. London: 1926. V. 62; 64; 65; 66
Seven Tales and Alexander. London: 1929. V. 64; 66
Something Short and Sweet. London: 1937. V. 62
The Spring Song and In View of the Fact That. London: 1927. V. 63; 64
The Story Without an End and The Country Doctor. London: 1932. V. 63; 66
A Threshing Day. London: 1931. V. 64; 66
Through the Woods. London: 1936. V. 62; 63; 65
Through the Woods. New York: 1936. V. 64
The Tree. London: 1930. V. 64
The Woman Who Had Imagination. London: 1934. V. 62; 64

BATES, J.
How to Find Fish and Make Them Strike. 1974. V. 67
Streamers and Bucktails. 1979. V. 67

BATES, JAMES
Quakero - Methodism; or, a Confutation of the First Principles of the Quakers and Methodists. London: 1740. V. 64

BATES, R. S. P.
Breeding Birds of Kashmir. London: 1952. V. 67

BATES, RALPH
Lean Men: an Episode in a Life. London: 1934. V. 63

BATES, ROBERT
Mountain Men. 1988. V. 64

BATES, WILLIAM
George Cruikshank: the Artist, the Humorist and the Man, With Some Account of His Brother. Houston: 1879. V. 65
George Cruikshank: the Artist, the Humorist and the Man, With Some Account of His Brother Robert. London: 1879. V. 64
Spiritual Perfection, Unfolded and Enforced. London: 1699. V. 63
Stars and Stripes in Rebeldom. Boston: 1862. V. 63
The Works.... London: 1700. V. 67

BATESON, FREDERICK WILSE
Cambridge Bibliography of English Literature. Cambridge: 1940-1957. V. 65
Cambridge Bibliography of English Literature. New York and Cambridge: 1941. V. 66
The Cambridge Bibliography of English Literature. Cambridge: 1966. V. 67

BATESON, WILLIAM
Materials for the Study of Variation. 1894. V. 64; 66
Materials for the Study of Variation. London: 1894. V. 62; 63; 65; 67
Mendel's Principles of Heredity. Cambridge: 1902. V. 62; 64; 65; 66; 67
Mendel's Principles of Heredity. Cambridge: 1909. V. 62; 64; 66
The Methods and Scope of Genetics. Cambridge: 1908. V. 66; 67
Notes on the Later Stages in the Development of Balanoglossus Kowalevskii. 1884. V. 67
Problems of Genetics. New Haven: 1913. V. 65
Reports to the Evolution Committee of the Royal Society. London: 1910. V. 65

BATH, WILLIAM PULTENEY, EARL OF
The Case of the Revival of the Salt Duty, Fully Stated and Considered, with Some Remarks on the Present State of Affairs. London: 1732. V. 62
An Enquiry into the Conduct of Our Domestick Affairs, from the Year 1721 to the Present Time. London: 1734. V. 66
An Epistle from Lord L---l to Lord C---d by Mr. P----. London: 1740. V. 63

BATHURST, HENRY
An Introduction to the Law Relative to Trials at Nisi Prius. London: 1785. V. 65

BATKIN, MAUREEN
Gifts for Good Children: the History of Children's China Part II: 1890-1990. London: 1995. V. 67

BATTELEY, JOHN
The Antiquities of Richborough and Reculver. London: 1774. V. 63

BATTEN, J.
The Best of Sheep Hunting. 1985. V. 64

BATTEN, JOHN H.
The Forest and the Plain. 1984. V. 67

BATTENBERG, LOUIS
Men-of-War Names. Their Meaning and Origin. London: 1908. V. 64

BATTERSBY, H. F. PREVOST
India Under Royal Eyes. London: 1906. V. 64

BATTERSBY, MARTIN
The Decorative Twenties. London: 1969. V. 62

BATTEY, THOMAS C.
The Life and Adventures of a Quaker Among the Indians. Boston: 1875. V. 67

BATTIE, WILLIAM
A Treatise on Madness and Remarks on Dr. Battie's Treatise on Madness. London: 1962. V. 63; 65

BATTIN, RICHARD H.
Astronautical Guidance. New York: 1964. V. 66

BATTINE, CECIL
The Crisis of the Confederacy, a History of Gettysburg and the Wilderness. London: 1905. V. 62; 63; 65

THE BATTLE of Fort Sumter and First Victory of the Soutehrn Troops, April, 13th, 1861. Charleston: 1861. V. 62; 63; 65

BATTLE of Shiloh. Official Report of the 2nd Brigade 1st Division April 6, 1862. Memphis: 1862. V. 63; 65

BATTY, BEATRICE
Forty-Two Years Among the Indians and Eskimo. London: 1893. V. 63; 66

BATZ DE TRANQUELLEON, CAROLINE
Le Pirate. Agen: 1826. V. 66

BAUCHER, F.
A New Method of Horsemanship, Including the Breaking and Training of Horses.... New York: 1850. V. 62

BAUDELAIRE, CHARLES
Les Fleurs du Mal. Paris: 1861. V. 63
Les Fleurs du Mal. New York: 1940. V. 64
Les Fleurs du Mal. Stockholm: 1946. V. 63; 66
Les Fleurs du Mal. Paris: 1958. V. 67
Flowers of Evil. New York and London: 1936. V. 67
Flowers of Evil. New York: 1940. V. 64
Flowers of Evil. New York: 1971. V. 65
Intimate Journals. London: 1930. V. 63; 64; 65
Spleen - Thirty-One Versions of Baudelaire's Je Suis Comme le Roi. London: 1973. V. 65
Twenty Prose Poems. London: 1946. V. 62

BAUDELOT DE DAIRVAL, CHARLES CESAR
L'Utilite des Voyages qui Concerne la Connoissance des Medailles, Inscriptions, Statues, Dieux Lares, Peintures Anciennes, et les Bas Reliefs, Pierres Precieuses et Gravees, Cahcets, Talismans, Anneaux Manuscrits.... Paris: 1693. V. 62

BAUDER, EMMA
Ruth and Marie. Chicago and Philadelphia: 1895. V. 63; 65

BAUDESSON, H.
Indo-China and its Primitive People. London: 1915. V. 62

BAUDIN, P.
Fetichism and Fetich Worshipers. New York: 1885. V. 64

BAUDRAND, MICHEL ANTOINE
Dictionaire Geographique et Historique Contenant Une Description Exacte de Tous les Etats, Royaumes, Provinces, Ville Bourgs, Montagnes, Caps, Isles. Paris: 1705. V. 67

BAUDRILLARD, JEAN
Systeme des Objets. Paris: 1968. V. 67

BAUER, FRED
Cake-Art-Craft. Chicago: 1932. V. 66

BAUER, JOHANN
Kafka and Prague. New York Washington London: 1971. V. 67

BAUER, LOUIS
Hip Disease. A Clinical Lecture Delivered at the Long Island College Hospital, of Brooklyn. Nashville: 1859. V. 64

BAUER, LOUIS HOPEWELL
Aviation Medicine. Baltimore: 1926. V. 63; 65

BAUER, MAX
Edelsteinkunde. eine Allgemein Vorstandiche Darstellung der Eigenschaften, des Verkommens und der Verwendung der Edelstein, Nebst Einer Einleitung zur Bestimmung Derselben fur Mineralogen Steinschleifer, Juweliere, etc. Leipzig: 1896. V. 64; 67

BAUER, PAUL
Himalayan Campaigns: the German Attack on Kangchenjunga, the Second Highest Mountain in the World. Oxford: 1937. V. 64
Himalayan Quest. 1938. V. 63; 65
Himalayan Quest. London: 1938. V. 63; 64

BAUER, R. T.
Crustacean Sexual Biology. New York: 1991. V. 65

BAUGHAN, PETER E.
North of Leeds. London: 1966. V. 62; 64; 65; 66

BAUGHMAN, ROBERT W.
Kansas in Maps. Topeka: 1961. V. 65

BAUGHMAN, THEODORE
The Oklahoma Scout. Chicago: 1886. V. 64

BAUHIN, C.
Catalogus Plantarum Cira Basilieam Sponte Nascentium. Basel: 1622. V. 62

BAUHIN, CASPAR
Pinax Theatri Botanici.... Basel: 1623. V. 63; 66
Pinax Theatri Botanici.... Basel: 1671. V. 64

BAUM, FRANK J.
The Laughing Dragon of Oz. Racine: 1935. V. 64

BAUM, LYMAN FRANK
American Fairy Tales. Chicago: 1901. V. 66
Babes in Birdland. Chicago: 1911. V. 65
Cinderella and Sleeping Beauty. Chicago: 1905. V. 65
The Daring Twins, a Story for Young Folk. Chicago: 1911. V. 66
Dorothy and the Wizard in Oz. Chicago: 1961. V. 64
Dot and Tot of Merryland. Indianapolis: 1901. V. 65
The Emerald City of Oz. Chicago: 1910. V. 62
The Enchanted Island of Yew. Indianapolis: 1903. V. 66
Father Goose: His Book. Chicago: 1899. V. 67
Glinda of Oz. Chicago: 1920. V. 62; 66
John Dough and the Cherub. Chicago: 1906. V. 62; 66
The Land of Oz. Chicago: 1904. V. 63
Little Dorothy and Toto. Chicago: 1913. V. 62
Little Wizard Stories of Oz. Chicago: 1914. V. 65
The Marvelous Land of Oz. Chicago: 1904. V. 65; 67
The New Wizard of Oz. Indianapolis: 1903. V. 66
Ozma of Oz. Chicago: 1907. V. 62; 63
The Patchwork Girl of Oz. Chicago: 1913. V. 62
Rinkitink in Oz. Chicago: 1916. V. 66
The Scarecrow of Oz. Chicago: 1915. V. 62
The Sea-Fairies. Chicago: 1911. V. 62; 66
Sky Island. Chicago: 1912. V. 64; 66
The Songs of Father Goose. 1900. V. 62; 63
The Songs of Father Goose: for the Kindergarten, the Nursery and the Tome. Indianapolis: 1909. V. 65
The Surprising Adventures of the Magical Monarch of Mo and His People. Indianapolis: 1903. V. 62
The Surprising Adventures of the Magical Monarch of Mo and His People. Chicago: 1913. V. 65
Tik-Tok of Oz. Chicago: 1914. V. 62
Two Songs of Father Goose. Chicago: 1900. V. 64
The Wizard of Oz. Chicago: 1903. V. 63
The Wizard of Oz Picture Book. Racine: 1939. V. 65
The Wizard of Oz Waddle Book. New York: 1934. V. 62; 64; 66

BAUMAN, GUSTAVE
Frijoles Canyon Pictographs. Santa Fe: 1939. V. 66

BAUMBACH, JONATHAN
Writers as Teacher/Teachers as Writers. New York: 1970. V. 63

BAUME, ERIC
Five Graves at Nijmegen. London: 1945. V. 66

BAUMER, LEWIS
Jumbles. London: 1905. V. 64

BAUMGARTNER, L.
A Bibliography of the Poem Syphilis Sive Morbus Gallicus by Giroloma Fracastoro of Verona. New Haven: 1935. V. 67

BAUMOL, WILLIAM J.
Welfare Economics and the Theory of the State. London: 1952. V. 65

BAUSCH, RICHARD
Mr. Field's Daughter. New York: 1989. V. 63

BAWDEN, EDWARD
Adam and Evelyn at Kew. London: 1930. V. 64
The Queen's Beasts.... 1953. V. 63
Travellers' Verse. London: 1946. V. 65

BAWDEN, NINA
Eyes of Green. New York: 1953. V. 62

BAWR, ALEXANDRINE, MADAME DE
Raoul ou l'Eneide. Paris: 1832. V. 66

BAX, ANDRE
The Mauritus Almanac and Commercial Handbook for 1929-1930. Port Louis: 1929. V. 64

BAX, CLIFFORD
Florence Farr, Bernard Shaw, and W. B. Yeats. 1941. V. 62; 65
Florence Farr, Bernard Shaw and W. B. Yeats. Dublin: 1941. V. 62

BAXT, GEORGE
The Affair At Royalties. New York: 1971. V. 67
The Dorothy Parker Murder Case. New York: 1984. V. 67
A Parade of Cockeyed Creatures. New York: 1967. V. 67

BAXTER, CHARLES
First Light. New York: 1987. V. 65; 67
Shadow Play. New York: 1993. V. 65; 67
The South Dakota Guidebook. New York: 1974. V. 62; 64; 67
Through the Safety Net Stories. New York: 1985. V. 66

BAXTER, DOREEN
Fairyland Frolics. Leicester: 1950. V. 62

BAXTER, E. H.
From Shikar and Safari. London: 1931. V. 67

BAXTER, EVELYN V.
The Birds of Scotland. London: 1953. V. 66

BAXTER, FRANCIS WILLOUGHBY
Percy Lockhart; or, the Hidden Will. London: 1872. V. 67

BAXTER, GLEN
Cranireons of Botya - Drawings. New York: 1974. V. 62; 67

BAXTER, JAMES PHINNEY
The British Invasion from the North. Albany: 1887. V. 66
The Introduction of the Ironclad Warship. Cambridge: 1933. V. 65

BAXTER, KATHERINE S.
In Bamboo Lands. New York: 1895. V. 64

BAXTER, LUCY
The Life of William Barnes. Poet and Philologist. London: 1887. V. 62; 64; 66

BAXTER, RICHARD
An Abridgment of Mr.. Baxter's History of His Life and Times. London: 1702. V. 62
A Call to the Unconverted To Turn and Live and Accept of Mercy While Mercy May be Had.... Northallerton: 1802. V. 64
Catholic Theologie: Plain, Pure, Peaceable.... London: 1675. V. 63
The Divine Life: in Three Treatises; the First, of the Knowledge of God, The Second, of Walking with God. The Third, Of Conversing with God In Solitude. 1664. V. 63
The Poetical Fragments. London: 1821. V. 62; 67

BAXTER, WILLIAM
British Phaenogamous Botany; or, Figures and Descriptions of the Genera of British Flowering Plants. Oxford: 1834-1843. V. 62

BAYARD, FERDINAND MARIE
Voyage dans l'Interieur des Etats-Unis, a Bath, Winchester, dans la Vallee de Shenandoah.... Paris: 1797. V. 66

BAYARD, SAMUEL J.
A Sketch of the Life of Com. Robert F. Stockton.... New York: 1856. V. 62; 63; 66

BAYER, WILLIAM
Peregrine. N.P: 1981. V. 67
Switch. New York: 1984. V. 65

BAYFIELD, H. W.
The Nova Scotia Pilot: South East Coast from Mars Head to Cape Casino, Including Sable Island. London: 1860. V. 64
The St. Lawrence Pilot; Comprising Sailing Directions for the Gulf and River. London: 1860. V. 64

BAYLE, PIERRE
Dictionnaire Historique et Critique.... Rotterdam: 1702. V. 67

BAYLEY, DIANA
Employment, the True Source of Happiness; or, the Good Uncle and Aunt. London: 1825. V. 63

BAYLEY, F. W. N.
Comic Nursery Tales.... London: 1844. V. 63

BAYLEY, HAROLD
The Lost Language of Symbolism. London: 1912. V. 65

BAYLEY, JOHN
The History and Antiquities of the Tower of London. London: 1825. V. 62
A Summary of the Law of Bills of Exchange, Cash Bills and Promissory Notes.... London: 1797. V. 63

BAYLEY, NATHAN
English and Latine Exercises for School Boys, Comprising all the Rules of Syntaxis. Boston: 1720. V. 63

BAYLEY, NICOLA
The Mouse Hole Cat. 1990. V. 67
Nicola Bayley's Book of Nursery Rhymes. London: 1975. V. 66

BAYLIS, H. A.
Fauna of British India Including Ceylon and Burma. Nematoda. London: 1936-1939. V. 66
Fauna of British India, Nematoda. 1936-1939. V. 63; 66
Fauna of British India, Nematoda. London: 1936-1939. V. 62

BAYLISS, MARGUERITE F.
Bolinvar. New York: 1937. V. 63; 66
The Yearbook of Show Horses. New York: 1936. V. 62; 66

BAYLISS, WILLIAM MADDOCK
The Vaso-Motor System. London: 1923. V. 65

BAYLOR, BYRD
Plink Plink Plink. Boston: 1971. V. 63

BAYLOR, GEORGE
Bull Run to Bull Run; or, Four Years in the Army of Northern Virginia. Richmond: 1900. V. 63

BAYLY, MARY
Workmen and Their Difficulties. London: 1861. V. 62

BAYNE, A. D.
Royal Illustrated History of Eastern England.... Great Yarmouth: 1873. V. 65

BAYNE, CHARLES S.
The Call of the Birds. London: 1945. V. 62
My Book of Best Fairy Tales. London: 1915. V. 63; 65

BAYNES, HELTON GODWIN
Mythology of the Soul: a Research into the Unconscious from Schizophrenic Dreams and Drawings. Baltimore: 1940. V. 65

BAYNES, JOHN
The Cotton Trade. Two Lectures on the Above Subject, Delivered Before the Members of the Blackburn Literary, Scientific and Mechanics Institution. 1857. V. 65

BAZIN, D.
Copper Deposits of Iran. Tehran: 1969. V. 67

BAZIN, G. A.
Le Livre Jaune Contenant Quelques Conversations sur les Logomachies, c'est-a-dire abus des Termes, Double Entente, Faux sens. Basle: 1748. V. 63

BAZLEY, THOMAS
A Lecture Upon Cotton, as an Element of Industry, Delivered at the Rooms of the Society of Arts, London, in Connexion with the Exhibition of 1851. London: 1852. V. 65

BEACH, A. H., MRS.
Women of Wyoming, Including a Short History of Some of the Early Activities of Women in Our State. Casper: 1927. V. 67

BEACH, CHARLES
Andrew Deverel; the History of an Adventurer in New Guinea. London: 1863. V. 67

BEACH, DAVID NELSON
Beach Family Reminiscences and Annals. Meriden: 1931. V. 63; 66

BEACH, REX
Oh, Shoot!. London: 1921. V. 67

BEACH, S. A.
The Apples of New York. Albany: 1905. V. 62

BEACH, SYLVIA
Les Annees Vingt. Les Ecrivains Americains a Paris et Leurs Amis 1920-1930. Paris: 1959. V. 63
Shakespeare and Company. 1960. V. 62; 65

BEACH, WOOSTER
Rise, Progress and Present State of the New York Medical Institution and Reformed Medical Society of the United States. New York: 1830. V. 62

BEACHWOOD Borough Directory, Who's Who and Year Book. New York: 1924. V. 66

BEADLE, DELOS WHITE
Canadian Fruit, Flower and Kitchen Gardener.... Toronto: 1872. V. 62

BEADLE, J. H.
Brigham's Destroying Angels. Salt Lake City: 1904. V. 64; 67
Life in Utah; or the Mysteries and Crimes of Mormonism.... Philadelphia: 1870. V. 63; 66
Western Wilds and the Men Who Redeem Them - an Authentic Narrative. Cincinnati: 1878. V. 65

BEADLE, R.
New Science Out of Old Books. Aldershot: 1995. V. 62

BEAGLE, PETER S.
A Fine and Private Place. New York: 1960. V. 63; 67
The Last Unicorn. New York: 1968. V. 63; 65

BEAGLEHOLE, J. C.
The Exploration of the Pacific. London: 1968. V. 63
The Life of Captain James Cook. London: 1974. V. 63
The Life of Captain James Cook. Stanford: 1974. V. 63; 64
Words for Music - Poems. Christchurch: 1938. V. 64

BEAL, ANTHONY
Selected Literary Criticism. London: 1955. V. 63

BEAL, M. D.
A History of Southeastern Idaho. Caldwell: 1942. V. 63
Inter-Mountain Railroads Standard and Narrow Gauge. Caldwell: 1962. V. 63

BEAL, WILLIAM JAMES
An American Pioneer in Science. The Life and Service of William James Beal. Amherst: 1925. V. 63

BEALE, LIONEL
Disease Germs. Their Nature and Origin. London: 1872. V. 67
How to Work with the Microscope. Philadelphia: 1870. V. 66
How to Work with the Microscope. London: 1880. V. 66
A Treatise on the Distortions and Deformities of the Human Body Exhibiting a Concise View of the Nature and Treatment of the Principal Malformations and Distortions of the Chest.... London: 1833. V. 64; 67

BEALE, R. L. T.
History of the 9th Virginia Cavalry. Richmond: 1899. V. 62; 63; 65

BEALE, REGINALD
Lawns for Sports. London: 1924. V. 64

BEALES, P.
Classic Roses. New York: 1985. V. 67
Classic Roses. New York: 1997. V. 67

BEALL, JOHN BRAMLETT
In Barrack and Field. Nashville: 1906. V. 62

BEAMAN, ARDERN
The Squadron. London: 1920. V. 64

BEAMISH, C. T. M.
Beamish: a Genealogical Study of the Family in County Cork and Elsewhere. 1950. V. 64

BEAN, L. L.
Hunting - Fishing and Camping. Freeport: 1942. V. 62

BEAN, W. J.
The Royal Botanic Gardens, Kew.... London: 1908. V. 62
Trees and Shrubs Hardy in the British Isles. London: 1936. V. 67
Trees and Shrubs Hardy in the British Isles. London: 1950. V. 67
Trees and Shrubs Hardy in the British Isles. 1950-1951. V. 65
Trees and Shrubs Hardy in the British Isles. London: 1970. V. 67
Trees and Shrubs Hardy in the British Isles. London: 1973. V. 67
Trees and Shrubs Hardy in the British Isles. London: 1992. V. 67

BEAR, GREG
The Wind from a Burning Woman. Sauk City: 1983. V. 62; 64; 66

THE BEAR-Cat Musketeer. Citizen's Military Training Camp. Camp Del Monte Calif. 1923. Chicago: 1923. V. 62

BEARDLOCK, JAMES
A Treatise Upon Tithes: Containing an Estimate of Every Titheable Article in Common Cultivation.... London: 1809. V. 66

BEARCROFT, PHILIP
An Historical Account of Thomas Sutton Esq. and of His Foundation in Charter-House. London: 1737. V. 66

BEARD, GEOFFREY
Craftsmen and Interior Decoration in England 1660-1820. London: 1986. V. 63

BEARD, GEORGE MILLER
Eating and Drinking: a Popular Manual of Food and Diet in Health and Disease. New York: 1871. V. 65; 67
A Practical Treatise on Nervous Exhaustion (Neurasthenia). American Nervousness: Its Causes and Consequences. The Psychology of the Salem Witchcraft Excitement of 1692 and its Practical Application to Our Own Time. New York: 1881-1882. V. 62
Sexual Neurasthenia (Nervous Exhaustion). Its Hygiene, Causes, Symptoms and Treatment.... New York: 1891. V. 63

BEARD, JAMES
Hors D'Oeuvre and Canapes. New York: 1940. V. 65

BEARD, PETER HILL
The End of the Game. London: 1965. V. 65

BEARD, W. E.
The Battle of Nashville. Nashville: 1913. V. 62; 63

BEARD, W. H.
Humor in Animals. New York: 1885. V. 67

BEARDSLEY, AUBREY VINCENT
Last Letters of Aubrey Beardsley. London: 1904. V. 62
Letters from Aubrey Beardsley to Leonard Smithers. London: 1937. V. 64
The Letters of Aubrey Beardsley. London: 1971. V. 62
A Second Book of Fifty Drawings. London: 1899. V. 64
The Story of Venus and Tannhauser in Which is Set Forth an Exact Account of the Manner of State Held by Madame Venus Goddess and Meretrix.... London: 1907. V. 62; 65
Under the Hill and Other Essays in Prose and Verse. London: 1904. V. 66
Under the Hill or the History of Venus and Tannhauser in Which is Set Forth an Exact Account of the Manner of State Held by Madam Venus, Goddess and Meretrix, Under the Famous Horseleap.... Paris: 1959. V. 62; 63
The Yellow Book. Volumes I-XIII. London: 1894-1897. V. 65

BEARING South: Antarctica, at Sea. 1991. V. 64

BEARMAN, F. A.
Fine and Historic Bookbindings from the Folger Shakespeare Library. Washington: 1992. V. 62

BEASLAI, PIARAS
Michael Collins and the Making of a New Ireland. 1926. V. 64
Michael Collins: Soldier & Stateman. Dublin & Cork: 1937. V. 67

BEASLEY, NORMAN
Main Street Merchant: the Story of the J. C. Penney Company. New York: 1948. V. 63

BEATH, ROBERT B.
History of the Grand Army of the Republic. New York: 1888. V. 67

BEATIE, RUSSELL
Saddles. Norman: 1981. V. 67

BEATON, CECIL
Ashcombe - the Story of a Fifteen Year Lease. London: 1949. V. 62
Cecil Beaton. Electa Editrice Portfolios. Milan: 1982. V. 67
The Face of the World - an International Scrapbook of People and Palces. London: 1957. V. 63; 65

BEATON, CECIL continued
The Face of the World, an International Scrapbook of People and Places. New York: 1957. V. 66
Far East. London: 1943. V. 65
The Glass of Fashion. London: 1954. V. 62
My Royal Past by Baroness Von Bulop...as told To Cecil Beaton. London: 1939. V. 63
Near East. London: 1943. V. 63
Time Exposure. New York: 1941. V. 65

BEATON, M. C.
Death of a Gossip. New York: 1985. V. 66; 67

BEATRIX
Jones Farrand (1872-1959), Fifty Years of American Landscape Architecture. Washington: 1982. V. 67

BEATSON, ROBERT
Naval and Military Memoirs of Great Britain from 1727 to 1783. London: 1804. V. 62
A Political Index to the Histories of Great Britain and Ireland; or, a Complete Register of the Hereditary Honours, Public Offices and Persons in Office, from the Earliest Periods to the Present Time. London: 1788. V. 66

BEATTIE, ANN
Chilly Scenes of Winter. New York: 1976. V. 62; 63; 65
Falling in Place. New York: 1980. V. 63
Love Always. New York: 1985. V. 67
Where You'll Find Me. New York: 1986. V. 65

BEATTIE, DAVID JOHNSTONE
Prince Charlie and the Borderland. Carlisle: 1928. V. 65

BEATTIE, GEORGE
John O' Arnha: to Which is Added The Murderit Mynstrell and Other Poems. Montrose: 1826. V. 66

BEATTIE, GEORGE WILLIAM
Heritage of the Valley, San Bernardino's First Century. Pasadena: 1939. V. 63; 66

BEATTIE, JAMES
Essays. On the Nature and Immutability of Truth, in Opposition to Sophistry and Scepticism. On Poetry and Music, as They Affect the Mind. On Laughter, and Ludicrous Composition. On the Utility of Classical Learning. Edinburgh: 1776. V. 65
The Minstrel; or, the Progress of Genius; and Other Poems. London: 1807. V. 64
The Minstrel; or the Progress of Genius; and Other Poems. London: 1819. V. 64
The Minstrel; or, the Progress of Genius, with Some Other Poems. London: 1805-1803. V. 65
Original Poems and Translations. London: 1760. V. 64; 66

BEATTIE, WILLIAM
The Castles and Abbeys of England from the National Records, Early Chronicles and Other Standard Authorities. London. V. 62; 66
Scotland: Illustrated in a Series of Views.... London: 1818. V. 65
Scotland Illustrated in a Series of Views.... London: 1842. V. 62
The Waldenses or Protestant Valleys of Piedmont, Dauphiny and Ban De La Roche. London: 1838. V. 63

BEAUCHAMPS, PIERRE FRANCOIS GODART DE
Recherches sur Les Theatres de France. Paris: 1735. V. 64

BEAUCLERK, DIANA
A Summer and Winter in Norway. London: 1868. V. 65

BEAUCLERK, HELEN
The Green Lacquer Pavilion. London: 1926. V. 62
The Love of the Foolish Angel. London: 1929. V. 67

BEAUFORT, L. F.
Fishes of the Eastern Part of the Indo-Australian Archipelago, With Remarks on Its Zoogeography. Amsterdam: 1913. V. 65

BEAUHARNAIS, FANNY DE
L'Abailard suppose ou Le Sentimen a l'Epreuve. Nilsson. V. 66

BEAUMONT, CYRIL W.
The Diaghilev Ballet in London - a Personal Record. London: 1945. V. 62
Impressions of the Russian Ballet 1918 (and) 1919. London: 1918-1919. V. 67
New Paths. Verse, Prose, Pictures 1917-1918. London: 1918. V. 62; 64
The Romantic Ballet in Lithographs of the Time. London: 1938. V. 66

BEAUMONT, FRANCIS
The Maids Tragedy. London: 1650. V. 62; 66
The Works. London: 1750. V. 62; 64

BEAUMONT, JOHN THOMAS BARBER
An Essay on Provident or Parish Banks, for the Security and Improvement of the Savings of Tradesmen, Artificers, Servants, &c.... London: 1816. V. 65
A Letter to the Right Honourable Lord Sidmouth...Shewing the Extreme Injustice to Individuals and Injury to the Public of the Present System of Public House Licensing.... London: 1817. V. 63

BEAUMONT, JOSEPH
Psyche, or Love's Mystery, in XXIV Cantos. Cambridge: 1702. V. 64

BEAUMONT, ROBERTS
Colour in Woven Design. London: 1890. V. 63
Woollen and Worsted. The Theory and Technology of the Manufacture of Woollen, Worsted and Union Yarns and Fabrics. London: 1919. V. 63

BEAUMONT, WILLIAM
Experiments and Observations on the Gastric Juice and the Physiology of Digestion. Plattsburgh: 1833. V. 63
Experiments and Observations on the Gastric Juice, and the Physiology of Digestion. Boston: 1834. V. 62; 66
The Physiology of Digestion, with Experiments on the Gastric Juice. Burlington: 1847. V. 62

BEAUNIER, ANDRE
Visages de Femmes. Paris: 1913. V. 63

BEAUREGARD, HENRY JOSEPH COSTA DE, MARQUIS
A Man of Other Days. London: 1877. V. 62

BEAUREGARD, P. G. T.
Beauregard's Official Report of The Battle of Manassas. Richmond: 1861. V. 62; 65; 66

THE BEAUTIES of Mrs. Siddons; or, a Review of Her Performance of the Characters of Belvidera, Zara, Isabella, Margaret of Anjou, Jane Shore and Lady Randolph. London: 1786. V. 66

THE BEAUTIES of the British Senate; taken from the Debates of the Lords and Commons, from the Beginning of the Administration of Sir Robert Walpole, to the End of the Second Session of the Administration of...William Pitt.... London: 1786. V. 67

THE BEAUTIES of the English Stage.... London: 1737. V. 63

BEAUTIFUL Britain, the Scenery and Splendours of the United Kingdom, Royal Residences, Homes of Princes and Noblemen.... Chicago: 1859. V. 67

BEAUTY and the Beast: To Which is added, the Punishment of Ingratitude. New York: 1935. V. 66

THE BEAUTY of Godly Government in a Church Reformed; or, a Platforme Government Consonant to the World of Truth.... London: 1641. V. 66

BEAUTY'S Awakening. A Masque of Winter and of Spring. London: 1899. V. 62

BEAUVOIR, SIMONE DE
The Blood of Others. New York: 1948. V. 63
Le Deuxieme Sexe. Paris: 1949. V. 63; 66
Le Force de l'Age. (The Prime of Life). Paris: 1960. V. 63
La Force des Choses. (Force of Circumstance). Paris: 1963. V. 63
L'Invitee. Paris: 1945. V. 63
La Longue Marche. (The Long March). Paris: 1957. V. 63
Les Mandarins. Paris: 1954. V. 63
The Mandarins. Cleveland and New York: 1956. V. 64
Memories d'une Jeune fille Rangee. (Memoirs of a Dutiful Daughter). Paris: 1958. V. 63
The Second Sex. New York: 1953. V. 65
Toute Compte Fait. (All Said and Done). Paris: 1972. V. 63

BEAVAN, PAUL W.
For the Welfare of Children. Springfield: 1955. V. 64; 67

BEAVAN, R.
Handbook of the Freshwater Fishes of India. 1877. V. 66
Handbook of the Freshwater Fishes of India. London: 1877. V. 63; 64

BEAVER, W. N.
Unexplored New Guinea; a Record of the Travels, Adventures and Experiences of a Resident Magistrate Amongst the Head-Hunting Savages and Cannibals of the Unexplored Interior of New Guinea. London: 1920. V. 64

BEAWES, WYNDHAM
Lex Mercatoria Redivia; or, the Merchant's Directory.... London: 1752. V. 65

BEAZLEY, J. D.
Paralipomena, Additions to Attic Black-figure Vase-painters and to Attic Red-Figure Vase Painters. Oxford: 1971. V. 65

BEAZLEY, SAMUEL
A General View of the System of Enclosing Waste Lands.... London: 1812. V. 65
The Roue. London: 1828. V. 67

BEBEL, AUGUST
Woman in the Past, Present and Future.... London: 188-. V. 64

BECANUS, MARTINUS
Analogia Veteris Ac Novi Testamenti. Lovanii: 1754. V. 64
Serenissimi Jacobi Angliae Regis, Apologiae & Monitoriae Praefationis ad Imperatorem, Reges & Principes, Refutatio. (with) Refutatio Torturae Torti.... Moguntium (Mainz): 1612. V. 66

BECCARI, O.
A Monographic Study of the Genus Pritchardia. Honolulu: 1921. V. 65
Wanderings in the Great Forests of Borneo; Travels and Researches of a Naturalist in Sarawak. London: 1904. V. 64

BECCARIA, CESARE
Dei Delitti e delle Pene. Livorno: 1764. V. 67
An Essay on Crimes and Punishments. London: 1767. V. 62; 65

BECCARIA, GIOVANNI BATTISTA
Dell' Elettricismo Artificiale, e Naturale Libri Due. Turin: 1753. V. 65; 66

BECHE, H. T. DE LA
A Geological Observer Manual. London: 1831. V. 62

BECHER, JOHANN JOACHIM
Magnalia Naturae, or the Philosophers-Stone. London: 1680. V. 64
Physica Subterranea Profundum Subterraneorum Genesin, e Principiis Hucusque Ignotis.... Leipzig: 1738. V. 64

BECHER, S.
Untersuchungen Ueber Echtfarbung der Zellkerne. Berlin: 1921. V. 67

BECHERVAISE, JOHN
Blizzard and Fire. A Year at Mawson, Antarctica. Sydney: 1963. V. 64; 66

BECHET, SIDNEY
Treat It Gentle. New York: 1960. V. 65

BECHSTEIN, J. M.
Cage and Chamber-Birds. London: 1853. V. 65; 67
Cage and Chamber-Birds. London: 1900. V. 63
The Natural History of Cage Birds: Their Management, Habits, Food, Diseases, Treatment, Breeding.... London: 1860. V. 63

BECHSTEIN, LUDWIG
As Pretty As Seven and Other Popular German Tales. London: 1872. V. 63
As Pretty As Seven and Other Popular German Tales. London: 1880. V. 63
The Rabbit Catcher and Other Fairy Tales. New York: 1962. V. 63

BECHTEL, H. P.
The Manual of Cultivated Orchid Species. Cambridge: 1981. V. 67

BECK, HENRY CHARLTON
Murder in the News Room. New York: 1931. V. 66

BECK, LEWIS C.
Botany, of the Northern and Middle States; or a Description of the Plants Found in the United States. Albany: 1833. V. 64

BECK, R. AND J., LTD
Beck Microscopes. London: 1926. V. 66

BECK, ROBERT
Pimp. The Story of My Life. Los Angeles: 1967. V. 64

BECK, S. WILLIAM
Gloves, Their Annals and Associations, a Chapter of Trade and Social History. London: 1883. V. 66

BECK, WILHELMINA VON, BARONESS, PSEUD.
Personal Adventures During the Late War of Independence in Hungary. London: 1851. V. 65

BECKE, LOUIS
By Reef and Palm. London: 1894. V. 67

BECKER, CARL
Kunstwerke und Geralhschaften des Mittelalters und der Renaissance. Frankfurt: 1852-1863. V. 65

BECKER, JUREK
Jakob der Lugner. Berlin: 1969. V. 67

BECKER, L.
Les Arachnides de Belgique. Brussels: 1882-1896. V. 62; 63; 65

BECKER, ROBERT H.
Designs on the Land: Disenos of California Ranchos and Their Makers. San Francisco: 1969. V. 63; 64

BECKET, ANDREW
Prose Miscellanies. London: 1838. V. 63

BECKETT, SAMUEL
All That Fall - a Play. London: 1957. V. 62
Assez. Paris: 1966. V. 62
Bing. Paris: 1966. V. 62
Cap au Pire. Paris: 1988. V. 62
Catastrophe et Autres Dramaticules: Cette Fois, Solo, Berceuse, Impromptu d'Ohio, Quoi Ou. Paris: 1986. V. 64
Comedie et Actes Divers. Paris: 1972. V. 64
Comment c'est. Paris: 1961. V. 65
Compagnie. Paris: 1980. V. 64
Le Depeupleur. Paris: 1970. V. 65
Eh Joe and Other Writings. London: 1967. V. 63
En Attendant Godot. Paris: 1952. V. 65; 67
En Attendant Godot. Paris: 1954. V. 62
Endgame - a Play in One Act Followed by Act Without Words a Mime for One Player. London: 1958. V. 65
Fin de Partie Suivi de Actes sans Paroles. (Endgame). Paris: 1957. V. 62; 65
Film - Suivi de Souffle. Paris: 1972. V. 62
First Love. London: 1973. V. 62
From an Abandoned Work. London: 1958. V. 62
Happy Days. London: 1962. V. 62
How It Is. New York: 1964. V. 63
How It Is. London: 1977. V. 64
Ill See Ill Said. Northridge: 1982. V. 63; 67
Imagination Dead Imagine. London: 1965. V. 63; 64; 66
Immobile. Paris: 1976. V. 62
L'Innommable. Paris: 1953. V. 65; 66
Krapp's Last Tape and Embers. London: 1959. V. 63
The Lost Ones. London: 1972. V. 63; 67
Malone Dies. London: 1958. V. 62
Malone Meurt. Paris: 1951. V. 62; 64; 65
Mercier et Camier. Paris: 1970. V. 65
Molloy. Paris: 1951. V. 62; 63; 66
Molloy. 1955. V. 65
Molloy. Paris: 1955. V. 62; 64
Molloy. Malone Dies. The Unnamable. Paris: 1959. V. 63; 64
Murphy. London: 1938. V. 65
Murphy. Paris: 1947. V. 62; 65
Murphy. London: 1951. V. 65
Murphy. New York: 1957. V. 67
Nohow On. New York: 1989. V. 65; 67
Nouvelles et Textes pour Rein. Paris: 1955. V. 62; 65
Nouvelles et Textes Pour Rien. Paris: 1981. V. 64
Oh Les Beau Jours. Paris: 1963. V. 65
Pas Suivi de Quatre Esquisses. Paris: 1984. V. 64
Poemes. Paris: 1968. V. 66
Premier Amour. Paris: 1970. V. 62; 64; 65
Proust. London: 1931. V. 65
Quad et Autres Pieces Pour la Television - Suivi de l'Epuise par Gilles Deleuze. Paris: 1992. V. 64
A Samuel Beckett Reader. London: 1967. V. 63
Sans. Paris: 1969. V. 66
Still. Milan: 1974. V. 64
Stirrings Still. New York and London: 1988. V. 64; 65
Waiting for Godot. New York: 1954. V. 62; 65; 67
Waiting for Godot. London: 1956. V. 65; 66
Waiting for Godot. London: 1957. V. 63
Waiting for Godot. London: 1965. V. 63
Watt. Paris: 1953. V. 63
Watt. Paris: 1958. V. 63; 65
Watt. New York: 1959. V. 65
Watt. Paris: 1968. V. 65
Whoroscope. Paris: 1930. V. 65; 67

BECKFORD, PETER
Thoughts on Hunting. Sarum: 1782. V. 62
Thoughts on Hunting. 1810. V. 62
Thoughts Upon Hare and Fox Hunting. London: 1931. V. 63

BECKFORD, WILLIAM
An Arabian Tale. London: 1786. V. 65; 67
Italy; with Sketches of Spain and Portugal. London: 1834. V. 62; 64; 65; 66
Recollections of an Excursion to the Monasteries of Alcobaca and Batalha. London: 1835. V. 63
The Travel Diaries of William Beckford of Fonthill. London: 1928. V. 63
Vathek. London: 1816. V. 66
Le Vathek. Paris: 1876. V. 65
Vathek. London: 1929. V. 64

BECLARD, P. A.
Additions to the General Anatomy of Xavier Bichat. Boston: 1823. V. 64
Elements of General Anatomy. Edinburgh: 1830. V. 66; 67

BECQUEREL, LOUIS ALFRED
Traite des Applications de l'Electricite a la Therapeutique Medicale et Chirurticale. Paris: 1860. V. 65

BECQUERET, CHARLES
Heures Royales, Contenant Les Offices, Vespres, Hymnes et Proses de l'Eglise. Paris: 1666. V. 63

BEDDARD, F. E.
Challenger Voyage Zoology. Parts 33 and 48 Isopoda. 1884 1886. V. 66
Contributions to the Anatomy of the Anthropoid Apes. 1893. V. 66
On Some Points in the Structure of Hapalemur Griseus (from Madagascar). 1884. V. 67

BEDDIE, M. K.
Bibliography of Captain James Cook. Sydney: 1970. V. 63; 64; 65

BEDDOES, THOMAS
Chemical Experiments and Opinions Extracts from a Work Published in the Last Century. Oxford: 1790. V. 65
Hygeia; or Essays Moral and Medical on the Causes Affecting the Personal State of Our Middling and Affluent Classes. Bristol: 1802-1803. V. 64

BEDDOES, THOMAS LOVELL
The Complete Works. London. V. 67
The Complete Works. London: 1928. V. 64; 66

BEDDOME, R. H.
The Ferns of Southern India, Being Descriptions and Plates of the Ferns of the Madras Presidency. Madras: 1864. V. 64

BEDE
The Ecclesiastical History of the English Nation. London: 1723. V. 67
Historiae Ecclesiasticae Gentis Anglorum. Cambridge: 1722. V. 64
The History of the Church of Englande. Oxford: 1930. V. 62; 64
The History of the Church of Englande. Stratford-Upon-Avon: 1930. V. 62
Homiliae...Hyemales, Quadragesimales, De Tempore Item & Sanctis, Nuc Denuo Summa Diligentia Restitutae. Coloniae: 1541. V. 66

BEDFORD, ARTHUR
The Great Abuse of Musick. London: 1711. V. 63
The Scripture Chronology Demonstrated by Astronomical Calculations... or, an Account of Time.... London: 1730. V. 67

BEDFORD, HERBERT
The Heroines of George Meredith. London. V. 62; 66

BEDFORD, HILORY G.
Texas Indian Troubles. Dallas: 1905. V. 62

BEDFORD, JOHN RUSSEL, 6TH DUKE OF
Outline Engravings and Descriptions of the Woburn Abbey Marbles. London: 1822. V. 67

BEDFORD, JOHN THOMAS
Robert; or, Notes from the Diary of a City Waiter. London: 1885. V. 67

BEDFORD, SYBILLE
Aldous Huxley - A Biography 1894-1963. London: 1973-1974. V. 64

BEDFORDSHIRE GENERAL LIBRARY
Catalogue of the Bedfordshire General Library; Established in July 1830. Bedford: 1831. V. 62

BEDIER, JOSEPH
German Atrocities from German Evidence. Paris: 1915. V. 64
How Germany Seeks to Justify Her Atrocities. Paris: 1915. V. 64

BEDINGER, MARGERY
Navajo Indian Silver-Work. Denver: 1936. V. 66

BEDRIAGA, J. VON
Beitrage zur Kenntnis der Amphibien und Reptilien der Fauna von Corsika. Berlin: 1883. V. 67
Przewalski's Expedition to Central Asia. Volume 3. St. Petersburg: 1898-1912. V. 62

THE BEDTIME Story Book. London: 1930. V. 67

BEDWORTH, THOMAS
The Power of Conscience Exemplified in the Genuine and Extraordinary Confession of Thomas Bedworth...the Night Before His Execution on Septemer 18, 1815 for the Murder of Elizabeth Beesmore, in Drury Lane. London: 1815. V. 63

BEE, CLAIR
Buzzer Basket. New York: 1962. V. 66
Comeback Cagers. New York: 1963. V. 66
Home Run Feud. New York: 1964. V. 66
Hungry Hurler. New York: 1966. V. 66

BEE, SUSAN
Talespin. New York: 1995. V. 64

BEEBE, LUCIUS
Great Railroad Photographs, U.S.A. Berkeley: 1964. V. 65
Mansions on Rails, the Folklore of the Private Railway Car. Berkeley: 1959. V. 65
Mr. Pullman's Elegant Palace Car. The Railway Carriage that Established a New Dimension of Luxury and Entered the National Lexicon as a Symbol of Splendor. New York: 1961. V. 67
Narrow Gauge in the Rockies. Berkeley: 1970. V. 65; 67

BEEBE, WILLIAM
The Arcturus Adventure, an Account of the New York Zoological Society's First Oceanographic Expedition. New York: 1926. V. 62; 63; 65; 67
Deep-Sea Fishes of the Bermuda Oceanographic Expeditions. New York: 1933. V. 65
Deep-Sea Fishes of the Bermuda Oceanographic Expeditions. New York: 1933-1936. V. 63
The Fishes of Port-Au-Prince Bay, Haiti. New York: 1928. V. 63
Galapagos; World's End. New York: 1924. V. 62; 63; 64; 66; 67
Galapagos; World's End. New York: 1926. V. 62
A Monograph of the Pheasants. London: 1918-1922. V. 62; 63; 64; 66
A Monograph of the Pheasants. 1990. V. 62
Pheasants, Their Lives and Homes. New York: 1926. V. 62; 63; 64; 66; 67
Pheasants, their Lives and Homes. Garden City: 1931. V. 67
Pheasants, Their Lives and Homes. Garden City: 1936. V. 63; 64; 67

BEECHER, CATHERINE E.
The American Woman's Home; or, Principles of Domestic Science.... New York: 1869. V. 62; 65
Letters to the People on Health and Happiness. London: 1855. V. 65
Miss Beecher's Domestic Receipt Book. New York: 1850. V. 67
Miss Beecher's Domestic Receipt Book. New York: 1852. V. 67

BEECHER, ELIZABETH
Walt Disney's Davy Crocket: King of the Wild Frontier. New York: 1955. V. 65

BEECHER, H. W.
Royal Truths. Boston: 1866. V. 66

BEECHEY, FREDERICK WILLIAM
An Account of a Visit to California. 1826-1827. San Francisco: 1941. V. 63; 66
Narrative of a Voyage to the Pacific and Beering's Strait to Co- Operate with the Polar Expeditions: Performed in His Majesty's Ship Blossom, Under the Command of Captain F. W. Beechey.... London: 1831. V. 66
Proceedings of the Expedition to Explore the Northern Coast of Africa, from Tripoli Eastward in MDCCCXXI and MDCCCXXII.... London: 1828. V. 64
A Voyage of Discovery Towards the North Pole.... London: 1843. V. 64

BEEDHAM, R. JOHN
Wood Engraving. Ditchling: 1929. V. 64
Wood Engraving. Hassocks: 1929. V. 62
Wood Engravings. Sussex: 1935. V. 67

BEEDING, FRANCIS, PSEUD.
The Secret Weapon. New York: 1940. V. 67

The Seven Sleepers. Boston: 1925. V. 67
The Six Proud Walkers. Boston: 1928. V. 67
The Ten Holy Horrors. New York and London: 1939. V. 66
The Two Undertakers. Boston: 1933. V. 67

BEEDOME, THOMAS
Select Poems Divine and Humane. London: 1928. V. 62

BEEKMAN, GEORGE C.
Early Dutch Settlers of Monmouth County, New Jersey. Freehold: 1901. V. 63

BEELER, JOE
Cowboys and Indians. Norman: 1960. V. 62
Cowboys and Indians. Norman: 1967. V. 63
The Joe Beeler Sketchbook. Flagstaff: 1974. V. 66

BEER, G. R. DE
The Development of the Vertebrate Skull. Oxford: 1937. V. 66

BEER, GEORGE JOSEPH
A Manual of the Diseases of the Human Eye, Intended for Surgeons Commencing Practice, from the Best National and Foreign Works.... Glasgow: 1821. V. 65

BEERBOHM, MAX
Around Theatres, More Theatres and Last Theatres. London: 1953-1970. V. 62
Cartoons. The Second Childhood of John Bull. London: 1911. V. 65
Catalogue of an Exhibition Entitled Ghosts. London: 1928. V. 65
A Christmas Garland. London: 1912. V. 63; 65
A Christmas Garland. London: 1932. V. 64
Fifty Caricatures. London: 1914. V. 62
The Happy Hypocrite. London: 1897. V. 62; 64; 67
The Happy Hypocrite. London: 1915. V. 62
Herbert Beerbohm Tree - Some Memories of Him and His Art Collected by Max Beerbohm. London: 1920. V. 62
Heroes and Heroines of Bitter Sweet. 1931. V. 65
Observations. London: 1925. V. 62; 64
Observations. London: 1926. V. 62
A Peep into the Past and Other Prose Pieces. London: 1972. V. 67
The Poet's Corner. London: 1904. V. 64
Rossetti and His Circle. London: 1922. V. 64; 65
Seven Men. London: 1919. V. 64
Things New and Old. London: 1923. V. 62; 64; 65
The Works of Max Beerbohm. London: 1896. V. 64
The Works of Max Beerbohm. New York: 1896. V. 64
The Works of Max Beerbohm. London: 1922-1924. V. 65
Zuleika Dobson. London: 1911. V. 64; 66
Zuleika Dobson. New York: 1960. V. 63
Zuleika Dobson. Oxford: 1975. V. 62; 65

BEERS, ANDREW
Beers' Almanac for the Year of Our Lord 1795 and 1811. Hartford: 1795. V. 65

BEERS, CLIFFORD WHITTINGHAM
A Mind That Found Itself: an Autobiography. New York: 1908. V. 65

BEERS, FRANK
The Green Signal or Life on the Rail. Kansas City: 1904. V. 65

BEERY, JESSE
Prof. Beery's Mail Course in Horsemanship. Pleasant Hill: 1908. V. 66
Prof. Jesse Beery's Saddle-Horse Instructions. Pleasant Hill: 1909. V. 66

BEESLEY, ALFRED
The History of Banbury.... London: 1841. V. 65

BEESON, JOHN
A Plea for the Indians: with Facts and Features of the Late War In Oregon. New York: 1858. V. 63

BEETHAM, GEORGE
The First Ascent of Mount Ruapehu, New Zealand and a Holiday Jaunt to Mounts Ruapehu, Tongario and Ngauruhoe. London: 1926. V. 64

BEETON, ISABELLA
Beeton's Every-Day Cookery and Housekeeping Book. London: 1890. V. 65
The Book of Household Management. London: 1861. V. 63; 65
The Book of Household Management. London: 1896. V. 63
The Book of Household Management. London: 1906. V. 62
The Book of Household Management. London: 1920. V. 62; 66
Mrs. Beeton's Book of Household Management. London: 1915. V. 65; 66
Mrs. Beeton's Dictionary of Every-Day Cookery. London: 1865. V. 66
Mrs. Beeton's Family Cookery. London: 1912. V. 63
Mrs. Beeton's Household Management: a Complete Cookery Book.... London: 1929. V. 62

BEETON, S. O.
Beeton's Book of Household Amusements and Family Recreation. London. V. 63
Beeton's Dictionary of Geography. London: 1868?. V. 67

BEEVER, WILLIAM HOLT
Notes on Fields and Cattle from the Diary of an Amateur Farmer. London: 1862. V. 63

BEGBIE, HAROLD
Great Men. London: 1901. V. 64

BEGLEY, JOHN
The Diocese of Limerick; Ancient and Mediaeval. 1993. V. 67
The Diocese of Limerick from 1691 to the Present Time. 1938. V. 67

BEGLEY, LOUIS
The Man Who Was Late. New York: 1992. V. 67
Wartime Lies. New York: 1991. V. 64; 66
Wartime Lies. New York: 1993. V. 64; 65; 67

BEHAN, BRENDAN
Borstal Boy. London: 1958. V. 64
Borstal Boy. New York: 1959. V. 66
Brendan Behan's Island - an Irish Sketch-Book. New York: 1962. V. 62
Hold Your Hour and Have Another. London: 1963. V. 63
The Hostage. London: 1958. V. 62
The Quare Fellow. 1956. V. 65

BEHIND the Scenes; or, an Expose of Oneida Community. Oneida: 1875. V. 62

BEHM, MARC
The Queen of the Night. Boston: 1977. V. 67

BEHN, APHRA
All the Histories and Novels.. London: 1751. V. 65
Love-Letters Between a Nobleman and His Sister.... London: 1708. V. 65
The Novels. London: 1905. V. 65
Poems Upon Several Occasions: with a Voyage to the Island Of Love. London: 1684. V. 65
The Ten Pleasures of Marriage and the Second Part The Confession - Attributed to Aphra Behn. London: 1922. V. 64
The Ten Pleasures of Marriage, and the Second Part, The Confession of the New Married Couple. 1922. V. 67
The Works. London: 1915. V. 62
The Works. London: 1992. V. 65

BEHREND, MOSES
Diseases of the Gallbladder and Allied Structures, Diagnosis and Treatment. Philadelphia: 1947. V. 66; 67

BEHRING SEA CLAIMS COMMISSION
Argument for the United States in Reply. Washington: 1897. V. 63

BEING and Doing. A Selection of Helpful Thoughts from Various Authors, Arranged for Daily Reading. Liverpool: 1901. V. 66

BEINHART, LARRY
No One Rides for Free. New York: 1986. V. 65; 66; 67

BEINING, GUY
Stoma. New York: 1984. V. 66

BEIRNE, BRYAN
British Pyralid and Plume Moths. London: 1954. V. 62

BEISER, ARTHUR
The Proper Yacht. London: 1978. V. 62

BEKASSY, FERENC
Adriatica and Other Poems. London: 1925. V. 64

BEKE, CHARLES T.
Discoveries of Sinai in Arabia and of Midian. London: 1878. V. 64

BEL, LANDON C.
The Old Free State: a Contribution to the History of Lunenburg County and Southside Virginia. Richmond: 1927. V. 66

BELASCO, DAVID
Fairy Tales. Told by the Seven Travellers at the Red Lion Inn. New York: 1906. V. 66

BELCHER, E.
The Last of the Arctic Voyages.... London: 1855. V. 63
Narrative of the Voyage of H.M.S. Samarang During 1843-1846. 1848. V. 66

BELCHER, HENRY
Illustrations of the Scenery on the Line of the Whitby and Pickering Railway, in the North Eastern Part of Yorkshire. London: 1836. V. 65

BELCHER'S Farmer's Almanack for the Province of Nova Scotia for the Year of Our Lord 1872. Halifax: 1872. V. 64

BELCHER'S Farmer's Almanack for the Province of Nova Scotia for the Year of Our Lord 1880. Halifax: 1876. V. 64

BELCHER'S Farmers' Almanack, for the Year of Our Lord 1867. Halifax: 1867. V. 64

BELCHER'S Farmers' Almanack for the Year of Our Lord 1852. Halifax: 1852. V. 63

BELDAM, GEORGE W.
Great Batsmen. Their Methods at a Glance. London: 1905. V. 67
Great Bowlers and Fielders. Their Methods at a Glance. London: 1907. V. 67
Great Golfers. London: 1904. V. 65; 66
Great Lawn Tennis Players. London: 1907. V. 62

BELDER, A. L.
The Fur Trade of America and Some of the Men Who Made and Maintain It.... New York: 1917. V. 63

BELFAST NATURALIST'S FIELD CLUB
Systematic Lists Illustrative of the Flora, Fauna, Palaeontology and Archaeology of the North of Ireland. Belfast: 1887-1911. V. 62

BELIDOR, BERNARD FORET DE
Architecture Hydraulique, ou l'Art de Conduire, d'Elever, et de Menager Les Eaux Pour les Differens Besoins de la vie. (and) Seconde Partie, qui Comprend l'art de Diriger les Eaux de la Mer & Des Rivieres a l'Avantage de la Defense des Places, du Commerc. Paris: 1737-1751. V. 65

BELISARIO, A. M.
A Report of the Trial of Arthur Hodge, Esquire. Middletown: 1812. V. 64

BELKIN, J. N.
The Mosquitoes of the South Pacific. Berkeley: 1962. V. 63; 66

BELKNAP, BILL
Fred Kabotie: Hopi Indian Artist. Flagstaff: 1977. V. 63; 64
Gunnar Widforss - Painter of the Grand Canyon. Flagstaff: 1969. V. 66

BELKNAP, CHARLES E.
History of the Michigan Organizations at Chickamauga, Chattanooga and Missionary Ridge 1863. Lansing: 1897. V. 65
History of the Michigan Organizations at Chickamauga, Chattanooga, and Missionary Ridge, 1863. Lansing: 1899. V. 65

BELKNAP, JEREMY
The Foresters, an American Tale: Being a Sequel to the History of John Bull the Clothier. Boston: 1792. V. 62

BELL, ALEXANDER G.
The Question of Sign Language & the Utility of Signs in the Instruction of the Deaf. Washington: 1898. V. 65

BELL, ANDREW
Extract of a Sermon on the Education of the Poor, Under an Appropriate System: Preached at St. Mary's, Lambeth 28t June 1807, for the Benefit of the Boys' Charity-School at Lambeth.... London: 1807. V. 63; 65

BELL, ANNE OLIVIA
Editing Virginia Woolf's Diary. Oxford: 1989. V. 65

BELL, BARBARA
Zuni - the Art and the People. Dallas: 1975-1977. V. 66

BELL, BENJAMIN
The Remains of Wimbleton. and The Story of a Romancer. Edinburgh: 1826. V. 65
A System of Surgery Extracted from the Works of Benjamin Bell of Edinburgh. Philadelphia: 1791. V. 64; 66; 67
Traite de la Theorie et de la Curation des Ulceres. Paris: 1789. V. 65
Traite Theorique et Pratique des Ulceres, Suivi d'une Dissertation sur les Tumeurs Blanches des Articulations, et Precede d'un Essai sur le Traitement Chirurgical de l'Inflammation.... Paris: 1788. V. 65
A Treatise on Gonorrhoea Virulenta and Lues Venerea. Edinburgh: 1797. V. 63
A Treatise on the Theory of Management of Ulcers; with a Dissertation on White Swellings of Joints. Edinburgh: 1791. V. 65

BELL, CHARLES
The Anatomy and Philosophy of Expression as Connected with the Fine Arts. London: 1872. V. 65
The Anatomy of the Brain, Explained in a Series of Engravings. London: 1802. V. 64; 66
Engravings from Specimens of Morbid Parts, Preserved in the Author's Collection, Now in Windmill Street.... London: 1813. V. 66
Engravings of the Brain and Nerves. Birmingham: 1984. V. 63
Essays on the Anatomy of Expression in Painting. London: 1806. V. 62; 63; 67
The Hand, Its Mechanism and Vital Endowments.... London: 1833. V. 62; 65
The Hand: Its Mechanism and Vital Endowments.... Philadelphia: 1833. V. 65
Letters...Selected from His Correspondence With His Brother George Joseph Bell. London: 1870. V. 65
Manuscript Drawings of the Arteries. 1971. V. 67
The Nervous System of Human Body Including the Papers Delivered Before the Royal Society on the Subject of Nerves. Washington: 1833. V. 64
A Series of Engravings Explaining the Course of the Nerves with an Address to Young Physicians on the Study of Nerves. Philadelphia: 1834. V. 67
Tibet, Past and Present. Oxford: 1924. V. 64

BELL, CHARLES DENT
The Four Seasons at the Lakes. London: 1880. V. 62; 66

BELL, CHARLES J.
Conquest of the Southern Plains - Uncensored Narrative of the Battle of the Washita and Custer's Southern Campaign. Oklahoma City: 1938. V. 65

BELL, CLIVE
Poems. London: 1921. V. 66

BELL, D.
Physiology and Biochemistry of the Domestic Fowl. London: 1971. V. 67

BELL, E. W.
The Scottish Deerhound. 1990. V. 62; 64
The Scottish Deerhound. London: 1990. V. 63

BELL, EVANS
The Great Parliamentary Bore. London: 1869. V. 64
Our Great Vassal Empire. London: 1870. V. 64

BELL, F. JEFFREY
Catalogue of the British Echinoderms in the British Museum. London: 1892. V. 67

BELL, FRANCIS DILLON
Reasons for Promoting the Cultivation of the New Zealand Flax. London: 1842. V. 63

BELL, GEORGE HAMILTON
Treatise on Cholera Asphyxia or Epidemic Cholera, as It Appeared in Asia and More Recently in Europe. Edinburgh: 1831. V. 64

BELL, GERTRUDE LOWTHIAN
Amurath to Amurath. London: 1911. V. 64

BELL, H. T. MAC KENZIE
A Forgotten Genius: Charles Whitehead - a Critical Monograph. London: 1884. V. 63

BELL, H. W.
Sherlock Holmes and Dr. Watson: The Chronology of Their Adventures. 1953. V. 66

BELL, HENRY NUGENT
The Huntingdon Peerage.... London: 1821. V. 66

BELL, HORACE
Reminiscences of a Ranger of Early Times in Southern California. Santa Barbara: 1922. V. 62

BELL, ISAAC
Foxiana. London: 1929. V. 67

BELL, J. H. B.
A Progress in Mountaineering. 1950. V. 63; 65
A Progress in Mountaineering. London: 1950. V. 62; 63; 64

BELL, JAMES B.
The Homoeopathic Therapeutics of Diarrhoea, Dysentery, Cholera, Cholera Morbus, Cholera Infantum and All Other Loose Evacuations of the Bowels. Philadelphia: 1881. V. 66; 67
The Homoeopathic Therapeutics of Diarrhoea, Dysentery, Cholera Morbus, Cholera Infantum, and All Other Loose Evacuations of the Bowels. New York: 1881. V. 67

BELL, JOHN
The Anatomy and Physiology of the Human Body. (and) The Anatomy and Physiology of the Brain and Nerves. New York: 1822. V. 63
The Anatomy of the Human Body. London: 1802. V. 66
Bell's British Theatre, Consisting of the Most Esteemed English Plays. London: 1776-1777. V. 64
Journey of John Bell, Esq. from St. Petersburgh to Pekin. Philadelphia: 1803. V. 62
The Principles of Surgery.... New York: 1810. V. 64
Travels from St. Petersburg in Russia. Glasgow: 1763. V. 64; 66

BELL, JOHN R.
The Journal of Captain John R. Bell, Official Journalist for Stephen H. Long Expedition to the Rocky Mountains 1820. Glendale: 1957. V. 64; 66

BELL, JULIAN
Winter Movement and Other Poems. London: 1930. V. 67
Work for the Winter and Other Poems. London: 1936. V. 63; 64

BELL, KATHARINE M.
Swinging the Censor - Reminiscences of Old Santa Barbara. Santa Barbara: 1931. V. 63; 66

BELL, LANDON C.
An Address at Johnson's Island: in Memory of the Confederate Soldiers Who While Prisoners Died and are Buried on the Island. N.P: 1929. V. 64
Sunlight on the Southside. Baltimore: 1974. V. 67

BELL, M. A.
The Evolutionary Biology of the Threespine Stickleback. Oxford: 1994. V. 63; 65

BELL, MAC KENZIE
Christina Rossetti. Boston: 1898. V. 64
Christina Rossetti. London: 1898. V. 64

BELL, MADISON SMARTT
All Soul's Rising. New York: 1995. V. 63; 66
Waiting for the End of the World. New York: 1985. V. 66
The Washington Square Ensemble. New York: 1983. V. 62; 63

BELL, MARCUS
Message of Love. Atlanta: 1860. V. 64

BELL, MARVIN
Things We Dreamt We Died For. Iowa City: 1966. V. 64; 67
Woo Havoc. Somerville: 1971. V. 63

BELL, QUENTIN
Victorian Artists. Cambridge: 1967. V. 62
Virginia Woolf - a Biography. London: 1972. V. 63; 65; 66

BELL, R. C.
Specious Token and Those Struck for General Circulation 1784-1804. Newcastle-upon-Tyne: 1968. V. 64
Tradesmen's Tickets and Private Tokens 1785-1819. Newcastle-upon-Tyne: 1966. V. 64

BELL, RAYMOND
Hacienda de Atotonillo. Durango: 1936. V. 63

BELL, ROBERT
Art and Song. London: 1867. V. 64

BELL, SAM H.
Summer Loanen and Other Stories. 1943. V. 67

BELL, T. HEDLEY
The Birds of Cheshire. (with) A Supplement to the Birds of Cheshire. Altrincham: 1962. V. 62

BELL, THELMA HARRINGTON
Black Face. Garden City: 1931. V. 66

BELL, THOMAS
The Anatomy, Physiology and Diseases of the Teeth. London: 1829. V. 62; 66
The Catalogue of 15,000 Volumes of Scarce and Curious Printed Books, and Unique Manuscripts, Comprised in the Unrivalled Library Collected by the late Thomas Bell, Esq. Between the Years 1797 and 1860. Newcastle-upon-Tyne: 1860. V. 66
A History of British Quadrupeds.... London: 1836-1837. V. 62
A History of British Reptiles. London: 1849. V. 66
A History of the British Stalk-Eyed Crustacea. London: 1853. V. 63; 64; 66
Observations on the Genus Cancer. Some Account of the Crustacea of the Coasts of South America. 1835. V. 66

BELL, W. A.
The Picton Coalfield, Nova Scotia. Ottawa: 1940. V. 65

BELL, W. D. M.
Bell of Africa. London: 1960. V. 62; 67
Karamojo Safari. 1949. V. 62; 66
Karamojo Safari. London: 1949. V. 63
The Wanderings of an Elephant Hunter. London: 1923. V. 62; 64; 65; 66; 67
The Wanderings of an Elephant Hunter. 1958. V. 63
The Wanderings of an Elephant Hunter. London: 1958. V. 67

BELL, W. S.
Old Fort Benton - What It Was and How It Came to Be. Helena: 1909. V. 65; 67

BELL, WILLIAM
A Dissertation on the Following Subject: What Causes Principally Contribute to Render a National Populous?. Cambridge: 1756. V. 65
Poetry from Oxford in Wartime. London: 1945. V. 65

BELL, WILLIAM A.
New Tracks in North America. London: 1870. V. 65
New Tracks in North America. Albuquerque: 1965. V. 63; 65; 67

BELL, WILLIAM GARDNER
Will James - the Life and Works of a Lone Cowboy. Flagstaff: 1987. V. 66

BELL, WILLIAM M.
Wm. M. Bell's Pilot. Chicago: 1920. V. 66

BELLA *Starr, the Bandit Queen, or the Female Jesse James....* Austin: 1960. V. 66

BELLAMY, DANIEL
The British Remembrancer; or, the Chronicles of the Kings of England Epitomized, for the Entertainment and Instruction of Younger Minds. London: 1757. V. 67
Ethic Amusements.... London: 1768. V. 62; 65

BELLAMY, EDWARD
Looking Backward. Hollywood: 1941. V. 62
Looking Backward 2000-1887. Boston: 1888. V. 62

BELLAMY, GEORGE ANNE
Memoirs of George Anne Bellamy.... London: 1785. V. 66

BELLARD, ALFRED
...Gone for a Soldier. The Civil War Memoirs of Private Alfred Bellard. Boston: 1975. V. 63; 66

BELLAY *Differentes Pensees d'Ornements Arabesques a Divers Usages... Premiere (-Seconde) Partie.* Paris: 1750. V. 64

BELLCHAMBERS, EDMUND
A Biographical Dictionary.... London: 1835. V. 65

BELLE, FRANCES P.
Life and Adventures of the Celebrated Bandit Joaquin Murrieta. Chicago: 1925. V. 63

BELLECOUR, ABBE
Academie Universelle des Jeux Contenant les Regles des Jeux de Cartes Permis; du Trictrac, des Echecs, de la Paulme, du Mail, du Billard & Autres. Paris: 1718. V. 64

BELLECROIX, ERNEST
La Chasse Pratique. Paris: 1879. V. 66; 67

BELLERBY, FRANCES
The Stuttering Water and Other Poems. Gillingham: 1970. V. 65

BELLET, ISAAC
Lettres Sur le Pouvoir de l'Imagination des femmes Enceintes. Paris: 1745. V. 65

BELLEW, C. D.
Catalogue of the Mount Bellew Library 1814. Dublin;: 1814. V. 62

BELLEW, FRANCIS
Trial of Francis Bellew, Esq., Youngest Son of Sir Patrick Bellew, Bart, for Appearing in Arms, with a Mob of Defenders, on the 26th of December 1792. Dublin: 1794. V. 63

BELLEW, HENRY WALTER
Afghanistan and the Afghans; Being a Brief Review of the History of the Country and Account of Its People.... London: 1879. V. 64
From the Indus to the Tigris; a Narrative of a Journey through the Countries of Balochistan, Afghanistan, Khorassan and Iran in 1872. London: 1874. V. 64

BELL-IRVING, D. J.
Tally-Ho. 1920. V. 64
Tally-Ho. Dumfries: 1920. V. 67

BELLITT, BEN
Graffiti. Princeton Junction: 1989. V. 62; 64
Graffiti. Washington: 1989. V. 64

BELLOC, HILAIRE
The Battle Ground. London: 1936. V. 65
Beasts from Belloc.... Portland: 1982. V. 64
Cautionary Tales for Children. London: 1908/. V. 64
Cromwell. London: 1934. V. 64
The Highway and Its Vehicles. London: 1926. V. 62
Jim Who Ran Away from His Nurse and Was Eaten by a Lion. Providence: 1995. V. 62
Lambkin's Remains. Oxford: 1900. V. 66
The Missing Masterpiece. London: 1929. V. 64; 67
The Modern Traveller. London: 1898. V. 65; 66
The Pyrenees. London: 1909. V. 67
Songs from the Bad Child's Book of Beasts. Duckworth: 1932. V. 62
The Verse of Hilaire Belloc. N.P: 1954. V. 63; 64
The Verse of Hilaire Belloc. London: 1954. V. 64
Verses. London: 1910. V. 64

BELLOSTE, AUGUSTIN
The Hospital Surgeon or a New, Gentle and Easie Way to Cure Speedily All Sorts of Wounds, and Other Diseases Belonging to Surgery.... London: 1713. V. 65
The Hosptial Surgeon. Volume II. London: 1729. V. 62

BELLOT, H. HALE
University College London, 1826-1926. London: 1929. V. 64

BELLOW, SAUL
The Adventures of Augie March. New York: 1953. V. 63; 67
Dangling Man. London: 1946. V. 66
Dangling Man. New York: 1947. V. 67
The Dean's December. New York: 1982. V. 63; 66
Henderson the Rain King. London: 1959. V. 63; 66
Henderson the Rain King. New York: 1959. V. 65; 67
Herzog. New York: 1964. V. 67
Humboldt's Gift. New York: 1975. V. 63
Mr. Sammler's Planet. New York: 1970. V. 66; 67
Mosby's Memoirs and Other Stories. New York: 1968. V. 67
Nobel Lecture. New York: 1979. V. 63; 64
Ravelstein. New York: 2000. V. 67
Seize the Day. New York: 1956. V. 67
Seize the Day. London: 1957. V. 65; 66
A Silver Dish. New York: 1979. V. 66
A Theft. New York: 1989. V. 62
The Victim. New York: 1947. V. 65; 66; 67
The Victim. London: 1948. V. 64; 66

BELLOWS, ALBERT J.
Philosophy of Eating. New York: 1867. V. 67

BELLOWS, GEORGE W.
His Lithographs. New York: 1928. V. 62; 65

BELL's British Theatre. London: 1791-1797. V. 66

BELLWOOD, PETER
Man's Conquest of the Pacific. New York: 1979. V. 63; 64; 65; 66

BELMAS, DENIS GENIE
Traite de la Cystotomie Sus-Pubienne. Paris: 1827. V. 65

BELMONTE, JUAN
Juan Belmonte, Killer of Bulls: Autobiography of a Matador as Told to Manuel Chaves Noages. London: 1937. V. 66

BELOE, WILLIAM
Anecdotes of Literature and Scarce Books. London: 1807-1812. V. 63
The Sexagenarian. London: 1817. V. 65
The Sexagenarian. London: 1818. V. 65

BELOFF, MINDY
I Am My Own Worst Anxiety. New York: 1998. V. 64

BELOIT COLLEGE
First Annual Report of the Trustees of Beloit College, Jan. 1849. Beloit: 1849. V. 63

BELON, PIERRE
De Arboribus Coniferis, Resiniferis, Aliis Quoque Nonnullis Sempiterna Fronde Virentibus.... Paris: 1553. V. 63; 66; 67
L'Histoire de la Natvre des Oyseavx. Paris: 1555. V. 63

BELOUS, RUSSELL E.
Will Soule.... 1969. V. 63
Will Soule.... Los Angeles: 1969. V. 62

BELOUSSOV, V.
Critical Aspects of the Plate Tectonics Theory. Athens: 1990. V. 67

BELSHAM, WILLIAM
History of Great Britain. 1802. V. 67

BELT, THOMAS
The Naturalist in Nicaragua. London: 1874. V. 64
The Naturalist in Nicaragua. London: 1888. V. 64

BELTRAMI, FRANCESCO
Il Forestiere Instruito Delle Cose Notabili Della Citta di Ravenna. Ravenna: 1783. V. 64

BELTRAMI, GIACOMO
A Pilgrimage in Europe and America, Leading to the Discovery of the Sources of the Mississippi. London: 1828. V. 66; 67

BEMAN, DAVID
The Mysteries of Trade, or the Great Sources of Trade, or the Great Sources of Wealth.... Boston: 1825. V. 66

BEMBO, PIETRO, CARDINAL
Della Historia Vinitiana...Libri XII. Venice: 1570. V. 62
Historiae Venetae Libri XII. Venice: 1551. V. 65

BEMELAMNS, LUDWIG
Are You Hungry, Are You Cold. Cleveland & New York: 1960. V. 62

BEMELMANS, LUDWIG
The Castle Number Nine. New York: 1937. V. 62
Father, Dear Father. New York: 1953. V. 65
Madeline and the Gypsies. 1958. V. 62
Madeline's Rescue. New York: 1953. V. 64; 65
Parsley. New York: 1955. V. 65
Quito Express. New York: 1938. V. 62; 66
A Tale of Two Glimps. New York: 1947. V. 64

BENAVIDES, ALONSO DE
Benavides' Memorial of 1630. Washington: 1954. V. 63; 64; 66
The Memorial of Fray Alonso de Benavides. Chicago: 1916. V. 63
The Memorial of Fray Alonso de Benavides. Albuquerque: 1965. V. 67

BENBOW, WILLIAM
The Crimes of the Clergy, or the Pillars of Priest-Craft Shaken, with an Appendix, Entitled the Scourge of Ireland.... London: 1823. V. 63
The Trial of William Benbow, for Publishing Certain Libels (alleged to be licentious) in The Rambler's Magazine.... London: 1822. V. 63

BENCE-JONES, MARK
Burke's Guide to Country Houses. Volume I. Ireland. 1978. V. 67
A Guide to Irish Country Houses. 1988. V. 65

BENCHLEY, PETER
Jaws. Garden City: 1974. V. 63; 64

BENCHLEY, ROBERT C.
Of All Things. New York: 1921. V. 66

BENDA, JULIEN
La Trahison des Clercs. Paris: 1927. V. 67

BENDA, W. T.
Masks. New York: 1944. V. 65

BENDER, AVERAM B.
The March of Empire Frontier Defence of the Southwest 1848-1866. Lawrence: 1952. V. 67

BENDER, HENRY E.
Uintah Railway: the Gilsonite Route. Berkeley: 1971. V. 67

BENDIRE, C.
Life Histories of North American Birds. Washington: 1892-1895. V. 62; 67
Life Histories of North American Birds.... Washington: 1895. V. 64; 67

BENEDEN, PIERRE JOSEPH VAN
Recherches sur l'Organisation et le Developpement des Linguatules (Pentastoma Rud.). Suivies de la Description d'une Espece Nouvelle Provenant d'un Mandrill. Brussels: 1849. V. 65

BENEDETTI, GIOVANNI BATTISTA
Speculationum Liber, in Quo Mira Subtilitate Haec Tractata Continentur. Venice: 1599. V. 66

BENEDETTI, MARIO
Esta Manana. Motevideo: 1949. V. 67

BENEDICT, CARL P.
A Tenderfoot Kid on Gyp Water. Austin: 1943. V. 63; 66

BENEDICT, E.
How to Analyze People on Sight. East Aurora: 1921. V. 67
How to Unlock Your Subconscious Mind. East Aurora: 1921. V. 67

BENEDICT, FRANCIS
The Physiology of Large Reptiles. Washington: 1932. V. 67

BENEDICT, G. G.
Vermont in the Civl War. Burlington: 1886. V. 64

BENEDICT, H. T. N.
Murray's English Grammar, Revised, Simplifed and Adapted to the Inductive and Explanatory Mode of Instruction. Frankfort: 1832. V. 66

BENEDICT, WILLIAM H.
New Brunswick in History. New Brunswick: 1925. V. 63; 66

BENEDICTUS, JOHANNES
Pindari Olympia, Pythia, Nemea, Isthmia. Salmuriii: 1620. V. 66

BENEDIKIT, MORIZ
Anatomical Studies Upon Brains of Criminals. New York: 1881. V. 64; 66; 67

BENEDIKT, MORIZ
Die Seelenkunde des Menschen als Reine Erfahrungswissenscahft. Leipzig: 1895. V. 65

BENEDIKT, R.
The Chemistry of Coal-Tar Colours. London: 1889. V. 66; 67

BENEDIT, F. G.
The Physiology of Large Reptiles. Amsterdam: 1973. V. 66

BENET, STEPHEN VINCENT
The Bishop's Beggar. Flemington: 1968. V. 62; 65
Heavens and Earth. A Book of Poems. New York: 1920. V. 63
James Shore's Daughter. New York: 1934. V. 63
John Brown's Body. Garden City: 1928. V. 62; 63
John Brown's Body. New York: 1928. V. 63; 67
Tiger Joy: a Book of Poems. New York: 1925. V. 63

BENEZET, ANTHONY
Observations on the Inslaving, Importing and Purchasing of Negroes.... Germantown: 1760. V. 66
Some Historical Account of Guinea, Its Situation, Practice and the General Disposition of its Inhabitants. Philadelphia: 1771. V. 64; 66

BENFORD, GREGORY
Timescape. 1980. V. 62; 64; 66

BENFORD, R. J.
The Heritage of Aviation Medicine. Washington: 1979. V. 63

BENGER, ELIZABETH OGILVIE
Memoirs of the Life of Mary Queen of Scots, with Anecdotes of the Court of Henry II, During Her Residence in France. London: 1823. V. 63

BEN-GURION, DAVID
Israel: A Personal History. New York: 1971. V. 64; 65; 67

BENHAM, GEORGE C.
A Year of Wreck by a Victim. New York: 1880. V. 67

BENIRSCHKE, K.
Primates. Road to Self-Sustaining Populations. New York: 1986. V. 64

BENISCH, ABRAHAM
The Sabbath of the Jews In Its Relation to the Sunday Question.... London: 1866. V. 63

BENITEZ, SANDRA
A Place Where the Sea Remembers. Minneapolis: 1993. V. 64; 67

BENJAMIN, ASHER
The American Builder's Companion; or, a System of Architecture. Boston: 1816. V. 64; 66
The American Builder's Companion; or, a System of Architecture. Boston: 1826. V. 66

BENJAMIN, EDWARD H.
California Mines and Minerals. San Francisco: 1899. V. 63

BENJAMIN, L. N.
The St. Albans Raid; or Investgation into the Charges Against Lieut. Bennett H. Young and Command for Their Acts at St. Albans, Vt. on the 19th Oct. 1864. Montreal: 1865. V. 63

BENJAMIN, MARCUS
John Bidwell Pioneer. Washington: 1907. V. 66
Washington During War Time. Washington: 1902. V. 67

BENJAMIN, PARK
Appleton's Cyclopaedia of Applied Mechanics. New York: 1896. V. 64
Shakings. Etchings from the Naval Academy. Boston: 1867. V. 64

BENJAMIN, S. G. W.
Art in America: a Critical and Historical Sketch. New York: 1880. V. 66
Persia and the Persians. London: 1887. V. 64

BENJAMIN, WALTER
Der Begriff der Kunstkritik in der deutschen Romantik. Berlin: 1920. V. 67
Einbahnstrasse. Berlin: 1928. V. 65
Illuminations. New York: 1968. V. 67
Ursprung Des Deutschen Trauerspiels. Berlin: 1928. V. 65

BENKARD, ERNST
Undying Faces - a Collection of Death Masks from the 15th Century to the Present Day. London: 1929. V. 64; 65

BENKOVITZ, MIRIAM J.
Aubrey Beardsley. An Account of His Life. New York: 1981. V. 67
A Bibliography of Ronald Firbank. Oxford: 1982. V. 67
Frederick Rolfe: Baron Corvo, a Bibliography. New York: 1977. V. 67
Ronald Firbank. A Biography. New York: 1969. V. 67

BENN, EDITH FRASER
An Overland Trek from Indian, by Side Saddle, Camel and Rail, the Record of a Journey from Baluchistan to Europe. London: 1909. V. 64

BENNET, S. S. R.
Thirty Seven Bamboos Growing in India. Dehra Dun: 1990. V. 63

BENNETT, A.
Case of Cerebral Tumour. London: 1885. V. 67

BENNETT, A. G.
Whaling in the Antarctic. Edinburgh: 1931. V. 64

BENNETT, A. W.
The Flora of the Alps.... New York: 1898. V. 64; 67

BENNETT, AGNES MARIA
The Beggar Girl and Her Benefactors. London: 1799. V. 65

BENNETT, ALAN
Forty Years On. London: 1969. V. 62
Writing Home. London: 1994. V. 63

BENNETT, ANNA MARIA
Rosa, ou la Fille Mendiante et ses Bienfaiteurs. Paris: 1798. V. 66

BENNETT, ARNOLD
Arnold Bennett's Letters to His Nephew. London: 1936. V. 67
The Card. London: 1911. V. 64
The Clayhanger Family. London: 1925. V. 67
Elsie and the Child. London: 1929. V. 66
The Grim Smile of the Five Towns. London: 1907. V. 62
Mediterranean Scenes: Rome-Greece-Constantinople. London: 1928. V. 64
The Old Wive's Tale. Oxford: 1941. V. 62
Venus Rising from the Sea. London: 1931. V. 63; 64; 65
Venus Rising from the Sea. London: 1951. V. 64

BENNETT, C. J. B.
The Galweys of Lota. 1909. V. 67

BENNETT, CHARLES
The Book of Blockheads. London: 1863. V. 64
Character Sketches, Development Drawings and Original Pictures of Wit and Humour. London. V. 67
Comic Shadows. London: 1860. V. 64
Funny Shadows. London: 1860. V. 64
London People Sketched from Life. London: 1863. V. 64
Nursery Fun-The Little Folks Picture Book. London: 1863. V. 64
Shadow and Substance. London: 1860. V. 64
Shadows. London: 1857. V. 64
Shadows. London: 1860. V. 64
Shadows. Philadelphia: 1860. V. 64

BENNETT, CHARLES H.
The Book of Blockheads. London: 1863. V. 62
Character Sketches, Development Drawings and Original Pictures of Wit and Humour. London: 1872. V. 65
The Nine Lives of a Cat: a Tale of Wonder. London: 1860. V. 62; 65
Old Nurse's Book of Rhymes, Jingles and Ditties. London: 1865. V. 62
Proverbs with Pictures. London: 1859. V. 63
The Stories that Little Breeches Told, and The Pictures Which Charles Bennet Drew for Them. London: 1863. V. 62

BENNETT, E. H.
The Sectional Anatomy of Congenital Coecal Hernia. London: 1888. V. 67

BENNETT, E. T.
The Gardens and Menagerie of the Zoological Society Delineated. 1830-1831. V. 62; 63; 64; 66; 67
The Gardens and Menagerie of the Zoological Society Delineated. Volume 2. Birds. London: 1831. V. 62

BENNETT, EDMUND H.
A Selection of Leading Cases in Criminal Law: with Notes. Boston: 1856. V. 67

BENNETT, EMERSON
The Outlaw's Daughter. Philadelphia: 1871. V. 62

BENNETT, FRED E.
Fred Bennett the Mormon Detective or Adventures in the Wild West. Chicago: 1887. V. 62

BENNETT, GEORGE
Wanderings in New South Wales, Batavia, Pedir Coast, Singapore and China.... London: 1834. V. 62

BENNETT, IAN
Oriental Rugs. Caucasian and Oriental. London: 1981. V. 64

BENNETT, JOHN
The Artificer's Complete Lexicon, for Terms and Prices, Adapted for Gentlemen, Engineers, Architects, Builders, Mechanists, Millwrights, Manufacturers, Tradesmen, Etc.... London: 1833. V. 65
Letters to a Young Lady, on a Variety of Useful and Interesting Subjects. Hartford: 1798. V. 65

BENNETT, JOHN WHITCHURCH
Ceylon and Its Capabilities; an Account of Its Natural Resources.... London: 1843. V. 62
A Selection of the Most Remarkable and Interesting of the Fishes Found on the Coasts of Ceylon. London: 1834. V. 65

BENNETT, LERONE
Confrontation: Black and White. Chicago: 1965. V. 64

BENNETT, PAUL A.
Elmer Adler in the World of Books. Reminiscences. 1964. V. 65

BENNETT, PAUL A. continued
Postscripts on Dwiggins. New York: 1960. V. 63

BENNETT, PETER B.
The Physiology and Medicine of Diving and Compressed Air Work. Baltimore: 1969. V. 66

BENNETT, RICHARD
The Story of Bovril. 1953. V. 65

BENNETT, W.
The History of Burnley. To 1400; 1400 to 1650; 1650-1850; from 1850. 1946-1951. V. 65
The History of Burnley. To 1400; 1400 to 1650; 1650-1850; from 1850. London: 1946-1951. V. 63

BENNETT, WENDELL C.
Tarahumara, an Indian Tribe of Northern Mexico. Chicago: 1935. V. 64

BENNETT, WHITMAN
A Practical Guide to American Book Collecting (1663-1940). New York: 1941. V. 66

BENNETT, WILLIAM A.
The First Baby in Camp. A Full Account of the Scenes and Adventures During Pioneer Days of '49. Salt Lake City: 1893. V. 67

BENOIS, ALEXANDRE
The Russian School of Painting. New York: 1916. V. 62

BENOIT, PIERRE
L'Atlantide Roman. Versailles: 1927. V. 64

BENSE, MAX
Quantenmechanik und Daseinsrelativität. Köln: 1938. V. 67

BENSEN, D. R.
Irene, Good-Night. New York: 1982. V. 63

BENSLEY, PIERCE
The Ploughman's Crede. London: 1814. V. 65

BENSON, A. E.
History of the Massachusetts Horticultural Society. N.P: 1929. V. 67

BENSON, ARTHUR CHRISTOPHER
Le Cahier Jaune. Poems. Eton: 1892. V. 66
The Diary of Arthur C. Benson. London. V. 67
The Isles of Sunset. London: 1904. V. 63
Lyrics. London: 1895. V. 67

BENSON, BERRY
Berry Benson's Civil War Book. Athens: 1962. V. 62; 63

BENSON, C. E.
Crag and Hound in Lakeland. London: 1902. V. 65; 67

BENSON, E. F.
Bensoniana. London: 1912. V. 64
The Book of Months. London: 1903. V. 65
The Freaks of Mayfair. London. V. 67
The Kaiser and English Relations. London: 1936. V. 64
Queen Victoria. London: 1935. V. 63
Spook Stories. London: 1928. V. 66

BENSON, EUGENE
Gaspara Stampa: Her Life with a Selection from Her Sonnets. Boston: 1881. V. 63; 67

BENSON, HENRY C.
Life Among the Choctaw Indians and Sketches of the Southwest. Cincinnati: 1860. V. 64

BENSON, IVAN
Mark Twain's Western Years. 1938. V. 63

BENSON, JOHN HOWARD
The First Writing Books. 1954. V. 62

BENSON, JOSEPH
A Defence of the Methodists, in Five Letters, Addressed to the Rev. Dr. Tatham...(with) A Farther Defence of the Methodists: in Five Letters.... London: 1793-1794. V. 64
A Farther Defence of the Methodists: In Five Letters, Addressed to the Rev. W. Russel.... London: 1794. V. 64
A Vindication of the People Called Methodists; in Answer to a "Report from the Clergy of a District in the Diocese of Lincoln.". London: 1800. V. 63

BENSON, MARIA
The Carriage. London: 1819. V. 65

BENSON, RAYMOND
The World is Not Enough. London: 1999. V. 65; 67

BENSON, THOMAS
Vocabularium Anglo-Saxonicum, Lexico Gul. Somneri Magna Parte Auctius. London: 1701. V. 66
Vocabularium Anglo-Saxonicum, Lexico Gul. Somneri Magna Parte Auctius. Oxoniae: 1701. V. 63; 64; 67

BENSUSAN, A. D.
Silver Images. History of Photography in Africa. Cape Town: 1966. V. 62

BENT, A. C.
Life Histories of North American Birds. Washington: 1916-1968. V. 65
Life Histories of North American Birds. New York: 1963-1968. V. 64
Life Histories of North American Cardinals, Grosbeaks, Buntings, Towhees, Finches, Sparrows and Allies.... Washington: 1968. V. 67
Life Histories of North American Diving Birds, Order Pygopodes. Washington: 1919. V. 67
Life Histories of North American Gulls and Terns, Order Longipennes. Washington: 1921. V. 67
Life Histories of North American Shore Birds. 1962. V. 67

BENT, J. THEODORE
The Ruined Cities of Mashonaland, Being a Record of Excavation and Exploration in 1891.... London: 1892. V. 64
The Sacred City of the Ethiopians. London: 1893. V. 64
Southern Arabia. London: 1900. V. 64

BENT, SILAS
Thermal Paths to the Pole. Saint Louis: 1872. V. 64

BENTHAM, GEORGE
The Botany of the Voyage of Sulphur. 1846. V. 66
Genera Plantarum, ad Exemplaria Imprimis in Herbariis Kewensibus Servata Definita. London: 1862-1883. V. 63; 64; 67
Handbook of the British Flora. A Description of the Flowering Plants and Ferns...in the British Isles. London: 1865. V. 64; 65; 67

BENTHAM, J. A.
Shoes. A Story for Children. London: 1920. V. 64

BENTHAM, JEREMY
Defence of Usury; Shewing the Impolicy of the Present Legal Restraints on the Terms of Pecuniary Bargains.... London: 1816. V. 62; 66
Defense of Usury; Shewing the Impolicy of the Present Legal Restraints on the Terms of Pecuniary Bargains. Philadelphia: 1796. V. 62
A Fragment on Government; or, a Comment on the Commentaries.... London: 1823. V. 64
An Introduction to the Principles of Morals and Legislation. London: 1823. V. 64
An Introduction to the Principles of Morals and Legislation. Oxford: 1879. V. 64
Jeremy Bentham to His Fellow-Citizens of France, on Houses of Peers and Senates. 1830. V. 64
Letters to Count Torono on the Proposed Penal Code, Delivered in by the Legislation Committee of the Spanish Cortes, April 25th 1821.... London: 1822. V. 65
Theorie des Peines et des Recompenses. London: 1811. V. 65
Theorie des Peines et des Recompenses, Ouvrage Extraits des Manuscrits de M. Jeremie Bentham.... Paris: 1818. V. 66
Traites de Legislation Civile et Penale, Precedes de Principes Generaux de Legislation.... Paris: 1802. V. 64

BENTIVOGLIO, GUIDO
Opere...Cio e Le Relationi di Fiandri, e di Francia, L'Historia della Guerra di Fiandra, e Le Lettere, Scritte nel Tempo Delle Sue Nuntiature.... Parigi: 1650. V. 67

BENTLEY, ARTHUR
The Deer of Australia. 1978. V. 62; 63; 64; 66; 67

BENTLEY, E. C.
Trent's Last Case. London: 1913. V. 62; 65

BENTLEY, EDMUND CLERIHEW
Biography for Beginners: Being a Collection of Miscellaneous Examples for the Use of the Upper Forms. London: 1930. V. 66

BENTLEY, G. E.
A Blake Bibliography. 1964. V. 66
A Blake Bibliography - Annotated Lists of Works, Studies and Blakeana. Minneapolis: 1964. V. 63

BENTLEY, GEORGE
After Business: Papers Written in the Intervals of Work. London: 1883. V. 65

BENTLEY, H. CUMBERLAND
A Dream's Fulfilment. London: 1895. V. 67

BENTLEY, JOHN
Portrait of Wycoller. Haunt of the Brontes; Valley of Ghosts; Home of the Cunliffes; Site of Historic Bridges. Nelson: 1975. V. 65

BENTLEY, RICHARD
The Bentley Ballads. London: 1861. V. 62
A Full and Ture Account of the Dreadful and Melancholy Earthquake, Which Happened Between Twelve and One O'Clock in the orning, on Thursday te Fifth Instant. London: 1750. V. 67

BENTON, FRANK
Cowboy Life on the Sidetrack. Denver: 1903. V. 64; 66

BENTON, JOSIAH H.
Voting in the Field. A Forgotten Chapter of the Civil War. Boston: 1915. V. 63
What Women Did for the War, and What the War Did for Women. A Memorial Day Address...The Soldier's Club at Wellesley, Mass., May 30, 1894. Boston: 1894. V. 63

BENTON, THOMAS HART
Thirty Years' View or, a History of the Working of the American Government for Thirty Years from 1820 to 1850.. New York: 1854. V. 63; 66
Thirty Years' View; or, a History of the Working of the American Government for Thirty Years from 1820 to 1850.... San Francisco: 1854. V. 63

BENVENISTE, ASA
5 X 5. An Anthology. London: 1981. V. 67

BENZENBERG, JOHANN FRIEDRICH
Die Sternschuppen. Hamburg: 1839. V. 65

BEOWULF
Beowulf. New York: 1932. V. 65
Beowulf. New York: 1939. V. 63
Beowulf. London: 1984. V. 65
Beowulf. Market Drayton: 1984. V. 64
Beowulf. London: 1999. V. 67
Beowulf. London: 2000. V. 66; 67
Beowulf. Translated by Seamus Heaney. London: 1999. V. 66

BERALDI, HENRI
Estampes et Livres 1872-1892. Paris: 1892. V. 62

BERANGER, PIERRE JEAN DE
The Songs of Beranger in English with a Sketch of the Author's Life. Philadelphia: 1844. V. 62

BERCE, M. E.
Faune Entomologique Francaise: (Papillons Description de tous les Lepidopteres qui se Trouvent en France).... Paris: 1867-1872. V. 64

BERCHTOLD, LEOPOLD, COUNT
An Essay to Direct and Extend the Inquiries of Patriotic Travellers; with Further Observations on the Means of Preserving the Life, Health and Property of the Unexperieced in Their Journies by Land and Sea. London: 1789. V. 64

BERDAN, F. F.
Codex Mendoza. Berkeley: 1992. V. 62

BERENDT, JOHN
Midnight in the Garden of Good and Evil. New York: 1994. V. 62; 63; 65; 66; 67

BERENDT, R. M.
Australian Aboriginal Art. New York and London: 1964. V. 62

BERENGARIO DA CARPI, GIACOMO
Isagogae Brevis P(er)lucide ac Uberrime in Anatomiam Humani Corporis. Bologna: 1523. V. 62; 66
Tractatus Perutilis et Completus de Fractura Cranei. Venice: 1535. V. 63

BERENGER, CHARLES RANDOM
Helps and Hints How to Protect Life and Property. London: 1835. V. 65

BERENS, JOHANN CHRISTOPH
Bonhomien, Geschrieben Bei Eroffnung der Neuerbauten Rigischen Stadsbibliothek. Mitan: 1792. V. 64

BERENSON, BERNARD
The Drawings of the Florentine Painters. Chicago: 1938. V. 62
A Sienese Painter of the Franciscan Legend. London: 1910. V. 67

BERENSON, MARY
Across the Mediterranean. Tipografia Giachetti: 1935. V. 67

BERESFORD, CHARLES
Nelson and His Time. London: 1898. V. 66

BERESFORD, J. D.
The Hapdenshire Wonder. London: 1911. V. 65
Revolution. London: 1921. V. 65

BERESFORD, JAMES
Bibliosophia; or, Book-Wisdom. London: 1810. V. 66

BERETARIO, P. SEBASTIANO
Vida del Padre Joseph de Ancheta de la Compania de Iesus, y Provincial del Brasil. Salamanca: 1618. V. 62

BEREWOOD, EDWARD
Enquiries Touching the Diversity of Languages and Religions through the Chief Parts of the World. London: 1674. V. 63

BERG, ELIZABETH
Durable Goods. New York: 1993. V. 64; 66; 67
Talk Before Sleep. New York: 1994. V. 67

BERG, LILLIE C.
Early Pioneers and Indians of Minnesota and Rice Country. San Leandro: 1959. V. 64; 67

BERGAN, RONALD
The United Artists Story. New York: 1986. V. 66

THE BERGEN
County Democrat's History of Hackensack N.J. Its Olden Story, Present Annals, Prospective Growth. Hackensack: 1898. V. 63; 66

BERGEN, TEUNIS G.
Register in Alphabetical Order, of the Early Settlers of Kings County, Long Island, New York, from Its First Settlement by Europeans to 1700.... New York: 1881. V. 66

BERGENGREN, RALPH
David the Dreamer His Book of Dreams. Boston: 1922. V. 63
Jane Joseph and John.... Boston: 1918. V. 62

BERGER, BRUCE
Hangin' On; Gordon Snidow Portrays the Cowboy Heritage. Flagstaff: 1980. V. 67

BERGER, JOHN
Art and Revolution - Ernst Neizvestny and the Role of the Artist in the U.S.S.R. London: 1969. V. 65

BERGER, K.
Gericault Drawings and Watercolors. New York: 1946. V. 65
Odilon Redon: Fantasy and Colour. London: 1964. V. 65

BERGER, SIDNEY E.
Printing and the Mind of Merker: a Bibliographical Study. New York: 1997. V. 64

BERGER, THOMAS
Crazy in Berlin. New York: 1958. V. 63
Little Big Man. New York: 1964. V. 62

BERGERON, LOUIS
Manuel du Tourneur, Ouvrage Dans Lequel on Enseigne Aux Amateurs la Maniere d'Executer sur le Tour a Pointes, a Lunettes.... Paris: 1816. V. 64
Manuel du Tourneur.... Paris: 1816-1842. V. 66

BERGH, LEONARD JOHN
On the Trail of the Pigmies, an Anthropological Exploration Under the Co-operation of the American Museum of Natural History and American Universities. London: 1922. V. 64

BERGIUS, PETER JONAS
Descriptiones Plantarum ex Capite Bonae Spei.... Stockholm: 1767. V. 63; 67

BERGMAN, RAY
Trout. London: 1950. V. 67

BERGMAN, ROBERT
A Kind of Rapture. New York: 1998. V. 63

BERGMAN, STEN
Sport and Exploration in the Far East. 1933. V. 67

BERGMAN, TORBERN
Afhandling, Om Bitter-Selzer-Spa-Och Pyrmonter-Vattens.... Upsala: 1776. V. 64

BERGSON, HENRI
Time and Free Will: an Essay on the Immediate Data of Consciousness. London: 1910. V. 67

BERINGTON, JOSEPH
The History of the Reign of Henry the Second and of Richard and John, His Sons.... Basil: 1793. V. 64

BERINGTON, SIMON
The Adventures of Signor Gaudentio di Lucas: Being the Substance of His Examination Before the Fathers of the Inquisition at Bologna in Italy. London: 1763. V. 66

BERJEAU, J. P.
The Homoeopathic Treatment of Syphilis, Gonorrhoea Spermatorrhoea, and Urinary Diseases. Philadelphia: 1870. V. 66; 67

BERKE, JOSEPH
Counter Culture. London: 1969. V. 65

BERKELEY, EDMUND
Autographs and Manuscripts: a Collector's Manual. New York: 1978. V. 63

BERKELEY, GEORGE
Historical Applications and Occasional Meditations Upon Several Subjects. London: 1798. V. 67
The Naval History of Britain from he Earliest Periods of Which There Are Accounts in History, to the Conclusion of the Year MDCCLVI. London: 1756. V. 62; 63; 66
A Treatise Concering the Principles of Human Knowledge. Dublin: 1710. V. 63

BERKELEY, GEORGE, BP. OF CLOYNE
Alciphron or the Minute Philosopher in Seven Dialogues. London: 1732. V. 62; 65; 67
Alciphron; or, the Minute Philosopher. (with) An Essay Towards a New Theory of Vision. Dublin: 1732. V. 64
Philosophical Commentaries, Generally Called the Commonplace Book. London: 1944. V. 64
Siris: a Chain of Philosophical Reflexions and Inquiries.... Dublin: 1744. V. 65
Siris: a Chain of Philosophical Reflexions and Inquiries.... London: 1744. V. 62; 65
The Works.... Dublin: 1784. V. 64
The Works.... Oxford: 1871. V. 62; 65

BERKELEY, HENRY ROBINSON
Four Years in the Confederate Artillery. Chapel Hill: 1961. V. 62; 63; 65

BERKELEY, M. J.
The Botany of the Antarctic Voyage...II Flora Novae Zelandiae, Part II Flowerless Plants (Fungi only). 1855. V. 62
Handbook of British Mosses. 1863. V. 66
Handbook of British Mosses. London: 1863. V. 64
Introduction to Crytogamic Botany. London: 1857. V. 67

BERKENHOUT, J.
Synopsis of the Natural History of Great Britain and Ireland. 1795. V. 63
Synopsis of the Natural History of Great Britain and Ireland. London: 1795. V. 62

BERKEY, C. P.
Geology of Mongolia.... New York: 1927. V. 63

BERKEY, WILLIAM A.
The Money Question. The Legal Tender Paper Monetary System of the United States. Grand Rapids: 1876. V. 64

BERKHEY, JOANNES LE FRANCQ VAN
Expositio Characteristica Structurae Florum Qui Dicuntur Compositi. Lugduni Batavorum: 1760. V. 67

BERKLEY, HENRY
A Treatise on Mental Disease Based Upon the Lecture Course at the Johns Hopkins University, 1899 and Designed for the Use of Practioners and Students of Medicine. New York: 1900. V. 64; 65; 67

BERKMAN, ALEXANDER
Prison Memoirs of an Anarchist. New York: 1912. V. 63

BERKNER, L. V.
Manual on Rockets and Satellites: Annals of the International Geophysical Year, Volume VI. London: 1958. V. 66

BERKO, PATRICK
Dictionary of Belgian Painters Born Between 1750 and 1875. Brussels: 1981. V. 62

BERKOWITZ, DAVID SANDLER
In Remembrance of Creation; Evolution of Art and Scholarship in the Medieval and Renaissance Bible. Waltham: 1968. V. 62

BERKSON, BILL
Recent Visitors. New York: 1973. V. 63

BERLAND, ANTHONY
Walk in Beauty: the Navajo and their Blankets. New York: 1977. V. 66

BERLANDER, JEAN L.
The Indians of Texas in 1830. Washington: 1969. V. 67

BERLANT, A.
Walk in Beauty: the Navajo and Their Blankets. Boston: 1977. V. 62

BERLEPSCH, H.
The Alps; or Sketches of Life and Nature in the Mountains. London: 1861. V. 64
Die Alpen in Natur- und Lebensbildern...Mit 16 Illustrationem und Einem Titelbilde.... Leipzig: 1861. V. 65

BERLESE, L.
Monographie du Genre Camellia et Traite Complet sur sa Culture, sa Description et sa Classification. Paris: 1840. V. 66; 67

BERLIN, IRVING
Songs from Top Hat. New York: 1935. V. 63

BERLIN, SVEN
I Am Lazarus. London: 1961. V. 65
Pride of the Peacock - The Evolution of an Artist. London: 1972. V. 65

BERLINGER, B.
Danger Down the Sights. 1964. V. 67

BERLYN, G. P.
Botanical Microtechnique and Cytochemistry. 1976. V. 67

BERMAN, T.
The Daily Growth Cycle of Phytoplankton.... Dordrecht: 1992. V. 65

BERNACCHI, LOUIS C.
The Polar Book. London: 1930. V. 64
Saga of the Discovery. London and Glasgow: 1938. V. 62; 63; 64
To the South Polar Regions; Expeditions of 1898-1900. London: 1901. V. 64
A Very Gallant Gentleman. London: 1933. V. 64

BERNAL, I.
Ancient Mexico in Colour. New York: 1968. V. 62
100 Great Masterpieces of the Mexican National Museum of Anthropology. New York: 1972. V. 63

BERNAL, LOUIS
Illustrated Catalogue of the Distinguished Collection of Works of Art and Vertue, from the Byzantine Period to that of Louise Seize, Collected by the Late Ralph Bernal, Esq. London: 1855. V. 67

BERNANOS, GEORGES
The Diary of a Country Priest. 1986. V. 65
The Diary of a Country Priest. New York: 1986. V. 62

BERNARD, APRIL
Prayers and Sermons for the Stations of the Cross. New York: 1983. V. 64

BERNARD, CLAUDE
Lecons de Physiologie Experimentale Appliquee a La Medecine Faites au College France. Paris: 1855-1856. V. 64; 66
Lecons sur La Chaleur Animale sur les Effets de la Chaleur et Sur la Fievre. Paris. 1876. V. 64; 66
Lecons sur la Physiologie et la Pathologie du Systeme Nerveux.... Paris: 1858. V. 62; 64; 66
Lecons sur les Effects De Substances Taxiques et Medicamenteuses. Paris: 1857. V. 64; 66
Lecons sur Les Properties des Tissus Vivants. Paris: 1866. V. 64; 66

BERNARD, EDWARD
Catalogi Librorum Manuscriptorum Angliae et Hiberniae in Unnum Collecti.... Oxoniae: 1697. V. 63
De Mensuris et Ponderibus Antiquis, Liber Tres. Oxoniae: 1688. V. 63; 67

BERNARD, FERNAND
A Travers Sumatra. Paris: 1904. V. 67

BERNARD, GEORGE S.
The Battle of the Crater in Front of Petersburg. July 30, 1864. Petersburg: 1890. V. 63; 65
War Talks of Confederate Veterans. Petersburg: 1892. V. 62; 63

BERNARD, JOHN
The Poets of the New York School. Philadelphia: 1969. V. 63
Retrospections of the Stage. London: 1830. V. 65

BERNARD, OF GORDON
Bern. Gordonii Opvs, Lilivm, Medicinae Inscriptum, de Morborum Prope Omnium Curatione, Septem Particulis Distributum.... Lvgduni Apud: 1559. V. 64

BERNARD, PHILIPPA
Antiquarian Books, a Companion for Booksellers, Librarians and Collectors. Philadelphia: 1994. V. 63

BERNARD, THOMAS
The Reports of the Society for Bettering the Condition and Increasing the Comforts of the Poor. London: 1811. V. 67
Spurinna or the Comforts of Old Age. London: 1816. V. 66

BERNARD, W. D.
Narrative of the Voyages and Services of the "Nemesis", from 1840 to 1843, and of the Combined Naval and Military Operations in China.... London: 1844. V. 64

BERNARDI, MARZIANO
Antonello in Sicilia. Torino: 1957. V. 62; 63; 64; 66

BERNARDIN DE SAINT PIERRE, JACQUES HENRI
Paul et Virginie. (with) *Chaumiere Indienne etc.* Paris: 1829. V. 62

BERNARDIS, CALOGERO DE
Insurrection in Sicily 1820. Sicily: 1820. V. 66

BERNATH, DESIRE DE
Cleopatra, Her Life and Reign. London: 1907. V. 62

BERNATZ, J. M.
Bilder aus dem Heiligen Lande.... Stuttgart. V. 62

BERNE, SUZANNE
A Crime in the Neighbourhood. Chapel Hill: 1997. V. 67

BERNERS, GABRIEL HUGH TYRWHITT WILSON
A Distant Prospect - a Sequel to First Childhood. London: 1945. V. 63

BERNERS, GERALD HUGH TYRWHITT WILSON
Poroy Wallingford and Mr. Pidger. Oxford: 1941. V. 64

BERNERS, JULIANA
The Treatyse of Fysshynge with an Angle. London: 1827. V. 63
A Treatyse of Fysshynge with an Angle. London: 1880. V. 67
A Treatyse of Fysshynge with an Angle. Chelsea: 1903. V. 65

BERNERS, LORD
The Camel. London: 1936. V. 62; 64
Count Omega. London: 1941. V. 66
A Distant Prospect. London: 1945. V. 67

BERNHARD, RUTH
Gift of the Commonplace. Carmel: 1996. V. 62

BERNHARD, THOMAS
Auf der Erde und in der Hoelle. Saltzburg: 1957. V. 67
Frost. Frankfurt: 1963. V. 67

BERNHARDT, C.
Indian Raids in Lincoln County, Kansas, 1864 and 1869.... Lincoln: 1910. V. 63; 64; 67

BERNHEIM, HIPPOLYTE
De la Suggestion dans l'Etat Hypnotique et dans l'etat de Veille. Paris: 1884. V. 65
De la Suggestion et de Sans Applications a la Therapeutique. Paris: 1886. V. 65
Die Suggestion und ihre Heilwirkung. Leipzig/Wien: 1888-1889. V. 62; 65
Die Suggestion und ihre Heilwirkung. Leipzig/Wien: 1896. V. 65

BERNHEIMER, CHARLES L.
Rainbow Bridge. New York: 1924. V. 63

BERNIER, J. E.
Master Mariner and Arctic Explorer. A Narrative of 60 Years at Sea from the Logs and Yarns of Captain J. E. Bernier. Ottawa: 1939. V. 63

BERNIERES, LOUIS DE
Corelli's Mandolin. New York: 1994. V. 62

BERNOULLI, DANIEL
Hydrodynamica, sive De Viribus et Motibus Fluidorum Commentarii, Opus Academicum. Strasburg: 1738. V. 62

BERNOULLI, JACOB
Ars Conjectandi, Opus Post-Human. Basel: 1713. V. 66
Dissertation e Gravitate Aetheris. (with) *Conamen Novi Systematis Cometarum, Pro Motu Eorum Sub Calculum Revocando & Apparitionibus Praedicendis.* Amsterdam: 1683-1682. V. 65

BERNOULLI, JOHANN
Opera Omnia.... Lausanne & Geneva: 1742. V. 63; 64

BERNSTEIN, ALINE
Three Blue Suits. New York: 1933. V. 64

BERNSTEIN, CARL
All the President's Men. New York: 1974. V. 62; 64

BERNSTEIN, CHARLES
Resistance. Windsor: 1983. V. 66

BERNSTEIN, LEONARD
The Joy of Music. New York: 1959. V. 63

BERQUIN, ARNAUD
Idylles. Paris: 1775. V. 64
The Looking-Glass for the Mind; or Intellectual Mirror.... London: 1821. V. 62
The Looking-Glass for the Mind; or Intellectual Mirror.... London: 1827. V. 64; 65

BERQUIN, JACQUES
Architectura of Wiskunstige Verhandeling om de Voornaamste Eigenschappen der Burgerlyke Bouwkonst.... Amsterdam: 1789-1790. V. 64

BERRA, YOGI
Yogi. It Ain't Over. New York: 1989. V. 66; 67

BERRIAULT, GINA
Descent. New York: 1960. V. 67
Short Story 1. New York: 1958. V. 63

BERRIGAN, DANIEL
Time Without Number. New York: 1957. V. 63

BERRIGAN, TED
Clear the Range. New York: 1977. V. 63
In the Early Morning Rain. London: 1970. V. 62; 63; 67
Many Happy Returns. Poems. New York: 1969. V. 64; 67
Red Wagon. Chicago: 1976. V. 63
So Going Around Cities: New and Selected Poems 1958-1979. Berkeley: 1980. V. 63; 66
The Sonnets. New York: 1964. V. 63

BERRY, CHARLES WALTER
In Search of Wine. London: 1935. V. 67

BERRY, DON
A Majority of Scoundrels - an Informal History of the Rocky Mountain Fur Company. New York: 1961. V. 64; 65

BERRY, GEOFFREY
Across Northern Hills. Long Distance Footpaths in the North of England. Kendal: 1975. V. 63; 65

BERRY, GERALD L.
The Whoop-Up Trail (Alberta-Montana Relationships). Edmonton: 1953. V. 67

BERRY, H. N.
Selections. Meridian: 1911. V. 65

BERRY, MARY
Social Life in England and France, from the French Revolution in 1789, to that of July 1830. London: 1831. V. 65
Some Account of the Life of Rachael Wriothesley Lady Russell.... London: 1819. V. 63; 66

BERRY, R.
The Caecal Folds and Fossae...of the Vermiform Appendix. Edinburgh: 1897. V. 67

BERRY, R. J.
Inheritance and Natural History. London: 1977. V. 65; 67
The Natural History of Shetland. London: 1980. V. 62; 63

BERRY, THOMAS FRANKLIN
Four Years with Morgan and Forrest. Oklahoma City: 1914. V. 63; 65

BERRY, WENDELL
The Broken Ground. New York: 1964. V. 65
Clearing. New York: 1977. V. 65
Collected Poems 1957-1982. 1985. V. 66
Collected Poems 1957-1982. Berkeley: 1985. V. 62
The Farm. Monterey: 1995. V. 62
The Gift of Good Land. San Francisco: 1981. V. 67
Harlan Hubbard, Life and Work. Lexington: 1990. V. 67
The Hidden Wound. Boston: 1970. V. 62; 63
Nathan Coulter. Boston: 1960. V. 62; 63
November Twenty Six Nineteen Hundred Sixty Three. New York: 1964. V. 63; 64; 67
Remembering. San Francisco: 1988. V. 67
Sabbaths. Monterey: 1987. V. 65
Sabbaths 1987. Monterey: 1991. V. 67
Sayings and Doings. Lexington: 1975. V. 64; 65; 67
Sayings and Doings and an Eastward Look. Frankfort: 1990. V. 63
Standing on Earth. Ipswich: 1991. V. 67
The Unforeseen Wilderness. Lexington: 1971. V. 64
The Unsettling of America: Culture and Agriculture. San Francisco: 1977. V. 64
Watch With Me. New York: 1994. V. 67

BERRY, WILLIAM
County Genealogies of Berkshire, Buckinghire and Surrey Families. 1837. V. 67

BERRY, WILLIAM D.
Deneki. An Alaskan Moose. New York: 1965. V. 65

BERRYMAN, JOHN
A Critical Supplement in Poetry. Chicago: 1949. V. 64
The Dispossessed. New York: 1948. V. 65
His Thoughts Made Pocket and the Plane Buckt. Pawlet: 1958. V. 64
His Toy, His Dream, His Rest. 308 Dream Songs. New York: 1968. V. 63
Homage to Mistress Bradstreet. New York: 1956. V. 62; 63; 64
Love and Fame. New York: 1970. V. 62; 64
Poems. 1942. V. 64
Poems. New York: 1942. V. 63
Poems. Norfolk: 1942. V. 64; 67
Stephen Crane. New York: 1950. V. 63; 67
Two Poems. N.P: 1970. V. 62
Two Poems. New York: 1970. V. 64

BERSENBRUGGE, MEI-MEI
Hiddenness. Poems. Richard Tuttle. Illuminations. New York: 1987. V. 64

BERSON, MORTON I.
Atlas of Plastic Surgery. New York: 1948. V. 66

BERTELSEN, E.
The Ceratioid Fishes, Ontogeny, Taxonomy, Distribution and Biology. Copenhagen: 1951. V. 63

BERTHA S. Goudy: First Lady of Printing. 1958. V. 64

BERTHIER, R. P. JOACHIM JOSEPH
La Plus Ancienne Danse Macabre au Klingenthal, a Bale. Paris: 1897. V. 67

BERTHOLD, VICTOR M.
The Pioneer Steamer California 1848-1849. Boston and New York. V. 65
The Pioneer Steamer, California 1848-1849. Boston: 1932. V. 63; 66

BERTHOLET, JOHANNES
Quem Praeses Totius Naturae Benigniffimus Deus ter Optimus Maximus Clementer a Nobis Avertere Velit Dirum Pectoris Hydropem. Basel: 1765. V. 66

BERTHOLLET, M.
Elements of the Art of Dyeing. 1791. V. 67

BERTHOLON DE SAINT LAZARE, NICOLLE PIERRE
De l'Electricite des Vegetaux. Lyon: 1783. V. 64
De l'Electricite des Vegetaux. Paris: 1783. V. 64
De L'Electricite du Corps Humain dans l'Etat de Sante et de Maladie. Lyon: 1780. V. 64; 67
De l'Electricite du Corps Humain dans l'Etat de Sante et de Maladie. Paris: 1786. V. 64
Die Elektricitat der Lufterscheinungen, Worinne von der Naturlichen Elektricitat Uberhaupt, und von den Lufterscheinungen Besonders Gehandelt Wird.... Liegnitz: 1792. V. 64

BERTHOUD, FERDINAND
Eclaircissemens sur l'Invention, la Theorie, la Construction, et les Epreuves des Nouvelles machines Proposees en France.... Paris: 1773. V. 66

BERTHRONG, DONALD J.
The Southern Cheyennes. Norman: 1963. V. 67

BERTI, DOMENICO
Il Processo Originale di Galileo Galilei Pubblicato per la Prima Volta. Roma: 1876. V. 64

BERTIE, WILLOUGHBY
Thoughts on the Letter of Edmund Burke, Esq. to the Sheriffs of Bristol, on the Affairs of America. Oxford: 1777?. V. 65

BERTON, B.
A Voyage on the Colorado - 1878. Los Angeles: 1953. V. 62

BERTON, FRANCIS
A Voyage on the Colorado - 1878. Los Angeles: 1953. V. 65

BERTRAM, CHARLES JULIUS
The Description of Britain.... London: 1809. V. 63; 65

BERTRAM, JAMES
North China Front. London: 1939. V. 67

BERTRAND, ADRIEN
Les Jardins de Priape, Poemes. Paris: 1915. V. 65

BERTRAND, LOUIS
Developpement Nouveau de la Partie Elementaire des Mathematiques. Geneva: 1778. V. 67

BERTRAND DE MOLEVILLE, ANTOINE FRANCOIS, MARQUIS DE
Private Memoirs Relative to the Last Year of the Reign of Lewis the Sixteenth, Late King of France. London: 1797. V. 66

BERWICK, EDWARD
Memoirs of the Life of the Elder Scipio Africanus, with Notes and Illustrations by.... London: 1817. V. 63

BERZELIUS, JONS JACOB
Essai Sur la Theorie des Proportions Chimiques et sur l'Influence Chimique de l'Electricite.... Paris: 1819. V. 64
Om Blasrorets Anvandande i kemien och Mineralogien. Stockholm: 1820. V. 62

BESANT, ANNIE
The Law of Population. Bound Brook: 1886. V. 63; 66

BESANT, W. H.
A Treatise on Hydrostatics and Hydrodynamics. Cambridge: 1859. V. 64

BESANT, WALTER
All in a Garden Fair; the Simple Story of Three Boys and a Girl. London: 1885. V. 67
Armorel of Lyonesse; a Romance of Today. London: 1894. V. 67
Beyond the Dreams of Avarice. London: 1895. V. 66
The Chaplain of the Fleet. London: 1881. V. 66
The Chaplain of the Fleet. London: 1884. V. 67
For Faith and Freedom. London: 1889. V. 66
The Golden Butterfly. London: 1890. V. 67
Herr Paulus. His Rise, His Greatness and His Fall. London: 1888. V. 66
In Deacon's Orders. London: 1895. V. 67

BESANT, WALTER continued
The Ivory Gate. London: 1892. V. 66
The Lady of Lynn. London: 1901. V. 67
London. London: 1900. V. 62
London in the Nineteenth Century. London: 1909. V. 62
The Master Craftsman. London: 1896. V. 67
The Orange Girl. London: 1899. V. 66
St. Katherine's by the Tower. London: 1891. V. 66
'Twas in Trafalgar's Bay and Other Stories. London: 1885. V. 67

BESCHKE, WILLIAM
The Dreadful Suffering and Thrilling Adventures of an Overland Party of Emigrants to California...Their Conflicts with Savage Tribes of Indians. New Orleans: 1946. V. 67

BESIER, RUDOLF
The Barretts of Wimpole Street. Boston: 1931. V. 66

BESKOW, ELSA
The Tale of the Wee Little Old Woman. New York: 1930. V. 63

BESSE, JOSEPH
An Abstract of the Sufferings of the People Call'd Quakers for the Testimony of a Good Conscience, from the Time First Distinguished by the Name, Taken from Original Records.... London: 1733-1738. V. 62

BESSEMER, HENRY
An Autobiography. London: 1905. V. 63; 66

BESSON, JACQUES
Theatre des Instrumens Mathematiques de Mechaniques. Geneva: 1500. V. 63; 64; 66

BESSON, MAURICE
The Scourge of the Indies. Buccaneers, Corsairs and Filibusters, from the Original Texts and Contemporary Engravings. London: 1929. V. 63; 66

THE BEST American Short Stories. 1987. Boston: 1987. V. 66

THE BEST American Short Stories 1988. Boston: 1988. V. 62

BEST, GERALD M.
Nevada Country Narrow Gauge. Berkeley: 1965. V. 67

BEST in Children's Books. New York: 1960. V. 62; 64
BEST in Children's Books. New York: 1961. V. 64

BEST, J. J.
Excursions in Albania.... London: 1842. V. 64

BEST, M. C., MRS.
Six Thousand Years Ago; or the Works of Creation Illustrated. Bath: 1844. V. 64; 65

BEST Poems of 1959. Palo Alto: 1961. V. 63

THE BEST Short Stories of 1931. London: 1932. V. 62

BEST, THOMAS
The Art of Angling, Confirmed by Actual Experience.... London: 1822. V. 64

BESTALL, ALFRED
A New Rupert Book. 1945. V. 65
A New Rupert Book. London: 1945. V. 64

BESTER, ALFRED
Who's He?. 1953. V. 64; 66

BESTERMAN, THEODORE
Old Art Books Collected and Catalogued by.... London: 1975. V. 63
The Pilgrim Fathers. Waltham St. Lawrence: 1939. V. 64; 65; 67
A World Bibliography of Bibliographies.... London: 1947-1949. V. 62
A World Bibliography of Bibliographies.... Lausanne: 1960. V. 65

BETHAM, WILLIAM
Irish Antiquarian Researches. Dublin: 1826-1827. V. 63

BETHAM EDWARDS, MATILDA
East of Paris. Sketches in the Gatinais, Bourbonnais, and Champagne. London: 1902. V. 67
Holidays Among the Mountains; or, Scenes and Stories of Wales. London: 1861. V. 67
Pearla. London: 1883. V. 65

BETHEL MISSION OF EASTERN EUROPE, INC.
From Darkness Into Light: the Remarkable Life Story of Mrs. Fanny Rosenberg. Los Angeles: 1949. V. 66

BETHEL, SLINGSBY
An Account of the French Usurpation Upon the Trade of England, and What Great Damage the English do Yearly Sustain by Their Commerce, and How the Same May be Retrenched and England Improved in Riches and Interest. London: 1679. V. 63
The World's Mistake in Oliver Cromwell; or a Short Political Discourse, Shewing, that Cromwell's Mal-Administration (During His Four Years, and Nine Months Pretended Protectorship) Layed the Foundation of Our Present Condition, in the Decay of Trade. London: 1668. V. 63; 67

BETHUNE, ALEXANDER
Practical Economy, Explained and Enforced. Edinburgh: 1839. V. 63

BETHUNE, M. DRINKWATER
The River Mole, or Emlyn Stream. 1839. V. 62; 66

BETHUNE, THOMAS GREENE
The Marvelous Musical Prodigy, Blind Tom, the Negro Boy Pianist.... Baltimore: 1866. V. 65

BETJEMAN, JOHN
Church Poems. London: 1980. V. 63
Collected Poems. London: 1970. V. 65
Collected Poems. Boston: 1971. V. 65
Collins Guide to English Parish Churches. London: 1958. V. 62
Continual Dew: a Little Book of Bourgeois Verse. London: 1937. V. 62; 63
English Cities and Small Towns. London: 1933. V. 65
English, Scottish and Welsh Landscape - 1700-c.1860. London: 1944. V. 63; 65
A Few Late Chrysanthemums. London: 1954. V. 63; 64; 65
Ghastly Good Taste. London: 1933. V. 62
Ground Plan to Skyline. London: 1960. V. 62
High and Low. London: 1966. V. 63
Letters - 1926 to 1951; 1951-1984. London: 1994-1995. V. 65
Mount Zion or In Touch with the Infinite. London: 1931. V. 62
Murray's Berkshire Architectural Guide. London: 1949. V. 63; 65
New Bats in Old Belfries. London: 1945. V. 62; 63; 66
A Nip in the Air. London: 1974. V. 63; 65
An Oxford University Chest. London: 1938. V. 66
Poems in the Porch. London: 1954. V. 64
A Ring of Bells. London: 1962. V. 62; 63; 66
Shell Guide to Cornwall. London: 1934. V. 62
Shropshire - a Shell Guide. London: 1951. V. 63
Summoned by Bells. 1960. V. 67
Summoned by Bells. London: 1960. V. 62; 64; 65
Uncollected Poems. London: 1982. V. 63

BETTENS, EDWARD D.
Picture Buying. New York: 1919. V. 66

BETTERSWORTH, JOHN K.
Mississippi in the Confederacy. Baton Rouge: 1961. V. 65

BETTRIDGE, WILLIAM
A Brief History of the Church in Upper Canada.... London: 1838. V. 65

BETTS, A. D.
Experiences of a Confederate Chaplain. Greenville: 1907. V. 62; 63; 65

BETTS, DORIS
The Gentle Insurrection. New York: 1954. V. 63

BETZINEZ, JASON
I Fought with Geronimo. Harrisburg: 1960. V. 67

BEUMERS, E.
Kings of Africa, Art and Authority in Central Africa. Maastricht: 1992. V. 62

BEUQUE, ETIENNETTE
Rebelles Au Martyrs? Roman Irlandais. 1928. V. 65

BEURDELEY, MICHEL
Chinese Ceramics. London: 1974. V. 64

BEVAN, EDWARD
The Honey-Bee: Its Natural History. London: 1827. V. 65
The Honey Bee. Its Natural History. London: 1870. V. 62

BEVAN, JOSEPH GURNEY
Memoirs of the Life and Travels, in the Service of the Gospel of Sarah Stevenson. London: 1807. V. 62

BEVAN, PHILIP
Descriptive Catalogue of the Anatomical and Pathological Museum of the Dublin School of Medicine. Dublin: 1847. V. 67

BEVAN, THEODORE F.
Toil, Travel and Discovery in British New Guinea. London: 1890. V. 64

BEVENS, WILLIAM E.
Reminiscences of a Private Company G, First Arkansas Regiment Infantry. May 1861 to April 1865. Newport: 1913. V. 63; 65

BEVERIDGE, ALBERT J.
Abraham Lincoln 1809-1858. Boston and New York: 1928. V. 62; 63; 66
The Life of John Marshall. Boston: 1916-1919. V. 65

BEVERIDGE, W. H.
Unemployment: a Problem of Industry. London: 1909. V. 63
Unemployment: A Problem of Industry. London: 1931. V. 64

BEVERIDGE, WILLIAM
Full Employment in a Free Society. London: 1944. V. 62

BEVERLEY, ROBERT
Histoire de la Virginie; Contenant, I. L'Histoire du Premier Establissement dans la Virginie.... Paris: 1707. V. 64; 67

BEVIER, ROBERT S.
History of the First and Second Missouri Confederate Brigades 1861- 1865. St. Louis: 1879. V. 63; 65

BEVILL, ROBERT
A Treatise on the Law of Homicide and of Larceny at Common Law. London: 1799. V. 62; 65

BEWICK, ELIZABETH
Comfort Me With Apples and Other Poems. Kent: 1987. V. 64

BEWICK, J.
Geological Treatise on the District of Cleveland, in North Yorkshire.... London: 1861. V. 64; 65; 66

BEWICK, THOMAS
Figures of British Land Birds Engraved on Wood.... Newcastle-upon-Tyne: 1800. V. 66; 67
A General History of Quadrupeds. Newcastle-upon-Tyne: 1790. V. 66
A General History of Quadrupeds. 1800. V. 64; 65
A General History of Quadrupeds. Newcastle-upon-Tyne: 1807. V. 62; 66; 67
A General History of Quadrupeds. 1811. V. 62; 63; 64; 66; 67
A General History of Quadrupeds. Newcastle-upon-Tyne: 1811. V. 66
A General History of Quadrupeds. Newcastle-upon-Tyne: 1820. V. 62; 66; 67
A General History of Quadrupeds. 1824. V. 67
A General History of Quadrupeds. Newcastle-upon-Tyne: 1824. V. 62
A General History of Quadrupeds. (with) History of British Birds. Newcastle: 1811-1832. V. 66
History of British Birds. Newcastle: 1797-1804. V. 66
History of British Birds. Newcastle: 1804. V. 62
A History of British Birds. Newcastle-upon-Tyne: 1805. V. 62; 67
A History of British Birds. Newcastle: 1816. V. 66; 67
A History of British Birds. Newcastle-upon-Tyne: 1832. V. 63; 67
A History of British Birds. Newcastle-upon-Tyne: 1847. V. 62
History of British Birds. (With) A General History of Quadrupeds. Newcastle-upon-Tyne: 1797-1804. V. 66
Memoir of Thomas Bewick. London: 1862. V. 64
A Memoir of Thomas Bewick. Newcastle-upon-Tyne, London: 1862. V. 63; 64
A Memoir of Thomas Bewick. 1887. V. 65
A Memoir of Thomas Bewick. 1924. V. 63
Memoir of Thomas Bewick. London: 1924. V. 62; 66
A Natural History of British Birds; Water Birds; Foreign Birds; Fishes; British Quadrupeds: Foreign Quadrupeds; Reptiles, Serpents and Insects. Alnwick: 1815. V. 62
Select Fables: With Cuts Designed and Engraved by Thomas and John Bewick. Newcastle: 1820. V. 66; 67
Ten Working Drawing Reproductions Shown with Impressions of the Corresponding Drawings. Chicago: 1972. V. 63; 65
21 Engravings. St. Charles: 1951. V. 64
The Watercolours and Drawings of Thomas Bewick and His Workshop. London: 1981. V. 63; 65
Wood Engravings of Thomas Bewick - Reproduced in Collotype. London: 1953. V. 63; 67

BEYE, CHARLES ROWAN
Epic and Romance in the Argonautica of Apollonius. Carbondale and Edwardsville: 1982. V. 66

BEYER, AUGUST
Memoriae Historico-Criticae Librorum Rariorum. Dresdae & Lipsiae: 1734. V. 63

BEYER, EDWARD
Album of Virginia.... 1980. V. 64

BEYER, HARTMANN
Qvaestiones Novae in Libellvm de Sphaera Ioannis de Sacro Bosco, in Gration Studiosae Iuuentutis Collectae ab Ariele Bicardo.... Parisiis: 1562. V. 63

BEYER, JOHANN HARTMANN
Stereometriae Inanivm Nova et Facilis Ratio, Geometricis Demonstrationibus Confirmata.... Frankfurt: 1602. V. 62

BEYER, W. F.
Deeds of Valor, How America's Heroes Won the Medal of Honor. Detroit: 1905. V. 65; 66

BEYLE, MARIE HENRI
Les Cenci. Paris: 1946. V. 62
Lucien Leuwen. London: 1931. V. 65

BEZA, THEODORE
Tatio De Repvdiis et Divortiis: In Qva Pieraeqve De Causis Matrimonialibus...Incidentes Controuersiae ex Verbo Dei Deciduntur. Genevae: 1569. V. 65
Tractatio de Plygamia...(with) Tractatio de Repudiis et Divortis.... Geneva: 1573. V. 64

BEZOUT, ETIENNE
Traite de Navigation. Paris: 1814. V. 66

BEZZERIDES, A. I.
Thieves' Market. New York: 1949. V. 63

BIAGI, GUIDO
The Book In Italy During the Fifteenth and Sixteenth Centuries Show in Fascimile Reproductions from the Most Famous Printed Volumes Collected.... New York: 1928. V. 64

BIANCHI, LEONARDO
The Functions of the Frontal Lobes. London: 1895. V. 65

BIANCHINI, FRANCESCO
Camera ed Inscrizioni Sepulcrali De' Liberti, Servi, et Ufficiali della Casa di Augusto.... Rome: 1727. V. 64

BIANCO, MARGERY WILLIAMS
The House that Grew Smaller. New York: 1931. V. 66

BIANCO, PAMELA
Little Houses Far Away. New York: 1951. V. 62

BIANCONI, GIOVANNI LODOVICO
Descrizione dei Circhi Particolarmente di Quello di Caracalla.... Rome: 1789. V. 64
Due Lettere di Fisica al Signor Marchese Scipione Maffei.... Venice: 1746. V. 66

BIAS, CLIFFORD
Trumpet Mediumship. How to Develop It. New York: 1945. V. 63

BIBB, GEORGE M.
An Exposition of the Meaning of the Clause in the Constitution of the United States.... Frankfurt: 1824. V. 63

BIBER, EDWARD
Christian Education, in a Course of Lectures, Delivered in London, in Spring 1829. London: 1830. V. 64

BIBER, GEORGE
E(dward) Henry Pestalozzi, and His Plan of Education.... London: 1831. V. 64

BIBIENA, BERNARDO DOVIZI DA
Calandra. Vinegia: 1562. V. 65

BIBLE. CHEROKEE - 1856
Genesis, or the First Book of Moses. Park Hill: 1856. V. 66

BIBLE. CHEROKEE - 1860
The New Testament. New York: 1860. V. 63

BIBLE. DUTCH - 1646
Biblia Sacra, Dat is de Geheele Heylighe Schrifture. Antwerp: 1657-1646. V. 67

BIBLE. EFIK - 1888
New Testament. Glasgow?: 1888. V. 65

BIBLE. ENGLISH
The Family Devotional Bible Containing the Authorised Version of the Old and New Testaments.... London. V. 64; 65
The Holy Bible. New York. V. 67

BIBLE. ENGLISH - 1583
The Bible. London: 1583-1584. V. 67

BIBLE. ENGLISH - 1589
The Text of the New Testament of Iesus Christ. London: 1589. V. 67

BIBLE. ENGLISH - 1591
The Whole Book of Psalmes. Collected into English.... London: 1591. V. 63

BIBLE. ENGLISH - 1598
The Text of the New Testament of Iesus Christ.... London: 1598. V. 65

BIBLE. ENGLISH - 1599
The Bible, That Is the Holy Scriptures Conteined in the Olde and Newe Testament. London: 1599. V. 67

BIBLE. ENGLISH - 1600
The New Testament of Jesus Christ Faithfuly Translated into English.... Antwerp: 1600. V. 64

BIBLE. ENGLISH - 1607
The Bible That Is, the Holy Scriptures Contained in the Old and New Testament. London: 1607. V. 64

BIBLE. ENGLISH - 1609
The Holie Bible Faithfully Translated into English Out of the Authentical Latin. Doway: 1609-1610. V. 62

BIBLE. ENGLISH - 1611
The Holy Bible.... London: 1611-1613. V. 66

BIBLE. ENGLISH - 1632
The Holy Bible Conteyning the Old Testament and the New. London: 1633. V. 66

BIBLE. ENGLISH - 1660
The Holy Bible, Containing the Old Testament and the New.... London: 1660. V. 62

BIBLE. ENGLISH - 1693
The Bible. London: 1693. V. 64

BIBLE. ENGLISH - 1709
The Holy Bible, Containing the Old Testament and the New. 1709. V. 65

BIBLE. ENGLISH - 1715
The Holy Bible Containing the Old Testament (only up to Malachi and Bound without the New Testament). London: 1715. V. 63

BIBLE. ENGLISH - 1720
The Whole Book of Psalms. London: 1720. V. 66

BIBLE. ENGLISH - 1761
The Psalms of David. New York: 1761?. V. 63

BIBLE. ENGLISH - 1769
The New Testament of Our Lord and Saviour Jesus Christ.... London: 1769. V. 62

BIBLE. ENGLISH - 1780
The Bible in Miniuture (sic), or a Concise History of the Old and New Testaments. London: 1780. V. 66

BIBLE. ENGLISH - 1785
The Holy Bible. Edinburgh: 1785. V. 67

BIBLE. ENGLISH - 1789
The Holy Bible. Cambridge: 1789. V. 67

BIBLE. ENGLISH - 1792
The Self-Interpreting Bible: Containing the Text of the Old and New Testament.... New York: 1792. V. 66

BIBLE. ENGLISH - 1793
The Holy Bible, Containing the Old and New Testaments.... Trenton: 1793-1794. V. 63; 64

BIBLE. ENGLISH - 1795
The Holy Bible. London: 1795. V. 63

BIBLE. ENGLISH - 1798
The Holy Bible.... Philadelphia: 1798. V. 64; 66

BIBLE. ENGLISH - 1800
(The Holy Bible) Embellished with Engravings from Pictures and Designs by the Most Eminent English Artists. London: 1800. V. 65

BIBLE. ENGLISH - 1804
The Holy Bible, containing the Old and New Testaments, and also the Apocrypha.... Birmingham: 1804-1805. V. 66

BIBLE. ENGLISH - 1811
The Holy Bible Abridged or the History of the Old and New Testament; for the Use of Children. Boston: 1811. V. 66
The Whole Book of Psalms. Oxford: 1811. V. 63

BIBLE. ENGLISH - 1813
The Devotional Diamond Pocket Bible.... London: 1813. V. 66
The Holy Bible Abridged or the History of the Old Testament and New Testament. Barnard: 1813. V. 62

BIBLE. ENGLISH - 1815
The Holy Bible, Containing the Old and New Testaments.... Oxford: 1815. V. 63

BIBLE. ENGLISH - 1817
The New Testament. London: 1817. V. 66

BIBLE. ENGLISH - 1821
The Holy Bible Containing the Old and New Testaments. Cambridge: 1821. V. 66
A Miniature History of the Holy Bible. Hartford: 1821. V. 63; 64

BIBLE. ENGLISH - 1823
The Holy Bible; Containing the Old and New Testaments.... Philadelphia: 1823. V. 62
The Holy Bible, Containing the Old and the New Testaments. Together with the Apocrypha. New York: 1823. V. 63; 66

BIBLE. ENGLISH - 1834
The Holy Bible, Containing the Old and New Testaments: Together with the Apocrypha.... Cooperstown: 1834. V. 66

BIBLE. ENGLISH - 1838
The Pictorial Bible: Being the Old and New Testaments According to the Authorized Version.... London: 1838. V. 64

BIBLE. ENGLISH - 1846
The Illuminated Bible, Containing the Old and New Testaments.... New York: 1846. V. 64

BIBLE. ENGLISH - 1847
Parables of Our Lord. London: 1847. V. 62

BIBLE. ENGLISH - 1848
The New Testament in English. London: 1848. V. 62
The New Testament of Our Lord and Saviour Jesus Christ.... Philadelphia: 1848. V. 64

BIBLE. ENGLISH - 1850
The Book of Ruth from the Holy Scriptures. London: 1850. V. 65

BIBLE. ENGLISH - 1851
New Testament...Literal Translation from the Syriac Peshito Version. New York: 1851. V. 63

BIBLE. ENGLISH - 1860
The New Testament. New York: 1860. V. 64

BIBLE. ENGLISH - 1861
The Psalms of David. Leeds: 1861. V. 64
The Psalms of David. (The Victoria Psalter). London: 1861. V. 62

BIBLE. ENGLISH - 1866
The Holy Bible. Paris: 1866. V. 64

BIBLE. ENGLISH - 1870
The Holy Bible, Containing the Old and New Testaments. London: 1870. V. 67

BIBLE. ENGLISH - 1880
Cassell's Family Bible.... London: 1880. V. 62

BIBLE. ENGLISH - 1897
The Book of Ruth and The Book of Esther. New York: 1897. V. 63
The Song of Solomon. London: 1897. V. 62; 67

BIBLE. ENGLISH - 1902
The Song of Songs. New York: 1902. V. 64

BIBLE. ENGLISH - 1903
The English Bible. Hammersmith: 1903-1905. V. 62

BIBLE. ENGLISH - 1909
The Song of Songs, Which is Solomon's. London: 1909. V. 65

BIBLE. ENGLISH - 1911
The Holy Bible Containing the Old and New Testament and the Apocrypha. London: 1911. V. 65
The Sermon on the Mount. London: 1911. V. 62; 67

BIBLE. ENGLISH - 1918
The Book of Job. East Sheen: 1918. V. 62

BIBLE. ENGLISH - 1922
The Song of Songs, Being Love Lyrics from Ancient Palestine. 1922. V. 62

BIBLE. ENGLISH - 1923
The Book of Ruth. London: 1923. V. 62; 64; 66; 67

BIBLE. ENGLISH - 1924
Genesis. London: 1924. V. 63
The Holy Bible, reprinted According to the Authorised Version 1611. Together with the Apocrypha. London: 1924-1925. V. 64; 66
The Holy Bible Reprinted According to the Authorised Version...1611. (with) The Apocrypha. London: 1925-1927-1924. V. 65
The Sermon on the Mount. San Francisco: 1924. V. 64

BIBLE. ENGLISH - 1925
The Birth of Christ from the Gospel According to Saint Luke. Waltham St. Lawrence: 1925. V. 64
Samson and Delilah. From the Book of Judges According to the Authorized Version. Waltham St. Lawrence: 1925. V. 64; 67
The Song of Songs called by Many the Canticle of Canticles. Waltham St. Lawrence: 1925. V. 62; 65; 66

BIBLE. ENGLISH - 1926
Passo Domini Nostri Jesu Christi: Being the 26th and 27th Chapters of Saint Matthew's Gospel from the Latin Text. Waltham St. Lawrence: 1926. V. 65

BIBLE. ENGLISH - 1930
The Sermon on the Mount. From the Gospel of St. Matthew. Sussex: 1930. V. 65
The Song of Solomon. Jerusalem: 1930. V. 62

BIBLE. ENGLISH - 1931
Canticum Canticorum Salomonis. 1931. V. 65

BIBLE. ENGLISH - 1932
Ecclesiasticus. Chelsea: 1932. V. 65
The Wisdom of Jesus The Son of Sirach Commonly Called Ecclesiasticus. Chelsea: 1932. V. 62; 64; 65

BIBLE. ENGLISH - 1933
The Lamentations of Jeremiah. Newtown: 1933. V. 62

BIBLE. ENGLISH - 1934
The Book of Ruth. Flansham: 1934. V. 62; 63; 64; 66
Ecclesiastes or the Preacher. Waltham St. Lawrence: 1934. V. 64

BIBLE. ENGLISH - 1936
The Song of Songs. Waltham St. Lawrence: 1936. V. 67

BIBLE. ENGLISH - 1939
The New Testament Translated by William Tyndale 1534.... London: 1939. V. 64

BIBLE. ENGLISH - 1941
Ecclesiastes. Cambridge: 1941. V. 62; 65

BIBLE. ENGLISH - 1944
The Twenty-Third Psalm. New York: 1944. V. 63; 64

BIBLE. ENGLISH - 1946
Bible in English. The Book of Job. 1946. V. 62

BIBLE. ENGLISH - 1949
The Holy Bible, Containing the Old and New Testaments.... Cleveland and New York: 1949. V. 65; 67

BIBLE. ENGLISH - 1950
The Song of Songs. 1950. V. 67

BIBLE. ENGLISH - 1955
The Newe Testamente. 1955. V. 65

BIBLE. ENGLISH - 1958
The New Testament of Our Lord and Saviour Jesus Christ. London and New York: 1958. V. 63

BIBLE. ENGLISH - 1962
The Holy Gospel According to Mathew, Mark, Luke and John. Verona: 1962. V. 62; 65

BIBLE. ENGLISH - 1963
The Book of Proverbs. New York: 1963. V. 62
The Holy Bible. The Authorized or King James Version of 1611, Now Reprinted with the Apocrypha. London: 1963. V. 62; 64; 65; 67

BIBLE. ENGLISH - 1965
Ecclesiastes, or the Preacher in the King James Translation of the Bible. New York: 1965. V. 63
The Twenty-Third Psalm. Worcester: 1965. V. 63

BIBLE. ENGLISH - 1974
The Book of Kells. Reproductions from the Manuscript in Trinity College. New York: 1974. V. 63

BIBLE. ENGLISH - 1977
The Sermon on the Mount. Oxford: 1977. V. 63; 64

BIBLE. ENGLISH - 1979
The Book of the Prophet Isaiah in the King James Version. London: 1979. V. 63
The Book of the Prophet Isaiah in the King James Version. New York: 1979. V. 62; 64; 66

BIBLE. ENGLISH - 1989
The First Book of Moses, Called Genesis. The King James Version. New York: 1989. V. 63; 65

BIBLE. ENGLISH - 1992
Ecclesiastes. 1992. V. 64
Words of the Teacher. Selections from Ecclesiastes. Colorado: 1992. V. 64

BIBLE. ENGLISH - 1995
The Song of Songs. London: 1995. V. 62

BIBLE. ENGLISH - 1996
The Book of Ruth. London: 1996. V. 62; 64
From the Revelation of St. John the Divine. Berkeley: 1996. V. 64

BIBLE. ENGLISH - 1997
The Book of Job. Market Drayton: 1997. V. 64

BIBLE. ENGLISH - 1999
The Holy Bible. New York: 1999. V. 66
The Holy Bible Containing All the Books of the Old and New Testaments. North Hatfield: 1999. V. 67

BIBLE. FRENCH - 1608
In Canticum Canticorum Salomonis. Paris: 1608. V. 67

BIBLE. FRENCH - 1668
Le Nouveau Testament de Notre Seigneur Jesus Christ.... Mons: 1668. V. 66

BIBLE. FRENCH - 1931
Cantique des Cantiques de Salomon. Paris: 1931. V. 64

BIBLE. FRENCH - 1952
Cantique Des Cantiques. Paris: 1952. V. 62

BIBLE. GERMAN - 1793
Biblia das ist: die Ganze Gittliche Heilige Schrift, Alten und Neuen Testaments.... Minden: 1793-1801. V. 63

BIBLE. GREBO - 1880
St. Mark's Gospel. 1880. V. 63

BIBLE. GREEK - 1516
Novum Instrumentum Omne, Diligenter ab ERasmo Roterodamo, Recognitum & Emendatum.... Basel: 1516. V. 63

BIBLE. GREEK - 1550
Novum Iesu Christi D. N. Testament. Lutetiae: 1550. V. 66

BIBLE. GREEK - 1569
Noveum Testamentum. Paris: 1569-1568. V. 62

BIBLE. GREEK - 1617
E Kaine Diatheke (Greek). Novum Testamentum. Geneva: 1617. V. 66

BIBLE. GREEK - 1632
(Greek type) Novum Testamentum. Cambridge: 1632. V. 62

BIBLE. GREEK - 1670
'E Kaine Diatheke (Greek). Novum Testamentum (Graecum). Amsterdam: 1670. V. 66

BIBLE. GREEK - 1685
Novum Testamentum. Amsterdam;: 1685. V. 66

BIBLE. GREEK - 1800
H. Kainh Iaokhk, Novum Testamentum. Wigorniae: 1800. V. 63

BIBLE. GREEK - 1843
(Greek Letter) Novum Testmaentum Graecum Edition. London: 1843. V. 65

BIBLE. GREEK - 1886
The New Testament in the Original Greek. New York: 1886. V. 63

BIBLE. HAWAIIAN - 1860
The New Testament. New York: 1860. V. 63

BIBLE. HEBREW - 1834
Bible. Leipzig: 1834. V. 67

BIBLE. HIEROGLYPHIC - 1791
A Curious Hieroglyphick Bible; or Select Passages in the Old and New Testaments, Represented with Emblematical Figures.... London: 1791. V. 67

BIBLE. HIEROGLYPHIC - 1855
A New Hieroglyphic Bible. Boston: 1855. V. 62

BIBLE. ITALIAN - 1596
Il Nuovo Testamento di Jesu Christo Nostro Signore. 1596. V. 65

BIBLE. LATIN - 1480
Biblia. Venice: 1480. V. 64

BIBLE. LATIN - 1486
(Bible in Latin). Strassburg: 1486. V. 67

BIBLE. LATIN - 1491
(Bible in Latin). Basel: 1491. V. 67

BIBLE. LATIN - 1532
Biblia. Paris: 1532. V. 64

BIBLE. LATIN - 1533
Novvm Testamentum. Basileae: 1553. V. 66

BIBLE. LATIN - 1534
Biblia. Breves in Eadem Annotationes, Ex Dictiss. Interpretationibus & Herbraeorum Commentariis. Antwerp: 1534. V. 67

BIBLE. LATIN - 1548
Testamenti Nova. Editio Vulgata. Lyons: 1548. V. 62; 65; 67

BIBLE. LATIN - 1587
Biblia Scara. Antwerp: 1587. V. 67

BIBLE. LATIN - 1602
Testamenti Veteris Biblia Sacra.... Hanau: 1602. V. 66; 67

BIBLE. LATIN - 1605
Testamenti Veteris et Novi Bibli Sacra.... Hanover: 1605. V. 65; 67

BIBLE. LATIN - 1729
Biblia Sacra. Parisiis: 1729-1745. V. 66

BIBLE. LATIN - 1961
Gutenberg Bible Facsimile. Paterson: 1961. V. 67

BIBLE. MANDARIN - 1905
New Testament (Luke). Shanghai: 1905. V. 65

BIBLE. MANX - 1819
Yv Vible Casherick ny yn Chenn Chonaant.... London: 1819. V. 62

BIBLE. MICMAC - 1863
Ae Buk Ov Samz (The Book of Psalms). Bath: 1863. V. 66

BIBLE. MICMAC - 1870
The Book of Exodus in MicMac. Halifax: 1870. V. 66

BIBLE. MICMAC - 1871
Pela Kesagunoodumumkawa Tan Tula Ukskumamenoo Westowoolkw Sasoogoole Clistawit Ootcnink...(The Gospel According to St. Mathew in MicMac.). Halifax: 1871. V. 66

BIBLE. MPONGWE - 1850
The Gospel of Matthew in the Mpongwe Language. Gabon: 1850. V. 66

BIBLE. POLYGLOT - 1516
Psalterium, Hebreum, Grecum, Arabicum & Chaldeum.... Genoa: 1516. V. 63

BIBLE. POLYGLOT - 1558
Biblia Sacra Veteris & Novi Testamenti Iuxta Vulgatum, Ovam Dicvnt.... Parisiis: 1558. V. 67

BIBLE. POLYGLOT - 1570
(Title in Greek, then): Novvm Textamentvm Iesv Christi Filii Del, Ex Versione Erasmi. Basileae: 1570. V. 66

BIBLE. POLYGLOT - 1571
The Gospels of the Fower Evangelistes Translated in the Olde Saxons Tyme Out of Latin Into the Vulgare Toung of the Saxons. London: 1571. V. 66

BIBLE. POLYGLOT - 1584
Biblia Hebraica. Eorundem Latina Interpretatio Xantis Pagnini Lucensis & Quorum Dam Aliorum Collato Studio, ad Hebraicam Dictionem Diligentissime Expensa...(Novum Testamentum Graecum, cum Vulgata Interpretatione Latina Graeci Contextu Lineis Inserta...). Antwerp: 1584. V. 62

BIBLE. POLYGLOT - 1602
Psaltervm Harmonicvm. Nuremberg: 1602. V. 64

BIBLE. POLYGLOT - 1710
Biblia Pentapla, Das ist: Die Bucher der Heiligen Schrift. Das Alten und Neuen Testaments, Nach funf-facher Deutscher Verdolmetschung.... Wandsbeck and Gottorf: 1710-1712. V. 62

BIBLE. POLYGLOT - 1845
The English Version of the Polyglot Bible Containing the Old and New Testament. Portland: 1845. V. 67

BIBLE. POLYGLOT - 1857
Parabola de Seminatore ex Evangelio Matthaei, in LXXII Europeas Linguas. London: 1857. V. 65

BIBLE. POLYGLOT - 1990
The Song of Songs. (Hebrew and English). Woodmere: 1990. V. 64

BIBLE. SWEDISH - 1851
New Testament. Stockholm: 1851. V. 65

BIBLE. TURKISH - 1827
The New Testament. Paris: 1827. V. 62

BIBLE. WELSH - 1799
Y Bibl Cyssegr-lan; sef, yr hen Testament a'r Newydd...(Preceded by) Hyfforddiadau i ymddygiad defosiynol a gweddus...a appwyntiwd gan eglwys loegr...(and) Llyfr Gweddi Gyffredin..(Followed by) Llyfr y Psalmau.... Rhydychen (i.e. Oxford): 1799. V. 66

BIBLIANDER, THEODORE
Temporum a Condito Mundo Usque ad Ultimam Ipsius Aetatem Supputatio, Partitio' que Exactior. Universae Quidem Historiae Divinae, Ecclesiasticae & Exterea Latinarum, Grecorum Aegyptiorum, Chaldaeorum, Germanorum & Aliarum Gentium Accomodata.... Basiliae: 1558. V. 66

THE BIBLIOGRAPHER. A Journal of Book-Lore. London: 1881. V. 66

BIBLIOGRAPHICA. Papers on Books, Their History and Art. London: 1895-1897. V. 66

BIBLIOGRAPHICAL SOCIETY OF AMERICA
Papers of the Bibliographical Society of America. New York: 1945-1988. V. 62; 63; 64

BIBLIOGRAPHICAL SOCIETY, LONDON.
Occasional Papers 1-8. London: 1958-1994. V. 62

BIBLIOGRAPHY of American Literature. Volume Two. New Haven;: 1957. V. 63

BIBLIOGRAPHY of Captain James Cook, R.N., F.R.S., Circumnavigator. Sydney: 1970. V. 62

A BIBLIOGRAPHY of the Writings of Harvey Cushing Prepared on the Occasion of His Seventieth Birthday.... Springfield: 1939. V. 64; 66

A BIBLIOGRAPHY of the Writings of Harvey Cushing Prepared on the Occasion of His Seventieth Birthday.... Park Ridge: 1993. V. 67

BIBLIOPHILE SOCIETY
Tenth Year Book of the Bibliophile Society. Boston: 1911. V. 63

BIBLIOTHEQUE Raphael Esmerian. Paris: 1972-1974. V. 65

BICARDUS, ARIEL
Quaestiones Novae in Libellm de Sphaera Ionnis de Sacro Bosco, in Gratia Studio sae Iuuen Tutis Collectae ab Ariele Bicardo.... Paris: 1552. V. 65

BICHAT, MARIE FRANCOIS XAVIER
Anatomie Generale, Appliquee a la Physiologie et a la Medecine. Paris: 1801. V. 65
Recherches Physiologiques sur la Vie et la Mort. Paris: 1822. V. 67
Traite des Membranes en General et de Diverse Membranes en Particulier. Paris: 1800. V. 64
Traite des Membranes en General, et de Diverses Membranes en Particulier.... Paris: 1802. V. 65

BICKEL, LENNARD
Shackleton's Forgotten Argonauts. South Melbourne: 1982. V. 65

BICKERDYKE, J.
Angling for Coarse Fish. 1922. V. 67
The Book of the All Round Angler. 1888. V. 65; 67

BICKERDYKE, JOHN
The Curiosities of Ale and Beer. London: 1886. V. 66

BICKERSTAFF, LAURA M.
Pioneer Artists of Taos. Denver: 1955. V. 62
Pioneer Artists of Taos. Denver: 1983. V. 63

BICKERSTETH, M.
Japan As We Saw It. London: 1893. V. 64

BICKHAM, GEORGE
The British Monarchy: or, a New Chorographical Description of all the Dominions Subject to the King of Great Britain Comprehending the British Isles, The American Colonies, The Electoral States, The African and Indian Settlements. London: 1748-1749. V. 64
Deliciae Britannicae; or the Curiosities of Kensington, Hampton Court and Windsor Castle Delineated.... London: 1755. V. 62; 66
A Description of All the Cities and Borough Towns. 1740. V. 67
The Drawing and Writing Tutor. London: 1760?. V. 66
The Universal Penman, or the Art of Writing Made Useful.... London: 1743. V. 65

BICKHAM, WARREN STONE
Operative Surgery Covering the Operative Technic Involved in the Operations of General and Special Surgery. Philadelphia: 1930. V. 66; 67

BICKMORE, ALBERT S.
Travels in the East Indian Archipelao. London: 1868. V. 64

BICKNELL, F.
Twelve Views of Bognor. Bognor: 1869. V. 62; 66

THE BICYCLE Boy. New York: 1896. V. 63

DIDAL, LILLIAN H.
Pisacah - a Place of Plenty. El Paso: 1995. V. 66
The Run of the Elk - a Biography of Angie Lydia Hendrix Cleve. El Paso: 1996. V. 66

BIDART, FRANK
The Book of the Body. New York: 1977. V. 63; 64
Golden State. New York: 1973. V. 67

BIDDLE, ELLEN M.
Reminiscences of a Soldier's Wife. Philadelphia: 1907. V. 63; 66; 67

BIDDLE, GEORGE
Tahitian Journal. N.P: 1968. V. 66

BIDDLE, NICHOLAS
The Journals of the Expedition Under the Command of Lewis and Clark. New York: 1962. V. 67

BIDDLE, RICHARD
Captain Hall in America. Philadelphia: 1830. V. 66

BIDDLE, TYRREL E.
The Corinthian Yachtsman, or Hints on Yachting. London: 1886. V. 63
Hints to Beginners in Amateur Yacht Designing.... London: 1890. V. 67

BIDDLECOMBE, GEORGE
The Art of Rigging Containing an Explanation of Terms and Phrases and the Progressive Method of Rigging Expressly Adapted for Sailing Ships. Salem: 1925. V. 63; 64

BIDEN, CHRISTOPHER
Naval Discipline. London: 1830. V. 62

BIDPAI
A Fable of Bidpai. West Burke: 1974. V. 63; 64

BIDWELL, CHARLES T.
The Isthmus of Panama. London: 1865. V. 65

BIDWELL, HARRY SHELFORD
The Outer Barrier, Hodbarrow Iron Mines, Millom, Cumberland. London: 1906. V. 65

BIDWELL, JOHN
Echoes of the Past.... Chico: 1914. V. 64; 67
A Journey to California with Observation About the Country, Climate and Route to this Country - a Day by Day Record of the Journey from May 18, 1841 to November 6, 1841. San Francisco: 1937. V. 65

BIEBER, RALPH
Marching With Army of the West 1846-1848. Glendale: 1936. V. 65
The Southwest Historical Series. Glendale: 1931-1943. V. 66

BIELER, LUDWIG
Ireland, Harbinger of the Middle Ages. 1963. V. 65

BIELFELD, JACOB FRIEDRICH, BARON
The Elements of Universal Erudition.... London: 1770. V. 63

BIELSCHOWSKY, A.
Lectures on Motor Anomalies. Hanover: 1940. V. 64; 67

BIER, AUGUST KARL GUSTAV
Hyperemia as a Therapeutic Agent.... Chicago: 1905. V. 63

BIERCE, AMBROSE
The Cynic's Word Book. New York: 1906. V. 62; 67
The Monk and the Hangman's Daughter. Chicago: 1892. V. 62; 64; 67
Seven Fables. 1986. V. 64
Tales of Soldiers and Civilians. San Francisco: 1891. V. 62
Ten Tales. London: 1925. V. 64

BIERSTADT, EDWARD HALE
Satan Was a Man. Garden City: 1935. V. 65

BIERSTADT, O. A.
The Library of Robert Hoe. New York: 1895. V. 62

BIESIUS, NICOLAUS
De Varietate Opinionum Liber Unus. Louvain: 1567. V. 62

THE BIG Book of Fables. New York: 1912. V. 64

BIG Book (Reading for Meaning RFM). Boston: 1950. V. 62

THE BIG Christmas Wonder Book a Real Feast!. London: 1937. V. 67

BIG Dogs, Little Dogs, Cats and Kittens. London: 1903. V. 63; 66

BIGELOW, H. B.
Fishes of the Western North Atlantic. New Haven: 1948-1989. V. 63
Fishes of the Western North Atlantic. Part 1. New Haven: 1948. V. 63
Fishes of the Western North Atlantic. Part 2. Sawfishes, Guitarfishes, Skates, Rays and Chimaeroids. New Haven: 1953. V. 63
Fishes of the Western North Atlantic. Part 3. Soft-Rayed Bony Fishes.... New Haven: 1963. V. 63

BIGELOW, H. E.
North American Species of Clitocybe. Berlin: 1982-1985. V. 66

BIGELOW, HENRY JACOB
Insensibility During Surgical Operations Produced by Inhalation. Boston: 1846. V. 62; 63; 64; 67

BIGELOW, JACOB
Florula Bostoniensis. Boston: 1814. V. 66
Florula Bostoniensis, a Collection of Plants of Boston and Its Vicinity. Boston: 1840. V. 67
A Treatise on the Materia Medica. Boston: 1822. V. 64

BIGELOW, JOHN
The Campaign of Chancellorsville: a Strategic and Tactical Study. New Haven: 1910. V. 63
On the Bloody Trail of Geronimo. Los Angeles: 1959. V. 64; 67

BIGGAR, H. P.
Voyages of Jacques Cartier. Ottawa: 1924. V. 67

BIGGER, RUBY VAUGHAN
My Miss Nancy. Macon: 1924. V. 67

BIGGERS, DON H.
Buffalo Guns and Barbed Wire. Austin: 1991. V. 65
From Cattle Range to Cotton Patch. Bandera: 1944. V. 63; 67
Shackelford County Sketches. Albany: 1974. V. 65

BIGGERS, EARL DERR
Charlie Chan Carries On. Indianapolis: 1930. V. 66
The Chinese Patriot. New York. V. 66
The House Without a Key. New York: 1925. V. 66
Love Insurance. Indianapolis: 1914. V. 66

BIGGLE, LLOYD
The Whirligig of Time. New York: 1979. V. 67

BIGGS, JAMES
The History of Don Francisco de Miranda's Attempt to Effect a Revolution in South American, in a Series of Letters. Boston: 1810. V. 66

BIGGS, JOSEPH
A Concise History of the Kehukee Baptist Association, From Its Original Rise to the Present Time. Tarborough: 1834. V. 63; 66

BIGGS, WILLIAM
The Military History of Europe, &c. From the Commencement of the War With Spain in 1739, to the Treaty of Aix-la-Chapelle in 1748.... London: 1755. V. 67

BIGG-WITHER, THOMAS P.
Pioneering in South Brazil: Three Years of Forest anf Prairie Life in the Province of Parana. New York: 1968. V. 65

BIGHAM, CLIVE
A Year in China 1899-1900. London: 1901. V. 64

BIGLAND, JOHN
The History of Spain, From the Earliest Period to the Close of the Year 1809. London: 1810. V. 67
Letters on Natural History; Exhibiting a View of the Power, Wisdom and Goodness of the Deity.... 1810. V. 64
A Natural History of Birds, Fishes, Reptiles and Insects. Philadelphia: 1831. V. 66; 67
A Natural History of Birds, Fishes, Reptiles and Insects. Philadelphia: 1844. V. 66

BIGMORE, F. C.
A Bibliography of Printing. London: 1969. V. 67

BIHALJI-MERIN, O.
Masters of Naive Art: a History. New York: 1970. V. 62; 65

BIJOU Picture of London, or, the Gems of the Metropolis. London. V. 66

LES BIJOUX des neuf Soeurs. Paris: 1884. V. 65

BIKEL, THEODORE
Theo. New York: 1994. V. 63

BILBO, JACK
An Autobiography. London: 1948. V. 66

BILDERBUCH Schoner Spiele. 1915. V. 64

BILES, JACK
Talk: Conversations with William Golding. New York: 1970. V. 62

BILLBERG, G. J.
Ekonomisk Botanik. Parts I and II. Stockholm: 1815-1816. V. 65

BILLET, ANNE LOUISE FRANCOISE DEFORME
Historical Memoirs of Stephanie Louise De Bourbon Coni. Newbern: 1801. V. 62

BILLINGS, ARCHIBALD
Practical Observations on Disease of the Lungs and Heart. London: 1832. V. 66

BILLINGS, JOHN S.
Circular No. 4 Report on Barracks and Hospitals with Descriptions of Military Posts. New York: 1974. V. 67
Circular No. 8 Report on the Hygiene of the United States With Descriptions of Military Posts and Circular No. 9 Report to the Surgeon General on Transportation of Sick and Wounded by Pack Animals. New York: 1974. V. 67
Selected Papers.... N.P: 1965. V. 63

BILLINGS, ROBERT WILLIAM
Architectural Illustrations, History and Description of Carlisle Cathedral. London: 1840. V. 66
The Baronial and Ecclesiastical Antiquites of Scotland. London: 1845-1852. V. 62; 66

BILLINGSLEY, JOHN
General View of the Agriculture in the County of Somerset.... London: 1794. V. 64

BILLMARK, CARL JOHAN
Aquarell-Lithograpier Och Tontryck. Stockholm: 1853-1864. V. 66
Chateau Royal d'Ulriksdal. Paris: 1871. V. 66
Voyage Pittoresque de Stockholm a Gothembourg. Stockholm. V. 64

BILLON, F. L.
Annals of St. Louis in the Territorial Days from 1804 to 1821. St. Louis: 1888. V. 64

BILLON, FRANCOIS DE
Le Fort Inexpugnable du Sexe Feminin. Paris: 1555. V. 66

BILLROTH, C. A. T.
Aphorismen zum Lehren und Lernen der Medicinisehen Wissenschaften. Vienna: 1886. V. 67

BILSON, THOMAS
The Survey of Christs Sufferings for Mans Redemption; and of His Descent to Hades or Hell for Our Deliverance.... London: 1604. V. 63

BILSTON, J.
Preparing for the Press, from an Ancient MS de Fucorum Ordinibus Continued by a Modern Hand.... 1752. V. 62

BINAGHI, O. A.
Opinion Upon the Edpidemic Cholera Morbus Observed at Warsaw.... New York: 1832. V. 62

BINDER, FRANK
Old World Japan, Legends of the Land of the Gods. London: 1895. V. 63

BINDON, DAVID
Some Thoughts on the Woollen Manufactures of England: in a Letter from a Clothier to a Member of Parliament. London: 1731. V. 63

BINET, ALFRED
The Development of Intelligence in Children. Baltimore: 1916. V. 66

BINFIELD, CLYDE
The History of the City of Sheffield 1843-1993. 1993. V. 65; 66

BING, ROBERT
Compendium of Regional Diagnosis in Affections of the Brain and Spinal Cord. St. Louis: 1927. V. 65
Compendium of Regional Diagnosis in Lesions of the Brain and Spinal Cord.... St. Louis: 1940. V. 65
A Textbook of Nervous Diseases for Students and Practising Physicians in Thirty Lectures. New York: 1915. V. 65

BINGAY, MALCOLM W.
Detroit Is My Home Town. Indianapolis: 1946. V. 67

BINGHAM, CLIFTON
The Airship in Animal Land. London: 1913. V. 65
The Animals Trip to Sea. London and New York: 1900. V. 63
Full of Fun. London: 1908. V. 66
Whirligig Pictures. London: 1898. V. 63

BINGHAM, DENIS ARTHUR
The Marriages of the Bourbons. London: 1890. V. 62

BINGHAM, HELEN
In Tamal Land. San Francisco: 1906. V. 63; 66

BINGHAM, HIRAM
A Residence of Twenty-One Years in the Sandwich Islands; or the Civil, Religious and Political History of Those Islands. Hartford: 1847. V. 65

BINGHAM, JOHN A.
Trial of the Conspirators for the Assassination of President Lincoln, etc., Argument of John A. Bingham, Special Judge Advocate.... Washington: 1865. V. 62

BINGHAM, JOSEPH
Origines Ecclesiasticae; or the Antiquities of the Christian Church. London: 1708-1722. V. 67
Origines Ecclesiasaticae: or the Antiquities of the Christian Church. London: 1710-1722. V. 63
The Works.... London: 1726. V. 62

BINGHAM, PEREGRINE
The Law and Practice of Judgments and Executions, Including Extents at the Suit of the Crown. London: 1815. V. 65

BINGLEY, W.
Animal Biography; or, Popular Zoology.... London: 1820. V. 66
Animal Biography...Authentic Anecdotes.... 1813. V. 66
Animal Biography...Authentic Anecdotes...of the Animal Creation. London: 1813. V. 63

BINGLEY, WILLIAM
Travels in North America. London: 1821. V. 63

BINION, CHARLES H.
An Introduction to El Paso's Scenic and Historic Landmarks. El Paso: 1970. V. 65

BINNEY, GEORGE
With Seaplane and Sledge in the Arctic. London: 1925. V. 63; 66

BINNEY, THOMAS
Sir Thomas Fowell Buxton, Bart. London: 1853. V. 67

BINNS, ARCHIE
Peter Skene Ogden: Fur Trader. Portland: 1967. V. 66

BINNS, RICHARD WILLIAM
A Century of Potting in the City of Worcester, Being the Story of the Royal Porcelain Works from 1751 to 1851.... Worcester: 1865. V. 64

BINSTOCK, R. C.
The Light of Home. New York: 1992. V. 66; 67

BINYON, LAURENCE
The Drawings and Engravings of William Blake. London: 1922. V. 62; 66
The Engraved Designs of William Blake. London: 1926. V. 62; 66
Landscape in English Art and Poetry. London: 1931. V. 63
The New World: Poems. London: 1918. V. 66
Painting in the Far East. London: 1923. V. 62; 63; 64; 66
Persephone. Oxford: 1890. V. 64

BIOGRAPHICAL and Genealogical History of Morris County, New Jersey. New York: 1899. V. 63; 66

THE BIOGRAPHICAL Encyclopedia of New Jersey of the Nineteenth Century. Philadelphia: 1877. V. 63; 66

BIOGRAPHICAL, Genealogical and Descriptive History of the First Congressional District of New Jersey. New York: 1900. V. 66

BIOGRAPHICAL Review...Containing...Life Sketches of Leading Citizens of Burlington and Camden Counties, New Jersey. Boston: 1897. V. 63; 66

BIOGRAPHICAL Sketches of the Hon. the Lord Provosts of Glasgow. Glasgow: 1883. V. 67

THE BIOLOGY of the Crustacea. 1982-1983. V. 66

BION, NICHOLAS
Traite de la Construction et Des Principaux Usages des Instruments de Mathematique. Paris: 1725. V. 63

BIOT, JEAN BAPTISTE
Traite Elementaire d'Astronomie Physique.... Paris et St. Petersbourg: 1810-1811. V. 65

BIOY-CASARES, ADOLFO
La Estatua Casera. Buenos Aires: 1936. V. 62
A Plan for Escape. New York: 1975. V. 62

BIRCH, A. G.
The Moon Terror and Other Stories. 1927. V. 62

BIRCH, ERIC
The Management of Coarse Fishing Waters. London: 1964. V. 67

BIRCH, H. CLARKSON
An Old Sailor's Yarn. Ipswich: 1914. V. 66

BIRCH, JAMES H.
History of the War in South Africa. New Brunswick: 1899. V. 67

BIRCH, JOHN
Examples of Labourer's Cottages, &c. London: 1871. V. 64

BIRCH, MARY
Letters Written by the Late Mrs. Birch of Barton Loge, in the Ninety-Ninth and Hundredth Years of Her Age. London: 1837?. V. 65

BIRCH, S.
Fac-similes of the Egyptian Relics, Discovered at Thebes in the Tomb of Queen Aah-Hotep (circa BC 1800) Exhibited in the International exhibition of 1862. London: 1863. V. 64

BIRCH, THOMAS
The Heads of Illustrious Persons of Great Britain. London: 1747-1752. V. 66
The History of the Royal Society of London.... London: 1756. V. 64
The History of the Royal Society of London.... Brussels: 1968. V. 62
The Life of Henry Prince of Wales, Eldest Son of King James I. London: 1760. V. 67
The Life of the Honourable Robert Boyle. London: 1744. V. 65
The Life of the Most Reverend Dr. John Tillotson, Lord Archbishop of Canterbury. London: 1752. V. 67
Memoirs of the Reign of Queen Elizabeth, from the Year 1581 till Her Death. London: 1754. V. 62; 67

BIRCHALL, EDWIN
The Lepidoptera of Ireland. London: 1867. V. 67

BIRCHLEY, S. W.
British Birds for Cages, Aviaries and Exhibition. London: 1909. V. 65

BIRD, ANNIE L.
Boise - the Peace Valley. Caldwell: 1934. V. 63; 66

BIRD, CYRIL KENNETH
The Changing Face of Britain. London: 1940. V. 63

THE BIRD *Fancier's Companion and Sure Guide.* 1762. V. 66

BIRD, G. W.
Wanderings in Burma. London: 1897. V. 64

BIRD, GEORGE FREDERICK
The Locomotives of the Great Northern Railway. London: 1910. V. 62

BIRD, JAMES
Cosmo, Duke of Tuscany: a Tragedy. London: 1822. V. 63
Dunwich: a Tale of the Splendid City. London: 1828. V. 66

BIRD, JAMES BARRY
The Laws Respecting Highways and Turnpike Roads. London: 1801. V. 66

BIRD, ROBERT MONTGOMERY
Nick of the Woods, or the Jibbenainosay. A Tale of Kentucky. Philadelphia: 1837. V. 64

BIRD, WILL R.
The Communication Trench. Amherst: 1933. V. 65

BIRDSONG, JAMES C.
Brief Sketches of the North Carolina State Troops in the War Between the States. Raleigh: 1894. V. 62; 63

BIRDWELL, CLEO
Amazons. New York: 1980. V. 63; 66
Amazons. Toronto: 1980. V. 66

BIRGE, JOHN KINGSLEY
The Bektashi Order of Dervishes. London: 1937. V. 64

BIRGE, JULIUS C.
The Awakening of the Desert. Boston: 1912. V. 67

BIRINGUCCIO, VANOCCIO
De La Pirotechnia. Venice: 1540. V. 67
The Pirotechnia.... New York: 1942. V. 62
La Pyrotechnie, ou Art du Feu, Contenant Dix Livres. Rouen: 1627. V. 62

BIRK, L. A.
The Paphiopedilum Grower's Manual. Santa Barbara: 1983. V. 67

BIRKBECK, MARY
An Epistle from the Quarterly Meeting for the County of York, Held at Leeds.... London: 1782. V. 65

BIRKBECK, MORRIS
Notes on a Journey in America, from the Coast of Virginia to the Territory of Illinois. London: 1818. V. 63; 66
Notes on a Journey through France, from Dieppe through Paris and Lyons, to the Pyrenees and Back through Toulouse, in July, August and September 1814.... London: 1815. V. 65

BIRKET-SMITH, K.
Ethnography of the Egedesminde District.... New York: 1976. V. 62
An Ethnological Sketch of Rennell Island. A Polynesian Outlier in Melanesia. Copenhagen: 1956. V. 62

BIRKETT, HENRY F.
The Story of Ulverston. Kendal: 1949. V. 63; 66

BIRKHOFF, GEORGE DAVID
Collected Mathematical Papers. New York: 1950. V. 65; 66

BIRKIN, ANDREW
J. M. Barrie and the Lost Boys. London: 1979. V. 67

BIRKMIRE, WILLIAM H.
Skeleton Construction in Buildings. New York: 1894. V. 67

BIRMINGHAM, G. A.
Irishmen All. 1913. V. 63

BIRNEY, EARLE
Down the Long Table. Toronto: 1955. V. 66

BIRNEY, HOFFMAN
Vigilantes. Philadelphia: 1929. V. 67

BIRNEY, JAMES G.
The American Churches, the Bulwarks of American Slavery. London: 1840. V. 63

BIRNIE, WILLIAM
The Blame of Kirk-Buriall Tending to Perswade Cemiteriall Civilitie. 1833. V. 67
The Blame of Kirk-Buriall Tending to Perswade Cemiteriall Civilitie. London: 1833. V. 62; 65

BIRRELL, AUGUSTINE
Frederick Locker-Sampson - a Character Sketch with a Small Selection from Letters Addressed to Him.... London: 1920. V. 62
Life of Charlotte Bronte. London: 1887. V. 66
Miscellanies. London: 1902. V. 65

BIRRELL, OLIVE M.
Justice Warren's Daughter: a Story of New England. London: 1883. V. 65

BIRTHS, *Marriages and Daths.* London: 1954. V. 63

BISBEE, WILLIAM HAYMOND
Through Four American Wars. The Impressions and Experience of Brigadier General William Haymond Bisbee. Boston: 1931. V. 67

BISCHOFF, ERNEST PHILIPP EDUARD
Microscopic Analysis of the Anastomoses Between the Cranial Nerves. Hanover: 1977. V. 66; 67

BISCHOFF, G. W.
Die Rhizokarpen und Lycopodeen, Organographisch, Phytonomisch und systematisch. Nurnberg: 1828. V. 66

BISCHOFF, HERMAN
Deadwood to the Big Horn 1877. Bismarck: 1931. V. 65

BISCHOFF, JAMES
Foreign Tariffs, their Injurious Effect on British Manufactures, Especially the Woollen Manufacture; with Proposed Remedies.... London: 1843. V. 63

BISCHOFF, WILLIAM N.
The Jesuits in Old Oregon. Caldwell: 1945. V. 64

BISGOOD, MARY
Powder and Jam. London: 1909. V. 65

BISHOP, ABRAHAM
Oration, in Honor of the Election of President Jefferson and the Peaceable Acquisition of Louisiana, Delivered at the National Festival in Hartford on the 11th of May, 1804. Hartford: 1804. V. 63; 66
An Oration on the Extent and Power of Political Delusion Delivered in New Haven...September 1800.... Newark: 1800. V. 66

BISHOP, C. K. K.
Notes on Church Organs. London: 1873. V. 62

BISHOP, CORTLANDT F.
The Cortlandt F. Bishop Library. New York: 1938-1939. V. 62

BISHOP, ELIZABETH
The Ballad of the Burglar of Babylon. New York: 1968. V. 65; 67
The Collected Prose. New York: 1984. V. 67
The Complete Poems. New York: 1969. V. 62; 63; 66
The Complete Poems 1927-1979. New York: 1983. V. 64
The Diary of Helena Morley. New York: 1957. V. 66
Geography III. New York: 1976. V. 62; 65; 66
North and South. Boston: 1946. V. 63
Poem. New York: 1973. V. 65
Poems. London: 1956. V. 64
Poems. North and South - a Cold Spring. Boston: 1955. V. 62; 64; 65
Questions of Travel. New York: 1965. V. 62; 65
Selected Poems. London: 1967. V. 62

BISHOP, FREDERICK
The Illustrated London Cookery Book.... London: 1852. V. 63

BISHOP, GEORGE
Every Woman Her Own Lawyer. A Private Guide in All Matters of Law, of Essential Interest to Women, and by the Aid of Which Every Female May... Understand Her Legal Course and Redress and Be Her Own Legal Adviser.... New York: 1858. V. 66

BISHOP, H. H.
Pictorial Architecture in Greece and Italy. London: 1887. V. 66
Pictorial Architecture of the British Isles. London: 1885. V. 66

BISHOP, ISABELLA LUCY BIRD
Among the Tibetans. New York: 1894. V. 64
The Englishwoman in America. London: 1856. V. 65
The Golden Chersonese and the Way Thither. London: 1883. V. 66
Journeys in Persia and Kurdistan.... London: 1891. V. 64
Korea and Her Neighbours; a Narrative of Travel with an Account of the Vicissitudes and Position of the Country. London: 1905. V. 64
A Lady's Life in the Rocky Mountains. New York: 1879-1880. V. 62; 65
Unbeaten Tracks in Japan. London: 1880. V. 64
Unbeaten Tracks in Japan. London: 1900. V. 66
Unbeaten Tracks in Japan.... London: 1990. V. 65
The Yangtze Valley and Beyond; an Account of Journeys in China.... London: 1899. V. 64

BISHOP, JOEL P.
Commentaries on the Law of Marriage and Divorce and Evidence in Matrimonial Suits. Boston: 1856. V. 66

BISHOP, JOHN
Beautifull Blossomes, Gathered...from the Best Trees of All Kyndes, Divine, Philosophicall, Astronomicall, Cosmographical, Historical & Humane.... London: 1577. V. 64
Pierce Egan's Account of the Trial of Bishop, Williams and May, for Murder...Including the Confessions of the Murderers; Their Execution and Dissection.. London: 1831. V. 63

BISHOP, JOHN GEORGE
The Brighton Chain Pier: in Memoriam. Its History from 1823 to 1896.... Brighton: 1897. V. 65
A Peep Into the Past Brighton in the Olden Time, with Glances at the Present. Brighton: 1892. V. 67

BISHOP, JOHN PEALE
Minute Particulars. New York: 1935. V. 62

BISHOP, LEANDER J.
A History of American Manufactures from 1608 to 1860. Philadelphia: 1864. V. 63

BISHOP, LEO V.
The Fighting Forty-fifth, the Combat Report of an Infantry Division. Baton Rouge: 1946. V. 65

BISHOP, MATTHEW
The Life and Adventures of Matthew Bishop of Deddington in Oxfordshire. London: 1744. V. 67

BISHOP, NATHANIEL H.
Four Months in a Sneak-Box. Edinburgh: 1880. V. 62
Voyage of the Paper Canoe. Boston: 1878. V. 67

BISHOP, RACHEL P. F.
Farmer and Field Families of Virginia. Columbia: 1983. V. 67

BISHOP, ROBERT
Centuries and Styles of the American Chair 1640-1970. New York: 1972. V. 63

BISHOP, ROBERT H.
Outlines of a Course of Lectures on Logic, Delivered in the Transylvania University. Lexington: 1807. V. 64

BISHOP, S. C.
Handbook of Salamanders, the Salamanders of the United States, of Canada and Lower California. Ithaca: 1943. V. 62; 63

BISHOP, SAMUEL
Feriae Poeticae.... Londini: 1766. V. 63

BISHOP, WILLIAM A.
Winged Warfare. New York: 1918. V. 63

BISHOP, ZEALIA
The Curse of Yig. Sauk City: 1953. V. 62

BISIAK, E. H.
Buccaner Ballads. London: 1910. V. 67

BISLAND, ELIZABETH
The Life and Letters of Lafcadio Hearn. 1906. V. 67

BISPHAM, GEORGE T.
The Principles of Equity: a Treatise on the System of Justice Administered in Courts of Chancery. Philadelphia: 1878. V. 65

BISSELL, RICHARD
Say, Darling. London: 1957. V. 65

BISSET, JAMES
The Second and Improved Edition of the Descriptive Guide of Leamington Priors. Coventry: 1816. V. 66

BISSET, PETER
The Book of Water Gardening. New York: 1907. V. 67

BITAUBE, PAUL JEREMIE
Joseph, en neuf Chants. Paris: 1768. V. 66

BITTING, KATHERINE
Gastronomic Bibliography. London: 1981. V. 66
Gastronomic Bibliography. Mansfield: 1995. V. 66

BIXBY-SMITH, SARAH
Adobe Days, a Book of California Memories. Cedar Springs: 1925. V. 64; 67

BIZARRI, PIETRO
Senatus Populique Genuensis Rerum...Historiae.... Antwerp: 1579. V. 66

BJORKMAN, FRANCES MAULE
Woman Suffrage: History Arguments and Results. New York: 1913. V. 67

BJORNSTROM, F.
Hypnotism: Its History and Present Development. New York: 1887. V. 67

BLAAUW, F. E.
A Monograph of the Cranes. Leiden and London: 1897. V. 63

BLAAUW, WILLIAM HENRY
The Barons' War Including the Battles of Lewes and Eversham. 1871. V. 64

BLACK, A.
Black's Guide to England and Wales Containing Plans of All the Principal Cities, Charts, Maps and Views and List of Hotels. Edinburgh: 1869. V. 67

THE BLACK Art; or Magic Made Easy. New York: 1869. V. 65

BLACK, CYRUS
Historical Record of the Posterity of William Black, Who Settled in This Country in the Year Seventeen Hundred and Seventy-five.... Amherst: 1885. V. 64

BLACK, DAVIDSON
Asia and the Dispersal of Primates. Peking: 1925. V. 66; 67

BLACK, ELANDRA
The Gold Rush Song Book - a Compilation of Famous Songs by the Men Who Came to California to Mine for Gold in 1849. San Francisco: 1940. V. 66

BLACK, GEORGE F.
A Gypsy Bibliography. London: 1914. V. 62
A Gypsy Bibliography. 1971. V. 65

BLACK, HENRY C.
A Treatise on the Law of Judgments, Including the Doctrine of Res Judicata. St. Paul: 1891. V. 67

BLACK, JAMES
Conversations Between James Black, Esq. and Millar, the editor of the Monthly Miscellany.... Ayr: 1817. V. 65

BLACK, JOHN
Life of Torquato Tasso; with an Historical and Critical Account of His Writings. London: 1810. V. 62

BLACK, JOHN LOGAN
Crumbling Defenses, or Memoirs and Reminiscences of John Logan Black, Colonel CSA. Macon: 1960. V. 63

BLACK, JOSEPH
On Acid Humor Arising From Foods and On White Magnesia. Minneapolis: 1973. V. 63; 64

BLACK Magic and Music. N.P: 1983. V. 66

BLACK, MARGARET
Three Brothers and a Lady. London: 1947. V. 63

BLACK Panthers of the 66th Division. N.P: 1945?. V. 65

BLACK, PETER
The Surgical Art of Harvey Cushing. Park Ridge: 1992. V. 66; 67

BLACK, R. HARRISON
An Etymological and Explanatory Dictionary of Words Derived from the Latin.... London: 1825. V. 64

BLACK, ROBERT C.
Island in the Rockies - the History of Grand County Colorado to 1930. Boulder: 1969. V. 66

BLACK, ROBERT CLIFFORD
The Railroads of the Confederacy. Chapel Hill: 1952. V. 63

BLACK, SAMUEL
A Journal of a Voyage from Rocky Mountain Portage in Peace River to the Sources of Finlays Branch and North West Ward in Summer 1824. London: 1955. V. 65

BLACK, WILLIAM
The Beautiful Wretch. The Four Macnichols. The Pupil of Aurelius. London: 1881. V. 62
Macleod of Dare. London: 1879. V. 67
The Privileges of the Royal Burrows as Contained in Their Particular Right and the Ancient Laws and Records of Parliament, and Their General Convention.... Edinburgh: 1707. V. 66
Sabina Zembra. London: 1887. V. 66
A Short View of Our Present Trade and Taxes, Compared With What These Taxes May Amount to After the Union. Edinburgh?: 1706?. V. 65
The Strange Adventures of a Phaeton. London: 1874. V. 66; 67
Sunrise: a Story of These Times. London: 1881. V. 66
White Heather. London: 1885. V. 66
White Wings; a Yachting Romance. London: 1880. V. 67

BLACK, WILLIAM HENRY
History and Antiquities of the Worshipful Company of Leathersellers. London: 1871. V. 62; 66

BLACK, WINIFRED
Dope. The Story of the Living Dead. New York: 1928. V. 66

BLACKADDER, H. HOME
Observations on Phagedaena Gangranenosa. In Two Parts.... Edinburgh: 1818. V. 66; 67

BLACKBEARD, BILL
Sherlock Holmes in America. New York: 1981. V. 65; 66

BLACKBURN, HUGH, MRS.
Birds Drawn from Nature. Edinburgh: 1862. V. 62

BLACKBURN, I. W.
Illustrations of the Gross Morbid Anatomy of the Brain in the Insane. Washington: 1908. V. 66; 67
Intracranial Tumors Among the Insane. Washington: 1902. V. 67
Intracranial Tumors Among the Insane. Washington: 1903. V. 65

BLACKBURN, JANE
Birds Drawn from Nature. Edinburgh;: 1862. V. 66; 67

BLACKBURN, JOHN
Blow the House Down. London: 1970. V. 66
Broken Boy. London: 1959. V. 67
The Gaunt Woman. London: 1962. V. 67
Nothing But the Night. London: 1968. V. 66
A Scent of New Mown Hay. New York: 1958. V. 67
A Sour Apple. 1959. V. 62; 64; 66

BLACKBURN, PAUL
The Dissolving Fabric. Palma de Mallorca: 1955. V. 62; 64
Early Selected Y Mas. Poems. Los Angeles: 1972. V. 63
Gin: Four Journal Pieces. Mt. Horeb: 1970. V. 67
In, On, or About the Premises. London: 1968. V. 63
The Journals: Blue Mounds Entries. Mt. Horeb: 1971. V. 67
The Nets. New York: 1961. V. 62
The Omitted Journals. Mt. Horeb: 1983. V. 67
The Reardon Poems. Mt. Horeb: 1967. V. 64
The Selection of Heaven. Mt. Horeb: 1980. V. 66
Three Dreams and an Old Poem. Buffalo: 1970. V. 63

BLACKBURN, THOMAS
The Feast of the Wolf. London: 1971. V. 66

BLACKBURN, WILLIAM
One and Twenty: Duke Narrative and Verse 1924-1946. Durham: 1945. V. 65
Under Twenty-Five - Duke Narrative and Verse 1945-1962. Durham: 1963. V. 62

BLACKBURNE, FRANCIS
Considerations on the Present State of the Controversy Between the Protestants and Papists of Great Britain and Ireland. London: 1768. V. 66
Remarks on Johnson's Life of Milton. London: 1780. V. 62

BLACKBURNE, JOHN
The Register Book of Ingleby Juxta Grennow as Much as Is Extant in the Old Booke. Canterbury: 1889. V. 66

BLACKER, CARLOS PATON
Birth Control and the State: a Plea and a Forecast. London: 1926. V. 65

BLACKETT, T. OSWALD
An Essay on the Use of the Spirit Level, as Applied to Engineering and Other Purposes. Newcastle-upon-Tyne: 1838. V. 63

BLACKFORD, CHARLES M.
Annals of the Lynchburg Home Guard. Lynchburgh: 1891. V. 62; 63; 65
Campaign and Battle of Lynchburg, Va. Lynchburg: 1901. V. 63; 65
An Historical Sketch of the Book of Common Prayer. Lynchburg;: 1893. V. 62

BLACKFORD, W. W.
War Years with Jeb Stuart. New York: 1945. V. 66

BLACKFORD, WILLIAM M.
Lines to My Daughter Lucy Landon. Lynchburg: 1881. V. 62

BLACK HAWK
Autobiography of Ma-Ka-Tai-Me-She-Kia-Kiak or Black Hawk. St. Louis: 1882. V. 67

BLACKIE'S Children's Annual 1907. 1907. V. 66

BLACKIE'S Children's Annual. 19th Year. 1922. V. 65

BLACKIE'S Children's Annual. 28th Year. 1931. V. 65

BLACKIE'S Children's Annual. 31st Year. 1934. V. 65

BLACKIE'S Children's Annual. 34th Year. 1937. V. 67

BLACKIE'S Children's Annual. 36th Year. 1939. V. 67

BLACKMAN, RAYMOND V. B.
Jane's Fighting Ships 1953-1954. New York: 1954. V. 66

BLACKMAR, FRANK W.
Kansas: a Cyclopedia of State History, Embracing Events, Institutions, Industries, Counties, Cities, Towns, Prominent Persons, Etc. Chicago: 1912. V. 66
The Life of Charles Robinson - The First State Governor of Kansas. Topeka: 1902. V. 64; 67

Spanish Institutions of the Southwest. Baltimore: 1891. V. 64

BLACKMORE, HOWARD L.
Guns and Rifles of the World. London: 1965. V. 67

BLACKMORE, JOHN
Views on the Newcastle and Carlisle Railway, from Original Drawings by J. W. Carmichael, with Details by John Blackmore. Newcastle: 1836-1838. V. 62

BLACKMORE, RICHARD
The Lay-Monastery. London: 1714. V. 65
Prince Arthur: an Heroick Poem. London: 1695. V. 62
A Treatise of Consumptions and Other Distempers Belonging to the Breast and Lungs. London: 1724. V. 64

BLACKMORE, RICHARD DODDRIDGE
Fringilla; or, Tales in Verses. Cleveland: 1895. V. 63; 64
Perlycross; a Tale of the Western Hill. London: 1894. V. 67

BLACKMUR, R. P.
The Double Agent: Essays in Craft and Elucidation. New York: 1935. V. 63
From Jordan's Delight. New York: 1937. V. 62

BLACKNER, JOHN
The History of Nottingham, Embracing Its Antiquities, Trade and Manufactures, from the Earliest Authentic Records to the Present Period. Nottingham: 1815. V. 65

BLACK'S General Atlas of the World, Embracing the Latest Discoveries, New Boundaries and Other Changes Accompanied by Introductory Letterpress and Index. Edinburgh: 1879. V. 65

BLACK'S Picturesque Guide to the Trossachs, Loch Catrine, Loch Lomond and Central Touring District of Scotland. Edinburgh: 1853. V. 62

BLACK'S Picturesque Guide to Yorkshire. Edinburgh: 1868. V. 65
BLACK'S Picturesque Guide to Yorkshire. Edinburgh: 1871. V. 62; 65

BLACKSTOCK, CHARITY
Dewey Death. London: 1956. V. 62

BLACKSTONE, ORIN
Index to Jazz I-IV. New Orleans: 1947. V. 67

BLACKSTONE, WILLIAM
Commentaries on the Laws of England. Oxford: 1766-1769. V. 62; 65
Commentaries on the Laws of England. Oxford: 1770. V. 67
Commentaries on the Laws of England. London: 1773. V. 63
Commentaries on the Laws of England. London: 1778. V. 62
Commentaries on the Laws of England. Oxford: 1778. V. 62
Commentaries on the Laws of England. London: 1783. V. 66
Commentaries on the Laws of England. London: 1876. V. 62
Commentaries on the Laws of England. Philadelphia: 1882. V. 62
Law Tracts. Oxford: 1762. V. 62
Tracts Chiefly Relating to the Antiquities and Laws of England. Oxford: 1771. V. 66
A Treatise on the Law of Descents in Fee-Simple. Oxford: 1759. V. 65

BLACKWALL, ANTHONY
An Introduction to the Classics: Containing a Short Discourse on Their Excellancies.... London: 1737. V. 64

BLACKWALL, J.
A History of the Spiders of Great Britain and Ireland. London: 1861-1864. V. 62; 66

BLACKWELDER, F
Research in China. Washington: 1907. V. 65; 66

BLACKWELDER, R. E.
Checklist of the Coleopterous Insects of Mexico, Central America, the West Indies and South America. 1982. V. 63; 66
Taxonomy, a Text and Reference Book. New York: 1967. V. 63

BLACKWELL, ALICE STONE
Lucy Stone, Pioneer of Woman's Rights. Boston: 1930. V. 65

BLACKWELL, ANNA
Poems. London: 1853. V. 65

BLACKWELL, ELISABETH
Herbarivm Blackwellianvm. Norimbergae: 1757. V. 66

BLACKWELL, ROBERT
Original Acrostics on All the States and Presidents of the United States.... Nashville: 1861. V. 63
Original Acrostics, on Some of the Southern States, Confederate Generals and Various Other Persons and Things. Baltimore: 1873. V. 66

BLACKWELL, SARAH ELLEN
A Military Genius. Washington: 1891. V. 65

BLACKWELL, THOMAS
An Enquiry into the Life and Writings of Homer. London: 1735. V. 62; 63
An Enquiry Into the Life and Writings of Homer. London: 1736. V. 64; 66

BLACKWOOD, ALGERNON
Jimbo. 1909. V. 62; 64; 66

BLACKWOOD, JOHN
A Selection from the Obituary Notices of the Late John Blackwood, Editor of Blackwood Magazine. Edinburgh: 1880. V. 67

BLACOW, RICHARD
Lancaster Summer Assizes 1821. The Trial of the Rev. Richard Blacow, for Libels on Her Late Majesty.... London: 1821?. V. 63
A Letter to William King, LL.D. Principal of St. Mary Hall in Oxford. London: 1755. V. 62; 65
The Substance of a Discourse Preached in St. Mark's Church, Liverpool, on...Nov. 26th 1821. On the Aspect of the Times. London: 1821?. V. 63

BLADES, WILLIAM
The Enemies of Books. London: 1880. V. 67

BLAGDON, F. W.
The Historical Memento Representing the Different Scenes of Public Rejoicing.... London: 1814. V. 62; 66

BLAGG, C. J.
A History of the North Staffordshire Hounds and Country 1825 to 1902. London: 1902. V. 62; 67

BLAGG, THOMAS M.
Abstracts of Nottinghamshire Marriage Licences. London: 1930-1935. V. 65

BLAGROVE, WILLIAM
The Elements of Chess; a Treatise Combining Theory with Practice.... Boston: 1805. V. 64; 66

BLAIKIE, FRANCIS
On the Conversion of Arable Land Into Pasture, and On Other Rural Subjects. London: 1817. V. 62; 66
On the Management of Farm-Yard Manure, and On Other Rural Subjects.... London: 1821. V. 62
A Treatise on the Management of Hedges and Hedge-Row Timber.... London: 1821. V. 62

BLAIKIE, JOHN ARTHUR
Madrigals, Songs and Sonnets. London: 1870. V. 65

BLAINE, DELABERE P.
An Encyclopaedia of Rural Sports or Complete Account of Hunting, Shooting, Fishing Racing &c &c. London: 1870. V. 67

BLAINE, JAMES G.
Twenty Years of Congress. Norwich: 1884. V. 65

BLAIR, DAVID
Outlines of Political Economy. Boston: 1828. V. 65
The Universal Preceptor, Being a General Grammar of Arts, Sciences and Useful Knowledge. Philadelphia: 1817. V. 65

BLAIR, F. C. HUNTER
Charters of the Abbey of Crosraguel. Edinburgh: 1886. V. 62

BLAIR, GORDON
Father Tabb: Poet, Priest, Soldie, Wit. Richmond: 1940. V. 64

BLAIR, HUGH
Lectures on Rhetoric and Belles Letters. Philadelphia: 1784. V. 67
Sermons. London. V. 62

BLAIR, JOHN
The Chronology and History of the World, From the Creation to the Year of Christ, 1790. London: 1790. V. 65

BLAIR, MARY ELLEN
Margaret Tafoya: a Tewa Potter's Heritage and Legacy. West Chester: 1986. V. 63

BLAIR, ROBERT
The Grave. London: 1808. V. 62
The Grave. London: 1870. V. 64
Scientific Aphorisms, Being the Outline of an Attempt to Establish Fixed Principles of Science.... Edinburgh and London: 1827. V. 65

BLAIR, SAMUEL
The Great Glory of God, Which is Display'd in the Gospel of Christ, with Its Sanctifying Efficacy Upon the Souls of Men. Boston: 1739. V. 63

BLAIR, WALTER A.
A Raft Pilot's Log: a History of the Great Rafting Industry on the Upper Mississippi 1840-1915. Cleveland: 1930. V. 64; 66

BLAKE, E. R.
Manual of Neotropical Birds. Volume I Sphenischidae (Penguins) to Laridae (Gulls). Chicago: 1977. V. 66; 67

BLAKE, EUPHEMIA VALE
Arctic Experiences: Containing Capt. George E. Tyson's Wonderful Drift on the Ice-floe, a History of the Polaris Expedition, the Cruise of the Tigress and Rescue of the Polaris Survivors. New York: 1874. V. 62; 65

BLAKE, FORRESTER
Riding the Mustang Trail. New York: 1935. V. 67

BLAKE, HENRY ARTHUR
China. London: 1909. V. 65

BLAKE, HERBERT CODY
Blake's Western Stories. N.P: 1929. V. 62

BLAKE, J. L.
Conversations on Vegetable Physiology.... Boston: 1830. V. 62

BLAKE, JOHN
The Private Instructor, and Young Gentleman's Pocket Companion.... Trenton: 1815. V. 63; 66

BLAKE, JOHN B.
A Short Title Catalogue of Eighteenth Century Printed Books in the National Library of Medicine. Bethesda: 1979. V. 65

BLAKE, JOSEPH A.
The Relation of the Trachea and Bronchi to the Thoracic Walls, as Determined by the Rontgen Rays. New York: 1899. V. 67

BLAKE, MRS.
The Realities of Freemasonry. London: 1879. V. 65

BLAKE, NELSON M.
William Mahone of Virginia. Soldier and Political Insurgent. Richmond: 1935. V. 65

BLAKE, NICHOLAS
Head of a Traveller. London: 1949. V. 65

BLAKE, PETER
An American Synagogue for Today and Tomorrow: a Guide Book to Synagogue Design and Construction. New York: 1954. V. 62; 65

BLAKE, S. F.
Geographical Guide to the Floras of the World. Washington: 1942-1961. V. 67

BLAKE, W. P.
Catalogue of Books for Sale. Boston: 1798. V. 62

BLAKE, WILLIAM
Auguries of Innocence. New York: 1968. V. 65
Auguries of Innocence. Providence: 1997. V. 62
Blake's Pencil Drawings: Second Series. N.P: 1956. V. 63; 64; 66
Blake's Pencil Drawings. Second Series. London: 1956. V. 62; 65; 66
The Book of Los. London: 1976. V. 67
The Book of Thel. London: 1965. V. 62
The Book of Urizen. London: 1958. V. 64; 66
The Complete Portraiture of William and Catherine Blake. London: 1977. V. 65
Illustrations of the Book of Job. London: 1825-1826. V. 64
The Illustrations of William Blake for Thornton's Virgil.... London: 1937. V. 64
Jerusalem. London: 1952. V. 62
The Land of Dreams: Twenty Poems by William Blake. New York: 1928. V. 65
The Letters of William Blake. London: 1968. V. 62
The Marriage of Heaven and Hell. London: 1960. V. 64; 66
The Marriage of Heaven and Hell. Oxford: 1975. V. 66
Milton - a Poem. London: 1967. V. 63
Pencil Drawings. N.P: 1927. V. 63; 64; 66
The Poems. London: 1893. V. 66
Poems. 1973. V. 62
The Poems. Cambridge: 1973. V. 64
Poems from William Blake's Songs of Innocence. London: 1967. V. 65
Poetical Sketches. London: 1868. V. 62; 63; 66
Poetical Sketches. London: 1899. V. 62; 63; 64; 66
XVII Designs to Thornton's Virgil Reproduced from the Original woodcuts MDCCCXXI. Portland: 1899. V. 62; 65
The Songs of Experience. London: 1899. V. 63
Songs of Innocence. London: 1954. V. 64
Songs of Innocence and Experience. London: 1868. V. 62; 67
Songs of Innocence and Experience. London: 1955. V. 64
Songs of Innocence and Experience, with Other Poems. London: 1866. V. 62; 65
Songs of Innocence and Other Poems. London: 1912. V. 64
Vala or the Four Zoas. Oxford: 1963. V. 62
Visions of the Daughters of Albion. London: 1959. V. 63
William Blake's Designs for Edward Young's Night Thoughts. London: 1980. V. 66
William Blake's Engravings. London: 1950. V. 62
William Blake's Writings. Oxford: 1978. V. 62
Writings. London: 1925. V. 62; 63; 65

BLAKELOCK, DENYS
Acting My Way. London: 1964. V. 64

BLAKENEY, WILLIAM R. N.
On the Coasts of Cathay and Cipango Forty Years Ago.... London: 1902. V. 64

BLAKER, RICHARD
Medal Without Bar. London: 1930. V. 64

BLAKESLEY, JOSEPH WILLIAMS
Four Months in Algeria: With a Visit to Carthage. Cambridge: 1859. V. 62

BLAKEY, DOROTHY
The Minerva Press 1790-1820. Oxford: 1939. V. 67

BLAKEY, ROBERT
Hints on Angling, with Suggestions for Angling Excursions in France and Belgium.... London: 1846. V. 63; 67

BLAKISTON, T. W.
Birds of Japan.... Tokyo: 1882. V. 62
Five Months on the Yang-Tsze; with a Narrative of the Exploration of Its Upper Waters, and Notices of the Present Rebellions in China.... London: 1862. V. 64

BLAKSTON, W. A.
The Illustrated Book of Canaries and Cage Birds, British and Foreign. London: 1877-1880. V. 64

BLAMIRES, DAVID
Margaret Pilkington: 1891-1974. Derbyshire: 1995. V. 64

BLANCH, JOHN
Observations on the Bill Now Depending in the House of Lords, with Relation to the Woollen Manufacture. London: 1731. V. 63

BLANCH, WILLIAM HARNETT
Ye Parish of Camerwell. London: 1875. V. 66

BLANCHAN, N.
The American Flower Garden. New York: 1909. V. 67
Nature's Garden, an Aid to Knowledge of Our Wild Flowers and Their Insect Visitors. New York: 1900. V. 67

BLANCHARD, AMY ELLA
Bonny Bairns. New York: 1888. V. 64
Wee Babies. New York: 1882. V. 64

BLANCHARD, EDWARD LITT LAMAN
The Legend of Vilikins and Dinah. London: 1854. V. 62

BLANCHARD, F. N.
A Revision of the King Snakes: Genus Lampropeltis. Washington: 1921. V. 63

BLANCHARD, SAMUEL LANMAN
Life and Literary Remains of L. E. L. London: 1841. V. 65
Lyric Offerings. London: 1828. V. 66

BLANCHERE, H. DE LA
La Peche aux Bains de Mer. Paris: 1850. V. 66

BLANCK, JACOB
Bibliography of American Literature. New Haven and London: 1955-1973. V. 64; 65
Merle Johnson's American First Editions. New York: 1936. V. 62; 63; 66

BLANCKLEY, THOMAS RILEY
Shewing and Explaining the Words and Terms of Art Belonging to Parts, Qualities and Proportions of Building, Rigging, Furnishing and Fitting a Ship for Sea. London: 1750. V. 62

BLAND, ALEXANDER
The Royal Ballet. London: 1981. V. 63

BLAND, DAVID
A History of Book Illustration. The Illuminated Manuscript and the Printed Book. London: 1958. V. 62
A History of Book Illustration. The Illuminated Manuscript and the Printed Book. London: 1959. V. 65
A History of Book Illustration: the Illuminated Manuscript and the Printed Book. London: 1969. V. 63

BLAND, ELEANOR TAYLOR
Dead Time. New York: 1992. V. 65

BLAND, PETER
Domestic Interiors: Poems. Wellington at the Wa-te-ata: 1964. V. 62; 63

BLAND, ROSAMUND E. NESBIT
The Man in the Stone House. London: 1934. V. 64

BLAND Tomtar Och Troll en Samling Sagor. Stockholm: 1922. V. 64
BLAND Tomtar Och Troll en Samling Sagor. Stockholm: 1923. V. 64

BLAND, WILLIAM
Letters to Charles Buller, Junior, Esq. M.P. from the Australia Patriotic Association. Sydney: 1849. V. 67

BLANDFORD, GEORGE FIELDING
Insanity and Its Treatment: Lectures on the Treatment, Medical and Legal of Insane Patients. Philadelphia: 1871. V. 65

BLANDING, STEPHEN F.
In the Defences of Washington; or the Sunshine in a Soldier's Life. Providence: 1889. V. 67
Recollections of a Sailor Boy, or the Cruise of the Gunboat Louisiana. Providence: 1886. V. 63

BLAND-SUTTON, J.
Man and Beast in Eastern Ethiopia, from Observations Made in British East Africa, Uganda and the Sudan. London: 1911. V. 64
Orations and Addresses. London: 1924. V. 67

BLANDY, MARY
The Genuine Trial at Large of Mary Blandy, Spinster, for Poisoning Her Late Father, Francis Blandy.... Edinburgh: 1752. V. 63
The Genuine Tryal at Large of Mary Blandy, Spinster, for Poisoning her Late Father Francis Blandy, Gent.... London: 1752. V. 62; 63; 65

BLANE, GILBERT
Elements of Medical Logick, Illustrated by Practical Proofs and Examples. London: 1821. V. 62

BLANKENSHIP, GEORGE, MRS.
Early History of Thursten County, Washington - Some Pioneer Trips Across the Plains in the 1840's. Olympia: 1914. V. 63

BLANTON, WYNDHAM B.
Medicine in Virginia in the 17th Century. Richmond: 1930. V. 63

BLASCHE, BERNHARD HEINRICH
Papyro-Plastics, or the Art of Modelling in Paper.... London: 1825. V. 62; 66

BLASINGAME, IKE
Dakota Cowboy (My Life in the Old Days). New York: 1958. V. 64; 67

BLASIUM, GERHARDUM
Exercitationes Anatomicae Duae de Structura et Usu Renum Ut Et Degustus Organo. Lugduni Bat: 1711. V. 65

BLATCHFORD, ROBERT
The Dolly Ballads. London: 1905. V. 62

BLATCHLEY, W. S.
An Illustrated Descriptive Catalogue of the Coleoptera or Beetles Known to Occur in Indiana. Indianapolis: 1910. V. 62; 66
Rhynchophora or Weevils of Eastern North America. Indianapolis: 1916. V. 64

BLATCHLY, JOHN
The Bookplates of Edward Gordon Craig. London: 1997. V. 65

BLATHERWICK, CHARLES
Miss Nancy Stocker. London: 1887. V. 67

BLATIN, HENRY
Traite des Maladies des Femmes, qui Determinent des Flueurs-Blanches, des Leucorrhees, ou Tout Autre Ecoulement Utero-Vaginal. Paris: 1842. V. 65

BLATTER, ETHELBERT
Beautiful Flowers of Kashmir. London: 1927-1928. V. 62
Beautiful Flowers of Kashmir. London: 1928. V. 64
Beautiful Flowers of Kashmir. Westminster: 1928. V. 67
Beautiful Flowers of Kashmir. London: 1928-1929. V. 63
Beautiful Flowers of Kashmir. London: 1929. V. 62
The Palms of British India and Ceylon. Dehra Dum: 1978. V. 67

BLATTY, WILLIAM PETER
The Exorcist. New York: 1971. V. 62

BLAU, FRED
The Orient Flight Lz 127-Graf Zeppelin: a Philatelic Handbook. 1980. V. 65

BLAVATSKY, H. P.
Isis Unveiled: a Master-Key to the Mysteries of Ancient and Modern Science and Theology. New York: 1893. V. 62

BLAXTER, J. H. S.
Advances in Marine Biology. London: 1985. V. 65

BLAYLOCK, JAMES P.
The Last Coin. Willimantic: 1988. V. 67
Night Relics. New York: 1994. V. 67

BLAYNEY, PETER W. M.
The First Folio of Shakespeare. Washington: 1991. V. 63

BLAZE, FRANCOIS HENRY
La Danse et Les Ballets Depuis Bacchus Jusu'a Mademoiselle Taglioni. Paris: 1832. V. 65

BLAZE DE BURY, MARIE PAULINE ROSE STEWART, BARONESS
Voyage en Autriche en Hongrie et en Allemagne Pendant les Evenements de 1848 et 1849. Paris: 1851. V. 65; 67

BLEANEY, B. I.
Electricity and Magnetism. Oxford: 1959. V. 63

BLEDSOE, A. J.
Indian Wars of the Northwest. A California Sketch. Oakland. V. 66

BLEDSOE, ALBERT T.
An Essay on Liberty and Slavery. Philadelphia: 1856. V. 63
An Examination of President Edwards' Inquiry Into the Freedom of the Will. Philadelphia: 1845. V. 63

BLEECK, OLIVER
The Brass Go-Between. New York: 1969. V. 62

BLEEK, W. H.
The Mantis and His Friends. Cape Town: 1910. V. 64
Reynard the Fox in South Africa; or, Hottentot Fables and Tales. London: 1864. V. 64
Specimens of Bushman Folklore. London: 1911. V. 64

BLEEKER, PIETER
Collected Fish Papers of Pieter Bleeker. The Hague: 1973-1976. V. 65

BLEGEN, THEODORE C.
Sherlock Holmes: Master Detective. 1952. V. 66

BLEGNY, ETIENE DE
Les Elemens ou Premieres Instructions de la Jeunesse. Paris: 1732. V. 64

BLEGNY, NICOLAS DE
Le Bon Usage du The, du Caffe et du Chocolat.... Paris: 1687. V. 62; 66

BLEGVAD, H.
Fishes of the Iranian Gulf. Copenhagen: 1944. V. 63

BLEMENBACH, JOHANN FRIEDRICH
Institutions Physiologiques.... Lyon: 1797. V. 65

BLENKINSOP, ADAM
A Transport Voyage to the Mauritius and Back, Touching at the Cape of Good Hope and St. Helena. London: 1851. V. 64

BLENNERHASSETT, ROSE
Adventures in Mashonaland.... London: 1894. V. 64

BLESH, RUDI
This is Jazz. San Francisco: 1943. V. 64

BLESSINGTON, JOSEPH P.
The Campaigns of Walker's Texas Division. New York: 1875. V. 62; 63

BLESSINGTON, MARGUERITE GARDINER, COUNTESS OF
The Book of Beauty; or, Regal Gallery. London: 1849. V. 65
Country Quarters. Tauchnitz: 1850. V. 65
Heath's Book of Beauty. London: 1838-1840. V. 65
Heath's Book of Beauty. Leipzig: 1850. V. 65
A Journal of Conversations with Lord Byron. Boston: 1859. V. 65
The Keepsake. London: 1845. V. 65
The Lottery of Life. Paris: 1842. V. 66
Meredith. Paris: 1843. V. 65
Strathern, or Life at Home and Abroad. Paris: 1845. V. 65
The Two Friends: a Novel. Paris: 1835. V. 65
The Victims of Society. Paris: 1837. V. 65

BLEULER, PAUL EUGEN
Affectivity, Suggestibility, Paranoia. Utica: 1912. V. 65
Dementia Praecox Oder Gruppen der Schizophrenien. Leipzig/Wien: 1911. V. 65
Dementia Praecox or the Group of Schizophrenias. New York: 1950. V. 65
Lehrbuch der Psychiatrie. Berlin: 1916. V. 65
Textbook of Psychiatry. New York: 1924. V. 65

BLEW, WILLIAM C. A.
A History of Steeple-Chasing. London: 1901. V. 67

BLEWETT, GEORGE
An Enquiry Whether a General Practice of Virtue Tends to the Wealth of Poverty, Benefit or Disadvantage of a People. London: 1725. V. 66

BLEWITT, JONATHAN
The Matrimonial Ladder. London: 1841. V. 65

BLIGH, STANLEY M.
The Direction of Desire. London: 1910. V. 63

BLIGH, WILLIAM
Voyage in the Resource from Coupang to Batavia, Together with the Log of His Subsequent Passage to England in the Dutch Packet Vlydt and His Remarks on Morison's Journal. Waltham St. Lawrence: 1937. V. 62; 65
A Voyage to the South Sea. London: 1792. V. 65; 66
A Voyage to the South Seas. Adelaide: 1974. V. 65
A Voyage to the South Seas. Adelaide: 1975. V. 62; 63; 64

BLIGHT, J. T.
Ancient Crosses and Other Antiquities in the East of Cornwall. London: 1858. V. 62; 66

BLIND, MATHILDE
A Selection from the Poems. London: 1897. V. 66

BLIN DE SAINMORE, ADRIEN MICHEL HYACINTHE
Lettres en Vers, ou Epitres Heoiques et Amoureuses. Paris: 1766. V. 62

BLINKY Bill. Racine: 1935. V. 63

BLINN, CAROL J.
On Becoming Three and Thirty. N.P: 1976. V. 63
On Becoming Three and Thirty. Easthampton: 1976. V. 66
A Poultry Piece. Easthampton: 1978. V. 66

BLINN, H. C.
The Life and Gospel Experience of Mother Ann Lee. East Canterbury: 1901. V. 63

BLISH, HELEN H.
A Pictographic History of Oglala Sioux. Lincoln: 1967. V. 63; 65; 67

BLISH, JAMES
A Clash of Cymbals. London: 1959. V. 62; 64; 66
Doctor Mirabilis. London: 1964. V. 62; 64
The Frozen Year. 1957. V. 62; 64; 66
More Issues at Hand - Critical Studies in Cotnemporary Science Fiction. Chicago: 1970. V. 64

BLISS, CAREY S.
Autos Across America: a Bibliography of Transcontinental Automobile Travel 1903-1940. Los Angeles: 1972. V. 64
A Leaf from the 1583 Rembert Dodoens Herbal Printed by Christopher Plantin. San Francisco: 1977. V. 62
A Pair on Printing: Atkyns' The Origins and Growth of Printing, and William Caslon and the First English Type Specimen Book. North Hills: 1982. V. 62
The Willow Dale Press, 1879. With Notes on the History of the Amateur Press in California. Los Angeles: 1975. V. 64

BLISS, DOUGLAS PERCY
Edward Bawden. Loxhill, Godalming. V. 64
Edward Bawden. London: 1969. V. 62
Edward Bawden. Godalming, Surrey: 1979. V. 63
Edward Bawden. Godalming: 1980. V. 64; 65

BLISS, ELIOT
Luminous Isle. London: 1934. V. 64

BLISS, MRS.
Practical Cook Book. Philadelphia: 1856. V. 64

BLISS, PHILIP
Bibliographical Miscellanies, Being a Selection of Curious Pieces. Oxford: 1813. V. 66

BLITH, WALTER
The English Improver Improved, or the Survey of Husbandry Surveyed Discovering the Improveableness of All Lands. London: 1652. V. 64

BLITS, H. I.
Professor H. Blits' Canning Fruits and Vegetables by Hot Air and Steam. Pittsburgh: 1890. V. 67
Professor H. I. Blits' Methods of Canning Fruits and Vegetables by Hot Air and Steam and Berries by the Compounding of Syrups and The Crystallizing and Candying of Fruits. New York: 1890. V. 62

BLITZ, ANTONIO
Life and Adventures of Signor Blitz.... Hartford: 1872. V. 67

BLOBEL, OSCAR
Little Herta's Christmas Dream. Inssbruck: 1911. V. 64

BLOCH, ERNST
Geist der Utopie. Munich & Leipzig: 1918. V. 67
Kritische Erorterungen Ueber Rickert und das Problem der Modernen Erkenntnistheorie. Ludwigshafen am Rhein: 1909. V. 67

BLOCH, M. E.
Allgemeine Naturgeschichte der Fische. Berlin: 1782-1795. V. 62
Allgemeine Naturgeschichte der fische. New York: 1993. V. 66
Systema Ichthyologiae. Berlin: 1801. V. 62

BLOCH, ROBERT
Blood Runs Cold. New York: 1961. V. 63
The Couch. Greenwich: 1962. V. 67
The Deadbeat. New York: 1960. V. 64; 67
The Eighth Stage of Fandom. 1962. V. 66
The First World Fantasy Convention: Three Authors Remember. 1980. V. 67
The King of Terrors. New York: 1977. V. 67
Lost in Time and Space with Lefty Feep. Pacifica: 1987. V. 67
The Opener of the Way. Sauk City: 1945. V. 62; 63; 64; 65; 66
Out of My Head. 1986. V. 64; 66
Pleasant Dreams - Nightmares. Sauk City: 1960. V. 63
Psycho. New York: 1959. V. 64
Psycho II. Binghamton: 1982. V. 65; 67
The Scarf. 1947. V. 64; 66
The Scarf. New York: 1947. V. 62
Screams. San Rafael: 1989. V. 65
Screams, Three Novels of Suspense. 1989. V. 62; 64; 66
The Skull of the Marquis de Sade. New York: 1965. V. 67
Unholy Trinity. 1986. V. 62; 64; 66

BLOCHWITZ, MARTIN
Anatomia Sambuci, Quae Non Solum Sambucum and Hujusdem Medicamenta Singulatim Delineat.... Leipzig: 1631. V. 62

BLOCK, ADRIENNE
Women in American Music: a Bibliography of Music and Literature. Westport: 1979. V. 65

BLOCK, HANS RASMUSSON
Horticultura Danica. Copenhagen: 1647. V. 62; 65

BLOCK, LAWRENCE
After Hours. Albuquerque: 1995. V. 66; 67
After Hours. Gallup: 1995. V. 65
Ariel. New York: 1980. V. 65; 66; 67
The Burglar in the Closet. New York: 1978. V. 67
The Burglar in the Library. Harpenden: 1997. V. 63
The Burglar in the Library. London: 1997. V. 64; 66; 67
The Burglar Who Liked to Quote Kipling. New York: 1979. V. 65; 67
The Burglar Who Painted Like Mondrian. New York: 1983. V. 65; 66; 67
The Burglar Who Studied Spinoza. New York: 1980. V. 65; 66; 67
The Burglar Who Traded Ted Williams. New York: 1994. V. 64; 67
Burglars Can't Be Choosers. New York: 1977. V. 65
The Canceled Czech. New York: 1994. V. 66; 67
Coward's Kiss. Unity: 1999. V. 67
A Dance at the Slaughterhouse. New York: 1991. V. 64
Ehrengraf for the Defense. 1994. V. 67
Eight Million Ways to Die. New York: 1982. V. 62; 65; 67
Even the Wicked. London: 1996. V. 64; 67
The Girl with the Long Green Heart. Unity: 1999. V. 67
In the Midst of Death. Delavan: 1995. V. 65; 66; 67
Mona. Unity: 1999. V. 67
One Night Stands. 1999. V. 64; 66
The Sins of the Fathers. Arlington Heights: 1992. V. 65
The Specialists. New York: 1969. V. 67
The Specialists. Aliso Viejo: 1996. V. 62; 65; 66; 67
A Stab in the Dark. New York: 1981. V. 66
The Thief Who Couldn't Sleep. 1994. V. 64; 66
The Thief Who Couldn't Sleep. New York: 1994. V. 66; 67
A Ticket to the Boneyard. New York: 1990. V. 67
Time to Murder and Create. Arlington Heights: 1993. V. 65
The Triumph of Evil. New York: 1971. V. 67
When the Sacred Gin Mill Closes. New York: 1986. V. 67

BLOCK, LAWRENCE continued
Writing the Novel: From Plot to Print. Cincinnati: 1979. V. 65; 66; 67

BLODGET, LORIN
North and South. Boston: 1946. V. 63

BLODGETT, JEAN
Kenojuak. Toronto: 1985. V. 63; 66

BLODGETT, MABEL FULLER
The Giant's Ruby and Other Fairy Tales. Boston: 1903. V. 63

BLOIS, JOHN T.
Gazetteer of the State of Michigan. Detroit and New York: 1838. V. 67

BLOMBERG, NANCY J.
Navajo Textiles - the William Randolph Hearst Collection. Tucson: 1988. V. 64; 67

BLOMFIELD, CHARLES JAMES
National Education. A Sermon Preached...on Sunday, Feb. 18, 1838 in Compliance with the Queen's Letter on Behalf of the National Society for Educating the Children of the Poor.... London: 1838. V. 65

BLOMFIELD, REGINALD
The Formal Garden in England. London: 1892. V. 62; 65; 66; 67

BLONDEL, DAVID
A Treatise of the Sibyls, So Highly Celebrated, As Well by the Antient Heathens, as the Holy Father of the Church.... London: 1661. V. 63; 64; 65

BLONDEL, JACQUES
Emily Bronte. 1955. V. 66

BLONDELLO, DAVID
De Ioanna Papissa: sive Farmousae Quaestionis.... Amsterdam: 1657. V. 65

BLOOD for Gold, or Death for Forgery, Proved to be Inexpedient, Unjust and Unscriptural. London: 1824. V. 64

BLOOM, AMY
Come to Me. New York: 1993. V. 67
Love Invents Us. New York: 1996. V. 67

BLOOM, EDWARD A.
Samuel Johnson in Grub Street. Providence: 1957. V. 63

BLOOMFIELD, J. A.
Lakes of New York State. New York: 1978. V. 65

BLOOMFIELD, NATHANIEL
An Essay of War, in Blank Verse; Honington Green, a Ballad; The Culprit an Elegy; and Other Poems. Bury St. Edmunds: 1803. V. 63
An Essay of War, in Blank Verse; Honington Green, a Ballad; The Culprit, an Elegy; and Other Poems. London: 1803. V. 66

BLOOMFIELD, ROBERT
The Banks of Wye: a Poem. London: 1811. V. 64; 65; 67
The Fakenham Ghost. London: 1813. V. 62
The Farmer's Boy; a Rural Poem. London: 1800. V. 66
The Farmer's Boy; a Rural Poem. London: 1801. V. 67
Good Tidings; or, News from the Farm. London: 1804. V. 66
Hazelwood-Hall: a Village Drama. London: 1823. V. 66
May Day with the Muses. London: 1822. V. 66
The Remains. 1824. V. 64
The Remains. London: 1824. V. 66
Rural Tales, Ballads and Songs. London: 1802. V. 63; 66
Wild Flowers; or, Pastoral and Local Poetry. London: 1806. V. 64; 65

BLOOR, ALFRED J.
Letters from the Army of the Potomac, Written During the Month of May 1864 to Several of the Supply Correspondents of the U.S. Sanitary Commission. Washington: 1864. V. 65

BLOOR, ELLA REEVE
We Are Many. New York: 1940. V. 63

BLORE, EDWARD
The Monumental Remains of Noble and Eminent Persons.... London: 1826. V. 66

BLOSSEVILLE, ERNEST DE
Histoire des Colonies Penales de l'Angleterre dans l'Australie. Paris: 1831. V. 66

BLOT, PIERRE
Hand-Book of Practical Cookery for Ladies and Professional Cooks. New York: 1868. V. 67

BLOTNER, JOSEPH
Faulkner: a Biography. New York: 1973. V. 62

BLOUNT, CHARLES
The Miscellaneous Works.... London: 1695. V. 64
The Oracles of Reason. London: 1693. V. 65

BLOUNT, THOMAS
Boscobel.... London: 1660. V. 62; 66
Boscobel.... London: 1725. V. 63
Fragmenta Antiquitates; or Antient Tenures of Land and Jocular Customs of Some Manors, Etc. York: 1784. V. 62
Glossographia; or a Dictionary, Interpreting the Hard Words of Whatsoever Language, Now Used in Our Refined Tongue.... London: 1674. V. 64
A Law Dictionary and Glossary, Interpreting Such Difficult and Obscure Words and Terms, as Are Found Either in Our Common or Statute, Ancient and Modern Laws. In the Savoy: 1717. V. 63

BLOUNT, THOMAS POPE
Censura Celebration Authorum: sive Tractatus in Quo Varia Virorum Doctorum de Clarissimis Cujusque Seculi Scriptoribu Judicia Traduntur.... London: 1690. V. 63
De Re Poetica; or, Remarks Upon Poetry. London: 1694. V. 62; 64; 66

BLOXAM, CHARLES LOUDON
Metals, Their Properties and Treatment. London: 1888. V. 64

BLOXAM, MATTHEW HOLBECHE
A Glimpse at the Monumental Architecture and Sculpture of Great Britain. London: 1834. V. 62; 67

BLUCHER, H.
Technischer Modellatlas. 15 Zerlegbare Modele aus den Gebeiten der Maschinen- und Verkehrstechnik mit Gemeinverstandlichen Erlauterungen. Leipzig and Vienna: 1915. V. 63

BLUE Beard; or, Fatal Curiosity. Yorkshire. V. 65

THE BLUE Book. N.P: 1936. V. 65

THE BLUE Laws of New Haven Colony.... Hartford: 1838. V. 63

BLUM, ANN S.
Picturing Nature. American Nineteenth Century Zoological Illustrations. Princeton: 1993. V. 67

BLUM, RICHARD
Utopiates. The Use and Uses of LSD-25. New York: 1964. V. 65

BLUMBERG, FANNIE BURGHEIM
Rowena Teena Tot and the Blackberries. Chicago: 1934. V. 62
Rowena Teena Tot and the Runaway Turkey. Chicago: 1936. V. 65

BLUME, CARL LUDWIG
Flora Javae nec Non Insularum Adjacentium...Volume I. Brussels: 1829-1830. V. 63; 66; 67
Flora Javae Nec Non Insularum Adjacentium...Volume III. Brussels: 1828-1851. V. 63
Flora Javae.... Brussels: 1828-1851. V. 67

BLUMENBACH, J. F.
A Manual of Comparative Anatomy.... London: 1827. V. 67

BLUMENBERG, HANS
Kopernikanische Wende. Frankfurt: 1965. V. 67

BLUMENTHAL, JOSEPH
Art of the Printed Book 1455-1955: Masterpieces Of Typography Through Five Centuries from the Collections of te Pierpont Morgan Library. New York: 1973. V. 63; 64; 66

BLUNDELL, DEREK
A Continent Revealed. The European Geotraverse. 1992. V. 67

BLUNDELL, NICHOLAS
Blundell's Diary. Comprising Selections from the Diary of Nicholas Blundell, Esq. from 1702 to 1728. Liverpool: 1895. V. 63; 66

BLUNDELL, R. H.
Trial of Buck Ruxton. London: 1937. V. 63; 64; 65

BLUNDEN, EDMUND
Christ's Hospital - a Retrospect. London: 1923. V. 62
Fall in, Ghosts - an Essay on a Battalion Reunion. London: 1932. V. 62
Japanese Garland. England: 1928. V. 62
Masks of Time. London: 1925. V. 62
Near and Far. London: 1929. V. 64; 66
The Poems of Edmund Blunden. London: 1930. V. 62
Retreat: New Sonnets and Poems. London: 1928. V. 64
A Summer's Fancy. London: 1930. V. 65
To Nature. 1923. V. 65
To Nature. London: 1923. V. 62; 64
To Themis - Poems on Famous Trials, With Other Pieces. London: 1931. V. 62; 65
Undertones of War. London: 1928. V. 62; 64
Verses to H.R.H. The Duke of Windsor. 1936. V. 63
Votive Tablets. London: 1931. V. 62; 63
Winter Nights. London: 1928. V. 67

BLUNDEVILLE, THOMAS
His Exercises, Containing Sixe Treatises, the Titles Whereof Are Set Down in the Next Printed Page.... London: 1594. V. 65

BLUNT, ANNE
Bedouin Tribes of the Euphrates. London: 1879. V. 64
Bedouin Tribes of the Euphrates. New York: 1879. V. 67
A Pilgrimage to Nejd; the Cradle of the Arab Race. London: 1881. V. 64

BLUNT, ANTHONY
Baroque and Rococo: Architecture and Decoration. London: 1978. V. 62; 65
Francois Mansart; and the Origins of French Classical Architecture. 1941. V. 67
Nicolas Poussin. New York: 1967. V. 62; 65

BLUNT, EDMUND M.
The American Coast Pilot; Containing Directions for the Principal Harbors, Capes and Headlands on the Coasts of North and South America.... New York: 1850. V. 62

BLUNT, JOHN
Practical Farriery. 1773. V. 62

BLUNT, JOHN HENRY
Dictionary of Sects, Heresies, Ecclesiastical Parties and Schools of Religious Thought. London: 1874. V. 64

BLUNT, JOHN JAMES
The Duties of the Parish Priest. London: 1858. V. 63

BLUNT, WILFRED
The Art of Botanical Illustration. London: 1950. V. 62; 63; 67
The Art of Botanical Illustration. London: 1955. V. 62; 67
The Art of Botanical Illustration. London: 1971. V. 66
Cockerell - Sydney Carlyle Cockerell, Friend of Ruskin and William Morris.... London: 1964. V. 64
England's Michelangelo. London: 1975. V. 67
Flora Superba. London: 1971. V. 63; 64
The Illustrated Herbal. New York: 1979. V. 67

BLUNT, WILFRID SCAWEN
In Vinculis. London: 1889. V. 64
The Love Lyrics and Songs of Proteus.... London: 1892. V. 65
The Love-Lyrics and Songs of Proteus.... 1892. V. 62
My Diaries, Being a Personal Narrative of Events 1888-1914. London: 1919-1920. V. 67
A New Pilgrimage and Other Poems. 1889. V. 63
A New Pilgrimage and Other Poems. London: 1889. V. 66
Sydney Carlyle Cockerell, Friend of Ruskin and William Morris and Director of the Fitzwlliam Museum, Cambridge. London: 1964. V. 63

BLY, ROBERT
Iron John. New York: 1990. V. 67
Iron John. Reading: 1990. V. 63
Mirabai Versions. New York: 1980. V. 64
Silence in the Snowy Fields. London: 1967. V. 62
The Teeth-Mother Naked At Last. Minnesota: 1970. V. 62
The Traveller Who Repeats His Cry. New York: 1982. V. 66

BLYTH, E.
The Natural History of the Cranes.... London: 1881. V. 67

BLYTH, MARY POPHAM
Antoinette. London: 1888. V. 65

BLYTHE, RONALD
Aldeburgh Anthology. 1972. V. 65
First Friends. Denby Dale: 1997. V. 62
First Friends. London: 1998. V. 65

BLYTON, ENID
Adventures of the Wishing Chair. London: 1937. V. 66
The Adventures of Mr. Pink-Whistle. London: 1942. V. 67
The Animal Book. London: 1927. V. 66
Benny and the Princess. 1951. V. 65
The Big Noddy Book. London: 1951. V. 65
Bom and the Rainbow. 1959. V. 66
Bom the Little Toy Drummer. 1956. V. 67
The Buttercup Farm Family. 1951. V. 67
The Castle of Adventure. London: 1952. V. 66
The Children of Cherry Tree Farm. London: 1941. V. 67
The Christmas Book. London: 1944. V. 66
The Circus of Adventure. 1952. V. 65
The Circus of Adventure. London: 1952. V. 66
Claudine at St. Clare's. London: 1944. V. 67
A Day with Noddy. London: 1956. V. 67
The Enchanted Wood. London: 1956. V. 66
The Enid Blyton Holiday Book. London: 1958. V. 67
Enid Blyton's Circus Book. 1949. V. 66
Enid Blyton's Daffodil Story Book. 1954. V. 67
Enid Blyton's Jolly Story Book. London: 1959. V. 67
Enid Blyton's Noddy Theatre. 1955. V. 65
The Famous Five Special. London: 1959. V. 66
Five Fall Into Adventure. 1950. V. 65
Five Fall Into Adventure. 1950. V. 66
Five Get Into a Fix. London: 1958. V. 66
Five Get Into Trouble. 1949. V. 65
Five Get Into Trouble. London: 1949. V. 66
Five Get Into Trouble. London: 1950. V. 67
Five Go Adventuring Again. London: 1949. V. 66
Five Go Down to the Sea. 1953. V. 65
Five Go Down to the Sea. London: 1953. V. 66
Five Go Off to Camp; The Seventh Story of the Adventures of the Four Children and Their Dog. London: 1951. V. 63
Five Go to Demon's Rocks. London: 1961. V. 66
Five Go to Mystery Moor. London: 1954. V. 66
Five Go to Smuggler's Top. London: 1959. V. 67
Five Have a Mystery to Solve. London: 1962. V. 66
Five Have a Wonderful Time. 1952. V. 65
Five on a Hike Together. London: 1951. V. 66
Five on a Secret Trail. London: 1956. V. 66
Five on a Treasure Island. 1949. V. 65
Five Run Away Together. London: 1949. V. 67
Good Old Secret Seven. 1960. V. 66
Heyo, Brer Rabbit!. London: 1942. V. 66
The Island of Adventure. 1944. V. 65
Let's Have a Story. 1952. V. 67
Look Out Secret Seven. 1962. V. 67
The Mountain of Adventure. 1949. V. 65
The Mountain of Adventure. London: 1954. V. 67
The Mystery of Banshee Towers. London: 1961. V. 65
The Mystery of Holly Lane. London: 1960. V. 67
The Mystery of the Invisible Thief. London: 1950. V. 65
The Mystery of the Invisible Thief. London: 1960. V. 67
The Mystery of the Pantomime Cat. London: 1961. V. 67
The Mystery of the Secret Room. London: 1957. V. 67
The Mystery of the Strange Bundle. London: 1952. V. 65
The Mystery of the Strange Messages. London: 1957. V. 65; 66
The Mystery of the Tally-Ho Cottage. London: 1954. V. 65
The Mystery of the Tally-Ho Cottage. London: 1957. V. 67
The Mystery of the Vanished Prince. London: 1956. V. 67
The Mystery that Never Was. London: 1961. V. 67
The Naughtiest Girl in the School. London: 1951. V. 67
The New Big Noddy Book. Number 4. London: 1954. V. 66
Noddy Goes to Toyland. London: 1949. V. 65
Noddy's New Big Book. Number 7. London: 1957. V. 65
Puzzle for the Secret Seven. 1958. V. 66
Rainy Day Stories. 1952. V. 67
The Rat-a-Tat Mystery. London: 1956. V. 66
The River of Adventure. London: 1955. V. 66
The Rockingdown Mystery. London: 1949. V. 66
Round the Year with Enid Blyton. 1950. V. 67
The Sea of Adventure. 1948. V. 65
The Secret Seven. Leicester: 1949. V. 66
The Secret Seven. London: 1949. V. 66
Secret Seven Fireworks. 1959. V. 66
The Ship of Adventure. London: 1950. V. 66
Silver and Gold. London: 1927. V. 66
Silver and Gold. 1930. V. 66
The Six Bad Boys. 1960. V. 67
Songs for Infants. London: 1949. V. 66
A Story Party at Green Hedges. London: 1949. V. 67
Tales About Toys. 1950. V. 67
The Teacher's Treasury. London: 1926. V. 66
The Toys Come to Life, an Enid Blyton Picture Book. 1943. V. 66
The Treasure Hunters. 1941. V. 65
The Valley of Adventure. 1947. V. 65
The Valley of Adventure. London: 1952. V. 67
Welcome Josie, Click and Bun!. London: 1952. V. 66
The Wishing Chair Again. London: 1967. V. 67

BOADEN, JAMES
An Inquiry into the Authenticity of Various Pictures and Prints, Which, From the Decease of the Poet of Our Own Times, Have Been Offered to the Public as Portraits of Shakespeare. London: 1824. V. 62; 67
The Life of Mrs. Jordan.... London: 1831. V. 63
Memoirs of the Life of John Philip Kemble. London: 1825. V. 64

BOAG, JOHN
The Imperial Lexicon of the English Language. London: 1850. V. 64
The Imperial Lexicon of the English Language. Edinburgh: 1852-1853. V. 64

BOARDMAN, PETER
The Shining Mountain. London: 1978. V. 64; 66

BOARDMAN, RUDY
Saint Tropez: Poems and a Drawing. London: 1932. V. 63

BOAS, FRANZ
The Mythology of the Bella Coola Indians. New York: 1898. V. 63
Tsimshian Texts. Washington: 1902. V. 65

BOAS, J.
Ohrknorpel und Ausseres Ohr der Saugtiere. Copenhagen: 1912. V. 67

BOASE, HENRY SAMUEL
The Philosophy of Nature. London: 1860. V. 65

BOBBY Bear's Annual for 1935. 1941. V. 67

BOBBY Bob Tail. Akron: 1910. V. 64

BOBROW, JILL
Classic Yacht Interiors. London: 1983. V. 62

BOB'S School Days. New York: 1870. V. 63

BOCALINI, TRAJANO
Iragguagli Di Parnasso, or Advertisements from Parnassus, in Two Centuries. London: 1674. V. 66

BOCCACCIO, GIOVANNI
Amorous Fiammetta. London: 1929. V. 63; 66
Il Decameron. Amsterdam: 1665. V. 63
Il Decameron. Amsterdam: 1703. V. 67
The Decameron. London: 1822. V. 62; 63

BOCCACCIO, GIOVANNI continued
Il Decameron. London: 1920. V. 62
The Decameron. London: 1921. V. 66
The Decameron. New York: 1925. V. 62; 64
The Decameron. London: 1930. V. 65
The Decameron. New York: 1930. V. 62; 64
The Decameron. Oxford: 1934-1935. V. 65
The Decameron. New York: 1940. V. 65
Il Decamerone. In Lione: 1555. V. 63
Il Decamerone. Venetia: 1588. V. 66
Il Decamerone. London: 1702. V. 66
Genealogiae Deorum. Venice: 1494-1495. V. 64
Life of Dante. New York: 1900. V. 64
Opera dell'Huomo Dotto et Famoso Giovanni Boccaccio Dalla Lingua Latina nel Thosco Idioma.... Venice?: 1530. V. 63

BOCHART, SAMUEL
Geographia Sacra. Frankfurt: 1681. V. 66

BOCK, CARL
The Head-Hunters of Borneo.... London: 1881. V. 62
The Head-Hunters of Borneo.... London: 1882. V. 64

BOCKEMUHL, L.
Odontoglossum, a Monograph and Iconograph. Hildesheim: 1989. V. 67

BOCKRIS, VICTOR
With William Burroughs: A Report from the Bunker. New York: 1981. V. 67

BOCKSTOCE, JOHN R.
American Whalers in the Western Arctic, the Final Epoch of the Great American Sailing Whaling Fleet. Fairhaven: 1983. V. 62; 63

BODDAM-WHETHAM, JOHN WHETHAM
Across Central America. London: 1877. V. 62; 67

BODDE, D.
An Essay to Show that Petroleum may be Used with Advantages in Manufacaturing Operations, for the Purpose of Heating Steam-Boilers and Generating Steam. Batavia: 1870. V. 62

BODDIE, JOHN B.
Southside Virginia Families. Redwood City: 1955. V. 67

BODDIE, WILLIAM WILLIS
History of Williamsburg. Columbia: 1923. V. 67

BODDING, P. O.
Studies in Santal Medicine and Connected Folklore. Calcutta: 1925-1940. V. 62

BODDINGTON, CRAIG
America, the Men and Their Guns that Made Her Great. Los Angeles: 1981. V. 67
Deer Hunting Coast to Coast. 1990. V. 62; 63; 66

BODDINGTON, L.
Landing Experiments with Undercarriagless Vampire Aircraft on a Flexible Deck. London: 1950. V. 64

BODENHEIM, MAXWELL
Minna and Myself. New York: 1918. V. 63

BODENSTEDT, FRIEDRICH
The Morning-Land; or a Thousand and One Days in the East. London: 1851. V. 64

BODFISH, H. H.
Chasing the Bowhead. Cambridge: 1936. V. 63; 64

BODKIN, THOMAS
Four Irish Landscape Painters. George Barret, Walter Osborne, Nathaniel Hone, James A. O'Connor. Dublin: 1920. V. 64
Hugh Lane and His Pictures. 1923. V. 63
Hugh Lane and His Pictures. 1932. V. 66

BODMER, KARL
Karl Bodmer's America. Japan: 1984. V. 63

BODONI, GIAMBATTISTA
Manuel Tipografico 1788. Verona: 1968. V. 62
Le Piu Pitture Parmensi Indicate Agli Amatori Delle Belle Arti. Parma: 1809. V. 66
Prosi e Versi Per Ornorare la Memoria de Livia Doria Caraffa.... Parma: 1784. V. 65

BODROGI, T.
Art in Africa. Corvina: 1968. V. 62
Art in the North-East New Guinea. Budapest: 1961. V. 62
Oceanian Art. Budapest: 1959. V. 62

BOECK, W.
Picasso. New York: 1955. V. 65

BOECKH, AUGUSTUS
The Public Economy of Athens.... London: 1842. V. 63

BOEHM, JACOB
Jacob Behmen's Theosophick Philosophy Unfolded; in Divers Considerations and Demonstrations, Shewing the Verity and Utility of the Several Doctrines or Propositions Contained in the Writings of that Divinely Instructed Author.... London: 1691. V. 63

BOEHME, JACOB
(XL Questions Concerning the) Soule. London: 1647. V. 62

BOEHME, SARAH E.
Seth Eastman: a Portfolio of North American Indians. Afton: 1995. V. 63; 66

BOEHN, MAX VON
Dolls and Puppets. London: 1932. V. 63

BOELTER, HOMER
Portfolio of Hopi Kachinas. Hollywood: 1969. V. 63; 64; 65; 66

BOERHAAVE, HERMANN
Aphorismi de Cognoscendis et Curandis Morbis in Usum Doctrinae Domesticae Digesti. Leyden: 1737. V. 63
Atrocis, nec Descripti Prius, Morbi Historia, Secundum Medicae Artis Leges Conscripta Ab Hermanno Boerhaave. (with) *Atrocis, Rarissimique Morbi Historia Altera. Conscripta ab Hermanno Boerhaave.* Leyden: 1724. V. 66
De Morbis Oculorum. Gottingae: 1750. V. 65
Elements Chemiae, Quae Anniversario Labore Docuit.... Paris: 1733. V. 65
Methodus Studii Medici. Amstelaedami: 1751. V. 67
Praelectiones Academicae De Morbis Nervorum Quas Auditorum Manuscriptis.... Venetiis: 1762. V. 66
Praxis Medica, Sive Commentarium in Aphorismos Hermanni Boerhaave De Cognoscendis & Curandis Morbis. London: 1738. V. 65; 66
A Treatise on the Powers of Medicines by the Late Learned Herman Boerhaave.... London: 1740. V. 65

BOESEN, GUDMUND
Old Danish Silver. Copenhagen: 1949. V. 67

BOETHIUS
Anglo-Saxon Version of the Metres of Boethius, with an English Translation.... London: 1835. V. 66
Dialecta Aristotelis, Boethio Severino Interprete, Ab. Ioan Raenerio Recognita.... 1543. V. 65
Interlatinos Aristotelis Interpretes & Aetate Primi & Doctrina Praecipui Dialectica. Venice: 1568. V. 67
King Alfred's Anglo-Saxon Version of the Metres of Boethius with an English Translation and Notes by the Rev. Samuel Fox. London: 1835. V. 62

BOGAINVILLE, LOUIS ANTOINE DE
A Voyage Round the World, Performed by Order of His Most Christian Majesty in the Years 1766 1767, 1768, and 1769. London: 1772. V. 66

BOGAN, LOUISE
The Blue Estuaries. Poems 1923-1968. New York: 1968. V. 62; 63
Body of This Death. New York: 1923. V. 63; 64
Collected Poems: 1923-1953. New York: 1954. V. 62; 63; 64
Poems and New Poems. New York: 1941. V. 62; 64

BOGAN, PHEBE M.
Yaqui Indian Dances of Tucson, Arizona. Tucson: 1925. V. 67

BOGAN, ZACHARY
(Greek title, then) Comparatio Homeri Cum Scriptoribus Sacris Quoad Normam Loquendi. Oxoniae: 1658. V. 64; 66

BOGARDE, DIRK
A Gentle Occupation - a Novel. London: 1980. V. 64
A Particular Friendship. New York: 1989. V. 64
A Postillion Struck by Lightning. London: 1977. V. 62
Snakes and Ladders. London: 1978. V. 64

BOGER, E., MRS.
Bygone Southark. London: 1895. V. 62

BOGERT, C. M.
A Preliminary Analysis of the Herpetofauna of Sonora. New York: 1945. V. 66

BOGG, EDMUND
The Golden Vale of Mowbray. London: 1900. V. 65
Lower Wharfeland: the Old City of York and the Ainsty, the Region of Historic Memories. London: 1904. V. 65
Nidderdale: and the Vale of the Nidd from Nun Monkton to Great Whernside. Leeds. V. 65
The Old Kingdom of Elmet: York and the Ainsty District.... London: 1902. V. 62; 65
A Thousand Miles in Wharfedale and the Wharfe. London. V. 62; 65
A Thousand Miles of Wandering Along the Roman Wall, the Old Border Region, Lakeland and Ribblesdale. Leeds: 1898. V. 62
Two Thousand Miles in Wharfedale. London: 1904. V. 63; 65
Two Thousand Miles of Wandering in the Border Country, Lakeland and Ribblesdale. Leeds: 1898. V. 62
The Vale of Mowbray. Volume I of Richmondshire and the Vale of Mowbray. London: 1908. V. 65

BOGGS & BUHL
Autumn & Winter Fashions, Catalogue 22. 1897-1898. Allegheny: 1898. V. 65

BOGGS, K. D.
Prints and Plants of Old Gardens. Richmond: 1932. V. 67

BOGGS, MAY HELEN BACON
My Playhouse Was a Concord Coach. Oakland: 1942. V. 62; 65

BOGGS, TOM
An American Anthology. 67 Poems Now In Anthology Form for the First Time. Prairie City: 1942. V. 64; 67

BOGGS, WILLIAM ROBERTSON
Military Reminiscences of General Wm. R. Boggs, C.S.A. Durham: 1913. V. 62; 63; 65

BOGIRA, STEVE
$144 a Month, Life in the Safety Net. Chicago: 1993. V. 62; 64

BOGUET, HENRY
An Examen of Witches Drawn from Various Trials of Many of This Sect in the District of Saint Oyan de Joux Commonly Known as Saint Claude in the County of Burgundy.... London: 1929. V. 65

BOHADSCH, H. B.
De Quibusdam Animalibus Marinis Eorumque Proprietatibus, Orbi Litterario Vel Nondum Vel Minus Notis Liber. Dresden: 1761. V. 66

BOHAN, PETER
The Peter T. Bohan Memorial Lectures on Medicine. First and Second Series. Lawrence: 1957-1969. V. 66

BOHATTA-MORPURGO, IDA
The Adventures of Mr. Pipweasel. Munich: 1934. V. 62

BOHLKE, J. E.
Fishes of the Bahamas and Adjacent Tropical Waters. 1968. V. 64
Fishes of the Bahamas and Adjacent Tropical Waters. Philadelphia: 1968. V. 66
Fishes of the Bahamas and Adjacent Tropical Waters. Wynnewood: 1968. V. 65

BOHN, CASIMIR
Bohn's Album and Autographs of the University of Virginia with a Short History.... Washington: 1859. V. 67

BOHN, HENRY G.
A Catalogue of Books. London: 1841. V. 65
A Cataogue of Books. New York: 1974. V. 66
The Handbook of Games.... London: 1850. V. 64

BOHROD, AARON
A Decade of Still Life. Madison: 1966. V. 62

BOHUN, EDMUND
An Address to the Free-Men and Free-Holders of the Nation. London: 1682. V. 63
The Diary and Autobiography of.... 1853. V. 62; 63

BOHUN, W.
The Law of Tithes: Shewing Their Nature, Kinds, Properties and Incidents; by Whom, to Whom, When and in What Manner Payable. London: 1744. V. 67

BOID, EDWARD
A Concise History and Analysis of All the Principal Styles of Architecture; Namely Egyptian, Grecian, Roman, that of the Dark Ages, of the Arabians and of the Normans.... London. V. 66
The History of the Spanish School of Painting; to Which is Appended, An Historical Sketch of the Rise and Progress of the Art of Miniature Illumination. London: 1843. V. 66

BOIJE AF GENNAS, FREDERIK CARL
Dessins et Croquis des Plus Celebres Maitres de Toutes les Ecoles, Calques sur Leurs Dessis Autographes qui se Trouvent dans le Musee Royale Suedois, Part 1. Stockholm: 1820. V. 66

BOILAU, I. T.
A Collection of Tables, Astronomical, Meteorological and Magnetical, Also for Determining the Altitudes of Mountains.... Umballa: 1850. V. 65

BOILEAU, DANIEL
Counsels at Home: Interspersed with Entertaining Tales and Interesting Anecdotes. London: 1831. V. 65

BOILEAU, JACQUES
A Just and Seasonable Reprehension of Naked Breasts and Shoulders. London: 1678. V. 62

BOILEAU-DESPREAUX, NICOLAS
Oeuvres. Paris: 1798. V. 63; 66
Oeuvres Diverses. Amsterdam: 1702. V. 67
The Works of Monsieur Boileau. London: 1712-1711. V. 62

BOISGELIN, LOUIS DE
Ancient and Modern Malta.... London: 1805. V. 64; 66

BOISSARD, JOHANN JACOB
Typographia Urbis Romae, Das ist: Eigentliche Beschreibung der Stadt Rom.... Frankfurt: 1681. V. 62

BOISSIER, PIERRE EDMOND
Flora Orientalis sive Enumeratio Plantarum in Oriente a Graecis et Aegypto ad Indiae Fines Hucusque Observatarum. Basel: 1867-1888. V. 63

BOLAM, G.
Wild Life in Wales. 1913. V. 67

BOLAN, MARC
The Warlock of Love. Plymouth: 1969. V. 66

BOLAND, EAVAN
Limitations. New York: 2000. V. 67

BOLAND, ROSITA
Muscle Creek. Dublin: 1991. V. 65

BOLANDER, JOHN ALFRED
Violin Bow Making. San Jose: 1969. V. 67

BOLDINGH, I.
The Flora of the Dutch West Indian Islands. Volume I. Leiden: 1909. V. 67

BOLIN, EDWARD H.
Catalog of The World's Finest Riding Equipment Accessories and Silver and Leather Goods. Hollywood: 1941. V. 65

BOLINGBROKE, HENRY SAINT JOHN, 1ST VISCOUNT
The History of England from the Minutes of Humphrey Oldcastle, Esq. London: 1747. V. 66
A Letter to Sir William Windham. II. Some Reflections on the Present State of the Nation. III. A Letter to Mr. Pope. London: 1753. V. 65; 66
Letters on the Spirit of Patriotism: on the Idea of a Patriot King....(with) A Familiar Epistle to the Most Impudent Man Living. London: 1749. V. 64; 65
Letters on the Study and Use of History. London: 1752. V. 65
Memoirs of the Life and Ministerial Conduct, with Some Free Remarks on the Political Writings of the Late Lord Visc. Bolingbroke. London: 1752. V. 65
The Philosophical Works. London: 1754. V. 66

BOLL, HEINRICH
The Bread of Those Early Years. New York: 1976. V. 63
The Lost Honor of Katharina Blum, or, How Violence Develops and Where It Can Lead. New York: 1975. V. 63

BOLLER, HENRY A.
Among the Indians Eight Years in the Far West 1858-1866 Embracing Sketches of Montana and the Far West. Philadelphia: 1868. V. 64; 67

BOLLES, ALBERT S.
Industrial History of the U.S. Norwich: 1881. V. 63

BOLLINGER, EDWARD T.
Rails that Climb, the Story of the Moffat Road. Santa Fe: 1950. V. 65

BOLOTIN, JAY
The Hidden Boy. Cincinnati: 1984-1985. V. 62
Jack and Eve: a Pre-History to That Which Is, by Mistake, Called the Fall of Man. Cincinnati: 1998. V. 62

BOLSTER, EVELYN
A History of the Diocese of Cork from the Reformation to the Penal Era. 1982. V. 67
A History of the Diocese of Cork from...Earliest Times to the Reformation. 1972. V. 64

BOLTANSKI, CHRISTIAN
El Caso. N.P: 1988. V. 65

BOLTON, CLAIRE
Awa Gami: Japanese Handmade Papers from Fuji Mills, Tokushima. Winchester: 1991. V. 64
The Compton Marbling Portfolio of Patterns. Oxford: 1992. V. 65
Delittle 1888-1988: the First Years in a Century of Wood Letter Manufacture. Oxford: 1988. V. 64
Maziarczyk Pasate Papers. Oxford: 1991. V. 64
Specimens of Wood Type Held at the Alembic Press. Oxford: 1993. V. 65

BOLTON, HERBERT EUGENE
Anza's California Expeditions. Berkeley: 1930. V. 62; 66
Coronado On the Turquoise Trail, Knight of Pueblo and Plains. Albuquerque: 1949. V. 62; 65
Cross Swords and Gold Plan. Los Angeles: 1936. V. 63; 66
The Geology of Rossendale. Bacup: 1890. V. 63; 65
Greater America. Berkeley: 1945. V. 66
New Spain and the Anglo-American West: Historical Contributions. Los Angeles: 1932. V. 64
Outpost of Empire. The Story of the Founding of San Francisco. New York: 1931. V. 65
Pageant in the Wilderness. The Story of the Escalante Expedition to the Interior Basin 1776. Salt Lake City: 1950. V. 63; 64; 67
Rim of Christendom: a Biography of Eusebio Francisco Kino, Pacific Coast Pioneer. New York: 1936. V. 62; 63; 65; 66
Texas in the Middle Eighteenth Century, Studies in Spanish Colonial History and Administration. Berkeley: 1915. V. 63

BOLTON, ISABEL
Do I Wake or Sleep. New York: 1946. V. 66

BOLTON, JAMES
Filices Britannicae.... Leeds: 1785. V. 64

BOLTON, JOHN
Geological Fragments Collected Principally from Rambles Among the Rocks of Furness and Cartmel. London: 1869. V. 65
Geological Fragments Collected Principally from Rambles Among the Rocks of Furness and Cartmell. Ulverston: 1869. V. 65; 66

BOLTON, ROBERT
An Answer to the Question, Where are Your Arguments Against What You Call, Lewdness, If You Make No Use of the Bible?. London: 1755. V. 65
On the Employment of Time. Three Essays. London: 1754. V. 63; 67

BOLTON, WILLIAM COMPTON
The Trial of Capt. William Compton Bolton, for an Alleged Violation of the Orders of Commodore Hull, in Returning from the Mediterranean to the United States in May 1841. Philadelphia: 1841. V. 64

BOLTZMANN, LUDWIG
Vorlesungen Uber Maxwell's Theorie der Elektricitat und des Lichtes. Leipzig: 1891-1893. V. 65

BOLUS, H.
The Orchids of the Cape Peninsula.... Cape Town: 1888. V. 62
The Orchids of the Cape Peninsula.... Cape Town: 1918. V. 62

BOMBAL, MARIA LUISA
House of Mist. New York: 1947. V. 67

BOMBERG, DAVID
Poems and Drawings from the First World War. London: 1992. V. 65
Russian Ballet. London: 1919. V. 64

BOMBOURG, J. DE
Recherche Crieuse de la Vie de Raphael Sansio d'Urbin, de ses Oeuvres, Peintures & Estampes.... Lyon: 1709. V. 64

BOMER, ANTON
Triumphus Novem Seculorum imperii Romano-Germanici.... Augsburg: 1725. V. 66

BOMMER, GEORGE
A New Method Which Teaches How to Make Vegetable Manure by a Course of High Fermentation in Fifteen Days.... New York: 1843. V. 64

BONAFOUS, MATTHIEU
Traite de l'Education des Vers a Soie et de la Culture du Murier, Suivi De Divers Memoires sur l'Art Sericicole. Paris: 1840. V. 67

BONARDO, GIOVANNI MARIA
La Grandezza, Larghezza, E Distanza di Tutte Le Sfere.... Venice: 1600. V. 64

BONARELLI DELLA ROVERE, GUIDUBALDO, CONTE
Filli Di Sciro Favola Pastorale. Ferrara: 1607. V. 66

BONATTI, WALTER
On the Heights. London: 1964. V. 63

BONAVENTURA, SAINT
Santi Bonaventure Tractatus et Libri Quamplurimi. 1489. V. 66
Vita e Fioreti di Sancto Francisco. Milan: 1495. V. 64

BONAVIA, E.
The Cultivated Oranges and Lemons, etc. of India and Ceylon.... Dehra Dun: 1973. V. 62

BOND, C.
Leaves from a Christmas Bough. London: 1867. V. 65

BOND, J. WESLEY
Minnesota and Its Resources. New York: 1854. V. 65

BOND, JAMES H.
From Out of the Yukon. Oregon: 1948. V. 67

BOND, JOHN
A Compleat Guide for Justices of Peace...in Two Parts. London: 1696. V. 67
A Complete Guide for Justices of the Peace, According to the best Approved Authors. London: 1687. V. 67

BOND, LARRY
Red Phoenix. New York: 1989. V. 67

BOND, MARY WICKHAM
How 007 Got His Name. London: 1966. V. 65; 66

BOND, NELSON
Lancelot Biggs; Spaceman. 1950. V. 64; 66
Lancelot Biggs: Spaceman. New York: 1950. V. 62

BOND, T. E. T.
Wild Flowers of the Ceylon Hills, Some Familiar Plants of the Up-Country Districts. London: 1953. V. 67

BONE, DAVID W.
The Brassbounder. New York: 1923. V. 64
Merchantman Rearmed. London: 1949. V. 62

BONE, GERTRUDE
The Hidden Orchis. London: 1928. V. 62

BONE, STEPHEN
The West Coast of Scotland: Skye to Oban - Shell Guide. London. V. 65

BONER, CHARLES
Chamois Hunting in the Mountains of Bavaria. 1853. V. 62; 63; 64
Chamois Hunting in the Mountains of Bavaria. London: 1853. V. 64
Forest Creatures. 1861. V. 62; 67

BONETT, JOHN
Dead Lion. London: 1949. V. 67

BONFIGLIOLI, KYRIL
Something Nasty in the Woodshed. London: 1976. V. 67

BONGE, LYLE
The Photographs of Lyle Bonge. North Carolina: 1982. V. 63
The Sleep of Reason. 1974. V. 63
The Sleep of Reason. North Carolina: 1974. V. 63

BONHAM, T.
Journal. Period October 1st 1890 to March 31st 1892. London: 1889. V. 66
Log Book. Mr. T. Bonham. H. M. S. Northumberland. Period 1st January 1889 to 30th September 1890. London: 1888. V. 66

BONHOTE, J. LEWIS
Birds of Britain. London: 1907. V. 66; 67

BONINGTON, R. P.
A Series of Subjects from the Works of the Late R. P. Bonington Drawn on Stone by J. D. Harding. London: 1829-1830. V. 66
A Series of Subjects from the Works of the Late R. P. Bonington, Drawn on Stone by J. P. Harding. London: 1829. V. 66

BONINI, WILLIAM E.
The Caribbean South American Plate Boundary and Regional Tectonics. 1984. V. 67

BONNARD, PIERRE
The Complete Graphic Work. New York: 1981. V. 64

BONNARDOT, A.
De la Reparation des Vielles Reliures Complement de l'Essai sur l'Art de Restaurer les Estampes et les Livres Suivi d'un Dissertation sur les Moyens d'Obtenir des Duplicata de Manuscrits. Paris: 1858. V. 63

BONNE, C.
Mosquitoes of Surinam, a Study of Neotropical Mosquitoes. Amsterdam: 1925. V. 63

BONNEFOY, YVES
Traite du Pianiste. Paris: 1946. V. 67

BONNELL, HENRY E.
Charlotte Bronte: George Eliot: Jane Austen: Stuies in their Works. London: 1902. V. 66

BONNEMAINS, JACQUELINE
Baudin in Australian Waters. The Artwork of the French Voyage of Discovery to the Southern Lands 1800-1804. Melbourne: 1988. V. 63; 64

BONNER, C. E. B.
Index Hepaticarum. Weineheim: 1962-1978. V. 62

BONNER, CINDY
Lily. Chapel Hill: 1992. V. 63; 64; 67

BONNER, HYPATIA BRADLAUGH
Charles Bradlaugh: Record of His Life and Work.... London: 1894. V. 64

BONNER, T. D.
The Life and Adventures of James P. Beckwourth. New York: 1856. V. 63, 64, 66

BONNET, CHARLES
Considerations Sur Les Corps Organises, ou l'on Traite de Leur Origine.... London: 1762. V. 64
Oeuvres d'Histoire Naturelle et de Philosophie. Neuchatel: 1779-1783. V. 62
Recherches sur l'Usage des Feuilles dans les Plantes.... Gottingen and Leiden: 1754. V. 62; 63; 64

BONNEY, CECIL
Looking Over My Shoulder - Seventy Five Years in the Pecos Valley. Roswell: 1971. V. 64; 67

BONNEY, ORRIN H.
Battle Drums and Geysers: the Life and Journals of Lt. Gustavus Cheney Doane, Soldier and Explorer of the Yellowstone and the Snake River Regions. Chicago: 1970. V. 67

BONNEY, THOMAS GEORGE
Outline Sketches in the High Alps of Dauphine. London: 1865. V. 62

BONNYCASTLE, JOHN
An Introduction to Astronomy. London: 1786. V. 66
An Introduction to Astronomy. London: 1796. V. 63
An Introduction to Astronomy. London: 1811. V. 65
The Scholar's Guide to Arithmetic; or a Complete Exercise Book for the Use of Schools. London: 1788. V. 65
A Treatise on Plane and Spherical Trigonometry.... London: 1806. V. 64

BONNYCASTLE, R. H.
The Canadas in 1841. London: 1842. V. 63
Spanish America; or a Descriptive, Historical and Geographical Account of the Dominions of Spain the Western Hemisphere. Philadelphia: 1819. V. 66

BONSAL, STEPHEN
Edward Fitzgerald Beale - a Pioneer in the Path of Empire 1822-1903. New York: 1912. V. 65

BONSER, WILFRID
Proverb Literature: a Bibliography of Works Relating to Proverbs. London: 1930. V. 64

BONTE, LOUISE QUARLES
ABC in Dixie: a Plantation Alphabet. London: 1904. V. 64

BONTEMPS, ARNA
Sad-Faced Boy. Boston: 1937. V. 64

BONVALOT, GABRIEL
Through the Heart of Asia; over the Pamir to India. London: 1889. V. 64

BONWICK, JAMES
Romance of the Wool Trade. London: 1887. V. 64

BOOK Collecting: Four Broadcast Talks. Cambridge: 1950. V. 64

A BOOK of Belgium's Gratitude. 1915. V. 62

THE BOOK of Bosh, With Which are Incorporated Some Amusing and Instructive Nursery Stories in Rhyme. London: 1896. V. 64

A BOOK of Christmas Carols Illuminated from Ancient Manuscripts in the British Museum. London: 1845?. V. 62

A BOOK of Christmas Verse. London: 1895. V. 64

THE BOOK of English Poetry; with Critical and Biographical Sketches of the Poets. London: 1855. V. 62

THE BOOK of English Trades and Library of the Useful Arts.... London: 1827. V. 64

BOOK of 50 Pictures. Concord: 1850. V. 64

BOOK of Games and Sports. London: 1856. V. 64

THE BOOK of Kells. Bern: 1951. V. 66

THE BOOK of Kells: Reproductions. London: 1974. V. 62

BOOK OF MORMON
Book of Mormon, printed in the Deseret Alphabet. Part I. New York: 1869.. V. 65

BOOK of Nonsense. Chicago: 1896,. V. 63

BOOK of Nursery and Mother Goose Rhymes. Garden City: 1954. V. 66

THE BOOK of Old English Ballads. London: 1910. V. 64

THE BOOK of Old English Songs and Ballads. London, New York, Toronto: 1915. V. 62

THE BOOK of Oz Cooper. An Appreciation of Oswald Bruce Cooper, With Characteristic Examples of His Art in Lettering, Type Designing and Such of His Writings as Reveal the Cooperian Typographica Gospel. Chicago: 1949. V. 63; 64

BOOK of Picture Alphabets - 1. Alphabet of Beasts. 2. Birds. 3. Nations. 4. Scripture Alphabet. London. V. 63

BOOK of Princeton Verse. Princeton: 1916. V. 63

A BOOK of Princeton Verse. Princeton: 1919. V. 64

BOOK of Simples. London: 1908. V. 66

A BOOK of Sundry Draughtes Principally Serving Glasiers.... London: 1898. V. 62

THE BOOK of the Bear - Being Twenty-One Tales from the Russian. London: 1926. V. 65

THE BOOK of the Coronation of Our Liege Lady Victoria. London: 1853. V. 65

THE BOOK of the Poets' Club. London: 1909. V. 65

THE BOOK of the Queen's Dolls' House Library. London: 1924. V. 66

THE BOOK of Trades, or the Library of the Useful Arts. Part I. London: 1810. V. 62

THE BOOK of Trades; or Young British Tradesmen.... London: 1835. V. 64

THE BOOK of Wedding Days. London: 1889. V. 62

BOOKANO Stories No. 4. London: 1937. V. 67

BOOKER, LUKE
Malvern, a Descriptive and Historical Poem. Dudley: 1798. V. 62

A BOOKFUL of Fun. London: 1905. V. 64

THE BOOKWORM. London: 1888-1894. V. 67

BOOLE, GEORGE
George Boole's Collected Logical Works. La Salle: 1952. V. 63
Studies in Logic and Probability. London: 1953. V. 62
A Treatise on Differential Equations. (with) Treatise on Differential Equations. Supplementary Volume. London: 1872-1865. V. 66

BOON, K. G.
Rembrandt, the Complete Etchings. New York: 1963. V. 62; 65; 66

BOONE, ELIZABETH HILL
The Codex Magliabechiano (with) The Book of the Life of the Ancient Mexicans. Berkeley: 1963. V. 63
The Codex Magliabechiano. (with) The Book of the Life of the Ancient Mexicans. Berkeley: 1983. V. 62; 64

BOOSEY, EDWARD J.
Foreign Bird Keeping. 1960. V. 67

BOOSEY, THOMAS
Anecdotes of Fish and Fishing. London: 1887. V. 63
Piscatorial Reminiscences and Gleanings by an Old Angler and Bibliopolist.... London: 1835-1836. V. 64

THE BOOT and Shoe-Maker's Assistant, Containing a Treatise on Clicking and the Form and Fitting-Up of Lasts Scientifically Considered.... Manchester: 1853. V. 66

BOOTH, ARTHUR JOHN
Robert Owen, the Founder of Socialism in England. London: 1869. V. 64

BOOTH, CHARLES
The Housing Question in Manchester. Notes on the Report of the Citizens' Association. Manchester: 1904. V. 67

BOOTH, E. E.
By Observations and Experiences in the United States Army. Los Angeles: 1944. V. 67

BOOTH, EDWARD CARTON
Australia. London: 1874-1876. V. 64

BOOTH, EDWIN
Edmund Booth (1810-1905) Forty-Niner, The Life Story of a Deaf Pioneer. Stockton: 1953. V. 65

BOOTH, JAMES
On the Application of a New Analytic Method to the Theory of Curves and Curved Surfaces. London and Liverpool: 1843. V. 65

BOOTH, JOHN T.
Booth's Manual of Domestic Medicine and Guide to Health and Long Life. Cincinnati: 1884. V. 62

BOOTH, MARY L.
History of the City of New York. New York: 1880. V. 67

BOOTH, MAUD BALLINGTON
Sleepy-Time Stories. New York: 1899. V. 64

BOOTH, N. K.
Residential Landscape Architecture, Design Process for the Private Residence. Upper Saddle River: 1991. V. 67

BOOTH, PHILIP
Letter from a Distant Land. New York: 1957. V. 63

BOOTH, STEPHEN
The Book Called Holinshed's Chronicle. San Francisco: 1968. V. 62

BOOTH, WILLIAM
In Darkest England. New York and London: 1890. V. 63; 64
In Darkest England and The Way Out. London: 1890. V. 63; 64; 66; 67

BOOTHBY, BROOKE
A Letter to the Right Honourable Edmund Burke. London: 1791. V. 65

BOOTHBY, GUY
Across the World for a Wife. London: 1898. V. 66
The Kidnapped President. London: 1902. V. 65; 67
The Lust of Hate. London: 1898. V. 66
Pharos the Egyptian. London: 1899. V. 64

BOOTHBY, WALTER M.
Respiratory Physiology in Aviation. Randolph Field: 1954. V. 63

BOOTHROYD, B.
The History of the Ancient Borough of Pontefract. Pontefract: 1807. V. 62; 64; 65

BOOTS, JOHN MERCER
Power Rider Invasion- War on the Rustlers in 1892. Los Angeles: 1923. V. 63

BOOTT, FRANCIS
Illustrations of the Genus Carex. London: 1858-1867. V. 66

BOR, N. L.
Some Beautiful Indian Climbers and Shrubs. Bombay: 1954. V. 67

BORCHGREVINK, C. E.
First on the Antarctic Continent. London: 1901. V. 64

BORCKE, HEROS VON
Memoirs of the Confederate War for Independence. Edinburgh and London: 1866. V. 62; 63; 65
Zwei Jahre Im Sattel Und Am Feinde.... Berlin: 1886. V. 62

BORDE, ANDREW
The Boke of the Introduction of Knowledge. London: 1814. V. 64

BORDELON, LOUIS
The Management of the Tongue. London: 1707. V. 63

BORDEN, ROBERT LAIRD
Robert Laird Borden: His Memoirs. Toronto: 1938. V. 64

BORDEN, SPENCER
The Arab Horse. New York: 1906. V. 62
What Horse for the Calvary?. Fall River: 1912. V. 66

BORDLEY, JOHN BEALE
Essays and Notes on Husbandry and Rural Affairs. Philadelphia: 1801. V. 62
Intimations; on Agriculture and Manufactures; and on New Sources of Trade.... N.P: 1796?. V. 62

BORDONE, BENEDETTO
Isolario...Nel Qual si Ragiona di Tutte l'Isole del Mondo.... Venice: 1547. V. 62

BOREIN, EDWARD
Edward Borein, Drawings and Paintings of the Old West. Volume I: the Indians. Flagstaff: 1968. V. 66
The Etchings of Edward Borein. San Francisco;: 1971. V. 62; 64
Etchings of the Far West. Santa Barbara. V. 62
Etchings of the West: Collected Etchings, Drawings and Water Colors of Western Life. Santa Barbara: 1950. V. 64

BORELLI, GIOVANNI ALPHONSO
De Vi Percussionis Liber. Bologna: 1667. V. 62; 66

BOREMAN, ROBERT
The Country-Mans Catechisme; or the Churches Plea for Tithes. London: 1652. V. 63

BOREMAN, T.
A Compendium of Zoology.... London: 1818. V. 64
A Description of More than Three Hundred Animals.... London: 1812. V. 62

BORENIUS, TANCRED
The Leverton Harris Collection. 1931. V. 67

BORG, CARL OSCAR
Cross Sword and Gold Pan. Los Angeles: 1936. V. 64

BORGES, JORGE LUIS
El Aleph. Buenos Aires: 1949. V. 67
The Aleph and Other Stories 1933-1969. London: 1971. V. 63
Antologia Personal. Buenos Aires: 1961. V. 65
The Congress. London: 1974. V. 65
Elogio de la Sombra. Buenos Aires: 1969. V. 65
Fervor de Buenos Aires. Buenos Aires: 1923. V. 67
Ficciones. London: 1962. V. 63; 65
Ficciones. N.P: 1984. V. 62; 63; 64; 66
Ficciones. New York: 1985. V. 63
Historia Universal de la Infamia. Buenos Aires: 1935. V. 65; 67
El Idioma de Los Argentinos. Buenos Aires: 1928. V. 62
El Jardin de Senderos Que Se Bifurcan. Buenos Aires: 1942. V. 65
El Libro de Arena. Buenos Aires: 1975. V. 65
A Personal Anthology. London: 1968. V. 62
Poems (1922-1943). Buenos Aires: 1943. V. 67
Selected Poems 1923-1967. London: 1972. V. 64
Siete Poemas Sajones/Seven Saxon Poems. Verona: 1974. V. 65

BORGHINI, RAFFAELLO
Il Riposo.... Florence: 1730. V. 62; 65

BORGLIN, J. N.
Chemistry of Terpenes and Resin Acids. Wilmington: 1942. V. 63
Treatise on Rosin. Wilmington: 1945. V. 65

BORGMAN, ALBERT S.
Thomas Shadwell: His Life and Comedies. New York: 1928. V. 62

BORHIDI, A.
Phytogeography and Vegetation Ecology of Cuba. Budapest: 1996. V. 62; 63

BORKENAU, FRANZ
The Spanish Cockpit: an Eye-Witness Account of the...Conflicts of the Civil War. London: 1937. V. 66

BORLASE, GEORGE
Cantabrigienses Graduati: sive Catalogus, Exhibens Nomina Eorum, Quos ab Anno 1659, Usque ad Annum 1800, Gradu Quocunque Ornavit.... Cambridge: 1800. V. 62

BORLASE, WILLIAM
Natural History of Cornwall. Oxford: 1758. V. 62

BORRER, W.
The Birds of Sussex. London: 1891. V. 62; 67

BORRICHIUS, OLAUS
Hermetis Aegyptiorum, et Chemicorum Sapientia ab Hermanni Conringii Animadversionibus Vindicata.... Hafniae: 1674. V. 67

BORRINGDON, JOHN PARKER, 2ND BARON
Trial Between Lord Borringdon and Sir A. Paget, K.B. for Criminal Conversation with the Plaintiff's Wife. Which Was Tried...July 19, 1808. London: 1808. V. 63

BORROW, GEORGE HENRY
The Bible in Spain. London: 1843. V. 62
The Bible in Spain. Philadelphia: 1843. V. 63
Celebrated Trials of all Countries and Remarkable Cases of Criminal Jurisprudence. Philadelphia: 1835. V. 63
Lavengro: the Scholar, The Gipsy, The Priest. 1936. V. 65
Lavengro. The Scholar, The Gipsy, The Priest. London: 1936. V. 62
The Romany Rye. London: 1857. V. 67
The Romany Rye. London: 1858. V. 66
The Zincali; or, an Account of the Gypsies of Spain. London: 1843. V. 66

BORSI, FRANCO
Leon Battista Alberti. New York: 1977. V. 63; 64

BORSNAN, CORNELIUS
Jason Lee Prophet of the New Oregon. New York: 1932. V. 67

BORTON, BENJAMIN
On the Parallels or Chapters of Inner History. A Story of the Rappahannock. Woodstown: 1903. V. 63; 66

BORUP, GEORGE
A Tenderfoot with Peary. New York: 1911. V. 64; 66

BORUWLASKI, JOSEPH
Memoirs of Count Boruwlaski.... Durham: 1820. V. 62; 66
Memoirs of the Celebrated Dwarf, Joseph Boruwlaski, a Polish Gentleman.... London: 1788. V. 62

BOSANQUET, CHARLES
A Letter to W. Manning, Esq. M.P. on the Causes of the Rapid and Progressive Depreciation of West India Property. London: 1807?. V. 63

BOSANQUET, EUSTACE F.
English Printed Almanacks and Prognostications. A Bibliographical History to the Year 1600. London: 1917. V. 64

BOSANQUET, S. R.
A New System of Logic and Development of the Principles of Truth and Reasoning.... London: 1839. V. 63

BOSANQUET, THEODORA
Henry James at Work. London: 1924. V. 62

BOSE, J. C.
Growth and Tropic Movements of Plants. London: 1929. V. 63

BOSE, T. K.
Floriculture and Landscaping. Calcutta: 1999. V. 67
Fruits: Tropical and Subtropical. Calcutta: 1990. V. 63
Propagation of Tropical and Subtropical Horticultural Crops. Calcutta: 1997. V. 63
Trees of the World. Orissa: 1998. V. 63
Tropical Horticulture. Calcutta: 1999. V. 63

BOSNAL, STEPHEN
Edward Fitzgerald Beale a Pioneer in the Path of Empire 1822-1903. New York: 1912. V. 62

BOSSCHERE, JEAN DE
Weird Islands. New York: 1922. V. 64

BOSSE, ABRAHAM
De La Maniere de Graver a l'Eau Forte et au Burin, et de la Gravure en Maniere Noire. Paris: 1758. V. 66
Traite des Pratiques Geometrales et Perspectives Enseignees dans l'Academie Royale de la Peinture et Sculpture. Paris: 1665. V. 62

BOSSERT, H. T.
Folk Art of Europe. London: 1954. V. 66
Ornament. London: 1924. V. 62

BOSSI, GIUSEPPE
Del Cenacolo di Leonardo da Vinci, Libri Quattro. Milan: 1810. V. 64

BOSSI, LOUIS
Guide des Etrangers a Milan et dans les Environs. Milan: 1819. V. 66

BOSSON, ABRAHAM
Specimen Medicum Inauqurale de Morbis ex Vermium in Primis Viis Nidulatione Oriundis.... Leyden: 1777. V. 66

BOSSUET, JACQUES BENIGNE
A Discourse on the History of the Whole World.... London: 1686. V. 63

BOSSUT, CHARLES
Traito Elementaire de Mecanique et de Dinamique, Applique Principalement Aux Mouvems des Machines. Charleville: 1763. V. 62

BOSTOCK, HUGH S.
Yukon Territory Selected Field Reports of the Geological Survey of Canada 1898 to 1933. Ottawa: 1957. V. 63

BOSTON ARTISTS' ASSOCIATION
Catalogue of Paintings of the Second Exhibition of the Boston Artists' Association, 1843, at Harding's Gallery, 22 School Street. Boston: 1843. V. 62; 64
The Constitution of the Boston Artists' Association, with a Catalogue of the First Public Exhibition of Paintings at Harding's Gallery. Boston: 1842. V. 62; 64

BOSTON ATHENAEUM
Catalogue of the Second Exhibition of Sculpture in the Athenaeum Gallery. Boston: 1840. V. 64

BOSTON FEMALE ANTISLAVERY SOCIETY
Report...with a Concico Statement of Events, Previous and Subsequent to the Annual Meeting of 1835. Boston: 1836. V. 66

BOSTON, L. M.
The Fossil Snake. London: 1975. V. 67
The Sea Egg. London: 1967. V. 67

BOSTON, LUCY
The Children of Green Knowe. London: 1954. V. 65

BOSTON SOCIETY OF LANDSCAPE ARCHITECTS
Year Book for 1929. Boston: 1929. V. 64

BOSTWICK, F. M.
Kohana San. Tokyo: 1900. V. 65

BOSTWICK, HENRY A.
Genealogy of the Bostwick Family in America, the Descendants of Arthur Bostwick, of Stratford, Connecticut. New York: 1901. V. 65

BOSTWICK, LUCY W.
Margery Daws' Home Confectionary. New York: 1891. V. 67

BOSWELL, EDWARD
The Civil Division of the County of Dorset.... Sherborne: 1795. V. 62; 65

BOSWELL, GEORGE
A Treatise on Watering Meadows. London: 1792. V. 63
A Treatise on Watering Meadows. London: 1801. V. 62

BOSWELL, JAMES
An Account of Corsica, the Journal of a Tour to that Island.... Glasgow: 1768. V. 62; 65; 66; 67
Boswell in Holland 1763-1764 - Including His Correspondence with Belle De Zuylen. New York: 1952. V. 65
Boswell's Note Book 1776-1777.... London: 1925. V. 62

BOSWELL, JAMES continued
The Correspondence of Boswell with James Bruce and Andrew Gibb, Overssers of the Auchinleck Estate. Edinburgh and New Haven: 1998. V. 62
Everybody's Boswell - Being the Life of Samuel Johnson Abridged from James Boswell's Complete Text and from the "Tour to the Hebrides". London: 1930. V. 63
The Journal of a Tour to the Hebrides. Dublin: 1785. V. 62; 64; 65; 66
The Journal of a Tour to the Hebrides. London: 1785. V. 64
The Journal of a Tour to the Hebrides. London: 1852. V. 62; 63
The Journal of a Tour to the Hebrides. Avon: 1974. V. 62
Journal of a Tour to the Hebrides. Bloomfield: 1974. V. 62; 64
A Letter to the People of Scotland, On the Present State of the Nation.... London: 1784. V. 64
Letters of James Boswell, Addressed to the Rev. W. J. Temple.... London: 1857. V. 65
Life of Johnson and Tour to the Hebrides. London: 1860. V. 62
Life of Johnson. Together with Boswell's Journal of a Tour to the Hebrides and Johnson's Diary of a Journey into North Wales. Oxford: 1934. V. 65
The Life of Samuel Johnson. London: 1791. V. 64; 65; 66; 67
The Life of Samuel Johnson. London: 1791-1793. V. 63
The Life of Samuel Johnson. London: 1793. V. 63; 66
The Life of Samuel Johnson. Boston: 1807. V. 63
The Life of Samuel Johnson. London: 1811. V. 62
The Life of Samuel Johnson. London: 1823. V. 67
The Life of Samuel Johnson. London: 1826. V. 62; 63; 67
The Life of Samuel Johnson. Oxford: 1826. V. 64; 65; 67
The Life of Samuel Johnson. London: 1835. V. 65
The Life of Samuel Johnson. London: 1839. V. 65; 67
The Life of Samuel Johnson. London: 1848. V. 62
The Life of Samuel Johnson. London: 1882. V. 66
The Life of Samuel Johnson. London: 1885. V. 63
The Life of Samuel Johnson. Oxford: 1887. V. 64
The Life of Samuel Johnson. London: 1901. V. 63
The Life of Samuel Johnson. London: 1912. V. 62
The Life of Samuel Johnson. New York: 1916. V. 62
The Life of Samuel Johnson. London: 1924. V. 66
The Life of Samuel Johnson. Bath: 1925. V. 65
The Life of Samuel Johnson. 1938. V. 62
On the Profession of a Player - three Essays. London: 1929. V. 64
Private Papers of James Boswell from Malahide Castle in the Collection of Lt. Colonel Ralph Heyward Isham. New York: 1928-1937. V. 63; 66
The Yale Editions of the Private Papers of James Boswell. London: 1951-1960. V. 67

BOSWELL, P. G. H.
The Middle Silurian Rocks of North Wales. 1949. V. 67

BOSWELL, ROBERT
Dancing in the Movies. Iowa City: 1986. V. 63

BOSWORTH, JOSEPH
A Compendious Anglo-Saxon and English Dictionary. London: 1848. V. 62; 65

BOSWORTH, T. O.
Geology of the Tertiary and Quaternary Periods in N.W. Peru, with an Account of the Palaeontology. 1922. V. 63; 66

THE BOTANICAL Magazine; or Flower-Garden Displayed. London: 1787-1815. V. 62

BOTCHKAREVA, MARIA
Yashka - My Life as Peasant, Exile and Soldier. London: 1919. V. 64

BOTFIELD, BERIAH
Notes on the Cathedral Libraries of England. Detroit: 1969. V. 67
Stemmata Botevilliana. Westminster: 1858. V. 63

BOTKIN, B. A.
Folk-Say a Regional Miscellany 1930. Norman: 1930. V. 66
Folk-Say IV - The Land is Ours. Norman: 1932. V. 66

BOTSCHANTZEVA, Z. P.
Tulips: Morphology, Cytology, Phytogeography and Physiology. Rotterdam: 1982. V. 63

BOTT, W.
A Description of Buxton, and the Adjacent Country, in Which Will Be Found a Correct Guide and Directory to all the Romantic and Charming Scenes.... Manchester: 1818. V. 62

BOTTA, CHARLES
History of the War of the Independence of the U.S.A. New Haven: 1837. V. 65

BOTTANI, GIOVANNI
Descrizione Storica Delle Pitture del Regio - Ducale Palazzo del Te, Fuori Della Porta di Mantova Detta Pusterla. Mantova: 1783. V. 64

BOTTO, ANTONIO
The Children's Book. Lisbon: 1935. V. 64

BOTTOME, PHYLLIS
Murder in the Bud. London: 1939. V. 66

BOTTOMLEY, GORDON
King Lear's Wife and Other Plays. London: 1920. V. 67
Laodice and Danae - a Play in One Act. Boston: 1916. V. 65

BOTTOMS, DAVID
Shooting Rats at the Bibb County Dump. New York: 1980. V. 63

BOTTRALL, RONALD
Collected Poems. London: 1961. V. 65
The Turning Path. London: 1939. V. 62

BOTTS, JOHN MINOR
Interesting and Important Correspondence Between Opposition Members of the Legislature of Virginia and Hon. John Minor Botts, Jan. 17, 1860. Washington: 1860. V. 64

BOUCARD, A.
Travels of a Naturalist, a Record of Adventures, Discoveries, History and Customs of Americans and Indians, Habits and Descriptions of Animals.... Bournemouth: 1894. V. 64

BOUCH, C. M. L.
The Lake Counties 1500-1830. Manchester: 1961. V. 65

BOUCHARDON, EDME
Etudes Prises dans le Bas Peuple ou les Cris de Paris, Premiere (- Cinquieme) Suitte. Paris: 1737-1746. V. 62

BOUCHER, CHAUNCEY SAMUEL
The Nullification Controversy in South Carolina. Chicago: 1916. V. 63

BOUDARD, JEAN BAPTISTE
Iconologie Tiree de Divers Auteurs. Parma: 1759. V. 66

BOUDIER DE VILLEMERT, PIERRE JOSEPH
Le Nouvel Ami des Femmes ou la Philosophie du Sexe. Amsterdam: 1779. V. 66

BOUDINOT, ELIAS
Address, of the New Jersey Bible Society in the Publick.... New Brunswick: 1810. V. 63; 66
Journal or Historical Recollections of American Events During the Revolutionary War. Philadelphia: 1894. V. 63
Memoirs of the Life of the Rev. William Tennent, Formerly Pastor of the Presbyterian Church at Freehold, in New Jersey.... Poughkeepsie: 1815. V. 63; 66
The Second Advent, or Coming of the Messiah in Glory.... Trenton: 1815. V. 63; 66
A Star in the West; or, a Humble Attempt to Discover the Long Lost Ten Tribes of Israel.... Trenton: 1816. V. 63; 66

BOUGAINVILLE, LOUIS ANTOINE DE COMTE
Voyage Autour du Monde, Par la Fregate du Roi La Boudreuse, et la Flute L'Etoile, en 1766, 1767, 1768 and 1769. Paris: 1772. V. 62

BOUGUER, PIERRE
De la Manoeuvre des Vaisseaux, ou Traite de Mechanique et de Dynamique, dans Lequel on Reduit a des Solutions tres Simples les Problemes de Marine les plus Difficiles qui Ont Pour Object le Mouvement du Navire. Paris: 1757. V. 67
Traite d'Optique sur la Gradation de la Lumiere: Ouvrage Posthume.... Paris: 1760. V. 63

BOUHOURS, DOMINIQUE
The Life of St. Ignatius, Founder of the Society of Jesus. London: 1686. V. 64

BOUILLART, JACQUES
Historie de l'Abbaye Royale de Saint Germain des Prez.... Paris: 1724. V. 62

BOUILLON, J. P.
Art Nouveau 1870-1914. 1985. V. 62
Art Nouveau 1870-1914. New York: 1985. V. 65

BOUILLON-LAGRANGE, EDME JEAN BAPTISTE
A Manual of a Course of Chemistry; or a Series of Experiments and Illustrations Necessary to form a Complete Course of that Science. London: 1800. V. 65

BOUILLY, JEAN NICHOLAS
Les Jeunes Femmes. Paris: 1785. V. 65
Les Jeunes Femmes. Paris: 1790?. V. 65

BOULANVILLIERS, H., COMTE DE
Etat de la France, Dans Lequel on Voit Tout ce qui Regarde le Gouvernement Ecclesiastique, le Militaire, la Justice, les Finances, le Commerce, les Manufactures, le Nombre des Habitans.... Londres: 1727-1728. V. 67
An Historical Account of the Antient Parliaments of France or States General of the Kingdom. London: 1739. V. 65; 67

BOULART, R.
Ornithologie du Salon...Oiseaux de Voliere Europeens et Exotiques. 1878. V. 62

BOULDIN, POWHATAN
The Old Trunk, or Sketches of Colonial Days. Danville: 1896. V. 63

BOULENGER, E. G.
Reptiles and Batrachians. London: 1914. V. 64

BOULENGER, G. A.
Catalogue of the Freshwater Fishes of Africa in the British Museum. London: 1909-1916. V. 62; 63; 65
Catalogue of the Freshwater Fishes of Africa in the British Museum (Natural History). London: 1909. V. 64
Catalogue of the Lizards in the British Musuem. London: 1885-1887. V. 64
Catalogue of the Perciform Fishes in the British Museum. 1895. V. 63
Catalogue of the Perciform Fishes in the British Museum. London: 1895. V. 65

BOULGER, DEMETRIUS CHARLES
The Life of Sir Stamford Raffles. London: 1897. V. 62

BOULNOIS, H. P.
The Construction of Carriageways and Footways. 1895. V. 67

BOULNOIS, HELEN MARY
Into Little Thibet. London: 1923. V. 64

BOULTON, M. P. W.
On Aerial Locomotion. London: 1864. V. 65

BOULTON, RICHARD
A Compleat History of Magick, Sorcery and Witchcraft.... London: 1715-1716. V. 63; 67

BOUQUERET, CHRISTIAN
Des Annees Folles Aux Annees Noire: La Nouvelle Vision Photographique En France 1920-1940. Paris: 1997. V. 65
Roger Parry: Le Meteore Fabuleux. Rome: 1995. V. 65

BOUQUET, MICHEL
The Tourist's Ramble in the Highlands.... London: 1850. V. 62; 66

BOURDIER DE VILLEMER
The Friend of Women. Philadelphia: 1803. V. 65

BOURDIEU, PIERRE
Sociologie de l'Algerie. Paris: 1958. V. 67

BOURDILLON, FRANCIS WILLIAM
Ailes d'Alouette (Second Series). London: 1902. V. 64
A Lost God. London: 1891. V. 64

BOURGEOIS, LOUISE
The Puritan. N.P: 1990. V. 65

BOURGET, JOHN
The History of the Royal Abbey of Bec, Near Rouen in Normandy. London: 1779. V. 66

BOURGET, PAUL
Pastels. Paris: 1895?. V. 62; 67

BOURGUET, LOUIS
Trait de Petrifcations. Paris: 1742. V. 62

BOURIGNON, ANTOINETTE
Le Nouveau Ciel et la Nouvelle Terre. (with) Les Pierres De La Nouvelle Jersulam. Amsterdam: 1679. V. 63
Le Nouveau Ciel et La Nouvelle Terre. (with) Les Pierres De la Nouvelle Jerusalem. Amsterdam: 1683. V. 65

BOURJAILY, VANCE
The End of My Life. New York: 1947. V. 62; 63

BOURKE, A. F. G.
Social Evolution in Ants. Princeton: 1995. V. 67

BOURKE, JOHN G.
An Apache Campaign in the Sierra Madre - An Account of the Expedition in Pursuit of the Hostile Chiricahua Apaches of 1883. New York: 1886. V. 66
Mac Kenzie's Last Fight with the Cheyennes. Bellevue: 1970. V. 67
On the Border with Crook. New York: 1891. V. 65; 66; 67
Scatalogic Rites of All Nations. New York: 1934. V. 66
The Snake Dance of the Moquis of Arizona.... London: 1884. V. 64
The Snake Dance of the Moquis of Arizona.... New York: 1884. V. 63; 65
With General Crook in the Indian War. Palo Alto: 1968. V. 67

BOURKE, THOMAS
A Concise History of the Moors in Spain, from Their Invasion of that Kingdom to Their Final Expulsion Of It. London: 1811. V. 67

BOURKE, ULICK J.
The College Irish Grammar. 1856. V. 62; 65

BOURKE-WHITE, MARGARET
Dear Fatherland, Rest Quietly: A Report on the Collapse of Hitler's Thousand Years. New York: 1946. V. 63
Eyes on Russia. New York: 1931. V. 65
Newsprint. Montreal: 1939. V. 65
Portrait of Myself. New York: 1963. V. 63, 65
Shooting the Russian War. New York: 1942. V. 64
They Called It Purple Heart Valley - A Combat Chronicle of the War in Italy. New York: 1944. V. 64

BOURNE, G. H.
The Rhesus Monkey. London: 1975. V. 64

BOURNE, GEORGE
The Spirit of the Public Journals; or, Beauties of the American Newspapers for 1805. Baltimore: 1806. V. 63

BOURNE, GEORGE, PSEUD.
Memoirs of a Surrey Labourer.... London: 1907. V. 64

BOURNE, H. R.
The Story of Our Colonies: with Sketches of Their Present Condition. London: 1869. V. 66

BOURNE, HENRY
Observations on Popular Antiquities, Including the Whole of Mr. Bourne's Antiquitates Vulgares, with an Addenda to Every Chapter of that Work.... London: 1810. V. 62; 66

BOURNE, HERMON
Flores Poetici. The Florist's Manual.... Boston: 1833. V. 64

BOURNE, JOHN
Examples of Steam, Air and Gas Engines of the Most Recent Approved Types as Employed in Mines, Factories, Steam Navigation.... London: 1878. V. 65
Indian River Navigation; A Report Addressed to the Committee of Gentlemen Formed for the Establishment of Improved Steam Navigation.... London: 1849. V. 64
A Treatise on the Screw Propeller.... London: 1852. V. 67

BOURNE, JOHN C.
Great Western Railway. London: 1970. V. 65
London and Birmingham Railway. London: 1970. V. 65

BOURNE, VINCENT
Miscellaneous Poems: Consisting of Originals and Translations. London: 1772. V. 62; 65; 66
Poematia. Oxonii: 1826. V. 67
Poematia. London: 1840. V. 62; 67

BOURRY, EMILE
Treatise on Ceramic Industries: a Complete Manual for Pottery, Tile and Brick Works. London: 1901. V. 65; 66

BOUSQUET, JACQUES
Mannerism: the Painting and Style of the Late Renaissance. New York: 1964. V. 62; 63; 64

BOUSSARD, J.
Constructions et Decorations Pour Jardins, Kiosques - Orangeries - Voliees - Abris Divers. Paris: 1881. V. 64

BOUTCHER, WILLIAM
A Treatise on Forest Trees. Edinburgh: 1778. V. 63; 66

BOUTELL, CHARLES
A Manual of British Archaeology. London: 1858. V. 64
The Monumental Brasses of England: a Series of Engravings Upon Wood, From Every Variety.... London: 1849. V. 62

BOUTET, CLAUDE
The Art of Painting in Miniature: Teaching the Speedy and Perfect Acquisition of that Art Without a Master. London: 1752. V. 66
Traite de la Peinture en Mignature...Corrige et Augmente.... La Haye: 1708. V. 64

BOUTWELL, GEORGE S.
A Manual of the Direct and Excise Tax System of the United States. Washington: 1863. V. 65

BOUVET, MARGUERITE
Sweet William. Chicago: 1890. V. 64

BOVA, BEN
Mars. 1992. V. 65

BOWDEN, CHARLES
Blue Desert. Tucson: 1986. V. 62; 64
Frog Mountain Blues. Tucson: 1987. V. 67
Street Signs Chicago. Chicago: 1981. V. 63; 64; 65; 66

BOWDEN, J.
The Naturalist in Norway; or, Notes on the Wild Animals, Birds, Fishes, and Plants, of that Country. London: 1869. V. 66

BOWDICH, T. E.
Taxidermy; or, the Art of Collecting, Preparing and Mounting Objects of Natural History for the Use of Museums and Travellers. London: 1835. V. 62

BOWDITCH, H. P.
The Growth of Children; a Supplementary Investigation. Boston: 1877-1879. V. 67

BOWDITCH, NATHANIEL
A History of the Massachusetts General Hospital (to August 5, 1851). Boston: 1872. V. 64; 66; 67
Mathematical Papers from the Fourth Volume of the Memoirs of the American Academy of Arts and Sciences. Boston: 1820. V. 64
Memoirs of Nathaniel Bowditch. Boston: 1840. V. 63
The New American Practical Navigator. Newburyport: 1802. V. 64
The New American Practical Navigator. New York: 1826. V. 63; 64

BOWDLER, CHARLES
The Punishment of Death, in the Case of Forgery; Its Injustice and Impolicy Demonstrated. London: 1819. V. 63

BOWDLER, JANE
Poems and Essays. Dublin: 1787. V. 65

BOWDLER, THOMAS
Sermons on the Doctrines and Duties of Christianity. Bath: 1811. V. 66

BOWDOIN COLLEGE
Catalogue of the Peucinian Library, Bowdoin College. Lewiston: 1859. V. 66

BOWEN, E.
Rambles in the Path of the Steam Horse: an Off-Hand Olla Podrida. Philadelphia and Baltimore: 1855. V. 65

BOWEN, ELIZABETH
Ann Lee's: and Other Stories. London: 1926. V. 65
Bowen's Court. 1964. V. 67
The Death of the Heart. 1938. V. 67
Encounters: Stories. London: 1926. V. 65
A World of Love. London: 1955. V. 62

BOWEN, F. W.
History of Port Elizabeth, Cumberland County, New Jersey, Down to the Present Time. Philadelphia: 1885. V. 63; 66

BOWEN, FRANK C.
The Golden Age of Sal Indiamen, Packets and Clipper Ships. London: 1925. V. 64

BOWEN, HAROLD
The Life and Times of Ali Ibn Isa; The Good Vizier. Cambridge: 1928. V. 64

BOWEN, JOHN JOSEPH
The Strategy of Robert E. Lee. New York: 1914. V. 63

BOWEN, MARJORIE
Brave Employments. London: 1931. V. 67

BOWEN, MURIEL
Irish Hunting. 1954. V. 64

BOWEN, PETER
Coyote Wind. New York: 1994. V. 65; 67
Kelly Blue. New York: 1991. V. 66
Yellowstone Kelly. 1987. V. 66
Yellowstone Kelly. Ottawa: 1987. V. 63; 65; 67

BOWEN'S New Guide to the City of Boston and Vicinity: State of Massachusetts. Boston: 1849. V. 66

BOWER, DONALD E.
Fred Rosenstock. A Legend in Books and Art. 1976. V. 67

BOWER, F. O.
Sixty Years of Botany in Britain (1875-1935) Impressions of an Eye-Witness. London: 1938. V. 67

BOWER, JOHN
Description of the Abbeys of Melrose and Old Melrose. Kelso: 1813. V. 62
Description of the Abbeys of Melrose and Old Melrose. Edinburgh: 1822. V. 66; 67

BOWERS, C. G.
Rhododendrons and Azaleas, their Origins, Cultivation and Development. New York: 1936. V. 62; 65; 67
Rhododendrons and Azaleas, Their Origins, Cultivation and Development. New York: 1960. V. 62

BOWERS, D. N.
Seventy Years in Norton County, Kansas. Norton: 1942. V. 66

BOWERS, EDGAR
The Form of Loss. Denver: 1956. V. 65

BOWERS, FREDSON
George Sandys, a Bibliographical Catalogue of Printed Editions in England to 1700.... New York: 1950. V. 63

BOWERS, G.
Canters in Crampshire. London. V. 64; 66; 67
Mr. Crop's Harriers. London: 1891. V. 67

BOWERS, JOHN Z.
Advances in American Medicine: Essays on the Bicentennial. New York: 1976. V. 65; 67

BOWERS, W. H.
Researches into the History of the Parish and Parish Church of Stone, Staffordshire. Birmingham: 1929. V. 63

BOWES, JAMES
Japanese Marks and Seals. London: 1882. V. 62
Japanese Marks and Seals. London: 1887. V. 66
Notes on Shippo. Liverpool: 1895. V. 62

BOWKER, DAVID E.
Lunar Orbiter Photographic Atlas of the Moon. Washington: 1971. V. 67

BOWKER, PIERPONT F.
The Indian Vegetable Family Instructer.... Boston: 1836. V. 63

BOWLBY, ANTHONY
Injuries and Diseases of Nerves. London: 1899. V. 67

BOWLES, CARRINGTON
The Artist's Assistant in Drawing, Perspective, Etching, Engraving, Mezzotinto-Scraping, painting on Glass, in Crayons, in Water-Colours and on Silks and Satins. London: 1807. V. 62

BOWLES, E. A.
A Handbook of Crocus and Colchicum for Gardeners. London: 1952. V. 67
My Garden in Spring, Summer, Autumn and Winter. 1914. V. 67
My Garden in Spring, Summer, Autumn and Winter. London: 1914-1972. V. 64
My Garden in Spring, Summer, Autumn and Winter. 1972. V. 63

BOWLES, FLORA GATLIN
A No Man's Land Becomes a County. Austin: 1958. V. 66

BOWLES, JANE
The Collected Works. New York: 1966. V. 66
Two Serious Ladies. New York: 1943. V. 67

BOWLES, JOHN
A Letter Addressed to Samuel Whitbread, Esq. M.P. London: 1807. V. 64
A Protest Against T. Paine's Rights of Man Addressed to the Members of a Book Society.... London: 1792. V. 62

BOWLES, PAUL
The Boy Who Set the Fire and Other Stories. Los Angeles: 1974. V. 63
Collected Stories 1939-1976. Santa Barbara: 1979. V. 67
Dear Paul, Dear Ned: the Correspondence of Paul Bowles and Ned Rorem. North Pomfret: 1997. V. 64
The Hours After Noon. London: 1959. V. 63; 65; 67
A Hundred Camels in the Courtyard. San Francisco: 1962. V. 63
In Touch: The Letters of Paul Bowles. New York: 1994. V. 62; 67
Let It Come Down. London: 1952. V. 62; 63; 65
Let It Come Down. New York: 1952. V. 62; 63; 66; 67
A Little Stone. London: 1950. V. 63
Morocco. New York: 1993. V. 62
Next to Nothing. Kathmandu: 1976. V. 64; 65
Photographs. How Could I Send a Picture to the Desert?. Zurich: 1994. V. 62
Scenes. Los Angeles: 1968. V. 65
The Sheltering Sky. 1949. V. 62
The Sheltering Sky. Connecticut: 1949. V. 66
The Sheltering Sky. London: 1949. V. 62
The Spider's House. London: 1957. V. 63; 67
Their Heads are Green and Their Hands are Blue. New York: 1963. V. 63; 64
The Thicket of Spring. Poems 1926-1969. Los Angeles: 1972. V. 63; 65
The Time of Friendship. New York: 1967. V. 62; 64
Too Far From Home. London: 1994. V. 63; 65; 66
Two Poems. New York: 1933. V. 65
Two Poems. New York: 1934. V. 67
Up Above the World. New York: 1966. V. 62; 63; 64; 65; 66
Up Above the World. London: 1967. V. 62
Without Stopping: an Autobiography. New York: 1972. V. 63
Yallah. New York: 1957. V. 63

BOWLES, SAMUEL
A Summer's Journey to the Rocky Mountains, the Mormons and the Pacific States.... Springfield: 1865. V. 62

BOWLES, WILLIAM LISLE
Sonnets and Other Poems. (with) Poems. Bath: 1805-1803. V. 62

BOWLEY, A. L.
Two Funny Fairies. London: 1925. V. 65
Wages and Income in the United Kingdom Since 1860. Cambridge: 1937. V. 65

BOWLEY, ARTHUR LYON
The Measurement of Groups and Series: a Course of Lectures... Delivered at the Institute of Actuaries, Staple Inn Hall, During the Session 1902-1903. London: 1903. V. 66

BOWLING, TOM
The Book of Knots. London: 1900. V. 64

BOWLING, W. K.
Cholera, as It Appeared in Nashville, in 1849, 1850, 1854 and 1866. Nashville: 1866. V. 63

BOWLKER, CHARLES
The Art of Angling; or, Compleat Fly-Fisher.... 1792. V. 67

BOWLT, JOHN E.
Twentieth Century Russian and East European Painting (in the) Thyssen-Bornemisza Collection. 1993. V. 67

BOWMAN, A. K.
The Life and Times of Sir William Mac Ewen. London: 1942. V. 64

BOWMAN, ANNE
The Bear-Hunters of the Rocky Mountains. London: 1861. V. 65
The Bear-Hunters of the Rocky Mountains. Boston: 1862. V. 64

BOWMAN, DAVID
Let the Dog Drive. 1992. V. 64; 66
Let the Dog Drive. New York: 1992. V. 63; 65; 66; 67
Let the Dog Drive. 1993. V. 62
Let the Dog Drive. New York: 1993. V. 65

BOWMAN, ELIZABETH SCAGGS
Land of High Horizons. Kingsport: 1951. V. 67

BOWMAN, F. H.
The Structure of the Wool Fibre, In Its Relation to the Use of Wool for Technical Purposes. Manchester: 1885. V. 63

BOWMAN, JAMES
Pecos Bill. The Greatest Cowboy Of All Time. Chicago: 1937. V. 64

BOWMAN, JAMES CLOYD
Tales from a Finnish Tupa. Chicago: 1936. V. 66

BOWMAN, MARY K.
Reference Book of Wyoming County History. Parsons: 1965. V. 67

BOWMAN, RICHARD G.
Walking in Beauty, The Art and Life of Gerald Curtis Delano. Niwot: 1990. V. 63

BOWMAN, S. M.
Sherman and His Campaigns: a Military Biography. New York and London: 1865. V. 64

BOWMAN, WILLIAM DODGSON
Charlie Chaplin - His Life and Art. London: 1931. V. 65

BOWNAS, SAMUEL
A Description of the Qualifications Necessary to a Gospel Minister, Containing Advice to Ministers and Elders, How to Conduct Themselves in Their Conversation and Various Services, According to their Gifts in the Church of Christ. London: 1767. V. 66
The Journals of the Lives and Travels of.... London: 1759. V. 65

BOWREY, THOMAS
The Papers of Thomas Bowrey, 1669-1713 Discovered in 1913 by John Humphreys, M.A., F.S.A.... London: 1927. V. 63

BOWRING, JOHN
(Serbian title) Serbian Popular Poetry. London: 1827. V. 65

BOWYER, JAMES T.
The Pollinctor. Richmond: 1895. V. 63
The Witch of Jamestown. Richmond: 1890. V. 63

BOX, EDGAR
Death in the Fifth Position. 1952. V. 66

BOX, MICHAEL JAMES
Captain James Box's Adventures and Explorations in New and Old Mexico. New York: 1869. V. 66

BOXALL, G. E.
The Story of the Australian Bushrangers. London: 1899. V. 64

BOXER, C. R.
Further Selections from the Tragic History of the Sea 1559-1565. Cambridge: 1968. V. 63
Jan Compagnie in Japan 1600-1817; an Essay on the Cultural, Artistic and Scientific Influences Exercised by the Hollanders in Japan from the Seventeenth to the Nineteenth Centuries. Hague: 1936. V. 64

THE BOY Who Was Turned into a Monkey, or, the Story of Mischievous Tom. London: 1856. V. 63

BOYCE, ANNE OGDEN
Records of a Quaker Family: The Richardsons of Cleveland. London: 1889. V. 63

BOYCE, M. S.
The Jackson Elk Herd, Intensive Wildlife Management in North America. Cambridge: 1989. V. 67

BOYCE, PETER
The Genus Arum. Kew: 1993. V. 67

BOYCE, S. MINERVA
Mother Moons Nursery Rhymes. La Park;: 1906. V. 65

BOYD, ANDREW
Boyd's Directory of Watertown, North Watertown and Juhelville, with a Business Directory of Jefferson Co...1863-1864. Watertown: 1864. V. 66

BOYD, ANDREW K. H.
Twenty-Five Years of St. Andrews September 1865 to September 1890. London: 1892. V. 62

BOYD, ARCHIBALD
The Cardinal. London: 1854. V. 65

BOYD, E.
Popular Arts of Spanish New Mexico. Santa Fe: 1974. V. 62; 63; 64; 66
Saints and Saint Makers of New Mexico. Santa Fe. V. 64
Saints and Saintmakers of New Mexico. Santa Fe: 1946. V. 67

BOYD, ERNEST A.
Ireland's Literary Renaissance. New York: 1922. V. 67

BOYD, J.
The Hebrides. London: 1990. V. 62

BOYD, JAMES
Drums. New York: 1928. V. 65
Long Hunt. New York: 1930. V. 64
Marching On. New York: 1927. V. 63; 65

BOYD, JAMES P.
Recent Indian Wars, Under the Lead of Sitting Bull and Other Chiefs; with a Full Account of the Messiah Craze and Ghost Dancers. 1891. V. 67

BOYD, JOHN M'NEILL
A Manual for Naval Cadets. London: 1860. V. 62

BOYD, LOUISE A.
The Coast of Northeast Greenland. New York: 1948. V. 64; 66

BOYD, MARTIN
Retrospect. Melbourne: 1920. V. 63

BOYD, MAURICE
Kiowa Voice, Myths, Legends and Folktales. Fort Worth: 1983. V. 63

BOYD, OPSEMUS, MRS.
Cavalry Life in Tent and Field. New York: 1894. V. 65; 67

BOYD, THOMAS
Simon Girty - The White Savage. New York: 1928. V. 67
Through the Wheat. New York and London: 1923. V. 62; 64; 67

BOYD, W.
Littondale Past and Present. Leeds: 1893. V. 64

BOYD, WILLIAM
Brazzaville Beach. London: 1990. V. 63; 67
A Good Man in Africa. London: 1981. V. 62; 65
A Good Man in Africa. New York: 1982. V. 62
On the Yankee Station. New York: 1982. V. 65
Protobiography. 1998. V. 63; 65
School Ties. London: 1985. V. 66
Stars and Bars. London: 1984. V. 65

BOYD, WILLIAM KENNETH
Some Eighteenth Century Tracts Concerning North Carolina. Raleigh: 1927. V. 67
The Story of Durham, City of the New South. Durham: 1925. V. 67

BOYD, ZACHARY
Four Letters of Comforts for the Deaths of the Earle of Hadingtoun and of the Lord Boyd 1640. Edinburgh: 1878. V. 66

BOYDEN, ANNA L.
Echoes from Hospital and White House, a Record of Mrs. Rebecca R. Pomroy's Experiences in War-Times. Boston: 1884. V. 65

BOYDEN, POLLY
The Pink Egg. Truro: 1942. V. 63

BOYDEN, SETH
Correspondence on the Subject of Atmospheric Electricity. Newark: 1868. V. 63; 66

BOYER, ABEL
The English Theophrastus; or, the Manners of the Age. London: 1702. V. 64
The History of Queen Anne.... London: 1735. V. 67
The History of the Life and Reign of Queen Anne.... London: 1722. V. 66
The History of the Life and Reign of Queen Anne.... London: 1740. V. 63
The Royal Dictionary. London: 1751. V. 67
The Royal Dictionary Abridged. London: 1728. V. 66
The Royal Dictionary, French and English and English and French. London: 1752-1753. V. 64
The Royal Dictionary, in Two Parts.... London: 1699. V. 67
The Royal Dictionary/Le Dictionnaire Royal, French and English and English and French.... London: 1796. V. 66
The Wise and Ingenious Companion, French and English. London: 1707. V. 63

BOYER, CHARLES S.
The Diatomaceae of Philadelphia. Philadelphia: 1916. V. 63; 65; 66
Early Forges and Furnaces in New Jersey. Philadelphia: 1931. V. 66
Early Forges and Furnaces in New Jersey. Philadelphia: 1963. V. 63
Old Inns and Taverns in the West Jersey. Camden: 1962. V. 66

BOYER, GLENN G.
I Married Wyatt Earp. The Recollections of Josephine Sarah Marcu. Tucson: 1976. V. 63; 66
Suppressed Murder of Wyatt Earp. San Antonio: 1967. V. 65

BOYER, NATHALIE ROBINSON
A Virginia Gentleman and His Family. Philadelphia: 1939. V. 63

BOYER, RICHARD L.
The Giant Rat of Sumatra. London: 1977. V. 66

BOYER, RICK
Billingsgate Shoal. 1982. V. 64

BOYER-FONFREDE, JEAN BAPTISTE
Des Moyens de Conserver les Antilles a la France, si Nous Avons Une Guerre Maritime. Paris: 1793. V. 64

BOYES, JOHN
King of the Wa-Kikuyu.... London: 1911. V. 64

BOYKIN, EDWARD
Ghost Ship of the Confederacy: the Story of the Alabama and Her Captain, Raphael Semmes. New York: 1957. V. 63; 65

BOYKIN, RICHARD M.
Captain Alexander Hamilton Boykin. New York: 1942. V. 62; 63; 65

BOYLE, ELEANOR VERE
Beauty and the Beast. London: 1875. V. 66
A Children's Summer. London: 1853. V. 67
Child's Play. London: 1852. V. 65
Child's Play. London: 1866. V. 62
A New Child's Play. London: 1877. V. 64
Ros Rosarum ex Horto Poetarum. London: 1885. V. 62

BOYLE, GERTRUDE M.
A Bibliography of Canadiana First Supplement. Toronto: 1959. V. 64

BOYLE, J. R.
The County of Durham: its Castles, Churches and Manor Houses. London: 1892. V. 63
The Early History of the Town and Port of Hedon, in the East Riding of the County of York. Hull and York: 1895. V. 63
The Regulations and Establishment of the Household of Henry Algernon Percy, the Fifth Earl of Northumberland, at his Castles of Wressle and Leckonfield in Yorkshire Begun Anno Domini MDXII. Hull: 1905. V. 63

BOYLE, JACK
Boston Blackie. 1919. V. 62; 64; 66

BOYLE, KAY
A Glad Day. Norfolk: 1938. V. 64
Pinky in Persia. New York: 1968. V. 63
Primer for Combat. 1942. V. 65
Short Stories. Paris: 1929. V. 64

BOYLE, ROBERT
A Continuation of New Experiments Physico-Mechanical, Touching the Spring and Weight of the Air, and Their Effects. Oxford: 1669. V. 63
An Essay About the Origine of Gems. London: 1672. V. 62
An Essay of the Great Effects of Even Languid and Unheeded Motion. London: 1685. V. 64; 66
The Excellency of Theology, Compar'd with Natural Philosophy. (with) *About the Excellency and Grounds of Mechanical Hypothesis.* London: 1674. V. 64; 66
Experimentorum Novorum Physico-Mechanicorum Continuatio Secunda. London: 1680. V. 64; 66
Experiments and Considerations About the Porosity of Bodies, in Two Essays. London: 1684. V. 65; 66
A Free Discourse Against Customary Swearing. London: 1695. V. 63
Hydrostataical Paradoxes, Made Out by New Experiments. Oxford: 1666. V. 64; 67
The Martyrdom of Theodora, and of Didymus. London: 1687. V. 67
Memoirs for the Natural History of Human Blood, Especially the Spirit of that Liquor. London: 1684. V. 66
New Experiments and Observations Touching Cold, or, an Experimental History of Cold, Begun, To Which are Added an Examen of Antiperistasis, and an Examen of Mr. Hobs's Doctrine About Cold. London: 1683. V. 65
Occasional Reflections Upon Several Subjects. London: 1665. V. 64; 65; 66; 67
The Philosophical Works.... 1725. V. 64
The Philosophical Works.... London: 1738. V. 64
Some Considerations Touching the Style of the H. Scriptures. (with) *Some Motives and Incentives to the Love of God, Pathetically Discours'd of In a Letter to a Friend.* London: 1663-1665. V. 65
Some Considerations Touching the Style of the Holy Scriptures. London: 1668. V. 62
Some Considerations Touching the Usefulnesse of Experimental Natural Philosophy Propos'd in a Familiar Discourse to a Friend... (with) *Some Considerations...Second Tome.* Oxford: 1664-1671. V. 67
Some Motives and Incentives to the Love of God, Pathetically Discours'd Of in a Letter to a Friend. London: 1661. V. 63
Some Motives and Incentives to the Love of God, Pathetically Discours'd of In a Letter to a Friend. London: 1665. V. 65
Tracts Consisting of Observations About the Saltness of the Sea.... London: 1674. V. 64; 67
The Works. London: 1669-1670. V. 66; 67

BOYLE, T. CORAGHESSAN
Budding Prospects. New York: 1984. V. 62; 65; 66; 67
Descent of Man. Boston: 1979. V. 62; 63; 64; 65; 66; 67
East is East. New York: 1990. V. 66; 67
Greasy Lake. New York: 1985. V. 63; 66; 67
If the River Was Whiskey. New York: 1989. V. 66; 67
The Road to Wellville. Franklin Center: 1993. V. 63; 65
The Road to Wellville. New York: 1993. V. 67
Tortilla Curtain. New York: 1995. V. 66; 67
Water Music. Boston: 1980. V. 67
Water Music. Boston-Toronto: 1981. V. 63; 65; 66; 67
Water Music. London: 1981. V. 67
World's End. New York: 1987. V. 65; 66; 67

BOYLE'S Fashionable Court and Country Guide and Town Visiting Directory. London: 1831. V. 62

BOYNTON, H. V.
Battle of Chickamauga, Georgia, September 19-20, 1863. Washington: 1895. V. 63

BOY'S Own Annual. 1894-1895. V. 66

BOY'S Own Annual. 1895-1896. V. 67
BOY'S Own Annual. 1897-1898. V. 67
BOY'S Own Annual. 1898-1899. V. 64; 67

BOY'S Own Annual. 1931-1932. V. 67
BOY'S Own Annual. 1935-1936. V. 67

BOYS, EDWARD
Boy's Captivity and Adventures. London: 1831. V. 66
The Narrative of a Sojourn Near Keswick in the Cumberland Lake District.... London: 1871. V. 64

THE BOY'S Holiday Book, For All Seasons.... London: 1850. V. 66

BOYS, JOHN
Substance of a Report of the Trial in an Action Between John Boys, Attorney, and Miss Mary Edmunds, Both of Margate, for Three Alleged Poetical Labels and Two Caricature Drawings. Tried at Maidstone...on Tuesday, the 18th of July, 1815. London: 1815. V. 63

THE BOY'S Picture Book (No. 7). Concord: 1843. V. 64

BOYS, THOMAS SHOTTER
London As It Is. Drawn from Nature Expressly for This Work and Lithographed by Thomas Shotter Boys.... London: 1842. V. 62; 63; 66

BOY'S Wife of Aldivalloch. To Which is Added, The Highland Plaid, Neil Gow's Fareweel, John Anderson, My Jo, Maria. London: 1823. V. 62

BRACE, CHARLES L.
The New West or California in 1867-69. New York: 1869. V. 65

BRACEGIRDLE, BRIAN
A History of Microtechnique. New York: 1978. V. 66; 67
The Microscopic Photographs of J. B. Dancer. Chicago: 1993. V. 66

BRACHER, T. W., & CO.
Catalogue of Hatters' Specialties. Stockport: 1929. V. 66

BRACHET, J.
The Cell: Biochemistry, Physiology, Morphology. New York: 1958-1964. V. 62

BRACHET, JEAN LOUIS
Traite Complet de l'Hypochondrie. Paris: 1844. V. 65

BRACK, O. M.
Writers, Books and Trade. An Eighteenth Century English Miscellany for William B. Todd. New York: 1994. V. 62

BRACKEN, HENRY
Farriery Improved; or, a Complete Treatise of the Art of Farriery.... Philadelphia: 1798. V. 66
The Traveller's Pocket-Farrier or a Treatise Upon the Distempers and Common Incidents Happening to Horses Upon a Journey. London: 1743. V. 66; 67

BRACKENRIDGE, HENRY
Views of Louisiana; Together with a Journal of a Voyage Up the Missouri River in 1811. Pittsburgh: 1814. V. 66

BRACKENRIDGE, HENRY MARIE
History of the Late War, Between the United States and Great Britain. Baltimore: 1817. V. 63
History of the Western Insurrection in Western Pennsylvania Commonly Called the Whiskey Insurrection, 1794. Pittsburgh: 1859. V. 64; 67

BRACKENRIDGE, HUGH HENRY
Modern Chivalry.... Philadelphia: 1804-1807. V. 63
Modern Chivalry.... Wilmington: 1813. V. 63

BRACKETT, ANNA C.
The Education of American Girls. New York: 1874. V. 65

BRACKETT, LEIGH
The Starmen. 1952. V. 64

BRADBEER, WILLIAM WEST
Confederate and Southern State Currency. Chicago: 1945. V. 63

BRADBURN, SAMUEL
Methodism set Forth and Defended in a Sermon, on Acts XXVII.22 Preached at the Opening of Portland-Chapel, Bristol, August 26, 1792. Bristol: 1792. V. 63; 65

BRADBURY, FREDERICK
History of Old Sheffield Plate. London: 1912. V. 62; 67

BRADBURY, JOHN
Travels in the Interior of America, in the Years 1809, 1810 and 1811.... Liverpool: 1817. V. 66

BRADBURY, MALCOLM
The History of Man. London: 1975. V. 64
Rates of Exchange. London: 1983. V. 63; 65

BRADBURY, RAY
Beyond 1984: Remembrance of Things Future. New York: 1979. V. 63; 67
Dandelion Wine. London: 1957. V. 66
Death is a Lonely Business. Franklin Center: 1985. V. 63
Fahrenheit 451. New York: 1953. V. 63; 64
Fahrenheit 451. New York: 1982. V. 66
The Golden Apples of the Sun. London: 1953. V. 63
I Sing the Body Electric. New York: 1969. V. 64; 66
The Martian Chronicles. Avon: 1974. V. 62
The Pedestrian. 1951. V. 66
Quicker than the Eye. Franklin Center: 1996. V. 63
S is for Space. New York: 1966. V. 67

BRADDON, E.
Thirty Years of Shikar. 1895. V. 62; 63; 64; 66; 67

BRADDON, LAURENCE
The Tryal of Laurence Braddon and Hugh Speke, Gent. Upon an Information of High-Misdemeanor and Spreading False Reports.... London: 1684. V. 62

BRADDON, MARY ELIZABETH
Aurora Floyd. London: 1864. V. 65
The Captain of the Vulture: a Novel. London: 1886. V. 65
The Cloven Foot. Leipzig: 1879. V. 65
The Cloven Foot. London: 1879. V. 66
Dead Love Has Chains. Leipzig: 1907. V. 65
Dead-Sea Fruit. London: 1875. V. 65
The Doctor's Wife. Leipzig: 1864. V. 65
The Doctor's Wife. London: 1864. V. 65
Eleanor's Victory. London: 1863. V. 65
Eleanor's Victory. London: 1880. V. 65
The Fatal Three. London: 1888. V. 65
Garibaldi and Other Poems. London: 1861. V. 65
The Golden Calf. London: 1885. V. 65
Hostages to Fortune: a Novel. London: 1884. V. 65
Hostages to Fortune: a Novel. London: 1892. V. 65
Ishmael. London: 1884. V. 65
Ishmael. London: 1885. V. 65
Joshua Haggard: a Novel. London: 1877. V. 65
Just As I Am. London: 1885. V. 65
Lady Audley's Secret. London: 1862. V. 65
The Lady's Mile. Leipzig: 1866. V. 65
Like and Unlike: a Novel. London: 1887. V. 65

BRADDON, MARY ELIZABETH continued
London Pride; or When the World Was Younger. London: 1896. V. 65
Only a Clod: a Novel. London: 1886. V. 65
An Open Verdict: a Novel. Leipzig: 1878. V. 65
Rough Justice. London: 1898. V. 65
Run to Earth: a Novel. Leipzig: 1869. V. 65
Run to Earth: a Novel. London: 1893. V. 65
The Story of Barbara: Her Splendid Misery and Her Gilded Cage. London: 1890. V. 65
A Strange World: a Novel. London: 1875. V. 65
To the Bitter End: a Novel. London: 1880. V. 65
Under Love's Rule. London: 1897. V. 65
The Venetians. London: 1892. V. 65

BRADDON, RUSSELL
Cheshire V.C. - A Study of War and Peace. London: 1954. V. 65

BRADFIELD, SCOTT
The History of Luminous Motion. London: 1989. V. 63
The History of Luminous Motion. New York: 1989. V. 63

BRADFIELD, WESLEY
Cameron Creek Village, a Saite in the Mimbres Area in Grant County New Mexico. Santa Fe: 1929. V. 63
Cameron Creek Village: a Site in the Mimbres Area in Grant County, New Mexico. Sante Fe: 1931. V. 63; 64

BRADFORD, ALDEN
History of Massachusetts, from 1764 (...to 1820). Boston: 1822-1829. V. 63; 66

BRADFORD, ALEXANDER
American Antiquities and Researches into the Origin and History of the Red Race. New York: 1841. V. 63

BRADFORD, E. E.
Lays of Love and Life. London: 1916. V. 62; 63
The New Chivalry and Other Poems. London: 1918. V. 62
The Romance of Youth and Other Poems. London: 1920. V. 63

BRADFORD, GAMALIEL
Confederate Portraits. Boston and New York: 1914. V. 63; 65
Lee the American. Boston: 1912. V. 63

BRADFORD, JOHN
Holy Meditations Upon the Lords Prayer, the Beleife and Ten Commandments, with Many Holy and Comfortable Prayers, for Sundry Purposes. London: 1614. V. 62

BRADFORD, RICHARD
Red Sky at Morning. Philadelphia: 1968. V. 63

BRADFORD, THOMAS L.
The Bibliographer's Manual of American History. Philadelphia: 1909. V. 62

BRADLAUGH, CHARLES
Labour and Law. London: 1891. V. 64
The Queen v. Charles Bradlaugh and Annie Besant. London: 1877. V. 64

BRADLEE, FRANCIS BOARDMAN CROWNINSHIELD
Blockade Running During the Civil War and the Effect of Land and Water Transportation on the Confederacy. Salem: 1925. V. 63; 65

BRADLEY, A.
A Philosophical Account of the Works of Nature. 1721. V. 66

BRADLEY, A. C.
A Miscellany. London: 1929. V. 63

BRADLEY, DAVID
South Street. New York: 1975. V. 63

BRADLEY, EDWARD
The Adventures of Mr. Verdant Green, an Oxford Freshman. (with) Little Mr. Bouncer and Tales of College Life. Boston: 1893. V. 64
The Adventures of Mr. Verdant Green. (and) The Further Adventures. (and) Married and Done For. London: 1856. V. 67
The Foxhound of the Twentieth Century. London: 1014. V. 62
Glencreggan; or, a Highland Home in Cantire. London: 1861. V. 64
Nearer and Dearer: a Tale Out of School.... London: 1857. V. 64
Photographic Pleasures Popularly Portrayed with Pen and Pencil. London: 1859. V. 63
The Rook's Garden. Essays and Sketches. London: 1865. V. 64

BRADLEY, F. H.
Appearance and Reality. London: 1893. V. 63
Essays on Truth and Reality. Oxford: 1914. V. 62

BRADLEY, GEORGE
Midden. New York: 1986. V. 67
Where the Blue Begins. New York: 1985. V. 64; 67

BRADLEY, GLENN D.
The Story of the Santa Fe. Boston: 1920. V. 63
Winning the Southwest - a Story of Conquest. Chicago: 1912. V. 67

BRADLEY, HAROLD WHITMAN
The American Frontier in Hawaii. The Pioneers 1789-1843. Stanford/London: 1944. V. 63

BRADLEY, HELEN
In the Beginning Said Great-Aunt Jane. London: 1974. V. 62; 65
Miss Carter Came With Us. London: 1973. V. 66

BRADLEY, JAMES H.
The March of the Montana Column: a Prelude to the Cluster Disaster. Norman: 1961. V. 63; 64; 65; 66; 67

BRADLEY, JOHN
A Narrative of Travel and Sport in Burmah, Siam and the Malay Peninsula. 1876. V. 64

BRADLEY, LONSDALE
An Inquiry into the Deposition of Lead Ore, in the Mineral Veins of Swaledale, Yorkshire. London: 1862. V. 64

BRADLEY, MARION ZIMMER
The Mists of Avalon. New York: 1982. V. 65

BRADLEY, MARY HASTINGS
Murder in Room 700. New York: 1931. V. 65

BRADLEY, OMAR
A Soldier's Story. New York: 1951. V. 63

BRADLEY, R. T.
The Outlaws of the Border or the Lives of Frank and Jesse James, Their Exploits, Adventures and Escapes, Down to the Present Time.... St. Louis: 1880. V. 64

BRADLEY, RICHARD
New Improvements of Planting and Gardening, Both Philosophical and Practical.... London: 1717-1718. V. 64

BRADLEY, SAMUEL MESSENGER
Manual of Comparative Anatomy and Physiology. London: 1875. V. 65

BRADLEY, TOM
The Esk. Leeds: 1892. V. 65
The Old Coaching Days in Yorkshire. Leeds: 1889. V. 64; 65; 66
The Ouse. Leeds: 1891. V. 65
Yorkshire Angler's Guide. 1894. V. 62; 63; 65; 67

BRADLEY, WILL
Peter Poodle Toymaker to the King. New York: 1906. V. 63

BRADLOW, EDNA
Thomas Bowler of the Cape of Good Hope. Cape Town and Amsterdam: 1955. V. 62; 66

BRADMAN, ARTHUR
The Jovial Beggar, a Comedy.... Portland: 1798?. V. 62

BRADSHAW, ANNIE
The Gates of Temptation; a Natural Novel. London: 1898. V. 67

BRADSHAW, GEORGE
Bradshaw's Railway Time Tables, and Assistant Railway Travelling.... London: 1889. V. 66

BRADSHAW, HENRY
Collected Papers. Cambridge: 1889. V. 63
Henry Bradshaw's Correspondence on Incunabula.... Amsterdam: 1966-1978. V. 63

BRADSHAW, PERCY V.
Art in Advertising: a Study of British and American Pictorial Publicity. London: 1925. V. 62
The Art of the Illustrator. London. V. 65
They Make Us Smile. London: 1942. V. 67

BRADSHAW, PERCY W.
Brother Savages and Guests - a History of the Savage Club 1857-1957. London: 1958. V. 63

BRADSTREET, ANNE
The Works of Anne Bradstreet in Prose and Verse. Charlestown: 1867. V. 64

BRADY, G. S.
Challenger Expedition. Zoology, Part 3, Ostracoda. London: 1880. V. 65
Challenger Voyage. Zoology. Part 3. Ostracoda. 1880. V. 66

BRADY, H. B.
Foraminifera. 1884. V. 66

BRADY, JAMES T.
Trial of Charles B. Huntington for Forgery. New York: 1857. V. 65

BRADY, JASPER EWING
Tales of the Telegraph - the Story of a Telegrapher's Life and Adventures in Railroad, Commercial and Military Work. New York: 1899. V. 67

BRADY, JOHN H.
The Visitor's Guide to Knole, in the County of Kent, with Catalogues of the Pictures. Sevenoaks: 1839. V. 62

BRADY, ROBERT
A Full and Clear Answer to a Book, Written by William Pettit, Esq. printed in the Year 1680. London: 1681. V. 67

BRADY, WILLIAM
Glimpses of Texas: its Divisions, Resources, Development and Prospects. Houston: 1871. V. 62

BRAGG, JEFFERSON DAVIS
Louisiana in the Confederacy. Baton Rouge: 1941. V. 62; 63; 65

BRAID, JAMES
Abstract of a Lecture on Electro-Biology Delivered at the Royal Institution, Manchester, on the 26th March 1851. Manchester: 1851. V. 64
Braid on Hypnotism. London: 1899. V. 66

BRAIDLEY, A.
The Complete English Cook; or, the Art of Cookery Made Plain and Easy.... London: 1786. V. 65

BRAIDWOOD, P. MURRAY
The Parramatta Times. Liverpool: 1886. V. 64

BRAIN, R.
Art and Society in Africa. London: 1980. V. 62

BRAINARD, JOE
I Remember. New York: 1975. V. 63
29 Mini-Essays. Calais: 1978. V. 66

BRAINE, JOHN
Room at the Top. Boston: 1957. V. 63; 67
The Vodi. London: 1959. V. 66

BRAINERD, C. N.
My Diary: Three Weeks on the Wing - a Peep At the Great West. New York: 1868. V. 65

BRAINERD, DAVID
An Abridgment of Mr. David Brainerd's Journal Among the Indians. London: 1748. V. 65

BRAITHWAITE, DEBORAH W.
Van Der Zee: Photographer 1886-1983. Washington: 1993. V. 63

BRAITHWAITE, E. R.
To Sir, with Love. Englewood Cliffs: 1959. V. 63
To Sir, With Love. London: 1959. V. 63

BRAITHWAITE, GEORGE FOSTER
The Salmonidae of Westmorland. 1884. V. 62; 63; 67
The Salmonidae of Westmorland. Kendal: 1884. V. 62; 64; 65; 66; 67
The Salmonidae of Westmorland. London: 1884. V. 65

BRAITHWAITE, J. W.
Guide to Kirkby Stephen, Appleby, Brought, Warcop, Ravenstonedale, Mallerstang &c. Kirkby Stephen: 1884. V. 66

BRAITHWAITE, JOSEPH BEVAN
Memoirs of Joseph John Gurney. Norwich: 1854. V. 67

BRAITHWAITE, ROBERT
The British Moss Flora. 1887-1905. V. 64; 67
The British Moss-Flora. London: 1887-1905. V. 62; 65
The Sphagnaceae or Peat Mosses of Europe and North America. 1880. V. 63

BRAITHWAITE, WILLIAM STANLEY
Anthology of Magazine Verse for 1923 and Yearbook of American Poetry. Boston: 1923. V. 64; 67
Our Lady's Choir. A Contemporary Anthology of Verse by Catholic Sisters. Boston: 1931. V. 64

BRALY, JOHN HYDE
Memory Pictures. Los Angeles: 1912. V. 63; 66

BRAM, R. A.
The Genus Culex in Thailand. 1967. V. 63; 66

BRAMLETT, JIM
Ride for the High Points - The Real Story of Will James. Missoula: 1987. V. 63; 66

BRAMLY, T. J.
Loans by Private Individuals to Foreign States Entitled to Government Protection, by the Fundamental Laws, as a Branch of Trade.... London: 1842. V. 63

BRAMMER, WILLIAM
The Gay Place. Boston: 1961. V. 65

BRAMSTON, JAMES
The Art of Politicks, in Imitation of Horace's Art of Poetry. London: 1729. V. 64; 65
The Man of Taste, Occasion'd by an Epistle of Mr. Pope's on that Subject. London: 1733. V. 66

BRAMWELL, BYROM
The Diseases of the Spinal Cord. Edinburgh: 1882. V. 67
Post-Graduate Demonstraions on Nervous Diseases. Edinburgh: 1915. V. 67
Studies in Clinical Medicine. Edinburgh and London: 1889. V. 65

BRAMWELL, J. MILNE
Hypnotism: Its History, Practice and Theory. New York: 1956. V. 66

BRANAGAN, THOMAS
Avenia, or a Tragical Poem, on the Oppression of the Human Species.... Philadelphia: 1810. V. 64
The Excellency of the Female Character Vindicated.... New York: 1807. V. 65
The Flowers of Literature. Trenton: 1806. V. 63; 66

BRANCA, GIOVANNI
Le Machine. Rome: 1629. V. 62; 63

BRANCH, DOUGLAS
The Cowboy and His Interpretors. New York: 1926. V. 63; 66
The Hunting of the Buffalo. New York: 1929. V. 67

BRANCH, EDGAR M.
Clemens of the Call, Mark Twain in San Francisco. Berekely: 1969. V. 63

BRAND Book of the North Dakota Stock Grower's Association for 1892. Mandan: 1892. V. 66

BRAND, ADAM
Relation du Voyage de Mr. Evert Isbrand Envoye de Sa Majeste Czarienne a l'Empereur de la Chine, en 1692, 1693 and 1694. Amsterdam: 1699. V. 67

BRAND, CHRISTIANNA
Brand X. London: 1974. V. 64
Fog of Doubt. New York: 1953. V. 67
Nurse Matilda Goes to Hospital. London: 1974. V. 63
The Rose in Darkness. London: 1979. V. 66
Suddenly at His Residence. London: 1947. V. 66; 67
The Three Cornered Halo. London: 1957. V. 66
Tour de Force. London: 1955. V. 66

BRAND, JOHANN CHRISTIAN
Zeichnungen Nach Dem Gemeinem Volk, Besonders; Der Kaufruf in Wien.... Vienna: 1775. V. 62

BRAND, MAX
Call of the Blood. New York: 1934. V. 66
Dr. Kildare Takes Charge. New York: 1941. V. 65; 66
The Killers. New York: 1931. V. 65
Red Devil of the Range. New York: 1934. V. 65
Timbal Gulch Trail. New York: 1934. V. 65
Valley Thieves. New York: 1946. V. 65

BRAND, SEBASTIAN
Stultifera Navis, qua Omnium Mortalium Narratur Stultitia...The Ship of Fooles.... London: 1570. V. 63

BRANDAU, R. S.
History of Homes and Gardens of Tennessee. Nashville: 1936. V. 64; 67

BRANDE, W. T.
A Descriptive Catalogue of the British Specimens Deposited in the Geological Collection of the Royal Institution. 1816. V. 62
A Manual of Chemistry. New York: 1825?. V. 65
Outlines of Geology. London: 1829. V. 63

BRANDER, A. A. D.
Wild Animals in Central India. London: 1923. V. 62

BRANDER, G.
Fossilia Hantoniensia Collecta, et in Musaeo Britannico. London: 1766. V. 65

BRANDERT, MICHAEL
The International Encyclopaedia of Shooting. London: 1972. V. 67

BRANDES, ERNST
Ueber die Weiber. Leipzig: 1787. V. 65

BRANDES, RAY
Troopers West, Military and Indian Affairs on the American Frontier. San Diego: 1970. V. 64; 67

BRANDIS, D.
The Forest Flora of North-West and Central India. 1874. V. 62

BRANDON, ISAAC
Fragments in the Manner of Sterne. London: 1797. V. 62

BRANDON, RAPHAEL
An Analysis of Gothic Architecture. Edinburgh: 1903. V. 63

BRANDRETH, JEREMIAH
The Trials of Jeremiah Brandreth, William Turner, Isaac Ludlam, George Weightman and Others for High Treason, Under a Special Commission at Derby, Thursday, the 16th-Saturday the 25th of Otober 1817. London: 1817. V. 63

BRANDT, BILL
Camera in London. 1948. V. 66
Camera in London. London: 1948. V. 62
Literary Britain. London: 1984. V. 63
Perspective of Nudes. New York: 1961. V. 63; 65
Shadow of Light. London: 1966. V. 62

BRANDT, GERARD
The History of the Reformation and Other Ecclesiastical Transactions In and About the Low Countries. London: 1720-1723. V. 67

BRANDT, HERBERT
Alaska Bird Trails. Adventures of an Expedition by Dog Sled to the Delta of the Yukon River at Hoper Bay. Cleveland: 1943. V. 66
Arizona and Its Bird Life. Cleveland: 1951. V. 64
Arizona and Its Bird Life. Cleveland: 1956. V. 63

BRANDT, J. F.
Spicilegia Ornithologica Exotica. St. Petersburg: 1839. V. 67

BRANDT, JOHN C.
The International Halley Watch Atlas of Large-Scale Phenomena. Boulder: 1992. V. 67

BRANDT, JOHN H.
Asian Hunter. New Mexico: 1989. V. 62; 67

BRANDT, REX
Into the Outside. Rex Brandt's Landscapes. Corona del Mar: 1994. V. 62
Rex Brandt's San Diego. Palm Desert: 1969. V. 63

BRANDT, RICHARD B.
Hopi Ethics, A Theoretical Analysis. Chicago: 1954. V. 63; 66

BRANHAM, BUD
Sourdough and Swahili, a Professional Hunter on Two Continents. Clinton: 1989. V. 65

BRANNER, JOHN CASPER
A Bibliography of Clays and Ceramic Arts. Columbus: 1906. V. 63
Casper Branner of Virginia and His Descendants. Stanford: 1913. V. 62

BRANNER, R.
Manuscript Painting in Paris During the Reign of Saint Louis. Berkeley: 1977. V. 62

BRANNON, G.
Graphic Delineations of the Most Prominent Objects in the Isle of Wight.... Isle of Wight: 1857. V. 62; 66

BRANNON, PETER A.
The Organization of the Confederate Post Office Deparatment at Montgomery and a Story of the Thomas Welsch Provisional Stamped Envelope.... Montgomery: 1960. V. 63

BRANSBY, JAMES HEWS
A Sketch of the History of Carnarvon Castle. Carnarvon: 1829. V. 66

BRANT, SEBASTIAN
Navis Stultifera...Primum Edificata: et Lepidissimis Teutonice Lingue Rithmis Decorata. Basel: 1506. V. 62

BRANTOME, PIERRE DE BORDEILLE, SEIGNEUR DE
Lives of Fair and Gallant Ladies. Paris: 1901-1902. V. 63

BRANTOME, PIERRE DE BOURDEILLE, SEIGNEUR DE
The Lives of the Gallant Ladies. Waltham St. Lawrence: 1924. V. 66
Spanish Rhodomontades. London: 1741. V. 64

BRAQUE, GEORGES
Cahier de Georges Braque 1917-1947. Paris: 1948. V. 64
Georges Braque: His Graphic Work. New York: 1961. V. 65

BRAQUEHAYE, JULES
De La Methode Graphique Appliquee a L'Etude du Traumatisme Cerebral. Paris: 1895. V. 64

BRARD, CYPRIEN PROSPER
Manuel du Mineralogiste et du Geologue Voyageur. Paris: 1808. V. 64

BRASH, J. C.
Cunningham's Text Book of Anatomy. New York: 1937. V. 64; 67

BRASHEAR, JOHN A.
John A. Brashear: the Autobiography of a man Who Loved the Stars. New York: 1924. V. 67

BRASHLER, WILLIAM
The Bingo Long Traveling All Stars and Motor Kings. New York: 1973. V. 63
Joan Gibson. A Life of Negro Leagues. New York: 1978. V. 67

BRASSAI
Camera in Paris. London: 1949. V. 63
Graffiti. Paris: 1993. V. 63

BRASSAVOLA, ANTONIO MUSA
Examen Omnium Catapotiorum.... Venice: 1543. V. 64
In Octo Libros Aphorismorum Hippocratis & Galeni, Commentaria and Annotationes. Basel: 1541. V. 62

BRASSEY, ANNIE ALLNUTT, BARONESS
Sunshine and Storm in the East. London: 1880. V. 65; 66
Tahiti.... London: 1882. V. 64; 65
A Voyage in the Sunbeam, Our Home on the Ocean for Eleven Months. London: 1880. V. 66

BRASSEY, THOMAS
Work and Wages in Continuation of Lord Brassey's "Work and Wages".... London: 1904-1914. V. 64

BRASSINGTON, W. SALT
Historic Bindings in the Bodleian Library, Oxford, with Reproductions of Twenty Four of the Finest Bindings. London: 1891. V. 63; 64
A History of the Art of Bookbinding, with Some Account of the Books of the Ancients. London: 1894. V. 62

BRASTEBERGER, GEBHARD ULRICH
Untersuchungen uber Kants Kritik der Pratisoehn Vernunst. Tubingen: 1792. V. 66

BRATHWAITE, RICHARD
Drunken Barnaby's Four Journeys in the North of England. London: 1723. V. 63; 64; 67
Drunken Barnaby's Four Journeys to the North of England. London: 1805. V. 64; 65
Drunken Barnaby's Four Journeys to the North of England. London: 1822. V. 66

BRATT, JOHN
Trails of Yesterday. Chicago: 1921. V. 63; 66

BRATTLEBORO LIBRARY ASSOCIATION
Catalogue of Books Belonging to the Brattleboro Library Association, Founded, October 1842. Brattleboro: 1844. V. 66

BRAUDEL, FERNAND
La Mediterranee et la Monde Mediterraneen a l'Epoque de Philippe II. Paris: 1949. V. 67

BRAUN, LILIAN JACKSON
The Cat Who Ate Danish Modern. New York: 1967. V. 66
The Cat Who Could Read Backwards. New York: 1966. V. 65
The Cat Who Turned On and Off. New York: 1968. V. 65

BRAUN, RICHARD EMIL
Bad Land. Penland: 1971. V. 63

BRAUN, J.
Illustrations of Furniture, Candelabra, Musical Instruments from the Great Exhibitions of London and Paris with Examples of Similar Articles from Royal Palaces and Noble Mansions. London: 1858. V. 64

BRAUTIGAN, RICHARD
The Abortion: an Historical Romance. New York: 1971. V. 63
All Watched Over by Machines of Loving Grace. San Francisco: 1967. V. 65
A Confederate General from Big Sur. New York: 1964. V. 65; 67
The Edna Webster Collection of Undiscovered Writings. Berkeley and Forest Knolls: 1999. V. 64; 67
The Galilee Hitch-Hiker. San Francisco,: 1966. V. 63
I Watched the World Glide Effortlessly Bye and Other Pieces. N.P: 1996. V. 63; 67
In Watermelon Sugar. New York: 1969. V. 63
June 30th, June 30th. New York: 1978. V. 65
Lay the Marble Tea. San Francisco: 1959. V. 62
Loading Mercury with a Pitchfork. New York: 1976. V. 62; 63
Loading Mercury with a Pitchfork. New York: 1979. V. 66; 67
Please Plant This Book. San Francisco: 1968. V. 63
Revenge of the Lawn. Stories 1962-1970. New York: 1971. V. 63; 65
Rommel Drives on Deep into Egypt. New York: 1970. V. 63; 66; 67
Sombrero Fallout. New York: 1976. V. 66; 67
The Tokyo-Montana Express. New York: 1979. V. 64; 67
The Tokyo-Montana Express. New York: 1980. V. 63; 66
Trout Fishing in America. London: 1970. V. 65
Willard and His Bowling Trophies. New York: 1975. V. 63

BRAVERMAN, KATE
Lithium for Medea. New York: 1978. V. 67
Palm Latitudes. New York: 1988. V. 65

BRAVO, FRANCISCO
The Opera Medicinalia.... Folkestone & London: 1970. V. 66

BRAWLEY, JAMES S.
Rowan Story 1753-1953. A Narrative History of Rowan County, North Carolina. Salisbury: 1953. V. 67

BRAWNE, FANNY
The Letters of Fanny Brawne to Fanny Keats 1820-1824. New York: 1937. V. 64

BRAY, ANNA ELIZA
Fitz of Fitz-Ford. London: 1830. V. 65
The Good St. Louis and Her Times. London: 1870. V. 65
Life of Thomas Stothard, R.A. London: 1851. V. 65; 66

BRAYBROOKE, PATRICK
The Amazing Mr. Noel Coward. London: 1933. V. 63

BRAYER, HERBERT
The Cattle Barons Rebellion Against Law and Order - First Eyewitness Accounts of the Johnson County War in Wyoming 1892. Evanston: 1955. V. 65
Pikes Peak...or Busted! Frontier Reminiscences of William Hawkins Hedges. Evanston: 1954. V. 67
To Form a More Perfect Union - the Lives of Charles Frances and Mary Clark from their Letters 1847-1871. Albuquerque: 1941. V. 65; 67
William Blackmore: the Spanish Mexican Land Grants of New Mexico and Colorado and Early Financing of the Denver and Rio Grande Railway and Ancillary Land Companies. Denver: 1949. V. 65

BRAYLEY, ARTHUR W.
Bakers and Baking in Massachusetts, Including the Flour, Baking Supply and Kindred Interests from 1620 to 1909. Boston: 1909. V. 63
History of the Granite Industry of New England Illustrated. Boston: 1913. V. 63

BRAYLEY, E. G.
History of Surrey. London. V. 63

BRAYLEY, EDWARD WEDLAKE
A Concise Account, Historical and Descriptive of Lambeth Palace. London: 1806. V. 62; 63; 66
The Graphic and Historical Illustrator, an Original Miscellany of Literary, Antiquarian and Topographical Information.... London: 1834. V. 62
Historical and Descriptive Accounts of the Theatres of London.... London: 1826. V. 66
The History of the Antient Palace and Late Houses of Parliament at Westminster. London: 1836. V. 67
Londiniana; or, Reminiscences of the British Metropolis.... London: 1829. V. 63

BRAYSHAW, THOMAS
A History of the Ancient Parish of Giggleswick. London: 1932. V. 64; 65; 66
Hurtley's Poems on the Natural Curiosities of Malham, in Craven, Yorkshire. Settle: 1917. V. 66

THE BRAZIER, a Pathetic Tale. New York: 1816. V. 62

BRAZIOLI, ANDREA
Discorso di Peste...Nelquale si Contengono Utilissime Speculationi Intorno Alla Natura, Cagioni, e Curatione della Peste, con un Catalogo di Tutte le Pesti Piu Notabili de' Tempi Passati. Venice: 1576. V. 63

BREAD and Honey. London: 1890. V. 65

BREAKENRIDGE, WILLAM M.
Helldorado Bringing the Law to the Mesquite. Boston: 1928. V. 63; 64; 65; 66

BREASTED, JAMES HENRY
The Edwin Smith Surgical Papyrus.... Chicago: 1930. V. 62

BREATHNACH, SARAH BAN
Mrs. Sharpe's Traditions. New York: 1990. V. 65

BREAZEALE, J. F.
The Pima and His Basket. Tucson: 1923. V. 63; 64; 66

BREBEUF, JEAN DE
Travels and Sufferings of Father Jean de Brebeuf Among the Hurons of Canada. Waltham St. Lawrence: 1938. V. 62; 64; 65; 66

BRECHT, BERTOLT
The Private Life of the Master Race - a Documentary Play. New York: 1944. V. 65

BRECK, J.
New Book of Flowers. New York: 1866. V. 67

BRECKINRIDGE, SOPHONISBA P.
Marriage and Civic Rights of Women. Chicago: 1931. V. 65

BREDER, C. M.
Modes of Reproduction in Fishes. Garden City: 1966. V. 65

BREDON, JULIET
Peking: a Historical and Intimate Description of its Chief Places of Interest. Shanghai: 1931. V. 65

BREE, CHARLES ROBERT
A History of the Birds of Europe, Not Observed in the British Isles. London: 1859-1863. V. 64; 67
A History of the Birds of Europe, Not Observed in the British Isles. London: 1863-1864. V. 62
A History of the Birds of Europe, Not Observed in the British Isles. London: 1875-1876. V. 67

BREEN, PATRICK
The Diary of Patrick Breen: Recounting the Ordeal of the Donner Party Snowbound in the Sierra 1846-1847. San Francisco: 1946. V. 64

BREEN, WALTER
Walter Breen's Encyclopedia of U.S. and Colonial Proof Coins 1722-1977. New York: 1977. V. 66

BREES, S. C.
Appendix to Railway Practice, Containing a Copious Abstract of the Whole of the Evidence Given Upon the London and Birmingham and Great Western Railway Bills.... London: 1839. V. 65
First (-Fourth) Series of Railway Practice: a Collection of Working Plans.... London: 1847. V. 65
Second Series of Railway Practice: a Collection of Working Plans and Practical Details of Construction in the Public Works of the Most Celebrated Engineers.... London: 1840. V. 65

BREEVOORT, J. C.
Notes on Some Figures of Japanese Fish.... Washington: 1856. V. 62

BREGEAULT, H.
La Chaine Du Mont-Blanc. Sep. 1920. V. 65

BREHM, ALFRED E.
Cassell's Book of Birds. London: 1869-1873. V. 63
From North Pole to Equator. 1895. V. 66
From North Pole to Equator. London and Edinburgh: 1895. V. 63

BREHME, HUGO
Mexico, Baukunst, Landschaft, Volksleben. Berlin: 1925. V. 65

BRELIN, JOHANNES
Anmarkningar, wid Byggnings-Konsten. Stockholm: 1763. V. 64

BREMER, FREDRIKA
The Home; or, Family Cares and Family Joys. London: 1843. V. 65
The Homes of the New World. New York: 1853. V. 64
Life, Letters and Posthumous Works of.... New York: 1868. V. 63
The President's Daughters; Including Nina.... London: 1843. V. 63

BREMNER, DAVID
The Industries of Scotland, Their Rise, Progress and Present Condition. Edinburgh: 1869. V. 63

BREMSER, BONNIE
For Love of Ray. London: 1971. V. 67

BRENAN, GERALD
Doctor Partridge's Almanack for 1935.... London: 1934. V. 62
A History of the House of Percy from the Earliest Times Down to the Present Century. London: 1902. V. 63
Jack Robinson - a Picturesque Novel. London: 1933. V. 62
The Literature of the Spanish People, from Roman Times to the Present Day. Cambridge: 1951. V. 66
The Literature of the Spanish People, from Roman Times to the Present Day. London: 1951. V. 64
Personal Record 1920-1972. London: 1974. V. 65
The Spanish Labyrinth: an Account of the Social and Political Background of the Civil War. Cambridge: 1943. V. 66
The Spanish Labyrinth: an Account of the Social and Political Background of the Civil War. London: 1943. V. 64

BRENCHLEY, JULIUS L.
Jottings During the Cruise of HMS "Curacoa" Among the South Sea Island in 1865. London: 1873. V. 64

BRENDEL, JOHANN PHILIPP
Consilia Medica Celeberrimorum Quorundam Germaniae Medicorum. Frankfurt am Main: 1615. V. 66

BRENNAN, JOSEPH PAYNE
The Borders Just Beyond. 1986. V. 64; 66
The Casebook of Lucius Leffing. 1973. V. 64; 66
The Casebook of Lucius Leffing. New Haven: 1973. V. 65
Nine Horrors and a Dream. Sauk City: 1958. V. 62; 63; 64; 66
Scream at Midnight. 1963. V. 62

BRENNAND, GEORGE
Walton's Delight. London: 1953. V. 67

BRENNER, ANITA
The Boy Who Could Do Anything and Other Mexican Folk Tales. New York: 1942. V. 62; 66
Idols Behind Altars. New York: 1929. V. 62
The Wind that Swept Mexico: The History of the Mexican Revolution. New York and London: 1943. V. 63; 65

BRENT, JOSEPH LANCASTER
Memoirs of Brigadier-General Joseph Lancaster Brent, C.S.A. New Orleans: 1940. V. 62; 63

BRENTANO, CLEMENS
The Tale of Gockel, Hinkel and Gackeliah. New York: 1961. V. 65

BRENTANO, FRITZ
Herzliebchens Bilderbuch (Sweetheart's Picture Book). 1910. V. 64

BRENTANO, JOSEPH AUGUSTIN
Catalogue d'une Precieuse Collection de Tableaux des Ecoles Hollandaise, Flamande et Italienne. Amsterdam: 1822. V. 64

BRENT DYER, ELINOR M.
Adrienne and the Chalet School. London: 1965. V. 66
Althea Joins the Chalet School. 1969. V. 67
The Chalet School Reunion. 1963. V. 67
The Chalet School Wins the Trick. London: 1961. V. 66
Challenge for the Chalet School. 1966. V. 67
The Exploits of the Chalet Girls. London: 1933. V. 66
A Genius at the Chalet School. London: 1956. V. 66
Jane and Chalet School. London: 1964. V. 66
A Leader in the Chalet School. London: 1961. V. 66
Mary Lou of the Chalet School. 1959. V. 66
Peggy of the Chalet School. London: 1950. V. 65
Prefects of the Chalet School. 1970. V. 67
Redheads at the Chalet School. London: 1964. V. 65; 66
Summer Term at the Chalet School. 1965. V. 66
Theodora and the Chalet School. 1959. V. 66
A Thrilling Term at Janeways. London. V. 67
Trials for the Chalet School. London: 1959. V. 66
Two Sams at the Chalet School. 1967. V. 67

BRENTON, EDWARD PELHAM
The Naval History of Great Britain, from the Year 1783 to 1836. London: 1837. V. 64

BRENTON, JAMES
Voices from the Press: a Collection of Sketches, Essays and Poems by Practical Printers. New York: 1850. V. 63; 65

BRERETON, F. S.
Jones of the 64th, a Story of the Battles of Assaye and Laswaree. 1908. V. 64

BRERETON, J. M.
The Horse in War. London: 1976. V. 67

BREREWOOD, EDWARD
Enquiries Touching the Diversity of Languages and Relgions through the Chief Parts of the World.... London: 1674. V. 64

BRES, JEAN PIERRE
Contes de Robert Mon Oncle. Paris: 1820. V. 67
La Dame Blanche. Chronique des Chevaliers a l'Ecusson Vert. Paris: 1828. V. 67

BRESHKOVSKY, CATHERINE
The Little Grandmother of the Russian Revolution.... Boston: 1919. V. 65

BRESSON, HENRI CARTIER
The Decisive Moment. New York: 1952. V. 66
Les Europeens. Paris: 1955. V. 66

BRETON, ANDRE
Mont de Piete. Paris: 1919. V. 67
Second Manifeste du Surrealisme. Paris: 1930. V. 65
Yves Tanguy. New York: 1946. V. 62; 63; 64

BRETON, NICHOLAS
The Twelve Moneths. Waltham St. Lawrence: 1927. V. 63; 65

BRETON, WILLIAM HENRY
Excursions in New South Wales, Western Australia and Van Diemen's Land, During the Years 1830, 1831, 1832 and 1833. London: 1833. V. 64
Scandanavian Sketches or a Tour in Norway. London: 1835. V. 66

BRETSCHNEIDER, E.
History of European Botanical Discoveries in China. Leipzig: 1962. V. 63
History of European Botanical Discoveries in China. Leipzig: 1981. V. 64

BRETT, WILLIAM
The Principles of Astronomy. Cambridge: 1832. V. 65

BREUER, JOSEF
Studien Uber Hysterie. Leipzig/Wien: 1895. V. 62
Studien Uber Hysterie. 1909. V. 62
Ueber den Psychischen Mechanismus Hysterischer Phanomene. Leipzig: 1893. V. 65

BREVAL, JOHN
The History of the Most Illustrious House of Nassau, Continued from the Tenth Century...to the Present Time.... London: 1734. V. 63
Remarks on Several Parts of Europe, Relating Chiefly to their Antiquities and History. London: 1738. V. 67

BREVINT, DANIEL
Missale Romanum, or the Depth and Mystery of (the) Roman Mass. Laid Open and Explained, for the Use of Both Reformed and Un-Reformed Christians. Oxford: 1672. V. 66
Saul and Samuel at Endor, or the New Waies of Salvation and Service.... Oxford: 1674. V. 63

BREVOORT, ELIAS
New Mexico. Her Natural Resources and Attractions. Santa Fe: 1874. V. 66

BREVOORT, J. C.
Notes on Some Figures of Japanese Fish Taken from Recent Specimens by the Artists of the U.S. James Expedition. Washington: 1856. V. 65; 67

BREWER, J. MASON
The Word on the Brazos. Austin: 1953. V. 63

BREWER, J. NORRIS
Histrionic Topography; or the Birth Places, Residences and Funeral Monuments of the Most Distinguished Actors. London: 1818. V. 65; 66

BREWER, JEUTONNE
Anthony Burgess: a Bibliography. Metuchen: 1980. V. 63

BREWER, LUTHER A.
My Leigh Hunt Library: the First Editions. Cedar Rapids: 1938. V. 62
Some Letters from My Leigh Hunt Portfolios. Cedar Rapids: 1929. V. 66

BREWER, W.
The Family Medical Reference Book.... London: 1840. V. 63

BREWER, WILLIAM HENRY
Such a Landscape! A Narrative of the 1864 California Geological Survey Exploration of Yosemite, Sequoia and Kings Canyon. Yosemite National Park: 1987. V. 63
Up and Down California in 1860-1864. New Haven: 1930. V. 66
Up and Down California in 1860-1864. New Haven: 1931. V. 63

BREWER'S Dictionary of Phrase and Fable. London: 1989. V. 63

BREWERTON, GEORGE DOUGLAS
Overland with Kit Carson: a Narrative of the Old Spanish Trail in '48. New York: 1930. V. 64; 66; 67

BREWINGTON, M. V.
The Peabody Museum Collection of Navigating Instruments With Notes on Their Makers. Gloucester/Staten Island. V. 63; 64; 65

BREWSTER, A. B.
The Hill Tribes of Fiji. London: 1922. V. 64

BREWSTER, ADEL
Free Man's Companion; a New and Original Work, Consisting of Numerous Moral, Political and Philosophical Views. Hartford: 1827. V. 64

BREWSTER, DAVID
The Life of Sir Isaac Newton. London: 1821. V. 64
The Life of Sir Isaac Newton. London: 1831. V. 62
The Martyrs of Science, or the Lives of Galileo, Tycho Brahe and Kepler. London: 1841. V. 66
Plates Illustrative of Ferguson's Astronomy and of the Twelve Supplementary Chapters. Philadelphia: 1817. V. 66
A Treatise on Magnetism.... Edinburgh: 1837. V. 64
A Treatise on Optics. London: 1831. V. 62; 64

BREWSTER, JOHN
The Parochial History and Antiquities of Stockton Upon Tees. London: 1796. V. 63

BREWSTER, PATRICK
The Seven Chartist and Military Discourses, Libelled by the Marquis of Abercorn, and Other Heritors of the Abbey Parish. Paisley: 1843. V. 64

BREYFOGLE, J. D.
Diary of J. D. Breyfogle Sr. Covering His Experiences During His Overland Trip to California During the Gold Rush in 1849. N.P. V. 65

BRIAN Wildsmith's ABC. London: 1962. V. 67

BRICE, GERMAIN
Description Nouvelle de la Ville de Paris et Recherche de Singularitez les Plus Remarquables. Paris: 1706. V. 67
A New Description of Paris. London: 1687. V. 67

BRICE, MITFORD
The King's Dogs. 1935. V. 67

BRICHARD, P.
Cichlids and All the Other Fishes of Lake Tanganyika. Neptune: 1989. V. 65

BRICHETEAU, I.
Medical Clinics of the Hospital Necker or Researches and Observations on the Nature, Treatment and Physical Causes of Diseases. Philadelphia: 1837. V. 64; 66

BRICK, C. J.
California-Album. Eine Erinnerung vom Strande des Stillen Meeres. San Francisco: 1883. V. 65

BRICKDALE, ELEANOR FORTESCUE
The Book of Old English Songs and Ballads. London: 1918. V. 64

BRICKELL, CHRISTOPHER
The American Horticultural Society Encyclopedia of Gardening. New York: 1993. V. 67
An English Florilegium. London: 1987. V. 62

BRICKELL, JOHN
The Natural History of North Carolina. Dublin: 1737. V. 63; 66

BRIDDON, JAMES
The Garden of England. Ventnor: 1875. V. 66

BRIDGE, CYPRIAN
W. L. Wyllie, R.A. London: 1907. V. 62

BRIDGEMAN, CHARLES
Stowe Gardens in Buckinghamshire, Belonging to the Right Honourable the Lord Viscount Cobham, Laid Out by Mr. Bridgeman.... London: 1987. V. 64; 67

BRIDGEMAN, L. J.
Kewts. New York and Boston: 1902. V. 62

BRIDGENS, R.
The Antiquities of Sefton Church. London: 1835. V. 66
Furniture with Candelabra and Interior Decoration. London: 1838. V. 64

BRIDGER, BOBBY
A Ballad of the West. Austin: 1983. V. 66

BRIDGES, A.
Alphonse Mucha: the Complete Graphic Works. New York: 1980. V. 65
Modern Salmon Fishing. 1939. V. 67

BRIDGES, E. LUCAS
Uttermost Part of the Earth. London: 1948. V. 64

BRIDGES, JOHN AFFLECK
Myrtle and Ivy. London: 1895. V. 67

BRIDGES, ROBERT
Carmen Elegiacum. London: 1876. V. 65
Eros and Psyche. Newtown: 1935. V. 64; 65; 66
Eros and Psyche. Waltham St. Lawrence: 1935. V. 65
The Feast of Bacchus. Oxford: 1889. V. 67
Hymns: the Yattendon Hymnal. Oxford: 1899. V. 64
Nero Part 2. London: 1894. V. 66
New Verse Written in 1921. Oxford: 1925. V. 62
New Verse Written in 1921. Oxford: 1926. V. 66
Poems. London: 1873. V. 66
Poems Written in the Year MCMXIII. 1914. V. 67
The Testament of Beauty. Oxford: 1929. V. 63

BRIDGES, THOMAS
A Burlesque Translation of Homer.... New York: 1809. V. 66

BRIDGES, VICTOR
The Happy Murderers. London: 1932. V. 66

BRIDGETT, R. C.
Tight Lines. 1926. V. 67

BRIDGING Normandy to Berlin. N.P: 1945. V. 62; 66

BRIDGMAN, FREDERICK ARTHUR
Winters in Algeria. New York: 1890. V. 66

BRIDGMAN, L. J.
Gulliver's Bird Book. Boston: 1902. V. 63
Mother Wild Goose and Her Wild Beast Show. Boston: 1900. V. 65
Mother Wild Goose and Her Wild Beast Show. Boston: 1900-1904. V. 63

BRIDGMAN, LEONARD
Jane's All the World's Aircraft 1942. New York: 1943. V. 64
Jane's All the World's Aircraft 1949-1950. New York: 1949. V. 65

BRIDSON, G. D. R.
Plant, Animal and Anatomical Illustration in Art and Science.... Winchester: 1990. V. 62; 67

BRIEF Biographical Sketch of the Living Curiosities and the Leading Wonders of Barnum's Traveling Museum and Menagerie. New York: 1871. V. 64

BRIEF History of the Introduction and Progress of the Trade of Woolen Weaving in England.... Manchester: 1810. V. 63

A BRIEF Inquiry Into the Present Condition of the Navy of Great Britain and Its Resources: Followed by Some Suggestions, Calculated to Remedy the Evils, the Existence of Which is Made Apparent in the Course of Investigation. London: 1804. V. 64

A BRIEF View of the London Hibernian Society, for Establishing Schools and Circulating the Holy Scriptures in Ireland. London: 1837. V. 62

BRIERLEY, HENRY
The Registers of Barton, Baptisms and Marriages 1666-1812, Burials 1666-1830. Kendal: 1917. V. 65
The Registers of Brough Under Stainmore 1556-1812. Kendal: 1923-1924. V. 64; 65; 66
The Registers of Crosthwaite. Volume II. 1600-1670. Penrith: 1930. V. 65
The Registers of Crosthwaite. Volume III. Penrith: 1930. V. 65
The Registers of Dacre, Cumberland, 1559-1716. Kendal: 1912. V. 65
The Registers of Kendal, Westmorland Part I: 1558-1587. Part II: Marriages and Burials 1558-1587, Baptisms 1591-1595; Part III: Baptisms 1596- 1599, Marriages and Burials, 1591-599, Baptisms 1607-31; Part IV: Marriages and Burials 1606-1631; Part IV: Ind. Kendal: 1921-1973. V. 65
The Registers of Kendal Westmorland, Part II. Marriages and Burials 1558-1587, Baptisms 1591-1595. Kendal: 1922. V. 65
The Registers of Milburn, Westmorland 1679-1812. Kendal: 1913. V. 65
The Registers of St. Michael's on Wyre 1659-1707 and Woodplumpton 1604-1659. Cambridge: 1906. V. 65
The Registers of the Parish Church of Skelton, Cumberland, 1580-1812. Kendal: 1918. V. 65

BRIERRE DE BOISMONT, ALEXANDRE J. F.
Hallucinations; or, the Rational History of Apparitions, Dreams, Ecstasy, Magnetism and Somnambulism. Philadelphia: 1853. V. 65

BRIERRE DE BOISMONT, ALEXANDRE J.F.
On Hallucinations: a History and Explanation of Apparitions, Visions, Dreams, Ecstasy, Magnetism and Somnambulism.... London: 1859. V. 64

BRIFFAULT, ROBERT
The Mothers. London: 1927. V. 65
The Mothers. New York: 1927. V. 66

BRIGGS, C. F.
Homes of American Authors. New York and London: 1853. V. 65
The Story of the Telegraph and a History of the Great. New York: 1858. V. 66

BRIGGS, D. E.
Malting and Brewing Science. London: 1918-1982. V. 67

BRIGGS, HAROLD
Frontiers of the Northwest. New York: 1940. V. 64; 65; 67

BRIGGS, JOHN
Letters Addressed to a Young Person in India.... London: 1828. V. 64
The Lonsdale Magazine, or, Provincial Repository.... Kendal: 1829-1822. V. 62; 65; 66
Poems on Various Subjects. Ulverston: 1818. V. 62; 66
The Remains of John Briggs.... Kirkby Lonsdale: 1825. V. 62

BRIGGS, JOSHUA F.
A Pioneer Missourian. Boston: 1939. V. 63

BRIGGS, LLOYD VERNON
Arizona and New Mexico 1882, California 1886, Mesico 1891. Boston: 1932. V. 64
Fifteen Months' Service on the Old Supervisory State Board of Insanity in Massachusetts 1913-1914. Boston: 1928. V. 65
Occupation as a Substitute for Restraint in the Treatment of the Mentally Ill: a History of the Passage of Two Bills through the Massachusetts Legislature. Boston: 1923. V. 65
Two Years' Service on the Reorganized State Board of Insanity in Massachusetts August 1914 to August 1916. Boston: 1930. V. 65
A Victory for Progress in Mental Medicine: Defeat of Reactionaries: the History of an Intrigue. Boston: 1924. V. 65

BRIGGS, RAYMOND
The Bear. 1904. V. 67
Father Christmas Goes on Holiday. London: 1975. V. 62
The Snowman. London: 1978. V. 67
When the Wind Blows. London: 1982. V. 64

BRIGGS, RICHARD
The English Art of Cookery.... London: 1791. V. 65
The New Art of Cookery.... Boston: 1798. V. 62; 64

BRIGGS, SOPHIA
The Gitana: a Tale. London: 1845. V. 65

BRIGGS, WALTER
Without Noise of Arms: the 1776 Dominquez Escalante Search for a Route from Sante Fe to Monterey. Flagstaff: 1976. V. 63; 66

BRIGGS, WILLIAM
Ophthalmographia, sive Oculi Ejusque Partium Descriptio Anatomica. London: 1687. V. 65

BRIGHAM, AMARIAH
Remarks on the Influence of Mental Cultivation and Mental Excitement Upon Health. Philadelphia: 1845. V. 64; 65

BRIGHAM, CLARENCE S.
Paul Revere's Engravings. Worcester: 1954. V. 64; 66

BRIGHAM, MARIAH
An Inquiry Concerning the Diseases and Functions of the Brain. The Spinal Cord and the Nerves. New York: 1840. V. 64

BRIGHT, JOHN
Speeches on Questions of Public Policy. London: 1868. V. 67

BRIGHT, RICHARD
Travels from Vienna through Lower Hungary; with Some Remarks on the State of Vienna During the Congress in the Year 1814. Edinburgh: 1818. V. 64

BRIGHT, TIMOTHY
A Treatise of Melancholie. London: 1586. V. 63

BRIGHTEYES Merry Book. London: 1922. V. 62

BRIGHTFIELD, MYRON F.
John Wilson Croker. 1940. V. 67

BRIGHTON, JOHN GEORGE
History of Rothwell, in the County of Northampton. Northampton: 1869. V. 62

BRIGHTWELL, CECILIA LUCY
Memorials of the Life of Amelia Opie. Norwich: 1854. V. 65

BRILL, CHARLES J.
Conquest of the Southern Plains, Uncensored Narrative of the Battle of the Washita and Custer's Southern Campaign. Oklahoma City: 1938. V. 67

BRILLAT-SAVARIN, JEAN ANTHELME
Brillat-Savarin's Physiologie du Gout. London: 1884. V. 63
The Handbook of Dining or Corpulency and Leanness Scientifically Considered. London: 1864. V. 64
Physiologie du Gout. Paris: 1826. V. 63
Physiologie du Gout.... Paris: 1829. V. 63
The Physiology of Taste. Philadelphia: 1854. V. 66
The Physiology of Taste. New York: 1949. V. 62
The Physiology of Taste. New York: 1971. V. 66

BRIM, CHARLES J.
Medicine in the Bible; the Pentateuch, Torah. New York: 1936. V. 63

BRIMLEY, C. S.
Insects of North Carolina. Raleigh: 1938. V. 64; 67

BRIMLOW, GEORGE F.
Cavalryman Out of the West - Life of General William Carey Brown. Caldwell: 1944. V. 65; 67
Harney County, Oregon and Its Range Land. Portland: 1951. V. 65

BRIN, DAVID
Brightness Reef. Norwalk: 1995. V. 65

BRINCKERHOFF, SIDNEY
Lancers for the King, A Study of the Frontier Military System of Northern New Spain with a Translation of the Royal Regulation of 1771. Phoenix: 1965. V. 66

BRINCKLE, WILLIAM D.
Hoffy's North American Pomologist.... Philadelphia: 1860. V. 64

BRINDLEY, G. W.
Crystal Structure of Clay Minerals and Their X-Ray Indentification. 1980. V. 67

BRINDLEY, H.
Some Cases of Caudal Abnormality in Mabula Carinata and Other Lizards. Bombay: 1898. V. 67

BRINDLEY, JOHN
The Marriage System of Socialism Freed from the Misrepresentations of Its Enemies.... Chester: 1840-1841. V. 63
Tract I. A Reply to Robert Owen's Fundamental Principles of Socialism, proving the Free Agency of Man. Birmingham: 1840. V. 63
Tract 2. Containing a Reply to Robert Owens's Attack Upon Marriage; in an Address to the Working Classes. Birmingham: 1840. V. 63

BRINE, MARY DOW
From Gold to Grey. New York, London, Paris: 1886. V. 63

BRINGHURST, R.
The Lyell Island Variations. Stockton: 1995. V. 62

BRINGLEY, JOHN
An Examination of Various Solutions of Kepler's Problem, and a Short Practical Solution of that Problem Painted Out.... Dublin: 1803. V. 62

BRININSTOOL, E. A.
Crazy Horse Greatest Fighting Chief of the Ogalala Sioux His Tragic End. Los Angeles: 1949. V. 65; 67
The Custer Fight, Captain Benteen's Story of the Little Big Horn June 25-26, 1876. Hollywood: 1933. V. 65; 67
Dull Knife. Hollywood: 1935. V. 65
Major Reno Vindicated. Hollywood: 1935. V. 67
Trail Dust of a Maverick. New York: 1914. V. 64
Troopers with Custer: Historic Incidents of the Battle of the Little Big Horn. Harrisburg: 1952. V. 64; 66

BRINKLEY, JOHN
Elements of Astronomy. Dublin: 1813. V. 62

BRINTON, DANIEL G.
American Hero-Myths: a Study in the Native Religions of the Western Continent. Philadelphia: 1882. V. 63; 64
Giordano Bruno: Philosopher and Martyr. Philadelphia: 1890. V. 64
The Laws of Health in Relation to the Human Form. Springfield: 1871. V. 64; 65
Rig Veda Americanus. Sacred Songs of the Anicent Mexicans.... Philadelphia: 1890. V. 67

BRIQUET, C. M.
Les Filigranes: Dictionaire Historique Des Marques Du Papier. New York: 1966. V. 64

BRISBANE, ALBERT
Social Destiny of Man; or, Association and Reorganization of Industry. Philadelphia: 1840. V. 66

BRISBIN, JAMES S.
The Beef Bonanza: or How to Get Rich on the Plains. Philadelphia: 1881. V. 63; 67

BRISCOE, JOHN POTTER
A Concise History of the Nottingham Castle...and a Guide to the Art Gallery and Museum (Nottingham Castle). Nottingham: 1888. V. 65

BRISEUX, CHARLES ETIENNE
Traite du Beau, Essentiel Dans les Arts, Applique Particulierement a l'Architecture.... Paris: 1752. V. 64

BRISSON, BARNABE
B. Brissonii I. C. et in Suprema Parisiensi Curia Advocati, De Ritu Nuptarum Liber Singularis. Paris: 1564. V. 65

BRISSON, MATHURIN JACQUES
Ornithologia sive Synopsis Methodica Sistens Avium Divisionem in Ordines, Sectiones, Genera, Species, Ipsarumque Varietates. Paris: 1760. V. 66; 67
Pesanteur Specifique des Corps. Paris: 1787. V. 67
Traite Elementaire ou Principes de Physique, Fondes sur les Connoissances les Plus Certaines tant Anciennes Que Modernes Confirmes par l'Experience. Paris. V. 67

BRISSOT DE WARVILLE, J. P.
New Travels in the U.S.A. Performed in 1788. London: 1792. V. 65

BRISTED, JOHN
An Oration on the Utility of Literary Establishments Delivered (at the Request of the Proprietors) at the Opening of the Literary Rooms in New York. New York: 1814. V. 62

BRISTER, BOB
Moss, Mallards and Mules and Other Hunting and Fishing Stories. New York: 1974. V. 65
Shotgunning: the Art and the Science. 1976. V. 67

BRISTOL, SHERLOCK
The Pioneer Preacher: an Autobiography. New York: 1898. V. 67

BRITAINE, WILLIAM LE
Human Prudence; or the Art by Which a Man May Raise Himself and His Fortune to Grandeur. London: 1739. V. 63

BRITE, POPPY Z.
The Seed of Lost Souls. Burton: 1999. V. 67

BRITISH ASSOCIATION FOR THE ADVANCEMENT OF SCIENCE
Report of the 48th Meeting Held at Dublin in August 1878. 1879. V. 65

THE BRITISH Aviary, and Bird Keeper's Companion.... London: 1840. V. 62

BRITISH Birds. 1840. V. 65

BRITISH Birds. The Water Birds. London: 1857. V. 67

BRITISH Birds, Their Haunts and Habits. London: 1868. V. 62

THE BRITISH Champion; or Honour Rewarded. York: 1795. V. 67

BRITISH Colonial Flags. Also Flags of All Nations. Glasgow: 1915. V. 63

BRITISH COLUMBIA FISHING & PACKING CO.
Sample Salmon Labels. Vancouver: 1921. V. 63

BRITISH COLUMBIA PIONEER SOCIETY
Constitution, By Laws and Rules of Order of the British Columbia Pioneer Society, Organized April 28, 1871. Victoria: 1874. V. 63

BRITISH COLUMBIA SOCIETY OF SPIRITUALISTS
By Laws of the First British Columbia Society of Spiritualists of Victoria, B.C. Victoria: 1891. V. 63

THE BRITISH Constitution Invulnerable. London: 1792. V. 62

THE BRITISH Crisis; or, the Disorder of the State at Its Height. London: 1797. V. 63

BRITISH Hunts and Huntsmen. The North East and Western Midlands of England and Wales. 1910. V. 62

BRITISH Hunts and Huntsmen. The South-East, East and Eastern Midlands. 1909. V. 62; 64

BRITISH Journal of Medical Psychology. 1920. V. 66

BRITISH Liberties or the Free-Born Subject's Inheritance; Containing the laws that Form the Basis of Those Liberties with Observations Thereon.... London: 1766. V. 62

THE BRITISH Martial; or an Anthology of Englis Epigrams; Being the Largest Collection Ever Published. London: 1806. V. 67

BRITISH MUSEUM
Bookbindings from the Library of Jean Grolier. Oxford: 1965. V. 62
Catalogue of Books, Manuscripts, Maps and Drawings. New York: 1992. V. 63; 64; 65; 67
A Catalogue of Engraved Gems in the British Museum. London: 1888. V. 65
Catalogue of the Books, Manuscripts, Maps and Drawings. London: 1903-1940. V. 62
Catalogue of the Ungulate Mammals in the British Museum. 1913-1916. V. 64
General Catalogue of Printed Books to 1955. New York: 1967-1987. V. 62
Greek Printing Types, 1465-1927. Facsimiles from an Exhibition of Books Illustrating the Development of Greek Printing Shown in the British Museum. London: 1927. V. 62
Poetry in the Making - Catalogue of an Exhibition of Poetry Manuscripts int he British Museum April-June 1967. London: 1967. V. 64

THE BRITISH Navy in the Present Year of Grace. London: 188-1886. V. 65

BRITISH Pharmacopoeia. London: 1864. V. 62

BRITISH Regional Geology. London: 1947-1950. V. 62

BRITISH Sea Weeds. Natural Specimens. London: 1870. V. 64

BRITISH SPELEOLOGICAL ASSOCIATION
Caves and Caving 1937-1938. Settle: 1937-1938. V. 64
Proceedings. Nos. 1-8. Settle: 1963-1970. V. 64; 65

BRITISH Sports and Sportsmen Past and Present. 1908. V. 67

THE BRITISH Theatre. London: 1791-1797. V. 63

BRITO FREIRE, FRANCISCO DE
Relacao da Viagem Que Fez ao Estado do Brazil a Armada da Companhia, anno 1655. Lisbon: 1657. V. 62

BRITTAIN, I. J.
Tragedy of Naomi Wise. Life of Andrew Jackson. The First English Baby in America. The Little Lost Girl. Mrs. David Caldwell. A Tory Beauty. Winston Salem: 1920. V. 66

BRITTAIN, LEWIS
Principles of the Christian Religion and Catholic Faith Investigated. London: 1790. V. 63

BRITTAIN, VERA
Halcyon or the Future of Monogamy. London: 1929. V. 65
The Women of Oxford - a Fragment of History. London: 1960. V. 63

BRITTEN, L. H.
Manual of Street Crowd Tactics. 1918. V. 63, 64

BRITTON, JOHN
The Authorship of the Letters of Junius Elucidated.... London: 1848. V. 67
The Beauties of England and Wales; or Delineations, Topographical, Historical and Descriptive. London: 1801. V. 62
An Historical and Architectural Essay on Redcliffe Church, Bristol.... London: 1843. V. 67
An Historical and Architectural Essay Relating to Redcliffe Church. London: 1813. V. 66
The History and Antiquities of the Abbey, and Cathedral Church of Peterborough.... London: 1836. V. 62; 66
Illustrations of the Early Domestic Architecure of England. London: 1846. V. 66
Memoir of John Aubrey, F.R.S. London: 1845. V. 67

BRITTON, N. L.
The Cactaceae.... Washington: 1937. V. 62; 67
The Cactaceae.... New York: 1963. V. 67
The Cactaceae.... 1964. V. 66
The Cactaceae.... Dover: 1964. V. 64

BRITTON, WILEY
The Civil War on the Border, a Narrative of the Operations in Missouri, Kansas, Arkansas and the Indian Territory During the Years 1861- 1862. New York: 1891. V. 63; 65
The (Five Civilized Indian Nations) Union Brigade in the Civil War. Kansas City: 1922. V. 62; 63; 65

BRITZMAN, HOMER
Charles M. Russell - the West in Bronze - a Pictorial Study of Bronzes. Los Angeles: 1950. V. 63

BRIZGUZ Y BRU, ATANASIO GENARO
Escuela de Arquitectura Civil.... Valencia: 1804. V. 64

BROAD, LOWTHER
The Jubilee History of Nelson from 1842 to 1892. London: 1892. V. 64

BROADFOOT, N. W.
Billiards. London: 1902. V. 64; 66

BROADFOOT, W.
The Career of Major George Broadfoot, CB in Afghanistan and the Punjab Compiled from His Papers and Those of Lords Ellenborough and Hardinge.... London: 1888. V. 64

BROCA, PAUL
Des Anevrysmes et de Leur Traitement. Paris: 1586. V. 66
On the Phenomena of Hybridity in the Genus Homo. London: 1864. V. 64; 67
Remarques sur le Siege, Le Diagnostic et la Nature De L'Aphemie. (with) Perte de La Parole: Ramolissement Chronique et Destruction Partielle du Lobe Anerieur Gauche du Cerveau. 1863. V. 64

BROCH, HERMANN
Die Schlafwandler. Munich: 1931. V. 67
Die Schlafwandler. Munich: 1931-1932. V. 67
The Sleepwalkers. A Trilogy. London: 1932. V. 67

BROCK, EDWIN
I Never Saw It Lit. Poems. Santa Barbara: 1974. V. 63

BROCK, HENRY IRVING
Colonial Churches in Virginia. Richmond: 1930. V. 63

BROCK, R. A.
Documents, Chiefly Unpublished, Relating to the Huguenot Emigration to Virginia and the Settlement of Manakin-Town. Richmond: 1886. V. 67
General Robert Edward Lee, Soldier, Citizen and Christian Patriot. Richmond: 1897. V. 62; 65

BROCK, SAMUEL
Injuries of the Skull, Brain and Spinal Cord. Baltimore: 1940. V. 65; 66

BROCKETT, JOHN TROTTER
A Glossary of North Country Words in Use. Newcastle-Upon-Tyne: 1825. V. 63
A Glossary of North Country Words in Use. Newcastle upon Tyne: 1846. V. 64; 65

BROCKETT, L. P.
The Silk Industry in America. A History: Prepared for the Centennial Exposition. N.P: 1876. V. 63; 66
Woman: Her Rights, Wrongs, Privileges, and Responsibilities. Hartford: 1870. V. 65

BROCKETT, PAUL
Bibliography of Aeronautics 1909-(1932). Washington: 1921-1936. V. 64

BROCKLEHURST, H. C.
Game Animals of the Sudan. 1931. V. 62; 63; 64
Game Animals of the Sudan. London: 1931. V. 63; 64

BROCKLEHURST, THOMAS
Mexico Today; a Country with a Great Future.... London: 1883. V. 64

BROCKLESBY, JOHN
Elements of Meteorology, With Questions for Examination, Designed for Schools and Academies. New York: 1857. V. 67

BROCKMAN, WILLIAM E.
Orange County, Virginia Families. Volume II. Minneapolis: 1956. V. 64

BROCKWELL, MAURICE W.
A Catalogue of Some of the Paintings of the British School in the Collection of Henry Edwards Huntington at San Marino California. New York: 1925. V. 67

BRODER, PATRICIA JANIS
American Indian Painting and Sculpture. New York: 1981. V. 62; 63; 64; 66
The American West: the Modern Vision. Boston: 1984. V. 64; 67
Bronzes of the American West. New York: 1973. V. 64; 66; 67
Hopi Painting: the World of the Hopis. New York: 1978. V. 62; 63; 64; 66
Taos: a Painter's Dream. New York: 1980. V. 63

BRODERIP, FRANCES FREELING
Tales of the Toys, Told by Themselves. London: 1869. V. 65

BRODIE, BENJAMIN COLLINS
Lectures Illustrative of Certain Local Nervous Affections. London: 1837. V. 62; 65
Pathological and Surgical Observations on Diseases of the Joints. London: 1822. V. 65
Pathological and Surgical Observations on Diseases of the Joints. London: 1834. V. 63; 65
The Works of.... London: 1863. V. 64; 66; 67
The Works of.... London: 1865. V. 66

BRODIE, WILLIAM
The Trial of William Brodie, Wright and Cabinet Maker in Edinburgh, and of George Smith, Grocer There, ...On the 27th and 28th Days of August 1788. Edinburgh: 1788. V. 63

BRODIGAN, THOMAS
A Botanical, Historical and Practical Treatise on the Tobacco Plant.... London: 1830. V. 63; 66

BRODKEY, HAROLD
A Poem About Testimony and Argument. New York: 1986. V. 62; 63

BRODMAN, ESTELLE
The Development of Medical Bibliography. 1954. V. 67

BRODRICK, GEORGE C.
English Land and English Landlords, an Enquiry into the Origin and Character of the English Land System with Proposals for Its Reform with an Index. London: 1881. V. 63

BRODSKY, JOSEPH
Less Than One: Selected Essays. New York: 1986. V. 64
A Part of Speech. New York: 1980. V. 63; 64
Stekotvoreni I Poemi. Washington: 1965. V. 64; 67
To Urania. New York: 1988. V. 64; 66
Verses on the Winter Campaign 1980. London: 1981. V. 62

BROGAN, JOHN
The Official Travis McGee Quiz Book. New York: 1984. V. 67

BROGGER, W. C.
Fridtjof Nansen. 1861-1893. London: 1896. V. 64; 65; 66

BROGNIART, ALEXANDRE
Traite Elementaire de Mineralogie. 1807. V. 62

BROINOWSKI, G. J.
The Birds of Australia.... Melbourne: 1887-1891. V. 64; 65; 66

BROMAN, IVAR
Normale und Abnorme Entwicklung des Menschen. Wiesbaden: 1911. V. 65

BROMBERG, PAUL
Practische Woning Inrichting.... Amsterdam: 1933. V. 65

BROMLEY, A. NELSON
A Fly Fisher's Reflections 1860-1930. London: 1930. V. 67

BROMLEY, GEORGE T.
The Long Ago and the Later On - Or Recollections of Eighty Years. San Francisco: 1904. V. 67

BROMLEY, WILLIAM
Remarks in the Grand Tour of France and Italy. London: 1692. V. 67
Remarks in the Grand Tour of France and Italy. London: 1705. V. 67

BROMME, TRAUGOTT
Illustriter Hand-Atlas der Geographie und Statistik. Stuttgart: 1862. V. 65

BROMSEN Lectures. *The First Seven Lectures Complete.* Boston: 1976-1981. V. 63

BRONAUGH, W. C.
The Younger's Fight for Freedom - A Southern Soldier's Twenty Years Campaign to Open Northern Prison Doors. Columbia: 1906. V. 63; 64; 65; 67

BRONDSTED, P. O.
Voyages et Recherches dans la Grece.... Paris: 1826-1830. V. 66

BRONK, WILLIAM
Five Cummington Poems 1939. Cummington: 1939. V. 64
Life Supports. New and Collected Poems. New Rochelle: 1981. V. 64
Light and Dark. Ashland: 1956. V. 62; 64; 67
Light In a Dark Sky. Ten Poems. Concord: 1982. V. 62
Six Duplicities. New York. V. 63

BRONOWSKI, J.
For Wilhelmina Queen of the Netherlands. Cambridge: 1929. V. 67

BRONSON, BERTRAND H.
Johnson and Boswell - Three Essays. Berkeley and Los Angeles: 1944. V. 62

BRONSON, EDGAR BEECHER
Cowboy Life on the Western Plains. New York: 1910. V. 67
In Closed Territory. Chicago: 1910. V. 64; 65
Reminiscences of a Ranchman. New York: 1908. V. 66

BRONTE, ANNE
Agnes Grey. Oxford: 1988. V. 63
The Complete Poems of.... New York: 1920. V. 63; 66
The Tenant of Wildfell Hall. New York: 1848. V. 65
The Tenant of Wildfell Hall. 1854. V. 66
The Tenant of Wildfell Hall. New York: 1857. V. 63
The Tenant of Wildfell Hall. London: 1859. V. 65
The Tenant of Wildfell Hall. London: 1880. V. 65
The Tenant of Wildfell Hall. New York: 1905. V. 63

BRONTE, CHARLOTTE
The Adventures of Ernest Alembert, a Fairy Tale. London: 1896. V. 66
An Autobiography. London: 1847. V. 66
The Complete Poems. London: 1923. V. 66
Five Novelettes. Passing Events. Julia. Mina Laury. Captain Henry Hastings. Caroline Vernon. London: 1971. V. 63
Jane Eyre. Boston: 1848. V. 62; 66
Jane Eyre. Leipzig: 1848. V. 65
Jane Eyre. London: 1848. V. 65; 66
Jane Eyre. New York: 1848. V. 67
Jane Eyre. London: 1855. V. 65
Jane Eyre. London: 1857. V. 65
Jane Eyre. New York: 1858. V. 65
Jane Eyre. Paris: 1859. V. 66
Jane Eyre. London: 1871. V. 65
Jane Eyre. Leipzig: 1881. V. 65
Jane Eyre. Chicago, NY, San Francisco: 1889. V. 64
Jane Eyre. London: 1899. V. 65
Jane Eyre. London: 1902. V. 63
Jane Eyre. Franklin Center: 1981. V. 63
Legends of Angria. New Haven: 1933. V. 66
Passing Events. Julia. Mina Laury. Captain Henry Hastings. Caroline Vernon. London: 1971. V. 64
Le Professeur. Paris: 1869. V. 63
The Professor. Leipzig: 1857. V. 65
The Professor. London: 1857. V. 62; 63; 64; 65; 66
The Professor. New York: 1857. V. 62; 63; 66; 67
The Professor. London: 1860. V. 63; 65; 66
The Professor. New York: 1865. V. 66
The Professor. New York: 1905. V. 63
Shirley. London: 1849. V. 66
Shirley. New York: 1850. V. 63; 66
Shirley. London: 1857. V. 64; 65
Shirley. London: 1860. V. 63
Shirley. New York: 1905. V. 63
The Spell, an Extravaganza. London: 1931. V. 66
The Twelve Adventurers and Other Stories. London: 1925. V. 62; 63; 66
Villette. Leipzig: 1853. V. 65
Villette. London: 1853. V. 65; 66; 67
Villette. New York: 1853. V. 62; 63; 66
Villette. London: 1855. V. 63; 65
Villette. London: 1857. V. 65
Villette. New York: 1858. V. 66
Villette. New York: 1905. V. 63
The Works. London. V. 62

BRONTE, EMILY
The Complete Poems. London: 1923. V. 63; 65
Gondal's Queen. Austin: 1955. V. 63
Les Hauts de Hurle-Vent. (Wuthering Heights). Paris: 1925. V. 63

BRONTE, EMILY continued
The Novels of.... London: 1895. V. 66
The Novels of.... London: 1965-1970. V. 66
Poemes. Paris: 1963. V. 63
Wuthering Heights. New York: 1862. V. 66
Wuthering Heights. New York: 1865. V. 65
Wuthering Heights. New York: 1905. V. 63
Wuthering Heights. London: 1931. V. 62; 63; 64
Wuthering Heights. New York: 1931. V. 63
Wuthering Heights. London: 1955. V. 62
Wuthering Heights. Boston: 1956. V. 66
Wuthering Heights. 1970. V. 63
Wuthering Heights. Franklin Center: 1975. V. 63
Wuthering Heights. New York: 1993. V. 65

BRONTE, PATRICK
Bronteana: His Collected Works and Life. London: 1898. V. 64
The Rev. Patrick Bronte. His Collected Works and Life. Bingley: 1898. V. 63

BRONTE, PATRICK BRANWELL
And the Weary Are at Rest. 1924. V. 65
And the Weary Are at Rest. London: 1924. V. 63; 66

BRONTE, THE SISTERS
Novels. Edinburgh: 1905. V. 66
Novels. London: 1905-1909. V. 63
Novels. Edinburgh: 1911. V. 62; 65; 67
Novels. Edinburgh: 1924. V. 65
Novels. Edinburgh: 1924. V. 62; 63
Novels. London: 1931-1933. V. 63
Poems. London: 1846-1848. V. 63
Poems. Philadelphia: 1848. V. 63
Poems. New York: 1902. V. 62; 66
Poems by Currer, Ellis and Acton Bell. Philadelphia: 1848. V. 64; 65
The Works. London: 1931-1936. V. 63
The Works. London: 1949. V. 67
Wuthering Heights and Agnes Grey. London: 1850. V. 65
Wuthering Heights and Agnes Grey. Leipzig: 1851. V. 65
Wuthering Heights and Agnes Grey. London: 1851. V. 63
Wuthering Heights and Agnes Grey. London: 1858. V. 65
Wuthering Heights and Agnes Grey. London: 1863. V. 65
Wuthering Heights and Agnes Grey. London: 1871. V. 65
Wuthering Heights and Agnes Grey. Leipzig: 1912. V. 65
Wuthering Heights and Jane Eyre. New York: 1943. V. 63

THE BRONTES - Their Lives, Friendships and Correspondence. London: 1932. V. 63

BROOK, A. W.
Witch's Hollow or the New Babes in the Wood. London: 1920. V. 67

BROOK, G.
Catalogue of the Madreporarian Corals in the British Museum. 1893-1928. V. 63; 66
Challenger Voyage. Zoology. Part 80. Antipatharia. 1889. V. 66

BROOK, HARRY E.
Land of Sunshine: Southern California. Los Angeles: 1893. V. 65

BROOK, JOHN R.
Civil Report of Manor-General John R. Brook, U.S. Army, Military Governor, Island of Cuba. Washington: 1900. V. 63

BROOK, RICHARD
The Cyclopaedia of Botany.... 1854. V. 67
New Cyclopaedia of Botany and Complete Book of Herbs.... 1853. V. 62

BROOKE, FRANCES
The History of Emily Montague. Dublin: 1786. V. 65

BROOKE, FULKE GREVILLE, 1ST BARON
Caelica. Nowtown: 1937. V. 65
Certaine Learned and Elegant Workes. London: 1633. V. 62; 65; 67

BROOKE, HENRY
Annals of the Revolution; or, a History of the Doans. Philadelphia: 1843. V. 64; 66
Annals of the Revolution; or, a History of the Doans. Philadelphia: 1848. V. 66
The Fool of Quality; or, the History of Henry Earl of Moreland. London: 1782. V. 64
Gustavus Vasa, the Deliverer of His Country. London: 1739. V. 65
The History of the Earl of Moreland. London: 1781. V. 64

BROOKE, JOCELYN
The Crisis in Bulgaria - Or Ibsen to the Rescue!. London: 1956. V. 65
The Flower in Season. London: 1952. V. 65
The Military Orchid. London: 1948. V. 65
Private View. London: 1954. V. 63; 65
The Wild Orchids of Britain. London: 1950. V. 62; 63; 64; 65; 67

BROOKE, L. LESLIE
Johnny Crow's New Garden. London: 1935. V. 62
The Three Little Pigs and Tom Thumb. London: 1930. V. 63

BROOKE, LORD
An Eye-Witness in Manchuria. London: 1905. V. 64

BROOKE, M.
The History of Henry, Earl of Moreland. 1815. V. 66

BROOKE, MRS.
A Dialogue Between a Lady and Her Pupils, Describing a Journey through England and Wales. London: 1800?. V. 65
A Dialogue Between a Lady and Her Pupils, Describing a Journey through England and Wales. London: 1808. V. 63

BROOKE, RALPH
A Catalogue and Succession of the Kings, Princes, Dukes, Marquesses, Earles and Viscounts of this Realm of England, Since the Norman Conquest.... 1622. V. 64

BROOKE, RALPHE
A Discoveries of Certaine Errours Published in Print in the Much Commended Britannia, 1594, Very Prejudicial to the Dissenters and Successions of the Ancient Nobilities of the Relame. London: 1723-1724. V. 66

BROOKE, RICHARD
Observations Illustrative of the Accounts Given by the Ancient Historical Writers of the Battle of Stoke Field, Between King Henry the Seventh and John de la Pole, Earl of Lincoln, in 1847. Liverpool: 1825. V. 65

BROOKE, RUPERT
The Collected Poems of Rupert Brooke. London: 1918. V. 62; 63; 66
The Collected Poems of Rupert Brooke. London: 1919. V. 63
The Collected Poems of Rupert Brooke. London: 1923. V. 62
The Complete Poems. London: 1932. V. 63
Democracy and the Arts. London: 1946. V. 63; 66
Fragments Now First Collected Some Being Hithero Unpublished. Hartford: 1925. V. 63; 66
John Webster and the Elizabethan Drama. London: 1916. V. 62; 65
Letters from America. London: 1916. V. 62; 65; 66
Lithuania. 1915. V. 65
Lithuania. Chicago: 1915. V. 63; 64; 66
Lithuania. Cincinnati: 1922?. V. 63
Lithuania. 1935. V. 65
1914 and Other Poems. London: 1915. V. 63; 64; 66
1914 and Other Poems. New York: 1915. V. 62; 64; 67
The Old Vicarage Grantchester. London: 1916. V. 62; 64
Poemes. Paris: 1947. V. 63; 66
Poems. London: 1911. V. 65
Selected Poems. London: 1917. V. 63
Two Sonnets: with a Memoir.... London: 1945. V. 62

BROOKE, SUSAN W.
Stately Progress A Tale of Ducal Profligacy and Providence. New York: 1980. V. 63

BROOKE, THOMAS HENRY
A History of the Island of St. Helena, from Its Discovery by the Portugese of the Year 1806.... London: 1808. V. 62

BROOKES, IVESON L.
A Discourse Investigating the Doctrine of Washing the Saints Feet: Delivered at Monticello. Macon: 1830. V. 66

BROOKES, RICHARD
Brooke's General Gazetteer Improved.... Philadelphia and Richmond: 1812. V. 63
The General Gazetteer; and Geographical Dictionary. London: 1070. V. 64
The General Gazetteer; or, Compendious Geographical Dictionary. London: 1820. V. 63
The General Practice of Physic.... London: 1763. V. 67
The General Practice of Physic.... Philadelphia: 1831. V. 66
An Introduction to Physic and Surgery. London: 1763. V. 66
A New and Accurate System of Natural History.... London: 1763. V. 62

BROOK HART, DENYS
British 19th Century Marine Painting. Woodbridge: 1974. V. 67

BROOKMAN, LESTER G.
The 19th Century Postage Stamps of the United States. New York: 1947. V. 66

BROOKNER, ANITA
The Genius of the Future: Studies in French Art Criticism. London: 1971. V. 62
Hotel du Lac. London: 1984. V. 63
A Start in Life. London: 1981. V. 62; 66

BROOKS, BRUCE
The Moves Make the Make. New York: 1984. V. 65
What Hearts. New York: 1992. V. 65

BROOKS, BRYANT B.
Memoirs of....Cowboy, Trapper, Lumberman, Stockman, Oilman, Banker and Governor of Wyoming. Glendale: 1939. V. 65; 67

BROOKS, CECIL R. L.
The Musicians and Other Sketches. Hampstead: 1901. V. 67

BROOKS, CHANDLER MC CUSKEY
The Historical Development of Physiological Thought.... Mansfield Center: 1999. V. 65

BROOKS, CHARLES WOLCOTT
Early Migration of the Chinese Race. San Francisco: 1876. V. 67
Origin of the Chinese Race.... San Francisco: 1876. V. 64

BROOKS, CLEANTH
Modern Poetry and the Tradition. Chapel Hill: 1939. V. 64

BROOKS, CLINTON E.
Forts and Forays, James A. Bennett. A Dragoon in New Mexico 1850- 1856. Albuquerque: 1948. V. 65; 67

BROOKS, CLIVE
The Memoirs of Professor Moriarty: Volume One. Southampton: 1990. V. 63; 66
Sherlock Holmes Revisited: Volume Two. Southampton: 1990. V. 63

BROOKS, ELISHA
A Pioneer Mother of California. San Francisco: 1922. V. 63; 65
A Pioneer Mother of California. New York: 1973. V. 66

BROOKS, GEORGE
Industy and Property; a Plea for Truth and Honesty in Economics, and for Liberty and Justice in Social Reform. 1892-1894. V. 62

BROOKS, GWENDOLYN
Annie Allen. New York: 1949. V. 63
A Street in Bronzeville. New York: 1945. V. 63; 64; 67
The Tiger Who Wore White Gloves. Chicago: 1974. V. 62; 63

BROOKS, H. ALLEN
Prairie School Architecture: Studies from The Western Architect. Toronto: 1975. V. 62; 65

BROOKS, HENRY
Natal, a History and Description of the Colony; Including Its Natural Features, Productions, Industrial Condition and Prospects. London: 1876. V. 64

BROOKS, JEROME E.
Tobacco: Its History Illustrated by the Books, Manuscripts and Engravings in the Library of George Arents, Jr.... New York: 1937-1969. V. 62

BROOKS, JOHN
A Discourse Delivered Before the Humane Society of the Commonwealth of Massachusetts, 9th June 1795. Boston: 1795. V. 63

BROOKS, JUANITA
On the Mormon Frontier - the Diary of Hosea Stout. Volume One 1844-1848. Volume Two 1848-1861. Salt Lake City: 1964. V. 66

BROOKS, NOAH
First Across the Continent - the Story of the Lewis and Clark Expedition in 1803-1805. New York: 1901. V. 63; 66

BROOKS, SHIRLEY
Sooner or Later. London: 1868. V. 65

BROOKS, U. R.
Butler and His Cavalry in the War of Secession 1861-1865. Columbia: 1909. V. 62; 63; 65
Stories of the Confederacy. Columbia: 1912. V. 62; 63; 65

BROOKS, VAN WYCK
The Ordeal of Mark Twain. London: 1922. V. 65

BROOKS, W. K.
Challenger Voyage. Zoology. Part 45. Stomatopoda. 1886. V. 66
Handbook of Invertebrate Zoology for Laboratories and Seaside Work. Boston: 1890. V. 64

BROOKS, WALTER
To and Again. New York: 1927. V. 63

BROOKS, WALTER R.
Freddy and the Ignoramus. New York: 1941. V. 64
Freddy and the Men from Mars. New York: 1954. V. 65
Freddy and the Pied Piper. New York: 1946. V. 62
Freddy the Pilot. New York: 1952. V. 62; 65

BROOKS, WILLIAM H.
Modern Practical Baking. Palo Alto: 1921. V. 66

BROOM, R.
The South African Fossil Ape-Men. Pretoria: 1946. V. 66

BROOME, WILLIAM
Poems on Several Occasions. London: 1727. V. 66
Poems on Several Occasions. London: 1750. V. 65; 66

BROOMHALL, MARSHALL
Martyred Missionaries of the China Indian Mission with a Record of the Perils and Sufferings of Some Who Escaped. London: 1901. V. 63

BROOMHEAD, FRANK
The Book Illustrations of Orlando Jewitt. London: 1995. V. 67

BROOM'S Authentic Account of the Attempt to Assinate...the Duke of Cumberland at His Apartments in St. James's Palace, on Thursday May 31, 1810, by Joseph Seillis, His Valet.... London: 1810?. V. 63

BROONZY, WILLIAM
Big Bill Blues. London: 1955. V. 63

BROPHY, BRIGID
The Finishing Touch. London: 1963. V. 63

BROPHY, JOHN
Somerset Maugham. London: 1952. V. 64

BROSNAN, C. J.
History of the State of Idaho. New York: 1918. V. 63

BROSSE, J.
Great Voyages of Exploration, the Golden Age of Discovery in the Pacific. 1983. V. 63

BROSTER, D. K.
Couching at the Door. London: 1942. V. 67

BROSTER, JOHN
A Walk Round the Walls and City of Chester. Chester: 1821. V. 65

BROSTER, JOSEPH
The Rivers of Axedge, a Loco-Descriptive Poem: and the Progress of Time, a Moral and Historical Poem. Macclesfield: 1818. V. 62; 65

BROTHERHEAD, W.
General Fremont and the Injustice Done Him by Politicians and Envious Military Men. Philadelphia: 1862. V. 64

BROTHERS, MARY HUDSON
A Pecos Pioneer. Albuquerque: 1943. V. 64; 66; 67

BROTHERS, SAMUEL
Strength and Symetry; or the Art of Dressing Boys, so as to Ensure the Perfect Development of the Bodily Organs. London: 1850. V. 65

BROUARDEL, P. C. H.
Death and Sudden Death. London: 1902. V. 64; 67

BROUGH, ROBERT
The Life of Sir John Falstaff. London: 1858. V. 67

BROUGH, ROBERT B.
A Cracker Bon-Bon for Christmas Parties.... London: 1861. V. 65
Funny Dogs with Funny Tails. London: 1857. V. 65
Which is Which? or, Miles Cassidy's Contract. London: 1860. V. 65

BROUGHAM, HENRY, BARON
Albert Lunel. London: 1872. V. 66

BROUGHAM, JOHN
Dombey and Son. Dramatized from Dickens' novel. New York: 1875. V. 62
Lotus Leaves. Boston: 1875. V. 63; 67

BROUGHAM AND VAUX, HENRY PETER BROUGHAM, 1ST BARON
An Inquiry into the Colonial Policy of the European Powers. Edinburgh: 1803. V. 63; 64
The Life and Times, Written by Himself. London: 1871. V. 62
Political Philosophy. London: 1842-1843. V. 64
The Speech...in the House of Lords, on Thursday May 21, 1835, on the Education of the People. London: 1838. V. 64
Speeches...Upon Questions Relating to Public Rights, Duties and Interests.... Edinburgh: 1838. V. 64

BROUGHTON, HUGH
An Epistle to the Learned Nobilitie of England...(with) Declaration of Generall Corruption of Religion, Scripture and all Learning.... Middlebrugh: 1597-1604. V. 63

BROUGHTON, JAMES
A Long Undressing. Collected Poems 1949-1969. New York: 1971. V. 63; 67
75 Life Lines. Highlands: 1988. V. 63; 67

BROUGHTON, RHODA
A Beginner. London: 1894. V. 65
Joan: a Tale. London: 1876. V. 65

BROUMAS, OLGA
Soie Sauvage. Port Townsend: 1979. V. 63

BROUSSAIS, FRANCOIS JOSEPH VICTOR
De l'Irritation et de La Folie, Ouvrage Dans Lequel les Rapports du Physique et du Moral Sont Etablis sur les Bases de la Medecine Physiologique.... Paris: 1828. V. 67
History of Chronic Phelgmasiae, or Inflammations, Founded on Clinical Experience and Pathological Anatomy Exhibiting a View of Different Varieties and Complications of These Diseases With their Various Methods of Treatment.... Philadelphia: 1831. V. 67

BROUSSEAU, KATE
Mongolism: a Study of the Physical and Mental Characteristics of Mongolian Imbelcils. Baltimore: 1928. V. 65

BROUWER, H. A.
Geological Expedition of the University of Amsterdam to the Lesser Sunday Islands. New York: 1937. V. 67

BROWENELL, CHARLES DE WOLF
The Indian Races of North and South America.... Hartford: 1864. V. 63

BROWER, DANIEL ROBERTS
A Practical Manual of Insanity for the Medical Student and General Practitioner. Philadelphia: 1902. V. 65

BROWER, J. H.
The Mills of Mammon. Joliet: 1909. V. 65

BROWER, JACOB V.
The Mississippi River and Its Source, a Narrative and Critical History of the Discovery of the River and Its Headwaters.... Minneapolis: 1893. V. 64
The Missouri River. St. Paul: 1897. V. 66

BROWER, KENNETH
The Wake of the Whale. San Francisco: 1979. V. 63; 64; 65

BROWN, A. G.
Illustrated Catalogue of Vertical Quadruple Expansion Engines.... Bolton: 1890. V. 66

BROWN, A. GORDON
South and East African Year Book and Guide. London: 1942. V. 63

BROWN, ALEXANDER
The Cabells and Their Kin: a Memorial Volume of History, Biography and Genealogy. Richmond: 1939. V. 64

BROWN, BARRON
Comanche the Sole Survivor of All the Forces in Custer's Last Stand, The Battle of the Little Big Horn. Kansas City: 1935. V. 67

BROWN, BENJAMIN
Testimonies for the Truth: a Record of Manifestations of the Power of God, Miraculous and Providential, Witnessed in the Travels and Experience of Benjamin Brown.... Liverpool: 1853. V. 62; 64

BROWN, BOB
Demonics. Cagnes-sur-Mer: 1931. V. 63
Gems - a Censored Anthology. Cagnes-sur-Mer: 1931. V. 63
Let There Be Beer. New York: 1932. V. 63
The Readies. 1930. V. 63

BROWN, C. B.
Reports on the Physical, Descriptive and Economic Geology of British Guiana. 1875. V. 66
Reports on the Physical, Descriptive and Economic Geology of British Guiana. London: 1875. V. 63

BROWN, CAMPBELL
The First Manassas: Correspondence Between Generals R. S. Ewell and G. T. Beauregard.... Nashville: 1885. V. 63; 65

BROWN, CARLETON
A Register of Middle English Religious and Didactic Verse. Oxford: 1916-1920.. V. 66

BROWN, CATHERINE HAYES
Letters to Mary. New York: 1940. V. 64; 67

BROWN, CHARLES BROCKDEN
An Address to the Government of the United States, on the Cession of Louisiana to the French.... Philadelphia: 1803. V. 66
Arthur Mervyn, or Memoirs of the Year 1793. Philadelphia: 1799. V. 63; 65
The British Treaty. Philadelphia: 1807. V. 63; 66

BROWN, CLAUDE
Manchild in the Promised Land. New York: 1965. V. 62

BROWN, CORNELIUS
The Annals of Newark-upon Trent Comprising the History, Curiosities, and Antiquities of the Borough. London: 1879. V. 65; 66
The Worthies of Nottinghamshire and Celebrated & Remarkable Men of the County from the Norman Conquest to A.D. 1882. London: 1882. V. 65

BROWN, D.
Considerazioni sulli Rapporti che Legano gli Uomini in Societa del D. Brown Ovvero Elementi dell'Organizzazione Sociale. Brescia: 1803. V. 63
Freshwater Snails of Africa and Their Medical Importance. London: 1994. V. 66

BROWN, D. A.
Tertiary Cheilostomatous Polyzoa of New Zealand. London: 1952. V. 63; 66

BROWN, D. K.
The Design and Construction of British Warships 1939-1945. London: 1995. V. 63

BROWN, DAVID
Invasion Europe. London: 1994. V. 66

BROWN, DAVID PAUL
The Forum, or Forty Years Full Practice at the Philadelphia Bar. Philadelphia: 1856. V. 64

BROWN, DEE A.
Bury My Heart at Wounded Knee, an Indian History of the American West. New York: 1970. V. 67

BROWN, DEE ALEXANDER
The Bold Cavaliers. Morgan's 2nd Kentucky Cavalry Raiders. Philadelphia: 1959. V. 63

BROWN, DOLORES CLINE
Yukon Trophy Trials. 1971. V. 67

BROWN, DON
Fragments 1971. Champaign: 1971. V. 64

BROWN, EDWARD
A Brief Account of Some Travels in Divers Parts of Europe, Viz, Hungaria, Servia, Bulgaria, Macedonia, Thessaly, Austria.... London: 1685. V. 62; 64; 66

BROWN, ELEANOR MC LAREN
John and Mary and Tommy. London: 1932. V. 63

BROWN, ELIZABETH CULLEN
Passion and Reason; or, the Modern Quintilian Brothers. London: 1832. V. 66

BROWN, F. M.
Jamaica and Its Butterflies. 1972. V. 63

BROWN, FREDERICK, MRS.
Little Margaret's Ride, or The Wonderful Rocking Horse. London: 1880. V. 64; 65

BROWN, FREDRIC
And the Gods Laughed. West Bloomfield: 1987. V. 65
Angels and Spaceships. New York: 1954. V. 62
Brother Monster. 1987. V. 67
The Case of the Dancing Sandwiches. New York: 1951. V. 66
The Case of the Dancing Sandwiches. Volcano: 1985. V. 65; 67
The Case of the Dancing Sandwiches. 1985. V. 62; 64; 66
Compliments of a Fiend. New York: 1950. V. 63; 67
The Far Cry. 1951. V. 66
Happy Ending. Missoula: 1990. V. 65; 67
His Name Was Death. 1954. V. 62; 66
His Name Was Death. New York: 1954. V. 64
Homicide Sanitarium. 1984. V. 62; 64
Knock 3-1-2- T.V. London and New York: 1959. V. 63; 66; 67
The Late Lamented. New York: 1959. V. 63; 67
The Lenient Beast. New York: 1956. V. 66
Nightmare in Darkness. Miami Beach: 1987. V. 65
The Office. New York: 1958. V. 67
The Office. Miami Beach: 1987. V. 67
One for the Road. New York: 1958. V. 66
Pardon My Ghoulish Laughter. 1986. V. 64; 65; 67
The Peak Show Murders. 1985. V. 64
The Pickled Punks. Hilo: 1991. V. 65; 67
Space on My Hands. 1951. V. 62; 64; 66; 67
Space on My Hands. Chicago: 1951. V. 66
Thirty Corpses Every Thursday. 1986. V. 64; 66
Three-Corpse Parlay. Missoula: 1988. V. 63; 65; 67
The Water-Walker. Missoula: 1990. V. 65; 67
What Mad Universe. 1948. V. 66
What Mad Universe. New York: 1949. V. 62; 64

BROWN, G.
European and Japanese Gardens. Philadelphia: 1902. V. 67

BROWN, G. H.
The East-India Register and Directory, for 1831.... London: 1831. V. 65

BROWN, GEORGE
Arithmetica Infinita, or the Accurate Accomptant's Best Companion Contriv'd and Calculated by.... Edinburgh: 1718. V. 65
Arithmetica Infinita or the Accurate Accomptant's Best Companion Contriv'd and Calculated.... 1717-1718. V. 62
Melanesians and Polynesians. Their Life Histories Described and Compared. London: 1910. V. 64

BROWN, GEORGE H.
On Foot Round Settle. Settle: 1888. V. 65
On Foot Round Settle. Settle: 1896. V. 64; 65
Over the Oldest Ground in Yorkshire. Settle: 1913. V. 65

BROWN, GEORGE MAC KAY
The Hooded Fisherman: a Story. Foss: 1985. V. 63
The Loom of Light. Nairn: 1986. V. 63
Orfeo - a Masque. Lastingham: 1995. V. 64
A Time to Keep and Other Stories. London: 1969. V. 62

BROWN, GEORGE S.
Yarmouth, Nova Scotia; a Sequel to Campbell's History. Boston: 1888. V. 67

BROWN, HENRY
The Cotton Fields and Cotton Factories.... London: 1840?. V. 66

BROWN, HORATIO F.
Drift. London: 1900. V. 64
Drift. London: 1901. V. 67
John Addington Symonds. London: 1895. V. 65; 67
John Addington Symonds. London: 1903. V. 67
Life on the Lagoons. London: 1904. V. 67
The Venetian Printing Press. London: 1891. V. 63

BROWN, INA CORINNE
The Story of the American Negro. New York: 1936. V. 63; 64; 67

BROWN, ISAAC V.
Memoirs of the Rev. Robert Finley, D.D. Late Pastor of the Presbyterian Congregation at Basking Ridge New Jersey.... New Brunswick: 1819. V. 63; 66

BROWN, IVOR J.
The Mines of Shropshire. London: 1976. V. 64; 65

BROWN, J.
Beatrix, the Gardening Life of Beatrix Jones Farrand 1872-1959. New York: 1995. V. 67

BROWN, J. E.
A Practical Treatise on Tree Culture in South Australia. Adelaide: 1881. V. 62

BROWN, J. L.
The Story of Kings County California. Berkeley: 1941. V. 62; 65

BROWN, J. MORAY
Polo. London: 1895. V. 66

BROWN, J. P. S.
Jim Kane. New York: 1970. V. 67

BROWN, J. T.
Among the Bantu Nomads, a Record of Forty Years Spent Among the Bechuana. London: 1926. V. 64

BROWN, JAMES
The Forester. A Practical Treatise on Planting and Rearing General Management of Forest Trees. Edinburgh: 1851. V. 67

BROWN, JAMES continued
The Importance of Preserving Unviolated the System of Civil Government in Every State.... London: 1793. V. 62

BROWN, JAMES BARRETT
Skin Grafting. Philadelphia: 1949. V. 63; 66

BROWN, JAMES BERRY
Journal of a Journey Across the Plains in 1859. San Francisco: 1970. V. 65; 66

BROWN, JAMES C.
Calabazas or Amusing Recollections of an Arizona City. San Francisco: 1882. V. 66

BROWN, JAMES H.
Catalogue of the Extensive Dramatic Collection of the Late James Brown Esq. of Malden, Mass. Boston: 1898. V. 63

BROWN, JAMES M.
Captives of Abb's Valley, a Legend of Frontier Life. Philadelphia. V. 67
The Captives of Abb's Valley: a Legend of Frontier Life. Burlington: 1943. V. 67

BROWN, JAMES S.
Life of a Pioneer, Being the Autobiography of.... Salt Lake City: 1900. V. 62

BROWN, JANE
Fulbrooks: the Sketchbook, Letters, Specification of Works and Accounts for a House by Edward Lutyens 1896-1899. 1989. V. 65

BROWN, JENNIE B.
Fort Hall on the Oregon Trail, a Historical Sketch. Caldwell: 1932. V. 65; 67

BROWN, JESSE
The Black Hills Trails - a History of the Struggles of the Pioneers in the Winning of the Black Hills. Rapid City: 1924. V. 65; 67

BROWN, JIM
Out of Bounds. New York: 1989. V. 63

BROWN, JOE
The Hard Years. London: 1967. V. 63
The Hard Years. 1979. V. 63; 65

BROWN, JOHN
The Elements of Medicine of John Brown, M.D. Portsmouth: 1803. V. 65
An Essay on Satire: Occasion'd by the Death of Mr. Pope. London: 1745. V. 62
Essay on the Characteristics. London: 1751. V. 62
An Estimate of the Manners and Principles of the Times. London: 1757. V. 66; 67
Horae Subsecivae. Locke and Sydenham with Other Occasional Papers. Edinburgh: 1858. V. 67
Letters of Dr. John Brown, with Letters from Ruskin, Thackeray and Others. London: 1907. V. 67
Occasional Suggestions Relative to Ireland and the Church of Ireland from 1818. Aberdeen: 1838. V. 65
On the Natural Duty of a Personal Service, in Defence of Ourselves and Country. A Sermon, Preached at St. Nicholas Church, in Newcastle on Occasion of a Late Dangerous Insurrection, at Hexham. Newcastle-upon-Tyne: 1761. V. 64

BROWN, JOHN H.
Indian Wars and Pioneers of Texas. Austin: 1896. V. 67
Indian Wars and Pioneers of Texas. 1988. V. 67

BROWN, JOHN HENRY
Life and Times of Henry Smith, the First American Governor of Texas. Dallas: 1887. V. 64; 65

BROWN, JOHN P.
Old Frontiers to Story of the Cherokee Indians from Earliest Times to the Date of Their Removal to the West in 1838. Kingsport: 1938. V. 63; 66

BROWN, JOHN ROSS
The Indians of California. San Francisco: 1944. V. 64

BROWN, JOHN WILLIAM
The Life of Leonardo da Vinci, with a Critical account of His Works. London: 1828. V. 66

BROWN, JONATHAN
Velazquez: Painter and Courtier. New Haven;: 1986. V. 66

BROWN, JOSEPH EMERSON
Correspondence Between the Secretary of War and Governor Brown, Growing Out of a Requisition Made Upon the Governor for the Reserve Militia of Georgia to Be Turned Over to Confederate Control. Milledgeville: 1865. V. 65
Message of His Excellency Joseph E. Brown to the Extra Session of the Legislature, Convened March 10th, 1864. Milledgeville: 1864. V. 62

BROWN, JOSEPH NEWTON
A Colonel at Gettysburg and Spotsylvania. Columbia: 1931. V. 62

BROWN, L. H.
Eagles, Hawks and Falcons of the World. New York: 1968. V. 64
Eagles, Hawks and Falcons of the World. London: 1979. V. 64

BROWN, LARRY
Big Bad Love. Stories. Chapel Hill: 1990. V. 64; 67
Dirty Work. 1989. V. 67
Eagles, Hawks and Falcons of the World. New York: 1968. V. 67
Facing the Music. Chapel Hill: 1988. V. 62; 63; 64; 65; 67

BROWN, LESLIE
Eagles, Hawks and Falcons of the World. New York: 1968. V. 62; 63
Eagles, Hawks and Falcons of the World. Secaucus: 1989. V. 63

BROWN, M. E.
The Physiology of Fishes. New York: 1957. V. 65

BROWN, MABEL WEBSTER
Neuropsychiatry and the War: a Bibliography with Abstracts. New York: 1918. V. 65

BROWN, MARCIA
Dick Whittington and His Cat. New York: 1950. V. 66

BROWN, MARGARET WISE
The Big Fur Secret. New York: 1944. V. 62
Country Noisy Book. New York: 1940. V. 62
The Dark Wood of the Golden Birds. New York: 1950. V. 62
Don't Frighten the Lion!. New York: 1942. V. 64
Little Fur Family. New York: 1946. V. 62; 66
Little Pig's Picnic. Boston: 1939. V. 65
Two Little Trains. New York: 1949. V. 63

BROWN, MARK H.
The Frontier Years and Before Barbed Wire. New York: 1955-1956. V. 65

BROWN, MONTY
Where Giants Trod. 1989. V. 67

BROWN, NORMAN D.
Journey to Pleasant Hill - The Civil War Letters of Captain Elijah P. Petty - Walker's Texas Division CSA. San Antonio: 1982. V. 65

BROWN, NORMAN O.
Hermes the Thief. The Evolution of a Myth. Madison: 1947. V. 67

BROWN, P.
New Illustrations of Zoology.... 1776. V. 66
New Illustrations of Zoology.... London: 1776. V. 65

BROWN, P. HUME
George Buchan, Humanist and Reformer. A Biography. Edinburgh: 1890. V. 62

BROWN, PAUL
Aintree Grand Nationals - Past and Present. New York: 1930. V. 62
Good Luck and Bad. New York: 1940. V. 62
Mick and Mack. New York: 1937. V. 62

BROWN, PERCY
Tours in Sikkim and the Darjeeling District. Calcutta: 1917. V. 64
Tours in Sikkim; and the Darjeeling District. Calcutta: 1922. V. 64

BROWN, PHILIP FRANCIS
Reminiscences of the War of 1861-1865. Roanoke: 1912. V. 62; 63; 65

BROWN, R.
A Brief Account of Microscopical Observations Made in the Months of June, July and August 1827, on the Particles Contained in the Pollen of Plants... (with) Additional Remarks.... Edinburgh: 1828-1830. V. 63
Chloris Melvilliana. 1823. V. 63
General Remarks, Geographical and Systematical, on the Botany of Terra Australia. 1814. V. 63; 64; 65; 66
The London Bookshop. 1971-1977. V. 62

BROWN, R. N. RUDMOSE
A Naturalist at the Poles; the Life, Work and Voyages of Dr. W. S. Bruce, the Polar Explorer. London: 1923. V. 64
The Voyage of the Scotia Being the Record of a Voyage of Exploration in the Antarctic Seas. London: 1906. V. 64

BROWN, RICHARD
Domestic Architecture Containing a History of the Science. London: 1842. V. 62; 67
A History of Accounting and Accountants. Edinburgh: 1905. V. 62; 63; 64
The Principles of Practical Perspective; or, Scenographic Projection.... London: 1815. V. 62
Sacred Architecture, Its Rise, Progress and Present State. London: 1845. V. 62

BROWN, RICHARD BLAKE
Miss Higgs and Her Silver Flamingo. London: 1931. V. 67

BROWN, RITA MAE
Six of One. New York: 1978. V. 67

BROWN, ROBERT
Notes on the Earlier History of Barton-on-Humber. 1906. V. 62

BROWN, ROBERT D.
Antler Development in Cervidae. 1983. V. 67

BROWN, ROBERT L.
Saloons of the American West. Denver: 1978. V. 64

BROWN, ROSELLEN
Tender Mercies. New York: 1978. V. 67

BROWN, S.
Alpine Flora of the Canadian Rocky Mountains. New York and London: 1907. V. 65; 67

BROWN, STERLING
The Collected Poems of Sterling Brown. New York: 1980. V. 64; 66
The Negro Caravan. New York: 1941. V. 63; 64

BROWN, STEWARDSON
Alpine Flora of the Canadian Rocky Mountains. New York: 1907. V. 66

BROWN, SUSAN ANNA
Mrs. Gilpin's Frugalities. New York: 1883. V. 67

BROWN, TARLETON
Memoirs of Tarleton Brown, A Captain in the Revolutionary Army.... New York: 1862. V. 66

BROWN, THOMAS
An Account of the People Called Shakers: Their Faith, Doctrines and Practice. Troy: 1812. V. 63
Amusements Serious and Comical Calculated for the Meridian of London. London: 1700. V. 63; 64
An Atlas of the Fossil Conchology of Great Britain and Ireland. 1889. V. 66
An Atlas of the Fossil Conchology of Great Britain and Ireland.... London: 1889. V. 62; 63
Book of Butterflies, Sphinxes and Moths. London and Edinburgh: 1832. V. 66
The Book of Butterflies, Sphinxes and Moths. London and Edinburgh: 1834. V. 66
Certain Miscellany Tracts. London: 1684. V. 62
A Collection of Dialogues, One of Them Entituled Democratici Vapulantes, Being a Dialogue Between Julian, and Others.... London: 1704. V. 65
The Englishman in Paris. London: 1819. V. 67
Illustrations of the Fossil Conchology of Great Britain and Ireland. London: 1849. V. 62
Illustrations of the Land and Fresh Water Conchology of Great Britain and Ireland. 1845. V. 66
Illustrations of the Recent Conchology of Great Britain and Ireland. 1844. V. 66
The Illustrations of the Recent Conchology of Great Britain and Ireland. London: 1844. V. 62
A Legacy for the Ladies, or Characters of the Women of the Age. London: 1705. V. 65
A Treatise on the Philosophy of the Human Mind, Being the Lectures of the Late Thomas Brown, M.D. Cambridge: 1827. V. 62; 67
The Works of Mr Thomas Brown, Serious and Comical, in Prose and Verse, with His Remains. London: 1760. V. 66
The Works.... London: 1760-1730-1715. V. 62

BROWN, THOMAS ALEXANDER
The Sphinx of Eaglehawk; a Tale of Old Bendigo. London: 1895. V. 64

BROWN, TOM
The Beauties of Tom Brown, Consisting of Humorous Pieces in Prose and Verse.... London: 1808. V. 62

BROWN, VARINA DAVIS
A Colonel at Gettysburg and Spotsylvania. Columbia: 1931. V. 65

BROWN, WALTER F.
Hail Columbia!. Providence: 1876. V. 63

BROWN, WILFRED GAVIN
Angler's Almanac. London: 1949. V. 67

BROWN, WILLIAM H.
The History of the First Locomotivs in America. New York: 1871. V. 63

BROWN, WILLIAM LAWRENCE
An Essay on the Natural Equality of Men; On the Rightd that Result from It.... Edinburgh: 1793. V. 63

BROWN, WILLIAM ROBINSON
The Horse of the Desert. New York: 1929. V. 62

BROWN, WILLIAM WELLS
Clotelle; or the Colored Heroine. Boston: 1867. V. 63

BROWNE, B.
The Conquest of Mount McKinley. 1913. V. 63; 65
The Conquest of Mount McKinley. 1956. V. 63; 65

BROWNE, D. J.
The Field Book of Manures; or the American Muck Book. New York: 1855. V. 62

BROWNE, E. G.
A Year Amongst the Persians. London: 1893. V. 64
A Year Amongst the Persians. Cambridge: 1927. V. 64

BROWNE, EDGAR
Phiz and Dickens as They Appeared to Edgar Browne. London: 1913. V. 62

BROWNE, FRANCES
My Share of the World. London: 1861. V. 66

BROWNE, FRANCIS FISHER
Every-Day of Abraham Lincoln. A Narrative and Descriptive Biography.... Chicago: 1913. V. 62; 63

BROWNE, G. WALDO
A Daughter of Maryland. New York: 1895. V. 63; 66
The New America and the Far East: a Picturesque and Historic Description of These Lands and Peoples.... Boston: 1901. V. 63

BROWNE, GEORGIANA
Water Babies' Circus and Other Stories. Boston: 1940. V. 65

BROWNE, GERALD
Slide. New York: 1976. V. 65

BROWNE, GORDON
Anon: Nobody and Somebody - Nobody's Scrapbook. 1900. V. 67
A Nobody's Scrap Book. London: 1900. V. 66

BROWNE, H. K.
Illustrations of the 5 Senses. London: 1852. V. 62

BROWNE, HAROLD
Warrior of the Dawn. 1943. V. 62

BROWNE, HOWARD
Halo for Satan. 1948. V. 64
Halo for Satan. Indianapolis: 1948. V. 62; 66
Halo in Blood. 1946. V. 64
Halo in Blood. Indianapolis: 1946. V. 62; 66
Halo in Brass. 1949. V. 64; 66
Halo in Brass. Indianapolis: 1949. V. 62
The Incredible Ink. Tucson: 1997. V. 65; 66
The Paper Gun. 1985. V. 64
The Paper Gun. Belen: 1985. V. 65; 66; 67
The Taste of Ashes. 1957. V. 62; 66
The Taste of Ashes. London: 1957. V. 64
Warrior of the Dawn. 1943. V. 64; 66

BROWNE, ISAAC HAWKINS
De Animi Immortalitate. Londini: 1754. V. 65
De Animi Immortalitate Poema.... London: 1811. V. 62
Poems Upon Various Subjects.... London: 1768. V. 63

BROWNE, J. STARK
Through South Africa with the British Association. London: 1906. V. 64

BROWNE, JOHN A.
Dissertatio Chirurgica Inauguralis de Morbo Coxae. Edinburghi: 1813. V. 62

BROWNE, JOHN ROSS
Crusoe's Island: a Ramble in the Footsteps of Alexander Selkirk. With Sketches of Adventure in California and Washoe. New York: 1867. V. 63; 65
The Indians of California. San Francisco: 1944. V. 63
A Peep at Washoe and Washoe Revisited. Balboa Island: 1959. V. 63; 64
Yusef; or the Journey of the Fangi. A Crusade in the East. New York: 1865. V. 62; 63; 64

BROWNE, JOSEPH
Institutions in Physick. London: 1714. V. 64; 66; 67

BROWNE, MAGGIE
Pleasant Work for Busy Fingers of Kindergarten at Home. London: 1891. V. 63

BROWNE, MARK
Irish Gallantry!. London: 1817. V. 63

BROWNE, MAURICE
Recollections of Rupert Brooke. Chicago: 1927. V. 64; 66

BROWNE, PETER
A Discourse of Drinking Healths. Dublin: 1716. V. 65
Things Divine and Supernatural Conceived by Analogy. 1733. V. 65

BROWNE, PETER A.
Trichologia Mammalium; or a Treatise on the Organization, Properties and Uses of Hair and Wool.... Philadelphia: 1853. V. 63

BROWNE, T. H.
History of the English Turf 1904-1930. London: 1931. V. 67

BROWNE, THOMAS
Certain Miscellany Tracts.... London: 1684. V. 64
Christian Morals.... London: 1756. V. 64
The Last Chapter of Urne Buriall. London: 1946. V. 62
A Letter to a Friend Upon Occasion of the Death of His Intimate Friend. Boston: 1971. V. 67
Pseudodoxia Epidemica; or, Enquiries into Very Many Received Tenents, and Commonly Presumed Truths. London: 1646. V. 63
Pseudodoxia Epidemica; or, Enquiries into Very Many Received Tenents and Commonly Presumed Truths. London: 1650. V. 62; 63
Pseudodoxia Epidemica; or, Enquiries into Very Many Received Tenents, and Commonly Presumed Truths. London: 1659. V. 64
Pseudodoxia Epidemica; or, Enquiries Into Very Many Received Tenents...Together with the Religio Medici. London: 1672. V. 62
Religio Medici. Argentorai: 1665. V. 64; 66; 67
Religio Medici. London: 1672. V. 64; 67
Religio Medici. London: 1678. V. 64; 66
Religio Medici. Canterbury: 1894. V. 65
The Works. London: 1686. V. 63; 64; 66; 67
The Works. Edinburgh: 1912. V. 64
The Works. London: 1928-1931. V. 67

BROWNE, THOMAS GUNTER
Hermes Unmasked; or the Art of Speech Founded on the Association of Words and Ideas. London: 1795. V. 65

BROWNE, WILLIS
Notitia Parliamentaria; or, an History of the Counties, Citie and Boroughs in England and Wales.... London: 1715-1716. V. 67

BROWNING, COLIN
The Convict Ship; a Narrative of the Results of Scriptural Instruction and Moral Discipline as These Appeared on Board the Earl Grey During the Voyage to Tasmania.... London: 1844. V. 64

BROWNING, ELIZABETH BARRETT
Aurora Leigh. London: 1857. V. 65
Aurora Leigh. New York: 1857. V. 62; 65
Aurora Leigh. London: 1859. V. 63

BROWNING, ELIZABETH BARRETT continued
Casa Guidi Windows. London: 1851. V. 65
A Drama of Exile: and Other Poems. New York: 1845. V. 62; 64; 65
The Earlier Poems... 1826-1833. London: 1878. V. 62
The Greek Christian Poets and English Poets. London: 1863. V. 65
Last Poems. London: 1862. V. 62; 65; 66
Napoleon III in Italy. And Other Poems. New York: 1860. V. 65
Poems. London: 1844. V. 66
Poems. London: 1853. V. 65
Poems. London: 1856. V. 65
Poems. London: 1862. V. 65
Poetical Works. London: 1870. V. 65
The Poetical Works. London: 1889. V. 65; 66
The Poetical Works. London: 1906. V. 63
The Seraphim and Other Poems. London: 1838. V. 65
Sonnets from the Portuguese. New Rochelle: 1901. V. 62
Sonnets from the Portuguese. New York and London: 1932. V. 62; 67

BROWNING, ROBERT
A Blot in the Scutcheon, and Other Poetic Dramas. London: 1896. V. 66
Browning's Essay on Chatterton. Cambridge: 1948. V. 65
Dramatic Romances and Lyrics. 1899. V. 62
Dramatis Personae. London: 1864. V. 63; 65; 67
Dramatis Personae. Hammersmith: 1910. V. 62; 64; 65; 67
Letters from Robert Browning to Various Correspondents. London: 1895. V. 63
Men and Women. Hammersmith: 1908. V. 65
Pacchiarotto and How He Worked in Distemper: With Other Poems. London: 1876. V. 62
Paracelsus. London: 1835. V. 67
Parleying with Certain People of Importance in Their Day.... London: 1887. V. 67
Pictor Ignotus, Fra Lippo Lippi, Andrea del Sarto. Waltham St. Lawrence: 1925. V. 65; 66
The Pied Piper of Hamelin. London: 1898. V. 62
The Pied Piper of Hamelin. Chicago: 1910. V. 62; 63; 66
The Pied Piper of Hamelin. London: 1928. V. 62
The Pied Piper of Hamelin. London: 1934. V. 62
The Pied Piper of Hamelin. London: 1939. V. 63; 66
Poems. 1969. V. 62
Poetical Works. London: 1888. V. 67
Poetical Works. London: 1889. V. 66
The Ring and the Book. London: 1868-1869. V. 67
La Saisiaz: the Two Poets of Croisic. London: 1878. V. 67
Saul. Boston: 1890. V. 63
Some Poems by Robert Browning. 1904. V. 62
Strafford: an Historical Tragedy. London: 1837. V. 62; 66

BROWNJOHN, ALAN
The Railings - Poems. London: 1961. V. 63

BROWNJOHN, JOHN
Miltiades Peterkin Paul, His Adventures. Boston: 1877. V. 63

BROWNLEE, CLAUDIA J.
Colonel Joe, the Last of the Rough Raiders. New York: 1978. V. 67

BROWNLEE, RICHARD S.
Gray Ghosts of the Confederacy. Baton Rouge: 1958. V. 63

BROWNLOW, WILLIAM GANNAWAY
A Political Register, Setting Forth the Principles (sic) of the Whig and Locofoco Parties in the United States.... Jonesborough: 1844. V. 63

BROWNRIG, RALPH
Twenty Five Sermons. London: 1685. V. 67

BROWNRIGG, LINDA L.
Making the Medieval Book: Techniques of Production. Los Altos Hills, London: 1995. V. 62
Medieval Book Production, Assessing the Evidence.... Los Altos Hills: 1990. V. 64

BROWN SEQUARD, CHARLES E.
Course of Lectures of the Physiology and Pathology of the Central Nervous System, Delivered at the Royal College of Surgeons of England in May 1858. Philadelphia: 1860. V. 64; 66
Experimental and Clinical Researches on the Physiology and Pathology of the Spinal Cord and Some Other Parts of the Nervous Centres. (with) Experimental Researches Applied to Physiology and Pathology. Richmond: 1855. V. 64; 66
Journal De La Physiologie De L'Homme et des Animaux. Paris: 1858-1862. V. 67
Lectures on the Diagnosis and Treatment of Functional Nervous Affections. Philadelphia: 1868. V. 64; 66

BROWNSON, O. A.
Essays and Reviews Chiefly on Theology, Politics. New York: 1852. V. 63

BROWSE, LILLIAN
Degas Dancers. London: 1949. V. 65

BROXBOURNE LIBRARY
Catalogue of Valuable Printed Books from the Broxbourne Library Illustrated the Spread of Printing.... London: 1977. V. 62; 63; 64; 66

BRUCCOLI, MATTHEW J.
F. Scott Fitzgerald - a Descriptive Bibliography. Pittsburgh: 1972. V. 65
Facts on File Bibliography of American Fiction 1919-1998. New York: 1991. V. 63
Kenneth Millar/Ross Macdonald: a Checklist. Detroit: 1971. V. 67
The Romantic Egoists. New York: 1974. V. 67
Ross Mac Donald - A Checklist. Detroit: 1971. V. 65; 66

BRUCE, ALEXANDER
Illustrations of the Nerve Tracts in the Mid and Hind Brain and the Cranial Nerves Arising Therefrom. Edinburgh;. V. 64
Review of Neurology and Psychiatry. Edinburgh: 1904-1908. V. 65

BRUCE, C. G.
The Assault on Everest. 1922. 1923. V. 63; 65
The Assault on Mount Everest 1922. London: 1923. V. 63
Himalayan Wanderer. 1934. V. 63; 65
Himalayan Wanderer. London: 1934. V. 63; 64
Twenty Years in the Himalaya. London: 1910. V. 64

BRUCE, EDWARD
Art in Federal Buildings: Illustrated Record of the Treasury Department's New Program in Painting and Sculpture. Volume I: Mural Designs 1934-1936. Washington: 1936. V. 67

BRUCE, GEORGE
The Land Birds in and Around St. Andrews, Including a Condensed History of the British Land Birds, with Extracts from the Poets and Observations and Anecdotes on Natural History. Dundee: 1895. V. 62; 63

BRUCE, H.
The Gardens of Witherhur in All Seasons. New York: 1968. V. 67

BRUCE, J. COLLINGWOOD
The Hand-Book to the Roman Wall. London: 1885. V. 66
The Roman Wall: a Historical, Topographical and Descriptive Account of the Barrier of the Lower Isthmus.... London: 1851. V. 63
The Wallet-book of the Roman Wall. London: 1863. V. 66

BRUCE, JAMES
Travels Between the Years 1765 and 1773.... London: 1805. V. 64

BRUCE, KATHLEEN
Virginia Iron Manufacture in the Slave Area. New York: 1931. V. 62

BRUCE, LENNY
How to Talk Dirty and Influence People. Chicago: 1965. V. 64

BRUCE, LEO
Furious Old Women. London: 1960. V. 67

BRUCE, MARJORY
The Book of Tales for Little Folks. London: 1932. V. 67

BRUCE, MICHAEL
The Works.... 1865. V. 65

BRUCE, MINER WAIT
Alaska: its History and Resources, Gold Fields, Routes and Scenery. Seattle: 1895. V. 62

BRUCE, PHILIP A.
Virginia, Rebirth of the Old Dominion. Chicago and New York: 1929. V. 62; 64

BRUCE, ROBERT
The Fighting Norths and Pawnee Scouts - Narratives and Reminiscences of Military Service on the Old Frontier. New York: 1932. V. 67

BRUCE, THOMAS
Southwest Virginia and Shenandoah Valley. Richmond: 1891. V. 62

BRUCE LOCKHART, ROBERT
My Rod My Comfort. London: 1957. V. 67

BRUCHAC, JOE
Walking With My Sons: New Poems. Madison: 1986. V. 66

BRUEGMANN, ROBERT
Holabird & Roche, Holabird & Root. An Illustrated Catalog of Works 1880-1940. New York and London: 1991. V. 67

BRUEHL, ANTON
Mexico. New York: 1933. V. 66

BRUFF, HAROLD JOHN LEXOW
T'ill An' T'oade Uns Upuv Greenho'. An Account of the Traditions, Life and Work of the Old Lead Miners of Greenhow Hill in Yorkshire. York: 1920. V. 64; 65
T'Miners. Character Sketches of Yorkshire Lead Miners. York: Sep. 1920. V. 64; 65

BRUFF, J. GOLDSBOROUGH
Gold Rush - The Journals, Drawings, and Other Papers of J. Goldsborough Bruff. New York: 1944. V. 66
Gold Rush: the Journals, Drawings and Other Papers of J. Goldsborough Bruff, Captain, Washington City and California Mining Association April 2, 1849- July 20, 1851. New York: 1949. V. 63

BRUFFY, GEORGE A.
Eighty-One Years in the West. Butte: 1925. V. 62; 65

BRUGIS, THOMAS
Vade Mecum; or a Companion for a Chirurgion, Fitted for Times of Peace or War. London: 1670. V. 65

BRUGUIERE, FRANCIS
Beyond This Point. London: 1928. V. 63; 65
San Francisco. San Francisco: 1918. V. 63; 65

BRUMBAUGH, FLORENCE
Donald Duck and His Nephews. Boston: 1940. V. 65

BRUMMIT, STELLA W.
Brother Van. New York: 1919. V. 65; 67

BRUMOY, PIERRE
Le Theatre des Grecs. Amsterdam: 1732. V. 67

BRUNACCIO, ATTILIO
Commentariorum Collegii Conimbricensis, E. Societate Iesu, Super Octo Libros Physicorum Aristotelis Stagiritae. Venetiis: 1616. V. 66

BRUNCK, R.
Analecta Veterum Poetarum Graecorum. Argentorati: 1772-1776. V. 65

BRUNDAGE, F.
The Cats' Pajamas. Rochester: 1932. V. 64
Kitty Cat. New York: 1927. V. 64

BRUNEL, ISAMBARD
The Life of Isambard Kingdom Brunel, Civil Engineer. London: 1870. V. 64

BRUNEL, M. I.
An Explanation of the Works of the Tunnel Under the Thames from Rotherhithe to Wapping. London: 1838. V. 65

BRUNET, PIERRE GUSTAVE
Bibliomania in the Present Day in France and England, or, Some Account of Celebrated Recent Sales.... New York: 1880. V. 62; 65

BRUNETTI, MR.
Description of the Model of Ancient Jerusalem, Illustrative of the Sacred Scriptures and the Writings of Josephus. Boston: 1849. V. 62

BRUNHOFF, JEAN DE
Babar and Father Christmas. London: 1940. V. 66
Babar and Father Christmas. London: 1944. V. 64
Babar and that Rascal Arthur. London: 1948. V. 64; 66
Babar at Home. London: 1942. V. 64
Babar's Friend Sephir. London: 1937. V. 64; 66
Babar's Travels. London: 1947. V. 64
Histoire de Babar, le Petit Elephant. Paris: 1931. V. 63
The Story of Babar the Little Elephant. London: 1939. V. 64

BRUNHOFF, LAURENT DE
The Babar Books. New York: 1935. V. 62
Babar et Le Pere Noel. New York: 1941. V. 62

BRUNKER, H. M. E.
Story of the Campaign in Eastern Virginia, Including "Stonewall Jackson" Operations in the Valley April 1861 to May 1863. London: 1904. V. 62

BRUNNER, A. W.
Cottages or Hints on Economical Building. New York: 1890. V. 62; 66

BRUNNER, ELIZABETH FARKAS
Mystic India Through Art. No publisher: 1935. V. 62

BRUNNER, R.
The Manufacture of Lubricants, Shoe Polishes and Leather Dressings. 1906. V. 67

BRUNS, LUDWIG
Die Geschwulste des Nervensystes. Hirngeschwulste. Ruckenmarksgeschwulste, Geschwulste der Peripheren Nerve. Berlin: 1897. V. 64

BRUNSCHWICG, LEON
Condorcet et Fontanes. Vers lus au Banquet de la Saint-Charlemagne le 30 Janvier 1886. Paris: 1886. V. 67
Qua Inesse Demonstraverit. Paris: 1897. V. 67

BRUNSCHWIG, HIERONYMUS
Buch der Cirurgia. 1970. V. 64; 66

BRUNSKILL, R. W.
Vernacular Architecture of the Lake Counties. London: 1974. V. 64; 65

BRUNTON, LAUDER
Collected Papers on Circulation and Respiration. London and New York: 1906. V. 65

BRUNTON, MARY
Discipline: a Novel. Edinburgh: 1814. V. 64; 65
Discipline; a Novel. London: 1832. V. 65
Discipline: a Novel. London: 1837. V. 65
Emmeline. Edinburgh: 1819. V. 65
Self-Control. Edinburgh: 1811. V. 62
Self-Control. London: 1832. V. 63; 65

BRUTUM Fulmen: or the Bull of Pope Pius V Concerning the Damnation, Excommunication and Desposition of Queen Elizabeth as Also the Absolution of Her Subjects.... London: 1681. V. 62

BRUUN, A. F.
Flying-Fishes (Exocoetidae) of the Atlantic, Systematic and Biological Studies. Copenhagen: 1935. V. 63

BRUYS, FRANC
L'Art de Connoitre Les Femmes, Avec des Pense-es Libres Sur Divers Sujets & une Dissertation sur l'Adultere. Amsterdam: 1749. V. 65

BRY, THEODOR DE
Discovering the New World. New York: 1976. V. 65

BRYAN, DANIEL
The Appeal for Suffering Genius.... Washington City: 1826. V. 62

BRYAN, EMMA L.
1860-1865: A Romance of the Valley of Virginia. Harrisonburg: 1892. V. 64

BRYAN, JOHN
Notes from Underground I. San Francisco: 1964. V. 65

BRYAN, JOHN STEWART
Joseph Bryan, His Time, His Family, His Friends, a Memoir. Richmond: 1935. V. 62; 63; 65

BRYAN, MARGARET
A Compendious System of Astronomy, in a Course of Family Lectures, In Which the Principles of that Science are Clearly Elucidated.... London: 1805. V. 66
A Comprehensive Astronomical and Geographical Class Book, for the Use of Schools and Private Families. London: 1815. V. 66

BRYAN, WILLIAM ALANSON
Natural History of Hawaii. Honolulu: 1915. V. 63

BRYAN, WILLIAM JENNINGS
The Fruits of the Tree. New York: 1910. V. 63

BRYANT, A. T.
Olden Times in Zululand and Natal; Containing Earlier Political History of the Eastern Nguni Clans. London: 1929. V. 64

BRYANT, CHARLES
Flora Diaetetica or History of Esculent Plants, Both Domestic and Foreign. London: 1783. V. 65

BRYANT, EDWIN
What I Saw in California. Santa Ana: 1936. V. 62; 63

BRYANT, HENRY G.
The Peary Auxiliary Expedition of 1894. Philadelphia: 1895. V. 64

BRYANT, JACOB
A New System, or, Analysis of Ancient Mythology. London: 1775-1776. V. 63; 67

BRYANT, JOSEPH
Captain Matthew Flinders R.N., His Voyages, Discoveries and Fortunes. London: 1928. V. 63

BRYANT, MR.
The New Skylark, or Theatrical Budget of Harmony.... London: 1824. V. 67

BRYANT, SARA CONE
Epaminodas and His Auntie. Boston: 1938. V. 64
Stories to Tell the Littles Ones. London: 1918. V. 67

BRYANT, WILLIAM CULLEN
An Address to the People of the United States in Behalf of the American Copyright Club. New York: 1843. V. 62
Poems. Cambridge: 1821. V. 64; 66
Thirty Poems. New York: 1864. V. 64; 65

BRYCE, JAMES
The American Commonwealth. London: 1888. V. 64
The American Commonwealth. London: 1889. V. 64
The American Commonwealth. London: 1893-1901. V. 64

BRYCE, T. H.
Contributions to the Study of the Early Development and Imbedding of the Human Ovum. Glasgow: 1908. V. 67

BRYCE ECHENIQUE, ALFREDO
Un Mundo Para Julius. Barcelona: 1970. V. 67

BRYDALL, ROBERT
Art in Scotland, It's Origin and Progress. Edinburgh and London: 1889. V. 67

BRYDEN, H. A.
Gun and Camera in Southern Africa. 1893. V. 66; 67
Gun and Camera in Southern Africa. London: 1893. V. 64
Nature and Sport in Britain. London: 1904. V. 67
Nature and Sport in South Africa. 1897. V. 66
Wild Life in South Africa. London: 1936. V. 67

BRYDEN, WILLIAM
Remedial Measures for Ireland.... 1837-1844. V. 62

BRYDGES, CHARLES JOHN
The Letters of Charles John Brydges 1883-1889. Winnipeg: 1981. V. 63

BRYDGES, SAMUEL EGERTON
The Autobiography, Times, Opinions and Contemporaries. London: 1834. V. 67
The Lake of Geneva, a Poem, Moral and Descriptive, in Seven Books. Geneva: 1832. V. 67
Letters on the Character and Poetical Genius of Lord Byron. London: 1824. V. 62; 66
Lex Terrae. A Discussion of the Law of England, Regarding Claims of Inheritable Rights of Peerage. Geneva: 1831. V. 64
Restituta; or, Titles, Extracts and Characters of Old Books in English Literature, Revived. London: 1814-1816. V. 66
Select Poems. London: 1814. V. 65

BRYDONE, PATRICK
A Tour through Sicily and Malta. London: 1773. V. 67
A Tour through Sicily and Malta. London: 1775. V. 62; 66

BRYDSON, A. P.
Sidelights on Mediaeval Windermere. Kendal: 1911. V. 62
Some Records of Two Lakeland Townships (Blawith and Nibthwaite) Chiefly from Original Documents. London. V. 65; 66
Some Records of Two Lakeland Townships (Blawith and Nibthwaite) Chiefly from Original Documents. Ulverston. V. 64

BRYDSON, THOMAS
A Summary View of Heraldry in Reference to the Usages of Chivalry and the General Economy of the Feudal System with an Appendix Respecting Such Distinctions of Rank as Have Place in the British Constitution. London: 1795. V. 63

BRYHER, WINIFRED
Civilians. Territet: 1927. V. 62

BRYMER, JOHN
Gammon and Spinach. London: 1901. V. 63
Two Merry Mariners. London: 1902. V. 65

BRYSON, H. COURTNEY
Rock Climbs Round London. 1936. V. 65

BUBBLES.. New York: 1892. V. 64

BUBENIK, G. A.
Betting on the Muse. Santa Rosa: 1996. V. 67
Horns, Pronghorns and Antlers, Evolution, Morphology, Physiology and Social Significance. New York: 1990. V. 67

BUBER, MARTIN
Die Geschichten des Rabbi nachman. Frankfurt am Main: 1906. V. 67

BUCHAN, ALEXANDER
A Handy Book of Meteorology. Edinburgh and London: 1867. V. 65

BUCHAN, ALEXANDER PETER
A Treatise on Sea Bathing with Remarks on the Use of the Warm Bath. London: 1810. V. 62
Venus Sine Concubitu. Unquam Aliud Natura Aliud Sapientia Dixit. London: 1822. V. 66

BUCHAN, JOHN
Andrew Jameson, Lord Ardwell. 1913. V. 62; 64
Augustus. 1937. V. 66
The Battle of Jutland. 1916. V. 62; 64
The Battle of the Somme. First Phase. London: 1917. V. 67
Battle of the Somme. Second Phase. 1917. V. 62
The Blanket of the Dark. 1931. V. 64
The Book of the Horace Club. 1901. V. 62
Canadian Occasions. 1940. V. 64
Castle Gay. London: 1930. V. 62
The Causal and the Casual in History. Cambridge: 1929. V. 63
Comments and Characters. 1940. V. 64; 66
The Courts of the Morning. London: 1929. V. 66
The Dancing Floor. 1926. V. 66
Episodes of the Great War. 1936. V. 62
Francis and the Riversdale Grenfell. 1920. V. 66
The Free Fishers. 1934. V. 62; 66
The Free Fishers. London: 1934. V. 62; 67
The Gap in the Curtain. 1932. V. 62
Gordon at Khartoum. London: 1934. V. 65
Greenmantle. London: 1916. V. 63
A History of the Great War. 1921-1922. V. 62; 64; 66
A History of the Great War. Boston and New York: 1922. V. 64
The History of the Royal Scots Fusiliers. 1925. V. 62; 64
The History of the South African Forces in France. 1920. V. 62; 64; 66
Homilies and Recreations. 1926. V. 64; 66
The House of Four Winds. 1935. V. 62; 66
Huntingtower. London: 1922. V. 64; 66
The Interpreter's House. 1938. V. 66
The Island of Sheep. 1919. V. 64
The Island of Sheep. London: 1936. V. 64; 66
The King's Grace. 1935. V. 62; 64; 66
The King's Grace. London: 1935. V. 67
The Last Secrets. 1923. V. 64; 66
The Last Secrets. London: 1923. V. 64; 66
The Long Traverse. 1941. V. 64; 66
The Long Traverse. London: 1941. V. 65
The Long Road to Victory. 1920. V. 64
The Margins of Life. 1933. V. 62
The Marquis of Montrose. 1913. V. 64; 66
The Massacre of Glencoe. 1933. V. 62; 66
The Massacre of Glencoe. London: 1933. V. 64
A Message from John Buchan. London: 1916. V. 62
Midwinter. 1923. V. 66
Mr. Standfast. 1919. V. 62
The Moon Endureth - Tales and Fancies. London. V. 65
Musa Piscatrix. 1896. V. 62
Naval Episodes of the Great War. 1938. V. 62
Nelson's History of the War. 1915-1919. V. 62; 66
The Pilgrim Fathers. 1898. V. 62
Poems Scots and English. 1917. V. 64
The Power-House. 1916. V. 64; 66
The Power-House. Edinburgh: 1916. V. 64; 65
The Power-House. London: 1916. V. 64
Prester John. 1910. V. 66
Prester John. London: 1910. V. 62
A Prince of the Captivity. 1933. V. 62; 66
Principles of Social Service. 1933. V. 62; 64
The Runagates Club. 1928. V. 66
Scholar Gipsies. 1896. V. 62
Sick Heart River. 1941. V. 66
Sir Quixote of the Moors. 1895. V. 62; 64; 66
Sir Quixote of the Moors. London: 1895. V. 64
Sir Quixote of the Moors. 1918?. V. 66
Sir Walter Raleigh. 1897. V. 62
Sir Walter Raleigh. 1911. V. 62; 64; 66
Sir Walter Scott. 1932. V. 62; 64; 66
Some Eighteenth Century Byways and Other Essays. 1908. V. 62; 64; 66
The Thirty-Nine Steps. 1915. V. 62
The Three Hostages. 1924. V. 64
Two Ordeals of Democracy. 1925. V. 62; 64; 66
The Watcher by the Threshold. 1902. V. 66

BUCHAN, P.
An Historical and Authentic Account of the Ancient and Noble Family of Keith. London: 1820?. V. 66

BUCHAN, WILLIAM
Domestic Medicine. Philadelphia: 1784. V. 66; 67
Domestic Medicine. Philadelphia: 1797. V. 64; 67
Domestic Medicine. Waterford: 1797. V. 66
Domestic Medicine. Halifax: 1864. V. 66
Every Man His Own Doctor; or a Treatise on the Prevention and Cure of Disease.... New Haven: 1816. V. 66; 67

BUCHANAN, CLAUDIUS
Christian Researches in Asia, with Notices of the Translation of the Scriptures Into the Oriental Languages. Lexington: 1813. V. 63
Colonial Ecclesiastical Establishment: Being a Brief View of the State of the Colonies of Great Britain.... London: 1813. V. 63

BUCHANAN, EDNA
Nobody Lives Forever. New York: 1990. V. 67

BUCHANAN, GEORGE
Camp Life; as Seen by a Civilian. Glasgow: 1871. V. 64
An Impartial Account of the Affairs of Scotland, from the Death of K. James the Fifth to the Tragical Exit of the Earl of Murray, Regent of Scotland. London: 1705. V. 63

BUCHANAN, H.
Nature into Art, a Treasury of Great Natural History Books. New York: 1979. V. 62; 67

BUCHANAN, JOSEPH R.
Manual of Psychometry, the Dawn of a New Civilization. Boston: 1885. V. 62

BUCHANAN, MABEL
The Land of the Christmas Stocking.... London: 1948. V. 67

BUCHANAN, R.
The Life and Adventures of John James Audubon. London: 1869. V. 64

BUCHANAN, ROBERT
The Book of Orm - a Prelude to the Epic. London: 1870. V. 64; 66
The Charlatan. Chicago;: 1895. V. 65
The Devil's Case: a Bank Holiday Interlude. London: 1896. V. 64
The Fleshly School of Poetry and Other Phenomena of the Day. London: 1872. V. 64; 66
The Piper of Hamelin: a Fantastic Opera in Two Acts. London: 1893. V. 64
Wayside Posies: Original Poems of the Country Life. London: 1867. V. 63

BUCHANAN, ROBERT WILLIAMS
The Heir of Linne. London: 1888. V. 67
A Marriage by Capture: a Romance of Today. 1896. V. 67
The Martydom of Madeline. 1891. V. 67
Matt: a Story of a Caravan. 1885. V. 67
The New Abelard; a Romance. 1892. V. 67

BUCHANAN, W.
Memoirs of Painting, with a Chronological History of the Importation of Pictures by the Great Masters Into England Since the French Revolution. London: 1824. V. 66

BUCHANAN JARDINE, JOHN
Hounds of the World. 1937. V. 62; 64
Hounds of the World. London: 1937. V. 67

BUCHAND, JAMES
Correspondence Relative to the Condition of Affairs in Utah Territory - 36t Congress 1st Session, House of Representatives. Washington: 1800. V. 66

BUCHAN TELFER, J.
Crimea and Transcaucasia; Being the Narrative of a Journey in the Kouban, in Gouria, Georgia, Armenia, Ossety, Imeritia, Swannety and Mingrelia and in the Tauric Range. London: 1876. V. 64

BUCHARD, JAMES
Correspondence Relative to the Condition of Affairs in Utah Territory.... Washington: 1800. V. 63

BUCHNER, ALEXANDER
Mechanical Musical Instruments. London: 1955. V. 67

BUCHNER, GEORG
Danton's Death: a Play. London: 1939. V. 62
The Plays of Georg Buchner. London: 1927. V. 65

BUC'HOZ, PIERRE JOSEPH
Manuel de Medecine Pratique, Royale et Bourgeoise; ou Pharmacopee Tiree des Trois Regnes, Appliquee Aux Maladies de Habitans des Villes. Paris: 1771. V. 66

BUCK, IRVING ASHBY
Cleburne and His Command. New York and Washington: 1908. V. 62; 65
Cleburne and His Command. Jackson: 1959. V. 63

BUCK, S.
The Castles, Abbeys and Priories of the County of Cumberland.... Carlisle: 1877. V. 62; 66

BUCKBEE, EDNA B.
The Saga of Old Tuolumme. New York: 1935. V. 62; 63; 65; 67

BUCKE, CHARLES
On the Life, Writings and Genius of Akenside; with Some Account of His Friends. London: 1832. V. 67

BUCKER, BENJAMIN
A Complete Vindication of the Mallard of All-Souls College, Against the Injurious Suggestions of the Rev. Mr. (John) Pointer. London: 1751. V. 64

BUCKERIDGE, A.
Jennings in Particular. London: 1968. V. 66

BUCKEYE Cookery with Hints on Practical Housekeeping. Minneapolis: 1883. V. 67

BUCKINGHAM, GEORGE VILLIERS, 1ST DUKE OF
Letters of the Duke and Duchess of Buckingham, Chiefly Addressed to King James I, of England. Edinburgh: 1834. V. 62

BUCKINGHAM, JAMES SILK
America, Historical, Statistic and Descriptive. London: 1841. V. 66; 67
Evidence. Drunkeness, Presented to the House of Commons, by the Select Committee Appointed by the House to Inquire into this Subject and Report the Minutes of Evidence.... London: 1834. V. 65
National Evils and Practical Remedies, with the Plan of a Model Town. London: 1849. V. 64
The Slave States of America. London: 1842. V. 66

BUCKINGHAM, JOHN SHEFFIELD, 1ST DUKE OF
The Works of John Sheffield, Earl of Mulgrave, Marquis of Normanby, and Duke of Buckingham. London: 1729. V. 63; 65

BUCKINGHAM, NASH
Blood Lines, Tales of Shooting and Fishing. New York: 1938. V. 65; 66
Mark Right! Tales of Shooting and Fishing. New York: 1936. V. 64; 66
Ole Miss'. New York: 1937. V. 63; 66

BUCKINGHAM, WILLIS J.
Emily Dickinson's Reception in the 1890's. Pittsburgh: 1989. V. 64

BUCKINGHAM & CHANDOS, RICHARD PLANTAGENET TEMPLE NUGENT BRYD
Memoirs of the Courts and Cabinets of William IV and Victoria. London: 1861. V. 64

BUCKLAND, FRANK
Log-Book of a Fisherman and Zoologist. London: 1891. V. 67

BUCKLAND, WILLIAM
Geology and Mineralogy Considered with Reference to Natural Theology. London: 1836. V. 65; 66; 67
Geology and Mineralogy Considered with Reference to Natural Theology. London: 1837. V. 64; 65
Reliquiae Diluvianae; or, Observations on the Organic Remains Contained in Caves, Fissures, and Diluvial Gravel and Other Geological Phenomena, Attesting the Action of an Universal Deluge. London: 1824. V. 65

BUCKLAND WRIGHT, JOHN
Baignouses. Donby Dale: 1995. V. 62; 65
Negen Houtsneden. (Nine Woodcuts). Eindhoven: 1940. V. 66
Surreal Times: the Abstract Engravings and Wartime Letters of.... Denby Dale: 2000. V. 66

BUCKLE, RICHARD
In Search of Diaghilev. London: 1956. V. 64

BUCKLER, BENJAMIN
A Philosophical Dialogue Concerning Decency. 1751. V. 66

BUCKLER, E. H.
Illustrations of the Collegiate Church of Southwell, in a Series of Ten Views of the Exterior and Interior.... London: 1853. V. 63

BUCKLER, WILLIAM
The Larvae of British Butterflies and Moths. 1886-1897. V. 65
The Larvae of British Butterflies and Moths. London: 1886-1897. V. 66
The Larvae of the British Butterflies and Moths. London: 1886-1901. V. 65

BUCKLEY, CHARLES BURTON
An Anecdotal History of Old Times...in Singapore. Singapore: 1902. V. 64

BUCKLEY, E. E.
Venoms. Washington: 1956. V. 66

BUCKLEY, RICHARD
The Proposal for Sending Back the Nobility and Gentry of Ireland. London: 1690. V. 62

BUCKLEY, T. E.
A Vertebrate Fauna of the Orkney Islands. Edinburgh: 1891. V. 62

BUCKLEY, W.
Big Game Hunting in Central Africa. 1930. V. 62; 63; 64
Big Game Hunting in Central Africa. London: 1930. V. 64

BUCKMASTER, HENRIETTA
Lucy and Loki. New York: 1958. V. 64

BUCKNALL, THOMAS SKIP DYOT
The Orchardist: or a System of Close Pruning and Medication, for Establishing the Science of Orcharding.... London: 1805. V. 65

BUCKNILL, JOHN A.
The Birds of Singapore Island. Singapore: 1927. V. 62
The Birds of Surrey. 1900. V. 67

BUCKNILL, JOHN CHARLES
A Manual of Psychological Medicine.... Philadelphia: 1858. V. 65
The Medical Knowledge of Shakespeare. London: 1860. V. 62; 66

BUCKRIDGE, A.
According to Jennings. London: 1954. V. 66
Jennings as Usual. 1954. V. 66

BUCKTON, ALICE MARY
Through Human Eyes. Poems. Oxford: 1901. V. 66

BUCKTON, G. B.
Monograph of British Aphids. London: 1876-1873. V. 64; 65; 67
Monograph of British Aphids. 1876-1883. V. 63
Monograph of British Aphids. London: 1876-1883. V. 65; 66

BUDD, A. C.
Budd's Flora of the Canadian Prairie Provinces. Hull: 1979. V. 63

BUDD, GEORGE
On Diseases of the Liver. London: 1852. V. 64

BUDD, LOUIS J.
Interviews with Samuel L. Clemens. Arlington: 1977. V. 63

BUDGE, ERNEST ALFRED WALLIS THOMPSON
Annals of the Kings of Assyria. London: 1902. V. 62
Baralam and Yewasef; Being the Ethiopian Version of a Christianized Recension of the Buddhist Legend of the Buddha and the Bodhisatva. Cambridge: 1923. V. 64
The Book of the Dead. London: 1898. V. 66
The Book of the Dead. London: 1899. V. 65
British Museum. A Guide to the Egyptian Galleries (Sculpture). London: 1909. V. 62; 65
Cook's Handbook for Egypt and the Sudan. London: 1905. V. 63
Egypt Under the Priest-Kings, Tanites and Nubians. London: 1902. V. 67
The Egyptian Sudan, Its History and Monuments. London: 1907. V. 64
From Fetish to God in Ancient Egypt. Oxford: 1934. V. 66
George of Lydda a Study of the Cultus of Sir George in Ethiopia. London: 1930. V. 64
The Gods of the Egyptians; or, Studies in Egyptian Mythology. London: 1904. V. 64
The Nile. London: 1907. V. 62
Syrian Anatomy Pathology and Therapeutics of the Book of Medicines. London: 1913. V. 66

BUDGELL, EUSTACE
Memoirs of the Life and Character of the Late Earl of Orrery, and of the Family of Boyles. London: 1732. V. 67

BUDGEN, L. M.
Episodes of Insect Life. 1849-1851. V. 67

THE BUDGET of Novelties Containing a Catalogue of Valuable Books and All the Latest Novelties and Curiosities for Everybody. N.P: 1874. V. 67

BUDLONG, CAROLINE GALE
Memories, Pioneer Days in Oregon and Washington Territory. Eugene: 1949. V. 67

BUDS and Blossom of Childish Life. London: 1870. V. 67

BUDWORTH, JOSEPH
A Fortnight's Ramble to the Lakes in Westmoreland, Lancashire, and Cumberland. London: 1792. V. 63

BUECHNER, THOMAS S.
Norman Rockwell, Artist and Illustrator. New York: 1970. V. 63; 64

BUEL, J. W.
Heroes of the Plains or Lives and Wonderful Adventures of Wild Bill, Buffalo Bill, Kit Carson, Capt. Payne, Capt. Jack, Texas Jack, California Joe and Other Celebrated Indian Fighters.... St. Louis: 1882. V. 65
Life and Marvelous Adventure of Wild Bill, the Scout.... Chicago: 1880. V. 63; 66
The Younger Brothers. The Notorious Border Outlaws. The Younger Brothers. Also Jesse and Frank James and Their Comrades in Crime. Baltimore. V. 63; 66

BUEL, JESSE
The Farmer's Companion.... Boston: 1840. V. 64
The Farmer's Companion.... New York: 1858. V. 64

BUELER, L. E.
Wild Dogs of the World. 1974. V. 63

BUELL, AUGUSTUS
The Cannoneer, Recollections of Service in the Army of the Potomac. Washington: 1890. V. 63

BUELL, MARJORIE HENDERSON
Little Lulu and the Organ Grinder Man. Springfield: 1946. V. 67

BUELL, P. L.
A Guide to Phrenology, Deisigned to Illustrate the Science of the Human Mind as Manifested through the Brain.... Woodstock: 1842. V. 63

BUERJA, ABEL
Der Mathematische maler, Oder Grundliche Anweisung zur Perspective... Nebst Einem Anhange Uber Die Theatralische Perspective.... Berlin: 1795. V. 64

BUFFALO Bill's Wild West and Congress of Rough Riders of the World. New York: 1895. V. 65

BUFFALO Bill's Wild West and Congress of Rough Riders of the World Official Program. N.P: 1907. V. 64; 67

BUFFET, EDWARD P.
The Layman Revato: a Story of a Restless Mind in Buddhist India at the Time of Greek Influence. New York: 1914. V. 62; 63; 64; 66

BUFFON, GEORGE LOUIS LECLERC
A Natural History, General and Particular.... London: 1834. V. 67

BUFFON, GEORGES LOUIS LECLERC
Oeuvres d'Histoire Naturelle.... Berne: 1792. V. 64

BUFFON, JEAN LOUIS LECLERC, COUNT DE
Natural History, General and Particular. London: 1791. V. 66
The Natural History of Birds. London: 1793. V. 65
A Natural History of British Birds. Alnwick: 1809. V. 66
A Natural History of Fishes. Alnwick: 1809. V. 66
A Natural History of Foreign Quadrupeds. British Birds, Water Birds, Foreign Birds, Fishes. Alnwick: 1809. V. 65; 66
Natural History of Oviparous Quadrupeds and Serpents. Edinburgh: 1802. V. 62
A Natural History of Water Birds. Alnwick: 1809. V. 66

Buffon's Natural History Abridged. London: 1792. V. 62

BUFFUM, GEORGE T.
On Two Frontiers. Boston: 1918. V. 64; 67

BUGLER, ARTHUR
HMS Victory. Building, Restoration and Repair. London: 1966. V. 65

BUHL, H.
Nanga Parbat Pilgrimage. 1956. V. 63; 65

BUIAL'SKII, IL'IA VASIL'EVICH
Tabulae Anatomico-Chirurgicae Operationes Ligandarum Arteriarum Maiorum Exponentes, ad Naturam Depictae et Aeri Incisae, Brevi cum Descriptione Earum Anatomica Succinctque.... St. Petersburg: 1828. V. 63

BUICK, T. LINDSAY
The Mystry of the Moa. New Plymouth: 1931. V. 62

BUISSERT, DAVID
From Sea Charts to Satellite Images: Interpreting North American History through Maps. Chicago: 1990. V. 65

BUIST, K. A.
Birds, Their Cages and Their Keep, Being a Practical Manual of Bird-Keeping and Bird-Rearing. London: 1874. V. 65

BUIST, ROBERT
The Rose Manual. Philadelphia: 1847. V. 64; 67
The Stormontfield Piscicultural Experiments 1853-1866. Edinburgh: 1866. V. 67

BUJOLD, LOIS MC MASTER
Mirror Dance. Norwalk: 1994. V. 65

BUKOWSKI, CHARLES
Barfly, the Continuing Saga of Henry Chinaski. Sutton West & Santa Barbara: 1984. V. 65; 67
Betting on the Muse, Poems and Stories. Santa Rosa: 1996. V. 62; 66
Bring Me Your Love. Santa Barbara: 1983. V. 66
The Captain Is Out to Lunch and the Sailors Have Taken Over the Ship. Santa Rosa: 1998. V. 66
Crucifix in a Deathhand. New York: 1965. V. 62; 65; 66
The Day It Snowed in L.A. Sutton West: 1986. V. 67
The Days Run Away Like Wild Horses Over the Hills. Los Angeles: 1969. V. 64; 66
Factotum. London: 1981. V. 63
Flower, Fist and Bestial Wall. Eureka: 1960. V. 65
Ham on Rye. Santa Barbara: 1982. V. 62; 63; 67
The Last Generation. Santa Barbara: 1982. V. 63; 64
The Last Night of the Earth Poems. Santa Rosa: 1992. V. 62; 67
Living on Luck, Selected Letters 1960's-1970's. Santa Rosa: 1995. V. 67
The Movie Barfly. Santa Rosa: 1987. V. 66
Notes of a Dirty Old Man. North Hollywood: 1969. V. 62
Now. Santa Rosa: 1992. V. 66
Post Office. Los Angeles: 1971. V. 66; 67
Pulp. Santa Rosa: 1994. V. 63; 65; 66
Run With the Hunted, A Charles Bukowski Reader. New York: 1993. V. 67
Screams from the Balcony. Santa Rosa: 1993. V. 62; 66; 67
Septuagenarian Stew. Santa Rosa: 1990. V. 66
War All the Time. Poems 1981-1984. Santa Barbara: 1984. V. 66; 67

BULFINCH, CHARLES
Report...The Committee to Whom Was Referred the Memorial of George Barrell and S.V.S. Wilder in Behalf of Themselves and Other Heirs of the Owners of the Ship Columbia and Sloop Washington, and the Heirs of Captain John Kendrick and Martha Gray, Widow of. Washington: 1852. V. 64

BULFINCH, STEPHEN GREENLEAF
Poems. Charleston: 1834. V. 62; 63; 67

BULFINCH, THOMAS
The Age of Fable. Boston: 1855. V. 65
The Age of Fable. Boston: 1856. V. 66

BULGAKOV, MIKHAIL
The Master and Margarita. London: 1967. V. 62
The White Guard. London: 1971. V. 62

BULGIN, E. J.
Bulgin's Best Blows on Romanism and Eddyism. Indianapolis: 1915. V. 62

BULKELEY, CATHARINE
The Bulkeley Case; or the Romance of Real Life. London: 1828?. V. 63

BULKELEY, JOHN
A Voyage to the South-Seas, in the Years 1740-1741. London: 1743. V. 66

BULKIN, ELLY
Lesbian Poetry. Watertown: 1981. V. 66

BULL, H. G.
Notes on the Birds of Herefordshire. 1888. V. 63; 66
Notes on the Birds of Herefordshire. London and Hereford: 1888. V. 62

BULL, J.
Birds of New York State. Garden City: 1974. V. 67

BULL, JOHN
Sermons on the Fifty First Psalm with Others on Doctrinal and Practical Subjects. London: 1824. V. 62; 65

BULL, MARCUS
A Defence of the Experiments to Determine the Comparative Value of the Principal Varities of Fuel Used in the United States and also in Europe. Philadelphia, London: 1828. V. 63
Experiments to Determine the Comparative Value of the Principal Varieties of Fuel Used in the United States and Also in Europe.... Philadelphia: 1827. V. 64; 66

BULL, WILLIAM PERKINS
From Medicine Man to Medical Man. Toronto: 1934. V. 66; 67

BULLAR, J.
A Winter in the Azores and at the Summer Baths of the Furnas. London: 1841. V. 62

BULLEID, ARTHUR
The Glastonbury Lake Village.... 1911-1917. V. 62

BULLEN, FRANK T.
The Cruise of the Cachalot Round the World after Sperm Whales. London: 1898. V. 62
The Cruise of the Cachalot Round the World After Sperm Whales. New York: 1899. V. 67

BULLEN, KEITH
Salamander. Cairo: 1942-1943. V. 65

BULLER, A. H. R.
Researches on Fungi. New York: 1958. V. 62

BULLER, FRED
Domesday Book of Mammoth Pike. 1979. V. 67
Pike. 1971. V. 67

BULLER, WALTER L.
Buller's Birds of New Zealand. London: 1967. V. 65; 67
A History of the Birds of New Zealand. New Zealand: 1967. V. 67

THE BULL-FINCH. London: 1788. V. 67

BULLFINCH, THOMAS
Legends of Charlemagne. New York: 1924. V. 62

BULLOCH, JAMES D.
The Secret Service of the Confederate States In Europe.... New York: 1884. V. 62; 63; 65

BULLOCH, JOSEPH GASTON BAILLIE
A History and Genealogy of the Habersham Family. Columbia: 1901. V. 67

BULLOCH, WILLIAM
The History of Bacteriology. London: 1938. V. 63

BULLOCK, HELEN
The Williamsburg Art of Cookery, or, Accomplish'd Gentlewoman's Companion.... Williamsburg: 1955. V. 66; 67

BULLOCK, W.
Six Months Residence and Travels in Mexico: Containing Remarks on the Present State of New Spain, Its Natural Productions, State of Society, Manufactures, Trade, Agriculture, Antiquities, etc. London: 1825. V. 66

BULLOCK, WILLIAM
Le Mexique en 1823 or Relation d'un Voyage dans la Nouvelle- Espagne.... Paris: 1824. V. 63; 64

BULLOCK, WILLIAM continued
Sketch of a Journey through the Western States of North America, from New Orleans by the Mississippi, Ohio, City of Cincinnati and Falls of Niagara to New York in 1827. London: 1827. V. 62; 64
Virginia Impartially Examined and Left to Publick View, to be Considered by all Judicios and Honest Men.... London: 1649. V. 63

BULLOCK, WYNN
Wynn Bllock. San Francisco: 1971. V. 63; 65

BULMER, T.
History, Topography and Directory of Cumberland. Preston: 1901. V. 66

BULMER, T., & CO.
History, Topography and Directory of Furness and Cartmel Comprising Its History and Archaeology, Physical and Geological Features.... Preston. V. 62; 65

BULMER, T. F.
History, Topography and Directory of East Cumberland, Comprising Its Ancient and Modern History.... Manchester: 1884. V. 63
History, Topography and Directory of Westmorland.... Preston: 1906. V. 63

BULOW, ERNIE
After Hours, Conversations with Lawrence Block. 1995. V. 63
Navajo Taboos. Gallup: 1991. V. 63; 64; 65; 66; 67

BULSTRODE, RICHARD
Memoirs and Reflections Upon the Reign and Government of King Charles the 1st and King Charles the IId. London: 1721. V. 66
Miscellaneous Essays.... London: 1715. V. 67

BULWER, HENRY LYTTON
The Monarchy of the Middle Classes, or France, Social, Literary, Political. Second Series. Paris: 1836. V. 64

BULWER, JOHN
Anthropometamorphosis: Man Transform'd. London: 1650. V. 63

BUM, ANTON
Therapeutisches Lexikon fur Praktische Arzte. Wien und Leipzig. 1891. V. 62

BUMGARDNER, GEORGE
Novelle Cinque: Tales from the Veneto. Barre: 1974. V. 62; 63; 64

BUMP, G.
The Ruffled Grouse, Life History, Propagation, Management. Albany: 1947. V. 64; 65; 67

BUNBURY, HENRY WILLIAM
An Academy for Grown Horsemen.... London: 1808. V. 64
An Academy for Grown Horsemen.... London: 1809. V. 62; 66

BUNBURY, SELINA
Coombe Abbey: an Historical Tale of the Reign of James the First. London: 1860. V. 65

BUNCE, DANIEL
Travels with Dr. Leichhardt in Australia. Melborne: 1859. V. 67

BUNCE, WILLIAM
Freight Train. New York: 1954. V. 63

BUNGIANA, or an Assemblage of What-dy'e call-em's, in Prose and Verse. London: 1756. V. 65

BUNIN, IVAN
Memories and Portraits. London: 1951. V. 64
The Well of Days. London: 1946. V. 64

BUNIVA, MICHELE FRANCESCO
Observations et Experiences sur la Maladie Epizootique des Chats, qui Regne Depuis Quelques Annees en France, en Allemange en Italie et en Angleterre. Paris: 1800. V. 63

BUNKER, EDWARD
The Animal Factory. New York: 1977. V. 66
No Beast So Fierce. New York: 1973. V. 66

BUNN, ALFRED
The Stage. London: 1840. V. 66

BUNNELL, LAFAYETTE H.
Discovery of the Yosemite and the Indian War of 1851 Which Led to that Event. Chicago: 1880. V. 63
Discovery of the Yosemite and the Indian War of 1851 Which Led to That Event. Los Angeles: 1911. V. 63; 65; 66

BUNNY o' The Cosy Corner. London: 1919. V. 62

BUNSEN, ROBERT
Gasometrische Methoden...Mit 60 in den Text Eingedruckten Holzschnitten. Braunschweig: 1857. V. 63

BUNT, CYRIL G. E.
The Watercolors of Sir Frank Brangwyn, R. A. Leigh-On-Sea: 1958. V. 64

BUNTING, BAINBRIDGE
John Gaw Meem Southwestern Architecture. Albuquerque: 1983. V. 63

BUNTING, BASIL
Basil Bunting: April 15-19, 1976. St. Andrews College. Laurinburg: 1976. V. 62
Basil Bunting in America. Laurinburg: 1976. V. 63
Briggflatts. 1966. V. 67
Briggflatts. London: 1966. V. 62; 64
Collected Poems. Oxford: 1978. V. 63

Descant On Rwathey's Madrigal. Lexington: 1968. V. 63
Loquitur. London: 1965. V. 64; 66
The Spoils. Newcastle-upon-Tyne: 1965. V. 62
What the Chairman Told Tom. Cambridge: 1967. V. 62

BUNTING, EVE
Smoky Night. New York: 1994. V. 65

BUNTON, MARY T.
A Bride On the Old Chisholm Trail in 1886. San Antonio: 1939. V. 65

BUNYAN, JOHN
A Discourse Upon the Pharisee and the Publicane. London: 1685. V. 64
Divine Emblems; or, Temporal Things Spiritualised. Coventry: 1806. V. 67
The Pilgrim's Progress. London: 1758. V. 64
The Pilgrim's Progress. London: 1766. V. 64
The Pilgrim's Progress. Boston: 1805. V. 62
Pilgrim's Progress. Burlington: 1805. V. 63; 66
Pilgrim's Progress. London: 1811. V. 62
The Pilgrim's Progress. London: 1830. V. 65; 67
The Pilgrim's Progress. London: 1840. V. 62; 63
Pilgrim's Progress. Philadelphia: 1844?. V. 66
The Pilgrim's Progress. London Edinburgh & Dublin: 1847. V. 64
The Pilgrim's Progress. London: 1849. V. 62
The Pilgrim's Progress. London: 1861. V. 65
The Pilgrim's Progress. London: 1880. V. 63
The Pilgrims Progress. London: 1899. V. 63
The Pilgrim's Progress. London: 1903. V. 67
The Pilgrim's Progress. London: 1928. V. 64; 66
The Pilgrim's Progress. London: 1947. V. 62
A Relation of the Imprisonment of Mr. John Bunyan, Minister of the Gospel at Bedford in November 1660. London: 1765. V. 64
A True Relation of the Holy War.... London: 1860. V. 64

BUNYARD, EDWARD
Old Garden Roses. London: 1936. V. 62

BUNZEL, RUTH L.
The Pueblo Potter: a Study of Creative Imagination in Primitve Art. New York: 1929. V. 66

BUONAIUTI, B. SERAFINO
Italian Scenery: Representing the Manners, Customs and Amusements of the Different States of Italy. London: 1806. V. 62; 66

BUONANNI, FILIPPO
Gabinetto Armonico Pieno d'Instromenti Sonori.... Rome: 1723. V. 63; 65; 66
La Gerarchia Ecclesiatica Considerata Nelle Vesti Sagre, E Civili Usate da Quelli.... Roma: 1720. V. 67

BUONAROTTI, MICHEL ANGELO
Rime...Raccolte da Michelagnolo suo Nipote. Florence: 1623. V. 62; 63; 67

BUONARROTI, MICHEL ANGELO
Sonnets and Madrigals. Cambridge: 1900. V. 62

BURBANK, LUTHER
His Methods and Discoveries and Their Practical Application, Prepared from His Original Field Notes.... New York and London: 1914. V. 64
How Plants are Trained to Work for Man. New York: 1921. V. 67
Luther Burbank, His Methods and Discoveries and Their Practical Application.... New York: 1914-1915. V. 64

BURBERRY, H. A.
The Amateur Orchid Cultivators' Guide Book. Liverpool: 1900. V. 67

BURBIDGE, F. W.
Cultivated Plants, Their Propagation and Improvement. Edinburgh: 1877. V. 65; 66

BURCH, JOHN C.
State Debt and State Finances: Re-Establishment of the State Bank Demanded. Nashville: 1878. V. 64

BURCH, JOHN P.
Charles W. Quantroll. Vega: 1923. V. 62; 63; 64; 67

BURCH, R. M.
Colour Printing and Colour Printers. London: 1910. V. 62; 67

BURCHARDUS DE BELLEVAUX
Apologia de Barbis. Cambridge: 1935. V. 64

BURCHERSH, or, The Pleasures of a Country Life. London: 1855. V. 66

BURCHETT, JOSIAH
A Complete History of the Most Remarkable Transactions at Sea, Etc. London: 1720. V. 64

BURCKHARDT, RUDY
Mobile Homes. Calais: 1979. V. 62; 64

BURCKMYER, CORNELIUS L.
The Burckmyer Letters March 1863 to June 1865. Columbia: 1926. V. 63

BURDEKIN, KATHERINE
The Rebel Passion. London: 1929. V. 64

BURDELL, HARVEY
Observations on the Structure, Physiology, Anatomy and Diseases of the Teeth. New York: 1838. V. 64; 66; 67

BURDEN, E. A. R.
A History of St. Enodoc Golf Club. Plymouth: 1965. V. 67

BURDEN, PHILIP D.
The Mapping of North America: a List of Printed Maps 1511-1670. Rickmansworth: 1996. V. 65

BURDETT, C. D., MRS.
English Fashionables Abroad. London: 1827. V. 65

BURDETT, CHARLES
Kit Carson - The Life and Adventures of Christopher Carson. Philadelphia: 1860. V. 62; 64; 65

BURDETT, FRANCIS
Sir Francis Burdett to His Consituents; Denying the Power of the House of Commons to Imprison the People of England. London: 1810. V. 63
Fairburn's Edition of the Trial of Sir F. Burdett, on a Charge of Seditious Libel Against His Majesty's Government, Including the Defence at Length. London: 1820. V. 63
The Trial of Sir Francis Burdett, Bart. at Leicester, on Thursday, March 23rd, 1820.... London: 1820. V. 63

BURDETTE, ROBERT J.
Gems of Modern Wit and Humor. Chicago: 1903. V. 65

BURDICK, USHER L.
David F. Barry's Indian Notes on The Custer Battle. Balitmore: 1949. V. 65; 67
The Last Battle of the Sioux Nation. Fargo: 1929. V. 65; 67
The Last Days of Sitting Bull, Sioux Medicine Chief. Baltimore: 1941. V. 65
Tales from Buffalo Land. The Story of George M. Newton, Old Time Buffalo Hunter of Dakota and Montana. Baltimore: 1939. V. 62; 67

BURDSALL, R.
Men Against the Clouds. 1935. V. 63

BURFORD, ROBERT
Description of a View of the Bay of Islands, New Zealand; and the Surrounding Country, Now Exhibiting at the Panorama, Leicester Square. London: 1838. V. 64

BURGEL, BRUNO H.
Astronomy for All. London: 1911. V. 63

BURGER, GOTTFRIED AUGUST
Lenore. London: 1900. V. 65

BURGER, J.
African Buffalo Trails. 1957. V. 62; 63
The Black Skimmer, Social Dynamics of a Colonial Species. New York: 1990. V. 67

BURGER, J. F.
African Jungle Memories. 1958. V. 64; 66

BURGER, JOHN
African Adventures. 1957. V. 66

BURGESS, ANTHONY
Any Old Iron. London: 1989. V. 65
Beard's Roman Women - a Novel. London: 1977. V. 65
A Clockwork Orange. London: 1962. V. 66
A Clockwork Orange. New York: 1963. V. 66
The Clockwork Testament or; Enderby's End. London: 1974. V. 64
Coaching Days of England. London: 1966. V. 66
Devil of a State. London: 1961. V. 63
Enderby's Dark Lady or No End to Enderby. London: 1984. V. 65
The Eve of St. Venus. London: 1964. V. 63
Flame Into Being - The Life and Work of D. H. Lawrence. London: 1985. V. 64
Inside Mr. Enderby. London: 1963. V. 65
Joysprick - an Introduction to the Language of James Joyce. London: 1973. V. 65
The Kingdom of the Wicked. Franklin Center: 1985. V. 67
Little Wilson and Big God. 1987. V. 67
Little Wilson and Big God. Franklin Center: 1987. V. 63
1985. London: 1978. V. 63; 65
Tremor of Intent. London: 1966. V. 63
Urgent Copy - Literary Studies. London: 1968. V. 62
The Wanting Seed. London: 1962. V. 65
The Worm and the Ring. London: 1961. V. 62; 65

BURGESS, C. M.
The Living Cowries. New York: 1970. V. 62; 66

BURGESS, EBENEZER
Address to the American Society for Colonizing the Free People of Colour of the United States. Washington: 1818. V. 65

BURGESS, GELETT
Are You a Bromide? or, the Sulphitic Theory. New York: 1906. V. 67
Goop Tales Alphabetically Told. New York: 1904. V. 65
The Lively City O' Ligg: a Cycle of Modern Fairy Tales for City Children. New York: 1899. V. 62

BURGESS, HENRY
A Petition to the Honourable the Commons House of Parliament, to Render Manifest the Errors, the Injustice, and the Dangers of the Measures of Parliament Respecting Currency and Bankers.... London: 1829. V. 64; 65

BURGESS, JOHN CART
An Easy Introduction to Perspective. London: 1828. V. 66; 67
An Easy Introduction to Perspective. London: 1840. V. 64

BURGESS, KENNETH FARWELL
Colonists of New England and Nova Scotia. Burgess and Heckman Families. 1956. V. 66

BURGESS, RENATE
Portraits of Doctors and Scientists in the Wellcome Institute of the History of Medicine, a Catalogue. London: 1973. V. 62

BURGESS, S.
The Hangman's Record. London: 1910. V. 63

BURGESS, THORNTON W.
The Adventures of Mr. Mocker. Boston: 1914. V. 62
Baby Possum's Queer Voyage. Racine: 1928. V. 64
Bedtime Nature Library. New York: 1940. V. 62
Bowser the Hound. Boston: 1920. V. 62
Buster Bear Invites Old Mr. Toad to Dine. New York: 1928. V. 62
The Feast at the Big Rock and Other Stories. New York: 1914. V. 63
Grandfather Frog Stays in the Smiling Pod. New York: 1922. V. 65
A Great Joke on Jimmy Skunk. Racine: 1928. V. 64
Happy Jack Squirrel Helps Unc' Billy. Racine: 1928. V. 64
Jerry Muskrat at Home. Boston: 1926. V. 62
Jerry Muskrat Wins Respect. New York: 1928. V. 62
Lightfoot the Deer. BostonL: 1921. V. 62; 65
Little Animal Books. New York: 1917. V. 62
Little Joe Otter. Boston: 1925. V. 65
Mother West Wind How Stories. Boston: 1916. V. 65
Mother West Wind When Stories. Boston: 1917. V. 62
Mother West Wind's Neighbors. Boston: 1913. V. 65
The Neatness of Bobby Coon. Racine: 1928. V. 64
Old Granny Fox. Boston: 1920. V. 64
Peter Rabbit Learns To Use His New Coat. New York: 1928. V. 65

BURGESS, W. E.
Atlas of Freshwater and Marine Catfishes. 1989. V. 64
Dr. Burgess's Atlas of Marine Aquarium Fishes. Neptune City: 1990. V. 65
Pacific Marine Fishes. 1971-1976. V. 66

BURGESS, WALTER W.
Bits of Old Chelsea. London: 1894. V. 63

BURGGREN, W. W.
Biology of the Land Crabs. New York: 1988. V. 65

BURGH, JAMES
The Art of Speaking. London: 1775. V. 64

BURGH, N. P.
Modern Marine Engineering. London: 1872. V. 64

BURGHART, GOTTFRIED HEINRICH
Die zum Allgemeinen Gebrauch Wohleingerichtete Destillier-Kunst... Neue Zusatze zu der Wohl Eingerichteten Destillier-Kunst...Neu Auflage. Breslau: 1754. V. 62

BURGHCLERE, WINIFREDE, LADY
Strafford. 1931. V. 62; 65

BURGIN, RICHARD
Conversations with Jorge Luis Borges. New York: 1969. V. 63; 64; 66

BURGOYNE, FRANK J.
Northumberland Manuscripts. London: 1904. V. 65

BURGOYNE, JOHN
A State of Expedition from Canada, as Laid Before the House of Commons...and Verified by Evidence; with a Collection of Authentic Documents.... London: 1780. V. 63; 64; 66

BURGUM, J. S.
Zezula or Pioneer Days in the Smoky Water Country. Valley City: 1937. V. 65; 67

BURHAN AL-DIN, AL-ZARNUJI
Enchiridion Studiosi, Arabice Conscriptum a Borhaneddino Alzernouchi, Cum Duplici Versione Latina, Altera a Friderico Rostgaard. Utrecht: 1709. V. 63

BURK, DALE
A Brush with the West. Missoula: 1980. V. 67

BURK, JOHN
The History of Virginia from Its First Settlement to the Present Day. Petersburg: 1804. V. 65

BURKE, A. L.
The Mayberry Murder Mystery of Bonito City. Alamogordo. V. 64; 67

BURKE, BERNARD
A Genealogical and Heraldic Dictionary of the Peerage and Baronetage, The Privy Council and Knightage. London: 1935. V. 64
Genealogical and Heraldic History of the Landed Gentry of Great Britain. London: 1921. V. 66
A Genealogical and Heraldic History of the Landed Gentry of Ireland. 1904. V. 63

BURKE, CLIFFORD
Bone Songs. Newark: 1992. V. 64
Printing Poetry: A Workbook in Typographic Reification. San Francisco: 1980. V. 62; 63; 64; 66

BURKE, DOREEN BOLGER
In Pursuit of Beauty: Americans and the Aesthetic Movement. New York: 1986. V. 64

BURKE, EDMUND
An Account of the European Settlements in America. London: 1765. V. 63; 66

BURKE, EDMUND continued
Correspondence of the Right Honourable Edmund Burke: Between the Year 1744 and the Period of His Decease in 1797. London: 1844. V. 63
An Impartial History of the War in America, Between Great Britain and Her Colonies.... London: 1780. V. 63; 66
A Philosophical Enquiry into the Origin of Our Ideas of the Sublime and Beautiful. London: 1757. V. 67
A Philosophical Enquiry into the Origin of Our Ideas of the Sublime and Beautiful. London: 1794. V. 67
A Philosophical Inquiry into the Origin of Our Ideas of the Sublime and Beautiful. Philadelphia: 1806. V. 63
Reflections on the Revolution in France and on the Proceedings in Certain Societies in London Relative to that Event.... London: 1790. V. 64; 65; 66
The Speeches of the Right Honourable Edmund Burke, in the House of Commons and in Westminster Hall. London: 1816. V. 63
Thoughts on the Cause of the Present Discontents. London: 1770. V. 63
A Vindication of Natural Society.... London: 1756. V. 62
The Works of Edmund Burke. (with) *The Letters of Edmund Burke.* 1925-1930. V. 67
The Works.... London: 1792. V. 64
The Works.... London: 1854. V. 64

BURKE, FRED
Illustrator II, the Art of Clive Barker. Forestville: 1993. V. 66

BURKE, J. BERNARD
Vicissitudes of Families. 1869. V. 67

BURKE, JACKSON
Prelum to Albion: a History of the Development of the Hand Press, from Gutenberg to Morris. San Francisco: 1940. V. 64

BURKE, JAMES LEE
Black Cherry Blues. Boston: 1989. V. 62; 63; 64; 65; 66; 67
Burning Angel. New Orleans: 1995. V. 65; 66
Cadillac Jukebox. New Orleans: 1996. V. 65; 66
Cimarron Rose. London: 1997. V. 62; 63; 64; 65; 66; 67
Cimarron Rose. New Orleans: 1997. V. 65; 66
The Convict. Baton Rouge: 1985. V. 62; 63; 64; 66; 67
The Convict and Other Stories. Boston: 1990. V. 66
Dixie City Jam. New York: 1994. V. 62; 64; 65; 66; 67
Half of Paradise. Boston: 1965. V. 62; 65; 66; 67
Heartwood. New Orleans: 1999. V. 65; 66; 67
Heaven's Prisoners. New York: 1988. V. 62; 63; 65; 66; 67
In the Electric Mist with the Confederate Dead. New York: 1993. V. 62; 66; 67
Lay Down My Sword and Shield. New York: 1971. V. 62; 65; 66
The Lost Get-Back Boogie. Baton Rouge and London: 1986. V. 63; 65; 66
The Lost Get-Back Boogie. New York: 1986. V. 67
A Morning for Flamingoes. Boston: 1990. V. 65; 66; 67
A Morning for Flamingoes. New York: 1990. V. 62; 63; 64; 65; 67
The Neon Rain. New York: 1987. V. 62; 63; 65; 66; 67
Purple Cane Road. London: 2000. V. 67
Purple Cane Road. New Orleans: 2000. V. 66; 67
A Stained White Radiance. New York: 1992. V. 67
Sunset Limited. Blakeney: 1998. V. 65; 66; 67
Texas City, 1947. Northridge. 1992. V. 65; 67
To The Bright and Shining Sea. New York: 1970. V. 66; 67
Two for Texas. New York: 1982. V. 64; 65; 67
Two for Texas. Huntington Beach: 1992. V. 62
Winter Light. Huntington Beach: 1992. V. 65; 66; 67

BURKE, JOHN BERNARD
Romantic Records of Distinguished Families. London: 1850. V. 62; 67

BURKE, MARIE LOUISE
Kamehameha. King of the Hawaiian Islands. San Francisco: 1939. V. 63

BURKE, PAULINE W.
Emily Donelson of Tennessee. Richmond: 1941. V. 65

BURKE, PETER
Celebrated Trials Connected with the Aristocracy, In the Relations of Private Life. London: 1849. V. 63
Recollections of the Court Room, or, Narratives, Scenes and Anecdotes from Courts of Justice. New York: 1859. V. 67

BURKE, THOMAS
The Best Stories of Thomas Burke. London: 1950. V. 64
Hibernia Dominicana. Cologne: 1762. V. 67
The History of the Ford Rotunda 1934-1962. Hicksville: 1977. V. 67
The Sun in Splendour. London: 1927. V. 62

BURKE, THOMAS N.
Ireland's Case Stated in Reply to Mr. Froude. New York: 1873. V. 67

BURKE, WILLIAM
An Examination of the Commercial Principles of the Late Negotiation Between Great Britain and France in MDCCLXI. London: 1762. V. 63
The Greek-English Derivative Dictionary.... London: 1806. V. 64
Horrid Murders in Edinburgh. The Trial of Wm Burke and Helen McDougal, on Wednesday, December 24th, 1828..on an Indictment for the Wilful Murder of Mary Patterson, James Wilson and Madgy McGonegal...for the Purpose of Sale to the Medical Faculty.... Manchester: 1829. V. 63

BURKE'S *Presidential Families of the United States of America.* London: 1975. V. 63

BURKHARDT, F.
A Calendar of the Correspondence of Charles Darwin 1821-1882, with Supplement. Cambridge: 1994. V. 64; 66

BURKILL, JOHN
Bolton Illustrated: a Series of Views of the Scenery Around Bolton Abbey, Wharfdale, Yorkshire.... London: 1848. V. 65; 66

BURKITT, LEMUEL
A Concise History of the Kehukee Baptist Association. Halifax: 1803. V. 63; 66

BURKLEY, FRANK J.
The Faded Frontier. Omaha: 1935. V. 62; 65

BURKLUND, C.
New Michigan Verse. Ann Arbor: 1940. V. 63

BURL, AUBREY
The Stone Circles of the British Isles. 1977. V. 67

BURLAND, C. A.
Magic Books from Mexico. London: 1953. V. 64; 65; 66; 67

BURLEIGH, WILLIAM G.
The Angel with the Flaming Sword. Parkersburg: 1828. V. 65

BURLEND, REBECCA
A True Picture of Emigration; or Fourteen Years in the Interior of North America.... London: 1848. V. 65

BURLINGHAM, RUSSELL
Forrest Reid; a Portrait and Study. 1953. V. 67

BURLINGTON FINE ARTS CLUB
Catalogue of a Collection of Pictures of the Umbrian School. London: 1910. V. 64
Catalogue of Bronzes and Ivories of European Origin Exhibited in 1879. London: 1879. V. 64

BURMAN, JOHANN
Thesaurus Zeylanicus, Exhibens Plantas in Insula Zeylana Nascentes.... Amsterdam: 1737. V. 63

BURMEISTER, H.
A Manual of Entomology. 1836. V. 66
The Organisation of Trilobites. London: 1846. V. 66

BURN, JACOB HENRY
A Descriptive Catalogue of the London Traders, Tavern and Coffee-House Tokens Current in the Seventeenth Century.... London: 1853. V. 62

BURN, JOHN
The History of the French, Walloon, Dutch and Other Foreign Protestant Refugees Settled in England, from the Reign of Henry VIII to the Revocation of the Edict of Nantes with Notices of their Trade and Commerce.... London: 1846. V. 64

BURN, JOHN SOUTHERDEN
Registrum Ecclesiae Parochialis. The History of Parish Registers in England, Also of the Registers of Scotland, Ireland, the East and West Indies, Foreign Countries, Dissenters, the Fleet, King's Bench, Mint, Chapel Royal &c.... London: 1829. V. 65

BURN, RICHARD
Ecclesiastical Law. London: 1767. V. 66
The History of the Poor Laws, with Observations. London: 1764. V. 63; 66
The Justice of the Peace and Parish Officer. London: 1762. V. 66
The Justice of the Peace, and Parish Officer. London: 1793. V. 63

BURN, ROBERT SCOTT
Mechanics and Mechanism.... London: 1853. V. 62
Modern Building and Architecture: a series of Working Drawings and Practical Designs.... Edinburgh: 1869. V. 65
Year-Book of Agricultural Facts for 1859. London: 1860. V. 62; 65

BURNABY, ANDREW
Travels through the Middle Settlements in North America in the Years 1759 and 1760. London: 1775. V. 63; 66

BURNABY, FRED
The High Alps in Winter; or, Mountaineering in Search of Health. London: 1883. V. 64
On Horseback through Asia Minor. London: 1877. V. 64

BURNABY, THOMAS FOWKE ANDREW
The Ordinance and Foundation of the Schools of Grammar and Song, at Newark-upon-Trent, by Mr. Thomas Magnus. Newark: 1855. V. 65

BURNAND, FRANCIS COWLEY
Happy Thoughts. London: 1890. V. 67
Mokeanna!. London: 1873. V. 67

BURNAND, R.
Reims La Cathedrale. Nancy: 1920. V. 67

BURNAP, WILLARD A.
One Man's Lifetime 1840-1920. Fergus Falls: 1929. V. 63; 66

BURNBY, JOHN
An Historical Description of the Cathedral and Metropolitical Church of Christ, Canterbury.... Canterbury: 1772. V. 63

BURNE, PETER
The Teetotaler's Companion; or a Plea for Temperance...(with) The Concordance of Scripture and Science Illustrated, with Reference to the Temperance Cause.... London: 1847. V. 63

BURNEAGLE COAL & COKE CORP.
Law Arguments. Roanoke: 1924. V. 65

BURNE-JONES, EDWARD
The Beginning of the World - Twenty-Five Pictures. London: 1902. V. 62; 63; 66
The Flower Book. 1905. V. 64; 67
The Flower Book. London: 1905. V. 65
Letters to Katie. London: 1924. V. 65
Letters to Katie. London: 1925. V. 63; 64
Little Holland House Album. 1981. V. 64

BURNELL, R. D.
The Oxford & Cambridge Boat Race 1829-1953. 1954. V. 67

BURNES, ALEXANDER
Cabool; a Personal Narrative of a Journey to and Residence in that City in the Years 1836, 1837 and 1838. London: 1842. V. 64
Travels in Bokhara; Being the Account of a Journey from India to Cabool, Tartary and Persia. London: 1834. V. 64

BURNESS, TED
Monstrous American Car Spotter's Guide 1920-1980. Osceola: 1986. V. 67

BURNET, FRANK MAC FARLANE
The Clonal Selection Theory of Acquired Immunity. Cambridge: 1959. V. 63
Virus as Organism. Evolutionary and Ecological Apsects of Some Human Virus Diseases. Cambridge: 1945. V. 63

BURNET, GILBERT, BP. OF SALISBURY
An Answer to Mr. Law's Letter to the Lord Bishop of Bangor in a Letter to Mr. Law. (with) A Full Examination of Several Important Points Relating to Church Authority.... London: 1717-1718. V. 64
Bishop Burnet's History of His Own Time.... London: 1724-1734. V. 63
Bishop Burnet's History of His Own Time.... Oxford: 1823. V. 63
A Discourse of the Pastoral Care. London: 1692. V. 64
A Discourse of the Pastoral Care.... London: 1713. V. 63; 64
An Essay on the Memory of the Late Queen. London: 1695. V. 63; 67
An Exposition of the Church Catechism, for the Use of the Diocese of Sarum.... London: 1710. V. 64
A Full Examination of Several Important Points Relating to Church- Authority, the Christian Priesthood, the Positve Institutions of the Christian Religion, and Church Communion. London: 1718. V. 67
The History of the Reformation of the Church of England. Oxford: 1865. V. 63
The History of the Rights of Princes in the Disposing of Ecclesiastical Benefices and Church Lands. London: 1682. V. 64
An Impartial Examination of Bishop Burnet's History of His Own Times. London: 1724. V. 66
The Letter Writ by the Last Assembly General of the Clergy of France to the Protestants, Inviting Them to Return to Their Communion. London: 1683. V. 64
The Life of John, Earl of Rochester. London: 1820. V. 65
Life of William Bedell, D.D. London: 1692. V. 64
The Lives of Sir Matthew Hale and John Earl of Rochester. London: 1820. V. 64
The Memoirs of the Lives and Actions of James and William Dukes of Hamilton and Castleherald &c. London: 1677. V. 66; 67
A Modest Survey of the Most Considerable Things in a Discourse Lately Published, Entitled Naked Truth. London: 1676. V. 65
Reflections on Mr. Varillas's History of the Revolutions that Have Happened in Europe in Matters of Religion. Amsterdam: 1686. V. 64
Some Letters. Containing an Account of What Seemed Most Remarkable in Switzerland, Italy &c.... Rotterdam: 1686. V. 65
Some Letters, Containing an Account of What Seemed Most Remarkable in Travelling through Switzerland, Italy, Some Parts of Germany &c. in the Years 1685 and 1686. (with) Three Letters Concerning the Present State of Italy, Written in the Year 1687. Rotterdam: 1687. V. 67
Some Passages of the Life and Death of the Right Honourable John Earl of Rochester, Who Died the 26th of July, 1680. London: 1680. V. 62; 65
A Supplement to Burnet's History of My Own Time.... Oxford: 1902. V. 63

BURNET, JACOB
Notes on the Early Settlement of the North-Western Territory. Cincinnati: 1847. V. 63
Notes on the Early Settlement of the North-Western Territory. New York: 1847. V. 67

BURNET, JOHN
Practical Essays on Various Branches of the Fine Arts. London: 1848. V. 66; 67
The Progress of a Painter in the Nineteenth Century.... London: 1854. V. 66
A Treatise on Painting. London: 1837. V. 66
A Treatise on Painting. London: 1864-1865. V. 66

BURNET, ROSS
A Bookseller's Diary. Katoomba: 1993. V. 64

BURNET, THOMAS
De Fide & Officiis Christianorum.... London: 1728. V. 62
De Statu Mortuorum and Resurgentium Tractatus. London: 1728. V. 65
De Statu Mortuorum et Resurgentium Liber. London: 1723. V. 65
The Necessity of Impeaching the Late Ministry. London: 1715. V. 65
The Sacred Theory of the Earth. 1816. V. 64
The Sacred Theory of the Earth. London: 1816. V. 64
The Sacred Theory of the Earth.... London: 1722. V. 67
The Theory of the Earth Containing an Account of the Original of the Earth.... London: 1684. V. 66

BURNET, W. HODGSON
Quite So Stories. London: 1918. V. 64

BURNETT, CHARLES H.
Conquering the Wilderness. The Building of the Adirondack and St. Lawrence Railroad by William Seward Webb, 1891-1892. Norwood: 1932. V. 62

BURNETT, DAVID
Root and Flower: Selected Poems. 1990. V. 62
Six Poems. Durham: 1995. V. 67
Vines. 1948. V. 65

BURNETT, FRANCES HODGSON
His Grace of Osmonde. New York: 1897. V. 64; 67
Little Lord Fauntleroy. London: 1886. V. 66
Little Lord Fauntleroy. New York: 1886. V. 63
Little Lord Fauntleroy. London: 1902. V. 65
Little Lord Fauntleroy. London: 1911. V. 63
A Little Princess. Philadelphia: 1963. V. 62
The Making of a Marchioness. New York: 1901. V. 62; 64; 67
The One I Knew Best of All. London: 1893. V. 65
Piccino and Other Child Stories. New York: 1894. V. 62
Rackety-Packety House. New York: 1906. V. 62
The Secret Garden. New York: 1911. V. 63
The Spring Cleaning. New York: 1908. V. 62
Two Little Pilgrim's Progress. London: 1895. V. 65

BURNETT, GEORGE
The Red Book of Menteith, Reviewed in Reply to Charges of Literary Discourtesy Made Against the Reviewer in a Letter to the Author of that Work. Edinburgh: 1881. V. 67

BURNETT, J. H.
The Vegetation of Scotland. Edinburgh: 1964. V. 63

BURNETT, J. J.
Sketches of Tennessee's Pioneer Baptist Preachers. Nashville: 1919. V. 64

BURNETT, M. A.
Plantae Utiliores; or Illustrations of Useful Plants. London: 1839-1846. V. 62
Plantae Utiliores; or Illustrations of Useful Plants Employed in the Arts and Medicine. 1842-1850. V. 65; 66

BURNETT, W. R.
The Asphalt Jungle. New York: 1949. V. 67
4 Novels. Little Caesar. The Asphalt Jungle. High Sierra. Vanity Row. London: 1984. V. 66
High Sierra. New York and London: 1940. V. 63; 67
Iron Man. New York: 1930. V. 63
Round the Clock at Volari's. Greenwich: 1961. V. 67
Underdog. New York: 1957. V. 67

BURNETT, WHIT
This is My Best in the Third Quarter of the Century. Garden City: 1970. V. 63

BURNETT, WILLIAM HICKLING
Views of Cintra. London: 1835. V. 66

BURNEY, CHARLES
An Eighteenth Century Musical Tour in France and Italy. London and New York: 1959. V. 66
A General History of Music, from the Earliest Ages to the Present Period. London: 1776-1789. V. 62; 66
Scholes: an Eighteenth-Century Musical Tour in France and Italy. London and New York: 1959. V. 66
With Critical and Historical Notes by Frank Mercer: a General History of Music. New York and London: 1957. V. 66

BURNEY, JAMES
A Chronological History of North-Eastern Voyages of Discovery; and of Early Eastern Navigations of the Russians. Amsterdam/New York: 1969. V. 63
A Chronological History of the Discoveries in the South Sea or Pacific Ocean. London: 1803-1817. V. 66

BURNEY, SARAH HARRIET
Tales of Fancy. London: 1816-1820. V. 65
Traits of Nature. London: 1812. V. 65

BURNHAM, ALAN
New York Landmarks: a Study and Index of Architecturally Notable Structures in Greater New York. Middletown: 1963. V. 65

BURNHAM, CARRIE S.
Woman Suffrage. The Argument of Carrie S. Burnham Before Chief Justice Reed, and Associate Justices Agnew, Sharswood and Mercur, of the Supreme Court of Pennsylvania.... Philadelphia: 1873. V. 67

BURNHAM, DANIEL H.
Plan of Chicago. New York: 1970. V. 62; 65

BURNHAM, DAVID
Last Act in Bermuda. New York: 1940. V. 67

BURNHAM, ELEANOR WARING
Justin Morgan the Romantic History of a Horse. New York: 1911. V. 64

BURNHAM, FREDERICK R.
Taking Chances. Los Angeles: 1904. V. 64

BURNHAM, GEORGE P.
American Counterfeits. Springfield: 1875. V. 66

BURNHAM, S. W.
Double Star Observations Made with the Thirty-Six Inch and Twelve- Inch Refractors of the Lick Observatory, from August 1888 to June 1892. Sacramento: 1894. V. 66

BURNLEY, JAMES
The History of Wool and Woolcombing. London: 1889. V. 63

BURNLY, JUDITH
Penguin Modern Stories 7. London: 1971. V. 66

BURN MURDOCH, WILLIAM GORDON
From Edinburgh to India and Burmah. London: 1910. V. 64

BURNS, EDWARD
The Letters of Gertrude Stein and Carl Van Vechten. New York: 1985. V. 66

BURNS, ESTHER
Mrs. Peregrine and the Yak. New York: 1938. V. 64

BURNS, INEZ E.
History of Blount Co., Tennessee from War Trail to Landing Strip 1795-1955. Maryville: 1957. V. 67

BURNS, JAMES DAWSON
Three Years Among the Working-Classes in the United States During the War. London: 1865. V. 64

BURNS, JAMES MC GREGOR
To Heal and to Build: the Programs of President Lyndon B. Johnson. New York: 1968. V. 63

BURNS, JOHN
The Principles of Midwifery.... New York: 1807. V. 67

BURNS, JOHN H.
Memoirs of a Cow Pony, as Told by Himself. Boston: 1906. V. 64; 67

BURNS, OLIVE ANNE
Cold Sassy Tree. New York: 1984. V. 62; 63; 66; 67

BURNS, RICHARD
Some Poems. London: 1976. V. 65

BURNS, ROBERT
Auld Lang Syne. London: 1859. V. 62
The Complete Writings. London: 1927. V. 65; 67
The Geddes Burns. Boston: 1918. V. 62
Illustrated Songs.... London: 1861. V. 62
The Merry Muses of Caledonia, a Collection of Favorite Scots Songs. N.P. Edinburgh?: 1911. V. 66
The Poems. New York: 1965. V. 64
Poems, Chiefly in the Scottish Dialect. Edinburgh: 1787. V. 62; 65
Poems, Chiefly in the Scottish Dialect. London: 1787. V. 63
Poems, Chiefly in the Scottish Dialect. Edinburgh: 1797. V. 64
Poems, Chiefly in the Scottish Dialect. Kilmarnock: 1870-1869-1869. V. 65
The Poetical Works. Alnwick: 1808. V. 65
The Poetical Works. Edinburgh: 1856. V. 64
The Poetical Works. London: 1958. V. 64
The Poetry. Edinburgh: 1896. V. 62
Reliques...Consisting Chiefly of Original Letters, Poems and Critical Observations on Scottish Songs. Philadelphia: 1809. V. 66
The Soldier's Return. London: 1857. V. 62
Songs. Waltham St. Lawrence: 1949. V. 66
Songs and Ballads. London. V. 64
Tam O'Shanter. London: 1855. V. 62
The Works. London: 1801. V. 67
The Works. London: 1819. V. 62
Wyoming Pioneer Ranches. Laramie: 1955. V. 65; 67

BURNS, STANLEY B.
Early Medical Photography in America 1839-1883. New York: 1983. V. 67

BURNS, T. E.
Van Dieman's Land Correspondence.... Tasmania: 1961. V. 62

BURNS, WALTER W.
The District of Columbia Coast Artillery, National Guard 1915-1919. Menasha: 1921. V. 65

BURNS, WILLIAM J.
The Crevice. New York: 1915. V. 67

BURNS BEGG, ROBERT
The Lochleven Angler. Kinross: 1874. V. 67

BURNSIDE, H. M.
The Childrens (sic) Wonderland. London: 1900. V. 63

BURNYEAT, JOHN
The Truth Exalted in the Writings of that Eminent and Faithful Servant of Christ John Burnyeat.... London: 1691. V. 64

BURPEE, LAWRENCE J.
The Search for the Western Sea: the Story of the Exploration of North Western America. Toronto: 1935. V. 63; 64; 66

BURR, AARON
The Trial of Col. Aaron Burr, on an Indictment for Treason, Before the Circuit Court of the United States, Held in Richmond, (Virginia) May Term 1807; Including the Arguments and Decisions On all the Motions Made During the Examination and Trial, and on. Washington City: 1807-1808. V. 65; 66

BURR, ANNA ROBESON
Alice James, Her Brothers - Her Journal. London: 1934. V. 66

BURR, CHARLES C.
Lectures of Lola Montez (Countess of Landsfeld), Including Her Autobiography. New York: 1858. V. 65

BURR, NELSON R.
Education in New Jersey 1630-1871. Princeton: 1942. V. 66

BURRAGE, A. M.
Don't Break the Seal. London: 1946. V. 65

BURRARD, GERALD
Big Game Hunting in the Himalayas and Tibet. 1925. V. 67
Big Game Hunting in the Himalayas and Tibet. London: 1925. V. 64
Big Game Hunting in the Himalayas and Tibet. 1927. V. 62; 63; 64
Fly-Tying: Principles and Practice. London: 1940. V. 67
In the Gunroom. London: 1930. V. 67
The Modern Shotgun. London: 1944. V. 67
The Modern Shotgun. 1959. V. 67
The Modern Shotgun. 1963. V. 62
The Modern Shotgun. London: 1985. V. 62; 67
Notes on Sporting Rifles for Use in India and Elsewhere. London: 1925. V. 67

BURRARD, WILLIAM DUTTON
Chronicles of an Eminent Fossil. 1896. V. 67

BURRELL, PHILLIPPA
He Was Like a Continent. London: 1947. V. 67

BURRIDGE, JOHN
A Narrative of an Interesting Trial at Law, (Founded on Mystery) with Hints to the Whigs, on the Close Borough System, and a Glance at the Borough of Lyme Regis.... Southampton: 1821. V. 63

BURRILL, KATHERINE
Amateur Cook. New York. V. 67

BURRISH, ONSLOW
Batavia Illustra, or, a View of the Policy and Commerce of the United Provinces. London: 1731. V. 63

BURRIS-MEYER, H.
Theatres and Auditoriums. New York: 1949. V. 65

BURRITT, ELIHU
Sparks from the Anvil. Together with Voice from the Forge. London. 1848. V. 67
A Walk from London to John O'Groats.... London: 1864. V. 62
A Walk from London to Land's end and Back with Notes by the Way. London: 1868. V. 62

BURROUGHS, CHARLES GORDON
Home. Chicago: 1987?. V. 67

BURROUGHS, EDGAR RICE
Apache Devil. 1933. V. 66
Back to the Stone Age. 1937. V. 62; 64; 66
Back to the Stone Age. Tarzana: 1937. V. 63; 66
Carson of Venus. 1939. V. 64; 66
Carson of Venus. Tarzana. 1939. V. 62; 63
The Deputy Sheriff of Comanche County. 1940. V. 66
The Deputy Sheriff of Comanche County. Tarzana: 1940. V. 62; 63; 65
The Deputy Sheriff of Comanche County. London: 1941. V. 64
The Deputy Sheriff of Comanche County. Tarzana: 1941. V. 63
Escape on Venus. 1946. V. 64
Escape on Venus. Tarzana: 1946. V. 63
A Fighting Man of Mars. 1931. V. 62
The Gods of Mars. 1918. V. 62
Jungle Girl. London: 1934. V. 65
Jungle Tales of Tarzan. 1919. V. 66
The Lad and the Lion. 1938. V. 64; 66
The Lad and the Lion. Tarzana: 1938. V. 62; 63
Land of Terror. 1934. V. 66
Land of Terror. 1944. V. 64
Land of Terror. Tarzana: 1944. V. 63
Llana of Gathol. 1948. V. 64
Llana of Gathol. Tarzana: 1948. V. 63
The Mad King. 1926. V. 64
The Monster Men. 1929. V. 64
The New Adventures of Tarzan. Chicago: 1935. V. 63
The Oakdale Affair and the Rider. Tarzana: 1937. V. 62; 66
Pirates of Venus. Tarzana: 1934. V. 63
A Princess of Mars. 1917. V. 62; 64
The Return of Tarzan. 1915. V. 62; 64; 66
The Son of Tarzan. 1917. V. 64; 66
The Son of Tarzan. 1918. V. 64; 66
Swords of Mars. Tarzana: 1936. V. 63
Synthetic Men of Mars. Tarzana: 1940. V. 63
Tanar of Pellucidar. New York: 1931. V. 67
Tarzan and the Ant-Men. London: 1925. V. 67
Tarzan and the City of Gold. 1933. V. 64; 66
Tarzan and the City of Gold. Tarzana: 1933. V. 63
Tarzan and the Forbidden City. 1938. V. 64; 66

BURROUGHS, EDGAR RICE *continued*
Tarzan and the Forbidden City. Tarzana: 1938. V. 63
Tarzan and the Foreign Legion. 1947. V. 64; 66
Tarzan and the Foreign Legion. Tarzana: 1947. V. 62
Tarzan and the Jewels of Opar. 1918. V. 64; 66
Tarzan and the Jewels of Opar. Chicago: 1918. V. 65
Tarzan and the Leopard Men. 1935. V. 64
Tarzan and the Leopard Men. Tarzana: 1935. V. 63
Tarzan and the Lost Empire. 1929. V. 62; 64; 66; 67
Tarzan and the Lost Empire. New York: 1929. V. 65
Tarzan and the Tarzan Twins. New York: 1963. V. 67
Tarzan of the Apes. 1915. V. 67
Tarzan: The Lost Adventure. Milwaukie, Oregon: 1995. V. 66
Tarzan the Untamed. Chicago: 1920. V. 64
Tarzan Triumphant. 1932. V. 64; 66
Tarzan Triumphant. Tarzana: 1932. V. 62; 63; 64
Tarzan's Quest. 1936. V. 64
Tarzan's Quest. Tarzana: 1936. V. 63

BURROUGHS, FRANKLIN
Compression Wood. Haverford: 1999. V. 66; 67

BURROUGHS, JOHN
The Complete Nature Writings of John Burroughs. New York: 1915. V. 62
Notes on Walt Whitman, as Poet and Person. New York: 1867. V. 65; 67
The Writings of John Burroughs. Boston and New York: 1904-1913. V. 67
The Writings of John Burroughs. Boston: 1904-1916. V. 66

BURROUGHS, JOHN R.
Guardians of The Grasslands. The First Hundred Years of the Wyoming Stock Growers Association. Cheyenne: 1971. V. 64; 67

BURROUGHS, LAURA LEE
Flower Arranging. A Fascinating Hobby. (with) *Flower Arranging. A Fascinating Hobby. Volume II.* Atlanta: 1940-1942. V. 62

BURROUGHS, SAMUEL
An Enquiry into the Customary Estates and Tenant Rights of Those Who Hold Lands of Church and Other Foundations, by the Tenure of Three Lives and Twenty-One Years. London: 1731. V. 62

BURROUGHS, STEPHEN
Sketch of the Life of the Notorious.... Hudson. V. 66

BURROUGHS, WILLIAM S.
The Adding Machine. London: 1985. V. 67
The Adding Machine. New York: 1986. V. 67
Ali's Smile/Naked Scientology. Gottingen: 1978. V. 67
Blade Runner (A Movie). Berkeley: 1976. V. 67
Blade Runner (A Movie). Berkeley: 1979. V. 66
The Book of Breathing. Berkeley: 1975. V. 67
The Book of Breathing. Berkeley: 1980. V. 62
The Burroughs File. San Francisco: 1984. V. 67
Cities of the Red Night. New York: 1981. V. 67
Cobble Stone Gardens. N.P: 1976. V. 67
Dead Fingers Talk. London: 1963. V. 66; 67
The Dead Star. San Francisco: 1969. V. 67
Doctor Benway. Santa Barbara: 1979. V. 67
Early Routines. Santa Barbara: 1981. V. 67
The Exterminator. San Francisco: 1960. V. 62; 67
Exterminator!. New York: 1973. V. 65
The Four Horsemen of the Apocalypse. Germany: 1984. V. 67
Ghost of a Chance. New York: 1991. V. 62; 64
Ghost of Chance. London: 1995. V. 67
The Job. Interviews with William S. Burroughs. New York: 1970. V. 64
Junkie. 1966. V. 64
The Last Words of Dutch Schultz. London: 1970. V. 66; 67
Letters to Allen Ginsberg 1953-1957. New York: 1982. V. 62; 64; 67
Mummies. Dusseldorf/New York: 1982. V. 66
The Naked Lunch. New York: 1959. V. 62; 63
The Naked Lunch. Paris: 1959. V. 62; 65; 66
The Naked Lunch. London: 1964. V. 66
Nova Express. London: 1966. V. 63
The Place of Dead Roads. New York: 1983. V. 62
The Place of Dead Roads. New York: 1984. V. 67
Ruski. Brooklyn: 1984. V. 67
The Seven Deadly Sins. New York: 1991. V. 63; 65
Sinki's Sauna. New York: 1982. V. 67
The Soft Machine. Paris: 1961. V. 62
The Third Mind. New York: 1978. V. 67
The Ticket that Exploded. Paris: 1962. V. 62; 67
The Ticket that Exploded. 1967. V. 62
The Ticket that Exploded. New York: 1967. V. 65
Tornado Alley. N.P: 1989. V. 67
White Subway. London: 1973. V. 67

BURROW, J. C.
'Mongst Mines and Miners; or Underground Scenes by Flashlight: a Series of Photographs, with Explanatory Letterpress, Illustrating Methods of Working in Cornish Mine. London and Camborne: 1893. V. 65

BURROWES, J. F.
The Piano-Forte Primer, Containing the Rudiments of Music.... London: 1823. V. 65

BURROWS, GEORGE
On Disorders of the Cerebral and Circulation and on the Connection Between Affections of the Brain and Diseases of the Hear. Philadelphia: 1848. V. 66

BURROWS, GEORGE MAN
Commentaries on the Causes, Forms, Symptoms and Treatment, Moral and Medical of Insanity. London: 1828. V. 65
An Inquiry Into Certain Errors Relative to Insanity; and Their Consequences, Physical, Moral and Civil. London: 1820. V. 65

BURROWS, GUY
The Curse of Central Africa. London: 1903. V. 62

BURROWS, MONTAGU
The Family of Brocas of Beaurepaire and Roche Court, Hereditary Masters of the Royal Buckhounds, with Some Account of the Englifmhissh Rule in Aquitaine. 1886. V. 67

BURROWS, SILAS E.
America and Russia. Correspondence 1818 to 1848. N.P: 1849. V. 63

BURRUS, ERNEST J.
Kino and the Cartography of Northwestern New Spain. Tucson: 1965. V. 62; 64; 65; 66

BURSCOUGH, WILLIAM
The Question About Eating Blood Stated and Examined.... Dublin: 1733. V. 65
A Sermon Preach'd in Christ's Church, Dublin; Before His Exellency John, Lord Carteret, Lord Lieutenant General, of Ireland. Dublin: 1725. V. 65

BURSLEM, ROLLO
A Peep Into Toorkistan. London: 1846. V. 64

BURT, GEORGE
Notes of a Three Months' Trip to Egypt, Greece, Constantinople and the Eastern Shores of the Mediterranean Sea. London: 1878. V. 64

BURT, JOHN T.
Results of the System of Separate Confinement, as Administered at the Pentonville Prison. London: 1852. V. 65

BURT, S. W.
The Rocky Mountain Gold Regions. Denver: 1962. V. 65; 67

BURTIS, THOMSON
Flying Blood. New York: 1932. V. 67

BURTON, ALFRED
The Adventures of Johnny Newcome in the Navy: a Poem. London: 1818. V. 62

BURTON, E. F.
Reminiscences of Sport in India. 1885. V. 62; 63; 64; 66; 67

BURTON, EDWARD
A Description of the Antiquities and Other Curiosities of Rome; from Personal Observation During a Visit to Italy in the Years 1818-1819. London: 1828. V. 66

BURTON, HARLY TRUE
The History of the J. A. Ranch. New York: 1966. V. 63

BURTON, ISABEL
The Life of Captain Sir Rich'd Burton.... London: 1893. V. 64

BURTON, J. A.
Owls of the World, their Evolution, Structre and Ecology. New York: 1973. V. 67

BURTON, J. W.
The Fui of To-Day. London: 1910. V. 64

BURTON, JOHN
Lectures on Female Education and Manners. Dublin: 1794. V. 64; 65
The Parish Priest; a Poem. London: 1800. V. 62; 65
The Present State of Navigation on the Thames Considered; and Certain Regulations Proposed. Oxford: 1767. V. 63

BURTON, JOHN HILL
The Book Hunter, Etc. Edinburgh: 1882. V. 63
Political and Social Economy.... Edinburgh: 1848. V. 64
Political and Social Economy.... Edinburgh: 1849. V. 64

BURTON, KATHERINE
A Memoir of Mrs. Curdelius. Edinburgh: 1879. V. 65
St. Columba with Part of a Poem by St. Columba. 1939. V. 67

BURTON, MILES
Early Morning Murder. London: 1945. V. 65; 67
Situation Vacant. London: 1945. V. 65
Situation Vacant. London: 1946. V. 65

BURTON, PHILIP
The Practice in the Office of Pleas of the Court of Exchequer Epitomised. London: 1770. V. 63

BURTON, R. G.
A Book of Man-Eaters. 1931. V. 64
The Tiger Hunters. 1936. V. 62; 63

BURTON, RICHARD
Admirable Curiosities, Rarities and Wonders in England, Scotland and Ireland. Westminster: 1811. V. 66

BURTON, RICHARD FRANCIS
Abeokuta and the Cameroons Mountains: an Exploration. London: 1863. V. 62; 67
The Book of the Sword. London: 1884. V. 64; 66; 67
The City of the Saints and Across the Rocky Mountains to California. London: 1862. V. 62; 67
The City of the Saints and Across the Rocky Mountains to California. New York: 1862. V. 66
Etruscan Bologna. London: 1876. V. 64; 67
First Footsteps in East Africa; or an Exploration of Harar. London: 1856. V. 64; 65
First Footsteps in East Africa, or Exploration of Harare. 1982. V. 63
Goa, and the Blue Mountains; or, Six Months of Sick Leave. London: 1851. V. 64
The Gold-Mines of Midian; and the Ruined Midianite Cities. London: 1878. V. 62; 64; 67
The Highlands of Brazil. London: 1869. V. 66; 67
The Jew, The Gypsy and El Islam. London: 1898. V. 64
The Kasidah of Haji Abdu Al-Yazdi. London: 1900. V. 64
The Kasidah of Haji Abdu el-Yenzdi. Portland: 1915. V. 64
The Kasidah of Haji Abdu El-Yezdi. Philadelphia: 1931. V. 67
Lake Regions of Central Africa. London: 1860. V. 64
The Land of Midian (Revisited). London: 1879. V. 62; 67
The Lands of Cazembe in 1798. London: 1873. V. 64
Letters from the Battle-fields of Paraguay. London: 1870. V. 62; 66; 67
A Mission to Gelele, King of Dahome. London: 1864. V. 64; 66; 67
A Mission to Gelele King of Dahome. London: 1893. V. 67
A New System of Sword Exercise for Infantry. London: 1876. V. 64
The Nile Basin. London: 1864. V. 62; 66
Personal Narrative of a Pilgrimage to El-Medinah and Meccah. London: 1855-1856. V. 62; 67
Personal Narrative of a Pilgrimage to Mecca and Medina. Leipzig: 1874. V. 62
Pilgrimage to Al-Madinah and Meccah. London: 1898. V. 64
Sind Revisited; with Notices of the Anglo-Indian Army: Railroads, Past, Present and Future. London: 1877. V. 66; 67
Ultima Thule; or, a Summer in Iceland. London: 1875. V. 63
Unexplored Syria. London: 1872. V. 66; 67
Voyage aux Grands Lacs de L'Afrique Orientale. Paris: 1862. V. 67
Wanderings in Three Continents. London: 1901. V. 67
Wanderings in West Africa. London: 1863. V. 62; 65; 67
Zanzibar: City Island and Coast. London: 1872. V. 64

BURTON, ROBERT
The Anatomy of Melancholy. Oxford: 1660. V. 62; 64; 66
The Anatomy of Melancholy. London: 1676. V. 65; 66
The Anatomy of Melancholy. London: 1827. V. 63; 64
The Anatomy of Melancholy. London: 1837. V. 64
The Anatomy of Melancholy. London: 1840. V. 63
The Anatomy of Melancholy. London: 1907. V. 63
The Anatomy of Melancholy. London: 1925. V. 65
Melancholy: as It Proceeds from the Disposition and Habit, the Passion of Love and the Influence of Religion. London: 1801. V. 66

BURTON, THOMA DE
Chronica Monasterii de Melsa, a Fundatione Usque ad Annum 1396. London: 1866-1868. V. 66

BURTON, THOMAS
Diary of Thomas Burton, Esq. Member in the Parliaments of Oliver and Richard Cromwell from 1656 to 1659.... London: 1828. V. 63

BURTON, WILLIAM
A Commentary on Antoninus, His Itinerary, or Journies of the Roman Empire, So Far As It Concerneth Britain.... London: 1658. V. 64; 67
A Pasquinade, on the Performers of the York Company. Leeds: 1801. V. 64

BURTON, WILLIAM E.
Bibliotheca Dramatica. Catalogue of the Theatrical and Miscellaneous Library of the Late William E. Burton.... New York: 1860. V. 63

BURTON, WILLIAM WESTBROOKE
The State of Religion and Education in New South Wales. London: 1840. V. 64

BURY, ADRIAN
Joseph Crawhall, the Man and the Artist. 1957. V. 67
Shadow of Eros: a Biographical and Critical Study of the Life and Works of Sir Alfred Gilbert. 1952. V. 62

BURY, CHARLOTTE SUSAN MARIA
Conduct is Fate. Edinburgh: 1822. V. 63; 65
Diary Illustrative of the Times of George the Fourth. London: 1838-1839. V. 62
The Divorced. London: 1837. V. 65
The Exclusives. London: 1830. V. 65
Journal of the Heart, by the Authoress of Flirtation. London: 1835. V. 63

BURY, G. WYMAN
Arabia Infelix; or the Turks in Yamen. London: 1915. V. 64

BURY, J. B.
The Cambridge Ancient History: Volume of Plates.... Cambridge: 1927-1939. V. 65

BURY, T. T.
Coloured Views on the Liverpool and Manchester Railway. Oldham: 1976. V. 62

BUSBEQUIUS, A. GISLENIUS
Omnia Quae Extant. Leyden: 1633. V. 66

BUSBY, CHARLES AUGUSTINE
A Series of Designs for Villas and Country Houses. London: 1808. V. 64

BUSBY, JAMES
Journal of a Recent Visit to the Principal Vineyards of Spain and France. New York: 1835. V. 66

BUSBY, SAMUEL
A Report of the Trial of Samuel Busby and Judith His Wife, Upon the Three Several Indictments for the Unnatural Treatment of Their Children... Tuesday 2d July, 1793.... Dublin: 1793. V. 63

BUSBY, T. L.
The Fishing Costume and Local Scenery of Hartlepool, in the County of Durham, Painted and Engraved from Nature. London: 1819. V. 66

BUSCAGLIA, LEO F.
The Way of the Bull. N.P: 1973. V. 66

BUSCH, FREDERICK
Breathing Trouble and Other Stories. London: 1973. V. 64
Domestic Particulars. A Family Chronicle. New York: 1976. V. 66
I Wanted a Year Without Fall. London: 1971. V. 63
Manual Labor. New York: 1974. V. 66

BUSCH, WILHELM
Schnaken & Schnurren. (Joking and Joking). Munchen: 1892-1895. V. 64

BUSH, GEORGE
Looking Forward. New York: 1987. V. 63; 65

BUSH, I. J.
Gringo Doctor. Caldwell: 1939. V. 67

BUSH, RICHARD J.
Reindeer, Dogs and Snow-Shoes; a Journal of Siberian Travel and Explorations Made in the Years 1865, 1866 and 1867. London: 1871. V. 64

BUSH, VANNEVAR
Pieces of the Action. New York: 1970. V. 63

BUSHELL, STEPHEN W.
Catalogue of the Morgan Collection of Chinese Porcelains. New York: 1910. V. 67
Oriental Ceramic Art Illustrated by Examples from the Collection of W. T. Walters. New York: 1980. V. 63

BUSHICK, FRANK H.
Glamorous Days. San Antonio: 1934. V. 64; 67

BUSHONG, MILLARD K.
Fightin' Tom Roster, C.S.A. Shippensburg: 1983. V. 66
General Turner Ashby and Stonewall's Valley Campaign. Verona: 1980. V. 66
Historic Jefferson County. Boyce. 1972. V. 64

BUSK, G.
A Monograph of the Fossil Polyzoa of the Crag. 1859. V. 63; 66
Note on a Ready Method of Measuring the Cubic Capacity of Skulls. 1870. V. 67

BUSK, HANS
The Rifle; and How to Use It. London: 1859. V. 64; 67

BUSK, RACHEL HENRIETTE
Sagas from the Far East; or Kalmouk and Mongolian Traditionary Tales. London: 1873. V. 67

BUSTER Brown. London: 1905. V. 62
BUSTER Brown. London: 1910. V. 65

THE BUSTLE; a Philosophical and Moral Poem. Boston: 1845. V. 62

BUSWELL, LESLIE
Ambulance No. 10, Personal Letters from the Front. Boston and New York: 1916. V. 63

BUTCHER, DAVID
The Stanbrook Abbey Press, 1956-1990. Herefordshire: 1992. V. 64
The Stanbrook Abbey Press 1956-1990. Lower Marston: 1992. V. 63

BUTCHER, E.
Sidmouth Scenery; or, Views of the Principal Cottages and Residences of the Nobility and Gentry.... Sidmouth: 1817. V. 66

BUTLER, ALBAN
The Lives of the Fathers, Martyrs and Other Principal Saints. Dublin: 1779-1880. V. 65
The Lives of the Fathers, Martyrs and Other Principal Saints. London: 1926. V. 64

BUTLER, ARTHUR G.
Birds of Great Britain and Ireland, Order Passeres. Hull and London: 1907-1908. V. 65
British Birds with Their Nests and Eggs. London: 1896-1898. V. 62; 63; 67
Foreign Finches in Captivity. Hull and London: 1899. V. 64; 67
Illustrations of Typical Specimens of Lepidoptera Heterocera in the Collection of the British Museums. London: 1878. V. 62

BUTLER, CATHARINE O'BRIEN
Some Particulars of the Case, Wherein the Lessee of Catharine O'Brien Butler was Plaintiff, and the Rev. A. Dunn, Defendant, Tried at the Trim Assizes, Aug. 24, 1802. Manchester: 1805. V. 63

BUTLER, CHARLES
The Feminine Monarchie; or the Historie of Bees. London: 1623. V. 64; 66
Historical Memoirs Respecting the English, Irish and Scottish Catholics. 1819. V. 67
The Life of Fenelon, Archbishop of Cambray. London: 1810. V. 62
Reminiscences of Charles Butler, Esq. 1827. V. 67
Reminiscences of Charles Butler, Esq. (with) A Letter to a Lady on Ancient and Modern Music. 1824-1827. V. 64

BUTLER, DAVID
The Quaker Meeting Houses of Britain. London: 1999. V. 64; 66

BUTLER, E.
An Essay On Our Indian Question. New York: 1882. V. 62; 65

BUTLER, ELLIS PARKER
Philo Gubb: Correspondence School Detective. Boston: 1918. V. 65; 67

BUTLER, FREDERICK
The Farmer's Manual...on the Art of Husbandry.... Weatherfield: 1821. V. 64

BUTLER, H. J.
The Black Book of Edgeworthtown and Other Edgeworth Memories 1585-1817. 1927. V. 65

BUTLER, HENRY
South African Sketches: Illustrative of the Wild Life of a Hunter on the Frontier of the Cape Colony. London: 1841. V. 66; 67

BUTLER, J. R.
Floralia, Garden Paths and By-Paths of the Eighteenth Century. Chapel Hill: 1938. V. 67

BUTLER, JAMES D.
Nebraska Its Characteristics and Prospects. N.P: 1873. V. 63

BUTLER, JOHN
Christian Liberty Asserted in Oposition (sic) to the Roman Yoke. Delivered in a Sermon Preached in His Majesties Royal Chapel of Windsor. The 8th of Decemb. 1678. London: 1678. V. 66
A Consultation on the Subject of a Standing Army, Held at the King's Arms Tavern, on the Twenty-Eighth day of February 1763. London: 1763. V. 63

BUTLER, JOSEPH
The Analogy of Religion, Natural and Revealed, to the Constitution and Course of Nature. London: 1736. V. 66

BUTLER, JOSEPHINE E.
Personal Reminiscences of a Great Crusade. London: 1911. V. 65

BUTLER, MANN
A History of the Commonwealth of Kentucky. Louisville: 1834. V. 66

BUTLER, MARY
The Tryal and Conviction of Mary Butler, Alias Strickland, at Justice-Hall in the Old-Baily, in London, on the 12th Day of October, 1699. London: 1700. V. 65

BUTLER, MATHEW C.
Speeches on the Race Problem. Gaffney: 1899. V. 65

BUTLER, RICHARD
Annals of Ireland. 1849. V. 64
Registrum Prioratus Omnium Sanctorum Juxta. Dublin: 1845. V. 64; 67
Some Notices of the Castle and of the Ecclesiastical Buildings of Trim. Dublin: 1861. V. 65

BUTLER, ROBERT OLEN
The Alleys of Eden. New York: 1981. V. 62; 63; 64; 65; 66; 67
Countrymen of Bones. New York: 1983. V. 62; 64; 65; 67
The Duece. New York: 1989. V. 64
A Good Scent from a Strange Mountain. New York: 1991. V. 67
A Good Scent from a Strange Mountain. 1992. V. 64; 65
A Good Scent from a Strange Mountain. New York: 1992. V. 65; 66; 67
Mr. Spaceman. New York: 2000. V. 67
On Distant Ground. New York: 1985. V. 65; 66; 67
Sun Dogs. New York: 1981. V. 66
Sun Dogs. New York: 1982. V. 62; 64; 65; 66
Tabloid Dreams. New York: 1996. V. 64; 67
They Whisper. Huntington Beach: 1994. V. 63; 66
Wabash. New York: 1987. V. 63; 64; 66; 67

BUTLER, SAMUEL
Butleriana. London: 1932. V. 63; 64; 65
Erewhon. 1923. V. 67
Erewhon. New York: 1934. V. 62
The Genuine Poetical Remains.... London: 1827. V. 67
The Genuine Remains in Verse and Prose of Mr. Samuel Butler, Author of Hudibras. London: 1759. V. 63; 67
Hudibras. London: 1663-1664. V. 62
Hudibras. London: 1674. V. 66
Hudibras. London: 1716. V. 67
Hudibras. Cambridge: 1744. V. 64
Hudibras. Dublin: 1744. V. 62
Hudibras. Glasgow: 1763. V. 62
Hudibras. London: 1764. V. 63
Hudibras. Troy: 1806. V. 62; 63
Hudibras. London: 1819. V. 62; 64; 65; 66; 67
The Posthumous Works. London: 1730. V. 62
The Posthumous Works. London: 1732. V. 64

BUTLER, SAMUEL, BP. OF LICHFIELD & COVENTRY
A Letter to Henry Brougham, Esq. M.P. On Certain Clauses in the Education Bills Now Before Parliament. Shrewsbury: 1820. V. 65

BUTLER, W. F. T.
Gleanings from Irish History. 1925. V. 67

BUTLER, WEEDEN
The Cheltenham Guide; or, Useful Companion, in the Journey of Health and Pleasure to the Cheltenham Spa. 1781. V. 65

BUTLER, WILLIAM ARCHER
Lectures on the History of Ancient Philosophy. London: 1856. V. 62

BUTLER, WILLIAM F.
Sir William Butler: an Autobiography. London: 1911. V. 63

BUTLER, WILLIAM FRANCIS
The Great Lone Land. London: 1872. V. 64
The Great Lone Land. London: 1874. V. 67

BUTLIN, MARTIN
The Paintings of J. M. W. Turner. New Haven: 1984. V. 67

BUTOR, MICHEL
Passage de Milan. Paris: 1954. V. 67

BUTT, KHAN S. J.
Shikar. 1963. V. 67

BUTTER, WILLIAM
A Treatise on the Disease Commonly Called Angina Pectoris. London: 1791. V. 65

BUTTERFIELD, CONSUL W.
An Historical Account of the Expedition Against Sandusky Under Col. William Crawford in 1782. Cincinnati: 1873. V. 65
Washington-Irvine Correspondence. The Official Letters Which Passed Between Washington and Brig. Gen. William Irvine...Concerning Military Affairs in the West from 1781 to 1783. Madison: 1882. V. 67

BUTTERFIELD, LINDSAY
Flora Forms in Historic Design. London. V. 62

BUTTIKER, W.
Fauna of Saudi Arabia. Basel: 1993. V. 66

BUTTRE, J. C.
Catalogue of Engravings by J. C. Buttre, Publisher, Engraver and Plate Printer. New York: 1870. V. 62

BUTTS, CHARLES
Geology of the Appalachian Valley in Virginia. 1941. V. 65

BUTTS, MARY
Ashe of Rings. London: 1933. V. 64
The Crystal Cabinet - My Childhood at Salterns. London: 1937. V. 62
Last Stories. 1938. V. 63
Scenes from the Life of Cleopatra. London: 1935. V. 66
Traps for Unbelievers. London: 1932. V. 62

BUXBAUM, EDWIN C.
Collector's Guide to the National Geographic Magazine. Wilmington: 1971. V. 66

BUXTON, CHARLES
Memoirs of Sir Thomas Bowell Buxton. London: 1855. V. 67

BUXTON, EDWARD NORTH
Short Stalks. 1892. V. 62; 64; 66
Short Stalks; or Hunting Camps North, South, East and West. London: 1893. V. 67
Short Stalks. Second Series. London: 1898. V. 67
Two African Trips. London: 1902. V. 66; 67

BUXTON, H. MAUDE
On Either Side of the Red Sea. London: 1895. V. 62

BUXTON, NOEL
Travel and Politics in Armenia. London: 1914. V. 64

BUXTON, THOMAS FOWELL
The African Slave Trade. London: 1839. V. 62; 65
The African Slave Trade and Its Remedy. London: 1840. V. 63
Memoirs.... London: 1852. V. 67
Memoirs.... London: 1860. V. 64; 67

BUXTORF, JOHANN
Lexicon Chaldaicum, Talmudicum et Rabbinicum. Basle: 1640. V. 62; 65
Synagoga Judaica Noviter Restaurata.... Frankfurt: 1728. V. 64

BUYALSKI, ILYA VASILEVICH
An Anatomical Description of Changes Found in the Human Body, to the Heart (etc.) Due to the Failure of the Spleen. St. Petersburg: 1829. V. 67

BYARS, BETSY
The Summer of the Swans. New York: 1970. V. 65

BYATT, A. S.
Angels and Insects. London: 1992. V. 63
Angels and Insects. New York: 1992. V. 67
Angels and Insects. Franklin Center: 1993. V. 62
Babel Tower. Franklin Center: 1996. V. 62
Babel Tower. London: 1996. V. 62; 67
Babel Tower. New York: 1996. V. 67
The Djinn in the Nightingale's Eye. London: 1994. V. 67
The Game. London: 1967. V. 62
Heavenly Bodies. Atlanta: 1999. V. 66
Possession. London: 1990. V. 62; 64

BYATT, A. S. *continued*
Possession. New York: 1990. V. 67
Still Life. New York: 1983. V. 67
Wordsworth and Coleridge in their Time. London: 1970. V. 62

BYE, JOHN O.
Back Trailing in the Heart of the Short Grass Country. N.P: 1956. V. 66

BYERS, S. H. M.
With Fire and Sword. New York: 1911. V. 62; 63; 65

BYFIELD, NATHANAEL
An Account of the Late Revolution in New England. Together with the Declartation of the Gentlemen, Merchants and Inhabitants of Boston and the Country Adjacent. London: 1689. V. 63; 66

BYLES, C. E.
The Life and Letters of R. S. Hawker (Sometime Vicar of Morwenstow) by His Son-in-Law. London: 1905. V. 62; 66

BYLLESBY, LANGDON
Observations on the Sources and Effects of Unequal Wealth.... New York: 1826. V. 62

BYNE, M. STAPLEY
The Sculptured Capital in Spain: a Series of Examples Dating from 6th to 16th Century. New York: 1926. V. 62; 65
Spanish Gardens and Patios. New York: 1924. V. 63

BYNG, ARTHUR H.
The Autobiography of an English Gamekeeper (John Wilkins of Stanstead Essex). London: 1892. V. 67

BYNG, JOHN
An Exact Copy of a Letter from Admiral Byng to the Right. Hon. W(illiam) P(itt), Esq., dated March 12, 1757, Two Days Before His Execution. London: 1757. V. 65
The Torrington Diaries. London: 1934-1938. V. 62

BYNNER, WITTER
Tiger. New York: 1913. V. 62; 66

BYRD, CECIL K.
A Bibliography of Illinois Imprints 1814-1858. Chicago. 1966. V. 64

BYRD, RICHARD EVELYN
Alone. New York: 1938. V. 63
Anarctic Discovery: the Story of the Second Byrd Antarctic Expedition. London: 1936. V. 64
Discovery. New York: 1935. V. 64; 66
Little America. New York: 1930. V. 63; 64; 66

BYRD, WILLIAM
Another Secret Diary of William Byrd of Westover 1739-1741.... Richmond: 1942. V. 67
The Westover Manuscripts.... Petersburg: 1841. V. 66
The Writings of Colonel William Byrd of Westover in Virginia. New York: 1901. V. 63; 66

BYRNE, BERNARD J.
A Frontier Army Surgeon...Colorado in the Eighties. Cranford: 1935. V. 65; 67

BYRNE, DAVID
Strange Ritual. San Francisco: 1995. V. 65

BYRNE, DAWSON
The Story of Ireland's National Theatre. Dublin: 1929. V. 67

BYRNE, DONN
Crusade. Boston: 1928. V. 67
Field of Honor. New York: 1929. V. 66
The Power of the Dog. 1929. V. 67

BYRNE, JAMES
Sketch of the Life and Unparalleled Suffings of James Bryne, Late Coachman to the Honourable John Jocelyn, Brother to the Father In God.... London: 1822. V. 63

BYRNE, JULIA CLARA BUSK
Curiosities of the Search-Room. London: 1880. V. 65
Realities of Paris Life. London: 1859. V. 64; 65
Undercurrents Overlooked. London: 1860. V. 62

BYRNE, L. S. R.
The Eton Book of the River with Some Account of the Thames and the Evolution of Boat-Racing. London: 1935. V. 65

BYRNE, OLIVER
The Handbook for the Artisan, Mechanic and Engineer. Philadelphia: 1863. V. 65

BYRNE, P. E.
Soldiers of the Plains. New York: 1926. V. 65; 67

BYRNES, THOMAS
1886 Professional Criminals of America. New York City: 1969. V. 63

BYROM, JOHN
A Catalogue of the Library of the Late John Byrom, Esq.... London: 1848. V. 65
The Universal English Short-Hand, or the Way of Writing English in the Most Easy, Concise, Regular and Beautiful Manner. Manchester: 1767. V. 67

BYRON, GEORGE GORDON NOEL, 6TH BARON
Beppo, a Venetian Story. London: 1818. V. 65
Byron - A Self Portrait: letters and Diaries 1798-1824. London: 1950. V. 65
Byron's Works. London. V. 62
Cain, a Mystery. London: 1822. V. 63
Childe Harold's Pilgrimage. London: 1812. V. 67
Childe Harold's Pilgrimage. London: 1812-1818. V. 62
Childe Harold's Pilgrimage. London: 1845. V. 66
Childe Harold's Pilgrimage. Paris and London: 1931. V. 63
The Complete Works. Mannheim: 1837-1838. V. 62
Correspondence of Lord Byron, with a Friend. Paris: 1825. V. 64
The Corsair. London: 1814. V. 63; 64; 66
Don Juan. London: 1819. V. 65
Don Juan. (Cantos I-V). London: 1822. V. 67
English Bards and Scotch Reviewers. London: 1809. V. 65
English Bards and Scotch Reviewers. London: 1810. V. 62; 67
The Genuine Rejected Addresses, Presented to the Committee...for Drury Lane Theatre.... London: 1812. V. 66
Hebrew Melodies. (with) The Prisoner of Chillon and Other Poems. London: 1815-1816. V. 64
Hours of Idleness, a Series of Poems, Original and Translated. Newark: 1807. V. 62; 65
The Island, or Christian and His Comrades. Philadelphia: 1823. V. 64
Lara, a Tale. Jacqueline, a Tale. London: 1814. V. 63
Letters and Journals of Lord Byron; with Notices of His Life. London: 1830. V. 67
Manfred. London: 1929. V. 64
Marino Faliero, Doge of Venice. London: 1821. V. 63; 65; 66; 67
Mazeppa. London: 1819. V. 65
Mazeppa. New York: 1819. V. 65
Poems. London: 1816. V. 62; 64
Poems, Consisting of the Giaour, the Bride of Abydos, the Corsair, Lara. London: 1846. V. 64; 65
The Poetical Works. London: 1851. V. 63
The Poetical Works. London: 1864. V. 64
The Poetical Works. London: 1873. V. 62; 67
The Poetical Works. London: 1879. V. 67
Prisoner of Chillon. London: 1816. V. 64
The Prisoner of Chillon. London: 1865. V. 65
Sardanapalus, a Tragedy. The Two Foscari, a Tragedy. Cain, a Mystery. London: 1821. V. 62; 63; 64; 65
The Siege of Corinth. A Poem. Parisina. A Poem. London: 1816. V. 62; 65
Tales and Poems. London: 1853. V. 65
Waltz; an Apostrohic Hymn. London: 1821. V. 62; 65
Werner, a Tragedy. London: 1823. V. 65
Works. London: 1815. V. 62
Works. London: 1816. V. 62
The Works. Philadelphia: 1816. V. 62
The Works. London: 1819. V. 62; 65
The Works. Philadelphia: 1825. V. 66
The Works. London: 1825-1826. V. 62; 64
The Works. London: 1827. V. 67
The Works. Paris: 1827. V. 62
The Works. London: 1834-1832-1833. V. 64
The Works. 1898-1901. V. 65
The Works. London: 1898-1904. V. 67

BYRON, JOHN
Byron's Journal of His Circum-Navigation 1764-1766. Cambridge: 1964. V. 63; 64; 66
The Narrative of the Honourable John Byron (Commodore in a Late Expediton Round the World).... London: 1768. V. 64
The Narrative of the Honourable John Byron, Containing an Account of the Great Distresses, Suffered by Himself and His Companions on the Coasts of Patagonia from the Year 1740. London: 1780. V. 64
The Universal English Short-Hand.... Manchester: 1767. V. 62
A Voyage Round the World in His Majesty's Ship the Dolphin.... London: 1767. V. 64

BYRON, MAY
The Adventures of Trooper Peek-a-Boo. London: 1916. V. 67
Barbara Peek-A-Boo's Holiday. London: 1920. V. 63
Cecil Aldin's Happy Family with Stories. London: 1912. V. 63
Cecil Aldin's Merry Party. London: 1913. V. 63
Humpty Dumpty Give a Fancy Dress Ball. London: 1913. V. 65
Jack and Jill. New York: 1914. V. 66
The Little Small Red Hen. London: 1910. V. 62
The Magic Map Book. New York. V. 63

BYRON, ROBERT
The Birth of Western Printing - a History of Colour, Form and Iconography.... London: 1930. V. 64
The Byzantine Achievement in Historical Perspective A.D. 330-1453. London: 1929. V. 64
First Russia Then Tibet. London: 1933. V. 64
Imperial Pilgrimage. London: 1937. V. 66
Innocence and Design. London: 1935. V. 65
Letters Home. London: 1991. V. 65
The Station. London: 1928. V. 62
The Station Athos, Treasures and Men. London: 1949. V. 66

BYRRNE, E. FAIRFAX
The Heir Without a Heritage. London: 1887. V. 65

BYSSHE, EDWARD
The Art of English Poetry. London: 1705. V. 64
The Art of English Poetry. London: 1718. V. 66
The Art of English Poetry. London: 1762. V. 64; 65

BYTHNER, VICTORINUS
Lyra Prophetica Davidis Regis. London: 1664. V. 66

C

C. A. T. *Spells Cat.* London: 1910. V. 62

C., E.,
The Worhsip of Bacchus a Great Delusion. London: 1876. V. 63

CABALA: Sive Scrinia Sacra. *Mysteries of State and Government of Letters of Illustrious Persons....* London: 1663. V. 65

CABANIS, PIERRE JEAN GEORGES
Rapports du Physique et du Moral de l'Homme.... Paris: 1855. V. 63

CABANNE, P.
The Brothers Duchamp: Jacques Villon, Raymond Duchamp-Villon, Marcel Duchamp. 1976. V. 62; 65

CABATON, A.
Java and the Dutch East Indies. London: 1912. V. 64

CABELL, JAMES BRANCH
The First Gentleman of America. 1942. V. 67
Jurgen. Waltham St. Lawrence: 1949. V. 62
Jurgen. Westport: 1976. V. 63; 64
The Music from Behind the Moon. 1926. V. 67
Smirt. 1934. V. 67
Some of Us: An Essay in Epitaphs. New York: 1930. V. 67
Sonnets from Antan with an Editorial Note.... New York: 1929. V. 66
Straws and Prayer Books. 1924. V. 67
The Way to Ecben. 1929. V. 67
The White Robe. 1928. V. 67

CABELL, JULIA
Sketches and Recollections of Lynchburg. Richmond: 1858. V. 64; 66

CABET, ETIENNE
Voyage en Icarie, Roman Philosophique et Social.... Paris: 1842. V. 62; 65

THE CABIN *Boy's Companion.* London: 1830. V. 62

CABINET *Maker's Album of Furniture; Comprising a Collection of Designs for the Newest and Most Elegant Styles of Furniture....* Philadelphia: 1868. V. 62; 64

THE CABINET *of Natural History, and American Rural Sports.* Philadelphia: 1830-1832. V. 64; 67

THE CABINET *of the Scottish Muses....* Edinburgh: 1808. V. 62

CABLE, GEORGE WASHINGTON
Dr. Sevier. A Novel. Edinburgh: 1884. V. 64
Old Creole Days. New York: 1879. V. 63; 66
The Southern Struggle for Pure Government. Boston: 1890. V. 63

CABOT, JAMES ELIOT
A Memoir of Ralph Waldo Emerson. Boston: 1887. V. 64

CABOT, L.
The Immature State of the Odonata. Part I. Subfamily Gomphina. Part II. Subfamily Aeschina. Cambridge: 1872-1881. V. 64; 65

CABRAL, PEDRO ALVARES
The Voyage of Pedro Alvares Cabral to Brazil and India. London: 1938. V. 63; 64

CABRERA INFANTE, G.
Asi en la Paz Como en La Guerra. Havana: 1960. V. 67
Infante's Inferno. New York: 1984. V. 63
Three Trapped Tigers. New York: 1971. V. 62; 67

CACHET, CHRISTOPHER
Pandora Bacchica Furens Medicis Armis Oppugnata, Hic Temulentiae Ortus et Progressus ex Antiquorum Monumentisi Investigatur. Toul: 1614. V. 64

THE CACIQUE *of Ontario, Being an Entertaining Moral and Instructive History of Two Lovers, Founded Upon Facts.* Stonington Port: 1799. V. 62

CADBURY, EDWARD
Sweating. London: 1907. V. 64

CADBURY, GEORGE
Town Planning, with Special Reference to the Birmingham Schemes. London: 1915. V. 64

CADBURY, RICHARD
Cocoa: All About It. London: 1896. V. 66; 67

CADELL, W. A.
A Journey in Carniola, Italy and France, in the Years 1817, 1818. Edinburgh: 1820. V. 66

CADFRYN-ROBERTS, JOHN
The Four Seasons of Sport. London: 1960. V. 64; 67

CADMAN, A.
Tales of a Wildfowler. 1957. V. 67

CADMAN, HENRY
Harry Druidale, Fisherman, from Manxland to England. London: 1898. V. 62; 63; 65

CADMAN, S. PARKES
The Parables of Jesus. Philadelphia: 1931. V. 64

CADOGAN, WILLIAM
A Dissertation on the Gout, and all Chronic Diseases. London: 1771. V. 65

CADY, HARRISON
A Great Feast on Butternut Hill. Racine: 1929. V. 64; 65
A Harrison Cady Picture Book. Racine: 1928. V. 65
Holiday Time on Butternut Hill. Racine: 1929. V. 63
Peter Rabbit: Series B-1 Story Painting and Crayon Book. New York: 1923. V. 64
Peter Rabbit: Series B-3 Story Painting and Crayon Book. New York: 1923. V. 64
Peter Rabbit: Series B-4 Story Painting and Crayon Book. New York: 1923. V. 64
Time on Butternut Hill. Racine: 1929. V. 65
When the Circus Comes to Town. Racine: 1928. V. 64

CADY, JOHN H.
Arizona's Yesterday. Patagonia: 1915. V. 64
Arizona's Yesterday. Patagonia: 1916. V. 64; 67

CAELIUS AURELIANUS
Caelius Aurelianus. On Acute Diseases and on Chronic Diseases. Chicago: 1950. V. 64
Liber Celerum el Acuturum Passionu(m).... Paris: 1533. V. 63

CAESAR, GAIUS JULIUS
C. Julii Caesaris Quae Exstant.... 1693. V. 66
C. Julii Caesaris Quae Extant. Accuratissime cum Libris Editis & MSSS Optimis Collata, Recognita & Correcta. London: 1712. V. 64
Commentaries. London: 1737. V. 67
The Commentaries. London: 1755. V. 66
The Commentaries. London: 1870. V. 62; 67
Commentaries. Waltham St. Lawrence: 1951. V. 62; 65
Commentarii. Venice: 1490. V. 62
Commentarios de Bello Gallico, ac Civili, Henrici Glareani Poetae Laureati Annotationes (with) In C. Iulii Caesarii Dictatoris viri Dissertissimi et Auli Hirtii, seu Oppii, Commentaria...Annotationes Io. Rhellicani Tigurini...(with) Francisci.... Lugduni: 1538-1543. V. 66
Commentariorum De Bello Gallico. Venetiis: 1571. V. 63
Commentariorum de Bello Gallico Libri Septem (and other works). Parisiis: 1755. V. 63
De Bellis Gallico et Civili Pompejano.... Leyden: 1737. V. 64
The Gallic Wars. London: 1954. V. 64
Quae Exstant.... 1693. V. 65
Quae Extant Omnia. Lugduni Batavorum: 1713. V. 65
(Opera) Quae Extant. Amstelodami: 1628. V. 65

CAESAR, PETE
Let There Be Light. N.P: 1984. V. 63

CAFEY, THOMAS E.
Battle-Fields of the South, from Bull Run to Fredericksburg.... London: 1863. V. 62; 63

CAFFYN, KATHLEEN
A Yellow Aster. London: 1894. V. 65

CAFKY, MORRIS
Colorado Midland. Denver: 1965. V. 65; 66
Rails Around Gold Hill. Denver: 1955. V. 64; 67

CAGE - Cunningham - Johns: *Dancers on a Plane.* New York: 1990. V. 63

CAGE, JOHN
Empty Words. Writings '73-'78. Middletown: 1979. V. 63

CAHILL, JAMES
An Index of Early Chinese Painters and Paintings. 1980. V. 62

CAHILL, ORLAND
Atlas of Human Cross-Sectional Anatomy. New York: 1990. V. 64; 67

CAHN, JOSEPH M.
The Teenie Weenies Book, the Life and Art of William Donahey. La Jolla: 1986. V. 63

CAHN, JULIUS
Official Theatrical Guide. New York: 1899. V. 65

CAHN, ROBERT
American Photographers and the National Parks. New York: 1981. V. 63

CAHN, W.
Romanesque Manuscripts: the Twelfth Century. London: 1996. V. 62

CAILLER, P.
Catalogue Raisonne de l'Oeuvre Lithographie et Grave Hans Erni... Volume I: Lithographs 1930-1957. Geneve: 1969. V. 65

CAILLIE, RENE
Travels through Central Africa to Timbuctoo: and Across the Great Desert to Morocco, Performed in the Years 1824-1828. London: 1830. V. 62

CAILLOIS, ROGER
Proces Intellectuel de l'Art. Marseille: 1935. V. 67

CAIN, JAMES M.
The Butterfly. New York: 1947. V. 63
Double Indemnity. New York: 1943. V. 66
Galatea. New York: 1953. V. 63; 65; 67
The Institute. London: 1977. V. 67
Jealous Woman. London: 1955. V. 66
Mignon. New York: 1962. V. 63
Mildred Pierce. New York: 1941. V. 63; 64; 65; 66
Mildred Pierce. London: 1943. V. 66
The Moth. New York: 1948. V. 63; 65; 67
Our Government. New York: 1930. V. 62; 64; 66
Past All Dishonor. New York: 1946. V. 63; 64; 67
The Postman Always Rings Twice. New York. V. 67
The Postman Always Rings Twice. London: 1934. V. 65; 66
Rainbow's End. New York: 1975. V. 63; 66
Sinful Woman. Cleveland: 1948. V. 65; 66
Three of a Kind. New York: 1943. V. 64
Three of a Kind. London: 1945. V. 65; 66

CAIN, JULIEN
Humanisme Actif: Melanges d'Art et de Litterature. Paris: 1968. V. 64

CAIN, PAUL
Fast One. Carbondale: 1978. V. 66

CAINE, CAESAR
Capella de Gerardegile or the Story of a Cumberland Chapelry (Garrigill). Haltwhistle: 1908. V. 66

CAINE, HALL
The Deemster. London: 1887. V. 66

CAINE, WILLIAM
Fish, Fishing and Fishermen. London: 1927. V. 67

CAIRD, JAMES
Our Daily Food, Its Price and Sources of Supply. London: 1868. V. 67

CAIRD, JOHN
Religion in Common Life. Edinburgh and London: 1855. V. 62

CAIRD, MONA
The Pathway of the Gods. London: 1898. V. 63

CAIRNES, JOHN ELLIOTT
The Character and Logical Method of Political Economy. London: 1875. V. 64
The Slave Power: Its Character, Career and Probable Designs.... London: 1862. V. 63
The Slave Power: Its Character, Career and Probable Designs.... London: 1863. V. 64

CAIRNS, JAMES
Report of the Trial of Cairns, Turnbull, Smith and Lamb, Before the High Court of Justiciary at Edinburgh, on Monday the 18th of December 1837, for the Crimes of Mobbing and Rioting, and Assault, Committed at Hawick on the Occasion of the Late Election o. Edinburgh: 1838. V. 63

CAJORI, FLORIAN
William Oughtred; A Great Seventeeenth Century Teacher of Mathematics. Chicago: 1916. V. 66

CALADO, MANOEL
O Valeroso Lucideno, e Triumpho da Liberdade.... Lisbon: 1648. V. 62

CALAMY, EDWARD
An Abridgement of Mr. Baxter's History of His Life and Times. London: 1702. V. 66

CALCOTT, GEORGE SYMES
A Descriptive Account of a Descent made into Penpark-Hole in the Parish of Westbury...in the Year 1775. Bristol: 1792. V. 66

CALCOTT, WELLINS
A Candid Disquisition of the Principles and Practices of the Most Ancient and Honourable Society of Free and Accepted Masons.... London: 1769. V. 64

CALDECOTT, RANDOLPH
The Complete Collection of Pictures and Songs. London: 1887. V. 63
The Complete Collection of Randolph Caldecott's Contributions to the Graphic. London: 1888. V. 64
Gleanings from the Graphic. London: 1889. V. 67
More Graphic Pictures. London: 1887. V. 67
R. Caldecott's Picture Book No. 3. London. V. 62
R. Caldecott's Second Collection of Pictures and Songs. London. V. 63
Randolph Caldecott's Graphic Pictures. London: 1883. V. 67
Randolph Caldecott's Painting Book. London: 1895. V. 65
A Sketch-Book of R. Caldecott's. London. V. 67
A Sketch-Book of R. Caldecott's. London: 1883. V. 65

CALDERARA, M.
Manuel de L'Aviateur-Constructeur. Paris: 1910. V. 66

CALDER MARSHALL, ARTHUR
A Crime Against Cania. London: 1934. V. 66
A Crime Against Cania. Waltham St. Lawrence: 1934. V. 63; 66

CALDERON, V. G.
The Lottery Ticket. Waltham St. Lawrence. V. 62
The Lottery Ticket. Waltham St. Lawrence: 1945. V. 66

CALDERON, W. F.
The Painting and Anatomy of Animals. London: 1936. V. 62; 65

CALDERON DE LA BARCA, FRANCIS ERSKINE INGLIS
Life in Mexico, During a Residence of Two Years in that Country. London: 1843. V. 66

CALDERON DE LA BARCA, PEDRO
Life's a Dream - a Play in Three Acts. London: 1968. V. 62
Six Dramas of Calderon. London: 1853. V. 65

CALDERWOOD, HENRY
Caffres and Caffre Missions, with Preliminary Chapters on the Cape Colony as a Field for Emigration and a Basis of Missionary Operation. London: 1858. V. 64

CALDERWOOD, W. L.
The Life of the Salmon. 1907. V. 67
Salmon. 1938. V. 67
The Salmon Rivers and Lochs of Scotland. London: 1909. V. 67

CALDINS, DICK
Buck Rogers: 25th Century Featuring Buddy and Allura in Strange Adventures in the Spider-Ship. Chicago: 1935. V. 64

CALDWELL, E.
Puss in Boots Picture Book. London: 1890. V. 64

CALDWELL, ERSKINE PRESTON
The Bastard. New York: 1929. V. 64
God's Little Acre. Franklin Center: 1979. V. 66
Hamrick's Polar Bear and Other Stories. Helsinki: 1984. V. 65
Journeyman. New York: 1938. V. 62; 64; 67
Kneel to the Rising Sun and Other Stories. New York: 1935. V. 64; 66
Say, Is This the U.S.A. New York and Boston: 1941. V. 63
We Are the Living. New York: 1933. V. 64

CALDWELL, H. R.
Blue Tiger. London: 1925. V. 64
South China Birds, a Complete and Popular and Scientific Account of nearly Five Hundred and Fifty Forms of Birds.... Shanghai: 1931. V. 67

CALDWELL, J. A.
Caldwell's Illustrated Combination Centennial Atlas of Washington Co., Pennsylvania. 1976. V. 66

CALDWELL, J. F. J.
History of a Brigade of South Carolinians Known First as Gregg's and Subsequently as MacGowan's Brigade. Philadelphia: 1866. V. 62
A History of a Brigade of South Carolinians Known First as Gregg's and Subsequently as McGowan's Brigade. Marietta: 1951. V. 63

CALDWELL, LEWIS A. H.
The Policy King. Chicago: 1945. V. 65

CALENDARIUM *Rotulorum Chartarum et Inquisitionum ad Quod Damnum.* London: 1803. V. 64

CALEPINUS, AMBROSIUS
Dictionarium (Octolingue).... Lugduni: 1647. V. 67

CALHOUN, FREDERICK S.
The Lawmen; United States Marshalls and Their Deputies, 1789-1989. Washington: 1989. V. 67

CALHOUN, JAMES S.
The Official Correspondence of James S. Calhoun. Washington: 1915. V. 64

CALHOUN, JOHN C.
The Works of John C. Calhoun. New York: 1864. V. 64

CALHOUN, WILLIAM LOWNDES
History of the 42nd Regiment, Georgia Volunteers. Atlanta: 1900. V. 62; 63; 65

CALIFORNIA
State Register and Yearbook of Facts: for the Year 1857. San Francisco: 1857. V. 63

CALIFORNIA. LEGISLATURE - 1854
Proceedings of a Public Meeting of the Democratic Members of the Legislature Held in the Senate Chamber at Benecia on Thursday Evening, Feb. 2, 1854. San Francisco: 1854. V. 62

CALIFORNIA and New Mexico: Message from the President of the United States. Washington: 1850. V. 63

THE CALIFORNIA Brand Book 1918. San Francisco: 1919. V. 63; 66

CALIFORNIA HISTORICAL SOCIETY
Drake's Plate of Brass; Evidence of His Visit to California in 1579. San Francisco: 1937. V. 63

CALIFORNIA MINERS' ASSOCIATION
California Mines and Minerals. San Francisco: 1899. V. 67

CALIFORNIA Mines and Minerals. San Francisco: 1899. V. 64

CALIFORNIA PERFUME CO.
Catalog. N.P: 1900. V. 63

CALL, JAN VAN
Admirandorum Quadruplex Spectaculum, Delectum Pictum et Aeri Incisum. Amsterdam: 1700. V. 62; 65

CALL, WILLIAM TIMOTHY
Blackmail. Brooklyn: 1915. V. 65

CALLAGHAN, MORLEY
No Man's Meat. Paris: 1931. V. 65
Strange Fugitive. New York: 1928. V. 63
That Summer in Paris - Memories of Tangled Friendships with Hemingway, Fitzgerald and Some Others. New York: 1963. V. 65

CALLAHAN, HARRY
Harry Callahan: Color. Providence: 1980. V. 63; 65; 66

CALLAHAN, JAMES MORTON
Diplomatic History of the Southern Confederacy. Baltimore: 1901. V. 62; 63

CALLAWAY, REV. CANON
Nursery Tales, Traditions and Histories Of the Zulus. London: 1868. V. 63

CALLCOTT, MARIA
A Short History of Spain. London: 1828. V. 65

CALLENDER, JAMES H.
History and Genealogy of the Cochran Family of Kirkcudbright and New York. 1932. V. 63

CALLENDER, L.
The Windmill - Stories, Essays, Poems and Pictures by Authors and Artists.... London: 1923. V. 63

CALLIACHI, NICOLAI
De Ludis Scenicis Mimorum & Pantomimrum. Padua: 1713. V. 62

CALLIMACHUS
Hymnes de Callimaque. Paris: 1775. V. 66
The Hymns of Callimachus. 1755. V. 65

CALLISON, JOHN J.
Bill Jones of Paradise Valley, Oklahoma, His Life and Adventures of Over Forty Years in the Great Southwest. Chicago: 1914. V. 63; 65

CALLON, J.
Lectures on Mining Delivered at the School of Mines, Paris. London: 1876-1881. V. 62

CALLOT, JAQUES
De Droeve Ellendigheden van den Oorloogh. Amsterdam: 1740. V. 62

CALLOW, EDWARD
Old London Taverns Historical Descriptive and Reminiscent: With Some Account of the Coffee Houses, Clubs, Etc. London: 1899. V. 63

CALLWELL, C. E.
Small Wars, Their Principles and Practice. London: 1909. V. 64

CALMANN, G.
Ehret, Flower Painter Extraordinary. Boston: 1977. V. 67

CALMEIL, LOUIS FLORENTINE
De La Paralysie Consideree Chez les Alienes, Recherches Faites dans le Service de Feu M. Royer-Colalrd et de M. Esquirol. Paris: 1826. V. 65

CALMOUR, ALFRED C.
Fact and Fiction About Shakespeare. Stratford-on-Avon: 1894. V. 66

CALNEK, W. A.
History of the County of Annapolis Including Old Port Royal and Acadia.... Toronto: 1897. V. 64

CALT, STEPHEN
King of the Delta Blues. The Life and Music of Charlie Patton. Newton: 1988. V. 67

CALTHORPE, SOMERSET JOHN GOUGH
Letters from Head-Quarters; or the Realities of the War in the Crimea. London: 1856. V. 65

CALTHROP, D. C.
The Charm of Gardens. London: 1910. V. 67
The Guide to Fairyland. London: 1905. V. 66

CALVERLEY, C. S.
Fly Leaves. Cambridge: 1890. V. 64
The Complete Works of.... London: 1905. V. 62

CALVERT, ALBERT F.
The Cameroons. London: 1917. V. 64
Exploration of Australia. London: 1895-1896. V. 64
Moorish Remains in Spain: the Alhambra.... London: 1907. V. 65
Nigeria and Its Tin Fields. London: 1910. V. 63
Southern Spain. London: 1907. V. 62
Southern Spain. London: 1908. V. 65; 66

CALVERT, FREDERICK
Calvert's Lithographic Drawing Book. No. III. London: 1825. V. 66
Theatre Versus Conventicle; or, the Drama Attacked and Defended. Hull: 1826. V. 67

CALVERT, GEORGE HENRY
Introduction to Social Science. A Discourse in Three Parts. New York: 1856. V. 64

CALVERT, M.
An Account of the Knaresborough Spaw.... Knaresborough: 1836. V. 65

CALVERT, ROBERT
Diatomaceous Earth. New York: 1930. V. 67

CALVERT, W. R.
Wild Life on Moor and Fell. 1937. V. 67

CALVIN, JOHN
An Abridgement of the Insitution of the Christian Religion.... Edinburgh: 1587. V. 65
Commentaries on the Twelve Minor Prophets. Edinburgh: 1846-1849. V. 66
Commentary on a Harmony of the Evangelists, Mathew, Mark and Luke. Edinburgh: 1845-1846. V. 66
Commentary on the Book of Psalms. Edinburgh: 1845-1849. V. 66
The Institutes of Christian Religion. Edinburgh: 1845. V. 66

CALVIN, ROSS
River of the Sun. Stories of the Storied Gila. Albuquerque: 1946. V. 64; 67

CALVINO, ITALO
Baron in the Trees. London: 1959. V. 63
The Castle of Crossed Destinies. New York: 1977. V. 62
Cosmicomics. London: 1969. V. 64
Prima Che Tu Dica Pronto. (Before You Say Hello.). Cottondale: 1985. V. 64
Time and the Hunter. London: 1970. V. 64

CALWELL, H. G.
Andrew Malcolm of Belfast 1818-1856, Physician and Historian. 1977. V. 67

CAMAC, C. N. B.
Epoch Making Contributions to Medicine, Surgery and Allied Sciences.... Philadelphia: 1909. V. 66

CAMBELL, MARY MASON
The New England Butt'ry Shelf Cookbook. New York: 1969. V. 64

CAMBIAIRE, CELESTIN P.
East Tennesse and Western Virginia Mountain Ballads. London: 1927. V. 63

CAMBLIN, GILBERT
The Town in Ulster. Belfast: 1951. V. 67

CAMBRENSIS, GIRALDI
Opera. 1861-1891. V. 65

THE CAMBRIDGE Modern History. Cambridge: 1902-1912. V. 66
THE CAMBRIDGE Modern History. Cambridge: 1934. V. 66

CAMBRIDGE, RICHARD
The Works. London: 1803. V. 62

CAMBRIDGE, RICHARD OWEN
A Dialogue Between a Member of Parliament and His Servant. London: 1752. V. 64
The Scribleriad: an Heroic Poem. London: 1751. V. 62; 63; 65; 66

CAMBRIDGE, W. G.
Familiar Illustrations of Language of Mathematics, or a New Picture Alphabet for Well-Behaved Undergraduates. (with) Cambridge Customs and Costumes. London: 1850. V. 62

CAMDEN, WILLIAM
Britannia; or, a Chorographical Description of Great Britain and Ireland, Together with the Adjacent Islands. London: 1722. V. 66
Britannia; or, a Chorographical Description of the Flourishing Kingdoms of England, Scotland and Ireland.... London: 1789. V. 66; 67
Britannia, Sive Florentiss. Regnorum Angliae, Scotiae, Hiberniae, Insularum. Amsterdam: 1639. V. 66
Britannia Sive Florentissimorum Regnorum, Angliae, Scotiae, Hiberniae, et Insularum. London: 1590. V. 66
Britannia: Sive Florentissimorvm Regnorvm, Angliae, Scotiae, Hiberniae et Insvlarvm. Francofvrdi: 1590. V. 63; 66
The History of the Most Renowned and Victorious Princess Elizabeth, Late Queen of England. London: 1675. V. 65
Reges, Reginae, Nobiles, et alij in Ecclesia Collegiata B. Petri Westmonasterii Sepulti, Usque ad Annum Reparatae Salutis 1600. 1600. V. 63
Remains Concerning Britain; their Languages, Names, Surnames, Allusions, Anagrams, Amories, Moneys. London: 1674. V. 66
Remains Concerning Britaine...Their Languages, Names, Syrnames, Allusions, Anagrammes, Armories, Moneys, Empresses, Apparel, Artillerie, Wise Speeches, Proverbes, Poesies, Epitaphs.... London: 1629. V. 64
A Second Edition of Camden's Description of Scotland, Containing a Supplement of These Peers, or Lords of Parliament.... Edinburgh: 1695. V. 63

CAMERA PICTORIALISTS OF LOS ANGELES
The Pictorialist. Los Angeles: 1931. V. 65

CAMERARIUS, JOACHIM
Symbolorvm et Emblematvm Centvriae Tres. I. Ex Herbis & Stirpibus. II. Ex Animalibus Quadrupedibus. III. Ex Volatilibus & Accessit Noviter Centvria. IV. Ex Aquatilibus & Reptilibus. Nuremberg: 1605. V. 63; 66

CAMERARIUS, PHILLIPUS
The Living Librarie or Meditations and Observations Historical, Natural, Moral, Political and Poetical.... London: 1625. V. 65

CAMERON, A.
The Greek Anthology from Meleager to Planudes. Oxford: 1993. V. 62

CAMERON, CHARLOTTE
A Cheechako in Alaska and Yukon. London: 1920. V. 64
Mexico in Revolution. London: 1925. V. 64

CAMERON, DONALD
A Saharan Venture; Being the Account of a Journey Across the Sahara from Kano to Algeria. London: 1928. V. 64
Thaumaturgus; or, the Wonders of the Magic Lantern. (with) Thaumaturgus; or, the Wonders of the Magic Lantern...II. Edinburgh: 1816. V. 64

CAMERON, ELIZABETH
A Book of White Flowers. 1980. V. 64

CAMERON, JAMES
Shorthorns in Central and Southern Scotland. Edinburgh and London: 1921. V. 63

CAMERON, JOHN
Celtic Man; The Senchus Mor and The Book of Aicill and the Traces of Early Gaelic System of Law in Scotland. 1937. V. 63
Researches in Craniometry. Halifax: 1928-1931. V. 66; 67

CAMERON, JULIA MARGARET
Victorian Photographs of Famous Men and Fair Women. London: 1926. V. 66
Victorian Photographs of Famous Men and Fair Women. New York: 1926. V. 63; 64

CAMERON, KENNETH NEILL
The Carl H. Pforzheimer Library: Shelley and His Circle 1773-1822. Cambridge: 1961. V. 62; 67

CAMERON, LUCY LYTTELTON
Englishwomen in Past and Present Times. London: 1841. V. 65

CAMERON, OWEN
The Owl and the Pussycat. New York: 1949. V. 67

CAMERON, P.
A Monograph of the British Phytophagous Hymenoptera. London: 1882-1893. V. 63; 64; 65; 66; 67
A Monograph of the British Phytophgous Hymenoptera. Volume II. Nematina. London: 1885. V. 64; 66

CAMERON, RODERICK
Pioneer Days in Kansas: a Homesteader's Narrative of Early Settlement and Farm Development on the High Plains Country of Northwest Kansas. Belleville: 1951. V. 63; 64; 66

CAMERON, VERNEY LOVETT
Across Africa. London: 1885. V. 67

CAMESASCA, E.
History of the House. New York: 1971. V. 65

CAMILLI, CAMILLO
Imprese Illustri di Diversi, Coi Discorsi. Venice: 1586. V. 64; 66

CAMINADE, MARC ALEXANDRE
Premiere Elemens de la Langue Francaise, ou Grammaire Usuelle et Complete,... Paris: 1803. V. 66

CAMM, DOM BEDE
Forgotten Shrines. London: 1910. V. 62; 66

CAMMACK, JOHN HENRY
Personal Recollection of John Henry Cammack: a Soldier of the Confederacy 1861-1865. Huntington: 1912. V. 65
Personal Recollections of Private John Henry Cammack, a Soldier of the Confederacy 1861-1865. Huntington: 1920. V. 62; 63; 65

CAMP, CHARLES A.
John Doble's Journal and Letters from the Mines: Mokelumne Hill, Jackson, Volcano and San Francisco. Denver: 1962. V. 63

CAMP, CHARLES C.
George C. Yount and His Chronicles of the West. Denver: 1966. V. 65
Muggins, the Cow Horse. Denver: 1928. V. 65

CAMP, CHARLES L.
James Clyman, Frontiersman. Portland: 1960. V. 62; 66
James Clyman, Frontiersman. Portland: 1966. V. 63; 66
Narrative of Nicholas Cheyenne Dawson, Overland to California in '41 and '49 and Texas in '51. San Francisco: 1933. V. 65; 67

CAMP, WALTER
American Football. New York: 1891. V. 63
Custer in '76, Walter Camp's Notes on the Custer Fight. Provo: 1976. V. 65

CAMPA, MIGUEL DE LA
A Journal of Explorations Northward Along the Coast from Monterey in the Year 1775. San Francisco: 1964. V. 63

CAMPAN, JEANNE LOUISE HENRIETTE
De l'Education, suivi des Conseils aux Jeunes Filles, d'un Theatre Pour Les Jeunes Personnes et de Quelques Essais de Morale. Paris: 1824. V. 63; 65; 66
The Private Journal of Madame Campan, Comprising Original Anecdotes of the French Court.... London: 1825. V. 63

CAMPBELL, A.
A Debate Between Rev. A. Campbell and Rev. N. L. Rice on the Action, Subject, Design and Administrator of Christian Baptism.... Lexington: 1844. V. 63

CAMPBELL, ALEXANDER
An Address to the Members of the Union Literary Society of the Miami University, Ohio. Bethany: 1844. V. 66
A Journey from Edinburgh through Parts of North Britain.... London: 1802. V. 62; 63; 66

CAMPBELL, ARCHIBALD
Reports Upon the Survey of the Boundary Between the Territory of the United States and the Possessions of Great Britain. Washington: 1878. V. 64
A Voyage Round the World from 1806 to 1812.... Amsterdam/New York: 1969. V. 63; 64; 65

CAMPBELL, BARBARA
The Story of Timothy Tabbycat. London: 1947. V. 66

CAMPBELL, BEBE MOORE
Your Blues Ain't Like Mine. New York: 1992. V. 66; 67

CAMPBELL, BERT
Arizona Highways. Phoenix: 1944-1953. V. 64

CAMPBELL, CHARLES
History of the Colony and Ancient Dominion of Virginia. Philadelphia: 1860. V. 62; 63; 64

CAMPBELL, DUGALD
Camels through Libya. London: 1930. V. 64
In the Heart of Bantuland: a Record of 29 Years' Pioneering in Central Africa Among the Banta Peoples.... London: 1922. V. 64

CAMPBELL, DUNCAN
Nova Scotia, in Its Historical, Mercantile and Industrial Relations. Montreal: 1873. V. 62; 67

CAMPBELL, EDWARD LIVINGSTON
Historical Sketch of the Fifteenth Regiment New Jersey Volunteers, First Brigade, First Division. Trenton: 1880. V. 63; 66

CAMPBELL, F. A.
A Year in the New Hebrides, Loyalty Islands and New Caledonia. Geelong: 1873. V. 64

CAMPBELL, GEORGE
Modern India: a Sketch of the System of Civil Government. London: 1853. V. 64

CAMPBELL, GEORGE L.
Miners' Thrift and Employers' Liability, a Remarkable Experience. Wigan: 1902. V. 64

CAMPBELL, GORDON
Captain James Cook, R.N., F.R.S. London: 1936. V. 63; 66

CAMPBELL, HELEN
Darkness and Daylight; or Lights and Shadows of New York Life. Hartford: 1891. V. 63
Darkness and Daylight; or Lights and Shadows of New York Life. Hartford: 1897. V. 63

CAMPBELL, J. J.
Legends of Ireland. 1955. V. 67

CAMPBELL, J. K.
Through Egypt, Palestine and Syria. London: 1884. V. 64

CAMPBELL, J. MENZIES
A Dental Bibliography British and American, 1682-1880. London: 1949. V. 62

CAMPBELL, J. R.
A History of the County of Yarmouth, Nova Scotia. Saint John: 1876. V. 64

CAMPBELL, J. W.
A History of Virginia, from its Discovery Till the Year 1781. Philadelphia: 1813. V. 66

CAMPBELL, JAMES HAVELOCK
McClellan: a Vindication of the Military Career of General George B. McClellan. New York: 1916. V. 62; 63; 65

CAMPBELL, JOHN
A Concise History of Spanish America.... London: 1741. V. 66
Lives of the Admirals and Other Eminent British Seamen.... 1742-1744. V. 65
Lives of the Admirals and Other Eminent British Seamen.... London: 1761. V. 65
Lives of the British Admirals.... London: 1785. V. 66
The Lives of the Lord Chancellors and Keepers of the Great Seal of England, from the Earliest Times Till the Death of King George IV. London: 1848-1850. V. 62
Maritime Discovery and Christian Missions: Considered in Their Mutual Relations. London: 1840. V. 64
A Political Survey of Britain.... London: 1774. V. 66
The Present State of Europe. London: 1750. V. 67
Travels in South Africa, Undertaken at the Request of the London Missionary Society.... London: 1822. V. 65

CAMPBELL, JOHN A.
Reminiscences & Documents Relating to the Civil War During the Year 1865. Baltimore: 1887. V. 65

CAMPBELL, JOHN CAMPBELL, 1ST BARON
The Lives of the Chief Justices of England. London: 1849. V. 63

CAMPBELL, JOHN F.
History and Bibliography of the New American Practical Navigator and the American Coast Pilot. Salem: 1964. V. 63

CAMPBELL, JOHN LORNE
Highland Songs of the Forty-Five. Edinburgh: 1933. V. 62

CAMPBELL, JOHN P.
Strictures on Two Letters. Lexington: 1805. V. 64

CAMPBELL, JOHN W.
Cloak of Aesir. Chicago: 1952. V. 67

CAMPBELL, KEN
In the Presence of My Enemy. Execution: the Book. N.P: 1990. V. 64

CAMPBELL, OLIVE ARNOLD
English Folk Songs from the Southern Appalachians. New York: 1917. V. 63

CAMPBELL, R. J.
Livingstone. London: 1920. V. 66

CAMPBELL, RAMSEY
The Count of Eleven. London: 1991. V. 62; 64; 66
Dark Feasts. London: 1987,. V. 67
The Height of the Scream. Sauk City: 1976. V. 67
The Inhabitants of the Lake and Less Welcome Tenants. Sauk City: 1964. V. 62; 64; 65; 67
New Tales of the Cthulhu Mythos. Sauk City: 1980. V. 63; 66
Scared Stiff. 1987. V. 62; 64; 66

CAMPBELL, REAU
Campbell's New Revised Complete Guide and Descriptive Book of Mexico. Chicago: 1909. V. 65

CAMPBELL, ROBERT
The Rocky Mountain Letters of Robert Campbell. 1955. V. 63; 66

CAMPBELL, ROBERT F.
Some Aspects of the Race Problem in the South. Asheville: 1899. V. 65

CAMPBELL, ROY
Broken Record - Reminiscences. Campden, Glouchestershire: 1934. V. 63
Choosing a Mast. London: 1931. V. 62
The Collected Poems of.... 1949. V. 67
The Flaming Terrapin: a Poem. London: 1924. V. 65
Flowering Reeds - Poems. London: 1931. V. 65
The Georgiad. 1931. V. 66
The Georgiad. Chipping, Campden: 1931. V. 63
The Georgiad. London: 1931. V. 62; 63
The Gum Trees. London: 1930. V. 63
Light on a Dark Horse - an Autobiography. London: 1951. V. 62
Mithraic Emblems - Poems. London: 1936. V. 65
Pomegranates. A Poems. Campden: 1932. V. 63

CAMPBELL, RUTH
Small Fry and the Winged Horse. Joliet: 1927. V. 63

CAMPBELL, STUART
Stories of King Arthur. London and Glasgow: 1935. V. 62; 65

CAMPBELL, THOMAS
Annals of Great Britain, from the Ascension of George III to the Peace of Amiens. Edinburgh: 1807. V. 66
Campbell's Poems. London: 1848. V. 62
Gertrude of Wyoming. London: 1809. V. 66
Life of Mrs. Siddons. London: 1834. V. 62
A Philosophical Survey of the South of Ireland, in a Series of Letters to John Watkinson, M.D. Dublin: 1778. V. 62; 66
The Poetical Works. London: 1837. V. 62
The Poetical Works. London: 1853. V. 63
Theodoric: a Domestic Tale, and Other Poems. London: 1824. V. 63

CAMPBELL, WALTER S.
The Book Lover's Southwest - a Gude to Good Reading. Norman: 1955. V. 67

CAMPBELL, WILFRED
Canada. 1907. V. 67
Canada. London: 1907. V. 65

CAMPBELL, WILL
Brother to a Dragonfly. New York: 1977. V. 63

CAMPBELL, WILLIAM A.
The Child's First Book. Richmond: 1864. V. 62

CAMPBELL, WILLIAM C.
From the Quarries of Last Chance Gulch: a News-History of Helena and Its Masonic Lodges. Butte & Helena: 1965-1964. V. 63; 64; 66

CAMPE, J. H.
Cortez; or, the Conquest of Mexico as Related by a Father to His Children; and Designed for the Instruction of Youth. London: 1819. V. 67

CAMPION, J. S.
On the Frontier Reminiscences of Wild Sports, Personal Adventures and Strange Scenes. London: 1878. V. 65; 67

CAMPION, THOMAS
Campion's Works. Oxford: 1909. V. 62
Selected Songs. Boston: 1973. V. 63; 67
The Works. London: 1889. V. 62; 65; 67

CAMPOMANES, PEDRO RODRIGUES, CONDE DE
Discurso Sobre el Fomento De La Industria Popular. Madrid: 1774. V. 63; 66

CAMUS, ALBERT
L'Envers et L'Endroit. Paris: 1958. V. 67
The Fall. New York: 1957. V. 67
The Fall. Kentfield: 1966. V. 63; 64; 66
La Peste. Paris: 1947. V. 67
The Stranger. London: 1971. V. 67
The Stranger. New York: 1971. V. 62; 63; 64; 66

CAMUS, JEAN
Isolement et Psychotherapie: Traitement de l'Hysterie et de la Neurasthenie Pratique de la Reeducation Morale et Physique. Paris: 1904. V. 65

CANADA. ROYAL COMMISSION ON INDIAN AFFAIRS
Report of the Royal Commission on Indian Affairs for the Province of British Columbia. Victoria: 1916. V. 63

CANADA. SUPREME COURT
No. 407 in the Supreme Court of Canada On Appeal from the Exchequer Court of Canada Nova Scotia Admiralty District. Between Compagne Generale Transatlantique (Plaintiff) Appellant and The Ship Emo Southern Pacific Whaling Company, Ltd. Halifax: 1920?. V. 64

THE CANADIAN Almanac and Repository of Useful Knowledge for the Year 1859. Toronto: 1859. V. 66

THE CANADIAN Almanac...for the Year 1860. V. 66

THE CANADIAN Almanac...for the Year 1861. V. 66

THE CANADIAN Almanac...for the Year 1862. V. 66

THE CANADIAN Almanac...for the Year 1863. V. 66

THE CANADIAN Almanac...for the Year 1864. V. 66

THE CANADIAN Almanac...for the Year 1865. V. 66

THE CANADIAN Almanac...for the Year 1866. V. 66

CANADIAN BANK OF COMMERCE
The Canadian Book of Commerce Charter and Annual Reports 1867-1907; 1908-1914. Toronto: 1907-1914. V. 63

THE CANADIAN Economist, A Book of Tried and Tested Recipes. Ottawa: 1881. V. 62

THE CANADIAN Handbook and Tourists' Guide, Giving a Description of Canadian Lake and River Scenery and Places of Historical Interest, with the Best Spots for Fishing and Shooting. Montreal: 1867. V. 64

CANADIAN PACIFIC RAILWAY
Annotated Time Table Information as to C.P.R. Transcontinental Routes, Corrected to May 16th, 1892. Montreal: 1892. V. 63
Challenge of the Mountains. Montreal: 1906. V. 66
Get Your Farm Home From the Canadian Pacific. A Hand Book of Information Regarding Alberta, Saskatchewan and Manitoba and the Opportunities Offered You by the Canadian Pacific Railway in These Provinces. Calgary: 1915. V. 64

CANALETTO, GIOVANNI ANTONIO DA CANALE
Fifty Drawings by Canaletto from the Royal Library, Windsor Castle. London: 1983. V. 65; 67

CANAVAN, MYRTELLE
Elmer Ernest Southard and His Parents. Cambridge: 1925. V. 67

A CANDID Review of Mr. Pitt's Twenty Resolutions. Addressed to the People of Ireland. London: 1785. V. 62

CANDIDUS DECEMBRIUS, PETRUS
De Genitura Hominis. Augsburg: 1498. V. 64

CANDLER, EDMUND
The Long Road to Baghdad. London: 1919. V. 64

CANDOLLE, ALPHONSE LOUIS PIERRE PYRAMUS DE
Origine des Plantes Cultivees. Paris: 1883. V. 64; 67

CANDOLLE, AUGUSTIN PYRAMUS DE
Note sur Quelques Plantes Observees en Fleurs au Mois de Janvier 1828, dans la Serre de M. Saladin, a Pregny. Geneva: 1828. V. 64; 67
Revue de la Famille des Cactees...Leur Vegetation et Leur Culture. Paris: 1829. V. 62

THE CANDY Maker. A Practical Guide to the Manufacture of the Various Kinds of Plain and Fancy Candy. New York: 1901. V. 66

CANE, CLAUDE
Summer and Fall in Western Alaska. The Record of a Trip to Cook's Inlet After Big Game. London: 1903. V. 64; 66

CANESTRELLI, PHILIP
A Kootenai Grammar. Spokane: 1959. V. 63; 66

CANETTI, ELIAS
Auto-de-Fe. London: 1946. V. 65; 67
Die Blendung. Vienna: 1936. V. 67
Die Blendung. Munich: 1948. V. 67

CANEUON Ceiriog Detholiad. Newtown: 1925. V. 62

CANFIELD, C. L.
The Diary of a Forty-Niner, An Authentic First-Hand Account of California Life in the Golden Days of '49. San Francisco: 1906. V. 63; 66

CANFIELD, FREDERICK A.
A History of Thomas Canfield and of Matthew Canfield with a Genealogy of Their Descendants in New Jersey. Dover: 1897. V. 63; 66

CANIN, ETHAN
The Emperor of the Air. Boston: 1988. V. 65; 67

CANIVELL, FRANCISCO
Tratado de Vendages y Apositos Para el Uso de Los Reales Colegios de Cirurgia. Madrid: 1785. V. 63
Tratado de Vendages y Apositos Para el Uso de los Reales Colegios de Cirurgia. Barcelona: 1763. V. 62

CANNECATTIM, BERNARDO MARIA DE
Colleccao de Observacoes Grammaticas Sobre a Lingua Bunda ou Angolense.... Lisbon: 1805. V. 62

CANNIFF, WILLIAM
The Medical Profession in Upper Canada 1783-1850. Toronto: 1894. V. 66

CANNING, RICHARD
An Account of the Gifts and Legacies, That Have Been Given and Bequeathed to Charitable Uses, in the Town of Ipswich.... Ipswich: 1819. V. 62; 65

CANNON, CORNELIA JAMES
The Fight for the Pueblo - the Story of Onate's Expedition and the Founding of Santa Fe 1598-1609. Boston: 1934. V. 67

CANNON, GEORGE Q.
The Life of Joseph Smith, the Prophet. Salt Lake City: 1888. V. 66

CANNON, J. P.
Inside of Rebeldom, the Daily Life of a Private in the Confederate Army. Washington: 1900. V. 63

CANNON, MILES
Toward the Setting Sun. Portland: 1953. V. 67
Waiilatpa, Its Rise and Fall 1836-1847.... Boise: 1915. V. 63; 67

CANNON, RICHARD
Historical Record of the Twenty-Second, or the Cheshire Regiment of Foot to 1849. London: 1849. V. 63
Historical Records of the British Army...The Forty-Sixth, or the South Devonshire, Regiment of Foot.... London: 1851. V. 63

CANOVA, ANTONIO
The Works of Antonio Canova.... London: 1822-1824. V. 64

CANTACUZINO, S.
New Uses for Old Buildings. 1975. V. 65

CANTON, FRANK
Frontier Tales, the Autobiography of Frank Canton. Boston: 1930. V. 65; 67

CANTWELL, JOHN J.
A Sermon of His Excellency, Most Reverend at Requiem Mass for Mr. Edward Laurence Doheny, Saint Vincent's Church, September 11th, Nineteen Hundred and Thirty-Five. San Francisco: 1935. V. 62

CANTY, THOMAS
A Monster at Christmas. West Kingston: 1985. V. 67

CAPA, CORNELL
Robert Capa Photographs. New York: 1985. V. 66

CAPEK, KAREL
Travels in the North. London: 1939. V. 65

CAPEL, ARTHUR
Letters Written by His Excellency Arthur Capel, Earl of Essex, Lord Lieutenant of Ireland in the Year 1675 to Which is Prefixed an Historical Account of His Life and Deplorable Death in the Tower of London. Dublin: 1770. V. 67

CAPEN, ELWIN A.
Oology of New England.... Boston: 1886. V. 64; 67

CAPERS, HENRY DICKSON
Life and Times of C. G. Memminger. Richmond: 1893. V. 62; 63

CAPERS, WALTER B.
The Soldier-Bishop. Ellison Capers. New York: 1912. V. 62

CAPONIGRO, PAUL
Megaliths. N.P: 1986. V. 63; 65

CAPOTE, TRUMAN
Answered Prayers. London: 1986. V. 63
Breakfast at Tiffany's. London: 1958. V. 65
Breakfast at Tiffany's. New York: 1958. V. 67
A Christmas Memory. New York: 1966. V. 67
The Grass Harp. New York: 1951. V. 66; 67
The Grass Harp. New York: 1952. V. 64
House of Flowers. New York: 1954. V. 66
House of Flowers. New York: 1968. V. 63; 65; 67
I Remember Grandpa. Atlanta: 1987. V. 66
In Cold Blood. New York: 1965. V. 65; 66; 67
In Cold Blood. London: 1966. V. 67
Local Color. New York: 1950. V. 63; 66
Miriam. Mankato: 1982. V. 63
The Muses are Heard. New York: 1956. V. 62; 66
Music for Chameleons. New York: 1980. V. 64; 65; 66
One Christmas. New York: 1983. V. 63; 66; 67
Other Voices, Other Rooms. New York: 1948. V. 62; 63
Other Voices, Other Rooms. Franklin Center: 1979. V. 63; 66
The Thanksgiving Visitor. New York: 1967. V. 65
A Tree of Night and Other Stories. New York: 1949. V. 62; 66

CAPPE, CATHERINE
Memoirs of the Life of the Late Mrs. Catherine Cappe. London: 1823. V. 66

CAPPE, NEWCOME
A Sermon Preach'd at York, to a Congregation of Protestant Dissenters on the 27th of November 1757, Just Upon Receiving the Account of the King of Prussia's Victory, on the Fifth of the Month. York: 1757. V. 67

CAPPER, HENRY D. R. N.
Royal Naval Warrant Officers' Manual 1910. Portsmouth: 1910. V. 65

CAPPONI, ALESSANDRO GREGORIO, MARCHESE
Catalogo della Libreria Cappni o sia de'Libri Italiani del fu Marchese Alessandro Gregorio Capponi.... Rome: 1747. V. 62

CAPRA, ALLEXANDRO
La Nuova Architettura Civile e Militare...Divisa in Due Tomi, in Questa Nuova Impressione Diligentemente Corretta.... Cremona: 1717. V. 66

CAPRIULO, G. M.
Ecology of Marine Protozoa. New York: 1990. V. 65

CAPRON, E. S.
History of California from Its Discovery to the Present Time: Comprising Also a Full Description of Its Climate, Surface, Soil, Rivers, Towns, Beasts, Birds, Fishes, State of Its Society, Agriculture, Commerce, Mines, Mining &c. Boston: 1854. V. 62; 63

CAPTIVITY Narrative of Hannah Duston Related by Cotton Mather, John Greenleaf Whittier, Nathaniel Hawthorne and Henry David Thoreau, Four Versions of Events in 1697. San Francisco: 1987. V. 62; 63; 64; 66

CAPUTO, PHILIP
A Rumor of War. New York: 1977. V. 67

THE CAR to Buy, Containing a Complete List of Motor Vehicles of All Classes with Full Particulars as to Prices, Records, etc.... London: 1907. V. 62

CARACCIOLI, LOUIS ANTOINE
Advice from a Lady of Quality to Her Children, in the Last State of a Lingering Illness. Boston: 1796. V. 65
Le Livre a la Mode. Paris: 1759. V. 65
Le Livre de Quatre Couleurs. Paris: 1760. V. 65; 66

CARASI, CARLO
Le Pubbliche Pitture di Pacenza. Piacenza: 1780. V. 64

CARBURI DE CEFFALONE, MARIN, LE COMTE
Monument Eleve a la Gloire de Pierre Le Grand, ou Relation des Travaux et des Moyens Mecaniques Qui Ont Ete Employes Pour Transporter a Petersbourg un Rocher de Trois Millions Peasant.... Paris: 1777. V. 65; 66

CARCO, FRANCIS
Vertes. New York: 1946. V. 65

CARD, ORSON SCOTT
The Folk on the Fringe. West Bloomfield: 1969. V. 67
The Memory of Earth. 1992. V. 62; 64; 66
Speaker for the Dead. New York: 1986. V. 62; 64

CARDANO, GIROLAMO
In Cl. Ptolemaei...aut, ut Vulgo Vocant, Quadripartitae Constructionis Libros Commnentaria. Basel: 1554. V. 62
Mediolanensis Proxeneta: Seu De Prudentia Civili Liber. Geneva: 1630. V. 64

CARDEN, ALLEN D.
The Missouri Harmony. Cincinnati: 1839. V. 63

CARDIGAN, JAMES THOMAS BRUDENELL, 7TH EARL OF
The Trial of James Thomas Earl of Cardigan Before the Right Honourable the House of Peers in Full Parliament for Felony, on Tuesday the 16th Day of February 1841. London: 1841. V. 66

CARDINELL, CHARLES
Adventures of the Plains. San Francisco: 1922. V. 63; 66

CARDOZO, BENJAMIN
What Medicine Can Do for Law. The Anniversary Discourse Delivered Before the New York Academy of Medicine November 1, 1928. New York: 1930. V. 67

CARDWELL, KENNETH H.
Bernard Maybeck: Artisan, Architect, Artist. Santa Barbara: 1977. V. 64

CARE, HENRY
English Liberties, or the Freeborn Subject's Inheritance, Containing Magna Charta...Habeas Corpus...and Several Other Statutes.... London: 1719. V. 62
The Grandeur and Glory of France, Drawn in the Triumphant Portraictures of Her Present Victorious Monarch and Most Illustrious Nobility. London: 1673. V. 62
The History of the Damnable Popish Plot, in Its Various Branches and Progress.... London: 1680. V. 64

CARELESS, JOHN, PSEUD.
The Old English Squire. London: 1821. V. 67

CARELESS, RONALD
Battleship Nelson. The Story of HMS Nelson. London: 1986. V. 63

CAREW, HAROLD D.
History of Pasadena and the San Gabriel Valley. St. Clark: 1930. V. 64

CAREW, THOMAS
A Rapture. Waltham St. Lawrence: 1927. V. 62
A Selection from the Poetical Works of.... London: 1810. V. 63

CAREY, BASIL
Secret Voyage. New York: 1933. V. 67

CAREY, FRANCES JANE
Journal of a Tour in France, in the Years 1816 and 1817. London: 1823. V. 65

CAREY, HENRY CHARLES
A Complete Historical, Chronological and Geographical American Atlas.... Philadelphia: 1822. V. 66
The Credit System in France, Great Britian and the United States. Philadelphia: 1838. V. 66
The Geography, History and Statistics of America and the West Indies.... London: 1823. V. 64

CAREY, LEWIS
My Gun and I. London: 1933. V. 67

CAREY, MATHEW
Catalogue of Books, Pamphlets, Maps and Prints Published by Mathew Carey, 118 Market Street, Philadelphia. Philadelphia: 1795. V. 62
The Crisis. An Appeal to the Good Sense of the Nation, Against the Spirit of Resistance, and Dissolution of the Union. Philadelphia: 1832. V. 62
The Olive Branch, or Faults on Both Sides, Federal and Democratic.... Philadelphia: 1815. V. 63
A Short Account of the Malignant Fever, Lately Prevalent in Philadelphia: with a Statement of the Proceedings...United States. Philadelphia: 1794. V. 67

CAREY, PATRICK
Trivial Poems and Triolets. London: 1820. V. 66

CAREY, PETER
The Fat Man in History. London: 1980. V. 63
Illywhacker. St. Lucia: 1985. V. 62
The Tax Inspector. London: 1991. V. 63; 66

CAREY, ROSA NOUCHETTE
Doctor Luttrell's First Patient. London: 1897. V. 65
The Key to the Unknown. London: 1909. V. 65
Life's Trivial Round. London: 1900. V. 65
Nellie's Memories. London: 1868. V. 65
Not Like Other Girls. London: 1884. V. 65
Not Like Other Girls. London: 1889. V. 66

CAREY, WILLIAM
A Grammar of the Mahratta Language, to Which are Added Dialogues on Familiar Subjects. Serampore: 1825. V. 66
Travel and Adventure in Tibet.... London: 1902. V. 64

CAREY HOBSON, MARY ANNE
At Home in the Transvaal. London: 1884. V. 65

CARGILL, MORRIS
Jamaica. London: 1965. V. 66

CARION, JOHANNES
The Three Bokes of Cronicles, Whyche John Carion.... colophon: 1550. V. 66

CARISBRICK, EDWARD
The Life of the Lady Warner of Parham in Suffolk. London: 1691. V. 66

CARL H. PFORZHEIMER LIBRARY
Interludes 1553-1576. New York: 1940. V. 62

CARLES, WILLIAM RICHARD
Life in Corea. London: 1888. V. 62; 64

CARLETON, DON E.
Who Shot the Bear?. Austin: 1984. V. 65

CARLETON, G. W., & CO.
Parlor Table Companion: a Home Treasury of Biography, Romance, Poetry, History.... New York: 1877. V. 67

CARLETON, H. A. R.
California Transient Service: Progress and Methods of Approach, August 1933-April 1935. San Francisco: 1935. V. 62

CARLETON, JAMES HENRY
Diary of an Excursion to the Ruins of Abo, Quarra and Gran Quivira in New Mexico. Washington: 1855. V. 63
Diary of an Excursion to the Ruins of Abo, Quarra and Gran Quivira in New Mexico. Santa Fe: 1965. V. 64
The Prairie Logbooks 1844-1845. Dragoon Campaigns to the Pawnee Villages in 1844 and to the Rocky Mountains in 1845. Chicago: 1943. V. 65; 67

CARLETON, JOHN WILLIAM
Recreations in Shooting.... London: 1846. V. 67

CARLETON, WILLIAM
The Fawn of Spring-Vale, the Clarionet and Other Tales. Dublin: 1841. V. 65
Traits and Stories of the Irish Peasantry. Second Series. London: 1833. V. 65

CARLEVALE, JOSEPH WILLIAM
Americans of Italian Descent in New Jersey. Clifton: 1950. V. 66

CARLILE, JANE
Report of the Trial of Mrs. Carlile, on the Attorney-General's Ex-Officio Information for the Protection of Tyrants.... London: 1821. V. 63

CARLING, JOHN R.
The Weird Picture. London: 1905. V. 66

CARLISLE, ANTHONY
An Essay on the Disorders of Old Age, and on the Means for Prolonging Human Life. Philadelphia: 1819. V. 66

CARLISLE, BILL
Bill Carlisle Lone Bandit. An Autobiography. Pasadena: 1946. V. 63; 64; 66
Bill Carlisle Lone Bandit, an Autobiography. Pasadena: 1950. V. 62

CARLISLE, EARL OF
Diary in Turkish and Greek Waters. London: 1854. V. 64

CARLISLE, JOHN G., MRS.
Mrs. John G. Carlisle's Kentucky Cook Book. Chicago: 1893. V. 67

CARLISLE NATURAL HISTORY SOCIETY
Transactions. Carlisle: 1909-1928. V. 62

CARLISLE, NICHOLAS
An Historical Account of the Origin of the Commission, Appointed to Inquire Concnering Charities in England and Wales. London: 1828. V. 66

CARLISLE, WILLIAM
An Essay on Evil Spirits; or Reasons to Prove Their Existence in Opposition to a Lecture. Bradford: 1825. V. 67

CARLOWITZ, HANS KARL VON
Sylvicultural Oconomica...(with) Historia Naturalis Arborum et Fruticum Sylvestrium Germaniae.... Leipzig: 1732. V. 64; 66; 67

CARLQUIST, S.
Island Life, a Natural History of the Islands of the World. New York: 1965. V. 62

CARLSON, PAUL H.
William A. Shaffer: Military Commander in the American West. N.P: 1973. V. 67

CARLTON, H. W.
Spaniels, Their Training for Sport and Field Trials. 1915. V. 67

CARLYLE, JANE WELSH
Letters and Memorials. London: 1883. V. 64
The Love Letters of Thomas Carlyle and Jane Welsh. London: 1909. V. 65
New Letters and Memorials. London: 1903. V. 65

CARLYLE, R. W.
A History of Mediaeval Political Theory in the West. New York: 1903-1936. V. 63

CARLYLE, THOMAS
Chartism. London: 1840. V. 64; 66
Complete Works. Boston: 1880. V. 62
Complete Works. Boston: 1884. V. 66
The French Revolution: a History. London: 1837. V. 64
German Romance: Specimens of Its Chief Authors; with Biographical and Critical Notices. Edinburgh: 1827. V. 65
Last Words of Thomas Carlyle. Edinburgh: 1882. V. 67
Latter-Day Pamphlets. London: 1850. V. 63; 65; 67
Latter-Day Pamphlets. London: 1858. V. 63
The Life of Friedrich Schiller. London: 1825. V. 67
The Life of John Sterling. Boston: 1851. V. 64; 65
The Life of John Sterling. London: 1852. V. 67
On Heroes, Hero-Worship, and the Heroic in History. London: 1842. V. 67
Past and Present. Boston: 1843. V. 65
Sartor Resartus. Boston: 1836. V. 66
Sartor Resartus. London: 1838. V. 62
Sartor Resartus. Hammersmith: 1907. V. 62; 67
Sator Resartus. 1907. V. 63
Shooting Niagara; and After?. London: 1867. V. 67

CARMER, CARL
The Hurricane's Children. New York: 1937. V. 64
Stars Fell on Alabama. New York: 1937. V. 64

CARMICHAEL, ANDREW BLAIR
The Law Scrutiny; or Attornies' Guide. Dublin: 1807. V. 63

CARMICHAEL, HOAGY
The Stardust Road. New York: 1946. V. 65

CARMICHAEL, ROBERT
A Treatise on the Calculus of Operations, Designed to Facilitate the Processes of the Differential and Integral Calculus and the Calculus of Finite Differences. London: 1855. V. 65

CARMONT, JAMES
The Crichton Royal Institution Dumfries. Leicester: 1896. V. 65

CARNAC, CAROL
Death of a Lady Killer. London: 1959. V. 66

CARNAP, RUDOLF
Der Raum. Ein Beitrag zur Wissenschaftslehre. Berlin: 1922. V. 67
The Unity of Science. London: 1934. V. 67

CARNARVON, EARL OF
Athens and the Morea. London: 1869. V. 64

CARNARVON, HENRIETTA HERBERT, COUNTESS OF
1745. A Tale. London: 1859. V. 65

CARNE, JOHN
Letters from Switzerland and Italy, During a Late Tour. London: 1834. V. 65
Letters from the East.... London: 1830. V. 66

CARNE, PETER
Deer of Britain and Ireland. 2000. V. 67

CARNEGIE, ANDREW
The Problems of To-Day, Wealth Labor Socialism. New York: 1909. V. 62
Triumphant Democracy; or Fifty Year's March of the Republic. New York: 1886. V. 63; 67

CARNEGIE, D.
Among the Matabele. London: 1894. V. 64

CARNEGIE, DAVID WYNFORD
Spinifex and Sand. A Narrative of Five Years' Pioneering and Exploration in Western Australia. London: 1898. V. 62

CARNEGIE INSTITUTION OF WASHINGTON
Papers from the Tortugas Laboratory of the Carnegie Institution of Washington. Volumes I-V. Washington: 1908-1914. V. 65
Papers from the Tortugas Laboratory of the Carnegie Institution of Washington. Volume II. Washington: 1908. V. 65
Papers from the Tortugas Laboratory of the Carnegie Institution of Washington. Volume VI. Washington: 1914. V. 65
Papers from the Department of Marine Biology of the Carnegie Institution of Washington. Volume VIII. Washington: 1915. V. 65
Papers from the Department of Marine Biology of the Carnegie Institution of Washington. Volume IX. Washington: 1918. V. 65
Papers from the Department of Marine Biology of the Carnegie Institution of Washington. Volume XI. Washington: 1917. V. 65
Papers from the Department of Marine Biology of the Carnegie Institution of Washington. Volume XII. Washington: 1918. V. 65
Papers from the Tortugas Laboratory of the Carnegie Institution of Washington. Volumes 28-29, 31, 33. Washington: 1934-1942. V. 65

CARNEGIE MUSEUM
Memoirs 1901-1911. Pittsbrugh: 1911. V. 65
Memoirs of the Carnegie Museum 1913-1914. Pittsburgh: 1914. V. 65
Memoirs of the Carnegie Museum 1919-1920. Pittsburgh;: 1920. V. 65

CARNELY, A. L.
Diagnosis an Treatment of Brain Ischemia CT Brain Blood Flow, Brain Hemodynamics and Carotid and Vertebral Artery Surgery. New York: 1981. V. 67

CARNEY, ANDREW
Diagnosis and Treatment of Brain Ischemia CT Brain Blood Flow, Brain Hemodynamics and Carootid and Vertebral Artery Surgery. New York: 1981. V. 64; 66

CARNOT, L. N. M.
De La Correlation des Figures the Geometrie. Paris: 1801. V. 66
Principes Fondamentaux de l'Equilibre et du Mouvement. Paris: 1803. V. 65

CARO, ANNIBALE
Rime Del Commendatore Annibal Caro. In Venetia: 1572. V. 66

CAROLINO, PEDRO
The New Guide of the Conversation in Portuguese and English. Boston: 1883. V. 63

CAROSSA, HANS
A Roumanian Diary. London: 1929. V. 63

CAROVE, FRIEDRICH W.
Story Without an End. Boston: 1836. V. 63

CARPENTER, EDWARD
Angels' Wings: a Series of Essays on Art and Its Relation to Life. London: 1908. V. 64
Angels' Wings: a Series of Essays on Art and Its Relation to Life. London: 1913. V. 62
The Art of Creation: Essays on the Self and Its Powers. London: 1904. V. 64
British Aristocracy and the House of Lords. London: 1908. V. 65
England's Ideal and Other Papers on Social Subjects. London: 1887. V. 64
Iolaus: an Anthology of Friendship. London: 1902. V. 64
Love's Coming-of-Age. Manchester: 1896. V. 65
My Days and Dreams, Being Autobiographical Notes. London: 1916. V. 64
My Days and Dreams, Being Autobiographical Notes. London: 1921. V. 64
Never Again! A Protest and a Warning Addressed to the People of Europe. London: 1916. V. 65
Three Ballads: an Intermezzo in War Time. N.P.: 1917. V. 63; 67
An Unknown People. London: 1897. V. 65

CARPENTER, FRANCES
Tales of a Russian Grandmother. Garden City: 1933. V. 64

CARPENTER, G. D. H.
A Naturalist in East Africa, Being Notes Made in Uganda, Ex-German and Portuguese East Africa. Oxford: 1923. V. 64
A Naturalist on Lake Victoria.... New York: 1920. V. 62; 63

CARPENTER, GEORGE
Golden Rules for Diseases of Infants and Children. Bristol and London: 1903. V. 66

CARPENTER, J. ESTLIN
The Life and Work of Mary Carpenter. London: 1881. V. 65

CARPENTER, JOHN
The Life and Death of John Carpenter, Alias Hell Fire Jack the Noted Horse Stealer, who Was Executed April 4, 1805; also the Particulars of Eliz. Barber, Alias Mrs. Daley, hanged for Murder. To Which is Added the Trial of J. Dransfield.... London: 1805. V. 63

CARPENTER, JOHN A.
Sword and Olive Branch - Oliver Otis Howard. Pittsburgh: 1964. V. 67

CARPENTER, MARY THORN
A Girl's Winter in India. New York: 1892. V. 66

CARPENTER, P. H.
Challenger Voyage. Zoology. Part 32. Crinoidea. The Stalked Crinoids. 1884. V. 66
Challenger Voyage. Zoology. Parts 32 and 60. Crinoidea. 1884-1888. V. 66

CARPENTER, STEPHEN
Memoirs of the Hon. Thomas Jefferson, Secretary of State, Vice President and President of the United States of America. New York: 1809. V. 67

CARPENTER, WILLIAM
Political Letters and Pamphlets, Published for the Avowed Purpose of Trying with the Government the Question of Law - Whether All Publications Containing News or Intelligence, However Limited in Quantity or Irregularly Issued.... London: 1830-1831. V. 63

CARPENTER, WILLIAM B.
Introduction to the Study of the Foraminifera. London: 1862. V. 63; 65; 66
The Microscope and Its Revelations. London: 1875. V. 63; 67
Microscope and Its Revelations. New York: 1883. V. 66
The Microscope and Its Revelations. London: 1891. V. 62; 64
The Microscope and Its Revelations. London: 1901. V. 64
On the Use and Abuse of Alcoholic Liquors, in Health and Disease. Boston: 1851. V. 64
Zoology; Being a Systematic Account of the General Structure, Habits, Instincts and Uses of the Principal Families of the Animal Kingdom.... London: 1858. V. 63

CARPENTER, WILLIAM W.
Travels and Adventures in Mexico: in the Course of Journeys Upward of 2500 Miles Performed On Foot. New York: 1851. V. 67

CARPENTIER, ALEJO
The Kingdom of This World. New York: 1957. V. 65
The Kingdom of This World. New York: 1987. V. 65
The Lost Steps. London: 1956. V. 67

CARPENTIER, JACQUES
Platonis Cum Ariototelo in Univerca Philosophia, Comparatio.... Parisiis: 1573. V. 65

CARPUE, J. C.
An Account of Two Successful Operations for Restoring a Lost Nose from the Integuments of the Forehead. Birmingham: 1981. V. 62; 63

CARR, A. H.
The True Likeness of John Wesley. London: 1930. V. 66

CARR, BENJAMIN
Lessons and Exercises in Vocal Music. Baltimore: 1810. V. 66

CARR, CALEB
The Alienist. New York: 1994. V. 63; 64; 66; 67
America Invulnerable. New York: 1988. V. 63; 64; 67
Casing the Promised Land. New York: 1980. V. 67
The Devil Soldier. New York: 1992. V. 66

CARR, CAMILLUS
A Cavalryman in Indian Country. Ashland: 1974. V. 65

CARR, CLARK E.
My Day and Generation. Chicago: 1908. V. 64; 67

CARR, COMYNS, MRS.
Sketches of Northern Italian Folk. London: 1878. V. 62

CARR, EZRA S.
The Patrons of Husbandry on the Pacific Coast. San Francisco: 1875. V. 64

CARR, FRANK G. C.
Vanishing Craft. London: 1934. V. 65

CARR, GLYN
Swing Away, Climber. New York: 1959. V. 66

CARR, J.
Analyses of New Works of Voyages and Travels. London: 1806. V. 64

CARR, J. L.
A Month in the Country. 1990. V. 62; 65
What Hetty Did. Kettering: 1988. V. 65

CARR, JOHN
Pioneer Days in California: Historical and Personal Sketches. Eureka: 1891. V. 63; 66
The Stranger in France; or, a Tour from Devonshire to Paris.... London: 1803. V. 66
The Stranger in Ireland. London: 1806. V. 64
A Vulcan Among the Argonauts, Being Vivid Excerpts from Those Most Original and Amusing Memoirs. Berkeley: 1936. V. 62

CARR, JOHN DICKSON
The Arabian Nights Murder. London: 1936. V. 64
The Dead Man's Knock. New York: 1958. V. 66
Deadley Hall. New York: 1971. V. 67
The Demoniacs. New York: 1962. V. 66
Dr. Fell, Detective and Other Stories. New York: 1947. V. 65
The Emperor's Snuff Box. New York: 1942. V. 66
Fatal Descent. New York: 1939. V. 67
Fell and Foul Play. New York: 1991. V. 67
He Who Whispers. New York: 1946. V. 66; 67
In Spite of Thunder. New York: 1960. V. 66

CARR, JOHN DICKSON continued
Lord of the Sorcerers. London: 1946. V. 66
The Man Who Could Not Shudder. New York: 1940. V. 65
The Murder of Sir Edmund Godfrey. New York: 1936. V. 66
My Late Wives. New York: 1946. V. 66
My Late Wives. London: 1947. V. 66
Panic in Box C. New York: 1966. V. 67
The Plague Court Murders. 1934. V. 62; 64
The Problem of the Wire Cage. New York: 1939. V. 67
The Punch and Judy Murders. 1937. V. 64
Scandal at High Chimneys. London: 1959. V. 67
The Sleeping Sphinx: a Doctor Fell Detective Story. New York: 1947. V. 63
The Third Bullet and Other Stories. London: 1954. V. 66
The Third Bullet and Other Stories. New York: 1954. V. 63; 64; 66
Till Death do Us Part. New York: 1944. V. 66
The White Priority Murders. 1934. V. 64

CARR, RICHARD
The Classical Scholar's Guide; an Original Treatise on Clasical Pronunciation &c. London: 1832. V. 63; 65; 66

CARR, WILLIAM
The Dialect of Craven, in the West-Riding of the County of York.... London: 1828. V. 64; 65; 66
Horae Momenta Cravenae, or, the Dialect of Craven.... London: 1824. V. 64; 65

CARRA, EMMA, PSEUD.
Viroqua; or, the Flower of the Ottawas. Boston: 1848. V. 64

CARRACCI, ANNIBALE
Historia del Testamento Vecchio. Roma: 1670?. V. 66

CARRICK, JOHN DONALD
The Laird of Logan; or, Anecdotes and Tales Illustrative of the Wit and Humour of Scotland. Glasgow: 1853. V. 67

CARRIER, CONSTANCE
The Middle Voice. Denver: 1955. V. 63

CARRIERI, RAFFAELE
Souvenir Caporal. Verona: 1946. V. 64

CARRIGAN, MINNE BOCE
Captured by the Indians - Reminiscences of Pioneer Life in Minnesota. Buffalo Lake: 1912. V. 63; 66

CARRIKER, ROBERT C.
Fort Supply Indian Territory, Frontier Outpost on the Plains. Norman: 1970. V. 65; 67

CARRINGTON, DORA
Carrington - Paintings, Drawings and Decorations. Oxford: 1978. V. 64

CARRINGTON, FRANCES C.
My Army Life and the Fort Phil Kearny Masacre. Philadelphia: 1911. V. 65; 67

CARRINGTON, FREDERICK AUGUSTUS
A Supplement to All the Modern Treatises on the Criminal Law. London: 1827. V. 65

CARRINGTON, HENRY B.
Some Phases of the Indian Question - An Address. Boston: 1909. V. 65; 67

CARRINGTON, HENRY E.
The Plymouth and Devonport Guide; with Sketches of the Surrounding Scenery. 1830. V. 63

CARRINGTON, MARGARET IRVIN
Absaraka Home of the Crows Being the Experiences of an Officer's Wife on the Plains. Philadelphia: 1878. V. 67

CARRINGTON, N. T.
Dartmoor; a Descriptive Poem. London: 1826. V. 62
Remarks on the Rev. R. Polwhele's Letter to the Rev. R. Hawker, D.D. Vicar of the Parish of Charles, Plymouth, Occasioned by His Late Expedition into Cornwall. Plym Dock: 1800?. V. 63

CARROL, JOHN
Fanaticism! Curelty!! Bigotry!!! The Particulars of the Horrible Murder of Catharine Sinnott, a Child Under Four Years of Age.... London: 1824. V. 63

CARROLL, B. R.
Historical Collections of South Carolina.... New York: 1836. V. 63

CARROLL, CAMPBELL
Three Bar. The Story of Douglas Lake. Vancouver: 1958. V. 66

CARROLL, H. BAILEY
The Texas Sante Fe Trail. Canyon: 1951. V. 65
Three New Mexico Chronicles. Albuquerque: 1942. V. 66

CARROLL, JIM
The Basketball Diaries. California: 1978. V. 65; 66
Forced Entries: The Downtown Diaries 1971-1973. New York: 1987. V. 65

CARROLL, JOHN M.
The Arrest and Killing of Sitting Bull - A Documentary. Glendale: 1986. V. 67
Bards of the Little Big Horn. Bryan: 1978. V. 64
The Benteen Golden Letters on Custer and His Battle. New York: 1974. V. 65; 67
The Black Military Experience in the American West. Fort Leavenworth: 1973. V. 66
Buffalo Soldiers West. Fort Collins: 1971. V. 65; 67
Camp Talk - the Very Private Letters of Frederick W. Benteen of the 7th Cavalry to His Wife 1871-1888. Mattituck: 1983. V. 67
Cavalry Scraps - The Writing of Frederick W. Benteen. Athens: 1979. V. 65; 67
Colonel Tommy Tompkins: a Military Heritage and Tradition. Mattitock;: 1984. V. 67
Custer in Texas: an Interrupted Narrative.... New York: 1975. V. 63; 64
Custer in the Civil War - His Unfinished Memoir. San Raphael: 1977. V. 67
Eggenhofer: The Pulp Years. Fort Collins: 1975. V. 63; 66
General Custer and the Battle of the Little Big Horn: the Federal View. New York: 1976. V. 65; 67
General Custer and the Battle of the Washita: the Federal View. Bryan: 1978. V. 65; 67
The Grand Alexis in the United States of America. New York: 1972. V. 65; 67
I, Varnum, the Autobiographical Reminiscences of Custer's Chief of Scouts. Mattituck. V. 67
Illustrations of the Black Soldier in the West. N.P: 1973. V. 66
Private Theodore Ewert's Diary of the Black Hills Expedition of 1874. Piscataway: 1986. V. 67
Roll Call On the Little Big Horn, June 28, 1876. Fort Collins: 1974. V. 65; 67
The Two Battles of the Little Big Horn. New York: 1974. V. 65; 67

CARROLL, JONATHAN
Outside the Dog Museum. London: 1991. V. 67
Sleeping in Flame. London: 1988. V. 67
Voice of Our Shadow. New York: 1983. V. 67

CARROLL, KENNETH
Quakerism on the Eastern Shore. Baltimore?: 1970. V. 67

CARROLL, PAUL
Odes. Chicago: 1969. V. 67
The Young American Poets - a Big Table Book. Chicago and New York: 1968. V. 64

CARRUTH, HAYDEN
Almanach du Printemps Vivarois. New York: 1979. V. 63
Journey to a Known Place. A Poem. Norfolk: 1961. V. 62; 63
The Norfolk Poems.... Iowa City: 1962. V. 63
The Oldest Killed Lake in North America, Poems: 1979-1981. Grenada: 1985. V. 62

CARRUTH, VANCE
Teton Sketches of Summer. Boulder: 1969. V. 63; 66

CARRUTHERS, DOUGLAS
Arabian Adventure. 1935. V. 66
Beyond the Caspian; a Naturalist in Central Asia. Edinburgh: 1949. V. 64
Unknown Mongolia; a Record of Travel and Exploration in North-West Mongolia and Dzungaria. London: 1913. V. 64
Unknown Mongolia: a Record of Travel and Exploration in North-West Mongolia and Dzungaria. London: 1914. V. 64

CARRUTHERS, FRANCIS, MRS.
Twentieth Century Home Cook Book. Chicago: 1906. V. 67

CARRYL, CHARLES
Davy and the Goblin, or what Followed Reading Alice's Adventures in Wonderland. Boston and New York: 1913. V. 64

CARRYL, GUY W.
Mother Goose for Grown-Ups. New York: 1900. V. 63

CARSE, ROBERT
Department of the South. Hilton Head Island in the Civil War. Columbia: 1961. V. 65

CARSE, ROLAND
The Pantomine ABC. London: 1902. V. 62

CARSON, C.
Letters from the Alphabet. Oldcastle: 1995. V. 62

CARSON, JAMES H.
Recollections of the California Mines - An Account of the Early Discoveries of Gold, with Anecdotes and Sketches of California and Miner's Life, and a Description of the Great Tulare Valley. Oakland: 1950. V. 65; 67

CARSON, JAMES PETIGRU
Life, Letters and Speeches of.... Washington: 1920. V. 63

CARSON, L.
The Stage Yearbook. London: 1908. V. 65

CARSON, RACHEL
The Edge of the Sea. Boston: 1955. V. 63; 64
The Sea Around Us. New York: 1980. V. 66
Silent Spring. Boston: 1962. V. 63; 64; 67

CARTARI, VINCENZO
Le Imagine con la Spositione de i Dei de Gli Antichi. Venice: 1556. V. 66

CARTAS Sobre la Educacion del Bello Sexo Por Una Senora Americana. Paris: 18-?. V. 63

CARTE, THOMAS
An History of the Life of James Duke of Ormonde, from His Birth in 1610, to His Death in 1688. London: 1736-1735. V. 66

CARTER, A. CECIL
The Kingdom of Siam. New York: 1904. V. 64

CARTER, ANGELA
Black Venus's Tale. London: 1980. V. 62
The Infernal Desire Machines of Doctor Hoffman. London: 1972. V. 65

CARTER, ANGELA continued
Shadow Dance. London: 1966. V. 65; 66; 67
Unicorn. Leeds: 1966. V. 63

CARTER, BENJAMIN F.
Historical Address. Woodbury and Vicinity...in M. E. Church, Woodbury, N.J. February 27th, 1872. Woodbury: 1873. V. 63; 66

CARTER, CHARLES ROOKING
Victoria, the British El-Dorado.... London: 1870. V. 62

CARTER, CLARENCE E.
Territorial Papers of the U.S. Volumes II and III. Northwest Territories 1781-1803. Washington: 1934. V. 64

CARTER, DENNY
Henry Farny. Japan: 1978. V. 63; 66
Henry Farny. New York: 1978. V. 62; 64; 65; 66

CARTER, ELIZABETH
Poems on Several Occasions. London: 1776. V. 65
A Series of Letters Between Mrs. Elizabeth Carter and Miss Catherine Talbot, from the Year 1741 to 1770.... London: 1819. V. 67

CARTER, EMILY BARKER
Hollywood: The Story of the Cahuengas. Hollywood: 1926. V. 62

CARTER, FORREST
The Education of Little Tree. N.P: 1976. V. 62
The Education of Little Tree. New York: 1976. V. 67

CARTER, FREDERICK
D. H. Lawrence and the Body Mystical. London: 1932. V. 65
The Dragon of the Alchemists. London: 1926. V. 62

CARTER, H. B.
Sir Joseph Banks (1743-1820). Winchester: 1987. V. 63; 67

CARTER, HARRY
Catalogue of the Edward Clark Library. Edinburgh: 1976. V. 64
A History of the Oxford University Press. Volume I to the Year 1780. Oxford: 1975. V. 63

CARTER, HARVEY LEWIS
Dear Old Kit The Historical Kit Carson. Norman: 1968. V. 66

CARTER, HENRY F.
Reports on Malaria and Mosquitoes, Ceylon. Colombo: 1914-1927. V. 62

CARTER, HOWARD
The Tomb of Tut Ankh Amen, Discovered by the Earl of Carnarvon and Howard Carter. London: 1923. V. 64

CARTER, JAMES
A Lecture on the Primitive State of Man, Read Before the Ipswich Mechanics' Institute on Sept. 15, and Before the Colchester Mechanics' Institute on Sept. 28, 1835. London: 1836. V. 67

CARTER, JAMES EARL
Always a Reckoning. New York: 1995. V. 64; 67
Everything to Gain. New York: 1987. V. 65
Keeping Faith. New York: 1982. V. 63; 65
Keeping Faith. Norwalk: 1982-1986. V. 65
Living Faith. New York: 1996. V. 66
An Outdoor Journal. New York: 1988. V. 65

CARTER, JOHN
A. E. Housman, an Annotated Checklist. London: 1940. V. 64
ABC for Book Collectors. London: 1952. V. 64
ABC for Book Collectors. New York: 1960. V. 64
After Ten Years. London: 1961. V. 64
Bibliography of the Rare Book Trade. 1954. V. 64
Binding Variants in English Publishing 1820-1900. London and New York: 1932. V. 63; 64
Binding Variants in English Publishing 1820-1900; More Binding Variants. London and New York: 1932-1938. V. 62
Books and Book-Collectors. London: 1956. V. 64
Catalogue of the Valuable Collection of Printed Books the Property of the Late John Carter.... London: 1976. V. 64
Clerihews; an Unofficial Supplement to Biography for Beginners. Cambridge: 1938. V. 64
Collecting Detective Fiction. London: 1938. V. 64
The Dry Martini. London: 1963. V. 64
An Enquiry Into the Nature of Certain Nineteenth Century Pamphlets. London: 1934. V. 62; 63; 67
The Forgeries of Tennyson's Plays. Oxford: 1967. V. 64
The Iniquity of Oblivion Foil'd; or, a Discourse of Certain Copies, Lately Found, or Urne Buriall and The Garden of Cyrus.... London: 1932. V. 64
The John Carter Collection of A. E. Housman. 1966. V. 64
Michael Sadleir: a Valediction. London: 1958. V. 64
More Binding Variants. London: 1938. V. 63; 64
New Paths in Book Collecting: Essays by Various Hands. New York: 1934. V. 64
Printing and the Mind of Man. London: 1963. V. 64; 65
Printing and the Mind of Man. London: 1967. V. 64
Printing and the Mind of Man. New York: 1967. V. 62; 63; 64
Printing and the Mind of Man. London: 1983. V. 64
Taste and Technique in Book-Collecting: a Study of Recent Developments in Great Britain and the United States. Cambridge: 1948. V. 64
William Ged and the Invention of Stereotype. London: 1960. V. 66

CARTER, MARY NELSON
North Carolina Sketches. Chicago: 1900. V. 67

CARTER, MATHEW
Honor Redivivus; or, the Analysis of Honor and Amory. London: 1673. V. 65

CARTER, MATTHEW
A Most True and Exact Relation of That as Honourable as Unfortunate Expedition of Kent, Essex and Colchester. London: 1650. V. 66

CARTER, R. G.
On the Border with Mackenzie of Winning West Texas from the Comanche. 1988. V. 65

CARTER, R. R.
Pictures and Engravings,. London: 1904. V. 66

CARTER, RAY
An Exhibition of Works by Sir John Betjeman from the Collection of Ray Carter. London: 1983. V. 63

CARTER, ROBERT B.
A Half-Hour with Religious, Charitable and Secular Institutions, Industries, Corporations, Societies and Mercantile and Professional Representatives, of Burlington, N.J. Beverly: 1881. V. 63; 66

CARTER, ROBERT G.
The Old Sergeant Story Winning the West from Fighting Indians and Bad men in Texas from 1870 to 1876. New York: 1926. V. 64
The Old Sergeant's Story - Fighting Indians and Bad Men in Texas from 1870 to 1876. Mattituck: 1982. V. 67
On the Border with Mac Kenzie or Winning West Texas from the Comanches. New York: 1961. V. 67

CARTER, SEBASTIAN
Miscellany 2. London: 1998. V. 62; 67
Rampant Lions Press. Miscellany 2. Cambridge: 1998. V. 65

CARTER, SUSAN
The Frugal Housewife, or Complete Woman Cook. London: 1790?. V. 65

CARTER, SUSANNAH
The Frugal Housewife; or Complete Woman Cook. Philadelphia: 1796. V. 64

CARTER, THOMAS FORTESCUE
A Narrative of the Boer War.... London: 1883. V. 64

CARTER, THOMAS FRANCIS
The Invention of Printing in China and Its Spread Westward. New York: 1925. V. 64
The Invention of Printing in China and Its Spread Westward. New York: 1931. V. 67
The Invention of Printing in China and Its Spread Westward. New York: 1955. V. 64

CARTER, W. H.
The History of Fort Robinson. Cranford: 1942. V. 65

CARTER, WILL
Clerihews - an Unofficial Supplement to Biography for Beginners. Cambridge: 1938. V. 63

CARTER, WILLIAM H.
From Yorktown to Santiago, with the Sixth Cavalry. Baltimore: 1900. V. 63; 67
The History of Fort Robinson. Crawford: 1942. V. 67
Horses, Saddles and Bridles. Leavensworth: 1906. V. 67
The Life of Lieutenant General Chaffee. Chicago: 1917. V. 64; 67
McCurtain County and Southeastern Oklahoma. Idabel: 1923. V. 63

CARTERET, PHILIP
Carteret's Voyage Round the world 1766-1769. Cambridge: 1965. V. 63

CARTIER-BRESSON, HENRI
About Russia. London: 1974. V. 65
The Decisive Moment. New York: 1952. V. 64
From One China to the Other. New York: 1956. V. 66
The People of Moscow. New York: 1955. V. 66; 67

CARTON, PAUL
L'Art Medical. L'Individualisation des Regles de Santo. Paris: 1930. V. 65

CARTWRIGHT, DAVID
Natural History of Western Wild Animals and Guide for Hunters, Trappers and Sportsmen; Embracing Observations on the Art of Hunting and Trapping. Toledo: 1875. V. 63; 66

CARTWRIGHT, FAIRFAX LEIGHTON
Olga Zanelli: a Tale of an Imperial City. London: 1890. V. 66

CARTWRIGHT, GEORGE
A Journal of Transactions and Events, During a Residence of Nearly Sixteen Years on the Coast of Labrador; Containing Many Interesting Particulars, Both of the Country and Its Inhabitants, Not Hitherto Known. Newark: 1792. V. 66

CARTWRIGHT, JULIA
Sacharissa. Some Account of Dorothy Sidney, Countess of Sutherland her Family and Friends 1617-1684. London. V. 65

CARTY, JAMES
Ireland (From the Flight of the Earls to the Treaty of 1921). 1949-1951. V. 63; 66
Ireland (From the Flight of the Earls to the Treaty of 1921). 1951-1952. V. 63; 66

CARUS, PAUL
The Mechanistic Principle and the Non-Mechanical. Chicago: 1913. V. 65

CARUTHERS, ELI WASHINGTON
Sketch of the Life and Character of the Rev. David Caldwell, D. D. Greensborough: 1842. V. 63; 66

CARUTHERS, WILLIAM ALEXANDER
The Cavaliers of Virginia, or the Recluse of Jamestown. New York: 1834-1835. V. 62

CARVER, JONATHAN
Three Years Travels through the Interior Parts of North America.... Philadelphia: 1784. V. 63; 66

CARVER, RAYMOND
All of Us: the Collected Poems. London: 1996. V. 65
At Night the Salmon Move. Santa Barbara: 1976. V. 62; 64; 66; 67
Carnations: a Play in One Act. Vineburg: 1992. V. 62; 63; 64; 66
Cathedral. New York: 1983. V. 62; 63; 65; 66; 67
Fires: Essays, Poems, Stories. Santa Barbara: 1983. V. 62; 64; 66
Furious Seasons and Other Stories. Santa Barbara: 1977. V. 62
A New Path to the Waterfall. New York: 1989. V. 67
No Heroics, Please. New York: 1992. V. 63; 67
The Painter and the Fish. Concord: 1988. V. 62; 63
Put Yourself in My Shoes. Santa Barbara: 1974. V. 62; 65
Two Poems. Salisbury: 1982. V. 62
Two Poems. Concord: 1986. V. 62
Ultramarine. New York: 1986. V. 62; 63; 64; 66
What We Talk About When We Talk About Love. New York: 1981. V. 62; 63; 65; 66
What We Talk About When We Talk About Love. London: 1982. V. 65
Where I'm Calling From. Franklin Center: 1988. V. 65; 67
Where I'm Calling From. London: 1988. V. 65
Where I'm Calling From. New York: 1988. V. 62; 65
Where Water Comes Together and Other Water. New York: 1985. V. 62; 66; 67
Where Water Comes Together With other Water. New York: 1986. V. 67
Will You Please Be Quiet, Please?. New York: 1976. V. 63; 65; 66
Will You Please Be Quiet, Please?. New York: 1978. V. 62
Winter Insomnia. Santa Cruz: 1970. V. 62; 64; 66

CARVOE, FREDERICK W.
Story without End. Boston: 1836. V. 66
The Story Without End. London: 1872. V. 66

CARY, JOHN
Cary's New Itinerary.... London: 1798. V. 63
Cary's New Itinerary.... London: 1802. V. 63
Cary's New Itinerary.... London: 1815. V. 64
Cary's New Map of England and Wales, with Part of Scotland. London: 1794. V. 62
Cary's Survey of the High Roads from London to Hampton Court, Bagshot, Oakingham, (etc.).... London: 1790. V. 62
Cary's Traveller's Companion, or, a Delineation of the Turnpike Roads of England and Wales.... London: 1824. V. 66
A Discourse Concerning the Trade of Ireland and Scotland, as They Stand in Competition with the Trade of England.... London: 1696. V. 62; 65
A New Elementary Atlas Containing Distinct Maps Of All the Principal Kingdoms and States Throughout the World Drawn from the Best Authorities. (with) New and Correct English Atlas.. London: 1813-1809. V. 66
New Itinerary: or an Accurate Delineation of the Great Roads, Both Direct and Cross. London: 1802. V. 66
Traveller's Companion; or a Delineation of the Turnpike Roads of England and Wales...(with) New Itinerary; or an Accurate Delineation of the Great Roads. 1814-1815. V. 66

CARY, JOYCE
The African Witch. London: 1936. V. 65
An American Visitor. London: 1933. V. 64
The Drunken Sailor. London: 1947. V. 62
A House of Children. London: 1941. V. 65
Illustrations by Joyce Cary for The Old Strife at Plant's. Oxford: 1956. V. 66

CARY, LORENE
Black Ice. New York: 1991. V. 67

CARY, MELBERT B.
Mademoiselle from Armentieres. New York: 1930. V. 62
Mademoiselle from Armentieres. New York: 1930-1935. V. 64

CARY, RICHARD MILTON
Skirmishers' Drill and Bayonet Exercise (as Now Used in the French Army), with Suggestions for the Soldier in Actual Conflict. Richmond: 1861. V. 62

CARY, S. F.
Ritual for the Admission of Females into the Order of the Sons of Temperance. Trenton: 1860. V. 63

CARY, VIRGINIA
Letters on Female Character, Address to a Young Lady.... Richmond: 1830. V. 62; 64; 67

CARYL, JOSEPH
An Exposition with Practical Observations Upon the Book of Job. London: 1676-1677. V. 67

CARYOPHILUS, BLASIUS
De Veterum Clypeis.... Lugduni Batavorum (Leiden): 1751. V. 66

CARYSFORT, JOHN JOSHUA, 1ST EARL
Copy of a Letter from the Right Honourable Lord Carysfort, to the Huntingdonshire Committee: to Which is Added, the Report of the Westminster Sub-Committee Respecting the Duration of Parliament.... N.P. London?: 1780. V. 67

Dramatic and Narrative Poems. London: 1810. V. 62

CASANOVA DE SEINGALT, GIROLAMO
Memoirs. Edinburgh: 1940. V. 67
The Memoirs. Haarlem: 1972. V. 62

CASAS, BARTOLOME DE LAS, BP. OF CHIAPA
An Account of the First Voyages and Discoveries made by the Spaniards in America. London: 1699. V. 64
Relation des Voyages et des De'Couvertes Que les Espagnols ont Fait dans les Indes Occidentales.... Amsterdam: 1698. V. 63

CASATI, GAETANO
Ten Years in Equatoria and the Return with Emin Pasha. London and New York: 1891. V. 64

CASAUBON, ISAAC
Animadversionvm in Athen Dipnosophitas Libri XV. Lvgdvni: 1621. V. 63

CASE, ARTHUR E.
A Bibliography of English Poetical Miscellanies 1521-1750. Oxford: 1935. V. 66

CASE, FRANK
Tales of a Wayward Inn. New York: 1938. V. 64

CASE, NELSON
History of Labette County, Kansas, from the First Settlement to the Close of 1892. Topeka: 1893. V. 63

THE CASE of Orphans Consider'd, from Antiquity. London: 1725. V. 62; 64

THE CASE of Our Fellow Creatures, the Oppressed Africans, Respectively Recommended to the Serious Consideration of the Legislature of Great Britain. London: 1784. V. 63

THE CASE of the Hon. Admiral Byng, Ingenuously Represented. London: 1757. V. 65

THE CASE of the Proprietors of East New Jersey, with Opinions of Counsel on the Same. Newark: 1825. V. 63

CASEMENT, DAN D.
Random Recollections - The Life and Times and Something On the Personal Philosophy of a 20th Century Cowman. Kansas City: 1955. V. 65

CASEMENT, ROGER
Sir Roger Casement's Diaries: His Mission to Germany and the Findlay Affair. Munich: 1922. V. 62; 65
Some Poems of.... 1918. V. 62; 65

CASEY, JOHN
An American Romance. New York: 1977. V. 62; 63; 65; 67
Spartina. New York: 1988. V. 62
Spartina. New York: 1989. V. 66
Testimony and Demeanor. New York: 1979. V. 63; 65; 67

CASEY, R.
The Ammonoidea of the Lower Greensand. 1960-1980. V. 62

CASEY, ROBERT J.
Baghdad and Points East. New York: 1928. V. 64

CASH, AGNES E.
Tufty, Teddy and Toots: the Adventures of Three Hold Bears. New York: 1916. V. 62

CASH, BARBARA
Fragments. Sweden, Maine: 1997. V. 62

CASH, W. J.
The Mind of the South. New York: 1941. V. 62; 64

CASHMORE, R. A., MRS.
Free-Arm Drawing as a Means of Development. London: 1895. V. 67

THE CASKET, a Miscellany, Consisting of Unpublished Poems. London: 1829. V. 64

CASKEY, L. D.
Catalogue of Greek and Roman Sculpture. Cambridge: 1925. V. 62
Geometry of Greek Vases: Attic Vases in the Museum of Fine Arts.... Boston: 1922. V. 62

CASLON, H. W., & CO., LTD.
Types, Borders and Initials. Catalogue of Printers' Joinery, etc. London: 1925. V. 66

CASPARY, VERA
Bedelia. London: 1945. V. 65; 66
Final Portrait. London: 1971. V. 66
The Husband. New York: 1957. V. 66
Laura. Boston: 1943. V. 67

CASSADY, CAROLYN
Heart Beat. My Life with Jack and Neal. Berkeley: 1976. V. 62; 64

CASSAVETES, JOHN
Minnie and Moskowitz. Los Angeles: 1973. V. 66

CASSELL, GEORGE F.
Clive Staples Lewis. Chicago: 1950. V. 63

CASSELL, GUSTAV
The Theory of Social Economy. London: 1923. V. 65

CASSELL'S Book of Birds. London: 1880. V. 62

CASSELL'S Book of Indoor Amusements. London: 1888. V. 66

CASSELL'S Children's Annual 1916. 1915. V. 65

CASSERES, BENJAMIN DE
The Shadow Eater. New York: 1923. V. 63

CASSIN, JOHN
Illustrations of the Birds of California, Texas, Oregon, British and Russian America.... Philadelphia: 1856. V. 67

CASSIN, R.
50 Years of Alpism. 1981. V. 65

CASSIODORUS, FLAVIUS MAGNUS AURELIUS
Variaravm Libri XII. De Anima Liber Vnvs. Augustae Vindelic: 1533. V. 63; 66

CASSON, S.
Sculpture of Today. London: 1939. V. 65

CASSON, STANLEY
Rupert Brooke and Skyros. London: 1921. V. 64

CASTANEDA, CARLOS
The Teachings of Don Juan. Berkeley and Los Angeles: 1968. V. 63; 65

CASTEL, ALBERT
General Sterling Price and the Civil War in the West. Baton Rouge: 1968. V. 63

CASTEL, DR.
Exposition des Attributs du Systeme Nerveux Refutation de la Doctrine de Charles Bell a Explication Des Phenomenes de la Paralysie. Paris: 1845. V. 64

CASTELL, ROBERT
The Villas of the Ancients Illustrated. London: 1728. V. 66

CASTELLANOS, ISRAEL
La Delincuencia Femenina en Cuba. Habana: 1929. V. 64

CASTELLANOS, ROSARIO
Balun Canan. Mexico City: 1957. V. 67

CASTELLI, CHARLES
The Theory of Options in Stocks and Shares. London: 1877. V. 64

CASTELLUM Huttonicum. Some Account of Sheriff-Hutton Castle, with Brief Notices of the Church of St. Helen, the Ancient Forst of Galtres, the Poet Gower of Stitenham. York: 1824. V. 62

CASTETTER, EDWARD F.
Pima and Papago Indian Agriculture. Albuqerque: 1942. V. 67

CASTIGLIONE, BALDASSARE
The Courtyer.... London: 1900. V. 66

CASTIGLIONI, ARTURO
Adventures of the Mind. Philadelphia: 1946. V. 67
A History of Medicine. New York: 1941. V. 62; 64; 65; 66; 67

CASTIGLIONI, LUIGI
Viaggio Negli Stati Uniti Dell' America Settentrionale, Fatto Negli Anni 1785, 1786 e 1787. Milan: 1790. V. 63

CASTILLO, ANA
So Far From God. New York: 1993. V. 67

CASTLE, AGNES
Our Sentimental Garden. London: 1914. V. 62

CASTLE, EGERTON, MRS.
My Little Lady Anne. London: 1896. V. 64

CASTLE, THOMAS
An Essay on Animal, Mineral and Vegetable Poisons.... 1822. V. 62

CASTLEMAN, JOHN BRECKENRIDGE
Active Service. Louisville: 1917. V. 62

CASTLEMAN, RIVA
American Impressions: Prints Since Pollack. New York: 1985. V. 65

CASTOR
A Century of Foxhunting with the Warwickshire Hounds.... London: 1891. V. 67

CASTRO, PEDRO DE
Causas Eficientes y Accidentales del Fluxo y Refluxo del mar. Madrid: 1694. V. 62

CASTRO ALVES, ANTONIO DE
Espumas Fluctuantes. Poesias. Bahia: 1870. V. 62

CASWALL, EDWARD
Characteristic Sketches of Young Gentlemen. London: 1835. V. 64

CASWAY, JERROLD I.
Owen Roe O'Neill and the Struggle for Catholic Ireland. Philadelphia: 1984. V. 67

CAT, CHRISTOPHER
The Lost Zoo. New York: 1940. V. 67

A CATALOGUE of All the Books, Printed in the United States, with the Prices, and Places Where Published, Annexed. Boston: 1804. V. 64

A CATALOGUE of Five Hundred Celebrated Authors of Great Britain, Now Living. London: 1788. V. 63

CATALOGUE of Morgan Horses Blue Ribbon Winners at Edgeview Farm. Brandon: 1919. V. 66

CATALOGUE of Rare and Curious Books, Including the Collection of M. Tross.... London: 1870. V. 66

CATALOGUE of the Museum of Flags, Trophies and Relics Relating to the Revolution, War of 1812, Mexican War, and the Present Rebellion, Forming the Most Complete and Interesting Collection Ever Brought Together in the United States. Philadelphia: 1864. V. 64

CATANEO, GIOVANNI
The Source, the Strength and the True Spirit of Laws.... London: 1753. V. 63

CATANEO, PIETRO
La Pratiche delle due Prime Matematiche.... Venice: 1559. V. 63; 66

CATCOTT, A.
A Treatise on the Deluge. London: 1768. V. 62

CATE, WIRT A.
Two Soldiers: the Campaign Diaries of Thomas J. Key, CSA Dec. 7, 1863 - May 7, 1865 and Robert J. Campbell, U.S.A. Jan 1 - July 1864. Chapel Hill: 1938. V. 62; 65

CATECHISMUS Romanus, ex Decreto Concilii Tridentini & Pii V...Nunc Vero Luculentis Quaestionibus, Quae Mox Rei Propositae Materiam Oculis Subijicant Distinctus, Brevibusque.... Antwerp: 1596. V. 62

CATESBY, MARK
The Natural History of Carolina, Florida and the Bahama Islands. Savannah: 1974. V. 65; 67

CATHCART, WILLIAM
The Ancient British and Irish Churches Including the Life and Labors of St. Patrick. Philadelphia: 1894. V. 64
The Baptist Encyclopedia. A Dictionary...of the Baptist Denomination.... Philadelphia: 1881. V. 66

THE CATHEDRALS of England and Wales. London: 1894. V. 62; 66

CATHER, WILLA SIBERT
April Twilights. Boston: 1903. V. 63; 67
April Twilights. New York: 1923. V. 63
Death Comes for the Archbishop. Lincoln: 1999. V. 67
December Night. New York: 1933. V. 63
Father Junipero's Holy Family. N.P: 1955. V. 67
A Lost Lady. New York: 1923. V. 65
Lucy Gayheart. New York: 1935. V. 62; 63; 64; 65; 67
My Mortal Enemy. New York: 1926. V. 62
Not Under Forty. New York: 1936. V. 62; 63; 64; 66
Obscure Destinies. New York: 1932. V. 63; 66
The Old Beauty and Others. New York: 1948. V. 66
The Professor's House. New York: 1925. V. 66
Saphira and the Slave Girl. New York: 1940. V. 62; 63; 64; 66; 67
Shadows on the Rock. New York: 1931. V. 62; 63; 64; 67

CATHERINE OF SIENNA, SAINT
Lettere Devotissime Della Beata Vergine Santa Caterina Da Siena.... Venetia: 1562. V. 66

CATHOLIC CHURCH. LITURGY & RITUAL
Index Librorum Prohibitorum. Rome. 1900. V. 64
Missae Episcopales Pro Sacris Ordinibus Conferendis Secundum Ritu(m) Sacrosancte Romane Ecclesie...Breve Compendium Diversorum Casuum.. Venice: 1563. V. 65
L'Officio di Maria Vergine. Vienna: 1672. V. 65
Officium B. Mariae Virginis, Nuper Reformatum.. Antwerp: 1731. V. 65

CATHOLIC CHURCH. LITURGY & RITUAL. BREVIARY
Breviarium Romanum. Lyon: 1548. V. 62
Breviarum Romanum. Lyon: 1507. V. 63
Breviarum Sanctae Lugdunensis Ecclesiae Primae Galliarum Sedis. Paris: 1780. V. 62

CATHOLIC CHURCH. LITURGY & RITUAL. HOURS
Heures A l'Usaige de Romme. Paris: 1515?. V. 64
Heures Choisies des Dames Chretiennes. Paris: 1874. V. 62
Heures Nouvelles Dediees a Madame Royale. Brussels: 1759. V. 66
Horae Beatae Virginis Mariae Juxta Ritum Sacri Ordinis Praedicatorum Jussu Editae. 1923. V. 67
Horae Beatae Virginis Mariae Juxta Ritum Sacri Ordinis Praedicatorum.... Ditchling, Sussex: 1923. V. 66
Horae Diue Virginis Marie Secundum vsum Romanum.... Paris: 1511. V. 67
Livre de Prieres, Tisse d'Apres les Enluminures des Manscrits Du XIVe au XVIe Siecle. Lyon: 1886. V. 67
Livre de Prieres, Tisse d'Apres les Enluminures des manuscrits du XIVe au XVIe Siecle. Lyon: 1887. V. 62
Officium b. Mariae Virginis Nuper Reformatum. Antwerp: 1677. V. 67
Officium Beatae Mariae Virginis.... Antwerp: 1622. V. 67

CATHOLIC CHURCH. LITURGY & RITUAL. MISSAL
Manuale Missalis Romani ex Decreto Sacrosancti Conciliium Tridentini Restituti, Nunc ad Literam Excerptum & Impressum. Coimbra: 1577. V. 62
Missal for the Use of the Laity.... London: 1847. V. 67
Missale Romanum. Tornaci: 1890. V. 64

CATHOLIC CHURCH. LITURGY & RITUAL. OFFICE
L'Office de la Quinzaine de Pasque, Latin-Francois, a l'Usage de Rome and de Paris. Paris: 1752. V. 67
L'Office de la Semaine-Sainte, a l'Usage de la Maison du Roy. Paris: 1748. V. 62
The Office of the Holy Week.... Baltimore: 1810. V. 64

CATHOLIC CHURCH. LITURGY & RITUAL. PONTIFICAL
Pontificale Romanum. Venice: 1543. V. 64

CATICH, EDWARD M.
Letters Redrawn from Trajan Inscription in Rome. Davenport: 1961. V. 64
The Origin of the Serif: Brush Writing and Roman Letters. Davenport: 1968. V. 63
Reed, Pen and Brush: Alphabets for Writing and Lettering. Davenport: 1972. V. 63; 64

CATLIN, GEORGE
Drawings of the North American Indians. Garden City: 1984. V. 63; 66
Letters and Notes on the Manners, Customs, and Condition of the North American Indians. New York: 1841. V. 66
North American Indians - Being Letters and Notes on Their Manners, Customs and Condition, Written During Eight Years Travel Amongst the Wildest Tribes of Indians in North America 1832-1839. Edinhurst: 1926. V. 67
Shut Your Mouth and Save Your Life. New York: 1875. V. 63

CATLIN, THOMAS
The Press Album - Published in Aid of the Journalists' Orpahn Fund. London: 1909. V. 64

CATLOW, A.
The Conchologist's Nomenclator. 1845. V. 66
Popular Conchology. 1843. V. 66

CATLOW, AGNES
The Children's Garden and What They Made Of It. London: 1865. V. 67
Popular Conchology. London: 1843. V. 62
Sketching Rambles; or, Nature in the Alps and Apennines. London: 1862. V. 62

CATLOW, JOSEPH PEEL
On the Principles of Aesthetic Medicine, or the Natural Use of Sensation and Desire in the Maintenance of Health and the Treatment of Disease, as Demonstrated by Induction from the Common Facts of Life. London: 1867. V. 65

CATO
Cato's Moral Distichs. Los Angeles: 1939. V. 64
Disticha, De Morbius Ad Filium.... Amstelaedami: 1754. V. 65

CATON, JOHN D.
The Antelope and Deer of America.... New York: 1877. V. 64
The Antelope and Deer of North America. 1881. V. 66; 67
The Antelope and Deer of North America. 1974. V. 67

CATTEAU-CALLEVILLE, JEAN PIERRE GUILLAUME
A General View of Sweden.... London: 1790. V. 64

CATTERMOLE, E. G.
Famous Frontiersman, Pioneers and Scouts, the Vanguards of American Civilization. Chicago. V. 67

CATULLUS, C. VALERIUS
The Carmina. London: 1894. V. 67
Catulli, Tibulli, Et Propertii Opera. Birminghamiae: 1772. V. 66
Catullus, Tibullus, and Propertius: Opera.... Cantabrigiae: 1702. V. 66
Catullus, Tibullus, Propertius (Opera) Multus in locis Restituti. Parisiis: 1534. V. 66

CAUGHEY, JOHN W.
The Indians of Southern California in 1852. San Marino: 1952. V. 64

CAULFIELD, JAMES
The Antiquity, Honor and Dignity of Trade, Particularly as Connected with the City of London. London: 1813. V. 63

CAULFIELD, RICHARD
Annals of St. Fin Barre's Cathedral, Cork. Cork: 1871. V. 62

CAULFIELD, S. F. A.
The Dictionary of Needlework. London: 1885. V. 62; 66
The Dictionary of Needlework, an Encyclopaedia of Artistic, Plain and Fancy Needlework. London: 1900. V. 65

CAUMONT DE LA FORCE, CHARLOTTE ROSE DE
Histoire Secrete de Marie de Bourgogne. Lyon: 1694. V. 66

CAUNTER, HOBART
Caunter's and Daniell's Oriental Annual, 1839. London: 1838. V. 62

CAUS, ISAAC DE
Hortus Penbrochianus. Le Jardin de Vuilton.... London: 1895. V. 64

CAUSLEY, CHARLES
The Ballad of Charlotte Dymond. Dartington Hall. V. 65
Hands to Dance. London: 1951. V. 63; 65
Hymn. N.P: 1983. V. 66
Johnny Alleluia. N.P: 1968. V. 65
Twenty-One Poems. London: 1986. V. 64; 65

CAUSTON, H. STAPLE
The Rights of Heirship; or the Doctrine of the Descents and Consanguity as Applied by the Laws of England to the Succession of Real Proeprty and Hereditaments.... London: 1842. V. 64

CAUTLEY, H. MUNRO
Suffolk Churches and Their Treasures. Ipswich: 1938. V. 63

CAVAFY, C. P.
The Complete Poems of C. P. Cavafy. London: 1961. V. 62
Fourteen Poems by C. P. Cavafy Chosen and Illustrated with Twelve Etchings by David Hockney. London: 1966. V. 64
Homage to Cavafy. Ten Poems by Constantine Cavafy. Danbury: 1978. V. 64; 65
Three Poems. Edinburgh: 1980. V. 67
Three Poems. West Chester: 1987. V. 63; 67

CAVALCANTI, GUIDO
The Sonnets and Ballate of Guido Cavalcanti. Boston: 1912. V. 64
Sonnets and Ballate of Guido Cavalcanti with Translations of Them.... London: 1912. V. 64

CAVALHO, S. N.
Incidents of Travel and Adventure in the Far West with Col. Fremont's Last Expedition. New York: 1857. V. 64

CAVALIERI, BONAVENTURA
Lo Specchio Ustorio, Trattato delle Sectioni Coniche, et Alcuni Loro Mirabili Effetti Intorno al lume, Caldo Freddo, Suono e Moto Abcora. Bologna: 1632. V. 66
Trigonometria Plana et Sphaerica, Linearis & Logarithmica. Bologna: 1643. V. 65

CAVALIERS & Pioneers: Abstracts of Virginia Land Patents and Grants. Richmond: 1992. V. 64

CAVALLO, TIBERIUS
A Complete Treatise on Electricity in Theory and Practice, with Original Experiments. London: 1782. V. 63
The History and Practice of Aerostation. London: 1785. V. 64

CAVALLY, FREDERICK L.
Mother Goose's Teddy Bears. Indianapolis: 1907. V. 62; 64

CAVANAGH, GEORGE A.
Model Aeroplanes and Their Motors. New York: 1916. V. 63

CAVE, A. J. E.
On the Human Crania from New Guinea. Kingswood: 1937. V. 66; 67

CAVE, C. J. P.
Roof Bosses in Medieval Churches: an Aspect of Gothic Sculpture. Cambridge: 1948. V. 62; 65

CAVE, F. O.
Birds of the Sudan. Edinburgh: 1955. V. 62; 67
Birds of the Sudan. London: 1955. V. 66

CAVE, HENRY W.
The Book of Ceylon; Being a Guide to Its Railway System and an Account of the Varied Attractions for the Visitor and Tourist. London et al: 1908. V. 65
The Ceylon Government Railway: A Descriptive and Illustrative Guide. London et al: 1910. V. 65
Golden Tips. London: 1901. V. 64
The Ruined Cities of Ceylon. London: 1897. V. 64

CAVE, JOHN
An Epistle to the Inhabitants of Gillingham, in the County of Dorset.... Brecon: 1781. V. 64

CAVE, RODERICK
Private Press. New York: 1971. V. 64; 65
Typographia Naturalis. 1967. V. 62

CAVE, WILL
Nez Perce Indian War of 1877 and Battle of the Big Hole. Missoula. V. 66

CAVE, WILLIAM
Antiquitates Apostolicae; or, the History of the Lives, Acts and Martyrdoms of the Holy Apostles of Our Saviour...(with) Apostolici; or, the History of the Lives, Acts, Death and Martyrdoms.... London: 1677. V. 62
Antiquitates Christianae; or the History of the Life and Death of Holy Jesus.... London: 1684. V. 65; 67
Ecclesiastici; or, the History of the Lives, Acts, Death and Writings of the Most Eminent Fathers of the Church, that Flourish in the Fourth Century...Historical Account of the State of Paganism Under the First Christian Emperours.... London: 1683. V. 66
Primitive Christianity; or the Religion of the Ancient Christians in the First Ages of the Gospel. London: 1676. V. 66
Primitive Christianity; or, the Religion of the Ancient Christians in the First Ages of the Gospel. London: 1682. V. 64

CAVENDISH, FREDERICK
Report of the Trial of an Action, Wherein the Honourable Frederick Cavendish was Plaintiff, and the Hope Insurance Comapany of London were Defendants.... Dublin: 1813. V. 63

CAVENDISH, GEORGE
The Life and Death of Thomas Woolsey, Cardinal. London: 1667. V. 64
The Life of Cardinal Wolsey and Metrical Visons.... Chiswick: 1825. V. 62
The Life of Thomas Wolsey, Cardinal Archbishop of York. 1893. V. 62
The Life of Thomas Wolsey, Cardinal Archbishop of York. London: 1893. V. 65
The Negotiations of Thomas Woolsey. London: 1641. V. 63; 66

CAVENDISH, HENRY
Observations on Mr. Hutchins's Experiments for Determining the Degree of Cold at Which Quicksilver Freezes. London: 1784. V. 63

CAW, JAMES L.
William McTaggart. A Biography and an Appreciation. Glasgow: 1917. V. 64

CAWEIN, MADISON
Accolon of Gaul with Other Poems. Louisville: 1889. V. 63
Minions of the Moon. Cincinnati: 1913. V. 62

CAWSE, JOHN
The Art of Painting Portraits, Landscapes, Animals, Draperies, Satins &c in Oil Colours.... London: 1840. V. 66; 67

CAWSTON, ABRAHAM W.
The Fortunate Youth; or, Chippenham Croesus; Containing the Commencement, Action and Denoucement of the Newmarket Hoax. London: 1818. V. 63

CAWSTON, ARTHUR
A Comprehensive Scheme for Street Improvements in London. London: 1893. V. 62; 64

CAWTHORN, JAMES
Poems. London: 1771. V. 62; 67

CAYLEY, CORNELIUS
A Letter to the Rev. Mr. Potter. In Answer to His Sermon Preach'd at Reymerston in Norfolk, Against the People Call'd Methodists. Norwich: 1758. V. 62; 65
The Seraphical Young Shepherd...To Which is Added...A Small Bunch of Violets.... London: 1779. V. 66

CAYLEY, N.
Australian Parrots. Sydney: 1938. V. 63; 64; 66; 67

CAYLUS, COMTE DE
Histoire de Joseph, Accompagnee de Dix Figures, Relatives aux Principaux Evenemens de la Vie de ce Fils du Patriarche Jacob et Gravees sur les Modeles du Fameux Reimbrandt.... Amsterdam: 1757. V. 65
Suite of Plates for the Oeuvres Badines Completes. Amsterdam and Paris: 1787. V. 62

CAZALET-KEIR, THELMA
Homage to P. G. Wodehouse. London: 1973. V. 62

CAZEAU, P.
Traite Theorique et Pratique de l'Art Des Accouchements Comprenant L'Historie Des Maladis.... Bruxelles: 1846. V. 64

CECI, CARLO
Piccoli Bronzi del Real Museo Borbonico.... Naples: 1854. V. 64

CECIL, The Orphan: or the Reward of Virtue: A Tale for the Young. New York: 1849. V. 63

CECIL, DAVID
Modern Verse In English 1900-1950. New York: 1950. V. 62; 64
A Portrait of Jane Austen. London: 1978. V. 66

CECIL, E.
A History of Gardening in England. 1910. V. 63
A History of Gardening in England. London: 1910. V. 62

CECIL, HENRY
Hunt the Slipper. London: 1977. V. 67

CECIL, RICHARD
A Friendly Visit to the House of Mourning. New Brunswick: 1801. V. 63

CELA, CAMILO JOSE
La Familia de Pascual Duarte. Madrid: 1991. V. 62

CELAN, PAUL
Nineteen Poems. Manchester: 1972. V. 63

CELEBRATED Actor-Folks' Cookeries. New York: 1916. V. 65

CELEBRATION of the Seventy-Fifth Anniversary of the Chatham Artillery of Savannah May 1, 1861. Savannah: 1861. V. 63; 65

CELENIA or the History of Hyempsal, King of Numidia. London: 1736. V. 63

CELINE, LOUIS FERDINAND
Journey to the End of the Night. 1934. V. 63
Voyage au Bout de la Nuit. Paris: 1932. V. 67

CELLAN Press Poems. Llitchin: 1972-1975. V. 64

CELLARIUS, CHRISTOPH
Georgia Antiqua: Being a Complete Set of Maps of Antient Geography.... London: 1785. V. 64

CELLARIUS, HENRI
Fashionable Dancing. London: 1847. V. 64

CELLINI, BENVENUTO
The Life.... London: 1771. V. 66; 67
The Life.... London: 1888. V. 65
The Life.... London: 1900. V. 65
The Life.... New York: 1906. V. 67
The Life.... 1937. V. 62; 65
Memoirs of Benvenuto Cellini, a Florentine Artist.... London: 1823. V. 67
Vita..da Lui Medesimo Scritta, Nella Quale Molte Curiose Particolarita si Toccano Appartenenti alle Arti e all' Istoria del suo Tempo, Tratta da un' Ottimo Manoscritto, e Dedicata all' Eccellenza di Mylord Riccardo Boyle Conte di Burlington, e Cork. Cologne: 1728. V. 63

CELSUS
Aurelii Cor. Celsi De Re Medica Libri VIII. Item Qu. Sereni Liber de Medicina. Qu. Rhemnii Fannii Palaemonis de Pond Mensuris Liber. Lugduni: 1554. V. 66
Aurelii Cornelii Celsi, De Re Medica... Q. Sereni Samonici Praecepta medica...Q. Rhemnii Fannii Palaemonis...Hos Libros D. Ioan. Caesarius.... Salingiaci: 1538. V. 66
Celsi De Medicina Libro Octo, Quibus Accedunt Indices Capitum Autorum et Rerum.... Edinburgi: 1814. V. 67
Medicinae Libri Octo Ex Recensione Leonardi Targa Editio Altera Accuratior, Cui Accedit Lexicon Celsainum. Verona: 1810. V. 64

CENATI, BERNARDINO
La Silvia Errante, Aricomedia Capricciosa Morale. Venetia: 1608. V. 65

THE CENTENARY of Kentucky. Proceedings at the Celebration by the Filson Club. Louisville: 1892. V. 67

CENTENNIAL Celebration of the Ordination and Induction of the Late Rev. Alexander Dick, Presbyterian Minister Maitland, Hants County, Nova Scotia June 21st and 23rd 1903. Truro: 1903. V. 65

CENTLIVRE, SUSANNAH
The Works of the Celebrated Mrs. Centlivre.... London: 1760-1761. V. 63

CENTRAL RAILROAD COMPANY OF NEW JERSEY
Twenty-Fifth Annual Report of the Board of Directors...1872. New York: 1872. V. 63; 66
Twenty-Fourth Annual Report of the Board of Directors...1871. New York: 1871. V. 63; 66

CENTRE GEORGES POMPIDOU
Salvador Dali Retrospective 1920-1980. 18 Dec. 1979-21 Avril 1980. V. 65

THE CENTURY Guild Hobby Horse. London: 1889-1890. V. 62

A CENTURY of Japanese Photography. New York: 1980. V. 64

CENTURY Review 1805-1905. Maury Co., Tennessee. Columbia: 1905. V. 62

CEREDI, GIUSEPPE
Tre Discorsi Sopra il Modo d'alzar Acque da' Luoghi Bassi. Parma: 1567. V. 62

CEREMONIES Attending the Unveiling of the Equestrian Statue to Major General George Armstrong Custer by the State of Michigan and Formally Dedicated at the City of Monore, Michigan, June Fourth, Nineteen Hundred and Ten. Detroit: 1911. V. 63

CERIMONIALI per la Solennita dell' Incoronazione di...Ferdinand I. Milan: 1838. V. 66

CERNOHORSKY, W. O.
Marine Shells of the Pacific. Sydney: 1971-1972. V. 62

CERTAIN Considerations Relating to the Royal African Company of England. In Which, the Original Growth and National Advantages of the Guiney Trade, are Demonstrated.... London: 1680. V. 66

CERTAIN Sermons or Homilies Appointed as to be Read in Churches, in the Time of Queen Elizabeth of Famous Memory.... London: 1673. V. 66

CERVANTES SAAVEDRA, MIGUEL DE
Adventures of Don Quixote De La Mancha. London: 1858. V. 67
Adventures of Don Quixote de La Mancha. London: 1866. V. 63
Cassell's Library Edition of Don Quixote. London: 1866. V. 63
Don Quixote de la Mancha. London: 1930. V. 62; 64
Don Quixote of the Mancha. London: 1906-1907. V. 67
Don Quixote the Ingenious Gentleman of La Mancha. New York: 1950. V. 64
The First (and Second) Part of the History of the Valorous and White Knight Errant Don Quixote of the Mancha. 1927-1928. V. 67
The History of Don Quixote. London and New York: 1880. V. 64; 65
The History of Don Quixote. London: 1896. V. 62
The History of Don Quixote. London: 1922. V. 62
El Ingenioso Hidalgo Don Quixote de la Mancha. Madrid: 1780. V. 63
El Ingenioso Hidalgo Don Quixote De La Mancha. Madrid: 1797. V. 62
El Ingenioso Hidalgo Don Quixote de la Mancha. Madrid: 1797-1798. V. 66
The Life and Exploits of Don Quixote of La Mancha. London: 1824. V. 65
The Life and Exploits of the Ingenious Gentleman Don Quixote de la Mancha. London: 1766. V. 64
The Much Esteemed History of the Ever Famous Knight, Don Quixote de la Mancha. London: 1716. V. 66
The Spanish Ladie and Two Other Stories. London: 1928. V. 62

CERVER, F. A.
Architectural Houses 3: Houses by the Sea. Barcelona: 1991. V. 62; 65

CESARE
One Hundred Cartoons. Boston: 1916. V. 66

CESCINSKY, HERBERT
Early English Furniture & Woodwork. London: 1922. V. 62
English and American Furniture. New York: 1929. V. 62
English Furniture from Gothic to Sheraton. Grand Rapids: 1929. V. 63
English Furniture of the Eighteenth Century. London: 1909-1911. V. 66
The Old World House, Its Furniture and Decoration. New York: 1924. V. 62; 65

CESNOLA, LUIGI PALMA DI
Cyprus: Its Ancient Cities, Tombs and Temples. New York: 1878. V. 62

CEULEN, LUDOLPH VAN
De Circulo & Adscriptis Liber. Leyden: 1619. V. 66
Van den Circkel, Daer in Gheleert Werdt te Winden de Naeste Propertie des Circkels Diameter Teghen Synen Omloop, Daer Door All Circkels.... Leyden: 1615. V. 66

CHABON, MICHAEL
The Mysteries of Pittsburgh. New York: 1988. V. 63; 67

CHABOUILLET, A.
Description des Antiquites et Objets d'Art Composant le Cabinet de M. Louis Fould. Paris: 1861. V. 64

CHACE, ARNOLD BUFFUM
The Rhind Mathematical Papyrus. Berlin: 1927. V. 66

CHACON, PEDRO
De Triclinio Sive de Modo Convivandi Apud Priscos Romanos.... Amsterdam: 1664. V. 66
De Triclinio sive de Modo Convivandi apud Priscos Romanos.... Amsterdam: 1689. V. 66

CHAD, GEORGE WILLIAM
A Narrative of the Late Revolution in Holland. London: 1814. V. 63

CHADRON
Chadron's Journal at Fort Clark 1834-1839. Pierre: 1937. V. 62

CHADWICK, DAVID
On the Rate of Wages in Manchester and Salford, and the Manufacturing Districts of Lancashire, During the Twenty Years from 1839 to 1859. (with) *On Working Men's Colleges.* (with) *Parliamentary Representation.* London: 1860. V. 63

CHADWICK, EDMUND
Reports on the Estate of Sir Andrew Chadwick and the Recent Proceedings of the Chadwick Association in Reference Thereto. London: 1881. V. 66

CHADWICK, EDWIN
Report from His Majesty's Commissioners for Inquiring Into the Administration and Practical Operation of the Poor Laws. London: 1834. V. 67

CHADWICK, ELLIS, MRS.
In the Footsteps of the Brontes. 1914. V. 63; 64
In the Footsteps of the Brontes. London: 1914. V. 66
Mrs. Gaskell. Haunts, Homes and Stories. 1913. V. 63

CHADWICK, F. E.
Report on the Training System for the Navy and Mercantile Marine of England, and on the Naval Training System of France.. Washington: 1880. V. 65

CHADWICK, J. W.
Out of the Heart, Poems for Lovers Young and Old. Boston: 1891. V. 65

CHADWICK, W. S.
Man-Killers and Marauders, Some Big Game Encounters of an African Hunter. London: 1929. V. 64

CHADWICK'S American Manual. New York: 1873. V. 65

CHAFFERS, WILLIAM
Collector's Handbook of Marks and Monograms on Pottery and Porcelain of the Renaissance and Modern Periods. London: 1877. V. 62; 65
Hall Marks on Gold and Silver Plate, with Tables of Annual Date Letters Employed in the Principal Assay Offices of England, Scotland and Ireland. London: 1863. V. 62
Marks and Monograms on European and Oriental Pottery and Porcelain. London: 1912. V. 63
Marks and Monograms on European and Oriental Pottery and Porcelain. London: 1974. V. 64
Marks and Monograms on Pottery and Porcelain.... London: 1876. V. 64

CHAFFIN, LORAH B.
Sons of the West - Biographical Account of Early Day Wyoming. Caldwell: 1941. V. 67

CHAGALL, MARC
Dessins Pour La Bible. Verve - Nos 37-38. Paris: 1960. V. 65
The Lithographs. Volume II. 1957-1962. Monte Carlo: 1963. V. 62; 65
Marc Chagall, His Graphic Work. New York: 1957. V. 62

CHAILLE, STANFORD
Historical Sketch of the Medical Department of the University of Louisiana: Its Professors and Alumni, from 1835 to 1862. New Orleans: 1861. V. 63; 65; 66

CHALCOGRAPHIMANIA; or the Portrait Collector and Printsellers Chronicle, With Infatuations of Every Description. London: 1814. V. 66

CHALDECOTT, F. M.
Jericho and Golf in the Early Days in Vancouver 1892-1905. Vancouver: 1935. V. 63

CHALFANT, W. A.
Outposts of Civilization. Boston: 1928. V. 62; 66
The Story of Inyo. Chicago: 1922. V. 63; 65

CHALIAPIN, FEODOR IVANOVICH
Chaliapin - an Autobiography as told to Maxim Gorky. London: 1968. V. 64

CHALIFOUR, J. E.
Atlas of Canada. Ottawa: 1915. V. 65

CHALKLEY, LYMAN
Chronicles of the Scotch-Irish Settlement in Virginia Extracted from the Original Court Records of Augusta Co. 1745-1800. Baltimore: 1974. V. 65

CHALMERS, GEORGE
An Estimate of the Comparative Strength of Great Britain During the Present and Four Preceding Reigns and of the Losses of Her Trade from Every War Since the Revolution.... London: 1786. V. 63; 64
An Historical View of the Domestic Economy of Britain and Ireland, from the Earliest to the Present Times.... Edinburgh: 1812. V. 62; 65
Opinions on Interesting Subjects of Public Law and Commercial Policy.... London: 1785. V. 63

CHALMERS, HENEAGE
An Apology for the Beleivers in the Shakespeare Papers. London: 1797. V. 65

CHALMERS, JAMES
Pioneer Life and Work in New Guinea 1877-1894. London: 1895. V. 65
Plain Truth: Addressed to the Inhabitants of America. London: 1776. V. 64
Work and Adventure in New Guinea. 1877 to 1885. London: 1885. V. 63

CHALMERS, JANE
Plain Truth: Addressed to the Inhabitants of America. London: 1776. V. 66

CHALMERS, JOHN P.
A Bookbinder's Florilegium. Austin: 1988. V. 64

CHALMERS, LIONEL
An Account of the Weather and Diseases of South Carolina. London: 1776. V. 63; 66

CHALMERS, PATRICK
Birds Ashore and Aforeshore. 1935. V. 67
The Cecil Aldin Book. 1932. V. 64
Field Sports of Scotland. 1936. V. 66
A Fisherman's Angles. London: 1931. V. 67
Forty Fine Ladies. London: 1929. V. 64
The Frequent Gun and Little Fishing. London: 1928. V. 67
Gun-Dogs. London: 1931. V. 64; 66; 67
The Horn. London: 1937. V. 67
Mine Eyes to the Hills. 1931. V. 64; 67
Mine Eyes Unto the Hills. London: 1931. V. 67
Rhymes of Flood and Field. London: 1931. V. 64
The Shooting Man's England. London: 1936. V. 67
Where the Spring Salmon Run. London: 1921. V. 67

CHALMERS, THOMAS
Considerations on the System of Parochial Schools in Scotland and on the Advantage of Establishing Them in Large Towns. Glasgow: 1819. V. 64
On Political Economy, in Connexion with the Moral State and Moral Prospects of Society. Glasgow: 1832. V. 64
On Political Economy, in Connexion with the Moral State and Moral Prospects of Society. New York: 1832. V. 67
On the Power, Wisdom and Goodness of God as Manifested in the Adaptation of External Nature to the Moral and Intellectual Constitution of Man. London: 1833. V. 65
On the Power, Wisdom, and Goodness of God As Manifested in the Adaptation of External Nature to the Moral and Intellectual Constitution of Man. London: 1834. V. 62
Political Economy in Connexion with the Moral State and Prospects of Society. Edinburgh: 1854. V. 64

CHAMBERLAIN, GEORGE A.
African Hunting Among the Thongas. 1923. V. 67

CHAMBERLAIN, M.
A Catalogue of Canadian Birds.... Saint John: 1887. V. 64

CHAMBERLAIN, RICHARD
The Complete Justice. London: 1681. V. 66

CHAMBERLAIN, SAMUEL
Sketches of Northern Spanish Architecture. New York: 1926. V. 64

CHAMBERLAIN, SAMUEL E.
My Confession. New York: 1956. V. 65

CHAMBERLAIN, SARAH
Alphabetarium. Vienna: 1982. V. 63
Bestiary. Boston: 1979. V. 63

CHAMBERLAIN, WILT
A View from Above. New York: 1991. V. 63

CHAMBERLAINE, WILLIAM W.
Memoirs of the Civil War Between the Northern and Southern Sections of the United States of America 1861 to 1865. Washington: 1912. V. 65

CHAMBERLAYNE, EDWARD
Angliae Notitia. London: 1684. V. 64
Angliae Notitia. Oxonii: 1686. V. 62
Angliae Notitia. London: 1704. V. 66

CHAMBERLAYNE, HAM
Ham Chamberlayne-Virginian. Letters and Papers of an Artillery Officer in the War for Southern Independence 1861-1865. Richmond: 1932. V. 62; 64

CHAMBERLAYNE, JOHN
Magnae Britanniae Notitia; or the Present State of Grat Britian.... London: 1737. V. 62; 66

CHAMBERLAYNE, THOMAS
The Complete Midwife's Practice Enlarged.... London: 1680. V. 63

CHAMBERLEN, HUGH
Papers Relating to a Bank of Credit, Upon Land Security; Proposed to the Parliament of Scotland. Edinburgh: 1693. V. 65

CHAMBERLIN, T. C.
Geology of Wisconsin. Survey of 1873-1879. Madison: 1883-1887-1880. V. 64

CHAMBERS, ANDREW J.
Recollections. N.P: 1947. V. 63; 65; 66; 67

CHAMBERS, DAVID
Cock-a-Hoop. A Sequel to Chanticleer, Pertelote and Cockalorum, Being a Bibliography of the Golden Cockerel Press September 1949-December 1961. Pinner, Middlesex: 1976. V. 62; 66

CHAMBERS, E.
Cyclopaedia. London: 1778-1786. V. 62

CHAMBERS, EPHRAIM
Cyclopaedia. London: 1728. V. 67
Cyclopaedia. London: 1738. V. 64

CHAMBERS, G. F.
Astronomy. London: 1913. V. 67

CHAMBERS, JAMES JULIUS
A Mad World and Its Inhabitants. New York: 1877. V. 65

CHAMBERS, LENOIR
Stonewall Jackson. New York: 1959. V. 62; 63; 65

CHAMBERS, MARGARET
Reminisences (sic). N.P: 1903. V. 63

CHAMBERS, ROBERT
Ancient Sea-Margins, as Memorials of Changes in the Relative Level of Sea and Land. London: 1848. V. 64
The Book of Days. London: 1866. V. 64
The Book of Days. London: 1883. V. 63
Illustrations of the Author of Waverley; Being Notices and Anecdotes of Real Characters, Scenes and Incidents.... Edinburgh: 1825. V. 62; 65
Vestiges of the Natural History of Creation. New York: 1845. V. 64; 66

CHAMBERS, ROBERT W.
Garden-Land. New York: 1907. V. 63
The Maker of Moons. 1896. V. 62; 64
Mountain-Land. New York: 1906. V. 63
The Mystery of Choice. New York: 1897. V. 63
River-Land. New York: 1904. V. 63

CHAMBERS, W.
Things As They Are in America. Philadelphia: 1854. V. 66

CHAMBERS, W. R.
Pictorial History of the Russian War 1854-1856. Edinburgh and London: 1856. V. 65

CHAMBERS, WALTER
Labor Unions and the American Public. New York: 1936. V. 67

CHAMBERS, WILLIAM
California: Bound in Chambers's Papers for the People. Volume IV. Edinburgh: 1850. V. 62
Chambers's Edinburgh Journal. Edinburgh: 1844-1848. V. 62
Chambers's Miscellany of Useful and Entertaining Tracts. Edinburgh: 1844-1847. V. 64
Dessins des Edifices Meubles, Habits, Machines et Ustensiles des Chinois. London: 1757. V. 64
A Dissertation on Oriental Gardening. London: 1773. V. 62
Memoir of Robert Chambers with Autobiographic Reminiscences of William Chambers. Edinburgh: 1872. V. 65
Memoir of William and Robert Chambers. Edinburgh: 1893. V. 65
A Treatise on Civil Architecture, In Which the Principles of that Art are Laid Down.... London: 1759. V. 63

CHAMEROVZOW, LOUIS ALEXIS
The New Zealand Question and the Rights of Aborigines. London: 1848. V. 64

CHAMFORT, SEBASTIAN ROCH NICHOLAS DE
Maxims and Considerations. Waltham St. Lawrence: 1926. V. 62; 65; 66

CHAMFORT, SEBASTIAN ROCH NICOLAS DE
Oeuvres. Paris: 1795. V. 67

CHAMIER, FREDERIC
The Life of a Sailor. London: 1833. V. 66
A Review of the French Revolution of 1848, from the 24th of February to the Election of the First President. London: 1849. V. 65
The Unfortunate Man. London: 1835. V. 66
Walsingham, the Gamester. London: 1837. V. 65
Walsingham, The Gamester. Philadelphia: 1838. V. 66

CHAMISSO, ADELBERT VON
A Sojourn at San Francisco Bay, 1816. San Francisco: 1936. V. 64

CHAMPION COATED PAPER CO.
A Book of Samples of Papers Manufactured to Print Properly All Kinds of Illustrations Together with a Book of the Same Papers Printed and Lithographed In All of the Principal Processes Used.... New York: 1922. V. 64

CHAMPION, F. W.
The Jungle in Sunlight and Shadow. London. V. 67

CHAMPION, IVAN F.
Across New Guinea from the Fly to the Sepik. London: 1932. V. 64

CHAMPION, L. C.
Lettre Sur les Accouchements Avec presentation du Gras. Paris: 1829. V. 65

CHAMPLAIN, SAMUEL DE
The Works of Samuel De Champlain. Toronto: 1971. V. 63

CHAMPNEY, ELIZABETH
Great Grandmother's Girls in New Mexico. Boston: 1888. V. 67

CHAMPNEYS, BASIL
Memoirs and Correspondence of Coventry Patmore. London: 1900. V. 65

CHAMPNEYS, W. WELDON
Marriage with a Deceased Wife's Sister. London: 1849. V. 67

CHAMPOMIER, P. A.
A Statement of the Sugar Crop, Made in Louisiana in 1861-1862, with an Appendix. New Orleans: 1862. V. 64

CHANCELLOR, E. BERESFORD
The History and Antiquities of Richmond, Kew, Petersham &c. Richmond: 1894. V. 66
Original Views of London, As It Is, by Thomas Shotter Boys, 1842. London: 1926. V. 66

CHANCELLOR, JOHN
The Martitime Paintings of John Chancellor. London: 1984. V. 67

CHANDLER, ELIZABETH MARGARET
The Poetical Works. Philadelphia: 1836. V. 65; 66

CHANDLER, GEORGE
Four Centuries of Banking. London: 1963-1968. V. 62; 65
Four Centuries of Banking. London: 1964-1968. V. 66
Liverpool. London: 1957. V. 62; 65

CHANDLER, LLOYD H.
A Summary of the Work of Rudyard Kipling, Including Items Ascribed to Him. New York: 1930. V. 62

CHANDLER, M. E. J.
The Lower Tertiary Floras of Southern England. 1961-1964. V. 64; 65; 66
The Lower Tertiary Floras of Southern England. London: 1961-1964. V. 65

CHANDLER, MELBOURNE C.
Garryowen in Glory the History of the Seventh United States Regiment of Cavalry. Annandale: 1960. V. 65; 67

CHANDLER, RAYMOND
Backfire. Santa Barbara: 1984. V. 62
The Big Sleep. Cleveland: 1946. V. 65
The Blue Dahlia. Carbondale: 1976. V. 65; 66
Farewell, My Lovely. New York: 1940. V. 67
The Finger Man and Other Stories. 1946. V. 62; 63
Finger Man and Other Stories. New York: 1946. V. 66; 67
The High Window. New York: 1942. V. 66
Killer in the Rain. 1964. V. 62; 64
Killer in the Rain. Boston: 1964. V. 66
The Lady in the Lake. New York: 1943. V. 62
The Lady in the Lake. London: 1944. V. 62; 64; 66
Letters: Raymond Chandler and James M. Fox. Santa Barbara: 1978. V. 65; 66
The Little Sister. 1949. V. 65; 66
The Little Sister. London: 1949. V. 62; 64; 66
The Long Goodbye. London: 1953. V. 64; 65; 66; 67
The Long Goodbye. Boston: 1954. V. 65
The Notebooks of Raymond Chandler and English Summer. New York: 1976. V. 66
Playback. 1958. V. 64
Playback. Boston: 1958. V. 62; 65
Playback. London: 1958. V. 62; 64; 65; 66
The Raymond Chandler Omnibus. New York: 1964. V. 64; 66
Raymond Chandler's Unknown Thriller: the Screenplay of Playback. New York: 1985. V. 66
Red Wind. Cleveland: 1946. V. 66
The Simple Art of Murder. Boston: 1950. V. 67
The Simple Art of Murder. New York: 1968. V. 67
Spanish Blood - a Collection of Short Stories. Cleveland and New York: 1946. V. 63
Stories and Early Novels and Later Novels and Other Writings. New York: 1995. V. 65

CHANDLER, RICHARD
The Life of William Waynflete, Bishop of Winchester, Lord High Chancellor of England in the Reign of Henry VI and Founder of Magdalen College, Oxford.... London: 1811. V. 64
Travels in Asia Minor or an Account of a Tour Made at the Expence of the Society of Dilettanti. Oxford: 1775. V. 62
Travels in Asia Minor; or, an Account of a Tour Made at the Expense of the Society of Dilettanti. London: 1776. V. 64

CHANDLER, SAMUEL
The History of Persecution, from the Patriarchal Age, to the Reign of George II.... Hull: 1813. V. 64

CHANDLER, THOMAS BRADBURY
The Life of Samuel Johnson, D.D. the First President of King's College in New York. New York: 1805. V. 66

CHANDRASEKHAR, S.
Selected Papers: Volume I: Stellar Structure and Stellar Atmospheres. Chicago: 1989. V. 67

CHANEY, EDWARD
Oxford, China and Italy _ Writings in Honour of Sir Harold Acton on His Eightieth Birthday. London: 1984. V. 65

CHANEY, J. M.
Poliopolis and Polioland. A Trip to the North Pole. Kansas City: 1900. V. 66

CHANG, S. T.
Tropical Mushrooms, Biological Nature and Cultivation Methods. Hong Kong: 1982. V. 63

CHANIN, NATHAN
Berele. New York: 1938. V. 64

CHANNEL BRIDGE AND RAILWAY COMPANY LTD.
Le Pont sur la Manche. London and Paris: 1892. V. 66

CHANNING, WALTER
A Physician's Vacation; or, a Summer in Europe. Boston: 1856. V. 64

CHANNING, WILLIAM ELLERY
Emancipation. Philadelphia: 1841. V. 67
Lectures on the Elevation of the Labouring Portion of the Community. London: 1840. V. 64
A Letter to the Hon. Henry Clay, on the Annexation of Texas to the United States. Boston: 1837. V. 66

CHANNING, WILLIAM ELLERY continued
Poems. Boston: 1843. V. 62; 63; 64
Slavery. Boston: 1835. V. 63; 67

CHANNON, HENRY
The Ludwigs of Bavaria. London: 1952. V. 64

CHANSLOR, ROY
The Ballad of Cat Ballou. Boston and Toronto: 1956. V. 66

CHANTER, CHARLOTTE
Ferny Combes. London: 1856. V. 62

CHAN-TOON, MABEL
A Marriage in Burmah: a Novel. London: 1905. V. 64
Told on the Pagoda: Tales of Burmah.... London: 1895. V. 64

CHANTRE, E.
Recherches Anthropologiques dans le Caucase. Paris: 1885-1887. V. 67

CHANTS et Chansons Populaires de la France. Paris: 1848. V. 66

CHAPEL, C. E.
Gun Care and Repair. New York: 1943. V. 67

CHAPELLE, HOWARD IRVING
American Small Sailing Craft. Their Design, Development and Construction. New York: 1951. V. 63
The Baltimore Clipper. Salem: 1930. V. 62; 63; 64
The Baltimore Clipper. Hatboro: 1965. V. 63; 65; 66

CHAPIN, ANNA ALICE
The Everyday Fairy Book. New York: 1915. V. 62; 63
The Now-a-Days Fairy Book. New York: 1911. V. 63

CHAPIN, HOWARD M.
Documentary History of Rhode Island Being the History of the Towns of Providence and Warwick to 1649 and to the Colony to 1647. Providence: 1916. V. 65

CHAPIN, JAMES P.
The Birds of the Belgian Congo. New York: 1932-1954. V. 62; 67

CHAPIN, LON
Art Work on Southern California. San Francisco Chicago: 1900. V. 62

CHAPIN, OLIVER W.
A History of the First Presbyterian Church of Hanover, 1718-1968. Hanover: 1968. V. 66

CHAPIN, WILLIAM
A Complete Reference Gazetteer of the United States of North America. New York: 1841. V. 66

CHAPLAIN, E. M.
A History of the 10th Regiment, Vermont Volunteers, with Biographical Sketches of the Officers Who Fell in Battle and a Complete Roster. 1870. V. 63

CHAPLIN, CHARLES
My Autobiography. London: 1964. V. 63

CHAPLIN, PATRICE
By Flower and Dean Street and The Love Apple. London: 1976. V. 63; 66

CHAPLIN, W. KNIGHT
Advance Endeavour!. Souvenir Report of the World's Convention of Christian Endeavour, London, 1900. London: 1900. V. 62

CHAPMAN, ABEL
Bird Life of the Borders. 1889. V. 67
Bird Life of the Borders. London: 1889. V. 63; 65
Bird Life of the Borders. London: 1907. V. 62; 66; 67
The Borders and Beyond. 1924. V. 62; 63; 67
The Borders and Beyond. London: 1924. V. 62; 63; 64; 67
First Lessons in the Art of Wildflowing. 1896. V. 63
Flora of the Southern United States.... New York: 1897. V. 66
Memories of Fourscore Years Less Two 1851-1929. 1930. V. 66
Memories of Fourscore Years Less Two 1851-1929. London: 1930. V. 62; 64; 67
Retrospect. London: 1928. V. 62; 67
Unexplored Spain. London: 1910. V. 66; 67

CHAPMAN, ALVAN WENTWORTH
Flora of the Southern United States: Containing Abridged Descriptions of the Flowering Plants and Ferns of Tennessee, North and South Carolina, Georgia, Alabama, Mississippi and Florida.... New York: 1872. V. 67

CHAPMAN, CHARLES
All About Ships and How to Make Models of Them. The Life and Duties of a Sailor.... London: 1869. V. 65
The First Ten Years of a Sailors Life at Sea. London: 1876. V. 62

CHAPMAN, EDWARD J.
Practical Mineralogy; or a Compendium of the Distinguishing Characters of Minerals. London: 1843. V. 62

CHAPMAN, ELIZABETH RACHEL
The New Godiva and Other Studies in Social Questions. London: 1885. V. 65

CHAPMAN, F.
Gun, Rod and Rifle. 1908. V. 63

CHAPMAN, F. SPENCER
Lhasa: the Holy City. London: 1938. V. 65

Watkins' Last Expedition. London: 1934. V. 64

CHAPMAN, FRANK M.
Bird Life. New York: 1898. V. 65; 67
Camps and Cruises of an Ornithologist. New York: 1908. V. 67
The Warblers of North America. New York: 1907. V. 65

CHAPMAN, GEORGE
A Treatise on Education. London: 1790. V. 63; 64

CHAPMAN, GUY
A Passionate Prodigality - Fragments of Autobiography. New York: 1966. V. 65

CHAPMAN, H. C.
The Placenta and Generative Apparatus of the Elephant. Philadelphia: 1880. V. 67

CHAPMAN, HAROLD
The Beat Hotel. Geneva: 1984. V. 67

CHAPMAN, HENRY CADWALDER
History of the Discovery of the Circulation of the Blood. Philadelphia: 1884. V. 67

CHAPMAN, HESTER W.
Diversion. London: 1946. V. 63

CHAPMAN, HILARY
The Wood Engravings of Ethelbert White. Netherton: 1992. V. 64

CHAPMAN, JAMES
Historical Notices of Saint Peter's Church, in the City of Perth Amboy. Elizabeth-Town: 1830. V. 63; 66

CHAPMAN, JOHN
Prostitution: Governmental Experiments in Controlling It. London: 1870. V. 65

CHAPMAN, JOHN RATCLIFFE
Instructions to Young Marksmen...The Improved American Rifle. New York: 1848. V. 63; 66

CHAPMAN, KENNETH M.
The Pottery of Santo Domingo Pueblo. Santa Fe: 1936. V. 62; 65; 67
The Pottery of Santo Domingo Pueblo. Santa Fe: 1953. V. 63; 64
The Pottery of Santo Domingo Pueblo. Albuquerque: 1977. V. 63

CHAPMAN, L. L.
Chapman's Principia; or, Nature's First Principles. Philadelphia: 1855. V. 66

CHAPMAN, N.
Discourses on the Elements of Therapeutics and Materia Medica. Philadelphia: 1817. V. 67

CHAPMAN, R. W.
Cancels. London: 1930. V. 62

CHAPMAN, WALTER
Dutchie Doings. London. V. 67

CHAPONE, HESTER
Letters on the Improvement of the Mind, Addressed to a Young Lady. Hagers-Town: 1815. V. 63
The Works.... London: 1793. V. 65

CHAPPE D'AUTEROCHE, JEAN
A Voyage to California, to Observe the Transit of Venus.... London: 1778. V. 64; 66

CHAPPELL, CARL L.
Seven Minus One: The Story of Astronaut Gus Gurssom. Madison. V. 67

CHAPPELL, EDWARD
Voyage of His Majesty's Ship Rosamond to Newfoundland and the Southern Coast of Labrador.... London: 1818. V. 63

CHAPPELL, FRED
The Inkling. New York: 1965. V. 62; 64
The World Between the Eyes. Baton Rouge: 1971. V. 63

CHAPPELL, GEORGE S.
The Cruise of the Kava. (with) *My Northern Exposure.* New York and London: 1923-1922. V. 64

CHAPPELL, LOUIS W.
Folk Songs of Roanoke and the Albemarle. Morganton: 1939. V. 63; 66
John Henry: a Folk-lore Study. Jena: 1933. V. 65

CHAPPELL, RUSSELL E.
Apollo. Washington: 1973. V. 63

CHAPPELL, WALTER
Walter Chappell: Vintage Photographs 1954-1978. New York: 2000. V. 67

CHAPPELL, WILLIAM
The Preacher, or the Art and Method of Preaching.... London: 1656. V. 64
Studies in Ballet. London: 1948. V. 64

CHAPPELLE, HOWARD L.
The History of the American Sailing Navy, the Ships and Their Development. 1950. V. 65

CHAPPLE, L. J. B.
Wangagnui. Hawera: 1939. V. 66

CHAPTAL, J. A.
Elements of Chemistry.... 1795. V. 62

CHAPTAL DE CHANTELOUP, JEAN ANTOINE CLAUDE, COMTE DE
Chimie Appliquee aux Arts. Paris: 1807. V. 65

THE CHARACTERS of Charles Dickens Portrayed in a Series of Original Water Colour Sketches by Kyd. London: 1900. V. 66

CHARAKA CLUB
Proceedings of.... New York: 1902-1985. V. 64; 66
The Proceedings of.... New York: 1910. V. 64; 66
The Proceedings of.... New York: 1916. V. 64; 66
Proceedings of.... New York: 1938. V. 64; 66
Proceedings of.... Baltimore: 1941. V. 65
Proceedings of.... New York: 1947. V. 65
Proceedings of.... New York: 1985. V. 64; 66

CHARAS, MOYSE
The Royal Pharmacopoea, Galenical and Chymical, According to the Practice of the Most Eminent and Learned Physitians of France. London: 1678. V. 66

CHARCOT, JEAN BAPTISTE ETIENNE AUGUSTE
The Voyage of the Why Not? in the Antarctic; The Journal of the Second French South Polar Expedition, 1908-1910. London: 1910. V. 64

CHARCOT, JEAN MARIE
Clinical Lectures of the Diseases of the Old Age. New York: 1881. V. 66
Clinical Lectures on Senile and Chronic Diseases. London: 1881. V. 64; 65; 66
Clinical Lectures on the Diseases of Old Age. New York: 1881. V. 65
Lectures on the Diseases of the Nervous System Delivered at la Salpetriere. Second Series. London: 1881. V. 65
Lectures on the Localisation of Cerebral and Spinal Diseases. London: 1877-1883. V. 64; 66
Neue Vorlesungen Uber die Krankheiten des Nervensystems Insbesondere Uber Hysterie. Leipzig/Wien: 1886. V. 62; 65
Poliklinische Vortrage. Leipzig/Wien: 1894-1895. V. 65

CHARDEL, CASIMIR
Esquisse de la Nature Humaine Expliquee par le Magnetisme Animal Procedee d'un Apercu du Systeme General de l'Univers, et Contenant l'Explication du Somnambulisem Magnetique et de Tous les Phenomenes du Magnetisme Animal. Paris: 1826. V. 66

CHARDHADI, DRISS BEN HAMED
A Life Full of Holes. London: 1964. V. 63; 65
A Life Full of Holes. New York: 1964. V. 64

CHARDIN, JOHN
Travels in Persia. London: 1927. V. 62

CHARDON, F. A.
Chardon's Journal at Fort Clark 1834-1839. Pierre: 1932. V. 65
Chardon's Journal at Fort Clark 1834-1839. Pierre: 1937. V. 65

CHARKE, CHARLOTTE
Theatrical Biography; or Memoirs of the Principal Performers of the Three Theatres Royal Drury Lane, Covent Garden, Hay Market. (with) A Narrative of the Life of Mrs. Charlotte Charke. London: 1772 1750. V. 65

CHARLES & CO.
Catalog of Fine Foods, Candies, Beverages, Tobaccos, etc. New York: 1926. V. 67

CHARLES, EDWIN
Keys to the Drood Mystery. London: 1908. V. 62

CHARLES, ELIZABETH
Chronicles of the Schonberg-Cotta Family. London: 1867. V. 65
Diary of Mrs. Kitty Trevylyan: a Story of the Times of Whitefield and the Wesleys. London: 1866. V. 65
On Both Sides of the Sea; A Story of the Commonwealth and the Restoration. London: 1868. V. 65
Our Seven Homes: Autobiographical Reminiscences. London: 1896. V. 65
The Victory of the Vanquished: a Tale of the First Century. London: 1871. V. 65

CHARLES Frederick Clark. A Brief Biography of a Great Character. London: 1945. V. 66

CHARLES, R. H.
Remarks on the Morphology of the Lumbar, Sacral and Caudal Regions of the Panjabi Calcutta: 1894. V. 67

CHARLES, ROBERT H.
A Roundabout Turn. London: 1930. V. 62; 65

CHARLES, TOM, MRS.
More Tales of the Tualrosa. Almagordo: 1961. V. 64; 67

CHARLES I, KING OF GREAT BRITAIN
His Majesties Instructions to His Commissioners of the Army, for the Severall Counties of England, and the Principality of Wales.... London: 1642. V. 63

CHARLESTON, SOUTH CAROLINA
Annual Report of the City Registrar, Comprising Return of Deaths, with a Classification of the Disease, Age, Sex, Status and Nativity of Each Case, for the Year Ending December 31, 1860. Together with Abstracts of the Barometer, Thermometer, Dewpoint, Wi. Charleston: 1861. V. 65

CHARLESWORTH, J. K.
Historical Geology of Ireland. 1963. V. 67
The Quaternary Era with Special Reference to its Glaciaton. London: 1957. V. 66

CHARLESWORTH, MARIA LOUISA
Ministering Children; a Tale Dedicated to Childhood. London: 1855. V. 67

CHARLEVOIX, P. F. X. DE
Histoire et Description Generale de la Nouvelle France avec le Journal Historique d'un Voyage fait par Ordre du Roi dans l'Amerique Septentrionale. Paris: 1744. V. 66
History and General Description of New France. Chicago: 1962. V. 67

CHARLTON Lectures on Art.... Oxford: 1925. V. 65

CHARLTON, THOMAS U. P.
The Life of Major General James Jackson. Atlanta: 1896. V. 66; 67

CHARM Of the Shadows. Cynthiana: 1945. V. 64

CHARNAS, SUZY MC KEE
The Vampire Tapestry. 1980. V. 62; 64; 66

CHARNAY, DESIRE
The Ancient Cities of the New World, Being Voyages and Explorations in Mexico and Central America from 1857-1882. New York: 1888. V. 65

CHARNOCK, RICHARD STEPHEN
Verba Nominalia; or, Words Derived from Proper Names. London: 1866. V. 64

CHARRIERE, ISABELLE, MME. DE
Bien-Ne. Nouvelles et Anecdotes. Apologie de la Flatterie. Paris: 1788. V. 63

CHARSLEY, F. A.
The Wild Flowers Around Melbourne. London: 1867. V. 64

CHARTERIS, LESLIE
The First Saint Omnibus. London: 1939. V. 65
Lady on a Train. Hollywood: 1945. V. 67
Meet -- The Tiger!. Garden City: 1929. V. 62
The Saint on Guard. Garden City: 1944. V. 67

CHARTERS, ANN
Kerouac - a Biography. London: 1974. V. 65

CHARYN, JEROME
Once Upon a Droshky. New York: 1964. V. 67

CHASE, CARROLL
The First Hundred Years of United States Territorial Postmarks 1787-1887. Federalsburg: 1950. V. 62; 65

CHASE, CHARLES M.
The Editor's Run in New Mexico and Colorado. Lyndon: 1882. V. 67

CHASE County Historical Sketches. Emporia: 1948-1980. V. 63

CHASE, ELIZA B.
Transcontinental Sketches, Legends, Lyrics and Romances Gleaned on Vacation Tours in North-Eastern and Middle Canada and the Pacific States. Philadelphia: 1909. V. 63; 64; 66

CHASE, LUCIEN B.
English Serfdom and American Slavery; or, Ourselves as Others See Us. New York: 1854. V. 67

CHASE, OWEN
Narratives of the Wreck of the Whale-Ship Essex of Nantucket Which as Destroyed by a Whale in the Pacific Ocean in the Year 1819. Waltham St. Lawrence: 1935. V. 62; 65

CHASE, PHILIP H.
Confederate Treasury Notes. The Paper Money of the Confederate States of America 1861-1865. Philadelphia: 1947. V. 65

CHASE, SAMUEL
The Answer and Pleas of Samuel Chase, One of the Associate Justices of the Supreme Court of the United States, to the Articles of Impeachment, Delivered Against Him.... Newburyport: 1805. V. 62
The Answer and Pleas of Samuel Chase, One of the Associate Justices of the Supreme Court of the United States, to the Articles of Impeachment, Delivered Against Him.... Washington City: 1805. V. 66

CHASEN, F. N.
A Handlist of Malaysian Birds.... Singapore: 1935. V. 67

CHASLES, MICHEL
Rapport sur les Progres de la Geometrie. Paris: 1870. V. 65

CHASLES, PHILARETE
Anglo-American Literature and Manners. New York: 1852. V. 65

CHASTELLUX, FRANCOIS JEAN, MARQUIS DE
An Essay on Public Happiness, Investigating the State of Human Nature, Under Each of Its Particular Appearances, Through the Several Periods of History, to the Present Times. London: 1774. V. 63
Travels in North America, in the Years 1780, 1781, 1782. Dublin: 1787. V. 66
Voyages de M. Le Marquis de Chastellux dans L'Amerique Septentrionale dans les Annees 1780, 1781 & 1782. Paris: 1786. V. 64

CHATAIGNE & GILLIS
Virginia Business Directory and Gazetteer and Richmond City Directory: 1877-1878. Richmond: 1877. V. 62

CHATEAUBRIAND, FRANCOIS AUGUSTE RENE, VICOMTE DE
Recollections of Italy, England and America.... London: 1815. V. 63
Souvenirs d'Italie, d'Angleterre et d'Amerique Suivis de Morceaux Divers De Morale et de Litterature. London: 1815. V. 67
Travels in Greece Palestine, Egypt and Barbary. Philadelphia: 1813. V. 65

CHATELAIN, CLARA DE PONTIGNY
The Child's Pictorial Vocabulary for Teaching Familiar Phrases in Three Languages by the Aid of Coloured Illustrations. London: 1865. V. 62
The Silver Swan. London: 1847. V. 62; 65

CHATELAIN, J. B.
Vues Diverses des Villages pres de Londres.... London: 1752. V. 66

CHATHAM AND ROCHESTER PHILOSOPHICAL AND LITERARY INSTITUTION
Rules and Regulations of the Philosophical and Literary Institution Established 1827. Rochester: 1828. V. 63

CHATHAM, JOHN PITT, 2ND EARL OF
General Regulations and Standing Orders for the Garrison of Gibraltar. Gibraltar: 1825. V. 62; 66

CHATHAM, KITTY
A Nursery Garland. New York: 1917. V. 62

CHATHAM, RUSSELL
Silent Seasons. New York: 1978. V. 67

CHATHAM, WILLIAM PITT, EARL OF
Correspondence.... London: 1838-1840. V. 62
Letters Written by the Late Earl of Chatham to His Nephew Thomas Pitt, Esq. 1804. V. 66

CHATTERBOX 1895. V. 67

CHATTERBOX 1896. V. 67

CHATTERBOX 1910. V. 67

CHATTERTON, EDWARD KEBLE
Down Channel in the Vivette. London: 1910. V. 67
Down Channel in the Vivette. London: 1912. V. 65
Old Sea Paintings. The Story of Maritime Art as Depicted by the Great Masters. London: 1928. V. 63; 64; 67
Sailing Models, Ancient and Modern. London: 1934. V. 65
Ship Models. London: 1923. V. 63; 64; 65
The Story of Maritime Art as Depicted by the Great Masters. London: 1928. V. 64
Through Holland in Vivette. London: 1910. V. 65
To the Mediterranean in Charmina. London: 1934. V. 67
Whalers and Whaling. London: 1925. V. 62

CHATTERTON, FENIMORE C.
Yesterday's Wyoming. The Intimate Memories of Fenimore C. Chitterton, Territorial Citizen, Governor, Statesman - an Autobiography. Denver: 1957. V. 65; 67

CHATTERTON, GEORGINA, LADY
The Lost Bride. London: 1875. V. 65
Rambles in the South of Ireland During the Year 1838. 1839. V. 62

CHATTERTON, THOMAS
Poems, Supposed to Have Been Written at Bristol, by Thomas Rowley and Others. London: 1777. V. 62; 64; 65
Poems, Supposed to Have Been Written at Bristol, by Thomas Rowley and Others. London: 1778. V. 63
Poems, Supposed to Have Been Written at Bristol, by Thomas Rowley and Others. London: 1782. V. 63
Poems Supposed to Have Been Written at Bristol by Thomas Rowley and Others. Cambridge: 1794. V. 62; 66
The Poetical Works of Thomas Chatterton. London: 1872. V. 65
The Rowley Poems. London: 1898. V. 65
The Works. London: 1803. V. 67

A CHATTO and Windus Almanack 1927. London: 1927. V. 67

CHATTO, W. A.
The Old English Squire. London: 1821. V. 66
Scenes and Recollections of Fly-Fishing in Northumberland, Cumberland and Westmoreland. 1834. V. 65; 67

CHATTOCK, R. S.
Wensleydale. London: 1872. V. 66

CHATWIN, BRUCE
In Patagonia. London: 1977. V. 62; 64; 65; 67; 67
In Patagonia. New York: 1977. V. 67
In Patagonia. New York: 1978. V. 62; 64; 66; 67
On the Black Hill. London: 1982. V. 62; 65; 66
On the Black Hill. New York: 1983. V. 67
Photographs and Notebooks. London: 1993. V. 67
The Songlines. Franklin Center: 1987. V. 65; 67
The Songlines. London: 1987. V. 63; 66
The Songlines. New York: 1987. V. 63; 67
Utz. London: 1988. V. 65
Utz. New York: 1988. V. 63
The Viceroy of Ouidah. London: 1980. V. 63; 64; 66
The Viceroy of Ouidah. New York: 1980. V. 63; 64; 66
What Am I Doing Here. London: 1989. V. 63

CHAUCER, GEOFFREY
The Canterbury Tales. Waltham St. Lawrence: 1929-1931. V. 65
The Canterbury Tales. New York: 1930. V. 64
The Canterbury Tales. Waltham St. Lawrence: 1931. V. 64
The Canterbury Tales. London: 1934. V. 64
Chaucer for Children. London: 1882. V. 63
The Ellesmere Chaucer Reproduced in Facsimile. Manchester: 1911. V. 66
The Flower and the Leaf. London: 1902. V. 67
The Prologue to the Tales of Canterbury. Chelsea: 1897. V. 65

Troilus and Cressida. London: 1939. V. 66
Troilus and Criseyde. Waltham St. Lawrence: 1927. V. 62
The Woorkes.... London: 1561. V. 64; 65
The Workes. London: 1542. V. 63
The Workes. London: 1602. V. 64
The Works. London: 1687. V. 64
The Works. London: 1721. V. 64
The Works. Hammersmith: 1896. V. 62; 66; 67
The Works. 1958. V. 64
The Works. Cleveland and New York: 1958. V. 63

CHAUDHARY, R. P.
Biodiversity in Nepal, Status and Conservation. Saharanpur: 1998. V. 63

CHAUDHURI, K. N.
Sport in Jhell and Jungle. Calcutta: 1918. V. 67

CHAUDHURI, NIRAD C.
A Passage to England. London: 1959. V. 63

CHAUDRON, A.
Chaudron's Spelling Book, Carefully Prepared for Family and School Use. Mobile: 1865. V. 62; 63; 65

CHAUNCY, CHARLES
Complete View of Episcopacy. Boston: 1771. V. 63
A Letter to a Friend, Containing Remarks on Certain Passages in a Sermon Preached By.... Boston: 1767. V. 63; 64; 66

CHAUNDY, LESLIE
A Bibliography of the First Editions of the Works of Maurice Baring. London: 1925. V. 64

CHAUVELIN
The Authentic State Papers Which Passed Between Monsieur Chauvelin, Minister Pleni-Potentiar from France and the Right Hon. Lord Greenville. London: 1793. V. 64

CHAUVENET, WILLIAM
A Manual of Spherical and Practical Astronomy.... Philadelphia: 1863. V. 66

CHAUVIN, ETIENNE
Lexicon Philosophicum Secundis Curis. Novum Opus. Leeuwarden: 1713. V. 62

CHAVES, AMADO
The Defeat of the Comanches in 1717. Santa Fe: 1906. V. 66

CHAVEZ, FRAY ANGELICO
My Penitente Land. Albuquerque: 1974. V. 65
My Penitente Land. Albuquerque: 1975. V. 63
Origins of New Mexico Families. Santa Fe: 1954. V. 62; 65

CHAWEROT in Erez Jisrael. Berlin: 1937. V. 67

CHAYTOR, A. H.
Essays Sporting and Serious. London: 1930. V. 67
Letters to a Salmon Fisher's Sons. 1910. V. 67
Letters to a Salmon Fisher's Sons. London: 1919. V. 67
Letters to a Salmon Fisher's Sons. London: 1925. V. 67
Letters to a Salmon Fisher's Sons. 1936. V. 67

THE CHEAP Magazine, a Work of Humble Import.... Haddington: 1813. V. 63
THE CHEAP Magazine, a Work of Humble Import.... Haddington: 1813-1814. V. 62

CHEATHAM, KITTY
A Nursery Garland. New York: 1917. V. 66

THE CHEATS of London Exposed; or, the Tricks of the Town Laid Open to Both Sexes.... London: 1772. V. 67

CHECCHETELLI, GIUSEPPE
Una Giornata di Osservazione nel Palazzo e Nella Villa di S.E. Il Sig. Principe D. Alessandro Torlonia. Rome: 1842. V. 64

CHEEK, HENRY
Cheek's Farriery: a Complete Treatise on the Causes and Symptoms of the Diseases of the Horse, and Their Remedies. Memphis: 1845. V. 66

CHEEKE, JOHN
The True Subject to the Rebell. Or the Hurt of Sedition.... Oxford: 1641. V. 64

THE CHEERFUL Warbler, or Juvenile Song Book. London: 1820. V. 66

CHEESEMAN, T. F.
Illustrations of the New Zealand Flora. Wellington: 1914. V. 62; 64
Manual of the New Zealand Flora. Wellington: 1925. V. 66

CHEESMAN, R. E.
In Unknown Arabia. London: 1926. V. 64

CHEETHAM, JAMES
The Life of Thomas Paine. New York: 1809. V. 64
A Narrative of the Suppression by Co. Burr, of the History of the Administration of John Adams.... New York: 1802. V. 63; 66

CHEEVER, GEORGE B.
The Dream; or the True History of Deacon Giles's Distillery, and Deacon Jones's Brewery. New York: 1859. V. 63
God Against Slavery; and the Freedom and Dusty of the Pulpit to Rebuke It, as a Sin Against God. Cincinnati: 1859. V. 64
Wanderings of a Pilgrim in the Shadow of Mont Blanc and the Jungfrau Alp. London. V. 63; 64

CHEEVER, GEORGE B. continued
Wanderings of a Pilgrim in the Shadow of Mont Blanc and the Jungfrau Alp. Aberdeen: 1848. V. 64
Wanderings of a Pilgrim in the Shadow of Mont Blanc and the Jungfrau Alp. Glasgow: 1860. V. 64

CHEEVER, HENRY T.
The Island World of the Pacific; Being the Personal Narrative and Results of Travel through the Sandwich or Hawaiian Islands.... Glasgow: 1850. V. 64
Life in the Sandwich Islands, or, the Heart of the Pacific, As It Was and Is. New York: 1851. V. 64

CHEEVER, JOHN
Atlantic Crossing. Cottondale: 1986. V. 64; 67
The Enormous Radio and Other Stories. New York: 1953. V. 62; 64; 65; 66
Expelled. N.P: 1987. V. 62; 64; 67
Falconer. New York: 1976. V. 62; 63; 66
Homage to Shakespeare. Stevenson: 1968. V. 64
The Stories of John Cheever. New York: 1978. V. 63; 64
The Wapshot Chronicle. New York: 1957. V. 62
The Way Some People Live. New York: 1943. V. 63; 66; 67

CHEEVER, LAWRENCE O.
The House of Morrell. Cedar Rapids: 1948. V. 67

CHEEVER, SUSAN
Looking for Work. New York: 1979. V. 63

CHEIRO, LOUIS HAMON
Cheiro's Guide to the Land. Chicago and New York: 1900. V. 63

CHEKE, VAL
The Story of Cheese Making in Britain. London: 1959. V. 62

CHEKHOV, ANTON
The House with the Mezzanine and Other Stories. New York: 1917. V. 66
The Letters of Anton Chekhov. London: 1973. V. 63
Russian Silhouettes: More Stories of Russian Life. New York: 1915. V. 66
The Short Stories of Anton Chekhov. Avon: 1973. V. 63; 64
Skazki Melpomeny (Fairy Tales of Melpomene). Moscow: 1884. V. 67
That Worthless Fellow Platonov. New York: 1930. V. 64
The Unknown Chekhov. New York: 1954. V. 67

CHELIUS, J. M.
A System of Surgery. Philadelphia: 1847. V. 63

CHELLIS, MARY DWINELL
Ten Cents. New York: 1877. V. 63

CHELSUM, JAMES
Remarks on the Two Last Chapters of Mr. Gibbon's History, of the Decline and Fall of the Roman Empire in a Letter to a Friend. London: 1776. V. 65

CHELUCCI, PAULINO
Institutiones Arithmeticae cum Appendice de Natura, Atque usu Logarithmorum. Rome: 1740. V. 65

CHEMI, JAMES M.
The George L. Leach Correspondence. Robbed by Highway-Men.... N.P: 1972. V. 66

CHEN, J. T. F.
A Synopsis of the Vertebrates of Taiwan. 1956. V. 65; 67

CHEN, S.
Native Orchids to China in Colour. Beijing: 1999. V. 65

CHEN, T. T.
Research in Protozoology. Oxford: 1967-1972. V. 66; 67

CHENERY, THOMAS
The Arabic Language: a Lecture Given on December 3, 1868. London: 1869. V. 63

CHENERY, WILLIAM H.
The Fourteenth Regiment Rhode Island Heavy Artillery (Colored), in the War to Preserve the Union, 1861-1865. Providence: 1898. V. 62

CHENEY, EDNA D.
Louisa May Alcott, the Children's Friend. Boston: 1888. V. 65

CHENEY, PETER
They Never Say When. London: 1944. V. 65

CHENG, TE, EMPEROR OF CHINA
The Rambles of the Emperor Ching Tih in Keang Nan. A Chinese Tale. London: 1843. V. 65

CHENGYUAN, MA
Ancient Chinese Bronzes. London: 1986. V. 66

CHENIER, ELISABETH SANTI L'HOMACA
Lettres Grecqus. Paris: 1879. V. 63

CHENIER, MARIE JOSEPH DE
Charles IX, ou l'Ecole de Rois, Tragedie.... paris: 1790. V. 65

CHEREPASHCHUK, A. M.
Highly Evolved Close Binary Stars; Part I: Catalog Part II: Finding Charts. Amsterdam: 1996. V. 67

CHEROKEE NATION
Address of the Committee and Council of the Cherokee Nation, in General Council Convened to the People of the United States. N.P: 1830. V. 63; 66

Laws of the Cherokee Nation; Adopted by the Council at Various Periods. (and) The Constitution and Laws of the Cherokee Nation Passed at Tahlequah. Tahlequah: 1852. V. 62; 66

CHERRINGTON, ERNEST H.
The Anti-Saloon League Year Book. Westerville: 1909-1920. V. 63

CHERRY-GARRARD, APSLEY
The Worst Journey in the World. Antarctic 1910-1913. London: 1922. V. 62
The Worst Journey in the World: Antarctic 1910-1913. London: 1937. V. 64; 65; 66

CHERRYH, C. J.
Cloud's Rider. Norwalk: 1996. V. 65

CHERTOK, HARVEY
Quotations from Charlie Chan. New York: 1968. V. 65; 66

CHESBRO, GEORGE C.
An Affair of Sorcerers. 1979. V. 66
The Beasts of Valhalla. 1985. V. 65; 66
City of Whispering Stone. New York: 1978. V. 67
Shadow of a Broken Man. 1977. V. 66
Shadow of a Broken Man. New York: 1977. V. 67

CHESEBROUGH, CAROLINE
The Fishermen of Gamp's Island. New York: 1865. V. 65

CHESELDEN, WILLIAM
The Anatomy of the Human Body. London: 1756. V. 66
The Anatomy of the Human Body. London: 1778. V. 64; 67
The Anatomy of the Human Body. Boston: 1795. V. 63
Osteographia or the Anatomy of Bones. London: 1753. V. 62

CHESHIRE, JOSEPH B.
Nonnula. Memories, Stories, Traditions, More or Less Authentic. Chapel Hill: 1930. V. 66; 67

CHESLEY, HARRY E.
Adventuring with the Old Times, Trails Travelled, Tales Told. Midland: 1979. V. 67

CHESNEY, CHARLES CORNWALLIS
Campaigns in Virginia and Maryland. London: 1864-1865. V. 62; 63; 65

CHESNEY, FRANCIS RAWDON
The Expedition for the Survey of the Rivers Euphrates and Tigris Carried on by Order of the British Government in the Years 1834, 1836 and 1837. 1969. V. 66
Narrative of the Euphrates Expedition Carried on by Order of the British Government During the Years 1835, 1836 and 1837. London: 1868. V. 62

CHESNEY, GEORGE TOMKYNS
The Dilemma. Edinburgh: 1876. V. 65

CHESNUTT, CHARLES W.
The Colonel's Dream. New York: 1905. V. 64; 66
The House Behind the Cedars. Boston: 1900. V. 64

CHESNUTT, HELEN M.
Charles Waddell Chesnutt. Pioneer of the Color Line. Chapel Hill: 1952. V. 66

CHESSHYRE, E.
Posthumous Songs, Etc. 1837. V. 65

CHESSON, NORA
Selected Poems. London: 1900. V. 63

CHESTER, ALFRED
Here Be Dragons: Stories. Paris: 1955. V. 66

CHESTER, GEORGE RANDOLPH
The Wonderful Adventures of Little Prince Toofat. New York: 1922. V. 63; 67

CHESTER, LEONARD
Federalism Triumphant in the Steady Habits of Connecticut Alone, or, the Turnpike Road to a Fortune, a Comic Opera, or, Political Farce in Six Acts. N.P: 1802. V. 66

CHESTER PLAYS
The Chester Play of the Deluge. Waltham St. Lawrence: 1927. V. 62; 65

CHESTERFIELD Burlesqued, or, School of Modern Manners. London: 1811. V. 65

CHESTERFIELD, PHILIP DORMER STANHOPE, 4TH EARL OF
Characters of Eminent Personages of His Own Time.... Holborn: 1777. V. 66
Correspondence with Various Ladies.... London: 1930. V. 63; 66
The Fine Gentleman's Etiquette; or Lord Chesterfield's Advice to His Son, Versified. London: 1776. V. 64
The Letters and Works. London: 1845-1853. V. 67
Letters of Philip, ... Earl of Chesterfield, to Several Celebrated Individuals of the Time of Charles II, James II, William III and Queen Anne, with Some of Their Replies. London: 1829. V. 63
Letters Written by the Late Right Honourable Philip Dormer Stanhope, Earl of Chesterfield to His Son. Dublin: 1774-1775. V. 63; 66
Letters Written...to His Son. Dublin: 1774. V. 62; 65; 66
Letters Written...to His Son.... London: 1774. V. 62; 63; 65; 66
Lettres du Comte de Chesterfield a son Fils Philippe Stanhope. Venice: 1811. V. 66
Miscellaneous Works.... London: 1779. V. 65
The Oeconomy of Human Life. London: 1751. V. 66
The Poetical Works of.... Montagnola: 1927. V. 67
Principles of Politeness and of Knowing the World.... Portsmouth: 1786. V. 62

CHESTERFIELD, RUTH
A New Version of Old Mother Hubbard. Boston: 1866. V. 64

CHESTERTON, GILBERT KEITH
The Ball and the Cross. London: 1910. V. 66
Chaucer. London: 1932. V. 65
The Club of Queer Trades. New York: 1903. V. 62
The Club of Queer Trades. 1905. V. 64
The Club of Queer Trades. New York: 1905. V. 66
The Coloured Lands. London: 1938. V. 66
The Crimes of England. London: 1915. V. 63
A G. K. Chesterton Omnibus. London: 1936. V. 65
Gloria in Profundis. New York: 1927. V. 62
The Incredulities of Father Brown. London: 1926. V. 66
The Incredulity of Father Brown. New York: 1926. V. 63
The Innocence of Father Brown. 1911. V. 67
London. London: 1914. V. 63
London. Minneapolis: 1914. V. 65
The Napoleon of Notting Hill. London: 1914. V. 64; 66
St. Thomas Aquinas. New York: 1933. V. 66
The Scandal of Father Brown. London: 1935. V. 63; 66
The Secret of Father Brown. London: 1927. V. 63

CHETHAM, JAMES
The Angler's Vade Mecum; or, a Compendious, Yet Full Discourse of Angling.... London: 1700. V. 62

CHETHAM, JOHN
A Book of Psalmody, Containing Variety of Tunes for all the Common Metres of the Psalms.... London: 1745. V. 62

CHETLAIN, AUGUSTUS L.
Recollections of Seventy Years. Galena: 1899. V. 64; 67

CHETTLE, E. M.
Jacks and Jills. London: 1890. V. 64

CHETWOOD, WILLIAM RUFUS
The Voyages and Adventures of Captain Boyle, in Several Parts of the World. London: 1781. V. 63; 67

CHETWYND, JAMES
A Treatise Upon Fines, Containing Their Nature, Antiquity and Definition, by Ancient Authors. London: 1774. V. 62

CHETWYND, JULIA
Janie: a Highland Love Story. London: 1870. V. 65

CHEUSE, ALAN
The Bohemians. Cambridge: 1982. V. 67

CHEVALLIER, A.
Manuel Pratique de l'Appareil de Marsh, ou Guide de l'Expert Toxicologiste. Paris: 1843. V. 66

CHEVES, LANGDON
Southern State Rights, Free Trade and Anti-Abolition Tract No. 1. Charleston: 1844. V. 66

CHEVEY, P.
Iconographie Ichthyologique de l'Indochine. Saigon: 1932. V. 62; 63; 65; 66

CHEVREUL, M. E.
The Laws of Contrast and Colour. London: 1861. V. 67
The Laws of Contrast of Color. London: 1859. V. 62
Lecons de Chimie Appliquee a la Teinture. Paris: 1829-1830. V. 66
The Principles of Harmony and Contrast of Colours. London: 1854. V. 67
The Principles of Harmony and Contrast of Colours. London: 1855. V. 65

CHEW, ROGER PRESTON
Military Operations in Jefferson County Virginia (and West Virginia) 1861-1865. Charlestown: 1911. V. 62

CHEYNE, GEORGE
The English Malady; or, a Treatise of Nervous Diseases of All Kinds. London: 1733. V. 63; 64; 65; 66
The English Malady; or, a Treatise of Nervous Diseases of All Kinds.... London: 1773. V. 64
An Essay of Health and Long Life. London: 1724. V. 65
An Essay of Health and Long Life. London: 1725. V. 62; 67
An Essay of the True Nature and Due Method of Treating the Gout. London: 1725. V. 62
An Essay on Regimen. Together with Five Discourses, Medical, Moral and Philosophical.... London: 1740. V. 65
The Natural Method of Cureing the Diseases of the Body, and the Disorders of the Mind Depending on the Body. London: 1742. V. 65
Philosophical Principles of Religion: Natural and Revealed. London: 1715. V. 65

CHEYNEY, PETER
Dark Hero. London: 1946. V. 65
The Dark Street. New York: 1944. V. 67

CHIABRANO, CHARLES
Six Sonates a Violon Seul et Basse Continue Dediees a Monseigneur Le Dauphin. Paris: 1754. V. 65

CHICAGO. WORLD'S COLUMBIAN EXPOSITION, 1893.
The Columbian Exposition Album Containing Views of the Grounds, Main and State Buildings, Statuary, Architectural Details, Interiors, Midway Plaisance Scenes, and Other Interesting Objects Which Had Place at the World's Columbian Exposition Chicago 1893. Chicago: 1893. V. 65

CHICHESTER, FRANCIS
The Lonely Sea and the Sky. London: 1964. V. 65

CHICKAMAUGA MEMORIAL ASSOCIATION
Proceedings at Chatanooga, Tennessee, and Crawfish Springs, Georgia, September 19 and 20, 1889. Chattanooga: 1889. V. 64

CHICKEN World. New York: 1910. V. 64

CHIDLAW, B. W.
The Story of My Life. Philadelphia: 1890. V. 67

CHIEF MAX BIG MAN
The Plains Absarokee. Billings: 1936. V. 66

CHIEF STANDING BEAR
My People, the Sioux. Boston: 1928. V. 67

CHILCOTE Park. London: 1860. V. 63

CHILD, HAMILTON
Gazetteer and Business Directory of Orleans County, New York for 1869. Syracuse: 1869. V. 65

CHILD, JOSIAH
A New Discourse of Trade.... London: 1694. V. 65
A New Discourse of Trade.... London: 1698. V. 66
A New Discourse of Trade.... Glasgow: 1751. V. 63

CHILD, JULIA
Mastering the Art of French Cooking. New York: 1961. V. 63

CHILD, LEE
Close to Home. Winston Salem: 1996. V. 63
Killing Floor. New York: 1997. V. 62; 67

CHILD, LYDIA MARIA FRANCIS
An Appeal in Favor of that Class of Americans Called Africans. Boston: 1833. V. 63; 64
The Girl's Own Book. London: 1858. V. 64
Letters from New York. New York and Boston: 1843. V. 66
Letters from New York. New York: 1844. V. 66
Letters from New York. (First Series). (and) (Second Series). New York and Boston: 1843-1845. V. 66
Letters from New York. Second Series. Boston: 1845. V. 62; 63; 66
A New Flower for Children. New York: 1856. V. 63
Philothea, a Romance. Boston and New York: 1836. V. 65

CHILD STUDY ASSOCIATION OF AMERICA
Read-To-Me Storybook. New York: 1947. V. 63

CHILD Torture in Scotland. Edinburgh: 1895. V. 64

CHILDERS, ERSKINE
The Framework of Home Rule. 1911. V. 62
The Riddle of the Sands. London: 1927. V. 62

CHILDISH, BILLY
Black Things Hidden in Dust. Poetry from 1981. Chatham: 1982. V. 67
Prity Thing. Poeting 1982. Chatham: 1982. V. 67
The Wild Breed is Here. Chatham: 1982. V. 67

THE CHILDREN in the Wood. London: 1835. V. 64

THE CHILDREN'S Hour. Boston: 1907. V. 62

THE CHILDREN'S King Arthur. London: 1905. V. 62

CHILDREN'S Toys, and Some Elementary Lessons in General Knowledge Which They Teach. London: 1877. V. 64

CHILDREN'S Treasury of Great Stories. London: 1910. V. 64

THE CHILDREN'S Wedding. 1890. V. 63

CHILDRESS, ALICE
Like One of the Family...Conversations from a Domestic's Life. Brooklyn: 1956. V. 64; 65

CHILDRESS, MARK
Crazy in Alabama. New York: 1993. V. 67
A World Made of Fire. New York: 1984. V. 62; 63

THE CHILD'S Book About Whales (No. 10). Concord: 1843. V. 64

THE CHILD'S Coloured Gift Book. London. V. 66

THE CHILD'S Garland, or Poetry for Young Minds. Boston: Sep. 1830. V. 64

CHILDS, GEORGE
English Landscape Scenery; an Advanced Drawing Book. London: 1860. V. 66; 67

THE CHILD'S Illustrated Alphabet. London: 1840. V. 65

CHILD'S Picture Book. Concord: 1849. V. 64

A CHILD'S Stamp Book of Old Verses, Picture Stamps. New York: 1915. V. 66

THE CHILD'S True Friend. London: 1808. V. 63

CHILTON, JOHN
A Digest of the Laws, Respecting Wills, Executors and Administrators, Jurisdiction and Practice of the Courts of Probate and Equity.... Vicksburg: 1846. V. 63

CHILTON, LANCE
New Mexico. A New Guide to the Colorful State. Albuquerque: 1974. V. 63; 66

CHIMMO, WILLIAM
On Euplectella Aspergillum Also on ...Phosphorescnet Animalcules; Sea-Sawdust (etc.). 1883. V. 67

CHINA Floral Encyclopaedia. 1993. V. 67

CHINA, the Country, History and People. London: 1860. V. 64

THE CHINESE Bronzes of Yunnan. London: 1983. V. 62

CHINESE Classical Gardens of Suzhou. New York: 1993. V. 67

THE CHINESE Economic Monthly. Volumes I-III. Peking: 1923-1926. V. 64

CHING, R.
New Zealand Birds, an Artist's Field Studies. Auckland: 1986. V. 63

CHIN-LIANG, N. A.
Chinese Seals: the Collection of Ralph C. Lee. Taiwan: 1966. V. 63

CHIPAULT, ANTOINE
Etudes de Chirurgie Medullaire. Paris: 1894. V. 64
Manuel D'Orthopedie Vertebale. Paris: 1904. V. 66

CHIPMAN, NATHANIEL
Sketches of the Principles of Government. Rutland: 1793. V. 63

CHIPPENDALE, JOHN
The Gentleman and Cabinet-Maker's Director. London: 1939. V. 62

CHIPPINDALL, W. H.
History of the Township of Gressingham. Kendal: 1919. V. 66
A Sixteen Century Survey and Year's Account of the Estates of Hornby Castle, Lancashire. Manchester: 1939. V. 65

CHIRICO, GIORGIO DE
Hebdomeros. Paris: 1929. V. 67

CHIROL, M. VALENTINE
Twixt Greek and Turk; or Jottings During a Journey through Thessaly, Macedonia, and Epirus in the Autumn of 1880. Edinburgh: 1881. V. 64
With Pen and Brush in Eastern Lands. London: 1929. V. 64

CHISHOLM, C. R., & BROS.
Chisholm's All Round Route and Panoramic Guide of the St. Lawrence. Montreal: 1875. V. 62; 66

CHISHOLM, JOE
Brewery Gulch, Frontier Days of Old Arizona - Last Outpost of the Great Southwest. San Antonio: 1949. V. 64; 67

CHISHOLM, LOUEY
The Enchanted Land: Tales Told Again. London: 1906. V. 62

CHISHULL, EDMUND
Antiquitates Asiaticae Christianam Aeram Antecedentes.... London: 1728. V. 65; 67

CHISOLM, J. JULIAN
A Manual of Military Surgery for the Use of Surgeons in the Confederate States Army; with an Appendix of the Rules and Regulations of the Medical Department of the Confederate States Army. Richmond: 1862. V. 63; 65

CHITTENDEN, F. J.
Dictionary of Gardening. London: 1956. V. 64; 65; 67

CHITTENDEN, HIRAM MARTIN
The American Fur Trade of the Far West. New York: 1902. V. 66
The American Fur Trade of the Far West. New York: 1935. V. 64, 65, 66
The American Fur Trade of the Far West. Stanford: 1954. V. 62
History of Early Steamboat Navigation on the Missouri River, Life and Adventures of Joseph Labarge. New York: 1909. V. 65; 67
Life, Letters and Travels of Father Pierre Jean De Smet.... New York: 1905. V. 65

CHITTENDEN, RUSSELL HENRY
A Study of Some Infant Foods in Comparison with Mothers' Milk.... New York: 1896. V. 67

CHITTENDEN, WILLIAM LAWRENCE
Ranch Verses. New York: 1893. V. 66

CHITTICK, JAMES
Silk Manufacturing and Its Problems. New York: 1913. V. 66

CHITTY, JOSEPH
Chitty's Treatise on Pleading and Parties to Actions, With a Second Volume Containing Modern Precedents of Pleadings & Practical Notes. Springfield: 1885. V. 63
Treatise on the Law of Bills of Exchange, Checks on Bankers, Promissory Notes, Bankers Cash Notes and Bank-Notes. Portland: 1807. V. 64
A Treatise on the Law of Contracts and Upon the Defences to Actions Thereon. Cambridge: 1874. V. 66

CHITTY, SUSAN
Antonia White. Diaries 1926-1957. London: 1991. V. 67

CHIVERS, THOMAS HOLLEY
Nacoochee; or the Beautiful Star, with Other Poems. New York: 1837. V. 64

CHOCOLATE Surprise Book of Nursery Rhymes. London: 1891. V. 62

CHOISEUL-MEUSE, FELICITE, COMTESSE DE
Entre Chien et Loup. Londres: 1894. V. 65

CHOISY, ABBE DE
Journal du Voyage de Siam fait en 1685 and 1686. Paris: 1687. V. 64; 66
Journal ou Suite du Voyage du Siam. Amsterdam: 1687. V. 67

CHOLMONDELEY, MARY
Moth and Rust; Together with Geoffrey's Wife and the Pitfall. London: 1902. V. 65
Prisoners: Fast Bound in Misery and Iron. New York: 1906. V. 65

CHOLMONDELEY-PENNELL, H.
The Angler Naturalist. 1863. V. 67
Fishing - Salmon and Trout. London: 1885. V. 62
Fishing. Salmon and Trout. Pike and Coarse Fish. 1889. V. 62
Fishing Gossip. 1866. V. 67
Fishing - Pike and Other Coarse Fish. London: 1886. V. 67
Fishing - Salmon and Trout. London: 1886. V. 67
Fishing - Salmon and Trout. London: 1912. V. 67
The Modern Practical Angler. 1870. V. 67
Pegasus Re-Saddled. London: 1878. V. 62
Puck of Pegasus. London: 1861. V. 62
Puck on Pegasus. London: 1868. V. 64

CHOMEI, KAMO NO
An Account of My Hut: The Hojoki of Kamo No Chomei. Pawlet: 1956. V. 63

CHOMEL, AUGUST FRANCOIS
Des Fievres et des Maladies Pestilientielles. Paris: 1821. V. 64

CHOMEL, NOEL
Dictionaire Oeconomique: or, the Family Dictionary. London: 1725. V. 64

CHOMSKY, NOAM
Syntactic Structures. The Hague: 1957. V. 63; 67

CHOPIN, KATE
The Awakening. New York: 1906. V. 62; 63
Bayou Folk. Boston: 1894. V. 62
Edna. Paris: 1952. V. 63

CHOPIN, M.
Russie. Paris: 1840. V. 65

CHOPRA, R. N.
Indigenous Drugs of India. Their Medical and Economic Aspects. Calcutta: 1933. V. 66

CHORLEY, HENRY F.
The Authors of England. London: 1838. V. 63
Memorials of Mrs. Hemans. Philadelphia: 1836. V. 65

CHORLTON, WILLIAM
American Grape Grower's Guide. New York: 1862. V. 66

CHOUKRI, MOHAMED
Tennesse Williams in Tangier. Santa Barbara: 1979. V. 62; 66

CHOULANT, LUDWIG
History and Bibliography of Anatomic Illustration. New York: 1945. V. 64; 66
History and Bibliography of Anatomic Illustration. Cambridge: 1993. V. 66

CHOWN, DAISY M.
Wayfaring in Africa: a Woman's Wanderings from the Cape to Cairo. London: 1927. V. 65

CHOYCE Drollery; Songs and Sonnets. Lincolnshire: 1876. V. 67

CHOYSELAT, PRUDENT
The Discours Oeconomique. 1951. V. 65

LE CHRETIEN Fortifie Dans Les Souffrances. Mons: 1761. V. 64

CHRISTIAN Lyrics: Chiefly Selected from Modern Authors. London: 1868. V. 62

CHRISMAN, HARRY E.
The Ladder of Rivers - the Story of I. P. (Print) Olive. Denver: 1965. V. 67

CHRIST, JAY FINLEY
Flashes by Flashlight. 1946. V. 67
Sherlock's Anniversaries. New York: 1961. V. 65

CHRISTENSEN, ERWIN E.
Primitive Art. New York: 1955. V. 64

CHRISTENSEN, LARS
My Last Expedition to the Antarctic 1936-1937. Oslo: 1938. V. 64
My Last Expedition to the Antarctic 1936-1937. Washington: 1940. V. 66
Such is the Antarctic. London: 1935. V. 63, 64

THE CHRISTIAN Almanack 1823 and 1824. Boston: 1823-1824. V. 65

THE CHRISTIAN Book of Concord, or Symbolical Books of the Evangelical Lutheran Church.... Newmarket: 1851. V. 67

THE CHRISTIAN Chaplet - A Wreath of Prose Poetry and Art. London: 1860. V. 64

CHRISTIAN, F. W.
The Caroline Islands: Travel in the Sea of the Little Lands. London: 1899. V. 64

CHRISTIAN, GEORGE L.
North Carolina and Virginia in the Civil War. Nashville: 1904. V. 62; 63; 65

A CHRISTIAN Library: Consisting of Extracts from the Abridgments of the Choicest Pieces of Practical Divinity, Which Have Been Published in the English Tongue. Burlington: 1774. V. 63; 64; 66

CHRISTIAN, W. ASBURY
Lynchburg and It's People. Lynchburg: 1900. V. 64

CHRISTIAN, W. ASBURY continued
Richmond: Her Past and Present. Richmond: 1912. V. 64

THE CHRISTIAN'S, Scholar's and Farmer's Magazine. Elizabeth-Town: 1790. V. 63; 64
THE CHRISTIAN'S, Scholar's and Farmer's Magazine. Elizabethtown: 1791. V. 66

CHRISTIE, AGATHA
The ABC Murders. London: 1936. V. 62
Absent in Spring. London: 1944. V. 63
The Adventure of the Christmas Pudding. London: 1960. V. 67
At Bertram's Hotel. London: 1965. V. 63
The Burden. London: 1956. V. 66
By the Pricking of My Thumbs. London: 1968. V. 67
A Caribbean Mystery. 1964. V. 64; 66
Cat Among the Pigeons. 1959. V. 64; 66
Death Comes at the End. London: 1945. V. 64; 67
Destination Unknown. 1954. V. 64
Destination Unknown. London: 1954. V. 62
Five Little Pigs. London: 1942. V. 63; 64; 65
4:50 from Paddington. London: 1957. V. 67
Hercule Poirot's Christmas. London: 1939. V. 65
The Hound of Death and Other Stories. London: 1933. V. 66; 67
The Labours of Hercules. London: 1947. V. 62; 64
Mrs. McGinty's Dead. New York: 1952. V. 64
The Moving Finger. London: 1943. V. 66; 67
The Murder at the Vicarage. 1930. V. 66
Murder in the Calais Coach. 1934. V. 62; 66
Murder in the Calais Coach. New York: 1952. V. 64
Murder in the Mews. London: 1937. V. 62
The Murder of Roger Ackroyd. New York: 1926. V. 65
The Pale Horse. London: 1961. V. 63
Partners in Crime. 1929. V. 66
Partners in Crime. New York: 1929. V. 64
Passenger to Frankfurt - an Extravaganza. London: 1970. V. 65
Peril at End House. 1932. V. 67
Sad Cypress. 1940. V. 67
Sad Cypress. London: 1940. V. 62
The Secret of Chimneys. London: 1925. V. 62
Sleeping Murder. London: 1976. V. 67
They Came to Baghdad. London: 1951. V. 62
They Do It With Mirrors. London: 1952. V. 64
Triple Threat. New York: 1943. V. 66
The Under Dog and Other Stories. New York: 1951. V. 62

CHRISTIE, ARCHIBALD
Traditional Method of Pattern Designing, an Introduction to the Study of Formal Ornament. Oxford: 1929. V. 67

CHRISTIE, ARCHIBALD, MRS.
Samplers and Stitches. London: 1934. V. 62

CHRISTIE, JAMES
A Disquisition Upon Etruscan Vases; Displaying Their Probable Connection, with the Shows at Eleusis.... London: 1806. V. 62; 65
An Essay on that Earliest Species of Idolatry, the Worship of the Elements. Norwich: 1814. V. 62; 63
An Inquiry Into the Antient Greek Game, Supposed to Have Been Invented by Palamedes, Antecedent to the Siege. London: 1801. V. 65

CHRISTIE, JAMES TRAILL
Concise Precedents of Wills, with an Introduction and Practical Notes. London: 1849. V. 62

CHRISTIE-MILLER, SYDNEY RICHARDSON
The Britwell Handlist, or, Short-Title Catalogue of the Principal Volumes from the Time of Caxton to the Year 1800 Formerly in the Library of Britwell Court, Buckinghamshire. London: 1933. V. 63

CHRISTINE DE SUEDE
Pensees. Paris: 1825. V. 66

CHRISTISON, DAVID
Early Fortifications in Scotland, Motes, Camps and Forts. Edinburgh: 1898. V. 63

CHRIST-JANER, ALBERT
Boardman Robinson. Chicago: 1946. V. 62; 63; 65

CHRISTLIEB, THEODORE
The Indo-British Opium Trade and Its Effect. London: 1879. V. 67

THE CHRISTMAS Book. New York: 1905. V. 62

CHRISTMAS Pictures by Children. London: 1922. V. 62

CHRISTMAS Play Book (Number 5799). USA: 1943. V. 66

CHRISTMAS Tales of Flanders. London: 1917. V. 66

CHRISTMAS With the Poets. London: 1872. V. 62

CHRISTO
The Umbrellas: the Accordion-Fold Book for Joint Project for Japan and U.S.A. San Francisco: 1991. V. 63
Wrapped Coast One Million Sq. Ft. Minnesota: 1969. V. 66

CHRISTOPHER, FREDERICK
A Textbook of Surgery by American Authors. Philadelphia: 1942. V. 67

CHRISTOPHER, SYDNEY A.
Big Game Shooting in Lower Burma. 1916. V. 62; 63; 64; 66

CHRISTY, DAVID
Pulpit Politics; or Ecclesiastical Legislation on Slavery, In Its Disturbing Influences on the American Union. Cincinnati: 1862. V. 65

CHRISTY, EDWIN P.
Christy's Nigga Songster, Containing Songs as Are Sung by Christy's Pierce's White's Sable Brothers and Dumbleton's Band or Minstrels. Boston: 1850. V. 62

CHRISTY, MILLER
The Bryant and May Museum of Fire-Making Appliances. Catalogue of the Exhibits.... London: 1926-1928. V. 62; 64; 66

CHRISTY, THOMAS
Thomas Christy's Road Across the Plains. Denver: 1959. V. 67
Thomas Christy's Road Across the Plains. Denver: 1969. V. 63

CHRONICUM Saxonicum ex MSS. Codicibus nunc Primum Integrum Edidit, a Lantinum Fecit. Oxonii: 1692. V. 63

CHRONIQUES de France. Joan the Maid of Orleans. San Francisco: 1938. V. 66

CHRONOLOGIST or the Present War; or General Historical and Political Register. London: 1797. V. 63

CHU, Y. T.
Fishes of East China Sea. 1963. V. 65

CHUBB, CHARLES
The Birds of British Guiana, Based on the Collection of Frederick Vavasour McConnell. London: 1916-1921. V. 67

CHU-CHIA-CHIEN
The Chinese Theatre. London: 1922. V. 66

CHUKOVSKY, KORNEI
Zaika. Moscow: 1929. V. 64

CHUMS: A Tale of the Queen's Navy. London: 1882. V. 65

CHUN, C.
Aus den Tiefen des Weltmeeres. Jena: 1903. V. 66

CHUNG WAH NAN
The Art of Chinese Gardens. Hong Kong: 1982. V. 67

CHURCH, ALFRED J.
The Chantry Priest of Barnet: a Tale of the Two Roses. London: 1885. V. 66

CHURCH, ARCHIBALD
My African Journey. London: 1908. V. 64

CHURCH, E. D.
A Catalogue of Books Relating to the Discovery and Early History of North and South America, Forming a Part of the Library of E.D. Church. 1995. V. 65

CHURCH, EDWARD
Notice on the Beet Sugar.... Norhtampton: 1837. V. 64

CHURCH OF ENGLAND
Articles Whereupon it was Agreed by the Archbishoppes and Bishoppes of Both Provinces and the Whole Cleargie, in the Convocation Holden at London in the Yere of Our Lorde God 1562...for the Avoiding of the Diversities of Opinions.... Colophon: 1571. V. 63
Certain Sermons or Homilies Appointed to be Read in Churches, in the Time of Queen Elizabeth of Famous Memory; and Now Thought Fit to Be Reprinted by Authority from the Kings Most Excellent Majesty. London: 1683. V. 63
Constitutions and Canons Ecclesiasticall: Treated Upon by the Archbishops of Canterbury and York.... London: 1640. V. 62
A Form of Prayer With Thanksgiving for the Safe Delivery of the Queen and Happy Birth of the Young Prince. London: 1688. V. 63
The Orthodox Communicant, By Way of Meditation on the Order for the Administration of the Lord's Supper, or Holy Communion, According to the Liturgy of the Church of England. London: 1721. V. 62

CHURCH OF ENGLAND. BOOK OF COMMON PRAYER
Book of Common Prayer. Oxford: 1693. V. 65
Book of Common Prayer. London: 1713. V. 64
The Book of Common Prayer. London: 1729. V. 66
Book of Common Prayer. Oxford: 1731. V. 62
Book of Common Prayer. Cambridge: 1760. V. 65
Book of Common Prayer. Cambridge: 1762. V. 65
Book of Common Prayer. Cambridge: 1788. V. 63
Book of Common Prayer. London: 1801. V. 62; 63
Book of Common Prayer. Cambridge: 1806. V. 63
Book of Common Prayer. Birmingham: 1829. V. 63
The Book of Common Prayer. London: 1844. V. 64
The Book of Common Prayer. Dublin: 1849-1850. V. 65
The Book of Common Prayer. Oxford: 1858-1860. V. 63
Book of Common Prayer. Oxford: 1862. V. 66
Book of Common Prayer. London: 1864. V. 62
The Book of Common Prayer. Oxford: 1890?. V. 66
The Book of Common Prayer. Oxford: 1894. V. 65
Book of Common Prayer. New York: 1904. V. 65
Book of Common Prayer and Administration of the Sacraments. London: 1678. V. 66

CHURCH OF ENGLAND. BOOK OF COMMON PRAYER continued
The Book of Common Prayer and Administration of the Sacraments. London: 1717. V. 62; 67
The Book of Common Prayer and Administration of the Sacraments. Cambridge: 1761. V. 63; 64; 65
The Book of Common Prayer, and Administration of the Sacraments. Cambridge: 1762. V. 64
The Book of Common Prayer and Administration of the Sacraments. Oxford: 1770. V. 64
The Book of Common Prayer and Administration of the Sacraments. London: 1848. V. 64
The Book of Common Prayer Noted by John Merbecke, 1550. London: 1844. V. 62
Book of Common Prayer Ornamented with Woodcuts from Designs of Albert Durer, Hans Holbein and Others. London: 1855. V. 65
Book of Common Prayer...Together with the Psalter or Psalms of David. London: 1737. V. 63
Liber Precum Publicarum seu Ministerii Ecclesiasticae Administrationis Sacramentorum...in Ecclesia Anglicana. 1574. V. 64
Liturgia, seu Liber Precum Communium et Administrationis Sacramentorum, Aliorumque Rituum Atque Ceremoniarum Ecclesiae, Juxta Usum Ecclesiae Anglcianae.... London: 1670. V. 64
Liturgia, Seu Liber Precum Communium, et Administrationis Sacramentorum Aliorumque Rituum Atque Ceremoniarum Ecclesiae Juxta Usum Ecclesiae Anglicanae.... Londini: 1685. V. 65

CHURCH OF ENGLAND. CATECHISMS AND CREEDS
Preces Catechismus et Hymni Graece et Latine. Londini: 1814. V. 62

CHURCH OF SCOTLAND. BOOK OF COMMON PRAYER
Book of Common Prayer...for the Use of the Church of Scotland. Edinburgh: 1637. V. 63; 66

CHURCH OF SCOTLAND. CATECHISMS AND CREEDS
Larger Catechism, Agreed Upon by the Assembly of Divines at Westminster, with the Assitance of Commissioners from the Church of Scotland. Raleigh: 1815. V. 66

CHURCH, RICHARD
Hurricane and Other Poems. London: 1919. V. 67
Philip and Other Poems. Oxford: 1923. V. 67

CHURCH, T. D.
Gardens are For People. New York: 1983. V. 67

CHURCH, WILLIAM CONANT
The Life of John Ericsson. New York: 1891. V. 64

CHURCHILL, CHARLES
The Apology. London: 1761. V. 67
Gotham, a Poem. Book III. London: 1764. V. 66
Poems. London: 1766. V. 66
The Poetical Works. London: 1844. V. 62; 67
The Works. London: 1774. V. 62; 65; 66

CHURCHILL, FLEETWOOD
Essays on the Puerperal Fever and Other Diseases Peculiar to Women. London: 1849. V. 62
A Manual for Midwives and Monthly Nurses. Dublin: 1867. V. 65

CHURCHILL, JENNY
The Reminiscences.... London: 1908. V. 65

CHURCHILL, RANDOLPH
Arms and the Covenant, Speeches by the Right Hon. Winston S. Churchill. London: 1938. V. 66

CHURCHILL, ROBERT
Game Shooting. London: 1955. V. 67

CHURCHILL, VICTOR, VISCOUNT
All My Sins Remembered. London: 1964. V. 63

CHURCHILL, WILLIAM
October, a Poem: Inscrib'd to the Fox-Hunters of Great Britain. London: 1717. V. 66

CHURCHILL, WINSTON
Divi Britannici.... London: 1675. V. 62

CHURCHILL, WINSTON LEONARD SPENCER
The Collected Works of.... London: 1973-1976. V. 66
A History of the English Speaking Peoples. London: 1956-1958. V. 63; 64; 66
Ian Hamilton's March. London: 1900. V. 63; 64
London to Ladysmith Via Pretoria. London: 1900. V. 62
Lord Randolph Churchill. London: 1906. V. 62; 66
Lord Randolph Churchill. London: 1907. V. 64
Marlborough His Life and Times. London: 1933. V. 62; 64
Marlborough His Life and Times. London: 1947. V. 64
My African Journey. London: 1908. V. 62; 64
The Second World War. London: 1949-1954. V. 62; 64
Story of the Malakand Field Force. London: 1898. V. 62; 64; 67
War Speeches. London: 1941-1946. V. 62
The War Speeches. London: 1951-1952. V. 63
The World Crisis 1911-1914. London: 1923. V. 64

CHURTON, RALPH
The Life of Alexander Nowell, Dean of St. Paul's.... London: 1809. V. 63

CHUSID, JOSEPH G.
Correlative Neuroanatomy and Functional Neurology. Los Altos. V. 66; 67

CHUTE, CAROLYN
The Beans. London: 1985. V. 67

CIAMPINI, GIOVANNI
De Sacris Aedificiis a Constantino Magno Constructis Synopsis Historica. Rome: 1693. V. 64

CIARDI, JOHN
The Monster Den, or Look What Happened at My House - and To It. Philadelphia: 1966. V. 63

CIBBER, COLLEY
Another Occasional Letter From Mr. Cibber to Mr. Pope. London: 1744. V. 63
An Apology for the Life of Colley Cibber, Comedian and Late Patentee of the Theatre Royal. Written by Himself. Waltham St. Lawrence: 1925. V. 62; 65
An Apology for the Life of Mr. Colley Cibber. London: 1822. V. 63
An Apology for the Life of Mr. Colley Cibber. London: 1889. V. 62; 63
The Tragicall History of King Richard III. London: 1700. V. 65

CIBBER, THEOPHILUS
An Apology for the Life of Theophilus Cibber, Comedian. London: 1740. V. 66
Theophilus Cibber to David Garrick Esq. With Dissertations on Theatrical Subjects. London: 1759. V. 65

CICERO, MARCUS TULLIUS
Ad Q. Fratrem Dialogi Tres De Oratore. Ex MSS. Cantabrigiae: 1716. V. 66
Cato Major, or Discourse on Old Age.... London: 1778. V. 63
Ciceronis Orationem.... Venitiis: 1518-1519. V. 66
The Correspondence of....With a Revision of the Text, a Commentary, and Introductory Essays.... Dublin: 1904. V. 66
De Officiis Libri Tres. Amsterdam: 1664. V. 66
De Oratore. Venice: 1470. V. 62; 65
De Oratore Libri Tres Ex Editione J. Aug. Ernesti Cum Notis Variorum. Londini: 1824. V. 65
Epistolae Familiares. Lvgdvni: 1550. V. 63; 66
Fragmentorum Tomi III, cum Andreae Patricii Adnotationibus, Irregular Pagination.... Venice: 1565. V. 63
The Letters of Marcus Tullius Cicero to Several of His Friends.... London: 1753. V. 64; 65
Officiorum... Cato Maior...Paradoxa Stoicorum...Somnium Scipionis... Additae sunt in Extremo Opere Variae Lectiones e Libris Manu Scriptis & ex Ingenio. Lutetiae (Paris): 1549. V. 66
Onomasticon Tullianum Continens M. Tulli Ciceronis Vitam Historiam Litterariam.... 1836. V. 65
Opera. Parisiis: 1539. V. 65
Opera. Parisiis: 1555. V. 65
Opera. Oxonii: 1783. V. 66
Opera Omnia. Amstelodami: 1661. V. 66
Opera Omnia Ex Recensione Jo. Aug. Ernesti cum Varietate Lectionis Gruterianae et Clave Ciceroniana. Halae et Berolini: 1820. V. 65
Opera Quae Supersunt Omnia. Amsterdam: 1724. V. 65
Opera Quae Supersunt Omnia. Glasguae: 1748-1749. V. 65; 66
Orationum. Venice: 1518. V. 65
Philosophicorum.... Hanoviae: 1606-1610. V. 65
La Rhetorique De Ciceron.... Paris: 1673. V. 65
Select Letters. Oxford: 1971. V. 66

CICHY, B.
The Great Ages of Architecture, from Ancient Greece. New York: 1964. V. 65

CICOGNINI, GIACINTO ANDREA
La Cadvta Del Gran Capitano Belisario. Bologna: 1666. V. 64

CIKOVSKY, N.
George Inness. New York: 1971. V. 65

CIMENT, MICHEL
John Boorman. London: 1986. V. 67
Kubrick. New York: 1983. V. 62; 63

CINDERELLA
Cinderella. London: 1840. V. 62
Cinderella. London: 1910. V. 65
Cinderella. New York: 1934. V. 63
Cinderella. New York: 1938. V. 62
Cinderella. New York: 1954. V. 62
Oskubuska Aefintyri Handa Bornum. Myndabaedkur Barnanna No. 2. Roykjavik: 1910. V. 64

CINDERELLA'S Dream and What is Taught Her. Melbourne: 1916-1920. V. 65

CINQUANTE Quatre: Flying Corps Sons. Cambridge: 1918. V. 63

CIPOLLA, BARTOLOMEO
Tractatus de Simulatione Co(n)tractum.... Venice: 1518. V. 62

CIPRIANI, LEONETTO
California and Overaldn Diary of Count Leonetto Cipriani from 1853 to 1871. Portland: 1962. V. 63; 66

A CIRCLE of Nations. Hillsboro: 1993. V. 62

CIRCUMNAVIGATION of the Globe. Edinburgh: 1837. V. 66

A CIRCUS Picture Book for Little Tots. 1959. V. 65

CIRCUS PLACE SCHOOL, EDINBURGH
First Annual Report of the Directors of the Circus-Place School, to the Subscribers, at the Annual Meeting Held Within the School-House, Upon Monday, the 15th Day of January 1827. (with) Regulations of the Circus-Place School. Edinburgh: 1827. V. 63

CISNEROS, ANTONIO
Comentarios Reales. Lima: 1964. V. 67

CISNEROS, SANDRA
The House of Mango Street. New York: 1994. V. 63
Woman Hollering Creek. New York: 1991. V. 63; 66; 67

CIST, LEWIS J.
Trifles in Verse: a Collection of Fugitive Poems. Cincinnati: 1845. V. 63

THE CITIZEN
and Farmer's Almanac, for the Year of Our Lord 1810.... Morris Town: 1809. V. 63

THE CITIZEN'S
Pocket Chronicle: Containing a Digest View of the History, Antiquity and Temporal Government of the City of London.... London: 1827. V. 64; 65

THE CITIZEN'S
Procession, or, the Smugler's Success and the Patriots Disappointment. London: 1733. V. 67

CITOIS, FRANCOIS
Abstinens Confolentanea.... Montpellier: 1602. V. 64

CITRI DE LA GUETTE, SAMUEL
The History of the Triumvirates. London: 1686. V. 63

CITY
Biography Containing Anecdotes and Memoirs of the Aldermen and Other Conspicuous Personages of the Corporation of London. London: 1800. V. 62

CITY
Cries; or a Peep at Scenes in Town. Philadelphia: 1851. V. 64; 66

THE CITY
Directory 1884-1885 of Seattle Washington...Also a Classified Business Directory of Seattle. Seattle: 1884. V. 64

THE CITY
of Denver and the State of Colorado. St. Louis: 1890. V. 64

THE CITY
of Elizabeth, New Jersey, Illustrated. Elizabeth: 1889. V. 63

CLAESEN, CHARLES
Recueil d'Ornements et de Sujets Pour Etre Appliques a l'Ornementation des Armes. Liege, Paris and Berlin: 1856. V. 64

CLAIBORNE, JOHN F. H.
Historical Account of Hancock County and the Sea Board of Mississippi. New Orleans: 1876. V. 63; 66

CLAIBORNE, NATHANIEL HERBERT
Notes on the War in the South.... Richmond: 1819. V. 63; 66

CLAIR, COLIN
The Spread of Printing. Amsterdam: 1969-1972. V. 63

CLAIR, HENRY ST.
The United States Criminal Calendar; or Awful Warning to the Youth of America.... Boston: 1840. V. 67

CLAIRIDGE, JOHN
General View of the Agriculture in the County of Dorset.... London: 1793. V. 64

CLAMPITT, AMY
A Homage to John Keats. New York: 1984. V. 62; 64; 67
The Isthmus. New York: 1981. V. 67
The Kingfisher. New York: 1983. V. 62; 63; 67
Manhattan, an Elegy, and Other Poems. Iowa City: 1990. V. 62; 64
Multitudes, Multitudes. New York: 1973. V. 64; 67

CLAMPITT, JOHN W.
Echoes from the Rocky Mountains. Chicago: 1889. V. 66

CLANCEY, P. A.
The Birds of Natal and Zululand. 1964. V. 63; 67
The Birds of Natal and Zululand. Edinburgh and London: 1964. V. 67
Gamebirds of Southern Africa. New York: 1967. V. 67
A Handlist of the Birds of Southern Mocambique. 1971. V. 66; 67

CLANCY, JAMES J.
Ireland: As She Is, As She Has Been & As She Ought to Be. New York: 1877. V. 64

CLANCY, TOM
Das Echo aller Furcht Roman. Aus dem Amerikanischen von Hardo Wickmann. Muchen: 1992. V. 62
The Hunt for Red October. Annapolis: 1984. V. 62
Patriot Games. New York: 1987. V. 67
Rainbow Six. New York: 1998. V. 62
Red Storm Rising. New York: 1986. V. 67
Submarine. New York: 1993. V. 66; 67
The Sum of All Fears. New York: 1991. V. 67
Without Remorse. New York: 1993. V. 64; 65

CLAPAREDE, JEAN LOUIS RENE ANTOINE EDOUARD
Recherches sur La Structure des Annelides Sedentaires. Geneva: 1873. V. 65

CLAPHAM, RICHARD
The Book of the Fox. London: 1936. V. 62
The Book of the Otter. London: 1922. V. 62; 63; 64; 65; 67
Rough Shooting for the Man of Moderate Means.... London: 1935. V. 67
Sport on Fell, Beck and Tarn. London: 1924. V. 67
Trout Fishing for the Beginner. London: 1922. V. 67

CLAPPE, LOUISE AMELIA KNAPP SMITH
California in 1851, the Letters of Dame Shirley. San Francisco: 1933. V. 63; 64; 67
The Shirley Letters from California Mines in 1851-1852. San Francisco: 1922. V. 62
The Shirley Letters from the California Mines 1851-1852. New York: 1949. V. 65

CLAPPERTON, C.
Quarternary Geology and Geomorphology of South America. Amsterdam: 1993. V. 67

CLAPPERTON, COMMANDER
Journal of a Second Expedition into the Interior of Africa, from the Bight of Benin to Soccatoo. London: 1829. V. 63; 66

CLAPPERTON, R. H.
Paper. An Historical Account of Its Making by Hand from the Earliest Times Down to the Present Day. Oxford: 1934. V. 62; 65

CLARAC, FREDERIC, COMTE DE
Fouille Fait a Pompei en Presence de S. M. la reine de Deux Siciles.... N.P: 1813. V. 66

CLARE, JOHN
A Cag of Swipes. Brighton: 1993. V. 62
The Poems. London: 1935. V. 62
Poems Chiefly from Manuscript. London: 1920. V. 63; 65
Poems Descriptive of Rural Life and Scenery.... London: 1820. V. 66
The Rural Muse. Poems. London: 1835. V. 66
Sketches in the Life of John Clare by Himself. London: 1931. V. 63; 65
The Village Minstrel, and Other Poems. London: 1821. V. 67
The Village Minstrel and Other Poems. London: 1823. V. 67

CLARE, MARTIN
The Motion of Fluids, Natural and Artificial: In Particular That of the Air and Water.... London: 1747. V. 65

CLARE, WALTER
A Report of the Trial of Walter Clare, Upon an Indictment for High Treason. Dublin: 1803. V. 63

CLARE, WILLIAM
A Compleat System of Grammar and English and Latin Wherein that Most Excellent Art is Plainly, Fully and Distinctly Taught.... London: 1699. V. 66

CLAREMONT, LEOPOLD
The Gem-Cutter's Craft. London: 1906. V. 63; 65

CLARENDON, EDWARD HYDE, 1ST EARL OF
A Brief View and Survey of the Dangerous and Pernicious Errors to Church and State in Mr. Hobbes's Book Entitled Leviathan. Oxford: 1676. V. 64
A Collection of Several Tracts of the Right Honourable Earl of Clarendon.... London: 1727. V. 63
The History of the Rebellion and Civil Wars in England. Oxford: 1702-1704. V. 64
The History of the Rebellion and Civil Wars in England. Oxford: 1717. V. 63
The History of the Rebellion and Civil Wars in England. London: 1839. V. 64
The Life of Edward, Earl of Clarendon. Oxford: 1826. V. 63; 66

CLARENDON, THOMAS
An Examination into the True Seat and Extent of the Powers of the Horse...Application in Draught and Burthen. Dublin: 1843. V. 67

CLARIDGE, JOHN
The Shepherd of Banbury's Rules to Judge of the Changes of the Weather.... London: 1744. V. 62; 65

CLARIDGE, R. T.
Hydropathy: or the Cold Water Cure as Practiced in Vincent Priessnitz, at Graefenberg, Silesia, Austria. London: 1842. V. 67

CLARIDGE, W.
Origin and History of the Bradford Grammar School, from Its Foundation to Christmas 1882. Bradford: 1882. V. 65

CLARIDGE, W. WALTON
A History of the Gold Coast and Ashanti, from the Earliest Times to the Commencement of the Twentieth Century. London: 1915. V. 64

CLARION, CLAIRE HYPPOLITE
Memoires de Mlle. Clairon, Actrice du Theatre Francais.... Paris: 1822. V. 67

CLARK, A. H.
The Invasion of New Zealand by People, Plants and Animals, the South Island. New Brunswick: 1950. V. 63
Monograph of the Exisiting Crinoids. Washington: 1915-1967. V. 62; 66

CLARK, A. J.
Comparative Physiology of the Heart. Cambridge: 1927. V. 67

CLARK, A. M.
The Echinoderms of Southern Africa. London: 1976. V. 66

CLARK, ALLEN C.
Greenleaf and Law in the Federal City. Washington: 1901. V. 65

CLARK, AMASA
Reminiscences of a Centenarian. Bandera: 1930. V. 65

CLARK, ANDREW
Practical Directions for Preserving the Teeth.... London: 1825. V. 64; 66; 67

CLARK, ATWOOD
Those Were the Days!. London: 1933. V. 67

CLARK, BADGER
Sun and Saddle Leather Including Grass Grown Trails and New Poems. Boston: 1922. V. 64

CLARK, BARZILLA W.
Bonneville County in the Making. Idaho Falls: 1941. V. 62; 65

CLARK, C. DUNNING
The Yankee Rajah; or, the Fate of the Black Sheriff. New York: 1881. V. 65

CLARK, C. M.
A Trip to Pike's Peak and Notes by the Way, Etc. San Jose: 1958. V. 63; 64

CLARK, CALVIN PERRY
Two Diaries. Denver: 1962. V. 63; 64; 65; 66

CLARK, CAROL
Thomas Moran - Watercolors of the American West. Austin: 1980. V. 65

CLARK, CHARLES B.
The Eastern Shore of Maryland and Virginia. New York: 1950. V. 67

CLARK, CHARLES E.
Prince and Boatswain: Sea Tales from the Recollection of Rear Admiral Charles E. Clark. Greenfield: 1915. V. 65

CLARK, CHARLES F.
Annual City Directory of the City of Detroit for 1867-1868. Detroit: 1868. V. 67
Annual City Directory of the City of Detroit for 1865-1866. Detroit: 1865. V. 65
Annual City Directory of the City of Detroit for 1868-1869. Detroit: 1868. V. 67
Annual City Directory of the City of Detroit for 1869-1870. Detroit: 1869. V. 67
Annual City Directory of the City of Detroit for 1870-1871. Detroit: 1870. V. 67
Annual City Directory of the City of Detroit for 1871-1872. Detroit: 1871. V. 67

CLARK, COLIN
The Conditions of Economic Progress. London: 1940. V. 65

CLARK, DANIEL
Proofs of the Corruption of Gen. James Wilkinson and of His Connexion with Aaron Burr, with Full Refutation of His Slanderous Allegations in Relation to the Character of the Principal Witness Against Him. Philadelphia: 1809. V. 66

CLARK, DAVID R.
Dry Tree, Poems. 1966. V. 67

CLARK, E. KITSON
The History of 100 Years of Life of the Leeds Philosophical and Literary Society. Leeds: 1924. V. 65

CLARK, FRANCIS E.
Our Journey Around the World. Hartford: 1895. V. 67

CLARK, G. C.
Life Histories of the South African Lycaenid Butterflies. Cape Town: 1971. V. 65; 66

CLARK, G. ORR
The Moon Babies. New York: 1900. V. 66

CLARK, GEORGE T.
Cartae et Alia Munimenta Quae ad Dominium de Glamorgancia Pertinent. Cardiff: 1910. V. 66
Leland Stanford: War Governor of California, Railroad Builder and Founder of Stanford University. Stanford: 1931. V. 67
Mediaeval Military Architecture in England. London: 1884. V. 62; 65; 66
Report to the General Board of Health on a Preliminary Inquiry Into the Sewerage, Drainage and Supply of Water, and the Sanitary Condition of the Inhabitants of the City and County of Bristol. London: 1850. V. 64

CLARK, H. L.
Catalogue of Recent Ophiurans: Based on the Collection of the Museum of Comparative Zoology. Cambridge: 1915. V. 64; 65
Echinoderms from Australia, Collections Made in 1929 and 1932. Cambridge: 1938. V. 66
Hawaiian and Other Pacific Echini. Cambridge: 1912. V. 64
Hawaiian and Other Pacific Echini. Cambridge: 1917. V. 64; 65

CLARK, HARTLEY
Bokhara, Turkoman and Afghan Rugs. London: 1922. V. 64; 66

CLARK, J. J.
The Manufacture of Pulp and Paper. New York & London: 1921. V. 65

CLARK, J. MAX
Colonial Days. Denver: 1902. V. 64

CLARK, J. W.
Order of the Proceedings at the Darwin Celebration...with a Sketch of Darwin's Life. Cambridge: 1909. V. 67

CLARK, JAMES
A Memoir of John Conolly, M.D.... London: 1869. V. 65
The Sanative Influence of Climate. London: 1846. V. 64; 65
Shoeing and Balancing the Light Harness Horse. Buffalo: 1916. V. 62

CLARK, JAMES H.
Cuba and the Fight for Freedom. Philadelphia: 1896. V. 67

CLARK, JANE INGLIS
Pictures and Memories. London: 1938. V. 62; 63; 64

CLARK, JIM
CS Ranch - Steer Roping and Art Exhibit Post, Texas October 2-3 1976. Post: 1976. V. 67

CLARK, JOHN WILLIS
The Life and Letters of the Rev. Adam Sedgwick, LL.D.... Cambridge: 1890. V. 62; 66

CLARK, KATE MC COSH
Maori Tales and Legends. London: 1896. V. 65

CLARK, KEITH
Terrible Trail: the Meek Cutoff 1845. Caldwell: 1966. V. 65

CLARK, KENNETH
A Catalogue of the Drawings of Leonardo Da Vinci in the Collection of His Majesty the King at Windsor Castle. New York: 1935. V. 62; 63; 64
A Commemorative Catalogue of the Exhibition of Italian Art Held in the...Royal Academy, Burlington House, 1930. London: 1931. V. 65
The Drawings of Leonardo Da Vinci at Windsor Castle in the Collection of Her Majesty the Queen. London: 1968-1969. V. 63; 66
Landscape Into Art. London: 1949. V. 65

CLARK, L. J.
Wild Flowers of the Pacific Northwest from Alaska to Northern California. Sidney: 1976. V. 63; 66

CLARK, LA VERNE HARRELL
They Sang for Horses. 1966. V. 63

CLARK, LARRY
Tulsa. New York: 1979. V. 65; 66

CLARK, LEONARD
Andrew Young - Prospect of a Poet - Essays and Tributes.... London: 1957. V. 62

CLARK, LEWIS
Wild Flowers of British Columbia. Sidney: 1973. V. 64

CLARK, MARGERY
The Poppy Seed Cakes. Garden City: 1924. V. 64; 65

CLARK, MARY
Lost Legends of the Nursery Songs. London: 1920. V. 67

CLARK, MARY HIGGINS
Where Are the Children?. New York: 1975. V. 62

CLARK, NATHANIEL G.
A Scale of Prices for Job Work on Old Ships, Carefully Arranged and Compiled by Nathaniel G. Clark, J. Mallett.... London: 1825. V. 63

CLARK, ROBERT JUDSON
The Arts and Crafts Movement in America 1876-1916.... Princeton: 1972. V. 62

CLARK, ROBERT STERLING
Through Shen-Kan. London: 1912. V. 62; 65; 66

CLARK, ROLAND
Gunner's Dawn. New York: 1937. V. 64; 65
Roland Clark's Etchings. New York: 1938. V. 64; 66
Stray Shots. New York: 1931. V. 66

CLARK, SAMUEL
The Lives of Sundry Eminent Persons in This Later Age. London: 1683. V. 62

CLARK, SUSIE C.
The Round Trip from the Hub to the Colorado Gate. Boston: 1890. V. 66

CLARK, THOMAS
Clark's Sixth Set of Hymn Tunes. London: 1775. V. 65
A Still Life. Dentdale: 1977. V. 63
Ways Through Bracken. Highlands: 1980. V. 63

CLARK, THOMAS BLAKE
Omai, First Polynesian Ambassador to England. San Francisco: 1940. V. 63
Omai, First Polynesian Ambassador to England. San Francisco: 1941. V. 63

CLARK, W. E.
Essays on Growth and Form Presented to D'Arcy Wentworth Thompson. Oxford: 1945. V. 66

CLARK, W. P.
The Indian Sign Language with Brief Explanatory Notes.... Philadelphia: 1885. V. 64; 67

CLARK, WALTER
Gen. James Johnston Pettigrew. N.P: 1920. V. 63
Histories of the Several Regiments and Battalions from North Carolina in the Great War 1861-1865. Raleigh. V. 62; 63
North Carolina at Gettysburg and Pickett's Charge a Misnomer. Raleigh: 1921. V. 62; 63

CLARK, WALTER E.
West Virginia Today: a Work for Newspaper and Library Reference. N.P: 1941. V. 66

CLARK, WALTER VAN TILBURG
The Ox-Bow Incident. New York: 1940. V. 67
The Watchful Gods and Other Stories. New York: 1950. V. 66

CLARK, WILLIAM
The Field Notes of Captain William Clark 1803-1805. New Haven: 1964. V. 66

CLARK, WILLIAM B.
Naval Documents of the American Revolution. Washington: 1964. V. 66

CLARK, WILLIAM S.
The Early Irish Stage. 1955. V. 67

CLARKE, A. H.
The Freshwater Molluscs of Canada. Ottawa: 1981. V. 62; 66

CLARKE, ADAM
The Bibliographical Miscellany: or Supplement to the Bibliographical Dictionary. London: 1806. V. 65

CLARKE, ADELE
Old Montreal. John Clarke: His Adventures, Friends and Family. Montreal: 1906. V. 66

CLARKE, ALLEN
Windmill Land. (with) More Windmill Land. London: 1916-1918. V. 65

CLARKE, ANNE
Mrs. Clarke's Cookery Book. Toronto: 1883. V. 62

CLARKE, ARTHUR
An Essay on Warm, Cold and Vapour Bathing, with Practical Observations on Sea Bathing, Diseases of the Skin, Bilious Liver Complaints and Dropsy. London: 1820. V. 62

CLARKE, ARTHUR C.
Against the Fall of Night. 1953. V. 62; 64
Beyond Jupiter: the Worlds of Tomorrow. Boston: 1972. V. 66
The Coming of the Space Age. 1967. V. 64
The Coming of the Space Age. New York: 1967. V. 66
The Deep Range. London: 1937. V. 67
The Deep Range. 1957. V. 62; 64; 66
Expedition to Earth. 1954. V. 62; 64
Expedition to Earth. London: 1954. V. 63; 64
Rendezvous with Rama. New York: 1973. V. 62
Report on Planet Three. 1974. V. 66
Report on Planet Three. New York: 1974. V. 64
The Sentinel. 1983. V. 64; 66
Tales from the White Hart. 1970. V. 64
Tales from the White Hart. New York: 1970. V. 62
Tales of Ten Worlds. 1962. V. 64; 66
2010: Odyssey Two. 1982. V. 62; 64

CLARKE, ASA B.
Travels in Mexico and California: Comprising a Journal of a Tour From Brazos Santiago, through Central Mexico, by Way of Monterey, Chihuahua.... Boston;: 1852. V. 65

CLARKE, AUSTIN
The Bright Temptation - a Romance. London: 1932. V. 63
The Collected Poems of.... New York: 1936. V. 67
Mnemosyne Lay in Dust. Dublin: 1966. V. 62; 63
Old Fashioned Pilgrimage and Other Poems. 1967. V. 67
Orphide and Other Poems. 1970. V. 67
The Singing-Men at Cashel. London: 1936. V. 63
The Sun Dances at Easter - a Romance. London: 1952. V. 63
The Vengeance of Fionn. Dublin and London: 1917. V. 62

CLARKE, BASIL
English Churches. London: 1964. V. 65

CLARKE, BRIAN
The Pursuit of Stillwater Trout. London: 1975. V. 67

CLARKE, C. B.
Illustrations of Cyperaceae. 1909. V. 62

CLARKE, C. E.
Speech of Hon. C. E. Clarke of New York, on the Bill Establishing the Boundary Between Texas and New Mexico. Washington: 1850. V. 65

CLARKE, CHARLES
Architectura Ecclesiastica Londini.... London: 1819. V. 66

CLARKE, CHARLES G.
The American Ship-Master's Guide and Commercial Assistant.... Boston: 1838. V. 64
The Men of the Lewis and Clark Expedition, a Biographical Roster of the 51 Members and a Composite Diary of their Activities from All Known Sources. Glendale: 1970. V. 65

CLARKE, CHARLES MANSFIELD
Observations on Those Diseases of Females, Which are Attended by Discharges.... London: 1821. V. 64; 66

CLARKE, DWIGHT L.
Stephen Watts Kearny - Soldier of the West. Norman: 1961. V. 63; 66

CLARKE, E. D.
Testimonies of Different Authors Respecting the Colossal Statue of Thebes Placed in the Vestibule of the Public Library at Cambridge. Cambridge: 1803. V. 63; 66

CLARKE, E. Y.
Illustrated History of Atlanta. Atlanta: 1875. V. 67

CLARKE, EDWARD DANIEL
The Life and Remains of Rev. Edward Daniel Clarke, LL.D. London: 1824. V. 62

CLARKE, EDWARD GOODMAN
The Modern Practice of Physic. London: 1805. V. 66

CLARKE, EDWARD H.
Visions: a Study of False Sight (Pseudopia). Boston: 1878. V. 65; 66; 67

CLARKE, EDWIN
The Human Brain and Spinal Cord. San Frnacisco: 1995. V. 65
The Human Brain and Spinal Cord. San Francisco: 1996. V. 64; 65; 66
An Illustrated History of Brain Function. Imaging the Brain from Antiquity to the Present. San Francisco: 1996. V. 64; 65; 66

CLARKE, G. F.
Six Salmon Rivers and Another in Canada. 1960. V. 67

CLARKE, G. R.
The History and Description of the Town and Borough of Ipswich, Including the Villages and Country Seats in Its Vicinity.... Ipswich: 1830. V. 66

CLARKE, GEORGE FREDERICK
Too Small a World: the Story of Acadia. Fredericton: 1958. V. 63

CLARKE, H. C.
Confederate States Almanac and Repository of Useful Knowledge for the Year 1865. Mobile: 1864. V. 63

CLARKE, H. L.
History of Sedbergh School 1525-1925. Sedbergh: 1925. V. 62

CLARKE, H. T.
The Chemistry of Penicillin Report on a Collaborative Investigation by American and British Chemists. Princeton: 1949. V. 64; 67

CLARKE, HAROLD GEORGE
Colour Pictures on Pot Lids and Other Forms of 19th Century Staffordshire Pottery. 1924-1927. V. 65

CLARKE, HEWSON
An Impartial History of the Naval, Military and Political Events in Europe.... Bungay: 1816. V. 63

CLARKE, J.
A Series of Twenty-Four Views Illustrative of the Holy Scriptures. London: 1817?. V. 62; 66

CLARKE, J. B. B.
An Account of the Infancy, Religious and Literary Life of the Rev. Adam Clarke. 1833. V. 63; 66

CLARKE, J. F.
Building Ships on the North East Coast. Whitley Bay: 1997. V. 67

CLARKE, J. F. G.
Catalogue of the Meyrick Types of Microlepidoptera in the British Museum. 1955-1970. V. 66

CLARKE, J. JACKSON
Congenital Dislocation of the Hip. London: 1910. V. 67

CLARKE, JAMES
History of Football in Kendal from 1871 to 1908. Kendal: 1908. V. 63
A Survey of the Lakes of Cumberland, Westmorland, and Lancashire.... London: 1789. V. 62; 65; 66

CLARKE, JAMES STANIER
The Life and Services of Horatio Viscount Nelson.... London: 1840. V. 62

CLARKE, JOHN
The London Practice of Widwifery; Including the Treatment During the Puerperal State and the Principal Infantile Diseases. Concord: 1826. V. 67
Treatise on the Mulberry Tree and Silkworm. Philadelphia: 1839. V. 63

CLARKE, JOHN COOPER
Directory 1979. London: 1979. V. 65

CLARKE, JOSEPH I. C.
My Life and Memories. New York: 1925. V. 65

CLARKE, LEWIS
Narrative of the Sufferings of Lewis Clarke, During a Captivity of More than Twenty-Five Years, Among the Algerines of Kentucky, One of the So Called Christian States of North America. Boston: 1845. V. 63; 66

CLARKE, M. V.
Fourteenth Century Studies. 1937. V. 67

CLARKE, MARY ANNE
The Rival Princes; or a Faithful Narrative of Facts.... London: 1810. V. 65

CLARKE, MARY COWDEN
The Girlhood of Shakespeare's Heroines: a Series of Fifteen Tales. London: 1884. V. 67

CLARKE, MARY WHATLEY
The Slaughter Ranches and Their Makers. Austin: 1979. V. 67

CLARKE, MATTHEW
Legislative and Documentary History of the Bank of the United States.... Washington: 1832. V. 62

CLARKE, MRS.
The Trial of Mrs. Clarke and Wrights the Upholsterers, for a Conspiracy Against Col. Wardle, at the Court of King's Bench, Monday, Dec. 11. Before Lord Ellenborough and a Special Jury. London: 1809. V. 62

CLARKE, OLIVE
Freddy Frizzy-Lock. London: 1910. V. 66

CLARKE, S. F.
Development of Amblystoma Punctatum. (Reptila) Part I (all published). Baltimore: 1879. V. 67

CLARKE, SAMUEL
A Collection of Papers Which Passed Between the Late Learned Mr. Leibnitz, and Dr. Clarke, in the Years 1715 and 1716. London: 1717. V. 62; 63
A Discourse Concerning the Being and Attributes of God, the Obligations of Natural Religion, and the Truth and Certainty of Christian Revelation. London: 1725. V. 67
The Marrow of Ecclesiastical History, Divided into Two Parts.... London: 1674. V. 66
The Scripture Doctrine of the Trinity. London: 1712. V. 67

CLARKE, STEPHEN
Fifteen Discourses Upon the Following Subjects.... London: 1727. V. 67

CLARKE, STEPHEN REYNOLDS
The New Lancashire Gazette, or Topographical Dictionary.... London: 1830. V. 65

CLARKE, T. H.
The Domestic Architecture of the Reigns of Queen Elizabeth and James the First. London: 1833. V. 66

CLARKE, THOMAS J.
Glimpses of an Irish Felon's Prison Life. Dublin and London: 1922. V. 67

CLARKE, WILLIAM
The Boy's Own Book: a Complete Encyclopedia of all the Diversions, Athletic, Scientific and Recreative, of Boyhood and Youth. London: 1864. V. 62
A Compleat System of Grammar English and Latin.... London: 1699. V. 64
Three Courses and a Dessert. London: 1830. V. 66

CLARKE, WILLIAM EAGLE
Studies in Bird Migration. London: 1912. V. 63; 67

CLARKE, WILLIAM MANSFIELD
The Determination of Hydrogen Ions. Baltimore: 1921. V. 67

CLARKSON, CHRISTOPHER
The History of Richmond. Richmond: 1814. V. 65

CLARKSON, HENRY M.
Evelyn: a Romance of The War Between the States.... Charleston: 1871. V. 62; 63

CLARKSON, PAUL
Bibliography of William Sydney Porter. Caldwell: 1938. V. 64; 67

CLARKSON, THOMAS
An Essay on the Slavery and Commerce of the Human Species, Particularly the African. Philadelphia: 1787. V. 67
A Portraiture of Quakerism, as Taken from a View of the Moral Education, Discipline, Peculiar Customs, Religious Principles.... London: 1806. V. 67

CLARY, WILLIAM W.
History of the Law Firm of O'Melveny & Myers, 1885-1965. Los Angeles: 1966. V. 62

CLATER, Youatt, Skinner & Mills: *Farmers' Barn-Book.* Philadelphia: 1857. V. 65

CLAUDET, F. G.
Gold: Its Properties, Modes of Extraction, Value &c. &c. Vancouver: 1958. V. 64

CLAUDIAN
Cl. Claudiani Quae Extant. Leiden: 1650. V. 64
Cl. Claudiani Quae Extant. Amstelodami: 1665. V. 66
Cl. Claudiani Quae Extant. Amsterdam: 1677. V. 66
Cl. Claudianus, Theod. Pulmanni Craneburgii Diligentia & Side Summa e Vetustis Codicibus Restitutus. Antwerpiae: 1571. V. 65
Opera Quae Extant, Omnia. Amstelodami: 1760. V. 66

CLAUDY, C. H.
Tell Me Why Stories. New York: 1912. V. 65

CLAUSEN, R. T.
Sedum of North America North of the Mexican Plateau. Ithaca: 1975. V. 64; 67
Sedum of North America North of the Mexican Plateau. Ithaca: 1976. V. 62

CLAUSEWITZ, KARL VON
Der Feldzug von 1813 His Zum Waffenstillstand. N.P: 1813. V. 67

CLAUSIUS, R.
The Mechanical Theory of Heat, with Its Applications to the Steam- Engine and to the Physical Properties of Bodies. London: 1867. V. 65

CLAVELL, JAMES
King Rat. Boston and Toronto: 1962. V. 63; 67
Shogun. New York: 1975. V. 65
Tai-Pan. New York: 1966. V. 62

CLAVERING, HENRY
The New and Complete Parish Officer, or a Perfect Guide to Churchwardens, Overseers, Constables, Headboroughs, Tithingmen, Sidesmen, Borsholders, Beadles and Other Parochial Officers.... London: 1812. V. 65

CLAVERING, ROBERT
An Essay on the Construction and Building of Chimneys.... London: 1779. V. 64

CLAVIUS, CHRISTOPHER
Epitome Arithmeticae Practicae Nunc Denuo ab Ipso Auctore Recognita. Rome: 1585. V. 62

CLAY, ALBERT T.
Business Documents of Murashu Sons of Nippur. Philadelphia: 1904. V. 62

CLAY, BEATRICE
Stories of King Arthur and the Round Table. London. V. 62

CLAY, C. H.
Design of Fishways and Other Fish Facilities. Ottawa: 1961. V. 67

CLAY, ENID
The Constant Mistress. Waltham St. Lawrence: 1934. V. 64; 66
Sonnets and Verses. Waltham St. Lawrence: 1925. V. 62; 65

CLAY, FELIX
Modern School Buildings, Elementary and Secondary: a Treatise on the Planning, Arrangement and Fitting of Day and Boarding Schools Having Special Regard to School Discipline, Organisation an Educational Requirements.... London: 1902. V. 64

CLAY, HENRY
Life and Speeches of Henry Clay. New York: 1842-1843. V. 66
Speech of the Hon. (Henry Clay Before the) American Colonization Society...with an Appendix. Washington: 1827. V. 64

CLAY, JEHU CURTIS
Annals of the Swedes on the Delaware from their First Settlement in 1636 to the Present Time. Philadelphia: 1858. V. 66

CLAY, JOHN
The City of the Hounds. Chicago: 1933. V. 66
My Life on the Range. Chicago: 1924. V. 62; 65
My Recollections of Ontario. Chicago: 1918. V. 65
Old Days Recalled. Chicago: 1915. V. 66
Twenty-Five Years - a Story of Success 1886-1911. Chicago: 1911. V. 65

CLAY, R.
The History of the Microscope. 1975. V. 67

CLAY, S.
The Present-Day Rock Garden. 1937. V. 63; 66
The Present-Day Rock Garden. London: 1937. V. 62

CLAY, VIRGINIA
Belle of the Fifties, Memoirs of Mrs. Clay of Alabama, Covering Social and Political Life in Washington and the South 1853-1866. New York: 1904. V. 62; 63

CLAY, WALTER LOWE
The Prison Chaplain: a Memoir of Rev. John Clay, Late Chaplain of Preston Gaol. Cambridge: 1861. V. 62; 64

CLAYPOOLE, H. G. C.
The Witchery of Water. 1970. V. 67

CLAYTON, AUGUSTIN S.
The Office and Duty of a Justice of the Peace, and a Guide to Clerks, Constables, Coroners...According to the Laws of the State of Georgia.... Milledgeville: 1819. V. 63

CLAYTON, ELLEN C.
Queen's of Song: Being Memoirs of Some of the Most Celebrated Female Vocalists.... New York: 1865. V. 63
The Soldier's Friend; or the Noble Deeds of a Heroic Woman. London: 1875?. V. 65

CLAYTON, JOHN
The Works of Sir Christopher Wren. London: 1848-1849. V. 66

CLAYTON, LAWRENCE
Watkins Reynolds Matthews: a Biography. Abilene: 1990. V. 65

CLAYTON, MURIEL
Catalogue of Rubbings of Brasses and Incised Slabs. London: 1929. V. 62

CLAYTON, POWELL
Aftermath of the Civil War in Arkansas. New York: 1915. V. 62; 63; 65

CLAYTON, W.
The Invisible Hand. London: 1815. V. 62

CLAYTON, W. F.
A Narrative of the Confederate States Navy. Weldon: 1910. V. 62; 63; 65

CLAYTON, W. WOODFORD
History of Bergen and Passaic Counties, New Jersey, with Biographical Sketches of Many of Its Pioneers and Prominent Men. Philadelphia: 1882. V. 63; 66
History of Union and Middlesex Counties, New Jersey, with Biographical Sketches of Many of their Pioneers and Prominent Men. Philadelphia: 1882. V. 63

CLAYTON, WILLIAM
Rural Discourses. Saffron Walden: 1814. V. 66

CLEARY, BEVERLY
Dear Mr. Henshaw. New York: 1983. V. 65

CLEAVELAND, AGNES MORLEY
Satan's Paradise. Boston: 1952. V. 67

CLEAVES, MARGARET ABIGAIL
The Autobiography of a Neurasthene as Told by One of Them and Recorded by Margaret A. Cleaves, M.D. Boston: 1910. V. 65

CLEEVE, BOURCHIER
A Scheme for Preventing a Further Increase of the National Debt and for Reducing the Same. London: 1756. V. 65

CLEGG, JOHN
The Freshwater Life of the British Isles. London: 1959. V. 62

CLEGHORN, THOMAS
The Hydro-Aeronaut, or Navigator's Life-Buoy. London: 1810. V. 63

CLEISHBOTHAM, PSEUD.
A Handbook of the Scottish Language. Edinburgh: 1858. V. 64

CLELAND, A. M.
Through Wonderland...Yellowstone Park. Northern Pacific Railway. N.P: 1910. V. 65

CLELAND, HENRY WILSON
(Essay) on the History and Properties Chemical and Medical of Tobacco.... Glasgow: 1840. V. 63

CLELAND, JOHN
An Inquiry Into the Variations of the Human Skull. 1869. V. 67
The Mechanism of the Gubernaculum Testis.... Edinburgh: 1856. V. 67
Memoirs of a Coxcomb. London: 1751. V. 63
Memoirs of a Coxcomb. Dijon: 1926. V. 67
Memoirs of a Coxcomb. London: 1926. V. 64

CLELAND, ROBERT GLASS
The Cattle on a Thousand Hills. San Marino: 1941. V. 65
The Cattle on a Thousand Hills. San Marino: 1951. V. 67
Pathfinders. Los Angeles: 1928. V. 63
The Place Called Sespe - the History of a California Ranch. Los Angeles: 1940. V. 66

CLELAND, THOMAS
The Socini-arian Detected: a Series of Letter to Barton W. Stone, On Some Important Subjects. Lexington: 1815. V. 64

CLEMENS, CLARA
My Father Mark Twain. New York: 1931. V. 63

CLEMENS, JERE
The Rivals: a Tale of the Times of Aaron Burr and Alexander Hamilton. Philadelphia: 1860. V. 63

CLEMENS, JEREMIAH
Bernard Lile: an Historical Romance, Embracing the Periods of the Texas Revolution and the Mexican War. Philadelphia: 1856. V. 66

CLEMENS, SAMUEL LANGHORNE
The Adventures of Huckleberry Finn. London: 1884. V. 63; 64
The Adventures of Huckleberry Finn. Montreal: 1885. V. 62
Adventures of Huckleberry Finn. New York: 1885. V. 62; 63; 64; 65; 66; 67
Adventures of Huckleberry Finn. New York: 1906. V. 63
Adventures of Huckleberry Finn. Detroit: 1983. V. 63
The Adventures of Tom Sawyer. Hartford: 1876. V. 62; 63; 64; 67
The Adventures of Tom Sawyer. New York: 1904. V. 64
The Adventures of Tom Sawyer. 1982. V. 65
The Adventures of Tom Sawyer. Washington: 1982. V. 63
Ah Sin a Dramatic Work.... San Francisco: 1961. V. 63
The American Claimant. London: 1892. V. 66
The American Claimant. New York: 1892. V. 63
A Boy's Adventure. New York: 1928. V. 65
The Celebrated Jumping Frog of Calaveras County and Other Sketches. New York: 1867. V. 63; 64; 65; 66
The Celebrated Jumping Frog of Calaveras County and Other Sketches. New York: 1868. V. 62
The Celebrated Jumping Frog of Calaveras County and Other Sketches. London: 1875. V. 63
A Champagne Cocktail and A Catastrophe. New York: 1930. V. 65
Christian Science with Notes Containing Corrections to Date. London New York: 1907. V. 62; 63
Coming Out. New York: 1921. V. 63; 64
A Connecticut Yankee in King Arthur's Court. New York: 1889. V. 65; 66
The Curious Republic of Gondour and Other Whimsical Sketches. New York: 1919. V. 63; 67
A Curtain Lecture Concerning Skating.... Denver: 1967. V. 63
The Diaries of Adam and Eve (Parts I and II). Hyattsville: 1990. V. 64
A Dog's Tale. New York: 1904. V. 63
A Double Barrelled Detective Story. New York: 1902. V. 63; 66; 67
English as She Is Taught. Boston: 1900. V. 63
Europe and Elsewhere. New York: 1923. V. 63
Following the Equator. Hartford: 1897. V. 63; 64
The Gilded Age. Hartford & San Francisco: 1873. V. 63
The Gilded Age. Hartford and Chicago: 1873. V. 63; 66
The Gilded Age. Hartford & Cincinnati: 1874. V. 63
The Gilded Age. Hartford and San Francisco: 1874. V. 63
The Gilded Age. London: 1883. V. 66
A Horse's Tale. New York: 1907. V. 63
How to Tell a Story and Other Essays. New York: 1897. V. 63
The Innocents Abroad. Hartford: 1869. V. 63
The Innocents Abroad. New York: 1962. V. 66
The Innocents Abroad. Chicago: 1998. V. 62; 64
Is Shakespeare Dead?. New York and London: 1909. V. 63; 64; 67
King Leopold's Soliloquy. Boston: 1905. V. 66
Letters from Honolulu Written for the Sacramento Union by Mark Twain. Honolulu: 1939. V. 63
Letters from the Sandwich Islands. San Francisco: 1937. V. 63
Letters from the Sandwich Islands. Stanford: 1938. V. 62
The Letters of Quintus Curtius Snodgrass. Dallas: 1946. V. 63
Life on the Mississippi. Boston: 1883. V. 62; 63; 64; 67
Life on the Mississippi. London: 1883. V. 64; 66
Life on the Mississippi. Montreal: 1883. V. 63
Life on the Mississippi. New York: 1888. V. 66
Life on the Mississippi. New York: 1891. V. 64; 65
Life on the Mississippi. New York: 1944. V. 63
The Loyalty of Friendship. New York: 1915. V. 66
The Man That Corrupted Hadleyburg. New York: 1900. V. 63; 65
Mark Twain-Howells Letters. Cambridge: 1960. V. 63
Mark Twain in Eruption. New York: 1940. V. 63
Mark Twain: San Francisco Correspondent. San Francisco: 1957. V. 63
Mark Twain the Letter Writer. Boston: 1932. V. 63
Mark Twain to Mrs. Fairbanks. San Marino: 1949. V. 63; 64
Mark Twain's Autobiography. New York: 1924. V. 63; 65
Mark Twain's (Burlesque) Autobiography and First Romance. New York: 1871. V. 62; 63; 64; 65; 67
Mark Twain's Birthday Report of the Celebration of the Sixty-Seventh Thereof at the Metropolitan Club. New York: 1903. V. 63
Mark Twain's Letter to the California Pioneers. Oakland: 1911. V. 63
Mark Twain's Letter to William Bowen. San Francisco: 1938. V. 63
Mark Twain's Letters. New York: 1917. V. 63
Mark Twain's Letters from the Sandwich Islands. Stanford and London: 1938. V. 63
Mark Twain's Letters in the Muscatine Journal. Chicago: 1942. V. 63
Mark Twain's Letters to Will Bowen. Austin: 1941. V. 63
Mark Twain's Letters. Volume I. 1853-1866. and Volume II. 1867-1868. Berkeley: 1988-1990. V. 63
Mark Twain's Library of Humor. New York: 1888. V. 63
Mark Twain's Library of Humor. New York: 1906. V. 63
Mark Twain's Notebook. New York: 1935. V. 63
Mark Twain's Rubaiyat. Austin and Santa Barbara: 1983. V. 63
Mark Twain's Scrapbook. New York: 1877. V. 66
Mark Twain's Sketches. London: 1872. V. 67
Mark Twain's Sketches. New York: 1874. V. 63; 64; 65
Mark Twain's Sketches New and Old. Hartford: 1875. V. 63; 66
Mark Twain's Speeches. New York: 1910. V. 63
Mark Twain's Speeches. New York: 1923. V. 63
Mark Twain's Travels with Mr. Brown. New York: 1940. V. 63
Merry Tales. New York: 1892. V. 62
The Mississippi Pilot. London: 1877. V. 66
More Tramps Abroad. London: 1897. V. 62; 63; 64
The Mysterious Stranger and Other Stories by Mark Twain. New York: 1922. V. 63
The New War-Scare. Santa Barbara: 1981. V. 63
Old Times on the Mississippi. Toronto: 1876. V. 63
The 1,000,000 Bank-Note and Other New Stories. New York: 1893. V. 62; 63; 64; 67
Personal Recollections of Joan of Arc. London: 1896. V. 62; 63; 64; 65
Personal Recollections of Joan of Arc. New York: 1896. V. 63
The Prince and the Pauper. Boston: 1882. V. 63
The Prince and the Pauper. Leipzig: 1882. V. 67
Pudd'nhead Wilson. London: 1894. V. 62; 64; 67
Pudd'nhead Wilson. New York: 1959. V. 63
Punch Brothers, Punch! And Other Sketches. New York: 1878. V. 63
The Quaker City Holy Land Excursion, an Unfinished Play. New York: 1927. V. 63; 65
Queen Victoria's Jubilee. New York: 1910. V. 63; 65
Rambling Notes of an Idle Excursion. Toronto: 1878. V. 63
Roughing It. Hartford: 1872. V. 63; 65
Roughing It. New York: 1907. V. 63
S.L.C. to C.T. New York: 1925. V. 63
Saint Joan of Arc. New York: 1919. V. 63; 64
Simon Wheeler, Detective. New York: 1963. V. 63; 67
1601. Conversation As It Was By the Social Fire-Side in the Time of the Tudors. Chicago: 1936. V. 65
1601. Conversation, As It Was by the Social Fireside, in the Time of the Tudors. Easthampton: 1978. V. 65
Sketches by Mark Twain. Toronto: 1876. V. 63
Sketches of the Sixties. San Francisco: 1926. V. 63; 66
Sketches of the Sixties. San Francisco: 1927. V. 63
Slovenly Peter. New York: 1935. V. 63
The Stolen White Elephant. New York: 1888. V. 65
The Suppressed Chapter of Life on the Mississippi. New York: 1913. V. 65
The $30,000 Bequest, and Other Stories by Mark Twain. New York: 1906. V. 63
Three Aces. Westport: 1929. V. 63
To the Person Sitting in Darkness. New York: 1901. V. 63
Tom Sawyer, a Drama. Washington: 1940. V. 64
Tom Sawyer Abroad. London: 1894. V. 62; 67
Tom Sawyer Abroad. New York: 1894. V. 63; 67
Tom Sawyer Abroad, Tom Sawyer Detective. New York: 1896. V. 63; 64; 65
Tom Sawyer Abroad, Tom Sawyer Detective. London: 1897. V. 64
Tragedy of Pudd'nhead Wilson. Hartford: 1894. V. 62; 64; 66; 67
A Tramp Abroad. Hartford: 1880. V. 63; 65; 66
A Tramp Abroad. London: 1880. V. 63; 66
A Tramp Abroad. Toronto: 1880. V. 63; 66
An Unexpected Acquaintance. New York and London: 1904. V. 63
The Washoe Giant in San Francisco. San Francisco:: 1938. V. 63
What Is Man?. New York: 1906. V. 65
What Is Man?. London: 1910. V. 63
The Writings of Mark Twain. London: 1899-1900. V. 63

CLEMENS, WILL
Famous Funny Fellows, Brief Biographical Sketches of American Humorists. Cleveland: 1882. V. 66
Mark Twain, His Life and Work. San Francisco: 1892. V. 63
Sixty and Six Chips from Literary Workshops. New York: 1897. V. 63

CLEMENT, HAL
Needle. 1950. V. 66
Needle. New York: 1950. V. 62
Needle. London: 1961. V. 66

CLEMENT, JOHN
Sketches of the First Emigrant Settlers in Newton Township, Old Gloucester County, West New Jersey. Camden: 1877. V. 63; 66

CLEMENT, LEWIS
Shooting Adventures, Canine Lore and Sea Fishing Trips. 1879. V. 63
Shooting and Fishing Trips. 1876. V. 63; 66; 67
Shooting and Fishing Trips. 1878. V. 67

CLEMENT, SAINT
Epistolae Duae and Corinthios, Interpretibus Patricio Junio, Gottifredo Venedlino & John. Bapt. Cotelerio.... London: 1694. V. 66

CLEMENTE, FRANCISCO
Pinxit. London: 1981. V. 64
The Pondicherry Pastels. London: 1986. V. 62
Watercolours. Zurich: 1982. V. 64

CLEMENTIS ALEXANDRINI
Clementis Alexandrini Opera Graece Et Latine Quae Extant.... Lutetiae: 1629. V. 66

CLEMENTS, FREDERIC E.
Minnesota Trees and Shrubs.... Minneapolis: 1912. V. 64

CLEMENT VIII, POPE
Caeromoniale Episcoporum Iussu Clementis VIII. Pont. Max. Reformatum. Parisiis. 1633. V. 66

CLEMENT XIV, POPE
Interesting Letters of Pope Clement XIV. Ganganelli (i.e. Giovanni Vincenzo Antonio, Cardinal). Dublin: 1777. V. 62

CLEMMER, JEAN
Canned Candies - The Exotic Women and Clothes of Paco Rabanne. London: 1969. V. 63

CLENCH, W. J.
Johnsonia, Monographs of the Marine Mollusks of the Western Atlantic. Cambridge: 1941-1959. V. 62; 63
Johnsonia, Monographs of the Marine Mollusks of the Western Atlantic. Cambridge: 1941-1974. V. 65
Johnsonia, Monographs of the Marine Mollusks of the Western Atlantic. Nos: 1-32. Cambridge: 1946-1975. V. 65

CLENDENING, LOGAN
Behind the Doctor. London: 1933. V. 66

CLERGUE, LUCIEN
Eros and Thanatos. Boston: 1985. V. 66
Genese. France: 1973. V. 64

CLERGYMAN, PSEUD.
Antipodes; or, the New Existence. London: 1855. V. 65

THE CLERGYMAN'S
Intelligencer; or, a Compleat Alphabetical List of All the Patrons in England and Wales, with the Dignities, Livings and Benefices in their Gift.... London: 1745. V. 67

CLERICUS
Rambles and Recollections of a Fly Fisher. 1854. V. 65; 67

CLERIHEW, E.
Biography for Beginners, Being a Collection of Miscellaneous Examples for the Use of Upper Forms. London: 1905. V. 62; 63

CLERK, JOHN
The Circumstances of Scotland Consider'd, With Respect to the Present Scarcity of Money.... Edinburgh: 1705. V. 65
An Essay on Naval Tactics, Systematical and Historical. London: 1790-1797. V. 66
An Essay on Naval Tactics, Systematical and Historical.... Edinburgh: 1804. V. 64; 65

CLERKE, AGNES
The Concise Knowledge of Astronomy. 1898. V. 67
Modern Cosmogonies. London: 1905. V. 67
Problems in Astrophysics. 1903. V. 65
The System of the Stars. 1890. V. 67
The System of the Stars. 1905. V. 65

CLERY, M.
A Journal of Occurrences at the Temple, During the Confinement of Louis XVI, King of France. London: 1798. V. 63; 66

CLEVELAND, DUCHESS OF
The Life and Letters of Lady Hester Stanhope. London: 1914. V. 64

CLEVELAND, GROVER
Public Papers...March 4, 1885 to March 4, 1889. Washington: 1889. V. 64

CLEVELAND, HENRY W.
Village and Farm Cottages. The Requirements of American Village Homes Considered and Suggested Cost. New York: 1856. V. 63

CLEVELAND, JOHN
The Character of a Country Committe-Man, with the Eare-Marke of a Sequstrator. London: 1649. V. 62; 65
The Idol of the Clownes, or Insurrection of Wat the Tyler, and His Fellow Kings of the Commons, Against the English Church, the King, the Lawes, Nobility and Gentry, in the Fourth Year of King Richard 2nd. Anno 1381. London: 1654. V. 65

CLEVELAND, NEHEMIAH
Green-Wood Illustrated in Highly Finished Line Engraving.... New York: 1847. V. 64

CLEVERDON, DOUGLAS
Fifty Years. Middlesex: 1978. V. 67
Stanley Morison and Eric Gill 1925-1933. London: 1983. V. 62

CLEWS, HENRY
Twenty-Eight Years in Wall Street. New York: 1888. V. 64; 66; 67

CLIFFORD, ANNE
The Diary of Lady Anne Clifford. London: 1923. V. 66

CLIFFORD, C.
How to Lower Ship's Boats. A Treatise on the Dangers and Defects in the System at present in Use and Their Remedy. London: 1859. V. 67

CLIFFORD, D.
A History of Garden Design. New York: 1963. V. 67

CLIFFORD, FREDERIC
The Agricultural Lock-Out of 1874.... Edinburgh: 1875. V. 64

CLIFFORD, HENRY B.
Rocks in the Road to Fortune or the Unsound Side of Mining. New York: 1908. V. 63

CLIFFORD, HUGH
Further India, Being the Story of Exploration from the Earliest Times in Burma, Malaya, Siam and Indo-China.. London: 1904. V. 64

CLIFFORD, ISIDORE
Crown, Bar, and Bridge-Work; New Methods of Permanently Adjusting Artificial Teeth Without Plates. London: 1887. V. 63

CLIFFORD, JERONIMY
The Case of Jeronimy Clifford, Merchant and Planter of Surinam. Colophon: 1711. V. 65

CLIFFORD, WILLIAM KINGDON
Mathematical Fragments.... London: 1881. V. 65

CLIFT, WILLIAM
The Tim Bunker Papers; or, a Yankee Farming. New York: 1868. V. 66

CLIFTON, FRANCIS
The State of Physick, Ancient and Modern Briefly Consider'd.... London: 1732. V. 65
Tabular Observations for the Improvement of Physick. London: 1731. V. 65

CLIFTON, LUCILLE
Ten Oxherding Pictures. Santa Cruz: 1988. V. 62; 64; 67

CLIFTON, MARK
They'd Rather Be Right. 1957. V. 62; 63; 64; 66

CLIFTON, VIOLET
The Book of Talbot. 1933. V. 67

CLIFTON TAYLOR, ALEC
Six English Towns - Six More English Towns - Another Six English Towns. 1978. V. 67

CLIMENSON, EMILY J.
Passages from the Diaries of Mrs. Philip Lybbe Powys of Hardwick House, Oxon 1756-1808. London: 1899. V. 67

CLINCH, GEORGE
Bloomsbury and St. Giles, Past and Present. 1890. V. 63
Bloomsbury and St. Giles's: Past and Present. London: 1890. V. 62
Marleybone and St. Pancras, Their History, Celebrities, Buildings and Institutions. 1890. V. 63

CLINE, GLORIA GRIFFIN
Exploring the Great Basin. Norman: 1963. V. 67

CLINE, WALTER M.
The Muzzle-Loading Rifle Then and Now. West Virginia: 1942. V. 67
The Muzzle-Loading Rifle...Then and Now. Huntington: 1944. V. 63; 66

CLINKENBEAR, ANNA D.
Across the Plains in '64 by Prairie Schooner to Oregon. New York: 1953. V. 63

CLINTON, DE WITT
Correspondence on the Importance & Practicability of a Rail Road, from New York to New Orleans, In Which is Embraced a Report on the Subject. New York: 1830. V. 63

CLINTON, HENRY
The Campaign in Virginia 1781. London: 1888. V. 63
A Letter from Lieut. Gen. Sir Henry Clinton to the Commissioners of Public Accounts, Relative to Some Observations.... London: 1784. V. 66

CLINTON, ISAAC
Household Baptism. Lowville: 1838. V. 66

CLINTON, JANE GREY
Happy Hours in an Irish Home. 1938. V. 62

CLIVE, CAROLINE
Nine Poems by V. London: 1928. V. 66
Poems. London: 1890. V. 66

CLIVE, ROBERT
Lord Clive's Speech in the...Commons, 30th March, 1772, On the Motion...for...a Bill for the Better Regulations of...the East India Company, and...Justice in Bengal. London: 1772. V. 66

CLOETE, STUART
The Third Way. Boston: 1947. V. 67

CLOQUET, M. JULES
Anatomical Dissections of the Parts Concerned in Inguinal and Femoral Hernia. London: 1835. V. 64

CLOSSY, SAMUEL
Observations on Some of the Diseases of the Parts of the Human Body, Chiefly Taken from the Dissections of the Morbid Bodies. London: 1763. V. 62

CLOUD, YVONNE
Beside the Seaside - Six Variations. London: 1934. V. 63

CLOUGH, ARTHUR HOUGH
The Bothies of Toper-na-Fuosich. A Long Vacation Pastoral. Oxford: 1848. V. 66

CLOUGH, ARTHUR HUGH
The Poems and Prose Remains. London: 1869. V. 64; 65

CLOUGH, ROBERT T.
The Lead Smelting Mills of the Yorkshire Dales. 1962. V. 65
The Lead Smelting Mills of the Yorkshire Dales. Keighley: 1962. V. 62; 64
The Lead Smelting Mills of the Yorkshire Dales. London: 1962. V. 62; 66
The Lead Smelting Mills of the Yorkshire Dales. 1980. V. 65
The Lead Smelting Mills of the Yorkshire Dales. Keighley: 1980. V. 62; 64
The Lead Smelting Mills of the Yorkshire Dales. London: 1980. V. 66

CLOUSTON, J. STORER
Carrington's Cases. Edinburgh and London: 1920. V. 63

CLOUSTON, THOMAS SMITH
Neuroses of Development Being the Morison Lectures for 1890. Edinburgh: 1891. V. 65

CLOUSTON, W. A.
Arabian Poetry for English Readers. Glasgow: 1881. V. 62

CLOUZOT, MARIANNE
Jeunesse. N.P: 1945. V. 64

CLOVER, SAMUEL T.
On Special Assignment. New York: 1965. V. 67

CLOWES, G. S. LAIRD
The Story of Sail. London: 1936. V. 67

THE CLOWN'S Frolics. Boston: 1910. V. 66

CLOWN'S Songster. Lockport: 1878. V. 67

CLUBBE, JOHN
Miscellaneous Tracts of the Rev. John Clubbe, Rector of Whatfield and Vicar of Debenham, Suffolk. Ipswich: 1770. V. 63; 67
Miscellaneous Tracts of the Rev. John Clubbe, Rector of Whatfield and Vicar of Debenham, Suffolk. London: 1770. V. 66

CLUM, JOHN P.
It All Happened in Tombstone. Flagstaff: 1965. V. 63; 66
The San Carlos Apache Police. Albuquerque: 1929. V. 65
Victorio Head Chief of the Warm Spring Apaches in 1877 at Ojo Caliente, New Mexico. Albuquerque: 1929. V. 62; 65

CLUM, WOODWORTH
Apache Agent - the Story of John P. Clum. Boston: 1936. V. 65

CLUTTERBUCK, HENRY
Observations on the Prevention and Treatment of the Epidemic Fever, at Present Prevailing in This Metropolis and Most Parts of the United Kingdom. London: 1819. V. 63

CLUTTERBUCK, WALTER J.
About Ceylon and Borneo.... London: 1892. V. 62

CLUVERIUS, PHILIPPUS
Introductio in Universam Goegraphiam Tam Veteram Quam Novam Tabulis Geographicas XLVI ac Notis Olim Ornata a Johanne Bunone.... Londini: 1711. V. 67

CLYDE, TODD W.
The Birds of the Santa Marta Region of Colombia. Lancaster: 1922. V. 64

CLYMAN, JAMES
James Clyman Frontiersman. Portland: 1960. V. 66

CLYNE, GERALDINE
The Jolly Jump-Ups Journey through Space. Springfield: 1952. V. 65

COACH and Sedan. London: 1925. V. 67

COAL and Reparation. N.P: 1923. V. 67

COATES, ROBERT
Eater of Darkness. Paris: 1926. V. 67

COATS, A. M.
The Book of Flowers, for Centuries of Flower Illustration. New York: 1973. V. 67
The Plant Hunters, Being a History of the Horticultural Pioneers.... New York: 1970. V. 67

COATS, ALICE M.
The Story of Horace. New York: 1939. V. 64

COATS, P.
Great Gardens of Western World. New York: 1963. V. 67
House and Garden Book of Garden Decoration. New York: 1870. V. 67

COBB, B.
Ferns, and Their Related Families of Northeastern and Central North America with a Section on Species Also Found in the British Isles and Western Europe. Norwalk: 1985. V. 67

COBB, BELTON
Double Detection. London: 1945. V. 67

COBB, DANIEL
The Medical Botanists and Expositor of Diseases and Remedies. Castile: 1846. V. 62

COBB, HOWELL
Governor Cobb to Governor Means, on the Boundary Between Georgia and South Carolina. Athens: 1852. V. 63

COBB, IRVIN S.
Down Yonder with Judge Priest. New York: 1932. V. 65

COBB, JAMES F.
Off to California. London: 1884. V. 64

COBB, STANLEY
A Preface to Nervous Disease. Baltimore: 1936. V. 64; 66; 67

COBB, THOMAS R. R.
An Inquiry into the Law of Negro Slavery in the United States of America, to which is prefixed, an Historical Sketch of Slavery. Philadelphia: 1858. V. 62; 64; 65

COBBE, FRANCES POWER
The Duties of Women. A Course of Lectures. London: 1881. V. 66

COBBETT, ANNE
English Housekeeper. London: 1836. V. 62

COBBETT, THOMAS
An Account of the Expedition of the British Fleet to Sicily in the Years 1718, 1719 and 1720. London: 1739. V. 62

COBBETT, WILLIAM
A' Protestans Reformatio' Historiaja Angliaban' Irlandban. Nagyvaradon: 1834. V. 62
The American Gardener; or, a Treatise on the Situation, Soil, Fencing and Laying-Out of Gardens.... London: 1821. V. 66
The American Gardener; or a Treatise on the Situation, Soil, Fencing and Laying-Out of Gardens.... New York: 1835. V. 62
A Bone to Gnaw for the Democrats. London: 1797. V. 62
Cobbett's Legacy to Labourers; or, What Is the Right Which the Lords, baronets and Squaires, Have to the Lands of England?. London: 1835. V. 62
Cobbett's Paper Against Gold.... London: 1817. V. 64
Cobbett's Tour in Scotland and in the Four Northern Counties of England, in the Autumn of the Year 1832. London: 1833. V. 62; 65; 66
Cobbett's Two-Penny Trash; or Politics for the Poor. London: 1830-1832. V. 62; 66
Cobbett's Two-Penny Trash, or, Politics for the Poor. London: 1831-1832. V. 63
Cottage Economy: Containing Information Relative to Brewing Beer.... London: 1823. V. 65
Cottage Economy: Containing Information Relative to the Brewing of Beer, Making of Bread, Keeping of Cows.... London: 1835. V. 64
Elements of Reform, or an Account of the Motives and Intentions of the Advocates for Parliamentary Reformation. London: 1809. V. 63
The English Gardener. 1829. V. 64
The English Gardener. Andover: 1829. V. 66
The English Gardener. London: 1838. V. 64; 66
A Full and Accurate Report of the Trial of William Cobbett, Esq....On Thursday July 7, 1831. London: 1831. V. 63
A Grammar of the English Language. London: 1826. V. 64; 66
A Grammar of the English Language.... London: 1836. V. 64
Historia da Reforma Protestante dem Inglaterra e Irlanda.... Lisboa: 1827. V. 63
History of the Regency and Reign of King George the Fourth. London: 1830-1834. V. 63; 64
A History of the Protestant Reformation in England and Ireland.... London: 1829. V. 63
A Kick for a Bite; or, Review Upon Review; with a Critical Essay of Mrs. S. Rowson. Philadelphia: 1796. V. 63
The Laws of Turnpikes; or, an Analytical Arrangement of and Illustrative Commentaries On all the General Acts Relative to Turnpike Roads in England. London: 1824. V. 66
Life and Adventures of Peter Porcupine, with Other Records of His Early Career in England and America. London: 1927. V. 63
Life of Andrew Jackson, President of the United States of America. London: 1834. V. 63
A New French and English Dictionary. London: 1833. V. 64; 66
Paper Against Gold; or, the History and Mystery of the Bank of England of the Debt of the Stocks, of the Sinking Fund and Of All the Other Tricks and Contrivances Carried on by Means of Paper Money. London: 1828. V. 62; 65
Proceedings of a General Court Martial Held at the Horse-Guards on the 24th and 27th of March 1792, for the Trial of Capt. Richard Powell, Lieut. Christopher Seton and Lieut. John Hall, of the 54th Regiment of Foot.... London: 1809. V. 65
A Prospect from the Congress-Gallery, During the Session Begun Decembr 7, 1795...with Occasional Remarks. Philadelphia: 1796. V. 62
Rural Rides. London: 1830. V. 66
Rural Rides. London: 1853. V. 66
Rural Rides. London: 1908. V. 63
Rural Rides. London: 1930. V. 63
Selections from Cobbett's Political Works.... London: 1835-1837. V. 64
The Soldier's Friend; or, Considerations on the Pretended Augmentation of the Subsistence of Private Soldiers. London: 1792. V. 65
A Treatise on Cobbett's Corn Containing Instructions for Propagating.... London: 1828. V. 62

COBBETT, WILLIAM continued
A Year's Residence in the United States of America. London: 1818-1819. V. 65
A Year's Residence, in the United States of America. London: 1828. V. 66

COBBIN, INGRAM
Elements of Arithmetic for Children, on a Plan Entirely New.... London: 1833. V. 63

COBBOLD, EDWARD
The Galley: a Poem, in Two Cantos, Descriptive of the Loss of a Naval Officer and Five Seamen off St. Leonards Nov. 20th, 1834. London: 1835. V. 63

COBBOLD, RICHARD
The Character of Woman, in a Lecture, Delivered at the Hanover Square Rooms, April 13th, 1848 for the Benefit of the Governesses Benevolent Institution. 1848. V. 66
The Character of Woman, in a Lecture, Delivered at the Hanover Square Rooms, April 13th, 1848 for the Benefit of the Governesses Benevolent Institution. London: 1848. V. 65
The History of Margaret Catchpole, a Suffolk Girl. London: 1847. V. 66

COBBOLD, THOMAS SPENCER
Entozoa; an Introduction to the Study of Helminthology.... 1864-1869. V. 63
Entozoa: an Introduction to the Study of Helminthology...(with) Entozoa, Being a Supplement.... London: 1864-1869. V. 62; 66
Observations on the Canal of Petit. Edinburgh: 1852. V. 64; 66; 67
Parasites: a Treatise on the Entozoa of Man and Animals.... London: 1879. V. 63

COBDEN, EDWARD
Poems on Several Occasions. London: 1748. V. 65

COBDEN, RICHARD
Russia. (with) England, Ireland, and America. Edinburgh: 1836. V. 67
Speeches on Questions of Public Policy. London: 1870. V. 63; 67

COBDEN-SANDERSON, THOMAS JAMES
The Arts and Crafts Movement. Hammersmith: 1905. V. 62; 67
Cobden-Sanderson and the Doves Press. San Francisco: 1929. V. 67
Cosmic Vision. Thaives Inn: 1922. V. 63
Credo. Hammersmith: 1908. V. 65
Four Lectures. San Francisco: 1974. V. 64
The Ideal Book or Book Beautiful. 1900. V. 63
The Journals of Thomas James Cobden-Sanderson 1879-1922. London: 1926. V. 63
The Journals of Thomas James Cobden-Sanderson 1879-1922. New York: 1926. V. 62; 63
London, A Paper Read at a Meeting of the Art Workers Guild...March 6 1891. Hammersmith: 1906. V. 62; 67
Shakespearia Punctuation - a Letter Addressed to the Editor of "The Times" October 26, 1911. V. 63

COBEN, HARLAN
Miracle Cure. Latham: 1991. V. 66; 67

COBEN, LAWRENCE
Japanese Cloissone. History, Technique and Appreciation. New York and Tokyo: 1982. V. 66

COBERN, CAMDEN M.
Recent Explorations in the Holy Land and Kadesh-Barnea, the "Lost Oasis" of the Sinaitic Peninsula. Meadville: 1915. V. 64

COBHAM, ALAN
Twenty Thousand Miles in a Flying-Boat. London: 1932. V. 66

COBLENTZ, STANTON A.
Villains and Vigilantes.... New York: 1936. V. 67

COBURN, ALVIN LANGDON
Alvin Langdon Coburn Photographer - an Autobiography. London: 1966. V. 62
Alvin Langdon Coburn: Photographer: an Autobiography. New York/Washington: 1966. V. 63
London. London: 1914. V. 65

COBURN, WALLACE DAVID
Rhymes from a Roundup Camp. New York: 1903. V. 62

COBURN, WALT
Pioneer Cattlemen in Montana   The Story of the Circle C Ranch. Norman: 1968. V. 66

COCCEIUS, JOHANNES
Summa Doctrina de Foedere et Testamento Dei.... Lugd. Batav: 1654. V. 66

COCCHI, ANTONIO
Discorso Primo Antonio Cocchi Sopra Ascelpiade. Firenze: 1758. V. 64

COCHIN, CHARLES NICHOLAS
Observations Upon the Antiquities of the Town of Herculaneum Discovered at the Foot of Mount Vesuvius. London: 1766. V. 67

COCHRAN, D. M.
Frogs of Columbia. Washington: 1970. V. 63; 66
Frogs of Southeastern Brazil. Washington: 1955. V. 67
The Herpetology of Hispaniola. 1941. V. 66
Poisonous Reptiles of the World: a Wartime Handbook. Washington: 1943. V. 66; 67

COCHRAN, JOHN H.
Dallas County - a Record of It's Pioneers and Progress. 1928. V. 66

COCHRAN, JOHN S.
Bonnie Belmont, a Historical Romance of the Days of Slavery and the Civil War. Wheeling: 1907. V. 66

COCHRANE, ALEXANDER BAILLIE
Ernest Vane. London: 1849. V. 67
Poems. London: 1838. V. 63

COCHRANE, CHARLES STUART
Journal of a Residence and Travels in Colombia During the Years 1823 and 1824. London: 1825. V. 66

COCHRANE, GORDON S.
Baseball, The Fan's Game. New York: 1939. V. 67

COCHRANE, JOHN GEORGE
Catalogue of the London Library, 12, St. James's Square, by John George Cochrane. London: 1847-1852. V. 65

COCHRANE, R. G.
Leprosy in Theory and Practice. Bristol: 1959. V. 66

COCK-A-DOODLE-DOO.. London. V. 67

COCK Robin. Akron: 1910. V. 65

COCK, S.
An Examination of the Report of the Bullion Committee; Shewing that the Present High Price of Bullion, Together with the Scarcity of Gold Coin.... London: 1810. V. 64

THE COCK, the Mouse, and the Little Red Hen. New York: 1946. V. 64

COCKALORUM.. Waltham St. Lawrence: 1950. V. 66

COCKALORUM. A Sequel to Chanticleer and Pertelote Being a Bibliography of the...Press June 1943-December 1948. Waltham St. Lawrence: 1949. V. 66

COCKAYNE, L.
The Vegetation of New Zealand. Leipzig: 1928. V. 64

COCKBURN, HENRY
An Examination of the Trials for Sedition which Have Hitherto Occurred in Scotland. Edinburgh: 1888. V. 63
Memorials of His Time. Edinburgh: 1874. V. 63

COCKBURN, HENRY THOMAS
Life of Lord Jeffrey, with a Selection from His Correspondence. Edinburgh: 1852. V. 62

COCKER, EDWARD
Cocker's Arithmetick. London: 1719. V. 65
Cocker's Arithmetick. London: 1734. V. 63; 66

COCKERAM, HENRY
The English Dictionarie; or, an Interpreter of Hard English Words. London: 1639. V. 64

COCKERELL, CHARLES ROBERT
Iconography of the West Front of Wells Cathedral.... London: 1851. V. 62; 66

COCKERELL, SYDNEY CARLISLE
The Gorleston Psalter. A Manuscript of the Beginning of the Fourteenth Century in the Library of C. W. Dyson Perrins, Described in Relation to Other East Anglican Books of the Period. London: 1907. V. 63
Old Testament Miniatures: a Medieval Picture Book with 283 Paintings from the Creation to the Story of David. New York: 1975. V. 62; 63

COCKERELL, SYDNEY CARLYLE
Some German Woodcuts of the Fifteenth Century. Hammersmith: 1897. V. 67

COCKLE, MAURICE J. D.
A Bibliography of the Military Books Up to 1642. London: 1957. V. 63

COCKROFT, BARRY
The Dale That Died.... London: 1975. V. 64; 65

COCKS, C.
Bordeaux et Ses Vins. Bordeaux: 1974. V. 67

COCKS, JOHN SOMERS
A Short Treatise on the Dreadful Tendency of Levelling Principles. London: 1793. V. 66

COCKTON, HENRY
The Life and Adventures of Valentine Vox, the Ventriloquist. London: 1840. V. 62; 67
The Life and Adventures of Valentine Vox the Ventriloquist. London: 1849. V. 66

COCLES, BARTOLOMEO
Physiognomiae and Chiromantiae Compendium. Argentorati: 1555. V. 63; 66

COCTEAU, JEAN
Romeo et Juliette, D'Apres Le Drame De William Shakespeare. Paris: 1926. V. 65
Le Sang d'un Poete. Monaco: 1957. V. 66

CODDINGTON, HENRY
An Elementary Treatise on Optics. Cambridge: 1825. V. 66

A CODE of Gentoo Laws, or, Ordinations of the Pundits. London: 1781. V. 63

CODE Penal ou Recueil des Principales Ordonnances, Edits et Declarations, sur les Crimes et Delits, avec un Essai sur l'Esprit and Les Motifs de la Procedure Criminelle. Paris: 1765. V. 63

CODMAN, JOHN
The Round Trip By Way of Panama through California, Oregon, Nevada, Utah, Idhao and Colorado. New York: 1881. V. 66

CODRESCU, ANDREI
A Serious Morning. Santa Barbara: 1973. V. 63; 64; 66

CODRINGTON, R. H.
The Melanesians, Studies in their Anthropology and Folk-Lore. Oxford: 1891. V. 62

CODRINGTON, ROBERT
The Life and Death of the Illustrious Robert (Third) Earle of Essex &c. London: 1646. V. 66

CODY, LIZA
1st Culprit - an Annual of Crime Stories. London: 1922. V. 63
Head Case. London: 1985. V. 65; 66

CODY, WILLIAM F.
Buffalo Bill's Wild West and Congress of Rough Riders of the World. Chicago: 1893. V. 66
Life and Adventures of Buffalo Bill. Chicago: 1917. V. 63; 64
The Life of Hon. William F. Cody Known as Buffalo Bill...an Autobiography. Hartford: 1879. V. 67
Story of the Wild West and Campfire Chats. N.P: 1888. V. 65
Story of the Wild West and Campfire Chats. Chicago: 1901. V. 66
True Tales of the Plains. New York: 1908. V. 65

COE, CHARLES H.
Juggling a Rope. Pendleton: 1927. V. 67

COE, ELMER
Fort Scott As I Knew It. Fort Scott: 1940. V. 63

COE, GEORGE W.
Frontier Fighter - The Autobiography of George W. Coe. Boston: 1934. V. 64; 67

COE, M. D.
In the Land of the Olmec. Austin: 1980. V. 62

COE, R. T.
Lost and Found Traditions: Native American Art, 1965-1985. 1986. V. 62; 65

COE, WILBUR
Ranch on the Ruidoso: The Story of a Pioneer Family in New Mexico 1871-1968. New York: 1968. V. 64

COEHOORN, BARON VAN
A Catalogue of a Valuable Collection of Prints, Drawings, Books of Prints &c. London: 1802. V. 64

COEL, MARGARET
The Eagle Catcher. 1995. V. 62
The Eagle Catcher. Boulder: 1995. V. 65; 66; 67
The Eagle Catcher. Niwot: 1995. V. 64; 67

COELEBS the Younger in Search of a Wife, or the Drawing Room Troubles of Moody Robinson Esquire. London: 1870. V. 64

COELHO, SIMAO
Compendio das Chronicas da Ordem de Nossa Senhora do Carmo. 1572. Primeira Parte...(and Livro Segundo). Lisbon: 1572. V. 62

COETLOGAN, DENNIS DE
Natural Sagacity the Principal Secret, If Not the Whole in Physick.... London: 1742. V. 64

COETZEE, J. M.
Dusklands. Johannesburg: 1974. V. 66
Dusklands. London: 1974. V. 62
Foe. New York: 1987. V. 63
From the Heart of the Country. New York: 1977. V. 63
The Life and Times of Michael K. London: 1983. V. 65

COEUROY, ANDRE
Le Jazz. Paris: 1926. V. 67

COFFEE, FRANK
Forty Years on the Pacific. Sydney/San Francisco: 1925. V. 63; 64

COFFEY, DIARMID
O'Neill and Ormond: a Chapter in Irish History. 1914. V. 66

COFFEY, GEORGE
Guide to the Celtic Antiquities of the Christian Period Preserved in the National Museum, Dublin. Dublin: 1910. V. 62

COFFEY, THOMAS M.
Agony at Easter, the 1916 Irish Uprising. New York: 1969. V. 67

COFFIN, CHARLES CARLETON
The Seat of Empire. Boston: 1870. V. 64

COFFIN, J. H., & CO.
Rural Homesteads. Franklin Tract. Superior Farm and Garden Lands. 20,000 Acres for Sale, on the Railroad Running from Philadelphia to Cape May... In Lots to Suit Purchasers.... Philadelphia: 1865. V. 63

COFFIN, LEVI
Reminiscences of Levy Coffin, the Reputed President of the Underground Ralroad.... Cincinnati: 1899. V. 62

COFFIN, MORSE H.
The Battle of Sand Creek. Waco: 1965. V. 65; 67

COFFIN, ROBERT P. TRISTRAM
Lost Paradise a Boyhood on a Maine Coast Farm. New York: 1934. V. 64; 67

COFFMAN, EDWARD M.
The Old Army, a Portrait of the American Army in Peacetime 1784-1898. New York: 1986. V. 67

COFFMAN, RAMON
Uncle Ray's Story of the Stone-Age People. Chicato: 1936. V. 67

COFIELD, THOMAS R.
Training the Hunting Retriever, Labrador, Chesapeake and Golden. London: 1959. V. 67

COGAN, THOMAS
Ethical Questions, or Speculations on the Principal Subjects of Controversy in Moral Philosophy. London: 1817. V. 63
A Philosophical Treatise on the Passions. Bath: 1802. V. 65

COGGER, H. G.
Reptiles and Amphibians of Australia. Ithaca: 1992. V. 62; 63

COGGESHALL, GEORGE
History of the American Privateers, the Letters of Marque, During Our War with England in the Years 1812, '13 and '14. New York: 1856. V. 62
Voyages to Various Parts of the World Made Between the Years 1799 and 1844. New York: 1851. V. 62; 64
Voyages to Various Parts of the World, Made Between the Years 1800 and 1831. Second Series of Voyages to Various Parts of the World Made Between the Years 1802 and 1841. New York: 1853-1852. V. 64; 65

COGGESHALL, WILLIAM T.
Poets and Poetry of the West: with Biographical and Critical Notes. Columbus: 1860. V. 62

COGHLAN, MARGARET
Memoirs of Mrs. Coghlan...Being Inerspersed with Anecdotes of the Late American and Present French War.... New York: 1795. V. 64; 65

COGLAN, THOMAS
An Improved System of Mnemonics; or Art of Assisting the Memory, Simplified and Adapted to the General Branches of Literature.... London: 1813. V. 63

COGROSSI, CARLO FRANCESCO
Nuova Idea Del Male Contagioso de'Buoi. New Theory on the Contagious Disease Among Oxen. Rome: 1953. V. 65

COHEN, BERNARD
Compendium of Finance.... London: 1822. V. 63

COHEN, GUSTAVE
Affaire Aldington Contre Lawrence d'Arabie. N.P: 1956. V. 67

COHEN, HENRI
Guide de l'Amateur de Livres a Gravures ud XVIII Siecle. 1998. V. 65
Guide de L'Amateur de Livres a Vignettes (et a Figures) du XVIIIe Siecle. Paris: 1880. V. 65

COHEN, HENRY
Guide de l'Amateur de Livres a Vignettes (et a Figures) du XVIIIe Siecle. 1880. V. 67

COHEN, I. B.
Introduction to Newton's Principia. Cambridge: 1971. V. 62

COHEN, LEONARD
Beautiful Losers. New York: 1966. V. 65
Selected Poems 1956-1968. London: 1969. V. 63
Stranger Music. New York: 1993. V. 63

COHEN, LEVY EMANUEL
Report of the Trial of the King v. Cohen, on the Prosecution of Wm. Courthope Mabbott, Esq...at the Lewes Summer Assizes, July 31, 1833. Brighton: 1833. V. 63

COHN, ALBERT M.
A Few Notes Upon Some Rare Cruikshankiana. London: 1915. V. 62
George Cruikshank: a Catalogue Raisonne of the Work Executed During the Years 1806-1877. New York: 1997. V. 62

COHN, DAVID L.
New Orleans and Its Living Past. Boston: 1941. V. 63

COHN, NORMA
Little People in a Big Country. New York: 1945. V. 64

COILLARD, FRANCOIS
On the Threshold of Central Africa; a Record of Twenty Years' Pioneering Among the Barotsi of the Upper Zambesi. New York: 1903. V. 65

COIMBRA UNIVERSIDADE
Estatutos da Universidade de Coimbra Compilados Debaixo da Immediata e Suprema Inspeccao de El-Rei D. Jose I. Lisbon: 1772. V. 62

COKE, EDWARD
An Abridgment of the First Part of My L'd Coke's Institutes.... Savoy: 1719. V. 66
The First Part of the Institutes of the Laws of England. Dublin: 1791. V. 64
The Fourth Part of the Institutes of the Laws of England. London: 1797. V. 65
The Second Part of the Institutes of the Laws of England. London: 1669. V. 66

COKE, HENRY J.
A Ride Over the Rocky Mountains to Oregon and California.... London: 1852. V. 64

COKE, ROGER
A Detection of the Court and State of England During the Four Last Reigns and the Inter-Regnum. London: 1697. V. 62

COKE, THOMAS
The Substance of a Sermon on the Godhead of Christ, Preached at Baltimore, in the State of Maryland, on the 26th Day of December, 1784 Before the General Conference of the Methodist Episcopal Church. London: 1785. V. 64

COKE, VAN DEREN
Photography in New Mexico - From the Daguerreotype to the Present. Albuquerque: 1979. V. 63; 66

COKER, JAMES LIDE
History of Company G, Ninth S.C. Regiment, Infantry, S.C. Army and Company E, Sixth S.C. Regiment, Infantry, S.C. Army. Charleston: 1899. V. 62; 63; 65

COKER, W. C.
Saprolegniaceae.... Chapel Hill: 1923. V. 64
Trees of Southeastern States, Including Virginia.... Chapel Hill: 1945. V. 67

COLAS, RENE
Bibliographie General do Costume et de la Mode. New York: 1963. V. 65
Bibliographie Generale Du Costume et de la Mode. 1994. V. 65

COLBATCH, JOHN
A Dissertation Concerning Mistletoe, a Most Wonderful Specifick Remedy for...Convulsive Distempers. London: 1730. V. 66

COLBECK, NORMAN
A Bookman's Catalogue: the Norman Colbeck Collection of Nineteenth Century and Edwardian Poetry and Belles Lettres in the Special Collections of the University of British Columbia. Vancouver: 1987. V. 62

COLBERG, NANCY
A Descriptive Bibliography of Wallace Stegner. Lewiston: 1990. V. 66

COLBERT, E.
Chicago. Historical and Statistical Sketch of the Garden City.... Chicago: 1868. V. 63

COLBORN, EDWARD F.
To Geyserland, Oregon Short Line Railroad to the Yellowstone National Park Connecting with Transcontinental Trains from All Points East and West Thence through the Park by Four-Horse Concord Coaches of the M-Y Stage Company. N.P: 1910. V. 65

COLBURN, ZERAH
A Memoir of Zerah Colburn: Written by Himself. Springfield: 1833. V. 65

COLCORD, CHARLES F.
The Autobiography of 1859-1934. N.P: 1970. V. 62; 65

COLDEN, CADWALLADER
An Explication of the first Causes of Action in Manner, and of the Cause of Gravitation. London: 1746. V. 66

COLDEN, CADWALLADER DAVID
The Life of Robert Fulton. New York: 1817. V. 62

COLDEN, JANE
Botanic Manuscript of Jane Colden 1724-1766. New York: 1963. V. 64; 67

COLDSTREAM, W.
Illustrations of Some of the Grasses of the Southern Punjab, Being Photo-Lithographs of Some of the Principal Grasses Found at Hissar.... 1889. V. 63

COLE, BENJAMIN THOMAS HALCOTT
The Renegade; and Other Poems. London: 1833. V. 63

COLE, CHRISTIAN
Memoirs of Affairs of State, Containing Letters Written by Ministers Employed in Foreign Negotiations, from the Year 1697 to the Latter End of 1708.... London: 1733. V. 67

COLE, CORNELIUS
California Three Hundred and Fifty Years Ago - Manuelo's Narrative. San Francisco: 1888. V. 63
Memoirs of...Ex Senator of the United States from California. New York: 1908. V. 66

COLE, DAVID
History of Rockland County, New York, with Biographical Sketches of Its Prominent Men. New York: 1884. V. 63; 66

COLE, EDWARD MAULE
Geological Rambles in Yorkshire Leeds to Scarboro', Filey, Whitby and Bridlington. London: 1883. V. 64; 65

COLE, ELIZABETH M.
Jottings from Overland Trip to Arizona and California. Poughkeepsie: 1908. V. 63

COLE, G. D. H.
Birthday Gifts and Other Stories. London: 1946. V. 67
The Blatchington Tangle. New York: 1926. V. 66

COLE, GILBERT L.
In the Early Days Along the Overland Trail in Nebraska Territory. Kansas City: 1905. V. 63; 64; 66

COLE, HARRY ELLSWORTH
Stage Coach and Tavern Tales of the Old Northwest. Cleveland: 1930. V. 66

COLE, JAMESON
A Killing in Quail Country. 1996. V. 66
A Killing in Quail County. New York: 1996. V. 63; 64; 65; 67

COLE, JOHN
A Bibliographical and Descriptive Tour from Scarborough to the Library of a Philobiblist In Its Neighbourhood. Scarborough: 1824. V. 63
Historical Sketches of Scalby, Burniston and Cloughton, with Descriptive Notices of Hayburn Wyke and Stainton Dale.... Scarborough: 1829. V. 62
The History and Antiquities of Filey in the County of York. Scarborough: 1828. V. 65; 66
The Scarborough Album of History and Poetry. Scarborough: 1825. V. 65
The Scarborough Collector and Journal of the Olden Time. Scarborough: 1828. V. 66
Scarborough Guide. London: 1825. V. 65
The Scarborough Souvenir. Scarborough: 1827. V. 65; 66
The Scarborough Repository and Mirror of the Season.... Scaraborough: 1824. V. 64
The Seraph; a New Selection of Psalm Tunes, Hymns and Anthems.... Baltimore: 1822. V. 62
Union Harmony; or, Music Made Easy: a New and Pleasing Selection of Psalm and Hymn Tunes.... Baltimore: 1829. V. 63; 66

COLE, JOSEPH
Early Recollections, Chiefly Relating to the Late Samuel Taylor Coleridge During His Long Residence in Bristol. London: 1837. V. 62

COLE, JULIE KRAMER
Interwoven. Loveland: 1995. V. 62; 63; 64; 66

COLE, K. M.
Biology of the Red Algae. Cambridge: 1995. V. 67

COLE, PETER
Rift. New York: 1986. V. 67

COLE, PHILIP G.
Montana in Miniature. Kalispell: 1966. V. 63; 64; 65; 66; 67

COLE, R. E. G.
History of the Manor and Township of Doddington, Otherwise Doddington-Pigot, in the County of Lincoln.... Lincoln: 1897. V. 62

COLE, R. V.
British Trees. London: 1907. V. 63; 67

COLE, REX VICAT
The Art and Life of Byam Shaw. London: 1932. V. 63

COLE, SELINA
First Impressions of Florence. Liverpool: 1906. V. 66

COLE, THOMAS HOLWELL
The Antiquities of Hastings and the Battlefield.... London: 1884. V. 62

COLE, TIMOTHY
Considerations on Engraving. New York: 1921. V. 62

COLE, WILLIAM
Philosophical Remarks on the Theory of Comets; to Which is Subjoined, a Dissertation on the Nature and Properties of Light. London: 1823. V. 63

COLEBROOKE, T. E.
Life of the Honourable Mountstuart Elphinstone. London: 1884. V. 67

COLEBY, R. J. W.
Regional Angling Literature. 1979. V. 67

COLEMAN, DOROTHY S.
A Collector's Book of Doll's Clothes. New York: 1975. V. 66
The Collector's Encyclopaedia of Dolls. New York: 1968. V. 62

COLEMAN, EDWARD
The Tryal of Edward Coleman for Conspiring the Death of the King and the Subversion of the Government of England. Edinburgh: 1888. V. 64

COLEMAN, J. WINSTON
Slavery Times in Kentucky. Chapel Hill: 1940. V. 66; 67

COLEMAN, JOHN
Charles Reade As I Knew Him. London: 1904. V. 67

COLEMAN, KENNETH
The American Revolution in Georgia 1763-1789. Athens: 1958. V. 67

COLEMAN, WANDA
Hand Dance. Santa Rosa: 1993. V. 67

COLEMAN, WILLIAM
A Collection of the Facts and Documents Relative to the Death of Major General Alexander Hamilton.... New York: 1804. V. 65

COLENSO, JOHN WILLIAM
The Pentateuch and Book of Joshua Critically Examined. London: 1863-1865. V. 64

COLERIDGE, EDITH
Memoirs and Letters of Sara Coleridge. London: 1873. V. 65

COLERIDGE, HARTLEY
Biographia Borealis; or Lives of Distinguished Northerns. Whitaker: 1833. V. 66
Essays and Marginalia. London: 1851. V. 65
Lives of Illustrious Worthies of Yorkshire. Hull: 1835. V. 63; 65

COLERIDGE, MARY ELIZABETH
Fancy's Following. Oxford: 1896. V. 65
Fancy's Guerdon. London: 1897. V. 64

COLERIDGE, SAMUEL TAYLOR
Aids to Reflection. London: 1848. V. 63
Aids to Reflection. London: 1861. V. 63
The Ancient Mariner. London and Edinburgh: 1906. V. 67
Biographia Literaria; or Biographical Sketches of My Literary Life and Opinions. London: 1817. V. 63
Christabel: Kubla Khan, a Vision; the Pains of Sleep. London: 1816. V. 62; 65; 67
Confessions of an Inquiring Spirit. London: 1840. V. 63
The Friend. London: 1818. V. 62
The Friend. Vermont: 1831. V. 63
The Friend. London: 1844. V. 62
Hints Towards the Formation of a More Comprehensive Theory of Life. London: 1848. V. 65

COLERIDGE, SAMUEL TAYLOR continued
The Letters of Samuel Taylor Coleridge. London: 1950. V. 65
Letters, Conversations and Recollections. London: 1836. V. 64
Notes and Lectures Upon Shakespeare and Some of the Old Poets and Dramatists with Other Literary Remains. London: 1849. V. 66
I. On the Constitution of the Church and State. II. Lay Sermons. London: 1839. V. 66
The Philosophical Lectures of Samuel Taylor Coleridge.... London: 1949. V. 62
Poems. London: 1797. V. 67
Poems. London: 1852. V. 62
Poems Chosen Out of the Works. 1896. V. 62; 66
Poems Chosen Out of the Works. London: 1896. V. 64
The Poems of Coleridge. London: 1907. V. 64
The Rime of the Ancient Mariner. 1899. V. 62; 67
The Rime of the Ancient Mariner. London: 1899. V. 67
The Rime of the Ancient Mariner. Oxford: 1930. V. 63
The Rime of the Ancient Mariner. New York: 1931. V. 64
The Rime of the Ancient Mariner. London: 1945. V. 64
The Rime of the Ancient Mariner. London: 1972. V. 65
The Rime of the Ancient Mariner. 1995. V. 62
Selected Poems. London: 1935. V. 65
Selected Poems. 1988. V. 62
Sibylline Leaves: a Collection of Poems. London: 1817. V. 64; 66
Specimens of the Table Talk. London: 1835. V. 62; 64; 65
Specimens of the Table Talk. London: 1836. V. 63; 66
Unpublished Letters of Samuel Taylor Coleridge.... London: 1932. V. 62
Zapolya: a Christmas Tale. London: 1817. V. 63

COLERIDGE, SAMUEL TAYLOR, MRS.
Minnow Among Tritons. Mrs. S. T. Coleridge's Letters to Thomas Poole 1799-1834. London: 1934. V. 65

COLERIDGE, SARA
Phantasmion, a Fairy Tale. London: 1874. V. 65

COLERIDGE-TAYLOR, S.
Twenty-Four Melodies Transcribed for the Piano. Op. 59. Boston: 1905. V. 62

COLES, BENJAMIN
A Memoir on the Subject of the Wheat and Flour of the State of New York. New York: 1820. V. 63

COLES, CHARLES
Game Birds. 1981. V. 64; 65; 67
Game Birds. Limpsfield: 1983. V. 67
Game Birds. New York: 1983. V. 65

COLES, ELISHA
An English Dictionary Explaining the Difficult Terms that Are Used in Divinity, Husbandry, Physick, Philosophy, Law, Navigation, Mathematicks and Other Arts and Sciences. London: 1713. V. 64

COLES, MANNING
Without Lawful Authority. Garden City: 1943. V. 67

COLES, ROBERT
Dorothea Lange: Photographs of a Lifetime. Millerton: 1982. V. 63
The Last and First Eskimos. Boston: 1978. V. 65; 66
The Old Ones of New Mexico. Albuquerque: 1973. V. 63

COLETTE, SIDONIE GABRIELLE
Break of Day. New York: 1983. V. 62; 63; 64; 66
The Cat. New York: 1936. V. 63
Chambre d'Hotel. Paris: 1940. V. 66
Duo. New York: 1935. V. 63
L'Ingenue Libertine. Paris: 1922. V. 63
Lettres a Ses Pairs. Paris: 1973. V. 63
Mes Cahiers. Paris: 1941. V. 63
Mitsou or How Girls Grow Wise. New York: 1930. V. 63
La Naissance du Jour. Paris: 1928. V. 66
The Pure and the Impure. New York: 1933. V. 67
The Pure and the Impure. New York: 1967. V. 62
Recaptured. New York: 1932. V. 63

COLGAN, N.
Contributions Towards a Cybele Hibernica.... Dublin: 1898. V. 66

COLHOUN, SAMUEL
An Essay on Suspended Animation. Philadelphia: 1823. V. 64; 67

COLINS, WILLIAM
The Poetical Works. London: 1800. V. 64

COLLADO, LUIS
Practica Manuale di Arteglieria; Nellaquale si Tratta Della Inventione di Essa dell'Ordine di Conduria & Piantarla Sotto a Qualunque Fortezza.... Venice: 1586. V. 62

COLLAER, P.
Music of the Americas. London: 1973. V. 62

COLLAR, N. J.
Threatened Birds of Africa and Related Islands. Cambridge: 1985. V. 67

COLLAS, ACHILLES
The Great Seals of England. London: 1837. V. 62

COLLECCAO *De Varias Poesias, Feitas por Differentes Engenhos....* Lisboa Occidental: 1729. V. 62

THE COLLECTED *Colorado Rail Annual - a Journal of Railroad History in the Rocky Mountain West.* Golden: 1974. V. 67

A COLLECTION *of Hymns for the Use of Native Christians of the Mohawk Language....* New York: 1832. V. 63

A COLLECTION *and Selection of English Prologues and Epilogues.* London: 1779. V. 66

COLLECTION *de Peintures Antiques, Qui Ornoient les Palais, Thermes, Mausolees, Chambres Sepulcrales des Empereurs Tite, Trajan, Adrien et Constantin et Autres Edifices tan a Rome qu'aux Environs Jusqu'aupres de Naples....* Rome: 1781. V. 64

A COLLECTION *of All the Declarations and Resolutions, Published by the Different Counties, Cities, Towns, Parishes, Incorporations, and Societies Throughout Scotland, Against a Proposed Repeal of the Statutes....* Edinburgh: 1780. V. 66

A COLLECTION *of Anthems Used in His Majesty's Chapel Royal and Most Cathedral Churches in England and Ireland.* London: 1769. V. 67

A COLLECTION *of Birds and Riddles.* London: 1820. V. 66

A COLLECTION *of Divine Sayings, in English and Bengalee.* Calcutta: 1819. V. 63

A COLLECTION *of Epigrams. To Which is Prefix'd, a Critical Dissertation on this Species of Poetry.* London: 1727. V. 66

A COLLECTION *of Fables, for the Instruction and Amusement of Little Misses and Masters.* London: 1825. V. 66

A COLLECTION *of Hymns, for the Use of the Tabernacles in Scotland.* Edinburgh: 1800. V. 62

COLLECTION *of Nebraska Pioneer Reminiscences.* Cedar Rapids: 1916. V. 66

COLLECCAO *of Papers Printed by Order of the Society for the Propogation of the Gospel in Foreign Parts: The Charter, The Qualifications of Missionaries...Instructions for School-Masters, Prayers for the Charity Schools....* London: 1788. V. 65

A COLLECTION *of Prints, Illustrative of English Scenery, from the Drawings and Sketches of Gainsborough in the Various Collections of....* London: 1802-1805. V. 66

A COLLECTION *of Testimonies Concerning Several Ministers of the Gospel Among the People Called Quakers, Deceased....* London: 1760. V. 62; 67

A COLLECTION *of the Principal Flags of All Nations of the World: From the Best Authorities.* Bungay: 1813. V. 62

A COLLECTION *of the Several Statutes and Parts of Statutes, Now in Force, Relating to High Treason, and Misprision of High Treason... (bound with) A Form and Method of Trail of Commoners, In Cases of High Treason...* London: 1709. V. 65

COLLECTS *of the Church of England.* London: 1871. V. 62; 67

COLLEDGE, J. J.
Ships of the Royal Navy: an Historical Index. London: 1969-1970. V. 63

COLLENETTE, S.
An Illustrated Guide to the Flowers of Saudi Arabia. 1985. V. 63
An Illustrated Guide to the Flowers of Saudi Arabia. London: 1985. V. 66; 67

COLLENUCIUS, PANDULPHUS
Del Compendio dell'Istoria del Regno di Napoli. Prima (Secunde) & Terza. Venetia: 1591. V. 67

COLLES, ABRAHAM
Lectures on the Theory and Practice of Surgery.... Dublin: 1850. V. 67

COLLES, H. C.
Grove's Dictionary of Music and Musicians. New York: 1947. V. 65

COLLES, RAMSAY
The History of Ulster from the Earliest Times to the Present Day. 1919. V. 62; 65

COLLETT, HENRY
On a Collection of Plants from Upper Burma and the Shan States. 1889. V. 62

COLLETTE, CHARLES HASTINGS
Dr. Newman and His Religious Opinions. London: 1866. V. 65

COLLIBER, SAMUEL
Columna Rostrata; or, a Critical History of the English Sea-Affairs.... London: 1727. V. 63; 66; 67

COLLIER, GEORGE
Selima & Azor, a Persian Tale, in Three Parts; as Performed at the Theatre Royal, Drury Lane. London: 1784. V. 65

COLLIER, HIRAM PRICE
England and the English from an American Point of View. New York: 1909. V. 62

COLLIER, JANE
An Essay on the Art of Ingeniously Tormenting, with Proper Rules for the Exercise of that Amusing Study. London: 1753. V. 63; 64; 66
An Essay on the Art of Ingeniously Tormenting; with Proper Rules for the Exercise of that Amusing Study. London: 1806. V. 64

COLLIER, JEREMY
An Ecclesiastical History of Great Britain.... London: 1840-1841. V. 63

COLLIER, JEREMY continued
An Essay Upon Gaming in a Dialogue Between Callimachus and Dolomedes. London. V. 66
Essays Upon Several Moral Subjects. London: 1698. V. 63; 67
Essays Upon Several Moral Subjects. London: 1703. V. 64
Essays Upon Several Moral Subjects. London: 1722. V. 64
A Short View of the Immorality and Profaneness of the English Stage.... London: 1698. V. 62
A Short View of the Immorality and Profaneness of the English Stage.... London: 1698-1699. V. 66
A Short View of the Immorality and Profaneness of the English Stage.... London: 1699. V. 63

COLLIER, JOHN
The Devil and All. 1934. V. 64
The Devil and All. London: 1934. V. 62; 66
Fancies and Goodnights. New York: 1951. V. 65
Fancies and Goodnights. New York: 1952. V. 62
Green Thoughts. London: 1932. V. 62; 64; 66
His Monkey Wife. London: 1930. V. 62; 67
His Monkey Wife. New York: 1931. V. 66
Presenting Moonshine. New York: 1941. V. 63
A View of the Lancashire Dialect.... London: 1746. V. 64
The Works of Tim Bobbin, Esq., in Prose and Verse.... Rochdale: 1819. V. 64; 65

COLLIER, JOHN PAYNE
A Bibliographical and Critical Account of the Rarest Books in the English Language Alphabetically Arranged. London: 1865. V. 65
Mr. J. Payne Collier's Reply to Mr. N.E.S.A. Hamilton's "Inquiry" into the Imputed Shakespeare Forgeries. London: 1860. V. 65
Punch and Judy. London: 1828. V. 64
Punch and Judy, with Twenty-Four Illustrations.... London: 1881. V. 65

COLLIER, ROBERT J.
In Memoriam Peter Fenelon Collier. New York: 1910. V. 66

COLLING, J. K.
Art Foliage. Boston: 1880. V. 64
Details of Gothic Architecture. London: 1856. V. 65

COLLINGRIDGE, GEORGE
The First Discovery of Australia and New Guiea.... Sydney: 1906. V. 64

COLLINGS, ELLSWORTH
The Old Home Ranch, Will Rogers Range in the Indian Territory. Stillwater: 1964. V. 67
The 101 Ranch. Norman: 1937. V. 63

COLLINGWOOD, C.
Rambles of a Naturalist on the Shores and Waters of the China Sea. 1868. V. 66

COLLINGWOOD, G. L. NEWNHAM
A Selection from the Public and Private Correspondence of Vice-Admiral Lord Collingwood.... London: 1829. V. 62

COLLINGWOOD, R. G.
The Roman Inscriptions of Britain. Oxford: 1965. V. 64

COLLINGWOOD, STUART DODGSON
The Life and Letters of Lewis Carroll. London: 1899. V. 67

COLLINGWOOD, W. G.
The Book of Coniston. Kendal: 1897. V. 64
Coniston Tales. Ulverston: 1889. V. 62; 65
Elizabethan Keswick. Kendal: 1912. V. 65
King William the Wanderer, an Old British Saga, From the Old French Versions. London: 1904. V. 64
The Lake Counties. London: 1932. V. 63; 65; 66
The Life and Work of John Ruskin. Cambridge: 1893. V. 62
The Limestone Alps of Savoy: a Study in Physical Geology. Orpington: 1884. V. 62
Northumbrian Crosses of the Pre-Norman Age. London: 1927. V. 62; 66
The Roman Inscriptions of Britain. Oxford: 1965. V. 66

COLLINS, ANNA MARIA
The Great Western Cook Book, or Table Receipts, Adapted to Western Housewifery. New York: 1857. V. 63

COLLINS, ANTHONY
A Discourse of Free Thinking, Occasion'd by the Rise and Growth of a Sect Call'd Free Thinkers. London: 1713. V. 64
A Philosophical Enquiry Concerning Human Liberty. London: 1717. V. 65
Priestcraft in Perfection, or a Detection of the Fraud of Inserting and Continuing This Clause in the Twentieth Article of the Articles of the Church of England. London: 1710. V. 62

COLLINS, CECIL
The Vision of the Fool. London: 1947. V. 65

COLLINS, CHARLES ALLSTON
At the Bar. London: 1866. V. 65

COLLINS, DENNIS
The Indians Last Fight or the Dull Knife Raid. Girard: 1915. V. 63; 66

COLLINS, F. S.
The Green Algae of North America. 1909-1912. V. 63

COLLINS, FRANCES
The Woodleighs of Amscote. London: 1881. V. 65

COLLINS, FRANCIS
Voyages to Portugal, Sicily, Asia Minor, Spain, Malta, Egypt from 1796 to 1801. London: 1813. V. 64

COLLINS
Guide in English Parish Churches Including the Isle of Man. London: 1959. V. 63

COLLINS, H. B.
The Far North - 2000 Years of American Eskimo and Indian Art. Washington: 1973. V. 62

COLLINS, HERBERT RIDGEWAY
Threads of History. Washington: 1979. V. 65

COLLINS, HUNT
Tomorrow's World. 1956. V. 62; 64; 66

COLLINS, J. H.
A Handbook to the Mineralogy of Cornwall and Devon. London: 1871. V. 66
The Hensbarrow Granite District; a Geological Description and a Trade History. Truro: 1878. V. 62
Observations on the West of England Mining Region. Plymouth: 1912. V. 64; 65

COLLINS, JOHN
The City and Scenery of Newport, Rhode Island. Burlington: 1957. V. 62
Commercium Epistolicum D. Johannis Collins et Aliorum de Analysi Promota.... London: 1712. V. 65

COLLINS, JOHN A.
Right and Wrong Among the Abolitionists of the United States.... Glasgow: 1841. V. 63

COLLINS, MARY
Pioneering in the Rockies. N.P: 1919. V. 67

COLLINS, MR.
The Chapter of Kings. London: 1818. V. 65

COLLINS, N. M.
The Conservation of Insects and Their Habitats. London: 1991. V. 64

COLLINS, PERRY MC DONOUGH
A Voyage Down the Amoor; with a Land Journey through Siberia, and Incidental Notices of Manchooria, Kamschatka and Japan. New York: 1860. V. 64

COLLINS, R. M.
Chapters from the Unwritten History of the War Between the States.... St. Louis: 1893. V. 62

COLLINS, ROBERT O.
Shadows in the Grass: Britain in the Southern Sudan 1918-1956. New Haven and London: 1983. V. 66

COLLINS, SAMUEL
The Present State of Russia. In a Letter to a Friend.... London: 1671. V. 66

COLLINS, VARNUM LANSING
The Continental Congress at Princeton. Princeton: 1908. V. 63; 66
President Witherspoon. A Biography. Princeton: 1925. V. 63

COLLINS, WILKIE
Antonina; or the Fall of Rome. London: 1850. V. 65
Armadale. London: 1866. V. 62; 65
Armadale. New York: 1866. V. 65
Armadale. London: 1869. V. 63
Basil. London: 1862. V. 66
Basil. London: 1865. V. 65
The Guilty River. Bristol: 1886. V. 65
Heart and Science. London: 1885. V. 65
Man and Wife. London: 1871. V. 65
Miss or Mrs?. London: 1873. V. 65
The Moonstone. New York: 1868. V. 66
New Magdalen. London: 1873. V. 65
No Name. London: 1862. V. 67
No Name. London: 1863. V. 65
Rambles Beyond Railways; or Notes in Cornwall Taken A-Foot. London: 1852. V. 62
Rambles Beyond Railways; or, Notes in Cornwall Taken A-Foot. London: 1861. V. 65
The Woman in White. London: 1860. V. 64; 65; 67
The Woman in White. New York: 1860. V. 64; 65
The Woman in White. London: 1890. V. 66

COLLINS, WILLIAM
The Poetical Works. London: 1827. V. 62

COLLINS, WILLIAM EDWARD
Archbishop Laud Commemoration, 1895. Lectures on Archbishop Laud together with a Bibliography of Laudian Literature and the Laudian Exhibition Catalogue. Barking: 1895. V. 66

COLLINS, WILLIAM LUCAS
The Education Question. Edinburgh and London: 1862. V. 63

COLLINSON, S.
Richard's Tower: an Idyll of Nottingham Castle and Other Poems. London: 1876. V. 65

COLLIS, SEPTIMA M.
A Woman's Trip to Alaska, Being an Account of a Voyage through the Inland Seas of the Sitkan Archipelago in 1890. New York: 1890. V. 63; 64

COLLMANN, H.
The Britwell Handlist or Short-title Catalogue of the Principal Volumes from the Time of Caxton to the Year 1800.... London: 1933. V. 62

COLLOT, PIERRE
P. Collot, Inventor. (with) Pieces d'Architecture, ou Sont Comprises Plusieurs Sortes de Cheminees Portes, Taernacles.... Paris: 1633. V. 66

COLLYMORE, FRANK A.
Thirty Poems. Bridgetown: 1944. V. 63

COLMAN, BENJAMIN
The Honour and Happiness of the Vertuous Woman.... Boston: 1716. V. 63

COLMAN, GEORGE
Broad Grins, My Nightgown and Slippers and Other Humourous Works, Prose and Poetical. London: 1871. V. 67

COLMAN, HELEN CAROLINE
Jeremiah James Colman, a Memoir, by One of His Daughters. London: 1905. V. 63

COLMAN, PAMELA
The Bijou Alphabet. Boston: 1846. V. 62

COLMENERO LEDESMA, ANTONIO
Della Cioccolata. Discorso Diviso in Quattro Parti. D'Antonio Colmenero Ledesma. Medico e Chirurgo Della d'Ecija nell'Andaluzia. Rome: 1667. V. 62

COLNETT, JAMES
A Voyage to the South Atlantic and Round Cape Horn Into the Pacific Ocean, for the Purpose of Extending the Spermaceti Whale Fisheries and Other Objects of Commerce.... London: 1798. V. 63

A Voyage to the South Atlantic and Round Cape Horn into the Pacific Ocean, for the Purpose of Extending the Spermaceti Whale Fisheries and Other Objects of Commerce.... Amsterdam: 1968. V. 64; 65

COLOMBIER, JEAN
Precepts sur la Sante des Gens de Guerre, ou Hygiene Militaire. Paris: 1775. V. 63

COLONNA, FRANCESCO
La Hypnerotomachia di Poliphilo, Cio' Pugna D'Amore in Sogno. Venice: 1545. V. 65; 67

THE COLOPHON: A Book Collector's Quarterly. No. 8. New York: 1931. V. 64

THE COLOPHON. New Series. 1935-1938. V. 63

COLORADO
First Annual Report of the Union Colony of Colorado, Including a History of the Town of Greeley.... New York: 1871. V. 65

COLORADO (TERRITORY). LAWS, STATUTES, ETC. - 1865
General Laws and Joint Resolutions, Memorials and Private Acts Passed at the Fourth Session of the Legislature Assembly of the Territory of Colorado. Denver: 1865. V. 65; 67

COLORADO (TERRITORY). LEGISLATURE - 1867
Council Journal of the Legislative Assembly of the Territory of Colorado Sixth Session. Central City: 1867. V. 65; 67

COLORED Atlas of Chinese Oceanic Fluids. Shanghai: 1975. V. 65

COLOUR Show Pictures of Ten Little Nigger Boys. London: 1950. V. 64

THE COLOURED Quintette...The Cleveland Gospel Quintette. Kilmarnock: 1937. V. 66

COLQUHOUN, ARCHIBALD R.
Across Chryse; Being the Narrative of a Journey of Exploration through the South China Border Lands from Canton to Mandalay. London: 1883. V. 64

China in Transformation. New York: 1898. V. 62

COLQUHOUN, JOHN
The Moor and the Loch. 1841. V. 62
The Moor and the Loch. Edinburgh: 1880. V. 62
The Moor and the Loch. 1888. V. 62; 63; 65; 66
Sporting Days. London: 1866. V. 67

COLQUHOUN, PATRICK
A New and Appropriate System of Education for the Labouring People.... London: 1806. V. 63

A Treatise on the Commerce and Police of the River Thames.... London: 1800. V. 63

A Treatise on the Functions and Duties of a Constable.... London: 1803. V. 65

A Treatise on the Police of London.... Philadelphia: 1798. V. 62

A Treatise on the Police of the Metropolis, Explaining the Various Crimes and Misdemeanors Which at Present are Felt as a Pressure Upon the Community.... London: 1796. V. 65; 66; 67

A Treatise on the Wealth, Power and Resources of the British Empire, in Eery Quarter of the World, Including the East Indies and the Rise and Progress of the Funding System Explained.... London: 1815. V. 66

COLSON, NATHANIEL
The Mariners New Kalender. London: 1729. V. 65

COLT, MIRIAM DAVIS
A Heroine of the Frontier, Miriam Davis Colt, Kansas 1856. Cedar Rapids: 1941. V. 62
Went to Kansas. Watertown: 1862. V. 62; 67

COLT, SAMUEL
Armsmear: the Home, the Arm and the Armory of Samuel Colt. New York: 1866. V. 66
Sam Colt's Own Record. Hartford: 1949. V. 63; 67

COLTER, ELI
The Adventures of Hawke Travis - Episodes in the Life of a Gunman. New York: 1931. V. 66

COLTON, J. H.
Colton's Octavo Atlas of the World. New York: 1865. V. 65
Colton's Traveler and Tourist's Guide-Book through the United States of America and the Canadas. New York: 1850. V. 62; 67

COLTON, M. R.
The Little-Known Small House Ruins in the Coconino Forest. Lanchester: 1918. V. 65

COLTON, RAY C.
The Civil War in the Western Territories. Norman: 1959. V. 67

COLTON, ROBERT
The Bye-Lanes and Downs of England, with Turf Scenes and Characters. London: 1850. V. 63
Pedestrian and Other Reminiscences at Home and Abroad; with Sketches of a Country Life. London: 1846. V. 66

COLTON, WALTER
Three Years in California. New York: 1850. V. 62; 63; 64; 67

COLTRANE, JAMES
A Good Day to Die. New York: 1999. V. 67

COLUM, PADRAIC
The Big Tree of Bunlahy: Stories of My Own Countryside. New York: 1933. V. 62
The Frenzied Prince, Being Heroic Stories of Ancient Ireland. Philadelphia: 1943. V. 62; 67
Irish Elegies. 1958. V. 67
Old Pastures. New York: 1930. V. 62; 66; 67
Orpheus - Myths of the World. New York: 1930. V. 63
Ten Poems. Dublin: 1957. V. 62
Wild Earth. New York: 1922. V. 66

COLUMBANI, P.
Vases and Tripods on Twelve Plates. London: 1775. V. 64

COLUMBIA UNIVERSITY
Catalogue of an Exhibition at Columbia University to Commemorate the One Hundredth Anniversary of the Birth of Lewis Carroll (Charles Lutwidge Dodgson) 1832-1898. New York: 1932. V. 64

COLUMBIAN EXPOSITION OF 1892
World's Columbian Exposition Department of New Mexico. Albuquerque: 1891. V. 65

COLUMBUS, CHRISTOPHER
Christopher Columbus His Own Book of Privileges 1502. London: 1893. V. 66
Codice Diplomatico Colombo-Americano. Genoa: 1823. V. 67
The History of the Voyages of Christopher Columbus, in Order to Discover America and the West Indies. London: 1772. V. 66
The Voyages of Christopher Columbus Being the Journals of His First and Third, and the Letters Concerning His First and Last Voyages, To Which is Added the Account of His Second Voyage.... London: 1930. V. 66

COLVIL, SAMUEL
The Whigs Supplication, or, the Scotch-Hudibras, a Mock-Poem. London: 1710. V. 63; 67

COLVILLE, HENRY
The Land of the Nile Springs. London: 1895. V. 64

COLVIN, H. M.
The History of the King's Works. London: 1963. V. 65

COLVIN, JOHN B.
The Magistrate's Guide and Citizen's Counseller.... Frederick Town: 1805. V. 64

COLWIN, LAURIE
Passion and Affect. New York: 1974. V. 67

COLYER, CHARLES N.
Flies of the British Isles. London: 1951. V. 62

COMAN, CAROLYN
What Jamie Saw. Arden: 1995. V. 65

COMB Making in America. An Account of the Origin and Development of the Industry of Which Leominster Has Become Famous. Boston: 1925. V. 67

COMBE, ANDREW
The Physiology of Digestion Considered with Relation to the Principles of Dietetics. Edinburgh: 1836. V. 63

COMBE, GEORGE
Elements of Phrenology. Edinburgh: 1841. V. 64
Essays on Phrenology, or an Inquiry Into the Principles and Utility of the System of Drs. Gall and Spurzheim and into the Objections Made Against It. Philadelphia: 1822. V. 65
Lectures on Phrenology.... New York: 1841. V. 63
The Life and Correspondence of Andrew Combe, M.D. Edinburgh: 1850. V. 66

COMBE, WILLIAM
Doctor Syntax in London; or the Pleasures and Miseries of the Metropolis. A Poem. London: 1820. V. 62
Doctor Syntax's Three Tours. London: 1868. V. 62
The English Dance of Death. London: 1815-1816. V. 62
The English Dance of Death. (with) the Dance of Life. London: 1815-1817. V. 64; 66
The First (Second & Third) Tour(s) of Doctor Syntax. London: 1880. V. 67
The History of Johnny Quae Genus. London: 1822. V. 66
The History of the Abbey Church of St. Peter's Westminster, Its Antiquities and Monuments. London: 1812. V. 62
Journal of Sentimental Travels in the Southern Provinces of France, Shortly Before the Revolution. London: 1821. V. 62; 64
Letters from Eliza to Yorick. London: 1775. V. 66
The Life, Adventures and Opinions of Col. George Hanger, Written by Himself. London: 1801. V. 76
Life of Napoleon. A Hudibrastic Poem in Fifteen Cantos, by Dr. Syntax. London: 1817. V. 66
The Three Tours of Dr. Syntax.... London: 1855. V. 62

COMBE, WILLIAM continued
The Tour of Doctor Syntax in Search of a Wife. Philadelphia: 1829. V. 66
The Tour of Doctor Syntax in Search of the Picturesque. London: 1819. V. 65
The Tour of Dr. Syntax: In Search of the Picturesque: in Search of Consolation; and In Search of a Wife. London: 1855. V. 62; 66
The Tour(s) of Doctor Syntax.... London: 1819-1821. V. 67

COMBER, THOMAS
A Companion to the Altar; or an Help to the Worthy Receiving of the Lords Supper.... London: 1681. V. 62

COMBERBACH, R.
The Report of Several Cases Argued and Adjudged in the Court of King's Bench at Westminster, fromt he First Year of King James the Second to the Tenth Year of King William the Third. London: 1724. V. 65

COMBINATION Atlas Map of Salem and Gloucester Counties. Philadelphia: 1876. V. 63; 66

COMBS, LOULA LONG
My Revelation. Lee's Summit: 1947. V. 64

COMDEN, BETTY
Applause. New York: 1971. V. 66

COMEAU, NAPOLEON A.
Life and Sport on the North Shore of the Lower St. Lawrence and Gulf.... Quebec: 1909. V. 67
Life and Sport on the North Shore of the Lower St. Lawrence and Gulf.... Quebec: 1923. V. 64

COMERT, PIERRE
Petain - Laval: the Conspiracy. London: 1942. V. 64

COMES, NATALIS
Natalis Comitvm Veneti de Venatione Libri IIII. Venetiis: 1551. V. 66

COMFORT, ALEX
I and That. New York: 1979. V. 67
Poems for Jane. New York: 1979. V. 67

COMFORT, ARTHUR
Pen and Ink Drawings. Halifax: 1900. V. 64; 66

COMFORT, J. W.
Thomsonian Practice of Midwifery and Treatment of Complaints Peculiar to Women and Children. Philadelphia: 1845. V. 66

COMFORT, WILL LEVINGTON
Apache. New York: 1931. V. 62; 67
Trooper Tales - a Series of Sketches of the Real American Private Soldier. New York: 1899. V. 67

THE COMIC Adventures of Old Mother Hubbard and Her Dog. London: 1820. V. 66

COMINIUS, JOANNES AMOS
Orbis Sensualium Pictus: (Visible World).... New York: 1810. V. 62
Orbis Pictus - Die Welt in Bildern. (The World in Pictures). Leipzig: 1860. V. 64

COMMELIN, CASPARUS
Beschryvinge Van Amsterdam. Amsterdam: 1726. V. 63; 66

COMMEMORATIVE Biographical Record of Fairfield Co., Connecticut. Chicago: 1899. V. 66

COMMERCE and Industry. London. V. 62

COMMERCIAL TRAVELERS' ASSOCIATION OF THE STATE OF CALIFORNIA
Constitution and By-Laws of the Commercial Travelers' Association of the State of California. Incorporated January 18th, 1878. San Francisco: 1878. V. 63

COMMINES, PHILIPPE DE
Les Memoires. Paris: 1572. V. 63; 66
Les Memoires. Geneva: 1593. V. 66
The Memoirs. London: 1712. V. 66

COMMUNICATIONS to the Board of Agriculture, on Subjects Relative to the Husbandry, and Internal Improvement of the Country. London: 1797-1813. V. 62

A COMPANION to Ragland Castle; or, a Familiar Description of That Beautiful and Interesting Ruin: with Biographical Notices.... Monmouth: 1833. V. 64; 65

A COMPANION to the Magdalen-Chapel. London: 1780?. V. 64

A COMPANION to the Theatre; or, a View of Our Most Celebrated Dramatic Pieces. London: 1747. V. 65

COMPARETTI, ANDRE
Occursus Medici de Vaga Aegritudine Infirmitatis Nervorum. Venetiis: 1780. V. 65

A COMPENDIOUS Geographical and Historical Grammar: Exhibiting a Brief Survey of the Terraqueous Globe. London: 1795. V. 62

A COMPENDIOUS Library of the Law, Necessary for Persons of All Degrees and Professions. London: 1740. V. 63

A COMPENDIOUS Library of the Law: Necessary for Persons of All Degrees and Professions. London: 1743. V. 62; 63

A COMPILATION of All the Acts, Resolutions, Reports and Other Documents in Relation to the Bank of the State of South Carolina Affording Full Information Concerning that Institution. Columbia: 1848. V. 66; 67

THE COMPLEAT Clerk, Containing the Best Forms of All Sorts of Presidents for Conveyances and Assurances.... London: 1677. V. 67

A COMPLEAT Collection of all the Verses, Essays, Letters and Advertisements, Which Have Been Occasioned by the Publication of Three Volumes of Miscellanies, by Pope and Company.... London: 1728. V. 62

THE COMPLEAT Drawing Book: Containing Many and Curious Specimens, Under the Following Heads. 1. Select Parts of the Human Body. 2. Heads, with the Various Passions of the Soul. 3. Academy and Groups of Figures. 4. Beasts and Birds of Various Kinds. 5. La. London: 1762. V. 63

A COMPLETE and Comprehensive Description of the Agricultural Stock Raising and Mineral Resources of Utah - also Statistics in Regard to Its Climate, Etc. St. Louis: 1893. V. 63

A COMPLETE Collection of State Trials and Proceedings Upon Impeachments for High Treason and Other Crimes and Misdemeanours; from the Reign of King Henry the Fourth, to the End of the Reign of Queen Anne, (George II). London: 1719-1735. V. 67

THE COMPLETE Farmer; or, a General Dictionary of Husbandry In All Its Branches. 1769. V. 62

THE COMPLETE Farmer; or, a General Dictionary of Husbandry in All Its Branches. London: 1796. V. 65

THE COMPLETE Grazier; or, Gentleman and Farmer's Directory. London: 1767. V. 66

A COMPLETE Guide to All Persons who Have Any Trade or Concern With the City of London and Parts Adjacent.... London: 1752. V. 63

COMPLETE Typophile Chap Book Commentaries: No. 1-30. New York: 1960. V. 64

COMPTON, DENIS
Denis Compton's Test Diary 1964. London: 1964. V. 63

COMPTON, HERBERT
The Twentieth Century Dog. London: 1904. V. 67

THE COMPTON Marbling Portfolio of Patterns. Oxford: 1992. V. 64

COMPTON-BURNETT, IVY
Dolores. Edinburgh and London: 1911. V. 62; 66
A Family and a Fortune. London: 1939. V. 66

COMPTON BURNETT, IVY
A Father and His Fate. London: 1957. V. 66

COMPTON-BURNETT, IVY
A House and Its Head. London: 1935. V. 66
Novels. London: 1972. V. 67
Pastors and Masters. A Study. London: 1925. V. 62; 67

COMRIE, J. D.
History of Scottish Medicine. London: 1932. V. 62

COMSTOCK, FRANCIS ADAMS
A Gothic Vision: F. L. Griggs and His Work. Oxford: 1966. V. 66

COMSTOCK, GEORGE C.
Report of the Comet Committee: Halley's Comet, 1909-1910. 1915. V. 67

COMSTOCK, J. A.
Butterflies of California.... 1927. V. 66
Butterflies of California.... London: 1927. V. 62
Butterflies of California.... Los Angeles: 1927. V. 62; 63; 64

COMSTOCK, J. H.
The Spider, a Manual for...America North of Mexico. New York: 1913. V. 62

COMSTOCK, J. L.
The Young Botanist.... New York: 1835. V. 63

COMSTOCK, W. P.
Butterflies of the American Tropics.... New York: 1961. V. 64
The Housing Book. New York: 1919. V. 65

COMTE, AUGUSTE
The Positive Philosophy. London: 1853. V. 64
The Positive Philosophy. London: 1875. V. 65
System of Positive Polity. London: 1875-1877. V. 64
Traite Elementaire de Geometrie Analytique a Deux et a Trois Dimensions.... Paris: 1843. V. 65

COMTE, T.
Illustrations of Baptismal Fonts. London: 1844. V. 62

COMYN, THOMAS DE
State of the Philippine Islands.... London: 1821. V. 62

CONANT, NORMAN F.
Manual of Clinical Mycology. Philadelphia &: 1944. V. 63

CONANT, R.
The Reptiles of Ohio. Notre Dame: 1938. V. 67

CONAWAY, JAMES
The Big Easy. London: 1971. V. 65

CONCERTS of Antient Music, Under the Patronage of Their Majesties: as Performed at the New Rooms, Tottenham Street. London: 1787-1789. V. 63

CONCIONES Sive Orationes Ex Graecis Latinisque Historicis Excerptae.... Geneva: 1570. V. 66

A CONCISE Description of Bury St. Edmunds and Its Environs With the Distance of Ten Miles.... London: 1827. V. 62; 67

A CONCISE History of Worcester, Containing an Ample and Authentic Description of Whatever is Worthy of Remark in that Ancient City.... Worcester: 1808. V. 63

A CONCISE Introduction to the Knowledge of the Most Eminent Painters.... London: 1778. V. 64

CONCORD, MASSACHUSETTS
Reports of the Selectmen and Other Officers of the Town of Concord, from March 5, 1860 to March 4, 1861. Concord: 1861. V. 63; 64

CONDER, C. R.
Heth & Moab: Explorations in Syria in 1881 and 1882. London: 1883. V. 65

CONDER, CLAUDE REIGNIER
Palestine. London: 1889. V. 62
Tent Work in Palestine. 1878-1879. V. 63

CONDER, FRANCIS R.
Personal Recollections of English Engineers, and of the Introduction of the Railway System Into the United Kingdom. London: 1868. V. 64

CONDER, JAMES
An Arrangement of Provincial Coins, Tokens and Medalets, Issued in Great Britain, Ireland and the Colonies Within the Last Twenty Years.... Ipswich: 1799. V. 63

CONDER, JOSIAH
The Associate Minstrels. London: 1810. V. 66
Landscape Gardening in Japan (with) Supplement to Landscape Gardening in Japan. Tokio: 1893. V. 63; 64
The Theory of Japanese Flower Arrangements. Kobe and London: 1935. V. 63

CONDILLAC, ETIENNE BONNOT DE
Traite des Sensations, a Madame la Comtesse de Vasse. London and Paris: 1754. V. 65

CONDIT, I. J.
The Fig. Waltham: 1947. V. 67

CONDIT, JOTHAM H.
Genealogical Record of the Condit Family. Descedants of John Cundit, a Native of Great Britain, Who Settled in Newark, N.J. N.P: 1916. V. 63; 66

CONDON, RICHARD
The Manchurian Candidate. 1959. V. 67
The Manchurian Candidate. New York: 1959. V. 65; 66

CONDORCET, MARIE JEAN ANTOINE NICOLAS DE CARITAT, MARQUIS DE
A Letter from M. Condorcet...to a Magistrate in Swisserland, Respecting the Massacre of Swiss Guards on the 10th of April, &c. With a Letter from Thomas Paine to the People of France.... New York: 1793. V. 62
The Life of M. Turgot.... London: 1787. V. 62
Vie de Monsieur Turgot. Londres i. e. Paris: 1786. V. 66

CONDRY, WILLIAM M.
The Natural History of Wales. London: 1981. V. 63
The Snowdonia National Park. London: 1966. V. 63; 64

THE CONDUCT of the Stage Consider'd. London: 1721. V. 62; 65

THE CONDUCT of the Tories Consider'd.... London: 1715. V. 66

CONDUCTOR Generalis, or the Office, Duty and Authority of Justices of the Peace.... Philadelphia: 1722. V. 66

CONDUITE Pour la Beinseance Civile et Chretienne.... Oud-Hollandt: 1895. V. 66

THE CONFEDERATE Reveille Memorial Edition. Raleigh: 1898. V. 62; 63

THE CONFEDERATE States Almanac..1862. Nashville: 1862. V. 62

THE CONFEDERATE States Almanac...1865. Macon: 1865. V. 62

CONFEDERATE STATES OF AMERICA. CONSTITUTION
Constitution of the Confederate States of America: Adopted by the Congress of the Confederate States at the City of Montgomery, Alabama, March 11th, 1861. New Orleans: 1861. V. 63; 65

CONFEDERATE STATES OF AMERICA. DEPT. OF THE ARMY
Army Regulations, Adopted for the Use of the Army of the Confederate State, in Accordance with Late Acts of Congress, Revised from the Army Regulations of the Old U.S. Army, 1857. New Orleans: 1861. V. 63
Regulations for the Army of the Confederate States 1862. Richmond: 1862. V. 63
Regulations for the Medical Department of the Confederate States Army. Richmond: 1863. V. 63; 66
Regulations of the Army of the Confederate States. Richmond: 1864. V. 63
Reports of the Operations of the Army of Northern Virginia, from June, 1862 to and Including the Battle of Fredericksburg, Dec. 13, 1862. Richmond: 1864. V. 63

CONFEDERATE STATES OF AMERICA. DEPT. OF THE NAVY
Ordnance Instructions for the Confederate States Navy Relating to the Preparation of Vessels of War for Battle to the Duties of Officers and Others When at Quarters, to Ordnance and Ordnance Stores and to Gunnery.... London: 1864. V. 65
Report of the Secretary of the Navy...November 5, 1864. Richmond: 1864. V. 65

CONFEDERATE STATES OF AMERICA. LAWS, STATUTES, ETC. - 1863
A Bill to Distribute Bounty. Granted as a Reward to the Officers and Men Serving on Board of the Virginia, Patrick Henry, Jamestown, Raleigh, Beaufort and Teazer, for Their Gallantry & Courage in the Naval Engagement with the Enemy' Vessels.... Richmond: 1863. V. 65

CONFEDERATE STATES OF AMERICA. LAWS, STATUTES, ETC. - 1864
A Bill to Be Entitled an Act to Consolidate and Amend the Laws Relative to Impressments. Richmond: 1864. V. 65
A Bill to Increase the Efficiency of the Army, by the Employment of the Free Negroes and Slaves in Certain Capacities. Richmond: 1864. V. 65
The Statutes at Large of the Confederate States of America, Passed at the Third Session of the First Congress, 1863. Richmond: 1864. V. 62
The Statutes at Large of the Provisional Government of the Confederate States of America, from the Institution of the Government Feb. 8, 1861, to Its Termination Feb. 18, 1862.... Richmond: 1864. V. 62

CONFEDERATE STATES OF AMERICA. LAWS, STATUTES, ETC. - 1865
A Bill to Provide for the Establishment of a Bureau for Special and Secret Service. Richmond: 1865. V. 65

CONFEDERATE STATES OF AMERICA. ORDNANCE DEPARTMENT
Regulations for the Government of the Ordnance Department of the Confederate States of America. Richmond: 1862. V. 63

CONFEDERATE STATES OF AMERICA. PRESIDENT
Correspondence Between the President and General Joseph E. Johnston. Together with that of the Secretary of War and the Adjutant and Inspector General During the Months of May, June and July 1863. Richmond: 1864. V. 65
Message of the President. Executive Department, Tallahassee, Dec. 9th, 1864. Richmond: 1864. V. 65
Message of the President. (Submitting the Report of the Commissioners to Confer with the President of the U.S. with a View to the Restoration of Peace). Richmond: 1865. V. 65
Message of the President, to the Senate and House of Representatives of the Confederate States of America. Richmond: 1865. V. 63

CONFEDERATE STATES OF AMERICA. STATE DEPARTMENT
Correspondence of the Department of State, in Relation to the British Consuls Resident in the Confederate States. Richmond: 1863. V. 63

CONFEDERATE STATES OF AMERICA. WAR DEPARTMENT
Army Regulations, Adopted for the Use of the Army of the Confederate State, In Accordance With Late Acts of Congress. New Orleans: 1861. V. 62
Army Regulations Adopted for the Use of the Army of the Confederate States in Accordance with Late Acts of Congress Revised from the Army Regulations of the Old U.S. Army 1857.... Richmond: 1861. V. 62
General Orders from Adjutant and Inspector-General's Office, Confederate States Army, From January, 1862 to December, 1863 (both inclusive). In Two Series. Columbia: 1864. V. 62
General Orders from Adjutant and Inspector-General's Office, Confederate States Army in 1862.... Charleston: 1864. V. 62
General Orders from the Adjutant and Inspector General's Office, Confederate States Army, for the Year 1863.... Richmond: 1864. V. 62
General Orders from the Adjutant and Inspector General's Office, Confederate States Army from Jan. 1, 1864 to July 1, 1864.... Columbia: 1864. V. 62
A Manual of Military Surgery Prepared for the Use of the C.S.A. Richmond: 1863. V. 62; 65
Regulations for the Army of the Confederate States, 1862. Richmond: 1862. V. 62
Regulations for the Army of the Confederate States, 1863. Richmond: 1863. V. 62
Regulations for the Medical Department of the C. S. Army. Richmond: 1863. V. 62
Report of the Secretary of War...November 3, 1864. Richmond: 1864. V. 65
Report of Vessels Sunk and Burnt in Thepamunkey River, by Captain Chas. S. Carrington.... Richmond: 1863. V. 62
Reports of the Operations of the Army of Northern Virginia, from June 1861 to and Including the Battle of Fredericksburg, Dec. 13, 1862. Richmond: 1864. V. 62

CONFEDERATED SOUTHERN MEMORIAL ASSOCIATION
History of the Unconfederated Memorial Associations of the South. New Orleans?: 1904. V. 66

A CONFESSION of Faith Owned and Consented to by the Elders and Messengers of the Churches in the Colony of Connecticut in New England. New London: 1760. V. 62; 64

CONFIGLIACHI, PIETRO
Giornale di Fisica, Chimica, Storia Naturale Medicina et Arti... Compilato dal Dott. Gaspare Brugnatelli. Decade Secondo Tomo II (-Decade II. Tomo II). Pavia: 1819-1820. V. 65

CONFUCIUS
The Confucian Analects. Washington: 1951. V. 62
The Morals of Confucius, a Chinese Philosopher. London: 1780. V. 67
The Unwobbling Pivot and the Great Digest. Bombay, Calcutta and Madras: 1949. V. 62

CONGRESSIONAL Directory for the First Session of the Nineteenth Congress of the United States. Washington: 1825. V. 65

CONGREVE, RICHARD
Essays, Political, Social and Religious (and Historical Lectures). London: 1874-1900. V. 64

CONGREVE, WILLIAM
The Way of the World, a Comedy. London: 1700. V. 64; 66
The Way of the World and Love for Love. London: 1929. V. 63
The Works. London: 1710. V. 66
Works. London: 1730. V. 64; 65
The Works. Birmingham: 1761. V. 62; 63; 64; 66; 67

CONKLING, MARGARET COCKBURN
The American Gentleman's Guide to Politeness and Fashion.... New York: 1860. V. 65

CONKLING, ROSCOE P.
The Butterfield Overland Mail.... Glendale: 1947. V. 63; 64; 66; 67

CONN, RICHARD
Native American Art in the Denver Museum. Denver: 1979. V. 63; 64

CONNAGHTON
An Authentic Report of the Speech of the Celebrated and Eloquent Irish Barrister, Mr. Phillips, Delivered at Roscommon Assizes, 1816, on a Trial for Seduction. London: 1816. V. 63

CONNECTICUT MEDICAL SOCIETY
Report of a Committee of the Connecticut Medical Society, Respecting an Asylum for the Insane, with the Constitution of the Society for Their Relief. Hartford: 1821. V. 64

CONNELL, EVAN S.
The Anatomy Lesson and Other Stories. New York: 1957. V. 62; 64; 66
The Connoisseur. New York: 1974. V. 64
The Diary of a Rapist. New York: 1966. V. 65
Mesa Verde. New York: 1993. V. 64; 67
Mrs. Bridge. New York: 1959. V. 65
Son of the Morning Star. San Francisco: 1984. V. 62; 63; 64; 65; 67

CONNELL, ROBERT
Arkansas. New York: 1947. V. 66

CONNELLEY, WILLIAM ELSEY
Doniphan's Expedition and the Conquest of New Mexico. Kansas City: 1907. V. 65
Doniphan's Expedition and the Conquest of New Mexico and California. Topeka: 1907. V. 62; 65
The Life of Preston B. Plumb 1837-1891. Chicago: 1913. V. 67
The Provisional Government of Nebraska Territory and the Journals of William Walker, Provisional Governor of Nebraska Territory. Lincoln: 1899. V. 67
Quantrill and the Border Wars. Cedar Rapids: 1910. V. 62; 63; 65; 66
War With Mexico 1846-1847. Doniphan's Expedition and the Conquest of New Mexico and California. Kansas City: 1907. V. 65
Wild Bild and His Era. New York: 1933. V. 65; 66

CONNELLY, MARC
The Green Pastures. New York: 1929. V. 64; 67

CONNELLY, MICHAEL
The Black Echo. Boston: 1992. V. 62; 63; 64; 65; 66; 67
The Black Ice. Boston: 1993. V. 67
Blood Work. Boston: 1997. V. 67
Blood Work. Tucson: 1997. V. 63; 65; 66
Blood Work. Tucson: 1998. V. 67
The Concrete Blonde. Boston: 1994. V. 67
The Last Coyote. Boston: 1995. V. 67
The Poet. Boston: 1996. V. 67
Void Moon. Tucson: 1999. V. 63; 65; 66; 67

CONNER, J. D.
Belgian Draft Horses. Volume V. National Register. Wabash: 1913. V. 66

CONNER, JAMES
Letters of General James Conner, C.S.A. Columbia: 1950. V. 62

CONNETT, EUGENE
Fishing a Trout Stream. 1934. V. 67
My Friend the Trout. 1961. V. 67

CONNEY, MRS.
A Ruthless Avenger. London: 1893. V. 65

CONNICK, CHARLES J.
Adventures in Light and Color. New York: 1937. V. 62; 65
Stained Glass. Adventures in Light and Color. New York: 1937. V. 62

CONNINGTON, J. J.
Gold Brick Island. Boston: 1933. V. 66
Jack-in-the Box. Boston: 1944. V. 66

CONNOLD, E. T.
British Oak Galls. London: 1908. V. 62
British Vegetable Galls. 1901. V. 66
British Vegetable Galls. London: 1901. V. 62
British Vegetable Galls. New York: 1902. V. 63; 66

CONNOLLY, CHRISTOPHER P.
The Devil Learns to Vote - the Story of Montana. New York: 1938. V. 64; 67

CONNOLLY, CYRIL
The Condemned Playground. Essays 1927-1944. London: 1945. V. 67
Enemies of Promise. London: 1938. V. 62; 64; 65; 67
Enemies of Promise. London: 1949. V. 67
The Golden Horizon. London: 1953. V. 64
Ideas and Places. London: 1953. V. 67
The Modern Movement, One Hundred Key Books from England, France and America 1880-1950. London: 1965. V. 62
Previous Convictions. Selected Writings of a Decade. New York and Evanston: 1963. V. 67
The Rock Pool. Paris: 1936. V. 62; 65
The Rock Pool. New York: 1937. V. 66
The Unquiet Grave. London: 1944. V. 62; 65
The Unquiet Grave. London: 1945. V. 66

CONNOLLY, JAMES
Erin's Hope. The Ends and the Means. Rutherglen: 1897?. V. 63; 66
The New Evangel. Dublin: 1917. V. 63
Socialism and Nationalism, a Selection from the Writings of James Connolly. 1948. V. 67

CONNOLLY, JOHN
Dark Hollow. London: 2000. V. 67
Every Dead Thing. London: 1999. V. 65; 66; 67

CONNOLLY, JOSEPH
Modern First Editions: Their Value to Collectors. London: 1987. V. 67

CONNOR, D. R.
BG Off the Record. A Bio/Discography of Benny Goodman. Fairless Hills: 1958. V. 65

CONNOR, ROBERT DIGGES WIMBERLY
Cornelius Harnett. An Essay in North Carolina History. Raleigh: 1909. V. 67

CONOLLY, JOHN
An Inquiry Concerning the Indications of Insanity with Suggestions. London: 1830. V. 62; 65
The Treatment of the Insane Without Mechanicl Restraints. London: 1856. V. 65

CONOR, WILLIAM
The Irish Scene. 1944. V. 62; 65

CONOVER, G. W.
Sixty Years in Southwest Oklahoma or the Autobiography of.... 1927. V. 67
Sixty Years in Southwest Oklahoma, or the Autobiography of.... Anadarko: 1927. V. 65

CONOVER, TED
Rolling Nowhere. New York: 1984. V. 63; 64; 66

CONRAD, DAVID H.
Memoir of Rev. James Chisholm, AM.M., Late Rector of St. John's Church, Portsmouth, Va.... New York: 1856. V. 67
Memoir of Rev. James Chisholm, AM.M. Late Rector of St. John's Church, Portsmouth, Va.... New York: 1857. V. 67

CONRAD, HOWARD LOUIS
Uncle Dick Wootten, the Pioneer Frontiersman of the Rocky Mountain Region. Chicago: 1890. V. 63; 64; 67

CONRAD, J. M.
Natural Resource Economics, Notes and Problems. Cambridge: 1987. V. 64

CONRAD, JESSIE
Handbook of Cookery for a Small House. Garden City: 1923. V. 67
Simple Cooking Precepts for a Little House. London: 1921. V. 62

CONRAD, JOSEPH
Arrow of Gold. New York: 1919. V. 67
Chance. London: 1914. V. 66
The Collected Works. Garden City: 1925. V. 63; 64
Conrad's Manifesto - Preface to a Career.... Philadelphia: 1966. V. 65
The Dover Patrol - a Tribute. Canterbury: 1922. V. 62
Five Letters by Joseph Conrad - Written to Edward Noble in 1895. London: 1925. V. 65
The Inheritors. London: 1901. V. 64; 66
The Inheritors. New York: 1901. V. 67
Last Essays. London: 1926. V. 64
Laughing Anne. London: 1923. V. 64
A Letter from John Galsworthy to Joseph Conrad. London: 1926. V. 64
Lord Jim. Edinburgh: 1906. V. 67
The Mirror of the Sea: Memories and Impressions. London: 1906. V. 62; 63; 66
The Mirror of the Sea: Memories and Impressions. New York: 1906. V. 66
Nostromo: a Tale of the Seaboard. London: 1904. V. 63; 64; 66
Notes by Joseph Conrad - Written in a Set of His First editions in the Possession of Richard Curle. London: 1925. V. 65
Notes on My Books. London: 1921. V. 64
Notes on My Books. New York and Toronto: 1921. V. 64
One Day More. London: 1919. V. 64
An Outcast of the Islands. London: 1896. V. 63; 65
The Point of Honor. New York: 1908. V. 62
The Rescue. London: 1920. V. 63
The Rover. London: 1923. V. 65; 67
The Secret Agent. London: 1907. V. 63
The Secret Agent. London: 1923. V. 65
The Secret Sharer. 1985. V. 62
A Set of Six. London: 1908. V. 63; 64; 66
The Shadow-Line: a Confession. London: 1917. V. 62; 63; 64; 66
The Sisters. New York: 1928. V. 63; 64; 65; 66
Suspense. Garden City: 1925. V. 63; 64; 66
Suspense. London and Toronto: 1925. V. 62; 65; 66
Suspense. New York: 1925. V. 62; 63
Tales of Hearsay. London: 1925. V. 63; 64
Tales of Unrest. Leipzig: 1898. V. 67
Tales of Unrest. London: 1898. V. 66
Typhoon. New York: 1902. V. 63; 64; 66
Typhoon and Other Stories. London: 1903. V. 62; 66; 67
Under Western Eyes. New York: 1911. V. 66
Within the Tides. London: 1915. V. 64
The Works. London and Edinburgh: 1925. V. 66
Youth: a Narrative and Two Other Stories. Edinburgh and London: 1902. V. 62; 67
Youth: a Narrative and Two Other Stories. Edinburgh: 1909. V. 67

CONRAD, L. J.
Bibliography of Antarctic Exploration Expedition Account from 1768 to 1960. Washington: 1999. V. 65; 66

CONRAD, THOMAS NELSON
Rebel Scout, a Thrilling History of Scouting Life in the Southern Army. Washington: 1904. V. 62; 63

CONRAD, TIMOTHY ABBOTT
A Geological Vision and Other Poems. Trenton: 1871. V. 63; 66

CONRADS, U.
The Architecture of Fantasy: Utopian Buildings and Planning. New York: 1962. V. 65

CONROY, FRANK
Stop-Time. New York: 1967. V. 63; 65

CONROY, J. W.
The Northern Barrage. Mine Force United States Atlantic Fleet the North Sea 1918. Annapolis: 1919. V. 64

CONROY, JACK
A World to Win. New York: 1935. V. 63

CONROY, PAT
Beach Music. New York: 1995. V. 63; 65; 67
The Boo. Verona: 1970. V. 62
The Boo. Atlanta: 1988. V. 63
The Great Santini. Boston: 1976. V. 62; 64; 67
Lords of Discipline. Boston: 1980. V. 62; 63; 64; 66; 67
The Prince of Tides. Boston: 1986. V. 63
Thomas Wolfe. Atlanta: 2000. V. 67
The White Paper. New York: 1958. V. 65

CONSELMAN, DIERDRE
Keedle. New York: 1940. V. 62

CONSEQUENCES - A Complete Story in the Manner of the Old Parlour Game in Nine Chapters. Waltham St. Lawrence: 1932. V. 63

THE CONSEQUENCES of a Scientific Education to the Working Classes of this Country Pointed Out and the Theories of Mr. Brougham on that Subject Confuted; in a Letter to the Marquess of Lansdown. London: 1826. V. 64

CONSETT, MATTHEW
A Tour through Sweden, Swedish-Lapland, Finland and Denmark. Stockton: 1789. V. 67
A Tour through Sweden, Swedish-Lapland, Finland and Denmark. Stockton: 1815. V. 66

CONSIDERATIONS Against Laying Any New Duty Upon Sugar; Wherein is Particularly Shewn, That a New Imposition Will be Ruinous to the Suga onies.... London: 1744. V. 63

CONSIDERATIONS in Favour of the Appointment of Rufus King, to the Senate of the United States. Submitted to the Republican Members of the Legislature of...New York. New York: 1819. V. 63

CONSIDERATIONS On the Danger and Impolicy of Laying Open the Trade with India and China; Including an Examination of the Objections Commonly Urged Against the East India Company's Commercial and Financial Management. London: 1812. V. 63

CONSIDERATIONS Upon a Proposal for Lowering the Interest Of All the Redeemable National Debts to Three Per Cent...to Give Immediate Ease to His Majesty's Subjects.... London: 1737. V. 63

CONSTABLE, HENRY
Poems and Sonnets. London: 1897. V. 62

CONSTABLE, JOHN
The Conversation of Gentlemen Considered in Most of the Ways, that Make Their Mutual Company Agreeable, or Disagreeable. London: 1738. V. 65
Correspondence. (with) Constable's Discourses. (and) Further Documents and Correspondence. London: 1975. V. 63
English Landscape Scenery: a Series of Forty Mezzotint Engravings on Steel, by David Lucas. London: 1855. V. 66

CONSTABLE, THOMAS
Archibald Constable and His Literary Correspondents.... Edinburgh: 1873. V. 65

CONSTABLE, W. G.
Canaletto. Oxford: 1976. V. 66

CONSTABLE, WILLIAM
The Early (and Later) Paintings and Drawings of John Constable. New Haven: 1996. V. 67

THE CONSTANT Lovers; or the Histories of Mr. Franklin and Miss Calden and Mr. Welford and Miss Byersley.... London: 178-?. V. 66

CONSTANT, SAMUEL VICTOR
Calls, Sounds and Merchandise of the Peking Street Peddlers. Newtown: 1993. V. 64

CONSTANT DE REBECQUE, FRANCOIS MARC SAMUEL
Instructions de Morale, a l'Usage des Enfans Qui Commencent a Penser. Londres (Paris?): 1785. V. 63

CONSTANTINE, K. C.
The Man Who Liked Slow Tomatoes. Boston: 1981. V. 62
The Man Who Liked Slow Tomatoes. Boston: 1982. V. 67
The Man Who Liked to Look at Himself. 1973. V. 65; 66
The Man who Liked to Look at Himself. New York: 1973. V. 65; 67
Upon Some Midnights Clear. London: 1985. V. 67

CONSTANTINE, MILDRED
Tina Modotti: a Fragile Life. New York: 1975. V. 63

CONSTANTINUS
Lexicon Graecolatinum Rob. Constantini Secunda hac Editione.... 1592. V. 66

CONSTANTINUS AFRICANUS
Constantini Africani Post Hippocratem et Galenvm Qvorum, Graece Lingvae Doctus Sedulus Suit Lector, Medicoru Nulli Prorsus.... Basilease: 1536. V. 62

CONSTITUTIONAL Charter of the Kingdom Of Poland in the Year 1815, With Some Remarks On the Manner in Which the Charter, and the Stipulations in the Treaties Relating to Poland, Have Been Observed...Sold for the Benefit of the Military Hospitals.... London: 1831. V. 67

CONSTITUTIONAL Letters, in Answer to Mr. Paine's Rights of Man. London: 1792. V. 64

CONTEMPORARY Art: Thirty Etchings and Chromolithographs After the Original Pictures by Eminent Artists of the Present Day. London: 1876. V. 64

THE CONTINENTAL SYSTEM and Its Relations with Sweden. London: 1813. V. 63

THE CONTINENTAL Tourist and Pictorial Companion.... London: 1840. V. 67

THE CONTINENTAL Tourist: Belgium and Nassau. London: 1840. V. 64

A CONTINUATION of the State of New England; Being a Farther Account of the Indian Warr.... London: 1676. V. 63

CONTRIBUTIONS to a History of the Richmond Howitzer Batallion. Richmond: 1886. V. 64

CONTRIBUTIONS to Medical and Biological Research Dedicated to Sir William Osler, in Honor of His Seventieth Birthday July 12, 1919.... New York: 1919. V. 63; 64; 67

CONTRIBUTIONS To the Medical Sciences in Honor of Dr. Emanuel Libman by His Pupils, Friends and Colleagues. New York: 1932. V. 63

CONVERSE, H. M.
Myths and Legends of the New York State Iroquois. 1908. V. 62

THE CONVIVIAL Jester, or Bane of Melancholy.... 1800. V. 66
THE CONVIVIAL Jester, or Bane of Melancholy.... London: 1800. V. 62

CONWAY, J. M.
Climbing On the Himalaya and Other Mountain Ranges. 1902. V. 63; 65

CONWAY, MARTIN
Catalogue of the Loan Exhibition of Flemish and Belgian Art, Burlington House.... London: 1927. V. 67
No Man's Land. Cambridge: 1906. V. 62
With Ski and Sledge over Arctic Glaciers. London: 1898. V. 64

CONWAY, MONCURE DANIEL
Barons of the Potomack and Rappanock. New York: 1892. V. 62
The Life of Thomas Paine with a History of His Literary Political and Religious Career in America, France and England. New York and London: 1892. V. 64
The Voysey Case, from an Heretical Stand Point. Ramsgate: 1871. V. 67

CONWAY, WILLIAM MARTIN
Aconcagua and Tierra Del Fuego. London: 1902. V. 63; 64
The Alps. London: 1904. V. 63; 64; 65; 66
The Alps from End to End. London: 1895. V. 62; 63; 64
The Alps from End to End. Westminster: 1895. V. 65
The Bolivian Andes. 1901. V. 63; 65
The Bolivian Andes; a Record of Climing and Exploration in the Cordillera Real in the Years 1898 and 1900. New York: 1901. V. 64
Climbing and Exploration in the Karakoram-Himalayas. 1894. V. 63; 65
Climbing and Exploration in the Karakoram-Himalayas. London: 1894. V. 63; 64
Episodes in a Varied Life. London: 1932. V. 64

CONWELL, RUSSELL H.
Woman and the Law. Boston: 1875. V. 65

CONYBEARE, FRED C.
The Dreyfus Case. London: 1898. V. 64

CONYBEARE, W. D.
Outlines of the Geology of England and Wales. 1822. V. 62; 64; 67
Outlines of the Geology of England and Wales. London: 1822. V. 64; 65; 66
Outlines of the Geology of England and Wales. 1882. V. 67

CONYERS, ANSLEY
Chesterleigh. London: 1873. V. 66

COODE, JOHN
Report to the Coleraine Town Improvement Commissioners. Coleraine: 1878. V. 63; 66

COOK, ARTHUR BERNARD
Zeus: a Study in Ancient Religion.... New York: 1964. V. 65

COOK, CHARLES
Among the Pimas or the Mission to the Pima and Maricopa Indians. Albany: 1893. V. 66
Personal Experiences in the Prisons of the World, with Stories of Crime, Criminals and Convicts. London: 1902. V. 63

COOK, CHARLES H.
The Book of the All-Round Angler. London: 1904. V. 67

COOK, CHARLES L.
Trial (Before the Municipal Court) of Charles L. Cook, Late Preacher of the Gospel of the Orthodox and Restorationist Denominations, for Receiving Stolen Goods. Boston: 1835. V. 66

COOK, CYRIL
The Life and Work of Robert Hancock. London: 1948. V. 62; 66

COOK, D. J.
Hands Up or Thirty-five Years of Detective Life in the Mountains and on the Plains. Denver: 1897. V. 63; 66

COOK, E. T.
The Life of John Ruskin. London: 1912. V. 65

COOK, ELLIOTT WILKINSON
Land Ho! - The Diary of a Forty-Niner. Baltimore: 1935. V. 65

COOK, F.
Invitation to the Garden, a Literary and Photographic Celebration. New York: 1992. V. 67

COOK, FREDERICK A.
My Attainment of the Pole. New York: 1911. V. 63
Through the First Antarctic Night 1898-1899. A Narrative of the Belgica. New York: 1900. V. 65
To the Top of the Continent. New York: 1908. V. 62

COOK, GEORGE H.
Geology of New Jersey. Newark: 1868. V. 63; 66

COOK, HARVEY TOLIVER
The Hard Labor Section. Greenville: 1924. V. 63
Rambles in the Pee Dee Basin, South Carolina. Volume I. (all published). Columbia: 1926. V. 63; 66; 67

COOK, JAMES
An Abridgment of Captain Cook's First and Second Voyages. London: 1788. V. 64
The Charts and Coastal Views of Captain Cook's Voyage. Volume One. The Voyage of the Endeavour 1768-1771. Volume Two. The Voyage of the Resolution and Adventure 1772-1775. London: 1988-1992. V. 63
A Complete Set of Cook's Voyages. London: 1773-. V. 66
James Cook Surveyor of Newfoundland. San Francisco: 1965. V. 66
The Journals of Captain James Cook on His Voyages of Discovery. Glasgow: 1961-1974. V. 66
The Journal of H.M.S. Resolution (1772-1775). Guildford: 1981. V. 64
A Voyage to the Pacific Ocean...1776, 1777, 1778, 1779 and 1780. London: 1785. V. 64
A Voyage Towards the South Pole and Round the World...in the Years 1772, 1773, 1774 and 1775. London: 1777. V. 64
Voyages Round the World, Performed by Captain James Cook, F.R.S. London: 1822. V. 62

COOK, JOHN R.
The Border and the Buffalo, an Untold Story of the Southwest Plains. Topeka: 1907. V. 64; 67

COOK, M. T.
Ecological Survey of the Flora of Porto Rico. Rio Pedras: 1928. V. 64

COOK, MARGARET
America's Charitable Cooks. Kent: 1971. V. 64

COOK, MOSES
The Manner of Raising, Ordering and Improving Forest and Fruit Trees, also, How to Plant, Make and Keep Woods, Walks, Avenues, Lawns, Hedges &c. Also Rules and Tables Shewing How the Ingenious Planter May Measure Superficial Figures. London: 1679. V. 63; 67

THE COOK Not Mad, or Rational Cookery.... Watertown: 1830. V. 63

COOK, OLIVE
Movement in Two Dimensions. London: 1963. V. 63; 66
The Sense of Continuity in a Heretfordshrie Parrish. A Study of Anstey. 1969. V. 63

COOK, ROBIN
The Legacy of the Stiff Upper Lip or Astonishing Social Hinterland of a Lapse. London: 1980. V. 64; 65

COOK, ROY B.
The Annals of Fort Lee. Charleston: 1935. V. 67
Lewis County in the Civil War 1861-1865. Charleston: 1924. V. 64
Washington's Western Lands. Strasburg: 1930. V. 66

COOK, SPRUILL
J. Frank Dobie Bibliography. Waco: 1968. V. 65

COOK, STANLEY
A Was an Angler. London: 1890. V. 64

COOK, T. A.
Twenty-Five Great Houses of France. London. V. 62; 65

COOK, TENNESSEE CELESTE
Constitutional Equality a Right of Woman; or a Consideration of the Various Relations which She Sustains as a Necessary Part of the Body of Society and Humanity. New York: 1871. V. 63; 64
Essays on Social Topics. Westminster, London: 1895?. V. 62

COOK, THOMAS, & SON
Egypt and the Nile. London: 1902. V. 64

COOK, THOMAS H.
The Orchids. Boston: 1982. V. 65; 66; 67

COOK, WARREN L.
Flood Tide of Empire, Spain and the Pacific Northwest - 1543-1819. New Haven: 1973. V. 67

COOKE, ALISTAIR
Garbo and the Night Watchmen.... London: 1937. V. 65

COOKE, CHARLES
Cooke's Pocket Edition of Select British Poets. London: 1795-1801. V. 67

COOKE, EDWARD
A Voyage to the South Sea, and Round the World Performed in the Years 1708, 1709, 1710 and 1711...Wherein an Account is Given of Mr. Alexander Selkirk.. London: 1712. V. 64; 66

COOKE, G. A.
A Topographical and Statistical Description of the County of Cumberland.... London. V. 66
A Topographical and Statistical Description of the County of Cumberland.... London: 1829. V. 62
A Topographical and Statistical Description of the County of Lancaster.... London: 1805. V. 62
A Topographical and Statistical Description of the County of Lancaster.... London: 1822. V. 65
Views in London and Its Vicinty. London: 1834. V. 63
Walks through London; or a Picture of the British Metropolis. London: 1833. V. 62

COOKE, GEORGE P.
Moolelo O Molokai: a Ranch Story of Molokai. Honolulu: 1949. V. 62; 65

COOKE, GILES B.
Just Before and After Lee Surrendered to Grant. Houston: 1922. V. 62; 63

COOKE, J. P.
First Principles of Chemical Philosophy. Cambridge: 1868. V. 62

COOKE, JOHN ESTEN
An Essay on the Invalidity of Presbyterian Ordination. Lexington: 1829. V. 66
Leather Stocking and Silk; or, Hunger John Myers and His Times.... New York: 1854. V. 62
A Life of Gen. Robert E. Lee. New York: 1871. V. 62; 63
The Life of Stonewall Jackson. New York: 1863. V. 65
The Life of Stonewall Jackson. Richmond: 1863. V. 62; 63; 65
Stonewall Jackson. New York: 1866. V. 64
Stonewall Jackson: a Military Biography. New York: 1876. V. 62; 63
Wearing of the Gray. New York: 1867. V. 63, 64
The Wearing of the Gray. Bloomington: 1959. V. 63

COOKE, LAYTON
The Agricultural Referee, and Guide to the Valuation of Real Property, Which Indicates the Rent and Probable Amount of Profit to be Derived from the Cultivation of the Various Descriptions of Land. London: 1850. V. 63

COOKE, M. C.
Microscopic Fungi. London: 1886. V. 62
A Plain and Easy Account of British Fungi.... Geneva: 1911. V. 62

COOKE, MAUDE C.
Great 20th Century Cook Book: Three Meals a Day. Chicago: 1902. V. 67

COOKE, NICHOLAS F.
Satan in Society. Cincinnati: 1872. V. 65

COOKE, PERCIVAL
The Confession of Percival Cooke and James Tomlinson, Who Were Executed on Friday April 10, 1812.... Nottingham: 1812. V. 63

COOKE, PHILIP ST. GEORGE
The Conquest of New Mexico and California. New York: 1878. V. 62
Exploring Southwestern Trails 1846-1854. Glendale: 1938. V. 64
Report of...Journal of Captain A. R. Johnston, First Dragoon. Washington: 1848. V. 64

COOKE, THOMAS
A Letter to Mar Milbank, Esq., M.P. of Thorp Hall, and Barningham, in the County of York.... London: 1823. V. 62

COOKE, WILLIAM
The Life of Samuel Johnson, LL.D. London: 1785. V. 64
Memoirs of Charles Macklin, Comedian. London: 1806. V. 65
A Practical and Pathological Enquiry into the Sources and Effects of Derangements of the Digestive Organs, Embracing Dejection and Some Afflictions of the Mind. London: 1828. V. 63

COOK'S Own Book and Housekeeper's Register. Boston: 1845. V. 67

COOKSON, WILLIAM
Agenda - An Anthology. The First Four Decades 1959-1993. Manchester and Riverdale-on-: 1994. V. 64

COOLBRITH, INA
Songs from the Golden Gate. New York: 1895. V. 62

COOLEY, G. E.
On the Reserve Cellulose of the Seeds of Liliaceae and of Some Related Orders. Boston: 1895. V. 63; 64

COOLEY, J. E.
Extracts from Humbugiana; or the World's Convention. Gotham (i.e. New York): 1847. V. 63

COOLEY, TIMOTHY MATHER
Sketches of the Life and Character of the Rev. Lemuel Haynes for Many Years Pastor of a Church in Rutland, Vt. and Late in Granville New York. New York: 1839. V. 63

COOLEY, W. D.
The History of Maritime and Inland Discovery. London: 1830. V. 67
The World Surveyed in the XIX Century.... London: 1845. V. 64

COOLEY'S Cyclopedia of Practical Receipt and Collateral Information on the Arts, Manufactures, Professions and Trades, Including Medicine, Pharmacy and Domestic Economy.... New York: 1891. V. 64

COOLIDGE, CALVIN
The Autobiography of Calvin Coolidge. New York: 1929. V. 63

COOLIDGE, D.
Arizona Cowboys. New York: 1938. V. 67
Old California Cowboys. New York: 1939. V. 67

COOLIDGE, H. J.
A Revision of the Genus Gorilla. Cambridge: 1929. V. 66

COOLIDGE, HAROLD J.
Three Kingdoms of Indochina. New York: 1933. V. 64

COOLIDGE, JULIAN LOWELL
The Mathematics of Great Amateurs. Oxford: 1950. V. 63

COOLIDGE, MARY R.
The Navajo Indians. Boston: 1930. V. 65

COOLIDGE, SUSAN
What Katy Did. London: 1873. V. 65

COOLIDGE, W. A. B.
The Alps in Nature and History. London: 1908. V. 64
The Central Alps of the Dauphiny. London: 1905. V. 62
Guide to Switzerland. London: 1901. V. 63; 64

COOMBE, FLORENCE
Islands of Enchantment. London: 1911. V. 64

COONEY, ROBERT
The Autobiography of a Wesleyan Methodist Missionary (formerly a Roman Catholic). Montreal: 1856. V. 67

COONEY, SEAMUS
The Black Sparrow Press: a Checklist of the First One Hundred Publications of the Black Sparrow Press. Los Angeles: 1971. V. 66

COONTS, STEPHEN
Flight of the Intruder. Annapolis: 1986. V. 63; 67

COOPER, A.
The Complete Domestic Distiller.... London: 1826. V. 62

COOPER, ASTLEY
The Anatomy and Surgical Treatment of Inguinal and Congenital Hernia. London: 1804. V. 66
Illustrations of the Diseases of the Breast...Part I. London: 1829. V. 65
A Series of Lectures on the Most Approved Principles and Practice of Modern Surgery.... Boston: 1823. V. 64; 66; 67
Oeuvres Chirurgicales Completes.... Brussels: 1835. V. 65

COOPER, BERNARD
Maps to Anywhere. Athens: 1990. V. 67

COOPER, BRANSBY B.
Lectures on the Principles and Practice of Surgery. Philadelphia: 1852. V. 67
The Life of Sir Astley Cooper, Bart.... London: 1843. V. 65
Surgical Essays: The Result of Clinical Observations Made at Guy's Hospital. London: 1843. V. 66; 67

COOPER, CHARLES HENRY
Athenae Cantabrigienses 1500-1609. Cambridge: 1858-1861. V. 62

COOPER, CLARENCE LEVI
The Farm. New York: 1967. V. 66
Weed. Illinois: 1961. V. 66

COOPER, DIANA
The Rainbow Comes and Goes. The Light of Common Day. Trumpets from the Steep. London: 1958-1960. V. 66

COOPER, DOUGLAS
Picasso Theatre. New York: 1987. V. 63; 64
The Work of Graham Sutherland. London: 1962. V. 63

COOPER, EDMUND
Muker: the Story of a Yorkshire Parish. London: 1948. V. 65

COOPER, EDWARD H.
Wyemarke and the Mountain Fairies. London: 1912. V. 67

COOPER, ELIZABETH
The Harim and the Purdah; Studies of Oriental Women. London: 1915. V. 64

COOPER, FRANK C.
Stirring Lives of Buffalo Bill and Pawnee Bill. New York: 1912. V. 67

COOPER, FREDERICK FOX
A Tale of Two Cities. London: 1885. V. 62

COOPER, G.
Permian Brachiopods of West Texas. Washington: 1972-1977. V. 62

COOPER, G. C.
Colchester Town Hall. A Brief History. 1988. V. 65

COOPER, GEORGE A.
Some Works of Art in the Possession Of.... London: 1903. V. 64

COOPER, J. C.
Military History of Yamhill County. McMinnville: 1899. V. 67

COOPER, J. W.
Game Fowls, Their Origin and History.... West Chester: 1869. V. 63; 67

COOPER, JAMES FENIMORE
The American Democrat, or Hints on the Social and Civic Relations of the United States of America. Cooperstown: 1838. V. 66
The Battle of Lake Erie, or Answers to Messrs. Burges, Duer, and MacKenzie. Cooperstown: 1843. V. 67
The Bravo: a Venetian Story. London: 1831. V. 62
The Bravo: a Venetian Story. London: 1834. V. 67
The Bravo: a Venetian Story. 1836. V. 67
The Deerslayer. Philadelphia: 1841. V. 62; 63; 64
The Deerslayer. London: 1841. V. 66
The Headsman; or, the Abbaye des Vignerons. London: 1833. V. 62; 67
The Heidenmauer; or the Benedictines. Philadelphia: 1832. V. 62; 64
The History of the Navy of the United States of America. London: 1839. V. 64
The History of the Navy of the United States of America. Philadelphia: 1839. V. 64
Homeward Bound; or the Chase. A Tale of the Sea. Philadelphia: 1838. V. 62; 64; 67
The Last of the Mohicans. Paris: 1826. V. 64
The Last of the Mohicans. New York: 1919. V. 63
Lionel Lincoln; or the Leaguer of Boston. London: 1825. V. 62; 64
Lucy Hardinge: a Second Series of Afloat and Ashore. London: 1854. V. 62; 65
Notions of the Americans: Picked Up by a Travelling Bachelor. London: 1828. V. 67
The Pathfinder; or, The Inland Sea. London: 1840. V. 65
The Pathfinder; or, the Inland Sea. Philadelphia: 1840. V. 63
The Pathfinder; or, the Inland Sea. London: 1850. V. 67
The Pilot. London: 1837. V. 67
The Pilot. London: 1849. V. 67
The Pioneers, or the Sources of the Susquehanna.... New York: 1823. V. 64
The Pioneers, or the Sources of the Susquehanna.... London: 1849. V. 67
The Prairie. London: 1827. V. 62
The Prairie. Philadelphia: 1827. V. 62; 64
The Prairie. London: 1836-1837. V. 67
The Red Rover; a Tale. London: 1848. V. 67
Sketches of Switzerland. Philadelphia: 1836. V. 62; 64; 67
The Spy, a Tale of the Neutral Ground. Leipzig: 1842. V. 67
The Two Admirals. Philadelphia: 1842. V. 62; 64; 67
The Two Admirals. London: 1844. V. 67
The Water Witch; or, The Skimmer of the Seas. London: 1850. V. 67
The Wept of Wish Ton-Wish: a Tale. Philadelphia: 1829. V. 62; 64; 67

COOPER, JANE
Letters Wrote by Jane Cooper, to Which is Prefixt Some Account of Her Life and Death. London: 1764. V. 64

COOPER, JOHN
Artists in Crime: an Illustrated Survey of Crime Fiction First Edition Dust Wrappers 1920-1970. Aldershot: 1995. V. 66
Detective Fiction: the Collector's Guide. Aldershot: 1994. V. 66; 67
A Report of the Proceedings Against Abraham Thornton, at Warwick Summer Assizes, 1817 for the Murder of Mary Ashford.... Warwick: 1818. V. 63
The Warwickshire Hunt, from 1795 to 1836.. London: 1837. V. 64

COOPER, JOHN GILBERT
Cursory Remarks on Mr. Warburton's New Edition of Mr. Pope's Works. London: 1751. V. 62

COOPER, JOSEPH
Domus Mosaicae; sive Legis Sepimentum. London: 1673. V. 63
The Lost Continent; or, Slavery and the Slave Trade in Africa 1875. London: 1875. V. 63; 64; 66; 67

COOPER, R.
Fifty Wonderful Portraits. London: 1827. V. 63

COOPER, SAMUEL
The First Lines of the Practice of Surgery.... Boston: 1828. V. 65

COOPER, SUSAN ROGERS
Houston in the Rearview Mirror. New York: 1990. V. 63; 64; 65; 66; 67
The Man in the Green Chevy. 1989. V. 62
The Man in the Green Chevy. New York: 1989. V. 64
The Man in the Green Chevy. New York: 1990. V. 66

COOPER, THOMAS
Address to the Graduates of the South Carolina College, at the Public Commencement, 1830. Columbia: 1831. V. 63; 66
The Bankrupt Law of America, Compared with the Bankrupt Law of England. Philadelphia: 1801. V. 66
Consolidation. An Account of Parties in the United States from the Convention of 1787 to the Present Period. Columbia: 1824. V. 66
Consolidation. An Account of Parties in the United States, from the Convention of 1787, to the Present Period. Columbia: 1830. V. 63
The Right of Free Discussion. New York: 1829. V. 64
The Scripture Doctrine of Materialism. Philadelphia: 1823. V. 64
Some Information Respecting America. London: 1794. V. 63; 66
Tracts on Medical Jurisprudence. Philadelphia: 1819. V. 65

COOPER, THOMAS continued
A View of Metaphysical and Physiological Arguments in Favor of Materialism. Philadelphia: 1824. V. 64

COOPER, W. D.
A New Roman History, from the Foundation of Rome, to the End of the Commonwealth. Philadlephia: 1809. V. 64

COOPER, W. HEATON
The English Lakes. London: 1908. V. 65
The Hills of Lakeland. London: 1938. V. 66
Lakeland Portraits. London: 1954. V. 65
The Lakes. London: 1966. V. 65
The Tarns of Lakeland. London: 1960. V. 65
The Tarns of Lakeland. Kendal: 1983. V. 65

COOPER, W. S.
Charters of the Royal Burgh of Ayr. Edinburgh: 1883. V. 62

COOPER, W. T.
A Portfolio of Australian Birds. Rutland: 1968. V. 65

COOPER, WILLIAM
A Sketch of the Life of the Late Henry Cooper, Barrister-at-Law of the Norfolk Circuit; as Also of His Father, by His Son William Cooper. London: 1856. V. 63
The Struggles of Albert Woods. London: 1952. V. 63
Yachts and Yachting Being a Treatise on Building, Sparring, Canvassing, Sailing and General Management of Yachts.... London: 1979. V. 65

COOPER, WILLIAM DURRANT
A Glossary of the Provincialisms in Use in the County of Sussex. London: 1853. V. 64

COOTE, C. H.
Johann Schoner, Professor of Mathematics at Nuremberg. London: 1888. V. 66

COOVER, ROBERT
Charlie in the House of Rue. Lincoln: 1980. V. 66
Gerald's Party. New York: 1986. V. 62
The Origin of the Brunists. New York: 1966. V. 62; 63; 67
The Origin of the Brunists. London: 1967. V. 62; 66
Pricksongs and Descants. New York: 1969. V. 63; 67
The Public Burning. New York: 1977. V. 63
Spanking the Maid. Bloomfield Hills, Columbia: 1981. V. 62; 66
The Stone Wall Book of Short Fictions. Iowa City: 1973. V. 62; 64
A Theological Position. Plays: The Kid, Love Scene, Rip Awake, a Theological Position. New York: 1972. V. 63
The Universal Baseball Association, Inc. J. Harry Waugh, Prop. New York: 1968. V. 63; 64; 65; 66; 67
The Water Pourer: an Unpublished Chapter from the Origins of the Brunists. Bloomfield Hills & Columbia: 1972. V. 62; 66

COPE, E. D.
Contribution to the Ichthyology of the Lesser Antilles. Philadelphia: 1871. V. 65
The Crocodilians, Lizards and Snakes of North America. Washington: 1900. V. 62; 63; 66
The Origin of the Fittest, Essays on Evolutions. New York: 1887. V. 63
A Review of the Modern Doctrine of Evolution. Salem: 1880. V. 62
Syllabus of Lectures on the Vertebrata.... Philadelphia: 1898. V. 63
Synopsis of the Cyprinidae of Pennsylvania.... Philadelphia: 1860. V. 65

COPE TOBACCO CO.
Smoker's Garland. Liverpool: 1889-1890. V. 63

COPE, WENDY
Being Boring. West Chester: 1998. V. 64
Making Cocoa for Kingsley Amis. London: 1985. V. 64
The River Girl. London: 1991. V. 64; 65
Serious Concerns. London: 1992. V. 64

COPELAND, E. B.
The Coco-nut. London: 1914. V. 67

COPELAND, R. M.
Country Life: a Handbook of Agriculture, Horticulture and Landscape Gardening. Boston: 1859. V. 64; 67

COPELAND, RICHARD
Introduction to the Practice of Nautical Surveying and the Construction of Sea-Charts. London: 1823. V. 62

COPELAND, TOM
Valuation. Speculation and Investing. New York: 1995. V. 64

COPEMAN, EDWARD
A Collection of Cases of Apoplexy.... London: 1845. V. 64

COPERNICUS, NICOLAUS
De Revolutionibus Orbium Coelestium, Libri VI. Basle: 1566. V. 65
De Revolutionibus Orbium Coelestium Libri VI. Thorun: 1873. V. 67

COPIES of the Depositions of the Witnesses Examined in the Cause of Divorce Now Pending in the Consistory Court of the Lord Bishop of London, at Doctor's-Commons. London: 1771. V. 65

COPINGER, WALTER A.
Heraldry Simplified: an Easy Introduction to the Science. Manchester: 1910. V. 63; 66

COPLAND, AARON
Music and Imagination. Cambridge: 1952. V. 63

COPLESTON, EDWARD
Advice to a Young Reviewer with a Specimen of the Art. Oxford: 1807. V. 63; 66
A Reply to the Calumnies of the Edinburgh Review Against Oxford. Oxford: 1810. V. 62
A Reply to the Calumnies of the Edinburgh Review Against Oxford. (with) A Second Reply to the Edinburgh Review. (with) A Third Rely to the Edinburgh Review. Oxford: 1810-1811. V. 63

COPLEY, ESTHER
Cottage Comforts, with Hints for Promoting Them, Gleaned from Experience.... London: 1844. V. 62
The Housekeeper's Guide; or a Plain and Practical System of Domestic Cookery. London: 1834. V. 65
The Housekeeper's Guide, or a Plain and Practical System of Domestic Cookery. London: 1845. V. 62
The Young Women of the Factory; or, Friendly Hints on Their Duties and Dangers. London: 1845?. V. 62

COPLEY, FRANK BARKLEY
Frederick W. Taylor, Father of Scientific Management. New York: 1923. V. 62

COPLEY, JOHN M.
A Sketch of the Battle of Franklin, Tennessee.... Austin: 1893. V. 63; 65

COPPARD, ALFRED EDGAR
Adam and Eve and Pinch Me. Waltham St. Lawrence: 1921. V. 64
Cherry Ripe. London: 1935. V. 64
Cherry Ripe. Windham: 1935. V. 64
Clorinda Walks in Heaven. Tales. Waltham St. Lawrence: 1922. V. 64
Count Stefan. Waltham St. Lawrence: 1928. V. 62; 63; 65; 66
Crotty Shinkwin and the Beauty Spot. Berkshire: 1932. V. 66
Crotty Shinkwin and The Beauty Spot. Waltham St. Lawrence: 1932. V. 64
Emergency Exit. New York: 1934. V. 63
Fearful Pleasures. Sauk City: 1946. V. 64; 66
The Field of Mustard. Tales. London: 1926. V. 64
Fishmonger's Fiddle. London: 1925. V. 64
Hips and Haws. Waltham St. Lawrence: 1922. V. 64; 66
The Hundredth Story. Waltham St. Lawrence: 1931. V. 62; 64; 65; 66
Nixey's Harlequin. London: 1931. V. 64
Pelagea and Other Poems. Waltham St. Lawrence: 1926. V. 62; 64; 65; 66; 67
Pink Furniture: a Tale for Lovely Children and Noble Natures. London: 1930. V. 64; 66
Silver Circus. London: 1926. V. 64
Silver Circus. London: 1928. V. 64; 65; 66
Tapster's Tapestry. Waltham St. Lawrence: 1938. V. 66
Yokohama Garland and Other Poems. 1926. V. 64; 66

COPPEE, FRANCOIS
Blessed are the Poor. London: 1894. V. 67

COPPEE, HENRY
A Gallery of English and American Women Famous in Song. Philadelphia: 1875. V. 67
A Gallery of Famous English and American Poets.... Philadelphia: 1859. V. 62; 66

COPPENS, AUGUSTIN
Perspectives des Ruines de la Ville de Bruxelles, Designees au Naturel. Brussels: 1695. V. 62

COPPENS, M.
Negro Sculpture: a Photographic Approach. Eindhoven: 1975. V. 62

COPPER RIVER OIL AND MINING COMPANY
The Copper River Oil and Mining Company, Main Offices; New Whatcom, Washington. New Whatcom: 1898. V. 63

COPPIN, L. J.
The Key to Scriptural Interpretation, or Expository Notes on Obscure Passages. Philadelphia: 1895. V. 65

COPPINGER, R. W.
Cruise of the Alert Four Years in Patagonian, Polynesian and Mascarene Waters. London: 1883. V. 62

COPPOCK, THOMAS
The Genuine Dying Speech of the Rev. Parson Coppock, Pretended Bishop of Carlisle.... Carlisle: 1746. V. 66

COPWAY, GEORGE
The Life, History and Travels of Kah-Ge-Ga-Gah-Bowh (George Copway), a Young Indian Chief of the Ojebwa Nation, a Convert to the Christian Faith.... Albany: 1847. V. 67

THE COQUET'S Surrender; or, the Humorous Punster. London: 1732. V. 65

CORBET, KATHERINE
Animal Land Where There Are No People. New York: 1897. V. 62

CORBET, P. S.
Dragonflies. London: 1960. V. 64
Dragonflies: Behaviour and Ecology of Odonata. 1999. V. 67
Dragonflies, Behaviour and Ecology of Odonata. Ithaca: 1999. V. 65

CORBETT, BERTHA L.
Baby Days: a Sunbonnet Record. New York: 1910. V. 62

CORBETT, E. T., MRS.
Wise Old Couples. London: 1881. V. 67

CORBETT, JULIAN STAFFORD
Kophetua the Thirteenth. London: 1889. V. 66

CORBETT, THOMAS B.
Colorado Mining Directory. Denver: 1879. V. 64

CORBETT MELCHER, BERTHA
What's On the Air?. Topanga: 1928. V. 62

CORBIERE, TRISTAN
Poems. N.P: 1947. V. 63

CORBIN, MARIE OVERTON
Urchins at the Pole. New York: 1901. V. 66

CORBIN, RICHARD WASHINGTON
Letters of a Confederate Officer to His Family in Europe. Paris: 1902. V. 62; 63; 65

CORBUSIER, WILLIAM T.
Verde to San Carlos, Recollections of a Famous Army Surgeon and His Observant Family on the Western Frontier 1869-1886. Tucson: 1968. V. 65; 67

CORDASCO, FRANCESCO
American Medical Imprints 1820-1910. Totawa: 1985. V. 66

CORDEAUX, JOHN
Birds of the Humber District. London: 1872. V. 62

CORDELL, EUGENE FAUNTLEROY
The Medical Annals of Maryland 1799-1899. Baltimore: 1903. V. 67

CORDER, WILLIAM
An Accurate Account of the Trial of William Corder, for the Murder of Maria Marten, of Polstead.... London: 1828. V. 63; 65
An Authentic and Faithful History of the Mysterious Murder of Maria Marten...to Which is Added, the Trial of William Corder.... London: 1828. V. 63
The Trial of William Corder, at the Assizes, Bury St. Edmunds, Suffolk, August 7th and 8th, 1828, for the Murder of Maria Marten, in the Red Barn, at Polstead.... London: 1828. V. 63

CORDIER, A. H.
Some Big Game Hunts. Kansas City: 1911. V. 64

CORDIER, HENRI
Bibliotheca Indosinica: Dictionnaire Bibliographique des Ouvrages Relatifs a la Penensule Indochinoise. 1998. V. 65

CORDINER, CHARLES
Antiquities and Scenery of the North of Scotland in a Series of Letters. London: 1780. V. 66
Remarkable Ruins and Romantic Prospects of North Britain. London: 1788. V. 66
Remarkable Ruins and Romantic Prospects of North Britain. London: 1795. V. 62; 63; 66

CORDION'S Song and Other Verses from Various Sources. London: 1894. V. 67

CORDLEY, RICHARD
A History of Lawrence Kansas, from the First Settlement to the Close of the Rebellion. Lawrence: 1895. V. 64; 67

CORDOVA, CORDELIA
Human Nature. London: 1816. V. 65

CORDY, T. A., MRS.
The Story of Marking the Santa Fe Trail. Topeka: 1915. V. 63

CORE, GEORGE
Southern Excursions. Charlotte: 1997. V. 67

CORELL, D. S.
Manual of the Vascular Plants of Texas. 1979. V. 66

CORELL, PHILIP
History of Union Coast Guard, 99th NYS Volunteers with Reminiscences from June 1st 1861 to June 19th 1863. New York: 1901. V. 62; 63

CORELLI, MARIE
Love - and the Philosopher: a Study in Sentiment. London: 1923. V. 65
The Murder of Delicia. London: 1896. V. 65
The Murder of Delicia. Philadelphia: 1896. V. 63
The Secret Power: a Romance of the Time. London: 1921. V. 65
The Sorrows of Satan, or the Strange Experience of One Geoffrey Tempest, Millionaire: a Romance. London: 1895. V. 65

COREMANS, P.
Van Eyck. The Adoration of the Mystic Lamb. Amsterdam: 1948. V. 63

CORK, BARRY
Laid Dead. London: 1990. V. 67

CORK, RICHARD
Vorticism and Abstract Art. London: 1976. V. 65

CORK & ORRERY, JOHN BOYLE, 5TH EARL OF
Letters from Italy in the Years 1754 and 1755. 1773. V. 63; 66
Letters from Italy in the Years 1754 and 1755. London: 1773. V. 65
Letters from Italy, in the Years 1754 and 1755. London: 1774. V. 63
Remarks on the Life and Writings of Dr. Jonathan Swift. London: 1752. V. 62; 64; 66; 67

CORK AND ORRERY, COUNTESS OF
The Orrery Papers. 1903. V. 65

CORKRAN, DAVID H.
The Creek Frontier 1540-1783. Norman: 1967. V. 67

CORKS and Curls. Charlottesville: 1895. V. 64

CORLE, EDWIN
Fig Tree John. New York: 1935. V. 64; 65
Fig Tree John. Los Angeles: 1955. V. 62
John Studebaker. An American Dream. New York: 1948. V. 63
People on the Earth. New York: 1937. V. 64; 65

CORLIN, AXEL
Cosmic Ultra-Radiation in Northern Sweden. Lund: 1934. V. 65

CORMACK, J. M. R.
Notes on the History of the Inscribed Monuments of Aphrodisias. 1955. V. 65

CORMAN, CID
Any How. Japan: 1976. V. 63; 64
Clocked Stone. Poems. Kyoto: 1959. V. 64
For Good. Kyoto: 1964. V. 62
Hearth. Kyoto: 1968. V. 64
In Good Time. Kyoto: 1964. V. 63
In No Time. Kyoto: 1963. V. 66
Of. Venice: 1990. V. 63; 64
Origin: Third Series. Kyoto: 1966-1971. V. 63; 64; 66
The Precisions. New York: 1955. V. 64
The Responses. Ashland: 1956. V. 63
'S. New Rochelle: 1976. V. 63; 64; 66
Stances and Distances. Ashland: 1957. V. 62; 64
A Thanksgiving Eclogue from Theocritus. Corona: 1954. V. 63; 64; 66
Words for Each Other. 1967. V. 62
Words for Each Other. London: 1967. V. 63

CORMIER, ROBERT
The Chocolate War. N.P: 1974. V. 63; 64; 66

CORN, ALFRED
A Call in the Midst of the Crowd. Poems. New York: 1978. V. 63
Somerset Alcaics. New York: 1988. V. 67
An Xmas Murder. New York: 1987. V. 66; 67

CORNARO, LUIGI
Discourses on a Sober and Temperate Life. London: 1768. V. 66
Sure and Certain Methods of Attaining a Long and Healthy Life.... London: 1737. V. 63

CORNEILLE, PIERRE
Heraclius Empereur d'Orient. Paris: 1647. V. 66
Le Menteur. Comedie. 1647. V. 66
Oeuvres De P. Corneille...Precedes De La Vie De L'Auteur.... Paris: 1875. V. 66
La Suite du Menteur. Comedie. 1648. V. 66

CORNELIUS, MARY HOOKER
The Young Housekeeper's Friend; or, a Guide to Domestic Economy and Comfort. Boston: 1852. V. 62

CORNELIUS, TEMPLE H.
Sheepherder's Gold. Denver: 1964. V. 67

CORNELIUS NEPOS
Liber Aemilii Probi, Seu Corn. Nepotis.... Lugduni: 1616. V. 66

CORNELL, JOSEPH
Joseph Cornell: Portfolio. New York: 1976. V. 67

CORNER, E. J. H.
A Monograph of Clavaria and Allied Genera. Oxford: 1950. V. 64
Wayside Trees of Malaya. Singapore: 1952. V. 63; 66

CORNER, JULIA
The History of Spain and Portugal: from the Earliest Periods to the Present Time. London: 1840. V. 64; 65

CORNER, WILLIAM
San Antonio De Bexar - A Guide and History. San Antonio: 1890. V. 62; 65

CORNFORD, FRANCES
Autumn Midnight. 1923. V. 62
Fifteen Poems from the French. London: 1976. V. 62
Mountains and Molehills. London: 1934. V. 62
On a Calm Shore - Poems. Cambridge: 1960. V. 62
On a Calm Shore. Poems. London: 1960. V. 63
Poems. Hampstead and Cambridge: 1910. V. 63
Spring Morning. London: 1915. V. 62

THE CORNHILL Gallery. London: 1864. V. 62; 64; 66

THE CORNHILL Magazine. London: 1860-1882. V. 64; 67

CORNILLIER, PIERRE EMILE
Contribution a l'Etude des Phenomenes de Mantes. Paris: 1929. V. 67

CORNISH, C. J.
The Naturalist on the Thames. London: 1902. V. 63

CORNISH, HENRY
The Tryals of Henry Cornish, Esq. for Conspiring the Death of the King...and John Fernley, William King and Elizabeth Gaunt.... London: 1685. V. 62
Under the Southern Cross. Madras: 1880. V. 64

CORNISH, VAUGHAN
The Travels of Ellen Cornish, Being the Memoir of a Pilgrim of Science. London: 1913. V. 64

CORNWALL, BRUCE
Life Sketch of Pierre Barlow Cornwall. San Francisco: 1906. V. 66

CORNWALLIS, JANE
Private Correspondence...1613-1644. London: 1842. V. 63

CORNWALLIS, WILLIAM
Essayes. London: 1600. V. 64

CORNWELL, BERNARD
Sharpe's Eagle. New York: 1981. V. 63
Sharpe's Gold. London: 1981. V. 63
Sharpe's Gold. New York: 1982. V. 66
Sharpe's Tiger. Blakeney: 1997. V. 65

CORNWELL, PATRICIA D.
All that Remains. London: 1992. V. 65; 66; 67
All that Remains. New York: 1992. V. 64
The Body Farm. New York: 1994. V. 67
Body of Evidence. New York: 1991. V. 62; 65; 66; 67
Cause of Death. New York: 1996. V. 62; 64; 65
Point of Origin. New York: 1998. V. 66
Postmortem. New York: 1990. V. 62; 65; 66; 67
Unnatural Exposure. New York: 1997. V. 66

CORONITI, SAMUEL C.
Planetary Electrodynamics.... New York: 1969. V. 67

CORP, HARRIET
Cottage Sketches; or Active Retirement. London: 1812. V. 65

CORPORATION FOR THE RELIEF OF WIDOWS AND CHILDREN OF CLERGY
The Charter of the Corporation for the Relief of Widows and Children.... New Brunswick: 1808. V. 63

CORPRON, CARLOTTA
Carlotta Corpron: Designer with Light. Fort Worth Austin London: 1980. V. 63

CORPUS *Francicae Historiae Veteris et Sincerae.* Hanau: 1613. V. 65

A CORRECT *Narrative of the Distressing Shipwrecks, that Unhappily Took Place in Seaford Bay, on Thursday Morning, Dec. the 7th 1809....* 1809. V. 63

A CORRECT *Narrative of the Distressing Shipwrecks that Unhappily Took Place in Seaford Bay, on Thursday Morning, Dec. the 7th 1809....* London: 1809. V. 67

CORRELL, D. S.
Flora of the Bahama Archipelago.... Vaduz: 1996. V. 63
Manual of the Vascular Plants of Texas. 1979. V. 63
Native Orchids of North America North of Mexico. Waltham: 1950. V. 67

CORRESPONDENCE in Relation to the Boundary of Texas. 1850. V. 65

CORRESPONDENCE Relative to Hostilities of the Araickanee Indians. Washington: 1823. V. 63

CORRESPONDENCE Relative to the Recent Disturbances in the Red River Settlements and Correspondence Relative to the Recent Expedition to the Red River Settlement with Journal of Operations. London: 1870-1871. V. 62

CORRIE, GEORGE ELWES
Brief Historical Notices of the Interference of the Crown with the Affairs of the English Universities. Cambridge: 1839. V. 66

CORRIGAN, DOMINIC JOHN
Ten Days in Athens. London: 1862. V. 64

CORRIGAN, DOUGLAS
That's My Story. New York: 1938. V. 63

CORRINGTON, JOHN WILLIAM
The Anatomy of Love and Other Poems. Fort Lauderdale: 1964. V. 63

CORRY, JOHN
The Life of Joseph Priestley, LL.D., F.R.S., &c. Birmingham: 1804. V. 63; 66

CORSARO, FRANK
The Love for Three Oranges. The Glyndebourne Version.... New York: 1984. V. 62; 65

CORSO, GREGORY
American Express. Paris: 1961. V. 65
(Ankh). New York: 1971. V. 62; 64
Elegiac Feelings American. New York: 1970. V. 65

CORSON, EUGENE
A Skiagraphic Study of the Normal Membral Eipiphyses at the Thirteenth Years. Philadelphia: 1900. V. 67

CORTAZAR, JULIO
Bestiario. Buenos Aires: 1951. V. 67
Casa Tomada. Buenos Aires: 1969. V. 62
End of the Game and Other Stories. New York: 1963. V. 66
End of the Game and Other Stories. New York: 1967. V. 62; 66
Prosa del Observatorio. Barcelona: 1972. V. 62
Los Reyes. Buenos Aires: 1949. V. 67
Silvalandia. Mexico: 1957. V. 65
62: Modelo Para Armar. Buenos Aires: 1968. V. 62
La Urna Griega en la Poesia de John Keats. Mendoza: 1946. V. 62; 67
The Winners. New York: 1965. V. 67

CORTE REAL, JERONIMO
Naufragio e Lastimoso Sucesso da Perdicam de Manoel de Sousa de Sepulveda & Dona Lianor de Sasua Mulher, e Filhos, Vindo da India Para Este Reyno na Nao Chamada o Galiao Grande S. Joao, Que se Peredeo No Cabo de Boa Esperanca.... Lisbon: 1594. V. 62

CORTES, HERNANDO
The Despatches of...the Conqueror of Mexico, Addressed to the Emperor Charles V. London: 1843. V. 65

CORTI, U. A.
Les Oiseaux Nicheurs d'Europe. Zurich: 1956. V. 67

CORVINUS, JOHANNES ARNOLDI
Elementa Juris Civilis. Amsterdam: 1645. V. 66

CORWIN, HUGH D.
The Kiowa Indians - Their History and Life Stories. Lawton: 1958. V. 63; 64; 66

CORWIN, THOMAS
Report of the Officers Constituting the Light-House Board, to Inquire Into the Condition of the Light-House Establishment of the United States. Washington: 1852. V. 66

CORY, CHARLES B.
The Birds of Haiti and San Domingo. Boston: 1885. V. 62; 64; 67
The Birds of Illinois and Wisconsin. Chicago: 1909. V. 67
Birds of the Bahama Islands.... Boston: 1880. V. 67
The Birds of the Bahama Islands.... Boston: 1890. V. 62; 67

CORY, CHARLES HENRY
James Cory and Susan Mulford. N.P: 1920? V. 66
Lineal Ancestors of Captain James Cory and of His Descendants. N.P: 1937. V. 66

CORY, ISAAC PRESTON
Ancient Fragments of the Phoenician, Chaldaen, Egyptian, Syrian, Carthaginian, India, Persian and Other Writers.... London: 1832. V. 63
Chronological Inquiry Into the Ancient History of Egypt. (with) Mythological Inquiry Into the Recondite Theology of the Heathens. London: 1837. V. 67
Cory's Ancient Fragments.... London: 1876. V. 63
Mythological Inquiry into the Recondite Theology of the Heathens. (with) Chronological Inquiry Into the Ancient History of Egypt. London: 1837. V. 64

CORY, WILLIAM JOHNSON
Hints for Eton Masters. London: 1898. V. 64
Ionica. London: 1858. V. 65

CORYAT, THOMAS
Coryat's Crudities. London: 1611. V. 64; 66
Coryat's Crudities. Glasgow: 1905. V. 63
Venice Visited Being a Dozen Extracts from the Journal of Thomas Coryat, Who, In the Early Seventeenth Century, Walked from Somerset to Venice and Back. Bath: 1999. V. 65

COSENTINO, F. J.
Edward Marshall Boehm, 1913-1969. Chicago: 1970. V. 62

COSGROVE, RACHEL R.
Hidden Valley of Oz. Chicago: 1951. V. 64; 66

COSIN, JAMES
The Names of the Roman Catholic, Nonjurors and Others Who Refus'd to Take the Oaths to His Late Majesty King George. London: 1745. V. 66

COSSE, MADAME DE
Catalogue d'une Belle Collection de Tableaux Originales des Trois Ecoles.... Paris: 1778. V. 64

COSSERY, ALBERT
Les Hommes Oublies de Dieu. Cairo, Alexandria: 1941. V. 67
If All Men Were Beggars. London: 1957. V. 65

COSSY, L. A.
Experimentale Et Clinique sur les Ventricules Lateraux. Paris: 1879. V. 64

COSTA, E. M. DA
A Natural History of Fossils. 1757. V. 65

COSTAKIS, GEORGE C.
Russian Avant-Garde Art. New York: 1981. V. 62

COSTANSO, MIGUEL
The Portola Expedition of 1769-1770. Diary of Miguel Costanso. Berkeley: 1911. V. 64; 66

COSTARD, G.
A Letter to Martin Folkes, Esq., President of the Royal Society, Concerning the Rise and Progress of Astronomy Amongst the Antients. London: 1746. V. 66

COSTE, JEAN BAPTISTE
Petites Fabriques Italiennes. Paris: 1809. V. 64

COSTE D'ARNOBAT, PIERRE
Voyage au Pays de Bambouc.... Bruxelles: 1789. V. 64

COSTELLO, LOUISA STUART
The Falls, Lakes and Mountains of North Wales. London: 1845. V. 65
Memoirs of an Eminent Englishwoman. London: 1844. V. 62
The Rose Garden of Persia. London: 1845. V. 63
The Rose Garden of Persia. London: 1888. V. 62
The Rose Garden of Persia. London: 1912. V. 62

COSTON, H. E.
River Management. London: 1936. V. 67

COSTUME of the Russian Empire. London: 1804. V. 64
COSTUME of the Russian Empire. London: 1811. V. 62

COSTUMES, or a Short Sketch of the Manners and Customs, of the Principal Foreign Inhabitants of the Globe. London: 1820. V. 64

COTES, HUMPHREY
An Enqviry Into the Condvct of a Late Right Honvrable Commoner. Dublin: 1766?. V. 65

COTGREAVE, ALFRED
A Contents-Subject Index to General and Periodical Literature. London: 1900. V. 65

COTHREN, MARION B.
Cher Ami: the Story of a Carrier Pigeon. Boston: 1935. V. 67

COTIN, CHARLES
Oeuvres Meslees de Mr. Cotin...(with) L'Uranie, ou la Metamorphose d'une Nymphe en Oranger.... Paris: 1659. V. 66

COTTAM, C.
Whitewings, the Life History, Status, and Management of the White-Winged Dove. Princeton: 1968. V. 67

COTTEN, KATHRYN
Saga of Scurry. San Antonio: 1957. V. 64

COTTERILL, C. C.
Human Justice for Those at the Bottom; An Appeal to Those at the Top. A Fragment. London: 1907. V. 62

COTTIN, MARIE SOPHIE RISTAUD
Oeuvres Completes. Paris: 1820. V. 66

COTTIN, SOPHIE
Malvina. London: 1804. V. 67

COTTLE, JOSEPH
Early Recollections, Chiefly Relating to the Late Samuel Taylor Coleridge During His Long Residence in Bristol. London: 1837. V. 66

COTTON, B. C.
The Molluscs of South Australia. Adelaide: 1938-1940. V. 63; 64

COTTON, CHARLES
The Compleat Gamester. Barre: 1970. V. 64
The Genuine Poetical Works. London: 1741. V. 64
The Genuine Poetical Works.... London: 1765. V. 62
The Planters Manual. London: 1675. V. 64
Poems on Several Occasions. London: 1689. V. 62; 63; 66
Scarronides; or Le Virgile Travesty. London: 1664. V. 63; 64; 65
Scarronnides, or, Virgile Travestie. London: 1709. V. 62

COTTON, CLEMENT
A Complete Concordance to the Bible of the Last Translation.... Amsterdam: 1635. V. 63

COTTON, HENRY
A Typographical Gazetteer, Attempted by the Rev. Henry Cotton.... Oxford: 1831. V. 62; 67

COTTON, JANE BALDWIN
Things is Goin as Usule. Boston: 1928. V. 67
Wall-Eyed Caesar's Ghost and Other Sketches. Boston: 1925. V. 67

COTTON, JOHN
The Song Birds of Great Britain.... London: 1835-1836. V. 65; 67

COTTON, NATHANIEL
Visions in Verse, for the Entertainment and Instruction of Younger Minds. London: 1798. V. 62

COTTON, ROBERT
Sir Thomas Roe His Speech in Parliament: Wherein He Sheweth the Cause of the Decay of Coine and Trade in This Land, Especially of Merchants Trade. London: 1641. V. 67

COTTON, ROBERT BRUCE
The Danger Wherein the Kingdome Now Standeth, and the Remedie. (bound after a defective copy of) A Short View of the Long Life and Raigne of Henry the Third, King of England. Presented to King James.... London: 1628-1627. V. 63
An Exact Abridgement of the Records in the Tower of London, from the Reign of King Edward the Second, Unto King Richard the Third.... London: 1689. V. 63

COTTON, W. B.
Sport in the Eastern Sudan. London. V. 64
Sport in the Eastern Sudan. 1912. V. 62; 63

COUBRO & SCRUTTON
Catalogue Ship Stores. London: 1912. V. 66

COUCH, JONATHAN
The History of Polperro, a Fishing Town on the South Coast of Cornwall.... Truro: 1871. V. 62; 65; 66
A History of the Fishes of the British Islands. London: 1862-1865. V. 63; 65
A History of the Fishes of the British Islands. 1864-1867. V. 66
A History of the Fishes of the British Islands. 1877. V. 65; 66

COUCHAUD, ANDRE
Choix d'Eglises Byzantines en Grece. Paris: 1841-1842. V. 64

COUCHOUD, PAUL LOUIS
Mythologie Asiatique Illustree. Paris: 1928. V. 65

COUES, ELLIOTT
Abstract of Results of a Study of the Genera Geomys and Thomomys.... Washington: 1875. V. 67
The Expeditions of Zebulon Montgomery Pike to Headwaters of the Mississippi River through Louisiana Territory and New Spain Paving the Years 1805-1806-1807. 1965. V. 67
The Expeditions of Zebulon Montgomery Pike to Headwaters of the Mississippi River through Louisiana Territory and New Spain, Paving the Years 1805-1806-1807. Minnesota: 1965. V. 64
Field and General Ornithology. 1890. V. 67
Forty Years a Fur Trader On the Upper Missouri. Personal Narrative of Larpenteur. New York: 1898. V. 65
History of the Expedition Under the Command of Lewis and Clark to the Sources of the Missouri River.... New York: 1893. V. 66
Key to North American Birds.... Boston: 1887. V. 64
Monographs of North American Rodentia. Washington: 1887. V. 62; 63; 66
New Light on the Early History of the Greater Northwest.... New York: 1897. V. 63; 66
On the Trail of a Spanish Pioneer. New York: 1900. V. 62; 63; 64; 66

COUGHLIN, JACK
Impressions of Bohemia. Carmel: 1986. V. 65

COUGHLIN, WILLIAM J.
The Stalking Man. New York: 1979. V. 65

COULTAS, H.
What May Be Learned from a Tree. Philadelphia: 1860. V. 64

COULTER, E. MERTON
Travels in the Confederate States. A Bibliography. Norman: 1948. V. 62; 63
William G. Brownlow, Fighting Parson of the Southern Highlands. Chapel Hill: 1937. V. 66

COULTER, JOHN
Adventures on the Western Coast of South America, and the Interior of California.... London: 1847. V. 63

COULTON, G. G.
Friar's Lantern. London: 1906. V. 64
A Victorian Schoolmasater: Henry Hart of Sedbergh. London: 1923. V. 65

COUNCE, S. J.
Developmental Systems: Insects. London: 1972-1973. V. 63

COUNCIL OF TRENT
Sacrosancti et Oecvmenici Concilii Tridentini...Canones et Decreta. Antverpiae: 1596. V. 64

THE COUNTIES of Nottingham and Lincoln Past and Present. Portsmouth: 1920. V. 65

COUNTRY Home. London: 1909. V. 67

COUNTRY Life. London: 1901-1915. V. 66

THE COUNTRY Life Annual for 1938. London: 1938. V. 62

COUNTRY Life Illustrated. Christmas Number 1900. London: 1900. V. 64

COUPER, ROBERT
Poetry Chiefly in the Scottish Language. Inverness: 1804. V. 65

COUPER, WILLIAM
History of the Shenandoah Valley. New York: 1952. V. 62; 64
The V.M.I. New Market Cadets. Charlottesville: 1933. V. 64

COUPLAND, DOUGLAS
Generation X: Tales for an Accelerated Culture. New York: 1991. V. 66

COUPLAND, R.
The Exploitation of East Africa 1856-1890. London: 1939. V. 64

COURAGE and Conflict. 1901. V. 67

COURCELLES, DAVID CORNELIUS DE
Icones Musculorum Capitis, Utpote Faciei, Aurium, Ocolorum Linguae, Pharyngis, Ossis Hyoidis, Colli, ut et Eorum, Qui Capiti Adnectuntur... (with) Icones Musculorum Plantae Pedis Eorumque Descriptio. Lungduni Batvorum (Leiden): 1743. V. 62

COURNOS, JOHN
The Mask. London: 1919. V. 62

COURNOT, ANTOINE AUGUSTIN
Exposition De La Theorie des Chances et Des Probabilités. Paris: 1843. V. 64

COURSEY, O. W.
Wild Bill James Butler Hickok. Mitchell: 1924. V. 64; 67

THE COURT and City Register. For the Year 1763. London: 1762-1763. V. 65

COURT Jobbery; or, The Black Book of the Palace.... London: 1848. V. 64

COURT, PIETER DE LA
The True Interest and Political Maxims of the Republic of Holland. London: 1746. V. 65; 66

COURTENAY, ELLEN
A Narrative by Miss Ellen Courenay of Most Extraordinary Cruelty, Perfidy and Depravity, Perpetrated Against Her by Daniel O'Connell.... London: 1832. V. 63

COURTENAY, JOHN
A Poetical Review of the Literary and Moral Character of the Late Samuel Johnson, LL.D. London: 1786. V. 62

COURTENAY, THOMAS PEREGRINE
A Letter to Lord Grenville on the Sinking Fund. London: 1828. V. 64

COURTET, ALEXANDRE VICTOR
La Science Politique Fondee sur la Science de l'Homme, ou Etude des Races Humaines Sous le Rapport Philosophique, Historique et Social. Paris: 1838. V. 63

COURTHION, PIERRE
Georges Roualt. New York: 1961. V. 63

COURTILZ, GATIEN, SIEUR DE SANDRAS
Memoirs of Monsieur d'Artagnan, Captain-Lieutenant of the 1st Company of the King's Musketers. London: 1925. V. 66
Testament Politiques de Messire Jean Baptiste Colbert, Ministre & Secretaire d'Etat. La Haye (The Hague): 1693. V. 66

COURTNEY, JAMES
James Dean, Back Creek Boy. 1990. V. 67

COURTNEY, WILLIAM PRIDEAUX
A Bibliography of Samuel Johnson. Oxford: 1925. V. 62
A Bibliography of Samuel Johnson. 1984. V. 67

THE COURTSHIP and Marriage of Cock Robin and Jenny Wren. London: 1890. V. 64

THE COURTSHIP, Marriage and Pic-nic Dinner of Cock Robin & Jenny Wren, with the Death and Burial of Poor Cock Robin. Harrisburg: 1840. V. 63; 65

COURVILLE, CYRIL B
Commotio Cerebri. Cerebral Concussions and the Postconcussion Sydrome in Their Medical and Legal Aspects. Los Angeles: 1953. V. 66; 67

COURVOISIER, FRANCOIS BENJAMIN
Extraordinary Particulars. The Horrible Murder of Lord William Russell.... London: 1840. V. 63
The Life, Trial, Confession, Copy of a Letter and Execution of Francois Benjamin Courvoisier for the Horrid Murder of Lord William Russell, Uncle to Lord John Russell.... London: 1840. V. 63

COUSIN, J. A. J.
Traite de Calcul Differentiel et de Calcul Integral. Paris: 1796. V. 67

COUSIN, JEAN
L'Art de Dessiner Augmente de Plusieurs Figures d'Apres l'Antique. Paris: 1802. V. 66

COUSIN, VICTOR
Elements of Psychology: Included in a Critical Examination of Locke's Essay on the Human Understanding. Hartford: 1834. V. 64
Jacqueline Pascal Premieres Etudes sur Les Femmes Illustres et la Societe du XVIIe Siecle. Paris: 1856. V. 66
Madame de Sable. Paris: 1854. V. 63
The Philosophy of Kant: Lectures. London: 1854. V. 64
Report on the State of Public Instruction in Prussia.... London: 1834. V. 64
La Societe Francaise au XVIIe Siecle d'Apres le Grand Cyrus de Mlle. de Scudery. Paris: 1866. V. 67

COUSINS, FRANK
The Colonial Architecture of Salem. Boston: 1919. V. 67

COUSINS, M.
20th Century Glass. Secaucus: 1989. V. 65

COUSINS, SHEILA
To Beg I Am Ashamed. London: 1938. V. 65

COUSTILLAS, PIERRE
Gissing's Writings on Dickens - a Bio-biliographical Survey - Together with Two Uncollected Reviews by George Gissing from the Times Literary Supplement. London: 1969. V. 65

COUTANT, C. C.
The History of Wyoming from Earliest Known Discoveries.... Laramie: 1899. V. 64; 67

COUTO, DIOGO DO
Decada Quinta da Asia.... Lisbon: 1612. V. 62

COUTS, CAVE
Hepah California! The Journal of Cave Couts. Tucson: 1961. V. 66

COUVREUR, JESSIE CATHERINE
Uncle Piper of Piper's Hill. London: 1889. V. 65

COUZYN, JENI
Twelve to Twelve. London: 1970. V. 62; 64

COVARRUBIAS, MIGUEL
The Eagle, the Jaguar and the Serpent. New York: 1954. V. 64
Indian Art of Mexico and Central America. New York: 1957. V. 65; 66

COVELL, THOMAS
Ickworth Survey Booke. 1893. V. 63

COVENTRY, FRANCIS
The History of Pompey the Little; or, the Life and Adventures of a Lap-Dog. London: 1751. V. 62; 64; 67
The History of Pompey the Little, or the Life and Adventures of a Lap-Dog. Waltham St. Lawrence: 1926. V. 66

COVENTRY, GEORGE
A Critical Inquiry Regarding the Read Authorship of the Letters of Junius.... London: 1825. V. 66

COVENTRY, HENRY
Philemon to Hydaspes; Relating Several Conversations with Hortensius Upon the Subject of False Religion. London: 1742. V. 63; 67

COVILLE, F. V.
Botany of the Death Valley Expedition. Washington: 1893. V. 64; 67

COWAN, ROBERT ERNEST
A Bibliography of the History of California 1510-1930. San Francisco: 1933. V. 63
A Bibliography of the History of California 1510-1930. Los Angeles: 1964. V. 64
A Bibliography of the History of California 1510-1930. 1998. V. 65

COWARD, NOEL
Bitter Sweet. London: 1929. V. 62; 64
Bon Voyage and Other Stories. London: 1967. V. 64
Cavalcade. New York: 1933. V. 64
Chelsea Buns. London: 1924-1925. V. 63
Chelsea Buns by Hernia Whittlebot. London: 1925. V. 64
Design for Living: a Comedy in Three Acts. London: 1933. V. 63
Design for Living: a Comedy in Three Acts. New York: 1933. V. 64
Fallen Angels: a Comedy in Three Acts. London: 1925. V. 64
Future Indefinite. London: 1954. V. 64
Hay Fever: a Light Comedy in Three Acts. London: 1925. V. 64
Home Chat. London: 1927. V. 64
The Noel Coward Songbook. London: 1953. V. 65
Not Yet the Dodo and Other Verses. New York: 1968. V. 64
The Plays...First Series: Sirocco; Home Chat; The Queen Was in the Parlour. New York: 1928. V. 64
Point Valaine. London: 1935. V. 63; 64
Pomp and Circumstance. London, Melbourne, Toronto: 1960. V. 65
Post-Mortem: a Play in Eight Scenes. London: 1931. V. 63; 64
Present Indicative. London: 1937. V. 63
Pretty Polly and Other Stories. New York: 1965. V. 64
Pretty Polly Barlow and Other Stories. London: 1964. V. 63
Private Lives: an Intimate Comedy in Three Acts. New York: 1930. V. 64
Quadrille - A Romantic Comedy in Three Acts. London: 1952. V. 63; 64
The Queen Was in the Parlour. London: 1926. V. 64
Sirocco. London: 1927. V. 64
Spangled Unicorn - an Anthology. London: 1932. V. 62; 64
Suite in Three Keys: a Song at Twilight; Shadows of the Evening; Come Into the Garden Maud: Three Plays. London: 1966. V. 64
Suite in Three Keys: a Song at Twilight, Shadows of the Evening, Come into the Garden Maude. Garden City: 1967. V. 63
Terribly Intimate Portraits. New York: 1922. V. 63; 64
Three Plays: The Rat Trap; The Vortex; Fallen Angels. London: 1925. V. 64
To Step Aside: Seven Short Stories. London: 1939. V. 63
Tonight at 8:30: Plays by.... London: 1936. V. 63
Tonight at Eight-Thirty. New York: 1936. V. 64
The Vortex: A Play in Three Acts. London: 1925. V. 62; 64
The Vortex: a Play in Three Acts. New York: 1925. V. 64
A Withered Nosegay. London: 1922. V. 64; 65

COWARD, T. A.
The Birds of the British Isles and Their Eggs. London: 1932-1934. V. 62

Cowboy Artists of America. Flagstaff: 1971. V. 63
Cowboy Artists of America. Flagstaff: 1972. V. 64

COWBOY Artists of America. Flagstaff: 1975. V. 63
COWBOY Artists of America. Phoenix: 1977. V. 67

COWBOY Artists of America. Phoenix: 1979. V. 67
COWBOY Artists of America. Flagstaff: 1986-1998. V. 64

COWDEN CLARKE, MARY
Many Happy Returns of the Day!. London: 1860. V. 65
Recollections of Writers. London: 1878. V. 65

COWDROY, JOAN A.
The Flying Dagger Murder. New York: 1932. V. 65

COWDRY, RICHARD
A Description of Pictures, Statues, Busto's, Basso Relievo's and Other Curiosities at the Earl of Pembroke's House at Wilton. London: 1752. V. 66; 67

COWELL, BENJAMIN
Spirit of '76 in Rhode Island: or, Sketches of the Efforts of the Government and People in the War of the Revolution. Boston: 1850. V. 63

COWELL, JOHN
The Interpreter; or Booke Containing the Signification of Words. Cambridge: 1607. V. 64
The Interpreter; or Booke Containing the Signification of Words. London: 1637. V. 64; 67

COWLES, JOHN CLIFFORD
The Whispering Buddha. Los Angeles: 1932. V. 67

COWLEY, ABRAHAM
The Mistress With Other Select Poems. London: 1926. V. 64
Prose Works.... London: 1826. V. 62; 63; 65
The Works. London: 1668. V. 64
The Works. London: 1710-1711. V. 65

COWLEY, CHARLES
Leaves from a Lawyer's Life Afloat and Ashore. Lowell: 1879. V. 63

COWLEY, HANNAH
The Runaway, A Comedy. London: 1776. V. 63

COWLEY, MALCOLM
Exile's Return. New York: 1981. V. 64; 65; 66

COWLING, ERIC T.
Rombalds Way. Otley: 1946. V. 64; 65

COWNING, FANNY
Harvestings: Sketches in Prose and Verse. Boston: 1855. V. 63

COWPER, FRANK
Sailing Tours: the Yachtsmans Guide to the Cruising Waters of the English Coast. Part II. The Coasts of Kent, Sussex, Hants, the Isle of Wight, Dorset, Devon, Cornwall and the Scilly Isles. London: 1899. V. 67
Sailing Tours 2: the Yachtsman's Guide to the Cruising Waters of the English Coast. Part II. The Coasts of Kent, Sussex, Hants, the Isle of Wight, Dorset, Devon, Cornwall and the Scilly Isle. The Nore to Tresco. London: 1893. V. 62
Sailing Tours: The Yachtman's Guide.... Volume 2 - The Coasts of Kent, Sussex, Hants, the Isle of Wight, Dorset, Devon, Cornwall and the Scilly Isles. London: 1909. V. 62
Sailing Tours 5: the Yachtsman's Guide to the Cruising Waters of the English and Adjacent Coast. Part V. The West Coasts of Scotland, the Orkneys and the West Coast of the North Sea. London: 1896. V. 62

COWPER, HENRY SWAINSON
Hawkshead: (the Northernmost Parish of Lancashire) Its History, Archaeology, Industries, Folklore, Dialect, Etc. Etc. London: 1899. V. 64; 65
The Hill of the Graves; a Record of Investigations Among the Trilitho and Megalithic Sites of Tripoli. London: 1897. V. 64; 66
Wind and Sun, Wastewater. London: 1899. V. 66

COWPER, WILLIAM
The Anatomy of the Humane Bodies.... Oxford: 1698. V. 62
The Correspondence. London: 1904. V. 62; 66
The Diverting History of John Gilpin. London: 1828. V. 65
The Diverting History of John Gilpin. New York London and Glasgow: 1888. V. 64
The Letters of the Late William Cowper, Esq. London: 1817. V. 67
Memoir of the Early Life of William Cowper, Esq. London: 1816. V. 67
Myotomia Reformata; or an Anatomical Treatise on the Muscles of the Human Body. London: 1724. V. 64; 66
Poems. London: 1786. V. 64
Poems. London: 1787. V. 63
Poems. London: 1799. V. 64
Poems. London: 1800. V. 62; 64
Poems. London: 1803. V. 62; 65
Poems. London: 1841. V. 62; 65
The Poetical Works. London: 1843. V. 62; 65
Private Correspondence of William Cowper. London: 1824. V. 62; 63; 67
The Task, a Poem in Six Books. Philadelphia: 1797. V. 66
The Works. London: 1835-1837. V. 67

COX, ALFRED J.
The Masking of the Book: a Sketch of the Bookbinding Art. New Castle: 1986. V. 64

COX, CHARLES
The Chronicles of the Collegiate Church of Free Chapel of All Saints, Derby. London: 1881. V. 66

COX, CHRISTOPHER C.
Female Education: a Poem Delivered Before The Frederick Female Seminary, at Its Annual Commencement July 8th, 1858. Frederick: 1858. V. 63

COX, DAVID
The Young Artist's Companion; or, Drawing-Book of Studies and Landscape Embellishments.... London: 1825. V. 64

COX, E. H. M.
Plant Hunting in China. 1945. V. 67
Plant Hunting in China. London: 1945. V. 64
The Plant Introductions of Reginald Farrer. London: 1930. V. 64; 66

COX, EDMUND C.
Police and Crime in India. London: 1911. V. 65

COX, EDWARD GODFREY
Reference Guide to the Literature of Travel. 1992. V. 65

COX, EDWARD YOUNG
The Art of Garnishing Churches at Christmas and Other Festivals. London: 1869. V. 63

COX, F. A.
The Baptists in America; a Narrative of the Deputation from the Baptist Union in England, to the United States and Canada. New York: 1836. V. 67

COX, GEORGE
Black Gowns and Red Coats, or Oxford in 1834. London: 1834. V. 65

COX, HARDING
Coursing and Falconry. London: 1892. V. 64; 67

COX, HIRAM
Reise in dem Innern des Reichs Burnham. Jena: 1822. V. 63

COX, J. CHARLES
The Chronicles of the Collegiate Church or Free Chapel of All Saints, Derby.... London: 1881. V. 62

COX, J. H.
Hawaiian Sculpture. Hawaii: 1974. V. 65

COX, J. M.
A Cultural Table of Orchidaceous Plants. Sydney: 1946. V. 67

COX, JAMES
Historical and Biographical Record of the Cattle Industry of Texas and Adjacent Territory. New York: 1959. V. 62; 66

COX, JOHN HERRINGTON
Folk-Songs of the South. Cambridge: 1925. V. 63; 67

COX, MARIAN ROLFE
Cinderella: Three Hundred and Forty-Five Variants of Cinderella, Catskin and Cap o'Rushes.... London: 1893. V. 65

COX, MARY L.
History of Hale County Texas. Plainview: 1937. V. 66

COX, MORRIS
Blind Drawings: Examples of an Exercise Investigating the Objective/ Subjective Principle of Graphic Art. 1978. V. 62
Forty-Five Untitled Poems. 1969. V. 65
An Impression of Spring (Summer, Autumn, Winter): a Landscape Panorama. 1965-1966. V. 62
Mummers' Fool. London: 1965. V. 64

COX, NICHOLAS
The Gentleman's Recreation: in Four Parts.... 1721. V. 64; 66; 67
The Gentleman's Recreation.... 1677. V. 62
The Gentleman's Recreation.... 1707. V. 62

COX, PALMER
The Brownies and Prince Florimel, or Brownieland, Fairyland and Demonland. New York: 1918. V. 63
The Brownies: Their Book. New York: 1887. V. 63; 66
The Brownies through the Union. New York: 1895. V. 66

COX, ROSS
Adventures on the Columbia River, Including the Narrative of a Residence of Six Years on the Western Side of the Rocky Mountains.... London: 1831. V. 66
The Columbia River. London: 1832. V. 65
The Columbia River. Norman: 1957. V. 66

COX, SAMUEL S.
Search for Winter Sunbeams in the Riviera, Corsica, Algiers and Spain. New York: 1870. V. 65

COX, SANDFORD C.
Recollections of the Early Settlement of the Wabash Valley. Lafayette: 1860. V. 67

COX, W. E.
The Book of Pottery and Porcelain. New York: 1944. V. 62

COX, WILLIAM E.
Our Family Genealogy. Raleigh: 1938. V. 63; 67

COX, WILLIAM R.
Address on the Life and Character of Maj. General Stephen D. Ramseur.... Raleigh: 1891. V. 62

COX, WILLIAM SANDS
A Memoir on Amputation of the Thigh, at the Hip-Joint. London: 1845. V. 65
A Synopsis of the Bones, Ligaments, Muscles, Blood-Vessels and Nerves of the Human Body. Birmingham: 1831. V. 65

COXE, EDWARD
Miscellaneous Poetry.... Bath: 1805. V. 65

COXE, JOHN REDMAN
Practical Observations on Vaccination; or Inoculation for the Cow- Pock. Philadelphia: 1802. V. 62

COXE, RICHARD SMITH
A New Critical Pronouncing Dictionary of the English Language.... Burlington: 1813. V. 63; 66

COXE, WILLIAM
Account of the Russian Discoveries Between Asia and America. London: 1787. V. 64; 65
Memoirs of the Administration of the Right Honourable Henry Pelham.... London: 1829. V. 62
Memoirs of the Kings of Spain of the House of Bourbon. London: 1815. V. 62
Memoirs of the Life and Administration of Sir Robert Walpole, Earl of Orford. London: 1800. V. 62
Travels in Poland, Russia, Sweden and Denmark. London: 1802. V. 62
Travels into Poland, Russia, Sweden and Denmark. London: 1784. V. 67
Travels into Poland Russia, Sweden and Denmark. London: 1785. V. 66
A View of the Cultivation of Fruit Trees.... Philadelphia: 1817. V. 62

COXHEAD, A. C.
Thomas Stothard, R.A. An Illustrated Monograph. London: 1906. V. 66

COY, OWEN C.
In the Diggins in '49, an Authentic Historical Account of the Gold Region. Los Angeles: 1948. V. 67

COZENS, ALEXANDER
Principles of a Beauty Relative to the Human Head. London: 1778. V. 66; 67

COZZENS, FREDERICK S.
Father Tom and the Pope, or a Night in the Vatican. New York: 1867. V. 66
The Sayings of Dr. Bushwacker and Other Learned Men. New York: 1867. V. 66

COZZENS, JAMES GOULD
Confusion. Boston: 1924. V. 67

CRABB, GEORGE
English Synonymes, with Copious Illustrations and Explanations. London: 1826. V. 67
The History and Postal History of Tristan Da Cunha. Ewell: 1980. V. 64; 66
The Order and Method of Instructing Children, with Strictures on the Modern System of Education. London: 1801. V. 62; 65

CRABB, JAMES
The Gipsies' Advocate. London: 1831. V. 66
The Gipsies' Advocate. London: 1832. V. 65

CRABB, RICHARD
Empire on the Platte. Cleveland: 1967. V. 62

CRABBE, GEORGE
The Borough: a Poem in Twenty-four Letters. London: 1810. V. 66; 67
An Outline of a System of Natural Theology. London: 1840. V. 67
Poems. London: 1807. V. 67
Poems. London: 1808. V. 67
Poems. Cambridge: 1905-1907. V. 65
The Poetical Works. London: 1834. V. 63
The Poetical Works. London: 1834-1836. V. 66
Tales. London: 1812. V. 66
Tales of the Hall. London: 1819. V. 64; 66
The Works. London: 1823. V. 63

CRABTREE, ADAM
Animal Magnetism, Early Hypnotism and Psychical Research, 1766-1925. Millwood: 1988. V. 65
Animal Magnetism, Early Hypnotism and Psychical Research 1766-1925. White Plains: 1988. V. 66

CRACE, JIM
Being Dead. London: 1999. V. 67

CRACE, JOHN D.
The Art of Colour Decoration: Being an Explanation of the Purposes to Be Kept in View and Means of Attaining Them. London: 1912. V. 62; 63; 64; 66

CRACE CALVERT, F.
On Protoplasmic Live, and the Action of Heat and Antiseptics Upon It. Manchester: 1873. V. 67

CRACKANTHORPE, HUBERT
Sentimental Studies and a Set of Village Tales. London: 1895. V. 67
Vignettes: a Miniature Journal of Whim and Sentiment. London: 1896. V. 64; 67
Wreckage-Seven Studies. London: 1893. V. 63; 67

CRACROFT, SOPHIA
Lady Franklin Visits Sitka, Alaska 1870. The Journal of.... Anchorage: 1918. V. 65

CRADDOCK, THOMAS
The Chemistry of the Steam-Engine Practically Considered.... London: 1847. V. 65

CRADOCK, H. C., MRS.
The House of Fancy. 1922. V. 66
Josephine Goes Travelling. London: 1940. V. 62
Josephine, John and the Puppy. London: 1920. V. 64
Josephine's Birthday. London: 1920. V. 62; 64
Josephine's Happy Family. London. V. 66

CRAFTON, ALLEN
Free State Fortress - the First Ten Years of the History of Lawrence Kansas. Lawrence: 1954. V. 67

CRAFTON, WILLIAM BELL
A Short Sketch of the Evidence for the Abolition of the Slave Trade. Philadelphia: 1792. V. 64
A Short Sketch of the Evidence for the Abolition of the Slave Trade (and) a Recommendation of the Subject to the Serious Attention of People in General. London: 1792. V. 66

CRAHAN, MARCUS ESKETH
Early American Inebrietatis. Review of the Development of American Habits in Drink and the National Bias Fixations Resulting Therefrom. Los Angeles: 1964. V. 67

CRAIG, C. H.
Catalogue of Books at Castle Point, Salcombe, South Devon. Salcombe: 1908. V. 66

CRAIG, CAMPBELL
The Trial at Bar Between Campbell Craig, Lessee of James Annesley, Esq., Plaintiff, and Richard Earl of Anglesey, Defedant, Before the...Barons of the Exchequer, at the King's Court, Dublin in...1743. London: 1744. V. 63

CRAIG, E. T.
An Irish Commune, The History of Ralahine. 1921. V. 64; 67

CRAIG, EDWARD GORDON
Henry Irving. London: 1930. V. 67
Henry Irving. Ellen Terry. A Book of Portraits. Chicago: 1899. V. 66
A Living Theatre. The Gordon Craig School. The Arena Goldoni. The Mask. Setting Forth the Aims and Objects of the Movement.... Florence: 1913. V. 65
The Mask. Florence: 1925. V. 67
Paris Diary 1932-1933. North Hills: 1982. V. 64
A Production Being Thirty-Two Collotype Plates of Designs Projected or Realised for the Pretenders of Henrik Ibsen and Produced at the Royal Theatre Copenhagen 1926. London: 1930. V. 63; 65

CRAIG, ELLEN GORDON
Edward Gordon Craig: the Last Eight Years 1958-1966. Glouchestershire: 1983. V. 64

CRAIG, G. Y.
Geology of Scotland. 1991. V. 67

CRAIG, H. STANLEY
Cumberland County (New Jersey) Marriages. Merchantville: 1932. V. 63; 66
South Jersey Marriages, Supplementing the Cape May, Cumberland, Gloucester and Salem County Marriage Records. Merchantville: 1930. V. 63; 66

CRAIG, JOHN
Britten's Aldeburgh. London: 1997. V. 64; 65
The Locks of the Oxford Canal. London: 1984. V. 65
New Universal Etymological, Technological and Pronouncing Dictionary of the English Language.... London: 1855. V. 62

CRAIG, LILLIAN K.
Reverend John Craig 1709-1774: Descendants and Allied Familes. New Orleans: 1963. V. 67

CRAIG, MAURICE
Dublin 1660-1860. 1952. V. 62
Irish Bookbindings 1600-1800. 1954. V. 62; 65
Irish Bookbindings 1600-1800. London: 1954. V. 62

CRAIG, PATRICIA
Julian Symons at 80: a Tribute. Helsinki: 1992. V. 64

CRAIG, R. MANIFOLD
The Sacrifice of Fools. London: 1896. V. 64

CRAIG, R. T.
The Mammillaria Handbook with Descriptions, Illustrations and Key to the Species of the Genus Mammillaria of the Cactaceae. Pasadena: 1945. V. 63; 66; 67

CRAIG, REGINALD S.
The Fighting Parson, The Biography of Colonel John M. Chivington. Los Angeles: 1959. V. 64; 67

CRAIG, W. M.
A Course of Lectures on Drawing, Painting and Engraving.... London: 1821. V. 66; 67
An Essay on the Study of Nature in Drawing Landscape. London: 1793. V. 64; 66

CRAIGE, JOHN H.
Cannibal Cousins. New York: 1934. V. 62; 64

CRAIGHEAD, MEINHEAD
The Mother's Birds. Worcester: 1976. V. 63; 65

CRAIGHILL, EDLEY
The Musketeers. Lynchburg: 1931. V. 67

CRAIGIE, PEARL MARY TERESA RICHARDS
A Bundle of Life. London: 1893. V. 64
A Bundle of Life. New York: 1894. V. 63
The Dream and the Business. London: 1906. V. 65
The Gods, Some Mortals and Lord Wickenham. London: 1895. V. 65
Some Emotions and a Moral. London: 1891. V. 64

CRAIK, DINAH MARIA MULOCK
The Adventures of a Brownie. Chicago: 1923. V. 63
Fair France: Impressions of a Traveller. London: 1871. V. 65
The Fairy Book. London: 1913. V. 62; 65
Hannah. London: 1872. V. 65
Is It True?. New York: 1872. V. 65
John Halifax, Gentleman. London: 1897. V. 65
Our Year: a Child's Book, in Prose and Verse. Cambridge: 1860. V. 65
An Unknown Country. New York: 1887. V. 62; 65
The Woman's Kingdom. New York: 1868. V. 64
The Woman's Kingdom. New York: 1869. V. 63
A Woman's Thoughts About Women. New York: 1858. V. 65

CRAIK, GEORGE LILLIE
The Romance of the Peerage, or Curiosities of Family History. London: 1848-1850. V. 67

CRAIK, GEORGIANA MARION
Diana. London: 1889. V. 65
Faith Unwin's Ordeal. London: 1865. V. 65

CRAIK, MRS.
The Little Lame Prince and His Traveling Cloak. London: 1875. V. 67

CRAIS, ROBERT
Free Fall. New York: 1993. V. 65; 66; 67
Indigo Slam. New York: 1997. V. 67
Lullaby Town. New York: 1992. V. 65
The Monkey's Raincoat. New York: 1987. V. 62; 65; 66; 67
The Monkey's Raincoat. London: 1989. V. 66
The Monkey's Raincoat. New York: 1993. V. 65; 66; 67
Stalking the Angel. New York: 1989. V. 65; 67
Sunset Express. New York: 1996. V. 67

CRAKER, L. E.
Herbs, Spices and Medicinal Plants.... New York: 1988-1995. V. 64; 66

CRAM, RALPH ADAMS
American Church Building of Today. New York: 1929. V. 66

CRAMBROOK, W. H. M.
Catalogue of Mathematical and Mechanical Puzzles, Deceptions and Magical Curiosities.... London: 1844. V. 62

CRAMER, GABRIEL
Introduction a L'Anaylse des Lignes Courbes Algebriques. Geneva: 1750. V. 66

CRAMER, ZADOCK
The Navigator.... Pittsburgh: 1811. V. 66

CRAMP, ARTHUR J.
Nostrums and Quackery. Chicago: 1921. V. 63
Nostrums and Quackery and Pseudo-Medicine. Chicago: 1936. V. 63

CRAMP, S.
Handbook of the Birds of Europe, the Middle East and North Africa. 1977. V. 66
Handbook of the Birds of Europe, the Middle East and North Africa. London: 1977. V. 64
Handbook of the Birds of Europe, the Middle East and North Africa. London: 1977-1994. V. 64
Handbook of the Birds of Europe, the Middle East and North Africa. London: 1980. V. 64
Handbook of the Birds of Europe, the Middle East and North Africa. London: 1985. V. 64
Handbook of the Birds of Europe, the Middle East and North Africa. The Birds of the Wester Palearctic. Volumes I and 2. Ostrichs to Bustards. London: 1977-1980. V. 62
Handbook of the Birds of Europe, the Middle East and North Africa, the Birds of the Western Palearctic. Volumes 1-7. Oxford: 1977-1993. V. 63
Handbook of the Birds of Europe, the Middle East and North Africa. The Birds of Western Palearctic. 1986-1988. V. 62
Handbook of the Birds of Europe, the Middle East and North Africa. Volume 2. Hawks to Bustards. London: 1982. V. 64
Handbook of the Birds of Europe, the Middle East and North Africa. Volume 3. 1983. V. 66

CRAMPTON, C. GREGORY
The Mariposa Indian War, 1850-1851. Salt Lake City: 1957. V. 63; 64; 67

CRAMPTON, GERTRUDE
Tottle. New York: 1945. V. 65

CRANBURNE, CHARLES
The Arraignments, Tryals and Condemnations of Charles Cranburne and Robert Lowick, for the Horrid and Exercrable Conspiracy to Assassinate His Sacred Majesty King William in Order to a French Invasion of This Kingdom.... London: 1696. V. 62

CRANDALL, ALLAN
Fisher of the Antelope Hills. Manhattan: 1949. V. 65

CRANDALL, BRUCE V.
Goldenhair and the Bettendorf Bears. Iowa: 1911. V. 64

CRANDALL, NORMA
Emily Bronte. 1957. V. 63

CRANDALL, WARREN D.
History of the Ram Fleet and the Mississippi Marine Brigade in the War for the Union...The Story of the Ellets and their Men. St. Louis: 1907. V. 65

CRANE, CLARKSON
Last Adventure. San Francisco in 1851. San Francisco: 1931. V. 62; 65

CRANE, E.
Bees and Beekeeping, Science, Practice and World Resources. Ithaca: 1990. V. 62

CRANE, FRANCES
The Applegreen Cat. Philadelphia: 1943. V. 66
Eaters of the Dead. New York: 1976. V. 67

CRANE, HART
The Bridge. New York: 1930. V. 63; 65
The Bridge. New York: 1981. V. 66
The Collected Poems of Hart Crane. London: 1938. V. 62
The Letters of Hart Crane - 1916-1932. New York: 1952. V. 64
Ten Unpublished Poems. New York: 1972. V. 62
Voyages, Six Poems. New York: 1957. V. 62; 66

CRANE, J.
Fiddler Crabs of the World. Princeton: 1975. V. 65

CRANE, JOAN
Guy Davenport: a Descriptive Bibliography 1947-1995. Haverford: 1996. V. 62; 67

CRANE, NATHALIA
The Janitor's Boy and Other Poems. New York: 1924. V. 63
Lava Lane and Other Poems. New York: 1925. V. 63

CRANE, P. R.
Evolution, Systematics, and Fossil History of the Hamanedidae. Oxford: 1989. V. 65; 66

CRANE, STEPHEN
George's Mother. New York and London: 1896. V. 62
Great Battles of the World. London: 1901. V. 65
The Little Regiment and Other Episodes of the American Civil War. New York: 1896. V. 62
Maggie. New York: 1893. V. 64
Maggie. London: 1896. V. 67
Maggie. London: 1918. V. 64
The Monster and Other Stories. New York and London: 1899. V. 62
The Open Boat and Other Stories. New York: 1898. V. 65
The O'Ruddy. New York: 1903. V. 62; 67
The Red Badge of Courage. New York: 1900. V. 64
The Red Badge of Courage. New York: 1931. V. 62; 63
Wounds in the Rain. London: 1900. V. 65

CRANE, W. J. E.
Bookbinding for Amateurs: Being Descriptions of the Various Tools and Appliances Required and Minute Instructions for Their Effective Use. London: 1903. V. 64; 66

CRANE, WALTER
Annie and Jack in London. London: 1874. V. 65
Baby's Bouquet, a Fresh Bunch of Old Rhymes and Tunes. London: 1878. V. 63
The Baby's Opera. New York. V. 63
A Flower Wedding.... London: 1905. V. 64
Grammar in Rhyme. London: 1868. V. 64
Hazelford Sketch Book; a Sampler with Autobiographical Notes.... Cambridge: 1937. V. 64
King Arthur's Knights. London: 1911. V. 66
The Little Pig Went to Market. London: 1870. V. 66
Mother Hubbard Her Picture Book Containing: Mother Hubbard, The Three Bears & The Absurd ABC. London and New York: 1897. V. 63
The Multiplication Table in Verse. London: 1874. V. 65
Of the Decorative Illustration of Books Old and New. London: 1896. V. 64
Princess Belle-Etoile. London: 1875. V. 65
Queen Summer or the Journey of the Lily and the Rose, Penned and Portrayed by Walter Crane. London: 1891. V. 62; 65; 66
Renascence. A Book of Verse. London: 1891. V. 62; 64
Triplets Comprising The Baby's Opera, The Baby's Bonquet, and The Baby's Own Aesop. London: 1899. V. 67
Walter Crane's Picture Book. London: 1874. V. 66

CRANE, WILLIAM E.
Bugle Blasts. Cincinnati: 1884. V. 67

CRANFIELD, SYDNEY W.
Houses for the Working Classes. London: 1904. V. 64

CRANFILL, J. B.
From Memory - Reminiscences, Recitals and Gleaming from a Bustling and Busy Life. Nashville: 1937. V. 66

CRANSTOUN, JAMES
Elevations, Sections and Details of the Chapel of Saint Bartholomew, Near Oxford. Oxford: 1844. V. 66

CRANTZ, DAVID
The History of Greenland: Including an Account of the Mission Carried On by the United Brethren in that Country.... London: 1820. V. 65

CRANWELL, EDWARD
An Index of the English Books Printed Before the Year MDC as Are Now in the Library of Trinity College, Cambridge. London: 1847. V. 64

CRANWORTH, LORD
Kenya Chronicles. 1939. V. 62; 63
Profit and Sport in British East Africa. London: 1919. V. 67

CRAPO, HENRY H.
The New-Bedford Directory.... Bedford: 1836. V. 62

CRAPSEY, ADELAIDE
Verse. Rochester: 1915. V. 63

CRARY, A. M.
The A. M. Crary Memoirs and Memoranda. Herington: 1915. V. 64; 67

CRASHAW, RICHARD
Caritas Nimia. Worcester: 1963. V. 63
Steps to the Temple and the Delight of the Muses, and Carmen Deo Nostro. London: 1670. V. 64

CRASHAW, WILLIAM
Decimarum & Oblationum Tabula. A Tything Table. London: 1658. V. 63

CRASTER, H. H. E.
The Parish of Corbridge. London: 1914. V. 65; 66

CRAUFURD, H. W.
The Russian Fleet in the Baltic in 1836. London: 1837. V. 64; 65

CRAUFURD, JAMES
The History of the House of Este, from the Time of Forrestus, Until the Death of Alphonsus the Last Duke of Ferrara.... London: 1681. V. 67

CRAVEN, AVERY
Edmund Ruffin Southerner; a Study in Secession. New York: 1932. V. 63

CRAVEN, ELIZABETH
A Journey through the Crimea to Constantinople in a Series of Letters from the Right Honourable...to His Serene Highness the Margrave of Brandenbourg, Anspach and Bareith. London: 1789. V. 65

CRAVEN, HENRY
English-Congo and Congo-English Dictionary. London: 1883. V. 64

CRAVEN, HENRY THORNTON
The Old Tune. Its History. London: 1876. V. 66

CRAVEN, JOSEPH
A Bronte Moorland Village and Its People: a History of Stanbury. Keighley: 1907. V. 64; 65; 66

CRAWFORD, ADAIR
Experiments and Observations on Animal Heat, and the Inflammation of Combustible Bodies.... London: 1788. V. 65

CRAWFORD, CHARLES
Observations Upon Negro-Slavery.... Philadelphia: 1790. V. 62

CRAWFORD, DONALD
Notes on Crawford v. Crawford, Queen's Proctor Intervening. Cinderford, Glos: 1886. V. 63

CRAWFORD, ELIZABETH
The Woman Suffrage Movement: a Reference Guide 1866-1928. London: 1919. V. 65

CRAWFORD, FRANCIS MARION
A Cigarette-Makers Romance. London: 1890. V. 63
Corleone: a Tale of Sicily. London: 1897. V. 66
Gleanings from Venetian History. London: 1905. V. 62; 67
Khaled: a Tale of Arabia. London: 1891. V. 66
Marzio's Crucifix. London: 1887. V. 67
The Novel: What It Is. New York: 1908. V. 67
Paul Patoff. London: 1887. V. 66
Pietro Ghisleri. London: 1893. V. 66
The Ralstons. New York: 1895. V. 66
Saracinesca. Edinburgh: 1887. V. 67
Saracinesca. London: 1887. V. 66
Taquisara. New York: 1896. V. 66
To Leeward. London: 1884. V. 66
With the Immortals. London: 1888. V. 66

CRAWFORD, J. B.
Wounds of the Brain an Essay. Wilkes Barre: 1885. V. 64; 66; 67

CRAWFORD, J. H.
From Fox's Earth to Mountain Tarn. London: 1907. V. 67

CRAWFORD, J. MARSHALL
Mosby and His Men: a Record of that Renowned Partisan Ranger, John S. Mosby. New York: 1867. V. 62; 63; 65

CRAWFORD, JACK
Lariattes - A Book of Poems and Favorite Recitations. Sigourney: 1904. V. 65

CRAWFORD, LEWIS F.
Badlands and Bronco Trails. Bismarck: 1922. V. 62; 67
Ranching Days in Dakota and Custer's Black Hills Expansion of 1874. Baltimore: 1950. V. 65; 67
Rekindling Campfires. The Exploits of Ben Arnold (Connor) (Wa-Si-Cu Tam-A-He-Ca). An Authentic Narrative of Sixty Years in the Old West As Indian Fighter, Gold Miner, Cowboy, Hunter and Army Scout. Bismark: 1926. V. 62; 65; 67

CRAWFORD, M. P.
An Address, Delivered Before the Lancaster Agricultural Society. Lancaster: 1854. V. 67

CRAWFORD, OSWALD
Dialogues of the Day. London: 1895. V. 65

CRAWFORD, ROBERT
Across the Pampas and the Andes. London: 1884. V. 63

CRAWFORD, STANLEY G.
Gascoyne. London: 1966. V. 63

CRAWFORD, WILLIAM
Remarks on the Late Earl of Chesterfield's Letter to His Son. London: 1776. V. 65

CRAWFURD, GEORGE
A Sketch of the Rise and Progress of the Trades' House of Glasgow, Its Constitution, Funds and Bye-Laws. Glasgow: 1858. V. 63

CRAWFURD, JOHN
Journal of an Embassy from the Governor-General of India to the Court of Ava. London: 1834. V. 64

CRAWHALL, JOSEPH
Chap-book Chaplets. London: 1883. V. 62
A Collection of Right Merrie Garlands for North Country Anglers. Newcastle-on-Tyne: 1864. V. 62; 65
Old Tayles Newlye Relayted. London: 1883. V. 67

CRAWLEY, W. J. C.
Camentaria Hibernica: Being the Public Constitutions that Have Served to Hold Together the Freemasons of Ireland. 1900. V. 63

CRAWSHAY, GEORGE
The Immediate Cause of the Indian Mutiny, as Set Forth in the Official Correspondence. London: 1857. V. 65

CRAWSHAY WILLIAMS, E.
Across Persia. London: 1907. V. 64

CRAYON, PORTE
Virginia Illustrated Containing a Visit to the Virginian Canaan. New York: 1857. V. 63
Virginia Illustrated: Containing a Visit to the Virginian Canaan and the Adventures of Porte Crayon and His Cousins. New York: 1871. V. 65

CREALOCK, HENRY HOPE
Deer Stalking in the Highlands of Scotland. 1892. V. 67

CREASEY, JOHN
Monarch of Skies. London: 1939. V. 65
Puzzle for Inspector West. London: 1951. V. 62

CREASY, EDWARD S.
The Fifteen Decisive Battles of the World. New York: 1969. V. 63; 64; 66

THE CREATION from the Book of Enoch - 5 1/2 Hours in Paradise. London: 1992. V. 62

CREATON & SON
Improvements at Westminster. Capital Building Materials. A Catalogue of the Very Excellent Materials Contained in two Substantial First-Rate Dwelling Houses. London: 1810. V. 62; 66

CREECH, SHARON
Walk Two Moons. New York: 1994. V. 65

CREED, PERCY R.
The Boston Society of Natural History 1830-1930. Boston: 1930. V. 67

CREED, R. S.
Reflex Activity of the Spinal Cord. 1938. V. 64

CREELEY, ROBERT
The American Dream: Collected Works of Robert Indiana. Los Angeles: 1999. V. 62
The Charm - Early and Uncollected Poems. N.P: 1967. V. 63
The Charm: Early and Uncollected Poems. Mt. Horeb: 1967. V. 67
The Charm: Early and Uncollected Poems. San Francisco: 1969. V. 63
Corn Close. Knotting: 1980. V. 62
Desultory Days. Knotting, Bedfordshire: 1978. V. 63
Divisions and Other Early Poems. Mt. Horeb: 1968. V. 64
Dreams. Madison: 1988. V. 63
For Love. Poems 1950-1960. New York: 1962. V. 63
A Form of Women. New York: 1959. V. 63; 67
Le Fou. Columbus: 1952. V. 64; 65; 67
Four Poems from a Form of Women. New York: 1959. V. 62; 67
The Gold Diggers. Palma de Mallorca: 1954. V. 63
Hello. Taylors Mistake, New Zealand: 1970. V. 63
If You. San Francisco: 1956. V. 62; 64
In London. Bolinas: 1970. V. 63
The Island. New York: 1963. V. 63
Later. West Branch: 1978. V. 67
Listen. Monoprints.... Los Angeles: 1972. V. 63
Myself. Knotting: 1977. V. 62
Numbers. 1968. V. 67
Numbers. Stuttgart-Schmela Dusseldorf: 1968. V. 62
Numbers. West Germany: 1968. V. 64
Personal. Berkeley: 1998. V. 62
Poems 1950-1965. London: 1966. V. 64
Thinking. Calais: 2000. V. 67
Thirty Things. Los Angeles: 1974. V. 63
Visual Poetics: the Art of Donald Sultan. Los Angeles: 1999. V. 62
The Whip. Worcester: 1957. V. 63; 64; 65
Words. Rochester: 1965. V. 62; 66
Words. New York: 1967. V. 64

CREENY, W. F.
Illustrations of Incised Slabs on the Continent of Europe, from Rubbings and Tracings. Norwich: 1891. V. 66

CREIGHTON, CHARLES
A History of Epidemics in Britain. Cambridge: 1891-1894. V. 64
Illustrations of Unconscious Memory in Disease Including a Theory of Alternatives. London: 1886. V. 65

CREIGHTON, JOHN
An Accurate Report of a Trial for Alledged Seduction Wherein John Creighton...was Plaintiff and Henry Dive Townshend.... Dublin: 1816. V. 63
Seduction!!! The Eloquent Speech of Mr. Phillips, of the Irish Bar, in the Case of Creighton v. Townsend, for Seduction. London: 1817. V. 63

CREIGHTON, W. S.
The Ants of North America. Cambridge: 1950. V. 63

CRELLIN, J. K.
Herbal Medicine Past and Present. Volume II. Durham: 1990. V. 67

CREMER, JOHN DORLAND
Records of the Dorland Family in America, Embracing the Principal Branches Dorland, Dorlon, Dorlan, Durland, Durling, in the United States and Canada. Washington: 1898. V. 63; 66

CREMER, LOTHAR
The Physcis of the Violin. Cambridge: 1984. V. 67

CREMER, ROBERT
Lugosi, the Man Behind the Cape. Chicago: 1976. V. 66
Lugosi, the Man Behind the Cape. 1976. V. 65

CREMER, W. H.
The Magician's Own Book. London: 1871. V. 66
The Secret Out, or, One Thousand Tricks in Drawing-Room or White Magic.... London: 1875. V. 63

CREMONY, JOHN C.
Life Among the Apaches. San Francisco: 1868. V. 67

CRENSHAW, A. H.
Campbell's Operative Orthopaedics. St. Louis: 1963. V. 67

THE CREOLE Tourist's Guide and Sketch Book to the City of New Orleans. New Orleans: 1910. V. 63

CREPAZ, ADELE
The Emancipation of Women and Its Probable Consequences.... London: 1893. V. 63; 66

CRERAR, ADAMS & CO.
Railway Supplies. Chicago: 1906. V. 67

CRESCENZI, PIETRO DE
Tradotto Novamente per M. Francesco Sansovino Nel Quale si Trattano le Cose Della Villa Con le Figure Delle Herbe Poste Nel Fine. Venice: 1564. V. 64; 66

CRESSWELL, BEATRICE F.
The Royal Progress of King Pepito. London: 1889. V. 62

CRESSY-MARCKS, VIOLET O.
Up the Amazon and Over the Andes. London: 1932. V. 64

CRESWELL, K. A. C.
A Bibliography of the Architecture, Arts and Crafts and Islam to Jan. 1, 1960. Cairo: 1961. V. 65
The Muslim Architecture of Egypt. New York: 1978. V. 62

CRESWICKE, LOUIS
South Africa and the Transvaal War. Edinburgh: 1900-1901. V. 65

CREVECOEUR, MICHEL GUILLAUME ST. JEAN DE
Letters from an American Farmer. Philadelphia: 1793. V. 66
Voyage Dans la Haute Pensylvanie (sic) et Dans L'Etat de New York. Paris: 1801. V. 64

CREWE, ROBERT CREWE-MILNES, MARQUESS OF
Lord Rosebery. London: 1931. V. 64

CREWS, HARRY
Blood and Grits. New York: 1979. V. 63; 65; 66
Car. London: 1973. V. 62; 66
A Childhood: a Biography of a Place. New York: 1978. V. 64; 65; 67
Feast of Snakes. New York: 1976. V. 64; 66; 67
Florida Frenzy. Gainesville: 1982. V. 66
The Gospel Singer. New York: 1968. V. 64
The Hawk is Dying. New York: 1973. V. 67
Karate is a Thing of the Spirit. New York: 1971. V. 63; 64; 65; 67
Two by Crews. Northridge: 1984. V. 65

CRIBB, P.
The Forgotten Orchids of Alexandre Brun. New York: 1992. V. 67

CRICHTON, CAPTAIN
In the Peculiar of the Dean and Chapter of Saint Paul's, Saturday, the 18th of July, 1801, Crichton agst. Crichton, Before the Worshipful John Fisher.. London: 1801. V. 63

CRICHTON, KYLE S.
Law and Order Ltd. The Rousing Life of Elfeso Baca of New Mexico. Santa Fe: 1928. V. 62; 63; 66

CRICHTON, MICHAEL
Airframe. Franklin Center: 1996. V. 63
Airframe. New York: 1996. V. 67
The Andromeda Strain. New York: 1969. V. 62; 65
Binary. New York: 1972. V. 65
Disclosure. Franklin Center: 1993. V. 63
Easy Go. New York: 1968. V. 65
Jurassic Park. New York: 1990. V. 62
Jurassic Park. London: 1991. V. 64
Jurassic Park. New York: 1991. V. 63; 67
Rising Sun. Franklin Center: 1992. V. 65
Scratch One. New York: 1967. V. 65
Sphere. New York: 1987. V. 67
The Terminal Man. New York: 1972. V. 67
Timeline. Franklin Center: 1999. V. 65
Travels. Franklin Center: 1988. V. 63; 65; 67

CRICK, THRONE, PSEUD.
Sketches from the Diary of a Commercial Traveller. London: 1847. V. 64

THE CRIES of Blood and Injured Innocence!!! Or, the Protection of Vice and Persecution of Virtue Exemplified in the Sufferings of Mary Neal and Her Unfortunate Family.... 1788. V. 63

THE CRIES of London, for the Information of Little Country Folks. London: 1830. V. 62; 66

CRILE, GEORGE W.
Anoci-Association. Philadelphia: 1915. V. 65

THE CRIMINAL Recorder, or Biographical Sketches of Notorious Public Characters.... London: 1804. V. 63

CRIMINAL Trials Illustrative of the Tale Entitled The Heart of Mid-Lothian.... Edinburgh: 1818. V. 63

CRIPPEN, ALICE HOTCHKISS
French Pastry Book. New York: 1926. V. 64

CRIPPS, ERNEST C.
Plough Court. London: 1927. V. 64

CRIQUI, ORVEL A.
Fifty Fearless Men, the Forsyth Scouts and Beechers's Island. Marceline: 1993. V. 67

CRISP, FRANK
Medieval Gardens. London: 1924. V. 62

CRISP, QUENTIN
How to Become a Virgin. London: 1981. V. 62
How to Have a Life Style. London: 1975. V. 65
The Naked Civil Servant. London: 1968. V. 65

CRISPIN, EDMUND
Holy Disorders. London: 1945. V. 65

CRISSO, W. D.
From Where the Sun Now Stands; Addresses by a Posse of Famous Western Speakers. Santa Fe: 1963. V. 63; 64; 66

CRISTIANO Occupato. Rome: 1762. V. 65

CRISWELL, ELIJAH HARDY
Lewis and Clark: Linguistic Pioneer. Mansfield: 2000. V. 67

CRISWELL, GROVER C.
Confederate and Southern State Currency. Pass-A-Grille Beach: 1957. V. 63

CRITCHETT & WOODS
The Post Office Directory for 1817. (with) a New Guide to Stage Coaches. London: 1817. V. 66

CRITCHFIELD, RICHARD
An American Looks at Britain. New York: 1990. V. 67

CRITCHLEY, MAC DONALD
The Parietal Lobes. London: 1953. V. 64; 66

CRITES, ARTHUR S.
Pioneer Days in Kern County. Los Angeles: 1951. V. 64; 67

CRITICISMS of the Folliad. Part the First. London: 1785. V. 63; 67

CRITTENDEN, EDWARD B.
The Entwined Lives of Miss Gabrielle Austin, Daughter of the Late Rev. Ellis C. Austin. And of Redmond, the Outlaw, Leader of the North Carolina Moonshiners. Philadelphia: 1880. V. 66

CRITTENDEN, H. H.
The Crittenden Memoirs. New York: 1936. V. 63; 66

CRITTENDEN, HIRMAN MARTIN
The Battle of Westport and National Memorial Park. Kansas City: 1938. V. 65

CROCE, ANDREA DALLA
Cirvgia Vniversale Eperfetta Di tutte le Parti Pertinenti all'Ottimo Chirurgo di Gio Andrea Dalla Croce. Venetia: 1583. V. 67

CROCE, FLAMINIO DELLA
Theatro Militare...La Seconda Volta Dato all'Impressione con l'Aggiunta di Molte Figure Molti Capitoli Nuovi & Gli Altri Ampliati. Antwerp: 1617. V. 65

CROCKATT, GILBERT
Scotch Presbyterian Eloquence Display'd: or, the Folly of Their Teaching Discover'd from their Books, Sermons and Prayers.... London: 1748. V. 67

CROCKER, ALAN
The Diaries of James Simmons, Paper Maker of Haslemere 1831-1868. Oxshott, Surrey: 1990. V. 62

CROCKER, BETTY
Betty Crocker's Picture Cook Book. Minneapolis: 1950. V. 66

CROCKER, JAMES F.
Prison Reminiscences. Portsmouth: 1906. V. 62; 63; 65

CROCKET, G. L.
Two Centuries in East Texas - a History of San Augustine County and Surrounding Territory. Dallas: 1932. V. 63

CROCKETT, ALBERT STEVENS
Old Waldorf Bar Days. New York: 1931. V. 67

CROCKETT, DAVID
Go Ahead!! The Crockett Almanac 1839. Volume II. No. 1. Nashville: 1838. V. 63
The Life of Martin Van Buren, Heir Apparent to the "Government".... Philadelphia: 1837. V. 62; 63
A Narrative of the Life of David Crockett of the State of Tennessee. Philadelphia: 1834. V. 64
Sketches and Eccentricities of Col. David Crockett of West Tennessee. New York: 1833. V. 65

CROCKETT, G. L.
Two Centuries in East Texas - a History of San Augustine County and Surrounding Territory. Dallas: 1932. V. 66

CROCKETT, SAMUEL RUTHERFORD
The Grey Man. London: 1896. V. 67
Lad's Love. London: 1897. V. 67
Mad Sir Uchtred of the Hills. 1894. V. 67

CROES, JOHN
A Discourse Delivered at Woodbury, in New Jersey, on the Twenty-Second of February Eighteen Hundred. Philadelphia: 1800. V. 66

CROFFUT, W. A.
Fifty Years in Camp and Field - Diary of Major General Ethan Allen Hitchcock, U.S.C. New York: 1909. V. 67

CROFT, HERBERT
The Abbey of Kilkhampton, or Monumental Records. London: 1780. V. 66
The Legacy of the Right Reverend Father of God, Herbert Lord Bishop of Hereford: to His Diocese. London: 1679. V. 65
Love and Madness. London: 1780. V. 63; 66
The Naked Truth. Or, the True State of the Primitive Church. London: 1675. V. 65

CROFT, JOHN
Memoirs of Harry Rowe: Constructed from Materials Found in an Old Box After His Decrease.... York: 1805. V. 62

CROFT, P. J.
Autograph Poetry in the English Language. London: 1973. V. 62

CROFTS, FREEMAN WILLS
Death of Train. London: 1946. V. 66
Double Tragedy. 1941. V. 67
Enemy Unseen. London: 1945. V. 66
Golden Ashes. London: 1940. V. 66
Silence for the Murderer. London: 1949. V. 64
Sir John Magill's Last Journey - an Inspector French Case. New York: 1930. V. 64

CROIL, JAMES
Steam Navigation and its Relation to the Commerce of Canada and the United States. Toronto: 1898. V. 65

CROIZAT, L.
Panbiogeography, or, an Introductory Synthesis of Zoogeography, Phytogeography and Geology. London: 1958. V. 63
Panbiogeography.... 1958. V. 66
Space, Time, Form: the Biological Synthesis. Caracas: 1962. V. 65

CROKE, ALEXANDER
A Report of the Case of Horner Against Liddiard, Upon the Question of What Consent is Necessary to the Marriage of Illegitimate Minors.... London: 1800. V. 65

CROKER, HENRY
Adventures in New Guinea.... London: 1876. V. 64

CROKER, JOHN WILSON
The Croker Papers. London: 1884. V. 64
The Croker Papers. London: 1885. V. 64
Familiar Epistles to Frederick (Jones) on the Present State of the Irish Stage. Dublin: 1804. V. 62; 65

CROKER, THOMAS CROFTON
Killarney Legends. 1831. V. 62; 65
The Popular Songs of Ireland. 1839. V. 63; 66
Popular Songs of Ireland. London: 1886. V. 66
Researches in the South of Ireland Illustrative of the Scenery, Architectural Remains and the Manners and Superstitions of the Peasantry.... 1824. V. 65
A Walk from London to Fulham. 1860. V. 62; 65
A Walk from London to Fulham. London: 1860. V. 62

CROLL, JAMES
Climate and Time in Their Geological Relations: a Theory of Secular Changes of the Earth's Climate. New York: 1875. V. 67

CROLY, DAVID
An Essay Religious and Political on Ecclesiastical Finance, as Regards the Roman Catholic Church in Ireland.... Cork: 1834. V. 62
Miscegenation: The Theory of the Blending of the Races Applied to the American White Man and Negro. New York: 1864. V. 62

CROLY, GEORGE
Gems, Principally from the Antique, Draw and Etched by Richard Dagley. London: 1822. V. 62
Salathiel. A Story of the Past and Present and Future. London: 1828. V. 63
Sermons Preached in the Chapel of the Foundling Hospital, With Others Preached in St. Stephen's Walbrook, in 1847. London: 1848. V. 63
Tales of the Great St. Bernard. 1828. V. 62; 65
Tales of the Great St. Bernard. London: 1829. V. 66

CROMARTY, D.
Picturesque Lancashire (North of the Ribble). London: 1908. V. 65

CROMBIE, ALEXANDER
An Essay on Philosophical Necessity. London: 1793. V. 63

CROMBIE, CHARLES
Laws of Cricket.... (Copyright of Perrier): 1906. V. 67

CROMBIE, JOHN
Rimbaud: Une Illumination. France: 1990. V. 64

CROME, JOHN
Etchings of Views in Norfolk by the Late John Crome, Founder of the Norwich Society of Artists, Together with a Biographical Memoir by Dawson Turner. Norwich: 1838-1850. V. 64

CROMEK, R. H.
Remains of Nithsdale and Galloway Song: with Historical and Traditional Notices Relative to the Manners and Custom of the Peasantry. London: 1810. V. 65

CROMER, EARL OF
Modern Egypt. London: 1908. V. 65

CROMMELIN, MAY
Joy or the Light of Cold-Home Ford. London: 1884. V. 67
Over the Andes from the Argentine to Chili and Peru. New York: 1896. V. 65

CROMMELIN-BROWN, J. L.
Wykehamical Poems and Parodies. Winchester: 1908. V. 64

CROMPTON, RICHMAL
Sweet William. 1936. V. 65
William. 1936. V. 67
William and A. R. P. 1939. V. 67
William and A.R.P. 1940. V. 65
William and the Masked Ranger. London: 1966. V. 65
William and the Pop Singers. London: 1965. V. 65
William and the Witch. 1964. V. 67
William and the Witch. London: 1964. V. 65
William - the Conqueror. 1936. V. 67
William - the Fourth. 1937. V. 67
William - the Showman. 1937. V. 65

CROMWELL, OLIVER
A Declaration of the Lord General and His Councel of Officers.... London: 1653. V. 62

CROMWELL, RICHARD
The Speech of His Highness the Lord Protector, Made to Both Houses of Parliament at Their First Meeting, on Thursday the 27th of January 1658.... London: 1659. V. 62

CROMWELL, THOMAS
History and Description of the Ancient Town and Borough of Colchester, in Essex. 1825. V. 62; 66
History and Description of the Ancient Town and Borough of Colchester in Essex. Colchester: 1825. V. 62
Oliver Cromwell and His Times. London: 1822. V. 65

CRONE, G. C. E.
Nederlansche Jachten, Binnenschepen Visschersvaartuigen en Daarmee Verwante Kleine Zeeschepen 1650-1900. Amsterdam: 1926. V. 67

CRONHELM, FREDERICK WILHELM
Double Entry by Single, a New Method of Book-Keeping, Applicable To all Kinds of Business.... London: 1818. V. 67

CRONICA DEL REY DON JUAN EL SEGUNDO
Comienca la Cronica del Serenissimo Rey Don Juan el Segundo. Logrono: 1517. V. 62

CRONIN, A. J.
The Citadel. London: 1937. V. 67

CRONISE, TITUS FEY
The Natural Wealth of California. New York: 1868. V. 66
The Natural Wealth of California. San Francisco: 1868. V. 62

CROOK, C.
Campanulas, Their Cultivation and Classification. 1951. V. 63; 66

CROOK, JOHN
Short History of the Life of John Crook, Containing His Spiritual Travails and Breathings After God, etc. London: Sep. 1790. V. 63

CROOKES, WILLIAM
Sur la Viscosite des Gaz tres Rarefies. Paris: 1882. V. 64

CROPPER, MICHAEL
Works of Arthur Conan Doyle: the Michael Cropper Collection. San Francisco: 1983. V. 65

CROSBY, ALEXANDER L.
Old Greenwood, Pathfinder of the West. Georgetown: 1967. V. 67

CROSBY, CARESSE
Painted Shores. Paris: 1927. V. 67
Poems for Harry Crosby by C.C. Paris: 1931. V. 63

CROSBY, ELIZABETH CAROLINE
Correlative Anatomy of the Nervous System. New York: 1962. V. 65

CROSBY, EVERETT U.
Susan's Teeth and Much About Scrimshaw. Nantucket Island: 1955. V. 62

CROSBY, GEORGE
Illustrated Guide to Scarborough. Scarborough: 1846. V. 65

CROSBY, HARRY
Anthology. Paris: 1923-1924. V. 63; 65
Antigua California. Albuquerque: 1994. V. 62; 63
Transit of Venus. Paris: 1929. V. 65

CROSBY, W. O.
Geology of the Boston Basin. Boston: 1893-1900. V. 63

CROSBY'S Caledonian Musical Repository: a Choice Selection of Esteemed Scottish Songs Adapted for the Voice, Violin, and German Flute. Edinburgh: 1811. V. 62; 63

CROSLAND, NEWTON, MRS.
Memorable Women. The Story of Their Lives. London: 1854. V. 65

CROSLAND, THOMAS W. H.
The First Stone: On Reading the Unpublished Parts of De Profundis. London: 1912. V. 64; 67
Iris and the Water Lilies. 1888?. V. 67
Last Poems. London: 1928. V. 67
The Motor Car Dumpy Book. London: 1904. V. 64
The Pink Book. Brighton: 1894. V. 67

CROSLEY, WILLIAM F.
The Trenton City Directory for 1869.... Trenton: 1869. V. 63; 66

CROSS, AMANDA
In the Last Analysis. New York: 1964. V. 63
The James Joyce Murder. New York: 1967. V. 63
The Question of Max. New York: 1976. V. 63
The Theban Mysteries. New York: 1971. V. 63

CROSS, ANDREW J.
A System of Ocular Skiametry. New York: 1903. V. 67

CROSS Child. New York: Sep. 1870. V. 64

CROSS, J. W.
George Eliot's Life as Related in Her Letters and Journals. Edinburgh: 1885. V. 65
George Eliot's Life as Related in Her Letters and Journals. New York: 1885. V. 65

CROSS, JEREMY
The Templars' Chart, or Hieroglyphic Monitor; Containing All the Emblems and Hieroglyphics Explained in the Valiant and Magnanimous Orders.... New York: 1856. V. 66

CROSS, JOE
Cattle Clatter - a History of Cattle from the Creation to the Texas Centennial in 1936. Kansas City: 1938. V. 63; 66

CROSS, JOHN KEIR
The Other Passenger - 18 Strange Stories. London: 1944. V. 63

CROSS, JONATHAN
Five Years in the Alleghanies. New York: 1863. V. 63; 66

CROSS, L.
The Book of Old Sundials and Their Mottoes. 1914. V. 63

CROSS, ODO
The Snail that Climbed the Eiffel Tower and Other Stories. London: 1947. V. 65

CROSS, R. W.
The True Masonic Chart or Hieroglyphic Monitor. New York: 1846. V. 64

CROSS, RALPH HERBERT
The Early Inns of California, 1844-1869. San Francisco: 1954. V. 63

CROSS, ROBERT
Vita Sackville-West: a Bibliography. New Castle: 1999. V. 67

CROSS, WILBUR L.
The Life and Times of Laurence Sterne. New Haven: 1925. V. 62

CROSSE, ANDREW F.
Round About the Carpathians. London: 1878. V. 64

CROSSE, CORNELIA
Red-Letter Days of My Life. London: 1892. V. 67

CROSSEN, FOREST
Western Yesterdays. Boulder: 1966-1969. V. 63; 66

CROSTHWAITE, PETER
A Series of Accurate Maps of the Principal Lakes of Cumberland, Westmorland and Lancashire. Newcastle-upon-Tyne: 1968. V. 62

CROSTON, JAMES
Buxton and Its Resources: with Excursions to Haddon, Chatsworth, Castleton, Matlock and Dove Dale. London: 1865. V. 66

CROTCH, WILLIAM
Six Etchings...of the Ruins of the Late Fire at Christ Church, Oxford. Oxford: 1809. V. 62

CROTTY, D. G.
Four Years Campaigning in the Army of the Potomac, by Color Sergeant D. G. Crotty, Third Michigan Volunteer Infantry. Grand Rapids: 1874. V. 65

CROTTY, DANIEL
At a General Court Martial, Held at Horsham Barracks on the 17th September 1806...Ensign Daniel Crotty, of the 2nd Battalion 90th Regiment of Foot.... N.P: 1806. V. 63

CROUCH, E. A.
An Illustrated Introduction to Lamarck's Conchology. 1827. V. 66

CROUCH, NATHANIEL
The English Hero; or Sir Francis Drake Reviv'd.... London: 1762. V. 65
A Journey to Jerusalem.... Hartford: 1796. V. 66
The Wars in England, Scotland and Ireland. London: 1681. V. 64

CROUSAZ, JEAN PIERRE DE
A New Treatise of the Art of Thinking; or a Compleat System of Reflections, Concerning the Conduct and Improvement of the Mind Illustrated with Variety of Characters and Examples Drawn from the Ordinary Occurrences of Life.... London: 1724. V. 64

CROW, JEFFERSON BRIM
Randolph Scott, the Gentleman from Virginia. Carrollton: 1987. V. 66

CROW, S. H.
Hampshire Avon Salmon. 1966. V. 67

CROWE, ANNE MARY
An Extraordinary Case in Chancery, Fairly Related.... Deptford: 1806. V. 64

CROWE, CAMERON
Fast Times at Ridgemont High. New York: 1981. V. 65

CROWE, CATHERINE
The Night Side of Nature; or Ghosts and Ghostseers. London: 1848. V. 66
The Night Side of Nature; or, Ghosts and Ghostseers. London: 1852. V. 65

CROWE, GEORGE
The Commission of H.M.S. Terrible 1898-1902. London: 1903. V. 65

CROWE, PAT
Spreading Evil - Pat Crowe's Autobiography. New York: 1927. V. 63; 66

CROWE, SAMUEL JAMES
Halsted of Johns Hopkins. The Man and His Men. Springfield: 1957. V. 65

CROWELL, BENEDICT
America's Munitions 1917-1918. Washington: 1919. V. 65
The Road to France. New Haven: 1921. V. 64

CROWELL, JOSEPH E.
The Young Volunteer. The Everyday Experiences of a Soldier Boy in the Civil War. New York: 1906. V. 63; 66

CROWFOOT, J. W.
Excavations in the Tyropoeon Valley, Jerusalem. London: 1929. V. 62

CROWHILL, ARTHUR
Tales for Children. London: 1864. V. 62

CROWLEY, ALEISTER
The Collected Works. Foyers: 1905-1907. V. 62
The Diary of a Drug Fiend. London: 1922. V. 67
Magick in Theory and Practice by the Master Therion. Paris: 1929. V. 64; 66
Moonchild: a Prologue. London: 1929. V. 66
The Stratagem and Other Stories. London: 1929?. V. 66
White Stains. The Literary Remains of George Archibald Bishop. Amsterdam: 1898. V. 64

CROWLEY, JOHN
Beasts. New York: 1976. V. 67

CROWLEY, MART
The Boys in the Band. New York: 1968. V. 63; 64; 66

CROWN, JOHN
Henry the Sixth, the First Part. (with) ...Part the Second. London: 1681. V. 62

CROWNOVER, SIMS
The Battle of Franklin. Nashville: 1955. V. 63; 65

CROWTHER, JONATHAN
A True and Complete Portraiture of Methodism; or, the History of the Wesleyan Methodists.... London: 1812. V. 64

CROXALL, SAMUEL
An Original Canto of Spencer; Design'd as Part of His Fairy Queen, but Never Printed. Now Made Publick, by Nestor Ironside. London: 1714. V. 66

CROXTON SMITH, A.
About Our Dogs. London. V. 67

CROZIER, E. W.
The Knoxville Blue Book of Selected Names of Knoxville and Suburban Towns. Knoxville: 1894. V. 64

CRUDEN, ALEXANDER
A Complete Concordance to the Holy Scripture of the Old and New Testament: In Two Parts. London: 1738. V. 66

CRUDEN, JOHN
Report on the Management of the Estates Sequestered in South Carolina, by Order of Lord Cornwallis in 1780-1782. Brooklyn: 1890. V. 63; 67

CRUICKSHANK, ALEX
Matsqui Prairie and Its Surroundings in the Province of British Columbia Dominion of Canada. Vancouver: 1899. V. 63

CRUICKSHANK, BRODIE
Eighteen Years on the Gold Coast of Africa, Including an Account at the Native Tribes, and Their Intercourse with Europeans. London: 1853. V. 64

CRUICKSHANK, T.
The Practical Planter.... Edinburgh: 1830. V. 63; 66

CRUIKSHANK, GEORGE
The Bottle and the Drunkard's Children in Sixteen Plates. London: 1847-1848?. V. 65
The British Bee Hive. London: 1867. V. 65

CRUIKSHANK, GEORGE continued
Catalogue of George Cruikshank's Own Original Collection of His Works. London: 1903. V. 65
A Catalogue Raisonne of the Work Executed During the Years 1806-1877. New York: 1997. V. 67
The Comic Almanack. London: 1854. V. 66
The Comic Almanack. London: 1870-1878. V. 65
The Comic Almanack for 1839 (-1842). London: 1843?. V. 65
Cruikshank at Home: a New Family Album. London: 1845. V. 62
A Few Remarks on the System of General Education as Proposed by the National Education League. With a Second Edition of A Slice of Bread and Butter, Upon the Same Subject. London: 1870. V. 65
George Cruikshank's Fairy Library. Hop-O'My-Thumb and the Seven-League Boots. London: 1860. V. 65
George Cruikshank's Fairy Library.... London: 1885. V. 63
George Cruikshank's Table-Book. London: 1845. V. 65
Hop-O'My Thumb and the Seven League Boots. London: 1860. V. 62
The House that Jack Built. London: 1853. V. 65
Illustrations of Popular Works. London: 1830. V. 65
Illustrations of Time. London: 1874. V. 65
London Characters. London: 1827-1906. V. 62
A Pop-Gun Fired Off by George Cruikshank. London: 1860. V. 65
Scraps and Sketches. London: 1881. V. 65
Six Illustrations to Cowper's Diverting History of John Gilpin.... London: 1828. V. 65
Stenelaus and Amylda: a Christmas Legend. London: 1858. V. 65
Sunday in London. London: 1833. V. 64

CRUIKSHANK, I. R.
Lessons of Thrift. London: 1820. V. 63

CRUIKSHANK, ROBERT
The Playfair Papers, or Brother Jonathan, the Smartest Nation in All Creation. London: 1841. V. 64
Sketches of Pumps, Handled by Robert Cruikshank. London: 1846. V. 65

CRUIKSHANK, WILLIAM CUMBERLAND
Anatomie des Vaisseaux Absorbans du Corps Humain. Paris: 1787. V. 66

CRUISE, FRANCIS R.
Observations on the Reduction Dislocations with the Description of a New Apparatus for Making Extension. Dublin: 1861. V. 67

CRUISE, RICHARD A.
Journal of a Ten Months' Residence in New Zealand. London: 1823. V. 64

CRUISE, WILLIAM
An Essay on the Nature and Operation of Fines and Recoveries. London: 1786. V. 65

CRULL, JODICUS
An Introduction to the History of the Kingdoms and States of Asia, Africa and America, Both Ancient and Modern, According the the Method of Samuel Puffendorf.... London: 1705. V. 67

CRULL, JOHN
The Antiquities of St. Peter's; or the Abbey Church of Westminster.... London: 1711. V. 66

CRUM, JOSIE MOORE
The Rio Grande Southern Railroad. Durango: 1961. V. 66
The Rio Grande Southern Story. Durango: 1957. V. 66

CRUM, MARGARET
First-Line Index of English Poetry 1500-1800 in Manuscripts of the Bodelian Library, Oxford. New York: 1969. V. 62
First-Line Index of English Poetry 1500-1800 in Manuscripts of the Bodelian Library Oxford. Oxford: 1969. V. 62; 65; 67

CRUMB, ROBERT
Sketchbook Volume 1. Seattle: 1992. V. 66
The Yum Yum Book. San Francisco: 1975. V. 62

CRUMLEY, JAMES
Border Snakes. New York: 1996. V. 67
Border Snakes. Tucson: 1996. V. 63; 64; 65; 66; 67
The Collection. London: 1991. V. 65; 66
Dancing Bear. New York: 1983. V. 63; 64; 65; 66; 67
Introduction to Kent Anderson's Sympathy for the Devil. Tacoma: 1997. V. 67
The Last Good Kiss. New York: 1978. V. 62; 63; 64; 65; 66; 67
The Mexican Pig Bandit. Mission Viejo: 1998. V. 67
The Mexican Pig Bandit. Royal Oak: 1998. V. 67
The Mexican Tree Duck. 1992. V. 64; 66
The Mexican Tree Duck. Bristol: 1993. V. 65
The Mexican Tree Duck. Huntington Beach: 1993. V. 65; 66
The Mexican Tree Duck. London: 1993. V. 62; 64; 66
The Muddy Fork (A Work in Progress). Northridge: 1984. V. 66
The Muddy Fork and Other Things. Livingston: 1991. V. 64; 65; 66; 67
One to Count Cadence. New York: 1969. V. 62; 63; 64; 65; 66; 67
One to Count Cadence. New York: 1978. V. 63
One to Count Cadence. London: 1994. V. 63
The Pigeon Shoot. Santa Barbara: 1987. V. 66
The Wrong Case. New York: 1975. V. 66; 67

CRUMMELL, ALEX
The Relations and Duties of Free Colored Men in America to Africa. Hartford: 1861. V. 62

CRUMMER, LE ROY
A Catalogue of Manuscripts and Medical Books Printed Before 1640, in the Library of Le Roy Crummer. Omaha;: 1927. V. 66

CRUMP, NORMAN
By Rail to Victory. London: 1947. V. 63

CRUMP, PAUL
Burn, Killer, Burn!. Chicago: 1962. V. 63

CRUMP, SPENCER
Henry Huntington and the Pacific Electric. A Pictorial Album. Los Angeles: 1970. V. 66

CRUMP, W. B.
Ancient Highways of the Parish of Halifax. Part VII - The York and Chester Highway. Part VIII Sowerby Highways. Part IX Heptonstall and Its Highways. Halifax: 1929. V. 65

CRUMPE, SAMUEL
An Essay on the Best Means of Providing Employment for the People. London: 1793. V. 65

CRUMRINE, BOYD
History of Washington Co., Pennsylvania, With Biographical Sketches of Many of Its Pioneers and Prominent Men. Philadelphia: 1882. V. 63

CRUSE, THOMAS
Apache Days and After. Caldwell: 1941. V. 63; 66; 67

CRUSIUS, LEWIS
The Lives of the Roman Poets. London: 1733. V. 66
The Lives of the Roman Poets. London: 1833. V. 62

CRUTCHLEY, BROOKE
A Printer's Christmas Books. Cambridge: 1974. V. 64
A Tally of Types. Cambridge: 1973. V. 65
Two Men. Walter Lewis and Stanley Morison at Cambridge. Cambridge: 1968. V. 62; 64; 65; 67

CRUTCHLEY, E. A.
A History and Description of the Pitt Press Erected...for the Use of the University Printing Press AD 1833. Altered and Restored AD 1937. London: 1938. V. 62

CRUTTENDEN, ROBERT
The Experience of Mr. R. Cruttenden, as Delivered Into a Congregation of Christ, in Lime-Street, Under the Pastoral Care of the Reverend Mr. Richardson. London: 1755. V. 64

THE CRYSTAL Palace, (Sale Catalogue). 1911. V. 62

CUBAS, ANTONIO GARCIA
The Republic of Mexico in 1876. Mexico: 1876. V. 62

CUBBIN, THOMAS
The Wreck of the Serica, a Narrative of 1868. London: 1950. V. 64

CUBBON, WILLIAM
A Bibliographical Account of Works Relating to the Isle of Man with Biographical Memoranda and Copious Literary References. London: 1933. V. 66
Island Heritage Dealing with Some Phases of Manx History. Manchester: 1952. V. 67

CUDWORTH, CHARLES
Fen and Flood. A Cantata for Soprano and Baritone Soli, Chorus and Orchestra. London: 1955. V. 67

CUDWORTH, RALPH
The True Intellectual System of the Universe.... London: 1678. V. 64
The True Intellectual System of the Universe.... London: 1743. V. 64

CUDWORTH, WILLIAM
Life and Correspondence of Abraham Sharp, the Yorkshire Mathematician and Astronomer and Assistant of Flamsteed. London: 1889. V. 64; 65; 66
Old Bradford Views. Bradford: 1897. V. 65

CUENDIAS, EMANUEL VON
Spanien und die Spanier.... Brussels & Leipzig: 1849. V. 64

CUEVAS, P. MARIANO
Monje y Marino: La Vida y los Tiempos de Fray Andres de Urdaneta. Mexico: 1943. V. 67

CUISIN, P.
Bouquet Offert a Mlle. Rachel. Paris: 1839. V. 67

CUISINE et la Patisserie Expliquees Du Cordon-Bleu. Paris. V. 67

LE CUISINIER Roial et Bourgeois. Paris: 1698. V. 64

CUITT, GEORGE
Wanderings and Pencillings Amongst the Ruins of the Olden Times: a Series of Seventy-Three Etchings.... London: 1838. V. 66
Wanderings and Pencillings Amongst the Ruins of the Olden Times; a Series of Seventy-Three Etchings.... 1848. V. 67

CULBERTSON, ELY
Contract Bridge Complete. London: 1954. V. 63

CULLEN, COUNTEE
Color. New York and London: 1925. V. 63; 64; 66

CULLEN, DR.
Isthmus of Darien Ship Canal: with a Full History of the Scotch Colony of Darien, Several Maps, Views of the County and Original Documents. London: 1853. V. 64

CULLEN, J.
The Orchid Book, a Guide to the Cultivated Orchid Species. Cambridge: 1992. V. 67

CULLEN, LUKE
Insurgent Wicklow 1798. 1948. V. 67

CULLEN, WILLIAM
Institutions of Medicine. Edinburgh: 1788. V. 63
A Treatise of the Materia Medica. New York: 1802. V. 65
The Works of William Cullen, M.D. Edinburgh: 1827. V. 64

CULLEY, JOHN H.
Cattle Horses and Men On the Western Range. Los Angeles: 1940. V. 64

CULLIS, CHARLES
Faith Cures; or, Answers to Prayer in the Healing of the Sick. Boston: 1879. V. 66

CULLUM, GROVE
Selection and Training of the Polo Pony with Comments on the Game.... New York: 1934. V. 66

CULLUM, RIDGEWELL
Sheets in the Wind. Philadelphia: 1932. V. 67

CULLYER, JOHN
The Gentleman and Farmer's Assistant.... Norwich: 1818. V. 67

CULPEPER, NICHOLAS
The British Herbal and Family Physician, to Which is Added a Dispensatory for the Use of Private Families. Halifax: 1818?. V. 64; 66
Complete Herbal and English Physician. 1805. V. 67
Culpeper's English Physician and Complete Herbal. London: 1790. V. 63; 67
The English Physitian. London: 1652. V. 65
The English Physitian Enlarged. London: 1653. V. 64
The English Physitian Enlarged. London: 1656. V. 64; 66
The English Physitian Enlarged. 1788. V. 63; 66
The English Physitian Enlarged. London: 1788. V. 64
Pharmacopoeia Londinensis; or the London Dispensatory.... London: 1683. V. 63; 67
Pharmacopoeia Londinensis; or the London Dispensatory.... London: 1654. V. 64
Pharmacopoeia Londinensis; or the London Dispensatory.... Boston: 1720. V. 64; 66
A Physical Directory.... London: 1651. V. 66

CULTURA Do Arroz. Porto Alegre: 1935. V. 66

CULVER, FRANCIS BARNUM
Blooded Horses of Colonial Days. Baltimore: 1922. V. 64

CULVER, R. K.
The Roosevelt Bears Abroad. New York: 1908. V. 62

CULVERWELL, NATHANAEL
An Elegant, and Learned Discourse of the Light of Nature With Several Other Treatises. London: 1661. V. 64

CUMBERLAND AND WESTMORLAND ANTIQUARIAN & ARCHAEOLOGICAL SOC.
Transactions - Old Series. Volumes 1-16. Kendal: 1874-1899. V. 66

CUMBERLAND, C. S.
Sport on the Pamirs and Turkistan Steppes. Edinburgh: 1895. V. 64
Sport on the Pamirs and Turkistan Steppes. 1989. V. 67

CUMBERLAND, GEORGE
An Attempt to Describe Hafod, and the Neighbouring Scenes About the Bridge of the Funack, Commonly Called the Devils Bridge, in the County of Cardigan.... London: 1796. V. 66
An Essay on the Utility of Collecting the Best Works of the Ancient Engravings of the Italian School.... London: 1827. V. 66
Outlines from the Antients, Exhibiting Their Principles of Composition in Figures, and Basso-Relievos Taken Chiefly from Inedited Mountains of Greek and Roman Sculpture.... London: 1829. V. 65

CUMBERLAND MUTUAL FIRE INSURANCE CO.
Charter and By-Laws of the Cumberland Mutual Fire Insurance Co. Ridgeton (i.e. Bridgeton): 1852. V. 63

CUMBERLAND, RICHARD
Anecdotes of Eminent Painters in Spain, During the Sixteenth and Seventeenth Centuries.... London: 1782. V. 62
The Brothers, a Comedy. London: 1770. V. 66
Calvary; or the Death of Christ. London: 1792. V. 62; 67
An Essay Towards the Recovery of the Jewish Measures and Weights, Comprehending Their Monies.... London: 1686. V. 63
John de Lancaster. London: 1809. V. 65
Original Tales. London: 1810. V. 65
A Treatise on the Laws of Nature. London: 1727. V. 63; 67

CUMING, E. D.
British Sport Past and Present. London: 1909. V. 67
With Horse and Hound: from British Sport Past and Present. 1911. V. 64

CUMINGS, SAMUEL
The Western Pilot, Containing Charts of the Ohio River, and of the Mississippi, from the Mouth of the Missouri to the Gulf of Mexico.... Cincinnati: 1832. V. 66

CUMMING, CONSTANCE FREDERICA GORDON
At Home in Fiji. Edinburgh and London: 1882. V. 65
Lady's Cruise in a French Man-of-War. Edinburgh: 1882. V. 65
Memories. Edinburgh: 1904. V. 65

CUMMING, T. G.
Description of the Iron Bridges of Suspension Now Erecting Over the Straight of Menai, at Bangor and over the River Conway, in North Wales.... London: 1824. V. 65

CUMMING, W. P.
The Discovery of North America. London: 1971. V. 62
The Southeast in Early Maps. Chapel Hill: 1998. V. 65

CUMMINGS, A. I.
The Lady's Present; or, Beauties of Female Character. Boston: 1852. V. 64; 66

CUMMINGS, A. L.
The Framed Houses of Massachusetts Bay 1625-1725. Cambridge: 1979. V. 65

CUMMINGS, BRYON
First Inhabitants of Arizona and the Southwest. Tucson: 1953. V. 63; 66
Kinishba. A Prehistoric Pueblo of the Great Pueblo Period. Tucson: 1940. V. 63; 64; 65; 66

CUMMINGS, CAREY
The Biorhythmic Holmes: a Chronological Perspective. Volume I. N.P: 1980. V. 66

CUMMINGS, D. C.
A Historical Survey of the Boiler Makers' and Iron and Steel Ship Builders' Society, from August 1834 to August 1904. Newcastle-on-Tyne: 1905. V. 64

CUMMINGS, EDWARD ESTLIN
Eimi. New York: 1933. V. 63; 65; 66; 67
The Enormous Room. New York: 1922. V. 67
The Enormous Room. London: 1928. V. 65; 66
50 Poems. New York: 1940. V. 63
Him. New York: 1927. V. 66; 67
Is 5. New York: 1926. V. 64; 66
A Miscellany. New York: 1958. V. 64
No Thanks. New York: 1935. V. 67
73 Poems. New York: 1963. V. 63
Tulips and Chimneys. New York: 1923. V. 64
Xaipe: Seventy-One Poems. New York: 1950. V. 65

CUMMINGS, JACOB ABBOT
School Atlas to Cummings' Ancient and Modern Geography. Boston: 1820. V. 62

CUMMINGS, M.
The Life, Travels and Gospel Labors of Eld. Joseph Thomas. New York: 1861. V. 62

CUMMINGS, RAY
The Girl in the Golden Atom. 1923. V. 66
Tales from the Scientific Crime Club. London: 1979. V. 65

CUMMINGS, SARAH
Autobiography and Reminiscences. New York: 1914. V. 63

CUMMINGS, THAYER
Seven on Sherlock: Some Trifling Observations on the Greatest of All rivate Consulting Detectives. 1968. V. 65

CUMMINGTON Poems 1939. Cummington: 1939. V. 62

CUMMINS, ELLA S.
The Story of the Files: a Review of Californian Writers and Literature. San Francisco: 1893. V. 62; 63

CUMMINS, MARIA S.
Haunted Hearts. Boston: 1864. V. 63; 66

CUMPSTON, J.
The History of Small-Pox in Australia, 1788-1908. Melbourne: 1914. V. 62

CUNARD, NANCY
Memories of George Moore. London: 1956. V. 63
Negro. An Anthology. London: 1934. V. 64
Nous Gens d'Espagne: Poems. 1949. V. 66
Parallax. London: 1925. V. 62; 63; 67
Poemes a la France - 1939-1944. Paris: 1947. V. 63
Poemes A La France 1934-1944. Paris: 1947. V. 64
Thoughts About Ronald Firbank. New York: 1971. V. 63

THE CUNARD White Star Quadruple-Screw Liner Queen Mary. London: 1972. V. 64

CUNDALL, H. M.
Birket Foster, R. W. S. London: 1906. V. 64

CUNEO, TERENCE
The Mouse and His Master. The Life and Work of Terence Cuneo. London: 1977. V. 67
The Railway Paintings of Terence Cuneo. London: 1984. V. 67

CUNEY-HARE, MAUD
Negro Musicians and Their Music. Washington: 1936. V. 62

CUNINGHAME, WILLIAM
Essays on Political Subjects. London: 1791. V. 67

CUNNINGHAM, ALLAN
The Lives of the Most Eminent British Painters, Sculptors and Architects. London: 1829-1833. V. 67

CUNNINGHAM, D. J.
Challenger Voyage Zoology. Part 16 Marsupialia. 1882. V. 66
Challenger Voyage, Zoology. Part 16. Marsupialia. London: 1882. V. 62

CUNNINGHAM, D. J. *continued*
The Lumbar Curve in Man and Apes.... 1886. V. 66
Report on the Scientific Results of the Voyage of HMS Challenger... Part XVI Report on the Marsupalia. 1882. V. 67
The Skeleton of the Irish Giant, Cornelius Magrath. Dublin: 1891. V. 67

CUNNINGHAM, EUGENE
Triggernometry. A Gallery of Gunfighters. Caldwell: 1941. V. 64
Triggernometry. A Gallery of Gunfighters. New York: 1934. V. 64; 67

CUNNINGHAM, F.
James David Forbes. Pioneer Scottish Glaciologist. Edinburgh: 1990. V. 67

CUNNINGHAM, FRANCIS
An Account of the Death of Philip John, Who Was Executed for the Murder of His Father, in the Island of Jersey, October 3, 1829. London: 1830. V. 63

CUNNINGHAM, FRANK
General Stand Waite's Confederate Indians. San Antonio: 1959. V. 62; 63
Knight of the Confederacy, General Turner Ashby. San Antonio: 1960. V. 62

CUNNINGHAM, H. H.
Doctors in Gray. The Confederate Medical Service. Baton Rouge: 1958. V. 63

CUNNINGHAM, HENRY STEWART
The Heriots. London: 1890. V. 66
Late Laurels. London: 1864. V. 66

CUNNINGHAM, IMOGEN
After Ninety. Seattle and London: 1977. V. 63
Photographs. Seattle: 1970. V. 62

CUNNINGHAM, J. V.
Doctor Drink. Poems. Cummington: 1950. V. 63
The Helmsman. San Francisco: 1942. V. 63; 64; 67
The Judge is Fury. New York: 1947. V. 63
The Literary Form of the Prologue to the Canterbury Tales. N.P: 1952. V. 62
Selected Poems. Mt. Horeb: 1971. V. 64
Some Salt. Mt. Horeb: 1967. V. 67

CUNNINGHAM, J. W.
The Velvet Cushion. London: 1814. V. 67
The Velvet Cushion. London: 1817. V. 66

CUNNINGHAM, JOHN
Poems Chiefly Pastoral. London: 1766. V. 66

CUNNINGHAM, JOHN BENEDICT
1919 The Death Bell. St. Albans: 1912. V. 62

CUNNINGHAM, MICHAEL
Flesh and Blood. New York: 1995. V. 67
Golden States. New York: 1984. V. 62; 63; 65
A Home at the End of the World. New York: 1990. V. 67
The Hours. New York: 1998. V. 62; 63; 64; 67

CUNNINGHAM, PETER
The Story of Nell Gwyn; and The Sayings of Charles the Second. London: 1852. V. 64

CUNNINGHAM, PETER MILLER
Two Years in New South Wales; Comprising Sketches of the Actual State of Society in that Colony.... London: 1827. V. 63

CUNNINGHAM, R. O.
Notes on the Natural History of the Strait of Magellan and West Coast of Patagonia, Voyage of H.M.S. Nassau in 1866-1869. Edinburgh: 1871. V. 62; 64
Notes on the Reptiles, Amphibia, Fishes, Mollusca and Crustacea Obtained During the Voyage of HMS Nassau in the Years 1866-1869 (in South America). 1870. V. 67

CUNNINGHAM, S. A.
Confederate Veteran Magazine. Wendell: 1984. V. 63

CUNNINGHAM, TIMOTHY
The Law of Bills of Exchange, Promissory Notes, Bank Notes and Insurances.... London: 1766. V. 62
A New and Complete Law Dictionary.... London: 1764. V. 67

CUNNINGHAM, WILLIAM
The Growth of English Industry and Commerce.... Cambridge: 1910-1912. V. 64

CUNYNGHAME, A.
Aide-de-Cam's Recollections of Service in China.... London: 1844. V. 64
Travels in the Eastern Caucasus, on the Caspian and Black Seas, Especially in Daghestan, and on the Frontiers of Persia and Turkey During the Summer of 1871. 1872. V. 63; 64; 66; 67

CUPID & PSYCHE
The Story of Cupid and Psyche. 1974. V. 65

CUPID'S Horn-Book. Songs and Ballads of Marriage and of Cuckoldry Written by Various Hands and Embellished with Cuts. Mt. Vernon: 1936. V. 66

CUPPLES, GEORGE
The Green Hand: a Sea Story. London: 1856. V. 65
Shadows on the Screen; or, An Evening With the Children. London: 1883. V. 65

CUREAU DE LA CHAMBRE, MARIN
Novae Methodi Pro Explicandis Hippocrate & Aristotele Specimen. Paris: 1662. V. 64

CURIALIA Miscellanea, or Anecdotes of Old Times: Regal, Nobel, Gentilitial & Miscellaneous. London: 1818. V. 67

CURIE, MARIE
Recherches sur les Substances Radioactives.... Paris: 1904. V. 64

CURIO, CAELIUS SECUNDUS
Pasquillorum Tomi Duo. Quorum Primo Versibus ac Rhythmis, Altero Soluta Oratione Conscripta Quamplurima Continentur.... Basle: 1544. V. 62
The Visions of Pasquin, or, a Character of the Roman Court., Religion and Practices.... London: 1689. V. 63

CURLE, ALEXANDER O.
The Treasure of Traprain. Glasgow: 1923. V. 62; 66

CURLE, JAMES
A Roman Frontier Post and Its People, the Fort of Newstead in the Parish of Melrose. Glasgow: 1911. V. 67

CURLE, RICHARD
Collecting American First Editions, Its Pitfalls and Its Pleasures. Indianapolis: 1930. V. 65

CURLEY, EDWIN A.
Nebraska, Its Advantages, Resources and Drawbacks. London: 1875. V. 65

CURLING, B. W. R.
British Racecourses. London: 1951. V. 63; 67

CURLING, THOMAS BLIZARD
A Treatise on Tetanus Being the Essay For Which the Jacksonian Prize for the Year 1834, was Awarded, by the Royal College of Surgeons in London. Philadelphia: 1837. V. 64; 67

CURLL, EDMUND
The Life of the Eminent Comedian Robert Wilks, Esq. London: 1733. V. 66

CURR, EDWARD M.
Pure Saddle-Horses, and How to Breed Them in Australia. Melbourne: 1863. V. 67

CURRAN, J. J.
Mr. Foley of Salmon a Story of Life in a California Village. San Jose: 1907. V. 63

CURRAN, WILLIAM HENRY
The Life of the Right Honourable John Philpot Curran, Late Master of the Rolls in Ireland. New York: 1820. V. 64

THE CURRENCY and Other Questions. The View of the Democracy Contrasted with Those of the Opposition!. Nashville: 1859-1860. V. 63

CURRENT, KAREN
Photography and the Old West. New York: 1978. V. 63

CURRENT, WILLIAM
Pueblo Architecture of the Southwest. Austin: 1971. V. 63

CURREY, LLOYD W.
Bibliography of Yosemite, the Central and the Southern High Sierra, and the Big Trees, 1839-1900. Los Angeles: 1992. V. 62; 63; 65
Science Fiction Fantasy Authors. 1979. V. 62

CURREY, RICHARD
Fatal Light. New York: 1988. V. 63

CURRIE, BARTON
Officer 666. New York: 1912. V. 67

CURRIE, MARY MONTGOMERIE LAMB SINGLETON, BARONESS
From Dawn to Noon. London: 1872. V. 66

CURRIE, P. J.
Encyclopaedia of Dinosaurs. 1997. V. 63; 66

CURRIER, THOMAS FRANKLIN
A Bibliography of Oliver Wendell Holmes. New York: 1953. V. 65

CURRY County, New Mexico. Dallas: 1978. V. 63

CURRY, GEORGE
George Curry 1861-1947 - an Autobiography. Albuquerque: 1958. V. 67

CURRY, JAMES
A Brief Sketch of the Causes Which First Gave Rise to the Late High Price of Grain in Great Britain.... London: 1815. V. 67

CURRY, JOHN
Elements of Bleaching. Dublin: 1779. V. 67

CURRY, MANFRED
Wind and Water. London: 1930. V. 65
Yacht Racing. London: 1930. V. 62

CURRY, ROBERT A.
Bahamian Lore. Paris: 1930. V. 64

CURSORY Remarks on the Subject of Reform, Addressed to the Members of the Reading Societies, Established by the Radicals; and Intended to be Read at Their Meetings. Newcastle: 1819. V. 67

CURTAIN, L. S. M.
By the Prophet of the Earth. Santa Fe: 1949. V. 63; 66

CURTIN, JEREMIAH
Irish Folk Tales. 1944. V. 67
Myths and Folk Tales of the Russians, Western Slavs and Magayrs. Boston: 1895. V. 65

CURTIN, L. S. M., MRS.
Healing Herbs of the Upper Rio Grande. Santa Fe: 1947. V. 64

CURTIS, BENJAMIN R.
Executive Power. Boston;: 1862. V. 64

CURTIS, C. H.
Orchids for Everyone. London: 1910. V. 67
Orchids, Their Description and Cultivation. 1950. V. 64
Orchids, Their Description and Cultivation. London: 1950. V. 67

CURTIS, CHARLES B.
Velazquez and Murillo. London: 1883. V. 62; 63

CURTIS, CHRISTOPHER PAUL
Bud, Not Buddy. New York: 1999. V. 65

CURTIS, EDWARD S.
In a Sacred Manner We Live. Barre: 1972. V. 63
Indian Days of the Long Ago. Yonkers-on-Hudson: 1915. V. 63; 65
The North American Indian: The Southwest. Santa Fe: 1980. V. 62; 63
Portraits from North American Indian Life. New York: 1972. V. 63

CURTIS, GEORGE
Nile Notes of a Howadji. New York: 1851. V. 63

CURTIS, GEORGE TICKNOR
A Treatise on the Law of Copyright in Books, Dramatic and Musical Compositions, Letters and Other Manuscripts, Engravings and Sculpture, as Enacted and Administered in England and America.... Boston: 1847. V. 63
A Treatise on the Law of Patents for Useful Inventions in the United States of America. Boston: 1854. V. 64

CURTIS, GEORGE WILLIAM
Nile Notes. London: 1851. V. 64

CURTIS, J.
Farm Insects. 1860. V. 65; 67
Farm Insects. London: 1860. V. 64

CURTIS, J. SYDNEY
The Story of the Marsden Mayoralty: with Sketch of the Mayor's Life.... Leeds: 1875. V. 63

CURTIS, JOHN
British Entomology: Illustrations and Descriptions of the Genera of Insects Found in Great Britain and Ireland. London: 1823-1840. V. 62
Farm Insects: Being the Natural History and Economy of the Insects Injurious to the Field Crops of Great Britain and Ireland. London: 1860. V. 66
Farm Insects: Being the Natural History and Economy of the Insects Injurious to the Field Crops of Great Britain and Ireland. London: 1883. V. 63
The Genera of British Lepidoptera.... 1858. V. 66
The Genera of British Lepidoptera.... London: 1858. V. 63

CURTIS, NATALIE
The Indian's Book. New York: 1907. V. 63; 64

CURTIS, PAUL A.
Guns and Gunning. London: 1934. V. 67

CURTIS, SAMUEL
A Monograph on the Genus Camellia. Guildford: 1965. V. 63; 66

CURTIS, WILLIAM
Flora Londinensis; or, Plates and Descriptions of Such Plants as Grow Wild in the Environs of London.... London: 1775-1798. V. 64
Lectures on Botany, as Delivered in the Botanic Garden at Lambeth. London: 1805. V. 65
Practical Observations on the British Grasses. 1805. V. 66
Practical Observations on the British Grasses. London: 1805. V. 64
A Short History of the Brown-Tail Moth. London: 1969. V. 64

CURTIS, WINIFRED
The Endemic Flora of Tasmania. 1967-1978. V. 62

CURTIS'S *Botanical Magazine; or Flower Garden Displayed.* 1835-1842. V. 63

CURTISS, MINA
Other People's Letters: a Memoir. Boston: 1978. V. 66

CURTIUS RUFUS, QUINTUS
Alexander Magnus Et in Illum Commentarius Samuel Pitisci...Editio Tertia Prioribus Ornatior and Compitor. Hagae: 1708. V. 66
De Rebus Gestis Alexandri Magni. Parisiis: 1543. V. 66
De Rebus Gestis Alexandri Magni. Lugduni Batavorum: 1696. V. 65; 66
Historiarum Libri Accuratissime Editi. Lugd. Batavorum: 1633. V. 65; 66
Historiarum Libri.... Lugd. Batavorum: 1663. V. 66
Q. Curtii Rufi Historiarum Libri, Accurantissimi Editi. Lugd. Batavorum: 1633. V. 65

CURWEN, HENRY
A History of Booksellers, The Old and The New. London: 1873. V. 62
A History of Booksellers. The Old and the New. London: 1874. V. 64; 66

CURWEN, JOHN F.
Architectural Facts and Figures. Kendal: 1902. V. 64
The Castles and Fortified Towers of Cumberland, Westmorland and Lancashire North-of-the-Sands.... Kendal: 1913. V. 64; 65; 66
Historical Description of Levens Hall. Kendal: 1898. V. 65
A History of the Ancient House of Curwen of Workington in Cumberland, and Its Various Brances.... Kendal: 1928. V. 62; 66
Records Relating to the Barony of Kendale. Volume 3. Kendal: 1926. V. 65

THE CURWEN Press Almanack. London: 1926. V. 62

THE CURWEN Press Miscellany. London: 1931. V. 63

CURWOOD, JAMES OLIVER
The Black Hunter. New York: 1926. V. 66
The Crippled Lady of Peribonka. Garden City: 1929. V. 65
The Great Lakes, The Vessels that Plough Them: Their Owners, Their Sailors and Their Cargoes.... Mattituck: 1967. V. 66
The Plains of Abraham. Garden City: 1928. V. 67

CURZON, COLIN
The Body in the Barrage Balloon. New York: 1942. V. 67

CURZON, GEORGE NATHANIEL, 1ST MARQUIS OF
British Government in India. London: 1925. V. 66

CURZON, ROBERT
Armenia; a Year at Erzeroom, and On the Frontiers of Russia, Turkey and Persia. London: 1854. V. 62; 65
Visits to Monasteries in the Levant. London: 1850. V. 62
Visits to Monasteries in the Levant. London: 1865. V. 64

CUSACK, DYMPHNA
Kanga-Bee and Kanga Bo. Sydney: 1945. V. 65

CUSACK, MARY F.
The History of Ireland, Social, Ecclesiastical, Biographical, Industrial and Antiquarian. 1876. V. 67
A History of the City and County of Cork. 1875. V. 64
Woman's Work in Modern Society. London: 1874. V. 65

CUSHING, FRANK
A Chant, A Myth, A Prayer Pai-Ya-Ti-Ma God of Dewand the Drum. San Francisco: 1955. V. 65
My Adventures with the Zuni. Santa Fe: 1941. V. 62
The Nation of Willows. Flagstaff: 1965. V. 65
Zuni Folk Tales. New York and London: 1901. V. 63; 65

CUSHING, HARVEY WILLIAMS
A Bio-Bibliography of Andreas Vesalius. New York: 1943. V. 64; 66
A Classification of the Tumors of the Glioma Group on a Histogenetic Basis with a Correlated Study of Prognosis. Philadelphia: 1926. V. 66
A Classification of the Tumors of the Glioma Group on a Histogenetic Basis with a Correlated Study of Prognosis. 1971. V. 64; 66
Further Concerning a Parasympathetic Center in the Interbrain. VII. The Effect of Intraventicularly-Injected Histamine. VIII. The Comparative Effects on Gastric Motility of Intramuscular and Intraventricular Pituttrin, Pilocarpine and Histamine. 1932. V. 66
The Harvey Cushing Collection of Books and Manuscripts. New York: 1943. V. 65; 66
Harvey Cushing. Selected Papers on Neurosurgery. New Haven: 1969. V. 64
Intracranial Tumours. Springfield: 1932. V. 64; 66
The Life of Sir William Osler. London: 1925. V. 64; 66
The Life of Sir William Osler. Oxford: 1925. V. 63; 64; 65; 66; 67
The Life of Sir William Osler. Oxford: 1940. V. 64; 67
The Life of Sir William Osler. Birmingham: 1988. V. 63
Meningiomas, Their Classification, Regional Behaviour, Lfe History and Surgical End Results. Springfield: 1938. V. 66
Meningiomas. Their Classification, Regional Behaviour, Life History and Surgical End Results. New York: 1969. V. 66
Papers Relating to the Pituitary Body, Hypothalamus and Parasympathetic Nervous System. Springfield: 1932. V. 66
The Pituitary Body and Its Disorders. Philadelphia: 1912. V. 66
Selected Papers on Neurosurgery. New Haven: 1969. V. 66
Studies in Intracranial Physiology and Surgery. The Third Circulation. The Hypophysis. The Gliomas. The Cameron Prize Lectures. London: 1926. V. 64
Studies in Intracranial Physiology and Surgery. The Third Circulation. The Hypophysis. The Gliomas. The Cameron Prize Lectures. Oxford: 1926. V. 66
The Surgical Mortality Percentages Pertaining to a Series of Two Thousand Verified Intracranial Tumors. 1932. V. 64
Tumors Arising from the Blood-Vessels of the Brain. Springfield: 1928. V. 66
Tumors of the Nervus Acusticus and the Syndrome of the Cerebellopontile Angle. Philadelphia: 1917. V. 64; 66
A Visit to Le Puy-En-Velay. Cleveland: 1986. V. 66

CUSHING, LUTHER S.
Manual of Parliamentary Practice. Boston: 1845. V. 62; 64
Rules of Proceeding and Debate in Deliberative Assemblies. Boston: 1864. V. 67

CUSHING, MARSHALL
The Story of Our Post Office. Boston: 1893. V. 62; 65

CUSHING, THOMAS
History of the Counties of Gloucester, Salem and Cumberland, New Jersey.... Philadelphia: 1883. V. 63; 66

CUSHMAN, CHARLES ROWLEY
Memorial Addresses Delivered Before the Two Houses of Congress on the Life and Character of Abraham Lincoln, James A. Garfield, William McKinley. Washington: 1903. V. 63; 64

CUSHMAN, H. B.
History of the Choctaw, Chickasaw and Natchez Indians. Stillwater: 1962. V. 63

CUSHMAN, J. A.
The Foraminifera of the Atlantic Ocean. Washington: 1918-1929. V. 65
Foraminifera of the Philippine and Adjacent Seas. 1921. V. 63; 66
Foraminifera of the Phillippine and Adjacent Seas. Washington: 1921. V. 65

CUSHMAN, J. A. continued
A Monograph of the Foraminifera of the North Pacific Ocean. Washington: 1910-1917. V. 65

CUSHMAN, ROBERT
A Sermon, Describing the Sin and Danger of Self Love Preached at Plymouth in New England 1621. Stockbridge: 1822. V. 65

CUSHMAN, SAMUEL
The Gold Mines of Gilpin County, Colorado. Central City: 1876. V. 66

CUSSANS, JOHN EDWIN
History of Hertfordshire.... London: 1879. V. 62

CUSSLER, CLIVE
The Mediterranean Caper and Iceberg. New York: 1995. V. 65
Night Probe!. New York: 1981. V. 65
Raise the Titanic. New York: 1976. V. 64; 65; 67

CUST, EDWARD
A Letter to Sir Robert Peel, Bart. M.P. on the Expedience of a Better System of Control Over Buildings Erected at the Public Expense.... London: 1835. V. 63

CUST, LADY
Invalid's Own Book: a Collection of Recipes. New York: 1853. V. 67

CUSTANCE, REGINALD
War at Sea. Modern Theory and Ancient Practice. Edinburgh and London: 1919. V. 64; 66

CUSTER, ELIZABETH B.
Boots and Saddles. New York: 1885. V. 62; 67
Following the Guidon. New York: 1890. V. 67
Tenting on the Plains or General Custer in Kansas and Texas. New York: 1887. V. 67
Tenting on the Plains or General Custer in Kansas and Texas. New York: 1889. V. 67

CUSTER, GEORGE ARMSTRONG
My Life on the Plains. New York: 1874. V. 65
Wild Life on the Plains and Horrors of Indian Warfare - General Crook and the Apaches. St. Louis: 1885. V. 65; 67

CUSTIS, G. W. PARKE
Collections and Private Memoirs of Washington. Washington: 1859. V. 65

CUTBUSH, EDWARD
Inaugural Dissertation on Insanity; Submitted to the Examination of...the Trustees and Medical Professors of the University of Pennsylvania.... Philadelphia: 1794. V. 64
Observations On the Means of Preserving the Health of Soldiers and Sailors.... Philadelphia: 1808. V. 64

CUTBUSH, JAMES
The American Artist's Manual, or Dictionary of Practical Knowledge in the Application of Philosophy to the Arts and Manufactures. Philadelphia: 1814. V. 62
Early American Papermaking: Two Treatises on Manufacturing Techniques. New Castle: 1990. V. 64

CUTCHINS, J. A.
A Famous Command: the Richmond Light Infantry Blues. Richmond: 1934. V. 62

CUTCLIFFE, H. C.
The Art of Trout Fishing on Rapid Streams. 1863. V. 67
The Art of Trout Fishing on Rapid Streams. London: 1900. V. 67

CUTHBERT, CHARLES
A Full and Accurate Report of the Trial, Cuthbert v. Browne, Being an Action for Deceit, Wherein Charles Cuthbert, Farmer of Bray...was Plaintiff, and John Browne Coast Officer of Excise...was Defendant...26th day of June 1823. Dublin: 1823. V. 63

CUTHBERTSON, BENNETT
Cuthbertson's System, for the Complete Interior Management and Oeconomy of a Battalion of Infantry. Bristol: 1776. V. 66
A System for the Compleat Interior Management and Oeconomy of a Battalion of Infantry. Dublin: 1768. V. 65

CUTHBERTSON, CATHERINE
Santo Sebastiano; or the Young Protector. London: 1806. V. 66

CUTHBERTSON, DAVID
Rosslyn Lyrics. Edinburgh: 1878. V. 65

CUTLER, BENJAMIN C.
Twelve Hours on the Wreck; or, The Stranding of the Sheffield. New York: 1844. V. 66

CUTLER, CARL C.
A Descriptive Catalogue of the Marine Collection at India House. Middleton: 1973. V. 64

CUTLER, D. F.
Anatomy of the Dicotyledons. Volume IV. 1998. V. 63

CUTLER, H. M. TRACY
Phillipia, a Woman's Question. 1886. V. 67

CUTLER, JERVIS
A Topographical Description of the State of Ohio, Indiana Territory and Louisiana. Boston: 1812. V. 63; 66

CUTTEN, GEORGE BARTON
The Silversmiths of North Carolina. Raleigh: 1948. V. 67

CUTTER, CHARLES, & SONS
The Gem Souvenir of Hot Springs, Arkansas. N.P. Hot Springs?: 1875?. V. 65

CUTTS, EDWARD L.
A Manual for the Study of the Sepulchral Slabs and Crosses of the Middle Ages. London: 1849. V. 63

CUTTS, JAMES MADISON
The Conquest of California and New Mexico by the Forces of the United States, in the Years 1846 and 1847. Philadelphia: 1847. V. 65

CUTTS, SIMON
Pianostool Footnotes. Highlands: 1982. V. 63

CUVIER, GEORGES, BARON
The Animal Kingdom, Arranged After its Organization.... London: 1859. V. 65; 66; 67
Animal Kingdom Insects. London: 1832. V. 62
A Classified Index and Synopsis of the Animal Kingdom. 1835. V. 63
A Discourse on the Revolutions of the Surface of the Globe and the Changes Thereby Produced in the Animal Kingdom. London: 1829. V. 62; 64
Essay on the Theory of the Earth. Edinburgh and London: 1813. V. 65
Essay on the Theory of the Earth. Edinburgh and London: 1822. V. 64; 65; 67
Essay on the Theory of the Earth. Edinburgh: 1827. V. 62
Rapport...sur un Memorie de M. Flourens, Intitule: Determination Des Proprietes du Systeme Nerveux. V. 64
Recherches sur les Ossemens Fossiles.... Paris: 1821-1823. V. 65
Recherches sur les Ossemens Fossiles.... 1821-1825. V. 62
Le Regne Animal Distribue d'Apres son Organisation.... Paris: 1829-1830. V. 63; 65

CUYLER, EMILY
The Church's Floral Kalendar. London: 1862. V. 67

CUYLER, THEODORE L.
From the Nile to Norway and Homeward. New York: 1882. V. 66

CYCLOPEDIA of Engineering. A General Reference Work on Steam Boilers, Steam Pumps, Steam Engines, Gas and Oil Engines, Marine and Locomotive Work.... Chicago: 1908. V. 64

CYNWAL, WILLIAM
In Defence of Woman. Waltham St. Lawrence: 1960. V. 62; 63; 64; 66; 67

CYPRIANUS, SAINT, BP. OF CARTHAGE
Sancti Caecilii Cypriani Opera. Parisiis: 1666. V. 66

CZERKAS, S. J.
Dinosaurs Past and Present. Los Angeles: 1987. V. 64

CZERMAK, JOHANN N.
Der Kehlkopfspiegel und Seine Verwerthung fur Physiologie und Medizine. Leipzig: 1860. V. 64

CZERNIN, OTTOKAR, COUNT
In the World. London: 1919. V. 63

CZICHOES, RAYMOND L.
Frederic Remington 1861-1909 He Knew the Horse. New York. V. 66

D

DABNEY, CHARLES W.
The Public School Problem in the South. N.P: 1901. V. 64

DABNEY, R. L.
Life and Campaigns of Lieut. Gen. Thomas J. Jackson (Stonewall Jackson). New York: 1866. V. 66
Life of Lieut. Gen. Thomas J. Jackson (Stonewall Jackson). London: 1864-1866. V. 63; 65
Syllabus and Notes of the Course of Systematic and Polemic Theology Taught in Union Theological Seminary, Virginia. Asbury Park: 1885. V. 63

D'ABRANTES, DUCHESS OF
Memoirs of Napoleon, His Court and Family. London: 1836. V. 62

D'ABRERA, B.
Birdwing Butterflies of the World. London: 1976. V. 63
Butterflies of the Afrotropical Region.... East Melbourne: 1980. V. 62
Butterflies of the Australian Region. 1971. V. 63; 66
Butterflies of the Australian Region. Melbourne: 1971. V. 66
Butterflies of the Australian Region. Melbourne: 1977. V. 62
Butterflies of the Neotropical Region. East Melbourne: 1981-1984. V. 62
Butterflies of the Oriental Region. Ferny Creek and Melbourne: 1982-1986. V. 62
Butterflies of the World. Melbourne: 1980-1994. V. 65

DACIER, ANDRE
The Life of Pythagoras, with His Symbols and Golden Verses. Together with the Life of Hierocles and His Commentaries Upon the Verses. London: 1707. V. 67

DACRE, ARABELA SULLIVAN
Recollections of a Chaperon. London: 1833. V. 63

DACUS, J. A.
Illustrated Lives and Adventures of Frank and Jesse James and the Younger Brothers. The Noted Western Outlaws. St. Louis: 1880. V. 67

DACUS, J. A. continued
Illustrated Lives and Adventures of Frank and Jesse James and the Younger Brothers, the Noted Western Outlaws. St. Louis: 1881. V. 62

DADDOW, SAMUEL HARRIES
Coal, Iron and Oil; or the Practical American Miner. Pottsville: 1866. V. 62; 64

DADDY'S Little Rhyme Book. London: 1913. V. 65

DAELLI, G.
A Relic of the Italian Revolution of 1849. New Orleans: 1850?. V. 63

DAELMAN, CAROLO GISLENO
Theologia seu Observationes Theologicae in Summam D. Thomae. Antverpiae: 1734. V. 67

DAFT, RICHARD
Kings of Cricket. Bristol: 1893. V. 62; 66

DAGGETT, DAVID
Count the Cost. An Address to the People of Connecticut, on Sundry Political Subjects, and Particularly on the Proposition for a New Constitution. Harford: 1804. V. 63; 66
Mr. Daggett's Argument, Before the General Assembly of the State of Connecticut, October 1804 in the Case of Certain Justices of the Peace. New Haven: 1804. V. 62
Sun-Beams May Be Extracted from Cucumbers, But the Process is Tedious. New Haven: 1799. V. 63

DAGGETT, MARSHA LEA
Pecos County History. Canyon: 1984. V. 63

DAGLEY, RICHARD
Death's Doings: Consisting of Numerous Original Compositions in Prose and Verse. London: 1826. V. 63
Death's Doings: Consisting of Numerous Original Compositions in Verse and Prose. Boston: 1828. V. 63
Takings; or the Life of a Collegian. London: 1821. V. 66

DAGLISH, ERIC FITCH
Birds of the British Isles. London: 1948. V. 64; 65; 67
The Book of the Dachshund. Manchester: 1937. V. 67

DAGLISH, ROBERT, & CO.
List of Bevel, Change, Mitre, Ratchet, Spur and Worm Wheel Patterns, Made on a Correct Principle and With Perfect Mechanical Accuracy. 1874. V. 65

DAGUE, R. A.
Henry Ashton. Alameda: 1903. V. 63

DAGUERRE, LOUIS JACQUES MANDE
The Hand-Book of Heliography, or the Art of Writing or Drawing by the Effect of Sun-Light. London: 1840. V. 62
Historique et Description Des Procedes du Daguerreotype et du Diorama. Paris: 1839. V. 66

D'AGUIAR, FRED
Dear Future. New York: 1996. V. 67
The Longest Memory. New York: 1994. V. 67

DAGUIN, PIERRE ADOLPHE
Traite Elementaire de Physique Theorique et Experimentale avec les Applications a la Meteorologie et aux arts Industriels.... Toulouse: 1861-1862. V. 67

DAHL, F.
Dutch Corantos 1618-1650: A Bibliography...and an Introductory Essay on 17th Century Stop Press News. The Hague: 1946. V. 62

DAHL, LOUIS H.
The Roman Camp and the Irish Saint at Burgh Castle. 1913. V. 67

DAHL, ROALD
The BFG. New York: 1982. V. 65; 67
Charlie and the Great Glass Elevator. New York: 1972. V. 65
Fantastic Mr. Fox. New York: 1970. V. 62
The Gremlins. New York: 1943. V. 66
The Gremlins from Walt Disney Production. London: 1944. V. 62
James and the Giant Peach. London: 1967. V. 66
Kiss Kiss. London: 1960. V. 62; 65; 66
My Uncle Oswald. London: 1979. V. 63; 64; 65; 67
Someone Like You. New York: 1953. V. 62
Someone Like You. London: 1954. V. 66
Switch Bitch. New York: 1974. V. 62
The Twits. 1980. V. 65
The Witches. London: 1983. V. 66

DAHLBERG, EDWARD
Bottom Dogs. New York: 1930. V. 63
Do These Bones Live. New York: 1941. V. 63
The Flea of Sodom. London: 1950. V. 64
The Leafless American. Sausalito: 1967. V. 63
The Sorrows of Priapus. Norfolk: 1957. V. 63; 64

DAHLE, L.
Specimens of Malagasay Folk-Lore. Faravohitra: 1877. V. 62

DAHLEN, BEVERLY
The Egyptian Poems. Berkeley: 1983. V. 63

DAHLGREN, B. E.
Index of American Palms. 1936. V. 62; 63

DAILEY, ABRAM H.
Mollie Fancher, the Brooklyn Enigma, an Authentic Statement of Facts in the Life of Mary J. Fancher.... Brooklyn: 1894. V. 66

DAILEY, M. D.
Ecology of the Southern California Blight.... Berkeley: 1993. V. 65

THE DAILY News History of Buchanan County and St. Joseph from the Year of the Platte Purchase to the End of the Year 1898. St. Joseph. V. 64; 67

DAILY Verses. London: 1840. V. 67

DAINELLI, GIOTTO
Buddhists and Glaciers of Western Tibet. London: 1933. V. 64

THE DAISY or Cautionary Stories in Verse Adapted to the Ideas of Children from Four to Eight Years. New York: 1850. V. 62

DAIX, P.
Picasso: the Blue and Rose Periods - a Catalogue Raisonne of the Paintings 1900-1906. 1967. V. 62; 65

DAKOTA TERRITORY. IMMIGRATION
Resources of Dakota 1887 - an Official Publication Compiled by the Commissioner of Immigration. Sioux Falls: 1887. V. 63; 66

DAKOTA TERRITORY. LAWS, STATUTES, ETC. - 1879
Laws of Dakota - 1879. Yankton: 1879. V. 63
Laws Passed at the Thirteenth Session of the Legislative Assembly of the Territory of Dakota. Yankton: 1879. V. 63; 66

DAKOTA TERRITORY. LAWS, STATUTES, ETC. - 1885
General and Special Laws Passed at the Sixteenth Session of the Legislative Assembly of the Territory of Dakota. Yankton: 1885. V. 63; 66

DAKOTA TERRITORY. LAWS, STATUTES, ETC. - 1887
Laws Passed at the Seventeenth Session of the Legislative Assembly of the Territory of Dakota. Bismarck: 1887. V. 63; 66

DALE, EDWARD EVERETT
Cow Country. 1942. V. 67
Cow Country. Norman: 1942. V. 63; 64; 66
The Range Cattle Industry. Norman: 1930. V. 65
The Range Cattle Industry. Norman: 1960. V. 64

DALE, HARRISON CLIFFORD
The Ashley-Smith Exploration and the Discovery of a Central Route to the Pacific 1822-1829. Cleveland: 1918. V. 63; 66

DALE, HENRY HALLETT
Adventures in Physiology with Excursions in Autopharmacology. London: 1965. V. 67

DALE, I. R.
Kenya Trees and Shrubs. 1961. V. 63; 66
Kenya Trees and Shrubs. Nairobi: 1961. V. 66

DALE, J.
Angling Days. 1895. V. 67

DALE, NELLIE
The Dale Readers: First and Second Primers. London: 1902. V. 66

DALE, PERRY
You Scratch My Back. New York: 1952. V. 67

DALE, R. W.
Impressions of Australia. London: 1889. V. 63

DALE, ROBERT
An Exact Catalogue of the Nobility of England. London: 1697. V. 65

DALE, RODNEY
Louis Wain the Man Who Drew Cats. London: 1968. V. 67

DALE, T. F.
The Fox. London: 1906. V. 62
Riding and Polo Ponies. London: 1902. V. 66

DALE, THOMAS
An Introductory Lecture Delivered in the University of London, Friday Octobr 24, 1828. London: 1828. V. 64

DALECHAMP, JACQUES
Histoire General des Plantes. Lyon: 1653. V. 63; 66

D'ALENCE, JOACHIM
Curieux Traitte de L'Aiman. Paris: 1712. V. 65

DALEY, BRIAN
Han Solo at Star's End. 1979. V. 64; 66

DAL FABBRO, MARIO
How to Build Modern Furniture. New York: 1951-1952. V. 65

DALGLIESH, ALICE
The Davenports and Cherry Pie. New York: 1949. V. 66

DALI, SALVADOR
Diners de Gala. New York: 1973. V. 62; 65; 66
The Secret Life of.... New York: 1942. V. 67
The Secret Life of.... London: 1949. V. 62

DALL, CAROLINE H.
Barbara Fritchie, a Study. Boston: 1892. V. 65
Patty Gray's Journey to the Cotton Islands: from Baltimore to Washington. Boston: 1876. V. 65

DALL, W. H.
List of the Birds of Alaska.... Chicago: 1869. V. 64
Notes on the Avifuana of the Aleutian Islands, from Unalashka, Eastward (west of Unalashka). 1873-1874. V. 62
Spencer Fullerton Baird, a Biography.... Philadelphia: 1915. V. 66

DALLAS, ENEAS SWEETLAND
Poetics: an Essay of Poetry. London: 1852. V. 65
Three Essays: I. Learning and Science. II. Science and Language. III. Language and Poetry. London: 1863. V. 65

DALLAWAY, JAMES
Series of Discourses Up on Archiecture in England from the Norman Era to the Close of the Reign of Queen Elizabeth. London: 1833. V. 65

DALLAWAY, R. C.
Observations on the Most Important Subjects of Education.... London: 1812. V. 63

DALLIERE, A.
Les Plantes Ornementales a Feuillage Panache et Colore.... Ghent: 1873-1874. V. 62

DALLIMORE, W.
A Handbook of the Coniferae Including Ginkgoaceae. 1948. V. 67

DALLING AND BULWER, HENRY
Sir Robert Peel. An Historical Sketch. London: 1874. V. 67

DALLING AND BULWER, WILLIAM HENRY LYTTON EARL BULWER, BARON
France, Social, Literary, Political. (with) The Monarchy of the Middle Classes. France, Social, Literary and Political. New York: 1835. V. 63

DALLMEIR, F.
Biodiversity Assement and Long-Term Monitoring, Lower Urbamba Region, Peru.... Washington: 1997-1999. V. 67

DALLY, JOSEPH W.
Woodbridge and Vicinity. New Brunswick: 1873. V. 63; 66

DALMENY, LADY
The Spanish Ladye's Love. London: 1846. V. 62

DALRYMPLE, CAMPBELL
Extracts from a Military Essay, Containing Reflections on the Raising, Arming, Clothing and Discipline of the British Infantry and Cavalry. Philadelphia: 1776. V. 64

DALRYMPLE, CHARLES JOHN
Report of the Trial of the Students on the Charge of Mobbing, Rioting and Assault at the College on January 11 and 12, 1838. Edinburgh: 1838. V. 63

DALRYMPLE, JOHN
An Essay Towards a General History of Feudal Property in Great Britain Under the Following Heads.... London: 1758. V. 63
Memoirs of Great Britain and Ireland. London: 1771. V. 67
Pathology of the Human Eye. London: 1852. V. 67
The Question Considered, Whether Wool Should Be Allowed to Be exported, when the Price is low at Home, on Paying a Duty to the Public. London: 1781. V. 62

THE DALTON
Brothers and Their Astounding Career of Crime by an Eyewitness. Chicago: 1892. V. 64

DALTON, EMMETT
When the Daltons Rode. New York: 1931. V. 62

DALTON, JAMES
The Gentleman in Black. London: 1831. V. 65

DALTON, JOHN
Experiments and Observation on the Combinations of Carbonic Acid and Ammonia.... Manchester: 1814. V. 62
Experiments and Observations on the Heat and Cold Produced by the Mechanical Condensation and Rarefaction of Air. Manchester: 1801. V. 62
Experiments and Observations on the Power of Fluids to Conduct Heat; with Reference to Count Rumford's Seventh Essay. Manchester: 1799. V. 62

D'ALTON, JOHN
History of the County of Dublin. 1838. V. 64; 67
Illustrations, Historical and Genealogical of King James Irish Army List (1689). 1861. V. 65
The Memoirs of the Archbishops of Dublin. 1838. V. 65

DALTON, JOHN
Meterological Observations and Essays. London: 1793. V. 65
A New System of Chemical Philosophy. Manchester: 1808-1827. V. 63

DALTON, JOHN C.
History of the College of Physicians and Surgeons in the City of New York, Medical Department of Columbia College. New York: 1888. V. 64
Topographical Anatomy of the Brain. Philadelphia: 1885. V. 64; 66
A Treatise on Physiology and Hygiene: for Schools, Families and Colleges. New York: 1876. V. 67

DALTON, KIT
Under the Black Flag. Memphis: 1914. V. 62; 63; 65

DALTON, MICHAEL
The Countrey Justice.... London: 1666. V. 63
The Country Justice: Containing the Practice of the Justices of the Peace Out of Their Sessions. London: 1690. V. 67

DALTON, MORAY
The Art School Murders. London: 1943. V. 67

DALTON, RICHARD
Remarks on Prints, That Were Published in the Year 1781, Relative to the Manners, Customs &c. of the Present Inhabitants of Egypt. London: 1790. V. 66

DALTON, WILLIAM
Phaulcon the Adventurer; or, the Europeans in the East. London: 1862. V. 62; 67

DALY, AUGUSTIN
Catalogue of a Valuable and Interesting Collection of Books Formed by a Prominent American Playwright. New York: 1878. V. 65

DALY, ELIZABETH
Somewhere in the House. New York: 1946. V. 65

DALY, LOUISE HASKELL
Alexander Cheves Haskell: the Portrait of a Man. Norwood: 1934. V. 62; 63; 65

DALY, MARCUS
Big Game Hunting and Adventure 1897-1936. 1937. V. 64

DALY, SEAN
Cork: a City in Crisis. 1978. V. 67

DALYELL, JOHN GRAHAM
Musical Memoirs of Scotland with Historical Annotations.... Edinburgh: 1849. V. 62
Musical Memoirs of Scotland with Historical Annotations.... London: 1849. V. 66
Shipwrecks and Disasters at Sea, or, Historical Narratives of the Most Noted Calamities and Providential Deliverances from Fire and Famine, on the Ocean. Manchester: 1837. V. 63; 66

DALZEL, ANDREAS
Analekta Hellenika (Greek) sive Collectanea Graeca.... Edinburgh: 1789. V. 66

DALZELL, GEORGE W.
The Flight from the Flag. Chapel Hill: 1940. V. 63

DALZIEL, HUGH
The St. Bernard: Its History, Points, Breeding, and Rearing. London: 1888. V. 67
The St. Bernard: Its History, Points, Breeding and Rearing. London: 1890. V. 63

DALZIEL, THE BROTHERS
The Brothers Dalziel. A Record of Fifty Years' Work in Conjunction with Many of the Most Distinguished Artists of the Period 1840-1890. London: 1901. V. 62; 66

DALZIELS' Bible Gallery. London: 1881. V. 64

D'AMBIVERE, FERRANTE, COMTE
In Occasione Della Partenza da Bergamo di Sua Eccelenza Elena Sagredo Buzzacarini, Elogio. Bergamo: 1791. V. 66

D'AMBROSIO, JOE
Daisies Never Tell. Sherman Oaks: 1982. V. 62; 67
David. Sherman Oaks: 1993. V. 62; 67
Oaxaca and the Saguaro Cactus. Phoenix: 1996. V. 62; 67

DAME *Girafe a Paris Adventures et Voyage de Cette Illustre Etrangere....* Paris: 1827. V. 66

DAME, LORIN
Typical Elms and Other Trees of Massachusetts. Boston: 1890. V. 67

DAME, WILLIAM M.
From the Rapidan to Richmond and the Spottsylvania Campaign. Baltimore: 1920. V. 66

DAME *Wonder's Multiplication Table.* New York: Sep. 1840. V. 65

DAME *Wonders' Picture Books: the Sailor Boy.* New York: 1865. V. 64

DAMER, G., MRS.
Diary of a Tour in Greece, Turkey, Egypt and the Holy Land. London: 1842. V. 64

D'AMICO, SILVIO
Enciclopedia Dello Spettacolo. Rome: 1954-1968. V. 67

DAMME, D. VAN
The Freshwater Mollusca of Northern Africa.... Dordrecht: 1984. V. 65

DAMON, ROBERT
Geology of Weymouth, Portland and Coast of Dorsetshire from Swanage to Bridport-on-Sea.... Weymouth: 1884. V. 63
Geology of Weymouth...With Notes on the Natural History. E. Stanford: 1880. V. 62
Handbook of the Geology of Weymouth and the Island of Portland, with Notes on the Natural History. E. Stanford: 1864. V. 62
Handbook to the Geology of Weymouth and the Island of Portland. London: 1864. V. 63

DAMON, S. FOSTER
A Note on the Discovery of a New Page of Poetry in William Blake's Milton. Boston: 1925. V. 63

DAMPIER, WILLIAM
A Collection of Voyages. London: 1729. V. 66

DAMPIER, WILLIAM JAMES
A Memoir of John Carter. London: 1850. V. 67
A Memoir of John Carter. London: 1875. V. 67

DANA, C. W.
The Garden of the World, or the Great West.... Boston: 1856. V. 63

DANA, CHARLES A.
Lincoln and His Cabinet. A Lecture Delivered Tuesday, March 10, 1896, Before the New Haven Colony Historical Society. New York: 1896. V. 62

DANA, CHARLES LOOMIS
Multiple Sclerosis (Disseminated Sclerosis).... New York: 1922. V. 65

DANA, E. S.
Textbook of Mineralogy with an Extended Treatise on Crystallography and Physical Mineralogy. 1932. V. 67

DANA, JAMES D.
Manual of Mineralogy and Lithology.... London: 1882. V. 67

DANA, RICHARD HENRY
Cruelty to Seamen. Berkeley: 1937. V. 65
Poems. Boston: 1827. V. 62
To Cuba and Back. Boston: 1859. V. 64
Two Years Before the Mast. London: 1844. V. 67
Two Years Before the Mast. New York: 1850. V. 66
Two Years Before the Mast. New York: 1947. V. 63; 64; 66
Two Years Before the Mast. Los Angeles: 1964. V. 62; 63; 64

DANBY, THOMAS, EARL OF
A Collection of Some Memorable and Weighty Transactions in Parliament, in the Year 1678 and Afterwards. London: 1695. V. 62
Memoirs Relating to the Impeachment of Thomas, Earl of Danby, now Duke of Leeds in the Year 1678. London: 1711. V. 66

DANCE, JAMES
Pamela: a Comedy. Dublin: 1742. V. 65

DANCE, PETER S.
The Art of Natural History. Animal Illustrators and Their Work. London: 1978. V. 67
The Art of Natural History, Animal Illustrators and Their Work. New York: 1978. V. 63; 65; 67
The Art of Natural History. Animal Illustrators and Their Work. Woodstock: 1978. V. 64
Classic Natural History Prints: Birds. New York: 1990. V. 67
Shell Collecting. London: 1966. V. 62

DANDOLO, EMILIO
The Italian Volunteers and Lombard Rifle Brigade, Being an Authentic Narrative of the Organization, Adventures and Final Disbanding of These Corps in 1848-1849. London: 1851. V. 65

DANDRIDGE, RAYMOND GARFIELD
Zalka Peetruza and Other Poems. Cincinnati: 1928. V. 62; 64

THE DANDY Book 1953. V. 66

DANDY, WALTER
Benign, Encapsulated Tumors in the Lateral Ventricles of the Brain, Diagnosis and Treatment. Baltimore: 1934. V. 66
Benign Tumors in the Third Ventricle of the Brain.... Springfield: 1933. V. 65
Benign Tumors in the Third Ventricle of the Brain.... Birmingham: 1991. V. 65
Benign Tumors in the Third Ventricle of the Brain.... London: 1933. V. 66
The Brain. Hagerstown: 1945. V. 66
Intracranial Arerial Aneurysms. Ithaca: 1945. V. 66
Intracranial Arterial Aneurysms. Ithaca: 1947. V. 64
Orbital Tumors Results Following the Transcranial Operative Attack. New York: 1941. V. 66
Selected Writings of Walter E. Dandy. Springfield: 1957. V. 66

DANE, RICHARD
Sport in Asia and Africa. London: 1921. V. 67

D'ANGELO, SERGIO
World Car Catalogue. Bronxville: 1968. V. 65

THE DANGER and Immodesty of the Present Too General Custom of Unnecessarily Employing Men-Midwives. London: 1772. V. 65

DANGERFIELD, THOMAS
The Information of...Delivered at the Bar of the House of Commons, Tuesday the Twentieth Day of October, in the Year of Our Lord 1680. Dublin: 1680. V. 62

DANIEL, EDMUND R.
Pleading and Practice of the High Court of Chancery. Boston: 1846. V. 65
Pleading and Practice of the High Court of Chancery. Boston: 1871. V. 65

DANIEL, FERDINAND E.
Recollections of a Rebel Surgeon. Austin: 1899. V. 62; 63

DANIEL, GABRIEL
Histoire de la Milice Francoise, et des Changemans qui s'y Sont Faits Depuis l'etablissement de la Monarchie Francoise dans les Gaules.... Paris: 1721. V. 67
A Voyage to the World of Cartesius. London: 1694. V. 65

DANIEL, GEORGE
Catalogue of the Most Valuable, Interesting and Highly Important Library of the Late George Daniel, Esq. London: 1864. V. 62
Merrie England in the Olden Time. London: 1842. V. 62; 67

DANIEL, JOHN M.
Daniel's Law Directory of the United States 1879. Volume Fifth. Baltimore: 1879. V. 64

DANIEL, SAMUEL
The Collection of the History of England. London: 1626. V. 64

DANIELEWSKI, MARK Z.
House of Leaves. New York: 2000. V. 66
The Whalestoe Letters. New York: 2000. V. 67

DANIELI, FEDELE
Trattato Della Divina Providencia Divisio in Tre Libri Composto dal P. Fedele Danieli della Compagnia de Giesu. Milan: 1615. V. 65

DANIELL, L. E.
Personnel of the Texas State Government with Sketches of Distinguished Texans. Austin: 1887. V. 62; 65
Types of Successful Men of Texas. Austin: 1890. V. 65

DANIELL, WILLIAM
The Oriental Annual or Scenes in India. 1834. V. 66
A Voyage Round Great Britain Undertaken Between the Years 1813 and 1823 and Commencing from the Land's End, Cornwall.... London: 1978. V. 66
A Voyage Round Great Britain Undertaken Between the Years 1814 and 1825. London: 1978. V. 62

DANIEL-ROPS, HENRY
The Misted Mirror. London: 1930. V. 64

DANIELS, JONATHAN
Thomas Wolfe: October Recollections. Columbia: 1961. V. 64

DANIELS, JOSEPHUS
The Wilson Era. Years of Peace 1910-1917. Chapel Hill: 1944. V. 67

DANIELSON, H.
The First Editions of the Writings of Thomas Hardy and Their Values.... London: 1916. V. 62

DANIEL-TYSSEN, AMHERST
The Church Bells of Sussex, with Inscriptions of all the Bells in the County. Sussex: 1864. V. 66

DANTE ALIGHIERI
Divina Commedia. Venice: 1491. V. 67
La Divina Commedia. Lyons: 1552. V. 65; 67
La Divina Commedia. Munchen: 1921. V. 67
La Divina Commedia. Berlin: 1925. V. 65
La Divina Commedia. London: 1928. V. 63; 64
La Divina Commedia or the Divine Vision.... N.P: 1928. V. 62
The Divine Comedy. New York: 1932. V. 62
Dante's Inferno. New York: 1985. V. 64
Dante's Inferno. Hopewell: 1993. V. 64; 65
L'Enfer. Pari: 1872. V. 67
La Purgatoire. La Paradis. Purgatoire: 1830. V. 67
The Stone Beloved: Six Poems. Austin: 1986. V. 62
The Vision of Hell. (with) The Vision of Purgatory and Paradise. London: 1903. V. 67
The Vision of Purgatory and Paradise. London. V. 62; 66

DANTICAT, EDWIDGE
Breath, Eyes, Memory. New York: 1994. V. 63; 64; 66; 67
Krik? Krak?. New York: 1995. V. 66

DANTO, ARTHUR C.
Analytical Philosophy of Knowledge. Cambridge: 1968. V. 67
Mapplethorpe. London: 1992. V. 63

DAPPER, OLFERT
Naukeurige Beschryving Van Asie: Behelsende de Gewesten Van Mesopotamie, Babylonie, Assyrie, Anatolie, of Klein Asie.... Amsterdam: 1680. V. 63

DARBY, ABIAH
Useful Instruction for Children, By Way of Question and Answer. London: 1763. V. 64

DARBY, CHARLES
Bacchanalia; or a Description of a Drunken Club. London: 1680. V. 62; 64

DARBY, JOHN N.
The Irrationalism of Infidelity, Being a Reply to Phases of Faith (by Francis W. Newman). London: 1853. V. 64

DARBY, JONATHAN GEORGE NORTON
A Practical Treatise on the Statutes of Limitations in England an Ireland. London: 1867. V. 63

DARBY, MADGE
Who Caused the Mutiny of the Bounty?. Sydney: 1965. V. 63

DARBY, WILLIAM
Darby's Universal Gazetteer. A Dictionary, Geographical, Historical and Statistical of the Various Kingdoms, States, Provinces, Cities, Towns, Forts, Harbors, Rivers, Lakes, Seas, Mountains, etc.... Philadelphia: 1845. V. 65
Emigrant's Guide to the Western and Southwestern States and Territories. New York: 1818. V. 63; 66
A Geographical Description of the State of Louisiana.... Philadelphia: 1816. V. 62; 63; 66; 67
Memoir of Geography and Natural and Civil History of Florida.... Philadelphia: 1821. V. 63

D'ARCY, ELLA
Modern Instances. London: 1898. V. 65

D'ARCY, W. G.
Solanaceae, Biology and Systematics. New York: 1986. V. 63

DARELL, W.
The History of Dover Castle. London: 1808. V. 66

DAREMBERG, CHARLES VICTOR
Histoire des Sciences Medicales. Paris: 1870. V. 64

DARK, S.
Sir William Orpen: Artist and Man. 1932. V. 62; 63; 66

DARLEY, GEORGE
Nepenthe - a Poem in Two Cantos. London: 1897. V. 62; 64

DARLING, F. FRASER
The Highlands and Islands. London: 1964. V. 62; 63
The Natural History in the Highlands and Islands. London: 1947. V. 62; 63
West Highlands Survey. 1955. V. 67

DARLING, ROGER
Benteen's - Scout to the Left - The Route from the Divide to the Morass (June 25, 1976). Spokane: 2000. V. 66; 67
Custer's Seventh Cavalry Comes to Dakota. El Segundo: 1989. V. 67
A Sad and Terrible Blunder, Generals Terry and Custer at the Little Big Horn; New Discoveries. Vienna: 1992. V. 67

DARLING, S.
Chicago Furniture: Art, Craft and Industry 1833-1983. New York and London: 1984. V. 65

DARLING, WILLIAM STEWART
Sketches of Canadian Life, Lay and Ecclesiastical. London: 1849. V. 64; 65

DARLINGTON & HOWGEGO
Printed Maps of London Circa 1553-1850. London: 1964. V. 67

DARLINGTON, E. M.
The Radcliffes of Leigh, Lancashire. Lutterworth: 1918. V. 66

DARLINGTON, WILLIAM
Address Delivered Before the Philadelphia Society for Promoting Agriculture at the Annual Exhibition, Held Oct. 17, 1844. Germantown: 1844. V. 66
American Weeds and Useful Plants. New York: 1859. V. 66
Flora Cestrica; an Herborizing Companion for the Young Botanists of Chester County, State of Pennsylvania. Philadelphia: 1853. V. 66; 67

DARNELL, A. W.
Hardy and Half Hardy Plants. 1930-1931. V. 63; 66

D'ARNOUX, CHARLES ALBERT
Les Infortunes de Touche-a-Tout. Paris: 1868. V. 65

DARNTON, ROBERT
Mesmerism and the End of the Enlightenment in France. Cambridge: 1968. V. 67

D'ARPENTIGNY, C. S.
La Chirognomonie ou L'Art de Reconnaitre les Tendaces del l'Intelligence d'apres les Formes De L Main. Paris: 1843. V. 66

DARRAH, H. Z.
Sport in the Highlands of Kashmir. 1898. V. 63; 67
Sport in the Highlands of Kashmir. London: 1898. V. 64

DARRAH, WILLIAM C.
The World of Stereographs. Gettysburg: 1977. V. 63

DARROW, CLARENCE SEWARD
Farmington. Chicago: 1904. V. 63
Resist Not Evil. Chicago: 1904. V. 63
The Story of My Life. New York: 1932. V. 67

DARROW, PIERCE
Scott's Militia Tactics.... Hartford: 1821. V. 63; 66

DART, JOHN
The History and Antiquities of the Cathedral Church of Canterbury, and the Once-Adjoining Monastery. London: 1726. V. 64

DARTMOUTH COLLEGE
A Catalogue of the Books in the Library of Dartmouth College... November 1825. Concord: 1825. V. 66

DARTNELL, GEORGE R.
A Brief Narrative of the Shipwreck of the Transport "Premier" Near the Mouth of the River St. Lawrence, on the 4th November 1843.... London: 1845. V. 65

DARTON, F. J. HARVEY
The Good Fairy; or, the Adventures of Sir Richard Whittington, R Crusoe, Esqre., Master Jack Horner and Others. Wells Gardner, Darton and Co: 1922. V. 65

DARTON, WILLIAM
Little Jack of All Trades; or, Mechanical Arts Described in Prose and Verse. London: 1823. V. 66

DARVILL, RICHARD
A Treatise on the Care, Treatment and Training of the English Race Horse, in a Series of Rough Notes. Edinburgh: 1762. V. 64
A Treatise on the Care, Treatment and Training of the English Race Horse, in a Series of Rough Notes. London: 1846. V. 65

DARWALL, JOHN
Plain Instructions for the Management of Infants, with Practical Observations on the Disorders Incident to Children. London: 1830. V. 63

DARWENT, C. E.
Shanghai; A Handbook for Travellers and Residents to the Chief Objects of Interest In and Around the Foreign Settlements and Native City. Shanghai: 1905. V. 64

DARWIN, BERNARD
Golf. London: 1954. V. 63
The Golf Courses of the British Isles. London: 1910. V. 62
Golfing By-Paths. London: 1946. V. 62
A History of Golf in Britain. London: 1952. V. 67
James Braid. London: 1952. V. 62
Oboli, Boboli and Little Joboli. London: 1938. V. 62
Second Shots. London: 1930. V. 62
The Tale of Mr. Tootleoo. London: 1925. V. 66

DARWIN, CHARLES ROBERT
Charles Darwin's Notebooks 1836-1844.... Ithaca: 1987. V. 64; 66
The Collected Works of Charles Darwin. London: 1986-1988. V. 62
Le Descendance de l'Homme et la Selection Sexuelle. Paris: 1873-1874. V. 64
The Descent of Man and Selection in Relation to Sex. London: 1871. V. 64; 66
The Descent of Man and Selection in Relation to Sex. 1875. V. 66
The Descent of Man and Selection in Relation to Sex. New York: 1880. V. 67
The Descent of Man and Selection in Relation to Sex. 1894. V. 66
The Different Forms of Flowers on Plants of the Same Species. London: 1884. V. 67
The Different Forms of Flowers on Plants of the Same Species. 1877. V. 66
The Different Forms of Flowers on Plants of the Same Species. New York: 1899. V. 63
The Effects of Cross and Self Fertilisation in the Vegetable Kingdom. London: 1876. V. 62; 65
The Effects of Cross and Self Fertilisation in the Vegetable Kingdom.... London: 1878. V. 67
The Expression of the Emotions in Man and Animals. London: 1872. V. 62; 65; 66; 67
The Expression of the Emotions in Man and Animals. New York: 1873. V. 66
The Formation of Vegetable Mould, through the Action of Worms.... London: 1881. V. 62; 63; 67
The Formation of Vegetable Mould, through the Action of Worms.... 1882. V. 67
Geological Observations on the Volcanic Islands and Parts of South America Visited During the Voyage of H.M.S. Beagle. 1876. V. 62
Geological Observations on the Volcanic Islands and Parts of South America Visited During the Voyage of H.M.S. Beagle. London: 1876. V. 67
Geological Observations on the Volcanic Islands and Parts of South America Visited During the Voyage of H.M.S. Beagle. London: 1891. V. 63
Geological Observations on the Volcanic Islands and Parts of South America Visited During the Voyage of H.M.S. Beagle. London: 1891. V. 65; 66
Insectivorous Plants. New York: 1875. V. 64; 67
Insectivorous Plants. London: 1876. V. 67
Insectivorus Plants. London: 1888. V. 62; 66
Journal of Researches into the Natural History and Geology of the Countries Visited During the Voyage of H.M.S. Beagle. New York: 1846. V. 63; 67
Journal of Researches into the Natural History and Geology of the Countries Visited During the Voyage of H.M.S. Beagle. London: 1860. V. 63; 64
Journal of Researches into the Natural History and Geology of the Countries Visited During the Voyage of H.M.S. Beagle. New York: 1956. V. 64
Naturwissenchaftliche Heisen. (Journal of Researches). Braunschweig. 1844. V. 63
The Life and Letters of Charles Darwin. 1887. V. 67
The Life and Letters of Charles Darwin. London: 1887. V. 65
The Life and Letters of Charles Darwin. New York: 1896. V. 65
The Movements and Habits of Climbing Plants. London: 1885. V. 67
The Movements and Habits of Climbing Plants. 1891. V. 66
The Movements and Habits of Climbing Plants. London: 1891. V. 62
Narrative of the Surveying Voyages of His Majesty's Ships Adventure and Beagle, Between the Years 1826 and 1836. London: 1839. V. 66
A Narrative of the Voyage of H.M.S. Beagle. London: 1977. V. 62; 64
A Naturalist's Voyage Journal of Researches...HMS Beagle...Sixteenth Thousand. London. 1884. V. 67
On the Origin of Species. London: 1859. V. 62; 63
On the Origin of Species. London: 1860. V. 62; 63; 66
On the Origin of Species. New York: 1860. V. 64
On the Origin of Species. New York: 1861. V. 64
On the Origin of Species. New York: 1871. V. 64
On the Origin of Species. London: 1872. V. 67
On the Origin of Species. London: 1882. V. 64
On the Origin of Species. Adelaide: 1963. V. 66
On the Various Contrivances by Which British and Foreign Orchids are Fertilised by Insects and on the Good Effects of Intercrossing. London: 1862. V. 62
The Origin of Species. 1872. V. 62
The Origin of Species. New York: 1884. V. 67
The Origin of the Species. London: 1861. V. 67
The Origin of the Species. London: 1872. V. 64
The Power of Movement in Plants. 1880. V. 66
The Power of Movement in Plants. London: 1880. V. 67
Selected Works of Charles Darwin. New York. v. 63; 66
The Structure and Distribution of Coral Reefs.... London: 1874. V. 67
The Variation of Animals and Plants Under Domestication. London: 1868. V. 62; 63; 64; 67
The Variation of Animals and Plants Under Domestication. London: 1875. V. 62; 66
The Variation of Animals and Plants Under Domestication. New York: 1876. V. 62
The Various Contrivances by Which Orchids are Fertilised by Insects. 1877. V. 66
The Various Contrivances by Which Orchids are Fertilised by Insects. London: 1877. V. 62
The Various Contrivances by Which Orchids are Fertilised by Insects. 1882. V. 66
The Various Contrivances by Which Orchids are Fertilised by Insects.... London: 1882. V. 67
The Works of.... 1968-1969. V. 65
The Works of.... London: 1986-1989. V. 62; 63; 66
The Zoology of the Voyage of H.M.S. Beagle. 1994. V. 63
The Zoology of the Voyage of H.M.S. Beagle. London: 1994. V. 62

DARWIN, ERASMUS
The Botanic Garden. 1973. V. 66

DARWIN, ERASMUS continued
The Botanic Garden. London: 1973. V. 63
Phytologia; or, the Philosophy of Agriculture and Gardening. 1800. V. 64; 65
Phytologia; or the Philosophy of Agriculture and Gardening. Dublin: 1800. V. 63
Phytologia; or, the Philosophy of Agriculture and Gardening. London: 1800. V. 67
A Plan for the Conduct of Female Education, in Boarding Schools. Derby: 1797. V. 65
Zoonomia; or, the Laws of Organic Life. London: 1801. V. 65

DARWIN, FRANCIS
The Life and Letters of Charles Darwin. New York: 1888. V. 64

DARY, DAVID
True Tales of the Old Time Plains. New York: 1979. V. 66

DARY, MICHAEL
Dary's Miscellanies: Being for the Most Part, a Brief Collection of Mathematical Theorems. London: 1669. V. 66

DARYUSH, ELIZABETH
Verses - Sixth Book. Boars Hill: 1938. V. 64

DAS, SARAT CHANDRA
Journey to Lhasa and Central Tibet. London: 1904. V. 64

DASENT, GEORGE WEBBE
The Story of Burnt Njal or Life in Iceland at the End of the Tenth Century. Edinburgh: 1861. V. 62

DASHWOOD, JAMES
Case of the Rector of Doddington. London: 1811. V. 63
Case of the Rector of Doddington. Wisbech: 1811. V. 63

D'ASSIGNY, MARIUS
An Antidote Against the Pernicious Errors of the Anabaptists or, of the Dipping-Sect.... London: 1708. V. 63; 65

DATER, JUDY
Imogen Cunningham: a Portrait. Boston: 1979. V. 63

DAUBENTON, L. J. M.
Observations on Indigestion: In Which is Satisfactorily Shewn the Efficacy of Ipecacuan, in Relieving This, as Well As Is Connected Train of Complaints Peculiar to the Decline of Life. London: 1809. V. 64

DAUBENY, CHARLES GILES BRIDLE
A Description of Active and Extinct Volcanos; with Remarks on Their Origin, Their Chemical Phaenomena and the Character of Their Products.... London: 1826. V. 65; 66
Sketch of the Geology of North America, Being the Substance of a Memoir Read Before the Ashmolean Society Nov. 26, 1838. Oxford: 1839. V. 62; 64

D'AUBIGNE, J. H. MERLE
History of the Reformation in Europe in the Time of Calvin. London: 1863. V. 66

DAUDET, ALPHONSE
My First Voyage: My First Life. London: 1901. V. 63
Port Tarascon. New York: 1891. V. 65
Recollections of a Literary Man. London: 1889. V. 63; 64
Tartarin of Tarascon. New York: 1930. V. 62; 63

DAUGHERTY, JAMES
The Picnic-A Frolic In Two Colors and Three Parts. New York: 1958. V. 64
Poor Richard. New York: 1941. V. 66

DAUGHTERS OF THE REPUBLIC OF TEXAS
Founders and Patriots of the Republic of Texas. Waco: 1985. V. 64

DAUGHTERY, JAMES
Abraham Lincoln. New York: 1943. V. 65
Daniel Boone. New York: 1939. V. 65

D'AULAIRE, INGRI
Abraham Lincoln. New York: 1939. V. 64; 65
Animals Everywhere. New York: 1940. V. 66
Columbus. Garden City: 1955. V. 64
Leif the Lucky. Garden City: 1941. V. 64
The Magic Meadow. Garden City: 1958. V. 62; 66
Nils. Garden City: 1950. V. 63
Ola and Blakken and Line, Sine, Trine. Garden City: 1933. V. 65
Pocahontas. Garden City: 1946. V. 64
Wings for Per. Garden City: 1944. V. 66

DAULBY, DANIEL
A Descriptive Catalogue of the Works of Rembrandt, and of His Scholars, Bol, Livens and Van Vliet.... Liverpool: 1796. V. 65

DAUMAL, RENE
Le Grande Beuverie. Paris: 1938. V. 67

DAUMAS, MAURICE
Scientific Instruments of the 17th & 18th Centuries and Their Makers. London: 1972. V. 67

DAUTERT, ERICH
Big Game in Antarctica. Bristol: 1937. V. 64

DAVAINE, CASIMIR JOSEPH
L'Oeuvre. Paris: 1889. V. 64

DAVENANT, CHARLES
Discourses on the Publick Revenues; and on the Trade of England, in Two Parts. (with) *Discourses on the Publick Revenues and on the Trade of England.* London: 1698. V. 64
Essays Upon I. Ballance of Power. II. The Right of Making War, Peace and Alliances. III. Universal Monarchy. To Which is Added, An Appendix.... London: 1701. V. 62; 64
Tom Double Return'd Out of the Country; or the True Picture of a Modern Whig.... London: 1702. V. 66

DAVENANT, WILLIAM
The Dramatic Works. Edinburgh: 1872-1878. V. 62

D'AVENANT, WILLIAM
Gondibert: an Heroick Poem. London: 1651. V. 65

DAVENANT, WILLIAM
The Works.... London: 1673. V. 62; 65

DAVENPORT, C. B.
Inheritance of Characteristics in Domestic Fowl. Washington: 1909. V. 62

DAVENPORT, CYRIL
English Embroidered Bookbindings. London: 1899. V. 64
English Heraldic Book-Stamps. London: 1909. V. 66
Mezzotints. New York: 1903. V. 63
Royal English Bookbindings. London: 1896. V. 67
Samuel Mearne, Binder to King Charles II. Chicago: 1906. V. 62; 63

DAVENPORT, GEORGE O.
Catalogue of Law Books Contained in the Ohio County Law Library and the Libraries of the Ohio County Bar. Wheeling: 1871. V. 65

DAVENPORT, GUY
The Antiquities of Ellis. N.P: 1971. V. 62
August. Tuscaloosa: 1986. V. 62; 64; 67
The Bicycle Rider. New York: 1985. V. 64; 67
The Bowmen of Shu. New York: 1983. V. 62; 64; 67
Do You Have a Poem Book on E. E. Cummings?. Penland: 1969. V. 63
Eclogues, Eight Stories: The Trees at Lystra, The Death of Picasso, The Daimon of Sokrates, Christ Preaching at the Henley Regatta, Mesoroposthonippidon, Lo Splendore della Luce at Bologna, Idyll & On Some Lines of Virgil. San Francisco: 1981. V. 63
Father Louie. New York: 1991. V. 62; 64; 67
50 Drawings. New York: 1996. V. 64; 67
Flowers and Leaves: Poema Vel Sonata Carmina Autumni Primaeque Veris Transformations. Highlands: 1966. V. 63; 64; 66
The Geography of the Imagination. San Francisco: 1981. V. 63
Goldfinch Thistle Star. New York: 1983. V. 66
Jonah. New York: 1986. V. 63; 64; 67
Jonathan Williams, Poet. Cleveland: 1969. V. 63
Maxims of the Ancient Egyptians. Louisville: 1983. V. 63
Maxims of the Ancient Egyptians. Louisville: 1984. V. 65
The Medusa. 1984. V. 62; 63
Pennant Key-Indexed Study Guide to Homer's Iliad. Philadelphia: 1967. V. 62
Ralph Eugene Meatyard. Millerton: 1974. V. 62
The Resurrection in Cookham Churchyard. New York: 1982. V. 62; 63; 64; 67
Robot. New York: 1972. V. 62; 64
Tatlin!. New York: 1974. V. 63
Trois Caprices. Louisville: 1981. V. 63

DAVENPORT, RICHARD ALFRED
Sketches of Imposture, Deception and Credulity. London: 1837. V. 62

DAVENPORT, W. BROMLEY
Sport in Prose and Verse. London: 1933. V. 67

DAVEY, F. H.
Flora of Cornwall Being an Account of the Flowering Plants and Ferns Found in the County of Cornwall. Penryn: 1909. V. 64; 65; 67

DAVEY, J. E.
Record of the Trial of the Rev. Prof. J. E. Davey by the Belfast Presbtery. 1927. V. 63

DAVEY, RICHARD
A History of Mourning. London: 1892?. V. 63

DAVID, A.
Abbe David's Diary.... Cambridge: 1949. V. 64

DAVID, DONALD
Brides of Reason. A Selection of Poems. Swinford: 1955. V. 65

DAVID, ELIZABETH
French Provincial Cooking. London: 1984. V. 67

DAVID, RICHARD
A Tailor's Poems. Pittsburgh: 1943. V. 63

DAVID, ROBERT BEEBE
Finn Burnett, Frontiersman - The Life and Adventures of an Indian Fighter, Mail Coach Driver, Pioneer, Cattleman, Participant in the Powder River Expedition, Survivor of the Hay Field Fight.... Glendale: 1937. V. 65; 67
Malcolm Campbell Sheriff. Casper: 1932. V. 65

DAVID, VILLIERS
The Guardsman and Cupid's Daughter and Other Poems. London: 1930. V. 62; 64

DAVIDIAN, H. H.
The Rhododendron Species. Volume II. Elepidotes. Part I. Arboreum Lactaeum. Portland: 1989. V. 67

DAVIDOFF, LEO
The Abnormal Pneumoencephalogram. Philadelphia: 1950. V. 67

DAVIDSON, ANDREW
The Neccesity & Inducements to Do Good: a Sermon Preached Before the Religious Tract Society; at Their First Annual Meeting Oct 30, 1812. Staunton: 1812. V. 65

DAVIDSON, BRUCE
The Bridge. New York: 1964. V. 63
Bruce Davidson Photographs. New York: 1978. V. 66

DAVIDSON, D.
The Great Pyramid - Its Divine Message. London: 1925. V. 64; 66

DAVIDSON, DIANE MOTT
Catering to Nobody. New York: 1990. V. 65; 67
The Cereal Murders. New York: 1993. V. 67
Dying for Chocolate. New York: 1992. V. 64; 65
The Last Suppers. New York: 1994. V. 67

DAVIDSON, DONALD
The Long Street. Nashville: 1961. V. 64

DAVIDSON, ELLIA A.
A Practical Manual of House Painting, Graining, Marbling and Sign- Writing. London: 1891. V. 66

DAVIDSON, FRANCES
Unstable as Water. London: 1875. V. 65

DAVIDSON, GEORGE
The Alaska Boundary. San Francisco: 1903. V. 66
The Glaciers of Alaska that Are Shown on Russian Charts of Mentioned in Older Narratives. San Francisco: 1904. V. 63

DAVIDSON, HAROLD G.
Ed Borein Cowboy Artist - The Life of John Edward Borein. New York: 1974. V. 65
Edward Borein - the Update - The Watercolors, Etchings and Drawings. Santa Barbara: 1991. V. 67

DAVIDSON, HOMER K.
Black Jack Davidson, a Cavalry Commander on the Western Frontier, the Life of General John W. Davidson. Glendale: 1974. V. 67

DAVIDSON, JOHN
Ballads and Songs. London: 1894. V. 65
Fleet Street Eclogues. London: 1893. V. 64
A Full and True Account of the Wonderful Mission of Earl Lavender, Which Lasted One Night and One Day.... London: 1895. V. 64
Mammon and His Message - Being the Second Part of God and Mamman - a Trilogy. London: 1908. V. 64
Miss Armstrong's and Other Circumstances. London: 1896. V. 64
Perfervid: the Career of Ninian Jamieson. London: 1890. V. 64
Plays. Being: an Unhistorical Pastoral: a Romantic Farce: Bruce A. Chronicle Play: Smith A Tragic Farce and Scaramouch in Naxos a Pantomine. London: 1894. V. 64
Seven Happy Days. London: 1913. V. 67
Smith: a Tragedy. Glasgow: 1888. V. 64
The Triumph of Mamon. London: 1907. V. 62

DAVIDSON, MARSHALL B.
The Original Water Colour Paintings by John James Audubon for the Birds of America. London: 1966. V. 64

DAVIDSON, PETER
The Mistletoe and Its Philosophy. 1898. V. 64

DAVIDSON, RANDALL T.
The Lambeth Conferences of 1867, 1878 and 1888. London: 1889. V. 63

DAVIDSON, THOMAS
British Fossil Brachiopoda. 1851-1856. V. 62; 63; 64; 65; 66; 67
British Fossil Brachiopoda. London: 1851-1886. V. 65
British Fossil Brachiopoda. VII. The Silurian Brachiopoda. 1866-1871. V. 63; 66
Challenger Expedition. Zoology Part I. Brachiopoda. London: 1880. V. 65
Classification der Brachiopoden.... Vienna: 1856. V. 64
Report on the Brachiopoda Dredged by HMS Challenger. 1880. V. 67

DAVIE, DONALD
Brides of Reason. Oxford: 1955. V. 65
Brides of Reason. Swinford: 1955. V. 62; 63; 65
Collected Poems - 1950-1970. London: 1972. V. 63
New and Selected Poems. Middletown: 1961. V. 65
Poems. Swinford: 1954. V. 62; 65
The Poems of Doctor Zhivago. Manchester: 1965. V. 64

DAVIE, IAN
Oxford Poetry - 1942-1943. Oxford: 1943. V. 65

DAVIE, JOHN CONSTANSE
Letters from Paraguay.... London: 1805. V. 67

DAVIE, OLIVER
Methods in the Art of Taxidermy. Philadelphia: 1900. V. 62
Reveries and Recollections of a Naturalist. Columbus: 1898. V. 67

DAVIE, W. GALSWORTHY
Old English Doorways. London: 1903. V. 62

DAVIES, A. M.
Solon H. Borglum: a Man Who Stands Alone. Chester: 1974. V. 65
Tertiary Faunas. A Text-Book for Oilfield Palaeontologists and Student's of Geology. 1971-1975. V. 67

DAVIES, ARTHUR
Thoughts on Colonization with the View of Suppressing the Slave Trade.... London: 1850. V. 64; 67

DAVIES, BENJAMIN
A New System of Modern Geography. Richmond: 1813. V. 67

DAVIES, CHARLES
Mathematical and Cyclopedia of Mathematical Science. New York: 1856. V. 67
Mathematical Dictionary and Cyclopedia of Mathematical Science. New York: 1857. V. 65

DAVIES, CHARLES G.
Shipping and Craft in Silhouette. Salem: 1929. V. 65

DAVIES, D. C.
A Treatise on Metalliferous Minerals and Mining. 1881. V. 64
A Treatise on Metalliferous Minerals and Mining. 1888. V. 64; 67
A Treatise on Metalliferous Minerals and Mining. London: 1888. V. 65

DAVIES, D. P.
A New Historical and Descriptive View of Derbyshire from the Remotest Period to the Present Time. Belper: 1811. V. 62

DAVIES, DAVID STUART
The Tangled Skein. Weymouth: 1992. V. 66

DAVIES, EDWARD
Celtic Reocearches on the Origin, Traditions and Language, of the Ancient Britons. 1804. V. 62
Celtic Researches, on the Origins, Traditions and Language of the Ancient Britons.... London: 1804. V. 64; 66
The Life of Bartoleme E. Murillo.... London: 1819. V. 64
The Mythology and Rites of the British Druids, Ascertained by National Documents.... London: 1809. V. 63

DAVIES, EDWARD WILLIAM LEWIS
Algiers in 1857. London: 1858. V. 65

DAVIES, ELLIS
The Prehistoric and Roman Remains of Denbighshire. Cardiff: 1929. V. 62

DAVIES, G. CHRISTOPHER
The Swan and Her Crew; or the Adventures of Three Young Naturalists & Sportsmen on the Broads and Rivers of Norfolk. V. 67

DAVIES, GLYN
Minera. Minera: 1964. V. 64; 65

DAVIES, GRIFFITH
Treatise on Annuities: with Numeorus Tables, Based on the Experience of the Equitable Society and on the Northampton Rate of Mortality. London: 1856. V. 66

DAVIES, J. SANGER
Dolomite Strongholds. London: 1896. V. 63; 64

DAVIES, J. SILVESTER
The Tropenell Catulary. London: 1908. V. 63

DAVIES, JOHN
The Civil Warres of Great Britain and Ireland. London: 1661. V. 62
The History of the Tahitian Mission 1799-1830. Cambridge: 1961. V. 64; 65
The History of the Tahitian Mission 1799-1830. Nendeln: 1974. V. 64
The Innkeeper's and Butler's Guide, or a Directory of making and Managing British Wines.... Leeds: 1809. V. 62
Orchestra, or a Poeme of Dancing. London: 1622. V. 66
The Original, Nature and Immortality of the Soul. London: 1714. V. 62

DAVIES, K. G.
Letters from Hudson Bay 1703-1740. London: 1965. V. 63

DAVIES, MARGARET SIDNEY
The Miss Margaret Sidney Davies Complete Collection of Special Gregynog Bindings. Antwerp: 1995. V. 62; 65

DAVIES, MARY CAROLYN
The Comic ABC Rendered Into English Verse. New York: 1922. V. 64

DAVIES, MELVYN
Worms Head and Mainland Caves 1-47. London: 1989. V. 64

DAVIES, MYLES
Eikon micro-biblikie (graece) Sive Icon Libellorum, or a Critical History of Pamphlets. London: 1715. V. 63

DAVIES, NINA
Egyptian Paintings. Harmondsworth: 1954. V. 62
Egyptian Paintings. London: 1954. V. 66; 67

DAVIES, R.
The Histories of the King's Manour House at York.... York: 1883. V. 62; 66

DAVIES, R. RICE
First Prize Essay on the Desirability and Advantages of Recreation Grounds for Swansea. Swansea: 1875. V. 64

DAVIES, RHYS
Arfon. London: 1931. V. 66
Daisy Matthews and Three Other Tales. Waltham St. Lawrence: 1932. V. 62; 64

DAVIES, RHYS continued
Rings on Her Fingers. London: 1930. V. 64; 66
A Woman. 1931. V. 66
A Woman. London: 1931. V. 64

DAVIES, RICHARD
An Account of the Convincement, Exercises, Services and Travels.... Philadelphia: 1770. V. 63; 66
An Account of the Convincement, Exercises, Services and Travels.... Newtown: 1928. V. 65; 66

DAVIES, ROBERT
A Memoir of the York Press, with Notices of Authors Printers and Staioners, in the Sixteenth, Seventeenth and Eighteenth Centuries. London: 1868. V. 66; 67
A New Welsh Grammar. Chester: 1808. V. 62

DAVIES, ROBERTSON
The Cunning Man. London: 1995. V. 62
An Introduction to the Twenty-First Toronto Antiquarian Book Fair. 1993. V. 67
Leaven of Malice. Toronto: 1954. V. 66
The Lyre of Orpheus. Franklin Center: 1988. V. 63; 65
The Lyre of Orpheus. Toronto: 1988. V. 63; 66
The Manticore. New York: 1972. V. 64
The Manticore. Toronto: 1972. V. 63
Murther and Walking Spirits. Franklin Center: 1991. V. 63
Murther and Walking Spirits. London: 1991. V. 63; 65; 66
The Table Talk of Samuel Marchbanks. Toronto: 1949. V. 62; 66
Tempest-Tost. New York: 1952. V. 66
A Voice from the Air. New York: 1960. V. 66
Why I Do Not Intend to Write an Autobiography. Toronto: 1993. V. 62

DAVIES, THEODORE
Losing to Win. New York: 1874. V. 63; 65

DAVIES, THOMAS
Dramatic Miscellanies.... London: 1784. V. 65
Leben von David Garrick. Aus dem Englischen.... Leipzig: 1782. V. 63
Memoirs of the Life of David Garrick. London: 1780. V. 66
Memoirs of the Life of David Garrick. London: 1781. V. 65; 66

DAVIES, W. P.
A Brand Plucked Out of the Fire? or a Brief Account of Robert Kendall.... Northampton: 1813. V. 64

DAVIES, WILLIAM
Plays Written for a Private Theatre. London: 1786. V. 66

DAVIES, WILLIAM HENRY
The Adventures of Johnny Walker, Tramp. London: 1926. V. 65
Forty-Nine Poems. London: 1928. V. 62
Selected Poems. Newtown: 1928. V. 62
True Travellers: a Tramp's Opera. London: 1923. V. 66

D'AVIGDOR, ELIM H.
Across Country, by Wanderer. London: 1882. V. 67

DAVILA, DON PEDRO
Catalogue Systematique et Raisone des Curiosites et de la Nature et de l'Art, Qui Composent le Cabient de M. Davila.... Paris: 1767. V. 65

DAVILA, H. C.
The Historie of the Civill Warres of France. London: 1647. V. 63; 65
The Historie of the Civill Warres of France. London: 1647-1648. V. 67

DAVILLIER, CHARLES
Le Cabinet du Duc d'Aumont et les Amateurs de Son Temps.... Paris: 1870. V. 66
Spain. New York: 1876. V. 62
Spain. London: 1881. V. 65

DAVIS, A. M.
The Journey of Moncacht-Ape, an Indian of the Yazoo Tribe, Across the Continent About the Year 1700. Worcester: 1883. V. 66

DAVIS, ANDREW JACKSON
The Philosophy of Spiritual Intercourse.... New York: 1851. V. 64

DAVIS, ANGELA Y.
If They Come In the Morning. New York: 1971. V. 63
The Soledad Brothers and Other Political Prisoners. New York: 1971. V. 66
Women, Race and Class. New York: 1981. V. 64; 66

DAVIS, BRITTON
The Truth About Geronimo. New Haven: 1929. V. 63; 66; 67

DAVIS, BURKE
Gray Fox. Robert E. Lee and the Civil War. New York: 1956. V. 62

DAVIS, C. C.
The Marine and Fresh-Water Plankton. East Lansing: 1955. V. 67

DAVIS, CHARLES B.
Report on Interoceanic Canals and Railroads Between the Atlantic and Pacific Oceans. Washington: 1867. V. 65

DAVIS, D. H. S.
Ecological Studies in Southern Africa. The Hague: 1964. V. 63

DAVIS, DAVID D.
The Principles and Pratice of Obstetric Medicine. London: 1836. V. 67

DAVIS, DUKE
Flashlights from Mountain and Plain. Bound Brook: 1911. V. 64

DAVIS, E. J.
Anatolica; or the Journal of a Visit to Some of the Ancient Ruined Cities of Caria, Phrygia, Lycia and Pisidia. London: 1874. V. 64
Life in Asiatic Turkey.... London: 1879. V. 64

DAVIS, E. O.
The First Five Years of the Railroad Era in Colorado. N.P: 1948. V. 64; 67

DAVIS, EDWARD HILL
Historical Sketches of Franklin County. Raleigh: 1948. V. 63; 67

DAVIS, EDWIN ADAMS
Fallen Guidon. The Forgotten Saga of General Jo Shelby's Confederate Command.... Santa Fe: 1962. V. 62; 63

DAVIS, ELLIS A.
Davis' Commercial Encyclopedia of the Pacific Southwest, California, Nevada, Utah and Arizona. Berkeley: 1914. V. 62; 63

DAVIS, ERWIN ADAMS
Fallen Guidion: The Forgotten Sage of General Jo Shelby's Confederate Command: The Brigade that Never Surrendered and Its Exhibition to Mexico. Santa Fe: 1962. V. 64

DAVIS, FRANCIS P.
Year Book: Los Angeles Architectural Club, 1910. Los Angeles: 1910. V. 62

DAVIS, FRANK MARSHALL
Jazz Interlude. Chicago: 1985. V. 67

DAVIS, GEORGE
Coming Home. New York: 1971. V. 62; 65
Love, Black Love. New York: 1978. V. 65

DAVIS, GEORGE T. B.
Metlakahtla. A True Narrative of the Red Man. Chicago: 1904. V. 65

DAVIS, GEORGE WESLEY
Sketches of Butte (From Vigilante Days to Prohibition). Boston: 1921. V. 66

DAVIS, H. B.
Life and Work of Cyrus Guernsey Pringle. Burlington: 1936-1937. V. 66; 67

DAVIS, H. H.
A Tee-Totaller's Album. Carlisle: 1838. V. 64

DAVIS, HENRY GEORGE
The Memorials of the Hamlet of Knightsbridge. London: 1859. V. 62

DAVIS, HENRY H.
The Fancies of a Dreamer. London: 1842. V. 62

DAVIS, HENRY HARRISON
An Excursion from Lancaster Up the Vale of Lune, and from Kirkby Lonsdale, to the Caves of Yorkshire. Kirkby Lonsdale: 1851. V. 64

DAVIS, HENRY T.
Solitary Places Made Glad, Being Observations and Experience for Thirty-Two Years in Nebraska with Sketches and Incidents. Cincinnati: 1890. V. 62; 65

DAVIS, J. A. G.
Treatise on Criminal Law, with an Exposition of the Office and Authority of Justices of the Peace in Virginia. Philadelphia: 1838. V. 66

DAVIS, J. B.
On Synoptic Crania Among the Aboriginal Race of Man. Haarlem: 1865. V. 67
On the Osteology and Peculiarities of the Tasmanians, a Race of Man Recently Become Extinct. Haarlem: 1874. V. 67
On the Peculiar Crania of the Inhabitants of Certain Groups of Islands in the Western Pacific. Haarlem: 1866. V. 67

DAVIS, J. W.
On the Fossil Fishes of the Carboniferous Limestone Series of Great Britain. Dublin: 1883. V. 66
West Yorkshire: an Account of Its Geology, Physcial Geography, Climatology and Botany. London: 1880. V. 64; 65

DAVIS, JAMES J.
The Iron Puddler, My Life in the Rolling Mills and What Came Of It. New York: 1922. V. 67

DAVIS, JAMES LUCIUS
The Trooper's Manual; or, Tactics for Light Dragoons and Mountd Riflemen. Richmond: 1861. V. 62; 63; 65
The Trooper's Manual; or, Tactics for Light Dragoons and Mounted Riflemen. Richmond: 1862. V. 62; 63; 65

DAVIS, JEFFERSON
His Letters, Papers and Speeches. Jackson: 1923. V. 67
The Rise and Fall of the Confederate Government. New York: 1881. V. 63; 65
The Rise and Fall of the Confederate Government. New York and London: 1912. V. 64

DAVIS, JOHN
The First Settlers of Virginia. Jamestown: 1806. V. 62
The First Settlers of Virginia. New York: 1806. V. 62; 64
Life and Times of the Late Rev. Harris Harding, Yarmouth, N.S. Charlottetown: 1866. V. 64

DAVIS, JOHN C. B.
The Massachusetts Justice: a Treatise Upon the Powers and Duties of Justices of the Peace. Worcester: 1847. V. 67

DAVIS, JOHN EDWARD
Notes on the Deep-Sea Sounding.... London: 1867. V. 64

DAVIS, JOHN FRANCIS
Hien Wun Shoo. Chinese Moral Maxims; with a Free and Verbal Translation.... London: 1823. V. 64

DAVIS, JOHN K.
With the Aurora in the Antarctic 1911-1914. London: 1919. V. 64

DAVIS, JOHN STAIGE
Plastic Surgery. Its Principles and Practice. Philadelphia: 1919. V. 63

DAVIS, JOSEPH
A Digest of Legislative Enactments, Relating to the Society of Friends, Commonly Called Quakers, in England.... Bristol: 1820. V. 64

DAVIS, JOSIAH G.
Memorial Services: Address of Welcome, Poem, Responses, Ceremonies and Oration at the Dedication of the Soldiers' Monument in Amherst, N.H. on the Reunion of the Tenth Regiment of N. H. Veterans, June 19, 1890. Manchester: 1890. V. 66

DAVIS, JULIA
Never Say Die: The Glengarry McDonalds of Virginia. Stafford: 1980. V. 64; 67

DAVIS, LAVINIA
A Bibliography of the Writings of Edith Wharton. Portland: 1933. V. 62

DAVIS, LINDSEY
A Dying Light in Corduba. Bristol: 1996. V. 63; 64
A Dying Light in Corduba. Bristol: 1996. V. 63; 64
A Dying Light in Corduba. London: 1996. V. 67
The Iron Hand of Mars. London: 1991. V. 66
The Iron Hand of Mars. London: 1992. V. 67
Last Act in Palmyra. London: 1994. V. 67
Shadows in Bronze. London: 1990. V. 65; 66; 67
The Silver Pigs. London: 1989. V. 62
Silver Pigs. New York: 1989. V. 65
Three Hands in the Fountain. London: 1997. V. 67
Time to Depart. London: 1995. V. 67
Venus in Copper. London: 1991. V. 63; 65; 66; 67

DAVIS, M. E. M.
An Elephant's Track and Other Stories. New York: 1897. V. 64; 65
The Little Chevalier. Boston and New York: 1903. V. 62
The Queen's Garden. Boston and New York: 1900. V. 64; 65

DAVIS, MARIANNA W.
Contributions of Black Women to America. Columbia: 1982. V. 65; 67

DAVIS, MARTHA ANN
Poems of Laura: an Original American Work. Petersburg: 1818. V. 63

DAVIS, MATTHEW L.
Memoirs of Aaron Burr. With Miscellaneous Selections from His Correspondence. New York: 1836. V. 66

DAVIS, N.
Carthage and Her Remains: Being an Account of the Excavations and Researches on the Site of the Phoenician Metropolis in Africa and Other Adjacent Places. London: 1861. V. 66
Ruined Cities Within Numidian and Carthaginian Territories. London: 1862. V. 66

DAVIS, NATHAN SMITH
History of Medicine with the Code of Medical Ethics. Chicago: 1903. V. 63

DAVIS, NICHOLAS A.
The Campaign from Texas to Maryland with the Battle of Fredericksburg. Austin: 1961. V. 63; 67

DAVIS, PAUL
Faces. New York: 1985. V. 62

DAVIS, R. C.
Encyclopedia of American Forest and Conservation History. New York: 1983. V. 66; 67

DAVIS, RICHARD C.
Lobsticks Stone Cairns: Human Landmarks in the Arctic. Calgary: 1996. V. 64
Sir John Franklin's Journals and Correspondence: the First Arctic Land Expedition 1819-1822. Toronto/Ottawa: 1965. V. 64

DAVIS, RICHARD HARDING
About Paris. New York: 1895. V. 64
The Adventures of My Freshman. Sketches in Pen and Pencil.... Bethlehem: 1883. V. 62
Cuba in War Time. New York: 1897. V. 67
The Rulers of the Mediterranean. New York: 1894. V. 66

DAVIS, ROBERT
Kendrew of York and His Chapbooks for Children. Wetherby, West Yorkshire: 1988. V. 62

DAVIS, ROBERT H.
Deep Diving and Submarine Operations (Parts I and II). Cwbran, Gwent: 1995. V. 62

DAVIS, ROBERT S.
History of the Rebel Steam Ram Atlanta Now on Exhibition at Foot of Washington Street, for the Benefit of the Union Volunteer Refreshment Saloon, Philadelphia. Philadelphia: 1863. V. 63; 65

DAVIS, ROGER
Kendrew of York and His Chapbooks for Children. Wetherby, West Yorkshire: 1988. V. 62; 65

DAVIS, SAMUEL B.
Escape of a Confederate Officer from Prison. Norfolk: 1892. V. 62; 63; 65

DAVIS, SUSAN L.
Authentic History: Ku Klux Klan 1865-1877. New York: 1924. V. 67

DAVIS, T.
The Architecture of John Nash. London: 1960. V. 65

DAVIS, VARINA H.
Jefferson Davis, Ex-President of the Confederate States of America, a Memoir. New York: 1890. V. 62; 64

DAVIS, VIRGINIA L. H.
Tidewater Virginia Families. Baltimore: 1989. V. 64

DAVIS, W. M.
The Coral Reef Problem. New York: 1928. V. 63; 66

DAVIS, WILLIAM
A Complete Treatise on Land Surveying, by the Chain, Cross and Offset Staffs Only. London: 1802. V. 62
Nimrod of the Sea. Boston: 1926. V. 64
An Olio Bibliographical and Literary Anecdotes and Memoranda. London: 1814. V. 64

DAVIS, WILLIAM C.
Breckinridge: Statesman, Soldier, Symbol. Baton Rouge: 1974. V. 66
The Image of War. New York: 1981-1984. V. 62

DAVIS, WILLIAM H.
Seventy-Five Years in California. San Francisco: 1929. V. 62; 64
Sixty Years in California. San Francisco: 1889. V. 63

DAVIS, WILLIAM J.
The Partisan Rangers of the Confederate States Army. Louisville: 1904. V. 63

DAVIS, WILLIAM WATTS HART
El Gringo; or New Mexico and Her People. Santa Fe: 1938. V. 63

DAVIS, WINFIELD J.
History of Political Conventions in California 1849-1892. 1893. V. 62; 63
An Illustrated History of Sacramento County California. New York: 1890. V. 63
An Illustrated History of Sacramento County California. San Francisco: 1890. V. 62

DAVISON, FRANCIS
Davison's Poetical Rhapsody. London: 1890. V. 65
The Poetical Rhapsody; to Which are Added Several Other Pieces.... London: 1826. V. 64

DAVISON, RICHARD ALLAN
Charles and Kathleen Norris: The Courtship Year. San Francisco: 1993. V. 64

DAVY Crockett's 1844 Almanac. Boston: 1843. V. 66

DAVY, DAVID
Kanzana. Lawrence: 1986. V. 65

DAVY, HUMPHRY
Collected Works. London: 1839-1840. V. 64
Elements of Agricultural Chemistry in a Course of Lectures for the Board of Agriculture. 1813. V. 67
Elements of Agricultural Chemistry in a Course of Lectures for the Board of Agriculture. London: 1813. V. 64; 65
Elements of Agricultural Chemistry, in a Course of Lectures for the Board of Agriculture. London: 1814. V. 63
Elements of Chemical Philosophy...Part I. Volume I. 1812. V. 62
On the Safety Lamp for Coal Miners. London: 1818. V. 62; 63; 67
On the Safety Lamp for Preventing Explosions in Mines, Houses, Lighted by Gas. London: 1825. V. 63
Salmonia; or Days of Fly Fishing. London: 1828. V. 66
Salmonia or Days of Fly Fishing. 1829. V. 65; 67
Salmonia; or Days of Fly Fishing. London: 1829. V. 66
Salmonia or Days of Fly Fishing. 1851. V. 65; 67
Six Discourses Delivered Before the Royal Society.... London: 1827. V. 62
Some New Researches on Flame. 1817. V. 62

DAVY, JOHN
The Angler and His Friend. 1855. V. 67
The Angler in the Lake District. 1857. V. 65; 67
The Angler in the Lake District. London: 1857. V. 63; 65; 66; 67
Lectures on the Study of Chemistry. London: 1849. V. 62
Memoirs of the Life of Sir Humphry Davy, Bart. 1836. V. 62
Notes and Observations on the Ionian Islands and Malta; with Some Remarks on Constantinople and Turkey and on the System of Quarantine as at Present Conducted. London: 1842. V. 65

DAVYS, PETER
Adminiculum Puerile; or an Help for School-Boys. Philadelphia: 1764. V. 64

DAWDY, DORIS O.
Artists of the American West - a Biographical Dictionary. Chicago/Athens: 1974-1985. V. 63

DAWE, WILLIAM CARLTON
Kakemonos: Tales of the Far East. New York and London: 1897. V. 67
Mount Desolation. London: 1892. V. 67

DAWES, BEN
The Trematoda of British Fishes. London: 1947. V. 67

DAWES, CHARLES G.
Ships of the Past. Salem: 1929. V. 66

DAWKINS, H. C.
Tropical Mois Forest Silviculture and Management.... Wallingford: 1998. V. 63

DAWKINS, W. BOYD
British Pleistocene Mammalia. 1902-1912. V. 65; 66
British Pleistocene Mammalia. British Pleistocene Felidae. 1866-1868. V. 64
Cave Hunting, Researches on the Evidence of Caves Respecting the Early Inhabitants of Europe. London: 1874. V. 62; 64
Inaugural Address to the Manchester Geological Society. Manchester: 1874. V. 67
On the Prehistoric Mammalia of Great Britain. N.P: 1869?. V. 67

DAWSON, CAROL
The Waking Spell. Chapel Hill: 1992. V. 63; 66

DAWSON, CHARLES
History of Hastings Castle. London: 1909. V. 62
Pioneer Tales of the Oregon Trail of Jefferson County. Topeka: 1912. V. 66

DAWSON, DANIEL
The Second Trial and Capital Conviction of Daniel Dawson, for Poisoning Horses, at Newmarket in 1809, Before Mr. Justice Heath at Cambridge on Wednesday the 22d July 1812. London: 1812. V. 63
The Trial of Daniel Dawson for Poisoning Mr. Adams' Mare, at Newmarket, in 1809...Cambridge, July 22, 1812.... London: 1812/. V. 63

DAWSON, FIELDING
On Duberman's Black Mountain and B. H. Friedman's Biography of Jackson Pollock. Toronto: 1973. V. 63

DAWSON, FRANCIS W.
Our Women in the War. Charleston: 1876. V. 62; 63; 65
Reminiscences of Confederate Service 1861-1865. Charleston: 1882. V. 62

DAWSON, G. M.
Report on the Queen Charlotte Islands 1878. Montreal: 1880. V. 64

DAWSON, HENRY B.
Battles of the United States by Sea and Land. New York: 1858. V. 63

DAWSON, JAMES
Hell Gate. New York: 1967. V. 67

DAWSON, JOHN WILLIAM
Acadian Geology. London: 1868. V. 64
Acadian Geology. London: 1878. V. 64
The Canadian Ice Age.... Montreal: 1893. V. 64
The Dawn of Life: Being the History of the Oldest Known Fossil Remains, and Their Relations to Geological Time and to the Development of the Animal Kingdom. Montreal: 1875. V. 64
Eden Lost and Won - Studies of the Early History and Final Destiny of Man as Taught in Nature and Revelation. London: 1895. V. 64
First Lessons in Scientific Agriculture For Schools and Private Instruction. Montreal and Toronto: 1864. V. 64
Fossil Men and Their Modern Representatives. An Attempt to Illustrate the Characters and Condition of Pre-Historic Men in Europe. London: 1883. V. 64
The Geology of Nova Scotia, New Brunswick and Prince Island, or Acadian Geology. London: 1891. V. 64
Handbook of Geology for the Use of Canadian Students. Montreal: 1889. V. 64
Lecture Notes on Geology and Outline of the Geology of Canada. Montreal: 1880. V. 63
Nature and the Bible. New York: 1875. V. 64
Points of Contact Between Revelation and Natural Science. London: 1889?. V. 64
Relics of Primeval Life. London: 1895. V. 64

DAWSON, KENNETH
Just an Ordinary Shoot. London: 1938. V. 67
Marsh and Mudflat. London: 1931. V. 67
Salmon and Trout in Moorland Streams. London: 1928. V. 67

DAWSON, LIONEL
Sport in War. 1936. V. 62; 64
Sport in War. London: 1936. V. 67

DAWSON, LUCY
Dogs As I See Them. London: 1936. V. 67

DAWSON, NICHOLAS
Narrative of Nicholas Cheyenne Dawson (Overland to California in '41 and '49 and Texas in '51). San Francisco: 1933. V. 64

DAWSON, PHILIP
Electric Railways and Tramways, Their Construction and Operation. London: 1897. V. 64

DAWSON, S.
Incidents in the Course of a Long Cycling Career. Lancaster: 1909. V. 62

DAWSON, S. J.
Report on the Exploration of the Country Between Lake Superior and the Red River Settlement. N.P: 1968. V. 64

DAWSON, THOMAS
Memoirs of St. George the English Patron, and of the Most Noble Order of the Garter. London: 1714. V. 65

DAWSON, W. H.
Social Switzerland. Studies of Present-Day Social Movements and Legislation in the Swiss Republic. London: 1897. V. 63

DAWSON, W. J.
Works. 1888-1897. V. 62

DAWSON, WARREN R.
A Leechbook, or Collection of Medical Recipes of the Fifteenth Century. London: 1934. V. 64; 66

DAWSON, WILLIAM, & SONS, LTD.
Medicine and Science: a Bibliographical Catalogue of Historical and Rare Books from the 15th to the 20th Century. (Catalog 91). London: 1958. V. 62

DAWSON, WILLIAM LEON
The Birds of California. San Diego: 1923. V. 62; 63; 64; 67
The Birds of California. New York: 1940. V. 62; 67
Birds of Ohio. Columbus: 1903. V. 64
The Birds of Washington. Seattle: 1909. V. 62; 67

DAY, A. GROVE
Coronado's Quest and the Discovery of the Southern States. Berkeley: 1940. V. 66

DAY at the Zoo. London: 1900. V. 65

DAY, CHARLES WILLIAM
Hints on Etiquette and the Usages of Society.... London: 1850. V. 64

DAY, FRANCIS
British and Irish Salmonidae. 1887. V. 62
British and Irish Salonidae. London: 1887. V. 65
The Fauna of British India...Fishes. 1889. V. 62
The Fishes of Great Britain and Ireland. 1880-1884. V. 65; 66
The Fishes of Great Britain and Ireland. London: 1880-1884. V. 62; 64
The Fishes of India.... London: 1878-1888. V. 65
The Fishes of Malabar. London: 1865. V. 65
Report on the Fresh Water Fish and Fisheries of India and Burma. Calcutta: 1873. V. 62; 64

DAY, J. H.
A Guide to Marine Life on South African Shores. Cape Town: 1969. V. 66
A Guide to Marine Life on South African Shores. Cape Town and Rotterdam: 1974. V. 64; 65
Polychaeta of Southern Africa. London: 1967. V. 66

DAY, J. WENTWORTH
British Birds of the Wild Places. 1961. V. 67
Farming Adventure. 1949. V. 67
Ghosts and Witches. 1954. V. 67
Harvest Adventure. 1948. V. 67
The New Yeomen of England. 1952. V. 67
Sporting Adventure. London: 1937. V. 67
Wild Wings and Some Footsteps. London: 1948. V. 67

DAY, JAMES W.
King George V as a Sportsman. 1935. V. 67

DAY, JEREMIAH
An Introduction to Algebra. New Haven: 1814. V. 63

DAY, L.
The Tragedy of the Klondike - This Book of Travel Gives the True Facts of What Took Place in the Gold Fields Under the British Rule. New York: 1906. V. 67

DAY, L. MEEKER
The Improved American Family Physician; or, Sick Man's Guide to Health.... New York: 1833. V. 64

DAY, ROBIN
Day By Day. A Dose of My Own Hemlock. London: 1975. V. 67

DAY, SAMUEL PHILLIPS
Down South; or, an Englishman's Experience at the Seat of the American War. London: 1862. V. 63; 65

DAY, THOMAS
The History of Sandford and Merton Intended for the Use of Children. 1816. V. 63

DAY, W.
The History of Little Jack, a Foundling; with The History of William, an Orphan. London: 1826. V. 62

DAYE, ELIZA
Poems, on Various Subjects. Liverpool: 1798. V. 65

DAYES, EDWARD
The Works of the Late Edward Dayes.... London: 1805. V. 62; 65; 66

DAY LEWIS, CECIL
Beechen Vigil and Other Poems. London: 1925. V. 62
Child of Misfortune - a Novel. London: 1939. V. 63
Collected Poems 1929-1933 and A Hope for Poetry. New York: 1935. V. 65
The Friendly Tree. London: 1936. V. 67
The Magnetic Mountain. London: 1933. V. 65
The Mind in Chains - Socialism and the Cultural Revolution. London: 1937. V. 63; 64

DAY LEWIS, CECIL continued
Minute for Murder. London: 1947. V. 62
Noah and the Waters. London: 1936. V. 65; 66
The Otterbury Incident. London: 1948. V. 63
Poems in Wartime. London: 1940. V. 64
Posthumous Poems. Andoversford: 1979. V. 62; 65
Ten Singers: an Anthology. London: 1925. V. 66
Thou Shell of Death. London: 1936. V. 64
A Time to Dance. London: 1935. V. 63; 65
Word Over All. London: 1943. V. 65

DAYS with the English Poets. London: 1915. V. 62

DAYTON, EDSON C.
Dakota Days May 1886-August 1898. Clifton Springs: 1937. V. 64; 67

D'AZEMAR, LEOPOLD MICHEL MARTIAL, LE BARON
Avenir de La Cavalerie. Paris: 1860. V. 64

THE DE La Cruz-Badiano Aztec Herbal of 1552. Baltimore: 1939. V. 65

DEACLE, WILLIAM GRANT
A Black Scene Opened: Being the True State of Mr. John Kendrick's Gifts to the Town of Reading.... Reading: 1791. V. 63

DEACON, A. B.
Malekula. A Vanishing People in the New Hebrides. London: 1934. V. 62

DEACON, C. W.
Deacon's Map of Yorkshire, with a History of the County and Geological Notes. London: 1885. V. 65

DEAKIN, JOHN
London Today. London: 1949. V. 67
Rome Alive. A Notebook. London: 1951. V. 67

DEAKIN, TERENCE J.
Catalogi Librorum Eroticorum. London: 1964. V. 67

DEAN, BASHFORD
Bashford Dean Memorial Volume: Archaic Fishes. New York: 1930-1942. V. 65
Chimaeroid Fishes and Their Development. Washington: 1906. V. 65

DEAN, G. A.
The Land Steward. London: 1851. V. 63

DEAN, JOHN
The Gray Substance of the Medulla Oblongata and Trapezium. Washington: 1864. V. 67

DEAN, WILLIAM
An Historical and Descriptive Account of Croome d'Abitot, the Seat of the Rt. Hon. the Earl of Coventry.... Worcester: 1824. V. 64

DE ANDRADE, CARLOS DRUMMOND
Souvenir of the Ancient World. New York: 1976. V. 66

DEANE, EDMUND
Spadacrene Anglica; or, the English Spaw. Leeds: 1736. V. 64; 65; 66
Spadacrene Anglica, or the English Spaw. Bristol: 1922. V. 65

DEANE, SAMUEL
The New England Farmer; or, Georgical Dictionary.... Worcester: 1790. V. 62

DEANE, SEAMUS
Selected Poems. Oldcastle, County Meath: 1988. V. 65

DE ANGELI, MARGUERITE
The Door in the Wall. Garden City: 1949. V. 66
Ted and Nina Go to the Grocery Store. Garden City: 1935. V. 62
Yone Wondernose. Garden City: 1944. V. 65

DEANS, JOSEPH
Melbourne Church. London: 1843. V. 65

DEAR Alec...A Tribute for His Eightieth Birthday from Friends Known and Unknown. London: 1972. V. 63

DEAR, MATTIE
The Writings of Mattie Dear. Clarksdale: 1944. V. 65

DEARING, J. S.
A Drummer's Experiences. Colorado Springs: 1913. V. 65

DEARMER, MABEL
A Noah's Ark Geography. London: 1900. V. 64
Round-About Rhymes. Glasgow and Dublin: 1898. V. 65
Round-About Rhymes. London: 1898. V. 64

DEARN, T. D. W.
Designs for Lodges and Entrances to Parks, Paddocks and Pleasure Grounds, in the Gothic, Cottage and Fancy Styles. London: 1823. V. 64

THE DEATH and Burial of Cock Robin. Lichfield: 1780. V. 62; 65
THE DEATH and Burial of Cock Robin. New York: 1820. V. 62
THE DEATH and Burial of Cock Robin. London: 1830. V. 62
THE DEATH and Burial of Cock Robin. London: 1850. V. 64; 65

THE DEATH and Burial of Cock Robin also The Pleasing Story of the House that Jack Built to Which is Added The Poetical Alphabet. London: 1791-1795. V. 67

DEATON, E. L.
Indian Fights on the Texas Frontier. Fort Worth: 1927. V. 67

DEATS, HIRAM E.
Marriage Records of Hunterdon County, New Jersey, 1795-1875. Flemington: 1918. V. 63; 66

DEAVER, JEFFREY
A Maiden's Grave. New York: 1995. V. 67
Praying for Sleep. New York: 1994. V. 67

DE BACA, MANUEL C.
Vicente Silva and His 40 Bandits. Washington: 1947. V. 63; 66

DE BAKEY, MICHAEL E.
Surgery of the Aorta. Summit: 1956. V. 63

DE BARRERA, ANITA
Gems and Jewels: Their History, Geography, Chemistry and Ana. London: 1860. V. 63

DE BARTHE, JOE
The Life and Adventures of Frank Grouard. St. Joseph: 1890. V. 65; 67

DE BAYE, J.
The Industrial Arts of the Anglo-Saxons. London: 1893. V. 62

DE BAZANCOURT, BARON
The Crimean Expedition to the Capture of Sebastropol. London: 1856. V. 64

DE BEER, G. R.
Alps and Men: Pages from Forgotten Diaries of Travellers and Tourists in Switzerland. 1932. V. 65
Alps and Men: Pages from Forgotten Diaries of Travellers and Tourists in Switzerland. London: 1932. V. 63

DE BELDER, R.
A Magnificent Collection of Botanical Books.... London: 1987. V. 64

DE BERA, ROMON
English Bhamorro Dialogues. Hong Kong: 1931. V. 66

DE BERNIERES, LOUIS
Captain Corelli's Mandolin. 1994. V. 63
Captain Corelli's Mandolin. London: 1994. V. 66
Corelli's Mandolin. New York: 1994. V. 62; 63
A Day Out for Mohmot Erbil. London: 1999. V. 64; 65
Labels. London: 1993. V. 64; 67
Senor Vivo and the Coca Lord. New York: 1991. V. 67
Senor Vivo and the Coca Lord. New York: 1993. V. 67
The Troublesome Offspring of Cardinal Guzman. London: 1992. V. 63
The Troublesome Offspring of Cardinal Guzman. New York: 1994. V. 67
The War of Don Emmanuel's Nether Parts. London: 1990. V. 63; 65
The War of Don Emmanuel's Nether Parts. New York: 1991. V. 64; 66
The War of Don Emmanuel's Nether Parts. (with) Senor Vivo & The Coca Lord. (with) The Troublesome Offspring of Cardinal Guzman. London: 1990-1991. V. 66

DE BLAS, C.
The Nutrition of the Rabbit. Wallingford: 1998. V. 67

DE BLOIS, S. W.
Historical Sketch of the 1st Horton Baptist Church, Wolfville, for the Period of One Hundred Years, from A.D. 1778 to A.D. 1878. Halifax: 1879. V. 63

DEBO, ANGIE
And Still Waters Run, the Betrayal of the Five Civilized Tribes. Princeton: 1940. V. 64; 67
The Cowman's Southwest - Being the Reminiscences of Oliver Nelson.... Glendale: 1953. V. 63
The Road to Disappearance. Norman: 1941. V. 64; 67
Tulsa, from Creek Town to Oil Capital. Norman: 1942. V. 65

DE BONO, EDWARD
The Use of Lateral Thinking. London: 1967. V. 64

DE BORN, EDITH
Daughter of the House. London: 1953. V. 67
The End of the Struggle. London: 1972. V. 67
A Question of Age. London: 1961. V. 67

DE BOSIS, LAURO
The Story of My Death. London: 1933. V. 64

DE BOURDEILLE, PIERRE
The Lives of Gallant Ladies. Waltham St. Lawrence: 1924. V. 66

DE BOURGADE LA DARDYE, E.
Paraguay; the Land and the People, Natural Wealth and Commercial Capabilities. London: 1892. V. 64

DE BOW, JAMES
Pacific Rail-Road. A Review of the Reports of the Committees of the Senate and House of Representatives of the Last Session. New Orleans: 1850. V. 63; 66

DE BOW, JAMES D. B.
The Interest in Slavery of the Southern Non-Slaveholder. Charleston: 1860. V. 62

DE BRY, THEODOR
Discovering the New World. New York: 1976. V. 63; 66

DE CALONNE, CHARLES ALEXANDER
A Catalogue of All that Nobel and Superlatively Capital Assemblage of Valuable Pictures, Drawings, Miniatures and Prints, the Property of.... London: 1795. V. 63; 65

DE CAMP, L. SPRAGUE
Demons and Dinosaurs. Sauk City: 1970. V. 64
The Great Monkey Trial. New York: 1968. V. 63
Rogue Queen. 1951. V. 66
Rogue Queen. New York: 1951. V. 64
The Tritonian Ring and Other Pusadian Tales. New York: 1953. V. 66
The Wheels of If. 1948. V. 62; 64; 66

DE CARO, VINCENZIO
Saggi Sulla Podagra. Naples: 1790. V. 65

DECAY of Trade. A Treatise Against the Abating of Interest. Or Reasons on Shewing the Inconveniencies Which Will Insue, by the Bringing Downe of Interest Money to Six or Five in the Hundred and Raising the Price of Land in this Kingdome. London: 1641. V. 65

DE CHAIR, SOMERSET
Divided Europe. London: 1931. V. 65
The First Crusade. Waltham St. Lawrence: 1945. V. 67
The Golden Carpet. London: 1943. V. 65
The Golden Carpet. Waltham St. Lawrence: 1943. V. 64
The Silver Crescent. London: 1943. V. 65
The Silver Crescent. Waltham St. Lawrence: 1943. V. 64

DE CHIMAY, JACQUELINE
The Life and Times of Madame Veuve Clicquot-Ponsardin. Reims: 1961. V. 66

DECKER, MATTHEW
An Essay on the Causes of the Decline of the Foreign Trade, Consequently of the Value of the Lands of Britain. London: 1750. V. 65
An Essay on the Causes of the Decline of the Foreign Trade, Consequently of the Value of the Lands of Britain. Edinburgh: 1756. V. 63; 66
Serious Considerations on the Several High Duties which the Nation in General (as well as it's (sic) Trade in Particular) Labours Under.... London: 1744. V. 64

DECKER, PETER
A Descriptive Checklist Describing Almost 7500 Items of Western Americana of the Important Library Formed by George F. Soliday. 1997. V. 65
The Diaries of Peter Decker - Overland to California in 1849 and Life in the Mines 1850-1851. Georgetown: 1966. V. 62; 65

DECLE, LIONEL
Three Years in Savage Africa. London: 1900. V. 64

THE DECORATOR'S Assistant. London: 1880. V. 66

DE CORDOBA, FRANCISCO H.
The Discovery of the Yucatan. Berkeley: 1942. V. 64

DE CORDOVA, RAFAEL J.
The Prince's Visit: a Humorous Description of the Tour of His Royal Highness, the Prince of Wales. New York: 1861. V. 67

DE COSSON, EMILIUS ALBERT
The Cradle of the Blue Nile, a Visit to the Court of King John of Ethiopia. London: 1877. V. 64

DECOU, GEORGE
Burlington: a Provincial Capital. Historical Sketches of Burlington, New Jersey and Neighbourhood. Philadelphia: 1945. V. 66

DECOURCEY, R.
Man Displayed in Four Parts...Anatomical and Physiological Structure.... Hamilton: 1857. V. 66; 67

DE COURTOT, CECILE, BARONESS
Memoirs of the Baroness Cecile de Courtot, Lady-in Waiting to the Princess de Lamballe, Princess of Savoy-Carignan. London: 1900. V. 67

DE CRAUZAT, E.
La Reliure Francaise de Mill Neuf Cent a Mil Neuf Cent Vingt-Cinq. Paris: 1932. V. 62

DECREMPS, HENRI
La Magie Blanche Devoilee ou Explication des Tours Supernnants, Qui sont Depuis eu l'Admiration de la Capitale et de la Province.... Paris: 1784. V. 66

DECREMPS, M.
Le Parisien a Londres, ou Avis aux Francais Qui Vont en Angleterre, Contenant la Parallele des Deux Plus Grandes Villes de l'Europe. Paris: 1789. V. 66

DEDICATION of the Palomar Observatory and the Hale Telescope: June 3, 1948, California Institute of Technology. San Francisco. V. 67

DEDMON, EMMETT
Fabulous Chicago. New York: 1981. V. 63

DEE, JOHN
John Dee's Library Catalogue. London: 1990. V. 63

DEE, JONATHAN
The Lover of History. New York: 1990. V. 67

DEEL, EERSTE
Reis Langs Den Rhijn. (Journey Along the Rhine). Haarlem: 1793. V. 66

DEEPING, WARWICK
Love Among the Ruins. London: 1904. V. 64

DEERING, CHARLES
Nottinghamia Vetus et Nova. Nottingham: 1751. V. 65

DEERING, JOHN R.
Lee and His Cause or Why and How of the War Between the States. New York and Washington: 1907. V. 62; 63

DEFENBACK, BRYON
Red Heroines of the Northwest. Caldwell: 1935. V. 63

DEFENDERS and Offenders. New York: 1885. V. 62; 65
DEFENDERS and Offenders. New York: 1888. V. 63

DEFOE, DANIEL
An Abstract of the Remarkable Passages in the Life of a Private Gentleman. Boston: 1744. V. 62
The Dissenters in England Vindicated from Some Reflections in a Late Pamphlet. N.P: 1707. V. 63
The Dumb Philosopher; or Great Britain's Wonder. London: 1719. V. 65
An Essay on the History and Reality of Apparitions. London: 1727. V. 64
The Evident Approach of War; and Something of the Necessity Of It, in Order to Establish Peace, and Preserve Trade. London: 1727. V. 64
The Evident Approach of War; and Something of the Necessity Of It, In Order to Establish Peace and Preserve Trade. London: 1999. V. 64
The Experiment; or the Shortest Way With the Dissenters Exemplified. London: 1705. V. 64
The History of the Union Between England and Scotland, with a Collection of Original Papers Relating Thereto.... London: 1786-1787. V. 64
A Hymn to the Pillory. London: 1703. V. 64
A Journal of the Plague Year. London: 1722. V. 65
A Journal of the Plague Year. Bloomfield: 1968. V. 63
A Journal of the Plague Year. New York: 1968. V. 63
Legion's New Paper: Being a Second Memorial to the Gentleman of the Late House of Commons. London: 1702. V. 65
The Life and Adventures of Robinson Crusoe. London: 1804. V. 64
The Life and Most Surprising Adventures of Robinson Crusoe, of York, Mariner. Edinburgh: 1769. V. 66
The Life and Most Surprising Adventures of Robinson Crusoe, of York, Mariner. Dublin: 1780. V. 67
The Life and Most Surprising Adventures of Robinson Crusoe, of York, Mariner. Edinburgh: 1781. V. 66
The Life and Strange Surprising Adventures of Robinson Crusoe. London: 1891. V. 65
The Life and Strange Surprising Adventures of Robinson, of York, Mariner. Ipswich: 1828. V. 66
The Life and Surprising Adventures of Robinson Crusoe. Halifax: 1810. V. 64
The Life and Surprising Adventures of Robinson Crusoe. London: 1831. V. 65
The Life and Surprising Adventures of Robinson Crusoe. London: 1869. V. 66
Minutes of the Negotiations of Monsr. Mesnager at the Court of England, Towards the Close of the Last Reign. London: 1717. V. 62; 63; 67
A New Voyage Round the World, by a Course Never Sailed Before. London: 1725. V. 66
Novels and Selected Writings. Oxford: 1927. V. 62
The Novels and Miscellaneous Works. Oxford: 1840-1841. V. 67
The Novels and Select Writings of Daniel Defoe. 1928. V. 66
The Re-Representation; or, a Modest Search After the Great Plunderers of the Nation.... London: 1711. V. 65
Remarks on the Speech of James Late Earl of Derwentwater, beheaded on Tower-Hill for High Treason, February 24, 1711-1712. London: 1716. V. 62
Robinson Crusoe. London: 1920. V. 63
Robinson Crusoe. Garden City: 1945. V. 65
Some Reasons Offered by the Late Ministry in Defence of Their Administration. London: 1715. V. 63
The Storm; or a Collection of the Most Remarkable Casualties and Disasters Which Happened in the Late, Dredful Tempest. London: 1704. V. 62
A System of Magic; or, a History of the Black Art. London: 1728. V. 67
A Tour thro' the Whole Island of Great Britain. London: 1927. V. 65
A Tour through the Island of Great Britain. London: 1778. V. 67
A Tour through the Whole Island of Great Britain. London: 1769. V. 62; 66
Vita e Avventura di Robinson Crusoe. Milan: 1866. V. 62
Der Vollstandige Robinson Crusoe. Constanz: 1829. V. 66
Die Wunderbare Lebensbeschribung, und Erstaunliche Begenbenheiten des Beruhmten Helden Robinson Crusoe. (Robinson Crusoe). Philadelphia: 1789. V. 64

DE FONTAINE, FELIX GREGORY
Marginalia, or Gleanings from an Army Note-Book. Columbia: 1864. V. 62; 63; 65

DE FONTPERTUIS, FROUT
Les Etats-Unis, De l'Amerique Septentrionale. Paris: 1872. V. 64

DE FOREST, EFFINGHAM
Moore and Allied Families. The Ancestor of William Henry Moore. New York: 1938. V. 63; 66

DE FOREST, JOHN WILLIAM
History of the Indians of Connecticut from the Earliest Known Period to 1850. Hartford: 1851. V. 64
History of the Indians of Connecticut from the Earliest Known Period to 1850. Hartford: 1852. V. 63
Honest John Vane. New Haven: 1875. V. 64

DE FOREST, LEE
Father of the Radio: the Autobiography of Lee de Forest. Chicago: 1950. V. 63

DE GAERTRINGEN, FRIDERICUS HILLER
Inscriptiones Atticae Euclidis Anno Anteriores.... Chicago: 1974. V. 65
Inscriptiones Atticae Euclidis Anno Anteriores.... Chicago: 1974-1979. V. 65

DEGELE, W. A.
Ansichten der Herrschaftlichen Schlosser und Garten von Hannover... Nach Zeichnungen und Kupfertischen von J. J. Muller und J. van Sasse.... Hannover: 1861. V. 64

DEGENER, OTTO
Flora Hawaiiensis or New Illustrated Flora of the Hawaiian Islands. 1946-1975. V. 64
Naturalist's South Pacific Expedition: Fiji. Honolulu: 1949. V. 64

DEGGE, SIMON
The Parsons Counsellor, with the Law of Tithes or Tithing. London: 1681. V. 65

DE GIVRY, GRILLOT
Witchcraft, Magic and Alchemy. London: 1931. V. 62

DE GOLYER, E.
Across Aboriginal America. The Journey of Three Englishmen Across Texas in 1568. El Paso: 1947. V. 62; 63; 66
The Development of the Art of Prospecting. Princeton: 1940. V. 62

DE GOUEY, LOUIS P.
Derrydale Book of Fish and Game. Lyon: 1937. V. 66

DE GRAZIA, TED
Padre Kino. Los Angeles: 1962. V. 63; 66

DE GRIJALVA, JUAN
The Discovery of New Spain in 1518. Berkeley: 1942. V. 64

DE GRUCHY, AUGUSTA
Under the Hawthorn and Other Verse. London: 1893. V. 64

DE GRUYTER, JULIUS A.
The Kanawha Spectators: Volume One. Charleston: 1953. V. 65; 66

DE HAMEL, CHRISTOPHER
A History of Illuminated Manuscripts. Boston: 1986. V. 64; 66

DE HAVILLAND, ROBERT J. LANGSTAFF
Enslaved. London: 1884. V. 67

DE HORTHY, EUGENE
The Sport of a Lifetime. London: 1939. V. 62; 67

DEIBLER, DAN GROVE
Historic Bridges in Virginia. Charlottesville: 1975. V. 66

DEIDER, ANTONIO
Dissertatio Medica De Morbis Venereis, Cui Adjungitur Dissertatio Medcio Chirurgica De Tumoribus. London: 1724. V. 66; 67

DEIDIER, L'ABBE
La Science des Geometres, ou la Theorie et la Pratique de la Geometrie.... Paris: 1739. V. 65

DEIGHTON, LEN
Action Cook Book. London: 1963. V. 66
Airshipwreck. London: 1978. V. 65
Basic French Cooking. London: 1979. V. 65
Billion-Dollar Brain. London: 1966. V. 65; 66
Charity. Franklin Center: 1996. V. 63
Close-Up. London: 1972. V. 65
Declarations of War. London: 1971. V. 65
Drinks-man-ship. Town's Album of Fine Wines and High Spirits. London: 1964. V. 62; 65
An Expensive Place to Die. London: 1967. V. 65; 66
Funeral in Berlin. London: 1964. V. 62; 63; 65; 66
Hope. Blakeney, Gloucestershire: 1995. V. 63
Hope. Franklin Center: 1996. V. 66
Horse Under Water. London: 1963. V. 62; 63; 64; 65; 66
The Ipcress File. London: 1962. V. 62; 64; 65; 66
The Ipcress File. 1963. V. 64; 66
Len Deighton's London Dossier. London: 1967. V. 62; 63; 65; 66
Only When I Larf. London: 1968. V. 62; 65
The Orient Flight L.Z. 127-Graf Zeppelin: a Philatelic Handbook. Westminster: 1980. V. 66
Pests. 1994. V. 65
Pests. London: 1994. V. 62
SS-GB: Nazi Occupied Britain 1941. London: 1978. V. 65
Yesterday's Spy. London: 1975. V. 65; 67

DEIHL, EDNA GROFF
The Little Kitten That Would Not Wash Its Face. New York: 1922. V. 66
The Little Pig That Would Not Get Up. New York: 1925. V. 64
The Teddy Bear that Prowled at Night. New York: 1924. V. 65

DEILER, J. HANNO
Zur Geschichte der Deutsch en Kirchengemeinden im Staate Louisiana. New Orleans: 1894. V. 67

DE JARNETTE, DANIEL C.
The Monroe Doctrine Speech of Hon. D. C. De Jarnette, of Virginia in the Confederate House of Representatives Jan. 30th, 1865.... Richmond?: 1865. V. 62

DEJERINE, JOSEPH JULES
Cahier Feuilles D'Autopsies Pour l'Etude des Lesions du Nevre. Paris: 1911. V. 64
Les Manifestations Fonctionelles des Psychonervroses; Leur Traitement. Paris: 1911. V. 65

DE JONG, MEINDERT
Along Came A Dog. New York: 1958. V. 63
The Little Cow and the Turtle. London: 1961. V. 65

DE JONGH, BERTHA
Rosa Noel. London: 1873. V. 65

DE KAY, J. E.
Sketches of Turkey in 1831 and 1832. New York: 1833. V. 63
Zoology of New York, or the New York Fauna. Part III. Reptiles and Ambphibia, Part IV. Fishes. Albany: 1842. V. 63; 65; 66
Zoology of New York: Part 2 Birds. Albany: 1843. V. 64
Zoology of New York: Part 2 Birds. Albany: 1844. V. 67
Zoology of New York, or the New York Fauna. Part V. Mollusca. Part VI. Crustacea. Albany: 1843-1844. V. 65

DEKKER, THOMAS
Foure Birds of Noah's Arke. Oxford: 1925. V. 63
The Wonderful Year 1603. London: 1989. V. 66

DE KNIGHT, FREDA
Date with a Dish. New York: 1948. V. 64; 67

DE KOVEN, ANNA FARWELL
By the Waters of Babylon. Chicago: 1901. V. 63

DE KROYFT, S. H.
A Place in Thy Memory. New York: 1850. V. 62

DE LA BECHE, H. T.
A Geological Manual. London: 1833. V. 65
The Geological Observer. 1853. V. 65
Report on the Geology of Cornwall, Devon and West Somerset. London: 1839-1903. V. 64; 65

DE LA BRETONNE, RESTIF
Sara. London: 1927. V. 65

DE LA CHAUSSE, MICHAEL ANGELUS CAUSEUS
Romanum Museum Sive Thesaurus Eruditae Antiquitatis in Quo Proponuntur.... Rome: 1746. V. 62

DELACOUR, JEAN
Birds of the Philippines. 1946. V. 67
Curassows and Related Birds. New York: 1973. V. 62; 63; 64
Les Oiseaux de l'Indochine Francaise. Paris: 1931. V. 67
The Pheasants of the World. London: 1951. V. 62; 64; 66
The Pheasants of the World. 1965. V. 63; 66
Pheasants of the World. London: 1965. V. 64
The Pheasants of the World. Surrey: 1977. V. 62
Pheasants of the World. London: 1984. V. 62
Waterfowl of the World. 1954-1956. V. 62; 67
The Waterfowl of the World. 1954-1964. V. 66
The Waterfowl of the World. London: 1954-1964. V. 62; 63; 64; 67
The Waterfowl of the World. 1954-1966. V. 66
The Waterfowl of the World. 1956. V. 63; 66
The Waterfowl of the World. 1956. V. 62
The Waterfowl of the World. London: 1964. V. 62
The Waterfowl of the World. 1966. V. 63
The Waterfowl of the World. London: 1966. V. 62
The Waterfowl of the World. London and New York: 1973. V. 65

DE LA CROIX, IRENEE A.
Rules and Regulations for the Field Exercise and Maneuvers of Infantry, Compiled and Adapted to the Organization of the Army of the United States. New York: 1820. V. 67

DE LA CROIX, ROBERT
Horizon - Cahiers de Litterature. Nantes: 1947. V. 65

DELAFAYE-BREHIER, JULIE
Les Enfans de la Providence ou Aventures de Trois Jeunes Orphelins. Paris: 1819. V. 63
Les Nouvelles de l'Enfance. Paris: 1815. V. 65

DELAGARDETTE, CLAUDE MATHIEU
Les Ruines de Paestum ou Posidonia Ancienne ville de la Grande Grece.... Paris: 1798-1799. V. 64

DE LAGUNA, F.
Chugach Pre-History. The Archaeology of Prince William Sound, Alaska. 1956. V. 62

DE LAHONTAN, BARON
New Voyages to North America. Chicago: 1905. V. 66

DELAISTRE, J. R.
Encyclopedie de l'Ingenieur, ou Dictionnaire des Ponts et Chaussees. Paris: 1812. V. 65

DE LALANDE, JOSEPH
The Art of Papermaking. Mountcashel: 1976. V. 64

DE LA MARE, WALTER
Behold This Dreamer of Reverie, Night Sleep, Dream, Love-Dreams, Nightmare, Death, the Unconscious, the Imagination, Divination, the Artist and Kindred Subjects. London: 1939. V. 63
The Connoisseur and Other Stories. London: 1926. V. 64
Crossings - a Fairy Play. London: 1923. V. 64
Desert Islands and Robinson Crusoe. London: 1930. V. 63
Down-Adown-Derry A Book of Fairy Poems. London: 1922. V. 66
Flora. London: 1919. V. 65

DE LA MARE, WALTER continued
Henry Brocken: His Travels and Adventures in the Rich, Strange, Scarce-Imaginable Regions of Romance. London: 1904. V. 64
Memoirs of a Midget. London: 1921. V. 63
Mr. Bumps and His Monkey. Chicago: 1942. V. 66
On the Edge - Short Stories. London: 1930. V. 65
Peacock Pie. A Book of Rhymes. London: 1946. V. 62
Poems. London: 1937. V. 62
The Printing of Poetry. A Paper Read Before the Double Crow Club. Cambridge: 1931. V. 65
The Riddle and Other Stories. London: 1923. V. 66
Self to Self. London: 1928. V. 65; 67
Songs of Childhood. London: 1902. V. 63
Stories from the Bible. London: 1961. V. 63
Stuff and Nonsense and So On. London: 1927. V. 64
This Year: Next Year. London: 1937. V. 64; 66
To Lucy. London: 1931. V. 64
The Traveller. London: 1946. V. 63
The Veil and Other Poems. London: 1921. V. 64

DELAMAYNE, THOMAS HALLIE
The Senators; or, a Candid Examination into the Merits of the Principal Performers of St. Stephen's Chapel. London: 1772. V. 65

DELAMERE, HENRY, BARON
Tryal of Henry Baron Delamere for High Treason...the 14th Day of Jan. 1685. London: 1686. V. 62

DE LA MOTRAYE, AUBRY
Travels through Europe, Asia and Into Part of Africa; With Proper Cutts and Maps. London: 1723-1732. V. 63

DE LA MOTTE, FREEMAN GAGE
A Primer of the Art of Illumination for the Use of Beginners.... London: 1874. V. 64; 65

DELAMOTTE, PHILIP H.
The Art of Sketching from Nature. London: 1871. V. 66

DELAND, CHARLES E.
The Sioux Wars: South Dakota Historical Collections. Volume XV. Pierre: 1930. V. 67
The Sioux Wars: South Dakota Historical Collections. Volumes XV & XVII. 1930-1934. V. 65

DELAND, MARGARET
The Awakening of Helen Ritchie. New York: 1906. V. 64

DELANO, ALONZO
Across the Plains and Among the Diggings. New York: 1936. V. 66
Across the Plains and Among the Diggings. New York: 1937. V. 67
Across the Plains and Among the Diggings. El Paso: 1947. V. 63
Alonzo Delano's California Correspondence. Sacramento: 1952. V. 62; 63
Pen-Knife Sketches or Chips of the Old Block. San Francisco: 1934. V. 64; 67
A Sojourn With Royalty and Other Sketches by Old Block. San Francisco: 1936. V. 64; 67

DELANO, AMASA
A Narrative of Voyages and Travels, in the Northern and Southern Hemispheres.... Boston: 1817. V. 64

DELANY, JOHN
A Report of Trials Before the Lord Chief Justice and Sir Wm. C. Smith, Bart, at the Special Commission, at Maryborough, Commencing on the 23rd May, and Ending on the 6th June. Dublin: 1832. V. 63

DELANY, PATRICK
Revelation Examined with Candour. London: 1745-1763. V. 67
The Tribune. 1729. V. 67

DELANY, SAMUEL R.
The Jewels of Aptor. 1976. V. 64
The Motion of Light in Water. Sex and Science Fiction Writing in the East Village 1957-1965. New York: 1988. V. 65
Nova. 1968. V. 66
Nova. New York: 1968. V. 64

DE LA PLACE, PIERRE ANTOINE
Tom Jones.... A Londres: 1767. V. 66

DE LA PORTE, M.
La Science des Negocians et Teneurs de Livres. Paris: 1748. V. 66

DE LA RAMEE, MARIE LOUISE
In Maremma: a Story. London: 1882. V. 65
Two Offenders. London: 1894. V. 65
Wanda. London: 1883. V. 65

DE LA REE, GERRY
Beauty and the Beasts. 1978. V. 65

DE LA RENAUDIERE, M.
Historia de Mejico, Tejas y Tuatemala...y la del Peru. Paris: 1846. V. 67

DE LA ROCHE, MAZO
The Song of Lambert. London: 1955. V. 67

DE LA SALE, ANTOINE
Les Quinze Joyes de Mariage. Haye: 1726. V. 65

DELASIAUVE, LOUIS JEAN FRANCOIS
D'une Forme mal Decrite de Delire Consecutif a l'Epilepsie. Paris: 1852. V. 65

DE LA SOUCHERE, DOR
Picasso In Antibes. New York: 1960. V. 62; 63; 64; 66

DELASSAUX, VICTOR
Street Architecture, a Series of Shop Fronts and Facades. London: 1855. V. 66

DE LA TOREE, LILLIAN
The Detections of Dr. Sam. Johnson. Garden City: 1960. V. 66; 67

DE LA TORRE, LILLIAN
Dr. Sam Johnson, Detector. New York: 1946. V. 63

DELAUNAY, CHARLES
Django Reinhardt. London: 1961. V. 63
Hot Discography. Paris: 1936. V. 63
Hot Discography. New York: 1940. V. 66

DELAUNAY, H.
Oeuvre de Jehan Foucquet. Paris: 1866-1867. V. 62

DELAUNE, THOMAS
Angliae Metropolis; or the Present State of London; with Memorials Comprehending a Full and Succinct Account of the Ancient and Modern State Thereof.... London: 1690. V. 66
De Laune's Plea for the Non-Conformists: Shewing the True State of Their Case.... London: 1706. V. 66

DELAVAN, EDWARD C.
Permanent Temperance Documents from 1831 to 1838. Boston: 1838. V. 64
A Report on the Trial of the Cause of John Taylor vs. Edward C. Delavan, Prosecuted for an Alledged Libel, Tried at the Albany Circuit, April 1840. Albany: 1840. V. 63

DE LA VOYE, MARIN J. GEORGE
The Pictorial Grammar for the Use of Children. London: 1848. V. 62

DELAWARE AND RARITAN CANAL CO.
Address of the Directors of the Camden and Amboy Rail Road and Delaware and Raritan Canal Companies, to the People of New Jersey. Trenton: 1846. V. 63
An Investigation into the Affairs of the Delaware & Raritan Canal and Camden & Amboy Rail Road Companies, in Reference to Certain Charges by.... Newark: 1849. V. 63
Report of Commissioners Appointed to Investigate Charges Made Against the Directors of the Delaware and Raritan Canal and Camden and Amboy Railroad and Transportation Companies. Trenton: 1850. V. 63; 66
Report of the Committee Appointed to Offer to the State of New Jersey the Delaware and Raritan Canal and Feeder and the Camden and Amboy Rail Road, with their Appendages. Princeton: 1836. V. 63

DELAWARE RIVER BAPTIST ASSOCIATION
Minutes of the Delaware River Baptist Association...1839 (1844, 1845, 1847). 1839-1847. V. 63

DELBANCO, NICHOLAS
The Writers' Trade and Other Stories. New York: 1990. V. 67

DELBREL, E.
Traite det Modeles D'Escaliers D'Art. Paris: 1890. V. 64

DE LEON, THOMAS C.
Belles Beaux and Brains of the 60's. New York: 1909. V. 62; 63; 65
South Songs: from the Lays of Later Days. New York: 1866. V. 63; 65

DELETANVILLE, THOMAS
A New French Dictionary in Two Parts. London: 1771. V. 64
A New French Dictionary in Two Parts. London: 1794. V. 64

DELEUZE, GILLES
David Hume. Sa Vie, Son Oeuvre. Avec un Expose de sa Philosophie. Paris: 1952. V. 67

DELEUZE, J. P. F.
Histoire et Description du Museum Royal d'Histoire Naturelle. Paris: 1823. V. 67

THE DELIGHTFUL Colored Picture Book. Philadelphia: 1855. V. 62

DE LILLE, JACQUES M.
Flore de l'Egypte. Paris: 1812-1826. V. 62
The Garden, a Poem. 1805. V. 63
Les Jardins...Poeme. Paris: 1791. V. 64

DELILLE, JACQUES M.
The Rural Philosopher: or French Georgics. Newbern: 1804. V. 62; 63; 66; 67

DELILLO, DON
Amazons: an Intimate Memoir by the First Woman Ever to Play in the National Hockey League. New York: 1980. V. 64; 67
Americana. Boston: 1971. V. 62; 64; 67
The Body Artist. New York: 2001. V. 67
The Day Room. New York: 1987. V. 62; 66; 67
End Zone. Boston: 1972. V. 62; 64; 65; 66
Great Jones Street. Boston: 1973. V. 62; 64; 65; 66; 67
Libra. New York: 1988. V. 62; 66; 67
Mao II. New York: 1991. V. 66; 67
The Names. New York: 1982. V. 63; 66; 67
Players. New York: 1977. V. 62; 65; 67
Ratner's Star. New York: 1976. V. 62; 65; 66
Running Dog. New York: 1978. V. 65; 66; 67
Underworld. New York: 1997. V. 62; 63; 64; 65; 66; 67
Valparaiso. New York: 1999. V. 67
White Noise. New York: 1985. V. 63; 67

DE L'ISLE-ADAMS, VILLIERS
Olympe and Henriette. Sherman Oaks: 1992. V. 64

DELIUS, CHRISTOPH TRAUGOTT
Anleitung zu der Bergbaukunst Nach Ihrer Theorie und Ausubung, Nebst Einer Abhandlung von den Grundsatzen der Berg-Kammeralwissenschft, fur die Kaiserl.... Vienna: 1773. V. 62

DELKE, JAMES ALMERIUS
History of the North Carolina Chowan Baptist Association, 1806-1881. Raleigh: 1882. V. 67

DELL, FLOYD
Looking at Life. New York: 1924. V. 63

DELL, J. H.
Nature Pictures. London: 1878. V. 63

DELLENBAUGH, FREDERICK S.
Fremont and '49. New York: 1914. V. 63
George Armstrong Custer. New York: 1917. V. 65
The North Americans of Yesterday. New York and London: 1901. V. 63; 64
The North Americans of Yesterday. New York: 1902. V. 65
The Romance of the Colorado River. New York: 1902. V. 62; 65

DEL MAR, ALEXANDER
History of the Montearly Systems. London: 1895. V. 65

DE LOLME, JEAN LOUIS
The Constitution of England. London: 1775. V. 62; 63
The Constitution of England. Dublin: 1770. V. 62
The Constitution of England. London: 1788. V. 65

DELONEY, THOMAS
The History of Thomas Reading; or the Six Worthy Yeomen of the West. London: 1827. V. 65

DE LONG, LIEUT. COMMANDER GEORGE
Voyage of the Jeannette. New York: 1886. V. 62; 64

DELORME, PHILIBERT
Le Premier Tome de l'Architecture. Paris: 1567. V. 64

DE LOUTHERBOURG, P. J.
The Romantic and Picturesque Scenery of England and Wales.... 1979. V. 66

DELPHINUS, PETRUS
Petri Delphini Veneti Prioris Sacre Eremi(tae) & Generalis Totius Ordinis Camaldulensis Episolatrum Volumen. Venice: 1524. V. 65

DEL REY, LESTER
And Some Were Human. 1948. V. 62; 64; 66
And Some Were Human. Philadelphia: 1948. V. 63
Mission to the Moor. Philadelphia: 1956. V. 66

DE LUC, JEAN ANDRE
Idees sur le Meterorologie. London and Paris: 1787. V. 65
Lettres Physiques et Morales sur les Montagnes et sur l'Hitoire de la Terre et de l'Homme: Adresses a la Reine de la Grande Bretange. The Hague: 1778. V. 65

DEL VECCHIO, JOHN
The 13th Valley. Toronto/New York: 1982. V. 63

DE MADARIAGA, SALVADOR
Don Quixote, an Introductory Essay in Psychology. Newtown: 1934. V. 62; 64

DE MAGELLAN, J. H.
A Description of a Glass-Apparatus for Making in a Few Minutes and at Very Small Expence, the Best Mineral Waters of Pyrmont, Spa, Seltzer, Seydschutz, Aix-la-Chapelle &c. Together with the Description of Two New Eudiometers. London: 1783. V. 65

DEMAISON, G.
Petroleum Geochemistry and Basin Evaluation. Tulsa: 1984. V. 67

DE MAISSE, ANDRE HURAULT, SIEUR
A Journal of All that Was Accomplished by Monsieur de Maisse, Ambassador in England from King Henri IV to Queen Elizabeth Anno Domini 1597. London: 1931. V. 63

DE MAISTRE, JOSEPH
Letters on the Spanish Inquisition: a Rare Work.... Boston;: 1843. V. 66

DE MALAN, CHAVIN
Histoire de Saint Francois d'Assise (1182-1226). Paris: 1890. V. 64

DE MAN, PAUL
Blindness and Insight. New York: 1971. V. 67

DEMAND, CARLO
Kuhne Manner Tolle Wagen, Die Gordon Bennett-Rennen 1900-1905. Stuttgart: 1987. V. 66

THE DEMAREST Family. A Record of the des Marets Family and of the Descendants of David des Marets.... Hackensack: 1964-1971. V. 63; 66

DEMAREST, MARY A.
The Demarest Family: David des Marets of the French Patent on Hackeck and His Descendants. New Brunswick: 1938. V. 63; 66

DEMARET, JIMMY
My Partner Ben Hogan. New York: 1954. V. 66

DE MARINIS, T.
La Legatura Aristica in Italia Nei Secoli XV e XVI.I: Napoli, Roma, Urbino, Firenze; II: Bologna, Cesena, Ferrara, Venezia. III: Verona, Milano e Pavia, Genova, Bergamo, Perugia. Florence: 1960. V. 62

DEMARQUAY, JEAN NICOLAS
De la Regeneration des Organes des Tissus. Paris: 1874. V. 65

DEMENTIEV, G. P.
Birds of the Soviet Union. Jerusalem: 1966-1970. V. 62
Birds of the Soviet Union. Springfield: 1966-1970. V. 62

DE MERS, JOE
Alice in Letterland. Hollywood: 1946. V. 66

DEMESSE, HENRI
Une Journee d'Enfant. Paris: 1889. V. 67

DEMEUNIER, J. N.
Encyclopedie Methodique. Paris: 1784-1788. V. 66

DEMIDOFF, PRINCE E.
After Wild Sheep in the Altai and Mongolia. 1900. V. 62; 63; 64
After Wild Sheep in the Altai and Mongolia. 1992. V. 62; 63; 64; 66
Hunting Trips in the Caucasus. 1898. V. 62; 63; 64
A Shooting Trip to Kamchatka.... London: 1904. V. 64

DE MILLE, NELSON
By the Rivers of Babylon. New York: 1978. V. 66; 67
Cathedral. New York: 1981. V. 65
The General's Daughter. Franklin Center: 1992. V. 63

DEMING, THERESA
Edwin Willard Deming. New York: 1925. V. 65

DEMING, WILLIAM CHAPMAN
Collected Writing and Addresses of William Chapman Deming. Glendale: 1946-1947. V. 67

DEMIROVIC, HAMDIJA
Twenty-Five Poems. Richmond: 1980. V. 63

DEMMIN, AUGUSTE
An Illustrated History of Arms and Armour from the Earliest Period to the Present. London: 1877. V. 62

THE DEMOCRATIC Book 1936. N.P: 1936. V. 63

DE MOIVRE, ABRAHAM
Annuities Upon Lives; or, the Valuation of Annuities Upon Any Number of Lives.... London: 1725. V. 64

DE MONVEL, MAURICE LOUIS BOUTET
La Civilite - Puerile et Honnete. Paris. V. 66; 67

DE MORGAN, AUGUSTUS
Arithmetical Books from the Invention of Printing to the Present Time Being Brief Notices of a Large Number of Works Drawn Up from Acutal Inspection. London: 1847. V. 65
A Budget of Paradoxes.... London: 1872. V. 63
The Connexion of Number and Magnitude; an Attempt to Explain the Fifth Book of Euclid. London: 1836. V. 62
An Essay on Probabilities and on their Application to Life Contingencies and Insurance Offices. London: 1838. V. 62; 63; 64; 65; 66
Essays on Practical Education.... London: 1836. V. 63; 66
Formal Logic or the Calculus of Interference, Necessary and Probable. London: 1847. V. 65
A Treatise on Problems of Maxima and Minima, Solved by Algebra. London: 1859. V. 65

DE MORGAN, MARY
On a Pincushion and Other Fairy Tales. 1900. V. 64
The Windfairies and Other Tales. London: 1900. V. 64

DE MORGAN, SOPHIA ELIZABETH
Threescore Years and Ten.... London: 1895. V. 67

DEMORO, HARRE
The Evergreen Fleet...A Pictorial History of Washington State Ferries. San Marino;: 1971. V. 66

DEMOSTHENES
Cinque Orationi di Demosthene, et Una di Eschine.... In Venetia: 1557. V. 63
Demosthenis Et Aeschinis Principum Graeciae Oratorum Opera.... Francofurti: 1604. V. 65
Habes Lector Demosthensis Graecorum Oratorum Omnium Facile Principis Orationes Duas & Sexaginta.... Basiliae: 1532. V. 63
Opera Cum...notis Illustrata, per Hieronymum Wolfium.... Genevae: 1607. V. 66
Selectae Orationes.... Etoniae: 1755. V. 66

DE MOUSTIER, CHARLES ALBERT
Lettres a Emile sur la Mythologie. Paris: 1797-1798. V. 64

DEMOUSTIER, CHARLES ALBERT
Lettres a Emile sur la Mythologie. Paris: 1804. V. 63

DEMPSEY, G. DRYSDALE
The Practical Railway Engineer; a Concise Description of the Engineering and Mechanical Operations and Structures Which are Combined in the Formation of Railways for Public Traffic.... London: 1855. V. 65

DEMPSEY, HUGH A.
History in Their Blood: the Indian Portraits of Nicholas de Grandmaison. New York: 1982. V. 63

DEMPSEY, JACK
Dempsey. By the Man Himself.... New York: 1960. V. 63

DEMPSTER, CHARLOTTE LOUISE
Blue Rose or Helen Malimofska's Marriage. London: 1877. V. 65
The Hotel du Petit St. Jean. London: 1869. V. 65

DE NADAILLAC, MARQUIS
Pre-Historic America. New York: 1884. V. 63

DE NAHLIK, A. J.
Wild Deer. London: 1959. V. 62; 67

DENBY, CHARLES
China and Her People: Being the Observations, Reminiscences and Conclusions of an American Diplomat. Boston: 1906. V. 63; 65

DENBY, EDWIN
Aerial. A Collection of Poetry. New York: 1981. V. 64
Collected Poems. New York: 1975. V. 63
Mediterranean Cities. Sonnets. New York: 1956. V. 62
Snoring in New York. New York: 1974. V. 64

DENCH, EDWARD BRADFORD
Diseases of the Ear. New York: 1896. V. 67

DENDY, WALTER COOPER
The Philosophy of Mystery. London: 1841. V. 65

DENE, NOEL
The Aftermath. London: 1885. V. 67

DENHAM, MAJOR
Narrative of Travels and Discoveries in Northern and Central Africa in the Years 1822, 1823 and 1824. London: 1828. V. 64

DENHAM, MICHAEL AISLABIE
The Denham Tracts. London: 1892-1895. V. 64

DENHARDT, ROBERT MOORMAN
The Horse of the Americas. Norman: 1947. V. 63; 67

DENHART, JEFFREY
Just Bones. Aurora: 1996. V. 65

THE DENHOLM Collection of Autograph Letters and Ancient and Curious Documents. Edinburgh: 1903. V. 62

DENHOLM, JAMES
A Tour to the Principal Scotch and English Lakes. Glasgow: 1804. V. 65

DENIS, ALBERTA J.
Spanish Alta California. New York: 1927. V. 64

DENIS, CHARLES
Select Fables. London: 1754. V. 65

DENISON, GEORGE T.
A History of Cavalry from the Earliest Times. London: 1913. V. 66

DENISON, MERRILL
Canada's First Bank. A History of the Bank of Montreal. Toronto, Montreal: 1966. V. 65

DENISON, WILLIAM
An Attempt to Approximate to the Antiquity of Man by Induction. Madras: 1865. V. 62

DENMAN, D. R.
Commons and Village Greens. London: 1967. V. 62

DENMAN, LESLIE VAN NESS
The Corn Maidens' Dance and Its Greek Analogies. Pai Ya Tu Ma, God of All Dance and His Customs of the Flute, Zuni Pueblo 1932. San Francisco: 1955. V. 63; 66
The Flute Ceremonial - Hotevila and Snake Antelope Ceremonial of the Hopi Mesas. San Francisco: 1956. V. 65
The Peyote Ritual - Visions and Descriptions of Monroe Tsa Take. San Francisco: 1957. V. 65
Sha' Lak'0 Mana - Ritual of Creation (Hopi). N.P: 1953. V. 67
Sha-Lak'o Mana - Ritual of Creation (Hopi). San Francisco: 1957. V. 67

DENMAN, THOMAS
An Introduction to the Practice of Midwifery.... London: 1832. V. 65

DENNE, KENNER, PSEUD.
Little Miss Fairfax. London: 1867. V. 65

DENNETT, R. E.
Notes on the Folklore of the fjort. London: 1898. V. 64

DENNIE, JOSEPH
The Lay Preacher; or Short Sermons for Idle Readers. Walpole: 1796. V. 64

DENNIS, C. J.
The Moods of Ginger Mick. Sydney: 1916. V. 63

DENNIS, JOHN
The Comical Gallant; or the Amours of Sir John Falstaffe. London: 1702. V. 66; 67
The Pioneer of Progress or the Early Closing Movement in Relation to the Saturday Half-Holiday and the Early Payment of Wages. London: 1861. V. 64
The Usefulness of the Stage to Religion and to Government: Shewing the Advantage of the Drama in all Nations Since Its First Institution. London: 1738. V. 63
The Usefulness of the Stage, to the Happiness of Mankind. London: 1698. V. 65; 66

DENNIS, JONAS
The Landscape Gardener.... London: 1835. V. 64

DENNIS, R. W. G.
British Cup Fungi and Their Allies. London: 1960. V. 62

DENNIS, WAYNE
Readings in the History of Psychology. New York: 1948. V. 67

DENNY BROWN, D.
The Motor Functions of the Agranular Frontal Cortex. 1947. V. 66
Selected Writings of Sir Charles Sherrington. London: 1939. V. 64; 66

DENSLOW, W. W.
Barn-Yard Circus. New York: 1904. V. 62
Denslow's 5 Little Pigs. New York: 1903. V. 64
Denslow's Little Red Riding Hood. New York: 1903. V. 64
Denslow's Old Mother Hubbard. New York: 1903. V. 64
Jack and the Beanstalk. New York: 1903. V. 62
Little Red Riding Hood. New York: 1903. V. 62
Mother Goose A B C. New York: 1904. V. 64
Pictures from the Wonderful Wizard of Oz. Chicago: 1930?. V. 65
Scarecrow and the Tin-Man. New York: 1904. V. 62
Simple Simon. New York: 1904. V. 62
Three Bears. New York: 1903. V. 62
Through Foreign Lands with Sunny Jim. Buffalo: 1910. V. 62
When I Grow Up. London: 1909. V. 65

DENSON, ALAN
Printed Writings by George W. Russell: a Bibliography. Evanston: 1961. V. 62; 65

DENSON, CLAUDE BAKER
An Address Delivered in Raleigh, N.C. on Memorial Day (may 10), 1895. Raleigh: 1895. V. 62; 63; 65

DENT, C. T.
Mountaineering. London: 1901. V. 63

DENT HARDWARE CO.
Refrigerator Trimmings & Similar Goods for Butchers Cooling Rooms, Grocers Ice Boxes, Beer Coolers, Cold Storage & Special Hardware. Fullerton: 1901. V. 65

DENT, HERBERT C.
Old English Bronze Wool-Weights. Norwich: 1927. V. 66

THE DENTISTS Register: Printed and Published Under the Direction of the General Council of Medical Education and Registration of the United Kingdom, Pursuant to an Act Passed in the Year XLI and XLII Victoriae, Cap. XXXIII.... London: 1895. V. 63

DENTON, B. E.
A Two-Gun Cyclone. Dallas: 1927. V. 64; 67

DENWOOD, JONATHAN M.
Idylls of a North Countrie Fair. Cockermouth: 1916. V. 64; 65

DE OSMA, G.
Mariano Fortuny, His Life and Work. 1980. V. 65

DE PALOL, PEDRO
Early Medieval Art in Spain. New York: 1966?. V. 63

DE PAOLA, TOMIE
Giorgio's Village. New York: 1982. V. 65

DEPERTHES, JEAN LOUIS HUBERT SIMON
Histoire des Naufrages, ou Recueil des Relations les plus Interessantes des Naufrages, Hivernemens, Delaissemens, Incendies et Autres Evenemens Funestres Arrives sur Mer. Paris: 1818. V. 65

DEPEW, CHAUNCEY M.
The Man in the Street Stories. New York: 1902. V. 66

DE PEYSTER, JOHN WATTS
Personal and Military History of Phillip Kearny Major General United States Volunteers. New York: 1869. V. 65; 67

DEPIERRIS, HIPPOLYTE ADEON
Le Tabac; qui Contient le Plus Violent des Poisons La Nicotine. Paris: 1898. V. 63

DEPONS, F.
Travels in Parts of South America, During the Years 1801, 1802, 1803 and 1804. London: 1806. V. 64
Travels in Parts of South America During the Years 1801, 1802, 1803 and 1804. London: 1906. V. 65
Travels in South America, During the Years 1801, 1802, 1803 and 1804. London: 1807. V. 66

DE PRADT, D. D.
Du Congres De Vienne.... Paris: 1815. V. 67

DE QUATREFAGES, A.
The Pygmies. London: 1895. V. 62

DE QUINCEY, THOMAS
The Collected Writings. Edinburgh: 1889-1890. V. 63
The Collected Writings. London: 1896-1897. V. 62; 63; 65
Confessions of an English Opium Eater. London: 1822. V. 62; 64; 65
Confessions of an English Opium Eater. Bridgetown: 1823. V. 66
Confessions of an English Opium Eater. Philadelphia: 1823. V. 63

DE QUINCEY, THOMAS continued
Confessions of an English Opium Eater. 1930. V. 65
Confessions of an English Opium Eater. London: 1930. V. 67
Confessions of an English Opium Eater. New York: 1930. V. 64
Confessions of an English Opium Eater. Oxford: 1930. V. 62
A Diary of Thomas De Quincey 1803.... London: 1928. V. 64
Klosterheim; or, the Masque. London: 1832. V. 62; 65
Works. Edinburgh: 1862-1863. V. 67
The Works. Edinburgh: 1862-1874. V. 67
The Works. Edinburgh: 1863. V. 66
The Works. Edinburgh: 1871. V. 67

DERANIYAGALA, P. E. P.
A Coloured Atlas of Some Vertebrates from Ceylon. Volume 1. Fishes. Albany: 1842. V. 63
A Coloured Atlas of Some Vertebrates from Ceylon. Volume I Fishes. Colombo: 1952. V. 66
Some Extinct Elephants, Their Relatives and The Two Living Species. Colombo: 1955. V. 62

DERBY, EDWARD GEORGE GEOFFREY STANLEY, 14TH EARL OF
The Speech of the Right Honble. Lord Stanley, in the House of Lords, on Monday, May 25th, 1846. London: 1846. V. 64

DERBY, GEORGE H.
Phoenixiana; or, Sketches and Burlesques. New York: 1856. V. 64
Phoenixiana; or Sketches and Burlesques. San Francisco: 1937. V. 63

DERCUM, FRANCIS XAVIER
A Clinical Manual of Mental Diseases. Philadelphia: 1913. V. 65

DEREN, MAYA
Divine Horsemen: The Living Gods of Haiti. London and New York: 1953. V. 63

DERHAM, WILLIAM
Astro-Theology. London: 1715. V. 63
Astro-Theology. London: 1726. V. 63
Physico-Theology. London: 1713. V. 62; 66
Physico-Theology. London: 1754. V. 63
Physico-Theology.... London: 1798. V. 64

DERING, EDWARD HENEAGE
The Ban of Maplethorpe. With a Memoir of the Author. London and Leamington: 1894. V. 66

DERLETH, AUGUST WILLIAM
The Adventure of the Orient Express. 1965. V. 62
And You, Thoreau!. Norfolk: 1944. V. 64
Any Day Now. Chicago: 1939. V. 64
A Boy's Way. 1947. V. 62; 64; 66
The Casebook of Solar Pons. Sauk City: 1965. V. 62; 66
Dark Things. Sauk City: 1971. V. 63
Here On a Darkling Plain. 1940. V. 62; 64; 66
In Re: Sherlock Holmes. 1945. V. 62; 63; 66
In Re: Sherlock Holmes. Sauk City: 1945. V. 63; 64; 65; 66
It's A Boy's World. 1948. V. 64; 66
Lonesome Places. Sauk City: 1962. V. 62; 63; 64
The Man On All Fours. 1934. V. 64; 66
The Mask of Cthulhu. 1958. V. 66
The Mask of Cthulhu. Sauk City: 1958. V. 62
The Memoirs of Solar Pons. 1951. V. 62; 66
The Memoirs of Solar Pons. Sauk City: 1951. V. 65; 66
The Narracong Riddle. New York: 1940. V. 67
Not Long for this World. Sauk City: 1948. V. 62; 64; 65
Over the Edge. Sauk City: 1964. V. 63
The Reminiscences of Solar Pons. 1961. V. 66
The Reminiscences of Solar Pons. 1981. V. 62
The Return of Solar Pons. 1958. V. 62; 66
Sentence Deferred. New York: 1939. V. 67
The Solar Pons Omnibus. Sauk City: 1982. V. 66
Some Notes on H. P. Lovecraft. Sauk City: 1959. V. 63
Someone in the Dark. Sauk City: 1941. V. 62; 64; 66
Something Near. Sauk City: 1945. V. 62; 64; 66
Three Problems for Solar Pons. 1952. V. 62; 63; 66
The Trail of Cthulhu. Sauk City: 1962. V. 62; 66
Wind Over Wisconsin. New York: 1938. V. 64
Wisconsin Murders. 1968. V. 64; 66

DERMODY, THOMAS
Poems, Moral and Descriptive. London: 1800. V. 66

DER NERSESSIAN, SIRAPIE
American Manuscripts in the Walters Art Gallery. Baltimore: 1973. V. 62

DE ROME, F. J.
Notes on the Harbour of Hong Kong. London: 1927. V. 67
Notes on the New Territories of Hong Kong. London: 1929. V. 67

DEROME, LEOPOLD
La Reliure De Luxe. Le Livre et l'Amateur. Paris: 1888. V. 67

DE ROPP, ROBERT S.
The Master Game: Pathways to Higher Consciousness Beyond the Drug Experience. New York: 1968. V. 66

DE ROS, JOHN FREDERICK FITZGERALD
Personal Narrative of Travels in the United States and Canada in 1826.... London: 1827. V. 64; 66

DERRICK, CHARLES
Memoirs of the Rise and Progress of the Royal Navy. London: 1806. V. 62

DERRICK, FREDA
A Day in Animal Town. London: 1938. V. 65

THE DERRICK'S Handbook of Petroleum....* Oil City: 1898-1900. V. 64

DERRIDA, JACQUES
Glas. Paris: 1974. V. 66
La Voix et le Phenomene. Paris: 1967. V. 67

DERRY, JOSEPH T.
Story of the Confederate States; or, History of the War for Southern Independence, Embracing a Brief but Comprehensive Sketch of the Early Settlement of the Country.... Richmond: 1895. V. 65

DES Imagistes: an Anthology. London: 1914. V. 62

DES LAURIERS
Prologues tant Serieux que Facetieux Avec Plusieurs Galimatias par le Sieur D. L. Paris: 1610. V. 62

DESAGULIERS, J. T.
Lectures of Experimental Philosophy. London: 1719. V. 65

DESAI, ANITA
Fasting, Feasting. London: 1999. V. 66
Voices in the City. London: 1965. V. 62

DESBORDES-VALMORE, MARCELINE
Poesies Completes. Paris: 1931-1932. V. 63
Poesies de Madame Desbordes Valmore. Paris: 1860. V. 66
Poesies Inedites. Geneve: 1860. V. 63

DES BRISAY, MATHERS
History of the County of Lunenburg. Toronto: 1895. V. 67

DESCARTES, RENE
Discours de la Methode Pour Bien Conduire sa Raison & Chercher la Verite dans les Sciences. Plus la Dioptrique, les Meteores, la Mechanique, et la Musique, Qui son des Essais de Cette Methode. Paris: 1668. V. 62
Epistolae. Amsterdam: 1682-1683. V. 66
Opera Philosophica. Amstordam: 1685. V. 62
Principia Philosophiae. Amsterdam: 1644. V. 62

DESCENDANTS of Solomon Cox of Cole Creek, Virginia and Other Cox Ancestry of the Cole Creek Coxs. N.P: 1955. V. 67

DESCH, JOHN MICHAEL
Midnight Revels. San Francisco: 1939. V. 62

DES CHARMES, PAJOT
The Art of Bleaching Piece-Goods, Cottons and Threads, of Every Description...to Which are Added the Most Certain methods of Bleaching Silk and Wool.... London: 1799. V. 67

DE SCHWEINITZ, G. E.
Diseases of the Eye. Philadelphia: 1896. V. 66; 67

DESCOURTILZ, J. T.
Pageantry of Tropical Birds. (with) Oiseaux Brillans et Remarquable du Bresil. Amsterdam and Rio: 1960. V. 66
Pageantry of Tropical Birds. (with) Oiseaux Brillants de Remarquables du Bresil.... London: 1960. V. 65

DESCRIPTION de la Ville de Florence et ses Environs. Florence: 1824. V. 66

DESCRIPTION des Principales Rejouissances, Faites a la Haye a l'Occasion du Couronnement de Sa Majeste Imperiale Francois I....* The Hague: 1747. V. 65

DESCRIPTION of Duncombe Park, Rivalx Abbey and Helmsley Castle, with Notices of Byland Abbey, Kirkdale Church &c. Kirkby Moorside: 1829. V. 64

DESCRIPTION of Mount Pilate With Its Legends, Popular Traditions, etc. Lucerne: 1865. V. 62

A DESCRIPTION of the Ancient Vessel Recently Found Under an Old Branch of the River Rother in Kent, with Various Conjectures Respecting Her Antiquity....* London: 1823. V. 66

A DESCRIPTIVE Catalogue of the Marine Collection to Be Found at India House. Middletown: 1873. V. 62

DESCRIPTIVE, Historical, Commercial, Agricultural and Other Important Information Relative to the City of San Diego, California. San Diego: 1874. V. 63

DESCRIZIONE delle cose Piu Notabili che Sono Nella Chiesa di S. Giustina di Padova de Monaci Casinensi. Padua: 1741. V. 64

DE SCUDERY, M.
Clelia. London: 1655. V. 66

DESCURET, JEAN BAPTISTE FELIX
La Medecine des Passions, ou Les Passions Considerees Dans Leurs Rapports Avec les Maladies.... Liege: 1844. V. 65

DESEINE, FRANCOIS
Nouveau Voyage d'Italie Contenant une Description Exacte de Toutes ses Provinces, Villes & Lieux Considerables & des Isles, Qui en Dependent, avec Les Routes, et Chemis Publics pour y Parvenir, la Distance des Lieux, et les Choses Remarquables. Lyons: 1699. V. 67

DESEJOUR, DIONIS
The Origin of the Graces. London: 1889. V. 67

DESERET UNIVERSITY
The Deseret Furst Bok by the Regents of th Yionivursiti. With The Deseret Second Bok by the Regents of th Deseret Yionivursiti. Salt Lake City: 1868. V. 66

DE SERVIEZ, JACQUES ROERGAS
The Lives and Amours of the Empresses, Consorts to the First 12 Caesars of Rome. London: 1723. V. 65

DE SHIELDS, JAMES T.
Border Wars of Texas. Tioga: 1912. V. 62; 65
Cynthia Ann Parker, the Story of Her Capture. St. Louis: 1886. V. 65; 67
Tall Men with Long Rifles. San Antonio: 1935. V. 62

DESHOULIERES, ANTOINETTE
Oeuvres de Madame de Mademoiselle Deshoulieres. Paris: 1764. V. 63

DESJARDINS, MARIE CATHERINE HORTENSE DE
The Unfotunate (sic) Heroes; or the Adventures of Ten Famous Men.... London: 1679. V. 67

DESMOND, HARRY W.
Stately Homes in America from Colonial Times to the Present Day. New York: 1903. V. 66

DESMOND, R.
Bibliography of British Gardens. Winchester: 1988. V. 67

DE SOUZA, BARETTO
Principles of Equitation. New York: 1925. V. 66

DESPARD, EDWARD MARCUS
Fairburn's Edition of the Trial at Large of Colonel Despard for High Treason.... London: 1803. V. 63
The Trial of Colonel Despard and Others, for High Treason, Before Lord Ellenborough, Monday Feburary 7,...1803. Chatham: 1803. V. 63

DESPAZE, JOSEPH
The Five Men; or a Review of the Proceedings and Principles of the Executive Directory of France.... London: 1797. V. 64

DESRUELLES, H. M. J.
Traite de la Coqueluche, D'Apres les Principes de la Doctrine Physiologique, Ouvrage Couronne Par la Societe Medico-Pratique de Paris. Paris: 1827. V. 64

D'ESTOURMEL, JOSEPH, COMTE DE
Journal d'un Voyage en Orient. Paris: 1844. V. 63

DESTUTT DE TRACY, ANTOINE LOUIS CLAUDE, COMTE
A Treatise on Political Economy. Georgetown: 1817. V. 66

DE TABLEY, JOHN BYRNE LEICESTER WARREN, 3RD BARON
Poems Dramatic and Lyrical. London: 1893. V. 64
Poems Dramatic and Lyrical. Second Series. London: 1895. V. 64
Poems Dramatic and Lyrical. (with) Poems Dramatic and Lyrical - Second Series. London: 1893-1895. V. 62

DETERMINATIONS of the Honourable House of Commons, Concerning Elections, and All Their Incidents. London: 1741. V. 62

DETERMINATIONS of the Honourable House of Commons Concerning Elections, and All Their Incidents. London: 1747. V. 63

DETMOLD, E. J.
Baby Animals of the Wild. London: 1920. V. 64
Twenty-Four Nature Pictures. London: 1919. V. 62

DETMOLD, MAURICE
Pictures from Birdland. London: 1899. V. 62

DE TOLNAY, CHARLES
History and Technique of Old Master Drawings. A Handbook. New York: 1943. V. 64

DETROIT Fire Historical Record 1825-1977. N.P: 1978. V. 67

DETROIT City Directory for 1881. Detroit: 1881. V. 65

DETROIT City Directory for 1884. Detroit: 1884. V. 65

DETROIT MUSEUM OF ART
Catalogue of the First Annual Exhibition of the Detroit Architectural Club in the Galleries of the Detroit Museum of Art, Jefferson Avenue, from April Twenty Eighth to May Twelfth 1900. V. 65

DEUTSCH, RICHARD R.
Northern Ireland: 1921-1974: a Select Bibliography. 1975. V. 67

DE VALERA, EAMON
Ireland's Stand, Being a Selection of Speeches of Eamon de Valera During the War 1939-1945. 1946. V. 62

DE VARGAS, JUAN
Les Aventures de Don Juan de Vargas, Racontees par Lui-Meme. Paris: 1853. V. 64

DEVAUCHELE, R.
La Reliure en France de ses Origines a Nos Jours. Paris: 1959-1961. V. 62

DEVENTER, HENDRICK VAN
Operationum Chirugicarum Novum Lumen Obstetricantibus. Leiden: 1733. V. 65

DE VERE, AUBREY
Sonnets. 1875. V. 67

DEVEREAUX, JOHN C.
The Most Material Parts of Kent's Commentaries, Reduced to Questions and Answers. New York: 1873. V. 66

DEVEREUX, G. R. M.
Etiquette for Men. London: 1919. V. 67

DEVEY, LOUISA
Life of Rosina, Lady Lytton, with Numerous Extracts from Her MS. Autobiography.... London: 1887. V. 65; 66

DEVILLE, NICOLAS
Historie des Plantes de l'Euroe.... Lyon: 1753. V. 64

DE VILLEROI, B.
Sub-Description for the Erection of a Monument to the Memory of the Brave and Unfortunate John Brown. Philadelphia: 1867. V. 63

DE VINCK, CHRISTOPHER
Only the Heart Knows How to Find Them. Precious Memories for a Faithless Time. New York: 1991. V. 67

DEVINE, T. M.
Ireland and Scotland, 1600-1850. 1983. V. 67

DE VINNE, THEODORE LOW
Modern Methods of Book Composition. New York: 1904. V. 66
Notable Printers of Italy During the Fifteenth Century. New York: 1910. V. 64
Title-Pages as Seen by a Printer. New York: 1901. V. 64

DE VITA, STEPHEN
The Apotheosis of William McKinley. Philadelphia: 1904. V. 64

DEVLIN, DENIS
Lough Derg and Other Poems. New York: 1946. V. 62

DEVLIN, ROBERT T.
Pebble Beach. Costa Mesa: 1980. V. 66

DEVNEY, EDWARD J.
Pictorial Highlights from the History of the 460th Bombardment Group, U.S. 15th Army Air Force. Cleveland: 1946. V. 67

DEVOL, GEORGE H.
Forty Years a Gambler on the Mississippi. Austin: 1967. V. 66

DE VOLPI, CHARLES
The Eastern Townships - a Pictorial Board. Montreal: 1962. V. 64
Newfoundland - a Pictorial Record Historical Prints and Illustrations of the Province of Newfoundland Canada 1497-1887. Toronto: 1972. V. 63

DE VOTO, BERNARD
The Letters of Bernard De Voto. New York: 1973. V. 67
Mark Twain at Work. Cambridge: 1942. V. 63
Mark Twain's America. Boston: 1932. V. 63
The Year of Decision. New York: 1947. V. 65

DE VRIES, P. J.
The Butterflies of Costa Rica, and Their Natural History. Princeton: 1987-1997. V. 66

DE VRIES, PETER
Angels Can't Do Better. New York: 1944. V. 65
But Who Wakes the Bugler?. Boston: 1940. V. 67
No But I Saw the Movie. Boston: 1952. V. 63

DEW, CHARLES B.
Ironmaker to the Confederacy. Joseph R. Anderson and the Tredegar Iron Works. New Haven: 1966. V. 62; 63

DE WAAL, L. C.
Ecology and Management of Invasive Riverside Plants. Chichester: 1994. V. 67

DE WAAL, RONALD BURT
The World Bibliography of Sherlock Holmes and Dr. Watson. Boston: 1974. V. 66

DEWAR, G. A. B.
The Book of the Dry Fly. 1910. V. 67
The Pageant of English Landscape. London: 1924. V. 65

DEWAR, JOHN
The Dewar Manuscripts. Glasgow: 1963. V. 67

DEWAR, MARGARET
Island Rhymes. London: 1937. V. 65

DEWEES, WILLIAM P.
A Compendious System of Midwifery. Philadelphia: 1826. V. 63
A Practice of Physic, Comprising Most of the Diseases Not Treated of in Diseases of Females and Diseases of Children. Philadelphia: 1833. V. 67
A Treatise on the Diseases of Females. Philadelphia: 1860. V. 63; 65
A Treatise on the Physical and Medical Treatment of Children. Philadelphia: 1826. V. 64

DEWEY, B.
A True and Concise Narrative of the Origin and Progress of the Church Difficulties in the Vicinity of Dartmouth College in Hanover. Hanover: 1815. V. 64

DEWEY, THOMAS B.
Draw the Curtain Close. 1947. V. 64; 66
Handle With Fear. 1951. V. 64; 66
Hue and Cry. New York: 1944. V. 65

DE WINDT, HARRY
From Peking to Calais by Land. London: 1892. V. 65
My Restless Life. London: 1909. V. 67
A Ride to India: Across Persia and Baluchistan. London: 1891. V. 64
Through the Gold-Fields of Alaska to Bering Straits. London: 1898. V. 65

DE WIT, AUGUSTA
Java: Facts and Fancies. London: 1905. V. 65

DE WITT, DAVID MILLER
The Assassination of Abraham Lincoln and Its Expiation. New York: 1909. V. 63
Judicial Murder of Mary E. Surratt. Baltimore: 1895. V. 63

DE WOLFF, J. H.
Pawnee Bill, His Experience and Adventures on the Western Plains.... N.P: 1901. V. 65; 67
Pawnee Bill (Major Gordon W. Lillie): His Experience and Adventures on the Western Plains. 1902. V. 64

DEWS, NATHAN
The History of Deptford in the Counties of Kent and Surrey. London and Deptford: 1884. V. 67

DEXTER, COLIN
The Daughters of Cain. London: 1994. V. 66; 67
The Dead of Jericho. London: 1981. V. 67
Death is Now My Neighbour. London: 1996. V. 66; 67
The Jewel That Was Ours. Bristol: 1991. V. 65; 66; 67
Last Bus to Woodstock. London: 1975. V. 65; 67
Last Seen Wearing. London: 1976. V. 65; 67
Morse's Greatest Mystery and Other Stories. London: 1993. V. 65; 66; 67
The Remorseful Day. London: 1999. V. 66
The Riddle of the Third Mile. London: 1983. V. 65; 66; 67
The Secret of Annexe 3. London: 1986. V. 62; 65; 66; 67
Service of the Dead. London: 1979. V. 67
The Silent World of Nicholas Quinn. London: 1977. V. 65; 67
The Way Through the Woods. Bristol: 1992. V. 65; 66; 67
The Way Through the Woods. London: 1992. V. 63
The Wench is Dead. London: 1989. V. 63; 66; 67
The Wench is Dead. New York: 1989. V. 63; 67

DEXTER, F. THEODORE
Forty-Two Years' Scrapbook of Rare Ancient Firearms. Los Angeles: 1954. V. 64

DEXTER, PETE
Brotherly Love. Franklin Center: 1991. V. 63
God's Pocket. New York: 1983. V. 62; 64; 65; 67
Paris Trout. New York: 1988. V. 63

DEY, BISHNU
Jamini Roy. Calcutta: 1944. V. 63

DEZALLIER D'ARGENVILLE, ANTOINE JOSEPH
L'Histoire Naturelle Eclaircie dans une de ses Parties Principales, la Conchyliologie.... Paris: 1757. V. 63; 65; 66
The Theory and Practice of Gardening.... London: 1712. V. 66

DEZALLIER D'ARGENVILLE, ANTOINE NICOLAS
Voyage Pittoresque de Paris. A Paris: 1765. V. 66
Voyage Pittoresque de Paris. Paris: 1778. V. 66

D'HERBELOT, BARTHELEMY
Bibliotheque Orientale ou Dictionaire Universel Contenant Generalement Tout ce qui Regarde la Connoissance des Peuples de l'Orient.... Paris: 1697. V. 62

A DIALOGUE Between a Country Gentleman and a Lawyer, Upon the Doctrine of Distress for Rent.... London: 1776. V. 66

A DIALOGUE Betwixt Sam, the Ferryman of Dochet, Will, a Waterman of London, and Tom, a Bargeman of Oxford. London: 1681. V. 66

DIALOGUES on Entomology, in Which the Forms and Habits of Insects are Familiarly Explained. London: 1819. V. 63

THE DIAMOND Fairy Book. London: 1918. V. 67

DIAMOND, J. M.
Avifauna of the Eastern Highlands of New Guinea. 1972. V. 67

DIAMOND, SEYMOUR
The Practicing Physician's Approach to Headache. Baltimore: 1979. V. 66; 67

DIAZ DEL CASTILLO, BERNAL
The True History of the Conquest of Mexico. New York: 1927. V. 66

DI BASSI, PIETRO ANDREA
The Labors of Hercules. 1971. V. 67

DIBDIN, CHARLES
The Professional Life of Mr. Dibdin. London: 1803. V. 67
Songs, Naval and National of the Late Charles Dibdin, with a Memoir and Addenda, Collected and Arranged by Thomas Dibdin. London: 1841. V. 63

DIBDIN, MICHAEL
Dark Spectre. London: 1995. V. 65; 66
The Last Sherlock Holmes Story. London: 1978. V. 65
A Rich Full Death. London: 1986. V. 65

DIBDIN, THOMAS COLMAN
Dibdin's Progressive Lessons in Water Colour Painting. London: 1848. V. 66

DIBDIN, THOMAS FROGNALL
Aedes Althorpianae; or an Account of the Mansion, Books and Pictures at Althorp, the Residence of George John Earl Spencer.... London: 1822. V. 64
A Bibliographical, Antiquarian and Picturesque Tour in France and Germany. London: 1829. V. 62; 64; 67
A Bibliogaphical, Antiquarian and Picturesque Tour in the Northern Counties of England and Scotland. London: 1838. V. 62; 63; 65
Bibliomania; or Book-Madness.... London: 1876. V. 63; 66
Bibliophobia. Remarks on the Present Languid and Depressed State of Literature and the Book Trade. London: 1832. V. 62; 65
Brief Remarks Upon the Preface and Notes of G. A. Crapelet.... London: 1821. V. 63
An Introduction to the Knowledge of Rare and Valuable Editions of Greek and Roman Classics. Glocester (sic): 1802. V. 62; 67
An Introduction to the Knowledge of Rare and Valuable Editions of the Greek and Latin Classics. London: 1827. V. 62
The Library Companion; or, the Young Man's Guide, and the Old Man's Comfort, in the Choice of a Library. London: 1824. V. 62; 65; 66
Poems. London: 1797. V. 65
Reminiscences of a Literary Life. London: 1836. V. 65
Typographical Antiquities or the History of Printing in England Scotland and Ireland.... London: 1810-1819. V. 63

DIBDIN, THOMAS JOHN
The Reminiscences of Thomas Dibdin, of the Theatres Royal, Covent Garden, Drury Lane, Haymarket &c. London: 1837. V. 62

DICEY, EDWARD
The Peasant State. An Account of Bulgaria in 1894. London: 1894. V. 64

DICK, ALEXANDRA
Macalastair Looks On. London: 1947. V. 67

DICK, JOHN
Lectures on Theology. Edinburgh: 1834. V. 66

DICK, PHILIP K.
Confessions of a Crap Artist. 1975. V. 64
The Crack in Space. New York: 1966. V. 62
A Handful of Darkness. London: 1955. V. 62; 66; 67
Time Out of Joint. London: 1961. V. 62

DICK, ST. JOHN
Flies and Fly Fishing for White and Brown Trout, Grayling and Coarse Fish. 1873. V. 63; 65

DICK, STEVEN J.
The Biological Universe; the Twentieth Century Extraterrestrial Life Debate and the Limits of Science. Cambridge: 1996. V. 67

DICK, THOMAS
On the Mental Illumination and Moral Improvement of Mankind; or, an Inquiry into the Means by Which a General Diffusion of Knowledge and Moral Principle May be Promoted. Glasgow: 1844. V. 64
The Practical Astronomer... (with) The Solar System...(with) The Atmosphere and Atmospherical Phenomena. Philadelphia: 1848-1849. V. 66

DICK Whittington (Aunt Louisa's London Toy Books). London: 1880. V. 65

DICK, WILLIAM
Dick Versus Dick; or, a Full and Curious Account of the Particular and Interesting Proceedings Instituted at Doctors' Commons by Rachel Dick Against Her Husband the Rev. William Dick, of West Cowes, in the Isle of Wight, for a Nullity of Marriage. London: 1811. V. 64

DICKASON, OLIVE PATRICIA
Indian Arts in Canada. Ottawa: 1972. V. 66

DICKENS, CHARLES
Address Delivered at the Birmingham and Midland Institute, on the 27th September 1869. Birmingham: 1869. V. 62
All the Year Round. London: 1859-1867. V. 62
All the Year Round. London: 1860-1873. V. 62
American Notes for General Circulation. London: 1842. V. 62; 65; 67
American Notes for General Circulation. New York: 1842. V. 62
Barnaby Rudge. London: 1841. V. 62
Barnaby Rudge. Philadelphia: 1842. V. 62
Barnaby Rudge. London: 1860?. V. 62
Barnaby Rudge. London: 1871. V. 62
The Bat Boy. New York: 1885. V. 63
The Battle of Life. London: 1846. V. 62; 66; 67
The Battle of Life. and The Haunted Man. Leipzig: 1856. V. 62
Bleak House. London: 1853. V. 62; 63; 64; 65; 66; 67
Bleak House. London: 1870. V. 62
Charles Dickens and Maria Beadnell Private Correspondence. Boston: 1908. V. 67
A Child's Dream of a Star. Boston: 1871. V. 64; 65
A Child's Dream of a Star. London: 1899. V. 62
A Child's History of England. London: 1852-1854. V. 62; 64; 66
A Child's History of England. Leipzig: 1853-1854. V. 62; 65
A Child's History of England. London: 1853-1854. V. 62
The Chimes. London: 1845. V. 62; 63; 64; 66; 67
The Chimes. Paris: 1845. V. 62

DICKENS, CHARLES continued

The Chimes. London: 1906. V. 64
The Chimes. London: 1913. V. 62
The Chimes. New York: 1931. V. 64
Christmas Books. London: 1852. V. 62; 63
Christmas Books. London: 1856. V. 62
Christmas Books. New York: 1861. V. 65
A Christmas Carol. Leipzig: 1843. V. 62
A Christmas Carol. London: 1843. V. 62; 66; 67
A Christmas Carol. London: 1844. V. 62; 66
A Christmas Carol. Philadelphia: 1844. V. 62; 65
A Christmas Carol. London: 1845. V. 62
A Christmas Carol. London: 1846. V. 62
A Christmas Carol. London: 1858. V. 62
A Christmas Carol. London: 1859. V. 66
A Christmas Carol. London: 1875. V. 62
A Christmas Carol. London: 1915. V. 62; 63
A Christmas Carol. London: 1922. V. 62
A Christmas Carol. Chicago: 1940. V. 62
A Christmas Carol. New York: 1971. V. 62
A Christmas Carol. New York: 1983. V. 65
Christmas Stories from All the Year Round. London: 1868. V. 62; 64; 65
Christmas Stories from Household Words and All the Year Round 1852-1867. London: 1852-1867. V. 62
Christmas Stories from Household Words and All the Year Round and Other Stories. London: 1880. V. 62
The Companion Dickens. Boston: 1884. V. 62
(Complete Works). London: 1895. V. 67
The Complete Works. London: 1901-1902. V. 62
The Complete Works and Letters. London: 1937-1938. V. 62; 63
The Cricket on the Hearth. London: 1846. V. 62; 64; 66
The Cricket on the Hearth. Waltham St. Lawrence: 1933. V. 65
A Curious Dance Round a Curious Tree. London: 1860. V. 62
Dame Durden, Little Woman. New York: 1855. V. 65
The Dickens-Kolle Letters. Boston: 1910. V. 67
Dombey and Son. New York: 1846-1848. V. 65
Dombey and Son. Leipzig: 1847-1848. V. 62
Dombey and Son. London: 1848. V. 62; 63; 64; 65; 66; 67
Dombey and Son. London: 1858. V. 62
Dombey and Son. London: 1865. V. 62
Dombey and Son. London: 1870. V. 62
Dombey and Son. (with) Barnaby Rudge. Philadelphia: 1848-1850. V. 62
Great Expectations. London: 1861. V. 62
Great Expectations. London: 1862. V. 62
Great Expectations. London: 1864. V. 62
Great Expectations. London: 1875?. V. 62
Great Expectations. London: 1876. V. 62
Great Expectations. London: 1880. V. 62
Great Expectations. Edinburgh: 1937. V. 62
Great Expectations. Oxford: 1993. V. 62
Great Expectations. with American Notes and Pictures from Italy. London: 1867. V. 62
Great Expectations. (with) The Old Curiosity Shop. London: 1876. V. 62
Great Expectations. (with) The Uncommercial Traveller. London: 1876-1877. V. 62
Hard Times. London: 1854. V. 62; 64; 65
Hard Times. and Pictures from Italy. London: 1866. V. 62
The Haunted Man. London: 1848. V. 62
The Haunted Man and the Ghost's Bargain. London: 1846. V. 62; 64
The Haunted Man and the Ghost's Bargain. London: 1848. V. 63; 64; 66; 67
Household Words. London: 1850-. V. 62
Household Words. A Weekly Journal. London: 1850-1855. V. 62
Household Words. A Weekly Journal. London: 1850-1859. V. 62
Hunted Down. With Some Account of Thomas Griffiths Wainewright, the Poisoner. London: 1871. V. 62
The Lamplighter: a Farce.... London: 1879. V. 62
The Lamplighter's Story: Hunted Down; the Detective Polic; and Other Novelettes. Philadelphia: 1861. V. 64; 65
The Lazy Tour of Two Idle Apprentices. No Thoroughfare. The Perils of Certain English Prisoners. London: 1890. V. 62
The Letters. London: 1880. V. 62
The Letters. London: 1880-1882. V. 62
The Life of Our Lord. London: 1934. V. 62; 64
The Life and Adventures of Martin Chuzzlewit. Leipzig: 1844. V. 62
The Life and Adventures of Martin Chuzzlewit. London: 1844. V. 62; 63; 64; 65; 66; 67
The Life and Adventures of Martin Chuzzlewit. Philadelphia: 1844. V. 62
The Life and Adventures of Martin Chuzzlewit. London: 1850. V. 62
The Life and Adventures of Martin Chuzzlewit. London: 1857. V. 62
The Life and Adventures of Martin Chuzzlewit. London: 1859. V. 62
The Life and Adventures of Martin Chuzzlewit. London: 1863. V. 62
The Life and Adventures of Martin Chuzzlewit. London: 1870. V. 62
The Life and Adventures of Martin Chuzzlewit. London: 1891. V. 62
The Adventures of Nicholas Nickleby. Philadelphia: 1839. V. 62; 66
The Life and Adventures of Nicholas Nickleby. London: 1838-1839. V. 62
The Life and Adventures of Nicholas Nickleby. London: 1839. V. 62; 63; 64; 65; 66; 67
The Life and Adventures of Nicholas Nickleby. Leipzig: 1843. V. 62
The Life and Adventures of Nicholas Nickleby. London: 1863. V. 62
The Life and Adventures of Nicholas Nickleby. London: 1875. V. 62
The Life and Adventures of Nicholas Nickleby. London: 1880. V. 62
The Life and Adventures of Nicholas Nickleby. London: 1910. V. 64
Little Dorrit. London: 1855. V. 62; 65
Little Dorrit. London: 1855-1857. V. 62; 64
Little Dorrit. London: 1857. V. 62; 63; 66; 67
Little Dorrit. Philadelphia: 1857. V. 64
Little Dorrit. London: 1863. V. 62
Little Dorrit. London: 1865. V. 62
Little Dorrit. London: 1880. V. 62
Lloyd's Sixpenny Dickens. London: 1909-1911. V. 62
Master Humphrey's Clock. London: 1840. V. 63
Master Humphrey's Clock. London: 1840-1841. V. 62; 64; 65; 66; 67
Master Humphrey's Clock. Calcutta: 1841-1842. V. 62
Master Humphrey's Clock. Leipzig: 1846. V. 62
Mr. Pickwick. Pages from the Pickwick Papers. London: 1910. V. 66
Mr. Pickwick. (Pages from the Pickwick Papers). London: 1911. V. 67
Mr. and Mrs. Charles Dickens: His Letters to Her. London: 1935. V. 62
Mr. Nightingale's Diary: a Farce in One Act. Boston: 1877. V. 62
The Mudfog Papers, etc. London: 1880. V. 62
Mugby Junction, the Extra Christmas Number of All the Year Round for Christmas 1866. London: 1866. V. 63; 66
The Mystery of Edwin Drood. London: 1870. V. 62; 63; 64; 65; 66; 67
The Mystery of Edwin Drood. London: 1872. V. 62
The Mystery of Edwin Drood. London: 1873?. V. 62
The Nine Christmas Numbers of All the Year Round. London: 1868. V. 62; 63
No Thoroughfare. London: 1867. V. 62
The Nonesuch Dickens. Bloomsbury: 1937-1938. V. 62; 65; 67
The Old Curiosity Shop. London. V. 62; 64; 66
The Old Curiosity Shop. London: 1841. V. 62
The Old Curiosity Shop. Philadelphia: 1841. V. 62; 66
The Old Curiosity Shop. London: 1913. V. 66; 67
The Old Curiosity Shop. Oxford: 1997. V. 62
Oliver Twist. London: 1838. V. 62; 64; 66; 67
Oliver Twist. New York: 1839. V. 66
Oliver Twist. London: 1841. V. 62
Oliver Twist. New York: 1842. V. 62
Oliver Twist. London: 1846. V. 62; 63; 66
Oliver Twist. London: 1850. V. 62
Oliver Twist. London: 1877. V. 62
Oliver Twist. London: 1895. V. 62
Oliver Twist. London: 1900?. V. 62
Oliver Twist. (with) Edwin Drood. London: 1870. V. 62
Our Mutual Friend. London: 1864-1865. V. 62
Our Mutual Friend. London: 1865. V. 62; 65; 66; 67
Our Mutual Friend. New York: 1865. V. 62
Our Mutual Friend. London: 1870. V. 62
The Oxford Illustrated Dickens. Oxford: 1987. V. 66
Paris et Londres en 1795. (A Tale of Two Cities). 1861. V. 62
The Personal History of David Copperfield. London: 1849. V. 64
The Personal History of David Copperfield. Leipzig: 1849-1850. V. 62
The Personal History of David Copperfield. London: 1850. V. 62; 63; 64; 66; 67
The Personal History of David Copperfield. London: 1863. V. 62
The Personal History of David Copperfield. London: 1865. V. 62
The Personal History of David Copperfield. London: 1880. V. 62
The Personal History of David Copperfield. London: 1911. V. 66; 67
The Personal History of David Copperfield. London: 1912. V. 62
La Petite Dorrit. Paris: 1858. V. 62
The Pic Nic Papers. London: 1841. V. 62; 63
The Pic Nic Papers. London: 1870?. V. 62
The Pic Nic Papers. (with) New Years' Stories. Philadelphia: 1870. V. 62
Pictures from Dickens. London. V. 64
Pictures from Italy. 1846. V. 67
Pictures from Italy. Leipzig: 1846. V. 62
Pictures from Italy. London: 1846. V. 62; 64; 66; 67
Pictures from Italy. Paris: 1846. V. 62
The Plays and Poems.... London: 1885. V. 62
The Poor Traveller: Boots at the Holly Tree Inn: and Mrs. Gamp. London: 1858. V. 62
The Posthumous Papers of the Pickwick Club. London: 1836. V. 62; 64
The Posthumous Papers of the Pickwick Club. London: 1837. V. 62; 63; 64; 65; 66; 67
The Posthumous Papers of the Pickwick Club. Philadelphia: 1838. V. 62
The Posthumous Papers of the Pickwick Club. New York: 1842. V. 62
The Posthumous Papers of the Pickwick Club. Philadelphia: 1846. V. 62
The Posthumous Papers of the Pickwick Club. London: 1866. V. 62
The Posthumous Papers of the Pickwick Club. London: 1867. V. 63
The Posthumous Papers of the Pickwick Club. London: 1875. V. 62
The Posthumous Papers of the Pickwick Club. London: 1883?. V. 62
The Posthumous Papers of the Pickwick Club. London: 1910. V. 62; 66
The Posthumous Papers of the Pickwick Club. London: 1911. V. 62
The Posthumous Papers of the Pickwick Club. London: 1912. V. 67
The Posthumous Papers of the Pickwick Club. London: 1932. V. 62
Sketches by Boz. London: 1836. V. 62; 66
Sketches by Boz. London: 1836-1837. V. 62

DICKENS, CHARLES continued
Sketches by Boz. London: 1837. V. 62
Sketches by Boz. Philadelphia: 1837. V. 62
Sketches by Boz. London: 1839. V. 62; 67
Sketches by Boz. London: 1863. V. 62
Sketches by Boz. London: 1874. V. 62
Sketches by Boz. London: 1880. V. 62
Sketches of Young Couples.... London: 1840. V. 62; 65
Sketches of Young Gentlemen. London: 1838. V. 62; 67
Speech of Charles Dickens Delivered at Gore House, Kensington, May 10, 1851. Boston: 1909. V. 67
Speeches Literary and Social. London: 1870. V. 62
Speeches Literary and Social. London: 1871. V. 62
Speeches Literary and Social. London: 1874. V. 62
The Story of Little Dombey. London: 1858. V. 62; 65; 67
The Strange Gentleman. London: 1871. V. 62
Sunday Under Three Heads. London: 1884. V. 62
Sunday Under Three Heads. Manchester: 1884. V. 62
A Tale of Two Cities. London: 1859. V. 62; 63; 67
A Tale of Two Cities. Philadelphia: 1859. V. 66
A Tale of Two Cities. London: 1860. V. 62
A Tale of Two Cities. London: 1866. V. 62
The Uncommercial Traveller. London: 1861. V. 62
The Uncommercial Traveller. London: 1880?. V. 62
Unpublished Letters...to Mark Lemon. London: 1927. V. 63; 66
The Village Coquettes. London: 1836. V. 62
The Village Coquettes. London: 1870. V. 62
The Village Coquettes. London: 1883?. V. 62
Works. London: 1858-1859. V. 62
Works. London: 1863-1866. V. 62
Works. London: 1866. V. 64; 65
Works. Boston: 1868. V. 64; 65
Works. London: 1871-1879. V. 62
Works. London: 1874-1876. V. 62
The Works. New York: 1880. V. 67
The Works. London: 1885?. V. 62
Works. London: 1890. V. 62
The Works. London: 1899-1901. V. 62
Works. New York: 1900. V. 65
Works. London: 1901-1902. V. 62
The Works. London: 1907. V. 62
The Works. London: 1912. V. 62

DICKENS, HENRY FIELDING
Memories of My Father. London: 1928. V. 67

DICKENS, MAMIE
My Father As I Recall Him. London: 1897. V. 67

DICKERSON, B. C.
The Old Rose Adventurer. Portland: 1999. V. 67

DICKERSON, EDWARD N.
The Navy of the United States. New York: 1864. V. 64

DICKERT, D. AUGUSTUS
History of Kershaw's Brigade, With Complete Roll of Companies. Newberry: 1899. V. 63; 65

DICKEY, CHARLEY
Backtrack. Clinton: 1977. V. 65

DICKEY, D. R.
The Birds of El Salvador. Chicago: 1938. V. 63

DICKEY, JAMES
Babel to Byzantium. New York: 1968. V. 67
Deliverance. Boston: 1970. V. 62; 63; 64; 67
Deliverance. London: 1970. V. 66; 67
Deliverance. Franklin Center: 1981. V. 66
The Owl King. New York: 1977. V. 62
Poems 1957-1967. London: 1967. V. 64
Poems 1957-1967. Middletown: 1967. V. 67
Scion. Deerfield: 1980. V. 63
Tucky the Hunter. New York: 1978. V. 66
The Zodiac. New York: 1976. V. 64

DICKEY, ROLAND
New Mexico Village Arts. Albuquerque: 1949. V. 63; 64; 66; 67

DICKEY, THOMAS S.
Field Artillery Projectiles of the American Civil War. Atlanta: 1980. V. 64; 67

DICKIE, G.
A Flora of Ulster and a Botanists Guide to the North of Ireland. Belfast: 1864. V. 64; 65; 67

DICKINSON, ANNA ELIZABETH
What Answer?. Boston: 1868. V. 62; 63

DICKINSON, CHARLES
Waltz in Marathon. New York: 1983. V. 62

DICKINSON, CHARLES M.
Reunion of the Dickinson Family, at Amherst, Augusts 8th and 9th 1883. Amherst: 1884. V. 62

DICKINSON, EMILY ELIZABETH
Bolts of Melody. New York and London: 1945. V. 62; 63; 64
Face to Face - Unpublished Letters - with Notes.... Boston: 1912. V. 62
Further Poems of Emily Dickinson. Boston: 1929. V. 62; 64; 67
Letters of Emily Dickinson. Boston: 1899. V. 63
The Manuscript Books of Emily Dickinson. Cambridge and London: 1981. V. 62
The Poems. Cambridge. V. 62
Poems. Boston: 1895. V. 65
Poems, Second Series. Boston: 1892. V. 64; 65
Poems, Third Series. Boston: 1896. V. 66
Two Poems. New York: 1968. V. 66
Unpublished Poems. Boston: 1935. V. 64
The World in a Frame. New York: 1989. V. 62

DICKINSON, ERIC
Laolus and Other Poems. 1924. V. 67

DICKINSON, F. A.
Lake Victoria to Khartoum, with Rifle and Camera. 1910. V. 63
Lake Victoria to Khartoum, with Rifle and Camera. London: 1910. V. 64

DICKINSON, H. W.
A Short History of the Steam Engine. Cambridge: 1938. V. 62

DICKINSON, HENRY C.
Diary of Capt. Henry C. Dickinson. Denver. V. 66

DICKINSON, JOHN NODES
A Letter to the Honourable the Speaker of the Legislative Council on the Formation of a Second Chamber in the Legislature of New South Wales. Sydney: 1852. V. 67

DICKINSON, JONATHAN
Familiar Letters to a Gentleman Upon a Variety of Seasonable and Important Subjects in Religion. Newark: 1797. V. 66

DICKINSON, PATRIC
Soldiers' Verse. London: 1945. V. 65

DICKINSON, WILLIAM
Antiquities Historical, Architectural, Chronological and Itinerary, in Nottinghamshire and the Adjacent Counties.... Newark: 1801. V. 65; 66
A Glossary of Words and Phrases of Cumberland. Whitehaven: 1859. V. 64

DICKISON, MARY ELIZABETH
Dickison and His Men. Reminiscences of the War in Florida. Louisville: 1890. V. 62

DICKSON, ARTHUR JEROME
Covered Wagon Days - a Journey Across the Plains in the Sixties, and Pioneer Days in the Northwest from the Private Journals of Albert Jerome Dickson. Cleveland: 1929. V. 64; 67

DICKSON, CHARLES
The Life of Michael Dwyer. 1945. V. 67

DICKSON, JOHN THOMPSON
Matter and Force Considered in Relation to Mental and Cerebral Phenomena. Lewes: 1869. V. 67
The Science and Practice of Medicine in Relation to Mind, the Pathology of Nerve Centres and the Jurisprudence of Insanity.... London: 1874. V. 65

DICKSON, LOVAT
Half-Breed; the Story of Grey Owl. London: 1939. V. 67

DICKSON, R. W.
The New Botanic Garden.... London: 1812. V. 67

DICKY Birds ABC. Boston: 1890. V. 64

DICTIONARIUM Rusticum, Urbanicum, Botanicum &c. Or, a Discovery of Husbandry, Gardening, Trade, Commerce and All Sorts of Country Affairs. London: 1726. V. 65

DICTIONARUM Concionatorum Pauperum Auctoritis Incogniti.... Coloniae: 1610. V. 66

DICTIONARY of National Biography. London: 1885-1912. V. 62; 66
DICTIONARY of National Biography. London: 1975. V. 66

A DICTIONARY of the Holy Bible.... London: 1759. V. 67

A DICTIONARY of the Law of Elections, With the Practice from the Issuing of the Writ to the Final Decision.... London: 1826. V. 64

THE DICTIONARY of Trade, Commerce and Navigation.... 1844. V. 64

A DICTIONARY to Enable Any Two Persons to Maintain a Correspondence, with a Secrecy, Which is Imposible for Any Other Person to Discover. Hartford: 1805. V. 62

DICTIONNAIRE Universel Francois et Latin, Contenant la Signification et la Definition Tant des Mots de l'une & de l'Autre Langue, avec Leurs Differents Usages.... Paris: 1721. V. 67

DICTIONNAIRE Universel Francois et Latin, Vulgairement Appele Dictionnaire de Trevoux, Contenant la Signification & la Definition des Mots de l'Une & de l'Autre Languae.... Paris: 1771. V. 62

DICTIONARY of American Naval Fighting Ships. Washington: 1964-1991. V. 67

DIDAY, P.
A Treatise on Syphilis on New-Born Children and Infants at the Breast. London: 1859. V. 66; 67

DIDEROT, DENIS
Memoires sur Differens Sujets de Mathematiques. Paris: 1748. V. 66

DIDION, JOAN
A Book of Common Prayer. New York: 1977. V. 67
A Book of Common Prayer. Franklin: 1981. V. 66
Democracy. New York: 1984. V. 67
Essays and Conversations. New York: 1984. V. 67
The Last Thing He Wanted. Franklin Center: 1996. V. 63; 67
The Last Thing He Wanted. New York: 1996. V. 63
Play It As It Lays. New York: 1970. V. 67
Run River. New York: 1963. V. 63; 67
Salvador. New York: 1982. V. 67
Slouching Towards Bethlehem. New York: 1968. V. 67
Telling Stories. Berkeley: 1978. V. 67
The White Album. New York: 1987. V. 67

DIEBERT, RALPH C.
A History of the Third United States Cavalry 1846-1937. Harrisburg. V. 67

DIEFENBAKER, JOHN G.
One Canada Memoirs of the Right Honourable John G. Diefenbaker. Toronto: 1975-1977. V. 63

DIEHL, CHARLES S.
The Staff Correspondent - How the News of the World is Collected and Dispatched by a Body of Trained Press Writers. San Antonio: 1931. V. 65; 67

DIEHL, EDITH
Bookbinding: Its Background and Technique. New York: 1946. V. 63; 64; 66

DIEHL, WILLIAM
Sharkey's Machine. New York: 1978. V. 65; 66

DIEMBERGER, KURT
Summits and Secrets. London: 1971. V. 62

DIEMERBROECK, YSBRAND VAN
Opera Omnia Anatomcia et Medica. Utrecht: 1685. V. 64; 66; 67

DIENST, KLAUS PETER
Rhinozeros. Hamburg: 1961. V. 65

DIEREVILLE, N. DE
Relation of the Voyage to Port Royal in Acadia or New France. Toronto: 1933. V. 66

DIETRICH, MARLENE
Marlene Dietrich's ABC. New York: 1962. V. 63

DIETZ, AUGUST
Dietz Confederate States Catalog and Handbook of the Postage Stamps and Envelopes of the Confederate States of America. Richmond: 1945. V. 63
Dietz Confederate States Catalog and Handbook of the Postage Stamps and Envelopes of the Confederate States of America. Richmond: 1959. V. 63; 65
The Postal Service of the Confederate States of America. Richmond: 1929. V. 62; 63; 65

DIGBY, BASSETT
The Mammoth and Mammoth Hunting in North-East Siberia. 1926. V. 67
The Mammoth and Mammoth Hunting in North-East Siberia. Witherby: 1926. V. 66
Tigers, Gold and Witch-Doctors. 1928. V. 63; 66; 67

DIGBY, KENELM
Eroffnung Unterschiedlicher Heimlichkeiten der Natur, Worbey viel... (with) Medicina Experimentalis Digbaeana, das Ist: Ausserlesene und Bewahrte Artzney-Mittle, Auss.... Frankfurt: 1671. V. 64
Journal of a Voyage into the Mediterranean of Sir Kenelm Digby. 1868. V. 64
A Late Discours Made in a Solemne Assembly of Nobles and Learned Men at Montepelier in France.... London: 1664. V. 64
Of Bodies and Man's Soul. London: 1669. V. 63
Private Memoirs.... London: 1827. V. 63; 66
Private Memoirs.... London: 1827-1828. V. 64; 66; 67
Two Treatises. In the One of Which the Nature of Bodies; in the Other, the Nature of Mans Soule; is Looked Into; in Way of Discovery, of the Immorality of Reasonable Soules. Paris: 1644. V. 63; 64; 66; 67

DIGBY, KENELM HENRY
The Broad Stone of Honour; or, Rules for the Gentleman of England. London: 1823. V. 65; 66

DIGBY, LETTICE
My Ancestors, Being the History of the Digby and Strutt Families. 1928. V. 62

DIGBY, W.
Natural Law in Terretrial Phenomena. 1902. V. 67

DIGGES, DUDLEY
The Unlawfulness of Subjects Taking Up Armes Against Their Soveraign, In What Case Soever. London: 1647. V. 63

DIGGES, LEONARD
A Geometrical Practical Treatise Named Pantometria, Divided into Three Bookes, Longimetra, Planimetra, and Stereometria.... London: 1591. V. 63
Pantometria. London: 1591. V. 67

DIGGES, THOMAS
Englands Defence. A Treatise Concerning Invasion; or, a Brief Discourse of What Orders Were Best for Repulsing of Foreign Forces.... London: 1680. V. 65

DIGGLES, SILVESTER
Companion to Gould's Handbook; or, Synopsis of the Birds of Australia. Brisbane: 1877. V. 66; 67

DIKS, R.
Igrushki. Moscow: 1911. V. 64

DILKE, CHARLES WENTWORTH
Greater Britain: a Record of Travel in English Speaking Countries During 1866 and 1867. New York: 1869. V. 64

DILKE, EMILIA
French Engravers and Draughtsmen of the XVIIth Century. London: 1902. V. 67

DILKE, O. A. W.
Roman Books and Their Impact. Leeds: 1977. V. 64

DILL, DAVID BRUCE
Life, Heat and Altitude. Physiological Effects of Hot Climates and Great Heights. Cambridge: 1938. V. 63

DILL, EDWARD M.
The Mystery Solved or Ireland's Miseries, The Grand Cause and Cure. 1852. V. 67

DILLARD, ANNIE
An American Childhood. New York: 1987. V. 64; 66
Holy the Firm. New York: 1977. V. 67
Life Class. Chapel Hill: 1972. V. 67
Pilgrim at Tinker Creek. New York: 1974. V. 62; 63; 64; 65; 66
Teaching a Stone To Talk. New York: 1982. V. 64; 67
Tickets for a Prayer Wheel. Columbia: 1974. V. 63; 65; 67

DILLARD, RICHARD
The Civil War in Chowan County, North Carolina. N.P: 1916. V. 62; 65

DILLE, ROBERT
Buck Rogers. 1970. V. 65

DILLEY, A. U.
Oriental Rugs and Carpets: a Comprehensive Study. New York: 1931. V. 65

DILLON, E. S.
A Manual of Common Beetles of Eastern North America. Evanston: 1961. V. 66

DILLON, JOHN F.
John Marshall: Life, Character and Judicial Services. Chicago: 1903. V. 64

DILLON, MYLES
The Celtic Realms. 1967. V. 67

DILLON, P.
Narrative and Successful Result of a Voyage in the South Seas, Performed by Order of the Government of British India, to Ascertain the Actual Fate of La Perouse's Expedition, Interspersed with Accounts of the Religion, Manners, Customs.... Amsterdam/New York: 1972. V. 64

DILLON, R. C.
The Lord Mayor's Visit to Oxford in the Month of July 1826. London: 1826. V. 66

DILLON, RICHARD
Images of Chinatown: Louis J. Stellman's Chinatown Photographs. San Francisco: 1976. V. 63
Siskiyou Trail. New York: 1975. V. 66
Texas Argonauts: Isaac H. Duval and the California Gold Rush. San Francisco: 1987. V. 64
William Henry Boyle's Personal Observations on the Conduct of the Modoc Wat. Los Angeles: 1959. V. 63

DILS, LENRE
Horny Toad Man. El Paso: 1966. V. 64

DILWORTH, THOMAS
New Guide to the English Tongue: in Five Parts. Philadelphia: 1797. V. 67
The Schoolmasters Assistant, Being a Compendium of Arithmetic, Both Practical and Theoretical. London: 1780. V. 64
The Schoolmaster's Assistant, Being a Compendium of Arithmetic, Both Practical and Theoretical. London: 1793. V. 67
The Young Book-Keeper's Assistant.... London: 1810. V. 64

THE DIMAGGIO Albums. New York. V. 62

DIMAGGIO, JOE
The Dimaggio Albums. New York: 1989. V. 63

DIMITRY, ADELAIDE STUART
War-Time Sketches, Historical and Otherwise. New Orleans: 1913. V. 62; 63; 65

DIMOCK, A. W.
Florida Enchantments. New York: 1908. V. 65
Florida Enchantments. London: 1909. V. 63; 64; 65
Florida Enchantments. Peekamose: 1915. V. 63

DIMOCK, J. F.
Illustrations of the Collegiate Church of Southwell (Notts) in a Series of Ten Views in Tinted Lithography from Drawings by E. H. Buckler.... London: 1854. V. 62; 66

DIMOND, WILLIAM
The Story of the Broken Sword, On Which is Founded the Popular Melo-Drama Now Performing at Covent Garden Theatre.... London: 1816. V. 63

DIMOND, WILLIAM continued
The Young Hussar, or Love and Mercy, an Operatic Piece in Two Acts.... Baltimore: 1808. V. 66

DIMSDALE, THOMAS
The Present Method of Inoculating for the Small-Pox. London: 1767. V. 65

DINE, JIM
Kali: Poems and Etchings. London: 1999. V. 64; 65
Nancy Outside in July: Etchings. West Islip: 1983. V. 62; 65

DINES, ELAINE
Paul Outerbridge: a Singular Aesthetic; Photographs and Drawings 1921-1941. Laguna Beach: 1981. V. 63; 65

DINES, H. G.
The Metalliferous Mining Region of South-West England. London: 1969. V. 62

DINESEN, ISAK
Last Tales. London: 1957. V. 66
Last Tales. New York: 1957. V. 67
Letters from Africa 1914-1931. Chicago: 1981. V. 63; 64
Seven Gothic Tales. New York: 1924. V. 64
Seven Gothic Tales. New York: 1934. V. 63

DINGER, CHARLOTTE
Art of the Carousel. Green Village: 1983. V. 64

DINGLE, H.
Migration, the Biology of Life on the Move. New York: 1996. V. 65; 66

DINGLER, MAX
Sonnenkinder Stuben. Oldenburg: 1925. V. 66

DINGLEY, ROBERT
Vox Coeli: Philosophical, Historicall and Theological Observations of Thunder. London: 1658. V. 63

DINGWALL, A. C.
Handling and Nursing the Game Cock. Chicago: 1928. V. 67

DINGWALL, ERIC
Four Modern Ghosts. London: 1958. V. 64

DINKINS, JAMES
Personal Recollections and Experiences in the Confederate Army. Cincinnati: 1897. V. 62; 63; 65

DINSDALE, FREDERICK P.
A Glossary of Provincial Words Used in Teesdale in the County of Durham. London: 1849. V. 66

DINWIDDIE, ROBERT
The Official Records of Robert Dinwiddie, Lieutenant-Governor of the Colony of Virginia 1751-1758. Richmond: 1883. V. 63; 64

DIODORUS SICULUS
Bibliothecae Historiae.... Lyons: 1552. V. 65
Bibliothecae Historicae Libri Qui Supersunt.... Amstelodami: 1746. V. 65
Historici Clarissimi, Bibliothecae, Seu Rerum Antiquarum Fabulosarum.... Parisiis: 1531. V. 65; 66

DIOGENES *Defictions.* Berkeley: 1994. V. 62

DIOGENES LAERTIUS
The Lives, Opinions and Remarkable Sayings of the Most Famous Ancient Philosophers.... London: 1688-1696. V. 67

DIOMEDI, ALEXANDER
Sketches of Modern Indian Life. Woodstock: 1894. V. 62

DION CASSIUS
Dionis Nicaei Rerum Romanarum...Epitome.... Lugduni: 1559. V. 65; 66
Romanarum Historiarum Libri XXIII, a XXXVI ad LVIII Usque.... Lutetiae (Paris): 1548. V. 66

DIONIS, PIERRE
Cours D'Operations de Chirurgie, De'Montrees au Jardin Royal.... Paris: 1740. V. 64

DIONIS DU SEJOUR, MLLE.
Origine des Graces (and Other Works). Paris: 1777. V. 66

DIONYSIUS CARTHUSIANUS
D. Dionysii A Rickel Carthusiani, Insigne Commentariourm Opus, In Psalmos Omnes Davidicos.... Coloniae: 1531. V. 66

DIONYSIUS LONGINUS
On the Sublime. London: 1739. V. 63

DIONYSIUS OF HALICARNASSUS
Antiquitatum Rom. Libris XI. 1592. V. 67
Antiquitatum Sive Originum Romanum Libri X. Basiliae: 1549. V. 65
Dionysii Halicarnassei Antiquitatum Romanarum. (with) Dionysii Halicarnassei de Compositione, Seu Orationis Partium Apta Inter se Collocatione.... Lutetiae: 1546-1547. V. 65
The Roman Antiquities. London: 1758. V. 67
(Greek title, then:) Scripta, Qvae Extant, Omnia, et Historica, et Rhetorica. Lipsiae: 1691. V. 63

DI PESO, CHARLES C.
Casas Grandes - A Fallen Trading Center of the Gran Chichimeca. Flagstaff: 1974. V. 63; 64; 67
Casas Grandes: a Fallen Trading Center of the Gran Chichimeca. Dragoon: 1974. V. 62

The Reeve Ruin of Southeastern Arizona - A Study of a Prehistoric Western Pueblo Migration into Middle San Pedro Valley. 1958. V. 65
The Reeve Ruin of Southeastern Arizona - a Study of a Prehistoric Western Pueblo Migration into Middle San Pedro Valley. Dragoon: 1958. V. 62
The Sobaipuri Indians of the Upper San Pedro River Valley, Southeastern Arizona. Dragoon: 1953. V. 62

DIPPIE, BRIAN W.
Bards of the Little Big Horn. Bryan: 1978. V. 63
Charles M. Russell, Word Painter: Letters 1887-1926. Fort Worth: 1993. V. 63
Remington and Russell. The Sid Richardson Collection. Austin: 1982. V. 64

DI PRIMA, DIANE
Combination Theatre Poem and Birthday Poem for Ten People. New York: 1965. V. 63
Loba as Eve. New York: 1975. V. 62
Loba. Part II. Pt. Reyes and Kathmandu: 1976. V. 62
Revolutionary Letters. New York: 1968. V. 63

DIRCKS, HENRY
The Life, Times and Scientific Labours of the Second Marquis of Worcester. London: 1865. V. 62
Perpetuum Mobile; or a History of the Search for Self-Motive Power. Amsterdam: 1968. V. 62

DIRCKS, RUDOLF
Sir Christopher Wren A.D. 1632-1723. London: 1923. V. 64; 66

A DIRECTORY for the Publique Worship of God, Throughout the Three Kingdoms of England, Scotland and Ireland. London: 1645. V. 63

DIRECTORY of New Brunswick, also Milltown, South River, Sayreville, South Amboy, Piscataway, Dunhamtown, Metuchen, Raritan River Road, Bound Brook. New Brunswick: 1901. V. 63; 66

DIRECTORY of Newark, for 1835-1836. Newark: 1835. V. 66

A DIRECTORY of Sheffield. Sheffield: 1889. V. 63; 65

DIRECTORY of the City of Newark for 1858-59. Newark. V. 63

DIRINGER, DAVID
The Alphabet. London: 1949. V. 64
The Alphabet. New York: 1968. V. 63
The Illuminated Book, Its History and Production. London: 1958. V. 62

DIRINGSHOFEN, HEINZ VON
Medical Guide for Flying Personnel. Toronto: 1940. V. 63

DIRR, M. A.
Dirr's Hardy Trees and Shrubs, an Illustrated Encyclopedia. Portland: 1997. V. 67

THE DIRTY Child. New York: 1867. V. 64

DISBROW, EDWARD D.
The Man Without a Gun - The Stories of Life in the Dakotas in the Early Nineties. Boston: 1936. V. 66

DISCH, THOMAS M.
Black Alice. London: 1969. V. 63
Camp Concentration. London: 1968. V. 64

DISCOVERY and Declaration. That the Judgement in Behalf of the Fundamental Deliverance of the Poor and Afflicted, the Faithful and Elect, Is Not at All to Begin with the Pope of Rome.... London: 1660. V. 66

A DISERTATION Upon Earthquakes, Their Causes and Consequences. London: 1750. V. 64

DISFARMER, MIKE
Disfarmer 1939-1946 Heber Springs Portraits from the Collections of Peter Miller and Julia Scully. Santa Fe: 1996. V. 63

DISNEY, JOHN
Memoirs of Thomas Brand-Hollis, Esq. F.R.S. and S.A. London: 1808. V. 62; 65
Museum Disneianum.... London: 1849. V. 64

DISNEY, WALT
Bambi Picture Book. USA: 1942. V. 66
The Big Bad Wolf and Little Red Riding Hood. New York: 1934. V. 62
The Cinderella Magic Wand Book. London: 1950. V. 62; 65; 66
The Cold-Blooded Penguin. New York: 1946. V. 62
The Disneyland Ark. London: 1955. V. 62
Donald Duck Has His Ups and Downs. Racine: 1937. V. 62
Donald Duck's Wonder Book. London: Sep. 1950. V. 65
Donald's Lucky Day. Racine: 1939. V. 62
Dumbo of the Circus. Garden City: 1941. V. 62
Father Noah's Ark from the Silly Symphony. London: 1934. V. 62
Ferdinand the Bull. Racine: 1938. V. 62
The Golden Touch. Racine: 1937. V. 62
Hiawatha. Racine: 1938. V. 62
Magic Movie Palette: Christmas Gift for Mickey Mouse. 1937. V. 62
Mickey Mouse Air Pilot. London: 1937. V. 66
Mickey Mouse and His Friends. Racine: 1936. V. 62; 66
Mickey Mouse Annual. London. V. 65; 66
Mickey Mouse Annual. London: 1951. V. 65
Mickey Mouse Annual. London: 1953. V. 66
Mickey Mouse Book. New York: 1930. V. 63
Mickey Mouse Cut Out Doll Book. (Number 980). Akron: 1933. V. 66

DISNEY, WALT continued
Mickey Mouse Has a Busy Day. Racine: 1937. V. 64
Mickey Mouse in King Arthur's Court. New York: 1933. V. 63
Mickey Mouse in Pigmyland. London: 1935. V. 66
Mickey Mouse in Pigmyland. Racine: 1936. V. 62
Mickey Mouse Sky High. London: 1937. V. 62; 66
Mickey Mouse Story Book. Philadelphia: 1931. V. 62
Mickey Mouse the Boat Builder. New York: 1938. V. 62
Mickey Mouse Waddle Book. New York: 1934. V. 62; 66
Mickey Mouse's Musical ABC. Australia: 1937. V. 65
Mickey Sees the U.S.A. Boston: 1944. V. 66
Mickey's Magic Hat Cookie Carnival. Racine: 1937. V. 62
Mickey's Wonder Book. London: Sep. 1950. V. 62
Une Partie de Polo. Partre: 1936. V. 65
Pastoral from Walt Disney's Fantasia. New York: 1940. V. 65
Pinocchio. New York: 1939. V. 62
Pinocchio's Christmas Party. Lancaster: 1939. V. 62
The Pop-Up Mickey Mouse. New York: 1933. V. 62
The Pop-Up Minnie Mouse. New York: 1933. V. 62
Santa's Workshop from the Walt Disney Silly Symphony. London: 1934. V. 65
6 Wee Little Books. Racine: 1934. V. 64
Sketch Book of Snow White and the Seven Dwarfs. London: 1938. V. 65
Snow White and the Seven Dwarfs. Philadelphia: 1937. V. 64
Snow White and the Seven Dwarfs. 1979. V. 66
Snow White Magic-Mirror Book and the Story of Snow white and the Seven Dwarfs. London: 1939. V. 66
The Story of Casey Jr. New York: 1941. V. 62; 66
The Story of Mickey Mouse and the Smugglers. Racine: 1935. V. 67
The Three Orphan Kittens. London: 1936. V. 66
Walt Disney Presents a Mickey Mouse ABC. Sydney: 1938. V. 65
Walt Disney Presents Twelve New Illustrations. 1950. V. 62
Walt Disney's Brave Little Tailor Paint and Crayon Book. Racine: 1938. V. 62
Walt Disney's Dumbo. New York: 1947. V. 64
Walt Disney's Famous Seven Dwarfs. Racine: 1938. V. 62
Walt Disney's Forest Friends from Snow White. New York: 1938. V. 64
Walt Disney's Mickey Mouse. Hollywood: 1937. V. 64
Walt Disney's Silly Symphony Annual. London: 1937. V. 65
Walt Disney's the Practical Pig. Garden City: 1940. V. 64
Walt Disney's Tiny Movie Stories. New York: 1950. V. 64; 66

DISORDERLY Girl. New York: 1865. V. 64

DISPENSER'S Formulary or Soda Water Guide. New York: 1915. V. 63; 66

DISRAELI, BENJAMIN
The Bradenham Edition of the Novels and Tales. 1926-1927. V. 67
Coningsby. London: 1849. V. 66
Endymion. London: 1880. V. 63; 64; 65; 66
England and Denmark. Speech of Mr. Disraeli in the House of Commons the 19th April, 1848, on the Danish Question. London: 1848. V. 64
England and France; or, a Cure for the Ministerial Gallomania. London: 1832. V. 64; 65
The Infernal Marriage. London: 1929. V. 67
The Letters of Runnymede. London: 1836. V. 64; 67
Lord Beaconsfield on the Constitution. London: 1884. V. 64
Lord George Bentinck; a Political Biography. London: 1852. V. 62; 63; 64
Lothair. London: 1850. V. 66
Lothair. London: 1870. V. 66
The Novels and Tales. London: 1890. V. 62
Parliamentary Reform. London: 1867. V. 64
Rumpal Stilts Kin. London: 1952. V. 64
Selected Speeches of the Late...Earl of Beaconsfield.... London: 1882. V. 64
Sybil; or, the Two Nations. London: 1845. V. 66
Tancred or the New Crusade. London: 1850. V. 66
Venetia. London: 1877. V. 67
Vindication of the English Constitution in a Letter to a Noble and Learned Lord. London: 1835. V. 67
The Voyage of Captain Popanilla. Philadelphia: 1828. V. 64; 65
The Young Duke. London: 1831. V. 63; 64

D'ISRAELI, ISAAC
The Calamities and Quarrels of Authors.... London: 1859. V. 65
Curiosities of Literature. London: 1834. V. 65
Curiosities of Literature. London: 1838. V. 64
Curiosities of Literature. London: 1859. V. 65
Curiosities of Literature. Cambridge: 1864. V. 63
Curiosities of Literature. (with) Amenities of Literature.... London: 1881. V. 62
The Invention of Printing (with) the First English Printer. Cincinnati: 1942. V. 62
The Literary Character; or the History of Men of Genius.... London: 1828. V. 64
Miscellanies of Literature. London: 1840. V. 65
Miscellanies of Literature. Paris: 1840. V. 65
Narrative Poems. London: 1803. V. 65
Works. London: 1859-1862. V. 62; 66

DISSERTATIONS by Eminent Members of the Royal Medical Society (of Edinburgh). Edinburgh: 1892. V. 62; 66

DISTRICT OF COLUMBIA
Letter from the President of the Board of Commissioners of the District of Columbia. Washington: 1908. V. 65

DISTRICT OF COLUMBIA PAPER MANUFACTURING CO.
Designs and Typography for Cover Papers. Washington: 1924. V. 62; 63; 64

DISTURNELL, J.
Influence of Climate in North and South America.... New York: 1867. V. 62

DITCHFIELD, P. H.
Vanishing England. London: 1910. V. 64

THE DIVINE Life; or, Christ Within Us. A Sermon on Rom. VIII. 6. To Be Carnally Minded in Death, but to be Spiritually Minded is Life and Peace. London: 1739. V. 64

THE DIVINE Right of Kings to Govern Wrong. London: 1821. V. 62

DIX, D. L.
Memorial to the Legislature of Massachusetts. Boston: 1843. V. 62; 64

DIX, DOROTHEA
Conversations on Common Things; or, Guide to Knowledge. Boston: 1841. V. 66

DIX, JOHN
The Life of Thomas Chatterton, Including His Unpublished Poems and Correspondence. London: 1837. V. 62; 67

DIX, JOHN A.
A Winter in Madeira & a Summer in Spain and Florence. New York: 1850. V. 65

DIX, JOHN HOMER
Treatise on Strabismus, or Squinting and the New Mode of Treatment. Boston: 1841. V. 63

DIX, THOMAS
A Treatise on Land-Surveying in Six Parts. London: 1799. V. 64

DIX, WILLIAM SPICER
Remarks on the Utility of a New-Invented Patent Machine for Clearing Grain from the Straw, Instead of Threshing It with the Flail. London: 1797. V. 66

DIXEY, ANNIE COATH
The Lion Dog of Peking. London: 1967. V. 67

DIXIE, FLORENCE
Across Patagonia. London: 1880. V. 65

DIXON, C.
The Game Birds and Wild Fowl of the British Islands. Sheffield: 1900. V. 67

DIXON, FRANKLIN W.
The Phantom Freighter. New York: 1947. V. 66
The Secret of Skull Mountain. New York: 1948. V. 66
The Secret Panel. New York: 1946. V. 66
The Sign of the Crooked Arrow. New York: 1949. V. 66

DIXON, FREDERICK
The Geology and Fossils of the Teritary and Cretaceous Formations of Sussex. London: 1850. V. 64; 65
The Geology of Sussex; or the Geology and Fossils of the Tertiary and Cretaceous Formations of Sussex. Brighton: 1878. V. 64; 65

DIXON, GEORGE
Voyage Autour du Monde: et Principalement a La Cote Nord-Ouest de l'Amerique. Paris: 1789. V. 63
A Voyage Round the World; but More Particularly to the North-West Coast of America; Performed in 1785, 1786, 1787 and 1788. London: 1789. V. 63

DIXON, H. H.
Saddle and Sirloin or English Farm and Sporting Worthies (Part North). London: 1870. V. 67
Silk and Scarlet. London: 1859. V. 62

DIXON, J. H.
Chronicles and Stories of the Craven Dales. London: 1881. V. 65

DIXON, J. M.
Kangaroos. London: 1973. V. 62

DIXON, JOSEPH K.
The Vanishing Race - the Last Great Indian Council. Philadelphia: 1914. V. 65

DIXON, JOSHUA
The Literary Life of William Brownrigg, M.D., F.R.S.... London: 1801. V. 66

DIXON, MAYNARD
Maynard Dixon Sketchbook. Flagstaff: 1967. V. 64

DIXON, MICHAEL M.
Life at the Flats. Detroit: 1987. V. 66

DIXON, MYLES C.
Sketch of an Extemporaneous Discourse, on West Indian Slavery.... Barnard Castle: 1834. V. 62

DIXON, ROBERT
The Stone Wall Book of Short Fictions. Iowa City: 1973. V. 67
A Treatise on Heat. Part I. The Thermometer: Dilation; Change of State; and Laws of Vapours. Dublin: 1849. V. 65

DIXON, ROBERT HEPWORTH
Robert Blake, Admiral and General at Sea. London: 1889. V. 66

DIXON, SAM HOUSTON
Romance and Tragedy of Texas History. Houston: 1924. V. 66; 67

DIXON, STEPHEN
14 Stories. Baltimore: 1980. V. 67
Quite Contrary. The Mary and Newt Story. New York: 1979. V. 67
Too Late. New York: 1978. V. 67

DIXON, THOMAS
The Clansman. New York: 1905. V. 64; 67
Leopard Spots. New York: 1903. V. 62

DIXON, WILLIAM GRAY
The Land of the Morning; an Account of Japan and Its People, Based on Four Years' Residence in that Country. Edinburgh: 1882. V. 64

DIXON, WILLIAM HEPWORTH
Diana, Lady Lyle. London: 1877. V. 66
Free Russia. London: 1870. V. 66
New America. London: 1867. V. 63; 66
Spiritual Wives. London: 1868. V. 63

DIXON, WILLIAM SCARTH
Fox Hunting in the Twentieth Century. London: 1925. V. 67
Hunting in the Olden Days. London: 1912. V. 64
In the North Countree. London: 1889. V. 64; 65

DJILAS, M.
Rise and Fall. New York: 1985. V. 63
Wartime. London: 1977. V. 63

DOANE, A. SIDNEY
Surgery Illustrated. New York: 1836. V. 63

DOANE, ISAIAH
Address of the Louisiana Native American Association, to the Citizens of Louisiana and the Inhabitants of the United States. New York: 1839. V. 66

DOBB, MAURICE
Welfare Economics and the Economics of Socialism. Cambridge: 1969. V. 65

DOBBS, ARTHUR
An Essay on the Trade and Improvement of Ireland. (with) An Essay on the Trade of Ireland. Part II. Dublin;: 1721-1731. V. 62

DOBBS, CAROLINE
Men of Champoeg. A Record of the Lives of the Pioneers Who Founded the Oregon Government. Portland: 1932. V. 64; 67

DOBBS, MICHAEL
Last Man to Die. London: 1991. V. 66

DOBELL, CLIFFORD
Antony van Leeuwenhoek and His Little Animals. New York: 1958. V. 62; 66

DOBELL, PETER
Travels in Kamchatka and Siberia; with a Narrative of a Residence in China. London: 1830. V. 67

DOBIE, JAMES FRANK
Apache Gold and Yaqui Silver. Boston: 1939. V. 65
Carl Sandburg and Saint Peter at the Gate. Austin: 1966. V. 65
Coronado's Children - Tales of the Lost Miner and Buried Treasure in the Southwest. Dallas: 1930. V. 64; 65
The Flavor of Texas. Dallas: 1936. V. 64; 67
Guide to Life and Literature of the Southwest with a Few Observations. Austin: 1943. V. 66
John C. Duval - First Texas Man of Letters. Dallas: 1939. V. 66
The Mustangs. Boston: 1952. V. 64
Mustangs and Cow Horses. Austin: 1940. V. 65
My Salute to Gene Rhodes. El Paso: 1947. V. 66
Pony Tracks. Norman: 1961. V. 64
The Seven Mustangs. Austin: 1948. V. 65
Southwestern Lore. Dallas: 1931. V. 63; 66
Texan Stomping Grounds. Austin: 1941. V. 64; 67

DOBIE, JOHN
John Dobie's Journal and Letters from the Mines 1851-1865. Denver: 1962. V. 66

DOBIE, ROWLAND
The History of the United Parishes of St. Giles in the Field. London: 1829. V. 62

DOBLIN, ALFRED
Die Ermordung Einer Butterblume und Anderer Erzahlungen. Munich: 1913. V. 67

DOBREZENSKY, JOACOBUS JOANNES WENCESLAUS
Nova, et Amaenior de Admirando Fontium Genio (ex Abditis Naturae Claustris in orbis Lucem Emanante) Philosophia.... Ferrara: 1659. V. 65

DOBSON, AUSTIN
The Ballad of Beau Brocade, and Other Poems of the XVIIIth Century. London: 1892. V. 62; 67
Eighteenth Century Vignettes. London: 1892. V. 62
Eighteenth Century Vignettes. (and) Eighteenth Century Vignettes. Second Series. London: 1892-1894. V. 62; 67
Four Frenchwomen.... New York: 1891. V. 66
Poems on Several Occasions. London: 1895. V. 64
Proverbs in Porcelain. London: 1877. V. 65
Proverbs in Porcelain. London: 1893. V. 63; 67

DOBSON, EDWARD
The Rudiments of Masonry and Stonecutting. London: 1873. V. 64

DOBSON, G.
On the Pteropiae of India and Its Islands. Calcutta: 1873. V. 67
Russia. London: 1913. V. 65
St. Petersburg. London: 1910. V. 65

DOBSON, MATTHEW
A Medical Commentary on Fixed Air.... London: 1787. V. 65

DOBSON, ROSEMARY
The Continuance of Poetry - Twelve Poems for David Campbell. Canberra: 1981. V. 62

DOBYNS, HENRY
Hepah California! the Journal of Cave Couts. Tucson: 1961. V. 63

DOBYNS, STEPHEN
Black Dog, Red Dog. Poems. New York: 1984. V. 63
Concurring Beasts. New York: 1971. V. 67
Concurring Beasts. New York: 1972. V. 63; 67

DOCKRILL, A. W.
Australian Indigenous Orchids. 1969. V. 67

DOCKSTADER, FREDERICK J.
Indian Art in America. Greenwich. V. 67

DR. S-----'s Real Diary; Being a True and Faithful Account of Himself, for that Week Wherein He is Traduc'd by the author of a Scandalous and Malicious Hue and Cry....* London: 1757. V. 66

DOCTOROW, E. L.
American Anthem. New York: 1982. V. 62
Billy Bathgate. Franklin Center: 1989. V. 63
Billy Bathgate. New York: 1989. V. 62; 67
The Book of Daniel. New York: 1971. V. 67
Jack London, Hemingway and the Constitution. New York: 1993. V. 67
Lives of the Poets. New York: 1984. V. 67
Loon Lake. New York: 1980. V. 63; 67
Ragtime. New York: 1975. V. 65; 67
The Waterworks. New York: 1994. V. 63
World's Fair. New York: 1985. V. 67

DOCUMENTARY
History of Banking and Currency in the United States. New York: 1983. V. 67

DOCUMENTS
Sur Les Falsifications des Matieres Alimentaires. Paris: 1882. V. 64

DOD, WILLIAM ARMSTRONG
History of the College of New Jersey, From Its Commencement, A.D. 1746 to 1783. Princeton: 1844. V. 66

DODD, BETHUEL L.
Genealogies of the Male Descendants of Daniel Dod, of Branford, Conn.,a Nature of England, 1646 to 1863. Newark: 1864. V. 63; 66

DODD, CHARLES
The Church History of England, from the Year 1500, to the Year 1688.... Brussels: 1737-1742. V. 62

DODD, DAVID O.
Letters of David O. Dodd. N.P: 1917. V. 63; 65

DODD, EPHRAIM SHELBY
Diary of Ephraim Shelby Dodd. Member of Company D, Terry's Texas Rangers, December 4 1862 - January 1, 1864. Austin: 1914. V. 62; 63; 65

DODD, GEORGE
The Textile Manufactures of Great Britain. London: 1851. V. 63

DODD, STEPHEN
An Historical and Topographical Account of the Town of Woburn, Its Abbey and Vicinity.... Woburn: 1818. V. 64; 66
History and Description of Woburn and Its Abbey. Woburn: 1845. V. 64

DODD, WILLIAM
The Beauties of History; or, Pictures of Virtue and Vice.... London: 1796. V. 67
The Laboring Classes of England, Especially Those Engaged in Agriculture and Manufactures; in a Series of Letters. Boston: 1847. V. 62; 65
Poems by Dr. Dodd. London: 1767. V. 63

DODDERIDGE, JOHN
The Lavves Resolvtions of Womens Rights; or, the Lavves Provision for Women. London: 1632. V. 65

DODDINGTON, GEORGE BUBB
The Diary of.... Salisbury: 1784. V. 64

DODDRIDGE, JOHN
An Historical Account of the Antient and Modern State of the Principality of Wales, Dutchy of Cornwall and Earldom of Chester.... London: 1714. V. 62

DODDRIDGE, JOSEPH
Notes on the Settlement and Indian Wars. Pittsburgh: 1912. V. 66

DODDRIDGE, P.
Some Remarkable Passages in the Life of the Honourable Col. James Gardiner.... London: 1748. V. 62; 63; 66

DODGE, GRENVILLE M.
The Battle of Atlanta and Other Campaign Addresses, etc. Council Bluffs: 1911. V. 67

DODGE, GRENVILLE M. continued
Biographical Sketch of James Bridger, Mountaineer, Trapper and Guide. Kansas City: 1904. V. 66
Fiftieth Anniversary of the Fourth Iowa Veteran Infantry, Dodge's Second Iowa Battery, Dodge's Band as Guests.... Council Bluffs: 1911. V. 65
General Dodge's Paper on the Transcontinental - Paper Read Before the Society of the Army of the Tennessee at the Twenty-First Annual Reunion at Toledo, O. Sept. 15, 1888. Together with Comments There on By Gen. Wm. T. Sherman. New York: 1899. V. 66
Indian Campaigns of the Winter of 1865-1865. Denver: 1907. V. 65; 67

DODGE, H.
A Historical Review of the Mollusks of Linnaeus. New York: 1952-1959. V. 65

DODGE, J. R.
West Virginia: Its Farms and Forests, Mines and Oil Wells. Philadelphia: 1865. V. 66

DODGE, ORVIL
Pioneer History of Coos and Curry Counties. Salem: 1898. V. 67

DODGE, RICHARD I.
The Black Hills. New York: 1876. V. 62; 65; 66
The Hunting Grounds of the Great West - a Description of the Plains, Game and Indians of the Great North American Desert. London: 1877. V. 65; 67
Our Wild Indians: Thirty Five Years Personal Experience Among the Red Men of the Great West. Hartford: 1882. V. 65
Our Wild Indians: Thirty Three Years Personal Experience Among the Red Men of the Great West. Hartford: 1886. V. 67

DODGE, THEODORE AYRAULT
Riders of Many Lands. New York: 1894. V. 64; 67

DODGSON, CAMPBELL
An Iconography of the Engravings of Stephen Gooden. London: 1944. V. 62
Old French Colour-Prints. London: 1924. V. 64

DODGSON, CHARLES LUTWIDGE
Alice au Pays des Merveilles. Liege: 1930. V. 65
Alice au Pays des Merveilles. Paris: 1939. V. 64
Alice au Pays des Merveilles and Alice a Travers le Miroir. Paris: 1948. V. 66
Alice I Underlandet. Stockholm: 1966. V. 65
Alice in Wonderland. London. V. 67
Alice in Wonderland. London: 1917. V. 66
Alice in Wonderland. Germany: 1922. V. 66
Alice in Wonderland. London: 1923. V. 62
Alice in Wonderland. Wien: 1923. V. 65
Alice in Wonderland. Paris: 1930. V. 63
Alice In Wonderland. London: 1932. V. 64
Alice in Wonderland. 1943. V. 67
Alice in Wonderland. London: 1948. V. 62
Alice in Wonderland. N.P: 1950. V. 64
Alice in Wonderland. London: 1960. V. 64
Alice in Wonderland. London: 1965. V. 65
Alice in Wonderland. Bologna: 1969. V. 64
Alice in Wonderland. London: 1969. V. 62
Alice in Wonderland and Through the Looking Glass. London: 1934. V. 65
Alice in Wonderland and Through the Looking Glass. Cleveland and New York: 1935. V. 62
Alice in Wonderland and Through the Looking Glass. Stockholm: 1945. V. 66
Alice in Wonderland and Through the Looking Glass. London: 1960. V. 65
Alices Abenteuer im Wunderland. Stuttgart. V. 62
Alice's Adventure in Wonderland and Through the Looking Glass and What Alice Found There. New York: 1932-1935. V. 65
Alice's Adventures in Wonderland. New York: 1866. V. 64
Alice's Adventures in Wonderland. Boston: 1869. V. 64; 65
Alice's Adventures in Wonderland. Boston: 1872. V. 62
Alice's Adventures in Wonderland. New York: 1900. V. 62
Alice's Adventures in Wonderland. London: 1901. V. 62
Alice's Adventures in Wonderland. London: 1907. V. 62; 65
Alice's Adventures in Wonderland. New York: 1907. V. 62; 66
Alice's Adventures in Wonderland. London: 1913. V. 62; 65
Alice's Adventures in Wonderland. London: 1914. V. 62; 64; 65
Alice's Adventures in Wonderland. London: 1915. V. 66
Alice's Adventures in Wonderland. London: 1916. V. 64; 66
Alice's Adventures in Wonderland. New York: 1917. V. 65
Alice's Adventures in Wonderland. London: 1919. V. 62
Alice's Adventures in Wonderland. London: 1922. V. 62; 65; 66
Alice's Adventures in Wonderland. Philadelphia: 1926. V. 66
Alice's Adventures in Wonderland. New York: 1929. V. 64
Alice's Adventures in Wonderland. New York: 1932. V. 64
Alice's Adventures in Wonderland. New York?: 1940. V. 62
Alice's Adventures in Wonderland. New York: 1969. V. 62; 66
Alice's Adventures in Wonderland and Through the Looking Glass. New York: 1900. V. 62
Alice's Adventures in Wonderland and Through the Looking Glass. Chicago and New York: 1916. V. 66
Alice's Adventures in Wonderland and Through the Looking Glass. New York: 1934. V. 65
Alice's Adventures in Wonderland and Through the Looking Glass. Racine: 1945. V. 62
Alice's Adventures in Wonderland and Through the Looking Glass. Stockholm and London: 1946. V. 62; 64
Alice's Adventures in Wonderland and Through the Looking Glass. London: 1954. V. 62; 65
Alice's Adventures in Wonderland. and Through the Looking Glass. London: 1993. V. 67
Alice's Adventures in Wonderland. (and) Through the Looking-Glass. Sydney: 1943. V. 64
Alice's Adventures in Wonderland. (and) Through the Looking-Glass and What Alice Found There. London: 1867-1872. V. 63
Alice's Adventures in Wonderland. (with) Through the Looking Glass. New York: 1902. V. 64
Alice's Adventures in Wonderland. (with) Through the Looking Glass. West Hatfield: 1982. V. 62
Alice's Adventures Under Ground.... London: 1886. V. 62; 63; 65
Alices Aventyr I Sagolandet. Stockholm: 1945. V. 62
Alicia in Terra Mirabili - Liber Notissimus Primum Abhinc Annis Centum Editus. London: 1964. V. 63
Aventures d'Alice au Pays de Merveilles. London: 1869. V. 66
Le Avventure D'Alice nel Paese Delle Meraviglie. Londra: 1872. V. 62
The Children's Alice. London: 1949. V. 65
The Complete Alice and The Hunting of the Snark. Topsfield: 1987. V. 63
La Chasse au Snark. Chapelle-Reanville: 1929. V. 62
Curiosa Mathematica. Part I. Part II. London: 1888-1893. V. 63; 65; 67
Feeding the Mind. London: 1907. V. 67
The Game of Logic. London: 1887. V. 62; 65
The Hunting of the Snark. London: 1876. V. 62; 63; 66
The Hunting of the Snark. London: 1898. V. 63
The Hunting of the Snark. London: 1910. V. 63
The Hunting of the Snark. Andoversford: 1975. V. 63; 65
The Hunting of the Snark. London: 1975. V. 62; 63
Lewis Carroll: Electa Editrice Portfolios. Milan: 1982. V. 65
The Lewis Carroll Picture Book. London: 1899. V. 64; 65
Logical Nonsense: the Works of Lewis Carroll. New York: 1934. V. 63; 64
The New Belfry of Christ Church, Oxford. Oxford: 1872. V. 63; 66
The Nursery Alice. London: 1890. V. 66
The Nursery Alice. London: 1891. V. 66
Phantasmagoria and Other Poems. London: 1869. V. 66
Rhyme? and Reason?. London: 1883. V. 63
Songs from Alice in Wonderland and Through the Looking Glass. London: 1921. V. 62
Sylvie and Bruno Concluded. London: 1893. V. 62; 64; 65; 67
Sylvie and Bruno. Syvlie and Bruno Concluded. London: 1899. V. 63
Three Sunsets and Other Poems.... London: 1898. V. 62
Through the Looking Glass. New York and London: 1902. V. 62
Through the Looking Glass. New York: 1905. V. 62
Through the Looking Glass and What Alice Found There. London: 1871. V. 63
Through the Looking Glass and What Alice Found There. London: 1872. V. 63; 65
Through the Looking Glass and What Alice Found There. New York: 1909. V. 65; 66
Through the Looking-Glass and What Alice Found There. West Hatfield: 1982. V. 66; 67
Useful and Instructive Poetry. London: 1954. V. 63

DODINGTON, GEORGE BUBB
The Diary of the Late George Bubb Dodington,.... Salisbury: 1784. V. 62; 62; 63; 66

DODOENS, REMBERT
Medicinalium Observationum Exempla Rara, Recognita & Aucta. Cologne: 1851. V. 62
A New Herball or Historie of Plants. 1595. V. 63; 65
A Niewe Herball, or Historie of Plantes.... London: 1578. V. 64
Stirpium Historiae Pemptades Sex. Antwerp: 1583. V. 64
Stirpium Historiae Pemptades Sex, Sive Libri XXX. Antwerp: 1616. V. 62

DODS, MARGARET
The Cook and Housewife's Manual: a Practical System of Modern Domestic Cookery and Family Management. Edinburgh: 1829. V. 67

DOD'S Peerage, Baronetage and Knightage of Great Britain and Ireland. 1904. V. 63

DODSLEY, ROBERT
The Art of Preaching. London: 1738. V. 63
The Chronicle of the Kings of England, from the Norman Conquest Unto the Present Time. Birmingham: 1777?. V. 64
A Collection of Poems, by Several Hands. London: 1748-1758. V. 65
A Collection of Poems by Several Hands. London: 1763. V. 67
A Collection of Poems in Four Volumes by Several Hands. London: 1783. V. 64
A Collection of Poems in Six Volumes. London: 1775. V. 67
A Collection of Poems in Six Volumes. London: 1782. V. 62; 66
A Collection of Poems in Six Volumes. London: 1782. V. 67
The Economy of Human Life. Manchester: 1797. V. 62; 65
Fugitive Pieces on Various Subjects. London: 1761. V. 65
The King and the Miller of Mansfield. London: 1738. V. 65
The Oeconomy of Human Life. Burlington: 1771. V. 66
Select Fables of Esop and Other Fabulists. London: 1776. V. 62

DODSON, C. H.
The Biology of Orchids. N.P: 1967. V. 67
Icones Plantarum Tropicarum. Series II. St. Louis: 1989. V. 64

DODWORTH, CHARLES R.
Gideons Band. Philadelphia: 1861. V. 63

DOE, JANET
A Bibliography of the Works of Ambroise Pare.... Chicago: 1937. V. 64; 66

DOERR, HARRIET
Consider This, Senora. New York: 1993. V. 64
Stones for Ibarra. New York: 1984. V. 64; 67

DOGEN, MATTHIAS
Architectura Militaris Moderna. Amstelodami: 1647. V. 63; 66

DOGGETT, MARGUERITE
Long Island Printing 1791-1830, a Checklist of Imprints. Brooklyn: 1979. V. 63

DOGGETT'S New York City Directory for 1850-1851. New York: 1850. V. 63

THE DOGS' Grand Dinner Party. London: 1855. V. 66

DOHENY, ESTELLE
The Estelle Doheny Collection. New York: 1987-1989. V. 62; 63; 64; 67

DOIG, IVAN
Bucking the Sun. New York: 1996. V. 67
Dancing at the Rascal Fair. New York. V. 67
English Creek. New York: 1984. V. 63; 64; 67
The Sea Runners. New York: 1982. V. 64
This House of Sky. New York: 1978. V. 62; 63; 64; 66; 67
This House of Sky. New York: 1992. V. 67
Winter Brothers. New York: 1980. V. 62; 64; 67

THE DOINGS of the Alphabet. New York. V. 63

DOISSIN, LUDOVICO
Scalptura Carmen. Milan: 1777. V. 64

DOKE, CLEMENT M.
The Lambas of Northern Rhodesia, a Study of Their Customs and Beliefs. London: 1931. V. 64

DOLBY, J.
Six Views of Eton College. Eton: 1838. V. 62; 66

DOLBY, THOMAS
The Shakespearian Dictionary.... London: 1832. V. 62

DOLCE, LUDOVICO
Aretino: a Dialogue on Painting. London: 1770. V. 66

DOLE, NATHAN HASKELL
America In Spitsbergen: the Romance of an Arctic Coal-Mine With an Introduction Relating the History and Describing the Land and the Flora and Fauna of Spitsbergen. Boston: 1922. V. 62; 63; 64

DOLLAR, ROBERT
Private Diary of Robert Dollar on His Recent Visits to China. London: 1847. V. 66

DOLLMAN, J. G.
Rowland Ward's Records of Big Game with Their Distribution, Characteristics, Dimensions, Weights and Horn and Tusk Measurements. London: 1928. V. 67

DOLLYLAND ABC. London: 1890. V. 64

DOLMEN PRESS
Six Prospectuses. Dublin: 1954-1978. V. 65

DOLMETSCH, H.
Der Ornamentenschatz, ein Musterbuch Stilvoller Ornamente aus Allen Kunstepochen. Stuttgart: 1889. V. 66

THE DOLPHIN: a Journal of the Making of Books. New York: 1933-1941. V. 64
THE DOLPHIN: a Journal of the Making of Books. New York: 1935. V. 63; 64

THE DOLPHIN: a Periodical For All People Who Find Pleasure in Fine Books. Parts I, II and III. New York: 1940. V. 62; 63, 64

DOMAN, HENRY
Songs in Shade. London: 1881. V. 63

THE DOME: A Quarterly Containing Examples of All the Arts. London: 1897-1898. V. 64

DOMENECH, E.
Missionary Adventures in Texas and Mexico, a Personal Narrative of Six Years' Sojourn in Those Regions. London: 1858. V. 64
Seven Years' Residence in the Great Deserts of North America. London: 1860. V. 62; 64

DOMESTIC Anecdotes of the French Nation, During the Last Thirty Years. London: 1794. V. 63

DOMINGUEZ, FRANCISCO ATANASIO
The Missions of New Mexico, 1776. Albuquerque: 1956. V. 63
The Missions of New Mexico, 1776. Albuquerque: 1975. V. 66

DOMINO, JOHN
The Fable of a Proud Poppy. Paris: 1934. V. 66

DOMJAN, J.
Thirty-Two Coloured Woodcuts. Budapest: 1956. V. 64

DOMMETT, W. ERSKINE
A Dictionary of Aircraft. London: 1918. V. 63

DOMVILLE, ERIC
A Concordance of the Plays of W. B. Yeats. Cornell: 1972. V. 64

DOMVILLE-FIFE, CHARLES W.
Submarines, Mines and Torpedoes in the War. London: 1914. V. 64

DONAGHY, LYLE
Into the Light, and Other Poems. Dublin: 1934. V. 64

DONAHEY, MARY DICKERSON
Down Spider Web Lane. New York: 1909. V. 62; 67

DONAHEY, WILLIAM
Alice and the Teenie Weenies. Chicago: 1927. V. 62
Monarch Teenie Weenie Sweets. Chicago: 1926. V. 62
Teenie Weenie Neighbors. New York: 1945. V. 62
Teenie Weenie Town. New York: 1942. V. 62; 66

DONAHUE, L. O
Encyclopedia of Batik Designs. East Brunswick: 1982. V. 62

DONALD, DAVID HERBERT
Lincoln at Home: Two Glimpses of Abraham Lincoln's Domestic Life. New York: 1999. V. 64

DONALD, JAY
Outlaws of the Border: a Complete and Authentic History of the Lives of Frank and Jesse James, The Younger Brothers and Their Robber Companions.... Cincinnati: 1882. V. 64; 67

DONALDSON, D. J.
Cajun Nights. New York: 1988. V. 65; 66

DONALDSON, FLORENCE
Lepcha Land or Six Weeks in the Sikhim Himalayas. London: 1900. V. 62; 66

DONALDSON, M. E. M.
Further Wanderings - Mainly in Argyll Recounting Highland History, Traditions, Ecclesiology, Archaeology, Romance, Present Conditions.... Paisley: 1926. V. 62; 63
Wanderings in the Western Highlands and Islands. Paisley: 1920. V. 62; 63

DONALDSON, NORMAN
In Search of Dr. Thorndyke. Bowling Green: 1971. V. 67

DONALDSON, STEPHEN
Forbidden Knowledge. New York: 1991. V. 64
The Gap Into Conflict: the Real Story. New York: 1991. V. 63

DONALDSON, THOMAS
The George Catlin Indian Gallery in the U.S. National Museum (Smithsonian Institution) with Memoir and Statistics. Washington: 1885. V. 66
Idaho of Yesterday. Caldwell: 1941. V. 64; 67
Indians the Six Nations of New York - Cayugas, Mohawks (Saint Regis), Oneidas, Onondagas, Senecas, Tuscaroras. Washington: 1892. V. 65
The Public Domain: Its History, With Statistics. Washington: 1884. V. 64

DONALDSON, WILLIAM
The Further Letters of Henry Root. London: 1980. V. 67

DONATO, MARCELLO
De Medica Historia Mirabili Libri Sex. Mantua: 1586. V. 62

DONDERS, F. C.
On the Anomalies Accomodation and Refraction of the Eye. London: 1864. V. 63; 67
On the Pathologeny of the Squint.... Dublin: 1864. V. 67

DONLEAVY, J. P.
The Beastly Beatitudes of Balthazar. New York: 1968. V. 67
The Ginger Man. Paris: 1955. V. 62; 63; 64; 66
The Ginger Man. Paris: 1958. V. 63; 66
The Ginger Man. Franklin Center: 1978. V. 63
The Lady Who Liked Clean Rest Rooms. New York: 1997. V. 62; 64
Shultz. New York: 1979. V. 67
A Singular Man. Boston: 1963. V. 67
A Singular Man. London: 1965. V. 62

DONN, J.
Hortus Cantabrigiensis; or an Accented Catalogue of Indigenous and Exotic Plants Cultivated in the Cambridge Botanic Garden. 1845. V. 67

DONNE, JOHN
An Anatomie of the World.... Shaftesbury: 1929. V. 63
A Defence of Women for Their Inconstancy & Their Paintings Made by Jack Donne.... London: 1930. V. 67
Donne's Sermon of Valediction at His Going Into Germany Preached at Lincoln's Inn, April 18, 1619. London: 1932. V. 63
Essays in Divinity. London: 1855. V. 63
The First Anniversarie. (with) The Second Anniversarie. London: 1926. V. 66
Ignatius His Conclave; or, His Inthronisation in a Late Election in Hell. London: 1635. V. 64
The Love Poems. Boston: 1905. V. 65
Love Poems. London: 1923. V. 63
Mud Walls. Excerpts from Sermons. Wakefield: 1986. V. 65
Paradoxes and Problemes. London: 1923. V. 67
Poems by J.D. with Elegies on the Authors Death. London: 1639. V. 63
The Poems of John Donne, From the Old Editions and Numerous Manuscripts. London: 1963. V. 66
A Sermon of Valediction at His Going into Germany...1619. London: 1932. V. 62; 67
X Sermons. London: 1923. V. 62; 64; 65

DONNE, T. E.
Red Deer Stalking in New Zealand. 1924. V. 62; 63; 64; 66
Rod Fishing in New Zealand Waters. London: 1927. V. 67

DONNELL, ROBERT
Thoughts on Various Subjects. Louisville: 1856. V. 65

DONNELLY, C. SHIRLEY
Historical Notes on Fayette Co., West Virginia. 1958. V. 66

DONNELLY, MONA
Chinese Junks and Other Native Craft. London: 1930. V. 62

DONNER HOUGHTON, ELIZA P.
The Expedition of the Donnor Party and its Tragic Fate. Los Angeles: 1920. V. 63

DONNISON, T. E.
The Jaw-Cracking Jingles. London: 1900. V. 64

DONOGHUE, STEPHEN
Just My Story. London: 1923. V. 63

DONOSO, JOSE
El Charleston. Santiago: 1960. V. 62
Charleston and Other Stories. Boston: 1977. V. 62
Coronacion. Santiago: 1957. V. 67
The Obscene Bird of Night. New York: 1973. V. 62
Tres Novelitas Burguesas. Barcelona: 1973. V. 62
Veraneo y Otros Cuentos. Santiago: 1955. V. 67

DONOVAN, DANIEL
Sketches in Carbery, County Cork. its Antiquities History, Legends and Topography. London: 1876. V. 66

DONOVAN, DICK
The Chronicles of Danevitch of the Russian Secret Service. London: 1897. V. 62; 65
In the Face of Night. London: 1908. V. 65
Young Lochinvar; a Tale of the Border Country. London: 1896. V. 67

DONOVAN, E.
The Natural History of British Fishes. London: 1802-1808. V. 62
The Natural History of British Shells. 1799-1803. V. 66
Natural History of the Insects of India. London: 1842. V. 64
The Naturalist's Repository. London: 1822-1834. V. 62

DONOVAN, MICHAEL
Domestic Economy. London: 1830-1845. V. 64
A Treatise on Chemistry. London: 1832. V. 67

DONOVAN, MIKE
The Science of Boxing Also Rules and Articles on Training Generalship in the Ring and Kindred Subjects. New York: 1893. V. 67

DOOIJES, D.
A History of the Dutch Poster, 1890-1960. Amsterdam: 1968. V. 65

DOOLAN, DENNIS
Crosshill Execution. The Life and Behaviour Since Condemnation, of Dennis Doolan and Patrick Redding.... Glasgow: 1842. V. 63

DOOLEY, JAMES H., MRS.
Dem Good Ole Times. New York: 1906. V. 63

DOOLING, RICHARD
White Man's Grave. New York: 1994. V. 67

DOOLITTLE, HILDA
Collected Poems of H.D. New York: 1925. V. 63
Hedylus. Boston: 1928. V. 66
Hedylus. Oxford: 1928. V. 66
Heliodora and Other Poems. London: 1924. V. 65
Kora and Ka. Dijon: 1930. V. 64
Kora and Ka. Paris: 1934. V. 62
Nights. Dijon: 1935. V. 64
Priest and A Dead Priestess Speaks. Port Townsend: 1983. V. 63
Red Roses for Bronze. New York: 1929. V. 63
Red Roses for Bronze. London: 1931. V. 62; 64
2 Poems by H.D. Berkeley: 1971. V. 63
The Usual Star. London: 1928. V. 64
What Do I Love?. London. V. 64
Within the Walls. Iowa City: 1993. V. 62; 64

DOORLY, ELEANOR
The Insect Man. 1946. V. 67

DOORLY, GERALD S.
The Voyages of the Morning. Banham: 1996. V. 64

DOPPING, ANTHONY
Modus Tenendi Parliamenta in Hibernia. Dublin: 1772. V. 63

DORAN, ADELAIDE LEMERT
Pieces of Eight Channel Islands: a Biographical Guide and Source Book. Glendale: 1980. V. 63

DORAN, DR.
Annals of the English Stage, From Thomas Betterton to Edmund Kean. London: 1864. V. 63
Habits and Men, With Remarks of Record Touching the Makers of Both. London: 1855. V. 63

DORAN, JOHN
London in the Jacobite Times. London: 1877. V. 63

DORE, BENJAMIN
Journal of Benjamin Dore 1849-1850. Berkeley: 1923. V. 66

DORE, GUSTAVE
London, a Pilgrimage. London: 1872. V. 62

DOREITH, VELMA
Pie Face. Racine: 1947. V. 63

DOREMUS, PHILIP
Reminiscences of Montclair with Some Account of Montclair's Part in the Civil War. Montclair: 1908. V. 63

DORF, P.
Liberty Hyde Bailey, an Informal Biography. Ithaca: 1956. V. 67

DORFMAN, ARIEL
El Absurdo Entre Cuatro Paredes, el teatro de Harold Pinter. Santiago: 1968. V. 67
The Last Song of Manuel Sendero. New York: 1987. V. 63

DORING, BIANCA
Tag Nacht Helles Verlies. (Day Night Light Dungeon). Gotha: 1995. V. 64

DORIVAL, BERNARD
Cezanne. Boston: 1949. V. 67

D'ORLEANS, HENRI, PRINCE
From Tonkin to India by the Sources of the Irawadi Jan. 95-Jan. 96. London: 1898. V. 64

DORMAN, RUSHTON M.
Origin of Primitive Superstitions and Their Development into the Worship of Spirits and the Doctrine of Spiritual Agency Among the Aborigines of America. Philadelphia: 1881. V. 63

DORMER, ELIZABETH ANNE
Lady Selina Clifford: a Novel. London: 1855?. V. 65

DORN, EDWARD
Captain Jack's Chaps or Houston/MLA. Madison: 1983. V. 63
From Gloucester Out. London: 1964. V. 62; 64
Geography. London: 1965. V. 63
The Newly Fallen. New York: 1961. V. 63
The North Atlantic Turbine. London: 1967. V. 63
What I See in the Maximus Poems. Ventura: 1960. V. 67

DORN, GUNTER
The Cavalry Regiments of Frederick the Great 1756-1763. West Chester: 1989. V. 66

DORNAN, S. S.
Pygmies and Bushmen of the Kalahari. London: 1925. V. 64

DORNBLASER, T. F.
My Life Story for Young and Old. N.P: 1930. V. 63

DORNBUSCH, C. E.
Regimental Publications and Personal Narratives of the Civil War - a Checklist. New York: 1961. V. 64; 67

DOROSHEVITCH, V.
The Way of the Cross. London: 1916. V. 65

DORRIS, MICHAEL
The Benchmark. From the Collection Working Men: Stories. New York: 1993. V. 63
The Broken Cord. New York: 1989. V. 64; 65; 66
The Crown of Columbus. New York: 1991. V. 67
Morning Girl. New York: 1992. V. 67
A Yellow Raft in Blue Water. New York: 1987. V. 62; 64; 66; 67

D'ORS, EUGENIO
Pablo Picasso. Paris: 1930. V. 64

DORSET, CATHERINE ANNE TURNER
The Peacock At Home a Sequel to The Butterfly's Ball. London: 1808. V. 62

DORSEY, GEORGE A.
The Pawnee - Mythology (Part 1). Washington: 1906. V. 66

DORSEY, JOHN SYNG
Elements of Surgery.... Philadelphia: 1813. V. 66

DORST, J.
The Life of Birds. New York: 1974. V. 63; 67

DOS PASSOS, JOHN RODERIGO
Airways, Inc. New York: 1928. V. 65
Brazil on the Move. New York: 1963. V. 63; 65
The 42nd Parallel. Boston: 1946. V. 66
The Garbage Man. New York: 1926. V. 65
The Grand Design. Boston: 1949. V. 65
Journeys Between Wars. New York: 1938. V. 65
Mid Century. Boston: 1961. V. 65
1919. New York: 1932. V. 62; 64; 65
Number One. Boston: 1943. V. 65
Number One. London: 1944. V. 64
Occasions and Protests. Chicago: 1964. V. 65
Three Soldiers. New York: 1921. V. 62
U.S.A. London: 1938. V. 63
U.S.A. Boston: 1946. V. 66

DOSS, JAMES D.
The Shaman Sings. New York: 1994. V. 64; 66; 67

DOSSIE, ROBERT
The Elaboratory Laid Open, or, the Secrets of Modern Chemistry and Pharmacy Revealed. London: 1758. V. 62; 66
The Handmaid to the Arts.... London: 1764. V. 66

DOSTOEVSKII, FYODOR MIKHAILOVICH
The Brothers Karamozov (in Russian). St. Petersburg: 1881,. V. 62; 63; 64; 66
Byesy. (i.e. The Possessed). St. Petersburg: 1873. V. 64; 66
Crime and Punishment. London: 1886. V. 67
Crime and Punishment. New York: 1948. V. 65
The Letters of Dostoyevsky to His Wife. London: 1930. V. 64
Prestupleniye i Nakazaniye. (Crime and Punishment). St. Petersburg: 1867. V. 66
A Raw Youth. Verona: 1974. V. 62; 63; 64; 65
The Short Novels of Dostoevsky. New York: 1945. V. 64; 66
Stavrogin's Confession. Richmond: 1922. V. 62
Stavrogin's Confession and The Plant of the Life of a Great Sinner.... London: 1922. V. 65; 66

DOTY, MARK
Favrile. New York: 1997. V. 62; 67
An Introduction to the Geography of Iowa. Fort Kent: 1979. V. 63
An Island Sheaf. New York: 1998. V. 63
Sweet Machine. New York: 1998. V. 63
Turtle Swan. Boston: 1987. V. 63

DOUAI, ADOLF
The Kindergarten. New York: 1872. V. 65

DOUBLE Acrostics by Various Authors. London: 1880. V. 64

DOUCE, FRANCIS
The Dance of Death Exhibited in Elegant Engravings on Wood.... London: 1833. V. 66
Holbein's Dance of Death Exhibited in Elegant Engravings..(with) Holbein's Bible Cuts. London: 1858. V. 66
Illustrations of Shakespeare and of Ancient Manners.... London: 1807. V. 62; 65; 66; 67

DOUCET, JEROME
Mon Ami Pierrot. Paris: 1890. V. 67
Tales of the Spinner. New York: 1902. V. 62

DOUGALL, JAMES DALZIELL
Shooting: Its Appliance, Practice and Purpose. 1875. V. 66
Shooting: Its Appliance, Practice and Purpose. New York: 1882. V. 64

DOUGALL, JOHN
Angling Songs and Poems, with Miscellaneous Pieces. Glasgow: 1901. V. 67

DOUGHTY, CHARLES MONTAGU
Mansoul or the Riddle of the World. London: 1923. V. 62; 65
Travels in Arabia Deserta. London: 1943. V. 62

DOUGHTY, J. H.
Hill Writings. Manchester: 1937. V. 63; 64

DOUGHTY, JOHN
The Cabinet of Natural History and American Rural Sports. Philadelphia: 1830-1832. V. 62; 64; 66

DOUGHTY, MARION
Afoot through the Kashmir Valleys. London: 1902. V. 62

DOUGLAS, ALFRED
The Collected Satires. London: 1926. V. 65
In Excelsis. London: 1924. V. 65
Nine Poems. London: 1926. V. 65
Perkin Warbeck and Some Other Poems. London: 1897. V. 64
Poemes. Paris: 1896. V. 64
Selected Poems. London: 1926. V. 64
Tails with a Twist. London: 1898. V. 64

DOUGLAS, AMANDA M.
In Trust; or, Dr. Bertrand's Household. Boston: 1866. V. 63; 66

DOUGLAS, ANN
The Feminization of American Culture. New York: 1977. V. 67

DOUGLAS, C. L.
Famous Texas Feuds. Dallas: 1936. V. 63; 66
The Gentleman in the White Hats. Dramatic Episodes in The History of the Texas Rangers. Dallas: 1934. V. 64
James Bowie - the Life of a Bravo. Dallas: 1944. V. 63; 67

DOUGLAS, CLARENCE B.
The History of Tulsa, Oklahoma. A City with a Personality. Chicago: 1921. V. 63; 66

DOUGLAS, DAVID
The Oregon Journals of David Douglas of His Travels and Adventures Among the Traders and Indians in the Columbia Williamette and Snake River Regions During the Years 1825, 1826 and 1827. Volume I. Ashland: 1972. V. 66

DOUGLAS, ELLEN
The Rock Cried Out. New York and London: 1979. V. 64; 67

DOUGLAS, GAVIN
Seamanship for Passengers. London: 1949. V. 64

DOUGLAS, HENRY KYD
I Rode with Stonewall. Chapel Hill: 1904. V. 63
I Rode With Stonewall. Chapel Hill: 1940. V. 62; 65

DOUGLAS, JAMES
The Advancement of Society in Knowledge and Religion. Edinburgh: 1836. V. 67
Descriptio Peritonaei Nec Non Illius Portiunculae Membranae Cellelaris Quae Exteriori Hujus Lateri Adjacet.... Leyden: 1737. V. 64
Myographiae Comparata Specimen; or, a Comparative Description of All the Muscles in a man and a Quadruped. London: 1707. V. 64
Nenia Britannica; or a Sepulchral History of Great Britain; from the Earliest Period to Its General Conversion to Christianity.... London: 1793. V. 66

DOUGLAS, JOHN, BP. OF SALISBURY
A Letter Addressed to Two Great Men, On the Prospect of Peace.... London: 1760. V. 64; 65

DOUGLAS, KEITH
Alamein to Zem Zem. London: 1946. V. 64
Alamein to Zem Zem. London: 1947. V. 66
Collected Poems. London: 1951. V. 62; 62; 66

DOUGLAS, NIEL
An Address to the Judges and Jury in a Case of Alleged Sedition, on 26th May, 1817, Which was Intended to be Delivered Before Passing Sentence. Glasgow: 1817. V. 63
Strictures on the Author's Trial, Declaration Before the Sheriff, Remarks on the Crown Evidence and Some Important Information Respecting the Cause of Reform. Glasgow: 1818. V. 63
The Trial of the Rev. Niel Douglas, Before the High Court of Justiciary at Edinburgh, on the 16th Mary, 1817, for Sedition. Edinburgh: 1817. V. 63

DOUGLAS, NORMAN
The Angel of Manfredonia. San Francisco: 1929. V. 63
Capri: Materials for a Description of the Island. Florence: 1930. V. 62
D. H. Lawrence and Maurice Magnus. Florence: 1924. V. 65
Experiments. Florence: 1925. V. 66
Fabio Giordano's Relation of Capri. Naples: 1906. V. 66
How About Europe?. Florence: 1929. V. 66
In the Beginning. Florence: 1927. V. 64; 66
In the Beginning. London: 1928. V. 64
In the Beginning. New York: 1928. V. 63
London Street Games. London: 1916. V. 62
London Street Games. London: 1931. V. 62; 67
Looking Back: an Autobiographical Excursion. London: 1934. V. 62
Nerinda. Florence: 1929. V. 63; 66
One Day. Chapelle-Reanville: 1929. V. 62; 66
Paneros. Florence: 1930. V. 62
Paneros. London: 1931. V. 63; 66
Some Antiquarian Notes. Naples: 1907. V. 66
South Wind. Chicago: 1929. V. 62
South Wind. 1932. V. 65
South Wind. New York: 1932. V. 63
Three of Them. London: 1930. V. 66
Unprofessional Tales by Normyx. London: 1901. V. 64; 65; 67

DOUGLAS, RONALD
The Irish Book; a Miscellany. 1936. V. 67

DOUGLAS, WILLIAM
Sermon Preached in the African Protestant Epsicopal Church of St. Thomas', Philadelphia. Philadelphia: 1854. V. 63

DOUGLAS, WILLIAM A.
America Challenged. Princeton: 1960. V. 63

DOUGLAS, WILLIAM O.
North from Malaya. Garden City: 1953. V. 63
Of Men and Mountains. New York: 1950. V. 63
Towards a Global Federalism. New York: 1968. V. 63; 67

DOUGLAS HAMILTON, IAIN
Among the Elephants. London: 1975. V. 67

DOUGLASS & Aikman's Almanack and Register for the Island of Jamaica: for the Year 1780. Kingston: 1779. V. 62

DOUGLASS, FREDERICK
Correspondence Between the Rev. Samuel H. Cox and Frederick Douglass. New York: 1846. V. 62
My Bondage and My Freedom. New York: 1857. V. 65
Narrative of the Life of Frederick Douglass, an American Slave. Boston: 1845. V. 63; 65; 66
Two Speeches...One on West India Emancipation...and the Other on the Dred Scott Decision. Rochester: 1857. V. 64

DOUTHIT, MARY
Souvenir of Western Women. Portland: 1905. V. 64; 67

DOUTHITT, KATHERINE CHRISTIAN
Romance and Dim Trails, a History of Clay County. Dallas: 1938. V. 64; 67

DOUTRE, JOSEPH
Constitution of Canada. The British North American Act, 1867; Its Interpretation, Gathering from the Decisions of the Courts, The Dicta of Judges, and Opinions of Statemen and Others.... Montreal: 1880. V. 67

DOVE, HEINRICH WILHELM
The Law of Storms, Considered in Connection with the Ordinary Movements of the Atmosphere. London: 1862. V. 67

DOVE, HEINRICH WILHELM *continued*
Remarks on His Recently Constructed Maps of the Monthly Isothermal Lines of the Globe and On Some of the Principal Conclusions in Regard to Climatology Deducible from Them. (with) Temperature Tables.... London: 1849-1848. V. 65

DOVE, RITA
Lady Freedmon Among Us. West Burke: 1994. V. 62; 64
Mother Love. New York: 1995. V. 63
Ten Poems. Lisbon: 1977. V. 64
Thomas and Beulah. Poems. Pittsburgh: 1986. V. 62; 64
Through the Ivory Gate. New York: 1992. V. 63
The Yellow House on the Corner. Pittsburgh: 1980. V. 65

DOVE, TONI
Mesmer: Secrets of the Human Frame. New York: 1993. V. 64

DOVE, VEE
Madison County Homes: a Collection of Pre-Civil War Homes and Heritages. 1975. V. 64

DOVER, C.
American Negro Art. 1967. V. 65

DOVER, THOMAS
The Ancient Physician's Legacy to His Country. London: 1733. V. 64
The Ancient Physician's Legacy to His Country. London: 1762. V. 62

DOVES PRESS
Catalogue Raisonne of Books Printed and Published at the Doves Press. Hammersmith: 1908. V. 64
Catalogue Raisonne of Books Printed and Published at the Doves Press, 1900-1911. Hammersmith: 1911. V. 62; 67

DOW, ALDEN B.
Reflections. Midland: 1970. V. 66

DOW, ETHEL C.
The Diary of a Birthday Doll. New York: 1908. V. 62; 66

DOW, GEORGE
Railway Heraldry and Other Insignia. London: 1973. V. 64; 66

DOW, GEORGE FRANCIS
The Arts and Crafts in New England 1704-1775. Topsfield: 1927. V. 62
Every Day Life in the Massachusetts Bay Colony. Boston;: 1935. V. 66
The Pirates of the New England and Coast 1630-1730. Salem: 1923. V. 65
Slave Ships and Slaving. Salem: 1927. V. 63; 66
Whale Ships and Whaling. Salem: 1925. V. 67

DOW, LORENZO
A Journey from Babylon to Jerusalem, or the Road to Peace and True Happiness.... Lynchburg: 1812. V. 66
Travels, Providential Experience, &c, &c. of Lorenzo Dow, in Europe and America. Dublin: 1806. V. 67

DOW, R. S.
The Physiology and Pathology of the Cerebellum. Minneapolis: 1958. V. 67

DOWDEY, CLIFFORD
Death of a Nation. The Story of Lee and His Men at Gettysburg. New York: 1958. V. 62

DOWELL, A.
Catalogue of the Very Extensive and Valuable Library of Books on Anatomy, Physiology, Medicine, Natural History...Which Belonged to the Late Professor Goodsir. Edinburgh: 1867. V. 67

DOWELL, COLEMAN
One of the Children is Crying. New York: 1968. V. 67
The Silver Swanne. New York: 1983. V. 63

DOWELL, STEPHEN
The History and Explanation of the Stamp Duties...and the Stamp Laws at Present in Force in the United Kingdom.... London: 1873. V. 64

DOWELL, W. C.
The Webley Story. 1962. V. 62; 63

DOWIE, MENIE MURIEL
A Girl in the Karpathians. London: 1891. V. 64

DOWLING, JOSEPH
The Important Trial of Capt. Harrower, at the Old Bailey, Feb. 17, 1816, on an Indictment for Marrying the Daughter of Mr. Giblet, the Celebrated Butcher, His Former Wife Being Alive, a Lunatic in India. London: 1816. V. 64

DOWLING, WILLIAM
Poets and Statesmen: Their Homes and Memorials in the Neighbourhood of Windsor and Eton. Eton: 1857. V. 62

DOWNES, HENRY
A Sermon Preach'd in Christ's Church, Dublin; Before His Excellency John, Lord Cartaret, Lord Lieutenant General, and General Governour of Ireland. On Sat. May 29, 1725. Dublin: 1725. V. 65
A Sermon Preach'd in Christ's-Church, Dublin on Friday, October 23d 1719/. Dublin: 1719. V. 65

DOWNES, JOHN
Roscius Anglicanus, or an Historical Review of the Stage. London: 1789. V. 63

DOWNES, OLIN
Symphonic Masterpieces. New York: 1935. V. 63

DOWNES, WILLIAM HOWE
John S. Sargent, His Life and Work. London: 1926. V. 62

DOWNEY, EDMUND
Clashmore. 1903. V. 67

DOWNEY, FAIRFAX
Fyfe, Drum and Bugle. Fort Collins: 1971. V. 66
Indian Fighting Army. New York: 1941. V. 65; 67

DOWNEY, WILLIAM SCOTT
Proverbs.... Boston: 1853. V. 63

DOWNHOWER, J. F.
The Biography of the Island Region of Western Lake Erie. Columbus: 1988. V. 63

DOWNIE, N. M.
The Beetles of Northeastern North America. Gainesville: 1996. V. 64

DOWNIE, WILLIAM
Hunting for Gold. Reminiscences of Personal Experinece and Research in the Early Days of the Pacific Coast from Alaska to Panama. San Francisco: 1893. V. 63; 66

DOWNING, ANDREW JACKSON
The Fruits and Fruit Trees of America.... New York: 1845. V. 62
The Horticulturist and Journal of Rural Art and Rural Taste.... Albany: 1847-1848. V. 62; 67
Rural Essays. New York: 1853. V. 63
Rural Essays, Horticulture Landscape-Gardening-Rural Architecture- Trees-Agriculture- Fruit, Etc. New York: 1890. V. 64; 67
A Treatise on the Theory and Practice of Landscape Gardening.... New York: 1844. V. 64; 67
A Treatise on the Theory and Practice of Landscape Gardening.... New York: 1859. V. 64

DOWNING, FANNY MURDAUGH
Nameless. Raleigh: 1865. V. 62; 64; 67

DOWNING, HARRIET
Remembrances of a Monthly Nurse. London: 1852. V. 65

DOWNING, JACK
Letters of Jack Downing, of the Downingville Militia. New York: 1865. V. 62

DOWNS, JANET B.
Mills of Rockingham Co. Harrisonburg: 1997-1998. V. 63

DOWNS, JOSEPH
American Furniture: Queen Anne and Chippendale Periods in the History Francis Du Pont Winterthur Museum. New York: 1952. V. 67

DOWNSHIRE, MARQUESS OF
Report on the Manuscripts of the Marquess of Downshire. 1924-1940. V. 63

DOWSETT, J. MOREWOOD
Big Game and Big Life. London: 1925. V. 64

DOWSON, ERNEST
Decorations: in Verse and Prose. London: 1899. V. 64
The Pierrot of the Minute. London: 1897. V. 65
The Poems of Ernest Dowson. Portland: 1902. V. 64
The Poems of Ernest Dowson. London: 1906. V. 64
Studies in Sentiment - Apple Blossom in Brittany - The Eyes of Pride - Countess Marie of the Angels - The Dying of Francis Donne. Portland: 1915. V. 62
Verses. London: 1896. V. 64

DOWSON, JOHN
An Essay on Warm and Cold Bathing for the Preservation of Health. Whitby: 1857. V. 64

DOYLE, ADRIAN CONAN
The Exploits of Sherlock Holmes. London: 1954. V. 62; 63; 65; 66; 67
The Exploits of Sherlock Holmes. New York: 1954. V. 67

DOYLE, ARTHUR CONAN
Adventures of Gerard. London: 1903. V. 62
The Adventures of Gerard. New York: 1903. V. 66
The Adventures of Sherlock Holmes. 1892. V. 62; 66
The Adventures of Sherlock Holmes. London: 1892. V. 62; 64; 65
Adventures of Sherlock Holmes. New York: 1892. V. 62; 63
The Adventures of Sherlock Holmes. London: 1893. V. 67
The Adventures of Sherlock Holmes. 1950. V. 62
The Adventures of Sherlock Holmes. New York: 1950. V. 66
The Annotated Sherlock Holmes - the Four Novels and Fifty-Six Short Stories. London: 1968. V. 65
The Black Doctor and Other Tales of Terror and Mystery. New York: 1919. V. 66
The Captain of the Polestar and Other Tales. London and New York: 1890. V. 66
The Casebook of Sherlock Holmes. London: 1927. V. 65; 67
The Croxley Master. New York: 1907. V. 67
The Croxley Master. New York: 1925. V. 65
Danger! and Other Stories. London: 1918. V. 66
The Doings of Raffles Haw. London: 1893. V. 66
The Exploits of Brigadier Gerard. London: 1896. V. 67
The Final Adventures of Sherlock Holmes. 1952. V. 62
His Last Bow: Some Reminiscences of Sherlock Holmes. London: 1917. V. 66; 67
A History of the Great War, the British Campaigns in France and Flanders 1914-1918. New York: 1917-1920. V. 65
The Hound of the Baskervilles. 1902. V. 62; 64; 65; 66
The Hound of the Baskervilles. London: 1902. V. 62; 63; 64; 65

DOYLE, ARTHUR CONAN *continued*
The Hound of the Baskervilles. San Francisco: 1985. V. 65
The Later Adventures of Sherlock Holmes. 1952. V. 62
The Lost World, Being an Account of the Recent Amazing Adventures of Professor George E. Challenger, Lord John Roxton, Professor Summerlee and Mr. E. D. Malone of the Daily Gazette. London: 1912. V. 67
The Maracot Deep. New York: 1929. V. 67
The Memoirs of Sherlock Holmes. London: 1894. V. 66; 67
Memoirs of Sherlock Holmes. New York: 1894. V. 64; 67
Memories and Adventures. 1924. V. 66
Memories and Adventures. Boston: 1924. V. 62
Memories and Adventures. 1988. V. 63
Micah Clarke. London and New York: 1889. V. 65
The Mystery of Cloomber. London: 1895. V. 66; 67
Our African Winter. London: 1929. V. 67
The Oxford Sherlock Holmes. Oxford: 1993. V. 63
The Parasite. Westminster: 1894. V. 65
The Parasite. London: 1897. V. 63
A Parasite. Westminster: 1897. V. 66
The Poison Belt. New York: 1913. V. 62
The Refugees; a Tale of Two Continents. London: 1893. V. 67
The Return of Sherlock Holmes. 1905. V. 62
The Return of Sherlock Holmes. London: 1905. V. 63
The Return of Sherlock Holmes. New York: 1905. V. 67
Rodney Stone. London: 1896. V. 65; 67
Rodney Stone. New York: 1896. V. 65
Rodney Stone. London: 1901. V. 67
Round the Fire Stories. 1908. V. 63; 66
Round the Red Lamp. London: 1894. V. 63; 66; 67
Sherlock Holmes: a Drama. London: 1922. V. 63
The Sign of the Four. London: 1892. V. 67
Sir Nigel. London: 1906. V. 67
Sir Nigel. Toronto: 1906. V. 66
Songs of the Road. London: 1911. V. 67
The Stark Munro Letters, Being a Series of Sixteen Letters Written by J. Stark Monro, M.B. to his Friend and Former Fellow Student, Herbert Swanborough...1881-1884. London: 1895. V. 67
A Study in Scarlet. London: 1891. V. 67
A Study in Scarlet. New York and London: 1960. V. 65
A Study in Scarlet. London: 1993. V. 66
Through the Magic Door. London: 1907. V. 66; 67
Through the Magic Door. New York: 1908. V. 62
Uncle Bernac. London: 1897. V. 65; 67
The Unknown Conan Doyle: Uncollected Stories. London: 1982. V. 66
The Valley of Fear. New York: 1914. V. 66
The Valley of Fear. London: 1915. V. 63
The Vital Message. London: 1919. V. 64
The White Company. Leipzig: 1891. V. 65
The White Company. London: 1892. V. 67
The White Company. New York: 1922. V. 65
The Works. London: 1903. V. 66

DOYLE, J. E. P.
Plymouth Church and Its Pastor. Hartford: 1874. V. 65

DOYLE, JAMES E.
A Chronicle of England BC 55 - AD 1485. London: 1864. V. 65

DOYLE, JOHN MILLEY
A Speech in the Court of Common Pleas, Dublin May 22, 1820 by Holwell Walshe, Esq. (of the Irish Bar) for the Plaintiff in an Action of Criminal Conversation, Brought by Sir John Milloy Doyle, versus George Peter Browne, Esq. London: 1820. V. 63

DOYLE, MARTIN
A Cyclopaedia of Practical Husbandry and Rural Affairs. 1844. V. 63
Hints for the Small Farmers of Ireland. Dublin: 1830. V. 66
The Illustrated Book of Domestic Poultry. Philadelphia: 1900. V. 63
Irish Cottagers. Dublin: 1800. V. 65
Practical Gardening. 1839. V. 62

DOYLE, RICHARD
The Foreign Tour of Messrs. Brown, Jones and Robinson. London: 1855. V. 67
The Foreign Tour of the Misses Brown, Jones and Robinson. London: 1880. V. 65
God's Englishmen: Forty Drawings by Richard Doyle From "Manners and Customs of ye Englyse: to Which be Added Some Extracts from Mr. Pips (sic) Hys Diary".... London: 1948. V. 64
In Fairyland, a Series of Pictures form the Elf-World.... London: 1870. V. 65
Jack the Giant Killer. London: 1888. V. 64; 66

DOYLE, RODDY
The Commitments. New York: 1987. V. 64; 66
The Commitments. New York: 1989. V. 66
The Giggler Treatment. London: 2000. V. 67
Paddy Clarke Ha Ha Ha. New York: 1993. V. 62; 64; 66; 67
A Star Called Henry. New York: 1999. V. 67
The Van. London: 1991. V. 66
The Van. New York: 1992. V. 66; 67
The Woman Who Walked Into Doors. London: 1996. V. 63

D'OYLY, CATHERINE
The History of the Life and Death of Our Blessed Saviour. Southampton: 1794. V. 65

A DOZEN All Told. 1894. V. 67

DRABBLE, MARGARET
London Consequences: a Novel. London: 1972. V. 66
The Middle Ground - a Novel. London: 1980. V. 65
A Natural Curiosity. London: 1989. V. 63
The Needle's Eye. New York: 1972. V. 63

DRAKE, DANIEL
Discourses Delivered by Appointment Before the Cincinnati Medical Library Association, January 9th and 10th, 1852. Cincinnati: 1852. V. 66; 67
A Systematic Treatise, Historical, Etiological and Practical on the Principal Diseases of the Interior Valley of North America. Cincinnati: 1850. V. 64; 67

DRAKE, EDWARD CAVENDISH
A New Universal Collection of Authentic and Entertaining Travels. London: 1769. V. 62

DRAKE, FRANCIS
Sir Francis Drake's West Indian Voyage 1585-1586. London: 1981. V. 63; 64; 66

DRAKE, FRANCIS S.
Dictionary of American Biography, Including Men of Our Times.... Boston: 1872. V. 65

DRAKE, JAMES MADISON
Historical Sketches of the Revolutionary and Civil Wars. New York: 1908. V. 63; 66
The History of the Ninth New Jersey Veteran Vols.: a Record of Its Service from Sept. 13th, 1861 to July 12th 1865. Elizabeth: 1889. V. 63; 66

DRAKE, JOSEPH RODMAN
The Culprit Fay and Other Poems. New York: 1923. V. 64

DRAKE, JUDITH
An Essay in Defence of the Female Sex, In Which are Inserted the Characters of a Pendant, a Squire, a Beau, a Vertuoso.... London: 1696. V. 65

DRAKE, SAMUEL ADAMS
The Heart of the White Mountains; Their Legend and Scenery. London: 1882. V. 64
The Heart of the White Mountains; Their Legends and Scenery. New York: 1882. V. 63

DRAKE, SAMUEL G.
Biography and History of the Indians of North America.... Boston: 1857. V. 63

DRAKE, STILLMAN
Mechanics in Sixteenth Century Italy. Madison: 1969. V. 63

DRAKE-BROCKMAN, RALPH E.
British Somaliland. London: 1912. V. 64

DRANNAN, WILLIAM F.
Captain W. F. Drannan, Chief of Scouts, As Pilot to Emigrant and Government Trains, Across the Plains of the Wild West of Fifty Years Ago. Chicago: 1910. V. 64
Thirty-One Years on the Plains and In the Mountains Or, the Last Voice from the Plains. Chicago: 1900. V. 64

DRAPARNAUD, JACQUES PHILIPPE RAYMOND
Histoire Naturelle des Mollusques Terrestres et Fluviatiles de la France. Paris: 1805. V. 64; 67

DRAPER, GEORGE
Beleigh (sic) Abbey, Essex. London: 1818. V. 62

DRAPER, JOHN W.
History of the Conflict Between Religion and Science. New York: 1875. V. 63

DRAPER, LYMAN C.
King's Mountain and Its Heroes. Cincinnati: 1881. V. 66

DRAPER, THEODORE
The 84th Infantry Division in the Battle of the Ardennes, Dec. 1944-Jan. 1945. Leige: 1945. V. 63

DRAPER, THOMAS
Vancouver City Directory - 1888. Victoria: 1888. V. 64

DRAPER, W. H.
The Morning Walk; or City Encompass'd. London: 1751. V. 63

DRAPER, WILLIAM H.
Adel and Its Norman Church. Leeds: 1909. V. 65

DRAUD, GEORG
Bibliotheca Librorum Germanicorum Classica... (with) Bibliotheca Exotica, sive Catalogus Officinalis Librorum. Frankfurt: 1611-1610. V. 63

DRAYTON, DANIEL
Personal Memoir of...For Four Years and Four Months a Prisoner.... Boston: 1853. V. 62; 64

DRAYTON, JOHN
Memoirs of the American Revolution, from Its Commencement to the Year 1776, Inclusive.... Charleston: 1821. V. 63; 66

DRAYTON, MICHAEL
Endimion and Phoebe Ideas Latmus. Stratford-upon-Avon: 1925. V. 63
Nimphidia and the Mvses Elizivm. London: 1896. V. 62
Poems. London: 1616. V. 62; 63
Poems. London: 1619. V. 63
Poems. Oxford: 1970. V. 63
The Works. London: 1748. V. 63

THE DREAM Song of Olaf Asteson. 1995. V. 62

DREAMS and Derisions. New York: 1927. V. 66

DREANY, E. JOSEPH
Cowboys in Pop-Up Action Pictures. London: 1951. V. 65

DREDGE, JAMES
A Record of the Transportation Exhibits at the World's Columbian Exposition of 1893. London: 1894. V. 65

DREDGE, W.
Description of Suspension Bridges on Dredge's Patent Taper Principle, with Diagrams.... Edinburgh: 1851. V. 65

DREIER, KATHERINE S.
Shawn the Dancer. New York: 1933. V. 63

DREIFUS, LEONARD S.
Mechanisms and Therapy of Cardiac Arrhythmias. New York: 1966. V. 63; 66

DREISER, THEODORE
An American Tragedy. New York: 1925. V. 63; 65; 66
An American Tragedy. New York: 1954. V. 65
The Bulwark. Garden City: 1946. V. 65
The Carnegie Works at Pittsburgh. Chelsea: 1927. V. 65
Chains. New York: 1927. V. 64; 67
Dawn. London: 1931. V. 62
Dawn. New York: 1931. V. 65
Dreiser Looks at Russia. London: 1928. V. 64
Dreiser Looks at Russia. New York: 1928. V. 65
Epitaph. New York: 1929. V. 66
Free and Other Stories. New York: 1918. V. 65
A Gallery of Women. New York: 1929. V. 63; 65
The Hand of the Potter. New York: 1918. V. 64; 65
Hey Rub-a-Dub-Dub: a Book of Mystery and Wonder and Terror of Life. New York: 1920. V. 65
A Hoosier Holiday. New York: 1916. V. 65; 66
Jennie Gerhardt: a Novel. New York and London: 1911. V. 64; 65
Moods Cadenced and Declaimed. New York: 1926. V. 64
Plays of the Natural and the Supernatural. New York: 1916. V. 65
Sister Carrie. New York: 1900. V. 63
Sister Carrie. New York: 1939. V. 63
The Stoic. Garden City: 1947. V. 65
The Titan. New York: 1914. V. 65
Twelve Men. New York: 1919. V. 65

DRENTTEL, WILLIAM
Paul Auster - A Comprehensive Bibliographic Checklist of Published Works 1968-1994. New York: 1994. V. 65

DRESSER, CHRISTOPHER
The Art of Decorative Design, with an Appendix.... London: 1862. V. 64
Popular Manual of Botany.... Edinburgh: 1860. V. 62
Unity in Variety, as Deduced from the Vegetable Kingdom.... London: 1860. V. 62

DRESSER, HENRY EELES
Eggs of the Birds of Europe.... 1910. V. 66
A History of the Birds of Europe.... London: 1878-1881. V. 67
A Manual of Palearctic Birds. London: 1902-1903. V. 62
A Monograph of the Meropidae, or Family of the Bee Beaters. London: 1884-1886. V. 67
Supplement to a History of the Birds of Europe.... London: 1895-1896. V. 67

DRESSLER, ALBERT
California Pioneer Mountaineer of Rabbit Creek. San Francisco: 1930. V. 63; 66

DREW, ANDREW
A Narrative of the Capture and Destruction of the Steamer "Caroline" and Her Descent Over the Falls of Niagara On the Night of the 29th of December, 1837. London: 1864. V. 64

DREW, SAMUEL
The Divinity of Christ and the Necessity of His Atonement, Vindicated from the Cavils of Mr. Thomas Prout (the pamphlet "The Unitarian's Serious Appeal") and His Associates. Penryn: 1814. V. 64
An Essay on the Identity and General Resurrection of the Human Body. London: 1809. V. 65
An Essay on the Identity and General Resurrection of the Human Body. Brooklyn: 1811. V. 65

DREW, THOMAS
John Brown Invasion, an Authentic History of the Harper's Ferry Tragedy. Boston: 1860. V. 65

DREW, WILLIAM
The Art of Making Coloured Crystals to Imitate Precious Stones. London: 1787. V. 65

DREW, WILLIAM A.
Glimpses and Gatherings During a Voyage and Visit to London and the Great Exhibition. Augusta: 1852. V. 66

DREWER, J. N.
A Topographical and Historical Description of Oxfordshire. London: 1810. V. 62

DREWES, WILLIAM K.
Fine Arts Insurance. New York: 1938. V. 67

DREWITT, F. D.
The Romance of the Apothecaries' Garden at Chelsea. London: 1922. V. 67

DREWRY, WILLIAM SIDNEY
The Southampton Insurrection. Washington: 1900. V. 67

DREXEL, JEREMIAS
Aeternitatis Prodromus Mortis Nuntius Quem Sanis, Aegrotis, Moribundis Sistit. Cologne: 1633. V. 67

DREYFUS, JOHN
Aspects of French Eighteenth Century Typography. Cambridge: 1982. V. 62
Bruce Rogers and American Typography. New York: 1959. V. 64
Eric Gill for Father Desmond. London: 1993. V. 64; 65
Eric Gill for Father Desmond. London: 1995. V. 67
Giovanni Mardersteig: an Account of His Work by John Dreyfus. Verona: 1966. V. 62
A History of the Nonesuch Press. London: 1981. V. 62; 64; 65; 67
Italic Quartet: a Record of the Collaboration Between Harry Kessler, Edward Johnston, Emery Walker and Edward Prince in Making the Cranach Press Italic. Cambridge: 1966. V. 66
The Personal Pleasures of a Private Press. Worcester: 1971. V. 67
The Survival of Baskerville's Punches. Cambrdige: 1949. V. 62; 64
A Typographical Masterpiece. 1991. V. 62
A Typographical Masterpiece. London: 1993. V. 65
William Caxton and His Quincentenary. San Francisco: 1976. V. 64; 66
The Work of Jan Van Krimpen. Haarlem: 1952. V. 65; 67

DRIBERG, J. H.
Initation. Waltham St. Lawrence: 1932. V. 63; 64; 65

DRIEBE, TOM
In Search of the Wild Indian: Photographs and Life Works by Carl and Grace Moon. Moscow: 1997. V. 63

DRIGGS, B. W.
History of the Teton Valley Idaho. Caldwell: 1926. V. 65

DRIGGS, FRANK
Black Beauty, White Heat. A Pictorial History of Classic Jazz. New York: 1982. V. 64; 66

DRIGGS, HOWARD R.
Mormon Trail: Pathway of Pioneers Who Made Deserts Bloom. New York: 1947. V. 63
Westward America - with Reproductions of Forty Water Color Paintings by William Henry Jackson. New York: 1942. V. 63

DRINKER, FREDERICK E.
Booker T. Washington, The Master Mind of a Child of Slavery. N.P: 1915. V. 63

DRINKWATER, JOHN
American Vignettes 1860-1865. Boston: 1931. V. 64
Claud Lovat Fraser. New York: 1923. V. 63
Cotswold Characters. New Haven and London: 1921. V. 63
From an Unknown Isle. London: 1924. V. 64
Persephone. New York: 1926. V. 62; 65
Selected Poems. London: 1922. V. 64

DRISKELL, DAVID
Harlem Renaissance: Art of Black America. New York: 1987. V. 65

DROST, WILLIAM E.
Clocks and Watches of New Jersey. Elizabeth: 1966. V. 63; 66

DROUGHT, J. B.
Successful Shooting. London: 1948. V. 67

DRUCKER, JOHANNA
Narratology: Historical Romance, Sweet Romance, Science Fiction, Romantic Suspense, Supernatural, Horror, Sensual Romance, Adventure, Thriller, Glitz. N.P: 1994. V. 64

DRUITT, HERBERT
A Manual of Costume as Illustrated by Monumental Brasses. Philadelphia. V. 64
A Manual of Costume as Illustrated by Monumental Brasses. London: 1906. V. 67

DRUMHELLER, DAN
Uncle Dan Tells Thrills of Western Tales in 1854. Spokane: 1925. V. 63

DRUMM, STELLA M.
Down the Santa Fe Trail and Into Mexico. New Haven: 1926. V. 63

DRUMMOND, ALEXANDER
Travels through Different Cities of Germany, Italy, Greece and Several Parts of Asia.... London: 1754. V. 62

DRUMMOND, GEORGE
Parochial Psalmody; or Seventy Psalm Tunes Arranged for the Organ and Piano Forte.... London: 1820. V. 65

DRUMMOND, HENRY
Histories of Noble British Familes with Biographical Notices of the Most Distinguished Individuals in Each. London: 1846. V. 67
Letter to Thomas Phillips, Esq. R.A. on the Connection Between the Fine Arts and Religion, and the Means of their Revivial. London: 1840. V. 67
The Monkey That Would Not Kill. London: 1898. V. 64
The Monkey that Would Not Kill. New York: 1925. V. 64
Speeches in Parliament and Some Miscellaneous Pamphlets of the Late Henry Drummond, Esq. London: 1860. V. 63

DRUMMOND, W. H.
The Large Game and Natural History of South and South-East Africa from the Journals of the Hon. W. H. Drummond. Edinburgh: 1875. V. 65

DRUMMOND, WILLIAM
The Poems of William Drummond of Hawthornden. London: 1791. V. 66

DRUMMOND, WILLIAM HAMILTON
The Battle of Trafalgar, an Heroic Poem. Charleston: 1807. V. 64; 66

DRURY, ANNA HARRIET
Annesley and Other Poems. London: 1847. V. 67
Eastbury; a Tale. London: 1851. V. 65

DRURY, AUBREY
John A. Hooper and California's Robust Youth. San Francisco: 1952. V. 67

DRURY, CLIFFORD M.
The Diaries and Letters of Henry H. Spaulding and Asa Bowen Smith Relating to the Nez Perce Mission 1838-1842. Glendale: 1958. V. 66
First White Woman Over the Rockies. Glendale: 1963-1966. V. 64
Henry Harmon Spalding, Pioneer of Old Oregon. Caldwell: 1936. V. 63; 66
Marcus and Narcissa Whitman and the Opening of Old Oregon. Glendale: 1973. V. 64; 65; 67
Nine Years with the Spokane Indians. The Diary 1838-1848 of Elkanah Walker. Glendale: 1976. V. 67

DRURY, H.
Reminiscences of Life and Sport in Southern India. 1890. V. 66
The Useful Plants of India. Madras: 1858. V. 62

DRURY, HENRY
A Catalogue of the Extensive and Valuable Library of the Rev. Henry Drury, M.A., Late Fellow of King's College, Cambridge and Rector of Fingest, Bucks. London: 1827. V. 64

DRURY, TOM
The End of Vandalism. Boston: 1994. V. 67
The End of Vandalism. New York: 1994. V. 67

DRURY, W. P.
The Peradventures of Private Pagett. London: 1911. V. 62

DRYANDER, J.
Anatomiae, Hoc est Corporis Humani Dissectionis. Marburg Eucharius Cervicornu: 1537. V. 67

DRYBROUGH, T. B.
Polo. London: 1898. V. 66

DRYDEN, JOHN
Alexander's Feast. 1904. V. 65
Alexander's Feast. Chipping Campden: 1904. V. 63
All for Love; or the World Well Lost. London: 1692. V. 62
All for Love, or The World Well Lost.... San Francisco: 1929. V. 64
All for Love, or the World Well Lost.... 1932. V. 65
All For Love, or the World Well Lost.... London: 1932. V. 67
The Dramatick Works. London: 1735-1750. V. 66
The Dramatic Works. London: 1931-1932. V. 62
The Dramatick Works. London: 1735. V. 64
The Dramatick Works. London: 1762-1763. V. 65
The Duke of Guise. London: 1587. V. 66
Fables Ancient and Modern. London: 1700. V. 66
Fables Ancient and Modern. London: 1721. V. 67
Fables Ancient and Modern...(with) Original Poems. Glasgow: 1776-1775. V. 63
Fables Antcient and Modern. London: 1755. V. 66
The Fables.... London: 1797. V. 63
The First Part of Miscellany Poems. London: 1727. V. 62; 65
Four Comedies/Four Tragedies. Chicago and London: 1967. V. 65
Miscellany Poems. London: 1716. V. 67
Miscellany Poems in Two Parts. (with) Sylvae; or the Second Part of Poetical Miscellanies. London: 1692. V. 66
Of Dramatick Poesie: an Essay 1668. London: 1928. V. 62; 63; 65
Original Poems and Translations. London: 1743. V. 65; 66
Poems. Oxford: 1958. V. 65
The Poetical Works. London: 1832-1833. V. 62; 66
Songs and Poems. Waltham St. Lawrence: 1957. V. 62; 64; 65; 67
Troilus and Cressida, or Truth Bound Too Late. London: 1679. V. 62; 65
The Works of the Late Famous Mr. John Dryden. London: 1701. V. 64

DRYFHOUT, JOHN
Augustus Saint-Gaudens. The Portrait Reliefs. New York: 1969. V. 65

DRYSDALE, WILLIAM
Auld Biggins of Stirling, Its Closes, Wynds and Nebour Villages. Stirling: 1904. V. 62; 63

DUANE, WILLIAM
An Examination of the Question, Who is the Writer of Two Forged Letters addressed to the President of the United States?. Washington?: 1803. V. 63; 66
Politics for American Farmers: Being a Series of Tracts.... Washington City: 1807. V. 62; 63
A Visit to Colombia in the Years 1822 and 1823, by Laguayra and Caracas, Over the Cordillera to Bogota, and Thence by the Magdalena to Cartagena. Philadelphia: 1826. V. 66

DUBARRY, ARMAND
Les Tueurs de Serpents. Adventures d'un Officier Francais au Lac Tchad. Paris: 1891. V. 64

DU BARTAS, GUILLAUME DE SALLUSTE, SEIGNEUR DE
Du Bartas His Divine Weekes and Workes.... London: 1633. V. 63

DU BARTAS, GUILLAUME DE SALUSTE, SEIGNEUR DE
Du Bartas His Divine Weekes and Workes.... London: 1613. V. 66
Les Oevvres. Paris: 1583. V. 66

DUBE-HEYNIG, A.
Kirchner, His Graphic Art. 1961. V. 62

DUBIE, NORMAN
Alehouse Sonnets. Pittsburgh: 1971. V. 63
The Funeral. Calais: 1998. V. 62; 63; 66; 67
Popham of the New Song and Other Poems. Port Townsend: 1975. V. 63
The Prayers of the North American Martyrs. Lisbon: 1975. V. 62; 63; 64; 66; 67

DUBLIN Delineated in 26 Views of the Principle Public Buildings. 1831. V. 63; 66

THE DUBLIN University Calendar MDCCCXXXIII. Corrected to November 20, 1832. Dublin;: 1833. V. 67

DUBNER, F.
Epigrammatum Anthologia Palatina Cum Planudeis et Appendice Nova Epigrammatum Veterum Ex Libris Et Marmoribus Ductorum.... Parisiis: 1864-1872. V. 65

DU BOCCAGE, MARIE ANNE LE PAGE
Letters Concerning England, Holland and Italy. London: 1770. V. 66
Recueil des Oeuvres. Lyon: 1770. V. 63

DU BOIS, A. J.
Science and the Supernatural. London: 1886. V. 67

DUBOIS, ALPHONSE
Synopsis Avium. Nouveau Manuel d'Ornithologie. Bruxelles: 1899-1904. V. 65
Synopsis Avium Nouveau Manuel d'Ornithologie. Bruxeles: 1902-1904. V. 67

DUBOIS, CHARLES G.
Kick the Dead Lion, a Casebook of the Custer Battle. Billings: 1954. V. 67

DUBOIS, EDWARD
My Pocket Book; or, Hints for a Right Merrie and Conceited Tour. 1808. V. 62; 65
My Pocket Book; or, Hints for A Ryghte Merrie and Conceitede Tour. London: 1808. V. 63
St. Godwin: a Tale of the Sixteenth, Seventeenth and Eighteenth Centuries. London: 1800. V. 62
The Wreath.... London: 1799. V. 64

DU BOIS, EUGENE FLOYD
Lane Medical Lectures: the Mechanism of Heat Loss and Temperature Regulation. Palo Alto: 1937. V. 66

DUBOIS, FELIX
Timbuctoo the Mysterious. London: 1897. V. 64

DU BOIS, JOHN VAN
Campaign in the West 1856-1861. The Journal of John Van Du Bois. Tucson: 1949. V. 65; 67

DU BOIS, JUNE
W. R. Leigh - the Definitive Illustrated Biography. Kansas City: 1977. V. 63; 66

DUBOIS, PAUL
Les Psychonervroses et Leur Traitement Moral; Lecons Faites a l'Universite de Berne. Paris: 1904. V. 65

DUBOIS, PIERRE
Histoire de l'Horlogerie Depuis son Origine Jusqu'a Nos Jours Precedee de Recherches sur la Mesure du Temps dans l'antiquite Suivie de la Biographie des Horlogers les Plus Celebres de l'Euopre.... Paris: 1849. V. 66

DU BOIS, W. E. B.
Black Folk: Then and Now. New York: 1939. V. 63
Black Reconstruction. New York: 1956. V. 63; 66
Dusk of Dawn. New York: 1940. V. 67
The Negroes of Farmville, Virginia. a Social Study. Washington: 1898. V. 65
The Souls of Black Folk. Chicago: 1903. V. 65
The Souls of Black Folk. London: 1905. V. 64; 66
The Souls of Black Folk. New York: 1953. V. 65

DU BOIS, WILLIAM PENE
The Three Policemen or Young Bottsford of Fabre Island. New York: 1938. V. 65

DU BOS, CHARLES
Approximations - Deuxieme Serie et Troisieme Serie. Paris: 1927-1929. V. 64

DU BOSC, JACQUES
The Excellent Woman Described by Her True Characters and their Opposites. London: 1692. V. 63
La Femme Heroique ou Les Heroines Comparees avec Les Heros en Tout Sorte de Vertus. Paris: 1645. V. 65

DU BOSE, JOHN WITHERSPOON
Alabama's Tragic Decade. Ten Years of Alabama 1865-1874. Birmingham: 1940. V. 67
General Joseph Wheeler and the Army of Tennessee. New York: 1912. V. 62; 63; 65

DUBOURDIEU, JOHN
An Historical Dissertation Upon the Thebean Legion, Plainly Proving It to be Fabulous. London: 1696. V. 67

DUBREUIL, JEAN
Bowle's Practice of Perspective; or, an Easy Method of Representing Natural Objects According to the Rules of Art.... London: 1782. V. 66
Perspective Practical, or a Plain and Easie Method of True and Lively Represresenting all Things to the Eye at a Distance by the Exact Rules of Art.... London: 1672. V. 64

DUBREUIL, JEAN continued
Practical Perspective.... London: 1765. V. 66

DU BREUIL, M.
The Science and Practice of Grafting, Pruning and Training Fruit Trees...In Profitable Cultivation of the Pear, Apple, Plum, Peach, Etc. 1862. V. 63

DU BROCA, LOUIS
Interesting Anecdotes of the Heroic Conduct of Women, Previous To, and During the French Revolution. Baltimore: 1804. V. 65

DUBUFFET, JEAN
Jean Dubuffet: Towards an Alternative Reality. New York: 1987. V. 66

DUBUS, ANDRE
Adultery and Other Choices. Boston: 1977. V. 62
Broken Vessels. Boston: 1991. V. 67
The Cage Keeper and Other Stories. New York: 1989. V. 63
Dancing After Hours. New York: 1996. V. 63; 65
Finding A Girl in America. Boston: 1980. V. 65
The Last Worthless Evening. Boston: 1986. V. 62
The Lieutenant. New York: 1967. V. 62; 63; 65; 66; 67
Meditations from a Movable Chair. New York: 1998. V. 67
Separate Flights. Boston: 1975. V. 65
The Times are Never So Bad. Boston: 1983. V. 65
Voices from the Moon. Boston: 1984. V. 62; 65
We Don't Live Here Anymore. New York: 1984. V. 62

DUBUS, R.
Reminiscences of Twenty Years Pigsticking in Bengal. 1893. V. 67

DUBUT, LOUIS AMBROISE
Architecture Civile. Maisons de Ville et de Campagne de Touts Formes et de Tous Genres.... Paris: 1802-1803. V. 66

DUCAMP, THEODORE
Traite des Retentions d'Urine Causees par le Retrecissement de l'Uretre.... Paris: 1825. V. 63

DU CANE, ELLA
The Flowers and Gardens of Japan. London: 1908. V. 64
The Flowers and Gardens of Madeira. London: 1909. V. 64
The Flowers and Gardens of Spain. London: 1908. V. 67

DU CANE, FLORENCE
The Canary Islands. London: 1911. V. 62
The Canary Islands. London: 1933. V. 65
The Flowers and Gardens of Madeira. London: 1909. V. 65; 67

DUCANGE, ANGLICUS, PSEUD.
The Vulgar Tongue; Comprising Two Glossaries of Slang, Cant, and Flash Words and Phrases, Principally Used in London at the Present Day. London: 1857. V. 64

DUCAT, A. C.
Memoir of.... Chicago: 1897. V. 65

DU CHAILLU, PAUL B.
Explorations and Adventures in Equatorial Africa.... London: 1861. V. 64
The Land of the Midnight Sun. New York: 1881. V. 62; 63
The Land of the Midnight Sun. New York: 1882. V. 64
The Land of the Midnight Sun. London: 1899. V. 62

DUCHAMP, MARCEL
The Almost Complete Works of Marcel Duchamp. London: 1968. V. 65
From the Green Box. New Haven: 1957. V. 66

DUCHARTRE, PIERRE LOUIS
The Italian Comedy. New York: 1929. V. 64

DUCHENNE DE BOULOGNE, GUILLAUME BENJAMIN AMAND
A Treatise on Localized Electrization, and Its Applications to Pathology and Therapeutics. Philadelphia: 1871. V. 65

DUCHESNE, JOSEPH DE
Tetrade Des Plvs Grieves Maladies De Tovt Le Cerveau. Paris: 1625. V. 66

DU CHOUL, GUILLAUME
Discours de la Religion des Anciens Romains. De la Castramentation & Discipline Militaire d'Iceux. Lyon: 1567. V. 66

THE DUCHOW Journal - a Voyage from Boston to California in 1852. San Francisco: 1959. V. 63

DUCK, STEPHEN
Poems on Several Occasions. London: 1736. V. 66
Poems on Several Occasions. London: 1738. V. 64

A DUCKLING and Some Dogs. London: 1920. V. 64

DUCKWORTH, JAMES
A Trip Round the World. Rochdale: 1890. V. 64

DUCKY Tales. London. V. 66

DU COMMUN, JEAN PIERRE NICHOLAS
L'Eloge des Tetons, Ouvrage Curieux, Galant et Badin.... Cologne: 1775. V. 65

DUCOUDRAY HOLSTEIN, H. L. V.
Memoirs of Simon Bolivar, President Liberator of the Republic of Colombia; and of His Principal Generals. Boston: 1829. V. 66
Memoirs of Simon Bolivar, President Liberator of the Republic of Columbia and of His Principal Generals. Boston: 1830. V. 66

DUCRUE, BENNO
Ducrue's Account of the Expulsion of the Jesuits from Lower California 1676-1769. St. Louis: 1967. V. 63

DU DEFFAND, MARIE DE VICHY-CHAMROND, MARQUISE
Correspondence Inedite. Paris: 1859. V. 63

DUDEVANT, JEAN F.
The History of the Harlequinade. London: 1915. V. 66

DUDGEON, D.
Inland Waters of Tropical Asia and Australia: Conservation and Management. Stuttgart: 1994. V. 64; 65

DUDIN, M.
The Art of the Bookbinder and Gilder, 1772. Leeds: 1977. V. 62; 65; 66

DUDLEY, DEAN
Officers of Our Union Army and Navy; Their Lives, Their Portraits. Boston: 1862. V. 66; 67

DUDLEY, EDGAR S.
A Reminiscence of Washington and Early's Attack in 1864. Cincinnati: 1884. V. 67

DUDLEY, JOHN WILLIAM WARD, 1ST EARL OF
Letters of the Earl of Dudley to the Bishop of Llandaff. London: 1840. V. 64

DUDLEY OBSERVATORY AND THE SCIENTIFC COUNCIL
Statement of the Trustees. Albany: 1858. V. 67

DUELLMAN, W. E.
Hylid Frogs of Middle America. 1970. V. 64
A Monographic Study of the Colubrid Snake Genus Leptodeira. New York: 1958. V. 66
The South American Herpetofauna: Its Origin, Evolution and Dispersal. London: 1931-1961. V. 62
The South American Herpetofauna: Its Origin, Evolution and Dispersal. Lawrence: 1979. V. 63; 66

DUER, WILLIAM ALEXANDER
The Life of William Alexander, Earl of Stirling, Major General in the Army of the United States, During the Revolution, with Selections from His Correspondence. New York: 1847. V. 63; 66

DUERDEN, J. E.
West Indian Madreporarian Polyps. Washington: 1902. V. 63

DUERER, ALBRECHT
Etliche Underricht, zu Befestigung der Stett, Schlosz, und Flecken. Nuremberg: 1527. V. 62; 63
The Humiliation and Exaltation of Our Redeemer in 32 Prints. London: 1856. V. 66
Institutionum Geometricarum...(with) De Urbibus, Arcibus, Castellisque Condendis... (Underweysung der Messung, mit dem Zirckel und Richtschyet.... Paris: 1532. V. 66
The Passion of Our Lord Jesus Christ.... London: 1844. V. 62
Passion Week. London: 1857. V. 66
Underweysung der Messung, mit dem Zirckel und Richtscheyt, in Linien Ebnen unnd Corporen...(with) Hierinn Sind Begriffen vier Bucher Von menschlicher Proportion. (bound before) Etliche Underricht, zu Befestigung der Stett, Schlosz, und Flecken. Nuremberg: 1525-1527. V. 65
Underweysung der Messung, mit dem Zirckel und Richtscheyt, in Linien Ebnen Unnd Gantzen Corporen...(with) Hierinn Sind Begriffen Vier Bucher von Menschlicher Proportion. (with) Etliche Underricht zu Befestigung der Stett, Schlosz, und flecken. Nuremberg: 1525-1528. V. 64

DUEZ, NATHANEL
Le Vray et Parfait Guidon de la Langue Francoise.... Amsterdam: 1669. V. 66

DU FAUR, FREDA
The Conquest of Mount Cook and Other Climbs. London: 1915. V. 63; 64; 66
The Conquest of Mount Cook and Other Climbs. London: 1936. V. 64

DUFF, CHARLES
Spain at War - A Monthly Journal of Facts and Pictures. London: 1938-1939. V. 62

DUFF, E. GORDON
The Printers, Stationers and Bookbinders of London and Westminster in the Fifteenth Century. London: 1899. V. 62

DUFF, P.
Geology of England and Wales. 1992. V. 67

DUFFET, THOMAS
The Spanish Rogue. London: 1674. V. 66

DUFFY, CHARLES G.
Conversations with Carlyle. 1982. V. 67

DUFFY, JOHN
A History of Public Health in New York City, 1625-1866. New York: 1968. V. 63

DUFIEF, N. G.
Nature Displayed in Her Mode of Teaching Langauge to Man.... Philadelphia: 1806. V. 62; 64; 67

DUFOUR, CHARLES L.
Nine Men in Gray. Garden City: 1963. V. 63

DUFOUR, JEAN ALEXANDER
Essai sur L'Hygiene des Hebreux. Montpelier: 1809. V. 63

DU FOUR, LE SIEUR
Recueil d'Epigrammes des Plus Fameux Poetes Latins. Paris: 1669. V. 64

DUFRAN, DORA
Low Down on Calamity Jane.... Rapid City: 1932. V. 62

DUFRENOY, ADELAIDE, MME. DE
Oeuvres Poetiqus.... Paris: 1826. V. 63

DUFRESNE, JOHN
Lethe, Cupid, Time and Love. Candia: 1994. V. 67
Louisiana Power and Light. New York and London: 1994. V. 63; 64; 66; 67
The Way That Water Enters Stone. New York: 1990. V. 62
The Way That Water Enters Stone. New York: 1991. V. 63; 64; 66
Well Enough Alone: Two Stories and Thirteen Poems. Candia: 1996. V. 63; 64; 67

DU FRESNOY, A.
L'Ecole d'Uranie ou l'Art de la Peinture. Paris: 1753. V. 66

DU FRESNOY, CHARLES ALPHONSE
L'Art de Peinture.... Paris: 1673. V. 62
The Art of Painting. London: 1750. V. 67
The Art of Painting. Dublin: 1783. V. 65
The Art of Painting. York: 1783. V. 64; 67
De Arte Graphica. The Art of Painting. London: 1695. V. 67

DUFRESNY, CHARLES, SIEUR DE LA RIVIERE
Amusements Serious and Comical; or a New Collection of Bons-Mots, Keen-Jests, Ingenious Thoughts, Pleasant Tales and Comical Adventures. London: 1719. V. 66

DUFTON, HENRY
Narrative of a Journey through Abyssinia in 1862-1863.... London: 1867. V. 64

DUFTON, WILLIAM
The Nature and Treatment of Deafness and Diseases of the Ear; and the Treatment of the Deaf and Dumb. London: 1844. V. 62

DUGAN, ALAN
Poems. New Haven: 1961. V. 63

DU GARD, ROGER MARTIN
Summer 1914. New York: 1941. V. 63; 64

DUGDALE, FLORENCE E.
The Book of Baby Beasts. London: 1911. V. 66
The Book of Baby Pets. London: 1910. V. 62

DUGDALE, R. L.
The Jukes. A Study in Crime, Pauperism, Disease and Heredity. New York: 1884. V. 67

DUGDALE, WILLIAM
The Antient Usage in Bearing of Such Ensigns of Honour as Are Commonly Call'd Arms. Oxford: 1682. V. 64
The Antiquities of Warwickshire Illustrated.... London: 1656. V. 62; 64; 65
The Baronage of England, or an Historical Account of the Lives and Memorable Actions of Our English Nobility in the Saxon Time. London: 1675-1676. V. 63
Monasticon Anglicanum: a History of the Abbies and Other Monasteries, Hospitals, Frieries and Cathedral and Collegiate Churches.... London: 1849. V. 63
A Short View of the Late Troubles in England.... Oxford: 1681. V. 62; 65

DUGES, ANTOINE LOUIS
Memoire sur la Conformite Organique dans l'Echelle Animale. Montpellier: 1832. V. 65

DUGGAN, ALFRED
Conscience of the King. London: 1951. V. 62

DUGGER, SHEPHERD MONROE
The Balsam Groves of the Grandfather Mountain: a Tale of the Western North Carolina Mountains. Banner Elk: 1892. V. 67
The War Trails of the Blue Ridge. Banner Elk: 1932. V. 63; 66; 67

DUGMORE, ARTHUR RADCLYFFE
Camera Adventures in the African Wilds. New York: 1910. V. 64
The Romance of the Newfoundland Caribou. 1913. V. 62; 63; 64; 66; 67
The Romance of the Newfoundland Caribou. Philadelphia: 1913. V. 67
The Wonderland of Big Game. London: 1925. V. 67

DUGRES, GABRIEL
Dialogi Gallico-Anglico-Latini. Oxford: 1639. V. 65

DU GUILLET, PERNETTE
Rymes de Gentile et Vertueuse Dame D. Pernette du Guillet, Lyonnoise. Lyon: 1856. V. 66

DUHAMEL, H.
The Central Alps of the Dauphiny. London: 1905. V. 64

DU HAMEL, J. B.
De Corpre Animato Libri Quatuor, Seu Promotae Per Experimenta Philosophiae Specimen Alterum. Paris: 1673. V. 64

DUHAMEL, JEAN MARIE CONSTANT
Cours D'Analyse de L'Ecole Polytechnique. Paris: 1841-1840. V. 67

DUHAMEL, PASCHAL
Perspectivus Tribus Libris Succincte Denuo Correcta, et Figuris Illustrata. Paris: 1556. V. 66

DUHAMEL DU MONCEAU, HENRI LOUIS
A Practical Treatise of Husbandry. 1759. V. 63
A Practical Treatise of Husbandry. London: 1759. V. 62; 66

DU HASSET, MADAME
The Private Memoirs of.... New York: 1827. V. 65

DUHEM, PIERRE MAURICE MARIE
Traite Elementaire de Mecanique Chimique Fondee sur la Thermodynamique.... Paris: 1897-1899. V. 65

DUINWAY, ABIGAIL SCOTT
David and Anna Matson. New York: 1876. V. 65

DUKE, BASIL W.
History of Morgan's Cavalry. Cincinnati: 1867. V. 62; 63; 65
A History of Morgan's Cavalry. Bloomington: 1960. V. 63
Morgan's Cavalry. New York and Washington: 1906. V. 62; 63
Reminiscences of General Basil W. Duke C.S.A. Garden City: 1911. V. 62; 63; 65

DUKE, EDWARD
Prolusiones Historicae; or Essays Illustrative of the Halle of John Halle, Citizen and Merchant of Salisbury in the Reigns of Henry IV and Edward IV with Notes.... Salisbury: 1827. V. 63

DUKE, J. A.
CRC Handbook of Nuts. Boca Raton: 1989. V. 62

DUKE, JOHN A.
The Columban Church. 1932. V. 63; 66

THE DUKE of Anjou's Succession Considered, As To Its Legality and Consequences...(with) The Duke of Anjou's Succession Further Consider'd As to the Danger that May Arise From it to Europe in General.... London: 1701. V. 64

DUKE of Cleveland's Fox Hounds. Operations of the Baby Pack. Richmond, Yorks: 1839. V. 64

DUKE-ELDER, W. STEWART
Text-Book of Ophthalmology. London: 1932-1954. V. 64

DULAC, EDMUND
Edmund Dulac's Fairy Book. London. V. 65
Edmund Dulac's Fairy Book. London: 1916. V. 62
Edmund Dulac's Picture-Book for the French Red Cross. London: 1914. V. 64
Edmund Dulac's Picture-Book for the French Red Cross. London: 1915. V. 63
Edmund Dulac's Picture Book for the French Red Cross. London: 1917. V. 64
Fairy Book. London: 1917. V. 64
A Fairy Garland Being Fairy Tales from the Old French. London: 1928. V. 62
The Legion Book. London: 1930. V. 64
Lyrics, Pathetic & Humorous from A to Z. London: 1908. V. 64
Lyrics Pathetic and Humorous from A to Z. London: 1909. V. 64

DULAU & CO.
A Catalogue of Foreign Books, Comprising Popular and Standard Works in the French and Other Foreign Languages. London: 1845. V. 62

DULLAERT, JEAN
Questiones Super Duos Libros Peri Hermenias Aristotelis. Salamanca: 1517. V. 62

DULLES, JOHN FOSTER
War or Peace. New York: 1950. V. 63; 67

DU LUC, JEAN ANDRE
Lettres Physiques et Morales sur l'Histoire de la Terre et de l'Homme. Paris & La Haye: 1779-1700. V. 65

DUMAREST, NOEL
Notes on Cochiti, New Mexico. Lancaster: 1919. V. 67

DUMAS, ALEXANDRE
La Bouillie de la Comtesse Berthe. Paris: 1845. V. 66
The Count of Monte Cristo. London: 1846. V. 65
La Dame Aux Camelias. Paris: 1872. V. 62
The Honey Stew of the Countess Bertha, A Fairy Tale. London: 1846. V. 66
The Memoirs. London: 1891. V. 67
(Novels). London: 1910-1911. V. 67
Pascal Bruno. London: 1837. V. 67
The Three Musketeers. New York: 1932. V. 64

DUMAS, F. RIBADEAU
These Moderns. London: 1932. V. 62

DU MAURIER, DAPHNE
Hospoda Jamajka. (Jamaica Inn). Prague: 1972. V. 65

DU MAURIER, GEORGE
Peter Ibbetson. London: 1892. V. 66; 67
Trilby. London: 1895. V. 62
Trilby. London: 1895. V. 67

DUMONT, ETIENNE
Recollections of Mirabeau, and of the Two First Legislative Assemblies of France. London: 1832. V. 64

DUMONT, GEORGES
Annales d'Electricite et de magnetisme (1889-1890) & (1891-1892).... Paris: 1890-1892. V. 65

DU MONT, JOHN S.
Custer Battle Guns. Fort Collins: 1974. V. 65; 67

DUMONT, P. J.
Narrative of Thirty-Four Years; Slavery and Travels in Africa. London: 1819. V. 64; 66

DUMONT DE MONTEUX, PIERRE LOUIS CHARLES
Testament Medical Philosophique et Litteraire.... Paris: 1865. V. 65

DU MOULIN, PETER
The Anatomy of the Mass... Together With a Learned Treatise of Traditions. Dublin: 1750. V. 63
Petri Molinaei...Poematum Libelli Tres. 1. Hymni in Symbolum Aposolorum. 2. Ecclesiae Gemitus. 3. Sylva Variorum.... London: 1670. V. 63

DUNANT, JEAN HENRI
A Memory of Solferino. Washington: 1939. V. 65
Un Souvenir de Solferino.... Geneva: 1862. V. 62; 64; 65

DUNAWAY, WAYLAND FULLER
Reminiscences of a Rebel. New York: 1913. V. 63

DUNBAR, ALICE
The Goodness of Saint Rocque. New York: 1899. V. 65

DUNBAR, JENNIE
Young Hopeful. London: 1932. V. 65

DUNBAR, PAUL LAURENCE
Candle-Lightin' Time. New York: 1901. V. 64; 66
The Fanatics. New York: 1901. V. 64
Folks from Dixie. New York: 1898. V. 64; 67
The Heart of Happy Hollow. New York: 1904. V. 64
Joggin' Erlong. New York: 1906. V. 66
Lyrics of Sunshine and Shadow. New York: 1905. V. 66
Lyrics of the Hearthside. New York: 1899. V. 62; 63
Speakin' O' Christmas. New York: 1914. V. 62; 64
The Strength of Gideon and Other Stories. New York: 1900. V. 65
The Uncalled. New York: 1898. V. 62; 64; 66; 67

DUNBAR, SEYMOUR
A History of Travel in America. Indianapolis: 11915. V. 64

DUNBAR-BRUNTON, JAMES
Big Game Hunting in Central Africa.... London: 1912. V. 62

DUNBAR-NELSON, ALICE MOORE
The Dunbar Speaker and Entertainer. Naperville: 1920. V. 62

DUNCAN, A.
Roll of the Officers and Members of the Georgia Hussars. Savannah: 1906. V. 62

DUNCAN, ALASTAIR
American Art Deco. New York: 1986. V. 65
Art Nouveau and Art Deco Bookbinding: French Masterpieces 1880-1940. New York: 1989. V. 62; 64; 65
Tiffany at Auction. New York: 1981. V. 62; 65

DUNCAN, ALEXANDER
The History of the Revolution 1688.... Edinburgh: 1790. V. 62
Miscellaneous Essays, Naval, Moral, Political and Divine. London: 1799. V. 66

DUNCAN, ANDREW
A Letter to Dr. James Gregory of Edinburgh, in Consequence of Certain Printed Papers.... Edinburgh: 1811. V. 62
A Tribute of Regard to the Memory of Sir Henry Raeburn, R.A. Portrait Painter to the King for Scotland.... Edinburgh: 1824. V. 67

DUNCAN, DANIEL
La Chymie Naturelle ou l'Explication Chymique et Mechanique de la Nourriture de l'Animal. Paris: 1683. V. 64

DUNCAN, DAVID
Goodbye Picasso. New York: 1974. V. 63
The Life and Letters of Herbert Spencer. London: 1908. V. 64

DUNCAN, DAVID JAMES
The Brothers K. New York: 1992. V. 67
The River Why. San Francisco: 1983. V. 63; 67

DUNCAN, F.
Canada in 1871; or, Our Empire in the West. London: 1872. V. 64

DUNCAN, FRANCIS
A Description of the Island of St. Helena.... London: 1805. V. 64

DUNCAN, GEORGE
Bibliography of Glass (From the Earliest Records to 1940). London: 1960. V. 62

DUNCAN, GEORGE JOHN C.
Memoir of the Rev. Henry Duncan, D.D. Minister of Ruthwell, Founder of the Savings Banks.... Edinburgh: 1848. V. 64

DUNCAN, HARRY
Doors of Perception: Essays in Book Typography. Austin: 1983. V. 62; 64

DUNCAN, HENRY
The Young South Country Weaver; or a Journey to Glasgow; a Tale for the Radicals. Edinburgh: 1821. V. 63

DUNCAN, ISADORA
My Life. New York: 1927. V. 66

DUNCAN, J.
The Natural History of Bees. Edinburgh: 1840. V. 66

DUNCAN, JONATHAN
The Bank Charter Act: Ought the Bank of England or the People of England to Receive the Profits of the National Circulation?. London: 1857. V. 64
The History of Russia from the Foundation of the Empire to the Close of the Hungarian War. London: 1854. V. 66

DUNCAN, P. M.
A Revision of Genera and Great Groups of the Echinoidea. London: 1889. V. 62

DUNCAN, PETER
A Letter of Exposure and Remonstrance, Respectfully Addressed to Isaac Taylor, Esq., in Which His Allegations Against the Integrity and Ecclesiastical Order of Wesleyan Methodism.... Bath: 1852. V. 64
Report of the Proceedings Under a Brieve of Idiotry, Peter Duncan Against David Yoolow, Tried at Coupar-Angus, 28-30 Jan. 1837. Edinburgh: 1837. V. 63

DUNCAN, PHILIP BURY
Essays and Miscellanea. Oxford: 1840. V. 62

DUNCAN, ROBERT
A Book of Resemblances - Poems 1950-1953. New Haven: 1966. V. 62
Caesar's Gate. Poems 1949-1950. Palma de Mallorca: 1955. V. 64; 65
The Cat and the Blackbird. San Francisco: 1967. V. 63
Faust Foutu. San Francisco: 1960. V. 62
From the Maginogion. N.P: 1963. V. 62; 64
Ground Work: Before the War. New York: 1984. V. 63
Letters. Highlands: 1958. V. 63; 64
Medieval Scenes 1950 and 1959. Kent: 1978. V. 62; 64
Notebook: Poems. San Francisco: 1991. V. 64
A Paris Visit. Five Poems. New York: 1985. V. 62; 64
Sets of Syllables. Sets of Words. Sets of Lines. Sets of Poems Addressing: Veil, Turbine, Cord & Bird. New York: 1979. V. 63
Six Prose Pieces. Rochester: 1966. V. 64
Stein Imitations - a Composition Book for Madison 1953. Albuquerque: 1964. V. 62
The Sweetness and Greatness of Dante's Divine Comedy 1265-1965. San Francisco: 1965. V. 62
The Truth and Life of Myth: an Essay in Essential Autobiography. New York: 1968. V. 63
The Years as Catches - First Poems (1939-1946). Berkeley: 1966. V. 62; 63

DUNCAN, SINCLAIR THOMSON
Journal of a Voyage to Australia by the Cape of Good Hope, Six Months in melbourne and Return to England by Cape Horn.... Edinburgh: 1884. V. 65

DUNCAN, STANLEY
The Complete Wildfowler. (Ashore and Afloat). London: 1950. V. 67

DUNCAN, THOMAS D.
Recollections of Thomas D. Duncan, a Confederate Soldier. Nashville: 1922. V. 62

DUNCAN, WILLIAM
Fairburn's Edition of the Trial of William Duncan for the Wilful Murder of William Chivers at Battersea, January 24, 1807. London: 1807. V. 63

DUNCAN, WINTHROP
A Narrative of the Captivity of Isaac Webster. Metuchen: 1927. V. 66

DUNCKER, ALEXANDER
Die Landlichen Wohnsitze, Schlosser und Residenzen der Ritterschaftlichen Grundbesitzer in der Preussischen Monarchie.... Berlin: 1857-1883. V. 64

DUNCOMBE, GILES
Tryals per Pais in Capital Matters.... London: 1702. V. 63

DUNCOMBE, J.
Dramatic Tales. Field of Forty Footsteps. 1825. V. 65
Dramatic Tales. Field of Forty Footsteps. London: 1825. V. 62

DUNCUM, BARBARA
The Development of Inhalation Anaesthesia. 1947. V. 64

DUNDONALD, THOMAS COCHRANE
The Autobiography of a Seaman. London: 1861. V. 67

DUNDONALD, THOMAS COCHRANE, 10TH EARL OF
The Autobiography of a Seaman. London: 1860. V. 62; 66
The Calumnious Aspersions Contained in the Report of the Sub- Committee of the Stock Exchange Exposed and Refuted, In So Far as Regards Lord Cochrane, the Hon. Cochrane Johnstone and R. G.... London: 1814. V. 63
A Letter to Lord Ellenborough from Lord Cochrane. London: 1815. V. 63
The Trial of Lord Cochrane and Others, for a Conspiracy. London: 1814. V. 63

DUNGLISON, ROBLEY
Medical Lexicon. Philadelphia: 1848. V. 63
On the Influence of Atmosphere and Locality, Change of Air and Climate, Seasons, Food, Clothing, Bathing, Exercise, Sleep, Corporeal & Intellectual Pursuits, &c.... Philadelphia: 1835. V. 65

DUNHAM, JOHN M.
The Vocal Companion and Masonic Register. Boston: 1802. V. 62

DUNHAM, K. C.
Geology of the Northern Pennine Orefield. Volume 1 - Tyne to Stainmore. London: 1967. V. 64; 65

DUNHEM, PIERRE MAURICE MARIE
Traite Elementaire de Mecanique Chimique Fondee sur la Thermodynamique. Paris: 1897-1899. V. 63

DUNIWAY, ABIGAIL SCOTT
David and Anna Matson. New York: 1876. V. 63

DUNKIN, EDWIN
The Midnight Sky: Familiar Notes on the Stars and Planets. London: 1869. V. 65

DUNKIN, JOHN
The History and Antiquities of Bicester.... London: 1816. V. 65; 66

DUNKIN, ROBERT
The Roedeer. London: 1904. V. 66
The Roedeer. Southampton: 1987. V. 62; 67

DUNKLE, JOHN J.
Prison Life During the Rebellion. Singer's Glen: 1869. V. 62; 63

DUNLAP, SUSAN
Karma. Toronto: 1981. V. 67

DUNLAP, WILLIAM
History of the New Netherlands, Province of New York and State of New York, to the Adoption of the Federal Constitution. New York: 1839-1840. V. 64
The Life of George Frederick Cook.... London: 1815. V. 66

DUNLOP, JOHN
The History of Fiction. London: 1814. V. 63; 64
The History of Fiction. London: 1816. V. 64
The History of Fiction. London: 1845. V. 62

DUNLOP, MADELEINE A. W.
How We Spent the Autumn; or Wanderings in Brittany. London: 1860. V. 65

DUNLOP, WILLIAM S.
S. Lee's Sharpshooters' or the Forefront of Battle. Little Rock: 1899. V. 65

DUNMORE, JOHN
The Expedition of the St. Jean Baptiste to the Pacific 1769-1770 from Journals of Jean de Surville and Guillaume Labe. London: 1981. V. 63; 64

DUNN, DOROTHY
American Indian Painting. Albuquerque: 1968. V. 63

DUNN, DOUGLAS
Elegies. London: 1985. V. 62
A Rumoured City - New Poets from Hull. Newcastle-upon-Tyne: 1982. V. 64

DUNN, HENRY
Principles of Teaching; or, the Normal School Manual. Hamilton: 1845. V. 66
Principles of Teaching; or, the Normal School Manual. London: 1845. V. 62

DUNN, HENRY T.
Recollections of Dante Gabriel Rossetti and His Circle or Cheyne Walk Life. 1984. V. 64

DUNN, J.
Perilous Trails of Texas. Dallas: 1932. V. 67

DUNN, J. P.
Massacres of the Mountains: a History of the Indian Wars in the Far West. New York: 1886. V. 63; 64; 65; 67

DUNN, JAMES
Essay on the Present State of Manners and Education Among the Lower Class of the People of Ireland, and the Means of Improving Them. Dublin: 1799. V. 65

DUNN, JOHN
The History, Antiquities and Present State of the Town of Nottingham.... Nottingham: 1807. V. 65

DUNN, JOSEPH
The Ancient Irish Epic Tale: Tain Bo Cualgne. 1914. V. 62

DUNN, KATHERINE
Attic. New York: 1970. V. 62; 63
Geek Love. New York: 1989. V. 63
Truck. New York: 1971. V. 62; 64; 65; 67

DUNN, MATTHIAS
An Historical, Geological and Descriptive View of the Coal Trade of the North of England.... Newcastle-upon-Tyne: 1844. V. 64

DUNN, SAMUEL
Memoirs of Mr. Thomas Tatham and of Wesleyan Methodism in Nottingham. 1847. V. 64

DUNN, THOMAS
A Discourse Delivered in the New Dutch Church, Nassau Street, on Tuesday, Oct. 21, 1794. New York: 1794. V. 67

DUNNE, EDWARD F.
Illinois, the Heart of the Nation. Chicago and New York: 1933. V. 67

DUNNE, J. W.
An Experiment with Time. London: 1927. V. 67
Sunshine and the Dry Fly. London: 1924. V. 67
Sunshine and the Dry Fly. 1926. V. 67

DUNNETT, DOROTHY
Dolly and the Bird of Paradise. London: 1983. V. 67

DUNNING, JOHN
Booked to Die. New York: 1992. V. 62; 63; 65; 66; 67
Booked to Die. London: 1993. V. 67
The Bookman's Wake. New York: 1994. V. 62; 64; 65; 67
The Bookman's Wake. New York: 1995. V. 67
The Bookscout. Minneapolis: 1998. V. 65; 67
Deadline. New York: 1981. V. 65
Deadline. Huntington Beach: 1995. V. 62; 63; 64; 65; 67
A Defence of the United Company of Merchants of England, Trading to the East-Indies and their Servants.... London: 1762. V. 62
Denver Now. Denver: 1982. V. 64; 65; 67
Dreamer. Huntington Beach: 1995. V. 63; 66; 67
On the Air. New York: 1998. V. 64; 66; 67
On the Air. Oxford: 1998. V. 67
The Torch Passes. Huntington Beach: 1995. V. 62
Tune in Yesterday. Englewood Cliffs: 1976. V. 66; 67
Tune in Yesterday. New York: 1976. V. 66; 67
Two O'Clock Eastern War Time. New York: 2000. V. 67
Two O'Clock, Eastern War Time. New York: 2001. V. 67

DUNPHIE, CHARLES JAMES
The Splendid Advantages of Being a woman, and Other Erratic Essays. New York: 1880. V. 63

DUNSANY, EDWARD JOHN MORETON DRAX PLUNKETT
Alexander, and Three Small Plays. 1926. V. 62; 64; 66
The Charwoman's Shadow. London: 1926. V. 63
The Compromise of the King of the Golden Isles. New York: 1924. V. 62; 64
The Curse of the Wise Woman. London: 1933. V. 66
The Fourth Book of Jorkens. London: 1947. V. 67
The Fourth Book of Jorkens. Sauk City: 1948. V. 64; 67
Guerilla. 1944. V. 67
If. 1922. V. 62; 64; 66
If I Were Dictator. London: 1934. V. 62; 64; 66
Rory and Bran. 1937. V. 62; 64; 66
Selections from the Writings of Lord Dunsany. Churchtown: 1912. V. 62; 63
The Sword of Welleran and Other Stories. London: 1908. V. 63
Tales of War. Dublin: 1918. V. 67
Unhappy Far-Off Things. 1919. V. 64

DUNSTERVILLE, G. C. K.
Orchid Hunting in the Lost World (and elsewhere in Venezuela). West Palm Beach: 1988. V. 67
Orchids of Venezuela. Cambridge: 1979. V. 67

DUNSTONE, N.
Behaviour and Ecology of Riparian Mammals. Cambridge: 1998. V. 64

DUNTHORNE, GORDON
Flower and Fruit Prints of the 18th and Early 19th Centuries.... Washington: 1938. V. 66; 67

DUNTON, JOHN
Athenian Sport, or, Two Thousand Paradoxes Merrily Argued.... London: 1707. V. 65
The Life and Errors of John Dunton. London: 1818. V. 62; 67
The Phenix; or, a Revival of Scarce and Valuable Pieces from the Remotest Antiquity Down to the Present Times. London: 1707-1708. V. 63; 67

DUPASQUIER, LOUIS
Monographie de Notre Dame du Brou, Texte.... Paris: 1850. V. 66

DUPIN, JACQUES
Fits and Starts. Weston: 1974. V. 62
Joan Miro: Life and Work. New York: 1962. V. 62; 63; 64; 66

DUPIN, LOUIS ELLIES
A Compleat History of the Canon and Writers, of the Books of the Old and New Testament.... London: 1699-1700. V. 67
A New History of Ecclesiastical Writers.... London: 1697-1699. V. 67

DUPLAIX, LILY
The White Bunny and His Magic. New York: 1945. V. 63

DU-PLAT-TAYLOR, F. M.
The Design, Construction and Maintenance of Docks, Wharves and Piers. London: 1928. V. 62; 66
The Design, Construction and Maintenance of Docks, Wharves and Piers. London: 1949. V. 62

DUPLEIX, SCIPION
La Curiosite Naturelle Redigee en Questions Selon l'Ordre Alphabetique. Rouen: 1648. V. 64

DUPLESSIS, GEORGES
Histoire de la Gravure en France. Paris: 1861. V. 63

DUPONT, INGE
Morgan Library Ghost Stories. Roslyn: 1990. V. 67

DU PONT, J. E.
Philippine Birds. Greenville: 1971. V. 67

DUPONT-AUBERVILLE
Industriel L'Ornement des Tissus. Recueil Historique et Pratique. Paris: 1877. V. 64

DUPPA, RICHARD
The Life of Michel Angelo Buonarroti, with His Poetry and Letters. London: 1807. V. 66

DUPREE, A. H.
Asa Gray 1810-1888. Cambridge: 1959. V. 67

DUPUY, R. ERNEST
St. Vith: Lion in the Way. Washington: 1949. V. 67

DURAN, ANTONIO
Cercos de Mocambique, Defendidos Por Don Estevan de Atayde.... Madrid: 1633. V. 62

DURAND, EDWARD
Wandering with a Fly-Rod. London: 1938. V. 67

DURAND, J. P. L.
A Voyage ot Senegal; or Historical, Philosophical and Political Memoirs.... London: 1806. V. 64

DURANTY, LOUIS EMILE
Theatre des Marionnettes. Paris: 1880. V. 65

DURAS, CLAIRE DE DURFORT, DUCHESSE DE
Ourika. Paris: 1824. V. 67
Ourika. 1977. V. 64
Ourika. Austin: 1977. V. 67

DURAS, MARGUERITE
The Ravishing of Lol Stein. London: 1966. V. 66

DURCAN, THOMAS J.
History of Irish Education from 1800. 1972. V. 67

DU REFUGE, EUSTACHE
Arcana Aulica; or Walsingham's Manual of Prudential Maxims for the States-Man and Courtier. London: 1694. V. 62; 64

DURFEE, JOB
The Panidea; or an Omnipresent Reason considered as the Creative and Sustaining Logos. Boston: 1846. V. 65

D'URFEY, THOMAS
The Marriage Hater Match'd: a Comedy. London: 1692. V. 65
New Opera's with Comical Stories and Poems on Several Occasions, Never Before Printed. London: 1721. V. 65
Tales Tragical and Comical. London: 1704. V. 65
Wit and Mirth; or Pills to Purge Melancholy Being a Collection of the Best Merry Ballads and Songs, Old and New. London: 1719-1720. V. 64

DURHAM, DICK
Our Strip of Land. A History of Daggett County, Utah. Lusk: 1947. V. 64

DURHAM, J. M. B. B.
Melton and Homespun. London: 1913. V. 67

DURHAM, JAMES
Clavis Cantici; or, an Exposition of the Song of Solomon. Glasgow: 1723. V. 63
The Collection of Pictures at Raynham Hall.... N.P: 1926. V. 64

DURHAM, JOHN GEORGE LAMBTON, 1ST EARL OF
The Report of the Earl of Durham, Her Majesty's High Commissioner and Governor-General of British North America. London: 1902. V. 64

DURHAM, MARY EDITH
The Struggle for Scutari. London: 1914. V. 64
Through the Lands of the Serb. London: 1904. V. 64
Twenty Years of Balkan Triangle. London: 1920. V. 64

DURICK, AGNES YORK
Father Bear, Mother Bears and Baby Bear to Read and Color. Cleveland: 1932. V. 64

DURLACHER, LEWIS
A Concise Treatise on Corns, Bunions and the Disorders of Nails with Advice for the General Management of the Feet. London: 1858. V. 62; 66; 67

DURLEY, THOMAS
A Tangled Yarn: Captain James Payen's Life Log. London: 1891. V. 62

DURLING, RICHARD J.
A Catalogue of Sixteenth Century Books in the National Library of Medicine. Bethesda: 1967. V. 62; 63

DURRANT, VALENTINE
The Cheveley Novels. A Modern Minister. London: 1878. V. 66
The Cheveley Novels. Saul Weir. London: 1879. V. 66

DURRELL, GERALD
The Bafut Beagles. New York: 1954. V. 63
Birds, Beasts and Relatives. New York: 1969. V. 63
Catch Me a Colobus. New York: 1972. V. 63
Fauna and Family. New York: 1978. V. 63
Menagerie Manor. London: 1964. V. 63
My Family and Other Animals. London: 1956. V. 63
The Picnic and Other Inimitable Stories. New York: 1980. V. 63

DURRELL, LAWRENCE GEORGE
The Alexandria Quartet. New York and London: 1957-1960. V. 66
The Alexandria Quartet. London: 1962. V. 63; 64; 65
The Alexandria Quartet. New York: 1962. V. 66; 67
Beccafico. La Licorne: 1963. V. 63
Beccafico. Le Becfigue. Montpellier: 1963. V. 62
Bitter Lemons. London: 1957. V. 63
The Black Book. Paris: 1938. V. 63
The Black Book. New York: 1960. V. 63; 65
Blue Thirst. Santa Barbara: 1975. V. 63; 64
Cities, Plains and People - Poems. London: 1946. V. 62; 63; 67
Collected Poems. London: 1960. V. 63
Collected Poems 1931-1974. 1980. V. 67
Collected Poems 1931-1974. London: 1980. V. 62; 63; 64
Deus Loci. Ischia: 1950. V. 62; 63
The Grey Penitents. London: 1973. V. 63
Groddeck. Wiesbaden: 1961. V. 62
The Ikons and Other Poems. London: 1966. V. 63
In Arcadia. 1968. V. 66
A Landmark Gone. Los Angeles: 1949. V. 63
Monsieur or the Prince of Darkness. London: 1974. V. 62
Mountolive. London: 1958. V. 67
Nothing is Lost, Sweet Self. 1967. V. 66
On Seeming to Presume. London: 1948. V. 63; 64
On the Suchness of the Old Boy. 1972. V. 64
The Plant-Magic Man. Santa Barbara: 1973. V. 62
A Private Country. London: 1943. V. 63
Quinx or the Ripper's Tale. London: 1985. V. 62
The Red Limbo Lingo. London: 1971. V. 67
Sappho. A Play in Verse. London: 1950. V. 63
Sauve Qui Peut. London: 1976. V. 63
Selected Poems. London: 1956. V. 63
Sicilian Carousel. London: 1977. V. 62
Six Poems from the Greek of Sekilianos and Seferis. Rhodes: 1946. V. 63
The Tree of Idleness and Other Poems. London: 1955. V. 63; 67
Vega and Other Poems. London: 1973. V. 63
White Eagles Over Serbia. London: 1957. V. 63

DURRENMATT, FRIEDRICH
The Pledge. London: 1959. V. 67
Der Richter und sein Henker. Einseideln: 1952. V. 67

DURRETT, REUBEN T.
Traditions of the Earliest Visits of Foreigners to North America. Louisville: 1908. V. 67

DURY, ANDREW
Le Porte Feuille Neccessaire a Tous Les Seigneurs qui Font le Tour D'Italie.... London: 1774. V. 65

DURY, THEODORE
The Monthly Teacher, Published During the Year 1831. Keighley: 1831. V. 64; 65

DUSARD, JAY
The North American Cowboy: a Portrait. Prescott: 1983. V. 63; 64; 66; 67

DUSEJOUR, DIONIS
The Origin of the Graces. London: 1895. V. 62
The Origin of the Graces. London: 1900. V. 66

DUSFRESNY, CHARLES RIVIERE
Amusemens Serieus et Comiques. Amsterdam: 1700. V. 66

DUSTIN, FRED
The Custer Fight. Hollywood: 1936. V. 65; 67
The Custer Tragedy - Events Leading Up to and Following the Little Big Horn Campaign of 1876. 1939. V. 65
The Custer Tragedy - Events Leading Up to and Following the Little Big Horn Campaign of 1876. El Segundo: 1987. V. 67

DU TEMPLE, JEAN LOUIS RIVALLON
Communications et Transmissions de la Pensee: l'Audition, la Vue, la Parole, les Sons, etc. etc. Paris: 1878. V. 67

THE DUTIES of a Lady's Maid.... London: 1825. V. 65

DUTIES Payable by Law on all Goods, Wares and Merchandise, Imported Into the United States of America, After the Last Day of June 1812. Washington?: 1812. V. 63

DUTTON, BERTHA P.
Sun Father's Way. The Kiva Murals of Kuaua. Albuquerque/Santa Fe: 1963. V. 63; 66

DUTTON, CHARLES J.
The Shadow of Evil. New York: 1930. V. 67

DUTTON, E. A. T.
The Basuto of Basutoland. London: 1923. V. 64
Kenya Mountain. London: 1929. V. 63; 64
Kenya Mountain. 1930. V. 63; 65

DUTTON, FRANCIS
South Australia and Its Mines, and an Historical Sketch of the Colony, Under Its Several Administrations, to the Period of Captain Grey's Departure. London: 1846. V. 65

DUTTON, GEOFFREY
Russell Drysdale. London: 1964. V. 65

DUTTON, LEWIS
Joan in Flowerland. London: 1935. V. 63

DUVAL, ELIZABETH W.
T. E. Lawrence. A Bibliography. New York: 1938. V. 64

DUVAL, ISAAC H.
Texas Argonauts: Isaac Duval and the California Gold Rush. San Francisco: 1988. V. 63

DUVAL, JOHN C.
The Adventures of Big-Foot Wallace - the Texas Ranger and Hunter. Macon: 1870. V. 63

DUVAL, MARY V.
The Queen of the South...a Drama. Grenada: 1901. V. 63

DUVAL, P.
The Art of Glen Loates. Ontario: 1977. V. 67

DU VAL, PIERRE
Geographia Universalis: the Present State of the Whole World.... London: 1685. V. 67

DUVERNOY, HENRI M.
Human Brainstem Vessels. Berlin: 1978. V. 66; 67

DUVIVIER, DU TILLE
Nouveau Calendrier Perpetuel, Compose en Faveur des Curieux.... Paris: 1747. V. 64

DUVOISIN, ROGER
Donkey-Donkey: The Troubles of a Silly Little Donkey. Racine: 1934. V. 66
Donkey-Donkey: the Troubles of a Silly Little Donkey. New York: 1940. V. 62

DUYCKINCK, EVERT A.
National History of the War for the Union. New York: 1861. V. 66
National Portrait Gallery of Eminent Americans.... New York: 1862. V. 65
Portrait Gallery of Eminent Men and Women of Europe and America. New York: 1872-1874. V. 62; 67

DUYCKINCK, WHITEHEAD CORNELL
The Duyckinck and Allied Families. New York: 1908. V. 63; 66

DUZGUNMAN, MUSTAPHA
(Turkish Marbling). Istanbul: 1989. V. 64

DWIGGINS, W. A.
The Books of WAD - a Bibliography of the Books Designed by W. A. Dwiggins. Baton Rouge: 1974. V. 65
MSS. by WAD - Being a Collection of the Writings of Dwiggins on Various Subjects, Some Critical, Some Philosophical, Some Whimsical. New York: 1947. V. 63
Millenium I. New York: 1945. V. 65
Paraphs. New York: 1928. V. 63
22 Printers' Marks and Seals Designed or Redrawn.... New York: 1929. V. 63

DWIGHT, J.
The Sequence of Plumages and Moults of the Passerine Birds of New York. London: 1900. V. 67

DWIGHT, JONATHAN
Memoirs of Rev. David Brainerd; Missionary to the Indians On the Borders of New York, New Jersey and Pennsylvania. New Haven: 1822. V. 64

DWIGHT, NATHANIEL
A Short but Comprehensive System of the Geography of the World.... Elizabeth Town: 1801. V. 66
A Short but Comprehensive System of the Geography of the World.... New York: 1808. V. 63; 66

DWIGHT, T.
The Anatomy of the Head with Six Lithographic Plates Representing Frozen Sections. Boston: 1876. V. 67
Description of the Balaenoptera Musculus in the Possession of the Boston Society of Natural History. Boston: 1871. V. 63

DWIGHT, THEODORE
The Northern Traveller, and Northern Tour, with Routes to the Springs, Niagara and Quebec, and the Coal Mines of Pennsylvania.... New York: 1830. V. 62
The Northern Traveller: Containing the Routes to Niagara, Quebec and the Springs.... New York: 1825. V. 62
An Oration Spoken Before The Connecticut Society, for the Promotion of Freedom and the Relief of Persons Unlawfully Holden in Bondage. Hartford: 1794. V. 66

DWIGHT, TIMOTHY
The Conquest of Canaan: a Poem in Eleven Books. London: 1788. V. 63
Greenfield Hill: a Poem, in Seven Parts. (with) The Triumph of Infidelity; a Poem. New York: 1794-1788. V. 62
Travels in New England and New York. New Haven: 1821-1822. V. 64; 66
Travels in New England and New York. London: 1823. V. 64

DWINELLE, JOHN W.
The Colonial History of the City of San Francisco. San Diego: 1924. V. 63

DWYER, ALEXANDER
A Discourse on the Structure of the Poetry of the Hebrews. Utica: 1830. V. 66

DWYER, K. R.
Dragonfly. New York: 1975. V. 62

DWYER, PHILIP
The Diocese of Killaloe from the Reformation to the Close of the 18th Century. 1878. V. 62; 65
The Siege of Londonderry in 1689. 1893. V. 62

DYBEK, STUART
Childhood and Other Neighborhoods. New York: 1980. V. 63

DYCHE, THOMAS
A New General English Dictionary. London: 1752. V. 64
A New General English Dictionary. London: 1759. V. 64

DYCK, PAUL
Brule, the Sioux People of the Rosebud. Flagstaff: 1971. V. 65; 67

DYE, JOHN SMITH
The Adder's Den; or Secrets of the Great Conspiracy to Overthrow Liberty in America. New York: 1864. V. 62

DYE, JON
Recollections of a Pioneer 1830-1852. Rocky Mountains, New Mexico, California. Los Angeles: 1951. V. 65

DYER, ALFRED S.
The European Slave Trade in English Girls. London: 1885. V. 65

THE DYER and Colour Maker's Companion.... Philadelphia: 1850. V. 64

DYER, ANTHONY
Classic African Animals: the Big Five. New York: 1973. V. 66; 67
The East African Hunters, the History of the East African Professional Hunters' Association. Clinton: 1979. V. 65

DYER, D. B., MRS.
Fort Reno or Picturesque Cheyenne and Arapahoe Army Life. Flagstaff: 1971. V. 67

DYER, FRANK L.
Edison, His Life and Inventions. New York: 1910. V. 63; 64; 66

DYER, FREDERICK H.
A Compendium of the War of the Rebellion. New York: 1959. V. 63; 65
A Compendium of the War of the Rebellion. 1994. V. 65

DYER, GILBERT
A Restoration of the Ancient Modes of Bestowing Names on the Rivers, Hills, Vallies, Plains and Settlements of Britain, ... Exeter: 1805. V. 66

DYER, JAMES
Three Learned Readings made Upon Three Very Useful Statutes; the First, by the Great and Eminent Sage of the Law, Sir Iames Dyer, of the Middle Temple, Upon the Statute of Wills. London: 1648. V. 65

DYER, JOHN
The Fleece: a Poem. London: 1757. V. 66
The Poems of John Dyer. 1903. V. 64
Poems. Viz. I. Grongar Hill. II. The Ruins of Rome. III. The Fleece. in Four Books. London: 1761. V. 63

DYER, MARY
The Rise and Progress of the Serpent from the Garden of Eden, to the Present Day, with a Discolosure of Shakerism. Concord: 1847. V. 63

DYER, THOMAS H.
Ancient Athens: Its History, Topography and Remains. London: 1873. V. 65
Pompeii Photographed. The Ruins of Pompeii.... London: 1867. V. 66

DYER, W. A.
The Rocking Chair: an American Institution. New York and London: 1928. V. 65

DYHRENFURTH, G. O.
To the Third Pole. The History of the High Himalaya. London: 1955. V. 63; 64

DYJA, THOMAS
Play for a Kingdom. New York: 1997. V. 67

DYK, WALTER
Son of Old Man Hat. New York: 1938. V. 67

DYKASTRA, ROBERT R.
The Cattle Towns. New York: 1968. V. 67

DYKEMAN, WILMA
The French Broad. New York: 1955. V. 63

DYKES, J. C.
Billy the Kid: the Bibliography of a Legend. Albuquerque: 1952. V. 66

DYKES, JEFF
Billy the Kid - the Biography of a Legend. Albuquerque: 1952. V. 64; 67
Fifty Great Western Illustrators - a Bibliographic Checklist. Flagstaff: 1975. V. 63; 64; 67

DYKES, OSWALD
English Proverbs, with Moral Reflexions.... London: 1709. V. 64
The Royal Marriage. King Lemuel's Lesson of 1. Chastity. 2. Temperance. 3. Charity. 4. Justice. 5. Education. 6. Industry. 7. Frugality. 8. Religion. 9. Marriage &c. London: 1722. V. 66

DYLAN, BOB
Tarantula. New York: 1971. V. 63
Whaaat?. N.P: 1984. V. 64

DYMOND, DAVID
The Register of Thetford Priory. Part I 1482-1517. Part II. 1518- 1540. London: 1995-1996. V. 63

DYMOND, JONATHAN
Essays on the Principles of Morality and on the Private and Political Rights and Obligations of Mankind.... London: 1830. V. 65; 66

DYON, WILLIAM
The Trial of William Dyon and John Dyon, for the Wilful Murder of John Dyon, Their Brother and Uncle.... Sheffield: 1828. V. 63

DYOTT, G. M.
Silent Highways of the Jungle; Being the Adventures of an Explorer in the Andes and Along the Upper Reaches of the Amazon. London: 1924. V. 65

DYRENFORTH, JAMES
Adolf in Blunderland. London: 1939. V. 65

DYSON, ANTHONY
Pictures to Print. London: 1984. V. 62; 64; 67

DYSON, FRANK
Eclipses of the Sun and Moon. Oxford: 1937. V. 66

E

E. ELEPHANT, Esq. Showman. New York: 1894. V. 62

E., E. P.
Poetry, &c. for Private Circulation. Brighton: 1867. V. 63

E., G.
Authentic Memoirs of the Life and Surprising Adventures of John Sheppard; Who Was Executed at Tyburn, November the 16th 1724. London: 1724. V. 65

E. M. MORSMAN. Omaha: 1942. V. 65

EACHARD, JOHN
The Grounds and Occasions of the Contempt of the Clergy and Religion Enquired into &c. Together with Some Observations Upon an Answer Thereto. London: 1685. V. 67

EACHARD, LAWRENCE
The Gazetteer's; or, Newsman's Interpreter. (with) *The Second Part.* London: 1724. V. 64

EAGER, SAMUEL W.
An Outline History of Orange County...Together with Local Traditions and Short Biographical Sketches of Early Settlers, etc. Newburgh: 1846-1847. V. 63; 66

EAGLE, A.
Eagle's Trees and Shrubs of New Zealand in Colour. Auckland: 1981. V. 67

EAGLE, H. M.
New Lyrics of Praise. Dalton: 1912. V. 65

EAGLESTONE, C. R.
A Girl-Artist. London: 1885. V. 65

EAGLETON, WELLS P.
Brain Abscess. Its Surgical Pathology and Operative Technic. New York: 1922. V. 66; 67

EAKIN, R. M.
The Third Eye. Berkeley: 1973. V. 65; 66

EALY, RUTH R.
Water in a Thirsty Land. N.P: 1955. V. 63

EARBERY, MATTHIAS
Impartial Reflections Upon Dr. Burnet's Posthumous History. London: 1724. V. 66

EARDLEY-WILMOT, SAINTHILL
Forest Life and Sport in India. New York: 1910. V. 65
Our Journal in the Pacific.... London: 1873. V. 66

EARL, CYRIL
Youth's Book on the Mind, Embracing the Outlines of the Intellect, the Sensibilities and the Will.... Portland: 1842. V. 64

EARL, GEORGE WINDSOR
The Ethnological Library Conducted by Edwin Norris, Esq. London: 1853. V. 62

EARL, MAUD
The Power of the Dog. London: 1911. V. 64; 66; 67

EARLE, ALICE MORSE
Early Prose and Verse. New York: 1893. V. 66
Sun-Dials and Roses of Yesterday. New York: 1902. V. 66
Two Centuries of Costume in America 1620-1820. New York: 1903. V. 65

EARLE, CYRIL
The Earle Collection of Early Staffordshire Pottery. 1915. V. 67

EARLE, F.
The Lyric Year. New York: 1912. V. 63

EARLE, JOHN
Microcosmographie or a Piece of the World Discovered in Essayes and Characters. Waltham St. Lawrence: 1928. V. 65

EARLE, PLINY
The Curability of Insanity: a Series of Studies. Philadelphia: 1887. V. 65
Memoirs of Pliny Earle, M.D., with Extracts from His Diary and Letters (1830-1892) and Selections from His Professional Writing (1839-1891). Boston: 1898. V. 65

EARLE, WILLIAM
Obi; or, the History of Three-Fingered Jack. Worcester: 1804. V. 64

EARLEY, TONY
Here We Are in Paradise. Boston: 1994. V. 67

EARLY Coastwise and Foreign Shipping of Salem. Salem;: 1934. V. 67

EARLY History of Atlantic County, New Jersey. Kutztown: 1915. V. 63; 66

EARLY, JOHN
A Collection of Hymns for Public, Social and Domestic Worship. Charleston: 1847. V. 66

EARLY, JUBAL ANDERSON
A Correspondence Between General Early and Mahone, in Regard to a Military Memoir of the Latter. Lynchburg: 1871. V. 65
Jackson's Campaign Against Pope in August 1862. Baltimore: 1883. V. 62; 63; 65
Lieutenant General Jubal Anderson Early, C.S.A. Autobiographical Sketch and Narrative of the War Between the States. Philadelphia & London: 1912. V. 63; 64; 65
A Memoir of the Last Year of the War for Independence, in the Confederate States of America.... Toronto: 1866. V. 62; 63; 65
A Memoir of the Last Year of the War for Independence, in the Confederate States of America.... Lynchburg: 1867. V. 63; 65
War Memoirs. Bloomington: 1960. V. 63; 65

EARLY, R. H.
The Family of Early... and Its Connections with Some Other Families. Lynchburg: 1920. V. 67

THE EASBY Abbey Breeding Stud. 1860. V. 64

EASON, T. W.
A Portrait of Michael Roberts. Chelsea: 1949. V. 63

EAST INDIA COMPANY
THE EAST INDIA Register and Directory for 1820, Corrected to the 25th March 1820.... London: 1820. V. 64
The Petition and Remonstrance of the Governour and Company of Merchants of London Trading to the East Indies. London: 1641. V. 63
Popular Topics; or, the Grand Question Discussed in Which the Following Subjects are Considered. Viz. The King's Prerogative, the Privileges of Parliament, Secret Influence and a System of Reform for the East-India Company. London: 1884. V. 65

EASTERN Pennington County Memories. Wall: 1965. V. 67

EASTLAKE, C. L.
Contributions to the Literature of the Fine Arts. London: 1848. V. 66

EASTLAKE, CHARLES L.
Hints on Household Taste in Furniture, Upholstery and Other Details. London: 1868. V. 64
Hints on Household Taste in Furniture, Upholstery and Other Details. London: 1869. V. 64

EASTLAKE, WILLIAM
The Bronc People. New York: 1958. V. 67
Dancers in the Scalp House. New York: 1975. V. 64; 66
Go in Beauty. New York: 1956. V. 64; 65; 67
The Long Naked Descent into Boston. New York: 1977. V. 63
Portrait of an Artist with 26 Horses. New York: 1963. V. 64; 67

EASTMAN, C. E.
Catalog of Fossil Fishes in the Carnegie Museum. Pittsburgh: 1911-1914. V. 66

EASTMAN, CHARLES
Indian Boyhood. New York: 1902. V. 65

EASTMAN, EDWIN
Seven and Nine Years Among the Camanches and Apaches. Jersey City: 1873. V. 63
Seven and Nine Years Among the Camanches and Apaches. Jersey City: 1874. V. 64; 66

EASTMAN, ELAINE C.
Pratt: the Red Man's Moses. Norman: 1935. V. 67

EASTMAN, HUBBARD
Noyesism Unveiled: a History of the Sect Self-Styled Perfectionists.... Brattleboro: 1849. V. 63

EASTMAN, MARY H.
Aunt Phillis's Cabin; or Southern Life As It Is. Philadelphia: 1852. V. 62; 67
The Romance of Indian Life. Philadelphia: 1853. V. 63

EASTMAN, W. R.
The Parrots of Australia, a Guide to Field Identification and Habits. Sydney: 1966. V. 63; 67

EASTMEAD, W.
Historia Rievallensis: Containing the History of Kirkby Moorside.... 1824. V. 63

EASTON, JOHN
An Unfrequented Highway through Sikkim and Tibet to Chumolaroi. London: 1928. V. 64; 67

EASTON, PHOEBE
Marbling, a History and a Bibliography. Los Angeles: 1983. V. 62

EASTWICK, MR.
Most Private and Confidential. Correspondence on the Removal of Mr. Eastwick from Tehran. London: 1864. V. 65

EASTWOOD, DOROTHEA
River Diary. 1950. V. 67

EASTWOOD, FREDERICK
Calumny. London: 1877. V. 67

AN EASY Introduction to the Game of Chess.... Philadelphia: 1817. V. 62; 63; 66

EASY Lessons for Infants and Short Stories.... London: 1822. V. 63

EASY Lessons; or, Leading Strings to Knowledge in Three Parts. 1838. V. 65

EASY Rhymes for Children from Five to Ten Years of Age. London: 1828. V. 63

EATON, ARTHUR WENTWORTH HAMILTON
The Elmwood Eatons. (with) *Memorial Sketch of William Eaton and The Olivestob Hamiltons.* New York: 1893-1895. V. 67
Families of Eaton-Sutherland Layton-Hill. (with) *The Cochran-Inglis Family of Halifax.* (with) *Lt.-Col. Otho Hamilton of Olivestob.* Halfiax: 1899. V. 67
The History of Kings County Nova Scotia, Heart of the Acadian Land. Salem: 1910. V. 67
Tales of Garrison Town. New York and St. Paul: 1892. V. 66

EATON, CHARLOTTE ANN
Narrative of A Residence in Belgium During the Campaign of 1815. London: 1817. V. 65

EATON, E. H.
Birds of New York. Albany: 1909-1914. V. 64; 65; 67

EATON, J. C.
70 Years Observations of a Trout Fisherman. 1937. V. 65
70 Years Observations of a Trout Fisherman. Richmond: 1937. V. 62; 63; 67

EATON, J. M.
A Treatise on the Art of Breeding and Managing Tame, Domesticated, Foreign and Fancy Pigeons. London: 1858. V. 65; 67
A Treatise on the Art of Breeding and Managing the Almond Tumbler; a Treatise on the Art of Breeding and Managing Tame Domesticated and Fancy Pigeons. London: 1851-1852. V. 62

EATON, L. K.
Landscape Artist in America: the Life and Work.... Chicago: 1964. V. 65

EATON, SEYMOUR
More About Teddy B. and Teddy G. The Roosevelt Bears. Philadelphia: 1907. V. 62; 65
The Roosevelt Bears Abroad. New York: 1908. V. 62
The Roosevelt Bears. Their Travels and Adventures. Philadelphia: 1906. V. 62; 65

EBAN, ABBA
Heritage: Civilization and the Jews. New York: 1984. V. 66
Voice of Israel. New York: 1957. V. 65

EBBS, ELOISE BUCKNER
A Record of the Ebbs Family of Western North Carolina. N.P: 1934. V. 67

EBEL, JOHANN GOTTFRIED
Instructions Pour un Voyageur Qui se Propose de Parcourir La Suisse. Basel: 1795. V. 66

EBELING, KLAUS
Ragamala Painting. London: 1973. V. 62

EBERHARDT, WALTER
The Jig-Saw Puzzle Murder. New York: 1933. V. 65

EBERHART, RICHARD
A Bravery of Earth. London: 1930. V. 63
A Bravery of Earth. New York: 1930. V. 62; 64
Brotherhood of Men. Pawlet: 1949. V. 62; 65
Chocorua. New York: 1981. V. 63
Collected Poems 1930-1960. New York: 1960. V. 63
Great Praises. London: 1957. V. 63
Hour: Gnats. New Poems. N.P: 1977. V. 66
Poems New and Selected. Norfolk: 1944. V. 64
The Quarry. New Poems. New York: 1964. V. 63
Reading the Spirit. New York: 1937. V. 63
Song and Idea: Poems. London: 1940. V. 66
Survivors. Brockport: 1979. V. 63
Thirty-One Sonnets. New York: 1967. V. 63; 64
Undercliff. Poems 1946-1953. New York: 1953. V. 64
A World-View. Tufts College Phi Beta Kappa Poem 1941. N.P: 1941. V. 62; 64

EBERLE, JOHN A.
A Treatise of the Materia Medica and Therapeutics. Philadelphia: 1822. V. 66

EBERLE, MATT
Rudy and Midge. Madison: 1998. V. 62

EBERLEIN, CHRISTIAN NIKOLAS
Beschreibung der Herzoglichen Bilder-Gallerie zu Salzthalum. Brunswick: 1776. V. 66

EBERLEIN, HAROLD DONALDSON
Manor Houses and Historic Homes of Long Island and Staten Island. Philadelphia: 1928. V. 67
Practical Book of Early American Arts and Crafts. Philadelphia and London: 1916. V. 64
The Practical Book of Garden Structure and Design. Philadelphia: 1937. V. 67

EBRINGTON, HUGH FORTESCUE
Memorandum of Two Conversations Between the Emperor Napoleon and Viscount Ebrington, at Porte Ferrajo on the 6th and 8th of December, 1814. London: 1823. V. 62

ECCLES, CHARLOTTE O'CONNOR
The Matrimonial Lottery. Leipzig: 1906. V. 63

ECCLES, J. C.
Sherrington His Life and Thought. 1979. V. 64

ECCLESHILL OLD MILL COMPANY
Abstract of the Co-Partnership Deed of the Eccleshill Old Mill Company, Now Carrying on the Trade of Scribbling and Fulling Millers, at Eccleshill, in the Parish of Bradford, in the County of York Under the Firm of Mutton, Thorntons and Co.... Bradford: 1861. V. 63

THE ECCLESIASTICAL and Architectural Topography of England. Diocese of Oxford. Oxford and London: 1849-1850. V. 67

THE ECCLESIASTICAL and Architectural Topography of England. Oxford and London: 1852. V. 66

ECCLESIASTICAL Gallantry; or, the Mystery Unravelled, a Tale. London: 1778. V. 65

ECCLESTON, ROBERT
The Mariposa Indian War 1850-1851. The Diaries of.... Salt Lake City: 1957. V. 63
Overland to California on the Southwestern Trail 1849. Berkeley & Los Angeles: 1950. V. 64; 65

ECCLESTONE, J.
The Way to Happiness. N.P: 1726. V. 67

ECHARD, LAURENCE
The History of England. London: 1720. V. 63
The History of England from the First Entrance of Julius Caesar and the Romans.... London: 1707-1718. V. 67

THE ECHO and Other Poems. New York: 1807. V. 63

ECHOES of Hellas - The Tale of Troy and the Story of Orestes from Homer and Aeschylus.... London: 1887. V. 65

ECHOES of the Aesthetic Society of Jersey City. New York: 1882. V. 63; 66

ECK, C.
Traite de Construction en Poteries et Fer, a l'Usage des Batimens Civils, Industriels et Militaires. Paris: 1836. V. 65
Traite de l'Application du fer, de la Fonte et de la Tole dans les Constructions Civiles, Industrielles et Militaires.... Paris: 1841. V. 65

ECKEL, JOHN C.
The First Editions of the Writings of Charles Dickens and Their Values. A Bibliography. London: 1932. V. 62
The First Editions of the Writings of Charles Dickens: Their Points and Values. New York: 1932. V. 62; 65
Prime Pickwick in Parts.... New York: 1928. V. 62

ECKERT, A. W.
The Owls of North America.... Garden City: 1974. V. 67

ECKERT, ROBERT P.
Edward Thomas - A Biography and a Bibliography. London: 1937. V. 62
Edward Thomas: a Biography and a Bibliography. New York: 1937. V. 66

ECKFELDT, JACOB
A Manual of Gold and Silver Coins of All Nations, Struck Within the Past Quarter Century. Philadelphia: 1842. V. 63; 64; 66
New Varieties of Gold and Silver Coins, Counterfeit Coins and Bullion, with Mint Values. Philadelphia: 1850. V. 62

ECKHARDT, GEORGE H.
Electronic Television. Chicago: 1936. V. 64

THE ECLECTIC Repertory and Analytical Review, Medical and Philosophical. Philadelphia: 1813. V. 67

ECO, UMBERTO
The Bomb and the General. London: 1989. V. 64
The Island of the Day Before. New York: 1995. V. 64; 66
Il Nome Della Rosa. Milan: 1980. V. 64
The Three Astronauts. London: 1989. V. 64

L'ECOLE des Demoiselles. Ou Memoires de Constance. Amsterdam et Leipzig: 1753. V. 66

THE ECONOMIC Housekeeping Book for Fifty-Two Weeks.... London: 1881-1892. V. 65

ECTON, JOHN
Liber Regis vel Thesaurus Rerum Ecclesiasticarum. London: 1786. V. 67
Liber Valorum and Decimarum; Being an Account of the Valuations and the Yearly Tenths of All Such Ecclesiastical Benefices in England and Wales as Now Stand Chargeable with the Payments of First-Fruits and Tenths. London: 1711. V. 66
Thesaurus Rerum Ecclesiasticarum.... London: 1742. V. 66

EDDINGTON, A. S.
Fundamental Theory. Cambridge: 1946. V. 63
Space Time and Gravitation - an Outline of the General Relativity Theory. 1920. V. 63

EDDINS, ROY
History of Falls Church, Texas. Falls Church: 1947. V. 63

EDDISON, E. R.
Mistress of Mistresses. 1935. V. 66
Mistress of Mistresses. London: 1935. V. 62
Mistress of Mistresses. New York: 1935. V. 62; 64
Poems, Letters and Memories of Philip Sidney Nairn. 1916. V. 62; 64; 66
Styrbiorn the Strong. 1926. V. 62; 64; 66

EDDISON, EDWIN
History of Worksop; with Historical, Descriptive and Discursive Sketches of Sherwood Forest and the Neighbourhood. London: 1834. V. 65

EDDY, A. J.
Cubists and Post-Impressionism. Chicago: 1914. V. 62; 65

EDDY, CLARENCE E.
The Pinnacle of Parnassus. Salt Lake City: 1902. V. 64

EDDY, CLYDE
Down the World's Most Dangerous River (the Colorado). New York: 1929. V. 63

EDDY, DANIEL CLARKE
Lectures to Young Ladies on Subjects of Practical Importance. Lowell: 1848. V. 64

EDDY, MARY BAKER GLOVER
Science and Health. Lynn: 1878. V. 62

EDE, B.
Wild Birds of America. Tuscaloosa and New York: 1991. V. 67

EDE, H. S.
Savage Messiah. London: 1931. V. 62

EDE, J.
A View of the Gold and Silver Coins of All Nations Exhibited in Above Four Hundred Copper Plate Engravings Correctly Executed by an Eminent Artist. London: 1808. V. 66

EDEL, LEON
The Diary of Alice James. London: 1965. V. 67
Henry James. 1953-1963. V. 67
Henry James. London: 1953-1972. V. 67
Henry James in Westminster Abbey. The Address by Leon Edel. Honolulu: 1976. V. 67
Some Memories of Edith Wharton. New York: 1993. V. 62; 67

EDELSTEIN, J. M.
Wallace Stevens - a Descriptive Bibliography. Pittsburgh: 1973. V. 65

EDELSTEIN, SIDNEY M.
Catalog of the Sidney M. Edelstein Collection of the History of Chemistry, Dyeing and Technology. Jerusalem: 1981. V. 63

EDEN, C. H.
Australia's Heroes.... 1875. V. 64
Japan Historical and Descriptive. London: 1877. V. 67

EDEN, EMILY
The Semi-Detached House. London: 1859. V. 65; 67
Up the Country: Letters Written to Her Sister from the Upper Provinces of India. London: 1866. V. 65

EDEN, LIZZIE SELINA
A Lady's Glimpse of the Late War in Bohemia. London: 1867. V. 65

EDGAR, MARRIOTT
Albert 'Arold and Others. London. V. 62

EDGAR, ROBERT
An Historical Sketch of the College of New Jersey. Philadelphia: 1859. V. 66

EDGAR, WILLIAM
Vectigalium Systema; or a New Book of Rates.... 1718. V. 67

EDGE, FREDERICK MILNES
An Englishman's View of the Battle Between the Alabama and the Kearsage. New York: 1864. V. 62

EDGECUMBE, E. R. PEARCE
Zephyrus; a Holiday in Brazil and on the River Plate. London: 1887. V. 67

EDGER, BOB
Brand of a Legend. Cody: 1978. V. 67

EDGERTON, CLYDE
Raney. Chapel Hill: 1985. V. 66; 67
Walking Across Egypt. Chapel Hill: 1986. V. 67
Walking Across Egypt. Chapel Hill: 1987. V. 67

EDGERTON, HAROLD E.
Flash!: Seeing the Unseen by Ultra High-Speed Photography. Boston: 1939. V. 63

EDGERTON, LINDA
Bopeep and Boy-Blue. London and Croydon: 1918. V. 65

EDGEWORTH, C. SNEYD
Memoirs of the Abbe Edgeworth.... 1815. V. 63

EDGEWORTH, MARIA
Belinda. London: 1801. V. 65
Belinda. London: 1811. V. 62
Castle Rackrent: an Hiberian Tale. London: 1782. V. 65
Castle Rackrent, an Hiberian Tale. Dublin: 1801. V. 65
Comic Dramas, in Three Acts. London: 1817. V. 63
Harrington. London: 1817. V. 65
Harry and Lucy Concluded. London: 1825. V. 63
Helen: a Tale. 1834. V. 62
Helen, a Tale. London: 1834. V. 65
Helen, a Tale. Paris: 1837. V. 65
Helen, a Tale. 1843. V. 65
Leonora. London: 1806. V. 62; 65
Letters of Maria Edgeworth and Anna Letitia Barbauld. Waltham St. Lawrence: 1953. V. 63
The Modern Griselda. London: 1805. V. 65
The Modern Griselda. (with) Letters for Literary Ladies. George Town: 1810. V. 65
Moral Tales. London: 1816. V. 65
Moral Tales for Young People. London: 1801. V. 65
The Novels. London: 1893. V. 63; 66
The Parent's Assistant; or Stories for Children. London: 1822. V. 63
The Parent's Assistant; or, Stories for Children. London: 1848. V. 65
Patronage. London: 1814. V. 65
Popular Tales. London: 1804. V. 65
Practical Education. London: 1798. V. 65
Practical Education. London: 1801. V. 64; 65
Tales and Miscellaneous Pieces. London: 1825. V. 63
Tales and Novels. London: 1832-1833. V. 66
Tales and Novels. London: 1848. V. 65
Tales of Fashionable Life. London: 1809. V. 65
Tales of Fashionable Life. London: 1812-1813. V. 65
Tales of Fashionable Life. London: 1824. V. 65
Tales of Fashionable Life. Paris: 1831. V. 65

EDGEWORTH, RICHARD LOVELL
An Essay on Irish Bulls. London: 1808. V. 63
An Essay on the Construction of Roads and Carriages. London: 1813. V. 63

EDGINGTON, T. B.
The Monroe Doctrine. Boston: 1905. V. 67

THE EDINBURGH Journal of Natural History and the Physical Sciences. Edinburgh: 1835-1836. V. 66

EDINGER, LUDWIG
Twelve Lectures on the Structure of the Central Nervous System for Physicians and Students. Philadelphia: 1891. V. 65; 66; 67

EDIS, ROBERT W.
Decoration and Furniture of Town Houses. London: 1881. V. 63

EDISON ELECTRIC LIGHT COMPANY
The Edison Incandescent Lamp Case. New York: 1891?. V. 63; 66

EDISON, JOHN SIBBALD
A Commentary on Lord Brougham's Character of George the Third. London: 1860. V. 67

EDKINS, J.
Opium: Historical Note, or the Poppy in China. Shanghai: 1898. V. 62

EDMOND, J. P.
The Aberdeen Printers, Edward Raban to James Nicol 1620-1736. Aberdeen: 1886. V. 62

EDMONDS, HARFIELD
Brook and River Trouting. 1980. V. 62

EDMONDS, RICHARD H.
Facts about the South. Baltimore: 1898. V. 65

EDMONDS, S. EMMA E.
Nurse and Spy in the Union ARmy.... Hartford: 1864. V. 65

EDMONDS, WALTER D.
The Matchlock Gun. New York: 1941. V. 64

EDMONDSTON, J.
The Dispersion of Knowledge: a Sermon, Preached at Salisbury, Before the Annual District Meeting of the Methodist Itinerant Preachers, of the Portsmouth District July 7, 1813. Portsea: 1813. V. 64

EDMONSTON, CATHERINE DEVEREUX
The Journal of Catherine Devereux Edmonstown 1860-1866. Mebane: 1954. V. 63

EDMUND and Albina, or Gothic Times, A Romance. London: 1801. V. 63

EDMUNDS, F. H.
Wells and Springs of Sussex. 1928. V. 67

EDMUNDS, ROBERT
The Cold-Blooded Penguin. New York: 1944. V. 65

EDSON, RUSSELL
The Brain Kitchen. Writings and Woodcuts. Stamford: 1965. V. 63
What A Man Can See. Ray Johnson Drawings. Penland: 1969. V. 63

EDWARD, DAVID
The History of Texas; or the Emigrant's Farmer's and Politician's Guide...from Personal Observation and Experience. Cincinnati: 1836. V. 63; 64

EDWARD, THOMAS
Chosen Essays. Newtown: 1926. V. 65

EDWARDS, AMELIA B.
Pharaohs, Fellahs and Explorers. New York: 1891. V. 67
Pharaohs, Fellahs and Explorers. New York: 1892. V. 66
Pharaohs, Fellahs and Explorers. London: 1893. V. 65
A Thousand Miles Up the Nile. Leipzig: 1878. V. 65
A Thousand Miles up the Nile. 1891. V. 62
A Thousand Miles Up the Nile. London: 1891. V. 65; 67
Untrodden Peaks and Unfrequented Valleys: a Midsummer Ramble in the Dolomites. London: 1873. V. 62; 65
Untrodden Peaks and Unfrequented Valleys: a Midsummer Ramble in the Dolomites. London: 1890. V. 65

EDWARDS, BRYAN
The History, Civil and Commercial, of the British West Indies.... London: 1819. V. 63

EDWARDS, CLARENCE E.
Camp-Fires of a Naturalist. London: 1893. V. 67

EDWARDS, E. I.
Desert Harvest. Los Angeles: 1962. V. 63
Desert Voices: a Descriptive Bibliography. Los Angeles: 1958. V. 63
Lost Oases Along the Carrizo. Los Angeles: 1958. V. 63
Lost Oases along the Carrizo. Los Angeles: 1961. V. 66

EDWARDS, EDWARD
A Letter to Benjamin Hawes, Esq. M.P. Being Strictures on the Minutes of Evidence Taken Before the Select Committee on the British Museum.... London: 1836. V. 65

EDWARDS, F. W.
British Blood Sucking Flies. London: 1939. V. 63

EDWARDS, FREDERICK
Our Domestic Fire-Places. London: 1870. V. 64

EDWARDS, GEORGE
An Attempt to Rectify Public Affairs, and Promote Private Prosperity, as Present Exigencies Require.... London: 1802. V. 62
Humble Petition, &c, &c. or, a Prospectus of Proposals for Rectifying Our Present Infinitely Distressed and Dangerous Situation.... Newcastle: 1817. V. 63
A Treatise on the Powers and Duties of Justices of the Peace and Town Officers in the State of New York. Bath: 1830. V. 63

EDWARDS, GEORGE W.
Constantinople, Istamboul. Philadelphia: 1930. V. 65

EDWARDS, H. SUTHERLAND
The Prima Donna. Her History and Surroundings from the Seventeenth to the Nineteenth Century. London: 1888. V. 65

EDWARDS, HARRY STILLWELL
His Defense and Other Stories. New York: 1899. V. 67

EDWARDS, HENRY
Marriage: a Poem. London: 1842. V. 66

EDWARDS, HUGH
All Night at Mr. Stonyhurst's. London: 1963. V. 65

EDWARDS, J.
The Hemiptera-Homoptera (Cicadina and Psyllina) of the British Islands. 1896. V. 66

EDWARDS, J. B.
Early Days in Abilene. Abilene: 1938. V. 62

EDWARDS, JENNIE
John N. Edwards. Biography, Memoirs, Reminiscences, and Recollections. Kansas City: 1889. V. 65

EDWARDS, JOHN
Letters to the British Nation, and to the Inhabitants of Every Other Country Who May Have Heard of the Late Shameful Outrages Committed in This Part of the Kingdom. Part I. London: 1791?. V. 65
Letters to the British Nation, and to the Inhabitants of Every Other Country Who May Have Heard of the Late Shameful Outrages Committed in This Part of the Kingdom. Part II. Birmingham: 1791. V. 65

EDWARDS, JOHN E.
The Confederate Solider: Being a Memorial Sketch of George N. and Bushrod W. Harris, Privates in the Confederate Army. New York: 1868. V. 62
Life of Rev. John Wesley Childs: for Twenty-Three Years an Itinerant Methodist Minister. Richmond & Louisivlle: 1852. V. 65

EDWARDS, JOHN FRANK
Army Life of Frank Edwards, Confederate Veteran, Army of Northern Virginia 1861-1865. La Grange: 1911. V. 62; 63; 65

EDWARDS, JOHN N.
John N. Edwards. Biography, Memoirs, Reminiscences and Recollections. Kansas City: 1889. V. 62; 63; 65
Noted Guerrillas, or the Warfare of the Border. St. Louis: 1877. V. 65
Shelby's Expeditions to Mexico an Unwritten Leaf of the War. Austin: 1964. V. 63; 66

EDWARDS, JONATHAN
An Account of the Life of the Rev. David Brainerd...Missionary to the Indians...and a Pastor of a Church of Christian Indians in New Jersey.... Newark: 1811. V. 63; 66
Catalogue of the Greek and Roman Coins in the Numistic Collection of Yale College. New Haven: 1880. V. 65
The Distinguishing Marks of a Work of the Spirit of God. London: 1774. V. 64
The Excellency of Christ. A Sermon on Revelations V. 5, 6. Boston: 1805. V. 63
A Faithful Narrative of the Suprising Work of God in the Conversion of Many Hundred Souls in Northampton and the Neighbouring Towns and Villages of New Hampshire and New England. Elizabeth Town: 1790. V. 63; 66
History of Spokane County, State of Washington. 1900. V. 62
The History of the Work of Redemption. New York: 1786. V. 63; 66
Memoirs of the Rev. David Brainerd: Missionary to the Indians on the Borders of New York, New Jersey, and Pennsylvania.... New Haven: 1822. V. 63; 66
A Preservative Against Socinianism. Oxford: 1693-1703. V. 63
A Treatise Concerning Religious Affections. New York: 1768. V. 62
A Treatise Concerning Religious Affections. Elizabeth-Town: 1787. V. 63; 66
The Works of President Edwards. Worcester: 1808-1809. V. 62

EDWARDS, K. C.
The Peak District. London: 1962. V. 63

EDWARDS, LAWRENCE
Bits of Memory. Montevallo: 1976. V. 67
Old Speedwell Families. N.P: 1955. V. 67

EDWARDS, LIONEL
Beasts of the Chase. London: 1950. V. 64; 67
Bridleways through History. London: 1936. V. 67
The Fox. London: 1949. V. 67
Horses and Riders. London: 1946. V. 67
My Irish Sketchbook. 1938. V. 62; 64
My Scottish Sketch Book. 1929. V. 66
Reminiscences of a Sporting Artist. London: 1947. V. 67
Scarlet and Corduroy. 1941. V. 64
Seen from the Saddle. 1937. V. 64
A Sportsman's Bag. London: 1937. V. 64; 66

EDWARDS, MARY STELLA
Time and Chance - Poems. London: 1926. V. 63

EDWARDS, MONICA
No Going Back. London: 1960. V. 67

EDWARDS, OWEN
Clych Atgof. Panodau yn Hanes Fy Addysg. Newtown: 1933. V. 63; 64; 65; 66

EDWARDS, OWEN DUDLEY
The Quest for Sherlock Holmes: a Biographical Study of Arthur Conan Doyle. Edinburgh: 1983. V. 66

EDWARDS, PERMELIA
Table and Its Service. Spokane. V. 67

EDWARDS, PHILIP LEGET
California in 1837 - Diary of Colonel Philip L. Edwards. Sacramento: 1890. V. 65
The Diary of Philip Leget Edwards, The Great Cattle Drive from California to Oregon in 1837. San Francisco: 1932. V. 66
Sketch of the Oregon Territory of Emigrant's Guide. Kansas City: 1951. V. 66

EDWARDS, R. D.
The Great Famine, Studies in Irish History 1845-1852. 1956. V. 64; 66

EDWARDS, RALPH
Dictionary of English Furniture from the Middle Ages to the Late Georgian Period. London: 1954. V. 64
The Dictionary of English Furniture from the Middle Ages to the Late Georgian Period by Percy Macquoid and Ralph Edwards. London: 1990. V. 65
Georgian Cabinet Makers c. 1700-1800. London: 1955. V. 67

EDWARDS, RICHARD
Edwards' Great West and Her Commercial Metropolis. New York: 1860. V. 65
Tao-Chi Landscape Album from the Poems of Tu-Pu. Tokyo: 1968. V. 62; 63; 64; 66

EDWARDS, RICHARD KEMBLE
The Mystery of the Miniature. Boston: 1908. V. 65

EDWARDS, ROBERT
Church and State in Tudor Ireland. 1935. V. 62; 65

EDWARDS, RUTH DUDLEY
Corridors of Death. London: 1981. V. 66

EDWARDS, SYDENHAM
Cynographia Britannica. 1800. V. 62

EDWARDS, T. A.
Daring Donald McKay, or the Last War Trail of the Modocs. Erie: 1888. V. 63

EDWARDS, T. L.
The Angler's Cast. London: 1960. V. 67

EDWARDS, THOMAS
An Account of the Trial of the Letter y alias Y. London: 1753. V. 64
The Canons of Criticism and Glossary, the Trial of the Letter Y(upsilon), alias Y and Sonnets. London: 1765. V. 64

EDWARDS, WELDON NATHANIEL
Memoir of Nathaniel Macon, of North Carolina. Raleigh: 1862. V. 63; 65

EDWARDS, WILLIAM
The Early History of the North Riding. London: 1924. V. 65
The Story of Colt's Revolver - The Biography of Col. Samuel Colt. Harrisburg: 1953. V. 64

EDWARDS, WILLIAM H.
Butterflies of North America. Boston: 1888-1884. V. 62
The Butterflies of North America. Third Series. Boston and New York: 1897. V. 63
Football Days. New York: 1916. V. 64

EDWARDS, WILLIAM J.
Twenty-five Years in the Black Belt. Boston: 1918. V. 66

EDWARDS, WILLIAM SEYMOUR
Through Scandinavia to Moscow. Cincinnati: 1906. V. 66

EDYE, JOHN
Calculations Relating to the Equipment, Displacement, Etc. of Ships and Vessels of War. London: 1832. V. 64

EELIES-DUPIN, LOUIS
The Universal Library of Historians...Their Lives...Histories... Style...Character...Catalogue of the Several Editions of their Works (etc.) Done into English.... London: 1709. V. 66

EELLS, MYRON
Father Eells or the Results of Fifty-Five Years of Missionary Labor in Washington and Oregon. A Biography of Rev. Cushing Eells. Boston: 1894. V. 63

EELLS, MYRON continued
Hymns in the Chinook Jargon Language. Portland: 1889. V. 64
Marcus Whitman, Pathfinder and Patriot. Seattle: 1909. V. 67

EELMS, CHARLES
The Pirates Own Book, or Authentic Narratives of the Lives, Exploits and Executions of the Most Celebrated Sea Robbers.... Portland: 1844. V. 67

THE EFFECTS of Atomic Weapons Prepared For and In Cooperation with the U.S. Department of Defense and the U.S. Atomic Energy Commission Under the Direction of te Los Alamos Scientific Laboratory. Washington: 1950. V. 65

EGAN, BERESFORD
Pollen - a Novel in Black and White. London: 1933. V. 62
The Sink of Solitude. London: 1928. V. 65

EGAN, ELEANOR FRANKLIN
The War in the Cradle of the World: Mesopotamia. London: 1918. V. 67

EGAN, FEROL
The El Dorado Trail - The Story of the Gold Rush Routes Across Mexico. New York: 1970. V. 67

EGAN, HOWARD
Pioneering the West 1846 to 1878. Richmond: 1917. V. 63

EGAN, PIERCE
Anecdotes (Original and Selected) of the Turf, the Chase, the Ring, and the Stage; the Whole Forming a Complete Panorama of the Sporting World.... London: 1827. V. 62
Boxiana; or, Sketches of Ancient and Modern Pugilism. London: 1818. V. 62; 67
A Complete History and Development of All the Extraordinary Circumstances and Events Connected With the Murder of Mr. Weare.... London: 1824. V. 65
Life in London. London: 1821. V. 62
Life in London. London: 1823. V. 62
The Life of an Actor. London: 1825. V. 62; 63; 66; 67
The Life of an Actor. London: 1892. V. 62; 65; 67
The Show Folks!. London: 1831. V. 66
Sporting Anecdotes, Original and Selected.... Sherwood: 1825. V. 65

EGAN, THOMAS J.
History of the Halifax Volunteer Battalion and Volunteer Companies 1859-1887. Halifax: 1888. V. 64

EGAN, WILLIAM M.
Pioneering the West 1846 to 1878. Major Eagan's Diary.... Salt Lake City: 1917. V. 63; 66

EGBERT, DONALD DREW
The Tickhill Psalter and Related Manuscripts: a School of Manuscript Illumination in England During the Early Fourteenth Century. New York: 1940. V. 62; 63; 64

EGE, RALPH
Pioneers of Old Hopewell with Sketches of Her Revolutionary Heroes. Hopewell: 1908. V. 63; 66

EGE, V.
Contributions to the Knowledge of the North Atlantic and the Mediterranean Species of the Genus Paralepis.... Copenhagen: 1930. V. 65
A Revision of the Genus Anguilla Shaw, a Systematic, Phylogenetic and Geographical Study. Copenhagen: 1939. V. 63

EGERER, J. W.
A Bibliography of Robert Burns. Edinburgh: 1964. V. 67

EGERTON, DANIEL THOMAS
Fashionable Bores; or Coolers in High Life. London: 1824. V. 63; 66

EGERTON, GEORGE
Keynotes. London: 1893. V. 65
Keynotes. London: 1894. V. 65

EGGELING, W. J.
The Indigenous Trees of the Uganda Protectorate. Entebbe: 1940. V. 64

EGGENHOFER, NICK
Horses, Horses, Always Horses - the Life and Art of Nick Eggenhofer. Cody: 1981. V. 63; 66
Wagons, Mules and Men. New York: 1961. V. 64; 67

EGGLESTON, GEORGE C.
American War Ballads and Lyrics. New York: 1889. V. 62
The History of the Confederate War. Its Causes and Its Conduct. A Narrative and Critical History. New York: 1910. V. 63; 65

EGGLESTON, J. D.
Southern Sketches (1-7). First Series. Charlottesville: 1835. V. 65

EGGLESTON, WILLIAM
The Democratic Forest. New York: 1989. V. 65

EGLINTON, JOHN
Two Essays on the Remnant. London: 1894. V. 65

EGOLF, TRISTAN
Lord of the Barnyard. London: 1998. V. 62

EHLE, JOHN
The Land Breakers. New York: 1964. V. 63; 64

EHRENBERG, C. G.
Sylvae Mycologicae Berolinenses. Berlin: 1818. V. 63; 66

EHRENS, SUSAN
Alma Lavenson: Photographs. Berkeley: 1990. V. 65

EHRLICH, BETTINA
Dolls. New York: 1963. V. 64
Trovato. London: 1960. V. 65

EHRLICH, GRETEL
Heart Mountain. New York: 1988. V. 62; 64; 65; 67
A Match to the Heart. New York: 1994. V. 66
The Solace of Open Spaces. New York: 1985. V. 62; 63; 64; 65; 67

EHRLICH, J. W.
Howl of the Censor. San Carlos: 1961. V. 63

EHRMANN, MARIANNE
Philosophie d'une Femme. N.P: 1787. V. 66

EICHHORST, HERMANN
Handbook of Practical Medicine. New York: 1886. V. 65

EICKEMEYER, CARL
Among the Pueblo Indians. New York: 1895. V. 63; 66

EICKEMEYER, RUDOLF
The Old Farm. New York: 1901. V. 63
Winter. New York: 1903. V. 65

EIDINOFF, MAXWELL LEIGH
Atomics. London: 1950. V. 65

EIFFEL, GUSTAVE
Notice sur la Viaduc de Garabit (Pres Saint-Flour). Ligne de Marvejols a Neussargues. Paris: 1888. V. 65
Notice sur le Pont du Douro, a Porto (Pont Maria-Pia). Clichy: 1879. V. 65

EIGENMANN, C. H.
American Characidae. Cambridge: 1917-1927. V. 64; 65
The American Characidae. Cambridge: 1917-1929. V. 63
American Characidae. Cambridge: 1918-1927. V. 64
The Cheirodontinae, a Subfamily of Minute Characid Fishes of South American. Pittsburgh: 1915. V. 66
Fishes of Western South America. Lexington: 1942. V. 62
The Fresh-Water Fishes of Patagonia and an Examination of the Archiplata-Arehhelenis Theory. (with) Catalogue of the Fresh-Water Fishes of Tropical and South Temperate America. Stuttgart: 1909-1910. V. 62
The Freshwater Fishes of British Guiana.... Pittsburgh: 1912. V. 65
Pimelodell and Typhlobargrus, Cheirodontinae and Pygidildae. Pittsburgh: 1915-1917. V. 64
Revision of the South American Nematognathi or Cat-Fishes. San Francisco: 1890. V. 64

EIGHT Oxford Poets. London: 1941. V. 62

EIGL, KURT
Der Neue Struwelpeter (sic). Wien: 1955. V. 66

EIGNER, LARRY
Air/The Trees. Los Angeles: 1968. V. 62; 63
Another Time in Fragments. London: 1967. V. 62; 63
The Breath of Once Live Things/In the Field with Poe. Los Angels: 1968. V. 63
Six Poems. N.P: 1967. V. 62; 64

EIKON BASILIKE
Basilika. The Workes of King Charles the Martyr. London: 1662. V. 66

EILAND, M. L.
Oriental Rugs, a Comprehensive Guide. 1976. V. 65

EILOART, ELIZABETH
My Lady Clare. London: 1882. V. 65

EILSHEMIUS, LOUIS M.
My Brother Victor. A Convalescent's Fancy. New York: 1912. V. 63; 66

EIMER, G. H. THEODOR
Organic Evolution as the Result of the Inheritance of Acquired Characters According to the Laws of Organic Growth. London: 1890. V. 67

EINSTEIN, ALBERT
Die Entwicklung Unserer Anschauungen Uber Das Wesen und Die Konstitution der Strahlung. Leipzig: 1909. V. 65
Entwurf Einer Verallgemeinerten Relativitatstheorie und Einer Theorie der Gravitation. Leipzig: 1913-1910. V. 65
The Evolution of Physics: the Growth of Ideas from Early Concepts to Relativity and Quanta. New York: 1938. V. 63
Die Formale Grundlage der Allgemeinen Relativitatstheorie. (and) Zur Allgemeinen Relativitatstheorie...(and) Die Feldgleichungen der Gravitation. Berlin: 1914-1915. V. 65
Die Grundlage der Allgemeinen Relativitats-Theorie. Leipzig: 1916. V. 66
Ideas and Opinions. New York: 1954. V. 63; 65
The Meaning of Relativity. Princeton: 1950. V. 65; 66
Out of My Later Years. New York: 1950. V. 63
Relativity. 1920. V. 65
Relativity: the Special and General Theory. New York: 1947. V. 65
Some Thoughts Concerning Education. Albany: 1936. V. 63
Theorie der Opaleszenz von Homogenen Flussigkeiten und Flussigkeitsgemischen in der Hahe des Kritischen Zustandes. Leipzig: 1910. V. 65
Vier Vorlesungen Uber Relativitaetstheorie Gehalten im Mai 1921 an der Universitat Princeton. Braunschweig: 1922. V. 66

EINSTEIN, ALBERT continued
The World As I See It. London: 1934. V. 64
Zum Gegenwartigen Stand des Strahlungsproblems. Leipzig: 1909. V. 65

EISENBERG, J. F.
Mammals of the Neotropics. Volume I. Chicago: 1989. V. 64

EISENBERG, RONALD L.
Radiology. An Illustrated History. St. Louis: 1992. V. 66; 67

EISENBERG, WILLIAM E.
The Lutheran Church in Virginia 1717-1962. Roanoke: 1967. V. 67

EISENHOWER, DWIGHT DAVID
At Ease: Stories I Tell to Friends. Garden City: 1967. V. 63
Crusade in Europe. Garden City: 1948. V. 63; 65
Mandate for Change, 1953-1956. New York: 1963. V. 62; 63; 64
The White House Years: Mandate for Change 1953-1956. (with) The White House Years: Waging Peace, 1956-1961. Garden City: 1963-1965. V. 63; 66

EISENSCHIML, OTTO
The Story of Shiloh. Chicago: 1946. V. 62
Why Was Lincoln Murdered. Boston: 1937. V. 62

EISENSTAEDT, ALFRED
Eisenstaedt: Aberdeen, Portrait of a City. Baton Rouge: 1984. V. 65
People. New York: 1973. V. 66

EISNER, LOTTE H.
Fritz Lang. New York: 1977. V. 63

EISSLER, K. R.
Goethe. A Psychoanalytic Study 1775-1786. Detroit: 1963. V. 62

EKELOF, GUNNAR
Selected Poems. New York: 1971. V. 65

EKEMAN, LORENZ
Zeichnungs-Buch zum Selbst-Unterricht im Baum und Landschafts- Zeichnen.... Munich: 1819. V. 66

ELAM, CHARLES
A Physician's Problems. London: 1869. V. 65

EL-BAZ, FAROUK
Astronaut Observations from the Apollo-Soyuz Mission. Washington: 1977. V. 67

ELBORN, GEOFFREY
Hand and Eye: an Anthology for Sacheverell Sitwell. Edinburgh: 1977. V. 62; 64
To John Piper on His Eightieth Birthday - 13 December 1983. London: 1983. V. 63; 65

ELDER, DEAN
Pianists at Play. Evanston: 1982. V. 67

ELDER, FRANK
The Book of the Hackle. Edinburgh: 1979. V. 67

ELDERKIN, JAMES D.
Biographical Sketches and Anecdotes of a Soldier of Three Wars. Detroit: 1899. V. 66

ELDERKIN, JOHN
A Brief History of the Lotos Club. New York: 1895. V. 65

ELDERSHAW, FINNEY
Australia as It Really Is: In Its Life, Scenery and Adventure.... London: 1854. V. 67

ELDERSHEIM, ALFRED
The Life and Times of Jesus the Messiah. Michigan: 1962. V. 66

ELDREDGE, ZOETH S.
The Beginning of San Francisco from the Expedition of Anza 1774 to the City of Charter of April 15, 1850. San Francisco: 1912. V. 63; 66
The March of Portoloa and the Log of San Carlos. San Francisco: 1909. V. 67

ELDRIDGE, ELLEANOR
Memoirs of Elleanor Eldridge. Providence: 1843. V. 63

ELDRIDGE, LEMUEL B.
The Torrent, or an Account of a Deluge Occasioned by an Unparalleled Rise of the New Haven River.... Middlebury: 1831. V. 63; 66

AN ELECTION Ball. In Poetical Letters, From Mr. Inkle at Bath to His Wife at Gloucester: with a Poetical Address to John Miller, Esq. Bath: 1776. V. 66

ELECTION Day. A Sketch from Nature. London: 1844. V. 62

ELECTRICTY as Applied to Submarines. Washington: 1918. V. 67

ELEGANT Arts for Ladies. London: 1856. V. 64; 65

ELEGANT Extracts: Being a Copious Selection...from the Most Eminent British Poets. Volume I. London: 1830. V. 64; 66

AN ELEGY on the Death and Burial of Cock Robin. London: 1820. V. 66

ELEGY to the Memory of the Late Most Excellent Lady Blackett.... Newcastle-upon-Tyne: 1759. V. 64

ELEMENTS Of Chess. Boston: 1805. V. 63

ELEMENTS of Geography. London: 1820. V. 62; 65

ELGARD, JIM
Snow Dog. London: 1949. V. 64

ELGEE, FRANK
Early Man in North-East Yorkshire. Gloucester: 1930. V. 64; 65; 66
The Moorlands of North-Eastern Yorkshire. London: 1912. V. 66

ELGOOD, GEORGE S.
Italian Gardens. 1907. V. 63
Italian Gardens. London: 1907. V. 64
Some English Gardens. London: 1904. V. 64
Some English Gardens. 1933. V. 63; 66
Some English Gardens. London: 1933. V. 67

ELIAS, EDITH L.
The Children's Robinson Crusoe. London: 1935. V. 65
The Story of Hiawatha. London: 1914. V. 63; 65

ELIAS, NORBERT
Uber den Prozess der Zivilisation. Soziogenetische und Psyvhogenetische Untersuchungen. Basel: 1939. V. 67

ELICE, FERDINANDO
Saggio sull' Elettricita. Genoa: 1817. V. 64

ELIOT, C.
Letters from the Far East. London: 1907. V. 67

ELIOT, CHARLES
Charles Eliot, Landscape Gardener. Boston: 1902. V. 66
The East African Protectorate. London: 1905. V. 62; 67
Vegetation and Scenery in the Metropolitan Reservations of Boston. Boston: 1898. V. 66

ELIOT, ELLSWORTH
West Point in the Confederacy. New York: 1941. V. 62; 63; 65

ELIOT, GEORGE, PSEUD.
Adam Bede. Edinburgh and London: 1859. V. 65; 66
Adam Bede. Leipzig: 1859. V. 65
Complete Works. With Life by J. W. Cross. Boston: 1900. V. 67
Daniel Deronda. Edinburgh and London: 1876. V. 62; 63; 64; 65; 67
Daniel Deronda. Leipzig: 1876. V. 65
Daniel Deronda. Montreal: 1876. V. 65
Daniel Deronda. London: 1877. V. 62
Early Essays. London: 1919. V. 65
Essays and Leaves from a Note-Book. Edinburgh and London: 1844. V. 66
Essays and Leaves from a Note-Book. Edinburgh and London: 1884. V. 63; 65
The Essays of George Eliot. New York: 1883. V. 65
Family Secrets. London: 1843?. V. 65
Felix Holt, the Radical. Edinburgh and London: 1866. V. 62; 65; 66
Fragments et Pensees. Geneve: 1877. V. 65
Fragments et Pensees. Geneve: 1879. V. 65; 66
George Eliot's Life as Related in Her Letters and Journals. London: 1885. V. 63; 66
George Eliot's Life as Related in Her Letters and Journals. Edinburgh and London: 1885-1886. V. 62
How Lisa Loved the King. Boston: 1869. V. 65
Impressions of Theophrastus Such. Edinburgh: 1879. V. 65
Impressions of Theophrastus Such. New York: 1879. V. 65
The Legend of Jubal and Other Poems. Boston: 1874. V. 64
The Legend of Jubal and Other Poems. Edinburgh and London: 1874. V. 65; 67
The Lifted Veil and Brother Jacob. Leipzig: 1878. V. 65
Middlemarch. Edinburgh: 1871. V. 65
Middlemarch. Edinburgh: 1871-1872. V. 63; 66
Middlemarch. Berlin: 1872. V. 65
Middlemarch. Edinburgh: 1873. V. 65
Middlemarch. Hamburg: 1880. V. 65
The Mill on the Floss. Edinburgh and London: 1860. V. 63; 65; 66
The Mill on the Floss. New York: 1860. V. 63; 64; 65
The Novels. Edinburgh & London: 1881-1883. V. 62
Novels. London: 1885. V. 65
The Novels. London: 1890. V. 62; 66
Novels. Edinburgh: 1900. V. 65
Romola. London: 1863. V. 67
Romola. London: 1880. V. 65
Scenes of Clerical Life. Edinburgh and London: 1858. V. 65
Scenes of Clerical Life. London: 1859. V. 65
Silas Marner, the Weaver of Raveloe. Edinburgh and London: 1861. V. 62; 63; 65; 66; 67
Silas Marner: the Weaver of Raveloe. New York: 1861. V. 65
Silas Marner, the Weaver of Raveloe. London: 1905. V. 63
Silas Marner. The Weaver of Raveloe. 1953. V. 62; 65; 67
The Spanish Gipsy. Boston: 1868. V. 65
The Spanish Gipsy. Edinburgh: 1868. V. 65
The Spanish Gipsy. Edinburgh: 1869. V. 65
The Works. Edinburgh: 1885?. V. 65
The Works. Edinburgh and London: 1901. V. 66

ELIOT, JACOB
Diary of Rev. Jacob Eliot, M.A. 1737-1764 Part II. 1944. V. 67

ELIOT, JOHN
The Indian Primer; or, The Way of Training Up of Our Indian Youth in the Good Knowledge of God, 1669.... Edinburgh: 1880. V. 67
The Parlement of Pratlers. London: 1928. V. 66

ELIOT, MONTAGUE
Too Weak. London: 1907. V. 65

ELIOT, SAMUEL A.
Letter to the President of Harvard College. Boston: 1849. V. 66

ELIOT, THOMAS STEARNS
After Strange Gods - a Primer of Modern Heresy - the Page-Barbour Lectures at the University of Virginia 1933. London: 1934. V. 62
The Aims of Poetic Drama. London: 1949. V. 65
Ash Wednesday. London: 1930. V. 64; 65
Ash Wednesday. New York: 1930. V. 62; 64; 65
A Choice of Kipling's Verse Made by T. S. Eliot.... London: 1941. V. 63
The Cocktail Party. London: 1950. V. 62; 64
La Cocktail Party. Paris: 1952. V. 65
Collected Plays. London: 1962. V. 65
Collected Poems 1909-1935. London: 1936. V. 62; 64; 65
Collected Poems 1909-1935. New York: 1936. V. 67
Collected Poems 1909-1962. London: 1963. V. 65
The Confidential Clerk. London: 1954. V. 63; 64; 65; 66
The Cultivation of Christmas Trees. London: 1954. V. 65
Dante. London: 1929. V. 65
East Coker. Burnt Norton. Dry Salvages. Little Gidding. London: 1940-1942. V. 62
Essays Ancient and Modern. London: 1936. V. 65
Ezra Pound: His Metric and Poetry. New York: 1917. V. 64
Ezra Pound: His Metric and Poetry. New York: 1918. V. 64; 65
The Family Reunion. London: 1939. V. 63; 65; 66
The Family Reunion. London: 1952. V. 63
For Lancelot Andrewes: Essay on Style and Order. London: 1928. V. 64; 65
Four Quartets. London: 1940-1942. V. 64
Four Quartets. New York: 1943. V. 65
Four Quartets. London: 1944. V. 62; 65
Four Quartets. London: 1960. V. 62; 64; 66; 67
Four Quartets. Cambridge: 1996. V. 62; 65
From Poe to Valery: a Lecture Delivered at the Library of Congress.... New York: 1949. V. 63; 66
Growl Tiger's Last Stand and Other Poems. London: 1986. V. 67
Homage to John Dryden: Three Essays on Poetry of the Seventeenth Century. London: 1924. V. 65; 66
The Idea of a Christian Society. London: 1939. V. 62; 64; 65
The Idea of a Christian Society. New York: 1940. V. 63
John Dryden: The Poet, The Dramatist, the Critic. New York: 1932. V. 64; 65
Knowledge and Experience in the Philosophy of F. H. Bradley. London: 1963. V. 62
Knowledge and Experience in the Philosophy of F. H. Bradley. London: 1964. V. 62; 63
Later Poems 1925-1935. London: 1941. V. 66
Letters of T. S. Eliot. Volume I 1898-1922. New York: 1989. V. 62; 64
Il Libro dei Gatti Tuttofare. (Old Possum's Book of Practical Cats). 1963. V. 63
The Literature of Politics. 1955. V. 66
Milton. Annual Lecture on a Master Mind. Henriette Hertz Trust of the British Academy 1947. Read 26 March 1947. London: 1947. V. 67
Meurtre Dans La Cathedrale. Paris: 1947. V. 65
Murder in the Cathedral. Canterbury: 1935. V. 65
Murder in the Cathedral. London: 1935. V. 64; 65
Murder in the Cathedral. London: 1937. V. 63
Notes Towards the Definition of Culture. London: 1948. V. 63; 64
Old Possum's Book of Practical Cats. London: 1939. V. 65; 67
Old Possum's Book of Practical Cats. London: 1953. V. 63
On Poetry and Poets. London: 1957. V. 66
Poemes 1910-1930.... Paris: 1947. V. 65
Poems. Richmond: 1919. V. 63
Poems 1909-1925. London: 1925. V. 62; 64; 65; 67
Poems Written in Early Youth. London: 1967. V. 63
Prufrock and Other Observations. London: 1917. V. 63; 65; 67
Quartets. London: 1996. V. 65
Religious Drama: Mediaeval and Modern. New York: 1954. V. 64; 65; 67
Reunion by Destruction. London: 1943. V. 65
The Rock: a Pageant Play. London: 1934. V. 62; 65; 66
The Sacred Wood: Essays on Peotry and Criticism. London: 1920. V. 64; 65; 66
Selected Essays. London: 1932. V. 62; 65
Selected Essays. London: 1934. V. 62
Selected Essays. New York: 1944. V. 66
Selected Poems. London: 1954. V. 65
Shakespeare and the Stoicism of Seneca. London: 1927. V. 64; 65
A Song for Simeon. London: 1928. V. 65; 67
Sweeney Agonistes. London: 1932. V. 62; 63; 65; 66
To Criticize the Critic and Other Writings. London: 1965. V. 64
To Criticize the Critic and Other Writings. New York: 1965. V. 64
Triumphal March. Ariel Poem No. 35. London: 1928. V. 62
The Undergraduate Poems of T. S Eliot Published While He Was At College in the Harvard Advocate. Cambridge: 1949. V. 62; 65; 67
The Waste Land. Richmond: 1923. V. 62
The Waste Land. London: 1961. V. 62; 64; 65
The Waste Land. London: 1962. V. 62
The Waste Land. London: 1971. V. 62; 64; 65
The Waste Land. New York: 1971. V. 63; 67
What Is a Classic?. London: 1944. V. 63

What Is a Classic?. London: 1945. V. 65

ELIOT, THOMS STEARNS
The Three Voices of Poetry. New York: 1954. V. 63

ELKIN, R. H.
The Children's Corner. London: 1914. V. 65
The Children's Corner. Philadelphia/London: 1915. V. 63
Little People. London. V. 64
Old Dutch Nursery Rhymes. 1917. V. 67
Old Dutch Nursery Rhymes. London/Philadelphia: 1917. V. 62; 63

ELKIN, STANLEY
A Bad Man. New York: 1967. V. 62
Boswell. New York: 1964. V. 67

ELKINS, AARON J.
The Dark Place. 1983. V. 62; 64; 66
The Dark Place. New York: 1983. V. 63; 66
A Deceptive Clarity. 1987. V. 64; 66
A Deceptive Clarity. New York: 1987. V. 67
Fellowship of Fear. 1982. V. 62; 64
Fellowship of Fear. New York: 1982. V. 63; 66
Murder in the Queen's Armes. New York: 1985. V. 62; 63; 65; 66
Murder in the Queen's Armes. London: 1990. V. 63

ELLENBECKER, JOHN G.
The Jayhawkers of Death Valley. Marysville: 1938. V. 63; 66
Oak Grove Massacre (Oak, Nebraska) Indian Raids On the Little Blue River in 1864. Maryville. V. 65; 67

ELLENBERGER, D. F.
History of the Basuto: Anicent and Modern. London: 1912. V. 67

ELLER, E. M.
Dictionary of American Naval Fighting Ships. Washington: 1959-1981. V. 67

ELLER, EVELYN
Forms of Communication. Forest Hills: 1997. V. 64
Reliquary for the Book. Forest Hills: 1996. V. 64

ELLERMAN, J. R.
Checklist of Palaearctic and Indian Mammals. London: 1951. V. 62; 63
Checklist of Palaearctic and Indian Mammals. London: 1966. V. 63
The Families and Genera of Living Rodents. London: 1940-1949. V. 63
The Families and Genera of Living Rodents. 1966. V. 66
The Families and Genera of Living Rodents. Oxford: 1966. V. 62; 65

ELLERY, HARRISON
The Pickering Genealogy: Being an Account of the First Three Generations of the Pickering Family of Salem, Mass. N.P. V. 67

THE ELLESMERE Family: a Tale of Unfashionable Life. Wellington, Salop: 1829. V. 62; 65

ELLESMERE, THOMAS EGERTON, BARON
Certaine Observations Concerning the Office of the Lord Chancellor.... London: 1651. V. 65

ELLET, ELIZABETH F.
The Women of the American Revolution. Williamstown: 1980. V. 65

ELLICE, EDWARD C.
Place-Names in Glengarry and Glenquoich and Their Origin. London: 1898. V. 62

ELLICOTT, ANDREW
The Journal of Andrew Ellicott, Late Commissioner on Behalf of the United States During Part of the Year 1796, the Years 1797, 1798, 1799 and part of the Year 1800. Philadelphia: 1803. V. 64; 66
The Journal of Andrew Ellicott..During Part of the Year 1796, the Years 1797, 1798, 1799 and Part of the Year 1800. Philadelphia: 1814. V. 63

ELLIN, STANLEY
The Key to Nicholas Street. 1952. V. 64; 66

ELLINGER, ESTHER PARKER
The Southern War Poetry of the Civil War. Philadelphia: 1918. V. 63; 65

ELLIOT, D. G.
A Classification and Synopsis of the Trochilidae. Washington: 1880. V. 62
The Gallinaceous Game Birds of North America.... New York: 1897. V. 63; 67
The Life and Habits of Wild Animals. London: 1874. V. 66; 67
The New and Heretofore Unfigured Species of the Birds of North America. New York: 1866-1869. V. 67
North American Shore Birds.... London: 1895. V. 63
North American Shore Birds.... New York: 1895. V. 65; 67
Review of the Ibidinae, or Subfamily of the Ibises. 1877. V. 62
A Review of the Primates. New York: 1912-1913. V. 66
A Review of the Primates. New York: 1913. V. 62; 64
The Wild Fowl of the United States and British Possessions.... New York: 1898. V. 63; 64; 67

ELLIOT, FRANCES
Old Court-Life in France. London: 1886. V. 65

ELLIOT, GEORGE FRANCIS SCOTT
A Naturalist in Mid-Africa. London: 1896. V. 67

ELLIOT, HENRY M.
Memoirs on the History, Folk-Lore, and Distribution of the Races of the North Western Provinces of India.... London: 1869. V. 67

ELLIOT, JAMES
The Poetical and Miscellaneous Works of James Elliot, Citizen of Guilford, Vermont and Late a Noncommissioned Officer in the Legion of the United States. Greenfield: 1798. V. 64

ELLIOT, ROBERT
Views in the East; Comprising India, Canton and the Shores of the Red Sea. London: 1833. V. 64

ELLIOT, STEPHEN
A Sketch of the Botany of South Carolina and Georgia. Charleston: 1821-1824. V. 63

ELLIOT, W. J.
The Spurs. Spur: 1939. V. 64

ELLIOTT, B.
The Country House Garden from the Archives of Country Life 1897-1939. London: 1995. V. 67

ELLIOTT BROS.
The Anschutz Gyro Compass. London: 1910. V. 63

ELLIOTT, CHARLES W.
Mysteries; or, Glimpses of the Supernatural. New York: 1852. V. 65

ELLIOTT, DAVID STEWART
Last Raid of the Daltons and Battle with the Bandits at Coffyville Kansas Oct. 5, 1892. Coffyville: 1892. V. 65

ELLIOTT, GEORGE
Parktilden Village. Boston: 1958. V. 63

ELLIOTT, GEORGE H.
Report of a Tour of Inspection of European Light-House Establishments, Made in 1873. Washington: 1874. V. 66

ELLIOTT, GRACE DALRYMPLE
Journal of My Life During the French Revolution. London: 1859. V. 63

ELLIOTT, HENRY W.
A Monograph of the Pribylov Group, or the Seal Islands of Alaska. Kingston: 1976. V. 66
Report on the Seal Islands of Alaska. N.P: 1884. V. 67

ELLIOTT, J. H.
Credit the Life of Commerce. London: 1845. V. 64

ELLIOTT, J. W.
National Nursery Rhymes and Nursery Songs, Set to Original Music.... London: 1902. V. 64; 67

ELLIOTT, JOHN
A Discourse Delivered on the First Sabbath After the Commencement of the Year 1802. Middletown: 1802. V. 65

ELLIOTT, MARY
The Rose, Containing Original Poems for Young People. London: 1824. V. 63; 65
Rustic Excursions to Aid Tarry-at-Home Travellers: for the Amusement and Instruction for Young Persons. London: 1825. V. 62

ELLIOTT, MAUD H.
Art and Handicraft in the Woman's Building of the World's Columbian Exposition, Chicago 1893. Paris and New York: 1893. V. 66

ELLIOTT, MRS.
Greedy Child Cured. New York: 1885. V. 63

ELLIOTT, R. H.
Gold, Sport and Coffee Planting in Mysore.... 1894. V. 66

ELLIOTT, RICHARD
A Song and A Diary for A. New York: 1973. V. 63

ELLIOTT, RICHARD S.
Notes Taken in Sixty Years. St. Louis: 1883. V. 67

ELLIOTT, STEPHEN
Vain is the Help of Man. A Sermon Preached in Christ Church, Savannah...September 15, 1864. Macon: 1864. V. 63

ELLIOTT, T. C.
Coming of the White Woman 1836 as Told in Letters and Journals of Narcissa Prentiss Whitman. Portland: 1937. V. 64; 67

ELLIOTT, W. H.
Block and Interlocking Signals. New York: 1896. V. 67

ELLIOTT, WILLIAM
Address to the Imperial and Central Agricultural Society of France. Read Before Them at Paris, the 4th July, 1855. Paris: 1855. V. 63
Carolina Sports, by Land and Water. Charleston: 1846. V. 66
Carolina Sports, by Land and Water. New York: 1859. V. 63; 66
Carolina Sports, by Land and Water. London: 1867. V. 63; 66; 67

ELLIS, A. B.
The Ewe-Speaking Peoples of the Slave Coast of West Africa. London: 1890. V. 67
The Yoruba-Speaking Peoples of the Slave Coast of West Africa; Their Religion, Manners.... London: 1894. V. 67

ELLIS, ALBERT F.
Ocean Island and Nauru. Sydney: 1936. V. 67

ELLIS, BRET EASTON
Less than Zero. New York: 1985. V. 62; 63; 66; 67

ELLIS, CHARLES THOMAS
Practical Remarks and Precedents of Proceedings in Parliament.... London: 1802. V. 65

ELLIS, E. A.
The Broads. London: 1965. V. 63

ELLIS, E. H.
International Boundary Lines Across Colorado and Wyoming. Boulder: 1966. V. 64; 66

ELLIS, EDWARD S.
Thrilling Adventures Among the American Indians. Washington: 1905. V. 67

ELLIS, F. S.
The History of Reynard the Fox.... London: 1894. V. 64

ELLIS, GEORGE E.
Extracts from a History of the Massachusetts General Hospital 1810- 1851....with a continuation 1851-1872. Boston: 1899. V. 64; 66
Memoir of Sir Benjamin Thompson, Count Rumford, with Notices of His Daughter. Boston: 1871. V. 62

ELLIS, HAVELOCK
Chapman, with Illustrative Passages. London: 1934. V. 62
The Resolution of Obscenity. Paris: 1931. V. 62
Sonnets, with Folk Songs from the Spanish. Waltham St. Lawrence: 1925. V. 62
A Study of British Genius. London: 1904. V. 64

ELLIS, HENRY
A General Introduction to the Domesday Book Accompanied by Indexes of the Tenants in Chief and Under Tenants.... London: 1833. V. 63
Journal of the Proceedings of the Late Embassy to China; Comprising a Correct Narrative of the Public Transactions of the Embassy of the Voyage to and from China and of the Journey from the Mouth of the Pei-Ho to the Return to Canton. Philadelphia: 1818. V. 65
Original Letters, Illustrative of English History.... London: 1825-1846. V. 63
A Voyage to Hudson's Bay, by the Dobbs Galley and California, in the Years 1746 and 1747.... London: 1748. V. 63; 66

ELLIS, HENRY HAVELOCK
Chapman. London: 1934. V. 65
Concerning Jude the Obscure. London: 1931. V. 66
The Criminal. New York: 1890. V. 65
Studies in the Psychology of Sex. Philadelphia: 1903-1913. V. 65

ELLIS, J. B.
The North American Pyrenomycetes. Newfield: 1892. V. 62

ELLIS, JOHN
The Necessity of a National Reformation of Manners.... London: 1701. V. 63

ELLIS, M. M.
The Gymnotid Eels of Tropical America. Pittsburgh: 1913. V. 66

ELLIS, PETER
Over the Hills and Far Away. Calcutta;: 1910. V. 66

ELLIS, RON
Ears of the City. London: 1998. V. 67

ELLIS, ROWLAND C.
Colonial Dutch Houses in New Jersey. Twenty Wood Engravings. Newark: 1933. V. 63; 66

ELLIS, S. M.
George Meredith; His Life and Friends in Relation to His Work. London: 1919. V. 67

ELLIS, SARAH STICKNEY
The Daughters of England, Their Position in Society, Character and Responsibilities. London: 1842. V. 65
Family Secrets or Hints to Those Who Would Make a Home Happy. London: 1841. V. 62; 63; 65
The Morning Call: a Table Book of Literature and Art. London: 1852. V. 65
The Mothers of England.... London: 1843. V. 64
Social Distinction; or Hearts and Homes. London: 1848-1849. V. 65
Summer and Winter in the Pyrenees. London: 1841. V. 65
Temper and Temperament; or Varieties of Character. London: 1846. V. 65
The Wives of England, Their Relative Duties, Domestic Influence and Social Obligations. London: 1843. V. 64
The Wives of England, Their Relative Duties, Domestic Influence and Social Obligations. London: 1848. V. 64
The Women of England, Their Social Duties and Domestic Habits. London: 1839. V. 65
The Women of England, Their Social Duties and Domestic Habits. London: 1840. V. 65

ELLIS, WILLIAM
Agriculture Improv'd; or, the Practice of Husbandry Displayed. London: 1745. V. 64
An Authentic Narrative of A Voyage Performed by Captain Cook and Captain Clerke, in His Majesty's Ships Resolution and Discovery During the Years 1776-1780; in Search of a North-West Passage Between the Continents of Asia and America. Amsterdam: 1969. V. 63
The Campagna of London.... London: 1791-1793. V. 62
An Essay on the Cure of the Veneral Gonorrhoea, in a New Method. London: 1771. V. 65
Lessons on the Phenomena of Industrial Life and the Conditions of Industrial Success. London: 1854. V. 63
The Modern Husbandman; or, the Practice of Farming; as It Is Now Carried On by the Most Accurate Farmers in Several Counties of England. Dublin: 1743-1744. V. 66

ELLIS, WILLIAM continued
Polynesian Researches. London: 1829. V. 62; 63; 66; 67
Polynesian Researches. New York: 1833. V. 66
Three Visits to Madagascar During the Years 1853-1854-1856. London: 1858. V. 62; 63
Three Visits to Madagascar During the Years 1853-1854-1856. New York: 1859. V. 65

ELLIS, WILLIAM CHARLES
A Treatise on the Nature, Symptoms, Causes and Treatment of Insanity, with Practical Observations on Lunatic Asylums and a Description of the Pauper Lunatic Asylum...at Hanwell.... London: 1838. V. 65

ELLISON, BERNARD C.
The Prince of Wales's Sport in India. 1925. V. 62; 63; 64; 66; 67
The Prince of Wales's Sport in India. London: 1925. V. 62

ELLISON, HARLAN
Approaching Oblivion. 1915. V. 66
Approaching Oblivion. 1974. V. 62; 64
Dangerous Visions. New York: 1967. V. 63; 67
Love Ain't Nothing but Sex Misspelled. 1968. V. 67
Rumble. New York: 1958. V. 65
Shatterday. Boston: 1980. V. 66
Spider Kiss. 1990. V. 62; 64
Strange Wine: Fifteen New Stories from the Nightside of the World. New York: 1977. V. 63; 66; 67

ELLISON, JOSEPH
California and the Nation 1850-1869: a Study of the Relations of a Frontier Community with the Federal Government. Berkeley: 1927. V. 64; 66

ELLISON, RALPH
Invisible Man. New York: 1952. V. 65
Invisible Man. Franklin Center: 1980. V. 63
The Writer's Experience. Washington: 1964. V. 62; 64

ELLISON, ROBERT S.
Fort Bridger, Wyoming - a Brief History. Sheridan: 1938. V. 67

ELLISON, W. G. H.
The Settlers of Vancouver Island. A Tale for Emigrants. London: 1908. V. 64

ELLMAKER, ELIAS E.
The Revelation of Rights. Columbus: 1841. V. 65

ELLMANN, RICHARD
The Backgrounds of Ulysses. 1954. V. 67
Henry James Among the Aesthetes. London: 1983. V. 64
James Joyce. 1959. V. 67
James Joyce. New York: 1982. V. 63
Oscar Wilde. London: 1987. V. 62
Ulysses on the Liffey. 1972. V. 62; 65

ELLROY, JAMES
Because the Night. New York: 1984. V. 65; 67
The Big Nowhere. New York: 1988. V. 65; 66; 67
The Black Dahlia. 1987. V. 64; 65; 66
The Black Dahlia. New York: 1987. V. 65; 66; 67
Blood on the Moon. New York: 1984. V. 65; 66; 67
Brown's Requiem. New York: 1981. V. 65; 66; 67
Brown's Requiem. London: 1984. V. 62; 65; 66
Brown's Requiem. New York: 1994. V. 67
Clandestine. London: 1984. V. 65
Crime Wave. London: 1999. V. 67
L. A. Confidential. New York: 1980. V. 67
L. A. Confidential. New York: 1990. V. 65; 67
My Dark Places. Blakeney, Gloucestershire: 1996. V. 63
Suicide Hill. New York: 1986. V. 65; 66

ELLSON, HAL
Reefer Boy - A Story of Teenage Drug Adicts. London: 1955. V. 64

ELLSWORTH, EPHRAIM ELMA
The Zouave Drill, Being a Complete Manual of Arms for the Use of the Rifled Musket, With Either the Percussion Cap, or Maynard Primer. Philadelphia: 1861. V. 64

ELLWANGER, GEORGE H.
Meditations on Gout, with a Consideration of its Cure through the Use of Wine. New York: 1897. V. 66

ELLWOOD, THOMAS
Sacred History; or the Historical Part of the Holy Scriptures.... Burlington: 1804. V. 63; 66

ELMAN, R.
Hunting. 1980. V. 67

ELMER, LUCIUS Q. C.
The Constitution and Government of the Province and State of New Jersey, with Biographical Sketches of Governors from 1776 to 1845.... Newark: 1872. V. 63; 66

ELMES, JAMES
A General and Bibliographical Dictionary of the Fine Arts...Principal Terms Used...Historical Sketches of.... London: 1826. V. 66
Memoirs of the Life and Works of Sir Christopher Wren with a Brief View of the Progress of Architecture in England from the Beginning of the Reign of Charles The First to the End of the Seventeenth Century. London: 1823. V. 64; 66; 67
A Practical Treatise on Ecclesiastical and Civil Dilapidations, Re- Instatements, Waste, &c. London: 1829. V. 62

A Scientific, Historical and Commercial Survey of the Harbour and Port of London. London: 1838. V. 64; 66

ELMHIRST, PENNELL
Fox-Hound Forest and Prairie. London: 1892. V. 63

ELMSLIE, KENWARD
Album. New York: 1969. V. 64
Motor Disturbance. New York & London: 1971. V. 63
Pavilions. Poems. New York: 1961. V. 62

ELOY, NICOLAS FRANCOIS JOSEPH
Dictionnaire Historique de la Medecine Ancienne et Moderne. Mons: 1778. V. 66

ELPHINSTONE, MOUNTSTUART
An Account of the Kingdom of Cabul and Its Dependencies in Persia, Tartary and India.... London: 1842. V. 64

ELSAM, RICHARD
Hints for Improving the Condition of the Peasantry.... London: 1816. V. 64

ELSASSER, W. M.
The Physical Foundation of Biology, an Analytic Study. London: 1958. V. 67

ELSEN, ALBERT
Paul Jenkins. New York: 1973. V. 66

ELSENSOHN, M. ALFREDA, SISTER
Pioneer Days in Idaho Country. Caldwell: 1947-1951. V. 64; 67

ELSHOLTZ, JOHANN SIGISMUND
Vom Garten-Baw: oder Unterricht von der Gartnerey auff das Clima der Chur-Marck Brandenburg, Wie Auch der Benachbarten Teutschen Lander Gerichtet.... Berlin: 1684. V. 62; 63

ELSON, HENRY W.
The Civil War through the Camera. Springfield: 1912. V. 63

ELSON, WILLIAM H.
Elson-Gray Basic Readers Book One. Chicago: 1936. V. 62

ELSTOB, ELIZABETH
An English-Saxon Homily on the Birth-day of St. Gregory.... London: 1709. V. 64
The Rudiments of Grammar for the English Saxon Tongue. London: 1715. V. 63

ELSTOB, PETER
The Armed Rehearsal. London: 1964. V. 66

ELSTOB, WILLIAM
Observations on an Address to the Public, Dated April 20, 1775, Superscribed Bedford Level and signed Charles Nelson Cole, Register. Lynn: 1776. V. 66

ELSYNGE, HENRY
The Ancient and Present Manner of Holding Parliaments in England; with Their Priviledges. London: 1663. V. 64
The Ancient Method and Manner of Holding of Parliaments in England. London: 1660. V. 65

ELTON, BEN
Popcorn. London: 1996. V. 65

ELTON, GODFREY
The Testament of Dominic Burleigh. Boston and New York: 1926. V. 63

ELTON, OLIVER
Sixteen Poems. Liverpool. V. 67

ELUARD, PAUL
Le Dur Desir De Durer. London: 1950. V. 64
Le Dur Desir de Durer; Poems. Philadelphia: 1950. V. 66
Lady Love - A Poem for Pat Thomas. Hayle Mill, Maidstone: 1983. V. 64
Poesie et Verite 1942 - Poetry and Truth 1942. London: 1944. V. 64
Thorns of Thunder - Selected Poems. London: 1936. V. 65

ELVIDGE, G. H.
Widow Wiselad's Son. London: 1883. V. 67

ELWES, HENRY JOHN
Memoirs of Travel, Sport and Natural History. London: 1930. V. 67

ELWIN, VERRIER
The Religion of an Indian Tribe. Bombay: 1955. V. 62
The Tribal World of Verrier Elwin. Bombay: 1964. V. 62

ELWOOD, ANNE KATHARINE
Memoirs of the Literary Ladies of England.... London: 1843. V. 62

ELWOOD, GEORGE S.
Some English Gardens. London: 1904. V. 67

ELY, TIMOTHY C.
Approach to the Site. New York: 1986. V. 64

ELYOT, THOMAS
The Boke, Named Governour. London: 1580. V. 66
The Castel of Helthe (1541)...Together with the Titlepage and Preface of the Edition of 1539. New York: 1937. V. 63

EMANUEL, HARRY
Diamonds and Precious Stones: their History, Value and Distinguishing Characteristics. London: 1867. V. 63

EMBICK, MILTON A.
Military History of the Third Division, Ninth Corps, Army of the Potomac. Harrisburg: 1913. V. 65

EMBODEN, WILLIAM A.
Jean Cocteau and the Illustrated Book. Northridge: 1990. V. 64

EMBREY, ALVIN T.
Waters of the State. Richmond: 1931. V. 62; 64

EMBURY, A. H.
The Dutch Colonial House: Its Origin, Design, Modern Plan and Construction. New York: 1913. V. 62; 65

EMBURY, EMMA C.
The Poems of Emma C. Embury. New York: 1869. V. 63

EMDEN, A. B.
A Biographical Register of the University of Oxford to A.D. 1500. Oxford: 1957-1959. V. 63

EMDEN, WALTER
Picturesque Westminster, a Collection of Sketches.... London: 1902. V. 62

EMECHETA, BUCHI
In the Ditch. London: 1972. V. 62

EMERSON, CAROLINE D.
Mickey Sees the U. S. A. Boston: 1944. V. 65
School Days in Disneyville. Boston: 1939. V. 65

EMERSON, EARL
Black Hearts and Slow Dancing. New York: 1988. V. 65

EMERSON, EDWARD WALDO
Henry Thoreau as Remembered by a Young Friend. Boston: 1917. V. 64; 65

EMERSON, G. B.
Manual of Agriculture for the School, the Farm and the Fireside. Boston: 1862. V. 64
A Report on the Trees and Shrubs Growing Naturally In the Forests of Massachusetts. Boston: 1903. V. 67

EMERSON, JAMES
A Picture of Greece in 1825; as Exhibited in the Personal Narratives of James Emerson, Esq. London: 1826. V. 67

EMERSON, M. FARLEY, MRS.
Woman in America: Her Character and Position as Indicated by Newspaper Editorials and Sustained by American Social Life. Cincinnati: 1857. V. 65

EMERSON, P. H.
Naturalistic Photography for Students of the Art. London: 1889. V. 65
Naturalistic Photography for Students of the Art. New York: 1899. V. 65

EMERSON, RALPH WALDO
An Address Delivered Before the Senior Class in Divinity College. Boston: 1838. V. 65
An Address Delivered in the Court-House in Concord Massachusetts, on 1st August, 1844.... Boston: 1844. V. 63; 67
English Traits. Boston: 1856. V. 66
The Essay on Self Reliance. East Aurora: 1905. V. 62
Essays. Boston: 1841. V. 65
Essays. Boston: 1847. V. 66
Essays. Hammersmith: 1906. V. 62; 65; 67
Essays. London: 1910. V. 62
Essays (First and Second Series). Boston: 1841-1844. V. 62
A Historical Discourse Delivered Before the Citizens of Concord. Concord: 1835. V. 64; 65
The Letters of Ralph Waldo Emerson. New York: 1939. V. 62; 64; 65
May-Day and Other Pieces. Boston: 1867. V. 64; 65
Nature. Boston: 1836. V. 65
Nature. Munich: 1929. V. 64; 66
An Oration Delivered Before the Phi Beta Kappa Society at Cambridge, August 31, 1837. Boston: 1837. V. 62
Poems. Boston: 1847. V. 62; 65
Success. Boston and New York: 1912. V. 67
The Works. Boston: 1883-1884. V. 62; 66

EMERSON, WILLIAM
The Doctrine of Fluxions; Not Only Explaining the Elements Thereof, But Also Its Application and Use in the Several Parts of Mathematics and Natural Philosophy. London: 1743. V. 65
The Mathematical Principles of Geography. (with) Dialling, or the Art of Drawing Dials, On All Sorts of Planes Whatsoever. London: 1770. V. 66
Old Bridges of France. New York: 1925. V. 65
The Principles of Mechanics. London: 1836. V. 65

EMERY, JACK
The Putney Debates. 1983. V. 65
The Putney Debates. Cambridge: 1983. V. 63

EMERY, K. O.
The Geology of the Atlantic Ocean. Berlin: 1984. V. 67

EMERY, M.
Furniture by Architects: 500 International Masterpieces of 20th Century Design and Where to Buy Them. New York: 1983. V. 62; 65

EMHEIM, DAVID
The Nondescript. Davey, Called the Man Bear. New York: 1882. V. 65

EMILIANE, GABRIEL D'
Observations on a Journey to Naples. London: 1691. V. 67

EMILIO, LUIS F.
Roanoke Island, Its Occupation Defense and Fall. New York: 1891. V. 62

EMINA, ERNESTO
La Donna in Roma Antica. 1890. V. 63

EMIN PASHA, MEHMED
Emin Pasha in Central Africa: Being a Collection of His Letters and Journals. London: 1888. V. 67

EMMERS, R.
A Stereotaxic Atlas of the Brain of the Squirrel Monkey. Madison: 1963. V. 67

EMMET, THOMAS ADDIS
Ireland Under English Rule, or a Plea for the Plaintiff. New York: 1909. V. 65
Memoir of Thomas Addis and Robert Emmet with Their Ancestors and Immediate Family. New York: 1915. V. 67

EMMETT, CHRIS
Shanghai Pierce, a Fair Likeness. Norman: 1953. V. 65

EMMONS, E.
Agriculture of New York.... Albany: 1843-1851. V. 62
Agriculture of North Carolina.... Raleigh: 1860. V. 62

EMMONS, SAMUEL B.
Every Man His Own Physician. The Vegetable Family Physician. Boston: 1836. V. 62

EMMONS, WILLIAM
Authentic Biography of Col. Richard M. Johnson, of Ky. New York: 1833. V. 63

EMMONS, WILLIAM HARVEY
The Enrichment of Ore Deposits. Washington: 1917. V. 64

EMORY, WILLIAM HEMSLEY
Notes of a Military Reconnaissance from Fort Leavenworth, in Missouri and San Diego in California. Washington: 1848. V. 62; 63; 64; 66; 67
Report on the United States and Mexican Boundary Survey. Washington: 1859. V. 65; 67
Report on the United States and Mexican Boundary Survey. Austin: 1987. V. 65; 66

EMPSON, PATIENCE
The Wood Engravings of Robert Gibbings with Some Recollections by the Artist. London: 1959. V. 62

EMPSON, WILLIAM
Seven Types of Ambiguity. London: 1930. V. 64

EMSLEY, M.
Rain Forests and Cloud Forests. New York: 1979. V. 62

EMSLIE, JOHN
Introduction to Natural Philosophy, Comprising a Popular Account of the Properties of Bodies.. London: 1850. V. 65

ENAULT, LOUIS
Angleterre, Ecosse, Irlande Voyage Pittoresque. Paris: 1859. V. 66
Londres. Paris: 1876. V. 66

ENCYCLOPAEDIA Britannica; or a Dictionary of Arts and Sciences.... 1972. V. 66

ENDE, MICHAEL
The Neverending Story. N.P: 1983. V. 62
The Neverending Story. Garden City: 1983. V. 65
Die Unendliche Geschichte. Stuttgart: 1979. V. 67

ENDEAVOUR FIRE COMPANY OF THE CITY OF BURLINGTON
Constitution and Act of Incorporation...Instituted 1795. Burlington: 1857. V. 66

ENDELL, FRITZ
Old Tavern Signs. Boston: 1916. V. 67

ENDICOTT, WILLIAM C.
Board on Fortifications or Other Defenses. Washington: 1886. V. 62

ENDLE, SIDNEY
The Kacharis. London: 1911. V. 67

THE ENDOWED Charities of the City of London.... London: 1829. V. 62

ENDRESS, P. K.
Diversity and Evolutionary Biology of Tropical Flowers. Cambridge: 1994. V. 65; 66

ENEROTH, OLOF
Herregardar Uti Sodermanland.... Stockholm: 1869. V. 62; 66

ENFANTIN, BARTHLEMY PROSPER
Religion Saint-Simonienne. Economie Politique et Politique. Articles Extraits du Globe. Paris: 1823. V. 66

ENFIELD, D. E.
L. E. L. - A Mystery of the Thirties. London: 1928. V. 62

ENFIELD, MARY
God First; or Hester Needham's Work in Sumatra, Her Letters and Diaries. London: 1899. V. 67

ENFIELD, WILLIAM
Biographical Sermons; or a Series of Discourse On the Principal Characters in Scripture. Boston: 1794. V. 67

ENFIELD, WILLIAM continued
Elementary View of the Fine Arts.... London: 1809. V. 63
Institutes of Natural Philosophy, Theoretical and Practical. Boston: 1802. V. 63

ENFIELD, WILLIAM, MRS.
Nottingham Sketches. London: 1854. V. 63

ENGEL, D. H.
Japanese Gardens for Today. Rutland/Tokyo: 1959. V. 62; 65

ENGEL, JOHAN JACOB
Ideen Zur Einer Mimik. Berlin: 1785-1786. V. 65

ENGEL, SAMUEL
Essai sur Cette Question; Quand et Comment L'Amerique a-t-elle Peuplee d'Hommes et d'Animaux?. Amsterdam: 1767. V. 62

ENGELBACH, LEWIS
Naples and the Campagna Felice: In a Series of Letters, etc. London: 1815. V. 62

ENGELBACH, WILLIAM
Endocrine Medicine. Springfield: 1932. V. 65

ENGELHARDT, ALEXANDER PLATONOVICH
A Russian Province of the North (Archangel). Westminster and Philadelphia: 1899. V. 67

ENGELHARDT, ZEPHYRIN
Mission San Gabriel Mission and the Beginnings of Los Angeles. San Gabriel: 1927. V. 65
Missions and Missionaries of California. San Francisco: 1908-1922. V. 64

ENGELS, FRIEDRICH
Die Lage der Arbeiten Klasse in England. Nach Eigner Anschauuing und Authentischen Quellen. Leipzig: 1845. V. 63

ENGELS, MICHEL
Die Feierlich Schlukprozession der Muttergottes-Octave zu Luxemburg. Luxembourg: 1893. V. 66

THE ENGINEER and Machinist's Assistant; Being a Series of Plans, Sections and Elevations, of Steam Engines, Spinning Machines, Mills for Grinding, Tools, etc.... Glasgow: 1856. V. 65

ENGINEERING RESEARCH ASSOCIATES
High Speed Computing Devices. New York: 1950. V. 64; 67

ENGLAND and Wales; or, the County Album.... London: 1841. V. 66

ENGLAND, GEORGE ALLAN
The Air Trust. 1915. V. 62; 64
The Golden Blight. New York: 1916. V. 65
Vikings of the Ice. New York: 1924. V. 63

ENGLAND, T. R.
Letters from the Abbe Edgeworth to His Friends (1777-1807). 1818. V. 62

ENGLANDER, NATHAN
For the Relief of Unbearable Urges. New York: 1999. V. 62; 67

ENGLAND'S Vanity; or the Voice of God Against Monstrous Sin of Pride, in Dress and Apparel: Wherein Naked Breasts and Shoulders, Antick and Fantastick Garbs, Patches and Painting.... London: 1683. V. 65

ENGLEFIELD, HENRY
A Description of the Principal Picturesque Beauties, Antiquities and Geological Phenomena of the Isle of Wight. London: 1816. V. 65; 67
On the Determination of the Orbits of Comets, According to the Methods of Father Boscovich and Mr. De La Place.... London: 1793. V. 62
A Walk through Southampton. London: 1801. V. 66
A Walk through Southampton. Southampton: 1805. V. 62; 66

ENGLEFIELD, J.
The Delightful Life of Pleasure on the Thames.... 1912. V. 65
Dry-Fly Fishing for Trout and Grayling. 1908. V. 65; 67

AN ENGLISH Florilegium.... New York: 1988. V. 64; 67

THE ENGLISH Lakes. London: 1859. V. 64

THE ENGLISH Matron; a Practical Manual for Young Wives. London: 1861. V. 67

THE ENGLISH Register; or the Irish Register Match'd. London: 1742. V. 63

ENGLISH Rustic Pictures. London: 1882. V. 64

THE ENGLISH Theophrastus; or, the Manners of the Age. London: 1702. V. 66

ENGLISH Lake Scenery. London: 1880. V. 62

ENGLISH, MARY KATHERINE J.
Prairie Sketches of Fugitive Recollections of an Army Girl of 1899. N.P: 1899. V. 65; 67

THE ENGLISHMAN'S Mirror; or, Corruption and Taxation Unmasked!. London: 1820. V. 63

ENGSTRAND, STUART
Beyond the Forest. New York: 1948. V. 66

ENNIS, JACOB
The Origin of the Stars, and the Causes of Their Motions and Their Light. New York: 1868. V. 66

ENOCUS
De Puerili Graecaru Literatum Doctrina Liber. Geneva: 1555. V. 66

ENOS, D. L.
The Arabian Art of Taming and Training Wild and Vicious Horses. Chicago: 1857. V. 64

AN ENQUIRY Relative to the Highways in the Shire of Berwick. Edinburgh?: 1770?. V. 65

ENRIGHT, ANNE
The Portable Virgin. London: 1991. V. 66

ENRIGHT, D. J.
Insufficient Poppy - a Novel. London: 1960. V. 63
Season Ticket. Alexandria: 1948. V. 62
The Year of the Monkey - a Farewell Edition. Kobe: 1956. V. 64

ENS, CASPAR
Deliciae Italiae et Index Viatoribus ab Urbe Roma ad Omnes in Italia. (with) Deliciae Galliae Sive Iterarium per Univrsam Galliam. Cologne: 1609. V. 62

ENSLIN, THEODORE
Forms. New Rochelle: 1970-1974. V. 63

THE ENTERTAINING History of Miss Patty Proud, or the Downfall of Vanity; with the Reward of Good-Nature. London: 1800. V. 63

THE ENTERTAINING Story of Little Red Riding Hood. London: 1820. V. 66

ENTICK, JOHN
Entick's New Spelling Dictionary. London: 1801. V. 64
Entick's New Spelling Dictionary. London: 1803. V. 64

ENTOMOLOGICAL SOCIETY OF AMERICA
Journal of Economic Entomology. 1955-1972. V. 67

ENTWISLE, E. A.
A Literary History of Wallpaper. London: 1960. V. 66

ENYEART, JAMES L.
Edward Weston's California Landscapes. Boston: 1984. V. 65

EPICTETUS
All the Works.... London: 1758. V. 65
Enchiridion. Amsterdam: 1670. V. 66
Enchiridion. Paris: 1782. V. 66
The Enchiridion. Austin: 1997. V. 62
Epicteti Enchiridion. Paris: 1623. V. 67
Epictetus His Morals. London: 1694. V. 66
The Golden Sayings. With the Hymn of Cleanthes. London: 1920. V. 62
Manvale et Cebetis Tabvla Graece et Latine. Leipzig: 1798. V. 66
The Works.... London: 1807. V. 64

EPICURIUS
Epicurius: the Extant Remains of the Greek Text. 1947. V. 65

EPINAY, LOUISE FLORENCE PETRONVILLE, MME. DE
L'Amitie de Deux Jolies Femmes Suivie de Un Reve de Mlle. Clairon.... Paris: 1885. V. 63
Les Conversations d'Emile. Hambourg: 1796. V. 64
The Conversations of Emily. London: 1815. V. 66

AN EPISODE at Schmeks; a Novel. London: 1895. V. 67

THE EPITOMIST: a Literary Miscellany and Record of Progress. London: 1854. V. 62

EPPERSON, HARRY A.
Colorado As I Saw It. Kaysville: 1944. V. 63; 66

EPPS, JOHN
Epilepsy, and Some Nervous Affections, Its Precursors: Being Twenty-Two Cases Successfully Treated. London: 1841. V. 65
The Life of John Walker, M.D. London: 1832. V. 66; 67

EPPSTEIN, JOHN
The Catholic Tradition of the Law of Nations. Washington: 1935. V. 66

EPSTEIN, BRIAN
A Cellarful of Noise. 1964. V. 67
A Cellarful of Noise. London: 1964. V. 65

EPSTEIN, JEAN
La Poesie d'Aujourd'hui un Nouvel Etat d'Intelligence. Lettre de Blaise Cendrars. Paris: 1921. V. 67

EQUITABLE Distribution of the Waters of the Rio Grande. Washington: 1898. V. 65

ERASMUS, DESIDERIUS
Adagiorum D. Erasmi Roterodamii Epitome. Amsterdam: 1663. V. 66
The Apothegms of the Ancients.... London: 1753. V. 63
Colloquiorum Familiarum. Londini: 1653. V. 62; 67
The Complaint of Peace; to Which is Added Antipolemus; or The Plea of Reason, Religion and Humanity Against War.... Boston: 1813. V. 66
Encomium Moriae i.e. Stultitiae Laus. Praise of Folly. Basle: 1931. V. 66
Exomologesis Sive Modus Confitendi. Basel: 1524. V. 65
Moriae Encomium (and other works). Basel: 1522. V. 65; 67
Moriae Encomium, Stultitiae Laus.... Basel: 1676. V. 62; 65
Parabolarum Sive Similium Liber. Strassburg: 1518. V. 62
The Pope Shut Out of His Heaven Gates; or, a Dialogue Between Pope Julius the 2d. His Genius and Saint Peter.... London: 1673. V. 66
Twenty-Two Select Colloquies Out of Erasmus.... London: 1725. V. 62

ERB, WILHELM HEINRICH
Handbook of Electro-Therapeutics. New York: 1883. V. 65

ERBEN, KARLA JAROMIRA
Tri Zlate Vlasy Deda Vseyeda. Pohadka. (Three Golden Hairs of the Wise Man. A Fairy Tale). Prague: 1914. V. 64

ERCOLANI, GIROLAMO
La Reggia Delle Vedove Sacre.... Bologna: 1682. V. 65

ERDRICH, LOUISE
Baptism of Desire. New York: 1989. V. 67
The Bingo Palace. New York: 1994. V. 63
Jacklight. New York: 1984. V. 63
Love Medicine. New York: 1984. V. 63; 64; 66; 67

ERFURT, JULIUS
The Dyeing of Paper Pulp. 1901. V. 67

ERICHSEN, JOHN
On Concussion of the Spine, Nervous Shock...in Their Clinical and Medico-Legal Aspects.... London: 1882. V. 67

ERICKSON, ARTHUR
The Architecture.... New York: 1988. V. 62; 65

ERICKSON, STEVE
Days Between Stations. New York: 1985. V. 62

ERKISON, ERIK
Gandhi's Truth: On the Origins of Militant Nonviolence. New York: 1969. V. 63

ERLE, WILLIAM
The Law Relating to Trade Unions. London: 1869. V. 63

ERLEIGH, EVA
The Little One's Log. Baby's Record. London: 1929. V. 67

ERMENTROUT, DANIEL
Our People in American History, an Oration. Reading: 1878. V. 62

ERNST, C. H.
Turtles of the World. Washington: 1989. V. 67

ERNST, MAX
A L'Interieur de la Vue. 8 Poemes Visibles. Paris: 1948. V. 66
Le Musee de l'Homme Suivi de la Peche Au Soleil Levant. Paris: 1965. V. 67

ERNUL, J. B.
Life of a Confederate Soldier in a Federal Prison. Vanceboro: 1910. V. 62; 63

ERRINGTON, HARRIET
The Trial of Mrs. Harriet Errington, Wife of George Errington, Esq. of the Adelphi, in the Bishop of London's Court,...for Committing Adultery.... London: 1785?. V. 63; 65

ERSKINE, ALBERT RUSSELL
History of the Studebaker Corporation. N.P: 1924. V. 62

ERSKINE, BEATRICE
Anna Jameson: Letters and Friendships (1812-1860). London: 1915. V. 65

ERSKINE, JOHN ELPHINSTONE
Journal of a Cruise Among the Islands of the Western Pacific, Including the Jeejees and Others Inhabited by the Polynesian Negro Races, in Her Majesty's Ship Havannah. London: 1853. V. 63; 67

ERSKINE, MICHAEL
The Diary of Michael Erskine.... Midland: 1979. V. 67

ERSKINE, PAYNE
The Harper and the King's Horse. Chicago: 1905. V. 67

ERSKINE, ROBERT
A Dissertation on Rivers and Tides, Intended to Demonstrate in General the Effect of Bridges, Cuttings, Remvoing of Shoals and Imbankments.... London: 1780. V. 65

ERSKINE, STEUART, MRS.
Vanished Cities of Northern Africa. London: 1920. V. 65

ERSKINE, THOMAS, 1ST BARON
A Letter... to An Elector of Westminster Author of A Reply to the Short Defence of the Whigs. London: 1819. V. 66

ERSKINE, WILLIAM
Scacchia Ludus; or, the Game of Chess. London: 1736. V. 65

ERWIN, ALLEN A.
The Southwest of John Horton Slaughter 1841-1922. Pioneer, Cattleman and Trail Driver of Texas, the Pecos and Arizona, Sheriff of Tombstone. Glendale: 1965. V. 64; 67

ERWIN, CHARLES H.
History of the Town and Village of Painted Post, and Village of Painted Post, and of the Town of Erwin.... Painted Post: 1874. V. 65

ERWIN, RICHARD E.
The Truth About Wyatt Earp. Carpinteria: 1992. V. 66

ERWITT, ELLIOT
Personal Exposures. New York/London: 1988. V. 63
Photographs and Anti-Photographs. London: 1972. V. 66

ESAKI, T.
Icones Heteroceroum Japonicorum in Coloribus Naturalibus. Osaka: 1969. V. 66

ESCHENBACH, WOLFRAM VON
The Romance of Parzival and the Holy Grail. 1990. V. 65

ESCHLE, FRANZ C. R.
Grundzuge der Psychiatrie. Berlin/Wien: 1907. V. 65

ESEQUIE del Divino Michelagnolo Buonarroti Celebrate in Firenze dall'Accademia de Pittori, Scultori and Architettori Nella Chiesa di S. Lorenzo il di 28. Giugno MDLXIIII. Florence: 1564. V. 62

ESHLEMAN, CLAYTON
Bearings. Santa Barbara: 1971. V. 64; 66
Brother Stones. Kyoto: 1968. V. 63
Caterpillar (1-20). New York: 1967-1973. V. 64
Caterpillar: Volumes 3-20. New York: 1968-1973. V. 63; 64; 66
The Gull Wall. Los Angeles: 1975. V. 63
Mexico and North. Tokyo: 1962. V. 63; 67
Our Lady of the Three Pronged Devil. New York: 1981. V. 64

ESMERALDA, AURORA
Life and Letters of a Forty-Niner's Daughter. San Francisco: 1929. V. 66

ESMOND, HENRY
A Life's Hazard; or the Outlaw of Wentworth Waste. London: 1880. V. 66

ESMONDE, THOMAS
Hunting Memories of Many Lands. 1925. V. 62; 63; 64
Hunting Memories of Many Lands. London: 1925. V. 67
More Hunting Memories. 1930. V. 62; 63; 67
More Hunting Memories. Dublin: 1930. V. 63

ESPENCE, CLAUDE D'
Traict' Contre L'Erreur Vieil Renouvelle, des Perdestinez. Lyons: 1548. V. 67

ESPER, EUGENIUS JOHANN CHRISTOPH
Naturgeschichte im Auszuge des Linneischen Systems.... Nuremberg: 1784. V. 64

ESPIARD DE LA BORDE, FRANCOIS IGNACE
The Spirit of Nations. London: 1753. V. 63

ESPIN, T.
Rudiments of English Grammar, Compiled by the Late T. Espin, F.S.A. Master of the English and Commercial Academy, Louth, Lincolnshire; and Further Enlarged by Extracts from Various Authors, by J. Hardwick, Master of the Commercial Academy, Grantham. Grantham: 1846. V. 66

ESPINASSE, ISAAC
A Digest of the Law of Actions of Trials at Nili Prius. Dublin: 1794. V. 63

ESPINOSA, J. MANUEL
First Expedition of Vargas into New Mexico 1692. Albuquerque: 1940. V. 65

ESPINOSA, JOSE E.
Saints in the Valleys, Christian Sacred Images in the History, Life and Folk Art of Spanish. Albuquerque: 1960. V. 65; 67

ESPOSITO, VINCENT
The West Point Atlas of American Wars. New York: 1959. V. 63
The West Point Atlas of American Wars. New York: 1960. V. 64

ESPY, WILLARD R.
Oysterville: Roads to Grandpa's Village. New York: 1977. V. 67

ESQUIROL, JEAN
Des Maladies Mentales Considerees Sous les Rapports Medical, Hygieniqe et medico-Legale. Paris: 1838. V. 65
Mental Maladies: a Treatise on Insanity. Philadelphia: 1845. V. 65

ESQUIVEL, LAURA
Como Agua Para Chocolate. (Like Water for Chocolate). Mexico City: 1989. V. 67
The Law of Love. New York: 1996. V. 67
Like Water for Chocolate. New York: 1992. V. 63; 65; 66; 67

ESSAI Theorique and Pratique sur la Phtisie. Senlis: 1759. V. 65

AN ESSAY for the Construction of Roads on Mechanical and Physical Principles. London: 1774. V. 65

AN ESSAY on Civil Government. In Two Parts: Part I. An Inquiry Into the Ends of Government, and the Means of Attaining Them. Part II. On the Government and Commerce of England; with Reflections on Liberty, and the Method of Preserving the Present Constit. London: 1743. V. 65

AN ESSAY on Mineral, Animal and Vegetable Poisons; in Which the Symptoms, Mode of Treatment and Tests of Each Particular Poison.... 1823. V. 63

ESSAY on Modern Martyrs with a Letter to General Burgoyne. London: 1780. V. 62

AN ESSAY On the Atonement, Being an Attempt to Answer the Question, Did Christ Die for All Mankind?. New York: 1811. V. 64

ESSAY on the Corn Laws; to Evince, on the Most Indubitable Ground, in Opposition to the Inflammatory memorial for the Merchants, Traders and Manufacturers of Glasgow.... Edinburgh: 1777. V. 63

ESSAY on the Uses and Abuses of Sabbath School Libraries. Philadelphia: 1838. V. 65

ESSAYS Honoring Lawrence C. Wroth. Portland: 1951. V. 63

ESSAYS on Gothic Architecture.... London: 1808. V. 63

ESSAYS on the Spirit of Legislation in the Encouragement of Agriculture, Population, Manufactures and Commerce. London: 1772. V. 65

ESSAYS on the Spirit of Legislation in the Encouragement of Agriculture, Population, Manufactures, and Commerce. Newark: 1800. V. 63; 66

ESSEN-MOLLER, ELIAS
La Reine Christine. Etude Medicale et Biologique. Paris: 1937. V. 65

ESSEX, ARTHUR CAPEL, EARL OF
Selections from the Correspondence of...1675-1677. London: 1913. V. 65

ESSEX COUNTY ABOLITION SOCIETY
Constitution and Officers of the Essex County Abolition Society, with an Address to Abolitionists. Salem: 1839. V. 62

THE ESSEX House Song Book.... Chipping Campden: 1905. V. 63; 65; 66

ESSEX, JOHN
The Young Ladies Conduct; or, Rules for Education, Under Several Heads; with Instructions Upon Dress, Both Before and After Marriage. London: 1722. V. 65

ESSEX, ROBERT DEVEREUX, 2ND EARL OF
An Apologie of the Earle of Essex, Against Those Which Jealously and Maliciously, Tax Him to the Hinderer of the Peace .... London: 1603. V. 66

ESSEX, ROBERT DEVEREUX, 3RD EARL OF
Famae Posthumae Excellentissimi Herois ac Domini Roberti Devereux, Comitas Essexiae, Vice-Comitis Herefordiae, &c. Generalis Belli, Pro Religione & Libertate Patria.... Londini: 1646. V. 66
Lawes and Ordinances of Warre, Established for the Better Conduct of the Army by His Excellency The Earle of Essex Lord Generall of the Forces raised by the Authority of the Parliamet, for the Defence of the King and Kingdom. London: 1642. V. 66
A Letter from His Excellency, Robert Earl of Essex, to the Honourable House of Commons: Concerning the Sending of a Commission Forthwith to Sir William Waller. London: 1644. V. 66

ESSLEMONT, DAVID
The Printer's Flowers. Montgomery: 1999. V. 65; 66

ESSLIN, MARTIN
Brecht - a Choice of Evils - a Critical Study of the Man, His Work and His Opinions. London: 1959. V. 63

ESTERGREEN, M. MORGAN
Kit Carson: a Portrait in Courage. Norman: 1962. V. 64; 66

ESTES, CLAUD
List of Field Officers, Regiments and Battalions in the Confederate States Army 1861-1865. Macon: 1912. V. 62; 63

ESTES, ELEANOR
The Moffats. New York: 1941. V. 62

ESTEVEN, JOHN
Graveyard Watch. New York: 1938. V. 65

ESTHETIQUE de la Photographie. Paris: 1900. V. 65

ESTIENNE, CHARLES
De Latinis et Graecis Nominibs Arborum, Fruticum, Herbarum, Piscium & Auium Liber. Lvtetiae: 1547. V. 63
De Re Hortensi Libellus. (and) Seminarivm et Plantarivm Fructiferarum. (and) Sylua Frutetum, Collis. (and) Arbustum, Fonticlvs, Spinetvm. (and) Pratum, Lacvs Arundinetum. Paris: 1539-1540-1538. V. 63
De Re Hortensi Libellus. (and) Seminarivm, et Plantarivm Fructiferarum. (and) Sylua, Frutetum, Collis. (and) Arbustum, Fonticvlvs, Spinetvm. (and) Pratum, Lacvs, Arundinetum. Paris: 1539. V. 66
Les Figures et Portraicts des Parties du Corps Humain. Paris: 1575. V. 63
Maison Rustique, or the Countrie Farme. London: 1600. V. 64
Paradoxes, Ce Sont Propos, Contre le Commune Opinion, Debutez en Forme de Declamations Foreses.... Paris: 1554. V. 66
Praedivm Rvsticvm. Paris: 1554. V. 63; 66
Pratum, Lacvs, Arundinetum. Paris: 1543. V. 63; 66

ESTIENNE, HENRI
Epigrammata Graeca, Selecta ex Anthologia. Geneva: 1570. V. 66

ESTIUS, GUILIELMUS
Absolutissima in Omnes Beati Pauli et Septem Catholicas Apostolorum Epistolas Commentaria Tribus Tomus Distincta.... Paris: 1679. V. 67

ESTLEMAN, LOREN D.
Motor City Blue. Boston: 1980. V. 62

ESTREES Bearneses. Pau: 1800. V. 66

ETAT General des Unions Faites des Biens et Revenus des Maladies, Leproseries, Aumoneries & Autres Lieux Pieux, Aux Hopitaux des Pauvres Malades.... Paris: 1705. V. 63

ETCHEBASTER, PIERRE
Pierre's Book. The Game of Court Tennis. Barre: 1971. V. 63

ETCHECOPAR, R. D.
The Birds of North Africa. 1967. V. 62; 63; 64; 67
The Birds of North Africa. Edinburgh: 1967. V. 62; 67

ETCHISON, DENNIS
Red Dreams. 1984. V. 64; 66

ETERNOD, AUGUSTE CHARLES FRANCOIS
Universite de Geneve. Faculte de Medecine, 1876-1896. Geneva: 1896. V. 65

ETHEL Jennings Newton 1885-1965. Dublin: 1966. V. 62

ETHERIDGE, R.
Lord Howe Island, Its Zoology, Geology and Physical Characters. Sydney: 1889. V. 63; 65

ETHERTON, P. T.
Across the Roof of the World; a Record of Sport and Travel through Kashmir, Gilgit, Hunza, the Pamirs, Chinese Turkistan, Mongolia and Siberia. London: 1911. V. 67
Manchuria; the Cockpit of Asia. London: 1932. V. 67

THE ETHIOPIAN Serenaders' Own Book. New York: 1847. V. 64

AN ETHNOGRAPHIC Bibliography of New Guinea. Canberra: 1968. V. 62

ETIENNE, CHARLES
Dictionarium Historicum, Geographicum, Poeticum, Gentium. Geneva: 1596. V. 64

ETIQUETTE for Gentlemen: With Hints on the Art of Conversation. London: 1838. V. 64

ETIQUETTE for Ladies. Eighty Maxims on Dress, Manners and Accomplishments. London: 1841. V. 64; 65

ETMULLER, MICHAEL
Etmullerus Abridg'd; or, a Complete System of the theory and Practice of Physic. London: 1703. V. 64

ETS, MARIE HALL
Nine Days to Christmas. New York: 1959. V. 65

ETZLER, J. A.
The New World or Mechanical System, to Perform the Labours of Man and Beast by Inanimate Powers, That Cost Nothing, for Producing and Preparing the Substances of Life. Philadelphia: 1841. V. 64

EUBULUS Oxoniensis Discipulus Suis. London: 1720. V. 65

EUCLIDES
Gli Elementi...Dal P. Dechales...Tradotto dal Francese. Bergao: 1749. V. 66
(Greek) Elementorum Eluclidis Libri Tredecim. Secundum Vetera Exemplaria Restituti. London: 1620. V. 65
Elementorum Libri XV Breviter Demonstrati.... Londini: 1659. V. 64; 65
The Elements Explain'd, in a New, but Most Easie Method.... Oxford: 1700. V. 64
The Elements or Principles of Geometrie. London: 1684. V. 66
Euclides' Elements.... London: 1632. V. 64
Euclides' Elements.... London: 1732. V. 66; 67
Euclidis Elementorum Libri Priores Sex.... Oxford: 1731. V. 65
Euclidis Elementorum Libri XV. Cologne: 1564. V. 65
Euclidis Elementorum Librir Priores Sex.... Oxford: 1747. V. 65
Euclidis Posteriores Libri IX. Accessit Libri XVI. De Solidorum Regularium...Omnes Perspicuis Demonstrationibus.... Frankfort: 1607. V. 65
The First Six Books of the Elements. London: 1847. V. 62
La Perspectiva, y Especularia de Euclides. Madrid: 1585. V. 62
Solo Introduttore Delle Scientie Mathematice: Diligentemente Reasettato, et alla Integrita Ridotto per Nicolo Tartalea.... Venice: 1543. V. 62; 67

EUDORA Welty: a Tribute. 13 April 1984. Winston-Salem: 1984. V. 62; 64; 67

EUGENIDES, JEFFREY
The Virgin Suicides. New York: 1993. V. 63; 67

EULER, LEONHARD
Briefe an Eine Deutsche Prinzessinn Uber Verschiedene Eegenstande aus der Physik und Philosophie. Leipzig: 1769-1773. V. 63
Elements of Algebra. London: 1810. V. 65; 66
Institutiones Calculi Differentialis cum Eius Usu in Analysi Finitorum ac Doctrina Serierum. St. Petersburg: 1755. V. 63
Introductio in Analysin Infinitorum. Lausanne: 1748. V. 65; 66
Introduction a l'Analyse Infinitesimale.... Paris: 1796-1797. V. 66
Letters on Different Subjects in Physics and Philosophy Addressed to a German Princess. London: 1802. V. 62; 66
Theoria Motuum Planetarum et Cometarum. Berlin: 1744. V. 63

THE EUPHORBIA Journal. Mill Valley: 1983-1985. V. 67

EUREKA TRICK & NOVELTY CO.
Eureka Trick and Novelty Co.'s Manual and Illustrated Price List of New Conjuring Tricks, Magician's Articles, Foreign and Domestic Novelties, Musicial Instruments, Scientific Toys, Automations, Smokers' Goods, Etc. New York: 1877. V. 63

EURIPIDES
The Bacchae: Dionysus, The God. Kentfield: 1972. V. 62; 63; 64
Choruses from the Iphigeneia in Aulis and the Hippolytus of Euripides. London: 1919. V. 63
Electra. Rome: 1545. V. 66
(Greek Leter) Euripidis Quae Extant Omnia. Tragoediae Nempe XX, Praeter Ultimam, Omnes Completae: Item Fragmenta Aliarum Plusquam LX Tragoedianrum; et Epistolae V.... Cantabrigia: 1694. V. 63
The Plays. 1931. V. 67
The Plays. Newtown: 1931. V. 62; 65
The Tragedies. London: 1781-1783. V. 64
The Tragedies of.... London: 1814. V. 62
Euripidis Quae Extant Omnia...Opera & Studio Josuae Barnes.... Cambridge: 1694. V. 65; 66
(The Works). Euripidou ta Sozomena (Transliterated from the Greek). Oxonii: 1778. V. 63

EUROPE'S Catechism. To which are added, The New Elect Catechis'd.... London: 1741. V. 65

EUSEBIUS
The Ancient Ecclesiasticall Histories of the First Six Hundred Years After Christ.... 1650. V. 66
Evangelicae Praeparationis. (with) Evangelicae Demonstationis. Lutetiae: 1544-1545. V. 66
Habes Opt. Lector Chronicon.. Basiliae: 1536. V. 65
Hystoria Ecclesiastica Venundatur. Parisius: 1520. V. 66

EUSTACE, J. S.
Traite d'Amitie, de Commerce et de Navigation, Entre s Majeste Britanique et les Etats Unis de Americaine.... Paris: 1796. V. 64

EUSTACE, JOHN CHETWODE
A Classical Tour through Italy, An MDCCCII. London: 1817. V. 67

EUSTACHIUS, BARTOLOMEO
Tabulae Antomocarum Clarissimi Viri Bartholomaei Eustachaei.... Rome: 1728. V. 62; 64

EUTROPIUS
Breviarium Historiae Romanae. Lutetiae Parisiorum: 1746. V. 66
Eutropii Breviarum Historiae Romanae, Cum Metaphrasi Graeca Paeanii.... Leiden: 1793. V. 65
Eutropii Breviarum Historiae Romanae, Ab Urbe Condita Ad Annum Eiusdem Urbis DCCCL. Etonae: 1813. V. 65
Eutropii Historiae Romanae Breviarum Ab Urbe Condita Usque Ad.... Parisiis: 1683. V. 65; 66
Historiae Romanae Breviarium Notis et Emendationibus Illustravit.... Oxonii: 1696. V. 67

EVANGELIARIO *Per Le Somennita Cristiane.* Verona: 1965. V. 65

EVANOVICH, JANET
One for the Money. New York: 1994. V. 63; 64; 65; 66; 67
Three to Get Ready. New York: 1997. V. 67
Two for the Dough. New York: 1996. V. 65; 67

EVANS, A. H.
A Fauna of the Tweed Area. Edinburgh: 1911. V. 62
A Vertebrate Fauna of the Shetland Islands. Edinburgh: 1899. V. 62

EVANS, ABEL
Vertumnus. An Epistle to Mr. Jacob Bobart, Botany Professor to the University of Oxford, and Keeper of the Physick Garden. Oxford: 1713. V. 65

EVANS, ARTHUR
The Palace of Minos at Knossos. London: 1921. V. 62
The Palace of Minos at Knossos. London: 1930. V. 62

EVANS, ARTHUR BENONI
The Cutter, In Five Lectures Upon the Art and Practice of Cutting Friends, Acquaintances and Relations. London: 1808. V. 62; 67
Fungusiana; or the Opinions and Table talk of the Late Barnaby Fungus.... London: 1809. V. 67

EVANS, C. S.
Cinderella. London: 1919. V. 62; 63; 65
The Sleeping Beauty. London: 1920. V. 63; 64; 66

EVANS, CHARLES
Chick Evans' Golf Book. N.P: 1985. V. 65
Report of the Trial of the Hon. Samuel Chase, One of the Associate Justices of the Supreme Court of the United States, Before the High Court of Impeachment, Composed of the Senate of the United States. Baltimore: 1805. V. 64

EVANS, CHRISTMAS
Sermons on Various Subjects. 1837. V. 65

EVANS, D.
Mather Brown, Early American Artist in England. 1982. V. 65

EVANS, D. MORIER
Facts, Failures and Frauds: Revelations, Financial, Mercantile, Criminal. London: 1859. V. 64
The History of the Commercial Crisis 1857-1858 and the Stock Exchange Panic of 1859. London: 1859. V. 64
Speculative Notes and Notes on Speculation, Ideal and Real. London: 1864. V. 64

EVANS, DAVID C.
Custer's Last Fight - The Story of the Battle of the Little Big Horn - Volume One. El Segundo: 1999. V. 66

EVANS, DONALD
Two Deaths in the Bronx. Philadelphia: 1916. V. 67

EVANS, E.
Puyallup Indian Reservation. Address Delivered Before the Tacoma Chamber of Commerce, May 17, 1892. Tacoma: 1892. V. 66

EVANS, EDMUND
The Illuminated Scripture Book. London: 1880. V. 67
The Reminiscences of Edmund Evans.... London: 1967. V. 64

EVANS, EDWARD
British Polar Explorers. London: 1933. V. 64

EVANS, ELWOOD
Oration, Portland, Oregon, July 4, 1865. Portland: 1965. V. 66
The Re-Annexation of British Columbia to the United States, Right, Proper and Desirable. Olympia: 1870. V. 63

EVANS, ERNESTINE
The Frescoes of Diego Rivera. New York: 1929. V. 62; 63; 64

EVANS, EVAN
Some Specimens of the Poetry of the Antient Welsh Bards. London: 1764. V. 64

EVANS, F. W.
Ann Lee (The Founder of the Shakers). A Biography With Memoirs of William Lee, James Whitaker, J. Hocknell, J. Meacham and Lucy Wright. London: 1871. V. 63

EVANS, FRANCIS
Furness and Furness Abbey.... Ulverston: 1842. V. 65

EVANS, G. P.
Big Game Shooting in Upper Burma. 1912. V. 67

EVANS, GEORGE BIRD
An Affair with Grouse. Old Hemlock: 1982. V. 65
The Bird Dog Book. Clinton: 1979. V. 65
Recollections of a Shooting Guest. Clinton: 1978. V. 65
The Ruffed Grouse Book. Clinton: 1977. V. 65
The Upland Gunner's Book. Clinton: 1979. V. 65
The Woodcock Book. Clinton: 1977. V. 65

EVANS, GEORGE EWART
Ask the Fellows Who Cut the Hay.... 1999. V. 65

EVANS, HENRY
Some Account of Jura Red Deer. 1993. V. 67

EVANS, HERBERT
Vital Need of the Body for Certain Unsaturated Fatty Acids. 1934. V. 66

EVANS, IVOR H. N.
The Negritos of Malaya. Cambridge: 1937. V. 67
Studies in Religion, Folk-Lore and Customs in British North Borneo and the Malay Peninsular. Cambridge: 1923. V. 67

EVANS, J.
Letters Written During a Tour through North Wales, in the Year 1798 and at other Times.... London: 1804. V. 66

EVANS, JAMES
Small River Fly Fishing. London: 1977. V. 67
The Speller and Interpreter, in Indian and English, for the Use of the Mission Schools and Such As May Desire to Obtain a Knowledge of the Ojibway Tongue. New York: 1837. V. 63

EVANS, JOHN
The Ancient Stone Implements, Weapons and Ornaments of Great Britain. London: 1872. V. 66
The Ancient Stone Implements, Weapons and Ornaments of Great Britain. London: 1897. V. 66
A Brief View of the Doctrines of the Christian Religon as Proffered by the Society of Friends, in the Form of Question and Answer.... London: 1810. V. 62
An Excursion to Windsor, in July 1810, through Battersea, Putney, Kew, Richmond, Twickenham, Strawberry Hill and Hampton Court.... London: 1817. V. 63; 66
Richmond and Its Vicinity, with a Glance at Twickenham, Strawberry Hill and Hampton Court. Richmond: 1824. V. 62; 63; 66

EVANS, KATHERINE
Friskey Margaret. Chicago: 1944. V. 62

EVANS, LIZ
Who Killed Marilyn Monroe?. London: 1997. V. 65

EVANS, MYFANWY
No Rubbish Here. London: 1936. V. 62

EVANS, NATHANIEL
Poems of Several Occasions with some Other Compositions. Philadelphia: 1772. V. 63; 66

EVANS, NICHOLAS
The Horse Whisperer. New York: 1995. V. 63; 64; 67

EVANS, OLIVER
The Young Mill-Wright & Miller's Guide. Philadelphia: 1795. V. 64

EVANS, SEBASTIAN
The High History of the Holy Graal. London and New York: 1903. V. 63

EVANS, T.
Old Ballads, Historical and Narrative, with Some of Modern Date. London: 1784. V. 66

EVANS, W. F.
British Libellulinae, or, Dragonflies. London: 1845. V. 62

EVANS, W. H.
A Catalogue of the American Hesperiidae in the British Museum. London: 1951-1955. V. 63

EVANS, WALKER
American Photographs. New York: 1938. V. 63
Incognito. New York: 1995. V. 63

EVANS, WILL F.
Border Skylines, Fifty Years of "Tallying Out" on the Bioys Roundup Ground - a History of the Bioys Cowboy Camp Meeting. Dallas: 1940. V. 65

EVANS, WILLIAM
The Mammalian Fauna of the Edinburgh District. 1892. V. 62; 63; 64; 66; 67
A New English-Welsh Dictionary. Carmarthen: 1771. V. 66

EVANS, WILLIAM JULIAN
The Sugar Planter's Manual, being a Treatise ont he Art of Obtaining Sugar from Sugar Cane. Philadelphia: 1848. V. 63

EVARTS, JEREMIAH
Essays on the Present Crisis in the Condition of the American Indians.... Philadelphia: 1830. V. 67

EVELYN, JOHN
Acetaria, a Discourse of Sallets. 1937. V. 63
The Charters of the City of London.... London: 1745. V. 65
The Diary Now First Printed in Full.... Oxford: 1955. V. 63
Diary of John Evelyn, F.R.S.... London: 1879. V. 63
Directions for the Gardiner at Says-Court.... London: 1932. V. 62; 64; 65; 67
Fumifufium; or, the Inconvenience of the Aer, and Smoake of London Dissipated Together with Some Remedies Humbly Proposed by John Evelyn Esq.... London: 1930. V. 62
The Life of Mrs. Godolphin. London: 1847. V. 67
The Life of Mrs. Godolphin. London: 1848. V. 62
Memories for My Grand-Son. London: 1926. V. 65
Memories for My Grand-son. Oxford: 1926. V. 65
The Miscellaneous Writings. London: 1825. V. 62; 63
Publick Employment and an Active Life with All Its Appanages.... London: 1667. V. 63; 66
Sculptura; or, the History and Art of Chalcography and Engraving in Copper.... London: 1769. V. 65
Silva; or, a Discourse of Forest Trees. London: 1729. V. 66; 67
Silva; or a Discourse of Forest Trees. York: 1776. V. 63
Sylva, or a Discourse of Forest Trees. London: 1664. V. 64
Sylva, or a Discourse of Forest Trees. London: 1679. V. 62; 65; 67
Sylva, or a Discourse of Forest Trees. 1973. V. 67

AN EVENING Conversation Between Four Very Good Old Ladies Over a Comfortable Game at Quadrille. N.P: 1790. V. 65

THE EVENING News and Hoboken. Hoboken: 1893. V. 66

EVENINGS at Derley Manor. London: 1850. V. 67

EVENSON, R. E.
Research and Productivity in Asian Agriculture. Ithaca: 1991. V. 65

EVERARD, GILES
Panacea or the Universal Medicine Being a Discovery of the Wonderful Vertues of Tobacco Taken in a Pipe.... London: 1659. V. 66

EVERARD, JOHN
Some Gospel Treasures or the Holiest of All Unvailing. Germantown: 1757. V. 62

EVERARD, THOMAS
Stereometry, or the Art of Gauging Made Easie, by the Help of a Sliding-Rule. London: 1705. V. 63; 66

EVERETT, EDWARD
The Discovery and Colonization of America and the Immigration to the United States. Boston: 1853. V. 62
A Lecture on the Workingmen's Party. Boston: 1830. V. 62
An Oration Delivered on the Battlefield of Gettysburg, (November 19, 1863), at a Consecration of the Cemetery Prepared for the Interment of the Remains of Those Who Fell in the Battles of July 1st, 2d and 3rd, 1863. New York: 1863. V. 65; 66
Speech of Mr. Everett of Massachusetts, on the Bill for Removing the Indians from the East to the West Side of the Mississippi. Washington: 1830. V. 63

EVERETT, FRANKLIN
Memorials of the Grand River Valley. Chicago: 1878. V. 66

EVERETT, JAMES
Historical Sketches of Wesleyan Methodism in Sheffield and Its Vicinity. Sheffield: 1823. V. 63

EVERETT, T. H.
Encyclopedia of Horticulture. New York: 1981-1982. V. 64
New Illustrated Encyclopedia of Gardening. New York: 1906-1963. V. 64; 67

EVERETT-GREEN, EVELYN
Six Stories. London. V. 64

EVERHART, RICHARD
Brotherhood of Men. Pawlet: 1949. V. 64

EVERMANN, B. W.
Fishes of Porto Rico. Washington: 1900. V. 62
Investigations of the Aquatic Resources and Fisheries of Porto Rico by the United States Fish Commission Steamer Fish Hawk in 1899. Washington: 1900. V. 63
Investigations of the Aquatic Resources and Fisheries of Porto Rico by the United States Fish Commission Steamer Fish Hawk in 1899. Washington: 1902. V. 65
Lake Maxinakuckee, a Physical and Biological Survey. Indianopolis: 1920. V. 65

EVERTS, TRUMAN C.
Thirty-Seven Days of Peril - A Narrative of the Early Days of the Yellowstone. San Francisco: 1923. V. 63

EVERY Lady's Guide to Her Own Greenhouse, Hothouse and Conservatory.... London: 1851. V. 67

EVERY Man's Pocket Companion; or, Hints Upon the Law Respecting Landlord and Tenant, Concerning Tenants at Will - the Nature of the Tenure - The Incidents To It - The Power of Determining Such Estates. London: 1778. V. 66

EVERYMAN. London: 1911. V. 63; 64; 65
EVERYMAN. London: 1930. V. 62

EWALD, ALEXANDER CHARLES
Leaders of the Senate: a Biographical History of the Rise and Development of the British Constitution. London: 1884-1885. V. 64
The Right Hon. Benjamin Disraeli, Earl of Beaconsfield and His Times. London: 1881-1882. V. 64
The Right Hon. Benjamin Disraeli, Earl of Beaconsfield, K.G. and His Times. London: 1882. V. 64

EWALD, C. A.
The Diseases of the Stomach. New York: 1893. V. 63

EWALD, JOHANNES
The Death of Balder. London: 1889. V. 62; 63

EWART, GAVIN
Poems and Songs. London: 1939. V. 62; 66
Throwaway Lines. London: 1964. V. 64
Twelve Apostles. Belfast: 1970. V. 64

EWBANK, THOMAS
The Spoon.... London: 1845. V. 66

EWELL, ALICE M.
A Virginia Scene of Life in Old Prince William. Lynchburg: 1931. V. 64

EWELL, R. S.
The Making of a Soldier. Letters of R. S. Ewell. Richmond: 1935. V. 62; 63

EWELL, THOMAS
Plain Discourses on the Laws of Properties of Matter.... New York: 1806. V. 62
Statement of Improvements in the Theory and Practice of the Science of Medicine. Philadelphia: 1819. V. 63; 66

EWERS, JOHN C.
Artists of the Old West. Garden City: 1973. V. 66
The Horse in Blackfoot Indian Culture. Washington: 1955. V. 63

EWING AND HOPEWELL VIGILANT SOCIETY
Articles of Association of the Ewing and Hopewell Vigilant Society... Revised November 28, 1885. Trenton: 1885. V. 63; 66

EWING, DOUGLAS C.
Pleasing the Spirits. New York: 1982. V. 66

EWING, EMMA P.
Cooking and Castle Building. Boston: 1880. V. 65

EWING, FINIS
A Series of Lectures, on the Most Important Subjects (i)n Divinity. Fayetteville: 1827. V. 66

EWING, J.
Earthquake Measurement. Tokyo: 1883. V. 62

EWING, J. H., MRS.
The Brownies and Other Stories. London: 1954. V. 67

EWING, JULIANA HORATIA
Blue Bells on the Lea and Ten Other Tales. London: 1885. V. 64
Old Fashioned Fairy Tales. London: 1882. V. 64

EXAMEN Miscellaneum. London: 1702. V. 66

THE EXAMINATION of Edward Fitzharris, Relating to the Popish Plot, Taken the Tenth Day of March 1681. London: 1681. V. 66

EXAMINATION of the Controversy Between Georgia and the Creeks. N.P: 1825. V. 66

EXERCISE at the Ordination of Five Missionaries.... Chicago: 1867. V. 65

EXERCISES in Reading and Recitation; Performed by the Pupils of Hill-Top School at Birmingham. Birmingham: 1814-1815. V. 62

EXERCISES Instructive and Entertaining, in False English.... Leeds: 1802. V. 64

THE EXHIBITION and Grand London Sights. London: 1851. V. 67

EXHIBITION of Paintings by Children from Bedales and Burgess Hill. London: 1945. V. 65

EXISTING Regulations Connected with the Commissariat Department in the Windward and Leeward Islands and Colonies in the West Indies, Condensed and Collected Up to the Present Date.... Bridge-Town: 1823. V. 65

EXLEY, FREDERICK
A Fan's Notes. New York: 1968. V. 62; 63; 67

EXNER, A. H.
Japan As I Saw It. London: 1912. V. 67
Japan As I Saw It. London: 1930. V. 62

EXPLANATION of the Pilgrim's Progress, &c &c. London: 1818. V. 63

EXPLANATIONS And Instructions Relative to the Pay and Allowances of Foot Soldiers Serving at Home. London: 1793. V. 63

L'EXPOSITION de Paris (1900). Paris: 1900. V. 67

EXQUEMELIN, ALEXANDRE OLIVIER
The Buccaneers of America. London/New York: 1893. V. 63

THE EXQUISITE Horse. Madison: 1997. V. 62; 64

EXTERIOR Decoration, a Treatise on the Artistic Use of Colors in the Ornamentation of Buildings and a Series of Designs Illustrating the Effects of Different Combinations of Colors in Connection with Various Styles of Architecture. New York: 1885. V. 66

EXTRACTS From Humbugiana; or, the World's Convention. New York: 1847. V. 64

EXTRACTS From Italian Prose Writers. London: 1828. V. 67

THE EXTRAORDINARY Red Book. London: 1816. V. 64; 65
THE EXTRAORDINARY Red Book. London: 1817. V. 64

EYB, ALBERTUS DE
Margarita Poetica. Basileae: 1503. V. 63; 66

EYLES, DESMOND
Royal Doulton Figures Produced at Burslem, c. 1890-1978. Stoke-on-Trent: 1978. V. 62

EYRE, ALICE
The Famous Fremonts and Their America. 1948. V. 63

EYRE, EDWARD JOHN
Journals of Expeditions of Discovery into Central Australia and Overland from Australia to King George's Sound, in the Years 1840-1841. London: 1845. V. 67

EYTON, T. C.
Osteologia Avium. 1867-1875. V. 63
Osteologia Avium. London: 1867-1875. V. 64

EZEKIEL, HERBERT
The History of the Jews of Richmond from 1769 to 1917. Richmond: 1917. V. 66

F

F. W. SHEPPERD CO.
Hand-Book of Water Works Statistics and Fire Department Equipment, 1896. New York: 1896. V. 67

FABER, HAROLD
The Kennedy Years. New York: 1964. V. 63

FABER, M.
Sketches of the Internal State of France.... London: 1811. V. 63

FABER, T.
Arne Jacobsen. London: 1964. V. 62; 65

FABES, GILBERT H.
The Autobiography of a Book. London: 1926. V. 63
Modern First Edition: Points and Values. London: 1929-1932. V. 62; 66

FABIAN, JENNY
Groupie. London: 1969. V. 63

FABIAN SOCIETY
Fabian Tracts. Numbers 1-181. 1884-1916. V. 67

FABLES Calculated for the Amusement and Instruction of Youth.... Taunton: 1789. V. 64

FABRE, J. A.
Traite Complet sur la Theorie et la Pratique du Nivellement. Draguignan: 1809. V. 65

FABRE, JEAN HENRI
Fabre's Book of Insects. New York: 1935. V. 66
FABRE'S Book of Insects. New York: 1937. V. 63
FABRE'S Book of Insects Retold from Alexander Teixeira De Matto's translation.... New York: 1936. V. 65

FABRE, M. H. L.
Dictionnaire Francais-Basque. Bayonne: 1870. V. 64

FABRE, PIERRE JEAN
Alle in Zwey Theile Verfassete Chymische Schriften.... Hamburg: 1713. V. 64

FABRICIUS, GEORGIUS
Roma, Liber ad Opt. Autorum Lectionem Apprime Utilis ac Necessarius.... Basel: 1551. V. 64

FABRICIUS, M. THEODOSIUS
Loci Communes D. Martini Lutheri Viri Dei et Prophetae Germanici.... Magdeburg: 1594. V. 66

FABRICUS, GEORGE
Roma Illustrata, Sive Antiquitatem Romanarum Breviarium.... Amsterdam: 1657. V. 66

FABRY VON HILDEN, WILHELM
Observationum et Curationum Chirurgicarum Centuriae.... Lyons: 1641. V. 65

FABYAN, ROBERT
The Chronicle of Fabyan.... London: 1559. V. 62; 63
The New Chronicles of England and France.... London: 1811. V. 62

FACCIOLATI, G.
Totius Latinitatis Lexicon.... Londini: 1828. V. 66

FACTS and Arguments Repsecting the Great Utility of an Extensive Plan of Inland Navigation in Ireland. Dublin: 1800. V. 62

FAENSEN, HUBERT
Early Russian Architecture. London: 1975. V. 67

FAETH Fiadha: the Breastplate of Saint Patrick. 1957. V. 63

FAGAN, LOUIS
The Life of Sir Anthony Panizzi.... London: 1880. V. 65

FAGAN, ROBERTA E.
Custer and His Times - Book Three. Arkansas: 1987. V. 67

FAGG, HELEN
Adventures in Americana 1492-1897.... New York: 1964. V. 64

FAGIOLO, M.
Roman Gardens, Villas of the Countryside. New York: 1997. V. 67

FAHEY, HERBERT
Early Printing in California from Its Beginning in the Mexican Territory to Statehood, September 9, 1850. San Francisco: 1956. V. 62; 64

FAHNESTOCK, WILLIAM BAKER
Worlds Within Worlds; or New and Wonderful Discoveries in Astronomy. Philadelphia: 1876. V. 63

FAHRNER, BARBARA
A Flower Like a Raven. New York: 1996. V. 64

FAHY, E.
Child of the Tides. 1985. V. 67

FAILLET, GEORGE
La Danse Macabre. Paris: 1920. V. 64

FAINLIGHT, HARRY
Selected Poems. London: 1986. V. 62

FAIR, LAURA D.
Official Report of the Trial of Laura D. Fair, for the Murder of Alex P. Crittenden, Including the Testimony, the Arguments of the Counsel, and the Charge of the Court.... San Francisco: 1871. V. 65

FAIRBAIRN, JAMES
Fairbairn's Book of Crests of the Families of Great Britain and Ireland. Edinburgh: 1892. V. 67
FAIRBAIRN'S Book of Crests of the Families of Great Britain and Ireland. 1905. V. 67

FAIRBAIRN, STEVE
On Rowing. London: 1951. V. 67

FAIRBAIRN, WILLIAM
Iron. Its History, Properties and Processes of Manufacture. Edinburgh: 1861. V. 65

FAIRBAIRN, WILLIAM ALEXANDER
Some Game Birds of West Africa. London: 1952. V. 67

FAIRBANK, ALFRED
Renaissance Handwriting, an Anthology of Italic Scripts. London: 1960. V. 62

FAIRBANK, CALVIN
Rev. Calvin Fairbank During Slavery Times. Chicago: 1890. V. 67

FAIRBANKS, DOUGLAS
Laugh and Live. New York: 1917. V. 65

FAIRBRIDGE, DOROTHEA
Lady Anne Barnard at the Cape of Good Hope 1797-1802. Oxford: 1924. V. 66

FAIRBURN, JAMES
The Vistors' Guide to Ripon, Harrogate and Adjoining Country.... Ripon: 1860. V. 65

FAIRBURN, JOHN
Fairburn's Authentic and Copious Account of the Extra-Ordinary Siamese Twins, Eng and Ching (sic) Now Exhibiting in London.... London: 1830. V. 63

FAIRBURN, WILLIAM ARMSTRONG
Merchant Sail. Center Lovell: 1945-1955. V. 65

FAIRCHILD, D.
Exploring for Plants, from Notes of the Allison Vincent Armour Expeditions for the United States Department of Agriculture, 1925-1926-1927. New York: 1930. V. 65

FAIRCLOUGH, HENRY RUSHTON
Some Aspects of Horace. San Francisco: 1935. V. 62

FAIRCLOUGH, M. A.
Ideal Cookery Book. London. V. 67

THE FAIRFAX Correspondence, Memoirs of the Reign of Charles the First. London: 1848. V. 63

THE FAIRFAX Correspondence. Memoirs of the Reign of Charles the First. (with) Memorial of the Civil War, Comprising the Correspondence of the Fairfax Family. London: 1848-1849. V. 63

FAIRFAX, JAMES GRIFFYTH
The Gates of Sleep and Other Poems. London: 1906. V. 62
The Horns of Taurus. London: 1914. V. 62
Poems. London: 1908. V. 62

FAIRFAX, JAMES GRIFFYTH continued
Sonnets and Lyrics at Home and Abroad 1914-1919. London: 1919. V. 62
The Temple of Janus - a Sonnet Sequence. London: 1917. V. 62

FAIRFAX, THOMAS
The Complete Sportsman; or Country Gentleman's Recreation. London: 1764. V. 66
A Declaration of His Excellency Sir Thomas Fairfax and His Councell of Warre.... London: 1647. V. 65
Short Memorials of Thomas Lord Fairfax. Written by Himself. London: 1699. V. 62

FAIRFAX BLAKEBOROUGH, J.
Country Life and Sport. London: 1926. V. 67

FAIRFIELD, ASA MERRILL
Fairfield's Pioneer History of Lassen County, Calfiornia. San Francisco: 1916. V. 62; 63; 65

FAIRFIELD, ULA K.
Pioneer Lawyer, A Story of the Western Slope Off Colorado. Denver: 1946. V. 65

FAIRHOLT, F. W.
A Dictionary of Terms in Art. London: 1854. V. 67
A Dictionary of Terms in Art. London: 1865. V. 67
Gog and Magog. The Giants in Guildhall. London: 1859. V. 66
Rambles of an Archaeologist Among Old Books and in Old Places.... London: 1871. V. 64; 65

FAIRLIE, GERARD
Bulldog Drummond Attacks. London: 1939. V. 65
Captain Bulldog Drummond. London: 1945. V. 67

FAIRMONT, ETHEL
Rhymes for Kindly Children. Joliet: 1927. V. 64; 66

THE FAIRY Book. London: 1923. V. 64

THE FAIRY Cabinet: Containing Fairy Tales. Boston: 1845. V. 63

THE FAIRY Family. London: 1857. V. 64

A FAIRY Garland Being Fair Tales from the Old French. London: 1928. V. 63; 64; 66

FAIRY Moonbeam Story Book Containing Cinderella, or the Little Glass Slipper; Hop O' My Thumb; The Three Bears; Aladdin, or the Wonderful Lamp; Sleeping Beauty in the Woods, and The Frog Who Would a Wooing Go. New York: 1884. V. 64

THE FAIRY Shoemaker and Other Fairy Tales. New York: 1928. V. 64

THE FAIRY Tale Omnibus. London: 1930. V. 62

FAIRY Tales of All Nations. Philadelphia: 1910. V. 66

FAIRYLAND ABC. New York: 1900. V. 65

FAIRYTALE Gems. London: 1920. V. 66

THE FAITHFUL, Yet Imperfect, Character of a Glorious King, King Charles I. His Country's and Religions Martyr. London: 1660. V. 62

FAITHFULL, EMILY
Three Visits to America. Edinburgh: 1884. V. 64

FAITHFULL, MARIANNE
Faithfull: an Autobiography. Boston: 1994. V. 63

FAITHORNE, WILLIAM
The Art of Graveing and Etching.... London: 1662. V. 64

FALCONER, J. D.
On Horseback through Nigeria; or, Life and Travel in the Central Sudan. London: 1911. V. 67

FALCONER, LANOE
The Hotel d'Angleterre and Other Stories. London: 1891. V. 65
Mademoiselle Ixe. London: 1891. V. 65

FALCONER, THOMAS
Letters and Notes on the Texas Santa Fe Expedition 1841-1842. New York: 1930. V. 62

FALCONER, WILLIAM
An Account of the Efficacy of the Aqua Mephitica Alkalina; or, Solution of Fixed Alkaline Salt, Saturated with Fixible Air, in Calculous Disorders and Other Complaints of the Urinary Passages. London: 1789. V. 67
The Poetical Works. London: 1836. V. 66
A Practical Dissertation on the Medicianl Effects of the Bath Waters. Bath and London: 1790. V. 65
The Shipwreck. London: 1764. V. 66
The Shipwreck. London: 1772. V. 65
The Shipwreck. London: 1811. V. 62; 64; 65; 66
An Universal Dictionary of the Marine.... London: 1769. V. 64

FALK, RICHARD A.
The Vietnam War and International Law. Princeton: 1968. V. 67

FALKENER, EDWARD
Ephesus, and the Temple of Diana. Bodon: 1862. V. 67
Games Ancient and Oriental and How to Play Them. London: 1892. V. 65

FALKLAND, LUCIUS CARY, VISCOUNT
The Draught of a Speech Concerning Episcopacy, by the Lord Viscount Falkland. London: 1644. V. 63

FALKNER, JOHN MEADE
A History of Oxfordshire. London: 1899. V. 64
The Lost Stradivarius. Edinburgh: 1895. V. 65
Temenos. Loanhead: 1993. V. 67

FALKUS, HUGH
Salmon Fishing, a Practical Guide. 1984. V. 67
Sea Trout Fishing. 1978. V. 67

THE FALL of Nineveh. The Sublime, Historical Bible Spectacle. Buffalo: 1892. V. 65

FALLEN Angels: a Disquisition Upon Human Existence, an Attempt to Elucidate Some of Its Mysteries.... London: 1894. V. 64

FALLON, W. J.
Practical Wildfowling. 1907. V. 63; 66

FALLON, WALTER J.
Practical Wildfowling. London: 1907. V. 63; 67

FALLOPPIO, GABRIELE
Observationes Anatomicae. Parisiis: 1562. V. 66

FALLS, D. W. C.
The Life and Adventures of General Spooley. A Story of a Toy Soldier. London: 1910. V. 65

FALRET, JEAN PIERRE
Considerations Generales sur les Maladies Mentales. Paris: 1843. V. 65
Observations sur le Projet de Loi Relatif aux Alienes. Paris: 1837. V. 65

FAME'S Trumpet: Twenty Rhymes. Brisbane: 1982. V. 64

FAMILY Pastime, or, Homes Made Happy, 1852. London: 1852. V. 67

FAMILY Prayers, and Moral Essays, In Prose and Verse. London: 1769. V. 62; 66

FAMILY Worship. Staunton: 1812. V. 65

FANCY Dress ABC. London: 1905. V. 66

FANE, JULIAN
Memoir in the Middle of the Journey. London: 1971. V. 64

FANE, JULIAN H. C.
Tannhauser; or, the Battle of the Bards. Mobile: 1863. V. 65

FANNING, EDMUND
Voyages and Discoveries in the South Seas 1792-1832. Salem: 1924. V. 65

FANNING, PETE
Great Crimes of the West. San Francisco;: 1929. V. 63

FANNING the Embers - History of Custer County Montana. Miles City: 1971. V. 62

FANTE, JOHN
Ask the Dust. New York: 1939. V. 66
The Road to Los Angeles. Santa Barbara: 1985. V. 67
Wait Until Spring, Bandini. New York: 1938. V. 66

FARADAY, MICHAEL
Chemical Manipulation.... London: 1829. V. 62
Diary. London: 1932-1936. V. 64
Experimental Researches in Chemistry and Physics. London: 1859. V. 64
Histoire d'une Chandele.... Paris: 1865. V. 64

FARADAY, PHILIP MICHAEL
Amasis, an Egyptian Princess. London: 1906. V. 64

FARCY, CHARLES
Essai sur le Dessin et la Peinture, Relativement a l'Enseignement. Paris: 1820. V. 66

FARELL, M. L.
Red Letter Days. London: 1933. V. 64

FAREY, JOHN
A Treatise on the Steam Engine.. London: 1971. V. 62

FARIA Y SOUSA, EMANUEL DE
The History of Portugal, From the First Ages of the World to the Late Great Revolution, Under King John IV in the Year MDCXL. London: 1698. V. 64; 67

FARINA, RICHARD
Been Down So Long It Looks Like Up to Me. New York: 1966. V. 65
Been Down So Long It Looks Like Up to Me. New York: 1983. V. 66
Long Time Coming and a Long Time Gone. New York: 1969. V. 63; 64

FARINGTON, JOSEPH
The Diary of Joseph Farington. 1978-1998. V. 66
The Diary of Joseph Farington. New Haven: 1978-1998. V. 65
The Farington Diary by Joseph Farington, A.A. July 13th 1793 to Dec. 30th 1821. 1923-1928. V. 65

FARIS, J. T.
Old Gardens in and About Philadelphia and Those Who Made Them. Indianapolis: 1932. V. 67

FARISH, THOMAS EDWIN
History of Arizona. Phoenix: 1915. V. 64
History of Arizona. Phoenix: 1915-1918. V. 67

FARJEON, ELEANOR
The Country Child's Alphabet. London: 1924. V. 62
Dream Songs for the Beloved. London: 1911. V. 67
Kaleidoscope. London: 1963. V. 62
Pan-Worship and Other Poems. London. V. 67
The Perfect Zoo. Philadelphia: 1929. V. 64
Perkin the Pedlar. London: 1932. V. 65; 67

FARJEON, J. JEFFERSON
The Oval Table. London: 1946. V. 67
Peril in the Pyrenees. London: 1946. V. 66; 67
Prelude to Crime. London: 1948. V. 65; 67

FARJON, A.
A Bibliography of Conifers.... 1990. V. 67

FARLEIGH, JOHN
Graven Image. London: 1940. V. 67

FARLEY, EDWARD
Imprisonment for Debt Unconstitutional and Oppressive, Proved from the Fundamental Principles of the British Constitution and the Rights of Nature. London: 1788. V. 62

FARLEY, JOHN
London Art of Cookery. London: 1796. V. 67

FARLEY, JOSEPH PEARSON
Three Rivers: the James, The Potomac, The Hudson. A Retrospect of Peace and War. New York and Washington: 1910. V. 62; 63; 65

FARLEY, WALTER
The Black Stallion Revolts. New York: 1953. V. 66

FARLOW, WILLIAM GILSON
Icones Farlowianae. Cambridge: 1929. V. 62; 66

FARM Reports, or Accounts of the Management of Select Farms. 1830-1835. V. 67

FARMAN, EDGAR
The Bulldog. A Monograph. London: 1985. V. 67

FARMER, CECILY
Dragons and a Bell. London: 1931. V. 63

FARMER, D. S.
Avian Biology. 1971-1975. V. 66

FARMER, FANNIE MERRITT
New Book of Cookery. Boston: 1912. V. 66

FARMER, HENRY T.
Imagination: the Maniac's Dream and Other Poems. New York: 1819. V. 62

FARMER, JOHN S.
The Public School Word-Book. London: 1900. V. 64
'Twixt Two Worlds: a Narrative of the Life and Works of William Eglinton.... London: 1886. V. 65

FARMER, NANCY
A Girl Named Disaster. New York: 1996. V. 65

FARMER, PHILIP JOSE
The Adventure of the Peerless Peer. Boulder: 1974. V. 66
The Alley of God. London: 1970. V. 62; 64
A Feast Unknown. 1969. V. 62
Flesh. 1968. V. 62
Flesh. New York: 1968. V. 64
Gods of Riverworld. 1983. V. 64
Lord of the Trees. London: 1982. V. 64
Lord Tyger. 1970. V. 66
Lord Tyger. New York: 1970. V. 62; 64
The Magic Labyrinth. 1980. V. 64
Tarzan Alive. New York: 1972. V. 67

FARMER, RICHARD
An Essay on the Learning of Shakespeare. Basil: 1800. V. 67
An Essay on the Learning of Shakespeare. London: 1821. V. 64, 65

THE FARMERS' Receipt Book; and Pocket Farrier. Concord: 1831. V. 66

THE FARMER'S and Mechanic's Guide, Containing Correct Precedents of Statements of Demand in a Variety of Actions.... Newark: 1829. V. 63

THE FARMER'S Friend. London: 1847. V. 63

THE FARMER'S Guide and Western Agriculturist. Cincinnati: 1832. V. 67

THE FARMER'S Lawyer; or Every Country Gentleman His Own Counsellor. London: 1774. V. 63

THE FARMER'S Night-Cap; or, the Parson's Pocket Companion. London: 1783. V. 62

FARNELL, LEWIS RICHARD
The Cults of the Greek States. Oxford: 1896-1909. V. 65

FARNER, D. S.
Avian Biology. Volume I. New York: 1971. V. 63

FARNHAM, ELIZA W.
California, In-Doors and Out; or, How We Farm, Mine and Live Generally in the Golden State. New York: 1856. V. 65

FARNHAM, LUTHER
A Glance at Private Libraries. Boston: 1855. V. 64

FARNHAM, THOMAS JEFFERSON
History of Oregon Territory. New York: 1845. V. 63
Life, Adventures and Travels in California... Travels in Oregon and History of the Gold Regions. New York: 1849. V. 65
Life Adventures and Travels in California...Travels in Oregon and History of the Gold Region. New York: 1850. V. 63; 66
Mexico: Its Geography - Its People - and Its Institutions. New York: 1846. V. 65

FARNOL, JEFFERY
The Money Moon. New York: 1911. V. 63

FARNSWORTH, N. R.
Thai Medicinal Plants Recommended for Primary Health Care System. Bangkok: 1992. V. 67

FARQUHAR, F. P.
History of the Sierra Nevada. Berkeley, Los Angeles: 1965. V. 63
Yosemite, the Big Trees and the High Sierra. Berkeley: 1948. V. 65; 66; 67

FARQUHAR, FERDINAND
The Relicks of a Saint. London: 1816. V. 62

FARQUHAR, GEORGE
The Beaux Stratagem. London: 1707. V. 66
The Beaux Stratagem. Bristol: 1929. V. 66
The Beaux Stratagem. London: 1929. V. 62
The Complete Works of George Farquhar. London: 1930. V. 67
The Recruiting Officer. London: 1926. V. 67

FARQUHAR, JOHN F.
Phyciologie Des Lobes Frontaux Et Du Cervelet Etude Experimentale et Clinique. Paris: 1953. V. 64

FARR, WILLIAM
A Treatise Explanatory of a Method Whereby Occult Cancer May Be Cured. London: 1825. V. 62

FARRAND, MAX
The Records of the Federal Convention of 1787. New Haven: 1911. V. 63

FARRAR, CHARLES A. J.
Through the Wilds, a Record of Sport and Adventure in the Forests of New Hampshire and Maine. Boston: 1892. V. 63

FARRAR, EMMIE F.
Old Virginia Houses - Shenandoah. Charlotte: 1976. V. 65
Old Virginia Houses Along the Fall Line. New York: 1971. V. 64; 66
Old Virginia Houses: the Mountain Empire. Charlotte: 1978. V. 64
Old Virginia Houses: The Northern Peninsulas. New York: 1972. V. 66
Old Virginia Houses: the Piedmont. Charlotte: 1975. V. 64

FARRAR, F. W.
Our English Minsters. London. V. 63

FARRAR, FERDINANDO RICHARD
Johnny Reb, the Confederate and Rip Van Winkle, or the Virginian that Slept Ten Years. Two Lectures. Richmond. 1869. V. 62

FARRAR, FREDERIC W.
Eric or Little by Little; a Tale of Roslyn School. Edinburgh: 1858. V. 66

FARRAR, TIMOTHY
Report of the Case of the Trustees of Dartmouth College Against William H. Woodward. Portsmouth: 1819. V. 66

FARRE, HENRY
Sky Fighters of France. Boston and New York: 1919. V. 64

FARRELL, JAMES GORDON
A Girl in the Head. London: 1967. V. 66

FARRELL, JAMES T.
A Father and His Son. London: 1943. V. 64
The League of Frightened Philistines and Other Papers. London: 1948. V. 64
A Misunderstanding. New York: 1949. V. 63
The Road Between. London: 1949. V. 62
When Time Was Born. N.P: 1966. V. 65

FARRELL, M. J.
Red Letter Days. 1933. V. 64

FARRELL, WILLIAM
Carlow in '98, the Autobiography of William Farrell of Carlow. 1949. V. 67

FARRER, REGINALD
Alpines and Bog-Plants. London: 1908. V. 62; 66
Among the Hills. 1927. V. 63
The Dolomites: King Laurin's Garden. London: 1913. V. 62
The English Rock Garden. 1919. V. 63; 66
The English Rock Garden. London: 1925. V. 64; 67
The English Rock Garden. London: 1948. V. 64

FARRER, REGINALD continued
The English Rock Garden. & Samson Clay's Present Day Rock Garden. London: 1954. V. 64; 65
The English Rock Garden. (with) *The Present Day Rock Garden.* 1919-1937. V. 66
Farrer's Last Journey, Upper Burma. 1926. V. 66
The Garden of Asia. London: 1904. V. 66
In a Yorkshire Garden. London: 1909. V. 65; 66
In a Yorkshire Garden. Rhode Island: 1979. V. 64; 65
On the Eaves of the World. London: 1917. V. 67
On the Eaves of the World. London: 1926. V. 65
The Plant Introductions of Reginald Farrer. 1930. V. 63
The Plant Introductions of Reginald Farrer. London: 1930. V. 62
The Rainbow Bridge. 1921. V. 63
The Rainbow Bridge. London: 1922. V. 64; 67
The Rainbow Bridge. 1926. V. 66
The Rainbow Bridge. London: 1926. V. 63; 67

FARRER, WILLIAM
The Chartulary of Cockersand Abbey of the Premonstratensian Order. London: 1898-1909. V. 66
Records Relating to the Barony of Kendale. Kendal: 1923. V. 62

FARRERE, CLAUDE
Thomas L'Agnelet Gentilhomme e Fortune. Paris: 1927. V. 66

FARRIER, GEORGE H.
Memorial of the Centennial Celebration of the Battle of Paulus Hook...with a History of the Early Settlement and Present Condition of Jersey City. Jersey City: 1879. V. 63; 66

FARRINGTON, CHISIE
Women Can Fish. 1951. V. 65; 67

FARRIS, JACK
A Man to Ride With. Philadelphia: 1957. V. 62; 65

FARRIS, JOHN
King Windom. New York: 1967. V. 66

FARROW, EDWARD S.
Camping On the Trail of Some of My Experiences in the Indian Country. Philadelphia: 1902. V. 64; 67

FARROW, G. E.
The Wallypug of Why. New York: 1896. V. 64

FARROW, JAMES
The Clumber Spaniel. 1991. V. 67

FARSON, NEGLEY
Going Fishing. London: 1942. V. 67

FARTHER Excursions of the Observant Pedestrian, Exemplified in a Tour to Margate. London: 1801. V. 67

THE FARWELL of the Zoo Pet. London: 1882. V. 67

THE FASHIONABLE American Letter Writer, or the Art of Polite Correspondence.... Totten: 1828. V. 63

FAST, HOWARD
Spartacus. New York: 1951. V. 66

THE FAT Boy from Dickens Pickwick. New York: 1882. V. 63

FATE of the Steam-Ship President, Which Sailed from New York March 11th, 1841, Bound for Liverpool. Boston: 1845. V. 62

FATHER TUCK'S Funny Friends. London: 1890. V. 65

FAU, J.
The Anatomy of te External Forms of Man; Intended for the Use of Artists, Painters and Sculptors.... London: 1849. V. 67

FAUCONNIER, HENRI
The Soul of Malaya. London: 1931. V. 67

FAUJAS SAINT FOND, BARTHELMY
Travels in England, Scotland and the Hebrides; Undertaken for the Purpose of Examining the State of the Arts, the Sciences, Natural History and Manners in Great Britain.... London: 1799. V. 65

FAULDER, R.
Catalogue of Five Hundred Celebrated Authors of Great Britain, Now Living.... London: 1788. V. 62

FAULK, ODIE B.
General Tom Green, Fighting Texan. Waco: 1963. V. 63; 66
Leather Jacket Soldier Spanish Military Equipment and Institutions of the Late 18th Century. Pasadena: 1971. V. 64; 67

FAULKNER, CHARLES JAMES
Speech of Charles Jas. Faulkner (of Berkeley) in the House of Delegates of Virginia, On the Policy of the State with Respect to Her Slave Population Delivered January 29, 1832. Richmond: 1832. V. 66

FAULKNER, D.
Living Corals. New York: 1979. V. 63; 65

FAULKNER, GEORGENE
Christmas Stories. Chicago: 1916. V. 62
Old English Nursery Tales. Chicago: 1916. V. 64
Old English Nursery Tales. Chicago: 1920. V. 62

FAULKNER, WILLIAM HARRISON
Absalom, Absalom!. London: 1936. V. 63
Absalom, Absalom!. New York: 1936. V. 62; 67
Absalom, Absalom!. New York: 1986. V. 63; 67
Absalon! Absalon! (Absalom, Absalom). Paris: 1953. V. 67
An Address Delivered by William Faulkner, Oxford, Mississippi at the Seventeenth Annual Meeting of Delta Council, May 15, 1952. Cleaveland: 1952. V. 62
Afternoon of a Cow. Iowa City: 1991. V. 66
L'Arbre Aux Souhaits. (The Wishing Tree). Paris: 1969. V. 67
Big Woods. New York: 1955. V. 62; 63; 66
Collected Stories of William Faulkner. New York: 1950. V. 64; 67
Descends, Moise. (Go Down, Moses). Paris: 1955. V. 67
Doctor Martino and Other Stories. London: 1934. V. 62
Doctor Martino and Other Stories. New York: 1934. V. 62; 64; 67
Le Domain. (The Mansion). Paris: 1962. V. 67
A Fable. New York: 1954. V. 62; 63; 64; 65; 67
A Fable. London: 1955. V. 62
Father Abraham. New York: 1983. V. 64; 67
Faulkner's County - Tales of Yoknapatawpha County. London: 1955. V. 62
Go Down, Moses and Other Stories. New York: 1942. V. 62
The Hamlet. New York: 1940. V. 65; 67
Histoires Diverses. Paris: 1967. V. 67
Intruder in the Dust. New York: 1948. V. 62; 64
Intruder in the Dust. London: 1949. V. 62
L'Intrus. (Intruder in the Dust). Paris: 1952. V. 67
L'Invaincu. (The Unvanquished). Paris: 1949. V. 67
Knight's Gambit. New York: 1949. V. 64
Les Larrons (The Reivers). Paris: 1964. V. 67
Light in August. New York: 1932. V. 65
The Mansion. New York: 1959. V. 64; 66; 67
Marionettes. Oxford: 1975. V. 66
Miss Zilphia Gant. N.P: 1932. V. 63; 64
Mosquitoes. New York: 1927. V. 64; 67
Mosquitoes. London: 1964. V. 62
Nobel Prize Speech. New York: 1951. V. 62; 65
Notes on a Horse Thief. Greenville: 1950. V. 62; 64; 67
Les Palmiers Sauvages. (Wild Palms). Paris: 1952. V. 67
Parabole. (A Fable). Paris: 1958. V. 67
Pylon. New York: 1935. V. 67
Le Rameau Vert. (A Green Bough). Paris: 1955. V. 67
The Reivers. London: 1962. V. 62
The Reivers. New York: 1962. V. 63; 66
Requiem for a Nun. New York: 1951. V. 62; 64; 67
Requiem for a Nun. London: 1953. V. 62
Sanctuary. New York: 1931. V. 64; 67
Sartoris. New York: 1929. V. 67
Sartoris. London: 1932. V. 62
Selected Short Stories. New York: 1961. V. 63
Sherwood Anderson and Other Famous Creoles. New Orleans: 1926. V. 62
Soldiers' Pay. London: 1930. V. 67
The Sound and the Fury. New York: 1929. V. 67
These Thirteen. New York: 1932. V. 62
Thinking of Home. William Faulkner's Letters to His Mother and Father 1918-1925. New York: 1992. V. 63
This Earth. New York: 1932. V. 62
The Town. New York: 1957. V. 64; 65
The Town. London: 1958. V. 63
The Unvanquished. New York: 1936. V. 62; 64; 67
The Unvanquished. New York: 1938. V. 62; 65
La Ville. (The Town). Paris: 1962. V. 67
The Wild Palms. New York: 1939. V. 67
William Faulkner's Letters to Malcolm Franklin. Irving: 1976. V. 62

FAULKS, SEBASTIAN
The Girl at the Lion D'Or. London: 1989. V. 63

FAULL, M. L.
West Yorkshire: an Archaeological Survey to A.D. 1500. Wakefield: 1981. V. 65; 66

THE FAUNA of British India, Including Ceylon and Burma. Mammalia. London: 1939-1941. V. 66

FAUNTLEROY, HENRY
Pierce Egan's Account of the Trial of Mr. Fauntleroy, for Forgery... on Saturday the 30th of October 1824.... London: 1824. V. 63
The Trial of Mr. Henry Fauntleroy, for Forgery on Saturday, October 30th, 1824...With the Whole of the Defence...Anecdotes of Mother Bang and Her Pals. London: 1824. V. 63

FAUQUIER, FRANCIS
An Essay on Ways and Means for Raising Money for the Support of the Present War, Without Increasing the Public Debts. London: 1756. V. 64
The Official Papers of Francis Fauquier, Lieutenant Governor of Virginia 1758-1768. Richmond: 1980-1983. V. 64

FAURE, ELIE
Antonin Raymond, His Work in Japan 1920-1935. Tokyo: 1936?. V. 67

FAURE, M.
Catalogue de Tableaux Modernes. Paris: 1878. V. 64

FAUSSETT, BRYAN
Inventorium Sepulchrale: an Account of Some Antiquities Dug Up at Gilton, Kingston, Sibertswold, Barfriston, Beakesbourne, Chartham and Crundale in the County of Kent from 1757 to 1773. London: 1856. V. 64

FAUST, SEYMOUR
The Lovely Quarry. New York: 1958. V. 62

FAUX, R.
High Ambition. 1982. V. 65

FAUX, W.
Memorable Days in America, Being a Journal of a Tour to the United States.... Cleveland: 1904. V. 64

FAVENC, ERNEST
The History of Australian Exploratin from 1788 to 1888. Sydney: 1888. V. 62

FAVOUR, ALPHEUS H.
Old Bill Williams - Mountain Man. Chapel Hill: 1936. V. 64; 67

FAVOURITE English Poems of Modern Times. London: 1862. V. 65

FAVOURITE Fables for Tiny Tots. London: 1899. V. 66

THE FAVOURITE Picture Book and Nursery Companion. London: 1865. V. 65

FAVRE, ABBE DE
Les Quatre Heures de la Toilette des Dames Poeme Erotique. Paris: 1880. V. 64

FAVYN, ANDRE
The Theater of Honour and Knight-Hood. London: 1623. V. 67

FAWCETT, CLARA H.
Dolls: Ramblings of a Vagabond Collector. N.P: 1960. V. 66

FAWCETT, F. BURLINGTON
Broadside Ballads of the Restoration Period from the Jersey Collection Known as the Osterley Park Ballads. London: 1930. V. 62; 64

FAWCETT, GRAHAM
Poems for Shakespeare 2. London: 1973. V. 62; 64

FAWCETT, JOSEPH W.
Journal of Joseph W. Fawcett. Chillicothe: 1944. V. 65

FAWCETT, MILLICENT GARRETT
Josephine Butler. London: 1927. V. 65
The Women's Victory and after; Personal Reminiscences 1911-1918. London. 1920. V. 65

FAWCETT, TREVOR
The Rise of English Provincial Art. Oxford: 1974. V. 67

FAWCETT, WILLIAM
Rules and Regulations for the Sword Exercise of the Cavalry. London: 1796. V. 62

FAWKES, FRANCIS
Original Poems and Translations. London: 1761. V. 63

FAXON, W.
Notes on the Crayfishes in the United States National Museum and the Museum of Comparative Zoology.... Cambridge: 1914. V. 64; 65

FAY, EDWIN H.
The Infernal War. Austin: 1958. V. 62; 63

FAY, ELIZA
Original Letters, from India: Containing a Narrative of a Journey through Egypt, and the Author's Imprisonment at Calicut, by Hyder Ally. Calcutta: 1821. V. 64

FAY, THEODORE SEDGWICK
Sydney Clifton: or, Vicissitudes in Both Hemispheres. New York: 1839. V. 62
Views in New York and Its Environs, from Accurate, Characteristic and Picturesque Drawings.... New York: 1831-1834. V. 62; 64

FAY, W. G.
The Fays of the Abbey Theatre; an Autobiographical Record. 1935. V. 67

FAYLE, C. ERNEST
History of the Great War - Seaborne Trade. London: 1920-1924. V. 64

FAYRER, JOSEPH
European Child-Life in Bengal. London: 1873. V. 67
The Natural History and Epidemiology of Cholera. London: 1888. V. 66; 67
On the Bael Fruit; on the Relation of Filaria Sanguinis Homins to the Endemic Diseases of India. 1878-1879. V. 67
The Royal Tiger of Bengal. His Life and Death. 1875. V. 63

THE FEARFUL Choice - a Debate on Nuclear Policy. London: 1958. V. 65

FEARING, KENNETH
The Big Clock. New York: 1946. V. 66; 67
Dead Reckoning. New York: 1938. V. 64
The Generous Art. New York: 1954. V. 67
The Loneliest Girl in the World. London: 1952. V. 64
Poems. New York: 1935. V. 62
Poems. New York: 1936. V. 67

FEARN, J.
A Letter to Professor Stewart on the Objects of General Terms and on the Anatomical Laws of Vision. London: 1818. V. 66

FEARNE, CHARLES
The Posthumous Works.... London: 1797. V. 63

FEARON, HENRY BRADSHAW
Sketches of America. London: 1818. V. 66

FEASEY, JESSE EATON
Robin Hood and Other Stories of Yorkshire. London: 1913. V. 67

THE FEATHER of the Finist the Falcon. Moscow: 1902. V. 66

FEATHER, JOHN
English Book Prospectuses. Newtown/Minneapolis: 1984. V. 64

FEATHERSTONHAUGH, GEORGE WILLIAM
A Canoe Voyage Up the Minnay Sotor.... London: 1847. V. 66
Geological Report of an Examination Made in 1834 of the Elevated Country Between the Missouri and Red Rivers. London: 1835. V. 62; 66

FEATLEY, DANIEL
Clavis Mystica; a Key Opening Divers Difficult and Mysterious Texts of Holy Scripture.... London: 1636. V. 63

FEATON, EDWARD HENRY
The Art Album of New Zealand Flora.... London: 1889. V. 67

FEBBESSY, RENA
Birds of the African Bush. London: 1975. V. 67

FEDDEN, ROBIN
The Land of Egypt. London: 1939. V. 64

FEDDEN, ROMILLY
The Basque Country. London: 1921. V. 67

FEDER, NORMAN
American Indian Art. New York: 1965. V. 66
American Indian Art. New York: 1969. V. 62; 63; 65; 66
American Indian Art. New York: 1982. V. 63

FEDERAL PARTY, NEW JERSEY
Proceedings and Address of the Second Convention of Delegates, Held at the City of Trenton, on the Fourth of July 1814 to the People of New Jersey. Trenton?: 1814. V. 63

FEDERMAN, RAYMOND
Among the Beasts, Parmi les Monstres. Paris: 1967. V. 67
Double or Nothing. Chicago: 1971. V. 67

FEE, CHESTER ANDERS
Chief Joseph. The Biograhy of a Great Indian. New York: 1936. V. 63; 67

FEELY, FRANK M.
The Criminal Law and Procedure (Ireland) Act 1887. 1888. V. 67

FEHER, JOSEPH
Hawaii: a Pictorial History. Honolulu: 1969. V. 65; 66

FEHR, W. R.
Principles of Cultivar Development. New York: 1987. V. 62

FEHRENBACH, T. R.
Lone Star: a History of Texas and the Texans. New York: 1968. V. 63; 64

FEIGL, FRITZ
Spot Tests in Organic Analysis. Amsterdam: 1956. V. 65

FEIN, HARRY H.
The Flying Chinaman. New York: 1938. V. 67

FEINAIGLE, GREGOR VON
The New Art of Memory, Founded Upon the Principles Taught by.... London: 1813. V. 63; 67

FEININGER, ANDREAS
Changing America - the Land As It Was and How Man Has Charged It. New York: 1955. V. 62

FEIST, UWE
Panzerkampfwagen Tiger. Retford Notts: 1992. V. 67

FELD, CHARLES
Picasso: His Recent Drawings 1966-1968. New York: 1977. V. 64; 66

FELDMAN, DAVID
Handbook of Irish Philately. 1968. V. 67

FELDMAN, F.
Andy Warhol Prints: a Catalogue Raisonne. Munich and New York: 1985. V. 65

FELDMAN, WALTER
The Alphabet Book ... WWII. A Short History of the Second World War.... Providence: 1996. V. 62

FELIBIEN, ANDRE
Tapisseries Du Roy, Ou Sont Representez Les Quatre Elemens et Les Quatre Saisons. (with) Relation De La Feste de Versailles. Paris: 1679. V. 66

FELICIANO, FELICE
Alphabetum Romanum. Verona: 1960. V. 62; 63; 65

FELINI, PIETRO M.
Trattato Nuovo delle Cose Maravigliose dell'Alma Citta di Roma. Rome: 1625. V. 62

FELIX the Cat Painting Book. London: 1961. V. 65

FELKIN, WILLIAM
A History of the Machine-Wrought Hosiery and Lace Manufacatures. Cambridge: 1867. V. 64

FELL, ALFRED
The Early Iron Industry of Furness and District.... Ulverston: 1908. V. 63; 66
A Furness Military Chronicle. Ulverston: 1937. V. 66

FELL, W. A., LTD.
Modern Wood Working Machinery. Catalog No. 37. Windermere: 1938. V. 64; 65; 66

FELLIG, ARTHUR
Naked City. Cincinnati: 1945. V. 63
Weegee's Creative Camera. Garden City: 1959. V. 63; 65
Weegee's People. New York: 1946. V. 62; 63

FELLOWES, EDMOND H.
The Tenbury Letters. Waltham St. Lawrence: 1942. V. 63; 64

FELLOWES, P. F. M.
First Over Everest; the Houston-Mount Everest Expedition 1933. London: 1933. V. 67

FELLOWES, ROBERT
A Brief Treatise on Death, Philosophically, Morally and Practically Considered. London: 1805. V. 65; 66

FELLOWES, W. D.
A Visit to the Monastery of La Trappe in 1817. London: 1818. V. 62
A Visit to the Monastery of La Trappe in 1817.... London: 1853. V. 66

FELLTHAM, OWEN
Resolves. A Duple Century. London: 1634. V. 62

FELTHAM, JOHN
A Guide to All the Watering and Sea-Bathing Places.... London: 1804. V. 65
A Guide to All the Watering and Sea-Bathing Places.... London: 1813. V. 67

FELTON, HENRY
A Dissertation on Reading the Classics, and Forming a Just Style. London: 1713. V. 64

FELTON, HENTY
A Dissertation on Reading the Classics and Forming a Just Style. London: 1730. V. 63

FELTON, MRS.
American Life. A Narrative of Two Years' City and Country Residence in the United States. London: 1842. V. 64
Life in America. Hull: 1838. V. 66

FELTON, REBECA LATIMER
Country Life in Georgia in the Days of My Youth. Atlanta: 1919. V. 63

FEMALE Excellence; or, Hints to Daughters. London: 1838. V. 65

THE FEMALE Mentor; or Select Conversations. Philadelphia: 1802. V. 65

FEMINIANA, or the Poets' Beauties. Edinburgh: 1835. V. 65

FENDT, TOBIAS
Monumenta Sepulcrorum cum Epigraphis Ingenio et Doctrina Excellentium Virorum Aloriorumque tam Prisci Quam Nostri Seculi Memorabilium Hominum de Archetypis Expressa.... Breslau: 1574. V. 64

FENELON, FRANCOIS SALIGNAC DE LA MOTHE, ABP.
The Adventures of Telemachus, the Son of Ulyses. London: 1773. V. 66
The Adventures of Telemachus, the Son of Ulysses. London: 1776. V. 66
Les Aventures de Telemaque. Paris: 1781. V. 63; 66
Les Aventures de Telemaque. Paris: 1785. V. 63
De l'Education Des Filles. Amsterdam: 1708. V. 65
A Demonstration of the Existence, Wisdom and Omnipotence of God, Drawn from the Knowledge of Nature, Particularly of Man and Fitted to the Meanest Capacity. London: 1714. V. 66
Dialogues Concerning Eloquence in General.... London: 1722. V. 64
A Patern of Christian Education, Agreable to the Precepts and Practice of Our Blessed Lord and Saviour Jesus Christ. Germantown: 1756. V. 63

FENGQIN, T.
The Blossoming Botanical Gardens of the Chinese Academy of Sciences. Beijing: 1997. V. 63

FENLEY, FLORENCE
Grandad and I - A Story of a Grand Old Man and Other Pioneers of Texas and the Dakotahs. Leakey: 1951. V. 64
Old Timers - Their Own Stories. Texas: 1939. V. 64

FENN, ALWARD
Fenn Family Brands and Their Historical Brands. N.P. V. 66

FENN, ELEANOR
Cobwebs to Catch Flies; or, Dialogues in Short Sentences Adapted to Children from the Age of Three to Eight Years. London: 1825. V. 62; 66
Juvenile Correspondence; or, Letters, Suited to Children, From Four to Above Ten Years of Age. London: 1783. V. 65
The Juvenile Tatler. London: 1790. V. 65
The Rational Dame, or Hints Towards Supplying Prattle for Children. London: 1786. V. 66

FENN, ELEANOR FRERE
Sketches of Little Boys; the Well-Behaved Little Boy, the Covetous, the Dilatory, the Exact, the Attentive, the Inattentive, the Quarrelsome and the Good Little Boy. London: 1850. V. 63; 65

FENN, FORREST
The Beat of the Drum and the Whoop of the Dance, a Story of the Life and Work of Joseph Henry Sharp. Santa Fe: 1983. V. 64

FENN, GEORGE MANVILLE
George Alfred Henry, the Story of an Active Life. 1907. V. 63; 67
The White Virgin. London: 1895. V. 65

FENN, JOHN
Sherlock Holmes and the Affair of the Amorous Aunt. New York: 1972. V. 66

FENNER, CAROL
Yolanda's Genius. New York: 1995. V. 65

FENNER, THOMAS P.
Religious Folk Songs of the Negro as Sung on the Plantations. Hampton 1909. V. 65

FENNING, DANIEL
The Ready Reckoner; or, Trader's Sure Guide. York: 1801. V. 64
The Royal English Dictionary. London: 1763. V. 64
The Royal English Dictionary.... London: 1775. V. 64

FENNING, ELIZABETH
Affecting Case of Eliza Fenning...(with) Thirty Original and Interesting Letters Written by the Late Elizabeth Fenning, Whilst in Prison and Under Sentence of Death. London: 1815. V. 63; 65
Circumstantial Evidence. The Extraordinary Case of Eliza Fenning, Who Was Executed in 1815.... London: 1830. V. 63
The Genuine Trial and Affecting Case of Eliza Fenning, Who Was Convicted of Attempting to Poison Mr. Turner and Family.... London: 1815. V. 63
The Important Results of an Elaborate Investigation into the Mysterious Case of Elizabeth Fenning.... London: 1815. V. 63

FENNO, HENRY
Our Police; the Official History of the Police Department of the City of Lynn from the First Constable to the Latest Appointee. Lynn: 1895. V. 62

FENOLLOSA, ERNEST
East and West - the Discover of America and Other Poems. New York and Boston: 1893. V. 63
Epochs of Chinese and Japanese Art - an Outline History of East Asiatic Design. London: 1913. V. 64
Noh: or, Accomplishment: a Study of the Classical Stage of Japan. New York: 1917. V. 66

FENTON, ELIJAH
Mariamne, a Tragedy. London: 1723. V. 63

FENTON, GEOFFREY
Golden Epistles, Contayning Carietie of Discourse, Both Morall, Philosphical and Divine.... London: 1582. V. 65

FENTON, JAMES
All the Wrong Places: Adrift in the Politics of Asia. London: 1989. V. 63
Children in Exile. Edinburgh: 1983. V. 62; 63; 64
Dead Soldiers. Oxford: 1981. V. 63
Manila Envelope. 1989. V. 65
The Memory of War: Poems 1968-1982. Edinburgh: 1982. V. 62; 64
Our Western Furniture. 1968. V. 64
Put Thou Thy Tears Into My Bottle. Oxford: 1969. V. 63
Terminal Moraine. 1972. V. 64
Terminal Moraine: Poems. London: 1972. V. 66
A Vacant Possession. London: 1978. V. 64

FENTON, RICHARD
A Historical Tour through Pembrokeshire. London: 1811. V. 65
A Tour in Quest of Genealogy through Several Parts of Wales, Somersetshire and Wiltshire, in a Series of Letters to a Friend in Dublin.... London: 1811. V. 62; 66

FENWICK, E. P.
The Inconvenient Corpse. 1943. V. 64; 66

FENWICK, GEORGE EDGEWORTH
Excision of the Knee-Joint with Report of Twenty-Eight Cases.... Montreal: 1883. V. 64; 66; 67

FENWICK, JOHN
Substance of the Speech of John Fenwick, at a General Meeting of the Various Denominations of Protestant Dissenter, of Newcastle Upon Tyne, on the 14th June 1825.... Newcastle upon Tyne: 1826. V. 65

FERBER, EDNA
Cimarron. Garden City: 1930. V. 62; 64
Emma Mc Chesney and Co. New York: 1915. V. 64; 66
Giant. Garden City: 1952. V. 67
Saratoga Trunk. Garden City: 1941. V. 62
Show Boat. Garden City: 1926. V. 66

FERDOWSI
Episodes from the Shah Nameh; or Annals of the Persian Kings, by Ferdoosee. London: 1815. V. 63

FERE, CHARLES
The Pathology of the Emotions: Phsyiological and Clinical Studies. London: 1899. V. 65

FERENCZI, SANDOR
Entwicklungsstufen des Wirklichkeitsinnes. Leipzig/Wien: 1913. V. 62

FERGUS, HENRY
The History of the United States. London: 1830-1832. V. 67

FERGUSON, ADAM
Essai sur l'Histoire de la Societe Civile.... Paris: 1783. V. 62; 65
The History of the Progress and Termination of the Roman Republic.... Basle: 1791. V. 64
Institutes of Moral Philosophy. Edinburgh: 1769. V. 63

FERGUSON, CHARLES D.
The Experiences of a '49er During the 34 Years Residence in California and Australia. Cleveland: 1888. V. 64; 65

FERGUSON, EDNA
Mexican Cookbook. Santa Fe: 1934. V. 66

FERGUSON, JAMES
Astronomy Explained Upon Sir Isaac Newton's Principles. London: 1757. V. 64
Astronomy Explained Upon Sir Isaac Newton's Principles and Made Easy to Those Who Have Not Studied Mathematics. London: 1772. V. 66
Lectures on Select Subjects in Mechanics, Hydrostatics, Pneumatics and Optics. London: 1760. V. 65
Lectures on Select Subjects in Mechanics, Hydrostatics, Pneumatics and Optics. London: 1770. V. 64

FERGUSON, JOHN
Bibliographical Notes on Histories of Inventions and Books of Secrets. London: 1981. V. 62
Bibliographical Notes on Histories of Inventions and Books of Secrets. 1998. V. 64
Bibliographical Notes on Histories of Inventions and Books of Secrets. Staten Island: 1998. V. 62
Bibliotheca Chemica. Mansfield Centre. V. 67
Bibliotheca Chemica. Glasgow: 1906. V. 66
Bibliotheca Chemica. London: 1954. V. 65
Bibliotheca Chemica. Mansfield Centre: 1997. V. 63
Some Aspects of Bibliography. Edinburgh: 1900. V. 63

FERGUSON, JOHN ALEXANDER
Bibliography of Australia. Cranberra: 1975-1986. V. 64
Bibliography of Australia 1784-(1900). Canberra: 1980-1986. V. 62

FERGUSON, KEN
Day at the Haces. Northumberland: 1996. V. 66

FERGUSON, LADY
Sir Samuel Ferguson in the Ireland of His Day. 1896. V. 66

FERGUSON, M.
The Printed Books in the Library of the Hunterian Museum in the University of Glasgow. Glasgow: 1930. V. 62

FERGUSON, M. C.
The Irish Before the Conquest. 1890. V. 62; 65

FERGUSON, O. J.
A Brief Biographical Sketch of I. A. Van Amburgh, and an Illustrated and Descriptive History of the Animals Contained in This Mammoth Menagerie and Great Moral Exhibition.... New York: 1860. V. 63

FERGUSON, RICHARD S.
Cumberland and Westmorland M.P.'s (sic). From the Restoration to the Reform Bill of 1867, (1660-1867). London: 1871. V. 62; 66

FERGUSON, ROBERT
Swiss Men and Swiss Mountains. London: 1854. V. 62; 63; 64

FERGUSON, SAMUEL
Hibernian Nights Entertainments. 1887-1897. V. 62; 65

FERGUSON, W. B. M.
The Pilditch Puzzle. New York: 1932. V. 65

FERGUSON, WILLIAM
Twelve Sketches of Scenery And Antiquities on the Line of the Great North of Scotland Railway. Edinburgh: 1883. V. 62

FERGUSSAN, BERNARD
Eton Portrait. London: 1937. V. 63

FERGUSSON, ADAM
The History of the Progress and Termination of the Roman Republic. London: 1783. V. 67

FERGUSSON, C. BRUCE
Place-Names and Places of Nova Scotia. Bellville: 1974. V. 63

FERGUSSON, EMA
New Mexico: a Pageant of Three Peoples. New York: 1951. V. 67

FERGUSSON, ERNA
Murder and Mystery in New Mexico. Santa Fe: 1991. V. 62

FERGUSSON, GORDON
Hounds are Home. 1979. V. 62; 64

FERGUSSON, JAMES
A History of Architecture In all Countries, from the Earliest Times to the Present Day. London: 1873-1874. V. 66

FERGUSSON, T. M.
Border Sport and Sportsmen. Hexham: 1932. V. 67

FERGUSSON, VERE H.
The Story of Fergie Bey (Awarauay). London: 1930. V. 67

FERGUSSON, W. N.
Adventure, Sport and Travel on the Tibetan Steppes. London: 1911. V. 65

FERGUSSON, WILLIAM
A System of Practical Surgery. Philadelphia: 1843. V. 63
A System of Practical Surgery. Philadelphia: 1848. V. 66

FERLINGHETTI, LAWRENCE
Endless Life. N.P: 1980. V. 67
Pictures of the Gone World. San Francisco: 1955. V. 62; 64; 67
La Quatrieme Personne Du Singulier. Paris: 1961. V. 67
The Sea and Ourselves at Cape Ann. Madison: 1979. V. 66
Starting from San Francisco. Norfolk: 1961. V. 63

FERMAT, PIERRE DE
Varia Opera Mathematica. Toulouse: 1679. V. 67

FERMIN DE MENDINUETA, PEDRO
Indian and Missin Affairs in New Mexico 1773. Santa Fe: 1965. V. 66

FERMOR, PATRICK LEIGH
Between the Woods and the Water - On Foot to Constantinople from the Hook of Holland: the Middle Danube to the Iron Gates. London: 1986. V. 65
Mani: Travels in the Southern Pelonnese. London: 1958. V. 63; 65
Roumeli - Travels in Northern Greece. London: 1966. V. 65
Three Letters from the Andes. London: 1991. V. 64

FERN, ALAN
The Complete Prints of Leonard Baskin. Boston: 1983. V. 65

FERNALD, JOSEPH
Lafayette Medical Mirror: Being a Narrative of a new and Most Infallibly Effectual Method Of Curing the Lingering Diseases of the Human System. Saco: 1827. V. 62

FERNANDEZ, JUSTINO
Danzas de los Cocheros en San Miguel de Allende. Mexico: 1941. V. 63

FERNANDEZ DE PALENCIA, DIEGO
Primera, y Segunda Parte de la Historica del Peru...Contiene la Primera, lo Succedido en la Nueva Espana y en el Peru, sobre la Execucion de las Nuevas Leyes.... Seville: 1571. V. 62

FERNEL, JEAN FRANCOIS
Therapevtices Vniversalis Sev medendi Rationalis. Libris Septem. Lyon?: 1569. V. 62, 64, 66
Universa Medicina: Ab Ipso Quidem Authore Ante Obitum Diligenter Recognita et Iustis Accessionibus Locupletata. Lugduni: 1615-1602. V. 62; 67

FERNETT, GENE
Next Time Drive Off the Cliff. Cocoa: 1968. V. 66

FERONI, LEOPOLDO
Viaggio di un Anno Dall' Ottobre 1821, All' Ottobre 1822. Firenze: 1822. V. 67

FERRAR, JOHN
A View of Ancient and Modern Dublin with Its Improvements to the Year 1796. (with) A Tour from Dublin to London in 1795. 1796. V. 67

FERRARI, ENRIQUE LAFUENTE
Goya: the Frescos in San Antonio De la Florida in Madrid. New York: 1955. V. 62; 63; 64; 66

FERRARI, GIROLAMO
Philosophia Sensuum Mechanica.... Brixiae: 1735-1736. V. 66
Philosophia Sensuum Mechanica.... Brescia: 1751-1752. V. 64

FERRARI, PHILIP
Lexicon Geographicum in Quo Universi Orbis Appida, Urbes, Regiones, Provinciae, Regna, Emporia, Academiae, Metropoles, Fontes, Flumina & Maria Antiquis Recentibusque.... London: 1657. V. 63

FERRARIO, GIULIO
Il Costume Antico e Moderno..No. 199. Milano: 1816. V. 62; 67
Monumenti Sacri e Profani dell'Imperiale e Reale Basilica di Sant'Ambrogio in Milano. Milan: 1824. V. 64
Storia ed Analisi Degli Antichi Romanzi di Cavelleria e Dei Poemi Romanzeschi d'Italia.... Milan: 1828-1829. V. 64

FERRARS, MAX
Burma. London: 1900. V. 67

FERRE, ROSARIO
Los Papeles de Pandora. Mexico City: 1976. V. 67
The Youngest Doll. Lincoln: 1991. V. 67

FERRELL, ANDERSON
Where She Was. New York: 1985. V. 63

FERRELL, MALLORY HOPE
Silver San Juan, The Rio Grande Southern Railroad. Boulder: 1973. V. 65

FERRER, MELCHOR G.
Tito's Hats. New York: 1940. V. 62

FERRERIUS, ZACHARIAS
Zacharias Ferrerius. In Die Festo Epiphaniae. Choriambicum Alphabeticum. Verona: 1968. V. 65

FERREY, BENJAMIN
A Series of Ornamental Timber Gables, from Existing Examples in England and France, of the Sixteenth Century. London: 1839. V. 66

FERRI, ENRICO
Criminal Sociology. New York and London: 190-. V. 63

FERRIAR, JOHN
An Essay Towards a Theory of Apparitions. London: 1813. V. 64
Illustrations of Sterne: with Other Essays and Verses. London: 1798. V. 63

FERRIER, DAVID
The Functions of the Brain. London: 1886. V. 65
The Functions of the Brain. New York: 1886. V. 65
On Tabes Dorsalis. The Lumleian Lectures Delivered Before the Royal College of Physicians, London, March 1906. New York: 1906. V. 65

FERRIER, SUSAN EDMONDSTONE
Destiny; or, the Chief's Daughter. Edinburgh: 1831. V. 65
Destiny; or the Chief's Daughter. Philadelphia: 1831. V. 62; 63; 65
Destiny; or, the Chief's Daughter. London: 1841. V. 65
The Inheritance. Edinburgh: 1824. V. 65
Marriage. Edinburgh and London: 1818. V. 63; 66
Marriage. Edinburgh: 1819. V. 65
Marriage. Edinburgh: 1826. V. 65
Memoir and Correspondence of Susan Ferrier 1782-1854.... London: 1898. V. 65

FERRIS, BENJAMIN
A History of the Original Settlements on the Delaware, From Its Discovery by Hudson to the Colonization Under William Penn. Wilmington: 1846. V. 63; 66
Utah and the Mormons - the History of Government, Doctrines, Customs and Prospects of the Latter-Day Saints. New York: 1854. V. 63

FERRIS, JACOB
The States and Territories of the Great West Including Ohio, Indiana, Illinois, Missouri, Michigan, Wisconsin, Iowa, Minnesota, Kansas, Nebraska. New York: 1856. V. 66

FERRIS, JOHN
Herbs of Lost Thyme. Shelburne: 1971. V. 67

FERRIS, WARREN ANGUS
Life in the Rocky Mountains. Denver: 1940. V. 64; 67
Life in the Rocky Mountains. Salt Lake City: 1940. V. 66
Life in the Rocky Mountains. Denver: 1983. V. 67

FERRISS, HUGH
The Metropolis of Tomorrow. New York: 1929. V. 66

FERRO, ANTONIO
Apparato della Statue, Nuovamente Trovate Nella Distrutta Cuma...et con la Descrittione del Tempio.... Naples: 1606. V. 64

FERRY, D. M., & CO.
Illustrated, Descriptive and Priced Catalogue of Garden, Flower and Agricultural Seeds. Detroit: 1879. V. 62

FERSEN, JACQUES D'ADELSWARD, COUNT
Curieux d'Amour. London: 1970. V. 67

FERTE, M. DE LA
Extrait des Differens Ouvrages Publies sur la Vie des Peintres. Paris: 1776. V. 64

FERUS, JOHANNES
Reverendi Patris D. Ioannis Feri, In Totam Genesim Nom Minus Eruditae, Quam Catholicae Enarrationes. Coloniae Agrippinae: 1572. V. 66

FESSENDEN, T. G.
An Essay on the Law of Patents for New Inventions. Boston: 1810. V. 63
The New American Gardener...Fruits and Vegetables.... Boston: 1828. V. 62

LE FESTE d'Apollo, Celebrate sul Treatro di Corte Nell' Agosto del MDCCLXIX Per le Auguste Seguite Nozze Tra il Reale Infante Don Ferdinando e la R. Arciduchessa Infanta Maria Amalia. Parma: 1769. V. 62

FESTEAU, PAUL
French Grammar: Being the Newest and Exactest Method Now Extant, for the Attaining to the Elegancy and Purity of the French Tongue.... London: 1679. V. 62; 66
Paul Festau's French Grammar.... London: 1685. V. 64

FESTSCHRIFT for Marianne Moore's Seventy-Seventh Birthday. London: 1966. V. 64

FETHERSTONHAUGH, T.
Our Cumberland Village. Carlisle: 1925. V. 65

FETIS, F. J.
Notice of Anthony Strandivari, the Celebrated Violin-Maker, Known by the Name of Stradivarius.... London: 1864. V. 64

FEUCHTERSLEBEN, ERNST, FREIHEER VON
The Principles of Medical Psychology.... London: 1847. V. 65

FEUCHTWANGER, LEWIS
A Treatise on Gems, in Reference to Their Practical and Scientific Value.... New York: 1838. V. 64

FEUERBACH, LUDWIG
The Essence of Christianity. London: 1881. V. 65

FEUERBACK, ANSELM
Narrative of Remarkable Criminal Trials. London: 1846. V. 63

FEUILLET, G.
Unterchidliche Kirchen und Closter Proten, Inventiert und Gezeichnet von G. Feuillet. Augsburg: 1730. V. 67

FEUILLET, OCTAVE
The Story of Mr. Punch. New York: 1929. V. 64

FEURIGE Kohlen Der Aufsteigenden Liebesflammen Im Lustspiel der Weisheit. Oeconomie: 1826. V. 66

A FEW Serious Observations Upon the Several Papers Lately Printed Upon the Subject of the Election of Magistrates. Edinburgh: 1725. V. 65

FEWKES, J. W.
The Tusayan Ritual: a Study of the Influence of Environment on Aboriginal Cults. and The Cliff Villages of the Red Rock Country and the Tusayan Ruins at Sikyatki and Awatobi, Arizona. 1885. V. 62

FEYDEAU, GEORGES
A Flea in Her Ear - a Farce. London: 1968. V. 65

FEYJOO Y MONTENEGRO, BENITO JERONIMO
Three Essays or Discourses on the Following Subjects, a Defence or Vindication of the Women, Church Music, a Comparison Between Ancient and Modern Music. London: 1778. V. 62; 66

FFIRTH, JOHN
Truth Vindicated; or, A Scriptural Essay, Wherein the Vulgar and Frivolous Cavils, Commonly Urged Against the Methodist Cavils, Commonly Urged Against the Methodist Episcopal Church, are Briefly Considered in a Letter to a Friend. New York: 1810. V. 66

FFOLLIOTT, ROSEMARY
The Pooles of Mayfield and Other Irish Families. 1958. V. 62

FICORONI, FRANCESCO
Dissertatio de Larvis Scenicis et Figuris Comicis Antiquroum Romanorum. 1754. V. 66

FIDDES, RICHARD
Fifty-Two Practical Discourses on Several Subjects. London: 1720. V. 63
Theologia Speculativa; or, The First Part of a Body of Divinity Under that Title Wherein are Explain'd the Principles of Natural and Reveal'd Religion. Dublin: 1718. V. 67

FIDELIS, LUDOVICUS
...De Militia Spirutali Libri Quatuor. Paris: 1540. V. 62

FIELD, A. E.
Peaks, Passes and Glaciers, by Members of the Alpine Club. London: 1932. V. 64

FIELD, BARON
Geographical Memoirs of New South Wales. London: 1825. V. 67
A Review of the Late Publications on Libel, of Messrs. George, Holt, Starkie and Jones; in Which the Authority of the Case of Rex v. Taylor, Upon Which the Late Attorney General Rested the Prosecution at Common Law, of D. I. Eaton, for Blasphemy, Is Expo. London: 1815. V. 63

FIELD, CYRIL
Britain's Sea Soldiers. Liverpool: 1924. V. 64

FIELD, D. J.
The Human House. Boston: 1939. V. 65

FIELD, EUGENE
Little Book of Tribune Verse. Denver: 1901. V. 62
A Little Book of Western Verse. Chicago: 1889. V. 63
The Love Affairs of a Bibliomaniac. London: 1896. V. 64
Lullaby-Land. London: 1898. V. 65
Poems of Childhood. New York: 1904. V. 63; 65
The Symbol and the Saint. London: 1924. V. 65

FIELD, GEORGE
Chromatics, or an Essay on the Analogy and Harmony of Colours. London: 1817. V. 67

FIELD, GEORGE W.
A Treatise on the Constitution and Jurisdiction of the Courts of the United States. Philadelphia: 1883. V. 62

FIELD, HENRY
Arabs of Central Iraq: their History, Ethnology and Physical Characters. Chicago: 1935. V. 67

FIELD, HENRY M.
Bright Skies and Dark Shadows. New York: 1890. V. 65
From the Lakes of Killarney to the Golden Horn. New York. V. 67
Gibraltar. New York: 1888. V. 65
Gibraltar. London: 1889. V. 67
History of the Atlantic Telegraph. New York: 1866. V. 67
Our Western Archipelago. New York: 1895. V. 63; 66

FIELD, HORACE
English Domestic Architecture of the XVII and XVIII Centuries. London: 1905. V. 64; 66

FIELD, J.
Prison Discipline. The Advantages of the Separate System of Imprisonment, as Established in the New County Gaol of Reading...(with) Separate Imprisonment. Report Read at the Berkshire Quarter Sessions by the Chaplain of the County Gaol.... London: 1846. V. 65

FIELD, KATE
Pen Photographs of Charles Dickens's Readings. Boston: 1871. V. 62

FIELD, LOUISE A.
Peter Rabbit and His Ma. Chicago: 1917. V. 64
Peter Rabbit and His Pa. Akron: 1916. V. 64
Peter Rabbit Goes to School. Akron: 1917. V. 64

FIELD, M.
City Architecture or Designs for Dwelling-Houses, Stores, Hotels, Etc. New York: 1853. V. 64

FIELD, MATTHEW C.
Prairie and Mountain Sketches. Norman: 1957. V. 64; 66

FIELD, MICHAEL
The Race of Leaves. London: 1901. V. 62

FIELD, MICHAEL, PSEUD.
Fair Rosamund. 1897. V. 65
Julia Domna. 1903. V. 65
Poems of Adoration. London and Edinburgh: 1912. V. 64
Sight and Song. London: 1892. V. 64; 65
Stephania: a Trialogue. London: 1892. V. 64
Underneath the Bough: a Book of Verses. London: 1893. V. 64
Wild Honey from Various Thyme. London: 1908. V. 64; 65

THE FIELD of Mars; Being an Alphabetical Digestion of the Principal Naval and Military Engagements, in Europe, Asia, Africa and America, Particularly of Great Britain and Her Allies, from the Ninth Century to the Present Period. London: 1781. V. 64

FIELD, RACHEL
Hitty Her First Hundred Years. New York: 1929. V. 64; 65
The Pointed People. New Haven: 1924. V. 64
Prayer for a Child. New York: 1944. V. 62; 65
The Yellow Shop. Garden City: 1931. V. 62

FIELD, ROBERT D.
The Art of Walt Disney. London: 1944. V. 66

FIELD, WILLIAM B. OSGOOD
Edward Lear On My Shelves. Munich: 1933. V. 64

FIELD & DEMPSTER, REALTORS
Nanaimo! Vancouver Island, B.C. Its Resources and Prospects. The Rising City of the Pacific Coast. The Newcastle of the Pacific. Nanaimo: 1891. V. 63

FIELDE, ADELE M.
A Corner of Cathay, Studies from Life Among the Chinese. New York: 1894. V. 67

FIELDHOUSE, R.
A History of Richmond and Swaledale. London: 1978. V. 64; 65; 66

FIELDING, HELEN
Bridget Jones's Diary. London: 1996. V. 62; 65
Cause Celeb. London: 1994. V. 62

FIELDING, HENRY
The Adventures of Joseph Andrews. London: 1832. V. 62; 65
Amelia. London: 1752. V. 63; 64; 65; 66
Apology for the Life of Mrs. Shamela Andrews.... Waltham St. Lawrence: 1926. V. 66
The Author's Farce; and the Pleasures of the Town. London: 1730. V. 66
An Enquiry Into the Causes of the Late Increase of Robbers, &c., with Some Proposals for Remedying This Growing Evil. London: 1751. V. 64; 66
The History of Amelia. London: 1832. V. 63; 65
The History of the Adventures of Joseph Andrews. London: 1742. V. 63
The History of the Adventures of Joseph Andrews, and His Friend Mr. Abraham Adams. Edinburgh: 1770. V. 62
The History of Tom Jones, a Foundling. London: 1749. V. 63; 65; 67
The History of Tom Jones, a Foundling. Philadelphia: 1810. V. 63
The History of Tom Jones, a Foundling. London: 1819. V. 65
The History of Tom Jones; a Foundling. London: 1834. V. 64
The Journal of a Voyage to Lisbon. London: 1755. V. 63; 64
Journal of a Voyage to Lisbon. Cambridge: 1902. V. 62
A Journey From This World to the Next. Waltham St. Lawrence: 1930. V. 62; 64; 65
The Life of Mr. Jonathan Wild the Great. Waltham St. Lawrence: 1932. V. 62; 65
The Mock Doctor; or the Dumb Lady Cured. London: 1794. V. 66
The Novels. Boston: 1926. V. 62
The Novels. London: 1926. V. 62
The Novels. Oxford: 1926. V. 66
Pasquin. London: 1736. V. 66
The Remarkable History of Tom Jones, a Foundling. Worcester: 1799. V. 63
A Serious Address to the People of Great Britain. London: 1745. V. 63
The Works. London: 1784. V. 67
The Works. London: 1871-1872. V. 62; 66
The Works. London: 1902. V. 64
The Works. London: 1920. V. 63
Works. (with) Miscellanies and Poems. London: 1871. V. 65

FIELDING, SARAH
The Adventures of David Simple.... London: 1744. V. 65
Familiar Letters Between the Principal Characters in David Simple, and Some Others. London: 1747. V. 67
The Governess, or, the Little Female Academy. London: 1968. V. 63; 66
The Lives of Cleopatra and Octavia. London: 1757. V. 64

FIELDING, T. H.
British Castles; or, a Compendious History of the Ancient Military Structures of Great Britain. London: 1821. V. 66
A Picturesque Description of the River Wye, from the Source to Its Junction with the Severn. London: 1841. V. 62; 66
A Picturesque Tour of the English Lakes. London: 1821. V. 62; 63; 66
Synopsis of Practical Perspective, Lineal and Aerial. London: 1836. V. 66

FIELDING, XAN
The Stronghold. London: 1953. V. 67

FIELDING-HALL, H.
Margaret's Book. London: 1913. V. 65

FIELDS, J. T.
Anniversary Poem. Boston;: 1838. V. 65

FIELDS, JOSEPH
My Sister Eileen. New York: 1941. V. 66
The Ponder Heart: a New Comedy. Adapted from a Story by Eudora Welty. New York: 1956. V. 67

FIELDS, W. S.
Disorders of the Developing Nervous System. Springfield: 1961. V. 67

FIENNES, NATHANAEL
A Speech of the Honorable...in Answer to the Third Speech of the Lord George Digby. Concerning Bishops and the City of Londons Petition...9th of Feb. 1640 (1)....In Which is Plainly Cleared...Objections Against the Londoners Petition.... London: 1641. V. 66

FIERA, BATTISTA
De Iusticia Pingenda - On the Painting of Justice, a Dialogue Between Mantegna and Momus.... 1957. V. 63

FIFE COOKSON, J. C.
Tiger Shooting in the Doon and Ulwar. 1887. V. 67

FIFTY Years in Chains. New York: 1858. V. 63

FIGG, ROYAL W.
Where Men Only Dare to Go!. Richmond: 1885. V. 63

FIGGIS, DARRELL
The Paintings of William Blake. 1925. V. 65
The Paintings of William Blake. London: 1925. V. 66
The Return of the Hero. 1923. V. 67

A FIGURE of Christ, Executed in Stained Glass, by John Gibson, for the Corporation of Newcastle, from a Painting by W. Dixon, and Inserted in the East Window of St. Nicholas' Church April 9, 1827. Newcastle: 1827. V. 65

FILCHER, J. A.
Untold Tales of California: Short Stories Illustrating Phases of Life Peculiar to the Early Days of the West. 1903. V. 66

FILD, HENRY M.
Bright Skies and Dark Shadows. New York: 1890. V. 63

FILHOL, ANTOINE MICHEL
Galerie Du Musee De France. Paris: 1814-1815. V. 67
Galerie du Musee Napoleon. Paris: 1804-1815. V. 62

FILIPPI, FILIPPO DE
The Ascent of Mount St. Elias (Alaska) by H.R.H. Prince Luigi Amedeo Di Savoia Duke of the Abruzzi. 1900. V. 63; 65
Karakoram and the Western Himalaya. 1912. V. 63; 65
Ruwenzori. 1908. V. 63; 65
Ruwenzori. London: 1908. V. 63; 64; 66
Il Ruwenzori. Milan: 1908. V. 64

FILIPPI, ROSINA
Duologues and Scenes, from the Novels of Jane Austen. London: 1895. V. 63

FILSON, JOHN
Histoire De Kentucke, Nouvelle Colonie a L'Ouest de La Virginie. Paris: 1785. V. 63; 64; 66

FINALLY, DAVID W.
Reminiscences of Yacht Racing and Some Racing Yachts. Glasgow: 1910. V. 62

FINBERG, ALEX J.
Turner's Watercolours at Farnley Hall. London. V. 66

FINCH, CHRISTOPHER
The Art of Walt Disney. New York: 1973. V. 66
The Story of Jack and the Giants. New York: 1973. V. 66

FINCH, EDWIN W.
The Frontier, Army and Professional Life of Edwin W. Finch, M.D. New Rochelle: 1909. V. 62; 63

FINCH, GEORGE INGLE
The Making of a Mountaineer. 1924. V. 63; 65
The Making of a Mountaineer. London: 1924. V. 64
The Making of a Mountaineer. London: 1927. V. 63; 64

FINCH, MARIANNE
An Englishwoman's Experience in America. London: 1853. V. 66

FINCHAM, A. A.
Aspects of Decapod Crustacean Biology. Oxford: 1988. V. 65

FINCHAM, JOHN
Directions for Laying Off Ships on the Mould Loft Floor Designed for Use of the Students in the School of Naval Architecture, Portsmouth Dockyard. Portsea: 1822. V. 64
A Treatise on Masting Ships and Mast Making Explaining Their Principles and Practical Operations.... London: 1982. V. 62

FINCH HATTON, HAROLD
Advance Australia!. London: 1885. V. 67

FINDEN, W.
Les Dames de Byron; or, Portraits of the Principal Female Characters in Lord Byron's Poems. London: 1836. V. 65

FINDEN, WILLIAM
Views of Ports and Harbours, Watering Places, Fishing Villages.... London: 1838. V. 62

FINDLAY, ALEXANDER G.
A Classical Atlas: to Illustrate Ancient Geography.... New York: 1860. V. 64

FINDLAY, FREDERICK RODERICK NOBLE
Big Game Shooting and Travel in Southeast Africa. London: 1903. V. 62; 66; 67

FINDLAY, W. P. K.
Wayside and Woodland Fungi. London: 1967. V. 62

FINDLEY, WILLIAM
History of the Insurrection in the Western Counties of Pennsylvania in the Year 1794. Philadelphia: 1796. V. 67

THE FINE Book a Symposium. Pittsburgh: 1934. V. 62

FINE, ORONCE
Opere...Divise in Cinque Parti; Arimetica, Geometria, Cosmografia & Orivoli.... Venice: 1587. V. 67

FINERTY, JOHN F.
War Path and Bivouac of the Conquest of the Conquest of the Sioux. Chicago: 1890. V. 65
War Path and Bivouac or the Conquest of the Sioux. Chicago: 1910. V. 67

FINGER, CHARLES J.
Frontier Ballads: Woodcuts by Paul Honore. Garden City: 1927. V. 64

FINGER, F. L.
Catalogue of the Incunabula in the Elmer Belt Library of Vincinana. Los Angeles: 1971. V. 65

FINGER, STANLEY
Origins of Neuroscience. a History of Explorations into Brain Function. New York: 1994. V. 67

FINGERHUTH, CARL ANTON
Monographia Generis Capsici. Dusseldorf: 1832. V. 62; 63

FINK, LARRY
Social Graces. New York: 1984. V. 66

FINKEL, DONALD
A Joyful Noise. Poems. New York: 1966. V. 63

FINLAY, IAN HAMILTON
Canal Game. London: 1967. V. 64
Ceolfrith 5. Sunderland: 1970. V. 64
Rapel: 10 Fauve and Suprematist Poems. Edinburgh: 1963. V. 62; 64

FINLAYSON, JOHN L.
It Happened Here. New York: 1948. V. 66

FINN, FRANK
Indian Sporting Birds. Calcutta: 1915. V. 65; 67

FINNEY, CHARLES G.
The Circus of Dr. Lao. New York: 1946. V. 62
The Circus of Dr. Lao. 1982. V. 62; 63; 64

FINNEY, JACK
About Time. New York: 1986. V. 63
5 Against the House. London: 1954. V. 67
House of Numbers. London: 1957. V. 67
Marion's Wall. New York: 1973. V. 66
The Third Level. New York: 1957. V. 67
Time and Again. New York: 1970. V. 62; 65; 67
The Woodrow Wilson Dime. New York: 1968. V. 67

FINNEY, PETER DAVENPORT
Doe ex d. Finney, v. Roylance and Others. A Full Report of the Trial of the Action of Ejectment Between P. D. Finney, Plaintiff, and Peter Roylance and Others, Defendants Before Mr. Justice Holroyd and a Special Jury, at the Assizes at Lancaster.... Manchester: 1825. V. 63

FINOT, JEAN
Prejuge et Probleme des Sexes. Paris: 1912. V. 65
Race Prejudice. London: 1906. V. 64

FINSCH, O.
Die Papageien.... Leyden: 1867-1868. V. 66

FINSTERBUSCH, C. A.
Cock Fighting All Over the World. Gaffney: 1929. V. 66; 67

FIOCCO, ANDREA DOMENICO LUCIUS
Fenestellae de Magistratibus Sacerdotiisq; Romanoru Libellus, Iam Primum Nitori Restitutus. Augsburg: 1533. V. 63; 65

FIOROVANTI, LEONARDO
De Capricci Medicinali Dell' Eccellente Medic & Cirugico Messer Leonardo Fioruanti Bolognese. Venetia: 1629. V. 66; 67

FIRBANK, RONALD
The Artificial Princess. London: 1934. V. 64; 65
The Complete Ronald Firbank. London: 1961. V. 67
Concerning the Eccentricities of Cardinal Pirelli. London: 1926. V. 66
Extravaganzas, Containing the Artificial Princess and Concerning the Eccentricities of Cardinal Pirelli. New York: 1935. V. 62; 65
The Flower Beneath the Foot, Being a Record of the Early Life of St. Laura de Nazianzi and the Times in Which She Lived. New York: 1924. V. 63; 65
Odette: a Fairy Tale for Weary People. London: 1916. V. 66
Odette D'Antrevernes and A Study in Temperament. London: 1905. V. 62; 63; 64; 67
Vainglory. New York: 1925. V. 66
Valmouth. London: 1956. V. 65
When Widows Love and A Tragedy in Green - Two Stories. London: 1980. V. 65
The Wind and the Roses. London: 1965. V. 65

FIRDOUSI
The Epic of Kings; Stories Retold from Firdusi.... London: 1882. V. 62
Roostum Zaboolee and Soohrab, from the History of Persia.... Calcutta: 1829. V. 65; 67

FIRISHTAH, MUHAMMAD QASIM HINDU SHAH ASTARABADI
The History of Hindostan, from the Earliest Account of Time to the Death of Akbar. London: 1768. V. 66

FIRMIN, PETER
The Winter Diary of a Country Rat. 1981. V. 67

FIRMINGER, T. A. C.
A Manual of Gardening for Bengal and Upper India. London: 1864. V. 62; 64; 67

FIRST American Artists' Congress 1936. New York: 1936. V. 62

FIRST Anniversary of the Proclamation of Freedom in South Carolina, Held at Beaufort, S.C. January 1, 1864. Beaufort: 1864. V. 66

FIRST EDITION CLUB
Bibliographical Catalogue of First Editions, Proof Copies of Manuscripts of Books by Lord Byron, Exhibited at the Fourth Exhibition Held by the First Edition Club Jan. 1925. London: 1925. V. 67

FIRST Exposition of Conservation and Its Builders. Knoxville: 1914. V. 65

THE FIRST Fleet. The Record of the Foundation of Australia from Its Conception to the Settlement at Sydney Cove. Waltham St. Lawrence: 1937. V. 67

FIRST Over Everest. The Houston-Mount Everest Expedition 1933. London: 1933. V. 63; 64

FIRST Reading Book. Philadelphia: 1835. V. 65

THE FIRST Spanish Entry Into San Francisco Bay, 1775. San Francisco: 1971. V. 63

FIRTH, WILLIAM
Remarks on the Recent State Trials, and the Rise and Progress of Disaffection in the Country.... London: 1818. V. 63

FISCHER & JIROUCH CO.
Catalog of Interior Decorative Ornament. Catalog No. 8. Cleveland. V. 66

FISCHER, AARON
Ted Berrigan: an Anotated Checklist. New York: 1998. V. 67

FISCHER, CARLOS
Les Costumes de l'Opera. Paris: 1931. V. 65

FISCHER, DONALD E.
Security Analysis and Portfolio Management. 1991. V. 64

FISCHER, EUGEN
Die Rehobother Bastards. Jena: 1913. V. 67

FISCHER VON ERLACH, JOHANN BERNHARD
Entwurff Einer Historischen Architektur, in Abbildung.... Leipzig: 1725. V. 64

FISH, DONALD
Airline Detective. London: 1962. V. 65; 66

FISH, HELEN DEAN
Animals of the Bible. London: 1956. V. 66
Butterfly Land.... New York: 1931. V. 65

FISH, ROBERT L.
The Incredible Schlock Homes. New York: 1966. V. 65
Kek Huuygens, Smuggler. New York: 1976. V. 63

FISH, WILLIAM
Betrayed by Bloodhounds, or the Barbarous Barber of Blackburn, Being a True and Graphic Account of His Life and Mysterious Parentage. London: 1885?. V. 63

FISH, WILLIAM A.
A Memoir of Butler Wilmarth, M.D.... New York: 1854. V. 64

FISHER, A. K.
The Hawks and Owls of the United States in Their Relation to Agriculture. Washington: 1893. V. 62; 67

FISHER, A. T.
Outdoor Life in England. 1896. V. 67

FISHER, CHARLES HAWKINS
Reminiscences of a Falconer. London: 1901. V. 62

FISHER, EDWARD
A Christian Caveat to the Old and New Sabbatarians. London: 1655. V. 63
Questions Prepatory to the Better, Free and More Christian Administration of the Lords Supper. London: 1655. V. 63

FISHER, F. H.
Reginald Farrer, Author, Traveller, Botanist and Flower Painter. London: 1932. V. 64

FISHER, HARRISON
Maidens Fair. New York: 1912. V. 63

FISHER, HENRY W.
Abroad with Mark Twain and Eugene Field. New York: 1922. V. 63

FISHER, J.
The Fulmar. London: 1952. V. 65
Sea Birds. 1954. V. 67
Sea Birds. London: 1954. V. 62

FISHER, J. R.
Camping in the Rocky Mountains. New York: 1880. V. 62

FISHER, JIM
Voices from the Rio Grande. Albuquerque: 1978. V. 63; 66

FISHER, JOHN D.
Description of the Distinct Confluent, and Inoculated Small Pox, Varioloid Disease, Cow Pox and Chicken Pox. Boston: 1829. V. 62

FISHER, LALA
Creek and Gully: Stories and Sketches Mostly of Bush Life. London: 1899. V. 65

FISHER, MARY FRANCES KENNEDY
Here Let Us Feast. New York: 1946. V. 65
Spirits of the Valley. New York: 1985. V. 62; 64

FISHER, O. C.
The Texas Heritage of the Fishers and Clarks. Salano: 1963. V. 62; 65

FISHER, ORECENTH
Baptismal Catechism; or a Scriptural View of the Nature, Mode and Subjects of Christian Baptism. Houston: 1849. V. 66

FISHER, OSMOND
Physics of the Earth's Crust. London: 1889. V. 67

FISHER, P.
The Angler's Souvenir. London: 1835. V. 67
The Angler's Souvenir. 1890. V. 67

FISHER, R. A.
The Design of Experiments. Edinburgh and London: 1942. V. 63; 64
A Digest of the Reported English Cases Relating to Patents, Trade Marks and Copyrights. Cincinnati: 1872. V. 66
The Genetical Theory of Natural Selection. Oxford: 1930. V. 67

FISHER, RAYMOND N.
Bering's Voyages. Wither and Why. Seattle and London: 1977. V. 64

FISHER, ROBERT
Flamborough: Village and Headland. Hull: 1894. V. 65

FISHER, ROY
Collected Poems. 1968. London: 1969. V. 63
Cultures. London: 1975. V. 67
The Cut Pages. London: 1971. V. 63

FISHER, RUTH B.
On the Borders of Pigmy Land. London: 1905. V. 65

FISHER, THEODORE WILLIS
Plain Talk About Insanity: Its Causes, Forms, Symptoms and the Treatment of Mental Diseases.... Boston: 1872. V. 65

FISHER, VARDIS
City of Illusion. New York: 1941. V. 66
Gold Rush and Mining Camps of Early American West. Caldwell: 1968. V. 64; 67
In Tragic Life. Caldwell: 1932. V. 66
Passions Spin the Plot. Caldwell and Garden City: 1934. V. 66
We Are Betrayed. Caldwell/Garden City: 1935. V. 66

FISHER, W. H.
The Top of the World. New York and Cincinnati: 1926. V. 65, 67

FISHER, W. K.
Asteroidea of the North Pacific and Adjacent Waters. Washington: 1911-1930. V. 62; 64
Asteroidea of the North Pacific and Adjacent Waters. Parts 2 and 3. 1928-1930. V. 63
Starfishes of the Philippine Seas and Adjacent Waters. Washington: 1919. V. 63; 66

FISHER, WALTER M.
The Californians. London: 1876. V. 62; 65

FISHER, WILLIAM
An Interesting Account of the Voyages and Travels of Captains Lewis and Clark, in the Years 1804, 1805 and 1806, Giving a Faithful Description of the River Missouri and Its Source.... Baltimore: 1812. V. 64

FISHER'S Drawing Room Scrap Book. London: 1831. V. 63; 67
FISHER'S Drawing Room Scrap Book. London: 1833. V. 63; 67
FISHER'S Drawing Room Scrap Book. London: 1834. V. 63; 67
FISHER'S Drawing Room Scrap Book. London: 1836. V. 63; 67
FISHER'S Drawing Room Scrap Book. London: 1837. V. 63; 67
FISHER'S Drawing Room Scrap Book. London: 1843. V. 63; 67
FISHER'S Drawing Room Scrap Book. London: 1845. V. 63; 67
FISHER'S Drawing Room Scrap Book. London: 1846. V. 63; 67
FISHER'S Drawing Room Scrap Book. London: 1847. V. 63; 67
FISHER'S Drawing Room Scrap Book. London: 1848. V. 63; 67

THE FISHES Grand Gala. London: 1808. V. 66

FISHES of the Western North Atlantic. New Haven: 1948-1977. V. 65; 66
FISHES of the Western North Atlantic. New Haven: 1957-1977. V. 63

FISHING MASTERS' ASSOCIATION
Fishermen of the Atlantic Fishing Master's Associaton. Boston: 1932. V. 64

FISHMAN, ALFRED P.
Circulation of the Blood, Men and Ideas. New York: 1964. V. 65

FISHWICK, HENRY
A History of Lancashire. London: 1887. V. 65
The History of the Parish of Bispham in the County of Lancaster. London: 1887. V. 64; 66
The History of the Parish of Kirkham in the County of Lancaster. London: 1874. V. 64; 65; 66
The History of the Parish of Poulton-Le-Fylde, in the Count of Lancaster. London: 1885. V. 64; 65; 66
The History of the Parish of Preston in Amounderness in the County of Lancaster. Rochdale: 1900. V. 62
Lancashire and Cheshire Church Surveys 1649-1655. London: 1879. V. 65
The Lancashire Library. London: 1875. V. 64; 65; 66
The Registers of the Parish Church of Rochdale in the County of Lancaster, from October 1582 to March 1641. Rochdale: 1888-1889. V. 65; 66
Rochdale Jubilee. A Record of Fifty Years Municipal Work 1856 to 1906. Manchester: 1906. V. 63; 65

FISK, JAMES L.
Expedition of Captain Fisk to the Rocky Mountains. Reports of Captain Fisk of His Late Expedition to the Rocky Mountains. Washington: 1864. V. 63

FISKE, D. T.
Faith Working by Love: as Exemplified in the Life of Fidelia Fiske. Boston: 1868. V. 65

FISKE, FRANK B.
Life and Death of Sitting Bull. Fort Yates: 1933. V. 65
The Taming of the Sioux. Bismarck: 1917. V. 67

FISKE, GEORGE
Fiske the Cloudchaser: Twelve Yosemite Photographs by George Fiske. Oakland: 1981. V. 63

FISKE, JOHN
The American Revolution. Boston and New York: 1896. V. 67
The Dutch and Quaker Colonies in America. London: 1899. V. 67
Outlines of Cosmic Philosophy, Based on the Doctrine of Evolution with Criticisms on the Positive Philosophy. London: 1874. V. 66
Tobacco and Alcohol. New York: 1869. V. 66

FITCH, A. J. H., MRS.
Memoir of Lieut. Edward Lewis Mitchell, Who Fell at the Battle of Shiloh, Aged Twenty-Two Years. New York: 1864. V. 62; 63; 65

FITCH, ELIJAH
The Beauties of Religion. Providence: 1789. V. 64

FITCH, GEORGE H.
Great Spiritual Writers of America. San Francisco: 1916. V. 63

FITCH, MICHAEL HENDRICH
Ranch Life and Other Sketches. Pueblo: 1914. V. 63; 66

FITCH, SAMUEL S.
Six Discourses on the Functions of the Lungs; and Causes, Prevention and Cure of Pulmonary Consumption, Asthma and Disease of the Heart.... New York: 1853. V. 67

FITCHEET, LAURA S.
Beverages & Sauces of Colonial Virginia 1607-1907. New York and Washington: 1906. V. 65

FITCHETT, JOHN
King Alfred a Poem. London: 1841-1842. V. 62

FITHIAN, PHILIP VICKERS
Philip Vickers Fithian Journal and Letters 1767-1774. Princeton: 1900. V. 63; 66

FITTLER, JAMES
Cartons (sic) of Raphael D'Urbin. London: 1797. V. 66

FITTON, EDWARD BROWN
New Zealand; Its Present Condition, Prospects, and Resources; Being a Description of the Country Mode of Life Among New Zealand Colonists, for the Information of Intending Emigrants. London: 1856. V. 67

FITTON, W. H.
The Silurian System: from the Edinburgh Review. Edinburgh: 1841. V. 62

FITZ, FRANCES ELLA
Lady Sourdough. New York: 1941. V. 66

FITZ-ADAM, ADAM
The World. London: 1767. V. 66

FITZCLARENCE, GEORGE AUGUSTUS FREDERICK
Journal of a Route Across India; through Egypt to England in the Latter End of the Year 1817 and the Beginning of 1818. London: 1819. V. 67

FITZENMEYER, FRIEDA, PSEUD.
Once Upon a Time. Book One. Easthampton: 1984. V. 66
Once Upon a Time. Book Two. Easthampton: 1985. V. 66

FITZ-GEFFREY, CHARLES
The Life and Death of Sir Francis Drake. Kent: 1819. V. 64; 65

FITZGERALD, D. J. L.
History of the Irish Guards in the Second World War. Aldershot: 1949. V. 64

FITZGERALD, E. A.
Climbs in the New Zealand Alps. London: 1890. V. 64
Climbs in the New Zealand Alps. 1896. V. 63; 65
The Highest Andes. 1899. V. 63; 65
The Highest Andes. London: 1899. V. 63; 64; 66

FITZGERALD, EDWARD
Euphranor. A Dialogue of Youth. London: 1851. V. 62; 63; 66
Euphranor, a Dialogue on Youth. London: 1855. V. 65
A Fitzgerald Friendship - Being Hitherto Unpublished Letters from Edward Fitzgerald to William Bodham Donne. London: 1932. V. 62
A Fitzgerald Friendship. Being Hitherto Unpublished Letters from Edward Fitzgerald to William Bodham Donne.... New York: 1932. V. 67
Letters. London: 1894. V. 65
The Letters. 1980. V. 65
Letters. (with) *More Letters.* London: 1894-1902. V. 62
Letters. (with) *More Letters; Letters...to Fanny Kemble 1871-1883. Some New Letters.* London: 1894-1923. V. 65
The Variorum and Definitive Edition of the Practical and Prose Writings of Edward Fitzgerald. New York: 1967. V. 64; 65
Works. Boston: 1887. V. 65

FITZGERALD, FRANCIS SCOTT KEY
All the Sad Young Men. New York: 1926. V. 62; 63; 65
The Beautiful and the Damned. New York: 1922. V. 66
The Beautiful and the Damned. London: 1950. V. 66
Bits of Paradise - 21 Uncollected Stories. London: 1973. V. 62; 65
F. Scott Fitzgerald's Ledger: a Facsimile. Washington: 1972. V. 65
F. Scott Fitzgerald's Preface to This Side of Paradise. Iowa City: 1975. V. 62; 64
Flappers and Philosophers. New York: 1920. V. 62
The Great Gatsby. New York: 1925. V. 62; 64; 65; 66
The Great Gatsby. London: 1948. V. 66
The Great Gatsby. Washington: 1973. V. 64
The Great Gatsby. N.P: 1980. V. 66
The Letters of F. Scott Fitzgerald. New York: 1963. V. 62
The Letters of F. Scott Fitzgerald. London: 1964. V. 66
The Pat Hobby Stories. New York: 1962. V. 65
The Stories of F. Scott Fitzgerald. New York: 1951. V. 65
Taps at Reveille. New York: 1935. V. 66
Tender is the Night. New York: 1934. V. 62; 63
Tender is the Night. London: 1953. V. 63; 65
Tender is the Night. New York: 1982. V. 66
The Vegetable, or From President to Postman. New York: 1923. V. 62; 65

FITZGERALD, PENELOPE
Human Voices. London: 1980. V. 63; 67

FITZGERALD, PERCY
Croker's Boswell and Boswell - Studies in the Life of Johnson. London: 1880. V. 65
The Garrick Club. London: 1904. V. 65
The Kembles. London: 1871. V. 67
The Life of Lawrence Sterne. London: 1864. V. 67
The Life of Mrs. Catherine Clive. London: 1888. V. 63
Mildrington the Barrister. London: 1863. V. 66

FITZGERALD, S. H. ADAIR
Dickens and the Drama. London: 1910. V. 62

FITZGERALD, THOMAS W. H.
A Popular History of Ireland. Chicago: 1910. V. 67

FITZGERALD, WILLIAM WALTER AUGUSTINE
Travels in the Coastlands of British East Africa and the Islands of Zanzibar and Pemba.... London: 1898. V. 62

FITZGERALD, ZELDA
Save Me the Waltz. New York: 1932. V. 67

FITZHERBERT, ANTHONY
The New Natura Brevium of the Most Reverend Judge, Mr. Anthony Fitz-Herbert.... London: 1687. V. 65
La Novel Natura Brevium.... London: 1635. V. 65

FITZHUGH, GEORGE
Cannibals All! Or, Slaves Without Masters. Richmond: 1857. V. 62; 64

FITZMAURICE, EDMOND
The Life of Granville George Leveson Gower, Second Earl Granville (1815-1891). New York: 1905. V. 67

FITZPATRICK, HUGH
A Report of the Trial of Mr. Hugh Fitzpatrick for a Libel Upon...The Duke of Richmond, Lord Lieutenant of Ireland, Plaintiff and Charles Kerr, Defendant.... London: 1819. V. 63

FITZPATRICK, J. P.
The Transvaal from Within. London: 1899. V. 67

FITZPATRICK, T. J.
Rafinesque, a Sketch of His Life with Bibliography. Des Moines: 1911. V. 64; 66

FITZPATRICK, W. J.
The Sham Squire and The Informers of 1798. Dublin: 1872. V. 67

FITZPATRICK, WILLIAM JOHN
Lady Morgan: Her Career Literary and Personal. London: 1860. V. 63
The Life of Charles Lever. London: 1879. V. 65
The Life of Charles Lever. London: 1884. V. 67

FITZROY, A. T.
Despised and Rejected. London: 1918. V. 67

FITZSIMMONS, CORTLAND
The Evil Men Do. New York: 1941. V. 67

FITZSIMONS, F. W.
The Monkey Folk of South Africa. 1911. V. 63; 66
The Monkey Folk of South Africa. London: 1911. V. 62; 67
The Natural History of South Africa - Mammals. London: 1919. V. 66
Snakes. 1932. V. 64; 66
The Snakes of South Africa.... Cape Town: 1919. V. 62

FITZSIMONS, V. F. M.
Fitzsimons' Snakes of Southern Africa. Johannesburg: 1983. V. 66
The Lizards of South Africa. Pretoria: 1943. V. 62
Snakes of Southern Africa. 1962. V. 63; 66
Snakes of Southern Africa. Cape Town: 1962. V. 64
Snakes of Southern Africa. London: 1962. V. 62

FITZSTEPHEN, WILLIAM
Fitz-Stephen's Description of the City of London, Newly Translated from the Latin Original.... London: 1772. V. 65

FITZWILLIAM MUSEUM
Cockerel Bindings 1894-1980, an Exhibition of Bindings and Conservation of Manuscripts and Printed Books. Cambridge: 1981. V. 63

FIVE *Cummington Poems. 1939.* Northampton: 1939. V. 67

FIVE *Hundred Curious and Interesting Narratives and Anecdotes; Comprising the Wonderful Book, the Anecdote Book, Sailors' Yarns, Salmagundi, and the Domestic Manners of the Americans.* Glasgow: 1844. V. 62

FIVE *Poets of the Pacific Northwest. Kenneth O. Hanson, Richard Hugo, Carolyn Kizer, William Stafford, David Wagoner.* Seattle: 1964. V. 63

FIVE *Points in the Record of North Carolina in the Great War of 1861-1865.* Goldsboro: 1904. V. 63; 65

FIXLMILLNER, PLACIDUS
Meridianus Speculae Astronomicae Cremifanensis seu Longitudo eius Geographica.... 1765. V. 62

FLACK, MARJORIE
The Tadpole and the Great Bullfrog. Garden City: 1934. V. 64; 66

FLACK, PETER
Heart of an African Hunter. 2000. V. 67

FLADER, LOUIS
Achievement in Photo-Engraving and Letter-Press Printing. Chicago: 1927. V. 62; 63

FLAGG, EDMUND T.
The Far West: or a Tour Beyond the Mountains, Embracing Outlines of Western Life and Scenery. New York: 1838. V. 63

FLAGG, FANNIE
Coming Attractions. New York: 1981. V. 64; 66
Fried Green Tomatoes at the Whistle Stop Cafe. New York: 1987. V. 63; 66

FLAGG, OSCAR H.
A Review of the Cattle Business in Johnson County Wyoming Since 1882 and the Causes that Led to the Recent Invasion. Cheyenne: 1967. V. 64; 67

FLAGG, WILLIAM J.
Three Seasons in European Vineyards. New York: 1869. V. 64

FLAMEN, ALBERT
Poissons Diverses Especies de Poissons de Mer (...de Poissons d'eau douce). Paris: 1664. V. 67

FLAMMARION, CAMILLE
Les Etoiles et les Curiosites du Ciel.... Paris: 1882. V. 67
Les Merveilles Celestes; Lectures Du Soir. Paris: 1897. V. 67
Les Terres Du Ciel; Description Astronomique, Physique, Climatologique, Geographique des Planetes Qui Gravitent Avec la Terre.... Paris: 1877. V. 67

FLAMMENBERG, LAWRENCE
The Necromancer; or the Tale of the Black Forest. London: 1927. V. 63

FLAMMER, GORDON H.
Stories of a Mormon Pioneering Community Linden, Arizona Mission 1878-1945. Provo: 1995. V. 67

FLAMSTEED, JOHN
A Letter Concerning Earthquakes, Written in the Year 1693.... London: 1750. V. 62

FLANAGAN, BUD
My Crazy Life - the Autobiography. London: 1961. V. 64

FLANDERS, HELEN HARTNESS
Looking Out of Jimmie. New York: 1927. V. 65

FLANDERS, HENRY
The Life of John Marshall. Philadelphia: 1905. V. 67

FLANIGAN, J. H.
Mormonism Triumphant! Truth Vindicated, Lies Refuted. The Devil Mad, and Priest Craft in Danger !!!. Being a Reply to Palmer's Internal Evidence Against the Book of Mormon. Liverpool: 1849. V. 65

FLANNER, JANET
Men and Monuments. New York: 1957. V. 62; 64

THE FLATEY Book and Recently Discovered Vatican Manuscripts Concerning America as Early as the Tenth Century. London: 1906. V. 63

FLAUBERT, GUSTAVE
Bouvard and Pechuchet. London: 1936. V. 65
Un Coeur Simple. 1901. V. 62; 63; 67
The Complete Works. London. V. 66
The Complete Works. London: 1926. V. 67
La Legende de Saint Julien L'Hospitalier. 1900. V. 62; 67
Madame Bovary. Paris: 1857. V. 62; 65; 66; 67
Madame Bovary. London: 1886. V. 67
Madame Bovary. London: 1904. V. 66
Madame Bovary. London: 1928. V. 62
Salambo. Paris: 1863. V. 65
Salambo. Waltham St. Lawrence: 1931. V. 62; 65
Salambo. 1960. V. 62
Salamammbo. New York: 1960. V. 63
Salammbo. Westminster. V. 64
Salammbo. London and New York: 1886. V. 66
A Simple Heart. Paris: 1895. V. 62
The Temptation of St. Anthony. London: 1895. V. 67

FLAVEL, JOHN
Husbandry Spiritualiz'd; or, the Heavenly Use of Earthly Things. London: 1714. V. 64

FLAXMAN, JOHN
Anatomical Studies of the Bones and Muscles for the Use of Artists from Drawings. London: 1833. V. 64
Eight Illustrations of the Lord's Prayer, from the Designs of the Late..., Drawn on Stone by Richard Lane.... London: 1835. V. 66
J. Flaxmani Picturae Lineares ad Homeri Iliadem. Lipsiae: 1804. V. 66
Lectures on Sculpture, as Delivered Before the President and Members of the Royal Academy. London: 1838. V. 62

FLAYDERMAN, NORMAN
Illustrated Catalogue of Arms and Military Goods Containing Regulations for the Uniform of the Army, Navy, Marine and Revenue Corps of the United States. New York: 1961. V. 66

FLECKENSTEIN, HENRY A.
Shore Bird Decoys. Pennsylvania: 1980. V. 67

FLECKER, JAMES ELROY
The Bridge of Fire - Poems. London: 1907. V. 62; 63; 65; 66
Forty-Two Poems. London: 1911. V. 62
The Last Generation: a Story of the Future. London: 1908. V. 63; 64; 66
The Letters of J. E. Flecker to Frank Savery. London: 1926. V. 62; 64
The Letters of J. E. Flecker to Frank Savery. Westminster: 1926. V. 63

FLEET, DOROTHY
Our Flight to Destiny. New York: 1964. V. 66

FLEETWOOD, WILLIAM
Chronicum Preciosum; or, an Account of English Money, the Price of Corn and Other Commodities; and of Stipends, Salaries, Wages, Jointures, Portions, Day-Labour &c. in England, for Six Hundred Years Last Past... London: 1745. V. 65
An Essay Upon Miracles. London: 1701. V. 66
The Relative Duties of Parents and Children, Husbands and Wives, Masters and Servants.... London: 1716. V. 65

FLEISCHMAN, SIS
The Whipping Boy. New York: 1986. V. 65

FLEITMANN, L. L.
The Horse in Art from Primitive Times to the Present. London: 1931. V. 66

FLEMING, A. B., & CO. LTD.
Specimens of High-Class Chromo-Litho and Poster Printing Inks. Edinburgh and London. V. 64

FLEMING, ALEXANDER
Penicillin: Its Practical Application. London: 1946. V. 63; 64

FLEMING, DAVID HAY
St. Andrews Cathedral Museum. 1931. V. 67
St. Andrews Cathedral Museum. London: 1931. V. 62

FLEMING, FRANCIS PATRICK
Kaffraria, and Its Inhabitants. London: 1853. V. 62

FLEMING, FRANCIS PHILLIP
Memoir of Capt. C. Seton Fleming, of the Second Florida Infantry, C. S.A. Jacksonville: 1884. V. 62; 63; 65

FLEMING, G.
Practical Horseshoeing. New York: 1872. V. 64

FLEMING, GEORGE, PSEUD.
Vestigia. London: 1884. V. 65

FLEMING, IAN LANCASTER
Casino Royale. London: 1953. V. 62; 67
Casino Royale. London: 1960. V. 65
The Diamond Smugglers. London: 1957. V. 66
Diamonds are Forever. London: 1956. V. 62
Dr. No. London: 1958. V. 66
For Your Eyes Only. London: 1960. V. 63; 64
From Russia with Love. London: 1957. V. 63
Goldfinger. New York: 1959. V. 63
Ian Fleming Introduces Jamaica. 1965. V. 63
Ian Fleming Introduces Jamaica. London: 1965. V. 65; 66
The Man With the Golden Gun. London: 1965. V. 63; 64; 65
The Man with the Golden Gun. New York: 1965. V. 65; 66
On Her Majesty's Secret Service. London: 1963. V. 63; 66
The Spy Who Loved Me. London: 1962. V. 62; 63; 66
Thrilling Cities. London: 1963. V. 64; 66
Thunderball. London: 1961. V. 62; 63; 65; 66
You Only Live Twice. London: 1964. V. 63; 64; 65; 66; 67

FLEMING, LINDSAY
History of Pagham in Sussex. 1949. V. 62

FLEMING, PATRICIA LOCKHART
Atlantic Canadian Imprints 1801-1820: a Bibliography. Toronto: 1991. V. 67

FLEMING, PAULA RICHARDSON
The North American Indians in Early Photographs. New York: 1986. V. 63

FLEMING, PETER
News from Tartary; a Journey from Peking to Kashmir. London: 1936. V. 65

FLEMING, SANDFORD
Report and Documents in Reference to the Canadian Pacific Railway. Ottawa: 1880. V. 65

FLEMING, VIVIAN MINOR
Campaigns of the Army of Northern Virginia Including the Jackson Valley Campaign 1861-1865. Richmond: 1928. V. 62; 63; 65

FLEMING, WALTER L.
Documentary History of Reconstruction. Cleveland: 1906. V. 63; 65
General W. T. Sherman as College President. Cleveland: 1912. V. 63; 65

FLEMMING, ERNST
Encyclopaedia of Textiles. London: 1958. V. 62

FLEROV, K. K.
Fauna of the U.S.S.R. Musk and Deer. 1960. V. 63; 64; 66; 67

FLETCHER, ALEXANDER
An Appeal to Public Opinion Against the Decision of the Associate Synod of Scotland, Arising Out of a Case Brought into the Court of King's Bench...(with) Trial of Rev. Alexander Fletcher. London: 1824-1825. V. 63
Trial of the Rev. Alexander Fletcher, A.M. Before the Lord Chief Justice of the Court of Common Sense.... London: 1825. V. 63

FLETCHER, ANDREW
An Account of a Conversation Concerning a Right Regulation of Governments for the Common Good of Mankind. Edinburgh: 1704. V. 62
A Speech Upon the State of the Nation. N.P: 1701. V. 62; 65

FLETCHER, BANISTER
A History of Architecture. London: 1975. V. 62

FLETCHER, C. R. L.
Historical Portraits 1400-1850. Oxford: 1909-1919. V. 66
An Introductory History of England from the Earliest Times to the Close of the Middle Ages. London: 1910. V. 62

FLETCHER, DANIEL C.
Reminiscences of California and the Civil War. Ayer: 1894. V. 63; 66

FLETCHER, ELLEN GORDON
A Bride on the Bozeman Trail - the Letters and Diary of Ellen Gordon Fletcher 1866. Medford: 1970. V. 64; 67

FLETCHER, F. A.
In the Days of the Tall Ships. London: 1928. V. 63

FLETCHER, F. N.
Early Nevada - the Period of Exploration 1776-1848. Reno: 1929. V. 62; 65

FLETCHER, H. R.
The Royal Botanic Garden Edinburgh 1670-1970. Edinburgh: 1970. V. 64; 67
The Story of the Royal Horticultural Society 1804-1968. London: 1969. V. 64; 67

FLETCHER, J. S.
Cobweb Castle. New York: 1928. V. 63
History of the St. Leger Stakes 1776-1926. London: 1927. V. 67
Memorials of a Yorkshire Parish. London: 1917. V. 65

FLETCHER, J. S. continued
Picturesque History of Yorkshire. London. V. 66
Safe Number Sixty-Nine. Boston: 1931. V. 65

FLETCHER, JOHN
Bible Arminianism & Bible Calvinism.... London: 1777. V. 64
Demetrius and Enanthe, Being the Humorous Lieutenant, a Play. London: 1830. V. 67
The Doctrines of Grace and Justice Equally Essential to the Pure Gospel.... London: 1777. V. 64
A Dreadful Phenomenon Described and Improved.... Bristol: 1774. V. 64
A Race for Eternal Life.... London: 1795. V. 64
A Vindication of the Rev. Mr. Wesley's Calm Address to the American Colonies. London: 1776. V. 64
A Vindication of the Rev. Mr. Wesley's Last Minutes: Occasioned by a Circular, Printed Letter, Inviting the Principal Persons, Both Clergy and Laity, as Well of the Dissenters as of the Established Church.... Bristol: 1771. V. 64

FLETCHER, JOHN GOULD
Fire and Wine. London: 1913. V. 63; 67

FLETCHER, JOSEPH SMITH
Where Highways Cross. London: 1895. V. 67

FLETCHER, RICHARD HOWE
Marjorie and Her Papa-How They Wrote a Story and Made Pictures. New York: 1891. V. 64

FLETCHER, ROBERT H.
Free Grass to Fences - The Montana Cattle Range Story. Helena and New York: 1960. V. 63; 64; 66; 67

FLETCHER, SAMUEL
Emblematical Devices with Appropriate Mottos. London: 1810. V. 66

FLETCHER, T. BAINBRIGGE
Some South Indian Insects and Other Animals of Importance.... Madras: 1914. V. 63; 66

FLETCHER, THOMAS
Arithmetick Made So Easy, That It May Be Learned Without a Master.... London: 1740. V. 65

FLETCHER, VALENTINE
Chimney Pots and Stacks. London: 1968. V. 64

FLETCHER, WILLIAM ANDREW
Rebel Private Front and Rear. Beaumont: 1908. V. 62; 63
Rebel Private Front and Rear. Austin: 1954. V. 65

FLETCHER, WILLIAM YOUNGER
Bookbinding in England and France. London: 1897. V. 62; 64
Bookbinding in France. London: 1894. V. 62; 63; 64; 66
Some Minor Arts as Practised in England.... London: 1894. V. 64

FLEURIEU, CHARLES PIERRE CLARET, COMTE DE
A Voyage Round the World, Performed During the Years 1790, 1791, and 1792. London: 1801. V. 66

THE FLEURON. London: 1923. V. 64

THE FLEURON. London, Cambridge: 1923-1930. V. 63

FLEURON.. 1925. V. 65
FLEURON. Cambridge: 1926. V. 65
FLEURON. Cambridge: 1928. V. 65

THE FLEURON. 1930. V. 63

FLEURON.. Cambridge: 1930. V. 65

FLEURON Anthology. London: 1973. V. 62

FLEURY, CLAUDE
The History, Choice and Method of Studies. London: 1695. V. 63; 67

FLEURY, PAUL
La Peinture en Equipages. Paris: 1893. V. 66

FLEXNER, ABRAHAM
Medical Education in the United States and Canada. A Report to the Carnegie Foundation for the Advancement of Teaching. Washington: 1960. V. 65

FLEXNER, J. T.
19th Century American Painting. New York: 1970. V. 65

FLICKINGER, ROBERT E.
The Choctaw Freedman and the Story of Oak Hill Industrial Academy. Pittsburg: 1914. V. 64

FLINDERS, MATTHEW
Narrative of His Voyage in the Schooner Francis: 1798. Waltham St. Lawrence: 1946. V. 62; 67
A Voyage to Terra Australis: Undertaken for the Purpose of Completing the Discovery of that Vast Country.... Adelaide: 1966. V. 67

FLINN, ANDREW
A Funeral Discourse Commemorative of the Rev. Isaac's Keith, D.D. Charleston: 1814. V. 63

FLINT, AUSTIN
A Practical Treatise on the Diagnosis, Pathology and Treatment of the Diseases of the Heart. Philadelphia: 1859. V. 66
A Treatise on the Principles and Practice of Medicine. Phiadlephia: 1886. V. 67

FLINT, CHARLES L.
Eighty Years Progress of the United States: a family record of American Industry, Energy and Enterprise. Hartford: 1869. V. 67
Milch Cows and Dairy Farming. Philadelphia: 1858. V. 64

FLINT, F. S.
Economic Equilibrium. London: 1940. V. 63
In the Net of the Stars. London: 1909. V. 63

FLINT, H. L.
Landscape Plants for Eastern North America Exclusive of Florida and the Immediate Gulf Coast. New York: 1983. V. 67

FLINT, THOMAS
Diary of Dr. Thomas Flint, California to Maine and Return 1851-1855. N.P: 1923. V. 66

FLINT, TIMOTHY
Biographical Memoir of Daniel Boone, the First Settler of Kentucky. Cincinnati: 1833. V. 63; 66
Francis Berrian or the Mexican Patriot. Boston: 1826. V. 65

FLINT, V. E.
A Field Guide to Birds of the USSR Including Eastern Europe and Central Asia. Princeton: 1984. V. 64

FLINT, WILLIAM RUSSELL
The Lisping Goddess. London: 1968. V. 62
The Lisping Goddess. Worcester: 1968. V. 62; 66
Minxes Admonished or Beauty Reproved. Waltham St. Lawrence: 1955. V. 62
Models of Propriety - Occasional Caprices for the Edification of Ladies and the Delight of Gentlemen. London: 1951. V. 62
Shadows in Arcady: The Angelus: The Brass Plate; An Alley in Languedoc; The Devil at La Charite. London: 1965. V. 62; 63; 64; 66

FLOCKHART, LOLITA L. W.
Art and Artists in New Jersey. Somerville: 1938. V. 63

FLOIRE ET JEANNE
Florus, King of Ausay. The Tale of King Florus and Fair Jehane. Hammersmith: 1893. V. 67
The Tale of King Florus and the Fair Jehane. 1893. V. 66

FLOOD, W. H. GRATTAN
Early Tudor Composers: Biographical Sketches of 32 Musicians 1485- 1555. Oxford: 1925. V. 64
The Story of the Bagpipe. London: 1911. V. 67

FLORA Europaea. Cambridge: 1964. V. 64

FLORA of China. Volume 18. Scrophulariaceae through Gesneriaceae. St. Louis: 1998. V. 67

FLORA of Tropical East Africa. London: 1952-1961. V. 64

FLORAL Cabinet and Magazine of Exotic Botany. 1837-1840. V. 65
FLORAL Cabinet and Magazine of Exotic Botany. London: 1837-1840. V. 66

THE FLORAL Offering. London: 1870. V. 66

FLORIAN, JEAN PIERRE CLARIS DE
Galatee, Roman Pastoral: Imite de Cervantes. Paris: 1793. V. 63; 66

FLORIDA, a Land Of Homes. Tallahassee: 1930?. V. 63

THE FLORIDA Pirate, or, an Account of a Cruise in the Schooner Esparanza! With a Sketch of the Life of Her Commander. New York: 1823. V. 64

FLORIO, JOHN
A Worlde of Wordes, or Most Copious and Exact Dictionarie in Italian and English. London: 1598. V. 65

FLORIS, JACOB
Compertimenta Pictoriis Flosculis Manubiisque Bellicis Variegata. Paris: 1660. V. 64

FLORIS, PETER
His Voyage to the East Indies in the "Globe" 1611-1615. London: 1934. V. 67

FLORUS, LUCIUS ANNAEUS
L. A. Florus Cum Notis Integris C. L. Salamsi Et Selectissimus Variorum Accurante S. M. D. C. Attitus Etiam L. Ampelius. Amstelodami: 1660. V. 65; 66
(Opera). Amstelodami: 1664. V. 65
Rerum Romanorum Epitome. Paris: 1674. V. 67

FLORY, S. P.
Fragments of Family History. London: 1896. V. 66

FLOURENS, MARIE JEAN PIERRE
Cours de Physiologie Comparee. Paris: 1856. V. 63
Histoire des Travaux et des Idees de Buffon. Paris: 1850. V. 64; 67

FLOWER, MARGARET
Victorian Jewellery. 1951. V. 67

FLOWER, ROBIN
Loves Bitter Sweet. 1925. V. 63; 66
Poems and Translations. 1931. V. 67

FLOWER, W. H.
Essays on Museums and Other Subjects Connected with Natural History. London: 1898. V. 64
An Introduction to the Study of Mammals, Living and Extinct. 1891. V. 63
An Introduction to the Study of Mammals Living and Extinct. London: 1891. V. 65; 66
The Native Races of the Pacific Ocean. London: 1878. V. 67

FLOWER, W. H. continued
Recent Memoirs on the Cetacea. London: 1866. V. 66

THE FLOWERING Plants of Africa. Pretoria and Ashford: 1977-. V. 67

THE FLOWERS and Gardens of Madeira. London: 1909. V. 63

FLOWERS for a Juvenile Garland. New Haven: 1840. V. 65

FLOWERS from Many Lands: a Christian Companion for Hours of Recreation. London: Sep. 1860. V. 62

THE FLOWERS of Autumn. Philadelphia: 1828. V. 66

FLOYD, JOHN
The Church Conquerant Over Humane Wit. (with) *The Totall Summe.* St. Omer: 1638-1639. V. 66

FLOYER, JOHN
Medicina Gerocomica; or the Galenic Art of Preserving Old Men's Health, Explain'd: in Twenty Chapters. London: 1724. V. 63; 67
Psychroloysia (Greek); or the History of Cold Bathing Both Ancient and Modern.... London: 1722. V. 62

FLYNN, ERROL
Showdown. London: 1952. V. 63

FLYNN, HENRY E.
A Glance at the Question of a Ship Canal Connected the Assylum Harbour at Kingstown with the River Anna Liffey at Dublin &c. Dublin: 1834. V. 63

FLYNN, VINCE
Term Limits. 1997. V. 65

FOA, E.
After Big Game in Central Africa. 1987. V. 62; 64

FOA, EUGENIE
Contes a ma Soeur Leonie. Heures de Recreation. Paris: 1825. V. 63

FOCHER, JUAN
Itinerarium Catholicum Profiscentium, ad Infideles Convertendos.... Seville: 1574. V. 62

FOCK, N.
Waiwai. Religion and Society of an Amazonian Tribe. Copenhagen: 1963. V. 62

FOCK, V.
The Theory of Space, Time and Graviation. New York: 1964. V. 65

FOCKE, WILHELM OLBERS
Die Pflanzen-Mischlinge Ein Beitrag Zur Biologie der Gewachse. Berlin: 1881. V. 65

FODEN, PETER
The Fell Imperial Quarto Book of Common Prayer. London: 1998. V. 66
The Fell Imperial Quarto Book of Common Prayer. Risbury: 1998. V. 64

FODERE, FRANCOIS EMMANUEL
Traite du Goitre et du Cretinisme.... Paris: 1800. V. 65

FOELIX, R. F.
Biology of Spiders. Cambridge: 1982. V. 67

FOERSTER, R. E.
The Sockeye Salmon, Oncorhynchus Nerka. Ottawa: 1968. V. 65

FOES, ANUCE
Oeconomia Hippocratis, Alphabeti Serie Distincta. Frankfurt: 1588. V. 66

FOGARTY, KATE HAMMOND
The Story of Montana. New York: 1916. V. 64

FOGAZZARO, ANTONIO
Eden Anto. San Francisco: 1930. V. 64

FOGEL, EDWIN M.
Beliefs and Superstitions of the Pennsylvania Germans. Philadelphia: 1915. V. 64

FOGERTY, JOSEPH
Mr. Jocko. London: 1891. V. 66

FOGHT, H. W.
The Trail of the Loup Being a History of the Loup River Region with Some Chapters on the State. 1976. V. 64

FOGLIETTA, UBERTO
Ex Universa Historia Rerum Europae Temporum Suorum. Coniuratio Ioannes Ludovici Flisci. Neapoli: 1571. V. 66

FOHMANN, VINCENZ
Das Saugadersystem der Wirbelthiere...Erstes heft. Das Saugadersystem der Fische. Heidelberg & Leipzig: 1827. V. 65

FOLENGO, TEOFILO
Opus Merlini Cocaii Poetae Mantuani Macaronicorum. Venetiis: 1581. V. 66
Opus Merlini Cocaii Poetae Mantuani Macaronicorum. Amsterdam: 1692. V. 62; 65

FOLEY, DANIEL
An English Irish Dictionary. 1855. V. 63; 66

FOLEY, ROBERT
Laws Relating to the Poor, from the Forty-Third of Queen Elizabeth to the Third of King George II. London: 1739. V. 63

FOLEY, THOMAS PHILIP
The Answer of the Rev. Thomas P. Foley, to the World, Who Hath Blamed His Faith in Believing It Was A Command from the Lord to Put in Print Such Parables.... Stourbridge: 1805. V. 63

FOLIO SOCIETY
Folio 21. A Bibliography of the Folio Society 1947-1967. (with) *Folio 1968-1971.* London: 1968-1972. V. 67

FOLKARD, ARTHUR CROUCH
A Monograph of the Family of Folkard of Suffolk. London: 1892-1897. V. 66

FOLKARD, H. C.
The Wildfowler. 1864. V. 62; 63

FOLKARD, HENRY COLEMAN
The Sailing Boat. London: 1863. V. 64; 66
The Sailing Boat. London: 1906. V. 62

FOLKARD, R.
Plant Lore, Legends and Lyrics. London: 1884. V. 62

FOLLEN, E. L., MRS.
Anti-Slavery Tracts. No. 8. To Mothers in the Free States. New York: 1855. V. 63

FOLLETT, KEN
The Bear Raid. London: 1976. V. 66; 67
The Gentlemen of 16 July. New York: 1978. V. 66
Lie Down with Lions. London: 1985. V. 67
The Man from St. Petersburg. London: 1982. V. 67
On Wings of Eagles. New York: 1983. V. 66; 67
The Shakeout. Lewes and London: 1975. V. 62
Triple. London: 1979. V. 66; 67

FOLLEY, W. W.
Romantic Wcyoller. A Haunt of the Brontes. Lancashire: 1949. V. 63

FOLMSBEE, STANLEY J.
Sectionalism and Internal Improvements in Tennessee 1796-1845. Knoxville: 1939. V. 67

FOLSOM, CHARLES FOLLEN
Mental Diseases. Boston?: 1886. V. 65

FOLSOM, GEORGE
The Dispatches of Hernando Cortes. New York: 1843. V. 65

FOLSOM, JOSEPH FULFORD
The Municipalities of Essex County, New Jersey 1666-1924. New York: 1925. V. 63; 66

FOLSOM, MONTGOMERY
Scraps of Song and Southern Scenes. Atlanta: 1889. V. 63

FOLWELL, WILLIAM M.
A History of Minnesota. St. Paul: 1921. V. 63; 66

FONBLANQUE, ALBANY
England Under Seven Administrations. London: 1837. V. 64

FONCECA, SIMON
Sketches in India, Chiefly from Nature. Madras: 1851-. V. 64

FONSECA, CHRISTOVAL DE
Devout Contemplations Expressed in Two and Fortie Sermons Upon All ye Quadragesimall Gospells Written in Spanish.... London: 1629. V. 64

FONSECA, JOSE NICOLAU DA
An Historical and Archaeological Sketch of the City of Goa. Bombay: 1878. V. 67

FONTAINE, JAMES
Memoirs of a Huguenot Family. New York: 1853. V. 67

FONTAINE, JOAN
No Bed of Roses. London: 1978. V. 65

FONTAINE, LAMAR
My Life and Lectures. New York: 1908. V. 62; 63; 65

FONTANA, BERNARD L.
Tarahumara; Where Night is the Day of the Moon. Flagstaff: 1979. V. 67

FONTANA, CARLO
Il Tempio Vaticano e Sua Origine, con Gli Edifitii Piu Cospicui Antichi e Moderni Fatti Dentro e Fuori di Esso.... Rome: 1694. V. 64

FONTANA, DOMENICO
Della Transportatione dell'Obelisco Vaticano et delle Fabriche di Nostro Signore Papa Sisto. V. Fatte dal Cavallier Domenico Fontana.... Naples: 1604. V. 62; 63

FONTANA, MARIANO
Della Dinamica Libri Tre. Pavia: 1790-1795. V. 65

FONTANES, LOUIS
Eloge Funebre de Washington: Prononce dans la Temple de Mars, le 20 Pluviose an 8. Paris: 1800. V. 65

FONTANIEU, PIERRE ELISABETH DE
Collection de Vases... Cette Collection a ete Faite Pour Servir aux Tourneurs a Ceux Qui Ornent les Vases, Comme Fondeurs et Ciseleurs. Paris: 1770. V. 64

FONTENELLE, BERNARD
Dialogues of Fontenelle. London: 1917. V. 64

FONTENELLE, BERNARD LE BOVIER DE
Conversations on the Plurality of Worlds. London: 1715. V. 62; 66
Elements de la Geometrie de l'Infini. Paris: 1727. V. 65
The History of the Oracles and the Cheats of the Pagan Priests. London: 1688. V. 63; 65
A Plurality of Worlds. London: 1929. V. 63; 65; 66
A Week's Conversation on the Plurality of Worlds. London: 1737. V. 63; 66

FONTEYN, MARGOT
Margot Fonteyn, an Autobiography. London: 1975. V. 67

FOOT, JOSEPH I.
An Historical Discourse, Delivered at West Brookfield, Mass., Nov. 27, 1828, on the Day of the Annual Thanksgiving. West Brookfield: 1843. V. 67

FOOT, MICHAEL
The Pen and the Sword. London: 1957. V. 65

FOOT, MIRJAM M.
The Henry Davis Gift: a Collection of Bookbindings.... London: 1978-1982. V. 62
Studies in the History of Bookbinding. Aldershot: 1993. V. 62
Studies in the History of Bookbinding. London: 1993. V. 64

FOOTE, ALEXANDER
Handbook for Spies. London: 1949. V. 63

FOOTE, ANDREW H.
Africa and the American Flag. New York: 1862. V. 67
The African Squadron: Ashburton Treaty: Consular Sea Letters Reviewed in an Address. Philadelphia: 1855. V. 64

FOOTE, HORTON
The Chase. New York and Toronto: 1956. V. 67
Harrison, Texas. New York: 1956. V. 64
The Young Man from Atlanta. New York: 1995. V. 66

FOOTE, JOHN
The Practioner's Pharmacopoeia and Universal Formulary.... New York: 1855. V. 65

FOOTE, MARY HALLOCK
The Led-Horse Claim. A Romance of a Mining Camp. Boston and New York: 1911?. V. 63

FOOTE, R. B.
The Geology of Baroda State. Madras: 1898. V. 62

FOOTE, SAMUEL
Bon Mots. London: 1894. V. 63
The Dramatic Works, To Which is Prefixed a Life of the Author. London: 1781-1795. V. 65

FOOTE, SHELBY
The Civil War: a Narrative (Red River to Appomattox). New York: 1974. V. 63; 67
Follow Me Down. New York: 1950. V. 65
Live in a Dry Season. New York: 1951. V. 65
Shiloh. New York: 1952. V. 65
Tournament. New York: 1949. V. 65

FOOTMAN, HENRY
Aspects and Retrospects, a Clergyman's Letter to His Sons. Lincoln: 1897. V. 65

FOOTNER, HULBERT
Dead Man's Hat. New York: 1932. V. 65

FOR *James Merrill: a Birthday Tribute.* New York: 1986. V. 67

FOR *Reynolds Price. 1 February 1983.* Winston-Salem: 1983. V. 62; 64; 67

FOR W. H. *Auden. February 21, 1972.* New York: 1972. V. 66

FORAKER, JOSEPH B.
Notes of a Busy Life. Cincinnati: 1916. V. 65

FORAN, R.
A Breath of the Wilds. 1958. V. 66; 67

FORAN, W. ROBERT
A Cuckoo in Kenya: the Reminiscenes of a Pioneer Police Officer in British East Africa. London: 1936. V. 67

FORBERG, FREDERICK CHARLES
Manual of Classical Erotology. Manchester: 1884. V. 64

FORBES, ALEXANDER
California: a History of Upper and Lower California. San Francisco: 1937. V. 62; 63

FORBES, B. C.
Automotive Giants of America. New York: 1926. V. 63

FORBES, BRYAN
International Velvet. London: 1978. V. 67

FORBES, DAVID CARL
Catch a Big Fish. 1967. V. 67

FORBES, DUNCAN
Some Considerations on the Present State in Scotland; in a Letter to the Commissioners and Trustees for Improving Fisheries and Manufactures. Edinburgh: 1744. V. 65

FORBES, E.
A History of British Mollusca and Their Shells. 1848-1853. V. 63
A History of British Mollusca and Their Shells. London: 1848-1853. V. 62
A History of British Mollusca and Their Shells. London: 1853. V. 62
A History of British Starfishes and Other Animals of the Class Echinodermata. London: 1841. V. 67
A Monograph of the British Naked-Eyed Medusae.... London: 1848. V. 66

FORBES, ESTHER
Johnny Tremain-A Novel for Old and Young. Boston: 1943. V. 66
A Mirror of Witches. 1928. V. 67

FORBES, F. E.
Five Years in China, from 1842 to 1847. London: 1848. V. 62; 63

FORBES, FRANCIS
The Improvement of Waste Lands, viz. Wet, Moory Land, Land Near Rivers and Running Waters, Peat Land and Propagating Oak and Other Timber.... London: 1778. V. 63

FORBES, FREDERICK E.
Dahomey and the Dahomans: Being the Journals of Two Missions of the King of Dahomey and Resistance at His Capital in the Years 1849 and 1850. London: 1851. V. 64

FORBES, GEORGE
David Gill, Man and Astronomer.... London: 1916. V. 67

FORBES, GORDON S.
Wild Life in Canara and Ganjam. London: 1885. V. 67

FORBES, H. O.
A Hand-Book to the Primates. 1896. V. 64; 67
A Hand-Book to the Primates. London: 1986. V. 65
A Naturalist's Wanderings in the Eastern Archipelago. London: 1885. V. 66
Naturalist's Wanderings in the Eastern Archipelago. New York: 1885. V. 66
Observations on the Development of the Rostrum in the Catacean Genus Mesoplodon. 1893. V. 67

FORBES, HUGH
Manual for the Patriotic Volunteer on Active Service in Regular and Irregular War. New York: 1855. V. 63

FORBES, J.
Travels through the Alps. 1900. V. 63; 65

FORBES, J. D.
Occasional Papers on the Theory of Glaciers. Edinburgh: 1859. V. 62; 63; 66
Travels through the Alps. London: 1900. V. 62

FORBES, JAMES D.
Occasional Papers on the Theory of Glaciers Now First Collected and Chronologically Arranged. Edinburgh: 1859. V. 65
Oriental Memoirs: Selected and Abridged from a Series of Familiar Letters Written During Seven Years Residence in India. London: 1813. V. 64; 66
Testimonials in Flavour of James D. Forbes...as a Candidate for the Chair of Natural Philosophy in the University of Edinburgh. Edinburgh: 1832. V. 62
Travels through the Alps of Savoy and Other Parts of the Pennine Chain with Observations.... Edinburgh: 1843. V. 64; 66

FORBES, JOHN
Memorandums Made in Ireland in the Autumn of 1852. London: 1853. V. 66
A Physician's Holiday or a Month in Switzerland in the Summer of 1848. London: 1850. V. 64
Sight-Seeing in Germany and the Tyrol in the Autumn of 1855. London: 1856. V. 67

FORBES, LESLIE
Bombay Ice. London: 1998. V. 66

FORBES, ROBERT H.
The Penningtons, Pioneers of Early Arizona. Lancaster: 1919. V. 62; 65

FORBES, ROSITA
Conflict: Angora to Afghanistan. London: 1931. V. 65
The Secret of the Sahara: Kufara. London: 1921. V. 65

FORBES, S. A.
The Fishes of Illinois. Urbana: 1908. V. 62; 63; 66

FORBIN, CLAUDE, COMTE DE
Memoirs of the Count de Forbin, Commodore in the Navy of France, and Knight of the Order of St. Lewis. London: 1731. V. 67

FORBUSH, EDWARD HOWE
Birds of Massachusetts and Other New England States. Boston: 1925. V. 67
Birds of Massachusetts and Other New England States. Boston: 1925-1929. V. 64
Birds of Massachusetts and Other New England States. 1929. V. 66
Birds of Massachusetts and Other New England States. Boston: 1929. V. 64
Game Birds, Wild-Fowl and Shore Birds of Massachusetts and Adjoining States. 1912. V. 62
Game Birds, Wild-Fowl and Shore Birds of Massachusetts and Adjoining States. 1916. V. 66
Game Birds, Wild-Fowl and Shore Birds of Massachusetts and Adjoining tates. Massachusetts: 1916. V. 67
The Gypsy Moth.... Boston: 1896. V. 65
A History of the Game Birds, Wild-Fowl and Shore Birds of Massachusetts and Adjacent States. Boston: 1912. V. 64
A Natural History of American Birds of Eastern and Central North America. New York: 1955. V. 62
A Natural History of American Birds of Eastern and Central North America. New York: 1970.

FORBUSH, T. B.
Florida: the Advantages and Inducements Which It Offers to Immigrants. Boston: 1868. V. 63; 66

FORCADEL, PIERRE
Arithmetique Entiere et Abregee. Paris: 1565. V. 66
L'Arithmetique par les Gects. Paris: 1558. V. 66

FORCE, PETER
Tracts and Other Papers, Relating Principally to the Origin, Settlement, and Progress of the Colonies in North America, from the Discovery of the Country to the Year 1776. Gloucester: 1963. V. 62

FORCE, WILLIAM G.
Force's Picture of the City of Washington & Its Vicinity. Washington: 1848. V. 65

FORCHE, CAROLYN
The Angel of History. New York: 1994. V. 67
The Country Between Us. Port Townsend: 1981. V. 62; 64
Gathering the Tribes. New Haven: 1976. V. 63

FORD, BORIS
The Cambridge Cultural History of Britain. 1995. V. 67

FORD, CHARLES HENRI
The Half-Thoughts, the Distance of Pain. New York: 1947. V. 62; 64
Silver Flower Coo. New York: 1968. V. 66

FORD, COREY
In the Worst Possible Taste. New York: 1932. V. 67

FORD, EDWARD
David Rittenhouse: Astronomer Patriot 1732-1796. Philadelphia: 1946. V. 66

FORD, FORD MADOX
Ancient Lights and Certain Reflections: Being the Memories of a Young Man. London: 1911. V. 64
The Bodley Head Ford Madox Ford. London: 1962-1971. V. 62
The Brown Owl; a Fairy Story. London: 1892-1891. V. 64
Christina's Fairy Book. London. V. 63
The Cinque Ports: a Historical and Descriptive Record. London: 1900. V. 62; 66
The Cinque Ports: A Historical and Descriptive Record. Edinburgh and London: 1990. V. 65
The Good Soldier; a Tale of Passion. London: 1915. V. 64
The Good Soldier: a Tale of Passion. New York: 1927. V. 64
The Great Trade Route. New York: 1937. V. 62; 63
Hans Holbein the Younger - a Critical Monograph. London: 1905. V. 65
Henry James - A Critical Study. London: 1913. V. 62
Ladies Whose Bright Eyes - a Romance. London: 1911. V. 62
The March of Literature - from Confucius to Modern Times. London: 1939. V. 64
New York Essays. New York: 1927. V. 62
No Enemy: a Tale of Reconstruction. New York: 1920. V. 64
No Enemy: a Tale of Reconstruction. New York: 1929. V. 63
No More Parades. London: 1925. V. 64
On Heaven and Other Poems Written On Active Service. London: 1918. V. 62; 63; 64
The Portrait. London: 1910. V. 63
Privy Seal: His Last Venture. London: 1907. V. 62
Provence - from Minstrels to the Machine. London: 1938. V. 63
Rossetti - a Critical Essay on His Art. London: 1902. V. 65
The Shifting of the Fire. London: 1892. V. 64; 66
The Soul of London, a Survey of a Modern City. London: 1905. V. 66
When the Wicked Man. New York: 1931. V. 63

FORD, G. M.
Cast In Stone. New York: 1996. V. 63
Who in Hell is Wanda Fuca?. New York: 1995. V. 62; 63; 64; 66; 67

FORD, GERALD R.
Portrait of the Assassin. New York: 1965. V. 63
A Time to Heal. New York: 1979. V. 63; 65
The War Powers Resolution: a Constitutional Crisis?. Oroville: 1992. V. 66

FORD, GUS L.
Texas Cattle Brands. Dallas: 1958. V. 66

FORD, HENRY J.
The Yellow Fairy Book. London: 1894. V. 67

FORD, HUGH
Nancy Cunard: Brave Poet, Indomitable Rebel. Philadelphia: 1968. V. 65

FORD, ISABELLA O.
Women's Wages and the Condition Under Which They are Earned. London: 1893. V. 65

FORD, JOHN
By Direction of...Old Park, Enfield, Catalogue of the Contents of the Mansion Furniture.... London: 1909. V. 64
The Dramtic Works.... London: 1827. V. 62
A Guide to the Diorama of the Campaigns of the Duke of Wellington. London: 1852. V. 62
Images of Brighton. Richmond-Upon-Thames: 1981. V. 66

FORD, JULIA ELLSWORTH
Imagina. New York: 1923. V. 62

FORD, LEWIS
The Variety Book, Containing Life Sketches and Reminiscences. Boston: 1892. V. 63

FORD, PAUL LEICESTER
The Journals of Hugh Gaine, Printer. New York: 1902. V. 62

FORD, RICHARD
Communist. Derry & Ridgewood: 1987. V. 66; 67
English Magnolias. An Exhibition of Mississippi Fiction Printed in England. University of Mississippi: 1992. V. 62; 67
A Guide to the Diorama of the Campaigns of the Duke of Wellington. London: 1852. V. 66
A Hand-book for Travellers in Spain and Readers at Home...with Notices on Spanish History. London: 1845. V. 64
Independence Day. London: 1995. V. 67
Independence Day. New York: 1995. V. 62; 63; 64; 65; 66; 67
Independence Day. Toronto: 1995. V. 64; 67
My Mother, In Memory. Elmwood: 1988. V. 67
A Piece of My Heart. New York: 1976. V. 62; 63; 64; 65; 66; 67
A Piece of My Heart. London: 1987. V. 62; 67
Rock Springs. New York: 1987. V. 63; 66; 67
The Sportswriter. London: 1986. V. 64
The Sportswriter. New York: 1986. V. 66; 67
The Ultimate Good Luck. Boston: 1981. V. 62; 64; 65; 66
The Ultimate Good Luck. London: 1989. V. 64; 67
Wildlife. Boston: 1990. V. 62; 67
Wildlife. New York: 1990. V. 62; 66; 67
Women with Men: Three Stories. New York: 1997. V. 62

FORD, ROBERT
A Blues Bibliography. Bromley: 1999. V. 65

FORD, THOMAS
A History of Illinois, from Its Commencement as a State in 1814 to 1847.... Chicago: 1854. V. 62; 64

FORD, WHITEY
Whitey and Mickey. An Autobiography of the Yankee Years. New York: 1977. V. 65

FORD, WILLIAM
A Description of Scenery in the Lake District Intended as a Guide to Strangers. Carlisle: 1840. V. 65; 66

FORDHAM, HALLAM
John Gielgud - an Actor's Biography in Pictures. London: 1952. V. 65

FORDYCE, GEORGE
Five Dissertations on Fever.... Boston: 1815. V. 66; 67

FORDYCE, JAMES
Sermons to Young Women. London: 1794. V. 65

FORDYCE, WILLIAM
The Great Importance and Proper Method of Cultivating and Curing Rhubarb in Britain, for Medicinal Uses.... London: 1792. V. 65

FOREL, AUGUSTE HENRI
The Social World of the Ants Compared with That of Man. London: 1928. V. 65

FOREMAN, CAROLYN THOMAS
Indians Abroad 1493-1938. Norman: 1943. V. 66
Oklahoma Imprints 1835-1907 - a History of Printing in Oklahoma Before Statehood. Norman: 1936. V. 63; 64; 66

FOREMAN, GRANT
Advancing the Frontier 1830-1860. Norman: 1933. V. 62; 65
Adventure on Red River - Report on the Exploration of the Red River by Captain Randolph B Marcy and Captain George B McClelland. Norman: 1937. V. 67
The Adventures of James Collier, First Collector of the Port of San Francisco. Chicago: 1937. V. 63; 66; 67
The Biography of an Oklahoma Town - Muskogee. Norman: 1943. V. 62; 66
The Five Civilized Tribes (Choctaw, Chickasaw, Creek, Seminole and Cherokee). Norman: 1934. V. 65; 67
Indian Justice, a Cherokee Murder Trail at Tablequah in 1840.... Oklahoma City: 1934. V. 63; 66
Indians and Pioneers. The Story of the American Southwest Before 1830. New Haven: 1930. V. 63
Marcy and the Gold Seekers.... Norman: 1930. V. 67
A Traveler in Indian Territory. Cedar Rapids: 1930. V. 67

FOREMAN, R. E.
Evolutionary Biology of Primitive Fishes. New York: 1985. V. 64; 65

FOREST, H. E.
The Vertebrate Fauna of North Wales. 1907. V. 62; 65; 66

THE FOREST Party. New York: 1930. V. 64

FORESTA, M. A.
George Tooker. N.P: 1983. V. 62; 65

FORESTANI, LORENZO
Pratica d'Arithmetica e Geometria. Sienna: 1682. V. 65

FORESTER, CECIL SCOTT
The Barbary Pirates. London: 1956. V. 65
The Bedchamber Mystery With Which is Included the Story of the Eleven Deckchairs and Modernity and Maternity. Toronto: 1944. V. 64
The Commodore. London: 1945. V. 65
The Earthy Paradise. London: 1940. V. 62
The Gun. London: 1935. V. 63
Poo-Poo and the Dragons. Boston: 1942. V. 62; 66

FORESTER, FANNY
Memoir of Sarah B. Judson, of the American Mission to Burmah. London: 1858. V. 65

FORESTER, FRANK
The Warwick Woodlands. 1990. V. 67

FORESTER, THOMAS
Norway in 1848 and 1849.... London: 1850. V. 62; 66
Rambles in the Islands of Corsica and Sardinia; with Notices of Their History, Antiquities and Present Condition. London: 1861. V. 67

FORGE, ANDREW
An Appreciation of Naum Gabo. Biddenden, Kent: 1985. V. 64

FORLONG, J. G. R.
Faiths of Man, A Cyclopedia of Religions. London: 1906. V. 67

A FORM of Prayer and Thanksgiving to Almighty God; to be Used on Tuesday the Nineteenth Day of December 1797, Being the Day Appointed by His Majesty's Royal Proclamation for a General Thanksgiving to Almighty God.... London: 1797. V. 62

FORMAN, HARRISON
Through Forbidden Tibet. London: 1936. V. 65

FORMILLI, C. T. G.
The Stones of Italy. London: 1927. V. 64

FORNERON, H.
Louise de Kerouaile, Duchess of Portsmouth 1649-1734 or How the Duke of Richmond Gained His Pension. London: 1887. V. 65

FORREST, EARLE R.
Arizona's Dark and Bloody Ground. Caldwell: 1936. V. 62; 64; 65
Lone War Trail of Apache Kid. Pasadena: 1947. V. 64; 65; 67
Missions and Pueblos in the Old Southwest: Their Myths, Legends, Fiesta, and Ceremonies.... Cleveland: 1929. V. 63; 64
Patrick Gass - Lewis and Clark's Last Man. Independence: 1950. V. 65

FORREST, EBENEZER
An Account of What Seemed Most Remarkable in the Five Days Peregrination of the Five Following Persons.... London: 1782. V. 62

FORREST, MARYANN
The Immaculate Misconception. London: 1972. V. 65

FORREST, THOMAS
A Voyage to New Guinea and the Moluccas, from Balambangan.... Dublin: 1779. V. 63

FORRESTER, ALFRED HENRY
Kindness and Cruelty; or the Grateful Ogre. London: 1859. V. 64
The Pictorial Grammar. London: 1842. V. 64
Seymour's Humorous Sketches. London: 1880. V. 65
Strange Surprising Adventures of the Venerable Gooroo Simple and His Five Disciples Noodle, Doodle, Wiseacre, Zany and Foozle. London: 1861. V. 67
Tales for Children. New York: 1864. V. 65
The Tutor's Assistant, or Comic Figures of Arithmetic.... London: 1843. V. 64

FORRESTER, MRS.
Diana Carew; or, For A Woman's Sake. London: 1876. V. 65

FORRY, SAMUEL
The Climate of the United States and Its Endemic Influences Based Chiefly on the Records of the Medical Department and Adjutant General's Office, United States Army. New York: 1842. V. 62

FORSHAW, JOSEPH M.
Australian Parrots. 1969. V. 67
Australian Parrots. Wynnewood: 1969. V. 64
Australian Parrots. Wynnewood: 1972. V. 64
Australian Parrots. Melbourne: 1981. V. 67
The Birds of Paradise and Bower Birds. Boston: 1979. V. 63; 67
Parrots of the World. Melbourne: 1973. V. 65; 67
Parrots of the World. Melbourne: 1978. V. 62

FORSTER, EDWARD MORGAN
Alexandria. 1922. V. 64
Commonplace Book. London: 1978. V. 65
The Development of English Prose Between 1918 and 1939. Glasgow: 1945. V. 64
The Eternal Moment and Other Stories. London: 1928. V. 62; 64
The Hill of Devi - Being Letters from Dewas State Senior. London: 1953. V. 65
Kabafes. Athens: 1971. V. 65
(Novels). London: 1996. V. 67
A Passage to India. London: 1924. V. 62; 63; 64; 65
Two Cheers for Democracy. London: 1951. V. 63
A View Without a Room. New York: 1973. V. 63
Virginia Woolf. New York: 1942. V. 65

FORSTER, EMILY L. B.
How to Become a Woman Doctor. London: 1918. V. 67

FORSTER, JOHANN GEORG ADAM
A Journey from Bengal to England.... London: 1808. V. 66
A Voyage Round the World in His Britannic Majesty's Sloop Resolution, Commanded by Capt. James Cook During the Years 1772, 1773, 1774 and 1775. London: 1777. V. 64; 66

FORSTER, JOHANN REINHOLD
The Resolution Journal of Johann Reinhold Forster 1772-1775. London: 1982. V. 63; 64

FORSTER, JOHN
The Life and Adventures of Oliver Goldsmith. London: 1848. V. 67
The Life of Charles Dickens. London: 1872-1874. V. 62; 67
The Life of Charles Dickens. London: 1911. V. 62

FORSTER, NICHOLAS
A Sermon Preach'd in Christ's Church Dublin; Before His Excellency John, Lord Cartaret, Lord Lieutenant General, and General Governour of Ireland, On Sat. May 19, 1725. Dublin: 1725. V. 65
A Sermon Preached in the Parish Church of St. Audeon, Dublin, Dec. 1st 1717. Dublin: 1717. V. 65

FORSTER, R. R.
New Zealand Spiders: an Introduction. Auckland: 1973. V. 64; 66
Spiders of New Zealand. 1967-1988. V. 63
Spiders of New Zealand. Dunedin: 1967-1988. V. 66

FORSTER, THOMAS
Observations on the Phenomena of Insanity. London: 1819. V. 67

FORSTER, THOMAS IGNATIUS
(Greek title) Arati Diosemea, Notis et Collatione Scriptorum Illustravit. London: 1815. V. 63
Original Letters of Locke; Algernon Sidney; and Anthony Lord Shaftesbury.... London: 1830. V. 63
Philosophia Musarum Containing Pan a Pastoral of the First Age with other Poems and Fragments...(with) Harmonia Musarum Containing Nugas Cantabrigenses, Florilegium Sanctae Aspirationis and Anthologis Borealis et Australis.... Bruges: 1843. V. 65
Researches About Atmospheric Phaenomena. London: 1815. V. 62
A Synoptical Catalogue of British Birds.... London: 1817. V. 63

FORSYTH, FREDERICK
The Day of the Jackal. London: 1971. V. 62; 66; 67
The Fourth Protocol. London: 1984. V. 67
No Comebacks and Other Stories. Helsinki: 1986. V. 63
The Phantom of Manhattan. Franklin Center: 1999. V. 66

FORSYTH, GEORGE A.
The Story of the Soldier. New York: 1900. V. 65; 67
Thrilling Days in Army Life. New York: 1902. V. 67

FORSYTH, J. S.
The Citizen's Pocket Chronicle.... London: 1827. V. 66

FORSYTH, JAMES
The Sporting Rifle and It's Projectiles. 1867. V. 62

FORSYTH, JOSEPH
Remarks on Antiquities, Arts and Letters During an Excursion in Italy in the Years 1802 and 1803. London: 1816. V. 63
Remarks on Antiquities, Arts and Letters During an Excursion in Italy in the Years 1802 and 1803. London: 1824. V. 66; 67

FORSYTH, ROBERT
Political Fragments. Edinburgh: 1830. V. 66
The Principles and Practice of Agriculture, Systematically Explained.... Edinburgh: 1804. V. 66; 67

FORSYTH, WILLIAM
An Epitome of Mr. Forsyth's Treatise on the Culture and Management of Fruit Trees. Philadelphia: 1803. V. 67
An Epitome of Mr. Forsyth's Treatise on the Culture and Management of Fruit Trees.... Philadelphia: 1804. V. 62; 64
History of the Captivity of Napoleon at St. Helena: from the Letters and Journals of the Late Lieut.-Gen. Sir Hudson Lowe and Official Documents Not Before Made Public. London: 1853. V. 67
A Treatise on the Culture and Management of Fruit Trees. London: 1802. V. 62
A Treatise on the Culture and Management of Fruit Trees. Philadelphia: 1802. V. 62; 64
A Treatise on the Culture and Management of Fruit Trees. 1803. V. 63
A Treatise on the Culture and Management of Fruit Trees. 1806. V. 63; 66

FORT Francis E. Warren Wyoming. Cheyenne: 1930. V. 67

FORTESCUE, HUGH, EARL OF
Public Schools for the Middle Classes. London: 1864. V. 64

FORTESCUE, J. B.
The Manuscripts of J. B. Fortescue Preserved at Dropmore. 1892-1927. V. 65

FORTESCUE, J. W.
A History of the British Army. Volume 13. 1852-1870. London: 1930. V. 66
A History of the British Army. Volume 5. 1803-1807. London: 1921. V. 66
The Story of a Red Deer. Newtown: 1935. V. 65

FORTESCUE, JOHN
De Laudibus Legum Angliae.... London: 1660. V. 66

FORTESQUE, JOHN
De Laudibus Legum Angliae.... London: 1672. V. 65

FORTNUM & MASON
275th Anniversary Catalogue. 1982. V. 63

FORTUGERRI, NICCOLO
Ricciardetto Di Nicolo Carteromaco. Londra: 1767. V. 63

THE FORTUNE Anthology - Stories, Criticism and Poems. London: 1942. V. 65

FORTUNE, R.
A Residence Among the Chinese...During a Third Visit to China from 1853 to 1856. London: 1857. V. 62; 63; 67

FORTUNE, R. continued
The Tea-Districts of China and India. London: 1853. V. 67
Three Years' Wanderings in the Northern Provinces of China. 1847. V. 66
Three Years' Wanderings in the Northern Provinces of China. London: 1847. V. 63; 67

FORTUNE, R. F.
Sorcerers of Dobu. London: 1932. V. 62; 63

FORTY, JEAN FRANCOIS
Oeuvres de Sculptures en Bronze Contenant Girandoles, Flambeaux, Feux de Cheminees. Pendules, Bras, Cartels, Barometres et Lustres.... Paris: 1780. V. 64

FORWOOD, GWENDOLEN
Filida and Corydon, with Other Stories. London: 1902. V. 65

FORWOOD, WILLIAM B.
Recollections of a Busy Life. Liverpool: 1910. V. 62

FOSBROKE, THOMAS DUDLEY
British Monachism; or Manners and Customs of the Monks and Nuns of England.... London: 1817. V. 62
Encyclopaediae of Antiquities, and Elements of Archaeology, Classical and Mediaeval. (with) Foreign Topography; or, an Encyclopedick Account, Alphabetically Arranged, of the Remains in Africa, Asia and Europe.... London: 1825-1828. V. 65
The Wye Tour, or Gilpin on the Wye. London: 1818. V. 63
The Wye Tour, or Gilpin on The Wye. 1838. V. 67
The Wye Tour, or Gilpin on The Wye. Ross: 1838. V. 66

FOSHAY, E. M.
Reflections of Nature, Flowers in American Art. New York: 1984. V. 67

FOSKETT, DAPHNE
Miniatures. London: 1990. V. 66

FOSLIE, M.
Contributions to a Monograph of Lithothamnia.... Trondheim: 1929. V. 64
Contributions to a Monograph of the Lithothamnia. 1970. V. 66

FOSS, ROBERT
Aubrey Beardsley. London: 1909. V. 62

FOSTER, BELINDA ATWATER
Family Memoirs: Atwater, Butler, Brown. Indianapolis: 1915. V. 67

FOSTER, BIRKET
Christmas with the Poets. London: 1872. V. 65; 67
Odes and Sonnets Illustrated. London: 1859. V. 65
The Rhine and Its Picturesque Scenery. London: 1856. V. 67

FOSTER, C. W.
The Parish Register of Brocklesby in the County of Lincoln 18538- 1837. 1912. V. 66

FOSTER, DAVID
The Scientific Angler. 1880. V. 67
The Scientific Angler. London: 1882. V. 67

FOSTER, ELIZABETH ANDROS
Motolinia's History of the Indians of New Spain. Albuquerque: 1950. V. 64; 65
Motolinia's History of the Indians of New Spain. Berkeley: 1950. V. 66

FOSTER, FRED W.
A Bibliography of Skating. London: 1898. V. 62

FOSTER, G. A.
Chemical Neroanatomy of the Prenatal Rat Brain.... Oxford: 1998. V. 62

FOSTER, GEORGE G.
New York in Slices; by an Experienced Carver. New York: 1848. V. 62

FOSTER, J. W.
Pre-Historic Races of the United States of America. Chicago: 1873. V. 67
Report on the Geology and Topography of a Portion of the Lake Superior Land District, in the State of Michigan. Washington: 1850. V. 66

FOSTER, JEREMIAH
An Authentic Report of the Testimony in a Cause at Issue in the Court of Chancery of the State of New Jersey. Philadelphia: 1831. V. 62

FOSTER, JOHN
An Essay on the Evils of Popular Ignorance. London: 1820. V. 63
Essays in a Series of Letters, on the Following Subjects. I. On a Man's Writing Memoirs of Himself. II. On Decision of Character. III. On the Application of the Epithet Romantic. IV. On some of the Causes by Which Evangelical Religion Has Been Rendered L. London: 1813. V. 62; 66

FOSTER, JOHN Y.
New Jersey and the Rebellion: a History of the Services of the Troops and People of New Jersey in Aid of the Union Cause. Newark: 1868. V. 63; 66

FOSTER, JOSEPH
Pedigrees of the County Familes of Yorkshire. London: 1874. V. 63
The Royal Lineage of Our Noble and Gentle Families. Together with Their Paternal Ancestry. London: 1883. V. 63

FOSTER, MICHAEL
Lectures on the History of Physiology During the Sixteenth, Seventeenth and Eighteenth Centuries. Cambridge: 1901. V. 67

FOSTER, MURIEL
Muriel Foster's Fishing Diary. London: 1980. V. 67

FOSTER, STEPHEN COLLINS
Foster-Hall Reproductions. Songs, Compositions, and Arrangements by.... Indianapolis: 1933. V. 63
Way Down Upon De Swanee Ribber. Boston: 1889. V. 65

FOSTER, STEPHEN S.
The Brotherhood of Thieves, or a True Picture of the American Church and Clergy. London: 1843. V. 64

FOSTER, WILLIAM
The Embassy of Sir Thomas Roe to the Court of the Great Mogul 1615- 1619, as Narrated in His Journal and Correspondence. London: 1899. V. 67
England's Quest of Eastern Trade. London: 1933. V. 67
The Journal of John Jourdain 1608-1617; Describing His Experiences in Arabia, India and the Malay Archipelago. Cambridge: 1905. V. 67
Pages from a Worker's Life. New York: 1939. V. 67
The Red Sea and Adjacent Countries at the Close of the Seventeenth Century; as Described by Joseph Pitts, William Daniel and Charles Jacques Poncet. London: 1949. V. 67
The Travels of John Sanderson in the Levant 1584-1602; with His Autobiography and Selections from His Correspondence. London: 1931. V. 67

FOSTER, WILLIAM EDWARD
The Royal Descents of the Fosters of Moulton and the Mathesons of Shinness and Lochalsh. London: 1912. V. 62

FOSTER, WILLIAM Z.
Misleaders of Labor. 1927. V. 63; 64

FOTHERGILL, ANTHONY
A New Experimental Enquiry into the Nature and Qualities of the Cheltenham Water.... Bath: 1785. V. 64

FOTHERGILL, AUGUSTA B.
Peter Jones and Richard Jones Genealogies. Richmond: 1924. V. 63

FOTHERGILL, GEORGE
A Gift to the State: the National Stud. 1916. V. 65
Hunting Racing Coaching and Boxing Ballads. London: 1920. V. 67
A North Country Album. Darlington: 1901. V. 62; 66
Notes from the Diary of a Doctor, Sketch Artist and Sportsman. York: 1901. V. 62; 66; 67
Twenty Sporting Designs with Selections from the Poets. Edinburgh: 1911. V. 67

FOTHERGILL, J.
History of the Rochdale Cricket Club 1824-1902. Rochdale: 1903. V. 64

FOTHERGILL, JESSIE
The Wellfields. London: 1880. V. 66

FOTHERGILL, JOHN
An Account of the Life and Travels in the Work of the Ministry, of John Fothergill. London: 1753. V. 62

THE FOTHERGILL Omnibus. London: 1931. V. 63

FOUCAULT, MICHEL
Folie et Deraison. Histoire de la Folie a l'Age Classique. Paris: 1961. V. 66

FOUCHE, LEO
Mapungubwe: Ancient Bantu Civilization on the Lumpopo. Cambridge: 1937. V. 67

FOUGASSE
Fun Fair. A Book of Collected Drawings. London: 1934. V. 65; 66

FOUGERA, KATHERINE G.
With Custer's Cavalry - From the Memoirs of the Late Katherine Gibson, Widow of Captain Francis Gibson of the 7th Cavalry. Caldwell: 1942. V. 65; 67

FOUINET, E.
Allan, Le Jeune Deporte a Botany-Bay. Paris: 1836. V. 66

FOULIS, ROBERT
A Catalogue of Pictures, Composed and Painted Chiefly by the Most Admired Masters of the Roman, Florentine, Parman, Bolognese, Venetian, Flemish and French Schools. London: 1776. V. 67

FOUNDATION, Statutes and Rules of Robert Gordon's Hospital in Aberdeen. Aberdeen: 1784. V. 65

THE FOUNDLING; or the History of Lucius Stanhope. London: 1825. V. 66

FOUNTAIN, PAUL
The Eleven Eaglets of the West. London: 1905. V. 65
The Eleven Eaglets of the West. London: 1906. V. 67
The River Amazon; from Its Source to the Sea. London: 1914. V. 67

FOUR Fictions. Kentfield: 1973. V. 63; 64

THE FOUR Gospels. Lexington: 1954-1955. V. 64

THE FOUR Gospels of Lord Jesus Christ According to the Authorized Version of King James I. Waltham St. Lawrence: 1931. V. 62; 65

THE FOUR Gospels of the Lord Jesus Christ. Wellingborough: 1988. V. 64

FOUR Letters by An Englishwoman on the Contagious Diseases' Acts. Bristol: 1871?. V. 65

FOURCROY, ANTOINE FRANCOIS DE
Elements of Chemistry and Natural History.... Edinburgh: 1800. V. 62
Elements of Natural History and Chemistry.... London: 1790. V. 64
Memoires et Observations de Chimie.... Paris: 1784. V. 64

FOURIER, JEAN BAPTISTE JOSEPH, BARON DE
The Analytical Theory of Heat. Cambridge: 1878. V. 63

FOURNIER, ALAIN
The Lost Domain. Oxford: 1986. V. 66

FOURNIER, D.
A Treatise on the Theory and Practice of Perspective. London: 1761. V. 66

FOURNIER, FRANCOIS IGNATIUS
Nouveau Dictionnaire Portatif de Bibliographie.... Paris: 1809. V. 67

FOURNIER, GEORGES
Hydrographie Contenant la Theorie et la Practique de Toutes les Parties de la Navigation. Paris: 1643. V. 65

FOURNIER, M. EDOUARD
Le Jeu de Paume, Son Histoire et sa Description. Paris: 1862. V. 62

FOURNIER, PIERRE SIMON
Manuel Typographique. Paris: 1764-1766. V. 63; 65; 66
The Manuel Typographique of Pierre-Simon Fournir le Jeune (1764/66). Together with Fournier on Typefounding. Darmstadt: 1995-1997. V. 66
Traites Historiques et Critiques sur l'Origine et les Progres de l'Imprimerie. (and) De L'Origine et des Productions de l'Imprimerie Primitive en Taille de Bois. (and) Observations sur un Ouvrage Intitule "Vindiciae Typographicae". (and) Remarques sur un. Paris: 1758-1763. V. 63

FOURNIR DE LEMPDES, FRANCOIS
Lithotritie Perfectionee. Paris: 1829. V. 65

FOURNIVAL, RICHARD DE
Master Richard's Bestiary of Love and Response. Northampton: 1985. V. 64

FOWLE, WILLIAM F.
Catalogue of the Choice Collection of Books Belonging to.... Cambridge: 1865. V. 64

FOWLER, CONNIE MAY
Sugar Cage. New York: 1992. V. 67

FOWLER, DAVID BURTON
The Practice of the Cort of Exchequer, Upon Proceedings in Equity. London: 1795. V. 65

FOWLER, EDWARD
An Answer to the Paper Delivered by Mr. Ashton at His Execution to Sir Francis Child: Sheriff of London &c. Together with the Paper It Self. London: 1691. V. 64

FOWLER, FRANK
Southern Lights and Shadows; Being Brief Notes of Three Years' Experience of Social, Literary and Political Life in Australia. London: 1859. V. 67

FOWLER, GEORGE
Papers on the Theory and Practice of Coal Mining. London: 1870. V. 63

FOWLER, H. W.
A Collection of Fishes from Sumatra. Philadelphia: 1904. V. 65
A Dictionary of Modern English Usage. Oxford and London: 1926. V. 63; 66
Fishes of Fiji. Suva: 1959. V. 63
The Fishes of New Jersey. 1905. V. 62; 63; 66
The Fishes of New Jersey. Trenton: 1906. V. 65
The Fishes of Oceania. Honolulu: 1928-1949. V. 66
The Fishes of Oceania. 1968. V. 62
The Fishes of the Groups Elasmobranchii, Holocephali, Isospondyli and Ostarophysi Obtained by the United States Bureau of Fisheries Steamer Albatross in 1907 to 1910.... Washington: 1941. V. 65
Fishes of the Red Sea and Southern Arabia. Jerusalem: 1956. V. 63; 65
The Marine Fishes of West Africa, Based on the Collection of the American Museum Congo Expedition 1909-1915. New York: 1936. V. 65
Study of the Fishes of the Southern Piedmont and Costal Plain. Philadelphia: 1945. V. 65

FOWLER, HARLAN D.
Three Caravans to Yuma. Glendale: 1980. V. 67

FOWLER, JACOB
The Journal of Jacob Fowler...Adventure from Arkansas through Indian Territory, Oklahoma, Kansas, Colorado, New Mexico, 1821-1822. New York: 1898. V. 63; 66

FOWLER, JOSEPH
Crim. Con. Between a Lawyer's Clerk and His Mistress. Fairburn's Edition of The Trial Between Joseph Fowler, an Attorney, and Chas. Hodgson, His Clerk, for Criminal Conversation with the Plaintiff's Wife...July 13, 1808. London: 1808. V. 63

FOWLER, O. S.
Fowler on Matrimony; or Phrenology and Physiology Applied to the Selection of Companions for Life.... New York: 1842. V. 66
Fowler's Practical Phrenology. New York: 1840. V. 66
Fowler's Practical Phrenology. New York: 1843. V. 63
A Home for All Or the Gravel Wall and Octagon Mode of Building New, Cheap, Convenient Superior and Adapted to Rich and Poor. New York: 1857. V. 64

FOWLER, W. W.
The Coleoptera of the British Islands. 1887-1913. V. 63

FOWLER, WILLIAM W.
Woman on the American Frontier. Hartford: 1880. V. 65

FOWLER & CO., JOHN (LEEDS) LTD.
Working Instructions for Fowler Road Rollers, and Traction Engines, With Hints on Their Maintenance and General Management. Leeds. V. 65

FOWLES, JOHN
The Aristos - a Self-Portrait in Ideas. Boston and Toronto: 1964. V. 62
The Collector. Boston: 1963. V. 62; 63; 64; 66; 67
The Collector. London: 1963. V. 63; 65
The Collector. Franklin Center: 1982. V. 63; 67
Daniel Martin. London: 1977. V. 62
The Ebony Tower. Boston: 1974. V. 62; 63; 64
The Enigma. Helsinki: 1987. V. 65; 67
The Enigma of Stonehenge. London: 1980. V. 63
The French Lieutenant's Woman. London: 1969. V. 62; 63
The French Lieutenant's Woman. Franklin Center: 1979. V. 63; 67
Land. Boston: 1985. V. 62
A Maggot. London: 1985. V. 62; 63; 64; 67
The Magus. Boston and Toronto: 1965. V. 62; 63; 66; 67
Mantissa. London: 1982. V. 63
Of Memoirs and Magpies. Austin: 1983. V. 62; 64
Poems. New York: 1973. V. 66
Poor Koko. Helsinki: 1987. V. 65
The Tree. London: 1979. V. 63
Wormholes. Essays and Occasional Writings. London: 1998. V. 62; 65
Wormholes. Essays and Occasional Writings. New York: 1998. V. 63

FOX, ALEY
Art Pictures from the Old Testament and Our Lord's Parables. 1905. V. 64

THE FOX and the Goose. London: 1888. V. 67

FOX, CHARLES H.
The Art of Making Up for Public and Private Theatricals. London: 1888. V. 64

FOX, CHARLES JAMES
The Heads of Mr. Fox's Speech: Containing the Arguments He Opposed to the Fourth Irish Proposition, in a Committee of the Whole House of Commons, May 23, 1785. London: 1785. V. 62
A History of the Early Part of the Reign of James the Second.... London: 1808. V. 65

FOX, CHARLES K.
Rising Trout. 1967. V. 67
Rising Trout. Carlisle: 1967. V. 66

FOX, CORNELIUS R.
Ozone and Antozone. Their History and Nature. London: 1873. V. 62

FOX, CYRIL
Pattern and Purpose. Cardiff: 1958. V. 62

FOX, FRANK
Australia. London: 1910. V. 67
The Balkan Peninsula. London: 1915. V. 67
Switzerland. London: 1914. V. 64

FOX, FRANKLIN
Glimpses of the Life of a Sailor. London: 1862. V. 62

FOX, GEORGE
Gospel-Truth Demonstrated, in a Collection of Doctrinal Books Given Forth by the Faithful Minister of Jesus Christ, George Fox.... London: 1706. V. 66
The History of Pontefract, in Yorkshire. Pontefract: 1827. V. 65
A Journal or Historical Account of the Life, Travels, Sufferings, Christian Experiences and Labour of Love. London: 1765. V. 64; 66
A Journal or Historical Account of the Life, Travels, Sufferings, Christian Experiences and Labour of Love. New York: 1800. V. 63; 64
A Journal or Historical Account of the Life, Travels, Sufferings, Christian Experiences and Labour of Love. Leeds: 1836. V. 63
The Line of Righteousness and Justice Stretched Forth Over All Merchants &c. London: 1661. V. 62

FOX, H.
Disease in Captive Wild Mammals and Birds. Philadelphia: 1923. V. 62

A FOX-HUNTING Anthology. London: 1928. V. 67

FOX, JAMES
White Mischief. London: 1982. V. 65

FOX, JOHN
Blue-Grass and Rhododendron. New York: 1901. V. 64
Hell Fer Sartain & Other Stories. New York: 1897. V. 64
The Little Shepherd of Kingdom Come. New York: 1931. V. 62; 63
Works. New York: 1909. V. 63

FOX, LORENE K.
Antarctic Icebreakers. New York: 1937. V. 66

FOX, MINNIE C.
The Blue Grass Cook Book. New York: 1904. V. 62

FOX, PAULA
The Slave Dancer. New York: 1973. V. 65

FOX, R. M.
History of the Irish Citizen Army. 1943. V. 67

FOX, UFFA
Racing, Cruising and Design. London: 1937. V. 62; 64; 65
Sail and Power. London: 1936. V. 62; 64; 65
Sailing, Seamanship and Yacht Construction. New York. V. 65

FOX, UFFA continued
Sailing, Seamanship and Yacht Construction. London: 1934. V. 62; 65
Sailing, Seamanship and Yacht Construction. London: 1943. V. 62; 63
Sailing, Seamanship and Yacht Construction. London: 1957. V. 64
Thoughts on Yachts and Yachting Design: Construction: Handling. London: 1938. V. 62; 64
Uffa Fox's Second Book. London: 1935. V. 62; 65

FOX, W. TILBURY
On Certain Endemic Skin and Other Diseases of India.... London: 1876. V. 62

FOX, WILLIAM F.
New York at Gettysburg. Albany: 1900. V. 65

FOXCROFT, THOMAS
Day of a Godly Man's Death, Better than the Day of His Birth. Boston: 1722. V. 66

FOX-DAVIES, A. C.
The Dangervile Inheritance. London: 1907. V. 64; 66
The Mauleverer Murders. 1907. V. 64; 66

FOXE, JOHN
Acts and Monuments of Matters Most Speciall and Memorable Happening in the Church.... London: 1641. V. 67
The Acts and Monuments...With a Life of the Martyrologist, and a Vindication of the Work, by the Rev. George Townsend, M.A. London: 1843-1849. V. 62; 64
A Continuation of the Histories of Forreine Martyrs; from the Happy Reign of the Most Renowned Queene Elizabeth to these Times.... London: 1641. V. 67

FOXON, D. F.
English Verse 1701-1750. Cambridge: 1975. V. 62

FOXON, DAVID
Pope and the Early Eighteenth Century Book Trade. Oxford: 1991. V. 62; 63

FOX'S
Book of Martyrs; or, the Acts and Monuments of the Christian Church.... Philadelphia: 1836. V. 63

FOX-STRANGWAYS, C.
The Geology of the Leicestershire and South Derbyshire Coalfield. 1907. V. 65

FOY, DANIEL
Clowning through Life. New York: 1928. V. 66

FRACASTORO, MARIO G.
An Atlas of Light Curves of Eclipsing Binaries. Turin: 1972. V. 67

FRACKELTON, WILL
Sagebrush Dentist. Pasadena: 1947. V. 67

FRAGONARD, ALEXANDRE
Recueil de Divers Sujets dans le Style Grec, Composes Dessines et Graves.... Paris: 1815. V. 64

FRAME, ELIZABETH
A List of MicMac Names of Places, Rivers, Etc. in Nova Scotia. Cambridge: 1892. V. 64

FRAME, JANET
Autobiography. London: 1983-1985. V. 65

FRAMJEE, DOSABHOY
Travels in Great Britain. Bombay: 1851. V. 66

FRAMPTON, JOHN
The Most Noble and Famous Travels of Marco Polo; Together with the Travels of Nicolo De Conti. London: 1937. V. 67

FRANCATELLI, CHARLES E.
The Modern Cook: A Practical Guide to the Culinary Art in All Its Branches.... London: 1855. V. 62
The Modern Cook: a Practical Guide to the Culinary Art In All Its Branches.... London: 1886. V. 65

FRANCE, ANATOLE
Balthasar. Paris: 1930. V. 66
Bee the Princess of the Dwarfs. London: 1912. V. 64
Memoires d'Un Volontaire. Paris: 1902. V. 62
Thais. London: 1905. V. 64

FRANCE, L. B.
Mountain Trails and Parks in Colorado. Denver: 1887. V. 64

FRANCES, MAY
Beyond the Argentine; or Letters from Brazil. London: 1890. V. 65

FRANCESCO D'ASSISI, SAINT
I Fioretti del Glorioso Poverello di Crist S. Francesco di Assisi. 1922. V. 62; 67
I Fioretti del Glorioso Poverello di Crist S. Francesco di Assisi. Chelsea: 1922. V. 65
Laudes Creaturarum. Hammersmith: 1910. V. 65
The Little Flowers of Saint Francis of Assisi. New York: 1930. V. 62

FRANCHERE, GABRIEL
Narrative of a Voyage to the Northwest Coast of America. New York: 1854. V. 66
Narrative of a Voyage to the Northwest Coast of America. New York: 1859. V. 62
Narrative of a Voyage to the Northwest Coast of America. Cleveland: 1904. V. 65

FRANCHI, COSTANTINO
Mille Miglia 1984. Brescia: 1984. V. 66

FRANCIS, A. M.
The Catskill Rivers. 1983. V. 67

FRANCIS, CLAUDE DE LA ROCHE
London Historic and Social. Philadelphia: 1902. V. 66

FRANCIS, DICK
Blood Sport. New York: 1967. V. 63; 65
Blood Sport. New York: 1968. V. 67
Bolt. London: 1986. V. 62; 63; 65; 67
Bonecrack. London: 1971. V. 62; 66
Break In. London: 1985. V. 62; 64; 67
The Danger. London: 1983. V. 64; 67
Driving Force. London: 1992. V. 67
The Edge. London: 1988. V. 64; 66
Enquiry. London: 1969. V. 65; 66
Field of 13. London: 1998. V. 65; 66; 67
Flying Finish. London: 1966. V. 65; 66; 67
Flying Finish. New York: 1966. V. 62; 65
Flying Finish. New York: 1967. V. 67
For Kicks. London: 1965. V. 66; 67
For Kicks. New York: 1965. V. 65; 67
Forfeit. London: 1968. V. 66; 67
Forfeit. New York and Evanston: 1969. V. 63; 67
High Stakes. London: 1975. V. 66; 67
In the Frame. London: 1976. V. 64; 66; 67
Knock Down. London: 1974. V. 62; 64; 66; 67
Lester. London: 1986. V. 67
Nerve. London: 1964. V. 62; 65
Odds Against. London: 1965. V. 65
Proof. London: 1984. V. 64
Rat Race. London: 1970. V. 62; 63; 64; 65; 66
Rat Race. New York: 1971. V. 64; 66
Reflex. London: 1980. V. 65; 66
Risk. London: 1977. V. 66; 67
Risk. New York: 1977. V. 67
Second Wind. Blakeney: 1999. V. 65; 66; 67
Shattered. London: 2000. V. 66; 67
Slay-Ride. London: 1973. V. 66
Smokescreen. London: 1972. V. 67
Smokescreen. New York: 1973. V. 67
The Sport of Queens. New York: 1969. V. 62; 66; 67
Straight. London: 1988. V. 67
To the Hilt. Blakeney: 1996. V. 63; 65; 66; 67
To the Hilt. London: 1996. V. 67
Trial Run. London: 1978. V. 67
Twice Shy. London: 1981. V. 64; 66; 67
Whip Hand. London: 1979. V. 64; 66
Wild Horses. London: 1994. V. 63; 65; 67

FRANCIS, E. T. B.
The Anatomy of the Salamander. Oxford: 1934. V. 64

FRANCIS, FRANCIS
A Book on Angling. 1867. V. 67
A Book On Angling. London: 1880. V. 66; 67
A Book on Angling. 1885. V. 67
By Lake and River. 1874. V. 67

FRANCIS, J. G.
A Book of Cheerful Cats and Other Animated Animals. New York: 1922. V. 65

FRANCIS, JOHN
History of the Bank of England, Its Times and Traditions from 1694 to 1844. New York: 1862. V. 64
A History of the English Railway: Its Social Relations and Revelations 1820-1845. London: 1850. V. 63

FRANCIS, JOHN W.
Old New York; or Reminiscences of the Past Sixty Years. New York: 1858. V. 62

FRANCIS, JOHN WAKEFIELD
Anniversary Discourse Before the New York Academy of Medicine Delivered in the Broadway Tabernacle, Nov. 10th, 1847. New York: 1847. V. 63; 65

FRANCIS, M.
The Meaning of Gardens. Cambridge: 1990. V. 67

FRANCIS, M. E.
The Duenna of a Genius. 1898. V. 67
Frieze and Fustian. London: 1896. V. 65
In a North Country Village. London: 1893. V. 65
Stepping Westward. London: 1907. V. 67
The Wild Heart. London: 1910. V. 65

FRANCIS, PHILIP
Letter from the Cocoa-Tree to the Country Gentlemen (and) An Address to the Cocoa-Tree. London: 1762. V. 63

FRANCIS, ROBERT
The Trouble with God. 1984. V. 62

FRANCIS, W. PHILIP
The Remarkable Adventures of Little Boy Pip. New York: 1907. V. 62

FRANCIS, W. PHILLIP
The Remarkable Adventures of Little Boy Pip. San Francisco: 1907. V. 64

FRANCIS, WILLIAM
The Gentleman's, Farmer's and Husbandman's Most Useful Assistant in Measuring and Expeditiously Computing the Amount of Any Quantity of Land.... London: 1818. V. 64

FRANCIS'S New Guide to the Cities of New York and Brooklyn.... New York: 1857. V. 65

FRANCISZKA Themerson, London 1941-1942. London: 1987. V. 67

FRANCK, HARRY A.
Glimpses of Japan and Formosa. London: 1924. V. 67
Tramping through Mexico, Guatemala and Honduras. New York: 1916. V. 64; 67

FRANCKE, A. H.
A History of Western Tibet: one of the Unknown Empires. London: 1907. V. 67

FRANCKEN, FRANZ
The Small 7 Acts of Mercy. London: 1728. V. 67

FRANCKLIN, WILLIAM
Observations Made on a Tour from Bengal to Persia in the Years 1786-1787. London: 1790. V. 62; 63

FRANCK VON FRANCKENAU, GEORG
Flora Francica.... Argentorati: 1685. V. 63; 66

FRANCL, JOSEPH
The Overland Journey of Joseph Francl. San Francisco: 1968. V. 66

FRANCOIS, ABBE LAURENT
Observations sur La Philosophie de l'Histoire et Le Dictionnaire Philosophique.... Paris: 1770. V. 65

FRANCOIS FRANK, CHARLES
Lecons sur les Fonctions Motrices du Cerveau Reactions Volontaires et Organiques et sur l'Epilepsie Cerebrale. Paris: 1887. V. 66

FRANCOME, JOHN
Eavesdropper. London: 1986. V. 64

FRANK. Yorkshire Fishing and Shooting. 1900. V. 67

FRANK, JEFF
A Fantasy Reader, The Seventh World Fantasy Convention. 1981. V. 62

FRANK, JOHANN PETER
Traite de Medecine Pratique. Paris: 1820-1823. V. 65

FRANK, LARRY
Historic Pottery of the Pueblo Indians 1600-1880. Boston: 1974. V. 63; 66
Indian Silver Jewelry of the Southwest 1868-1930. Boston: 1978. V. 63; 66

FRANK, RICHARD
A Catalogue of the Extensive and Valuable Library Collected by Richard Frank, Esq.... Doncaster: 1833. V. 62

FRANK, ROBERT
The Americans. New York: 1969. V. 63; 66
The Americans. New York: 1978. V. 63
The Lines of My Hand. Tokyo: 1972. V. 66
New York to Nova Scotia. Boston and Houston: 1986. V. 66

FRANK, ROBERT WERNER BISCHOF
From Incas to Indios. New York: 1956. V. 63

FRANKAU, GILBERT
One of Us. London: 1917. V. 67
The Poetical Works of Gilbert Frankau. London: 1923. V. 64

FRANKE, AUGUSTUS HERMANN
Nicodemus; or, a Treatise on the Fear of Man. Bristol: 1767. V. 64

FRANKENHAEUSER, FERDINAND
Die Nerven der Gebaermutter und Ihre Endigung in den Glatten Muskelfasern.... Jena: 1867. V. 63

FRANKENSTEIN, ALFRED
William Sidney Mount. New York: 1975. V. 62; 65

FRANKENSTEIN, GUSTAVUS
The Little Boy and the Elephant. Philadelphia: 1904. V. 65

FRANKFORT, H.
Cylinder Seals. London: 1939. V. 66

FRANKFORT, HENRY
The Art and Architecture of the Ancient Orient. London: 1954. V. 64

FRANKL, PAUL
Principles of Architectural History: the Four Phases of Architectural Style 1420-1900. 1968. V. 65

FRANKLAND, J. C.
Fungi and Environmental Change. Cambridge: 1996. V. 64

FRANKLAND, WILLIAM
The Speech of Wm. Frankland, Esq. in the House of Commons on Friday the 29th of March 1811, on the Second Reading of Several Hills, Brought in by Sir Samuel Romilly, for Making Alterations in the Criminal Law. London: 1811. V. 63

FRANKLIN, BENJAMIN
Autobiography.... Philadelphia: 1868. V. 64
Experiments and Observations on Electricity, Made at Philadelphia in America.... London: 1769. V. 65; 66
Experiments and Observations on Electricity, Made at Philadelphia in America.... London: 1774. V. 65
The Life of Benjamin Franklin. Philadelphia: 1874. V. 63
The Life of Doctor Benjamin Franklin, Written by Himself. Together with Essays, Humourous, Moral and Literary.... New London: 1798. V. 63
The Life of the Late Dr. Benjamin Franklin. Philadelphia: 1811. V. 67
New Experiments and Observations on Electricity Made at Philadelphia in America. London: 1754. V. 66
The Pennsylvania Gazette. Philadelphia: 1764. V. 63
The Works of Benjamin Franklin. Chicago: 1882. V. 63
The Works of Dr. Benjamin Franklin. Chiswick: 1824. V. 67
The Works of Dr. Benjamin Franklin.... Cincinnati: 1838. V. 67

FRANKLIN, COLIN
The Ashendene Press. Dallas: 1986. V. 62; 64; 65
Bookselling. A Memoir from 1980. Cleveland: 1999. V. 66
Doves Press: the Start of Worry. Dallas: 1983. V. 62; 63
Emery Walker. Some Light on His Theories of Printing and on His Relations with William Morris and Cobden-Sanderson. Cambridge: 1973. V. 62; 65
Fond of Printing: Gordon Craig as Typographer and Illustrator. London: 1980. V. 64
Printing and the Mind of Morris - Three Paths to Kelmscott Press. Cambridge: 1986. V. 63; 64

FRANKLIN, J. J.
Triumphs of Justice Over Unjust Judges. London: 1817. V. 63

FRANKLIN, JOHN
Narrative of a Journey to the Shores of the Polar Sea in the Years 1819-1820-1821-1822. London: 1824. V. 62; 63
Narrative of a Second Expedition to the Shores of the Polar Sea, in the Years 1825, 1826 and 1827. Edmonton: 1971. V. 63
A Resolution of This Case, viz Whether It Be Lawful to Separate from the Publick Worship of God in the Parochial Assemblies of England, Upon the New Preference, Which Some Men Make.... London: 1683. V. 62
Sir John Franklin's Journals and Correspondence: the Second Arctic Land Expedition 1825-1827. Toronto: 1998. V. 64

FRANKLIN, KENNETH J.
Joseph Barcroft 1872-1947. Oxford: 1953. V. 65

FRANKLIN, THOMAS
The Green Tragic Theatre.... London: 1777. V. 66

FRANKLYN, H. MORTIMER
A Glance at Australia in 1880; or Food from the South.... Melbourne: 1881. V. 62

FRANKS, J. M.
Seventy Years in Texas - Memories of Pioneer Days, Indian Depredations and the Northeast Cattle Trail. Gatesville: 1924. V. 67

FRARY, I. T.
Thomas Jefferson, Architect and Builder. Richmond: 1939. V. 62; 65

FRASCELLA, LARRY
The American Cowboy. New York: 1990. V. 62; 65

FRASCONI, ANTONIO
Against the Grain. New York & London: 1974. V. 67
Woodcuts. New York: 1957. V. 64
The Work of.... Cleveland: 1953. V. 62; 64

FRASER, A. Z.
Livingstone and Newstead. London: 1913. V. 67

FRASER, AGNES
Poor Margaret. London: 1855. V. 62

FRASER, ALEC
Inaugural Address Delivered at the Opening Meeting of the Royal College of Surgeons' Scientific Association. Dublin: 1887. V. 67

FRASER, ALEXANDER CAMPBELL
Essays in Philosophy. Edinburgh: 1856. V. 62

FRASER, ALEXANDER, MRS.
A Leader of Society: a Novel. London: 1887. V. 66

FRASER, ANDREW H. L.
Among Indian Rajahs and Ryots. London: 1911. V. 65

FRASER, CLAUD LOVAT
Characters from Dickens. London: 1925. V. 64

FRASER, D.
Torres Straits Sculpture: a Study in Oceanic Primitive Art. New York: 1978. V. 62

FRASER, EDWARD
Soldier and Sailor Words and Phrases. London: 1925. V. 64

FRASER, G. M.
The Old Deeside Road (Aberdeen to Braemar). Aberdeen: 1921. V. 62

FRASER, G. S.
Impressions of Japan and Other Essays. Tokyo: 1952. V. 62
Leaves Without a Tree. Tokyo: 1953. V. 62

FRASER, G. S. continued
Poetry Now - An Anthology. London: 1956. V. 64

FRASER, GEORGE MAC DONALD
Flash for Freedom from the Flashman Papers 1848-1849. London: 1971. V. 67
Flashman. London: 1969. V. 63; 67
Flashman and the Angel of the Lord. Bristol: 1994. V. 62
Flashman and the Angel of the Lord. London: 1994. V. 65; 66
Flashman and the Dragon. London: 1985. V. 67
Flashman and the Mountain of Light. London: 1990. V. 65; 67
Flashman and the Redskins. London: 1982. V. 65; 67
Flashman and the Tiger. London: 1999. V. 67
Flashman at the Charge. London: 1973. V. 65; 67
Flashman from the Flashman Papers 1839-1842. London: 1969. V. 62; 66
Flashman in the Great Game. London: 1975. V. 67
Flashman's Lady: From the Flashman Papers 1842-1845. London: 1977. V. 63; 65; 67
The Pyrates. London: 1983. V. 67
The Pyrates. London: 1993. V. 67
Royal Flash. London: 1970. V. 67
Royal Flash. New York: 1970. V. 63; 64
The Steel Bonnets. London: 1986. V. 66

FRASER, HUGH
Amid the High Hills. London: 1923. V. 67
Amid the High Hills. 1934. V. 67

FRASER, JAMES
Schools Inquiry Commissions. Report to the Commissioners...to Inquire Into the Education Given in Schools in England Not Comprised Within.... London: 1867. V. 66

FRASER, JAMES B.
Dark Falcon; a Tale of the Attruck. London: 1844. V. 67

FRASER, LOVAT
India: Under Curzon and After. London: 1911. V. 67
Pirates. London. V. 66

FRASER, N. C.
In the Shadow of the Dinosaur.... Cambridge: 1994. V. 63

FRASER, P. M.
Ptolemaic Alexandria. Oxford: 1972. V. 65

FRASER, P. P.
Notes of a Tour Round the World. Melbourne: 1885. V. 62

FRASER, ROBERT W.
The Kirk and the Manse. Edinburgh: 1857. V. 62; 64

FRASER, WILLIAM
Coila's Whispers. Edinburgh: 1869. V. 65
The Knight of Morar. Coilas's Whispers. Edinburgh & London: 1869. V. 62

FRASER, WILLIAM AUGUSTUS
Poems by the Knight of Morar. London: 1867. V. 67

FRASER-MAC DONALD, A.
Our Ocean Railways, or the Rise, Progress and Development of Ocean Steam Navigation. London: 1893. V. 64

FRAYN, MICHAEL
Headlong. New York: 1999. V. 67
Headlong. London: 2000. V. 67
On the Outskirts. London: 1964. V. 64
The Tin Men. London: 1965. V. 65

FRAZAR, DOUGLAS
Practical Boat Sailing. Boston: 1879. V. 65

FRAZER, JAMES GEORGE
The Golden Bough. London: 1926. V. 65
The Golden Bough. London: 1936. V. 65
The Golden Bough. London: 1955. V. 63
The Gorgon's Head and Other Literary Pieces. London: 1927. V. 63

FRAZER, LADY
The Singing Wood. London: 1941. V. 67

FRAZER, R. W.
Silent Gods and Sun Steeped Lands. 1895. V. 67

FRAZIER, CHARLES
Cold Mountain. London: 1997. V. 64
Cold Mountain. New York: 1997. V. 62; 63; 64; 65; 66; 67

FRAZIER, CHARLES H.
Surgery of the Spine and Spinal Cord. New York: 1918. V. 66; 67

FRAZIER, IAN
Dating Your Mom. New York: 1986. V. 65; 67
Great Plains. New York: 1989. V. 65; 67

FRAZIER, PAUL W.
Antarctic Assault. New York: 1958. V. 67

FREAKS and Frolics of Little Boys. New York: 1887. V. 62

FREDEMAN, WILLIAM E.
Victorian Poets After 1850. Detroit: 1985. V. 62

FREDENHEIM, CARL FREDRIC
Ex Museo Regi Sueciae Antiquarum e Mamore Statuarum Apollinis Musagetae Minervae Paciferae ac Novem Musarum Series Integra.... Stockholm: 1794. V. 64

FREDERIC, HAROLD
The Copperhead. New York: 1893. V. 66
Curtmantle: a Play. London: 1961. V. 66
Mrs. Albert Grundy: Observations in Phlistia. New York: 1896. V. 66
Seth's Brother's Wife: a Study of Life in the Greater New York. New York: 1887. V. 66

FREDERICK, J. L.
Ben Holliday - the Stagecoach King, A Chapter in the Development of Transcontinental Transportation. Glendale: 1940. V. 62; 66

FREDERICKSON, A. D.
Ad Orientem. London: 1889. V. 63; 66; 67

FREE and Impartial Remarks Upon the Letters Written by the Late Honourable Philip Dormer Stanhope, Earl of Chesterfield to His Son Philip Stanhope.... London: 1774. V. 66

THE FREE South. Beaufort: 1864. V. 65

FREE Thoughts on Seduction, Adultery and Divorce. London: 1771. V. 63

FREECE, HANS P.
The Letters of an Apostate Mormon to His Son. New York: 1908. V. 65; 67

FREED, FRED
The Decision to Drop the Bomb. New York: 1965. V. 67

FREEDLEY, EDWIN T.
Opportunities for Industry and the Safe Investment of Capital; or, a Thousand Chances to Make Money. London: 1859. V. 64
Philadelphia & Its Manufactures: A Hand-Book Exhibiting the Development, Variety, & Statistics of the Manufacturing Industry of Philadelphia in 1857. Philadelphia: 1858. V. 65
A Practical Treatise on Business; or How to Get, Save, Spend, Give, Led and Bequeath Money.... Philadelphia: 1852. V. 63

FREEDLEY, GEORGE
Theatrical Designs from the Baroque through Neoclassicism. New York: 1940. V. 65

FREEDMAN, RUSSELL
A Dibliography of Wendell Darry. Lexington: 1990. V. 62; 64; 65; 66; 67

FREELING, ARTHUR
The Gentleman's Pocket Book of Etiquette. London: 1840?. V. 64

FREELING, NICOLAS
The Kitchen. New York: 1970. V. 67

FREEMAN, BUD
If You Know of a Better Life! Please Tell Me. Dublin: 1976. V. 64

FREEMAN, D. DENNIS
The Road to Bordeaux. London: 1940. V. 62

FREEMAN, DON
The Guard Mouse. New York: 1967. V. 62

FREEMAN, DOUGLAS SOUTHALL
A Calendar of Confederate Papers. Richmond: 1908. V. 62; 63
George Washington: a Biography. New York: 1948. V. 65
The Last Parade. Richmond: 1932. V. 62; 63; 65
Lee's Lieutenants - a Study in Command. New York: 1942-1943. V. 65; 67
Lee's Lieutenants, a Study in Command. New York: 1946. V. 62
R. E. Lee: a Biography. New York: 1934-1935. V. 63
R. E. Lee: a Biography. New York: 1935. V. 66
R. E. Lee: A Biography. New York: 1936. V. 62; 63; 65
R. E. Lee: a Biography. New York and London: 1940. V. 67

FREEMAN, EDWARD AUGUSTUS
The Preservation and Restoration of Ancient Mounuments: a Paper Read Before the Archaeological Institute at Bristol, July 29, 1851. Oxford and London: 1852. V. 66

FREEMAN, GAGE EARLE
Practical Falconry; to which Is Added, How I Became a Falconer. 1868. V. 62

FREEMAN, HARRY C.
A Brief History of Butte, Montana, the World's Greatest Mining Camp. Chicago: 1900. V. 63; 66

FREEMAN, IRA S.
A History of Montezuma County, Colorado Land of Fulfilment, Being a Review. Boulder: 1968. V. 62; 65

FREEMAN, JAMES
Remarks on the American Universal Geography. Boston: 1793. V. 64

FREEMAN, JAMES W.
Prose and Poetry of the Livestock Industry of the United States. New York: 1959. V. 63; 66

FREEMAN, JOHN F.
A Guide to Manuscripts Relating to the American Indian in the Library of the American Philosophical Society. Philadelphia: 1980. V. 63; 64

FREEMAN, JOHN R.
On the Proposed Use of a Portion of the Hetch Hetchy, Eleanor and Cherry Valleys...Boundaries of the Stanislaus U. S. National Forest Reserve. San Francisco: 1912. V. 65

FREEMAN, LEWIS R.
The Colorado River: Yesterday, Today and Tomorrow. New York: 1923. V. 63
Down the Yellowstone. New York: 1922. V. 67

FREEMAN, MARGARET B.
Herbs for the Mediaeval Household for Cooking, Healing and Divers Uses. New York: 1943. V. 63

FREEMAN, R. AUSTIN
The D'Arblay Mystery. New York: 1926. V. 64; 66
Felo De Se?. London: 1937. V. 64; 66
John Thorndyke's Cases. London: 1909. V. 66
Mr. Pottermack's Oversight. New York: 1930. V. 66
The Mystery of Angelina Frood. London: 1924. V. 64
The Mystery of Angelina Frood. 1925. V. 62
The Red Thumb Mark. London: 1907. V. 63; 64; 66
The Red Thumb Mark. 1911. V. 66
The Uttermost Farthing. Philadelphia: 1914. V. 67

FREEMAN, R. B.
The Works of Charles Darwin. London: 1965. V. 67

FREEMAN, STRICKLAND
The Art of Horsemanship.... London: 1806. V. 64

FREEMAN, WALTER
The Columnar Arrangement of the Primary Afferent Centers in the Brain Stem of Man. Dorpat: 1925. V. 65
Neuropathology: The Anatomical Foundation of Nervous Diseases. Philadelphia: 1933. V. 65
Psychosurgery In the Treatment of Mental Disorders and Intractable Pain. Springfield: 1950. V. 64; 66
Psychosurgery, Intelligence, Emotion and Social Behavior Following Prefrontal Lobotomy for Mental Disorders. Springfield: 1942. V. 64

FREEMANTLE, BRIAN
Clap Hands, Here Comes Charlie. London: 1978. V. 63

FREEMANTLE, W. T.
A Bibliography of Sheffield and Vicinity. Sheffield: 1911. V. 66

FREEMASONS
The Constitution of the Free-Masons. London: 1723. V. 64
Proceedings of the Grand Council of Alabama, at the Annual Convocation, Held in the City of Montgomery, Commencing December 6th, 1865. Montgomery: 1866. V. 63
Proceedings of the M. W. Grand Lodge of Ancient, Free and Accepted Masons, of the State of Oregon, at Its Ninth Annual Communication. Portland: 1859. V. 63
Proceedings of the Most Woshipful Grand Lodge of Free and Accepted Masons of the State of California. San Francisco: 1853. V. 66

FREER, ADAMUS
Dissertatio Medica in Auguralis. De Syphilide Venerea.... Edinburgh: 1767. V. 67

FREER, MARTHA WALTER
The Married Life of Anne of Austria, Queen of France, Mother of Louis XIV, and Don Sebastian, King of Portugal. London: 1864. V. 65

FREES, HARRY WHITTIER
Animal Land on the Air. Boston: 1929. V. 64
The Little Folks of Animal Land. Boston: 1915. V. 64

FREESTON, CHARLES L.
The High-Roads of the Alps: a Motoring Guide to One Hundred Mountain Passes. London: 1910. V. 65

FREESTON, EWART C.
Prisoner of War Ship Mdoels 1775-1825. Lymington, Hampshire: 1973. V. 62

FREGE, GOTTLOB
Grundgesetze der Arithmetik. Begriffsschriftlich Abgeleitet. Jena: 1893-1903. V. 66

FREIBURG IM BREISGAU
Nuwe Stattrechten und Statuten der Statt Fryburg im Pryszgow Gelegen. Basle: 1520. V. 64; 66

FREIND, JOHN
Emmenologia. Londini: 1717. V. 64
Emmenologia. Parisiis: 1727. V. 65
Emmenologia. London: 1729. V. 64; 67
Opera Omnia Medica. Paris: 1735. V. 62; 64

FREIRE DE ANDRADA, JACINTO
The Life of Dom John de Castro, the Fourth Vice-Roy of India. London: 1664. V. 67

FRELINGHUYSEN, THEODORE
Speech of Mr. Frelinghuysen, of New Jersey, Delivered in the Senate of the United States, April 6, 1830, on the Bill for an Exchange of Lands with the Indians Residing in any of the States or Territories, and for Their Removal West of the Mississippi. Washington: 1830. V. 63

FREMANTLE, ARTHUR JAMES L.
Three Months in the Southern States: April-June 1863. Edinburgh & London: 1863. V. 63
Three Months in the Southern States: April-June, 1863. Mobile: 1864. V. 62; 63; 65
Three Months in the Southern States: April-June 1863. New York: 1864. V. 63

FREMANTLE, T. F.
The Book of the Rifle. 1901. V. 62

FREMONT, JOHN CHARLES
The Expeditions of John Charles Fremont. Urbana: 1970-1983. V. 63
The Exploring Expedition to the Rocky Mountains, Oregon and California...with Recent Notices of the Gold Reigion. Buffalo: 1852. V. 62
Geographical Memoir Upon Upper California. Washington: 1848. V. 62; 65
Geographical Memoir Upon Upper California in Illustration of His Map of Oregon and California. Washington: 1849. V. 63
Memoirs of My Life...Including in the Narrative Five Journeys of Western Exploration During the Years 1842, 1843-1844, 1845-1846-1847, 1848- 1849, 1853-1854.... Chicago: 1887. V. 65
Memories of My Life. New York: 1887. V. 63; 66
Narrative of the Exploring Expedition to the Rocky Mountains in the Year 1842 and to Oregon and North California in the Years 1843-1844. Washington: 1845. V. 67
Narrative of the Exploring Expedition to the Rocky Mountains, in the Year 1842; and to Oregon and North California, in the Years 1843-1844. New York: 1849. V. 63
A Report of an Expedition of the Country Lying Between the Missouri River and the Rocky Mountains on the Line of the Kansas and Great Platte Rivers. Washington: 1843. V. 64; 67
Report of the Exploring Expedition to the Rocky Mountains and to Oregon and North California in the Years 1843-1844. Washington: 1845. V. 62; 63; 65; 66

FRENCH, ALBERT
Billy. New York: 1993. V. 64

FRENCH, ALICE
An Adventure in Photography. New York: 1893. V. 65
The Lion's Share. Indianapolis: 1907. V. 65
The Missionary Sheriff. New York: 1897. V. 65
Stories of a Western Town. New York: 1893. V. 63

FRENCH, ALLEN
The Day of Concord and Lexington. Boston: 1925. V. 67

FRENCH, CECIL
Between Sun and Moon - Poems and Woodcuts. London: 1922. V. 62

FRENCH, FRANCES J.
The Abbey Theatre Series of Plays: a Bibliography. 1969. V. 67

FRENCH, GILBERT JAMES
The Life and Times of Samuel Crompton, Inventor of the Spinning Machine Called the Mule. London: 1859. V. 64
The Life and Times of Samuel Crompton, Inventor of the Spinning Machine Called The Mule.... Manchester and London: 1860. V. 62; 63
Remarks on the Mechanical Structure of Cotton Fibre. Manchester: 1857. V. 63

FRENCH, JAMES
Wild Jim - the Texas Cowboy and Saddle King with Wild Jim, Captain W. J. French, Texas Ranger, The Texas Cowby and Saddle King. Antioch/Chicago: 1890. V. 62
Wild Jim, Capt. W. J. French, Texas Ranger, The Texas Cowboy and Saddle King. Chicago. V. 64

FRENCH, JAMES C.
The Trip of the Steamer Oceanus to Fort Sumter & Charleston, S.C. Brooklyn: 1865. V. 67

FRENCH, JAMES WEIR
Modern Power Generators. London: 1908. V. 62; 65; 66

FRENCH, JANIE P. C.
Notable Southern Families, the Crockett Family and Connecting Lines. Bristol: 1928. V. 62

FRENCH, L. H.
Seward's Land of Gold. Five Seasons Experience with the Gold Seekers in Northwestern Alaska. New York: 1905. V. 62

FRENCH, LARRY L.
Notes for the Curious: a John Dickson Carr Memorial Journal. 1978. V. 66

FRENCH, NICCI
Killing Me Softly. London: 1999. V. 65; 66
The Memory Game. London: 1997. V. 65; 66

FRENCH, SAMUEL G.
Two Wars: an Autobiography. Nashville: 1901. V. 62; 63; 65

FRENCH, SARAH
Letters to a Young Lady, on Leaving School and Entering the World. Boston: 1855. V. 64

FRENCH, WILLIAM
Further Recollections of a Western Ranchman, New Mexico 1883-1899. New York: 1965. V. 65; 66
Some Recollections of a Western Ranchman - New Mexico 1883-1899. New York: 1928. V. 62; 64; 67

FRENCH SHELDON, M.
Sultan to Sultan: Adventures Among the Mawai and Other Tribes of East Africa. Boston: 1892. V. 65

FRENEAU, PHILIP
Poems Written and Published During the American Revolutionary War, and Now Republished from the Original Manuscripts. Philadelphia: 1809. V. 66
Poems Written Between the Years 1768 and 1794. Monmouth: 1795. V. 64

FRENEY, JAMES
The Life and Adventures of James Freney; Together with an Account of the Actions of Several Other Noted Highwaymen. Dublin: 1861. V. 63

FRERE, M.
Old Deccan Days; or Hindoo Fairy Legends, Current in Southern India. London: 1868. V. 67

FRERE, W.
Graduale Sarisburiense. A Reproduction in Facsimile of a Manuscript of the 13th century.... London: 1894. V. 62

FRESCHOT, CASIMIR
The Compleat History of the Treaty of Utrecht, also that of Gertruydenberg. London: 1715. V. 67
Remarques Historiques et Critiques Faites Dans un Voyage d'Italie en Hollande dans l'Annee 1704. Cologne: 1705. V. 67

FRESHFIELD, DOUGLAS W.
The Exploration of the Caucasus. 1896. V. 63; 65
Round Kangchenjunga a Narrative of Mountain Travel and Exploration. London: 1903. V. 62
Travels in the Central Caucasus and Bashan.... London: 1869. V. 64

FRESMAN, M. P.
The Dread Apache - The Early Day Scourge of the Southwest. Tucson: 1915. V. 67

FRETTER, VERA
British Prosobranch Molluscs. London: 1962. V. 62
British Prsobranch Molluscs. London: 1994. V. 67

FREUCHEN, PETER
Arctic Adventure. London: 1936. V. 62

FREUD, SIGMUND
Beobachtungen Uber Gestaltung und Feineren Bau der Als Hoden Beschlebenen Lappenorganen des Aals. Wien: 1877. V. 62; 65; 67
Beyond the Pleasure Principle. London and Vienna: 1922. V. 62
Collected Papers. London: 1950. V. 66; 67
Drei Abhandlungen zur Sexualtheorie. Leipzig/Wien: 1905. V. 62; 65
Group Psychology and the Analysis of the Ego. London: 1922. V. 62; 65
Group Psychology and the Analysis of the Ego. New York: 1922. V. 63
Die Infantile Cerebrallahmung. Specielle Pathologie und Therapie Herausgegeben von Hermann Nothnagel IX. Band II. Theil II. Abtheilung. Wien: 1897. V. 62; 65
The Interpretation of Dreams. London: 1913. V. 62; 65
Klinische Studie Uber die Halbseitige Cerebrallahmung der Kinder. Wien: 1891. V. 62; 65
Neue Folge der Vorlesungen zur Einfuhrung in Die Psychoanalyse. Wien: 1933. V. 62
New Introductory Lectures. New York: 1933. V. 62
On Aphasia: a Critical Study. London: 1953. V. 65
The Problem of Lay-Analyses. New York: 1927. V. 62
A Psycho-Analytic Dialogue: the Letters of Sigmund Freud and Karl Abraham. New York: 1965. V. 62
Psychoanalysis and the War Neuroses. Leipzig: 1921. V. 62
Psychopathology of Everyday Life. New York: 1914. V. 62
Reflections on War and Death. New York: 1918. V. 62
Selbstdarstellung. (Autobiography). Vienna: 1936. V. 62; 64; 65
Standard Edition of the Complete Psychological Works of Sigmund Freud. London: 1953-1974. V. 65
Totem and Taboo: Some Resemblances Between Psychic Lives of Savages and Neurotics. New York: 1918. V. 62
Die Traumdeutung. Leipzig/Wien: 1900. V. 62; 65
Die Traumdeutung. 1909. V. 62
Die Traumdeutung. Leipzig/Wien: 1909. V. 65
Die Traumdeutung. Leipzig/Wien: 1911. V. 65
Uber Coca. Wien: 1885. V. 62
Uber den Ursprung der Hinteren Nervenwurzeln im Ruckenmark von Ammocoetes. Wien: 1877. V. 62; 65
Uber Psychoanalyse. Leipzig/Wien: 1924. V. 62
Vorlesungen zur Einfuhrung in Die Psychoanalyse. Leipzig und Wien: 1916-1917. V. 65
Vorlesungen zur Einfuhrung in die Psychoanalyse 31 - 45. Tausend. Wien: 1930. V. 62
Wit and the Unconscious. New York: 1916. V. 62
Zur Auffassung der Aphasien: Eine Kritische Studie. Leipzig/Wien: 1891. V. 62; 65
Zur Kenntnis der Cerebralen Diplegien des Kindesalters.... Leipzig und Wien: 1893. V. 65
Zur Psychopathologie des Alltagslebens. Berlin: 1907. V. 62
Zur Psychopathologie des Alltagslebens. Berlin: 1910. V. 62
Zur Psychopathologie des Alltagslebens. Wien: 1929. V. 62

FREUND, GISELE
Gisele Freund: Photographer. New York: 1985. V. 63
James Joyce In Paris; His Final Years. 1965. V. 67

FREUNDLICH, ERWIN
The Foundations of Einstein's Theory of Gravitation.... Cambridge: 1920. V. 65

FREWEN, MORETON
Melton Mowbray and Other Memories. London: 1924. V. 67

FREY, HEINRICH
The Miscroscope and Microscopical Technology. New York: 1872. V. 62

FREYER, DERMOT
Night on the River and Other Stories. Cambridge: 1923. V. 64

FREYTAG, GUSTAV
Our Forefathers. London: 1873. V. 66

FREZIER, AMEDEE FRANCOIS
A Voyage to the South-Sea, and Along the Coasts of Chili and Peru in the Years 1712, 1713 and 1714. London: 1717. V. 62; 67

FRICK, GEORGE
A Treatise on the Diseases of the Eye, Including the Doctrine and Practice of the Most Eminent Modern Surgeons and Particularly Those of Professor Beer. London: 1826. V. 65; 66

FRICKE, R.
Revision of the Indo-Pacific Genera and Species of the Dragonet Family Callionymidae. Braunschweig: 1983. V. 65
Tripterygiid Fishes of the Western and Central Pacific. Koenigstein: 1997. V. 63

FRICKER, KARL
The Antarctic Regions. London: 1900. V. 65
The Antarctic Regions. London: 1904. V. 67

FRIDGE, IKE
History of the Chisum Way of Life of Ike Fridge Stirring Events of Cowboy Life on the Frontier. Electra: 1927. V. 65

FRIEBOES, WALTHER
Aulus Cornelius Celsus uber Die Arzneiwissenschaft in Acht Buchern. Braunschweig: 1906. V. 63

FRIEDAN, BETTY
The Feminine Mystique. New York: 1963. V. 63

FRIEDENWALD, HARRY
Jewish Luminaries in Medical History and a Catalogue of Works Bearing on the Subject of Jews and Medicine from the Private Library of Harry Friedenwald. Baltimore: 1946. V. 63
The Jews and Medicine. Baltimore: 1944. V. 63

FRIEDLAENDER, JOHNNY
Oeuvre 1961-1965. New York: 1970. V. 62; 64

FRIEDLAENDER, WALTER
Nicolas Poussin: a New Approach. New York: 1960. V. 66

FRIEDLANDER, LEE
The American Movement. New York: 1976. V. 63
The Jazz People of New Orleans. London: 1992. V. 63; 66
Letters from the People. New York: 1993. V. 65
Nudes. New York: 1991. V. 63

FRIEDMAN, KINKY
Elvis, Jesus and Coca Cola. New York: 1993. V. 67
Frequent Flyer. New York: 1989. V. 67
God Bless John Wayne. New York: 1995. V. 67
Greenwich Killing Time. 1986. V. 64; 66
Greenwich Killing Time. New York: 1986. V. 63; 65; 67
Musical Chairs. New York: 1991. V. 65; 67
When the Cat's Away. New York: 1988. V. 64; 67

FRIEDMANN, H.
Birds Collected by the Childs Frick Expedition to Ethiopia and Kenya Colony. Washington: 1930-1937. V. 67

FRIEDRICH II, EMPEROR OF GERMANY
The Art of Falconry. Stanford: 1943. V. 62
The Art of Falconry. Stanford: 1961. V. 63; 67
The Art of Falconry. 1969. V. 62; 64; 67

FRIEL, BRIAN
The Loves of Cass Mc Guire. 1967. V. 63; 66

THE FRIEND. Colombo: 1839-1840. V. 63

FRIEND, JOHN
The Arraignment, Tryal and Condemnation of Sir John Friend, Knight for High Treason, In Endeavouring to Procure Forces from France ot Invade This Kingdom.... London: 1696. V. 62

FRIEND, L.
Graphic Design. New York and London: 1936. V. 65

FRIEND, LERENA
Sam Houston. The Great Designer. Austin: 1954. V. 67

FRIENDS at the Farm. London. V. 67

FRIENDS of Far Eastern Art Exhibition of Chinese Art. 1934. V. 62

FRIENDSHIP Progress Civilisation. London: 1943. V. 65

FRIES, ADELAIDE LISETTA
Forsyth County. Winston: 1898. V. 66; 67

FRIGERIO, AMBROGIO
Vita Gloriosissima, et Miracoli Eccelsi del Beato Confessore Santo Nicola di Tolentino. In Ferrara: 1588. V. 63

FRIGGE, KARLI
Marbled Streamers. N.P: 1988. V. 64

FRINGS, KETTI
Look Homeward, Angel. New York: 1958. V. 66

FRINK, ELIZABETH
Etchings Illustrating Chaucer's Canterbury Tales. London: 1972. V. 62

FRINK, MAURICE
When Grass Was King - Contributions ot the Western Range Cattle Industry Study. Boulder: 1956. V. 64; 67

FRISBIE, CHARLOTTE J.
Navajo Medicine Bundles or Jish. Albuquerque: 1987. V. 64

FRISI, PAOLO
Cosmographiae Physicae, et Mathematicae Pars Prior (Pars Altera) Motuum Periodiocrum Theorium Contiens. Milan: 1775. V. 65

FRISI, PAUL
A Treatise on Rivers and Torrents; with the Method of Regulating Their Course and Channels.... London: 1818. V. 62

FRISKEY, MARGARET
Diving Ducks. Philadelphia: 1940. V. 63

FRISON-ROCHE, R.
The Lost Trail of the Sahara. New York: 1952. V. 64; 66

FRISTOE, WILLIAM
A Concise History of the Ketock Baptist Association. Staunton: 1808. V. 63; 66

FRITH, C. B.
The Birds of Paradise: Paradisaediae. Oxford: 1998. V. 63

FRITH, WALTER
The Sack of Monte Carlo. Bristol;: 1897. V. 65

FRITH, WILLIAM POWELL
John Leech. His Life and Work. London: 1891. V. 62; 67

FRITZ, PERCY S.
Colorado The Centennial State. New York: 1941. V. 67

FRIZZELL, L., MRS.
Across the Plains to California in 1852 from the Little Wabash River in Illinois to the Pacific Springs of Wyoming...Journal of.... New York: 1915. V. 66

FRODIN, D. G.
Guide to Standard Floras of the World. Cambridge: 1984. V. 67

THE FROG Princess. (Title in Russian). Moscow: 1901. V. 64; 66

THE FROG Who Would a Wooing Go. London: 1880. V. 65

FROHAWK, F. W.
British Birds with Their Nests and Eggs. 1896-1899. V. 67
Natural History of British Butterflies. London: 1914. V. 62
Natural History of British Butterflies.... London: 1924. V. 62; 64
Varieties of British Butterflies. London: 1946. V. 64

FROHMAN, DANIEL
Memories of a Manager. Reminiscences of the Old Lyceum and of Some Players of the Last Quarter Century. Garden City: 1911. V. 64

FROISSART, JOHN
Chronicles of England, France, Spain and the Adjoining Countries, from the Latter Part of the Reign of Edward II to the Coronation of Henry IV. London: 1808. V. 65

FROLICH, ERASMUS
Der Rhein von Mannheim bis Dusseldorf. Mannheim: 1840. V. 65

FROM Nursery Land. London: 1908. V. 63

FROM the Nile to the Jordan. London: 1873. V. 66

FRONTINUS
S. Julii Frontini Libri Quatuor Strategematicon...Curante Francisco Oudendorpio.... Lugduni Batavorum: 1731. V. 66

FROST, ANNIE
The Ladies' Guide to Needle Work, Embroidery, Etc. New York: 1877. V. 64

FROST, CHARLES
Notices Relative to the Early History of the Town and Port of Hull.... London: 1827. V. 64

FROST, DONALD
General Ashley - the Overland Trail and South Pass. Barre: 1945. V. 67
Notes on General Ashley, the Overland Trail and South Pass. Worcester: 1945. V. 64

FROST, H. GORDON
The Gentleman's Club. El Paso: 1983. V. 63; 66
I'm Frank Hammer: The Life of a Texas Peace Officer. Austin: 1968. V. 63

FROST, J.
The Mexican War and Its Warriors. New Haven and Philadlephia: 1848. V. 65
The Mexican War and Its Warriors. New Haven and Philadelphia: 1849. V. 66

FROST, JOHN
Thrilling Adventures Among the Indians Comprising the Most Remarkable Personal Narratives of Events in the Early Indian Wars.... Boston and Philadelphia: 1849. V. 64

FROST, LAWRENCE A.
The Custer Album - a Pictorial Biography of General George A. Custer. Seattle: 1964. V. 67
Custer's 7th Cavalry and the Campaign of 1873. El Segundo: 1986. V. 65
General Custer's Libbie. Seattle: 1976. V. 62; 67
General George Armstrong Custer. Dundee: 1968. V. 65
With Custer in '74. Provo: 1979. V. 67

FROST, ROBERT LEE
The Augustan Books of Poetry: Robert Frost. London: 1932. V. 62
A Boy's Will. London: 1913. V. 63
A Boy's Will. New York: 1915. V. 62; 63; 64; 65; 67
Collected Poems. New York: 1930. V. 64
Complete Poems of Robert Frost. New York: 1949. V. 64
The Complete Poems of Robert Frost. New York: 1950. V. 64
Complete Poems of Robert Frost. London: 1951. V. 65
In the Clearing. New York: 1962. V. 62; 63; 64; 67
A Masque of Mercy. New York: 1947. V. 67
A Masque of Reason. New York: 1945. V. 62
Mountain Interval. New York: 1916. V. 65
New Hampshire. A Poem with Notes and Trace Notes. New York: 1923. V. 64; 65
North of Boston. New York: 1915. V. 65
One Favored Acorn. Ripton: 1969. V. 66
Selected Poems. London: 1923. V. 65
Selected Poems. New York: 1923. V. 65
Selected Poems. New York: 1926. V. 65
Selected Poems. London: 1936. V. 63
Steeple Bush. New York: 1947. V. 62
West-Running Brook. New York: 1928. V. 62; 63; 64; 65; 67
A Witness Tree. New York: 1942. V. 62

FROST, TED
From Tree to Sea, the Building of a Wooden Steam Drifter. Lavenham: 1985. V. 67

FROST, THOMAS
The Secret Socieites of the European Revolution, 1776-1876. London: 1876. V. 64

FROUDE, JAMES ANTHONY
The English in Ireland in the Eighteenth Century. London: 1872. V. 64
The English in the West Indies, or the Bow Ulysses. London: 1888. V. 65
English Seamen in the Sixteenth Century. London: 1895. V. 63
English Seamen of the Sixteenth Century. London: 1911. V. 62
History of England from the Fall of Wolsey to the Defeat of the Spanish Armada. London: 1870. V. 62
The Nemesis of Faith. London: 1849. V. 63; 65
Thomas Carlyle. A History of His Life in London 1834-1881. London: 1885. V. 66
Thomas Carlyle. A History of the First Forty Years of His Life 1795-1835. London: 1882. V. 66
The Two Chiefs of Dunboy. 1889. V. 67

FRUIT of the Valley. Los Angeles: 1942. V. 63

FRY, CAROLINE
The Listener. London: 1831. V. 63; 65
The Listener. London: 1832. V. 64; 65
The Listener. London: 1836. V. 66

FRY, CHARLES BURGESS
The Book of Cricket. London: 1899. V. 66

FRY, CHRISTOPHER
Curtmantle. 1961. V. 65
A Phoenix Too Frequent. Helsinki: 1985. V. 63
Thor, with Angels. Canterbury: 1948. V. 64
A Yard of Sun: a Summer Comedy. London: 1970. V. 66

FRY, EDMUND
Pantographia.... London: 1799. V. 63

FRY, JAMES B.
McDowell and Tyler in the Campaign of Bull Run 1861. New York: 1884. V. 62; 63

FRY, JOHN
The Case of Marriages Between Near Kindred Particularly Considered.... London: 1773. V. 64

FRY, KATHARINE
Memoir of the Life of Elizabeth Fry, With Extracts from Her Journal and Letters. London: 1847. V. 65

FRY, LAWRENCE A.
Military Miscellanies. New York: 1889. V. 65

FRY, M.
Tropical Architecture in the Humid Zone. London: 1964. V. 65

FRY, ROGER
The Artist and Psycho-Analysis. London: 1924. V. 66
Giovanni Bellini. London: 1899. V. 62
A Sampler of Castile. Richmond: 1923. V. 63

FRY, ROGER ELIOT
Letters. New York: 1972. V. 64

FRY, W. G.
The Biology of Porifera. 1970. V. 63

FRYE, NORTHROP
Fearful Symmetry, a Study of William Blake. Princeton: 1947. V. 67

FRYER, JANE EAYRE
The Mary Frances Cook Book, or Adventures Among the Kitchen People. Philadelphia: 1912. V. 63; 67
Mary Frances Knitting and Crocheting Book. Philadelphia: 1918. V. 67
The Mary Frances Sewing Book or Adventures Among the Thimble People. Philadelphia: 1913. V. 62; 63; 67
The Mary Francis First Aid Book. Philadelphia: 1916. V. 66

FRYER, JOHN
A New Account of East-India and Persia; in Eight Letters, Being Nine Years Travels Begun 1672. London: 1698. V. 67

FRYKE, CHRISTOPHER
A Relation of Two Several Voyages Made into the East-Indies.... London: 1700. V. 67

FUCHS, ERNEST
Text-Book of Ophthalmology. New York: 1893. V. 67
Text-Book of Ophthalmology. New York: 1896. V. 64; 66; 67

FUCHS, LEONHARD
Alle Kranckheyt der Augen.... Strassburg: 1539. V. 63
De Historia Sitrpium Commentarii Insignes, Maximis Impensis et Vigilis Elaborati, Adiectis Earundem Vivis Plusquam.... Basel: 1542. V. 63

THE FUDGE Family in Edinburgh, in a Series of Poetical Epistles.... Edinburgh: 1820. V. 62; 66

FUELL, MELISSA
Blind Boone, His Early Life and Achievements. Kansas City: 1915. V. 63

FUENTES, CARLOS
Christopher Unborn. New York: 1989. V. 63
The Hydra Head. New York: 1978. V. 62
La Region mas Transparente. Mexico City: 1958. V. 67
Terra Nostra. New York: 1976. V. 62

FUERTES, LOUIS AGASSIZ
Abyssinian Birds and Mammals. Chicago: 1930. V. 67
Artist and Naturalist in Ethiopia. Garden City: 1936. V. 67
A Fuertes Portfolio of Texas Birds. Austin: 1977. V. 66

FUGATE, FRANCIS
The Spanish Heritage of the Southwest. El Paso: 1952. V. 63

FUGGER, WOLFGANG
Handwriting Manual. 1955. V. 64

FUGITIVES. An Anthology of Verse. New York: 1928. V. 64

FUHLROTT, J. K.
Menschliche Ueberreste Aus Felsengrotte des Dusselthals. Eine Beitrag Zur Frage Uber Die Existenz Fossiler Menschen. Bonn: 1859. V. 62; 64; 67

FUHRMAN, CHRIST
The Dangerous Lives of Altar Boys. Athens and London: 1994. V. 64; 66

FUJIKAWA, GYO
Mother Goose Portfolio of Prints. New York: 1960. V. 63

FUJIMOTO, T.
The Nightside of Japan. London: 1927. V. 67

FUJIWARA, KANESUKE
The Lady Who Loved Insects. London: 1929. V. 64

FULCHER, G. W.
Life of Thomas Gainsborough. 1856. V. 66

FULKE, WILLIAM
A Defense of the Sincere and True Translations of the Holie Scriptures into the English Tong, Against the Manifolde Cauils.... London: 1583. V. 63; 66

A FULL Report of the Case of Stacy Decow, and Joseph Henrickson, vs. Thomas L. Shotwell. Decided at a Special Term of the New Jersey Court of Appeals...Embracing the Decision of the Court of Chancery...the Arguments of the Counsel... Philadelphia: 1834. V. 63; 66

A FULL Statement of the Reasons Which Were in Part Offered to the Committee of the Legislature of Massachusetts...Respecting Abolitionits (sic) and Anti-Slavery Societies. Boston: 1836. V. 64

FULLAM, GEORGE TOWNLEY
Journal of George Townley Fullam, Boarding Officer of the Confederate Sea Raider Alabama. Mobile: 1973. V. 63; 65

FULLARTON, WILLIAM
A Letter, Addressed to the Right Hon. Lord Carrington, President of the Board of Agriculture. London: 1801. V. 63

FULLER, A. M.
Studies on the Flora of Wisconsin. Part I. The Orchids, Orchidaceae. Milwaukee: 1933. V. 67

FULLER, A. S.
The Grape Culturist; a Treatise on the Cultivation of the Native Grape. New York: 1967. V. 64

FULLER, ALFRED
Little People's Animal Book. London and New York: Sep. 1880. V. 65

FULLER, BUCKMINSTER
Intuition. New York: 1972. V. 63
Nine Chains to the Moon. Philadelphia and New York: 1938. V. 63
Untitled Epic Poem on the History of Industrialization. Highlands: 1962. V. 63
Untitled Epic Poem on the History of Industrialization. New York: 1962. V. 63

FULLER, CHARLES
A Soldier's Play. New York: 1982. V. 66

FULLER, CLAUD E.
Fire-arms of the Confederacy. Huntington: 1944. V. 62

FULLER, E.
Extinct Birds. London: 1987. V. 62; 64
The Great Auk. 1998. V. 63
Kiwis, a Monograph of the Family Apterygidae. Shrewsbury: 1991. V. 67

FULLER, GEORGE W.
A Bibliography of Bookplate Literature. Spokane: 1926. V. 64
A History of the Pacific North-West. New York: 1931. V. 64; 66

FULLER, HARLIN M.
The Journal of Captain John R. Bell, Official Journalist for Stephen H. Long Expedition to the Rocky Mountains. Glendale: 1967. V. 63

FULLER, HENRY C.
The Adventures of Bill Longley, Captured by Sheriff Milton Mart and Deputy Bill Burrows, Near Keatchie, Louisiana in 1877 and Was Executed at Giddings Texas in 1878. Nacagdoches. V. 65

FULLER, HENRY WILLIAM
On Diseases of the Lungs and Air-Passages; Their Pathology, Physical, Diagnosis, Symptoms and Treatment. Philadelphia: 1867. V. 67

FULLER, JOHN
A Bestiary. London: 1974. V. 62
Selected Poems 1954-1982. London: 1985. V. 63

FULLER, MARGARET
The Love-Letters of Margaret Fuller 1845-1846. New York: 1903. V. 63
The Works of Margaret Fuller. Boston: 1874. V. 63

FULLER, ROY
Brutus's Orchard - Poems. London: 1957. V. 64
Buff. London: 1965. V. 67
Catspaw. London: 1966. V. 67
Collected Poems 1936-1961. London: 1962. V. 67
Epitaphs and Occasions. London: 1949. V. 67
Fantasy and Fugue. London: 1954. V. 67
From the Joke Shop. London: 1975. V. 67
An Ill Governed Coast. Sunderland: 1976. V. 67
The Joke Shop Annexe. Edinburgh: 1975. V. 63
A Lost Season. London: 1944. V. 67
New Poems. London: 1968. V. 67
Off Course. London: 1969. V. 67
An Old War. Edinburgh: 1974. V. 63
The Other Planet and Three Other Fables. London: 1979. V. 64
The Other Planet and Three Other Fables. Surrey: 1979. V. 67
Owls and Artificers. London: 1971. V. 67
Poems. London: 1940. V. 62; 66; 67
Poor Boy. London: 1977. V. 67
The Reign of Sparrows. London: 1980. V. 67
The Second Curtain. London: 1953. V. 62
The Second Curtain. New York: 1956. V. 67
Song Cycle from a Record Sleeve. Oxford: 1972. V. 62
Strange Gold. A Story of Adventure. London: 1946. V. 67
Tiny Tears. London: 1973. V. 67
With My Little Eye. London: 1948. V. 67
With My Little Eye. New York: 1957. V. 67
The World through the Window. London: 1989. V. 67

FULLER, SAMUEL
A Serious Reply to...Abusive Queries Proposed to...the People Called Quakers, etc. Dublin: 1729. V. 62

FULLER, SARAH M.
Summer on the Lakes in 1843. Boston: 1844. V. 62; 65

FULLER, THOMAS
Abel Redivivus; or the Dead Yet Speaking. The Lives and Deaths of the Moderne Divines. London: 1651. V. 64
Anglorum Speculum, or the Worthies of England, in Church and State. London: 1684. V. 62; 63
The Church History of Britain from the Birth of Jesus Christ Until the Year MDCXLVIII. (with) The History of the University of Cambridge Since the Conquest. London: 1655. V. 66
The Church History of Britain, from the Birth of Jesus Christ Until the Year MDCXLVIII.... London: 1842. V. 63
The Church-History of Britain; from the Birth of Jesus Christ, Until the Year MDCXLVIII. London: 1845. V. 63
Gnomologia: Adagies and Proverbs.... London: 1732. V. 63; 64
The Historie of the Holy Warre... (wtih) The Holy State (The Profane State). Cambridge: 1651-1663. V. 63
The History of the Holy War. London: 1840. V. 62; 65
The History of the University of Cambridge, from the Conquest to the Year 1634. Cambridge: 1840. V. 66
The History of the Worthies of England.... London: 1811. V. 62
Pharmacopoeia Extemporanea; or, a Body of Medicines.... London: 1714. V. 65

FULLER, TIMOTHY
Reunion With Murder. Boston: 1941. V. 66

FULLER, WILLIAM
Architecture of the Brain. Grand Rapids: 1896. V. 64
A Plain Proof of the True Father and Mother of the Pretended Prince of Wales.... London: 1700. V. 62; 66

FULLERTON, GEORGIANA
Laurentia; a Tale of Japan. London: 1861. V. 65

FULLERTON, JAMES
Autobiography of Roosevelt's Adversary. Boston: 1912. V. 63

FULMAN, WILLIAM
Rerum Anglicarum Scriptorum Veterum. Oxoniae: 1684. V. 63
Rerum Anglicarum Scriptorum Veterum.... Oxoniae: 1684-1691. V. 66

FULOP-MILLER, RENE
The Russian Theatre. Its Character and History with Especial Reference to the Revolutionary Period. Philadelphia: 1930. V. 63

FULTON, A. R.
The Red Men of Iowa: Being a History of the Various Aboriginal Tribes Whose Homes Were in Iowa.... Des Moines: 1882. V. 65

FULTON, FRANCES I. SIMS
To and Through Nebraska. Lincoln: 1884. V. 63

FULTON, JOHN
Palestine: the Holy Land As It Was and As It Is. Philadelphia: 1900. V. 67

FULTON, JOHN FARQUHAR
A Bibliography of the Honourable Robert Boyle. Oxford: 1932. V. 64; 66; 67
The Bibliography of the Honourable Robert Boyle. Oxford: 1961. V. 62
A Bibliography of the Honourable Robert Boyle. (with) Addendum. 1932-1933. V. 67
Contribution to the Study of Tumors in the Region of the Third Ventricle: Their Diagnosis and Relation to Pathological Sleep. 1929. V. 67
Frontal Lobotomy and Affective Behavior. New York: 1951. V. 65
The Great Medical Bibliographers. Philadelphia: 1951. V. 64; 66
Harvey Cushing. A Biography. Springfield: 1947. V. 66
Harvey Cushing: a Biography. New York: 1991. V. 65
Michael Servetus Humanist and Martyr. New York: 1953. V. 64; 66
Selected Readings in the History of Physiology. Springfield: 1930. V. 65; 66
The Sign of Babinski. Springfield: 1932. V. 64; 65; 66; 67

FULTON, MAURICE G.
History of the Lincoln County War. Tucson: 1968. V. 64; 67

FULTON, ROBERT
Epic of the Overland. San Francisco: 1924. V. 64
The Illustrated Book of Pigeons.... London: 1876?. V. 65

FUN at the Circus. London: 1890. V. 64

FUNDAMENTALS of Hyperbaric Medicine. Washington: 1966. V. 66

FUNNY Picture Stories in the Struwwelpeter Manner. London: 1874-1876?. V. 66

FUR, Feather and Fin. The Fox. 1906. V. 67

FUR, Feather & Fin. The Hare. 1896. V. 67

FUR, Feather and Fin. Snipe and Woodcock. 1903. V. 67

FURBANK, P. N.
E. M. Forster; a Life. London: 1977-1978. V. 66

FURLONG, LAWRENCE
The American Coast Pilot.... Newburyport: 1798. V. 62

FURMAN, JAMES C.
Sermon on the Death of Rev. James M. Chiles, Preached at Horeb Church, Abbeville District, S.C. On Sunday 29th of March 1863. Greenville: 1863. V. 66

FURMAN, MOORE
The Letters of Moore Furman, Deputy Quarter-Master General of New Jersey in the Revolution. New York: 1912. V. 63; 66

FURMAN, WOOD
History of the Charleston Association of Baptist Churches in the State of South Carolina.... Charleston: 1811. V. 63; 66

FURNAS, ROBERT W.
Nebraska Her Resources - Adventures Advancement and Promises. New Orleans: 1885. V. 65

FURNEAUX, J. H.
Glimpses of India, a Grand Photographic History of the Land of Antiquity, the Vast Empire of the East. London: 1896. V. 63

FURNESS Year Book. Ulverston: 1896. V. 65
FURNESS Year Book. Ulverston: 1898. V. 66

FURNESS Year Book. Ulverston: 1899. V. 66
FURNESS Year Book. Ulverston: 1901. V. 65; 66
FURNESS Year Book. Ulverston: 1902. V. 65; 66
FURNESS Year Book. Ulverston: 1903. V. 66
FURNESS Year Book. Ulverston: 1904. V. 66
FURNESS Year Book. Ulverston: 1908. V. 66

FURNESS Year Book. Ulverston: 1909. V. 65

FURNESS, CLIFTON JOSEPH
Walt Whitman's Workshop. Cambridge: 1928. V. 66

FURNESS RAILWAY
Tours through Lake-Land. Barrow. V. 65

FURNESS, WILLIAM
History of Penrith from the Earliest Record to the Present Time. Penrith: 1894. V. 62; 65

FURNESS, WILLIAM HENRY
The Island of Stone Money; UAP of the Carolines. Philadelphia: 1910. V. 67

FURNISS, HARRY
The Confessions of a Caricaturist. New York and London: 1902. V. 66
Famous Crimes Past and Present. London: 1905. V. 63
Paradise in Picadilly, the Story of Albany. London: 1925. V. 62
The Two Pins Club. London: 1925. V. 67

FURNISS, NORMAN F.
The Mormon Conflict 1850-1859. New Haven: 1960. V. 65

FURNIVALL, FREDERICK J.
Anatomy of the Abuses in England in Shakespeare's Youth A.D. 1583. London: 1877-1879. V. 66
The Babees' Book.... New York: 1969. V. 63

FURNLEY, MAURICE
The Bay and Padie Book. Kiddie Songs. Melbourne-Sydney: 1918. V. 65

FURST, HERBERT
The Decorative Art of Frank Brangwyn: a Study of the Problems of Decoration with Special Reference to the Work of this Artist. London: 1924. V. 62; 63; 64
The Woodcut, an Annual. London: 1927. V. 63
The Woodcut, an Annual. London: 1927-1930. V. 64
The Woodcut. An Annual. London: 1929. V. 64

FURST, JILL LESLIE
Pre-Columbian Art of Mexico. New York: 1980. V. 62; 63; 64

FURST, VIKTOR
The Architecture of Sir Christopher Wren. London: 1956. V. 64

FURTHER and Still More Important Suppressed Documents. Boston: 1808?. V. 66

FURTTENBACH, JOSEF
Architectura Univeralis. Ulm: 1635. V. 64

FUSON, HARVEY H.
Ballads of the Kentucky Highlands. London: 1931. V. 63

FUSSELL, G. E.
The Old English Farming Books 1523 to 1730. (with) More Old English Farming Books 1731-1793. London: 1947-1950. V. 67
The Old English Farming Books from Fitzherbert to Tull 1523-1730. London: 1947. V. 65

FUSSELL, JAMES
A Refutation of Several Charges Alledged Against the Late J. Wesley, A.M. by the Rev. W. Ward, A.M. of Diss.... Diss: 1820. V. 64

FUSSELL, L.
A Journey Round the Coast of Kent.... London: 1818. V. 62

FUTURE Days, a Series of Letters to My Pupils. London: 1844. V. 65

FYFE, ANDREW
A Compendious System of Anatomy. Philadelphia: 1792. V. 64
One Hundred and Fifty-Eight Plates to Illustrate the Anatomy of the Human Body.... Edinburgh: 1830. V. 63

FYFE, HERBERT C.
Submarine Warfare, Past, Present and Future. London: 1902. V. 64

FYFIELD, FRANCES
A Question of Guilt. London: 1988. V. 66
Shadows on the Mirror. London: 1989. V. 66
Trial by Fire. London: 1990. V. 66

FYLEMAN, ROSE
The Katy Kruse Dolly Book. New York: 1927. V. 64
Katy Kruse Play Book. Philadelphia: 1930. V. 62
The Rose Fyleman Fairy Book. London: 1923. V. 62; 66

FYSON, P. F.
The Flora of the Nilgiri and Pulney Hill-Tops (Above 6500 Feet). Madras: 1954-1972. V. 62

G

G., C.
An Elegie Upon the Most Lamented Death of the Right Honourable and Truly Valiant, Robert Earle of Essex, &c. London: 1646. V. 66

G., W.
The Alphabet of Virtues in Verse. London: 1852. V. 65

G., W. E.
Odds and Ends from the Portfolio of an Amateur. London: 1820. V. 66

GABO, NAUM
Of Divers Arts. London: 1962. V. 63

GABRIELI, VITTORIO
Sir Kenelm Digby. Roma: 1957. V. 66; 67

GABRIELSON, I. N.
The Birds of Alaska. Harrisburg: 1959. V. 62; 63; 64; 65
Birds of Oregon. 1940. V. 65; 67
Western American Alpines. New York: 1932. V. 67

GACON DUFOUR, MARIE ARMANDE JEANNE
Moyens de Conserver la Sante des Habitans des Campagnes et de les Preserver de Maladies dans leurs Maisons et dans les Champs. Paris: 1806. V. 66

GADD, C. J.
Iraq. Volume VIII. 1946. London: 1946. V. 67

GADDIS, MAXWELL P.
Last Words and Old-Time Memories. New York: 1880. V. 67

GADDIS, WILLIAM
A Frolic of His Own. New York: 1994. V. 63; 66
J.R. New York: 1975. V. 62; 64; 65
The Recognitions. New York: 1955. V. 62; 63; 64; 67
The Recognitions. 1962. V. 63

GADOW, HANS
In Northern Spain. London: 1897. V. 65

GAEDE, MARC
Sundance: the Robert Sundance Story. La Canada: 1994. V. 67

THE GAELIC Choir. London. V. 62
THE GAELIC Choir. Paisley. V. 62

GAETAN, ANGELIQUE ROSE
Le Merite des Hommes. Poeme. Paris: 1801. V. 63

GAEVSKAYA, N. S.
The Role of Higher Aquatic Plants in the Nutrition of the Animals of Fresh-Water Basins. 1969. V. 65; 67

GAG, FLAVIA
Chubby's First Year. New York: 1960. V. 64
Sing a Song of Seasons. New York: 1936. V. 64

GAG, WANDA
The ABC Bunny. New York: 1933. V. 64
The Funny Thing. New York: 1929. V. 62
Millions of Cats. New York: 1928. V. 62
Millions of Cats. New York: 1933. V. 63
Nothing At All. New York: 1941. V. 62; 66

GAGE, JACK
The Johnson County War Ain't A Pack of Lies (Back to Back With) Is a Pack of Lies. Cheyenne: 1967. V. 65

GAGE, JOHN
The History and Antiquities of Hengrave, in Suffolk. London: 1822. V. 66
The History and Antiquities of Suffolk, Thingoe Hundred. 1838. V. 65

GAGE, S. H.
Life History of the Vermillion-Spotted Newt. Salem: 1891. V. 67
The Microscope and Microscopical Methods. Part I of the Microscope and Histology. Ithaca: 1894. V. 67

GAGE, THOMAS
A New Survey of the West India's, or the English American His Travail by Sea and Land.... London: 1655. V. 66

GAGNAEIUS
Grevissima Et Facillima in Omnes Pauli Epistolas Scholia, Ultra Priores Editiones.... Parisiis: 1563. V. 66

GAIL, OTTO WILLI
Mit Rakentenkraft Ins Weltenall. Stuttgart: 1928. V. 64; 67

GAIMAN, NEIL
Angels and Visitations: a Miscellany. Minneapolis: 1993. V. 65

GAINES, ERNEST J.
In My Father's House. New York: 1978. V. 67
A Lesson Before Dying. New York: 1993. V. 63; 66; 67
The Turtles. San Francisco: 1956. V. 62; 64; 67

GAINES, MARY LOUISE
I Heah de Voices Callin'. Atlanta: 1916. V. 67

GAINSBOROUGH, THOMAS
The Letters. London: 1961. V. 62; 67

GAIRDNER, JAMES
Lollardy and the Reformation in England, an Historical Survey. London: 1908-1913. V. 63

GAITSKILL, MARY
Bad Behavior. New York: 1988. V. 63; 65

GALBRAITH, JAMES
City Poems and Songs. Glasgow: 1868. V. 66

GALBRAITH, JOHN KENNETH
The Affluent Society. Boston: 1958. V. 63

GALBRAITH, JOHN S.
The Hudson's Bay Company as an Imperial Factor 1821-1869. Berkeley and Los Angeles: 1957. V. 62; 65

GALE, GEORGE
Upper Mississippi: or, Historical Sketches of the Mould Builders, the Indian Tribes, and the Progress of Civilization in the North West.... Chicago: 1867. V. 62

GALE, NORMAN
All Expenses Paid. Chicago: 1896. V. 66
Cricket Songs. London: 1894. V. 64
Songs for Little People. Westminster: 1896. V. 64

GALE, ROGER
Registrum Honoris de Richmond: Exhibens Terrarum and Villarum Quae Quondam Fuerunt Edwini Comitis Infra Richmundshire Descriptionem.... London: 1722. V. 63; 65; 66

GALE, THOMAS
Historiae Britannicae Saxinicae, Anglo-Danicae, Scriptores XV. Oxonia: 1691. V. 67
Historiae Poeticae Scriptores Antiqui. Parisiis: 1675. V. 63
Opuscula Mythologica Physica et Ethica. Amsterdam: 1688. V. 64

GALE, THOMAS A.
The Wonder of the Nineteenth Century, Rock Oil in Pennsylvania and Elsewhere. 1935. V. 67

GALEANO, EDUARDO
Memory of Fire. Genesis. Memory of Fire. Faces and Masks. Memory of Fire. Century of the Wind. New York: 1985. V. 66

GALELLA, RON
Jacqueline. New York: 1974. V. 67

GALENUS
Cl. Galeni Pergameni Omnia Quae Extant, In Latinem Sermonem Conversa.... 1562-1561. V. 65
Claudii Galeni De Simplificium Medicamentorum Facultatibus, Libri XI. Lugduni: 1561. V. 65; 66
Epitome Galeni Pergame ni Opervm, In Qvatvor Partes Digest.... Basilaea: 1551. V. 62; 66
Galen on Anatomical Procedures.... London: 1956. V. 64; 66
Galen on Medical Experience. London: 1944. V. 64
Galen on the Usefulness of the Parts of the Body. Ithaca: 1968. V. 64; 66
In Hippocratis Librum de Humoribus, Commentarii Tres.... Venetiis: 1562. V. 64; 66; 67
On Medical Experience. London: 1946. V. 63; 65
A Translation of Galen's Hygiene. Springfield: 1951. V. 65

GALERIE du Musee Napoleon.... Paris: 1804-1815. V. 64

GALERIE Theatrale, Ou Collection des Portraits en Pied, des Principaux Acteurs des Trois Premiers Theatres de la Capitale. Paris: 1812-1834. V. 65

GALET, JULES
El Cuerpo del Hombre o la Anatomia y Fisiologia Humanas, Puestas al Alcance de Todas las Clases de la Sociedad.... Barcelona: 1844-1846. V. 65

GALIANI, FERDINANDO
Della Perfetta Conservazione del Grano, Discorso di bartolommeo Intieri. Naples: 1754. V. 64

GALIBERT, LEON
L'Algeria Antica e Moderna, Dai Primi Ordini de'Cartaginesi Inso Alla Presa della Samala d'aB-el-Kader. Napoli: 1846. V. 66

GALILEI, GALILEO
Dialogo...Dove ne i Congressi di Quattro Giornate si Discorre Sopra i due Massimi Sistemi del Mondo Tolemaico, e Copernicano.... Fiorenza: 1710. V. 63
Dialogo...sopra i Due Massimi Sistemi del Mondo Tolemaico, e Copernicano.... Florence: 1632. V. 62; 63; 66
Istoria e Dimostrazioni Intorno alle Macchie Solari e Loro Accidenti Comprese in Tre Lettere Scritte all'Illustrissimo Signor Mateo Velseri Linceo.... Rome: 1613. V. 63
Opere....Coll' Aggiunta di Vari Trattati dell' Istesso Autore non Piu Dati Alle Stampe. Florence: 1718. V. 67

GALINDO, CATHERINE
Mrs. Galindo's Letter to Mrs. Siddons.... London: 1809. V. 62

GALITZINE, PRINCE GEORGE
Imperial Splendour: Palaces and Monasteries of Old Russia. New York: 1991. V. 67

GALL, F. J.
Des Dispositions Innees de l'Ame et de l'Esprit, du Materialisme, du Fatalisme et de la Liberte Morale avec des Reflexions sur l'Education.. Paris. 1811. V. 65
Recherches sur Le Systeme Nerveux en General, et Sur Celui Du Cerveau En Particulier.... Paris: 1809. V. 64; 67

GALLAEI, SERVATIUS
Sibyllina Oracula. Amstelodami: 1689. V. 65

GALLAGHER, FRANK
The Indivisible Island: History of the Partition of Ireland. 1957. V. 64; 67

GALLAGHER, M.
The Birds of Oman. London: 1980. V. 64

GALLAGHER, STEPHEN
Chimera. New York: 1982. V. 62; 65

GALLAGHER, TESS
Amplitude. St. Paul: 1987. V. 62
A Concert of Tenses. Ann Arbor: 1986. V. 62
Stepping Outside. Lisbon: 1974. V. 64
Stepping Outside. Lisbon: 1975. V. 64; 67
Willingly. Port Towsend: 1984. V. 63

GALLAHER, DE WITT CLINTON
A Diary Depicting the Experiences of De Witt Clinton Gallaher in the War Between the States. Charleston: 1961. V. 63

GALLANT, MAVIS
Green Water Green Sky. London: 1960. V. 65
The Other Paris. Boston: 1956. V. 63; 64

GALLATIN, A. E.
American Water-Colourists. New York: 1922. V. 62; 65

GALLATIN, ALBERT
Views of the Public Debt, Receipts and Expenditures of the United States. New York: 1800. V. 62

GALLATIN, ALBERT EUGENE
Notes on Some Rare Portraits of Whistler - With Six Examples Hitherto Unpublished. New York and London: 1916. V. 64
Paul Manship, a Critical Essay on His Sculpture and an Iconography. New York: 1917. V. 66
Portraits of Whistler. New York: 1918. V. 66

GALLE, F. C.
Azaleas. Portland: 1987. V. 67

GALLEGO, JULIAN
Zurbaran 1598-1664. Biography and Critical Analysis. Catalogue of the Works. London: 1977. V. 64

GALLENGA, GUY HARDWIN
Gun, Rifle and Hound in East and West. 1894. V. 62; 63; 67

GALLICHAN, WALTER M.
Fishing and Travel in Spain. 1904. V. 67
The Trout Waters of England. London: 1908. V. 67

GALLO, AGOSTINO
Le Vinte Giorni Sull'Agricoltura et de' Piaceri Della Villa. In Venetia: 1596. V. 63; 64; 66
Le Vinti Giornate Dell'Agricoltura et de Piaceri Della Villa. In Venetia: 1622. V. 63; 66

GALLOE, O.
Natural History of the Danish Lichens.... Copenhagen: 1927. V. 67

GALLON, M.
Arte de Convertier el Cobre en Laton por Medio de la Piedra Calamina.... Madrid: 1779. V. 64; 66

GALLOWAY, ELIJAH
History and Progress of the Steam Engine. London: 1830. V. 62

GALLOWAY, F. C.
Objects in the Museum of the Bronte Society at Haworth. 1896. V. 64
Objects in the Museum of the Bronte Society at Haworth. Bradford: 1896. V. 63

GALLOWAY, JOSEPH
A Letter to the Right Honourable Lord Viscount H---e on His Naval Conduct in the American War. London: 1779. V. 64

GALLOWAY, R. L.
Annals of Coal Mining and the Coal Trade. London: 1898-1904. V. 62

GALLOWAY, SAMUEL
Ergonomy; or, Industrial Science. Princeton: 1853. V. 66

GALLOWAY, VINCENT
The Oils and Mural of Sir Frank Brangwyn, R.A., 1867-1956. Leigh-on-Sea: 1962. V. 63; 64

GALLUCCI, PAOLO
Della Fabrica et Uso di Diversi Stromenti di Astronomia, et Cosmographia, oue si uede la Somma Della Teorica, et Practica di Queste due Nobilissime Scienze. Venice: 1598. V. 63

GALLUP, DONALD
Ezra Pound - a Bibliography. Charlottesville: 1983. V. 65
T. S. Eliot - a Bibliography. London: 1952. V. 63

GALLUP, JOSEPH A.
Outlines of the Institutes of Medicine: Founded on the Philosophy of the Human Economy in Health and Disease. Boston: 1839. V. 63; 66

GALLUS, HEINRICH
Delcaratio Instrumenti Astronomici Novi Quo Non Solum Horae Cuiuscunque Generis Interdiu Noctuque Dignosci.... Erfurt: 1574. V. 62

GALOIS, EVARISTE
Oeuvres Mathematiques d'Evariste Galois. (bound with) Manuscrits de Evariste Galois publies par Jules Tannery. Paris: 1897-1908. V. 65

GALSWORTHY, JOHN
Flowering Wilderness. London: 1932. V. 64
The Forsyte Saga. London: 1922. V. 62
From the Four Winds. London: 1897. V. 64; 66
The Man of Property. New York: 1964. V. 63; 66
A Modern Comedy. London: 1929. V. 64
The Plays of John Galsworthy. London: 1932. V. 64
Plays: Sixth Series. The Forest. Old English. The Show. London: 1925. V. 64
Swan Song. London: 1928. V. 62; 64
The White Monkey. London: 1924. V. 63

GALT, EDWIN
The Camp and the Cutter; or a Cruise to the Crimea. London: 1856. V. 67

GALT, JOHN
Annals of the Parish; or the Chronicle of Dalmailing.... Edinburgh: 1821. V. 64; 65; 66
The Ayrshire Legatees; or the Pringle Family. Edinburgh: 1821. V. 62; 65
Bogle Corbet; or, the Emigrants. London: 1831. V. 65
Lawrie Todd; or, the Settlers in the Woods. London: 1830. V. 65
The Life and Studies of Benjamin West, Esq. London: 1816. V. 67
The Life and Studies of Benjamin West, Esq. Philadelphia: 1816. V. 63; 64; 66
The Radical: an Autobiography. London: 1832. V. 67
Ringan Gilhaize; or the Convenanters. Edinburgh: 1823. V. 62; 65; 66
The Spaewife; a Tale of the Scottish Chronicles. Edinburgh: 1823. V. 66
The Works of.... Edinburgh: 1936. V. 63

GALTON, DOUGLAS
Healthy Hospitals. Oxford: 1893. V. 63

GALTON, FRANCIS
Essays in Eugenics. London: 1909. V. 64; 65
Finger Prints. London: 1892. V. 62
Fingerprint Directories. London: 1895. V. 62
Hereditary Genius; an Inquiry into Its Laws and Consequences. London: 1869. V. 64
Inquiries into Human Faculty and Its Development. London: 1883. V. 65
An Inquiry into the Physiognomy of Phthisis by the Method of Composite Portraiture. 1885. V. 67
Natural Inheritance. London: 1889. V. 62; 64
Vacation Tourists and Notes of Travel in 1860 and 1861. London: 1861-1862. V. 63

GALTON, JOHN CHARLES
The Myology of the Upper and Lower Extremities of Orycteropus Capensis (Aardvark). 1868. V. 67

GALVANI, ALOYSII
Aloysii Galvani de Manzoliniana Supellectili Oratio Habita in Scientiarum et Artium Institute Cum ad Anatomen in Tabulis ab Anna Manzolina Perfectis Publice Tradendam Aggrederetur. Bologna. 1777. V. 65

GALVANI, LUIGI
Commentary on the Effect of Electricity on Muscular Motion. Cambridge: 1953. V. 65

GALVIN, JOHN
The Etching of Edward Borein, a Catalog of His Work. San Francisco: 1981. V. 63
Through the Country of the Comanche Indians in the Fall of the Year 1845. The Journal of U.S. Army Expedition Led by Lt. James W. Abert. San Francisco: 1970. V. 63; 66

GAMA, J. P.
Traite Des Plaises de Tete et de L'Encephalite, Principalement de Celle Qui Leur Est Consecutive.... Paris: 1835. V. 64

GAMA, JOSE BASILIO DA
O Uraguay, O Poema.... Lisbon: 1769. V. 62

GAMBA, PIETRO, COUNT
A Narrative of Lord Byron's Last Journey to Greece. London: 1825. V. 62

GAMBLE, DAVID
The Descendants of Roger Gower. 1897. V. 63; 66

GAMBLE, GEORGE
The Halls. London: 1899. V. 67

GAMBLE, J. S.
The Bambuseae of British India. Calcutta: 1896. V. 63; 66

GAMBLE, SIDNEY GOMPERTZ
A Practical Treatise on Outbreaks of Fire.... London: 1931. V. 64

GAMBOA, FRANCISCO XAVIER DE
Commentaries on the Mining Ordinances of Spain.... London: 1830. V. 65

GAMBRILL, RICHARD
Sporting Stables and Kennels. New York: 1925. V. 64

GAME Pie - a Guinness Indoor Sportfolio. Dublin: 1955. V. 65

GAMES for Playtime and Parties for Children of All Ages. London. V. 63

GAMES of Skill and Conjuring Including Draughts, Dominoes, Chess..., Conjuring, Legerdemain, Tricks with Apparatus, Tricks with Cards.... London: 1861. V. 63

GAMING Houses. The Trial of the King Against Rich. Bennett, Fred. Oldfield, John Phillips and Thomas Carlos and of the King Against Charles Edward Rogier and William Southwell Humphries, for Misdemeanors in Keeping Common Gaming Houses.... London: 1823. V. 63

GAMMAGE, R. G.
History of the Chartist Movement 1837-1854. Newcastle-on-Tyne: 1894. V. 64

GAMMOND, PETER
A Bibliographical Companion to Betjeman. London: 1997. V. 65

GANE, DOUGLAS M.
Tristan da Cunha. London: 1932. V. 67

GANF, R. W.
Marsupials of Australia. Melbourne: 1979-1988. V. 62; 63; 65; 66

GANGOLLY, S. R.
The Mango. New Delhi: 1957. V. 66

GANGWERE, S. K.
The Bionomics of Grasshoppers, Katydids and Their Kia. Wallingford: 1997. V. 63

GANILH, CHARLES
An Inquiry into the Various Systems of Political Economy; Their Advantages and Disadvantages.... London: 1812. V. 63; 64

GANN, A. W.
The New Zealand Emigrants Bradshaw, or, Guide to the Britain of the South. London: 1858. V. 67

GANNETT, RUTH STILES
My Father's Dragon. New York: 1948. V. 65

GANSSER, EMIL B.
History of the 126th Infantry in the War with Germany. Grand Rapids: 1920. V. 65

GANT, ROLAND
Steps to the River. London: 1994. V. 65

GANTILLON, SIMON
Maya. Waltham St. Lawrence: 1930. V. 64; 65; 66

GANTT, E.
Handbook of Phycological Methods. Cambridge: 1980. V. 65

GANTT, W. HORSLEY
A Medical Review of Soviet Russia. London: 1928. V. 67

GANTZHORN, VOLKMAR
The Christian Oriental Carpet. 1991. V. 63

GARBER, VIRGINIA A.
The Armistead Family 1635-1910. Richmond: 1910. V. 63; 67

GARBETT, H.
The History of Harthill-w-Woodall and Its Hamlet Kiveton Park (the Latter Until A.D. 1868 When It Became Part of Wales Parish). Ilfracombe: 1950. V. 65

GARCES, FRANCISCO
A Record of Travels in Arizona and California, 1775-1776. San Francisco: 1965. V. 65
A Record of Travels in Arizona and California, 1775-1776. San Francisco: 1967. V. 63; 64

GARCIA, ANDREW
Tough Trip through Paradise 1878-1879. Boston: 1967. V. 64; 67

GARCIA, CRISTINA
Dreaming in Cuban. New York: 1992. V. 62; 64; 65; 66

GARCIA LORCA, FEDERICO
Antologia Poetica (1918-1936).... Buenos Aires: 1943. V. 65
Poemas Postumos: Canciones Musicales Divan del Tamarit. Mexico: 1945. V. 66
Poeta en Nueva York. Mexico City: 1940. V. 66
Sonnets of Dark Love. 1989. V. 65; 66
Sun and Shadow. London: 1972. V. 65

GARCIA MARQUEZ, GABRIEL
El Amor en Los Tiempos del Colera. Bogota: 1985. V. 62
El Amor en Los Tiempos Del Colera. (Love in the Time of Cholera). Buenos Aires: 1986. V. 64; 66
The Autumn of the Patriarch. New York: 1976. V. 65
La Aventura de Miguel Littin Clandestino en Chile. Colombia: 1986. V. 65
Cronica de Una Muerte Anunciada. Bogata: 1981. V. 65
El Coronel No Tiene Quien le Escriba. Medellin: 1961. V. 62; 63; 64; 66
Entre Cachacos, Volume I. Buenos Aires: 1988. V. 62
Entre Cachacos. Volume II. Buenos Aires: 1989. V. 62
Los Funerales de la Mama Grande. Xalapa: 1962. V. 62
Los Funerales de la Mama Grande. Mexico City: 1986. V. 62
El General en su Laberinto. Mexico City. 1989. V. 62
The General in His Labyrinth. New York: 1990. V. 65
The General in His Labyrinth. London: 1991. V. 63; 66
The General in His Labyrinth. New York: 1993. V. 62
La Hojarasca. Bogota: 1955. V. 65; 67
La Hojarasca. Mexico City: 1986. V. 62
In Evil Hour. New York: 1979. V. 64
Innocent Erendira and Other Stories. New York: 1978. V. 63; 67
Love in the Time of Cholera. New York: 1988. V. 62
La Mala Hora. Madrid: 1962. V. 66
No One Writes to the Colonel. New York: 1968. V. 67
No One Writes to the Colonel. London: 1971. V. 67
El Olor de la Guayaba. Bogota: 1982. V. 62
One Hundred Years of Solitude. New York & Evanston: 1970. V. 62; 64; 65; 67
The Solitude of Latin American. Nobel Lecture. New York: 1984. V. 64

GARCILASSO DE LA VEGA, INCA
The Royal Commentaries of Peru, In Two Parts. London: 1688. V. 67

GARD, E. CHAPIN
Palmer Lake and Environments. Palmer Lake: 1895. V. 65

GARD, WAYNE
Along the Early Trails of the Southwest. Austin: 1969. V. 63; 66
The Chisholm Trail. Norman: 1954. V. 64
Sam Bass. Boston: 1936. V. 63; 64; 67

GARDEN, ALEXANDER
Anecdotes of the American Revolution. Charleston: 1828. V. 63; 66
Anecdotes of the American Revolution. Brooklyn: 1865. V. 63
Anecdotes of the Revolutionary War in America.... Charleston: 1822. V. 63; 66
Six Letters to the Rev. Mr. George Whitefield. Boston: 1740. V. 66

THE GARDEN *Magazine....* New York: 1905-1907. V. 67

THE GARDEN *of Caresses.* Waltham St. Lawrence: 1934. V. 64

THE GARDEN *of the Night - Twenty-Six Sufi Poems.* Andoversford: 1979. V. 65

THE GARDENER'S *New Kalendar....* London: 1758. V. 67

GARDENIER, ANDERSON A.
The Successful Stockman and Manual of Husbandry. Canada: 1899. V. 64; 67

GARDENIER, ANDREW A.
The Successful Stockman and Manual of Husbandry. Springfield: 1899. V. 66

GARDENING *Illustrated.* London: 1908-1912. V. 67

GARDENS *in Edwardian England.* Woodbridge: 1985. V. 67

GARDENSHIRE, SAMUEL M.
The Long Arm. New York: 1906. V. 65

GARDI, R.
African Crafts and Craftsmen. New York: 1969. V. 62

GARDINER, ALAN
Egyptian Grammar, Being an Introduction to the Study of Hieroglyphs. London: 1950. V. 64

GARDINER, DOROTHY
Raymond Chandler Speaking. 1962. V. 67
Raymond Chandler Speaking. Boston: 1962. V. 65

GARDINER, FREDERIC JOHN
History of Wisbech and Neighbourhood, During the Last Fifty Years 1848-1898. 1898. V. 63

GARDINER, HOWARD C.
In Pursuit of the Golden Dream, Reminiscences of San Francisco and the Northern and Southern Mines 1849-1857. San Francisco: 1970. V. 64

GARDINER, J. STANLEY
The Fauna and Geography of the Maldive and Laccadive Archipelagoes.... Cambridge: 1901-1906. V. 67
The Natural History of Wicken Fen. Cambridge: 1923-1932. V. 62; 63

GARDINER, JOHN
An Inquiry into the Nature, Cause and Cure of the Gout and Some of the Diseases with Which It Is Connected. Edinburgh: 1792. V. 62

GARDINER, ROBERT
The Complete Constable. London: 1728. V. 62; 63

GARDINER, SAMUEL RAWSON
History of the Commonwealth and Protectorate 1649-1656. London: 1903. V. 64
History of the Commonwealth and Protectorate, 1649-1660. London: 1897. V. 66
Oliver Cromwell. London: 1899. V. 62; 63; 65; 67

GARDINER, WILLIAM
The Music of Nature...of the Animated World. Boston: 1838. V. 66
Twenty Lessons on British Mosses; First Steps to a Knowledge of the Beautiful Tribe of Plants. London: 1848. V. 64

GARDNER, ALAN, MRS.
Rifle and Spear with the Rajpoots. 1895. V. 63

GARDNER, ARTHUR
The Art and Sport of Alpine Photography. London: 1927. V. 62; 63; 64

GARDNER, C. A.
The Toxic Plants of Western Australia. Perth: 1956. V. 64; 66

GARDNER, CHARLES
Court Martial Proceedings of a General Court Martial, Held at Fort Independence, (Boston Harbor), for the Trial of Major Charles K. Gardner, of the Third Regiment Infantry, Upon Charges of Misbehaviour.... Boston: 1816. V. 63; 66

GARDNER, ERLE STANLEY
The Case of the Amorous Aunt. 1963. V. 67
The Case of the Angry Mourner. 1951. V. 67
The Case of the Backward Mule. 1946. V. 67
The Case of the Baited Hook. 1940. V. 66
The Case of the Beautiful Beggar. 1965. V. 67
The Case of the Black-Eyed Blonde. 1944. V. 67
The Case of the Black-Eyed Blonde. New York: 1944. V. 65
The Case of the Careless Cupid. New York: 1968. V. 67
The Case of the Demure Defendant. 1956. V. 67
The Case of the Drowning Duck. 1942. V. 66
The Case of the Dubious Bridegroom. 1949. V. 67
The Case of the Duplicate Daughter. 1960. V. 67
The Case of the Fiery Fingers. 1951. V. 67
The Case of the Foot-Loose Doll. 1958. V. 67

GARDNER, ERLE STANLEY continued
The Case of the Gilded Lily. 1956. V. 67
The Case of the Half-Wakened Wife. 1945. V. 67
The Case of the Horrified Heirs. 1964. V. 67
The Case of the Lucky Loser. 1957. V. 67
The Case of the Moth Eaten Mink. 1952. V. 67
The Case of the Negligent Nymph. 1950. V. 67
The Case of the One-Eyed Witness. New York: 1950. V. 67
The Case of the Reluctant Model. 1961. V. 67
The Case of the Screaming Woman. 1957. V. 67
The Case of the Shapely Shadow. 1960. V. 67
The Case of the Terrified Typist. 1956. V. 67
The Case of the Vagabond Virgin. 1948. V. 67
The Case of the Wayland Wolf. 1959. V. 67
The Court of Last Resort. New York: 1952. V. 65
Cut Thin to Win. 1965. V. 67
The D. A. Breaks a Seal. New York: 1946. V. 65
The D. A. Breaks an Egg. 1949. V. 67
Neighbourhood Frontiers. 1954. V. 66
Turn on the Heat. New York: 1940. V. 66

GARDNER, HAMILTON
History of Lehi Including a Biographical Section. Salt Lake City: 1913. V. 65

GARDNER, ISABELLA
That Was Then. New and Selected Poems. New York: 1979. V. 63

GARDNER, J. D.
Catalogue of the Principal Portion of the Valuable Library of John Dunn Gardner, Esq. of Chatteris, Cambridgeshire, Removed from His Late Residence, Bottisham Hall, Near Newmarket. London: 1854. V. 62

GARDNER, JOHN
The Alliterative Morte Arthure, The Owl and the Nightingale and Five Other Middle English Poems in a Modernized Version with Comments on the Poems and Notes. Carbondale and Edwardsvile: 1971. V. 66
The Art of Fiction. New York: 1984. V. 62
Cold. London: 1996. V. 65; 66
The Construction of Christian Poetry in Old English. Carbondale & Edwardsville: 1975. V. 66
The Construction of the Wakefield Cycle. Carbondale & Edwardsville: 1974. V. 66
Dragon, Dragon and Other Tales. New York: 1975. V. 66
The Forms of Fiction. New York: 1962. V. 63; 64
Frankenstein. 1979. V. 65
Frankenstein. Dallas: 1979. V. 66
The Gawain-Poet Notes. Lincoln: 1967. V. 66
Grendel. New York: 1971. V. 66; 67
Grendel. London: 1972. V. 62; 66
Licence Renewed. London: 1981. V. 64; 66; 67
Le Morte D'Arthur Notes. Lincoln: 1967. V. 66
MSS. Spring 1981. Dallas: 1981. V. 66
Nobody Lives For Ever. London: 1986. V. 63
On Becoming a Novelist. New York: 1983. V. 62
On Moral Fiction. New York: 1978. V. 66
Poems. Northridge: 1978. V. 66
The Poetry of Chaucer. Carbondale & Edwardsville: 1977. V. 62; 66
The Resurrection. New York: 1966. V. 67
Rumpelstiltskin. 1979. V. 65
Rumpelstiltskin. Dallas: 1979. V. 66
The Sunlight Dialogues. New York: 1972. V. 64; 67
The Sunlight Dialogues. London: 1973. V. 64
The Temptation Game. N.P: 1980. V. 66
Vlemk. The Box-Painter. Northridge: 1979. V. 66
William Wilson. Dallas: 1979. V. 66; 67
The Wreckage of Agathon. New York: 1970. V. 62; 66

GARDNER, LEONARD
Fat City. New York: 1969. V. 63; 67

GARDNER, MARTIN
The Wizard of Oz and Who He Was. East Lansing: 1957. V. 66

GARDNER, PERCY
Sculptured Tombs of Hellas. London: 1896. V. 65

GARDNER, THOMAS
A Pocket Guide to the English Traveller.... London: 1719. V. 66

THE GARDYNERS Passetaunce. (c. 1512). London: 1985. V. 66

GARELICK, MAY
Down to the Each. New York: 1973. V. 64

GARFIELD & Arthur Campaign Song Book. 1880. V. 66

GARFIELD, BRIAN
Death Wish. New York: 1972. V. 66

GARFITT, ALAN
The Book for the Police. London: 1958. V. 66

GARGA, D. P.
From My Big Game Diaries. Calcutta: 1944. V. 62; 63

GARGIULO, RAFFAELE
Recueil des Monumens les Plus Interessans du Musee national de Naples. Naples: 1874. V. 66

GARIMBERTO, HIERONIMO
Problemi Naturali, e Morali. Venice: 1549. V. 62

GARIS, HOWARD R.
The Adventures of Uncle Wiggily. Newark: 1924. V. 64
The Adventures of Uncle Wiggily the Bunny Rabbit Gentleman with the Twinkling Pink Nose. New York: 1924. V. 63
Uncle Wiggily's Arabian Nights. Chicago: 1917. V. 65
Uncle Wiggily's Friends. New York: 1939. V. 62
Uncle Wiggily's Holidays. New York: 1919. V. 63

A GARLAND for Jake Zeitlin on the Occasion of His 65th Birthday and the Anniversary of His 40th Year in the Book Trade. Los Angeles: 1967. V. 64

GARLAND, H. P.
The Water Buffalo.... Maine: 1922. V. 67

GARLAND, HAMLIN
The Book of the American Indian. New York: 1923. V. 64; 65; 67
A Daughter of the Middle Border. New York: 1921. V. 67

GARLAND, RICHARD
A Tour in Teesdale.... York: 1813. V. 65
A Tour in Teesdale.... London: 1848. V. 65

GARLAND, T.
Toxic Plants and Other Natural Toxicants. Wallingford: 1998. V. 63; 67

GARMAN, P.
Guide to the Insects of Connecticut. Part V. The Odonata or Dragonflies of Connecticut. Hartford: 1927. V. 67

GARMAN, S.
The Plagiostomia. Cambridge: 1913. V. 64

GARNER, ALAN
The Aimer Gate. 1978. V. 65
Granny Reardun. 1977. V. 65
Granny Reardun. London: 1977. V. 62
The Owl Service. London: 1967. V. 62

GARNER, R.
The Natural History of the County of Stafford. 1844. V. 62; 65; 66
The Natural History of the County of Stafford. London: 1844. V. 62; 63

GARNER, R. L.
Gorillas and Chimpanzees. 1896. V. 62; 63; 64; 66

GARNER, THOMAS
The Domestic Architecture of England During the Tudor Period. New York: 1929. V. 67

GARNETT, DAVID
Beany-Eye. London: 1935. V. 65; 66
Go She Must!. London: 1927. V. 63
The Grasshoppers Come. London: 1931. V. 65; 66
Lady into Fox. London: 1922. V. 63
A Man in the Zoo. London: 1924. V. 62
No Love. London: 1929. V. 62; 66
A Rabbit in the Air, Notes from a Diary Kept While Learning to Handle and Aeroplane. London: 1932. V. 66
The Sailor's Return. London: 1925. V. 65
The Sons of the Falcon. London: 1972. V. 64

GARNETT, EDWARD
An Imaged World: Poems in Prose. London: 1894. V. 64
Paradox Club. London: 1888. V. 63
The Trial of Jeanne d'Arc. London: 1912. V. 62
Turgenev - a Study. London: 1917. V. 62

GARNETT, JAMES M.
Lectures on Female Education.... Richmond: 1825. V. 65

GARNETT, JOHN
Keswick and Its Neighbourhood: a Hand-Book for the Use of Visitors.... Windermere: 1852. V. 63
The Scenery and Antiquities of the South West of Craven; or, Rambles in that Beautiful District. Skipton: 1853. V. 63; 64

GARNETT, LOUISE AYRES
The Muffin Shop. Chicago;: 1908. V. 62

GARNETT, LUCY MARY JANE
The Women of Turkey and Their Folklore. London: 1890-1891. V. 63

GARNETT, PORTER
A Documentary Account of the Beginnings of the Laboratory Press, Carnegie Institute of Technology. Pittsburgh: 1927. V. 63
Stately Homes of California. Boston: 1915. V. 62; 65; 67

GARNETT, RICHARD
A Chaplet from the Greek Anthology. London: 1892. V. 64
Iphigenia in Delphia: a Dramatic Poems. London: 1890. V. 64
Poems. London: 1893. V. 64
The Twilight of the Gods, and Other Tales. London: 1888. V. 64

GARNETT, RICHARD continued
The Twilight of the Gods and Other Tales. London: 1924. V. 65

GARNETT, T.
Observations on a Tour Through the Highlands and Part of the Western Isles of Scotland.... London: 1811. V. 62; 63
Outlines of a Course of Lectures on Chemistry. London: 1801. V. 64

GARNETT, TAY
Man Laughs Back. New York: 1935. V. 67

GARNETT, THOMAS
Animals of Philosophy, Natural History, Chemistry, Literature, Agriculture and the Mechanical and Fine Arts for the Year 1800 1801. London: 1801-1802. V. 65
Essays on Natural History and Agriculture. 1883. V. 67
A Lecture on the Preservation of Health. London: 1800. V. 65

GARNETT, W. J.
Freshwater Microscopy. London: 1953. V. 67

GARNIER, PHILIPPE
Gemmulae Gallicae Linguae, Latine & Germanice Adornatae.... Strasburg: 1634. V. 63

GARNIER, PIERRE
A Medical Journey in California. Los Angeles: 1967. V. 63; 64; 66

GARRARD, LEWIS
Wah-To-Yah and the Taos Trail. Cincinnati: 1850. V. 64; 66
Wah-To-Yah and The Taos Trail. San Francisco: 1936. V. 66
Wah-to-Yah and the Taos Trail. Glendale: 1938. V. 64

GARRARD, T.
Gold of Africa, Jewelry and Ornaments from Ghana, Cote D'Ivoire, Mali and Senegal. Munich: 1989. V. 62

GARRATT, B. COPSON
Many Physcially, Mentally and Spiritually Considered. London: 1884. V. 67

GARRET, DANIEL
Designs and Estimates of Farm Houses &c for the County of York, Northumberland, Cumberland, Westmoreland and Bishoprick of Durham. London: 1747. V. 64

GARRETSON, F. V. D.
Carmina Yalensia. New York: 1867. V. 65

GARRETSON, MARTIN S.
The American Bison - the Story of Its Extermination as a Wild Species and its Restoration Under Federal Protection. New York: 1938. V. 66

GARRETT, EDMUND
Elizabethan Songs in Honour of Love and Beautie. Boston: 1895. V. 62; 66

GARRETT, WILLIAM ROBERTSON
History of the South Carolina Cession and the Northern Boundary of Tennessee. Nashville: 1884. V. 67

GARRICK, DAVID
Memoirs of the Life of David Garrick, Esq. London: 1808. V. 62
An Ode Upon Dedication a Building and Erecting a Statue, to Shakespeare at Stratford Upon Avon. London: 1769. V. 65

GARRISON, F. G.
An Introduction to the History of Medicine and Medical Chronology, Suggestions for Study and Bibliographic Data. Philadelphia: 1929. V. 64; 66

GARRISON, G. R.
Mexican Houses: A Book of Photographs and Measured Drawings. New York: 1930. V. 62; 65

GARRISON, WENDEL PHILLIPS
The New Gulliver. Jamaica: 1898. V. 66

GARRISON, WILLIAM LLOYD
An Address Delivered Before the Free People of Color, in Philadelphia, New York, and Other Cities, During the Month of June 1831. Boston: 1831. V. 64
Thoughts on African Colonization; or an Impartial Exhibition of the Doctrines, Principles and Purposes of the American Colonization Society.... Boston: 1832. V. 64

GARROD, ALFRED HENRY
The Collected Scientific Papers. London: 1887. V. 65

GARTH, J. S.
Brachyura of the Pacific Coast of America, Oxyrhynca. 1958. V. 66

GARTH, SAMUEL
The Dispensary. London: 1726. V. 62

GARTON, GEORGE
Colt's S.A.A. Postwar Models. North Hollywood: 1979. V. 67

GARTON, R. V.
Lure of the Lochs. 1972. V. 67

GARWOOD, E. J.
The Lower Carboniferous Succession in the North West of England. 1912. V. 62

GARZONI, TOMMASO
L'Hospidale de' Pazzi Incurabili...Contre Capitoli in Fine Sopra la Pazzia. Venice: 1589. V. 63
L'Hospidale de' Pazzi Incvrabili. (bound after) *Il Theatro de Vari, e Diversi Cervelli Mondani.* In Venetia: 1589-1588. V. 63

GASCOIGNE, BAMBER
Images of Richmond. Richmond-upon-Thames: 1978. V. 63
Images of Twickenham. Richmond-upon-Thames: 1981. V. 66

GASCOIGNE, CAROLINE
Dr. Harold's Note-Book. London: 1869. V. 65

GASCOIGNE, GEORGE
Princely Pleasures with the Masque Intended to be Presented before Queen Elizabeth at Kenilworth Castle in 1575.... London: 1821. V. 63
The Queen Majesty's Entertainment at Woodstock 1575. Oxford: 1903-1910. V. 64; 66

GASCOINE, HENRY BARNETT
Gascoine's Path to Naval Fame. Warwick: 1825. V. 66

GASCOYNE, DAVID
Journal 1936-1937 - Death of an Explorer - Leon Chestov. London: 1980. V. 65
Journals 1936-1939. London: 1978-1980. V. 63
Man's Life Is This Meat. London: 1936. V. 64
Night Thoughts. London: 1956. V. 63
Poems 1937-1942. London: 1943. V. 62; 65; 66
Poems 1937-1942. London: 1944. V. 66
Selected Poems. London: 1994. V. 63
A Short Survey of Surrealism. 1935. V. 65
The Sun at Midnight - Notes on the Story of Civilisation Seen as the History of the Great Experimental Work of the Supreme Scientist. London: 1970. V. 65
Three Poems. N.P: 1976. V. 63
A Vagrant and Other Poems. London: 1950. V. 64

GASCOYNE, THOMAS
The Tryal of Sr Tho. Gascoyne Bar. for High-Treason, in Conspiring the Death of the King, the Subversion of the Government, and Alteration of Religion on Wednesday the 11th of February 1679...Before...Sir William Scroggs.... London: 1680. V. 62

GASH, JONATHAN
Firefly Gadroon. London: 1982. V. 66
The Gondola Scam. 1984. V. 66
The Grail Tree. London: 1979. V. 63; 65; 66
Jade Woman. London: 1988. V. 66
The Judas Pair. London: 1977. V. 66
The Judas Pair. New York: 1977. V. 62
The Lies of Fair Ladies. Bristol: 1991. V. 66
Moonspender. London: 1986. V. 66
Pearlhanger. 1985. V. 66
The Sleepers of Erin. London: 1983. V. 65; 66
Streetwalker. London: 1959. V. 65
Streetwalker. 1960. V. 66
Streetwalker. New York: 1960. V. 65
The Tartan Ringers. 1986. V. 66

GASKELL, CATHERINE MILNES
Lady Ann's Fairy Tales. London: 1914. V. 67

GASKELL, ELIZABETH CLEGHORN
Cranford. London: 1853. V. 63; 65
Cranford. London: 1864. V. 63; 65; 66
Cranford. London: 1891. V. 66; 67
Cranford. London: 1898. V. 63
A Dark Night's Work. London: 1867. V. 65
The Fairy Godmothers and Other Tales. London: 1851. V. 65
The Fairy Godmothers and Other Tales. London: 1860. V. 65
The Letters Of.... Manchester: 1966. V. 64; 66
The Life of Charlotte Bronte. London: 1857. V. 63; 64; 65; 66
Life of Charlotte Bronte. New York: 1857. V. 63; 65; 66
The Life of Charlotte Bronte. London: 1858. V. 66
Life of Charlotte Bronte. London: 1860. V. 63
Life of Charlotte Bronte. London: 1873. V. 63; 64
Marie Barton. Paris. V. 63
Marie Barton. Paris: 1856. V. 64
Mary Barton. London: 1849. V. 65
Mary Barton. London: 1877. V. 65
The Moorland Cottage. London: 1850. V. 65
My Diary. 1923. V. 63
My Diary. London: 1923. V. 65; 66
My Lady Ludlow and Other Tales.... London: 1861. V. 63; 66
North and South. London: 1855. V. 63; 65; 66
Novels and Tales. London: 1880. V. 65
Novels and Tales. London: 1881-1893. V. 64
Pocket Edition of Mrs. Gaskell's Works. London: 1897?. V. 65
Right at Last and Other Tales. London: 1860. V. 65
Right at Last and Other Tales. New York: 1860. V. 64
Round the Sofa. London: 1859. V. 65
Ruth. Leipzig: 1853. V. 63
Ruth. Paris: 1856. V. 64
Sylvia's Lovers. London: 1898. V. 66
Wives and Daughters. London: 1866. V. 63; 66
Wives and Daughters. London: 1877. V. 65
The Works. London: 1890. V. 64
Works. London: 1890-1893. V. 62
The Works. London: 1906. V. 66

GASKELL, ELIZABETH CLEGHORN continued
The Works. London: 1925. V. 63

GASKELL, ERNEST
Westmorland and Cumberland Leaders. Privately published: 1910. V. 66

GASKELL, G. A.
A Dictionary of the Sacred Language of All Scriptures and Myths. London: 1923. V. 64

GASKELL, JANE
All Neat in Black Stockings. London: 1966. V. 64; 66
Attic Summer. London: 1963. V. 64; 66
The City. London: 1966. V. 62; 64; 66
Strange Evil. London: 1957. V. 62; 64; 66

GASKELL, P.
The Manufacturing Population of England, Its Moral, Social and Physical Conditions and the Changes Which Have Arisen from the Use of Steam Machinery.... London: 1833. V. 64

GASKELL, W. H.
The Involuntary Nervous System. London: 1916. V. 65
On the Relations Between the Function, Structure, Origin and Distribution of the Nerve Fibres. London: 1888. V. 67
The Structure Distribution and Function of the Nerves Which Innervate the Viscera and Vascular System. 1885. V. 67

GASKIN, ARTHUR J.
A Book of Pictured Carols. London: 1893. V. 64

GASPAR DE MADRE DE DEOS, FATHER
Memorias Para a Historia da Capitania de S. Vicente, Hoje Chamada de S. Paulo do Estado do Brasil. Lisbon: 1797. V. 62

GASPARIN, ADRIEN ETIENNE PIERRE DE
Manuel d'Art Veterinaire, a l'Usage des Officiers de Cavalerie, des Agriculteurs et des Artistes Veterinaires. Paris and Geneva: 1817. V. 65

GASPER, HOWLAND
The Complete Sportsman. New York: 1893. V. 67

GASPERETTI, J.
The Snakes of Arabia. Basel: 1988. V. 63; 66

GASPEY, THOMAS
The History of England: Under the Reign of George III, George IV, William IV and Queen Victoria. London: 1852-1859. V. 66
The Lollards: a Tale Founded on the Persecutions Which Marked the Early Part of the Fifteenth Century. London: 1822. V. 65

GASQUET, CARDINAL
His Holiness Pope Pius XI. 1922. V. 63

GASS, PATRICK
A Journal of the Voyages and Travels of a Corps of Discovery Under the Command of Capt. Lewis and Capt. Clarke (sic).... Pittsburgh: 1807. V. 63
A Journal of the Voyages and Travels of Lewis and Clarke...1804, 1805 and 1806. Minneapolis: 1958. V. 67

GASS, WILLIAM H.
Culp. New York: 1985. V. 62; 64; 67
Fiction and Figures of Life. New York: 1970. V. 67
In the Heart of the Heart of the Country. New York: 1968. V. 63; 65
Omensetter's Luck. New York: 1966. V. 63; 67
Omensetter's Luck. London: 1967. V. 63; 67
The Tunnel. New York: 1995. V. 63; 66
Willie Masters' Lonesome Wife. N.P: 1968. V. 62
Willie Masters' Lonesome Wife. New York: 1971. V. 65

GASSIER, PIERRE
The Life and Complete Work of Francisco Goya with a Catalogue Raisonne of the Paintings, Drawings and Engravings. New York: 1971. V. 62; 63

GASSNER, JOHN
20 Best Film Plays. 1943. V. 65

GATAKER, THOMAS
Of the Nature and Use of Lots: a Treatise Historical and Theological. London: 1627. V. 64

GATCHET, ALBERT S.
The Karankawa Indians and the Coast People of Texas. Cambridge: 1891. V. 67

GATE, ETHEL MAY
Tales from the Enchanted Isles. New Haven: 1926. V. 63

GATENBY, J. B.
The Microtomist's Vade-Mecum (Bolles Lee). London: 1937. V. 67

GATES, BILL
The Road Ahead. New York: 1995. V. 63

GATES, ELEANOR
Good Night. New York: 1907. V. 65

GATES, R. R.
A Botanist in the Amazon Valley.... London: 1927. V. 63

GATEWOOD, JAMES D.
Naval Hygiene. Philadelphia: 1909. V. 65

GATHE, CARL E.
Pueblo Pottery Making, a Study of the Village of San Ildefonso. New Haven: 1925. V. 67

A GATHERING of Memories - a History of the Big Sandy Community Chouteau County, Montana. N.P: 1990. V. 65

GATHORNE HARDY, A. E.
Autumns in Argyleshire with Rod and Gun. London: 1900. V. 67
The Salmon. London: 1898. V. 67

GATHORNE-HARDY, ROBERT
The Native Garden. London: 1961. V. 62
Saint Francis and the Wolf of Gubbio. N.P: 1958. V. 64
Traveller's Trio. London: 1963. V. 67

GATKE, H.
Heligoland as an Ornithological Observatory.... Edinburgh: 1895. V. 62; 63; 66

GATTI, A.
Killers All!. 1951. V. 67

GATTINGER, A.
The Flora of Tennessee and a Philosophy of Botany. Nashville: 1901. V. 67
The Tennessee Flora; with Special Reference to the Flora of Nashville. Nashville: 1887. V. 67

GATTY, HORATIA K. F.
Aunt Judy's Annual Volume. London: 1883. V. 65

GATTY, MARGARET SCOTT
A Book of Emblems, with Interpretations Thereof. London: 1872. V. 65
The Book of Sun Dials. 1872. V. 66
British Sea-Weed. London: 1863. V. 64; 65; 67
British Sea-Weeds. 1872. V. 62; 63; 66
Parables from Nature. London: 1896. V. 64
The Poor Incumbent: a Tale. London: 1858. V. 65

GAUBIUS, H. D.
Libellus de Methodo Concinnandi Formulas Medicamentorum. Neapoli: 1763. V. 63

GAUDEN, JOHN
A Discourse of Auxiliary Beauty.... London: 1656. V. 62
Hiera Dakrua (Greek) Ecclesia Anglicanae Suspiria. The Tears, Signs, Complaints and Prayers of the Church of England. London: 1639. V. 66
Hiera Dakrua (Greek) Ecclesia Anglicanae Suspiria. The Tears, Signs, Complaints and Prayers of the Church of England.... London: 1659. V. 62
The Whole Duty of a Communicant.... London: 1716. V. 64

GAUGE, ISAAC
Four Years With Five Armies - Army of the Frontier, Army of the Potomac, Army of the Missouri, Army of the Ohio, Army of the Shenandoah. New York: 1908. V. 65

GAUGER, NICOLAS
Fires Improv'd: Being a New Method of Building Chimneys.... London: 1715. V. 64
Fires Improved; or a New Method of Building Chimnies, So as to Prevent Their Smoking in Which a Small Fire Shall Warm a Room Much Beter than a Large One Made the Common Way.... London: 1736. V. 65

GAUGHAN, ANTHONY J.
Doneraile. 1970. V. 63; 66

GAUGIN, PAUL
The Intimate Journals of Paul Gaugin. London: 1922. V. 65

GAUL, HARRIET
John Alfred Brashear: Scientist and Humanitarian 1840-1920. Philadelphia: 1940. V. 66

GAULT, WILLIAM CAMPBELL
Country Kill. New York: 1962. V. 67

GAUNTLETT, HENRY
Letters to the Stranger in Reading. London: 1810. V. 63

GAUNTLETT, HENRY JOHN
The Comprehensive Tune Book, Arranged in Vocal Score.... London: 1846. V. 62

GAUSE, ISAAC
Four Years with Five Armies. New York: 1908. V. 62; 63; 65

GAUSS, KARL F.
Recherches Arithmetiques. Paris: 1807. V. 65; 67

GAUTIER, EMILE JUSTIN ARMAND
L'Alimentation et les Regimes Chez l'Homme Sain et Chez les Malades. Paris: 1904. V. 65

GAUTIER, HUBERT
Traite de la Construction des Chemins, ou Il Est Parle de Ceux des Romains & de Ceux des Modernes, Suivant qu'on Les Pratique en France de leurs Figures.... Paris: 1721. V. 65

GAUTIER, THEOPHILE
Jean and Jeanette. Paris: 1895. V. 62; 67
King Candaules. Paris: 1895. V. 62; 67
Mademoiselle de Maupin. London: 1889. V. 67
Mademoiselle de Maupin. Waltham St. Lawrence: 1938. V. 62; 64; 65
A Night of Cleopatra. Paris: 1895. V. 62; 67
Le Roi Candaule. Paris: 1893. V. 62
Voyage en Espagne - Tras los Montes.... Paris: 1873. V. 64

GAUTIER D'AGOTY, JACQUES FABIEN
Anatomie de la Tete, en Tableaux Imprimes...D'Apres les Pieces Dissequees et Preparees par M. Duverney. Paris: 1748. V. 62
Chroa-Genesie ou Generation des Couleurs, Contre le Systeme de Newton. Paris: 1750-1751. V. 62

GAUTREAUX, TIM
Same Place, Same Things. New York: 1996. V. 66; 67

GAVARNI D'Apres Nature. Paris. V. 66

GAVIN, ANTONIO
A Master-Key to Popery: in Five Parts.... London: 1773. V. 62; 66

GAVORSE, JOSEPH
The Story of Phaethon, Son of Apollo. New York: 1932. V. 67

GAWAIN AND THE GREEN KNIGHT
Sir Gawain and the Green Knight. London: 1952. V. 62
Sir Gawain and the Green Knight. Waltham St. Lawrence: 1952. V. 65

GAWLER, JOHN BELLENDEN
The Trial of John Belenden Gawler, Esq. for Adultery, with the Lady of Lord Valentia (Sister to Lord Courtenay) on the Court of King's Bench... May 19, 1796. N.P: 1796?. V. 63

GAWSWORTH, JOHN
Annotations on Some Minor Writings of T. E. Lawrence. London: 1935. V. 65

GAY, CLAUDIO
Historia Fisica y Politica de Chile, Segun Documentos Adquiridos en Esta Republica Durante Doce Anos de Reisencia en Ella.... Paris: 1844-1871. V. 62

GAY, DELPHINE
Essais Poetiques. Paris: 1824. V. 63

GAY, FRANCO
The Cruiser Bartolomeo Colleoni. London: 1987. V. 67

GAY, HARRY, PSEUD.
The Proclamation; or, the Meeting of the Gothamites. London: 1792. V. 62

GAY, J. DREW
From Pall Mall to the Punjaub; or, with the Prince in India. London: 1876. V. 67

GAY, JOHN
Achilles. An Opera. London: 1733. V. 62; 64
The Beggar's Opera. London: 1728. V. 62; 66
The Beggar's Opera. London: 1921. V. 62
The Beggar's Opera. Paris: 1937. V. 62
The Distress'd Wife. London: 1743. V. 64
Fables. London: 1792. V. 63; 67
Fables. London: 1793. V. 62; 63; 65; 66
Fables. Paris: 1800. V. 62
Gay's Fables Epitomized with Short Poems.... London: 1767. V. 67
The Poems of John Gay. Chiswick: 1820. V. 63
Poems on Several Occasions. London: 1720. V. 64; 66
Trivia; or, the Art of Walking the London Streets. London: 1922. V. 63
Trivia; or the Art of Walking the Streets of London. London: 1716. V. 65
Trivia, or the Art of Walking the Streets of London. London: 1730. V. 62

GAY, MARY ANN HARRIS
Life in Dixie During the War. Atlanta: 1892. V. 62; 63

GAY, SOPHIE
Un Mariage sous l'Empire. Paris: 1832. V. 66

GAY, THERESSA
James W. Marshall - The Discoverer of California Gold. Georgetown: 1967. V. 62; 63; 65

GAY, WILLIAM
The Long Home. Denver: 1999. V. 65; 67

GAYA, LOUIS DE
Marriage Ceremonies; as Now Used in All Parts of the World. London: 1704. V. 65

GAYTON, EDMUND
Festivous Notes on the History and Adventures of the Renowned Don Quixote.... London: 1771. V. 65
Pleasant Notes Upon Don Quixot. London: 1654. V. 63

GAZE, HAROLD
Coppertop: the Queer Adventures of a Quaint Child. New York: 1924. V. 62
The Merry Piper, or, the Magical Trip of the Sugar Bowl Ship. London: 1925. V. 62; 66

GEARINO, G. D.
Counting Coup. New York: 1997. V. 67

GEBHARD, D.
200 Years of American Architectural Drawing. 1977. V. 65

GEDDES, JAMES
An Essay on the Composition and Manner of Writing of the Antients, Particularly Plato. Glasgow: 1748. V. 65

GEDDES, MICHAEL
Miscellaneous Tracts. London: 1709-1715. V. 62

GEDDES, NORMAN BEL
A Project for a Theatrical Presentation of the Divine Comedy of Dante Alighieri. New York: 1924. V. 65

GEDDES, PATRICK
A Synthetic Outline of the History of Biology. Edinburgh: 1886. V. 67

GEDDIE, JAMES
Notes of a Trip to the Mediterranean. Edinburgh: 1880. V. 67

GEDDIE, JOHN
Beyond the Himalayas. London: 1884. V. 67
The Lake Regions of Central Africa. London: 1883. V. 62

GEDGE, J. DENNY
The History of a Village Community (Methwold) in the Eastern Counties. Norwich: 1893. V. 65

GEE, CHRISTINE SOUTH
Some of the Descendants of Daniel Martin (1745-1829) of Laurens County, South Carolina, and the Allied Families of Hudgens, McNeese, Rodgers and Saxon. Greenville: 1963. V. 67

GEE, ERNEST R.
The American Shooter's Manual. New York: 1928. V. 62; 63; 66; 67
The Sportsman's Library. 1940. V. 62

GEE, JOSHUA
The Trade and Navigation of Great Britain Considered. London: 1767. V. 63; 67

GEE, MAGGIE
Dying, In Other Words. Brighton: 1981. V. 67

GEELHAAR, C.
Paul Klee and the Bauhaus. 1973. V. 62; 65

GEEN, PHILIP
Days Stolen for Sport. London. V. 67
Days Stolen for Sport. 1900. V. 67
What I Have Seen While Fishing and How I Have Caught My Fish. Richmond: 1905. V. 67

GEERE, H. VALENTINE
By Nile and Euphrates, a Record of Discovery and Adventure. Edinburgh: 1904. V. 67

GEERLINGS, G. K.
Metal Crafts in Architecture.... New York: 1929. V. 62; 65

GEERTSEN, I.
Greenlandic Masks. Copenhagen: 1988. V. 62

GEERTZ, CLIFFORD
The Religion of Java. Glencoe: 1960. V. 67

GEFFS, MARY L.
Under Ten Flags - a History of Weld County, Colorado. Greeley: 1938. V. 66

GEHENNA PRESS
A List of Gehenna Press Books. 1967. V. 65

GEIGER, MAYNARD
The Life and Times of Fray Junipera Serra or the Man Who Never Turned Back. Washington: 1959. V. 63; 66

GEIKIE, A.
The Ancient Volcanoes of Great Britain. 1897. V. 63; 66; 67
The Ancient Volcanoes of Great Britain. London: 1897. V. 62; 64; 65; 67
Annals of the Royal Society Club. The Record of a London Dining-Club in the Eighteenth and Nineteenth Centuries. London: 1917. V. 67
The Founders of Geology. London: 1905. V. 66
Geological Sketches at Home and Abroad. 1882. V. 67
Life of Sir Roderick I. Murchison. 1875. V. 62
Life of Sir Roderick I. Murchison. London: 1875. V. 64
On the Carboniferous Volcanic Rocks of the Basin of the Firth of Forth. Edinburgh: 1879. V. 62
The Scenery of Scotland. London and Cambridge: 1865. V. 62
Text-Book of Geology. London: 1862. V. 64
Text-Book of Geology. London: 1903. V. 64; 67

GEIKIE, J.
The Antiquity of Man in Europe, Being the Munro Lectures. Monro: 1914. V. 63
Fragments of Earth Lore. Edinburgh: 1893. V. 64; 66
Prehistoric Europe. A Geological Sketch. 1881. V. 67
Prehistoric Europe, a Geological Sketch. London: 1881. V. 64

GEIL, WILLIAM EDGAR
A Yankee on the Yangtze; Being a Narrative of a Journey from Shanghai through the Central Kingdom to Burma. London: 1904. V. 67

GEILER, JOHANN
Navicula sive Speculum Fatuorum. Strassburg: 1511. V. 65

GEISEL, THEODORE SEUSS
And to Think That I Saw It On Mulberry Street. New York: 1937. V. 63; 64
The Butter Battle Book. New York: 1984. V. 62
The Cat in the Hat Comes Back. New York: 1958. V. 63; 64; 65; 66
Dr. Seuss's Sleep Book. New York: 1962. V. 63
Happy Birthday To You!. New York: 1961. V. 63
Hunches in Bunches. New York: 1982. V. 65
On Beyond Zebra!. New York: 1955. V. 63; 65
One Fish, Two Fish, Red Fish, Blue Fish. New York: 1960. V. 63; 64
The Seven Lady Godivas. New York: 1939. V. 63; 64
The Seven Lady Godivas. New York: 1987. V. 65

GEISEL, THEODORE SEUSS continued
Sneetches and Other Stories. New York: 1961. V. 63; 65
This is Ann-She's Dying to Meet You. Washington: 1943. V. 64
Yertle the Turtle and Other Stories. New York: 1958. V. 63; 65

THE GEISHA. Or Happy Little Jappies. London: 1900. V. 65

GEIST, O. W.
Archaeological Excavations at Kukulik, St. Lawrence Island, Alaska. 1936. V. 62

GEKOSKI, R. A.
William Golding - a Bibliography 1934-1993. London: 1994. V. 62; 63; 64; 65

GELDART, HANNAH RANSOME
Memorials of Samuel Gurney. London: 1857. V. 64; 65

GELL, WILLIAM
The Geography and Antiquities of Ithaca. London: 1807. V. 64
Pompeiana: the Topography.... London: 1832. V. 62; 66
The Topography of Troy, and Its Vicinity.... London: 1804. V. 63; 65
The Unedited Antiquities of Attica.... London: 1817. V. 65

GELLERT, LEON
Songs of a Campaign. Sydney: 1917. V. 62

GELLIUS, AULUS
The Attic Nights of Aulus Gellius. 1795. V. 66
Auli Gelii Luculentis-Simi Scriptoris Notces Atticae. Lugduni: 1555. V. 65
Auli Gelii Luculentissimi Scriptoris Notces Atticae.... 1555. V. 66
Noctes Atticae. Lyon: 1537. V. 63

GEMMA, CORNELIUS
De Naturae Divinis Characterismis. Antverpiae: 1575. V. 63

GEMS Of American Wit and Anecdote, or the American Joe Miller. London: 1839. V. 64; 65; 66

GENARD, P.
Les Peintures Monumentales de l'Hotel et du Chateau de Schilde. Anvers: 1879. V. 64

GENATH, JOHANN JACOB
Decas I-VII. Disputationem medicarum Select.... Basle: 1618-1631. V. 64

GENAUER, EMILY
Chagall at the Met. New York: 1971. V. 62; 63; 64; 65

GENDEL, EVELYN
Tortoise and Turtle. New York: 1960. V. 64; 66

GENEALOGIES of Virginia Families: From the William and Mary College Quarterly Historical Magazine. Baltimore: 1982. V. 64

THE GENEALOGY and Chronological History of the Illustrious Family of Guelph or Welph; one of the Sons of Isenberd.... London: 1716?. V. 62

GENEBRIER, M. DE
Histoire de Carausius, Empereur de la Grande-Bretagne, Collegue de Diocletien.... Paris: 1740. V. 67

GENERAL CONFERENCE OF THE CONGREGATIONAL CHURCHES OF CONN.
Centennial Papers Published by Order of the General Conference of the Congregational Churches of Connecticut. Hartford: 1877. V. 65

GENERAL ELECTRIC SUPPLY CORP.
Lighting Equipment for Commercial Industrial and Floodlighting Requirements. Catalog 35L. Bridgeport: 1934. V. 66
Lighting Equipment for Commercial, Industrial and Floodlighting Requirements. Lighting Book 37L. Bridgeport: 1936. V. 65

A GENERAL History of Negro Slavery, Collected from the Most Respectable Evidence and Unquestionable Authorities.... Cambridge: 1826. V. 64

THE GENERAL Stud Book, Containing Pedigrees of Race Horses...from the Earliest Accounts to the year 1821 Inclusive. London: 1820. V. 62

GENERAL Taylor's Old Rough and Ready Almanac 1847. Lancaster. V. 65

GENET, JEAN
Journal du Voleur. N.P: 1949. V. 64
Les Negres. Clownerie. Paris: 1958. V. 63; 64
Querelle de Brest. N.P: 1947. V. 65

GENGA, BENARDINO
Anatomia Chirurgica Cioe Istoria Anatomica dell'Ossa e Muscoli del Corpo Umano con la Descrittione de' Vasi.... Rome: 1686. V. 62; 63

GENGENBACH, ERNEST DE
Judas ou Le Vampire surrealiste. Paris: 1949. V. 64

GENIN, THOMAS H.
The Napolead. In Twelve Books. St. Clairsville: 1833. V. 63

GENLIS, STEPHANIE FELICITE DUCREST DE ST. AUBIN, COMTESSE DE
Adele et Theodore, ou Lettres sur l'Education. Londres: 1796. V. 65
Adele et Theodore, ou Lettres sur l'Education. Paris: 1827. V. 66
Le Club des Dames, ou le Retour de Descartes. Paris: 1784. V. 66
Le Comte de Corke, Surnomme Le Grande, ou la Seduction sans Artifice. Paris: 1805. V. 64; 67
Memoirs of the Countess de Genlis. London: 1825-1826. V. 63
A New Method of Instruction for Children from Five to Ten Years Old, Including Moral Dialogues, The Children's Island, a Tale, Models of Composition.... London: 1800. V. 64; 65
Nouveaux Romans. London: 1802. V. 66
Religion Considered as the Only Basis of Happiness and of True Philosophy. London: 1787. V. 66
Saintclair, or the Victim of the Arts and Sciences; and Hortense, or the Victom to Novels and Travel. Georgetown: 1813. V. 62
Tales of the Castle, or Stories of Instruction and Delight. London: 1785. V. 65
Tales of the Castle; or, Stories of Instruction and Delight. London: 1806. V. 62; 63
Theatre of Education. Dublin: 1783. V. 65
Les Voeux Temeraires of L'Enthousiasme. Hambourg: 1798. V. 65

GENT, B. E.
A New Dictionary of the Terms Ancient and Modern of the Canting Crew. London: 1899. V. 65

GENT, THOMAS
The Antient and Modern History of the Loyal Town of Rippon. York: 1733. V. 66
Gent's History of Hull. Hull: 1869. V. 63
The Life of Mr. Thomas Gent, Printer, of York. London: 1832. V. 62; 65

GENTHE, ARNOLD
As I Remember. New York: 1936. V. 63
Isadora Duncan - Twenty-Four Studies.... New York: 1929. V. 64
Old Chinatown. New York: 1913. V. 65

GENTIL, FRANCOIS
Dissertation sur le Caffe, et sur les Moyens Propres a Prevenir les Effets qui Resultent de sa Preparation Communement Vicieuse.... Paris: 1787. V. 66

GENTILE, MARIA
Italian Cook Book. New York: 1919. V. 67

THE GENTLEMAN and Lady's Key to Polite Literature; or a Compendious Dictionary of Fabulous History.... London: 1783. V. 62

THE GENTLEMAN and Lady's Key to Polite Literature, or Compendious Dictionary of Fabulous Things. London: 1796. V. 63; 64

GENTLEMAN OF ELVAS
The Discovery of Florida.... San Francisco: 1946. V. 64
True Relation of the Hardships Suffered by Governor Hernando de Soto and Certain Portuguese Gentlemen During the Discovery of the Province of Florida. Deland: 1933. V. 63

THE GENTLEMAN'S Toilet. London: 1845. V. 66

GENTRY, THOMAS G.
Life Histories of the Birds of Eastern Pennsylvania. Philadelphia and Salem: 1876-1877. V. 67
Nests and Eggs of Birds of the United States. Philadelphia: 1882. V. 63; 64

A GENUINE Account of the Life and Actions of James Maclean, Highwayman, to the Time of His Trial and Receiving Sentence at the Old- Bailey. London: 1750. V. 65

THE GENUINE Account of the Life and Trial of Eugene Aram, for the Murder of Daniel Clark, Late of Knaresborough in the County of York. London: 1759. V. 65

A GENUINE Narrative of the Enterprise Against the Stores and Shipping at St. Maloes. Dublin: 1758. V. 63

GEO. H. Morrill Co., Printing and Lithographic Inks, Head Office: Norwood, Mass. Boston, New York, Chicago, San Francisco, London. Founded 1840. Norwood: 1914. V. 62

GEOGRAPHICA Classica: The Geography of the Ancients So Far Describ'd As It Is Contained in the Greek and Latin Classicks.... London: 1736. V. 62

GEOGRAPHICAL Fun; Being Humourous Outlines of Various Countires.... London: 1869. V. 66

GEOLOGICAL SOCIETY OF AMERICA
Treatise on Invertabrate Paleontology. Part N. Mollusca 6 Bivalvia. 1969-1989. V. 66
Treatise on Invertebrate Paleontolgy. Part O. Arthropoda 1. Trilobita, Revised. 1997. V. 66

GEOLOGICAL SOCIETY OF LONDON
Transactions of the Geological Society of London. Volume I, first series - Volume VII, part the fourth, second series. London: 1811-1856. V. 63

GEOLOGY of the County of Cape May, State of New Jersey. Trenton: 1857. V. 63; 66

GEORGE, ABRAHAM
International Finance Handbook. Volume 2. Foreign Investments. New York: 1983. V. 64

GEORGE, ANDREW L.
A Texas Prisoner - Sketches at the Penitentiary, Convict Farms and Railroads etc. N.P: 1895. V. 65
A Texas Prisoner - Sketches at the Penitentiary, Convict Farms and Railroads, etc. Charlotte: 1895. V. 62

GEORGE, ELIZABETH
A Great Deliverance. New York: 1988. V. 65; 66

GEORGE, ERNEST
Etchings in Belgium with Descriptive Letterpress. London: 1883. V. 66

GEORGE, GEORGE, PSEUD.
Public School, or, Boys Slaves to Boys. Salisbury: 1861. V. 63

GEORGE, GERTRUDE A.
Eight Months with the Women's Royal Air Force - (Immobile). Heath Cranton: 1920. V. 64

GEORGE, H. B.
The Oberland and Its Glaciers: Explored and Illustrated with Ice-Axe and Camera. 1866. V. 63; 65
The Oberland and Its Glaciers Explored and Illustrated with Ice-Axe and Camera. London: 1866. V. 62

GEORGE, HENRY
History of the 3d, 7th, 8th and 12th Kentucky, C.S.A. Louisville: 1911. V. 62; 63
Progress and Poverty. San Francisco: 1879. V. 66
Progress and Poverty. London: 1890. V. 66
Progress and Poverty. New York: 1898. V. 64

GEORGE, J. N.
English Guns and Rifles. 1947. V. 63
English Guns and Rifles. Harrisburg: 1947. V. 62; 66; 67
English Guns and Rifles. Plantersville: 1947. V. 64; 67
English Pistols and Revolvers. 1938. V. 62; 64; 66; 67

GEORGE, JEAN CRAIGHEAD
Julie of the Wolves. New York: 1972. V. 65

GEORGE, TODD M.
Just Memories and Twelve Years with Cole Younger. N.P: 1959. V. 67

GEORGE, WILLIAM
Some Account of the Oldest Plans of Bristol, and an Enquiry Into the Date of the First Authentic One.... Bristol: 1881. V. 66

GEORGI, CHRISTIAN SIGISMUND
Wittenbergischte Jubel-Geschichte.... Wittenberg: 1756. V. 65

GEORGIA Scenes, Characters, Incidents, Etc. in the First Half of the Century of the Republic. New York: 1840. V. 63

GEORGIA. LAWS, STATUTES, ETC. - 1862
Acts of the General Assembly of the State of Georgia, Passed in Milledgeville, at an Annual Session in Nov. and Dec. 1861. Milledgeville: 1862. V. 62

GEORGIA. LAWS, STATUTES, ETC. - 1864
Acts of the General Assembly of the State of Georgia, Passed in Milledgeville at an Annual Session in Nov. and Dec. 1863. Milledgeville: 1864. V. 63

GEORGIA. LAWS, STATUTES, ETC. - 1865
Acts of the General Assembly of the State of Georgia Passed in Milledgeville at an Annual Session in Nov. 1864, Also, Extra Session of 1865, at Macon. Milledgeville: 1865. V. 63

GEORGIA. LEGISLATURE - 1860
Report on the Address of a Portion of the Members of the General Assembly of Georgia. Charleston: 1860. V. 63

GEORGIA. LEGISLATURE - 1861
Journal of the Public and Secret Proceedings of the Convention of the People of Georgia, Held in Milledgeville and Savannah in 1861. Milledgeville: 1861. V. 63

GEORGIA. SENATE - 1861
Journal of the Senate of Georgia at the Annual Session of the General Assembly Begun and Held in Milledgeville.... Milledgeville: 1861. V. 63

THE GEORGIAN Period, a Collection of Papers Dealing with "Colonial" or XVIII Century Architecture in the United States. Boston: 1899-1902. V. 66

GEPHART, RONALD M.
Revolutionary America 1763-1789. A Bibliography. Washington. 1984. V. 65

GEPRIESENES Andencken von Erfindung der Buchdruckerey Wie Solches in Leipzig Beym Schluss des Dritten Jahrhunderts von den Gesammten Buchdruckern Daselbst Geseyrt Worden. Leipzig: 1740. V. 65

GERARD, FRANCES
Picturesque Dublin Old and New. 1898. V. 65

GERARD, JEAN IGNANCE ISIDORE
Un Autre Monde. Paris: 1844. V. 64

GERARD, JOHN
Gerard's Herball. London. 1927. V. 64
The Herball or Generall Historie of Plantes. London: 1597. V. 63; 67

GERARD, JOSEPH
Causes and Treatment of Sterility in Both Sexes. Boston: 1891. V. 64

GERARD, JULES
Lion Hunting and Sporting Life in Algeria. London: 1880. V. 67

GERARD, M.
Dali. New York: 1968. V. 62; 65

GERARD, MARC ANTOINE
Les Oeuvres. 1668. V. 65

GERARD DE NERVAL, GERARD LABRUNIE, KNOWN AS
Dreams and Life - Le Reve et la Vie. London and Manaton: 1933. V. 62

GERAULT, CARL FRIEDRICH
Geschichte Zweyer Merkwurdigen Bekehrungen zur Katholischen Religion.... N.P: 1787. V. 64

GERBAULT, ALAIN
The Gospel of the Sun. London: 1933. V. 67

GERDES, DANIEL
Florilegium Historico-Criticum Librorum Rariorum Cui Multa Simul Scitu Jucunda Adsperguntur Historiam Omnem Litterariam, and Cumprimis Refomrationis Ecclesiasticam Illustrantia. Groningae & Bremae: 1763. V. 65

GERDTS, WILLIAM H.
American Still-Life Painting. New York: 1971. V. 62; 65

GERHARD, PETER
Pirates on the West Coast of New Spain 1575-1742. Glendale: 1960. V. 63; 64; 66

GERHARDI, WILLIAM
The Romanovs - Evocation of the Past as a Mirror for the Present. London: 1940. V. 64

GERHART, ISAAC
Choral Harmonie. Harrisburg: 1818. V. 62
Choral Harmonie. Harrisburg: 1822. V. 63; 66

GERICAULT, THEODORE
Etudes de Chevaux. Paris: 1822. V. 62; 66

GERIN, WINIFRED
Charlotte Bronte: the Evolution of Genius. Oxford: 1967. V. 65

GERLI, AGOSTINO
Opuscoli. Parma: 1785. V. 63; 66

THE GERM. London: 1901. V. 63

GERMAN-REED, T.
Bibliographical Notes on T. E. Lawrence's Seven Pillars of Wisdom and Revolt in the Desert. London: 1928. V. 64

GERMISHUIZEN, G.
Transvaal Wild Flowers. Johannesburg: 1982. V. 67

GERNING, J. I.
Reise Durch Oestreich und Italien. Frankfurt: 1802. V. 66

GERNSHEIM, HELMUT
Creative Photography: Aesthetic Trends 1839-1960. London: 1962. V. 63
The History of Photography. London: 1969. V. 62
The History of Photography. New York: 1969. V. 62
L. J. M. Daguerre. The History of the Diorama and the Daguerrotype. London: 1956. V. 62
Lewis Caroll, Photographer. London: 1949. V. 63
Lewis Carroll Photographer. New York: 1950. V. 62; 63; 64

GEROW, JOSHUA R.
Alder Lake. A Symposium of Nostalgic and Natural Observation. Liberty: 1953. V. 64

GERRALD, JOSEPH
The Trial of Joseph Gerrald, Delegate from the London Corresponding Society, to the British Convention. Edinburgh: 1794. V. 63; 65

GERRISH, THEODORE
Army Life - a Private's Reminiscences of the Civil War. Portland: 1882. V. 67
Life in the World's Wonderland. Biddeford. V. 67

GERSDORFF, HANS VON
Feldbuch der Wundtartzney. Strassburg: 1535. V. 62
Feldbuch Der Wundtartzney.... 1970. V. 64; 66

GERSHOY, A.
Studies in North American Violets. Burlington: 1928-1934. V. 66

GERSTAECKER, FRIEDRICH WILHELM CHRISTIAN
Western Lands and Western Waters. London: 1864. V. 67
Wild Sports in the Far West. London: 1854. V. 67

GERSTLE, SARA
Four Ghost Stories. San Francisco: 1951. V. 62
Three Houses. San Francisco: 1952. V. 62

GERSTNER, FRANZ JOSEPH RITTER VON
Handbuch der Mechanik. Erster Band. Mechanik Fester Korper. Zweiter Band. Mechanik Flussiger Korper. Dritter Band. Beschreibung und Berechnung Grosserer Maschinenanlagen, Vorzuglich Jenet, Welche bey Dem Bau-, Berg- und Huttenwesen Vorkommen. Prague and Vienna: 1831 1834. V. 65

GERTRUDE, SAINT
Insinuationum Di Vinae Pietatis Exercitia Nonnulla. Parisiis: 1578. V. 65

GERVASUTTI, G.
Gervasutti's Climbs. 1957. V. 63

GESCHICKTER, CHARLES F.
Tumors of Bone. Philadelphia: 1949. V. 65

GESCHWIND, NORMAN
Selected Papers on Language and the Brain. Boston: 1976. V. 66; 67

GESELL, ARNOLD
Wolf Child and Human Child; Being a Narrative Interpretation of the Life History of Kamala, the Wolf Girl. New York and London: 1941. V. 65

GESNER, ABRAHAM
The Industrial Resources of Nova Scotia. Halifax: 1849. V. 64
A Practical Treatise on Coal, Petroleum and Other Distilled Oils. New York: 1861. V. 66; 67
Remarks on the Geology and Mineralogy of Nova Scotia. Halifax: 1836. V. 62; 63

GESNER, KONRAD
Evonymus De Remediis Secretis, Liber Secundus.... Zurich: 1569. V. 64

GESSNER, SALOMON
Mort D'Abel. Paris: 1793. V. 63; 66
Oeuvres. Paris: 1795. V. 64

GESTA Romanorum; or, Entertaining Moral Stories.... New York: 1872. V. 67

GETTMANN, ROYAL A.
A Victorian Publisher. A Study of the Bentley Papers. Cambridge: 1960. V. 67

GETTY, J. PAUL
My Life and Fortunes. London: 1964. V. 63

GEVARTIUS, JOHANN CASPARUS
Pompa Introitus Honori Serenissimi Principis Fernandi Austriaci Hispaniarum Infantis XV Kal. Maii Anno 1635. Antwerp: 1642. V. 62

GEWEHR, WESLEY M.
The Great Awakening in Va. 1740-1790. Durham: 1930. V. 63

GEYER, ANDREA
Grundlicher Abriss der Jenigen Zimmer in Welchen bey Noch Furwahrendem Reiches-Tag der an 1663 Angefangen und Biss Dato Continuiret.... Regensburg: 1722. V. 64

GHISI, LORENZO AGOSTINO
Telegrafia Elettrica Ossia Descrizione Dei Telegrafi Elettro- Magnetici Loro Modo Di Agire E Loro Applicazioni Agli Usi Sociali.... Milan: 1850. V. 64

GHOSE, SUDHIN N.
Folk Tales and Fairy Stories from India. Waltham St. Lawrence: 1961. V. 62; 66

GIANNESTRAS, NICHOLAS J.
Foot Disorders - Medical and Surgical Management. Philadelphia: 1967. V. 67

GIANNONE, PIETRO
Anecdotes Ecclesiastiques. Amsterdam: 1738. V. 66

GIANT Talk. New York: 1975. V. 62

GIBB, GEORGE DUNCAN
Carcinoma of the Larynx, Supervening Upon Subglottic Gouty Infiltration Necessitating Tracheotomy. London: 1868. V. 67
On the Diseases and Injuries of the Hyoid or Tongue Bone. London: 1862. V. 67
On Throat Cough: Its Causes and Treatment. London: 1865. V. 67
The Physical Condition of Centenarians, as Derived from Personal Observation in Nine Genuine Examples. London: 1072. V. 67
Stone Implements and Fragments of Pottery from Canada. London: 1873. V. 67
Ultra Centenarian Longevity. London: 1875. V. 67

GIBB, ROBERT SHIRRA
A Farmer's Fifty Years in Lauderdale. London: 1927. V. 64

GIBBINGS, ROBERT
Coconut Island or the Adventures of Two Children in the South Seas. London: 1936. V. 66
Coming Down the Wye. 1947. V. 67
Fourteen Wood Engravings.... Waltham St. Lawrence: 1932. V. 62; 65
Iorana! A Tahitian Journal. Boston: 1932. V. 64; 67
Iorana! A Tahitian Journal. London: 1932. V. 62; 63; 65
Lovely is the Lee. London: 1945. V. 67
Over the Reefs. 1948. V. 63
Sweet Thames Run Softly. 1940. V. 63; 66
The Wood Engravings of Robert Gibbings with Some Recollections by the Artist. London: 1959. V. 62; 66

GIBBON, CHARLES
By Mead and Stream: a Novel. London: 1886. V. 67
In Love and War. London: 1877. V. 67

GIBBON, EDWARD
The Decline and Fall of the Roman Empire. London: 1886?. V. 67
The Decline and Fall of the Roman Empire. London: 1983-1990. V. 66
An Essay on the Study of Literature. London: 1764. V. 63
The History of the Decline and Fall of the Roman Empire. London: 1776-1788. V. 64
The History of the Decline and Fall of the Roman Empire. London: 1782-1788. V. 64
The History of the Decline and Fall of the Roman Empire. London: 1828. V. 66
The History of the Decline and Fall of the Roman Empire. London: 1846. V. 66
The History of the Decline and Fall of the Roman Empire. London: 1854. V. 62
The History of the Decline and Fall of the Roman Empire. London: 1896-1900. V. 66; 67
The History of the Decline and Fall of the Roman Empire. London: 1897. V. 66
The History of the Decline and Fall of the Roman Empire. London: 1900-1901. V. 65
The History of the Decline and Fall of the Roman Empire. London: 1908. V. 62
The Library of Edward Gibbon - a Catalogue of His Books. London: 1940. V. 62
Miscellaneous Works with Memoirs of His Life and Writings. London: 1796. V. 62; 63; 64; 67

GIBBON, LLOYD, MRS.
A Treatise on the Use and Effect of Anatomical Stays, as a Means of Giving an Effectual Support to the Chest, and Abdomen, or Bowels, of Females.... Brentford: 1809. V. 65

GIBBON, MONK
The Branch of the Hawthorn Tree. 1927. V. 63
Netta. 1960. V. 67

GIBBONS, A. ST. H.
Exploration and Hunting in Central Africa 1895-1896. London: 1898. V. 67

GIBBONS, ALFRED RINGOLD
Recollections of an Old Confederate Soldier. Shelbyville: 1930. V. 62; 63; 65

GIBBONS, FLOYD
The Red Napoleon. New York: 1929. V. 66

GIBBONS, J. J.
In the Suan Juan, Colorado, Sketches. N.P: 1898. V. 63; 66

GIBBONS, J. S.
The Banks of New York, Their Dealers, the Clearing House, and the Panic of 1857. New York: 1859. V. 63

GIBBONS, KAYE
Ellen Foster. Chapel Hill: 1987. V. 62; 63; 64; 66; 67
Family Life. Rocky Mount: 1990. V. 64
A Virtuous Woman. Chapel Hill: 1989. V. 62; 64; 66; 67

GIBBONS, STELLA
The Bachelor. London: 1948. V. 67
Fort of the Bear. A Romance. London: 1953. V. 67
Here Be Dragons. London: 1953. V. 67
A Pink Front Door. London: 1959. V. 67
The Swiss Summer. London: 1951. V. 67
Ticky. London: 1943. V. 67

GIBBONS, WILLIAM
A Reply to Sir Lucius O'Brien, Bart, in Which that Part of His Letter to the Author Which Most Particulary Respects the Present State of the Iron Trade Between England and Ireland is Considered. Bristol: 1785. V. 63

GIBBS, FREDERICK ANDREWS
Atlas of Electroencephalography. N.P: 1941. V. 65

GIBBS, FREDERICK T. M.
The Illustrated Guide to the Royal Navy and Foreign Navies; also Mercantile Marine Steamers Available as Armed Cruisers and Transports.... London: 1896. V. 62

GIBBS, GEORGE
The Triangle Man. New York: 1939. V. 65; 66

GIBBS, JAMES
Bibliotheca Radcliviana: or, a Short Description of the Radcliffe Library at Oxford. London: 1747. V. 64
Rules for Drawing the Several Parts of Architecture, in a More Exact and Easy Manner Than Has Been Heretofore Practised, by Which All Fractions in Dividing the Principal Members of their Parts, are Avoided. London: 1732. V. 64; 66

GIBBS, JAMES G.
Who Burnt Columbia?. Newberry: 1902. V. 62

GIBBS, JIM
Disaster Log of Ships. Seattle: 1971. V. 65; 66

GIBBS, JOSIAH
Lights and Shadows of Mormonism. Salt Lake City: 1909. V. 65
The Mountain Meadows Massacre. Salt Lake City: 1910. V. 62; 66

GIBBS, JOSIAH W.
A Manual Hebrew and English Lexicon Including the Biblical Chaldee. New Haven: 1832. V. 62

GIBBS, MAY
Gum-Blossom Babies. Sydney: 1916. V. 62

GIBBS, PHILIP
The Adventures of an Arch-Rogue. London: 1897. V. 62

GIBBS, VICARY
The Speech...in Defence of J. H. Tooke, Esq. Tried by Special Commission on a Charge of High Treason. London: 1795. V. 63

GIBERNE, AGNES
A Lady of England: the Life and Letters of Charlotte Maria Tucker. London: 1896. V. 65

GIBNEY, V. P.
The Hip and Its Diseases. New York and London: 1884. V. 65

GIBSON, ARRELL M.
The Chickasaws. Norman: 1971. V. 67

GIBSON, C. B.
Historical Portraits, or, Irish Chieftains and Anglo-Norman Knights. 1871. V. 62; 65
The History of the County and City of Cork. 1861. V. 63; 67

GIBSON, CHARLES DANA
The Education of Dr Pipp. New York: 1900. V. 64
London, as Seen by.... New York: 1897. V. 62
The Social Ladder. New York: 1902. V. 64; 65

GIBSON, EDMUND
Chronicon Saxonicum ex MSS. Codicibus Nunc Primum Integrum Edidit ac Latinum Fecit. Oxonii: 1692. V. 64

GIBSON, EVA KATHERINE
Zauberlinda; the Wise Witch. Chicago: 1901. V. 62

GIBSON, FRANCIS
The Poetical Remains, with Other Detached Pieces. Whitby: 1807. V. 62; 65

GIBSON, GEORGE ROUTLEDGE
Journal of a Soldier Under Kearny and Doniphan 1846-1847 by George Ruthledge Gibson. Glendale: 1935. V. 65; 67

GIBSON, J. W.
The Colored American: from Slavery to Honorable Citizenship. Cincinnati: 1902. V. 64
Recollections of a Pioneer. St. Joseph: 1912. V. 63; 64

GIBSON, JAMES
Hand-Book to the Lakes; To Which is Appended an Account of Furness Abbey, the Pile of Fouldrey, Rampside, etc. London: 1852. V. 64
Report of Trial of the Issues, in the Action of Damages for Libel in the Beacon, James Gibson of Ingliston...Against Duncan Stevenson, Printer in England. Edinburgh: 1822. V. 63

GIBSON, JAMES E.
Dr. Bodo Otto and the Medical Background of the American Revolution. Springfield: 1937. V. 65

GIBSON, JOHN
My Evening with Sherlock Holmes. London: 1981. V. 65; 66

GIBSON, JOHN MASON
A Condensation of Matter Upon Anatomy, Surgical Operations and Treatment of Diseases of the Eye. Baltimore: 1832. V. 62; 64

GIBSON, KATHARINE
The Goldsmith of Florence: a Book of Great Craftsmen. New York: 1929. V. 62; 63; 64

GIBSON, PATRICK
A Letter to the Right Honourable the Lord Provost of Edinburgh, on the Subject of the Proposed New Streets and Approaches to the City.... Edinburgh: 1825. V. 62; 65

GIBSON, R. W.
Francis Bacon. A Bibliography of His Works and of Baconiana to the Year 1750. Oxford: 1950. V. 62; 64; 65; 66

GIBSON, THOMAS
The Anatomy of Humane Bodies Epitomized. London: 1703. V. 62
Legends and Historical Notes on Places of North Westmoreland. London: 1887. V. 62

GIBSON, W.
Geology of North Staffordshire Coalfields. 1905. V. 63

GIBSON, W. H.
Our Native Orchids.... New York: 1905. V. 67

GIBSON, WALTER B.
A Blonde for Murder. New York: 1948. V. 65; 66
The New Magician's Manual: Tricks and Routines with Instructions for Expert Performance by the Amatuer. New York: 1936. V. 67

GIBSON, WALTER MURRAY
The Prison of Weltevreden, and a Glance at the East Indian Archipelago. New York: 1855. V. 66

GIBSON, WILFRID WILSON
The Early Whistler. New York: 1927. V. 62; 64
Home. A Book of Poems. London: 1920. V. 62; 64
On the Threshold. London and Guildford: 1907. V. 67
The Stonefolds. London and Guildford: 1907. V. 67

GIBSON, WILLIAM
Burning Chrome. New York: 1986. V. 63
The Difference Engine. New York: 1991. V. 65; 67
The Farrier's Dispensatory. London: 1721. V. 66
The Farrier's Dispensatory. London: 1729. V. 66
Idoru. London: 1996. V. 63
The Miracle Worker: A Play for Television. New York: 1957. V. 62
Mr. Gibson's Short Practical Method of Cure for Horses, Extracted from His New Treatise on Their Diseases.... London: 1755. V. 67
Mona Lisa Overdrive. London: 1988. V. 62; 63; 65
Neuromancer. London: 1984. V. 63
Neuromancer. New York: 1984. V. 64
Neuromancer. 1986. V. 62
Neuromancer. West Bloomfield: 1986. V. 67
A New Treatise on the Diseases of Horses.... London: 1751. V. 63
Virtual Light. London: 1993. V. 63

GIBSON, WILLIAM SIDNEY
The History of the Monastery Founded at Tynemouth in the Diocese of Durham, to the Honour of God.... London: 1846. V. 65; 66
Tynemouth Priory. North Shields: 1870. V. 64

GIDDINGS, JOSHUA R.
The Exiles of Florida: or, the Crimes Committed by Our Government Against the Maroons, Who Fled from South Carolina and Other Slave States, Seeking Protection Under Spanish Laws. Columbus: 1858. V. 67

GIDDY-Go-Round. The Tale of a Wooden Horse. London: 1900. V. 65

GIDE, ANDRE
Montaigne - an Essay in Two Parts. London and New York: 1929. V. 63
Oscar Wilde, a Study. Oxford: 1905. V. 67
Oscar Wilde. In Memoriam (Souvenirs) Le De Profundis. Paris: 1910. V. 67
Persephone. New York: 1949. V. 63
Works of Andre Gide. London: 1948-1953. V. 63

GIDVANI, M. M.
Shah Abdul Latif. London: 1922. V. 66

GIEDION, S.
Spatbarocker und Romantischer Klassizismus. Munich: 1922. V. 67

Walter Gropius, Work and Teamwork. New York: 1954. V. 65

GIENANDT, FRITZ L.
Twentieth Century Book for the Progressive Baker, Confectioner, Ornamenter and Ice Cream Maker. Boston: 1912. V. 64

GIERACH, JOHN
Dances with Trout. New York: 1994. V. 67
Where Trout Are As Long as Your Leg. New York: 1991. V. 64; 67

GIEURE, MAURICE
G. Braque. New York: 1956. V. 62

GIFFARD, A. H.
Who Was My Grandfather?. 1865. V. 63

GIFFARD, WILLIAM
Cases in Midwifry. London: 1734. V. 65

GIFFEN, HELEN S.
The Story of El Tejon. Los Angeles: 1942. V. 62; 63
Trail Blazing Pioneer Colonel Joseph Ballinger Chiles. San Francisco: 1969. V. 63; 66

GIFFEN, LILIAN
The Ghost of the Belle-Alliance Plantation and Other Stories. N.P: 1901. V. 63

GIFFORD, BARRY
Jack's Book - an Oral Biography of Jack Kerouac.... New York: 1978. V. 65
Kerouac's Town. On the Second Anniversary of His Death. Santa Barbara: 1973. V. 63

GIFFORD, EDWARD W.
California Indian Nights Entertainments. Glendale: 1930. V. 66

GIFFORD, JOHN
A History of the Political Life of the Right Honourable William Pitt.... London: 1809. V. 66

GIFFORD, WILLIAM
The Baviad, a Paraphrastic Imitation of the first Satire of Perseus. London: 1791. V. 65

THE GIFT. 1839. V. 63; 64

A GIFT to the State: the National Stud. 1916. V. 62

GIGER, H. R.
Necronomicon. 1977. V. 65

GIGGLE Water Including Eleven Famous Cocktails of the Most Exclusive Club of New York. New York: 1928. V. 67

GILB, DAGOBERTO
The Magic of Blood. Albuquerque: 1993. V. 67
Winners on the Pass Line and Other Stories. El Paso: 1985. V. 63; 66

GILBANKS, W. F.
The Registers of the Parish Church of St. Giles, Great Orton, Cumberland, 1568-1812. Kendal: 1915. V. 65

GILBAR, STEVEN
L. A. Noir. Chico: 1999. V. 67

GILBART, JAMES WILLIAM
The Letters of Nehemiah; Relating to the Laws Affecting Joint Stock Banks, and the Effects Likely to be Produced, by the Measures of Sir Robert Peel.. London: 1845. V. 65
A Practical Treatise on Banking. London: 1856. V. 64

GILBERT, ANN TAYLOR
My Mother, a Poem. Philadelphia: 1837. V. 66

GILBERT, BENNETT
A Leaf from the Letters of St. Jerome First Printed by Sixtus Reissinger, Rome c. 1466-1467. Los Angeles: 1981. V. 62; 64

GILBERT, C. H.
The Fishes of Panama Bay. San Francisco: 1904. V. 63

GILBERT, CHRISTOPHER
Furniture at Temple Nesam and Lotherton Hall. London: 1978. V. 64

GILBERT, D. L.
Squid as Experimental Animals. New York: 1990. V. 65

GILBERT, DAVIES
On the Expediency of Assigning Specific Names...an Investigation of the Machine Moved by Recoil and Observations on the Steam Engine. 1827. V. 62

GILBERT, E. W.
The Exploration of Western America 1800-1850 - an Historical Geography. Cambridge: 1933. V. 65

GILBERT, G. K.
Report on the Geology of the Henry Mountains. Washington: 1880. V. 67

GILBERT, GEOFFREY
An Historical View of the Court of Exchequer and of the King's Revenues, There Answered. London: 1738. V. 63
The Law and Practice of Distresses and Replevin, by the Late Lord Chief Baron Gilbert. London: 1794. V. 65

GILBERT, H. A.
The Tale of a Wye Fisherman. 1929. V. 67

GILBERT, HENRY
King Arthur's Knights: the Tales Re-Told for Boys and Girls. Edinburgh; and London: 1911. V. 64

GILBERT, HENRY continued
Robin Hood and the Men of the Greenwood. London: 1912. V. 66
Robin Hood and the Men of the Greenwood. New York: 1912. V. 64

GILBERT, J. WARREN
The Blue and the Gray. A History of the Conflicts During Lee's Invasion and Battle of Gettysburg. Gettysburg: 1922. V. 63

GILBERT, JACK
Kochan. Syracuse: 1984. V. 64
Love: a Diptych. Asheville: 1994. V. 62; 64
Monolithos: Poems 1962 and 1982. New York: 1982. V. 62
Views of Jeopardy. New Haven and London: 1962. V. 62; 64; 67

GILBERT, JOHN M.
Hunting and Hunting Reserves in Medieval Scotland. Edinburgh: 1979. V. 67

GILBERT, JOHN T.
Chartularies of St. Mary's Abbey, Dublin.... 1884. V. 65
History of Dublin. 1903. V. 65
A Jacobite Narrative of the War in Ireland. 1688-1691. 1972. V. 67
Narratives of the Detention, Liberations and Marriage of Maria Clementina Stuart. 1970. V. 67
Register of the Abbey of St. Thomas. 1889. V. 65

GILBERT, JUDSON BENNETT
Disease and Destiny: A Bibliography of Medical References to the Famous. London: 1962. V. 66; 67

GILBERT, L.
The Royal Botanic Gardens, Sydney, a History 1816-1985. Melbourne: 1986. V. 67

GILBERT, MICHAEL
The Crack in the Teacup. London: 1966. V. 67
The Final Throw. London: 1982. V. 67
Game Without Rules. New York: 1967. V. 67
Trouble. London: 1987. V. 67
Young Petrella. London: 1988. V. 67

GILBERT, O. P.
Men in Women's Guise. London: 1926. V. 62

GILBERT, W. S.
Foggerty's Fairy and Other Tales. London: 1890. V. 65

GILBERT, WILLIAM
The City: an Inquiry into the Corporation, Its Livery Companies.... London: 1877. V. 64
Contrasts Dedicated to Ratepayers of London. London: 1873. V. 64
De Magnete, Magneticisque Corporibus et de Magno Magnete Tellure.... London: 1600. V. 65; 66
The Magic Mirror. London: 1866. V. 65; 66
The Wizard of the Mountain. London: 1867. V. 66

GILBERT, WILLIAM SCHWENCK
The Bab Ballads.... London: 1960. V. 62
Dan'l Druce, Blacksmith. N.P: 1876. V. 64
Her Majesty's Ship Pinafore; or, the Lass that Loved a Sailor. New York: 1879. V. 64
The Mikado. London: 1928. V. 64
The Pinafore Picture Book. 1908. V. 67
Savoy Operas. London: 1909. V. 64
Selected Bab Ballads. London: 1955. V. 62
Songs of a Savoyard. London: 1890. V. 62; 64
Songs of Two Savoyards. London: 1890. V. 66
The Story of H. M. S. Pinafore. London: 1913. V. 66
The Story of the Mikado. London: 1921. V. 66

GILBERTSON, JEAN
Two Men at the Helm, the First 100 Years of Crowley Maritime Corporation 1892-1992. Oakland: 1992. V. 67

GILBEY, WALTER
George Morland. His Life and Works. London: 1907. V. 66
Hounds in Old Days. Hindhead: 1979. V. 67

GILCHRIST, ALEXANDER
Life of William Blake.... London: 1863. V. 64; 66
The Life of William Blake.... London: 1880. V. 62; 64; 66; 67

GILCHRIST, D.
Journal of a High Country Hunter. 1992. V. 66; 67
On Bears and Bear Hunting. Clinton: 1984. V. 65

GILCHRIST, ELLEN
In the Land of Dreamy Dreams. Fayetteville: 1981. V. 63; 67
The Land Surveyor's Daughter. Fayetteville: 1979. V. 63
Two Stories. New York: 1988. V. 63
Victory Over Japan. Boston: 1984. V. 63

GILCHRIST, JOHN
A Collection of Ancient and Modern Scottish Ballads, Tales and Songs.... London: 1815. V. 66

GILCHRIST, ROBERT
Gothalbert and Hisanna With Other Poems. Newcastle: 1822. V. 65

GILCHRIST, ROBERT C.
Confederate Defence of Morris Island, Charleston Harbor, by the Troops of South Carolina, Georgia and North Carolina, in the Late War Between the States. Charleston: 1884. V. 62; 63

GILDER, HELENA DE KAY
A Letter on Woman Suffrage from One Woman to Another. New York: 1894. V. 63

GILDER, RICHARD W.
The New Day: a Poem in Songs and Sonnets. New York: 1876. V. 65

GILDER, WILLIAM H.
Ice-Pack and Tundra. New York: 1883. V. 62
Schwatka's Search. Sledging In the Arctic in Quest of the Franklin Records. Ann Arbor: 1966. V. 62; 64

GILDERDALE, JOHN SMITH
Disciplina Rediviva; or, Hints and Helps for Youths Leaving School. London: 1856. V. 65

GILDON, CHARLES
A New Miscellany of Original Poems, On Several Occasions. London: 1701. V. 66

GILES, BARBARA
Upright Downfall. Oxford: 1983. V. 67

GILES, CARL
Giles Sunday Express and Daily Express Cartoon Annuals. London: 1946-1995. V. 66

GILES, HERBERT A.
An Introduction to the History of Chinese Pictorial Art. London: 1918. V. 67

GILES, LEONIDAS BLANTON
Terry's Texas Rangers. Austin: 1911. V. 62; 63; 65

GILES, PIERRE
De Topographical Constantinopoleos, et de Illius Antiquitatibus Libri Quatuor. (with) De Bosporo Thracio Libri III. Lyon: 1561. V. 64

GILES, WILLIAM
A Collection of Poems on Divine and Moral Subjects, Selected from Various Authors. London: 1775. V. 62

GILES, WILLIAM B.
Plain Matters of Fact, Undenied and Undeniable, One at a Time Constructive Journies. Richmond: 1828. V. 66

GILFILLAN, ARCHER B.
Sheep. Boston: 1929. V. 66

GILFILLAN, GEORGE
A Memoir of Thomas Ebenezer Taylor. London: 1864. V. 63

GILHAM, WILLIAM
Manual of Instruction for the Volunteers and Milita of the Confederate States. Richmond: 1861. V. 62
Manual of Instruction for the Volunteers and Militia of the Confederate States. Richmond: 1862. V. 62

GILKIE, JAMES
Every Man His Own Procurator, or, the Country Gentleman's Vade-mecum. Edinburgh: 1778. V. 62

GILL, ERIC
Art and Prudence. Waltham St. Lawrence: 1928. V. 62; 64
Art-Nonsense and Other Essays. London: 1929. V. 62
Clothes. London: 1931. V. 62
Drawings from Life. 1940. V. 63
The Engravings. Wellingborough: 1983. V. 62; 67
Eric Gill. London: 1927. V. 62
An Essay on Typography. London: 1931. V. 62
First Nudes. 1954. V. 63; 65
From the Palestine Diary. 1949. V. 65
From the Palestine Diary. London: 1949. V. 62
Id Quod visum Placet. A Practical Test of the Beautiful. 1926. V. 67
The Inscriptions. A Descriptive Catalogue. London: 1994. V. 67
The Lord's Song. Waltham St. Lawrence: 1934. V. 62; 64; 65
Sculpture an Essay, on Stone-Cutting.... Hassocks, Ditchling, Sussex: 1924. V. 62; 65
Songs without Clothes.... Ditchling, Sussex: 1921. V. 62; 65
Unholy Trinity. London: 1938. V. 65

GILL, ISOBEL
Six Months in Ascension: an Unscientific Account of a Scientific Expedition. London: 1878. V. 65

GILL, JAMES
In the Exchequer of Pleas. A Verbatim Report of the Proceedings in an Action for Crim. Con. Between James Gill, Esq. Plaintiff and H. P. T. Aubrey, Esq. Defendant Tried at Lancaster Spring Assizes, April 4, 1820.... Hereford: 1820. V. 63

GILL, T.
Arrangement of Familes of Fishes, or Classes Pisces, Marsipobranchii and Leptocardii. (with) Catalogue of the Fishes of the East Coast of North America. Washington: 1872-1873. V. 63

GILL, THOMAS
Vallis Eboracensis; Comprising the History and Antiquities of Easingwold and Its Neighbourhood. London: 1852. V. 66

GILL, W.
The River of the Golden Sand; Being the Narrative of a Journey through China and Eastern Tibet to Burmah.... London: 1880. V. 67

GILL, WILFRED AUSTIN
Edward Cracroft Lefroy - His Life and Poems Including a Reprint of Echoes from Theocritus. London: 1897. V. 63; 64; 67

GILLAM, BEATRICE
The Wiltshire Flora. Newbury: 1993. V. 67

GILLAND, THOMAS
The Trap: a Moral, Philosophical, and Satirical Work.... London: 1809. V. 64

GILLESPIE, ALEXANDER
An Historical Review of the Royal Marine Corps, from Its Original Institution Down to the Present Era. Birmingham: 1803. V. 62; 65

GILLESPIE, C. C.
Dictionary of Scientific Biography. New York: 1970-1975. V. 65

GILLESPIE, JOSEPH HALSTEAD
Elsinore and Other Poems. Raleigh: 1888. V. 67

GILLET, C. C.
Les Hymenomycetes ou Description de Tous les Champignons (Fungi) Qui Croissent en France.... 1874-1891. V. 62

GILLETT, JAMES B.
Six Years with Texas Rangers 1875-1881. Austin: 1921. V. 65; 67

GILLETTE, F. L., MRS.
White House Cook Book. Chicago: 1889. V. 64

GILLETTE, MARTHA HILL
Overland to Oregon and the Indian Wars of 1853. Ashland: 1971. V. 67

GILLHAM, SARAH
Memoirs of Sarah Gillham, During Seven Years of Severe Affliction.... London: 1813. V. 67

GILLIARD, E. T.
Birds of Paradise and Bower Birds. 1969. V. 63; 66
Birds of Paradise and Bower Birds. Garden City: 1969. V. 67

GILLIES, HAROLD DELF
Plastic Surgery of the Face Based on Selected Cases of War Injuries of the Face Including Burns. London: 1920. V. 62

GILLIES, JOHN
The History of Ancient Greece, Its Colonies, and Conquests; from the Earliest Accounts Till the Division of the Macedonian Empire in the East. Basle: 1790. V. 64
Memoirs of the Life of Rev. George Whitefield, M.A., Late Chaplain to the Right Hon. The Countess of Huntingdon.... London: 1772. V. 63

GILLILAND, MAUDE T.
Rincon (Remote Dwelling Place). A Story of Life on a South Texas Ranch at the Turn of the Century. Brownsville: 1964. V. 62; 64; 67

GILLING, ISAAC
A Sermon Preach'd at Lyme Regis in the County of Dorset, at a Quarterly Lecture, Appointed for the Promoting the Reformation of Manners. Exon (i.e. Exeter): 1705. V. 65

GILLINGHAM, ROBERT C.
The Rancho San Pedro: The Story of a Famous Rancho in Los Angeles County and Of Its Owners, the Dominguez Family. 1961. V. 63
The Rancho San Pedro: the Story of a Famous Rancho in Los Angeles County and Of Its Owners, The Dominguez Family. Los Angeles: 1961. V. 62; 64

GILLIS, WILLIAM R.
Memories of Mark Twain and Steve Gillis. Sonora: 1924. V. 63

GILLISPIE, CHARLES COULSTON
Lazare Carnot Savant. Princeton: 1971. V. 67

GILLISS, WALTER
The Story of a Motto and Mark. Being a Brief Sketch of a Few Printers' Marks and Containing the Facts Concerning the Mark of the Gilliss Press. New York: 1932. V. 63

GILLMAN, JAMES
The Life of Samuel Taylor Coleridge. London: 1838. V. 64; 66

GILLMORE, PARKER
The Great Thirst Land: a Ride through Natal, Orange Free State, Transvaal and Kalahari Desert. London: 1878. V. 67
Gun Rod and Saddle: a Record of Personal Experiences. London: 1893. V. 67
The Hunter's Arcadia. London: 1860. V. 67
On Duty: a Ride through Hostile Africa. London: 1880. V. 67
Through Gasa Land; and the Scene of the Portuguese Aggression. The Journey of a Hunter in Search of Gold and Ivory. London: 1890. V. 67
Travels War and Shipwreck. New York: 1883. V. 66

GILLOW, JOSEPH
A Literary and Biographical History, Or Bibliographical Dictionary of English Catholics from the Breach with Rome. London: 1885-1902. V. 62

GILLS, W. R.
Gold Rush Days with Mark Twain. New York: 1930. V. 62

GILLY, WILLIAM STEPHEN
Narrative of an Excursion to the Mountains of Piemont, in the Year MDCCCXXIII and Researches Among the Vaudois.... London: 1826. V. 65
Narrative of an Excursion to the Mountains of Piemont, in the Year MDCCCXXIII and Researches Among the Vaudois.... London: 1827. V. 63

GILMAN, BENJAMIN IVES
Hopi Songs - a Journal of American Ethnology and Archaeology. Boston: 1908. V. 65

GILMAN, CAROLINE HOWARD
Recollections of a Southern Matron. New York: 1838. V. 62; 63; 64; 66

GILMAN, CHARLOTTE PERKINS STETSON
The Crux. New York: 1911. V. 66
The Home: Its Work and Its Influence. New York: 1903. V. 64
In This Our World. Boston: 1898. V. 65
The Man-Made World, or, Our Androcentric Culture. New York: 1911. V. 66
Women and Economics, a Study of the Economic Relation Between Men and Women as a Facator in Social Evolution. Boston: 1898. V. 65

GILMAN, S. C.
The Conquest of the Sioux. San Francisco: 1900. V. 67

GILMER, JOHN H.
Letter Addressed to Hon. Wm. C. Rives, by John H. Gilmer, on the Existing Status of the Revolution &c. Richmond: 1864. V. 63

GILMOR, HARRY
Four Years in the Saddle. New York: 1866. V. 62; 63; 65

GILMORE, C. W.
Fossil Lizards of North America. Washington: 1928. V. 62; 64; 66
The Fossil Turtles of the Uinta Formation. Pittsburgh: 1916. V. 66

GILMOUR, MARGARET
Ameliaranne at the Circus. London: 1931. V. 67
Ameliaranne Gives A Concert. London: 1944. V. 67

GILPATRICK, NOREEN
The Piano Man. New York: 1991. V. 62; 66; 67

GILPIN, JOSHUA
A Monument of Parental Affection to a Dear and Only Son. Wellington: 1808. V. 66

GILPIN, LAURA
The Enduring Navaho. Austin: 1968. V. 63; 64; 66
The Enduring Navaho. Santa Fe. 1968. V. 66
The Pueblos - a Camera Chronicle. New York: 1941. V. 63; 65; 66; 67
The Rio Grande - River of Destiny. New York: 1949. V. 62; 63; 65
Temples in Yucatan: a Camera Chronicle of Chicken Itza. New York: 1948. V. 63

GILPIN, THOMAS
Exiles in Virginia: with Observations on the Conduct of the Society of Friends, During the Revolutionary War. Philadelphia: 1848. V. 64

GILPIN, WILLIAM
An Essay on Prints. London: 1792. V. 62; 66
An Essay on Prints. London: 1802. V. 63
Observations on Several Parts of the Counties of Cambridge, Norfolk, Suffolk and Essex. London: 1809. V. 63; 67
Observations on the Coasts of Hampshire, Sussex and Kent, Relative Chiefly to Picturesque Beauty.... London: 1804. V. 66; 67
Observations on the River Wye, and Several Parts of South Wales &c. London: 1782. V. 63; 66; 67
Observations on the River Wye and Several Parts of South Wales, &c. London: 1789. V. 62; 63
Observations on the River Wye, and Several Parts of South Wales. &c. London: 1792. V. 66
Observations on the River, Wye and Several Parts of South Wales, &c. London: 1800. V. 66
Observations on the Western Parts of England, Relative Chiefly to Picturesque Beauty.... London: 1798. V. 66
Observations on the Western Parts of England, Relative Chiefly to Picturesque Beauty.... London: 1808. V. 66; 67
Observations, Relative Chiefly to Picturesque Beauty, Made in the Year 1772.... London: 1788. V. 63
Observations Relative Chiefly to Picturesque Beauty, Made in the Year 1772.... London: 1792. V. 67
Observations Relative Chiefly to Picturesque Beauty, Made in the Year 1772.... London: 1808. V. 66; 67
Observations Relative Chiefly to Picturesque Beauty, Made in the Year 1776.... London: 1789. V. 62; 63; 66; 66; 67
Remarks On Forest Scenery and Other Woodland Views. London: 1791. V. 63
Remarks on Forest Scenery and Other Woodland Views. London: 1791. V. 62
Remarks on Forest Scenery and Other Woodland Views. London: 1794. V. 62; 64; 66; 67
Remarks on Forest Scenery and Other Woodland Views. London: 1808. V. 64; 66; 67
Remarks on Forest Scenery and Other Woodland Views. Edinburgh: 1834. V. 62
Three Essays: on Picturesque Beauty; on Picturesque Travel; and on Sketching Landscape: to Which is added a Poem, on Landscape Painting. London: 1794. V. 66
Three Essays: on Picturesque Beauty; on Picturesque Travel; and on Sketching Landscape, to Which is added a Poem, on Landscape Painting. London: 1808. V. 66; 67

GILSAN, RODNEY
Journal of Army Life. San Francisco: 1874. V. 67

GILTAY, J. W.
Bow Instruments, their Form and Construction. London. V. 67

GIMSON, ERNEST
His Life and Work. Oxford: 1924. V. 65

GINGLE, JACOB
The Oxford Sermon Versified. London: 1729. V. 65
The Several Depositions Concerning the Late Riot in Oxford. London: 1716. V. 62

GINGLE, JOHN
The Oxford Sermon Versified. London: 1729. V. 62

GINGRICH, ARNOLD
The Gordon Garland. New York: 1965. V. 64

GINSBERG, ALLEN
Airplane Dreams: Compositions from Journals. Toronto: 1968. V. 62; 67
Bixby Canyon/Ocean Path/Word Breeze. New York: 1972. V. 62; 64
Careless Love. Madison: 1978. V. 67
Collected Poems 1947-1980. 1985. V. 63
Collected Poems 1947-1985. Harmondsworth, Middlesex: 1995. V. 64
Erwachen (Waking In). Gotha: 1996. V. 64
First Blues. New York: 1975. V. 65
The Gates of Wrath - Rhymed Poems: 1948-1952. Bolinas: 1972. V. 63
Howl. San Francisco: 1956. V. 62; 64
Howl. San Francisco: 1971. V. 62
Howl. Original Draft Facsimile, Transcript and Variant Versions. New York: 1986. V. 63; 64
Illuminated Poems. New York: 1996. V. 62; 64; 65; 67
Indian Journals: March 1962 - May 1963. San Francisco: 1970. V. 62; 63; 64
Kaddish and Other Poems 1958-1960. San Francisco: 1961. V. 64
Photographs. Altadena: 1990. V. 64
Reality Sandwiches 1953-1960. San Francisco: 1963. V. 62; 65
Sad Dust Glories. Berkeley: 1975. V. 62
Scrap Leaves: Tasty Scribbles. New York: 1968. V. 66
T. V. Baby Poems. London: 1967. V. 62
Wales - a Visitation July 29th 1967. London: 1968. V. 65
White Shroud. Madras: 1984. V. 64

GINSBERG, LOUIS
History of the Jews of Petersburg, 1789-1950. Petersburg: 1854. V. 65

GINUENE, P. L.
Hisoire Litteraire d'Italie. Paris: 1811. V. 64

GIOIA, DANA
Daily Horoscope. St. Paul: 1986. V. 63
Formal Introductions: an Investigative Anthology. West Chester: 1994. V. 63
Journeys in Sunlight. Six Poems. Cottondale: 1987. V. 64
Letter to the Bahamas: Remebering Ronald Perry. Omaha: 1983. V. 63
Planting a Sequoia. West Chester: 1991. V. 63; 67

GIONO, JEAN
The Hussar on the Roof. London: 1953. V. 65

GIORGI, FELICE
Descrizione Istorica del Teatro di Tor di Nona. Rome: 1795. V. 64

GIOSEFFI, DANIELA
Eggs in the Lake. Poems. Brockport: 1979. V. 63

GIOVANNI, NIKKI
Black Feeling, Black Talk. N.P: 1968. V. 62; 64

GIOVIO, PAOLO, BP. OF NOCERA
Dialogo Dell'Imprese Militari et Amorose di Monsignor Giouio Vescouo di Nocera.... Lyone: 1574. V. 66

GIOVIO, PAULO, BP. OF NOCERA
Pauli Iovii Comensis Medici de Romanis Piscibus.... Basle: 1531. V. 62

GIPSON, LAWRENCE H.
Lewis Evans. Philadelphia: 1939. V. 62

GIRAFFI, ALEXANDER
An Exact Historie of the Late Revolutions in Naples. London: 1650. V. 63; 66

GIRALDUS CAMBRENSIS
The Itinerary of Archbishop Baldwin through Wales, A.D. MCLXXXVIII. London: 1806. V. 65; 66
Itinerum Cambriae Seu Labriosae Baldvini Cantuariensis Archiepiscopi Per Walliam Legationis Accurata Descriptio Auctore Silv. Giraldo Cambrense. 1806. V. 66
Proposals for Enriching the Principality of Wales; Humbly Submitted to the Consideration of His Countrymen.... Glo(u)cester: 1762. V. 67

GIRARD, ALBERT
Invention Nouvelle en l'Algebre. Leyden: 1884. V. 67

GIRARD, C.
Contributions to the Fauna of Chile. Washington: 1855. V. 66
Contributions to the Fauna of Chile - Reptiles, Fishes and Crustacea from the U.S. Naval Astronomical Expedition. Washington: 1855-1851. V. 66
United States Pacific Railroad Survey: Fishes. Washington: 1857-1858. V. 65

GIRARD, JAMES PRESTON
The Late Man. New York: 1993. V. 63

GIRARDIN, STANISLAS XAVIER, COMTE DE
Promenade ou Itineraire des Jardins d'Ermenonville, Auquel on a Joint Vingt-Cinq de Leurs Principales Vues, Dessinees et Gravees par J. Merigot fils. Paris: 1788. V. 62

GIRAUD, FRANCIS F.
A Visitor's Guide to Faversham.... Faversham: 1876. V. 67

GIRAUD, P. F. F. J.
The Campaign of Paris in 1814; to Which is Prefixed a Sketch of the Campaign of 1813. London: 1815. V. 65

GIRAUD, S. LOUIS
Bookano Stories with Pictures That Spring Up in Model Form: No. 1. London: 1934. V. 65
Bookano Stories No. 3. London: 1936. V. 65
Bookano Stories with Pictures that Spring Up in Model Form: No. 4. London: 1937. V. 63; 65
Bookano Stories with Pictures that Spring Up in Model Form. No. 9. London: 1942. V. 64; 65
Bookano Stories. No. 11. London: 1944. V. 63
Bookano Stories. No. 13. London: 1946. V. 62
Bookano Stories. Number 14. London: 1947. V. 64
Old Rhymes and New Stories. No. 2. London: 1934. V. 65
Old Rhymes and New Stories No. 3: Bookano Living Picture Series. London: 1935. V. 64
Old Rhymes and New Stories. No. 4. London: 1934. V. 65

GIRAUDOUX, J.
La Grande Bourgeoisie ou Toute Femme a la Vocation. Paris: 1928. V. 64

GIRDLER, J. S.
Observations on the Pernicious Consequences of Forestalling, Regrating and Ingrossing, with a List of the Statutes, &c.... London: 1800. V. 64

GIRLS and Boys Come Out to Play. London: 1910. V. 62

GIRLS' and Boys' Primer (Part II). Concord: 1850. V. 64

GIRL'S Own Annual 1890-1891. V. 67

THE GIRL'S Realm. 1903. V. 67

GIROD-CHANTRANS, JUSTIN
Experiences Faites sur les Proprietes des Lezards.... Besancon: 1805. V. 65

GIRONI, ROBUSTIANO
Le Danze dei Greci, Descitte e Pubblicate.... Milan: 1820. V. 66
Saggio Intorno Alle Costumanze Civili dei Greci. Milan: 1823. V. 64

GIROUARD, MARK
Stowe. London: 1983. V. 67

GIRTIN, THOMAS
Naturae or a Collection of Prints from the Drawings of Thomas Girtin.... London: 1883. V. 64

GIRTY & ELLIOTT
Descriptive Catalogue of Agricultural and Horticultural Implements and Machinery, Field, Garden and Flower Seeds, Fruit and Ornamental Trees, Shrubs, Roses, Vines and Plants.... Cleveland: 1851. V. 62

GISBORNE, THOMAS
An Enquiry into the Duties of Men in the Higher and Middle Classes of Society in Great Britain. London: 1797. V. 64; 67
An Enquiry into the Duties of the Female Sex. London: 1797. V. 63; 66
An Enquiry Into the Duties of the Female Sex. London: 1798. V. 62; 64; 65

GISSING, GEORGE
Demos: a Story of English Socialism. London: 1886. V. 66
The Emancipated: a Novel. London: 1890. V. 65
Human Odds and Ends: Stories and Sketches. London: 1898. V. 65
The Nether World. London: 1889. V. 65; 67
New Grub Street. London: 1891. V. 65; 66
The Private Papers of Henry Ryecroft. New York: 1903. V. 63; 64
The Private Papers of Henry Ryecroft. Westminster: 1903. V. 62
Sleeping Fires. London: 1895. V. 64
The Town Traveller. London: 1898. V. 65; 66
Veranilda; a Romance. London: 1904. V. 65

GISSING, T. W.
The Ferns and Fern Allies of Wakefield and Its Neighbourhood. Wakefield: 1862. V. 64; 65; 66

GITTINGS, JOHN G.
Personal Recollections of Stonewall Jackson, also Sketches and Stories. Cincinnati: 1899. V. 62; 63; 65

GIUDICE, G.
The Sea Urchin Embryo, a Developmental Biological System. Berlin: 1986. V. 63

GIUSTINIAN, LEONARDO
Strambotti E. Canzonette D'Amore. Verona: 1945. V. 65

GIUSTINIANA, LODOVICO
Vita Del B. Filippo Benizi Nobil Fiorentino Quinto Generale E Propagatore Del Sacr' Ordine De' Serui Di Maria Vergine. Bologna: 1668. V. 66

GIUSTINIANI, VINCENZO
Galleria Giustiniani. Genoa: 1750. V. 62

GIUSTINIANO, AGOSTINO
Castigatissimi Annali Com la Loro Copiosa Tavola Della Eccelsa & Illustrissima Republi di Genoa, da Fideli & Approvati Scritori.... Genoa: 1537. V. 62

GIVEN, META
Meta Givens' Modern Encyclopedia of Cooking. Chicago: 1959. V. 67

GLADSTONE, HUGH S.
The History of the Dumfriesshire and Galloway Natural History and Antiquarian Society. Dumfries: 1913. V. 62
Record Bags and Shooting Records; Together with Some Account of the Evolution of the Sporting Gun, Markmanship and the Speed and Weight of Birds. London: 1922. V. 67

GLADSTONE, R. J.
The Pineal Organ.... London: 1940. V. 62

GLADSTONE, THOMAS H.
Kansas; or, Squatter Life and border Warfare in the Far West. London: 1857. V. 64

GLADSTONE, W. E.
Ecce Homo. London: 1868. V. 66
The Odes of Horace. London: 1894. V. 63

GLADWIN, HAROLD S.
Excavations at Snake Town. Globe: 1937-1948. V. 63
Excavations At Snaketown, Material Culture. Tucson: 1965. V. 62; 65
A History of the Ancient Southwest. Portland: 1957. V. 66
A Review and Analysis of the Flagstaff Culture. Lancaster: 1943. V. 65

GLADWIN, WINIFRED
Some Southwestern Pottery Types - Series III. 1933. V. 65

GLAESSNER, MARTIN F.
Principles of Micropalaeontology. New York: 1967. V. 67

GLAISTER, ELIZABETH
The Perfect Path, a Novel. London: 1884. V. 65

GLANVILL, JOSEPH
Scepsis Scientifica; or, Confest Ignorance, the Way to Science... (with) - Sciri Tuum Nihil Est: The Authors Defence of the Vanity of Dogmatizing.... London: 1665. V. 63
The Way of Happiness: Represented in Its Difficulties and Incouragements.... London: 1670. V. 66

GLANVILLE, JOHN
Reports of Certain Cases, Determined and Adjudged by the Commons in Parliament, in the Twenty-First and Twenty-Second Years of the Reign of King James the First.... London: 1775. V. 62

GLAPTHORNE, HENRY
The Plays and Poems. London: 1874. V. 65

GLAREANUS, HEINRICH LORITZ
De Geographia Liber Unus, ab Ipso Authore iam Novissime Recognitus. Freiburg: 1539. V. 62

GLASFURD, A. I. R.
Musings of an Old Shikari. 1928. V. 62; 63; 64; 66; 67

GLASGOW ARCHAEOLOGICAL SOCIETY
Transactions of the Glasgow Archaeological Society. Glasgow: 1868-1890. V. 65

GLASGOW ASYLUM FOR THE BLIND
Statements of the Education, Employments and Internal Arrangements, Adopted at the Asylum for the Blind, Glasgow. Glasgow: 1846. V. 64

GLASGOW COLONIAL SOCIETY
Selected Correspondence of the Glasgow Colonial Society 1825-1840. Toronto: 1994. V. 66

GLASGOW, ELLEN
Barren Ground. Garden City: 1925. V. 63
The Descendent. New York: 1897. V. 62
The Voice of the People. New York: 1902. V. 64; 67
The Woman Within. New York: 1954. V. 63

GLASGOW PHILOSOPHICAL SOCIETY
The Daily Exhibitor, Printed at the Philosophical Society's Exhibition of Models, Manufactures, Natural History, Works of Art.... Glasgow: 1847. V. 64

GLASIER, J. BRUCE
Socialism in Song. Manchester. V. 64

GLASNER, JOHN
20 Best Film Plays. 1943. V. 63

GLASPELL, SUSAN
Alison's House. New York: 1930. V. 66
A Jury of Her Peers. London: 1927. V. 65; 66; 67

GLASS, CHARLES GORDON
Stray Leaves from Scotch and English History, with the Life of Sir William Wallace, Scotland's Patriot, Hero and Political Martyr. Montreal: 1876. V. 64

GLASS, E. L. N.
The History of the Tenth Cavalry 1866-1921. Fort Collins: 1972. V. 66

GLASS, MARK
Ancient Song. New York: 1980. V. 64

GLASSCOCK, C. B.
The Death Valley Chuch-Walla: a Magazine for Men. Greenwater: 1990. V. 62

GLASSE, HANNAH
The Art of Cookery, Made Plain and Easy.... London: 1784. V. 64; 66
The Art of Cookery Made Plain and Easy.... Alexandria: 1805. V. 64

GLASSE, SAMUEL
Advice from a Lady of Quality to Her Children, in the Last Stage of a Lingering Illness in a Series of Evening Conferences on Most Interesting Subjects. London: 1778. V. 63
The Magistrate's Assistant; or a Summary of Those Laws, Which Immediately Respect the Conduct of a Justice of the Peace.... Glocester: 1788. V. 63
A Narrative of Proceedings, Tending Towards a National Reformation, Previous To and Consequent Upon, His Majesty's Royal Proclamation.... London: 1787. V. 65

GLASSII, SALOMONIS
Opuscula. Leiden: 1700. V. 64

GLASSMAN, S. F.
A Revison of Dahlgren's Index to American Palms. Lehre: 1972. V. 67

GLASSNER, JOHN
Best Film Plays 1943-1944. 1945. V. 63; 65

GLATZ, PAUL
Dyspepsies Nerveuses et Neurasthenie. Bale et Geneve: 1898. V. 65

GLAZIER, WILLARD
Three Years with the Federal Cavalry. New York: 1873. V. 67

GLEANINGS from Books on Agriculture and Gardening. 1802. V. 63; 66

GLEASON, H. A.
Manual of Vascular Plants of Northeastern United States and Adjacent Canada. New York: 1963. V. 67
The New Britton and Brown Illustrated Flora of the Northeastern States and Adjacent Canada. New York: 1968. V. 66

GLEASON, OSCAR
Gleasons' Veterinary Handbook and System of Horse Taming. Chicago: 1900. V. 64

GLEED, CHARLES S.
The Kansas Memorial. A Report of the Old Settlers' Meeting. Held at Bismarck Grove, Kansas, Sept. 15th and 16th. 1879. Kansas City: 1880. V. 63

GLEESON, JOHN
History of the Ely O'Carroll Territory, or, Ancient Ormonde Situated in Northern Tipperary and North Western King's County. 1915. V. 62; 65

GLEICHEN, COUNT
Journal of Our Mission to Fez. (1909). London: 1909. V. 67

GLEIG, GEORGE ROBERT
Allan Breck. London: 1834. V. 64
The Country Curate. London: 1830. V. 63
The Family History of England. London: 1836. V. 66
The Family History of England. London: 1854. V. 65
The Hussar. London: 1837. V. 65
A Narrative of the Campaigns of the British Army at Washington and New Orleans, Under Generals, Ross, Pakenham and Lambert, in the Years 1814 and 1815. London: 1826. V. 66

GLEN, JAMES
A Description of South Carolina.... London: 1761. V. 63

GLENELG, CHARLES GRANT, 1ST BARON
Lord Glenelg's Despatches to Sir F. B. Head, Bart., During His Administration of the Governement of Upper Canada. London: 1839. V. 65

GLENISTER, A. G.
The Birds of the Malay Peninsula, Singapore and Penang. Oxford: 1951. V. 67

GLENN, C. W.
Jim Dine Drawings. New York: 1985. V. 65

GLENN, JOHN
P.S. I Listened to Your Heartbeat: Letters to John Glenn. Houston: 1964. V. 63

GLENNIE, K. W.
Introduction to the Petroleum Geology of the North Sea. 1984. V. 67

GLINES, CARROLL V.
Doolittle's Tokyo Raiders. New Jersey. 1964. V. 63

GLISSON, FRANCIS
anatomia Hepatis Cui Praemittuntur Quaedam ad Rem Anatomicam Spectantia. Amstelodami: 1665. V. 65

A GLOSSARY of Terms Used in Grecian, Roman, Italian and Gothic Architecture. Oxford: 1850. V. 65

GLOSSOP, E. R. M.
Sporting Trips of a Subaltern. 1906. V. 67

GLOUCESTER CARRIAGE AND WHEEL WORKS
Catalogue B. 1901. V. 64

GLOUCESTER CITY
Charter of Gloucester City and By Laws for the Government of the City Council.... Camden: 1868. V. 63; 66

GLOUCESTER MANUFACTURING CO.
Charter and By-Laws of the Gloucester Manufacturing Company of New Jersey. Philadelphia: 1862. V. 63

GLOVER, DOROTHY
Victorian Detective Fiction - a Catalogue of the Collection Made by Dorothy Glover and Graham Greene.... London: 1966. V. 62; 62; 63

GLOVER, RICHARD
Leonidas a Poem. London: 1737. V. 63; 64; 67

GLOVER, ROBERT MORTIMER
On Mineral Waters; Their Physical and Medicinal Properties. London: 1857. V. 62

GLOVER, ROLFE E.
Blairs of Richmond, Virginia. The Descendants of Reverend John Durburrow Blair and Mary Winston Blair, His Wife. Richmond: 1933. V. 63

GLOVER, T. R.
Corner of Empire; the Old Ontario Strand. Cambridge: 1937. V. 67

GLUBB, JOHN B.
Britain and the Arabs: a Study of Fifty Years 1908-1958. London: 1959. V. 67

GLUCK, LOUISE
Ararat. New York: 1990. V. 67
Descending Figure. New York: 1980. V. 64
The First Four Books of Poems: Firstborn, The House on Marshaland, Descending Figure, The Triumph of Achilles. Hopewell: 1995. V. 63; 67
Firstborn. New York: 1968. V. 64; 67
The Garden. N.P: 1976. V. 62; 64; 67
The House of Marshland. New York: 1975. V. 64; 67
The Triumph of Achilles. New York: 1985. V. 64

GLUCKMAN, ARCADI
United States Martial Pistols and Revolvers. Buffalo: 1939. V. 63; 66
United States Muskets, Rifles and Carbines. Buffalo: 1948. V. 63; 67

GLUTCH, JOHN MATHEW
A Lytell Geste of Robin Hode with Other Ancient and Modern Ballads and Songs Relating to this Celebrated Yeoman. London: 1847. V. 65

GLYDENSTOLPE, N.
Birds Collected by the Swedish Zoological Expedition to Siam 1911- 1912. Stockholm: 1913-1916. V. 64

GLYN, ELINOR
Three Weeks. New York: 1907. V. 67

GMELIN, JOANNE GEORGIO
Flora Fibirica Sive Historia Plantarum Sibirlae. St. Petersburg: 1747-1749. V. 63; 66

GNOMES.. 1977. V. 67

GNUDI, MARTHA TEACH
Life and Times of Gaspare Tagliacozzi, Surgeon of Bologna, 1545-1599. Milan: 1950. V. 66
The Life and Times of Gaspare Tagliacozzi, Surgeon of Bologna 1545-1599. New York: 1950. V. 66

GO Ahead! Davy Crockett's 1838 Almanack of Wild Sports in the West, Life in the Backwoods, Sketches of Texas and Rows on the Mississippi. Nashville: 1837. V. 64

GO Ahead! The Crockett Almanac 1839. Volume I. No. 1. Nashville: 1838. V. 66

GOADBY, PETER
Big Fish and Blue Water. 1970. V. 63; 65; 67

GOBAT, SAMUEL
Journal of Three Years in Abyssinia. London: 1847. V. 67
Journal of Three Years' Residence in Abyssinia.... New York: 1851. V. 65

GOBINEAU, JOSEPH ARTHUR DE, COUNT
The Moral and Intellectual Diversity of Races, with Particular Reference to Their Respective Influence in the Civil and Political History of Mankind. Philadelphia: 1856. V. 65

GOBRIGHT, L. A.
Recollection of Men and Things at Washington, During the Third of a Century. Philadelphia: 1869. V. 63

GOCAR, JOSEF
Josef Gocar. Geneva: 1930. V. 65

GOD is Love. London: 1890. V. 67

GODART, J. B.
Histoire Naturelle des Lepidopteres ou Papillons de France. Paris: 1820-1844. V. 65; 66

GODBEY, J. E.
Lights and Shadows of Seveny Years. St. Louis: 1913. V. 64; 67

GODDARD, FREDERICK B.
Where to Emigrate and Why - Homes and Fortunes in the Boundless West and the Sunny South. Philadelphia: 1869. V. 63

GODDARD, JOHN
Still Water Flies, How and When to Fish Them. 1982. V. 67
Trout Flies of Stillwater. 1969. V. 67

GODDARD, PAUL
The Anatomy, Physiology and Pathology of the Human Teeth.... Philadelphia: 1844. V. 62; 66; 67
Plates of the Arteries, with References.... Philadelphia: 1839. V. 62

GODDARD, PLINY EARLE
Jicarilla Apache Texts. New York: 1911. V. 64
San Carlos Apache Texts. New York: 1919. V. 64; 65
White Mountain Apache Texts. New York: 1920. V. 64

GODDARD, ROBERT H.
Rockets. New York: 1946. V. 63

GODDARD, RUTH
Portiro Salinas. Austin: 1975. V. 66

GODDARD, THOMAS H.
A General History of the Most Prominent Banks in Europe.... New York: 1831. V. 64; 66

GODDARD, WILLIAM G.
An Address to the People of Rhode-Island, Delivered at Newport...on the Occasion of the Change in Civil Government.... Providence: 1843. V. 64; 66

GODDEN, GEOFFREY
Coalport and Coalbrookdale Porcelains. New York: 1970. V. 63
The Illustrated Guide to Lowestoft Porcelain. London: 1969. V. 64
The Illustrated Guide to Mason's Patent Ironstone China and Related Wares - Stone China, New Stone, Granite China.... New York: 1971. V. 63

GODEFROY, J.
Supplement a l'Histoire des Guerres Civiles de Flandre Sous Philippe II.... Amsterdam: 1729. V. 65

GODEY'S Lady's Book. Volumes XXVIII January-June XXIX July- December. Philadelphia: 1844. V. 67

GODFRAY, HUGH
An Elementary Treatise on the Lunar Theory; with a Brief Sketch of the History of the Problem Up to the Time of Newton. Cambridge: 1853. V. 67

GODFREY, CARLOS E.
The Commander-in-Chief's Guard. Revolutionary War. Washington: 1904. V. 63; 66

GODFREY, E. L. B.
History of the Medical Profession of Camden County, N.J. Philadelphia: 1896. V. 63; 66

GODFREY, EDWARD SETTLE
An Account of Custer's Last Campaign and Battle of the Little Big Horn. Palo Alto: 1968. V. 63
The Field Diary of Lt. Edward Settle Godfrey, Commanding Company K 7th Cavalry Regiment Under Lt. Colonel George Armstrong Custer in the Sioux Encounter at the Battle of Little Big Horn. Portland: 1957. V. 65; 67

GODFREY, J. H.
Netherlands East Indies. London: 1944. V. 67

GODFREY, JOHN T.
Manuscripts Relating to the County of Nottingham in the Possession of Mr. James Ward, Nottingham. London: 1900. V. 65
Notes on the Churches of Nottinghamshire. London: 1887. V. 65
Notes on the Parish Registers of St. Mary's Nottingham 1566 to 1812. Nottingham: 1901. V. 65

GODFREY, THOMAS
Juvenile Poems on Various Subjects. Philadelphia: 1765. V. 62; 66

GODINE, DAVID R.
Lyric Verse. Lunenburg: 1966. V. 66

GODKIN, J.
The Rights of Ireland. Dublin: 1845. V. 66

GODMAN, ERNEST
Norman Architecture in Essex. London: 1905. V. 62

GODMAN, F. DU CANE
A Monograph of the Petrels (Order Tubinares). London: 1907-1910. V. 62

GODMAN, JOHN D.
Addresses Delivered on Various Public Occasions.... Philadelphia: 1829. V. 67
American Natural History. Philadelphia: 1831. V. 63; 66

GODON, JULIEN
Painted Tapestry and Its Application to Interior Decoration. 1879. V. 62; 66

GODREJ, PHEROZA
Scenic Splendours: India through the Printed Image. London: 1989. V. 67

GODSPEED, T. HARPER
Plant Hunters in the Andes. London: 1941. V. 64

GODWIN, BENJAMIN
The Substance of a Course of Lectures on British Colonial Slavery, Delivered at Bradford, York and Scarborough. London: 1820. V. 67
The Substance of a Course of Lectures on British Colonial Slavery, Delivered at Bradford, York and Scarborough. London: 1830. V. 63

GODWIN, FAY
Land. Boston: 1985. V. 62; 64; 67

GODWIN, FRANCIS
Annales of England. London: 1630. V. 64
De Praesulibus Angliae Commentarius, Omnium Episcoporum Necnon et Cardinalium Eiusdem Gentis Nomina, Tempora, Seriem, Atque Actiones Maxime Memorabiles Ab Ultima Antiquitate Repetita.... Cantabrigiae: 1743. V. 66

GODWIN, G. N.
The Civil War in Hampshire (1642-1645) and the Story of Basing House. London: 1882. V. 63

GODWIN, GAIL
The Perfectionists. New York: 1970. V. 63; 66

GODWIN, HENRY
Stonehenge, or, the Romans in Britian. London: 1842. V. 65

GODWIN, PARKE
Popular View of the Doctrines of Charles Fourier. New York: 1844. V. 66

GODWIN, THOMAS
Romanae Historiae Anthologia. (with) *Synopsis Antiquitatum Hebraicarum.* Oxford: 1620. V. 63

GODWIN, WILLIAM
Caleb Williams.... London: 1831. V. 64
The Enquirer. Reflections on Education, Manners and Literature. London: 1797. V. 62; 63; 65
Enquiry Concerning Political Justice and Its Effect on Morals and Happiness. London: 1796. V. 66

GODWIN, WILLIAM continued
An Enquiry Concerning Political Justice and Its Influence on General Virtue and Happiness. London: 1793. V. 64
Enquiry Concerning Political Justice, and Its Influence on Moral Happiness. London: 1798. V. 64
Essay on Sepulchres; or, a Proposal for Erecting Some Memorial of the Illustrious Dead In All Ages on the Spot Where Their Remains Have Been Interred. London: 1809. V. 64
The History of the Life of William Pitt, Earl of Chatham. London: 1783. V. 63
History of the Commonwealth of England. London: 1824-1828. V. 64
The History of the Life of William Pitt, Earl of Chatham. London: 1783. V. 62
Life of Geoffrey Chaucer, the Early English Poet.... London: 1803. V. 67
Memoirs of Mary Wollstonecraft. London: 1927. V. 63
Of Population. London: 1820. V. 63
St. Leon: a Tale of the Sixteenth Century. Alexandria: 1801. V. 62; 66
Things As They Are; or, the Adventures of Caleb Williams.... London: 1796. V. 64
Vie et Memoires de Marie Wollstonecraft Godwin. Paris: 1802. V. 63

GOEBEL, K.
Organography of Plants, Especially of the Archegoniatae and Spermophyta. Oxford: 1900-1905. V. 64

GOEDAERDT, JOHANNES
De Insectis, in Methodum Redactus; cum Notularum Additione. Londini: 1685. V. 65

GOEDDAEUS, CONRADUS
Laus Ululae Ad Conscriptos Ululantium Patres and Patrones. Claucopoli: 1642. V. 63

GOELICKE, ANDREASE OTTOMAR
Historia Chirurgiae Antiqua, Seu Conspects Plerorumque, si Non Omnium Scritorum Veterum Qui a Primis Artis Medicae Incunabulis Usque ad Seculum Decimum Quintum Inclusive Chirurgicen Operibus Suis Exornarunt.... Halle: 1713. V. 64; 66

GOEREE, H. W.
Derde Deel, of Tweede Vervolgh of De Republyk der Hebreen, of Gemeenebest der Joden Onder de Priester-Ordening.... Amsterdam: 1683. V. 66

GOES, DAMIAO DE
De Bello Cambaico Ultimo Commentarii Tres. Louvain: 1549. V. 62

GOETGHEBUER, PIERRE JACQUES
Choix des Monuments, Edifices et Maisons les Plus Remarquables du Royaume des Pays-Bas.... Ghent: 1827. V. 64

GOETHE, JOHANN WOLFGANG VON
Auserlesene Lieder Gedichte und Balladen. Ein Strauss. Hammersmith: 1916. V. 62; 67
Faust. Stuttgart & Tubingen: 1825. V. 65
Faust. Stuttgart and Tubingen: 1833. V. 62
Faust. Hammersmith: 1906. V. 62
Faust. Hammersmith: 1906-1910. V. 67
Faust. London: 1908. V. 64
Faust. London: 1925. V. 62
Goethe's Faust - Parts I and II.... London: 1951. V. 63
Goethe's Theory of Colours. London: 1840. V. 62; 63
Iphigenie Auf Tauris: Ein Schauspeil. Hammersmith: 1912. V. 62; 67
Italian Journey (1786-1788). New York: 1962. V. 62; 64; 65
Die Leiden des Jungen Werthers. Leipzig: 1774. V. 65; 67
Reineke Fuchs.... Munich: 1846. V. 65
The Sorrows of Werter: a German Story. Dublin: 1780. V. 62
The Sorrows of Werther; a German Story. London: 1784. V. 66
Les Souffrances du Jeune Werther. Paris: 1809. V. 65; 67
Wilhelm Meister's Apprenticeship. Edinburgh: 1824. V. 66
Werke. Leipzig und Wien: 1901-1908. V. 67
Works. London: 1892. V. 62

GOETZMANN, WILLIAM H.
Explorations and Empire. The Explorer and the Scientist in Winning of the American West. New York: 1966. V. 65; 67
Karl Bodmer's America. N.P: 1984. V. 65

GOFF, BRUCE
Architecture. Billings: 1978. V. 62

GOFF, G. L.
Historical Records of the 91st Argyllshire Highlanders, Now the 1st Battalion Princess Louise's Argyll and Sutherland Highlanders. London: 1891. V. 66

GOFF, RICHARD
Century in the Saddle. Boulder: 1967. V. 67

GOFFART, M. AUGUSTE
The Ensilage of Maize and Other Green Fodder Crops. New York: 1879. V. 64

GOGARTY, OLIVER ST. JOHN
As I Was Going Down Sackville Street. New York: 1937. V. 63
Elbow Room. 1939. V. 63; 66
Elbow Room. Dublin: 1939. V. 64

GOGARTY, T.
The Council Book of the Corporation of Drogheda 1649-1734. 1988. V. 67

GOGGIN, JIM
Turk Murphy. Just for the Record. San Francisco: 1982. V. 63

GOGH, VINCENT VAN
The Complete Letters. 1958. V. 67
The Complete Letters of. Greenwich: 1958. V. 65
Complete Letters with Reproductions of All the Drawings in the Correspondence. Greenwich: 1959. V. 65
Letters to an Artist - from Vincent Van Gogh to Anton Ridder van Rappard 1881-1885. London: 1936. V. 63

GOGOL, NIKOLAI
The Diary of a Madman. London: 1929. V. 62
The Diary of a Madman. New York: 1998. V. 64
The Overcoat. Verona: 1975. V. 65
Vechera na Khutore bliz Dikan'ki. (Eveings on a Farm Near Dikanka). N.P: 1831-1832. V. 67

GOGUET, ANTOINE YVES
De l'Origine des Loix, des Arts, et des Sciences, et de Leurs Progres chez les Anciens Peuples. Paris: 1758. V. 62

GOINES, DAVID L.
A Constructed Roman Alphabet. Boston and London: 1982. V. 66

GOISSEAUD, ANTONY
Garages et Salles d'Exposition. Paris: Sep. 1930. V. 65

GOLD, THOMAS D.
History of Clarke County Virginia and Its Connection with the War Between the States. Berryville: 1914. V. 62; 63; 65

GOLDBERG, ISAAC
George Gershwin. A Study in American Music. New York: 1931. V. 64

GOLDBERG, WHOOPI
Book. New York: 1997. V. 67

GOLDBERGER, PAUL
The Skyscraper. New York: 1981. V. 65

GOLDEN Book of Famous Women. London: 1919. V. 66

GOLDEN Nuggets of Pioneer Days - a History of Garfield County. Panguitch: 1949. V. 67

GOLDEN, ARTHUR
Memoirs of a Geisha. New York: 1987. V. 64
Memoirs of a Geisha. New York: 1997. V. 62; 62; 66

GOLDEN Book of Famous Women. London: 1919. V. 62; 64

GOLDEN Book of Songs and Ballads. London: 1919. V. 64

GOLDEN, CHRISTOPHER
Cut: Horror Writers on Horror Film. Baltimore: 1992. V. 67

GOLDEN COCKEREL PRESS
A Bibliography of the Golden Cockerel Press, April 1921 - December 1927. Waltham St. Lawrence: 1928. V. 62
Cockalorum. A Sequel to Chanticleer and Pertelote. Waltham St. Lawrence: 1950. V. 62
Peretlote, a Sequel to Chanticleer. Waltham St. Lawrence: 1943. V. 67

GOLDEN, HARRY
Carl Sandburg. Cleveland: 1961. V. 67

GOLDEN, RICHARD L.
Sir William Osler: an Annotated Bibliography with Illustrations. San Francisco: 1988. V. 62; 65

THE GOLDEN Story Book. London: 1956. V. 63

THE GOLDEN Year Annual the Fourth. London: 1924. V. 67

GOLDENSOHN, BARRY
Saint Venus Eve. West Branch and Iowa City: 1971. V. 62

GOLDER, F. A.
Russian Expansion on the Pacific 1641-1850 - An Account of the Earliest and Later Expeditions Made by the Russians Along the Pacific Coast of Asia and North America. Cleveland: 1914. V. 64

GOLDICUTT, JOHN
Specimens of Ancient Decorations from Pompeii. London: 1825. V. 64

GOLDIE, HUGH
Calabar and its Mission. Edinburgh: 1890. V. 67

GOLDILOCKS and the Three Bears. New York: 1934. V. 63
GOLDILOCKS and the Three Bears. London: 1952. V. 64

GOLDING, BENJAMIN
An Historical Account of St. Thomas's Hospital Southwark. London: 1819. V. 62

GOLDING, LOUIS
Luigi of Cantanzaro. London: 1926. V. 65; 66
Magnolia Street. London: 1932. V. 67
Terrace in Capri: an Imaginary Conversation with Norman Douglas. London: 1934. V. 67

GOLDING, WILLIAM
The Brass Butterfly. London: 1958. V. 64; 66
The Brass Butterfly. London: 1963. V. 66
Close Quarters. London: 1987. V. 62; 66
Darkness Visible. London: 1979. V. 62; 66; 67
The Double Tongue. London: 1995. V. 67
An Egyptian Journal. London: 1985. V. 62
Fire Down Below. London: 1989. V. 62; 63
Free Fall. London: 1959. V. 62; 63; 66; 67

GOLDING, WILLIAM continued
The Hot Gates. London: 1965. V. 62; 66
The Inheritors. London: 1955. V. 65; 66; 67
The Inheritors. London: 1959. V. 66
Lord of the Flies. London: 1954. V. 66; 67
Lord of the Flies. New York: 1955. V. 64; 67
A Moving Target. London: 1982. V. 62
Nobel Lecture. 7 December 1983. Leamington Spa: 1984. V. 62; 63; 67
The Paper Men. London: 1984. V. 62; 66
Pincher Martin. London: 1956. V. 65; 66
Pincher Martin. London: 1961. V. 67
The Pyramid. London: 1967. V. 63; 64; 66; 67
Rites of Passage. London: 1980. V. 66
Rites of Passage. New York: 1980. V. 62
Rites of Passage. Close Quarters. Fire Down Below. New York: 1980-1989. V. 66
The Scorpion God. London: 1971. V. 62; 67
The Spire. London: 1964. V. 62; 64; 66; 67
To the Ends of the Earth. London: 1991. V. 62

GOLDMAN, E. A.
Biological Investigations in Mexico. Washington: 1951. V. 63

GOLDMAN, EDWIN E.
Vitalfarbung Am Zentralnervensystem Beitrag zur Phsiio-Pathologie des Plexus Chorioideus und der Hirnhaute. Berlin: 1913. V. 64

GOLDMAN, EMMA
Living My Life. New York: 1931. V. 64

GOLDMAN, LOUIS
Luigi of Cantanzaro. London: 1926. V. 67

GOLDMAN, WILLIAM
Magic. New York: 1976. V. 67
The Marathon Man. New York: 1974. V. 67
No Way to Treat a Lady. New York: 1968. V. 67
The Princess Bride. New York: 1973. V. 62; 65
Soldier in the Rain. New York: 1960. V. 63

GOLDONI, CARLO
Commedie Scelte di Carlo Goldoni Advocato Veneto. London: 1795. V. 65
The Liar - a Comedy in Three Acts. London: 1922. V. 62

GOLDSBOROUGH, WILLIAM W.
The Maryland Line in the Confederate Army 1861-1865. Baltimore: 1900. V. 62; 63; 65

GOLDSCHMIDT, E. P.
Gothic & Renaissance Bookbindings. London: 1928. V. 64
Old Books on Various Subjects...A Collection of Early Photographs and Books Commemorating the Centenary of Fox Talbot and Daguerre, 1839-1939. London: 1939. V. 63
The Printed Book of the Renaissance: Three Lectures on Type, Illustration, Ornament. 1950. V. 67
The Printed Book of the Renaissance: Three Lectures on Type, Illustration, Ornament. Cambridge: 1950. V. 62

GOLDSCHMIDT, LUCIEN
The Truthful Lens. New York: 1980. V. 63; 65

GOLDSMID, EDMUND
Bibliotheca Curiosa. Edinburgh: 1886-1888. V. 62
Bibliotheca Curiosa. Edinburgh: 1888. V. 62; 65

GOLDSMITH, JOHN
An Almanack for the Year of Our Lord God MDCCCXXIX. London: 1829. V. 62

GOLDSMITH, MILTON
The Adventure of Walter and the Rabbits, a Story for Children. New York: 1908. V. 63
Romantic Bears. New York: 1908. V. 64

GOLDSMITH, OLIVER
An Abridgement of the History of England. London: 1802. V. 67
An Abridgement of the History of England. Alexandria: 1811. V. 64
An Abridgment of the History of England. London: 1783. V. 62
An Abridgment of the History of England. London: 1796. V. 62
Choice Works. 1890. V. 67
The Citizen of the World. London: 1762. V. 64
The Citizen of the World. London: 1774. V. 64
The Citizen of the World. London: 1800. V. 62
Collected Works. 1966. V. 66
Le Cure de Wakefield. Dublin: 1797. V. 65
Dalziel's Illustrated Goldsmith.... London: 1865. V. 62
The Deserted Village. London: 1770. V. 62; 64; 67
The Deserted Village. N.P. Possibly Belfast: 1775. V. 66
The Deserted Village. 1927. V. 67
Dr. Goldsmith's Roman History Abridged by Himself for the Use of Schools. London: 1793. V. 62
An Enquiry into the Present State of Polite Learning in Europe. London: 1774. V. 62; 64
Essays. London: 1765. V. 62
Essays. London: 1766. V. 65
Essays and The Bee. Boston: 1820. V. 63
Goldsmith's History of British and Foreign Birds. London: 1838. V. 65; 67
Goldsmith's Natural History. London: 1803. V. 62
The Good Natur'd Man. London: 1768. V. 63; 66
Goody Two-Shoes. London: 1882. V. 63
An History of England, in a Series of Letters from a Nobleman to His Son. London: 1764. V. 65
The History of England, in a Series of Letters from a Nobleman to His Son. London: 1770. V. 65
The History of Little Goody Twoshoes.... Worcester: 1787. V. 63; 64
The History of the Earth, and Animated Nature. London: 1774-1790. V. 62
A History of the Earth and Animated Nature. London: 1791. V. 66; 67
A History of the Earth and Animated Nature. Glasgow: 1832. V. 64
A History of the Earth and Animated Nature. London: 1837-1840. V. 64
A History of the Earth and Animated Nature. London: 1848. V. 67
A History of the Earth and Animated Nature. London: 1851. V. 63
A History of the Earth and Animated Nature. Glasgow: 1854. V. 66
A History of the Earth and Animated Nature. Edinburgh and London: 1855. V. 64; 65; 67
A History of the Earth and Animated Nature. London: 1866. V. 63
A History of the Earth and Animated Nature. 1870. V. 67
The History of Greece, from the Earliest State to the Death of Alexander the Great. London: 1809. V. 66
The History of Rome from the Foundation of the City of Rome, to the Destruction of the Western Empire. Edinburgh: 1812. V. 65
The Life of Richard Nash of Bath, Esq. 1762. V. 66
The Life of Richard Nash of Bath, Esq. London: 1762. V. 62; 64
The Miscellaneous Works. London: 1784. V. 65
The Miscellaneous Works. Edinburgh: 1791. V. 63
The Miscellaneous Works. London: 1812. V. 67
The Miscellaneous Works. Glasgow: 1816. V. 64
The Miscellaneous Works. London: 1823. V. 62; 64
The Poetical and Dramatic Works. London: 1780. V. 63
The Poetical and Prose Works of Oliver Goldsmith.... 1880. V. 67
Poetical Effusions from Celebrated Authors. London: 1836. V. 66
The Poetical Works. Hereford: 1794. V. 67
The Poetical Works. London: 1811. V. 63; 66
The Poetical Works. 1877. V. 67
She Stoops to Conquer. London: 1773. V. 66
She Stoops to Conquer. London: 1912. V. 62; 63; 64; 66; 67
A Survey of Experimental Philosophy, Considered in Its Present State of Improvement. London: 1776. V. 64; 65
The Traveller. London: 1770. V. 63
The Traveller. London: 1816. V. 62
The Traveller. London: 1860. V. 63
The Vicar of Wakefield. Salisbury: 1766. V. 63; 66
The Vicar of Wakefield. London: 1773. V. 66
The Vicar of Wakefield. Berlin: 1784. V. 62
The Vicar of Wakefield. London: 1789. V. 62
The Vicar of Wakefield. Hereford: 1798. V. 64; 65
The Vicar of Wakefield. Dublin: 1800. V. 62
The Vicar of Wakefield. London: 1817. V. 64
The Vicar of Wakefield. London: 1886. V. 63
The Vicar of Wakefield. London: 1890. V. 67
The Vicar of Wakefield. London: 1906. V. 62
The Vicar of Wakefield. London: 1914. V. 64
The Vicar of Wakefield. 1926. V. 63
The Vicar of Wakefield. London: 1929. V. 62; 63; 65; 66
The Works of.... New York: 1881. V. 63

GOLDSTEIN, KURT
Language and Language Disturbances. New York: 1948. V. 64; 66
The Organism: a Holistic Approach to Biology Derived from Pathological Data in Man. New York: 1939. V. 65

GOLDSTONE, ADRIAN H.
The Adrian H. Goldstone Collection of Mystery and Detective Fiction. San Francisco: 1981. V. 62
John Steinbeck Bibliogrpahy. Austin: 1974. V. 62

GOLDWATER LIBRARY OF PRIMITIVE ART
Catalogue of the Robert Goldwater Library of Primitive Art. Boston: 1982. V. 62

GOLDWATER, R.
Artists on Art from the XIV to XX Century. New York: 1947. V. 66; 67

GOLTERMAN, H. L.
Physiological Limnology, an Approach to the Physiology of Lake Ecosystems. Amsterdam: 1975. V. 64

GOMERSALL, WILLIAM
Hunting In Craven. Skipton: 1889. V. 64

GOMEZ, MADELEINE ANGELIQUE POISSON DE
Le Belle Assemblee; or,t he Adventures of Six Days.... London: 1725. V. 67

GOMEZ, PEDRO
Breve Raltione della Gloriosa Morte di Paolo Michi, Giovanni Goto e Giacomo Thisai Martiri Giapponesi della Compagnia di Giesu Seguita in Nangasachi al 5. di Febraro 1597. Rome: 1628. V. 62

GOMME, GEORGE LAURENCE
The Gentleman's Magazine Library: Being a Classified Collection of the Chief Contents of the Gentleman's Magazine from 1731 to 1868. Romanao- British Remains: Parts I and II. London: 1887. V. 62

GOMPERTZ, BENJAMIN
The Principles and Application of Imaginary Quantities.... London: 1817-1818. V. 65; 67

GOMPERTZ, G. ST. G. M.
The Gordon Setter. History and Character. 1976. V. 66; 67

GOMPERTZ, M. L. A.
Magic Ladakh; an Intimate Picture of a Land of Topsy-Turvy Customs and Great Natural Beauty. London: 1928. V. 67
The Road to Lamaland; Impressions of a Journey to Western Thibet. London: 1916. V. 67
The Road to Lamaland: Impressions of a Journey to Western Tibet. London: 1920. V. 65

GONCHAROV, IVAN ALEKSANDROVICH
Obyknovennais, Istoriia. Roman v Dvukh Chastiakh. (The Same Old Story: a Novel in Two Parts). St. Petersburg: 1883. V. 65; 67

GONCOURT, EDMOND DE
La Femme au Dix-Huitieme Siecle. Paris: 1862. V. 63
Sophie Arnould d'Apres sa Correspondance et ses Memoires Inedits. Paris: 1885. V. 67

GONNELLI, GIUSEPPE
Monumenti Sepolcrali Della Toscana. Firenze: 1819. V. 62

GONZALES, AMBROSE E.
Laguerre: a Gascon of the Black Border. Columbia: 1924. V. 63; 64; 67
With Aesop Along the Black Border. Columbia: 1924. V. 63

GONZALES, BABS
I, Paid My Dues. East Orange: 1967. V. 63

GONZALES, NARCISO GENER
In Darkest Cuba. Columbia: 1922. V. 67

GONZALEZ, N. V. M.
Seven Hills Away. Denver: 1947. V. 62

GONZALEZ DE MENDOZA, JUAN
Rerum Morumque in Regno Chinensi Maxie Notablium Historia ex Ipsis Chinensium Libris & Religiosorum, Qui in Illo Primi Fuerunt Literis ac Relatione Concinnata.... Antwerp: 1655. V. 63

GOOCH, BRYAN N. S.
A Shakespeare Music Catalogue. Oxford: 1991. V. 62

GOOCH, E. H.
A History of Spalding. Spalding: 1840. V. 63

GOOCH, RICHARD
Nuts to Crack, or Quips, Quirks, Anecdotes and Facetiae of Oxford and Cambridge Scholars. London: 1835. V. 66

GOOCH, ROBERT
An Account of Some of the Most Important Diseases Peculiar to Women. 1829. V. 62
An Account of Some of the Most Important Diseases Peculiar to Women. London: 1829. V. 63

THE GOOD Citizen's Alphabet. London: 1953. V. 63

GOOD Company for Every Day of the Year. Boston: 1866. V. 64

A GOOD Expedient for Innocence and Peace, Being an Essay Concerning the Great Usefulness and Advantage of Laying Aside Publick Oaths. Edinburgh: 1704. V. 65

THE GOOD Girl (Number 1). Greenfield: 1845. V. 64

GOOD, PETER P.
The Family Flora and Materia Medica Botanica.... Elizabethtown: 1851?. V. 63

GOOD Things to Eat. Dayton: 1904. V. 64

GOODACRE, J. A.
Buxton Old and New: a Study of Its Rise and Growth During Two Thousand Years. Buxton: 1928. V. 63

GOODALL, EDWIN
The Croonian Lectures on Modern Aspects of Certain Problems in the Pathology of Mental Disorders. London: 1914?. V. 65

GOODE, D.
Cycads of Africa. Cape Town: 1989. V. 62

GOODE, G. B.
Catalogue of the Collection to Illustrate the Animal Resources and the Fisheries of the United States. Washington: 1879. V. 65
Fisheries and Fishery Industries of the United States. Section 1. Natural History of Useful Aquatic Animals. Washington: 1884. V. 62; 63; 65; 66
Ichthyology, a Treatise on the Deep-Sea and Pelagic Fishes of the World.... Washington: 1895. V. 62
Oceanic Ichthyology. Washington: 1895. V. 62; 65

GOODE, G. BROWN
The Published Writings of Philip Lutley Sclater 1844-1896. Washington: 1896. V. 67

GOODE, WILLIAM H.
Outposts of Zion. Cincinnati: 1863. V. 66

GOODELL, WILLIAM
Come-Outerism. The Duty of Secession from a Corrupt Church. New York: 1845. V. 64
The Old and the New; or the Changes of Thirty Years in the East, with Some Allusions to Oriental Customs as Elucidating Scripture. New York: 1853. V. 66

GOODEN, MONA
The Poet's Cat: an Anthology. London: 1946. V. 63

GOODEN, STEPHEN
An Iconography of the Engravings of Stephen Gooden. London: 1944. V. 63; 65

GOODENOUGH, JAMES GRAHAM
Journal of Commodore Goodenough During His Last Command as Senior Officer on the Australian Station. London: 1876. V. 67

GOODHOLME, TODD S.
Goodholme's Domestic Cyclopaedia of Practical Information. New York: 1889. V. 62

GOODHUGH, WILLIAM
The English Gentleman's Library Manual.... London: 1827. V. 65
The Gate to the Hebrew, Arabic and Syriac, Unlocked by a New and Easy Method of Acquiring the Accidence. London: 1828. V. 62; 65

GOODIS, DAVID
Behold this Woman. New York and London: 1947. V. 64
The Burglar. New York: 1991. V. 63
Street of No Return. New York: 1991. V. 63

GOODISON, J. W.
Reynolds Stone, His Early Development as an Engraver on Wood. Cambridge: 1947. V. 64

GOODISON, NICHOLAS
Ormolu: the Work of Matthew Boulton. London: 1974. V. 63

GOODLAKE, THOMAS
The Courser's Manual - or Stud Book. 1828. V. 62
The Courser's Manual or Stud-Book. Liverpool: 1828. V. 66

GOODLANDER, C. W.
Early Days of Fort Scott, Memoirs and Recollections of.... Fort Scott: 1900. V. 67
Memoirs and Recollections of C. W. Goodlander of the Early Days of Fort Scott from April 29, 1858 to January 1, 1870.... Fort Scott: 1900. V. 67

GOODLOE, ALBERT THEODORE
Some Rebel Recollections from the Seat of War. Nashville: 1893. V. 62

GOODMAN, ALLEGRA
The Family Markowitz. New York: 1996. V. 67
Total Immersion. New York: 1989. V. 63; 67

GOODMAN, BENNY
Benny: King of Swing. New York: 1979. V. 63
The Kingdom of Swing. New York: 1939. V. 67

GOODMAN, DAVID MICHAEL
A Western Panorama 1848-1875. Glendale: 1966. V. 67

GOODMAN, JOHN D.
American Natural History. Philadelphia: 1846. V. 67

GOODMAN, JOHN K.
Ross Stefan: an Impressionistic Painter of the Contemporary Southwest. Flagstaff: 1977. V. 64

GOODMAN, NELSON
The Structure of Appearance. Cambridge: 1951. V. 67

GOODMAN, PAUL
The Grand Piano, or, the Almanac of Alienation. N.P: 1942. V. 63; 64; 66

GOODMAN, RICHARD M.
Genetic Diseases Among Ashkenazi Jews. New York: 1979. V. 63
Genetic Disorders Among the Jewish People. Baltimore: 1979. V. 63

GOODMAN, S. M.
The Birds of Egypt. Oxford and New York: 1989. V. 62; 67

GOODNIGHT, CHARLES
Pioneer Days in the Southwest from 1850 to 1879. Guthrie: 1909. V. 62; 65

GOODNO, WILLIAM C.
The Practice of Medicine with Sections on Diseases of the Nervous System by Clarence Bartlett M.D. Philadelphia: 1894-1897. V. 66; 67

GOODRICH, ANDREW T.
Catalogue of Maps and Other Geographical Works.... New York: 1823. V. 62

GOODRICH, CHARLES A.
Lives of the Signers to the Declaration of Independence. New York: 1829. V. 65

GOODRICH, L.
Max Weber. New York: 1949. V. 62
Thomas Eakins. Washington: 1982. V. 63

GOODRICH, SAMUEL GRISWOLD
The Captive of Nootka; or, the Adventures of John R. Jewett. (sic). Philadelphia: 1869. V. 63
Les Contes de Pierre Parley sur l'Amerique. Boston: 1832. V. 64
Famous Men of Ancient Times by the author of Peter Parley's Tales. Boston: 1843. V. 63
Johnson's Natural History, Comprehensive, Scientific and Popular. 1870. V. 63
Peter Parley's Tales About China and the Chinese. London: 1843. V. 66
A Winter Wreath of Summer Flowers. New York: 1861. V. 64; 66

GOODSELL, FRED FIELD
John Service - Pioneer. Waban: 1945. V. 63

GOODSPEED, CHARLES ELIOT
Angling in America: Its Early History and Literature. Boston: 1939. V. 64

GOODSPEED, T. HARPER
Plant Hunters in the Andes. New York: 1941. V. 63; 64

GOODSPEED, WESTON A.
Counties of Whitley and Noble, Indiana: Historical and Biographical. Evansville: 1970. V. 67

GOODWIN, C. C.
The Comstock Club. Washington: 1891. V. 62

GOODWIN, CARDINAL
John Charles Fremont and Explanation of His Career. Stanford: 1930. V. 65

GOODWIN, CHARLES C.
As I Remember Them. Salt Lake City: 1913. V. 63; 64

GOODWIN, F.
Domestic and Cottage Architecture. London: 1843. V. 64

GOODWIN, GRENVILLE
The Social Organization of the Western Apache. Chicago: 1942. V. 63; 66

GOODWIN, H. M.
The Suggestive Method. An Address Delivered Before the Teachers' Institute at Rockton, Illinois, October 18, 1850. Chicago: 1850. V. 63

GOODWIN, HARRY
Through the Wordsworth Country. London: 1887. V. 65

GOODWIN, HARVEY
Education for Working Men. An Address Delivered in the Town Hall of Cambridge on the Evening of October 20, 1855. Cambridge: 1855. V. 64

GOODWIN, NAT C.
Nat Goodwin's Book. Boston: 1914. V. 64; 67

GOODWIN, RALPH A.
The Stoenberg Affair. New York: 1913. V. 65

GOODWIN, WILLIAM B.
The Ruins of Great Ireland in New England. Boston: 1946. V. 67

GOODY Two-Shoes. New York: 1881-1882. V. 62
GOODY Two-Shoes. London: 1882. V. 62
GOODY Two-Shoes. New York: 1897. V. 63
GOODY Two-Shoes. New York: 1898. V. 64

GOODYEAR, CHARLES
A Centennial Volume of the Writings of Charles Goodyear and Thomas Hancock. Boston: 1939. V. 62

GOODYEAR, W. A.
The Coal Mines of the Western Coast of the United States. San Francisco: 1877. V. 65

GOOSE, PHILIP H.
The Canadian Naturalist, a Series of Conversations on the Natural History of Lower Canada. 1840. V. 62
A Naturalist's Rambles on the Devonshire Coast. 1853. V. 62

GORDAN, JOHN D.
Arnold Bennett: The Centenary of His Birth: an Exhibition in the Berg Collection. New York: 1968. V. 64

GORDIMER, NADINE
The Black Interpreters, Notes on African Writing. Johannesburg: 1973. V. 62; 63; 67
The House Gun. New York: 1998. V. 65
Jump and Other Stories. Franklin Center: 1991. V. 63
Livingstone's Companion - Stories. London: 1972. V. 65
A Soldier's Embrace. Stories. London: 1980. V. 63
A Sport of Nature. New York: 1987. V. 62

GORDON, A. C.
Befo De War. Echoes in Negro Dialect. New York: 1888. V. 63

GORDON, ADAM LINDSAY
Poems of the Late Adam Lindsay Gordon. Melbourne: 1880?. V. 65

GORDON, ALBIE
Dawn in Golden Valley. N.P: 1971. V. 64

GORDON, ALISON
Night Game. Toronto: 1992. V. 67
Striking Out. Toronto: 1995. V. 67

GORDON, ANNA A.
The Beautiful Life of Frances E. Willard. Chicago: 1898. V. 63

GORDON, ARMISTEAD C.
Memories and Memorials of William Gordon Mc Cabe. Richmond: 1925. V. 62; 63; 65

GORDON, CAROLINE
Aleck Maury, Sportsman. New York: 1934. V. 62; 64
The Forest of the South. New York: 1945. V. 62; 64; 66
The Malefactors. New York: 1956. V. 63; 64
Old Red and Other Stories. New York: 1963. V. 63
The Strange Children. New York: 1951. V. 62; 66

GORDON, CHARLES
Old Time Aldwych, Kingsway & Neighbourhood. London: 1903. V. 65

GORDON, CHARLES ALEXANDER
Our Trip to Burmah; with Notes on that Country. London: 1875. V. 67

GORDON, ELINOR
Collecting Chinese Export Porcelain. New York: 1977. V. 63

GORDON, ELIZABETH
Bird Children. Chicago: 1912. V. 62
Flower Children. Chicago: 1910. V. 64
Four Footed Folk or the Children of the Farm and Forest. New York: 1914. V. 65
Wild Flower Children. Chicago: 1918. V. 64

GORDON, ERIC A.
Mark the Music, the Life and Work of Marc Blitzstein. New York: 1989. V. 67

GORDON, G.
The Pinetum. 1880. V. 66

GORDON, GEORGE
The Annals of Europe for the Year 1739-1743. London: 1740-. V. 67
Trial of George Gordon, Esquire, Commonly called Lord George Gordon. for High Treason at the Bar of the Court of King's Bench, on Monday, February 5th, 1781. (Parts I and II). London: 1781. V. 65

GORDON, GEORGE ALEXANDER
The Complete English Physician, or, an Universal Library of Family Medicines. London: 1785. V. 63

GORDON, GRANVILLE
Sporting Reminiscences. London: 1902. V. 67

GORDON, HAMPDEN
The Golden Keys. London: 1932. V. 66
Rhymes of the Red Triangle. London: 1920. V. 66

GORDON, J. E.
Six Letters on the Subject of Irish Education, Addressed To.... 1832. V. 62; 65

GORDON, JAMES D.
The Last Martyrs of Eromanga: Being a Memoir of the Rev. George N. Gordon and Ellen Catherine Powell, His Wife. Halifax: 1863. V. 63

GORDON, JOHN
Memoirs of the Life of John Gordon of Glencat, in the County of Aberdeen in Scotland.... London: 1734. V. 65
My Six Years with the Black Watch 1881-1887. Boston: 1929. V. 67

GORDON, JOHN BROWN
Reminiscences of the Civil War. New York: 1903. V. 63; 65

GORDON, LOCKHART
Fairburn's Edition of the Trial of Lockhart and Loudon Gordon, for Forcibly and Feloniously Taking Rachel Fanny Antonia Lee, from Her House, Against Her Will.... London: 1804. V. 63

GORDON, MARY
Final Payments. New York: 1978. V. 63

GORDON, MAURICE BEAR
Aesculapius Comes to the Colonies: The Story of the Early Days of Medicine in the Thirteen Original Colonies. Ventnor: 1949. V. 63; 66

GORDON, PRYSE LOCKHART
Personal Memoirs; or Reminiscences of Men and Manners at Home and Abroad, During the Last Half Century. London: 1830. V. 64

GORDON, ROBERT
Monet. New York: 1983. V. 64

GORDON, SAMUEL
The Watering Places of Cleveland.... Redcar: 1869. V. 64; 65

GORDON, SETON
Amid Snowy Wastes, Wild Life on the Spitsbergen Archipelago. London: 1922. V. 63
The Cairngorm Hills of Scotland. 1925. V. 67
The Cairngorm Hills of Scotland. London: 1925. V. 62; 63
Wanderings of a Naturalist. London: 1921. V. 62; 63

GORDON, T. E.
The Roof of the World.... Edinburgh: 1876. V. 67

GORDON, THOMAS
A Dedication to a Great Man Concering Dedications. London: 1719. V. 62
The Humourist: Being Essays on Several Subjects, viz. New Writers, Enthusiasm, The Spleen, Country Entertainments, Love, The History of Miss Manage, Ambition and Pride, Idleness, Fickleness of Human Nature, Prejudice, Witchcraft, Ghosts and Apparations.. London: 1724. V. 63; 67

GORDON, THOMAS F.
The History of New Jersey, from Its Discovery by Europeans, to the Adoption of the Federal Constitution. (with) A Gazetteer of the State of New Jersey.... Trenton: 1834. V. 63
The War on the Bank of the United States; or a Review of the Measures of the Administration Against the Institution and the Property of the Country. Philadelphia: 1834. V. 66

GORDON, W. J.
Perseus the Gorgon Slayer. London: 1883. V. 62

GORDON CUMMING, CONSTANCE FREDERICA
From the Hebrides to the Himalayas; a Sketch of Eighteen Months' Wanderings in Western Isles and Eastern Highlands. London: 1876. V. 64

GORDON-CUMMING, CONSTANCE FREDERICA
Granite Crags. Edinburgh: 1884. V. 63

GORDON CUMMING, CONSTANCE FREDERICA
The Inventor of the Numeral Type for China.... London: 1899. V. 66
Two Happy Years in Ceylon. New York: 1892. V. 66
Wanderings in China. Edinburgh: 1886. V. 64
Wanderings in China. Edinburgh: 1888. V. 66

GORDON CUMMING, ROUALEYN GEORGE
Five Years' of a Hunter's Life in the Far Interior of South Africa.... 1851. V. 66

GORE, AL
Earth in the Balance. Boston: 1992. V. 67
Earth in the Balance. Boston: 1995. V. 64

GORE, CATHERINE
Castles in the Air. Leipzig: 1847. V. 65
Cecil; or, the Adventures of a Coxcomb. London: 1841. V. 65
The Fair of May Fair. London: 1832. V. 65
Heckington. Leipzig: 1858. V. 65
The Inundation; or, Pardon and Peace.... London: 1860. V. 65
Mothers and Daughters: a Novel. London: 1834. V. 65; 67
Paris in 1841. London: 1841. V. 65
Self; or, the Narrow, Narrow World. London: 1856. V. 65
Transmutation; or, the Lord and the Lost. London: 1854. V. 65
The Two Aristocracies. London: 1857. V. 65

GORE, GEORGE
The Art of Scientific Discovery or the General Condition and Methods of Research in Physics and Chemistry. London: 1878. V. 63

GORE, J. A.
Alternatives in Regulated River Management. Boca Raton: 1989. V. 64; 65

GORE, JAMES H.
My Mother's Story: Despise Not the Day of Small Things. Philadelphia: 1923. V. 64

GORE, JOHN
Arithmetic Fairly Laid Open; or, the Trader's Sure Guide. Liverpool: 1769. V. 62; 66

GORE, M. E. J.
The Birds of Korea. Seoul: 1971. V. 63; 64; 67

GORE, MRS.
The Rose Fancier's Manual. London: 1838. V. 64; 67

GORE-BROWN, ROBERT
Murder of an M.P.!. London: 1927. V. 63

GORER, EDGAR
Chinese Porcelain and Hard Stones. London: 1911. V. 64

GORER, GEOFFREY
Africa Dances - A Book About West African Negroes. London: 1949. V. 64
Himalayan Village; an Account of the Lechas of Sikim. London: 1938. V. 67

GORES, JOE
Dead Skip. New York: 1972. V. 67
Final Notice. New York: 1973. V. 65; 66
Interface. New York: 1974. V. 65
A Time of Predators. New York: 1969. V. 67

GOREY, EDGAR
The Curious Sofa. New York: 1961. V. 63

GOREY, EDWARD
Amphigorey Also. New York: 1983. V. 63; 64
Artist of Mystery - Original Works by Edward Gorey. San Francisco: 1993. V. 62
The Awdrey-Gore Legacy. New York: 1972. V. 63
The Black Doll. A Silent Film. New York: 1973. V. 63
The Blue Aspic. New York: 1968. V. 63
Dogear Wryde Postcards. Neglected Murderesses Series. New York: 1980. V. 66
The Doubtful Guest. London: 1958. V. 67
The Gilded Bat. New York: 1966. V. 63
A Gorey Festival. New York: 1968. V. 63
Gorey Games. San Francisco: 1979. V. 66
The Hapless Child. New York: 1961. V. 63
The Improvable Landscape. New York. V. 67
Leaves from a Mislaid Album. New York: 1972. V. 62; 64
The Loathsome Couple. New York: 1977. V. 63
The Object Lesson. Garden City: 1958. V. 64
The Prune People. New York: 1983. V. 63
The Prune People II. New York: 1985. V. 63
The Secrets: Volume One. The Other Statue. New York: 1968. V. 63
The Unstrung Harp. New York/Boston: 1953. V. 62; 63; 64
The Utter Zoo. New York: 1967. V. 63
The Water Flowers. New York: 1982. V. 63

GORGAS, JOSIAH
The Civil War Diary of General Josiah Gorgas. 1947. V. 67

GORGES, RAYMOND
The Story of a Family through Eleven Centuries. Boston: 1944. V. 64

GORHAM CO.
Gorham Altars, Stained Glass, Church Appointments and Interior Decorations, Memorials in Metals, Mosaics, Marble, Granite or Wood. New York: 1925. V. 63

GORHAM, GEORGE CORNELIUS
The History and Antiquities of Eynesbury and St. Neot's in Huntingdonshire and of St. Neot's in the County of Cornwall. London: 1820-1824. V. 62

GORHAM, HARRY M.
My Memories of the Comstock. Los Angeles: 1939. V. 63; 66

GORHAM, MAURICE
The Local. 1939. V. 64

GORKI, MAXIM
Foma Gordyeff. New York: 1901. V. 66
Reminiscences of Leonid Andreyev. London: 1922. V. 64
Reminiscences of My Youth. London: 1924. V. 66

GORMAN & MILLER
Finest Quality Hand-Forged Gaffs. Catalog 5. Indianapolis: 1900. V. 67

GORMAN, ED
Invitation to Murder. Arlington Heights: 1991. V. 67

GORMAN, JEAN WRIGHT
The Peterborough Anthology. New York: 1923. V. 63

GORMAN, R. C.
R. C. Gorman: The Graphic Works. Albuquerque: 1987. V. 63
The Radiance of My People. Albuquerque: 1992. V. 63

GORSCH, RUDOLPH V.
Proctolobic Anatomy. Baltimore: 1953. V. 66; 67

GORSE, A.
Les Pyrenees Monumentales et Pittoresques Dessinees d'Apres Nature et Lithographiees.... Luchon: 1850. V. 62; 66

GORTER, JOHANNES DE
Medicina Hippocratica Exponens Aphorismos Hippocratis.... Patavii: 1768. V. 67

GORTON, BENJAMIN
A Scriptural Account of the Millenium: Being a Selection from the Prophechies Concerning Christ's Second Coming.... Troy: 1802. V. 64

GORTON, DAVID ALLYN
The History of Medicine. New York: 1910. V. 64; 66

GORTON, JOHN
A General Biographical Dictionary. London: 1833. V. 64
A General Biographical Dictionary. London: 1841. V. 66

GOSLING, PAULA
Fair Game. New York: 1978. V. 65
Hoodwink. London: 1988. V. 63
Loser's Blues. London: 1980. V. 63
The Woman in Red. London: 1983. V. 63
The Wychford Murders. London: 1986. V. 63

GOSLING, WILLIAM GILBERT
The Life of Sir Humphrey Gilbert, England's First Empire Builder. London: 1911. V. 65

GOSNELL, H. T.
The Science of Bird Nesting. 1947. V. 67

GOSNELL, HARPUR ALLEN
Before the Mast in the Clippers. New York: 1937. V. 64
Rebel Raider. Chapel Hill: 1948. V. 63

GOSNELL, R. E.
British Columbia. A Digest of Reliable Information Regarding its Natural Resources and Industrial Possibilities. Vancouver: 1890. V. 63
The Year Book of British Columbia and Manual of Provincial Information. To Which is Added A Chapter Containing Much Special Information Respecting the Canadian Yukon and Northern Territory Generally. Victoria: 1897. V. 64

GOSS-CUSTARD, J. D.
The Oystercatcher, from Individauls to Populations. Oxford: 1996. V. 65; 67

GOSSE, EDMUND
The Allies' Fairy Book. London: 1916. V. 65
Inter Arma - Being Essays Written in Time of War. London: 1916. V. 62
The Secret of Narcisse - a Romance. London: 1892. V. 64
The Unfortunate Traveller or the Life of Jack Wilton. London: 1892. V. 66

GOSSE, PHILIP HENRY
Actinologia Britanica. A History of the British Sea-Anemones and Corals. London: 1860. V. 62; 66; 67
The Aquarium: an Unveiling of the Wonders of the Deep Sea. 1854. V. 64
The Birds of Jamaica. London: 1847. V. 65; 67
The Canadian Naturalist. London: 1840. V. 66
Evenings at the Microscope.... London: 1859. V. 64; 65; 66; 67
Evenings at the Microscope.... New York: 1860. V. 66
An Introduction to Zoology. London: 1844. V. 63
Letters from Alabama, Chiefly Relating to Natural History. London: 1859. V. 64
A Manual of Marine Zoology, for the British Isles. London: 1855-1856. V. 66
The Monuments of Ancient Egypt, and Their Relation to the Word of God. London: 1855. V. 64
Natural History - Birds. London: 1849. V. 62
A Naturalist's Rambles on the Devonshire Coast. London: 1853. V. 66
Omphalos: an Attempt to Untie the Geological Knot. London: 1857. V. 64

GOSSE, PHILIP HENRY continued
The Pirates' Who's Who - Giving Particulars of the Lives and Deaths of the Pirates and Buccaneers. London: 1924. V. 63
Popular British Ornithology.... London: 1853. V. 66
The Romance of Natural History. London: 1861-1862. V. 63
The Romance of Natural History. Second Series. London: 1862. V. 66
The Romance of Natural History. (with) Second Series. London: 1861. V. 67
Tenby: a Sea-Side Holiday. London: 1856. V. 66

GOSSELIN, LOUIS LEON THEODORE
Two Royalist Spies of the French Revolution. London: 1924. V. 66

GOSSIP, G. H. D.
The Chess-Player's Manual. A Complete Guide to Chess. London: 1875. V. 63

GOSTLING, G.
Extracts from the Treaties Between Great Britain and Other Kingdoms and States of Such Articles as Relate to the Duty and Conduct of the Commanders of His Majesty's Ships of War. London: 1792. V. 64

GOSTLING, WILLIAM
A Walk in and About the City of Canterbury, with many Observations Not to be Found in Any Description Hitherto Published. Canterbury: 1777. V. 65

GOTCH, FRANCIS
Croonian Lecture. On the Mammalian Nervous System, Its Functions and Their Localisation Determined by an Electrical Method. 1891. V. 64

GOTFRYD, BERNARD
Anton the Dove Fancier and Other Tales of the Holocaust. New York: 1990. V. 64; 66

GOTHAM BOOK MART
We Moderns: Gotham Book Mart 1920-1940. New York: 1940. V. 62

GOTHEIN, M. L.
A History of Garden Art. 1928. V. 66

GOTHER, JOHN
A Practical Caechism in Fifty Two Lessons.... London: 1735. V. 62
Prayers for Sundays and Holy-Days and Other Festivals, from the Firt Sunday of Advent to Whitsuntide. London: 1718. V. 64

GOTTFREDSON, PETER
History of Indian Depredations in Utah. Salt Lake City: 1919. V. 66

GOTTLIEB, GERALD
Early Children's Books and Their Illustration. New York: 1975. V. 62

GOTTLIEB, SAM
Overbooked in Arizona. Scottsdale: 1994. V. 67

GOTTSCHALK, LOUIS
Lafayette and the Close the American Revolution. Chicago: 1942. V. 67
Lafayette Joins the American Army. Chicago: 1938. V. 67

GOUAN, A.
Historia Piscium. Histoire des Poissons.... Srassbourg: 1770. V. 63; 65; 66

GOUDAUX, ARMAND
The Exterior of the Horse. Philadelphia: 1904. V. 66

GOUDE, JEAN PAUL
Jungle Fever. New York: 1981. V. 66

GOUDEKET, MAURICE
Close to Colette. London: 1957. V. 63

GOUDGE, ELIZABETH
The Valley of Song. London: 1951. V. 67

GOUDY, FREDERIC WILLIAM
The Alphabet. New York: 1918. V. 64

GOUDY Greek. Easthampton: 1976. V. 64

GOUFFE, JULES
The Royal Cookery Book. London: 1883. V. 62; 66

GOUGAUD, LOUIS
Christianity in Celtic Lands. 1932. V. 64; 67
Christianity in Celtic Lands. 1992. V. 67

GOUGE, WILLIAM M.
A Short History of Paper Money and Banking in the United States. Philadelphia: 1833. V. 63; 64; 66

GOUGES, OLYMPE DE
L'Homme Genereux. Paris: 1786. V. 66

GOUGH, E.
W. Centaur; or the Turn Out. London: 1878. V. 64

GOUGH, JOHN
A New and Compendious Expositor of English Words Derived from the Latin, Greek and French. Dublin: 1760. V. 66

GOUGH, JOHN B.
Sunlight and Shadow or Gleanings from My Life-Work. London: 1881. V. 64

GOUGH, RICHARD
A Short Genealogical View of the Family of Oliver Cromwell. London: 1785. V. 62

GOULD, A. A.
The Naturlist's Library.... Boston: 1856. V. 67

GOULD, CHESTER
Dick Tracy: The Capture of Boris Arson. Chicago: 1935. V. 63; 64

GOULD, DOROTHY FAY
Beyond the Shining Mountains - 36 Northwest Adventures. Portland: 1938. V. 67

GOULD, ELIZABETH
Anne Gilchrist and Walt Whitman. Philadelphia: 1900. V. 62
The Little Women Play. Boston: 1900. V. 66
The Little Women Play. Philadelphia: 1900. V. 62

GOULD, G. M.
Anomalies and Curiosities of Medicine. Philadelphia: 1897. V. 64; 66; 67
Anomalies and Curiosities of Medicine. New York: 1937. V. 65
Anomalies and Curiosities of Medicine. London: 1958. V. 64; 66; 67
Cyclopedia of Practical Medicine and Surgery with Particular Reference to Diagnosis and Treatment. Philadelphia: 1912. V. 65

GOULD, GLEN
Period Lighting Fixtures. New York: 1928. V. 67

GOULD, HANNAH F.
New Poems. Boston: 1850. V. 67

GOULD, JOHN
Birds of Australia. 1967. V. 67
The Birds of Australia. 1992. V. 65
The Birds of Australia. 1993. V. 65
The Birds of Australia, and the Adjacent Islands. Melbourne: 1979. V. 63
Birds of Australia. Volume II. London: 1993. V. 64
Birds of Europe. 1966. V. 67
Birds of Europe. Birds of Australia. Birds of Asia. Birds of New Guinea. Birds of South America. London: 1966-1972. V. 62; 64
Birds of New Guinea. 1970. V. 67
The Birds of New Guinea. Volume II. 1993. V. 64; 65
The Birds of South America. London: 1972. V. 67
Hummingbirds. Secaucus: 1990. V. 63
An Introduction to the Birds of Great Britain. London: 1873. V. 67
John Gould, the Bird Man, a Chronology and Bibliography. Melbourne: 1982. V. 62
Kangaroos. 1973. V. 63; 66
A Monograph of the Macropodidae, or Family of Kangaroos. Melbourne: 1981. V. 63
A Monograph of the Trogonidae, or Family of Trogons. London: 1835-1838. V. 67
A Synopsis of the Birds of Australia, and the Adjacent Islands. London: 1837. V. 67

GOULD, LAURENCE M.
Cold. The Record of an Antarctic Sledge Journey. New York: 1931. V. 66
Cold. The Record of An Antarctic Sledge Journey. N.P: 1984. V. 64

GOULD, ROBERT
Poems Chiefly Consisting of Satyrs and Satyrical Epistles. 1689. V. 65; 67
Poems Chiefly Consisting of Satyrs and Satyrical Epistles. London: 1689. V. 63; 65

GOULD, ROBERT FREKE
The History of Freemasonry.... London: 1883. V. 62

GOULD, RUPERT T.
The Marine Chronometer. Its History and Development. London: 1960. V. 63

GOULD, STEPHEN JAY
Dinosaur in a Haystack. New York: 1996. V. 67
Ontogeny and Phylogeny. Cambridge: 1977. V. 65

GOULDEN, SHIRLEY
Tales from Japan. London. V. 67

GOULDEN'S Illustrated Scripture Alphabet. Canterbury: 1850. V. 66

GOULDER, W. A.
Reminiscences of a Pioneer, Incidents in the Life of a Pioneer in Oregon and Idaho. Boise: 1909. V. 63; 66

GOULDSBURY, C. E.
Tiger Slayer by Order. 1915. V. 67

GOULIMIS, CONSTANTINE N.
Wild Flowers of Greece. Kifissia: 1968. V. 62; 67

GOURARD, CHARLES
Socialism Unmasked; a Plain Lecture, from the French. London: 1850. V. 64

GOURBILLON, M.
Travels in Sicily and to Mount Etna in 1819. London: 1820. V. 65

GOURMONT, REMY DE
L'Ombre d'Une Femme. Paris: 1923. V. 64

GOUVEA, ANTONIO DE
Relacam em Que se Tratam as Guerras e Grandes Victorias Que Alcancou o Grande Rey da Persia Xa Abbas do Grao Turco Mahometto.... Lisbon: 1611. V. 62

GOVE, JESSE
The Utah Expedition 1857-1858. Letters of Capt. Jesse Gove, 10th Infantry USA. Concord: 1928. V. 64

GOVENAR, ALAN
The Blues and Jives of Dr. Hepcat. Racine: 1993. V. 64

GOVENAR, ALAN *continued*
Midnight Song. Racine: 1998. V. 64

GOVER, ROBERT
Getting Pretty on the Table. Santa Barbara: 1975. V. 63

GOW, A. S. F.
The Greek Anthology. Cambridge: 1965-1981. V. 65
Theocritus. Cambridge: 1952. V. 65

GOWER, RICHARD HALL
A Treatise on the Theory and Practice Seamanship Together with a System of Naval Signals. London: 1808. V. 62

GOWERS, WILLIAM RICHARD
Diagnosis of Diseases of the Brain and of the Spinal Cord. New York: 1885. V. 64
The Diagnosis of Diseases of the Spinal Cord. London: 1881. V. 64; 65; 66
Epilepsy and Other Chronic Convulsive Disorders. New York: 1885. V. 64; 66; 67
Lectures on the Diagnosis of Diseases of the Brain Delivered at University College Hospital. Philadelphia: 1887. V. 65
A Manual of Diseases of Nervous System. Philadelphia: 1892. V. 64; 66
A Manual of Diseases of the Nervous System. Philadelphia: 1893. V. 65
A Manual of Diseases of the Nervous System. Birmingham: 1981. V. 65

GOWING, EMILIA AYLMER BLAKE
Sita and Other Poems. London: 1895. V. 62

GOYEN, WILLIAM
Precious Door. New York: 1981. V. 66

GOYTISOLO, JUAN
Juegos de Manos. Barcelona: 1954. V. 67
The Young Assassins. London: 1960. V. 67

GRABA, JOHANN ANDREAS
Elaphographia (in Greek) sive Cervi Descripti Physico-Medico-Chymica, in Qua Tam Cervi in Genere, Quam in Specie Ipsius Partium Consideratio Theorico-Practica.... Jena: 1668. V. 62

GRABAU, A. W.
The Permian of Mongolia. New York: 1931. V. 62; 63; 65; 66
Stratigraphy of China. Peking: 1928. V. 67
Stratigraphy of China. Part I. Palaeozoic and Older. Peking: 1923-1924. V. 64; 67

GRABER, HENRY WILLIAM
Life Record of H. W. Graber, A Terry Texas Ranger 1861-1865. Dallas?: 1916. V. 62; 63; 65
A Terry Texas Ranger - The Life Record of H. W. Graber. N.P: 1916. V. 63; 66

GRABHAM, OXLEY
Yorkshire Potteries, Pots and Potters. London: 1971. V. 64

GRABHORN, JANE B.
A California Gold Rush. San Francisco: 1934. V. 63; 66

GRABHORN PRESS
Nineteenth Century Type Displayed in 18 Fonts Cast by United States Founders Now in the Cases of the Grabhorn Press. San Francisco: 1959. V. 63

GRABHORN, ROBERT
A Short Account of the Life and Work of Wynkyn de Worde, with a Leaf from the Golden Legend printed by Him...in 1527. 1949. V. 66

GRABLE, F. C.
Colorado the Bright Romance of American History. Denver: 1911. V. 65

GRACE, A. F.
A Course of Lessons in Landscape Painting in Oils. London: 1881. V. 66

GRACE, SHEFFIELD
Memoirs of the Family of Grace. London: 1823. V. 63

GRACE, TOM
Spyder Web. Dexter: 1997. V. 65

GRACE, W. G.
Cricket. Bristol: 1891. V. 66; 67
W. G. Cricketing Reminiscences and Personal Recollections. London: 1899. V. 63

GRACIAN, BALTASAR
The Art of Prudence; or, a Companion for a Man of Sense. London: 1705. V. 62; 64
The Art of Prudence; or, a Companion for a Man of Sense. London: 1714. V. 67
The Courtier's Manual Oracle, or the Art of Prudence. London: 1685. V. 67
The Courtier's Oracle; or the Art of Prudence. London: 1694. V. 64

GRACIE, ARCHIBALD
The Truth about Chickamauga. Boston: 1911. V. 63

GRACIE, THOMAS GRIERSON
Songs and Rhymes of a Lead Miner. Dumfries: 1921. V. 64

GRADUS ad Cantabrigiam; or New University Guide to the Academical Customs, and Colloquial or Cant Terms Peculiar to the University of Cambridge; Observing Wherein It Differs from Oxford.... 1824. V. 67

GRADY, BENJAMIN FRANKLIN
The Case of the South Against the North: or Historical Evidence Justifying the Southern States of the American Union in Their Long Controversy with the Northern States. Raleigh: 1899. V. 62

GRADY, G. S.
Challenger Voyage. Zoology. Part 23. Copepoda. 1883. V. 66

GRADY, JAMES
Shadow of the Condor. New York: 1975. V. 65
Six Days of the Condor. New York: 1974. V. 65; 67

GRAEME, BRUCE
Blackshirt the Audacious. London: 1935. V. 66
Passion, Murder and Mystery. Garden City: 1928. V. 67

GRAEME, LOUISA G.
Or and Sable. A Book of the Graemes and Grahams. Edinburgh: 1903. V. 65

GRAF, A. B.
Exotic Plant Manual.... East Rutherford: 1976. V. 64
Exotica. Series 3. Rutherford: 1980. V. 64

GRAFF, SIGMUND
The Endless Road. London: 1930. V. 64

GRAFFENRIED, ADOLF
Architecture Suisse, ou Choix de Maisons Rustiques des Alpes du Canton de Berne. Berne: 1844. V. 64

GRAFFIGNY, FRANCOISE, MME. DE
Recueil de ces Messieurs. Amsterdam: 1745. V. 63

GRAFFMAN, CARL SAMUEL
Skottska Vuer Tecknade efter Naturen Under en Resa i Skottland Ur 1830.... Stockholm: 1833. V. 62

GRAFIGNY, FRANCOISE
Oeuvres de Theatre. Paris: 1766. V. 67

GRAFTON, AUGUSTUS HENRY FITZROY, 3RD DUKE OF
Intrigues a-la-mode. London: 1812?. V. 67

GRAFTON, RICHARD
A Chronicle at Large and Meere History of the Affayres of Englande and Kinges of the Same, Deduced from the Creation of the Worlde.... London: 1569. V. 63
Grafton's Chronicle; or, History of England. London: 1809. V. 64

GRAFTON, SUE
A is for Alibi. London: 1982. V. 62
A is for Alibi. New York: 1982. V. 66
A is for Alibi. London: 1986. V. 63
B is for Burglar. London: 1985. V. 63
B is for Burglar. New York: 1985. V. 62; 66
B is for Burglar. London: 1986. V. 62
C is for Corpse. London: 1986. V. 63
C is for Corpse. New York: 1986. V. 63; 66
D is for Deadbeat. London: 1987. V. 63
D is for Deadbeat. New York: 1987. V. 63; 66
E is for Evidence. London: 1988. V. 63
E is for Evidence. New York: 1988. V. 63; 66
F is for Fugitive. London: 1989. V. 63
F is for Fugitive. New York: 1989. V. 63; 64; 65; 66; 67
Keziah Dane. 1967. V. 64; 66
Keziah Dane. New York: 1967. V. 65; 66
Kinsey and Me. Santa Barbara: 1991. V. 63
Kinsey and Me. Santa Monica: 1991. V. 66
The Lolly Madonna War. London: 1969. V. 66
M is for Malice. New York: 1996. V. 67

GRAFTON SMITH, ADELE
A Railway Foundling. London: 1890. V. 67

GRAGLIA, G. A.
A Collection of Italian Letters, Moral, Historical &c.... London: 1808. V. 63

GRAHAM, A.
Eyelids of Morning, the Mingled Destinies of Crocodiles and Men.... Greenwich: 1973. V. 66

GRAHAM, ALEXANDER
Travels in Tunisia with a Glossary, a Map, a Bibliography.... 1887. V. 65
Travels in Tunisia with a Glossary, a Map, a Bibliography.... Dulau: 1887. V. 62

GRAHAM, ANDREW
Andrew Graham's Observations on Hudson's Bay 1767-1791. London: 1969. V. 66

GRAHAM, BENJAMIN
Security Analysis. New York: 1934. V. 62
Security Analysis. New York: 1962. V. 64

GRAHAM, CAROLINE
Death of a Hollow Man. London: 1989. V. 66
The Envy of the Stranger. London: 1984. V. 63; 66

GRAHAM, ELEANOR
The Night Adventures of Alexis. London: 1925. V. 66

GRAHAM, FRANK
The New York Yankees. New York: 1943. V. 64

GRAHAM, GEORGE FARQUHAR
The Songs of Scotland.... Edinburgh;: 1854. V. 64

GRAHAM, GEORGE W.
The Mecklenburg Declaration of Independence May 20, 1775 and Lives of Its Signers. New York: 1905. V. 66; 67

GRAHAM, HARRY
Ruthless Rhymes for Heartless Homes. London: 1899. V. 63

GRAHAM, HOWE
Paul Outerbridge Jr.: Photographs. New York: 1980. V. 63; 65

GRAHAM, J. D.
Report...on Mason and Dixon's Line. Chicago: 1862. V. 64

GRAHAM, JAMES
A Game for Heroes. London: 1970. V. 65; 66

GRAHAM, JEAN
Tales of the Osage River County. Clinton: 1929. V. 67

GRAHAM, JOHN
Condition of the Border at the Union. London: 1907. V. 62

GRAHAM, JOHN W.
Neaera; a Tale of Ancient Rome. London: 1886. V. 66

GRAHAM, JORIE
Erosion. Princeton: 1983. V. 62
The Turning. Atlanta: 1994. V. 66

GRAHAM, MARIA
Journal of a Residence in Chile During the Year 1822. And a Voyage from Chile to Brazil in 1823. London: 1824. V. 66
Journal of a Residence in India. Edinburgh: 1812. V. 63; 64; 65

GRAHAM, MARY W.
Reminiscences of the Farmington Hunt Club, Albemarle County, Virginia. Crozet: 1970. V. 64

GRAHAM, PETER ANDERSON
The Red Scaur; a Novel of Manners. London: 1896. V. 67

GRAHAM, RIGBY
Kippers and Sawdust. 1992. V. 62
Slipper Orchids, the Art of Rigby Graham. Frenchs Forest: 1983. V. 67

GRAHAM, ROBERT BONTINE CUNNINGHAME
The Conquest of New Granada; Being the Life of Gonzalo Jimenez de Quesada. London: 1922. V. 67
The Conquest of the River Plate. London: 1924. V. 67

GRAHAM, STEPHEN
Pay as You Run. London: 1955. V. 67

GRAHAM, SYLVESTER
Lectures on the Science of Human Life. Boston: 1839. V. 62

GRAHAM, T.
Elements of Chemistry. London: 1842. V. 62
Elements of Chemistry.... London: 1850-1858. V. 62
Experiments on the Absorption of Vapours by Liquids. Edinburgh: 1828. V. 62
On Phosphuretted Hydrogen...Read 1st December 1834. Edinburgh: 1835. V. 62
On the Diffusion of Liquids. London: 1850. V. 62
On the Influence of the Air in Determining the Crystallization of Saline Solutions...read 17th December 1827. Edinburgh: 1828. V. 62
On the Tendancy of Air and the Different Gases to Mutual Penetration.... Glasgow: 1830. V. 62; 63

GRAHAM, THOMAS J.
Sure Methods of Improving Health, and Prolonging Life; or a Treatise on the Art of Living Long and Comfortably.... London: 1831. V. 67
A Treatise on Indigestion. London: 1828. V. 65

GRAHAM, W. A.
Abstract of the Official of Proceeding of the Reno Court of Inquiry. Harrisburg: 1954. V. 65; 67
The Custer Myth - a Source Book of Custeriana. New York: 1953. V. 67
The Story of the Little Big Horn. New York: 1926. V. 66

GRAHAM, W. S.
Cage Without Grievance - Poems. Glasgow: 1942. V. 65
Letters and Heads: Poems. 1993. V. 62
The Nightfishing. London: 1955. V. 62; 63; 64; 66
The Seven Journeys. Glasgow: 1944. V. 63

GRAHAM, WILLIAM
The Jordan and the Rhine; Being the Result of Five Years' Residence in Syria. London: 1854. V. 67

GRAHAM, WILLIAM A.
Revolutionary History of North Carolina. Raleigh: 1853. V. 63; 66

GRAHAM, WINIFRED
The Enemey of Woman. London: 1910. V. 65; 66
The Zionists. London: 1902. V. 65

GRAHAME, JAMES
The Birds of Scotland, with Other Poems. London: 1806. V. 66
British Georgics. Edinburgh: 1809. V. 64
An Inquiry Into the Principle of Population: Including an Exposition of the Causes and the Advantages of a Tendency to Exuberance of Numbers in Society, a Defence of the Poor-Laws.... Edinburgh: 1816. V. 65
Poems. London: 1807. V. 66
The Sabbath; a Poem. London: 1804. V. 66

GRAHAME, KENNETH
Bertie's Escapade. London: 1949. V. 67
The Cambridge Book of Poetry for Children. 1932. V. 63
Dream Days. New York and London: 1898. V. 63
Dream Days. London and New York: 1902. V. 63
First Whisper of The Wind of the Willows. London: 1944. V. 62
Fun O' the Fair. London: 1929. V. 67
The Golden Age. London: 1915. V. 67
The Golden Age. London: 1928. V. 62; 64
Pagan Papers. London: 1894. V. 66
The Wind in the Willows. London: 1927. V. 62; 66
The Wind in the Willows. New York: 1940. V. 65
Wind in the Willows. London: 1971. V. 64

GRAINGE, WILLIAM
The Battles and Battle Fields of Yorkshire.... York: 1854. V. 65
The Castles and Abbeys of Yorkshire: a Historical and Descriptive Account of the Most Celebrated Ruins in the County. York: 1855. V. 65
Daemonologia: a Discourse on Witchcraft. Harrogate: 1882. V. 65
The History and Topography of Harrogate and The Forest of Knaresbro'. London: 1871. V. 66
The History and Topography of the Townships of Little Timble, Great Timble and the Hamlet of Snowden, in the West Riding of the County of York. Otley: 1895. V. 66
Nidderdale; or, an Historical, Topographical and Descriptive Sketch of the Valley of the Nidd.... Pateley Bridge: 1863. V. 64
Yorkshire Longevity; or, Records and Biographical Anecdotes of Persons Who Have Attained to Extreme Old Age Within that County. Pateley Bridge: 1864. V. 66

GRAINGER, EDWARD
Medical and Surgical Remarks, Including a Description of a Simple and Effective method of Removing Polypi from the Uterus, Tonsils from the Throat, &c.... London: 1815. V. 65

GRAMATKY, HARDIE
Little Toot on the Thames. New York: 1964. V. 66

GRAMINAEUS, THEODORUS
Uberior Enarratio Eorum Quae a Ioanne de Sacro Bosco Proponuntur. Cologne: 1567. V. 64

GRAMMAR
Schools Considered, With Reference to a Case Lately Decided by the Lord Chancellor. London: 1820. V. 66

GRANBROOK, G. G. H.
Malaysia. Oxford: 1988. V. 63

GRANBY, MARQUESS
The Trout. London: 1899. V. 67

THE GRAND
Hall of Conviviality; Being a Collection of Rational, Manly, Humorous and Other Songs.... London: 1808. V. 62

GRAND, GORDON
The Silver Horn. London: 1934. V. 67

GRAND, SARAH
Babs the Impossible. London: 1901. V. 65
The Beth Book. New York: 1897. V. 63
The Heavenly Twins. London: 1893. V. 65
Our Manifold Nature. London: 1894. V. 65

GRAND, W. JOSEPH
Illustrated History of the Union Stockyards - Sketch Book of Familiar Faces and Places at the Yard. Chicago: 1896. V. 67

GRAND CARTERET, JOHN
La Femme e Allemagne. Paris: 1887. V. 63

GRANDIDIER, A.
Histoire Physique, Naturelle et Politique de Madagascar: Oiseaux. Paris: 1876-1937. V. 62
Histoire Physique, Naturelle et Politque de Madgascar. Paris: 1886. V. 65

GRAND'MAISON, MARIE DE
En Automobile. Paris: 1905. V. 66

GRANDMAMMA
Easy's Merry Multipication. London: 1840. V. 65

GRANDMAMMA
Easy's New Story About Old Daddy Long-Legs. London: 1845. V. 67

GRANDMAMMA
Easy's Stories about the Alphabet. Albany: 1851-1854. V. 66

GRANDMAMMA
Easy's Toy Shop. Albany: 1855-1857. V. 65

GRANDPRE, LOUIS MARIE JOSEPH DE
A Voyage in the Indian Ocean and to Bengal, Undertaken in the Years 1789 and 1790.... London: 1803. V. 62

GRANDVILLE, J. J.
Carte Vivante du Restauranteur. Paris: 1832. V. 62
Comical People. London: 1852. V. 62
Comical People, Illustrated with Sixteen Pictures. London: 1861. V. 65
Les Etoiles. Paris: 1849. V. 66

GRANDVILLE, JEAN IGNACE ISIDORE GERARD
The Flowers Personified: Being a Translation of Grandville's Les Fleurs Animees. New York: 1847. V. 66

GRANGE, RED
Zupke of Illinois. Chicago: 1937. V. 63

GRANGER, FRANK STEPHEN
Notes on the Psychological Basis of Fine Art. Nottingham: 1887. V. 65

GRANGER, J.
A Biographical History of England, from Egbert the Great to the Revolution. London: 1824. V. 65; 66

GRANGER'S Index to Poetry. New York: 1953-1957. V. 67

GRANNIE'S Little Rhyme Book. London: 1913. V. 65

GRANT, ANNE MAC VICAR
Letter from the Mountains: Being the Real Correspondence of a Lady; Between the Years 1773 and 1807. London: 1807. V. 65
Memoirs of an American Lady; with Sketches of Manners and Scenery in America.... London: 1808. V. 66
Memoirs of an American Lady.... New York: 1901. V. 65
Poems on Various Subjects. Edinburgh: 1803. V. 62; 65

GRANT, BLANCHE C.
Kit Carson's Own Story of His Life. Taos: 1925. V. 65
Kit Carson's Own Story of His Life. Taos: 1926. V. 64
Taos Indians. Taos: 1925. V. 64
When Old Trails Were New. New York: 1934. V. 65

GRANT, BREWIN
Christianity and Secularism. London: 1853. V. 67

GRANT, C. F.
Twixt Sand and Sea; Sketches and Studies in North Africa. London. V. 67

GRANT, CAMPBELL
The Rock Paintings of the Chumash. Santa Barbara: 1993. V. 65

GRANT, CHARLES L.
The Sound of Midnight. 1978. V. 64
The Sound of Midnight. London: 1978. V. 66
The Sound of Midnight. New York: 1978. V. 62

GRANT, D. S. O.
Before Port Arthur in a Destroyer. London: 1907. V. 65

GRANT, E. M.
Guide to Fishes. Brisbane: 1972. V. 65

GRANT, GEORGE MONRO
Our Picturesque Northern Neighbor. Chicago: 1899. V. 64
Picturesque Canada: the Country As It Was and Is. Toronto: 1882. V. 64

GRANT, HENRY
Mariquita, a Collection of Poetry. London: 1863. V. 65

GRANT, HUGH DUNCAN
Cloud and Weather Atlas. New York: 1944. V. 67

GRANT, J. C. BOILEAU
A Method of Anatomy Descriptive and Deductive. Baltimore: 1938. V. 67

GRANT, JAMES
The Bench and the Bar. London: 1837. V. 63
Jack Chaloner or the Fighting Forty-Third. London: 1883. V. 67
The Life of a Literary Man. London: 1843. V. 67
The Master of Aberfeldie. London: 1884. V. 67
Random Recollections of the House of Lord from the Year 1830 to 1835, Including the Personal Sketches of the Leading Members. London: 1836. V. 64
Rufus or the Red King: a Romance. London: 1838. V. 65
Thoughts on the Origin and Descent of the Gael.... Edinburgh: 1814. V. 64
Travels in Town. London: 1839. V. 67

GRANT, JOAN
Lord of the Horizon. London: 1943. V. 64

GRANT, JOHN PETER
Essays Towards Illustrating Some Elementary Principles Relating to Wealth and Currency. London: 1812. V. 64

GRANT, MAXWELL
Norgil the Magician. New York: 1977. V. 66; 67
The Shadow Laughs, a Detective Novel. New York: 1931. V. 66

GRANT, MICHAEL
T. S. Eliot - the Critical Heritage. London: 1982. V. 62

GRANT, R. G.
M15/M16 Britain's Security and Secret Intelligence Services. New York: 1989. V. 67

GRANT, ROBERT
The Expediency Maintained of Continuing the System by Which the Trade and Government of India are Now Regulated. London: 1813. V. 62; 63
History of Physical Astronomy, from the Earliest Ages to the Midde of the Nineteenth Century. London: 1848-1852. V. 65
History of Physical Astronomy, from the Earliest Ages to the Middle of the Nineteenth Century. London: 1852. V. 65

GRANT, SYBIL
The Land of Let's Pretend. Princess Mary's Gift Book. London: 1914. V. 64

GRANT, U. S.
Catalogue of the Marine Pliocene and Pleistocene Mollusca of California and Adjacent Regions. San Diego: 1931. V. 63; 66

GRANT, ULYSSES S.
The Papers of.... Carbondale: 1967-1973. V. 66
Personal Memoirs of U. S. Grant. New York: 1885-1886. V. 63; 64; 65
Personal Memoirs of U.S. Grant. New York: 1885. V. 63; 64; 66; 67

GRANT FORBES, G.
Another Wicked Woman. London: 1895. V. 67

GRANT FRANCIS, COLONEL
The Smelting of Copper in the Swansea District of South Wales, from the Time of Elizabeth to the Present Day. London: 1881. V. 66

GRANTHAM, JOHN
Ocean Steam Navigation, with a View to Its Further Development. London: 1869. V. 66

GRANTHAM, THOMAS
An Historical Account of Some Memorable Actions, Particularly in Virginia. Richmond: 1882. V. 67

GRANVILLE, ARTHUR
Transatlantic and Coastwise Steamship Funnel Marks, House Flags, and Private Signals.... New York: 1875. V. 62

GRANVILLE, AUGUSTUS DOZZI
An Historical and Practical Treatise on the Internal Use of Hydro- Cyanic (Prussic) Acid in Pulmonary Consumption and Other Diseases of the Chest.... London: 1820. V. 62
The Invalid's and Visitor's Hand-Book, to the Hot Springs of Bath. London: 1841. V. 66
St. Petersburgh. A Journal of Travels To and From that Capital.... London: 1828. V. 66
St. Petersburgh: a Journal of Travels to and from that Capital.... London: 1829. V. 65

GRANVILLE, GEORGE
Heroick Love: a Tragedy. London: 1698. V. 66

GRAPALDI, FRANCESCO MARIO
De Partibus Aedium. Parma: 1516. V. 63; 64
De Partibus Aedium. Turin: 1516. V. 62

GRAPEL, WILLIAM
Sources of the Roman Civil Law: an Introduction to the Institutes of Justinian. Philadelphia: 1857. V. 63

GRAPES and Grape Vines of California. New York: 1980. V. 64; 67
GRAPES and Grape Vines of California. New York: 1981. V. 66

GRASS, GUNTER
Die Blechtrommel. Darmstadt: 1959. V. 67
Cat and Mouse - a Novel. London: 1963. V. 62
The Flounder. New York: 1985. V. 64
Die Vorzuge der Windhuhner. Berlin: 1956. V. 67

GRASSET DE SAINT SAUVEUR, JACQUES
Costumes des Representans du Peuple.Membres des Deux Conseils, du Directoire Executif Representans du Peuple.... Paris: 1795. V. 64

GRASSMANN, THOMAS
The Mohawk Indians and Their Valley: Being a Chronological Documentary Record to the End of 1693. Fonda: 1969. V. 66

GRASSUS, BENEVENUTUS
De Oculis Eorumque Egritudinibus et Curis. Birmingham: 1905. V. 63

GRASTY, JOHN S.
A Noble Testimony. N.P: 1864. V. 63

GRATTAN, HENRY
The Speeches of the Rt. Hon. Henry Grattan in the Irish and Imperial Parliament. 1822. V. 63; 66

GRATTAN, THOMAS COLLEY
Civilized America. London: 1859. V. 64
High-Ways and By-Ways; or Tales of the Roadside, Picked Up in the French Provinces by a Walking Gentleman. Second Series. London: 1825. V. 65
Highways and By-Ways; or Tables of the Road-Side Picked Up in the French Provinces, by a Walking Gentleman. London: 1833. V. 67
The History of the Netherlands. London: 1830. V. 63
Legends of the Rhine and of the Low Countries. London: 1832. V. 67

GRATTAN, WILLIAM
Adventures with the Connaught Rangers 1809-1814. 1902. V. 65

GRATULATIO Academiae Cantabrigiensis Natales Auspicatissimos Georgii Walliae Principis Augustissimi Georgii III Magnae Britanniae Regis et Charlottae Reginae.... Cantabrigiae: 1762. V. 64

GRAUPNER, GOTTLIEB
Rudiments of the Art of Playing on the Piano Forte Containing Elements of Music Preliminary Remarks on Fingering with Examples.... Boston: 1819. V. 62

GRAUTOFF, OTTO
Die Entwicklung der Modernen Buchkunst in Deutschland. Leipzig: 1901. V. 66

GRAVELY, F. H.
Shells and Other Animal Remains Found on the Madras Beach. Madras: 1941-1942. V. 67

GRAVES, CHARLES L.
Life and Letters of Alexander Macmillan. London: 1910. V. 65

GRAVES, GEORGE
British Ornithology.... London: 1811-1813. V. 65; 67
The Naturalist's Companion.... London: 1824. V. 63
The Naturalist's Pocket-Book, or Tourist's Companion.... 1817. V. 62
The Naturalist's Pocket-Book, or Tourist's Companion.... London: 1818. V. 63

GRAVES, IDA
Epithalamion. A Poem. Higham, Colchester: 1934. V. 62; 65

GRAVES, J. A.
Out of Doors. California and Oregon. Los Angeles: 1912. V. 64; 67

GRAVES, JOHN
The Last Running. Austin: 1974. V. 62

GRAVES, RICHARD
Euphrosyne; or Amusements on the Road of Life. London: 1776-1780. V. 63
The Festoon: a Collection of Epigrams, Ancient and Modern. London: 1766. V. 65
Lubrications Consisting of Essays, Reveries &c in Prose and Verse. London: 1786. V. 63
The Spiritual Quixote: or, the Summer's Ramble of Mr. Geoffrey Wildgoose. London: 1783. V. 63
The Spiritual Quixote; or, the Summer's Ramble of Mr. Geoffrey Wildgoose. London: 1792. V. 62

GRAVES, RICHARD PERCEVAL
A. E. Housman - The Scholar-Poet. London: 1979. V. 63

GRAVES, ROBERT
Adam's Rib. London: 1955. V. 62; 64
Adam's Rib. N.P: 1958. V. 64; 66
Ann at Highwood Hall - Poems for Children. London: 1964. V. 63
Antigua, Penny, Puce. 1936. V. 63; 66
The Antigua Stamp. New York: 1937. V. 65
At the Gate: Poems. London: 1974. V. 62; 64
Beyond Giving. London: 1969. V. 62; 63; 64; 67
Collected Poems 1914-1947. London: 1948. V. 63
Colophon to Love Respelt: Poems. London: 1967. V. 63; 64
Count Belisarius. London: 1938. V. 62
Country Sentiment. London: 1920. V. 63; 64
The English Ballad: a Short Critical Survey. London: 1927. V. 66
The Feather Bed. London: 1923. V. 62
El Fenomeno del Turismo. Madrid: 1964. V. 62
Food for Centaurs: Stories, Talks, Critical Studies, Poems. Garden City: 1960. V. 63; 64; 66
The Golden Fleece. London: 1944. V. 66
Goliath and David. London: 1916. V. 64
Good-Bye To All That. London: 1929. V. 64; 66; 67
Goodbye to All That. London: 1957. V. 65
The Green-Sailed Vessel. London: 1971. V. 64
Hebrew Myths - the Book of Genesis. Garden City: 1964. V. 62
I, Claudius. London: 1977. V. 64; 65
I, Claudius. (with) Claudius the God and His Wife Messalina. 1934. V. 63
I, Claudius. (with) Claudius the God and His Wife Messalina. London: 1934. V. 64; 66
Impenetrability or the Proper Habit of English. London: 1927. V. 67
John Kemp's Wager - a Ballad Opera. Oxford: 1925. V. 62; 64
Lars Porsena; or the Future of Swearing. 1927. V. 64
Lars Porsena, or the Future of Swearing and Improper Language. London: 1972. V. 67
Life of the Poet Gnaeus Robertulus Gravesa. Deia: 1995. V. 66
Love Respelt. 1965. V. 64
Love Respelt Again. New York: 1969. V. 62; 64; 67
Majorca Observed. London: 1965. V. 63
Man Does, Woman Is. London: 1964. V. 64
Mockbeggar Hall. London: 1924. V. 64; 65
The More Deserving Cases - Eighteen Old Poems for Reconsideration. London: 1962. V. 62
The More Deserving Cases. Eighteen Old Poems for Reconsideration. 1962. V. 63; 64
My Head! My Head!. 1925. V. 64
Occupation: Writer. London: 1951. V. 65
Old Soldier Sahib. New York: 1936. V. 65
On English Poetry. London: 1922. V. 62; 64; 66; 67
Over the Brazier. London: 1916. V. 64
The Owl - No. 1. London: 1919. V. 65
Poems 1914-1926. London: 1927. V. 62; 66
Poems (1914-1927). London: 1927. V. 62; 64
Poems 1926-1930. London: 1931. V. 62; 64; 66
Poems. New York: 1980. V. 66
Poetic Unreason and Other Studies. London: 1925. V. 62
The Real David Copperfield. London: 1933. V. 62
Sergeant Lamb's America. New York: 1940. V. 65
Seventeen Poems Missing from Love Respelt. 1966. V. 64
The Shout. London: 1929. V. 62; 64
The Story of Marie Powell Wife to Mr. Milton. London: 1943. V. 65
Timeless Meeting: Poems. London: 1973. V. 64; 65; 66
Treasure Box. N.P: 1919. V. 64
Welchman's Hose. London: 1925. V. 63
White Goddess. London: 1948. V. 62
The White Goddess. New York: 1948. V. 63; 64; 66
The Winter Owl. London: 1923. V. 63
Work in Hand: Poems. London: 1942. V. 66

GRAVES, THOMAS
The Graves Papers and Other Documents Relating to the Naval Operations of the Yorktown Campaign July to October 1781. New York: 1916. V. 66

GRAVES, W. W.
Life and Letters of Fathers Ponziglione, Schoenmakers and Other Early Jesuits at Osage Mission.... St. Paul: 1916. V. 66

GRAVESANDE, WILLEM JACOB VAN S'
Mathematical Elements of Natural Philosophy, Confirmed by Experiments.... London: 1726. V. 65
Philosophiae Newtonianae Institutiones, In Usus Academicos. Leidae & Amstelodami: 1728. V. 62
Physices Elementa Mathematica, Experimentis Confirmata.... Leyden: 1748. V. 64

GRAVINA, VINCENZO
Della Ragion Poetica, Libri Due. Roma: 1718. V. 67

GRAY, ALASDAIR
Lanark. Edinburgh: 1981. V. 66
Lanark. Edinburgh: 1985. V. 66
1982 Janine. London: 1984. V. 65
Poor Things: Episodes From the Early Life of Archibald McCandless, M. D. New York: 1992. V. 63

GRAY, ALEXANDER HILL
Sixty Years Ago: Wanderings of a Stonyhurst Boy in Many Lands. London: 1925. V. 67

GRAY, ANNE AUGUSTA
Wendeline and Her Lady-Bug. Boston: 1846. V. 64

GRAY, ASA
Elements of Botany. New York: 1836. V. 62
Plantae Wrightianae Texano-Neo-Mexicanae: an Account of a Collection of Plants Made by Charles Wright.... Washington: 1852-1853. V. 66

GRAY, CAMILLA
The Great Experiment: Russian Art 1863-1922. New York: 1962. V. 62; 65
Hans Richter. London: 1971. V. 62

GRAY, CURME
Murder in Millenium VI. Chicago: 1951. V. 64

GRAY, ELIZABETH JANET
Adam of the Road. New York: 1942. V. 64

GRAY, F. W.
Mining and Transportation. A General Description. Toronto: 1909. V. 65

GRAY, G. R.
A Fasciculus of the Birds of China. 1871. V. 65
Hand List of Genera and Species of Birds.... London: 1869-1871. V. 63

GRAY, GEORGE G.
A Bibliography of the Works of Sir Isaac Newton Together with a List of Books Illustrating His Works. Cambridge: 1907. V. 62

GRAY, GEORGE J.
The Earlier Cambridge Stationers and Bookbinders and the First Cambridge Printer. London: 1904. V. 67

GRAY, HAROLD
Little Orphan Annie and Jumbo, the Circus Elephant. Chicago: 1935. V. 64

GRAY, HENRY
Anatomy. London: 1883. V. 67
Anatomy. London: 1887. V. 67
Anatomy. London: 1913. V. 67
Anatomy, Descriptive and Surgical. Philadelphia: 1870. V. 63
Anatomy, Descriptive and Surgical. Philadelphia: 1887. V. 66; 67

GRAY, I. W. D.
A Sermon Upon the Death of His Late Majesty, William IV. Saint John: 1837. V. 63

GRAY, J. E.
Catalogue of Monkeys, Lemurs and Fruit Eating Bats in the Collection of the British Museum. London: 1870. V. 64

GRAY, JANE
The Matrimonial Preceptor, or Instructive Hints to Those Who Are and Those Who are Like to Be Married. New Haven: 1829. V. 67

GRAY, JOHN
The Country-Solicitor's Practice in the High Court of Chancery; to Which is Added the Country Practice in Matters Conducted in the Crown Office of the Court of Queen's Bench.... London: 1837. V. 63
Doctor Price's Notions of the Nature of Civil Liberty, Shown to Be Contradictory to Reason and Scripture. London: 1777. V. 65
Lectures on the Nature and Use of Money. Delivered Before the Member of the Edinburgh Philosophical Institution. Edinburgh: 1848. V. 65
Liber Usualis: Missae et Officii Pro Dominicis et Festis.... Tornaci: 1920. V. 64
Silverpoints. London: 1893. V. 64

GRAY, JOHN HENRY
China; a History of the Laws, Manners and Customs of the People.... London: 1878. V. 67

GRAY, JOHN M.
David Scott, R.S.A. and His Works. Edinburgh & London: 1884. V. 64

GRAY, JOHN PERDUE
Insanity: Its Dependence on Physical Disease. Utica: 1871. V. 65

GRAY, JOHN S.
Cavalry and Coaches: The Story of Camp and Fort Collins. Fort Collins: 1978. V. 63; 64; 66
Centennial Campaign, The Sioux War of 1876. Fort Collins: 1976. V. 67

GRAY, LANDON CARTER
A Treatise on Nervous and Mental Diseases for Students and Practioners. Philadelphia: 1895. V. 65

GRAY, LOUIS HERBERT
The Mythology of all Races. New York: 1964. V. 65

GRAY, MARIA EMMA
Figures of Molluscous Animals.... London: 1874. V. 64; 65

GRAY, MARY W.
Gloucester Co., (Va.). Richmond: 1936. V. 63

GRAY, NICOLETE
Lettering on Buildings. London: 1960. V. 62
The Paintings of David Jones. London: 1989. V. 62

GRAY, P. N.
Records of North American Big Game. 1990. V. 67

GRAY, ROBERT
The Birds of the West of Scotland. Glasgow: 1871. V. 62; 67
The Birds of the West of Scotland Including the Outer Hebrides. Glasgow: 1871. V. 65; 66

GRAY, S. F.
A Natural Arrangement of British Plants. London: 1821. V. 62

GRAY, S. O.
British Sea-Weeds: an Introduction to the Study of Marine Algae of Great Britain, Ireland and the Channel Islands. 1887. V. 67

GRAY, THOMAS
Designs by Mr. Bentley, for Six Poems by Mr. Gray. London: 1753. V. 62; 63
An Elegy Written in a Country Church Yard. London: 1751. V. 62; 64
An Elegy Written in a Country Church Yard. London: 1756. V. 62
An Elegy Written in a Country Church Yard. London: 1763. V. 62
An Elegy Written in a Country Church Yard. London: 1868. V. 62
Elegy Written in a Country Church Yard. London: 1869. V. 64
Elegy Written in a Country Church Yard. Oxford: 1927. V. 66
Elegy Written in a Country Church Yard. London: 1938. V. 62
Elegy Written in a Country Church Yard. London: 1938. V. 65
Elegy Written in a Country Church Yard. New York: 1938. V. 63; 64; 66
Elegy Written in a Country Church Yard. Waltham St. Lawrence: 1946. V. 62; 65
An Elegy Written Originally in a Country Church Yard. London: 1753. V. 62
Gray's Elegy. London: 1846. V. 62; 64; 65
Ode on the Pleasure Arising from Vicissitude. San Francisco: 1933. V. 65
Odes by Mr. Gray. Strawberry Hill. 1757. V. 66
Odes by Mr Gray. 1757. V. 63
Poems. London: 1768. V. 62; 65; 66
The Poems. London: 1775. V. 62; 64; 66
The Poems. York: 1775. V. 63; 66
Poetical Works of Thomas Gray. London: 1853. V. 67

GRAY, WILLIAM
Travels in Western Africa in the Years 1818, 1819, 1820, 1821, from the River Gambia, through Woolli, Bondoo, Galam, Kasson, Kaarta and Foolidoo.... London: 1825. V. 62

GRAY, WILLIAM S.
Basic Pre-Primer Dick and Jane. Chicago: 1936. V. 62
The Elson Readers Pupil's Hand Chart. Chicago: 1921. V. 62
Fun with Dick and Jane. Chicago: 1940. V. 62; 67
Funny, Funny Sally: a First Grade Play. Chicago: 1955. V. 62
Guidebook for Friends and Neighbors. Chicago: 1946. V. 62; 65
Guidebook for Our New Friends. Chicago: 1946. V. 64
Guidebook for the Basic Primer Fun With Dick and Jane. Chicago: 1946. V. 62; 65
Guidebook To Accompany Guess Who. Chicago: 1951. V. 66
Guidebook to Accompany Our New Friends. Chicago: 1952. V. 65
More Dick and Jane Stories. Chicago: 1934. V. 62
The New Before We Read. Chicago: 1956. V. 62
The New Friends and Neighbors. Chicago: 1956. V. 62
The New Fun with Dick and Jane. Chicago: 1951. V. 62
The New Fun with Dick and Jane. Chicago: 1956. V. 62
The New Our New Friends. Toronto. V. 62
The New Our New Friends. Chicago: 1956. V. 62; 66
The New We Come and Go. Chicago: 1956. V. 62; 64; 65
The New We Look and See. Chicago: 1956. V. 62; 65
The New We Work and Play. Chicago: 1956. V. 64; 65
Our New Friends. Chicago: 1940. V. 62; 65
Teacher's Guidebook for the Elson Basic Readers Pre-Primer and Primer. Chicago: 1931. V. 62
Think-and-Do Book to Accompany Fun with Dick and Jane. Chicago: 1946. V. 62
Think-and-Do Book to Accompany Guess Who. Chicago: 1951. V. 62

We Look and See. Toronto. V. 62
We Look and See. Chicago: 1946. V. 62; 65
We Work and Play. Chicago: 1940. V. 62; 66
We Talk, Spell and Write: Sample Lessons for Grades One and Two. Chicago: 1952. V. 62

GRAYBILL, FLORENCE CURTIS
Edward Sheriff Curtis: Visions of a Vanishing Race. New York: 1976. V. 63

GRAYSON, CHARLES
The Sportsman's Hornbook. New York: 1933. V. 64
The Sportsman's Hornbook. London: 1953. V. 64

GRAYSON, DAVID
I Brake for Delmore Schwartz. 1983. V. 66

GRAYSON, WILLIAM JOHN
The Hireling and the Slave, Chicora and Other Poems. Charleston: 1856. V. 67

GRAZEBROOK, O. F.
Studies in Sherlock Holmes. New York: 1981. V. 66

GRAZIANI, ANTONIO MARIA
The History of the War of Cyprus. London: 1687. V. 67

GRAZIOSI, PAOLO
Palaeolithic Art. New York: 1960. V. 62; 63; 64

GRAZZINI, ANTONIO FRANCESCO, CALLED IL LASCA
The Story of Doctor Manente. Florence: 1929. V. 62

GREACEN, LAVINIA
Chink, a Biography (Eric Dorman-Smith or O'Gowan). 1989. V. 67

GREACEN, ROBERT
The Art of Noel Coward. Aldington: 1953. V. 63

GREAT BRITAIN
Report of the United Kingdom Shipyward Mission to the Government of India. London: 1950. V. 64

GREAT BRITAIN. ADMIRALTY - 1857
Instructions for the Exercise and Service of Great Guns & Shells on Board Her Majesty's Ships. 1857. V. 67

GREAT BRITAIN. ADMIRALTY - 1909
Rate Book and Authorised List of Naval Stores 1909-1910. London: 1909. V. 67

GREAT BRITAIN. ADMIRALTY - 1913
Report of a Committee Appointed by the Admiralty to Examine... Evidence Relating to the Tactics Employed by Nelson at the Battle of Trafalgar. London: 1913. V. 66; 67

GREAT BRITAIN. ADMIRALTY - 1937
Uniform Regulations for Officers of the Fleet 1937. London: 1937. V. 64

GREAT BRITAIN. ARMY - 1822
General Regulations and Orders for the Army. London: 1822. V. 65

GREAT BRITAIN. BOARD OF AGRICULTURE - 1795
Account of the Experiments Tried by the Board of Agriculture in the Composition of Various Sorts of Bread. London: 1795. V. 65
Report of the Committee of the Board of Agriculture, Appointed to Extract Information from the County Reports and Other Authorities Concerning The Culture and Use of Potatoes. London: 1795. V. 65

GREAT BRITAIN. BOARD OF AGRICULTURE - 1796
List of Members of the Board of Agriculture. London: 1796. V. 65

GREAT BRITAIN. CHALLENGER OFFICE - 1880
Report on the Scientific Results of the Voyage of H.M.S. Challenger During the Years 1872-1876, The Complete Zoology.... 1880-1889. V. 65

GREAT BRITAIN. CHALLENGER OFFICE - 1884
Challenger Voyage. Zoology. Parts 32 and 60. 1884-1888. V. 65

GREAT BRITAIN. COLONIAL OFFICE - 1858
Copies or Extracts of Corespondence Relative to the Discovery of Gold in Fraser's River District, in British North America. London: 1858. V. 64

GREAT BRITAIN. COURT OF STAR CHAMBER - 1637
A Decree of Star Chamber Concerning printing, Made July 11, 1637. New York: 1637. V. 65

GREAT BRITAIN. EDUCATION COMMISSION - 1861
Report of the Commissioners Appointed to Inquire Into the State of Popular Education in England. London: 1861. V. 65

GREAT BRITAIN. GEOLOGICAL SURVEY - 1846
Memoirs. 1846-1881. V. 65; 66

GREAT BRITAIN. LAWS, STATUTES, ETC. - 1576
Magna Charta, cum Statutis, Tum Antiquis, Tum Recentibus, Maximopere, Animo Tenendis Nunc Demum ad Vitum, Tipis Aedita, Per Richardum Tottell. London: 1576. V. 64

GREAT BRITAIN. LAWS, STATUTES, ETC. - 1704
Act of Queen Anne's Bounty. London: 1704. V. 66

GREAT BRITAIN. LAWS, STATUTES, ETC. - 1731
Act of Parliament in Favour of the Maiden Hospital..Rules and Constitutions for Governing and Managing the Maiden-Hospital Founded by the Company of Merchants, and Mary Erskine in Anno 1695. Edinburgh: 1731. V. 62; 63

GREAT BRITAIN. LAWS, STATUTES, ETC. - 1745
An Act for Making the Surgeons of London and the Barbers of London Two Separate and Distinct Corporations. London: 1745. V. 62

GREAT BRITAIN. LAWS, STATUTES, ETC. - 1749
An Act for the Further Encouragement and Enlargment of the Whale Fishery...and for the Naturalization of Such Foreign Protestants as shall Serve on Board Such Ships as Shall be Fitted Out for the Said Fishery (29th November 1748). London: 1749. V. 62

GREAT BRITAIN. LAWS, STATUTES, ETC. - 1765
Anno Quinto Georgii III Regis...an Act for Granting and Applying Certain Stamp Duties and Other Duties in the British Colonies and Plantations in America, Toward Further Defraying the Expences of Defending, Protecting and Securing the Same.... London: 1765. V. 62
Statutes at Large, Concerning the Turnpike Roads &c. of This Kingdom. From the Fifth Year of the Reign of King George I, to the Fifth Year of the Reign of King George III, Inclusive. London: 1765. V. 67

GREAT BRITAIN. LAWS, STATUTES, ETC. - 1787
An Act for Altering and Extending the Line of Cut or Canal...from the Forth to the...Clyde at Dalmuir Burnfoot...and a Collateral Cut from the Same to the City of Glasgow.... London: 1787. V. 65

GREAT BRITAIN. LAWS, STATUTES, ETC. - 1809
An Act for Building a Bridge Across the River Thames, from or Near Vauxhall Turnpike, in the Parish of Saint Mary Lambeth, in the County of Surrey.... London: 1809. V. 62

GREAT BRITAIN. LAWS, STATUTES, ETC. - 1816
An Act (Passed 10th June 1816) to Enable the Vestrymen of the Parish o Saint Mary-le-Bone, in the County of Middlesex, to Build a New Parish Church and Two or More Chapels.... London: 1816. V. 67

GREAT BRITAIN. LAWS, STATUTES, ETC. - 1837
Act for Registering Births, Deaths and Marriages in England. and The Act for Marriages in England Passed 17th August 1836. London: 1837. V. 63

GREAT BRITAIN. LAWS, STATUTES, ETC. - 1869
Acts of Parliament Relating to the Assay of Gold and Silver Wares. Birmingham: 1869?. V. 63

GREAT BRITAIN. LAWS, STATUTES, ETC. - 1886
The Public General Acts Passed in the 49th and 50th Years of the Reign of Queen Victoria.... London: 1886. V. 66

GREAT BRITAIN. NAVY - 1828
A List of the Flag Officers and Other Commissioned Officers of His Majesty's Fleet with the Dates of Their Respective Commissions. London: 1828. V. 63

GREAT BRITAIN. PARLIAMENT - 1628
The Priviledges and Practice of Parliaments in England. N.P: 1628. V. 64

GREAT BRITAIN. PARLIAMENT - 1642
A Declaration and Resolution of the Lords and Commons Assembled in Parliament, Concerning His Majesties Late Proclamation for the Suppressing of the Present Rebellion, Under the Command of Robert Earle of Essex.... London: 1642. V. 66

GREAT BRITAIN. PARLIAMENT - 1643
An Ordinance by the Lords and Commons Assembled in Parliament, for the Preservation and Keeping Together for Publique Use, Such Books, Evidences, Records and Writings Sequestered or Taken by Distresse or Otherwise.... London: 1643. V. 65

GREAT BRITAIN. PARLIAMENT - 1646
An Ordinance of the Lords and Commons Assembled in Parliament Authorizing Commissioners (sic) at Setle and Regulate the Heralds Office, and to Suppy the Offices of Constable and Marshall of England in Matters of Armes. London: 1646. V. 65

GREAT BRITAIN. PARLIAMENT - 1649
A Declaration of the Parliament of England Expressing the Grounds of their Late Proceedings and of Settling the Present Governement in the Way of a Free State. London: 1649. V. 65

GREAT BRITAIN. PARLIAMENT - 1742
A Further Report from the Committee...Appointed to Enquire into the Conduct of Robert, Earl of Orford, During His Ten Years of His Being First Commissioner of the Treasury, and Chancellor and Under Treasurer of His Majesty's Exchequer Delivered the 30th. London: 1742. V. 64; 65

GREAT BRITAIN. PARLIAMENT - 1806
Substance of the Debates on a Resolution for Abolishing the Slave Trade, Which Was Moved in the House of Commons on the 10th June, 1806, and in the House of Lords on the 24th June 1806. London: 1806. V. 64

GREAT BRITAIN. PARLIAMENT - 1844
Report from the Selection Committee on Tobacco Trade; Together with Minutes of Evidence, Appendix and Index. London: 1844. V. 64

GREAT BRITAIN. PARLIAMENT - 1890
Parliamentary Papers Relating to Kashmir. London: 1890. V. 67
United States. No. 2. (1890). Correspondence Respecting the Behring Sea Seal-Fisheries: 1886-1900. London: 1890. V. 63

GREAT BRITAIN. PARLIAMENT - 1901
Report from the Joint Select Committee of the House of Lords and House of Commons on London Underground Railways, Together with the Proceedings of the Committee, Minutes of Evidence, Appendix and Index. London: 1901. V. 62

GREAT BRITAIN. PARLIAMENT - 1911
Report of the Departmental Committee Appointed by the President of the Local Government Board with Respect to the Orders Relating to the Administration of Outdoor Relief. London: 1911. V. 67

GREAT BRITAIN. PARLIAMENT. HOUSE OF COMMONS - 1648
A Declaration of the House of Commons in Parliament Assembled Declaring 1. That the People are Under God the Originall of All Just Power. 2. That the Commons of England in Parliament Assembled Being Chosen by and Representing the People, Have the Supream. London: 1648. V. 64

GREAT BRITAIN. PARLIAMENT. HOUSE OF COMMONS - 1681
An Exact Collection of the Most Considerable Debates in the Honourable House of Commons, at the Parliament Held at Westminster The One and Twentieth of October 1680. London: 1681. V. 67

GREAT BRITAIN. PARLIAMENT. HOUSE OF COMMONS - 1729
A Report from the Committee Appointed to Enquire Into the State of the Goals of This Kingdom, Relating to the Fleet Prison. London: 1729. V. 65

GREAT BRITAIN. PARLIAMENT. HOUSE OF COMMONS - 1784
The Resolutions of the House of Commons, on the Great and Constitutional Questions Between the Privileges of the House of Commons and the Prerogative of the Crown; from the 17th of December 1783, to the 10th of March 1784. London: 1784. V. 67

GREAT BRITAIN. PARLIAMENT. HOUSE OF COMMONS - 1792
The Debate of a Motion for the Abolition of the Slave-Trade in the House of Commons on Monday, the Second of April, 1792, Reported in Detail. London: 1792. V. 66

GREAT BRITAIN. PARLIAMENT. HOUSE OF COMMONS - 1815
Report from Committee on the State of Mendicity in the Metropolis (Command 473). London: 1815. V. 67

GREAT BRITAIN. PARLIAMENT. HOUSE OF COMMONS - 1816
Committee on the State of the Police of the Metropolis. Report from the Committee on the State of the Police of the Metropolis.... London: 1816. V. 63
Report from the Select Committee of the House of Commons on the Earl of Elgin's Collection of Sculptured Marbles &c. London: 1816. V. 62; 63; 65

GREAT BRITAIN. PARLIAMENT. HOUSE OF COMMONS - 1822
Report from Select Committee on (the) Morpeth and Edinburgh Road. London: 1822. V. 66

GREAT BRITAIN. PARLIAMENT. HOUSE OF COMMONS - 1828
First (and Second) Report from the Select Committee on the State of Smithfield Market. London: 1828. V. 62

GREAT BRITAIN. PARLIAMENT. HOUSE OF COMMONS - 1830
Report from the Select Committee on the Settlements of Sierra Leone and Fernando Po. London: 1830. V. 64

GREAT BRITAIN. PARLIAMENT. HOUSE OF COMMONS - 1839
Palace of Westminster Report from the Select Committee on Lighting the House, Together with the Minutes of Evidence, Appendix and Index. London: 1839. V. 62

GREAT BRITAIN. PARLIAMENT. HOUSE OF COMMONS - 1875
Debates in the House of Commons on Sir Robert Peel's Bank Bills of 1844 and 1845. London: 1875. V. 62

GREAT BRITAIN. PARLIAMENT. HOUSE OF COMMONS - 1885
Report from the Select Committe on Westminster Hall Restoration; Together with the Proceedings of the Committee, Minutes of Evidence and Appendix. London: 1885. V. 65

GREAT BRITAIN. PARLIAMENT. HOUSE OF LORDS - 1695
The Humble Address of the Right Honourable the Lords Spiritual and Temporal in Parliament Assembled, Presented to His Majesty on the Sixteenth of December, 1695. London: 1695. V. 62

GREAT BRITAIN. PARLIAMENT. HOUSE OF LORDS - 1748
A Genuine and Complete Collection of all the Protests Made in the House of Lords, Against Things Suppos'd Injurious to the Publick.... Edinburgh: 1748. V. 63

GREAT BRITAIN. PARLIAMENT. HOUSE OF LORDS - 1838
Proceedings, Digest of the Evidence, Before the Committees of the House of Lords and Commons in the Year 1837 on the National System of Education in Ireland. London: 1838. V. 65

GREAT BRITAIN. PARLIAMENT. HOUSE OF LORDS - 1854
Report from the Select Committee of the House of Lords Appointed to Inquire into the Possibility of Improving the Ventilation and the Lighting of the House, and the Contiguous Chambers, Galleries, and Passages.... London: 1854. V. 62

GREAT BRITAIN. PARLIAMENT. HOUSE OF LORDS - 1885
Report from the Select Committee of the House of Lords on the Poor Law Guardian (Ireland) Bill; with Proceedings and Minutes of Evidence. 1885. V. 65

GREAT BRITAIN. PRIVY COUNCIL - 1711
The Several Declarations, Together with the Several Depositions Made in Council on Monday, the 22d of October, 1688. London: 1711. V. 65

GREAT BRITAIN. ROYAL COMM. FOR METROPOLITAN IMPROVEMENT
First Report of the Commissioners Appointed by Her Majesty to Inquire into and Consider the Most Effectual Means of Improving the. London: 1844. V. 62

GREAT BRITAIN. ROYAL COMM. ON HISTORICAL MONUMENTS - 1922
An Inventory of the Historical Monuments in Essex. 1916-1922. V. 65

GREAT BRITAIN. ROYAL COMMISSION ON THE ANCIENT AND HISTORIC
An Inventory of the Historical Monuments in Westmorland. London: 1936. V. 66

GREAT BRITAIN. ROYAL COMMISSION ON THE POOR LAWS AND RELIEF
Report of the Royal Commission on the Poor Laws and Relief of Distress. London: 1909. V. 62; 66

GREAT BRITAIN. STANDARDS COMMISSION - 1869
Second-(Fifth) Report of the Commissioners Appointed to Inquire into the Condition of the Exchequer (now Board of Trade) Standards. On the Question of the Introduction of the Metric System of Weights and Measures into the United Kingdom. London: 1869. V. 62

GREAT BRITAIN. TREATIES, ETC. - 1738
Treaty of Navigation and Commerce Between the Most Serene and Most Potent Princess Anne, by the Grace of God, Queen of Great Britain, France and Ireland, Defender of the Faith &c. London: 1738. V. 66

GREAT BRITAIN. TREATIES, ETC. - 1758
Extracts from the Several Treaties Subsisting Between Great Britain and Other Kingdoms and States of Such Articles and Clauses, as Relate to the Duty and Conduct of the Commanders of His Majesty's Ships of War. London: 1758. V. 64

GREAT BRITAIN. TREATIES, ETC. - 1919
The Treaty of Peace Between the Allied and Associated Powers and Germany. The Protocol Annexed Thereto, the Agreement Respecting the Military Occupation of the Territories of the Rhine, and the Treaty Between France and Great Britain.... London: 1919. V. 64

GREAT BRITAIN. WAR OFFICE - 1909
Treatise of Service Ordnance.... London: 1909. V. 65

THE GREAT Defects in the Theological Department of the Scotch Universities Pointed Out in a Letter Addressed to the Reverend Members of the Royal University Commission. Edinburgh: 1827. V. 63

GREAT Domesday Book. The County Edition. Buckinghamshire. London: 1987-1988. V. 65

THE GREAT Earthquake of 1923 in Japan. Tokyo: 1926. V. 64

THE GREAT GUN Exercise. Abstract. 1844. V. 65

THE GREAT Illegitimate!! Public and Private Life of That Celebrated Actress, Miss Bland, Otherwise Mrs. Ford, or Mrs. Jordan; Late Mistress of H. R.H. the D...of Clarence; Now King William IV. London: 1831. V. 65

GREAT NORTHERN RAILWAY
Town's Line. Hougham to Newark Contract. Drawings as Specimens of Works Contemplated. 1845. V. 63

GREAT Register of the County of Mono, State of California. San Francisco. 1877. V. 63

GREAT Teachers of Surgery in the Past. Bristol: 1969. V. 66

THE GREAT Wheel. New York: 1957. V. 64

GREATER American - Heroes, Battles, Camps - Dewey Islands, Cuba and Puerto Rico. New York. 1898. V. 63

GREAT EXHIBITION OF THE WORKS OF ALL NATIONS, 1851.
Official Catalogue of.... London: 1851. V. 62

GREATRAKES, VALENTINE
A Brief Account of Mr. Valentine Greatrak's and Divers of the Strange Cures by Him Lately Performed. London: 1666. V. 62

GREAVES, JOHN
The Origine and Antiquity of Our English Weights and Measures Discover'd By Their Near Agreement with Such Standards that are Now Found in One of the Egyptian Pyramids. London: 1706. V. 63

GRECO, GIOACHINO
The Royall Game of Chesse-Play. Sometimes The Recreation of the Late King.... London: 1656. V. 63; 64

GREEF, GUILLAUME JOSEPH DE
La Transformisme Social. Essai sur le Progress et le Regres des Soietes. Paris: 1895. V. 65

GREEGE, THOMAS
The True and Perfecte Newes of the Worthy and Valiaunt Exploytes Performed and Done by that Valiant Knight Syr Francis Drake, etc., 1587. Hartford: 1955. V. 63

THE GREEKS: a Poem. London: 1813. V. 62

GREELEY, A. W.
A Handbook of Polar Discoveries. Boston: 1907. V. 64
Three Years of Arctic Service. New York: 1886. V. 62; 63; 64

GREELEY, HORACE
Essays Designed to Elucidate the Science of Political Economy.... Boston: 1871. V. 62
The Tribune Almanac 1858-1869. New York. V. 65

GREELY, A. W.
International Polar Expedition, Report On the Proceedings of the United States, Expedition to Lady Franklin.... Washington: 1888. V. 65

GREEN, ANNA KATHARINE
A Difficult Problem. New York: 1900. V. 65

GREEN, ARCHIE
Only a Miner. Studies in Recorded Coal-Mining Songs. Urbana: 1972. V. 67

GREEN, ASHBEL
Discourses, Delivered, in the College of New Jersey, Addressed Chiefly to Candidates for the First Degree in the Arts.... Philadelphia: 1822. V. 63

GREEN, B. W.
Word Book of Virginia Folk-Speech. Richmond: 1899. V. 62

GREEN, BEN K.
Back to Back: Texas Cow Horses and the Vermont Maid. Austin: 1970. V. 63; 64; 67
Ben Green Tales. Flagstaff: 1974. V. 67
Biography of the Tennessee Walking Horse. Shelbyville: 1960. V. 66
The Color of Horses. Flagstaff: 1974. V. 62
The Color of Horses. N.P: 1983. V. 66
Horse Conformation as to Soundness and Performance. Cumby: 1969. V. 64; 65
The Last Trail Drive through Downtown Dallas. Flagstaff: 1971. V. 65
A Thousand Miles of Mustangin'. Flagstaff: 1972. V. 65
Wild Cow Tales. New York: 1969. V. 64; 66

GREEN, BENJAMIN RICHARD
Illustrations of Perspective, Being a Popular Explantion of the Science and Its Application to Design Generally. London: 1840. V. 64

GREEN, BERIAH
Four Sermons Preached in the Chapel of the Western Reserve College. Cleveland: 1833. V. 63
Things for Northern Men to Do; a Discourse...July 17, 1836. New York: 1836. V. 62; 64

GREEN, CHARLES FREDERICK
Shakespeare's Crab Tree, with Its Legend and a Descriptive Account.... London: 1862. V. 62; 65

GREEN, CHARLES R.
Green's Historical Series, Early Days in Kansas, in Keokuks Time on the Kansas Reservation. Kansas: 1913. V. 66

GREEN, CHRISTOPHER
The European Avant-Gardes. 1995. V. 67

GREEN, DAVID
Grinling Gibbons. His Work as Carver and Statuary 1648-1721. London: 1964. V. 62

GREEN, E. R. R.
The Industrial Archaeology of County Down. 1963. V. 63

GREEN, EDWIN L.
George McDuffie. Columbia: 1936. V. 67
A History of Richland County. Columbia: 1932. V. 63; 66; 67

GREEN, ELSA GOODWIN
Raiders and Rebels in South Africa. London: 1898. V. 64

GREEN, FRANCES
Might and Right: by a Rhode Islander. Providence: 1844. V. 62

GREEN, GEORGE DAWES
The Caveman's Valentine. New York: 1994. V. 63; 64; 65; 67

GREEN, HANNAH
I Never Promised You a Rose Garden. New York: 1964. V. 66

GREEN, HARRY CLINTON
A Record of the More Notable Women of the Early Days of the Country, and Particularly of the Colonial and Revolutionary Periods. New York: 1912. V. 67

GREEN, HENRY
Back. London: 1946. V. 62; 65; 66
Caught. London: 1943. V. 63
Concluding. 1948. V. 66
Concluding. London: 1948. V. 62; 64
Doting. London: 1952. V. 62; 64
Living. London: 1929. V. 63
Living. New York: 1929. V. 66
Loving. London: 1945. V. 62
Nothing. London: 1950. V. 62; 62; 64
Pack My Bag. London: 1940. V. 62; 65

GREEN, HORACE
Selections from Favorite Prescriptions of Living American Practitioners. New York. 1858. V. 66; 67

GREEN, J. BARCHAM
Papermaking by Hand in 1953. London: 1953. V. 64
Papermaking by Hand in 1967. Maidstone: 1967. V. 64

GREEN, J. H.
A Letter to Sir Astley Cooper, Bart. F.R.S. Surgeon to the King...of Certain Proceedings Connected with the Establishment of an Anatomical and Surgical School at Guy's Hospital. London: 1825. V. 64

GREEN, JOHN
Considerations on the Expediency of Making, and Manner of Conducting the Late Regulations at Cambridge (University). London: 1751. V. 63

GREEN, JOHN RICHARD
History of the English People. London: 1895. V. 66
The Making of England. London: 1885. V. 67

GREEN, JOHN WILLIAMS
Johnny Green of the Orphan Brigade. The Journal of a Confederate Soldier. Lexington: 1956. V. 62

GREEN, JONATHAN
Chasing the Sun: Dictionary Makers and the Dictionaries They Made. London: 1996. V. 62
On the Utility and Safety of the Fumigating Bath as a Remedial Agent in Complaints of the Skin, Joints, Rheumatism, Gout and Disorder of the Digestive Organs. London: 1847. V. 64

GREEN, LOUISA MEIGS
Brother of the Birds. Philadelphia: 1929. V. 64

GREEN, MATTHEW
The Spleen and Other Poems. London: 1796. V. 66

GREEN, N. W.
Mormonism: Its Rise, Progress and Present Condition. Hartford: 1870. V. 65

GREEN, PAUL
The Common Glory. A Symphonic Drama of American History with Music.... Chapel Hill: 1948. V. 67

GREEN, PAUL continued
The Hawthorn Tree. Chapel Hill: 1943. V. 67

GREEN, RALPH
The Iron Hand Press in America.... Rowayton: 1948. V. 63

GREEN, RENA M.
Mavericks Authentic Account of the Term. San Antonio: 1937. V. 67

GREEN, RICHARD LANCELYN
Arthur Conan Doyle on Sherlock Holmes. London: 1981. V. 63

GREEN, ROBERT B.
On the Arkansas Route to California in 1849 - The Journal of Robert B. Green of Lewisburg, Pennsylvania. Lewisburg: 1955. V. 63

GREEN, ROBERT M.
History of the Hundred and Twenty-Fourth Regiment Pennsylvania Volunteers in the War of the Rebellion 1862-1863. Philadelphia: 1907. V. 62; 63

GREEN, ROGER LANCELYN
Holmes, This Is Amazing: Essays in Unorthodox Research. London: 1975. V. 65
The Lost July. London: 1946. V. 64

GREEN, S. G.
In Memoriam John Rylands. Born February 7, 1801, Died December 11, 1888. Manchester: 1899. V. 64; 65

GREEN, SAMUEL G.
Swiss Pictures Drawn with Pen and Pencil. London: 1891. V. 64

GREEN, THOMAS
The Case of Capt. Tho. Green, Commander of the Ship Worcester, and His Crew, Tried and Condemned for Pyracy & Murther, in the Hight Court of Admiralty of Scotland. London: 1705. V. 65
Some Cursory Remarks on a Late Printed Paper, Called, the Last Speeches and Dying Words of Capt. Thomas Green, Commander of the Ship Worcester.... Edinburgh: 1705. V. 65
The Universal Herbal; or, Botanical, Medical and Agricultural Dictionary. Liverpool: 1816-1820. V. 64; 66
The Universal Herbal; or, Botanical, Medical and Agricultural Dictionary. Liverpool: 1816-1824?. V. 66; 67
The Universal Herbal, or Botanical, Medical and Agricultural Dictionary. 1825. V. 65

GREEN, THOMAS HILL
Lectures on the Principles of Political Obligation. London: 1895. V. 62

GREEN, THOMAS MARSHALL
The Spanish Conspiracy: A Review of Early Spanish Movements in the South-West. Cincinnati: 1891. V. 63; 64; 66

GREEN, VALENTINE
The History and Antiquities of the City and Suburbs of Worcester. London: 1796. V. 66
The History and Antiquities of the City and Suburbs of Worcester. (with) *An Account of the Discovery of the Body of King John, in the Cathedral Church of Worcester, July 17th, 1797....* London: 1797. V. 63
A Review of the Polite Arts in France.... London: 1782. V. 62

GREEN, W. SPOTSWOOD
Notes on Rockall Island and Bank. Dublin: 1897. V. 67

GREEN, WHARTON J.
Recollections and Reflections: an Auto(biography) of Half a Century and More. Raleigh: 1906. V. 62; 63

GREEN, WILLIAM
The Art of Living in London, a Poem. London: 1811. V. 62
A Description of a Series of Sixty Small Prints, Etched by William Green. 1814. V. 67
A Description of a Series of Sixty Small Prints, Etched by William Green. Ambleside: 1814. V. 66
The Excursionist's Guide to Nottingham, Grantham, Sleaford, Boston and the German Ocean. Boston: 1859. V. 65
The Instructive Monitor.... London: 1812. V. 64
A New Translation of the Prayer of Habakkuk, the Prayer of Moses and the CXXXIX Psalm.... Cambridge: 1755. V. 62
Selections, Moral and Religious. London: 1823. V. 66
The Song of Deborah, Reduced to Metre.... Cambridge: 1753. V. 62
The Tourist's New Guide. Kendal: 1819. V. 65; 66

GREEN, WILLIAM S.
Among the Selkirk Glaciers: Being the Account of a Rough Survey in the Rocky Mountain Regions of British Columbia. London: 1890. V. 65

GREENACRE, JAMES
The Edgeware-Road-Tragedy. Fairburn's Edition of the Trials of Greenacre and Gale, for the Horrible Murder and Mutilation of Hannah Brown... With a Life of Greenacre written by himself. London: 1837. V. 63
The Life and Career of James Greenacre, Partly Written by Himself.... London: 1837. V. 63
The Paddington Tragedy. A Circumstantial Narrative of the Lives and Trial of James Greenacre and the Woman Gale, for the Murder of Mrs. Hannah Brown.... London: 1837. V. 63

GREENAWAY, KATE
Almanack for 1883. London: 1883. V. 66
Almanack for 1884. London: 1883. V. 65
Almanack for 1886. London: 1885. V. 65
Almanack for 1886. London: 1886. V. 62; 64; 66
Almanack for 1890. London: 1890. V. 64; 65; 66
Kate Greenaway's Almanack and Diary for 1897. London: 1897. V. 64
Kate Greenaway's Almanack for 1928. London. V. 66
Almanack for 1929. London. V. 62
Almanacks 1883-1895. (with) *Almanack and Diary for 1897.* (with) *Alphabet c. 1885.* London: 1882-1896. V. 63
A Apple Pie. London. V. 63; 66
Apple Pie. London: 1886. V. 65
The April Baby's Book of Tunes with the Story of How They Came to Be Written. London: 1900. V. 65
Calendar of the Seasons 1881. London. V. 62
Calendar of the Seasons: 1882. London: 1882. V. 65
Calendar of the Seasons 1882. London. V. 62
Dame Wiggins of Lee and Her Seven Wonderful Cats: a Humorous Tale Written Principally by a Lady of Ninety. Orpington: 1885. V. 66
A Day in a Child's Life. London. V. 62; 66
A Day in a Child's Life. London: 1881. V. 62
The Favourite Album of Fun and Fancy. London: 1884. V. 65
Kate Greenaway's Alphabet. London. V. 66
Kate Greenaway's Alphabet. London: 1885. V. 65
Kate Greenaway's Book of Games. London: 1889. V. 62; 64
Language of Flowers. London: 1884. V. 62; 64; 65
Marigold Garden. London: 1885. V. 63; 65; 66
Mother Goose or the Old Nursery Rhymes. London: 1881. V. 65
Under the Window. London. V. 62; 66
Under the Window. New York: 1880. V. 66
Under the Window. New York: 1885. V. 66

GREENAWAY, THOMAS
The Trial of Weeping Billy, for the Wilful Murder of Ann Webb. London: 1807. V. 63

GREENBERG, C.
Mid-Century Modern: Furniture of the 1950's. New York: 1984. V. 62; 65

GREENBERG, G.
Comparative Psychology, a Handbook. New York: 1998. V. 65; 66

GREENBERG, SAMUEL
Poems by Samuel Greenberg. New York: 1947. V. 63

GREENBIE, SYDNEY
Frontiers and the Fur Trade. New York: 1929. V. 63; 66

GREENBLATT, S. H.
A History of Neurosurgery in Its Scientific and Professional Contexts. Park Ridge: 1997. V. 64; 66

GREENBURG, DAN W.
Book of the Governors. N.P: 1926. V. 64
Greenburg's Gazeteer - Featuring Casper, Natrona County and Environs - Its Resources and Assets in Wonderful Wyoming. Volume I No. 1 June 1928. Casper. V. 65
Sixty Years a Brief Review, the Cattle Industry in Wyoming. Cheyenne: 1932. V. 63; 66

GREENE, A. C.
The Last Captive. Austin: 1972. V. 62; 67

GREENE, C. W.
Birds: Their Homes and Their Habits.... Philadelphia: 1887. V. 63; 67

GREENE, FRANCIS V.
The Revolutionary War and the Military Policy of the United States. New York: 1911. V. 67

GREENE, GEORGE WASHINGTON
Historical View of the American Revolution. Boston: 1865. V. 67

GREENE, GRAHAM
A La Recherche d'un Personnage. (In Search of a Character). France: 1961. V. 63
The Annotated Library of Graham Greene. London: 1993. V. 63
Another Mexico. New York: 1939. V. 62; 64; 66
Babbling April. Oxford: 1925. V. 63; 66
The Basement Room and Other Stories. London: 1935. V. 62; 63; 64
The Bear Fell Tree. London: 1935. V. 63
Brighton Rock. London: 1938. V. 62; 63; 64
Brighton Rock. New York: 1938. V. 63
British Dramatists. London: 1942. V. 63
A Burnt-Out Case. London: 1961. V. 62; 63; 65
The Captain and the Enemy. Canada: 1988. V. 63
The Captain and the Enemy. London: 1988. V. 66
Carving a Statue - a Play. London: 1964. V. 63
Collected Essays. London: 1969. V. 62
Collected Stories. New York: 1973. V. 62
The Comedians. New York: 1966. V. 62; 63
The Complaisant Lover. London: 1959. V. 64
The Complaisant Lover. New York: 1959. V. 62
The Complaisant Lover. New York: 1961. V. 64
Dear David, Dear Graham: a Bibliographic Correspondence. Oxford: 1989. V. 62; 66
Doctor Fischer of Geneva or The Bomb Party. London: 1980. V. 63
Doctor Fischer of Geneva or The Bomb Party. New York: 1980. V. 63
The End of the Affair. London: 1951. V. 63
Essais Catholiques. Paris: 1953. V. 63
Getting to Know the General. London: 1984. V. 63; 64; 66
The Great Jowett. London: 1981. V. 62; 63
The Heart of the Matter. London: 1948. V. 63
The Heart of the Matter. New York: 1948. V. 63; 64; 66

GREENE, GRAHAM continued
How Father Quixote Became a Monsignor. USA: 1980. V. 63
The Human Factor. London: 1978. V. 66; 67
In Search of a Character. New York: 1961. V. 63; 66
Introduction to Three Novels. Norway: 1962. V. 63
Introduction to Three Novels. Stockholm: 1962. V. 64; 66
It's a Battlefield. Garden City: 1934. V. 66; 67
It's a Battlefield. London: 1934. V. 63
Journey Without Maps. London: 1936. V. 63; 66
Der Kleine Pferdebus. (The Little Horse Bus). Dusseldorf: 1955. V. 65
Die Kleine Lok. (The Little Train). Dusseldorf: 1953. V. 65
Die Kleine Trein. (The Little Train). N.P: 1954. V. 65
The Labyrinthine Ways. New York: 1940. V. 62; 63
L'Agent Secret. (The Confidential Agent). Paris: 1948. V. 63
Land Benighted. A Story of Liberia. London: 1938. V. 63
The Lawless Roads, a Mexican Journey. London: 1939. V. 62; 63; 65; 66
The Little Fire Engine. London: 1950. V. 62; 63; 66
The Little Horse Bus. London: 1952. V. 63
The Little Horse Bus. London: 1974. V. 65
The Little Steamroller. London: 1953. V. 63
The Little Steamroller. London: 1974. V. 65
The Living Room - A Play in Two Acts. London: 1953. V. 64
Loser Takes All. London: 1955. V. 63
The Man Within. 1929. V. 63
The Man Within. New York: 1929. V. 64; 66
May We Borrow Your Husband?. London: 1967. V. 63; 64; 67
Ministry of Fear. London: 1942. V. 62
Mr. Visconti - an Extract from Travels With My Aunt. London: 1969. V. 63; 64; 66
Monsignor Quixote. London: 1982. V. 63; 66
Monsignor Quixote. New York: 1982. V. 64; 67
The Monster of Capri. Helsinki: 1985. V. 63
The Name of Action. London: 1930. V. 62; 63; 66
The New House. Helsinki: 1988. V. 63
19 Stories. London: 1947. V. 63; 65
19 Stories. New York: 1949. V. 64; 66
The Old School: Essays by Divers Hands. London: 1934. V. 63; 66
Our Man in Havana. London: 1958. V. 62; 63; 64; 66
The Pleasure-Dome, the Collected Film Criticism 1935-1940 of Graham Greene. London: 1972. V. 63
The Potting Shed - a Play in Three Acts. London: 1957. V. 62
The Potting Shed - A Play in Three Acts. New York: 1957. V. 64
The Potting Shed - a Play in Three Acts. London: 1958. V. 64
The Power and the Glory. London: 1940. V. 63
A Quick Look Behind. USA: 1983. V. 63
The Quiet American. London: 1955. V. 63
Reflections on Travels with My Aunt. New York: 1989. V. 63
The Return of A. J. Raffles. London: 1975. V. 62; 63; 66
The Revenge: an Autobiographical Fragment. London: 1963. V. 62; 63; 66
Rumour at Nightfall. 1931. V. 63
A Sense of Reality. London: 1963. V. 62; 63; 64; 67
I Sista Rummet. (The Living-Room). Sweden: 1952. V. 63
A Sort of Life. London: 1971. V. 63; 67
The Spy's Bedside Book. London: 1957. V. 63; 64; 66
Stamboul Train. London: 1932. V. 62; 63; 64; 66
The Third Man. New York: 1950. V. 65; 67
The Third Man. Helsinki: 1988. V. 63
The Third Man and the Fallen Idol. London: 1950. V. 63
Travels With My Aunt. London: 1969. V. 64; 66
Travels with My Aunt. New York: 1969. V. 67
Tueur a Gages. (A Gun for Sale). Paris: 1947. V. 62
The Virtue of Disloyalty. London: 1972. V. 63; 66
A Visit to Morin. London: 1959. V. 63; 64; 66
A Visit to Morin. London: 1960. V. 62
Ways of Escape. Canada: 1980. V. 63
Ways of Escape. London: 1980. V. 63
A Wedding Among the Owls: an Extract from the Human Factor. London: 1977. V. 63; 66
A Weed Among the Flowers. USA: 1990. V. 63
Why the Epigraph?. London: 1989. V. 63
Yes and No. Helsinki: 1983. V. 62; 63; 65
Yes and No. (and) For Whom the Bell Chimes. London: 1983. V. 63

GREENE, HOMER
Burnham Breaker. London: 1888. V. 65

GREENE, HON. MRS.
The Grey House on the Hill. London: 1906. V. 62

GREENE, JOHN
The Privileges of the Lord Mayor and Aldermen of the City. London: 1722. V. 64

GREENE, JONATHAN H.
A Desperado in Arizona 1858-160, or the Life, Trial, Death and Confession of Samuel H. Calhoun.... Santa Fe: 1964. V. 64

GREENE, KATHERINE G.
Winchester, Virginia and its Beginnings 1743-1814. Strasburg: 1926. V. 63

GREENE, KATHLEEN CONYNGHAM
China Cats and Other Beasts in Rhyme. London: 1927. V. 67

GREENE, ROBERT
Dramatic Works. London: 1831. V. 62; 65

GREENE, S. N.
Sacred Songs and Hymns. Oklahoma City: 1944?. V. 67
Songs that Last. Healdton: 1955. V. 67

GREENE, TALBOT
American Nights' Entertainments.... Jonesborough: 1860. V. 62; 67

GREENE, W. T.
Birds I Have Kept in Years Gone By.... London: 1885. V. 63; 67

GREENE, WILLIAM B.
Remarks On the Science of History. Boston: 1849. V. 64

GREENE, WILLIAM HOWE
The Wooden Walls Among the Ice Floes Telling the Romance of the Newfoundland Seal Fishery. London: 1933. V. 65

GREENER, W. W.
The Breech-Loader and How to Use It. London: 1892. V. 67
The Breech-Loader and How to Use It. 1893. V. 62; 63
The Breech-Loader and How to Use It. 1899. V. 62; 63
The Gun and it's Development. 1881. V. 63
The Gun and Its Development. London: 1899. V. 66; 67
Modern Shot Guns. 1888. V. 62

GREENEWALT, CRAWFORD
Hummingbirds. 1960. V. 62; 63; 64; 66; 67
Hummingbirds. Garden City: 1960. V. 63; 67
Hummingbirds. New York: 1960. V. 63; 66

GREENFIELD, JOSEPH GODWIN
The Cerebro-Spinal Fluid in Clinical Diagnosis. London: 1925. V. 65

GREENHILL, BASIL
The Coastal Trade. 1975. V. 64
The Schooner Bertha L. Downs. London: 1995. V. 67

GREENHILL, ELIZABETH
Elizabeth Greenhill Bookbinder. A Catalogue Raisonne. 1986. V. 66

GREENHOW, ROBERT
The History of Oregon and California and the Other Territories on the Northwest Coast of North America. Boston: 1845. V. 65

GREENISH, HENRY G.
A Text Book of Materia Medica. London: 1929. V. 64

GREENLEAF, LAWRENCE N.
King Sham. New York: 1868. V. 66

GREENLEAF, SIMON
A Collection of Cases Overruled, Denied, Doubted or Limited in Their Application, Taken from American and English Reports. New York: 1840. V. 65

GREENLEAF, STEPHEN
State's Evidence. New York: 1982. V. 67

GREENOUGH, G. B.
A Critical Examination of the First Principles of Geology. London: 1819. V. 62

GREENOUGH, SARAH
Alfred Stieglitz: Photographs and Writings. Washington: 1983. V. 63
Robert Frank: Moving Out. Washington: 1994. V. 63

GREENOUGH, SARAH DANA
Treason at Home. London: 1865. V. 65

GREENUP, GWORDIE
Cumbria Rhymes.... Workington: 1876. V. 65
Cumbria Rhymes.... Dumfries: 1921. V. 64

GREENWALT, EMMETT
The Point Loma Community in California 1897-1942. Berkeley: 1955. V. 63; 65

GREENWAY, J. C.
Extinct and Vanishing Birds of the World. New York: 1958. V. 67

GREENWELL, DORA
The Patience of Hope. Boston: 1862. V. 66
Poems. London: 1848. V. 67

GREENWELL, G. C.
A Practical Treatise on Mine Engineering. Newcastle-upon-Tyne: 1855. V. 65; 66
A Practical Treatise on Mine Engineering. London: 1869. V. 64; 65; 67
A Practicl Treatise on Mine Engineering. Newcastle: 1892. V. 62

GREENWELL, WILLIAM
British Barrows. Oxford: 1877. V. 62; 66

GREENWICH HOSPTIAL
Commission. London: 1695. V. 62

GREENWOOD, GEORGE W.
Golf Really Explained. London. V. 64

GREENWOOD, ISAAC J.
The Revolutionary Services of John Greenwood of Boston and New York. New York: 1922. V. 66; 67

GREENWOOD, JAMES
Curiosities of Savage Life. London: 1863. V. 62; 67
The Hatchet Throwers. London: 1866. V. 63; 66
Journeys through London or Byways of Modern Babylon. London: 1876?. V. 62
Legends of Savage Life. London: 1867. V. 62
Legends of Savage Life. London: 1869. V. 62
The London Vocabulary, English and Latin. London: 1782. V. 66
Wild Sports of the World. 1870. V. 66; 67

GREENWOOD, JEREMY
Omega Cuts. London: 1998. V. 62
Omega Cuts. Woodbridge, Suffolk: 1998. V. 62

GREENWOOD, JOHN
Greenwood's Picture of Hull. Hull: 1835. V. 66
The Revolutionary Services of John Greenwood of Boston and New York. New York: 1922. V. 63

GREENWOOD, MARTIN
The Designs of William De Morgan. A Catalogue. Ilminster: 1989. V. 66

GREENWOOD, P. H.
The Haplochromine Fishes of the East African Lakes. Ithaca: 1981. V. 65

GREENWOOD, ROBERT
The California Outlaw Tiburcio Vasquez. Los Gatos: 1960. V. 63; 64; 66

GREENWOOD, THOMAS
Grace Montrose. London: 1886. V. 67
Public Libraries: a History of the Movement and a Manual for the Organization and Management of Rare-Supported Libraries. London: 1890. V. 65

GREENWOOD, W.
The Redmans of Levens and Harewood. Kendal: 1905. V. 64; 66

GREENWOOD, WALTER
Standing Room Only. London: 1936. V. 66

GREEPE, THOMAS
The True and Perfecte Newes of the Woorthy and Valiaunt Exploytes, Performed and Doone by the Valiant Knight Syr Frauncis Drake.... Hartford: 1955. V. 62; 63; 64

GREER, GERMAINE
The Female Eunuch. New York: 1971. V. 65

GREER, JAMES K.
Bois D'Arc to Barbed Wire, Ken Cary Southwestern Pioneer 1850-1896. Dallas: 1936. V. 64; 67
Buck Barry Texas Ranger. Dallas: 1932. V. 63; 66
Colonel Jack Hays. New York: 1952. V. 63; 66
Early in the Saddle. Dallas: 1936. V. 64; 67

GREER, ROBERT
The Devil's Hatband. New York: 1996. V. 67

GREEVER, IDA R.
Sketches of Early Burke's Garden. Radford: 1974. V. 63

GREFUSIS, VIOLET
Don't Look Round: Her Reminiscences. London: 1952. V. 64

GREG, R. P.
Manual of the Mineralogy of Great Britain and Ireland. 1858. V. 62

GREG, ROBERT HYDE
A Letter (to) the Right Hon. Henry Labouchere, on the Repeal of the Corn Laws and Sliding Scale, More especially Upon the Manufacturing Interests and Productive Classes. London: 1842. V. 62

GREG, W. W.
A Bibliography of the English Printed Drama to the Restoration. London: 1939,. V. 66

GREG, WILLIAM RATHBONE
Enigma of Life. London: 1873. V. 64

GREGER, DEBORA
Cartography. Lisbon: 1980. V. 66
Provisional Landscapes: Picture Postcards. Lisbon: 1974. V. 64

GREGG, HILDA CAROLINE
An Uncrowned King; a Romance of High Politics. Edinburgh: 1896. V. 67

GREGG, JACOB RAY
Pioneer Days in Malheur County. Los Angeles: 1950. V. 67

GREGG, JOSIAH
Commerce of the Prairies. New York: 1844. V. 66
Commerce of the Prairies. Norman: 1954. V. 66
Diaries and Letters of Josiah Gregg. Volume I. Southwest Enterprises 1840-1847. Volume II. Excursions in Mexico and California. 1847-1850. Norman: 1941-1944. V. 65

GREGG, KATE L.
The Road to Santa Fe.... Albuquerque: 1952. V. 67

GREGG, LINDA
Eight Poems. Port Townsend: 1982. V. 63

GREGG, R. E.
The Ants of Colorado, with Reference to Their Ecology, Taxonomy and Geographic Distribution. Boulder: 1963. V. 63

GREGG, THOMAS
How to Raise Fruits. New York: 1877. V. 64

GREGO, JOSEPH
Pictorial Pickwickiana, Charles Dickens and His Illustrators. London: 1899. V. 62; 64
The Royal Naval Exhibition. Humorous Art; the Social Aspects of Life in the Royal Navy. London: 1891. V. 65

GREGORIE, ANNE KING
Thomas Sumter. Columbia: 1931. V. 66

GREGORIUS I
Dialogi. Vita. (In Italian). Venice: 1475. V. 62

GREGOROVIUS, FERDINAND
Corsica: Picturesuqe, Historical and Social.... Philadelphia: 1855. V. 65
Wanderings in Corsica: Its History and Its Heroes. Edinburgh: 1855. V. 66

GREGORY, ALYSE
Hester Craddock. London: 1931. V. 64

GREGORY, DAVID
The Elements of Physical and Geometrical Astronomy. London: 1726. V. 66

GREGORY, DICK
Dick Gregory's Political Primer. New York: 1972. V. 66

GREGORY, G.
A Dictionary of Arts and Sciences. London: 1806-1807. V. 64

GREGORY, GEORGE
Facts and Important Information of Young Men on the Subject of Masturbation with Its Causes, Prevention and Cure. Boston: 1846. V. 62

GREGORY, ISABELLA AUGUSTA PERSE
Gods and Fighting Men. 1904. V. 65
Ideals in Ireland. 1901. V. 62; 65
The Kiltartan History Book. Dublin;: 1909. V. 63
The Kiltartan Poetry Book: Prose Translations from the Irish. Dublin: 1918. V. 62
The Kiltartan Wonder Book. 1910. V. 62
The Kiltartan Wonder Book. London: 1910. V. 65
Kincora; a Drama in Three Acts. New York: 1905. V. 66
Lady Gregory's Journals 1916-1930. 1946. V. 67
Mr. Gregory's Letter-Box 1813-1830. 1898. V. 62
Visions and Beliefs in the West of Ireland. New York and London: 1920. V. 66

GREGORY, J. W.
Dalradian Geology. The Dalradian Rocks of Scotland and Their Equivalents in Other Countries. 1931. V. 67
The Dead Heart of Australia; a Journey Around Lake Eyre in the Summer of 1901-1902.... London: 1906. V. 67
The Rift Valleys and Geology of East Africa. 1921. V. 67

GREGORY, JAMES
Conspectus Medicinae Theoreticae: or a View of the Theory of Medicine. Edinburgh: 1833. V. 64

GREGORY, JOHN
A Comparative View of the State and Faculties of Man With those of the Animal World. London: 1766. V. 63; 67
Elements of the Practice of Physic. Edinburgh and London: 1788. V. 65
A Father's Legacy to His Daughter. London: 1788. V. 63

GREGORY, JOHN WALTER
Australasia. London: 1907-1908. V. 62

GREGORY, JOSEPH W.
Gregory's Guide for California Travellers Via the Isthmus of Panama. San Francisco: 1949. V. 63; 66

GREGORY, SINDA
Private Investigations: the Novels of Dashiell Hammett. Carbondale: 1985. V. 67

GREGORY, WILLIAM
Animal Magnetism or Mesmerisim and its Phenomena. London: 1909. V. 63

GREGORY, WILLIAM K.
Evolution Emerging, a Survey of Changing Patterns from Primeval Life to Man. New York: 1951. V. 63
The Henry Cushier Raven Memorial Volume. The Anatomy of the Gorilla. New York: 1950. V. 66
In Quest of Gorillas. New Bedford: 1937. V. 66

GREGORY, WINIFRED
List of the Serial Publications of Foreign Governments 1815-1931. New York: 1932. V. 62

GREGORY NAZIANENSIS, SAINT
Operum Gregorii Nazianzeni Tomi Tres...Qua Interpretationem, Qua Veteres ad Libros Collationem, Elaborata est per Ioannem Levvenklaium.... Basiliae: 1571. V. 66

GREGORY THE GREAT, SAINT
Beatissimi Gregorii Pape Totius Ecclestie Luminis Preclarissimi: In Septe Psalmos Penietetiales Explanatio Admodum Vtilis cu Tabula Materiarum. Lyons: 1516. V. 62
Pastoralis Cure Liber Diui Gregorii Pape in Qua Tuor Tantum Divid fus Partes. Lyons: 1516. V. 62

GREGSON, MATTHEW
History of Lancashire. Liverpool: 1817-1824. V. 66
Portfolio of Fragments Relative to the History and Antiquities, Topography and Genealogies of the...Duchy of Lancaster. London: 1869. V. 65

GREGYNOG PRESS
The Miss Margaret Sidney Davies Complete Collection of Special Gregynog Bindings. 1995. V. 67

GREIG, ALEXANDER M.
Fate of the Blenden Hall; East Indiaman, Bound to Bombay, with an Account of Her Wreck and Sufferings and Privations Endured by the Survivors, for Six Months.... New York: 1847. V. 67

GRELLMANN, HENRICH MORITZ GOTTLIEB
Dissertation on the Gipsies.... London: 1787. V. 66

GRENFELL, JOYCE
George - Don't Do That. London: 1977. V. 65

GRENFELL, JULIAN
Pages From a Family Journal. London: 1916. V. 66

GRENFELL PRESS
The Grenfell Press, Typefaces &c. New York: 1980. V. 62; 64

GRENFELL, WILFRED THOMASON
Adrift on an Ice-Pan. London/Boston: 1910. V. 63
Forty Years for Labrador. Boston and New York: 1932. V. 64
Forty Years For Labrador. London: 1933. V. 64
A Labrador Doctor. London: 1920. V. 62
Labrador: the Country and the People. New York: 1922. V. 63
The Romance of Labrador. New York: 1934. V. 64
What Christ Means to Me. Boston and New York: 1927. V. 64

GRENVILLE, WILLIAM WYNDHAM GRENVILLE, BARON
Considerations on the Establishment of a Regency.... London: 1788. V. 62
Essay on the Supposed Advantages of a Sinking Fund. London: 1828. V. 64; 66

GRESE, R. E.
Jens Jensen, Maker of Natural Parks and Gardens. Baltimore: 1992. V. 67

GRESHAM, OTTO
The Greenbacks or the Money that won the Civil War and the World War. Chicago: 1927. V. 65

GRESHAM, WILLIAM LINDSAY
Limbo Tower. 1949. V. 67

GRESLEY, RICHARD N.
A Treatise on the Law of Evidence in the Courts of Equity. Philadelphia: 1848. V. 67

GRESLEY, WILLIAM
Church-Clavering; or, the Schoolmaster. London: 1843. V. 67
The Forest of Arden: a Tale Illustrative of the English Reformation. London: 1842. V. 67

GRESTY, JOHN
Gresty's Illustrated Chester, Consisting of Eight Large Chromolithographic Views from Photos, with a Plan of the City, Descriptive Letterpress.... Chester: 1862. V. 62; 66

GRESWEL, W.
The Forests and Deer Parks of Somerset. Taunton: 1905. V. 62

GRESWELL, WILLIAM PARR
Annals of Parisian Typography. London: 1818. V. 64; 66

GREUB, SUZANNE
Art of Northwest New Guinea. New York: 1992. V. 64

GREVILLE, CHARLES C.
Past and Present: Policy of England Towards Ireland. London: 1845. V. 67

GREVILLE, CHARLES CAVENDISH FULKE
The Greville Memoirs. London: 1874-1885. V. 64
The Greville Memoirs. London: 1888. V. 62
A Journal of the Reign of Queen Victoria from 1837 to 1852. London: 1885. V. 64

GREVILLE, FULKE
Maxims, Characters and Reflections, Critical, Satyrical and Moral. London: 1756. V. 64
Maxims, Characters and Reflections, Critical, Satyrical and Moral. London: 1757. V. 63; 67
Selected Poems. London: 1968. V. 62

GREVILLE, R. K.
Scottish Cryptogamic Flora, or...A Continuation of (Sowerby's) English Botany. Edinburgh: 1823-1828. V. 64; 65; 66

GREVILLE, VIOLET
Ladies in the Field. Sketches of Sport. London: 1900. V. 63

GREW, JOSEPH
Ten Years in Japan. New York: 1944. V. 67

GREW, NEHEMIAH
Anatomie des Plantes qui Contient une Description Exacte de Leurs Parties & de Leurs Usages.... Paris: 1675. V. 65
Anatomie des Plantes Qui Contient une Description Exacte de Leurs Parties & de Leurs Usages.... Cambridge: 1901-1906. V. 67
The Anatomy of Plants.... 1682. V. 63
The Anatomy of Plants.... London: 1682. V. 62
An Idea of a Phytological History Propounded Together with a Continuation of the Anatomy of Vegetables.... London: 1673. V. 64
Musaeum Regalis Societatis. 1681. V. 65; 66
Musaeum Regalis Societatis. London: 1681. V. 62; 65

GREY, C.
The Early Years of His Royal Highness the Prince Consort Compiled Under the Direction of Her Majesty the Queen. London: 1867. V. 66

GREY, CHARLES HENRY
Hardy Bulbs. 1937-1938. V. 62
Hardy Bulbs.... London: 1937-1938. V. 64; 67

GREY, EARL
Ireland. The Cause of Its Present Condition and the Measures Proposed for Its Improvement. 1888. V. 63

GREY, EDWARD GREY, 1ST VISCOUNT
Fly Fishing. London: 1899. V. 67

GREY, ELIZABETH CAROLINE
Passages in the Life of a Young Lady. London: 1862. V. 65
Two Hearts: a Tale. London: 1858. V. 65

GREY, GEORGE
Journals of Two Expeditions of Discovery in North-West and Western Australia; During the Years 1837, 1838 and 1839.... London: 1841. V. 67

GREY, HENRY GEORGE, 3RD EARL OF
Parliamentary Government Considered With Reference to a Reform of Parliament. London: 1858. V. 64

GREY, HERACLITUS
Playing Trades. London: 1870. V. 62

GREY, LOREN
Zane Grey's Odyssey. 1991. V. 67

GREY, RICHARD
Memoria Technica; or a New Method of Artificial Memory Applied to.... Wolverhampton. 1790. V. 62
A System of English Ecclesiastical Law. In the Savoy: 1762. V. 65

GREY, ZACHARY
Remarks Upon a Late Edition of Shakespear, with a Long List of Emendations Borrowed by the Celebrated Editor, from the Oxford Edition.... London: 1751. V. 62

GREY, ZANE
Adventures of a Deep Sea Angler. 1991. V. 62; 63; 65; 67
An American Angler in Australia. 1991. V. 62; 63; 65; 67
The Arizona Clan. New York: 1958. V. 66
The Fugitive Trail. New York: 1957. V. 66
Horse Heaven Hill. New York: 1959. V. 66
The Last of the Plainsmen. London: 1908. V. 62
The Story of Buffalo Jones - the Last of the Plainsmen. New York: 1908. V. 62
Tales of an Angler's Eldorado - New Zealand. 1991. V. 62; 63; 65; 67
Tales of Fishes. 1991. V. 62; 63; 65; 67
Tales of Fishing Virgin Seas. 1990. V. 62; 63; 65; 67
Tales of Fresh-Water Fishing. New York: 1928. V. 63
Tales of Southern Rivers. 1991. V. 62; 63; 65
Tales of Swordfish and Tuna. 1927. V. 67

GRIBBLE, FRANCIS
The Early Mountaineers. London: 1899. V. 63

GRIBBLE, R. B.
Black, but Comely; or Glimpses of Aboriginal Life in Australia. London: 1884. V. 67

GRIDLEY, MARION E.
Indians of Yesterday. Chicago: 1940. V. 67

GRIEG, JOHN
Scots Minstrelsie, a National Monument of Scottish Song. Edinburgh: 1893. V. 67

GRIERSON, GEORGE A.
An Introduction to the Maithili Language of North Bihar. Calcutta: 1882. V. 63

GRIERSON, M.
An English Florilegium, Flowers, Trees, Shrubs, Fruits, Herbs, the Tradescant Legacy. 1987. V. 63; 66
An English Florilegium, Flowers, Trees, Shrubs, Fruits, Herbs, the Tradescant Legacy. London: 1987. V. 64

GRIERSON, THOMAS
Autumnal Rambles Among the Scottish Mountains or Pedestrian Tourist's Friend. Edinburgh: 1850. V. 62; 63

GRIESINGER, WILHELM
Mental Pathology and Therapeutics. London: 1867. V. 65

GRIEVE, CHRISTOPHER MURRAY
Burns Today and Tomorrow. Edinburgh: 1959. V. 62
A Centenary Study. Glasgow. V. 62
Cunninghame Graham - A Centenary Study. Glasgow: 1952. V. 65
Early Lyrics. Preston, Lancashire: 1968. V. 62
The Fire of the Spirit. Glasgow: 1965. V. 62
The Islands of Scotland - Hebrides, Orkneys and Shetlands. London: 1939. V. 62
The Kind of Poetry I Want: a Long Poem. Edinburgh: 1961. V. 62
A Kist of Whistles: New Poems. Glasgow: 1947. V. 63

GRIEVE, CHRISTOPHER MURRAY continued
A Lap Of Honour. London: 1967. V. 63
The Lucky Bag. Edinburgh: 1927. V. 63
Northern Numbers.... London and Edinburgh: 1920. V. 64
Sangshaw. Edinburgh and London: 1925. V. 65
Scots Unbound and Other Poems. Stirling: 1932. V. 63
Scottish Eccentrics. London: 1936. V. 65
Second Hymn to Lenin. Thakeham: 1932. V. 63
Selected Poems. Glasgow: 1944. V. 63
Stony Limits and Other Poems. London: 1934. V. 65
Sydney Goodsir Smith. Edinburgh: 1963. V. 62
To Circumjack Cencrastus, or the Curly Snake: a Long Poem. Edinburgh and London: 1930. V. 66

GRIEVE, JAMES
The History of Kamtschatka and the Kurilski Islands; with the Countries Adjacent. Glocester: 1764. V. 67

GRIEVE, M., MRS.
A Modern Herbal. New York: 1971. V. 64

GRIEVE, SYMINGTON
The Great Auk or Garefowl.... London: 1885. V. 62

GRIFF
Surrendered - Some Naval War Secrets. 1920. V. 66

GRIFFEN, GEORGE BUTLER
Documents from the Sutro Collection. Los Angeles: 1891. V. 63

GRIFFIN, CHARLES E.
Traveling with a Circus. New York: 1892. V. 65

GRIFFIN, EDWARD
Strictures Upon a Publication Entitled A Brand Plucked Out of the Fire, or a Brief Account of Robert Kendall, Who Was Executed at Northampton, 13th August 1813. Nottingham: 1813. V. 62

GRIFFIN, GERALD
Card Drawing, the Half Sir, Suil Dhuv the Coiner. (Second Series). Dublin: 1857. V. 67
The Invasion. London: 1832. V. 66
Tales of My Neighborhood. London: 1835. V. 65

GRIFFIN, H. L.
An Official in British New Guinea. London: 1925. V. 67

GRIFFIN, JOHN HOWARD
The Devil Rides Outside. London: 1953. V. 63

GRIFFIN, JOHN S.
A Doctor Comes to California - The Diary of John S. Griffin, Assistant Surgeon with Kearney's Dragoons 1846-1847. San Francisco: 1943. V. 65; 67

GRIFFIN, L. C. L.
Naini Tal A Historical and Descriptive Account 1927. Allahabad;: 1928. V. 62

GRIFFIN, L. E.
The Anatomy of Nautilus Pompilius. Washington: 1898. V. 63
The Anatomy of Nautilus Pompilius. Washington: 1900. V. 62

GRIFFIN, MARTIN
Stephen Moylan, Muster-Master General, Secretary and Aide-de-Camp to Washington, Quartermaster General, Colonel of the Fourth Pennsylvania Light Dragoons and Brigadier General of the War for American Independence, the First and Last President of the Frie. Philadelphia: 1909. V. 64

GRIFFIN, ROBERT
Interest Tables on an Improved Plan. London: 1775. V. 65

GRIFFING, GORDON, & CO.
Atlas of Darke County, Ohio. Philadelphia: 1888. V. 66

GRIFFIS, JOSEPH K.
Tahan Out of Savagery into Civilization - an Autobiography. New York: 1915. V. 66

GRIFFIS, WILLIAM ELLIOT
The Mikado's Empire. New York: 1876. V. 65
The Mikado's Empire. New York: 1903. V. 62

GRIFFITH, A. KINNEY
The First Hundred Years of Nino Chochise, the Untold Story of an Apache Indian Chief. New York: 1971. V. 66

GRIFFITH, ARTHUR
Resurrection in Hungary, a Parallel for Ireland. 1918. V. 67

GRIFFITH, ELIZABETH
A Series of Genuine Letters Between Henry and Frances. London: 1757. V. 62; 65

GRIFFITH, ERNEST S.
The Modern Development of City Government in the United Kingdom and the United States. London: 1927. V. 64

GRIFFITH, GEORGE
Going to Markets and Grammar Schools, Being a Series of Autobiographical Records and Sketches of Forty Years Spent in the Midland Counties from 1830 to 1870. London: 1870. V. 62; 64
Olga Romanoff or the Syren of the Skies.... London: 1894. V. 62

GRIFFITH, J. W.
The Micrographic Dictionary. London: 1860. V. 67
The Micrographic Dictionary. 1883. V. 66
The Micrographic Dictionary. London: 1883. V. 62; 64

GRIFFITH, JOHN
A Journal of the Life, Travels and Labours in the Work of the Ministry of John Griffith. London: 1779. V. 63; 67
A Journal of the Life, Travels and Labours in the Work of the Ministry of John Griffith. London: 1780. V. 63

GRIFFITH, L. W.
Spring of Youth. London: 1935. V. 63

GRIFFITH, R.
Notice Respecting the Fossils of the Mountain Limestone of Ireland, as Compared with Those of Great Britain. Dublin: 1842. V. 62

GRIFFITH, S. Y.
Griffith's New Historical Description of Cheltenham and Its Vicinity. Cheltenham: 1826. V. 62; 66

GRIFFITH, WILLIAM
History of Kansas City - Illustrated in Three Decades. Kansas City: 1900. V. 64; 67

GRIFFITHS, ARTHUR
The Chronicles of Newgate. London: 1884. V. 63
Memorials of Millbank, and Chapters in Prison History. London: 1875. V. 63; 65
Mysteries of Police and Crime. New York: 1899. V. 64
Mysteries of Police and Crime. London: 1902. V. 63

GRIFFITHS, MAJOR ARTHUR
Ford's Folly, Ltd. London: 1900. V. 66

GRIFFITHS, MAURICE
Little Ships and Shoal Waters. London: 1937. V. 62

GRIFFITHS, ROGER
A Description of the River Thames &c. with the City of London's Jurisdiction and Conservancy Thereof Proved in Point of Right and Usage by Presecription, Charters, Acts of Parliament, Decrees Upon Hering Before the King, Letters Patent, &c.... London: 1758. V. 63

GRIFFITHS, SAMUEL
Important Case. Report of a Trial Which Took Place at the Guildhall County Court, London, on Friday, July 13, 1849. The Public and Medical Men. Griffiths v. Walford. Wolverhampton: 1849. V. 63

GRIFFITHS, W. H.
Lessons on Prescriptions and the Art of Prescribing. London: 1880. V. 67

GRIGGS, GEORGE
History of the Mesilla Valley or the Gadsden Purchase. Mesilla: 1930. V. 65

GRIGGS, NATHAN K.
Lyrics of the Lariat. Chicago: 1893. V. 62; 65

GRIGGS, R. F.
The Valley of Ten Thousand Smokes. Washington: 1922. V. 64

GRIGSBY, HUGH BLAIR
Letters by a South Carolinian. Norfolk: 1827. V. 63; 66
The Virginia Convention of 1776. A Discourse Delivered Before the Virginia Alpha of the Phi Beta Kappa Society. Richmond: 1855. V. 63

GRIGSON, G.
Recollections Mainly of Writers and Artists. London: 1984. V. 63

GRIGSON, GEOFFREY
About Britain. London: 1951. V. 66
The Englishman's Flora. London: 1955. V. 62
A Master of Our Time - a Study of Wyndham Lewis. London: 1951. V. 62
Visionary Poems and Passages; or, the Poet's Eye. London: 1944. V. 65

GRIMALDI, JOSEPH
Memoirs of Joseph Grimaldi. London: 1838. V. 62; 64; 65; 66; 67
Songs, Choruses, &c. In the New Pantomime Called Harlequin and Mother Goose or the Golden Egg. London: 1807. V. 66

GRIMALDI, STACEY
A Suit of Armour for Youth. London: 1824. V. 67

GRIMALKIN
Cats. London: 1901. V. 62

GRIMBLE, AUGUSTUS
Highland Sport. 1894. V. 62
More Leaves From My Game Book. London: 1917. V. 67
The Salmon Rivers of England and Wales. 1913. V. 67
The Salmon Rivers of England and Wales and Scotland. London: 1913. V. 64
The Salmon Rivers of Ireland. London: 1913. V. 62
The Salmon Rivers of Scotland. London: 1913. V. 67
Shooting and Salmon Fishing. London: 1892. V. 67

GRIMBLE, SAMUEL
A Treatise on Deportment, Fencing &c. Including the Science of Horesemanship.... Derby: 1829. V. 66

GRIMES, ABSALOM
Absalom Grimes, Confederate Mail Runner. New Haven: 1926. V. 62; 63; 65

GRIMES, BRYAN
Extracts of Letters of Major-Gen'l. Bryan Grimes to His Wife, Written While in Active Service in the Army of Northern Virginia. Raleigh: 1883. V. 62; 63; 65
Notes on Colonial North Carolina 1700-1750. Raleigh: 1905. V. 63

GRIMES, J. STANLEY
The Mysteries of Human Nature Explained, by a New System of Nervous Physiology.... Buffalo: 1857. V. 66

GRIMES, MARTHA
The Old Fox Deceiv'd. Boston: 1982. V. 63

GRIMKE, THOMAS S.
Address on the Patriot Character of the Temperance Reformation. Charleston: 1833. V. 63
Oration on the Principal Duties of Americans.... Charleston: 1833. V. 63; 66

GRIMM, THE BROTHERS
Fairy Tales from Grimm. London: 1894. V. 67
The Fairy Tales of the Brothers Grimm. New York: 1909. V. 64
Faithful John. London: 1998. V. 62; 67
The Gay Tales from Grimm. New York: 1943. V. 62
German Popular Stories. London: 1823-1826. V. 64
German Popular Stories. London: 1882. V. 64
German Popular Stories. London: 1892. V. 63
The Golden Bird and Other Fairy Tales of the Brothers Grimm. New York: 1962. V. 67
Grimm's Fairy Tales. London: 1907. V. 64
Grimm's Fairy Tales. London: 1911. V. 62
Grimm's Fairy Tales. New York: 1914. V. 63; 66
Grimm's Fairy Tales. London: 1920. V. 64
Hansel and Gretel. New York: 1925. V. 63; 65
Household Stories. London: 1882. V. 64
Household Tales. London: 1946. V. 63
The Juniper Tree and Other Tales from Grimm. New York: 1973. V. 62
The Juniper Tree and Other Tales from Grimm. London: 1974. V. 65
Little Brother and Little Sister and Other Tales. London: 1917. V. 63
Little Brother and Little Sister and Other Tales. New York: 1917. V. 63; 64
More Tales from Grimm. New York: 1947. V. 62; 66
Rapunzel. New York: 1982. V. 65
Rumpelstiltskin. A Tale Told Long Ago by the Brothers Grimm. New York: 1973. V. 63
Rumpelstiltskin. New York: 1986. V. 65
Six Fairy Tales.... 1970. V. 63
Snowdrop and Other Tales. New York: 1923. V. 63
Tales from Grimm. New York: 1936. V. 64
Three Gay Tales from Grimm. London: 1946. V. 62
The Water of Life. New York: 1986. V. 65

GRIMM, WILHELM
Dear Mili - an Old Tale. New York: 1988. V. 65

GRIMSHAW, BEATRICE
From Fiji to the Cannibal Islands. London: 1907. V. 66; 67
In the Strange South Seas. London: 1907. V. 67
Isles of Adventure. London: 1930. V. 63

GRIMSHAW, ISAAC
Tables and Explanations Necessary To Be Got by Heart by Every Pupil Studying Arithmetic. New York: 1815. V. 64

GRIMWOOD, KEN
Breakthrough. Garden City: 1970. V. 65
Elise. New York: 1979. V. 63

GRINDLAY, MELVILLE
A View of the Present State of the Question as to Steam Communication with India.... London: 1837. V. 62

GRINDON, LEO H.
Figurative Language, Its Origin and Constitution. London: 1879. V. 64
The Manchester Flora; a Descriptive List of the Plants Growing Wild Within Eighteen Miles of Manchester. London and Manchester: 1859. V. 62

GRINDROD, MRS.
Siam; General and Medical Features. Bangkok: 1930. V. 67

GRINFIELD, E. W.
An Apology for the Septuagint, In Which Claims to Biblical and Canonical Authority are Briefly Stated and Vindicated. London: 1850. V. 67

GRINNELL, GEORGE BIRD
American Duck Shooting. New York: 1901. V. 64
American Duck Shooting. New York: 1918. V. 65
American Game Bird Shooting. New York: 1910. V. 65
Beyond the Old Frontier. New York: 1913. V. 63; 65; 66
Blackfeet Indian Stories. New York: 1913. V. 65
By Cheyenne Campfires. New Haven: 1926. V. 63
The Cheyenne Indians, Their History and Ways of Life. New Haven: 1923. V. 65; 67
The Cheyenne Indians, Their History and Ways of Life. New York: 1962. V. 65
The Fighting Cheyenne. New York: 1915. V. 65
The Fighting Cheyenne. Norman: 1915. V. 67
Hunting Trails on Three Continents. New York: 1933. V. 67
Pawnee Hero Stories and Folk Tales. New York: 1889. V. 64; 67
The Story of the Indian. New York: 1895. V. 65
When Buffalo Ran. New Haven: 1923. V. 64
The Wolf Hunters, A Story of the Buffalo Plains. New York: 1924. V. 65

GRINNELL, JOSEPH
Animal Life in the Yosemite, an Account of the Mammals, Birds, Reptiles, and Amphibians in a Cross-Section of the Sierra Nevada. Berkeley: 1924. V. 64
The Biota of the San Bernardino Mountains. Berkeley: 1908. V. 63
A Distributional Summation of the Ornithology of Lower California. Berkeley: 1928. V. 64
Gold Hunting in Alaska. Elgin: 1901. V. 63; 66

GRINSTEIN, ALEXANDER
The Index of Psychoanalytic Writings. New York: 1956-1975. V. 66

GRISCOM, JOHN
A Year in Europe. Comprising a Journal of Observations in England, Scotland, Ireland, France, Switzerland, The North of Italy and Holland in 1818 and 1819. New York: 1823. V. 63; 64

GRISCOM, L.
The Warblers of America, a Popular Account of the Wood Warblers as They Occur in the Western Hemisphere. New York: 1957. V. 67

GRISEBACH, A. H. R.
Flora of the British West Indian Islands. London: 1864. V. 65

GRISHAM, JOHN
The Brethren. New York: 2000. V. 67
The Chamber. New York: 1994. V. 63
The Client. New York: 1993. V. 67
The Firm. New York: 1991. V. 62; 64; 65; 66
The Firm. New York: 1993. V. 63
The Pelican Brief. New York: 1992. V. 67
The Runaway Jury. New York: 1996. V. 67

GRISON, THEOPHILE
Le Teinturier au XIX Siecle. Rouen: 1860. V. 67

GRISSO, W. D.
From Where the Sun Now Stands; Addresses by a Posse of Famous Western Speakers. Santa Fe: 1963. V. 64

GRISSOM, BETTY
Starfall. New York: 1974. V. 67

GRISSOM, MARY ALLEN
The Negro Sings a New Heaven. Chapel Hill: 1930. V. 66

GRISWOLD, M.
The Golden Age of American Gardens, Proud Owners, Private Estates, 1890-1940. New York: 1991. V. 64; 67

GRISWOLD, P. R.
Colorado's Loneliest Railroad, The San Louis Southern. Boulder: 1980. V. 66

GRISWOLD, RUFUS WILMOT
The Female Poets of America. New York: 1873. V. 67
The Poets and Poetry of America. Philadelphia: 1842. V. 65
The Republican Court; or American Society in the Days of Washington. New York: 1855. V. 64

GRIT and Go. New York: 1902. V. 67

GRIVAS, THEODORE
Military Governments in California 1846-1850. Glendale: 1963. V. 63

GRIVOLIN, JEANNE AURELIE
Breviary of Love:...Private Journal Written at Lyon and Cherbourg During the Years 1802-1803. London: 1938. V. 64

THE GROANS of the Talents.... London: 1807. V. 62

GROBERT, J. F. L.
Description des Travaux Executes Pour le Deplacement, Transport et Elevation des Groupes de Coustou.... Paris: 1795-1796. V. 65

GROCE, GEORGE C.
The New York Historical Society's Dictionary of Artists in America 1564-1860. New Haven: 1957. V. 63
The New York Historical Society's Dictionary of Artists in America, 1564-1860. New Haven: 1969. V. 62

THE GROCER'S Companion and Merchant's Handbook. Boston: 1883. V. 63

GROENEN, LIEVIN
Illustrated Marine Encyclopedia English - French - Dutch. Antwerp: 1926. V. 64

GROENING, MATT
Life in Hell. 1982. V. 65

GROENVELT, JOHN
The Rudiments of Physick Clearly and Accurately Describ'd and Explain'd, In the Most Easy and Familiar Manner.... London: 1753. V. 66

GROGAN, EMMETT
Ringolevio - a Life Played for Keeps. Boston and Toronto: 1972. V. 64

GROGAN, EWART S.
From the Cape to Cairo, the First Traverse of Africa from South to North. London: 1900. V. 67

GROHMANN, WILL
Paul Klee. New York: 1954. V. 66
Wassily Kandinsky. Leipzig: 1924. V. 63

GROHMANN, WILL continued
Wassily Kandinsky. New York: 1958. V. 62; 63
Das Werk Ernst Kirchner. Munich: 1926. V. 66

GROLIER, JEAN
Bookbindings from the Library of Jean Grolier. London: 1965. V. 67

GROLIER CLUB, NEW YORK.
The Books of Antonio Frasconi, a Selection 1945-1995. New York: 1996. V. 62
Catalogue of Original and Early Editions of Some of the Poetical and Prose Works of English Writers from Wither to Prior. New York: 1905. V. 62
A Description of the Early Printed Books Owned by the Grolier Club with a Brief Account of Their Printers and the History of Typography in the Fifteenth Century. New York: 1895. V. 62
An Exhibition Illustrative of the Text of Shakespeare's Plays. New York: 1916. V. 62
Fifty-Five Books Printed Before 1515, Representing the Works of England's First Printers. An Exhibition from the Collection of Paul Mellon. Jan. 17 - March 3, 1968. New York: 1968. V. 66
Lists of Publications 1884-1905 Exhibition Catalogues 1886-1905. New York: 1906. V. 65
One Hundred Books Famous in Medicine. New York: 1995. V. 63; 65
Printers' Choice: Catalogue of an Exhibition Held at the Grolier Club, New York December 19, 1978-February 3, 1979. Austin: 1983. V. 64

GROMEK, R. H.
Remains of Nithsdale and Galloway Song; with Historical and Traditional Notices Relative to the Manners and Customs of the Peasantry. London: 1810. V. 63

GROMME, O. J.
Birds of Wisconsin. Madison: 1963. V. 64; 67

GROOM, ARTHUR
Gran'Pop's Annual. London: 1950. V. 63; 65

GROOM, WINSTON
As Summers Die. New York: 1980. V. 67
Better Times Than These. New York: 1978. V. 63
Forrest Gump. Garden City: 1986. V. 67
Forrest Gump. New York: 1986. V. 66
Gump and Co. Franklin Center: 1995. V. 63

GROSBOIS, CHARLES
Shunga: Images of Spring, Essay on Erotic Elements in Japanese Art. Geneva: 1964. V. 66

GROSE, D.
The Flora of Wiltshire. 1957-1975. V. 63; 66
The Flora of Wiltshire. London: 1957-1975. V. 64

GROSE, FRANCIS
Advice to the Officers of the British Army.... London: 1783. V. 63
The Antiquities of England and Wales. London: 1773-1777. V. 63
The Antiquities of Ireland. 1791-1795. V. 67
The Antiquities of Ireland. London: 1796. V. 67
The Antiquities of Scotland. London: 1797. V. 67
A Classical Dictionary of the Vulgar Tongue. London: 1785. V. 67
A Classical Dictionary of the Vulgar Tongue. London: 1788. V. 64
A Classical Dictionary of the Vulgar Tongue. London: 1796. V. 66
Classical Dictionary of the Vulgar Tongue, Revised and Corrected.... London: 1823. V. 64
A Classical Dictionary of the Vulgar Tongue.... London: 1931. V. 63; 64
A Glossary of Provincial and Local Words Used in England. London: 1839. V. 64
Lexicon Balatronicum. A Dictionary of Buckish Slang, University Wit, and Pickpocket Eloquence. London: 1811. V. 64
Military Antiquities Respecting a History of the English Army. (with) A Treatise on Ancient Armour and Weapons. London: 1801. V. 65
The Olio; Being a Collection of Essays, Dialogues, Letters, Biographical Sketches, Anecdotes, Pieces of Poetry, Parodies, Bon Mots, Epigrams, Epitaphs &c. London: 1792. V. 62
The Olio; Being a Collection of Essays, Dialogues, Letters, Biographical Sketches, Anecdotes, Pieces of Poetry, Parodies, Bon Mots, Epigrams, Epitaphs &c. London: 1796. V. 63; 64
A Provincial Glossary, with a Collection of Local Proverbs and Popular Superstitions. London: 1787. V. 64
A Provincial Glossary: with a Collection of Local Proverbs, and Popular Superstitions. London: 1790. V. 66
A Provincial Glossary; with a Collection of Local Proverbs and Popular Superstitions. London: 1811. V. 64; 66
Rules for Drawing Caricaturas; with an Essay on Comic Painting. London: 1800. V. 64

GROSE, MARQUIS OF
Horrid Mysteries. London: 1927. V: 63

GROSECLOSE, DAVID A.
A Bibliography of James Michener. Austin: 1996. V. 63; 64; 67

GROSER, THOMAS SIDNEY
The Lure of the Golden West.... London: 1927. V. 67

GROSH, A. B.
Washingtonian Pocket Companion.... Utica: 1842. V. 64

GROSJEAN, PAUL
A Catalogue of Incunabula in the Library of Milltown Park, Dublin. Dublin: 1912. V. 63

GROSLEY, PIERRE JEAN
New Observations on Italy and Its Inhabitants. London: 1759. V. 66

GROSS, A. O.
The Heath Hen. Boston: 1928. V. 64

GROSS, ALEXANDER, MRS.
Happy Billy Bunny. London. V. 63

GROSS, ROBERT E.
The Surgery of Infancy and Childhood. Philadelphia: 1953. V. 66; 67

GROSS, SAMUEL D.
Autobiography of Samuel D. Gross.... Philadelphia: 1887. V. 64
A Practical Treatise on Foreign Bodies in the Air Passages. Philadelphia: 1854. V. 66

GROSS, SAMUEL W.
Practical Treatise on Impotence, Sterility and Allied Disorders of the Male Sexual Organ. Philadelphia: 1881. V. 63

GROSS, SIDNEY W.
Diagnosis and Treatment of Head Injuries. New York: 1940. V. 66

GROSS, WARREN LEE
Recollections of a Private - a Story of the Army of the Potomac. New York: 1890. V. 67

GROSSE, ERNST
Casa Rossa: Phantasie Uber das Bild von Niklaus Stoecklin. Verona: 1927. V. 62

GROSSMAN, SID
Journey to the Cape. New York: 1959. V. 63

GROSSMANN, EDITH SEARLE
A Knight of the Holy Ghost. London: 1907. V. 65

GROSSMITH, GEORGE
The Diary of a Nobody. London: 1940. V. 62

GROSSMITH, JOHN
Government Upon first Principles, Proved and Illustrated Analogically. London: 1860. V. 63

GROSVENOR, BENJAMIN
Health. An Essay on Its Nature, Value, Uncertainty, Preservation and Best Improvement. London: 1716. V. 65

GROSVENOR, EDWIN A.
Constantinople. Boston: 1900. V. 65

GROSVENOR, J. DU V.
Model Yachts and Boats, their Designing, Making and Sailing. London: 1886. V. 62

GROSZ, GEORGE
George Grosz. London: 1948. V. 65
George Grosz. New York: 1948. V. 64
A Post War Museum: Drawings. 1931. V. 63
A Post-War Museum: Drawings. London: 1931. V. 66

GROTE, GEORGE
History of Greece. London: 1851-1856. V. 62
The Minor Works. London: 1873. V. 64
Posthumous Papers.... London: 1874. V. 64

GROTE, HARRIET
The Case of the Poor Against the Rich Fairly Considered. N.P: 1850. V. 64

GROTIUS, HUGO
De Mare Libero et Merula de Maribus. Leyden: 1633. V. 66
De Veritate Religionis Christianae. Amstelodami: 1662. V. 63; 66
De Veritate Religionis Christinae. Amsterdam: 1680. V. 66
...Of the Law of Warre and Peace with Annotations...and Memorials of the Author's Life and Death. London: 1654. V. 64; 66
Sensus Librorum Sex, Quos Pro Veritate Religionis Christianae.... Leyden: 1727. V. 66
The Truth of the Christian Religion. London: 1719. V. 66

GROTIUS, WILLIAM
De Principis Juris Naturalis Enchiridion. Hagae-Comitis: 1667. V. 64; 66

GROUT, A. J.
Mosses with Hand Lens and Miscroscope. New York: 1903. V. 63

GROUX, EUGENE
Abhandlungen und Notizen Uber E. A. Groux's Fissura Sterni Congenita. Hamburg: 1857. V. 65

GROVE, D. C.
Ancient Chalcatzingo. Austin: 1987. V. 62

GROVE, H. M.
Moscow. London: 1912. V. 67

GROVE, HENRY
A Discourse Concerning the Nature and Design of the Lord's Supper. Boston: 1793. V. 67

GROVE, JOSEPH
The Lives of the Earls and Dukes of Devonshire Descended from the Renowned Sir William Cavendish.... London: 1764. V. 67

GROVE, MISS
Spithead and Portsmouth. 1845. V. 62
Spithead and Portsmouth. London: 1845. V. 66

GROVER, EULALIE OSGOOD
Kittens and Cats: A Book of Tales. Boston: 1911. V. 64
Mother Goose. Chicago: 1915. V. 63
The Overall Boys, a First Reader. Chicago: 1915. V. 63
Sunbonnet Babies A B C Book: a Modern Hornbook. New York: 1929. V. 65

GROVER, EULALIE OSGOOD continued
The Sunbonnet Babies in Holland. Chicago: 1915. V. 65

GROVER, L.
Art Glass Nouveau. Rutland: 1968. V. 65

GROVER, RAY
English Cameo Glass. New York: 1980. V. 62

GROVES, JAMES
The British Charophyta. London: 1920-1924. V. 65; 67

GROVES, WILLIAM H.
The History of Mansfield. Nottingham: 1894. V. 65

GROVES, WILLIAM JOHN
Echoes from Egypt; or, the Type of Antichirst. London: 1857. V. 63

GROWOLL, A.
Three Centuries of English Booktrade Bibliography. London: 1964. V. 67

GRUBB, DAVIS
The Night of the Hunter. New York: 1953. V. 65

GRUBB, ISABEL
J. Ernest Grubb of Carrick-on-suir. 1928. V. 67

GRUBB, MARY B.
Our Alphabet Toys. Cleveland: 1932. V. 64

GRUBB, SARAH
Some Account of the Life and Religious Labours of Sarah Grubb.... Trenton: 1795. V. 66

GRUBB, W. BARBROOKE
An Unknown People in an Unknown Land: an Account of the Life and Customs of the Lengua Indians of the Paraguayan Chaco.... Philadelphia: 1911. V. 65

GRUBER, BERNHARD
Horographia Trigonometrica seu methodus Accuratissima Arithmetice per Sinus et Tangentes Horologia Quaevis Solaria.... Prague: 1718. V. 62

GRUBER, FRANCES
William Rainey, Painter of the Early West. New York: 1962. V. 67

GRUBER, FRANK
Bugles West. New York: 1954. V. 67
Fighting Man. New York: 1948. V. 67
The Highwayman. New York: 1955. V. 67
Johnny Vengeance. New York: 1954. V. 67
The Silver Jackass. New York: 1941. V. 67
Smoky Road. New York: 1949. V. 67
The Talking Clock. New York: 1946. V. 62

GRUELLE, JOHN B.
Beloved Belindy. Joliet: 1926. V. 63
Friendly Fairies. Chicago: 1919. V. 63; 65
The Little Brown Bear. Chicago: 1920. V. 64
The Magical Land of Noom with Sundry and Mondry Illustrations. Chicago: 1922. V. 63
Marcella Stories. Joliet: 1929. V. 63
Raggedy Ann and Andy. Akron: 1944. V. 65
Raggedy Andy Stories. Chicago: 1920. V. 63
Raggedy Ann and Andy and the Nice Fat Policeman. New York: 1942. V. 63
Raggedy Ann and Maizie Moocow. N.P: 1937. V. 63
Raggedy Ann at the End of the Rainbow. New York: 1947. V. 63
Raggedy Ann Picture Story Book. Akron: 1947. V. 63
Raggedy Ann's Joyful Songs. New York: 1937. V. 63
Raggedy Ann's Magical Wishes. Joliet: 1928. V. 62
Wooden Willie. Joliet: 1927. V. 62; 66

GRUELLE, JUSTIN
A Mother Goose Parade. Joliet: 1929. V. 63

GRUFFYDD, W. J.
Caniadau. Newtown: 1932. V. 65

GRUINNESS, LUCY E.
Across India at the Dawn of the 20th Century. London: 1898. V. 65

GRUMBACH, DORIS
The Short Throat, the Tender Mouth. New York: 1964. V. 65

GRUND, JOHANN GOTTFRIED
Afbildning of Nordmands-Dalen, i den Kongelige Lyst-hauge ved Fredensborg. Copenhagen: 1773. V. 64

GRUNDYM, G. B.
Thucydides and the History of His Age. Oxford: 1948. V. 65

GRUNER, L.
The Decorations of the Garden Pavilion...Buckingham Palace. London: 1846. V. 66
The Green Vaults, Dresden: Illustrations of the Choicest Works in that Museum of Art. Dresden: 1862. V. 64

GRUNSKY, CARL EWALD
Stockton Boyhood, Being the Reminiscences Carl Ewald Grunsky, Which Covers the Years from 1855 to 1877. N.P: 1959. V. 67

GRUPPE, O.
Griechische Mythologie und Religionsgeschichte.... Muchen: 1906. V. 65

GRZIMEK, B.
Animal Life Encyclopaedia. Volume 3. Mollusks and Echinoderms. 1974. V. 66

THE GUARDS. London: 1827. V. 67

GUARE, JOHN
Six Degrees of Separation. New York: 1990. V. 62; 64

GUARINI, GIOVANNI BATTISTA
The Faithful Shepherd. London: 1736. V. 63; 67
Il Pastor Fido. London: 1676. V. 62
Il Pastor Fido. Londra: 1718. V. 67

GUARINI-FORESIO, EMILE
Transmission de l'Energie Electrique par un fil et Sans Fil (par l'Ether). Application du Systeme aux Communications Telephoniques et Telegraphiques et aux Signaux Electriques en General. Liege: 1899. V. 64

GUARMANI, CARLO
Northern Najd; a Journey from Jerusalem to Aniaza in Qasim. London: 1938. V. 67

GUELLETTE, THOMAS SIMON
Chinese Tales.... London: 1726. V. 62

GUENARD, ELISABETH
Histoire de Madame Elisabeth de France, Soeur de Louis XVI. Paris: 1802. V. 63
Les Matinees du Hameau; ou Contes d'un Grand-Pere a Ses Petits Enfans. A Paris: 1808. V. 67

GUENON, FRANCOIS
Treatise Upon Milch Cows.... Dublin: 1851. V. 62

GUERIN, LEON
Histoire Maritime de France, Contenant l'Histoire des Provinces et Villes Maritimes, des combats de Mer Depuis La Fondation de Marseille 600 Ans Avant J. C. Paris: 1851-1856. V. 66

GUERIN, PIERRE
Traite sur les Maladies des Yeux, dans Lequel l'Auteur Apres Avoir Expose les Differentes Methodes de Faire l'Operation de la Catarcte, Propse un Instrument Nuveau qui Fixe l'Oeil Tout a la Fois & Opere la Section de la Cornee. Lyons: 1769. V. 64; 66

GUERINI, V.
A History of Dentistry from the Most Ancient Times Until the End of the Eighteenth Century. Philadelphia: 1909. V. 64; 66; 67

GUERNSEY, CHARLES A.
Wyoming Cowboy Days. New York: 1936. V. 66

GUERNSEY, ORRIN
History of Rock County and Transactions of the Rock County Agricultural Society and Mechanics' Institute. Janesville: 1856. V. 63

GUERNSEY, WILLIAM JEFFERSON
The Homoeopathic Therapeutics of Haemorrhoids. Philadelphia: 1892. V. 66; 67

GUERRA, FRANCISCO
American Medical Bibliography 1639-1783. New York: 1962. V. 65
Iconografia Medica Mexicana: Catalogo Grafico Descriptivo de los Impresos Medicos Mexicanos de 1552 a 1833 Ordenados Cronologicamente. Mexico City: 1955. V. 64

GUERRANT, EDWARD O.
The Galax Gatherers: The Gospel Among the Highlanders. Richmond: 1910. V. 65

GUERSANT, PAUL LOUIS BENOIT
Surgical Diseases of Infants and Children. Philadelphia: 1873. V. 64; 67

GUESS, PSEUD.
Scenes from the Life of Nickleby Married. London: 1840. V. 62

GUEST, BARBARA
Musicality. June Felter, Drawings. N.P: 1988. V. 64
Outside of This, That Is. Calais: 1999. V. 62; 66; 67
Port - a Murder in One Act. New York: 1964. V. 65

GUEST, MONTAGUE
List of Members of the Royal Yacht Squadron and Their Yachts: from Its Foundation in 1815 to 1897. London: 1897. V. 63
The Royal Yacht Squadron, Memorials of Its Members with an Enquiry into the History of Yachting and Its Development. London: 1903. V. 63

GUEST, RICHARD
The British Cotton Manufactures and a Reply to an Article on the Spinning Machinery.... Manchester: 1828. V. 63; 65

GUEULLETTE, THOMAS SIMON
Tartarian Tales; or a Thousand and One Quarters of Hours. London: 1759. V. 62; 63; 67

GUEVARA, ALVARO
St. George at Silene. N.P: 1928. V. 63

GUEVARA, ANTONIO DE
The Praise ad Happinesse of the Countrie Life. Newtown: 1938. V. 62

GUEVARA, ERNESTO CHE
Episodes of the Revolutionary War. Havana: 1967. V. 64
Reminiscences of the Cuban Revolutionary War. London: 1968. V. 65

GUGGENHEIM, PEGGY
Out of this Century: the Informal Memoirs. New York: 1946. V. 65

GUGLIELMINI, DOMICO
Opera Omnia. Mathematica, Hydraulica, Medica, et Physica. Geneva: 1719. V. 65

GUIA de Nueva York y los Estados Unidos, Para Uso de Los Espanoles Y Sudamericanos Donde se Esplica Cuanto Puede Interesar a un Viajero. Nueva York: 1856. V. 66

GUICCIARDINI, FRANCESCO
Della Istoria d'Italia...Libri XX. Venice: 1738. V. 63
The Historie of Guicciardin.... London: 1599. V. 63
The History of Italy, from the Year 1490 to 1532.... London: 1753-1761. V. 67

GUIDE de la Ville de Florence Avec la Description de la galerie et du Palais Pitte Ornee de Vues et Statues. Florence: 1827. V. 67

A GUIDE Or Hand-Book to the Shap Spa, Westmoreland. London: 1866. V. 64

GUIDE to Belfast and the Adjacent Counties by the Belfast Naturalist Field Club. 1874. V. 65

GUIDE to Government Situations. Shewing the Extent, Nature and Value of the Government Civil Patronage, at Here or Abroad with the Manner of Its Disposal. London: 1845. V. 62

THE GUIDE to Great Yarmouth: Containing Its Early History.... Great Yarmouth: 1862. V. 63

A GUIDE to Stage Coaches, Mails, Dilligences, Waggons, Carts, Coasting Vessels, Barges, and Boats. London: 1789. V. 66

GUIDE to the Church Congress and Ecclesiastical Art Exhibition Held in Barrow-in-Furness September 29, October 1, 2, 3, 4 and 5, 1906. 1906. V. 63

GUIDE to the City of New York.... New York: 1840. V. 63

A GUIDE to the Fortifications and Battlefields Around Petersburg. Petersburg: 1866. V. 64

A GUIDE to the Town, Abbey and Antiquities of Bury St. Edmunds.... Ipswich: 1821. V. 62

A GUIDE to the Vertebrate Fauna of the Eastern Cape Province. Grahamstown: 1931-1937. V. 66

GUIDO DE MONTE ROCHERII
Manipulus Curatorum. Venice: 1507. V. 66

GUIDONI, E.
Primitive Architecture. Milan: 1975. V. 62

GUIDOTT, THOMAS
A Collection of Treatises Relating to the City and Waters of Bath. London: 1725. V. 63
A Discourse of Bathe, and the Hot Waters There. London: 1676. V. 64

GUILBERT, ABBE PIERRE
Description Historique du Chateau Bourg et Forest de Fontainebleau. Paris: 1731. V. 66

GUILD, GEORGE B.
A Brief Narrative of the Fourth Tennessee Cavalry Regiment. Nashville: 1913. V. 65

GUILD, J. C.
Old Times in Tennessee: With Historical, Personal and Political Scraps and Sketches. Knoxville: 1971. V. 67

GUILD, THELMA S.
Kit Carson, a Pattern for Heroes. Lincoln: 1984. V. 67

GUILDFORD GRAMMAR SCHOOL
A Catalogue of the old Library of the Guildford Grammar School. Guildford: 1900. V. 67

GUILDHILL Studies in London History. London: 1973-1981. V. 67

GUILELLUS, PANSIEMSIS
Postilla Super Epistolas et Evangelia. Nurenberg: 1493. V. 67

GUILFORD BATTLE GROUND CO.
A Memorial Volume of the Guilford Battle Ground Co. Greensboro: 1893. V. 65

GUILLAIN, GEORGES
J. M. Charcot 1825-1893. His Life, His Work. London: 1959. V. 65

GUILLAIN, SIMONE
Vita de San Diego, Dipinta Nella Capella di Giacomo de Spagnuoli in Roma da Anibale Caracci, Delineata et Intagliata de Simone Guillain.... Rome: 1646. V. 66

GUILLAUME, P.
Primitive Negro Sculpture. New York: 1926. V. 62

GUILLEMARD, F. H. H.
The Cruise of the Marchesa to Kamschatka and New Guinea. London: 1886. V. 63; 65; 66; 67
The Cruise of the Marchesa to Kamschatka and New Guinea. London: 1889. V. 62; 65
On the Endemic Haematuria of Hot Climates Caused by Bilharzia Haematobia. London: 1882. V. 67

GUILLEMIN, AMEDEE
The Heavens. London: 1867. V. 65
The Heavens. 1886. V. 67

GUILLET, PETER
Timber Merchant's Guide. Baltimore: 1823. V. 66

GUILLET DE SAINTE GEORGE, GEORGES
Les Arts de l'Homme D'Epee, ou Le Dictionnaire du Gentilhomme Premiere Partie. Paris: 1678. V. 65

GUINN, J. M.
A History of California and An Extended History of Its Southern Coast. Los Angeles: 1907. V. 64; 67
History of the State of California and Biographical Record of the San Joaquin Valley, California. Chicago: 1905. V. 62; 63; 65

GUINNESS, DESMOND
Irish Houses and Castles. 1971. V. 63; 66
Irish Houses and Castles. New York: 1974. V. 62; 65

GUINNESS Sportfolio. London: 1956. V. 67

GUIRALDES, RICARDO
Cuentos de Muerte y de Sangre, Seguidos de aventras Grotescas y una Trilogia Cristiana. Buenos Aires: 1915. V. 67

GUIREY, WILLIAM
The History of Episcopacy, in Four Parts, from its Rise to the Present Day. Raleigh?: 1799?. V. 66

GUIRY, SACHA
Lucien Guitry: Sa Carriere et sa Vie Racontees par Sacha Guitry et Illustrees de Photographies de Ch. Gerschel. Paris: 1930. V. 66

GUISNEE
Application de l'Algebre a la Geomerie, ou Methode de De'Montrer par l'Algebre, Les Theoremes de Geometrie.... Paris: 1705. V. 65

GUITEAU, CHARLES J.
The Truth: a Companion to the Bible. Boston: 1879. V. 65

GUIZOT, FRANCOIS
Democracy in France. January 1849. London: 1849. V. 65
Washington. London: 1840. V. 67

GULIANO, EDWARD
Lewis Carroll Observed - a Collection of Unpublished Photographs, Drawings, Poetry and New Essays. New York: 1976. V. 62

GULICK, BILL
Chief Joseph Country, Land of the Nez Perce. Caldwell: 1981. V. 66

GULL, C. RANGER
The Woman in the Case. London: 1909. V. 65

GULLICK, THOMAS JOHN
Painting Popularly Explained.... London: 1859. V. 67

GULLY, JOHN
New Zealand Scenery Chromolithographed After Original Water-Color Drawings by John Gully. London: 1877. V. 62

GULSTON, JOSEPH
The School for Fathers. London: 1852. V. 65

GUMILLA, JOSEPH
Histoire Naturelle Civile et Geographique de l'Orenoque, et des Principales Rivieres qui s y Jettent.... Avignon: 1758. V. 66

GUMPERTZ, SYDNEY G.
Jewish Legion of Valor. New York: 1946. V. 63

GUNN, GEORGE W.
The Sunbonnet Series at Work/At Play. Chicago: 1904. V. 65

GUNN, JOHN C.
Gunn's Domestic Medicine, or Poor Man's Friend. Madisonville: 1835. V. 66
Gunn's Domestic Medicine, or Poor Man's Friend.... Springfield: 1835. V. 63
Gunn's Domestic Medicine, or Poor Man's Friend.... Springfield: 1836. V. 66
Gunn's New Family Physician, or Home Book of Health. Louisville: 1871. V. 65

GUNN, JOHN M.
Schat-Chen: History, Traditions and Narratives of the Queres Indians of Laguna and Acoma. Albuquerque: 1917. V. 63

GUNN, LEWIS C.
Records of a California Family. Journals and Letters of Lewis C. Gunn and Elizabeth Le Breton Gunn. San Diego: 1928. V. 62; 63

GUNN, M.
Ritual Arts of Oceania. Geneva: 1997. V. 62

GUNN, NEIL M.
Hidden Doors. Edinburgh: 1929. V. 63

GUNN, THOM
At the Barriers (Dore Alley Fair). New York: 1989. V. 63
Dancing David. Kripplebush: 1995. V. 63
Death's Door. 1989. V. 64
The Explorers. Bow, Crediton, Devon: 1969. V. 62
Fighting Terms. Oxford: 1954. V. 62; 64; 66
Fighting Terms. New York: 1958. V. 63
The Garden of the Gods. Cambridge: 1968. V. 62
A Geography. Iowa City: 1966. V. 62
The Hurtless Trees. New York: 1986. V. 62; 66; 67
Jack Straw's Castle. London: 1976. V. 63
Mandrakes. London: 1973. V. 62; 64
The Menace. San Francisco: 1982. V. 62
The Mixed Beat. Newark: 1976. V. 64
Moly. London: 1971. V. 63
My Sad Captains and Other Poems. London: 1961. V. 65; 66
Old Stories. New York: 1992. V. 62
Selected Poems 1950-1975. London and Boston: 1979. V. 63

GUNN, THOM continued
The Sense of Movement. London: 1957. V. 65; 66
Sidewalks. New York: 1985. V. 63
Songbook. New York: 1973. V. 63
Sunlight. New York: 1969. V. 63
Unsought Intimacies: Poems of 1991. Berkeley: 1993. V. 62

GUNNING, HENRY
Reminiscences of the University, Town and County of Cambridge, from the Year 1780. London: 1855. V. 62; 66

GUNNING, SUSANNAH
A Letter from Mrs. Gunning: Addressed to His Grace the Duke of Argyll. London: 1791. V. 62; 67

GUNNISON, J. W.
The Mormons, or the Latter-Day Saints, in the Valley of the Great Salt Lake: a History of Their Rise and Progress, Peculiar Doctrines, Present Condition and Prospects Dervied from Personal Observation.... London: 1852. V. 63

GUNTHER, A.
An Account of the Fishes of the States of Central America, Based on Collections Made by Capt. J. M. Dow, F. Godman, Esq. and O. Salvin, Esq. London: 1866. V. 63
Biologia Centrali-Americana - Reptilia and Batrachia. London: 1885-1902. V. 62
Catalogue of the Fishes in the British Museum. London: 1859-1870. V. 63
Catalogue of the Fishes in the Collection of the British Museum. 1937. V. 63; 66
Catalogue of the Fishes in the Collection of the British Museum. London: 1937. V. 62; 65
Catalouge of the Fishes of the British Museum. London: 1964. V. 64
Challenger Expedition. Zoology. Part 78, Pelagic Fishes. London: 1889. V. 65
Challenger Voyage. Zoology. Part 78, Pelagic Fishes. 1889. V. 66
Challenger Voyage. Zoology. Parts 6, 57 and 78. Fishes. 1880-1889. V. 66
An Introduction to the Study of Fishes. Edinburgh: 1880. V. 64; 65; 66

GUNTHER, GEORG CHRISTOPH
Praktische Anweisung zur Pastellmahlerey. Nuremberg: 1762. V. 66

GUNTHER, R. T.
Early Science in Cambridge. London: 1969. V. 66
Early Science in Oxford. Oxford: 1923. V. 65
Early Science in Oxford. London: 1923-1967. V. 64
Early Science in Oxford. Volume XI. Oxford Colleges and Their Men of Science. Oxford: 1937. V. 63

GUOMEI, F.
Rhododendrons of China. Volume II. New York: 1992. V. 63; 67

GUOYT, E. G.
Nouvelles Recreations Physiques et Mathematiques, Contenant ce Qui a Ete Imagine de Plus Curieux Dans ce Genre.... Paris: 1772-1775. V. 65

GUPPY, DARIUS
First Set: Blue Jade - A Book of Poetry from Oxford and Cambridge. Marlborough: 1984. V. 64

GUPPY, H. B.
Observations of a Naturalist in the Pacific Between 1896 and 1899. London: 1889. V. 62

GUPPY, H. B.
Observations of a Naturalist in the Pacific Between 1896 and 1899. London: 1903. V. 67

GUPPY, H. B.
Observations of a Naturalist in the Pacific, Between 1896 and 1899. 1903-1906. V. 63
The Solomon Islands and Their Natives. London: 1887. V. 66
Studies in Seeds and Fruits, an Investigation With the Balance. London: 1912. V. 63

GUPTA, A. P.
Morphogenetic Hormones of Arthropods. New Brunswick: 1990-1991. V. 63; 66

GURALNICK, PETER
The Listener's Guide to the Blues. 1982. V. 64
Searching for Robert Johnson. New York: 1989. V. 67

GURDON, P. R. T.
The Khasis. London: 1914. V. 67

GURGANUS, ALLAN
Breathing Lessons. 1981. V. 62; 64; 67
Breathing Lessons. North Carolina: 1981. V. 67
Good Help. Rocky Mount: 1988. V. 63; 66
Oldest Living Confederate Widow Tells All. London: 1989. V. 62
Oldest Living Confederate Widow Tells All. New York: 1989. V. 63; 64; 67

GURNEY, GOLDSWORTHY
A Course of Lectures on Chemical Science, As Delivered at the Surrey Institution. London: 1823. V. 62

GURNEY, IVOR
Severn and Somme. London: 1917. V. 64

GURNEY, J. H.
The Gannett. 1913. V. 67
Rambles of a Naturalist in Egypt; and Other Countries; with an Analysis of the Claims of Certain Foreign Birds to Be Considered British and Other Ornithological Notes. London: 1876. V. 67

GURNEY, JOSEPH JOHN
Memoirs with Selections From His Journal and Correspondence. London: 1854. V. 65
Memoirs...with Selections from His Journal and Correspondence. Norwich: 1854. V. 65
Notes Made on a Visit Made to Some of the Prisons in Scotland and the North of England, in Company with Elizabeth Fry.... 1819. V. 63

GURNEY, PRISCILLA
Hymns Selected from Various Authors, and Chiefly Intended for the Instruction of Young Persons. 1818. V. 67

GURNEY, S. GAMZU
From Generation to Generation. London: 1970. V. 64; 65

GURTEEN, S. HUMPHREYS
The Arthurian Epic - a Comparative Study of the Cambrian, Breton and Anglo-Norman Versions of the STory and Tennyson's Idylls of the King. London: 1895. V. 65

GUSLER, WALLACE B.
Furniture of Williamsburg and Eastern Virginia 1710-1790. Richmond: 1979. V. 63

GUSSOW, H. T.
Mushrooms and Toadstools: an Account of the More Edibile and Poisonous Fungi of Canada. Ottawa: 1927. V. 64

GUSTAFSON, RALPH
Flight into Darkness - Poems. New York: 1944. V. 62

GUSTAFSSON, RICHARD
Zemnoi Globus Papy. Moscow: 1913. V. 64

GUSTAV VON BERG, BARON
From Kapuvar to California. 1893. San Francisco: 1979. V. 66

GUTCH, JOHN
Collectanea Curiosa; or Miscellaneous Tracts, Relating to the History and Antiquities of England and Ireland, the Universities of Oxford and Cambridge.... Oxford: 1781. V. 63

GUTCH, JOHN MATHEW
A Lytell Geste of Robyn Hode and His Meiny.... San Francisco: 1932. V. 63; 66

GUTENBERG-Jahrbuch. Mainz: 1978-1981. V. 65

GUTERSON, DAVID
The Country Ahead of Us, the Country Behind. New York: 1989. V. 62; 63; 65; 67
East of the Mountains. New York: 1999. V. 63
Family Matters: Why Homeschooling Makes Sense. New York: 1992. V. 66
Snow Falling on Cedars. 1994. V. 62; 64; 66
Snow Falling on Cedars. New York: 1994. V. 62; 63; 64; 65; 67
Snow Falling on Cedars. London: 1995. V. 63; 64; 65; 67

GUTHRIE, A. B.
The Big Sky. New York: 1947. V. 62; 65; 67
Fair Land, Fair Land. Boston: 1982. V. 67
The Genuine Article. Boston: 1977. V. 67
Playing Catch-Up. Boston: 1985. V. 67
These Thousand Hills. Boston: 1956. V. 67
The Way West. New York: 1949. V. 63; 65; 67
Wild Pitch. Boston: 1973. V. 67

GUTHRIE, CHARLES GARDNER
On Cataract and Its Appropriate Treatment by the Operation Adapted for Each Peculiar Case. London: 1845. V. 65

GUTHRIE, ELLEN EMMA
The Old Houses of Putney. Putney: 1870. V. 65

GUTHRIE, G. J.
On Gun-Shot Wounds of the Extremities Requiring the Different Operations of Amputations. London: 1815. V. 66; 67

GUTHRIE, GEORGE W.
History of Lodge No. 45 F. & A. M. 1785-1910. Pittsburgh: 1912. V. 65

GUTHRIE, JAMES
The Elf. Winter Number. Sussex: 1904. V. 65
His Book of Bookplates, Consisting of 24 Original Designs. Edinburgh: 1907. V. 63
James Guthrie: His Book of Book-Plates, Consisting of 24 Original Designs. Edinburgh: 1907. V. 67

GUTHRIE, JESSE
The American Schoolmaster's Assistant. Paris: 1823. V. 66

GUTHRIE, MARIA
A Tour, Performed in the Years 1795-17965, through the Taurida or Crimea the Antient Kingdom of Bosphorus.... London: 1802. V. 65

GUTHRIE, THOMAS
Autobiography of Thomas Guthrie.... 1875-1876. V. 62
Seed-Time and Harvest of Ragged Schools, or a Third Plea, with New Editions of the First and Second Pleas. Edinburgh: 1860. V. 64

GUTHRIE, THOMAS ANSTEY
Baboo Jabberjee B.A. London: 1897. V. 62
A Bayard from Bengal, Being Some Account of the Magnificent and Spanking Career of Chunder Bindabun Bhosh.... London: 1902. V. 67
The Brass Bottle. London: 1900. V. 62; 67
The Pariah. London: 1889. V. 62
The Statement of Stella Maberly. London: 1896. V. 62
Tourmalin's Time Cheques. Bristol: 1891. V. 67
Voces Populi. London: 1890. V. 62
Voces Populi. Second Series. London: 1892. V. 62
Voces Populi...First (Second) Series. London: 1901. V. 67

GUTHRIE, TYRONE
A New Theatre. New York: 1964. V. 62

GUTHRIE, WILLIAM
Abrege de la Geographie Universelle, Descriptive, Historique, Industrielle et Commerciale des Quartre Parties du Monde. Paris: 1808. V. 65
The Christian's Great Interest, in Two Parts. South Hanover: 1834. V. 64
A General History of Scotland, from the Earliest Accounts to the Present Time. London: 1767-1768. V. 64
A New System of Modern Geography; or a Geographical, Historical and Commercial Grammar; and Present State of the Several Kingdoms. London: 1782. V. 67

GUTHRIE SMITH, H.
Birds of the Water, Wood and Waste. 1910. V. 67

GUTTERY, D. R.
From Broad-Glass to Cut Crystal. London: 1956. V. 66

GUTTMAN, SAMUEL A.
A Concordance to the Standard Edition of the Complete Psychological Works of Sigmund Freud. New York: 1984. V. 62

GUTTMANN, OSCAR
Monumenta Puleris Pyril, Reproductions of Ancient Pictures Concerning the History of Gunpowder. London: 1906. V. 64

GUTZLAFF, CHARLES D.
China Opened; or, a Display of the Topography, History, Customs, Manners, Arts, Manufactures, Commerce, Literature, Religion, Jurisprudence, etc. of the Chinese Empire. London: 1838. V. 67

GUY, ROSA
Bird at My Window. Philadelphia and New York: 1966. V. 62

GUYER, JAMES S.
Pioneer Life in West Texas. Brownwood: 1938. V. 67

GUYER, S.
My Journey Down the Tigris; a Raft-Voyage through Dead Kingdoms. London: 1925. V. 67

GUY OF WARWICK
The Romances of Sir Guy of Warwick and Rembrun His Son. Edinburgh: 1840. V. 65

GUYON, JEANNE MARIE BOUVIER DE LA MOTTE
An Extract of the Life of Madamde Guion. London: 1776. V. 64

GUYONNEAU DE PAMBOUR, FRANCOIS MARIE, COMTE
Practical Treatise on Locomotive Engines Upon Railways.... Philadelphia: 1836. V. 64

GUYOT, CHARLES
La Toison d'or Et Quelques Autres Contes de la Grece Ancienne. Paris: 1921. V. 62

GWATHMEY, JOHN H.
Historical Register of Virginians in the Revolution; Soldiers, Sailors, Marines (1775-1783). Richmond: 1838. V. 67
Historical Register of Virginians in the Revolution: Soldiers, Sailors, Marines, 1775-1783. Richmond: 1938. V. 63

GWILT, CHARLES PERKINS
Notices Relating to Thomas Smith of Campden and to Henry Smith.... London: 1836. V. 62

GWILT, JOSEPH
An Encyclopaedia of Architecture Historical, Theoretical and Practical. London: 1881. V. 64
An Encyclopaedia of Architecture, Historical, Theoretical and Practical. London: 1899. V. 63

GWILYM, DAFYDD
Selected Poems. Dublin: 1944. V. 62

GWYNN, ALBINIA
History of the Honourable Edward Mortimer. London: 1785. V. 65

GWYNN, DENIS
Duellist, Adventurer and Politician. 1934. V. 67
Tribute to Thomas Davis. 1947. V. 65

GWYNN, STEPHEN
Fishing Holidays. London: 1904. V. 67
River to River. London: 1937. V. 67

GWYNNE, JOHN
An Essay on Design; Including Proposals for Erecting a Public Academy.... London: 1749. V. 63

GYLDENSTOLPE, N.
Birds Collected by the Swedish Zoological Expedition to Siam 1911-1912. Stockholm: 1913-1916. V. 66

GYLLENBORG, CARL GREFVE
Letters Which Passed Between County Gyllenborg, the Barons Gortz, Sparre and Others.... London: 1717. V. 63

GYMNOPAEDIAE.. 1989. V. 62

GYP, PSEUD.
Le Monde a Cote. Paris: 1884. V. 63

H

H., Y.
Eight Years' Residence of an Englishman in the Ottoman Empire.... Newcastle-upon-Tyne: 1870. V. 62

HAANEL, B. F.
Facts About Peat. & Final Report of the Peat Committee. 1924-1925. V. 67

HAARDT, GEORGES MARIE
Le Raid Citroen. La Premiere Traversee du Sahara en Automobile. Paris: 1924. V. 64

HAAS, ERNST
The Creation. New York: 1981. V. 63

HAAST, JULIUS
Geology of the Provinces of Canterbury and Westland, New Zealand. Christchurch: 1879. V. 67
Report of a Topographical and Geological Exploration of the Western Districts of the Nelson Province, New Zealand. Nelson: 1861. V. 67

HABE, T.
Systematics of Mollusca in Japan, Bivalvia and Scaphopoda. Tokyo: 1977. V. 66

HABERLY, LLOYD
Daneway. 1929. V. 63

HABERLY, LOYD
Anne Boleyn and Other Poems. Newtown: 1934. V. 65
The Fourth of July; or an Oregon Orator. St. Louis: 1942. V. 64
Verses on Mans Mortalitie. Long Crendon: 1925. V. 67

HABERMAS, JURGEN
Das Absolute und die Geschichte von der Zwiespaltigkeit in Schellings Denken. Inaugural Dissertation zur Erlangung der Doktorwurde der Philosophischen Fakultaat. Bonn: 1954. V. 67

HABITS of Good Society. London: 1859. V. 64

THE HABITS of Good Society. New York: 1866. V. 67

HACHISUKA, M.
The Birds of the Philippine Islands. London: 1931-1935. V. 63

HACK, MARIA BARTON
English Stories. London: 1820. V. 65
Harry Beaufoy; or, the Pupil of Nature. London: 1824. V. 65
Stories of Animals Intended for Children Between Five and Seven Years Old. London: 1837. V. 67

HACKELEY, WOODFORD B.
The Little Fork Rangers - a Sketch of Company "D" Forth Virginia Cavalry. Richmond: 1927. V. 63; 66

HACKER, LILIAN PRICE
Susan. London: 1912. V. 62

HACKER, MARILYN
Presentation Piece. New York: 1974. V. 63; 67
Separations. New York: 1976. V. 66

HACKET, JOHN
Scrinia Reserata; a Memorial Offer'd to the Great Deservings of John Williams, D.D. London: 1693. V. 63

HACKETT, CHARLES WILSON
New Spain and the Anglo-American West. Lanchester: 1932. V. 66
Revolt of the Pueblo Indians of New Mexico and Otermin's Attempted Reconquest 1680-1682. Albuquerque: 1942. V. 63; 64; 65
Revolt of the Pueblo Indians of New Mexico and Otermin's Attempted Reconquest 1680-1682. Albuquerque: 1970. V. 65

HACKETT, JOHN
Select and Remarkable Epitaphs on Illustrious and Other Persons, in Several Parts of Europe. London: 1757. V. 64

HACKETT, R. G.
South African War Books. London: 1994. V. 62; 65

HACKLEY, WOODFORD BROADUS
The Little Fork Rangers. Richmond: 1927. V. 63

HACKMAN, JAMES
The Case and Memoirs of the Late Rev. Mr. James Hackman, and of the Acquaintance with the Late Miss Martha Reay.... London: 1779. V. 63

HADAMARD, J.
Four Lectures on Mathematics. New York: 1915. V. 67

HADDLE, JAN
The Complete Book of the Appaloosa. S. Brunswick: 1975. V. 62

HADER, BERTA
Little Appaollosa. New York: 1949. V. 62
Picture Book of the States. New York: 1932. V. 63
The Runaways. New York: 1956. V. 63; 66

HADFIELD, E.
Among the Natives of the Loyalty Group. London: 1920. V. 67

HADFIELD, JOHN
Georgian Love Songs. London: 1949. V. 63; 65; 67
Restoration Love Songs. 1950. V. 62; 67

HADFIELD, M.
Topiary and Ornamental Hedges, Their History and Cultivation. New York: 1971. V. 64

HAEBLER, KONRAD
The Study of Incunabula. New York: 1933. V. 63

HAECKEL, ERNST
Arabische Korallen. Ein Ausflug nach den Korallenbanken des Rothen Meers und eine Blick in das Leben der Korallenthiere. Berlin: 1876. V. 62
Challenger Voyage. Zoology Part 12. Deep Sea Medusae. 1882. V. 66
Challenger Voyage. Zoology. Part 77, i.e. Vol. 28. Report on the Siphonophorae. 1888. V. 66
Challenger Voyage. Zoology. Part 82. Deep Sea Keratosa. 1889. V. 66
The Evolution of Man: a Popular Scientific Study. New York: 1905. V. 66
The Last Link, Our Present Knowledge of the Descent of Man.... London: 1899. V. 67
Report on the Siphonophorae Collected by H.M.S. Challenger (Zoology). 1888. V. 67
Das System der Medusen. Jena: 1879-1881. V. 62; 65; 66
Wanderbilder; die Naturwunder der Tropenwelt, Ceylon und Insulinde. Gera-Untermhaus: 1910. V. 67

HAEFTEN, BENEDICTUS
Regia Via Crucis. Antverpiae: 1728. V. 63
Schola Cordis, Sive Aversi A deo Cordis, Ad Evmdem Redvctio, Et Instrvctio. Antverpiae: 1635. V. 66

HAEGER, KNUT
The Illustrated History of Surgery. New York: 1990. V. 67

HAEN, ANTONIO DE
Difficultates Circa Modernorum System, De Sensibilitate et Irriabilitate Humani Corporis, Orbi Medico Propositae or Antonio de Haen.... Viennae: 1761. V. 64

HAESER, HENRICUS
Bibliotheca Epidemiographica Sive Catalogus Librorum de Historia Morborum Epidemicorum Tam Generali Quam Speciali Conscriptorum. Jenae: 1843. V. 64

HAFEN, LE ROY
Analytical Index to the Southwest Historical Series. Glendale: 1943. V. 64
Broken Hand. The Life Story of Thomas Fitzpatrick, Chief of the Mountain Men. Denver: 1931. V. 64; 66
Broken Hand, the Story of Thomas Fitzpatrick. Denver: 1973. V. 64; 67
The Far West and Rockies - General Analytical Index and Supplement to the Journals of Forty-Niners - Salt Lake to Los Angeles. Glendale: 1955. V. 63
The Far West and Rockies - General Analytical Index to the Fifteen Volume Series and Supplement to the Journals of Forty-Niners Salt Lake City to Los Angeles. Glendale: 1961. V. 66
Far West and Rockies Historical Series 1820-1875. Glendale: 1954-1961. V. 62; 63
Fort Laramie and the Pageant of the West 1834-1890. Glendale: 1938. V. 65; 67
Fremont's Fourth Expedition - A Documentary Account of the Disasters of 1848-1849. Glendale: 1960. V. 63; 66
The Mountain Men and the Fur Trade of the Far West. Glendale: 1965-1972. V. 62; 65; 66
Old Spanish Trail - Santa Fe to Los Angeles - Diaries of Antonio Amijo and Orville Pratt. Glendale: 1954. V. 66
The Overland Mail 1816-1860. Cleveland: 1926. V. 64; 66
Overland Routes to the Gold Fields 1859 from Contemporary Diaries. Glendale: 1942. V. 64; 66
Pike's Peak Gold Rush Guide Books. Glendale: 1991. V. 66
Powder River Campaign and Sawyer Expedition of 1865. Glendale: 1961. V. 63; 64; 66; 67
Relations with the Indians of the Plains 1857-1861 - a Documentary Account of the Military Campaigns and Negotiations of Indian Agents.... Glendale: 1959. V. 66
Reports from Colorado - The Wildman Letters 1859-1865. With Other Related Letters and Newspaper Reports 1859. Glendale: 1961. V. 63; 64; 66
To the Rockies and Oregon 1839-1842 with Diaries and Accounts. Glendale: 1955. V. 66
Western America - the Exploration, Settlement and Development of the Region Beyond the Mississippi. New York: 1943. V. 67

HAFEN, MARY ANN
Recollections of a Hand Cart Pioneer of 1860. Denver: 1938. V. 65

HAFORD, GUSTAV
The Short-Timers. New York: 1970. V. 63

HAFTMANN, W.
Painting in the 20th Century. New York: 1960. V. 65

HAGAN, C. S. C.
Exactly in the Right Place, a History of Old Fort C. F. Smith - Montana Territory 1866-1868. El Segundo: 1999. V. 67

HAGEDORN, HERMANN
Leonard Wood, a Biography. New York: 1931. V. 64; 67
Roosevelt in the Badlands. Boston: 1921. V. 64; 67

HAGELSTANGE, RUDOLF
Venezianisches Credo. Verona: 1945. V. 62

HAGEMAN, JOHN F.
History of Princeton and Its Institutions. Philadelphia: 1879. V. 66

HAGEMANN, E. R.
Fighting Rebels and Redskins, Experiences in the Army Life of Colonel George B. Sanford 1861-1892. Norman: 1969. V. 67

HAGEN, OSKAR
The Birth of the American Tradition in Art. New York and London: 1940. V. 65

HAGEN, WALTER
The Walter Hagen Story. New York: 1956. V. 65

HAGER, ALICE ROGERS
Big Loop and Little The Cowboy's Story. New York: 1937. V. 64

HAGER, ANNA MARIE
The Zamorano Index to the History of California. Los Angeles: 1985. V. 63

HAGER, BENGT
Ballets Suedois (The Swiss Ballet). New York: 1990. V. 63; 64

HAGER, JEAN
The Grandfather Medicine. New York: 1989. V. 63; 65

HAGERBAUMER, D.
Selected American Gamebirds. 1980. V. 67
Waterfowling these Past Fifty Years. 1998. V. 67

HAGERTY, DONALD
Desert Dreams: the Art and Life of Maynard Dixon. Layton: 1993. V. 63
Leading the West - One Hundred Contemporary Painters and Sculptors. Flagstaff: 1997. V. 66

HAGGADAH
Haggada. Woodmere. V. 64
An Only Kid. New York: 1998. V. 64

HAGGARD, ANDREW
Sporting Yarns Spun Off the Reel. London: 1903. V. 67

HAGGARD, HENRY RIDER
Allan Quatermain. London: 1887. V. 66
Allan's Wife and Other Tales. London: 1889. V. 66
Ayesha. 1905. V. 64; 66
Beatrice - a Novel. London: 1890. V. 64; 65
Belshazzar. Garden City: 1930. V. 63; 64
Benita - an African Romance. London: 1906. V. 64
Black Heart and White Heart and Other Stories. London: 1900. V. 62
The Brethren. London: 1904. V. 67
Cetwayo and His White Neighbours, or Remarks on Recent Events in Zululand, Natal and the Transvaal. London: 1882. V. 62
Cleopatra.... London: 1889. V. 64; 65
Colonel Quaritch, V.C. A Tale of Country Life. London: 1889. V. 64
Dawn. London: 1887. V. 67
Doctor Therne. London: 1898. V. 67
Fair Margaret. London: 1907. V. 67
Heart of the World. London: 1896. V. 62; 64
Joan Haste. London: 1895. V. 62; 64
King Solomon's Mines. London: 1912. V. 62
King Solomon's Mines. Barre: 1970. V. 63
The Last Boer War. London: 1899. V. 67
Mr. Meeson's Will. London: 1888. V. 65
Montezuma's Daughter. London: 1894. V. 67
Moon of Israel. Tale of the Exodus. London: 1918. V. 66
Nada the Lily. London: 1892. V. 62; 67
Pearl Maiden, a Tale of the Fall of Jerusalem. London: 1903. V. 67
The People of the Mist. London: 1894. V. 67
Queen Sheba's Ring. London: 1910. V. 67
Regeneration; Being an Account of the Social Work of the Salvation Army in Great Britain. London: 1910. V. 67
Rural Denmark and Its Lessons. London: 1911. V. 63
She. London: 1887. V. 64; 66
Stella Fregelius - a Tale of Three Destinies. London: 1904. V. 64; 67
Swallow: a Tale of the Great Trek. London: 1899. V. 63; 65
The Way of the Spirit. London: 1906. V. 67
When the World Shook. New York: 1919. V. 66

HAGGARD, LILIAS RIDER
I Walked by Night. 1935. V. 67
The Rabbit Skin Cap. London: 1950. V. 67

HAGOOD, JOHNSON
Meet Your Grandfather. Columbia: 1947. V. 63; 65; 66
Memoirs of the War of Secession. Columbia: 1910. V. 62; 63; 65

HAGUE, RENE
The Death of Hector. London: 1973. V. 64

HAHN, GEORGE H.
The Catawba Soldier of the Civil War. Hickory: 1911. V. 63; 65

HAHNEMANN, SAMUEL
Organon of Homoeopathic Medicine. New York: 1843. V. 62; 64

HAHON, NICHOLAS
Selected Papers on the Pathogenic Rickettsiae. Cambridge: 1968. V. 63

HAIG, DOUGLAS
Sir Douglas Haig's Despatches (Dec. 1915-April 1919). London: 1920. V. 63

HAIG, JAMES
Philosophy; or, the Science of Truth. London: 1861. V. 65

HAIG BROWN, R.
The Western Angler. 1947. V. 67

HAIGH, JAMES
The Dier's Assistant in the Art of Dying Wool and Woolen Goods. New York: 1813. V. 66

HAIGHT, GORDON S.
George Eliot and John Chapman, with Chapman's Diaries. Hamden: 1969. V. 65

HAIGHT, THERON WILBUR
Three Wisconsin Cushings. A Sketch of the Lives of Howard B., Alonzo H. and William B. Cushing, Children of a Pioneer Family of Waukesha County, Wisconsin. 1910. V. 66
Three Wisconsin Cushings. A Sketch of the Lives of Howard B. Alonzo, H. and William B. Cushing, Children of a Pioneer Family of Waukesha County, Wisconsin. Waukesha County: 1910. V. 63

HAIGHTON, JOHN
A Syllabus of the Lectures on Midwifery, Delivered at Guy's Hospital and at Dr. Haighton's Theatre, in St. Saviour's Church Yard, Southwark. London: 1808. V. 66

HAIG THOMAS, D.
I Leap Before I Look. 1936. V. 67

HAILE, BERNARD
Head and Face Masks in Navaho Ceremonialism. St. Michaels: 1947. V. 63; 66
A Manual of Navaho Grammar. St. Michaels: 1926. V. 62

HAILEY, J. P.
The Baxter Trust. New York: 1988. V. 65
The Naked Typist. New York: 1990. V. 65

HAILEY, JOHN
History of Idaho. Boise: 1910. V. 63; 66

HAILS, WILLIAM ANTHONY
An Enquiry Concerning the Invention of the Life Boat. Gateshead: 1806. V. 67
Plain Strictures on the Controversy Between Mess. Briggs and Jamieson. Newcastle-upon-Tyne: 1817. V. 64

HAILSTONE, SAMUEL
A Dose for the Doctor; or a Bitter Pill for George Mossman... (with) a Dose for the Doctor Repeated.... London: 1796. V. 62

HAINES, HELEN
History of New Mexico, from the Spanish Conquest to the Present Time 1530-1980. New York: 1891. V. 65

HAINES, HERBERT
A Manual of Monumental Brasses.... Oxford and London: 1861. V. 65

HAINES, JOHN
Where the Twilight Never Ends. Boise: 1994. V. 62

HAINES, WILLIAM WISTER
Command Decision. Boston: 1947. V. 65

HAINING, PETER
Movable Books - an Illustrated History. London: 1979. V. 66; 67

HAIR, T. H.
Sketches of the Coal Mines in Northumberland and Durham. London: 1969. V. 65; 66

HAJEK, L.
Japanese Woodcuts. Early Period. London. V. 62

HAJOS, E. M.
Berliner Architektur der Nachkriegszeit. Berlin: 1928. V. 65

HAJRA, P. K.
Flora of India. Calcutta: 1996. V. 64
Plant Wealth of Nanda Devi Biosphere Reserve. Calcutta: 1955. V. 63

HAKE, A. EGMONT
Gordon in China and the Soudan. London: 1896. V. 67

HAKE, EDWARD
Newes Out of Powles Churchyarde Written in English Satyrs. London: 1872. V. 64

HAKE, LUCY
Something New on Men and Manners. Hailsham: 1828. V. 65

HAKE, THOMAS GORDON
The Poems of Thomas Gordon Hake.... London: 1894. V. 62

HAKEWILL, GEORGE
An Apologie or Declaration of the Power and Providence of God in the Government of the World. Oxford: 1635. V. 66

HAKEWILL, JAMES
An Attempt to Determine the Exact Character of Elizabethan Architecture.... London: 1836. V. 62; 63
A Series of Views of the Neighbourhood of Windsor, Including the Seats of Several of the Nobility and Gentry. London: 1820. V. 66

HAKKILA, P.
Utilization of Residual Forest Biomass. Berlin: 1989. V. 64; 66

HAKLUYT, RICHARD
A Discourse Concerning Western Planting Written in the Year 1584. Cambridge: 1877. V. 67
The Original Writings and Correspondence of the Two Richard Hakluyts. London: 1935. V. 64

HAKOLA, JOHN
Frontier Omnibus. Helena: 1962. V. 65; 67

HALAS, GEORGE
Halas by Halas. New York: 1979. V. 63

HALDANE, JOHN SCOTT
Methods of Air Analysis. London: 1912. V. 63

HALE, EDWARD E.
Kanzas and Nebraska. Boston: 1854. V. 66
The Life and Letters of Edward Everett Hale. Boston: 1917. V. 63

HALE, G. E.
Little Flower People. Boston: 1895. V. 67

HALE, JOHN
California as It Is. San Francisco: 1954. V. 66

HALE, KATHLEEN
Henrietta the Faithful Hen. London: 1967. V. 67
Manda. London: 1963. V. 67
Orlando. London: 1949. V. 66
Orlando (The Marmalade Cat) Becomes a Doctor. London: 1944. V. 63
Orlando (the Marmalade Cat) Keeps a Dog. London: 1949. V. 62; 63
Orlando's Magic Carpet. London: 1958. V. 65

HALE, LAURA VIRGINIA
Four Vailiant Years in the Lower Shenandoah Valley 1861-1865. Strasburg: 1968. V. 62; 63

HALE, MATTHEW
Contemplations Moral and Divine: in Two Parts. London: 1704-1705. V. 66
The Primitive Origination of Mankind, Considered and Examined According to the Light of Nature. London: 1677. V. 63

HALE, N. C.
Embrace of Life: the Sculpture.... New York: 1968. V. 62; 65

HALE, NATHAN
Remarks on the Practicability and Expediency of Establishing a Rail Road on One or More Routes from Boston to the Connecticut River. Boston: 1827. V. 63

HALE, P. M.
The Woods and Timbers of North Carolina. Raleigh: 1883. V. 63; 67

HALE, SALMA
History of the United States of America: With a Brief Account of Some of the Principal Empires and States of Ancient and Modern Times. Keene: 1820. V. 66

HALE, SARAH JOSEPHA
The Happy Changes. New York: 1860. V. 67
The Happy Changes. New York: 1842. V. 65
Mrs. Hale's New Cookbook. Philadelphia: 1857. V. 66
Woman's Record: or, Sketches of All Distinguished Women.... New York: 1853. V. 65
Woman's Record; or Sketches of All Distinguished Women.... New York: 1874. V. 63

HALE, THOMAS
A Compleat Body of Husbandry. 1755-1756. V. 64
A Compleat Body of Husbandry. London: 1758. V. 64
Social Harmony Consisting of a Collection of Songs and Catches.... London: 1763. V. 64; 65

HALES, JOHN
Golden Remains of Ever Memorable Mr. John Hales of Eton College &c. London: 1673. V. 65

HALES, NORMAN
The Spider in the Cup. New York: 1955. V. 63

HALES, STEPHEN
An Account of a Useful Discovery to Distill Double the Usual Quantity of Sea-Water, by Blowing Showers of Air Up through the Distilling Liquor.... London: 1756. V. 62; 63; 66
An Account of Some Experiments and Observations on Tar-Water: Wherein is Shown the Quantity of Tar That is Therein. London: 1747. V. 66
Haemastatique, ou La Statique des Animaux.... Geneva: 1744. V. 66
Philosophical Experiments.... London: 1739. V. 63; 67
Some Considerations on the Causes of Earthquakes Which were Read Before the Royal Society, April 5, 1750. London: 1750. V. 65
Statical Essays: Containing Vegetable Staticks; or, an Account of Som Statical Experiments on the Sap in Vegetables... (with) Statical Essays: Containing Haemastaticks; or, an Account of Some Hydraulick and Hydrostataical Experiments Made on the Blood. London: 1731. V. 65
La Statique des Vegetaux, et l'Analyse de l'Air. (with) Haemastatique, ou la Statique des Animaux.... Paris: 1735. V. 66

HALEVY, LUDOVIC
L'Abbe Constantin. Paris: 1888. V. 66

HALEY, ALEX
The Autobiography of Malcolm X. New York: 1965. V. 62; 64
Roots. Garden City: 1976. V. 63; 64; 67
Roots. New York: 1976. V. 65; 66

HALEY, ANDREW G.
Rocketry and Space Exploration: the International Story. Princeton: 1959. V. 67

HALEY, JAMES EVETTS
The Alamo Misson Bell. Midland: 1974. V. 65
Charles Goodnight, Cowman and Plainsman. Boston: 1936. V. 64; 67
A Day with Dan Casement. Kansas City: 1949. V. 63; 66
The Flamboyant Judge James D. Hamlin. Canyon: 1972. V. 65; 66
Fort Concho and the Texas Frontier. San Angelo: 1952. V. 64; 67
George W. Littlefield, Texan. Norman: 1943. V. 63; 64; 65
The Heraldry of the Range, Some Southwestern Brands. Canyon: 1949. V. 62
Jeff Milton, a Good Man with a Gun. Norman: 1948. V. 62; 66
A Log of Texas California Cattle Trail 1854. Austin: 1932. V. 64
Rough Times-Tough Fiber: a Fragmentary Family Chronicle. Canyon: 1976. V. 64; 66; 67
Some Southwestern Trails. San Angelo: 1948. V. 62; 65
The XIT Ranch of Texas. Norman: 1953. V. 67
The XIT Ranch of Texas. Chicago: 1929. V. 63; 66

HALFER, JOSEF
The Progress of the Marbling Art: from the Technical Scientific Principles. Buffalo: 1893. V. 64

HALFORD, FREDERIC M.
An Angler's Autobiography. 1903. V. 67
Dry Fly Fishing, Theory and Practice. 1902. V. 67
Dry-Fly Fishing in Theory and Practice. London: 1889. V. 67
Floating Flies and How to Dress Them. 1974. V. 67
Floating Flies and How to Dress Them. London: 1886. V. 67
Floating Flies and How to Dress Them. 1993. V. 67
Making a Fishery. 1902. V. 62; 67
Modern Development of the Dry Fly. London: 1910. V. 62; 66; 67

HALFORD, H. ST. JOHN
The Art of Shooting with the Rifle. 1888. V. 66

HALFORD, HENRY
Essays and Orations, Read and Delivered at the Royal College of Physicians.... London: 1833. V. 62; 63; 65
Essays and Orations, Read and Delivered at the Royal College of Physicians.... London: 1842. V. 67

HALFPENNY, JOSEPH
Fragmenta Vetusta or the Remains of Ancient Buildings in York. York: 1807. V. 66; 67

HALFPENNY, WILLIAM
Chinese and Gothic Architecture Properly Ornamented.... London: 1752. V. 64
Practical Architecture, or a Sure Guide to the True Working According to the Rules of that Science Representing the Five Orders, with Their Several Doors and Windows Taken from Inigo Jones and Other Celebrated Architects to Each Plate.... London: 1736. V. 63

HALIBURTON, THOMAS
An Extract of the Life and Death of Mr. Thomas Haliburton. London: 1741. V. 64

HALIBURTON, THOMAS CHANDLER
The Attache; or, Sam Slick in England. London: 1843. V. 64; 66
The Attache; or Sam Slick in England. London: 1844. V. 66
The Attache; or, Sam Slick in England. London: 1857. V. 67
The Clockmaker; or the Sayings and Doings of Sam Slick, of Slickville. Paris: 1839. V. 67
The Clockmaker; or the Sayings and Doings of Samuel Slick of Slickville. London: 1839 1840. V. 66
The Clockmaker; or the Sayings and Doings of Samuel Slick of Slickville. Philadelphia: 1839-1840. V. 62
The Clockmaker; or, the Sayings and Doings of Samuel Slick, of Slickville. First-Third Series. New York: 1840. V. 63; 66
The Clockmaker; or, the Sayings and Dowings of Samuel Slick of Slickville. London: 1857. V. 67
The Letter-Bag of the Great Western; or Life in a Steamer. London: 1853. V. 67
Nature and Human Nature. London: 1859. V. 66; 67
Sam Slick's Wise Saws and Modern Instances; or, What He Said, Did, Or Invented. London: 1853. V. 65
Traits of American Humour, by Native Authors. London: 1852. V. 65

HALIBURTON, WILLIAM DOBINSON
Ten Lectures on Biochemistry of Muscle and Nerve. Philadelphia: 1904. V. 65

HALIFAX, CHARLES
Familiar Letters on Various Subjects of Business and Amusement.... London: 1755. V. 64

HALIFAX, CHARLES MONTAGU, EARL OF HALIFAX
The Works and Life of.... London: 1715. V. 63

HALIFAX, GEORGE SAVILE, 1ST MARQUIS OF
The Character of a Trimmer, His Opinion of I. The Laws and Government. II. Protestant Religion. III. The Papists. IV. Foreign Affairs. London: 1688. V. 64
Miscellanies.... London: 1704. V. 65
Miscellanies.... London: 1717. V. 62

HALKETT, JOHN
Statement Respecting the Earl of Selkirk's Settlement of Kildonan, Upon the Red River, Its Destruction in 1815 and 1816.... London: 1817. V. 62

HALKETT, SAMUEL
Dictionary of Anonymous and Pseudonymous English Literature. London: 1926-1956. V. 65

HALL, A. D.
The Genus Tulipa. 1940. V. 66
The Genus Tulipa. London: 1940. V. 63

HALL, A. M.
Ireland Picturesque. Boston. V. 63; 66

HALL, A. VINE
Rainbow Houses for Boys and Girls. London: 1923. V. 62

HALL, ABRAHAM OAKEY
The Manhattaner in New Orleans; or, Phases of "Crescent City" Life. New York: 1851. V. 63

HALL, ADAM
The 9th Detective. London: 1966. V. 67
The Volcanoes of San Domingo. New York: 1963. V. 63; 67
The Warsaw Document. London: 1971. V. 67

HALL, AL
Petersen's Book of Man in Space. Los Angeles: 1974. V. 67

HALL, ALLEN
Observations on the Weather.... Chesterfield: 1777. V. 65
Observations on the Weather.... Lincoln: 1788. V. 65

HALL, ANGELO
Forty-One Thieves, a Tale of California. Boston: 1919. V. 63

HALL, ANNA MARIA FIELDING
Marian; or, a Young Maid's Fortunes. New York: 1840. V. 62; 64
Midsummer Eve: a Fairy Tale of Love. London: 1848. V. 64; 65
Stories of Irish Peasantry. Edinburgh: 1855. V. 65

HALL, BASIL
Extracts from a Journal, Written on the Coasts of Chili, Peru and Mexico, in the Years 1820, 1821, 1822. Edinburgh: 1824. V. 63; 63; 66
Forty Etchings from Sketches Made with the Camera Lucida, in North America in 1827 and 1828. Edinburgh and London: 1829. V. 66
Fragments of Voyages and Travels, Including Anecdotes of a Naval Life. Edinburgh: 1831-1832. V. 66
Schloss Hainfeld; or a Winter in Lower Styria. Edinburgh: 1836. V. 65
Travels in North America, in the Years 1827 and 1828. Edinburgh: 1829. V. 62
Travels in North America in the Years 1827 and 1828. Edinburgh: 1830. V. 66

HALL, BERT
One Man's War. New York: 1929. V. 65
Round-Up Years Old Mundy to the Black Hills. Pierre: 1954. V. 65

HALL, CARROLL
Bierce and the Poe Hoax. San Francisco: 1934. V. 63
Donner Miscellany. San Francisco: 1947. V. 62
Heraldry of New Helvetia - With Thirty Two Cattle Brands and Ear Marks. San Francisco: 1945. V. 63; 66
The Terry-Broderick Duel. San Francisco: 1939. V. 65

HALL, CHARLES A.
Plant-Life. London: 1915. V. 63

HALL, CHARLES B.
Military Records of General Officers of the Confederate States of America 1861-1865. Austin: 1963. V. 62

HALL, CHARLES F.
Life with the Esquimaux. A Narrative of Arctic Experience in Search of Survivors of Sir John Franklin's Expedition. Rutland: 1970. V. 63
Narrative of the North Polar Expedition. U.S. Ship Polaris, Captain Charles Francis Hall Commanding. Washington: 1876. V. 63
Narrative of the Second Arctic Expedition made by Charles Hall.... Washington: 1879. V. 62; 65; 66

HALL, CHARLES HENRY
Sermons Preached Before the University of Oxford at St. Mary's Church in the Year MDCCXCVII. Oxford: 1799. V. 62

HALL, CHARLES S.
Life and Letters of Samuel Holden Parsons.... Binghamton: 1905. V. 65

HALL, DANIEL
The Genus Tulipa. 1940. V. 64

HALL, DONALD
The Harvard Advocate Anthology. New York: 1950. V. 64; 67
Here at Eagle Pond. New York: 1990. V. 67
The Man Who Lived Alone. Boston: 1984. V. 63
1 2 3 4 Stories. Sweden, Maine: 1989. V. 67
Ox-Cart Man. New York: 1979. V. 66
Ric's Progress. Easthampton: 1996. V. 63; 65; 67
A Roof of Tiger Lilies. London: 1964. V. 63
Seasons at Eagle Pond. New York: 1987. V. 67
To the Loud Wind and Other Poems. Cambridge: 1955. V. 63
The Town of Hill. Boston: 1975. V. 62

HALL, EDWARD
Hall's Chronicle, Containing the History of England, During the Reign of Henry the Fourth, and the Succeeding Monarchs, to the End of the Reign of Henry the Eighth.... London: 1809. V. 63

HALL, EDWARD T.
The Silent Language. Garden City: 1959. V. 67

HALL, F. G.
The Bank of Ireland 1783-1946. 1949. V. 64; 67

HALL, FRANK
History of the State of Colorado. Chicago;: 1889. V. 63

HALL, FREDERIC
The History of San Jose and Surroundings with Biographical Sketches of Early Settlers. San Francisco: 1871. V. 62

HALL, GEORGE FRANKLIN
A Study in Bloomers; or the Model New Woman. Chicago, Philadelphia: 1895. V. 67

HALL, GRANVILLE D.
The Rending of Virginia. Chicago: 1902. V. 65

HALL, H. M.
Compositae of Southern California. Berkeley: 1907. V. 63

HALL, H. R.
Aegean Archaeology, an Introduction to the Archaeology of Prehistoric Greece. London: 1915. V. 67

HALL, HERBERT BYNG
Scottish Sports and Pastimes. 1850. V. 63
The Sportsman and His Dog, or Hints on Sporting, Together with Scottish Sports and Pastimes. 1850-1851. V. 63

HALL, J. H.
Temperance Songs. Dayton: 1910. V. 66

HALL, JAMES
Essay on the Origin, History and Principles of Gothic Architecture. London: 1813. V. 67
Legends of the West. New York: 1854. V. 63
Report of the Committee Appointed by the Citizens of Cincinnati, April 26, 1838 to Enquire into the Causes of the Explosion of the Moselle and to Suggest Such Preventive Measures as May be Best Calculated to Guard Hereafter Against Such Occurrences. Cincinnati: 1838. V. 63
The West: Its Commerce and Navigation. Cincinnati: 1848. V. 66

HALL, JAMES KING
One Hundred Years of American Psychiatry. New York: 1944. V. 65

HALL, JAMES NORMAN
The Lafayette Flying Corps. Boston and New York: 1920. V. 66

HALL, JAMES W.
Under Cover of Daylight. New York: 1987. V. 65; 66; 67

HALL, JIM
Tales of Pioneer Practice - Being Reminiscences of the Ways and By- Ways of the Early Day Medical Fraternity in Colorado. Denver: 1937. V. 67

HALL, JOHN F.
The Daily Union History of Atlantic City and County, New Jersey. Atlantic City: 1900. V. 63; 66

HALL, JOHN GEORGE
Notices of Lincolnshire Being an Historical and Topographical Account of Some Villages in the Division of Lindsey. Hull: 1890. V. 62

HALL, JOHN LINVILLE
Around the Horn in '49 - the Journal of the Hartford Union Mining and Trading Company.... San Francisco: 1928. V. 62; 63; 65

HALL, JOHN R. CLARK
A Concise Anglo-Saxon Dictionary for the Use of Students. London: 1894. V. 64

HALL, JOSEPH
Episcopacie by Divine Right. Asserted. London: 1640. V. 66
An Humble Remonstrance to the High Court of Parliament, by a Dutiful Sonne of the Church. London: 1640. V. 62; 63; 67
Satires. 1824. V. 67
The Works. London: 1647,. V. 66

HALL, LOWIE
Fifty-Six Waterloo Cups. 1922. V. 62

HALL, MARSHALL
A Descriptive, Diagnostic and Practical Essay on Disorders of the Digestive Organs and General Health, and Particularly of Their Numerous Forms and Complications. Kenne: 1823. V. 63
Lectures on the Nervous System and Its Diseases. Philadelphia: 1836. V. 64

HALL, MARTHA H.
The Confederate Army of New Mexico. Austin: 1978. V. 64; 67

HALL, MARTIN HARDWICK
Sibley's New Mexico Campaign. Austin: 1960. V. 63

HALL, MARY
A Woman in the Antipodes and in the Far East. London: 1904. V. 65
A Woman's Trek from the Cape to Cairo. London: 1907. V. 65

HALL, PARNELL
Detective. New York: 1986. V. 67

HALL, R. N.
The Ancient Ruins of Rhodesia. London: 1902. V. 67
Great Zimbabwe, Mashonaland, Rhodesia: an Account of Two Years' Examination Work in 1902-1904 on Behalf of the Government of Rhodesia. London: 1905. V. 67

HALL, RADCLYFFE
The Master of the House. London: 1932. V. 62
The Well of Loneliness. London: 1928. V. 65

HALL, ROBERT H.
Light Shining in Darkness. Lecture on Physiology, Psychology and Psychological Questions. Huntington: 1897. V. 65

HALL, SAMUEL CARTER
The Baronial Halls and Ancient Picturesque Edifices of England. New York: 1881. V. 64
Ireland, Its Scenery and Character. 1841-1843. V. 67
Ireland: Its Scenery, Character &c. London. V. 66

HALL, SAMUEL R.
Lectures on School Keeping. Boston: 1829. V. 62

HALL, SPENCER TIMOTHY
Biographical Sketches of Remarkable People.... London: 1873. V. 67
Mesmeric Experience. London: 1845. V. 67
The Phreno-Magnet and Mirror of Nature: a Record of Facts, Experiments and Discoveries in Phrenology, Magnetism &c. London: 1843. V. 63

HALL, T.
The Queen's Royal Cookery; or Expert and Ready Way for the Dressing of all Sorts of Flesh, Fowl, Fish.... London: 1713. V. 65

HALL, T. WALTER
Pedigree of Hall, and Others. Second Series. N.P: 1912. V. 63
Sheffield Pedigrees. 1915. V. 63

HALL, THOMAS
The Fortunes and Adventures of Baby Rattler, and His Man Floss. London: 1846. V. 66

HALL, TREVOR H.
A Bibliography of Books on Conjuring in English from 1580 to 1850. Minneapolis: 1957. V. 64; 66
The Creation of a Magical Effect: Methods of Evolution in the Past and the Application of These Principles to Development in the Future.... London: 1952. V. 64
The Last Case of Sherlock Holmes: Ivy Johnson Bull of Borley. Rockville Centre: 1986. V. 64
New Day Necromancy: a Lecture Delivered Before the Magic Circle. London: 1948. V. 64
Nothing is Impossible. Croydon: 1946. V. 64
Old Conjuring Books: a Bibliographical and Historical Study with a Supplementary Check-List. London: 1972. V. 64
Search for Harry Price. London: 1978. V. 64
Sherlock Holmes and His Creator. London: 1978. V. 67
Some Aspects of Presentation and Pattern: Report of a Lecture... Delivered Before the Magic Circle. London: 1947. V. 64
Some Printers and Publishers of Conjuring Books and Other Ephemera 1800-1850. Leeds: 1976. V. 64
The Spiritualists: the Story of Florence Cook and William Crookes. London: 1962. V. 64
The Strange Case of Edmund Gurney. London: 1964. V. 64
The Testament of Ralph W. Hull. 1946. V. 64
The Winder Sale of Old Conjuring Books. Leeds: 1975. V. 64

HALL, W. H.
The Romans on the Riveria and the Rhone, a Sketch of the Conquest of Liguia and the Roman Province. London: 1898. V. 67

HALL, WILLIAM
The Shoelace Robin. New York: 1945. V. 64
Telltime the Rabbit. New York: 1943. V. 64

HALLAHAN, WILLIAM H.
The Dead of Winter. Indianapolis: 1972. V. 65

HALLAM, HENRY
The Constitutional History of England from the Accession of Henry VII to the Death of George II. New York: 1854. V. 65
Introduction to the Literature of Europe in the Fifteenth, Sixteenth and Seventeenth Centuries. Paris: 1839. V. 64
Introduction to the Literature of Europe, in the Fifteenth, Sixteenth and Seventeenth Centuries. London: 1843. V. 64
View of the State of Europe During the Middle Ages. Paris: 1835. V. 65
View of the State of Europe During the Middle Ages. London: 1841. V. 62; 66

HALLBERG, J. H.
Motion Picture Electricity. New York: 1914. V. 67

HALL-DUNCAN, NANCY
The History of Fashion Photography. New York: 1979. V. 63

HALLECK, FITZ-GREENE
Fanny. New York: 1819. V. 62; 64

HALLENBECK, CLEVE
Alvar Nunez Cabeza De Vaca - Journey and Route of the First European to Cross the Continent of North America 1534-1536. Glendale: 1940. V. 64
The Journey of Fray Marcos de Niza. Dallas: 1949. V. 62; 64; 65
Land of the Conquistadores. Caldwell: 1950. V. 63; 66
Legends of the Spanish Southwest. Glendale: 1938. V. 64; 65
Spanish Missions of the Old Southwest. Garden City: 1926. V. 62; 63; 64

HALLER, ALBRECHT VON, BARON
Biblotheca Chirurgica, qua Scripta, Ad Artem Chirurgicam Facientia a Rearum Initiis Recensentur. Bernae: 1774-1775. V. 66
First Lines of Physiology. Troy: 1803. V. 64
Histoire des Plantes Suisses, ou Matiere Medicale et de l'Usage Economique des Plantes. Berne: 1791. V. 63
Letters from Baron Haller to His Daughter, on the Truths of the Christian Religion. London: 1780. V. 62

HALLER, ALBRECHT VON, BARON *continued*
Letters from Baron Haller to His Daughter on the Truths of the Christian Religion. London: 1793. V. 64; 65
Nothiger Unterricht, Wie bey den Herrschenden Bosartigen Fiebern die Krankheit Abgewandt, Oder aufs Zuverlaszigste geheilt Wenden Konne.... Bern: 1765. V. 65

HALLEUR, G. HERMANN
The Art of Photography.... London: 1854. V. 67

HALLEY, EDMOND
Astronomical Tables with Precepts Both in English and Latin for Computing the Places of the Sun, Moon, Planets and Comets. London: 1752. V. 66

HALLEY, EDMUND
Miscellanea Curiosa. London: 1708. V. 64

HALLEY, ROBERT
Lancashire: Its Puritanism and Nonconformity. Manchester: 1872. V. 65

HALLIDAY, BRETT
The Private Practice of Michael Shayne. 1940. V. 62; 64

HALLIDAY, HANNAH
Mrs. Hannah Halliday's Letter to John Maddox, Esq., One of His Majesty's Justices of the Peace for the County of Somerset. London: 1752. V. 64

HALLIDAY, R. B.
Mites of Australia, a Checklist and Bibliography. 1998. V. 67

HALLIDAY, R. J.
Practical Azalea Culture, a Treatise on the Propagation and Cultivation of the Azalea Indica. Baltimore: 1880. V. 67

HALLIFAX, CHARLES
Familiar Letters on Various Subjects of Business and Amusement.... London: 1755. V. 62

HALLING, SOLOMON
The Messiah, a Poem: Attempted in English Blank Verse.... Georgetown: 1810. V. 63

HALLIWELL-PHILLIPPS, JAMES ORCHARD
A Collection of Letters Illustrative of the Progress of Science in England from the Reign of Queen Elizabeth to that of Charles the Second. London: 1841. V. 62
The Literature of the Sixteenth and Seventeenth Centuries. London: 1851. V. 66
Nugae Poeticae. London: 1844. V. 64
Palatine Anthology.... London: 1850. V. 66
Popular Rhymes and Nursery Tales.... London: 1849. V. 64

HALLMAN, G. VICTOR
Personal Financial Planning. New York: 1987. V. 64

HALLOWELL, ANNA DAVIS
James and Lucretia Mott. Life and Letters. Boston: 1884. V. 65

HALLS, J. J.
The Life and Correspondence of Henry Salt, Esq. London: 1834. V. 66

HALL-STEVENSON, JOHN
Makarony Fables, Fables for Grown Gentlemen; Lyrick Epistles and Several Other Poems. Dublin: 1772. V. 63; 65

HALLWARD, REGINALD FRANCIS
Flowers fo Paradise. London: 1889. V. 64

HALPER, ALBERT
The Foundry. London: 1934. V. 63; 67
Union Square. New York: 1933. V. 63; 64

HALPERT, SAM
When We Talk About Raymond Carver. Layton: 1991. V. 63

HALSELL, H. H.
Cowboys and Cattleland. Nashville: 1937. V. 67
Cowboys and Cattleland. Nashville: 1944. V. 66
My Autobiography. Dallas: 1948. V. 64; 67

HALSEY, DON P.
A Sketch of the Life of Capt. Don P. Halsey of the Confederate States Army. London: 1904. V. 63
A Sketch of the Life of Capt. Don P. Halsey of the Confederate States Army. Richmond: 1904. V. 62

HALSEY, FRANCIS W.
The Pioneers of Unadila Village 1784-1840 and Reminiscences of Village Life and of Panama and California from 1849-1850. Unadila: 1902. V. 64; 67

HALSEY, HARLAN PAGE
Macon Moore, the Southern Detective. New York: 1881. V. 63; 66
Phil Scott, the Indian Detective: a Tale of Startling Mysteries. New York: 1882. V. 64; 66

HALSEY, JACOB LAFAYETTE
Thomas Halsey of Hertfordshire, England and Southampton, Long Island 1591-1679 with his American Descendants to the Eighth and Ninth Generations. Morristown: 1895. V. 63; 66

HALSEY, WILLIAM F.
Admiral Halsey's Story. New York: 1947. V. 63

HALSMAN, PHILLIPE
Phillipe Halsman's Jump Book. New York: 1959. V. 65

HALSTEAD, B. W.
Poisonous and Venomous Marine Animals of the World. Washington: 1965-1970. V. 62; 63; 66

HALSTEAD, WARD C.
Brain and Intelligence. Chicago: 1947. V. 67

HALSTED, CAROLINE A.
The Obligations of Literature to the Mothers of England. London: 1840. V. 67

HALSTED, EDWARD PELLEW
Iron-Cased Ships. London: 1861. V. 65

HALSTED, WILLIAM
A Digested Index to the Decisions of the Superior Courts of the State of New Jersey. Trenton: 1830. V. 66

HALSTED, WILLIAM STEWART
Contributions to the Surgery of the Bile Passages, Especially of the Common Bile Duct.. V. 67
The Cure of the More Difficult as Well as the Simpler Inguinal Ruptures. Baltimore: 1903. V. 67
Surgical Papers of William Stewart Halsted. Baltimore: 1952. V. 64; 66; 67

HALTER, ERNEST J.
Collecting First Editions of Franklin Roosevelt. Chicago: 1949. V. 66

HALVERSON, DORCAS
Lookin' Back Again - Big Horn Country. Hardin: 1992. V. 67

HALY ABBAS
Liber Totius Medicine Necessaria Continens Quem Sapientissimus Haly Filius Abbas Discipulus Abimeher Muysi Filii Sejar Editit.... Lugduni: 1523. V. 62

HALY, R. STANDISH
Impressment: an Attempt to Prove Why It Should and How It Could be Abolished. Poole: 1822. V. 62

HAMADAY, MARY LAIRD
Selected Poems 1973-1980. Springfield: 1982. V. 63

HAMADY, WALTER
For the Hundredth Time. Minor Confluence: 1981. V. 64
Journal Liftings. Madison: 1987. V. 63
Neopostmodernism or Gabberjab Number 6. Mt. Horeb: 1988. V. 62; 64
The Plumfoot Poems. Mt. Horeb: 1967. V. 66
Travelling. Mt. Horeb: 1966. V. 62

HAMAYA, HIROSHI
Landscapes. New York: 1982. V. 63; 64; 65

HAMBLY, W. D.
Source Book for African Anthropology. 1937. V. 62

HAMBOURG, DARIA
Richard Doyle His Life and Work. 1948. V. 67

HAMBURGER, MICHAEL
Orpheus Street, London, S.E.5. 1967. V. 63
Travelling. London: 1969. V. 63

HAMBY, WALLACE
The Case Reports and Autopsy Records of Ambroise Pare. Springfield. V. 64; 66

HAMDAN Stables Stud Book of Arabian Horses. Volume I. Cairo: 1969. V. 64

HAMEL, FRANK
Lady Hester Lucy Stanhope: a New Light on Her Life and Love Affairs. London: 1913. V. 67

HAMELN, GLUCKEL VON
Denkwurdigkeiten der Fluckel Von Hameln. Berlin: 1923. V. 67

HAMENOPOULOS, CONSTANTINO
Legum Procherion Cum Delectu Ac Compendio Ext Toto Iure Colelctum ac Digestum, a Pervenerando Constantino Harmenopulo.... Coloniae: 1555. V. 66

HAMERTON, PHILIP GILBERT
Contemporary French Painters. An Essay. London: 1868. V. 64

HAMILIN, PERCY GATLING
Old Bald Head (General R. S. Ewell). The Portrait of a Soldier. Strasburg: 1940. V. 63; 65

HAMILL, ALFRED E.
The Decorative Work of T. M. Cleland, a Record and Review. New York: 1929. V. 63

HAMILL, H. M.
The Old South. A Monograph. Nashville: 1904. V. 63

HAMILL, PETE
The Gift. New York: 1973. V. 62

HAMILTON, A.
Maori Art. London and New York: 1972-1977. V. 62

HAMILTON, ALEXANDER
Hamilton's Itinerarium, Being a Narrative of a Journey from Annapolis, Maryland, Through Delaware, Pennsylvania, New York, New Jersey, Connecticut, Rhode Island.... St. Louis: 1907. V. 64
Letters to Dr. William Osborn. Edinburgh: 1792. V. 66
A New Account of the East Indies.... London: 1930. V. 62

HAMILTON, ALEXANDER continued
Observations on Certain Documents Contained in No. V and VI of The History of the United States for the Year 1796 In Which the Charge of Speculation Against Alexander Hamilton, Late Secretary Treasury is Fully Refuted. Philadelphia: 1797. V. 64
Official Reports on Publick Credit, a National Bank, Manufactures and a Mint. Philadelphia: 1821. V. 66
A Treatise on the Management of Female Complaints and of Children in Early Infance. New York: 1972. V. 65
The Works of Alexander Hamilton. New York: 1904. V. 64

HAMILTON, ALLAN MCLANE
Clinical Electro-Therapeutics Medical and Surgical. New York: 1973. V. 62

HAMILTON, ANGUS
Korea: Its History, its People and Its Commerce. Boston: 1910. V. 67

HAMILTON, ANTHONY
Grammont's Memoirs of the Court of Charles the Second. London: 1906. V. 65
Memoires du Comte de Grammont. Londres: 1793. V. 63
Memoirs of Count Grammont. London: 1794. V. 62; 66; 67
Memoirs of Count Grammont. London: 1885. V. 62
Memoirs of the Life of Count de Grammont.... London: 1714. V. 67
Memories of Count Grammont. Philadelphia: 1888. V. 67

HAMILTON, ARCHIBALD
Report of the Trial by Jury of the Action of Damages for a Libel in the Beacon Newspaper; Lord Archibald Hamilton, Against Duncan Stevenson, Printer in Edinburgh. Edinburgh: 1822. V. 63

HAMILTON, AUGUSTA
Marriage Rites, Customs and Ceremonies of the Nations of the Universe. London: 1822. V. 64; 65

HAMILTON, BRUCE
Too Much of Water. London: 1958. V. 65

HAMILTON, DOUGLAS
Records of Sport in Southern India. 1892. V. 67

HAMILTON, EDMOND
The Star Kings. 1949. V. 64

HAMILTON, ELIZABETH
The Cottages of Glenburnie.... Edinbrugh: 1808. V. 65
The Cottages of Glenburnie.... Edinburgh: 1815. V. 65
Letters on the Elementary Principles of Education. Bath: 1801-1802. V. 62; 66
Letters on the Elementary Principles of Education. London: 1810. V. 65
Memoirs of Modern Philosophers. Bath: 1800. V. 62
Memoirs of Modern Philosophies. London: 1801. V. 66
Memoirs of the Life of Agrippina, the Wife of Germanicus. Bath: 1804. V. 63; 65
A Series of Popular Essays, Illustrative of Principles Essentially Connected with the Improvement of the Understanding, the Imagination and the Heart. Edinburgh: 1813. V. 63
Translation of the Letters of a Hindoo Rajah. London: 1796. V. 63; 65

HAMILTON, FRANCIS
An Account of the Fishes Found in the River Ganges and Its Branches. Edinburgh: 1822. V. 63
An Account of the Fishes Found in the River Ganges and Its Branches. 1972. V. 63

HAMILTON, GEORGE
The Elements of Drawings in Various Branches, for the Use of Students.... London: 1827. V. 64

HAMILTON, GEORGE ROSTREVOR
The Greek Portrait. London: 1934. V. 62; 65
The Latin Portrait. London: 1929. V. 64

HAMILTON, GERALD
Jacaranda. London: 1961. V. 64

HAMILTON, HAMISH
Majority 1931-1952 - an Anthology of 21 Years of Publishing. London: 1952. V. 63

HAMILTON, HARLAN
A Silhouette of William Combe. Bowling Green: 1969. V. 66

HAMILTON, HENRY A.
Reminiscences of a Veteran. Concord: 1897. V. 63; 66

HAMILTON, HENRY W.
The Sioux of the Rosebud, a History in Pictures. Norman: 1971. V. 65; 67

HAMILTON, HUGH
An Attempt to Prove the Existence and Absolute Perfection of the Supreme Unoriginated Being, in a Demonstrative Manner. Dublin: 1784. V. 62; 65
De Sectionibus Conicis. Tractatus Geometricus. In Quo ex Natura Ipsius Coni Sectionum Affectioens (sic) Facillime Duducuntur. Methodo Novo. Londini: 1758. V. 63

HAMILTON, IAN
Jean - a Memoir. London: 1941. V. 62
A Staff Officer's Scrap-Book During the Russo-Japanese War. London: 1905-1907. V. 67

HAMILTON, J. G. DE ROULHAC
Reconstruction in North Carolina. New York: 1914. V. 63

HAMILTON, JAMES
From Wilderness to Statehood, a History of Montana. Portland: 1957. V. 67
The History, Principles, Practice and Results of the Hamiltonian System, for the Last Twelve Years.... Manchester: 1829. V. 62; 64

Observations on the Use and Abuse of Mercurial Medicines in Various Diseases. Edinburgh: 1819. V. 62; 63
Observations on the Utility and Administration of Purgative Medicines in Several Diseases. Edinburgh: 1805. V. 63

HAMILTON, JANE
The Book of Ruth. New York: 1988. V. 62; 63; 64; 65; 66; 67
A Map of the World. New York: 1994. V. 63; 64; 66; 67
The Short History of a Prince. Franklin Center: 1998. V. 63
The Short History of a Prince. New York: 1998. V. 67

HAMILTON, JOHN
A Complete Body of Perspective, In All Its Branches. London: 1749. V. 65

HAMILTON, MYRA
Kingdoms Curious. London: 1905. V. 65

HAMILTON, PATRICK
Hangover Square. London: 1941. V. 67
Money with Menaces and To the Public Danger. London: 1939. V. 67
The Slaves of Solitude. London: 1947. V. 62

HAMILTON, R.
Game. Madras: 1881. V. 67
The Natural History of the Amphibious Carnivora. Edinburgh: 1839. V. 62

HAMILTON, RICHARD VESEY
Letters and Papers of Admiral of the Fleet Sir Thomas Byam Martin. London: 1903-1898-1901. V. 62

HAMILTON, ROBERT
An Inquiry Concerning the Rise and Progress, the Redemption and Present State and the Management of the National Debt of Great Britain. Edinburgh: 1813. V. 64
The May Flower. 1846. V. 63

HAMILTON, SCHUYLER
History of the National Flag of the United States of America. Philadelphia: 1852. V. 65

HAMILTON, SINCLAIR
Early American Book Illustrators and Wood Engravers 1670-1870. Princeton: 1968. V. 63

HAMILTON, STEVE
A Cold Day in Paradise. New York: 1998. V. 66; 67

HAMILTON, THOMAS
Men and Manners in America. Edinburgh: 1833. V. 67
Men and Manners in America. Edinburgh: 1834. V. 66
The Youth and Manhood of Cyril Thornton. London: 1829. V. 66
The Youth and Manhood of Cyril Thornton. Edinburgh: 1927. V. 63

HAMILTON, VIRGINIA
In the the Beginning (Creation Stories from Around the World). New York: 1988. V. 65
M. C. Higgins, the Great. New York: 1974. V. 65

HAMILTON, W. F.
Military Annals of Carroll County. Carrollton: 1906. V. 63

HAMILTON, W. T.
My Sixty Years on the Plains, Trapping, Trading, Indian Fighting. New York: 1905. V. 64
My Sixty Years on the Plains, Trapping, Trading, Indians. New York: 1975. V. 67

HAMILTON, WALTER
Dated Book-Plates (Ex-Libris), with a Treatise on Their Origin and Development. London: 1895. V. 66

HAMILTON, WILLIAM
Collection of Engravings from Ancient Vases Mostly of Pure Greek Workmanship Discovered in Sepulchres in the Kingdom of the Two Sicilies But Chiefly in the Neighbourhood of Naples During the Course of the Years MDCCLXXXIX and MDCCLXXXX no in the Possessi. Naples: 1791-1795. V. 63; 64
Discussions on Philosophy and Literature, Education and University Reform. London: 1853. V. 64
The Exemplary Life and Character of James Bonnell, Esq., Late Accomptant General of Ireland. London: 1807. V. 67
Letters Concerning the Northern Coast of the County of Antrim. London: 1786. V. 63

HAMILTON, WILLIAM J.
Researches in Asia Minor, Pontus and Armenia; with Some Account of Their Antiquities and Geology. London: 1842. V. 67

HAMILTON, WILLIAM RICHARD
Historical Notices of the Society of Dilettanti.... London: 1855. V. 64

HAMILTON, WILLIAM ROWAN
Elements of Quaternions. London: 1866. V. 63

HAMILTON, WILLIAM T.
A Word for the African. A Sermon for the Benefit of the American Colonization Society Delivered in the Second Presbyterian Church, Newark, July 24, 1825. Newark: 1825. V. 63; 66

HAMILTON BROWNE, G.
With the Lost Legion in New Zealand. London: 1911. V. 67

HAMLETT, W. C.
Sharks, Skates and Rays, the Biology of Elasmobranch Fishes. Baltimore: 1999. V. 63; 65

HAMLEY & CO.
Hamley Cowboy Catalog. Pendelton: 1931. V. 64

HAMLEY, EDWARD BRUCE
Lady Lee's Widowhood. Edinburgh: 1854. V. 67

HAMLIN, AUGUSTUS CHOATE
Martyria; or, Andersonville Prison. Boston: 1866. V. 63

HAMLIN, RALPH C.
Winning the Desert Race. Syracuse: 1912. V. 66

HAMMELL, GEORGE M.
The Passing of the Saloon. Cincinnati: 1908. V. 64; 66

HAMMELMAN, HANS
Book Illustrators in Eighteenth Century England. New Haven and London: 1975. V. 63

HAMMER, ARMAND
The Armand Hammer Collection: a Loan Exhibition for the Benefit of the Smithsonian Institution. 1970. V. 65

HAMMER, KEN
Custer in '76, Walter Camp's Notes on the Custer Fight. Provo: 1976. V. 67
Men With Custer. Fort Collins: 1972. V. 65; 67
Men With Custer. 1996. V. 67

HAMMER, LAURA V.
Light 'N Hitch; a Collection of Historical Writing Depicting Life on the High Plains. Dallas: 1958. V. 67

HAMMER, MINA FISHER
History of the Kodak and Its Continuations: The First Folding Panoramic Cameras: Magic Lantern, Kodak, Movie; Closeup of the Inventor and the Kodak Stato. New York: 1940. V. 63

HAMMER, S.
The Genus Conophytum. London: 1993. V. 64

HAMMER, VICTOR
Some Fragments for C. R. H. Lexington: 1967. V. 62

HAMMETT, DASHIELL
The Adventures of Sam Spade. New York: 1944. V. 65
The Battle of the Aleutians. 1944. V. 63; 64; 66
The Big Knockover. New York: 1965. V. 67
The Big Knockover. New York: 1966. V. 65; 67
The Continental Op. New York: 1945. V. 66; 67
The Continental Op. New York: 1974. V. 66; 67
The Dain Curse. New York: 1929. V. 64; 65; 66
The Dashiell Hammett Omnibus. London: 1950. V. 65; 67
The Dashiell Hammett Story Omnibus. London: 1966. V. 65; 67
Dead Yellow Women. New York: 1947. V. 67
The Glass Key. London: 1931. V. 64; 66
The Glass Key. New York: 1931. V. 64; 65
Hammett Homicides. New York: 1946. V. 67
Modern Tales of Horror. London: 1932. V. 66
The Return of the Continental Op. New York: 1945. V. 65
Secret Agent X9. New York: 1976. V. 65
Secret Agent X9. Princeton: 1990. V. 65
The Thin Man. 1934. V. 66
The Thin Man. New York: 1934. V. 65; 67

HAMMETT, G. A.
Philosophy of Space and Time. Newport: 1849. V. 64

HAMMOND, C. O.
The Dragonflies of Great Britain and Ireland. 1983. V. 66
The Dragonflies of Great Britain and Ireland. London: 1983. V. 64

HAMMOND, ERICSSON, MRS.
Swedish American Cookbook. New York: 1918. V. 66

HAMMOND, GEORGE P.
Captain Charles M. Weber - Pioneer of the San Joaquin and Founder of Stockton, California. Berkeley: 1966. V. 66
Coronado Cuarto Centennial Publications 1540-1940. Volume II - Narratives at the Coronado Expedition. Albuquerque: 1940. V. 66
The Discovery of New Mexico 1580-1954. Albuquerque: 1966. V. 66
Don Juan de Oñate: Colonizer of New Mexico 1595-1628. N.P: 1953. V. 66
The Duchow Journal a Voyage from Boston to California in 1852. San Francisco: 1959. V. 66
The Larkin Papers for the History of California. Berkeley: 1951-1964. V. 65
New Mexico in 1602, Juan De Montoya's Relation of the Discovery of New Mexico. Albuquerque: 1938. V. 66
Onate - Colonizer of New Mexico 1595-1628. Albuquerque: 1953. V. 65
The Rediscovery of New Mexico 1580-1594; The Explorations of Chamuscado, Espejo, Castano de Sota, Morlete and Leyva de Bonilla and Humana. Albuquerque: 1966. V. 64

HAMMOND, HENRY
Charis Kai 'Eiph'nh (Graece), or a Pacifick Discourse of Gods, Grace and Decrees in a Letter, of Full Accordance; Written to the Reverend and Most Learned, Dr. Robert Sanderson... (with) Some Profitable Directions Both for Priest and People.... London: 1660. V. 67
A Letter of Resolution to Six Quaeres, of Present Use in the Church of England. London: 1653. V. 67
Of the Power of the Keyes; or, Of Binding and Loosing. London: 1647. V. 65
Sermons Preached.... London: 1675. V. 67
Thirty-One Sermons Preached on Several Occasions. Parts I & II. The Miscellaneous Theological Works, to Which is Prefixed, The Life of the author by John Fell and a Practical Catechism. Oxford: 1847-1850. V. 67

HAMMOND, J. R.
Herbert George Wells, an Annotated Bibliography of His Works. New York and London: 1977. V. 63

HAMMOND, JAMES
Catalogue of James Hammond's Circulating Library. Newport: 1844?. V. 63
Love Elegies, Written in the Year 1732. London: 1751. V. 66

HAMMOND, JOHN FOX
A Surgeon's Report on Socotto, New Mexico: 1852. Together with Comments by Other Early Travellers through Socorro. Santa Fe: 1966. V. 64

HAMMOND, JOHN HAYS
The Autobiography of John Hays Hammond. New York: 1935. V. 67

HAMMOND, JOHN MARTIN
Colonial Mansions of Maryland and Delaware. Philadelphia: 1914. V. 66
Quaint and Historic Forts of North America. Philadelphia: 1915. V. 63

HAMMOND, L. M.
Trials and Triumphs of an Orphan Girl; or the Biography of Mrs. Deiadamia Chase.... 1859. V. 64

HAMMOND, NATALIE
A Woman's Part in a Revolution. New York: 1897. V. 63

HAMMOND, R. A.
The Life and Writings of Charles Dickens. Toronto: 1871. V. 62

HAMMOND, W. G.
J. R. R. Tolkien. A Descriptive Bibliography. Winchester: 1993. V. 62

HAMMOND, WILLIAM
Masonic Emblems with Jewels, Treasures at Freemasons' Hall, London. London: 1917. V. 62
On Certain Conditions of Nervous Derangement. New York: 1881. V. 62; 64
Physics and Physiology of Spiritualism. New York: 1871. V. 65
Physiological Memoirs. Philadelphia: 1863. V. 64
Sleep and Its Derangements. Philadelphia: 1873. V. 65
Spinal Irritation. New York: 1870. V. 65
A Treatise on Diseases of the Nervous System. New York: 1871. V. 64
A Treatise on Insanity In Its Medical Relations. New York: 1883. V. 64; 65

HAMMOND, WILLIAM A.
Robert Severne His Friends and His Enemies. Philadelphia: 1867. V. 66

HAMNER, EARL
Spencer's Mountain. New York: 1962. V. 66

HAMNETT, NINA
Laughing Torso - Reminicences. London: 1932. V. 63

HAMOR, RAPHE
A True Discourse of the Present Estate of Virginia, and the Succese of the Affaires There Till the 18 of June 1614. Together With a Relation of Several English Townes and Fortes.... Albany: 1860. V. 67

HAMPDEN, PSEUD.
Genuine Book of Nullification.... Charleston: 1831. V. 66

HAMPSON, G. F.
Catalogue of the Lepidoptera Phalaenae in the British Museum. 1898-1920. V. 65; 66
Catalogue of the Lepidoptera Phalaenae in the British Museum. London: 1898-1920. V. 64
Illustrations of Typical Specimens of Lepidoptera Heterocera in the Collection of the British Museum. Part 9 - Macrolepidoptera Heterocera of Ceylon. London: 1893. V. 62

HAMPSON, JOHN
A Bag of Stones - a Novel. London: 1952. V. 63
The Larches. London: 1938. V. 63
O Providence. London: 1932. V. 64
Saturday Night at the Greyhound. London: 1931. V. 63
Two Stories - the Mare's Nest: the Long Shadow. London: 1931. V. 63

HAMPSON, WALTER
A Wheel in Wharfeland. London: 1918. V. 62; 65

HAMPSTEAD ANTIQUARIAN AND HISTORICAL SOCIETY
Transactions for the Year(s) 1898, 1899, 1900, 1901, 1902-03. Hampstead: 1899-1905. V. 62

HAMPTON & SON'S
Illustrated Designs of Cabinet Furniture, Engraved from Photographs of Stock, at Their New Premises and Manufactory, 8 Pall Mall East and 1, 2, 3, Dorset Place, Charing Cross. London: 1902. V. 67

HAMPTON, CHRISTOPHER
Poems for Shakespeare. London: 1972. V. 62

HAMPTON, O. P.
Wounds of the Extremities in Military Surgery. St. Louis: 1951. V. 66; 67

HANAFORD, PHEBE A.
The Life and Writings of Charles Dickens. Augusta: 1871. V. 62

HANBRIDGE, MARY
The Memories of William Hanbridge. 1939. V. 65

HANBRIDGE, WILLIAM
The Memories of William Hanbridge. 1939. V. 63

HANBURY, ADA
Advanced Studies in Flower Painting. London: 1895. V. 66

HANBURY, D.
Science Papers, Chiefly Pharmacological and Botanical. 1876. V. 66
Science Papers, Chiefly Pharmacological and Botanical. London: 1876. V. 64

HANBURY, WILLIAM
A Complete Body of Planting and Gardening.... London: 1770-1771. V. 63
The History of the Rose and Progress of the Charitable Foundations at Church-Langton; Together with the Different Deeds of Trust of that Establishment. London: 1767. V. 63

HANCOCK, H. IRVING
Jiu-Jitsu Combat Tricks: Japanese Feats of Attack & Defence in Personal Encounter. New York and London: 1904. V. 67

HANCOCK, J.
The Herons of the World. New York: 1978. V. 63; 64

HANCOCK, JAMES
The Herons of the World. London: 1978. V. 62

HANCOCK, JOHN
Observations on the Climate, Soil and Productions of British Guiana, and On the Advantages of Emigration to and Colonizing the Interior of, That Country.... London: 1840. V. 66

HANCOCK, SAMUEL
The Narrative of Samuel Hancock of His Overland Journey to Oregon in 1845. New York: 1927. V. 64; 67

HANCOCK, THOMAS
A Centennial Volume of the Writings of Charles Goodyear and Thomas Hancock. Boston: 1939. V. 67

HANCOCK, WILLIAM NEILSON
Three Lectures on the Questions, Should the Principles of Political Economy be Disregarded at the Present Crisis?. Dublin: 1847. V. 63

THE HAND Book of North Devon, with a Trip on the Crediton and North Devon Railways. Exeter: 1856?. V. 63

HAND Book of the First Presbyterian Church. Wilmington, NC 1892-1913. Being a Continuation of the Memorial Volume of 1892. Wilmington: 1913. V. 67

THE HAND-BOOK for the Man of Business, Applicable to All Departments of Commerical Engagement. London: 1865. V. 66

A HAND-BOOK for Visitors to Oxford. Oxford: 1847. V. 62

THE HANDBOOK for Torquay and Its Neighbourhood, with Natural History of the District. London: 1854. V. 63

A HANDBOOK of Abyssinia. London: 1917. V. 64

THE HANDBOOK of Amherst. Amherst: 1891. V. 65

HANDBOOK of the Birds of the World. Volume 2. Stockholm: 1913-1916. V. 66

THE HANDBOOK of the Man of Fashion. Philadelphia: 1847. V. 65

HANDEL, GEORGE FRIDERIC
Messiah-the Wordbook for the Oratoro. New York: 1992. V. 65

HANDERSON, H. E.
The School of Salernum. An Historical Sketch of Medieval Medicine. New York: 1883. V. 64

HANDLEY, L.
Hunter's Moon. 1923. V. 67

HANDLEY, M. A., MRS.
Roughing It In Southern India. 1911. V. 67
Roughing It In Southern India. London: 1911. V. 65

HANDLEY-TAYLOR, GEOFFREY
C. Day-Lewis, the Poet Laureate: a Bibliography. 1968. V. 62
C. Day-Lewis, the Poet Laureate: a Bibliography. London: 1968. V. 65

HANDLIN, W. W.
American Politics, a Moral and Political Work, Treating of the Causes of the Civil War, the Nature of Government, and the Necessity for Reform. New Orleans: 1864. V. 62

HANDY, ISAAC W. K.
The Terrible Doings of God. Portsmouth: 1856. V. 66
U.S. Bonds; or Duress by Federal Authority. Baltimore: 1874. V. 65

HANDY, MARY O.
History of Fort Sam Houston. San Antonio: 1951. V. 64; 67

HANFF, HELENE
84 Charing Cross Road. New York: 1970. V. 65
84 Charing Cross Road. 1994. V. 66; 67

HANGER, GEORGE
The Life, Adventures and Opinions of Col. George Hanger. London: 1801. V. 66

THE HANGMAN'S Record, the Books of the Century.... London: 1903. V. 63

HANKE, KEN
Charlie Chan at the Movies: History, Filmography and Criticism. Jefferson: 1989. V. 67

HANKINSON, C. F. J.
Debrett's Peerage, Baronetage, Knightage and Companionage. London: 1936. V. 63
Debrett's Peerage, Baronetage, Knightage and Companionage. 1947. V. 63

HANKS, N. C.
Up the Hills. Chicago: 1921. V. 63; 66

HANLEY, JAMES
Aria and Finale. London: 1932. V. 66
Captain Bottell. London: 1933. V. 62; 66
Drift: a Novel. London: 1930. V. 66
Ebb and Flood - a Novel. London: 1932. V. 63
Grey Children: a Study in Humbug and Misery. London: 1937. V. 66
Hollow Sea. London: 1938. V. 66
Men in Darkness - Five Stories. London: 1931. V. 63; 66
The Ocean; a Novel. London: 1941. V. 66
The Secret Journey. London: 1936. V. 66
Stoker Haslett. Chipping Camden: 1932. V. 64
Stoker Haslett. London: 1932. V. 63; 66
The Welsh Sonata; Variations on a Theme. London: 1954. V. 67

HANLEY, PATRICK
Tiger Trails in Assam. 1961. V. 67

HANLY, J. FRANK
A Day in the Siskiyous - an Oregon Extravaganza. 1916. V. 65

HANMER, THOMAS
The Garden Book of Sir Thomas Hanmer Bart. London: 1933. V. 65

HANNA, G. D.
Miocene Marine Diatoms from Maria Madre Island, Mexico. 1926-1932. V. 62

HANNA, WILLIAM
Memoirs of the Life and Writings of Thomas Chalmers. Edinburgh: 1852-1854. V. 62

HANNAFORD, D. R.
Spanish Colonial or Adobe Architecture of California 1800-1850. New York: 1931. V. 62; 65

HANNAH, BARRY
Boomerang. Boston: 1989. V. 63
Captain Maximus. Stories. New York: 1985. V. 63
Geronimo Rex. New York: 1972. V. 65
Hey Jack!. New York: 1987. V. 63; 67
Nightwatchmen. New York: 1973. V. 62; 63; 64; 66; 67
The Tennis Handsome. New York: 1983. V. 63

HANNAHFORD, SAMUEL
Sea and River-Side Rambles in Victoria.... Geelong: 1860. V. 62

HANNAY, JAMES
The History of Acadia, from Its First Discovery to Its Surrender to England by the Treaty of Paris. St. John: 1879. V. 67
History of New Brunswick. St. John: 1909. V. 67
History of the War of 1812, Between Great Britain and the United States of America. St. John: 1901. V. 67
The Life and Times of Sir Leonard Tilley Being A Political History of New Brunswick for the Past Seventy Years. St. John: 1897. V. 66

HANNEMAN, AUDRE
Ernest Hemingway - a Comprehensive Bibliography. Princeton: 1967. V. 63
Ernest Hemingway: a Comprehensive Bibliography. Princeton: 1969. V. 66

HANNUM, ALBERTA
Roseanna McCoy. 1947. V. 67

HANOVER, J. W.
Genetic Manipulation of Woody Plants. New York: 1987. V. 67

HANRAHAN, JAMES STEPHEN
Space Biology. New York: 1960. V. 63

HANRAHAN, JOYCE Y.
Works of Maurice Sendak 1947-1994. A Collection with Comments. Portsmouth: 1995. V. 67

HANS, FRED
The Great Sioux Nation. Chicago: 1907. V. 65; 67

HANSARD, GEORGE AGAR
Trout and Salmon Fishing in Wales. London: 1834. V. 63

HANSARD, LUKE
The Auto-biography of Luke Hansard, Written in 1817. Wakefield: 1991. V. 64; 66

HANSARD, P.
The Art of Raymond Ching. New York: 1982. V. 62

HANSARD, THOMAS CURSON
Typographia: an Historical Sketch of the Origin and Progress of the Art of Printing: With Practical Directions for Conducting Every Department in an Office.... London: 1825. V. 62

HANSBERRY, LORRAINE
Les Blancs: The Collected Last Plays of Lorraine Hansberry. New York: 1972. V. 63
The Movement: Documentary of a Struggle for Equality. New York: 1964. V. 63

HANSCOMB, BRIAN
Cornwall. Herefordshire: 1992. V. 64
Cornwall. London: 1992. V. 65

HANSEN, AL
A Primer of Happenings and Time/Space Art. New York: 1965. V. 63

HANSEN, GLADYS C.
The Chinese in California, a Brief Bibliographical History. Portland: 1970. V. 62

HANSEN, HANS JURGEN
Art and the Seafarer. A Historical Survey of the Arts and Crafts of Sailors and Shipwrights. New York: 1968. V. 64; 66
Studies on Arthropoda. Copenhagen: 1921-1930. V. 66

HANSEN, HARVEY
Wild Oats in Eden - Sonoma County in the 19th Century. Santa Rosa: 1962. V. 65

HANSEN, JOSEPH
Fadeout. 1970. V. 66
Fadeout. New York: 1970. V. 65
Strange Marriage. 1965. V. 66

HANSEN, NEIL
Presences of Nature. Carlisle: 1982. V. 64; 67

HANSEN, RON
The Assassination of Jesse James by the Coward Robert Ford. New York: 1981. V. 67
The Assassination of Jesse James by the Coward Robert Ford. New York: 1984. V. 64
Desperadoes. New York: 1979. V. 62; 63; 65; 67
Mariette in Ecstasy. New York: 1991. V. 67
Nebraska. New York: 1989. V. 67

HANSON, F. D.
The Origin and Early Evolution of Animals. Middletown: 1977. V. 63

HANSON, H. C.
The Giant Canada Goose. Carbondale: 1965. V. 64

HANSON, H. J.
Ianthe Cruises: Ushant - Gironde. 1950. V. 63
Off the Irish Coast. Ianthe: 1933. V. 63

HANSON, HARRY
The Canal Boatman 1760-1914. Manchester: 1975. V. 64; 66

HANSON, J. A.
Spirits in the Art, from the Plains and Southwest Cultures. Kansas City: 1994. V. 62; 67

HANSON, JOHN W.
Historical Sketch of the Old Sixth Regiment of Massachusetts Volunteers. Boston: 1866. V. 64; 67

HANSON, JOSEPH
The Whole Proceedings on the Trial of an Indictment Against Joseph Hanson, Esq. for a Conspiracy to Aid the Weavers of Manchester in Raising Their Wages.... London: 1809. V. 63

HANSON, JOSEPH M.
The Conquest of the Missouri Being the Story of the Life and Exploits of Captain Grant Marsh. Chicago: 1909. V. 65; 67

HANSON, L. W.
Contemporary Printed Sources for British and Irish Economic History 1701-1750. Cambridge: 1963. V. 62

HANSON, MARGERY FRANCES DAY
Day unto Day A Study of the Day Family in America. N.P: 1978. V. 66

HANSON, S. C.
Merry Melodies for the School Room and Social Circle. Williamsport: 1887. V. 65

HANWAY, JONAS
An Account of the Society for the Encouragement of the British Troops, in Germany and North America. London: 1760. V. 64; 65
Advice from Farmer Trueman to His Daughter Mary, Upon Her Going Into Service. London: 1810. V. 64
Common Sense; in Nine Conferences, Between a British Merchant and a Candid Merchant of America, in Their Private Capacities as Friends.... London: 1775. V. 65
Midnight the Signal. London: 1779. V. 65
Proposal for County Naval Free Schools, To Be Built On Waste Lands.... London: 1783. V. 62
Virtue in Humble Life.... London: 1777. V. 62; 64; 65

HANZLICEK, C. G.
Living In It. Iowa City: 1971. V. 66

HAPPER, WILHELMINA
The Gunniwolf and Other Merry Tales.... London: 1937. V. 67

HAPPY Bears ABC. New York: 1920. V. 62

HAPPY Family. New York: 1880. V. 62

THE HAPPY Rock, a Book About Henry Miller. Berkeley: 1945. V. 65

HARA, H.
The Flora of Eastern Himalaya.... Japan: 1966. V. 65

HARADA, JIRO
The Lesson of Japanese Architecture. London: 1936. V. 63

HARASZTHY, AGOSTIN
Grape Culture, Wines and Wine Making.... New York: 1862. V. 62

HARASZTHY, ARPAD
Wine Making in California. San Francisco: 1978. V. 66

HARBAUGH, H.
The Birds of the Bible. Philadelphia: 1854. V. 67

HARBIN, GEORGE
The Hereditary Right of the Crown of England Asserted; and the History of the Succession Since the Conquest Clear'd.... London: 1713. V. 66; 67

HARBISON, MASSY
A Narrative of the Sufferings of Massy Harbison, from the Indian Barbarity.. Pittsburgh: 1825. V. 63

HARBORD, J. B.
Glossary of Navigation. London and Edinburgh: 1863. V. 65; 67

HARBOUR, HENRY
Where Flies the Flag. London and Glasgow: 1904. V. 65

HARCOURT, EDWARD VERNON
Sporting in Algeria. Hastings: 1859. V. 62

HARCOURT, JOHN
Original Jests, Comprising an Unpublished Collection of Bonmots, Jeux d'Esprit Repartees, Bulls &c. London: 1828. V. 67

HARCOURT, ROBERT
A Relation of a Voyage to Guiana. London: 1928. V. 67

HARCOURT-SMITH, SIMON
The Last of Uptake or the Estranged Sisters. London: 1942. V. 62; 64

HARCUS, WILLIAM
South Australia; Its History, Resources and Productions. London: 1876. V. 63; 67

HARDAKER, JOSEPH
The Bridal of Tomar; and Other Poems. London: 1831. V. 64; 65

HARDCASTLE, GEORGE
Wanderings in Wensleydale, Yorkshire. Sunderland: 1864. V. 65
Wanderings in Wensleydale, Yorkshire. 1865. V. 64

HARDEE, WILLIAM J.
Hardee's Tactics. Hardee's Rifle and Light Infantry Tactics. Philadelphia: 1861. V. 64
Rifle and Infantry Tactics Revised and Improved.... Raleigh: 1862. V. 62
Rifle and Light Infantry Tactics; for the Exercise and Manoeuvers of Troops.... Memphis: 1861. V. 62; 63
Rifle and Light Infantry Tactics: for the Exercise and Manoeuvres of Troops.... Nashville: 1861. V. 62
Rifle and Light Infantry Tactics; for the Exercise and Manoeuvres of Troops.... Richmond: 1861. V. 62; 63; 65

HARDESTY, HENRY
Historical Hand Atlas of the United States (Jefferson and Berkeley Co., West Virginia). Chicago: 1883. V. 67

HARDIE, JAMES
The History of the Tread-Mill, Containing an Account of Its Origin, Construction, Operation, Effects as It Respects the Health and Morals of the Convicts.... New York: 1824. V. 63

HARDIE, MARTIN
The Etched Work of W. Lee-Hankey, R.E. from 1904 to 1920. London: 1920?. V. 63
Water-Colour Painting in Britain. London: 1975. V. 62; 66

HARDIE, WILLIAM
Scottish Painting 1837-1939. London: 1976. V. 67

HARDIN, JOHN WESLEY
The Life of John Wesley Hardin as Written by Himself. Sequin: 1896. V. 64

HARDIN, PHILOMELIA ANNA MARIA ANTOINETTE
Every Body's Cook and Receipt Book: but More Particularly Designed for Buckeyes, Hoosiers, Wolverines, Corncrackers, Suckers and All Epicures Who Wish to Live with the Present Times. Cleveland: 1842. V. 63; 66

HARDING, ANNE
Bibliography of Articles and Papers on North American Art. Washington: 1940. V. 65

HARDING, C. T.
Harding's Fables for Young Folks. Treating of Flowers, Animals, Birds, Insects, &c. London: 1940. V. 65

HARDING, COLIN
In Remotest Barotseland: Being an Account of a Journey of Over 8000 Miles through the Wildest and Remotest Parts of Lewanika's Empire. London: 1904. V. 65

HARDING, E. W.
The Flyfisher and the Trout's Point of View, New Light on Flyfishing Theory and Practice. 1931. V. 67

HARDING, GEORGE L.
Don Agustin V. Zamorano, Statesman, Soldier, Craftsman and California's First Printer. Los Angeles: 1934. V. 62; 63

HARDING, J.
Songs for a Printers' Way Goose. New York: 1904. V. 64

HARDING, J. D.
Elementary Art, or the Use of the Chalk and Lead Pencil, Advocated and Explained. London: 1846. V. 66; 67
Lessons on Trees. London: 1865. V. 66

HARDING, SAMUEL BANNISTER
Life of George R. Smith - Founder of Sedalia, Mo. Sedalia: 1904. V. 64; 67

HARDINGE, EMMA
Outline of a Plan for a Self-Sustaining Institution for Homeless and Outcast Females, in Which they Can be Employed and Instructed in a Progressive System of Horticulture. New York: 1859. V. 67

HARDINGE, GEORGE
Winter's Crimes 1. London: 1969. V. 66

HARDISTY, M. W.
The Biology of Lampreys. London: 1971-1972. V. 63

HARDIVILLER, CHARLES ACHILLE D'
Souvenirs des Highlands. Paris: 1835. V. 62; 66

HARDOUIN, E.
Tooneelen uit Het Leven, Karakterschetsen en Kleederdragten van Java's Bewoners.... Leiden: 1855. V. 62; 66

HARDWICK, ELIZABETH
The Ghostly Lover. New York: 1945. V. 64; 67
The Simple Truth. New York: 1955. V. 63

HARDWICK, MICHAEL
Four Sherlock Holmes Plays. London: 1964. V. 63
The Game's Afoot: Sherlock Holmes Plays. London: 1969. V. 63

HARDY, A.
The Open Sea; Its Natural History. Boston: 1956-1959. V. 65

HARDY, CAMPBELL
Forest Life in Acadie: Sketches of Sport and Natural History in the Lower Provinces of the Canadian Dominion. London: 1869. V. 65

HARDY, CHARLES FREDERICK
The Hardys of Barbon and Some Other Westmorland Statesman.... London: 1913. V. 62; 64; 65; 66

HARDY, EVELYN
Survivors of the Armada. 1966. V. 67

HARDY, LADY D.
Through Cities and Prairie Lands - Sketches of an American Tour. New York: 1881. V. 63; 66

HARDY, R. W. H.
Travels in the Interior of Mexico in 1825, 1826, 1827 and 1828. London: 1829. V. 66

HARDY, SPENCE
Notices of the Holy Land and Other Places Mentioned in the Scriptures: Visited in 1832-1833. London: 1835. V. 65

HARDY, THOMAS
A Changed Man, the Waiting Summer, and Other Tales Concluding with the Romantic Tales of a Milkmaid. London: 1913. V. 64
The Dynasts. London: 1904-1908. V. 65; 66
The Dynasts. London: 1927. V. 62; 64; 66
The Famous Tragedy of the Queen of Cornwall at Tintagel in Lyonesse. London: 1923. V. 62; 66
Far from the Madding Crowd. New York: 1874. V. 62
Far From the Madding Crowd. 1958. V. 62
Far From the Madding Crowd. New York: 1958. V. 63
Human Shows, Far Phantasies: Songs and Trifles. London: 1925. V. 62; 63; 64; 65
Jude the Obscure. London: 1896. V. 62; 63; 64; 66; 67
Jude the Obscure. New York: 1969. V. 62
Late Lyrics and Earlier, with Many More Verses. London: 1922. V. 62; 64; 65; 67
Life's Little Ironies. London: 1894. V. 66
Life's Little Ironies. New York: 1894. V. 66
Life's Little Ironies. London: 1895. V. 63
The Mayor of Casterbridge. New York: 1964. V. 63; 64; 65; 66
Poems of the Past and the Present. London and New York: 1902. V. 64
The Return of the Native. London: 1878. V. 62
The Return of the Native. New York: 1929. V. 63
Selected Poems. London: 1921. V. 63
Tess of the D'Urbervilles. New York: 1892. V. 64; 65
Tess of the D'Urbervilles. New York: 1956. V. 63
The Three Wayfarers. New York: 1930. V. 63; 64; 66
The Three Wayfarers. Dorchester: 1935. V. 63
The Trumpet-Major. London: 1880. V. 62
The Trumpet-Major. London: 1896. V. 63
Under the Greenwood Tree. London: 1873. V. 66
Under the Greenwood Tree. London: 1876. V. 66
Under the Greenwood Tree. London: 1891. V. 66
Under the Greenwood Tree. London: 1940. V. 63
The Well Beloved. 1897. V. 62
Wessex Poems and Other Verses. London and New York: 1898. V. 63; 64
Wessex Poems and Other Verses. New York and London: 1899. V. 64
Wessex Tales Strange, Lively and Commonplace. London: 1888. V. 62
Winter Words in Various Moods and Metres. London: 1928. V. 62; 63; 65
Winter Words in Various Moods and Metres. New York: 1928. V. 63

HARDY, THOMAS DUFFUS
A Description of the Close Rolls in the Tower of London with an Account of the Early Courts of Law and Equity, and Various Historical Illustrations. London: 1833. V. 64

Memoirs of the Right Honourable Henry, Lord Langdale. London: 1852. V. 63

HARDY, W. G.
Alberta, a Natural History. Alberta: 1967. V. 65; 67

HARDY, WILLIAM
The Charters of the Duchy of Lancaster. London: 1845. V. 66
The Miner's Guide; or, Compleat Miner. Sheffield: 1748. V. 66

HARDYNG, JOHN
The Chronicle.... London: 1812. V. 62; 63

HARDY'S Anglers' Guide. Alnwick: 1928. V. 67

HARDY'S Angler's Guide. 1954. V. 67

HARE, AUGUSTUS J. C.
Biographical Sketches Being Memorials of Arthur Penrhyn Stanley, Dean of Westminster, Henry Alford, Dean of Canterbury, Mrs. Duncan Stewart, etc. London: 1895. V. 65
The Life and Letters of Maria Edgeworth. London: 1894. V. 65
Memorials of a Quiet Life. London: 1884-1876. V. 66
The Story of My Life. London: 1896-1900. V. 63
The Story of Two Noble Lives. London: 1893. V. 62; 67

HARE, C. E.
The Language of Sport. London: 1939. V. 67

HARE, CYRIL
An English Murder. London: 1951. V. 66
Tragedy at Law. New York: 1943. V. 66

HARE, FRANCIS
The Works. London: 1746. V. 63

HARE, FRANCIS AUGUSTUS
The Last of the Bushrangers; an Account of the Capture of the Kelly Gang. London: 1892. V. 67

HARE, JULIUS CHARLES
Fragments of Two Essays in English Philology. London: 1873. V. 64

HARE, R.
An Examination of the Question....the Discordancy Between the Characteristics of Mechanical Electricity and the Galvanic or Voltaic Fluid.... Philadelphia: 1836. V. 62
Experimental Observations and Improvements in Apparatus and Manipulation; with Theoretical Suggestions Respecting the Causes of Tornadoes.... Philadelphia: 1836. V. 62

HARE, ROBERT
On Electricity. Philadelphia: 1826. V. 63

HARE, THOMAS
Physiological Views of the Structure, Functions and Disorders of the Stomach and Alimentary Organs of the Human Body. London: 1824. V. 67

HAREWOOD, H.
A Dictionary of Sports...or Companion to the Field, the Forest and the Riverside.... 1835. V. 62
A Dictionary of Sports..or Companion to the Field, the Forest and the Riverside.... London: 1835. V. 65

HARFORD, JOHN SCANDRETT
Some Account of the Life, Death and Principles of Thomas Paine, Together with Remarks in His Writings.... Bristol: 1819. V. 65

HARFORD-BATTERSBY, CHARLES
Pilkington of Uganda. London: 1898. V. 67

HARGRAVE, LYNDON LANE
Report on Archaeological Reconnaissance in the Rainbow Plateau Area of Northern Arizona and Southern Utah.... Berkeley: 1935. V. 65

HARGREAVES, JACK
Fishing for a Year. 1951. V. 67

HARGROVE, E.
The History of the Castle, Town and Forest of Knaresborough, With Harrogate and it's Medicinal Springs.... York: 1798. V. 64; 65; 66
The History of the Castle, Town and Forest of Knaresborough, with Harrogate, and It's Medicinal Waters.... York: 1775. V. 65
The History of the Castle, Town and Forest of Knaresborough, with Harrogate and It's Medicinal Waters.... Knaresborough: 1789. V. 65
The Yorkshire Gazetteer, or, a Dictionary of the Towns, Villages and Hamlets; Monasteries and Castles; Principal Mountains, Rievers &c. in the County of York, and Ainsty, or County of the City, of York.... Knaresborough: 1812. V. 65

HARGROVE, WILLIAM
History and Description of the Ancient City of York.... London: 1818. V. 67
History and Description of the Ancient City of York.... York: 1818. V. 63
The York Poetical Miscellany: Being Selections from the Best Authors. York: 1835. V. 67

HARING, J. VREELAND
The Hand of Hauptmann. The Handwriting Expert Tells the Story of the Lindbergh Case. Plainfield: 1937. V. 66

HARINGTON, JOHN
The Metamorphosis of Ajax. London: 1927. V. 65
Nugae Antiquae.... 1769. V. 63

HARIOT, THOMAS
A Briefe and True Report of the New Found Land of Virginia. New York: 1871. V. 64

HARISTON, ELIZABETH S.
The Hairstons and Penns and Their Relations. Roanoke: 1940. V. 63

HARK, ANN
The Story of the Pennsylvania Dutch. New York: 1943. V. 64

HARKER, A.
The Tertiary Igneous Rocks of Skye. London: 1904. V. 62

HARKER, BAILEY J.
The Buxton of Yorkshire. London. V. 65
Philip Neville of Garriton. A Yorkshire Tale. London: 1875. V. 64
Rambles in Upper Wharfedale.... Skipton: 1869. V. 64; 65; 66

HARKNESS, MISS
Toilers in London; or, Inquiries Concerning Female Labour in the Metropolis. London: 1889. V. 62

HARKNESS, RUTH
The Lady and the Panda. 1938. V. 67

HARLAN, JACOB W.
California 46 to 48. San Francisco: 1888. V. 63; 66

HARLAN, ROBERT D.
Chapter Nine: The Vulgate Bible and Other Unfinished Projects of John Henry Nash. San Francisco: 1982. V. 62; 63; 64; 66
The Two Hundredth Book: a Bibliography of the Books Published by the Book Club of California 1958-1993. San Francisco: 1993. V. 64

HARLAND, HENRY
Grey Roses. London: 1895. V. 64

HARLAND, J.
Historical Account of the Cistercian Abbey of Salley in Craven, Yorkshire, founded AD 1147. London: 1853. V. 65

HARLAND, JOHN
Ballads and Songs of Lancashire Ancient and Modern. London: 1875. V. 62
Lancashire Folk-Lore: Illustrative of the Superstitions, Beliefs and Practices, Local Customs and Usages of the People of the County Palatine. Manchester: 1867. V. 62; 65
Lancashire Legends, Traditions, Pageants, Sports, &c. London: 1882. V. 62; 65

HARLAND, MARION
Common Sense in the Household. Toronto: 1879. V. 66

THE HARLEIAN Miscellany; or a Collection of Scarce, Curious and Entertaining Pamphlets and Tracts.... London: 1744-1745. V. 63

HARLEQUIN'S Invasion. London: 1790. V. 67

HARLEY, J. B.
Cartography in Prehistoric, Ancient and Medieval Europe and the Mediterranean. Chicago: 1987. V. 63

HARLEY, LEWIS R.
Francis Lieber. His Life and Political Philosophy. New York: 1899. V. 64

HARLEY, WILLIAM
The Harleian Dairy System; and an Account of the Various Methods of Dairy Husbandry Pursued by the Dutch. London: 1829. V. 63

HARLING, ROBERT
Notes on the Wood Engravings of Eric Ravilious. London: 1946. V. 67

HARLOW, ALVIN F.
Old Towpaths: the Story of the American Canal Era. New York: 1926. V. 63; 64
Old Waybills: the Romance of the Express Companies. New York: 1934. V. 63; 64; 66; 67

HARLOW, FRANCIS H.
Modern Pueblo Pottery. Flagstaff: 1977. V. 66

HARLOW, NEAL
Maps and Surveys of the Pueblo Lands of Los Angeles. Los Angeles: 1976. V. 63; 64; 65
Maps and Surveys of the Pueblo Lands of Los Angeles. Los Angeles: 1987. V. 62

HARLOW, REX
Oklahoma Leaders Biographical Sketches of the Foremost Living Men of Oklahoma. Oklahoma City: 1928. V. 65

HARLOW, V. T.
The Founding of the Second British Empire 1763-1793. London: 1964. V. 66
Ralegh's Last Voyage, Being an Account Drawn Out Of Contemporary Letters and Relations, Both Spanish and English.... London: 1932. V. 64; 65

HARMAN, APPLETON MILO
The Journal of Appleton Milo Harman. Glendale: 1946. V. 63; 66

HARMAN, FRED
The Great West in Painting. Chicago: 1969. V. 66

HARMAN, JOHN N.
Annals of Tazewel County, Virginia from 1800 to 1924. Richmond: 1922-1925. V. 64

HARMAN, SAMUEL W.
Hell on the Border. Fort Smith: 1920. V. 67
Hell on the Border. Lincoln: 1992. V. 66

HARMER, S. F.
Cambridge Natural History. London: 1922-1932. V. 64
Cambridge Natural History. 1959. V. 63

HARMON, DANIEL WILLIAMS
Harmon's Journal. Toronto: 1904. V. 64; 67

HARMON, J. C.
Crazy - the Kid or the Cowboy Scout. Sioux City: 1921. V. 62; 65

HARMON, NOLAN B.
The Famous Case of Myra Clark Gaines. Baton Rouge: 1946. V. 66

HARMON, R. W.
Bibliography of Animal Venoms. Gainesville: 1948. V. 62

HARMS, EMILIE
Caledonia. Von der Verfasserin der Sommerstunden. Hamburg: 1802-1804. V. 63

HARMSEN, DOROTHY
Harmsen's Western Americana. Flagstaff: 1971. V. 67
Harmsen's Western Americana. Denver: 1977-1978. V. 63

HARMSEN, TYRUS
Joseph Arnold Foster, Printer. Pasadena: 1998. V. 64

HARMSWORTH, ALFRED C.
Motors and Motor-Driving. London: 1902. V. 62
Motors and Motor-Driving. London: 1904. V. 67

HARNER, PHILIP M.
Tennessee: a History. New York: 1933. V. 66

HARPER, CHARLES
The Manchester and Glasgow Road, This Way to Gretna Green. London: 1907. V. 63

HARPER, HARRY
Dawn of the Space Age. London: 1946. V. 67

HARPER, HENRY H.
A Journey in Southwestern Mexico: Narrative of Experiences and Observations on Agricultural and Industrial Conditions. Boston: 1910. V. 64
The Psychology of Speculation. Boston: 1926. V. 65

HARPER, IDA
The Life and Work of Susan B. Anthony. Indianapolis and Kansas City: 1899-1908. V. 63

HARPER, J. RUSSELL
Paul Kane's Frontier, Including Wanderings of an Artist Among the Indians of North America. Forth Worth: 1971. V. 62; 63; 64
Portrait of a Period. A Collection of Notman Photographs 1856-1915. Montreal: 1967. V. 64

HARPER, MINNIE
Old Ranches. Dallas: 1936. V. 67

HARPER, ROBERT GOODLOE
Observations on the Dispute Between the United States and France. Philadelphia: 1797. V. 63
Observations on the Dispute Between the United States and France. London: 1798. V. 67

HARPER, WILLIAM
The Antiquity, Innocence and Pleasures of Gardening in a Sermon Preach'd at the Parish Church of Malpas in the County of Chester, at a Meeting of Gardners and Florists April 18, 1732. London: 1732. V. 66
The Pro-Slavery Argument; as Maintained by the Most Distinguished Writers of the Southern States.... Charleston: 1852. V. 62

HARPER'S Household Handbook. New York: 1913. V. 67

HARR, JONATHAN
A Civil Action. New York: 1995. V. 62; 64; 65; 66

HARRADEN, BEATRICE
Ships That Pass in the Night. Boston: 1893?. V. 65
Ships that Pass in the Night. New York: 1900. V. 63

HARRALL, THOMAS
Picturesque Views of the Severn: with Historical and Topographical Illustrations by Thomas Harral. London: 1824. V. 66; 67

HARRER, HEINRICH
Seven Years in Tibet. London: 1953. V. 62
Seven Years in Tibet. New York: 1993. V. 65
The White Spider. London: 1960. V. 63

HARRIGAN and Hart's End Men Joker. New York: 1890. V. 65

HARRIMAN ALASKA EXPEDITION
Alaska. Volume VIII. Insects. Part I. Volume IX. Insects Part 2. New York: 1904. V. 66

HARRINGTON, CHARLES
Summering in Colorado. Denver: 1874. V. 64; 66

HARRINGTON, CONYERS
An Impartial History of the Life and Reign of Her Late Majesty Queen Anne of Immortal Memory.... Cambridge: 1744. V. 65

HARRINGTON, ELIZABETH STILL STANHOPE, COUNTESS OF
Poems by.... London: 1874. V. 63
The Storks. The False Prince. London: 1875. V. 63

HARRINGTON, JAMES
The Oceana and Other Works.... London: 1737. V. 66
The Rota: or, a Model of a Free State, or Equall Common-Wealth.... London: 1660. V. 64

HARRINGTON, JOHN
Saint George's Chapel, Windsor. London: 1872. V. 66

HARRINGTON, JOHN W.
The Adventures of Admiral Frog. New York: 1902. V. 65

HARRINGTON, KENT
Dia De Los Muertos. Tucson: 1997. V. 66; 67

HARRIOTT, W. H.
The Cato Street Conspiracy. London: 1820. V. 62

HARRIS, A. C.
Alaska and the Klondike Gold Fields. N.P: 1897. V. 65

HARRIS, ALBERT W.
The Blood of the Arab. Chicago: 1944. V. 64
The Cruise of a Schooner. Chicago: 1911. V. 63; 66

HARRIS, ALEX
A World Unsuspected. Portraits of Southern Childhood. Chapel Hill: 1987. V. 67

HARRIS, ALEXANDER
Martin Beck; or, the Story of an Australian Settler. London: 1852. V. 67
Settlers and Convicts; or Recollections of Sixteen Years' Labour in the Australian Backwoods. London: 1852. V. 67

HARRIS, BERNICE KELLY
Pates Siding. London: 1939. V. 67

HARRIS, BURTON
John Colter, His Years in the Rockies. New York: 1952. V. 64

HARRIS, C. J.
Otters, a Study of the Recent Lutrinae. London: 1968. V. 64

HARRIS, CLIVE
The History of the Birmingham Gun-Barrel Proof House. Birmingham: 1946. V. 67

HARRIS, DEAN
By Path and Trail. Chicago: 1909. V. 63; 66
The Catholic Church in the Utah 1776-1909. Salt Lake City: 1909. V. 66

HARRIS, ELIZABETH
The Art of Medal Engraving: a Curious Chapter in the Development of 19th Century Printing Process. Newtown: 1991. V. 64
The Common Press: Being a Record, Description & Delineation of the Early Eighteenth Century Handpress in the Smithsonian Institution. Boston: 1978. V. 62; 63; 64; 66

HARRIS, FRANK
Elder Conklin and Other Stories. London: 1895. V. 65
My Life and Loves. Nice: 1922-1927. V. 66
New Preface to The Life and Confessions of Oscar Wilde. London: 1925. V. 67
The Yellow Ticket and Other Stories. London: 1914. V. 62; 64

HARRIS, FRANKLIN STEWART
The Fruits of Mormonism. New York: 1925. V. 63

HARRIS, G. F.
Catalogue of the Tertiary Mollusca...Part I (all published). London: 1897. V. 63; 66

HARRIS, GERTRUDE
A Tale of Men Who Knew No Fear - Sibley's Campaign of 1863. San Antonio: 1935. V. 67

HARRIS, HELENA J.
Southern Sketches. Cecil Gray, or the Soldier's Revenge (and) Rosa Sherwood; or the Avenger. New Orleans: 1866. V. 63

HARRIS, J. M.
Koobi Fora Research Projects. 1983. V. 66

HARRIS, J. R.
An Angler's Entomology. 1952. V. 62; 63; 65; 67

HARRIS, JAMES
Hermes or a Philosophical Inquiry Concerning Universal Grammar. London: 1794. V. 62; 64
Philisophical Arrangements. London: 1775. V. 62
Three Treatises. The First Concerning Art. The Second Concerning Music, Painting and Poetry. The Third Concerning Happiness. London: 1744. V. 64; 66; 67

HARRIS, JOEL CHANDLER
Aaron in the Wildwoods. Boston and New York: 1897. V. 62; 67
Balaam and His Master and Other Sketches and Stories. Boston and New York: 1891. V. 62
Free Joe and Other Georgian Sketches. New York: 1887. V. 62
Joel Chandler Harris, Editor and Essayist. Miscellaneous Literary, Political and Social Writings. Chapel Hill: 1931. V. 62
A Little Union Scout. New York: 1904. V. 65
Mingo and Other Sketches in Black and White. Boston: 1884. V. 62
Nights with Uncle Remus. Boston: 1883. V. 62; 64; 67
Nights with Uncle Remus. London: 1884. V. 62; 64; 65; 67
The Story of Aaron (so named) The Son of Ben Ali Told by His Friends and Acquaintances. Boston: 1896. V. 62
Tales of the Home Folks in Peace and War. Boston and New York: 1898. V. 62; 64; 67
The Tar Baby and Other Rhymes of Uncle Remus. New York: 1904. V. 64
Uncle Remus. Boston: 1908. V. 65
Uncle Remus. London: 1920. V. 65
Uncle Remus. 1939. V. 65
Uncle Remus and Brer Rabbit. New York: 1907. V. 64
Uncle Remus and His Friends. Boston: 1892. V. 66
Uncle Remus and His Legends of the Old Plantation. London: 1881. V. 64
Uncle Remus: His Songs and Sayings. New York: 1881. V. 62; 63; 64; 65
Uncle Remus: His Songs and Sayings. New York: 1934. V. 63
Uncle Remus: His Songs and Sayings. New York: 1957. V. 63
Uncle Remus or the Story of Mr. Fox and Brer Rabbit. London. V. 64
Wally Wanderoon and His Story Telling Machine. New York: 1903. V. 62

HARRIS, JOHN
Illustrations of the History of France. Walworth: 1810. V. 66

HARRIS, JOHN H.
Dawn in Darkest Africa. London: 1912. V. 67

HARRIS, JOSEPH
The Description and Use of the Globes, and the Orrery. London: 1731. V. 64
The Description and Use of the Globes and the Orrery. London: 1740. V. 65
The Description and Use of the Globes and the Orrery. London: 1768. V. 63; 67

HARRIS, LAURA
Animated Noah's Ark. New York: 1945. V. 62
The Happy Little Choo-Choo. New York: 1944. V. 65

HARRIS, LEE
Home Grown #1-10. London: 1977-1981. V. 66

HARRIS, MALCOLM H.
History of Louisa, County, Virginia. Richmond: 1963. V. 64
Old New Kent County, Some Account of the Planters, Plantations and Places in New Kent County. West Point: 1977. V. 64

HARRIS, MARK
Mark the Glove Boy or, the Last Days of Richard Nixon. New York: 1964. V. 65
A Ticket for a Seamstitch. New York: 1957. V. 67

HARRIS, MARTHA DOUGLAS
History and Folklore of the Cowichan Indians. Victoria: 1901. V. 66

HARRIS, MAX
The Vegetative Eye. Melbourne: 1943. V. 66

HARRIS, MELVIN
The True Face of Jack the Ripper. London: 1994. V. 67

HARRIS, ROBERT
Enigma. London: 1995. V. 66; 67
Fatherland. London: 1992. V. 66; 67

HARRIS, ROSEMARY
The King's White Elephant. London: 1973. V. 65

HARRIS, SEALE
Woman's Surgeon. The Life Story of J. Marion Sims. New York: 1950. V. 65

HARRIS, SHELDON
Blues Who's Who. New Rochelle: 1979. V. 65; 67

HARRIS, T. M.
The Assassination of Lincoln. Boston: 1892. V. 63; 65

HARRIS, T. W.
A Treatise on Some of the Insects Injurious to Vegetation. Boston: 1862. V. 62
A Treatise on Some of the Insects Injurious to Vegetation. New York: 1862. V. 66
A Treatise on Some of the Insects of New England Which are Injurious to Vegetation. Boston: 1852. V. 66

HARRIS, THOMAS
Black Sunday. New York: 1975. V. 62; 63; 65; 66; 67
Red Dragon. New York: 1981. V. 67
Red Dragon. London: 1982. V. 64
The Silence of the Lambs. New York: 1988. V. 62; 64; 67

HARRIS, W. CORNWALLIS
Portraits of the Game and Wild Animals of Southern Africa. 1986. V. 62; 66; 67
The Wild Sports of South Africa. 1852. V. 65

HARRIS, WALTER B.
The Land of an African Sultan; Travels in Morocco 1887, 1888 and 1889. London: 1889. V. 65

HARRIS, WILLIAM
Elements of the Chaldee Language Intended as a Supplement to the Hebrew Grammars, and As a Supplement to the Hebrew Grammars, and as a General Introduction to the Aramean Dialects. New York: 1823. V. 66
An Historical and Critical Account of the Life and Writings of Charles I. London: 1772. V. 64; 66
An Historical and Critical Account of the Life and Writings of James I, King of Great Britian. London: 1753. V. 62
An Historical and Critical Account of the Life of Oliver Cromwell, after the Manner of Mr. Bayle. London: 1762. V. 66
An Historical and Critical Account of the Life of Oliver Cromwell, Lord Protector of the Commonwealth of England, Scotland and Ireland. London: 1772. V. 63
The History of the Radical Party in Parliament. London: 1885. V. 64

HARRIS, WILSON
Companions of the Day and Night. London: 1975. V. 62; 66
Da Silva da Silva's Cultivated Wilderness and Genesis of the Clowns. London: 1977. V. 63

HARRISON, ADA
Examples of San Bernadino of Siena. London: 1926. V. 62

HARRISON, CHARLES
A Treatise on the Culture and Mangement of Fruit Trees. London: 1823. V. 62; 67

HARRISON, CONSTANCE CARY
A Bachelor Maid. New York: 1894. V. 63
Recollections Grave and Gay. New York: 1911. V. 62

HARRISON, D. L.
The Mammals of Arabia. 1964. V. 63; 66
The Mammals of Arabia. London: 1964. V. 64

HARRISON, EDWARD
An Address Delivered to the Lincolnshire Benevolent Medical Society at Their Anniversary Meeting in 1809. London: 1810. V. 64

HARRISON, FAIRFAX
The John's Island Stud (South Carolina) 1750-1788. Richmond: 1931. V. 63; 66
Landmarks of Old Prince William. Berryville: 1964. V. 64
Landmarks of Old Prince William. Baltimore: 1987. V. 63

HARRISON, FLORENCE
Elfin Song. New York: 1912. V. 63

HARRISON, HARRY
Bill, the Galactic Hero. New York: 1965. V. 64
The Technicolor Time Machine. 1967. V. 66

HARRISON, HENRY
Instructions for the Mixture of Water-Colours, Adapted to Various Styles of Miniature Painting...to Which is Added, The Elements of Painting in Water Colours. London: 1833. V. 65

HARRISON, J.
The Etymological Enchiridion; or, Practical Analyzer.... Preston: 1823. V. 64

HARRISON, J. E.
Greek Vase Painting. London: 1894. V. 66

HARRISON, J. M.
The Birds of Kent. 1953. V. 62; 65
A Handlist of the Birds of the Sevenoaks or Western District of Kent. 1942. V. 67

HARRISON, JAMES M.
Bristow and the Hastings Rarities Affair. 1968. V. 67

HARRISON, JIM
After Ikkyu and Other Poems. Boston: 1996. V. 62; 63; 64; 66; 67
The Boy Who Ran to the Woods. New York: 2000. V. 67
Dalva. New York: 1988. V. 67
Farmer. New York: 1976. V. 62; 62; 64
5 Blind Men. Michigan: 1969. V. 67
A Good Day to Die. New York: 1973. V. 67
Julip. Boston and New York: 1994. V. 62; 66
Just Before Dark. Livingston: 1991. V. 62; 63; 64; 66; 67
Legends of the Fall. New York: 1979. V. 62; 63; 66
Legends of the Fall. London: 1980. V. 67
Legends of the Fall: (I) Revenge. (II) The Man Who Gave Up His Name. (III) Legends of the Fall. New York: 1978-1979. V. 66; 67
Legends of the Fall, Revenge, and the Man Who Gave Up His Name. New York: 1978. V. 64; 66
Legends of the Fall, Revenge, The Man Who Gave Up His Name. New York: 1979. V. 62
Letters to Yesenin. Fremont: 1973. V. 62
Locations. New York: 1968. V. 66
Locations. New York: 1978. V. 67
Outlyer and Ghazals. New York: 1971. V. 62; 64; 67
The Road Home. New York: 1998. V. 62; 63; 64; 65; 66; 67
Selected and New Poems. New York: 1982. V. 62, 63, 65, 67
Selections from the Shape of the Journey. Port Townsend: 1998. V. 63
The Shape of the Journey: New and Collected Poems. Port Townsend: 1998. V. 63; 63; 64; 67
Sumac. Fremont: 1968-1971. V. 66
Sundog. New York: 1984. V. 66; 67
The Theory and Practice of Rivers. Seattle: 1986. V. 62; 63; 66
The Theory and Practice of Rivers. Livingston: 1989. V. 64; 66
Warlock. New York: 1981. V. 62; 63; 64; 65; 66; 67
The Woman Lit by Fireflies. Boston: 1990. V. 66; 67
The Woman Lit by Fireflies. London: 1991. V. 67

HARRISON, JOHN
An Exact and Perfect Survey and View of the Manor of Sheffield with Other Lands. London: 1908. V. 63

HARRISON, JOSEPH
The Locomotive Engine and Philadelphia's Share in Its Early Improvements. Philadelphia: 1972. V. 63
A Scriptural Exposition of the Church-Catechism.... London: 1735. V. 62

HARRISON, KATHRYN
Exposure. New York: 1993. V. 63

HARRISON, LOU
About Carl Ruggles. Section Four of a Book on Ruggles. New York: 1946. V. 64

HARRISON, MARTIN
Brian Clarke. London: 1981. V. 62

HARRISON, MARY ST. LEGER KINGSLEY
The History of Sir Richard Calmady. London: 1901. V. 65
The Wages of Sin. London: 1891. V. 65

HARRISON, MICHAEL
In the Footsteps of Sherlock Holmes. London: 1958. V. 65; 67

HARRISON, NELLIE FORTESCUE
For One Man's Pleasure. London: 1883. V. 67

HARRISON, R. G.
Hybrid Zones and the Evolutionary Process. New York: 1993. V. 66

HARRISON, ROBERT
The Dublin Dissector.... Dublin: 1831. V. 67

HARRISON, SUSANNA
Songs in the Night: by a Young Woman Under Heavy Afflictions. Ipswich: 1788. V. 67

HARRISON, TONY
Anno Forty Two: Seven New Poems. London: 1987. V. 64
Bow Down. London: 1977. V. 63
Continuous. 1981. V. 64
Dramatic Verse 1973-1985. London: 1985. V. 65
Earthworks. Leeds: 1964. V. 64
Earthworks. London: 1964. V. 63
The Loiners. London: 1970. V. 63; 66
Losing Touch. 1990. V. 64
Losing Touch: In Memoriam George Cukor Died 24.1.83: (a poem). London: 1990. V. 63
The Mother of the Muses. 1989. V. 64
Ten Poems from the School of Eloquence. London: 1976. V. 64
V. Newcastle-upon-Tyne: 1985. V. 64

HARRISON, W. H.
The Tourist in Portugal (Landscape Annual). London: 1839. V. 62

HARRISON, W. JEROME
Geology of the Counties of England and of North and South Wales. 1882. V. 67

HARRISON, WILLIAM
Burton and Speke. New York: 1982. V. 66
The Substance of the Speech of William Harrison, Esq. Before the Select Committee of the House of Commons, on East India-Built Shipping on Monday April 18, 1814. (with) The Substance of the Reply of William Harrison, Esq. before the Select Committe of th. London: 1814. V. 62

HARRISON, WILLIAM HENRY
The Life of Major General William Henry Harrison.... Philadelphia: 1840. V. 66

HARRISSE, HENRY
Bibliotheca Americana Vetustissima; A Description of Works Relating to America Published Between the Years 1492-1551.... 1998. V. 65
Decouverte et Evolution Cartographique de Terre-Neuve et des Pays Circonvoisins 1497-1501-1769. Ridgewood: 1968. V. 66

HARROD, W.
The History of Mansfield and Its Environs, in Two Parts. Mansfield: 1801. V. 65

HARRODS LIMITED
Harrods' General Catalogue for 1928-1929. London: 1928. V. 64

HARROGATE *Vistor's Handbook....* Ripon: 1845. V. 65

HARROP, DOROTHY
A History of the Gregynog Press. London: 1980. V. 66
A History of the Gregynog Press. Middlesex: 1980. V. 62; 63; 64; 66
The Old Stile Press...in the Twentieth Century, a Bibliography 1979-1999. London: 2000. V. 67

HARRRISON, FRANK MOTT
A Bibliography of the Works of Bunyan. London: 1932. V. 67

HARRSEN, META
Central European Manuscripts in the Pierpont Morgan Library. New York: 1958. V. 62; 63; 64
Italian Manuscripts in the Pierpont Morgan Library. New York: 1953. V. 62; 63; 64
Italian Manuscripts in the Pierpont Morgan Library. New York: 1953. V. 63
The Nekcsei-Lipocz Bible, a Fourteenth Century Manuscript from Hungary in the Library of Congress, Ms. Pre-Accession I, a Study. Washington: 1949. V. 63

HARRY *Rountree's Annual.* London: 1907. V. 67

HARSHBERGER, J. W.
The Botanists of Philadelphia and Their Work. Philadelphia: 1899. V. 67
The Vegetation of the New Jersey Pine-Barrens. Philadelphia: 1916. V. 63; 66; 67

HART, ADOLPHUS M.
History of the Discovery of the Valley of the Mississippi. St. Louis: 1852. V. 64

HART, ALBERT B.
Theodore Roosevelt Cyclopedia. New York: 1941. V. 65

HART, ALBERT BUSHNELL
The Varick Court of Inquiry to Investigate the Implication of Colonel Varick. Boston: 1907. V. 66

HART, CYRIL
The Verderers and Forest Laws of Dean. 1971. V. 67

HART, ERNEST
Hypnotism, Mesmerism and the New Witchcraft. London: 1896. V. 66

HART, FRANCIS RUSSELL
The Siege of Havanna. Boston and New York: 1931. V. 64

HART, FRED H.
The Sazerac Lying Club: a Nevada Book. San Francisco: 1878. V. 64

HART, FREEMAN H.
The Valley of Virginia in the American Revolution 1763-1789. Chapel Hill: 1942. V. 66; 67

HART, GEORGE
The Violin, Its Famous Makers and Their Imitators. London: 1875. V. 64
The Violin: Its Famous Makers and Their Imitators. London: 1885. V. 62; 66

HART, HANK
Bud and Sue the Barefoot Kids - Alive with Animation Created and Designed by Hank Hart. New York: 1946. V. 65

HART, HEBER L.
Women's Suffrage and National Danger. London: 1889. V. 65

HART, HENRY CHICHESTER
Some Account of the Fauna and Flora of Sinai, Petra and Wady 'Arabah. London: 1891. V. 62

HART, HORACE
Notes on a Century of Typography at the University Press Oxford 1693-1794. Oxford: 1970. V. 64

HART, I. R. G.
Torture Island. New York: 1928. V. 67

HART, J. L.
Pacific Fishes of Canada. Ottawa: 1973. V. 63; 65

HART, JULIA C.
Tonnewonte, or the Adopted Son of America. Exeter: 1831. V. 64

HART, MADGE
Eating and Drinking. London. V. 63

HART, MOSS
Act One. New York: 1959. V. 67

HART, STEPHEN HARDING
Overland to the Pacific. Denver: 1932. V. 66
Zebulon Pike's Arkansaw Journal: In Search of the Southern Louisiana Boundary Line. Denver: 1932. V. 65

HART, W. O.
A Boy's Recollection of the War. Oxford: 1912. V. 63

HART, WILLIAM S.
The Golden West Boys, Injun and Whitey Strike Out for Themselves. Boston: 1921. V. 65
My Life East and West. Boston: 1929. V. 63; 65; 67

HARTCLIFFE, JOHN
A Compleat Treatise of Moral and Intellectual Virtues...Under the Following Heads...viz. Ethicks...Fortitude...Temperance...Liberality... Comity, Veracity, Urbanity...Justice...Art...Prudence (etc.). London: 1722. V. 63

HART DAVIS, H. V.
Chats on Angling. London: 1906. V. 67

HART DAVIS, RUPERT
The Arms of Time: a Memoir by.... London: 1979. V. 67
The Lyttelton Hart-Davis Letters: Correspondence of George Lyttelton and Rupert Hart-Davis. London: 1979-1987. V. 66

HARTE, BRET
Colonel Starbottle's Client and Some other People. London: 1892. V. 67
The Complete Works. London: 1890-1896. V. 65
The Complete Works. London: 1896. V. 63
East and West. Boston: 1871. V. 67
East and West. London: 1872. V. 67
Excelsior. New York: 1877. V. 62; 65
Gabriel Conroy. Hartford: 1876. V. 62; 63; 67
The Heathen Chinee, Fac-simile of the Original Manuscript.... San Francisco: 1871. V. 62
In a Hollow of the Hills. London: 1895. V. 64
The Lectures of Bret Harte. Brooklyn: 1909. V. 63
The Luck of Roaring Camp and Other Sketches. Boston: 1870. V. 62
Maruja. London: 1885. V. 65
A Millionaire of Rough and Ready. Kentfield: 1955. V. 64
Mliss, a Story by Bret Harte.... San Francisco: 1948. V. 62
Outcroppings: Being Selections of California Verse. San Francisco: 1866. V. 63
The Pliocene Skull. Washington: 1871. V. 62; 64
Poems. Boston: 1871. V. 62
A Protege of Jack Hamlin's Etc. London: 1894. V. 67
The Queen of the Pirate Isle. London: 1886. V. 65
Selected Poems. Tokyo: 1926. V. 62
Tales of Trail and Town. Boston: 1898. V. 62
Tennessee's Partner. San Francisco and New York: 1907. V. 62; 67

HARTE, GLYNN BOYD
A Weekend in Dieppe. London: 1981. V. 64

HARTE, WALTER
An Essay on Reason. London: 1735. V. 63
Essays on Husbandry. 1764. V. 63
Essays on Husbandry. London: 1764. V. 64

HARTHAN, JOHN
The History of the Illustrated Book. The Western Tradition. London: 1981. V. 67

HARTING, JAMES EDMUND
Bibliotheca Accipitraria. A Catalogue of Books Anicent and Modern Relating to Falconry, with Notes, Glossary and Vocabulary. 1999. V. 65
The Birds of Shakespeare. 1871. V. 66
British Animals Extinct Within Historic Times With Some Account of British Wild White Castle. London: 1880. V. 65
British Animals Extinct Within Historic Times with Some Account of British Wild White Cattle. 1880. V. 64; 67
Handbook of British Birds. 1901. V. 67
Hints on the Management of Hawks. London: 1898. V. 62
Rambles in Search of Shells, Land and Freshwater. London: 1875. V. 64
The Zoologist: a Monthly Journal of Natural History. London: 1886-1895. V. 63

HARTJE, ROBERT G.
Van Dorn, The Life and Times of a Confederate General. Nashville: 1967. V. 66

HARTL, HANS
Hermann Oberth; Vorkamper der Weltraumfahrt. Hannover: 1958. V. 67

HARTLAND, MICHAEL
Frontier of Fear. London: 1988. V. 65
The Third Betrayal. London: 1986. V. 65

HARTLEY, CECIL B.
Heroes and Hunters of the West: Comprising Sketches and Adventures of Boone, Kenton, Brady, Logan Whetzel, Fleehart.... Philadelphia: 1853. V. 63

HARTLEY, DOROTHY
Water in England. London: 1964. V. 62

HARTLEY, FLORENCE
Ladies' Book of Etiquette and Manual of Politeness. Philadelphia: 1860. V. 66

HARTLEY, GILFRID
Wild Sport; with Gun Rifle and Salmon-Rod. London: 1903. V. 67

HARTLEY, L. P.
The Boat. London: 1949. V. 66
Eustace and Hilda. London: 1947. V. 65
The Go-Between. 1953. V. 65
The Go-Between. London: 1953. V. 64
Simonetta Perkins. London: 1925. V. 66
Two for the River. London: 1961. V. 66
The White Wand and Other Stories. London: 1954. V. 63

HARTLEY, LEONARD LAWRIE
Catalogue of the Library of the Late Leonard Lawrie Hartley. London: 1885-1887. V. 63

HARTLEY, MARIE
Life and Tradition in the Yorkshire Dales. London: 1968. V. 63; 65
Life and Tradition in West Yorkshire. London: 1976. V. 65
Life in the Moorlands of North-East Yorkshire. London: 1972. V. 65
The Old Hand-Knitters of the Dales. 1951. V. 65

HARTLIB, SAMUEL
His Legacie; or an Enlargement of the Discourse of Husbandry Used in Brabant and Flaunders. London: 1652. V. 65

HARTMAN, C. V.
Archaeological Researches in Costa Rica. Stockholm: 1901. V. 64

HARTMAN, ROBERT
About Fishing. London: 1935. V. 67

HARTMANN, PHILIPP CARL
Der Geist des Menschen in Seinen Verhaltnissen zum Physischen Leben, Oder Grundzuge zu Einer Physiologie des Denkens.... Wien: 1820. V. 65

HARTNER, WILLY
Oriens-Occidens. Hildesheim: 1968. V. 66

HARTNOLL, PHYLLIS
The Grecian Enchanted. Waltham St. Lawrence: 1952. V. 62

HARTSHORNE, ANNA C.
Japan and Her People. Philadelphia: 1902. V. 65; 66

HARTSHORNE, C. H.
The Book Rarities in the University of Cambridge. London: 1829. V. 62

HARTWIG, G.
The Tropical World: Aspects of Man and Nature in the Equitorial Regions of the Globe. 1873. V. 65

HARTZENBUSCH, JUAN EUGENIO
Lovers of Teruel: a Drama in Four Acts in Prose and Verse. Newtown: 1938. V. 62; 65

HARUF, KENT
Plainsong. New York: 1999. V. 67
The Tie that Binds. New York: 1984. V. 65; 66
Where You Once Belonged. New York: 1990. V. 65

THE HARVARD Advocate. Volume CV. Number 4. February 1972. Cambridge: 1972. V. 66

HARVARD UNIVERSITY
A Catalogue of the Officers and Students of Harvard University..1855-1856. Cambridge: 1855. V. 63
The Harvard College Library Department of Printing and Graphic Arts Catalogue of Books and Manuscripts. Part II. Italian 16th Century Books. Cambridge: 1974. V. 62
The Houghton Library 1942-1967 a Selection of Books and Manuscripts in Harvard Collections. Cambridge: 1967. V. 66
University Library Catalogue of Arabic, Persian and Ottoman Turkish Books.... Cambridge: 1968. V. 66

HARVESTER, SIMON
Let Them Prey. London: 1942. V. 65

HARVEY, ANDREW
Burning Houses. London: 1986. V. 67

HARVEY, ANNIE JANE
Our Cruise in the Claymore, with a Visit to Damascus and the Lebanon. London: 1861. V. 67

HARVEY, CHARLES
Jazz Parody (Anthology of Jazz Fiction). London: 1948. V. 63

HARVEY, CHRISTOPHER
The School of the Heart (of Itself Gone Away from God) Brought Back Again to Him and Instructed by Him. London: 1778. V. 67

HARVEY, CORNELIUS BURNHAM
Genealogical History of Hudson and Bergen Counties, New Jersey. London: 1900. V. 63
Genealogical History of Hudson and Bergen Counties, New Jersey. New York: 1900. V. 66

HARVEY Cushing's Seventieth Birthday Party April 8, 1839. Speeches, Letters and Tributes. Springfield: 1939. V. 65; 66

HARVEY, DANIEL WHITTLE
A Letter to the Burgesses of Colchester, Containing a Plain Statement of Proceedings Before the Benchers of the Inner Temple, Upon His Application be Be Called to the Bar.... London: 1822. V. 63

HARVEY, FRED
First Families of the Southwest. Kansas City: 1908. V. 66

HARVEY, GEORGE
Women, etc. New York: 1908. V. 65

HARVEY, GIDEON
The Conclave of Physicians, Detecting Their Intrigues, Frauds and Plots, Against Their Patients. London: 1683. V. 65

HARVEY, HENRY
History of the Shawnee Indians, from the Year 1681 to 1854 Inclusive. Cincinnati: 1855. V. 63

HARVEY, J.
The Gothic World 1100-1600: a Survey of Architecture and Art. London: 1950. V. 65

HARVEY, JAMES
A Collection of English Precedents, Relating to the Office of Justice of the Peace.... London: 1751. V. 62

HARVEY, JOHN
Cutting Edge. London: 1991. V. 65
Cutting Edge. New York: 1991. V. 64
Rough Treatment. London: 1990. V. 66

HARVEY, L. A.
Dartmoor. London: 1953. V. 63

HARVEY, MOSES
Newfoundland in 1897; Being Queen Victoria's Diamond Jubilee Year and the Four Hundredth Anniversary of the Discovery of the Island by John Cabot. London: 1897. V. 63
Newfoundland in 1900. New York & St. John's: 1900. V. 65

HARVEY, W. C.
Sensibility, the Stranger and Other Poems. London: 1818. V. 65

HARVEY, W. H.
A Manual of the British Marine Algae. 1849. V. 63; 66
A Manual of the British Marine Algae. London: 1849. V. 64
Nereis Boreali-Americana or Contributions to a History of the Marine Algae of North America. Washington: 1851. V. 63
Nereis Boreali-Americana, or Contributions to a History of the Marine Algae of North America. Washington: 1851-1858. V. 65; 66
Phycologia Britannica, or, a History of British Sea-Weeds. London: 1846-1851. V. 64; 65; 67

HARVEY, W. S.
William Symington, Inventor and Engine Builder. London: 1980. V. 64

HARVEY, WILLIAM
The Anatomical Exercises. London: 1673. V. 62
The Anatomical Exercises. London: 1928. V. 62; 63; 65; 66
The Anatomical Exercises. London: 1953. V. 67
Anatomical Exercitations Concerning the Generation of Living Creatures. London: 1653. V. 64
Exercitationes de Generatione Animalium. Amstelodami: 1651. V. 64; 66
Exercitationes de Generatione Animalium. Patavii (Padua): 1666. V. 64
Portraits of Dr. William Harvey. Oxford: 1913. V. 66; 67
Prelectiones Academiae Universalis. London: 1886. V. 65

Scottish Chapbook Literature. Paisley: 1903. V. 65

HARVEY, WILLIAM FRYER
The Beast with Five Fingers. New York: 1947. V. 67

HARVIE-BROWN, J. A.
A Fauna of the Moray Basin. Edinburgh: 1895. V. 62; 63
A Fauna of the North-West Highlands and Skye. Edinburgh: 1904. V. 64
A Fauna of the Tay Basin and Strathmore. Edinburgh: 1906. V. 63; 64; 66
A Fauna of the Tay Basin and Strathmore. London: 1906. V. 62
A Vertebrate Fauna of Argyll and the Inner Hebrides. Edinburgh: 1892. V. 64
A Vertebrate Fauna of Sutherland, Caithness and West Cromarty. 1887. V. 66
A Vertebrate Fauna of the Moray Basin. 1895. V. 62; 64; 66
A Vertebrate Fauna of the Moray Basin. London: 1895. V. 63
A Vertebrate Fauna of the Orkney Islands. 1891. V. 67
Vertebrate Fauna of Sutherland, Caithnes and West Cromarty. 1887. V. 64

HARWELL, RICHARD
Confederate Hundred. Urbana: 1964. V. 65
Confederate Music. Chapel Hill: 1950. V. 62; 63; 65
The Confederate Reader. New York: 1957. V. 63

HARWOOD, ANTHONY
Ten Poems. Venice: 1950. V. 66

HARWOOD, BUSICK
A Synopsis of a Course of Lectures on Comparative Anatomy and Physiology. Cambridge: 1807. V. 62

HARWOOD, EDWARD
Biographia Classica; The Lives and Characters of the Greek and Roman Classics. London: 1778. V. 64
A View of the Various Editions of the Greek and Roman Classics. London: 1790. V. 64

HARWOOD, GEORGE H.
The History of Wesleyan Methodism in Nottingham and Its Vicinity. Nottingham: 1859. V. 65

HARWOOD, ISABELLA
Kathleen. London: 1869. V. 65

HARWOOD, JOHN JAMES
History and Description of the Thirlmere Water Scheme. Manchester: 1895. V. 65

HARWOOD, LEE
The White Room. London: 1968. V. 65

HARWOOD, WILLIAM
On the Curative Influence of the Southern Coast of England, Especially that of Hastings with Observations on Diseases in which a Residence of the Coast is Most Beneficial. London: 1828. V. 67

HASCARD, GREGORY
A Discourse About the Charge of Novelty Upon the Reformed Church of England, Made by the Papists Asking of Us the Question, Where Was Our Religion Before Luther?. London: 1683. V. 62

HASEK, JAROSLAV
Good Soldier Schweik. New York: 1930. V. 67

HASELDEN, THOMAS
The Seaman's Daily Assistant, Being a Short, Easy and Plain Method of Keeping a Journal at Sea.... London: 1764. V. 63

HASELL, F. H. E.
Canyons and Caravans. London: 1930. V. 67

HASELLER, H.
A Series of Views of Sidmouth and its Neighbourhood, Drawn from Nature and on Stone. Sidmouth: 1825. V. 66

HASERICK, E. C.
The Secrets of the Art of Dyeing Wool, Cotton and Linen, Including Bleaching and Coloring Wool and Cotton Hosiery and Random Yarns. A Treatise Based on Economy and Practice. Cambridge: 1869. V. 64; 67

HASKEL, DANIEL
Complete Descriptive and Statistical Gazetteer of the U.S. of America. New York: 1844. V. 63

HASKELL, THOMAS NELSON
The Indian Question - Young Konkaput, the King of Utes and Shawsheen His Maiden Queen - a Legend of Twin Lakes the Ute-Meeker Massacre. Denver: 1889. V. 64; 65

HASKETT, WILLIAM J.
Shakerism Unmasked, or the History of the Shakers. Pittsfield: 1828. V. 62

HASKETT SMITH, W. P.
Climbing in the British Isles. London: 1894-1895. V. 66
Climbing in the British Isles 1-England. London: 1894. V. 64

HASKINS, JIM
James Van Der Zee: The Picture-Takin' Man. New York: 1979. V. 63

HASKINS, R. W.
New England and the West. Buffalo: 1843. V. 66

HASKINS, SAM
Photo Graphics. Geneve: 1980. V. 66

HASKINS, SAMUEL
African Image. New York: 1967. V. 63

HASLAM, JOHN
Observations on Madness and Melancholy.... London: 1809. V. 65
Sound Mind: or, Contributions to the Natural History and Physiology of the Human Intellect. London: 1819. V. 62; 65

HASLEHURST, ERNEST W.
Our Beautiful Homeland. London: 1921. V. 65

HASLEM, JOHN
The Old Derby China Factory: the Workmen and Their Productions. London: 1876. V. 62; 66

HASLER, H. G.
Harbours and Anchorages of the North Coast of Brittany. London: 1952. V. 62

HASLEWOOD, CONSTANCE
The Dear Old Nursery Rhymes. London: 1880. V. 64

HASLEWOOD, JOSEPH
Green Room Gossip; or, Gravity Gallinipt; a Gallimaufry, Consisting of Theatrical Anecdotes.... London: 1809. V. 66
Mirror for Magistrates in Five Parts. London: 1815. V. 64
The Secret History of the Green Room. London: 1792. V. 66
Some Account of the Life and Publications of the Late Joseph Ritson. London: 1824. V. 65

HASLUCK, PAUL
Cassell's Cyclopaedia of Mechanics.... London: 1908. V. 62

HASLUND, HENNING
Men and Gods In Mongolia. New York: 1935. V. 65

HASPER, WILHELM
Handbuch der Buchdruckerkunst.... Carlsruhe and Baden: 1835. V. 63

HASS, ROBERT
Field Guide. New Haven & London: 1973. V. 67
Praise. New York: 1979. V. 63
Sun Under Wood. New Poems. Hopewell: 1996. V. 63
Winter Morning in Charlottesville. Knotting, Bedfordshire: 1977. V. 63

HASSALL, ARTHUR HILL
Adulterations Directed or Plain Instructions for the Discovery of Frauds in Food and Medicine. London: 1861. V. 64

HASSALL, CHRISTOPHER
Christ's Comet. 1937. V. 65
Devil's Dyke with Compliment and Satire. 1936. V. 65

HASSALL, JOHN
Ding! Dong! Dell!. London: 1910. V. 63

HASSALL, W. O.
The Holkham Library. Oxford: 1970. V. 67

HASSE, ADELAIDE R.
A Narrative of an Attempt Made by the French of Canada Upon the Mohaque's Country Reproduced in Facsimile from the First Edition printed by William Bradford, 1693. New York: 1903. V. 64

HASSELL, J.
Excursions of Pleasure and Sports on the Thames. London: 1823. V. 62
Picturesque Rides and Walks, with Excursions by Water, Thirty Miles Round the British Metropolis. London: 1817-1818. V. 62
Tour of the Grand Junction, Illustrated in a Series of Engravings with an Historical and Topographical Description of Those Parts of the Counties.... London: 1819. V. 66

HASSELL, WILLIAM
The Retail Spirit Dealer's Sure Guide.... London: 1803. V. 64

HASSENFRATZ, J. H.
La Siderotechnie, ou l'Art de Traiter les Minerais de Fer Pour en Obtenir de la Fonte, du Feur, ou de l'Acier. Paris: 1812. V. 65

HASSLER, EDGAR W.
Old Westmoreland: a History of Western Pennsylvania During the Revolution. Pittsburg: 1900. V. 65

HASSLER, R. STEPHAN H.
Evolution of the Forebrain, Phylogensis and Ontogensis of the Forebrain. New York: 1967. V. 66; 67

HASSLER, WARREN W.
General George B. McClellan, Shield of the Union. Baton Rouge: 1957. V. 62

HASSLER, WILLIAM WOODS
A. P. Hill, Lee's Forgotten General. Richmond: 1957. V. 63; 65

HASSON, JAMES
The Banquet of the Immortals. Edinburgh: 1948. V. 67

HASSRICK, PETER
Frederic Remington: Paintings, Drawings and Sculpture in the Amon Carter Museum and the Sid W. Richardson Foundation Collections. New York: 1973. V. 64; 64; 65

HASTAIN, RONALD
White Coolie. London: 1947. V. 66

HASTED, J. E.
Racing Demon. London: 1936. V. 64

HASTINGS, A. C. G.
Nigerian Days. London: 1925. V. 67

HASTINGS, FRANK S.
A Ranchman's Recollections, an Autobiography. Chicago: 1921. V. 62; 65

HASTINGS, JAMES
Encyclopedia of Religion and Ethics. Edinburgh: 1908-1926. V. 65

HASTINGS, JAY E. A.
A Glimpse on the Tropics; or, Four Months' Cruising in the West Indies. London: 1900. V. 67

HASTINGS, THOMAS
The Book of the Wars of Westminster.... London: 1784. V. 62

HASTINGS, WARREN
The Defence of Warren Hastings, Esq. (Late Governor General of Bengal), at the Bar of the House of Commons, Upon the Matter of Several Charges of High Crimes and Miseamenors, Presented Against Him in the Year 1786. London: 1786. V. 63

HASTON, D.
The Eiger. 1974. V. 65

HASWELL, FRANCIS
The Parish Registers of Brougham 1645-1812. Penrith: 1943. V. 65
The Registers of St. Andrews Parish Church, Penrith. Volumes 1-5, 1556-1812. Penrith: 1938-1942. V. 66
The Registers of Bolton 1647-1812. Penrith: 1944. V. 65
The Registers of Cliburn 1565-1812. Penrith: 1932. V. 65
The Registers of Crosby Garrett, Westmorland 1559-1812. Penrith: 1945. V. 65
The Registers of Crosthwaite-Cum-Lyth 1569-1812. Penrith: 1925. V. 65
The Registers of Lamplugh 581-1812. Penrith: 1933. V. 65
The Registers of Lowther 1540-1812. Penrith: 1933. V. 65
The Registers of Millom, Cumberland. 1591-1812. Kendal: 1925. V. 65
The Registers of Newbiggen (Westmorland) 1571-1812. Penrith: 1927. V. 65
The Registers of Newton Reigny 1571-1812. Kendal: 1934. V. 65
The Registers of St. Andrews Parish Church Penrith. Volumes 1-5. 1556-1812. Penrith: 1938-1942. V. 65
The Registers of Whicham 1569-1812. Penrith: 1926. V. 65

HASWELL, JOHN H.
The Assassination of Abraham Lincoln, Late President of the United States of America, and the Attempted Assassination of William H. Seward, Secretary of State, and Frederick W. Seward, Assistant Secretary on the Evening of the 14th of April, 1865. Washington: 1867. V. 63

HATAI, K. M.
The Cenozoic Brachiopoda of Japan. 1940. V. 63

HATCH, ALDEN
Full Tilt. The Sporting Memoirs of Foxhall Keene. New York: 1938. V. 63

HATCH, BENTON L.
A Check List of the Publications of Thomas Bird Mosher of Portland Maine, MDCCCXCI-MDCCCCXXIII. N.P. 1966. V. 62; 66

HATCH, ERIC
Five Days. Boston: 1933. V. 66

HATCH, FREDERICK H.
The Gold Mines of the Rand Being a Description of the Mining Industry of Witwatersrand South African Republic. London: 1895. V. 62; 67

HATCH, J.
Morecambe, Lancaster and District. London: 1909. V. 62; 66

HATCH, LEWIS M.
Platt's Patent Grist Mill, Sold by Lewis M. Hatch. Charleston: 1853. V. 63

HATCHER, J. B.
The Ceratopsia. Washington: 1907. V. 63; 66

HATCHER, J. S.
The Book of the Garand. Washington: 1948. V. 67
Hatcher's Notebook. 1966. V. 67
Text Book of Pistols and Revolvers. 1935. V. 62; 63; 64; 66; 67

HATCHER, O. LATHAM
A Mountain School. Richmond: 1930. V. 66

HATCHER, VIRGINIA SNEAD
The Sneads of Fluvanna. Fort Union: 1959. V. 63

HATCHETT, WILLIAM
A Chinese Tale. London: 1740. V. 62

HATFIELD, C. W.
Catalogue of the Bonnell Collection in the Bronte Parsonage Museum. London: 1932. V. 63

HATFIELD, EDWIN A.
History of Elizabeth, New Jersey.... New York: 1868. V. 63; 66

HATFIELD, L. D.
The True Story of the Hatfield and Mc Coy Feud. Charleston: 1944. V. 67

HATHAWAY, ELLA C.
Battle of the Big Hole in August 1877.... N.P: 1919. V. 66

HATTON, EDWARD
An Intire System of Arithmetic In All Its Parts. London: 1721. V. 65
The Merchant's Magazine; or Trades Man's Treasury. London: 1719. V. 64

HATTON, JOSEPH
Cigarette Papers for After-Dinner Smoking. London: 1892. V. 62; 65

HATTON, JOSEPH continued
Newfoundland; the Oldest British Colony, Its History, Its Present Condition and Its Prospects in the Future. London: 1883. V. 67
Provincial Papers, Being a Collection of Tales and Sketches. London: 1861. V. 67

HATTON, THOMAS
A Bibliography of the Periodical Works of Charles Dickens. London: 1933. V. 62; 65

HAUBER, E. C.
Beschreibung der Stadt Kopenhagen und der Koniglichen Landschlosser.. Copenhagen: 1777. V. 64

HAUDICQUER DE BLANCOURT, FRANCOIS
The Art of Glass.... London: 1699. V. 64

HAUFF, WILHELM
Dwarf Long-Nose. New York: 1960. V. 62
Dwarf Long-Nose. London: 1984. V. 65

HAUGHTON, GRAVES CHAMNEY
Rudiments of Bengali Grammar. London: 1821. V. 67

HAUGHTON, HENRY LAURENCE
Sport and Folklore in the Himalaya. London: 1913. V. 62

HAUGHTON, SAUL
Sport and Travel. Dublin: 1916. V. 67

HAUGUM, J.
A Monograph of the Birdwing Butterflies.... Klampenborg: 1978-1985. V. 64

HAUPTMANN, FREDERICK D.
Bread and Cake Bearing. Pittsburgh: 1877. V. 67

HAUPTMANN, T.
A Day in the Life of Petronella Pig. New York: 1982. V. 63

HAURY, EMIL W.
The Hohokam - Desert Farmers and Craftsman - Excavations at Snaketown. Tucson: 1976. V. 66
Recently Dated Pueblo Ruins in Arizona. Washington: 1931. V. 67
Roosevelt: 9:6 a Hohokam Site of the Colonial Period. 1932. V. 63

HAUSDING, A.
A Handbook on the Winning and Utilization of Peat. London: 1921. V. 67

HAUSMAN, L.
Atlas I-III Atlases of the Spinal Cord and Brainstem and the Forebrain (7th printing) Atlas of Consecutive Stages in the Reconstruction of the Nervous System (5th printing). Atlas III. Illustrations of the Nervous System Clinical Neuroanatomy with a Met. Springfield: 1963. V. 66; 67

HAUSNER, A.
Manufacture of Preserved Foods and Sweetmeats. London: 1902. V. 67

HAUSSEZ, CHARLES LEMERCHER DE LONGPRE, BARON D'
Great Britain in 1833. Philadelphia: 1833. V. 64

HAUTMAN, PETE
Bad Beat. With Joe Crow's Rules for Poke and Life. Minneapolis: 1998. V. 64
Drawing Dead. New York: 1993. V. 64; 66; 67

HAUY, RENE JUST, ABBE
Traite Elementaire de Physique. Paris: 1806. V. 64

HAVEL, VACLAV
Largo Desolato: a Play in Seven Scenes. New York: 1987. V. 66

HAVELL, E. B.
The Ancient and Medieval Architecture of India: a Study of Indo-Aryan Civilisation. London: 1915. V. 67
Indian Architecture its Psychology, Structure and History from the First Muhammadan Invasion to the Present Day. London: 1927. V. 63

HAVELL, WILLIAM
A Series of Picturesque Views of the River Thames from the Drawings of William Havell. Guildford: 1970. V. 63

HAVELOCK, HENRY
Narrative of the War in Affghanistan in 1838-1839. London: 1840. V. 66

HAVEN, ALICE NEAL
All's Not Gold that Glitters, or the Young Californian. New York: 1853. V. 67

HAVEN, CHARLES C.
...Washington and His Army During Their March through the Return to New Jersey, in December 1776, and January 1777. Trenton: 1856. V. 63

HAVEN, CHARLES T.
A History of the Colt Revolver and Other Arms Made by Colt's Patent Fire Arms Manufacturing Patent Fire Arms Manufacturing Company from 1836 to 1940. New York: 1940. V. 63

HAVEN, GILBERT
Our Next-Door Neighbor: a Winter in Mexico. New York: 1875. V. 65

HAVEN, JASON
A Sermon Preached to the Ancient and Honorable Artillery Company in Boston, New England June 1, 1761. Boston: 1761. V. 62

HAVERGAL, FRANCES RIDLEY
Songs of the Master's Love. London. V. 62
Swiss Letters and Alpine Poems. London: 1882. V. 62

HAVERSCHMIDT, F.
Birds of Surinam. Edinburgh: 1968. V. 65; 67
Birds of Surinam. Wynnewood: 1968. V. 63
Birds of Surinam. 1994. V. 63

HAVILAND, LAURA S.
A Woman's Life Work: Labors and Experiences. Cincinnati: 1881. V. 65

HAVILAND, MAUD D.
A Summer of the Yenesei. London: 1915. V. 67

HAWAIIAN Cook Book. Honolulu: 1896. V. 64

HAWARDEN, EDWARD
An Answer to Dr. Clark and Mr. Whiston, Concerning the Divinity of the Son, and of the Holy Spirit. London: 1729. V. 67

HAWEIS, HUGH R.
Mark Twain... American Humorists. New York: 1883. V. 63

HAWEIS, MARY ELIZA
The Art of Beauty. London: 1878. V. 65

HAWES, C. H.
In the Uttermost East: Being an Account of Investigations Among the Natives and Russian Convicts of the Island of Sakhalin, with Notes of Travel in Korea, Siberia and Manchuria. London: 1903. V. 67

HAWES, WILLIAM POST
Sporting Scenes and Sundry Sketches: Being the Miscellaneous Writings of J. Cypress, Jr. New York: 1842. V. 63; 66

HAWK, JOHN
The House of Sudden Sleep. New York: 1930. V. 64

HAWKER, G.
The Life of George Grenfell, Congo Missionary and Explorer. London: 1904. V. 62

HAWKER, PETER
The Diary of Colonel Peter Hawker. 1893. V. 67
Instructions to Young Sportsmen in All that Relates to Guns and Shooting. London: 1824. V. 62
Instructions to Young Sportsmen in All That Relates to Guns and Shooting. 1825. V. 62
Instructions to Young Sportsmen in all that Relates to Guns and Shooting. London: 1844. V. 67
Instructions to Young Sportsmen in All that Relates to Guns and Shooting. 1859. V. 66
The Sportsman's Pocket Companion. 1980. V. 66

HAWKER, ROBERT
Misericordia; or, Compassion to the Sorrows of the Heart. Plymouth: 1795. V. 63
A Poor Man's Commentary of the Bible. Plymouth Dock: 1802-1805?. V. 63

HAWKER, ROBERT STEPHEN
The Cornish Ballads and Other Poems. London: 1869. V. 64; 66
Ecclesia: a Volume of Poems. Oxford: 1840. V. 65
Footprints of Former Men in Far Cornwall. London: 1870. V. 62
Footprints of Former Men in Far Cornwall. London, Exeter: 1908. V. 64
The Poetical Works.... London: 1879. V. 64; 65

HAWKES, JOHN
The Beetle Leg. New York: 1951. V. 66
The Blood Oranges. New York: 1971. V. 67
Death, Sleep and the Traveler. New York: 1974. V. 67
The Innocent Party. New York: 1967. V. 66
The Lime Twig. Norfolk: 1961. V. 65
Lunar Landscapes. Stories and Short Novels 1949-1963. New York: 1969. V. 67
The Passion Artist. New York: 1979. V. 63
Travesty. New York: 1976. V. 63

HAWKESWORTH, JOHN
An Account of the Voyages Undertaken...for Making Discoveries in the Southern Hemisphere and Successively Undertaken by Commodore Byron, Captain Wallis, Captain Carteret and Captain Cook. London: 1773. V. 64
Almoran and Hamet; an Oriental Tale. London: 1761. V. 62

HAWKINS, ANTHONY HOPE
The Chronicles of Count Antonio. London: 1895. V. 66
The Dolly Dialogues. London: 1894. V. 63; 64
The Great Miss Driver. London: 1908. V. 67
The King's Mirror. London: 1899. V. 66
Mrs. Maxon Protests. London: 1911. V. 67
The Prisoner of Zenda. Bristol: 1894. V. 62
Quisante. London: 1900. V. 67
Rupert of Netzau. Bristol: 1898. V. 66
Second String. London: 1910. V. 67
A Servant of the Public. London: 1905. V. 67
Tristram of Blent. London: 1901. V. 67

HAWKINS, B. WATERHOUSE
The Science of Drawing Simplified; or the Elements of Form Demonstrated by Models. London: 1843. V. 67

HAWKINS, BISSET
Germany; the Spirit of Her History, Literature, Social Condition and National Economy.... London: 1838. V. 64

HAWKINS, DEAN
Skull Mountain. Garden City: 1941. V. 67

HAWKINS, FREDERICK W.
The Life of Edmund Kean. London: 1869. V. 66

HAWKINS, ISAAC
An Essay for the Discovery of the Longitude at Sea, by Several New Methods.... London: 1714. V. 62

HAWKINS, JOHN
The Life of Samuel Johnson, LL.D. Dublin: 1787. V. 63
The Life of Samuel Johnson, LL.D. London: 1787. V. 62
The Young Clerk's Tutor Enlarged.... In the Savoy: 1717. V. 64

HAWKINS, JOHN SIDNEY
Ignoramus Comoedia: Scriptorio Georgio Ruggle. London: 1787. V. 66

HAWKINS, RICHARD
The Observations of Sir Richard Hawkins. London: 1933. V. 65

HAWKINS, SHERMAN
Seven Princeton Poets: Louise Coxe, George Garrett, Theodore Holmes, Galway Kinnell, William Meredith, W. S. Merwin, Bink Noll. Princeton: 1963. V. 64

HAWKINS, WILLIAM
A Treatise of the Pleas of the Crown; or a System of the Principal Matters Relating to that Subject, Digested Under their Proper Heads. London: 1724-1721. V. 64; 66

HAWKS, E.
Pioneers of Plant Study. London: 1928. V. 67

HAWKS, FRANCIS LISTER
The Adventures of Daniel Boone, the Kentucky Rifleman. New York: 1844. V. 65
The Early History of the Southern States. Philadelphia: 1832. V. 64
The Monuments of Egypt; or, Egypt a Witness for the Bible. New York: 1850. V. 62

HAWKS, WELLS
The Kinship of the Circus. New York: 1926. V. 67

HAWKSMOOR, NICHOLAS
The Town of Cambridge as It Ought to Be Reformed. London: 1955. V. 67

HAWLEY, ROBERT EMMETT
Skgeemus, or Pioneer Days on the Nooksack Being a Series of Personal Memoir. Bellingham: 1945. V. 64

HAWLEY, W. A.
Oriental Rugs, Antique and Modern. New York: 1925. V. 65

HAWORTH, SAMUEL
(Greek) or, a Philosophic Discourse Concerning Man, Being the Anatomy Both of His Soul and Body.... London: 1680. V. 66

HAWTHORNE, H.
The Lure of the Garden. New York: 1911. V. 67

HAWTHORNE, JULIAN
A Fool of Nature. New York: 1896. V. 66
Humors of the Fair. Chicago: 1893. V. 65

HAWTHORNE, NATHANIEL
The Blithedale Romance. Boston: 1852. V. 62; 67
The Complete Greek Stories of Nathaniel Hawthorne - from the Wonder Book and Tanglewood Tales. London: 1963. V. 65
The Complete Writings. Boston and New York: 1900. V. 62
The Complete Writings. Boston and New York: 1900-1902. V. 66
Doctor Grimshawe's Secret. Boston: 1883. V. 65
Doctor Grimshawe's Secret. Cambridge: 1883. V. 66
Famous Old People: Being the Second Epoch of Grandfather's Chair. Boston;: 1841. V. 65
Hawthorne's Wonder Book. London: 1922. V. 66
Hawthorne's Wonder Book. New York: 1922. V. 63
The House of the Seven Gables. Boston: 1851. V. 62; 64; 65
The House of the Seven Gables. Boston: 1857. V. 64
Life of Franklin Pierce. Boston: 1852. V. 62; 63
The Marble Faun; or, the Romance of Monte Beni. Boston: 1860. V. 63
Mosses from an Old Manse. New York: 1846. V. 66
Our Old Home: a Series of English Sketches. Boston: 1863. V. 62; 64; 65; 67
Passages from the American Note-Books. Boston: 1868. V. 65
Passages from the English Notebooks. Boston: 1870. V. 66
Passages from the French and Italian Note-Books. London: 1871. V. 62; 64
Passages from the French and Italian Note-Books. Boston: 1872. V. 66
The Scarlet Letter. Boston: 1850. V. 62; 64; 65; 67
The Scarlet Letter. London: 1851. V. 67
The Scarlet Letter. Boston: 1860. V. 64
The Scarlet Letter. New York: 1904. V. 63
Septimius Felton; or the Elixir of Life. Boston: 1872. V. 62; 64
Sights from a Steeple. Bremain and New York: 1988. V. 62
The Snow Image and Other Tales. London: 1851. V. 62; 64; 67
Tanglewood Tales for Boys and Girls: Being a Second Wonder Book. Boston: 1853. V. 63
True Stories from History and Biography. Boston: 1851. V. 62
A Wonder Book for Boys and Girls. Boston: 1893. V. 63; 64

HAWTREY, VALENTINA
A Ne'er-do-weel. 1903. V. 67

HAXTHAUSEN, AUGUST, BARON VON
The Russian Empire. London: 1856. V. 62
Transcaucasia; Sketches of the Nations and Races Between the Black Sea and the Caspian. London: 1854. V. 67

HAY, D. R.
The Science of Beauty, as Developed in Nature and Applied in Art. Edinburgh & London: 1856. V. 65

HAY, GEORGE
A Treatise on Expatriation. Washington: 1814. V. 66

HAY, JOHN
A Narrative of Procedure Before the Court of Session, and Circumstances Connected Therewith, in the Trial of John Hay.... Edinburgh: 1822-1823. V. 63
Nicholson's New Carpenter's Guide.... London: 1850. V. 62; 66
The Pike County Ballads. Boston: 1912. V. 65
A Private History. New York: 1947. V. 63

HAY, MARLEY FOTHERINGHAM
Secrets of the Submarine. New York: 1917. V. 64

HAY, PHILIP C.
Our Duty to Our Coloured Population. A Sermon for the Benefit of the American Colonization Society, Delivered in the Second Presbyterian Church, Newark, July 23, 1826. Newark: 1826. V. 63; 66

HAY, ROBERT
Geology and Mineral Resources of Kansas. Topeka: 1893. V. 62

HAY, THOMAS ROBSON
Hood's Tennessee Campaign. New York: 1929. V. 62; 63; 65

HAY, WILLIAM
Mount Caburn. A Poem. London: 1730. V. 66

HAYASHI, TAKASHI
Neurophysiology and Neurochemistry of Convulsion. Tokyo: 1959. V. 65

HAYDEN, F. V.
Preliminary Report of the United States Geological Survey of Montana and Portions of Adjacent Territories.... Washington: 1872. V. 65
Preliminary Report of the United States Geological Survey of Wyoming and Portions of Contiguous Territories. Washington: 1871. V. 62
United States Geological Survey of Colorado and New Mexico. Washington: 1869. V. 66

HAYDN, JOSEPH
Dictionary of Dates and Universal Reference Relating to All Ages and Nations.... London: 1853. V. 62

HAYDON, A. L.
The Riders of the Plains. Chicago: 1910. V. 65; 67
The Trooper Police of Australia, a Record of Mounted Police Work in the Commonwealth from the Earliest Days of Settlement to the Present Time. London: 1911. V. 67

HAYDON, ARTHUR
Spode and His Successors, a History of the Pottery, Stoke on Trent 1765-1865. London: 1929. V. 67

HAYDON, B. R.
Painting and the Fine Arts.... Edinburgh: 1838. V. 67

HAYDON, F. STANSBURY
Aeronautics in the Union and Confederate Armies. Baltimore: 1941. V. 63; 65

HAYEK, F. A.
Capitalism and the Historians. London: 1954. V. 62

HAYES, AUGUSTUS A.
New Colorado and the Santa Fe Trail. New York: 1880. V. 65
New Colorado and the Santa Fe Trail. London: 1881. V. 66

HAYES, BENJAMIN
Pioneer Notes from the Diaries of Judge Benjamin Hayes 1849-1875. Los Angeles: 1929. V. 65
Pioneer Notes from the Diary of Judge...1849-1875. Los Angeles: 1925. V. 62; 65

HAYES, BILLY
Midnight Express. New York: 1977. V. 65

HAYES, CHARLES
A Treatise of Fluxions; or, An Introduction to Mathematical Philosophy.... London: 1704. V. 66

HAYES, CHARLES H.
Directory of the Officers and Privates, Attached to the Fourteenth Regiment Heavy Artillery, Massachusetts Volunteers. Lawrence: 1862. V. 65

HAYES, CHARLES WELLS
William Wells of Southold and His Descendants, A. D. 1638 to 1878. Buffalo: 1878. V. 63
William Wells of Southold and His Descendants, A.D. 1638 to 1878. New York: 1878. V. 66

HAYES, HELEN
On Reflection: an Autobiography. New York: 1968. V. 63

HAYES, ISAAC I.
An Arctic Boat-Journey in the Autumn of 1854. London: 1860. V. 64
The Land of Desolation: Being a Personal Narrative of Observation and Adventure in Greenland. New York: 1872. V. 65

HAYES, JOHN L.
The Angora Goat: Its Origin, Culture and Products. New York: 1882. V. 64

HAYES, LOUIS M.
Reminiscences and Some of Its Local Surroundings from the Year 1840. London: 1905. V. 64

HAYES, MRS.
The Horsewoman. London: 1893. V. 62

HAYES, RICHARD
Ireland and Irishmen in the French Revolution. 1932. V. 64; 67
Old Links With France, Some Echoes of Exiled Ireland. 1940. V. 64; 67

HAYES, SAMUEL
The Deluge: a Poem. London: 1790. V. 62
Duelling: a Poem. Cambridge: 1775. V. 62
The Exodus. Cambridge: 1785. V. 62
Hope: a Poem. Cambridge: 1783. V. 62
The Nativity of Our Saviour: a Poem. Cambridge: 1778. V. 62
Prayer: a Poem. Cambridge: 1777. V. 62
Prophecy: a Poem. Cambridge: 1777. V. 62
Verses on His Majesty's Recovery. London: 1789. V. 63

HAYES, WALTER
The Captain from Nantucket and the Mutiny on the Bounty, a Recollection of Mayhew Folger, Mariner, Who Discovered the Last Mutineer and His Family on Pitcairn's Island... (with) Letters and Documents.... Ann Arbor: 1996. V. 65

HAYES, WILLIAM
An Introduction to Conveyancing, and the New Statutes Concerning Real Property; with Precedents an Pratical Notes. London: 1839. V. 63
Portraits of Rare and Curious Birds, with Their Descriptions, from Menagery of Osterly Park, in the County of Middlesex. London: 1794-1799. V. 67

HAYES MC COY, G. A.
Captain Myles Walter Keogh - USA 1840-1976. 1965. V. 67

HAYFORD, JOHN F.
A Text-Book of Geodetic Astronomy. New York: 1898. V. 66

HAYGARTH, JOHN
A Sketch of a Plan to Exterminate the Casual Small Pox from Great Britain and to Introduce General Inoculation.... London: 1793. V. 65

HAYGARTH, WILLIAM
Greece, a Poems, in Three Parts.... London: 1814. V. 62

HAYLEY, WILLIAM
Ballads, Founded on Anecdotes Relating to Animals, with prints, Designed and Engraved by William Blake. Chichester: 1805. V. 65; 66
Epistle to a Friend, on the Death of John Thornton, Esq. London: 1780. V. 62
Essai Satirique et Amusant sur les Vieilles Filles. Paris: 1788. V. 63
An Essay on History; in Three Epistles to Edward Gibbon, Esq. London: 1780. V. 66
An Essay on Painting, in a Poetical Epistle to an Eminent Painter. (with) An Essay on History, in Three Epistles to Edward Gibbon...(with) The Triumphs of Temper. Dublin: 1781. V. 62
An Essay on Painting in Two Epistles to Mr. Romney. London: 1781. V. 64
An Essay on Sculpture, in a Series of Epistles to John Flaxman, with Notes. London: 1800. V. 56/62
The Life and Posthumous Writings of William Cowper, Esq. Chichester: 1803-1804. V. 63
The Life and Posthumous Writings of William Cowper, Esq. Chichester: 1803-1806. V. 62
A Philosophical, Historical and Moral Essay on Old Maids. London: 1785. V. 63; 65
A Philosophical, Historical and Moral Essay on Old Maids. Dublin: 1786. V. 65
A Philosophical, Historical and Moral Essay on Old Maids. London: 1786. V. 62
A Poetical Epistle to an Eminent Painter. London: 1778. V. 62
The Triumph of Music: a Poem. Chichester: 1804. V. 62
Triumphs of Temper. London: 1781. V. 64; 65
The Triumphs of Temper. London: 1801. V. 65
The Triumphs of Temper. Chichester: 1803. V. 65; 67
The Triumphs of Temper. Chichester: 1817. V. 63; 66

HAYMAKER, WEBB
Bing's Local Diagnosis in Neurological Diseases. St. Louis: 1956. V. 65
Peripheral Nerve Injuries, Principles of Diagnosis. Philadelphia: 1953. V. 66; 67

HAYMAN, JAMES
An Appeal to Tradesmen, Relating to Sundry Abuses Deeply Affecting their Interests.... London: 1863. V. 63

HAYMAN, JOHN
Gielgud. London: 1971. V. 65

HAYNE, JOHANN
Trifolium Medicum, Oder Drey Hochst Nutzliche Tractatlein, Deren Erstes von Astralischen Kranckheiten.... Frankfurt am Main: 1683. V. 64; 66

HAYNE, PAUL H.
Sonnets and Other Poems. Charleston: 1857. V. 63; 64

HAYNES, DAVID
Live At Five. Minneapolis: 1996. V. 63

HAYNES, DRAUGHTON STITH
The Field Diary of a Confederate Solider. Darien: 1963. V. 62; 63

HAYNES, RIC
Rejected Mars. New York: 1995. V. 64

HAYNES, THOMAS
An Essay on the Soils and Composts Indispensably Necessary in the Propagation and Culture of the More Rare and Valuable Ornamental Trees, Shrubs, Plants and Flowers of the Pleasure Garden, Flower Garden and Green House Collection. London: 1821. V. 66; 67
A Treatise on the Improved Culture of the Strawberry, Raspberry and Gooseberry. London: 1812. V. 65

HAYNES, WILLIAM
A Journal of the Proceedings of the Flying Squadron. Devonport: 1871. V. 67

HAYS, FRANCES
Women of the Day. A Biographical Dictionary of Notable Contemporaries. London: 1885. V. 63; 67

HAYS, H. A.
A Little Maryland Garden. New York: 1909. V. 67

HAYS, ISAAC
Select Medico-Chirurgical Transactions. Philadelphia: 1831. V. 66; 67

HAYS, MARGARET
Grace G. Wiederseim Babykins. New York: 1914. V. 62
Kiddie Land. Philadelphia: 1910. V. 62

HAYTER, GEORGE
A Descriptive Catalogue of the Great Historical Picture, Painted by Mr. George Hayter...Representing the Trial of Her Late Majesty Queen Caroline of England. London: 1823. V. 66

HAYTER, HENRY HEYLYN
Handbook to the Colony of Victoria. Prepared Under the Direction of the Victorian Government. Melbourne: 1884. V. 67

HAYTER, SPARKLE
What's A Girl Gotta Do?. 1994. V. 64
What's a Girl Gotta Do?. New York: 1994. V. 65

HAYTER, THOMAS
An Essay on the Liberty of the Press, Chiefly As It Respects Personal Slander. Dublin: 1755. V. 65
An Essay on the Liberty of the Press Chiefly as It Respects Personal Slander. London: 1755. V. 62

HAYWARD, ABRAHAM
The Art of Dining, or, Gastronomy and Gastronomers. London: 1852. V. 63

HAYWARD, GEORGE
Surgical Reports and Miscellaneous Papers in Medicine Subjects. Boston: 1855. V. 64

HAYWARD, I. M.
The Adventive of Flora of Tweedside. Arbroath: 1919. V. 66

HAYWARD, J. F.
The Art of the Gunmaker. 1500-1830. London: 1965. V. 62; 67
Virtuoso Goldsmiths and the Triumph of Mannerism 1540-1620. New York: 1976. V. 63

HAYWARD, JOHN
English Poetry - an Illustrated Catalogue of First and Early Editions Exhibited in 1947 at 7 Ablemarle Street London. London: 1950. V. 62
The Lives of the III Normans, Kings of England: William the First, William the Second, Henrie the First. (with) The Life and Raigne of King Edward the Sixth.... London: 1613. V. 64
Prose Literature Since 1919. London: 1947. V. 64

HAYWARD, P. J.
Antarctic Cheilostomatous Bryozoa. Oxford: 1995. V. 64; 66
Handbook of the Marine Fauna of North-West Europe. New York: 1995. V. 65

HAYWARD, RICHARD
In Praise of Ulster. 1946. V. 67
Munster and the City of Cork. 1964. V. 67

HAYWOOD, C. WIGHTWICK
To the Mysterious Lorian Swamp; an Adventurous and Arduous Journey of Exploration through the Vast Waterless Tracts of Unknown Jubaland. London: 1927. V. 67

HAYWOOD, GAR ANTHONY
Fear of the Dark. New York: 1988. V. 65; 66; 67

HAYWOOD, JOHN
The Civil and Poltical History of the State of Tennessee.... Knoxville: 1823. V. 63

HAYWOOD, MARSHALL DE LANCEY
Lives of the Bishops of North Carolina. Raleigh: 1910. V. 67

HAZARD and Heroism. 1903. V. 67

HAZARD, NATHAN
Observations on the Peculiar Case of the Whig Merchants, Indebted to Great Britain at the Commencement of the Late War.... New York: 1785. V. 62; 66

HAZELWOOD SCHOOL
Laws of Hazelwood School. London: 1829. V. 62

HAZEN, ALLEN T.
A Catalogue of Horace Walpole's Library. 1969. V. 67
A Catalogue of Horace Walpole's Library. Oxford: 1969. V. 62

HAZEN, EDWARD
The Panorama of Professions and Trades; or Every Man's Book. Philadelphia: 1839. V. 62
Popular Technology; or Professions and Trades. New York: 1845. V. 67

HAZEN, JASPER
The Primary Instructer, and Improved Spelling Book...In Two Parts. Windsor: 1822. V. 63

HAZEN, R. W.
History of the Pawnee Indians. Fremont: 1893. V. 65

HAZEN, WILLIAM B.
Our Barren Lands. Cincinnati: 1875. V. 67

HAZLITT, WILLIAM
An Abridgment of the Light of Nature Pursued, by Abraham Tucker, Esq. London: 1807. V. 67
Characters of Shakespear's Plays. London: 1817. V. 63; 64
The Complete Works.... London: 1930-1934. V. 62
Conversations of James Northcote. London: 1830. V. 64
Criticisms on Art. London: 1844. V. 67
The Eloquence of the British Senate.... London: 1808. V. 65
An Essay on the Principles of Human Action. London: 1805. V. 67
Lectures on the Dramatic Literature of the Age of Elizabeth; Delivered at the Surrey Institution.... London: 1820. V. 64
Lectures on the English Comic Writers. London: 1819. V. 63; 67
Literary Remains of the Late William Hazlitt. London: 1836. V. 67
Notes of a Journey through France and Italy. London: 1826. V. 62
Oliver Cromwell. London: 1857. V. 65
The Plain Speaker: Opinions on Books, Men and Things. London: 1826. V. 63; 65
A Reply to Z. London: 1923. V. 65
Select Poems of Great Britain. London: 1825. V. 66
Selected Essays of William Hazlitt 1778-1830. London: 1930. V. 63
The Table Talk or Familiar Discourse of Martin Luther. London: 1848. V. 65
Table Talk, or Original Essays on Men and Manners. London: 1824. V. 62; 66
A View of the English Stage; or a Series of Dramatic Criticisms. London: 1818. V. 63; 65

HAZLITT, WILLIAM CAREW
Collections and Notes 1867-1876. (with) Second - Third & Final Series. London: 1876. V. 67
Hand-Book to the Popular, Poetical and Dramatic Literature of Britain, From the Invention of Printing to the Restoration. London: 1867-1868. V. 67
Joe Miller in Motley. London: 1892. V. 66
A Roll of Honour. London: 1908. V. 62
A Select Collection of Old English Plays. London: 1874. V. 67

HAZZLEDINE, GEORGE DOUGLAS
The White Man in Nigeria. London: 1904. V. 67

HEAD, FRANCIS BOND
Bubbles from the Brunnens of Nassau. London: 1834. V. 64; 65
Bubbles from the Brunnens of Nassau. Paris: 1834. V. 67
Descriptive Essays Contributed to the Quarterly Review. London: 1857. V. 62; 65
The Emigrant. London: 1846. V. 63
A Fortnight in Ireland. 1852. V. 64; 67
A Narrative. London: 1839. V. 63; 64; 67
Rough Notes Taken During Some Rapid Journey Across the Pampas and Among the Andes. London: 1826. V. 63

HEAD, GEORGE
A Home Tour through the Manufacturing Districts of England, in the Summer of 1835. London: 1836. V. 64
Rome. A Tour of Many Days. London: 1849. V. 65

HEAD, H. NUGENT
The Hoghunters' Annual. Volume 1. Allahabad: 1928. V. 67

HEAD, HENRY
Aphasia and Kindred Disorders and Speech. Cambridge: 1926. V. 64; 66
Aphasia and Kindred Disorders of Speech. New York: 1926. V. 65
On Disturbances of Sensation with Especial Reference to Pain of Visceral Disease. 1893. V. 67
Studies in Neurology. Oxford: 1920. V. 64; 66

HEADLAND, ISAAC TAYLOR
Chinese Mother Goose Rhymes. New York: 1900. V. 63

HEADLAND, ROBERT K.
Chronological List of Antarctic Expeditions and Related Historical Events. Cambridge: 1993. V. 63

HEADLEY, J. T.
The Chaplains and Clergy of the Revolution. Springfield: 1861. V. 67

HEADLEY, JOHN W.
Confederate Operations in Canada and New York. New York & Washington: 1906. V. 63; 65

HEADLEY, RUSSEL
The History of Orange County, New York. Middletown: 1908. V. 64

HEADS of the People, or Portraits of the English. London: 1840. V. 63

HEAL, AMBROSE
The English Writing-Masters and Their Copy-Books 1570-1800, a Biographical Dictionary and a Bibliography. Cambridge: 1931. V. 63
The English Writing-Masters and their Copy-Books 1570-1800. A Biographical Dictionary and Bibliography. London: 1931. V. 62
The London Goldsmiths 1200-1800. 1935. V. 65
London Tradesmen's Cards of the XVIII Century. An Account of Their Origin and Use. London: 1925. V. 63; 64
The Signboards of Old London Shops.... London: 1947. V. 66

HEALE, THEOPHILUS
New Zealand and the New Zealand Company.... London: 1842. V. 64; 65

HEALES, ALFRED
The Records of Merton Priory in the County of Surrey Chiefly from Early and Unpublished Documents. London: 1898. V. 62

HEALY, JEREMIAH
Blunt Darts. London: 1986. V. 67

HEALY, JOHN
Ireland's Ancient Schools and Scholars. 1893. V. 67
Maynooth College, Its Centenary History. 1895. V. 62; 65; 67

HEALY, T. M.
Letters and Leaders of My Day. 1928. V. 67

HEANEY, HOWELL J.
Thirty Years of Bird and Bull: a Bibliography 1958-1988. 1988. V. 62
Thirty Years of Bird and Bull: a Bibliography, 1958-1988. Newtown: 1988. V. 64

HEANEY, SEAMUS
After Summer. Old Deerfield and Dublin: 1978. V. 62
Audensque. Paris: 1998. V. 64
Beowulf. London: 1999. V. 65
A Boy Driving His Father to Confession. Frensham, Farnham: 1970. V. 62
Commencement Address: the University of North Carolina at Chapel Hill May 12, 1996. Chapel Hill: 1996. V. 64; 67
The Cure at Troy - a Version of Sophocles' Philoctetes. Lawrence Hill, Derry: 1990. V. 62; 63; 66
Death of a Naturalist. New York: 1965. V. 62
Death of a Naturalist. London: 1966. V. 62; 64
Door into the Dark. 1969. V. 65
Door into the Dark. London: 1969. V. 62
Door into the Dark. New York: 1969. V. 62; 63; 64
Eleven Poems. Belfast: 1965. V. 65; 67
Eleven Poems. Belfast: 1966. V. 62
A Family Album. N.P: 1979. V. 62
Field Work. London: 1979. V. 62; 63
Field Work. New York: 1979. V. 62
From the Republic of Conscience. Dublin: 1985. V. 62; 66
The Government of the Tongue - The 1986 T. S. Eliot Memorial Lectures and Other Critical Writings. London: 1988. V. 62; 63
Hailstones. Dublin: 1984. V. 62; 66
The Haw Lantern. London: 1987. V. 62; 66
Hedge School - Sonnets from Glanmore. Salem: 1979. V. 62
Hedge School. Sonnets from Glanmore. Newark: 1979. V. 62; 64
In Their Element.... Belfast: 1977. V. 62
Into the Dark. London: 1969. V. 64
Keeping Going. Poems. Concord: 1993. V. 62; 64; 67
A Lough Neagh Sequence. Didsbury: 1969. V. 62
A Lough Neagh Sequence. Phoenix: 1969. V. 64
The Midnight Verdict. Oldcastle: 1993. V. 62
New Selected Poems 1966-1987. London: 1990. V. 62; 64; 67
North. London: 1975. V. 62; 64
North. New York: 1976. V. 62; 64
Opened Ground. Poems 1966-1996. London: 1998. V. 63; 64; 67
Opened Grounds: Selected Poems 1966-1996. New York: 1998. V. 63
The Place of Writing. Atlanta: 1989. V. 64
Poems 1965-1975: Death of a Naturalist, Door into the Dark, Wintering Out, North. New York: 1980. V. 66
Poems and a Memoir. 1982. V. 62; 65
Poems and a Memoir. New York: 1982. V. 62; 64; 66
Pre-Occupations - Selected Prose 1968-1978. London: 1980. V. 62
Preoccupations: Selected Prose 1968-1978. New York: 1980. V. 66
The Redress of Poetry. New York: 1995. V. 66
Responses. Great Britain: 1971. V. 62
Robert Lowell - a Memorial Address and an Elegy. London: 1978. V. 62; 65
The School Bag. London: 1997. V. 62; 64
Seeing Things. London: 1991. V. 62
Selected Poems 1965-1975. London: 1980. V. 62; 63; 64
Selected Poems 1966-1987. New York: 1990. V. 62
The Sounds of Rain. Atlanta: 1988. V. 62; 66; 67
The Spirit Level. London: 1996. V. 62; 64; 67
The Spirit Level. New York: 1996. V. 62; 66
Station Island. London: 1984. V. 62; 63
Sweeney Astray. Derry: 1983. V. 62; 67
Sweeney Astray. New York: 1984. V. 63; 66
Sweeney Praises the Trees. New York: 1981. V. 62; 64
Sweeney's Flight.... London: 1992. V. 62
The Tree Clock. Belfast: 1990. V. 62
Verses for a Fordham Commencement. New York: 1984. V. 62; 67
Wintering Out. London: 1972. V. 62; 64; 67

HEAP, DAVID P.
Report on the International Exhibition of Electricity Held at Paris, August to Nov. 1881. Washington: 1884. V. 62

HEAP, GWINN HARRIS
Central Route to the Pacific: with Related Material on Railroad Explorations and Indian Affairs. Glendale: 1957. V. 64; 66

HEAPHY, THOMAS
A Wonderful Ghost Story, Being Mr. H.'s Own Narrative.... London: 1882. V. 62; 65

HEARD, H. F.
The Great Fog and Other Weird Tales. New York: 1946. V. 67
The Lost Cavern and Other Stories of the Fantastic. New York: 1948. V. 64
Murder by Reflection. New York: 1942. V. 67
The Notched Hairpin. New York: 1949. V. 67
The Notched Hairpin. London: 1951. V. 65

HEARD, ISAAC V. D.
History of the Sioux War and Massacres of 1862 and 1863. New York: 1864. V. 64

HEARD, JAMES
A Practical Grammar of the Russian Language. St. Petersburg: 1827. V. 64; 67

HEARN, ARTHUR
Shooting and Gunfitting. London: 1945. V. 67

HEARN, LAFCADIO
Appreciations of Poetry. London: 1919. V. 65
The Buddhist Writings of Lafcadio Hearn. Santa Barbara: 1977. V. 64
Chin Chin Kobakama. Tokyo: 1899. V. 65
Gibbeted; Execution of a Youthful Murderer...Shocking Tragedy at Dayton...A Broken Rope and a Double Hanging...Sickening Scenes Behind the Scaffold-Screen.... Los Angeles: 1933. V. 64
Gleanings in Buddha-Fields: Studies of Hand and Soul in the Far East. Boston: 1897. V. 63; 64
Japan. An Attempt at Interpretation. New York and London: 1904. V. 62; 64; 67
Japanese Fairy Tales. Tokyo: 1898-1925. V. 65
Japanese Fairy Tales. New York: 1924. V. 64
Japanese Lyrics. Boston: 1915. V. 66
Kokoro, Hints and Echoes of Japanese Inner Life. Boston and New York: 1896. V. 65
Kotto. New York and London: 1902. V. 62; 64; 66
Kotto. New York: 1903. V. 66
Leaves from the Diary of an Impressionist. Early Writings. Boston and New York: 1911. V. 62; 67
The Romance of the Milky Way and Other Studies of Stories. Boston and New York: 1905. V. 62; 63; 64
Shadowings. Boston: 1900. V. 62; 64; 65
Some Chinese Ghosts. Boston: 1887. V. 62; 66
Stray Leaves from Strange Literature. Boston: 1884. V. 62; 63; 64; 67

HEARN, WILLIAM EDWARD
Plutology; or the Theory of the Efforts to Satisfy Human Wants. Melbourne and Sydney: 1863. V. 62; 65
Plutology: or the Theory of the Efforts to Satisfy Human Wants. London: 1864. V. 65

HEARNE, SAMUEL
A Journey from Prince of Wales's For in Hudson Bay to the Northern Ocean. Amsterdam/New York: 1968. V. 62; 64

HEARNE, T.
Bibliotheca Hearneiana. London: 1848. V. 62

HEARNE, THOMAS
A Collection of Curious Discourses, Written by Eminent Antiquaries Upon Several Heads in Our English Antiquities.... Oxford: 1720. V. 66
Gloucester's Chronicle. Oxford: 1724. V. 63
Historia Vitae et Regni Ricardi II...a Monacho Quodam de Evesham Consignata Accesserunt.... Oxoniae: 1729. V. 63
Thomae Sprottii Chronica. Oxford: 1719. V. 66

HEARNE, VICKI
Nervous Horses. (Poems). Austin & London: 1980. V. 62

HEARON, SHELBY
Armadillo in the Grass. New York: 1968. V. 62

THE HEART of Man, Either A Temple of God, or a Habitation of Satan. Harrisburg: 1853. V. 62

THE HEART of the Continent. Chicago: 1882. V. 65

HEART of the Land. Essays on Last Great Places. New York: 1994. V. 63; 66

HEARTFIELD, JOHN
John Heartfield. New York: 1992. V. 67

HEARTMAN, CHARLES F.
American Primers, Indian Primers, Royal Primers, and Thirty-Seven Other Types of Non-New-England Primers Issued Prior to 1830. Highland Park: 1935. V. 63

HEARTSEASE and Honesty. Waltham St. Lawrence: 1935. V. 64

HEARTSILL, WILLIAM WILLISTON
Fourteen Hundred and 91 Days in the Confederate Army. Marshall: 1874-1876. V. 62; 63

HEAT, J.
The Moths and Butterlifes of Great Britain and Ireland. 1976-1989. V. 66

HEATH, A. H.
Sketches of Vanishing China. London: 1927. V. 67

HEATH, A. S.
Consumption, Diseases of the Heart, Cancer and Chronic Diseases, Their Prevention and Cure.... New York: 1860. V. 66

HEATH, AMBROSE
Good Drinks. London: 1939. V. 62
More Good Food. London: 1933. V. 67

HEATH, CHARLES
The Shakespeare Gallery, Containing the Principal Female Characters in the Plays of the Great Poet. London: 1836-1837. V. 65

HEATH, F. GEORGE
Autumnal Leaves. London: 1885. V. 64
The English Pesantry. London: 1874. V. 62

HEATH, H.
Old Way's and New Way's. London: 1830?. V. 67
Omnium Gatherum. 1830?. V. 67

HEATH, JOHN
The Moths and Butterflies of Great Britain. 1983-1996. V. 62

HEATH, LABAN
Heath's Infallible Government Counterfeit Detector at Sight. Boston and Washington: 1878. V. 63; 67

HEATH, ROBERT
A Natural and Historical Account of the Islands of Scilly.... London: 1750. V. 64

HEATH, SIDNEY
Old English Houses of Alms. London: 1910. V. 62

HEATH, THOMAS
Aristarchus of Samos, the Ancient Copernicus: a History of Greek Astronomy to Aristarchus.... Oxford: 1913. V. 62

HEATH, WILLIAM
Memoirs of Major-General William Heath, by Himself. New York: 1901. V. 66; 67

HEATHCOTE, RALPH
The Irenarch; or, Justice of the Peace's Manual. London: 1774. V. 63
Sylva; or, the Wood; Being a Collection of Anecdotes, Dissertations, Characters, Apophthegms, Original Letters Bon Mots and Other Little Things. London: 1786. V. 65

HEATHCOTE, WILLIAM
Catalogue of Books in the Library of...at Hursley Park in the County of Southampton. London: 1865. V. 63

HEATHER, J. F.
A Treatise on Mathematical Instruments.... London: 1849. V. 64

HEATHERINGTON, A.
A Practical Guide for Tourists, Miners and Investors, and all Persons Interested...Gold Fields of Nova Scotia. Montreal: 1868. V. 63

HEATON, CHARLES, MRS.
Masterpieces of Flemish Art.... London: 1869. V. 64

HEAVISIDES, EDWARD MARSH
The Poetical and Prose Remains. Stockton: 1850. V. 62

HEAVISIDES, HENRY
The Annals of Stockton-on-Tees.... Stockton-on-Tees: 1865. V. 65

HEAWOOD, EDWARD
Watermarks, Mainly of the 17th and 18th Centuries. Hilversum: 1950. V. 66

HEBARD, GRACE R.
The Bozeman Trail. Glendale: 1922. V. 63
The Bozeman Trail. Glendale: 1960. V. 65; 67
Washakie: an Account of Indian Resistance of the Covered Wagon and Union Pacific Railroad Invasions of their Territory. Cleveland: 1930. V. 64; 65; 67

HEBARD, HIPPOLYTE
De la Phthisie Pulmonaire.... Paris: 1867. V. 65

HEBER, GEORG
Elektrotherapie. Die Technik und Anwendung Elektrischer Apparte in der Arzlichen Praxis. Berlin & Leipzig: 1906. V. 65

HEBER, REGINALD
The Life of The Rt. Rev. Jer. Taylor, D.D.... Hartford: 1832. V. 64

HEBER, RICHARD
Bibliotheca Heberiana. Catalogue of the Library of the Late Richard Heber. Part the Fourth. London: 1984. V. 65

HEBERDEN, WILLIAM
Commentaries on the History and Cure of Diseases. London: 1816. V. 65

HEBER PERCY, ALGERNON
Moab, Ammon and Gilead. London: 1896. V. 67

HEBERT, FRANK
40 Years Prospecting and Mining in the Black Hills of South Dakota. Rapid City: 1921. V. 66

HEBERT, WALTER H.
Fighting Joe Hooker. Indianapolis: 1944. V. 62

HEBRA, FERDINAND
On the Diseases of the Skin, Including Exanthemata. 1866-1880. V. 64

HEBREW Customs, or the Missionary's Return. Richmond: 1872. V. 66

HECHT, ANTHONY
Aesopic: Twenty-Four Couplets. Northampton: 1967. V. 62; 64
Millions of Strange Shadows. New York: 1977. V. 63
The Presumptions of Death. 1995. V. 64
A Summoning of Stones. New York: 1954. V. 63; 64; 67
The Venetian Vespers. Boston: 1979. V. 64

HECHT, BEN
The Cat that Jumped Out of the Story. Philadelphia: 1947. V. 64
The Kingdom of Evil. Chicago: 1924. V. 67

HECK, ARCH O.
Descendants of Hezekiah Davis I, a Settler in North Eastern Tennessee in the Later part of the 1700's. Columbus: 1965. V. 62

HECKER, J. F. C.
The Black Death of the Fourteenth Century. (with) The Epidemics in the Middle Ages. London: 1833. V. 63
The Epidemics of the Middle Ages. Philadelphia: 1837. V. 65

HECKFORD, N.
Practical Sailing Directions and Coasting Guide from the Sand Heads to Rangoon, Maulmain, Akyab and Vice Versa.... London: 1859. V. 62

HECKSTALL-SMITH, BROOKE
A Catalogue of Prints, Portraits and Oil Paintings...of the Royal Thames Yacht Club. London: 1938. V. 67
The Complete Yachtsman. London: 1921. V. 62
Dixon Kemp's Manual of Yacht and Boat Sailing and Yacht Architecture. London: 1913. V. 62

HECLAWA
In the Heart of the Bitter Root Mountains - The Story of The Carlin Hunting Party. New York: 1895. V. 64; 67

HECO, JOSEPH
The Narrative of a Japanese. Yokahama: 1873-1892. V. 62
The Narrative of a Japanese. San Francisco: 1950. V. 65

HECQUET, MME.
The History of a Savage Girl, Caught Wild in the Woods of Champagne.... London: 1784. V. 65

HECTOR Protector, and As I Went Over the Water. London: 1967. V. 65

HECTOR, WILLIAM
Selections from the Judicial Records of Renfreshire. Paisley: 1876. V. 62; 66

HEDDERWICK, JAMES
Hedderwick's Miscellany of Instructive and Entertaining Literature. London and Glasgow: 1863. V. 64

HEDELIN, FRANCOIS
The Whole Art of the Stage. London: 1684. V. 67

HEDERICH, BENJAMIN
Graecum, Lexicon Manual. London: 1739. V. 63
Progymnasmata Architectonica, Oder Vor-Ubungen in Beyderley Bau- Kunst, und Zwar in der Civili.... Leipzig: 1730. V. 66

HEDEVIND, BERTIL
The Dialect of Dentdale in the West Riding of Yorkshire, Studia, Anglistica Upsaliensis. 1967. V. 64

HEDGECOE, JOHN
Henry Moore. New York: 1968. V. 62

HEDGEPETH, DON
The Art of Tom Lovell, an Invitation to History. Trumbull: 1993. V. 66
From Broncs to Bronzes - The Life and Work of Grant Speed. Flagstaff: 1979. V. 67
New Western Images - The Hillin Collection of the Cowboy Artists of America. Flagstaff: 1978. V. 64
Spurs Weve-a-Jinglin - A Brief Look at the Wyoming Range Cattle County. Flagstaff: 1975. V. 67

HEDGES, ISAAC A.
Sorgo or the Northern Sugar Plant. Cincinnati: 1863. V. 65

HEDGES, WILLIAM HAWKINS
Pike's Peak...or Busted! Frontier Reminiscences of William Hawkins Hedges. Evanston: 1954. V. 63; 64

HEDGPETH, J. W.
Treatise on Marine Ecology and Paleoecology. Volume I. Ecology. 1957. V. 62; 63

HEDIN, SVEN
Central Asia and Tibet Towards the Holy City of Lassa. London and New York: 1903. V. 67
Forskningar I Lop-Nor-Omradet: Tillagsband Till en Fard Genom Asien 1895-1897. Stockholm: 1902. V. 66
Jehol, City of Emperors. New York: 1933. V. 64
My Life as an Explorer. New York: 1925. V. 64
My Life as an Explorer. London: 1926. V. 62
Through Asia. London: 1898. V. 67
Trans-Himalaya, Discoveries and Adventures in Tibet. London: 1909-1910. V. 64
Von Peking Nach Moskau. Leipzig: 1924. V. 66

HEDINGER, J. M.
A Short Description of Castleton, in Derbyshire.... Derby: 1800. V. 64; 65; 66

HEDIO, CASPAR
Ein Ausselessne Chronick von Anfang der Welt bis Auff das Iar Nach Christi Unsers Eynigen Heylands Gepurt M.D. xxxiv.... Strasbourg: 1539. V. 65

HEDLEY, JOHN
A Practical Treatise on the Working and Ventilation of Coal Mines, with Suggestions for Improvements in Mining. 1851. V. 65
A Practical Treatise on the Working and Ventilation of Coal Mines; with Suggestions for Improvements in Mining. London: 1851. V. 62; 64
Tramps in Mongolia. London: 1910. V. 65

HEDREN, PAUL
First Scalp for Custer, the Skrimish at War Bonnet Creek, Nebraska July 17 1876, with A Short History of the War Bonnet Battlefield. Glendale: 1980. V. 67

HEDRICK, ULYSSES P.
The Cherries of New York. Albany: 1915. V. 62
Cyclopedia of Hardy Fruits. New York: 1922. V. 62
The Grapes of New York. Albany: 1908. V. 62
A History of Horticulture in America to 1860. New York: 1950. V. 67
Peaches of New York. Albany: 1917. V. 62; 64; 67
The Pears of New York. Albany: 1921. V. 62
The Plums of New York. Albany: 1911. V. 62
The Small Fruits of New York. Albany: 1925. V. 62
Sturtevant's Notes on Edible Plants. Albany: 1919. V. 66; 67
The Vegetables of New York. Albany: 1928-1937. V. 62

HEEBNER, MARY
Island: Journey from Iceland. Santa Barbara: 1997. V. 64
Scratching the Surface: a Visit to Lascaux and Rouffignac. Santa Barbara: 1997. V. 64

HEEDLESS Harry's Day of Disasters. London: 1855. V. 64

HEEMANS, FORBES
Thirteen Stories of the Far West. Syracuse: 1887. V. 64; 67

HEEREN, A. H.
A Manual of the History of the Political System of Europe and Its Colonies. Oxford: 1834. V. 66

HEEREN, ARNOLD A. H.
Historical Researches into the Politics, Intercourse and Trade of the Carthaginians, Ethiopians and Egyptians.... Oxford: 1838. V. 63

HEFELE, CHARLES JOSEPH
A History of the Christian Councils from the Original Translation from German with the Author's Approbation. Edinburgh: 1872-1896. V. 63

HEGEL, G. W. F.
System der Wissenschaft; Erster Thiel, Die Phaenomenologie des Geistes. Bamberg und Wurzburg: 1807. V. 63; 64

HEGEMANN, ELIZABETH COMPTON
Navaho Trading Days. Albuquerque: 1963. V. 63; 66

HEGEMANN, W.
City Planning Housing. Volume III: a Graphic Review of City Art, 1922-1937. New York: 1938. V. 65
Facades of Buildings. London: 1929. V. 66

HEGENETIUS, GOTTFRIED
Itinerarium Frisio-Hollandicum et Itinerarium Gallo-Brabanticum. Leyden: 1630. V. 66

HEGESIPUS
Historiographi...De Rebus A Iudaeorum Principibus in Obsidione Fortiter Gestis, Deque Excidio Hierosolymorum.... Cologne: 1530. V. 66

HEGI, URSULA
Floating in My Mother's Palm. New York: 1990. V. 65; 67
Unearned Pleasures and Other Stories. Moscow: 1988. V. 65; 67

HEIDEN, JAN VANDER
Beschryving Der Nieuwlyks Uitgevonden en Geoctrojeerde Slang-Brand- Psuiten en Haare Wyze vn Brand-Blussen, Tegenwoordig Binnen Amsterdam in Gebruik Zijnde.... Amsterdam: 1735. V. 62; 65

HEILNER, V. C.
Duck Shooting. 1951. V. 62; 63
Duck Shooting. London: 1951. V. 67

HEILPRIN, A.
Town Geology: the Lesson of the Philadelphia Rocks. Philadelphia: 1885. V. 63

HEIM, A.
The Throne of Gods. 1939. V. 63; 65

HEIM, R.
Les Champignons Hallucinogenes du Mexique. (with) Nouvelles Investigations sur les Champignons Hallucinogenes. Paris: 1958-1967. V. 63; 67

HEIMANN, JIM
Out With the Stars: Hollywood Nightlife in the Golden Era. New York: 1985. V. 65

HEIN, O. L.
Memories of Long Ago...Before and After the Civil War 1855-1865... Western Frontier...in Early Seventies and Eighties. New York: 1925. V. 65; 67

HEINE, HEINRICH
Atta Troll. London: 1913. V. 62; 66
Ausgewaehlte Lieder Heines. Chipping Campden: 1903. V. 65
Florentine Nights. London: 1927. V. 66

HEINE, HEINRICH continued
Gedichte. Berlin: 1822. V. 65; 67
The Prose and Poetical Works of Heinrich Heine. New York: 1910. V. 62

HEINE, JOHANN AUGUST
Traite des Batiments Propres a Loger les Animaux, Qui Sont Neccessaires a l'Economie Rurale.... Leipzig: 1802. V. 64

HEINEMANN, JAMES H.
P. G. Wodehouse, a Centenary Celebration 1881-1981. New York: 1981. V. 63

HEINEMANN, LARRY
Close Quarters. New York: 1977. V. 67
Paco's Story. New York: 1986. V. 63

HEINLEIN, ROBERT ANSON
Assignment in Eternity. Reading: 1953. V. 66
Between Planets. New York: 1951. V. 64
Double Star. London: 1958. V. 64
Farmer in the Sky. New York: 1930. V. 64
Farmer in the Sky. New York: 1950. V. 66
Farmer in the Sky. London: 1962. V. 66
Farnham's Freehold. 1964. V. 64; 66
The Green Hills of Earth. Chicago: 1951. V. 64; 66
The Man Who Sold the Moon. 1950. V. 66
The Man Who Sold the Moon. Chicago: 1950. V. 64
Methuselah's Children. 1958. V. 64; 66
Orphans of the Sky. London: 1963. V. 64; 66
Red Planet. London: 1963. V. 64; 66
Revolt in 2100. Chicago: 1953. V. 66
Rocket Ship Galileo. New York: 1947. V. 66
Sixth Column. 1949. V. 63; 64; 66
A Sixth Column. New York: 1949. V. 66
Space Cadet. London: 1966. V. 64; 66
The Star Beast. New York: 1954. V. 64; 66
Starman Jones. 1953. V. 64
Starman Jones. New York: 1953. V. 62; 66
Stranger in a Strange Land. 1961. V. 64
Time for the Stars. 1956. V. 66
Time for the Stars. New York: 1956. V. 64
Tunnel in the Sky. New York: 1955. V. 67
Waldo and Magic, Inc. Garden City: 1950. V. 66

HEIRS of Hippocrates. Iowa City: 1980. V. 67
HEIRS of Hippocrates. Iowa City: 1990. V. 64

HEISTER, LORENZ
Compendio Anatomico...Nel Quale si Contiene Tutta la Dottrina Anatomica Tradotto in Italiano Dalla Quarta Edizione Latina d'Altorf, Molto iu Corretta.... Naples: 1774. V. 65
Compendium Anatomicum Totam Rem Anatomicam Brevissime Complectens. Altdorf & Nuremberg: 1727. V. 66

HEITMAN, FRANCIS B.
Historical Register and Dictionary of the U.S. Army 1789-1903. Urbana: 1965. V. 62; 67
Historical Register and Dictionary of the U.S. Army 1789-1903. 1988. V. 67

HEJINIAN, LYN
Two Stein Talks. Santa Fe: 1995. V. 62; 64

HELD, JULIUS S.
Rembrandt and the Book of Tobit. Northampton: 1964. V. 62

HELICZER, PIERO
The Soap Opera. London: 1967. V. 63

HELIODORUS
Historia Ethiopica. Antwerp: 1554. V. 62

HELL, M.
Adjumentum Manuale, Seu Tabilae Succinctae Historico-Chronoligico- Genealogicae.... Munich & Ingolstadt: 1763. V. 66

HELL, RICHARD
Artifact. Madras/New York: 1990. V. 62

HELLE, ANDRE
La Boite a Jouyjoux. Paris: 1926. V. 66

HELLEBUST, J. A.
Handbook of Phycological Methods. Cambridge: 1978. V. 65

HELLER, JOSEPH
Catch 22. New York: 1961. V. 63; 65; 67
Catch 22. London: 1962. V. 62
Catch 22. Franklin Center: 1978. V. 63; 66
Catch 22. New York: 1994. V. 63; 65
Closing Time. Franklin Center: 1994. V. 62; 65
Closing Time. New York: 1994. V. 65
God Knows. New York: 1984. V. 62; 63; 66
Good as Gold. New York: 1979. V. 66
Now and Then: from Coney Island to Here. Franklin Center: 1998. V. 65
Picture This. New York: 1988. V. 66
Portrait of an Artist, as an Old Man. New York: 2000. V. 66
Something Happened. New York: 1974. V. 62; 63; 66
We Bombed in New Haven. New York: 1968. V. 66

HELLER, JULES
Papermaking: the White Art. Scottsdale: 1980. V. 63; 64; 66

HELLER, MORRIS
American Hunting and Fishing Books Volume I. 1997. V. 67

HELLINGA, WYTZE
Copy and Print In the Netherlands: an Atlas of Historical Bibliography. Amsterdam: 1962. V. 64

HELLMAN, LILLIAN
Another Part of the Forest. New York: 1947. V. 63
Candide. New York: 1957. V. 62
The Collected Plays. Boston: 1972. V. 62; 64
The Little Foxes. New York: 1939. V. 62
Pentimento. A Book of Portraits. Boston: 1973. V. 67
Three. Boston: 1979. V. 62
Toys in the Attic. New York: 1960. V. 62; 64
An Unfinished Woman - A Memoir. Boston: 1969. V. 62; 64; 67
Watch on the Rhine - a Play.... New York: 1942. V. 63

HELLOT, M.
L'Art de La Teinture des Laines, et des Etoffes de Laine, en Grand et Petit Teint. Paris: 1750. V. 66

HELLWIG, C. VON
Der Curieuse und Wohl-Erfahrne Chymist, Welcher Nicht Alleine die aus Dem Mineral.... Leipzig & Arnstadt: 1738. V. 64
Nosce te Ipsum vel Anatomicum Vivum, oder, Kurtz Gefasstes Doch Richtig Gestelltes Anatomisches Werck. Erfurt: 1716. V. 66

HELM, KATHERINE
The True Story of Mary, Wife of Lincoln. New York: 1928. V. 63

HELM, M.
Man of Fire: J. C. Orozco. New York: 1952. V. 62; 64
Modern Mexican Painters. New York: 1941. V. 62

HELMAN, ISIDORE STANISLAUS HENRI
Abrege Historique des Principaux Traits de la Vie de Confucius Celebre Philosophe Chinois Orne de 24 Estampes.... Paris: 1788. V. 62
Faits Memorables des Empereurs de la Chine, Tires des Annales Chinoises.... Paris: 1788. V. 64

HELMAN, JAMES A.
History of Emmitsburg, Maryland. Frederick: 1906. V. 63

HELME, ELIZABETH
The Farmer of Inglewood Forest; or an Affecting Portrait of Virtue and Vice. Newcastle-upon-Tyne: 1824. V. 65
Instructive Rambles Extended in London and the Adjacent Villages. London: 1806. V. 65
Saint-Clair des Isles ou Les Exiles a l'Isle de Barra.... Paris: 1809. V. 65

HELME, WILLIAM
Curious Miscellaneous Fragments on Various Subjects More Particularly Relative to English History from the Year 1050 to the Year 1701.... Brentford: 1815. V. 63

HELMHOLTZ, HERMANN VON
Die Lehre von Den Tonempfindungen, Als Physiologische Grundlage fur die Theorie der Musick. Braunschweig: 1863. V. 65

HELMHOLZ, HERMANN VON
On the Sensations of Tone, as a Physiological Basis for the Theory of Music. London: 1885. V. 63
Treatise on Physiological Optics.... Birmingham: 1985. V. 63
Uber die Erhaltung der Kraft, Eine Physikalische Abhandlung, Vorgetragen in der Sitzung der Physikalischen Gesellschaft zu Berlin am 23 sten Juli 1847. Berlin: 1847. V. 63
Ueber die Methoden, Kleinste Zeittheile zu messen, und Ihre Anwendung fur Physiologisch Zwecke.... Konigsberg: 1850. V. 63

HELMONT, FRANCISCUS MERCURIUS VAN
Alphabeti Vere Naturalis Hebraici Brevissima Delineatio.... Sulzbach: 1667. V. 64; 66

HELMUTH, J. HENRY C.
A Short Account of the Yellow Fever in Philadelphia for the Reflecting Christian. Philadelphia: 1794. V. 66; 67

A HELP to Elocution. Containing Three Essays.... London: 1780. V. 64

HELPER, HINTON ROWAN
The Impending Crisis of the South: How to Meet It. New York: 1857. V. 63; 67
The Land of Gold. Baltimore: 1855. V. 62; 63; 66
Nojoque: a Question for a Continent. New York: 1867. V. 67
Oddments of Andean Diplomacy, and Other Oddments. St. Louis: 1879. V. 67

HELPRIN, MARK
A City in Winter. New York: 1996. V. 63
A Dove of the East and Other Stories. New York: 1975. V. 63; 67
Ellis Island and Other Stories. New York: 1981. V. 63
Refiner's Fire. New York: 1977. V. 65
Refiner's Fire. London: 1978. V. 63; 64

HELPS, ARTHUR
Casimir Maremma. London: 1870. V. 66
The Claims of Labour. London: 1844. V. 63
The Claims of Labour. London: 1845. V. 63
The Conquerors of the New World and Their Bondsmen. London: 1848-1852. V. 63

HELPS, ARTHUR continued
Essays Written in the Intervals of Business. London: 1842. V. 67
A Letter from One of the Special Constables in London on the Late Occasion of Their Being Called Out to Keep the Peace. London: 1848. V. 67
Life and Labours of Mr. Brassey 1805-1870. London: 1872. V. 63; 67
The Life of Las Casas, The Apostle of the Indies. London: 1868. V. 67
The Spanish Conquest in America and Its Relation to the History of Slavery and to the Government of Colonies. London: 1855-1861. V. 66

HELSHAM, RICHARD
A Course of Lectures in Natural Philosophy. Dublin: 1778. V. 65
A Course of Lectures in Natural Philosophy.... Philadelphia: 1802. V. 66

HELU, ANTONIO
La Obligacion de Asesinar (The Compulsion to Murder). Mexico City: 1946. V. 66; 67

HELVETIUS, CLAUDE ADRIEN
De l'Esprit. Paris: 1758. V. 63
De l'Homme, de ses Facultes Intellectuelles et de son Education. Amsterdam: 1774. V. 63

HELVICK, JAMES
Beat the Devil. Philadelphia and New York: 1951. V. 65; 67

HELWICH, CHRISTOPHER
The Historical and Chronological Theatre.... London: 1687. V. 67

HELY-HUTCHINSON, JOHN
The Commercial Restraints of Ireland Considered in a Series of Letters to a Noble Lord. Dublin: 1779. V. 62; 65

HEMANS, FELICIA DOROTHEA BROWNE
The Domestic Affections and Other Poems. London: 1840. V. 65
The Forest Sanctuary and Other Poems. London: 1825. V. 65
Poems. Edinburgh: 1854. V. 63
Poetical Works. London: 1875. V. 62
Records of Woman; and Other Poems. Edinburgh: 1828. V. 63; 65
The Siege of Valencia; a Dramatic Poem. London: 1823. V. 65
Songs of the Affections with Other Poems. Edinburgh: 1835. V. 65
The Works. London: 1839. V. 66

HEMENWAY, ROBERT E.
Zora Neal Hurston: a Literary Biography. Urbana: 1977. V. 63

HEMINGWAY, ERNEST MILLAR
Across the River and Into the Trees. London: 1950. V. 63; 66
By-Line: Ernest Hemingway. New York: 1967. V. 64; 65
Death in the Afternoon. London: 1932. V. 62
Death in the Afternoon. New York: 1932. V. 62; 65
Ernest Hemingway Selected Letters 1917-1961. New York: 1981. V. 66
A Farewell to Arms. New York: 1929. V. 62; 63
The Fifth Column: a Play in Three Acts. New York: 1940. V. 65
The Fifth Column and Four Stories of the Spanish Civil War. New York: 1969. V. 62; 66
The Fifth Column and the First Forty-Nine Stories. London: 1939. V. 63
For Whom the Bell Tolls. New York: 1940. V. 65; 66
For Whom the Bell Tolls. London: 1941. V. 63
God Rest You Merry Gentlemen. New York: 1933. V. 62
Hokum. Wellesley Hills: 1978. V. 62; 66; 67
In Our Time. London: 1926. V. 64
Men Without Women. New York: 1927. V. 62; 64; 65; 66
A Moveable Feast. London: 1964. V. 62; 64; 65; 66; 67
The Nick Adams Stories. New York: 1972. V. 65; 66; 67
The Old Man and the Sea. London: 1952. V. 62; 63; 64; 66
The Old Man and the Sea. 1953. V. 67
The Old Man and the Sea. London: 1953. V. 65
The Old Man and the Sea. New York: 1990. V. 65
Selected Letters 1917-1961. New York: 1980. V. 62
Selected Letters 1917-1961. New York: 1981. V. 67
To Have and Have Not. New York: 1937. V. 63; 67
The Torrents of Spring. London: 1933. V. 64
The Wild Years. New York: 1962. V. 65
Winner Take Nothing. New York: 1933. V. 62; 63; 65; 66

HEMM, J. P.
Portraits in Penmanship of the Royal Family. Nottingham: 1831. V. 66

HEMMETER, JOHN C.
Diseases of the Intestines: Their Special Pathology, Diagnosis and Treatment. Philadelphia: 1901. V. 66
Master Minds in Medicine. New York: 1927. V. 66

HEMMING, JOHN
Monuments of the Incas. Boston: 1982. V. 63

HEMMING, PETER
Windmills in Sussex, a Description of the Construction and Operation of Windmills Exemplified by Up-to-Date Notes on the Still Existing Windmills in Sussex. London: 1828. V. 67
Windmills in Sussex, a Description of the Construction and Operation of Windmills Exemplified by Up-to-Date Notes on the Still Existing Windmills in Sussex. 1936. V. 67

HEMON, LOUIS
Maria Chapdelaine. Paris: 1922. V. 65

HEMPEL, AMY
At the Gates of the Animal Kingdom. Stories. New York: 1990. V. 63

HEMPEL, CARL FRIEDRICH
Sitten, Gebrauche, Trachten, Mundart, Hausliche und Landwirthschaftliche Einrichtung der Altenburgischen Bauern, Dritte Auflage. Altenburg: 1839. V. 66

HEMPEL, CARL GUSTAV
Der Typusbegriff im Lichte der Neuen Logik. Leiden: 1936. V. 67

HENAULT, CHARLES JEAN FRANCOIS
Nouvel Abrege Chronologique de l'Histoire de France, Conteenant Les Evenements de Notre Histoire Depuis Clovis Jusqu'a La Mort De Louis XIV. Les Guerres, Les Batailles, Les Sieges, Nos Lois, Nos Moeurs, Nos Usages, Etc. Paris: 1768. V. 64

HENDERSON, A.
Field Guide to the Palms of the Americas. Princeton: 1995. V. 63; 67
The Palms of the Amazon. New York: 1995. V. 63; 67

HENDERSON, ALEXANDER
The History of Ancient and Modern Wines. London: 1824. V. 63

HENDERSON, ALICE CORBIN
Brothers of Light; the Penitentes of the Southwest. New York: 1937. V. 64

HENDERSON, ARCHIBALD
O. Henry, a Memorial Essay. Raleigh: 1914. V. 62
Old Homes and Gardens of North Carolina. Chapel Hill: 1939. V. 63; 64; 67

HENDERSON, DAVID H.
Covey Rises and Other Pleasures. Clinton: 1983. V. 65
Men and Whales at Scammon's Lagoon. Los Angeles: 1972. V. 64
On Point, a Bedside Reader for Hunters and Fisherman. Clinton: 1990. V. 65
Sundown Covey. Clinton: 1986. V. 65

HENDERSON, EBENEZER
Iceland; or the Journal of a Residence in that Island During the Years 1814 and 1815. Edinburgh: 1818. V. 62

HENDERSON, FRANK V.
How to Make a Violin Bow. Seattle: 1977. V. 67

HENDERSON, G. F. R.
Stonewall Jackson and the American Civil War. London: 1902. V. 64

HENDERSON, GEORGE
Stonewall Jackson and the American Civil War. London, New York, Bombay: 1898. V. 62; 63

HENDERSON, HALTON
Artistry in Single Action. Dallas: 1989. V. 65

HENDERSON, HARRY
The Technicolor Time Machine. New York: 1967. V. 64

HENDERSON, J.
Economic Mammalogy. 1932. V. 63
Economic Mammalogy. London: 1932. V. 62

HENDERSON, J. B.
The Cruise of the Tomas Barrera.... New York: 1916. V. 64

HENDERSON, J. R.
Challenger Voyage. Zoology. Part 69. Anomura. 1888. V. 66

HENDERSON, J. W.
Frijoles: a Hidden Valley in the New World. Santa Fe: 1946. V. 63; 64

HENDERSON, JAMES
Notes by the Way. Tientsin: 1874. V. 64

HENDERSON, JEFF S.
100 Years in Montague County, Texas. N.P: 1958. V. 65; 67

HENDERSON, JOHN
A Full Report of the Trial of John Henderson for the Murder of Mr. Millie,...Perth, September 1830....(with) supplement. Perth: 1830. V. 63
Letters and Poems by the Late John Henderson. London: 1786. V. 62
The West Indies. London: 1905. V. 63

HENDERSON, JULIAN
Colorado: Short Studies of Its Past and Present. Boulder: 1927. V. 63

HENDERSON, L. R. S., MRS.
The Magic Aeroplane, a Fairy Tale. Chicago: 1911. V. 63

HENDERSON, MARC ANTONY, PSEUD.
The Song of Milgenwater. Cincinnati: 1856. V. 63

HENDERSON, PAUL C.
Landmarks of the Oregon Trail. New York: 1953. V. 65

HENDERSON, W.
My Life as an Angler. 1880. V. 67

HENDERSON, WILFRED
Seamanship. Portsmouth: 1907. V. 64

HENDERSON, WILLIAM
Nolachucky Jack (Gov. John Sevier). Knoxville: 1873. V. 67
Notes on the Folk-Lore of the Northern Counties of England and the Borders. London: 1879. V. 65

HENDERSON, WILLIAM continued
Trial of William Gardiner. London: 1934. V. 62

HENDERSON, WILLIAM AUGUSTUS
The Housekeeper's Instructor; or, Universal Family Cook. London: 1793. V. 62

HENDERSON, ZENNA
Pilgrimage: the Book of the People. 1961. V. 66
Pilgrimage: The Book of the People. New York: 1961. V. 64

HENDEY, N. I.
An Introductory Account of the Smaller Algae of British Coastal Waters. Part 5. Bacillariophyceae (diatoms). 1964. V. 66
An Introductory Account of the Smaller Algae of British Coastal Waters. Part 5. Bacillariophyceae (Diatoms). London: 1964. V. 62

HENDRICK, BURTON J.
The Lees of Virginia. Biography of a Family. Boston: 1935. V. 67
The Life and Letters of Walter H. Page. London: 1923-1925. V. 66

HENDRICKS, GORDON
Albert Bierstadt: Painter of the American West. New York: 1973. V. 64; 65; 66
Albert Bierstadt: Painter of the American West. New York: 1988. V. 63; 66
The Photographs of Thomas Eakins. New York: 1974. V. 63

HENDRICKS, ROBERT J.
Bethel and Aurora - an Experiment in Communism as Practical Christianity. New York: 1933. V. 64; 67

HENDRY, J. F.
The New Apocalypse - an Anthology of Criticism, Poems and Stories. London: 1940. V. 63

HENFREY, A.
Botanical and Physiological Memoirs.... London: 1853. V. 63

HENING, WILLIAM WALLER
The New Virginia Justice. Richmond: 1810. V. 62; 66
The New Virginia Justice. Richmond: 1820. V. 65; 66
Principia Legis et Aequitatis: Being an Alphabetical Collection of Maxims. Richmond: 1824. V. 63
Statutes of Virginia. Charlottesville: 1975. V. 66; 67
The Virginia Justice, Comprising the Office and Authority of a Justice of the Peace.... Richmond: 1825. V. 65; 66

HENKEL, AMBROSE
Das Kleine ABC Buch Oder Erste Anfangs-Buchlein.... New Market: 1819. V. 66

HENKEL, PAUL
Der Christliche Catechismus.... Neu-Market: 1816. V. 63; 66
Church Hymn Book: Consisting of Hymns and Psalms, Original and Selected. Harrisonburg: 1850. V. 65

HENLEY, HENRY HOSTE
A Catalogue of the Genuine Guns, and Natural History of the Late Henry Hoste Henley, at Sandringham Hall, Near Lynn, Norfolk.... Cambridge: 1834. V. 63

HENLEY, THOMAS
A Pacific Cruise: Musings and Opinions on Island Problems. Sydney: 1930. V. 67

HENLEY, TONY
Round the Camp Fire. V. 67

HENLEY, W. E.
A Book of Verses. London: 1888. V. 67
A London Garland. London and New York: 1895. V. 66
London Types. London: 1898. V. 62; 63

HENNELL, THOMAS
Poems. London: 1936. V. 62

HENNEN, JOHN
Principles of Military Surgery, Comprising Observations on the Arrangement, Police and Practice of Hospitals, and on the History, Treatment and Anomalies of Vriola and Syphilis. Edinburgh: 1820. V. 65

HENNEPIN, LOUIS
A Discovery of a Large, Rich and Plentiful Country, in the North.... London: 1720. V. 66
Nouveau Voyage d'un Pair Plus Grand que L'Europe/avec Les Reflections des Entreprises du Sieur de la Salle, sur les Mines de St. Barbe etc. Autrecht: 1698. V. 66

HENNESSEY, TOM
Feathers 'N Furs. N.P: 1989. V. 65

HENNESSY, W. B.
History of North Dakota - Embracing a Relation of the History of the State from the Earliest Times Down to the Present Day. Bismarck: 1910. V. 62; 65

HENNESSY, WILLIAM M.
The Annals of Ulster: 431-1378 A.D. 1889-1895. V. 65
Chronicum Scotorum. A Chronicle of Irish Affairs from the Earliest Times to A.D. 1150. 1866. V. 62; 65

HENNICKE, C. R.
Die Raubvogel Mitteleuropas. Halle: 1903. V. 66

HENNIG, HELEN KOHN
Columbia. Capital City of South Carolina 1786-1936. Columbia: 1936. V. 67

HENNIKER, FLORENCE
Arthur Henniker: a Little Book for His Friends. 1912. V. 66
Sowing the Sand. New York: 1898. V. 65

HENNIKER, JOHN HENNIKER, BARON
Two Letters on the Origin, Antiquity, and History of Norman Tiles, Stained with Armorial Bearings. London: 1794. V. 66

HENNING, CARL
Freilicht: Lyrisch-Lehrhaft-Launige Reimbilder. Wien: 1909. V. 62

HENNINGS, EMMY
Die Letzte Freude. Leipzig: 1913. V. 67

HENOCH, EDUARD
Vorlesungen uber Kinderkrankheiten. Berlin: 1883. V. 66

HENOT, GEORGES
Will. London: 1888. V. 67

HENRARD, J. T.
A Monograph of the Genus Aristida (Gramineae). Leiden: 1929-1932. V. 63

HENRETTA, J. E.
Kane and the Upper Allegheny. Philadelphia: 1929. V. 67

HENREY, BLANCHE
British Botanical and Horticultural Literature Before 1800. London: 1975. V. 62; 64; 65; 66
British Botanical and Horticultural Literature Before 1800. London: 1999. V. 64; 67

HENRIQUES DE SOUSA, JOAO
Discurso Politico Sobre o Juro do Dinheiro. Lisbon: 1786. V. 62

HENRY & NATHAN RUSSELL & DAY
Illustrated Catalog of Polished Brass Library Lamps #14. New York: 1888. V. 66

HENRY, ALEXANDER
The Manuscript Journals of Alexander Henry, Fur Trader of the Northwest Company, and of David Thompson, Official Geographer and Explorer of the Same Company. Minneapolis: 1965. V. 64
Travels and Adventures in Canada and the Indian Territories, Between the Years 1760 and 1776. New York: 1809. V. 65
Travels and Adventures in Canada and the Indian Territories Between the Years 1760-1776.... Boston: 1901. V. 64; 67

HENRY, DAVID
An Historical Account of the Curiosities of London and Westminster, in Three Parts. London: 1760. V. 62

HENRY E. HUNTINGTON LIBRARY AND ART GALLERY
Fine Books: an Exhibition of Written and Printed Books Selected for Excellence of Design, Craftsmanship and Materials. San Marino: 1936. V. 63

HENRY, FRANCOIS
Irish Art During the Viking Invasions 800-1020. 1967. V. 67
Irish Art in the Early Christian Period. 1940. V. 62; 65
Irish Art in the Early Christian Period. 1965. V. 64
Irish Art in the Early Christian Period (to 800 A.D.). London: 1965. V. 65
Irish Art in the Romanesque Period 1020-1170. 1965. V. 62
La Sculpture Irlandaise Pendant les Douze Premiers Siecles de l'ere Chretienne. Paris: 1933. V. 65

HENRY, GUY V.
Military Record of Civilian Appointment in the United States Army. New York: 1869. V. 62

HENRY, JOHN
County Map of Virginia 1770. Charlottesville: 1977. V. 65

HENRY, JOSEPH
The Papers of Joseph Henry. City of Washington: 1972-1996. V. 64; 66
Report of the Trial of Joseph Henry, Esq. in the Sherrif's Court, on...Jan. 20, 1809 for Criminal Conversation with Lady Emily Best. London: 1809. V. 63

HENRY, MARC
Beyond the Rhine. Memories of Art and Life in Germany Before the War. London: 1918. V. 64

HENRY, MARGUERITE
Auno Tauno: a Story of Finland. Chicago: 1940. V. 64
Black Gold. Chicago: 1957. V. 65
Justin Morgan Had a Horse. Chicago: 1954. V. 65
King of the Wind. Chicago: 1948. V. 65

HENRY, MATTHEW
An Account of the Life and Death of Mr. Matthew Henry, Minister of the Gospel at Hackney, who dy'd June 22, 1714, in the 52d year of his Age. London: 1716. V. 62
The Works of.... London: 1726. V. 66

HENRY, PAUL
An Irish Portrait. 1951. V. 67

HENRY PAULSON & CO.
Material and Supplies for Watchmakers, Jewelers and Opticians. Chicago;: 1928. V. 64

HENRY, ROBERT SELPH
First with the Most Forrest. Indianapolis: 1944. V. 63

HENRY, STUART
Conquering Our Great American Plains. New York: 1930. V. 63; 66

HENRY, THOMAS CHARLTON
Letters to an Anxious Inquirer.... Charleston: 1827. V. 66

HENRY, W.
The Elements of Experimental Chemistry.... 1829. V. 62

HENRY, WALTER
Events of a Military Life: Being Recollections After Service in the Penisular War, Invasion of France, the East Indies, St. Helena, Canada, Elsewhere. London: 1843. V. 64; 66
Trifles from My Port-Folio, or Recollections of Scenes and Small Adventures During Twenty-Nine Years of Military Service In the...Upper and Lower Canada. Quebec: 1839. V. 64

HENRY, WARREN
The Confessions of a Tenderfoot Coaster: a Trader's Chronicle of Life on the West African Coast. London: 1927. V. 67

HENRY, WILL
Alias Butch Cassidy. New York: 1967. V. 64; 65

HENRY, WILLIAM
An Estimate of the Philosophical Character of Dr. Priestley...Read to the First Meeting of the British Association for the Promotion of Science at York, September 28th, 1831. York: 1832. V. 65

HENSCHEN, FOLKE
The Human Skull. A Cultural History. London: 1965. V. 66

HENSCHEN, SALOMON E.
Klinische und Anatomische Beitrage zur Pathologie des Gehirns.... Stockholm: 1930. V. 65

HENSHAW, J. P. K.
Memoir of the Life of the Rt. Rev. Richard Channing Moore, D.D. Philadelphia: 1843. V. 64

HENSHAW, JULIA W.
Mountain Wild Flowers of America, a Simple and Popular Guide to the Names and Descriptions of the Flowers that Bloom Above the Clouds. Boston: 1906. V. 67
Mountain Wild Flowers of Canada. Toronto: 1906. V. 67
Wild Flowers of the North American Mountains. New York: 1915. V. 62; 63; 64; 67

HENSHAW, S.
Some Chinese Vertebrates. Cambridge: 1912. V. 62; 63; 65; 66

HENSHAW, SARAH
An Address to Females; on the Duties God Enjoins on Them; the Importance of Serving Him.... East Bennington: 1849. V. 62

HENSON, WILLIAM S.
The Great Facts of Modern Astronomy, with an Exposition of What They Teach Comprising the Formation of the Sun and Stars, the Cause of Rotary Motion...Theory of Light, and the Sun Spots. Newark: 1871. V. 63; 66

HENTY, C.
For the Peoples' Pleasure. New York: 1989. V. 67

HENTY, GEORGE ALFRED
At Aboukir and Acre. New York: 1898. V. 67
At Aboukir and Acre. 1899. V. 64
At Agincourt. 1897. V. 64; 67
At Agincourt. London: 1897. V. 63
At the Point of the Bayonet. 1902. V. 64; 67
Beric the Briton. 1893. V. 67
Beric the Briton. London: 1893. V. 63
Both Sides the Border. 1899. V. 63; 64; 67
The Boy Knight. Boston: 1883. V. 67
The Brahmin's Treasure. Philadelphia: 1900. V. 63; 67
The Bravest of the Brave. London: 1887. V. 63
By Conduct and Courage. 1905. V. 64; 67
By Conduct and Courage. London: 1905. V. 63; 66
By England's Aid, or, The Freeing of the Netherlands (1585-1604). London: 1891. V. 62
By Pike and Dyke. 1889. V. 64
By Pike and Dyke. London: 1890. V. 63
By Right of Conquest. London: 1891. V. 62
Captain Bayley's Heir. 1889. V. 63
The Cat of Bubastes. 1889. V. 67
The Cat of Bubastes. London: 1889. V. 63
A Chapter of Adventures. London: 1891. V. 62; 63
Colonel Thorndyke's Secret. London: 1899. V. 64; 67
Condemned as a Nihilist. London: 1893. V. 62
Courage and Conflict. 1901. V. 63
The Dash for Khartoum. 1892. V. 64
Dorothy's Double. Chicago: 1893-1895. V. 67
Dorothy's Double. London: 1895. V. 67
The Dragon and the Raven; or the Days of King Alfred. New York. V. 64; 66
Fighting the Saracens. Boston. V. 67
For Name and Fame. New York. V. 64; 66
For Name and Fame. London: 1886. V. 63
For the Temple. 1887. V. 64
For the Temple. 1888. V. 64; 67
Friends, Though Divided. 1883. V. 63; 64; 67
Friends though Divided. 1891. V. 67
A Girl of the Commune. New York. V. 67
Hazard and Heroism. New York. V. 64
Hazard and Heroism. 1904. V. 64
Held Fast for England. 1892. V. 64
Held Fast for England. 1982. V. 67
A Hidden Foe. Toronto. V. 67
In Freedom's Cause. 1885. V. 67
In Greek Waters. 1893. V. 67
In Greek Waters. London: 1893. V. 62
In the Days of the Mutiny. Toronto: 1895. V. 67
In the Hands of the Cave-Dwellers. 1900. V. 64
In the Hands of the Cave-Dwellers. New York: 1900. V. 63
In the Hands of the Cave-Dwellers. London: 1902. V. 66
In the Hands of the Malays. 1905. V. 64; 67
In the Hands of the Malays. London: 1905. V. 63
In the Heart of the Rockies. 1895. V. 67
In the Heart of the Rockies. London: 1895. V. 62
In the Irish Brigade. New York: 1900. V. 67
In the Irish Brigade. 1901. V. 64
In the Irish Brigade. London: 1901. V. 63
In the Reign of Terror. 1887. V. 64; 67
In the Reign of Terror. London: 1888. V. 63
Jack Archer. London: 1889. V. 64
Jack Archer. London: 1893. V. 67
A Jacobite Exile. 1894. V. 62; 64; 67
A Knight of the White Cross. New York: 1895. V. 67
A Knight of the White Cross. 1896. V. 63
The Lion of St. Mark. 1889. V. 63; 64
The Lion of the North. 1886. V. 63
The Lost Heir. 1899. V. 64
The Lost Heir. London: 1899. V. 63
The Lost Heir. Toronto: 1899. V. 67
The Lost Heir. New York: 1900. V. 67
Maori and Settler. 1891. V. 63
A March on London. New York: 1897. V. 67
A March on London. 1898. V. 64
A March On London. London: 1898. V. 67
A Night of the White Cross. 1896. V. 64
No Surrender. New York: 1899. V. 67
No Surrender. 1900. V. 63; 64; 67
On the Irrawaddy. New York: 1896. V. 67
On the Irrawaddy. 1897. V. 64; 67
One of the 28th. 1889. V. 64
One of the 28th. 1890. V. 64
Orange and Green. 1888. V. 64
Out on the Pampas. 1871. V. 67
Out on the Pampas. 1910. V. 67
Out with Garibaldi. New York: 1900. V. 67
Out with Garibaldi. 1901. V. 64
Peril and Prowess. New York. V. 63
Queen Victoria, Scenes from Her Life and Reign. 1901. V. 63
The Queen's Cup. New York: 1898. V. 63
A Roving Commission. 1900. V. 67
Rujub, the Juggler. London: 1893. V. 64
Rujub, the Juggler. London: 1894. V. 67
Rujub, the Juggler. London: 1899. V. 64
Rujub, the Juggler. London: 1903. V. 63; 67
Saint Bartholomew's Eve. 1894. V. 63; 64; 67
Seaside Maidens. London: 1880. V. 64
A Soldier's Daughter. 1906. V. 67
Steady and Strong. 1905. V. 64
Sturdy and Strong. 1888. V. 63; 64
Tales of Daring and Danger. 1890. V. 67
Those Other Animals. London. V. 67
Through Russian Snows. 1896. V. 67
Through the Fray. 1886. V. 64
Through the Fray. 1889. V. 64
Through the Sikh War. 1894. V. 64
Through Three Campaigns. 1904. V. 64
The Tiger of Mysore. New York: 1895. V. 67
The Tiger of Mysore. 1896. V. 64; 67
To Herat and Cabul. 1892. V. 63
To Herat and Cabul. 1902. V. 64; 67
The Treasure of the Incas. New York: 1902. V. 67
The Treasure of the Incas. 1903. V. 64; 67
The Treasure of the Incas. London: 1903. V. 65
True to the Old Flag. London. V. 63
True to the Old Flag. 1885. V. 67
Under Drake's Flag. 1883. V. 63
Under Wellington's Command. 1899. V. 63; 64; 67
Under Wellington's Command. London: 1899. V. 66
Venture and Valour. 1900. V. 64
When London Burned. New York: 1894. V. 67
When London Burned. London: 1895. V. 65
Winning His Spurs. London: 1888. V. 63
Winning His Spurs. London: 1891. V. 63
Winning His Spurs. London: 1893. V. 63
Winning His Spurs. London: 1896. V. 67
With Buller in Natal. New York: 1900. V. 67
With Buller in Natal. 1901. V. 64; 67
With Buller in Natal. London: 1901. V. 66
With Clive in India. 1884. V. 64; 67

HENTY, GEORGE ALFRED continued
With Clive in India. 1888. V. 64
With Clive in India. London: 1894. V. 63
With Cochrane the Dauntless. New York: 1896. V. 67
With Cochrane the Dauntless. 1897. V. 64; 67
With Cochrane the Dauntless. London: 1897. V. 63
With Frederick the Great. New York: 1897. V. 67
With Frederick the Great. 1898. V. 64
With Kitchener in the Soudan. New York: 1902. V. 67
With Kitchener in the Soudan. 1903. V. 64; 67
With Kitchener in the Soudan. London: 1903. V. 63
With Lee in Virginia. 1889. V. 64
With Lee in Virginia. 1890. V. 67
With Moore at Corunna. 1898. V. 63; 64; 67
With Moore at Corunna. London: 1898. V. 65; 66
With Roberts to Pretoria. 1902. V. 64; 67
With Roberts to Pretoria. London: 1902. V. 62
With the Allies to Pekin. 1903. V. 64
With the Allies to Pekin. 1904. V. 67
With the Allies to Pekin. London: 1904. V. 63
With the British Legion. 1903. V. 64; 67
With Wolfe in Canada; or the Wininng of a Continent. London: 1887. V. 65
A Woman of the Commune. 1895. V. 63; 64; 67
A Woman of the Commune. London: 1895. V. 63
A Woman of the Commune. 1896. V. 64
A Woman of the Commune. 1897. V. 63; 67
Won by the Sword. 1900. V. 67
Wulf the Saxon. 1895. V. 67
The Young Buglers. 1880. V. 63
The Young Buglers & The Young Franc-Tireurs. Preston. V. 67
The Young Carthaginian. London: 1887. V. 62
The Young Colonists. London: 1892. V. 67
The Young Franc-Tireurs. London: 1872. V. 67
The Young Franc-Tireurs. London: 1910. V. 67
Yule Logs. New York: 1898. V. 63
Yule Logs. London: 1901. V. 63
Yule-Tide Yarns. London: 1899. V. 63

HENTZ, CAROLINE LEE
Robert Graham. A Novel. Philadelphia: 1855. V. 67

HENTZLER, PAUL
A Journey into England in the Year 1598. London: 1770. V. 66

HENZELL, H. P.
Fishing for Sea Trout. London: 1949. V. 67

HEPBURN, A. BARTON
The Story of an Outing. New York and London: 1913. V. 64

HEPBURN, ALICE
Pollie and Jack. London: 1875. V. 65

HEPBURN, IAN
Flowers of the Coast. London: 1952. V. 62

HEPEL, CHARLES J.
The Homoeopathic Domestic Physician. London: 1846. V. 62

HEPPENSTALL, RAYNER
Sebastian. London: 1937. V. 62

HEPPER, F. N.
Royal Botanic Gardens, Kew, Gardens for Science and Pleasure. London: 1982. V. 67

HEPWORTH, BARBARA
A Pictorial Autobiography. London: 1970. V. 63

HEPWORTH, GEORGE H.
Starboard and Port: the Nettie Along Shore. New York: 1876. V. 66

HEPWORTH, J.
Resist Much, Obey Little - Some Notes on Edward Abbey. Salt Lake City: 1985. V. 64; 66

HERACLITUS Ridens; or a Discourse Between Jest and Earnest, Where Many a True Word is Pleasantly Spoken in Opposition to all Libellers Against the Government. 1713. V. 67

HERAIL, JEAN AUGUSTE
Essai sur Le Tic Douloureux de la Face. Montpelier: 1818. V. 64

HERALDIC Visitation of Westmoreland, Made in the Year 1615, By Sir Richard St. George, Knt., Norroy King at Arms. London: 1853. V. 64; 65; 66

HERALDS' Commemorative Exhibition 1484-1934 Held at the College of Arms. Guildford: 1890-1891. V. 62

HERALDS' Commemorative Exhibition 1484-1934, Held at the College of Arms. London: 1936. V. 66

THE HERALDY of Nature, or Instructions for the King at Arms; Comprising, The Arms, Supporters, Crests and Mottos, in Latin.... London: 1785. V. 63

HERBARIUM: British Mosses. 1850. V. 64

HERBARUM Imagines Vivae.... N.P: Sep. 1970. V. 65

HERBERT, A. P.
The Bomber Gipsy and Other Poems. London: 1918. V. 62; 66

HERBERT, AGNES
Two Dianas in Somaliland; the Record of Shooting Trip by Agnes Herbert. London: 1908. V. 67

HERBERT, ARTHUR STANLEY
The Hot Springs of New Zealand. London: 1921. V. 67

HERBERT, AUBERON EDWARD WILLIAM MOLYNEUX
The Right and Wrong of Compulsion by the State. London: 1885. V. 66

HERBERT, AUBREY
Ben Kendim; a Record of Eastern Travel. London: 1924. V. 67

HERBERT, EDWARD
The Autobiography of Edward Lord Herbert of Cherbury. Newtown: 1928. V. 65
The Life and Reign of King Henry the Eighth. London: 1672. V. 63

HERBERT, EDWARD HERBERT, BARON
The Life of.... London: 1770. V. 62
The Life of.... London: 1817. V. 62

HERBERT, FRANK
The Dragon in the Sea. New York: 1956. V. 64; 66
The Dragon in the Sea. London: 1960. V. 64; 66
Dune. London: 1967-1966. V. 67
Dune. New York: 1984. V. 63
God Emperor of Dune. 1981. V. 64

HERBERT, GEORGE
The Pattern Poems. Marcham: 1997. V. 67
The Remains. London: 1848. V. 65
The Temple. London: 1709. V. 62
The Temple. London: 1850. V. 62; 63
The Temple. London: 1927. V. 62; 63; 64; 65; 67

HERBERT, HENRY WILLIAM
Frank Forester's Field Sports of the United States and British Provinces of North America. New York: 1849. V. 63; 66
My Shooting Box. Philadelphia: 1846. V. 62; 64

HERBERT, J. A.
Illuminated Manuscripts. 1911. V. 63; 66

HERBERT, PAUL D.
The Sincerest Form of Flattery. an Historical Survey of Parodies, Pastiches and Other Imitative Writings of Sherlock Holmes 1891-1980. Bloomington: 1983. V. 66

HERBERT, WILLIAM
Amaryllidaceae.... London: 1837. V. 63
Antiquities of the Inns of Court and Chancery.... London: 1804. V. 66
The History of the Twelve Great Livery Companies of London.... London: 1837-1836. V. 63

HERBERT, ZBIGNIEW
Babarzynca w Ogrodzie. Warsaw: 1962. V. 67

HERBERTSON, AGNES GROZIER
Teddy and Trots in Wonderland. New York: 1910. V. 62

HERBIG, G. H.
Spectroscopic Astrophysics; an Assessment of the Contributions of Otto Struve. Berkeley: 1970. V. 67

HERBRAND, JACQUES
Theses Presentees a la Faculte des Sciences de Paris Pour Obetenir le Grade de Docteur en Sciences Mathematiques.... Warsaw: 1930. V. 66; 67

HERBST, JOSEPHINE
Rope of Gold. New York: 1939. V. 67

HERCIK, E.
Folk Toys. Prague: 1951. V. 62; 65

HERD, DAVID
Ancient and Modern Scottish Songs, Heroic Ballads, etc. Glasglow: 1869. V. 62; 66

HERD, RICHARD
Scraps of Poetry. Kirby Lonsdale: 1837. V. 64

HERDER, J. G.
The Spirit of Hebrew Poetry. Burlington: 1833. V. 62

HERDMAN, W.
Challenger Voyage. Zoology. Parts 17, 38 and 76 Tunicata. 1882-1888. V. 66
Pictorial Relics of Ancient Liverpool. Liverpool: 1878. V. 66

HERDMAN, W. A.
Fishes and Fisheries of the Irish Sea and Especially of the Lancashire and Western Sea-Fisheries District. London: 1901. V. 64; 65

HERDMAN, W. G.
Pictorial Relics of Ancient Liverpool. Liverpool: 1878. V. 64; 65

HERDMAN'S Liverpool. London: 1968. V. 62; 63; 65

HERFORD, OLIVER
An Alphabet of Celebrities. Boston: 1899. V. 66
A Child's Primer of Natural History. New York: 1899. V. 65

HERHOLDT, JOHAN DANIEL
Beschreibung Sechs menschlicher Misgeburten mit 14 Ausgemalten Kupfern. Copenhagen: 1830. V. 63

HERING, GEORGE EDWARDS
Sketches on the Danube, in Hungary and Transylvania. London: 1838. V. 62

HERITEAU, J.
Glorious Gardens, Designing, Creating, Nuturing. New York: 1996. V. 67

HERKLOTS, G. A. C.
Hong Kong Birds. Hong Kong: 1953. V. 64

HERLIHY, JAMES LEO
Midnight Cowboy. New York: 1965. V. 65; 66
The Sleep of Baby Filbertson. New York: 1959. V. 66
Stop, You're Killing Me: Three Short Plays. New York: 1970. V. 66

HERMANN, ISAAC
Memoirs of a Veteran Who Served as a Private in the 60's in the War Between the States. Atlanta: 1911. V. 63; 65

HERMANN, OSCAR
Living Dramatists: Pinero, Ibsen, D'Annunzio. New York: 1905. V. 63; 64

HERMANN, RICHARD
Julien Dubuque - His Life and Adventures. Dubuque: 1922. V. 65

HERMANT, ABEL
Les Confidences d'une Aieule (1788-1863). Paris: 1900. V. 64

HERMES TRISMEGISTUS
Pimandras Utraque Lingua Restitutus. Bordeaux: 1754. V. 64

HERMINGHAUSEN, F. W.
A Tragedy of the Platte Valley. Kansas City: 1915. V. 63

THE HERMIT of the Forest, and the Wandering Infants, a Rural Fragment. London: 1794. V. 62

THE HERMIT Of the Grove; or, the Fatal Effects of Gaming. London: 1804. V. 65

HERMITE, CHARLES
Oeuvres de Charles Hermite Publiees.... Paris: 1905-1917. V. 65

HERNANDEZ, FELISBERTO
La Cara de Ana. Mercedes: 1930. V. 67

HERNANDEZ, FORTUNATO
Los Razas Indigenas de Sonora y la Guerra del Yaqui. Mexico: 1902. V. 62

HERNDON, SARAH R.
Days of the Road Crossing the Plains in 1865. New York: 1902. V. 64; 67

HERNDON, WILLIAM H.
Herndon's Lincoln: the True Story of a Great Life. Chicago, New York, and S.F: 1889. V. 63; 66
Lincoln and Ann Rutledge and the Pioneers of New Salem. Herrin: 1945. V. 62; 63

HERNDON, WILLIAM LEWIS
Exploration of the Valley of the Amazon, Made Under the Direction of the Navy Department. Washington: 1853. V. 63; 67

HERNE, BRIAN
Tanzania Safaris. Clinton: 1981. V. 64
Uganda Safaris. Clinton: 1979. V. 65

HERNE, SAMUEL
Domus Carthusiana; or an Account of the Most Noble Foundation of the Charter-House near Smithfield in London. London: 1677. V. 62

HERO, OF ALEXANDRIA
Gli Artificiosi, e Curiosi Moti Spiritali.... Bologna: 1647. V. 64
The Pneumatics.... London: 1851. V. 63
Spiritalium Liber. A Federico Commandino Urbinate, ex Graeco, Nuper in Latinum Conversus. Urbino: 1575. V. 63

HERODOTUS
(Greek Title, then) Halicarnassei Historiarim Librix IX Codicem Sancrofti Manuscriptum.... Oxford: 1830. V. 62
Herodoti Musae.... Lipsiae: 1830. V. 66
Herodian of Alexandria His History of Twenty Roman Caesars and Emperors.... 1629. V. 66
Herodian's History of His Own Times, or of the Roman Empire After Marcus.... London: 1749. V. 67
Herodoti Libri Novem.... Basiliae: 1541. V. 65
Herodoti Musae. Londini: 1830. V. 65
His History of Twenty Roman Caesars and Emperors (of His Time). London: 1629. V. 62
Histor. Lib. VIII. Cum Angeli Politiani Interpretatione & Huius Partim Supplemento, Partim Examine Henrici Stephani.... Geneva: 1581. V. 66
Historia. 1570. V. 65
Historiarum. Geneva: 1592. V. 65
Historiarum Libri 8. Oxoniane: 1678. V. 66
The Histories. New York: 1958. V. 64
(Greek title, them:) Histor(iarum) Lib(ri) VIII. Lvgduni: 1611. V. 63; 66
Historiographi.... Cologne: 1526. V. 65
The History of Herodotus.... London: 1935. V. 62; 65

HEROLD, J. M.
Entwicklungsgeschichte der Schmetterlinge, Anatomisch und Physiologische Bearbeitet. Cassel & Marburg: 1815. V. 62

HERON, ROBERT
Scotland Described; or, a Topographical Description of all the Counties of Scotland.... Edinburgh: 1797. V. 62

HERON, ROY
Cecil Aldin the Story of a Sporting Artist. London: 1981. V. 63
Tom Firr of the Quorn, Huntsman Extraordinary. London: 1984. V. 67

HERON-ALLEN, E.
Barnacles in Nature and Myth. London: 1928. V. 66
Violin Making As It Was and Is, Being a Historical Theoretical and Practical Treatise. New York: 1885?. V. 67

HERONDAS
The Mimes of Herondas. San Francisco: 1981. V. 62; 63
The Mimiambs of Herondas. London: 1926. V. 67

HERON DE VILLEFOSSE, A. M.
Atlas de la Richesse Minerale.... 1838. V. 62

HERPF, HENRICUS
Espelho de Perfeycam. Coimbra: 1533. V. 62

HERR, MICHAEL
Dispatches. New York: 1977. V. 63; 64; 66

HERRE, H.
The Genera of the Mesembryanthemaceae. Cape Town: 1971. V. 64; 66

HERRENSCHWAND, JOHANN FRIEDRICH VON
Traite des Principales et des Plus Frequentes Maladies Externes et Internes. Berne: 1788. V. 65

HERREY, ROBERT F.
Two Right Profitable and Fruitfull Concordances, or Large Ample Tables Alphabeticall. 1592. V. 63

HERRICK, C. L.
Synopsis of the Entomostraca of Minnesota, with Descriptions of Related Species.... St. Paul: 1895. V. 65

HERRICK, CHARLES JUDSON
The Brain of the Tiger Salamander (Ambystoma Tigrinum). Chicago: 1948. V. 65

HERRICK, CHRISTINE TERHUNE
Consolidated Library of Modern Cooking and Household Recipes. New York: 1905. V. 66
Modern Domestic Science. Akron: 1909. V. 64; 67

HERRICK, F. H.
The American Lobster. Washington: 1895. V. 64; 66
Audubon the Naturalist. New York: 1917. V. 64
Natural History of the American Lobster. Washington: 1911. V. 64; 66

HERRICK, JAMES B.
A Short History of Cardiology. Springfield: 1942. V. 66

HERRICK, ROBERT
The Hesperides and Noble Numbers. London: 1891. V. 66
One Hundred and Eleven Poems. London: 1955. V. 63; 64
One Hundred and Eleven Poems. Waltham St. Lawrence: 1955. V. 62; 65; 66
The Poetical Works. London: 1825. V. 63
The Poetical Works. London: 1928. V. 62; 63
Select Poems from the Hesperides, or Works both Human and Divine.... Bristol: 1810. V. 64; 65

HERRIES, JOHN CHARLES
A Reply to Some Financial Mistatements In and Out of Parliament. London: 1803. V. 64

HERRING, FRANCES
The Gold Miners. London: 1914. V. 66

HERRING, RICHARD
Paper and Paper Making, Ancient and Modern. London: 1856. V. 62

HERRING, ROBERT
Adam and Evelyn at Kew, or Revolt in the Gardens. London: 1930. V. 62

HERRINGSHAW, THOMAS W.
Poets of America. 1890. V. 67

HERRINGTON, LEE
Carry My Coffin Slowly. New York: 1951. V. 63

HERRLINGER, ROBERT
Geschichte der edizinischen Abbildung. Von der Antike Bis um 1600 Sweite Verbesserte Auflage. Munchen: 1967. V. 64
History of Medical Illustration from Antiquity to 1600. 1970. V. 64; 66
History of Medical Illustration from Antiquity to A.D. 1600. New York: 1970. V. 63

HERRMANN, First Prestidigitateur from the Great European Theatres, With Commence in His Grand Performances, at the Academy of Music Dec. 2d, 1861.... New York: 1861. V. 67

HERROD-HEMPSALL, W.
Bee Keeping New and Old. London: 1930-1937. V. 64

HERRON, DON
Reign of Fear. 1988. V. 62; 64; 66

HERSCHEL, JOHN FREDERICK WILLIAM
A Catalogue of 10,300 Multiple and Double Stars, Arranged in the Order of Right Asension. London: 1874-1875. V. 66
Familiar Lectures on Scientific Subjects. London: 1871. V. 65
Ocherki Astronomii (in Cyrillic). Moscow: 1862. V. 65
Outlines of Astronomy. London: 1849. V. 66
Outlines of Astronomy. London: 1865. V. 65; 66
Physical Geography. Edinburgh: 1861. V. 65; 66
A Preliminary Discourse on the Study of Natural Philosophy. London: 1842?. V. 65
Traite d'Astronomie.... Paris: 1834. V. 63
Traite de la Lumiere.... Paris: 1829. V. 65
Traite de la Lumiere.... Paris: 1829-1833. V. 64

HERSEY, JOHN
Antonietta. New York: 1991. V. 63
A Bell for Adano. New York: 1944. V. 63; 65
The Wall. New York: 1950. V. 66

HERSHEY, JOHN
The Sign of the Four: a Sherlock Holmes Adventure in One Act. New York: 1937. V. 67

HERSHKOVITZ, P.
Living New World Monkeys. Chicago: 1977. V. 64; 66

HERTER, G. L.
Professional Fly-Tying and Tackle Making Manual and Manufacturer's Guide. 1950. V. 67

HERTRICH, WILLIAM
Camellias in the Huntington Gardens. San Marino: 1954. V. 64; 67
The Huntington Botanical Gardens 1905-1949. San Marino: 1949. V. 67

HERTS, B. RUSSELL
The Decoration and Furnishing of Apartments: the Artistic Treatment of Apartments Ranging from the Small 2 Room Suite to the Elaborate Duplex and Triplex. New York and London: 1915. V. 62; 65

HERTWIG, R.
Challenger Voyage. Zoology. Parts 15 and 73. Actinaria with the Supplement. 1882. V. 66

HERTZ, EMMANUEL
The Hidden Lincoln. New York: 1938. V. 63; 65

HERTZ, HEINRICH
Electric Waves Being Researches on the Propagation of Electric Action with Finite Velocity through Space. London: 1893. V. 62
Gesammelte Werke. Leipzig: 1895-1894. V. 64

HERTZA, THEODOR
Freeland: a Social Anticipation. London: 1891. V. 67

HERTZBERG, FRANCIS
Denis McLoughlin - Master of Light and Shade. Brooklyn: 1995. V. 62

HERTZLER, ARTHUR E.
The Peritoneum: Structure and Function in Relation to the Principles of Abdominal Surgery. St. Louis: 1919. V. 65
Surgical Operations with Local Anesthesia. New York: 1916. V. 63

HERTZOG, CARL
Swinburnian Coincidences. El Paso: 1960. V. 62

HERVEY, A. B.
Sea Mosses, a Collector's Guide and an Introduction to the Study of Marine Algae. Boston: 1881. V. 65; 66
Wayside Flowers and Ferns. Boston: 1899. V. 67

HERVEY, JAMES
Meditations and Contemplations. London: 1807. V. 62

HERVEY, JOHN
Lady Suffolk, the Old Grey Mare of Long Island. New York: 1936. V. 63; 66
Memoirs of the Reign of King George II. London: 1931. V. 66
Racing in America 1922-1936. New York: 1937. V. 62

HERVEY, THOMAS
A Complaint on the Part of the Hon. Thomas Hervey.... London: 1767. V. 62

HERVIEU, PAUL
Theroigne de Mericourt. Piece en Six Actes en Prose. Paris: 1902. V. 63

HERZFELD, ERNST E.
Iran in the Ancient East, Archaeological Studies Presented in the Lowell Lectures at Boston. London: 1941. V. 67

HERZL, THEODOR
Der Judenstaat. Leipzig & Vienna: 1896. V. 62

HERZOG, T.
Pneumatic Structures: a Handbook of Inflatable Architecture. New York: 1976. V. 65

HESELTINE, PHILIP
Merry-Go-Down. A Gallery of Gorgeous Drunkards through the Ages. 1929. V. 67

HESELTINE, WILLIAM
The Life of the Plantagenets.... London: 1829. V. 65

HESILRIGE, ARTHUR
Lieut. Colonel J. Lilburn Tryed an Cast; or His Case and Craft Discovered. London: 1653. V. 64

HESILRIGE, ARTHUR G.
Debrett's Peerage, Baronetage, Knightage and Companionage. London: 1915. V. 63
Debrett's Peerage, Baronetage, Knightage and Companionage. London: 1926. V. 63
Debrett's Peerage, Baronetage, Knightage and Companionage. London: 1935. V. 63

HESIOD
Hesiodi Ascrei Opera, Qvae Qvidem Extant. Basileae: 1550. V. 64; 66
Le Opera. Rome: 1826. V. 66
Opera et Dies Theogonia. Scvtvm Hercvlis. Venice: 1537. V. 66
Opuscula Inscripta. Parisiis: 1543. V. 64
The Remains of Hesiod the Ascraean. London: 1809. V. 65

HESKE, FRANZ
German Forestry. New Haven: 1938. V. 67

HESKI, THOMAS M.
Icastinyanka Cikala Hanzi The Little Shadow Catcher: D. F. Barry, Celebrated Photographer of Famous Indians. Seattle: 1978. V. 63; 67

HESLER, L. R.
North American Species of Hygrophorus. Knoxville: 1963. V. 63

HESS, D.
Die Blute eine Einfuhrung in Sturktur und Funktion Okologie und Evolution der Bluten. Stuttgart: 1983. V. 66

HESS, JOAN
Strangled Prose. New York: 1986. V. 63

HESS, JOSEPH F.
Out of Darkness Into Light - an Autobiography of Joseph F. Hess. Toronto: 1888. V. 66

HESSE, HERMANN
Das Glasperlenspiel. Zurich: 1943. V. 65
Knulp: Dres Geschichten Aus Dem Leben Knulps. Berlin: 1915. V. 64; 66
My Belief. Essays on Life and Art. New York: 1974. V. 67
Steppenwolf. Westport: 1977. V. 62; 63; 64; 66
Eine Stunde Hinter Mitternacht. Leipzig. V. 65

HESSE, KAREN
Out of the Dust. New York: 1997. V. 63

HESSELGRAVE, RUTH AVELINE
Lady Miller and the Batheaston Literary Circle. New Haven: 1927. V. 63

HESSELTINE, WILLIAM BEST
Civil War Prisons, a Study in the War Psychology. Columbus: 1930. V. 62; 63; 65

HESSEMER, FRIEDRICH M.
Arabische und Alt-Italienische Bau-Verzierungen.... Berlin: 1852-1853. V. 64

HESSE WARTEGG, CHEVALIER DE
Tunis: the Land and the People. London: 1882. V. 65

HESTON, ALFRED M.
...Heston's Hand-Book. Atlantic City. V. 66
Jersey Waggon Jaunts: New Stories of New Jersey. N.P: 1926. V. 63; 66
South Jersey. A History 1664-1924. New York: 1924. V. 63; 66

HETHERINGTON, BARRY
A Chronicle of Pre-Telescopic Astronomy. Chichester: 1996. V. 66

HETHERINGTON, GULLIFER
Paul Nugent - Materialist. London: 1890. V. 67

HETLEY, C., MRS.
The Native Flowers of New Zealand Illustrated in Colours.... London: 1887-1888. V. 62; 63

HEUCHER, M. J. H.
Magic Plants: Being a Translation of a Curious Tract Entitled De Vegetalibus Magicis. Edinburgh: 1886. V. 67

HEUSINGER, EDWARD W.
Early Explorations and Mission Establishments in Texas. San Antonio: 1936. V. 63

HEUSSER, ALBERT H.
The History of the Silk Dyeing Industry in the United States. Paterson: 1927. V. 63

HEUZE, GUSTAVE
Les Plantes Industrielles. Paris: 1859-1860. V. 64; 67

HEWAT, ALEXANDER
Historical Account of the Rise and Progress of the Colonies of South Carolina and Georgia. London: 1779. V. 63; 66

HEWER, H. R.
British Seals. 1974. V. 67

HEWETT, EDGAR L.
Landmarks of New Mexico. Albuquerque: 1940. V. 63
Mission Monuments of New Mexico. Albuquerque: 1943. V. 64; 65
Mission Monuments of New Mexico. N.P: 1946. V. 63; 64; 66
Pajarito Plateau and Its Ancient People. 1938. V. 63; 66

HEWITSON, A.
Our Country Churches and Chapels. London: 1872. V. 62
Stonyhurst College Present and Past: Its History, Discipline, Treasures and Curiosities. Preston: 1878. V. 62

HEWITT, ABRAMS
Sire Lines. N.P: 1877. V. 64
HEWITT, EDWARD RINGWOOD
Secrets of the Salmon. New York: 1925. V. 67
Telling on the Trout. 1926. V. 67
HEWITT, GRAILY
Lettering for Students and Craftsmen. London: 1930. V. 62; 65
The Pen and Type Design. London: 1928. V. 66
HEWITT, JOHN
Interest Compleated in Three Parts.... London: 1723. V. 67
HEWITT, RANDALL H.
Across the Plains. New York: 1906. V. 65
HEWITT, THOMAS
The Sitting Companion; or, Country Auctioneer's Guide.... Whitby: 1803. V. 62
HEWITT, W.
An Essay on the Encroachment of the German Ocean Along the Norfolk Coast, with a Design to Arrest Its Further Depredations.... Norwich: 1844. V. 64; 65
HEWLETT, MAURICE HENRY
A Masque of Dead Florentines. London: 1895. V. 62
Quattrocentisteria: How Sandro Botticelli Saw Simonetta in Spring. New York: 1937. V. 64
Quattrocentisteria: How Sandro Botticelli Saw Simonetta in the Spring. New York: 1921. V. 62
The Wreath 1894-1914. London: 1914. V. 62
HEXHAM, HENRY
A Tongue-Combat, Lately Happening Between Two English Souldiers in the Tilt-Boat at Gravesend.... London: 1623. V. 63
HEXHAM, LIONEL J. F.
Harry Roughton; or, Reminiscences of a Revenue Officer. London: 1859. V. 67
HEY, RICHARD
A Dissertation on Suicide. Cambridge: 1785. V. 64
HEY, WILLIAM
Practical Observations in Surgery.... London: 1803. V. 64
HEYDEMARCK, HAUPT
War Flying in Macedonia. London. V. 64
HEYEN, WILLIAM
Depth of Field. Poems. Baton Rouge: 1970. V. 63; 67
The Elm's Home. Derry: 1977. V. 62
The Mower. 1970. V. 63
Of Palestine: a Meditation. Omaha: 1976. V. 62
The Swastika Poems. New York: 1977. V. 63; 64
HEYER, GEORGETTE
No Wind of Blame. New York: 1939. V. 65
HEYERDAHL, THOR
The Art of Easter Island. Garden City: 1975. V. 64
HEYLYN, PETER
Cosmographie in Four Books. London: 1657. V. 63
Cosmographie, in Four Books. London: 1682. V. 66
Ecclesia Restaurata; or the History of the Reformation of the Church of England.... 1849. V. 63
The Undeceiving of the People in the Point of Tithes. London: 1651. V. 63
HEYMAN, MAX L.
Prudent Soldier - a Biography of Major General E. A. Canby 1817-1875. Glendale: 1959. V. 67
HEYMANN, BRUNO
Robert Koch. Erste Teil 1843-1882. Leipzig: 1932. V. 63
HEYMERING, HENRY
On the Horse's Foot, Shoes and Shoeing: the Bibliographic Record: and a Brief Timeline History of Horseshoeing. Cascade: 1990. V. 66
HEYNEN, JIM
The Man Who Kept Cigars in His Cap. Port Townsend: 1979. V. 63
HEYRICK, ELIZABETH
Immediate, Not Gradual Abolition; or, an Inquiry into the Shortest, Safest and Most Effectual Means of Getting Rid of West Indian Slavery. London: 1825. V. 64
HEYSINGER, ISAAC W.
Antietam and the Maryland and Virginia Campaigns of 1862. New York: 1912. V. 62; 63; 65
HEYWARD, DOROTHY
Porgy. A Play in Four Acts. Garden City: 1927. V. 64
HEYWARD, DU BOSE
Angel. New York: 1926. V. 64
Carolina Chansons. Legends of the Low Country. New York: 1922. V. 64
Fort Sumter 1861-1865. New York: 1938. V. 63
Mamba's Daughters. New York: 1929. V. 64
Mamba's Daughters. New York: 1939. V. 64
Porgy. New York: 1925. V. 64

HEYWOOD, GERALD G. P.
Charles Cotton and His River. Manchester: 1928. V. 67
HEYWOOD, SAMUEL
A Digest of the Law Respecting County Elections. London: 1790. V. 65
HEYWOOD, THOMAS
A Marriage Triumphe Solemnized in an Epithalamium in Memorie of the Happie Nuptials Betwixt the High and Mightie Prince Count Palantine and the Most Excellent Princesse the Lady Elizabeth. Bristol: 1936. V. 63
...; or, Nine Bookes of Various History. Concerninge Women; Inscribed by ye Names of Ye Nine Muses.... London: 1624. V. 64
HEYWOOD, V. H.
Flowering Plants of the World. New York: 1978. V. 67
HIAASEN, CARL
A Death in China. New York: 1984. V. 65; 66; 67
Double Whammy. 1987. V. 64; 66
Double Whammy. New York: 1987. V. 62; 67
Lucky You. New Orleans: 1997. V. 65; 66; 67
Native Tongue. New York: 1991. V. 67
Powder Burn. New York: 1981. V. 66; 67
Skin Tight. 1989. V. 64; 66
Skin Tight. New York: 1989. V. 62; 63; 64; 65; 67
Strip Tease. New York: 1993. V. 67
Team Rodent: How Disney Devours the World. New York: 1998. V. 67
Tourist Season. New York: 1986. V. 62; 63; 65; 66; 67
Trap Line. London: 1993. V. 63; 64
What Dead, Again?. Baton Rouge: 1979. V. 67
HIATT, CHARLES
Picture Posters: a Short History of the Illustrated Placard, With Many Reproductions.... London: 1895. V. 64
HIATT, JOHN
The Test of Loyalty. Indianapolis: 1864. V. 63
HIBBEN, FRANK C.
Kiva Art of the Anasazi at Pottery Mound. Las Vegas: 1975. V. 65
HIBBEN, SALLY
The New Official James Bond Movie Book. New York: 1989. V. 67
The Official James Bond 007 Movie Poster Book. London: 1987. V. 65
HIBBERD, SHIRLEY
History of the Extinct Volancos of the Basin of Neuwied on the Lower Rhine. Edinburgh: 1832. V. 62
The Ivy, a Monograph. London: 1872. V. 62
Rustic Adornments for Homes of Taste. 1895. V. 64
HIBBERT, GERALD K.
The New Pacifism. London: 1936. V. 63
HIBBERT, SAMUEL
Sketches of the Philosophy of Apparitions. Edinburgh: 1824. V. 62
HICHBORN, PHILIP
Report On European Dock-Yards. Washington: 1886. V. 65
HICHENS, ROBERT
The Green Carnation. London: 1894. V. 63
HICKERINGILL, EDMUND
Gregory, Father-Greybears with his Vizard off; or, News from the Cabal in Some. London: 1673. V. 63
The Survey of the Earth, in Its General Vileness and Debauch. London: 1706?. V. 63
HICKEY, J. J.
Peregrine Falcon Populations, Their Biology and Decline. Madison: 1969. V. 66
HICKEY, MICHAEL M.
The Death of Warren Baxter Earp - a Closer Look. Honolulu: 2000. V. 67
HICKEY, WILLIAM
Hints Originally Intended for the Small Farmers of the County of Wexford.... Dublin: 1830. V. 62
HICKIN, N. E.
Caddis Larvae. 1967. V. 67
HICKLIN, JOHN
The Ladies of Llangollen, as Sketched by Many Hands; With Notices of Other Objects of Interest in "That Sweetest of Vales". Chester: 1847. V. 65
HICKMAN, J. C.
The Jepson Manual, Highter Plants of California. Berkeley: 1993. V. 63
HICKMAN, WILLIAM
A Treatise on the Law and Practice of Naval Courts-Martial. London: 1851. V. 63
HICKOK, LAURENS P.
The Logic of Reason. Boston: 1875. V. 67
A System of Moral Science. Schenectady: 1853. V. 62
HICKS, ALBERT W.
The Life, Trial, Confession and Execution of Albert W. Hicks, the Pirate and Murderer, Executed on Bedloe's Island, New York Bay.... New York: 1860. V. 67

HICKS, ELIAS
Observations on the Slavery of the Africans and Their Descendants and on the Use of the Produce of Their Labour. New York: 1814. V. 66

HICKS, F. C.
Forty Years Among the Wild Animals of India from Mysore to the Himalayas. Madras: 1911. V. 66

HICKS, FREDERICK C.
High Finance in the Sixties. New Haven;: 1929. V. 65

HICKS, GRANVILLE
One of Us. The Story of John Reed. New York: 1935. V. 63

HICKS, J. R.
Value and Capital. An Inquiry into Some Fundamental Principles of Economic Theory. Oxford: 1939. V. 62

HICKS, J. STEPHEN
The Encyclopaedia of Poultry. London. V. 62
The Encyclopaedia of Poultry. 1930. V. 67

HICKSON, SYDNEY J.
A Naturalist in North Celebes; a Narrative of Travels in Minahassa, the Sangir and Talaut Islands, with Notices of the Fauna, Flora and Ethnology of the Districts Visited. London: 1889. V. 67

HIDGSON, W. EARL
Trout Fishing. London: 1908. V. 67

HIEB, LOUIS A.
A Bibliography of Charles Bowden. Santa Fe. 1994. V. 63; 64; 66
A Bibliography of Tony Hillerman. Tucson: 1990. V. 63; 64
Collecting Tony Hillerman. Santa Fe: 1992. V. 67
Tony Hillerman: a Bibliography. Tucson: 1988. V. 63

HIERONYMUS
Vitas Patrum. Lyon: 1512. V. 64

HIGDEN, WILLIAM
A Defence of the View of the English Constitution with Respect to the Sovereign Authority of the Prince, and the Allegiance of the Subject. (with) A View of the English Constitution. London: 1710. V. 67
A View of the English Constitution, with Respect to the Sovereign Authority of the Prince and the Allegiance of the Suject. London: 1709. V. 64

HIGGINS, AILEEN CLEVELAND
Dream Blocks. New York: 1908. V. 63; 64

HIGGINS, BRIAN
The Only Need: Poems. London: 1960. V. 66

HIGGINS, COLIN
Harold and Maude. Philadelphia: 1971. V. 66

HIGGINS, DICK
Jefferson's Birthday: Postface. New York: 1964. V. 66

HIGGINS, F. R.
Arable Holdings: Poems. Dublin: 1933. V. 62; 65
The Dark Breed - a Book of Poems. London: 1927. V. 64; 65
The Gap of Brightness - Lyrical Poems. London: 1940. V. 64

HIGGINS, GEORGE V.
The Friends of Eddie Coyle. London: 1972. V. 63
Old Earl Died Pulling Traps. Columbia: 1984. V. 65

HIGGINS, GODFREY
Anacalypsis, an Attempt to Draw Aside the Veil of the Saitic Isis; or, an Inquiry into the Origin of Languages, Nations and Religions. 1972. V. 65

HIGGINS, JACK
Day of Judgment. London: 1978. V. 67
Day of Reckoning. London: 2000. V. 66
Drink With the Devil. London: 1996. V. 67
Exocet. London: 1983. V. 66; 67
The Khufra Run. London: 1972. V. 66
The Last Place God Made. New York: 1972. V. 67
Night Judgement at Sinos. London: 1970. V. 65
A Prayer for the Dying. London: 1973. V. 65
Touch the Devil. London: 1982. V. 67

HIGGINS, WILLIAM
An Essay on the Theory and Practice of Bleaching, Wherein the Sulphuret of Lime is Recommended for Pot-Ash. London: 1799. V. 64
The House Painter; or Decorator's Companion. London: 1841. V. 62
The Philosophy of Sound and History of Music. London: 1838. V. 63

HIGGINSON, A. H.
As Hounds Ran. 1930. V. 64
British and American Sporting Authors. Berryville: 1949. V. 63; 64
British and American Sporting Authors. 1951. V. 62; 64
The Fox that Walked on the Water. London: 1939. V. 67

HIGGINSON, FRED H.
A Bibliography of the Works of Robert Graves. Hamden: 1966. V. 64

HIGGINSON, THOMAS WENTWORTH
Army Life in a Black Regiment. New York: 1890. V. 65

Woman's Rights Tracts...No. 4. Woman and Her Wishes. New York: 1853. V. 63

THE HIGH *History of the Holy Graal.* London: 1903. V. 64

HIGHAM, DAVID
They're Never Far Away. London: 1964. V. 66

HIGHAM, ROBIN
A Guide to the Sources of United States Military History. Hamden: 1975. V. 66

HIGHLAND SOCIETY OF SCOTLAND
Report of the Committee of the Highland Society of Scotland, To whom the Subject of Shetland Wool was Referred. Edinburgh: 1790. V. 62

HIGHMORE, ANTHONY
A Digest of the Doctrine of Bail: in Civil and Criminal Cases. London: 1783. V. 62; 65
A Succinct View of the History of Mortmain: The Statutes Relative to Charitable Uses. London: 1787. V. 67

HIGHMORE, NATHANIEL
Corporis Humani Disquisitio Anatomica; in Qua Sanguinis Circulationem in Quavis Corporis Particula Plurimis Typis Novis, ac Aenygmatum Medicorum Succincta Dilucidatione Ornatum Prosequutus est. The Hague: 1651. V. 65

HIGHSMITH, PATRICIA
The Boy Who Followed Ripley. London: 1980. V. 66
The Boy Who Followed Ripley. New York: 1980. V. 65; 66
A Dog's Ransom. London: 1972. V. 67
Little Tales of Misogyny. New York: 1986. V. 67
People Who Knock on the Door. London: 1983. V. 65
People Who Knock on the Door. New York: 1985. V. 67
Plotting and Writing Suspense Fiction. Boston: 1966. V. 67
Ripley Under Water. London: 1991. V. 62; 64; 65; 66
Ripley's Game. New York: 1974. V. 67
Slowly, Slowly in the Wind. New York: 1985. V. 67
Where the Action Is and Other Stories. Helsinki: 1989. V. 65
Where the Action Is and Other Stories. Helsinki, 1991. V. 65

HIGHTON, HUGH P.
Shooting Trips in Europe and Algeria. 1921. V. 62; 63
Shooting Trips in Europe and Algeria. London: 1921. V. 62; 67

HIGHTOWER, LYNN S.
Satan's Lambs. New York: 1993. V. 65

HIGHWATER, JAMAKE
Fodor's Indian America. New York: 1975. V. 63; 64; 66
Kiowa Indian Art. Santa Fe: 1979. V. 62; 63; 64
Pueblo Indian Painting. Santa Fe: 1973. V. 63
Song from the Earth, American Indian Painting. Boston: 1976. V. 63

HIGINBOTHAM, JOHN D.
When the West Was Young. Toronto: 1933. V. 67

HIGSON, DANIEL
Seafowl Shooting Sketches. 1909. V. 62

HIJEULOS, OSCAR
The Mambo Kings Play Songs of Love. New York: 1989. V. 65; 67

HIJUELOS, OSCAR
Our House in the Last World. New York: 1982. V. 66
Our House in the Last World. New York: 1983. V. 63

HIL, THEOPHILUS HUNTER
Hesper and Other Poems. Raleigh: 1861. V. 63

HILDERBRAND, SAMUEL S.
Autobiography of Samuel S. Hilderbrand. The Renowned Missouri "Bushwacker" and Inconquerable Rob Roy of America. Jefferson City: 1870. V. 65

HILDRETH, A. G.
The Lengthening Shadow of Dr. Andrew Taylor Still. Macon: 1938. V. 66; 67

HILDRETH, RICHARD
Japan as It Was and Is. Boston: 1855. V. 65
The Slave; or Memoirs of Archy Moore. Boston: 1840. V. 62; 66
The Slave; or Memoirs of Archy Moore. Boston: 1846. V. 66

HILDROP, JOHN
An Essay on Honour in Several Letters, Lately Published in the Miscellany. London: 1741. V. 66

HILER, HILAIRE
Bibliography of Costume. 1994. V. 65

HILL, AARON
The Works of the Late Aaron Hill, Esq. London: 1753. V. 65

HILL, ALEX
The Plan of the Central Nervous System, a Thesis of the Degree of Doctor of Medicine. Cambridge: 1885. V. 67

HILL, ALEXANDER S.
From Home to Home, Autumn Wanderings in the Northwest in the Years 1881, 1882, 1883, 1884. New York: 1966. V. 67

HILL, ALICE POLK
Tales of the Colorado Pioneers. Denver: 1884. V. 65

HILL, ARCHIBALD VIVIAN
Muscular Movement in Man: The Factors Governing Speed and Recovery Fatigue. New York: 1927. V. 65

HILL, BENJAMIN L.
Lectures on the American Electic System of Surgery. Cincinnati: 1850. V. 64

HILL, BRAD SABIN
Hebraica. N.P: 1989. V. 62

HILL, BRIAN
A Little Nonsense and Nonsense Again. 1974-1977. V. 67
Observations and Remarks in a Journey through Sicily and Calabria in the Year 1791.... London: 1792. V. 62

HILL, CONSTANCE
Maria Edgeworth and Her Circle in the Days of Buonaparte and Bourbon. London: 1910. V. 65

HILL, D. S.
Agricultural Entomology. Portland: 1994. V. 64

HILL, DANIEL HARVEY
Bethel to Sharpsburg. Raleigh: 1926. V. 62; 63; 65

HILL, DENIS
Electroencephalography: a Symposium on Its Various Aspects. London: 1950. V. 65

HILL, EMMA SHEPARD
Foundation Stones. Denver: 1926. V. 67

HILL, F.
Salmon Fishing. 1948. V. 67

HILL, FREDERICK TREVOR
Washington, the Man of Action. New York: 1914. V. 65

HILL, GENE
A Gallery of Waterfowl and Upland Birds. Los Angeles: 1978. V. 65
A Listening Walk...and Other Stories. Clinton: 1985. V. 65
Sunflight and Shadows, Essays and Stories on the Out-of-Doors. Los Angeles: 1990. V. 65
The Whispering Wings of Autumn. Clinton: 1981. V. 65

HILL, GEOFFREY
The Enemy's County - Words, Contexture and Other Circumstances of Language. Oxford: 1991. V. 65
For the Unfallen - Poems 1952-1958. London: 1959. V. 63; 65; 66; 67
For the Unfallen, Poems 1952-1958. N.P: 1960. V. 67
King Log: Poems. London: 1968. V. 66
The Mystery of the Charity of Charles Peguy. London: 1983. V. 63
Preghiere. Leeds: 1964. V. 62; 67
Somewhere is Such a Kingdom - Poems 1952-1971. Boston: 1975. V. 65
Tenebrae. London: 1978. V. 63

HILL, GEORGE F.
Drawings by Pisanello. Paris & Brussels: 1929. V. 64

HILL, GRACE L.
Crimson Roses. Philadelphia and London: 1928. V. 67

HILL, GRAHAM
Leaves from the Calvert Papers. London: 1894. V. 63

HILL, IRA
An Abstract of a New Theory of the Formation of the Earth. Baltimore: 1823. V. 66

HILL, J. B.
The Geology of Falmouth and Truro and the Mining District of Camborne and Redruth. Sheet 352. 1906. V. 65; 67

HILL, JAMES
The Trial of James Hill, Alias John the Painter, for Wilfully and Maliciously Setting Fire to the Rope-House, in the King's Yard at Portsmouth, Tried at Winchester, March 6th, 1777.... London: 1777. V. 63

HILL, JASON
The Curious Gardener. London: 1932. V. 62

HILL, JOHN
Arithmetick, both in Theory and Practice, Made Plain and Easy in All the Common and Useful Rules.... London: 1750. V. 65
The British Herbal.... 1756. V. 63
The British Herbal.... London: 1756. V. 62; 65
The Construction of Timber, from Its Early Growth; Explained by the Microscope, and Proved from Experiments, in a Great Variety of Kinds.... London: 1770. V. 63
A History of Plants. London: 1751. V. 63
Lucina Sine Concubitu. London: 1750. V. 63; 64; 67
Lucina Sine Concubitu. Waltham St. Lawrence: 1930. V. 65; 67
A Series of Progressive Lessons, Intended to Elucidate the Art of Flower Painting in Water Colours. Philadelphia: 1836. V. 64
A Short Authentic Account of the Late Decision on the Bull Baiting Question, in the Case of the King Against John Hill. Dudley: 1827. V. 63
The Story of Elizabeth Canning Considered...with Remarks.... London: 1753. V. 63

HILL, JOHN A.
Stories of the Railroad. New York: 1900. V. 67

HILL, JOSEPH
Memorials of Methodism in Bramley. Bramley: 1859. V. 65

HILL, JOSEPH J.
The History of Warner's Ranch and Its Environs. Los Angeles: 1927. V. 62; 63; 64; 65; 66

HILL, L.
The Vicarage Children. 1961. V. 67

HILL, M. F.
Permanent Way: the Story of the Kenya and Uganda Railway. Nairobi: 1949. V. 67

HILL, M. N.
The Sea. New York: 1962-1963. V. 65

HILL, MATTHEW DAVENPORT
Plans for the Government and Liberal Instruction of Boys in Large Numbers. London: 1822. V. 62

HILL, OCTAVIA
Life of Octavia Hill, as Told in Her Letters. London: 1914. V. 64

HILL, OLIVER
English Country Houses. Caroline. 1625-1685. London: 1966. V. 64

HILL, RALPH
Penguin Music Magazine. 1946-1949. V. 63

HILL, REGINALD
Another Death in Venice. London: 1976. V. 63; 65; 66
Captain Fantom. London: 1978. V. 65; 66
The Castle of the Demon. London: 1971. V. 66
Death of a Dormouse. London: 1987. V. 63
Dream of Darkness. London: 1989. V. 63
The Forging of Fantom. London: 1979. V. 66
Pictures of Perfection. Bristol: 1993. V. 63; 65
Recalled to Life. Bristol: 1992. V. 65
There Are No Ghosts in the Soviet Union. London: 1987. V. 66
Under World. London: 1988. V. 65; 66
The Wood Beyond. Blakeney: 1996. V. 65
The Wood Beyond. London: 1996. V. 63

HILL, RICHARD
An Address to Persons of Fashion Relating to Balls; with a Few Occasional Hints Concerning Play-Houses, Card-Tables, &c. Shrewsbury: 1771. V. 62; 64; 66
The Blessings of Polygamy Displayed, in an Affectionate Address to the Rev. Mr. Madan, Occasioned by His Late Work.... London: 1781. V. 62; 65

HILL, ROBERT T.
Geography and Geology of the Black and Grand Prairies, Texas. Washington: 1901. V. 64
The Present Condition of Knowledge of the Geology of Texas. Washington: 1887. V. 63

HILL, ROBIN
Australian Birds. 1967. V. 67

HILL, S. S.
Travels in Egypt and Syria. London: 1866. V. 67
Travels in Peru and Mexico. London: 1860. V. 64

HILL, SUSAN
A Bit of Singing and Dancing. London: 1973. V. 64

HILL, THEOPHILUS HUNTER
Hesper and Other Poems. Raleigh: 1861. V. 62

HILL, THOMAS
The Arte of Gardening. London: 1608. V. 64; 67
A Treatise, Upon the Utility of a Rail-Way, from Leeds to Selby and Hull, with Observations and Estimates Upon Rail-Ways Generally as Being Pre- eminent to All Other Modes of Conveyance for Dispatch and Economy. (with) A Supplement to the Short Treatise. Leeds: 1827-1829. V. 65

HILL, TRACIE L.
Thompson: the American Legend, the First Submachine Gun. Cobourg: 1996. V. 65

HILL, W. A.
Historic Hays. Hays: 1938. V. 63

HILL, W. C. O.
Comparative Anatomy and Taxonomy Primates. Edinburgh: 1953-1960. V. 67
Primate Studies, Osman Hill. 1932-1966. V. 66
Primates, Comparative Anatomy and Taxonomy. Edinburgh: 1953-1966. V. 64
Primates, Comparative Anatomy and Taxonomy. London: 1953-1970. V. 64; 66
Primates. Comparative Anatomy and Taxonomy. Volume 2. Edinburgh: 1964. V. 66
Primates. Comparative Anatomy and Taxonomy. Volume 4. Cebidae Part A. Edinburgh: 1960. V. 66
Primates. Comparative Anatomy and Taxonomy. Volume 7. Cynopithecinae, Crocebus, Macaca, Cynopithecus. Edinburgh: 1974. V. 66

HILL, WILLIAM
A History of the Rise, Progress, Genius and Character of American Presbyterianism. Washington: 1839. V. 66

HILL, WILLIAM HENRY
The Violin Makers of The Guarneri Family (1626-1762). London: 1965. V. 65

HILL, WOODMAN
Lectures. Machinery and Appliances used in Engineering Works, Delivered at the School of Military Engineering, Chatham. Chatham: 1886. V. 65

HILLARD, GEORGE STILLMAN
Six Months in Italy. London: 1853. V. 67

HILLARY, WILLIAM
An Appeal to the British Nation on the Humanity and Policy of Forming a National Institution for the Preservation of Lives and Property from Shipwreck. London: 1823. V. 65
Observations on the Changes of the Air and the Concomitant Epidemical Diseases, in the Island of Barbadoes. London: 1766. V. 63; 67

HILLEBRAND, W.
Flora of the Hawaiian Islands.... Heidelberg: 1888. V. 63

HILLER, D. E.
Collector's Guide to Air Rifles. 1986. V. 67

HILLERMAN, BRENDA
Fortress. Middletown: 1989. V. 63

HILLERMAN, TONY
The Blessing Way. London: 1970. V. 62; 64; 66
The Blessing Way. New York: 1970. V. 63; 65; 66; 67
The Blessing Way. New York: 1989. V. 62; 64; 65
The Blessing Way. New York: 1990. V. 63
The Boy Who Made Dragonfly: a Zuni Myth. New York: 1972. V. 63
Canyon de Chelly. California: 1998. V. 62; 65
Coyote Waits. New York: 1990. V. 63; 66
Dance Hall of the Dead. New York: 1973. V. 62; 63; 67
Dance Hall of the Dead. New York: 1991. V. 63; 64; 67
The Dark Wind. New York: 1982. V. 62; 63; 65; 66; 67
The Fallen Man. New York: 1996. V. 62; 63
Finding Moon. New York: 1995. V. 63
The First Eagle. New York: 1998. V. 63
The Fly on the Wall. New York: 1971. V. 63; 66
The Ghostway. New York: 1984. V. 67
The Ghostway. San Diego: 1984. V. 63; 65; 66; 67
The Ghostway. London: 1985. V. 62; 65; 66
The Ghostway. New York: 1985. V. 63; 63; 65; 66; 67
The Great Taos Bank Robbery. Albuquerque: 1973. V. 63; 64; 65; 66; 67
Hillerman Country. 1991. V. 64; 66
Hillerman Country. New York: 1991. V. 63; 65; 66
Indian Country: America's Sacred Land. Flagstaff: 1987. V. 63
The Jim Chee Mysteries. New York: 1989. V. 64; 67
The Jim Chee Mysteries. New York: 1990. V. 62
The Joe Leaphorn Mysteries. New York: 1989. V. 63; 66; 67
Listening Woman. New York: 1978. V. 63; 67
Listening Woman. London: 1979. V. 65; 66
Listening Woman. New York: 1994. V. 63
New Mexico. Portland: 1974. V. 63
New Mexico, Rio Grande and Other Essays. Portland: 1992. V. 63
People of Darkness. New York: 1980. V. 63; 66; 67
People of Darkness. London: 1988. V. 66
People of Darkness. New York: 1994. V. 63
Rio Grande. Portland: 1975. V. 63; 66; 67
Rio Grande. Portland: 1995. V. 63; 64; 67
Sacred Clowns. New York: 1993. V. 62; 63; 64; 65; 67
Skinwalkers. New York: 1986. V. 63; 66; 67
Skinwalkers. New York: 1987. V. 62; 66; 67
The Spell of New Mexico. New York: 1976. V. 64
The Spell of New Mexico. Albuquerque: 1976. V. 63; 65; 66; 67
Talking God. New York: 1989. V. 63; 66
Talking Mysteries. Albuquerque: 1991. V. 63; 64; 65; 66
A Thief of Time. New York: 1988. V. 62; 63; 64; 66; 67
Words, Weather and Wolfmen. Gallup: 1989. V. 63; 65; 66; 67
Words, Weather and Wolfmen. New York: 1989. V. 64; 67

HILLIER, BEVIS
Punorama. Andoversford: 1974. V. 64; 65
The Style of the Century 1900-1980. London: 1983. V. 62

HILLIER, JACK
The Art of Hokusai in Book Illustration. London: 1980. V. 64
The Art of the Japanese Book. London: 1987. V. 64

HILLS, A. C.
Matrimonial Brokerage in the Metropolis.... New York: 1859. V. 64

HILLS, J. W.
The Golden River. Sport and Travel in Paraguay. 1922. V. 65
A History of Fly Fishing for Trout. 1973. V. 67
River Keeper. The Life of William James Lunn. 1934. V. 67

HILLS, MONSON
A Treatise on the Operation of Cupping. London: 1839. V. 63

HILLYARD, M. B.
The New South. Baltimore: 1887. V. 65

HILPRECHT, HERMAN V.
Explorations in Bible Lands During the 19th Century. Philadelphia: 1903. V. 66

HILSOP, HERBERT R.
An Englishman's Arizona - the Ranching Letters of Herbert R. Hislop 1876-1878. Tucson: 1965. V. 63; 66

HILTON, JAMES
The Dawn of Reckoning. London: 1925. V. 64
Goodbye Mr. Chips. London: 1934. V. 65
Lost Horizon. New York: 1933. V. 63
To You Mr. Chips. London: 1938. V. 62
Twilight of the Wise. 1949. V. 63

HILTON, JOHN
Notes on Some of the Developmental and Functional Relations of Certain Portions of the Cranium. London: 1855. V. 64

HILTON, JOHN BUXTON
Death in Midwinter. London: 1969. V. 67

HIMES, CHARLES F.
Leaf Prints; or Glimpses of Photography. Philadelphia: 1868. V. 63; 65

HIMES, CHESTER
Blind Man With a Pistol. New York: 1969. V. 63
A Case of Rape. New York: 1980. V. 63
If He Hollers Let Him Go. Garden City: 1945. V. 64; 66
If He Hollers Let Him Go. New York: 1945. V. 67
Pinktoes. New York: 1965. V. 66
Plan B. Jackson: 1993. V. 67
The Primitive. New York: 1956. V. 67
The Quality of Hurt: the Autobiography of Chester Himes. Volume I. Garden City: 1972. V. 62; 63; 64; 66
The Real Cool Killers. London: 1985. V. 65
Run Man Run. London: 1967. V. 67

HIMES, VERA C.
Ola and Runaway Bread. New York: 1932. V. 64

HINCHCLIFF, THOMAS WOODBINE
Over the Sea and Far Away. London: 1876. V. 67

HINCHLIFFE, JOHN
Sermons. London: 1796. V. 63; 65

HINCKLEY, MARY H.
Notes on the Peeping Frog, Hyla Pickeringh. 1884. V. 67

HINCKS, T.
A History of the British Hydroid Zoophytes. 1868. V. 66
A History of the British Hydroid Zoophytes. London: 1868. V. 64

HIND, A. M.
A Catalogue of Rembrandt's Etchings. London: 1923. V. 62

HIND, ARTHUR
Engraving in England in the Sixteenth and Seventeenth Centuries. A Descriptive Catalogue.... Cambridge: 1952-1964. V. 63
An Introduction to a History of Woodcut, With a Detailed Survey of Work Done in the Fifteenth Century. New York: 1963. V. 63

HIND, HENRY YOULE
Territoire du Nord-Ouest. Toronto: 1859. V. 65

HINDE, G. J.
Catalogue of the Fossil Sponges in the Geological Department of the British Museum (Natural History) with Descriptions of New and Little Known Species. 1883. V. 64; 67
Catalogue of the Fossil Sponges in the Geological Department of the British Museum (Natural History) with Descriptions of New and Little Known Species. London: 1883. V. 65

HINDE, R. A.
Bird Vocalizations, Their Relation to Current Problems in Biology and Psychology.... Cambridge: 1969. V. 64

HINDE, S. L.
The Last of the Masai. London: 1901. V. 67

HINDERWELL, THOMAS
The History and Antiquities of Scarborough and the Vicinity. York: 1811. V. 65

HINDLEY, CHARLES
The History of the Catnach Press. London: 1886. V. 66
The History of the Catnach Press. London: 1887. V. 62

THE HINDOOS. London: 1834. V. 64

HINDS, JAMES PITCAIRN
Bibliotheca Jacksoniana. Catalogue. Kendal: 1909. V. 66

HINDS, ROY W.
The Treasure of Caricar. Philadelphia: 1927. V. 65; 66

HINDS, WILLIAM A.
American Communities: Brief Sketches of Economy, Zoar, Bethel, Aurora, Amana, Icaria, the Shakers. Oneida: 1878. V. 63

HINDUS, MAURICE
Red Bread. New York: 1931. V. 67

HINE, DARYL
Five Poems, 1954. Toronto: 1954. V. 64

HINE, REGINALD L.
The History of Hitchin. London: 1927. V. 62; 63

HINE, THOMAS CHAMBERS
Nottingham. Its Castle, A Military Fortress, A Royal Palace, a Dual Mansion, Blackened Ruin, a Museum and Gallery of Art. Nottingham: 1876-1879. V. 65

HINES, DAVID THEO
The Life, Adventures and Opinions of David Theo. Hines, of South Carolina, Master of Arts and Sometimes, Doctor of Medicine.... New York: 1840. V. 64; 66

HINES, GORDON
Alfalfa Bill: an Intimate Biography. Oklahoma City: 1932. V. 67

HINES, GUSTAVUS
Life on the Plains of the Pacific. Oregon: Its History, Condition and Prospects. Auburn: 1851. V. 64
Life on the Plains of the Pacific. Oregon: Its History, Condition and Prospects. New York: 1851. V. 64

HINGSTON, JAMES
Guide for Excursionists from Melbourne. Melbourne: 1868. V. 62

HINGSTON, R. W. G.
A Naturalist in the Guiana Forest. London: 1932. V. 64
A Naturalist in the Guiana Forest. New York: 1932. V. 66

HINKLE, JAMES F.
Early Days of a Cowboy on the Pecos. Roswell: 1937. V. 63; 66
Early Days of a Cowboy on the Pecos. Santa Fe: 1965. V. 64

HINMAN, S. D.
Journal...Missionary to the Santee Sioux Indians. Philadelphia: 1869. V. 63

HINSHAW, GLENNIS
A Bibliography of the Writings and Illustrations By Tom Lea. El Paso: 1971. V. 62; 63; 64

HINSHAW, WILLIAM W.
Encyclopedia of American Quaker Genealogy. Baltimore: 1973. V. 63

HINTON, MILT
Over Time. The Jazz Photographs of Milt Hinton. San Francisco: 1991. V. 64

HINTON, PERCIVAL
Eden Phillpotts. A Bibliography of First Editions. Birmingham: 1931. V. 66

HINTON, S. E.
The Outsiders. New York: 1967. V. 66

HINTS for Holidays in Southern Sunshine. London: 1933. V. 64

HINTS on Commercial Travelling. Glasgow: 1837. V. 63

HINTS to Some Churchwardens. London: 1825. V. 62

HINTS to the Purchasers of Horses. London: 1825. V. 62

HIORT, JOHN WILLIAMS
A Practical Treatise on the Construction of Chimneys...(with) Supplement to Mr. Hiort's Treatise on the Architectural Construction of Chimneys...(with) Note for the Information of the Public, Resultig from the Experience in Practical Application of Mr. H. London: 1828. V. 64

HIPPOCRATES
De Morbis Popularibus Liber Primus & Tertius. His Accomodavit Novem de Frebribus Commentarios Johannes Freind. London: 1717. V. 65
The Genuine Works of Hippocrates. London: 1849. V. 64; 66
Hippocrates Contractus in Quo Magni Hippocrates...Opera Omnia... Studio & Opera Thomas Burnet.... Venetiis: 1751. V. 67
Hippocratis Aphorismi, Ad Fidem Veterum Monimentorum Castigati. Parisiis: 1779. V. 65
Magni Hipporatis Medicorum Omnium Facile Principis, Opera Omnia Quae Extant.... Francofurti: 1621. V. 66
The Prognostics and Prorrhetics. London: 1788. V. 64; 66
Upon Air, Water and Situation: Upon Epdemical Diseases.... London: 1734. V. 66

HIPPOLYTUS Redivivus, Id Est, Remedium Contemnendi Sexum Muliebrem. N.P: 1644. V. 63

HIRASE, S.
A Collection of Japanese Shells. Tokyo: 1938. V. 62; 63

HIRD, FRANK
Lancashire Stories. London. V. 65

HIROSE, SADAO
Celebration Volume for Emeritus Professor Sadao Hirose. Tokyo: 1983. V. 65

HIRSCH, EDWARD
For the Sleepwalkers. New York: 1981. V. 66

HIRSCHFELD, AL
Hirschfeld On Line. New York: 1999. V. 65

HIRSCHFELD, LUDOVIC
Traite et Iconographie du Systeme Nerveux, et Des Organes Des Sens.... Paris: 1866. V. 64

HIRSCHMAN, JACK
Cantillations. Santa Barbara: 1974. V. 63

HIRSHBERG, LEONARD KEENE
What You Ought to Know About Your Baby. New York: 1910. V. 65

HIRST, BARTON COOKE
Human Monstrosities Illustrated with Photographic Reproductions and Wood Engravings. Edinburgh: 1892-1893. V. 64

HIRST, DAMIEN
Absolut Originals. Stockholm: 1998. V. 65

HIRT, LUDWIG
The Diseases of the Nervous System. New York: 1893. V. 64

HIRTZLER, VICTOR
Hotel St. Francis Book of Recipes and Model Menus, L'Art Culinaire. San Francisco: 1910. V. 67

HISLOP, HERBERT R.
An Englishman's Arizona: the Ranching Letters of.... Tucson: 1965. V. 62

HISSEY, JAMES JOHN
The Charm of the Road: England and Wales. London: 1910. V. 62
An English Holiday with Car and Camera. London: 1908. V. 62
A Leisurely Tour in England. London: 1913. V. 62
An Old-Fashioned Journey through England and Wales. London: 1884. V. 62
The Road and the Inn. London: 1917. V. 62
Through Ten English Counties. London: 1894. V. 66
Untravelled England. London: 1906. V. 62

HISTOIRE De Charles Price, Fameux Escroc de Londres, Connie Sous Differens Noms. Londres: 1787. V. 65

HISTOIRE De La Dragone, Contenant Les Actions Militaires & Les Avantures de Genevieve Premoy.... Geneve: 1703. V. 65

THE HISTORIC Gallery of Portraits and Paintings or Biographical Review Containing a Brief Account of the Lives of the Most Celebrated Men.... London: 1808. V. 62

HISTORIC Houses of the United Kingdom, Descriptive, Historical, Pictorial. London: 1892. V. 62; 65

HISTORIC, Military and Naval Anecdotes of Personal Valour, Bravery and Particular Incidents Which Occurred to the Armies of Great Britain and Her Allies.... London: 1818. V. 64

AN HISTORICAL Account of the Circumnavigation of the Globe and of the Progress of Discovery in the Pacific Ocean. New York: 1837. V. 67

HISTORICAL and Biographical Atlas of the New Jersey Coast. Philadelphia: 1878. V. 63; 66

AN HISTORICAL and Descriptive Account of Brimham Rocks, in the West Riding of Yorkshire. Ripon: 1838. V. 67

AN HISTORICAL, Antiquarian and Picturesque Account of Kirkstall Abbey.... London: 1827. V. 65

HISTORICAL Collections, or a Brief Account of the Most Remarkable Transactions of the Two Last Parliaments Held and Dissolved at Westminster and Oxford. London: 1681. V. 62; 66

HISTORICAL Collections Relating to Northamptonshire Family Histories, Pedigrees, Biographies, Tracts on Witches, Historical Antiquities, Reprints of Rare and Unique Tracts &c&c. Northampton: 1896. V. 66

THE HISTORICAL Family Library. Devoted to the Republication of Standard History. Volume 1. (all published). Cadiz: 1835-1836. V. 67

AN HISTORICAL Narrative of the Great and Terrible Fire of London, Sept. 2nd 1666; with Some Parallel Cases...(and) An Historical Narrative of the Great Plague at London, 1665, with an Abstract of...Opinions Concerning...that Disorder...Other Remarkable P. London: 1769. V. 63

HISTORICAL SOCIETY OF MONTANA
Collections of the Historical Society of Montana. Boston: 1966. V. 67
Contributions to the Historical Society of Montana. Volume II. Helena: 1896. V. 65; 67
Contributions to the Historical Society of Montana. Volume IV. Helena: 1903. V. 65; 67
Contributions to the Historical Society of Montana - Volume X. Helena: 1940. V. 63
Historical Society of Montana. Volume V. Helena: 1904. V. 67

HISTORICAL SOCIETY OF NEW MEXICO
Old Santa Fe. Santa Fe: 1913. V. 63

HISTORICAL SOCIETY OF FARIFAX COUNTY, VIRGINIA
Yearbooks. Fairfax: 1962-1992. V. 64

THE History and Adventures of Julia, the Curate's Daughter of Elmwood.... London: 178-?. V. 66

THE HISTORY and Description of Guildford, the County-Town of Surrey. London: 1790. V. 66

HISTORY and Description of the Cathedral Church of York...Now First Compiled from Authentic Resources.... York: 1825. V. 67

HISTORY and Medical Description of the Two headed Girl Told in Her Ow n Peculiar Way. Buffalo: 1870. V. 65

THE HISTORY, Debates and Proceedings of Both Houses of Parliament of Great Britain, from the Year 1743 to the year 1774.... London: 1792. V. 67

THE HISTORY of a Savage Girl, Caught Wild in the Woods of Champagne. London: 1760?. V. 64

THE **HISTORY** of a Savage Girl, Caught Wild in the Woods of Champagne. London: 1784. V. 63

HISTORY of Alameda County, California Including Its Geology, Topography, Soil and Productions. Oakland: 1883. V. 62; 63

THE HISTORY of Ali Cogia. Salem: 1808. V. 62

HISTORY of Arizona Territory, Showing and Advantages, Etc. Flagstaff: 1964. V. 63; 66

HISTORY of Bay County Michigan. Chicago;: 1883. V. 66

HISTORY of Bayard, the Good Chevalier, sans Peur et Sans Reproche. London: 1883. V. 67

HISTORY of Charles Nestel, Surnamed Commodore Foote and Joseph Huntler, Surnamed Colonel Small, the Two Smallest Men Living. New York: 1862. V. 65

HISTORY of Clear Creek and Boulder Valleys, Colorado. Chicago: 1880. V. 66

HISTORY Of Clear Creek and Boulder Valleys, Colorado. Evansville: 1971. V. 65

HISTORY of Contra Costa County California with Biographical Sketches. Los Angeles: 1926. V. 62; 65

HISTORY of Cripple Creek - Mining and Business Directory. Cripple Creek: 1894. V. 66

HISTORY of Custer Power River, Garfield Counties - April 1931. Miles City: 1931. V. 62

THE HISTORY of Don Francisco De Miranda's Attempt to Effect a Revolution in South America in a Series of Letters by a Gentleman Who Was an Officer Under that General .... Boston: 1810. V. 64

THE HISTORY of Giles Gingerbread, a Little Boy, Who Lived Upon Learning. London: 1820. V. 66

HISTORY of Goody Two Shoes. New York: 1865. V. 62

HISTORY of Howard and Cooper Counties, Missouri Written and Compiled from the Authentic Official and Private Sources.... St. Louis: 1889. V. 63; 66

HISTORY of Jackson County, Missouri - 1881. 1881. V. 67
HISTORY of Jackson County, Missouri - 1881. Kansas City: 1881. V. 64

THE HISTORY of John and the Oak Tree. London: 1850. V. 65

HISTORY of Kirkstall Abbey, Containing a Description of the Ruins, and Other Interesting Particulars.... Leeds: 1830. V. 65

HISTORY of Kirkstall Abbey, Containing a Description of the Ruins and Other Interesting Particulars.... Leeds: 1845. V. 65

HISTORY of Kirkstall Abbey, Near Leeds, Yorkshire.... Leeds: 1830. V. 65

THE HISTORY of Little Red Riding-Hood. London: 1825. V. 66

THE HISTORY of Little Tom Tucker. London: 1820. V. 66

THE HISTORY of Luna County. Deming: 1978. V. 64

HISTORY of Monmouth County, New Jersey 1664-1920. New York: 1922. V. 63; 66

A HISTORY of Morris County, New Jersey. Embracing Upwards of Two Centuries, 1710-1913. New York: 1914. V. 63

HISTORY of Morris County, New Jersey, with Illustrations and Biographical Sketches of Prominent Citizens and Pioneers. Morristown: 1967. V. 63; 66

HISTORY of Morris County, New Jersey.... New York: 1882. V. 63; 66

THE HISTORY of North America. London: 1776. V. 63

THE HISTORY of Origins. London: 1824. V. 66

HISTORY of Oswego County, New York. Philadelphia: 1877. V. 63

HISTORY of Preston, in Lancashire: Together with The Guild Merchant and Some Account of the Duchy and County Palatine of Lancaster. London: 1822. V. 64; 65

HISTORY of Printing. London: 1855. V. 64

THE HISTORY of Punch and Judy. London: 1870?. V. 66

THE HISTORY of Ripon: With Descriptions of Studley-Royal, Fountains Abbey, Newby, Hackfall &c. Ripon: 1806. V. 64; 65

HISTORY of San Luis Obispo County, California, with Illustrations and Biographical Sketches of Its Prominent Men and Pioneers. Oakland: 1883. V. 65

A HISTORY of Shrewsbury School from the Blakeway Mss., and Many Other Sources. Shrewsbury: 1889. V. 64

HISTORY of Southern and Central Africa.... London: 1875. V. 62

HISTORY of Southwestern Dakota Its Settlement and Growth. Sioux City: 1881. V. 65

THE HISTORY of the A Apple Pie Written by Z. London: 1808. V. 62; 67

THE HISTORY of the Abbey Church of St. Peter's Westminster, Its Antiquities and Monuments. London: 1812. V. 64

THE HISTORY of the Amours and Gallantry of Several Noble and Polite Persons at Rome and Syracuse Interpers'd with Curious Observations Moral and Political. London: 1728. V. 66

HISTORY of the Bath Free Library. Established 1875. London: 1875. V. 67

HISTORY of the Bible. Lansingburg: 1825. V. 66
HISTORY of the Bible. New London: 1831. V. 62

HISTORY of the Cattleman of Texas. Austin: 1991. V. 64

THE HISTORY of the Children in the Wood. Harrisburg: 1835. V. 63
THE HISTORY of the Children in the Wood. Harrisburg: 1840. V. 63

HISTORY of the City of Denver, Arapahoe County and Colorado.... Chicago: 1880. V. 64; 66

A HISTORY of the City of Newark, New Jersey, Embracing Practically Two and a Half Centuries 1666-1913. New York: 1913. V. 63; 66

HISTORY of the Foundations in Manchester of Christ's College, Chetham's College, and the Free Grammar School. London: 1834. V. 67

HISTORY of the Great Kanawha Valley. Madison: 1891. V. 65

A HISTORY of the Greatest Crime of the Century and of the Search for the Missing Pitezal Children by Detective Frank P. Geyer of the...Police Department...of Philadelphia.... N.P: 1896. V. 65

THE HISTORY of the Inhuman and Unparalleled Murders of Mr. William Galley, a Custom-house Officer, and Mr. Daniel Chater, a Shoemaker, by Fourteen Notorious Smugglers. Portsea: 1820. V. 62

THE HISTORY of the Life and Actions of Gustavus Vasa, Deliverer of His Country. London: 1739. V. 66

THE HISTORY of the Life and Death of Sultan Solyman the Magnificent Emperor of the Turks and of His Son Mustapha. London: 1739. V. 65

THE HISTORY of the London Burkers; Containing a Faithful and Authentic Account of the Horrid Acts of the Noted Resurrectionists, Bishop, Williams, May &c. and Their Trial and Condemnation.... London: 1832. V. 65

THE HISTORY of the Mitre (Francis Atterbury, Bishop of Rochester) and Purse (Simon Harcourt, Lord Chancellor), in Which the First and Second Parts of the Secret History of the White Staff are Fully Considered.... London: 1714. V. 65

HISTORY of the Peace Negotiations, Documentary and Verbal Between China and Japan, March-April, 1895. Tientsin. 1895. V. 62

A HISTORY of the Pottery Industry and Its Evolution as Applied to Sanitation with Unique Specimens and Facimile Marks from Ancient to Modern Foreign and American Wares. Trenton: 1910. V. 63; 66

HISTORY of the Revolution of the 18th Fructidor (September 4th 1797), and of the Deportations to Guiana...(with) Secret Anecdotes of the Revolution of the 18th Fructidor.... London: 1800-1799. V. 62

A HISTORY of the Royal Abbaye of Sainte Denis, with an Account of the Tombs of the Kings and Queens of France.... London: 1795. V. 63; 67

HISTORY of the Seige of Blair Castle in 1746. 1874. V. 67

THE HISTORY of Tom Jones, a Changeling. 1941. V. 65

THE HISTORY of Tommy and Harry. London: 1830. V. 66

A HISTORY of Trenton 1679-1929. Princeton: 1929. V. 63; 66

THE HISTORY of Whittington and His Cat. York: 1820. V. 66
THE HISTORY of Whittington and His Cat. Albany: 1851-1854. V. 66

THE HISTORY of Wisbech, with an Historical Sketch of the Fens, and Their Former and Present Aspect. Wisbech: 1834. V. 62

A HISTORY of Wonderful Animals: Containing an Account of the Most Remarkable Fishes, Beasts and Birds. London: 1818. V. 62

HISTORY, Resources, Possibilities, Exhibit at the World's Fair and a Description of Montana. Butte: 1893. V. 65

HISTORY, Topography and Directory of Derbyshire, Comprising His History and Archaeology.... London: 1895. V. 63

HISTORY, Topography and Directory of East Yorkshire (with Hull) Comprising Its Ancient and Modern History.... Preston: 1892. V. 63

HISTORY, Topography and Directory of Westmoreland, and the Hundreds of Lonsdale and Amounderness in Lancashire.... Beverely: 1851. V. 63

THE HISTORY of Prince Lee Boo, a Native of the Pelew Islands. London: 1822. V. 62; 65

HITCHCOCK, A. S.
The North American Species of Panieum. Washington: 1910. V. 67

HITCHCOCK, CHAMPION INGRAHAM
The Dead Men's Song: Being the Story of a Poem and a Reminiscent Sketch of the Author, Young Ewing Allison. Louisville: 1914. V. 67

HITCHCOCK, DAVID K.
Vindication of Russia and the Emperor Nicholas. Boston: 1844. V. 64; 66

HITCHCOCK, E.
Ichnology of New England. Boston: 1858. V. 62
Sketch of the Scenery of Massachusetts. Northampton: 1842. V. 64

HITCHCOCK, ENOS
The Farmer's Friend, or the History of Mr. Charles Worthy. Boston: 1793. V. 63; 65
Memoirs of the Bloomsgrove Family. Boston: 1790. V. 63; 66

HITCHCOCK, FRANK
Thrilling Chase and Capture of Frank Rande. Peoria: 1897. V. 63; 66

HITCHIN, W. E.
Surrey at the Opening of the Twentieth Century - Contemporary Biographies. Brighton: 1906. V. 62; 66

HITCHINGS, J. M.
In the Heart of the Sierras, the Yosemite Valley.... 1888. V. 65

THE HITOPADESHA: a Collection of Fables and Tales in Sanscrit. Calcutta: 1830. V. 63

HITT, THOMAS
A Treatise of Fruit-Trees. London: 1757. V. 62
A Treatise on Fruit Trees. London: 1768. V. 64

HITTEL, JOHN S.
The Resources of California, Comprising Agriculture, Mining, Geography, Climate, Commerce...and the Past and Future Development of the State. San Francisco: 1863. V. 65

HITTELL, JOHN S.
The Resources of California: Comprising Agriculture, Mining, Geography, Climate, Commerce, Etc. San Francisco: 1874. V. 62; 64; 65

HITTORFF, J. J.
Architecture Moderne de la Sicile, ou Recueil des plus Beaux Monumens Religieux et des Edifices Publics et Particuliers les Plus Remarquables de la Sicile.... Paris: 1835. V. 64
Description de la Rotonde des Panoramas, Elevee dans les Champs Elysees. Paris: 1842. V. 62; 66

THE HIVE. A Collection of the Most Celebrated Songs. London: 1724. V. 63; 66
THE HIVE. A Collection of the Most Celebrated Songs. London: 1726. V. 66

HIXON, ADRIETTA APPLEGATE
On to Oregon! A True Story of a Young Girl's Journey into the West. Weiser: 1947. V. 63; 66

HIYAMA, Y.
Living Fishes of the Japanese Coastal Waters. Tokyo: 1972. V. 66
Marine Fishes of the Pacific Coast of Mexico. Odawara: 1937. V. 62

HJORT, J.
Currents and Pelagic Life in the Northern Ocean. 1899. V. 63

HJORTSBERG, WILLIAM
Alp. New York: 1969. V. 63

HJORTSBURG, WILLIAM
Falling Angel. 1978. V. 64

HOAGLAND, EDWARD
Cat Man. Boston: 1956. V. 63
The Circle Home. New York: 1960. V. 62; 66
The Peacock's Tail. New York: 1965. V. 66
Red Wolves and Black Bears. New York: 1976. V. 62

HOAR, ALLEN
The Submarine Torpedo Boat - Its Characteristics and Modern Development. New York: 1916. V. 64

HOAR, W. S.
Fish Physiology. New York: 1969-1988. V. 65

HOARD, SAMUEL
The Churches Authority Asserted in a Sermon Preached at Chelmsford at the Metro-Political Visitation of the Most Reverend Father in God, William (Laud), Lord Arch-bishop of Canterbury his Grace and March 1, 1636. London: 1737. V. 63

HOARE, CLEMENT
Practical Treatise on the Cultivation of the Grape Vine On Open Walls. London: 1841. V. 62; 66

HOARE, J. DOUGLAS
Arctic Exploration. New York: 1906. V. 62

HOARE, RICHARD COLT
A Collection of Forty-Eight Views...in North and South Wales. London: 1806. V. 62; 66
A Tour through the Island of Elba. London: 1814. V. 62

HOBAN, RUSSELL
Kleinziet. London: 1974. V. 65
Riddley Walker. London: 1980. V. 62

HOBART, D.
Recollections of My Life - Fifty Years of Itinerancy in the Northwest. Redwing: 1885. V. 65

HOBART, DAVID BAYNE
The Clue of the Leather Noose. 1929. V. 65; 66

HOBART, DONALD BAYNE
Hunchback House. Racine: 1929. V. 67

HOBART, HENRY
The Reports of the Reverend and Learned Judge...Lord Chief, Justice of His Majesties Court of Common Pleas.... London: 1678. V. 65

HOBART, NOAH
An Attempt to Illustrate and Confirm the Ecclesiastical Constitution of the Consociated Churches, in the Colony of Connecticut. New Haven: 1765. V. 63

HOBART-HAMPDEN, AUGUSTUS C.
Never Caught. Personal Adventures Connected with Twelve Successful Trips in Blockade-Running During the American Civil War 1863-1864. London: 1867. V. 62; 65
Never Caught: Personal Adventures Connected with Twelve Successful Trips in Blockade-Running During the American Civil War 1863-1864. Mobile: 1876. V. 63
Never Caught: Personal Adventures Connected with Twelve Successful Trips in Blockade-Running During the American Civil War 1863-1864. New York: 1908. V. 62; 63; 65

HOBBES, JAMES R.
The Picture Collector's Manual, Being a Dictionary of Painters, Together with an alphabetical Arrangement of the Scholars, Imitators and Copyists of the Various Masters, and a Classification of Subjects.... London: 1849. V. 64

HOBBES, THOMAS
De Mrabilibus Pecci: Being the Wonders of the Peak in Darby-shire, Commonly Called The Devil's Arse of Peak. London: 1678. V. 64
Elementa Philosophica De Cive. Amsterdam: 1669. V. 66
Humane Nature; or the Fundamental Elements of Police. London: 1650. V. 66
Leviathan. London: 1651. V. 67
Leviathan. London: 1680. V. 66; 67

HOBBS, JAMES
Wild Life in the Far West. Hartford: 1873. V. 64
Wild Life in the Far West. Hartford: 1875. V. 63; 64; 67

HOBBS, ROBERT
Edward Hopper. New York: 1987. V. 65

HOBBS, WILLIAM HERBERT
Peary. New York: 1936. V. 64; 66

HOBBY, WILLIAM J.
Remarks Upon Slavery: Occasioned by Attempts Made to Circulate Improper Publications in the Southern States. Augusta: 1835. V. 63

HOBHOUSE, JOHN CAM
Historical Illustrations of the Fourth Canto of Childe Harold.... London: 1818. V. 67
A Journey through Albania and Other Provinces of Turkey in Europe and Asia to Constantinople During the Years 1809 and 1810.... London: 1813. V. 62; 67

HOBLER, J. PAUL
The Words of the Favourite Pieces, as Performed at the Glee Club, Held at the Crown and Anchor Tavern, Strand. London: 1794. V. 65

HOBLEY, C. W.
Kenya from Chartered Company to Crown Colony: Thirty Years of Exploration and Administration in British East Africa. London: 1929. V. 67

HOBLYN, RICHARD D.
A Dictionary of Terms Used in Medicine and the Collateral Sciences. Philadelphia: 1846. V. 63

HOBSON, ANNE
In Old Alabama, Being the Chronicls of Miss Mouse, the Little Black Merchant. New York: 1903. V. 67

HOBSON, ANTHONY
Apollo and Pegasus: an Inquiry into the Formation and Dispersal of a Renaissance Library. Amsterdam: 1975. V. 62; 63
Cyril Connolly as a Book Collector. Edinburgh: 1983. V. 67
Great Libraries. New York: 1970. V. 66
Humanists and Bookbinders: the Origins and Diffusion of the Humanistic Bookbinding 1459-1559.... Cambridge: 1989. V. 62; 63
Italian and French 16th Century Bookbindings. N.P: 1991. V. 62; 63

HOBSON, CHARLES
Shipwreck Stories: Facts and Fictions. San Francisco;: 1998. V. 62

HOBSON, E. W.
The Domain of Natural Science. The Gifford Lectures Delivered in the University of Aberdeen in 1921-1922. Cambridge: 1923. V. 66

HOBSON, G. D.
Bindings in Cambridge Libraries. Cambridge: 1929. V. 62
Blind-Stamped Panels in the English Book Trade c. 1485-1555. London: 1944. V. 62
Maioli, Canevari and Others. London: 1926. V. 62
Thirty Bindings. London: 1926. V. 62; 67

HOBSON, ROBERT LOCKHART
A Catalogue of Chinese Pottery and Porcelain in the Collection of Sir Percival David Bt., F.S.A. London: 1934. V. 65
Chinese Art. New York: 1927. V. 62
Chinese Corean and Japanese Parties: Descriptive Catalogue of Loan Exhibition of Selected Examples.... New York: 1914. V. 67
Chinese Pottery and Porcelain. London: 1915. V. 64
Pottery and Porcelain, an Account of the Potters Art in China from Primitive Times to the Present Day. 1915. V. 67

HOCH, EDWARD D.
Leopold's Way Detective Stories by Edward D. Hoch. Carbondale: 1985. V. 67
The Thefts of Nick Velvet. New York: 1978. V. 67

HOCHBAUM, H. B.
Travels and Traditions of Waterfowl. 1955. V. 67

HOCK, LEICHTER, PSEUD.
Crinoline In Its Bissextile Phases. London: 1864. V. 65

HOCKEN, EDWARD OCTAVIUS
A Treatise on Amaurosis and Amaurotic Affections. Philadelphia: 1842. V. 64; 67

HOCKEN, T. M.
A Bibliography of the Literature Relating to New Zealand. Wellington: 1909. V. 65

HOCKEY, P.
Waders of Southern Africa. Cape Town: 1995. V. 63

HOCKING, SILAS K.
Her Benny. London: 1879. V. 67
Her Benny. London: 1890. V. 67

HOCKLEY, WILLIAM BROWN
Pandurang Hari, or Memoirs of a Hindoo. London: 1883. V. 65

HOCKNEY, DAVID
Paintings, Prints and Drawings 1960-1970. Boston: 1970. V. 66
72 Drawings - Chosen by the Artist. London: 1971. V. 63
72 Drawings by David Hockney. New York: 1972. V. 66

HODDER, FRANK HEYWOOD
The Present State of the European Settlements on the Mississippi. Cleveland: 1906. V. 66

HODDER, GEORGE
Sketches of Life and Character: Taken at the Polic Court, Bow Street. London: 1845. V. 62

HODDER, JAMES
Hodder's Arithmetick; or, the Necessay Art Made Most Easy. London: 1720. V. 65

HODEL, D. R.
The Palms and Cycads of Thailand. 1998. V. 63; 66
The Palms of New Caledonia/Les Palmiers de Nouvelle Caledonie. 1998. V. 66

HODGE, ARCHIBALD A.
The Life of Charles Hodge, D.D. LL.D. New York: 1880. V. 63; 66

HODGE, DAVID
Angling Days on Scotch Lochs. 1884. V. 62; 65
The Quest of the Gilt-Edged Girl. London: 1897. V. 64

HODGE, FREDERICK WEBB
Fray Alonso De Benavides' Revised Memorial of 1630. Albuquerque: 1945. V. 63; 64
Handbook of American Indians North of Mexico. Washington: 1954. V. 63
Handbook of American Indians North of Mexico. New York: 1959. V. 63
Handbook of American Indians North of Mexico. Totowa: 1975. V. 63
Handbook of American Indians North of Mexico. Part I and II. Washington: 1912. V. 67
History of Hawikah, New Mexico, One of the So-Called Cities of Cibola. Los Angeles: 1937. V. 62; 65
The Plea and the Pioneers in Virginia. Richmond: 1905. V. 67
Spanish Explorers in the Southern United States 1528-1543. New York: 1907. V. 65; 67

HODGE, GENE MEANY
The Kachinas are Coming - Pueblo India Kachina Dolls with Related Folk Tales. Los Angeles: 1936. V. 62
The Kachinas Are Coming - Pueblo Indian Kachina Dolls with Related Folktales. Flagstaff: 1967. V. 66

HODGE, HIRAM C.
Arizona As It Is, or the Coming Country.... New York: 1877. V. 63; 64; 66

HODGES, CHARLES CLEMENT
Ecclesia Hagustaldensis, The Abbey Church of St. Andrew, Hexham; a Monograph. 1888. V. 62
Ecclesia Hagustaldensis. The Abbey Church of St. Andrew, Hexham, a Monograph. London: 1888. V. 63

HODGES, MARGARET
Saint George and the Dragon. Boston: 1984. V. 65

HODGES, WILLIAM ROMAINE
Carl Wimar: a Biography. Galveston: 1908. V. 64

HODGINS, J. E.
The Veterinary Science. Detroit: 1907. V. 66

HODGINS, J. GEORGE
Documentary History of Education in Upper Canada from the Passing of the Constituional Act of Toronto 1791 to the Close of Rev. Dr. Ryerson's Administration of the Education Department in 1876. Toronto: 1894-1910. V. 67

HODGKIN, JOHN
A Companion to Hodgkin's Introduction to Writing and Grammar.... London: 1827. V. 63

HODGKIN, JOHN ELIOT
Examples of Early English Pottery Names, Dated and Inscribed. London: 1881. V. 64; 66
Rariora Being Notes on Printed Books, Manuscripts. London: 1901. V. 66

HODGKIN, R. H.
A History of the Anglo Saxons. 1952. V. 67

HODGKINSON, T. W.
The Director System for Cutting Ladies' Garments. London: 1920. V. 66

HODGSON, CHRISTOPHER
An Account of the Foundation, the Progress and Present State of Marlborough College. London: 1867. V. 63

HODGSON, E.
Glimpes of Witherslack. Kendal: 1937. V. 66

HODGSON, FRED T.
Hodgson's Low-Cost American Homes. Chicago: 1904. V. 63

HODGSON, H. R.
The Society of Friends in Bradford. Bradford: 1926. V. 65

HODGSON, HENRY W.
A Bibliography of the History and Topography of Cumberland and Westmorland. Carlisle: 1968. V. 62; 65
A Bibliography of the History and Topography of Cumberland and Westmorland. London: 1968. V. 67

HODGSON, J. E.
The History of Aeronautics in Great Britain from the Earliest Times to the Latter Half of the Nineteenth Century. London: 1924. V. 62

HODGSON, J. F.
The Churches of Austin Canons. London. V. 62

HODGSON, JOHN
History of Northumberland. Volume II. Newcastle-upon-Tyne: 1973. V. 65
History of Northumberland. Volume IV. Newcastle-upon-Tyne: 1974. V. 65
A Picture of Newcastle Upon Tyne.... Newcastle: 1807. V. 64; 65; 66
A Topographical And Historical Description of the County of Westmoreland.... London: 1820. V. 65; 66
Trial of William Wemms, James Hartegan, William M'Cauley.... Boston: 1770. V. 66

HODGSON, JOSEPH
The Cradle of the Confederacy; or, the Times of Troup, Quitman and Yancey. Mobile: 1876. V. 63
A Treatise on the Diseaes of Arteries and Veins, Containing the Pathology and Treatment of Aneurisms and Wounded Arteries. (with) Engravings Intended to Illustrate some of the Diseases of Arteries. London: 1815. V. 65

HODGSON, RALPH
The Last Blackbird and Other Stories. London: 1907. V. 63
The Skylark and Other Poems. London: 1958. V. 62

HODGSON, RANDOLPH L.
On Plain and Peak. London: 1898. V. 67

HODGSON, W. B.
Creek Indian History as Comprised in Creek Confederacy and The Creek Country. Americus: 1938. V. 63; 66

HODGSON, W. E.
Trout Fishing. 1904. V. 67

HODGSON, W. EARL
Unrest; or the Newer Republic. London: 1887. V. 66

HODGSON, WILLIAM HOPE
Deep Waters. Sauk City: 1967. V. 63
The House on the Borderland. Sauk City: 1946. V. 64
The Night Land. London. V. 66

HODNETT, EDWARD
English Woodcuts, 1480-1535. Oxford: 1973. V. 66; 67

HODSON, A. W.
Trekking the Great Thirst. 1912. V. 62; 63; 64
Trekking the Great Thirst. London: 1912. V. 67
Trekking the Great Thirst. 1913. V. 63; 64; 67
Trekking the Great Thirst. London: 1913. V. 62; 66
Trekking the Great Thirst. London: 1914. V. 67

HODSON, JOHN
A Widow Indeed. Wednesbury: 1816. V. 64

HODSON, MARGARET
Wallace; or, the Fight for Falkirk; a Metrical Romance. London: 1810. V. 67

HODSON, T. C.
The Meitheis. London: 1908. V. 67

HODY, HUMPHREY
De Bibliorum Textibus Originalibus, Versionibus Graecis & latina Ulgata.... Oxford: 1705. V. 65; 66
De Graecis Illustribus Linguae Graecae Literarumque Humaniorum Instauratoribus, Eorum Vitis.... Londini: 1742. V. 65

HOE, ROBERT
Catalogue of the Library of Robert Hoe of New York. New York: 1911-1912. V. 63
A Lecture on Bookbinding as a Fine Art. New York: 1886. V. 62

HOEFLER, PAUL L.
Africa Speaks: a Story of Adventure. London: 1930. V. 67

HOEG, PETER
Smilla's Sense of Snow. New York: 1993. V. 63; 66

HOEHNE, F. C.
Flora Brasilica: Orchidaceae. Sao Paulo: 1940-1953. V. 66

HOEK, P. P. C.
Challenger Voyage. Zoology. Parts 25 and 28 Cirripedia. 1883-1884. V. 66

HOELLERING, GEORGE
The Film of Murder in the Cathedral. London: 1952. V. 62; 63

HOEVEN, C. PRUYS VAN DER
De Historia Medicinae, Liber Singularis, Auditorum in Usum Editus. Lugduni Batavorum: 1842. V. 64

HOFER, PHILIP
The Universal Penman. New York: 1941. V. 64

HOFF, E. C.
A Bibliography of Aviation Medicine. Springfield: 1942. V. 64; 66; 67

HOFFMAN, ABBIE
Steal This Book. New York: 1971. V. 64
Woodstock Nation. New York: 1969. V. 65

HOFFMAN, ABRAHAM
Vision or Villainy; Origins of the Owens Valley-Los Angeles Water Con roversy. College Station: 1981. V. 63

HOFFMAN, ALICE
Angel Landing. New York: 1980. V. 65
The Drowning Season. New York: 1979. V. 65
Illumination Night. New York: 1997. V. 66
Property Of. New York: 1974. V. 67
Property Of. New York: 1977. V. 64
Seventh Heaven. Franklin Center: 1990. V. 63; 66; 67
Turtle Moon. Franklin Center: 1992. V. 63
White Horses. New York: 1982. V. 67

HOFFMAN, BARRY
Gauntlet 2. 1992. V. 62

HOFFMAN, CHARLES F.
A Winter in the Far West. London: 1835. V. 62; 65
A Winter in the West. New York: 1835. V. 63; 66

HOFFMAN, HEINRICH
Der Struwwelpeter. Stuttgart. V. 63

HOFFMAN, IRWIN D.
Irwin D. Hoffman. New York: 1936. V. 66

HOFFMAN, RICHARD J.
A Decorative Divertissement: the Foundry and Monotype Typographic Piece Borders and Ornaments as Well as the Linotype Border Matrices and Border Matrix Slides...Together with the First Supplement to "A Gathering of Types".... Van Nuys: 1980. V. 64
When a Printer Plays: a Showing of Printers' Flowers and Typographic Fleurons Arranged in Arabesque Patterns. Van Nuys: 1987. V. 64

HOFFMAN, WERNER
The Earthly Paradise: Art in the Nineteenth Century. New York: 1961. V. 63

HOFFMANN, ERNST THEODOR AMADEUS
Nutcracker. London: 1984. V. 63; 65
Nutcracker and Mouse King and the Educated Cat. London: 1892. V. 64

HOFFMANN, FREDERICK J.
The Little Magazine: a History and a Bibliography. Princeton: 1946. V. 62

HOFFMANN, G.
Dekorative Turen. Stuttgart: 1977. V. 65

HOFFMANN-DONNER, HEINRICH
The English Struwwelpeter. London. V. 64
The English Struwwelpeter. London: 1885. V. 62
The English Struwwelpeter. London: 1890. V. 64; 65
Pierino Porcospno. Milano. V. 63
Struwelpeter. 1900. V. 67
Der Struwwelpeter. Berlin: 1984. V. 66
Der Struwwelpeter. Berlin: 1994. V. 66
Struwwelpeter. London: 1950. V. 66
Struwwelpeter. Berkeley: 1999. V. 64

HOFFMEISTER, WERNER
Travels in Ceylon and Continental India. Edinburgh: 1848. V. 62

HOFFY, ALFRED
Hoffy's North American Pomologist. Philadelphia: 1860. V. 63; 64; 66

HOFLAND, BARBARA HOOLE
Moderation. A Tale. London: 1825. V. 65
A Season at Harrogate.... Knaresborough: 1812. V. 65
A Season at Harrogate. Knaresborough: 1818. V. 65
Tales of the Priory. London: 1820. V. 65
The Young Cadet; or Henry Delamere's Voyage to India, His Travels in Hindostan and the Wonders of Elora. London: 1836. V. 62

HOFLAND, T. C.
The British Angler's Manual, or, the Art of Angling in England, Scotland, Wales and Ireland.... London: 1839. V. 67

HOFMAN, CAROLINE
The Little Red Balloon. Chicago: 1918. V. 63

HOFMANN, A. W.
Introduction to Modern Chemistry...Twelve Lectures Delivered in the Royal College of Chemistry. London: 1865. V. 62

HOFMANN, E.
Die Gross-Schmetterlinge Europas. Stuttgart: 1887. V. 65; 66
Die Gross-Schmetterlinge Europas. & Die Raupen. Stuttgart: 1893-1894. V. 65; 66

HOFMANN, HANS
Hans Hofmann....& Five Essays. New York: 1963. V. 65

HOFMANN, JOHAN JACOB
Lexicon Universale, Historiam Sacram Et Profanum Omnis Aevi, Oniumque Gentium.... Lugduni Batavorum: 1698. V. 65; 66

HOFMANN, WERNER
The Earthly Paradise: Art in the Nineteenth Century. New York: 1961. V. 64
Gustav Klimt. Greenwich: 1971. V. 62; 63; 66

HOFSTADTER, DOUGLAS R.
Godel, Escher, Bach: an Eternal Golden Braid. New York: 1979. V. 67

HOFSTATTER, H. H.
Jugendstil: Graphik und Druck-kunst. Halle: 1985. V. 65

HOG, WILLIAM
Satyra Sacra in Vanitatem Mundi et Rerum Humanarum Sive Parapharasis in Ecclesiasten Poetica. N.P: 1686. V. 64

HOGAN, DAVID
The Four Glorious Years. 1953. V. 64; 67

HOGAN, EDMUND
Onomasticon Goedelicum...an Index with Identifications, to the Gaelic Names of Places and Tribes. 1910. V. 66

HOGAN, INEZ
Nicodemus and His Little Sister. New York: 1932. V. 62
Nicodemus and His New Shoes. New York: 1937. V. 65
Nicodemus and the Gang. New York: 1939. V. 64

HOGAN, JAMES
Ireland in the European System Volume I 1500-1557. 1920. V. 67

HOGAN, JAMES FRANCIS
The Sister Dominions, through Canada to Australia by the New Imperial Highway. London: 1896. V. 67

HOGARTH, GEORGE
Memoirs of the Musical Drama. London: 1838. V. 63

HOGARTH, WILLIAM
The Analysis of Beauty. London: 1753. V. 62
The Works. London: 1768. V. 63
The Works.... Philadelphia: 1900. V. 66

HOGDSON, SOLOMON
The Hive of Ancient and Modern Literature. Newcastle: 1806. V. 67

HOGG, CHARLES E.
Equity Principles: a Practical Treatise on the Principle Rules and Doctrines of Equity Jurisprudence. Cincinnati: 1900. V. 65

HOGG, JABEZ
The Microscope: Its History, Construction and Application. London: 1770. V. 63
The Microscope: Its History, Construction and Application. London: 1854. V. 62
The Microscope. Its History, Construction and Application. London: 1859. V. 66
The Microscope: Its History, Construction and Application. London: 1861. V. 62
The Microscope. Its History, Construction and Application. London: 1867. V. 67

HOGG, JAMES
The Jacobite Relics of Scotland. Edinburgh: 1819. V. 63
The Jacobite Relics of Scotland. Edinburgh: 1819-1821. V. 62; 65
Kilmeny. London and Edinburgh: 1911. V. 67
The Pilgrims of the Sun: A Poem. London: 1815. V. 62
The Songs of the Ettrick Shepherd. London and Edinburgh. V. 65
Tales and Sketches, by the Ettrick Shepherd.... Glasgow: 1836. V. 66
The Three Perils of Man; or War, Women and Witchcraft. London: 1822. V. 66
Winter Evening Tales, Collected Among the Cottagers in the South of Scotland. Philadelphia: 1836. V. 66

HOGG, ROBERT
A Selection of the Eatable Funguses of Great Britain. London. V. 62
A Selection of the Eatable Funguses of Great Britain. London: 1866. V. 64

HOGG, THOMAS
A Concise and Practical Treatise on the Growth and Culture of the Carnation, Pink, Auricula, Polyanthus, Ranunculus, Tulip, Hyacinth, Rose and Other Flowers. London: 1832. V. 64
A Concise and Practical Treatise on the Growth and Culture of the Carnation, Pink, Auricula...Rules and Regulations of the Islington and Chelsea Florists' Society. London: 1820. V. 62

HOGG, THOMAS JEFFERSON
The Athenians. Waltham St. Lawrence: 1943. V. 67

HOGNER, W.
Isophotometric Atlas of Comets: in Two Parts. Berlin: 1980. V. 67

HOHNEL, L. VON
Discovery of Lakes Rudolf and Stefanie. 1968. V. 62; 64; 66; 67
Discovery of Lakes Rudolf and Stefanie. London: 1968. V. 63

HOISINGTON, H. R.
The Oriental Astronomer: Being a Complete System of Hindu Astronomy, Accompanied with a Translation and Numerous Explanatory Notes. Jaffna: 1848. V. 62; 66

HOKE, HELEN
The Fuzzy Kitten. New York: 1941. V. 64

HOLBACH, PAUL HENRY DIETRICH VON, BARON
Systeme de la Nature. Ou des Loix du Monde Physique & du Monde Moral. London: 1770. V. 66

HOLBEIN, HANS
L'Alfabeto Della Morte. Paris: 1856. V. 67
The Dance of Death. London: 1816. V. 66
The Dance of Death. London: 1825. V. 66
The Dance of Death. London: 1886. V. 66
The Dance of Death. London: 1947. V. 66
The Dances of Death, Through the Various Stages of Human Life. London: 1803. V. 66
Holbein's Dance of Death with an Historical and Literary Introduction. London: 1849. V. 67
Imitations of Original Drawings by Hans Holbein. London: 1812. V. 65

HOLBEIN, HANS continued
Der Todten Tanz...La Danse des Morts. Basel: 1843. V. 67

HOLBERG, LUDVIG, BARON
An Introduction to Universal History. London: 1758. V. 64
A Journey to the World Under-Ground. London: 1742. V. 64

HOLBROOK, J. H.
Ten Years Among the Mail Bags: or Notes from the Diary of a Special Agent of the Post Office Department. Philadelphia: 1855. V. 67

HOLBROOK, JOHN EDWARDS
Ichthyology of South Carolina. Charleston: 1860. V. 63

HOLBROOK, JOSIAH
A Familiar Treatise on the Fine Arts, Painting, Sculpture and Music. Boston;: 1833. V. 65

HOLBROOK, MERRILL & STETSON
Catalogue C. #118 Sanitary Plumbing Fixtures & Supplies. San Francisco: 1905. V. 63

HOLBROOK'S Newark City and Business Directory for the Year Ending May I, 1888. Newark: 1887. V. 63; 66

HOLBROOK'S Newark City and Business Directory for the Year Ending May 1, 1889. Newark: 1888. V. 63; 66

HOLBROOK'S Newark City and Business Directory...for the Year Ending May 1, 1891. Newark: 1890. V. 63; 66

HOLCIK, J.
The Freshwater Fishes of Europe. Volume I, Pt. I - Petromyzontiformes. Pt. II - General Introduction to Fishes. Wiesbaden: 1986-1989. V. 63; 65

HOLCOMB, RICHMOND C.
A Century with Norfolk Naval Hospital 1830-1930. Portsmouth: 1930. V. 65

HOLCOMBE, HENRY
Sermon, Occasioned by the Death of Lieutenant-General George Washington, Late President of the United States of America...First Delivered in the Baptist Church, Savannah, Georgia, Jan. 19th 1800.... Savannah: 1800. V. 66

HOLCOMBE, R. D.
Modern Sea Angling. London: 1921. V. 67

HOLCOMBE, RETURN IRA
An Account of the Battle of Wilson's Creek, or Oak Hills. Springfield: 1883. V. 62; 63

HOLCROFT, THOMAS
The Life of Baron Trenck.... Halifax: 1841. V. 67
Memoirs of the Late.... London: 1816. V. 63
A Plain and Succinct Narrative of the Late Riots and Disturbances in the Cities of London and Westminster, and Borough of Southwark. London: 1780. V. 66
Travels from Hamburgh, through Westphalia, Holland and the Netherlands to Paris. Glasgow: 1804. V. 67

HOLDEN, EDWARD S.
Publications of the Lick Observatory: Volume I 1887. Sacramento: 1887. V. 66

HOLDEN, G. H.
Canaries and Cage-Birds. New York: 1883. V. 65

HOLDEN, HORACE
A Narrative of the Shipwreck, Captivity and Sufferings of Horace Holden and Bnj. H. Nute, Who Were Cast Away in the American Ship Mentor, on the Pelew Islands, in the Year 1832. Boston: 1836. V. 66

HOLDEN, INEZ
Born Old Died Young. London: 1932. V. 63

HOLDEN, WILLIAM
History of the Colony of Natal South Africa.... London: 1855. V. 67

HOLDEN, WILLIAM CURRY
Alkali Trails or Social and Economic Movements of the Texas Frontier 1846-1900. Dallas: 1930. V. 64; 67
Hill of the Rooster. New York: 1956. V. 62; 65
A Ranching Saga. The Lives of William Electious Halsell and Ewing Halsell. San Antonio: 1976. V. 67
Rollie Burns or an Account of the Ranching Industry on the South Plains. Dallas: 1932. V. 67
The Spur Ranch - A Study of the Inclosed Ranch Phase of the Cattle Industry in Texas. Boston: 1934. V. 62; 65

HOLDER, C. F.
Big Game at Sea. 1908. V. 67
The Channel Islands of California, a Book for the Angler, Sportsman and Tourist. Chicago: 1910. V. 64; 65

HOLDERLIN, FRIEDRICH
Selected Poems of Friedrich Holderlin. London: 1944. V. 64

HOLDGATE, M. W.
Antarctic Ecology. London and New York: 1970. V. 65; 66

HOLDING, T. H.
British Liveries. London: 1894. V. 63

HOLE, HUGH MARSHALL
The Jameson Raid. London: 1930. V. 67
The Making of Rhodesia. London: 1926. V. 62

HOLE, WILLIAM
The Ornaments of Churches Considered, with a Particular View to the Late Decoration of the Parish Church of St. Margaret Westminster. Oxford: 1761. V. 66

Quasi Cursores. Edinburgh: 1884. V. 62; 66

HOLIDAY, BILLIE
Lady Sings the Blues. Garden City: 1956. V. 67

HOLIDAY, F. W.
River Fishing for Sea Trout. London: 1960. V. 67

THE HOLIDAY Present: Containing Anecdotes of Mr. and Mrs. Jennet, and Their Little Family.... Worcester: 1787. V. 66

HOLINSHED, RAPHAEL
Holinshed's Chronicles of England, Scotland and Ireland. London: 1807-1808. V. 66

HOLKHAM Bible Picture Book. London: 1954. V. 64

HOLL, HENRY
The White Favour. London: 1866. V. 66

HOLLAND: a Jaunt to the Principal Places in That Country. London: 1775. V. 65

HOLLAND, CECIL FLETCHER
Morgan and His Raiders. New York: 1942. V. 63

HOLLAND, ELIZABETH VASSALL, LADY
The Journal of Elizabeth Lady Holland, 1791-1811. London: 1908. V. 63; 64; 66
A Memoir of the Reverend Sydney Smith. London: 1855. V. 62

HOLLAND, HENRY
Chapters on Mental Physiology. London: 1852. V. 65
Chapters on Mental Physiology. London: 1858. V. 65
Essays on Scientific and Other Subjects Contributed to the Edinburgh at Quarterly Reviews. London: 1862. V. 66
General View of the Agriculture of Cheshire. London: 1808. V. 62
General View of the Agriculture of Cheshire. London: 1813. V. 64; 65; 67
Resolutions of the Associated Architects' With the Report of a Committee by Them Appointed to Consider the Causes of the Frequent Fires and the Best Means of Preventing the Like in Future. London: 1793. V. 62; 66

HOLLAND, HENRY RICHARD VASSALL FOX, 3RD BARON
Further Memoirs of the Whig Party, 1807-1821. London: 1905. V. 62
Memoirs of the Whig Party During My Time. London: 1852. V. 64

HOLLAND, JOHN
The History and Description of Fossil Fuel, the Collieries, and Coal Trade of Great Britain. London: 1835. V. 65; 66
The History and Description of Fossil Fuel, the Collieries and Coal Trade of Great Britain. London: 1841. V. 62
The History, Antiquities and Description of the Town and Parish of Worksop.... Sheffield: 1826. V. 62, 65

HOLLAND, MARGARET
My Winter of Discontent Under Indian Skies. Belfast: 1926. V. 63; 66

HOLLAND, P.
Select Views of the Lakes in Cumberland, Westmorland and Lancashire.... Liverpool: 1792. V. 65; 66

HOLLAND, RAY P.
Shotgunning in the Lowlands. New York: 1945. V. 64; 67

HOLLAND SOCIETY OF NEW YORK
Year Book of the Holland Society of New York. 1913-(1915). New York: 1913-1915. V. 63

HOLLAND, VYVYAN
XVIII Century French Romances. London: 1925-1928. V. 64
Son of Oscar Wilde. London: 1954. V. 64
Time Remembered.... London: 1966. V. 64
The Year Boke of the Sette of Odd Volumes an Annual Record of the Transactions of the Sette. Fiftieth Year 1927-1928. Oxford: 1929. V. 67

HOLLAND, W.
History of West Cork and the Diocese of Ross. 1949. V. 66

HOLLANDER, BERNARD
In Search of the Soul and the Mechanism of Thought, Emotion and Conduct: a Treatise in Two Volumes.... London: 1920. V. 65
The Revival of Phrenology. The Mental Functions of the Brain. London: 1901. V. 64

HOLLANDER, EUGEN
Karikatur und Satir in der Medizin. Stuttgart: 1921. V. 65

HOLLANDER, JOHN
Blue Wine and Other Poems. Baltimore and London: 1979. V. 64
A Crackling of Thorns. New Haven: 1958. V. 63
An Entertainment for Elizabeth Being a Most Excellent Princely Maske of the Seven Motions or Terpischore Unchain'd. 1972. V. 63
I. A. Richards: Essays in His Honor. New York: 1973. V. 63
The Immense Parade on Supererogation Day and What Happened To It. New York: 1972. V. 63
In Place. A Sequence. Omaha: 1978. V. 63; 64
Kinneret. New Haven: 1986. V. 64
Looking Ahead. New York: 1982. V. 63
Looking East in Winter. New York: 1990. V. 63
Poems of Our Moment. New York: 1968. V. 63
Reflections on Espionage: the Question of Cupcake. New York: 1976. V. 63
Some Fugitives Take Cover. New York: 1986. V. 66; 67
Tales Told of the Fathers. Poems. New York: 1975. V. 63
Types of Shape. New Haven and London: 1991. V. 64

HOLLANDER, JOHN *continued*
Vision and Resonance: Two Senses of Poetic Form. New York: 1975. V. 64
The Wind and the Rain: an Anthology of Poems for Young People. Garden City: 1961. V. 63

HOLLANDER, NICOLE
My Father Was Always Sleeping, Shh, Henry's Sleeping. Racine: 1996. V. 64

HOLLANDS, D.
Eagles, Hawks and Falcons of Australia. Melbourne: 1984. V. 67

HOLLBROOK, CHARLES W.
Teacher's Manual Explaining the Use of Chas. W. Holbrook's Lunar Tellurian. Hartford: 1888. V. 66

HOLLENBACK, FRANK R.
Pikes Peak by Rail. Denver: 1962. V. 65

HOLLERAN, ANDREW
Dancer for the Dance. New York: 1978. V. 67

HOLLES, DENZIL HOLLES, BARON
Lord Hollis (sic) His Remains: Being a Second Letter to a Friend, Concerning the Judicature of the Bishops in Parliament, in the Vindication of What He Wrote in His First.... London: 1682. V. 63
Memoirs...from the Year 1641 to 1648. London: 1699. V. 64

HOLLEY, FRANCES CHAMBERLAIN
Once Their Home. Chicago: 1892. V. 65; 67

HOLLEY, GEORGE W.
Niagara: Its History and Geology, Incidents and Poetry. New York City: 1872. V. 64

HOLLEY, MARY AUSTIN
Texas. Lexington: 1836. V. 66

HOLLICK, FREDERICK H.
A Popular Treatise on Venereal Diseases in All Their Forms. New York: 1852. V. 65

HOLLIDAY, JOHN
A Short Account of the Origin, Symptoms and Most Approved Method of Treating the Putrid Bilious Yellow Fever, Vulgarly Called the Black Vomit.... Falmouth: 1795. V. 65

HOLLING, HOLLING CLANCY
Claws of the Thunderbird. A Tale of Three Lost Indians. Joliet: 1928. V. 62
Little Buffalo Boy. New York: 1939. V. 63
Pago. Boston: 1957. V. 62; 63
Seabird. Boston: 1948. V. 66

HOLLINGHURST, ALAN
The Swimming Pool Library. London: 1988. V. 64; 67

HOLLINGS, J. F.
The History of Leicester During the Great Civil War; a Lecture Delivered to the Members of the Leicester Mechanics' Inst. Nov. 4, 1839. Leicester: 1840. V. 62

HOLLINGSHEAD, JOHN
The Story of Leicester Square. London: 1892. V. 62

HOLLINGSWORTH, JOHN MC HENRY
The Journal of Lieutenant John McHenry Hollingsworth of the First New York Volunteers (Stevenson's Regiment) September 1846-August 1849. San Francisco: 1923. V. 62; 63

HOLLINS, THOMAS
Hollins' Hand-Book for Harogate.... Harrogate: 1861. V. 65

HOLLIS, A. C.
The Nandi; Their Language and Folk-Lore.... Oxford: 1909. V. 67

HOLLIS, MARGERY
Emma. London: 1893. V. 65

HOLLIS, THOMAS
Memoirs of Thomas Hollis, Esq. (with) Appendix. London: 1780. V. 62; 64
The Monumental Effigies of Great Britain.... London: 1840-1842. V. 64

HOLLISTER, OVANDO JAMES
Boldly They Rode. A History of the First Regiment of Volunteers. Lakewood: 1949. V. 67
The Resources and Attractions of the Territory of Utah - 1879. Omaha: 1879. V. 63; 66

HOLLISTER, P. M.
Famous Colonial Houses. Philadelphia: 1921. V. 62; 65

HOLLISTER, URIAH S.
The Navajo and His Blanket. Denver: 1903. V. 65

HOLLO, ANSELM
& It Is a Song. Poems. Birmingham: 1965. V. 63
The Claim. London: 1965. V. 63

HOLLOWAY, JAMES
The Free and Voluntary Confession and Narrative Written With His Own Hand and Delivered by Himself to Mr. Secretary Jenkins.... London: 1684. V. 63

HOLLOWAY, JOHN
The Euing Collection of English Broadside Ballads in the Library of the University of Glasgow. Glasgow: 1971. V. 63
Fairburn's Second Edition of the Trial of John Holloway and Owen Haggerty for the Wilful Murder of Mr. Steele...and of Elizabeth Godfrey, for Stabbing Rd. Prince in the Eye.... London: 1807. V. 63
The Very Remarkable Trial of John Holloway, and Owen Haggerty, Who Were Found Guilty...February 20, 1807, of the Wilful Murder of Mr. J. C. Steele.... London: 1807. V. 63

HOLLOWAY, LAURA C.
The Ladies of the White House, or in the House of the Presidents Being a Complete History of the Social and Domestic Lives of the Presidents from Washington to the Present Time - 1789-1881. Philadelphia: 1881. V. 67

HOLLOWAY, MARK
Norman Douglas - a Biography. London: 1976. V. 62

HOLLOWAY, WILLIAM
A General Dictionary of Provincialisms.... 1839. V. 64
The Peasant's Fate. A Rural Poem. Boston: 1802. V. 66

HOLLOWELL, J. M.
War-time Reminiscences and Other Selections. Goldsboro: 1939. V. 62; 63; 65

HOLM, C. G.
Glimpses of Old Japan from Japanese Colour Prints: Birds and Flowers. London: 1930. V. 66

HOLMAN, ALBERT
Pioneering in the Northwest - Niobrara Virginia City Wagon Road. Sioux City: 1924. V. 67

HOLMAN, BOB
Cupid's Cashbox. Poems. N.P: 1988. V. 63

HOLMAN, DAVID
Buckskin and Homespun. Austin: 1979. V. 62
Letters of Hard Times in Texas. Austin: 1974. V. 64

HOLMAN, FREDERICK V.
Dr. John McLoughlin, the Father of Oregon. Cleveland: 1907. V. 64; 67

HOLMAN, JAMES
The Narrative of a Journey, Undertaken in the Years 1819, 1820 and 1821 through France, Italy, Savoy, Switzerland and Parts of Germany.... London: 1822. V. 66; 67
Travels in Madras, Ceylon, Mauritius, Cormoro Islands, Zanzibar, Calcutta, etc., etc. London: 1840. V. 67

HOLMAN, JOSEPH GEORGE
A Statement of the Differences Subsisting Between the Proprietors and Performers of the Theatre Royal Covent Garden.... London: 1800. V. 64

HOLMAN, SHERI
A Stolen Tongue. New York: 1997. V. 67

HOLMAN-HUNT, DIANA
Latin Among Lions: Alvaro Guevara. London: 1974. V. 64

HOLME, C. G.
Etching of Today. London: 1930. V. 62; 65
Glimpses of Old Japan from Japanese Colour Prints: Birds and Flowers. London: 1930. V. 64

HOLME, CHARLES
Colour Photography and Other Recent Developments of the Art of the Camera. London: 1908. V. 65
English Water-Colour With Reproductions of Drawings by Eminent Painters. London: 1902. V. 64
English Water-Colour With Reproductions of Drawings by Eminent Painters. New York: 1902. V. 64
Modern British Architecture and Decoration. London: 1901. V. 67
Modern Pen Drawings: European and American. London: 1901. V. 67

HOLME, CONSTANCE
Crump Folk Going Home. London: 1913. V. 64
Four One-Act Plays. Kirkby Lonsdale W. M. and H: 1932. V. 64
He Who Came?. London: 1930. V. 64; 65
The Splendid Fairing. London: 1919. V. 64
The Things Which Belong.... London: 1925. V. 64; 65

HOLMES, ABIEL
American Annals; or a Chronological History of America from its Discovery in MCCCCXCII to MDCCCIV. Cambridge: 1805. V. 63; 64

HOLMES, BAYARD
The Surgery of the Head. New York: 1930. V. 66; 67

HOLMES, C. J.
Constable and His Influence on Landscape Painting. London: 1902. V. 62; 66

HOLMES, CHARLES
Art in Photography: with Selected Examples of European and American Work. London: 1905. V. 63
Pen, Pencil and Chalk, a Series of Drawings by Contemporary European Artists. London: 1911. V. 63

HOLMES, E. BURTON
Burton Holmes Travelogues With Illustration from Photographs by the Author. Volume Six. New York: 1908. V. 63

HOLMES, EDMOND
The Silence of Love. London: 1899. V. 66

HOLMES, F.
Following the Roe. 1974. V. 67

HOLMES, FRANCIS S.
Remains of Domestic Animals Discovered Among the Post-Pliocene Fossils in South Carolina. Charleston: 1858. V. 63
The Southern Farmer and Markert Gardener. Charleston: 1842. V. 63; 66

HOLMES, J. H.
In Primitive New Guinea. London: 1924. V. 67
Way Back in Papua. London: 1926. V. 67

HOLMES, J. H. H.
A Treatise on the Coal Mines of Durham and Northumberland.... London: 1816. V. 63

HOLMES, JOHN CLELLON
Get Home Free. New York: 1964. V. 62
Go. New York: 1952. V. 64
The Horn. London: 1959. V. 62

HOLMES, JULIA ARCHIBALD
A Bloomer Girl on Pike's Peak 1858. Denver: 1949. V. 66

HOLMES, MAURICE G.
From New Spain by Sea to the Californis 1519-1668. Gelndale: 1963. V. 63

HOLMES, OLIVER WENDELL
Astraea. Boston: 1850. V. 63
Astraea. Boston: 1860. V. 67
The Autocrat of the Breakfast Table. Boston: 1858. V. 62; 64; 66
The Autocrat of the Breakfast Table. Boston: 1859. V. 64; 66; 67
The Autocrat of the Breakfast Table.. Edinburgh: 1859. V. 67
The Autocrat of the Breakfast Table. New York: 1955. V. 63; 64; 66
Border Lines of Knowledge in Some Province of Medical Science. Boston: 1862. V. 62; 63
Boylston Prize Dissertations for the Years 1836 and 1837. Boston: 1838. V. 62
Currents and Counter-Currents in Medical Science. Boston: 1861. V. 62
Dorothy Q Together With a Ballad of the Boston Tea Party and Grandmother's Story of Bunker Hill Battle. Boston: 1893. V. 64
Elsie Venner. Boston: 1861. V. 66; 67
Fair Play. Waltham: 1875. V. 62
The Guardian Angel. Boston: 1867. V. 66; 67
Holmes-Pollock Letters. Correspondence of Mr. Justice Holmes and Sir Frederick Pollock 1874-1932. Cambridge: 1941. V. 62
An Introductory Lecture, Delivered at the Massachusetts Medical College Novr. 3, 1847. Boston: 1847. V. 64
The Last Leaf. Cambridge: 1886. V. 64; 66
Mechanism in Thought and Morals: an Address Delivered Before the Phi Beta Kappa Society of Harvard University June 29, 1870.... Boston: 1871. V. 65
A Mortal Antipathy. Boston: 1885. V. 66; 67
The Oliver Wendell Holmes Year Book. Boston: 1894. V. 67
Our Hundred Days in Europe. Boston: 1887. V. 64
Over the Teacups. Boston and New York: 1891. V. 63
Poems. Boston and New York: 1886. V. 62; 64
Poems. London: 1846. V. 62; 64
The Poet at the Breakfast Table. Boston: 1872. V. 62; 63
The Poetical Works. Boston: 1884. V. 64; 66
The Professor at the Breakfast Table. Boston: 1860. V. 64; 66; 67
Puerperal Fever as a Private Pestilence. Boston: 1855. V. 62
The School Boy. Boston: 1879. V. 64
Speeches. Boston: 1900. V. 63
Speeches. Boston: 1918. V. 63
Touched with Fire. Civil War Letters and Diary of Oliver Wendell Holmes, Jr. Cambridge: 1946. V. 63
Urania: a Rhymed Lesson. Boston: 1846. V. 62; 64; 66; 67

HOLMES, RICHARD
Shelley - the Pursuit. London: 1974. V. 62

HOLMES, RICHARD R.
Naval and Military Trophies. London: 1896. V. 62; 66
Queen Victoria. 1897. V. 63
Queen Victoria. London and Paris: 1897. V. 65; 66

HOLMES, ROBERT
Keighley, Past and Present; or, an Historical, Topographical and Statistical Sketch.... London: 1858. V. 65

HOLMES, SAMUEL JACKSON
A Bibliography of Eugenics. Berkeley: 1924. V. 65

HOLMES, W. H.
Archaeological Studies Among the Ancient Cities of Mexico. 1895-1897. V. 62

HOLMES, WILLIAM RICHARD
Sketches on the Shores of the Caspian. London: 1845. V. 67

HOLMS, G. RANDOLPH
The Hounds of the Vatican; or, Holmes's Last Bow. New York: 1986. V. 66

HOLROYD, EDWARD
Observations Upon the Case of Abraham Thornton, Who Was Tried at Warwick, August 8, 1817, for the Murder of Mary Ashford.... London: 1819. V. 63

HOLROYD, MICHAEL
Bernard Shaw. 1988-1991. V. 67
Bernard Shaw. 1988-1992. V. 64; 67
Hugh Kingsmill - a Critical Biography. London: 1964. V. 65

HOLST, SPENCER
Thirteen Essays, Sixty Drawings. N.P: 1960. V. 67

HOLT, A. J.
Pioneering in the Southwest. Nashville: 1923. V. 67

HOLT, ARDERN
Fancy Dresses Described. London. V. 66
Fancy Dresses Described. London: 1882. V. 63

HOLT, DAVID
A Lay of Hero Worship and Other Poems. London: 1850. V. 63

HOLT, E. EMMETT
The Diseases of Infancy and Childhood. New York: 1899. V. 66; 67

HOLT, E. L.
Use of Drift Nets for the Capture of Salmon. 1908. V. 67

HOLT, GAVIN
Ivory Ladies. London: 1937. V. 67

HOLT, J. HOWARD
The Truth About Crime: Its Causes, Its Effects, Its Prevention, Its Cure. Wheeling?: 1920?. V. 63

HOLT, JOHN
Characters of the Kings and Queens of England, Selected from Different Histories.... Dublin: 1789. V. 65
General View of the Agriculture of the County of Lancaster; with Observations on the Means of Its Improvement. London: 1795. V. 67

HOLT, LUTHER EMMETT
The Care and Feeding of Children. New York: 1894. V. 63

HOLT, R. D.
Schleicher County; or, Eighty Years of Development in Southwest Texas. Eldorado: 1930. V. 64; 65

HOLT, ROSA BELLE
Rugs. Oriental and Occidental, Antique and Modern. Chicago: 1901. V. 62

HOLTBY, WINIFRED
The Astonishing Island.... London: 1933. V. 63
South Riding, an English Landscape. London: 1936. V. 62; 63; 65

HOLTHUSEN, HENRY F.
James W. Wadsworth, Jr. A Biographical Sketch. New York: 1926. V. 63

HOLTON, ISAAC F.
New Granada. 1857. V. 62; 63; 64; 66; 67

HOLT-WHITE, RASHLEIGH
The Life and Letters of Gilbert White of Selborne. London: 1901. V. 62; 66

HOLTZ, MATHILDE EDITH
Glacier National Park Its Trails and Treasures. New York: 1917. V. 65

HOLTZAPFFEL & CO.
Printing Apparatus for the Use of Amateurs, Containing Full and Practical Instructions for the Use of Cowper's Parlour printing Press. London: 1846. V. 62

HOLTZAPFFEL, CHARLES
Turning and Mechanical Manipulation. London: 1875-1891. V. 62

HOLWELL, J. B. L.
Breathlessness. Proceedings of an International Symposium Held on 7 and 8 April 1965 Under Auspices of the University of Manchester. Oxford: 1966. V. 66

HOLWELL, JOHN
A Sure Guide to the Practical Surveyor. London: 1678. V. 64

HOLWELL, JOHN Z.
An Address to the Proprietors of East-India Stock. London: 1764. V. 66
A Genuine Narrative of the Deplorable Deaths of English Gentlemen, and Others Who Were Suffocated in the Black-Hole in Fort William, at Calcutta, in the Kingdom of Bengal, in the Night Succeeding the 20th Day of June, 1756. London: 1758. V. 63

HOLYOAKE, GEORGE JACOB
Bygones Worth Remembering. London: 1905. V. 64
The Last Trial for Atheism in England. London: 1871. V. 63

HOLYROYD, ABRAHAM
A Garland of Poetry. London: 1873. V. 66

HOLZWORTH, JOHN M.
The Wild Grizzlies of Alaska; a Story of the Grizzly and Big Brown Bears of Alaska, Their Habits, Manners and Characteristics, Together with Notes on Mountain Sheep and Caribou.... New York and London: 1930. V. 65

HOMAGE to Henri Matisse. New York: 1970. V. 62

HOMAGE to Marc Chagall. New York: 1969. V. 62; 64

HOMAGE to Picasso on His 70th Birthday: Drawings and Watercolors Since 1893. London: 1951. V. 62; 63; 64

HOMANS, J. SMITH
Cyclopedia of Commerce and Commercial Navigation. New York: 1974. V. 66

THE HOME Cook Book. Toronto: 1877. V. 67

HOME, FRANCIS
Clincial Experiments, Histories and Dissections. London: 1780. V. 64
Clinical Experiments, Histories and Dissections. London: 1782. V. 62; 66

HOME, GORDON
The Evolution of an English Town. London: 1905. V. 63; 65
France. London: 1918. V. 66
Yorkshire Coast and Moorland Painted and Described. London: 1904. V. 62; 63; 65

HOME, GORDON *continued*
Yorkshire Dales and Fells. London: 1906. V. 65

HOME, HENRY
The Gentleman Farmer. Edinburgh: 1776. V. 66

HOME, JOHN
Douglas; a Tragedy. London: 1757. V. 65
Douglas: a Tragedy. Edinburgh: 1798. V. 62

HOME, ROBERT
Select Views in Mysore, the Country of Tippoo Sultan, from Drawings Taken On the Spot.... London: 1794. V. 64

HOMER, HENRY SACHEVERELL
An Enquiry Into the Means of Preserving and Improving the Publick Roads of This Kingdom. Oxford: 1767. V. 65

HOMER, PHILIP BRACEBRIDGE
The Garland: a Collection of Poems. Oxford: 1788. V. 62

HOMER, WILLIAM I.
Alfred Stieglitz and the Photo-Seccession. Boston: 1983. V. 63

HOMERUS
A Burlesque Translation of Homer. London: 1797. V. 67
Carmina Homerica, Ilias et Odyssea. (Works). Londini: 1820. V. 65
Homeri Ilia et Ulyssea Cum Interpretatione.... Basiliae: 1535. V. 65
Homeri Odyssea. 1567. V. 65
Homeri Opera Graeco-Latina.... Basileae: 1567. V. 65; 66
Homeri Opera Quae Extant Omnia. Amstelaedami: 1707. V. 66
Homeri Quae Extant Omnia Ilias, Odyssea, Batrachyomachia, Hymni, Poematia Aliquot. Basileae: 1606. V. 65
(title Greek, then): *Homeri et Homeridarum Opera et Reliquiae*. (Works in Greek). Lipsiae: 1804-1807. V. 65
Homer's Odyssey.... London: 1675. V. 64
The Homeric Hymn to Aphrodite. Waltham St. Lawrence: 1948. V. 62; 67
Hymnus in Cererem (in Greek). Lugduni Batavorum: 1808. V. 65
Homeri Ilias Cum Brevi Annotatione Curante G. Heyen. Lipsiae: 1804. V. 65
Homeri Ilias Graece et Lainte.... Londini: 1729-1732. V. 67
Homeri Ilias Seu Potius Omnia Eius Quae Extant Opera.... Argentorati: 1572. V. 66
The Iliad. London: 1715-1720. V. 63
Iliad. Boston: 1846. V. 64
The Iliad. N.P: 1931. V. 64
The Iliad (and) The Odyssey. London: 1931. V. 62; 63
The Iliad of Homer, the First Twelve Staves.... London: 1928. V. 63
The Iliad of Homer Translated by Mr. Pope. London: 1715. V. 67
The Iliad of Homer. (with) The Odyssey. Haarlem: 1931. V. 64
Ilias et Odyssea. (Greek Letter). London: 1831. V. 66
L'Iliade. A Paris: 1714. V. 64
Ilias. Parisiis: 1538. V. 66
Ilias. Glasguae: 1778. V. 64
Ilias. Oxonii et Londini: 1881. V. 66
Ilias & Odyssea, et in Easdem Scholia, sive Interpretatio Didymi. Amstelodami: 1656. V. 66
Ilias and Odysseae. (The Works in Greek and Latin). Cantabrigiae: 1711. V. 66
Ilias (and) Odysseae. (The Works in Greek and Latin). Londini: 1729-1740. V. 64
Ilias; Odyssea. London: 1818. V. 65
Ilias (The Iliad in Latin). Venetiis: 1502. V. 64
Ilias (The Iliad in Latin). Parisiis: 1538. V. 64
(Title in Greek, then): *Ilias & Odysseae*. (Works in Greek and Latin). Cantabrigiae: 1711. V. 64
(Title in Greek, then) *Ilias and Odysseae*. Oxonii: 1743-1750. V. 64
Nausikaa. (Translation of the Sixth Rhapsody of the Odyssey). Paris: 1899. V. 66; 67
Odyssea. (in Greek). Oxonii: 1827. V. 65
Odyssea (The Works in Latin). Lugduni: 1538. V. 64
Odyssea. Argentorati: 1572?. V. 64
Odysseae. Parisiis: 1581. V. 64; 66
L'Odyssée. (and) L'Iliade.... Paris: 1716-1719. V. 64; 66
(Greek Title): *Omhpoy Odysseia*. Oxford: 1909. V. 64
L'Odyssee D'Homere.... Paris: 1777. V. 64; 66
The Odyssey. Antwerp: 1528. V. 64
The Odyssey. London: 1725-1726. V. 67
The Odyssey. London: 1760. V. 63
The Odyssey. Cambridge: 1929. V. 64
The Odyssey. 1932. V. 65
The Odyssey. London: 1932. V. 66
The Odyssey. London: 1935. V. 62; 63; 64
The Odyssey. New York: 1981. V. 63; 64; 66
The Odyssey in Greek. Oxford: 1800. V. 65
Les Oeuvres D'Homere. Leiden: 1766. V. 64; 66
(*Opera*). Glasguae: 1756-1758. V. 66
Opera Graeco-Latina. Basel: 1567. V. 64
Opera Omnia (Iliad).... (with) Odyssea.... Amstelaedami: 1650. V. 65
Opvs Vtrvmqve Homeri... (The Works in Greek). Basileae: 1541. V. 64
Pages from the Iliad. Iowa City: 1976. V. 66
Il Primo Canto Del L'Iliade D'Omero (The First Two Books of the "Iliad" in Italian). Londra: 1736. V. 63; 66
Le Ulyxea. (Odyssey). Antwep: 1556. V. 62

HOMES, A. M.
Jack. New York: 1989. V. 62
The Safety of Objects. New York: 1990. V. 67

HOMES of American Authors. New York: 1854. V. 65

HOMES of American Statesmen: With Anecdotical, Personal and Descriptive Sketches by Various Writers. New York: 1854. V. 63; 64; 66

HONACKI, J. H.
Mammal Species of the World.... Lawrence: 1982. V. 62

HONE, JOSEPH
The Love Story of Thomas Davis told in the Letters of Annie Hutton. 1945. V. 65
The Moores of Moore Hall. 1939. V. 67

HONE, PHILIP
Diary 1828-1851. New York: 1889. V. 67
The Diary of Philip Hone, 1828-1851. New York: 1927. V. 66

HONE, WILLIAM
Ancient Mysteries Described, Especially the English Miracle Plays.... London: 1823. V. 63; 64; 65
Bartholomew Fair Insurrection: and the Pie-Bald Poney Plot!. London: 1817. V. 65
The Englishman's Mentor. London: 1819. V. 66
Facetiae and Miscellanies.... London: 1827. V. 66
Hone's Popular Political Tracts. London: 1823. V. 62
The Political A, Apple Pie or the Extraordinary Red Book Versified. London: 1820. V. 64; 65; 66
A Political Christmas Carol Set to Music. London. V. 65
Select Popular Political Tracts: Consisting of the House that Jack Built, Queen's Matrimonial Ladder, Non mi Ricordo, Right Divine of Kings to Govern Wrong, Political Showman, Man in the Moon, The Queen's Form of Prayer and a Slap at Slop. London. V. 66
Sixty Curious Authentic Narratives and Anecdotes Respecting Extraordinary Characters.... London: 1822. V. 63
The Three Trials of William Hone, for Publishing Three Parodies.... London: 1818. V. 63
The Year Book of Daily Recreation and Information...and a Perpetual Key to the Almanck. London: 1841. V. 66

HONEY, RICHARD
A Full Report of the Evidence Given Before the Coroner's Inquest on the Body of Richard Honey, who Was Slain by the Military, During the Progress of Her Late Majesty's Funeral Procession through London on Tuesday, August 14, 1821. London: 1821. V. 63

HONEY, WILLIAM BOWYER
European Ceramic Art from the End of the Middle Ages to About 1815. London: 1949-1952. V. 66

HONEYMAN, A. VAN DOREN
History of Union County, New Jersey 1664-1923. New York: 1923. V. 63; 66
Joannes Nevius. Schepen and Third Secretary of New Amsterdam under the Dtuch...and His Descendants, A.D. 1627-1900. Plainfield: 1900. V. 63

HONEYMAN, ROBERT
The Honeyman Collection of Scientific Books and Manuscripts. London: 1978-1981. V. 62

HONEYWOOD, ST. JOHN
Poems by...with Some Pieces in Prose. New York: 1801. V. 63

HONIG, LOUIS O.
James Bridger: The Pathfinder of the West. Kansas City: 1951. V. 63; 64
The Pathfinder of the West, James Bridger. Kansas City: 1951. V. 64; 67
Westport Gateway to the Early West. N.P: 1950. V. 62

HONIG, PIETER
Science and Scientists in the Netherland Indies. New York: 1945. V. 62; 67

HOOD, J. B.
Advance and Retreat: Personal Experiences in the United States and Confederate States Armies. New Orleans: 1880. V. 66

HOOD, J. DENNIS
Waterspouts on the Yorkshire Wolds. Cataclysm at Langtoft and Driffield. Driffeld: 1892. V. 64; 65; 66

HOOD, JAMES W.
Smith, Grant and Irons Families of New Jesey's Shore Counties, Including the Related Families of Willets and Birdsall. New Haven: 1955. V. 66

HOOD, JOHN
Australia and the East; Being a Journal Narrative of a Voyage to New South Wales, in an Emigrant Ship with a Residence of Some Months in Sydney and the Bush and the Route Home by Way of Indian and Egypt in the Years 1841 and 1842. London: 1843. V. 67
Index of Colonial and State Laws Between the Years 1663 and 1877 Inclusive. Trenton: 1877. V. 63; 64
Index of Titles of Corporations Chartered Under General and Special Laws by the Legislature of New Jersey, Betewen the Years 1693 and 1869, Inclusive. Trenton: 1870. V. 66

HOOD, JOHN BELL
Advance and Retreat. Personal Experiences in the United States and Confederate States Armies. New Orleans: 1880. V. 62; 63

HOOD, ROBERT
To the Arctic by Canoe 1819-1821. The Journal and Paintings of Robert Hood. Montreal and London: 1974. V. 62

HOOD, THOMAS
The Comic Annual. London: 1836. V. 65
The Dream of Eugene Aram. Knaresborough: 1875. V. 64

HOOD, THOMAS continued
The Headlong Career and Woeful Ending of Precocious Piggy. London: 1859. V. 64
Hood's Own; or Laughter from Year to Year. London: 1868-1862. V. 67
Miss Kilmansegg and Her Precious Leg. London: 1870. V. 62
Miss Kilmansegg and Her Precious Leg. Chipping Campden, Gloucester: 1904. V. 62
Thomas Hood (Poems). London: 1870. V. 63
Tom Tucker and Little Bo-Peep. New York: 1891. V. 64
Up the Rhine. London: 1840. V. 63; 64; 65

HOOK, JAMES W.
Smith, Grant and Irons Families of New Jersey's Shore Counties, Including the Related Families of Willets and Birdsall. New Haven: 1955. V. 63

HOOK, SIDNEY
The Metaphysics of Pragmatism. Chicago: 1927. V. 67

HOOK, THEODORE
Births, Deaths and Marriages. Paris: 1839. V. 67
The Choice Humorous Works, Ludicrous Adventures, Bon Mots, Puns and Hoaxes.... London: 1889. V. 67
Gurney Married: a Sequel to Gilbert Gurney. Paris: 1839. V. 67
Precepts and Practice. Paris: 1840. V. 67
Reminiscences of Michael Kelly, of the King's Theatre, ant Theatre Royal Drury Lane. London: 1826. V. 62

HOOK, THEODORE EDWARD
The Life and Remains. London: 1849. V. 66

HOOK, WALTER FARQUHAR
Lives of The Archbishops of Canterbury. London: 1860-1876. V. 63, 64

HOOKE, ANDREW
An Essay on the National Debt, and National Capital.... London: 1750. V. 65

HOOKE, NORMAN
Modern Shipping Disasters 1963-1987. London: 1989. V. 67

HOOKE, ROBERT
Lectiones Cutlerianae, or a Collection of Lectures; Physical, Mechanical, Geographical and Astronomical. London: 1679. V. 65
Micrographia (1665). Lincolnwood: 1987. V. 67
Micrographia; or Some Physiological Descriptions of Minute Bodies Made by Magnifying Glasses. London: 1665. V. 62; 67
Micrographia Restaurata; or, the Copper-Plates of Dr. Hooke's Wonderful Discoveries by the Microscope.... London: 1745. V. 64

HOOKER, JOHN DALTON
Handbook of the New Zealand Flora. 1867. V. 63
Lecture on Insular Floras, Delivered Before the British Association. London: 1896. V. 67

HOOKER, JOSEPH DALTON
The Botany of the Antarctic Voyage.... 1855. V. 62
Himalayan Journals. Glasgow. V. 62
Himalayan Journals. London: 1854. V. 67
Himalayan Journals. London: 1891. V. 66
Journal of a Tour in Morocco and the Great Atlas. 1878. V. 66
The Rhododendrons of Sikkim-Himalaya.... London: 1849-1851. V. 66

HOOKER, RICHARD
Of the Lawes of Ecclesiastical Politie.... London: 1676. V. 66
Of the Laws of Ecclesiastical Politie. London: 1636. V. 66; 67
The Works. London: 1682. V. 63
The Works. Oxford: 1793. V. 62
Works. London: 1803. V. 62
Works. Oxford: 1874. V. 63

HOOKER, W. J.
The Hookers of Kew 1785-1811. 1967. V. 66

HOOKER, WILLIAM FRANCIS
The Prairie Schooner. Chicago: 1918. V. 64; 67

HOOKER, WILLIAM JACKSON
The Botany of Captain Beechey's Voyage. Weineheim: 1965. V. 63
A Century of Ferns... (with) A Second Century of Ferns.... London: 1854-1861. V. 64
Flora Boreali-Americana; or the Botany of the Northern Parts of British America. London: 1833. V. 64
Garden Ferns. London: 1862. V. 62
Journal of a Tour in Iceland in the Summer of 1809. Yarmouth: 1813. V. 62
Synopsis Filicum.... London: 1868. V. 62
Synopsis Filicum.... 1874. V. 63

HOOKER, WORTHINGTON
Lessons from the History of Medical Delusions. New York: 1850. V. 67

HOOLA VAN NOOTEN, B.
Fleurs, Fruits et Feuillages Choisis de la Flore et la Pomone de l'Ile de Java.... Brussels: 1866. V. 63

HOOLE, BARBARA
A Season at Harrogate.... Knaresborough: 1812. V. 66
A Season at Harrogate.... Knaresborough: 1818. V. 64

HOOLE, CHARLES
The Common Accidence Examined and Explained, by Short Questions and Answers.... London: 1711. V. 64

HOOLE, HENRY E., & CO. LTD.
(Trade Catalogue of Fireplaces and Lanterns). Sheffield: 1910. V. 64

HOOLE, JOHN
Journal Narrative Relative to Doctor Johnson's Last Illness. Iowa City: 1972. V. 66

HOOPER, CHARLES EDWARD
The Country House: a Practical Manual of the Planning and Construction of the American Country Home and Its Surroundings. New York: 1909. V. 65

HOOPER, EDWARD JAMES
Hooper's Western Fruit Book: a Compendious Collection of Facts, from the Notes and Experience of Successful Fruit Culturists.... Cincinnati: 1857. V. 66
The Practical Farmer, Gardener and Housewife; or, Dictionary of Agriculture, Horticulture and Domestic Economy. Cincinnati: 1839. V. 64

HOOPER, GEORGE
Down the River. Or, Practical Lessons Under the Code Duello. New York: 1874. V. 62

HOOPER, JAMES
African Art from the James Hooper Collection. London: 1976. V. 62

HOOPER, JOHN
A Declaration of Christe and of His Offyce.... Zurych: 1547. V. 63

HOOPER, JOHNSON JONES
Some Adventures of Captain Simon Suggs, Late of the Tallapoosa Volunteers.... Philadelphia: 1846. V. 62

HOOPER, ROBERT
The Anatomist's Vade-Mecum.... Windsor: 1809. V. 62
A Compendious Medical Dictionary.,... London: 1798. V. 65
Lexicon Medicum; or Medical Dictionary.... London: 1825. V. 63
The Physician's Vade Mecum.... Albany: 1809. V. 66

HOOPER, W. H.
Ten Months Among the Tents of the Tuski. London: 1853. V. 66

HOOPER, WILLIAM
Fifty Years Since: an Address, Delivered Before the Alumni of the University of North Carolina, on the 7th of June, 1859. Chapel Hill: 1861. V. 67
Rational Recreations, In Which the Principles of Numbers and Natural Philosophy are Clearly and Copiously Elucidated, by a Series of Easy, Entertaining, Interesting Experiments Among Which Are All those Commonly Performed with the Cards. London: 1774. V. 66

HOORNBEEK, JOHANNE
Theologiciae Practicae Pars Prior. Ultrajecti: 1689. V. 66

HOOTON, EARNEST ALBERT
The Indians of Pecos of Pueblo: a Study of Their Skeletal Remains. New Haven: 1930. V. 63; 64

HOOVER, H. A.
Early Days in the Mogollons. El Paso: 1958. V. 66

HOOVER, HERBERT
American Individualism. New York: 1922. V. 64
Campaign Speeches of 1932. New York: 1933. V. 63
Memoirs 1920-1933. New York: 1952. V. 64
The Ordeal of Woodrow Wilson. New York: 1958. V. 63; 66

HOOVER, J. EDGAR
A Study of Communism. New York: 1962. V. 63

HOOVER, K. L.
Use of Small Fish Species in Carcinogenicity Testing. Bethesda: 1984. V. 65

HOPALONG Cassidy Lends a Helping Hand. Kenosha: 1950. V. 65

HOPE, A. D.
Poems. New York: 1961. V. 63

HOPE, ARTHUR
A Manual of Sorrento & Inlaid Work for Amateurs with Original Designs. Chicago: 1876. V. 67

HOPE, ASCOTT R.
Redskin and Paleface Romance and Adventures on the Plain. London: 1900. V. 67
Stories of the Wild West. Edinburgh: 1886. V. 67

HOPE, F. W.
The Coleopterist's Manual.... 1837-1838. V. 66

HOPE, J. F.
A History of Hunting in Hampshire. 1950. V. 62; 64

HOPE, JAMES
A Treatise on the Diseases of the Heart and Great Vessels, and on the Affections Which May be Mistaken for Them.... Philadelphia: 1846. V. 62; 66

HOPE, JOHN
A Letter to Francis Jeffrey, Esq. Editor of the Edinburgh Review. Edinburgh;: 1811. V. 65

HOPE, PEYTON H.
Moses Drury Hoge: Life and Letters. Richmond: 1899. V. 65

HOPE, THOMAS
Household Furniture and Interior Decoration, Executed from Designs by.... London: 1807. V. 64

HOPE, WILLIAM H. ST. JOHN
The Abbey of St. Mary in Furness, Lancashire. Kendal: 1902. V. 66

HOPE, WILLIAM H. ST. JOHN continued
Cowdray and Easebourne Priory. London: 1919. V. 62; 66
The History of the London Charterhouse. London: 1925. V. 67
Windsor Castle. London: 1903. V. 62

HOPEWELL SMITH, A.
Dental Microscopy. London and Philadelphia: 1899. V. 67
The Histology and Patho-Histology of the Teeth. London: 1903. V. 67

HOPKIN-JAMES, LEMUEL J.
The Celtic Gospels, Their Story and Their Text. 1934. V. 62

HOPKINS, A. I.
In the Isles of King Solomon, an Account of Twenty-Five Years Spent Amongst the Primitive Solomon Islanders. London: 1928. V. 67

HOPKINS, ALBERT A.
A Dickens Atlas, Including Twelve Walks in London with Charles Dickens. New York: 1923. V. 62
Magic Stage Illusions and Scientific Diversions. London: 1897. V. 63

HOPKINS, ALFRED
Modern Farm Buildings. New York: 1913. V. 63

HOPKINS, CHARLES
Boadicea Queen of Britain. London: 1697. V. 66

HOPKINS, GARLAND EVANS
The First Battle of Modern Naval History. Richmond: 1943. V. 62; 63; 65

HOPKINS, GERARD MANLEY
The Correspondence of Gerard Manley Hopkins and Richard Watson Dixon. London: 1935. V. 62
The Correspondence of Gerard Manley Hopkins and Richard Watson Dixon. London: 1955. V. 63
Further Letters of Gerard Manley Hopkins Including His Correspondence with Coventry Patmore. London: 1938. V. 63
The Journals and Papers of.... London: 1959. V. 62
The Letters of Gerard Manley Hopkins to Robert Bridges. London: 1935. V. 62
The Letters of Gerard Manley Hopkins to Robert Bridges, the Correspondence - Including His Correspondence with Coventry Patmore and Richard Watson Dixon. London: 1935-1938. V. 65
Pied Beauty. 1994. V. 65
Poems. London: 1930. V. 63; 65; 66
Poems, Now First Published. London: 1918. V. 64
Selected Poems. London: 1954. V. 62; 64; 64; 65
A Vision of the Mermaids: a Prize Poem dated Christmas 1862.... London: 1929. V. 64

HOPKINS, J. CASTELL
Life and Work of the Rt. Hon. Sir. John Thompson, P.C. K.C.M.G. Q.C. Brantford: 1895. V. 64

HOPKINS, JOHN A.
Economic History of the Production of Beef Cattle in Iowa - Iowa Economnic History Series. Iowa City: 1928. V. 67

HOPKINS, JOHN HENRY
Essay on Gothic Architecture, with Various Plans and Drawings for Churches.... Burlington: 1836. V. 63; 66

HOPKINS, KENNETH
Forty-two Poems. London: 1961. V. 66

HOPKINS, LUTHER W.
From Bull Run to Appomattox, a Boy's View. Baltimore: 1911. V. 63; 65

HOPKINS, R. H. E.
An Illustrated Catalogue of the Rothschild Collection of Fleas (Siphonaptera) in the British Museum. 1953-1971. V. 66

HOPKINS, SAMUEL
An Inquiry Concerning the Future State of Those Who Die in Their Sins.... Newport: 1783. V. 66

HOPKINS, SARAH WINNEMUCCA
Life Among the Piutes: Their Wrongs and Claims. Boston: 1883. V. 64; 67

HOPKINS, THOMAS SMITH
Colonial Furniture of West New Jersey. Haddonfield: 1936. V. 63; 66

HOPKINS, WALTER L.
Leftwich-Turner Families of Virginia and Their Connections. Richmond: 1931. V. 67

HOPKINSON, TOM
The Transitory Venus - Nine Stories. London: 1948. V. 64

HOPLEY, C. C.
Snakes. 1882. V. 63

HOPLEY, CATHERINE COOPER
Life in the South from the Commencement of the War.... New York: 1971. V. 66

HOPPER, NORA
Ballads in Prose. London: 1894. V. 64
Rambles and Gambols. London. V. 62
Under Quicken Boughs. London: 1896. V. 64

HOPPIN, AUGUSTUS
Nothing to Wear; a Poem of Transatlantic Origin. London: 1859. V. 62; 66
Two Compton Boys. Boston: 1885. V. 62

HOPPUS, EDWARD
The Gentleman's and Builder's Repository. London: 1738. V. 62

HOPPUS, MARY ANNE MARTHA
A Great Treason. London: 1883. V. 66

HOPTOCK, C.
Norwegian Design, from Viking Age to Industrial Revolution. Oslo: 1955. V. 62; 65

HOPTON, ARTHUR
A Concordancy of Yeares, Containing a New, Easie and Most Exact Computation of Time, According to the English Account.... London: 1615. V. 63

HOPWOOD, AUBREY
The Bunkum Book. London: 1900. V. 63

HORACE
Wells, Dentist. Father of Surgical Anesthesia. Proceedings of Centenary Commemorations of Wells' Discovery in 1844 and Lists of Wells memorabilia.... 1948. V. 64; 66

HORACE
Wells, Dentist. Father of Surgical Anesthesia. Proceedings of Wells' Discovery in 1844 and Lists of Wells Memorabilia. Hartford: 1948. V. 67

HORAE, C. A.
The Trypanosomes of Mammals, a Zoological Monograph. Oxford and Edinburgh: 1972. V. 67

HORAE, RICHARD COLT
Monastic Remains of the Religious Houses at Witham, Bruton and Stvordale, com somerset. Crockers: 1824. V. 67

HORAN, JAMES D.
The Life and Art of Charles Schreyvogel, Painter, Historian of the Indian Fighting Army of the American West. New York: 1969. V. 63
The McKenney-Hall Portrait Gallery of American Indians. New York: 1972. V. 62; 63
Timothy O'Sullivan: America's Forgotten Photographer. Garden City: 1966. V. 63

HORAN, ROBERT
A Beginning. New Haven: 1948. V. 63

HORATIUS FLACCUS, QUINTUS
Carmina Alcaica. 1903. V. 67
Carmina Alcaica. London: 1903. V. 65; 66
Carmina Sapphica. 1903. V. 62
Epitolae ad Pisones, et Augustum. London: 1776. V. 62
Horatii Tursellini, Romani Historiarum Ab Originer Mundi, Usque ad Annum a Christo Nato MDXCVIII. Ultrajecti: 1730. V. 65
The Odes. Oxford: 1838. V. 67
The Odes. London: 1843. V. 67
The Odes, Epodes, and Carmen Seculare of Horace. London: 1743-1746. V. 66
(*Opera*). Amstelodami: 1676. V. 63
Opera. London: 1733-1737. V. 63; 64; 66
(*Opera*). Birminghamiae: 1770. V. 65
(*Opera*). London: 1826. V. 62
Opera. Heidelburgiae et Spirae: 1827. V. 65
Opera. Paris: 1855. V. 62
Opera Cum Quibusdam Annotationibus. Strassburg: 1498. V. 64; 66
Opera, Cum Variis Lectionibus, Notis Variorum, et Indice Locupletissimo. Londoni: 1792-1793. V. 66; 67
Opera Dionys(ii) Lambini Monstroliensis Emendatus.... Lutetiae: 1567. V. 65
Opera Omnia. London: 1910. V. 65
A Poetical Translation of the Odes of Horace.... London: 1750. V. 62
A Poetical Translation of the Works of Horace.... London: 1749. V. 66
Q. Horatii Flacci, Quae Supersunt Recensuit et Notulis Instruxit Gilbertus Wakefield. London: 1794. V. 64; 66
Q. Horatius Flaccus: Cum Commentariis & Enarrationibus Commentatoris Veteris. 1611. V. 65
Q. Horatius Flaccus, Ex Antiquissimis Undecim Lib. M.S. et Schedis Aliquot Emendatus.... Antverpiae: 1579. V. 65
Q. Horatius Flaccus, Ex Recensione & cum Notis Atque Emendationibus Richardi Bentlii. Cantabrigiae: 1711. V. 66
Quinti Horati Flacci Carmina Alcaica. Chelsea: 1903. V. 65
Quinti Horatii Flacci Opera. London: 1733-1737. V. 66
Six Satires of Horace.... Ipswich: 1795. V. 63
Traduction des Oeuvres d'Horace en Vers Francois.... Paris: 1752. V. 64; 66
Works. Londini: 1820. V. 65
The Works of Horace, Translated Into English prose (along with the Latin Text) By C. Smart. London: 1790. V. 66

HORDER, GARRETT
The Treasury of American Sacred Songs. London and New York: 1896. V. 64; 65

HORE, J. P.
Sporting and Rural Records of the Chevely Estate. Newmarket: 1899. V. 67

HORGAN, PAUL
Approaches to Writing. New York: 1973. V. 67
The Centuries of Santa Fe. New York: 1956. V. 66
From the Royal City of the Holy Faith of St. Francis of Assisi Being Five Accounts of Life in that Place: the Captain General 1690. the Evening Air 1730. Triumphal Entry 1780. Bittersweet Waltz 1846. And Frock Coats and the Law 1878. Santa Fe: 1936. V. 63; 64
The Habit of Empire. Santa Fe: 1939. V. 62; 65
Lamy of Santa Fe. New York: 1975. V. 63
Mexico Bay. New York: 1982. V. 67
The Return of the Weed. Flagstaff: 1980. V. 63; 64
The Saintmaker's Christmas Eve. New York: 1955. V. 67

HORGAN, PAUL continued
Songs After Lincoln. New York: 1965. V. 62
Under the Sangre de Cristo. Santa Fe: 1982. V. 63; 64
Under the Sangre de Cristo. Santa Fe: 1985. V. 66

HORKHEIMER, MAX
Kants Kritik der Urteilskraft als Bindeglied Zwischen Theoretischer und Praktischer Philosophie. Frankfurt: 1925. V. 67

HORLER, SYDNEY
High Stakes. Boston: 1935. V. 67

HORLOCK, K. W.
Letters on the Management of Hounds. 1852. V. 67
The Squire of Beechwood. London: 1857. V. 66

HORN, CALVIN
New Mexico's Trouble Years: the Story of the Early Territorial Governors. Albuquerque: 1963. V. 63; 66

HORN, HOSEA B.
Horn's Overland Guide to California. New York: 1852. V. 66

HORN, ISOBEL
King George and the Turkish Knight - Old Sussex Play. Ditchling, Sussex: 1921. V. 62

HORN, J.
A History or Description, General and Circumstantial of Burghley House. Shrewsbury: 1797. V. 66

HORN, MADELINE DARROUGH
Log Cabin Family. New York: 1930. V. 63

HORN, STANLEY F.
The Army of the Tennessee. Norman: 1942. V. 62; 63
The Decisive Battle of Nashville. Baton Roge: 1956. V. 63
Gallant Rebel. The Fabulous Cruise of the C.S.S. Shenadoah. New Brunswick: 1947. V. 63

HORN, TOM
Life of Tom Horn, Government Scout and Interpretor. Denver: 1904. V. 62; 65; 66

HORN, W. DONALD
Witnesses for the Defense of General George Armstrong Custer. Short Hills: 1981. V. 65; 67

HORN, WALTER
The Plan of Gall, a Study of the Architecture and Economy of and Life in a Paradigmatic Carolingian Monastery. Berkeley: 1979. V. 66

HORNADAY, WILLIAM T.
Camp Fires on Desert and Lava. New York: 1909. V. 65
Camp-Fires in the Canadian Rockies. New York: 1906. V. 63; 64; 66
Camp-Fires on Desert and Lava. New York: 1908. V. 63
The Extermination of the American Bison.... Washington: 1889. V. 64
Two Years in the Jungle.... New York: 1885. V. 62

HORNBY, CHARLES H. ST. JOHN
A Descriptive Bibliography of the Books Printed at the Ashendene Press MDCCCXCV-MCMXXXV. 1935. V. 62

HORNBY, EDMUND, MRS.
In and Around Stamboul. Philadelphia: 1859. V. 67

HORNBY, EMILY
A Nile Journal. Liverpool: 1908. V. 67

HORNBY, NICK
Fever Pitch. London: 1992. V. 62; 66; 67
High Fidelity. London: 1995. V. 63

HORNE, GEORGE
A Fair, Candid and Impartial State of the Case Between Sir Isaac Newton and Mr. Hutchinson. Oxford: 1753. V. 63
A Letter to Adam Smith...On the Life, Death and Philosophy of His Friend David Hume.... London: 1813. V. 63
Letters on Infidelity. Oxford: 1786. V. 62
A Picture of the Female Character, As It Out to Appear When Formed. Poughnill, near Ludlow: 1801. V. 67

HORNE, HERBERT P.
The Binding of Books: an Essay in the History of Gold Tooled Bindings. London: 1894. V. 62; 63; 64; 67
Diversi Colores. London: 1891. V. 64

HORNE, JOHN
The Diversions of an Autograph Hunter. London: 1894. V. 63
Many Days in Morocco. London: 1925. V. 65

HORNE, M. J.
The Adventures of Naufragus. London: 1828. V. 65

HORNE, R. H.
A New Spirit of the Age. London: 1844. V. 64

HORNE, THOMAS HARTWELL
An Introduction to the Study of Bibliography. London: 1814. V. 63; 65; 67
The Lakes of Lancashire, Westmorland, and Cumberland.... London: 1816. V. 65; 66; 67

HORNECKER, MARTIN
Buffalo Hunting on the Texas Plains in 1879. N.P: 1929. V. 65

HORNER, GEORGE R. B.
Medical Topography of Brazil and Uruguay with Incidental Remarks. Philadelphia: 1845. V. 64

HORNER, J.
Bilder Des Griechischen Alterthums Oder Darstellung der Berghumtesten Gegenden Und Der Wichetigsten Kunstwerke Des Alten Griechenlandes. Zurich: 1823. V. 65

HORNER, JOHN WILLARD
Silver Town. Caldwell: 1950. V. 63

HORNER, LEONARD
Memoirs and Correspondence of Francis Horner.... London: 1843. V. 62

HORNER, R. A.
Sea Ice Biota. Boca Raton: 1985. V. 65

HORNIBROOK, MURRAY
Dwarf and Slow Growing Conifers. London: 1923. V. 67

HORNOR, WILLIAM S.
This Old Monmouth of Ours. Freehold: 1932. V. 66
This Old Monmouth of Ours. Cottonport: 1974. V. 63; 66

HORNUNG, CLARENCE P.
Trademarks. New York: 1930. V. 67
Treasury of American Design. New York: 1976. V. 67

HORNUNG, E. W.
Dead Men Tell No Tales. New York: 1899. V. 63; 64; 66
Mr. Justice Raffles. London: 1909. V. 66

HORNYOLD, HENRY
Genealogical Memoirs of the Family of Strickland of Sizergh. Kendal: 1928. V. 66

HORODISCH, ABRAHAM
Pablo Picasso als Buchkunstler. Frankfurt am Main: 1957. V. 63
Picasso as a Book Artist. London: 1962. V. 62

HORRAX, GILBERT
Neurosurgery - an Historical Sketch. Springfield: 1952. V. 64; 65; 66

HORRY, ELIAS
Address Respecting the Charleston and Hamburg Rail-Road.... Charleston: 1833. V. 66

HORSFALL, SAMUEL
Sermons on Different Subjects. Barnsley: 1800. V. 64

HORSFALL, THOMAS
Notes on the Manor of Well and Snape in the North Riding of the Coutny of York. Leeds: 1912. V. 65

HORSFIELD, T.
A Catalogue of the Mammalia in the Musuem of the Hon. East-India Company. London: 1851. V. 62

HORSFORD, EBEN NORTON
The Discovery of the Ancient City of Norumbega. Cambridge: 1889. V. 63; 66; 67

HORSIN-DEON, SIMON
De la Conservation et de la Restauration des Tableaux.... Paris: 1851. V. 66

HORSLEY, J. SHELTON
Surgery of the Stomach and Small Intestine. New York: 1926. V. 67

HORSLEY, JOHN
Britannia Romana, or the Roman Antiquities of Britain. Newcastle upon Tyne: 1974. V. 64
The Case of John Horsley, Esq. late Captain in the Royal Regiment of Horse Guards Blue. London: 1805. V. 63

HORSTI, GREGOR
Centvria Problematvm Medicorvm (Greek text). Continens Gravissimorum Affectuum Cognitionem & Curationem. Norigergae: 1636. V. 67

HORT, RICHARD
The Embroidered Banner, and Other Marvels. London: 1850. V. 66
Penelope Wedgebone: the Supposed Heiress. London: 1850. V. 67

HORTEGA, PIO DEL
The Microscopic Anatomy of Tumors of the Central and Peripheral Nervous System. Springfield: 1962. V. 66

HORTICULTURAL SOCIETY OF LONDON
Transactions. 1820-1835. V. 65

HORTON, DAVID
Celestial Wondering. 1995. V. 64

HORTON, LYDIARD HENEAGE WALTER
Dream Problem and the Mechanism of Thought Viewed from the Biological Standpoint. Philadelphia: 1926. V. 65

HORTON, ROBERT WILMOT
Speech of the Right Honble R. Wilmot Horton, in the House of Commons on the 6th of March, 1828, on Moving for the Production of the Evidence, Taken Before the Privy Council, Upon an Appeal Against the Compulsory of Slaves in Demerara and Berbice, with No. London: 1828. V. 66

HORTON, W. T.
A Book of Images. London: 1898. V. 64
William Thomas Horton (1864-1929) - a Selection of His Work. London: 1929. V. 63

HORWITZ, E. L.
Contemporary American Folk Artists. Philadelphia and New York: 1975. V. 65

HORWITZ, JONATHAN
Mock and Absurd Philosophy: a Word to the Reasonable. Boston: 1811. V. 64

HORWOOD, A. R.
British Wild Flowers in Natural Haunts. London: 1919. V. 64

HOSACK, DAVID
An Inaugural Discourse, Delivered at the Opening of Rutgers Medical College, in the City of New York. New York: 1826. V. 62; 65
The Memoir of De Witt Clinton with an Appendix. New York: 1829. V. 64

HOSE, CHARLES
The Field-Book of a Jungle Wallah. London: 1929. V. 67
Fifty Years of Romance and Research or a Jungle Wallah at Large. London: 1927. V. 62
The Pagan Tribes of Borneo; a Description of their Physical, Moral and Intellectual Condition, with Some Discussion of Their Ethnic Relations. London: 1912. V. 67

HOSIE, ALEXANDER
Manchuria; Its People, Resources and Recent History. London: 1901. V. 67
On the Trail of the Opium Poppy; a Narrative of Travel in the Chief Opium-Producing Provinces of China. London: 1914. V. 67

HOSIE, LADY
Portrait of a Chinese Lady. London: 1929. V. 67

HOSIER, JOHN
The Mariner's Friend, or a Treatise on the Stars.... London: 1809. V. 65

HOSKING, WILLIAM
A Guide to the Proper Regulation of Buildings in Towns as a Means of Promoting and Securing the Health, Comfort and Safety of the Inhabitants. London: 1848. V. 65

HOSKINS, W. G.
The Common Lands of England and Wales. London: 1963. V. 63

HOSKYN, RICHARD
Sailing Directions for the Coast of Ireland. Part II. 1887. V. 67

HOSKYNS, CHANDOS WREN
Talpa; or the Chronicles of a Clay Farm. London: 1857. V. 65

HOSMER, JAMES K.
The Color Guard. Boston: 1864. V. 63; 66

HOSMER, WILLIAM H. C.
Yonnondio, or Warriors of the Genesee; a Tale of the Seventeenth Century. New York: 1844. V. 62

HOSTE, WILLIAM
Memoirs and Letters. London: 1833. V. 63

HOSTETTER & SMITH
Hostetter's Illustrated United States Almanac. Pittsburgh: 1875. V. 67

HOTCHKISS, JEDEDIAH
Virginia: a Geographical and Political Summary. Richmond: 1876. V. 65

HOTMAN, ANTOINE
Traicte De La Dissolution Du Marriage, Pour l'Impuissance & Froideur de l'Homme ou de la Femme. (with) Second Traicte de la Dissolution du Marriage, Pour l'Impuissance de l'Homme ou de la Femme. Paris: 1610. V. 65

HOTSON, LESLIE
Shakespeare Versus Shallow. London: 1931. V. 65

HOTTEN, JOHN CAMDEN
Abyssinia and Its People; or Life in the Land of Prester John.... London: 1868. V. 62
Charles Dickens: the Story of His Life. London: 1870. V. 62
A Dictionary of Modern Slang, Cant and Vulgar Words, Used at the Present Day in the Streets of London.... London: 1859. V. 64; 67
The Original Lists of Persons of Quality: Emigrants, Religious Exiles, Political Rebels; Serving Men Sold for a term of Years 1600-1700. New York: 1874. V. 67
The Piccadilly Annual of Entertaining Literature. London: 1870. V. 66
Sarcastic Notices of the Long Parliament...Giving Many Famous Particulars.... London: 1863. V. 66
The Slang Dictionary. London: 1864. V. 62; 64
The Slang Dictionary. London: 1872. V. 64

HOTTENROTH, FREDERIC
Le Costume. Les Armes. Les Bijoux. La Cermaique. Les Utensils, Qutils, Objets, Mobiliers, Etc.... Paris: 1885. V. 64

HOTTON, N.
The Ecology and Biology of the Mammal-like Reptiles. Washington: 1986. V. 67

HOUDINI, HARRY
Miracle Mongers and Their Methods. New York: 1920. V. 64
The Unmasking of Robert-Houdin. New York: 1908. V. 63; 65

HOUFE, SIMON
The Dictionary of British Book Illustrators and Caricaturists 1900- 1914. 1978. V. 63

HOUGH, EMERSON
The Story of Cowboy. New York: 1897. V. 63; 66

HOUGH, FRANKLIN B.
Report Upon Forestry. Washington: 1878. V. 63
Washingtoniana; or, Memorials of the Death of George Washington.... Roxbury: 1865. V. 67

HOUGH, RICHARD
The BP Book of the Racing Campbells. London: 1960. V. 62

HOUGH, S. B.
Sweet Sister Seduced. London: 1968. V. 67

HOUGH, SAMUEL J.
The Beinecke Lesser Antilles Collection at Hamilton College. Gainesville: 1994. V. 64; 65; 66

HOUGH, WALTER
The Hopi Indians. Cedar Rapids: 1915. V. 63; 64

HOUGHTON, ARTHUR A.
Books and Manuscripts from the Library of Arthur A. Houghton, Jr. London: 1979. V. 66
The Collection of Miniature Books Formed by Arthur A. Houghton, Jr. London: 1979. V. 66

HOUGHTON, CLAUDE
The Beast. Belfast: 1936. V. 66
Three Fantastic Tales. London: 1934. V. 67

HOUGHTON, FREDERICK W.
The Story of the Settle-Carlisle Line. Bradford: 1948. V. 63; 64; 65
The Story of the Settle-Carlisle Line. Huddersfield: 1965. V. 64

HOUGHTON, GEORGE
Golfers' ABC - Golphabet for Addicts. London: 1953. V. 64

HOUGHTON, GEORGE L.
Appealed Cases - a History of Certain Court Corruptions in the U.S. and State Courts of Dakota. Vermillion: 1895. V. 62; 65

HOUGHTON, JOHN
A Collection of Letters for the Improvement of Husbandry and Trade. London: 1681. V. 64
Husbandry and Trade Improv'd.... London: 1728. V. 62; 63

HOUGHTON, RICHARD MONCKTON MILNES, 1ST BARON
The Real Union of England and Ireland. London: 1845. V. 65

HOUGHTON, THOMAS
Royal Institutions: Being Proposals for Articles to Establish and Confirm Laws, Liberties, and Customs of Silver and Gold Mines, To All the King's Subjects, in Such Parts of Africa and America.... London: 1694. V. 66

HOUGHTON, W.
British Fresh Water Fishes. 1879. V. 65; 66
British Fresh Water Fishes. London: 1879. V. 62; 64; 65
British Freshwater Fishes. 1895. V. 63; 66
British Freshwater Fishes. London: 1895. V. 62
Country Walks of a Naturalist with his Children. London: 1870. V. 64; 65

HOUGHTON, WILLIAM ROBERT
Two Boys in the Civil War and After. Montgomery: 1912. V. 62; 63; 65

HOUGLAN, WILLARD
Santos - a Primitive American Art. New York: 1946. V. 62; 65

HOULGATE, DEKE
Frans Nelson - a Biography. Los Angeles: 1940. V. 67

HOULIHAN, D. F.
Gills. Cambridge: 1982. V. 65

HOULIHAN, PATRICK T.
Lummis in the Pueblos. Flagstaff: 1986. V. 63

HOUSE, BOYCE
Oil Field Fury. San Antonio: 1954. V. 62

HOUSE, EDWARD M.
Philip Dru: Administrator, a Story of Tomorrow 1920-1935. New York: 1920. V. 63

HOUSE, HOMER D.
Wild Flowers of New York, in Two Parts. Albany: 1918. V. 63; 64; 65

HOUSE, M. R.
The Ammonoidea, the Evolution, Classification, Mode of Life and Geological Usefulness of a Major Fossil Group. New York: 1981. V. 65

THE HOUSE That Jack Built. 1823. V. 66
THE HOUSE That Jack Built. Philadelphia: 1835. V. 64
THE HOUSE That Jack Built. New York: 1889. V. 64

THE HOUSE that Jack Built. New York: 1891. V. 63

THE HOUSE That Jack Built. London: 1950. V. 63

THE HOUSEHOLD Domestic Hygiene, Foods and Drinks, Common Diseases, Accidents and Emgergencies and Useful Hints and Recipes. Battle Creek: 1875. V. 64

HOUSEHOLD, GEOFFREY
Rogue Male. London: 1939. V. 64
The Salvation of Pisco Gabar. London: 1938. V. 67

THE HOUSEHOLD Manual of Domestic Hygiene, Foods and Drinks, Common Diseases, Accidents and Emgergencies, and Useful Hints and Recipes. Battle Creek: 1875. V. 66

THE HOUSEHOLD Narrative of Current Events.... London: 1850-1853. V. 62

HOUSERIGHT, DAVID
Penance. Woodstock: 1995. V. 62; 64; 66; 67

HOUSMAN, ALFRED EDWARD
Last Poems. London: 1922. V. 65
More Poems. London: 1936. V. 63
A Morning with the Royal Family. London: 1955. V. 66
A Shropshire Lad. London: 1898. V. 67
A Shropshire Lad. Waterville: 1946. V. 65

HOUSMAN, C., MRS.
Letter to Dr. Spry, in Vindication of the Word of God Against Every Species of Scientific Opposition. London: 1839. V. 67

HOUSMAN, CLEMENCE
The Were-Wolf. London: 1896. V. 62; 63; 64; 66; 67

HOUSMAN, JOHN
A Descriptive Tour and Guide to the Lakes, Caves, Mountains and Other Natural Curiosities in Cumberland, Westmoreland, Lancashire. Carlisle: 1802. V. 63
A Descriptive Tour and Guide to the Lakes, Caves, Mountains and Other Natural Curiosities, in Cumberland, Westmoreland, Lancashire.... 1808. V. 64; 65; 66
A Descriptive Tour and Guide to the Lakes, Caves, Mountains and Other Natural Curiosities in Cumberland, Westmoreland, Lancashire.... Carlisle: 1812. V. 65

HOUSMAN, LAURENCE
Alice in Ganderland - A One Act Play. London: 1911. V. 64
All-Fellows: Seven Legends of Lower Redemption. London: 1896. V. 64
An Englishwoman's Love-Letters. London: 1900. V. 64
A Farm in Fairyland. London: 1894. V. 64; 65
The Field of Clover. London: 1898. V. 64
The Field of Clover. New York: 1902. V. 66
Gods and Their Makers. New York and London: 1897. V. 64
The House of Joy. London: 1895. V. 64
A Modern Antaeus. New York: 1901. V. 63
Princess Badoura. London: 1912. V. 66
Princess Badoura. London: 1913. V. 62
Prunella or Love in a Dutch Garden. London: 1906. V. 62; 67
Rue. London: 1899. V. 64
Stories from the Arabian Nights. London: 1907. V. 65; 66; 67
Stories from the Arabian Nights. New York: 1907. V. 65
Trimblerigg. New York: 1925. V. 64

HOUSTON, A. ROSS
War Papers - Read Before the Commanderty of the State of Wisconsin, Military Order of the Loyal Legion of the United States. Volume I. Milwaukee: 1891. V. 65; 67

HOUSTON, ANDREW JACKSON
Texas Independence. Houston: 1938. V. 67

HOUSTON, JAMES D.
Three Songs for My Father. Santa Barbara: 1974. V. 63

HOUSTON, PAM
Cowboys are My Weakness. London: 1983. V. 65
Cowboys are My Weakness. New York: 1992. V. 62; 63; 65; 66; 67
Cowboys are My Weakness. London: 1993. V. 67
A Little More About Me. New York: 1999. V. 67
Waltzing the Cat. New York: 1998. V. 66; 67
Women on Hunting. Hopewell: 1994. V. 67
Women on Hunting. New York: 1994. V. 63

HOUSTON, SAM
Ever Thine Truly. Austin: 1975. V. 63
Speech of General Sam Houston of Texas Refuting Calumnies Produced and Circulated Against His Character as Commander-in-Chief of the Army of Texas. Washington: 1859. V. 64

HOUTTUYN, MARTINUS
Houtkunde, Behelzende de Afbeeldingen van Meest alle Bekund in en Uitlandsche Houten.... Amsterdam: 1773-1791. V. 66

HOVELL-THURLOW, T. J.
Trade Unions Abroad and Hints for Home Legislation.... London: 1870. V. 64

HOVENDEN, R., & SONS
Album of Historical Coiffures with Technical Descriptions and Biographical Details. London: 1911. V. 64

HOVEY, HORACE
Celebrated American Caverns, Especially Mammoth, Wyandot and Luray. Cincinnati: 1882. V. 66

HOVGAARD, G. W.
Submarine Boats. London: 1887. V. 64

HOW Can the Young Lady Hood of England Assist in Improving the Condition of the Working Classes?. Bristol: 185-. V. 64

HOW to Abolish Slavery in America, and to Prevent a Cotton Famine in England with Remarks Upon Collie and African Emigration. London: 1858. V. 67

HOW to Catch Trout. Edinburgh: 1888. V. 64

HOW to Hunt Ducks, Geese, Turkeys, Grouse, Woodcock, Quail and Complete Directions for Mounting Specimens in Your Own Home by an Experienced Taxidermist. London. V. 67

HOW to Read Character: a New Illustrated Hand-Book on Phrenology and Physiognomy. New York: 1871. V. 64; 66; 67

HOW, WILLIAM
Phytologia Britannica.... London: 1650. V. 62

HOWARD, A. E. DICK
Commentaries on the Constitution of Virginia. Charlottesville: 1974. V. 67

HOWARD, ALICE WOODBURY
Ching-Li and the Dragons. New York: 1931. V. 66

HOWARD, BENJAMIN
Report of the Decision of the Supreme Court of the United States and the Opinions of the Judges Thereof, in the Case of Dred Scott Versus John F. Sandford. Washington: 1857. V. 63; 65

HOWARD, C.
Howard's Art of Computation and Golden Rule for Equation of Payments. San Francisco: 1881. V. 67

HOWARD, EDWARD
Rattlin, the Reefer. London: 1850. V. 67

HOWARD, F.
Imitative Art, or the Means of Representing the Pictorial Appearances of Objects, as Governed by Aerial and Linear Perspective.... London: 1842. V. 66; 67

HOWARD, F. E.
English Church Woodwork. London: 1917. V. 65
English Church Woodwork. London: 1927. V. 67
English Church Woodwork. London: 1933. V. 62

HOWARD, FRANK
Colour as a Means of Art.... London: 1838. V. 62
The Science of Drawing. London: 1839-1840. V. 65

HOWARD, GEORGE
Lady Jane Grey and Her Times. London: 1822. V. 67

HOWARD, H. ELIOT
The British Warblers, a History With Problems of Their Lives. London: 1907-1915. V. 62; 67

HOWARD, HELEN ADDISON
War Chief Joseph. Caldwell: 1941. V. 64

HOWARD, HENRY
The Anatomy, Physiology and Pathology of the Eye. Montreal: 1850. V. 65
A Defensatiue Against the Poyson of Supposed Prophesies. London: 1583. V. 64; 66
The Original Poems of Henry Howard. London: 1929. V. 63; 64; 66

HOWARD, HUTTON
A Treatise on the Complaints Peculiar to Females.... Columbus: 1832. V. 64

HOWARD, JOHN
An Account of the Principal Lazarettos in Europe.... Warrington: 1789. V. 62
The Illustrated Scripture History, for the Young. New York: 1845. V. 62
The State of the Prisons in England and Wales. Warrington: 1780. V. 63
The State of the Prisons in England and Wales.... Warrington: 1777. V. 63
The State of the Prisons in England and Wales.... Warrington: 1780. V. 63
The Works of John Howard; the State of the Prisons in England and Wales.... London: 1792-1791. V. 65

HOWARD, JOHN E.
Examination of Pavon's Collection of Peruvian Barks Contained in the British Museum. 1853. V. 62
Strayed Shots and Frayed Lines. Clinton: 1981. V. 65
Strayed Shots and Frayed Lines. Clinton: 1982. V. 65

HOWARD, L. O.
A History of Applied Entomology. Washington: 1930. V. 62

HOWARD, MARY MATILDA
Hastings, Past an Present; with Notices of the Most Remarkable Places in the Neighbourhood.... Hastings: 1855. V. 65

HOWARD, MC HENRY
Recollections of a Maryland Confederate Soldier and Staff Officer Under Johnston, Jackson & Lee. Baltimore: 1914. V. 64

HOWARD, MISSION
Little Wanderer's Friend. New York: 1868. V. 67

HOWARD, O. O.
Autobiography of.... New York: 1908. V. 63
Famous Indian Chiefs I Have Known. New York: 1908. V. 65; 67
My Life and Experiences Among Our Hostile Indians. Hartford: 1907. V. 64; 65; 67
Nez Perce Joseph. Boston: 1881. V. 67

HOWARD, RICHARD
Alone With America: Essays on the Art of Poetry in the United States Since 1950. New York: 1969. V. 66
Family Values. Poems. New York: 1998. V. 62; 64; 66; 67
Findings. New York: 1971. V. 63; 67
Like Most Revelations: New Poems. New York: 1994. V. 63
Misgivings. New York: 1979. V. 63; 67
Try These on for Size. East Hampton: 1997. V. 67
Try These On for Size. New York: 1997. V. 62
Two-Part Inventions. Poems. New York: 1974. V. 63; 67

HOWARD, ROBERT
Four New Plays, viz. The Surprisal, The Committee (Comedies). The Indian Queen, The Vestal Virgin (Tragedies), as They Were Acted by His Majesties Servants at the Theatre Royal. London: 1665. V. 62; 66

The Life and Reign of King Richard the Second. London: 1681. V. 67

Saturnian Religion, the Shield of Health; Showing That Diseases are Propagated and the Rites of Christianity Violated by the Modern Systems of Diet and Medicine. London: 1851. V. 63

Treatise on Salt, Showing Its Hurtful Effects on the Human Body and Mind of Man and on Animals; Its Tendency to Cause Diseases, Especially Consumption.... London: 1850. V. 62

HOWARD, ROBERT E.
Always Come Evening. 1957. V. 66
Always Come Evening. Sauk City: 1957. V. 64
Conan the Conqueror. 1950. V. 64; 66
A Gent from Bear Creek. 1965. V. 64; 66
King Conan. 1953. V. 64; 66
The Pride of Bear Creek. 1966. V. 64; 66
The Sword of Conan. 1952. V. 64; 66

HOWARD, ROBERT MILTON
Reminiscences. Columbus: 1912. V. 62; 63

HOWARD, ROBERT MOWBRAY
Record and Letters of the Family of the Longs of Longville, Jamaica and Hampton Lodge, Surrey. London: 1925. V. 67

HOWARD, SARAH ELIZABETH
Pen Pictures of the Plains. Denver: 1902. V. 63; 65

HOWARD, THOMAS
On the Loss of Teeth; and on the Best Means of Restoring Them. London: 1857. V. 62
On the Loss of Teeth; and on the Best Means of Restoring Them. London: 1858. V. 64

HOWARD-BURY, C. K.
Mount Everest. The Reconnaissance, 1921. 1922. V. 63

HOWARTH, HERBERT
Images from the Arab World; Fragments of Arab Literature. London: 1944. V. 67

HOWARTH, PATRICK
Special Operations. London: 1955. V. 65

HOWAY, F. W.
Voyages of the Columbia to the Northwest Coast 4787-1790 and 1790-1793. Boston: 1941. V. 64; 66
The Work of the Royal Engineers in British Columbia, 1858-1863. Victoria: 1910. V. 66

HOWBERT, A.
Reminiscences of the War. Springfield: 1888. V. 66

HOWBERT, IRVING
Memories of a Lifetime. New York: 1925. V. 67

HOWBERT, R. A.
Reminiscences of the War. Springfield: 1888. V. 63

HOWE, ALEXANDER HAMILTON
A Theoretical Inquiry into the Physical Cause of Epidemic Diseases Accompanied with Tables. London: 1865. V. 65

HOWE, BARBARA
The Undersea Farmer. Pawlet: 1948. V. 67

HOWE, EDGAR WATSON
The Story of a Country Town. Atchison: 1883. V. 64; 67

HOWE, ELLIC
The London Bookbinders 1780-1806. London: 1950. V. 64

HOWE, GORDON
Hockey...Here's Howe!. N.P: 1963. V. 66

HOWE, HENRY
Historical Collections of Ohio. Cincinnati: 1847. V. 65
Historical Collections of Ohio. Cincinnati: 1908. V. 63
Historical Collections of Virginia. Charleston: 1845. V. 62
Historical Collections of Virginia. Charleston: 1856. V. 64

HOWE, JOHN
The Christian's Pocket Companion. Enfield: 1826. V. 62; 63
A Funeral Sermon for Mrs. Esther Sampson, the Late Wife of Henry Sampson, Dr. of Physick, Who died Nov. 24 MDCLXXXIX. London: 1690. V. 65

HOWE, JULIA W.
Later Lyrics. Boston: 1866. V. 63

HOWE, M. A.
The Marine Algae of Peru. N.P: 1914. V. 67

HOWE, OCTAVIUS T.
American Clipper Ships 1833-1858. New York: 1967. V. 63
Argonauts of '49. History and Adventures of Emigrant Companies from Massachusetts 1849-1850. Cambridge: 1923. V. 65

HOWE, PAUL STURTEVANT
Mayflower Pilgrim Descendants in Cape May County, New Jersey...1620-1920.... Cape May: 1921. V. 63; 66

HOWE, S.
The Causes of Idiocy.... Edinburgh: 1858. V. 64

HOWE, SAMUEL GRIDLEY
An Essay on Separate and Congregate Systems of Prison Discipline.... Boston: 1846. V. 64

HOWE, SUSAN
Incloser. An Essay. Santa Fe: 1992. V. 64; 67
The Nonconformist's Memorial. New York: 1992. V. 67

HOWE, W. H.
The Butterflies of North America. Garden City: 1975. V. 64

HOWE, W. W.
Kinston, Whitehall and Goldsboro (North Carolina) Expedition December 1862. New York: 1890. V. 62; 63; 65

HOWLETT'S *Victoria Golden Almanack for 1853.* London: 1852. V. 67

HOWELL, G.
In Vogue: 60 Years of International Celebrities and Fashion from British Vogue. New York: 1976. V. 65
In Vogue: 60 Years of International Celebrities and Fashion from British Vogue. New York: 1978. V. 62

HOWELL, GEORGE
The Conflicts of Capital and Labour Historically and Economically Considered, Being a History and Review of the Trade Unions of Great Britain.... London: 1878. V. 64

HOWELL, J. B. L.
Breathlessness. Oxford: 1966. V. 65

HOWELL, JAMES
A Discourse Concerning the Precedency of Kings: Wherein the Reasons and Arguments of the Three Greatest Monarks of Christendom.... London: 1668?. V. 66
Dodona's Grove, or, the Vocall Forrest. London: 1640. V. 64; 66
Epistolae Ho-Elianae: Familiar Letters Domestic and Foreign.... London: 1726. V. 66; 67
Epistolae Ho-Elianae or the Familiar Letters. Boston: 1907. V. 63
Londinopolis, an Historical Discourse or Perlustration of the City of London, The Imperial Chamber, and Chief Emporium of Great Britain. London: 1657. V. 65
The Pre-Eminence and Pedigree of Parlement. London: 1645. V. 66

HOWELL, JOHN W.
Stories for My Children. Washington: 1930. V. 63; 66

HOWELL, LAURENCE
The Orthodox Communicant, by Way of Meditation on the Order for the Administration of Lord's Supper, or Holy Communion.... London: 1721. V. 64

HOWELL, WILLIAM
Medulla Historiae Anglicanae. London: 1694. V. 63
Some Interesting Particulars of the Second Voyage Made by the Missionary Ship, the Duff.... Knaresborough: 1809. V. 67

HOWELLS, WILLIAM DEAN
Atlantic Monthly. Boston: 1858. V. 64
A Boy's Town. New York: 1890. V. 62; 66
A Hazard of New Fortunes. New York: 1890. V. 62
Italian Journeys. London: 1901. V. 64
Miss Bellard's Inspiration. New York: 1905. V. 67
My Mark Twain. Reminiscences and Criticisms. New York: 1910. V. 63
Their Silver Wedding Journey. New York and London: 1899. V. 66
The Undiscovered Country. Boston: 1880. V. 66; 67
Venetian Life. Boston;: 1887. V. 66

HOWES, BARBARA
In the Cold Country. New York: 1954. V. 66
The Triumph of Love. Poems. New York: 1980. V. 66
The Undersea Farmer. Pawlet: 1948. V. 63

HOWES, JAMES VIRGIL
The Modern Gunsmith. London: 1944. V. 67

HOWES, WRIGHT
U.S. iana. Mansfield. V. 63
U.S. Iana. (1700-1950). New York: 1954. V. 64
U.S. Iana (1650-1950). New York: 1988. V. 62; 65

HOWIE, EDITH
Murder for Christmas. New York: 1941. V. 66

HOWISON, NEIL
Oregon. Report of Lieut. Neil M. Howison, United States Navy to the Commander of the Pacific Squadron; Being the Result of an Examination in the Year 1846 of the Coast, Harbors, Rivers, Soil, Productions, Climate and Population of the Territory of Oregon. Washington: 1848. V. 64

HOWISON, ROBERT R.
A History of Virginia from Its Discovery and Settlement. Philadelphia and Richmond: 1846-1848. V. 64

HOWITT, MARY
Jacob Bendixen, the Jew. London: 1852. V. 65
No Sense Like Common Sense; or Some Passages in the Life of Charles Middleton, Esq. London: 1843. V. 65
The Seven Temptations. London: 1834. V. 65

HOWITT, WILLIAM
A Boy's Adventures in the Wilds of Australia; or, Herbert's Note Book. London: 1855. V. 66

HOWITT, WILLIAM continued
The Hall and the Hamlet; or Scenes and Characters of Country Life. London: 1848. V. 67
Land, Labor and Gold; or Two Years in Victoria with Visits to Sydney and Van Diemen's Land. London: 1855. V. 67
The Life and Adventures of Jack of the Mill; Commonly Called Lord Othmill.... London: 1844. V. 67
Madam Dorrington of the Dene. The Story of a Life. London: 1852. V. 66
The Rural Life of England. London: 1838. V. 62
Stories of English and Foreign Life. London: 1853. V. 67
Visits to Remarkable Places: Old Halls, Battle Fields, and Scenes Illustrative of Striking Passages in English History and Poetry. London: 1840. V. 62

HOWLAND, E. P.
A Tale of Home and War. Portland: 1888. V. 64

HOWLAND, RICHARD H.
The Architecture of Baltimore: a Pictorial History. Baltimore: 1953. V. 65

HOWLETT, BARTHOLOMEW
A Selection of Views in the County of Lincoln; Comprising the Principal Towns and Churches, the Remains of Castles and Religious Houses, and Seats of the Nobility and Gentry, with Topographical and Historical Accounts of Each View. London: 1805. V. 65

HOWLETT, JOHN
An Enquiry Concerning the Influence of Tithes Upon Agriculture, Whether in the Hands of the Clergy or the Laity. London: 1801. V. 67

HOWLETT'S Victoria Golden Almanack for 1853. London: 1852. V. 67

HOWLEY, JAMES P.
The Beothucks or Red Indians. Cambridge: 1915. V. 62; 67

HOWSHIP, JOHN
Practical Observations on the Symptoms Discrimination & Treatment... Diseases of the Lower Intestines & Anus.... Philadelphia: 1821. V. 67

HOWSON, WILLIAM
An Illustrated Guide to the Curiosities of Craven. London: 1850. V. 64; 66

HOY, PATRICK C.
A Brief History of Bradford's Battery, Confederate Guards Artillery. Pontotoc: 1982. V. 62; 65

HOYEM, ANDREW
Picture/Poems: An Illustrated Catalogue of Drawings and Related Writings: 1961-1974. San Francisco: 1975. V. 64; 66

HOYER, MARIA A.
Good Dame Fortune. London: 1894. V. 65

HOYLAND, WILLIAM
Poems by the Reverend Mr. Hoyland. 1769. V. 65

HOYLE, EDMUND
Hoyle's Games Improved.... London: 1782. V. 62
A Short Treatise of the Game of Brag. London: 1751. V. 63; 64

HOYLE, ZOE
The Peek-A-Boos' Desert Island. New York: 1922. V. 64

HOYLE'S Games: Containing Established Rules and Practice of Whist, Quadrille, Chess...Draughts...Cricket...Billiards...Tennis, Goff or Golf.... Philadelphia: 1845. V. 66

HOYLE'S Games Improved and Enlarged. London: 1835. V. 62

HOYT, ELISABETH
Santa Claus' Dolls. Boston and Chicago: 1911. V. 62

HOYT, HENRY
A Frontier Doctor. Boston: 1929. V. 64

HOYT, JAMES A.
Palmetto Riflemen, Co. B. Fourth Regiment S.C. Volunteers Co. C, Palmetto Sharp Shooters. Greenville: 1886. V. 62

HOZIER, H. M.
The Franco-Prusian War: Its Causes, Incidents and Consequences. London: 1871 1872. V. 62; 65
The Seven Weeks' War. London: 1867. V. 65

HRDLICKA, ALEX
Early Man in South America. Washington: 1912. V. 66
Melanesians and Australians and the Peopling of America. Washington: 1933. V. 66; 67
Physiological and Medical Observations Among the Indians of Southwestern United States and Northern Mexico. Washington: 1908. V. 66; 67
Skeletal Remains Suggesting or Attributed to Early Man in North America. Washington: 1907. V. 67
Tuberculosis Among Certain Tribes of the United States. Washington: 1909. V. 66; 67

HROTSVIT, OF GANDERSHEIM
Abraham, a Play. 1922. V. 63
Callimachus. 1923. V. 63

HUARD, C. L.
Livre d'Or de l'Exposition. Paris: 1889. V. 67

HUARTE DE SAN JUAN, JUAN
Examen de Ingenios. The Examination of Mens Wits. London: 1604. V. 64; 66

HUBBACK, T. R.
Elephant and Seladang Hunting in the Federated Malay States. London: 1905. V. 67
To Far Western Alaska for Big Game. 1994. V. 66

HUBBARD, ARTHUR JOHN
Neolithic Dew-Ponds and Cattle-Ways. London: 1916. V. 62

HUBBARD, ELBERT
Advertising and Advertisements. East Aurora: 1929. V. 63
Little Journeys to the Homes of Famous Women. East Aurora: 1908. V. 67
The Man of Sorrows, Little Journey to the Home of Jesus of Nazareth. 1916. V. 66
A Message to Garcia. East Aurora: 1899. V. 67
So Here Then Are the Preachments Entitled the City of Tagaste, and a Dream and a Prophecy. East Aurora: 1910. V. 67

HUBBARD, JEREMIAH
Forty Years Among the Indians. Miami: 1913. V. 62; 65

HUBBARD, L. RON
Battlefield Earth: a Saga of the Year 3000. New York: 1982. V. 62
Death's Deputy. 1948. V. 64; 66
Death's Deputy. Los Angeles: 1948. V. 66
Dianetics. 1950. V. 63; 64; 66
Final Blackout. 1948. V. 62; 64; 66
Final Blackout. Providence: 1948. V. 65
The Kingslayer. 1949. V. 63; 64; 66
Science of Survival. 1951. V. 63
Self-Analysis in Dianetics - a Simple Self-Help Volume of Texts and Exercises. London: 1952. V. 63
Self-Analysis in Scientology. 1953. V. 64; 66
Slaves of Sleep. Chicago: 1948. V. 63; 64; 66
Triton. 1949. V. 63
Triton and Battle of Wizards. Los Angeles: 1949. V. 66
Typewriter in the Sky and Fear. 1951. V. 63; 64; 66
Typewriter in the Sky/Fear. New York: 1951. V. 63

HUBBARD, T. O'B.
Tomorrow is a New Day - a Fantasy. London: 1934. V. 63

HUBBARD, WILLIAM
A Narrative of the Indian Wars in New England, from the First Planting Thereof in the Year 1607 to the Year 1677.... Worcester: 1801. V. 66

HUBBELL, LINDLEY WILLIAMS
The Birth of the Diatom a Nativity Play. Pawlet: 1949. V. 63

HUBBELL, ROSE STRONG
Quacky Doodles' and Danny Daddles' Book. Chicago: 1916. V. 66

HUBBLE, EDWIN
The Realm of the Nebulae. New Haven: 1937. V. 67

HUBBS, C. L.
Fishes of the Yucatan Peninsula. Washington: 1936. V. 63

HUBER, FRANCOIS
Nouvelles Observations sur les Abeilles, Addresses a M. Charles Bonnet. A Geneve: 1792. V. 64

HUBER, J. W.
Vues Pittoresques des Ruines les Plus Remarquables de l'Ancienne Ville de Pompei. Zurich: 1824. V. 62

HUBER, JEAN PIERRE
The Natural History of Ants. London: 1820. V. 64

HUBER, MARIE
Lettres sur la Religion Essentielle a l'Homme, Distinguee de ce Qui n'en est Que l'Accessoire. Londres: 1756. V. 63
The World Unmasked, or the Philosopher the Greatest Cheat.... London: 1736. V. 65

HUBER, P.
The Natural History of Ants. 1820. V. 63

HUBER, PETER
Cerebral Angiography. Stuttgart: 1982. V. 67

HUBIN, ALLEN J.
Crime Fiction 1740-1980, a Comprehensive Bibliography. New York and London: 1984-1988. V. 62

HUC, EVARISTE REGIS
The Chinese Empire; Forming a Sequel to the Work entitled Recollections of a Journey through Tartary and Thibet. London: 1855. V. 67
Christianity in China, Tartary and Thibet. London: 1857-1858. V. 64
Recollections of a Journey through Tartary, Thibet and China, During the Years 1844, 1845 and 1846. London: 1852. V. 64

HUCKEL, J. F.
American Indians, First Families of the Southwest. Kansas City: 1926. V. 67

HUCKEL, WALTER
Theoretical Principles of Organic Chemistry. Amsterdam: 1955-1958. V. 63

HUDDART, JOSEPH
Memoir of the Late Captain Joseph Huddart, F.R.S. etc. London: 1821. V. 62; 65; 66

HUDDESFORD, GEORGE
The Poems of.... London: 1801. V. 64; 66
Salmagundi: a Miscellaneous Combination of Original Poetry.... London: 1791. V. 63; 65

HUDDLESTON, EUGENE L.
The Allegheny: Lima's Finest on the Chesapeake and Ohio and the Virginian. Edmunds: 1984. V. 67

HUDELBURG, CHARLES
The Bird Princess. New York: 1938. V. 64

HUDLESTON, C. ROY
An Armorial for Westmorland and Lonsdalde. Kendal: 1975. V. 64; 65; 66
Cumberland Families and Heraldry with a Supplement to an Armorial for Westmorland and Lonsdale. Kendal: 1978. V. 64; 65; 66
The Registers of Morland. Part I. 1538-1742. Durham: 1957. V. 65

HUDSON, ARTHUR PALMER
Folksongs of Mississippi. Chapel Hill: 1936. V. 63; 64

HUDSON, C. T.
The Rotifera or Wheel-Animalcules. 1886-1889. V. 66
The Rotifera or Wheel-Animalcules. London: 1886-1889. V. 62; 64

HUDSON, CHARLES
History of the Town of Lexington, Middlesex County...from Its First Settlement to 1868. Boston: 1913. V. 64

HUDSON, DAVID
A History of Jemima Wilkinson, a Preacheress of the Eighteenth Century.... New York: 1821. V. 66
Memoir of Jemima Wilkinson, a Preacheress of the Eighteenth Century. Bath: 1844. V. 62

HUDSON, DEREK
Arthur Rackham: His Life and Work. London: 1960. V. 66
Arthur Rackham, His Life and Work. New York: 1973. V. 63

HUDSON, ELIZABETH
A Bibliography of the First Editions of the Works of E. Oe Somerville and Martin Ross. New York: 1942. V. 65

HUDSON, G. V.
New Zealand Moths and Butterflies. 1898. V. 63

HUDSON, JAMES
Testimonials for an Official Appointment in the University of London. London: 1838. V. 64

HUDSON, JOHN
A Complete Guide to the English Lakes.... London: 1842. V. 64; 65; 66
Photographs of the Giant's Causeway with Descriptive Letterpress. Glasgow, London, Dublin: 1874. V. 63

HUDSON, JOSHUA HILARY
Sketches and Reminiscences. Columbia: 1903. V. 63

HUDSON, MARIANNE SPENCER
Almack's: a Novel. London: 1826-1827. V. 65
Almack's: a Novel. London: 1827. V. 65

HUDSON, MIKE
Private Impressions: a Collection of Four Monographs About Printing and Other Book Arts. Katoomba: 1995-1996. V. 62

HUDSON, NOEL
Early English Version of Hortus Sanitatis. London: 1954. V. 62

HUDSON, STEPHEN
Celeste and Other Sketches. London: 1930. V. 66

HUDSON, SUE F.
Background of Ho-Ho-Kus History. Ho-Ho-Kus: 1953. V. 66

HUDSON, WILLIAM
Flora Anglica.... London: 1778. V. 65; 66

HUDSON, WILLIAM HENRY
Birds in a Village. London: 1893. V. 62
Birds in London. London: 1898. V. 62; 65; 66
Birds of La Plata. 1920. V. 66
Birds of La Plata. London: 1920. V. 64; 67
Birds of la Plata. New York: 1920. V. 63; 67
British Birds. 1902. V. 67
The Collected Works. London: 1922-1923. V. 67
A Crystal Age. London: 1887. V. 62; 65
El Ombu. London: 1902. V. 63; 64
Green Mansions: a Romance of the Tropical Forest. London: 1904. V. 62
Letters to R. B. Cunninghame Grahame. Waltham St. Lawrence: 1941. V. 62; 64
A Little Boy Lost. London: 1921. V. 63; 64; 66
The Naturalist in La Plata. London: 1892. V. 63; 65
The Naturalist in La Plata. London and Toronto: 1923. V. 65
Nature in Downland. London: 1900. V. 62

HUDSON'S BAY COMPANY
Claim of the Mission of St. James, Vancouver, Washington Territory, to 640 Acres of Land. N.P: 1863. V. 66
Cumberland and Hudson House Journals 1775-1779 and 1775-1782. London: 1951-1952. V. 65
Hudson's Bay Company 1670-1870. Volume I: 1670--1763. Volume II: 1763-1820. Toronto: 1960. V. 66
Hudson's Bay Copy Book of Letters, Commissions, Instructions Outward 1688-1696. London: 1957. V. 65
Hudson's Bay Miscellany 1670-1870. Winnipeg: 1975. V. 64; 66
Letters from Hudson Bay 1703-1740. London: 1965. V. 64; 66
Minutes of the Hudson's Bay Company. London: 1945. V. 66
Moose Fort Journals 1783-1785. London: 1783-1785. V. 64
Moose Fort Journals, 1783-1785. London: 1954. V. 63; 66
Northern Quebec and Labrador Journals and Correspondence 1819-1835. London: 1963. V. 65; 66

HUDSPETH, THOMAS B.
M. F. H. Fox and Wolf Hounds. Sibley: 1914. V. 67

HUEBLER, DOUGLAS
Variable Piece 4. Secrets. New York: 1973. V. 67

HUEFFER, OLIVER MADOX
The Book of Witches. London: 1908. V. 66; 67
A Vagabond in New York. London: 1913. V. 65

HUELSENBECK, RICHARD
Die Newyorker Kantaten/Cantates New-Yorkaises. New York and Paris: 1952. V. 66

HUENE, HOYNINGEN
African Mirage. London: 1938. V. 67

HUESSER, ALBERT H.
The History of the Silk Dyeing Industry in the United States. Paterson: 1927. V. 66

HUET, CHRISTOPHE
Singeries ou Differentes Actions de la Vie Humaine, Representees par des Singes. Paris: 1750. V. 64

HUET, J.
The Dance, Art and Ritual of Africa. New York: 1978. V. 62

HUEY, PENNOCK
A True History of the Charge of the Eighth Pennsylvania Cavalry at Chancellorsville. Philadelphia: 1883. V. 62; 63

HUFFAKER, C. B.
Ecological Entomology. New York: 1984. V. 65

HUFFMAN, JAMES
Ups and Downs of a Confederate Soldier. New York: 1940. V. 62; 63

HUFHAM, J. D.
Memoir of Rev. John L. Prichard, Late Pastor of the First Baptist Church, Wilmington, N.C. Raleigh: 1867. V. 67

HUGGINS, WILLIAM
The Royal Society or Science in the State and in the Schools. New York: 1906. V. 67

HUGH
Lowthian Bell. A Record and Some Impressions. Middlesbrough: 1928. V. 64; 65

HUGHEL, AVVON CHEW
The Chew Bunch in Browns Park. San Francisco: 1970. V. 66

HUGHES, CHARLES EVANS
The Pathway of Peace. Representative Addresses Delivered During His Term as Secretary of State (1921-1925). New York: 1925. V. 67

HUGHES, CHARLES R.
Old Chape Clarke County, Virginia. Berryville: 1906. V. 64

HUGHES, DOROTHY B.
Ride the Pink Horse. 1946. V. 66

HUGHES, E. R.
The Invasion of China by the Western World. London: 1937. V. 67

HUGHES, EDWARD
The Equity Draftsman Being a Selection of Forms of Pleadings in Suits in Equity. New York: 1842. V. 67
North Country Life in the Eighteenth Century. Volume I. The North-East 1700-1750. Oxford: 1952. V. 62; 65
North Country Life in the Eighteenth Century. Volume II: Cumberland and Westmorland 1700-1830. London: 1965. V. 62

HUGHES, H. D.
A History of Durham Cathedral Library. Durham: 1925. V. 64

HUGHES, H. HAROLD
The Old Churches of Snowdonia. Bangor: 1924. V. 62

HUGHES, HARRIET
Memoir of the Life and Writings of Mrs. Hemans. Edinburgh: 1840. V. 65
Memoir of the Life and Writings of Mrs. Hemans. Edinburgh: 1841. V. 65

HUGHES, J.
Australia Revisited in 1890 and Excursions in Egypt, Tasmania and New Zealand.. London and Bangor: 1891. V. 62

HUGHES, JEREMIAH
A Brief Sketch of Maryland: Its Geography, Boundaries, History, Government, Legislation, Internal Improvements, Etc. Annapolis: 1845. V. 65

HUGHES, JOHN
The Boscobel Tracts, Relating to the Escape of Charles the Second After the Battle of Worcester.... Edinburgh: 1830. V. 62
Doniphan's Expedition.... Cincinnati: 1848. V. 62; 64; 65
Doniphan's Expedition.... Washington: 1914. V. 65
The Ecstasy. An Ode. London: 1720. V. 66
The Siege of Damascus. London: 1720. V. 67

HUGHES, LANGSTON
Ask Your Mamma - 12 Moods for Jazz. New York: 1961. V. 63
The Big Sea. New York: 1940. V. 65
Black Magic. A Pictorial History of the Negro in American Entertainment. New York: 1967. V. 67
The Book of Negro Folklore. New York: 1959. V. 66
The Collected Poems. New York: 1994. V. 63
Fields of Wonder. New York: 1947. V. 64; 65
The First Book of Negroes. New York: 1952. V. 65
The First Book of Rhythms. New York: 1954. V. 64; 65
Four Negro Poets. New York: 1927. V. 64
Freedom's Plow. New York: 1943. V. 63
The Langston Hughes Reader. New York: 1958. V. 66
The Negro Mother and Other Dramatic Recitations. New York: 1931. V. 62
A New Song. New York: 1938. V. 64; 66
The Panther and the Lash: Poems of Our Times. New York: 1967. V. 63
A Pictorial History of the Negro in America. New York: 1956. V. 65
The Sweet Flypaper of Life. New York: 1955. V. 64; 65
The Weary Blues. New York: 1926. V. 64; 67

HUGHES, LEWIS
Certaine Grievances Well Worthy the Serious Considerations of the Right Honourable and High Court of Parliament. Amsterdam: 1640. V. 66

HUGHES, MARY
The Orphan Girl; a Moral Tale, Founded on Facts. London: 1819. V. 63
Stories for Children; Chiefly Confined to Words of Two Syllables. London: 1819. V. 63

HUGHES, NATHANIEL C.
General William J. Hardee. Old Reliable. Baton Rouge: 1965. V. 63; 65

HUGHES, PENNETHORNE
Kent - A Shell Guice. London: 1969. V. 65

HUGHES, PHILIP
The Reformation in England. London: 1952-1954. V. 62; 64

HUGHES, RICHARD
Confessio Juvenis - Collected Poems. London: 1926. V. 62; 65
The Fox in the Attic - the Human Predicament - Volume One. London: 1961. V. 64
Gipsy-Night and Other Poems. Waltham St. Lawrence: 1922. V. 63; 65
A High Wind in Jamaica. London: 1929. V. 62; 63; 64; 65; 66
How Green Was My Valley. London: 1939. V. 65
The Innocent Voyage. New York: 1944. V. 65
The Spider's Palace - and Other Stories. London: 1931. V. 65
The Wooden Shepherdess. London: 1973. V. 63

HUGHES, RICHARD B.
Pioneer Years in the Black Hills. Glendale: 1957. V. 63; 64; 65; 66; 67

HUGHES, ROBERT
Amish, the Art of the Quilt. New York: 1990. V. 63
Coberley Hall. A Gloucestershire Tale of the Fourteenth Century. Cheltenham: 1824. V. 62; 63

HUGHES, ROBERT M.
General Johnston. New York: 1893. V. 62

HUGHES, SUKEY
Washi: the World of Japanese Paper. Tokyo, New York, and S.F.: 1978. V. 62

HUGHES, TED
Adam and the Sacred Nine. London: 1978. V. 62
Animal Poems. Bow, Crediton, Devon: 1967. V. 62; 64
The Best Worker in Europe: a Poem. London: 1985. V. 62
Birthday Letters. London: 1998. V. 62; 63; 64; 66; 67
The Burning of the Brothel. London: 1966. V. 62; 64
Chiasmadon. Baltimore: 1977. V. 62; 64; 67
The Coming of the Kings and Other Plays. London: 1970. V. 62
A Conversation with Ted Hughes About the Arvon Foundation. Hebden Bridge and Beaworthy: 1978. V. 63
Crow. From Life and Songs of the Crow. London: 1970. V. 62; 67
Crow. From the Life and Songs of the Crow. London: 1973. V. 63; 65
The Dreamfighter and Other Creation Tales. London: 1995. V. 62; 65
Earth Dances: Poems. 1994. V. 62
Earth-Moon. London: 1976. V. 62; 64
The Earth-Owl and Other Moon-People. London: 1963. V. 62; 63
Eat Crow. London: 1971. V. 63
Eclipse. Knotting, Bedfordshire: 1976. V. 62; 64
A Few Crows. Exeter: 1970. V. 62
A Few Crows. London: 1970. V. 64
Five Autumn Songs for Children's Voices. 1968. V. 64
Five Autumn Songs for Children's Voices. Bow, near Crediton: 1968. V. 63
Five Autumn Songs for Children's Voices. Devonshire: 1968. V. 62; 64
Five Autumn Songs for Children's Voices. Bow: 1968-1969. V. 63
Flowers and Insects. Some Birds and a Pair of Spiders. New York: 1986. V. 65
Fly Inspects. Devon: 1983. V. 62; 65
Four Tales Told by an Idiot. Knotting, Bedfordshire: 1979. V. 62; 64
Gaudete. London: 1977. V. 62
Gaudete. New York: 1977. V. 63
Giant Dream of Elephants. Devn: 1982. V. 65
Groom's Dream. Northampton: 1957. V. 64; 67
Groom's Dream. Northampton: 1959. V. 62
The Hawk in the Rain. London: 1957. V. 62; 64; 66
The Hawk in the Rain. New York: 1957. V. 67
Henry Williamson: a Tribute by Ted Hughes, Given at the Service of Thanksgiving at the Royal Parish Church of St. Martin-in-the-Fields, 1 December, 1977. London: 1979. V. 62; 67
Howls and Whispers. Hadley: 1998. V. 64; 65
The Iron Woman. London: 1993. V. 65
Lupercal. New York: 1960. V. 63
The Martyrdom of Bishop Farrar. Bow, Crediton, Devon: 1970. V. 62
Mice Are Funny Little Creatures. Devon: 1983. V. 62; 65
Moortown. London: 1979. V. 64
Moortown Elegies. Cambridge: 1978. V. 63
Orts. London: 1978. V. 62; 64
A Primer of Birds. Lurley in Devon: 1981. V. 62; 64; 65
Prometheus On His Crag. 21 Poems. London: 1973. V. 67
Rain - Charm for the Duchy and Other Laureate Poems/The Unicorn. London: 1992. V. 66
Recklings. London: 1966. V. 62; 64
Remains of Elmet. London: 1979. V. 62; 63; 64; 65; 67
Roosting Hawk. Northampton: 1959. V. 64; 67
Sean, the Fool, the Devil and the Cats. Chicago: 1974. V. 62
Selected Poems 1957-1981. London: 1982. V. 67
Shakespeare's Ovid. 1995. V. 63
Shakespeare's Ovid. London: 1995. V. 62; 64; 67
Shakepeare's Poem. London: 1971. V. 62; 63; 64
A Solstice. Knotting, Bedfordshire: 1978. V. 62; 64
Spring, Summer, Autumn, Winter. London: 1973. V. 64
The Story of Vasco. London: 1974. V. 62
Sunstruck. Knotting, Bedfordshire: 1977. V. 62; 64
T. S. Eliot: a Tribute. London: 1987. V. 63; 65
Tales from Ovid. London: 1997. V. 62; 64; 66; 67
Tales from Ovid. London: 1998. V. 63
Weasels at Work. Devon: 1983. V. 62; 65
Wodwo: Poems. London: 1967. V. 62; 67
Wolf-Watching. Devon: 1982. V. 62

HUGHES, THOMAS
The Ascension: a Poetical Essay. Cambridge: 1780. V. 62
Early Memories for the Children. London: 1899. V. 66
G.T.T. Gone to Texas. London: 1884. V. 65; 67
A Lecture on the Slop-System, Especially As It Bears Upon the Females Engaged In It. Delivered at the Library and Mechanics' Institution at Reading on February 3rd, 1852. Exeter: 1852. V. 64; 65
Memoir of a Brother. London: 1873. V. 65
Memoir of Daniel Macmillan. London: 1882. V. 65
Mental Furniture; or the Adaptation of Knowledge for Man. London: 1857. V. 63
Rugby Tennessee, Being Some Account of the Settlement Founded on the Cumberland Plateau by the Board of Aid to Land Ownership.... London: 1881. V. 65
The Scouring of the White Horse. Cambridge: 1859. V. 62; 65
Tom Brown at Oxford. Cambridge: 1861. V. 65; 66
Tom Brown's School Days. London: 1865. V. 65
Tom Brown's School Days. London: 1871. V. 65
Tom Brown's School Days by an Old Boy. London: 1896. V. 63

HUGHES, THOMAS SMART
Travels in Sicily, Greece and Albania. London: 1820. V. 62

HUGHES, W. J.
Rebellious Ranger. Rip Ford and the Old Southwest. Norman: 1964. V. 62; 63; 65; 67

HUGHES, W. R.
New Town. A Proposal in Agricultural, Industrial, Educational, Civic and Social Reconstruction. London: 1919. V. 64; 66; 67

HUGHES, WENDELL L.
Reconsructive Surgery of the Eyelids. St. Louis: 1943. V. 63; 66

HUGHES, WILLIAM CARTER
The American Miller and Millwrights' Assistant. Detroit: 1850. V. 64

HUGHES PARRY, J.
Fishing Fantasy. London: 1949. V. 67

HUGHES STANTON, PENELOPE
The Wood Engravings of Blair Hughes Stanton. London: 1991. V. 67

HUGHEY, ANN
Edmund Dulac-His Book Illustrations. Potomac: 1995. V. 65

HUGO Black and the Supreme Court: a Symposium. New York: 1967. V. 63

HUGO, HERMANN
Pia Desideria; or Divine Addresses, in Three Books. London: 1690. V. 63

HUGO, RICHARD
Death and the Good Life. New York: 1995. V. 67
Good Luck in Cracked Italian. New York and Cleveland: 1969. V. 64
The Lady in Kicking Horse Reservoir. New York: 1973. V. 62
A Run of Jacks. Minneapolis: 1961. V. 62; 63; 64; 67
What Thou Lovest Well Remains American. New York: 1975. V. 62; 64

HUGO, THOMAS
The Bewick Collector: A Supplement to a Descriptive Catalogue of the Works of Thomas and John Bewick.... London: 1868. V. 64
Bewick's Woodcuts; Impressions of Upwards of Two Thousand Wood- Blocks, Engraved, For the Most Part, by Thomas and John Bewick.... 1870. V. 67
A Descriptive Catalogue of the Works of Thomas and John Bewick. London: 1866. V. 66
An Illustrated Itinerary of the Ward of Bishopsgate in the City of London. London: 1862. V. 63

HUGO, VICTOR
The Hunchback of Notre Dame. Philadelphia: 1834. V. 62; 65
The Hunchbank, or Bell Ringer of Notre Dame. London: 1840. V. 66
The Last Days of a Condemned from French...with Observations on Capital Punishment by Sir P. Hesketh Fleetwood Bart, M.P. London: 1840. V. 66
Les Miserables. Bruxelles: 1862. V. 67
Les Miserables. New York: 1862. V. 67
Les Miserables. New York: 1863. V. 65
Napoleon the Little. London: 1852. V. 63
Notre-Dame de Paris. Paris: 1930. V. 64
The Toilers of the Sea. 1960. V. 62
The Toilers of the Sea. London: 1960. V. 67

HUGO DE SANCTO VICTORE
Opera. ?Paris: 1526. V. 66

HUIE, WILLIAM B.
The Klansman. New York: 1967. V. 67
Mud on the Stars. New York: 1958. V. 63

HUISH, ROBERT
Memoirs of Her Late Majesty Caroline, Queen of Great Britain.... London: 1821. V. 65
Memoirs of Her Late Royal Highness Charlotte Augusta, Princess of Wales &c.... London: 1818. V. 66
A Treatise on the Nature, Economy and Practical Management of Bees. 1817. V. 63; 66
A Treatise on the Nature, Economy and Practical Management, of Bees.... London: 1817. V. 66

HULBERT, ARCHER BUTLER
Pioneer Roads and Experiences of Travelers. Cleveland: 1904. V. 67
Southwest on the Turquoise Trail: The First Diaries on the Road to Santa Fe. Denver: 1933. V. 64; 65
Where Rolls the Oregon - Prophet and Pessimist Look Northwest. Denver: 1933. V. 64

HULBERT, HOMER B.
In Search of a Siberian Klondike. New York: 1903. V. 65
The Passing of Korea. London: 1906. V. 67

HULIT, L.
The Salt Water Angler. 1924. V. 67

HULKE, J. W.
On Fractures and Dislocations of the Vertebral Column. The Bradshaw Lecture Delivered at the Royal College of Surgeons of England.... London: 1892. V. 67

HULL, CLARK L.
Hypnosis and Suggestibility, an Experimental Approach. New York: 1933. V. 66

HULL, DENISON B.
Thoughts on American Fox-Hunting. 1958. V. 62

HULL, E.
Contributions to the Physical History of the British Isles. 1882. V. 62

HULL, EDWARD
The Coal-Fields of Great Britain.... 1881. V. 63; 66; 67
The Coal-Fields of Great Britain.... London: 1905. V. 64

HULL, ELEANOR
Cuchulain, the Hound of Ulster. 1911. V. 67

HULL, LINDLEY M.
A History of Central Washington - Part One - The Story of Pioneer Settlements - Part Two - The Development Period. Spokane: 1929. V. 66

HULL, RICHARD
The Ghost It Was. New York: 1937. V. 66

HULL, SUSAN
Boy Soldiers of the Confederacy. New York: 1905. V. 62; 63; 65

HULL, WILLIAM
Report of the Trial of Brig. General William Hull: Commanding the North-Western Army...by a Court Martial held at Albany.... New York: 1814. V. 64; 66

HULLAH, MARY E.
In Hot Haste. London: 1888. V. 67

HULLEY, T.
Six Views of Cheltenham, from Drawings Made by Mr. T. Hulley. Price, in Colours. London: 1813. V. 66

HULLMANDEL, CHARLES JOSEPH
The Art of Drawing on Stone, Giving a Full Explanation of the Various Styles, of the Different Methods to be Employed to Ensure Success.... London: 1824. V. 65

HULME, F. E.
The Flags of the World. London: 1890. V. 63

HULME, F. EDWARD
Familiar Garden Flowers. London: 1882-1886. V. 62
Familiar Garden Flowers. London: 1891. V. 62
Familiar Wild Flowers. London: 1880. V. 62
A Series of Sketches from Nature of Plant Form. 1868. V. 63; 66

HULSIUS, LEVINUS
XII Primorum Caesarum et LXIIII Ipsorum Uxorum et Parentum ex Antiquis Numismatibus.... Frankfurt-am-main: 1597. V. 62

HULSKER, J.
The Complete Van Gogh: Paintings, Drawings, Sketches. New York: 1980. V. 62; 65

HULTEN, E.
Flora of Alaska and Yukon. Lund and Liepzig: 1940-1946. V. 67

HULTEN, K. G. PONTUS
The Machine as Seen at the End of the Mechanical Age. New York: 1968. V. 62

HULTON, PAUL
Luigi Blugani's Drawings of African Plants. From the Collection Made by James Bruce of Kinnaird on His Travels to Discover the Source of the Nile 1767-1773. New Haven/Rotterdam: 1991. V. 64

THE HUMAN Experience. Contemporary American and Soviet Fiction and Poetry. New York: 1989. V. 66

HUMBER, R. D.
Game Cock and Countryman. London: 1966. V. 67

HUMBER, WILLIAM
A Complete Treatise on Cast and Wrought Iron Bridge Construction, Including Iron Foundations. London: 1870. V. 65
A Comprehensive Treatise on the Water Supply of Cities and Towns with Numerous Specifications of Exisiting Waterworks. London: 1876. V. 62; 66
A Practical Treatise on Cast and Wrought Iron Bridges and Girders, as Applied to Railway Structures, and to Buildings Generally.... London: 1857. V. 64; 65

HUMBERT, L. M.
Memorials of the Hospital of St. Cross and Alms House of Noble Poverty. London: 1868. V. 66

HUMBLE, B. H.
On Scottish Hills. London: 1946. V. 62

THE HUMBLE Petition and Representation of the Gentry, Ministrs and Others of the Counties of Cumberland and Westmoreland. London: 1642. V. 62

HUMBOLDT, FRIEDRICH HEINRICH ALEXANDER, BARON VON
Ansichten der Natur, mit wissenschaftlichen Erlauterungen. Stuttgart and Tubingen: 1849. V. 64
Cosmos: a Sketch of a Physical Description of the Universe. New York: 1850. V. 64
Cosmos. Essai d'une Description Physique du Monde. Paris: 1848. V. 64
A Geognostical Essay on the Superposition of the Rocks, in Both Hemispheres. London: 1823. V. 62
Letters of Alexander Von Humbolt to Varnhagen von Ense, 1827-1858. New York: 1860. V. 62
Melanges de Geologie et de Physique Generale. Paris: 1854. V. 65
Personal Narrative of Travels in the Equinoctial Regions of the New Continent, During the Years 1799-1804. Philadelphia: 1815. V. 65; 66
Selections from the Works of the Baron De Humboldt, Relating to the Climate, Inhabitants, Productions and Mines of Mexico. London: 1824. V. 64
Tableaux de la nature ou Considerations sur les Deserts, sur la Physionomie des Vegetaux, sur les Cataractes de l'Orenoque, sur la Structure et l'Action des Volcans dans les Differentes Regions de la Terre. Paris: 1828. V. 65
Voyage aux Regions Equinoxiales du Nouveau Continent, fait en 1799- 1804. Amsterdam and New York: 1971-1973. V. 66

HUMBOLDT, WILHELM, BARON VON
Thoughts and Opinions of a Statesman. London: 1850. V. 64

HUMBOLT, ALEXANDRE
Ensayo Politico Sobre el Reyno de Nueva Espana. Madrid: 1818. V. 63

HUME, A.
The Game Birds of India, Burmah and Ceylon. Calcutta: 1879-1881. V. 67

HUME, ABRAHAM
The Learned Societies and Printing Clubs of the United Kingdom. 1853. V. 62; 65
The Learned Societies and Printing Clubs of the United Kingdom. London: 1853. V. 64

HUME, C.
From the Wild. Toronto: 1986. V. 63

HUME, DAVID
The Beauties of Hume and Bolingbroke. London: 1782. V. 67
Bring 'Em Back Dead. New York: 1936. V. 67
Dialogues Concerning Natural Religion. London: 1779. V. 63; 65
An Enquiry Concerning the Principles of Morals. London: 1751. V. 64
Essays and Treatises on Several Subjects. London: 1753-1754. V. 62
Essays and Treatises on Several Subjects. London: 1760. V. 67
Essays and Treatises on Several Subjects. Edinburgh: 1793. V. 64
Four Dissertations. I. The Natural History of Religion. II. of the Passions. III. Of Tragedy. IV. Of the Standard of Taste. London: 1757. V. 63; 64
Histoire de la Maison de Stuart sur Le Trone d'Angleterre. Londres: 1766. V. 67
The History of England. London: 1754-1762. V. 67
The History of England, from the Earliest Period to the Present Time. London: 1870. V. 63; 66
The Imperial History of England from the Earliest Records to the Present Time. London: 1891. V. 67
My Own Life. Stanford Dingley: 1927. V. 66

HUME, DAVID continued
Philosophical Essays Concerning Human Understanding. London: 1748. V. 62; 64
Political Discourses. Edinburgh: 1752. V. 67

HUME, E. E.
Ornithologists of the United States Army Medical Corps. Baltimore: 1942. V. 65

HUME, EDGAR
General Washington's Correspondence Concerning the Society of the Cincinnati. Baltimore: 1941. V. 67

HUME, FERGUS
Chronicles of Fairyland. Philadelphia: 1911. V. 63
The Crime of the Liza Jane. London: 1895. V. 66
The Mystery of a Hansom Cab. London: 1887. V. 63; 64; 66
The Mystery of the Shadow. London: 1906. V. 63; 67
The Sealed Message. London: 1908. V. 67

HUME, H. HAROLD
Citrus Fruits and Their Culture. Jacksonville: 1904. V. 67

HUME, JOHN R.
The Industrial Archaeology of Scotland. Batsford: 1976-1977. V. 67

HUME, R. D.
Salmon of the Pacific Coast.... San Francisco: 1893. V. 63

HUME, R. W.
Old Songs. Edinburgh: 1850. V. 62
Old Songs. Leith: 1850. V. 63

HUME, SOPHIA
An Exhortation to the Inhabitants of the Province of South Carolina.... Bristol: 1750. V. 66
An Exhortation to the Inhabitants of the Province of South Carolina. London: 1752. V. 63; 66
An Exhortation to the Inhabitants of the Province of South Carolina.... Philadelphia: 1747. V. 63

HUME, W. F.
Geology of Egypt. Cairo: 1925-1937. V. 64
Geology of Egypt. London: 1925-1937. V. 65

HUMFEVILLE, J. LEE
Twenty Years Among the Hostile Indians. New York: 1903. V. 65

HUMORIST'S Own Book: a Cabinet of Original and Selected Anecdotes, Bon Mots, Sports of Fancy and Traits of Character. Philadelphia: 1833. V. 66

HUMPHERY, G.
The Land of the Amazons. London: 1901. V. 67

HUMPHREY, JEFFREY A.
Englewood. Its Annals and Reminiscences. New York: 1899. V. 63; 66

HUMPHREY, MABEL
Gallant Little Patriots. New York: 1899. V. 65

HUMPHREY, OMAR J.
Wreck of the Rainier. Portland: 1887. V. 67

HUMPHREY, S. D.
A Practical Manual of the Collodion Process, Giving in Detail a Method for Producing Postive and Negative Pictures on Glass and Paper. New York: 1857. V. 63

HUMPHREY, WILLIAM
Home from the Hill. New York: 1958. V. 63; 66
The Last Husband and Other Stories. London: 1953. V. 66
The Last Husband and Other Stories. New York: 1953. V. 66; 67
My Moby Dick. New York: 1978. V. 67
The Ordways. New York: 1965. V. 66

HUMPHREYS, A. A.
The Virginia Campaign of 1864 and 1865. New York: 1883. V. 67

HUMPHREYS, ARTHUR L.
Old Decorative Maps and Charts. London and New York: 1926. V. 64

HUMPHREYS, CHARLES A.
Field, Camp, Hospital and Prison in the Civil War 1863-1865. Boston: 1918. V. 66

HUMPHREYS, DAVID
An Historical Account of the Incorporated Society for the Propagation of the Gospel in Foreign Parts. London: 1730. V. 64
The Miscellaneous Works. New York: 1790. V. 64

HUMPHREYS, DESMOND, MRS.
A Husband of No Importance. London: 1894. V. 65

HUMPHREYS, HENRY NOEL
Ancient Coins and Medals. London: 1850. V. 62; 66; 67
British Moths and Their Transformations. 1843-1851. V. 65; 66
Hans Holbein's Celebrated Dance of Death.... London: 1868. V. 66
A History of the Art of Printing.... London: 1867. V. 62
Illuminated Illustrations of Froissart. London: 1844-1845. V. 65
Maxims and Percepts of the Saviour. N.P: 1848. V. 63
Ocean Gardens: the History of the Marine Aquarium and the Best Methods Now Adopted For Its Establishment and Preservation. (with) River Gardens.... London: 1857. V. 62; 66
The Origin and Progress of the Art of Writing.... London: 1853. V. 64
Stories by an Archaeologist and His Friends. London: 1856. V. 66

HUMPHREYS, JAMES
The Irish Widow: in Two Acts, as It Is Performed at the Theatre Royal in Drury Lane. Philadelphia: 1773?. V. 67

HUMPHREYS, JOSEPHINE
Dreams of Sleep. New York: 1984. V. 62; 65

HUMPHREYS, MILTON W.
Captain Thomas A. Bryan. Bryan's Battery, 13th Battalion Virginia Artillery, C.S.A. 1862-1865. Richmond: 1911. V. 65
A History of the Lynchburg Campaign by Milton W. Humphreys, Member of the King's Artillery, C.S.A. Charlottesville: 1924. V. 62; 63

HUMPHREYS, P. S.
Birds of Isla Grande (Tierra del Fuego). Lawrence: 1970. V. 67

HUMPHREY SMITH, CECIL R.
General Armory Two. Baltimore: 1974. V. 67

HUMPHRIES, ROLFE
New Poems by American Poets. New York: 1953. V. 63

HUMPHRIES, SYDNEY
Oriental Carpets. London: 1910. V. 62; 66

HUMPHRIS, EDITH
Adam Lindsay Gordon and His Friends in England and Australia. London: 1912. V. 66; 67

HUMPHRY, GEORGE MURRAY
Old Age. The Results of Information Received Respecting Nearly Nine Hundred Persons Who Had Attained the Age of Eighty Years, Including Seventy- Four Centenarians. Cambridge. 1889. V. 65; 66

HUMPHRYS, JAMES
Sleeping Partner. London: 2000. V. 66

HUMPHRYS, MILTON W.
A History of the Lynchburg Campaign by Milton W. Humphreys, Member of the King's Artillery, C.S.A. Charlottesville: 1924. V. 65

HUMPRHEYS, JOSEPHINE
Dreams of Sleep. New York: 1984. V. 67

HUMPTY Dumpty. Akron: 1910. V. 62

HUMPTY Dumpty's Tales: the History of Cinderella or the Little Glass Slipper. London: 1850. V. 64

HUN, HENRY
An Atlas of the Differential Diagnosis of the Diseases of the Nervous System. Troy: 1914. V. 65

HUNEKER, JAMES
Ivory Apes and Peacocks. New York: 1915. V. 63

HUNER, J. V.
Crustacean and Mollusk Aquaculture in the United States. New York: 1985. V. 65

HUNGERFORD, EDWARD
The Story of the Baltimore and Ohio Railroad. 1827-1927. New York: 1928. V. 65

HUNT, ALBERT B.
Houseboats and Houseboating. New York: 1905. V. 63

HUNT, AURORA
The Army of the Pacific: Its Operations in California, Texas, Arizona, New Mexico, Utah, Nevada, Oregon, Washington, Plains Region, Mexico Etc. 1860-1866. Glendale: 1951. V. 63; 64
Major General James Henry Carleton 1814-1873. Glendale: 1958. V. 62

HUNT, CHARLES C.
A Genealogical History of the Robert and Abigail Pancoast Hunt Family. Dixon: 1906. V. 62

HUNT, ELMER M.
The Gold Rush Diary of Moses Pearson Cooswell of New Hampshire. Concord: 1949. V. 63; 66

HUNT, ELVID
History of Fort Leavenworth 1827-1927. Fort Leavenworth: 1926. V. 65; 67
History of Fort Leavenworth 1827-1927. 1937. V. 67

HUNT, FRAZIER
Custer, the Last of the Cavaliers. New York: 1928. V. 67

HUNT, FREEMAN
Worth and Wealth: A Collection of Maxims, Morals and Miscellanies for Merchants and Men of Business. New York: 1857. V. 64

HUNT, G. H.
Outram & Havelock's Persian Campaign. London: 1858. V. 62

HUNT, HARRIOT K.
Glances and Glimpses; or Fifty Years Social, Including Twenty Years Professional Life. Boston: 1856. V. 63

HUNT, HENRY
A Copious Report of the Trial of Henry Hunt, Esq. and Others...held at the Castle, York, on Thursday March 16, 1820...for Conspiracy and Riot.... Hull: 1820. V. 63
An Impartial Report of the Proceedings in the Cause of the King Versus Henry Hunt, Joseph Johnson, John Knight (& others) for a Conspiracy... at York Spring Assizes on the 16th-27th March 1820. Manchester: 1820. V. 63
Investigation at Ilchester Gaol, in the County of Somerset, into the Conduct of William Bridle, the Gaoler, Before the Commissioners Appointed by the Crown. London: 1821. V. 63

HUNT, HENRY continued
The Trial of Henry Hunt, Esq. Jno Knight, Jos. Johnson, Jno. Thacker (& others)...for an Alledged Conspiracy to Overturn the Government &c. by Threats and Force of Arms..at the York Lent Assizes 1820. London: 1820. V. 63

HUNT, IRENE
Up a Road Slowly. New York: 1966. V. 65

HUNT, J. D.
The Anglo-Dutch Garden in the Age of William and Mary. 1988. V. 63

HUNT, J. H.
Nourishment and Evolution in Insect Societies. Boulder: 1994. V. 66

HUNT, JAMES H.
Mormonism: Embracing the Origin, Rise and Progress of the Sect, with an Examination of the Book of Mormon.... St. Louis: 1844. V. 62

HUNT, JOHN
The Ascent of Everest. London: 1953. V. 64
The Conquest of Everest. New York: 1954. V. 67
Irish Medieval Figure Sculpture 1200-1600. 1974. V. 63; 66
Report of the Cause of the King v. John Hunt, for a Libel on the House of Commons, in the Examinder; Tried...Feb. 21st, 1821. London: 1821. V. 63

HUNT, JOHN H.
The Honest Man's Book of Finance and Politics, Showing the Cause and Cure of Artificial Poverty, Dearth of Employment and Dullness of Trade. New York: 1862. V. 67

HUNT, LEIGH
Classic Tales, Serious and Lively; with Critical Essays on the Merits and Reputation of the Authors. London: 1807. V. 62
A Jar of Honey from Mount Hybla. London: 1848. V. 64
Leigh Hunt's Letter on Hogg's Life of Shelley with Other Papers. Cedar Rapids: 1927. V. 63
Men, Women and Books: a Selection of Sketches, Essays and Critical Memoirs, From His Uncollected Prose Writings. London: 1847. V. 62
The Old Court Suburb: Memorials of Kensington.... London: 1902. V. 62
Sir Ralph Esher; or, Adventures of a Gentleman of the Court of Charles II. London: 1832. V. 62
Stories from the Italian Poets; with Lives of the Writers. London: 1846. V. 62
The Town: Its Memorable Characters and Events. London: 1848. V. 62; 64
Wit and Humor, Selected from the English Poets. London: 1846. V. 64; 65

HUNT, LESLIE C.
The Prisoner's Progress. London: 1941. V. 66

HUNT, RACHEL MC MASTERS MILLER
Catalogue of Botanical Books in the Collection of.... London: 1958-1961. V. 62
Catalogue of Botanical Books in the Collection of.... Pittsburgh: 1958-1961. V. 62; 66
Catalogue of Botanical Books in the Collection of.... New York: 1991. V. 62

HUNT, RICHARD CARLEY
Salmon in Low Water. New York: 1950. V. 64

HUNT, ROCKWELL D.
California and Californians. San Francisco, Chicago, L.A: 1926. V. 62
California and Californians. San Francisco, Chicago, L.A: 1932. V. 63
John Bidwell, Prince of California Pioneers. Caldwell: 1942. V. 63; 66

HUNT, T. STERRY
Canada. A Geographical, Agricultural and Mineralogical Sketch. Quebec: 1865. V. 62
Report of...On the Gold Region of Nova Soctia. Ottawa: 1868. V. 64

HUNT, THOMAS P.
The Wedding Days of Former Times. Philadelphia: 1845. V. 65

HUNT, URIAH
An Atlas Accompanying Worcester's Epitome of Geography. Philadelphia: 1828. V. 64

HUNT, VIOLET
The Tiger Skin. London: 1924. V. 65

HUNT, WILLIAM GIBBES
An Address, Delivered at Nashville, Tennessee, April 6, 1831, at the Request of the Literary Societies of the University of Nashville. Nashville: 1831. V. 66

HUNT, WILLIAM HOLMAN
Pre-Raphaelitism and the Pre-Raphaelite Brotherhood. 1913. V. 64

HUNT, WILSON PRICE
The Overland Diary of Wilson Price Hunt. Ashland: 1973. V. 63; 64; 66

HUNTER, ADAM
A Lecture on the Sulphur Waters of Harrogate Read at the Promenade. York: 1806. V. 64; 65
A Treatise on the Mineral Waters of Harrogate and Its Vicinity. London: 1830. V. 64; 65
The Waters of Harrogate and Its Vicinity. London: 1838. V. 64; 65

HUNTER, ALEXANDER
Culina Famulatrix Medicinae; or, Receipts in Modern Cookery. York: 1806. V. 65
Culina Famulatrix Medicinae; or, Receipts in Modern Cookery.... York: 1807. V. 67
Georgical Essays. 1773. V. 63
Georgical Essays. York: 1777. V. 63; 66
The Huntsman of the South. New York and Washington: 1908. V. 63
Johnny Reb and Billy Yank. New York and Washington: 1905. V. 62; 63; 65
Outlines of Agriculture, Addressed to Sir John Sinclair, Bart. President of the Board of Agriculture. York: 1797. V. 65

HUNTER, CYRUS L.
Sketches of Western North Carolina, Historical and Biographical. Raleigh: 1877. V. 63; 66

HUNTER, DARD
My Life with Paper: an Autobiography. New York: 1958. V. 64
Papermaking by Hand in America. Chillicothe: 1950. V. 62; 64; 66
Papermaking by Hand in India. New York: 1939. V. 64
Papermaking: the History and Technique of Ancient Craft. New York: 1957. V. 64
Papermaking through Eighteen Centuries. New York: 1930. V. 64; 65

HUNTER, EVAN
The Blackboard Jungle. New York: 1954. V. 66
A Matter of Convinction. New York: 1959. V. 67
Second Coming. New York: 1956. V. 66

HUNTER, F. M.
An Account of the British Settlement of Aden in Arabia. London: 1877. V. 67

HUNTER, FRAZIER
I Fought With Custer. The Story of Sergeant Windolph. New York: 1947. V. 67

HUNTER, GEORGE LELAND
Tapestries of Clarence H. MacKay. New York: 1925. V. 62; 63; 64

HUNTER, H. L.
Leaves of Gold. London: 1951. V. 63

HUNTER, J. V.
Crustacean and Mollusk Aquaculture in the United States. New York: 1985. V. 64

HUNTER, JAMES
Fala and Soutra, Including a History of the Ancient "domus de Soltre" with Its Masters and Great Revenues, and Of Other Historical Associations and Buildings. Edinburgh: 1892. V. 62

HUNTER, JOHN
An Historical Journal of the Transactions at Port Jackson and Norfolk Island.... London: 1793. V. 67
Hunterian Reminiscences: Being the Substance of a Course of Lectures on the Principles and Practice of Surgery.... London: 1833. V. 66
The Natural History of the Human Teeth.... London: 1798. V. 66
The Natural History of the Human Teeth.... London: 1803. V. 64
The Natural History of the Human Teeth.... Birmingham: 1980. V. 62; 63
Traite des Maladies Veneriennes... (A Treatise on the Veneral Disease.). Paris: 1787. V. 64; 66
A Treatise of the Blood Inflamation and Gun-Shot Wounds. Philadelphia: 1817. V. 64; 66; 67
A Treatise on the Veneral Disease. London: 1788. V. 65
A Treatise on the Veneral Disease. Philadlephia: 1791. V. 64
A Treatise on the Veneral Disease. Philadelphia: 1853. V. 66
The Works of John Hunter F.R.S. with Notes. London: 1835-1837. V. 65

HUNTER, JOHN D.
Memoirs of Captivity Among the Indians of North America. London: 1824. V. 63

HUNTER, JOHN MARVIN
The Album of Gunfighters. Bandera: 1951. V. 62
The Album of Gunfighters. Bandera: 1955. V. 65
A Brief History of Bandera County, Covering More than Eighty Years of Intrepid History. Bandera: 1936. V. 66
Peregrinations of a Pioneer Printer: an Autobiography. Prairie: 1954. V. 67
The Trail Drivers of Texas. Nashville: 1925. V. 64; 65

HUNTER, JOSEPH
The Hallamshire Glossary. London: 1829. V. 64
Hallamshire. The History and Topography of the Parish of Sheffield in the County of York.... London: 1819. V. 66

HUNTER, MARY Y.
The Clyde River and Firth, Described by Neil Munro. London. V. 67

HUNTER, R. M. T.
Address to the Alumni of the University of Virginia at Charlottesville. Richmond: 1875. V. 63
Observations on the History of Virginia. Washington: 1855. V. 65
Speech of Hon. R. M. T. Hunter of Virginia, Against Increasing the Appropriation for the Collins Line of Steamers. Washington: 1852. V. 63

HUNTER, ROBERT E.
Shakespeare and Stratford-upon-Avon "A Chronicle of the Time".... London: 1864. V. 62; 65

HUNTER, ROGER
A Peep Into the Cottage at Windsor, or Love Among the Roses. London: 1820. V. 66

HUNTER, STEPHEN
The Day Before Midnight. New York: 1989. V. 62; 65; 66
The Master Sniper. New York: 1980. V. 62; 65; 66; 67
Point of Impact. New York: 1993. V. 65
The Second Saladin. New York: 1982. V. 62; 65; 66; 67
The Spanish Gambit. New York: 1985. V. 65; 67

HUNTER, THOMAS
Reflections Critical and Moral on the Letters of the Late Earl of Chesterfield. London: 1776. V. 65
Reflections: Critical and Moral on the Letters of the Late Earl of Chesterfield. Boston: 1780. V. 67
Report of the Trial of Thomas Hunter, Peter Hacket, Richard McNeil, James Gibb, and William McLean, Operative Cotton Spinners in Glasgow... January 3, 1838...for the Crimes of Illegal Conspiracy and Murder.... Edinburgh: 1838. V. 63

HUNTER, W. W.
Orissa. London: 1872. V. 65

HUNTFORD, ROLAND
Scott and Amundsen. The Race to the South Pole. New York: 1980. V. 65
Shackleton. New York: 1986. V. 64; 66

HUNTINGTON, BILL
Acres High. Billings: 1966. V. 62
Good Men and Salty Cusses. Billings: 1952. V. 66
They Were Good Men and Salty Cusses. Billings: 1952. V. 62

HUNTINGTON, D. C.
The Landscapes of Frederic Edwin Church: Vision of the American Era. New York: 1966. V. 65

HUNTINGTON, DWIGHT W.
Big Game, A Book for Sportsmen and Nature Lovers. 1904. V. 67

HUNTINGTON, E.
The Climatic Factor as Illustrated in Arid America. Washington: 1914. V. 63

HUNTINGTON, GEORGE
Robber and Hero - The Story of the Raid on the First National Bank of Northfield, Minnesota, by the James Younger Band of Robbers in 1876. Northfield: 1895. V. 63

HUNTINGTON, HELEN
The Solitary Path. New York: 1902. V. 63

HUNTINGTON, JONATHAN
Classical Sacred Musick. With a Concise System of Rudiments. Boston: 1812. V. 63

HUNTINGTON, MARGARET WENDELL
Told in a Hammock. London: Sep. 1880. V. 64

HUNTINGTON, RANDOLPH
General Grant's Arabian Horses, Leopard and Linden Tree an Their Sons Beale and Hegira. Philadelphia: 1885. V. 64

HUNTLEY, JAMES GORDON
A Summary of Controversies. St. Omer: 1618. V. 63; 66

HUNTON, ADDIE
Two Colored Women with the American Expeditionary Forces. Brooklyn: 1920. V. 64

HUNTTING, JAMES M.
A Sermon Containing a General History of the Parish of Westfield, N. J. Preached Jan 1, 1839, in the Presbyterian Church of the Place. Westfield: 1904. V. 63

HURD, EDITH THACHER
Nino and His Fish. New York: 1954. V. 66

HURD, HENRY MILLS
The Institutional Care of the Insane in the United States and Canada. Baltimore: 1916-1917. V. 65

HURD, JOHN
A National Bank, or No Bank; an Appeal to the Common Sense of the People of the United States: Especially of the Laboring Classes. New York: 1842. V. 66

HURDIS, JAMES
Tears of Affection, a Poem; Occasioned by the Death of a Sister.... London: 1794. V. 66
The Village Curate. London: 1788. V. 66
The Village Curate. Bishopstone, Sussex: 1797. V. 62

HURLBERT, WILLIAM H.
Ireland Under Coercion: The Diary of an American. 1888. V. 62; 65
Ireland Under Coercion: The Diary of an American. Edinburgh: 1888. V. 67

HURLEY, F. JACK
Russell Lee Photographer. Dobbs Ferry: 1978. V. 63; 65

HURLEY, FRANK
Argonauts of the South. London: 1925. V. 63
The Holy City; a Camera Study of Jerusalem and Its Surroundings. Sydney: 1949. V. 67

HURLEY, MICHAEL
Irish Anglicanism 1869-1969. 1970. V. 67

HURRELL, GEORGE
The Hurrell Style. New York: 1976. V. 66

HURRY, IVES, MRS.
Artless Tales. London: 1808. V. 65

HURST, ALEX A.
Anton Otto Fischer, Marine Artist. His Life and Work. Brighton: 1977. V. 67
Thomas Somerscales, Marine Artist, His Life and Work. Brighton: 1988. V. 67

HURST, C. C.
Experiments in Genetics. Cambridge: 1925. V. 62; 63

HURST, E.
The Poison Plants of New South Wales. Sydney: 1942. V. 63; 64; 66

HURST, JOHN THOMAS
A Hand-Book of Formulae, Tables and Memoranda for Architectural Surveyors.... London: 1866. V. 64

HURST, SAM N.
The Virginia Form Book. Pulaski City: 1905. V. 66

HURST, VICTOR, MRS.
Ponies and Riders. London: 1948. V. 67

HURST, WESLEY R.
Frontier Photographer Stanley J. Marrows Dakota Years. 1956. V. 67

HURSTHOUSE, CHARLES FLINDERS
New Zealand, or Zealandia, The Britain of the South. London: 1857. V. 62

HURSTON, ZORA NEALE
Moses: Man of the Mountain. Philadelphia: 1939. V. 63
Mules and Men. Philadelphia: 1939. V. 64
Seraph on the Suwanee. New York: 1948. V. 64
Their Eyes Were Watching God. Philadelphia: 1937. V. 66

HURTADO, ALBERTO
Mechanisms of Natural Acclimatization. Studies on the Native Resident of Morochocha, Peru at an Altitude of 14,900 Feet. Randolph Air Force Base: 1956. V. 63

HURTLEY, THOMAS
A Concise Account of Some Natural Curiosities, in the Environs of Malham, in Craven, Yorkshire. London: 1786. V. 62

HURTON, WILLIAM
A Voyage from Leith to Lapland; or, Pictures of Scandinavia in 1850. London: 1852. V. 66

HUSAIN ALI, KIRMANI
The History of Hydur Naik, Otherwise Styled Shums Ul Moolk, Ameer Ud Dowla Nawaub Hydur All Khan Bahadoor, Hydur Jung.... London: 1842. V. 64

HUSE, CALEB
The Supplies for the Confederate Army. Boston: 1904. V. 62

HUSKISSON, WILLIAM
The Speeches, with a Biographical Memoir, Supplied to the Editor from Authentic Sources. London: 1831. V. 64

HUSON, THOMAS
Round About Helvellyn. London: 1895. V. 62, 64, 65, 66

HUSSERL, EDMUND
L'Origine de la Geometrie. Paris: 1962. V. 67

HUSSEY, C.
The Life of Sir Edwin Lutyens. 1953. V. 66

HUSSEY, CHARLES
The Trial of Charles Hussey for the Murder of Mr. Bird and His House-Keeper at Greenwich, Tried at Maidstone, on Friday July 31, 1818.... London: 1818. V. 63

HUSSEY, CHRISTOPHER
Clarence House. The Home of Her Royal Highness, the Princess Elizabeth, Duchess of Edinburgh and of His Royal Highness, The Duke of Edinburgh. London: 1949. V. 62
English Country Houses. Early Georgian 1715-1760. London: 1967. V. 64
English Country Houses. Late Georgian 1800-1840. London: 1966. V. 64
English Country Houses. Mid Georgian 1760-1800. London: 1967. V. 64
English Gardens and Landscapes 1700-1750. New York: 1967. V. 64

HUSSEY, JOHN A.
The History of Fort Vancouver and Its Physical Structure. Portland: 1957. V. 65
The Voyage of the Racoon. A Secret Journal of a Visit to Oregon, California and Hawaii 1813-1814. San Francisco: 1958. V. 63

HUSSEY, JOSEPH
The Glory of Christ Vindicated, in the Excellency of His Person, Righteousness, Love and Power.... London: 1761. V. 65

HUSSEY, S. M.
Reminiscences of an Irish Land Agent. 1904. V. 63

HUSSEY, WILLIAM
Letters from an Elder to a Younger Brother, on the Conduct to be Pursued in Life. London: 1814. V. 64

HUSTON, JOHN
Frankie and Johnny. New York: 1930. V. 62; 63

HUTCHEON, L. F.
War Flying. Boston: 1917. V. 64

HUTCHESON, ARCHIBALD
The Two Last Treatises Published by Mr. Hutcheson. London: 1723. V. 67

HUTCHESON, FRANCIS
An Essay on the Nature and Conduct of the Passions and Affections. London: 1742. V. 63
An Inquiry into the Original Of Our Ideas of Beauty and Virtue, in Two Treatises. London: 1729. V. 65
An Inquiry into the Original of Our Ideas of Beauty and Virtue, in two Treatises. London: 1738. V. 62
A System of Moral Philosophy in Three Books.... Glasgow and London: 1755. V. 65

HUTCHINGS, J. M.
In the Heart of the Sierras: the Yosemite Valley, Both Historical and Descriptive and Scenes by the Way, Big Tree Groves, the High Sierra.... Yosemite Valley/Oakland: 1886. V. 64; 65
Scenes of Wonder and Curiosity in California. San Francisco: 1861. V. 62

HUTCHINGS, R. S.
The Western Heritage of Type Design: A Treasury of Currently Available Typefaces Demonstrating the Historical Development and Diversification of Form of Printed Letters. London: 1963. V. 63

HUTCHINGS, RICHARD HENRY
Hutchings Bonner Wyatt, an Intimate Family History. Utica: 1937. V. 67

HUTCHINGS, WILLIAM S.
The Lightning Calculator: a New Readable and Valuable Book.... New York: 1868. V. 63

HUTCHINS, B. L.
A History of Factory Legislation.... London: 1911. V. 64

HUTCHINS, JAMES S.
The Papers of Edward S. Curtis - Relating to the Curtis Fight. El Segundo: 2000. V. 67

HUTCHINS, JOHN
The History and Antiquities of the County of Dorset. 1774. V. 65

HUTCHINS, MAUDE PHELPS
Diagrammatics. New York: 1932. V. 62

HUTCHINSON, BENJAMIN
Cases of Tic Douloureux Successfully Treated. London: 1820. V. 66

HUTCHINSON, FRANCIS
An Historical Essay Concerning Witchcraft. London: 1720. V. 64

HUTCHINSON, FRANK
New South Wales: The Mother Colony of the Australias 1896. Sydney: 1896. V. 67

HUTCHINSON, G. E.
A Treatise on Limnology. Volume I Geography, Physics and Chemistry. New York: 1957. V. 65

HUTCHINSON, GEORGE THOMAS
From the Cape to the Zambesi. London: 1905. V. 67

HUTCHINSON, HAROLD F.
London Transport Posters. London: 1963. V. 63

HUTCHINSON, HORACE G.
Big Game Shooting. London: 1905. V. 67
Fishing. 1904. V. 67
Golf. London: 1890. V. 67
Golf. London: 1911. V. 64
Shooting. 1903. V. 67

HUTCHINSON, J.
A Botanist in Southern Africa. London: 1946. V. 64
British Wild Flowers. Newton Abbot: 1972. V. 62
The Genera of Flowering Plants (Angiospermae) Based Principally on the Genera Plantarum. Oxford: 1964-1967. V. 67

HUTCHINSON, J. R.
Reminiscences, Sketches and Addresses, Selected from My Papers During a Ministry of Forty-Five Years in Mississippi, Louisiana and Texas. Houston: 1874. V. 65

HUTCHINSON, JOHN A.
Land Titles in Virginia and West Virginia. Cincinnati: 1887. V. 62

HUTCHINSON, JOHN WALLACE
Story of the Hutchinsons. Boston: 1896. V. 64

HUTCHINSON, JONATHAN
The Pedigree of Disease.... London: 1884. V. 65

HUTCHINSON, JULIUS
Memoirs of the Life of Colonel Hutchinson, Governor of Nottingham Castle and Town.... London: 1808. V. 66

HUTCHINSON, LUCY
Memoirs of the Life of Colonel Hutchinson Governor of Nottingham by His Widow Lucy. London: 1885. V. 64; 65

HUTCHINSON, P.
An Art and Gardening Journal. Provincetown: 1987. V. 66

HUTCHINSON, T. C.
Effects of Acid Precipitation on Terrestrial Ecosystems. New York: 1980. V. 63

HUTCHINSON, THOMAS
Ballades and Other Rhymes of a Country Bookworm. London: 1888. V. 66
The History of the Colony of Massachusetts Bay, from the First Settlement...in 1628, Until the Incorporation...in 1691. London: 1765. V. 62
History of the Province of Massachusetts Bay, from 1749 to 1774.... London: 1828. V. 62

HUTCHINSON, THOMAS JAMES
The Parana; with Incidents of the Paraguayan War, and South American Recollections, from 1861-1868. London: 1868. V. 67

HUTCHINSON, VERONICA S.
Fireside Poems. New York: 1930. V. 64

HUTCHINSON, W. H.
A Bar Cross Man: the Life and Personal Writing of Eugene Manlove Rhodes. Norman: 1956. V. 64; 66
A Note Book of the Old West. Chicago: 1947. V. 67

HUTCHINSON, WILLIAM
An Excursion to the Lakes in Westmoreland and Cumberland August 1773. London: 1774. V. 62
An Excursion to the Lakes in Westmoreland and Cumberland; with a Tour through Part of the Northern Counties, in the Years 1773 and 1774. London: 1776. V. 63; 65
The History of the County of Cumberland, and Some Places Adjacent. Carlisle: 1794. V. 66
The Spirit of Masonry. London: 1775. V. 63

HUTCHISON, I. W.
On Greenland's Closed Shore; the Fairyland of the Arctic. London: 1930. V. 67

HUTH, ALFRED HENRY
A Catalogue of the Woodcuts and Engravings in the Huth Library. London: 1910. V. 66

HUTNER, MARTIN
The Making of the Book of Common Prayer 1928. N.P: 1990. V. 62

HUTTON, CHARLES
The Compendius Measurer, Being a Brief Yet Comprehensive Treatise on Mensuration and Practical Geometry.... London: 1786. V. 62
Elements of Conic Sections; with Select Exercises in Various Branches of Mathematics and Philosophy. London: 1787. V. 63
A Mathematical and Philosophical Dictionary.... London: 1795. V. 65
Mathematical Tables: Containing Common, Hyperbolic and Logistic Logarithms. London: 1785. V. 65
Tracts on Mathematical and Philosophical Subjects.... London: 1812. V. 67

HUTTON, EDWARD
The Cosmati. London: 1950. V. 66

HUTTON, F. W.
Catalogue of the Marine Mollusca of New Zealand. Wellington: 1873. V. 62; 63; 66
Fishes of New Zealand, Catalogue with Diagnoses of the Species, and Notes on the Edible Fishes of New Zealand.... Wellington: 1872. V. 65
Manual of the New Zealand Mollusca (Marine and Land). Wellington: 1880. V. 62; 63

HUTTON, J. A.
The Life History of the Salmon. Aberdeen: 1924. V. 67
Rod Fishing for Salmon on the Wye. 1920. V. 67
Wye Salmon and Other Fish. 1949. V. 67

HUTTON, J. H.
The Angami Nagas; with Some Notes on Neighbouring Tribes. London: 1921. V. 67
The Sema Nagas. London: 1921. V. 67

HUTTON, JAMES
Biographical Account of the Late Dr. James Hutton. Edinburgh: 1805. V. 66

HUTTON, JOHN
A Tour to the Caves, in the Environs of Ingleborough and Settle, in the West Riding of Yorkshire. London: 1781. V. 64; 65; 66

HUTTON, S. K.
Among the Eskimos of Labrador; a Record of Five Years' Close Intercourse with the Eskimo Tribes of Labrador. London: 1912. V. 67

HUTTON, W.
The Battle of Bosworth Field, Between Richard the Third and Henry Earl of Richmond, Austust 22, 1485, Wherein is Described the Approach of Both Armies, with Plans of the Battle, Its Consequences, the Fall, the Treatment and Character of Richard. London: 1813. V. 62
The Book of Nature Laid Open, In a Popular Survey of the Phenomena and Constitution of the Universe.... Georgetown: 1822. V. 64
A Journey from Birmingham to London. Birmingham: 1785. V. 62
The Scarborough Tour in 1803. London: 1804. V. 62

HUTTON, WILLIAM
Courts of Requests: Their Nature, Utility, and Powers Described, with a Variety of Cases, Determined in that of Birmingham. Birmingham: 1787. V. 65; 66
An History of Birmingham, to the End of the Year 1780. Birmingham: 1781. V. 64; 66
The History of Derby; from the Remote Ages of Antiquity to the Year MDCCXCI. London: 1791. V. 63
The Life of William Hutton. London: 1816. V. 62

HUTTON, WILLIAM R.
California 1847-1852. San Marino: 1956. V. 62

HUXHAM, JOHN
An Essay on Fevers. London: 1750. V. 65
An Essay on Fevers. London: 1764. V. 62
An Essay on Fevers. London: 1767. V. 63; 67
Observations on the Air and Epidemic Diseases from the Year MDCCXXVIII to MDCCXXXVII Inclusive, Made by Dr. Huxham, at Plymouth.... London: 1759-1767. V. 62; 65

HUXLEY, ALDOUS LEONARD
Along the Road. Notes and Essays of a Tourist. New York: 1925. V. 62
Antic Hay. London: 1923. V. 63
Arabia Infelix and Other Poems. New York: 1929. V. 64
Beyond the Mexique Bay. London: 1934. V. 62
Brave New World. Garden City: 1932. V. 62; 64; 67
Brave New World. London: 1932. V. 63; 64; 65; 67
Brave New World. New York: 1974. V. 62; 64
The Burning Wheel. Oxford: 1916. V. 66
Crome Yellow. London: 1921. V. 67
The Defeat of Youth and Other Poems. Oxford: 1918. V. 66
The Doors of Perception. London: 1954. V. 64
Eyeless in Gaza. London: 1936. V. 63; 65; 66; 67
Holy Face and Other Essays. London: 1929. V. 65
Leda. London: 1920. V. 66
Little Mexican and Other Stories. London: 1924. V. 65
Music at Night and Other Essays. London: 1931. V. 67
Music at Night and Other Essays. New York: 1931. V. 62; 67
On the Margin: Notes and Essays. London: 1923. V. 63

HUXLEY, ALDOUS LEONARD continued
The Perennial Philosophy. London: 1946. V. 63
Point Counter Point. London: 1928. V. 62; 64
Point Counter Point. London: 1931. V. 62
T. H. Huxley as a Man of Letters. London: 1932. V. 65
Those Barren Leaves. London: 1925. V. 64
Words and Their Meanings. Los Angeles: 1940. V. 65
The World of Light. London: 1931. V. 62; 63; 64

HUXLEY, LEONARD
Life and Letters of Joseph Dalton Hooker.... London: 1918. V. 65

HUXLEY, THOMAS HENRY
Address to the British Associaton for the Advancement of Science... Delivered by the President...at Liverpool. London: 1870. V. 67
Evidence As to Man's Place in Nature. London: 1863. V. 62
Evidence as to Man's Place in Nature. New York: 1863. V. 62; 63; 64
Further Observations Upon Hyperodapedon Gordoni. 1887. V. 67
Lectures on the Elements of Comparative Anatomy.... London: 1864. V. 64
The Oceanic Hydrozoa.... London: 1859. V. 66
On a Collection of Fossil Vertebrata from the Jarrow Colliery, County of Kilkenny. Dublin: 1867. V. 67
On a New Labyrinthodont from Bradford. 1869. V. 67
On the Characters of the Pelvis in the Mammalia, and the Conclusions Respecting the Origin of Mammals Which may be Based on Them. 1879. V. 67
On the Classification and the Distribution of the Crayfishes. 1878. V. 67
On the Upper Jaw of Magalosarus. 1869. V. 67
T. H. Huxley's Diary of the Voyage of HMS Rattleonake. London: 1935. V. 67

HUYBERTS, ADRIAN
A Corner-Stone Laid Towards the Building of a New Colledge (That Is To Say, A New Body of Physicians) in London, Upon the Occasion of the Vexatiuous and Oppressive Proceedings Acted in the Name of the Society Called the Colledge of Physicians.... London: 1675. V. 65

HUYETTE, M. C.
Reminiscences of a Soldier in the American Civil War. Buffalo: 1908. V. 65

HUYGENS, CHRISTIAAN
The Celestial Worlds Discover'd: or, Conjectures Concerning the Inhabitants, Plants and Productions of the Worlds in the Planets. London: 1698. V. 64
Oeuvres Completes de Christiaan Huygens. Hague: 1888-1937. V. 65
Opera Varia. Leiden: 1724. V. 66
Opuscula Postuma, Quae Continent Dioptricam. Leiden: 1703. V. 66
Traite de la Lumiere. Leiden: 1690. V. 65; 66

HUYSHE, G. L.
The Red River Expedition. London, New York: 1871. V. 62

HUYSMANS, J. K.
A Rebours. Paris: 1884. V. 65
Pages Catholiques. Paris: 1899. V. 62

HYAMS, E.
The Orchard and Fruit Garden. 1961. V. 66

HYAMS, EDWARD
Capability Brown and Humphry Repton. London: 1971. V. 62
Irish Gardens. 1967. V. 62; 65
The Orchard and Fruit Gardener.... London: 1961. V. 62; 64

HYATT, A.
Genesis of the Arietidae. 1889. V. 66
Genesis of the Arietidae. Cambridge: 1889. V. 64; 65
Genesis of the Arietidae. Washington: 1889. V. 63
The Triassic Cephalopod Genera of America. Washington: 1905. V. 65; 66

HYATT, HARRY MIDDLETON
Folklore from Adams County Illinois. N.P: 1965. V. 63
Hoodoo - Conjuration - Witchcraft - Rootwork. 1970. V. 63

HYATT, LLOYD
Furniture Weaving Projects. Milwaukee: 1922. V. 65

HYDE, D.
Catalogue of the Books and Mansucripts Comprising the Library of the Late Sir John T. Gilbert. Dublin: 1918. V. 62

HYDE, GEORGE E.
The Early Blackfeet and Their Neighbors. Denver: 1933. V. 65
The Pawnee Indian. Denver: 1934. V. 65
Pawnee Indians. Denver: 1951. V. 65
Red Cloud's Folk - a History of the Ogalala Sioux. Norman: 1937. V. 65; 67
A Sioux Chronicle. Norman: 1956. V. 67
Spotted Tail's Folk, a History of the Brule Story. Norman: 1961. V. 67

HYDE, HARFORD MONTGOMERY
Oscar Wilde. A Biography. London: 1977. V. 67
The Other Love. London: 1970. V. 67
The Quiet Canadian. London: 1989. V. 67
Solitary in the Ranks. London: 1987. V. 67
The Story of Lamb House Rye. The Home of Henry James. Rye, Sussex: 1966. V. 67
A Tangled Web. London: 1986. V. 67
Their Good Names. Twelve Cases of Libel and Slander with Some Introductory Reflections on the Law. London: 1970. V. 67

HYDE, J. A. LLOYD
Oriental Lowestoft. Chinese Export Porcelain. Porcelaine de la Cie, des Indes, with Special Reference to the Trade with China and the Porcelain Decorated for the American Market. Newport: 1964. V. 67

HYDE Nugent. London: 1827. V. 67

HYDE, PHILIP
Drylands: the Deserts of North America. New York: 1987. V. 63

HYDE, RALPH
Gilded Scenes and Shining Prospects. Panoramic Views of British Towns 1575-1900. New Haven: 1985. V. 64
The Regents Park Colosseum. London: 1982. V. 66

HYDE, THOMAS
Veterum Persarum et Parthorum et Medorum Religionis Historia. Oxford: 1760. V. 63

HYGINUS, CAIUS JULIUS
Poeticon Astronomicon. Colophon: 1517. V. 63
The Poeticon Astronomicon. 1985. V. 62

HYLTON, J. DUNBAR
The Bride of Gettysburg. An Episode of 1863. Palmyra: 1878. V. 63; 66

HYMAN, L. H.
Invertebrates. New York: 1940-1967. V. 66

HYMAN, LOUIS
The Jews of Ireland from the Earliest Times to the Year 1910. 1972. V. 67

HYMNS Ancient and Modern, together with the Book of Common Prayer. London: 1920. V. 66

HYMNS and Prayers for Use at the Marriage of Michael Hornby and Nicolette Ward at St. Margaret's Church, Westminster. 1928. V. 62; 67

HYMNS and Prayers for Use at the Marriage of Michael Hornby and Nicolette Ward at St. Margaret's Church, Westminster, November XV 1928. London: 1928. V. 64; 66

HYMNS and Prayers for Use at the Marriage of Roger Anthony Hornby and Veronica Blackwood at St Paul's Church, Knightsbridge. London: 1931. V. 62, 67

HYMNS for the Use of Native Christians. Calcutta: 1826. V. 62

HYMNS on Select Passages of Scripture; with Others Usually Sung at Camp-Meetings &c. Poughkeepsie: 1811. V. 62

HYNDMAN, HENRY MAYERS
The Record of an Adventurous Life. London: 1911. V. 64

HYNE, CHARLES JOHN CUTLIFFE WRIGHT
Adventures of Captain Kettle. London: 1898. V. 67
Four Red Nightcaps. London: 1890. V. 67
Further Adventures of Captain Kettle. London: 1899. V. 67
Honour of Thieves; a Novel. London: 1895. V. 67
Mc Todd. London: 1903. V. 67

HYSLOP, THEOPHILUS BULKELEY
Mental Physiology: Especially in Its Relations to Mental Disorders. Philadelphia: 1895. V. 65

HYSON, TIMOTHY
A Letter to Mr. Richard Twining, Tea Dealer and One of the Candidates for the Present Vacancy in the East India Direction. London: 1827. V. 67

I

IACOCCA, LEE
Iacocca, an Autobiography. New York: 1984. V. 67

IANNONE, DOROTHY
Danger in Dusseldorf, (of) I am Not What I Seem. Stuttgart: 1973. V. 66

IBANEZ, VICENTE BLASCO
Fleur-de-Mal. Paris: 1920. V. 66
The Mob. London: 1927. V. 63

IBBETSON, JAMES
The Heinous Nature of Rebellion. London: 1746. V. 67
Public Virtue, the Great Cause of the Happiness and Prospertiy of Any People. York: 1746. V. 67

IBBETSON, JOHN HOLT
Specimens in Eccentric Circular Turning with Practical Instructions for Producing Corresponding Pieces in the Art. London: 1835. V. 65; 66

IBBETSON, JULIUS
A Picturesque Guide to Bath, Bristol Hot-Wells, the River Avon, and the Adjacent Country. 1793. V. 67
A Picturesque Guide to Bath, Bristol Hot-Wells, the River Avon, and the Adjacent Country. London: 1793. V. 62; 66

IBN TUFAYL, MUHAMMAD
The History of Hai Eb'n Yockdan, an Indian Prince; or the Self-Taught Philosopher. London: 1686. V. 67

IBRAHIM-HILMY, PRINCE
The Literature of Egypt and the Soudan to 1885: a Bibliography. 1994. V. 65

IBSEN, HENRIK
Brand: a Version for the English Stage. London: 1978. V. 63
Bygmester Solness. (Master Builder). Copenhagen: 1892. V. 64
The Collected Works. London: 1919. V. 62
Digte. Kobenhavn: 1871. V. 66
Hedda Gabler. Kobenhavn: 1890. V. 65; 66
Hedda Gabler. Adapted by John Osborne. London: 1972. V. 66
John Gabriel Borkman. New York: 1897. V. 65
Little Eyolf: a Play in Three Acts. London: 1895. V. 66
Peer Gynt. London: 1936. V. 62; 64; 66
The Pillars of Society and Other Plays. London: 1888. V. 64
Three Plays - an Enemy of the People. The Wild Duck (and) Hedda Gabler. New York: 1964. V. 63
Vildanden. (The Wild Duck). Copenhagen: 1884. V. 62
The Works of.... New York: 1911-1912. V. 63

ICKIS, ALONZO FERDINAND
Bloody Trails Along the Rio Grande: a Day By Day Diary...(1836-1917). Denver: 1958. V. 64

IDDINGS, J. P.
Ingenous Rocks, Composition, Texture and Classifaction, Description and Occurrence. New York: 1909-1913. V. 63; 66

IDE, JOHN JAY
The Portraits of John Jay (1745-1829). New York: 1938. V. 67

IDELER, KARL WILHELM
Biographien Geisteskranker in Ihrer Psychologischen Entwicklung. Berlin: 1841. V. 65

IDRIESS, ION L.
In Crocodile Land: Wanderings in Northern Austrlia. Sydney: 1946. V. 67

IGNATOW, DAVID
Rescue the Dead. Poems. Middletown: 1968. V. 63
Sunlight: a Sequence for My Daughter. Brockport: 1979. V. 63

IJZERMAN, R.
Outline of the Geology and Petrology of Surinam (Dutch Guiana). Utrecht. V. 63; 66

ILES, FRANCIS
Before the Fact. London: 1932. V. 67

I'LL Take My Stand, The South and the Agrarian Tradition. New York and London: 1930. V. 63; 64

ILLINGWORTH, A. H.
More Reminiscences. 1936. V. 62; 63; 65

THE ILLUMINATED A B C. New York: 1850. V. 62

THE ILLUSTRATED A B C. New York: 1856. V. 65

ILLUSTRATED Annual of the Federation of State Societies of Southern California. Los Angeles: 1914. V. 63

ILLUSTRATED Atlas of Oakland County, Michigan. Racine: 1896. V. 67

THE ILLUSTRATED Book of Natural History.... Glasgow: 1845. V. 66; 67

ILLUSTRATED Exhibitor and Magazine of Art. London: 1852. V. 65

ILLUSTRATED Guide to Fairmont Park and the Centennial Exhibition Grounds and Buildings. Philadelphia: 1876. V. 65

AN ILLUSTRATED Itinerary of the County of Lancashire. London: 1842. V. 62

THE ILLUSTRATED London Spelling Book. London: 1849. V. 65

ILLUSTRATIONS, Historical and Descriptive of the Oxford Newdigate Prize Poems, With Engravings. Oxford: 1824. V. 67

ILLUSTRATIONS of Napa County California with Historical Sketch. Fresno: 1974. V. 66

ILLUSTRATIONS of Northern Antiquities, from the Earlier Teutonic and Scandinavian Romances.... London: 1814. V. 66

ILLUSTRATIONS to Scott's British Field Sports.... London: 1821. V. 66

IMAGE.. 1949-1952. V. 65

IMAGE DU MONDE
The Mirrour of the World. Kentfield: 1964. V. 62

IMAGE, SELWYN
The Poems of.... London: 1932. V. 62

IMAGES from the Great West. 1990. V. 63

AN IMAGINARY Conversation Between President Jackson and the Ghost of Jefferson. Columbia: 1831. V. 63

IMAGIST Anthology 1930. London: 1930. V. 62

IMES, BIRNEY
Juke Joint. Jackson: 1990. V. 62; 64; 67

IMISON, JOHN
The School of Arts, or, an Introduction to Useful Knowledge.... London: 1790?. V. 65

IMITATIO CHRISTI
The Christian's Pattern; or a Tratise of the Imitation of Jesus Christ.... London: 1700. V. 62
Counsels Selected from the Imitation of Christ. London: 1866. V. 66
De Imitatione Christi. Lugduni: 1658. V. 63; 66
De Imitatione Christi. Paris: 1764. V. 63
De Imitatione Christi. Paris: 1789. V. 63
De Imitatione Christi. Paris: 1919. V. 62
Imitation de Jesus Christ. Paris: 1885?. V. 65; 67
L'Imitation de Jesus Christ. Paris: 1856-1858. V. 62; 66
Of the Imitation of Christ. London: 1890. V. 67
Of the Imitation of Jesus Christ. London: 1851. V. 62

IMLAY, GILBERT
A Topographical Description of the Western Territory of North America.... London: 1792. V. 66
A Topographical Description of the Western Territory of North America.... London: 1793. V. 62; 66

IMMELMANN, FRANZ
Immelmann, the Eagle of Lille. London: 1935. V. 63; 67

AN IMPARTIAL and Exact Accompt of the Divers Popish Books, Beads and Crucifixes and Images, Taken at the Savoy, by Sr. William Waller...and Burnt by Order, in the New Palace-yard Westminster: the 11th of February. London: 1678. V. 63

AN IMPARTIAL History of the Late Revolution in France, From Its Commencement to the Death of the Queen, and the Execution of the Deputies of the Gironde Party. Boston: 1794. V. 66

IMPARTIAL Reflections on the Case of Mr. Byng, as Stated in an Appeal to the People, and Letter to a Member of Parliament, &c. London: 1756. V. 65

AN IMPARTIAL View of the Two Late Parliaments: Their Proceedings, and the Late Ministry, Fully Justify'd. London: 1711. V. 67

THE IMPERIAL First 100 Years. Tokyo: 1990. V. 66

IMPERIAL Fresno: Resources, Industries and Scenery Illustrated and Described. Fresno: 1897. V. 65

IMPERIALI, GIUSEPPE RENATO, CARDINAL
Bibliothecae Josephi Renati: Imperialis...Catalogus Secundum Auctorum Cognomina Ordine Alphabetico Dispositus.... Rome: 1711. V. 63

IMPEY, JOHN
The Office of Sheriff: Shewing Its History, Antiquity, Powers and Duties.... London: 1800. V. 65

IMPORTANT Custer, Indian War and Western Memorabilia. N.P: 1995. V. 65

IMPRESSIONS...of Animals, Birds, &c...Illustrative of British Field Sports; from a Set of Silver Buttons. London: 1821. V. 66

IMRIE, DAVID
Lakeland and Gamekeeper. London: 1949. V. 67

IN Albert Schweitzer's Realms, a Symposium. Cambridge: 1962. V. 63

IN Memoriam - Edwin R. Purple. New York: 1881. V. 63

IN Memoriam: Edwin Grabhorn 1889-1968. San Francisco: 1969. V. 64

IN Memoriam Sir Edmund A. H. Lechmere, Baronet. London: 1895. V. 67

IN Memoriam. William Frederick Havemeyer, Mayor of the City of New York, 1845-'46, 1848-'49, 1872-'74. New York: 1881. V. 62

IN Memoriam William Loring Andrews MDCCCXXXVII-MCMXX. New York: 1921. V. 63

IN Praise of Patterned Paper. London: 1997. V. 62; 67
IN Praise of Patterned Paper. Oldham: 1997. V. 62

IN Principio. Hammersmith: 1911. V. 66
IN Principio. London: 1929. V. 64

IN the Clutch of Circumstance, My Own Story. New York: 1922. V. 65

IN the Shadow of the Rockies - A History of the Augusta Area. N.P: 1978. V. 66

IN Tribute to Fred Anthoensen, Master Printer. Portland: 1952. V. 64

INAYAT, NOOT
Twenty Jataka Tales. Philadelphia: 1939. V. 64

INCHBALD, ELIZABETH
A Simple Story. London: 1799. V. 65
A Simple Story. London: 1833. V. 65

INCHBOLD, STANLEY
Lisbon and Cintra with Some Account of Other Cities and Historical Sites in Portugal. London: 1907. V. 63

INDAGINE, JOHANNES ROSENBACH
Chiromantia. 1. Physionomia, ex Aspectu Membrorum Hominis. 2. Periaxiomata de Faciebus Signorum. 3 Canones Astrologici, de Iudicitis Aegritudinum. 4. Astrologia Naturalis. 5. Complexionum Notitia Iuxta Dominium Planetarum. Paris: 1546. V. 64; 67

THE INDEX Expurgatorius of Martial, Literally Translated.... London: 1868. V. 62

INDEX Kewensis. Supplements I to XV. Oxford: 1901-1974. V. 65; 66

INDEX Librorum Prohibitorum Innoc. XI. P.M. Iussu Editus Usque ad Annum 1681. Rome: 1704-1734. V. 62

INDEX Librorum Prohibitorum Sanctissimi Domi Nostri Benedcti XIV... Jussu Recognitus, Atque Editus.... Rome: 1764. V. 62

INDIA HOUSE
A Descriptive Catalogue of the Marine Collection to be Found at India House. N.P: 1935. V. 63; 66
A Descriptive Catalogue of the Marine Collection to be Found at India House. Middletown: 1935. V. 63

INDIAN Anecdotes. Concord: 1850. V. 64

THE INDIAN Guide to Health, or Valuabale Vegetable Medical Prescriptions for the Use of Families or Young Practioners. Lafayette: 1845?. V. 63

INDIAN Tribes of Texas. Waco: 1971. V. 63

INDOOR Games and Amusements: a Book of Diversions for the Young and Old. New York: 1900. V. 63

INDUSTRIAL Rivers of the United Kingdom; Namely the Thames, Mersey, Tyne, Tawe, Clyde, Wear, Taff, Avon.... London: 1888. V. 64

INDUSTRIAL Trenton and Vicinity. Wilmington: 1900. V. 63; 66

THE INDUSTRIES of Los Angeles, California. Los Angeles: 1888. V. 63

INDUSTRIES of New Jersey. Part IV. Middlesex, Somerset and Union Counties. New York: 1882. V. 63; 66

INDUSTRY, a Tale of Real Life; Consisting of Interesting Occurrences, Illustrative of Felicity, Accruing from a Steady Perseverance in Diligence and Economy. London: 1825. V. 66

INFORMATION and Observations Respecting the Proposed Improvements at York Castle. 1823. V. 67

INGALLS, ALBERT G.
Amateur Telescope Making. New York: 1974. V. 63

INGALLS, FAY
About Dogs - and Me. Hot Springs: 1939. V. 64

INGALLS, RACHEL
Binstead's Safari. London: 1983. V. 64
Black Diamond. London: 1992. V. 64
Mrs. Caliban. London: 1982. V. 63; 64

INGE, WILLIAM
Bus Stop. New York: 1955. V. 66
Come Back, Little Sheba. New York: 1950. V. 62; 64
4 Plays by William Inge. New York: 1958. V. 66
Summer Brave and Eleven Short Plays. New York: 1962. V. 63

INGEGNIEROS, JOSE
Simulation de la Locura Ante la Sociologia Criminal y la Clinica Psiquiatrica. Buenos Aires: 1903. V. 65

INGELOW, JEAN
Mopsa the Fairy. New York: 1927. V. 63

INGER, R. F.
The Systematic and Zoogeography of the Amphibia of Boreno. London: 1966. V. 62

INGERSOLL, CHARLES JARED
A Discourse Concerning the Influence of America on the Mind.... Philadelphia: 1823. V. 66

INGERSOLL, CHESTER
Overland to California in 1847 - Letters Written En Route to California, West from Independence, Missouri, to the Editor of the Juliet Signal. Chicago: 1937. V. 63

INGERSOLL, E.
Birds' Nesting.... Salem: 1882. V. 62

INGERSOLL, ERNEST
Gold Fields of the Klondike and the Wonders of Alaska. St. John: 1897. V. 66

INGERSOLL, ROBERT G.
The Writings of Robert G. Ingersoll. New York: 1912. V. 63

INGERSOLL-RAND, C.
The Story of Hoover Dam (Boulder Dam). New York: 1931-1935. V. 65

INGHAM, HARNEY
The Northern Border Brigade. N.P: 1926. V. 67

INGHAM, THOMAS G.
Digging Gold Among the Rockies of Exciting Adventures of Wild Camp Life.... N.P: 1882. V. 64

INGLE, R. W.
British Crabs. London: 1980. V. 63

INGLIS, HENRY DAVID
The Channel Islands: Jersey, Guernsey, Alderney &c. London: 1834. V. 63
A Journey Throughout Ireland, During the Spring, Summer and Autumn of 1834. London: 1836. V. 66
Rambles in the Footsteps of Don Quixote. London: 1837. V. 65
Spain in 1830. London: 1831. V. 66

INGLIS, JAMES
Sport and Work on the Nepal Frontier. 1878. V. 67

INGPEN, ROGER
The Glory of Belgium. London: 1920. V. 64

INGRAHAM, EDWARD DUNCAN
A Sketch of the Events Which Preceded the Capture of Washington, by the British, on the Twenty-Fourth of August, 1814. Philadelphia: 1849. V. 66; 67

INGRAHAM, FRANC D.
Spina Bifida and Cranium Bifidum. Boston: 1944. V. 66; 67
Subdural Hematoma in Infancy. 1944. V. 64

INGRAHAM, JOSEPH
Joseph Ingraham's Journal of the Brigantine Hope on a Voyage to the Northwest Coast of North America 1790-1792. Barre: 1971. V. 62; 63; 64; 66

INGRAHAM, JOSEPH HOLT
Alice May and Bruising Bill. Boston: 1845. V. 63; 66
Fleming Field, or the Young Artisan. New York: 1845. V. 66
Lafitte: Pirate of the Gulf. New York: 1836. V. 63; 64; 66
The Seven Knights; or Tales of Many Lands. Boston: 1845. V. 66

INGRAHAM, P.
Seventy Years on the Old Frontier - Alexander Major.... Denver: 1893. V. 63

INGRAM, JAMES
Memorials of Oxford. Oxford: 1837. V. 62; 63; 67

INGRAM, JOHN H.
Oliver Madox Brown. London: 1883. V. 67

INGRAM, ROBERT ACKLOM
A Sermon Preached in the Parish-Church of St. James, Colchester on Sunday the 24th of August, 1788 for the Benefit of the Charity School. Colchester: 1788. V. 65

INGRAM, THOMAS DUNBAR
A History of the Legislative Union of Great Britain and Ireland. 1887. V. 67

INGRAMS, W. H.
Zanzibar; Its History and Its People. London: 1931. V. 67

INITIATION Amoureuse avec des Illustrations Originales par une Artiste Celebre. A Buenos Ayres: 1950. V. 64

INMAN, HENRY
Buffalo Jones' Forty Years of Adventure. Topeka: 1899. V. 64
The Great Salt Lake Trail. New York: 1898. V. 66
The Great Salt Lake Trail. Topeka: 1898. V. 65; 67
The Great Salt Lake Trail. Topeka: 1899. V. 65
The Old Santa Fe Trail - the Story of a Great Highway. New York: 1897. V. 67
Stories of the Old Santa Fe Trail. Kansas City: 1881. V. 65
Tales of the Trail. Short Stories of Western Life. Topeka: 1898. V. 65; 67

INNES, C. L.
Canterbury Sketches; or, Life from the Early Days. Christchurch: 1879. V. 67

INNES, HAMMOND
Dead and Alive. London: 1946. V. 63

INNES, MICHAEL
Appleby and the Ospreys. London: 1986. V. 62
Appleby Talking. London: 1954. V. 62
Carson's Conspiracy. London: 1984. V. 62
Death at the President's Lodging. London: 1936. V. 64
Honeybath's Haven. London: 1977. V. 67
Sheiks and Adders. London: 1982. V. 62

INNES, WILLIAM
Notes of Conversations with Hugh M'Donald, Neil Sutherland and Hugh M'Intosh, Who were Executed at Edinburgh on the 22d of April 1812 During the Time They Were Under Sentence of Death.... Edinburgh: 1812. V. 66

INNIS, BEN
Bloody Knife!. Fort Collins: 1973. V. 67

INNIS, HAROLD A.
The Fur Trade in Canada, an Introduction to Canadian Economic History. New Haven: 1930. V. 64
Peter Pond. Fur Trader and Adventurer. Toronto: 1930. V. 63; 64

INOUE SHINKODO
Hogei Zushiki. N.P: 1889. V. 66

INQUIRIES of Norfolk and Suffolk, Business Review. Birmingham: 1890. V. 63

AN INQUIRY Into the Policy of the Penal Laws, Affecting the Popish Inhabitants of Ireland. London: 1775. V. 66

THE INSECTS of Virginia. Blacksburg: 1969-1976. V. 66

INSKIPP, CAROL
A Guide to the Birds of Nepal. 1985. V. 67

INSTITOR, HEINRICH
Malleus Maleficarum. Nuremberg: 1500?. V. 64

INSTITUTE OF RADIO ENGINEERS
Proceedings of the IRE, Fiftieth Anniversary. New York: 1962. V. 66

INSTRUCTIONS for Officers and Non-Commissioned Officers on Outpost and Patrol Duty and Troops in Campaign. Washington: 1863. V. 63; 65

INSTRUCTIONS for Surgeons Under the Commissioners for Conducting His Majesty's Transport Service, for Taking Care of Sick and Wounded Seamen, and for the Care and Custody of Prisoners of War. London: 1809. V. 64

INSTRUCTIONS for the Exercise and Service of Great Guns &c. on Board Her Majesty's Ships. London: 1858. V. 62

THE INSTRUCTIVE Gift: a Premium for all Good Children. Philadelphia: 1852. V. 63

INSURRECTION Against the Military Government in New Mexico and California 1847-1848. Washington: 1900. V. 63

INTERCOLONIAL Railway and Prince Edward Island Railway of Canada. 1908. V. 65

THE INTEREST in Slavery of the Southern Non-Slaveholder. The Right of Peaceful Secession, Slavery in the Bible. Charleston: 1860. V. 66

INTERESTING Extracts from the Minutes of Evidence Taken Beofre the Committe of the Whole House, To Whom It Was Referred to Consider of the Affairs of the East India Company, in the Sessions of 1813.... London: 1814. V. 62

THE INTERESTING Trials of the Pirates for the Murder of William Little, Captain of the Ship American Eagle. Newburyport: 1796. V. 67

INTERIORS of the Italian Renaissance. N.P: Sep. 1890. V. 62; 65

INTERNATIONAL AND GREAT NORTHERN RAILROAD
Homes in Texas of the International and Great Northern R.R. 1880- 1881. Buffalo: 1880. V. 63

THE INTERNATIONAL Competition for a New Administration Building for the Chicago Tribune, 1922, Containing all the Designs Submitted.... 1923. V. 65

INTERNATIONAL INSTITUTE OF CHINA
Constitution of the International Institute of China. Shanghai: 1907. V. 63

INTERNATIONAL MEDICAL CONGRESS
Transactions of the International Medical Congress. Seventh Session Held in London August 2nd to 9th 1881.... London: 1881. V. 64; 67

INTERNATIONAL Policy. Essays on Foreign Relations of England. London: 1866. V. 62

INTERNATIONAL SNOW LEOPARD SYMPOSIUM
Proceedings. 1992. V. 67

INTERNATIONAL UNION FOR CO-OPERATION IN SOLAR RESEARCH
Transactions of the International Union for Co-Operation in Solar Research. Manchester: 1906-1914. V. 63

INTERNATIONAL UNION OF AMERICAN REPUBLICS
Commercial Directory of the American Republics.... Washington: 1897-1898. V. 65

THE INTRIGUING Courtiers; or, the Modish Gallants...Wherein the Secret Histories of Several Persons are...Represented. London: 1732. V. 63

AN INVESTIGATION into the Affairs of the Delaware and Raritan Canal and Camden and Amboy Rail Road Companies, in Reference to Certain Charges by A Citizen of Burlington. December 1848. Newark: 1849. V. 66

INVESTORS INTELLIGENCE INC.
The 1971 Encyclopedia of Stock Market Techniques. Larchmont: 1970. V. 64

INVESTORS' Supplement of the Commercial and Financial Chronicle. New York: 1888. V. 63

INWARDS, R.
The Temple of the Andes. London: 1884. V. 67

INWOOD, HENRY WILLIAM
The Erechtheion at Athens, Fragments of Athenian Architecture and a Few Remains in Attica, Megara and Epirus.... London: 1827. V. 64

IOBST, RICHARD W.
The Bloody Sixty. The Sixth North Carolina Regiment Confederate States of America. Raleigh: 1965. V. 65

IOLO Manuscripts. A Selection of Ancient Welsh Manuscripts, in Prose and Verse.... Liverpool: 1888. V. 66

IONESCO, EUGENE
Macbett. Paris: 1972. V. 63
Le Roi Se Meurt. Paris: 1963. V. 66

IOWA. GENERAL ASSEMBLY - 1866
H. R. Journal of...the 11th General Assembly of the State of Iowa. Des Moines: 1866. V. 65

IOWA. UNIVERSITY
Heirs of Hippocrates. Iowa City: 1990. V. 65

IRBY, A. H.
The Diary of a Hunter from the Pubjab to the Karakorum Mountains. 1863. V. 63

IREDALE, TOM
Birds of New Guinea. Melbourne: 1956. V. 67
Birds of Paradise and Bower Birds. Melbourne: 1950. V. 62; 63; 64; 66; 67
A Monograph of the Australian Loricates. Sydney: 1927. V. 66

IRELAND. DEPARTMENT OF LANDS AND FISHERIES - 1930
The Angler's Guide to the Irish Free State. Dublin: 1930. V. 67

IRELAND, ALEXANDER
The Book-Lover's Enchiridion.... London: 1884. V. 65

IRELAND, ANNIE E.
Life of Jane Welsh Carlyle. London: 1891. V. 65

IRELAND, GORDON
Boundaries, Possessions and Conflicts in Central and North America and the Caribbean. (with) Boundaries, Possessions and Conflicts in South America. Cambridge: 1941-1938. V. 63

IRELAND, JOHN
Hogarth Illustrated. London: 1793. V. 66

IRELAND, M. W.
The Medical Department of the United States Army in the World War. Washington: 1921-1929. V. 66

IRELAND, SAMUEL
Miscellaneous Papers and Legal Instruments Under the Hand and Seal of William Shakespeare.... London: 1796. V. 63
A Picturesque Tour through Holland, Brabant, and Part of France; Made in the Autumn of 1789. London: 1796. V. 67
Picturesque Views of the Severn. (with) Historical and Topographical Illustrations.... London: 1824. V. 63; 66
Picturesque Views on the River Medway, from the Nore to the Vicinity of Its Source in Sussex.... London: 1793. V. 66; 67
Picturesque Views on the River Thames, From Its Source in Gloucestershire to the Nore. London: 1801-1802. V. 64
Picturesque Views, with an Historical Account of the Inns of Court, in London and Westminster. London: 1800. V. 62

IRELAND, WILLIAM HENRY
All the Blocks! or, an Antidote All the Talent. London: 1807. V. 63; 66
The Confessions.... London: 1805. V. 63
Scribbleomania, or the Printer's Devil's Polychronicon, a Sublime Poem. London: 1815. V. 63
Stultitia. Stultifera Navis: Qua Omnium Mortalium Narratur. The Modern Ship of Fools. London: 1807. V. 67
Vortigern; an Historical Play. London: 1832. V. 62

IRELAND, WILLIAM W.
The Blot Upon the Brain: Studies in History and Psychology. Edinburgh: 1893. V. 66; 67

IRIARTE, TOMAS
Glorias Argentinas y Recuerdos Historicos. 1818-1825. Buenos Aires: 1858. V. 66

IRIGARAY, LUCE
Speculum de l'Autre Femme. Paris: 1974. V. 67

IRISH Economic and Social History. 1974-1993. V. 67

THE IRISH Protest to the Ministrial Manifesto, Contained in the Address of the British Parliament to the King. Dublin: 1785. V. 62

THE IRISH Statutes...3rd Edward II to the Union 1310-1800. 1995. V. 67

IRONSIDE, R.
Pre-Raphaelite Painters. London: 1948. V. 62; 65

IRVINE, ALEXANDER
The Illustrated Handbook of British Plants. London: 1858. V. 67
A Treatise on the Game Laws of Scotland. Edinburgh: 1850. V. 63

IRVINE, CHRISTOPHER
Historiae Scoticae Nomenclatura Latino-Vernacula: Multis Flosculis, ex Antiquis Albinorum Monumentis.... Edinbruchii: 1682. V. 65

IRVINE, F. R.
The Fishes and Fisheries of the Gold Coast. 1947. V. 63
Woody Plants of Ghana with Special Reference to Their Uses. London: 1961. V. 65

IRVINE, JAMES C.
Jack London at Yale. Westwood: 1906. V. 65

IRVINE, JOHN
By Winding Roads. 1950. V. 67

IRVING, CHRISTOPHER
A Catechism of Jewish Antiquites: Containing an Account of the Classes, Institutions, Rites, Ceremonies, Manners, Customs &c. of the Ancient Jews. New York: 1824. V. 66

IRVING, CONSTANCE
A Child's Book of Hours. 1920. V. 66

IRVING, EDWARD
Trial of Rev. Edward Irving, M. A. London: 1823. V. 63

IRVING, HENRY
The Collection of Theatrical Relics...Formed by the Late Sir Henry Irving. The Collection of Pictures and Drawings. Catalogue of the Valuable Library. London: 1905. V. 62

IRVING, JOHN
The Cider House Rules. Franklin Center: 1985. V. 62; 65; 67
The Cider House Rules. New York: 1985. V. 64; 66; 67
The Hotel New Hampshire. New York: 1981. V. 63; 66; 67
The Imaginary Girlfriend. London: 1996. V. 62
The Imaginary Girlfriend. Toronto: 1996. V. 67
A Prayer for Owen Meaney. Franklin Center: 1989. V. 62; 65
A Prayer for Owen Meany. New York: 1989. V. 62; 65; 66; 67
A Prayer for Owen Meany. Toronto: 1989. V. 67
Setting Free the Bears. New York: 1968. V. 63
A Son of the Circus. London: 1994. V. 67

IRVING, JOHN continued
A Son of the Circus. New York: 1994. V. 62; 64; 65; 67
Trying to Save Piggy Sneed. Toronto: 1993. V. 62; 63; 67
The Water Method Man. New York: 1972. V. 66; 67
A Widow for One Year. Media: 1997. V. 65
A Widow for One Year. 1998. V. 66
A Widow for One Year. Media: 1998. V. 62; 67
A Widow for One Year. New York: 1998. V. 63; 64; 66; 67
The World According to Garp. New York: 1978. V. 63; 65

IRVING, JOHN B.
A Day on Cooper River. Columbia: 1932. V. 63; 66

IRVING, JOSEPH
The Book of Dumbartonshire.... Edinburgh and London: 1879. V. 64

IRVING, PIERRE M.
The Life and Letters of Washington Iriving. New York: 1862-1864. V. 62

IRVING, WASHINGTON
Abbotsford and Newstead Abbey. Philadelphia: 1835. V. 67
Adventures of Captain Bonneville; or Scenes Beyond the Rocky Mountains of the Far West. London: 1840?. V. 67
The Adventures of Captain Bonneville, U.S.A. New York: 1856. V. 64
The Alhambra. London: 1832. V. 62
The Alhambra. Paris: 1832. V. 63
The Alhambra. Philadelphia: 1832. V. 63
The Alhambra. London: 1896. V. 64
Astoria. London: 1836. V. 63; 67
Astoria. Philadelphia: 1836. V. 63; 66
Astoria,. New York: 1851. V. 66
Astoria. New York: 1897. V. 62
Bracebridge Hall. London: 1822. V. 65
Bracebridge Hall. Paris: 1834. V. 63
Bracebridge Hall. London: 1895. V. 63
Christmas at Bracebridge Hall. London: 1906. V. 64
A Chronicle of the Conquest of Granada. London: 1829. V. 63; 65
A Chronicle of the Conquest of Granada. Paris: 1829. V. 63
Chronicle of the Conquest of Granada. New York: 1893. V. 62
A History of New York from the Beginning of the World to the End of the Dutch Dynasty.... New York: 1809. V. 64
A History of the Life and Voyages of Christopher Columbus. London: 1828. V. 65; 67
A History of the Life and Voyages of Christopher Columbus. Paris: 1829. V. 63
A Humorous History of New York.... London: 1820. V. 65
A Humorous History of New York.... London: 1821. V. 65
The Legend of Sleepy Hollow. New York: 1897. V. 64
The Legend of Sleepy Hollow. London: 1928. V. 65
The Legend of Sleepy Hollow. Hyattsville: 1983. V. 64
Legends of the Conquest of Spain. London: 1835. V. 67
Legends of the Conquest of Spain. London: 1836. V. 67
Letters of Jonathan Oldstyle, Gent. London: 1824. V. 67
The Life of Mahomet. Leipzig: 1850. V. 67
Mr. Irving's Notes and Journal of Travel in Europe, 1804-1805. New York: 1921. V. 64
Old Christmas. From the Sketchbook of Washington Irving. London: 1876. V. 62
Rip Van Winkle. London: 1850. V. 65
Rip Van Winkle. New York: 1869. V. 62; 64
Rip Van Winkle. New York: 1897. V. 62
Rip Van Winkle. East Aurora: 1905. V. 67
Rip Van Winkle. Philadelphia: 1921. V. 64; 65
Salmagundi: or, the Whim-Whams and Opinions of Launcelot Landstaff, Esq. Paris: 1824. V. 63
Salmagundi; or the Whim-Whams and Opinions of Launcelot Langstaff, Esq. London: 1811. V. 62
The Sketch Book of Geoffrey Crayon, Gent. Paris: 1831. V. 63
The Sketch-Book of Geoffrey Crayon, Esq. London: 1834. V. 67
The Sketch-Book of Geoffrey Crayon, Gent. New York and London: 1895. V. 63
Tales of a Traveller. London: 1824. V. 63
Tales of a Traveller. Paris: 1834. V. 63
A Tour on the Prairies. London: 1835. V. 63
A Tour on the Prairies. Philadelphia: 1835. V. 62; 65
Voyage d'un Americain a Londres, ou Esquisse sur les Moeurs Anglaises et Ameriaines... (The Sketchbook of Geoffrey Crayon). Paris: 1822. V. 66
Voyage to the Eastern Part of Terra Firma, or the Spanish main, in South America.... New York: 1806. V. 62
Voyages and Discoveries of the Companions of Columbus. Paris: 1831. V. 63
Wolfert's Roost and Other Papers, Now First Collected. New York: 1855. V. 67

IRWIN, EYLES
A Series of Adventures in the Course of a Voyage Up the Red Sea, On the Coasts of Arabia and Egypt.... London: 1780. V. 62

IRWIN, JOHN R.
The Story of Marcellus Moss Rice and His Big Valley Kinsmen. Montevallo: 1963. V. 67

IRWIN, RICHARD B.
History of the Nineteenth Army Corps. New York: 1892. V. 64

ISA, ALI IBN
Memorandum Book of a Tenth-Century Oculist for the Use of Modern Ophthalmologists. Birmingham: 1985. V. 63

ISAAC, BERT
The Landscape Within. 1992. V. 62

ISAAC, FRANK
English and Scottish Printing Types 1501-1535, 1508-1541. London: 1930. V. 64

ISAAC, PETER
William Bulmer: The Fine Printer in Context 1757-1830. London: 1993. V. 62; 64; 65
William Bulmer: the Fine Printer in Context 1757-1830. London: 1995. V. 62

ISAAC, S.
Aspects of Tropical Mycology. Cambridge: 1993. V. 64

ISAACS, ANNE
Swamp Angel. New York: 1994. V. 65

ISAACSON, HENRY
Saturni Ephemerides sive Tabula Historico-Chronologica. London: 1633. V. 66

ISABEY, JEAN BAPTISTE
Divers Essais Lithographiques.... Paris. V. 66
Voyage en Italie en 1822. Paris. V. 62; 66

ISAHAKIAN, AVETIK
Abu Lala Mahari. Yerevan: 1975. V. 64

ISARD, A. P.
The Model Shipbuilder's Manual Of Fittings and Guns. London: 1946. V. 63; 66

ISBELL, F. A.
Mining and Hunting in the Far West. San Francisco: 1940. V. 64

ISEMONGER, R. M.
Snakes and Snake Catching in Southern Africa. Cape Town: 1955. V. 66

ISHAM, NORMAN
Early Connecticut Houses, an Historical and Architectural Study. Providence: 1900. V. 67

ISHERWOOD, CHRISTOPHER
Christopher and His Kind 1929-1939. New York: 1976. V. 64; 67
Christopher and His Kind. 1929-1939. New York: 1977. V. 67
Commonplace Book: Being Some Quotations Christopher Isherwood Gathered and Recorded in His Lifetime. 1993. V. 64
The Condor and the Cows. London: 1949. V. 63
Goodbye to Berlin. London: 1939. V. 65
Goodbye to Berlin. New York: 1939. V. 64
How to Know God, the Yoga Aphorisms of Patanjali. New York: 1953. V. 65
Lions and Shadows - an Education in the Twenties. London: 1938. V. 64; 66
The Memorial: Portrait of a Family. London: 1932. V. 65; 66
My Guru and His Disciple. London: 1980. V. 62; 66
The Repton Letters. Settrington: 1997. V. 62; 64
Sally Bowles. London: 1937. V. 67
Vedanta for Modern Man. New York: 1951. V. 62; 64
Vedanta for the Western World. Hollywood: 1945. V. 65
The World in the Evening. London: 1954. V. 63
The World in the Evening. New York: 1954. V. 65

ISHIGURO, KAZUO
An Artist of the Floating World. London: 1986. V. 62; 67
An Artist of the Floating World. New York: 1986. V. 63; 66
A Pale View of Hills. London: 1982. V. 63; 66
The Remains of the Day. London: 1989. V. 62; 64; 66
The Remains of the Day. New York: 1989. V. 66
The Unconsoled. London: 1995. V. 62
The Unconsoled. New York: 1995. V. 63; 64; 67

ISHIKAWA, C.
Studies of Reproductive Elements. I. Spermatogenesis, Ovogenesis and Fertilization in Diaptomus. Tokyo: 1891. V. 67

ISHIZAKI, A.
Morphological, Physiological and Silvicultural Characteristics of Some Important Varieties of Cryptomeria Japonica D. Don in Kyushu. Tokyo: 1965. V. 67

ISLA, JOSE FRANCISCO DE
The History of the Famous Preacher Friar Gerund de Campazas; Otherwise Gerund Zotes. London: 1772. V. 62; 66

ISOCRATES
Isocratis Panegyricus, Areopagiticus, Ad Philippum, Et Archidamus. Ingolstadii: 1600. V. 65
Isocratis Scripta, Quae Quidem Nunc Extant Omnia, Graecolatina.... Basiliae: 1571. V. 65
(Omnia Opera). Basle: 1570. V. 66
Orationes & Epistolae. Parisiis: 1621. V. 66
The Orations and Epistles of Isocrates. London: 1752. V. 67

ISTVANFFI DE CSIK MADEFALVA, GYULA
A Clusius-Code Mykologi Meltatasa Adatokkal Clusius.... Budapest: 1900. V. 66

ISUMBRAS
Syr Ysambrace. 1897. V. 64

ITARD, JEAN MARC GASPARD
De l'Education d'un Homme Sauvage, ou Des Premiers Developpemens Physiques et Moraux du Jeune Sauvage de l'Aveyron...(with) Rapport Fait a Son Excellence le Ministre de l'Interieur sur les Nouveaux Developpment et l'Etat Actual du Sauvage.... Paris: 1801. V. 65

ITINERANT METHODISTS PREACHERS' ANNUITANT SOCIETY
Rules and Regulations of an Institution, Called the Itinerant Methodist Preachers' Annuitant Society, Formed in Liverpool, August 12, 1813. London: 1814. V. 64

IVENS, T. C.
Still Water Fly-Fishing. London: 1975. V. 67

IVERNOIS, FRANCIS
An Historical and Political View of the Constitution and Revolutions of Geneva, in the Eighteenth Century. Dublin: 1784. V. 64

IVES, BURL
Wayfaring Stranger. London: 1952. V. 64

IVES, JOHN M.
New England Book of Fruits. Salem: 1847. V. 62

IVES, JOSEPH C.
Report Upon the Colorado River of the West. Washington: 1861. V. 66

IVES, SIDNEY
The Parkman Dexter Howe Library. Gainesville: 1983-1995. V. 66

IVINS, VIRGINIA WILCOX
Pen Pictures of Early Western Days. N.P: 1908. V. 63; 66

IVY, R.
Poems for a Campaign. Thorpe Bay. V. 64

IWAMA, G. K.
Fish Stress and Health in Aquaculture. Cambridge: 1997. V. 64; 65

IWAMIYA, T.
Imperial Gardens of Japan. New York: 1970. V. 64

IZLAR, WILLIAM VALMORE
A Sketch of the War Record of the Edisto Rifles 1861-1865. Columbia: 1914. V. 62; 63; 65

IZZARD, SEBASTIAN
One Hundred Masterpieces from the Collection of Dr. Walter A. Compton. London: 1992. V. 64

IZZI, EUGENE
The Take. New York: 1987. V. 65

J

J., A.
An Apology for Camp Meetings, Illustrative of Their Good Effects and Answering the Principal Objections Urged Against Them. New York: 1810. V. 66

J., M. L.
Phebe of Plasthwaite. London: 1875. V. 67

J., T. E.
Lines on Chapel Island, in Morecambe Bay. Ulverston: 1847. V. 63; 65

JACINTO DE DEUS, FR.
Escudo dos Cavalleiros das Ordens Militares. Lisbon: 1670. V. 62
Vergel de Plantas e Flores da Provincia de Madre de Deos dos Capuchos Reformados. Lisbon: 1690. V. 62

JACK and Jill and Old Dame Gill. 1820. V. 66

JACK and Jill and Other Nursery Rhymes. 1900. V. 66

JACK and the Beanstalk. New York: 1888. V. 63
JACK and the Beanstalk. Chicago: 1936. V. 65

JACK and the Beanstalk and Hop O'my Thumb. London: 1962. V. 65
JACK and the Beanstalk and Hop O'my Thumb. London: 1965. V. 63

JACK and the Giants. London: 1851. V. 62

JACK Dandy's Delight, or, the History of the Birds and Beasts. York: 1820. V. 66

JACK, FLORENCE B.
The Woman's Book. 1935. V. 67

JACK in the Box. London: 1880. V. 65

JACK Jingle and Sucky Shingle. York: 1825. V. 66

JACK, MARIAN
The Adventures of Budgy Billy - a Nonsense Book. Philadelphia: 1920. V. 64; 65

JACK Spratt. New York: 1860. V. 62

JACK the Giant Killer. N.P: 1973. V. 63

JACKSON, A. B.
Catalogue of the Trees and Shrubs (Excluding Rhododendrons) at Borde Hill, Sussex.... Oxford: 1935. V. 62

JACKSON, A. J.
Blackburn Aircraft Since 1909. London: 1968. V. 62; 66

JACKSON, A. T.
Picture Writing of Texas Indians. Austin: 1938. V. 67

JACKSON, ALBERT
Official Report of the Trial of the Hon. Albert Jackson, Judge of the Fifteenth Judicial Circuit, Before the Senate, Composing the High Court of Impeachment of the State of Missouri. Jefferson City: 1859. V. 66; 67

JACKSON, ALFRED
Times from an Amateur's Palette; or a Few Stray Lines of Thought. London: 1849. V. 62

JACKSON, ALLEN W.
The Half-Timber House. New York: 1919. V. 67

JACKSON, C. E.
Bird Illustrators. 1975. V. 64
Bird Illustrators. London: 1975. V. 62; 66
Wood Engravings of Birds. 1978. V. 63

JACKSON, CATHERINE HANNAH CHARLOTTE
Works (on French History). London: 1899. V. 62

JACKSON, CHARLES JAMES
An Illustrated History of English Plate, Ecclesiastical and Secular. London: 1911. V. 62; 66; 67

JACKSON, CHARLES LORING
The Gold Point and Other Strange Stories. Boston: 1926. V. 63

JACKSON, CHARLES ROSS
Quintus Oakes. New York: 1904. V. 67

JACKSON, CHARLES T.
Remarks on Mineralogy and Geology of Nova Scotia. Cambridge: 1833. V. 63

JACKSON, CHARLES TENNEY
My Brother's Keeper. Indianapolis: 1910. V. 66

JACKSON, CLARENCE
Pageant of the Pioneers: Veritable Art of William H. Jackson. Minden: 1958. V. 63
Picture Maker of the Old West, William Henry Jackson. New York: 1947. V. 64; 66

JACKSON, DONALD
Letters of the Lewis and Clark Expedition - With Related Documents 1783-1854. Urbana: 1978. V. 65

JACKSON, E. NEVILLE
Silhouette, Notes and Dictionary.... London: 1938. V. 64

JACKSON, EDGAR
Three Rebels Write Home. Franklin: 1955. V. 62; 63; 65

JACKSON, F. HAMILTON
Rambles in the Pyrenees, and the Adjacent Districts, Gascony, Pays de Foix and Roussillion. New York: 1912. V. 65

JACKSON, F. J.
Notes on the Game Birds of Kenya and Uganda. London: 1926. V. 63

JACKSON, FREDERICK GEORGE
The Great Frozen Land (Bolshaia Zmelskija Tundra). London: 1895. V. 67

JACKSON, FREDERICK JOHN
The Birds of Kenya Colony and the Uganda Protectorate. London: 1938. V. 67
Notes on the Game Birds of Kenya and Uganda.... London: 1926. V. 67

JACKSON, GEORGE
Blood in My Eye. New York: 1972. V. 63

JACKSON, GEORGE A.
Jackson's Diary of 59. Idaho Springs: 1929. V. 63

JACKSON, GEORGE P.
Spiritual Folk-Songs of Early America: 250 Tunes and Texts, With an Introduction and Notes. New York: 1937. V. 66
White Spirituals in the Southern Uplands. 1933. V. 63; 67

JACKSON, HELEN HUNT
Ah-Wah-Ne-Days: a Visit to the Yosemite Valley in 1872. San Francisco: 1971. V. 63
Bits of Travel. Boston: 1872. V. 64
Ramona. Boston: 1900. V. 62
Ramona. Los Angeles: 1959. V. 63
Sonnets and Lyrics. Boston: 1886. V. 64
Verses. Boston: 1870. V. 64
Zeph. A Posthumous Story. Boston: 1885. V. 63

JACKSON, HENRY
About Edwin Drood. Cambridge: 1911. V. 62

JACKSON, HENRY R.
Tallulah and Other Poems. Savannah: 1850. V. 64; 66

JACKSON, HOLBROOK
A Catalogue for Typophiles of Books of Typographical Interest. 1932. V. 65
The Eighteen Nineties: a Review of Art and Ideas at the Close of the Nineteenth Century. New York: 1914. V. 66
Great English Novelists. London: 1908. V. 66
Maxims of Books and Reading. London: 1934. V. 67

JACKSON, HOWELL E.
Address of Hon. Howell E. Jackson. Delivered Before the State Teachers' Associaton at Jonesboro, TN on August 5, 1885.... Nashville: 1885. V. 64

JACKSON, I. R.
A Sketch of the Life and Public Services of William Henry Harrison. Lexington: 1836. V. 66

JACKSON, I. W.
An Elementary Treatise on Optics. Schenectady: 1852. V. 66

JACKSON, ISAAC R.
A Sketch of the Life and Public Services of William Henry Harrison, Commander in Chief of the North Western Army During the War of 1812, etc. New York: 1836. V. 65

JACKSON, J. E.
History of St. George's Church, Doncaster. Destroyed by Fire, February 28, 1853. London: 1855. V. 67

JACKSON, J. J.
Nonsense for Girls. New York: 1874. V. 63

JACKSON, J. Q.
Valuable Receipts; or, Secrets Revealed!. Boston: 1846. V. 66

JACKSON, J. R.
Minerals and Their Uses in a Series of Letters to a Lady. London: 1849. V. 64

JACKSON, JAMES
An Eulogy on the Character of John Warren, M.D. Delivered at the Request of...the Massachusetts Medical Society. Boston: 1815. V. 63

JACKSON, JEAN JONES
To Remember JJJ. N.P: 1985. V. 67

JACKSON, JOHN
An Address to Time with Other Poems. Macclesfield: 1808. V. 62
The Improved Tailors'.... London: 1831. V. 64
Journey from India; Towards England, in the Year 1797.... London: 1799. V. 67
Rational Amusement for Winter Evenings.... London: 1821. V. 62
A Treatise on Wood Engraving, Historical and Practical. London: 1839. V. 64; 67
A Treatise on Wood Engraving, Historical and Practical. London: 1861. V. 66

JACKSON, JOHN BAPTIST
An Essay on the Invention of Engraving and Printing in Chiaro Oscuro, as Practised by Albert Durer.... London: 1754. V. 66; 67

JACKSON, JOHN HUGHLINGS
Cases of Disease of the Nervous System in Patients the Subjects of Inherited Syphillis. London: 1868. V. 66
Neurological Fragments. London: 1925. V. 67
Selected Writings of John Hughlings Jackson.... London: 1931-1932. V. 64

JACKSON, JON A.
The Blind Pig. New York: 1978. V. 62; 63; 64; 66
Dead Folk. Tucson: 1995. V. 63; 66
The Diehard. New York: 1977. V. 63; 66; 67
Grootka. Woodstock: 1990. V. 64
Ridin' with Ray. Santa Barbara: 1995. V. 65; 66; 67

JACKSON, JULIAN R.
What to Observe, or the Traveller's Remembrancer. London: 1861. V. 67

JACKSON, KATHRYN
Big Farmer Big and Little Farmer Little. New York: 1948. V. 64

JACKSON, LEROY F.
The Peter Patter Book. London: 1918. V. 65

JACKSON, MAHALIA
Mahalia Jackson Cooks Soul. Nashville: 1970. V. 67

JACKSON, MARIA ELIZABETH
The Florist's Manual, or Hints for the Construction of a Gay Flower Garden.... London: 1822. V. 64

JACKSON, MARY ANNA
Julia Jackson Christian. Charlotte: 1910. V. 63
Memoirs of Stonewall Jackson. Louisville: 1895. V. 63

JACKSON, MARY E.
The Life of Nellie C. Bailey: or a Romance of the West. Topeka: 1885. V. 64
The Life of Nellie C. Bailey or a Romance of the West. Chicago: 1887. V. 66
Topeka Pen and Camera Sketches. Topeka: 1890. V. 65

JACKSON, MASON
The Pictorial Press. Its Origin and Progress. London: 1885. V. 67

JACKSON, R.
The Concise Dictionary of Artists' Signatures. London: 1980. V. 65

JACKSON, R. M. S.
The Mountain. Philadelphia: 1860. V. 66

JACKSON, R. T.
Phylogeny of the Echini. Boston: 1912. V. 63; 65; 66

JACKSON, ROBERT
An Exposition of the Practice of Affusing Cold Water on the Surface of the Body, as a Remedy for the Cure of Fever. Edinburgh: 1808. V. 64

JACKSON, ROBERT H.
The Struggle for Judicial Supremacy: a Study of a Crisis in American Power Politics. New York: 1941. V. 63

JACKSON, S. W.
A Fair Rebel's Interviews with Abraham Lincoln. New York: 1917. V. 63

JACKSON, SHIRLEY
The Bird's Nest. New York: 1954. V. 65
Hangsaman. 1951. V. 66
Hangsaman. New York: 1951. V. 65
Life Among the Savages. 1953. V. 66
Life Among the Savages. New York: 1953. V. 65
Magic Wishes. New York: 1963. V. 62
The Sundial. London: 1958. V. 64
The Sundial. New York: 1958. V. 66; 67
We Have Always Lived in Castles. 1962. V. 66
We Have Always Lived in the Castle. New York: 1962. V. 64

JACKSON, T. G.
The Church of St. Mary the Virgin, Oxford. Oxford: 1897. V. 62; 65

JACKSON, THEODORE
A Serious Address to the Queen, Prince of Wales and the Pacific at Large.... London: 1788. V. 62

JACKSON, WILFRID SCARBOROUGH
Nine Points of the Law. London: 1903. V. 65

JACKSON, WILLIAM
An Annotated List of the Publications of the Reverend Thomas Frognall Dibdin, D.D.... Cambridge: 1965. V. 62
Book-Keeping, in the True Italian Form of Debtor and Creditor, by Way of Double Entry.... New York: 1811. V. 64; 66
Papers and Pedigrees Mainly Relating to Cumberland and Westmorland. London: 1892. V. 66

JACKSON, WILLIAM A.
Records of the Court of the Stationers' Company 1602-1640. London: 1957. V. 66

JACKSON, WILLIAM HENRY
The Pioneer Photographer: Rocky Mountain Adventures with Camera. Yonkers-on-Hudson: 1929. V. 65
Time Exposure - The Autobiography of William Henry Jackson. New York: 1940. V. 63; 65; 66
William Henry Jackson's Rocky Mountain Railroad Album: Steam and Steel Across the Great Divide. Silverton: 1976. V. 62; 63

JACME, JEAN
A Litil Boke the Whiche Traytied and Reherced Many Gode Thinges Necessarie for the...Pestilence.... Manchester: 1910. V. 65

JACOB, GILES
The Compleat Court Keeper, or, Land-Steward's Assistant.... London: 1713. V. 65
The Compleat Court-Keeper; or, Land-Steward's Assistant.... London: 1715. V. 62
The Compleat Sportsman. London: 1718. V. 66
Every Man His Own Lawyer; or a Summary of the Laws of England in a new and Instructive Method.... London: 1740. V. 62
Every Man His Own Lawyer, or, a Summary of the Laws of England in a New and Instructive Method.... London: 1750. V. 62; 63
A New Law Dictionary; Containing, the Interpretation and Definition of Words and Terms Used in the Law.... London: 1744. V. 67
The Poetical Register; or, the Lives and Characters of all the English Poets. London: 1723. V. 67

JACOB, HAROLD F.
Kings of Arabia; the Rise and Set of the Turkish Sovranty in the Arabian Peninsula. London: 1923. V. 67

JACOB, JOHN J.
A Biographical Sketch of the Late Captain Michael Cresap. Cincinnati: 1866. V. 66

JACOB, NED
Exhibition Catalog - National Cowboy Hall of Fame. N.P: 1972. V. 65

JACOB, P. L.
La Perle ou Les Femmes Litteraires. Paris: 1832. V. 67

JACOB, WILLIAM
Tracts Relating to the Corn Trade and Corn Laws.... London: 1828. V. 62

JACOBACCI, VINCENZO
A Giambatista Bodoni, Che Gli fe 'Dono Dell 'Orazio Stampato Co' Suoi Caratteri. Paria: 1791. V. 65

JACOBI, ABRAHAM
Contributions to Pediatrics. New York: 1909. V. 66

JACOBI, CARL
Revelations in Black. 1947. V. 66
Revelations in Black. Sauk City: 1947. V. 63; 64; 65

JACOBI, JOHANN CHRISTIAN
Psalmodia Germanica, or, German Psalmod. Part II. London: 1725. V. 63; 66

JACOBS, JANE
The Death and Life of Great American Cities. New York: 1961. V. 63; 67

JACOBS, JOSEPH
The Book of Wonder Voyages. London: 1896. V. 62

JACOBS, JOSEPH continued
Celtic Fairy Tales. London: 1892. V. 64
English Fairy Tales. London: 1890. V. 64
More Celtic Fairy Tales. London: 1894. V. 64
More English Fairy Tales. London: 1894. V. 64

JACOBS, ORANGE
Memoirs of.... Seattle: 1908. V. 64

JACOBS, W. W.
Dialstone Lane. London: 1906. V. 67
Salthaven. London: 1908. V. 67
Salthaven. New York: 1908. V. 67
Sea Whispers. New York: 1926. V. 65

JACOBS-BOND, CARRIE
Tales of Little Cats. Joliet: 1918. V. 63

JACOBSEN, H.
Handbook of Succulent Plants. 1960. V. 66
Handbook of Succulent Plants. London: 1960. V. 64
Lexicon of Succulent Plants. 1974. V. 66
Lexicon of Succulent Plants. London: 1974. V. 64
Succulent Plants. London: 1935. V. 64

JACOBSON, J. Z.
Art of Today: Chicago 1933. Chicago: 1932. V. 62; 65
Thirty-five Saints and Emil Armin. Chicago: 1929. V. 65

JACOBSON, O. B.
Kiowa Indian Art. Santa Fe: 1979. V. 62

JACOBSON, SHERWOOD A.
The Post Traumatic Syndrome Following Head Injury Mechanism and Treatment. Springfield: 1963. V. 67

JACOBUS DE VARAGINE
In the State of Innocensye. Beckenham, Kent: 1988. V. 62

JACOUBET, T.
Atlas General de la Ville, es Fauborgs et des Monuments de Paris.... Paris: 1836. V. 66

JACQUES, DAVID
Fisherman's Fly and Other Studies. London: 1965. V. 67

JACQUES, FLORENCE PAGE
Francis Lee Jacques: Artist of the Wilderness World. New York: 1973. V. 63

JACSON, FRANCES
Isabella.... London: 1823. V. 66

JAEGER, HENRIK
The Life of Henrik Ibsen. London: 1890. V. 66

JAFFE, IRMA B.
John Trumbull - Patriot-Artist of the American Revolution. Boston: 1975. V. 63; 64

JAGERSKIOLD, AXEL LEONARD KRISTER EDVARD
Results of the Swedish Zoological Expedition to Egypt and the White Nile 1901.... Uppsala: 1904-1928. V. 67

JAGGER, MARY A.
The History of Honley and Its Hamlets from the Earliest Time to the Present. Huddersfield: 1914. V. 65

JAGO, RICHARD
Edge-Hill, or, the Rural Prospect Delineated and Moralized. London: 1767. V. 66
Poems, Moral and Descriptive...To Which is Added, Some Account of the Life and Writings of Mr. Jago. London: 1784. V. 66

JAHODA, GLORIA
Annie. Boston: 1960. V. 65

JAHRBUCH fur Psychoanalytische und Psychopathologische Forschungen.
Leipzig/Wien: 1909-1914. V. 62

JAKAB, IRENE
Conscious and Unconscious Expressive Art: Theory, Methodology, and Pathographies. Psychiatry and Art Volume 3. Basel: 1971. V. 65

JAKOBOVITS, IMMANUEL
Jewish Medical Ethics. New York: 1959. V. 63

JAKUBOWSKI, MAXIM
A Celebration of Crime Writing. Blakeney, Gloucestershire: 1996. V. 62
No Alibi. Blakeney: 1995. V. 62; 65
No Alibi. Manchester: 1995. V. 63

JALOVEC, KAREL
Beautiful Italian Violins. London: 1963. V. 65
German and Austrian Violin Makers. London: 1967. V. 65
Italian Violin Makers. New York: Sep. 1960. V. 65
The Violin Makers of Bohemia Including Craftsmen of Moravia and Slovakia. London. V. 65

JAMAICA. LAWS, STATUTES, ETC. - 1684
The Laws of Jamaica Passed by the Assembly and Confirmed by His Majesty in Council, April 17, 1864. To which is added, The State of Jamaica, As It Is Now. London: 1684. V. 64; 66

JAMBLICHUS OF CHALCIS
De Mysteriis Aegyptiorum, Chaldaeorum, Assyriorum. Lugduni: 1549. V. 66

JAMES, BILL
The Lolita Man. London: 1986. V. 65
You'd Better Believe It. London: 1985. V. 65

JAMES Broderna. St. Paul. V. 66

JAMES, C. L. R.
Beyond a Boundary. London: 1963. V. 64

JAMES, CHARLES
Hints Founded on Facts; or a Cursory View of Our Several Military Establishments.... London: 1791. V. 65
A New and Enlarged Military Dictionary in French and English.... London: 1810. V. 64
A New and Enlarged Military Dictionary, or Alphabetical Explantion of Technical Terms.... London: 1802. V. 63

JAMES, EDGAR
The Allen Outlaws and Their Career of Crime in the Mountains of Virginia. The Trilling Tragedy of Hillville Court House. Baltimore: 1912. V. 64

JAMES, EDWIN
Account of an Expedition from Pittsburgh to the Rocky Mountains. London: 1823. V. 66
Account of an Expedition from Pittsburgh to the Rocky Mountains. Barre: 1972. V. 67

JAMES Forbes; a Tale, Founded on Facts. London: 1824. V. 67

JAMES, GEORGE PAYNE RAINSFORD
Beauchamp; or, the Error. Leipzig: 1846. V. 67
Charles Tyrell; or, the Bitter Blood. London: 1839. V. 67
The Commissioner, or De Lunatic Inquirendo. Dublin: 1843. V. 66; 67
The Convict. A Tale. (with) Charles Tyrrell; or, the Bitter Blood. London: 1851-1852. V. 67
Delaware; or, the Ruined Family. Edinburgh: 1833. V. 67
Gowrie; or, The King's Plot. London: 1848-1849. V. 66
The History of Chivalry. London: 1830. V. 64
The Jacquerie; or, the Lady and the Page; an Historical Romance. London: 1841. V. 67
The King's Highway. London: 1840. V. 63; 67
The Last of the Fairies. London: 1848. V. 63
Russell: a Tale of te Reign of Charles II. London: 1847. V. 67
Sir Theodore Broughton; or, Laurel Water. London: 1848. V. 67
The Vicissitudes of a Life. London: 1853. V. 67

JAMES, GEORGE WHARTON
California, Romantic and Beautiful.... Boston: 1914. V. 65
California, Romantic and Beautiful.... Boston: 1921. V. 65
Exposition Memories: Panama California Exposition, San Diego 1916. Pasadena: 1917. V. 62; 63; 65
Francisco Palou's Life and Apostolic Labors of the Venerable Father Junipero Serra.... Pasadena: 1913. V. 65
Fremont in California. Los Angeles: 1903. V. 64
The Grand Canyon of Arizona How to See It. Boston: 1910. V. 63
Heroes of California, the Story of the Founders of the Golden State. Boston: 1910. V. 65
In and Around the Grand Canyon, The Grand Canyon of the Colorado River in Arizona. Boston: 1900. V. 66
In and Out of the Old Missions of California. Boston: 1905. V. 66
In and Out of the Old Missions of California. Boston: 1914. V. 65
Indian and Other Basketmaking. New York: 1903. V. 63
Indian Blankets and Their Makers. Chicago: 1914. V. 64
Indians of the Painted Desert Region. Boston: 1903. V. 63; 64
The Indians of the Painted Desert Region. Boston: 1905. V. 65
Mark Twain, an Appreciation of His Pioneer Writings on Fasting and Health. Pasadena: 1919. V. 63
New Mexico: The Land of the Delight Makers. Boston: 1920. V. 64
Practical Basket Making. Pasadena: 1925. V. 64
Rose Hartwick Thrope and the Story of Curfew Must Not Ring To-Night. Pasadena: 1916. V. 65
Through Ramona's Country. Boston: 1913. V. 65
Utah - the Land of the Blossoming Valleys. Boston;: 1922. V. 65
What the White Race May Learn from the Indian. Chicago: 1908. V. 66

JAMES, HENRY
Account of the Observations of the Principal Triangulation and of Figure, Dimensions and Mean Specific Gravity of the Earth as Dervied Therefrom. London: 1858. V. 65
The Ambassadors. New York and London: 1903. V. 65
The American. Boston: 1877. V. 65
The American Scene. New York and London: 1907. V. 62; 65; 66
The Aspern Papers. Louisa Pallant. The Modern Warning. London: 1888. V. 63; 66
The Awkward Age. London: 1899. V. 62; 65
The Beast in the Jungle. Kentfield: 1963. V. 63; 64
The Better Sort. London: 1903. V. 62; 65
The Bostonians. London: 1886. V. 65
Confidence. Boston: 1880. V. 62; 65
Daisy Miller. New York: 1879. V. 65; 66
Daisy Miller. Boston: 1883. V. 66
Daisy Miller. London: 1883. V. 63
Daisy Miller. Paris: 1886. V. 65
Daisy Miller. Boston & New York: 1899. V. 62
Daisy Miller. Cambridge: 1969. V. 66
Daisy Miller and an International Episode. New York: 1892. V. 64
Embarrassments. London: 1896. V. 62; 65

JAMES, HENRY continued
English Hours. Cambridge: 1905. V. 65
English Hours. London: 1905. V. 65
Essays in London and Elsewhere. London: 1893. V. 65
The Europeans. Boston: 1879. V. 65
The Finer Grain. London: 1910. V. 62; 63; 65; 66
French Poets and Novelists. London: 1878. V. 62; 65
Gabrielle de Bergerac. New York: 1918. V. 62
The Golden Bowl. London: 1905. V. 65
Hawthorne. London: 1879. V. 66
Instructions for Taking Meterological Observations. 1861. V. 62
Italian Hours. London: 1909. V. 62
The Ivory Tower. London: 1917. V. 65
The Ivory Tower. New York: 1917. V. 64; 65
A Landscape Painter. New York: 1919. V. 62; 65
The Lesson of the Master. London: 1892. V. 66
The Lesson of the Master. New York: 1892. V. 62; 65
The Letters of Henry James. London: 1920. V. 66
A Little Tour in France. Boston: 1885. V. 65
A Little Tour in France. Boston and New York: 1897. V. 65
A Little Tour in France. London: 1900. V. 62; 65
A London Life. The Patagonia. The Liar. Mrs. Temperly. London: 1889. V. 63
The Madonna of the Future and Other Tales. Boston: 1880. V. 65
The Middle Years. London: 1917. V. 62; 65; 66
A Most Unholy Trade. Cambridge: 1923. V. 64; 65
Notes and Reviews. Cambridge: 1921. V. 63
Notes of a Son and Brother. London: 1914. V. 66
Notes on Novelists, with Some Other Notes. New York: 1914. V. 65; 66
The Novels and Tales of Henry James. New York: 1907-1909-. V. 66
The Other House. London: 1896. V. 66
The Outcry. London: 1911. V. 64; 65
Partial Portraits. London: 1888. V. 62; 65
A Passionate Pilgrim and Other Tales. Boston: 1875. V. 65
Picture and Text. New York: 1893. V. 63; 64; 66
The Portrait of a Lady. London: 1881. V. 65
The Portrait of a Lady. Boston: 1882. V. 62; 63
The Portrait of a Lady. London: 1883. V. 65; 66
The Princess Casamassima: a Novel. London: 1887. V. 65
The Question of Our Speech, The Lesson of Balzac: Two Lectures. Boston and New York: 1905. V. 65
The Reverberator. London and New York: 1888. V. 62; 63; 65
Roderick Hudson. (with) Eugene Pickering. The Diary of a Man of Fifty. Leipzig: 1879-1880. V. 65
The Sacred Fount. London: 1901. V. 65
The Sacred Fount. New York: 1901. V. 62; 65
The Siege of London, the Pension Beaurepas, and the Point of View. Boston: 1883. V. 65
A Small Boy and Others. London: 1913. V. 65
The Soft Side. 1900. V. 64
The Soft Side. London: 1900. V. 65; 66
The Soft Side. New York: 1900. V. 65; 66
The Spoils of Poynton. Boston and New York: 1897. V. 62; 64; 65
The Spoils of Poynton. London: 1897. V. 65
Stories Revived. London: 1885. V. 65
Tales of Three Cities. London: 1884. V. 62; 65
Theatricals. (First Series). Two Comedies: Tenants, Disengaged. London: 1894. V. 65
Theatricals. (First and Second Series). New York: 1894-1895. V. 65
Theatricals. Second Series: the Album, the Reprobate. New York: 1894. V. 62
Three Letters from Henry James to Joseph Conrad. London: 1926. V. 64
The Tragic Muse. London and New York: 1890. V. 63
The Tragic Muse. Boston and New York: 1897. V. 65
Transatlantic Sketches. Boston: 1875. V. 64
Travelling Companions. New York: 1919. V. 62
The Two Magics: The Turn of the Screw, Covering End. London: 1898. V. 65; 66
Washington Square. The Pension Beaurepas. A Bundle of Letters. London: 1881. V. 62; 65
Watch and Ward. Boston: 1870. V. 65
What Maisie Knew. London: 1898. V. 65
William Wetmore Story and His Friends.... Boston: 1903. V. 63; 64; 65; 66
The Wings of the Dove. Westminster: 1902. V. 65; 66
Within the Rim and Other Essays 1914-1915. London: 1918. V. 65
Within the Rim and Other Essays 1914-1915. London: 1919. V. 62; 65

JAMES, JOHN H.
A History and Survey of the Cathedral Church of S.S. Peter, Paul, Dubritius, Teilo and Oudoceus, Llandaff. Cardiff: 1898. V. 66

JAMES, JOHN THOMAS
The Italian Schools of Painting with Observations on the Present State of Art. London: 1820. V. 65
Journal of a Tour in Germany, Sweden, Russia, Poland, During the Years 1813 and 1814. London: 1816. V. 62
Journal of a Tour in Germany, Sweden, Russia, Poland in 1813-1814. London: 1817. V. 65
Journal of a Tour in Germany, Sweden, Russia, Poland in 1813-1814. London: 1819. V. 62

JAMES, KAREN I.
The Cathedral Libraries Catalogue. Books Printed Before 1701 in the Libraries of the Anglican Cathedrals of England and Wales. London: 1984. V. 63

JAMES, M. R.
Abbeys. Paddington Station: 1926. V. 62
Ghost Stories of an Antiquary. London: 1950. V. 65

JAMES, MARQUIS
Cherokee Strip: a Tale of an Oklahoma Boyhood. New York: 1945. V. 64

JAMES, MERVYN
Mountains. Wymondham: 1972. V. 62; 65

JAMES, MONTAGUE RHODES
A Descriptive Catalogue of the McClean Collection of Manuscripts in the Fitzwilliam Museum. Cambridge: 1912. V. 64

JAMES, P. D.
The Black Tower. London: 1975. V. 65
The Black Tower. New York: 1975. V. 65
A Certain Justice. London: 1997. V. 63; 67
Cover Her Face. London: 1962. V. 66
Death of an Expert Witness. London: 1977. V. 65
Devices and Desires. London: 1989. V. 65; 66; 67
Innocent Blood. London: 1980. V. 65; 66; 67
A Mind to Murder. London: 1963. V. 66
The Skull Beneath the Skin. London: 1982. V. 63; 66; 67
The Skull Beneath the Skin. New York: 1982. V. 67
Unnatural Causes. London: 1967. V. 66
Unnatural Causes. New York: 1967. V. 62; 64; 65
An Unsuitable Job for a Woman. London: 1972. V. 64
An Unsuitable Job for a Woman. New York: 1972. V. 63; 64

JAMES, ROBERT
A Dissertation on Fevers, and Inflammatory Distempers. London: 1778. V. 63
Pharmacopoeia Universalis; or, a New Universal English Dispensatory. London: 1747. V. 62
A Treatise on Canine Madness. London: 1760. V. 65

JAMES, S. P.
A Monograph of the Anopheles Mosquitoes of India. Calcutta: 1904. V. 67

JAMES Sherman Kimball: a Sketch. Boston: 1865. V. 66

JAMES, T. H., MRS.
The Cub's Triumph. Tokyo. V. 63

JAMES, THOMAS
The Beauties of the Poets: Being a Collection of Moral and Sacred Poetry, from Eminent Authors. London: 1800?. V. 65
Captain Thomas James's Strange and Dangerous Voyage in His Intended Discovery of the North West Passage into the South Sea. N.P. V. 63
Three Years Among the Mexicans and Indians. St. Louis: 1916. V. 65
A Treatise of the Corruption of Scripture, Councils and Fathers by the Prelats, Pastors and Pillars of the Church of Rome, for Maintenance of Popery.... London: 1688. V. 67

JAMES, WILL
All in the Day's Riding. New York: 1933. V. 65
Cow Country. New York: 1927. V. 62; 66
Cowboy in the Making. New York: 1937. V. 63
Cowboys North and South. New York: 1924. V. 63
Cowboys North and South. New York: 1925. V. 65
The Dark Horse. New York: 1939. V. 63; 66
Horses I've Known. New York: 1940. V. 63; 66
Lone Cowboy. New York: 1930. V. 64
My First Horse. New York: 1940. V. 63; 66
Young Cowboy. New York: 1935. V. 63

JAMES, WILLIAM
A Full and Correct Account of the Chief Naval Occurrences of the Late War Between Britain and the United States of America.... London: 1817. V. 66
The Letters of William James. Boston: 1920. V. 63
The Naval History of Great Britain from the Declaration of War by France in 1793 to the Accession of George IV.... London: 1837. V. 67
The Principles of Psychology. New York: 1890. V. 62

JAMES, WILLIAM DOBEIN
A Sketch of the Life of Brig. Gen. Francis Marion.... Charleston: 1821. V. 66

JAMES, WILLIAM F.
Saint Patrick of England. San Francisco: 1955. V. 67

JAMES I, KING OF ENGLAND
His Maiesties Speach in the Upper House of Parliament on Munday the 26 of March 1621. London: 1621. V. 67
The Workes of the Most High and Mightly Prince, James, by the Grace of God Kinge of Great Brittaine, France and Ireland.... London: 1616. V. 64
Works of James the First. Glasgow: 1825. V. 66

JAMES I, KING OF SCOTLAND
The Kingis Quair. 1903. V. 65; 67
Kingis Quair. London: 1903. V. 62; 65
Poetical Remains. Edinburgh: 1783. V. 62

JAMES II, KING OF GREAT BRITIAN
Papers of Devotion of James II, Being a Reproduction of the Ms. in the Handwriting of James the Second, Now in the Possession of Mr. B. R. Townley Balfour. Oxford: 1925. V. 62

JAMESON, ANNA BROWNELL MURPHY
Characteristics of Women, Moral, Poetical and Historical. London: 1836. V. 65
Characteristics of Women, Moral, Poetical and Historical. London: 1858. V. 65
Diary of an Ennuyee. London: 1826. V. 62
The First, or Mother's Dictionary. London: 1825. V. 64
The History of Our Lord as Exemplified in Works of Art: with That of His Types. London: 1872. V. 65
Memoirs of Celebrated Female Sovereigns. London: 1831. V. 66
Memoirs of the Beauties of the Court of Charles the Second with Their Portraits. London: 1838. V. 66
Social Life in Germany. London: 1840. V. 65
Visits and Sketches at Home and Abroad. London: 1834. V. 65
Visits and Sketches at Home and Abroad. London: 1835. V. 65

JAMESON, HORATIO GATES
A Treatise on Epidemic Cholera. Philadelphia: 1855. V. 66

JAMESON, JAMES S.
Story of the Rear Column of the Emin Pasha Relief Expedition. London: 1890. V. 66

JAMESON, ROBERT
Mineralogy of the Scottish Isles.... Edinburgh: 1800. V. 63

JAMESON, THOMAS
Essays on the Changes of the Human Body, At Its Different Ages.... London: 1811. V. 64

JAMETEL, MAURICE
L'Encre de Chine. son Histoire et sa Fabricatin d'apres des Documents Chinois. Paris: 1882. V. 66

JAMIESON, FRANCES
Popular Voyages and Travels Throughout the Continents and Islands of Asia, Africa and America. London: 1820. V. 66

JAMSHEED, RASHID
Memories of a Sheep Hunter. 1996. V. 62; 63; 64; 67

JAN, GIORGIO
Iconographie Generale des Ophidiens. Weinheim: 1961. V. 67

JANE, CECIL
Select Documents Illustrating the Four Voyages of Columbus. Volume II. The Third and Fourth Voyages. London: 1933. V. 63
Select Documents Illustrating the Four Voyages of Columbus. Volumes I and II. London: 1930-1933. V. 63

JANE, FRED T.
All the World's Aircraft. London: 1912. V. 64
All the World's Aircraft. London: 1919. V. 64
All The World's Fighting Ships. London: 1898. V. 65
Blake of the Rattlesnake or the Man Who Saved England. London: 1895. V. 63
The British Battlefleet to Inception and Growth throughout the Centuries to the Present Day. London: 1915. V. 64

JANE'S Fighting Ships 1921. London: 1921. V. 65

JANE'S Fighting Ships 1939. 1939. V. 65

JANE'S Fighting Ships 1940. London: 1940. V. 63

JANE'S Fighting Ships 1942. 1942. V. 65
JANE'S Fighting Ships 1942. London: 1943. V. 66

JANE'S Fighting Ships 1947-1948. 1948. V. 65

JANET, PIERRE
The Major Symptoms of Hyotoria: Fifteen Lectures Given in the Medical School of Harvard University. New York: 1907. V. 65
Psychological Healing: a Historical and Clinical Study. London: 1925. V. 65

JANNEY, SAMUEL M.
The Last of Lenape and Other Poems. Philadelphia & Boston: 1839. V. 63
Memoirs of Samuel M. Janney: Late of Lincoln, Loudoun Co., Virginia. Philadelphia: 1881. V. 64

JANNOTIUS
Donati Iannotii Florentini Dialogi de Repub. Ventiorum. Lugd. Batav: 1631. V. 66

JANOWTIZ, TAMA
American Dad. New York: 1981. V. 65

JANSEN, CORNELIUS
Paraphrasis in Omnes Psalmos Davidicos Cum Argumentis et Annotationibus.... Antwerp: 1614. V. 66
Tetrateuchus Sive Commentarius in Sancta Jesu Christa Evangelia. Bruxellis: 1728. V. 64

JANSON, TOVE
The Happy Moomins. Indianapolis: 1952. V. 63

JANSSONUS, JOANNIS
Novus Atlas, Sive Theatrum Orbis Terrarum: In Quo Orbis Antiquus, Seu Geographia Vetus, Sacra & Profana Exhibetur Tomus Sextus. Amstelodami: 1658?. V. 64; 66

JAPAN INSTITUTE OF HOSPITAL ARCHITECTURE
Hospital Design in Japan. N.P: 1975. V. 62; 63; 66

THE JAPANESE Fairy Book. London: 1908. V. 65

THE JAPANESE Telephone and Business Directory of Southern California No. 37. Los Angeles: 1963. V. 65

JAPANESE GOVERNMENT RAILWAYS
An Official Guide to Japan, with Preparatory Explanations on Japanese Customs, Language, History, Religion, Literature, Fine Art, Architecture, Music, Drama, Etc., Etc. Tokyo: 1933. V. 65

JAPP, A. H.
Thoreau: His Life and Aims, a Study. Boston: 1877. V. 64

JAQUES, FAITH
Kidnap in Willobank Wood. London: 1982. V. 67

JAQUES, FLORENCE PAGE
Francis Lee Jaques: Artist of the Wilderness World. New York: 1973. V. 62; 64

JARAMILLO, CLEOFAS M.
Shadows of the Past. Santa Fe: 1941. V. 63; 64

JARDINE, ALEXANDER
Letters from Barbary, France, Spain, Portugal &c. London: 1790. V. 67

JARDINE, WILLIAM
The Birds of Great Britain and Ireland. 1876. V. 67
Birds of Great Britain and Ireland. Volume III. 1842. V. 67
Birds of Great Britain and Ireland. Volume III. Gallinaceous Birds. 1843. V. 67
Contributions to Ornithology for 1848-1852. Edinburgh: 1848-1852. V. 67
The Natural History of Game-Birds. Edinburgh: 1834. V. 63
The Natural History of Humming Birds. Edinburgh: 1833. V. 62; 66
The Natural History of Humming-Birds. Edinburgh: 1840. V. 62
The Naturalists' Library. Edinburgh: 1833-1843. V. 63
The Naturalist's Library - Game Birds. 1834. V. 63
The Naturalist's Library. Entomology. British Moths, Sphinxes, etc. Edinburgh and London: 1860. V. 65; 66
The Naturalist's Library. Ichthyology. Volume I. The Perch Family. Edinburgh: 1835. V. 65
The Naturalist's Library. Mammalia. British Quadrupeds. Edinburgh: 1850. V. 65
The Naturalist's Library. Mammalia. Marsupialia or Pouched Animals. Edinburgh: 1841. V. 65; 66
The Naturalist's Library. Ornithology. Flycatchers. Edinburgh: 1843. V. 65
Ruminating Animals - Deer, Antelopes, Camels &c. 1835. V. 63; 64
Sun-Birds. Edinburgh: 1843. V. 62

JARMAN, THOMAS
A Treatise on Wills. London: 1844. V. 62

JARMAN, W.
Hell on Earth or Uncle Sam's Abscess. Exeter: 1884. V. 65

JARNAC, PHILIPPE DE ROHAN CHABOT, COMTE DE
Cecile; or, the Pervert. London: 1851. V. 65
Rockingham; or, The Younger Brother. London: 1849. V. 65

JARRAUD, ROBERT
Les Gordini. 1983. V. 66

JARRELL, RANDALL
The Animal Family. New York: 1965. V. 65
The Animal Family. London: 1967. V. 65
The Bat-Poet. New York: 1964. V. 65
Blood for a Stranger. New York: 1942. V. 62; 64; 67
The Complete Poems. New York: 1969. V. 63; 64; 66
Fly By Night. New York: 1976. V. 62; 65
The Gingerbread Rabbit. New York: 1964. V. 62
Little Friend, Little Friend. New York: 1945. V. 64
Losses. New York: 1948. V. 63
The Lost World. New Poems. New York: 1965. V. 64
Pictures from an Institution. London: 1954. V. 62; 66
A Sad Heart at the Super Market. New York: 1962. V. 64
Selected Poems. New York: 1955. V. 62; 64
Selected Poems. London: 1956. V. 64
The Seven-League Crutches. New York: 1951. V. 62; 63
The Woman at the Washington Zoo. Poems and Translations. New York: 1960. V. 62; 64

JARRIN, G. A.
The Italian Confectioner; or Complete Economy of Deserts.... London: 1829. V. 62; 66

JARS, G.
Voyages Metallurgiques, ou Recherches et Observations sur les Mines & Forges de fer...en Allemagne, Suede, Norwege, Angleterre et Ecosse. Lyon: 1781. V. 62

JARVES, JAMES JACKSON
History of the Hawaiian Islands: Embracing Their Antiquities, Mythology, Legends, Discovery.... Honolulu: 1847. V. 62; 64
Parisian Sights and French Principles, Seen Through American Spectacles. London: 1853. V. 62

JARVIS, RUPERT C.
The Jacobite Risings of 1715 and 1745. Carlisle: 1954. V. 62; 64; 65; 66

JASPERS, KARL THEODOR
General Psychopathology. Chicago: 1963. V. 65

JASTROW, MORRIS
The Civilization of Babylonia and Assyria. Philadelphia: 1915. V. 67

JAUBERT, JEAN BAPTISTE
Richesses Ornithologiques du Midi de la France, ou Description Methodique de Tous les Oiseaux Observes en Provence et dans les Departements Circonvoisins. Marseille: 1859. V. 67

JAVELLE, EMILE
Alpine Memories. London: 1899. V. 63

JAVORKA, S.
Iconographia Florae Partis Austro-Orientalis Europae Centralis. Budapest: 1991. V. 65; 66

JAY, CYRUS
The Law: What I Have Seen, What I Have Heard,. London: 1868. V. 63

JAY, J. C.
A Catalogue of Recent Shells with Descriptions of New or Rare Species in the Collection. New York: 1836. V. 66
A Catalogue of Shells..in the Collection of.... New York: 1839. V. 62; 63; 66

JAY, LEONARD
Of the Making of Many Books There is No End. Birmingham: 1931. V. 64; 65; 66

JAY, WILLIAM
The Life of John Jay: With Selections from His Correspondence. New York: 1833. V. 63; 64
Morning Exercises for the Closet; for Every Day in the Year. London: 1833. V. 63
A View of Action of the Federal Government in Behalf of Slavery. New York: 1839. V. 64

JAYBERT, B.
Les Apres-Soupes par L'Auteur de Trois Dizains de Contes Gaulois. Paris: 1883. V. 64; 65
Trois Dizains de Contes Gaulois. Paris: 1882. V. 64; 65

JEAFFRESON, JOHN CORDY
A Book About Doctors. London: 1861. V. 67
Brides and Bridals. London: 1873. V. 64; 65
Novels and Novelists from Elizabeth to Victoria. London: 1858. V. 66

JEAN, MARCEL
The History of Surrealist Painting. London: 1960. V. 65

JEAN AUBRY, G.
Joseph Conrad; Life and Letters. New York: 1927. V. 67

JEANNE D'Arc. Paris: 1896. V. 65

JEANNERET-GRIS, CHARLES EDOUARD
My Work. London: 1960. V. 62
Urbanisme. Paris: 1925. V. 64

JEANNET DES LONGROIS, JEAN BAPTISTE CLAUDIUS
Conseils aux Femmes de Quarante Ans. Paris: 1787. V. 67

JEANS, JAMES
Through Space and Time. Based on the Royal Institution Lectures Christmas 1933. Cambridge: 1934. V. 67

JEANS, THOMAS
The Tommiebeg Shootings or a Moor in Scotland. 1861. V. 63

JEBB, BERTHA
Some Unconventional People. Edinburgh: 1896. V. 67

JEBB, GEORGE
A Guide to the Church of S. Botolph with Notes on the History and Antiquities of Boston and Shirbeck. Boston: 1903. V. 66

JEBB, HENRY GLADWYN
Out of the Depths. The Story of a Woman's Life. Cambridge: 1859. V. 63

JEBB, SAMUEL
The Life of Robert, Earl of Leicester, the Favourite of Queen Elizabeth. London: 1727. V. 67

JEDLICKA, VIKTOR
Ladovy Vesele Ucebnice Brouchi a Hmyz III, (Merry Textbook of Beetles and Insects). Praha (Prague): 1932. V. 64

JEFERIES, RICHARD
The Life of the Fields. London: 1908. V. 65

JEFFARES, A. NORMAN
Restoration Comedy. London: 1974. V. 64

JEFFERDS, CHARLES M.
Trial of Charles M. Jefferds for Murder, at New York, December 1861. New York: 1862. V. 63; 67

JEFFERIES, RICHARD
After London; or, Wild England. London: 1885. V. 63
Amaryllis at the Fair. London: 1887. V. 63; 67
Amaryllis at the Fair. 1908. V. 67
The Amateur Poacher. 1881. V. 66; 67
The Amateur Poacher. 1985. V. 63
Bevis: the Story of a Boy. London: 1882. V. 63; 66
Country Vignettes. Derbyshire: 1991. V. 64
The Dewy Morn. London: 1884. V. 62
Field and Hedgerow, Being the Last Essays of.... London: 1880. V. 63
The Gamekeeper at Home. 1878. V. 63; 66
Hodge and His Masters. London: 1880. V. 62; 63; 64; 66
The Life of the Fields. London: 1884. V. 62
Nature Near London. London: 1883. V. 67
The Open Air. 1885. V. 63
The Open Air. London: 1885. V. 62
Round About a Great Estate. London: 1880. V. 62; 66
The Toilers of the Field. 1892. V. 67
The Toilers of the Field. London: 1892. V. 64

Wild Life in a Southern Country. London: 1879. V. 63; 67
Wood Magic, a Fable. London: 1881. V. 66; 67

JEFFERS, LE ROY
The Call of the Mountains; Rambles Among the Mountains and Canyons of the United States and Canada. London: 1923. V. 67

JEFFERS, ROBINSON
Be Angry at the Sun. New York: 1941. V. 63; 64; 66
Brides of the South Wind: Poems 1917-1922. N.P: 1974. V. 63
Californians. New York: 1916. V. 65
Cawdor. New York: 1928. V. 64
Cawdor. N.P: 1983. V. 62; 63; 64; 66
Dear Judas and Other Poems. New York: 1929. V. 64; 65; 67
Descent to the Dead. New York: 1931. V. 62; 63; 64; 67
The Desert. Los Angeles: 1976. V. 66
The Double Axe and Other Poems. New York: 1948. V. 63
Give Your Heart to the Hawks and Other Poems. New York: 1933. V. 63; 64; 65
Medea. New York: 1946. V. 63; 67
Rhythm and Rhyme. Monterey: 1966. V. 66
Solstice and Other Poems. New York: 1935. V. 63
Songs and Heroes.... Los Angeles: 1988. V. 62
Stars. Pasadena: 1930. V. 64
Such Counsels You Gave to Me and Other Poems. New York: 1937. V. 63; 64
Themes in My Poems. San Francisco: 1956. V. 64
Thurso's Landing. New York: 1932. V. 65
Tragedy Has Obligations. Santa Cruz: 1973. V. 62; 63; 64; 66
The Women at Point Sur. New York: 1927. V. 64; 65

JEFFERS, UNA
A Book of Gaelic Airs for Una's Melodeon. San Francisco: 1989. V. 64
Jeffers at Work. Los Angeles: 1988. V. 66

JEFFERSON COUNTY HISTORICAL SOCIETY
With Pride in Heritage: History of Jefferson County. Portland: 1966. V. 66

JEFFERSON, GEOFFREY
The Invasive Adenomas of the Anterior Pituitary. Springfield: 1972. V. 67
Selected Papers. London: 1960. V. 66

JEFFERSON, JOSEPH
Industry, and a Pious Submission, Charity, and a Strict Oeconomy, Recommended and Enforced, as the Best Means of Alleviating the Present Distress. London: 1800. V. 65

JEFFERSON, ROBERT L.
A New Ride to Khiva. London: 1899. V. 67

JEFFERSON, SAMUEL
The History and Antiquities of Allerdale Ward, Above Derwent in the County of Cumberland.... Carlisle: 1842. V. 65; 66
The History and Antiquities of Leath Ward, in the County of Cumberland.... Carlisle: 1840. V. 65; 66

JEFFERSON, T. H.
Accompaniment to the Map of the Emigrant Road from Independence, Mo. to San Francisco, California. San Francisco: 1945. V. 65

JEFFERSON, THOMAS
A Manual of Parliamentary Practice for the Use of the Senate of the United States. George Town: 1812. V. 64
Memoir, Correspondence and Miscellanies from the Papers of Thomas Jefferson. Charlottesville: 1829. V. 65; 67
Notes on the State of Virginia. London: 1787. V. 63
Notes, on the State of Virginia.... New York: 1801. V. 63
The Papers of Thomas Jefferson. Princeton: 1950-1998. V. 63; 64

JEFFERYS, THOMAS
The Natural and Civil History of the French Dominions in North and South America. London: 1760. V. 67
The West-India Atlas: or, A Compendious Description of the West Indies. London: 1775. V. 67

JEFFREY, ALEXANDER
A Guide to the Antiquities and Picturesque Scenery of the Border. Edinburgh: 1838. V. 63

JEFFREYS, GEORGE
Edwin: a Tragedy. London: 1724. V. 63

JEFFREYS, JOHN G.
British Conchology, or an Account of the Mollusca Which Now Inhabit the British Isles and the Surrounding Seas. 1862-1869. V. 65
British Conchology, or an Account of the Mollusca Which Now Inhabit the British Isles and the Surrounding Seas. London: 1862-1869. V. 64; 67
British Conchology or an Account of the Mollusca Which Now Inhabit the British Isles and the Surrounding Seas. London: 1904-1863-1869. V. 62

JEFFRIES, DAVID
A Treatise on Diamonds and Pearls. London: 1751. V. 65

JEFFRIES, THOMAS FAYETTE
Crippled Fayette of Rockingham, Detailing His Times and Giving His R hymes. Mountain Valley: 1857. V. 64

JEKYLL, GERTRUDE
Garden Ornament. London: 1918. V. 64
Garden Ornament. London: 1927. V. 64; 65; 67
A Gardener's Testament. 1937. V. 63

JEKYLL, GERTRUDE continued
A Gardener's Testament. London: 1937. V. 67
Gardens for Small Country Houses. 1927. V. 63; 66
Gardens for Small Country Houses. 1981. V. 67
Home and Garden. London: 1910. V. 63
Lilies for English Gardens, A Guide to Amateurs. London: 1901. V. 64
Old West Surrey. London: 1904. V. 63; 64; 66
Wall and Water Gardens. London: 1901. V. 64
Wood and Garden, Notes and Thought, Practical and Critical, of a Working Amateur. London: 1899. V. 64; 67

JELGERSMA, GERBRANDUS
Atlas Anatomicum Cerebri Humani. 168 Sections of the Human Brain. Amsterdam: 1931. V. 65

JELLETT, E. C.
Germantown, Old and New. Germantown: 1904. V. 64

JELLETT, JOHN HEWITT
An Elementary Treatise on the Calculus of Variations. Dublin: 1850. V. 65

JELLICOE, ANN
Shelley, or the Idealist. London: 1966. V. 65

JELLICOE, J.
The Studies of a Landscape Designer Over 80 Years. Woodbridge: 1993-1996. V. 64

JELLIFFE, SMITH ELY
Diseases of the Nervous System: a Text Book of Neurology and Psychiatry. Philadelphia: 1915. V. 65

JEMMY and His Mother, a Tale for Children. And Lucy; or, the Slave Girl of Kentucky. Cincinnati: 1858. V. 65

JEN, GISH
Typical American. Boston: 1991. V. 64; 67

JENCKS, CHARLES
Towards a Symolic Architecture: the Thematic House. New York: 1985. V. 65

JENCKS, E. N.
The History and Philosophy of Marriage; or Polygamy and Monogamy Compared. Boston: 1869. V. 63

JENE, EDGAR
Surrealistische Publikationen. Vienna: 1950. V. 65

JENKIN, DAVID
A Discourse Touching the Inconveniences of a Long Continued Parliament. London: 1647. V. 65

JENKINS, A. O.
Olive's Last Round-Up. Loup City. V. 64

JENKINS, CHARLES FRANCIS
Button Gwinnett, Signer of the Declaration of Independence. Garden City: 1926. V. 63; 67

JENKINS, D.
Llanelly Pottery. Swansea: 1968. V. 62

JENKINS, E. VAUGHAN
Water Divining. London: 1902. V. 66

JENKINS, I.
The Hawaiian Calabash. Honolulu: 1995. V. 62

JENKINS, J.
The Naval Achievements of Great Britain from the Year 1793 to 1817. London: 1816-1817. V. 67

JENKINS, J. GERAINT
Nets and Coracles. London: 1974. V. 67

JENKINS, J. T.
The Sea Fisheries. London: 1920. V. 64
Whales and Modern Whaling. London: 1932. V. 62

JENKINS, JOHN
The Art of Writing, Reduced to Seven Books. Cambridge: 1813. V. 63; 66
A Selection of Architectural and Other Ornament, Greek, Roman and Italian, Drawn from the Originals in Various Museums and Buildings in Italy. London: 1827. V. 66

JENKINS, JOHN EDWARD
The Captain's Cabin: a Christmas Yarn. London: 1877. V. 67
The Devil's Chain. London: 1877. V. 67
Jobson's Enemeies. London: 1882. V. 66
Lord Bantam. London: 1872. V. 67

JENKINS, JOHN H.
Basic Texas Books, an Annotated Bibliography of Selected Works for a Research Library. Austin: 1983. V. 63
I'm Frank Hamer, The Life of a Texas Peace Officer. Austin: 1968. V. 64

JENKINS, LADY
Sport and Travel in both Tibets. London: 1909. V. 67

JENKINS, SIMON
Images of Hampstead. Richmond-upon-Thames: 1982. V. 62; 66

JENKINS, WARREN
The Ohio Gazetteer and Traveler's Guide.... Columbus: 1839. V. 66

JENKINSON, HENRY IRWIN
Practical Guide to the English Lake District. London: 1875. V. 65
Practical Guide to the English Lake District. London: 1876. V. 63; 65

JENKS, WILLIAM F.
Handbook of South American Geology. 1956. V. 67

JENNENS, WILLIAM
The Great Jennens Case: Being an Epitome of the History of the Jennens Family.... Sheffield: 1879. V. 63

JENNER, HENRY
A Handbook for the Cornish Language, Chiefly in Its Latest Stages.... London: 1904. V. 64

JENNER, THOMAS
That Goodly Mountain and Lebanon; being the Narrative of a Ride through the Countries of Judea, Samaria and Galilee, into Syria, in the Month of August 1872.... London: 1873. V. 67

JENNER, WILLIAM
An Inquiry into the Causes and Effects of the Variolae Vaccine. A Disease Discovered in Some of the Western Counties of England, Particularly, Gloucestershire and Known by the Name of Cow Pox. London: 1800. V. 62
Lectures and Essays on Fevers and Diptheria 1849 to 1879. New York: 1893. V. 64; 67

JENNESS, DIAMOND
The Copper Eskimos. Ottawa: 1923. V. 65
The Life of the Copper Eskimos. Ottawa: 1922. V. 62

JENNEWEIN, J. LEONARD
Black Hills Book Trails. Mitchell: 1962. V. 64; 65; 66

JENNINGS, AL
Number 30664 by Number 31539 - A Sketch in the Lives of William Sidney Porter (O. Henry) and Al Jennings, the Bandit. Hollywood: 1941. V. 66

JENNINGS, BERNARD
A History of Nidderdale. Huddersfield: 1967. V. 65

JENNINGS, BRENDAN
Michael O'Cleirigh, Chief of the Four Masters and His Associates. 1936. V. 63; 66

JENNINGS, D.
Our Work. No. V. Manners and Customs of the Indians of Simpson District, B.C. Toronto: 1890?. V. 63

JENNINGS, D. H.
The Physiology of Fungal Nutrition. Cambridge: 1995. V. 64

JENNINGS, ELIZABETH
Let's Have Some Poetry!. London: 1960. V. 64
Poems. Swinford, Eynsham: 1953. V. 62
A Sense of the World. London: 1958. V. 62; 63; 64
Song for a Birth or a Death and Other Poems. London: 1961. V. 63

JENNINGS, HARGARE
Rosicrucians, Their Rites and Mysteries. London: 1887. V. 63

JENNINGS, J. ELLIS
Color-Vision and Color-Blindness. Philadelphia: 1896. V. 66; 67

JENNINGS, JAMES
The Dialect of the West of England.... London: 1869. V. 64
Observations on Some of the Dialects in the West of England.... London: 1825. V. 64
A Practical Treatise on the History, Medical Properties, and Cultivation of Tobacco. London: 1830. V. 67

JENNINGS, JOHN
Theatrical and Circus Life; or, Secrets of the Stage, Green-Room and Sawdust Arena. St. Louis: 1882. V. 66

JENNINGS, MAUREEN
Except the Dying. New York: 1997. V. 65; 67

JENNINGS, N. A.
A Texas Ranger. Dallas: 1930. V. 63

JENNINGS, OBADIAH
Debate on Campbellism: Held at Nasville, Tennessee. Pittsburgh: 1832. V. 62

JENNINGS, OSCAR
Early Woodcut Initials, Containing Over Thirteen Hundred Reproductions of Ornamental Letters of the Fifteenth and Sixteenth Centuries. London: 1908. V. 63

JENSEN, A. S.
The Zoology of the Faroes. Copenhagen: 1928-1971. V. 66

JENSEN, J. MARINUS
History of Provo, Utah. Provo: 1924. V. 63; 66

JENSEN, JENS
The Clearing. Chicago: 1949. V. 64

JENSEN, LAURA
Bad Boats. New York: 1977. V. 63

JENSON, NICOLAS
The Last Will and Testament of the Late Nicolas Jenson, Printer, Who Departed This Life at the City of Venice in the Month of September A.D. 1480. Chicago: 1928. V. 62; 63; 64
The Last Will and Testament of the Late Nicolas Jenson, Printer, Who Departed This Life at the City of Venice in the Month of September A.D. 1480. Chicago: 1929. V. 66

JENYNS, SOAME
Miscellaneous Pieces, in Two Volumes. London: 1761. V. 66
A Scheme for the Coalition of Parties, Humbly Submitted to the Publick. London: 1772. V. 65

JENYS, SOAME
A View of the Internal Evidence of the Christian Religion. Boston: 1793. V. 62

JEPHSON, HARRIET JULIA
A Canadian Scrap-Book. London: 1897. V. 65

JEPHSON, HENRY
Notes on Irish Questions. Dublin: 1870. V. 67
The Platform, Its Rise and Progress. London: 1892. V. 64

JEPHSON, MAURICE DENHAM
An Anglo-Irish Miscellany: Some Records of the Jephsons of Mallow. 1964. V. 62; 65

JEPHSON, ROBERT
Braganza. A Tragedy. London: 1775. V. 67
Roman Portraits. 1794. V. 64; 67
Roman Portraits, a Poem, in Heroick Verse; Wit Historical Remarks and Illustrations. London: 1794. V. 62; 65; 66

JEPPE, C. BICCARD
Gold Mining on the Witwaterstrand. Cape Town: 1946. V. 65

JEPSON, EDGAR A.
Sibyl Falcon: a Study in Romantic Morals. London: 1895. V. 67

JEPSON, RALPH
The Expounder Expounded; or, Annotations Upon that Incomparable Piece, Intitled, A Short Account of God's Dealings with the Rev. Mr. G----e W---f---d. London: 1740. V. 64

JEPSON, SELWYN
Big Game Encounters. 1936. V. 67
A Noise in the Night. London: 1957. V. 67

JEPSON, WILLIS LINN
A Flora of California. Berkeley: 1922-1936. V. 66
The Silva of California. Berkeley: 1910. V. 62

JERDEN, WILLIAM
Leaflets of Memory by the Editor of the Oriental Annual. New York: 1858. V. 64

JERDON, T. C.
The Birds of India. Calcutta: 1862-1863. V. 67
The Birds of India. Calcutta: 1877. V. 64; 66
The Mammals of India. 1874. V. 62; 66
The Mammals of India. London: 1874. V. 62; 63

JEREMY, GEORGE
A Treatise on the Equity Jurisdiction of the High Court of Chancery. Philadelphia: 1830. V. 65

JERMY, A. C.
The Phylogeny and Classification of the Ferns. 1973. V. 63

JERNIGAN, E. WESLEY
Jewelry of the Prehistoric Southwest. Santa Fe/Albuquerque: 1978. V. 65

JERNINGHAM, EDWARD
The Nun: an Elegy. London: 1764. V. 62
The Nunnery. London: 1762? V. 62
Poems. London: 1779. V. 63
Poems. London: 1786. V. 66

JERNINGHAM, HUBERT E. H.
Life in a French Chateau. London: 1867. V. 64; 65
Norham Castle. Edinburgh: 1883. V. 64; 65

JEROME, IRENE E.
Sun Prints in Sky Tints, Original Designs with Appropriate Selections. Boston: 1893. V. 66

JEROME, JEROME K.
The Idle Thoughts of an Idle Fellow. London: 1886. V. 64
My Uncle Podger, a Picture Book. Boston: 1975. V. 67
The Second Toughts of an Idle Fellow. London: 1898. V. 67
Stage Land: Curious Habits and Customs of Its Inhabitants. London: 1890. V. 67

JEROME, JOSEPH
Montague Summers - a Memoir. London: 1965. V. 64

JERRARD, P.
The Humming Bird Keepsake. 1861. V. 62

JERROLD, BLANCHARD
The Life of George Cruikshank. London: 1882. V. 64; 65

JERROLD, DOUGLAS WILLIAM
Cakes and Ale. London: 1842. V. 66
The Chronicles of Clovernook; with Some Account of the Hermit of Bellyfulle. London: 1846. V. 67
Heads of the People; or, Portraits of the English. London: 1840. V. 67
Men of Character. London: 1841. V. 66
Men of Character. London: 1851. V. 67
Mrs. Caudle in Crinoline. London: 1858. V. 62
Punch's Letters to His Son. London: 1843. V. 67

JERROLD, WALTER
Bon Mots of Charles Lamb and Douglas Jerrold. London: 1893. V. 64
Bon-Mots of Samuel Foote and Theodore Hook. London: 1894. V. 64; 65
Bon-Mots of Sydney Smith and R. Brinsley Sheridan. London: 1893. V. 64

JERROLD, WILLIAM BLANCHARD
The Life and Remains of Douglas Jerrold. London: 1859. V. 62
London, a Pilgrimage. London: 1872. V. 62

JERSEY, FRANCES, COUNTESS OF
*Deathbed Confessions of the Late Countess of Guernsey, to Lady Anne H.**** Developing a Series of Mysterious Transactions....* London: 1821?. V. 67

JERSEY, GEORGE VILLIERS, 4TH EARL OF
The Correspondence Between the Earl and Countess of Jersey, and the Rev. Dr. Randolph, Upon the Subject of Some Letters Beloning to H.R.H. the Princess of Wales.... London: 1796. V. 62

JERVEY, SUSAN
Two Diaires from Middle St. John's, Berkeley, South Carolina. Feb.- May 1865. St. John's: 1921. V. 63

JERVIS, JOHN JERVIS WHITE
A Refutation of M. M. de Montgaillard's Calumnies Against British Policy.... London: 1812. V. 62

JERVOISE, E.
The Ancient Bridges of the North of England. London: 1931. V. 65

JESSE, EDWARD
An Angler's Rambles, 1836. V. 65; 67
Gleanings in Natural History, with Local Recollections. London: 1832-1834. V. 67

JESSE, F. TENNYSON
The Alabaster Cup. London: 1950. V. 66
Solange Stories. New York: 1931. V. 67

JESSE HANEY & CO.
The Soap-Maker's Manual, a Complete and Practical Guide to the Manufacture of All Kinds of Plain and Fancy Soaps, Washing Fluids, Medicinal Soaps, Etc. New York: 1869. V. 63

JESSE, J. HENEAGE
London: Its Celebrated Characters and Remarkable Places. London: 1871. V. 65

JESSEN, BURCHARD HEINRICH
W. N. MacMillan's Expeditions and Big Game Hunting in Southern Sudan, Abyssinia and East Africa. London: 1906. V. 67

JESSEN, H.
Trachten aus Alt-Hamburg. Hamburg: 1850. V. 66

JESSETT, MONTAGUE GEORGE
The Key to South Africa: Delagoa Bay. London: 1899. V. 67

JESSOP, WILLIAM R. H.
Flindersland and Sturtland; or, the Inside and Outside of Australia. London: 1862. V. 67

JESSUP, RICHARD
The Cincinnati Kid. Boston and Toronto: 1963. V. 63; 65; 66
Cincinnati Kid. London: 1964. V. 66

JESUP, THOMAS S.
Extract from a Report Written by an Officer of the United States Army and Addressed to the Secretary of War, Dated Washington City, March 31, 1820. Washington: 1820. V. 64
System of Accountability for Clothing and Camp Equipage Issued to the Army of the United States. Washington: 1827. V. 64

JET Propulsion; a Reference Text. 1946. V. 66

JETER, JEREMIAH B.
Campbellism Examined. New York: 1855. V. 62

JETER, K. W.
Wolf Flow. 1992. V. 64

JETT, STEPHEN C.
House of Three Turkeys: Anasazi Redoubt. Santa Barbara: 1977. V. 63; 64

JETZLEBENDES Italia, Das Ist Kurtze Doch Grundtliche Beschreibung des Welschlands, Wie es Jetziger Zeit Beschaffen.... Lindau: 1681. V. 64

JEVONS, WILLIAM STANLEY
The Coal Question; An Inquiry Concerning the Progress of the Nation and the Possible Exhauston of Our Coal-Mines. London and Cambridge: 1865. V. 65; 66
The Coal Question; an Inquiry Concerning the Progress of the Nation, and the Probable Exhaustion of Our Coal-Mines. London: 1866. V. 64
Investigations in Currency and Finance. London: 1884. V. 64
Methods of Social Reform and Other Papers. London: 1883. V. 66
Money and the Mechanism of Exchange. New York: 1875. V. 67
Pure Logic and Other Minor Marks. London: 1890. V. 64
The State in Relation to Labour. London: 1887. V. 64
The State in Relation to Labour. London: 1894. V. 64
Studies in Deductive Logic, a Manual for Students. London: 1880. V. 62; 63
The Theory of Political Economy. London: 1879. V. 64; 66
The Theory of Political Economy. London: 1888. V. 63
The Theory of Political Economy. London: 1911. V. 64

JEWEL, JOHN
A Defence of the Apologie of the Churche of Englande.... London: 1567. V. 64

JEWELL, JOHN
The Tourist's Companion, or the History and Antiquities of Harewood in Yorkshire.... Leeds: 1822. V. 65

JEWETT, JOHN HOWARD
Baby Finger Play and Stories. London: 1900. V. 62
The Stories the Baby Bears Told. London: 1914. V. 62
The Three Baby Bears. London. V. 63

JEWETT, MOSES
Jewett's Family Physician. Columbus: 1838. V. 66

JEWETT, PAUL
New England Farrier; or a Compendium of Earriery (sic), in Four Parts. Newburyport: 1795. V. 62

JEWETT, SARAH ORNE
Country By-Ways. Boston: 1881. V. 65
The Country of the Pointed Firs. Boston and New York: 1896. V. 66
Deephaven. Cambridge: 1894. V. 64; 67
A Native of Winby and Other Tales. Boston and New York: 1894. V. 62
The Queen's Twin and Other Stories. Boston and New York: 1899. V. 62; 64; 66
The Tory Lover. Boston and New York: 1901. V. 64; 65; 66
The White Heron. Boston: 1886. V. 64

JEWETT, SOPHIE
The Pilgrim and Other Poems. New York: 1896. V. 64; 67

JEWITT, JOHN HOWARD
Con the Wizard. 1900. V. 65
Con the Wizard. London: 1900. V. 67

JEWITT, JOHN R.
A Narrative of the Adventures and Sufferings of John R. Jewitt.... Middletown: 1815. V. 64
Narrative of the Adventures and Sufferings of John R. Jewitt.... Ithaca: 1849. V. 64; 65; 66

JEWITT, LLEWELLYN
The Ceramic Art of Great Britain from Pre-Historic Times Down to the Present Day. London: 1878. V. 65

JEWRY, MARY
Warne's Every-Day Cookery. 1889. V. 67

JEWSBURY, GERALDINE ENDSOR
Selections from the Letters to Jane Welsh Carlyle. London: 1892. V. 65

JEWSBURY, MARIA JANE
Phantasmagoria; or, Sketches of Life and Literature. London: 1825. V. 65

JEX-BLAKE, SOPHIA
Medical Women. Edinburgh: 1886. V. 65
Medical Women. Edinburgh: 1888. V. 67

JEYES, SAMUEL HENRY
The Life and Times of the...Marquis of Salisbury: a History of the Conservative Party During the Last Forty Years. London: 1895-1896. V. 64

JHABVALA, RUTH PRAWER
Esmond in India. New York: 1958. V. 67
The Householder. London: 1960. V. 62
Like Birds, Like Fishes - and Other Stories. London: 1963. V. 64
The Nature of Passion. London: 1956. V. 62

JIMENEZ, JUAN RAMON
Primeras Prosas. Madrid: 1962. V. 63; 64

JIN, HA
Ocean of Words, Army Stories. Cambridge: 1996. V. 65
Under the Red Flag. Athens: 1997. V. 66; 67
Waiting. New York: 1999. V. 65; 66

JISI, LUMIR
Tibetan Art. London: 1956. V. 64

JOAN, NATALIE
Cosy-Time Tales. London: 1922. V. 66
Tales for Teeny Wee. London: 1930. V. 62
Tales for Teeny Wee. Racine: 1935. V. 62

JOAO DOS PRAZERES, FR.
Principe dos Patriarcas S. Bento. Primeiro Tomo de Sua Vida, Discursada em Emprezas Politicas, e Predicaueis.... Lisbon: 1683-1690. V. 62

JOBSON, JOHN
The Best of John Jobson. 1982. V. 64

JOBSON, RICHARD
The Golden Trade or a Discovery of the River Gambra and the Golden Trade of the Aethiopians.... Teignmouth, Devonshire: 1904. V. 63
The Golden Trade or a Discovery of the River Gambra and the Golden Trade of the Aethiopians.... London: 1932. V. 65

JOCELIN, SIMEON
The Chorister's Companion.... New Haven: 1788. V. 63

JOCELYN, PERCY
The Bishop!! Particulars of the Charge Against the Hon. Percy Jocelyn, Bishop of Clogher, for an Abominable Offence with John Movelley, a soldier of the First Regiment of Foot Guards.... London: 1822. V. 63

JOCELYN, STEPHEN P.
Mostly Alkali. Caldwell: 1953. V. 64; 67

JOCHMANN, CARL GUSTAV
Die Hierarchie und Ihre Bundesgenossen in Frankreich. Arrau: 1823. V. 67

JOCKNICK, SIDNEY
Early Days on the Western Slope of Colorado and Campfire, Chats with Otto Mears, the Pathfinder from 1870 to 1883. Denver: 1913. V. 64

JOCOSERIUS, WAHRMUND
Wol-geschliffener Narren-Spiegel Worinnen Hundert und Vierzehn Arten Allerley Narren Ihr Eben-Bild und Ungestaltes Wesen Ersehen.... ?Nuremberg: 1730. V. 64

JOGENSEN, LISBET BALSLEV
Danmarks Arkitektur. Denmark: 1979. V. 67

JOHANNSEN, ALBERT
The House of Beadle and Adams and Its Dime and Nickle Novels. Norman: 1950. V. 63; 66

JOHANSEN, FREDERICK HJALMAR
With Nansen in the North. London: 1899. V. 62; 66

JOHL, MAX G.
The United States Commemorative Stamps of the Twentieth Century. New York: 1947. V. 66

JOHN, ADAMS
Butterflies of California: a Popular Guide to a Knowledge of the Butterflies of California Embracing all of te 477 Species.... Los Angeles: 1927. V. 66

JOHN, AUGUSTUS
Fifty-Two Drawings.... London: 1957. V. 64

JOHN DEERE & CO.
John Deere Quality Farm Equipment and How to Use It. Moline: 1928. V. 67

JOHN *Gilpin.* London: 1880. V. 65

JOHN, JEAN FREDERIC
Tableaux Chimiques du Regne Animal, ou Apercu des Resultats de Toutes les Analyses Faites Jusqu-a ce Jour sur les Animaux.... Paris: 1816. V. 64

JOHN *Lewis and the International Union: United Mine Workers of America.* N.P: 1952. V. 63

JOHN *Maynard Keynes 1883-1946.* 1949. V. 67

JOHN OF GADDESDEN
Rosa Anglica Practica medicine a Capite ad Pedes Navite Impress and Per Que Diligentissime Emdendata. Venice: 1502. V. 62

JOHN *Pounds, Mender of Shoes and Teacher of Children.* Boston: 1843. V. 66

JOHN OF THE CROSS, SAINT
The Song of the Soul. 1927. V. 64
The Song of the Soul. Abergavenny: 1927. V. 66

JOHNS, C. A.
Flowers of the Field. London: 1907. V. 64

JOHNS, JASPER
Jasper Johns Drawings. Oxford: 1978. V. 63

JOHNS, W. E.
Biggles' Second Case. London: 1948. V. 67
Biggles and the Leopards of Zinn. 1960. V. 67
Biggles Hunts Big Game. 1948. V. 67
The Biggles Omnibus. London: 1938. V. 67
The Cockpit - Flying Adventures for Young Pilots. London: 1934. V. 67
Comrades in Arms. London: 1947. V. 67
The Rustlers of Rattlesnake Valley. 1948. V. 67
Some Milestones of Aviation. London: 1935. V. 65

JOHNSGARD, P. A.
The Avian Brood Parasities, Deception at the Nest. New York: 1997. V. 65
Grouse and Quails of North America. Lincoln: 1973. V. 63; 67
The Hummingbirds of North America. Washington: 1983. V. 67
The Plovers, Sandpipers and Snipes of the World. Lincoln: 1981. V. 67

JOHNSON, A. B.
The Physiology of the Senses; or, How and What We See, Hear, Taste, Feel and Smell. New York: 1856. V. 66

JOHNSON, A. F.
One Hundred Title Pages 1500-1800. London: 1928. V. 64
Selected Essays on Books and Printing. Amsterdam: 1970. V. 62; 64
Selected Essays on Books and Printing. Amsterdam: 1970-1971. V. 67

JOHNSON, A. W.
The Birds of Chile and Adjacent Regions of Argentina, Bolivia and Peru. Buenos Aires: 1965-1972. V. 64; 67

JOHNSON, ADAM RANKIN
The Partisan Rangers of the Confederate States Army. Louisville: 1904. V. 62

JOHNSON, ALEXANDER B.
An Inquiry into the Nature of Value and of Capital and Into the Operation of Government, Loans, Banking Institutions and Private Credit. New York: 1813. V. 64

JOHNSON, ALFRED
History and Genealogy of One Line of Descent from Captain Edward Johnson. Boston: 1914. V. 67

JOHNSON, ALFRED FORBES
A Catalogue of Engraved and Etched English Title-pages Down to the Death of William Faithorne, 1691. London: 1934. V. 66
Decorative Initial Letters. London: 1931. V. 66

JOHNSON, AMANDUS
The Swedish Settlements on the Delaware, Their History and Relation to the Indians, Dutch and English, 1638-1664. Philadelphia: 1911. V. 63; 66

JOHNSON and Garrick. London: 1816. V. 62

JOHNSON, ANDREW
Trial of Andrew Johnson, President of the U.S....on Impeachment by the House of Representatives for High Crimes and Misdemeanors. Washington: 1868. V. 67

JOHNSON, ANNA C.
The Cottages of the Alps; or, Life and Manners in Switzerland. London: 1860. V. 65

JOHNSON, AUDREY
Furnishing Dolls' Houses. London: 1972. V. 62

JOHNSON, B. S.
All Bull: the National Servicemen. London: 1973. V. 62; 63; 66
Aren't You Rather Young to be Writing Your Memoirs?. London: 1973. V. 63; 64
Christie Malry's Own Double Entry. London: 1973. V. 64; 65; 66
A Dublin Unicorn. Nottingham: 1965. V. 64
Everyone Knows Somebody Who's Dead. London: 1973. V. 64
House Mother Normal. London: 1971. V. 63; 64; 66
Poems Two. 1972. V. 63
See the Old Lady Decently. London: 1975. V. 63
Statement Against Corpses: Short Stories. London: 1964. V. 64; 66
Travelling People. London: 1963. V. 63; 64; 66
Trawl. London: 1966. V. 63; 64
The Unfortunates. London: 1969. V. 62; 64; 66
Universities' Poetry Two. 1959. V. 64
You Always Remember the First Time. London: 1975. V. 63; 64

JOHNSON, BOB
History of Wayne County North Carolina. Goldsboro: 1979. V. 67

JOHNSON, BRADLEY TYLER
Memoir of the Life and Public Service of Joseph E. Johnston. Baltimore: 1891. V. 62; 64

JOHNSON, BURGES
Pleasant Tragedies of Childhood. New York: 1905. V. 67

JOHNSON, CHARLES
Black Humor. Chicago: 1970. V. 62; 67
The Complete Art of Writing Letters. London: 1770. V. 65
English Court Hand A.D. 1066-1500 Illustrated Chiefly from Public Records. New York: 1967. V. 64
Faith and the Good Thing. New York: 1974. V. 67
Middle Passage. New York: 1990. V. 66
The Sorcerer's Apprentice. New York: 1986. V. 63
The Victim. Dublin: 1727. V. 67
The Village Opera as It Is Acted at the Theatre Royal.... London: 1729. V. 63
The Wife's Relief; or, the Husband's Cure. London: 1712. V. 63

JOHNSON, CHARLES PLUMPTRE
Hints to Collectors of Original Editions of the Works of Charles Dickens. London: 1885. V. 66

JOHNSON, CHARLES S.
Ebony and Topaz. New York: 1927. V. 67
Patterns of Negro Segregation. London: 1944. V. 65

JOHNSON, CLIFTON
Highways and Byways of the Mississippi Valley. New York: 1906. V. 65; 66
An Unredeemed Captive. Holyoke: 1897. V. 63; 66

JOHNSON, D.
Palms for Human Needs in Asia.... Rotterdam: 1991. V. 62

JOHNSON, D. L.
The Architecture.... Adelaide: 1977. V. 65

JOHNSON, DANIEL
Sketches of Indian Field Sports.... London: 1827. V. 66

JOHNSON, DAVID F.
The American Historical Buttons. New Market: 1942. V. 65

JOHNSON, DENIS
Angels. New York: 1983. V. 63; 67
Fiskadoro. New York: 1985. V. 67
The Incognito Lounge and Other Poems. New York: 1982. V. 63; 64; 67
The Man Among the Seals. Iowa City: 1969. V. 62; 63; 67
Resuscitation of a Hanged Man. New York: 1990. V. 63

JOHNSON, DIANA L.
Fantastic Illustration and Design in Britain 1850-1930. Providence: 1979. V. 62

JOHNSON, EDGAR
Charles Dickens - His Tragedy and Triumph. London: 1953. V. 65

JOHNSON, EDWARD
Results of Hydropathy; or, Constipation Not a Disease of the Bowels.... London: 1848. V. 64

JOHNSON, ELISABETH B.
Rappahannock County, Virginia: a History. Orange: 1981. V. 64

JOHNSON, G. L.
Photographic Optics and Colour Photography. London: 1909. V. 67

JOHNSON, GEORGE W.
The Cottage Gardener.... London: 1849. V. 64
A Dictionary of Modern Gardening. London: 1846. V. 63
Memoirs of John Selden and Notices of the Political Contest During His Time. London: 1835. V. 62

JOHNSON, HAROLD
Who's Who in Major League Baseball. Chicago: 1933. V. 63

JOHNSON, HARRY
A History of Anderson County Kansas. Garnett: 1936. V. 65
Night and Morning in Dark Africa. London: 1902. V. 67
Night and Morning in Dark Africa. London: 1905. V. 62

JOHNSON, HENRY T.
The Ape Man. London: 1900. V. 67

JOHNSON, J. E.
An Address to the Public, on The Advantages of Steam Navigation to India. London: 1824. V. 65

JOHNSON, J. ROSAMOND
Utica Jubilee Singers Spirituals: as Sung at the Utica Normal and Industrial Institute of Mississippi. New York: 1930. V. 63

JOHNSON, JAMES
Change of Air, or the Pursuit of Health...(with) An Essay on Indigestion. London: 1831. V. 63
The Influence of Civic Life, Sedentary Habits and Intellectual Refinement, on Human Health, and Human Happiness.... London: 1818. V. 65
The Influence of Tropical Climates.... London: 1815. V. 62
Panegyrical Essays Upon the Prayer Lord, Pity the People, the Only Words of William I Prince of Orange.... London: 1716. V. 62
A Treatise on Derangements of the Liver, Internal Organs, Nervous System. Concord: 1832. V. 65

JOHNSON, JAMES D.
A Century of Chicago Streetcars 1858-1958. Wheaton: 1964. V. 63

JOHNSON, JAMES WELDON
The Autobiography of an Ex-Coloured Man. Boston: 1912. V. 63
The Autobiography of an Ex-Coloured Man. Garden City: 1927. V. 63
The Book of American Negro Poetry.... New York: 1922. V. 63
The Book of American Negro Spirituals. New York: 1925. V. 62
Negro Americans, What Now?. New York: 1934. V. 62; 64

JOHNSON, JOHN
The Clergyman's Vade Mecum; or an Account of the Ancient and Present Church of England.... London: 1709. V. 62
The Defense of Charleston Harbor, Including Fort Sumter and the Adjacent Islands 1863-1865. Charleston: 1890. V. 63; 65
Typographia or the Printer's Instructor. London: 1824. V. 64; 66

JOHNSON, JOHN J.
Directions for Using the Patent Excelsior Tanning Process. Russell: 1865. V. 67

JOHNSON, JOHN L.
The University Memorial Biographical Sketches of Alumni of the University of Virginia Who Fell in the Confederate War. Baltimore: 1871. V. 65

JOHNSON, JOHN LIPSCOMB
Autobiographical Notes. Boulder: 1958. V. 62; 63

JOHNSON, KENNETH M.
Aerial California: an Account of Early Flight in Northern and Southern California 1849 to World War One. Los Angeles: 1961. V. 63
The New Almaden Quicksilver Mine. Georgetown: 1963. V. 67
The Sting of the Wasp: Political and Satirical Cartoons from the Truculent Early San Francisco Weekly.... San Francisco: 1967. V. 64

JOHNSON, L. F.
Famous Kentucky Tragedies and Trials. New York: 1916. V. 65

JOHNSON, LAURA WINTHROP
Eight Hundred Miles in an Ambulance. Philadelphia: 1889. V. 65; 66

JOHNSON, LIONEL
The Art of Thomas Hardy. London: 1894. V. 64
Poems. London: 1895. V. 64
Reviews and Critical Papers. London: 1921. V. 66
Three Poems. Ysleta: 1928. V. 65

JOHNSON, LOUISA
Every Lady Her Own Flower Gardener, Addressed to the Industrious and Economical Only. London: 1845. V. 64

JOHNSON, M. L.
Trail Blazers - A True Story of the Struggles with Hostile Indians or the Frontier of Texas. Dallas: 1935. V. 67

JOHNSON, MARTIN
Lion. African Adventure with the King of Beasts. 1929. V. 67

JOHNSON, MERLE
American First Editions - Bibliographic Check Lists of the Works of 146 American Authors. New York: 1932. V. 63
American First Editions. Bibliographic Check Lists of the Works of One Hundred and Five American Authors. New York: 1929. V. 66
High Spots of American Literature. New York: 1929. V. 63; 66

JOHNSON, NEIL R.
The Chickasaw Rancher. Stillwater: 1961. V. 65

JOHNSON, OLGA WEYDEMEYER
The Story of the Tobacco Plains Country. The Autobiography of a Community. N.P: 1950. V. 62

JOHNSON, OSA
I Married Adventure: the Lives and Adventures of Martin and Osa Johnson. London: 1940. V. 67

JOHNSON, OWEN
The Variant. A Lawrenceville Story. Boston: 1930. V. 63

JOHNSON, P. DEMAREST
Claudius, the Cowboy of Ramapo Valley. Middletown: 1894. V. 63; 66

JOHNSON, PHIL
Life on the Plains. Chicago: 1888. V. 63

JOHNSON, PHILIP
Philip Johnson Writings. New York: 1979. V. 63

JOHNSON, R. H.
A Hand Book for Visitors to the Isle of Man. Douglas: 1849. V. 63; 66

JOHNSON, R. S.
Travelling People. London: 1963. V. 66

JOHNSON, RICHARD
Aristarchus Anti-Bentleianus Quadraginta Sex Bentleii Erroes Super Q. Horatii Flacci.... Nottinghamiae: 1717. V. 65
Blossoms of Morality. London: 1796. V. 62; 66
Juvenile Trials for Robbing Orchards, Telling Fibs and Other Heinous Offences. Boston: 1797. V. 64; 66
A New History of England. London: 1785. V. 62
A New History of the Grecian States; from Their Earliest Period to Their Extinction by the Ottomans.... Lansingburgh: 1794. V. 64; 66
A New Roman History, from the Foundation of Rome to the End of the Common-wealth. London: 1770. V. 62
The Picture Exhibition.... Worcester: 1788. V. 64

JOHNSON, RICHARD W.
A Soldier's Reminiscences in Peace and War. Philaldelphia: 1886. V. 62; 64; 67

JOHNSON, ROBERT
Nova Britannia. New York: 1867. V. 67

JOHNSON, ROBERT G.
An Historical Account of the First Settlement of Salem, in West Jersey.... Philadelphia: 1839. V. 66

JOHNSON, ROBERT U.
Battles and Leaders of the Civil War. New York: 1884-1887. V. 62; 65
Battles and Leaders of the Civil War. New York: 1884-1888. V. 62
Battles and Leaders of the Civil War. S. Brunswick: 1956. V. 63; 66

JOHNSON, RONALD
Aficionado's Southwestern Cooking. Albuquerque: 1968. V. 66
A Line of Poetry, a Row of Trees. Highlands: 1964. V. 62; 63; 64; 67
Songs of the Earth. San Francisco: 1970. V. 62
The Spirit Walks, The Rocks Will Talk. Eccentric Translations from Two Eccentrics. New York: 1969. V. 63
Sports and Divertissments. Urbana: 1969. V. 63; 67

JOHNSON, SAMUEL
The Adventurer. London: 1770. V. 62
An Archaeological Dictionary; or Classical Antiquities of the Jews, Greeks and Romans.... London: 1793. V. 65
The Beauties.... London: 1797. V. 62
A Diary of a Journey into North Wales, in the Year 1774. London: 1816. V. 65; 66
A Dictionary of the English Language. London: 1755. V. 66
A Dictionary of the English Language. London: 1755-1756. V. 64
Dictionary of the English Language. London: 1756. V. 63
A Dictionary of the English Language. London: 1760. V. 63; 64
A Dictionary of the English Language. London: 1766. V. 64
A Dictionary of the English Language. Dublin: 1768. V. 62; 66
A Dictionary of the English Language. London: 1770. V. 63; 64
A Dictionary of the English Language. London: 1773. V. 64; 65
A Dictionary of the English Language. London: 1783. V. 64
A Dictionary of the English Language. London: 1784. V. 64
A Dictionary of the English Language. London: 1785. V. 64
A Dictionary of the English Language. London: 1792. V. 62
A Dictionary of the English Language. London: 1794. V. 64
A Dictionary of the English Language. Philadelphia: 1805. V. 63; 66
A Dictionary of the English Language. London: 1806. V. 64
A Dictionary of the English Language. London: 1807. V. 66
A Dictionary of the English Language. London: 1810. V. 64
A Dictionary of the English Language. Philadelphia: 1813. V. 62
A Dictionary of the English Language. London: 1818. V. 62
A Dictionary of the English Language. London: 1823. V. 62
A Dictionary of the English Language.... London: 1799. V. 64
The False Alarm. London: 1770. V. 65
The Harleian Miscellany. London: 1744. V. 66
The History of Rasselas, Prince of Abyssinia. Whittingham: 1822. V. 67
The History of Rasselas, Prince of Abyssinia. Oxford: 1927. V. 64
The Idler. London: 1767. V. 67
The Idler. London: 1783. V. 62
The Idler. London: 1790. V. 62
Irene. London: 1749. V. 62
Irene. London: 1781. V. 66
Johnson, Boswell and Mrs. Piozzi, a Suppressed Passage Restored. Oxford: 1929. V. 66
Johnsoniana; or, Supplement to Boswell.... London: 1836. V. 64
Johnson's Dictionary of the English Language. London: 1807. V. 64
Johnson's Dictionary of the English Language in Miniature. London: 1799. V. 64
Johnson's Dictionary of the English Language in Miniature. London: 1805. V. 62
Johnson's Dictionary of the English Language in Miniature. London: 1811. V. 64
Johnson's English Dictionary as Improved by Todd. Philadelphia: 1859. V. 67
Johnson's Proposals for His Edition of Shakespeare 1756. London: 1923. V. 65
A Journey to the Western Islands of Scotland. Dublin: 1775. V. 62
A Journey to the Western Islands of Scotland. London: 1775. V. 64
A Journey to the Western Islands of Scotland. Baltimore, Boston, Albany: 1810. V. 62
A Journey to the Western Islands of Scotland. Glasgow: 1817. V. 62; 65
Letters to and from the Late Samuel Johnson, LL.D. Dublin: 1788. V. 62
Letters To and From the Late Samuel Johnson, LL.D. London: 1788. V. 62; 64; 65
The Letters...with Mrs. Thrale's Genuine Letters to Him. Oxford: 1952. V. 65
The Lives of the English Poets: and a Criticism on Their Works. Dublin: 1780-1781. V. 64
The Lives of the English Poets; and a Criticism on Their Works. Dublin: 1781. V. 64
The Lives of the Most Eminent English Poets. London: 1781. V. 62; 64
The Lives of the Most Eminent English Poets. London: 1790. V. 66
The Lives of the Most Eminent English Poets. London: 1800-1801. V. 63
The Lives of the Most Eminent English Poets. London: 1806. V. 65
The Lives of the Most Eminent English Poets. London: 1810. V. 66
The Lives of the Most Eminent Poets.... London: 1824. V. 62
The Lives of the Poets. Dublin: 1795-1802. V. 62
Lives of the Poets. London: 1825. V. 62
Lives of the Poets. Oxford: 1905. V. 65
London: a Poem and the Vanity of Human Wishes. London: 1930. V. 64
Miscellaneous and Fugitive Pieces. London: 1774. V. 62
Mr. Johnson's Preface to His Edition of Shakespeare's Plays. London: 1765. V. 64
A New Prologue.... Oxford: 1925. V. 66
Notes Upon the Phoenix Edition of the Pastoral Letter. Part 1. London: 1694. V. 63
Oriental Religions and Their Relation to Universal Religion. Boston: 1872. V. 63
Papers Written by Dr. Johnson an Dr. Dodd in 1777. Oxford: 1926. V. 66
Poems. New Haven and London: 1964. V. 65
The Poetical Works. London: 1785. V. 62; 66
The Poetical Works. Burlington: 1816. V. 66
Political Tracts. Dublin: 1777. V. 62
Prayers and Meditations. London: 1785. V. 62; 64
Prayers and Meditations. London: 1807. V. 66
Prefaces, Biographical and Critical to the Works of the English Poets.... London: 1779-1781. V. 62; 64
The Prince of Abissinia. London: 1759. V. 65; 67
The Prince of Abissinia. London: 1766. V. 62
Proposal for Printing...The Dramatick Works of William Shakespeare. Oxford: 1925. V. 66
Proposals for the Publisher. Oxford: 1930. V. 66
The Rambler. London: 1752. V. 64
The Rambler. London: 1763. V. 66
The Rambler. London: 1767. V. 62
Rasselas; a Tale. Dinarbas; a Tale. London: 1823. V. 65
Thoughts on the Late Transactions Respecting Falkland's Islands. London: 1771. V. 64
Le Vallon Fourtune, ou Rasselas et Dinarbas. Paris: 1817. V. 65
The Vanity of Human Wishes. London: 1749. V. 64
The Vanity of Human Wishes. London: 1927. V. 66
The Vanity of Human Wishes. Cambridge: 1984. V. 63
The Vanity of Human Wishes. London: 1984. V. 66
The Works. With an Essay on His Life and Genius by Arthur Murphy. Dublin: 1793. V. 66
The Works. With an Essay On His Life and Genius by Arthur Murphy. New York: 1835. V. 66
The Works.... London: 1779-1781. V. 66
The Works.... London: 1787. V. 62

JOHNSON, SAMUEL R.
California: a Sermon Preached in St. John's Church, Brooklyn, New York on Sunday, Feb. 11, 1849. New York: 1849. V. 65

JOHNSON, SIDNEY SMITH
Texas Who Wore the Gray. Tyler: 1907. V. 62

JOHNSON, T.
A Catalogue of Law Books. Philadelphia: 1856. V. 65
Opuscula Omnia Botanica...Nusperrime Edita a T. S. Ralph. 1847. V. 62

JOHNSON, T. W.
Sparrow, Fungi in Oceans and Estauries. 1961. V. 64

JOHNSON, THEODORE T.
Sights in the Gold Region and Scenes by the Way. New York: 1850. V. 62
Sights in the Gold Region and Scenes by the Way. New York: 1949. V. 63

JOHNSON, THOMAS BURGELAND
Physiological Observations on Mental Susceptibility.... London: 1838. V. 64
The Shooter's Companion. 1830. V. 62; 63; 66; 67
The Shooter's Companion. 1834. V. 63

JOHNSON, UNA E.
Isabel Bishop. Prints and Drawings 1925-1964. New York: 1964. V. 62

JOHNSON, UWE
Speculations About Jakob. New York: 1963. V. 67

JOHNSON, VIRGINIA W.
The Unregimented General. Boston: 1962. V. 67

JOHNSON, W. R.
Easter. Philadelphia: 1970. V. 63
The History of England in Easy Verse: from the Invasion of Julius Caesar to the Close of the Year 1809. London: 1812. V. 62
Narcissus. Vermont: 1990. V. 62

JOHNSON, WARREN B.
From the Pacific to the Atlantic Being an Account of a Journey Overland from Eureka, Humbolt County, California to Webster County, Massachusetts. Webster: 1887. V. 63

JOHNSON, WILLIAM
The Practical Mechanic's Journal. Volumes 1-8, Second Series Volumes 1-9. (lacking volume 6). Third Series Volumes 1-4. Glasgow. 1848. V. 65
Sketches of the Life and Correspondence of Nathanel Greene, Major General of the Armies of the United States, in the War of the Revolution. Charleston: 1822. V. 63

JOHNSON, WILLIAM S.
W. Eugene Smith: Master of the Photographic Essay. Millerton: 1981. V. 65

JOHNSTON & CO.
Johnston & Co. General Dealers in Farm Machinery & Carriages, Fredericton, N.B. Fredericton: 1888. V. 64

JOHNSTON, ALASTAIR
A Biliography of the Auerhahn Press and its Successor Dave Haselwood Books.... Berkeley: 1976. V. 62

JOHNSTON, ALEX KEITH
Atlas to Alison's History of Europe. Edinburgh: 1875. V. 65
Dictionary of Geography, Descriptive, Physical, Statistical and Historical.... London: 1851. V. 64

JOHNSTON, ANNIE FELLOWS
The Land of the Little Colonel, Reminiscence and Autobiography.... Boston: 1929. V. 63
The Little Colonel's Good Times Book. Boston: 1909. V. 63

JOHNSTON, D. C.
The Galaxy of Wit; or Laughing Philosopher. Boston: 1830. V. 64
Scraps No. 1. 1849. New Series. V. 67

JOHNSTON, DENIS
Collected Plays. London: 1960. V. 66

JOHNSTON, FREDERICK
Terracina Cloud: Poems. Verona: 1936. V. 62

JOHNSTON, G.
A History of British Sponges and Lithophytes. Edinburgh: 1842. V. 63
A History of the British Zoophytes. 1847. V. 63; 66; 67
A History of the British Zoophytes. London: 1847. V. 64

JOHNSTON, H. B.
Annotated Catalogue of African Grasshoppers. Cambridge: 1956-1968. V. 63; 66

JOHNSTON, HARRY H.
Britain: Across the Seas Africa. London: 1930. V. 67
British Central Africa.... London: 1897. V. 67
British Central Africa.... London: 1898. V. 65
George Grenfell and the Congo: a History and Description of the Congo Independent State and Adjoining Districts of Congoland.... London: 1908. V. 62; 66; 67
The Kilimanjaro Expedition: a Record of Scientific Exploration in Easter Equatorial Africa.... London: 1886. V. 67
Liberia. London: 1906. V. 67
Pioneers in Australasia. London: 1913. V. 67
Pioneers in Canada. London: 1912. V. 67
The River Congo, From Its Mouth to Bolobo; with a General Description of the Natural History of Anthropology of its Western Basin. London: 1884. V. 65
The Uganda Protectorate. London: 1902. V. 67

JOHNSTON, I. H.
Birds of West Virginia, their Economic Value and Aesthetic Beauty. Charleston: 1923. V. 67

JOHNSTON, J.
Notes of Visit to Walt Whitman: Etc. in July 1890. Bolton: 1890. V. 64

JOHNSTON, J. F. W.
Report on the Agricultural Capabilities of the Province of New Brunswick. Fredericton: 1850. V. 67

JOHNSTON, J. W.
Letter to the Granville Street Church, Halifax, N.S. Halifax: 1867. V. 63

JOHNSTON, JAMES FINLAY
The Chemistry of Common Life.... Edinburgh and London: 1880. V. 65

JOHNSTON, JAMES HOUSTOUN
Western and Atlantic Railroad of the State of Georgia. Atlanta: 1932. V. 63

JOHNSTON, JOHN
Historiae Naturalis de Avibus Libri VI. Amsterdam: 1657. V. 67

JOHNSTON, JOSEPH EGGLESTON
Narrative of Military Operations. New York: 1874. V. 62; 63

JOHNSTON, LORAND V.
Selected References Relating to the Ancestry of William and John Johnston Colonial Friends (Quakers) of Virginia. Shaker Heights: 1972. V. 67

JOHNSTON, MARTIN
Camera Trails in Africa. 1924. V. 67

JOHNSTON, MARY
Audrey. Boston: 1902. V. 64
Cease Firing. Boston and New York: 1912. V. 62; 63; 64
Lewis Rand. Boston and New York: 1908. V. 64; 67
The Long Roll. Boston: 1911. V. 63
Sir Mortimer. New York and London: 1904. V. 64; 67

JOHNSTON, NATHANIEL
The Assurance of Abby and Other Church-Lands in England to the Possessors Cleared from the Doubts...About the Danger of Resumption. London: 1687. V. 66
The King's Visitatorial Power Asserted, Being an Impartial Relation of the Late Visitation of St. Mary Magdalen College in Oxford. London: 1688. V. 64

JOHNSTON, PAUL
Biblio-Typographica. A Survey of Contemporary Fine Printing Style. New York: 1930. V. 63; 64

JOHNSTON, PRISCILLA
The Mill Book. Ditchling and Hammersmith: 1917. V. 62

JOHNSTON, R.
Parnell and the Parnells. A Historical Sketch. 1888. V. 67

JOHNSTON, R. F.
Feral Pigeons. New York: 1995. V. 67

JOHNSTON, RALPH
Buffalo Bill. Boston: 1938. V. 64

JOHNSTON, ROBERT
An Authentic Account of the Trial, Sentence and Execution of Robert Johnston, Who Was Executed at Edinburgh, on Wednesday the 30th December 1818 for Assault and Robbery.... Edinburgh;: 1819. V. 63
Travels through Part of the Russian Empire and the Country of Poland.... London: 1815. V. 64

JOHNSTON, WILLIAM PRESTON
The Life of Gen. Albert Sydney Johnston. New York: 1878. V. 63; 65; 66; 67
The Life of General Albert Sidney Johnston. New York: 1880. V. 63

JOHNSTONE, ANNE
Deans Gift Book of Bible Stories. London: 1974. V. 67

JOHNSTONE, CHARLES
Chrysal; or, the Adventures of a Guinea. London: 1761-1768. V. 62
Chrysal; or, the Adventures of a Guinea. London: 1771. V. 62
Chrysal; or, the Adventures of a Guinea. London: 1785. V. 62
The History of Arsaces, Prince of Betlis. Dublin: 1774-1775. V. 62

JOHNSTONE, CHEVALIER DE
Memoirs of the Rebellion in 1745 and 1746. London: 1822. V. 62; 66

JOHNSTONE, CHRISTIAN ISOBEL
The Edinburgh Tales. Edinburgh: 1845-1846. V. 65

JOHNSTONE, EDITH
The Douce Family. London: 1896. V. 64

JOHNSTONE, G. H.
Asiatic Magnolias in Cultivation. London: 1955. V. 63; 64

JOHNSTONE, GEORGE
The Speech of Mr. Johnstone, on the Third Reading of the Bill for Preventing the Gold Coin of the Realm from Being Paid or Accepted for a Greater Value than the Current Value of Such Coin.... London: 1811. V. 67

JOHNSTONE, IAIN
The World is Not Enough: a Companion. London: 1999. V. 67

JOHNSTONE, JAMES
Antiquitates Celto-Normannicae... (with) Antiquitates Celto- Scandicae. Copenhagen: 1786. V. 63; 66
British Fisheries, Their Administration and Their Problems. London: 1905. V. 64
Historical and Descriptive Account of George Heriot's Hospital. Edinburgh: 1827. V. 62; 66
An Historical Dissertation Concerning the Malignant Epidemical Fever of 1756. London: 1758. V. 65
My Experiences in Manipur and the Naga Hills. 1896. V. 66
My Experiences in Manipur and the Naga Hills. London: 1896. V. 67
A Treatise on the Malignant Angina; or Putrid and Ulcerous Sore- Throat, to Which are Added, Some Remarks on the Angina Tracheatis. Worcester: 1774. V. 65
A Treatise on the Malignant Angina; or, Putrid and Ulcerous Sore- Throat to Which are Added, Some Remarks on the Angina Tracheatis. Worcester: 1779. V. 65

JOHNSTONE, JOHN
An Account of the Approved Mode of Draining Land. Dublin: 1800. V. 63
An Account of the Most Approved Mode of Draining Land.... Edinburgh: 1797. V. 64
An Account of the Most Approved Mode of Draining Land.... Edinburgh: 1801. V. 64
Reply to Dr. James Carmichael Smyth, Containing Remarks on His Letter to Mr. Wilberforce and a Further Account of the Discovery of the Power of Mineral Acids in a State of Gas to Destroy Contagion. London: 1805. V. 62

JOHNSTONE, JOHN K.
The Isle of Axholme; its Place-Names and River-Names. Epworth: 1886. V. 63

JOHNSTONE, W. G.
The Nature Printed British Sea-Weeds. London: 1859-1860. V. 64

JOHNSTONE, WILLIAM
Paintings by William Johnstone. Newcastle upon Tyne: 1963. V. 64

JOHNSTON-LAVIS, H. J.
Bibliography of the Geology and Eruptive Phenomena of the More Important Volcanoes of Southern Italy. London: 1918. V. 64; 66

JOINVILLE, JOHN
The History of Saint Louis. Newtown: 1937. V. 64

JOKELSON, PAUL
One Hundred of the Most Important Paperweights. London: 1960. V. 67

JOLAS, EUGENE
Mots-Deluge - Hypnologues. Paris: 1933. V. 64
Transition 4. Paris: 1927. V. 63
Vertical. Paris. V. 63

JOLAS, MARIA
A James Joyce Yearbook. Paris: 1949. V. 62; 65

JOLIFFE, THOMAS R.
Letters from Palestine, Descriptive of a Tour through Galilee and Judaea, with Some Account of the Dead Sea and of the Present State of Jerusalem. London: 1819. V. 66

JOLINE, ADRIAN HOFFMAN
The Diversions of a Book-Lover. New York and London: 1903. V. 64

JOLLY Companions. London: 1896. V. 62

THE JOLLY Jump-Ups ABC Book. Springfield: 1948. V. 65

THE JOLLY Jump-Ups, See the Circus, Jingling Bros.... Springfield: 1944. V. 63

JOLY, H. L.
Legend in Japanese Art. London: 1908. V. 62

JOMINI, HENRI
Napoleon in the Other World. London: 1827. V. 64

JONES, A. BASSETT
Malingering or the Simulation of Disease.... London: 1917. V. 62; 63; 66

JONES, BENJAMIN WASHINGTON
Under the Stars and Bars. Richmond: 1909. V. 62; 63

JONES, BOBBY
Down the Fairway: the Golf Life and Play of Robert T. Jones, Jr. New York: 1927. V. 63; 65

JONES, C. N.
Early Days in Cooke County 1848-1873. Gainesville: 1936. V. 63

JONES, CAROLYN
Twice Upon a Time. New York: 1971. V. 63

JONES, CHARLES C.
The Battle of Honey Hill. Augusta: 1885. V. 63
Cathechism, of Scripture Doctrine and Practice.... Savannah: 1837. V. 66
The Dead Towns of Georgia. Savannah: 1878. V. 63; 66
Defence of Battery Wagner, July 18th, 1863. Augusta: 1892. V. 63
General Sherman's March from Atlanta to the Coast. Augusta: 1884. V. 62; 63
The History of Georgia. Boston: 1883. V. 63; 64
The Life and Services of Commodore Josiah Tatnall. Savannah: 1878. V. 62; 63; 65
The Religious Instruction of Negroes in the United States. Savannah: 1842. V. 64; 66
The Siege of Savannah in December 1864 and the Confederate Operations in Georgia...During General Sherman's March from Atlanta to the Sea. Albany: 1874. V. 62

JONES, CHARLES H.
Appletons' Hand-Book of American Travel, Southern Tour. New York: 1873. V. 63
Historical Atlas of the World Illustrated. Chicago: 1875. V. 67

JONES, CHARLES HANDFIELD
Clinical Observations on Functional Nervous Disorders. Philadelphia: 1867. V. 65
Studies on Functional Nervous Disorders. London: 1870. V. 65

JONES, D. J.
The Prints of Rockwell Kent: a Catalogue Raisonne. Chicago: 1975. V. 65

JONES, DANIEL W.
Forty Years Among the Indians. Salt Lake City: 1890. V. 64

JONES, DAVID
Anathemata - Fragments of an Attempted Writing. London: 1952. V. 62; 63; 66
A Compleat History of the Turks, from their Origin in the Year 755 to the Year 1701.... London: 1701. V. 67
The Fatigue: a Poem. Cambridge: 1965. V. 66
In Parenthesis. London: 1937. V. 64
In Parenthesis. London: 1961. V. 62; 64; 65
In Parenthesis. New York: 1961. V. 62
The Secret History of White-Hall, from the Restoration of Charles II, Down to the Abdication of the Late K. James. London: 1697. V. 66

JONES, E. ALFRED
The Loyalists of New Jersey. The Memorials, Petitions, Claims, etc. from English Records. Newark: 1927. V. 63; 66

JONES, EDWARD ALFRED
The Old Royal Plate of the Tower of London. Oxford: 1908. V. 63

JONES, ELECTA F.
Stockbridge, Past and Present; or, Records of an Old Mission Station. Springfield: 1854. V. 66

JONES, EMERYS
Atlas of London and the London Region. 1968. V. 62

JONES, ERASMUS
A Trip through London; Containing Observations on Men and Things.... London: 1728. V. 65

JONES, FAYETTE
Old Mining Camps of New Mexico 1854-1904. Santa Fe: 1964. V. 64

JONES, FRANKLIN D.
Ingenious Mechanisms for Designers and Inventors. New York: 1948-1951. V. 66

JONES, FREDERICK CONINGSBY
The Attorney's and Solicitor's New Pocket Book, and Conveyancer's Assistant.... London: 1850. V. 63

JONES, G. N.
A Botanical Survey of the Olympic Peninsula, Washington. Seattle: 1916. V. 67

JONES, GEORGE
Observations on the Zodiacal Light from April 2, 1853 to April 22, 1855 Made Chiefly On Board the United States Steam-Frigate Mississippi, During Her Late Cruise in Eastern Seas, and Her Voyage Homeward, With Conclusions from the Data thus Obtained. Washaington: 1856. V. 66
United States Japan Expedition. Observations On the Zodiacal Light from April 2, 1853 to April 22, 1855. Washington: 1856. V. 64

JONES, GEORGE W.
Catalogue of the Library of George W. Jones at the Sign of the Dolphin Next to Dr. Johnson's House in Gough Square, Fleet Steet, London E.C. 4. London: 1938. V. 63
The Message of One of England's Greatest Poets to a Printer and Printers, Especially Those Who Possess Love of Craft. London: 1931. V. 62

JONES, GERALD
Taking Stock: Painting and Sculpture by G. Harvey. Houston: 1986. V. 66

JONES, GLYN
The Saga of Llywarch the Old. Waltham St. Lawrence: 1955. V. 66

JONES, GWYN
The Green Island. Waltham St. Lawrence: 1946. V. 62; 66
The Welsh Review - Volume IV, No. 4. London: 1945. V. 63

JONES, H. J.
The Chrysanthemum Album. Lewisham: 1896. V. 64

JONES, H. S. V.
Spenser's Defence of Lord Grey. Urbana;: 1919. V. 67

JONES, HANNAH MARIA
Gretna Green; or the Elopement of Miss D---- With a Gallant Son of Mars. London: 1823. V. 65
A History of England from Julius Caesar to the Present Time. London: 1835?. V. 65

JONES, HAROLD
The Enchanted Night. London: 1947. V. 65
The Forest. London: 1981. V. 66
The Visit to the Farm. London: 1939. V. 65

JONES, HENRY
Card Essays, Clay's Decisions and Card Table Talk. New York: 1880. V. 62; 63; 64; 66

JONES, HORACE
The Story of Early Rice County. N.P: 1928. V. 65
The Story of Early Rice County. Wichita: 1928. V. 62

JONES, HOWARD
Illustrations of the Nests and Eggs of the Birds of Ohio. Circleville: 1879-1886. V. 67

JONES, HOWARD M.
The Harp that Once - a Chonicle of the Life of Thomas Moore. New York: 1937. V. 65

JONES, HUGH OWEN
A Review of the Past and Present Treatment of Disease in the Hip, Knee and Angle Joints with Their Deformities. Liverpool: 1878. V. 67

JONES, I.
A History of Printing and Printers in Wales to 1810 and of Successive and Related Printers to 1923. Also, a History of Printing and Printers in Monmouthshire to 1923. Cardiff: 1925. V. 62

JONES, ISAAC H.
Equilibrium and Vertigo. Philadelphia: 1918. V. 65

JONES, J.
Investigations Relative to Certain American Vertebrata. Washington: 1856. V. 62; 63; 64

JONES, J. O.
A Cowman's Memoirs. Fort Worth: 1953. V. 66

JONES, J. P.
Flora Devoniensis. London: 1829. V. 64

JONES, J. ROY
Saddle Bags in Siskiyou. Yreka: 1953. V. 63

JONES, J. W.
The Salmon. 1958. V. 67
The Salmon. London: 1959. V. 67

JONES, J. WILLIAM
Army of Northern Virginia Memorial Volume. Richmond: 1880. V. 62; 63
The Davis Memorial Volume: of Our Dead President, Jefferson Davis and The World's Tribute to His Memory. Richmond: 1890. V. 67
The Davis Memorial Volume, or Our Dead President, Jefferson Davis. Denver and Philadelphia: 1890. V. 63

JONES, JAMES
From Here to Eternity. New York: 1951. V. 62; 63; 66
From Here to Eternity. London: 1952. V. 66
The History and Antiquites of Harewood, in the County of York. London: 1859. V. 63
The Thin Red Line. New York: 1962. V. 64; 65

JONES, JAMES ATHEARN
Reft Rob; or, the Witch of Scot-Muir, Commonly Called Madge the Snoover. London: 1817. V. 65
Tales of an Indian Camp. London: 1829. V. 63

JONES, JENKIN
Pros and Cons, for Cupid and Hymen: in a Series of Metrical Satiric Dialogues. London: 1807. V. 63; 64; 65

JONES, JOHN
Attempts in Verse. London: 1831. V. 62
The History and Antiquities of Harewood, in the County of York.... London: 1859. V. 66
Medical, Philosophical and Vulgar Errors, of Various Kinds, Considered and Refuted. London: 1797. V. 66

JONES, JOHN BEAUCHAMP
A Rebel War Clerk's Diary at the Confederate States Capital. New York: 1935. V. 63

JONES, JOHN P.
Borger the Little Oklahoma. N.P. V. 62; 65

JONES, JOHN T.
Account of the War in Spain and Portugal and in the South of France from 1808 to 1814, Inclusive. London: 1818. V. 62

JONES, JOHN WILLIAM
Army of Northern Virignia Memorial Volume. Richmond: 1880. V. 62
Life and Letters of Robert Edward Lee. Soldier and Man. New York: 1906. V. 62

JONES, JOSEPH
Explorations of the Aboriginal Remains of Tennessee. Washington: 1876. V. 67
Medico-Legal Evidence Relating to the Detection of Human Blood Presenting the Alterations Characteristic of Malarial Fever, on the Clothing of a Man Accused of the Murder of Narcisse Arrieux, Dec. 27, 1876, Near Donaldsonville. New Orleans: 1878. V. 66

JONES, JOSEPH S.
A Defence of the Revolutionary History of the State of North Carolina from the Aspersions of Mr. Jefferson. Boston: 1834. V. 62
Life of Jefferson S. Batkins, Member from Cranberry Centre. Boston: 1871. V. 63

JONES, KATHARINE
Heroines of Dixie. New York: 1955. V. 62; 63; 65
Ladies of Richmond. Indianapolis: 1962. V. 63
The Plantation South. Indianapolis: 1957. V. 67

JONES, KENNETH
Stone Soup. Portland: 1985. V. 64

JONES, L. H.
Captain Roger Jones, or London and Virginia. Albany: 1891. V. 62

JONES, LEONARD A.
A Treatise on the Law of Liens, Common Law, Statutory, Equitable and Maritime. Boston and New York: 1888. V. 62

JONES, MARCUS E.
Contributions to Western Botany. No. 18. Claremont: 1935. V. 64

JONES, MARGARET BELLE
Bastrop: a Compilation of Material Relating to the History of the Town of Bastrop with Letters Written by Terry's Rangers. Bastrop: 1936. V. 62

JONES, O.
A Gamekeeper's Note Book. 1910. V. 67

JONES, OLIVE M.
Bibliography of Colorado Geology and Mining.... Denver: 1914. V. 67

JONES, OWEN
Examples of Chinese Ornament Selected from Objects in the South Kensington Museum and Other Collections. London: 1867. V. 63; 64
The Pslams of David. London: 1861. V. 67

JONES, OWEN GLYNNE
Rock Climbing in the English Lake District. London: 1897. V. 64
Rock Climbing in the English Lake District. Keswick: 1900. V. 63; 65; 66
Rock Climbing in the English Lake District. 1973. V. 65

JONES, PETER
Collection of Hymns for the Use of Native Christians of the Iroquois. New York: 1827. V. 65

JONES, PETER R.
Woodblock Engravings. 1991. V. 62

JONES, RICHARD
Literary Remains, Consisting of Lectures and Tracts on Political Economy.... London: 1859. V. 62; 65

JONES, RICHARD L.
Dinwiddie County: Carrefour of the Commonwealth. Richmond: 1976. V. 64

JONES, RICHARD R.
The Animal Kingdom Illustrated and Sketches Descriptive of the Beasts and Birds contained in Forepaugh's Menagerie. Buffalo: 1880. V. 65
The Animal Kingdom Illustrated and Sketches Descriptive of the Beasts and Birds Contained in Forepaugh's Menagerie. Buffalo: 1881. V. 64

JONES, ROBERT
The Muses Gardin for Delights; or, the Fift Booke of Ayres, Only for the Lute, the Base-Vyoll and the Voice. Oxford: 1901. V. 62; 64

JONES, ROBERT F.
African Twilight. 1994. V. 67

JONES, ROBERT HUHN
The Civil War in the Northwest. Norman: 1960. V. 63

JONES, S.
Fishes of the Laccadive Archipelago. Trivandrum: 1980. V. 66

JONES, S. C.
Reminiscences of the Twenty-Second Iowa Volunteer Infantry. Iowa City: 1907. V. 65

JONES, S. S.
Northumberland and Its Neighbour Lands. Hexham: 1871. V. 62; 66

JONES, SAMUEL
The Siege of Charleston and the Operations on the South Atlantic Coast in the War Between the States. New York: 1911. V. 62; 63; 65

JONES, SHIRLEY
Etched in Autumn 1997. Llanhamlach, Wales: 1997. V. 62
Falls and Shadow: Six Essays. 1995. V. 62
Falls the Shadow. Llanhamlach, Wales: 1995. V. 62
Impressions: Eight Aquatints to Accompany Eight Poems and Prose Pieces. 1984. V. 62
The Same Sun: Nine Poems and Nine Etchings. 1978. V. 62

JONES, STEPHEN
Sheridan Improved. London: 1806. V. 64
Sheridan Improved. London: 1812. V. 64

JONES, T. R.
A Monograph of the Tertiary Entomostraca of England. (with) A Monograph of the Fossil Estheriae. 1849-1863. V. 63

JONES, THOM
The Pugilist at Rest. Boston: 1993. V. 63; 66; 67
The Pugilist at Rest. New York: 1993. V. 67

JONES, THOMAS
The Gregynog Press. A Paper Read to the Double Crown Club on 7 April, 1934. London: 1954. V. 64
The Rise and Progress of the Most Honourable and Loyal Society of Antient Britons, Established in Honour of Her Royal Highness's Birth-Day, and the Principality of Wales, on St. David's Day, the First of March, 1714-1715. London: 1717. V. 62

JONES, THOMAS GOODE
Last Days of the Army of Northern Virginia. Richmond?: 1893. V. 62; 63; 65

JONES, THOMAS H.
Experience and Personal Narrative of Uncle Tom Jones.... Boston: 1855?. V. 64

JONES, THOMAS WARTON
A True Relation of the Life and Death of William Bedell. London: 1872. V. 65

JONES, TOM
The Fantasticks. New York: 1964. V. 63

JONES, VIRGIL C.
The Civil War at Sea. New York: 1960. V. 66
Gray Ghosts and Rebel Raiders. New York: 1956. V. 63; 66
Roosevelt's Rough Riders. New York: 1971. V. 67

JONES, W. F.
The Experiences of a Deputy U.S. Marshal of the Indian Territory. Tulsa: 1937. V. 67

JONES, W. H. S.
The Doctor's Oath. An Essay in the History of Medicine. Cambridge: 1924. V. 64; 67

JONES, W. NORTHEY
The History of St. Peter's Church in Perth Amboy...From an Organization in 1698 to the Year of Our Lord 1923...also a Genealogy of the Families Buried in the Churchyard. Perth Amboy: 1924. V. 63; 66

JONES, WILLIAM
A Course of Lectures on the Figurative Language of the Holy Scripture, and the Interpretation of It from the Scripture Itself. London: 1789. V. 62

Letters.... Oxford: 1970. V. 63; 65

The Muse Recalled, an Ode, Occasioned by the Nuptials of Lord Viscount Althorp and Miss Lavinia Bingham, Eldest Daughter of Charles Lord Lucan, March VI, 1781. Strawberry Hill: 1781. V. 67

Personal Reminiscences, Anecdotes and Letters of Gen. Robert E. Lee. New York: 1875. V. 63

Poems, Consisting Chiefly of Translations from the Asiatick Languages. London: 1777. V. 62; 65

A Popular Sketch of the Various Proposed Systems of Atmospheric Railway.... London: 1845. V. 65

A Prize Essay, in English and Welsh on the Character of the Welsh as a Nation, in the Present Age. London: 1841. V. 62

The Theological, Philosophical and Miscellaneous Works.... London: 1801. V. 63

JONG, ERICA
Fear of Flying. New York: 1973. V. 64; 65

JONSON, BEN
Ben Jonson, His Volpone; or, The Foxe. London: 1898. V. 64

A Croppe of Kisses. Waltham St. Lawrence: 1937. V. 65; 67

The Divell is an Asse. London: 1641. V. 65

The English Grammar Made by Ben Jonson for the Benefit of All Strangers Out of His Observation of the English Language.... London: 1928. V. 63

The Poems of Ben Jonson. Oxford: 1936. V. 63

The Poems of Ben Jonson. Oxford: 1937. V. 63

Volpone. Berlin: 1910. V. 66

The Workes.... London: 1616. V. 64

The Workes.... London: 1640. V. 64

JONSTON, JOHN
An History of the Constancy of Nature. London: 1657. V. 65

JONSTONE, JOHN
An History of the Wonderful Things of Nature. London: 1657. V. 63

JOPLIN, THOMAS
An Examination of Sir Robert Peel's Currency Bill of 1844, in a Letter to the Bankers of the United Kingdom. London: 1845. V. 65

Outlines of a System of Political Economy. Newcastle-upon-Tyne: 1823. V. 65

JORAY, MARCEL
Vasarely. 1965. V. 65

Vasarely IV: Plastic Arts of the Twentieth Century. Switzerland: 1979. V. 63

JORDAN, CHARLES EDWARD
A Letter from Charles Edward Jordan to His Family and Friends. Charlottesville: 1932. V. 62

JORDAN, CORNELIA J. M.
Corinth and Other Poems of the War. Lynchburg: 1865. V. 62

Flowers of Hope and Memory. Richmond: 1861. V. 62; 63; 65

JORDAN, DAVID STARR
The Aquatic Resources of the Hawaiian Islands. Part 3. Washington: 1906. V. 66

Contributions to North American Ichthyology. III. A. On the Distribution of the Fishes of the Alleghany Region of South Carolina, Georgia and Tennessee. B. A Synopsis of the Family Catostomidae. Washington: 1878. V. 65

The Days of a Man, Being Memories of a Naturalist, Teacher and Minor Propet of Democracy. Yonkers-on-Hudson: 1922. V. 63; 65

The Fishes of North and Middle America. Washington: 1896. V. 67

The Fishes of North and Middle America. Washington: 1896-1900. V. 65

The Fishes of Samoa.... Washington: 1906. V. 63

The Fishes of Sinaloa. Palto Alto: 1895. V. 65

The Fur Seals and Fur Seal Islands of the North Pacific Ocean. Washington: 1898. V. 63

Fur Seals and Fur Seal Islands of the North Pacific Ocean. Washington: 1898-1899. V. 62

The Genera of Fishes: a Contribution to the Stability of Scientific Nomenclature. Stanford: 1917-1920. V. 63; 65

The Genera of Fishes and a Classification of Fishes. Stanford: 1963. V. 65

Matka dn Kotik. A Tale of the Mist-Islands. San Francisco: 1897. V. 64

Synopsis of the Fishes of North America. Washington;: 1883. V. 64

JORDAN, EDWARD
An Interesting Trial of Edward Jordan, and Margaret His Wife Who Were Tried at Halifax N.S. Nov. 15th 1809.... Boston: 1809. V. 67

JORDAN, J.
The Workman's Testimony to the Sabbath; or the Temporal Advantages of that Day of Rest Considered in Relation to the Working Classes.... Edinburgh: 1853. V. 67

JORDAN, JOHN
Poetry Ireland 5. Dublin: 1965. V. 62

Welcombe Hills, Near Stratford Upon Avon, a Poem, Historical and Descriptive. London: 1777. V. 62

JORDAN, MICHAEL
Rare Air: Michael on Michael. San Francisco: 1993. V. 63

JORDAN, MILDRED
The Shoo-Fly Pie. New York: 1944. V. 63

JORDAN, NEIL
Night in Tunisia. New York: 1980. V. 66; 67

JORDAN, WILLIAM C.
Some Events and Incidents During the Civil War. Montgomery: 1909. V. 62; 63; 65

JORGE, EDWARD
Briefe aus Den Uereinigten Staaten Von Nord Amerika. Leipzig: 1853. V. 63

JORGENSEN, CHRISTINE
A Love to Die For. New York: 1994. V. 67

JORGENSEN, DANIEL B.
Air Force Chaplains 1917-1960. Washington: 1961. V. 65

JORGENSON, CHESTER
Uncle Tom's Cabin as Book and Legend. A Guide to an Exhibition. Detroit: 1952. V. 67

JORPES, J. ERIK
Jac. Berzelius, His Life and Work. Stockholm: 1966. V. 64

JOSEPH
Delteil. *Essays in Tribute.* London: 1962. V. 62

JOSEPH, DON JOHN
A Chemical Analysis of Wolfram; and Examinations of a New metal Which Enters Into Its Composition. London: 1785. V. 65

JOSEPHSON, HANNAH
Golden Threads: New England's Mill Girls and Magnates. New York: 1949. V. 63

JOSEPHUS, FLAVIUS
The Whole Genuine Complete Works of.... New York: 1792-1794. V. 64

Flavii Iosephi Hebraei, Historiographi Clariss, Opera, ad Multorum Codicum Latinorum.... 1524. V. 66

The Works. London: 1702. V. 67

The Works. London: 1708. V. 67

The Works. London: 1841. V. 63

JOSEPHUS, MICHAEL
Michaelis Josephus Morei Carmina. Rome: 1740. V. 66

JOSEPHUS DE JULIIS
Manuductio Ad Linguam Graecam Abbati Stephano Gradio Bibliothecae Vaticanae Praefecto Nuncupata. Romae: 1681. V. 66

JOSEPHY, ALVIN M.
Black Hills, White Sky - Photographs from the Collection of Arvada Center Foundation. New York: 1978. V. 63

500 Nations an Illustrated History of North American Indians. New York: 1994. V. 64

JOSIPOVICI, GABRIEL
Four Stories. London: 1977. V. 67

JOSLIN, SESYLE
What Do You Do, Dear?. London: 1963. V. 65

What Do You Say Dear! A Book of Manners for All Occasions. New York: 1986. V. 64

JOUIN DE SAUSEUIL, JEAN NICOLAS
An Analysis of the French Orthography; or the True Principles of the French Pronunciation.... London: 1772. V. 64

The Brachygraphy of the French Verbs; or An Easy and Speedy Method of Conjugating Them.... London: 1772. V. 64

JOURDAIN, MARGARET
English Interior Decoration 1500 to 1830. London: 1950. V. 62

Regency Furniture 1795-1820. London: 1948. V. 67

The Work of William Kent, Artist, Painter, Designer and Landscape Gardener. London: 1948. V. 62

JOURDANET, DENIS
Influence de la Pression de l'Air sur la Vie de l'Homme. Paris: 1875. V. 63

JOURNAL of an African Cruiser. New York: 1853. V. 65

JOURNAL of Applied Microscopy. Rochester: 1898-1903. V. 67

THE JOURNAL of Nervous and Mental Diseases. Special Number Dedicated to Howard C. Naffziger, M.D...by the Members of the Staff of the University of California Medical School on the Occasion of His Sixtieth Birthday May 6, 1944. Volume 99 issue 5. 1944. V. 64

A JOURNAL of the Life, Travels and Sufferings of William Edmundson. Dublin: 1820. V. 67

THE JOURNEY of Dr. Robert Bongout, and His Lady, to Bath. Performed in the Year 177-. London: 1778. V. 66

JOURNEYS.. Rockville: 1996. V. 65; 66; 67

JOUSSE, MATHURIN
Le Secret d'Architecture Decouvrant Fidelement les Traits Geometriques Necessaires dans les Bastiments. A La Fleche: 1642. V. 66

JOUTEL, HENRI
Journel of the Last Voyage Perform'd by Monsr. De La Salle, to the Gulph of Mexico, to Find Out the Mouth of the Mississippi.... London: 1714. V. 63; 66

JOWETT, WILLIAM
Christian Researches in Syria and the Holy Land, in MDCCCXXIII and MDCCCXXIV in Furtherance of the Objects of the Church Missionary Society.... London: 1825. V. 67

JOWSEY, JOAN
Curtis of Colchester. 1980. V. 67

THE JOY Book Children's Annual 1925. Manchester: 1924. V. 67

JOY, NORMAN H.
A Practical Handbook of British Beetles. 1976. V. 66

JOYCE, GEORGE HENRY
Some Records of Troutbeck. Staveley: 1924. V. 63; 65

JOYCE, JAMES
Anna Livia Plurabelle. New York: 1928. V. 65
Anna Livia Plurabelle. London: 1930. V. 62
El Artista Adolescente (Retrato). Madrid: 1926. V. 62
Chamber Music. Boston: 1918. V. 63; 65
Chamber Music. London: 1918. V. 66
Chamber Music. London: 1923. V. 62; 63; 65
Chamber Music. New York: 1954. V. 62
Collected Poems. New York: 1936. V. 62; 64; 65
The Dublin Book of Irish Verse 1728-1909. Dublin and London: 1909. V. 66
Dubliners,. London: 1914. V. 62
Dubliners. New York: 1916. V. 67
Dubliners. New York: 1986. V. 62; 64; 65; 66
Epiphanies. Buffalo: 1956. V. 62; 64
Exiles - a Play in Three Acts. London: 1952. V. 63
Finnegans Wake. London: 1939. V. 62; 66
Finnegans Wake. New York: 1939. V. 65
Gens de Dublin. (Dubliners). Paris: 1939. V. 64
Giacomo Joyce. New York: 1968. V. 66
Haveth Childers Everywhere. New York: 1930. V. 64
Haveth Childers Everywhere. Paris: 1930. V. 62; 64; 67
Haveth Childers Everywhere. London: 1931. V. 62; 66
Ibsen's New Drama. (and) James Clarence Mangan. London: 1930. V. 62
Joyce's Ulysses Notesheets in the British Museum. Charlottesville: 1972. V. 65
Letters of James Joyce. London: 1957. V. 65
The Mime of Mick, Nick and the Maggies - a Fragment from Work In Progress. The Hague and London: 1934. V. 64
Pomes Penyeach. Paris: 1927. V. 64
Pomes Penyeach. London: 1933. V. 65; 66
A Portrait of the Artist as a Young Man. New York: 1916. V. 67
A Portrait of the Artist as a Young Man. New York: 1968. V. 62
Stephen Hero. 1944. V. 62; 65
Stephen Hero. London: 1944. V. 63
Stephen Hero. New York: 1944. V. 62; 64
Stephen Le Heros. Paris: 1948. V. 62
Storiella as She is Syung. London: 1937. V. 62; 66
Storiella as She is Syung. London: 1973. V. 62
Tales Told of Shem and Shaun. Paris: 1929. V. 62; 65; 66
Two Tales of Shem and Shaun. Fragments from Work in Progress,. London: 1932. V. 66
Ulysses. Paris: 1942. V. 66
Ulysses. Paris: 1922. V. 62
Ulysses. Paris: 1925. V. 62
Ulysses. N.P: 1927. V. 64
Ulysses. Basel: 1927. V. 62
Ulysses. Paris: 1927. V. 67
Ulysses. London: 1930. V. 64
Ulysses. Hamburg: 1932. V. 63; 65; 66
Ulysses. New York: 1934. V. 65; 66
Ulysses. 1935. V. 62
Ulysses. Hamburg: 1935. V. 63
Ulysses. New York: 1935. V. 65; 67
Ulysses. 1936. V. 62; 65
Ulysses. London: 1936. V. 65
Ulysses. London: 1937. V. 62; 64
Ulysses. Amsterdam: 1969. V. 62
Ulysses: a Facsimile of the Manuscript. (with) Ulysses: the Manuscript and First Printings Compared. London: 1975. V. 64
Ulysses (in) Two Worlds Monthly. New York: 1926-1927. V. 62
Verbannte. Zurich: 1919. V. 62; 64; 65

JOYCE, JEREMIAH
An Account of Mr. Joyce's Arrest for Treasonable Practices His Examination Before His Majesty's...Privy Council.... London: 1795. V. 63

JOYCE, JOHN A.
A Checkered Life. Chicago: 1883. V. 64
Jewels of Memory. Washington: 1895. V. 64

JOYCE, PATRICK W.
The Origin and History of Irish Names of Places. Dublin: 1871. V. 64
The Origin and History of Irish Names of Places. 1902. V. 63

JOYCE, STANISLAUS
Le Journal de Dublin. Paris: 1967. V. 66

JOYCE, T.
Mexican Archaeology. An Introduction to the Archaeology of the Mexican and Mayan Civilizations of Pre-Spanish America. London: 1914. V. 62

JOYCE, WILLIAM
Santa Calls. New York: 1993. V. 64; 67

JOYCE, WILLIAM BROOKE
National Socialism Now. London: 1937. V. 62

JOYFUL Tales for Little Folks. New York: 1869. V. 62

JOYNES, WILLIAM T.
An Essay Upon the Act of the General Assembly of Virginia, Passed April 3, 1838, Entitled An Act Amending the Statute of Limitations.... Richmond: 1844. V. 65

JOZE, VICTOR
La Tribu d'Isidore. Paris: 1897. V. 66

JUAN Y SANTACILIA, JORGE
Dissertacion Historica y Geographica Sobre el meridiano de Demarcacion Entre los Dominios de Espana y Portugal y Los Parages Por Donde Passa en la America Meridional.... Madrid: 1749. V. 62

JUBILEE of Acadia College and Memorial Exercises. Halifax: 1889. V. 65

THE JUBILEE of 1809, Containing a Poetical Epistle, from John Lump, to His Brother in Yorkshire. London: 1809. V. 65

JUDAH, SAMUEL B. H.
Gotham and the Gothamites, a Medley. New York: 1823. V. 62
A Tale of Lexington: a National Comedy. New York: 1823. V. 62

JUDD, NEIL M.
The Material Culture of Pueblo Bonito. Washington: 1954. V. 62; 63; 67
Pueblo Del Arroyo Chaco Canyon New Mexico. Washington: 1959. V. 65

JUDD, WILLIAM BOTSFORD
A Tale of Three Villages, Bernardsville, Basking Ridge, Mendham. Bernardsville: 1899. V. 63; 66

JUDGE, A. W.
Engineering Workshop Practice. London: 1948. V. 67

JUDGES, A. V.
The Elizabethan Underworld. London: 1930. V. 66

JUDSON, A.
English and Burmese Dictionary.... Rangoon: 1877. V. 64

JUDSON, E. Z. C.
The Mysteries and Miseries of New York. New York: 1848. V. 62; 66

JUDSON, HELENA
Butterick Cook Book. New York: 1911. V. 67

JUETTNER, OTTO
Daniel Drake and His Followers: Historical and Biographical Sketches 1785-1909. Cincinnati: 1909. V. 67

JUGAKU, BUNSHO
Paper-Making by Hand in Japan. Tokyo: 1959. V. 63

JUGLAR, CLEMENT
A Brief History of Panics and Their Periodical Occurrence in the United States. New York: 1893. V. 63

JUILLET, GEORGES
L'Histoire d'Yuon. Paris: 1946. V. 65

JUKES, H. R.
Loved River. 1935. V. 67

JUKES, JOSEPH BEETE
Her Majesty's Geological Survey...and Its Connection with the Museum of Irish Industry in Dublin.... Dublin: 1867. V. 62
Narrative of the Surveying Voyage of H.M.S. Fly.... London: 1847. V. 62

JULIAN Symons Remembered. Tributes from Friends. Council Bluffs: 1996. V. 67

JULIANUS, FLAVIUS CLAUDIUS, EMPEROR
Juliani Imperatoris Opera Quae Extant Omnia. Parisiis: 1583. V. 66
(Greek title - then:) Opera, Qvae Wviden Reperiri Portvervnt, Omnia. Parisiis: 1630. V. 64; 66

JULIARD-HARTMANN, G.
Iconographie des Champignons Superieurs. Epinal: 1919. V. 65; 66

JULIEN, ADOLPHE
Histoire du Costume au Theatre Depuis les Origines du Theatre en France Jusqu'a Nos Jours Ouvrages Orne de Vignt-Sept Gravures et Dessins Originaux Tires de ARchives de l'Opera et Reproduits en Fac-Simile. Paris: 1880. V. 64

JULIEN, CARL
Beneath So Kind a Sky. Columbia: 1947. V. 67

JULIEN, ROCH JOSEPH
Catalogue General des Meilleures Cartes Geographiques & Topographiques; Plans de Villes, Sieges and Batailles.... Paris: 1752. V. 62

JULLIAN, P.
The Symbolists. London: 1973. V. 65

JULLIAN, PHILIPPE
Chateau-Bonheur. London: 1962. V. 64

JUNG, CARL GUSTAV
Collected Works of C. G. Jung. New York: 1957-1983. V. 65
Contributions to Analytical Psychology. London: 1928. V. 65
Der Inhalt der Psychose. Adademischer Vortrag, Gehalten im Rathause der Stadt Zurich am 16. Ajnner 1908. Leipzig/Wien: 1908. V. 65
Psychologische Typen. Zurich: 1921. V. 65
The Psychology of Dementia Praecox. New York: 1909. V. 67

JUNG, CARL GUSTAV continued
Studies in Word-Association: Experiments in the Diagnosis of Psychopathological Conditions Carried Out at the Psychiatric Clinic of the University of Zurich Under the Direction of C. G. Jung. London: 1918. V. 65
Symbols of Transformation: an Analysis of the Prelude to a Case of Schizophrenia. New York: 1956. V. 65

JUNGER, SEBASTIAN
The Perfect Storm: a True Story of Men Against the Sea. New York: 1997. V. 66

JUNGMAN, BEATRIX
Holland. London: 1904. V. 65
Norway. London: 1905. V. 65

JUNG-STILLING, JOHANN H.
Theory of Pneumatology: in Reply to the Question Waht Ought to be Believed or Disbelieved Concerning Presentiments, Visions and Apparitions. New York: 1854. V. 63

JUNIUS, FRANCISCUS
Etymologicum Anglicanum. Oxonii: 1743. V. 64

JUNIUS, PSEUD.
A Letter to an Honourable Brigadier General, Commander in Chief of His Majesty's Forces in Canada. London: 1841. V. 65
The Letters. London: 1791. V. 62
(Letters). London: 1799. V. 67
The Letters. London: 1801. V. 66
The Letters. Philadelphia: 1804. V. 66
The Letters. London: 1810. V. 67
The Letters. London: 1820. V. 62; 63
Stat Nominis Umbra. London: 1772. V. 64
Stat Nominis Umbra. London: 1794. V. 63
Stat Nominis Umbra. London: 1799. V. 63; 64; 65
Stat Nominis Umbra. London: 1801. V. 62; 66
Stat Nominis Umbra. London: 1812. V. 62

JUNKER, WILHELM
Travels in Africa; During the Years 1875-1878. London: 1890. V. 67
Travels in Africa During the Years 1875-1878. London: 1890-1892. V. 67
Travels in Africa During the Years 1882-1886. London: 1892. V. 66

JUNKIN, D. X.
The Life of Winfield Scott Hancock: Personal Military and Political. New York: 1880. V. 66

JURICH, JEFF
Are Blue Cats Dancing on the Eggs for Fun and Guess How High I Jumped to Kiss the Laughing Moon's Nose and Other Motion Stories. La Jolla: 1984. V. 66

JUSSERAND, J. J.
The English Novel in the Time of Shakespeare. London: 1890. V. 64
English Wayfaring Life in the Middle Ages,. London: 1889. V. 64
Le Roman d'un Roi d'Ecosse. Paris: 1895. V. 66

JUSSIEU, A. DE
Botanique. Paris: 1842. V. 66
Genera Plantarum Secundum Ordines Natrales Disposita Juxta Methodum in Horto Regio.... Paris: 1789. V. 64

JUSSIM, ESTELLE
Slave to Beauty: The Eccentric Life and Controversial Career of F. Holland Day, Photographer, Publisher, Aesthete. Boston: 1981. V. 63

A JUST Narrative of the Hellish New Counter-Plots of the Papists, to Cast the Odium of Their Horrid Treasons Upon the Presbyterians.... London: 1679. V. 62

JUST One More: 1954-1985. Los Angeles: 1954-1985. V. 65

JUSTE, MICHAEL
Shoot and Be Damned. London: 1935. V. 67

JUSTICE, DONALD
Banjo Dog. Poems and Linocut Illustrations. Riverside: 1995. V. 62
Departures. Iowa City: 1973. V. 64
From a Notebook. Iowa City: 1972. V. 63
L'Homme Qui Se Ferme. Iowa City: 1973. V. 66
A Local Storm. Iowa City: 1963. V. 62
Selected Poems. New York: 1979. V. 66
Sixteen Poems. Iowa City: 1970. V. 64
The Summer Anniversaries. Middletown: 1959. V. 63; 65
The Summer Anniversaries. Middletown: 1960. V. 62

JUSTINIAN I, EMPEROR
Codicis D. N. Justiniani Sacratiis. Principis PP. Aug Repetita Praelectionis Libri XII.... Lugduni;: 1593. V. 66
Institvtiones.... Venetiis: 1593. V. 64; 66
Institutiones D. Justiniani SS. Princ. Typis Variae; Rubris Nucleum Exhebentibus.... Amstelodami: 1676. V. 66
Novellarum Constitutionu(m). Paris: 1562. V. 66

JUSTINIANUS, LAURENTIUS
Doctrina della Vita Monastica. Venice: 1494. V. 64

JUSTINOPOLITANO, MUTIO
Il Gentilhuomo. Venetia: 1571. V. 66

JUSTINUS, MARCUS JUNIANUS
De Historicis Philippicis, Et Totius Mundi Originibus.... Parisiis: 1677. V. 65; 66

Historiae Philippicae cum Integris Commentariis Iac. Bongarsii, Franc. Modii, Matth. Bernecceri.... Leyden: 1760. V. 65
Historiae Philippicae, Ex Recensione Joannis Georgii Graevii. Amstelaedami: 1722. V. 65
Historiae, Phillipicae. Lugd. Batavorum: 1701. V. 65
Historiarum Philippicarum, Ex Historia Trogi Pompeii.... Amstelodami: 1638. V. 65; 66
History of the World from the Assyrian Monarchy Down to the Time of Augustus Caesar. London: 1719. V. 63
Iustini Historiarum Ex Trogo Pompeio Lib XLIV Cum Notis Isaaci Vossii. Lugd. Batavorum: 1640. V. 66

JUSTUS, MAY
Gabby Gaffer. Joliet: 1929. V. 62

JUVENALIS, DECIMUS JUNIUS
D. Junii Juvenalis Aquinatis Satyrae, Scoliis Veterum & Sere Omnium Eruditorum.... Ultrajecti: 1685. V. 66
Iunii Iuvenalis Aquinatis Satyrae Decem Et Sex. Antwerpiae: 1519. V. 66
Iuvenal Tradotto Di Latino in volgar Linguae Per Georgio Summaripa Veronese.... 1525. V. 66
Juvenal's Sixteen Satyrs, or, a Survey of the Manners and Actions of Mankind. London: 1647. V. 67
Satirae XVI. Oxonii: 1808. V. 65
The Satires of Decimus Junius Juvenalis. London: 1693. V. 66
Satyrae. 1494. V. 63

THE JUVENILE Scrap-Book. A Gage d'Amour for the Young. London: 1848. V. 62

K

KABOTIE, FRED
Designs from the Ancient Mimbrenos with a Hopi Interpretation. Flagstaff: 1982. V. 63
Fred Kabotie: Hopi Indian Artist. Flagstaff: 1977. V. 63; 65

KACHI Kachi Mountain. Tokyo: 1900. V. 66

KAEFFER & CO.
Chalets Suyises Bois Decoupes. Paris: 1867-1884. V. 64

KAEWERT, JULIE WALLIN
Unsolicited. New York: 1994. V. 66; 67

KAFKA, FRANZ
Amerika. Munich: 1927. V. 65
Betrachtung (Meditation). Leipzig: 1913. V. 65; 67
Conversation with the Supplicant. Vermont: 1971. V. 62
Description of a Struggle and The Great Wall of China. London: 1960. V. 63
The Diaries of Franz Kafka. New York: 1949. V. 67
The Great Wall of China and Other Pieces. London: 1946. V. 65
The Metamorphosis. London: 1937. V. 67
Metamorphosis. New York: 1984. V. 65
The Trial. London: 1950. V. 62
Das Urteil. Leipzig: 1916. V. 65

KAGAN, ANDREW
Trova. St. Louis: 1987. V. 63

KAGAN, SOLOMON R.
American Jewish Physicians of Note: Biographical Sketches. Boston: 1942. V. 63
Jewish Contributions to Medicine in America, (1656-1934), with Medica Chronology, Bibliography and Sixty-Nine Illustrations. Boston: 1934. V. 63
Jewish Medicine. Boston: 1952. V. 63
Leaders of Medicine. Boston: 1941. V. 63
Life and Letters of Fielding H. Garrison. Boston: 1938. V. 66
Victor Robinson Memorial Volume. Essays on History of Medicine, in Honor of Victor Robinson on His Sixtieth Birthday August 16, 1946. New York: 1948. V. 63

KAGEY, DEEDIE
When Past is Prologue: a History of Roanoke County. Roanoke: 1988. V. 63

KAGITCI, MEHMED ALI
Historical Study of Paper Industry in Turkey. Istanbul: 1976. V. 64

KAHL, VIRGINIA
Away Went Wolfgang!. New York: 1954. V. 63
The Baron's Booty. New York: 1958. V. 63
The Duchess Bakes a Cake. New York: 1955. V. 63
Plum Pudding for Christmas. New York: 1956. V. 63

KAHLENBERG, MARY HUNT
The Navajo Blanket. Los Angeles: 1972. V. 63

KAHLER, CHARLES
How to Treat Your Own Feet. A Treatise on the Human Foot. New York: 1893. V. 66

KAHLER, PETER
Dress and Care of the Feet. New York: 1899. V. 66

KAHN, DAVID
The Codebreakers. New York: 1967. V. 62

KAHN, HERMAN
On Thermonuclear War. Princeton: 1960. V. 67

KAHN, WILLIAM B.
An Adventure of Oilock Combs: the Succored Beauty. San Francisco: 1964. V. 63

KAHN-MAGOMEDOV, SELIM O.
Rodchenko: The Complete Work. Cambridge: 1987. V. 63

KAHRL, WILLIAM L.
The California Water Atlas. Sacramento: 1979. V. 62

KAINEN, JACOB
John Baptist Jackson: 18th Century Master of the Color Woodcut. Washington: 1962. V. 63

KAINS JACKSON, CHARLES PHILIP
Our Ancient Monuments and the Land Around Them. London: 1880. V. 67

KAKONIS, TOM
Michigan Roll. New York: 1988. V. 65

KAKUZO, OKAKURA
Book of Tea. Edinburgh: 1919. V. 67

KALB, LAURIE B.
Crafting Devotions - Tradition in Contemporary New Mexico Santos. Albuqerque: 1994. V. 66

KALFATOVIC, MARTIN R.
Nile Notes of a Howadji: a Bibliography of Travelers' Tales from Egypt, from the Earliest Time to 1918. Metuchen: 1992. V. 65

KALIDASA
A Circle of the Seasons - a Translation of the Ritu-Samhara of Kalidasa Made from Various European Sources by E. Powys Mathers. Waltham St. Lawrence: 1929. V. 62; 63; 66
Kalidasa Sacontala; or, the Fatal Ring; an Indian Drama. London: 1792. V. 67

KALLIR, O.
Grandma Moses. New York: 1973. V. 62; 66

KALM, PETER
Travels in North America. New York: 1937. V. 66; 67
Travels into North America. London: 1772. V. 63

KALOS, VICTOR
The Double-Backed Beast. Black Mountain College: 1952. V. 64

KALTENBORN, H.
Kaltenborn Edits the News. New York: 1937. V. 63

KALTER, SUZY
The Complete Book of M.A.S.H. New York: 1984. V. 67

KAMERA, WILLY DAVID
A Descriptive Index of the Characters in Anthony Powell's Music of Time: a Thesis.... Cornell: 1974. V. 66

KAMES, HENRY HOME, LORD
Elements of Criticism. Edinburgh: 1765. V. 64
Elements of Criticism. Edinburgh: 1807. V. 65
The Gentleman Farmer. Edinburgh: 1776. V. 64
The Gentleman Farmer. Edinburgh: 1779. V. 64
Sketches of the History of Man. Edinburgh: 1778. V. 64; 67
Sketches of the History of Man. Edinburgh: 1788. V. 64
Versuche Uber die Geschichte des Menschen. Vienna: 1790. V. 64

KAMINSKY, STUART M.
Bullet for a Star. 1977. V. 66
A Cold Red Sunrise. 1988. V. 66
Death of a Dissident. New York: 1981. V. 67
Exercise in Terror. New York: 1985. V. 67
A Fine Red Rain. 1987. V. 66
The Howard Hughes Affair. 1979. V. 66
Murder on the Yellow Brick Road. 1977. V. 63; 64; 66
Never Cross a Vampire. 1980. V. 66
Never Cross a Vampire. New York: 1980. V. 64
Red Chameleon. New York: 1985. V. 66
You Bet Your Life. New York: 1978. V. 64; 66

KAMOHARA, T.
Descriptions of the Fishes from the Provinces of Toss and Kishu, Japan. Tokyo: 1950. V. 65

KANAMORI, TOKUJIRO
Celebrated Dolls East and West. Kyoto: 1951. V. 63

KANDINSKY, WASSILY
The Art of Spiritual Harmony. London: 1914. V. 64
Der Blaue Reiter. Munchen: 1914. V. 66
Uber das Geistige in der Kunst. Munich: 1912. V. 67

KANE, ELISHA KENT
Arctic Explorations in Search of Sir John Franklin. London: 1882. V. 64
Arctic Explorations, The Second Grinnell Expedition in Search of Sir John Franklin 1853, 1854, 1855. Philadelphia: 1856. V. 63; 64; 65; 67
Arctic Explorations: the Second Grinnell Expedition...Sir John Franklin. Philadelphia: 1857. V. 66
The U.S. Grinnell Expedition in Search of Sir John Franklin. New York: 1854. V. 63; 64; 65

KANE, PAUL
Paul Kane's Frontier - Including Wanderings of an Artist Among the Indians of North America. Austin: 1971. V. 63; 66
Paul Kane's Frontier Including Wandering of an Artist Among the Indians of North America. Fort Worth & Ottawa: 1971. V. 66

KANE, ROBERT
Elements of Chemistry.... Dublin: 1849. V. 62
The Industrial Resources of Ireland. Dublin: 1844. V. 65
The Industrial Resources of Ireland. 1845. V. 66
The Industrial Resources of Ireland. Dublin: 1845. V. 64; 65

KANE, SAMUEL E.
Thirty Years with the Philippine Head Hunters. London: 1934. V. 67

KANE, THOMAS LEIPER
The Private Papers and Diary of Thomas Leiper Kane, a Friend of the Mormons. San Francisco: 1937. V. 63

KANIN, GARSON
Born Yesterday. New York: 1946. V. 66

KANON, JOSEPH
Los Alamos. New York: 1997. V. 62

KANSAS. STATE BOARD OF AGRICULTURE - 1876
Fourth Annual Report of the State Board of Agriculture to the Legislature of the State of Kansas. Topeka: 1876. V. 62

KANT, IMMANUEL
Allgemeine Naturgeschichte und Theorie des Himmels Oder Versuch von der Verfassung und dem Mechanischen Ursprunge des Ganzen Weltgebaudes Nach Newtonischen Grundsatzen Abgehandelt. Konigsberg and Leipzig: 1755. V. 66
Critik der Reinen Vernunft. Riga: 1781. V. 62; 63; 64; 66
Critik der Reinen Vernunft. Riga: 1787. V. 62; 63
Gedanken von der Wahren Schatzung der Lebendigen Krafte und Beurtheilung der Beweise Derer Sich Herr von Leibnitz und Andere Mechaniker in Dieser.... Konigsberg: 1746-1749. V. 63

KANTCHBULL-HUGESSEN, E. H.
Friends and Foes from Fairyland. Boston: 1886. V. 63

KANTOR, J. R. K.
Grimshaw's Narrative: Being the Story of Life and Events in California During Flush Times, Particularly the Years 1848-1850. Scaramento: 1964. V. 63

KANTOR, MACKINLAY
Andersonville. Cleveland and New York: 1955. V. 63
The Voice of Bugle Ann. 1935. V. 67

KAPLAN, HAROLD I.
Comprehensive Textbook of Psychiatry. Baltimore/London: 1980. V. 65

KAPLAN, MARGARET L.
The West of Buffalo Bill; Frontier Art, Indian Crafts, Memorabilia from the Buffalo Bill Historical Center. New York: 1974. V. 67

KAPLAN, N.
In the Land of the Reindeer. Lennigrad: 1974. V. 62

KAPLAN, WENDY
The Art That Is Life: The Arts and Crafts Movement in America, 1875-1920. Boston: 1987. V. 64

KAPP, FRIEDRICH
Aus Und Uber Amerika. Berlin: 1876. V. 64

KAPPEL, A. W.
British and European Butterflies and Moths. 1895. V. 66
British and European Butterflies and Moths. New York: 1895. V. 62

KAPPLER, CHARLES J.
Indian Treaties 1778-1883. New York: 1973. V. 65

KAPR, A.
The Art of Lettering. The History, Anatomy and Aesthetics of the Roman Letter Forms. Munich: 1983. V. 62

KARALUS, K. E.
The Owls of North America.... Garden City: 1974. V. 62

KARDINER, ABRAM
The Bio-Analysis of the Epileptic Reaction. Albany: 1932. V. 65

KARL ORT COMPANY
Aeronautical Supplies. York: 1937. V. 67

KAROLIK, M.
M. & M. Karolik Collection of American Water Colors and Drawings 1800-1875. Boston: 1962. V. 63

KARP, IVAN C.
Doobie Doo. Garden City: 1965. V. 63

KARPINSKI, LOUIS CHARLES
Bibliography of Mathematical Works Printed in America through 1850. Ann Arbor: 1940. V. 62; 65
The History of Arithmetic. Chicago and New York: 1925. V. 63

KARR, ALPHONSE
Les Femmes. Paris: 1855. V. 67
Voyage Autour de Mon Jardin. Paris: 1845. V. 64

KARR, H. W. SETON
Shores and Alps of Alaska. London: 1887. V. 67

KARR, MARY
Abacus. Middletown: 1987. V. 62
The Liar's Club. New York: 1995. V. 62; 67

KASCHNITZ, MARIE LUISE
Gedichte. Hamburg: 1947. V. 67

KASFIR, S. L.
West African Masks and Cultural Systems. 1988. V. 62

KASLO, British Columbia. The Mineral Metropolis of the World. Kaslo: 1899. V. 66

KASNER, DAVID
Andrew Jackson. The Gentle Savage. New York: 1929. V. 67

KASSNER, THEODORE
My Journey from Rhodesia to Egypt.... London: 1911. V. 62

KASTNER, ABRAHAM GOTTHELF
Anmerkungen Uber die Markscheidekunst. Nebst Einer Abhandlung von Hohenmessungen durch das Barometer. Gottingen: 1775. V. 62

KASTNER, ERICH
Der Gestiefelte Kater. Munchen: 1950. V. 66

KASTON, B. J.
Spiders of Connecticut. 1948. V. 63; 66

KATALOG der Ornamentstichsammlung der Staatlichen Kunstbibliothek Berlin. 1998. V. 65

KATES, GEORGE N.
Chinese Household Furniture.... New York: 1948. V. 62; 65

KATZ, D. MARK
Custer in Photographs. Gettysburg: 1985. V. 65; 67

KATZ, WILLIAM L.
The Black West - a Documentary and Pictorial History. New York: 1971. V. 67

KATZELNELBOGEN, SOLOMON
The Cerebrospinal Fluid and Its Relation to the Blood.... Baltimore: 1935. V. 65

KATZENBACH, L.
The Practical Book of American Wallpaper. Philadelphia and New York: 1951. V. 62; 65

KATZENSTEIN, CAROLINE
Lifting the Curtain, the State and National Woman Suffrage Campaigns in Pennsylvania as I Saw Them. Philadelphia: 1955. V. 65

KAUDERN, W.
Games and Dances in Celebes. Results of the Author's Expedition to Celebes 1917-1920. Goteborg: 1929. V. 62

KAUFELD, C.
Snakes and Snake Hunting. New York: 1957. V. 67

KAUFFMAN, RICHARD
Gentle Wilderness: the Sierra Nevada. San Francisco: 1967. V. 63

KAUFMAN, GEORGE S.
The Man Who Came to Dinner. New York: 1939. V. 66

KAUKOL, MARIA CLEMENT
Christlicher Seelen-Schatz Ausserlesener Gebetter. N.P: 1729?. V. 67

KAULBACH, WILLIAM
Schiller Gallery. New York. V. 66

KAUP, J. J.
Catalogue of Apodal Fish, in the Collection of the British Museum. London: 1856. V. 65

KAVAN, ANNA
A Bright Green Field and Other Stories. London: 1958. V. 65
Goose Cross. London: 1936. V. 63
Ice. London: 1967. V. 66
Who Are You?. 1963. V. 63

KAVANAGH, ARTHUR
The Cruise of the R.Y.S. Eva. Dublin: 1865. V. 65

KAVANAGH, DAN
Putting the Boot In. London: 1985. V. 62; 63

KAVANAGH, JULIA
Adele, a Tale. Leipzig: 1858. V. 63
Forget-me-Nots. London: 1878. V. 65
John Dorrien. Leipzig: 1875. V. 65
Rachel Gray. Leipzig: 1856. V. 65
Women of Christianity, Exemplary for Acts of Piety and Charity. London: 1852. V. 65

KAVANAGH, P. J.
A Happy Man. London: 1972. V. 66

KAVANAGH, PATRICK
Collected Poems. London: 1964. V. 62; 64
Come Dance with Kitty Stobling and Other Poems. London: 1960. V. 63
The Great Hunger. Dublin: 1942. V. 62; 64

A Soul for Sale - Poems. London: 1947. V. 63
Tarry Flynn. 1948. V. 63

KAVENEY, ROZ
Tales from the Forbidden Planet. London: 1987. V. 64

KAWAGUCHI, SHRAMANA EKAI
Three Years in Tibet: with the Original Japanese Illustrations. Madras: 1909. V. 67

KAWAKITA, M.
Contemporary Japanese Prints. Tokyo/Palo Alto: 1967. V. 65

KAY County, Oklahoma. Ponca City: 1919. V. 64; 67

KAY & BROTHER
Catalogue of the National and Pennsylvania Law Publications. Philadelphia: 1853. V. 65

KAY, GERTRUDE ALICE
When the Sand-man Comes. New York: 1916. V. 63

KAY, JOSEPH
The Education of the Poor in England and Europe. London: 1846. V. 64

KAY, SUSAN
Legacy. London: 1985. V. 62

KAYE, WALTER JENKINSON
A Brief History of the Church and Parish of Gosberton in the County of Lincoln. London: 1897. V. 62

KAYSEN, SUSANNA
Asa, As I Knew Him. New York: 1987. V. 63
Far Afield. New York: 1990. V. 63

KAY-SHUTTLEWORTH, JAMES
Four Friends of Public Education as Reviewed in 1832-1839-1846-1862. London: 1862. V. 64
Letter to Earl Granville, K.G. on the Revised Code of Regulations Contained in the Minutes of the Committe of Council on Education July 29th 1861. London: 1861. V. 66
The Life and Work of.... London: 1923. V. 64
Ribblesdale or Lancashire Sixty Years Ago. London: 1874. V. 66
Scarsdale; or Life on the Lancashire and Yorkshire Border, Thirty Years Ago. London: 1860. V. 66
Thoughts and Suggestions on Certain Social Problems Contained Chiefly in Addresses to Meetings of Workmen in Lancashire. London: 1873. V. 64

KAZANTZAKIS, NIKOS
Christopher Columbus. Kentfield: 1972. V. 63; 64
The Rock Garden. New York: 1963. V. 67
The Saviors of God: Spiritual Exercises. New York: 1960. V. 66

KEACH, BENJAMIN
War with the Devil; or the Young Man's Conflict with the Powers of Darkness. London: 1776. V. 65

KEAN, ROBERT GARLICK HILL
Inside the Confederate Government. The Diary of Robert Garlick Hill Kean, Head of the Bureau of War. New York: 1957. V. 62; 63; 65

KEANE, A. H.
Africa. London: 1895. V. 62

KEANE, JOHN F.
My Journey to Medinah; Describing a Pilgrimage to Medinah.... London: 1881. V. 67

KEARFOTT, ROBERT R.
Kerfoot, Kearfott and Allied Families in America. 1948. V. 64

KEARNEY, HUGH F.
Strafford in Ireland 1633-1641. 1961. V. 67

KEARNEY, P. J.
The Private Case. London: 1981. V. 62

KEARNEY, T. H.
Flowering Plants and Ferns of Arizona. Washington: 1942. V. 64
Report on a Botanical Survey of the Dismal Swamp Region. Washington: 1901. V. 63

KEARSLEY, GEORGE
Kearsley's Gentleman and Tradesman's Pocket Ledger for the Year 1790. London: 1790. V. 63; 67
Kearsley's Tax Tables, for 1808. London: 1808. V. 64

KEATE, GEORGE
An Account of the Pelew Islands. Basil (Basel): 1789. V. 67
The Distressed Poet. London: 1787. V. 65
An Epistle from Lady Jane Gray to Lord Guildford Dudley, Supposed to Have Been Written in the Tower, a Few Days Before They Suffered. London: 1762. V. 65

KEATING, H. R. F.
The Man Who - Stories by Detection Club Authors. Bristol: 1992. V. 63

KEATING, J.
The General History of Ireland. 1841. V. 67

KEATING, JOHN MC LEOD
A History of the Yellow Fever. Memphis: 1879. V. 63

KEATING, WILLIAM H.
Narrative of an Expedition to the Source of St. Peter's River, Lake Winnepeek, Lake of the Woods.... Philadelphia: 1824. V. 64; 66

KEATING, WILLIAM H. *continued*
Narrative of an Expedition to the Source of the St. Peter's River; Lake Winnepeek, Lake of the Woods, etc., Performed in the Year 1823.... London: 1825. V. 67

KEATINGE CLAY, WILLIAM
Liturgical Services: Liturgies and Occasional Forms of Prayer Set Forth in the Reign of Queen Elizabeth. Cambridge;: 1847. V. 66

KEATS, JOHN
Endymion. London: 1818. V. 62; 64; 65; 66
Endymion. 1902. V. 62
Hyperion. 1945. V. 62
Isabella or the Pot of Basil. Edinburgh and London. V. 62
Isabella or the Pot of Basil. Philadelphia: 1898. V. 64
Keats (i.e. Selected Poems). Hammersmith: 1914. V. 62; 67
Lamia, Isabella, The Eve of St. Agnes and Other Poems. London: 1820. V. 63; 64; 65; 67
Lamia, Isabella, the Eve of St. Agnes and Other Poems. New York: 1927. V. 66
Letters of John Keats to Fanny Brawne Written in the Years 1819 and 1820. London: 1878. V. 63
The Letters.... London: 1931. V. 63
Odes, Sonnets and Lyrics. Oxford: 1895. V. 64
The Poems. 1894. V. 64
Poems. London: 1897. V. 62
The Poems. London: 1904. V. 62
Poems. London: 1907. V. 65
The Poems. Cambridge: 1966. V. 64
The Poetical and Other Writings of John Keats. New York: 1938-1939. V. 62; 64
The Poetical Works. London: 1854. V. 64
The Poetical Works. London: 1907. V. 63
The Poetical Works. London: 1924. V. 66
The Poetical Works. New York: 1938. V. 64
Poetry and Prose of John Keats.... London: 1890. V. 66
The Sonnets. London?: 1900?. V. 62; 67
Three Essays by John Keats. London: 1889. V. 64

KEATS, M.
Sancho and His Stubborn Mule. New York: 1946. V. 62

KEBLE, JOHN
The Christian Year: thoughts in Verse for the Sundays and Holydays throughout the Year. Oxford: 1865. V. 67
Occasional Papers and Reviews. Oxford and London: 1877. V. 65

KEE, ROBERT
A Sign of the Times. London: 1955. V. 63

KEELER BRASS CO.
Furniture Hardware. Grand Rapids: 1962. V. 63

KEELER, HARRY STEPHEN
The Book with the Orange Leaves. London: 1943. V. 67
The Green Jade Hand. New York. V. 67
The Magic Ear-Drums. London: 1939. V. 66
The Tiger Snake. London: 1931. V. 67

KEELER, JAMES EDWARD
Photographs of Nebulae and Clusters, Made with the Crossley Reflector. Sacramento: 1908. V. 67

KEELING, ELSA D'ESTERRE
Three Sisters; or Sketches of a Highly Original Family. London: 1884. V. 65

KEELY, ROBERT N.
In Arctic Seas - the Voyage of the Kite. Philadelphia: 1892. V. 64; 66

KEEN, A. M.
Sea Shells of Tropical West America.... Stanford: 1971. V. 62

KEEN, ARTHUR
Charing Cross Bridge. London: 1930. V. 62

KEEN, GREGORY B.
The Descendants of Joran Kyn of New Sweden. Philadelphia: 1913. V. 63; 66

KEEN, RALPH HOLBROOK
Little Ape and Other Stories. London: 1921. V. 62; 66

KEEN, WILLIAM W.
Address in Surgery Delivered at the Semi-Centennial Meeting of the AMA at Philadelphia... (with) On the Surgical Complications of...Continued Fevers. Chicago: 1897. V. 64
Addresses and Other Papers. Philadelphia: 1905. V. 64; 66; 67
On Resection of the Gasserian Ganglion with a Pathological Report on Seven Ganglia. 1898. V. 64; 66; 67

KEENE, DAY
Naked Fury.... 1952. V. 62
Seed of Doubt. 1961. V. 64; 66

KEENE, DEREK
Survey of Medieval Winchester. Oxford: 1985. V. 62

KEENE, J. HARRINGTON
Fly-Fishing and Fly-Making for Trout, Bass, Salmon, Etc. New York: 1891. V. 62

KEEPE, HENRY
Monumenta Westmonasteriensia; or an Historical Account of the Original, Increase and Present State of St. Peter's, or the Abbey Church of Westminster. London: 1682. V. 62

KEES, WELDON
The Collected Poems of Weldon Kees. Iowa City: 1960. V. 64
The Last Man. San Francisco: 1943. V. 64
Limericks to Friends. N.P: 1985. V. 66
Poems 1947-1954. San Francisco: 1954. V. 64
The Waiting Room. Colorado Springs: 1999. V. 64

KEESE, JOHN
The Floral Keepsake. New York: 1854. V. 64
The Poets of America: Illustrated by One of Her Painters. New York: 1840. V. 62

KEESHAN, ROBERT
She Loves Me...She Loves Me Not.... New York: 1963. V. 64

KEESON, A.
Monts de Piete and Pawnbroking. 1854. V. 67

KEET, ALFRED ERNEST
Stephen Crane: in Memoriam. New York: 1930. V. 67

KEEVIL, J. J.
Medicine and the Navy 1200-1900. Edinburgh: 1957-1963. V. 64; 66

KEGLEY, F. B.
Kegley's Virginia Frontier: the Beginning of the Southwest, the Roanoke of Colonial Days 1740-1783. Roanoke: 1938. V. 66
Kegley's Virginia Frontier, the Beginning of the Southwest, the Roanoke of Colonial Days 1740-1783. Roanoke: 1970. V. 65

KEGLEY, MAX
Loot of a Desert Rat. Phoenix: 1938. V. 63; 66

KEIFER, SARAH J. HARRIS
Genealogical and Biographical Skekches of the New Jersey Branch of the Harris Family, in the United States. Madison: 1888. V. 63; 66

KEIGHLEY, WILLIAM
Keighley, Past and Present. Keighley; 1879. V. 65

KEIGHTLEY, THOMAS
An Account of the Life, Opinions and Writings of John Milton.... London: 1855. V. 62; 66
The Crusaders; or, Scenes, Events and Characters from the Times of the Crusades. London: 1833. V. 65
The Fairy Mythology.... London: 1900. V. 64
Notes on the Bucolics and Georgics of Virgil.... London: 1846. V. 62
Secret Societies of the Middle Ages; The Assasins of the East, the Knight Templars and the Fehm-Gerichte, or Secret Tribunals of Westphalia. London. V. 67
Tales and Popular Fictions. Their Resemblance and Transmission from Country to Country. London: 1834. V. 64

KEILL, JAMES
Essays on Several Parts of the Animal Oeconomy. London: 1717. V. 65

KEILL, JOHN
An Introduction to Natural Philosophy; or, Philosophical Lectures Read in the University of Oxford, Anno Dom 1700. London: 1726. V. 66
An Introduction to True Astronomy; or, Astronomical Lectures, Read in Astronomical School of the University of Oxford. London: 1721. V. 65
An Introduction to True Astronomy; or, Astronomical Lectures Read in the Astronomical School of the University of Oxford. London: 1730. V. 65

KEILLOR, GARRISON
Happy to Be There. 1982. V. 63; 65
Happy to be There. New York: 1982. V. 62

KEIM, B. RANDOLPH DE
Sheridan's Troopers on the Borders: a Winter Campaign On the Plains. Philadelphia: 1885. V. 67

KEIR, SUSANNAH HARVEY
Histoire de Miss Julie Greville. Lausanne: 1793. V. 67

KEITH, ARTHUR
The Antiquity of Man. Philadelphia: 1927. V. 64
Menders of the Maimed. London: 1919. V. 64

KEITH, C. H.
Flying Years. London: 1937. V. 64

KEITH, E. C.
A Countryman's Creed. 1938. V. 67
Shots and Shooting. 1951. V. 67

KEITH, ELIZABETH
Eastern Windows: an Artist's Notes of Travel in Japan, Hokkaido, Korea, China and the Philippines. Boston and New York: 1928. V. 66

KEITH, ISAAC STOCKTON
Sermons, Addresses and Letters. Charlestown: 1816. V. 67

KEITH, J. GRAY
The Human Eye; Diagrams and Descriptions. London: 1912. V. 67

KEITH, JAMES
Addresses on Several Occasions. Richmond: 1917. V. 62; 63

KEITH, THOMAS
An Introduction to the Theory and Practice of Plane and Spherical Geometry and the Orthographic and Tereographic Projections of the Sphere.... London: 1801. V. 62
New Treatise on the Use of the Globes.... London: 1860. V. 63

KEITH, WILLIAM
Two Papers, On the Subject of Taxing the British Colonies in America. London: 1767. V. 66

KEITHAHN, EDWARD L.
Monuments in Cedar. Ketchikan: 1945. V. 64

KELEHER, WILLIAM A.
The Fabulous Frontier. Santa Fe: 1945. V. 65; 67
Maxwell Land Grant, a New Mexico Item. Santa Fe: 1942. V. 63; 64
Turmoil in New Mexico 1846-1868. Santa Fe: 1957. V. 63; 66
Violence in Lincoln County, 1869-1881. Albuquerque: 1957. V. 63; 64; 65; 66

KELEMEN, P.
Medieval American Art. New York: 1943. V. 62

KELK, JOHN
The Scarborough Spa, Its New Chemical Analysis and Medicinal Uses to Which is Added, on the Utility of the Bath. London: 1860. V. 62

KELL, JOHN MC INTOSH
Recollection of a Naval Life, Including the Cruises of the Confederate States Steamers Sumter and Alabama. Washington: 1900. V. 62; 63; 65

KELLAND, PHILIP
Lectures on the Principles of Demonstrative Mathematics. Edinburgh: 1843. V. 65; 66

KELLER, ALLAN
Morgan's Raid. Indianapolis & New York: 1961. V. 63

KELLER, BETTY
To You, Walt Whitman. New York: 1997. V. 62; 64

KELLER, DAVID H.
The Devil and the Doctor. New York: 1940. V. 64
The Solitary Hunter and the Abyss. 1948. V. 64; 66
The Solitary Hunter and the Abyss. Philadelphia: 1948. V. 62

KELLER, GOTTFRIED
A Village Romeo and Juliet. London: 1915. V. 65

KELLER, HELEN
Midstream: My Later Life. Garden City: 1929. V. 63
My Religion. London: 1927. V. 62
Our Duties to the Blind. Boston: 1904. V. 63
Peace at Eventide. London: 1932. V. 67

KELLER, JUDITH
Walker Evans: the Getty Museum Collection. Malibu: 1995. V. 63

KELLER, JULIUS
German Jews Fought Back. New York: 1975. V. 67

KELLER, RONALD
Typographycs. Bremen and New York: 1994. V. 62; 64

KELLERMAN, FAYE
The Ritual Bath. New York: 1986. V. 62

KELLERMAN, JONATHAN
Blood Test. 1986. V. 64
The Butcher's Theater. 1988. V. 62; 64; 66
When the Bough Breaks. 1985. V. 64; 67
When the Bough Breaks. London: 1985. V. 66
When the Bough Breaks. New York: 1985. V. 62

KELLEY, E. G.
A Popular Treatise on the Human Teeth and Dental Surgery, Being a Practical Guide for the Early Management of the Health and Teeth of Children; the Preservation of the Adult Teeth.... Boston: 1843. V. 66

KELLEY, JOSEPH
Thirteen Years in the Oregon Penitentary. Portland: 1908. V. 64
Thirteen Years in the Oregon Penitentiary. Portland: 1918. V. 62; 65

KELLEY, ROBERT F.
Racing in America 1937-1959. New York: 1960. V. 62

KELLEY, WILLIAM D.
The New Northwest: An Address on the Northern Pacific Railway, In Its Relations to the Development of the Northwestern Section of the United States and to the Industrial and Commercial Interests of the Nation. Philadelphia: 1871. V. 66

KELLEY, WILLIAM MELVIN
Dancers on the Shore. New York: 1964. V. 65

KELLIE, J.
Remarks on the Cause of Epdiemic Cholera with Suggestions for Its Prevention in Marching Regiments. N.P: 1844. V. 67

KELLNER ET SES FILS
Album de la Maison (Voitures de Luxe). Paris: 1890. V. 67

KELLOG, JAY C.
Broncho Buster Busted and Other Messages. Wheeling: 1932. V. 65

KELLOGG, J. H.
Ladies' Guide in Health and Disease. Battle Creek: 1891. V. 65

KELLOGG, LOUISE P.
The British Regime in Wisconsin and the Northwest. Madison: 1935. V. 67

KELLOGG, M. G.
The Hygienic Family Physician: a Complete Guide for the Preservation of Health.... Battle Creek: 1873. V. 62

KELLOGG, SANFORD C.
The Shenandoah Valley and Virginia 1861-1865: a War Study. New York and Washington: 1903. V. 64

KELLOGG, V.
Darwinism Today. London: 1907. V. 67

KELLY, A. LINDSAY
Kelly's Directory of Bedfordshire, Huntingdonshire and Northamptonshire. London: 1928. V. 65

KELLY, CHARLES
Miles Goodyear, First Citizen of Utah - Trapper, Trader and California Pioneer. Salt Lake City: 1937. V. 65
Old Greenwood: the Story of Caleb Greenwood - Trapper, Pathfinder and Early Pioneer of the West. Salt Lake City: 1936. V. 63; 66
Outlaw Trail, a History of Butch Cassidy and His Wild Bunch. Salt Lake City: 1938. V. 65
Salt Desert Trails - a History of the Hastings Cutoff and Other Early Trails Which Crossed the Great Salt Desert Seeking a Shorter Road to California. Salt Lake City: 1930. V. 62; 65

KELLY, ERIC P.
The Trumpeter of Krakow. New York: 1928. V. 65

KELLY, FRED C.
One Thing Leads to Another. The Growth of an Industry. Boston: 1936. V. 63; 64; 66
The Wright Brothers. New York: 1943. V. 63

KELLY, GEORGE H.
Legislative History of Arizona 1864-1912. Phoenix: 1926. V. 64; 67

KELLY, HOWARD A.
Dictionary of American Medical Biography. New York: 1928. V. 64; 66
Some American Medical Botanists.... Troy: 1914. V. 62; 65; 67
The Vermiform Appendix and Its Diseases. Philadelphia: 1905. V. 62; 66; 67

KELLY, J. E.
On a Case of Polydactylism. Dublin: 1876. V. 67

KELLY, JOHN
French Idioms, with the English Adapted. London: 1736. V. 63

KELLY, JOHN L.
Fact and Fiction!. Manchester: 1853. V. 63

KELLY, L. V.
The Range Men - The Story of Ranchers and Indians of Alberta. Toronto: 1913. V. 66

KELLY, LAWRENCE
Navajo Roundup: Selected Correspondence of Kit Carson's Expedition Against the Navajo. Boulder: 1970. V. 63; 64; 66

KELLY, LEROY V.
The Range Men. Toronto: 1913. V. 63

KELLY, LUTHER S.
Yellowstone Kelly. New Haven: 1926. V. 66

KELLY, MICHAEL
Reminiscences of Michael Kelly, of the King's Theatre and Theatre Royal, Drury Lane.... London: 1826. V. 65

KELLY, PATRICK
A Practical Introduction to Spherics and Nautical Astronomy. London: 1805. V. 65
The Universal Cambist and Commercial Instructor.... London: 1811. V. 64; 65
The Universal Cambist, and Commercial Instructor.... London: 1826. V. 64

KELLY, R. TALBOT
Egypt. London: 1903. V. 64

KELLY, ROB ROY
American Wood Types 1828-1900: Volume One. Kansas City: 1964. V. 64

KELLY, ROBERT
Axon Dendron Tree. New York: 1967. V. 63
A Joining: a Sequence for H.D. San Francisco: 1967. V. 65
Report of the Trial of Robert Kelly, for the Murder of Head-Constable Talbot at the City of Dublin Commission Court, October 1871. Dublin: 1873. V. 63

KELLY, SUSAN
The Gemini Man. New York: 1985. V. 66

KELLY, WALT
Pogo. New York: 1951. V. 63
The Pogo Peek-A-Book. New York: 1955. V. 64; 66
Ten Ever-Loving Blue-Eyed Years with Pogo. New York: 1959. V. 64

KELLY, WAYNE SCOTT
Lariats and Chevrons or Corporal Jack Wilson, U.S.V.A., R. R. "Ante Lucem". Guthrie: 1905. V. 63

KELLY'S Directory of Barnet, Hadley, Potters Bar, South Mimms, Totteridge, Whetstone.... 1930. V. 62

KELLY'S Directory of Berkshire. London: 1928. V. 66

KELLY'S Directory of Cambridgeshire. London: 1925. V. 63; 66

KELLY'S Directory of Cumberland and Westmorland. London: 1894. V. 66

KELLY'S Directory of Derbyshire. London: 1928. V. 62
KELLY'S Directory of Derbyshire. London: 1932. V. 65

KELLY'S Directory of Durham. London: 1894. V. 63

KELLY'S Directory of Durham and Northumberland. London: 1910. V. 63; 65

KELLY'S Directory of Essex. London: 1894. V. 63

KELLY'S Directory of Herefordshire and Shropshire. 1917. London: 1917. V. 63

KELLY'S Directory of Leicestershire and Rutland. 1928. London: 1928. V. 63

KELLY'S Directory of Lincolnshire. London: 1900. V. 62; 63
KELLY'S Directory of Lincolnshire. London: 1913. V. 63
KELLY'S Directory of Lincolnshire. London: 1922. V. 63
KELLY'S Directory of Lincolnshire. London: 1930. V. 62

KELLY'S Directory of Norfolk and Suffolk. London: 1892. V. 66

KELLY'S Directory of Somersetshire. London: 1931. V. 63

KELLY'S Directory of Suffolk. 1900. V. 65
KELLY'S Directory of Suffolk. London: 1929. V. 66

KELLY'S Directory of the Counties of Cambridge, Norfolk and Suffolk. London: 1937. V. 63; 66

KELLY'S Directory of the Counties of Derby, Nottingham, Leicester and Rutland. London: 1916. V. 63

KELLY'S Directory of the Counties of Norfolk and Suffolk. London: 1922. V. 63
KELLY'S Directory of the Counties of Norfolk and Suffolk. London: 1929. V. 63

KELLY'S Directory of Wiltshire. London: 1935. V. 63

KELLY'S Handbook to the Titled, Landed and Official Classes for 1895. London: 1895. V. 64; 66

KELMAN, JAMES
The Busconductor Hines. Edinburgh: 1984. V. 63

KELMAN, JOHN
The Holy Land; Painted by John Fulleylove. London: 1902. V. 67

KELMSCOTT PRESS
A Chronological List of Books Printed at the Kelmscott Press, With Illustrative Material from a Collection Made by William Morris and Henry C. Marillier. Boston: 1928. V. 63; 64

KELSALL, CHARLES
Classical Excursion from Rome to Arpino. Geneva: 1820. V. 64
The Last Pleadings of Marcus Tullius Cicero Against Caius Verres.... London: 1812. V. 63

KELSALL, J. E.
The Birds of Hampshire and the Isle of Wight. 1905. V. 63; 66
The Birds of Hampshire and the Isle of Wight. London: 1905. V. 62; 65; 67

KELSEY, ALBERT WARREN
Autobiographical Notes and Memoranda by Albert Warren Kelsey 1840-1910. Baltimore: 1911. V. 62; 63

KELSEY, D. M.
History of Our Wild West and Stories of Pioneer Life. Chicago: 1901. V. 62

KELSEY, HENRY
The Kelsey Papers. Ottawa: 1929. V. 64; 66

KELSON, GEORGE M.
The Salmon Fly; How to Dress It and How to Use It. London: 1895. V. 67

KELTON, ELMER
The Art of James Bama. New York: 1993. V. 66

KELTY, MARY ANNE
The Favourite of Nature. London: 1822. V. 65

KELVIN, WILLIAM THOMSON, 1ST BARON
Notes of Lectures on Molecular Dynamics and the Wave Theory of Light.... Baltimore: 1884. V. 64
Sketch of Elementary Dynamics. Edinburgh: 1863. V. 65

KELYNG, JOHN
A Report of Divers Cases in Pleas of the Crown, Adjudged and Determined; in the Reign of the Late King Charles II. London: 1708. V. 63

KEMAL, YASHAR
Memed, My Hawk. London: 1961. V. 67

KEMBLE, EDWARD W.
Comical Coons. New York: 1898. V. 65
Kemble's Pickaninnies - a Collection. New York: 1901. V. 65
Kemble's Sketch Book. New York: 1899. V. 63

KEMBLE, FRANCES ANNE
Journal. London: 1835. V. 65
Journal. Philadelphia: 1835. V. 65
Journal of a Residence on a Georgian Plantation in 1838-1839. New York: 1863. V. 62; 63; 65
Poems. Boston: 1859. V. 63; 65
Records of a Girlhood. New York: 1883. V. 65
A Year of Consolation. (with) Record of a Girlhood. (with) Records of Later Life. (with) Further Records 1848-1883. (with) Poems. London: 1878. V. 65

KEMBLE, JOHN
Horae Ferales; or, Studies in the Archaeology of the Northern Nations. London: 1863. V. 62

KEMBLE, JOHN HASKELL
Side-Wheelers Across the Pacific. San Francisco: 1942. V. 66

KEMBLE, JOHN P.
Macbeth and King Richard the Third. London: 1817. V. 66
Shakespeare's King Henry the Fifth, a Historical Play. London: 1806. V. 66

KEMELMAN, HARRY
The Nine Mile Walk. New York: 1967. V. 67

KEMMERER, DONALD L.
Path to Freedom. The Struggle for Self Government in Colonial New Jersey 1703-1776. Princeton: 1940. V. 63; 66

KEMP, A.
The Birds of Prey of Southern Africa. Johannesburg: 1980. V. 63
The Birds of Southern Africa. Johannesburg: 1982. V. 63
The Owls of Southern Africa. Cape Town: 1987. V. 65; 67

KEMP, DIXON
A Manual of Yacht and Boat Sailing. London: 1882. V. 64; 67
A Manual of Yacht and Boat Sailing. London: 1888. V. 66
A Manual of Yacht and Boat Sailing. London: 1891. V. 64
A Manual of Yacht and Boat Sailing and Naval Architecture. London: 1878. V. 62; 67
The Yacht Racing Calendar and Review for 1893. London: 1893. V. 65

KEMP, DONALD C.
Colorado's Little Kingdom. 1949. V. 66

KEMP, EARL
The Illustrated Presidential Report of the Commission on Obscenity and Pornography. San Diego: 1970. V. 66

KEMP, EMILY G.
Wanderings in Chinese Turkestan. London: 1914. V. 67

KEMPE, MARTIN
Philologema De Osculo. Jena: 1665. V. 64

KEMP'S Nine Daies Wonder: Performed in a Daunce from London to Norwich. London: 1840. V. 66

KEMPTON, MURRAY
Rebellions, Perversities and Main Events. New York: 1994. V. 62

KEMSEY, W.
The British Herbal; or, a Practical Tratise on the Uses and Application of the Common Herbs of Great Britain. Bristol: 1818. V. 64

KENAN, THOMAS S.
Sketch of the Forty-Third Regiment North Carolina Troops. Raleigh: 1895. V. 63; 65

KENCHINGTON, FRANK
Dick Whittington. Salonika: 1916. V. 65

KENDAL, E. A.
Parental Education; or, Domestic Lessons.... London: 1803. V. 64

KENDALL, EDWARD AUGUSTUS
An Argument for Construing Largely the Right of an Appellee of Murder to Insist on Trial by Battle, and also for Abolishing Appeals.... London: 1818. V. 63
Keeper's Travels in Search of His Master. London: 1798. V. 65
Keeper's Travels in Search of His Master. Dublin: 1824. V. 64
Travels through the Northern Parts of the United States in the Years 1807 and 1809. New York: 1809. V. 67

KENDALL, ELIZABETH
A Wayfarer in China: Impressions of a trip across West China and Mongolia. Boston and New York: 1913. V. 65

KENDALL, GEORGE
Henry Alken. London: 1929. V. 67

KENDALL, GEORGE W.
Narrative of the Texas Santa Fe Expedition. New York: 1844. V. 66

KENDALL, M. G.
Bibliography of Statistical Literature Pre-1940 (1940-1949, 1950-1958). Edinburgh and London: 1968-1962. V. 62

KENDALL, PAUL G.
Polo Ponies: Their Training and Schooling. New York: 1933. V. 67

KENDALL, PERCY FRY
Geology of Yorkshire. 1924. V. 62; 66
Geology of Yorkshire. Leeds: 1924. V. 63; 64; 65
Geology of Yorkshire. London: 1924. V. 64

KENDALL, W. C.
The Fishes of New England. Part 2. The Salmons. 1935. V. 62; 63
The Fishes of New England. The Salmon Family. Part 2. Boston: 1935. V. 65; 66

KENDERDINE, THADDEUS S.
A California Tramp and Later Footprints; or, Life on the Plains and in the Golden State Thirty Years Ago. Newtown: 1888. V. 62

KENDON, FRANK
Each Silver Fly. Cambridge: 1946. V. 64

KENDON, FRANK continued
The Small Years. Cambridge: 1930. V. 66
The Time Piece: Poems. Cambridge: 1945. V. 66

KENDRICK, A. F.
Hand-Woven Carpets, Oriental and European. London: 1922. V. 62; 65; 66

KENDRICK, BAYNARD
Blind Allies. New York: 1954. V. 65
Blind Man's Bluff. Boston: 1943. V. 66

KENEALLY, ARABELLA
The Human Gyroscope. London: 1934. V. 65

KENEALLY, THOMAS
The Chant of Jimmie Blacksmith. New York: 1972. V. 65
The Fear. Melbourne Victoria: 1965. V. 63
The Place at Whitton. London: 1964. V. 66
Schindler's Ark. London: 1982. V. 63; 66
Schindler's List. New York: 1982. V. 65

KENEALY, EDWARD
Brallaghan, or the Deipnosophists. 1845. V. 65

KENEDY, R. C.
Grotesques. London: 1975. V. 66

KENLY, JOHN R.
Memoirs of a Maryland Volunteer. War with Mexico, in the Years 1846-1847-1848. Philadelphia: 1873. V. 65

KENNA, MICHAEL
Le Desert de Retz: Le Jardin Pittoresque de Monsieur de Monville (A Late Eighteenth Century French Folly Garden). San Francisco: 1995. V. 65

KENNAN, GEORGE
Memoirs 1925-1950. (and) Memoirs 1950-1963. Boston: 1967-1972. V. 63
The Salton Sea - an Account of Harriman's Fight with the Colorado River. New York: 1917. V. 63
Siberia and the Exile System. London: 1891. V. 66
Siberia, and the Exile System. New York: 1891. V. 64; 66
Tent Life in Siberia, a New Account of an Old Undertaking, Adventures Among the Koraks and Other Tribes in Kamchatka and Northern Asia. London: 1928. V. 67

KENNARD, A. S.
Synonymy of the British Non-Marine Mollusca. London: 1926. V. 66

KENNE, CAROLYN
The Secret of the Old Clock. New York: 1930. V. 63

KENNEDY, A. W. M. C.
The Birds of Berkshire and Buckinghamshire. Eton and London: 1868. V. 67

KENNEDY, ALEXANDER
Petra; Its History and Monuments. London: 1925. V. 67

KENNEDY, ARTHUR CLARK
Erotica. London. V. 64

KENNEDY, BART
A Tramp in Spain: from Andalusia to Andorra. London: 1920. V. 67

KENNEDY, DICK
Fun from France. New York: 1919. V. 64
Soldier's Jokes and Stories. N.P: 1917. V. 66

KENNEDY, E. B.
Thirty Seasons in Scandinavia. 1908. V. 62; 65; 67

KENNEDY, ELIJAH R.
The Contest for California in 1861: How Colonel E. D. Baker Saved the Pacific States to the Union. New York: 1912. V. 64

KENNEDY, G. W.
The Pioneer Campfire in Four Parts. Portland: 1914. V. 63

KENNEDY, GRACE
Anna Ross, a Story for Children. Edinburgh: 1824. V. 63
Dunallan; or Know What You Judge. Edinburgh: 1825. V. 65
Dunallan; or, Know What You Judge. New York: 1828. V. 62

KENNEDY, J. H.
Early Days of Mormonism - Palmyra, Kirtland and Nauvoo. New York: 1888. V. 63

KENNEDY, JACQUELINE BOUVIER
One Special Summer. New York: 1974. V. 66

KENNEDY, JAMES
Essays Ethnological and Linguistic. London: 1861. V. 64
The History of Contagious Cholera; with Facts Explanatory of Its Origins and Laws and a Rational Method of Cure. London: 1831. V. 62; 66
The History of the Contagious Cholera; with Facts Explanatory of Its Origin and Laws, and of a Rational Method of Cure. London: 1832. V. 65
A New Description of the Pictures, Statues, Bustos, Basso-Relievos and Other Curiosities at the Earl of Pembroke's House at Wilton. Salisbury: 1758. V. 66; 67
A New Description of the Pictures, Statues, Bustos, Basso-Relievos and Other Curiosities at the Earl of Pembroke's House at Wilton. Salisbury: 1771. V. 65
A New Description of the Pictures, Statutes, Bustos, Basso-Relievos and Other Curiosities in the Earl of Pembroke's House at Wilton. Salisbury: 1776. V. 62

KENNEDY, JOHN
As Others See Us!. London: 1932. V. 62

KENNEDY, JOHN FITZGERALD
Profiles in Courage. New York: 1956. V. 63; 64
The Unspoken Speech of John F. Kennedy at Dallas - November 22, 1963. N.P: 1964. V. 63
Why England Slept. London: 1940. V. 66

KENNEDY, JOHN P.
Memoirs of the Life of William Wirt. Philadelphia: 1849. V. 62

KENNEDY, JOHN PENNDLETON
Autograph Leaves of Our Country's Authors. Baltimore: 1864. V. 66

KENNEDY, LEWIS
The Present State of the Tenancy of Land in Great Britain.... London: 1828. V. 65

KENNEDY, LUDOVIC
Truth to Tell - the Collected Writings. 1991. V. 65

KENNEDY, MICHAEL
The Sea Angler's Fishes. London. V. 67

KENNEDY, MICHAEL S.
The Red Man's West - True Stories of the Frontier Indians from Montana. New York: 1964. V. 66
The Red Man's West: True Stories of the Frontier Indians from Montana. New York: 1965. V. 64

KENNEDY, R. EMMET
Mellows: a Chronicle of Unkown Singers. New York: 1924. V. 67

KENNEDY, RANKIN
The Book of the Motor Car. London: 1915. V. 62

KENNEDY, RICHARD
A Boy at the Hogarth Press. Andoversford: 1972. V. 63
A Boy at the Hogarth Press. London: 1972. V. 63; 66

KENNEDY, ROBERT F.
The Enemy Within. New York: 1960. V. 63
Just Friends and Brave Enemies. New York: 1962. V. 63
To Seek a Newer World. Garden City: 1967. V. 63; 66

KENNEDY, RUTH WEDGWOOD
Four Portrait Busts by Francesco Laurana. Northampton: 1962. V. 66

KENNEDY, SHIRLEY
Pucci, a Renaissance in Fashion. New York: 1991. V. 65

KENNEDY, WILLIAM
Billy Phelan's Greatest Game. New York: 1978. V. 64; 66
Charlie Malarkey and the Belly-Button Machine. Boston: 1986. V. 63; 67
The Flaming Corsage. Franklin Center: 1996. V. 63
The Flaming Corsage. New York: 1996. V. 67
The Ink Truck. New York: 1969. V. 62; 63; 66; 67
The Ink Truck. London: 1970. V. 64
The Ink Truck. 1983. V. 67
The Ink Truck. New York: 1984. V. 63
Ironweed. New York: 1983. V. 65; 66; 67
Legs. New York: 1975. V. 62; 63; 64; 67
Quinn's Book. New York: 1988. V. 67
Very Old Bones. New York: 1992. V. 67

KENNEDY, WILLIAM D.
Pythian History: Containing the Life, Death and Burial of the Founder of the Order, Justus H. Rathbone; The Birth and Progress of the Order. Chicago: 1904. V. 67

KENNEDY-FRASER, MARJORY
Songs of the Hebrides. London: Sep. 1920. V. 62

KENNER, HUGH
Paradox in Chesterton. London: 1948. V. 67

KENNET, E. HILTON YOUNG, LORD
A Bird in the Bush. London: 1936. V. 62

KENNETT, WHITE
Parochial Antiquities Attempted in the History of Ambrosden, Burcester and Other Adjacent Parts in Counties of Oxford and Bucks.... Oxford: 1695. V. 62; 63
A Sermon Preach'd at the Funeral of the Right Noble William Duke of Devonshire, in the Church of All-Hallows in Derby...Sept. 5th MDCCVII. London: 1708. V. 63

KENNEY, C. E.
Catalogue of the Celebrated Collection...of C. E. Kenney. London: 1965-1968. V. 62

KENNEY, JAMES F.
The Sources for the Early History of Ireland; Ecclesiastical. 1993. V. 67

KENNEY, MICHAEL
The Sea Angler's Fishes. London: 1979. V. 67

KENNICOTT, BENJAMIN
A Proposal for Establishing a Professorship of the Persian Language in the University of Oxford. N.P: 1767. V. 62; 64
The Ten Annual Accounts of the Collation of Hebrew Mss. of the Old Testament, Begun in 1760 and Compleated in 1769 by Benj. Kennicott.... Oxford: 1770. V. 62

KENNION, EDWARD
An Essay on Trees in Landscape; or, an Attempt to Shew the Propriety and Importance of Charactersitic Expression in this Branch of Art, and the Means of Producing It: with Examples. London: 1844. V. 62; 66

KENNION, GEORGE
Observations on the Medicinal Springs of Harrogate. London: 1867. V. 65

KENRICK, THOMAS
The British Stage and Literary Cabinet, July 1821. London: 1821. V. 67

KENRICK, W.
The New American Orchardist.... Boston: 1844. V. 62

KENSLEY, B.
Sea Shells of Southern Africa. Volume I. Gastropods. Cape Town: 1973. V. 66

KENT, ALEXANDER
The Flag Captain. New York: 1971. V. 67

KENT, ANDERSON
Night Dogs. Tucson: 1996. V. 63

KENT, CHARLES N.
History of the Seventeenth Regiment, New Hampshire Volunteer Infantry 1862-1863. Concord: 1898. V. 66

KENT, CHARLES W.
The Unveiling of the Bust of Edgar Allan Poe in the Library of the University of Virginia, October the 7th, Eighteeen Hundred and Ninety-Nine. Lynchburg: 1899?. V. 67

KENT, JAMES
An Anniversary Discourse, Delivered Before the New York Historical Society, Dec. 6, 1828. New York: 1829. V. 66

KENT, NATHANIEL
Hints to Gentlemen of Landed Property. London: 1775. V. 63; 65
Hints to Gentlemen of Landed Property. London: 1776. V. 62; 64

KENT, ROCKWELL
A Birthday Book. New York: 1931. V. 66
The Bookplates and Marks. New York: 1929. V. 62
Later Bookplates and Marks. New York: 1937. V. 62; 67
N by E. New York: 1930. V. 64; 66; 67
Rockwell Kent's Greenland Journal. New York: 1962. V. 62; 64; 67
Salamina. New York: 1935. V. 63

KENT, S. H.
Gath to the Cedars, Travels in the Holy Land Palmyra. London: 1000. V. 67

KENT, WILLIAM SAVILLE
The Great Barrie Reef of Australia: Its Products and Potentialities. London: 1893. V. 62
A Manual of the Infusoria. 1881-1882. V. 63; 66
A Manual of the Infusoria. London: 1881-1882. V. 64
The Naturalist in Australia. London: 1897. V. 62; 63; 66

KENTISH, MRS.
The Two Friends or the Dying Fawn.... London: 1832. V. 62; 65

KENTON, EDNA
The Indians of North America. New York: 1927. V. 63
Simon Kenton: His Life and Period 1755-1836. Garen City: 1930. V. 64

KENTUCKY Writing. Morehead: 1954. V. 63

KEPHART, CYRUS J.
Life of Rev. Isaiah L. Kephart, D. D. Dayton: 1909. V. 67

KEPHART, HORACE
Our Southern Highlanders. New York: 1922. V. 67

KEPLER, JOHANNES
Ad Vitellionem Paralipomena, Quibus Astronomiae Pars Optica Traditur.... Frankfurt: 1604. V. 62; 63
Ausszug Auss der Uralten Messe Kunst Archimedis und Deroselben Newlich in Latein Aussgangenr Ergentzung, Betreffend Rechnung der Corperlichen Figuren, Holen Gefessen und Weinfasser. Linz: 1616. V. 62; 63
Kepler's Somnium. The Dream, or Posthumous Work on Lunar Astronomy. Madison: 1967. V. 63
Narratio de Observatis a se Quatuor Iouis Satellitibus Erronibus Quos Galilaeus Galilaeus Mathematicus Florentinus iure Inventionis Medicaea Sidera.... Florence: 1611. V. 62; 63

KEPPEL, FREDERICK
The Gentle Art of Resenting Injuries - Being Some Unpublished Correspondence Addressed to the Author of "The Gentle Art of Making Enemies". New York: 1904. V. 65

KEPPEL, GEORGE
Personal Narrative of a Journey from India to England by Bussourah, Bagdad, the Ruins of Babylon, Curdistan, the Court of Persia, the Western Shore of the Caspian Sea, Astrakhan, Nishney Novogorod Moscow and St. Petersburgh in the Year 1824. London: 1827. V. 65

KEPPEL, HENRY
A Sailor's Life Under Four Sovereigns. London and New York: 1899. V. 64; 65
A Visit to the Indian Archipelago; in HM Ship Meander.... London: 1853. V. 67

KEPPLER, HERBERT
The Nikon Way, Including Nikkormat. London and Boston: 1982. V. 63

KEPPLER, P.
Wanderfahrten und Wallfahrten im Orient. Freiburg: 1895. V. 67

KER, DAVID
On the Road to Khiva. London: 1874. V. 67

KER, JOHN
The Memoirs of John Ker, of Kersland in North Britain Esq. London: 1726. V. 64
The Memoirs of John Ker, or Kersland in North Britain Esq. London: 1783. V. 64

KER, N. R.
Fragments of Medieval Manuscripts Used as Pastedowns in Oxford Manuscripts with a Survey of Oxford Binding c. 1515-1620. Oxford: 1954. V. 63

KERBY, ROBERT L.
The Confederate Invasion of New Mexico and Arizona 1861-1862. Los Angeles: 1958. V. 63

KERCHEVAL, SAMUEL
A History of the Valley of Virginia. Strasburg: 1925. V. 63

KERCKRING, THEODOR
Spicelegium Anatomicum. (with) Anthropogeniae Ichnographia. Amsterdam: 1670-1671. V. 63; 67

KEREKES, J. J.
Aquatic Birds in the Tropic Web of Lakes. Netherlands: 1994. V. 64

KERFOOT, J. B.
American Pewter. Boston: 1924. V. 67

KERLEY, CHARLES GILMORE
Treatment of Diseases of the Children. Philadelphia: 1908. V. 66; 67

KERN, C. M.
Practical Landscape Gardening. Cincinnati: 1855. V. 62

KERN, JEROME
The Library of Jerome Kern. New York: 1929. V. 62

KERN, ROBERT
Thrilling Locations: a Supplement for the James Bond 007 Game. New York: 1985. V. 67

KERNAHAN, COULSON
Captain Shannon. London: 1897. V. 66

KERNER, A.
Flowers and Their Unbidden Guests.... 1878. V. 67

KERNER, ROBERT J.
Northeastern Asia: a Selected Bibliography.... 1968. V. 65

KERNER VON MARILAUN, ANTON
The Natural History of Plants. London: 1896-1897. V. 63
The Natural History of Plants. London: 1902. V. 62

KERNODLE, GEORGE R.
From Art to Theatre. Form and Convention in the Renaissance. Chicago: 1947. V. 64

KEROUAC, JACK
Big Sur. New York: 1962. V. 64; 65; 66
The Dharma Bums. New York: 1958. V. 62; 66
Doctor Sax. New York: 1959. V. 62
Doctor Sax. London: 1977. V. 66
The Great Western Bus Ride. N.P: 1984. V. 62
Jan 1st 1959: Field Castro. N.P: 1959. V. 62
Last Words and Other Writings. N.P: 1985. V. 62
Mexico City Blues. New York: 1959. V. 66; 67
On the Road. New York: 1957. V. 62; 65; 66; 67
Pic, A Novel. New York: 1971. V. 62
Pull My Daisy. New York: 1961. V. 64; 67
Selected Letters 1957-1969. New York: 1999. V. 64
The Subterraneans. New York: 1958. V. 63
The Town and the City. New York: 1950. V. 62; 63; 64; 67
Visions of Cody. New York: 1972. V. 64; 66
Visions of Cody. London: 1973. V. 65
Visions of Gerard. New York: 1963. V. 67

KERR, ANDREW WILLIAM
History of Banking in Scotland. Glasgow: 1884. V. 67

KERR, CHARLES
History of Kentucky. Chicago and New York: 1922. V. 67

KERR, HUGH
A Poetical Description of Texas. New York: 1838. V. 64

KERR, J. G.
A Naturalist in the Gran Chaco. Cambridge: 1950. V. 62; 63

KERR, J. M. M.
Historical Review of British Obstetrics and Gynaecology 1800-1950. Edinburgh: 1954. V. 66; 67

KERR, JOHN
Curling in Canada and the United States. Edinburgh: 1904. V. 62

KERR, PHILIP
The Berlin Noir Trilogy. 1989-1991. V. 63
A German Requiem. 1991. V. 63
A German Requiem. London: 1991. V. 66
March Violets. London: 1989. V. 66

KERR, ROBERT
The Gentleman's House; or, How to Plan English Residences from the Parsonage to the Palace. London: 1864. V. 64; 67
Memoirs of the Life, Writings and Correspondence of William Smellie.... Edinburgh: 1811. V. 64; 67

KERRIGAN, ANTHONY
At the Front Door of the Atlantic. 1969. V. 64; 67

KERSEY, JOHN
Dictionarium Anglo-Britannicum; or, a General English Dictionary.... London: 1715. V. 64

KERSH, GERALD
An Ape, a Dog, and a Serpent. London: 1945. V. 62
Brain and Ten Fingers. London: 1943. V. 62
The Brazen Bull. London: 1952. V. 62
Clean, Bright and Slightly Oiled. London: 1946. V. 62
The Dead Look On. London: 1943. V. 62
Faces in a Dusty Picture. London: 1944. V. 62
Fowler's End. New York: 1957. V. 65
Guttersnipe. London: 1954. V. 62
The Horrible Dummy. London: 1944. V. 62
Neither Man Nor Dog. London: 1946. V. 62
Prelude to a Certain Midnight. London: 1947. V. 62
Sad Road to the Sea. London: 1947. V. 62
The Ugly Face of Love. London: 1960. V. 62

KERSHAW, S. W.
Art Treasures of the Lambeth Library. London: 1873. V. 67

KERSSING, HARRY
Cook. New York: 1965. V. 67

KERTESZ, ANDRE
Day of Paris. New York: 1945. V. 65
Kertesz on Kertesz. New York: 1983. V. 63

KESEY, KEN
Kesey's Garage Sale. New York: 1973. V. 62; 63; 65
Last Go Round. New York: 1994. V. 65
One Flew Over the Cuckoo's Nest. New York: 1962. V. 67
Sailor Song. New York: 1992. V. 63
Sometimes a Great Notion. New York: 1964. V. 64; 65; 67

KESSELL, E. L.
Festschirft for George Sprague Myers, in Honor of His Sixty-Fifth Birthday. San Francisco: 1970. V. 65

KESSELL, JOHN L.
The Missions of New Mexico Since 1776. Albuquerque: 1980. V. 64

KESSLER, LEO
Death Match. London: 1988. V. 67

KESWANI, N. H.
The Science of Medicine and Physiological Concepts in Ancient and Medieval India. New Delhi. V. 67

KETCHUM, PHILIP
Death in the Library. 1943. V. 64

KETTERING PERMANENT BENEFIT BUILDING SOCIETY
Rules of the Kettering Permanent Benefit Building Society, Established Pursuant to Act of Parliament...Commenced April 13th 1869. Office: The Temperance Hall, Kettering. Kettering: 1869. V. 66

KETTILBY, MARY
A Collection of Above Three Hundred Receipts in Cookery, Physick and Surgery for the Use of All Good Wives. London: 1719. V. 62
A Collection of Above Three Hundred Receipts in Cookery, Physick and Surgery for the Use Of all Good Wives. 1734. V. 67
A Collection of Above Three Hundred Receipts in Cookery, Physick and Surgery; for the Use of all Good Wives. London: 1734. V. 62

KETTON-CREMER, R. W.
Thomas Gray - a Biography. Cambridge: 1955. V. 64

KEULEMANS, J. G.
A Natural History of Cage Birds. 1871. V. 62

KEVERNE, RICHARD
At the Blue Gates. London: 1932. V. 66
Crook Stuff, Some Stories of Crime and Detection. London: 1935. V. 66

KEY, FRANCIS SCOTT
Poems. New York: 1857. V. 62; 64; 66
The Star Spangled Banner. Garden City: 1942. V. 65

KEYES, EDWARD L.
Lewis Atterbury Stimson, M.D. New York: 1918. V. 62; 63

KEYNES, GEOFFREY
The Apologie and Treatise of Ambroise Pare.... Chicago: 1952. V. 64; 66; 67
A Bibliography of Dr. Robert Hooke. Oxford: 1960. V. 62
A Bibliography of Henry King D.D., Bishop of Chichester. London: 1977. V. 62
A Bibliography of John Donne. Cambridge: 1932. V. 62; 66
The Bibliography of John Ray. London: 1951. V. 62
A Bibliography of Sir Thomas Browne. Cambridge: 1924. V. 64; 67
A Bibliography of Sir Thomas Browne. Oxford: 1968. V. 62; 65
A Bibliography of William Blake. New York: 1921. V. 62
Bibliotheca Bibliographici, a Catalogue of the Library Formed by Geoffrey Keynes. London: 1964. V. 62; 63; 66
Blake Studies. Notes on His Life and Works in Seventeen Chapters. London: 1949. V. 63; 66
The Complete Portraiture of William and Catherine Blake. London: 1977. V. 64
Engravings by William Blake. Dublin: 1956. V. 65
The Gates of Memory. 1981. V. 67
The Gates of Memory. London: 1981. V. 64
The Gates of Memory. Oxford: 1981. V. 66
Jane Austen: a Bibliography. London: 1929. V. 63; 65; 66
The Life of William Harvey. Oxford: 1966. V. 64
The Personality of William Harvey. The Linacre Lecture. Cambridge: 1949. V. 62; 67
The Portraiture of William Harvey. London: 1949. V. 65
The Portraiture of William Harvey. London: 1985. V. 67
A Study of the Illuminated Books of William Blake, Poet, Printer, Prophet. London and Paris: 1964. V. 63
William Blake's Illuminated Books, a Census. New York: 1953. V. 63
William Pickering Publisher - a Memoir and Handlist of His Editions. London: 1924.. V. 62

KEYNES, JOHN MAYNARD, 1ST BARON
Can Lloyd George Do It? An Examination of the Liberal Pledge. London: 1929. V. 63
The Economic Consequences of the Peace. London: 1919. V. 63; 64
The Economic Consequences of the Peace. New York: 1920. V. 65
The End of Laissez-Faire. London: 1926. V. 63
Essays in Biography. London: 1933. V. 62; 64; 66
Essays in Persuasion. 1931. V. 65
General Theory of Employment, Interest and Money. London: 1936. V. 62; 63; 64; 66; 67
The General Theory of Employment Interest and Money. New York: 1936. V. 64
How to Pay for the War. London: 1940. V. 62; 64
How to Pay for the War. Melbourne: 1940. V. 66
The Means to Prosperity. London: 1933. V. 65
A Revision of the Treaty. London: 1922. V. 62
A Revision of the Treaty. Toronto: 1922. V. 65
A Treatise on Money.... London: 1930. V. 62; 64; 67
A Treatise on Money.... New York: 1930. V. 65
A Treatise on Probability. London: 1921. V. 64; 65

KEYNES, JOHN NEVILLE
The Scope and Method of Political Economy. London: 1891. V. 64

KEYS, JOHN
A Treatise on the Breeding and Management of Bees, to the Greatest Advantage. London: 1814. V. 63; 64

KEYS, THOMAS E.
The History of Surgical Anesthesia. New York: 1945. V. 64; 66; 67

KEYSERLING, HERMANN, COUNT
Activity Through Silence. 1937. V. 63; 66

KEYSSLER, JOHANN GEORG
Antiquitates Selectae Septentrionaes et Celticae.... Hanover: 1720. V. 64
Travels through Germany, Bohemia, Hungary, Switzerland, Italy and Lorrain. London: 1756-1757. V. 64
Travels through Germany, Bohemia, Hungary, Switzerland, Italy and Lorrain.... London: 1757. V. 67

KHAN-MAGOMEDOV, S. O.
Alexandr Vesnin & Russian Constructivism. New York: 1986. V. 65

KHARMS, DANIEL
Hindrance. New York St. Petersburg: 1998. V. 62

KHATCHATRIANZ, I.
Armenian Folk Tales. Philadelphia: 1946. V. 64

KHERDIAN, DAVID
Homage to Adana. Mt. Horeb: 1970. V. 66

KHOURY, HENEINE B.
Glimpses Behind the Veil. London: 1935. V. 67

KICKNOSWAY, FAYE
The Cat Approaches. Grindstone City: 1978. V. 63

KIDD, J. H.
Personal Recollections of a Cavalryman With Custer's Michigan Cavalry Brigade in the Civil War. Grand Rapids: 1969. V. 65; 67

KIDD, JOHN
On the Adaptation of External Nature to the Physical Condition of Man. London: 1836. V. 67
On the Adaptation of External Nature to the Physical Condition of Man. London: 1852. V. 66

KIDD, SAMUEL
China; or Illustrations of the Symbols, Philosophy, Antiquities, Customs, Superstitions, Laws, Government, Education and Literature. London: 1841. V. 67

KIDD, W.
Kidd's Practical Hints for the Use of Young Carvers.... London: 1836. V. 66

KIDD, WILLIAM
Kidd's Guide to Dundee, Its Streets, Squares, Public Institutions.... Dundee: 1901. V. 62

KIDDER, ALFRED VINCENT
An Introduction to the Study of Southwestern Archaeology, with a Preliminary Account of the Excavations at Pecos. New Haven: 1924. V. 64; 66
Pecos, New Mexico: Archaeological Notes. Andover: 1958. V. 63

KIDDER, D. P.
Brazil and the Brazilians, Portrayed in Historical and Descriptive Sketches. Philadelphia: 1857. V. 62

KIDDER, EDWARD J.
Japanese Temples. Tokyo and Amsterdam: 1964. V. 66

KIDDER, FREDERIC
Military Operations in Easter Main and Nova Scotia During the Revolution....and a memoir of Col. John Allan. Albany: 1867. V. 67

KIDDER, J. EDWARD
Japanese Temples, Sculpture, Paintings, Gardens and Architecture. Tokyo and Amsterdam: 1964?. V. 63

KIDDER, PEABODY & CO. INC.
Ore-Ida Food Inc. New York: 1961. V. 64

KIDD'S Picturesque Pocket Companion to Brighton, Worthing, Bognor, etc. London. V. 66

KIDGELL, JOHN
The Card. London: 1755. V. 62; 65
A Genuine and Succinct Narrative of a Scandalous, Obscene and Exceedingly Profane Libel Entitled, an Essay on Woman, as Also of Other Poetical Pieces, Containing the Most Atrocious Blasphemies.... London: 1763. V. 62

THE KIDNAPPED Clergyman; or Experience the Best Teacher. Boston: 1839. V. 64

KIEFER, WARREN
Lingala Code. New York: 1972. V. 65

KIEFFER, HENRY M.
Some of the First Settlers of "The Forks of the Delaware" & Their Descendants...The First Reformed Church of Easton, Pennsylvania from 1760- 1852. Easton: 1902. V. 65

KIELY, BENEDICT
The Captain with the Whiskers. London: 1960. V. 63
The Cards of the Gambler - a Folktale. London: 1953. V. 63
Dogs Enjoy the Morning - a Novel. London: 1968. V. 63

KIEPERT, HENRY
Atlas Antiquus. Berlin: 1886. V. 63
Atlas Antiquus. Berlin: 1893. V. 64

KIERKEGAARD, SOREN
Af en Endnu Levendes Papirer (From the Papers of One Still Living. On Andersen as a Novelist with Constant Reference to His Work, Only a Fiddler). Copenhagen: 1838. V. 67
Enten-Eller. Copenhagen: 1843. V. 65
Kierkegaard. London: 1955. V. 67

KIERNAN, JOHN
Hints of Horse-Shoeing: Being an Exposition of the Dunbar System, Taught to the Farriers of the United States, Army.... Washington: 1871. V. 66

KIESLER, FREDERICK
Contemporary Art Applied to the Store and Its Display. New York: 1930. V. 66

KIJEWSKI, KAREN
Katapult. New York: 1990. V. 62; 65
Katwalk. New York: 1989. V. 62; 66
Wild Kat. Huntington Beach: 1994. V. 63; 64; 66

KIKUCHI, CHARLES
The Kikuchi Diary: Chronicle from an American Concentration Camp, The Tanforan Journals of Charles Kikuchi. Urbana Chicago London: 1973. V. 64

KIKUCHI, SADAO
A Treasury of Japanese Wood Block Prints Ukiyo-E. New York: 1969. V. 62

KILBY, T.
Original Designs and Sketches from Life by an Amateur. Southampton: 1828. V. 66

KILGOUR, WILLIAM T.
Twenty Years on Ben Nevis. Paisley: 1906. V. 62; 63

KILHMAN, CHARLES
Legend Into History, the Custer Mystery - an Analytical Study of the Battle of the Little Big Horn. Harrisburg: 1952. V. 67

KILLANIN, LORD
The Shell Guide to Ireland. 1971. V. 67

KILLEBREW, J. B.
Tobacco Leaf, Its Culture and Cure, Marketing and Manufacture. New York: 1897. V. 62
Wheat Culture in Tennessee. Nashville: 1877. V. 67

KILLED Without Inquest, the Masonic Tragedy of West Virginia. Chicago: 1890. V. 63

KILLENS, JOHN OLIVER
And Then We Heard the Thunder. New York: 1963. V. 62

KILLICK, JOHN
The Flora of Oxfordshire. Newbury: 1998. V. 67

KILLIGREW, THOMAS
Chit-Chat, a Comedy. As It Is Acted at the Theatre Royal in Drury Lane, by His Majesty's Servants. London: 1719. V. 64

KILLINGLY-GIBBONS, R.
Some Accounts of H. M. Ships in the Old Rivers, Gold Coast, etc. Accra: 1893. V. 63

KILLINGTON, F. J.
A Monograph of the British Neuroptera. London: 1936-1937. V. 63; 64; 66

KILLION, TOM
The Coast of California. Boston: 1988. V. 62; 65
Fortress Marin: An Aesthetic and Historical Description of the Coastal Fortifications of Southern Marin County. N.P: 1977. V. 64
Walls: a Journey Across Three Continents. Santa Cruz: 1990. V. 62; 64

KILLPACK, W. B.
The History and Antiquities of the Collegiate Church of Southwell.... London: 1839. V. 65

KILLPATRICK, JAMES
An Impartial Account of the Late Expedition Against St. Augstine Under General Oglethorpe. London: 1742. V. 66

KILMER, JOYCE
The Circus and Other Essays and Fugitive Pieces. New York: 1921. V. 64; 67
Trees and Other Poems. 1914. V. 67
Trees and Other Poems. New York: 1914. V. 65

KILNER, J.
The Account of Pythagoras's School in Cambridge; as in Mr. Grose's Antiquities of England and Wales, and Other Notices. Cambridge: 1783?. V. 63; 65; 66

KILNER, MARY ANN
Memoirs of a Peg-Top. London: 1790. V. 66

KILPATRICK, FREDERICK JACK
Sequoyah of Earth and Intellect. Austin: 1965. V. 63; 67

KILROE, J. R.
Description of the Soil Geology of Ireland. 1907. V. 67

KILVERT, FRANCIS
The Curate of Clyro: Extracts from the Diary of the Reverend Francis Kilvert. 1983. V. 65
A View of Kilvert: Passages from the Diary.... Glasgow: 1979. V. 62

KIMBALL, CHARLES P.
The San Francisco City Directory, September 1, 1850. San Francisco: 1850. V. 65

KIMBALL, FRANCIS P.
The Capital Region of New York State. New York: 1942. V. 67

KIMBALL, J. P.
Notes on the Geology of Western Texas and of Chihuahua, Mexico. New Haven: 1869. V. 62

KIMBALL, JOHN F.
Kimball and James' Business Directory, for the Mississippi Valley: 1844. Cincinnati: 1844. V. 63

KIMBALL, MARIA B.
A Soldier - Doctor of Our Army - James P. Kimball. Boston: 1917. V. 65; 67

KIMBALL, SOLOMON F.
Life of David P. Kimball and Other Sketches. Salt Lake City: 1918. V. 63

KIMBER, ISAAC
The Life of Oliver Cromwell, Lord Protector of the Common-Wealth. London: 1724. V. 62

KIME, D. E.
Endocrine Disruption in Fish. Boston: 1998. V. 65

KIMES, BEVERLY RAE
Packard, a History of the Motor Car and the Company. New York: 1978. V. 66

KIMES, WILLIAM F.
John Muir: a Reading Bibliography. Palo Alto: 1977. V. 62
John Muir: a Reading Bibliography. Fresno: 1986. V. 62; 63; 65

KIMMELL, J. A.
Twentieth Century History of Findlay and Hancock County, Ohio and Representative Citizens. Chicago: 1910. V. 66

KINAHAN, G. H.
The Geology of Ireland. London: 1878. V. 62
Manual of the Geology of Ireland. 1878. V. 67

KINCAID, JAMAICA
Annie, Gwen, Lilly, Pam and Tulip. New York: 1986. V. 64
Annie, Gwen, Lilly, Pam and Tulip. New York: 1989. V. 63
Annie John. New York: 1985. V. 63
At the Bottom of the River. New York: 1983. V. 62; 63

KINDERLEY, NATHANIEL
The Ancient and Present State of the Navigation of the Towns of Lyn, Wiseach, Spalding and Boston; of the Rivers that Pass through Those Places and the Countries that Border Thereupon, Truly Faithfully, and Impartially Represented. London: 1751. V. 66

KINDERSLEY, JEMIMA
Letters from the Island of Teneriffe, Brazil, the Cape of Good Hope and the East Indies. London: 1777. V. 62

KINDGON WARD, FRANCIS
Plant Hunter's Paradise. London: 1937. V. 67

KINDIG, R. H.
Pictorial Supplement to Denver South Park and Pacific. Denver: 1959. V. 66

KING Albert's Book. A Tribute to the Belgium King and People from Representative Men and Women. London: 1914. V. 64

KING, ALEXANDER W.
An Aubrey Beardsley Lecture. London: 1924. V. 62

THE KING and the Abbot. London: 1875. V. 65

KING, C. W.
Antique Gems: Their Origin, Uses and Value as Interpreters of Ancient History and as Illustrative of Ancient Art with Hints to Gem Collectors. London: 1860. V. 67
The Handbook of Engraved Gems. London: 1866. V. 63
The Natural History, Anicent and Modern of Precious Stones and Gems of the Precious Metals. London: 1865. V. 65
The Natural History of Gems or Decorative Stones. London: 1867. V. 66

KING, CHARLES
The British Merchant; or, Commerce Preserved. London: 1721. V. 64
Campaigning with Crook and Stories of Army Life. New York: 1890. V. 67

KING, CLARENCE
Botany. Washington: 1871. V. 63
Mountaineering in the Sierra Nevada. London: 1947. V. 62; 63; 64

KING, CORETTA SCOTT
My Life with Martin Luther King, Jr. New York: 1969. V. 66

KING, DANIEL
The Vale Royal of England or the County Palatine of Chester Illustrated. London: 1656. V. 62
The Vale Royal of England, or the County Palatine of Chester Illustrated. London: 1852. V. 66

KING, DAVID H.
Catalogue of Master Works by Distinguished Painters of the French, English, Dutch and Flemish Schools.... New York: 1896. V. 65

KING, DOROTHY N.
Count the Kittens. N.P: 1949. V. 64
Santa's Cuckoo Clock. U.S.A: 1954. V. 65

KING, ELIZABETH
Lord Kelvin's Early Home. 1909. V. 67

KING, FRANK M.
Longhorn Trail Drives. Burbank: 1940. V. 66
Mavericks: the Salty Comments of an Old-time Cowpuncher. Pasadena: 1947. V. 66; 67
Pioneer Western Empire Builders - a True Story of the Men and Women of Pioneer Days. Pasadena: 1946. V. 66

KING, G.
A Second Century of New and Rare Indian Plants. Calcutta: 1901. V. 65
The Species of Ficus of the Indo-Malayan and Chinese Countries. 1969. V. 64
The Species of Ficus of the Indo-Malayan and Chinese Countries. Calcutta: 1969. V. 66

KING, HARRIET BARBARA
The Bridal and Other Poems. London: 1844. V. 65

KING, HENRY
Poems. London: 1925. V. 62; 63
Poems and Pslams. Oxford: 1843. V. 62

KING, HENRY C.
The History of the Telescope. Cambridge: 1955. V. 66

KING, J. S.
Keighley Corporation Transport. Huddersfield: 1964. V. 64; 65

KING, JAMES T.
War Eagle - a Life of General Eugene A. Carr. Lincoln: 1963. V. 67

KING, JEFF
Where The Two Came To Their Father: a Navaho War Ceremonial. New York and Princeton: 1943-1991. V. 64
Where the Two Came To Their Father: a Navajo War Ceremonial. Princeton: 1969. V. 64

KING, JESSIE
How Cinderella Was Able to Go to the Ball. London: 1924. V. 64
Kirkcudbright. A Royal Burgh: a Book of Drawings with Letterpress. London: 1934. V. 63

KING, JOHN
The American Family Physician; or, Domestic Guide to Health Arranged in Two Divisions. Indianapolis: 1873. V. 63
Thoughts on the Difficulties and Distresses in Which the Peace of 1783 has Involved the People of England.... London: 1783. V. 64

KING, JOHN H.
The Supernatural: Its Origin, Nature and Evolution. New York: 1892. V. 65

KING, JOHN W.
The China Pilot; the Coasts of China, Korea, and Tartary; the Sea of Japan, Gulf of Tartary and Amur, and Sea of Okhotsk.... London: 1861. V. 67

KING, JOSEPH
W. G. Lawes of Savage Island and New Guinea. London: 1909. V. 67

KING, JOSEPH L.
History of the San Francisco Stock Exchange Board. San Francisco: 1910. V. 64

KING, KATHARINE
The Bubble Reputation. London: 1878. V. 65
Ethel Mildmay's Follies. London: 1872. V. 62
Our Detachment. London: 1875. V. 65
Sweet is True Love. London: 1888. V. 65

KING, LAURIE R.
The Beekeeper's Apprentice. New York: 1994. V. 62; 64; 66; 67
A Grave Talent. New York: 1992. V. 63; 64; 65; 66
A Grave Talent. 1993. V. 66
A Grave Talent. New York: 1993. V. 62; 63; 64
A Grave Talent. London: 1995. V. 62; 64
To Play the Fool. New York: 1995. V. 62

KING, LEONARD W.
A History of Sumer and Akkad, An Account of the Early Races of Babylonia from Prehistoric Times to the Foundation of the Babylonian Monarchy. London: 1910. V. 67

KING, LESTER C.
The Morphology of the Earth. 1967. V. 67

KING, MARTIN LUTHER
Daddy King. An Autobiography. New York: 1980. V. 64; 66
Strength to Love. New York: 1963. V. 67
Stride Toward Freedom. The Montgomery Story. New York: 1958. V. 63; 65; 66
Where Do We Go From Here: Chaos or Community?. New York: 1967. V. 63; 67

KING, MAUDE EGERTON
Round About a Brighton Coach Office. London: 1896. V. 65

KING, MOSES
King's Handbook of New York City. Boston: 1893. V. 66

KING, MURIEL
Let's Play Sailors and W.R.N.S. London: 1943. V. 62

KING, PETER
The Shooting Field. London: 1985. V. 67

KING, R. C.
Insect Ultrastructure. New York: 1984. V. 64

KING, RICHARD
Narrative of a Journey to the Shores of the Arctic Ocean in 1833, 1834 and 1835; Under the Command of Capt. Black, R.N. London: 1836. V. 64

KING, RICHARD JOHN
Handbook to the Cathedrals of England. London: 1861-1869. V. 62; 65

KING, ROSS
Ex-Libris. London: 1998. V. 65

KING, ROY
The World of Curier and Ives. New York: 1968. V. 65

KING, RUFUS
Design in Evil. Garden City: 1942. V. 66

KING, STEPHEN
Carrie. Garden City: 1974. V. 63; 67
Christine. New York: 1983. V. 66
Christine. West Kingston: 1983. V. 67
Danse Macabre. New York: 1981. V. 62; 65; 66
The Dark Half. London: 1989. V. 66
The Dark Half. New York: 1989. V. 66
The Dark Tower II: The Drawing of the Three. Hampton Falls: 1987. V. 66
The Dark Tower II: The Drawing of the Three. West Kingston;: 1987. V. 66
The Dark Tower III: The Wastelands. Hampton Falls: 1991. V. 66; 67
The Dark Tower IV; Wizard and Glass. Hampton Falls: 1997. V. 67
The Dead Zone. New York: 1979. V. 66
Desperation. Hapton Falls: 1996. V. 63
Different Seasons. New York: 1982. V. 66
Dolan's Cadillac. Northridge: 1989. V. 66
The Eyes of the Dragon. Bangor: 1984. V. 62; 64; 66; 67
Fantasy and Science Fiction. New York: 1978-1981. V. 66
Firestarter. New York: 1980. V. 66
Four Past Midnight. New York: 1990. V. 66
Gerald's Game. New York: 1992. V. 63; 66
The Green Mile. Part I. The Two Dead Girls. New York: 1996. V. 62
Insomnia. New York: 1994. V. 63
Insomnia. Shingletown: 1994. V. 67
It. New York: 1986. V. 64
Misery. New York: 1987. V. 66; 67
My Pretty Pony. New York: 1988. V. 65
My Pretty Pony. New York: 1989. V. 66
Needful Things. New York: 1991. V. 63; 66
Night Shift. 1978. V. 64
Night Shift. New York: 1978. V. 62
Nightmares in the Sky: Gargoyles and Grotesques. New York: 1988. V. 66
The Regulators. New York: 1996. V. 63
Rose Madder. New York: 1995. V. 63

KING, STEPHEN continued
Salem's Lot. Garden City: 1975. V. 62; 63; 65; 67
The Shining. Garden City: 1977. V. 62
The Stand. Garden City: 1978. V. 67
The Stand. New York: 1978. V. 65
The Stand. London: 1990. V. 66
The Stand. New York: 1990. V. 66
Storm of the Century. New York: 1999. V. 62
The Talisman. New York: 1984. V. 66
The Talisman. West Kingston & Boston: 1984. V. 62; 67
Thinner. New York: 1984. V. 65; 66
The Tommyknockers. New York: 1987. V. 63; 66

KING, W. J. HARDING
A Search for the Masked Tawareks. London: 1903. V. 67

KING, W. KENT
Massacre - the Custer Cover-Up - The Original Maps of Custer's Battlefield. El Segundo: 2000. V. 67

KING, W. R.
Campaigning in Kaffirland; or Scenes and Adventures in the Kaffir War of 1851-1852. London: 1853. V. 62; 67
The Sportsman and Naturalist in Canada.... London: 1866. V. 65; 67

KING, WILLIAM
The Art of Cookery, in Imitation of Horace's Art of Poetry. London: 1708. V. 66
The Art of Love.... London: 1708. V. 63
Doctor King's Apology, or, Vindication of Himself from the Several Matters Charged on Him by the Society of Informers. Oxford: 1755. V. 66
Epistola Objurgatoria Ad Guilielmum King, LL.D. London: 1744. V. 62
An Historical Account of the Heathen Gods and Heroes.... London: 1750. V. 63
Opera Gul. King. London: 1763. V. 62
Political and Literary Anecdotes of His Own Times. London: 1819. V. 63
The State of the Protestants of Ireland Under the Late King James Government. 1768. V. 66
The State of the Protestants of Ireland Under the Late King James Government. Bagnell, Cork: 1768. V. 63
A Translation of the Latin Epistle in the Dreamer. London: 754. V. 65
Useful Miscellanies; Containing. I. A Preface of the Publisher of the Tragi-Comedy of Joan of Hedington. II. The Tragi-Comedy of Joan of Hedington. III. Some Account of Horace His Behaviour During His Stay at Trinity College, Cambridge.... London: 1712. V. 66
Useful Transactions in Philosophy, and Other Sorts of Learning, for the Months of January and February 1708-1709...for the Month of March and April 1709...for the Months of May, June July, August and September 1709.... London: 1709. V. 66

KING COUNTY MEDICAL SOCIETY, SEATTLE
Constitution and By-Laws of the King County Medical Society, Seattle, Washington. Adopted August 11, 1889. Seattle: 1889. V. 63

KINGDON, J.
East African Mammals. 1971. V. 62; 63; 64; 66
East African Mammals. 1971-1982. V. 62
East African Mammals. London: 1971-1982. V. 66

KINGDON, J. A.
The Strife of the Scales: an Attempt to Explain How the King's Weigh-House and Beams Within the City of London Came Into the Charge of the Worshipful Company of Grocers. London: 1905. V. 62

KINGDON WARD, FRANCIS
Burma's Icey Mountains. London: 1949. V. 64
The Land of the Blue Poppy. Cambridge: 1913. V. 63
The Land of the Blue Poppy. London: 1973. V. 64
Pilgrimage for Plants. 1960. V. 63
Plant Hunter's Paradise. London: 1937. V. 64; 65
Plant Hunting on the Edge of the World. 1930. V. 63
Plant Hunting on the Edge of the World. London: 1930. V. 62
Return to the Irrawaddy. 1956. V. 63
Return to the Irrawaddy. London: 1956. V. 62; 64
The Romance of Plant Hunting. London: 1924. V. 64

KING HALL, EDITH
Adventures in Toyland. London: 1897. V. 67

KINGLAKE, ALEXANDER WILLIAM
Eothen, or Traces of Travel Brought Home from the East. New York: 1845. V. 64; 65
Eothen; or Traces of Travel Brought Home from the East. London: 1913. V. 64
The Invasion of the Crimea; Its Origin and an Account of Its Progress Down to the Death of Lord Raglan. Edinburgh and London: 1877. V. 63

KINGLAKE, WILLIAM
A Translation of the Latin Epistle in the Dreamer. London: 1845. V. 62

KINGLE, ROGER D.
The Complete Encyclopedia of Popular Music and Jazz 1900-1950. New Rochelle: 1974. V. 64

KINGMAN, LEE
Ilenka. Boston: 1945. V. 63
The Magic Christmas Tree. New York: 1956. V. 66

KINGSFORD, WILLIAM
The Canadian Canals: their History and Cost, with an Inquiry into the Policy Necessary to Advance the Well-Being of the Province. Toronto: 1865. V. 63

KINGSLEY, CHARLES
Alton Locke, Tailor and Poet. London: 1850. V. 65
Alton Locke, Tailor and Poet. London: 1851. V. 65
The Application of Associative Principles and Methods to Agriculture: a Lecture, Delivered on Behalf of the Society for Promoting Working Men's Associations on Wednesday May 28, 1851. London: 1851. V. 64
At Last: a Christmas in the West Indies. New York: 1871. V. 65
From Death to Life: Fragments of Teaching to a Village Congregation with Letters on the Life After Death. London: 1887. V. 65
Glaucus; or the Wonders of the Shore. Cambridge: 1855. V. 65
Glaucus; or, the Wonders of the Shore. London: 1859. V. 65; 66
Glaucus; or, the Wonders of the Shore. London: 1890. V. 62
The Heroes; or, Greek Fairy Tales for My Children. Cambridge: 1855. V. 62; 63
Miscellanies. London: 1860. V. 65
Out of the Deep. London: 1880. V. 65
Out of the Deep. London: 1885. V. 65
Prose Idylls, New and Old. London: 1884. V. 65
The Saint's Tragedy; or the True Story of Elizabeth Hungary, Landravine of Thuringia, Saint of the Romish Calendar. London: 1848. V. 64; 65
The Water Babies. London: 1863. V. 65
The Water Babies. London: 1886. V. 65
The Water Babies. London: 1898. V. 62
The Water Babies. London: 1916. V. 65; 66
The Water Babies. New York: 1916. V. 63
The Water Babies. London: 1935. V. 64
The Water Babies. London: 1961. V. 65
Westward Ho!. New York: 1947. V. 62; 64
Yeast: a Problem. London: 1851. V. 65; 66

KINGSLEY, HENRY
Austin Elliot. London: 1863. V. 67
The Recollections of Geoffry Hamlyn. Cambridge: 1859. V. 63; 67

KINGSLEY, J. S.
Nature's Wonderland or Short Talks on Natural History for Young and Old. New York: 1891. V. 63; 64
The Standard Natural History. Boston: 1884-1885. V. 66

KINGSLEY, MARY H.
West African Studies. 1899. V. 62; 63; 64; 66

KINGSLEY, ZEPHANIAH
A Treatise on the Patriarchal, or Co-Operative System of Society as It Exists in some Governments and Colonies in America, and in the United States, Under the Name of Slavery with Its Necessity and Advantages. Tallahassee: 1829. V. 63; 66

KINGSOLVER, BARBARA
Animal Dreams. New York: 1990. V. 62; 63; 64; 67
Another America. Seattle: 1992. V. 62; 63; 64; 66
The Bean Trees. New York: 1988. V. 62; 63; 65; 66; 67
The Bean Trees. London: 1989. V. 62; 64; 65; 66
High Tide in Tucson. New York: 1995. V. 62; 64; 67
Holding the Line. Ithaca: 1989. V. 62; 63; 64; 66; 67
Homeland. New York: 1989. V. 62; 63; 64; 65; 66; 67
Pigs in Heaven. New York: 1993. V. 63
The Poisonwood Bible. New York: 1998. V. 63; 66; 67
Prodigal Summer. New York: 2000. V. 66

KINGSTON, ALFRED
Hertfordshire During the Great Civil War and the Long Parliament. London: 1894. V. 63

THE KINGSTON
Atlantis; or, Woodward's Miscellany. London: 1731. V. 62

KINGSTON, ELIZABETH PIERREPOINT, DOWAGER DUCHESS OF
The Trial of Elizabeth Duchess Dowager of Kingston for Digamy, Before the Right Honourable the House of Peers in Westminster-Hall...April 1776. London: 1776. V. 62

KINGSTON, JAMAICA. CHAMBER OF COMMERCE - 1780
Minutes of the Proceedings of the Chamber of Commerce, at Kingston in Jamaica. Kingston: 1780. V. 62

KINGSTON, MAXINE HONG
China Men. New York: 1980. V. 63

KINGSTON, WILLIAM H. G.
In the Wilds of Florida. London: 1880. V. 63
Marmaduke Merry the Midshipman or My Early Days At Sea. London: 1864. V. 65
Saved from the Sea; or, The Loss of the "Viper" and the Adventures of Her Crew in the Great Sahara. London: 1876. V. 65
The Three Lieutenants; or Naval Life in the Nineteenth Century. London: 1878. V. 67
Western Wanderings; or, a Pleasure Tour in the Canadas. London: 1856. V. 67

KINHARDT, DOROTHY
Little Ones. New York: 1935. V. 66

KINKLE, ROGER D.
The Complete Encyclopedia of Popuar Music and Jazz. New Rochelle: 1974. V. 63; 65; 67

KINLOCH, A. A. A.
Large Game Shooting in Thibet and the North West. 1869. V. 62; 63
Large Game Shooting in Thibet and the North West. London: 1869. V. 64
Large Game Shooting in Thibet, the Himalayas, Northern and Central India. 1892. V. 67

KINLOCH, ARCHIBALD GORDON
The Trial of Sir Archibald Gordon Kinloch, of Gilmerton, Bart. for the Murder of Sir Francis Knloch, Bart, his Brother-German. Edinburgh: 1795. V. 63

KINMONT, ALEXANDER
Twelve Lectures on the Natural History of Man and the Rise and Progress of Philosophy. Cincinnati: 1839. V. 66

KINNAIRD, LAWRENCE
History of the Greater San Francisco Bay Region. New York: 1966. V. 63

KINNEAR, GEORGE
Anti-Chinese Riots at Seatte (sic), WN. February 8th, 1886. Seattle: 1911. V. 66

KINNEAR, JOHN
The Trial of John Kinnear, Lewis Levy and Mozely Woolf, Indicted with John Meyer and Others, for a Conspiracy at Guildhall, London, Before Lord Chief Justice Abbott, and a Special Jury, on the 20th and 21st Days of April 1819. London: 1819. V. 64

KINNEIR, DAVID BAYNE
A New Essay on the Nerves, and the Doctrine of Animal Spirits Rationally Considered. London: 1739. V. 63; 67

KINNELL, GALWAY
The Avenue Bearing the Initial of Christ into the New World. Poems 1946-1964. Boston: 1974. V. 63
Black Light. Boston: 1966. V. 63
Body Rags. Boston: 1968. V. 63
The Book of Nightmares. Boston: 1971. V. 63
First Poems 1946-1954. Mt. Horeb: 1970. V. 64
Flower Herding on Mount Momadnock. Boston: 1964. V. 63
The Fundamental Project of Technology. Concord: 1983. V. 63
The Hen Flower. Frensham, Farnham, Surrey: 1969. V. 62; 63
How the Alligator Missed Breakfast. Boston: 1982. V. 63; 65
The Last Hiding Places of Snow. Madison: 1980. V. 67
The Mind. Concord: 1984. V. 62
Mortal Acts, Mortal Words. Boston: 1980. V. 62
The Past. Boston: 1985. V. 63; 64
Remarks on Accepting the American Book Award for Poetry...April 28th, 1983. Concord: 1984. V. 63
The Seekonk Woods. Concord: 1985. V. 63
Selected Poems. Boston: 1982. V. 63
There Are Things I Tell to No One. New York: 1979. V. 63
Two Poems. New York: 1981. V. 66
What a Kingdom It Was. Boston: 1960. V. 63

KINNEY, J. KENDRICK
A Law Dictionary and Glossary. Chicago: 1893. V. 64

KINSELLA, THOMAS
Another September. 1958. V. 65; 67
Another September. Dublin: 1958. V. 62; 64
Downstream. 1962. V. 65
Downstream. London: 1962. V. 63
The Good Fight - a Poem for the Tenth Anniversary of the Death of John F. Kennedy. Dublin: 1973. V. 62
Her Vertical Smile. Dublin: 1985. V. 64
The Messenger. Dublin: 1978. V. 64
Nightwalker. 1967. V. 64
Nightwalker. 1968. V. 67
Notes from the Land of the Dead. 1972. V. 64
Notes from the Land of the Dead. Dublin: 1972. V. 63
One. Dublin: 1974. V. 63
Poems and Translations. New York: 1961. V. 63
A Selected Life. Dublin: 1972. V. 63
Song of the Night and Other Poems. Dublin: 1978. V. 64
Songs of the Psyche. Dublin: 1985. V. 64
Tear. Cambridge: 1969. V. 62
A Technical Supplement. Dublin: 1976. V. 64
Thomas Kinsella. Cecil King. West Germany: 1981. V. 64
The Train. London and New York: 1970. V. 62; 64
Vertical Man: a Sequel to a Selected Life. Dublin: 1973. V. 63
Wormwood. 1966. V. 64
Wormwood. Dublin: 1966. V. 63

KINSELLA, W. P.
Dance Me Outside. 1977. V. 65
The First and Last Annual Six Towns Area Old Timers' Baseball Game. Minneapolis: 1991. V. 64
The Iowa Baseball Confederacy. Boston: 1986. V. 62; 63; 64; 66
Shoeless Joe. Boston: 1982. V. 62; 64; 65; 66; 67

KINSEY, ALFRED
Sexual Behavior in the Human Male. Philadelphia: 1948. V. 63

KINSEY, CHARLES
Abridgment of Decisions of the Supreme Court of New Jersey, on Certiorari to Courts for the Trial of Small Causes. From May Term 1806 to February Term 1813, Inclusive. Burlington: 1815. V. 63; 66

KINSEY, WILLIAM MORGAN
Portugal Illustrated: in a Series of Letters. London: 1829. V. 62; 66

KINYON, EDWARD
The Northern Mines - Where Swept the Upper Tide of the Gold Rush. Grass Valley, Nevada City: 1949. V. 63

KINZIE, JULIETTE A.
Wau-Bun, the Early Days in the Northwest. New York: 1856. V. 66

KIP, JOANNES
Nouveau Theatre de la Grande Bretagne. London: 1724. V. 64

KIP, LAURENCE
Army Life on the Pacific - a Journal of the Expedition Against the Northern Indians - The Tribes of the Coeur d'Alenes, Spokans and Pelouses in the Summer 1858. New York: 1859. V. 65; 67

KIP, WILLIAM INGRAHAM
Early Days of My Episcopate. New York: 1892. V. 63; 66

KIPLING, RUDYARD
Barrack-Room Ballads and Other Verses. London: 1892. V. 62; 67
The Brushwood Boy. London: 1910. V. 67
Captains Courageous. London: 1897. V. 66
Captains Courageous. New York: 1897. V. 62; 65
The Collected Works. New York: 1941. V. 62; 64; 67
The Day's Work. London: 1898. V. 63; 64; 66
Debits and Credits. London: 1926. V. 63
Departmental Ditties. Lahore: 1886. V. 65
Departmental Ditties. Calcutta: 1890. V. 67
Departmental Ditties. Calcutta: 1891. V. 67
Departmental Ditties. Calcutta: 1895. V. 67
Departmental Ditties, Barrack Room Ballads and Other Verses. New York: 1890. V. 62
A Diversity of Creatures. London: 1917. V. 63
The Five Nations. London: 1903. V. 67
A Fleet in Being. Notes of Two Trips with the Channel Squadron. London: 1898. V. 63
40 Nord 50 Vest. (40 North 50 West). Moscow - Leningrad: 1931. V. 64
From Sea to Sea. New York: 1899. V. 62; 63; 64; 66; 67
From Sea to Sea. London: 1900. V. 66
Histoires Comme ca Pour Les Petits. (Just So Stories). Paris: 1934. V. 63
In Black and White. Allahabad: 1888. V. 62
Independence. Rectorial Address. London: 1923. V. 63
The Jungle Book. (with) The Second Jungle Book. London: 1894-1895. V. 63; 64; 65
The Light That Failed. London: 1890. V. 62
Many Inventions. London: 1893. V. 67
Many Inventions. New York: 1893. V. 63
The Naulahka. A Story of West and East. London: 1892. V. 63
The Phantom Rickshaw and Other Eerie Tales. London. V. 62
Plain Tales from the Hills. London: 1889. V. 65
Puck of Pook's Hill. London: 1906. V. 62; 64
Rewards and Fairies. Garden City: 1910. V. 64; 66
Rudyard Kipling's Verse Inclusive Edition 1885-1918. London: 1919. V. 62; 63; 64; 67
Sea and Sussex, from Rudyard Kipling's Verse. London: 1926. V. 62
Sea Warfare. London: 1916. V. 64; 65
The Second Jungle Book. London: 1895. V. 63
The Servant A Dog. London: 1930. V. 63
The Seven Seas. London: 1896. V. 63; 67
Soldier Tales. London and New York: 1896. V. 62; 64
Something of Myself for My Friends Known and Unknown. London: 1973. V. 63
Stalky and Co. London: 1899. V. 63; 67
The Sussex Edition of the Complete Works in Prose and Verse. Volume One only. London: 1937. V. 63
They. London: 1905. V. 67
Toomai of the Elephants. London: 1937. V. 67
Traffics and Discoveries. London: 1904. V. 63; 64
Twenty Poems from Rudyard Kipling. London: 1918. V. 64
The War in the Mountains. Garden City: 1917. V. 67
With the Night Mail. New York: 1909. V. 63
The Works. Garden City: 1925. V. 64

KIPPIS, ANDREW
The Life of Captain James Cook. London: 1788. V. 66
A Sermon Preached at the Old Jewry, on the Fourth of November 1788, Before the Society for Commemorating the Glorious Revolution.... London: 1788. V. 67

KIRA, ALEXANDER
Bathroom. New York: 1976. V. 67

KIRBY, JACK
Heroes and Villains. New York: 1987. V. 67

KIRBY, JOHN
The Capacity and Extent of the Human Understanding, Exemplified in the Extraordinary Case of Automathes, a Younge Nobleman, Who Was Accidentally Left in His Infancy, Upon a Desolate Island.... Dublin: 1746. V. 62
The Suffolk Traveller. Ipswich: 1735. V. 63
The Suffolk Traveller. 1764. V. 65

KIRBY, JOSHUA
Dr. Brook Taylor's Method of Perspective Made Easy, Both in Theory and Practice. Ipswich: 1755. V. 62

KIRBY, M.
Birds of Gay Plumage: Sun Birds. 1875. V. 62; 63; 64; 66; 67

KIRBY, M. continued
The Talking Bird.... London: 1856. V. 67

KIRBY, R. G.
Mexican Landscape Architecture: from the Street and From Within. 1972. V. 65

KIRBY, R. S.
The Wonderful and Scientific Museum; or, Magazine of Remarkable Characters.... London: 1803-1815. V. 66

KIRBY, WILLIAM
On the Power Wisdom and Goodness of God as Manifested in the Creation of Animals and In Their History Habits and Instincts. London: 1835. V. 67

KIRBY, WILLIAM F.
European Butterflies and Moths. 1882. V. 65; 66
European Butterflies and Moths. London: 1882. V. 62; 66
European Butterflies and Moths. London: 1889. V. 62
Handbook to the Order Lepidoptera. London: 1896-1897. V. 62; 64
An Introduction to Entomology. London: 1815-1826. V. 62
An Introduction to Entomology. 1816-1826. V. 63
An Introduction to Entomology. London: 1828. V. 65; 66
An Introduction to Entomology. London: 1857. V. 67
An Introduction to Entomology. London: 1858. V. 62

KIRCHER, ATHANASIUS
(Mundus Subterraneus). D'Vonder-Aardse Weereld in Haar Goddelijk Maaakel en Wonderbare Uitwerkselen Aller Dingen. Amsterdam: 1682. V. 64
Romani Collegii Societatis Jesu Musaeum Celeberrimum, Cujus Magnum Antiquariae Rei, Statuarum, Imaginum, Picturarumque Partem.... Amsterdam: 1678. V. 65

KIRK, ROBERT
The Secret Commonwealth of Elves, Fauns, and Fairies: a Study in Folk-Lore and Psychical Research. London: 1893. V. 65

KIRK, RUSSELL
Edmund Burke, a Genius Reconsidered. New Rochelle: 1967. V. 67
St. Andrews. London: 1954. V. 65

KIRK, T.
The Forest Flora of New Zealand. Wellington: 1889. V. 62; 65

KIRKBRIDE, JOHN
The Northern Angler, or Fly-Fisher's Companion. 1840. V. 67

KIRKBY, JOHN
Arithmetical Institutions Containing a Compleat System of Arithmetic Natural, Logarithmical and Algebraical In All their Branches.... London: 1735. V. 65

KIRKER, H.
California's Architectural Frontier: Style and Tradition in the 19th Century. 1960. V. 65

KIRKHAM, NELLIE
Derbyshire Lead Mining through the Centuries. Truro: 1968. V. 63

KIRKLAND, CAROLINE MATILDA STANSBURY
The Evening Book. New York: 1853. V. 63; 65
Forest Life. New York: 1842. V. 63; 66
A New Home - Who'll Follow?. New York: 1840. V. 62

KIRKLAND, JOHN
The Modern Baker Confectioner and Caterer. London: 1924. V. 67

KIRKLAND, THOMAS
Observations Upon Mr. Pott's General Remarks on Fractures &c. (with) An Appendix to the Observations.... London: 1770-1771. V. 65
A Treatise on Child-Bed Fevers, and On the Methods of Preventing Them. London: 1774. V. 65

KIRKMAN, F. B.
The British Bird Book. London: 1911-1913. V. 66
British Sporting Birds. London: 1924. V. 67
British Sporting Birds. London: 1936. V. 67

KIRKMAN, JAMES THOMAS
Memoirs of the Life of Charles Macklin, Esq. London: 1799. V. 63; 64, 66

KIRKPATRICK, B. J.
A Bibliography of Edmund Blunden. Oxford: 1979. V. 67
A Bibliography of Virginia Woolf. Oxford: 1980. V. 62

KIRKPATRICK, JOHN ERVIN
Timothy Flint: Pioneer, Missionary, Author, Editor 1780-1840. Cleveland: 1911. V. 64; 66

KIRKPATRICK, T. W.
The Mosquitoes of Egypt. Cairo: 1925. V. 66

KIRKPATRICK, THOMAS JEFFERSON, MRS.
Modern Cook Book. Springfield: 1890. V. 67

KIRKPATRICK, W. T.
Alpine Days and Nights. London: 1932. V. 66

KIRKUP, JAMES
Scenes from Sesshu. 1977. V. 66
The Submerged Village and Other Poems. London: 1951. V. 67

KIRKUS, A. M.
Robert Gibbings, a Bibliography. 1962. V. 64

KIRKWOOD, JAMES
A Chorus Line. New York: 1995. V. 66

KIRSCH, ABBY GAIL
Teen Cuisine. New York: 1969. V. 67

KIRSTEIN, L.
Elie Nadelman. New York: 1973. V. 62; 65

KIRSTEIN, LINCOLN
The Photographs of Henri Cartier-Bresson. New York: 1947. V. 64

KIRSTEN, L.
Tchelitchev. 1994. V. 65

KIRWAN, JOSEPH
A Descriptive and Historical Account of the Liverpool and Manchester Railway.... Glasgow: 1831. V. 62

KIRWAN, L. P.
The White Road. A Survey of Polar Exploration. London: 1959. V. 64

KIRWAN, RICHARD
Elements of Mineralogy. London: 1784. V. 63
The Manures Most Advantageously Applicable to the Various Sorts of Soils and the Causes of Their Beneficial Effect in Each Particular Instance. London: 1796. V. 62

KIRWIN, A. D.
Johnny Green of the Orphan Brigade. Lexington: 1956. V. 62

KISCH, MARTIN S.
Letters and Sketches from Northern Nigeria. London: 1910. V. 62

KISHINOUYE, K.
Contributions to the Comparative Study of the So-Called Scombroid Fishes. Tokyo: 1923. V. 63

KISSINGER, HENRY
The Troubled Partnership: a Reappraisal of the Atlantic Alliance. New York: 1965. V. 63
The White House Years. Boston: 1979. V. 63
The White House Years. London: 1979. V. 65
Years of Upheaval. Boston: 1982. V. 63

THE KIT Book for Soldiers, Sailors and Marines. Chicago: 1943. V. 63; 64

KITCHENER, H. H.
Photographs of Biblical Sites. London: 1874-1878. V. 63; 66

KITCHIN, C. H. B.
The Book of Life. London: 1960. V. 66
Steamers Waving. London: 1925. V. 63; 65
Ten Pollitt Place. London: 1957. V. 66

KITCHIN, T.
The Artists Assistant in Drawing, Perspecive (sic), Etching, Engraving, Mezzotint Scraping, Paining on Glass, in Crayons, in Water-Colours and on Silks and Satins.... London: 1775. V. 63

KITCHINER, WILLIAM
Cook's Oracle. Edinburgh and London: 1821. V. 66
The Cook's Oracle. Boston: 1822. V. 63
The Cook's Oracle. London: 1829. V. 67
Cook's Oracle. New York: 1830. V. 66
The Cook's Oracle. 1831. V. 62
The Cook's Oracle. London: 1831. V. 63
The Economy of the Eyes.... London: 1824. V. 63
The Housekeeper's Oracle; or the Art of Domestic Management.... London: 1829. V. 62; 66
The Traveller's Oracle, or Maxims for Locomotion.. London: 1826-1827. V. 62; 67

KITE, OLIVER
A Fisherman's Diary. 1969. V. 67
Nymph Fishing in Practice. 1963. V. 63

KITELEY, BRIAN
I Know Many Songs, But I Cannot Sing. New York: 1996. V. 67

KITT, FRED J.
Minor Rhymes in Mining Times. Whitley Bay: 1904. V. 64

KITTENBURGER, KALAMAN
Big Game Hunting and Collected in East Africa 1903-1926. London: 1929. V. 67

KITTO, JOHN V.
The Accounts of the Churchwardens of St. Martin-in-the-Fields 1525- 1605. London: 1901. V. 62

KITTON, FREDERIC GEORGE
Charles Dickens by Pen and Pencil. With A Supplement to Charles Dickens by Pen and Pencil. London: 1890. V. 62

KITTREDGE, WILLIAM
A Hole in the Sky. New York: 1992. V. 66
Lost Cowboys (but not forgotten). New York: 1992. V. 64
We Are Not in This Together. Port Townsend: 1984. V. 62

KITZINGER, E.
Byzantine Art in the Making: Main Lines of Stylistic Development in Mediterranean Art, 3rd-7th Century. Cambridge: 1977. V. 65

KIU TAI YU
Time in Pocket. Hong Kong: 1992. V. 67

KIZER, CAROLYN
The Ungrateful Garden. Bloomington: 1961. V. 63; 66

KJAERBOLLING, NIELS
Ornithologia Danica. Danmarks Fugle i 304 Afbildninger af de Gamle Hamner. (with) *rnithological Danica. Danmarks Fugle i 252 Afbildninger af de Dragtskiftende....* Copenhagen: 1854. V. 67

KLAH, HASTEEN
Navajo Creation Myth. The Story of the Emergence. Santa Fe: 1942. V. 62

KLAPP, H. MINOR
Krider's Sporting Anecdotes, Illustrative of the Habits of Certain Varieties of American Game. Philadelphia: 1853. V. 63; 66

KLAPROTH, JULIUS VON
Travels in the Caucasus and Georgia; Performed in the Years 1807 and 1808, by Command of the Russian Government.... London: 1814. V. 67

KLAPROTH, MARTIN HENRY
Observations Relative to the Mineralogical and Chemical History of the Fossils of Cornwall. London: 1787. V. 65

KLAUBER, L. M.
Rattlesnakes, Their Habits, Life Histories, and Influence on Mankind. Berkeley: 1956. V. 65; 66
Rattlesnakes, Their Habits, Life Histories and Influence on Mankind. Berkeley: 1997. V. 63

KLAUER KLATTOWSKY, WILHELM
The German Manual for Self Tuition. London: 1831. V. 67

KLAVAN, ANDREW
Face of the Earth. New York: 1980. V. 67
The Scarred Man. New York: 1990. V. 67

KLEE, PAUL
The Inward Vision: Watercolors, Drawings and Writings. New York: 1959. V. 62; 65
Pedagogical Sketchbook. London: 1953. V. 66

KLEIN, ADRIAN BERNARD
Colour-Music, the Arat of Light. London: 1926. V. 64

KLEIN, D.
In the Deco Style. New York: 1986. V. 65

KLEIN, JACOB THEODOR
Stemmata Avivm. Lipsiae: 1759. V. 64; 66

KLEIN, WILLIAM
New York: Life is Good and Good for You in New York Trance Witness Reveals. Paris: 1956. V. 66
Torino '90. Milano: 1990. V. 67

DAS KLEINE Lust-Gartlein Oder Schone Auserlesener Gebeter und Lieder zum Gebrauch der Jugend, Sowohol in der Schule als zu Hause. Canto: 1824. V. 64

KLEINGROTHE, C. J.
Malay Peninsula.... Singapore: 1920. V. 62

KLEINZAHLER, AUGUST
A Calendar of Airs. Toronto: 1978. V. 66
On Johnny's Time. Durham: 1988. V. 66

KLEIST, FRANZ ALEXANDER VON
Sappho. Ein Dramatisches Gedicht. Berlin: 1793. V. 63; 66

KLEMP, EGON
America in Maps Dating from 1500 to 1856. New York: 1976. V. 63

KLETT, MARK
Revealing Territory: Photographs of the Southwest. Albuquerque: 1992. V. 63; 65

KLEY, HEINRICH
Sammel-Album. Munchen: 1930. V. 65

KLINE, OTIS ADELBERT
The Planet of Peril. N.P: 1929. V. 67

KLINEFELTER, WALTER
Ex Libris A. Conan Doyle, Sherlock Holmes. Chicago: 1938. V. 67

KLINGER, FREDRICH MAXIMILIAN VON
Travels Before the Flood, an Interesting Oriental Record of Men and Manners in the Antediluvian World.... London: 1797. V. 65

KLINGSBERG, HARRY
Doowinkle, D. A. New York: 1940. V. 67

KLIPPART, JOHN H.
The Wheat Plant: Its Origin, Culture, Growth, Development, Composition, Varieties, Diseases, Etc. Etc. Cincinnati: 1860. V. 62; 64

KLOPSTOCK, FRIEDRICH
Memoirs of Frederick and Margaret Klopstock. Bath: 1808. V. 63; 66
The Messiah. Elizabeth Town: 1788. V. 67

KLOSOVSKII, B. N.
Blood Circulation in the Brain. Jerusalem: 1963. V. 64; 67

KLOSS, C. BODEN
In the Andamans and Nicobars; the Narrative of a Cruise in the Schooner Terrapin.... London: 1903. V. 62; 67

KLOSS, GENE
Gene Kloss Etchings. Santa Fe: 1981. V. 66

KLOSS, PHILIPS
The Great Kiva: a Poetic Critique of Religion. Santa Fe: 1980. V. 66

KLOSSOWSKI, PIERRE
Sade Mon Prochaine. Paris: 1947. V. 67

KLUCKHORN, CLYDE
To the Foot of the Rainbow. London: 1928. V. 63; 65

KLUNZINGER, C. B.
Die Korallthiere des Rothen Meeres. Berlin: 1877-1879. V. 62

KLUVER, HEINRICH
Mescal. London: 1928. V. 66

KNAPP, A. W.
Cocoa and Chocolate, Their History from Plantation to Consumer. London: 1920. V. 64

KNAPP, DAVID
The Confederate Horseman. New York: 1966. V. 63

KNAPP, GEORG FRIEDRICH
The State Theory of Money. London: 1924. V. 63; 65

KNAPP, JOHN LEONARD
The Journal of a Naturalist. London: 1829. V. 64

KNAPP, TRACEY
Match in a Bottle. North Andover: 1997. V. 62

KNATCHBULL-HUGESSEN, E. H.
Higgledy-Piggledy. London: 1875. V. 65
The Mountain Sprite's Kingdom and Other Stories. London: 1881. V. 63

KNAUSS, WILLIAM H.
The Story of Camp Chase. Nashville: 1906. V. 62; 63

KNAUSS, ZANE
Conversations with Jazz Musicians, Volume II. Detroit: 1977. V. 65; 67

KNEEDLER, H. S.
Through Storyland to Sunset Seas. Chicago: 1895. V. 62; 65
Through Storyland to Sunset Seas. Cincinnati: 1896. V. 63; 65

KNEELAND, SAMUEL
The Wonders of the Yosemite. 1872. V. 65
The Wonders of the Yosemite Valley and of California. Boston and New York: 1872. V. 63

KNEVELS, GERTRUDE
Out of the Dark. Philadelphia: 1932,. V. 67

KNIBBS, S. G.
The Savage Solomons: as They Were and Are. London: 1929. V. 67

THE KNICKERBOCKER Gallery: a Testimonial to the Editor of the Knickerbocker Magazine. New York: 1855. V. 64

KNIFFIN, GILBERT C.
Assault and Capture of Lookout Mountain. Washington: 1895. V. 66

KNIGHT, ARTHUR WINFIELD
The Beat Book - the Unspeakable Visions of the Individual - Volume 4. 1974. V. 65

KNIGHT, C. MORLEY
Hints on Driving. London: 1895. V. 67

KNIGHT, CHARLES
Capital and Labour, Including the Results of Machinery. London: 1845. V. 67
Essays on Practical Education, Selected from the Works of Ascham, Milton, Locke and Butler &c. London: 1835. V. 64
Knight's Dictionary of Arts, Commerce and Manufactures. London: 1851. V. 64
Knowledge is Power: a View of the Productive Forces of Modern Society, and the Results of Labour, Capital and Skill. London: 1855. V. 64
London. London: 1841-1844. V. 63; 66
Mind Amongst the Spindles. London: 1844. V. 62
Old England: a Pictorial Museum of Regal, Ecclesiastical, Municipal, Baronial and Popular Antiquities. London. V. 66
Old England, a Pictorial Museum of Regal, Ecclesiastical, Municipal, Baronial and Popular Antiquities. London: 1844. V. 63
Old England: a Pictorial Museum of Regal, Ecclesiatical, Baronial, Municipal, and Popular Antiquities. London: 1845. V. 63; 66
The Old Printer and the Modern Press. London: 1854. V. 62; 65
Once Upon a Time. London: 1854. V. 67
Passages of a Working Life During Half a Century: with a Prelude of Early Reminiscences. London: 1864. V. 62; 65; 66
Passages of a Working Life During Half a Century: with Prelude of Early Reminiscences. London: 1864-1865. V. 66
Shadows of the Old Booksellers. London: 1865. V. 65
William Caxton the First English Printer: a Biography. London: 1844. V. 67
The Windsor Guide, with a Brief Account of Eton. Windsor: 1825. V. 67
The Working-Man's Companion. London: 1831. V. 66

KNIGHT, E. F.
With the Royal Tour; a Narrative of the Recent Tour of the Duke and Duchess of Cornwall and York. London: 1902. V. 67

KNIGHT, ELLIS CORNELIA
Autobiography of Miss Cornelia Knight, Lady Companion to the Princess Charlotte of Wales. London: 1861. V. 65
A Description of Latium or la Campagna di Roma, with Etchings by Author. London: 1805. V. 62; 66
Dinarbas, a Tale. London: 1790. V. 62; 64

KNIGHT, K. W.
The Book of the Rabbit.... London: 1889. V. 62

KNIGHT, O. W.
The Birds of Maine. Bangor: 1908. V. 67

KNIGHT, OLIVER
Following the Indian Wars. The Story of the Newspaper Correspondents Among the Indian Campaigners. Norman: 1960. V. 67

KNIGHT, RICHARD PAYNE
An Analytical Essay on the Greek Alphabet. London: 1791. V. 64; 66
The Landscape; a Didactic Poem. London: 1794. V. 66
The Progress of Civil Society. London: 1796. V. 62

KNIGHT, T. A.
On the Origin and Office of the Alburnum of Trees (and) On the Inconvertibility of Bark into Alburnum. London: 1808. V. 63
Pomona Herefordiensis. London: 1811. V. 62
A Treatise on the Culture of the Apple and Pear, and on the Manufacture of Cider and Perry. Ludlow: 1809. V. 65

KNIGHT, THOMAS IRELAND
An Exact Abridgement in English of all the Reports of that Learned and Reverend Judge Sir James Dyer Knight. London: 1651. V. 63

KNIGHT, WILLIAM
Lord Monboddo and Some of His Contemporaries. London: 1900. V. 66
Through the Wordsworth Country. London: 1887. V. 66

KNIGHT, WILLIAM HENRY
Diary of a Pedestrian in Cashmere and Thibet. London: 1863. V. 62; 67

KNIGHT, WYNTER E.
Early Lost, Late Found. London: 1884. V. 67

KNIGHTS *Cyclopaedia of Manufactures....* London: 1851. V. 62

KNIGHT'S *Tourist's Companion through the Land We Live In.* London: 1853. V. 62

KNOBEL, F.
Field Key to the Land Birds. Boston: 1899. V. 67

KNOLLES, RICHARD
The Generall Historie of the Turkes, from the First Beginning of that Nation.... London: 1638. V. 64
The Turkish History, Comprehending the Origin of that Nation and the Growth of the Othoman Empire.... London: 1701. V. 64; 66

KNOPF, ADOLPH
The Mother Lode System of California. Washington: 1929. V. 64

KNOPF, F. I.
Ecology and Conservation of Great Plains Vertebrates. New York: 1997. V. 64

KNOPF, S. ADOLPHUS
Birth Control In its Medical, Social, Economic and Moral Aspects. New York: 1919. V. 67

KNORR, EMIL
Die Polnischen Ausstände seit 1830 in ihrem Zusammenhange mit den Internationalen Emsturzbestrebungen. Berlin: 1880. V. 63

KNORR, G. W.
Vergnugen der Augen und des Gemuths...Sammlung von Muscheln. Nuremburg: 1757-1772. V. 62

KNOTT, CARGILL GILSTON
Life and Scientific Work of Peter Guthrie Tait. Cambridge: 1911. V. 63

KNOTT, J. F.
An Essay on the Pathology of the Oesophagus. Dublin: 1878. V. 67

KNOWER, DANIEL
The Adventures of a Forty-Niner. Albany: 1894. V. 64; 67

KNOWLES, E. H.
The Castle of Kenilworth. A Hand-Book for Visitors. Warwick: 1872. V. 64

KNOWLES, HORACE J.
Countryside Treasures. 1946. V. 64; 67

KNOWLES, JAMES S.
The Dramatic Works. 1841. V. 62; 65
The Dramatic Works. 1859. V. 67
The Wife: a Tale of Mantua. (and) The Beggar of Bethnal Green. 1833-1834. V. 62

KNOWLES, JOHN
A Separate Peace. New York: 1960. V. 63; 65

KNOWLES, R. B. SHERIDAN
Glencoonoge. 1891. V. 65

KNOWLTON, CHARLES
Fruits of Philosophy. Sheffield: 1878. V. 65

KNOWLTON, ELIZABETH
The Naked Mountain. London: 1933. V. 64
The Naked Mountain. London: 1934. V. 63

KNOX, A. E.
Autumns on the Spey. 1872. V. 67

KNOX, CHARLES H.
Harry Mowbray. London: 1843. V. 65
Softness: a Novel. London: 1842. V. 65

KNOX, E. V.
Blue Feathers. London: 1929. V. 67

KNOX, GEORGE
Catalogue of the Tiepolo Drawings in the Victoria and Albert Museum. London: 1960. V. 67

KNOX, R. A.
Proving God - a New Apologetic. London. V. 65

KNOX, ROBERT
A Manual of Artistic Anatomy for the Use of Sculptors, Painters, and Amateurs. London: 1832. V. 64; 67
A Manual of Human Anatomy. London: 1853. V. 67

KNOX, RONALD
Bridegroom and Bride. London. V. 67
Enthusiasm. Oxford: 1950. V. 63
Essays in Satire. London: 1928. V. 62
Reunion All Round; or, Jael's Hammer Laid Aside, and the Milk of Human Kindness Beaten Up into Butter and Serv'd in a Lordly Dish.... London: 1914. V. 63

KNOX, SEYMOUR H.
To B. A. and Back 1932. Buffalo: 1933. V. 64

KNOX, THOMAS W.
The Boy Travellers in Great Britain and Ireland. New York: 1891. V. 63; 66; 67
The Boy Travellers in the Far East (Part Third). New York: 1882. V. 62; 63
The Voyage of the Vivian. To the North Pole and Beyond. Adventures of Two Youths in the Open Polar Sea. New York: 1885. V. 63

KNOX, VICESIMUS
Liberal Education; or, a Practical Treatise on the Method of Acquiring Useful and Polite Learning. London: 1781. V. 62; 66
The Spirit of Despotism. Morris-Town: 1799. V. 63; 66

KNOX, WILLIAM
The Controversy Between Great Britain and Her Colonies Reviewed.... London: 1769. V. 63

KNUTH, P.
Handbook of Flower Pollination. Oxford: 1906-1909. V. 64

KNUTSSON, BENGT
A Litil Boke the Whiche Traytied and Reherced Many Goode Things Necessaries for the...Pestilence...Made by the...Bisshop of Arusiens.... Manchester: 1910. V. 67

KNUTT, FRIGIDA
The Snow-Angel. New York: 1866. V. 66

KNUTTEL, GERARD
The Letter as a Work of Art: Observations and Confrontations with Contemporaneous Expressions of Art from Roman Times to the Present Day. Amsterdam: 1951. V. 64

KOBEL, JACOB
Den Stab Jacob ku(nst)lich und Gerecht Zemachen und Gebrauchen. Frankfurt: 1531. V. 67

KOBER, GEORGE M.
Reminiscences of.... Washington: 1930. V. 65; 67

KOCH, C.
Tenebrionidae of Angola. Lisboa: 1958. V. 64

KOCH, CARL LUDWIG CHRISTIAN
Die Myriapoden. Halle: 1863. V. 66

KOCH, G. S.
Statistical Analysis of Geological Data. New York. 1970-1971. V. 65; 66

KOCH, KENNETH
The Duplications. New York: 1977. V. 62
Guinevere, or the Death of the Kangaroo. New York: 1961. V. 63; 65
Interlocking Lives. New York: 1970. V. 63
The Pleasures of Peace and Other Poems. New York: 1969. V. 63
Poems - from 1952 and 1953. Los Angeles: 1968. V. 65
When the Sun Tries to Go On. Los Angeles: 1969. V. 65

KOCH, MICHAEL
The Shay Locomotive, Titan of the Timber. Denver: 1971. V. 66

KOCH, PETER
Ur-Text Volume I. Berkeley: 1994. V. 62
Ur-Text Volume 3. Berkeley: 1994. V. 62

KOCH, ROBERT A.
Joachim Patinir. Princeton: 1968. V. 64; 66

KOCH, RUDOLF
Die Geschichte vom Weihnachtsstern. (The Story of the Christmas Star). Offenbach: 1919. V. 64

KOCH, RUDOLF continued
The Typefoundary in Silhouette: How Printing Type is Developed at Klingspor Bros. in Offenbach. San Francisco: 1982. V. 62; 63; 64; 66

KOCH, STEPHEN
Andy Warhol Photographs. New York. V. 65; 66

KOCIEJOWSKI, MARIUS
The Testament of Charlotte B. 1988. V. 65
The Testament of Charlotte B. Marlborough: 1988. V. 63

KOCK, CHARLES PAUL DE
Memoirs of Paul De Kock, Written by Himself. London: 1899. V. 66

KOCK, K. H.
Antarctic Fish and Fisheries. Cambridge: 1992. V. 65

KOEBEL, W. H.
In the Maoriland Bush. London: 1912. V. 63; 64; 66
Modern Chile. London: 1913. V. 67

KOECHLIN, R.
Oriental Art: Ceramics, Fabrics, Carpets. New York: 1930. V. 62

KOELLE, H. H.
Handbook of Astronautical Engineering. New York: 1961. V. 67

KOENINGSBURG, M.
King News, an Autobiography. Philadelphia: 1941. V. 67

KOERNER, GUSTAVE
Memoirs of Gustave Koerner 1809-1896. Life Sketches Written at the Suggestion of His Children. Cedar Rapids: 1909. V. 65

KOESTER, FRANK
Modern City Planning and Maintenance. New York: 1914. V. 67

KOESTLER, ARTHUR
The Act of Creation. London: 1964. V. 63
The Age of Longing. London: 1951. V. 62
Arrival and Departure. London: 1943. V. 64
Darkness at Noon. New York: 1941. V. 62
Darkness at Noon. Franklin Center: 1979. V. 63
Scum of the Earth. London: 1941. V. 63
Spanish Testament. London: 1937. V. 65
Thieves in the Night. London: 1946. V. 62
Twilight Bar - an Escapade in Four Acts. London: 1945. V. 63

KOHEN, DEBORAH
Beauty and the Beast. La Jolla: 1980. V. 62

KOHL, J. G.
Travels in Ireland. London: 1844. V. 67

KOHLER, ARTHUR
Stilkunde: Kurzer Abriss der Stilkunde.... Bern/Basel: 1942. V. 65

KOHLHANS, JOHANN CHRISTOPH
Cometa Generalis cum Speciali, oder Cometen-Konig, Welcher im 1664 und 1665 Jahr am Himmel Erschienen, und Sich Prachtig hat Sehen Lassen.... Nurnberg: 1665. V. 63

KOHN, A. J.
Type Specimens and Identity of the Described Species of Conus 1758- 1810. 1959-1981. V. 66

KOHN, LEO
The Constitution of the Irish Free State. 1932. V. 67

KOICHI, MACHIDA
Buddhist Statues in Yamato. Japan: 1988. V. 62; 63; 64

KOIZUMI, GUNJI
Lacquer Work. London: 1925. V. 66

KOKOSCHKA, OSKAR
Oskar Kokoschka. Boston: 1948. V. 64

KOLB, ELLSWORTH L.
Through the Grand Canyon from Wyoming to Mexico. New York: 1914. V. 67

KOLBEN, PETER
The Present State of the Cape of Good Hope; or a Particular Account of the Several Nations of the Hottentots.... London: 1731. V. 67

KOLDEWAY, CAPTAIN
The German Arctic Expedition of 1869-1870; and Narrative of the Wreck of the Hansen in the Ice. London: 1874. V. 67

KOLFF, DIRK HENDRIK
Voyages of the Dutch Brig of War Dourga through the Southern and Little-Known Parts of the Moluccan Archipelago and Along the Previously Unknown Southern Coast of New Guinea.... London: 1840. V. 67

KOLLIST, E. J.
The Complte Patissier. London: 1950. V. 62

KOLLMAN, PAUL
The Victoria Nyanza; the Land, the Races and Their Customs, with Specimens of Some of the Dialects. London: 1899. V. 62; 67

KOLODNY, ANATOLE
Bone Sarcoma. The Primary Malignant Tumors of Bone and the Giant Cell Tumor. Chicago: 1927. V. 63

KOMISARJEVSKY, T.
Settings and Costumes of the Modern Stage. London: 1933. V. 62; 65

KONEWKA, PAUL
Silhouettes. New York: 1870. V. 64

KONIG, PAUL
Voyage of the Deutschland. The First Merchant Submarine. New York: 1916. V. 64

KONIGSBURG, E. L.
The View from Saturday. New York: 1996. V. 62; 63; 65

KONINGS, A.
Konings's Book of Cichlids and Other Fishes of the Lake Malawi. Neptune City: 1990. V. 65

KONOW, STEN
Norway: Official Publication for the Paris Exhibition 1900. Kristiania: 1900. V. 67

KONSTNARSODE, ETT
Carl Oscar Borg. Stockholm: 1953. V. 63; 66

KOONTZ, DEAN R.
Cold Fire. New York: 1991. V. 66
The Door to December. London: 1987. V. 65
Dragonfly. 1975. V. 66
Dragonfly. New York: 1975. V. 62; 64; 65
The Face of Fear. Indianapolis: 1977. V. 65
The Face of Fear. London: 1978. V. 65
Fear Nothing. New York: 1998. V. 67
Hanging On. 1973. V. 64; 66
Hanging On. New York: 1973. V. 65
How to Write Best Selling Fiction. 1981. V. 62; 63; 65
The Mask. London: 1989. V. 65
Night Chills. 1976. V. 64; 65; 66
Nightmare Journey. 1975. V. 67
The Servants of Twilight. 1988. V. 64
Shattered. New York: 1973. V. 65
Strange Highways. Baltimore: 1995. V. 66
Ticktock. London: 1996. V. 65
Watchers. New York: 1987. V. 66
Winter Moon. London: 1994. V. 67

KOOPS, MATTHIAS
Historical Account of the Substances Which Have Been Used to Describe Events, and to Convey Ideas, from the Earliest Date to the Invention of Paper. London: 1800. V. 67
Historical Account of the Substances which Have Been Used to Describe Events, and to Convey Ideas, from the Earliest Date to the Invention of Paper. 1801. V. 67

KOOSER, TED
The Blizzard Voices. Mineapolis: 1986. V. 64

KOPPELMAN, DOROTHY
Poems and Prints. New York: 1998. V. 65

KOPS, BERNARD
Barricades in West Hampstead: Poems. London: 1989. V. 66

KORAN
Al-Coranus S. Lex Islamitica Muhammedis, Filii Abdallae Pseudoprophete.... Hamburg: 1694. V. 62
The Alcoran of Mahomet. London: 1688. V. 67
The Koran. New York: 1935. V. 63
The Koran, Commonly Called the Alcoran of Mahomet. Springfield: 1808. V. 63
The Koran; Commonly Called the Alcoran of Mahomet. London: 1824. V. 66
The Koran, Commonly Called the Alcoran of Mohamet. Springfield: 1806. V. 63
The Koran, Commonly Called the Alcoran of Mohammed. London: 1734. V. 62; 65
The Koran; Commonly Called the Alcoran of Mohammed. London: 1850. V. 67

KOREN, NATHAN
Jewish Physicians. Jerusalem: 1973. V. 63

KORMAN, EZRA
Yidishe Dikhterins: Antologye. Detroit: 1928. V. 67

KORN, GRANINO A.
Electronic Analog Computers (D-c Analog Computers). New York: 1952. V. 65
Electronic Analog Computers (D-c Analog Computers). New York: 1956. V. 65

KORNBLUTH, CYRIL M.
The Mindworm. London: 1955. V. 63; 64; 66
Takeoff. Garden City: 1952. V. 63

KORNS, J. RODERIC
West from Fort Bridger: the Pioneering of the Immigrant Trails Across Utah 1846-1850; Original Diaries and Journals. Salt Lake City: 1951. V. 64

KORSMO, E.
Weed Seeds. Oslo: 1935. V. 64

KORSTEN, F.
A Catalogue of the Library of Thomas Baker. Cambridge: 1990. V. 62

KORTRIGHT, FANNY AIKIN
On Latmos. London: 1881. V. 67

KOSHTOYANTS, K. S.
Essays on the History and Physiology in Russia. Washington: 1964. V. 65

KOSINSKI, JERZY
Being There. New York: 1970. V. 65
Der Bemalte Vogel. (The Painted Bird). Munchen: 1965. V. 63
Cockpit. London: 1975. V. 62
The Devil Tree. New York: 1973. V. 63
The Future Is Ours, Comrade. Garden City: 1960. V. 63; 64; 66; 67
The Painted Bird. Boston: 1976. V. 66
Passion Play. New York: 1979. V. 62

KOSTELANETZ, RICHARD
In the Beginning: a Novella. Somerville: 1971. V. 63

KOSTER, JOHN THEODORE
Description of a New or Improved Method of Constructing Wheel- Carriages.... Liverpool: 1819. V. 63

KOTZEBUE, AUGUST VON
Sketch of the Life and Literary Career of Augustus von Kotzebue; with His Journal of His Tour to Paris at the Close of the Year 1790. London: 1800. V. 62

KOTZEBUE, OTTO VON
A Voyage of Discovery into the South Sea and Berring's Straits, for the Purpose of Exploring a North-East Passage Undertaken in the Years 1815- 1818...in the Ship Rurick.... London: 1821. V. 67

KOTZWINKLE, WILLIAM
Hermes 3000. New York: 1972. V. 64
The Hot Jazz Trio. Boston: 1989. V. 67
The Midnight Examiner. Boston: 1989. V. 67

KOURY, MICHAEL J.
Arms for Texas: a Study of the Weapons of the Republic of Texas. Fort Collins: 1973. V. 64
Diaries of the Little Big Horn. N.P: 1970. V. 67
Military Posts of Montana. Bellevue: 1970. V. 65
Military Posts of Montana. Fort Collins: 1970. V. 64; 67

KOVACS, ERNIE
Zoomar. New York: 1957. V. 66

KOVALEVSKY, SONYA
Recollections of Childhood. New York: 1895. V. 67

KOVEL, R.
American Country Furniture, 1780-1875. New York: 1965. V. 65

KOVIC, RON
Around the World in Eight Days. San Francisco: 1984. V. 62; 65
Born on the Fourth of July. New York: 1976. V. 66

KOZISEK, JOSEF
A Forest Story. New York: 1929. V. 63; 64
The Magic Flutes. New York: 1929. V. 65

KOZLOWSKI, T. T.
Fire and Ecosystems. New York: 1974. V. 63

KRAAY, COLIN M.
Greek Coins.... New York: 1965. V. 65

KRAEPELIN, EMIL
Dementia Praecox and Paraphrenia. Edinburgh: 1919. V. 65
Lectures on Clinical Psychiatry. New York: 1913. V. 65
Psychiatry: a Textbook for Students and Physicians. Canton: 1990. V. 65
Psychologische Arbeiten. Bande 1-9. Leipzig: 1896-1928. V. 65

KRAFFT, J. C.
Plans, Coupes et Elevations de Diverses Productions de l'Art de la Charpente Executees Tant en France que dans les Pays Etrangers. Paris: 1805. V. 65

KRAFFT, MICHAEL
The American Distiller, or, the Theory and Practice of Distilling, According to the Latest Discoveries and Improvements.... Philadelphia: 1804. V. 64; 66

KRAFT, LOUIS
Custer and the Cheyenne, George Armstrong Custer's Winter Campaign on the Southern Plains. El Segundo: 1995. V. 67

KRAKAUER, JON
Into Thin Air. New York: 1997. V. 62; 64; 66; 67

KRAKEL, DEAN
James Borein - a Study in Discipline. Flagstaff: 1968. V. 66
The Saga of Tom Horn, The Story of a Cattleman's War with Personal Narratives, Newspaper Accounts and Official Documents and Testimonies. Laramie: 1954. V. 62; 65
Seasons of the Elk. Kansas City: 1976. V. 63; 66
South Platte Country. A History of the Old Welch County 1739-1900. Laramie: 1954. V. 64; 65; 67
Tom Ryan - a Painter of Four Sixes Country. Northland: 1901. V. 67
Tom Ryan: a Painter in Four Sixes Country. Flagstaff: 1971. V. 63; 67

KRAMER, H.
Richard Lindner. 1975. V. 62; 65

KRAMER, JANE
Allen Ginsberg in America. New York: 1969. V. 63

KRAMER, WILHELM HEINRICH
Elenchus Vegetabilium et Animalium per Austriam Inferiorem Oservatorum. Viennea: 1756. V. 67

KRANS, HORATIO SHEAFE
William Butler Yeats and the Irish Literary Revival. New York: 1904. V. 66

KRAPF, J. LEWIS
A Dictionary of the Suahili Language. London: 1882. V. 67

KRASHENINNIKOV, STEPAN P.
Explorations of Kamchatka; North Pacific Scimitar. Report of a Journey Made to Explore Eastern Siberia in 1735-1741, by Order of the Russian Imperial Government. Portland: 1972. V. 64

KRASNER, WILLIAM
The Gambler. New York: 1950. V. 67

KRASSILNIKOV, N. A.
Ray Fungi, Higher Forms. Volume 2. Washington: 1981. V. 66

KRAUS, HANS P.
A Rare Book Saga. New York: 1978. V. 63
A Rare Book Saga. London: 1979. V. 64
Sir Francis Drake. Amsterdam: 1970. V. 64

KRAUS, KARL
Die Demolirte Literatur. Vienna: 1897. V. 67

KRAUSE, GREGOR
Borneo. N.P: 1927. V. 62

KRAUSE, HERBERT
Custer's Prelude to Glory, a Newspaper Account of Custer's 1874 Expedition to the Black Hills. Sioux Falls: 1974. V. 67

KRAUSS, JOHANN
Oeconomisches Haus-und Kunst-Buch, oder Sammlung Ausgesuchter Vorschriften.... Allentown: 1819. V. 66

KRAUSS, RUTH
Charlotte and The White Horse. New York: 1955. V. 64; 65
Charlotte and the White Horse. London: 1977. V. 65
A Hole Is to Dig. New York: 1969. V. 64

KRAVCHINSKY, SERGEI M.
The Career of a Nihilist. New York: 1889. V. 66

THE KRAY Portfolio. Surrey: 1993. V. 66

KRECICI, P.
Plecnik: the Complete Works. 1993. V. 65

KREIBORG, SVEN
Crouzon Syndrome. Copenhagen: 1981. V. 64

KREIDOLF, ERNST
Die Wiesenzwerge. (The Little People in the Meadow). Coln: 1902. V. 64

KRESKEN, H. ACOSTA
Wonders of the Flora. The Preservation of Flowers in Their Natural State and Colors. Dayton: 1879. V. 62

KRESS LIBRARY
The Kress Library of Business and Economics. Boston: 1993. V. 65

KRESSING, HARRY
Cook. New York: 1965. V. 64

KRETSCHMER, ERNST
Physique and Character: an Investigation of the Nature of Constitution and of the Theory of Temperament. New York: 1936. V. 65

KREYMBORG, ALFRED
Funnybone Alley. New York: 1927. V. 66
Others: an Anthology of the New Verse (1917). New York: 1917. V. 63

KRIDER, J.
Krider's Sporting Anecdotes. V. 67

KRIEG, WENDELL J. S.
Functional Neuroanatomy. Philadelphia: 1953. V. 65

KRIEGER, ALEX D.
Culture Complexes and Chronology in Northern Texas; with Extension of Puebloan Datings to the Mississippi Valley. Austin: 1947. V. 65

KRIEGER, L. C. C.
Catalogue of the Mycological Library of Howard A. Kelly. Baltimore: 1924. V. 67

KRIGE, E. J.
The Social System of the Zulus. London: 1936. V. 67

KRIMS, LES
The Deerslayers. Buffalo: 1972. V. 63

KRIVATSKY, PETER
A Catalogue of Seventeenth Century Printed Books in the National Library of Medicine. Mansfield Centre. V. 62; 65

KROEBER, A. L.
Handbook of the Indians of California. Washington: 1925. V. 66
Zuni Kin and Clan. New York: 1917. V. 63

KROEBER, THEODORA
The Inland Whale. Covelo: 1987. V. 62

KROEKER, MARVIN
Great Plains Command - William B. Hazen in the Frontier West. Norman: 1976. V. 67

KROG, HELGE
Three Plays - The Conch, Triad, The Copy. Boriswood: 1934. V. 64

KROGH, AUGUST
The Anatomy and Physiology of Capillaries. New York: 1959. V. 63
The Comparative Physiology of Respiratory Mechanisms. Philadelphia: 1941. V. 66

KROHN, J. A.
The Walk of Colonial Jack. Keene: 1910. V. 62

KROLL, ERNEST
Fifty Fraxioms. Omaha: 1973. V. 63
Marianne Moore at the Dial Commissions an Article on the Movies. 1989. V. 64

KRONFELD, PETER C.
The Human Eye in Anatomical Transparencies. New York: 1944. V. 67
The Human Eye in Anatomical Transparencies. New York: 1945. V. 64; 66; 67

KRONHEIM, J. M.
A Description of the Colosseum as Re-Opened in MDCCCXLV.... London: 1845. V. 62

KROPOTKIN, PETER
Memoirs of a Revolutionist. London: 1899. V. 64

KRUDENER, BARBARA JULIANE VON VIETINGHOF
Valerie. Paris: 1878. V. 67

KRUEGER, M.
Pioneer Life in Texas. An Autobiography. San Antonio: 1930. V. 63

KRUGER, MARCUS SALOMONIDES
Bibliographia Botanica. Handbuch der Botanischen Literatur.... Berlin: 1841. V. 65

KRUMBOLD, JOSEPH
...And Now Miguel. New York: 1953. V. 65

KRUMMEL, D. W.
The Literature of Music Bibliography, an Account of the Writings on the History of Music Printing and Publishing. Berkeley: 1992. V. 63

KRUPP, FRIED
Fried Krupp Ag Essen-Ruhr 1812-1912. Essen: 1912. V. 65

KRUSCHKE, E. P.
Contributions to the Taxonomy of Crategus. Milwaukee: 1965. V. 67

KUBASTA, VOITECH
How Columbus Discovered America. London: 1960. V. 64
Peter and Sally on the Farm. London: 1961. V. 63
Ricky the Rabbit. London. V. 65
The Runaways and the Robbers. London: 1960. V. 66
Sing a Song of Sixpence and Other Nursery Rhymes. London: 1960. V. 63
The Six Singers. London: 1964. V. 65
Sleeping Beauty. London: 1961. V. 65
Table Lay Yourself!. London: 1960. V. 65
There Was One White Daisy. London: 1963. V. 64

KUBITZKI, K.
The Families and Genera of Vascular Plants.... Berlin: 1990. V. 65

KUBLER, GEORGE
The Religious Architecture of New Mexico. Colorado Springs: 1940. V. 63

KUGLER, FRANZ
Handbook of Italian Painting. London: 1851. V. 66

KUGLER, FRANZ THEODOR
The Schools of Painting in Italy. London: 1851. V. 67

KUGY, JULIUS
Alpine Pilgrimage. London: 1934. V. 63

KUHLMAN, CHARLES
Custer and the Gall Saga. Billings: 1940. V. 65
Legend Into History, The Custer Mystery - An Analytical Study of the Battle of Little Big Horn. Harrisburg: 1952. V. 65

KUHN, K. G.
Medicorum Graecorum Opera Quae Exstant. Leipzig: 1821-1833. V. 64

KUKKENDALL, IVAN LEE
Ghost Riders of the Mogollon. San Antonio: 1954. V. 67

KULL, IRVING S.
New Jersey. A History. New York: 1930. V. 63; 66

KULTERMANN, UDO
The New Sculpture, Environments and Assemblages. New York: 1968. V. 63

KUMADA, TOSHIO
Illustrations of Edible Aquatic Fauna of the South Seas. N.P.: 1951. V. 62; 65
Poisonous Aquatic Fauna of the South Seas. Tokyo: 1943. V. 62; 65

KUMLIEN, LUDWIG
The Birds of Wisconsin. Milwaukee: 1903. V. 65
Contributions to the Natural History of Arctic America, made in Connection with the Howgate Polar Expediton 1877-1878. Washington: 1879. V. 65

KUMM, H. KARL W.
From Hausaland to Egypt, through the Sudan. London: 1910. V. 66

KUMMEL, B.
Handbook of Paleontological Techniques. San Francisco: 1965. V. 65

KUMMER, FREDERIC ARNOLD
Design for Murder. Boston: 1936. V. 67

KUNCKEL, JOHANN
Ars Vitraria Experimentalis, oder Volkommene Glasmacher-Kunst, Lehrende als in Einem aus Unbetruglicher.... Frankfurt and Leipzig: 1679. V. 64; 66
Philosophia Chemica Experimentis Confirmata.... Amsterdam: 1694. V. 64

KUNDERA, MILAN
Identity. New York: 1998. V. 65; 66
The Joke. New York: 1969. V. 63; 67
Life is Elsewhere. New York: 1974. V. 67
The Unbearable Lightness of Being. New York: 1984. V. 67

KUNHARDT, CHARLES P.
Small Yachts, Their Design and Construction.... London: 1891. V. 62

KUNHARDT, DOROTHY
The Telephone Book. New York: 1942. V. 63

KUNIKE, FRIEDRICH ADOLF
Die Bader Bohmens und Dere Umgebungen. Karlsbad, Toplitz, Franzensbrunn, Marienbad u Bilin. Vienna: 1830. V. 62; 66

KUNITZ, STANLEY
The Collected Poems. New York: 2000. V. 67
Intellectual Things. Garden City: 1930. V. 63
Intellectual Things. New York: 1930. V. 67

KUNKEL, R.
Elephants. New York: 1982. V. 63

KUNSTLER, WILLIAM M.
The Minister and the Choir Singer. The Hall-Mills Murder Case. New York: 1964. V. 63; 64

KUNZ, F. C.
Report on the Blackwell's Island Bridge (Queensboro Bridge). Steelton: 1909. V. 62

KUNZ, GEORGE FREDERICK
The Magic of Jewels and Charms. Phiadelphia/London: 1915. V. 63
Rings for the Finger, from the Earliest Known Times to the Present.... 1917. V. 64

KURCK, ARVID
Skanska Folkdragter Tecknade of O. Wallgren. Stockholm: 1872. V. 66

KURDOV, VALENTIN IVANOVICH
Kavaleirya (Cavalry). Leningrad: 1931. V. 64

KURODA, NAGAMICHI
Birds in Life Colours. Tokyo: 1935-1939. V. 64; 67
Birds of the Island of Java. Tokyo: 1933. V. 67
Birds of the Island of Java. Tokyo: 1933-1936. V. 67
Geese and Ducks of the World (Kari to Kamo). Tokyo: 1939. V. 62

KURTEN, B.
Pleistocene Mammals of North America. New York: 1980. V. 63

KURTZ, HENRY I.
The Art of the Toy Soldier. New York: 1987. V. 66

KURTZ, O. L.
Micro-Analytical Entomology for Food Sanitation Control. Washington. V. 67

KURUTZ, GARY F.
The California Gold Rush: a Descriptive Bibliography of Books and Pamphlets Covering the Years 1848-1853. San Francisco: 1997. V. 63; 65; 66
An Essay on Robert E. Cowan's A Bibliography of California and the Pacific West 1510-1906. San Francisco: 1993. V. 64

KURZ, RUDOLPH FRIEDERICK
Journal of Rudolph Friederick Kurz. An Account of His Experiences Along Fur Traders and American Indians On the Mississippi and the Upper Missouri Rivers During the Years 1846-1852. Washington: 1937. V. 66; 67

KURZBECK, JOSEPH NOBLE DE
Nouveau Guide par Vienne Pour les Etrangers et les Nationales de l'an 1792.... Vienna: 1792. V. 64

KURZWELL, ALLEN
A Case of Curiosities. Franklin Center: 1992. V. 63; 66

KUSHNER, ELLEN
Thomas the Rhymer. 1990. V. 64; 66

KUSHNER, TONY
Angels in America: a Gay Fantasia on National Themes. Part One: Millennium Approaches. New York: 1993. V. 62; 64

KUTTNER, HENRY
Ahead of Time. 1953. V. 64; 66

KUUT, J.
The Biology of Parasitic Flowering Plants. Berkeley: 1969. V. 63

KUYKENDALL, IVAN LEE
Ghost Riders of the Mogollon. San Antonio: 1954. V. 63; 64

KUYKENDALL, W. L.
Frontier Days, a True Narrative of the Striking Events on the Western Frontier. Los Angeles: 1917. V. 65; 67

KUYPER, J.
Afbeeldingen..., Tableaux des Habillemens, des Coutmes en Hollande, au Commencement du Dix-Neuvieme Siecle. Amsterdam: 1811. V. 66

KUZARA, STANLEY A.
Black Diamonds of Sheridan - a Facet of Wyoming History. Sheridan: 1977. V. 64

KUZENTSOV, YURY
Dutch Painting in Soviet Museums. New York: 1982. V. 63

KUZNECOV, ERAST DAVIDOVIC
L'Illustrazione del Libro Per Bambini e L'Avanguardia Russa. Firenze: 1991. V. 64

KUZNICKI, PHILIP
Alphabet Book. Berkeley: 1991. V. 62

KVITKO, L.
Loshadka. Moscow: 1944. V. 64

KYAN, JOHN H.
On the Elements of Light and Their Identity with Those of Matter, Radiant and Fixed. London: 1838. V. 66

KYD, STEWART
Arrangement, Under Distinct Titles, Of all the Provisions of the Several Acts of Parliament Relating to the Assessed Taxes. London: 1799. V. 65
A Treatise in the Law of Bills of Exchange and Promissory Notes. Albany: 1800. V. 63

KYD, THOMAS
The Tragedie of Solimon and Perseda. London: 1800. V. 67

KYLE, ROBERT A.
Medicine and Stamps. N.P: 1970. V. 63

KYOKAI, N. T.
Ming, Blue and White and Enamelled Porcelain. Tokyo: 1952. V. 62

KYUSHIN, K.
Fishes of the Indian Ocean. Tokyo: 1977. V. 65; 66

L

L., D.
The Plain Case of Great-Britain, Fairly Stated, in a Letter to a Member of the...House of Commons. Edinburgh?: 1712. V. 62

LA SANTA *Casa Di Loreto. Spiegazione Delli Quattro Prospetti dei Bassi Rilievi in Marmo Che Circondano la Mura Della S. Casa....* Loreto: 1792. V. 64

LA BARRE DE BEAUMARCHAIS, ANTOINE
Le Temple Des Muses, Orne de LX. Tableaux ou Sont Representes les Evenemens les Plus Remarquables de l'Antiquite Fabuleuse. Amsterdam: 1742. V. 64

LABAT, JEAN BAPTISTE
Nouveau Voyage aux Isles de l'Amerique, Contenant l'Histoire Naturelle de ces Pays.... Paris: 1722. V. 63

LABAW, GEORGE WARNE
Preakness and the Preakness Reformed Church, Passaic County, New Jersey. A History, 1695-1902. New York: 1902. V. 63; 66

LABELYE, CHARLES
A Description of Westminster Bridge. London: 1751. V. 62

LABILLARDIERE, JACQUES JULIEN HOUTON DE
Relation du Voyage a La Recherche de La Perouse, Fait par Ordre de l'Assemblee Constituante, Pendant les Annees 171, 1792 et Pendant a lere et la 2e Annee de la Republique Francoise. Paris: 1800. V. 62

LABILLIERE, PETER
The Christian Political Mouse-Trap!. London: 1789. V. 62
Death at Our Windows! Together with Oppression!. London: 1790?. V. 62

LABOR *Leaders Betray Tom Mooney.* San Francisco: 1931. V. 64

DAS LABORATORIUM: *Eine Sammlung von Abbildungen und Beschreibungen der Besten und Neuesten Apparate zum Behuf der Practischen und Physicalischen Chemie.* Weimar: 1825-1840. V. 64

LABORDE, BENJAMIN DE
Choix de Chansons Mises en Musique.... Paris: 1773. V. 62

LABORDE, LEON DE
Journey through Arabia Petraea to Mount Sinai and the Excavated City of Petra, the Edom of the Prophecies. London: 1836. V. 62; 66
Voyage de l'Arabie Petree par Leon de Laborde et Linant. Paris: 1830. V. 62; 67

LABOULAYE, EDOUARD
Fairy Tales. London: 1909. V. 62

LABOURERS' FRIENDLY SOCIETY
Articles for the Government and Regulation of the Labourers' Friendly Society, Held in the Vestry-Room at Frisby-on-the-Wreak, in the County of Leicester, Instituted April 2nd 1839. Melton-Mowbray: 1856. V. 67

LABROUSTE, H.
Analyse des Graphiques: Resultant de la Superposition de Sinuosoides. Paris: 1943. V. 64

LA BRUYERE, JEAN DE
Les Characteres de Theophraste...Avec les Caracteres ou Les Moeurs de Ce Siecle. Paris: 1694. V. 64; 66
The Works.... London: 1713. V. 64

LACAILLE, NICOLAS LOUIS
Lecons Elementaires de Mecanique, out Traite Abrege du Mouvement et de l'Equilibre. Paris: 1765. V. 67

LACAN, JACQUES
De la Pychose Paranoiaque. Paris: 1932. V. 67

LACANTIUS, L. C. F.
A Rolation of the Death of the Primitive Persecutors, Written Originally in Latin. Amsterdam: 1687. V. 63

LACEPEDE, COMTE DE
The Natural History of Ordinary Cetacea or Whales. Edinburgh: 1837. V. 67
Oeuvres Comprenant l'Histoire Naturelle des Quadrupedes, Ovipares, des Serpents, des Poissons et des Cetaces. Paris: 1826-1833. V. 62

LACERDA, FRANCISCO JOSE MARIA DE
The Lands of Cazembe Lacerda's Journey to Cazembe in 1798.... London: 1873. V. 66

LACHAMBRE, HENRI
Andree's Balloon Expedition in Search of the North Pole. New York: 1898. V. 64

LA CHAPELLE, VINCENT
The Modern Cook.... London: 1744. V. 65

LACHIOTTE, ALBERTA
Rebel Senator Strom Thurmond of South Carolina. New York: 1966. V. 67

LACKINGTON, JAMES
The Confessions of J. Lackington, Late Bookseller. London: 1804. V. 65; 66
Memoirs of the First Forty-five Years of the Life of James Lackington.... London: 1791. V. 62; 63; 66
Memoirs of the Forty-Five First Years of the Life of James Lackington, Bookseller. Written by Himself. London: 1827. V. 64
Memoirs of the Forty-Five Years of the Life of James Lackington, the Present Bookseller, Finbury-Square, London. London: 1794. V. 64

LACLOS, PIERRE AMBROISE FRANCOIS CHODERLOS DE
Dangerous Connections: a Series of Letters.... London: 1812. V. 65
Les Liaisons Dangereuses. Brussels: 1869. V. 62
Les Liaisons Dangereuses. Paris: 1929. V. 65

LACOMBE, J. M.
Abrege Chronologique de l'Histoire du Nord, ou es Etats de Dannemarc, de Russie, de Suede, de Pologne, de Prusse, de Courlande &c.... Paris: 1762. V. 66
Le Spectacle des Beaux Arts, ou Considerations Touchant leur Nature, Leurs Objets, Leurs Effets & leurs Regles Principales.... Paris: 1761. V. 67

LACOMBE, JEAN DE
A Compendium of the East.... London: 1937. V. 62; 65; 67
A Compendium of the East. Waltham St. Lawrence: 1937. V. 62

LA CONTERIE, LE VERRIER DE
Vernerie Normande ou l'Ecole de la Chasse Aux Chiens Courants. Rouen: 1778. V. 62

LA COUPRIERE
Manuel de l'Amateur des Oiseaux de Chambre. Paris: 1832. V. 67

LACOUR, LEOPOLD
Trois Femmes de la Revolution. Paris: 1900. V. 66

LACOUR, LOUIS
La Question des Femmes a l'Academie Francaise. Paris: 1865. V. 67

LACOUR, PIERRE
The Manufacture of Liquors, Wines and Cordials, with the Aid of Distillation. New York: 1843. V. 64; 67

LA COUR, TAGE
Ex Bibliotheca Holmesiana: the First Editions of the Writings of Sherock Holmes. Copenhagen: 1951. V. 65

LACRETELLE, PIERRE LOUIS DE
De L'Etablissement des Connoissances Humaines, et de l'Instruction Publique, dans La Constitution Francaise.... Paris: 1791. V. 62

LA CROIX, ARDA
Billy the Kid. New York: 1907. V. 65

LA CROIX, JEAN FRANCOIS
Dictionnaire Portatif des Femmes Celebres, Contenant l'Histoire des Femmes Savantes, des Actrices & Generalement des Dames qui se Sont Rendues Fameuses dans Tous les Siecles.... Paris: 1788. V. 67

LACROIX, PAUL
The Arts of the Middle Ages and at the Period of the Renaissance. London: 1875. V. 64
Contes du Bibliophile Jacob a ses Petits-enfans. Paris: 1831. V. 66
Le Moyen Age et la Renaissance, Histoire et Description des Moeurs et Usages, du Commerce et de l'Industrie, des Sciences, des Arts, des Litteratures et des Beaux-Arts en Europe. Paris: 1848-1851. V. 64
Vie Militaire et Religieuse au Moyen Age et l'Epoque de la Renaissance. Paris: 1873. V. 67

LACROIX, SYLVESTRE FRANCOIS
Elemens de Geometrie, Precedes de Reflexions sur l'Ordre a Suivre dans ces Elemens, sur la Maniere de les Ecrire et sur la methode en Mathematiques. Paris: 1799. V. 65
An Elementary Treatise on the Differential and Integral Calculus. Cambridge: 1816. V. 65; 66
Traite des Differences et des Series, Faisant Suite au Traite du Calcul Differentiel et du Calcul Integral. Paris: 1800. V. 65
Traite du Calcul Differntiel et du Calcul Integral.. Paris: 1810-1819. V. 65

LA CROIX DE CHEVRIES DE SAINT VALIER, JEAN BAPTISTE
Catechisme du Diocese de Quebec. Paris: 1702. V. 62

LA CROIX-LAVAL, FERDINAND ANTOINE
Collection De La Croix-Laval: Album de Soixante et Onze Reproductions de Reliures d'Art Executees sur des Editions De Grand Luxe par Les Meilleurs Maitres Contemporains. Paris: 1902. V. 64

LACTANTIUS, LUCIUS CAECILIUS FIRMIANUS
Opera. Paris: 1513. V. 64; 66

LACY, FLOYD H.
Hallelujah! Unique Gospel Songs and Spirituals as Sung by the Lacys. Kansas City: 1958. V. 63

LACY, GEORGE
Pictures of Travel, Sport and Adventure. 1899. V. 62; 63; 64; 66; 67
Pictures of Travel, Sport and Adventure. London: 1899. V. 67

LADA-MOCARSKI, VALERIAN
Bibliography of Books on Alaska Published Before 1868. 1998. V. 65
Bibliography of Books on Alaska Published Before 1868. Mansfield Centre: 1998. V. 64

LADD, B. F.
History of Vineland. Its Soil, Products, Industries and Commercial Interests. Vineland: 1881. V. 63; 66

LADD, HORATIO A.
The Story of New Mexico. Boston: 1891. V. 64

THE LADIES' Letter Writer or Complete Guide to Epistolary Correspondence....
Glasgow: 1840-1850. V. 66

LADIES of Toronto and Chief Cities and Towns in Canada Home Cook Book.
Toronto: 1877. V. 67

THE LADIES' Work-Table Book.... London: 1846. V. 67

LADIES' RELIEF SOCIETY OF THE CITY OF SEATTLE, WASHINGTON
Articles of Incorporation of the Ladies' Relief Society.... Seattle: 1884. V. 63

LADNER, MILDRED
O. C. Seltzer, Painter of the Old West. Norman: 1979. V. 65; 67

A LADY'S Religion. In Two Letters to the Honourable Lady Howard. London: 1748. V. 65

LAENNEC, RENE THEOPHILE HYACINTHE
De L'Auscultation Mediate ou Traite du Diagnostic des Maladies des Poumons et du Coeur, Fonde Principalement sur ce Nouveau Moyen d'Exploration. Paris: 1819. V. 62; 65; 66; 67
Propositions sur La Doctrine D'Hippocrate Relativement a La Medecine-Pratique, Presentees et Soutenues a l'Ecole de Medecine de Paris l3 22 Prairia an xii. Paris: 1923. V. 67
A Treatise on Diseases of the Chest and on Mediate Auscultation. London: 1834. V. 64

LAET, JOANNES DE
Portugallia Sive de Regis Portugalliae et Opibus Commentarius. Leiden: 1641. V. 64

LA FARGE, JOHN
An Artist's Letter from Japan. New York: 1897. V. 62; 63; 64

LA FARGE, MME.
Memoires de Marie Cappelle, veuve Lafarge. Paris: 1841. V. 63

LA FARGE, OLIVER
The Changing Indian. Norman: 1942. V. 67

LA FAYETTE, MARIE JOSEPH PAUL YVES ROCH GILBERT DU MOTIER
View Privee, Impartiale Politique Militaire et Domestique du Marquis de La Fayette, General des Bleuets, Pour Servir.. Paris: 1790. V. 62

LAFAYETTE, MARIE MADELEINE PIOCHE DE LA VERGNE, COMTESSE DE
Histoire de Madame Henriette d'Angleterre, Premiere Femme de Philippe de France, duc d'Orleans.... Paris: 1853. V. 63
Memoires de Mme. de la Fayette. Paris: 1890. V. 67
La Princesse de Cleves. Paris: 1741. V. 67
La Princesse de Cleves Suivie de la Princesse de Montpensier. (with) Zayde. Paris: 1826. V. 67
Zayde, Histoire Espagnole. Amsterdam: 1700. V. 67

LAFEVER, MINARD
The Modern Builder's Guide.... New York: 1833. V. 62

LAFFAN, R. G. D.
The Guardians of the Gate: Historical Lectures on the Serbs. Oxford: 1918. V. 67

LAFFAN, THOMAS
Tipperary's Families: Being the Hearth Money Records for 1665-1666-1667. 1911. V. 62

LAFFERTY, JOHN J.
An Editor for Twenty Years 1874-1894. N.P: 1894. V. 63

LAFITAU, JOSEPH FRANCOIS
Moeurs des Sauvages Ameriquains, Comparees aux Moeurs des Premiers Temps.... Paris: 1724. V. 64; 66

LAFITE, MARIE ELISABETH BOUEE, DE
Lettres sur Divers Sujets. La Haye: 1775. V. 63

LA FOLLETTE, ROBERT H.
Eight Notches and Other Stories of Nuevo Mexico and the Land of Yaqui and Yucca. Albuquerque: 1957. V. 67
Eight Notches/In an Upside Down World. Albuquerque: 1950. V. 67

LA FONT, DON
Rugged Life in the Rockies. Casper: 1951. V. 63; 66

LA FONTAINE, JEAN DE
The Amours of Cupid and Psyche.. London: 1759. V. 64
Choix de Fables....Tome Second. Tokio: 1894. V. 66
Contes. Paris: 1929. V. 63
Contes et Nouvelles. Amsterdam: 1699-1696. V. 65
Contes et Nouvelles en Vers. Amsterdam: 1762. V. 64; 66
Les Contes et Nouvelles en Vers de Jean De La Fontaine. Paris: 1930. V. 67
Fables. Paris: 1789. V. 64; 66
Fables. Valence: 1812. V. 66
Fables.... Paris: 1883. V. 62
Fables and Tales.... London: 1734. V. 62; 64
Fables Choisies. Paris: 1715. V. 64
Fables Choisies.... Paris: 1818. V. 65
Fables Choisies, Mises en Vers. Paris: 1765-1775. V. 64; 66
Fables de la Fontaine. Paris: 1820. V. 67
Fables de La Fontaine. Paris: 1838. V. 63
The Fables of Jean De La Fontaine. London: 1931. V. 62
The Fables of Jean de la Fontaine. London: 1933. V. 62
The Fables of La Fontaine. New York: 1954. V. 62; 64
La Fontaine's Tales. London: 1814. V. 64
The Loves of Cupid and Psyche; in Verse and Prose. London: 1744. V. 66
The Raven and the Fox and Other Fables. London: 1986. V. 62
Tales and Novels in Verse of.... Paris: 1883. V. 62

LAFOY, J. B.
The Complete Coiffeur or an Essay on the Art of Adorning Natural and of Creating Artificial Beauty. (with) Essai Sur l'Art de Parer la Beaute Naturelle et de crer la Beaute Factice.... New York: 1817. V. 65

LAFRENTZ, F. W.
Cowboy Stuff. Poems. New York: 1927. V. 64

LA GARDE, LOUIS A.
Gunshot Injuries, How They Are Inflicted, Their Complications and Treatment. London: 1917. V. 66

LAGNEAU, LOUIS VIVANT
Expose des Diverses Methodes de Traiter la Maladie Venerienne, et Leurs Differentes Modifications.... Paris: 1803. V. 65

LA GOURNERIE, J. DE
Traite de Perspective Lineaire. Paris: 1859. V. 64

LAGRANGE, JOSEPH LOUIS, COMTE DE
Mechanique Analitique. Paris: 1788. V. 63; 67
Theorie des Fonctions Analytiques, Cotnenant les Principes du Calcul Differentiel, Degages det Tout Consideration d'Infiniment Petits, d'Evanouissans de Limites et de Fluxions et Reduits a l'Analyse Algebrique des Quantites Finies. Paris: 1813. V. 67

LAGUERRE, JOHN
Hob in the Well. London: 1740?. V. 63

LAHONTAN, LOUIS ARMAND, BARON DE
New Voyages to North America. London: 1703. V. 67

LAING, ALEXANDER
The Donean Tourist: Giving an Account of the Battles, Castles, Gentlemen's Seats, Families, with their Origin, Armorial Ensigns, Badges of Distinction. Aberdeen: 1828. V. 62; 65

LAING, ALLAN M.
More Prayers and Graces. London: 1957. V. 67
Prayers and Graces. A Little Book of Extraordinary Piety. London: 1944. V. 63; 67

LAING, D.
Hints for Dwellings: Consisting of Original Designs for Cottages, Farmhouses, Villas &c. Plain and Ornamental.... London: 1804. V. 67

LAING, DAVID
A Compendious Book of Psalms and Spiritual Songs, Commonly Known as The Guide and Godlie Ballates. Edinburgh: 1868. V. 62

LANDON, LETITIA ELIZABETH
Francesca Carrara. London: 1834. V. 65
The Golden Violet, with Its Tales of Romance and Chivalry: and Other Poems. London: 1827. V. 65; 67
Poetical Works. London: 1853. V. 65

LANDON, PERCEVAL
Nepal. London: 1928. V. 67
The Opening of Tibet: an Account of Lhasa and the Country and People of Central Tibet and of the Progress of the Mission Sent There by the English Government in the Year 1903-1904. New York: 1905. V. 65

LANDOR, ARNOLD HENRY SAVAGE
Across Coveted Lands; or, a Journey from Flushing (Holland) to Calcutta, Overland. New York: 1903. V. 65
Across Unknown South America. Boston: 1913. V. 65
Across Widest Africa. London: 1907. V. 62
China and the Allies. New York: 1901. V. 63
In the Forbidden Land. London: 1898. V. 65
In the Forbidden Land. London: 1899. V. 62
In the Forbidden Land. London: 1904. V. 62
Tibet and Nepal. London: 1905. V. 62; 65

LANDOR, L. ELIZABETH
Flowers of Loveliness: Twelve Groups of Female Figures, Emblematic of Flowers. London: 1838. V. 63

LANDOR, WALTER SAVAGE
Citation and Examination of William Shakespeare...Before the Worshipful Sir Thomas Lucy. London: 1834. V. 62
Epicurus, Leontion and Ternissa. London: 1896. V. 65
The Hellenics Comprising Heroic Idyls &c. Edinburgh: 1859. V. 67
Imaginary Conversations. New York: 1936. V. 63
A Modern Greek Idyl. London: 1917. V. 66
Pericles and Aspasia. London: 1836. V. 62; 65
Pericles and Aspasia. London: 1890. V. 62

LANDRETH, JAMES
A Grampian Diary. 1920. V. 62; 63; 65

LANDRETH, MARSHA
The Holiday Murders. New York: 1992. V. 67

LANDRIANI, MARSIGLIO, COUNT
Opuscula Fisico-Chimici. Milan: 1781. V. 62

LANDSEER, EDWIN
Engravings of Lions, Tigers, Panthers, Leopards, Dogs &c. London: 1853. V. 67
The Landseer Gallery. London: 1871. V. 67

LANDSEER, JOHN
Lectures on the Art of Engraving, Delivered at the Royal Institution of Great Britain. London: 1807. V. 67

LANDTMAN, G.
The Kiwai Papuans of British New Guinea. London: 1927. V. 62

LANE, ARTHUR
Dancing in the Dark. 1977. V. 63

LANE, CYRIL GRANT
Adventures in the Big Bush in the Haunts of the Aboriginal. London: 1920. V. 67
Adventures in the Big Bush; in the Haunts of the Aboriginal. London: 1928. V. 67

LANE, ELEANOR MACARTNEY
The Life of Nancy Stair. N.P: 1904. V. 67

LANE, JEREMY
Like a Man. New York: 1928. V. 65

LANE, JOSCELYN
Lake and Loch Fishing. London: 1955. V. 67

LANE, LYDIA S.
I Married a Soldier or Old Days in the Old Army. Philadelphia: 1893. V. 67
I Married a Soldier or Old Days in the Old Army. Albuquerque: 1964. V. 67

LANE, MARGARET
The Tale of Beatrix Potter: a Biography. London and New York: 1946. V. 64

LANE, RICHARD
Studies of Figures by Gainsborough, Executed in Exact Imitation of the Originals by Richard Lane. London: 1825. V. 64

LANE, THOMAS
The Student's Guide through Lincoln's Inn.... London: 1814. V. 63

LANE, W. ARBUTHNOT
Cleft Palate and Hare Lip. (with) Operative Treatment of Chronic Constipation. London: 1905-1904. V. 67
The Operative Treatment of Chronic Constipation. (with) The Kink of the Ileum in Chronic Intestinal Statis. London: 1909-1910. V. 66

LANE, WALTER P.
Adventures and Recollections of General Walter P. Lane.... Marshall: 1887. V. 62; 63; 65; 66
The Adventures and Recollections of General Walter P. Lane. Marshall: 1928. V. 62; 63; 64; 67

LANE, WHEATON J.
From Indian Trail to Iron Horse, Travel and Transportation in New Jersey 1620-1860. Princeton: 1939. V. 63; 66

LANE, YOTI
African Folk Tales. London: 1946. V. 63

LANES, SELMA G.
The Art of Maurice Sendak. London: 1981. V. 65

LANG, A.
Angling Sketches. 1891. V. 67
Angling Sketches. London: 1895. V. 62

LANG, ANDREW
The Annesley Case. 1912. V. 67
The Arabian Nights Entertainments. London: 1898. V. 63
Ballads and Lyrics of Old France With Other Poems. Portland: 1898. V. 62
The Blue Poetry Book. London: 1891. V. 67
The Book of Dreams and Ghosts. London: 1897. V. 65
Books and Bookmen. London: 1886. V. 62
The Brown Fairy Book. London: 1904. V. 62; 63; 64; 65
The Crimson Fairy Book. New York: 1903. V. 63; 66
The Green Fairy Book. London: 1892. V. 63; 64; 66
The Grey Fairy Book. London: 1900. V. 63
Helen of Troy, Her Life and Translation Done Into Rhyme from the Greek Books. Portland. V. 66
The Library. London: 1892. V. 66
My Own Fairy Book.... New York: 1895. V. 62
A New Friendship's Garland. London: 1899. V. 62
Old Friends Among the Fairies. London: 1926. V. 65
The Olive Fairy Book. London: 1907. V. 62; 63; 65; 66
The Orange Fairy Book. London: 1906. V. 62; 63
The Pink Fairy Book. New York: 1904. V. 63
Prince Charles Edward. London: 1900. V. 65
Prince Prigio. London: 1889. V. 63
The Princess Nobody. London: 1884. V. 64
The Red Book of Heroes. London, Bombay, & Calcutta: 1909. V. 64
The Red Fairy Book. London: 1890. V. 63
The Secret Comonwealth of Elves, Fauns and Fairies. London: 1893. V. 67
XXXII Ballades in Blue China. London: 1907. V. 62
The Valet's Tragedy and Other Stories. London: 1903. V. 67

LANG, CECIL
The Mighty Mahseer and Other Fish; or Hints to Beginners on Indian Fishing. Madras: 1890. V. 65

LANG, JOHN D.
Report of a Visit to Some of the Tribes of Indians Located West of the Mississippi River. New York: 1843. V. 66

LANG, JOHN DUNMORE
Cooksland; in North-Eastern Australia, the Future Cotton-Field of Great Britain.... London: 1847. V. 67

LANG, JOSEPH
Artis Mathematicae Nimitum Logisticae Astronomicae, Geometricae, Astronomiae, Sphaericae, theoricae Planetarum, Geographiae. Frieburg: 1617. V. 66

LANG, LEONORA BLANCHE
The All Sorts of Stories Book. London: 1911. V. 65; 66
The Book of Princes and Princesses. London: 1908. V. 65
The Strange Story Book. New York: 1913. V. 64

LANG, WALTER B.
The First Overland Mail - Butterfield Trail/San Francisco to Memphis 1858-1861. Washington: 1945. V. 64

LANGA LANGA
Up Against Nigeria. London: 1922. V. 67

LANGBRIDGE, FREDERICK
The Queen of Dolls. London: 1885. V. 66

LANGDALE, CHARLES
Memoirs of Mrs. Fitzherbert; with an Account of Her Marriage with H.R.H. the Prince of Wales, Afterwards King George the Fourth. London: 1856. V. 64

LANGDALE, HENRY BICKERSTETH
Substance of a Speech Delivered...in the House of Lords on the 13th Day of June, 1836, on the Motion Made by the Lord Chancellor for the Second Reading of the Bill for the Better Administration of Justice in the High Court of Chancery. London: 1836. V. 63

LANGDALE, THOMAS
A Topographical Dictionary of Yorkshire; Containing the Names of All the Towns and Villages, Hamlets, Gentlemen's Seats, &c. in the County of York.... Northallerton: 1822. V. 65

LANGDON, JERVIS
Samuel Langhorne Clemens, Some Reminiscences and Some Excerpts from Letters and Unpublished Manuscripts. Elmira: 1938. V. 63

LANGDON, MARY
Ida May: a Story of Things Actual and Possible. Boston: 1854. V. 65

LANGDON, WILLIAM B.
A Descriptive Catalogue of the Chinese Collection Now Exhibiting at St. George's Place, Hyde Park Corner.... London: 1843. V. 62; 66

LANGE, CHARLES H.
Cochiti - a New Mexico Pueblo Past and Present. Austin: 1959. V. 63; 67

LANGE, HELENE
Higher Education of Women in Europe. New York: 1897. V. 65

LANGE, JOACHIM
Medicine Mentis, Qua Praemissa mentis medica Seur Philosophica, Detectaque ac Rejecta Philomoria.... Halae Magdeburgicae: 1718. V. 65

LANGELLIER, JOHN P.
Myles Keogh, the Life and Legend of an Irish Dragoon in the Seventh Cavalry. El Segundo: 1991. V. 67

LANGEN, EUGEN
Chemins de fer Suspendus a Rail Unique. Nurnberg: 1902. V. 65

LANGENSPIEN, B.
The Ottoman Steam Navy 1828-1928. London: 1995. V. 67

LANGFELD, WILLIAM R.
Washington Irving. A Bibliography. New York: 1933. V. 67

LANGFORD, ABRAHAM
A Catalogue of the Large and Valuable Freehold Estate of the Most Noble William, Duke of Powis, Deceased, Situate in the County of Northampton.... London: 1758. V. 63

LANGFORD, JOHN ALFRED
A Century of Birmingham Life; or a Chronicle of Local Events, from 1741 to 1841. Birmingham: 1870. V. 63; 65
Modern Birmingham and Its Institutions: a Chronicle of Local Events from 1841 to 1871. Birmingham: 1873-1877. V. 64

LANGFORD, NATHANIEL PITT
The Discovery of Yellowstone Park, 1870. The Complete Story of the Washburn Expedition to the Headquarters of the Yellowstone and Firehole Rivers in the 1870. St. Paul: 1923. V. 65
Vigilante Days and Ways - The Pioneers of the Rockies - Makers and Making of Montana, Idaho, Oregon, Washington and Wyoming. Boston: 1890. V. 62

LANGHAM, WILLIAM
The Garden of Health. London: 1633. V. 64

LANGHORN, RICHARD
The Tryall of Richard Langhorn, Esq...for Conspiring the Death of the King.... London: 1679. V. 63

LANGHORNE, JOHN
Frederic and Pharamond or the Consolations of Human Life. London: 1769. V. 64
The Poetical Works.... London: 1804. V. 63
Solyman and Almena. London: 1762. V. 62

LANGHORNE, MAURICE
An-As-Tar-Ta; or a Trip to Ould Nick's Land. Washington: 1879. V. 63

LANGLAND, WILLIAM
Pierce and the Ploughman's Crede. London: 1814. V. 66
The Vision and the Creed of Piers Ploughman. London: 1842. V. 63; 64; 67
The Vision of William Concerning Piers the Plowman. Oxford: 1886. V. 62
The Vision of William Concerning Piers the Plowman. London: 1901. V. 65
The Vision of William Concerning Piers the Plowman. London: 1924. V. 66

LANGLE, JOSEPH ADOLPHE FERDINAND
Les Contes du Gay Scavoir. Paris: 1828. V. 67

LANGLEY, BATTY
Ancient Architecture Restored and Improved, by a Great Variety of Grand and Useful Designs, Entirely New in the Gothick Mode.... London: 1741-1742. V. 66
The Builder's Jewel.... London: 1741. V. 62
The Builder's Jewel.... London: 1746. V. 62
The Builder's Jewel.... London: 1757. V. 62
Gothic Architecture, Improved by Rules and Proportions. London: 1747. V. 64
The London Prices of Bricklayers Materials and Works, Both of New Buildings and Repairs, Justly Ascertained.... London: 1749. V. 62

LANGLEY, HUGH
The Tides Ebb Out to the Night.... London: 1896. V. 66

LANGLEY, J. N.
Preliminary Account of the Arrangement of the Sympathetic Nervous System. London: 1893. V. 67

LANGLEY, NOEL
Desbarollda: the Waltzing Mouse. London: 1947. V. 64
An Elegance of Rebels; a Play in Three Acts. London: 1960. V. 66

LANGLEY, S. P.
The Internal Work of the Wind. Washington: 1908. V. 66

LANGLEY, WILLIAM
Observationes et Historiae Omnes and Singulae e Guiljelmi Harvei Libello De generatione Animalium Exceptae & in Accuratissimum Ordinem Redactae. Amsterdam: 1674. V. 65

LANGLIER, JOHN D.
Myles Keogh. The Life and Legend of an Irish Dragoon in the Seventh Cavalry. El Segundo: 1991. V. 65

LANGLOIS DE FANCAN, FRANCOIS
The Favourites Chronicle. London: 1621. V. 64; 65

LANGMAID, ROWLAND
The King's Ships through the Ages. Portsmouth: 1937. V. 62

LANGMAN, I. K.
A Selected Guide to the Literature on the Flowering Plants of Mexico. Philadelphia: 1964. V. 63

LANGRAND, O.
Guide to the Birds of Madagascar. New Haven: 1990. V. 67

LANGSDORFF, GEORG HEINRICH VON
Remarks and Observations on a Voyage Around the World from 1803 to 1807. Kingston/Fairbanks: 1993. V. 64
Voyages and Travels in Various Parts of the World During the Years 1803, 1804, 1805, 1806 and 1807. Amsterdam: 1968. V. 63

LANGSTON, GEORGE, MRS.
History of Eastland County, Texas. Dallas: 1904. V. 66

LANGSTON, JOHN M.
From the Virginia Plantation to the National Capitol or the First and Only Negro Representative in Congress from the Old Dominion. Hartford: 1894. V. 66

LANGTON, JANE
The Transcendental Murder. New York: 1964. V. 65

LANGTRY LYNAS, J.
Psychological Satyr or the Hounds of Hell. Belfast: 1928. V. 64; 67

LANGUAGE and Sentiment of Flowers. London: 1867. V. 63

THE LANGUAGE of Flowers. Philadelphia: 1835. V. 64

LANGUET, THOMAS
Cooper's Chronicle Contenynge the Whole Discourse of the Histories as Well of Hys Realme as All Other Countrees with the Succession of Theyr Kynges.... London: 1565. V. 64; 66

LANIER, SIDNEY
The Centennial Meditation of Columbia. New York: 1876. V. 65
Poems. Philadelphia: 1877. V. 62

LANIER, VIRGINIA
Death in Bloodhound Red. Sarasota: 1995. V. 63; 65

LANINGHAM, ANNE W.
Early Settlers of Lee Co., Virginia and Adjacent Counties. Greensboro: 1977. V. 63; 64; 67

LANK, D. M.
The Light and the Love, the Art and Life of Leo-Paul Robert. Montreal: 1996. V. 63

LANKESTER, EDWIN
Memorials of John Ray.... London: 1846. V. 62
On Food. London: 1861. V. 63; 65; 67
Vegetable Substances Used for the Food of Man. London: 1832. V. 62

LANKESTER, EDWIN RAY
Extinct Animals. 1905. V. 67
On the Heart Described by Professor Owen in 1841; on the Right Cardiac Valve of the Specimens of Apteryx Dissected by Sir Richard Owen in 1841. 1885. V. 67

LANMAN, CHARLES
Adventures of an Angler in Canada. Nova Scotia and the United States. London: 1848. V. 63
Letters from the Alleghany Mountains. New York: 1849. V. 65
A Tour to the River Saguenay, in Lower Canada. Philadelphia: 1848. V. 66

LANNING, C. M.
A Grammar and Vocabulary of the Blackfoot Language.... Fort Benton: 1882. V. 63

LANNING, JOHN TATE
The Spanish Missions of Georgia. Chapel Hill: 1935. V. 67

LANSDALE, JOE R.
The Boar. Burton: 1998. V. 66
By Bizarre Hands. Shingletown: 1989. V. 66
Cold in July. Shingletown: 1990. V. 65
A Fist Full of Stories (and Articles). Baltimore: 1996. V. 66
The Good, the Bad and the Indifferent. Burton: 1997. V. 66
The Long Ones. Orlando: 1999. V. 66
The Magic Wagon. Garden City: 1986. V. 65; 66
Mucho Mojo. New York: 1994. V. 65
Razored Saddles. 1989. V. 62
Savage Season. Shingletown: 1990. V. 65
The Two Bear Mambo. 1995. V. 64; 66
The Two Bear Mambo. New York: 1995. V. 67
Writer of the Purple Rage. 1994. V. 64
Writer of the Purple Rage. Baltimore: 1994. V. 66

LANSDOWNE, GEORGE GRANVILLE, BARON
Poems Upon Several Occasions. London: 1726. V. 62

LANSDOWNE, J. F.
Birds of the Northern Forest. Boston and Toronto: 1966. V. 67
Birds of the West Coast. Boston: 1976-1980. V. 65; 67

LANSDOWNE, MARQUIS OF
Glanerought and the Petty-Fitzmaurices. 1937. V. 65

LANUZA, JOSE LUIS
The Gaucho. London: 1968. V. 65

LA PEROUSE, JEAN FRANCOIS
The Journal of....1785-1788. London: 1994. V. 64
Le Voyage de La Perouse sur Les Cotes de L'Alaska et de la Californie. Baltimore: 1937. V. 65

LAPHAM, WILLIAM B.
History of Paris, Maine, from Its Settlement to 1880. Paris: 1884. V. 63

LAPLACE, PIERRE SIMON
Mecanique Celeste. Boston: 1829-1839. V. 62; 63; 64; 67
The System of the World. London: 1809. V. 65
Theorie Analytique des Probabilities. Paris: 1814. V. 66
Traite de Mecanique Celeste.... Paris: 1798-1802. V. 65; 66

LA PORT, M. DE
La Science des Negocians et Teneurs de Livres, Ou Instruction Generale Pour Tout ce Qui se Pratique Dans Les Comptoirs des Negocians.... Paris: 1769. V. 62

LAPORTE, JOHN
The Progress of a Water-Coloured Drawing.... London: 1802. V. 64

LA QUINTINYE, JEAN DE
The Compleat Gard'ner; or Directions for Cultivating and Right Ordering of Fruit-Gardens and Kitchen Gardens.... London: 1693. V. 64

LARA, BENJAMIN
Dictionary of Surgery; or the Young Surgeon's Pocket Assistant. London: 1796. V. 64; 67

LARCOM, HENRY
Distressing Narrative of the Loss of the Ship Margaret of Salem. N.P: 1810. V. 64

LARDEN, WALTER
Argentine Plains and Andine Glaciers. London: 1911. V. 63; 64; 67
Recollections of an Old Mountaineer. 1910. V. 63; 65
Recollections of an Old Mountaineer. London: 1910. V. 63; 64; 67

LARDER, ALFRED
A Sinner's Sentence. London: 1891. V. 66

LARDNER, DIONYSIUS
Steam Communication with India by the Red Sea Advocated in a Letter to the Right Honourable Lord Viscount Melbourne. London: 1837. V. 62; 63

LARDNER, E. G. D.
Soldiering and Sport in Uganda. 1912. V. 66

LARDNER, RING W.
Bib Ballads. Chicago: 1915. V. 67
June Moon. New York: 1930. V. 63

LARG, DAVID
Giuseppe Garibaldi - A Biography. London: 1934. V. 65

LARGE, DOROTHY M.
Talk in the Townlands. Dublin: 1937. V. 67

LARGE Letters for the Little Ones. London: 1890. V. 64

LARIMER, WILLIAM H. H.
Reminiscences of General William Larimer and of His Son, William H. H. Larimer - Two of the Founders of Denver. Lancaster: 1918. V. 64; 67

LARISON, CORNELIUS W.
The Class Abrod. A Descripshun ov the Tenting Tur mad bi the Techerz and Students ov the Academi ov Siens and Art at Ringos. Ringoes: 1888. V. 63; 66
The Larisun Famili: a Biografic Scetch ov te Desendants ov Jon Larisun, the Dan, thru hiz Sun Jamz Larisun, and hiz Grandsun Andru Larisun. Ringos: 1888. V. 66
Reminissensez ov Scul Lif. Ringoes: 1896. V. 66
Silvia Dublis (Now 116 Yer Old) A Biografy of the Slav who Whipt Her Mistres and Gand Her Fredom. Ringoes: 1883. V. 63; 66
The Tenting School: A Description of the Tours Taken and of the Field Work Done...in the Academy of Science and Art at Ringos, N.J. During the Year 1882. Ringos: 1883. V. 63; 66

LA RIVE, AUGUSTE DE
Notice sur la Vie et las Ouvrages de A. P. de Candolle. Geneva: 1845. V. 64

LA RIVERS, I.
Fishes and Fisheries of Nevada. Carson City: 1962. V. 65

LARKE, JULIAN K.
General Grant and His Campaigns. New York: 1864. V. 64

LARKIN, PHILIP
All What Jazz - a Record Diary 1961-1968. London: 1985. V. 65
All What Jazz - a Record Diary 1961-1971. London: 1985. V. 62
All What Jazz: a Record Diary 1961-1968. London: 1970. V. 66
Aubade. Salem: 1980. V. 62; 64
Collected Poems. London: 1988. V. 65
Femmes Damnees. Oxford: 1978. V. 62; 63
High Windows. London: 1974. V. 62; 63; 65; 66
High Windows. New York: 1974. V. 62
Jill. London: 1964. V. 64
The Less Deceived. Hessle, East Yorkshire: 1955. V. 62; 64
The Less Deceived. London: 1955. V. 65
The Less Deceived. Hessle: 1956. V. 62
The Less Deceived. New York: 1958. V. 65
The North Ship. London: 1945. V. 62
The North Ship. London: 1965. V. 63
The North Ship. London: 1966. V. 62; 67
Philip Larkin - the Fantasy Poets - Number Twenty One. Swinford, Eynsham: 1954. V. 62
Required Writing - Miscellaneous Pieces 1955-1982. London: 1983. V. 64; 65
Selected Letters of Philip Larkin 1940-1985. London: 1992. V. 64
The Whitsun Weddings. London: 1964. V. 62; 65

LARKING, C.
Bandobast and Khabar. 1888. V. 63; 64

LARMINIE, WILLIAM
West Irish Folk Tales and Romances. 1893. V. 65

LARNED, J. N.
The Literature of American History: a Bibliographical Guide. Columbus: 1953. V. 66

LA ROCHE, MARIE SOPHIE DE GUTTERMANN DE
Memoires de Mademoiselle de Sternheim. La Haye: 1773. V. 63

LA ROCHE, R.
Pneumonia Its Supposed Connection, Pathological and Etiological with Autumnal Fevers. Philadelphia: 1854. V. 66; 67

LA ROCHEFOUCAULD, FRANCOIS, DUC DE
The Duke de la Rochefoucalt's Celebrated Maxims and Moral Reflections.... London: 1799. V. 66
Maximes et Reflections Morales. Paris: 1827. V. 63
Maxims and Moral Reflections. Edinburgh: 1775. V. 67
Moral Maxims: by the Duke de la Roche Foucault. Dublin: 1751. V. 66

LA ROCHEFOUCAULD-LIANCOURT, FRANCOIS ALEXANDRE FREDERIC
Voyage Dans les Etats-Unis d'Amerique, Fait en 1795, 1796, et 1797. Paris: 1799. V. 62; 64

LARREY, BARON
Observations on Wounds and Their Complications by Erysipelas, Gangrene and Tetanus and the Principal Diseases and Injuries of the Head, Ear and Eye.... Philadelphia: 1832. V. 66

LARROQUE, MATTHIEU DE
The History of the Eucharist. London: 1684. V. 67

LARSEN, ELLOUISE
American Historical Views on Staffordshire China. New York: 1939. V. 63

LARSEN, JEANNE
Silk Road. New York: 1989. V. 67

LARSEN, SOFUS
Danish Eighteenth Century Bindings 1730-1830. Copenhagen: 1930. V. 62

LARSON, ANDREW G.
Report on Franklin Mining Camp and North Fork of Kettle River. N.P: 1914. V. 66

LARSON, JAMES
Sergeant Larson 4th Calvary. San Antonio: 1935. V. 63

LARSON, ROGER K.
Controversial James: an Essay on the Life and Work of George Wharton James. San Francisco: 1991. V. 65

LARSSON, CARL
Larsson - Ett Album Bestaende of 32 Malningar Och Med Text Teckningar. Stockholm: 1902. V. 65

LARTIGUE, J. H.
Boyhood Photos of J. H. Lartigue: the Family Album of a Gilded Age. Lausanne: 1966. V. 63

LARWOOD, JACOB
The Story of the London Parks. London. V. 66

LA SALLE, JEAN BAPTISTE DE SAINT
Les Regles de la Bienseance et de la Civilite Chretienne, Divisees en deux Parties. Reims: 1782. V. 66

LASATER, LAURENCE M.
The Lasater Philosophy of Cattle Raising. El Paso: 1972. V. 64

LASCARIS, EVADNE, PSEUD.
The Golden Bed of Kydno. Waltham St. Lawrence: 1935. V. 64; 66

LAS CASES, EMANUEL, COMTE DE
Journal of the Private Life and Conversations of the Emperor Napoleon at Saint Helena. London: 1825. V. 67

LASCELLES, EDWARD
Scenes from the Life of Edward Lascelles. Dublin: 1837. V. 65

LASCELLES, MARY
The Adversaries and Other Poems. Cambridge: 1971. V. 63

LASCELLES, ROWLEY
The Ultimate Remedy for Ireland. 1831. V. 67
The University and City of Oxford.... London: 1821. V. 65

LASERON, CHARLES FRANCIS
South with Mawson. Reminiscences of the Australasian Antarctic Expedition 1911-1914. Sydney/London: 1947. V. 64

LA SERRE, JEAN PUGET DE
The Secretary in Fashion; or, an Elegant and Compendious Way of Writing All Manner of Letters. London: 1654. V. 65

LASHLEY, KARL SPENCER
The Neuropsychology of Lashley: Selected Papers of.... New York: 1960. V. 65

LASINIO, GIOVANNI PAOLO
Pitture a Fresco del Camposanto di Pisa.... Florence: 1832. V. 62; 66

LASKEY, J.
A General Account of the Hunterian Museum. Glasgow: 1813. V. 64

LA SPINA, GREYE
Invaders from the Dark. Sauk City: 1960. V. 64; 66

LASSAIGNE, JACQUES
Chagall. Paris: 1957. V. 64
Marc Chagall. Drawings and Water Colors for the Ballet. New York: 1969. V. 64
Marc Chagall. The Ceiling of the Paris Opera. New York: 1966. V. 64

LASSELS, RICHARD
An Italian Voyage, or a Compleat Journey through Italy. London: 1697. V. 67
An Italian Voyage, or a Compleat Journey through Italy. London: 1698. V. 64

LASSWELL, MARY
John Henry Kirby: Prince or the Pines. Austin: 1967. V. 64

THE LAST of the Medici. Florence: 1930. V. 66

LASTEYRIE DU SAILLANT, CHARLES PHILIBERT, COMTE DE
Du Pastel, de l'Indigotier, et des autres Vegetaux dont on Peut Extraire une Couleur Bleue.... Paris: 1811,. V. 67

LASTRI, MARCO
L'Etruria Pittrice Ovvero Storia Della Pittura Toscana Dedotta dai Suoi Monumenti.... Florence N. Pagni and G. Bar: 1791-1795. V. 62

LA SUZE, HENRIETTE DE COLIGNY, MME. LA COMTESSE DE
Recueil de Pieces Galantes, en Prose et en Vers de Madame la Comtesse de la Suze, et de Monsieur Pelisson, Augmentee de Plusieurs Pieces Nouvelles de Divers Autheurs. Lyon: 1695. V. 67

LATARJET, A.
Anatomie Chirurgicale Du Crane et De L'Encephale. Paris: 1938. V. 64

LATEEF, YUSEF A.
A Night in the Garden of Love. New York: 1988. V. 66

LATHAM, GEORGE
The History of Stydd Chapel and Preceptory, Near Ribchester, Lancashire. London: 1853. V. 66

LATHAM, HIRAM
Trans-Missouri Stock Raising: the Pasture Lands of North America, Winter Grazing. Denver: 1962. V. 63; 64; 65; 66; 67

LATHAM, JOHN
A General Synopsis of Birds. London: 1781-1785. V. 67
On Rheumatism, and Gout: a Letter Addressed to Sir George Baker. London: 1796. V. 65

LATHAM, JOHN HERBERT
The Construction of Wrought Iron Bridges; Embracing the Practical Application of the Principles of Mechanics to Wrought Iron Girder Work. Cambridge: 1858. V. 64

LATHAM, WILFRID
The States of the River Plate: Their Industries and Commerce. London: 1866. V. 67

LATHAN, ROBERT
Historical Sketch of the Battle of King's Mountain. Yorkville: 1880. V. 63; 66

LATHBURY, MARY A.
The Birthday Week, Pictures and Verses. New York: 1884. V. 65

LATHBURY, R. H.
The History of Denham Bucks.... Uxbridge: 1904. V. 66

LATHBURY, THOMAS
Guy Fawkes; or, The Gunpowder Treason, A.D. 1605.... London: 1840. V. 62; 66

LATHROP, DOROTHY
The Dog in the Tapestry Garden. New York: 1962. V. 62
The Little White Goat. New York: 1933. V. 65
Puppies for Keeps. New York: 1943. V. 66
Who Goes There?. New York: 1935. V. 62

LATHROP, ELISE
Early American Inns and Taverns. New York: 1926. V. 63; 67
Historic Houses of Early America. New York: 1927. V. 64; 67

LATHROP, GEORGE
Some Pioneer Recollections Being the Autobiography of George Lathrop. Philadelphia: 1927. V. 62; 65

LATHROP, GILBERT A.
Little Engines and Big Men. Caldwell: 1954. V. 66

LATHROP, JOHN
Compendious Treatise on the Use of the Globes and of Maps. Boston: 1812. V. 63

LATIMER, JOHN
The History of the Society of Merchant Venturers of the City of Bristol with Some Account of the Anterior Merchant's Guilds. Bristol: 1903. V. 62

LATIMER, JONATHAN
Black is the Fashion for Dying. New York: 1959. V. 65
The Dead Don't Care. Garden City: 1938. V. 62
The Mink-Lined Coffin. London: 1960. V. 65
Red Gardenias. 1939. V. 67
Sinners and Shrouds. London: 1956. V. 66
Solomon's Vineyard. Santa Barbara: 1982. V. 65
The Westland Case. Garden City: 1937. V. 65

LATIMORE, SARAH BRIGGS
Arthur Rackham: a Bibliography. Los Angeles: 1936. V. 64

LA TOUCHE, JOHN
Ballet Ballads. New York: 1949. V. 67

LATOUCHE, JOHN
Travels in Portugal.... London: 1875. V. 65; 67

LATOUR, A. LACARRIERE
Historical Memoir of the War In West Florida and Louisiana in 1814- 1815. Philadelphia: 1816. V. 67

LATROBE, BENJAMIN HENRY BONEVAL
Characteristic Anecdotes, and Miscellaneous Authentic Papers, Tending to Illustrate the Character of Frederic II, Late King of Prussia. London: 1788. V. 66

LATROBE, CHARLES JOSEPH
The Alpenstock; or, Sketches of Swiss Scenery and Manners. (with) The Pedestrian.... London: 1829-1832. V. 67
A Journal of a Visit to South Africa, With Some Account of the Missionary Settlements of the United Brethren, near the Cape of Good Hope. London: 1821. V. 65
The Rambler in Mexico. London: 1836. V. 63; 64; 67

LATROBE, CHRISTIAN IGNATIUS
Journal of a Visit to South Africa in 1815 and 1816. New York: 1818. V. 64

LATROBE BATEMAN, JOHN FREDERICK
History and Description of the Manchester Waterworks. London: 1884. V. 66

LATTA, F. F.
Handbook of Yokuts Indians. Bakersfield: 1949. V. 63; 65
Tailholt Tales. Santa Cruz: 1976. V. 66

LATTA, M. L.
The History of My Life and Work. Raleigh, etc: 1920. V. 65

LATTA, ROBERT R.
Reminiscences of Pioneer Life. Kansas City: 1912. V. 64; 67

LATTIMORE, ELEANOR HOLGATE
Turkistan Reunion. London: 1927. V. 67

LATYMER, LORD
Stalking in Scotland and New Zealand. 1935. V. 62; 63; 64

LAUBREAUX, ALIN
Happy Glutton; or, How to Eat and How to Cook. London: 1931. V. 66

LAUD, WILLIAM
The History of the Troubles and Tryal.... London: 1695. V. 63
A Relation of the Conference Betweene William Lawd, Then Lrd. Bishop of St. Davids.... London: 1639. V. 63

LAUDAMUS, LEIF
The Leif Laudamus Atomic Energy Collection Commemorating the 50th Anniversary of the Discovery of Nuclear Fission. Amherst: 1989. V. 65

LAUDER, THOMAS DICK
An Account of the Great Floods of August 1829 in the Province of Moray and Adjoining Districts. 1830. V. 62
An Account of the Great Floods of August 1829, in the Province of Moray and Adjoining Districts. Edinburgh: 1830. V. 66
Parrots. Edinburgh: 1833. V. 67

LAUDER, WILLIAM
An Essay on Milton's Use and Imitation of the Moderns, in His Paradise Lost. London: 1750. V. 63

LAUDERDALE, JAMES MAITLAND, EARL OF
An Inquiry into the Nature and Origin of Public Wealth and Into the Means and Causes of Its Increase. Edinburgh: 1804. V. 62

LAUFER, BERTHOLD
Archaic Chinese Jades Collected in China by A. W. Bahr. New York: 1927. V. 66

THE LAUGHING Philosopher; or Repository of Wit; Containing Original Jests, Smart Puns, Irish Bulls, Satirical Epigrams, Diverting Poetry, Humorous Jokes, Lively Repartees, Punny Anecdotes, and Above Five Hundred Good Things.... 1800. V. 62; 66

LAUGHLIN, CLARENCE JOHN
Ghosts Along the Mississippi: an Essay in the Poetic Interpretation of Louisiana's Plantation Architecture. New York: 1961. V. 63; 65

LAUGHLIN, JAMES
Angelica. Fragment from an Autobiography. New York: 1993. V. 66
Gists and Piths: a Memoir of Ezra Pound. Iowa City: 1982. V. 64
Report on a Visit to Germany (American Zone). 1948. Lausanne: 1948. V. 62
Some Natural Things. New York: 1945. V. 63
Tabellae. New York: 1986. V. 66
The Wild Anemone & Other Poems. New York: 1957. V. 67

LAUGHLIN, S. B.
The Atlas of Breeding Birds of Vermont. Hanover: 1985. V. 67

LAUGHTON, JAMES W.
The General Receipt-Book, Containing an Extensive Collection of Valuable Receipts, Connected with Domestic Economy. London: 1838. V. 67

LAUGHTON, JOHN KNOX
Letters and Despatches of Horatio, Viscount Nelson, K.B., Selected and Arranged by.... London: 1886. V. 67

LAUGHTON, L. G. CARR
Old Ship Figure-Heads and Sterns. London: 1925. V. 64; 66

LAUGIER, MARC ANTOINE
Maniere de Bien Juger des Ouvrages de Peinture.... Paris: 1771. V. 67

LAUNSPACH, CHARLES W. L.
Tales of the Fantastic. London: 1948. V. 63

THE LAUREAT; or, the Right Side of Colley Cibber, Esq. London: 1740. V. 66

LAURENCE, EDWARD
The Duty and Office of a Land Steward: Represented Under Several Plain and Distinct Articles.... London: 1731. V. 66
The Duty of a Steward to His Lord. London: 1727. V. 62; 64; 67
The Young Surveyor's Guide; or a New Introduction to the Whole Art of Surveying Land.... London: 1716. V. 64; 66

LAURENCE, JANET
A Deepe Coffyn. London: 1989. V. 62; 65
Deepe Coffyn. New York: 1990. V. 67
Hotel Morgue. London: 1991. V. 65
A Tasty Way to Die. London: 1990. V. 62; 65

LAURENCIN, MARIE
Marie Laurencin. Paris: 1928. V. 63

LAURENT et Perrot *Les Femmes de l'Asie, ou Description de Leure Physionomie, Moeurs, Usages et Costumes.* Paris: 1830. V. 66

LAURENT, JEAN
Abrege Pour les Arbres Nains et Autres.... Paris: 1683. V. 64

LAURENTS, ARTHUR
Home of the Brave. New York: 1946. V. 63

LAURETTA, PSEUD.
A Drum for the Ears of the Drowsy. Philadelphia: 1814. V. 63; 66

LAURIE, DAVID
Hints Regarding the East India Monopoly, Submitted to the British Legislature. London: 1813. V. 65

LAURIE, JOSEPH
The Homoeopathic Domestic Medicine. London: 1851. V. 62
The Homoeopathic Domestic Medicine. London: 1857. V. 64

LAUSANNE, MR. DE
Elemens du Magnetisme Animal, ou Exposition Succincte des Procedes, de Phenomenes.... Paris: 1818. V. 65

LAUT, AGNES C.
The Blazed Trail of the Old Frontier. New York: 1926. V. 63; 66
The Fur Trade of America. New York: 1921. V. 67
Heralds of Empire, Being the Story on One Ramsay Stanhope, Lieutenant to Pierre Radissonn, the Northern Fur Trader. New York: 1902. V. 64; 67
The Story of the Trapper. New York: 1902. V. 64

LAUTERBACH, ANN
Closing Hours. New York: 1983. V. 66
A Clown, Some Colors, a Doll, Her Stories, A Song, A Moonlit Cove. New York: 1995. V. 64
Many Times, But Then. Austin: 1979. V. 62
Sacred Weather. New York: 1984. V. 66; 67
Thripsis. Calais: 1998. V. 62; 66; 67

LAUTREAMONT, ISIDORE DUCASSE, COMTE DE
The Lay of Maldoror. London: 1924. V. 62

LAUVRIERE, EMILE
The Strange Life and Strange Loves of Edgar Allan Poem. Philadelphia: 1935. V. 66

LAVATER, JOHANN CASPAR
Over de Physiognomie der J. C. Lavater. Tweede Druk. Amsterdam: 1783. V. 66

LAVATER, LUDWIG
De Spectris, Lemuribus et Magnis Atque Insolitis Fragoribus. Geneva: 1580. V. 67

LAVELLE, PATRICK
The Irish Landlord Since the Revolution. 1870. V. 65

LAVENDER, DAVID
The Fist in the Wilderness: a Narrative History of the American Fur Trade. New York: 1964. V. 64; 66

LAVERACK, EDWARD
The Setter. 1872. V. 66

LAVER GIBBS, CHRISTINE
The Early Years of Griffen Mill 1986-1998. Marcham: 1999. V. 67

LAVERY, BRIAN
The Ship of the Line 1650-1850. London: 1883-1884. V. 63

LAVERY, FELIX
Irish Heroes in the War. 1917. V. 63; 66

LAVIN, MARY
The House on Clewe Street. Boston: 1945. V. 62
In the Middle of the Fields and Other Stories. London: 1967. V. 62

LAVINGTON, GEORGE
The Enthusiasm of Methodists and Papists Compared. (with) Part II. London: 1752. V. 64
The Moravians Compared and Detected. London: 1755. V. 64; 65

LAVOISNE, M.
A Complete Genealogical, Historical, Chronological and Geographical Atlas. Philadelphia: 1821. V. 67

LA VOY, LAMBERT, M.
Bay Settlement of Monroe County, Michigan. N.P: 1971. V. 65

LAW, ALICE
Emily Jane Bronte and the Authorship of Wuthering Heights. Accrington: 1928. V. 66

THE LAW Instructor, or Farmer's and Mechanic's Guide.... Bridgeton: 1824. V. 63

LAW, JOHN
Het Groote Tafereel der Dwaasheid, Vertoonende de Opkomst Voortgang en Ondergang der Actie. Amsterdam: 1720. V. 62

LAW, JOHN, PSEUD.
Out of Work. London: 1888. V. 64

LAW, PHILLIP G.
Anare: Australia's Antarctic Outposts. Melbourne: 1957. V. 64

LAW, ROBERT
Memorialls; or the Memorable Things that Fell Out Within This Island of Brittain from 1638 to 1684.... Edinburgh: 1818. V. 63

LAW Tracts. Edinburgh: 1770. V. 62

LAW, WILLIAM
The Absolute Unlawfulness in the Stage Entertainment Fully Demonstrated. London: 1726. V. 64
A Collection of Letters on the Most Interesting and Important Subjects, and on Several Occasions. London: 1760. V. 64
The Grounds and Reasons of Christian Regeneration, or the New Birth. London: 1739. V. 65
An Humble, Earnest and Affectionate Address, to the Clergy. London: 1774. V. 64
The Nature and Design of Christianity. London: 1793. V. 64
The Oxford Methodists: Being an Account of Some Young Gentlemen in the City, in Derision so Called; Setting Forth Their Rise and Designs. London: 1738. V. 64
(A Practical Treatise on Christian Perfection). The Nature and Design of Christianity. Bristol: 1746. V. 64
A Practical Treatise on Christian Perfection. Newcastle-upon-Tyne: 1743. V. 64
A Practical Treatise Upon Christian Perfection. London: 1726. V. 64
Remarks On the Fable of the Bees. Cambridge: 1844. V. 64
A Second Letter to the Bishop of Bangor; Wherein His Lordship's Notion of Benediction, Absolution and Church Communion Are Prov'd to be Destructive of Very Institution of the Christian Religion. (with) A Reply to the Bishop of Bangor's Answer to the Repr. London: 1717-1719. V. 64
A Serious Call to a Devout and Holy Life. London: 1732. V. 64
A Serious Call to a Holy Life. Newcastle-upon-Tyne: 1744. V. 64
A Short but Sufficient Confutation of the Reverend Dr. Warburton's Projected Defence (As He Calls It) of Christianity, In His Divine Legation of Moses. In a Letter of the Right Reverend the Lord Bishop of London. London: 1757. V. 64

LAWES, W. G.
Grammar and Vocabulary of the Language Spoken by the Motu Tribe (New Guinea). Sydney: 1888. V. 63

LAWFORD, G. L.
The Telcon Story. 1850-1950. London: 1950. V. 62; 65

LAWFUL Amusements. Harrisonburgh: 1813. V. 65

LAWLER, JOHN
Book Auctions in England in the Seventeenth Century (1676-1700). London: 1898. V. 67

LAWLESS, EMILY
Grania: the Story of an Island. London: 1892. V. 65; 66

LAWLEY, ARTHUR
Tours: the First Tour of Coimbatore and Salem Districts 23 Sept. to 4 Oct. 1906; the Second Tour of Mysore State and North Arcot and Chingleput Districts 12-26 Oct. and 3 Nov. 1906; the Fourth Tour of Cochin and Travancore 25 Jan. to 14 Feb. 1907, the Fi. Madras: 1908-1911. V. 67

LAWLOR, HENRY CAIRNES
The Monastery of St. Mochaoi of Nendrum. 1925. V. 65
Ulster and Its Archaeology and Antiquities. 1928. V. 66
Ulster and Its Archaeology and Antiquities. London: 1928. V. 63

LAWLOR, P. A.
The Mystery of Maata - Katherine Mansfield Novel. Wellington: 1946. V. 64

LAWN, BUXTON
The Corn Trade Investigated. Salisbury: 1801. V. 64

LAWRENCE Gowing. London: 1983. V. 67

LAWRENCE, A. B.
A History of Texas, or the Emigrant's Guide to the New Republic.... New York: 1844. V. 63; 66

LAWRENCE, A. W.
T. E. Lawrence, by His Friends. London: 1937. V. 65

LAWRENCE, ADA
Young Lorenzo - Early Life of D. H. Lawrence.... Florence: 1932. V. 65

LAWRENCE, C. E.
The Iron Bell. London: 1921. V. 66

LAWRENCE, DAVID HERBERT
Amores: Poems. London: 1916. V. 63
Birds, Beasts and Flowers. New York: 1923. V. 62
Birds, Beasts and Flowers. London: 1930. V. 62
The Boy in the Bush. London: 1924. V. 65
The Boy in the Bush. New York: 1924. V. 62
The Collected Letters of D. H. Lawrence. London: 1965. V. 66
A Collier's Friday Night. London: 1934. V. 65
David. A Play. London: 1926. V. 66
England, My England. London: 1924. V. 65
Fantasia of the Unconscious. New York: 1922. V. 67
Fantasia of the Unconscious. London: 1923. V. 63
Fire and Other Poems. San Francisco: 1940. V. 62; 63; 64; 66
Kangaroo. London: 1923. V. 65
Kangaroo. New York: 1923. V. 63; 64; 66
Lady Chatterley's Lover. Florence: 1928. V. 63; 66
L'Arc-en Ciel. (The Rainbow). Paris: 1939. V. 63
Last Poems. Florence: 1932. V. 63; 67
Letters from D. H. Lawrence to Martin Secker 1911-1930. Bridgefoot Iver: 1970. V. 67
The Letters of D. H. Lawrence. London: 1932. V. 63
The Lost Girl. London: 1920. V. 65
Love Among the Haystacks and Other Pieces. London: 1930. V. 64; 65; 66
Love Poems and Others. London: 1913. V. 62
The Lovely Lady. London: 1932. V. 62; 65
The Man Who Died. London: 1931. V. 62; 65
The Man Who Died. London: 1935. V. 62
The Man Who Died. 1992. V. 63
A Modern Lover. London: 1934. V. 62
My Skirmish With Jolly Roger. New York: 1929. V. 62; 63; 64; 65; 66
Nettles. London: 1930. V. 62
The Paintings of D. H. Lawrence. London: 1929. V. 65
Pansies. London: 1929. V. 62; 63; 64; 67
The Plumed Serpent. London: 1926. V. 65
The Prussian Officer. And Other Stories. London: 1914. V. 62
The Rainbow. London: 1915. V. 62
Reflections on the Death of a Porcupine and Other Essays. Philadelphia: 1925. V. 65
St. Mawr. (with) The Princess. London: 1925. V. 62
Sea and Sardinia. New York: 1921. V. 64
Sex Locked Out. London: 1928. V. 62
The Ship of Death and Other Poems. London: 1933. V. 62
Sons and Lovers. London: 1913. V. 62
Sons and Lovers. Avon: 1975. V. 64
Sun. Paris: 1928. V. 62
Tortoises. New York: 1921. V. 64
The Trespassers. New York: 1912. V. 64; 65
The Virgin and the Gipsy. Florence: 1930. V. 62
The Virgin and the Gypsy. New York: 1930. V. 65
We Need One Another. New York: 1933. V. 62
The White Peacock. London: 1911. V. 64
The White Peacock. New York: 1911. V. 62; 63
The Woman Who Rode Away and Other Stories. London: 1928. V. 65
Women in Love. New York: 1920. V. 62

LAWRENCE, ELIZABETH
The Inca's Bride. Memphis: 1855. V. 63

LAWRENCE, ELIZABETH A.
His Very Silence Speaks - Comanche, The Horse Who Survived Custer's Last Stand. Detroit: 1989. V. 67

LAWRENCE, FRIEDA
Not I, But the Wind. Santa Fe: 1934. V. 64; 67

LAWRENCE, G. N.
Birds of Southwestern Mexico Collected by by Francis E. Sumichrast. Washington: 1876. V. 67

LAWRENCE, GEORGE ALFRED
Guy Livingston; or Thorough. London: 1857. V. 67

LAWRENCE, HEATHER
Yorkshire Pots and Potteries. London: 1974. V. 64; 65

LAWRENCE, JEROME
Inherit the Wind. New York: 1955. V. 63; 66

LAWRENCE, JOHN
British Field Sports.... London: 1818. V. 62; 66; 67
Good Babies, Bad Babies. 1986. V. 62
Good Babies, Bad Babies. Fullerton: 1986. V. 64
The New Farmer's Calendar; or Monthly Remembrancer for All Kinds of Country Business. London: 1801. V. 65; 67
The Slavery Question. Dayton: 1854. V. 65

LAWRENCE, JOSHUA
A Patriotic Discourse, Delivered by the Rev. Joshua Lawrence, at the Old Church in Tarborough, North Carolina, on Sunday the 4th of July 1830. Tarborough: 1830. V. 66

LAWRENCE, MARGARET
Hearts and Bones. New York: 1996. V. 67

LAWRENCE, MARGERY
Number Seven Queer Street. 1969. V. 64; 66

LAWRENCE, R. DE T.
History of Bill Yopp. N.P: 1920. V. 62

LAWRENCE, RICHARD
The Complete Farrier, and British Sportsman.... London: 1833. V. 66
Elgin Marbles, from the Parthenon at Athens.... London: 1818. V. 62; 66

LAWRENCE, ROBERT C.
The State of Robeson. Lumberton: 1939. V. 63; 66

LAWRENCE, THOMAS EDWARD
The Best of Friends - Further Letters to Sydney Carlyle Cockerell. London: 1956. V. 65
Cats and Landladies' Husbands. Denby Dale: 1995. V. 65
Cats and Landladies' Husbands. London: 1995. V. 67
Crusader Castles. Waltham St. Lawrence: 1936. V. 62; 64; 66
A Day Book of the R.A.F. London: 1955. V. 66
Diary of T. E. Lawrence MCMXI. 1937. V. 64
Diary of T. E. Lawrence MCMXI. London: 1937. V. 62
The Home Letters of T. E. Lawrence and His Brothers. Oxford: 1954. V. 65
The Letters of T. E. Lawrence. London: 1938. V. 62; 64
Letters to E. T. Leeds. Andoversford: 1988. V. 64
Men in Print. London: 1940. V. 63
Men in Print. Waltham St. Lawrence: 1940. V. 62; 64; 65
The Mint. Garden City: 1955. V. 64
The Mint. London: 1955. V. 62; 64; 66
More Letters from T. E. Shaw to Bruce Rogers. New York: 1936. V. 64
Oriental Assembly. London: 1939. V. 64; 67
Revolt in the Desert. New York: 1927. V. 62
Secret Dispatches from Arabia. London: 1939. V. 67
Secret Dispatches from Arabia. Waltham St. Lawrence: 1939. V. 62; 64; 65
Seven Pillars of Wisdom. Garden City: 1935. V. 62; 63; 64; 66
Seven Pillars of Wisdom. London: 1935. V. 62; 63; 64; 65; 66; 67
Seven Pillars of Wisdom. Fordingbridge, Hampshire: 1997. V. 62; 63
Shaw-Ede. T. E. Lawrence's Letters to H. S. Ede 1927-1935. Waltham St. Lawrence: 1942. V. 65
T. E. Lawrence: Letters to E. T. Leeds. London: 1988. V. 65
T. E. Lawrence to His Biographer, Liddell Hart: Information About Himself.... London: 1938. V. 66
T. E. Lawrence to His Biographer, Robert Graves. (with) T. E. Lawrence to His Biographer, Liddell Hart. New York: 1938. V. 62; 64; 66; 67
T. E. Lawrence to His Biographers, Robert Graves and Liddell Hart. London: 1963. V. 62

LAWRENCE, WILLIAM
Lectures on Physiology, Zoology and the Natural History, Delivered at the Royal College of Surgeons. London: 1819. V. 62
Lectures on Physiology Zoology and the Natural History of Man. 1819. V. 67
Lectures on Physiology, Zoology, and the Natural History of Man, Delivered at the Royal College of Surgeons. Benbow: 1822. V. 65
Lectures on Physiology, Zoology, and the Natural History of Man, Delivered at the Royal College of Surgeons. Salem: 1828. V. 64
Pictures in Color of the Lakes of Killarney and South of Ireland. 1905. V. 67
A Treatise on the Diseases of the Eye. Philadelphia: 1843. V. 62
A Treatise on the Diseases of the Eye. London: 1844. V. 63
A Treatise on the Diseases of the Eye. Philadelphia: 1854. V. 63

LAWRENCE, WILLIAM BEACH
The Origin and Nature of the Representataive and Federative Institutions of the United States. New York: 1832. V. 63; 66
Visitation and Search. Boston: 1858. V. 64

LAWRIE, W. H.
International Trout Flies. 1969. V. 65; 67

THE LAWS Concerning Travelling, &c. London: 1718. V. 64

LAWS of the Sea. The Rights of Seamen, Coaster's and Fisherman's Guide, and Master's and Mate's Manual. Boston: 1856. V. 66

LAWS, R. M.
Antarctic Seals. Research Method and Techniques. Cambridge: 1993. V. 64

THE LAWS Respecting Pews or Seats in Churches. London: 1826. V. 63

LAWSON, A.
The Modern Farrier; or, the Art of Preserving the Health and Curing the Diseases of Horses, Dogs, Oxen, Cows, Sheep and Swine. London: 1833. V. 66

LAWSON, G. W.
The Marine Algae and Coastal Environment of Tropical West Africa. Stuttgart: 1987. V. 65

LAWSON, HENRY
The Auld Shop and the New. Katoomba: 1992. V. 64

LAWSON, J. A.
Wanderings in the Interior of New Guinea. London: 1875. V. 65

LAWSON, JOHN
Lectures Concerning Oratory. Dublin: 1759. V. 67

LAWSON, JOHN HOWARD
Loud Speaker. New York: 1927. V. 63

LAWSON, JOHN PARKER
The Booth of Perth.... Edinburgh: 1847. V. 62

LAWSON, LADY
Highways and Homes of Japan. London: 1910. V. 67

LAWSON, PETER, & SON
Treatise on the Cultivated Grasses and other Herbage and Forage, Plantes, with the Kinds of Seeds for Sowing Down Land to Alternative Husbandry, Permanent Pasture, Lawns &c. Edinburgh and London: 1843. V. 66

LAWSON, ROBERT
Dick Whittington and His Cat. New York: 1949. V. 66
I Discover Columbus. Boston: 1941. V. 66
Rabbit Hill. New York: 1944. V. 64; 65
Smeller Martin. New York: 1950. V. 63
They Were Strong and Good. New York: 1940. V. 65
The Tough Winter. New York: 1954. V. 63; 66

LAWSON, WILLIAM
New Orchard and Garden. London: 1927. V. 66
Ten Years of Gentleman Farming at Blennerhasset, with Co-operative Objects. London: 1874. V. 62

LAWSON, WILLIAM PINKNEY
The Log of a Timber Cruiser. New York: 1915. V. 63

LAWTON, JOHN
Old Flames. London: 1996. V. 66

LAWYER, SARAH R.
The Jonathan and Hannah Steelman Family. Elkton: 1952. V. 63; 66

LAX, ROBERT
The Circus of the Sun. New York: 1959. V. 62

LAY, WILLIAM
A Narrative of the Mutiny, on Board the Ship Globe, of Nantucket, in the Pacific Ocean, Jan. 1824. New London: 1828. V. 66

LAYARD, ARTHUR
The Alphabet of Musical Bogeys. London: 1899. V. 64

LAYARD, AUSTEN HENRY
Nineveh and Its Remains. London: 1849. V. 67
Nineveh and Its Remains. New York: 1849. V. 64; 66
Nineveh and Its Remains. New York: 1849-1850. V. 63
Nineveh and Its Remains. London: 1849-1853. V. 67
Nineveh and Its Remains. New York: 1853. V. 64

LAYARD, E.
The Birds of South Africa.... Cape Town?: 1875-1884. V. 62

LAYARD, GEORGE SOMES
Catalogue Raisonne of Engraved British Portraits from Altered Plates.... London: 1927. V. 62
Mrs. Lynn Linton: Her Life, Letters and Opinions. London: 1901. V. 65

LAYARD, JOHN
Stone Men of Malekula: Vao. London: 1942. V. 67

LAYCOCK, J. W.
Methodist Heroes in the Great Haworth Round 1734 to 1784. Memorials. Keighley: 1909. V. 64; 65

LAYCOCK, SAMUEL
Warblin's Fro' an Own Songster. London: 1893. V. 66

LAYER, CHRISTOPHER
The Whole Proceeding Upon the Arraignment, Tryal, Conviction and Attainder of Christopher Layer, Esq. London: 1722. V. 62; 63

LAYMAN, RICHARD
Dashiell Hammett: a Descriptive Bibliography. Pittsburgh: 1979. V. 65; 67

LAYMAN, WILLIAM
The Pioneer, or Strictures on Maritime Strength and Economy.... London: 1821. V. 64

LAYNE, J. GREGG
Annals of Los Angeles from the Arrival of the First White Men to the Civil War 1769-1861. San Francisco: 1935. V. 62; 65

LAYNG, HENRY
The Rod, a Poem. Oxford: 1754. V. 66

LAYTON, IRVING
The Improved Binoculars. Highlands: 1956. V. 63
A Laughter in Mind. Highlands: 1958. V. 63
A Red Carpet for the Sun. Highlands: 1959. V. 63

LAZAR, NICOLAS
Israel. New York: 1958. V. 64

LAZAREV, V.
Old Russian Murals and Mosaics, from XI to the XVI Century. London: 1966. V. 62; 65

LAZARILLO, DE TORMES
The Life and Adventures of Lazarillo de Tormes. London: 1789. V. 62

LAZARUS, HENRY
The English Revolution of the Twentieth Century.... London: 1897. V. 64

LAZER, HANK
On Equal Terms. Poems by Charles Bernstein, David Ignatow, Denise Levertov, Louis Simpson, Gerald Stern. Tuscaloosa: 1984. V. 64

LE RAY'S *Poughkeepsie City Directory for the Year Ending May 1, 1887....* Poughkeepsie: 1886. V. 67

LEA, HENRY CHARLES
Materials Toward a History of Witchcraft. New York and London: 1957. V. 65

LEA, I.
Observations on the Genus Unio. Philadelphia: 1832. V. 66
Observations on the Genus Unio. Philadelphia: 1874. V. 67
A Synopsis of the Family of Naiades.... Philadelphia: 1838. V. 67
A Synopsis of the Family of Naiads. Philadelphia: 1836. V. 66
A Synopsis of the Family Unionidae. Philadelphia: 1870. V. 66

LEA, J. E.
Catalogue of the Circulating Library of J. E. Lea, Bookseller, Stationer, Music Seller, Printer and Vender of Patent Medicines (Near the Tolsey).... Gloucester: 1840. V. 62

LEA, TOM
The Art of Tom Lea. College Station: 1989. V. 62
87 Paintings and Drawings by Tom Lea. Austin: 1971. V. 64
87 Paintings and Drawings by Tom Lea. El Paso: 1971. V. 62; 63
The King Ranch. Boston: 1957. V. 66
The King Ranch. Kingsville: 1957. V. 67
Old Mount Franklin. El Paso: 1968. V. 62
A Picture Gallery: Paintings and Drawings. Boston: 1968. V. 62; 63; 66
A Selection of Paintings and Drawings from the Nineteen Sixties. Austin: 1969. V. 64
A Selection of Paintings and Drawings from the Nineteen Sixties. San Antonio: 1969. V. 62; 63; 64
Western Beef Cattle. Austin: 1967. V. 62
Western Beef Cattle. Dallas: 1967. V. 63; 66
Western Beef Cattle. El Paso: 1967. V. 67
The Wonderful Country. Boston: 1952. V. 66

LEACH, A. J.
Early Day Stories. The Overland Trail. Norfolk: 1916. V. 63; 64; 66
A History of Antelope County Nebaraska, from Its First Settlement in 1868 to the Close of the Year 1883. Chicago: 1909. V. 62; 65

LEACH, ARTHUR FRANCIS
Early Yorkshire Schools. Yorkshire: 1899-1903. V. 66

LEACH, JOSIAH GRANVILLE
Genealogical and Biographical Memorials of the Reading, Howell, Yerkes, Watts, Latham and Elkins Families. Philadelphia: 1898. V. 63; 66

LEACH, WILLIAM ELFORD
Malacostraca Podophthalmata Britanniae.... London: 1815 1820. V. 62

LEADBEATER, MARY
Memoirs and Letters of Richard and Elizabeth Shackleton, Late of Ballitore. 1822. V. 67
Memoirs and Letters of Richard and Elizabeth Shackleton, Late of Ballitore. 1849. V. 62; 65

LEADBITTER, MIKE
Nothing But Blue Skies. London: 1971. V. 64

LEADER, JOHN DANIEL
The Records of the Burgery of Sheffield, Commonly Called the Town Trust.... London: 1897. V. 62; 65

LEAF, MUNRO
Being an American Can Be Fun. Philadelphia: 1964. V. 63
Fair Play. New York: 1939. V. 64
Gordon the Goat. Philadelphia: 1944. V. 64
Lucky You. New York: 1955. V. 62; 63
Noodle. New York: 1937. V. 66
Noodle. London: 1938. V. 67
The Story of Simpson and Sampson. New York: 1941. V. 65
Turnabout. Philadelphia: 1967. V. 62
Wee Gillis. New York: 1938. V. 63

LEAKE, CHAUNCEY D.
Some Founders of Physiology. Washington: 1956. V. 64; 67

LEAKE, JOHN
The Life of Sir John Leake, Knt. Admiral of the Fleet &c. London: 1750. V. 62
The Scholar's Manual Being a Collection of Meditations, Reflections and Reasonings, Design'd for Establishing and Promoting Christian Principles and Practice.... London: 1733. V. 63; 67

LEAKEY, L. S. B.
White African. London: 1937. V. 67

LEAR, EDWARD
A Book of Nonsense. London: 1885. V. 63
The Book of Nonsense. London: 1905. V. 63
The Complete Nonsense of Edward Lear. London: 1947. V. 66
The Dong With a Luminous Nose. New York: 1969. V. 63
Edward Lear's ABC. London. V. 65
Illustrations of the Family of Psittacidae, or Parrots, the Greater Part of Them Species Hitherto Unfigured. London and New York: 1978. V. 67
Journals of a Landscape Painter in Albania &c. London: 1851. V. 66
More Nonsense. London: 1888. V. 67
Nonsense Songs, Stories, Botany and Alphabets. London: 1871. V. 62
Nonsense Songs, Stories, Botany and Alphabets. London: 1875. V. 63
On My Shelves. Munich: 1933. V. 62
Two Nonsense Stories: The Story of the Four Little Children Who Went Round the World. and The History of the Seven Families of the Late Pipple-Popple. 1989. V. 62
Views in the Seven Ionian Islands. London: 1863. V. 67

LEAR, P. G.
The Strange and Striking Adventures of Four Authors in Search of a Character. London: 1926. V. 67

LEARNER, RICHARD
Astronomy Through the Telescope; the 500 Year Story of the Instruments, the Inventors and Their Discoveries. New York: 1981. V. 67

LEARY, TIMOTHY
Flashbacks: an Autobiography. Los Angeles: 1983. V. 63
Interpersonal Diagnosis of Personality. New York: 1957. V. 62
Psychedelic Prayers. Kerhonkson: 1966. V. 64; 67

LEARY, W. A., & CO.
Valuable Historical, Theological and Miscellaneous Books. Philadelphia: 1850. V. 65

LEATHAM, A. E.
Sport in Five Continents. 1912. V. 63; 64; 66

LEATHER, STEPHEN
The Bombmaker. London: 1999. V. 67
The Chinaman. London: 1992. V. 66; 67
The Double Tap. London: 1996. V. 67
The Long Shot. London: 1994. V. 66
The Vets. New York: 1993. V. 67

LEAVEN for Doughfaces; or Threescore and Ten Parables Touching Slavery. Cincinnati: 1856. V. 64

LEAVIS, F. R.
Revaluation - Tradition and Development in English Poetry. London: 1936. V. 64

LEAVITT, DAVID
Family Dancing. New York: 1984. V. 63
Saturn Street. Amsterdam: 1996. V. 62; 64
While England Sleeps. New York: 1993. V. 66

LEAVITT, JONATHAN
A Summary of the Laws of Massachusetts, Relative to the Settlement, Support, Employment and Removal of Paupers. Greenfield: 1810. V. 66

LEAVITT, RICHARD
The World of Tennessee Williams. New York: 1978. V. 63; 67

LEBEDEV, LEV
Rendezvous in Space; Soyuz Apollo: an Account of the First Soviet-American Space Experiment, 1975. Moscow: 1979. V. 67

LEBEDEV, VALENTIN
Diary of a Cosmonaut; 211 Days in Space. Texas: 1988. V. 67

LEBEL, ROBERT
Marcel Duchamp. New York: 1959. V. 62; 65

LEBER, FERDINANDI
Praelectiones Anatomicae. Edinburgh: 1790. V. 67

LEBLANC, GEORGETTE
The Girl Who Found the Blue Bird: a Visit to Hellen Keller. New York: 1914. V. 63

LE BLANC, M.
Traite Historique Des Monnoies de France.... 1690. V. 66

LEBLANC, MAURICE
Arsene Lupin, Gentleman Burglar. Chicago: 1910. V. 67
Arsene Lupin Versus Herlock Sholmes. Chicago: 1910. V. 66
The Confessions of Arsene Lupin. Garden City: 1913. V. 67
The Golden Triangle: the Return of Arsene Lupin. New York: 1917. V. 65
The Hollow Needle. 1910. V. 64
The Hollow Needle. New York: 1910. V. 63
The Teeth of the Tiger. Garden City: 1914. V. 67
The Teeth of the Tiger. London: 1915. V. 64
The Tremendous Event. New York: 1922. V. 67

LEBLANC, P.
Description d'un Pont Suspendu de 198 Metres d'Ouverture et de 39m, 70 de Hauteur audessus des Basses Mers, Construit sur la Vilaine, a La Roche-Bernard, Route de nantes a Brest. Paris: 1841. V. 62

LE BOSSU, RENE
Monsieur Bossu's Treatise of the Epick Poem.... London: 1695. V. 64

LEBOUR, M. V.
The Dinoflagellates of Northern Seas. Plymouth: 1925. V. 64
The Planktonic Diatoms of Northern Seas. London: 1930. V. 63

LE BOURSIER DU COUDRAY, ANGELIQUE MARGUERITE
Abbrege de l'Art des Accouchemens. A Saintes: 1769. V. 64; 66

LE BRETON, ANNA LETITIA
Memoir of Mrs. Barbauld. London: 1874. V. 65

LE BRUN, CORNEILLE
Voyages De Corneille Le Brun par la Moscovie, en Perse, et Aux Indes Orientales. Amsterdam: 1718. V. 66

LE CARRE, JOHN
Call for the Dead. New York: 1962. V. 62
The Clandestine Muse. Newark: 1986. V. 62; 64; 67
The Clandestine Muse. Portland: 1986. V. 65; 66
The Honourable Schoolboy. London: 1977. V. 63
Le Carre Omnibus. London: 1964. V. 66
The Little Drummer Girl. New York: 1983. V. 67
The Looking-Glass War. London: 1965. V. 63; 64; 65; 66; 67
A Murder of Quality. London: 1962. V. 67
The Naive and Sentimental Lover. London: 1971. V. 66; 67
The Naive and Sentimental Lover. New York: 1972. V. 63
Nervous Times. 1998. V. 62
Nervous Times. London: 1998. V. 66
The Night Manager. London: 1993. V. 65; 66; 67
The Night Manager. New York: 1993. V. 67
Our Game. Franklin Center: 1995. V. 62; 67
Our Game. London: 1995. V. 63; 65; 66
Our Game. New York: 1995. V. 66
A Perfect Spy. 1986. V. 64
A Perfect Spy. London: 1986. V. 62; 63; 65
A Perfect Spy. New York: 1986. V. 67
The Russia House. 1989. V. 64
The Russia House. London: 1989. V. 65; 66; 67
The Russia House. New York: 1989. V. 62; 67
Sarratt and the Draper of Watford and Other Unlikely Stories About Sarratt from International Authors. Watford: 1999. V. 65; 66
The Secret Pilgrim. London: 1991. V. 66
The Secret Pilgrim. New York: 1991. V. 67
Single and Single. Franklin Center: 1999. V. 65; 67
Single and Single. London: 1999. V. 62; 64; 66; 67
A Small Town in Germany. London: 1968. V. 62; 63; 66
Smiley's People. London: 1979. V. 65; 67
Smiley's People. London: 1980. V. 63; 66
The Spy Who Came in from the Cold. London: 1963. V. 62; 63; 66; 67
The Tailor of Panama. London: 1996. V. 65
Tinker, Tailor, Soldier, Spy. London: 1974. V. 62
Tinker, Tailor, Soldier, Spy. New York: 1974. V. 67

LE CHAU, GERAUD DE
Dissertation sur Les Attributs de Venus. aris: 1780. V. 65

LECKENBY, CHARLES H.
The Tread of Pioneers. Steamboat Springs: 1945. V. 62; 63; 66

LECKIE, ROBERT
The Buffalo Soldiers - a Narrative of the Negro Cavalry in the West. Norman: 1967. V. 67

LECKIE, WILLIAM H.
The Military Conquest of the Southern Plains. Norman: 1963. V. 67

LECKY, HALTON STIRLING
The King's Ships Together with the Important Historical Episodes Connected with Successive Ships of the Same Name from Remote Times. London: 1913-1914. V. 62; 66

LECKY, S.
Bright Pages for Children of all Ages. London: 1890. V. 67

LECKY, S. T. S.
Wrinkles in Practical Navigation. London: 1900. V. 63

LECKY, WILLIAM EDWARD HARTPOLE
Democracy and Liberty. London and Bombay: 1896. V. 67
The Rise and Influence of the Spirit of Rationalism in Europe. London: 1865. V. 67

LE CLERC, CHARLES GABRIEL
The Compleat Surgeon; or, the Whole Art of Surgery Explain'd in a Most Familiar Method. London: 1714. V. 65
A Description of Bandages and Dressings, According to the Most Commodious Ways Now Used in France.... London: 1727. V. 65

LE CLERC, JEAN
Logica; Sive, Ars Ratiocinandi. (with, as issued) Ontologia; sive de Ente in Genere. London: 1692. V. 63

LE CLERC, SEBASTIEN
Practical Geometry; or a New and Easy Method of Treating the Art. London: 1742. V. 62
Pratique de la Geometrie, sur le Papier et sur le terrain. Paris: 1669. V. 66
Principles of Drawing, in Fifty-Two Plates. London: 1765. V. 66

LE CLERCQ, CHRISTIEN
New Relation of Gaspesia With the Customs and Religion of the Gaspesian Indians. Toronto: 1910. V. 66

LE CLERT, LOUIS
Le Papier. Recherches et Notes Pour Servir a L'Histoire du Papier, Principalement a Troyes et Aux Environs Depuis le Quatrozieme Siecle. Paris: 1926. V. 62

LE COMTE, LOUIS
Memoirs and Observations Made in a Late Journey through the Empire of China. London: 1698. V. 65
Nouveaux Memoires sur l'Etat Present de la Chine. Amsterdam: 1698. V. 67

LE CONTE, JOSEPH
A Journal of Ramblings through the High Sierra of California by the University Excursion Party. San Francisco: 1875. V. 63
A Journal of Ramblings through the High Sierra of California by the University Excursion Party. San Francisco: 1930. V. 62; 63
'Ware Sherman. A Journal of Three Months' Personal Experience in the Last Days of the Confederacy. Berkeley: 1937. V. 63

LE CONTE, MICHEL
Les Trophees de l'Amour Divin au Tres-Saint Sacrement de l'Autel. Charleville: 1645. V. 65

LE COQ, ALBERT VON
Buried Treasure of Chinese Turkestan, An Account of the Activities and Adventures of the Second and Third German Turfan Expeditions. New York: 1929. V. 67

LE COURAYER, PETER FRANCIS
A Defence of the Validity of the English Ordinations and of the Succession of the Bishops in the Church of England. Dublin: 1725. V. 62

LE COUVREUR, FRANK
From East Prussia to the Golden Gate. New York: 1906. V. 62; 65; 67

LECTURES to Ladies on Practical Education. Cambridge: 1857. V. 63

LECTURES to Ladies on Practical Subjects. Cambridge: 1855. V. 62; 65

LEDERER, WILLIAM J.
The Ugly American. New York: 1958. V. 63; 67

LEDFORD, PRESTON LAFAYETTE
Reminiscences of the Civil War 1861-1865. Thomasville: 1909. V. 62; 65

LEDIARD, THOMAS
The Life of John, Duke of Marlborough, Prince of the Roman Empire.... London: 1743. V. 62

LE DRAN, HENRI FRANCOIS
Traite ov Reflexions Tirees de la Pratique sur les Playes d'Armes a Seu. Paris: 1737. V. 66; 67

LEDRU, NICHOLAS PHILIPPE
Rapport de MM. Cosnier, Maloet, Darcet, Philip, Le Preux, Desessartz & Paulet, Docteurs-Regents de la Faculte de Medecine de Paris.... Paris: 1783. V. 64

LEDUC, STEPHANE
Electric Ions and Their Use in Medicine. London: 1908. V. 65

LEDWIDGE, FRANCIS
Songs of the Fields. London: 1916. V. 64; 67

LEE, AMY FREEMAN
Hobby Horses. New York: 1940. V. 66

LEE, ARTHUR
Extract from an Address in the Virginia Gazette, of March 19, 1767. Philadelphia: 1770. V. 63

LEE, BRIAN NORTH
The Bookplate Designs of Rex Whistler. Pinner: 1973. V. 64
Bookplates by Simon Brett. Wakefield: 1989. V. 64, 65
British Royal Bookplates and Ex-Libris of Related Families. Aldershot: 1992. V. 63; 64

LEE, C. Y.
The Flower Drum Song. New York: 1957. V. 63

LEE, CHANG RAE
Native Speaker. New York: 1995. V. 63; 64; 67

LEE, CHARLES HENRY
The Judge Advocate's Vade Mecum. Richmond: 1863. V. 63

LEE, DAVID
Wayburn Pig. Waldron Island: 1997. V. 63; 64; 66

LEE, EDMUND
The Story of a Sister's Love. London: 1891. V. 67

LEE, EDWIN
Report Upon the Phenomena of Clairvoyance or Lucid Somnambulism (From Personal Observation). London: 1843. V. 67

LEE, FITZHUGH
General Lee. New York: 1894. V. 62; 65

LEE, FRANCIS BAZLEY
Genealogical and Personal Memorial of Mercer County, New Jersey. New York: 1907. V. 63; 66
History of Trenton, New Jersey. Trenton: 1895. V. 63; 66
History of Trenton, New Jersey. Trenton: 1895-1898. V. 63
New Jersey as a Colony and as a State. New York: 1902. V. 63; 66
New Jersey as a Colony and as a State. New York: 1903. V. 63

LEE, FRED J.
Casey Jones. Kingsport: 1939. V. 63; 64

LEE, G. HERBERT
An Historical Sketch of the First Fifty Years of the Church of England in the Province of New Brunswick (1783-1833). St. John: 1880. V. 64

LEE, GREGORY V.
Bermuda Pocket Almanack Guide and Directory...1893. Hamilton: 1892. V. 67

LEE, GYPSY ROSE
The Strip-Tease Murders. London: 1942. V. 66

LEE, HARPER
To Kill a Mocking Bird. London: 1960. V. 62; 63; 64; 65
To Kill a Mockingbird. Philadelphia and New York: 1960. V. 63; 65; 67
To Kill a Mockingbird. New York: 1995. V. 62; 65; 66

LEE, HARRIET
The New Peerage; or, Our Eyes May Deceive Us. Dublin: 1788. V. 63

LEE, HENRY
The Vegetable of Tartary; a Curious Fable of the Cotton Plant. London: 1887. V. 64

LEE, HOLME
Legends from Fairyland. London. V. 67

LEE, IDA
The Coming of the British to Australia 1788 to 1829. London: 1906. V. 67

LEE, J. C.
The Amphibians and Reptiles of the Yucatan Peninsula. Ithaca: 1996. V. 64

LEE, J. S.
The Geology of China. London: 1939. V. 64

LEE, JACK H.
Power River, Let'er Buck. Boston: 1930. V. 65

LEE, JAMES
An Introduction to Botany. London: 1788. V. 64; 66

LEE, JAMES K.
The Volunteer's Handbook.... Richmond: 1861. V. 62

LEE, JAMES S.
The Underworld of the East: Being Eighteen Years' Actual Experiences of the Underworlds.... London: 1935. V. 66

LEE, JOHN
The Man They Could Not Hang. London: 1908. V. 63
A Narrative of a Singular Gouty Case; with Observations. London: 1782. V. 65

LEE, JOHN D.
A Mormon Chronicle: the Diaries of John D. Lee 1848-1876. San Marino: 1955. V. 62; 65
The Mormon Menace - Being the Confession of.... New York: 1905. V. 63

LEE, JOHN EDWARD
Delineations of Roman Antiquities Found at Caer Leon (the Ancient Isca Silurum) and the Neighbourhood. London: 1845. V. 63

LEE, JOHN THOMAS
The Authorship of Gregg's Commerce of the Prairies. Cedar Rapids: 1930. V. 67

LEE, JOSEPH
The Indian Mutiny. Events at Cawnpore by J. Lee late of H.M.'s 53rd Regt. also a Narrative of His Visit to England and America in 1883.... Cawnpore: 1886. V. 64

LEE, K. F.
Big Game Hunting and Markmanship. 1941. V. 67

LEE, KATE
Ten Thousand Goddam Cattle - A History of the American Cowboy in Song, Story and Verse. Flagstaff: 1976. V. 67

LEE, KATHARINE
Love or Money. London: 1891. V. 65
A Western Wildflower. London: 1882. V. 65

LEE, L. P.
History of the Spirit Lake Massacre! 8th March 1857 and Miss Abigail Gardiner's Three Months Captivity Among the Indians. New Britain: 1857. V. 64; 67

LEE, LAURIE
Cider with Rosie. 1959. V. 67
Cider with Rosie. London: 1959. V. 62; 66
Land at War: the Official Story of British Farming 1939-1944. London: 1945. V. 66
A Moment of War. New York: 1991. V. 62
Peasants' Priest - a Play. Canterbury: 1947. V. 63; 65
A Rose for Winter: Travels in Andalusia. London: 1955. V. 62; 66
The Sun My Monument. London: 1944. V. 62; 67
Two Women - a Book of Words and Pictures. London: 1983. V. 63
The Voyage of Magellan - a Dramatic Chronicle for Radio. London: 1948. V. 62

LEE, LAWRENCE
A Hawk from Cuckoo Tavern. Gaylordsville: 1930. V. 65

LEE, MARY
It's a Great War!. London: 1930. V. 62; 64

LEE, NATHANIEL
Constantine the Great, a Tragedy. London: 1684. V. 62
Mithriades King of Pontus, a Tragedy. London: 1685. V. 67
The Tragedy of Nero, Emperor of Rome.... London: 1675. V. 66

LEE, R.
A History and Description of the Modern Dogs of Great Britain and Ireland. The Terriers. 1896. V. 62; 64

LEE, R. H.
Draveil:, or the Life of Harriet Pebble. Philadelphia: 1876. V. 65

LEE, R., MRS.
Trees, Plants and Flowers; their Beauties, Uses and Influences. 1854. V. 63

LEE, R. W.
Antique Fakes and Reproductions. Framingham Centre: 1938. V. 65

LEE, RICHARD H.
Life of Arthur Lee, LL.D. Boston: 1829. V. 63
Observations on the Writings of Thomas Jefferson. Philadelphia: 1839. V. 64

LEE, ROBERT
Clinical Midwifery; with the Histories of Four Hundred Cases of Difficult Labor. London: 1842. V. 67

LEE, ROBERT E.
Lee's Dispatches. New York and London: 1915. V. 62
Lee's Dispatches. New York: 1957. V. 65
Recollections and Letters of General Robert E. Lee. New York: 1904. V. 62

LEE, SOPHIA
The Recess; or a Tale of Other Time.... Dublin: 1791. V. 65

LEE, STEPHEN DILL
Campaign of Generals Grant and Sherman Against Vicksburg in December 1862.... N.P: 1901. V. 62

LEE, WILLIAM H.
Standard Domestic Science Cook Book. Chicago: 1908. V. 67

LEE, WILLIAM MACK
History of the Life of Rev. Wm. Mack Lee. Norfolk: 1918. V. 65

LEE, WILLIS T.
The Manzano Group of the Rio Grande Valley, New Mexico. Washington: 1909. V. 63

LEE, YAN PHOU
When I Was A Boy in China. London: 1888. V. 67

LEECH, BOSDIN
History of the Manchester Ship Canal from Its Inception to Its Completion. London: 1907. V. 62

LEECH, J. H.
British Pyralides, Including the Pterophoridae. 1886. V. 66

LEECH, JOHN
Follies of the Year. London: 1866. V. 65
Pictures of Life and Character. London: 1854. V. 62
Pictures of Life and Character. London: 1887?. V. 63

LEECH, SAMUEL V.
The Drunkard, a Poem. Baltimore: 1862. V. 63

LEECHMAN, DOUGLAS
The Autocar Handbook: a Guide to the Motor Car. London: 1906. V. 64

LEEDS, E. T.
Celtic Ornament in the British Isles Down to AD 700. Oxford: 1933. V. 65

LEEDS, LEWIS W.
Lectures on Ventilation: Being a Course Delivered in the Franklin Institute of Philadelphia During the Winter of 1866-1867. New York: 1868. V. 67

LEEK, MICHAEL E.
The Art of Nautical Illustration. London: 1988. V. 67

LEENE, J. E.
The Portunidae of the Siboga-Expedition I. Leiden: 1938. V. 63; 65

LEEPER, D. R.
The Argonauts of Forty-Nine - Some Recollections of the Plains and the Diggings. 1894. V. 64; 67

LEEPER, WESLEY THURMAN
Rebels Valiant. Second Arkansas Mounted Rifles (Dismounted). Little Rock: 1964. V. 62; 63

LEES, EDWIN
The Affinities of Plants with Man and Animals, Their Analogies and Associations: a Lecture, Delivered Before the Worcestershire Natural History Society, November 26, 1833.... London: 1834. V. 64; 67

LEES, JAMES
Dana's Seamen's Friend.... London: 1900. V. 66

LEESER, ISAAC
The Book of Daily Prayers for Every Day in the Year According to the Custom of the German and Polish Jews. Philadelphia: 1848. V. 62
The Jews and the Mosaic Law. Philadelphia: 1834. V. 62

LEES-MILNE, JAMES
The Age of Adam. London: 1947. V. 62
Baroque in Italy. London: 1959. V. 62
Baroque in Spain and Portugal and Its Antecedents. London: 1960. V. 62
English Country Houses. Baroque 1685-1715. London: 1970. V. 64
Harold Nicolson: a Biography. London: 1980. V. 66
Saint Peter's - the Story of Saint Peter's Basilica in Rome. London: 1967. V. 62
William Beckford. Tisbury: 1976. V. 63
Worcestershire - A Shell Guide. London: 1964. V. 65

LEESON, F.
Identification of Snakes of the Gold Coast. London: 1950. V. 64

LEESON, M. A.
History of Montana. Chicago: 1885. V. 65

LEET, FRANK R.
The Clown's Acrobatic Alphabet. Cleveland: 1928. V. 62

LEEUWENHOEK, ANTONY VAN
Antony Van Leeuwenhoek and His "Little Animals".... New York: 1598. V. 66
Ontledingen en Ontdekkingen...(with) Register...Van alle de Werken... Verdeeld in Twee Deelen (Vol. 1 only).... Leiden: 1686. V. 62

LE FANU, JOSEPH SHERIDAN
Checkmate. London: 1899. V. 66
The Cock and Anchor, Being a Chronicle of Old Dublin City. Dublin: 1845. V. 66
Green Tea and Other Ghost Stories. Sauk City: 1945. V. 64

LE FANU, W. R.
A Bio Bibliography of Edward Jenner. London: 1951. V. 62

LEFEVRE, G. SHAW
Peel and O'Connell; a Review of the Irish Policy of Parliament. 1887. V. 67

LE FEVRE, GEORGE
An Eastern Odyssey: the Third Expediton of Haardt and Audouin- Dubreuil. London: 1935. V. 67

LEFEVRE, RAOUL
The Destruction of Troy, in Three Books. London: 1708. V. 64

LEFEVRE, THEOTISTE
Guide Pratique de Compositeur D'Imprimerie. Paris: 1855. V. 64

LEFEVRE D'ESAPLES, JACQUES
In hoc Opere Contine(n)tur Totius Philosophie Naturalis Paraphrases... (&) Introductio Metaphysica. Paris: 1501. V. 62

LEFFINGWELL, WILLIAM B.
Wild Fowl Shooting. Chicago: 1890. V. 62; 63; 66; 67

LE FORS, JOE
Wyoming Peace Officer - an Autobiography. Laramie: 1953. V. 64; 67

LEFROY, ANNA AUSTEN
Jane Austen's Sanditon: a Continuation by Her Niece, Together with Reminiscences of Aunt Jane. Chicago: 1983. V. 64

LEFROY, W. CHAMBERS
The Ruined Abbeys of Yorkshire. London: 1883. V. 63

A LEGACY of Affection, Advice and Instruction, from a Governess, to the Present Pupils of an Establishment for Female Education.... London: 1827. V. 65

LE GALLIENNE, RICHARD
The Book-Bills of Narcissus, an Account Rendered. Derby, Leicester and Notting: 1891. V. 62
English Poems. London: 1892. V. 62; 64
George Meredith - Some Characteristics. London: 1890. V. 62
Omar Repentant. London: 1908. V. 64
Orestes, a Tragedy. New York: 1910. V. 66
The Quest of the Golden Girl. London and New York: 1896. V. 62
The Silk-Hat Soldier and Other Poems. London: 1915. V. 64

LEGALLOIS, JULIEN JEAN CESAR
Experiences sur la Principe de la Vie. Paris: 1812. V. 67

LE GALLOIS, JULIEN JEAN CESAR
Experiments on the Principle of Life, and Particularly on the Principle of the Motions of the Heart, and on the Seat of This Principle.... New York: 194. V. 65

LE GEAR, CLARA
United States Atlases: a List of National, State, County, City and Regional Atlases in the Library of Congress. 1998. V. 65

LEGENDRE, ADRIEN MARIE
Essai Sur la Theorie des Nombres. Paris: 1797. V. 65

LEGER, ALEXIS SAINT LEGER
Anabasis. London: 1930. V. 65
Chronique. New York: 1961. V. 64
Exile. New York: 1949. V. 65
Winds. New York: 1953. V. 67

LEGG, THOMAS
Low-Life; or One Half of the World, Knows Not How the Other Half Live.... London: 1764. V. 62; 63

LEGGATT, ASHLEY
Stalking Reminiscences 1914-1920. London: 1921. V. 67

LEGGE-BOURKE, HARRY
Some Things Badly. Cairo: 1941. V. 67

LEGH, CROCUS FORSTER
My Cousin Percy. London: 1879. V. 65

LEGH, PETER
The Music of the Eye; or, Essays on the Principles of the Beauty and Perfection of Architecture. London: 1831. V. 65

THE LEGION of Liberty! and Force of Truth. New York: 1843. V. 64

LE GIVRE, P.
Arcanum Acidularum. Amsterdam: 1682. V. 65

LEGOUVE, ERNEST
La Question des Femmes. Paris: 1881. V. 63

LEGOUVE, GABRIEL
Le Merite des Femmes, et Autres Poesies. Paris: 1813. V. 63

LEGOYT, ALFRED
Le Suicide Ancien et Moderne. Etude Historique Philosophique, Morale et Statistique. Paris: 1881. V. 65

LE GRAND, ANTONII
Antonii le Grand Institutio Philosophiae, Secundum Principia Domni Renati Descartes: Nova Methodo Adornata & Explicata. 1672. V. 66

LEGRAND, AUGUSTIN
Cosmographie, ou Connoisances Astronomiques Appliquees a la Geographie et Rendues Sensibles sur Douze Tableaux. Paris: 1865. V. 66

LE GRAND, JULIA
Journal of Julia Le Grand. New Orleans 1862-1863. Richmond: 1911. V. 62; 63

LE GRAND, M.
Fabliaux, or Tales. London: 1796-1800. V. 62
Fabliaux, or Tales, Abridged from French Manuscripts of the XII and XIIIth Centuries. London: 1815. V. 66; 67

LE GRAND D'AUSSY, PIERRE JEAN BAPTISTE
Fabliaux or Tales.... London: 1800. V. 65

LEGROUX, A.
De L'Aphasie. These Presentee au Concours...Faculte de Medecine de Paris. Paris: 1875. V. 64

LE GUIN, URSULA K.
The Farthest Shore. London: 1973. V. 63

LEHANE, DENNIS
Darkness, Take My Hand. New York: 1996. V. 66; 67
A Drink Before the War. New York: 1994. V. 62; 64; 65; 66; 67
Sacred. New York: 1997. V. 67

LEHMAN, ANTHONY L.
Paul Landacre: a Life and a Legacy. Los Angeles: 1983. V. 62

LEHMAN, J. P.
Etude Complementaire des Poissons de l'Eotrias de Madagascar. Stockholm: 1952. V. 65

LEHMANN, JOHN
Evil Was Abroad. London: 1938. V. 63
New Writing - V. London: 1938. V. 63
New Writing and Daylight. London: 1946. V. 64
New Writing, New Writing (New Series). London: 1972. V. 62
The Noise of History. London: 1934. V. 63; 64
The Penguin New Writing. 1940-1950. V. 63
Prometheus and the Bolsheviks. London: 1937. V. 63

LEHMANN, ROSAMOND
Dusty Answer. London: 1982. V. 66

LEHMANN, V. W.
Forgotten Legions, Sheep In the Rio Grande Plain Texas. El Paso: 1964. V. 67

LEHMANN-HAUPT, HELLMUT
The Book in America. New York: 1939. V. 62
Bookbinding in America: Three Essays. Portland: 1941. V. 63
An Introduction to the woodcut of the Seventeenth Century. New York: 1977. V. 63
Peter Schoeffer of Gernsheim and Mainz.... Rochester: 1950. V. 67

LE HOUX, JEAN
(Songs Of) The Vaux de Vire of Maistre Jean Le Houx. London: 1875. V. 67

LEIBER, FRITZ
Bazaar of the Bizarre. West Kingston;: 1978. V. 67
Heroes and Horrors. Browns Mills: 1978. V. 67
Night Monsters. London: 1974. V. 66
Night's Black Agents. 1947. V. 66
Night's Black Agents. Sauk City: 1947. V. 63; 64

LEIBNIZ, GOTTFRIED WILHELM
Collectanea Etymologica Illustrationi Linguarum, Veteris Celticae, Germanicae, Gallicae.... Hanover: 1717. V. 63
Novissima Sinica Historiam Nostri Temporis Illustrata in Quibus De Christianismo Publica Nunc Primum.... N.P: 1699. V. 63

LEIBOVITZ, ANNIE
Photographs. New York: 1983. V. 62; 63

LEICESTER, PETER
Arthur of Britanny, an Historical Tale. London: 1831. V. 65

LEICESTER, ROBERT DUDLEY, EARL OF
Secret Memoirs. 1706. V. 65

LEICESTER GALLERIES
Catalogue of the Exhibitions. London: 1924. V. 66

LEICHHARDT, F. W. LUDWIG
The Letters of W. Ludwig Leichhardt. Cambridge: 1968. V. 64; 65

LEICHIUS, I. HEINRICHIUS
De Origine et Incrementis Typographiae Lipsiensis Liber Singularis Ubi Varia De Litterariis Urbis Studiis et Viris Doctis.... Leipzig: 1740. V. 65

LEIDENFROST, JOHANN GOTTLOB
Opuscula Physico-Chemica et Medica. Lemgoviae: 1797-1798. V. 65

LEIDING, HARRIETE KERSHAW
Charleston, Historic and Romantic. Philadelphia: 1931. V. 63

LEIDY, J.
The Ancient Fauna of Nebraska. 1853. V. 63
Fresh-Water Rhizopods of North America. Washington: 1879. V. 66
Memoir on the Extinct Species of American Ox. Washington: 1852. V. 65
Urnatella Gracilis; a Fresh-Water Polyzoan. Philadelphia c: 1885. V. 67

LEIFCHILD, JOHN R.
Cornwall: Its Mines and Miners. London: 1855. V. 65

LEIGH, AGNES
Tommy's Tiny Tales. London: 1907. V. 67

LEIGH, CHARLES
The Natural History of Lancashire, Cheshire and the Peak in Derbyshire. Oxford: 1700. V. 62; 64

LEIGH, EGERTON
Ballads and Legends of Cheshire. London: 1867. V. 63; 66
The Glossary of Words Used in the Dialect of Cheshire. London: 1877. V. 64

LEIGH, EVAN
The Science of Modern Cotton Spinning.... Manchester: 1873. V. 65

LEIGH, FLORENCE
Greedy Federick. London: 1899. V. 63

LEIGH, M. A.
Leigh's Guide to the Lakes and Mountains of Cumberland, Westmorland and Lancashire. London: 1832. V. 64

LEIGH, PERCIVAL
Comic Arithmetic. London: 1844. V. 64
The Comic Latin Grammar.... London: 1840. V. 64
Paul Prendergast; or, the Comic Schoolmaster. London: 1859. V. 64

LEIGH, SAMUEL
New Pocket Road-Book of England and Wales, and Part of Scotland.... London: 1826. V. 63

LEIGH, WILLIAM R.
The Western Pony. New York: 1933. V. 62

LEIGHLY, JOHN
California as an Island: an Illustrated Essay. San Francisco: 1972. V. 62; 63

LEIGHTON, CLARE
Four Hedges. New York: 1935. V. 64
Where Land Meets Sea. The Tide Line of Cape Cod. New York: 1954. V. 67
Woodcuts. London: 1930. V. 62

LEIGHTON, G. R.
The Life History of British Serpents and Their Local Distribution in the British Isles. Edinburgh: 1901. V. 66; 67

LEIGHTON, J. & J., BOOKSELLERS
Catalogue: Early Printed Books Arranged by Presses. 1910. V. 64

LEIGHTON, JOHN
Christmas Comes But Once a Year. London: 1850. V. 65

LEIGHTON, ROBERT
The Whole Works. London: 1830. V. 67

LEIGHTON, W. A.
The British Species of Angiocarpous Lichens, Elucidated by Their Spares. London: 1851. V. 64; 65; 67

LEINSTER, MURRAY
Operation Outer Space. 1954. V. 64
Sidewise in Time. Chicago: 1950. V. 64

LEIPNIK, F. L.
A History of French Etching from the Sixteenth Century to the Present Day. London: 1924. V. 62; 64

LEIRIS, MICHEL
Francis Bacon: Full Face and in Profile. New York: 1987. V. 63

LEITFRED, ROBERT H.
Death Cancels the Evidence. New York: 1938. V. 67

LEITHAUSER, BRAD
Equal Distance. New York: 1985. V. 63

LEITNER, G. W.
Anthropological Observations on the Following Dards and Kafirs in Dr. Leitner's Service. Calcutta?: 1890. V. 67

LE JEUNE, J. M.
Elements of Shorthand. Kamloops: 1891. V. 66
Prayers in Thompson. Kamloops: 1894. V. 66

LEJEUNE, RITA
The Legend of the Roland in the Middle Ages. London: 1971. V. 63

LEKSELL, LARS
Stereotaxis and Radiosurgery. An Operative System. Springfield: 1971. V. 64

LELAND, CHARLES G.
The Algonquin Legends of New England or Myths and Folk Lore of the MicMac, Passamaquoddy and Penobscot Tribes. Boston: 1884. V. 64
The Gypsies. London: 1882. V. 66
Johnnykin and the Goblins. London: 1877. V. 65
Ye Book of Copperheads. Philadelphia: 1863. V. 63

LELAND, EFFIE WILLIAMS
Crossin' Over. Columbia: 1937. V. 67

LELAND, JOHN
A View of the Principal Deistical Writers That Have Appeared in England in the Last and Present Century.... London: 1755. V. 66

LELAND, THOMAS
The History of Ireland, from the Invasion of Henry II. Dublin: 1774. V. 65
The History of the Life and Reign of Philip King of Macedonia, the Father of Alexander. London: 1748. V. 64
Longsword, Earl of Salisbury. An Historical Romance. London: 1762. V. 63

LELEK, A.
The Freshwater Fishes of Europe. Volume 9. Threatened Fishes of Europe. Wiesbaden: 1987. V. 65

LELIEVRE, J. F.
Nouveau Jardinier de la Louisiane.... Nouvelle Orleans: 1838. V. 64

LELLENBERG, JON L.
Irregular Records of the Early 'Forties: an Archival History of the Baker Street Irregulars. January 1941-March 1944. New York: 1991. V. 66

LE MAINGRE DE BOUCICAULT, DON LUIS
Les Amazones Revoltees. Rotterdam: 1737. V. 63

LE MAISTRE, J. G.
Frederic Latimer; or, the History of a Young Man of Fashion. Cork: 1801. V. 67

LEMAITRE, JULES
ABC - Petits Contes. (Little ABC Stories). Tours: 1919/. V. 64

LE MAOUT, EMMANUEL
Lecons Elementaires de Botanique Fondees sur l'Analyse de 50 Plantes Vulgaires et Formant un Traite Complet d'Organographie et de Physiologie Vegetale. Paris: 1844. V. 64

LEMARCHAND, JACQUES
Genevieve. London: 1947. V. 65

LE MARCHAND, MADAME, PSEUD.
Le Marchand's Fortune Teller, and Dreamer's Dictionary... Interpretation of Each Dream.... New York: 1863. V. 63

LE MAY, ALAN
The Searchers. New York: 1954. V. 66

LEMEE, FRANCOIS
Traite des Statues. Paris: 1688. V. 64

LEMERCHER DE LONGPRE, CHARLES
Great Britain in 1833. London: 1833. V. 66
Great Britain in 1833. Philadelphia: 1833. V. 66

LEMERY, NICOLAS
A Course of Chymistry. London: 1677. V. 62; 66
New Curiosities in Art and Nature.... London: 1711. V. 66
Traite Universel Des Drogues Simples.. Paris: 1714. V. 65

LEMNIUS, LEVINUS
De Miraculis Occultus Naturae Libri III. Jenae: 1588. V. 62

LEMOINE, HENRY
Typographical Antiquities, History, Origin and Progress of the Art of Printing.... London: 1797. V. 62; 66; 67

LEMON, GEORGE WILLIAM
English Etymology; or, a Derivative Dictionary of the English Language in Two Alphabets. London: 1783. V. 62

LEMON, MARK
Fairy Tales. London: 1868. V. 64
The Heir of Applebite and Our Lodgers. London: 1856. V. 67
The Jest Book.... London: 1864. V. 67
Legends of Number Nip. London: 1864. V. 62; 66
A Shilling's Worth of Nonsense. London: 1843. V. 67
Up and Down the London Streets. London: 1867. V. 62; 66

LE MOYNE, L. V.
Country Residences in Europe and America. New York: 1921. V. 63

LE MOYNE, PIERRE
The Gallery of Heroick Women. London: 1652. V. 62; 64
Of the Art Both of Writing and Judging of History with Reflections Upon Ancient as Well as Modern Historians Shewing through What Defects There Are So Few Good.... London: 1695. V. 66

LEMPERLY, PAUL
A List of Book-Plates Engraved on Copper by Mr. Edwin Davis French. Cleveland: 1899. V. 63

LE NAIN DE TILLEMONT, LOUIS SEBASTIAN
An Account of the Life of Apollonius Tyaneus. London: 1702. V. 62

LENEHAN, MICHAEL
The Essence of Beeing. Chicago: 1992. V. 62

LENERO, VICENTE
La Polvareda. Mexico City: 1959. V. 67
La Voz Adolorida. Mexico City: 1961. V. 67

LENG, SAM
Experiences and Reminiscences of a Cliff-Climber with Description of Flamborough, Bempton and Speeton Cliffs and the Birds that Inhabit them. Manchester: 1931. V. 64

L'ENGLE, MADELEINE
A Ring of Endless Light. New York: 1980. V. 65
A Wrinkle in Time. New York: 1962. V. 63

LENGLET, DUFRESNOY, N.
Le Cabinet Satyrique, ou Recueil de Vers Piquans & Galliards de ces Temps. Amsterdam?: 1697. V. 67

LENHOFF, H. M.
The Biology of Hydra and of Some Other Coelenterates. Coral Gables: 1961. V. 67

LENIHAN, DANIEL J.
Final Report of the National Reservoir Induation Study. Santa Fe: 1981. V. 63; 66

LENIN, VLADIMIR IL'ICH
Collected Works. Moscow: 1960-1980. V. 67
Lessons of the Russian Revolution. London: 1918. V. 67
Sag Vpered Dva Saga Nazad. Geneva: 1904. V. 63

LENNEP, WILLIAM VAN
The London Stage 1660-1800. Carbondale: 1965. V. 63

LENNON, JOHN
Bag One. New York: 1970. V. 66
In His Own Write. London: 1964. V. 64; 66
In His Own Write and a Spaniard in the Works. New York: 1965. V. 66
In His Own Write and A Spaniard in the Works. London: 1981. V. 65
A Spaniard in the Works. London: 1965. V. 65; 66

LENNOX, CHARLOTTE RAMSEY
The Female Quixote, or the Adventures of Arabella. London: 1810. V. 63

LENORMANT, FRANCOIS
Catalogue d'une Collection d'Antiquites Egyptiennes.... 1857. V. 64

LENSKI, LOIS
Bound Girl of Cobble Hill. New York: 1938. V. 65
Flood Friday. Philadelphia: 1956. V. 64
Grandmother Tippytoe. New York: 1931. V. 63
High Rise Secret. Philadelphia: 1966. V. 62
Let's Play House. New York: 1944. V. 63
The Little Farm. New York: 1942. V. 65
The Little Fire Engine. New York: 1946. V. 63
The Little Train. New York: 1940. V. 65
Prairie School. Philadelphia: 1951. V. 63
San Francisco Boy. Philadelphia: 1955. V. 65
Strawberry Girl. Philadelphia: 1945. V. 63; 65
Surprise for Mother. New York: 1934. V. 64
Susie Mariar. New York: 1939. V. 63
We Live in the North. Philadelphia: 1965. V. 63

LENZ, E. C.
Muzzle Flashes. Five Centuries of Firearms and Men. 1944. V. 66; 67

LENZ, P. H.
Zooplankton: Sensory Ecology and Physiology. Amsterdam: 1996. V. 64

LEON, MODENA
The History of the Rites, Customes, and Manner of Life of the Present Jews, Throughout the World. London: 1650. V. 63

LEON & BROTHER
First Editions of American Authors. New York: 1885. V. 63

LEONARD, ARTHUR GLYN
How We Made Rhodesia. London: 1896. V. 62

LEONARD, ELMORE
City Primeval. New York: 1980. V. 66
Dutch Treat. 1977. V. 64; 66
Fifty-Two Pickup. London: 1974. V. 67
Fifty-Two Pickup. New York: 1974. V. 65
Forty Lashes Less One. New York: 1972. V. 67
Get Shorty. New York: 1990. V. 66
Glitz. New York: 1985. V. 62
Gunsights. New York: 1979. V. 65
Hombre. New York: 1961. V. 65; 66; 67
The Hunted. New York: 1977. V. 66
The Moonshine War. Garden City: 1969. V. 67
The Moonshine War Exhibitor's Merchandising Manual for MGM. Culver City: 1970. V. 67
Notebooks. Northridge: 1990. V. 65
Notebooks. Northridge: 1991. V. 66
Rum Punch. Hastings-on-Hudson: 1992. V. 65
Split Images. New York: 1981. V. 66; 67
Swag. New York: 1976. V. 62; 65; 66; 67
The Switch. London: 1979. V. 65; 66; 67
Unknown Man No. 89. London: 1977. V. 67
Unknown Man No. 89. New York: 1977. V. 66

LEONARD, IRVING ALBERT
The Mecurio Volante of Don Carlos De Siquenza Y Gongora - An Account of the First Expedition of Don Diego De Vargas into New Mexico in 1692. Los Angeles: 1932. V. 65

LEONARD, R. M.
The Pageant of English Poetry. London: 1909. V. 62

LEONARD, THOMAS H.
From Indian Trail to Electric Rail. History of the Atlantic Highlands, Sandy Hook and Original Portland Point.... Atlantic Highlands: 1923. V. 63; 66

LEONARD, TOM
If Only Bunty Was Here. Glasgow: 1979. V. 63

LEONARD, ZENAS
Leonard's Narrative: Adventures of Zenas Leonard, Fur Trader and Trapper 1831-1836. Cleveland: 1904. V. 67

LEONARDI, CAMILLO
The Mirror of Stones; in Which the Nature, Generation, Properties, Virtues and Various Species of More than 200 Different Jewels, Precious and Rare Stones.... London: 1750. V. 63

LEONARDI, DOMENICO FELICE
Le Delizie della Villa di Castellazzo Descritte in Verso. Milan: 1743. V. 66

LEONARDI, PIERO
Le Dolomiti. Geologia dei Monti tra Isarco e Piave Premio Nazionaledei Lincei 1958 per Geologia e la Paleontologia. Trento: 1967. V. 67

LEONARDO DA VINCI
The Notebooks of Leonardo da Vinci. London: 1938. V. 65
Trattato Della Pittura.... Paris: 1651. V. 63
A Treatise on Painting Faithfully Translated.... London: 1802. V. 66

LEONARDUS, CAMILLUS
The Mirror of Stones. London: 1750. V. 63

LEONI, MICHELE
Prose. Lugano: 1829. V. 64

LEOPOLD, ALDO
Game Management. 1933. V. 62
Sand County Almanac and Sketches Here and There. New York: 1949. V. 67

LEOPOLD, JACOB
Theatrum Machinarum Molarium, Oder Schau-Platz Der Muhlen-Bau-Kunst. Leipzig: 1735. V. 66

LE PAYS, RENE
Les Nouvelles Oeuvres. Amsterdam: 1690. V. 66

LE PELLIER, JEAN
L'Alkaest ou Le Dissolvant Universel de Van-Helmont. Rouen: 1706. V. 65

LE PETRE, WILLIAM
The Bolshevik. London: 1930?. V. 63

LE PLUCHE, NOEL ANTOINE
The Truth of the Gospel Demonstrated from the Dispensations of Providence Preparative to it.... London: 1751. V. 62

LE PRADE, RUTH
Debs and the Poets. Pasadena: 1920. V. 63

LE PRINCE DE BEAUMONT, JEANNE MARIE
Magasin de Adolescentes ou Dialogues d'une Sage Gouvernante avec ses Eleves de la Premiere Distinction. Lyon: 1778. V. 67
Magasin des Enfan(t)s; ou, Dialogues d'une Sage Gouvernante, avec ses Eleves de la Premiere Distinction. London: 1806. V. 67
Magasin ou Instructions Pour les Jeunes Dames Qui Entrent dans le Monde et se Marient; Leurs Devoirs dans cet etat, et Envers leurs Enfants. Lyon: 1776. V. 67
Magazin des Enfants; or the Polite Tutoress, and Young Lady's Instructor. Dublin: 1770-1776. V. 62
Memoires de Madame la Baronne de Batteville, ou La Veuve Parfaite. Lyon et Liege: 1766. V. 63

LEPSIUS, C. R.
Standard Alphabet for Reducing Unwritten Languages and Foreign Graphic System to a Uniform Orthography in European Letters. London: 1863. V. 64

LEPSIUS, RICHARD
Letters from Egypt, Ethiopia and the Peninsula of Sinai.... London: 1853. V. 67

LE QUEUX, WILLIAM
Behind the Bronze Door. New York: 1923. V. 67
The Bond of Black. London: 1899. V. 64; 66
The Closed Book. 1904. V. 64; 66
Confessions of a Ladies Man. London: 1905. V. 64
The Czar's Spy. London: 1905. V. 64; 66
The Elusive Four. London: 1921. V. 65
The Great War in England in 1897. London: 1894. V. 66
Guilty Bonds. 1895. V. 64; 66
Hidden Hands. London: 1926. V. 63; 64; 66
The Place of Dragons. London: 1919. V. 67
Rasputinism in London. London: 1919. V. 65
Stolen Souls. 1895. V. 64; 66
The Temptress. London: 1895. V. 64
Treasure of Israel. London: 1910. V. 63
Zoraida. London: 1895. V. 63; 64; 66

LERMAN, LEO
The Museum, One Hundred Years and the Metropolitan Museum of Art. New York: 1969. V. 63

LERMONTOV, MIKHAIL
A Hero of Our Days. London: 1854. V. 67

LERNER, ALAN JAY
Camelot. New York: 1961. V. 66
My Fair Lady: a Musical in Two Acts. New York: 1956. V. 62
The Street Where I Live. London: 1978. V. 67
The Street Where I Live. New York: 1978. V. 66

LEROUX, GASTON
The Mystery of the Yellow Room. New York: 1908. V. 65
The Perfume of the Lady in Black. New York: 1909. V. 65
The Phantom of the Opera. 1911. V. 63
The Phantom of the Opera. New York: 1911. V. 65

LE ROUX, JEAN
La Clef de Nostradamus.... Paris: 1710. V. 64

LE ROY, CHARLES
Traite de l'Orthographe Francoise, en Forme de Dictionnaire.... A Poitiers: 1765. V. 65

LE ROY, JULIEN DAVID
Les Ruines des Plus Beaux Monuments de la Grece. Paris: 1758. V. 62; 64

LEROY, L. ARCHIER
Wagner's Music Drama of the Ring. London: 1925. V. 62

LE SAGE, ALAIN RENE
The Adventures of Gil Blas of Santillane. London: 1773. V. 62
The Adventures of Gil Blas of Santillane. London: 1785. V. 62
The Adventures of Gil Blas of Santillane. London: 1807. V. 66
The Adventures of Gil Blas of Santillane. London: 1819. V. 64; 66
The Adventures of Gil Blas of Santillane. London: 1830. V. 67
Aventuras de Gil Blas de Santillana Robadas a Espana...Que Nosufre se Burlen de su Nacion. Valencia: 1788-1789. V. 64
The Bachelor of Salmanaca. London: 1881. V. 62
The Devil Upon Two Sticks. London: 1824. V. 65
Il Diavolo Zoppo. (The Devil in a Bottle). Turin: 1840. V. 66

LESBIAN
Poetry. Watertown: 1981. V. 63

LESCARBOURA, AUSTIN C.
Behind the Motion-Picture Screen. New York: 1919. V. 65

LESIEUTRE, ALAIN
The Spirit and Splendour of Art Deco. New Jersey: 1974. V. 62

LESLEY, CRAIG
Winterkill. Boston: 1984. V. 62; 64; 65; 67

LESLEY, JOANNE
De Origine Moribus & Rebus Gestis Scotorum Libri Decem.... 1675. V. 66

LESLEY, LEWIS BURT
Uncle Sam's Camels.... Cambridge: 1928. V. 64; 67

LESLIE, ALFRED
100 Views Along the Road. New York: 1988. V. 65

LESLIE, C. R.
A Hand-Book for Young Painters. London: 1855. V. 62
Life and Times of Sir Joshua Reynolds.... London: 1865. V. 62

LESLIE, DAVID
Among the Zulus and Amatongas; with Sketches of the Natives, their Language and Customs; and the Country, Products, Climate, Wild Animals etc. Edinburgh: 1875. V. 67

LESLIE, ELIZA
Miss Leslie's New Receipts for Cooking. Philadelphia: 1854. V. 64

LESLIE, JOHN
De Illustrium Foeminarum in Republica Adminstranda ac Ferendis Legibus Authoritatae Libellus.... Reims: 1580. V. 65

Elements of Natural Philosophy...Volume 1st.... Edinburgh: 1823. V. 65

The Philosophy of Arithmetic; Exhibiting a Progressive View of The Theory and Practice of Calculation.... Edinburgh: 1817. V. 66

The Philosophy of Arithmetic: Exhibiting a Progressive View of the Theory and Practice of Calculation.... Edinburgh: 1820. V. 62; 65; 67

Rudiments of Plane Geometry, Including Geometrical Analysis and Plane Trigonometry. Edinburgh: 1828. V. 65

LESLIE, JOHN HENRY
The History of Landguard Fort, in Suffolk. London: 1898. V. 62

LESLIE, LIONEL
Wilderness Trails in Three Continents. London: 1931. V. 67

LESLIE, SHANE
The Cantab. London: 1926. V. 67

The Cuckoo Clock and Other Poems. 1987. V. 64

The Greek Anthology. 1929. V. 64; 67

The Greek Anthology. London: 1929. V. 66

Mark Sykes; His Life and Letters. London: 1923. V. 67

The Rubaiyat of the Mystics. Dublin: 1950. V. 67

Songs of Oriel. Dublin: 1908. V. 67

LESLIE'S Official History of the Spanish American War. New York: 1899. V. 67

LESNE, MATHURIN MARIE
La Reliure, Poeme Didactique en Six Chants... (with) Lettre d'un Relieur Francais a un Bibliographe Anglais. Paris: 1822-1823. V. 63

LESQUEREUX, L.
Contributions to the Fossil Flora of the Western Territories. Part II. Washington: 1878. V. 66

LESSING, DORIS
Children of Violence. Martha Quest.(with) A Proper Marriage. A Ripple from the Storm. (with) Landlocked. The Four Gated City. New York: 1964-1969. V. 65

The Good Terrorist. London: 1985. V. 62; 66

The Grass is Singing. London: 1950. V. 62

The Grass is Singing. New York: 1950. V. 63

The Habit of Loving. London: 1957. V. 62

Love, Again. New York: 1995. V. 67

The Memoirs of a Survivor. New York: 1975. V. 63

A Small Personal Voice: Essays, Reviews and Interviews. New York: 1974. V. 66

Three Stories. Helsinki: 1988. V. 65

Walking in the Shade, Volume Two of My Autobiography. New York: 1997. V. 67

LESSING, GOTTHOLD
Hamburgische Dramaturgie. Hamburg: 1767. V. 62

LESSIUS, LEONARD
Sir Walter Rawleigh's Ghost; or His Apparition. London: 1651. V. 64

LESSON, RENE PRIMEVERE
Histoire Naturelle des Oiseaux - Mouches; Histoire Naturelle des Colibris...; Les Trochilidees ou les Colibris et les Oiseaux-Mouches.... Paris: 1829-1830. V. 67

Histoire Naturelle des Oiseaux de Paradis et des Epimaques. Paris: 1834-1835. V. 67

LESSONS Of Thrift Published for General Benefit. London: 1820. V. 64

LESTER, CHARLES EDWARDS
The Gallery of Illustrious Americans, Containing the Portraits and Biographical Sketches of Twenty Four of the Most Eminent Citizens of the Republic.... New York: 1850. V. 64

The Glory and Shame of England. London: 1841. V. 64

The Glory and Shame of England. New York: 1866. V. 64

The Life of Sam. Houston. Philadelphia: 1860. V. 64

LESTER, HORACE FRANCIS
Queen of the Hamlet. London: 1894. V. 67

LESTER, JOHN ERASTUS
The Atlantic to the Pacific. London: 1873. V. 64; 65

LESTER, JULIUS
John Henry. New York: 1994. V. 65

LESTER, THOMAS
Opposition Dangerous. London: 1798. V. 64

LESTER, W. W.
A Digest of the Military and Naval Laws of the Confederate States.... Columbia: 1864. V. 63

LESTER, WILLIAM STEWART
The Transylvania Colony. Spence: 1935. V. 63; 64

LESTERMAN, JOHN
The Adventures of Trafalgar Lad - a Tale of the Sea. London: 1926. V. 63

L'ESTRANGE, A. G.
The Friendships of Mary Russell Mitford as Recorded in Letters from Her Literary Correspondents. London: 1882. V. 65

The Life of Mary Russell Mitford, Related in a Selection from Her Letters to Her Friends. London: 1870. V. 65

LE STRANGE, G.
Baghdad During the Abbasid Caliphate from Contemporary Arabic and Persian Sources. Oxford: 1900. V. 67

L'ESTRANGE, ROGER
An Answer to a Letter to a Dissenter Upon Occasion of His Majesties Late Gracious Declaration of Indulgence. London: 1687. V. 62

Discovery Upon Discovery: In Defence of Doctor Oates Against B. W.'s Libellous Vindication of Him, in His Additional Discovery.... London: 1680. V. 62

A Further Discovery of the Plot.... London: 1681. V. 62

LESUEUR, MERIDEL
Corn Village. Sauk City: 1970. V. 67

LESY, MICHAEL
Wisconsin Death Trip. New York: 1973. V. 66

LESZNAI, ANNA
De Reise Des Kleinen Schmetterlings Durchleszna und Nach Den Benachbarten Reenreichen. (Voyage of a Small Butterfly). Wien: 1912. V. 64

LETCHER, OWEN
The Bonds of Africa. 1913. V. 67

LETCHWORTH, WILLIAM PRYOR
The Insane in Foreign Countries. New York and London: 1889. V. 65

LETHABY, W. R.
Ernest Gimson His Life and Work. Oxford: 1924. V. 67

LETHBRIDGE, ALAN
West Africa the Elusive. London: 1921. V. 67

LETHEM, JONATHAN
Gun, with Occasional Music. 1994. V. 64; 66

Gun, with Occasional Music. New York: 1994. V. 63; 65; 66; 67

Motherless Brooklyn. New York: 1999. V. 67

LETI, GREGORIO
The Amours of Messalina Late Quee of Albion.... London: 1689. V. 65

Il Cardinalismo di Santa Chiesa; or the History of the Cardinals of the Roman Church, from the Time of Their First Creation, to the Election of the Present Pope, Clement the Ninth.... London: 1670. V. 62

LETOURNEAU, CHARLES
Sociology Based Upon Ethnography. London: 1881. V. 64

LETT, LEWIS
Knights Errant of Papua. London: 1935. V. 67

A LETTER from a Gentleman at Edinburgh to His Correspondent at London. London: 1745. V. 66

A LETTER from Beelzebub, Addressed to a Christian Church in Edinburgh; or, a Supplement to a Pamphlet, Entitled, Christ the True Rest; or, the Jewish Sabbath a Type of Christ. Chester: 1792. V. 65

LETTER on the Importance of Steam Navigation to the British Navy. London: 1821. V. 62

A LETTER on the Subject of the Succession. London: 1679. V. 65

A LETTER to a Country Gentleman, Shewing the Inconveniences, Which Attend the Last Part of the Act for Triennial Parliaments. London: 1716. V. 63

A LETTER to a Gentleman in the Country, from His Friend in London; Giving an Authentick and Circumstantial Account of the Confinement, Behaviour and Death of Admiral Byng, as Attested by the Gentlemen Who Were Present. London: 1757. V. 65

A LETTER to Lord Robert Bertie, Relating to Conduct in the Mediterranean and His Defence of Admiral Byng. London: 1757. V. 65

A LETTER to the Right Hon. William Wyndham, on His Late Opposition to the Bill to Prevent Bull-Baiting, by a Member of Parliament. London: 1800. V. 63

A LETTER to the Right Honourable Sir William Scott on His Clergy- Farmer's Bill. London: 1803. V. 66

A LETTER to the Right Honourable William Pitt, Esq., Being an Impartial Vindication of the Conduct of the Ministry, from the Commencement of the Present War to This Time. London: 1756. V. 65

LETTERS Addressed to the Merchants and Inhabitants of the Town of Liverpool, Concerning a Free Trade to the East Indies. Liverpool: 1812. V. 62

LETTERS and Papers on Agriculture, Planting &c. Selected from the Correspondence Book of the Society Instituted, at Bath for the Encouragement of Agriculture, Arts, Manufactures and Commerce.... Bath: 1783. V. 63; 67

LETTERS from an Irish Student in England to His Father in Ireland. London: 1809. V. 63

LETTERS from India and Kashmir: Written 1870: Illustrated and Annotated 1873. London: 1874. V. 63

LETTERS from Old Friends. Cheyenne: 1923. V. 65

LETTERS from the Mountains, Being the Real Correspondence of a Lady, Between the Years 1773 and 1807. London: 1813. V. 67

THE LETTERS from the True Zeta, to the Earl of Durham and Others, as Published in the True Sun in 1833-1834-1835. Chelsea: 1835. V. 62

LETTERS of Neptune and Gracchus, Addressed to the P(rince) of W(ales), and Other Distinguished Characters.... London: 1784. V. 63

LETTERS of the Gold Rush Discovery. 1948. V. 62

LETTERS to a Fiction Writer. New York: 1999. V. 62

LETTOW VORBECK, PAUL VON
Meine Erinnerungen Au Ostafrika. Leipzig: 1920. V. 67

LETTS, J. M.
California Illustrated: Including a Description of the Panama and Nicaragua Routes. New York: 1853. V. 63; 66
A Pictorial View of California.... New York: 1853. V. 62

LETTSOM, JOHN COAKLEY
Hints Respecting the Distresses of the Poor. London: 1796. V. 66
History of the Origin of Medicine: an Oration, Delivered at the Anniversary Meeting of the Medical Society of London, Jan. 19, 1778 and Printed at Their Request. London: 1778. V. 64
Memoirs of John Fothergill, M.D. London: 1786. V. 63
The Naturalist's and Traveller's Companion. London: 1799. V. 65

LETTY, C.
Wild Flowers of the Transvaal. Pretoria: 1962. V. 64; 66

LEUNCLAVIUS, JOANNES
Iuris Graeco Romanai Tam Canonici Quam Civilis Tomi Duo. 1971. V. 66

LEUPOLD, JACOB
Theatrum Machinarum Molarium, Oder Schau-Platz der Muhlen-Bau-Kunst. Leipzig: 1735. V. 64
Theatrum Pontificiale. Leipzig: 1726. V. 62; 66; 67

LEUPP, FRANCIS E.
The Latest Phase of the Southern Ute Question: a Report. Philadelphia: 1895. V. 63

LEVAILLANT, FRANCOIS
Histoire Naturelle d'une Partie D'Oiseaux Nouveaux et Rares de l'Amerique et des Indes.... Paris: 1801-1802. V. 67

LE VAILLANT, M.
Travels into the Interior Parts of Africa by the Way of the Cape of Good Hope, in the Years 1780, 1781, 1782, 1783, 1784 and 1785. London: 1796. V. 65

LEVAYER DE BOUTIGNY, ROLAND
Tarsis et Zelie. Paris: 1774. V. 62

LEVELING, HEINRICH
Anatomische Erklarung der Original-Figuren von Andreas Vesal, Samt Einer Anwendung der Winslowischen Zergliederungslehre in Sieben Buchern. Ingoldstadt: 1783. V. 64
Dissertatio de Pyloro Carcinomatoso.... Anglipoli: 1777. V. 65

LEVER, CHARLES JAMES
Arthur O'Leary; His Wanderings and Ponderings in Many Lands. London: 1845. V. 67
Arthur O'Leary; His Wanderings and Ponderings in Many Lands. New York: 1845. V. 63
Charles O'Malley, the Irish Dragoon. Dublin: 1841. V. 65
Confessions of Con. Cregan: the Irish Gil Blas. London: 1849. V. 65
The Confessions of Harry Lorrequer. Dublin: 1839. V. 66
A Day's Ride: a Life's Romance. London: 1864. V. 66
Diary and Notes of Horace Templeton, Esq. London: 1848. V. 66
The Dodd Family Abroad.... London: 1854. V. 62
The Knight of Gwynne. London: 1846-1847. V. 65
The Knight of Gwynne. London: 1858. V. 67
Luttrell of Arran. London: 1865. V. 65
Nuts and Nutcrackers. London: 1844. V. 65
The O'Donoghue; a Tale of Ireland Fifty Years Ago. Dublin: 1845. V. 67
Roland Cashel. London: 1854. V. 67
St. Patrick's Eve. London: 1845. V. 65; 66
That Boy of Norcott's. London: 1869. V. 65

LEVER, DARCY
The Young Officer's Sheet Anchor; or, a Key to the Leading of Rigging and to Practical Seamanship. Philadelphia: 1819. V. 62; 64
The Young Sea Officer's Sheet Anchor; or, a Key to the Leading of Rigging and to Practical Seamanship. London: 1808. V. 64; 66

LEVERING, H. BROOKE
The Story of Dolly and Dan and the Dimpledees. New York: 1916. V. 63

LEVERTOV, DENISE
Batterers. West Burke: 1996. V. 62; 64
Conversation in Moscow. N.P. 1973. V. 62
El Salvador: Requiem and Invocation. Boston: 1983. V. 62
Embroideries. Los Angeles: 1969. V. 62
Footprints. New York: 1972. V. 62; 67
Here and Now. San Francisco: 1957. V. 64; 66
In the Night. New York: 1968. V. 62
The Jacob's Ladder. London: 1965. V. 64
Life in the Forest. New York: 1978. V. 62; 66
Mad Cow. London: 1994. V. 67
A Marigold from North Viet Nam. New York: 1968. V. 62
The Menaced World. Concord: 1985. V. 62; 67
Modulations for Solo Voice. San Francisco: 1977. V. 62; 64; 67
A New Year's Garland for My Students. MIT 1969/1970. Mt. Horeb: 1970. V. 67
O Taste and See. New Poems. Norfolk: 1964. V. 66
On Equal Terms. University of Alabama: 1984. V. 67
Overland to the Islands. Highlands: 1958. V. 64; 66; 67
Pig Dreams. Woodstock: 1981. V. 62; 67
Three Poems. Mt. Horeb: 1968. V. 67
To Stay Alive. New York: 1971. V. 67
Two Poems. Concord: 1983. V. 62; 67
With Eyes at the Back of Our Heads. New York: 1959. V. 67

LEVESON, H. A.
The Forest and the Field. London: 1867. V. 64
The Forest and the Field. London: 1874. V. 67
Sport in Many Lands. 1890. V. 63
Sport in Many Lands. London: 1890. V. 62; 67

LEVESQUE DE POUILLY, LOUIS JEAN
The Theory of Agreeable Sensations. London: 1774. V. 63; 66

LEVI, A. J.
Conversion of Mr. and Mrs. Levi. New York: 1852. V. 63; 66

LEVI, CARLO
The Watch. New York: 1951. V. 66

LEVI, ELIPHAS
The History of Magic. 1922. V. 65

LEVI, LEONE
The History of British Commerce and of the Economic Progress of the British Nation 1763-1870. London: 1872. V. 65
The History of British Commerce and of the Economic Progress of the British Nation 1763-1878. London: 1880. V. 66

LEVI, PETER
Ruined Abbeys. Northwood: 1968. V. 62

LEVI, W. M.
The Pigeon. Sumter: 1963. V. 63; 64; 67

LEVICK, GEORGE MURRAY
Antarctic Penguins. London: 1914. V. 65; 67

LEVIN, HOWARD M.
Dorothea Lange: Farm Security Administration Photographs 1935-1939. Glencoe: 1980. V. 63

LEVIN, IRA
A Kiss Before Dying. New York: 1953. V. 65
Rosemary's Baby. New York: 1967. V. 62; 65; 66
The Stepford Wives. New York: 1972. V. 65

LEVINAS, EMMANUEL
La Theorie de l'Intuition dans la Phenomenologie de Husserl. Paris: 1930. V. 67

LEVINE, DAVID
Pens and Needles. Literary Caricatures by David Levine. Boston: 1969. V. 66

LEVINE, LEO
Ford: the Dust and the Glory, a Racing History. New York: 1968. V. 65

LEVINE, PHILIP
Ashes. Poems New and Old. Port Townsend: 1979. V. 62
The Bread of Time: Toward an Autobiography. New York: 1994. V. 67
Dreaming in Swedish. Los Angeles: 1994. V. 62; 67
The Names of the Lost. Poems. Iowa City: 1976. V. 62; 64; 67
New Season. Port Townsend: 1968. V. 62
New Season. Port Townsend: 1975. V. 62; 67
1933. New York: 1974. V. 62
Not This Pig. Middletown: 1968. V. 62; 63
On the Edge. Iowa City: 1963. V. 64; 65
On the Edge. Iowa City: 1964. V. 63
Pili's Wall. Santa Barbara: 1971. V. 66
The Poem of Chalk. Huntington Woods: 1995. V. 64
Red Dust. Poems. Santa Cruz: 1971. V. 66
Smoke. 1997. V. 62; 67
Uncollected Poems. Santa Cruz: 1997. V. 64; 67
A Walk with Tom Jefferson. New York: 1988. V. 62

LEVINSON, ANDRE
Bakst: the Story of the Artist's Life. London: 1923. V. 62

LEVINSON, JOHN L.
Frank Morrison Pixley of the Argonaut. San Francisco: 1989. V. 63

LEVINZ, CRESWELL
Les Reports de Sr. Creswell Levinz, Jades un del Justices del Common Bank, en trois Parts, Commencant.... London: 1702. V. 66

LEVIS, H. C.
Baziliologia, a Booke of Kings. New York: 1913. V. 62

LEVIS, LARRY
The Afterlife. Iowa City: 1977. V. 66
Elegy With a Thimbleful of Water in the Cage. Poem. Richmond: 1994. V. 62; 64; 67
The Rain's Witness. Iowa City: 1975. V. 64

LEVISON, WILLIAM H.
Professor Julius Caesar Hannibal's Scientific Discourses. New York: 1852. V. 62

LEVI STRAUSS, CLAUDE
La Vie Familiale et Sociale des Indiens Nambikwara. Paris: 1948. V. 67

LEVITAS, MICHAEL
American in Crisis. New York: 1969. V. 65

LEVITT, HELEN
Mexico City: with an Essay by James Oles. New York: 1997. V. 65
A Way of Seeing. New York: 1965. V. 63
A Way of Seeing. New York: 1981. V. 62; 63; 64; 67

LEVON, O. U.
Caverns. New York: 1940. V. 62

LEVRON, JACQUES
Charme Du Val De Loire. Paris: 1955. V. 65

LEVY, AMY
A Minor Poet and Other Verses. London: 1884. V. 65
Reuben Sachs. A Sketch. London: 1888. V. 63

LEWENHAUPT, C.
Sport Across the World. 1933. V. 67

LEWES, CHARLES LEE
Comic Sketches; or, the Comedian His Own Manager. London: 1804. V. 67
Memoirs, Containing Anecdotes, Historical and Biographical of the English and Scottish Stages, During a Period of Forty Years. London: 1805. V. 67

LEWES, GEORGE HENRY
The Biographical History of Philosophy, from Its Origin in Greece Down to the Present Day. London: 1857. V. 64
The Life of Maximilian Robespierre.... London: 1849. V. 65
The Physiology of Common Life. Edinburgh: 1859-1860. V. 67
Ranthorpe. Leipzig: 1847. V. 65
Ranthorpe. London: 1860?. V. 65
The Story of Goethe's Life. London: 1873. V. 65

LEWES, JOHN LEE
Poems. Liverpool: 1811. V. 67

LEWIN, F. G.
Rhymes of ye Olde Sign Boards. Bristol: 1911. V. 64

LEWIN, MICHAEL Z.
Ask the Right Question. New York: 1943. V. 66
Ask the Right Question. 1971. V. 66
The Way We Die Now. 1973. V. 66

LEWIN, WILLIAM
The Birds of Great Britian.... London: 1795-1796. V. 67

LEWINE, J.
Bibliography of Eighteenth Century Art and Illustrated Books. London: 1898. V. 65

LEWIS, A. H.
South Vancouver Past and Present; an Historical Sketch.... Vancouver: 1920. V. 66

LEWIS, ALETHEA BRERETON
Rhoda; a Novel. London: 1816. V. 63

LEWIS, ALFRED HENRY
Confessions of a Detective. New York: 1906. V. 65

LEWIS, ALUN
Inward Where All the Battle Is. 1997. V. 65

LEWIS, ANGELO JOHN
Every Boy's Book of Sport and Pastime. London: 1897. V. 62
Modern Magic. London: 1876. V. 66
More Magic. New York: 1895. V. 67
Puzzles Old and New. London and New York: 1893. V. 64; 66

LEWIS, ARTHUR, MRS.
Salthurst. London: 1878. V. 65

LEWIS, CHARLES LEE
David Glasgow Farragut - Admiral in the Making. Annapolis: 1941. V. 67

LEWIS, CHARLES THOMAS COURTNEY
The Picture Printer of the Nineteenth Century, George Baxter 1804- 1867. London: 1911. V. 64
The Story of Picture Printing in England During the Nineteenth Century, or Forty Years of Wood and Stone. London: 1928. V. 64

LEWIS, CLIVE STAPLES
Cheap and Contented Labor, the Picture of a Southern Mill Town in 1929. N.P: 1929. V. 66
Dymer. London: 1926. V. 63
English Literature in the Sixteenth Century Excluding Drama. London: 1954. V. 65
A Grief Observed. London: 1961. V. 63
Hero and Leander. London: 1952. V. 63
The Hideous Strength, a Modern Fairy-Tale for Grown-ups. London: 1945. V. 65
The Horse and His Boy. London: 1954. V. 63
The Horse and His Boy. New York: 1954. V. 66
The Last Battle. London: 1956. V. 62; 64
The Last Battle. New York: 1956. V. 66
Le Lion et la Sorciere Blanche. (The Lion, The Witch and the Wardrobe). Paris: 1952. V. 62
The Lion, The Witch and the Wardrobe. London: 1950. V. 63
The Lion, The Witch and the Wardrobe. New York: 1950. V. 66
The Magician's Nephew. London: 1955. V. 63
The Magician's Nephew. New York: 1955. V. 66
Out of the Silent Planet. London: 1938. V. 62; 65
Perelandra. London: 1943. V. 62; 64
Perelandra. New York: 1944. V. 66
The Pilgrim's Regress - an Allegorical Apology for Christianity Reason and Romanticism. London: 1933. V. 62
Prince Caspian. The Return to Narnia. London: 1951. V. 62; 63; 65
Prince Caspian, The Return to Narnia. New York: 1951. V. 66
Rehabilitations and Other Essays. London: 1939. V. 62
The Screwtape Letters and Screwtape Proposes a Toast. London: 1961. V. 65
The Silver Chair. New York: 1953. V. 66
Surprised by Joy - the Shape of My Early Life. London: 1955. V. 65
That Hideous Strength, a Modern Fairy-Tale for Grown-Ups. London: 1945. V. 62
Till We Have Faces. London: 1956. V. 64; 65
Till We Have Faces. New York: 1957. V. 62
The Voyage of the Dawn Trader. New York: 1952. V. 66
The Weight of Glory. London: 1942. V. 62

LEWIS, EDWARD
Edward Carpenter; an Exposition and an Appreciation. London: 1915. V. 64
The Patriot King Displayed: in the Life and Reign of Henry VIII King of England.... London: 1769. V. 62

LEWIS, ETHELREDA
Aloysius Horn; the Ivory Coast in the Earlies. London: 1927. V. 67

LEWIS, F. C.
Scenery of the River Dar, Being a Series of Thirty-Five Views. London: 1821. V. 66

LEWIS, G. GRIFFIN
The Practical Book of Oriental Rugs. Philadelphia: 1921. V. 66

LEWIS, G. R.
The Ancient Font of Little Walsingham, in Norfolk, Drawn and Illustrated with a Descriptive Interpretation. London: 1843. V. 62
Illustrations of Kilpeck Church, Herefordshire.... London: 1842. V. 66

LEWIS, GEORGE CORNEWALL
An Essay on the Government of Dependencies. London: 1841. V. 64
A Glossary of Provincial Words Used in Herefordshire and Some of the Adjoining Counties. London: 1839. V. 64

LEWIS, GEORGE E.
Tho Indiana Company 1763 1798: a Study in Eighteenth Century Frontier Land Speculation and Business Venture. Glendale: 1941. V. 64; 66

LEWIS, H. E.
Embalmer's Guide. Chicago: Sep. 1890. V. 63

LEWIS, H. H.
Thinking of Russia. Holt: 1932. V. 67

LEWIS, HARRY
Pulsars. Chesterfield: 1974. V. 63

LEWIS, HENRY C.
Papers and Notes on the Glacial Geology of Great Britain and Ireland. 1894. V. 63; 65
Papers and Notes on the Glacial Geology of Great Britain and Ireland. London: 1894. V. 63
Report on the Terminal Moraine in Pennsylvania and Western New York. Harrisburg: 1884. V. 63

LEWIS, HOMER P.
The A B C Primer. Philadelphia: 1910. V. 63

LEWIS, HUBERT
Principles of Conveyancing Explained and Illustrated by Concise Precedents. London: 1863. V. 63

LEWIS, JAMES OTTO
The American Indian Portfolio - an Eyewitness History 1823-1828. Kent: 1980. V. 64; 67

LEWIS, JANET
The Earth-Bound, 1924-1944. Aurora: 1946. V. 62

LEWIS, JENNY
Catalogue of an Exhibition of Poetry Manuscripts in the British Museum - April-June 1967. London: 1967. V. 65

LEWIS, JERRY A.
Silent Crossing. Clinton: 1988. V. 65

LEWIS, JOHN
Anatomy of Printing. The Influence of Art and History of Its Design. New York: 1970. V. 62
A Complete Guide to the Places of Amusement, Objects of Interest, Parks, Clubs, Markets, Docks, Principal Railway Routes, Leading Hotels...and also A Directory.... London: 1876. V. 63
A Complete History of Several Translations of the Holy Bible and New Testament into English.... London: 1739. V. 63
The History of the Life and Sufferings of the Reverend and Learned John Wiclif, D.D. Oxford: 1820. V. 63; 67
John Nash, the Painter as Illustrator. 1978. V. 65
John Nash: the Painter as Illustrator. Loxhill: 1978. V. 63; 66
Pratt Ware. London: 1984. V. 64
Printed Ephemera. The Changing Uses of Types and Letterforms in English and American Printing. Ipswich: 1962. V. 67

LEWIS, JOHN DELAWARE
Sketches of Cantabs. London: 1850. V. 67

LEWIS, JOHN H.
Recollections from 1860 to 1865. Washington: 1895. V. 62; 63

LEWIS, JOHN W.
The Life, Labors and Travels of Elder Charles Bowles, of the Free Will Baptist Denomination.... Watertown: 1852. V. 64

LEWIS, JOSEPH N.
Old Things and New; or, Ancient Fables and Modern Men. Baltimore: 1835. V. 62

LEWIS, MARGARET LYNN
The Common-Place Book of Margaret Lynn Lewis. Marlinton: 1924. V. 63

LEWIS, MARY S.
Antonio Gardano, Venetian Music Printer, 1538-1549.... New York and London: 1988. V. 63

LEWIS, MATTHEW GREGORY
Ambrosio; or the Monk. London: 1800. V. 63
The Monk: a Romance. London: 1797. V. 62; 65
Tales of Wonder. London: 1801. V. 62

LEWIS, MERIWETHER
History of the Expedition of Captains Lewis and Clark 1804-1805-1806. Chicago: 1902. V. 66

LEWIS, NORMAN
Sand and Sea in Arabia. London: 1938. V. 65; 67

LEWIS, OSCAR
The First 75 Years: The Story of the Book Club of California 1912- 1987. San Francisco: 1987. V. 62
Hearn and His Biographers. San Francisco: 1930. V. 67
Lola Montez. San Francisco: 1938. V. 62; 64; 67

LEWIS, SAMUEL
The History and Topography of the Parish of St. Mary, Islington in the County of Middlesex. London: 1842. V. 62
Topographical Dictionary of Ireland. 1837. V. 63
Topographical Dictionary of Scotland. London: 1851. V. 62

LEWIS, SAMUEL E.
The Treatment of Prisoners-of-War 1861-1865. Richmond: 1910. V. 63; 65

LEWIS, SARAH
Woman's Mission. London: 1839. V. 64
Woman's Mission. London: 1840. V. 65

LEWIS, SINCLAIR
Ann Vickers. London: 1933. V. 62; 63
Ann Vickers. New York: 1933. V. 66
Arrowsmith. New York. 1925. V. 65
Babbitt. New York: 1922. V. 66
Dodsworth. New York: 1929. V. 65; 66
Elmer Gantry. New York: 1927. V. 63
Free Air. New York: 1919. V. 66
Gideon Planish. New York: 1943. V. 65
John Dos Passos' Manhattan Transfer. New York: 1926. V. 65
Kingsblood Royal. New York: 1947. V. 66
Main Street. New York: 1920. V. 65
Main Street. Chicago: 1937. V. 63
Mantrap. New York: 1926. V. 67
Our Mr. Wrenn. New York: 1914. V. 63; 65
Selected Short Stories. Garden City: 1935. V. 66
Work of Art. Garden City: 1934. V. 66
Work of Art. New York: 1934. V. 66

LEWIS, T. PERCY
The Trade's Cake Book. 1930. V. 67

LEWIS, THOMAS
The History of the Parthian Empire. London: 1728. V. 64; 66
The Mechanism and Graphic Registration of the Heart Beat. London: 1920. V. 65
Seasonable Considerations on the Indecent and Dangerous Custom of Burying in Churches and Church-Yards. London: 1721. V. 65
The Soldier's Heart and the Effort Syndrome. New York: 1919. V. 63; 65
Vascular Disorders of the Limbs. New York. 1936. V. 63; 66; 67

LEWIS, TRACY HAMMOND
Along the Rio Grande. New York: 1916. V. 66

LEWIS, W.
Chess Problems, Being a Selection of Original Positions; to Which are Added, Others Extracted from Rare and Valuable Works.... London: 1833. V. 63

LEWIS, W. M.
Eutrophication and Land Use, Lake Dillon, Colorado. New York: 1984. V. 65

LEWIS, W. R. SUNDERLAND
Cubwood. London: 1924. V. 67

LEWIS, WILLE NEWBURY
Between Sun and Sod. Oxford: 1939. V. 66; 67

LEWIS, WILLIAM
Commercium Philosophico-Technicum; or the Philosophical Commerce of Arts.... London: 1763. V. 64
The New Dispensatory.... London: 1770. V. 67
A Second Series of Lessons on the Game of Chess, Written Expressly for the Use of the Higher Class of Players.... London: 1834. V. 65

LEWIS, WYNDHAM
The Apes of God. London: 1930. V. 62; 66
The Apes of God. 1955. V. 67
The Apes of God. London: 1955. V. 62
The Art of Being Ruled. London: 1926. V. 62
The Art of Wyndham Lewis.... London: 1951. V. 64
The Childermass: Section 1. London: 1928. V. 64
Count Your Dead - They Are Alive!. London: 1937. V. 63; 65; 66
The Diabolical Principle and the Dithyrambic Spectator. London: 1931. V. 64
The Enemy of the Stars. London: 1932. V. 65
Francois Villon. New York: 1928. V. 65
Harold Gilman - an Appreciation. London: 1919. V. 63
Left Wings Over Europe; or How to Make a War About Nothing. London: 1936. V. 66
Men Without Art. London: 1934. V. 64
The Mysterious Mr. Bull. London: 1938. V. 64
The Old Gang and the New Gang. London: 1933. V. 62; 66
One-Way Song. London: 1933. V. 63
The Red Priest. London: 1956. V. 62
The Roaring Queen. London: 1973. V. 64
Rotting Hill. London: 1951. V. 65
Rude Assignment: a Narrative of My Career Up-to-Date. London: 1950. V. 64
Satire and Fiction. London: 1930. V. 65
Self Condemned. London: 1954. V. 66
Snooty Baronet. London: 1932. V. 65
Tarr. London: 1918. V. 64; 66; 67
Tarr. London: 1928. V. 62
Thirty Personalities and a Self-Portrait. Harmsworth: 1932. V. 67
Thirty Personalities and a Self-Portrait. London: 1932. V. 65
Time and Western Man. London: 1927. V. 62; 64
Tyros and Portraits Catalogue of an Exhibition of Paintings and Drawings by Wyndham Lewis. London: 1921. V. 63
The Wild Body - a Soldier of Humour and Other Stories. London: 1927. V. 64; 66

LEWISOHN, LUDWIG
The Case of Mr. Crump. Paris: 1926. V. 65

LEWIS'S
Liverpool Directory for 1790. Liverpool: 1890. V. 62

LEWYS, GEORGES
Epic of Verdun and Ballads of France and Other War Poems.... New York: 1928. V. 63

LEXINGTON, ROBERT SUTTON
The Lexington Papers; or, Some Account of the Courts of London and Vienna at the Conclusion of the Seventeenth Century. London: 1851. V. 62

LEY, MURRAY HICKEY
A is All - a Myth for Time. San Francisco: 1953. V. 63

LEY, WILLY
Rockets: the Future of Travel Beyond the Stratosphere. New York: 1944. V. 66

LEYBOURN, WILLIAM
Arithmetick. London: 1684. V. 64; 66
Arithmetick. London: 1700. V. 65
The Line of Proportion or Numbers, Commonly Called Gunter's Line, Made Easie. London: 1726. V. 64; 66

LEYCESTER, GEORGE HANMER
A Disputation in Logic, Arguing the Moral and Religious Uses of a Devil. London: 1797. V. 66

LEYCESTERS
Common wealth: Conceived, Spoken and Published with the Most Earnest Protestation of All Dutifull Good Will and Affection Towards This Realme.... London: 1641. V. 64

LEYDEN, JOHN
A Historical and Philosophical Sketch of the Discoveries and Settlements of the Europeans in Northern and Western Africa.... Edinburgh: 1799. V. 66
The Poetical Remains. London: 1819. V. 67

LEYEL, C. F., MRS.
Magic of Herbs. London: 1932. V. 67

LEYLAND, FRANCIS
The Bronte Family. London: 1886. V. 62; 63; 66

LEYLAND, JOHN
Views of Ancient Buildings Illustrative of the Domestic Architecture of the Parish of Halifax. Halifax: 1879. V. 62; 66
The Yorkshire Coast and the Cleveland Hills and Dales. London: 1892. V. 65

LEYMARIE, JEAN
The Jerusalem Windows. New York: 1962. V. 62

LEYS, JOHN K.
The Black Terror. London: 1899. V. 65

L'HERITIER DE BRUTELLE
Sertum Anglicanum, Seu Plantae Rariores Quae in Hortis Juxta Londinum, Imprimis in Horto Regio Kewensi Excoluntur Ab Anno 1786 ad Annum 1787 Observatae. Paris. V. 65

L'HOSPITAL, GUILLAUME FRANCOIS ANTOINE DE
An Analytick Treatise of Conick Sections, and Their Use for Revolving of Equations in Determinate and Indeterminate Problems. London: 1723. V. 65

LI, HUI-LIN
Floristic Relationships Between Eastern Asia and Eastern North America. Philadelphia: 1952. V. 67

LIARDET, FRANCIS
The Midshipmen's Companion. London: 1851. V. 62

LIBANUS PRESS
Daylight Jobbery - Ephemera to 1985 by the Libanus Press. Marlborough, Wiltshire: 1985. V. 65

LIBBY, O. G.
The Arikara Narrative of the Campagin Against the Hostile Dakotas June 1876. Bismarck: 1920. V. 65; 67

LIBEL Suit of Chief Justice Ames Against Thomas R. Hazard. Providence: 1862. V. 63

LIBELLUS de Modo Penite(n)di and Co(n)fitendi. Paris: 1494. V. 64

LIBER Amicorvm Romain Rolland. Paris and Zurich: 1926. V. 64

LIBER Regalis, or the Coronation. London: 1821. V. 66

THE LIBERAL. Verse and Prose from the South. London: 1822. V. 64

LIBERMAN, ALEXANDER
The Art and Technique of Color Photography. New York: 1951. V. 63

LIBES, ANTOINE
*Le Monde Physique et le Monde Moral, ou Lettre a Mme. de **** Ouvrage Specialement Destine Aux Personnes Qui Veulent, Sans le Secors de la Gometrie....* Paris: 1822. V. 65

THE LIBRARY of Fiction, or Family Story-Telelr, Consisting of Original Tales, Essays and Sketches of Character. London: 1836-1837. V. 62

LIBRARY OF CONGRESS
American Prints in the Library of Congress, a Catalog of the Collection. Baltimore and London: 1970. V. 63
Catalogue of the John Boyd Thacher Collection of Incunabula. Washington: 1915-1931. V. 63
Children's Books in the Rare Book Division of the Library of Congress. Totowa: 1975. V. 63
The Lessing J. Rosenwald Collection. Washington: 1977. V. 63
Vision of a Collector: The Lessing J. Rosenwald Collection in the Library of Congress. Washington: 1991. V. 64

LIBRI, M. GUGLILMO
Catalogue of the Extraordinary Collection of Splendid Manuscripts Chiefly Upon Vellum, in Various Languages of Europe and the East, Formed by.... London: 1859. V. 65

LICHLITER, ASSELIA S.
Pioneering with the Belville and Related Families in South Carolina, Georgia and Florida. Washington: 1982. V. 67

LICHTENSTEIN, HENRY
Travels in Southern Africa in te Years 1803, 1804, 1805 and 1806. London: 1812. V. 65

LICK, ROSEMARY
The Generous Miser - The Story of James Lick of California. 1967. V. 66

LICK OBSERVATORY
Studies of the Nebulae, Made at the Lick Observatory, University of California, at Mount Hamilton, California and Santiago Chile. Berkeley: 1918. V. 67

LIDDELL, DONALD M.
Chessmen. London: 1938. V. 62

LIDDELL, HENRY G.
A History of Rome from the Earliest Times to the Establishment of the Empire. London: 1855. V. 66

LIDDELL, ROBERT
Lay of the Last Angler in Five Cantos, also Jack's Dangers and Deliverances. Kelso: 1888. V. 66

LIDDELL, T. HODGSON
China, Its Marvel and Mystery. London: 1909. V. 65

LIDDELL-HART, B. H.
T. E. Lawrence, Aldington and the Truth. London: 1955. V. 67
Why Don't We Learn from History?. London: 1946. V. 63

LIDDIC, BRUCE R.
Camp on Custer - Transcribing the Custer Myth. Spokane: 1995. V. 65; 67
I Buried Custer, the Diary of Pvt. Thomas W. Coleman, 7th U.S. Cavalry. College Station: 1979. V. 65; 67

LIDDLE, R. A.
The Geology of Venezuela and Trinidad. Texas: 1928. V. 62; 63

LIEBERMAN, M. M.
Maggot and Worm and Eight Other Stories. West Branch: 1969. V. 62

LIEBIG, JUSTUS VON
Animal Chemistry, or Chemistry in Its Application to Physiology and Pathology. London: 1843. V. 65
Animal Chemistry, or Organic Chemistry.... Cambridge: 1842. V. 62
Animal Chemistry, or Organic Chemistry in Its Application to Physiology and Pathology. London: 1842. V. 62; 64
Chemische Briefe. Heidelberg: 1845. V. 64
Nouvelles Lettres sur la Chimie Consideree dans ses Applications a l'Industrie, a la Physiologie et a l'Agriculture.... Paris: 1852. V. 64
Organic Chemistry in Its Applications to Agriculture and Physiology.... Cambridge: 1841. V. 64
Researches on the Chemistry of Food, and the Motion of the Juices in the Animal Body. Lowell: 1848. V. 62

LIECHTENSTEIN, MARIE, PRINCESS
Holland House. London: 1874. V. 66; 67

LIECHTI, P.
The Geology of Sarawak, Brunei and the Western Part of North Borneo. Sarawak: 1960. V. 67

LIEDERMAN, EARLE
The Science of Wrestling and the Art of Jiu-Jitsu. New York: 1926. V. 63

LIEDTKE, WALTER
The Royal Horse and Rider. Painting, Sculpture and Horsemanship 1500-1800. New York: 1989. V. 64

LIEF, ALFRED
The Firestone Story, a History of the Firestone Tire and Rubber Company. New York: 1951. V. 63

LIENHARD, HEINRICH
A Pioneer of Sutter's Fort 1846-1850. The Adventures of Heinrich Lienhard. Los Angeles: 1941. V. 63

LIETZE, ERNST
Modern Heliographic Processes. New York: 1888. V. 65

LIEUTAUD, JOSEPH
Historia Anatomico-Medica.... Longosallisae: 1786-1787. V. 65
Precis de la Matiere Medicale. Paris: 1781. V. 65
Precis de la Medecine Pratique.... Paris: 1759. V. 65
Synopsis Universae Praxeos Medicae.... Paris: 1770. V. 65

LIEVRE, EDOUARD
Works of Art in the Collections of England.... London: 1880. V. 62

THE LIFE and Actions of Lewis Dominique Cartouche; Who Was Broke Alive Upon the Wheel at Paris Nov. 28, 1721. London: 1722. V. 65

THE LIFE and Adventures of Lady Anne, the Little Pedlar. London: 1823. V. 62

THE LIFE and Adventures of that Most Eccentric Character James Hirst. London: 1840. V. 62

THE LIFE and Adventures of that Most Eccentric Character James Hirst of Rawcliffe, Yorkshire.... Knottingley: 1870. V. 64; 65; 67

THE LIFE and Death of Jenny Wren. 1820. V. 66

THE LIFE and Eccentricities of Lionel Scott Pilkington, Alias Jack Hawley. Doncaster: Sep. 1870. V. 64; 65

THE LIFE and Exploration of David Livingstone. London: 1879. V. 64

THE LIFE and History of George Barnwell; Who From the Highest Character and Credit, Fell to the Lowest Depth of Vice, Through the Artful Startagems of a Woman of the Town.... London: 1825. V. 62

THE LIFE and Memoirs of Mr. Ephraim Tristram Bates, Commonly Called Corporal Bates. London: 1756. V. 64; 65

LIFE and Public Services of Gen. Z. Taylor. New York: 1846. V. 65

LIFE and Remarkable Adventures of Israel R. Potter. Providence: 1824. V. 63

LIFE and Travels of Tom Thumb. Philadelphia: 1849. V. 62

LIFE in Space. Alexandria: 1983. V. 67

LIFE in the West: Back-wood Leaves and Prairie Flowers: Rough Sketches on the Borders of the Picturesque, the Sublime, and Ridiculous, Extracts from the Note Book of Morleigh in Search of an Estate. London: 1843. V. 67

THE LIFE of a Midshipman, a Tale Founded on Facts; and Intended to Correct an Injudicious Predilection in Boys for the Life of a Sailor. London: 1829. V. 65

THE LIFE of Bartolome E. Murillo. London: 1819. V. 66

THE LIFE of David Livingstone, LL.D. 1882. V. 64

THE LIFE of General George Armstrong Custer. Boston: 1959. V. 63

THE LIFE Of James Fitz-James, Duke of Berwick, Marshal, Duke and Peer of France.... London: 1738. V. 66

LIFE of James W. Jackson, The Alexandria Hero.... Richmond: 1862. V. 62

THE LIFE of Mahomet; or the History of the Imposture Which Was Begun, Carried On, and Finally Established by Him in Arabia.... Worcester: 1802. V. 62; 64

THE LIFE of Mohammed Ali, Viceroy of India. London: 1841. V. 64

THE LIFE of Thomas Paine, Interspersed with Remarks and Reflections by Peter Porcupine. Philadlephia: 1797. V. 65

THE LIFE, Speeches and Public Services of Abraham Lincoln. New York: 1860. V. 64

LIFE'S Sunny Hours. London: 1900. V. 64

LIGHT, ALEXANDER W.
A Plan for the Amelioration of the Condition of the Poor of the United Kingdom. 1830. V. 62

LIGHTING for Concealed Sources. New York: 1919. V. 67

LIGHTMAN, ALAN
Einstein's Dreams. London: 1993. V. 65; 67
Einstein's Dreams. New York: 1993. V. 64; 67

LIGHTMAN, ALAN continued
Time Travel and Pap Joe's Pipe. New York: 1984. V. 62; 65

LIGHTON, WILLIAM R.
Lewis and Clark. Portland: 1905. V. 66

LIGNE, CHARLES, PRINCE DE
Catalogue Raisonne des Desseins Originaux, du Cabinet de Feu.... Vienna: 1794. V. 64
Mon Refuge; ou Satyre sur les Abus des Jardins Modernes.... London: 1801. V. 64

LIGON, RICHARD
A True and Exact History of the Island of Barbadoes.... London: 1673. V. 62; 63

LIGOTTI, THOMAS
Weird Tales. Philadelphia: 1991. V. 66

LILBURNE, JOHN
A Defensive Declaration of Lieut. Col. John Lilburn, Against the Unjust Sentence of His Banishment, by the Late Parliament of England; Directed in An Epistle from His House in Bridges in Flanders, May 14, 1653. N.P: 1653. V. 64
The Legall, Fundamentall Liberties of the People of England Revived, Asserted and Vindicated. London: 1649. V. 64
The Out-Cryes of Oppressed Commons. N.P: 1647. V. 64

LILE, WILLIAM H.
Brief Making and the Use of Law Books. St. Paul: 1914. V. 65

LILFORD, THOMAS LITTLETON POWYS, 4TH BARON
Coloured Figures of the Birds of the British Islands. London: 1885-1897. V. 63; 64; 66
Lord Lilford, a Memoir by His Sister. London: 1900. V. 62
Lord Lilford on Birds.... London: 1903. V. 67

LILIENFELD, ABRAHAM M.
Chronic Diseases and Public Health. Baltimore: 1966. V. 65

LILJEGREN, S. B.
The Irish Element in the Valley of Fear. Uppsala: 1964. V. 65

LILLEGRAVEN, J. A.
Mesozoic Mammals. Berkeley: 1979. V. 67

LILLEY, W. O.
Bound for Australia, on Board the Orient a Passenger's Log. London: 1885. V. 67

LILLIE, ARTHUR
Croquet Up to Date. London: 1900. V. 62

LILLIE, GORDON W.
Life Story of Pawnee Bill. N.P: 1916. V. 66

LILLINGSTON, LUKE
Reflections on Mr. Burchet's Memoirs. 1704. V. 62

LILLY, E.
Prehistoric Antiquities of Indiana. 1937. V. 62

LILLY, WILLIAM
William Lilly's History of His Life and Times, From the Year 1602 to 1681. London: 1822. V. 63

LILLY, WILLIAM SAMUEL
A Century of Revolution. London: 1890. V. 64

LILY, WILLIAM
Short Introduction of Grammar Generally to Be Used...to which are added Useful Observations by Way of Comment Out of Ancient and Late Grammarians.... Oxford: 1714. V. 64; 66

LIMA, E. DA CRUZ
Mammals of Amazonia. Rio de Janeiro: 1945. V. 64

LIMB, GEORGE DENISON
The Register of the Parish Church of Addingham, County York, 1612- 1812. 1920. V. 65

LIMBOUR, GEORGES
Soleils Bas: Poemes. Paris: 1924. V. 66

LIMEBEER, ENA
To a Proud Phantom. Richmond: 1923. V. 65, 66

LIMITED EDITIONS CLUB
Quarto Millenary The First 250 Publications and the First 25 Years 1929-1954 of the Limited Editions Club; a Critique, a Conspectus, a Bibliography, Indexes. New York: 1954. V. 64

LIMON, MARTIN
Jade Lady Burning. New York: 1992. V. 65

LINCK, WENCESLAUS
Wenceslaus Linck's Diary of His 1766 Expedition to Northern Baja California. Los Angeles: 1966. V. 63

LINCOLN, ABRAHAM
Abraham Lincon: His Speeches and Writings. New York: 1946. V. 63
Complete Works. New York: 1894. V. 64
Political Debates Between Hon. Abraham Lincoln and Hon. Stephen A. Douglas in the Celebrated Campaign of 1858 in Illinois. Columbus: 1860. V. 62; 64

LINCOLN, MARY JOHNSON BAILEY
Mrs. Lincoln's Boston Cook Book. Boston: 1884. V. 63; 66
Mrs. Lincoln's Boston Cook Book. Boston: 1891. V. 67
What to Have for Luncheon. New York: 1904. V. 67

LINCOLN, WALDO
American Cookery Books 1742-1860. Worcester: 1954. V. 62

LINCOLN LUNATIC ASYLUM
State of the Lincoln Lunatic Asylum. Lincoln: 1829. V. 65
State of the Lincoln Lunatic Asylum (Instituted Nov. 4, 1819). 1841. Lincoln: 1841. V. 65

LIND, JAKOV
Eine Seele uas Holz. Berlin: 1962. V. 67
Soul of Wood and Other Stories. New York: 1965. V. 67

LIND, JAMES
An Essay On Diseases Incidental to Europeans in Hot Climates. London: 1788. V. 62
An Essay on Diseases Incidental to Europeans in Hot Climates. London: 1792. V. 65
Three Letters Relating to the Navy, Gibraltar and Porthmahon. London: 1757. V. 65

LIND, L. R.
Studies in Pre-Vasalian Anatomy, Biography, Translations, Documents. Philadelphia: 1975. V. 66
Studies in Pre-Vasalian Anatomy, Biography, Translations, Documents. Philadelphia: 1978. V. 64

LINDBERG, G. U.
Fishes of the Sea of Japan and the Adjacent Areas of the Sea of Okbotsk and the Yellow Sea. Part 1. Jerusalem: 1967. V. 65

LINDBERGH, ANNE MORROW
Listen! The Wind. New York: 1938. V. 63; 64
North to the Orient. London: 1936. V. 65
The Steep Ascent. New York: 1944. V. 66

LINDBERGH, CHARLES A.
The Spirit of St. Louis. London: 1953. V. 62; 64
The Spirit of St. Louis. New York: 1953. V. 63; 64
We. New York and London: 1927. V. 63; 65

LINDBERGH, REEVE
John's Apples. Mt. Horeb: 1995. V. 64

LINDEMAN, M. H.
The Quarter Horse Breeder. Wichita Falls: 1959. V. 66

LINDEN, DIEDERICK WESSEL
A Treatise on the Origin, Nature and Virtues of Chalybeat Waters and Natural Hot-Baths. London: 1755. V. 65

LINDEN, JOHANNES ANTOINE VAN DER
De Scriptis Medicis Libri Dvo. Amsterdam: 1662. V. 66

LINDEN, L.
Les Orchidees Exotiques et Leur Culture en Europe. Brussels: 1894. V. 65; 66

LINDER, LESLIE
A History of the Writings of Beatrix Potter.... London: 1971. V. 62; 65; 66; 67

LINDERMAN, FRANK B.
American - the Life Story of a Great Indian, Plenty-Coups, Chief of the Crows. New York: 1930. V. 65; 67
Blackfeet Indians. St. Paul: 1935. V. 63; 66
Bunch-Grass and Blue-Joint. New York: 1921. V. 66
Indian Old-Man Stories: More Sparks from War Eagler's Lodge-Fire. New York: 1920. V. 63; 64
Indian Why Stories. New York: 1915. V. 63; 66
Old Many Coyote (Crow). New York: 1932. V. 63
On the Passing Frontier - Sketches from the Northwest. New York: 1920. V. 64
Red Mother the Life Story of Pretty Shield, a Medicine Woman of the Crows. New York: 1932. V. 65; 67

LINDERMAN, GRANT B.
Indian Old Man Stories More Sparks from War Eagle's Lodge Fire. New York: 1920. V. 66

LINDERN, FRANZ BALTHASAR VON
Medicinischer Passe Par Tout Oder haupt Schlussels Zwenter Theil.... Strassburg: 1741. V. 65

LINDGREN, WALDEMAR
The Tertiary Gravels of the Sierra Nevada of California. Washington: 1911. V. 64

LINDLEY, AUGUSTUS
After Ophir; or, a Search for the South African Gold Fields. London: 1870. V. 62; 65
The Log of the Fortuna: a Cruise in Chinese Waters. London: 1871. V. 67

LINDLEY, ELIZABETH
The Diary of a Book Agent. New York: 1912. V. 66

LINDLEY, JOHN
Elements of Botany, Structural, Physiological, Systematical and Medical. London: 1841. V. 62
An Introduction to the Natural System of Botany; or, A Systematic View of the...Vegetable Kingdom. New York: 1831. V. 64
Ladies Botany; or a Familiar Introduction to the Study of the Natural System of Botany. London: 1839. V. 66
Rosarum Monographia; or a Botanical History of Roses. 1820. V. 62
Rosarum Monographia; or, a Botanical History of Roses. London: 1830. V. 62
The Theory of Horticulture. 1840. V. 63; 66
The Theory of Horticulture. New York: 1852. V. 64
The Vegetable Kingdom or the Structure, Classification and Uses of Plants.... London: 1853. V. 64

LINDLEY, WALTER
California of the South: Its Physical Geography, Climate, Resources, Routes of Travel and Health Resorts.... New York: 1888. V. 65

LINDMAN, MAJ
Snipp, Snapp, Snurr, and The Red Shoes. Chicago: 1934. V. 65

LINDO, A. A.
A Retrospect of the Past, as Connected With and Preparatory to a Faithful Exposition Intended to Be Given of the Divine Will and Dispensation Disclosed in the Sacred Books Received as Authority by the Jews. Cincinnati: 1848. V. 64

LINDQUIST, H. L.
The Stamp Specialist. Volumes 1-20. New York: 1939-1948. V. 63

LINDSAY, DAVID
Sphinx. London: 1923. V. 63

LINDSAY, DAVID M.
Camp-Fire Reminiscences. 1912. V. 67

LINDSAY, HOWARD
Happy Hunting. New York: 1957. V. 63
State of the Union. New York: 1946. V. 66

LINDSAY, IAN G.
Inverary and the Dukes of Argyll. Edinburgh: 1973. V. 62

LINDSAY, J. SEYMOUR
Iron and Brass Implements of English House. 1964. V. 67

LINDSAY, JACK
Fleas in Amber. London: 1930. V. 67
Helen Comes of Age. London: 1927. V. 67
The London Aphrodite - a Miscellany of Poems, Stories and Essays, by Various Hands.... London: 1929. V. 63
Propertius in Love. London: 1927. V. 67
William Blake. Creative Will and Poetic Image. London: 1927. V. 62; 64; 67

LINDSAY, JOHN
Notices of Remarkable Greek, Roman and Anglo-Saxon and Other Medieval Coins in the Cabinet of the Author. Cork: 1860. V. 63; 66

LINDSAY, LADY
About Robins. London: 1890. V. 62; 64

LINDSAY, MARTIN
Sledge, the British Trans-Greenland Expedition 1934. London: 1935. V. 67

LINDSAY, NICHOLAS VACHEL
Collected Poems. New York: 1923. V. 62
Collected Poems. New York: 1925. V. 62
General William Booth Enters into Heaven and Other Poems. New York: 1913. V. 63
A Handy Guide for Beggars. New York: 1916. V. 62
A Handy Guide for Beggars. New York: 1923. V. 63

LINDSAY, PATRICK
The Interest of Scotland, Considered with Regard to Its Police in Imploying of the Poor.... Edinburgh: 1733. V. 62

LINDSAY, PHILIP
There is No Escape. London: 1590. V. 66

LINDSAY, W. LAUDER
A Popular History of British Lichens. London: 1856. V. 63

LINDSAY, W. S.
History of Merchant Shipping and Ancient Commerce. New York: 1965. V. 62; 66

LINDSEY, DAVID L.
Heat from Another Sun. New York: 1984. V. 62

LINDSLEY, JOHN B.
The Military Annals of Tennessee. Confederate First Series: Embracing a Review of Military Operations with Regimental Histories and Memorial Rolls. Nashville: 1886. V. 64

LINDSLEY, KATHLEEN
The Country Life. London: 1997. V. 67
Pub Signs for Samuel Webster. 1983. V. 65

LINDUSKA, J. P.
Waterfowl Tomorrow. 1964. V. 67

LINES, KATHLEEN
Dick Whittington. London: 1970. V. 63
Lavender's Blue. London: 1954. V. 62

LING, NICHOLAS
Politeuphia, Wits Common-wealth. London: 1650. V. 63

LINGARD, JOHN
The History and Antiquities of the Anglo-Saxon Church.... London: 1845. V. 62; 63

LINK, HENRY FREDERICK
Travels in Portugal, and through France and Spain. London: 1801. V. 67

LINKLATER, ERIC
The Impregnable Women. London: 1938. V. 66

LINN, JOHN J.
Reminiscences of Fifty Years in Texas. New York: 1883. V. 64

LINN, WILLIAM ALEXANDER
The Story of the Mormons, from the Date of Their Origin to the Year 1901. New York: 1923. V. 67

LINNE, CARL VON
Entomologia Fauna Suecicae. Lugduni: 1789. V. 66
The Families of Plants, with Their Natural Characters.... 1787. V. 62
Flora Lapponica Exhibens Plantas per Lapponiam Crescentes.... Amsterdam: 1737. V. 64; 66
A Generic and Specific Description of British Plants.... Kendal: 1775. V. 66
Hortus Cliffortianus Plantas Exhibens Quas in Hortis Tam Vivis Quam.... Amsterdam: 1737. V. 64; 66
An Introduction to Botany. 1788. V. 63
Species Plantarum, Exhibentes Plantas Rite Cognitas cum Differentiis Specifiis Nominibus Trivialibus.... Stockholm: 1762-1763. V. 66
A System of Vegetables. Litchfield: 1782. V. 67
A System of Vegetables. Litchfield: 1782-1785. V. 64; 65
A System of Vegetables. Lichfield: 1783. V. 63
Systema Vegetablilium. Gottingae: 1825-1828. V. 65; 66

LINNE, S.
Zapotecan Antiquities, and the Paulson Collection in the Ethnographical Museum of Sweden. 1938. V. 62

LINNEHAN, JOHN W.
The Driving Clubs of Greater Boston. Boston: 1914. V. 63; 65

LINSLEY, D. C.
Morgan Horses.... New York: 1857. V. 62

LINSLEY, E. G.
Cerambycidae of North America. Los Angeles: 1961-1984. V. 66
Cerambycidae of North America. Los Angeles: 1961-1997. V. 66

LINSLEY, JOHN S.
Jersey Cattle in America. New York: 1885. V. 64

LINSSEN, E. F.
Beetles of the British Isles. First and Second Series. London: 1959. V. 62

LINSTRUM, DEREK
Historic Architecture of Leeds. Newcastle-upon-Tyne: 1969. V. 65

LINTON, ELIZA LYNN
The Lake Country. London: 1864. V. 66
My Literary Life. London: 1899. V. 65
Paston Carew, a Millionaire and Miser: a Novel. London: 1888. V. 65
Witch Stories. London: 1861. V. 62; 66
The World Well Lost. London: 1877. V. 65

LINTON, JOHN
A Handbook of the Whitehaven and Furness Railway, Being a Guide to the Lake District of West Cumberland and Furness. London: 1852. V. 64

LINTON, W. J.
The Ferns of the English Lake Country. Windermere: 1878. V. 64; 65

LINWOOD, MISS
Miss Linwood's Gallery of Pictures in Worsted, Leicester Square. 1812. V. 66

LIPKIND, WILL
The Christmas Bunny. New York: 1953. V. 64

LIPMAN, A.
Divinely Elegant: the World.... London: 1989. V. 65

LIPMAN, JEAN
American Folk Art in Wood, Metal and Stone. New York: 1948. V. 67
Calder's Circus. New York: 1972. V. 63

LIPPARD, L. R.
Eva Hesse. New York: 1976. V. 65

LIPPERHEIDE, FRANZ VON
Katalog der Freiherrlich von Lipperheide'schen Kostumbiliothek. 1996. V. 65

LIPPINCOTT, BENJAMIN
From Fiji through the Philippines with the Thirteenth Air Force. San Angelo: 1948. V. 67

LIPPINCOTT, J. G.
Design for Business. Chicago: 1947. V. 65

LIPPMANN, FRIEDRICH
The Art of Wood Engraving in Italy in the Fifteenth Century. London: 1888. V. 62

LIPPMANN, WALTER
Public Opinion. New York: 1922. V. 63

LIPPS, OSCAR H.
A Little History of the Navajos. Cedar Rapids: 1909. V. 67

LIPSCHUTZ, PEGGY
The World of Peggy Lipschutz. A Portfolio of Her Graphic Work. Chicago. V. 67

LIPSCOMB, GEORGE
Observations on Asthma; and the Cause of It Proved to Depend on Acidity in the System. London: 1805. V. 62

LIPSETT, CALDWELL
Where the Atlantic Meets the Land. London: 1896. V. 64

LIPSIUS, JUSTUS
Epistolarum Selectarum, Centuria Prima Miscellanea. Antwerp: 1611-1614. V. 66
Poliorceticon sive de Machinis. Tormentis. Telis.... Antverpiae: 1596. V. 66
Poliorceticon sive de Machinis. Tormentis. Telis. Libri Quinque...Dissertatiuncula Paud Principes...(with) De Vesta et Vestalibus Syntagma. (with) De Bibliothecis Syntagma. Antverpiae: 1599. V. 62; 66
Politicorum Sive Civilis Doctrinae Libri Sex. Qui Ad Principatum Maxime Spectant. Lugduni Batavorum: 1634. V. 63

LIPSON, E.
The Economic History of England. London: 1947-1949. V. 64

LISCOMBE, RHODRI W.
The Church Architecture of Robert Mills. Easley: 1985. V. 67

LISH, GORDON
Genesis West: a Garden to Grow the World Again. Burlingame: 1962-1964. V. 62; 64

LISLE, EDWARD
Observations in Husbandry. London: 1757. V. 66

LISNEY, A. A.
A Bibliography of British Lepidoptera 1608 to 1799. 1960. V. 63
A Bibliography of British Lepidoptera 1608 to 1799. London: 1960. V. 62

LISSAUER, FRANK
A Visit to Ireland. Leicester: 1975. V. 65

A LIST of the Viscounts or High Sheriffs of the County of York, from the Time of William I. N.P: 1782. V. 67

LISTER, A.
A Monograph of the Mycetozoa. London: 1911. V. 64
Monograph of the Mycetozoa. London: 1925. V. 66

LISTER, JOSEPH
The Collected Papers. Birmingham: 1979. V. 62; 63
On the Coagulation of the Blood. The Croonian Lecture Delivered Before the Royal Society of London 11th June 1863. London: 1863. V. 65

LISTER, R.
Antique Firearms, Their Care, Repair and Restoration. 1969. V. 67

LISTER, R. J.
A Catalogue of a Portion of the Library of Edmund Gosse. London: 1893. V. 66

LISTER, RAYMOND
Books at Bedtime, Being a List of Bedside Literature Suitable for Ladies and Gentlemen of all Tastes, Even the Most Fastidious. Linton: 1953. V. 67
Hammer and Hand. An Essay on the Ironwork of Cambridge. Cambridge: 1969. V. 62
Samuel Palmer - a Biography. London: 1974. V. 63

LISTER, THOMAS
A Mirror for Princes, in a Letter to His Royal Highness the Prince of Wales. London: 1797. V. 62
The Rustic Wreath. Poems, Moral, Descriptive and Miscellaneous. Leeds: 1834. V. 62
Stainborough and Rockley, their Historical Associations and Rural Attractions. London: 1853. V. 63

LISTER, THOMAS HENRY
Granby. A Novel. London: 1826. V. 63; 64; 66
Herbert Lacy. London: 1828. V. 62; 65; 67

LISTON, JOHN
Paul Pry; in which are all the Peculiairites, Irregularities, Singularities, Pertinacity, Loquacity and Audacity of Paul Pry, as Performed by Mr. Liston, at the Theatre Royal, Haymarket.... London: 1826. V. 62

LISTON, ROBERT
Elements of Surgery. Philadelphia: 1837. V. 64; 67

LITCHFIELD, HENRIETTA EMMA
Emma Darwin, Wife of Charles Darwin. A Century of Family Letters. Cambridge: 1904. V. 66

LITCHFIELD, P. W.
Autumn Leaves, Reflections of an Industrial Lieutenant. Cleveland: 1945. V. 62

THE LITERARY and Pictorial Souvenir. London: 1845-1850. V. 66

THE LITERARY Guillotine. New York/London: 1903. V. 65

THE LITERARY Museum; or, Ancient and Modern Repository. London: 1792. V. 64; 65

THE LITERATURE of Persia. The Literature of Japan. New York: 1899-1900. V. 63

LITHGOW, DAVID
Wm. C. Grimes Patent Perpetual Water Indicator and Steam Pressure Gauge. Philadelphia: 1858. V. 67

LITTLE Red Riding Hood and Other Tales. London: 1917. V. 63

LITTLE, A. G.
Liber Exemplorum ad Usum Praedicantium. Aberdeen: 1908. V. 65

LITTLE, A. J.
Through the Yang-Tse Gorges; or, Trade and Travel in Western China. London: 1888. V. 67

LITTLE Alfred's Visit to Wombell's Meangerie. London: 1875. V. 62

LITTLE, ARCHIBALD
In the Land of the Blue Gown. London and Leipsic: 1908. V. 65

LITTLE, ARCHIBALD, MRS.
Intimate China: the Chinese as I Have Seen Them. London: 1899. V. 67
Round About My Peking Garden. London: 1905. V. 67

LITTLE, BENTLY
The Mailman. London: 1994. V. 67
The Revelation. New York: 1990. V. 67

LITTLE Bo-Peep. London: 1920. V. 66

A LITTLE Book for Little Readers. London: 1838. V. 65

LITTLE Boy Blue. London: 1880. V. 65

LITTLE Child's Home ABC Book. New York: 1870. V. 64

THE LITTLE Dutch Book. New York: 1909. V. 62

LITTLE Dutchy-Nursery Songs from Holland. London: 1925. V. 64

LITTLE, E. L.
Common Trees of Puerto Rico and the Virgin Islands. Washington: 1964. V. 67

LITTLE Folks 1879. (Volume 9). V. 67

LITTLE Folks 1902. V. 67

LITTLE Folks 1908. V. 67

LITTLE Folks 1916. V. 67

LITTLE Frank's Almanack to Show Little Boys and Girls Their Play Days. Concord: 1832. V. 65

LITTLE, GEORGE
The American Cruisers Own Book. Philadelphia: 1859. V. 66
A History of Lumsden's Battery, C.S.A. Tuskaloosa: 1905. V. 62

LITTLE Innocents - Childhood Reminiscences. London: 1932. V. 64

LITTLE Jacob and How He Became Fat. New York: 1872. V. 64

LITTLE, JAMES A.
From Kirtland to Salt Lake City. Salt Lake City: 1890. V. 62; 65
Jacob Hamblin. Salt Lake City: 1881. V. 65
Jacob Hamblin. 1909. V. 65
What I Saw On the Old Santa Fe Trail - a Condensed Story of Frontier Life Half a Century Ago. Plainfield: 1904. V. 64; 67

LITTLE Katie's Picture Book. London: 1882. V. 67

LITTLE Lulu and Her Pals. Philadelphia: 1939. V. 64

LITTLE Lulu on Parade. Philadelphia: 1941. V. 65

LITTLE, MILES
Round Trip. Melbourne: 1977. V. 67

LITTLE Miss Giant. New York: 1875. V. 64

LITTLE Pets. A Panorama Picture Book of Animals. London: 1896. V. 62; 64

LITTLE Pigs. New York: 1890. V. 64

A LITTLE Present for a Good Child. (No. 4). Greenfield: 1848. V. 64

LITTLE Red Riding Hood. New York: 1890. V. 63
LITTLE Red Riding Hood. London: 1910. V. 62

THE LITTLE Sisters. New York: 1880. V. 64

LITTLE Songs of Long Ago. London: 1912. V. 65

LITTLE Susie Sunbonnet and How Her Year Was Spent. New York: 1907. V. 63

LITTLE, THOMAS
Confessions of an Oxonian. London: 1826. V. 63

LITTLE, THOMAS, MRS.
Domestic Institutes of Young Mothers.... London: 1824. V. 66

THE LITTLEST Ones. New York: 1898. V. 64

LITTLETON, ADAM
Linguae Latinae Liber Dictionarius...Latino Dictionary in Four Parts.... London: 1703. V. 63
Sixty One Sermons Preached Mostly on Publick Occasions.... London: 1680. V. 67

LITTLETON, THOMAS
Les Tenures du Monsier Littleton, Ouesque Certen Cases.... London: 1577. V. 64

LITTROW, JOSEPH JOHANN VON
Analytische Geometrie. Viena: 1823. V. 65

LITTROW, KARL LUDWIG VON
Erlauterungen zu J. J. Littrow's Vorlesungen Uber Astronomie. Vienna: 1842. V. 65

LIVELY, PENELOPE
Moon Tiger. London: 1987. V. 67

LIVERMORE, MARY A.
My Story of the War: a Woman's Narrative of the Four Years Personal Experience as Nurse in the Union Army. Hartford: 1889. V. 67

LIVERMORE, WILLIAM ROSCOE
The American Kriegspiel. A Game for Practicing the Art of War Upon a Topographical Map. Boston: 1882. V. 64

LIVES of the Most Remarkable Criminals Who Have Been Condemned and Executed for Murder, the Highway &c. London: 1927. V. 63

LIVING Blues 1:2. 1970. V. 66

LIVINGSTON, EDWARD
Project of a New Penal Code for the State of Louisiana. London: 1824. V. 65
Rapport sur le Projet d'un Code Penal, Fait a l'Assemblee Generale de l'Etat de la Louisiane.... Paris: 1825. V. 64
Remarks on the Expediency of Abolishing the Punishment of Death. Philadelphia: 1831. V. 62

LIVINGSTON, J. A.
Birds of the Eastern Forest. Boston and Toronto: 1968-1970. V. 65; 67

LIVINGSTON, JOHN
Livingston's Law Register. New York: 1851. V. 63

LIVINGSTON, LUTHER S.
Franklin and His Press at Passy: an Account of the Books, Pamphlets, and Leaflets Printed There, Including the Long-Lost "Bagatelles". New York: 1914. V. 62; 64

LIVINGSTON, PETER
Poems and Songs:...and Letters on Dr. Dick, the Christian Philosopher and Sir J. Franklin and the Arctic Regions. Dundee: 1865. V. 62

LIVINGSTON, ROBERT R.
Essay on Sheep: Their Varieties...Raising a Flock in the United States...Sheep and Woollen Manufactures. Concord: 1813. V. 64

LIVINGSTON, WILLIAM
A Funeral Elogium on the Reverend Mr. Aaron Burr, Late President of the College of New Jersey. Boston: 1758. V. 66

LIVINGSTONE, DAVID
The Last Journals of David Livingstone, in Central Africa, from 1865 to His Death.... London: 1874. V. 66; 67
Livingstone's Travels and Researches in South Africa. Philadelphia: 1859. V. 67
Missionary Travels and Researches in South Africa.... London: 1857. V. 64; 65; 67
Missionary Travels and Researches in South Africa.... New York: 1858. V. 62
Narrative of an Expedition to the Zambesi and Its Tributaries. London: 1865. V. 63; 67
Narrative of an Expedition to the Zambesi and Its Tributaries.... New York: 1866. V. 62
Narrative of an Expedition to the Zambesi and Its Tributaries. New York: 1886. V. 65
A Popular Account of Missionary Travels and Researches in South Africa. London: 1861. V. 66

LIVINGSTONE, W. P.
Laws of Livingstonia; a Narrative of Missionary Adventure and Achievement. London: 1918. V. 67

LIVINGSTONE-LEARMONTH, DAVID
The Horse in Art. London: 1958. V. 62; 67

LIVIUS
Historiarum ab Urbe Condita. Oxford: 1708. V. 65
Historiarum Ab Urbe Condita. Edinburgi: 1751. V. 64; 66
Historiarum Que Supersunt, ex Recensione Arn Drakenborchii. Oxford: 1800. V. 65
The Roman History.... London: 1686. V. 62
T. Livii Patavini Conciones, Cum Argumentis et Annotationbus Ioachimi Perionii.... Parisiis: 1532. V. 65
T. Livii Patavini Historiae Romanae Principis Decades Tres Cum Dimidia.... Lutetiae Parisiorum: 1552. V. 65
T. Livii Patavini Historiarum Ab Urbe Condita Libri Qui Supersunt Omnes.... Oxonii: 1821. V. 65
T. Livii Patavini Historicorum Omnium Romanorum Longe Uberrimi.... 1588. V. 65
Titi Livii Patavini Historiarum Ab Urbe Condita Libri Qui Supersunt XXXV. Parisiis: 1775. V. 65
Titi Livii Qui extant Historiarum Libri. Cantabrigiae: 1679. V. 65; 66

LIVRE de Prieres a l'Usage des Chretiens de l'Eglise Orthodoxe Catholique d'Orient. Paris: 1852. V. 66

LIVRE des Routes d'italie a l'Isage des Seigneurs Qui Voyagent Par La Poste.... N.P: 1780. V. 66

LIVRES des Livres. N.P: 1993. V. 64

LLEWELLYN, RICHARD
How Green Was My Valley. London: 1939. V. 65
None But the Lonely Heart. London: 1943. V. 62; 65

LLIMONA, MERCEDES
El Muneco de Papel. Madrid. V. 65

LLOYD, A. B.
In Dwarf Land and Cannibal Country; a Record of Travel and Discovery in Central Africa. London: 1899. V. 67
Uganda to Khartoum Life and Adventure on the Upper Nile. 1911. V. 64; 66

LLOYD, ARTHUR
New English Reader. Numbers 1-5. Tokyo: 1902. V. 65

LLOYD, DAVID
State Worthies. Or, the States-Men and Favourites of England Since the Reformation. London: 1670. V. 64

LLOYD, E.
A Visit to the Antipodes; with Some Reminiscences of a Sojourn in Australia by a Squatter. London: 1846. V. 67

LLOYD, E. W.
Artillery: Its Progress and Present Position. Portsmouth: 1893. V. 65

LLOYD, F. E.
The Carnivorous Plants. 1942. V. 63

LLOYD, H. E.
The German Tourist. London: 1837. V. 67

LLOYD, HENRY HUMPHREYS EVANS
A Political and Military Rhapsody, on the Invasion and Defence of Great Britain and Ireland.... London: 1792. V. 62

LLOYD, J. U.
Drugs and Medicines of North America, a Publication.... Cincinnati: 1930-1931. V. 63

LLOYD, JEREMY
Captain Beaky. London: 1976. V. 65

LLOYD, JESSIE SALE
Scamp. London: 1887. V. 67

LLOYD, JOHN URI
Stringtown on the Pike, a Tale of Northernmost Kentucky. New York: 1900. V. 66
Warwick of the Knobs, a Strong of Stringtown County, Kentucky. New York: 1901. V. 66

LLOYD, L.
Field Sports of the North of Europe.... London: 1831. V. 62; 66; 67
The Game Birds and Wild Fowl of Sweden and Norway.... London: 1867. V. 64; 65
Scandinavian Adventures, During a Residence of Upwards of Twenty Years.... London: 1854. V. 66

LLOYD, N.
Garden Craftmanship in Yew and Box. London: 1925. V. 64

LLOYD, NATHANIEL
History of the English House from Primitive Times to the Victorian Period. London: 1949. V. 62

LLOYD, NELSON
The Robberies Company Ltd. New York: 1906. V. 67

LLOYD, ROBERT
The Poetical Works. (with) The Life and Writings of the Author. London: 1774. V. 63

LLOYD, T. IVESTER
Hounds. 1934. V. 62; 64

LLOYD, THOMAS
An Essay on the Literary Beauties of the Scriptures. Chester: 1784. V. 64

LLOYD, W.
Sketches of Indian Life. London: 1890. V. 67

LLOYD, WILLIAM
A Seasonable Discourse Shewing the Necessity of Maintaining the Established Religion in Opposition to Popery. London: 1673. V. 66

LLOYD, WILLIAM P.
History of the First Regiment Pennsylvania Reserve Cavalry. Philadelphia: 1864. V. 65

LLOYD BROTHERS & CO.
Recollections of the Great Exhibition, 1851. London: 1851. V. 66

LLOYDS, F.
Practical Guide to Scene Painting and Painting in Distemper. London: 1860. V. 64; 65
Practical Guide to Scene Painting and Painting in Distemper. London: 1875. V. 66

LLOYDS REGISTER OF SHIPPING
Anchors- Approved Designs. London: 1945. V. 67

LOBB, THEOPHILUS
Medical Practice in Curing Fevers; Correspondent to Rational Methods &c.... London: 1735. V. 62; 66

LOBBAN, C. S.
Seaweed Ecology and Physiology. Cambridge: 1994. V. 64; 65

LOBEL, ANITA
On Market Street. New York: 1981. V. 65

LOBEL, ARNOLD
Fables. New York: 1980. V. 63; 65

LOBEL, MATTHIAS DE
In G. Rondelletii...Pharmaceuticam Officinam Animadversiones.... London: 1605. V. 64

LOBENSTINE, WILLIAM
Extracts from the Diary of William C. Lobenstine, December 31, 1851-1858. N.P: 1920. V. 62; 65

LO BIANCO, SALVATORE
Uova, Larve e Stadi Giovanili de Teleostei. Rome and Berlin: 1931-1956. V. 65

LOBLEY, J. L.
Mount Vesuvius, a Descriptive, Historical and Geological Account.... 1889. V. 63

LOBO, JERONYMO
A Voyage to Abyssinia. London: 1735. V. 63; 66
A Voyage to Abyssinia. Edinburgh: 1789. V. 62
A Voyage to Abyssinia. London: 1789. V. 64

LOBSTEIN, J. F. DANIEL
A Treatise Upon the Semeiology of the Eye, for the Use of Physicians, and of the Countenance for Criminal Jurisprudence. New York: 1830. V. 63; 64; 66

LOCATION Register of Twentieth-Century English Literary Manuscripts and Letters. Boston: 1988. V. 63

LOCH, JAMES
An Account of the Improvements on the Estates of the Marquess of Stafford, in the Counties of Stafford and Salop, and on the Estate of Sutherland. London: 1820. V. 66

LOCHER, A.
With Star and Crescent; a full an Authtentic Account of a Recent Journey with a Caravan from Bombay to Constantinople.... Philadelphia: 1890. V. 67

LOCHER, J. L.
M. C. Escher: His Life and Complete Graphic Work. New York: 1981. V. 62; 63; 64

LOCK, JOHN
A Man of Sorrow, The Life, Letters and Times of the Rev. Patrick Bronte. London: 1965. V. 63

LOCK, M. A.
Perspectives in Running Water Ecology. New York: 1981. V. 64; 65

LOCKARD, FRANK M.
Black Kettle. Goodlands: 1924. V. 64; 67

LOCKE, ALAIN
Plays of Negro Life. New York: 1927. V. 66

LOCKE, HAROLD
A Bibliographical Catalogue of the Published Novels and Ballads of William Harrison Ainsworth. London: 1925. V. 65

LOCKE, J.
The Game Laws.... 1849. V. 63

LOCKE, JAMES
Tweed and Don. 1860. V. 65
Tweed and Don. Edinburgh: 1860. V. 62; 66; 67

LOCKE, JOHN
An Abridgment of Mr. Locke's Essay Concerning Human Understanding. London: 1737. V. 62
An Abridgment of Mr. Locke's Essay Concerning Human Understanding. Edinburgh: 1778. V. 62
An Abridgment of Mr. Locke's Essay Concerning Human Understanding. Boston: 1794. V. 63
A Common-place Book to the Holy Bible: or, the Scriptures Sufficiency Practically Demonstrated. London: 1697. V. 63; 64
Essai Philosophique Concernant L'Entendement Humain, ou l'On Montre Quelle est l'Etendue de Nos Connoissances Certaines, et la Maniere Dont Nous y Parvenons.... Amsterdam: 1742. V. 65
An Essay Concerning Human (sic) Understanding. London: 1710. V. 64
An Essay Concerning Human Understanding. London: 1726. V. 62
An Essay Concerning Human Understanding and a Treatise on the Conduct of the Understanding. Philadelphia: 1831. V. 65
An Essay Concerning Humane Understanding. London: 1690. V. 67
An Essay on Human Understanding. London: 1753. V. 65
Histoire de la Navigation, Son Commencement, Son Progres & Ses Decouvertes Jusqu'a Present. Paris: 1722. V. 66
The Philosophical Works of John Locke. London: 1894. V. 62
Some Considerations of the Consequences of the Lowering of Interest, and Raising the Value of Money. (with) Short Observations on a Printed Paper, Intituled, For Encouraging the Coining Silver Money In England, and After for Keeping It Here. London: 1692-1695. V. 64
Some Familiar Letters Between Mr. Locke and Several of His Friends. London: 1708. V. 62
Some Thoughts Concerning Education. London: 1695. V. 64
Some Thoughts Concerning Education. London: 1809. V. 63
Two Treatises of Government: in the Former, the False Principles and Foundation of Sir Robert Filmer and His Followers.... London: 1698. V. 63
The Works. London: 1714. V. 65
The Works. London: 1740. V. 62
The Works in Ten Volumes. London: 1801. V. 67

LOCKE, RICHARD
The Circle Squared. To Which is Added, a Problem to Discover the Longitude Both at Land and Sea. London: 1730. V. 63

LOCKE, WILLIAM E.
A Centennial Discourse, Containing a History of the Scotch Plains Baptist Church, New Jersey, During the First Century of Its Ecclesiastical Existence. New York: 1847. V. 63; 66

LOCKER, ARTHUR
Sir Goodwin's Folly: a Story of the Year 1795. London: 1864. V. 67

LOCKER, EDWARD HAWKE
Views in Spain. London: 1824. V. 62

LOCKER, FREDERICK
A Selection from the Works of Frederick Locker. London: 1865. V. 62

LOCKER-LAMPSON, FREDERICK
London Lyrics. London: 1857. V. 65
London Lyrics. London: 1870. V. 65

LOCKET, G. H.
British Spiders. London: 1951-1974. V. 62
British Spiders. London: 1968. V. 66
British Spiders. London: 1974-1975. V. 62
British Spiders. London: 1978-1981. V. 64

LOCKHART, GEORGE
Memoirs Concerning the Affairs of Scotland, from Queen Anne's Accession to the Throne to the Commencement of the Union of the Two Kingdoms of Scotland and England in May 1707.... (With) A Key to the Memoirs of the Affairs of Scotland. London: 1714. V. 62
Memoirs Concerning the Affairs of Scotland, From Queen Anne's Accession to the Throne, to the Commencement of the Union of the Two Kingdoms of Scotland and England in May 1707. London: 1714. V. 66

LOCKHART, JOHN GIBSON
The History of Matthew Wald. Edinburgh: 1824. V. 66
Memoirs of the Life of Sir Wlater Scott, Bart. Edinburgh Robert Cadell; Lon: 1837-1838. V. 66
Reginald Dalton. London: 1823. V. 62; 65
Valerius: a Roman Story. Edinburgh: 1821. V. 63

LOCKLEY, R.
The Secrets of Natural New Zealand. Auckland: 1987. V. 63

LOCKLEY, R. M.
Dream Island. London: 1931. V. 62

LOCKMAN, MR.
Travels of the Jesuits, Into Various Parts of the World. London: 1743. V. 67

LOCKRIDGE, RICHARD
One Lady, Two Cats. London: 1968. V. 65

LOCKWOOD, A. G. B.
Gardens of Colony and State, Gardens and Gardeners of the American Colonies and Of the Republic Before 1840. New York: 1931-1934. V. 64

LOCKWOOD, C. B.
The Early Development of the Pericardium, Diaphram, and Great Veins. 1888. V. 67
Hunterian Lectures on the Development and Transition of the Testis. London and Edinburgh: 1888. V. 67

LOCKWOOD, CHARLES
The Estates of Beverly Hills, Holmby Hills, Bel Air, Beverly Park. Beverley Hills: 1989. V. 62

LOCKWOOD, FRANK C.
The Apache Indians. New York: 1938. V. 63; 67
Arizona Characters. Los Angeles: 1928. V. 67
Life in Old Tucson 1854-1864. Los Angeles: 1943. V. 65
The Life of Edward E. Ayer. Chicago: 1929. V. 63
Pioneer Days in Arizona - from the Spanish Occupation to Statehood. New York: 1932. V. 62; 65
Tucson - the Old Pueblo. Phoenix: 1920. V. 67

LOCKWOOD, JAMES D.
Life and Adventures of a Drummer Boy or Seven Years a Soldier. Albany: 1863. V. 65
Life and Adventures of a Drummer Boy or Seven Years a Soldier. Albany: 1893. V. 67

LOCKWOOD, LUKE VINCENT
Colonial Furniture in America. New York: 1913. V. 64

LOCKWOOD MARSH, W.
Aeronautical Prints and Drawings. London: 1924. V. 62

LOCKYER, J. NORMAN
The Chemistry of the Sun. London: 1887. V. 66
The Dawn of Astronomy. London: 1894. V. 63

LODGE, DAVID
The Man Who Wouldn't Get Up and Other Stories. 1998. V. 63; 65; 66
The Novelist at the Crossroads and Other Essays on Fiction and Criticism. London: 1971. V. 65
The Picturegoers. London: 1960. V. 64

LODGE, EDMUND
Illustrations of British History, Biography and Manners, in the Reigns of Henry VIII, Edward VI, Elizabeth and James I.... London: 1838. V. 63
Portraits of Illustrious Personages of Great Britain. Bohn: 1849-1850. V. 62
Portraits of Illustrious Personages of Great Britian. London and New York: 1860. V. 62

LODGE, GEORGE E.
Memoirs of an Artist Naturalist. London: 1946. V. 64; 65; 67

LODGE, HENRY C.
The War With Spain. New York and London: 1899. V. 67

LODGE, MRS.
George Elvaston. London: 1883. V. 65

LODGE, OLIVER
Electrons or the Nature and Properties of Negative Electricity. London: 1906. V. 65; 67

LOEB, JACQUES
The Mechanistic Conception of Life: Biological Essays.... Chicago: 1912. V. 63

LOEBER, E. G.
Paper Mould and Mouldmaker. Amsterdam: 1982. V. 64

LOEHR, CHARLES T.
War History of the Old First Virginia Infantry Regiment, Army of Northern Virginia. Richmond: 1884. V. 62; 63; 65

LOEWENFELD, LEOPOLD
Die Moderne Behandlung der Nervenschwache (Neurasthenie) der Hysterie und Verwandter Leiden. Wiesbaden: 1904. V. 65
Die Psychischen Zwangserscheinungen. Wiesbaden: 1904. V. 65

LOEWENFELD, LEOPOLD continued
Sexualleben und Nervenleiden: Die Nervosen Storungen Sexuellen Ursprungs. Wiesbaden: 1906. V. 65

LOFFLER, F.
Otto Dix: Life and Work. New York and London: 1982. V. 65

LOFT, CAPEL
Remarks on the Letter of the Rt. Hon. Edmund Burke, Concerning the Revolution in France, and on the Proceedings in Certain Societies in London, Relative to that Event. Dublin;: 1791. V. 65

LOFTIE, ARTHUR G.
A History of the Parishes of Wetheral and Warwick. Carlisle: 1923. V. 65

LOFTIE, W. J.
English Lake Scenery from Original Drawings by T. L. Rowbotham.... London: 1875. V. 64
Kensington: Picturesque and Historical. London: 1888. V. 62; 63
Orient Line Guide 1888. Chapters for Travellers by Sea and by Land. London: 1888. V. 66
Orient Line Guide 1895. Chapters for Travellers by Sea and Land. London: 1891. V. 66
The Rural Deanery of Gosforth, Diocese of Carlisle, Its Churches and Endowments. Kendal: 1889. V. 65

LOFTING, HUGH
About Doctor Doolittle. London: 1924. V. 63
Doctor Dolittle and the Secret Lake. Philadelphia and New York: 1948. V. 62
Doctor Dolittle and the Secret Lake. London: 1949. V. 65
Doctor Dolittle in the Moon. New York: 1928. V. 63
Doctor Dolittle's Caravan. New York: 1926. V. 62
Doctor Dolittle's Zoo. New York: 1925. V. 63; 64
Gub Gub's Book: an Encyclopedia of Food in Twenty Volumes. New York: 1932. V. 63; 65
The Story of Mrs. Tubbs. New York: 1923. V. 64

LOFTUS, W. R.
The Wine Merchant. London: 1865. V. 62

LOGAN, H. C.
Pictorial History of the Under Hammer Gun. 1960. V. 67

LOGAN, HERSCHEL C.
The American Hand Press: Its Origin, Development and Use. Whittier: 1980. V. 64

LOGAN, JACK ROBERT
Northmost Australia: Three Centuries of Exploration, Discovery and Adventure In and Around the Cape York Peninsula, Queensland. London: 1921. V. 67

LOGAN, JOHN
The Bridge of Change. Brockport: 1978. V. 66
Ghosts of the Heart - New Poems. Chicago: 1960. V. 62
The House that Jack Built or a Portrait of the Artist as a Sad Sensualist.... Omaha: 1974. V. 66
Poems. London: 1781. V. 64
Poems. London: 1782. V. 62
Sermons by the Late Reverend John Logan, F.R.S. Edin(burgh), One of the Ministers of Leith. Edinburgh: 1793. V. 66

LOGAN, JOHN A., MRS.
Reminicences of a Soldier's Wife, an Autobiography. New York: 1913. V. 65; 67

LOGAN, KATE VIRGINIA COX
My Confederate Girlhood, the Memoirs of Kate Virginia Cox Logan. Richmond: 1932. V. 63

LOGAN, OLIVE
Apropos of Women and Theatres. With a Paper or Two on Parisian Topics. New York: 1869. V. 65
Before the Footlights and Behind the Scenes.... Philadelphia: 1870. V. 65

LOGAN, RAYFORD
What the Negro Wants. Chapel Hill: 1944. V. 67

LOGAN, W.
Observations on the Effects of Sea Water in the Scurvy and Scrophula.... London: 1771. V. 62

LOGAN, W. E.
Geological Survey of Canada. Report of Progress 1863-1866. Ottawa: 1866. V. 67
Notes on the Gold of Eastern Canada.... Montreal: 1864. V. 64

LOGAN, WILLIAM BENNETT
Dress of the Day - War-and-After Reminiscences of the British Navy. London: 1930. V. 62

LOGGAN, DAVID
Cantabrigia Illustrata Sive Omnium Celeberrimae Istius Universitatis Collegiorum Aularum, Bibliothecae Academicae, Scholarum Publicarum.... Cambridge: 1690. V. 65

LOGSDON, JOHN M.
The Decision to Go to the Moon; Project Apollo and the National Interest. Cambridge: 1970. V. 67

LOGUE, CHRISTOPHER
The Man Who Told His Love - 20 Poems.... London: 1958. V. 62

LOGUE, MARY
A House in the Country. Minneapolis: 1994. V. 62; 64

LOGUE, ROSCOE
Tumbleweeds and Barb Wire Fences. Amarillo: 1936. V. 64; 67

LOHRLI, ANNE
Household Words.... Toronto: 1973. V. 62

LOHSE, JOHANNE
Mistaken Views on the Education of Girls. Christchurch: 1884. V. 65

LOMAX, ALAN
Mister Jelly Roll. New York: 1950. V. 62

LOMAX, GEORGE
Mr. Plausible Prate; or, the Adventures of an Assurance Agent. London: 1855. V. 64

LOMAX, JOHN A.
Cow Camps and Cattle Herds. Austin: 1967. V. 63; 67
Negro Folk Songs as Sung by Lead Belly. New York: 1936. V. 66
Songs of the Cattle Trail and Cow Camp. New York: 1919. V. 67

LOMAX, JOHN T.
Digest of the Laws Respecting Real Property...in the United States... in Virginia. Richmond: 1885. V. 62
A Treatise on the Law of Executors and Administrators, Generally in Use in the United States. Philadelphia: 1841. V. 63; 65; 67

LOMAX, LOUIS E.
The Negro Revolt. New York: 1962. V. 66

LOMAZZO, GIOVANNI PAOLO
Trattato dell' Arte de la Pittura, Diviso in Sette Libri.... Milan: 1584. V. 64

LOMBARDUS, PETRUS
Liber Sententiarum. Nuremberg: 1481. V. 64

LOMBROSO, CESARE
The Female Offender.... London: 1895. V. 63; 66

LOMMIUS, JODOCUS
Commentarii de Sanitate Tuenda in Primum Librum De Re Medica Aurel Cornelii Celsi.... Amsterdam: 1745. V. 63

LONCHAMP, FREDERIC CHARLES
Bibliographie Generale des Ouvrages Publies Ouillustres en Suisse et a L'Etranger de 1475 a 1914. 1995. V. 65

LONDON. GREAT EXHIBITION OF THE WORKS OF INDUSTRY
The Industry of All Nations 1851. The Art Journal Illustrated Catalogue. London: 1851. V. 66
Remembrances of the Great Exhibition. A Series of Views Beautifully Engraved on Steel, from Drawings Made on the Spot. London: 1851. V. 65

LONDON. IMPROVEMENTS AND TOWN PLANNING COMMITTEE
Reconstruction in the City of London. London: 1944. V. 64

LONDON *Almanack for the Year of Christ 1793.* London: 1793. V. 65

LONDON *Almanack for the Year of Christ 1797.* London: 1797. V. 65

LONDON *Almanack for the Year of Christ 1798.* London: 1797. V. 66

LONDON *Almanack for the Year of Christ 1812.* London: 1811. V. 65

LONDON *Almanack for the Year of Christ 1861.* London: 1860. V. 62

LONDON *Almanack for the Year of Our Lord 1735.* London: 1734. V. 65

LONDON *Catalogue of Books, with Their Sizes, Prices and Publishers.* London: 1827. V. 63; 65

THE LONDON *Catalogue of Books...from 1814 to 1846.* London: 1846. V. 65

THE LONDON *Censorship 1914-1919, by Members of the Staff Past and Present.* London: 1919. V. 63; 67

LONDON *Cries.* Birmingham: 1830. V. 62

A LONDON *Garland.* New York: 1895. V. 64

LONDON, H. STANFORD
The Queen's Beasts. London: 1953. V. 66

LONDON *Illustrated: a Complete Guide to the Places of Amusement, Objects of Interest, Parks, Clubs, Markets, Docks, Principal Railway Routes, Leading Hotels and also A Directory....* London: 1883. V. 62

LONDON, JACK
The Abysmal Brute. New York: 1913. V. 62; 63
The Acorn Planter. New York: 1916. V. 63
Adventure. New York: 1911. V. 65
Before Adam. New York: 1907. V. 62
Burning Daylight. New York: 1910. V. 65
The Call of the Wild. New York: 1903. V. 62
Children of the Frost. New York: 1902. V. 67
The Cruise of the Snark. New York: 1911. V. 63
A Daughter of the Snows. Philadelphia: 1902. V. 64
The Faith of Men. New York: 1904. V. 64
The Game. New York: 1905. V. 62; 66
The Iron Heel. New York: 1908. V. 66
John Barleycorn. New York: 1913. V. 63
The Kempton-Wace Letters. New York: 1903. V. 63; 64; 66
The Little Lady of the Big House. 1916. V. 62
Little Lady of the Big House. New York: 1916. V. 67
Lost Face. New York: 1910. V. 65
Love of Life. New York: 1907. V. 65; 67
Martin Eden. New York: 1909. V. 63; 64
Moon-Face. New York: 1906. V. 63; 64; 65; 66
The Mutiny of the Elsinore. New York: 1914. V. 63

LONDON, JACK continued
The People of the Abyss. Toronto: 1903. V. 64
The Sea Wolf. New York: 1904. V. 65
Smoke Bellew. New York: 1912. V. 63
A Son of the Sun. Garden City: 1912. V. 62; 65
South Sea Tales. New York: 1911. V. 65
The Star Rover. New York: 1915. V. 64
Theft. New York: 1910. V. 62; 63
The Turtles of Tasman. New York: 1916. V. 63
War of the Classes. New York: 1905. V. 65
When God Laughs. New York: 1911. V. 65; 67
White Fang. New York: 1906. V. 64
White Fang. London: 1907. V. 66
White Fang. Paris: 1916. V. 63

LONDON Liberties; or the Opinions of Those Great Lawyers, the Late Famous Lord Chief Justices Wild and Mr. Serjeant Maynard. London: 1683. V. 65

LONDON Library Catalogue. 1913-1950. V. 65

THE LONDON New Battledore. Whitehorn, Penryn: 1830. V. 65

LONDON: The Illustrated Hand-Book to London and Its Environs. London: 1853. V. 63

LONDON AND BIRMINGHAM RAILWAY
Book of Reference, Cotnaining the Names of Owners, or Reputed Owners and Occupiers of the Lands In or through Which the Said Railway is Intended to Pass.... Birmingham: 1833. V. 62
Observations on Railways Particularly on the Proposed London and Birmingham Railway. London: 1831. V. 62

LONDON CORRESPONDING SOCIETY
The Address Published by the London Corresponding Society at the General Meeting Held at the Globe Tavern, Strand, on Monday the 20th Day of Jan. 1794...to the People of Great Britain and Ireland. London: 1794. V. 62

LONDONDERRY, MARCHIONESS OF
The Magic Ink-Pot. 1928. V. 63; 66

LONDON PEACE SOCIETY
A Letter from the Committe of the London Peace Society; Respectfully Addressed to the Ministers of the Christian Religion, of Every Denomination and In Every Place. London: 1845. V. 66

LONG, A. L.
Memoirs of Robert E. Lee. New York: 1886. V. 62
Memoirs of Robert E. Lee. New York: 1887. V. 65

LONG, C. CHAILLE
Central Africa; Naked Truths of Naked People. London: 1876. V. 67

LONG, CATHERINE
The First Lieutenant's Story. London: 1853. V. 65

LONG, E. A.
Ornamental Gardening for Americans.... New York: 1885. V. 64

LONG, FRANK BELKNAP
The Hounds of Tindalos. Sauk City: 1946. V. 63

LONG, GEORGE
An Introduction to the Study of Grecian and Roman Geography. Charlottesville: 1829. V. 64
The Mills of Man. London: 1931. V. 62

LONG, HANIEL
Interlinear to Cabeza de Vaca. Santa Fe: 1936. V. 64
Malinche (Dona Marina). Santa Fe: 1939. V. 67
Pittsburg Memoranda. Santa Fe: 1935. V. 64; 65; 66

LONG, HUEY P.
Every Man a King. New Orleans: 1932. V. 64; 65
Every Man a King. New Orleans: 1933. V. 63

LONG Island Fauna and Flora. Brooklyn: 1913-1916. V. 65

LONG, JAMES
Farming in a Small Way. London: 1881. V. 63

LONG, JOHN
Voyages and Travels of an Indian Interpreter and Trader, Describing the Manners and Customs of the North American Indians.... London: 1791. V. 63; 65; 66
Voyages chez Differentes Nations Sauvages de l'Amerique Septentrionale.... Paris: 1794. V. 64; 66

LONG, JOHN LUTHER
Billy-Boy: a Study in Responsibilities. New York: 1906. V. 65

LONG, JOHN ST. JOHN
A Critical Exposure of the Ignorance and Mal-Practice of Certian Medical Practitioners, in Their Theory and Treatment of Disease, Likewise Observations on the Primary Cause of Ailments, Connected with the Discoveries of the Author. London: 1831. V. 64

LONG, JOSEPH ABRAHAM
The Oestrous Cycle in the Rat and Its Associated Phenomena. Berkeley: 1922. V. 63; 65

LONG, JOSEPH R.
A Treatise on the Law of Domestic Relations. St. Paul;: 1905. V. 64

LONG, JOSEPH W.
American Wild-Fowl Shooting. New York: 1874. V. 66

LONG, MARGARET
The Oregon Trail. Denver: 1954. V. 66
The Santa Fe Trail - Following the Old Historic Pioneer Trails On the Modern Highways. Denver: 1954. V. 64; 66; 67
The Shadow of the Arrow. Caldwell: 1941. V. 66
The Smoky Hill Trail, Following the Old Historic Pioneer Trails On the Modern Highways. Denver: 1947. V. 65

LONG, MASON
The Life of Mason Long, the Converted Gambler. Chicago: 1878. V. 64

LONG, SAMUEL P.
Art: Its Laws and the Reasons for Them, Collected, Considered and Arranged for General and Education Purposes. Boston: 1876. V. 67

LONG, STEPHEN H.
Voyage in a Six-Oared Skiff to the Falls of Saint Anthony in 1817. Philadelphia: 1860. V. 67

LONG, THOMAS
The History of the Donatists. London: 1677. V. 65

LONGACRE, EDWARD G.
The Cavalry at Gettysburg. Rutherford: 1986. V. 63
From Union Stars to Top Hat - a Biography of the Extraordinary General James Harrison Wilson. Harrisburg: 1972. V. 67

LONGDON, HENRY ISHAM
Administrations of the Archdeaconry of Northampton 1546-1676. London: 1935. V. 66

LONGEVILLE, HARCOUET DE
Long Livers, a Curious History of Such Persons of Both Sexes Who Have Liv'd Several Ages. London: 1722. V. 63

LONGFELLOW, HENRY WADSWORTH
Aftermath. Boston: 1873. V. 67
Alcune Poesie.... Padova: 1866. V. 63
The Birds of Killingworth. Bremen and New York: 1974. V. 62
The Courtship of Miles Standish. Boston: 1858. V. 62; 65; 66
The Courtship of Miles Standish. London: 1858. V. 62
The Courtship of Miles Standish. Boston: 1920. V. 65
The Divine Tragedy. Boston: 1871. V. 67
Evangeline. Boston: 1847. V. 64; 65
Evangeline. Boston: 1848. V. 66
Evangeline. London: 1856. V. 62
Evangeline. Boston: 1867. V. 67
Evangeline. New York: 1903. V. 62
Flower-De-Luce. Boston: 1867. V. 64; 65
The Golden Legend. London: 1851. V. 63; 66
The Golden Legend. London: 1910. V. 67
The Hanging of the Crane. Boston: 1916. V. 63
Hyperion, a Romance. New York: 1839. V. 62; 64; 66; 67
Kavanagh, a Tale. Boston: 1849. V. 62
The Longfellow Birthday-Book. Boston: 1881. V. 62
Longfellow's Earliest Poetry. Houston: 1977. V. 66
Michael Angelo, a Dramatic Poem. Boston and New York: 1884. V. 64; 65
The New England Tragedies. Boston: 1868. V. 67
Poems. Boston: 1850. V. 63
Poems on Slavery. Cambridge: 1843. V. 64
The Prose Works. (and) The Poetical Works. Boston: 1866. V. 63
Saggi De' Novellieri Italiani D'Ogni Socolo: Tratti da Piu Celebri Scrittori.... Boston: 1832. V. 62
The Seaside and the Fireside. Boston: 1850. V. 62; 63; 64; 67
The Song of Hiawatha. Boston: 1855. V. 62; 64; 65; 66
The Song of Hiawatha. London: 1855. V. 62
The Song of Hiawatha. London: 1856. V. 67
The Song of Hiawatha. London: 1911. V. 64
The Song of Hiawatha. London: 1912. V. 62
The Song of Hiawatha. (with) The Song of Drop o'Wather. London: 1855-1856. V. 67
The Spanish Student. Cambridge: 1843. V. 63
Tales of a Wayside Inn. Boston: 1863. V. 62; 64
Voices of the Night. Cambridge: 1839. V. 63
The Waif: a Collection of Poems. Cambridge: 1845. V. 66
The Wreck of the Hesperus. Boston: 1845?. V. 66
The Writings. Cambridge: 1886. V. 62; 64

LONGFIELD, CYNTHIA
The Dragonflies of the British Isles. London: 1937. V. 62
The Dragonflies of the British Isles. London: 1949. V. 62; 64

LONGFORD, ELIZABETH
Images of Chelsea. Richmond-upon-Thames: 1980. V. 66

LONGHI, GIUSEPPE
La Calcografia. Milano: 1830. V. 67

LONGHURST, MARGARET H.
Catalogue of Carvings in Ivory. London: 1927-1929. V. 62; 67

LONGINUS
De Sublimitate Commentarius: Ceteraque, Quae Reperiri Potuere.... 1694. V. 66
Dionysii Longini De Sublimi Libellus Graece Conscriptus; Latino, Italico & Gallico Sermone Reditus.... Veronae: 1733. V. 65
The Works of.... London: 1712. V. 63; 67

LONGLEY, MICHAEL
An Exploded View - Poems - 1968-1972. London: 1973. V. 63
The Ghost Orchid. London: 1995. V. 63
Lares - Poems. Woodford Green: 1972. V. 64
No Continuing City - Poems 1963-1968. London: 1969. V. 63
Ten Poems. Belfast: 1965. V. 63

LONGMAN, C. J.
Archery. London: 1894. V. 67

LONGMAN, HURST, REES, ORME & BROWN
A General Catalogue of Valuable and Rare Old Books, in the Ancient and Modern Languages, and Various Classes of Literature... Parts I-IV for 1814. London: 1814. V. 62

LONGMAN, WILLIAM
A History of the Three Cathedrals Dedicated to Saint Paul in London. London: 1873. V. 67

LONGMATE, BARAK
The Arms, Crests and Supporters of the Baronets of Great Britain. London: 1786. V. 63; 66

LONGMORE, THOMAS
A Treatise on Gunshot Wounds.... Philadelphia: 1863. V. 65

LONGOLIUS, CHRISTOPHORUS
Orationes Duae Pro Defensione Sua (and other works). Florentiae: 1524. V. 63; 66

LONGRIGG, ROGER
The History of Horse Racing. London: 1972. V. 67

LONGSHORE-POTTS, ANNA M.
Discourses to Women on Medical Subjects. London: 1890. V. 65

LONGSTAFF, G. B.
Butterfly Hunting in Many Lands.... London: 1912. V. 62

LONGSTAFF, TOM
This My Voyage. London: 1950. V. 63; 64

LONGSTAFFE, W. HYLTON
Richmondshire, Its Ancient Lords and Edifices: A Concise Guide to the Localities of Interest to the Tourists and Antiquary.... London: 1852. V. 65

LONGSTREET, AUGUSTUS BALDWIN
Georgia Scenes, Characters, Incidents &c. in the First Half Century of the Republic. New York: 1840. V. 63
Georgia Scenes, Characters, Incidents, etc. in the First Half Century of the Republic.... New York: 1860. V. 66
A Voice from the South: Comprising Letters from Georgia to Massachusetts, and to the Southern States. Baltimore: 1847. V. 63

LONGSTREET, HELEN
Lee and Longstreet at Hightide. Gainesville: 1905. V. 63; 65

LONGSTREET, JAMES
From Manassas to Appomattox. Philadelphia: 1896. V. 62; 63
From Manassas to Appomattox. Philadelphia: 1912. V. 62; 63; 65

LONGSTREET, T. MORRIS
Murder at Belly Butte and Other Mysteries from the Records of the Mounted Police. New York: 1931. V. 65

LONGSTRETH, R.
On the Edge of the World: Four Architects in San Francisco at the Turn of the Century. 1983. V. 65

LONGSWORTH, BASIL N.
Diary of Basil Longsworth March 15, 1853 to January 22, 1854 Covering His Migration from Ohio to Oregon. Denver: 1927. V. 63; 66

LONGUE, LOUIS PIERRE DE
Les Princesses Malabares, ou Le Celibat Philosophique Ouvrage Interessant.... Paris: 1734. V. 63

LONGUEVILLE, T.
Falklands. 1897. V. 67

LONGUS
Les Amours Pastorales de Daphnis et de Chloe.... A Paris: 1757. V. 66
Daphnis and Chloe. London: 1893. V. 64; 66
Daphnis and Chloe. Waltham St. Lawrence: 1923. V. 62
Daphnis et Chloe. Londres: 1878. V. 62
Daphnis et Chloe. Paris: Sep. 1930. V. 63
Longoi Poimenikon, ton Kala Daphnin Kai Kloe (Greek) Longi Pastoralium de Daphnide et Chloe.... Franekerae: 1660. V. 64; 66
The Pastoral Loves of Daphnis and Chloe. London: 1924. V. 64
Pastoralium, De Daphnide et Chloe. Lutetiae Parisorum: 1754. V. 64

LONGWELL, DENNIS
Steichen: the Master Prints 1895-1914. New York: 1978. V. 63

LONGWORTH, ISRAEL
Life of S. G. W. Archibald. Halifax;: 1881. V. 64

LONGWORTH, J. A.
A Year Among the Circassians. London: 1840. V. 67

LONN, ELLA
Desertion During the Civil War. New York: 1928. V. 62; 63; 65
Foreigners in the Union Army and Navy. Baton Rouge: 1951. V. 65
Reconstruction in Louisiana After Eighteen Hundred and Sixty Eight. New York: 1918. V. 62

LONSDALE, HENRY
A Sketch of the Life and Writings of Robert Knox, the Anatomist. London: 1870. V. 64; 65; 66; 67

LONSDALE, JOHN
Memoir of the Reign of James II. York: 1808. V. 62

LOOK at the U.S.A. Boston: 1955. V. 62

A LOOKING-Glass for England. London: 1667. V. 62

LOOMES, BRIAN
Lancashire Clocks and Clockmakers. London: 1975. V. 62

LOOMIS, ALFRED
Lectures on Fevers. New York: 1881. V. 67

LOOMIS, ANDREW
Figure Drawing For All Its Worth. New York: 1958. V. 63
Fun With a Pencil. New York: 1944. V. 67

LOOMIS, E.
Copy of the Journal of E. Loomis, Hawaii 1824-1826. N.P: 1937. V. 66

LOOMIS, EBEN J.
An Eclipse Party in Africa: Chasing Summer Across the Equator in the U.S.S. Pensacola. Boston: 1896. V. 64

LOOMIS, ELIAS
Elements of Algebraic Geometry and of the Differential and Integral Caculus. Shanghai: 1859. V. 62

LOOMIS, LEANDER V.
A Journal of the Birmingham Emigration Company. Salt Lake City: 1928. V. 62; 65

LOOMIS, NOEL
Pedro Vial and The Roads to Santa Fe. Norman: 1957. V. 64

LOOS, ANITA
Gentlemen Prefer Blonds. New York: 1925. V. 62
Gigi. New York: 1952. V. 66
Twice Over Lightly; New York Then and Now. New York: 1972. V. 62

LOPE DE VEGA
The Star of Seville. Newtown: 1935. V. 64

LOPES DE CASTANHEDA, FERNAO
Historia del Descubrimiento y Conquista della India por Los Portugueses.... Antwerp: 1554. V. 62

LOPEZ, BARRY
Arctic Dreams. New York: 1986. V. 65; 66; 67
Crossing the Open Ground. New York: 1988. V. 65; 67
Crow and Weasel. San Francisco: 1990. V. 62; 65; 65; 67
Desert Notes: Reflections in the Eye of a Raven. Kansas City: 1976. V. 63
Field Notes. New York: 1994. V. 65
Giving Birth to Thunder Sleeping With His Daughter. Kansas City: 1978. V. 62
Light Action in the Caribbean. New York: 2000. V. 67
Looking in a Deeper Lair: a Tribute to Wallace Stegner. Eugene: 1996. V. 66
Of Wolves and Men. New York: 1978. V. 62; 63; 64; 65; 66
River Notes. The Dance of Herons. Kansas City: 1979. V. 62; 64; 66; 67
Winter Count. New York: 1981. V. 62; 65

LOPEZ DE LETONA, JUAN
Alonso y Cora o la Abolicion del Culto del sol Sacada de la Historia de los Incas.... Valladolid: 1834. V. 66

LOPEZ MADERA, GREGORIO
Excelencias de la Monarchia y Reyno de Espana. Valladolid: 1597. V. 62

LORAC, E. C. R.
Death Came Softly. New York: 1943. V. 66

LORAIN, JOHN
Nature and Reason Harmonized in the Practice of Husbandry. Philadelphia: 1825. V. 63

LORANT, STEFAN
The New World. The First Pictures of America. New York: 1946. V. 64

LORD, G. A.
A Short Narrative and Military Experience of Corp. G. A. Lord (125th NYV). Troy?: 1862. V. 67

LORD, I. ELYSE
Masters of the Colour Print. London: 1927. V. 63; 64

LORD, JAMES
Alberto Giacometti Drawings. Greenwich: 1971. V. 62; 63; 64
The Theory and Practice of Conveyancing; with Precedents; an Analytical Table of Real Property.... London: 1844. V. 63

LORD, JOHN
Frontier Dust. Hartford: 1926. V. 67
Memoir of John Kay of Bury, County of Lancaster, Inventor of the Fly-Shuttle, Metal Reeds, etc., etc. with a Review of the Textile Trade and Manufacture from Earliest Times. Rochdale: 1903. V. 63; 65

LORD, JOHN KEAST
At Home in the Wilderness. London: 1876. V. 66
The Naturalist in Vancouver Island and British Columbia. London: 1866. V. 67

LORD, JOHN R.
Contributions to Psychiatry, Neurology and Sociology Dedicated to the Late Sir Frederick Mott. London: 1929. V. 65

LORD John Ten, a Celebration. Northridge: 1988. V. 65

LORD, JOSEPH
The Militiaman's Pocket Companion.... New York: 1822. V. 63

LORD, JOSEPH L.
A Defence of Mr. Charles T. Jackson's Claims to the Discovery of Etherization. Boston: 1848. V. 64; 66

LORD, SAMUEL
Elementary Treatises on the Fundamental Principles of Practical Mathematics for the Use of Students. Oxford: 1801. V. 67

LORD, W. B.
Shifts and Expedients of Camp Life, Travel and Exploration. London: 1871. V. 67

LORDE, AUDRE
The First Cities. New York: 1968. V. 64

LORENTZ, HENDRIK ANTOON
The Theory of Electrons and Its Applications to the Phemnomena of Light and Radiant Heat. Leipzig: 1909. V. 65
Versuch Einer Theorie der Electricshen und Optischen Erscheinungen in Bewegten Korpern. Leiden: 1895. V. 65; 66

LORENZINI, CARLO
The Adventures of Pinocchio. New York: 1925. V. 63
La Avventure di Pinocchio. Florence: 1900. V. 62
Pinocchio. New York: 1937. V. 66
Pinocchio. New York: 1946. V. 64
Pinocchio di Collodi. Milano. V. 63
Pinocchio: Put-Together Book. New York: 1937. V. 62
Pinocchio: The Story of a Marionette. Philadelphia: 1972. V. 65
Pinocchio the Story of a Puppet. Philadelphia: 1916. V. 63

LORIMER, E. O.
Language Hunting in the Karokoram. 1939. V. 67

LORIMER, NORMA
By the Waters of Africa. 1917. V. 62; 63

LORNE, JOHN DOUGLAS SUTHERLAND CAMPBELL, MARQUIS OF
A Trip to the Tropics and Home through America. London: 1867. V. 63

LORRAIN, CLAUDE
The Drawings. Berkeley: 1968. V. 64

LORTON, WILLIAM B.
Over the Salt Lake Trail in the Fall of '49. Los Angeles: 1957. V. 63; 66

LORT-PHILLIPS, F.
The Wander Years. 1931. V. 63; 64

LORY, GABRIEL
Voyage Pittoresque de Geneve a Milan par le Simplon. Basel: 1819. V. 66

LOS Angeles Athletic Club and Allied Clubs. Fifty Three Years.... Los Angeles. 1934. V. 65

LOS Angeles City Directory 1906.... Los Angeles: 1906. V. 65

LOS Angeles City Directory Including San Pedro, Wilmington, Palms, Van Nuys and Owensmouth. Los Angeles: 1917. V. 62

LOS Angeles City Directory, 1927. Los Angeles. 1920. V. 62

LOS ANGELES COUNTY MUSEUM OF ART
Irving Gill, 1870-1936. 1958. V. 62

LOS Angeles from the Mountains to the Sea. Chicago and New York. V. 62; 63

LOS Fierros Del Rancho Los Cerritos. Long Beach. V. 65

LOSE, G. W.
From Acorn to Oak: a Home Missionary Story. Columbus: 1899. V. 67

LOSS of the Travers, Indiaman, Captain Collins, Commander, which Struck on a Rock Detached from Sunken Island November 7, 1809. London: 1810. V. 64

LOSSING, BENSON JOHN
A Brief Catalogue of Books. New York: 1885. V. 66
The Hudson; from the Wilderness to the Sea. Troy: 1866. V. 67
The Pictorial Field Book of the Civil War. Hartford: 1877. V. 65
Pictorial Field Book of the Revolution. New York: 1851. V. 67
The Pictorial Field-Book of the Revolution. New York: 1851-1852. V. 67
The Pictorial Field-Book of the Revolution.... New York: 1859. V. 63
The Pictorial Field-Book of the Revolution. New York: 1860. V. 63; 65

LOTHROP, CHARLES H.
A History of the First Regiment Iowa Cavalry. N.P. V. 65

LOTI, PIERRE
The Book of Pity and Death. London: 1892. V. 64
An Iceland Fisherman. New York: 1931. V. 62; 64
La Maison des Aieules, Suivie de Mademoiselle Anna Tres Humble Poupee. Paris: 1927. V. 65
Le Marriage de Loti. 1898. V. 66

LOTOS Leaves. Boston: 1875. V. 65

LOTSY, J. P.
Voyages of Exploration to Judge of the Bearing of Hybridization on Evolution. 1928. V. 63

LOTT, BRET
The Man Who Owned Vermont. New York: 1987. V. 63; 67

LOTTINI, GIOVAN FRANCESCO
Avvedimenti Civili...al Serenissimo D. Francesco Medici. Florence: 1574. V. 64; 66

LOTZE, RUDOLF HERMANN
Medizinische Psychologie Oder Physiologie der seele. Leipzig: 1852. V. 65

LOUBAT, ALPONSE
The American Vine Dresser's Guide. New York: 1872. V. 63

LOUDON, CHARLES, MRS.
Philanthropic Economy; or the Philosophy of Happiness.... London: 1835. V. 62

LOUDON, JANE
Botany for Ladies; or, a Popular Introduction to the Natural System of Plants. London: 1842. V. 66; 67
British Wild Flowers. London: 1849. V. 64
Facts from the World of Nature, Animate and Inanimate. London: 1848. V. 64; 65
Instructions in Gardening for Ladies. London: 1840. V. 63
The Ladies' Companion to the Flower-Garden. London: 1864. V. 65
The Ladies' Flower-Garden of Ornamental Annuals. London: 1849. V. 64
The Ladies Magazine of Gardening. 1842. V. 62
The Lady's Country Companion, or How to Enjoy a Country Life Rationally. London: 1846. V. 65
Mrs. Loudon's Entertaining Naturalist. 1867. V. 66
Mrs. Loudon's Entertaining Naturalist. London: 1867. V. 64
Works. 1849-1858. V. 62

LOUDON, JOHN CLAUDIUS
Arboretum et Fruiticetum Britannicum; or, the Trees and Shrubs of Britain. 1844. V. 62
Arboretum et Fruticetum Britannicum; or the Trees and Shrubs of Britain.... London: 1844. V. 66; 67
An Encyclopaedia of Agriculture.... London: 1831. V. 62
An Encyclopaedia of Agriculture.... London: 1857. V. 62
An Encyclopaedia of Gardening.... London: 1822. V. 64
An Encyclopaedia of Gardening.... London: 1848. V. 66
An Encyclopaedia of Plants. 1829. V. 66
Encyclopaedia of Plants. 1880. V. 63
Hints on the Formation of Gardens and Pleasure Grounds with Designs in Various Styles of Rural Embellishment.... London: 1812. V. 64
Hortus Britannicus. London: 1830. V. 65
Hortus Britannicus. 1832. V. 63
Hortus Britannicus. 1832-1850. V. 65
Hortus Britannicus. 1839. V. 63; 66
Self-Instruction for Young Gardeners, Foresters, Bailiffs, Land-Stewards and Farmers. London: 1845. V. 66; 67

LOUIS, ANTOINE
Recueil D'Observations D'Anatomie et de Chirurgie, Pour Servir de Base a la Theorie des Lesions de la tete.... Paris: 1766. V. 66

LOUIS, P. C. A.
Anatomical, Pathological and Therapeutic Researches on the Yellow Fever of Gibraltar of 1828. Boston: 1839. V. 66
Recherches Anatomico-Pathologiques sur la Phthisie. Paris: 1825. V. 64

LOUISIANA. LAWS, STATUTES, ETC. - 1808
The Laws of the Territory of Louisiana. St. Louis: 1808. V. 64

LOUISIANA, Statistics and Information Showing the Agricultural and Timber Resources. St. Louis: 1891. V. 63

LOUNSBERRY, A.
A Guide to the Trees. New York: 1900. V. 67
Southern Wild Flowers and Trees. New York: 1901. V. 64; 66

LOUNSBERRY, CLEMENT A.
Early History of North Dakota - Outlines of American History. Washington: 1919. V. 66
North Dakota, a History and People. Chicago: 1916. V. 67

LOURBET, JACQUES
La Femme Devant la Science Contemporaine. Paris: 1896. V. 67

LOURENCO DA RESURREICAO, FR.
Ceremonial dos Religiosos Capuchos da Provincia de Santo Antoio do Brasil, em o Qual com Toda a Claresa se Trata do Modo.... Lisbon: 1708. V. 62

LOUSLEY, J. E.
Wild Flowers of Chalk and Limestone. London: 1950. V. 62

LOUTHERBOURG, PHILLIPPE JACQUES DE
The Romantic and Picturesque Scenery of England and Wales. London: 1805. V. 62

LOUVET, JEAN BAPTISTE
An Account of the Dangers to Which I Have Been Exposed, since the 31st of May 1793. Perth: 1795. V. 62

LOUYER VILLERMAY, JEAN BAPTISTE L.
Traite des Maladies Nerveuses ou Vapeurs et Particulierement de l'Hysterie et de l'Hypochondrie. Paris: 1816. V. 65

LOUYS, PIERRE
Aphrodite. Paris: 1901. V. 64
La Femme et le Pantin. Paris: 1903. V. 62
The Songs of Bilitis. New York: 1926. V. 66
Trois Filles de Leur Mere. 1956. V. 66
Twilight of the Nymphs. London: 1928. V. 62; 67

LOVE, A. E. H.
A Treatise on the Mathematical Theory of Elasticity. Cambridge: 1892-1893. V. 62
A Treatise on the Mathematical Theory of Elasticity. Cambridge: 1906. V. 63

LOVE, ALBERT G.
The Geneva Red Cross Movement European and American Influence On Its Development. Carlisle Barracks: 1942. V. 63

LOVE, CHRISTOPHER
Heaven's Glory: Hell's Terror. Glasgow-College: 1738. V. 66

LOVE, EDMUND G.
The 27th Infantry Division in World War II. Washington: 1949. V. 67

LOVE, JAMES
Poems on Several Occasions. Edinburgh: 1754. V. 66

LOVE, JOHN
Geodaesia; or the Art of Surveying and Measuring Land Made Easy. London: 1768. V. 65
Geodaesia; or the Art of Surveying and Measuring Land Made Easy.... New York: 1796. V. 64; 66

LOVE, NAT
The Life and Adventures of Nat Love. New York: 1968. V. 67

LOVE, ROBERTUS
The Rise and Fall of Jesse James. New York: 1926. V. 62; 65

LOVECHILD, MRS.
A Talk About Indians. Concord: 1849?. V. 65

LOVECRAFT, H. P.
Beyond the Wall of Sleep. 1943. V. 66; 67
Beyond the Wall of Sleep. Sauk City: 1943. V. 62
The Case of Charles Dexter Ward. London: 1951. V. 63; 64
Collected Poems. Sauk City: 1963. V. 66
The Dark Brotherhood and Other Pieces. Sauk City: 1966. V. 63
The Dunwich Horror and Others. Sauk City: 1963. V. 63
The Horror in the Museum and Other Revisions. Sauk City: 1970. V. 63
Lovecraft at Last. Arlington: 1975. V. 66
The Lurker at the Threshold. 1945. V. 63; 66
The Lurker at the Threshold. Sauk City: 1945. V. 62; 66
Marginalia. Sauk City: 1955. V. 65
The Outsider and Others. 1939. V. 66
The Outsider and Others. Sauk City: 1939. V. 62; 67
Selected Letters. Sauk City: 1965-1976. V. 63
The Shuttered Room and Other Pieces. Sauk City: 1959. V. 65
Something About Cats. 1949. V. 66
Something About Cats. Sauk City: 1949. V. 62; 65
Supernatural Horror in Literatuare. 1945. V. 62; 66
The Survivor and Others. Sauk City: 1957. V. 63
3 Tales of Horror. Sauk City: 1967. V. 66
The Watchers Out of Time and Others. Sauk City: 1974. V. 63

LOVEDAY, JAMES THOMAS
London Waterside Surveys for the Use of Fire Insurance Companies.... London: 1857. V. 62

LOVEJOY, JOSEPH C.
Memoir of the Rev. Elijah P. Lovejoy, Who Was Murdered in Defence of the Liberty of the Press at Alton, Illinois Nov. 7, 1837. New York: 1838. V. 63

LOVEJOY, OWEN
An Agricultural Poem...Delivered Before the Bureau County Atricultural Society, October 1859. Princeton;: 1862. V. 66

LOVELACE, RICHARD
Lucasta et Cetera. Mount Vernon: 1948. V. 64; 66
Poems. Oxford: 1925. V. 62; 65

LOVELASS, PETER
The Law's Disposal or a Person's Estate Who Dies Without Will or Testament.... Dublin: 1789. V. 63

LOVELESS, GEORGE
The Victims of Whiggery; Being a Statement of the Persecutuions Experienced by the Dorchester Labourers.... London: 1837. V. 64

LOVELING, BENJAMIN
Latin and English Poems. Oxford: 1741. V. 67

LOVELL, A. C. B.
Meteor Astronomy. Oxford: 1954. V. 66

LOVELL, DEVORA
Edgar Allan Poe Memorial. Muse Anthology of Contemporary Poets. New York: 1938. V. 66

LOVELL, JAMES
An Oration Delivered April 2D, 1771. At the Request of the Inhabitants of the Town of Boston; to Commemorate the Bloody Tragedy of the 5th of March 1770. Boston: 1771. V. 67

LOVEN, MOE
The Lotus Position: Living on Your Back in the Great Northwest. Vancouver. V. 66

LOVER, SAMUEL
Handy Andy: a Tale of Irish Life. London: 1842. V. 65
Legends and Stories of Ireland: 2nd Series. London: 1837. V. 67
The Parson's Hand-Book. Dublin: 1831. V. 67
Treasure Trove: the First of a Series of Accounts of Irish Heirs.... London: 1845. V. 66

THE LOVER'S Harmony, Being an Enitre New and Choice Collection of the Most Admired Songs, Sung at All Public Places of Amusement. London: 1838. V. 63

LOVE'S Young Dream. Indianapolis: 1909. V. 66

LOVESEY, PETER
The Last Detective. Bristol: 1991. V. 63
Swing, Swing Together. London: 1976. V. 65

LOVETT, RICHARD
Irish Pictures; Drawn with Pen and Pencil. London: 1888. V. 65
James Chalmers: His Autobiography and Letters. London: 1902. V. 67
United States Pictures Drawn with Pen and Pencil. London: 1891. V. 62

LOVETT, WILLIAM
The Life and Struggle of William Lovett.... London: 1876. V. 64

LOVING, J. C.
The Loving Brand Book. Austin: 1965. V. 65

LOVOOS, JANICE
Millard Sheets: One-Man Renaissance. Flagstaff: 1984. V. 63

LOW, A. P.
Cruise of the Neptune: Report on the Dominion Government Expedition to Hudson Bay and Arctic Islands on Board the D.G.S. Neptune 1903-1904. Ottawa: 1906. V. 62
Rapport de L'Expedition Du Gouvernement du Canada a la Baie d'Hudson et Aux Iles Arctiques a Bord du Navire du Gouvernement du Canada "Le Neptune" 1903-1904. Ottawa: 1912. V. 64; 65
Report on the Dominion Government Expedition to Hudson Bay and Arctic Islands on Board the D.G.S. Neptune 1903-1904. Ottawa: 1906. V. 64

LOW, CHARLES RATHBONE
Britannia's Bulwarks: an Historical Poem, Descriptive of the Deeds of the British Navy. London: 1895. V. 65

LOW, DAVID
Elements of Practical Agriculture. 1867. V. 67
On Landed Property and the Economy of Estates.... London: 1844. V. 64
On Landed Property and the Economy of Estates.... London: 1856. V. 64

LOW, FRANCES H.
Queen Victoria's Dolls. London: 1894. V. 66

LOW, GEORGE
Fauna Orcadensis; or the Natural History of the Quadrupeds, Birds, Reptiles and Fishes of Orkney and Shetland. Edinburgh: 1813. V. 65; 67

LOW, HUGH
Sarawak, its Inhabitants and Productions.... 1848. V. 66
Sarawak: Its Inhabitants and Productions.... London: 1848. V. 67

LOW, JOSEPH
The Present State of England in Regard to Agriculture, Trade and Finance.... London: 1823. V. 65

LOW, ROSEMARY
Lories and Lorikeets, the Brush Tongued Parrots. 1977. V. 67

LOW, S. M.
An Index and Guide to Audubon's Birds of America. New York: 1988. V. 64; 67

LOW, SAMPSON
The Charities of London in 1861. London: 1862. V. 66

LOW, SIDNEY
The Call of the East. Bombay: 1908. V. 67

LOWE, CONSTANCE
Changing Pets. London: 1895. V. 63
Dolls at Home. London: 1910. V. 64

LOWE, EDWARD JOSEPH
Beautiful Leaved Plants. 1861. V. 63
Beautiful Leaved Plants. 1864. V. 63
The Conchology of Nottingham. London: 1853. V. 62
Fern Growing. New York: 1898. V. 64
Ferns: British and Exotic. London: 1856-1860. V. 65
Ferns: British and Exotic. London: 1857-1862. V. 62
A Natural History of British Grasses. London: 1862. V. 64
A Natural History of New and Rare Ferns.... London: 1862. V. 66
A Natural History of New and Rare Ferns.... London: 1865. V. 65
A Treatise on Atmospheric Phaenomena. London: 1846. V. 65

LOWE, F. A.
The Heron. 1954. V. 67

LOWE, JOHN
Epochs of a Pioneer Life in Western Virginia. Clarksburgh: 1917. V. 63

LOWE, JOSEPH
The Present State of England in Regard to Agriculture, Trade and Finance.... London: 1822. V. 63; 64

LOWE, PERCIVAL G.
Five Years a Dragoon ('49 to '54) and Other Adventures On the Great Plains. Kansas City: 1906. V. 63; 67

LOWE, PETER
A Discourse of the Whole Art of Chyrurgery. London: 1654. V. 62

LOWE, R. T.
A Manual of the Flora of Madeira. 1857-1868. V. 63; 66

LOWE, ROBERT
General View of the Agriculture of the Counties of Nottingham, With Observations on the Means of Its Improvement. London: 1798. V. 63; 65

LOWE, SOLOMON
Arithmetic in Two Parts.... London: 1749. V. 65

LOWE, T. S. C.
The Air-Ship City of New York: a Full Description of the Air-Ship and the Apparatus to Be Employed in the Aerial Voyage to Europe.... New York: 1859. V. 64

LOWE, WILLOUGHBY P.
The Trail that is Always New. 1932. V. 67

LOWELL, AMY
John Keats. Boston: 1925. V. 67
Sword Blades and Poppy Seed. New York: 1914. V. 62

LOWELL Connector: Lines & Shots from Kerouac's Town. West Stockbridge: 1993. V. 67

LOWELL, JAMES RUSSELL
The Biglow Papers. Cambridge: 1848. V. 64; 65
The Biglow Papers.... London: 1859. V. 62; 65
The Cathedral,. Boston: 1870. V. 62
Class Poem. Cambridge: 1838. V. 62; 64
The Complete Writings of James Russell Lowell. Cambridge: 1904. V. 64
Fireside Travels. Boston: 1864. V. 64
The Present Crisis. Eugene: 1941. V. 62
Three Memorial Poems. Boston;: 1877. V. 65

LOWELL, MARIA
Letter of Maria White Lowell to Sophia Hawthorne. N.P: 1914. V. 65
The Poems. Cambridge: 1907. V. 62; 64; 65; 67
The Poems.... Providence: 1936. V. 62

LOWELL, PERCIVAL
The Evolution of Worlds. New York: 1909. V. 67
Mars as the Abode of Life. New York: 1909. V. 67

LOWELL, ROBERT
For the Union Dead. New York: 1964. V. 62; 64; 66
For the Union Dead. New York: 1965. V. 62
4 by Robert Lowell. Cambridge: 1969. V. 62; 64
Land of Unlikeness. Cummington: 1944. V. 63
Life Studies. New York: 1959. V. 62; 64
Lord Weary's Castle. New York: 1946. V. 62; 63; 64
A Memorial Address and an Elegy. London: 1978. V. 66
The Mills of the Kavanaughs. New York: 1951. V. 64; 66
Notebook 1967-1968. New York: 1969. V. 67
Poems 1938-1949. London: 1950. V. 62; 64

LOWENFELS, WALTER
Lands of Roseberries. Mexico City: 1965. V. 63
Some Deaths. Highlands: 1964. V. 63

LOWER, MARK ANTONY
Chronicles of Pevensey; with Notices, Biographical, Topographical and Antiquarian for Visitors. London: 1863. V. 63
English Surnames. London: 1849. V. 66
The Worthies of Sussex: Biographical Sketches.... Lewes: 1865. V. 62; 66

LOWER, RICHARD
Tractatus De Corde. Amstelodami: 1669. V. 66
Tractus de Corde. London: 1669. V. 67

LOWINSKY, RUTH
Lovely Food - A Cookery Notebook - with Table Decorations.... London: 1931. V. 62

LOWITH, KARL
Das Individuum in der rolle des Mitmenschen. Munich: 1928. V. 67

LOWMAN, AL
Printing Arts in Texas. N.P: 1975. V. 62
Remembering Carl Hertzog: a Texas Printer and His Books. Dallas: 1985. V. 63; 64

LOWMAN, PAUL D.
Space Panorama. Zurich: 1968. V. 67

LOWNDES, HANNAH MARIA JONES
Gretna Green or, the Elopement of Miss D-- with a Gallant Son of Mars. London: 1821. V. 63

LOWNDES, MARIE BELLOC
Jenny Newstead. London: 1932. V. 66
The Uttermost Farthing. London: 1908. V. 66

LOWNDES, WILLIAM
A Report Containing an Essay for the Amendment of the Silver Coins. London: 1695. V. 63

LOWNDES, WILLIAM THOMAS
The Bibliographer's Manual of English Literature. London: 1834. V. 65
The Bibliographer's Manual of English Literature. London: 1857-1864. V. 66
The Bibliographer's Manual of English Literature. London: 1865. V. 62; 67
The Bibliographer's Manual of English Literature. London: 1880. V. 63

LOWNDES'S London Directory, for the Year 1785. London: 1785. V. 64

LOWNE, B. T.
The Anatomy and Physiology of the Blow-Fly (Musca Vomitoria, Linn.). 1870. V. 63

LOWRY, D.
Conversations on Mineralogy. 1822. V. 62
Conversations on Mineralogy. London: 1826. V. 63

LOWRY, FLORA
Autobiography of Miss Flora Lowry. Tyrone: 1885. V. 65

LOWRY, LOIS
Number the Stars. Boston: 1989. V. 64

LOWRY, MALCOLM
Au-Dessous du Volcan. Paris: 1949. V. 62
Dark As the Grave Wherein My Friend is Laid. New York: 1968. V. 67
Dark as the Grave Wherein My Friend is Laid. London: 1969. V. 65
Hear Us O Lord from Heaven thy Dwelling Place. London: 1962. V. 65
Lunar Caustic. Paris: 1963. V. 65
Ultramarine. London: 1933. V. 64
Ultramarine. Philadelphia & New York: 1962. V. 62; 64; 67
Under the Volcano. London: 1947. V. 63
Under the Volcano. New York: 1947. V. 62; 65

LOWRY, THOMAS
Personal Reminiscences of Abraham Lincoln. London & Minneapolis: 1910. V. 65; 66

LOWSLEY, BARZILLAI
A Glossary of Berkshire Words and Phrases. London: 1888. V. 64

LOWTH, ROBERT
De Sacra Poesi Hebraeorum Praelectiones Academicae Oxonii Habitae. Oxonii: 1753. V. 67
The Life of William of Wykeham, Bishop of Winchester. London: 1758. V. 62; 66
A Sermon Preached Before the Honourable and Right Reverend Richard, Lord Bishop of Durham, the Honourable Henry Bathurst, and the Honourable Sir Joseph Yates, at the Assizes, Holden at Durham, August 15, 1764. Newcastle: 1764. V. 65
A Short Introduction to English Grammar, with Critical Notes. London: 1763. V. 62
A Short Introduction to English Grammar: With Critical Notes. London: 1787. V. 66

LOWTHE, H. C.
From Pillar to Post. 1911. V. 67

LOWTHER, ALICE
When It Was June. Richmond: 1923. V. 67

LOWTHER, BARBARA J.
Bibliography of British Columbia. Victoria: 1968-1975. V. 65

LOWTHER, CHARLES C.
A Tale of the Kansas Border. New York: 1949. V. 67

LOWTHER, GEORGE
The Adventures of Superman. New York: 1942. V. 63

LOWTHER, JOHN
The Correspondence of Sir John Lowther of Whitehaven 1693-1698. London: 1983. V. 62

LOY, MINA
The Last Lunar Baedeker. Highlands: 1982. V. 63; 67
Luna Baedeker and Time-Tables. Selected Poems. Highlands: 1958. V. 62; 64; 65; 67
Lunar Baedecker. Paris: 1923. V. 65; 67

LOYOLA, IGNACIO DE SAINT
Viti Beati. Rome: 1609. V. 66

LOZANO, PEDRO
A True and Particular Relation of the Dreadful Earthquake Which Happen'd at Lima, the Capital of Peru, and the Neighbouring Port of Callao, on the 28th of October 1746. London: 1748. V. 67

LOZIER, ROY
Cowboys on the Green River Circa 1918. Wilson: 1682. V. 67

LUBBOCK, BASIL
Adventures by Sea from Art of Old Time. London: 1925. V. 63; 64

LUBBOCK, J.
A Contribution To Our Knowledge of Seedlings. London: 1892. V. 64

LUBBOCK, J. G.
Aspects of Art and Science. Leicester: 1969. V. 63; 65
From the Snows to the Seas. 1986. V. 62
Love for the Earth. Cambridge: 1990. V. 62
Perceptions of the Earth. Cambridge: 1977. V. 63
Reflections from the Sea. Leicester: 1971. V. 63

LUBE, D. G.
An Analysis of the Principles of Equity Pleading.... New York: 184. V. 65.

LUCANUS, MARCUS ANNAEUS
De Bello Civili. Amsterdam: 1658. V. 63
De Bello Civili, vel Pharsaliae. Lipsiae: 1589. V. 62
Lucan's Pharsalia. London: 1720. V. 65
Lucan's Pharsalia. London: 1722. V. 64
M. Annaei Lucani Phrasalia Cum Notis Hugonis Grotii, et Ricardi Bentleii.... Strawberry Hill: 1760. V. 66
Pharsalia. Venice: 1486. V. 64; 66
Pharsalia. London: 1718. V. 62; 63
Pharsalia. Leyden: 1728. V. 66
Pharsalia. Leyden: 1728. V. 62
Pharsalia. Strawberry Hill: 1760. V. 65

LUCAS, A. H. S.
The Seaweeds of South Australia. Adelaide: 1936-1947. V. 63; 66

LUCAS, C. E.
On the Principles of Inflammation and Fever. London: 1822. V. 63

LUCAS, CHARLES
An Address to the...Lord Mayor, the Board of Aldermen, the Sheriffs, Commons, Citizens and Freeholders of Dublin, Relating to the Intended Augmentation of the Military Force in the Kingdom of Ireland. Dublin: 1768. V. 62
The Fenman's World. Norwich: 1930. V. 63; 66

LUCAS, E. V.
Another Book of Verses for Children. London: 1907. V. 63
As the Bee Sucks - Essays. London: 1937. V. 63
Four and Twenty Toilers. London: 1900. V. 63; 66
Mr. Punch's County Songs. London: 1928. V. 62
Playtime and Company. London: 1925. V. 62; 65
Traveller's Luck: Essays and Fantasies. London: 1930. V. 66
Twelve Songs from Playtime and Company. London: 1926. V. 67
Willow and Leather; a Book of Praise. Bristol: 1898. V. 67

LUCAS, F. L.
The Golden Cockerel Greek Anthology. Waltham: 1937. V. 64; 65; 66
Hero and Leander. N.P: 1949. V. 62

LUCAS, FRED W.
Appendiculae Historicae; or, Shreds of History Hung on a Horn. London: 1891. V. 66

LUCAS, JOCELYN
Hunt and Working Terriers. 1931. V. 64
Hunt and Working Terriers. London: 1931. V. 66

LUCAS, JOHN
History of Warton Parish. Kendal: 1931. V. 66

LUCAS, JOSEPH
Studies in Nidderdale; Upon Notes and Observations Other than Geological.... London. V. 62
Studies in Nidderdale: Upon Notes and Observations Other than Geological, Made During the Progress of the Government Geological Survey of the District 1867-1872. London: 1878. V. 65
Studies in Nidderdale: Upon Notes and Observations Other Than Geological, Made During the Progress of the Government Geological Survey of the District 1867-1872. London: 1882. V. 66

LUCAS, KEITH
The Conduction of the Nervous Impulse. London: 1917. V. 64; 66; 67

LUCAS, MATTIE DAVIS
A History of Grayson County, Texas. Sherman: 1936. V. 66

LUCAS, RACHEL
Remarkable Account of Mrs. Rachel Lucas, Daughter of Mr. James Hinman, of Durham (Conn.). Boston: 1811. V. 63

LUCAS, RICHARD
The Influence of Conversation; with the Regulation Thereof, Being a Sermon Preach'd at Saint Clement Dane, to a Religious Society. 1707. V. 67
(I) An Inquiry After Happiness...(II) Humane Life; or a Second Part of the Enquiry...(III) Religious Perfection, or a Third Part of the Enquiry. London: 1692-1696. V. 67

LUCAS, S.
In Praise of Toadstools. London: 1997. V. 62
In Praise of Toadstools. Volume 2. 1997. V. 63

LUCAS, SAMUEL
Dacoitee in Excelsis; or, the Spoilation of Oude, by the East India Company.... London: 1857. V. 62

LUCAS, SILAS E.
The Powell Family of Norfolk and Elizabeth City Counties, Virginia. N.P: 1961. V. 62

LUCAS, THOMAS J.
Camp Life and Sport in South Africa: Experiences of Kaffir Warfare with the Cape Mounted Rifles. London: 1878. V. 65
The Zulus and the British Frontiers. London: 1879. V. 65

LUCAS, WILLIAM JOHN
The Aquatic (Naiad) Stage of the British Dragonflies (Paraneuroptera). London: 1930. V. 62
British Dragonflies (Odonata). London: 1899. V. 64
British Dragonflies (Odonata). London: 1900. V. 62; 66
A Monograph of the British Orthoptera. London: 1920. V. 62; 63; 66

LUCCOCK, JOHN
The Nature and Properties of Wool.... Leeds: 1805. V. 63

LUCE, A. A.
Fishing and Thinking. 1959. V. 67

LUCE, EDWARD S.
Keogh, Comanche and Custer. N.P: 1939. V. 65; 67
Keogh, Comanche and Custer. Ashland: 1974. V. 65; 67

LUCE, NANCY
A Complete Edition of the Works of Nancy Luce, of West Tisbury, Duke County, Mass. New Bedford: 1875. V. 64

LUCIAN SAMOSATENSIS
Dialogorum Selectorum Libri Duo Graecolatini. Ingolstadii: 1605. V. 66
Dialogues Des Courtisanes. Paris: 1900. V. 64
The Dialogues of Lucian. London: 1930. V. 65
The Mimes of Courtesans. New York: 1928. V. 66
Opera. Amstelodami: 1743-1746. V. 65
Opera Omnia.... Salmurii: 1619. V. 65
The True Historie of Lucian the Samosatenian. Waltham St. Lawrence: 1927. V. 64; 66
(Greek Letter) Luciani Samosatensis Opera.... Basileae: 1563. V. 65

LUCIDUS, JOANNES
Opusculum de Emdendationibus Temporum ab Orbe Condito ad Usque Hanc Aetatem Nostram. Venice: 1537. V. 62

LUCIEN-GRAUX, DOCTEUR
L'Agneau du Moghreb. 1942. V. 65

LUCIE-SMITH, EDWARD
A Girl Surveyed - Five Poems. 1971. V. 63

LUCILLE Cook Book. 1892. V. 66

LUCKE, A.
Der Mohr von Bern. N.P: 1868. V. 64; 65

LUCKHOFF, C. A.
The Stapelieae of Southern Africa. Cape Town: 1952. V. 64

LUCKOCK, JOSEPH
Essays on the Theory of the Tides, The Figure of the Earth, the Atomical Philosophy and the Moon's Orbit. London: 1817. V. 62

LUCKY Bucky in Oz. Chicago: 1942. V. 65

LUCKY, ROCHELLE
Cookery in the Middle Ages. Fallbrook: 1978. V. 66

LUCRETIUS CARUS, TITUS
De Rerum Natura.... Lugduni Batavorum: 1725. V. 65
De Rerum Natura. Birminghamiae: 1772. V. 65
De Rerum Natura.... Londini: 1824. V. 65
De Rerum Natura. Oxford: 1950. V. 65
De Rerum Natura. Libri Sex. London: 1712. V. 62; 65
De Rerum Natura Libri Sex. Birminghamiae: 1773. V. 66
De Rerum Natura Libri Sex. Glasguae: 1813. V. 66
De Rerum Natura Libri Sex. London: 1913. V. 64; 65
His Six Books of Epicurean Philosophy, Done Into English Verse.... London: 1683. V. 64
The Nature of Things.... London: 1813. V. 67
Of the Nature of Things. London: 1714. V. 65; 66
Of the Nature of Things. London: 1715-1714. V. 66

LUCUBRATIONS of an Heir Apparent. London: 1795. V. 62

LUCY, MARY ELIZABETH
The Private Journal of a Tour on the Continent in the Years 1841- 1843. London: 1845. V. 65

LUDERS, ALEXANDER
Reports of the Proceedings in Committees of the House of Commons Upon Controverted Elections...During the Present Parliament. London: 1785-1790. V. 65

LUDLOW, FITZ H.
The Heart of the Continent: a Record of Travel Across the Plains and in Oregon with an Examination of the Mormon Principle. New York: 1870. V. 64

THE LUDLOW Guide, Containing an Historical Account of the Castle and Town.... Ludlow: 1808. V. 66

LUDLOW, WILLIAM
Report of a Reconnaissance from Carroll Montana Territory...to the Yellowstone National Park.... Washington: 1876. V. 62
Report of a Reconnaissance of the Black Hills of Dakota, Made in the Summer of 1874 by Captain William Ludlow, Corps of Engineers. Washington: 1875. V. 65; 67

LUDLUM, ROBERT
The Osterman Weekend. Cleveland: 1972. V. 65
The Road to Gandolfo. New York: 1975. V. 63; 67
The Scarlatti Inheritance. Cleveland: 1971. V. 65
The Scarlatti Inheritance. London: 1971. V. 63
The Scarlatti Inheritance. New York: 1971. V. 63

LUDOLF, HIERONYMUS
Die in Der Medicine Siegende Chymie.... Erfurt: 1746-1749. V. 64

LUDOVICUS PRUTHENUS
Trilogium Animae. Nuremberg: 1498. V. 62; 63

LUDVIGSEN, KARL
The Mercedes-Benz Racing Cars. 1971. V. 66

LUDWIG, CHRISTIAN
A Dictionary English, German and French.... Leipzig: 1706. V. 62

LUDWIG, H.
Asteroidea of Albatross Expedition to Tropical Pacific 1899-1900. Cambridge: 1905. V. 66

LUEBKE, FREDERICK
Mapping the North American Plains. Norman: 1987. V. 64

LUGAR, ROBERT
Plans and Views of Buildings Executed in England and Scotland, in the Castellated and Other Styles.... London: 1811. V. 64
Villa Architecture: a Collection of Views with Plans of Buildings Executed in England, Scotland &c. London: 1828. V. 66

LUGARD, F. D.
The Rise of Our East African Empire: Early Efforts in Nyasaland and Uganda. London: 1893. V. 67

LUGRIN, N. DE B.
A Handbook of Vancouver Island. Victoria: 1918. V. 64

LUGS, J.
Firearms Past and Present. 1973. V. 63; 64; 66; 67

LUHAN, MABEL DODGE
Intimate Memories: Background. New York: 1933. V. 66
Movers and Shakers. Volume 3 of Intimate Memories. New York: 1936. V. 66
Taos and Its Artists. New York: 1947. V. 63; 66

LUIKEN, JAN
Des Menschen Begin, Midden en Einde: Vertoonende het Kinderlyk Bedryf en Aanwasch. Amsteldam, 1758. V. 66

LUIS DE GRANADA
An Exhortation to Alms-Deeds. London: 1775. V. 62
A Memorial of a Christian Life, Compendiously Containing All That a Soul, Newly Converted to God, Ought to Do, That It May Attain to the Perfections, After Which It Ought to Aspire. London: 1688. V. 66
A Memoriall of a Christian Life. Rouen: 1586. V. 63

LUKACH, HARRY CHARLES
The Fringe of the East: a Journey through Past and Present. London: 1913. V. 66; 67

LUKE, HARRY
More Moves on an Eastern Chequerboard. London: 1935. V. 67

LUKIS, WILLIAM C.
An Account of Church Bells; with Some Notices of Wiltshire Bells and Bell-Founders. London and Oxford: 1857. V. 63

LULL, RAMON
The Order of Chivalry. (with) L'Ordene de Chevalerie. 1893. V. 62

LULLABIES and Ditties for Little Children. London: 1873. V. 63

LUM, EDWARD H.
Genealogy of the Lum Family. Somerville: 1927. V. 63; 66

LUMBOLTZ, CARL
New Trails in Mexico. New York: 1912. V. 66

LUMBY, EDWIN
Edwin Lumby's Illustrated Catalogue of Wrought Welded Boilers, Cisterns &c. West Grove Works, Halifax. Halifax: 1861. V. 65

LUMHOLTZ, CARL
Among Cannibals: an Account of Four Year's Travels in Australian and of Camp Life with the Aborigines of Queensland. London: 1889. V. 65
New Trails in Mexico. New York: 1912. V. 63
Through Central Borneo, an Account of Two Years' Travel in the Land of the Head Hunters Between the Years 1913 and 1917. New York: 1920. V. 67
Unknown Mexico. New York: 1902. V. 64
Unknown Mexico. London: 1903. V. 62

LUMLEY, BRIAN
Hero of Dreams. 1986. V. 64; 66

LUMMIS, CHARLES F.
General Crook and the Apache Wars. Flagstaff: 1966. V. 67
Mesa, Canon and Pueblo. New York: 1925. V. 66

LUMPKIN, WILSON
The Removal of the Cherokee Indians from Georgia. Wormsloe: 1907. V. 63

LUMPKINS, WILLIAM
La Casa Adobe. Santa Fe: 1961. V. 65

LUMSDAINE, J. P.
The Prints of Adolf Dehn...a Catalogue Raisonne. St. Paul: 1987. V. 65

LUMSDEN, PETER S.
Lumsden of the Guides, a Sketch of the Life of Lieut. Gen. Sir Harry Burnett Lumsden.... London: 1990. V. 63

LUNDBORG, EINAR
The Arctic Rescue. How Nobile Was Saved. New York: 1929. V. 64

LUNDELL, C. L.
Flora of Texas. Renner: 1967-. V. 67

LUNDIN, LEONARD
Cockpit of the Revolution. The War for Independence in New Jersey. Princeton: 1940. V. 63; 66

LUNEL, G.
Histoire Naturelle des Poissons du Bassin du Leman. Lausanne: 1975. V. 66

LUNN, JOHN
The Tyldesleys of Lancashire. Altrincham: 1966. V. 66

LUNT, DOLLY SUMNER
Woman's War-Time Journal. Macon: 1927. V. 65

LUNT, GEORGE
Spiritualism Show As It Is!. Boston: 1859. V. 62

LUPING, D. M.
Kinabalu, Summit of Borneo. Kota Kinabalu: 1978. V. 66

LUPTON, DONALD
The Glory of Their Times. Or the Lives of ye Primitive Fathers.... London: 1640. V. 63; 64; 66

LURANI, GIOVANNI
Mille Miglia 1927-1957. 1981. V. 66

LURIA, ALEKSANDR ROMANOVICH
The Nature of Human Conflicts or Emotion, Conflict and Will.... New York: 1932. V. 65

LURIE, ALISON
Love and Friendship. New York: 1962. V. 65
The Nowhere City. London: 1965. V. 62
Only Children. London: 1979. V. 62
The War Between the Tates. New York: 1974. V. 65

LUSBY, THOMAS C.
The Lives and Times of Illustrious and Representative Irishmen. New York: 1877. V. 62

LUSCINIUS, OTHMAR
Musurgia Seu Praxis Musicae. Strasburg: 1536. V. 65

LUSH, TOM
Allard...the Inside Story. Surrey: 1977. V. 66

LUSHINGTON, CHARLES, MRS.
Narrative of a Journey from Calcutta to Europe; by Way of Egypt in the Years 1827 and 1828. London: 1829. V. 67

LUST, H. C.
The Complete Graphics and Fifteen Drawings. New York: 1970. V. 62; 65

LUSTGARTEN, EDGAR
One More Unfortunate. New York: 1947. V. 67
Turn the Light Out as You Go. London: 1978. V. 67

LUSTIG, ALVIN
The Collected Writings.... New Haven: 1958. V. 62

LUTHER, MARTIN
A Commentarie Upon the Fiftene Psalmes, Called Psalmi Graduum, That Is, The Psalmes of Degrees.... London: 1577. V. 64
A Commentarie Vpon the Epistle of S. Paule to the Galathians. London: 1580. V. 64; 66
Dris Martini Lutheri Colloquia Mensalia; or, Divine Discourses at His Table.... London: 1652. V. 66
Das Jhesus Christus Eyn Geborner Jude Sey. Wittenberg: 1523. V. 62
Thirty Four Speciall and Chosen Sermons of Doctor Martin Luther.... London: 1652. V. 62

LUTHER, SETH
An Address to the Working Men of New England, on the State of Education, and on the Condition of the Producing Classes in Europe and America. New York: 1833. V. 62; 66

LUTHER, T.
Custer High Spots. Fort Collins: 1972. V. 65; 67

LUTKE, FYODOR P.
Voyage Autour du Monde, Execute par Ordre de sa Majeste Nicolas.... Amsterdam/New York: 1971. V. 66

LUTKEN, C.
The Danish Ingolf Expedition. Volume II. The Ichthyological Results. Copenhagen: 1898. V. 65

LUTTIG, JOHN C.
Journal of a Fur Trading Expedition on the Upper Missouri 1812-1813. St. Louis: 1920. V. 65

LUTTRELL, HENRY
Advice to Julia. A Letter in Rhyme. London: 1820. V. 66

LUTYENS, E. L.
Houses and Gardens. 1913. V. 63

LUTZ, EARLE
A Richmond Album, a Pictorial Chronicle of an Historic City's Outstanding Events and Palaces. Richmond: 1937. V. 63

LUTZ, FRANCIS E.
Chesterfield: an Old Virginia Co. Richmond: 1954. V. 64

LUTZ, JOHN
Bonegrinder. New York: 1977. V. 65

LUTZE, ARTHUR
Lehrbuch der Homoopathie. Cothen: 1867. V. 65

LUXEMBURG, ROSA
Sozialreform oder Revolution? Mit Einem Anhang: Mitiz und Militarismus. Leipzig: 1899. V. 67

LUYKEN, JAN
Afbeelding der menschelyke Bezigheden Bestaande in Hondert Onderscheiden Printverbeeldingen Vertonende Allerhande Stantspersonen.... Amsterdam: 1695. V. 65

LUYS, GEORGE
Contribution a l'Etude des Fractures du Crane. Des Blessures Des Sinus De La Dure-Mere (Sinus Longitudinal Superieur et sinus Lateral). Paris: 1900. V. 64

LYALL, EDNA
The Autobiography of Slander. London: 1892. V. 64
The Hinderers: a Story of the Present Time. London: 1902. V. 65
In the Golden Days. London: 1885. V. 66

LYCETT, JOHN
British Fossil Trigoniae, Together with the Supplement. 1872-1883. V. 66

LYCOPHRON
Cassandra. Cambridge: 1806. V. 65

LYDE, SAMUEL
An Appeal for the Ansyreeh of Northern Syria; Being a Report on Their Present State to the Right Rev. Dr. Gobat. London: 1853. V. 67

LYDEKKER, RICHARD
Animal Portraiture. 1912. V. 62
Catalogue of Fossil Birds. London: 1891. V. 64
Catalogue of Fossil Mammalia in the British Museum. London: 1885-1887. V. 64
Catalogue of the Fossil Reptilia and Amphibia in the British Museum. 1888-1890. V. 62
Catalogue of the Fossil Reptilia and Amphibia in the British Museum. London: 1888-1890. V. 64
Catalogue of the Heads and Horns of Indian Big Game.... London: 1913. V. 67
Catalogue of the Ungulate Mammals in the British Museum. 1913-1916. V. 63; 65; 66
Catalogue of the Ungulate Mammals in the British Museum. London: 1913-1916. V. 64; 67
The Game Animals of Africa. 1926. V. 62; 63; 66
The Game Animals of Africa. London: 1926. V. 62
The Game Animals of India, Burma, Malaya and Tibet. 1907. V. 62; 64
The Great and Small Game of India, Burma and Tibet. 1900. V. 63; 64; 66; 67
A Hand-Book to the Marsupialia and Monotremata. 1894. V. 63
A Hand-Book to the Marsupialia and Monotremata. London: 1894. V. 62
A Hand-Book to the Marsupialia and Monotremata. London: 1896. V. 67
A Handbook to the Carnivora. Part I. 1896. V. 62; 63; 64; 66; 67
The Horse and Its Relatives. 1912. V. 64
Library of Natural History. New York: 1901. V. 63
Mostly Mammals, Zoological Essays. London: 1903. V. 67
The Royal Natural History. London: 1893-1894. V. 66
Royal Natural History. 1893-1896. V. 66
The Royal Natural History.... London: 1893-1896. V. 62
The Sheep and Its Cousins. London: 1912. V. 64
Wild Life of the World. 1916. V. 63; 66
Wild Life of the World. London: 1916. V. 64; 66

LYDON, A. F.
English Lake Scenery. London: 1880. V. 63; 66
Scottish Loch Scenery. London: 1882. V. 62; 66

LYDON, F. A.
The Coloured Drawing Book for Young Painters. Part III Only (of 3). 1860. V. 67

LYDON, JOHN
Rotten - No Irish, No Blacks, No Dogs. New York: 1994. V. 63

LYDSTON, G. FRANK
The Diseases of Society (The Vice and Crime Problem). Philadelphia and London: 1904. V. 66
Panama and the Sierras - a Doctors Wander Days. Chicago: 1900. V. 63

LYE, EDWARD
Dictionarium Saxonico et Gothico-Latinum.... Edinburgh: 1772. V. 64

LYELE, R. C.
Royal Newmarket. London: 1945. V. 67

LYELL, CHARLES
Elements of Geology. 1838. V. 62
Elements of Geology. London: 1838. V. 64; 65; 66; 67
Elements of Geology. Boston: 1841. V. 65
The Geological Evidences of the Antiquity of Man. London: 1863. V. 62; 63; 64; 65; 66; 67
The Geological Evidences of the Antiquity of Man. London: 1873. V. 64
Life, Letters and Journals. London: 1881. V. 62
A Manual of Elementary Geology. New York: 1855. V. 67
Principles of Geology. London: 1835. V. 64; 65; 67
Principles of Geology. London: 1838. V. 65
Principles of Geology. 1847. V. 63
Principles of Geology. London: 1850. V. 64; 65; 67
Principles of Geology. London: 1853. V. 62; 67
Principles of Geology. New York: 1853. V. 64
Principles of Geology.... 1867-1868. V. 63; 66
Principles of Geology. London: 1872. V. 64; 65; 67
Principles of Geology. New York: 1872. V. 64
A Second Visit to the United States of America. London: 1849. V. 63
A Second Visit to the United States of North America. New York: 1849. V. 62; 64
A Second Visit to the United States of North America. London: 1850. V. 66
The Student's Elements of Geology. London: 1871. V. 62
Travels in North America, Canada, and Nova Scotia. London: 1845. V. 63; 64; 66; 67
Travels in North America in the Years 1841-1842; With Geological Observations on the United States, Canada and Nova Scotia. New York: 1845. V. 64

LYELL, DENIS D.
African Adventures. Letters from Big Game Hunters. 1935. V. 62; 63; 64; 66
The African Elephant and Its Hunters. London: 1924. V. 64; 65
The Hunting and Spoor of Central African Game: with Life-Size Illustrations of Most of the Game Tracks. London: 1929. V. 67
Memories of an African Hunter. 1990. V. 64

LYELL, JAMES P. R.
Early Book Illustration in Spain. London: 1926. V. 63

LYFORD, C. P.
The Mormon Problem - An Appeal to the American People. New York: 1886. V. 64

LYMAN, CHESTER S.
Around the Horn to the Sandwich Islands and California 1845-1850. New Haven: 1924. V. 64; 66

LYMAN, DARIUS
Leaven for Dough-Faces; or Threescore and Ten Parables Touching Slavery. Cincinnati: 1856. V. 65

LYMAN, HENRY M.
Hawaiian Yesterdays. Chapters from a Boy's Life in the Islands in the Early Days. Chicago: 1906. V. 63

LYMAN, JOSEPH B.
The Philosophy of House-Keeping: a Scientific and Practical Manual for the Preparation of All Kinds of Food, the Making Up of All Articles of Dress, the Presentation of Health.... Hartford: 1867. V. 63

LYMAN, ROBERT
The Beecher Island Annual. 1917. V. 65; 67
The Beecher Island Annual. 1930. V. 67

LYMAN, T.
Challenger Voyage. Zoology. Part 14. Ophiuroidea. 1882. V. 64; 66

LYNCH, BOHUN
A History of Caricature. London: 1926. V. 64

LYNCH, H. F. B.
Armenia; Travels and Studies. London: 1901. V. 67

LYNCH, HANNAH
George Meredith: a Study. London: 1891. V. 67

LYNCH, JAMES
With Stevenson in California 1846. Tierra Redonda: 1896. V. 62; 63; 65

LYNCH, JAMES D.
The Bench and Bar of Texas. St. Louis: 1885. V. 65

LYNCH, JOHN
Cambrensis Eversus. 1848. V. 67

LYNCH, JOHN R.
The Facts of Reconstruction. New York: 1913. V. 63

LYNCH, PATRICK
Guiness's Brewery in the Irish Economy 1759-1876. 1960. V. 67

LYNCH, STANISLAUS
Echoes of the Hunting Horn. 1946. V. 67

LYNCH, T. K.
A Visit to the Suez Canal. London: 1866. V. 62

LYNCH, W. F.
Narrative of the United States' Expedition to the River Jordan and the Dead Sea. Philadelphia: 1849. V. 65

LYNCH ROBINSON, C.
Intelligible Heraldry. 1948. V. 67

LYND, SYLVIA
The Enemies: Poems. London: 1934. V. 66

LYNDE, FRED C.
Descriptive Illustrated Catalogue of the Sixty-Eight Competitive Designs for the Great Tower of London. London: 1890. V. 65

LYNDWOOD, WILLIAM
Provinciale (seu Constitutiones Angliae) Constitutiones Provinciales Quatuordecim Archiepiscoporum Cantuariensium.... Oxford: 1679. V. 67

LYNE, MICHAEL
Horses, Hounds and Country. 1938. V. 62
A Parson's Son. Sporting Artist. 1974. V. 62; 64

LYNN ALLEN, B. G.
Short-Gun and Sunlight; the Game Birds of East Africa. London: 1951. V. 67

LYNX, LINNAEUS, PSEUD.
Parson-ography; or the Book of Parsons. London: 1857. V. 67

LYON, DANNY
The Bikeriders. Santa Fe: 1997. V. 66
Knave of Hearts. Santa Fe: 1999. V. 66; 67
Memories of the Southern Civil Rights Movement. 1992. V. 66
Photo Film 1959-1990. Essen: 1991. V. 66

LYON, DAVID JOHN
The Denny List. London: 1975. V. 66

LYON, GEORGE FRANCIS
A Brief Narrative of an Unsuccessful Attempt to Reach Repulse Bay.... London: 1825. V. 67
Journal of a Residence and Tour in the Republic of Mexico in the Year 1826. London: 1826. V. 64
Journal of a Residence and Tour in the Republic of Mexico in the Year 1826. London: 1828. V. 67
A Narrative of Travels in Northern Africa in the Years 1818, 1819 and 1820. London: 1821. V. 66
The Private Journal of Captain G. F. Lyon of H.M.S. Hecla During the Recent Voyage of Discovery Under Captain Parry. 1821-1823. Barre: 1970. V. 64; 66

LYON, P.
Observations on the Barrenness of Fruit Trees and the Means of Prevention and Cure. Edinburgh: 1813. V. 64; 65
A Treatise on the Physiology and Pathology of Trees; with Observations on the Barrenness and Canker of Fruit Trees, the Means of Prevention and Cure. Edinburgh: 1816. V. 66; 67

LYONS, ALBERT MICHAEL NEIL
Hookey: Being a Relation of Some Circumstances Surrounding the Early Life of Miss Josephine Walker. London: 1902. V. 66

LYONS, ARTHUR
All God's Children. 1975. V. 64; 66
The Killing Floor. 1976. V. 64; 66

LYONS, AUGUSTA LOUISE
Sir Philip Hetherington. London: 1851. V. 65

LYRA Apostolica. Derby: 1836. V. 63

THE LYRIC Year, One Hundred Poems. New York: 1912. V. 65

LYSAGHT, A. M.
The Book of Birds. 1974. V. 67
The Book of Birds. London: 1975. V. 64; 67
Joseph Banks in Newfoundland and Labrador 1766. Berkeley: 1971. V. 62; 63; 64

LYSONS, DANIEL
The Environs of London: Being an Historical Account of the Towns, Villages and Hamlets, Within Twelve Miles of that Capital.... London: 1792-1811. V. 63
An Historical Account of Those Parishes in the County of Middlesex.... London: 1800. V. 66
Magna Britannia.... London: 1816. V. 62; 65; 66
A Sketch of the Life and Character of the Late Charles Brandon Trye, Esq. Gloucester: 1812. V. 65

LYSONS, SAMUEL
A Collection of Gloucestershire Antiquities. London: 1804. V. 66
Our Vulgar Tongue. London: 1868. V. 64

LYTLE, ANDREW
Bedford Forrest and His Critter Company. New York: 1931. V. 62; 64
The Long Night. Indianapolis and New York: 1936. V. 62

LYTTELTON, GEORGE LYTTELTON, 1ST BARON
Considerations Upon the Present State of Our Affairs, at Home and Abroad. London: 1739. V. 66
Dialogues of the Dead. London: 1755. V. 62
Dialogues of the Dead. London: 1760. V. 62; 66; 67
A Gentleman's Tour through Monmouthshire and Wales in the Months of June and July. London: 1794. V. 66
To the Memory of a Lady Lately Deceased. London: 1747. V. 65

LYTTLETON, GEORGE COURTNEY
The History of England, from the Earliest Dawn of Authentic Record, to the Commencement of Hostilities in the Year 1803. London: 1803. V. 63

LYTTON, EDWARD GEORGE EARLE LYTTON BULWER-LYTTON, 1ST BARON
Caxtoniana: a Series of Essays on Life, Literature and Manners. Leipzig: 1864. V. 63
Falkland. London: 1827. V. 66
Kenelm Chillingly: His Adventures and Opnions. London: 1873. V. 66
King Poppy. London: 1892. V. 62
The Last Days of Pompeii. New York: 1834. V. 65
My Novel. London: 1853. V. 66
Pelham Novels. New York: 1831-1833. V. 62
The Student, a Series of Papers. London: 1835. V. 67

LYTTON, EDWARD ROBERT BULWER LYTTON, 1ST EARL OF
Poems. Boston: 1881. V. 64

The Rightful Heir: a Drama in Five Acts. London: 1868. V. 62
Serbski Pesme; or, National Songs of Serbia. London: 1861. V. 63

M

M., W.
The Queen's Closet Opened. London: 1686. V. 65

MAAR, INGRID
The American Cowboy. Washington: 1983. V. 64

MAASKAMP, E.
Vues Remaraquables, Edifices, Monuments et Statues dans les Provinces Septentrionales du Royaume des Pays-Bas. Amsterdam: 1816. V. 62; 67

MABIE, PETER
The A to Z Book. Racine: 1929. V. 62

MABIN, M. P.
Life in the American Army from Frontier Days to Army Distaff Hall. Washington: 1967. V. 66

MABINOGION
Mabinogion. Waltham St. Lawrence: 1948. V. 62; 64; 66; 67
Tales from the New Mabinogion. London: 1923. V. 63

MABLY, GABRIEL BONNOT, ABBE DE
The Principles of Negotiations; or, an Introduction to the Public Law of Europe Founded on Treatises &c. London: 1758. V. 63

MAC ALISTER, A.
A Descriptive Catalogue of Muscular Anomalies in Human Anatomy. Dublin;: 1872. V. 67
A Monograph on the Anatomy of Chlamydophorus Trancatus.... Dublin: 1873. V. 67
The Myology of the Chieroptera. 1872. V. 67
On the Cranium of a Native of Lord Howe's Island; Further Evidence as to Existence of Horned Men in Africa; on the Crania of Natives of the Solomon Islands (etc.).... Dublin: 1883. V. 67
A Text-Book of Human Anatomy. London: 1889. V. 67

MAC ALISTER, ETHEL FLORENCE BOYLE
The Misdeeds of Maria Together with Seventeen Other Poems. London: 1926. V. 64

MAC ALISTER, R.
The Book of Ui Maine, Otherwise Called "The Book of the O'Kelly's". Dublin: 1942. V. 62

MAC ALISTER, R. A. S.
Ecclesiastical Vestments: Their Development and History. 1896. V. 67

MAC ALPINE, I.
Schizophrenia 1677. London: 1956. V. 66

MACARDY, JOSEPH
A Practical Essay on Banking: in Which the Operations of the Bank of England.... London: 1834. V. 64

MAC ARTHUR, BLANCHE
Lessons in Figure Painting in Water Colours. 1885. V. 67

MAC ARTHUR, CHARLES
War Bugs. London: 1929. V. 64

MAC ARTHUR, DOUGLAS
Military Demolition's. Fort Leavenworth: 1909. V. 64
Reminiscences: General of the Army. New York: 1964. V. 63; 65

MAC ARTHUR, MILDRED YORBA
California-Spanish Proverbs.... San Francisco: 1954. V. 63

MAC ARTHUR, ROBERT C.
Room at the Mark, a History of the Development of Yachts, Yacht Clubs, Yacht Racing and Racing Rules. Boston: 1991. V. 67

MACARTNEY, JAMES
A Lecture on the Uses of Anatomy and Physiology. Dublin: 1826. V. 67
On the Minute Structure of the Brain in the Chimpanzee and of the Human Idiot, Compared with that of the Perfect Brain of Man.... Dublin: 1842. V. 67

MAC ASKILL, WALLACE R.
Out of Halifax: a Collection of Sea Pictures. New York: 1937. V. 63; 64

MACASSEY, L. LIVINGSTON
Belfast Water Supply. Report on the Present Supply of Water to the City of Belfast and the Suburban Districts.... Belfast: 1891. V. 66

MACAULAY, AULAY
Polygraphy; or, Short-Hand Made Easy to the Meanest Capacity.... London: 1747. V. 66

MACAULAY, DAVID
Black and White. Boston: 1990. V. 65

MACAULAY, JAMES
Plea for Mercy to Animals. London: 1875. V. 66

MACAULAY, ROSE
Crewe Train. London: 1926. V. 62

MACAULAY, ROSE continued
The Lee Shore. London: 1912. V. 62
Orphan Island. New York: 1925. V. 64
The Writings of E. M. Forster. London: 1938. V. 64

MACAULAY, THOMAS BABINGTON MACAULAY, 1ST BARON
Critical and Historical Essays. London: 1843. V. 62
Critical and Historical Essays. London: 1848. V. 65
Critical and Historical Essays. London: 1858. V. 64
Critical and Historical Essays. London: 1860. V. 62; 66
Critical and Historical Essays. London: 1865. V. 64
The History of England from the Accession of James the Second. London: 1854. V. 65
The History of England from the Accession of James the Second. London: 1913-1914. V. 67
Lays of Ancient Rome. London: 1842. V. 63; 65; 67
Pompeii. Cambridge: 1819. V. 67
The Works. London: 1898. V. 66

MAC BAIN, ALEXANDER
Celtic Mythology and Religion: With Chapters on Druid Circles and Celtic Burial. 1917. V. 65

MAC BEAR, ALEXANDER
A Dictionary of the Bible or an Explanation of the Proper Names and Difficult Words in the Old and New Testament. Worcester: 1798. V. 66

MAC BETH, GEORGE
The Broken Places - Poems. Lowestoft, Suffolk: 1963,. V. 63
Lecture to the Trainees. Oxford: 1962. V. 63
Noah's Journey. London: 1966. V. 65

MAC BRIDE, DAVID
Experimental Essays on Medical and Philosophical Subjects. London: 1767. V. 63; 65
Experimental Essays on Medical and Philosophical Subjects. London: 1776. V. 63
A Methodical Introduction to the Theory and Practice of Physic. London: 1772. V. 65

MAC CABA, ALASDAIR
The Irish Year Book. 1938. V. 67

MAC CAIG, NORMAN
The Sinai Sort. London: 1957. V. 64

MAC CALL, WILLIAM
The Elements of Individualism. London: 1847. V. 64
The Newest Materialism: Sundry Papers on the Books of Mill, Comte, Bain, Spencer, Atkinson and Feuerbach. London: 1873. V. 64

MAC CARTHY, DESMOND
Experience. London: 1935. V. 65

MACCLESFIELD, GEORGE, EARL OF
Remarks Upon the Solar and Lunar Years. London: 1750. V. 62

MACCLESFIELD, THOMAS, EARL OF
The Tryal of Thomas, Earl of Macclesfield in the House of Peers for High Crimes and Misdeameanours; Upon an Impeachment by the Knights Citizens and Burgesses in Parliament in the Name of Themselves and of All the Commons of Great Britain. London: 1725. V. 67

MAC COLL, HUGH
Ednor Whitlock. London: 1891. V. 67

MAC CORMAC, DEARMER
Patty Who Believed in Fairies. New York: 1928. V. 65

MAC COWN, EUGENE
Paintings - Drawings - Gouaches. Paris: 1930. V. 63

MAC CULLOCH, DONALD B.
The Wondrous Isle of Staffa. Glasgow: 1934. V. 62

MAC CULLOCH, JOHN
A Description of the Western Islands of Scotland Including the Isle of Man. London: 1819. V. 62; 64
The Highlands and Western Isles of Scotland.... London: 1824. V. 62; 63

MAC CURDY, JOHN THOMPSON
War Neuroses. Utica: 1918. V. 65

MAC DERMOT, E. T.
The Devon and Somerset Staghounds 1907-1936. London: 1936. V. 62
The History of the Forest of Exmoor. Taunton: 1911. V. 62; 64

MAC DONAGH, DONAGH
Twenty Poems. Dublin: 1934. V. 62
Veterans and Other Poems. Dublin: 1941. V. 62

MAC DONAGH, THOMAS
Literature in Ireland. 1919. V. 67
Lyrical Poems. Dublin: 1913. V. 66

MAC DONALD, BETTY
Mrs. Piggle Wiggle. Philadelphia: 1947. V. 63
Mrs. Piggle-Wiggle's Farm. Philadelphia: 1954. V. 63

MAC DONALD, C. OCHILTREE
The Coal and Iron Industries of Nova Scotia. Halifax: 1909. V. 64

MAC DONALD, DAVID
The Land of the Lama. London: 1929. V. 62
Twenty Years in Tibet: Intimate and Personal Experiences of the Closed Land Among All Classes of Its People.... London: 1932. V. 62

MAC DONALD, DONALD
A Treatise on the Holy Ordinance of Baptism. Charlottetown: 1845. V. 64

MAC DONALD, E. T.
History of the Great Western Railway. London: 1927-1931. V. 64; 66

MAC DONALD, GEORGE
At the Back of the North Wind. New York: 1871. V. 62
At the Back of the North Wind. Philadelphia: 1919. V. 64
A Book of Strife. London: 1901. V. 62
Good Words for the Young. London: 1869-1872. V. 62
The Light Princess. New York: 1893. V. 64
The Light Princess. New York: 1969. V. 65
Phanatastes; a Faerie Romance for Men and Women. London: 1858. V. 67
Phantastes, a Faerie Romance for Men and Women. Boston: 1870. V. 65
The Princess and Curdie. New York: 1930. V. 62
The Princess and the Goblin. London: 1872. V. 62
Rampolli: Growths from a Long Planted Root. London: 1897. V. 64
Ranald Bannerman's Boyhood. London: 1872. V. 64
Wilfrid Cumbermede, an Autobiographical Story. New York: 1872. V. 65
Within and Without. London: 1855. V. 62
Within and Without. New York: 1872. V. 65

MAC DONALD, JOHN D.
The Annex and Other Stories. Helsinki: 1987. V. 65; 66; 67
Bright Orange for the Shroud. Philadelphia: 1972. V. 63
Cancel All Our Vows. New York: 1953. V. 66
Condominium. 1977. V. 66
Condominium. Philadelphia: 1977. V. 64
The Crossroads. New York: 1959. V. 63; 67
Darker than Amber. Greenwich: 1966. V. 65
Dead Low Tide. London: 1976. V. 65; 66
Deadly Shade of Gold. Philadelphia and New York: 1974. V. 63; 64; 66
A Deadly Shade of Gold. Philadelphia: 1975. V. 67
The Deep Blue Good-Bye. 1975. V. 66
The Deep Blue Good-Bye. Philadelphia: 1975. V. 63; 64
The Dreadful Lemon Sky. Philadelphia & New York: 1974. V. 63; 65; 66; 67
Dress Her in Indigo. Philadelphia: 1971. V. 63
The Empty Trap. London: 2000. V. 67
The End of the Night. London: 1964. V. 66; 67
The Executioners. 1958. V. 64; 66
A Flash of Green. 1962. V. 62
The Girl in the Plain Brown Wrapper. 1973. V. 66
The Girl in the Plain Brown Wrapper. Philadelphia: 1973. V. 63; 64
The Girl, the Gold Watch and Everything. London: 1974. V. 65; 67
The House Guests. New York: 1965. V. 67
Judge Me Not. London: 1999. V. 66; 67
A Key to the Suite. Greenwich: 1962. V. 67
The Last One Left. New York: 1967. V. 67
The Long Lavender Look. London: 1972. V. 65; 66; 67
The Long Lavender Look. Philadelphia: 1972. V. 63; 64; 65; 66
The Moving Target. New York: 1949. V. 67
Murder for the Bride. London: 1977. V. 65; 66
Nightmare in Pink. Philadelphia: 1976. V. 63; 64; 65; 67
One Fearful Yellow Eye. 1977. V. 66
One Fearful Yellow Eye. Philadelphia: 1977. V. 63; 64
Pale Gray for Guilt. 1971. V. 64
Pale Gray for Guilt. Philadelphia: 1971. V. 63
Please Write for Details. 1959. V. 64; 66; 67
Please Write for Details. New York: 1959. V. 67
A Purple Place for Dying. New York: 1976. V. 66
A Purple Place for Dying. Philadelphia: 1976. V. 63; 64; 65; 66; 67
The Quick Red Fox. Philadelphia: 1964. V. 66
The Quick Red Fox. Philadelphia: 1974. V. 63
Reading for Survival. Washington: 1987. V. 67
The Scarlet Ruse. Greenwich: 1973. V. 67
The Scarlet Ruse. London: 1975. V. 65
The Scarlet Ruse. 1980. V. 66
The Scarlet Ruse. Philadelphia: 1980. V. 63; 64
Seven. London: 1974. V. 65
A Tan And Sandy Silence. Greenwich: 1972. V. 67
A Tan and Sandy Silence. London: 1973. V. 65; 66; 67
A Tan and Sandy Silence. 1979. V. 66
A Tan and Sandy Silence. Philadelphia: 1979. V. 63; 64; 67
Three for McGee. 1967. V. 66
Three for McGee. Garden City: 1967. V. 65
Three for McGee. New York: 1967. V. 63; 64
The Turquoise Lament. 1973. V. 66
The Turquoise Lament. Philadelphia: 1973. V. 63; 64
Wine of the Dreamers. 1951. V. 64; 66
You Live Once. London: 1976. V. 65; 66

MAC DONALD, JOHN HAY
Our Trip to Blunderland or Grand Excursion to Blundertown and Back by Jean Jambon. Edinburgh: 1877. V. 64

MAC DONALD, JOHN ROSS
The Name is Archer. 1955. V. 62

MAC DONALD, MARIANNE
Death's Autograph. London: 1996. V. 62
Death's Autograph. 1997. V. 64
Ghost Walk. London: 1997. V. 63

MAC DONALD, PHILIP
Death and Chicanery. Garden City: 1962. V. 65
The List of Adrian Messenger. London: 1959. V. 65

MAC DONALD, ROSS
Black Money. New York: 1966. V. 66
Blue. New York: 1947. V. 65
Blue City. New York: 1947. V. 66; 67
The Chill. New York: 1964. V. 65; 67
A Collection of Reviews. 1979. V. 64; 66
A Collection of Reviews. Northridge: 1979. V. 65; 66; 67
The Doomsters. New York: 1958. V. 66
The Far Side of the Dollar. New York: 1964. V. 64
Find a Victim. London: 1955. V. 63
The Goodbye Look. New York: 1969. V. 66
The Instant Enemy. 1968. V. 66
The Instant Enemy. New York: 1968. V. 64; 67
Lew Archer Private Investigator. 1977. V. 64; 66
Meet Me at the Morgue. New York: 1953. V. 65; 67
The Moving Target. New York: 1949. V. 67
Self Portrait: Ceaselessly into the Past. Santa Barbara: 1981. V. 66
Sleeping Beauty. New York: 1973. V. 67
The Three Roads. New York: 1948. V. 65; 66
Trouble Follows Me. New York: 1946. V. 67
The Zebra-Striped Hearse. New York: 1962. V. 67

MAC DONALD, WILLIAM
Contributions to the History of Development in Animals. Edinburgh: 1868. V. 67

MAC DONALD CLARK, JANET
Legends of King Arthur and His Knights. London: 1914. V. 65

MAC DONNELL, A. G.
England Their England. London: 1942. V. 62
Napoleon and His Marshals. London: 1934. V. 62

MAC DOUGALL, CARL
A Scent of Water. London: 1975. V. 62

MAC DOUGALL, P. L.
The Theory of War: Illustrated by Numerous Examples from Military History. London: 1856. V. 62

MAC DOUGALL, W. B.
The Eerie Book. London: 1898. V. 64

MAC DUFF, ALISTAIR
Lords of the Stone an Anthology of Eskimo Sculpture. North Vancouver: 1982. V. 63; 66

MAC EVILLY, JOHN
An Exposition of the Gospels. 1898-1902. V. 67

MAC EWEN, MARGARET
Narcissus: a Poem. London and Toronto. 1914. V. 67

MAC EWEN, WILLIAM
Atlas of Head Sections. New York: 1893. V. 66
The Growth and Shedding of the Antler of the Deer. Glasgow: 1920. V. 64; 66
The Growth of Bone. Glasgow: 1912. V. 66
Pyogenic Infective Diseases of Brain and Spinal Cord. Glasgow: 1893. V. 64; 65; 66

MAC FADZEAN, JAMES
The Parallel Roads of Glenroy; Their Origin and Relation to the Glacial Period and the Deluge. Edinburgh: 1882. V. 67

MAC FALL, HALDANE
Aubrey Beardsley: the Man and His Work. London: 1928. V. 64
The Book of Lovat. London: 1923. V. 66; 67
The French Pastellists of the Eighteenth Century. London: 1909. V. 66
The Masterfolk. London: 1903. V. 62
The Splendid Wayfaring. London: 1913. V. 62
The Wooings of Jezebel Pettyfer. London: 1898. V. 62; 64

MAC FARLAND, F. M.
Studies of Opisthobranchiate Mollusks of the Pacifc Coast of North America. San Francisco: 1966. V. 63

MAC FARLANE, A.
Himalaya and Tibet. Mountain Roots to Mountain Tops. 1999. V. 67

MAC FARLANE, CHARLES
Our Indian Empire: Its History and Present State, from the Earliest Settlement of the British in Hindostan to the Close of the Year 1843. London: 1844. V. 65

MAC FARLANE, JAMES
An American Geological Railway Guide, Giving the Geological Formation at Every Railway Station. New York: 1879. V. 63

MAC FARLANE, WALTER, & CO.
Illustrated Catalogue of MacFarlane's Castings. Glasgow: Sep. 1870. V. 65

MAC FIE, MATTHEW
Vancouver Island and British Columbia. London: 1865. V. 66

MAC FIE, ROBERT ANDREW
Recent Discussions on the Abolition of Patents for Inventions in the United Kingdom, France, Germany and the Netherlands. London: 1869. V. 64

MAC GEORGE, A.
William Leighton Leitch, Landscape Painter. A Memoir. London: 1884. V. 67

MAC GILL, PATRICK
Songs of the Navy. Windsor: 1911. V. 63

MAC GILL, THOMAS
An Account of Tunis: of Its Government, Manners, Customs and Antiquities.... Glasgow: 1811. V. 62

MAC GILLIVRAY, J.
Narrative of the Voyage of H.M.S. Rattlesnake.... London: 1852. V. 63

MAC GILLIVRAY, PITTENDRIGH
Pro Patria. Edinburgh: 1915. V. 66

MAC GILLIVRAY, W.
Descriptions of the Rapacious Birds of Great Britain. Edinburgh: 1836. V. 62; 67
A History of British Birds. London: 1837-1840. V. 65; 67
A History of British Birds. London: 1837-1852. V. 62
Lives of Eminent Zoologists from Aristotle to Linnaeus. Edinburgh: 1834. V. 62

MAC GOEGHEGAN, ABBE
The History of Ireland, Ancient and Modern, Taken from the Most Authentic Records.... New York: 1868. V. 63

MAC GOWAN, JOHN
Infernal Conference; or Dialogues of Devils on the many Vices Which Abound in the Civil and Religious World. London: 1813. V. 66
The Shaver's New Sermon for the Fast Day.... New York: 1796. V. 63

MAC GOWAN, S. DOUGLAS
New Brunswick's Fighting 26th a History of the 26th New Brunswick Battalion, C.E.F. 1914-1919. Saint John: 1994. V. 65

MAC GRATH, HAROLD
Deuces Wild. Indianapolis: 1913. V. 65; 66
The Lure of the Mask. Indianapolis: 1908. V. 66
The Wolves of Chaos. Garden City: 1929. V. 65

MAC GREGOR, ANGUSINE
Maxims for Mice and Others. London: 1915. V. 64

MAC GREGOR, BARRINGTON
King Longbeard, or Annals of the Golden Dreamland. London: 1898. V. 65

MAC GREGOR, DUNCAN
A Narrative of the Loss of the Kent East Indiaman, by Fire, in the Bay of Biscay on the 1st March 1825. Edinburgh: 1825. V. 62; 63; 67

MAC GREGOR, GEORGE
The History of Burke and Hare and of the Resurrectionist Times. a Fragment From the Criminal Annals of Scotland. Glasgow: 1884. V. 63

MAC GREGOR, J.
The Rob Roy on the Baltic: a Canoe Cruise through Norway, Sweden, Denmark. London: 1867. V. 66

MAC GREGOR, JESSIE
Christmas Eve at Romney Hall. London: 1900. V. 62

MAC GREGOR, JOHN
Through the Buffer State. A Record of Recent Travels through Borneo, Siam and Cambodia. London: 1806. V. 64; 65

MAC GREGOR, MIRIAM
Diary of an Apple Tree. Herefordshire: 1997. V. 64
Diary of an Apple Tree. London: 1997. V. 65
Diary of an Apple Tree. Risbury: 1997. V. 64

MACH, ERNST
Die Mechanik in Ihrer Entwickelung Historisch-Kritisch Dargestellt. Leipzig: 1901. V. 64

MACHADO, ANTONIO
Canciones. West Branch: 1980. V. 63

MACHADO, JOSE AGUSTIN ANTONIO
The Machados and Rancho La Ballona: The Story of the Land and Its Ranchero with a Genealogy of the Machado Family by Sister Mary Ste. Therese Wittenberg. Los Angeles: 1973. V. 63; 64

MACHELL, HUGH
John Peel Famous in Sport and Song. Heath Cranton: 1926. V. 65
John Peel Famous in Sport and Song. London: 1926. V. 64; 67

MACHEN, ARTHUR
The Anatomy of Tobacco; or Smoking Methodised, Divided and Considered After a New Fashion. London: 1894. V. 65

MACHEN, ARTHUR continued
The Bowmen and Other Legends of the War. New York and London: 1915. V. 64
Bridles and Spurs. Cleveland: 1951. V. 64
The Chronicle of Clemendy. 1923. V. 64; 66
The Chronicle of Clemendy; or, the History of the IX. Joyous Journeys. New York: 1923. V. 64
Dreads and Drolls. London: 1926. V. 67
Fantastic Tales. 1923. V. 64; 66
Fantastic Tales. Carbonnek: 1923. V. 65
The London Adventure or The Art of Wandering. London: 1924. V. 65
Ornaments in Jade. New York: 1924. V. 63; 64; 66
The Shining Pyramid. London: 1925. V. 63
Strange Roads and with the Gods in Spring. London: 1924. V. 66
The Terror. London: 1917. V. 66
Tom O'Bedlam and His Song. 1930. V. 62; 64; 66

MACHIAVELLI, NICCOLO
The Arte of Warre. London: 1588. V. 64
Machiavel's Discourses, Upon (sic) the First Decade of T. Livius.... London: 1636. V. 64
Opere Inedite di Niccolo Machiavelli. Londra: 1760. V. 64
The Prince. New York: 1954. V. 65
The Works of Nicolas Machiavel, Citizen and Secretary of Flornece.... London: 1720. V. 62

MACHSOR (Prayers for the Holidays). Pt. II. Vienna: 1836. V. 67

MAC ILWAIN, GEORGE
Memoirs of John Abernethy, F.R.S., with a View of His Lectures.... New York: 1853. V. 66; 67
Memoirs of John Abernethy, F.R.S., with a View of His Lectures.... London: 1854. V. 65

MAC INNES, C. M.
In the Shadow of the Rockies. London: 1930. V. 66

MAC INNES, COLIN
Absolute Beginners. London: 1959. V. 65
England, Half English. London: 1961. V. 65

MAC INTYRE, ALASDAIR
The Unconscious, a Conceptual Study. London: 1958. V. 67

MAC INTYRE, D.
Hindu-Koh: Wanderings and Wild Sport On and Beyond the Himalayas. London: 1889. V. 62
Hindu-Koh: Wanderings and Wild Sport On and Beyond the Himalayas. 1891. V. 67
Round the Seasons on a Grouse Moor. 1924. V. 67

MAC INTYRE, W. IRWIN
Colored Soldiers. Macon: 1923. V. 63

MACIRONE, FRANCIS
A Few Specimens of the Ars Logica Copleiana or Solicitor General's Logic as Exhibited in the Cause Macirone v. Murray, tried...December 10, 1819. London: 1820. V. 63

MAC IVER, SUSANNA
Cookery and Pastry. London: 1787. V. 66

MACK, EFFIE MONA
Mark Twain in Nevada. New York: 1947. V. 63
Nevada - A History of the State from the Earliest Times through the Civil War. Glendale: 1974. V. 65

MACK, JAMES LOGAN
The Border Line from the Solway Firth to the North Sea, along the Marches of Scotland and England. London: 1926. V. 62; 65

MACK, JULIAN E.
The Photographic Process. New York: 1939. V. 62

MACK, ROBERT ELLICE
All Round the Clock. New York: 1890. V. 62
Under the Mistletoe. New York: 1890. V. 63

MACKAIL, JOHN WILLIAM
An Address on Morris. 1902. V. 65
Homer: an Address Delivered on Behalf of the Independent Labor Party. London: 1905. V. 62
The Life of William Morris. London: 1899. V. 62
Socialism and Politics: an Address and a Programme. London: 1903. V. 64
William Morris. An Address Delivered at Kelmscott House Before the Hammersmith Socialist Society. Hammersmith: 1901. V. 62; 64; 65; 67

MACKALL, WILLIAM W.
A Son's Recollections of His Father. New York: 1930. V. 62; 63; 65

MACKANESS, GEORGE
The Life of Vice-Admiral William Bligh, R. N., F.R.S. New York/Toronto: 1931. V. 63; 64; 66

MAC KAY, ALEXANDER
Western World; or, Travels in the United States in 1846-1847.... London: 1849. V. 66
Western World; or Travels in the United States in 1846-1847.... Philadelphia: 1849. V. 66

MAC KAY, ANGUS M.
The Brontes Fact and Fiction. 1897. V. 63

MAC KAY, CHARLES
A Dictionary of Lowland Scotch with an Introductory Chapter on the Poetry, Humour and Literary History of the Scottish Language.... Edinburgh: 1888. V. 64
The Life of Charles Bradlaugh. London: 1888. V. 64
Memoirs of Extraordinary Popular Delusions and the Madness of Crowds. London: 1841. V. 65
The Thames and Its Tributaries; or Rambles Among the Rivers. London: 1840. V. 67

MAC KAY, HENRY
An Abridgement of the Excise-Laws and of the Custom-Laws Therewith Connected, Now in Force in Great Britain. Edinburgh: 1779. V. 62

MAC KAY, IAN
The Real Mac Kay - Being Essays by Ian Mac Kay. London: 1953. V. 63

MAC KAY, JAMES
Nursery Antiques, Toys, Dolls, Games and Puzzles, China, Books, Clothing Etc., described by James MacKay. London: 1976. V. 67

MAC KAY, JAMES A.
Tristan Da Cunha. Its Postal History and Philately. Ewell: 1965. V. 64; 66

MAC KAY, MALCOLM S.
Cow Range and Hunting Trail. New York: 1925. V. 64; 66

MAC KAY, THOMAS
The Thames and Its Tributaries; or, Rambles Among the Rivers. London: 1840. V. 66

MAC KAY SMITH, ALEXANDER
Foxhunting in North America. Virginia: 1985. V. 66

MACKCOULL, JAMES
Memoir of the Life and Trial of James Mackcoull, or Moffat, Whoe Died in the County Jail of Edinburgh on the 22d December 1820.... Edinburgh: 1822. V. 63

MACKCOULL, JOHN
Abuses of Justice, Illustrated by My Own Case.... London: 1812. V. 63

MACKEN, WALTER
God Made Sunday and Other Stories. 1962. V. 67
Rain on the Wind. 1950. V. 67

MAC KENIZE, EDWARD LOGAN
The New Whole Art of Confectionary. Otley: 1837. V. 64

MAC KENNAL, ALEXANDER
Homes and Haunts of the Pilgrim Fathers. London: 1899. V. 64

MACKENROT, A.
Secret Memoirs of the Honourable Andrew Cochrane Johnstone of...Sir Alex Forrester Cochrane, and of Sir Thomas John Cochrane.... London: 1814. V. 63

MAC KENZIE, ALEXANDER
Voyages from Montreal On the River St. Laurence, Through the Continent of North America to the Frozen and Pacific Oceans, in the Years 1789 and 1793. London: 1801. V. 66
Voyages from Montreal through the Continent of North America to the Frozen and Pacific Oceans in 1789 and 1793.... New York: 1902. V. 63; 66

MAC KENZIE, ALEXANDER SLIDELL
The American in England. Aberdeen: 1848. V. 67

MAC KENZIE, CHARLES
Notes On Haiti, Made During a Residence in that Republic. London: 1830. V. 67

MAC KENZIE, COMPTON
My Life and Times. London: 1963-1966. V. 64
My Life and Times. London: 1963-1970. V. 66
Poems. Oxford and London: 1907. V. 62
Santa Claus in Summer. London: 1924. V. 65

MAC KENZIE, DAN
The Infancy of Medicine. An Enquiry into the Influence of Folk-Lore Upon the Evolution of Scientific Medicine. London: 1927. V. 63

MAC KENZIE, GEORGE
Essays Upon Several Moral Subjects, viz. The Religious Stoic. London: 1713. V. 67
The Institutions of Scotland.... Edinburgh: 1699. V. 64
The Institutions of the Law of Scotland. Edinburgh: 1706. V. 62
Memoirs of the Affairs of Scotland from the Restoration of King Charles II A.D. MDCLX. Edinburgh: 1821. V. 62
Observations on the Acts of Parliament, Made by King James the First, King James the Second, King James the Third, King James, the Fourth King James, the Fifth, Queen Mary, King James the Sixth, King Charles the First, King Charles the Second.... Edinburgh: 1686. V. 62
Observations Upon the Laws and Customs of Nations as to Precedency... (with) The Science Of Herauldry, Treated as Part of the Civil Law and Law of Nations. Edinburgh: 1680. V. 62
A Vindication of the Government in Scotland During the Reign of King Charles II, Against Mis-Representations Made in Several Scandalous Pamphlets. London: 1691. V. 62

MAC KENZIE, GEORGE STEUART
Travels in the Island of Iceland, During the Summer of the Year MDCCCX. Edinburgh: 1812. V. 63; 64

MAC KENZIE, HENRY
Julia de Roubigne, a Tale. London: 1777. V. 63; 67
Julia de Roubigne, a Tale. London: 1782-1781. V. 63
The Man of Feeling. London: 1771. V. 62
The Man of Feeling. London: 1778. V. 62
A Man of Feeling. London: 1791. V. 62; 66
The Man of Feeling. London: 1794. V. 62
The Miscellaneous Works. Edinburgh: 1819. V. 66

MAC KENZIE, JAMES
Diseases of the Heart. London: 1925. V. 63
The History of Health and the Art of Preserving It.... Edinburgh: 1759. V. 62
Principles of Diagnosis and Treatment in Heart Affections. London: 1923. V. 63
The Study of the Pulse, Arterial, Venous and Hepatic and the Movements of the Heart. London: 1902. V. 65

MAC KENZIE, JOHN GORDON
Dissertatio medica Inauguralis de Typho.... Glasgow: 1801. V. 65

MAC KENZIE, JOHN WHITEFORD
Catalogue of the...Very Extensive and Valuable Library of Rare and Curious Books of the Late John Whiteford Mackenzie, Esq. Edinburgh: 1886. V. 62

MAC KENZIE, MORELL
The Fatal Illness of Frederick the Noble. London: 1888. V. 67

MAC KENZIE, PETER
An Exposure of the Spy System Pursued in Glasgow, During the Years 1816-1817-1818-1819 and 1820 with Copies of the Original Letters.... Glasgow: 1832. V. 63

MAC KENZIE, R. SHELTON
Life of Charles Dickens. Philadelphia: 1870. V. 62

MAC KENZIE, RANALD S.
Ranald S. Mackenzie's Official Correspondence Relating to Texas 1871-1877 and 1873-1879. Lubbock: 1967-1968. V. 62

MAC KENZIE, RODERICK
Strictures on Lt. Col. Tarleton's History of the Campaigns of 1780 and 1781 in the Southern Provinces of North America. London: 1787. V. 66

MAC KENZIE, W. M.
Pompeii. London: 1910. V. 66

MAC KENZIE, WILLIAM
A Practical Treatise on the Diseases of the Eye.... London: 1854. V. 67

MACKERELL, BENJAMIN
A New Catalogue of the Books in the Public Library of the City of Norwich, in the Year 1732. Norwich;: 1733. V. 65

MAC KERROW, P. E.
A Brief History of the Coloured Baptists of Nova Scotia, and Their First Organization as Churches A.D. 1832. Halifax: 1895. V. 63

MACKESY, PIERS
Statesmen at War: the Strategy of Overthrow 1798-1799. New York: 1974. V. 66

MACKEY, GORDON
Tall Tale'n and Oration. San Antonio: 1939. V. 63

MACKEY, WILLIAM
The Bewick's Scrap Book. Newcastle-Upon-Tyne. V. 65

MACKIE, CHARLES
Historical Description of the Abbey and Town of Paisley.... Glasgow: 1835. V. 62; 64
The History of the Abbey, Palace and Chapel-Royal of Holyrood House.... Edinburgh: 1819. V. 62
The History of the Abbey, Palace and Chapel-Royal of Holyrood House.... Edinburgh: 1821. V. 64

MACKIE, L. W.
Turkman, Tribal Carpets and Traditions. Washington: 1980. V. 65

MACKIE, PETER JEFFREY
The Keeper's Book. London: 1910. V. 67
The Keeper's Book. London: 1929. V. 67

MAC KINNEY, LOREN
Medical Illustrations in Medieval Manuscripts. London: 1965. V. 64; 66; 67

MAC KINNEY, FRANK DOUGLAS
Grand Larceny, Being the Trial of Jane Leigh Perrot, Aunt of Jane Austen. London: 1937. V. 63

MAC KINNON, JOHN
A Sketch Book Comprising Historical Incidents, Traditions, Tales and Translations. St. John: 1915. V. 66

MAC KINSTRY, ELIZABETH
The Fairy Alphabet as Used by Merlin. New York: 1933. V. 64

MAC KINTOSH, CHARLES RENNIE
Haus Eines Kunstfreundes. Glasgow: 1991. V. 67

MAC KINTOSH, H. W.
Notes on the Myology of the Coati-Mondi (Nasua Narica). Dublin: 1874. V. 67
On the Muscular Anatomy of Choloepus Didactylus. Dublin: 1874. V. 67

MAC KINTOSH, HAROLD
Early English Figure Pottery. London: 1938. V. 62; 66

MAC KINTOSH, JAMES
The Miscellaneous Works.... London: 1846. V. 63
Vindiciae Gallicae. Defence of the French Revolution and Its English Admirers Against the Accusations of the Right Hon. Edmund Burke.... Philadelphia: 1792. V. 64

MACKLEY, GEORGE
Confessions of a Woodpecker. Surrey: 1981. V. 64
Engraved in Wood: a Collection of Wood Engravings by George Mackley. London: 1968. V. 66

MACKMURDO, A. H.
Wren's City Churches. Orpington: 1883. V. 67

MAC KNIGHT, THOMAS
The Right Honourable Benjamin Disraeli, M.P. London: 1854. V. 64

MACKWORTH, HUMPHREY
A Vindication of the Rights of the Commons of England. London: 1701. V. 65

MACKWORTH PRAED, CYRIL WINTHROP
Birds of Eastern and North Eastern Africa. London: 1957-1955. V. 65; 67
Birds of Eastern and North Eastern Africa. 1980. V. 66
Birds of Eastern and North Eastern Africa. London: 1980. V. 64
Birds of the Southern Third of Africa. London: 1962-1963. V. 65; 67

MAC LACHLAN, PATRICIA
Sarah Plain and Tall. New York: 1985. V. 65

MAC LAGAN, T.
Captain Jinks. Philadelphia: 1860. V. 63

MAC LAGAN, T. J.
Rheumantism. Its Nature, Its Pathology and Its Successful Treatment. New York: 1886. V. 64; 66; 67

MAC LAREN, CHARLES
A Sketch of the Geology of Fife and the Lothians Including Detailed Descriptions of Arthur's Seat and Pentland Hills. Edinburgh: 1866. V. 67

MAC LAREN, JAMES
A Sketch of the History of the Currency; Comprising a Brief Review of the Opinions of the Most Eminent Writers on the Subject. London: 1858. V. 65

MAC LAREN-ROSS, JULIAN
Memoirs of the Forties. London: 1965. V. 62; 65
Of Love and Hunger. London: 1947. V. 66
The Stuff to Give the Troops.... London: 1944. V. 63

MAC LAURIN, COLIN
An Account of Sir Isaac Newton's Philosophical Discoveries, in Four Books. London: 1748. V. 63; 64; 65
An Account of Sir Isaac Newton's Philosophical Discoveries in Four Books. London: 1750. V. 65; 66
A Treatise on Fluxions.... London: 1801. V. 65

MAC LAURUINN, C.
Ainmeanna Cliuteach, Chriosd: Slabbruidh Oir A Chreidmhich; AGus An T'Slighe Chumhann, Do Neamh. 1832. V. 65

MACLAY, EDWARD STANTON
A History of the United States Navy. New York: 1895. V. 64; 66

MAC LEAN, ALISTAIR
The Guns of Navarone. London: 1957. V. 62; 66
H. M. S. Ulysses. London: 1955. V. 62
The Last Frontier. London: 1959. V. 63

MAC LEAN, CAROLINE
The Adventures of Maidlilie. San Francisco: 1926. V. 67

MAC LEAN, FITZROY
Holy Russia, an Historical Companion to European Russia. London: 1978. V. 67

MAC LEAN, HECTOR
The Watermillock and Matterdale Parish Registers. Kendal: 1908. V. 65; 66

MAC LEAN, JOHN
History of the College of New Jersey, from Its Origin in 1746 to the Commencement of 1854. Princeton: 1829. V. 66
History of the College of New Jersey, from Its Origin in 1746 to the Commencement of 1854. Philadelphia: 1877. V. 63
A Lecture on a School System for New Jersey, Delivered January 23, 1828, in the Chapel of Nassau Hall, Before the Literary and Philosophical Society of New Jersey. Princeton: 1829. V. 63

MAC LEAN, L.
An Inquiry into the Nature, Causes and Cure of Hydrothorax: Illustrated by Interesting Cases. Hartford: 1814. V. 66

MAC LEAN, NORMAN
A River Runs Through It and Other Stories. Chicago: 1976. V. 62; 65

MAC LEAN, VIRGINIA
A Short-title Catalogue of Household and Cookery Books Published in the English Tongue 1701-1800. 1981. V. 67

MAC LEISH, ARCHIBALD
Land of the Free. New York: 1938. V. 67
Nobodaddy. Cambridge: 1926. V. 62
The Pot of Earth. Boston: 1925. V. 62
Public Speech. New York: 1936. V. 63
Streets in the Moon. Boston and New York: 1926. V. 65
Tower of Ivory. New Haven: 1917. V. 62

MAC LEOD, A.
On India. London: 1872. V. 62

MAC LEOD, ALEX W.
Parlicot and How He Sets Out to Find a Playmate. London: 1943. V. 67

MAC LEOD, CHARLOTTE
Cirak's Daughter. New York: 1982. V. 67
Rest You Merry. Garden City: 1978. V. 65; 66

MAC LEOD, DONALD
A Treatise on the Second Sight, Dreams and Apparitions.... Glasgow: 1819. V. 62

MAC LEOD, GEORGE
Notes on the Surgery of the War in the Crimea with Remarks on the Treatment of Gunshot Wounds. Richmond: 1862. V. 62; 63; 65

MACLEOD, HENRY DUNNING
The Elements of Political Economy. London: 1858. V. 64
The Principles of Economical Philosophy. London: 1879. V. 65

MAC LEOD, HENRY DUNNING
The Theory and Practice of Banking.... London: 1883. V. 63

MAC LEOD, R. C.
The Book of Dunvegan, Being Documents from the Monument Room of the MacLeods of MacLeod at Dunvegan Castle, Isle of Skye. Aberdeen: 1938. V. 67

MACLISE, J.
Surgical Antomy. London: 1851. V. 62

MACLURE, W.
Observations on the Geology of the United States of America. Philadelphia: 1817. V. 62

MACLURE, WILLIAM
Opinions on Various Subjects, Dedicated to the Industrious Producers. New Harmony: 1831. V. 64; 66
Opinions on Various Subjects, Dedicated to the Industrious Producers. New Harmony: 1831-1838. V. 62

MAC MAHON, CANDACE
Elizabeth Bishop - a Bibliography 1927-1979. Charlottesville: 1980. V. 62

MAC MAHON, T. W.
Cause and Contrast: an Essay on an American Crisis. Richmond: 1862. V. 62

MAC MAHON, THOMAS O'BRIEN
The Candor and Good Nature of the Englishmen Exemplified, in Their Deliberate, Cautious and Charitable Way of Characterizing Customs, Manners, Constitution and Religion of Neighbouring Nations.... London: 1777. V. 65

MAC MECHAN, ARCHIBALD
Red Snow on Grand Pre. Toronto: 1931. V. 67

MAC MICHAEL, WILLIAM
The Gold-Headed Cane. London: 1827. V. 62
The Gold-Headed Cane. London: 1828. V. 66; 67
The Gold-Headed Cane. New York: 1932. V. 63
The Gold-Headed Cane. London: 1968. V. 63
Lives of British Physicians. London: 1830. V. 64

MAC MILLAN, DONALD B.
Four Years in the White North. Boston and New York: 1925. V. 63; 64

MAC MILLAN, H. F.
Tropical Planting and Gardening. London: 1943. V. 64

MAC MILLAN, HUGH
The Highland Tay from Tyndrum to Dunkeld. London: 1901. V. 62; 63

MAC MILLAN, TERRY
Mama. Boston: 1987. V. 67

MAC MINN, G. R.
The Theater of the Golden Age in California. Caldwell: 1941. V. 63; 66

MAC MUNN, G. F.
The Armies of India. London: 1911. V. 66

MAC NAB, DUNCAN
An Exact Description of the Island and Kingdom of Sicily, Its Provinces, Towns and Remarkable Places.... Falkirk: 1784. V. 65

MAC NAB, FRANCES
British Columbia for Settlers. Its Mines, Trade and Agriculture. London: 1898. V. 63

MACNAE, W.
A Natural History of Inhaca Island, Mocambique. Johannesburg: 1969. V. 67

MAC NAGHTEN, FRANCIS WORKMAN
Poor Laws-Ireland. Observations Upon the Report of George Nicholls, Esq. London: 1838. V. 62

MAC NAIR, PETER
The Geology and Scenery of the Grampians and the Valley of Strathmore. Glasgow: 1908. V. 64; 65; 66; 67

MAC NALLAY, LEONARD
Tristram Shandy, a Sentimental, Shandean Bagatelle. London: 1783. V. 62; 67

MAC NAMARA, N. C.
The Story of an Irish Sept; Their Character and Struggle to Maintain Their Lands in Co. Clare. 1896. V. 63; 66

MAC NAMARA, R.
Report Upon Contagious Pleuro-Pneumonia...by Direction of the Committee of the Irish Cattle Trade Defence Association. Dublin: 1877. V. 67

MAC NAMEE, JAMES J.
History of the Diocese of Ardagh. 1954. V. 63; 66

MAC NAUGHTON, MARGARET
Overland to Cariboo. An Eventful Journey of Canadian Pioneers to the Gold-Fields of British Columbia in 1862. Toronto: 1896. V. 64

MAC NEICE, LOUIS
Astrology. 1964. V. 67
Astrology. London: 1964. V. 63
Autumn Journal: a Poem. London: 1939. V. 62
Autumn Sequel - a Rhetorical Poem in XXVI Cantos. London: 1954. V. 64
Blind Fireworks. London: 1929. V. 62
Collected Poems of Louis Mac Neice. London: 1966. V. 63
The Earth Compels - Poems. London: 1938. V. 63
Holes in the Sky - Poems 1944-1947. London: 1948. V. 63
The Mad Islands and The Administrator. London: 1964. V. 65
Meet the U.S. Army. London: 1943. V. 63
Out of the Picture - a Play in Two Acts. London: 1937. V. 63; 65
Plant and Phantom - Poems. London: 1941. V. 65
Poems. London: 1935. V. 63; 65
Poems. London: 1937. V. 62
Roundabout Way. London: 1932. V. 66
Selected Poems. London: 1940. V. 66
The Sixpence that Rolled Away. London: 1956. V. 63
Ten Burnt Offerings. London: 1952. V. 63
Varities of Parable. Cambridge: 1965. V. 63
Zoo. London: 1938. V. 63

MAC NEIL, J. G. S.
The Constitutional and Parliamentary History of Ireland Till the Union. Dublin;. V. 66

MAC NEILL, HECTOR
The Poetical Works. London: 1801. V. 67

MAC NEILL, JOHN
Remarks on the Proposed Railway Between Birmingham and London, Proving by Facts and Arguments That They Would Cost Seven Millions and a Half.... London: 1831. V. 64; 65
Tables for Calculating the Cubic Quantity of Earth Work in the Cuttings and Embankments of Canals, Railways and Turnpike Roads. London: 1833. V. 65

MAC NISH, ROBERT
Philosophy of Sleep. Glasgow: 1830. V. 65
The Philosophy of Sleep. Glasgow: 1834. V. 62

MAC NUTT, FRANCIS AUGUSTUS
Bartholemew De Las Casas: His Life, Apostolate and Writings. Cleveland: 1909. V. 64; 67

MACOMB, ALEXANDER
Treatise on Martial Law and Courts Martial.... Charleston: 1809. V. 66

MACON, ALETHEA
Gideon Macon of Virginia and Some of His Descendants. Macon: 1956. V. 67

MACON, THOMAS J.
Reminiscences of the First Company of Richmond Howitzers. Richmond: 1909. V. 62; 63; 65

MACONCHIE, ALLAN
Directions for Preparing Manure from Peat. Instructions for Foresters. Edinburgh: 1815. V. 63

MACOUN, JOHN
Catalogue of Canadian Plants. Montreal & Ottawa: 1883-1890. V. 63
Manitoba and the Great North-West. The Field for Investment. The Home of the Emigrant. London: 1883. V. 64

MAC PHERSON, H. A.
The Birds of Cumberland. Carlisle: 1886. V. 62; 67
The Birds of Cumberland. St. Paul: 1899. V. 64
The Grouse. London: 1895. V. 67
The Hare. London: 1896. V. 67
History of Fowling. 1897. V. 63
The Partridge. London: 1894. V. 67
The Red Deer Natural History, Deer Stalking, Stag Hunting and Cookery. London: 1896. V. 67
Vertebrate Fauna of Lakeland.... 1892. V. 63

MAC PHERSON, J.
Geological Sketch of the Province of Cadiz.... Cadiz: 1873. V. 62

MAC PHERSON, JAMES
Dana Oisein Mhic Fhinn, Air an Cur Amach Airson Maith Coitcheannta Muinntir na Gaeltachd. Dunedin: 1818. V. 65
Fingal, an Ancient Epic Poem in Six Books...(with) Temora, an Ancient Epic Poem.... London: 1762-1763. V. 62
The Poems of Ossian. Edinburgh: 1830. V. 62
The Poems of Ossian. London: 1926. V. 65
Temora, an Ancient Epic Poems.... Dublin: 1763. V. 62

MAC PHERSON, MISS
My Experineces in Australia. London: 1860. V. 65

MAC QUARRIE, GORDON
Stories of the Old Duck Hunters and Other Drivel. (with) The Last Stories of the Old Duck Hunters. (and) More Stories of the Old Duck Hunters. Oshkosh: 1985. V. 65

MAC QUEEN, DANIEL
Letters on Mr. Hume's History of Great Britain. Edinburgh: 1756. V. 66

MAC QUEEN, PETER
In Wildest Africa. Boston: 1909. V. 64

MAC QUER, P. J.
Elements of the Theory and Practice of Chemistry.... 1775. V. 62

MAC QUOID, KATHERINE S.
Sir James Appleby, Bart. London: 1886. V. 63; 66

MACRAY, WILLIAM DUNN
A Manual of British Historians to AD 1600. London: 1845. V. 62; 65; 67

MACREADY, CATHERINE F. B.
Cowl and Cap; or, the Rival Churches; and Minor Poems. London: 1865. V. 64; 65

MACRO, COX
A Catalogue of Ancient Manuscripts Chiefly Antiquarian and Historical of Ancient Manuscripts.... London: 1820. V. 62

MACROBIUS
Aur. Theodosii Macrobii V. Cl. & Inlustris Opera. 1694. V. 66
Aurelii Macrobii Ambrosii Theodosii V. C. & Inlustris Quae Exstant Omnia.... Patavii: 1736. V. 66
In Somnium Scipionis Libri II. Eivsdem Conuiuiorum Saturnaliorum Libri VII. Parissis: 1585. V. 64
Opera. London: 1694. V. 65
Somnium Scipionis ex Ciceronis Libro de Republica Excerptum. (and) Saturanlia. Venice: 1500. V. 62

MAC SWINEY, OWEN
Tombeaux des Princes des Grands Capitaines et Autres Hommes Illustres Qui Ont Fleuri dans la grande Bretagne Vers la Fin Du XVII & Le Commencement du XVIII Siecle. Paris: 1741. V. 62

MAC SWINEY, TERENCE
The Principles of Freedom. 1921. V. 67

MAC VICAR, ANGUS
The Canisbay Conspiracy. London: 1966. V. 66

MADAN, FALCONER
The Early Oxford Press. A Bibliography of Printing and Publishing at Oxford 1468-1640. Oxford: 1895. V. 62; 63

MADAN, MARTIN
Thelyphthora; or, a Treatise on Female Ruin, In Its Causes, Effects, Consequences, Prevention and Remedy. London: 1780. V. 64
Thelyphthroa; or a Treatise on Female Ruin, In Its Causes, Effects, Consequences, Prevention and Remedy.... London: 1780-1781. V. 65

MADARIAGA, SALVADOR DE
Don Quioxte. An Introductory Essay in Psychology. Newtown: 1934. V. 65

MADDEN, FREDERICK
Privy Purse Expenses of the Princess Mary...with a Memoir of the Princess.... London: 1831. V. 66

MADDEN, HENRY MILLER
German Travelers in California. San Francisco: 1958. V. 64
Xantus, Hungarian Naturalist in the Pioneer West. Palo Alto: 1949. V. 64

MADDEN, HENRY RIDEWOOD
On the Relation of Therapeutics to Modern Physiology. London and Manchester: 1871. V. 67

MADDEN, R. R.
The Literary Life and Correspondence of the Countess of Blessington. London: 1855. V. 66

MADDEN, RICHARD R.
The Shrines and Sepulchres of the Old and New World. 1851. V. 62
The Shrines and Sepulchres of the Old and New World. London: 1851. V. 64

MADDENS, E. E.
Rambles in an Old City Comprising Antiquarian, Historical, Biographical and Political Associations. London: 1853. V. 62

MADDISON, A. R.
Lincolnshire Wills. First Series A.D. 1500-1600 (and) Second Series A.D 1600-1617. Lincoln: 1888-1891. V. 65

MADDOCK, ALFRED BEAUMONT
Practical Observations on Mental and Nervous Disorders. London: 1857. V. 65

MADDOCK, JAMES
The Florist's Directory. London: 1792. V. 64
The Florist's Directory. London: 1822. V. 67

MADDOW, BEN
Edward Weston: His Life and Photographs. New York: 1979. V. 62
Faces: a Narrative History of the Portrait in Photography. Boston: 1977. V. 63
The Photography of Max Yavno. Berkeley Los Angeles London: 1981. V. 63

MADDOX, WILLIAM A.
Historical Cravings in Leather. San Antonio: 1940. V. 67

MADEIRA, CRAWFORD CLARK
The Delaware and Raritan Canal. A History. East Orange: 1941. V. 63

MADEIRA, PERCY C.
Hunting in British East Africa. Philadelphia and London: 1909. V. 64

MADISON, JAMES
The Papers of James Madison Purchased by Order of Congress; Being His Correspondence and Reports of Debates During the Congress of the Confederation and His Reports of Debates in the Federal Convention. Washington: 1840. V. 64

MADOC, H. W.
Bird-Life in the Isle of Man. London: 1934. V. 62

MADOX, THOMAS
The History and Antiquities of the Exchequer of the Kings of England. London: 1711. V. 66; 67
The History and Antiquities of the Exchequer of the Kings of England. New York: 1969. V. 63

MADSEN, BRIGHAM D.
The Bannock of Idaho. Caldwell: 1958. V. 63

MAETERLINCK, MAURICE
The Essays and Plays of Maeterlinck. New York: 1901-1919. V. 62
The Intelligence of Flowers. New York: 1907. V. 62
News of Spring and Other Nature Studies. New York: 1913. V. 64
Pelleas et Melisande. Bruxelles: 1920. V. 62

MAFFEI, FRANCESCO SCIPIONE
A Compleat History of Ancient Amphitheatres, More Particularly Regarding the Architecture of Those Buildings.... London: 1730. V. 65

MAFFEI, PAOLO ALESSANDRO
Gemme Antiche Figurate.... Roma: 1707-1709. V. 67

MAFFEI, SCIPIONE
Compendio Della Verona Illustrata, Principalmente ad Uso de Forestieri, Coll-Aggiunta del Museo Lapidario.... Verona: 1795. V. 62; 67

MAFFITT, EMMA MARTIN
The Life and Services of John Newland Maffitt. New York and Washington: 1906. V. 62; 63

MAFFITT, JOHN N.
Tears of Contrition, or Sketches of the Life of John W. Maffitt.... New London: 1821. V. 63

MAGALOTTI, LORENZO
Travels of Cosmo the Third, Grand Duke of Tuscany, through England, During the Reign of King Charles the Second (1669). London: 1821. V. 62; 67

MAGATI, CESARE
De Rara Medicatione Vulnerum Seu de Vulneribus Rarb Tractandis Libri Duo.... Venice: 1676. V. 65

MAGEE, DAVID
Catalogue of Some Five Hundred Examples of the Printing of Edwin and Robert Grabhorn 1917-1960. San Francisco: 1961. V. 64
The Hundredth Book. N.P: 1958. V. 67

MAGEE, DOROTHY
Bibliography of the Grabhorn Press, 1940-1956. San Francisco: 1957. V. 64

MAGEE'S Centennial Guide of Philadelphia. Philadelphia: 1876. V. 65

MAGENDIE, FRANCOIS
An Elementary Treatise on Human Physiology, On the Basis of the Precis Elementaire de Physiologie. New York: 1844. V. 64; 66; 67
Formulary for the Preparation and Mode of Employing Several New Remedies.... Philadelphia: 1824. V. 65
Precis Elementaire de Physiologie. Paris: 1816-1817. V. 64, 66
Precis Elementaire de Physiologie. Paris: 1825. V. 64
Recherches Physiologiques et Medicales sur les Causes, les Symptomes et le Traitement de la Gravelle.... Paris: 1828. V. 65

MAGGI, GIROLAMO
Anglarensis de Tintinnabulis Liber Postumus. (and) Anglarensis de Equuleo Liber Postumus. (and, as part of the second work) Appendix De Eculei Tormento, ex Signoii Gallonii & Jureti Scriptis. Amstelodami: 1664. V. 64

MAGGIORE, LUIGI
Struttura, Comportamento e Signifacto del Canale di Schlemm nll'Occhio Umano in Condizioni Normali e Patholgiche. Roma: 1916. V. 65

MAGGS BROS.
Shakespeare and Shakespeareana Selected from the Stock of Maggs Bros. London: 1927. V. 63; 64; 66
Voyages and Travels in All Parts of the World. A Descriptive Catalogue by F. B. Maggs. Volume II. London: 1946. V. 66

MAGIC Fairy Tales: Alice in Wonderland. Springfield: 1943. V. 66

THE MAGIC Horse. London: 1930. V. 63

THE MAGICIAN'S Own Book; or the Whole Art of Conjuring. New York: 1857?. V. 66

MAGIRUS, JOHANNES
Physiologicae Peripateticae Libri Sex Cum Commentariis.... Cambridge: 1642. V. 64; 67

MAGNEE, R. M. H.
Willem M. Dudok. Amsterdam: 1954. V. 65

MAGNER, D.
Magner's Standard Horse and Stock Book. Akron: 1915. V. 64

MAGNUSSENN, DANIEL O.
Peter Thompson's Narrative of the Little Big Horn Campaign 1876. Glendale: 1974. V. 67

MAGOFFIN, SUSAN SHELBY
Down the Santa Fe Trail and Into Mexico - the Diary of.... New Haven: 1926. V. 64; 66; 67

MAGONIGLE, H. VAN HUREN
Architectural Rendering in Wash. New York: 1921. V. 65

MAGOON, E. L.
The Modern Whitfield, Sermons of the Rev. C. H. Spurgeon of London. New York: 1856. V. 67

MAGOUN, F. ALEXANDER
The Frigate Constitution and Other Historic Ships (Viking Ships, the Santa Maria, Mayflower, Flying Cloud and the Fishing Schooner Bluenose). Salem: 1928. V. 65

MAGOUN, HORACE WINCHELL
Neurophysiology. Washington: 1959. V. 65

MAGOWAN, ROBIN
JM: A Remembrance. New York: 1996. V. 67

MAGRATH, JOHN RICHARD
The Obituary Book of Queen's College, Oxford. Oxford: 1910. V. 62; 66
The Queen's College. Oxford: 1921. V. 62

MAGUIRE, GREGORY
Wicked, the Life and Times of the Wicked Witch of the West. New York: 1995. V. 67

MAGUIRE, ROCHFORT
The Journal of Rochfort Maguire 1852-1854. London: 1988. V. 64; 65; 66

MAHAFFEY, MERRILL
Merrill Mahaffey - Monumental Landscapes. Flagstaff: 1979. V. 66

MAHAFFY, J. P.
Greek Pictures Drawn with Pen and Pencil. London: 1890. V. 65

MAHAN, ALFRED THAYER
The Embodiment of the Sea Power of Great Britain. London: 1898. V. 66
Great Commanders. Admiral Farragut. New York: 1892. V. 66
The Gulf and Inland Waters. New York: 1883. V. 64
The Influence of Sea Power Upon History 1660-1783. London: 1889. V. 65
The Influence of Sea Power Upon History 1660-1783. London: 1890. V. 63; 65
Letters and Papers of Alfred Thayer Mahan 1847-1914. Annapolis: 1975. V. 64; 66
The Life of Nelson. The Embodiment of the Sea Power of Great Britain. Boston: 1897. V. 62; 64; 67
The Major Operations of the Navies in the War of American Independence. London: 1913. V. 64

MAHAN, ASA
Modern Mysteries, Explained and Exposed. Boston: 1855. V. 62

MAHAN, BRUCE E.
Old Fort Crawford and the Frontier. Iowa City: 1926. V. 67

MAHAN, DENNIS HART
An Elementary Course of Civil Engineering. Edinburgh: 1846. V. 62
An Elementary Treatise on Advanced-Guard, Out-Post, and Detachment Service of Troops.... New Orleans: 1861. V. 62
A Treatise on Field Fortification.... Richmond: 1862. V. 62; 63; 65

MAHMOUD, FATMA MOUSSA
William Beckford of Fonthill 1760-1844 Bicentenary Essays. Cairo: 1960. V. 67

MAHOLY-NAGY, LASZLO
Portrait of Eton. London: 1949. V. 63

MAHOMED, S. D.
Shampooing; or, Benefits Resulting from the Use of Indian Medicated Vapour Bath. Brighton: 1826. V. 67

MAHON, DEREK
Poems 1962-1978. Oxford: 1979. V. 63
Twelve Poems. Belfast: 1965. V. 63; 64

MAHONEY, JAMES W.
The Cherokee Physician; or, Indian Guide to Health, as Given by Richard Foreman, a Cherokee Physician. New York: 1857. V. 63

MAHONY, FRANCIS
The Reliques of Father Prout.... London: 1860. V. 67

MAHONY, FRANCIS SYLVESTER
Facts and Figures from Italy. London: 1847. V. 62

MAHOOD, RUTH I.
Photographer of the Southwest: Adam Clark Vroman 1856-1916. Los Angeles: 1961. V. 63
Photographer of the Southwest, Adam Clark Vroman 1856-1916. Los Angeles: 1969. V. 64; 67

MAHR, ADOLPH
Christian Art in Ancient Ireland. 1932-1941. V. 65

THE MAID of Renmore; or Platonic Love; a Mock Heroic Romance in Verse.... London: 1810. V. 62

MAIDEN, CECIL
Speaking of Mrs. McCluskie. New York: 1962. V. 66

MAIDEN HOSPITAL
The Rules and Constitutions for Governing and Managing the Maiden Hospital, Founded by the Company of Merchants, and Mary Erskine in Anno 1695. Edinburgh: 1731. V. 65

MAIDEN, J. H.
The Flowering Plants and Ferns of New South Wales. Sydney: 1895-1898. V. 62; 63; 66
A Manual of the Grasses of New South Wales. Sydney: 1898. V. 63
The Useful Native Plants of Australia (Including Tasmania). Sydney: 1889. V. 62

MAIDMENT, JAMES
A Book of Scotish Pasquils 1568-1715. Edinburgh: 1868. V. 62

MAIDWELL, LEWIS
A Scheme for a Public Academy, Some Reasons for Its Institution, the Common Objections Answer'd, with the Easie Method of Its Support.... London: 1699. V. 65

MAILER, NORMAN
Advertisements for Myself. New York: 1959. V. 62; 66
Ancient Evenings. Boston: 1983. V. 66
Cannibals and Christians. New York: 1966. V. 62
Deaths for the Ladies (and Other Disasters). New York: 1962. V. 62
The Deer Park. New York: 1955. V. 62
The Deer Park. London: 1957. V. 64
The Deer Park. New York: 1967. V. 65
The Executioner's Song. Boston: 1979. V. 66
The Faith of Graffiti. New York: 1974. V. 62
Genius and Lust. A Journey through the Major Writings of Henry Miller. New York: 1976. V. 66
The Naked and the Dead. New York: 1948. V. 63; 65; 67
The Naked and the Dead. London: 1949. V. 62
The Naked and the Dead. Franklin Center: 1979. V. 63; 66
Of a Fire on the Moon. Boston: 1970. V. 63
Picasso. Portrait of Picasso as a Young Man. New York: 1995. V. 66
The Prisoner of Sex. Boston: 1971. V. 62; 66
Tough Guys Don't Dance. New York: 1984. V. 66

MAILLART, ELLA K.
Forbidden Journey: from Peking to Kashmir. London and Toronto: 1937. V. 65
Turkestan Solo: One Woman's Expedition from the Tien Shan to the Kizil Kum. London: 1938. V. 65

MAILLET, BENOIT DE
Telliamed; or, Discourses Between an Indian Philosopher and a French Missionary.... London: 1750. V. 62

MAILS, THOMAS
The People Called Apache. Eaglewood Cliffs: 1974. V. 62
The Pueblo Children of the Earth Mother. New York: 1983. V. 62

MAILS, THOMAS E.
Dog Soldiers, Bear Men and Buffalo Women. Engelwood Cliffs: 1973. V. 63; 64; 66
The Mystic Warriors of the Plains. Garden City: 1972. V. 63; 64
The People Called Apache. Eaglewood Cliffs: 1974. V. 63; 64; 66
The Pueblo Children of the Earth Mother. Garden City: 1983. V. 63; 64; 66
Sundancing at Rosebud and Pine Ridge. N.P.: 1978. V. 67
Sundancing at Rosebud and Pine Ridge. Lake Mills: 1978. V. 65; 67

MAIMBOURG, L. S. J.
The History of the League. London: 1684. V. 63

MAIN, JAMES
Popular Botany. London: 1835. V. 67

MAINARDI, MATTEO
Opere Mercantili, et Economiche di Matteo Mainardi, Che Contengono la Forma Regolata Della Scrittura Mercantile.... Bologna: 1646. V. 66

MAINDRON, ERNEST
Marionnettes et Guignols. Paris: 1900. V. 65

MAINE
Plan for Shortening the Time of Passage Between New York and London. Printed for Order of the Legislature of Maine. Portland: 1850. V. 67

MAINE, FLOYD S.
Lone Eagle...the White Sioux. Albuquerque: 1956. V. 67

MAINE, GEORGE F.
The Wind in the Pines: a Celtic Miscellany. Edinburgh: 1922. V. 64

MAINE, HENRY SUMNER
The Early History of the Property of Married Women, as Collected from Roman and Hindoo Law. Manchester: 1873. V. 67

MAINS & Fitzgerald's Trenton, Chambersburg, Millham and Mercer County Directory 1879. Trenton: 1879. V. 63; 66

MAINTENON, MADAME DE
The Letters of Madame de Maintenon; and Other Eminent Persons of the Age of Lewis XIV. Dublin: 1753. V. 65
Memoirs from the History of Madame de Maintenon and of the Last Age. London: 1757. V. 63
The Secret Correspondence of Madame de Maintenon, with the Princess des Ursins; from the Original Manuscripts in the Possession of the Duke de Choiseul. 1827. V. 66

MAINWARING, H. G.
A Soldier's Shikar Trips. 1920. V. 67

MAINWARING, JOHN
Memoirs of the Late George Frederic Handel.... London: 1760. V. 62; 63

MAIR, JOHN
Book-Keeping Methodiz'd; or, a Methodical Treatise of Merchant- Accompts, According to the Italian Form. Edinburgh: 1763. V. 64
Book-Keeping Modernised; or, Merchant Accounts by Double Entry.... Edinburgh: 1789. V. 63
The Tyro's Dictionary, Latin and English.... Edinburgh: 1763. V. 64

MAISON, K. E.
Honore Daumier: Catalogue Raisonne of the Paintings and Watercolours and Drawings. New York: 1968. V. 62; 63

MAITLAND, BARRY
The Marx Sisters. London: 1994. V. 66

MAITLAND, C.
The Tribute.... Norwich: 1832. V. 63

MAITLAND, EDWARD
The Perfect Way; or the Finding of Christ. London: 1882. V. 65

MAITLAND, FOWLER
Building Estates. A Rudimentary Treatise on the Development, Sale, Purchase and General Management of Building Land Including the Formation of Streets and Sewers.... London: 1883. V. 67

MAITLAND, JOHN
Observations on the Impolicy of Permitting the Exportation of British Wool, and of Preventing the Free Importation of Foreign Wool. London: 1818. V. 63

MAITLAND, WILLIAM
The History of London, From Its Foundation by the Romans to the Present Time.... London: 1739. V. 67
The History of London from Its Foundation to the Present Time.... London: 1756. V. 62

MAITTAIRE, MICHAEL
Stephanorum Historia, Vitas Ipsorum ac Libros Complectens. London: 1709. V. 66

MAIUS, JUNIANUS
De Priscorum Proprietate Verborum. Venice: 1490. V. 62

MAJNO, GUIDO
The Healing Hand. Man and Wound in the Ancient World. Cambridge: 1975. V. 65

MAJOR, RALPH H.
Classic Descriptions of Disease with Biographical Sketches of the Authors. Springfield: 1932. V. 62; 65; 67
Classic Descriptions of Disease with Biographical Sketches of the Authors. Springfield: 1939. V. 67
Classic Descriptions of Disease with Biographical Sketches of the Authors. Springfield: 1943. V. 64; 66; 67
Classic Descriptions of Disease with Biographical Sketches of the Authors. Springfield: 1945. V. 67
A History of Medicine. Springfield: 1954. V. 64; 66; 67

MAJORS, ALEXANDER
Seventy Years on the Frontier, Alexander Majors Memoirs. Chicago: 1893. V. 65

MAJORS, GERRI
Black Society. Chicago: 1976. V. 64; 66

MAKAR, NAGUIB
Urological Aspects of Bilharziasis in Egypt. Cairo: 1955. V. 67

MAKARS *Dream and Other Stories.* London: 1892. V. 64

A MAKE-Belief *of Funny Beasts.* New York: 1910. V. 64

MAKINE, ANDREI
Dreams of My Siberian Summers. New York: 1997. V. 62

MAKINS, GEORGE HENRY
Surgical Experiences in South Africa 1899-1900.... London: 1913. V. 67

MAKINSON, R. L.
Green and Green: the Passion and the Legacy. Salt Lake City: 1998. V. 63
Greene and Greene: Architecture as a Fine Art. Salt Lake City: 1977. V. 65

MAKOWER, STANLEY V.
Perdita: a Romance in Biography. London: 1908. V. 67

MALAMUD, BERNARD
The Assistant. New York: 1957. V. 62
Dubin's Lives. New York: 1979. V. 62
The Fixer. New York: 1966. V. 62
Idiots First. New York: 1963. V. 64
The Magic Barrel. New York: 1958. V. 67
The Natural. New York: 1952. V. 67
The Natural. London: 1963. V. 65
The Stories. New York: 1983. V. 67
The Tenants. New York: 1971. V. 62; 66

MALAN, S. C.
Aphorisms on Drawing. London: 1856. V. 66

MALARME, CHARLOTTE DE BOURNON, COMTESSE
La Famille Tilbury, ou la averne de Wokey. Paris: 1816. V. 67
Theobald Leymour, ou la Maison Muree. Paris: 1799. V. 67

MALBERG, BERTIL
Ake and His World. New York: 1940. V. 66

MALCOLM, ALEXANDER
A New System of Arithmetic, Theoretical and Practical. London: 1730. V. 66
A Treatise of Book-Keeping, or Merchant's Accounts in the Italian method of Debtor and Creditor. London: 1731. V. 65
A Treatise of Musick, Speculative, Practical and Historical. London: 1730. V. 67

MALCOLM, FIONA
My Fairyland. London: 1916. V. 66

MALCOLM, J. P.
An Historical Sketch of the Art of Caricature (Principally in England).... London: 1813. V. 62; 65; 67

MALCOLM, JOHN
The Godwin Sideboard. London: 1984. V. 67
Whistler in the Dark. London: 1986. V. 67

MALCOLM, W.
Gold Fields of Nova Scotia. Ottawa: 1929. V. 64

MALCOLM, WILLIAM
General View of the Agriculture of the County of Buckingham, with Observations on the Means of Its Improvement. London: 1794. V. 65

MALCOLMSON, ANNE
Song of Robin Hood. Boston: 1947. V. 66

MALCOLM X
The Autobiography of Malcolm X. New York: 1965. V. 63; 65

M'ALEER, P.
Townland Names of County Tyrone, with Their Meanings. 1936. V. 67

MALET, LUCAS
The Wages of Sin. London: 1891. V. 63

MALET, R.
When the Red Gods Call. 1934. V. 62; 63

MALEY, W.
The Story of the Celtic. Glasgow: 1939. V. 65

MALEZIEUX, EMILE
Travaux Publics des Etats-Unis d'Amerique en 1870. Rapport de Mission. Paris: 1873. V. 62

MALFILATRE, JACQUES CHARLES LOUIS DE CLINCHAMP DE
Narcisse Dans l'Isle de Venus. Paris: 1769. V. 64; 66

MALHAM DEMBLEBY, J.
The Key to the Bronte Works. London: 1911. V. 66

MALIBRAN, H.
Guide a L'Usage des Artistes et des Costumiers Contenant La Description des Uniformes de l'Armee Francaoise de 1780 a 1848. (with) Album Du Guide.... Paris: 1904-1907. V. 65

MALING, E. A.
A Handbook for Ladies on In-Door Plants, Flowers for Ornament and Song Birds. London: 1867. V. 64

MALING, PETER
Early Charts of New Zealand 1542-1851. Wellington: 1969. V. 64

MALINOWSKI, BRONISLAW
Argonauts of the Western Pacific, an Account of Native Enterprise and Adventure in the Archipelagoes of Melanesian New Guinea. New York: 1953. V. 66

MALINS, D. C.
Biochemical and Biophysical Perspectives in Marine Biology. London: 1974. V. 65

MALKIN, BENJAMIN HEATH
The Scenery, Antiquities and Biography of South Wales.... London: 1804. V. 66

MALKIN TITLE WORKS CO. LTD.
(Trade Catalogue). London: 1900. V. 64

MALL, F. P.
The Anatomical Course and Laboratory of the Johns Hopkins. Baltimore: 1896. V. 67

MALLALIEU, H. B.
On the Berlin Lakes and Other Poems. Edinburgh: 1988. V. 67

MALLARD, R. Q.
Plantation Life Before the Emancipation. Richmond: 1892. V. 63

MALLARME, STEPHANE
L'Apres-Midi d'un Faune. Waltham St. Lawrence: 1956. V. 62
L'Art Pour Tous. Aurora: 1942. V. 62

MALLESON, F. A.
Holiday Studies of Wordsworth by Rivers, Woods and Alps. London: 1890. V. 66

MALLET, C. E.
A History of the University of Oxford. New York: 1924. V. 63; 65

MALLET, DAVID
Alfred; a Masque. London: 1740. V. 66
Amyntor and Theodora, or the Hermit, a Poem. London: 1747. V. 66

MALLET, ROBERT
Report on the Railroad Constructed from Kingstown to Dalkey in Ireland, Upon the Atmospheric System, and Upon the Application of This System to Railroads in General. London: 1844. V. 64

MALLETT, D. T.
Mallett's Index of Artists: International - Biograpical. New York: 1948. V. 62; 65

MALLOCH, ARCHIBALD
Finch and Baines - a Seventeenth Century Friendship. Cambridge: 1917. V. 67

MALLOCH, P. D.
Life History and Habits of the Salmon, Sea Trout, and Other Freshwater Fish. 1910. V. 67
Life History and Habits of the Salmon, Sea Trout, and Other Freshwater Fish. London: 1910. V. 65
Life History and Habits of the Salmon, Sea Trout, and Other Freshwater Fish. 1912. V. 67

MALLOCK, W. H.
Social Equality. London: 1882. V. 62

MALLOCK, WILLIAM HURRELL
The Heart of Life. London: 1895. V. 67
Memoirs of Life and Literature. London: 1920. V. 67
The New Paul and Virginia or Positivism on an Island. London: 1878. V. 66
The New Republic; or, Culture, Faith and Philosophy in an English Country House. London: 1877. V. 62; 67

MALLORY, ARTHUR
The Fiery Serpent. New York: 1929. V. 66

MALLOY, WILLIAM M.
Treaties, Conventions, International Acts, Protocols and Agreements Between the U.S.A. and other Powers 1776-1909. Washington: 1910. V. 66

MALMESBURY, JAMES HARRIS, 1ST EARL OF
Diaries and Correspondence.... London: 1845. V. 62

MALO, CHARLES
Paris et Ses Environs. Promenades Pittoresques. Paris: 1827. V. 67

MALOFF, I. G.
Electron Optics in Television: with Theory and Application of Television Cathode-Ray Tubes. New York and London: 1938. V. 64

MALONE, ANDREW
The Irish Drama, 1896-1928. 1929. V. 67

MALONE, EDMOND
An Inquiry into the Authenticity of Certain Miscellaneous Papers and Legal Instruments. New York: 1970. V. 62

MALONE, EDMUND
Historical Account of the Rise and Progress of the English Stage.... Basil: 1800. V. 62

MALONE, JAMES H.
The Chicksaw Nation, a Short Sketch of a Noble People. Louisville: 1922. V. 63; 66

MALONE, MICHAEL
Painting the Roses Red. New York: 1974. V. 65
Time's Witness. Boston;: 1989. V. 66

MALONEY, ALICE BAY
Fur Brigade to the Bonaventura: John Work's California Expedition 1832-1833.... San Francisco: 1945. V. 67

MALORY, THOMAS
Le Morte D'Arthur. London: 1920. V. 64
Le Morte D'Arthur. London: 1927. V. 65
La Morte d'Arthur. New York: 1936. V. 63; 64; 67
The Romance of King Arthur and His Knights of the Round Table. New York: 1917. V. 67
Works. Oxford: 1948. V. 62; 65

MALOT, HECTOR
Nobody's Boy. New York: 1916. V. 63

M'ALPIE, JAMES
Certain Curious Poems Written at the Close of the XVIIth and Beginning of the XVIIIth Century.... Paisley: 1818. V. 62

M'ALPINE, JOHN
Genuine Narratives and Concise Memoirs of Some of the Most Interesting Exploits and Singular Adventures of John M'Alpine.... Greenock: 1985. V. 67

MALRAUX, ANDRE
The Walnut Trees of Altenburg. London: 1952. V. 64

MALTBY, W. J.
Captain Jeff or Frontier Life in Texas with the Texas Rangers. Colorado: 1906. V. 62

MALTHUS, FRANCOIS DE
Traite des Feux Artificials Pour la Guerre & Pour la Recreation. Paris: 1640. V. 64

MALTHUS, THOMAS ROBERT
Additions to the Fourth and Former Editions of an Essay on the Principle of Population. London: 1817. V. 62; 63
An Essay on the Principle of Population. London: 1798. V. 63; 64; 65; 67
An Essay on the Principle of Population. London: 1803. V. 63; 64
An Essay on the Principle of Population. London: 1806. V. 64; 67
An Essay on the Principle of Population. London: 1807. V. 64; 66
An Essay on the Principle of Population. London: 1817. V. 63; 64
An Essay on the Principle of Population. London: 1826. V. 63; 64
An Essay on the Principle of Population. London: 1872. V. 64
Principles of Political Economy. London: 1820. V. 64; 65; 67
Principles of Political Economy. Boston: 1821. V. 63
Principles of Political Economy. London: 1836. V. 62; 64

MALTON, JAMES
The Young Painter's Maulstick.... London: 1800. V. 62; 64; 66

MALTON, THOMAS
Views of Oxford. London: 1810. V. 62; 67

MALTZ, ALBERT
The Cross and the Arrow. Boston: 1944. V. 66

MALVEZZI, VIRGILIO, MARCHESE
Discourses Upon Corenlius Tacitus.... London: 1642. V. 62; 66

MAMA'S Visit, With Her Little Ones to the Great Exhibition. London: 1852. V. 62

MAMET, DAVID
American Buffalo. New York: 1978. V. 62; 64
Bar Mitzvah. El Segundo: 1999. V. 62
Glengarry Glen Ross. New York: 1984. V. 66
Lakeboat. New York: 1981. V. 62; 66; 67
Oleanna. New York: 1992. V. 62; 66
Passover. New York: 1995. V. 67
Speed-the-Plow. New York: 1987. V. 62
The Water Engine. New York: 1978. V. 62; 66
The Woods. New York: 1979. V. 62; 64

MAMMON In London, or the Spy of the Day. London: 1823. V. 66

THE MAN In the Moon and Another Tale for Children at Christmastime. London: 1882. V. 64

MAN, JOHN
The Stranger in Reading, in a Series of Letters from a Traveller to His Friend in London. Reading: 1810. V. 63

THE MAN Who...Stories by Detection Club Authors. Bristol: 1992. V. 67

MANASSES, CONSTANTINUS
Annales. Lvgdvni Batavorvm: 1616. V. 64

MANBY, GEORGE WILLIAM
An Essay on the Preservation of Shipwrecked Persons, with a Descriptive Account of the Apparatus and Manner of Applying It. London: 1812. V. 63; 66
Plan for Saving the Lives of Shipwrecked Mariners. London: 1810-1813. V. 64

MANCERON, GENEVIEVE
The Deadlier Sex. New York: 1961. V. 62

MANCHESTER AND SALFORD SANITARY ASSOCIATION
Health Lectures for the People. Health Lectures Delivered in Manchester - 1875-1876, 1876-1877, 1877-1878, 1878-1879-1880. Manchester: 1878-1880. V. 63

MANCHESTER, DUKE OF
Court and Society, Elizabeth to Anne. London: 1864. V. 66

MANCHESTER, HENRY MONTAGU, EARL OF
Manchester at Mondo. London: 1658. V. 64

MANCHESTER LITERARY CLUB
The Papers and Proceedings of the Society for the Sessions 1876-1877. Manchester: 1877-1891. V. 64
The Papers with Proceedings of the Society for the Session 1876-1877. Manchester: 1877. V. 63

MANCHESTER UNIVERSITY. LIBRARY
Catalogue of the Medical Books in Manchester University Library 1480-1700. Manchester: 1972. V. 64

MANCHESTER, WILLIAM C.
Songs of Zion, or Conference Hymns, Selected and Original. Providence: 1831. V. 64

MANDAT-GRANCEY, EDMOND, BARON DE
La Breche Aux Buffles Un Ranch Francais Dans Le Dakota. Paris: 1889. V. 66

MANDELSTAM, OSIP
Journey to Armenia. London: 1980. V. 63
Kamen'. St. Petersburg: 1913. V. 67

MANDERSON, CHARLES F.
The Twin Seven-Shooters. New York and London: 1902. V. 64

MANDERSON, JAMES
Twelve Letters, Addressed to the Right Honourable Spencer Perceval. London: 1812. V. 63

MANDEVILLE, BERNARD DE
An Enquiry into the Origin of Honour and the Usefulness of Christianity in War. London: 1732. V. 62
The Fable of the Bees; or, Private Vices, Publick Benefits. London: 1723. V. 65
The Fable of the Bees; or, Private Vices, Publick Benefits. London: 1724. V. 62
The Fable of the Bees; or, Private Vices, Publick Benefits. London: 1729-1730. V. 63
The Fable of the Bees; or, Private Vices, Publick Benefits. London: 1732. V. 66
Free Thoughts on Religion, The Church and National Happiness. London: 1720. V. 67

MANDEVILLE, JOHN
The Voiage and Travayle.... London: 1887. V. 63; 65

MANDEY, VENTURUS
Mechanic Powers; or the Mystery of Nature and Art Unvail'd. Shewing what Great Things May Be Peformed by Mechanic Engines.... London: 1709. V. 63; 67

MANEC, J. P.
Traite Theorique et Pratique de La Ligature Des Arteres. Paris: 1836. V. 64

MANESE, DENIS JOSEPH
Traite sur la Maniere D'Empailler et des Conserver les Animaux, Les Pellereries et les Laines.... Paris: 1787. V. 64

MANGAM, D. WILLIAM
The Clarks - an American Phenomenon. New York: 1941. V. 62; 63; 65

MANGAN, JAMES CLARENCE
Poems of.... Dublin and London: 1903. V. 62

MANGAN, TERRY W.
Colorado on Glass: Colorado's First Half Century as Seen by the Camera. Denver: 1975. V. 65

MANGAN, WILLIAM
Colorado on Glass, Colorado's First Half Century As Seen by Camera. Denver: 1975. V. 63

MANGOLD, GEORGE B.
Problems of Child Welfare. New York: 1914. V. 66

MANGUM, NEIL C.
Battle of the Rosebud, Prelude to the Little Big Horn. El Segundo: 1987. V. 67

MANHATTAN SURGICAL INSTRUMENT CO.
Catalog 1 Surgical Instruments of Superior Quality, 1941. New York. 1941. V. 66

MANHEIM, FREDERICK
Affecting History of the Dreadful Distresses of Frederick Manheim's Family. Exeter: 1793. V. 66

MANHOFF, BILL
The Owl and the Pussycat. Garden City: 1965. V. 66

MANHOOD, H. A.
Bread and Vinegar. London: 1931. V. 62

MANIERE D'Ouvir et de Traiter les Absces, A Portee De La Main Du Chirurgien et des Secours de La Chirurgie. Paris: 1765. V. 64

MANILIUS, MARCUS
The Five Books of M. Manilius, Containing a System of Ancient Astronomy and Astrology; Together with the Philosophy of the Stoicks. London: 1697. V. 64

MANILLI, GIACOMO
Villa Borghese Fuori di Porta Pinciana Descritta. Roma: 1650. V. 67

MANION, JOHN S.
General Terry's Last Statement to Custer. Monroe: 1933. V. 65; 67

MANLEY, MARY DE LA RIVIERE
Secret Memoirs and Manners of Several Persons of Quality.... London: 1709. V. 63; 66; 67

MANLY, WILLIAM LEWIS
Death Valley in '49, Important Chapter of California Pioneer History, the Autobiography of a Pioneer. San Jose: 1894. V. 63

MANN, ALBERT W.
History of the Forty-Fifth Regiment, Massachusetts Volunteer Militia. Dept. of North Carolina. The Cadet Regiment. Boston: 1908. V. 62

MANN, ETTA D.
Four Years in the Governor's Mansion in Virginia 1910-1914. Richmond: 1937. V. 63

MANN, HERMAN
The Female Review; or Memoirs of an American Young Lady.... Dedham; printed by Nathaniel: 1797. V. 62

MANN, JAMES
Medical Sketches of the Campaigns of 1812, 18183, 1814, To Which Are Added, Surgical Cases, Observations on Military Hospitals.... Dedham: 1816. V. 64

MANN, LEONARD
Murder in Sydney. London: 1937. V. 65

MANN, MARY
Juanita: a Romance of Real Life in Cuba: Fifty Years Ago. Boston: 1887. V. 66

MANN, PATRICK
Dog Day Afternoon. New York: 1974. V. 65

MANN, SALLY
Immediate Family. London: 1992. V. 66

MANN, STEPHEN JOHN
Sketches and Reminiscences, Prose and Verse, Consisting of Railway Trips.... Nottingham: 1856. V. 63

MANN, THOMAS
The Beloved Returns. New York: 1940. V. 62; 65
Buddenbrooks. Berlin: 1901. V. 67
Buddenbrooks. New York: 1924. V. 67
Doktor Faustus. Stockholm: 1947. V. 62; 64; 66
Joseph and His Brothers. New York: 1934-1944. V. 65
Joseph and His Brothers. London: 1956. V. 65
Joseph und seine Bruder. Berlin: 1933-1943. V. 65
Der Kleine Herr Friedmann. Berlin: 1898. V. 67
Der Kleine Herr Friedmann. Berlin: 1903. V. 65
Koenigliche Hoheit. Berlin: 1909. V. 65
Lotte in Weimar. Stockholm: 1939. V. 63; 64; 66
Nocturnes. New York: 1934. V. 63
A Sketch of My Life. Paris: 1930. V. 65
Stories of Three Decades. New York: 1936. V. 63
The Transposed Heads. Kentfield: 1977. V. 62; 63; 65
Tristan. Berlin: 1903. V. 65

MANN, WILLIAM
Six Years' Reisdence in the Australian Provinces, Ending in 1839.... London: 1839. V. 62

MANNERING, E.
Flower Portraits. 1961. V. 63; 66
Flower Portraits. London: 1961. V. 62

MANNERING, GEORGE EDWARD
With Axe and Rope in the New Zealand Alps. London: 1891. V. 63; 64

MANNERS and Customs of the French. London: 1893. V. 64

THE MANNERS of the Times: a Satire. Philadelphia: 1762. V. 62

MANNERS, CATHERINE REBECCA
Poems. London: 1793. V. 62
Review of Poetry, Ancient and Modern. London: 1799. V. 65

MANNERS, J. HARTLEY
The Harp of Life. New York: 1921. V. 66

MANNERS, JOHN
Notes of an Irish Tour in 1846. 1881. V. 63

MANNERS, VICTORIA
John Zoffany, R.A. His Life and Works 1735-1810. London and New York: 1920. V. 64

MANNEX & WHELLAN
Hictory, Gazottoor and Directory of Cumberland.... Bovorloy: 1847. V. 65; 66
History, Gazetttteer and Directory of Cumberland.... Beckermet: 1974. V. 65

MANNEX, P., & CO.
History and Directory of Furness and Cartmel. Preston: 1882. V. 64
History, Topography and Directory of Westmorland and Lonsdale, North of the Sands in Lancashire. London: 1849. V. 65; 66
Topography and Directory of North and South Lonsdale Amounderness, Leyland and the Town of Southport.... Preston: 1866. V. 64; 65; 66

MANNHEIM, KARL
Strukturanalyse der Erkenntnistheorie. Berlin: 1922. V. 67

MANNHEIMER, E.
Morbus Caeruleus; an Analysis of 114 Cases of Congenital Heart Disease with Cyanosis. Basle: 1949. V. 67

MANNIN, ETHEL
Connemara Journal. 1947. V. 67

MANNING, ANNE
The Chronicle of Ethelfled. London: 1861. V. 65
Family Pictures. London: 1861. V. 65
The Ladies of Bever Hollow. London: 1858. V. 65
A Noble Purpose Nobly Won. London: 1862. V. 65
Some Account of Mrs. Clarinda's Singleheart. London: 1855. V. 65
Village Belles. London: 1833. V. 65
The Year Nine. London: 1858. V. 66

MANNING, EDWARD WINDHAM
The Law of Bills of Exchange, Promissory Notes, Bank Notes, Banker's Notes, Drafts, and Checks.... London: 1812. V. 65

MANNING, FREDERIC
Eidola. London: 1917. V. 62
Her Privates We. London: 1930. V. 62; 64
The Middle Parts of Fortune - Somme and Ancre, 1916. London: 1929. V. 62; 64; 67
Poems. London: 1910. V. 62
Scenes and Portraits. London: 1909. V. 62
The Vigil of Brunhild - a Narrative Poem. London: 1907. V. 62; 64

MANNING, FREDERICK GEORGE
The Bermondsey Murder. London: 1849. V. 63

MANNING, HENRY EDWARD
Sermons. London: 1845-1850. V. 63

MANNING, HUGO
Buenos Aires. Buneos Aires: 1942. V. 63

MANNING, IAN
With a Gun in Good Country. 1995. V. 64

MANNING, JAMES ALEXANDER
Lives of the Speakers of the House of Commons. London: 1850. V. 62

MANNING, OLIVIA
The Danger Tree. The Battle Lost and Won. The Sum of Things. London: 1977-1980. V. 66
The Great Fortune. London: 1959. V. 62; 65
A Romantic Hero and Other Stories. London: 1967. V. 63
The Spoilt City. London: 1962. V. 65

MANNING, R.
Book of Fruits.... Salem: 1838. V. 63

MANNING, R. B.
Hunters and Poachers. London: 1993. V. 67

MANNING, ROBERT
A Plain and Rational Account of the Catholic Faith...(with) The Reform'd Churches Proved Destitute of a Lawful Ministry. Rouen: 1721-1722. V. 63

MANNING, SAMUEL
American Pictures Drawn with Pen and Pencil. London: 1885. V. 65
Spanish Pictures Drawn with Pen and Pencil. London: 1890. V. 65

MANNINGHAM, RICHARD
The Symptoms, Nature, Causes and Cure of the Febricula or Little Fever.... London: 1750. V. 67

MANNING-SAUNDERS, RUTH
Children by the Sea. London: 1938. V. 63

MANRY, JOE EDGAR
Curtain Call; the History of the Theater in Austin, Texas 1839 to 1905. Austin: 1985. V. 67

MANSBRIDGE, MICHAEL
John Nash: A Complete Catalogue. New York: 1991. V. 66

MANSEL, ROBERT
A Defense of the Drama. New York: 1826. V. 64

MANSEL-PLEYDELL, J. C.
The Birds of Dorsetshire, a Contribution to the Natural History of the County. Dorchester: 1889. V. 65

MANSERGH, NICHOLAS
The Coming of the First World War; A Study in European Balance 1878-1914. 1949. V. 67
Ireland in the Age of Reform and Revolution 1840-1921. 1940. V. 67

MANSFIELD ASSOCIATION FOR THE APPREHENDING AND PROSECUTING
Rules of a Society Called the Equitable Associaton of the Inhabitants of Mansfield and Neighbourhood for the Apprehending and Prosecuting of Felons, and Receivers of Stolen Goods, and Other Offenders Against the Law. Mansfield: 1842. V. 65

MANSFIELD, EDWARD D.
Exposition of the Natural Position of Mackinaw City.... Cincinnati: 1857. V. 63; 66
The Legal Rights, Liabilities and Duties of Women. Salem and Cincinnati: 1845. V. 63
The Mexican War: a History of Its Origin and Detailed Account of the Victories. New York: 1848. V. 67

MANSFIELD, KATHERINE
The Aloe. New York: 1930. V. 62; 64; 67
The Doves' Nest. London: 1923. V. 63; 64; 65
The Garden Party and Other Stories. London: 1922. V. 62; 64
The Garden Party and Other Stories. London: 1939. V. 62
In a German Pension. London: 1911. V. 62; 64
Je Ne Parle Pas Francais. Hampstead: 1919. V. 64
The Letters. London: 1928. V. 62; 65; 66
Poems. New York: 1924. V. 65
Prelude. London: 1918. V. 65
The Scrapbook. London: 1939. V. 62; 65
Something Childish and Other Stories. London: 1924. V. 62; 63; 66
Something Childish and Other Stories. Toronto: 1924. V. 66

MANSFIELD, KENNETH
The Art of Angling. London: 1957. V. 67

MANSON, GRANT CARPENTER
Frank Lloyd Wright to 1910: the First Golden Age. New York: 1958. V. 62; 63

MANSON, J. B.
The Life and Work of Edward Degas. London: 1927. V. 64

MANSON, MARSDEN
The Yellow Peril in Action. San Francisco: 1907. V. 62

MANSON, PATRICK
Tropical Diseases. A Manual of the Diseases of Warm Climates. London: 1898. V. 63; 67

MANT, RICHARD
Sermons, for Parochial and Domestic Use, Designed to Illustrate and Enforce, in a Connected View, the Most Important Articles of Christian Faith and Practice. London: 1832. V. 62

MANTELL, GIDEON ALGERNON
The Geology of the South-East of England. London: 1833. V. 62
The Journal of Gideon Mantell. London: 1940. V. 62; 64; 65; 67
A Pictorial Atlas of Fossil Remains. London: 1850. V. 62; 64; 65; 66
Thoughts on a Pebble, or a First Lesson in Geology. London: 1849. V. 62; 65; 66
Thoughts on Animalcules; or, a Glimpse of the Invisible World Revealed by Microscope. London: 1846. V. 64; 66
The Wonders of Geology. London: 1866. V. 65; 66

MANTLE, MICKEY
The Mick. Garden City: 1985. V. 63

MANTZ, RUTH ELVISH
The Critical Bibliography of Katherine Mansfield. London: 1931. V. 62

A MANUAL of Catholic Prayers. Philadelphia: 1774. V. 62

A MANUAL of Military Surgery Prepared for the Use of the C.S.A. Richmond: 1863. V. 63

MANUAL of Seamanship for Boys' and Seamen of the Royal Navy 1904. London: 1905. V. 64; 65

A MANUAL of the Ceremonies Used in the Catholic Church (Book I). Boston: 1833. V. 64

A MANUALL; or, Analecta. London: 1641. V. 62

MANUEL, KING OF PORTUGAL
Early Portuguese Books 1489-1600 in the Library of His Majesty the King of Portugal. London: 1929-1935. V. 62

MANUTIO, PAOLO
Lettere Volgari di Diversi Nobilissimi Huomini. Venice: 1558. V. 65

MANUZIO, ALDO
Institvtionvm Grammaticarvm Libri Qvatvor. Venetiis in aedibus Francisc: 1549. V. 64

MANWARING, G. E.
A Bibliography of British Naval History. London: 1970. V. 67
My Friend the Admiral. The Life, Letters and Journals of Rear Admiral James Burney, F.R.S. London: 1931. V. 64; 66

MANYPENNY, GEORGE W.
Our Indian Wards. Cincinnati: 1880. V. 64; 67

MANZOLI, PIETRO ANGELO
Zodiacus Vita. Basileae: 1621. V. 66

MANZONI, ALESSANDRO
Tragedie. Il Conte di Carmagnola e l'Adelchi. Paris: 1826. V. 66

MAPLET, J.
A Greene Forest or a Natural Historie.... 1930. V. 63; 66
A Greene Forest or a Natural Historie.... London: 1930. V. 62

MAPLETOFT, D. J.
Select Proverbs, Italian, Spanish, French, English, Scotish, British &c. London: 1707. V. 63; 67
Wisdom from Above; or, Considerations Tending to Explain, Establish and Promote the Christian Life or that Holiness, Without Which No Man Shall See the Lord. London: 1714-1717. V. 62

MAPS, Reports, Estimates &c. Relative to Improvements of the Navigation of the River St. Lawrence and a Proposed Canal Connecting the River St. Lawrence and Lake Champlain Canal. Toronto: 1856. V. 67

MARAINI, F.
Karakoram. 1961. V. 63; 65
Where Four Worlds Meet. New York: 1964. V. 63; 64

MARAN, RENE
Batouala. New York: 1922. V. 64; 66
Batouala. New York: 1932. V. 65

MARANA, GIOVANNI PAOLO
Letters Writ by a Turkish Spy, Who Liv'd Five and Forty Years Undiscover'd at Paris.... London: 1734. V. 62

MARAT, JANE
Conversations on Botany. 1818. V. 67

MARBURG, OTTO
Hydrocephalus. Its Symptomatology, Pathology, Pathogensis and Treatment. New York: 1940. V. 67

MARCEL, GUILLAUME
Chronological Tables of Europe from Nativity of Our Saviour to the Year 1714. London: 1714. V. 62

MARCELIN, PIERRE
The Pencil of God. Boston: 1951. V. 63

MARCELLINUS, AMIANUS
The Roman Historie, Containing Such Acts and Occurrents as Passed Under Constantius, Iulianus, Iovianus, Valentinianus and Vlanes, Emperours.... London: 1609. V. 64

MARCET, JANE
Conversations on Political Economy.... London: 1821. V. 64; 65
Conversations on Political Economy.... London: 1824. V. 64; 65
Willy's Holidays; or, Conversations on Different Kinds of Governments. London: 1836. V. 64

MARCGRAVE, JORGE
Historia Natural do Brasil. Sao Paulo: 1942. V. 64

MARCH, DANIEL
Night Scenes in the Bible. Philadelphia: 1870. V. 62

MARCH, EDGAR J.
Sailing Drifters, the Story of the Herring Luggers of England, Scotland and the Isle of Man. London: 1952. V. 62

MARCH, ELEANOR
Little White Barbara. London: 1902. V. 66

MARCH, JOHN
The Jolly Angler or Waterside Companion. 1833. V. 63; 65
The Jolly Angler or Waterside Companion. London: 1836. V. 64

MARCH, JOSEPH M.
The Wild Party. Chicago: 1928. V. 65

MARCH, RICHARD
T. S. Eliot - a Symposium. London: 1948. V. 62

MARCH, WALTER
Shoepac Recollections: a Way-Side Glimpse of American Life. New York: 1856. V. 66

MARCH, WILLIAM
The Bad Seed. New York and Toronto: 1954. V. 65

MARCHAM, FREDERICK GEORGE
Louis Agassiz Fuertes and The Singular Beauty of Birds. New York: 1971. V. 63

MARCHAND, JEAN
Le Roman de Jean de Paris. Paris: 1924. V. 65

MARCHAND, JEAN HENRI
Mon Radotage, et Celui des Autres Recuelli par un Invalide.... 1760. V. 65

MARCHANT, GUYOT
La Grande Danse Macabre des Hommes et des Femmes.... Troyes: 1728. V. 67

MARCHANT, PETER
Tribunal Sacramentale et Visibile Animaruum in hac vita Mortali Tomis Duobus Explicatum.. Gandavi: 1642. V. 66

MARCHANTIUS, JACOBUS
Iac. Marchantii Flandria Commentariorum. Antverpiae: 1596. V. 66

MARCHETTI, ANGELO
Breve Introduzione ala Cosmografia. Pistoja: 1738. V. 62

MARCHINGTON, J.
A Portrait of Shooting. 1979. V. 66

MARCHINI, G.
Italian Stained Glass Windows. London: 1957. V. 62
Le Vetrate Italiane. Milano: 1956. V. 64

MARCHIO, VINCENZO
Il Forestiere Informato Delle Cose di Lucca. Lucca: 1721. V. 64

MARCOS, SUBCOMANDANTE
The Story of Colors. El Paso: 1999. V. 64; 67

MARCOU, JULES
Letter on Some Points of the Geology of Texas, New Mexico, Kansas and Nebraska: Adressed (sic) to Messrs. F. B. Meek and V. V. Hayden. Zurich: 1858. V. 62

MARCOY, PAUL
Travels in South America from the Pacific Ocean to the Atlantic Ocean. London: 1875. V. 67

MARCUS Ward's Golden Picture Book of Lays and Legends. London: 1880. V. 62

MARCUS, JACOB R.
Communal Sick-Care in the German Ghetto. Cincinnati: 1947. V. 63

MARCUS AURELIUS, ANTONINUS, EMPEROR OF ROME
The Thoughts of an Emperor. London: 1897. V. 62

MARCUSE, HERBERT
Hegel's Ontologie, und die Grundlegung einer Theorie der Geschichtlichkeit. Frankfurt: 1932. V. 67

MARCY, RANDOLPH BARNES
Exploration of the Red River of Louisiana in the Year 1852. Washington: 1853. V. 63
Exploration of the Red River of Louisiana in the Year 1852. Washington: 1854. V. 62
The Prairie Traveler. A Handbook for Overland Expeditions. London: 1863. V. 62
The Prairie Traveller - a Handbook for Overland Expeditions. New York: 1859. V. 66

MARDEN, ORISON S.
The Home Lovers' Library. New York and Washington: 1906. V. 64

MARDER, ARTHUR J.
Fear God and Dread Nought. London: 1952-1959. V. 66

MARDER, WILLIAM
Anthony, the Man, the Company, the Cameras: an American Photographic Pioneer: 140 Year History of a Company from Anthony to Ansco to GAF. N.P: 1982. V. 63

MARDERSTEIG, GIOVANNI
Giovanni Mardersteig on G. B. Bodoni's Type Faces. Verona: 1968. V. 65
The Officina Bodoni: an Account of the Work of a Hand Press 1923- 1977. Verona: 1980. V. 62; 65
On G. B. Bodoni's Type Faces. Verona: 1968. V. 64
The Treatise of Gerard Mercator, Literaum Latinarum, Quas Italicas.... Verona: 1930. V. 62

MARDRUS, J. C.
Le Paradis Musulman. Selon Le Texte et La Traduction du Dr. J. C. Mardrus. Paris: 1930. V. 65

MARETZEK, MAX
Crotchets and Quavers; or, Revelations of an Opera Manager in America. New York: 1855. V. 65

MAREY, E. J.
Animal Mechanism: a Treatise on Terrestrial and Aerial Locomotion. London: 1883. V. 63

MARGERISON, SAMUEL
The Registers of the Parish Church of Calverley, in the West Riding of the County of York.... Bradford: 1880-1887. V. 66

MARGERY, PIERRE
Decouvertes et Etablissements des Francais dans l'Ouest et dans le Sud de l'Amerique Septentrionale (1614-1754). Paris: 1876-1886. V. 66

MARGE'S Little Lulu Plays Pirate. Springfield: 1946. V. 65

MARGOLIN, PHILLIP
Gone, But Not Forgotten. New York: 1993. V. 67
The Last Innocent Man. New York: 1981. V. 66

MARGUERITE D'ANGOULEME, QUEEN OF NAVARRE
L'Heptameron. Paris: 1879. V. 63
The Heptameron. London: 1894. V. 62

MARIA Morevena. Moscow: 1903. V. 66

MARIANI, A.
Coca and its Therapeutic Application. New York: 1892. V. 64

MARIANI, JOHN
America Eats Out. New York: 1991. V. 67

MARIANI, PAUL
Timing Devices. Easthampton: 1977. V. 64

MARIE Laurencin. Paris: 1986. V. 66

MARIE, PIERRE
Essays on Acromegaly. London: 1891. V. 65
Lecons sur les Maladies De La Moelle. Paris: 1892. V. 64
Lectures on Diseases of the Spinal Cord. London: 1895. V. 65
Travaux et Memoires. Paris: 1928. V. 64

MARIE, QUEEN OF ROMANIA
The Dreamer of Dreams. London: 1915. V. 65
The Story of Naughty Kildeen. London: 1922. V. 65; 67
The Story of Naughty Kildeen. New York: 1922?. V. 66

MARIETT, PAUL
The Poems of.... New York: 1913. V. 63

MARILLIER, H. C.
A Brief Sketch of the Morris Movement and of the Firm Founded by William Morris to Carry Out His Designs and the Industries Revived or Started by Him. 1911. V. 64
Dante Gabriel Rossetti. London: 1899. V. 64

MARIN, MICHEL ANGEL
The Perfect Religious: a Work Designed for the Assistance of Those Who Aspire After Perfection in a Religious State.... Doway: 1762. V. 62

MARINARO, V. C.
A Modern Dry Fly Code. 1970. V. 67

MARINELLI, GIOVANNI
Gli Ornamenti delle Donne. Venice: 1562. V. 62

THE MARINER'S Chronicle.... New Haven: 1836. V. 66

MARINETTI, F. T.
Futurist Cookbook. San Francisco: 1989. V. 67

MARINHO DE AZEVEDO, LUIS
Apologeticos Discursos Offerecidos a Magestade del Rei Dom Ioam Nosso Senhor Quarto do Nome.... Lisbon: 1641. V. 62

MARINONI, GIOVANNI GIACOMO
De Astronomica Specula Domestica et Organico Apparatu Astronomico Libri Duo Reginae. Vienna: 1745. V. 62; 66

MARIO, QUEENA
Death Drops Delilah. New York: 1944. V. 63

MARION
Mummy's Bedtime Story Book. London: 1929. V. 63

MARION COUNTY HISTORICAL SOCIETY, INC.
A History of Marion County, West Virginia 1985. Fairmont: 1986. V. 66

MARIOTTE, EDME
Traite du Mouvement des Eaux et des Autres Corps Fluides. Paris: 1718. V. 62

MARITAIN, JACQUES
The Philosophy of Art. Ditchling: 1923. V. 65

MARITAIN, RAISSA
Patriarch Tree, Thirty Poems by Raissa Maritian. Worcester: 1965. V. 64; 66

A MARITIME History of New York. Garden City: 1941. V. 63

MARIUS, RICHARD
The Coming of Rain. New York: 1969. V. 63; 66

MARIVAUX, PIERRE CARLET DE CHAMBLAIN DE
Le Paysan Parvenu; or, the Fortunate Peasant. London: 1735. V. 63

MARJORIBANKS, E.
The Life of Lord Carson. 1932-1936. V. 63; 66

MARK, A. F.
New Zealand Alpine Plants. Wellington: 1973. V. 64

MARK, ENID
An Afternoon at Les Collettes. Wallingford: 1988. V. 62; 64

MARK, JAN
Fun with Mrs. Thum. 1993. V. 67

MARK, MARY ELLEN
Passport. New York: 1974. V. 66

MARK, P.
The Wild Bull and Sacred Forest. Cambridge: 1992. V. 62

MARK, VERNON
Violence and the Brain. New York: 1970. V. 66; 67

MARKHAM, ALBERT HASTINGS
The Great Frozen Sea; a Personal Narrative of the Voyage of the "Alert" During the Arctic Expedition of 1875-1876. London: 1878. V. 64
A Polar Reconnaissance. London: 1881. V. 66
A Whaling Cruise to Baffin's Bay and the Gulf of Boothia. London: 1875. V. 62

MARKHAM, CHRISTOPHER A.
The Records of the Borough of Northampton. London: 1898. V. 66

MARKHAM, CLEMENTS ROBERT
The Conquest of New Granada. New York: 1912. V. 63; 64; 66
Markham: the Church and Parish. London: 1882. V. 65
Travels in Peru and India While Superintending the Collection of Chinchona Plants and Seeds in South America.... London: 1862. V. 64; 65

MARKHAM, EDWIN
California the Wonderful. New York: 1914. V. 67
The Younger Choir. New York: 1910. V. 63

MARKHAM, GERVASE
Cheape and Good Husbandry for the Well Ordering of all Beasts and Fowles and for the General Cure of Their Diseases. London: 1631. V. 64
Country Contentments: or, the Husbandmans Recreations. London: 1631. V. 64
Country Contentments: or, the Husbandsmans Recreations. London: 1654. V. 64

MARKHAM, WILLIAM
An Introduction to Spelling and Reading English.... Alnwick. V. 63; 64; 66

MARKINO, YOSHIO
My Recollections and Reflections. London: 1913. V. 65

MARKLAND, ABRAHAM
Sermons Preach'd at the Cathedral Church of Winchester. London: 1729. V. 67

MARKLOVE, H.
Views of Berkeley Castle, Taken on the Spot, and Drawn on Stone. London: 1840. V. 62; 67

MARKMANN, CHARLES LAM
The Book of Sports Cars. London: 1960. V. 62; 66

MARKOPOULOS, GREGORY J.
Chaos Phaos. Florence: 1971. V. 66

MARKOVITS, RODION
Siberian Garrison. London: 1929. V. 64

MARKS, DAVID
The Life of David Marks to the 26th Year of His Age. Limerick: 1831. V. 64
A Treatise on the Faith of the Freewill Baptists.... Dover: 1834. V. 63

MARKS, HENRY STACEY
Pen and Pencil Sketches. London: 1894. V. 64

MARK's History of Little Dame Crump and Her Little White Pig. London: 1840. V. 62

MARKS, J. J.
The Peninsula Campaign in Virginia, or Incidents and Scenes on the Battle-Fields and In Richmond. Philadelphia: 1864. V. 64

MARKS, KURT
After Barbed Wire: Cowboys of Our Time. Pasadena: 1985. V. 64

MARKS, LILLIAN
Saul Marks and the Plantin Press: the Life and Work of a Singular Man. Los Angeles: 1980. V. 63; 64

MARKS, MARILLA
Memoirs of the Life of David Marks, Minister of the Gospel. Dover: 1847. V. 63

MARKS, PAULA M.
And Die in the West. The Story of the OK Corral Gunfight. New York: 1989. V. 65

MARKS, RICHARD
The Retrospect...and an Address to Naval Officers. Boston: 1822. V. 66

MARKSON, DAVID
The Ballad of Dingus Magee. New York: 1965. V. 67
Going Down. New York: 1970. V. 67

MARKUS, KURT
After Barbed Wire: Cowboys of Our Time. Pasadena: 1985. V. 63; 66

MARLBOROUGH, SARAH JENNINGS CHURCHILL, DUCHESS OF
An Account of the Conduct of the Dowager Duchess of Marlborough, From Her First Coming to Court, to the Year 1710. London: 1742. V. 63

MARLOTH, RUDOLF
The Flora of South Africa.... Capetown: 1913-1932. V. 63

MARLOWE, CHRISTOPHER
The Complete Works. Cambridge: 1973. V. 64
Hero and Leander. London: 1893-1894. V. 64
The Life and Death of Tamburlaine the Great.... London: 1930. V. 65; 66
The Tragical History of Doctor Faustus. N.P: 1903. V. 62; 63; 64; 66
The Works. London: 1850. V. 64
The Works. London: 1870. V. 62
The Works. London: 1885. V. 63

MARLOWE, DAN J.
Doorway to Death. New York: 1959. V. 67
Shake a Crooked Town. New York: 1961. V. 67

MARLOWE, G. S.
I Am Your Brother. London: 1935. V. 63

MARMELSZADT, WILLARD
Musical Sons of Aesculapius. New York: 1946. V. 62; 66

MARMET, PIERRE DE
Entertainments of the Cours; or Academical Conversations. London: 1658. V. 65

MARMION, ANTHONY
The Ancient and Modern History of te Maritime Ports of Ireland. London: 1855. V. 66

MARMONTEL, JEAN FRANCOIS
Belisaire. Paris: 1767. V. 64
Belisarius. London: 1767. V. 63
Les Contes Moraux. Paris: 1765. V. 64; 66
A New Collection of Moral Tales.... Perth: 1792. V. 62

MARMORA, ANDREA
Della Historia di Corfu Libri Otto. Venice: 1672. V. 64

MAROLLES, LEWIS DE
An Essay on Providence. London: 1790. V. 63; 67

MAROLOIS, SAMUEL
Geometria Theoretica ac Practica.... Amsterdam: 1647. V. 63

MARON, MARGARET
Bootlegger's Daughter. 1992. V. 67
Bootlegger's Daughter. New York: 1992. V. 62

MAROT, JEAN
Le Magnifique Chasteau de Richelieu, en General et en Particulier.... Paris: 1660. V. 64

MARQUAND, JOHN P.
Wickford Point. Boston: 1939. V. 62

MARQUIS, DON
Chapters for the Orthodox. Garden City: 1934. V. 62
Full and By, Being Verses in Praise of Drinking. London: 1925. V. 67
Master of the Revels. Garden City: 1934. V. 62

MARQUIS, DONALD M.
In Search of Buddy Bolden. First Man of Jazz. Baton Rouge: 1978. V. 67

MARQUIS, THOMAS B.
Custer, Cavalry and Crows, the Story of William White As Told to.... Fort Collins: 1975. V. 65; 67
Memoirs of a White Crow Indian. New York: 1928. V. 64; 65; 67

MARRACCI, LODOVICO
Rimedio Per Curare la Vanita' Feminile Composto Tre Ingresienti. Roma: 1680. V. 65

MARRAKECH.. Milano: 1992. V. 66

MARRIAGE A-La-Mode. London: 1858. V. 62

THE MARRIAGE of Cock Robin and Jenny Wren. London: 1880. V. 65

MARRIOTT, ALICE
These Are the People: Some Notes on the Southwestern Indians. New Mexico: 1949. V. 63; 64

MARRIOTT, CHARLES
The Cooperative Principle Not Opposed to a True Political Economy, or Remarks on Some Recent Publications on Subjects.... Oxford: 1855. V. 64

MARRIOTT, EDME
The Motion of Water and Other Fluids. London: 1718. V. 64; 66

MARRIOTT, ERNEST
Jack B. Yeats: His Pictorial and Dramatic Art. London: 1911. V. 63

MARRIOTT, WILLIAM
A Collection of English Miracles Plays of Mysteries. Basel: 1838. V. 66
The Country Gentleman's Lawyer, and the Farmer's Complete Law Library.... London: 1812. V. 65

MARROT, H. V.
William Bulmer, Thomas Bensley, a Study in Transition. London: 1930. V. 63; 64

MARRYAT, FLORENCE
The Blood of the Vampire. Leipzig: 1897. V. 65

MARRYAT, FRANK S.
Borneo and the Indian Archipelago. London: 1848. V. 64
Mountains and Mole-Hills: or Recollections of a Burnt Journal. London: 1855. V. 62
Mountains and Molehills or Recollections on a Burnt Journal. New York: 1855. V. 66

MARRYAT, FREDERICK
A Diary in America, with Remarks on Its Institutions, with Part Second. Paris: 1839-1840. V. 65
The Dog Fiend; or, Snarleyyow. London: 1862. V. 67
The Floral Telegraph; or Affection's Signals. London: 1850. V. 67
Japhet, in Search of a Father. Trenton: 1835. V. 63
Japhet, in Search of a Father. London: 1836. V. 67
Japhet, in Search of a Father. London: 1854. V. 67
Masterman Ready; or, the Wreck of the Pacific. London: 1841. V. 63
Masterman Ready; or, the Wreck of the Pacific. London: 1841-1842. V. 66
The Pirate; and the Three Cutters. London: 1836. V. 66
The Settlers in Canada. London: 1844. V. 66
Valerie, an Autobiography. 1857. V. 67

MARS, F. ST.
The Prowlers. 1913. V. 67

MARS, JAMES
Life of James Mars, a Slave Born and Sold in Connecticut. Written by Himself. Hartford: 1864. V. 63; 66

MARSAN, C. AJMONE
Seizure Atlas. Electroencephalography and Clinical Neurophysiology: an International Journal Supplement 15. Montreal: 1960. V. 65

MARSDEN, KATE
On Sledge and Horseback to Outcast Siberian Lepers. London: 1892. V. 62
On Sledge and Horseback to Outcast Siberian Lepers. London: 1893. V. 65

MARSDEN, WILLIAM
A Brief Memoir of the Life and Writings.... London: 1838. V. 64

MARSH, ANDREW
Marsh's Manual of Reformed Phonetic Short-Hand. San Francisco: 1868. V. 65

MARSH, ANNE
Two Olde Men's Tales. The Deformed and The Admiral's Daughter. London: 1004. V. 66

MARSH, BOWER
Alumni Carthusiani. London: 1913. V. 62; 66

MARSH, C. C.
A Course of Practice in Single Entry Book-Keeping, Improved by a Proof or Balance and Applied to Partnership Business. New York: 1859. V. 67

MARSH, CHARLES
The Clubs of London; with Anecdotes of Their Members, Sketches of Their Character and Conversations. London: 1828. V. 63
Recollections 1837-1910. Chicago: 1910. V. 64; 67

MARSH, E. L.
Where the Buffalo Roamed. Toronto: 1980. V. 64; 67

MARSH, GEORGE
Twelve Sermons Preach'd on Several Publick Occasions. London: 1737. V. 67

MARSH, GEORGE P.
The Camel: His Organization, Habits and Uses Considered with Reference to His Introduction into the U.S. Boston: 1856. V. 67

MARSH, HONORIA
Jane Austen and Her Times. London: 1905. V. 66
Shades from Jane Austen. London: 1975. V. 63

MARSH, JOHN
Decimal Arithmetic Made Perfect; or, the Management of Infinite Decimals Displayed. London: 1742. V. 65

MARSH, NGAIO
Death of a Peer. Boston: 1940. V. 67
Final Curtain. London: 1947. V. 66
Singing in the Shrouds. Boston: 1958. V. 67
Singing in the Shrouds. London: 1959. V. 67
Swing, Brother Swing. London: 1949. V. 66

MARSH, O. C.
Dinocerata. A Monograph of an Extinct Order of Gigantic Mammals. Washington: 1886. V. 65
Dinocerata; a Monograph of an Extinct Order of Gigantic Animals. Washington: 1884. V. 62; 65
Odontornithes: a Monograph on the Extinct Toothed Birds of North America.... Washington: 1880. V. 65
On Some Characters of the Genus Coryphodon, Owen. New Haven: 1876. V. 67
On Some Characters of the Tillodontia. New Haven: 1876. V. 67
On the Odontornithes or Birds with Teeth; Notice of New Odontornithes. New Haven: 1875-1876. V. 67
Principal Characters of the Dinocerata. New Haven: 1876. V. 67

MARSHAK, SAMUEL
Master-Lomaster. Leningrad: 1930. V. 64
Pudel. (Poodle). Leningrad: 1927. V. 64
Vanka-Vstanka. Moscow: 1944. V. 64

MARSHAL, ANDREW
Morbid Anatomy of the Brain, in Mania ad Hydrophobia.... London: 1815. V. 64

MARSHALL, AGNES B.
Mrs. A. B. Marshall's Cookery Book. London. V. 63
Mrs. A. B. Marshall's Cookery Book. London: 1899?. V. 65

MARSHALL, ALFRED
Elements of Economics of Industry Being the First Volume of Elements of Economics. London and New York: 1892. V. 66
Money Credit and Commerce. London: 1923. V. 66
Official Papers. London: 1926. V. 64
Principles of Economics. London: 1891. V. 62
Principles of Economics...Volume I. London: 1895. V. 63

MARSHALL, C.
An Introduction to the Knowledge and Practice of Gardening. 1798. V. 63; 66

MARSHALL Cavendish *Encyclopaedia of Gardening.* 1968-1970. V. 66

MARSHALL, CHARLES
An Aide-De-Camp of Lee. Boston: 1927. V. 65

MARSHALL, E.
The Heart of the Hunter. 1957. V. 67
Shikar & Safari. 1950. V. 67

MARSHALL, FRANCES
Old English Embroidery: Its Technique and Symbolism. London: 1894. V. 62

MARSHALL, GEORGE
Epistles in Verse, Between Cynthio and Leonora. Newcastle: 1812. V. 63

MARSHALL, H. RISSIK
Coloured Worcester Porcelain of the First Period (1751-1783). Newport: 1954. V. 66

MARSHALL, HUMPHRY
Arbustrum Americanum: the American Grove, or an Alphabetical Catalogue of Forest Trees and Shrubs.... Philadelphia: 1785. V. 63; 66

MARSHALL, J. T.
The Farmers and Emigrants Complete Guide or a Hand Book.... Cincinnati: 1857. V. 63

MARSHALL, JACK
Journey Among Men. London: 1962. V. 65

MARSHALL, JOHN
Atlas to Marshall's Life of Washington. Philadelphia: 1832. V. 64; 67
Life of George Washington. London: 1804-1807. V. 66
The Life of George Washington. Philadelphia: 1804-1807. V. 63; 64; 65
The Royal Navy Biography; or, Memoirs of the Services of All the Flag Officers, Superannuated Rear Admirals, Retired-Captains, Post-Captains and Commanders, Whose Names Appeared on the Admiralty List of Sea Officers at the Commencement of the Present Yea. London: 1823-1835. V. 67
The Village Paedagogue: a Poem, and Other Lesser Pieces; Together with a Walk from Newcastle to Keswick. Newcastle: 1817. V. 65

MARSHALL, JOHN A.
American Bastille. Philadelphia: 1869. V. 63
American Bastille. Philadelphia: 1884. V. 63

MARSHALL, JOHN DRUMMOND
Notes on the Statistics and Natural History of the Island of Rathlin, Off the Northern Coast of Ireland. Dublin: 1836. V. 62

MARSHALL, JOSEPH, PSEUD.
Travels through Holland, Flanders, Germany, Denmark, Sweden, Lapland, Russia, the Ukraine and Poland in the Years 1768, 1769 and 1700. London: 1772. V. 67

MARSHALL, JULIAN
The Annals of Tennis. London: 1878. V. 63

MARSHALL, JULIAN, MRS.
The Life and Letters of Mary Wollstonecraft Shelley. London: 1889. V. 67

MARSHALL, NINA L.
Mushroom Book. New York: 1903. V. 67

MARSHALL, PAULE
The Chosen Place, the Timeless People. New York: 1969. V. 62
Soul Clap Hands and Sing. New York: 1961. V. 64

MARSHALL, PETER
Let's Keep Christmas. New York: 1953. V. 64

MARSHALL, RACHEL
Archibald. London: 1915. V. 63

MARSHALL, THOMAS HAY
The History of Perth, from the Earliest Period to the Present Time. Perth: 1849. V. 62

MARSHALL, W. P.
Description of the Patent Locomotive Steam Engine of Messrs. Robert Stephenson and Co. London: 1838. V. 65; 66

MARSHALL, W. T.
Cactaceae. Pasadena: 1941. V. 66

MARSHALL, WILLIAM
Minutes, Experiments, Observations and General Remarks on Agriculture in the Southern Counties. To Which is prefixed, A Sketch of the Vale of London and an Outline of Its Rural Economy.... London: 1799. V. 65
Planting and Ornamental Gardening: a Practical Treatise. London: 1785. V. 64; 66
Planting and Rural Ornament. London: 1796. V. 63; 65
A Review of the Landscape, a Didactic Poem: Also of an Essay on the Picturesque.... London: 1795. V. 66

MARSHALL, WILLIAM continued
The Rural Economy of Gloucestershire.... 1796. V. 63; 66
The Rural Economy of Gloucestershire.... London: 1796. V. 62
The Rural Economy of the Midland Counties.... London: 1790. V. 65
The Rural Economy of the Midland Counties.... London: 1796. V. 65
The Rural Economy of the Southern Counties.... London: 1798. V. 65
The Rural Economy of the West of England. London: 1796. V. 62; 65
The Rural Economy of the West of England. Dublin: 1797. V. 64
The Rural Economy of Yorkshire. London: 1788. V. 63

MARSIGLI, L. F. DE
Histoire Physique de la Mer.... Amsterdam: 1724. V. 66

MARSOLLIER, JACQUES
The Life of St. Francis of Sales, Bishop of Prince of Geneva, Founder of the Order of the Visitation. London: 1737. V. 62

MARSON, CYRIL DARBY
Fishing for Salmon. London: 1929. V. 67

MARSTON, ANNE LEE
Records of a California Family, Journals and Letters of Lewis C. Gunn and Elizabeth Le Breton Gunn. San Diego: 1928. V. 66

MARSTON, CHARLES DALLAS
Poems. Cambridge: 1849. V. 66

MARSTON, E.
An Amateur Angler's Days in Dove Dale, or How I Spent My Three Weeks Holiday (July 24-Aug. 14, 1884). London: 1884. V. 63
Easy Chair Memories and Rambling Notes. London: 1911. V. 67
Frank's Ranch or My Holiday in the Rockies. Boston: 1886. V. 63; 66

MARSTON, EDWARD
After Work: Fragments from the Workshop of an Old Publisher. London: 1904. V. 65

MARSTON, JOHN
The Metamorphosis of Pigmalion's Image. Waltham St. Lawrence: 1926. V. 62; 64; 65

MARSTON, R. B.
Walton and Some Earlier Writers on Fish and Fishing. London: 1894. V. 67
Walton and Some Earlier Writers on Fish and Fishing. 1903. V. 67

MARTEAU, LUDOVICUS RENATUS
Quaestio Diaetetica...an Ad Sanitatem Musice?. Paris: 1743. V. 65

MARTENS, FREDERICK H.
Little Picture Songs. London. V. 62

MARTHOLD, J. DE
Le Grand Napoleon des Petits Enfans. Paris: 1893. V. 64

MARTIAL, LYDIE
La Femme et la Liberte. Le Feminisme. La Grandeur de son But. Femme Integrale. Paris: 1901. V. 63

MARTIALIS, MARCUS VALERIUS
Epigrammata. Lugd(uni) Batavorum: 1670. V. 64
Epigrammata. 1823-1822. V. 65
Epigrammata ad Optimas Editiones Collata. Biponti (i.e. Zweibrucken): 1784. V. 65
Epigrammata cum Notis Farnabaii et Variorum Gemino Indice tum Rerum tum Auctorum.... Lugd. Batavorum: 1661. V. 65; 66
Epigrammaton Libri XIIII. Lugdini: 1549. V. 65; 66
The Epigrams of M. Val. Martial, In Twelve Books. With a Comment by James Elphinston.... London: 1782. V. 65; 66; 67
Epigrammatum Libri XIV. Paris: 1601. V. 66

MARTIN, A. R.
Franciscan Architecture in England. London: 1937. V. 62

MARTIN, BENJAMIN
Biographia Philosophica Being an Account of the Lives, Writings, Inventions of the Most Eminent Philosophers and Mathematicians Who Have Flourished from the Earliest Ages of the World to the Present Time. London: 1764. V. 65
The Philosophical Grammar.... London: 1748. V. 62; 66

MARTIN, BENJAMIN ELLIS
The Stones of Paris in History and Letters. New York: 1899. V. 62; 67

MARTIN, BRIAN
Sporting Birds of the British Isles. 1984. V. 67

MARTIN, CECIL P.
Prehistoric Man In Ireland. 1935. V. 63; 66

MARTIN, CHARLES WYKEHAM
The History and Description of Leeds, Castle, Kent. London: 1869. V. 67

MARTIN, CLAIRE
The Race of the Golden Apples. New York: 1991. V. 65

MARTIN, E. S.
Martin's System of Practical Penmanship Taught in 24 Lessons at His Writing and Book Keeping Academy.... Worcester: 1847. V. 66
Martin's System of Practical Penmanship Taught in 24 Lessons at His Writing and Book Keeping Academy.... Worcester: 1848. V. 64

MARTIN, EDWARD A.
A Bibliography of Gilbert White.... London: 1934. V. 63
A Bibliography of Gilbert White.... London: 1970. V. 62

MARTIN, EDWARD SANDFORD
Abroad with Jane. Boston: 1918. V. 62; 63

MARTIN, EUSTACE MEREDYTH
A Tour through India in Lord Canning's Time. London: 1881. V. 65

MARTIN, F.
Martin's Natural History. New York. V. 66
Martin's Natural History. New York: Sep. 1850. V. 65

MARTIN, F. X.
The Scholar Revolutionary: Eoin MacNeill 1867-1945 and the Making of New Ireland. 1973. V. 67

MARTIN, FRANK
Newhaven Dieppe Recollections and Some History of the Town of Dieppe. London: 1996. V. 62; 67
The Wood Engravings of Frank Martin. London: 1998. V. 66

MARTIN, FREDERICK
The Life of John Clare. London and Cambridge: 1865. V. 66

MARTIN, GREGORY
A Discoverie of the Manifold Corruptions of the Holy Scriptures by the Heretikes of Our Daies, Specially the English Sectaries, and Of Their Foule Dealing Herein, by Partial and False Translations to the Advantage of Their Heresies, in their English Bibl. Rheims: 1582. V. 64

MARTIN, H. BRADLEY
The Library of H. Bradley Martin. New York: 1989. V. 63; 64; 66
The Library of H. Bradley Martin. New York: 1989-1990. V. 63; 67

MARTIN, H. G.
Sunset from the Main. 1951. V. 67

MARTIN, HELEN EASTMAN
The History of Los Angeles County Hospital (1878-1968) and the Los Angeles County University of Southern California Medical Center (1968-1978). Los Angeles: 1968-1978. V. 63

MARTIN, ISAAC
A Journal of the Life, Travels, Labours and Religious Exercises of Isaac Martin, Late of Rahway, in East Jersey, Deceased. Philadelphia: 1834. V. 63; 66
The Tryal and Sufferings of Mr. Isaac Martin, Who was put into the Inquisition in Spain, for the Sake of the Protestant Religion.... London: 1723-1724. V. 65

MARTIN, J. W.
My Fishing Days and Fishing Ways. 1906. V. 62; 63
Roach, Rudd and Bream Fishing in Many Waters. 1905. V. 63
The Trent Otter's Little Angling Book. 1910. V. 67

MARTIN, JACK
Border Boss - Captain John R. Hughes Texas Ranger. San Antonio: 1942. V. 62

MARTIN, JACQUELINE BRIGGS
Snowflake Bentley. Boston: 1998. V. 65

MARTIN, JAMES C.
Maps of Texas and the Southwest 1530-1900. Albuquerque: 1984. V. 62

MARTIN, JOHN
America Dancing. New York: 1936. V. 67
A Bibliographical Catalogue of Books Privately Printed.... London: 1834. V. 62
Characters of Trees.... London: 1817. V. 64
Illustrations of the Bible. By Westall and Martin. London: 1835-1836. V. 65

MARTIN, JONATHAN
The Life of Jonathan Martin, of Darlington, Tanner. Written by Himself. Lincoln: 1828. V. 63
Report of the Trial of Jonathan Martin, for Having, on the Night of the First of February 1829, Set Fire to York Minster. London: 1829. V. 63
The Trial of Jonathan Martin, at the Castle of York, on Tuesday, March 31, 1829, for Setting Fire to York Minster. York: 1830. V. 64

MARTIN, JOSEPH
A New and Comprehensive Gazetteer of Virginia and the District of Columbia. Charlottesville: 1835. V. 65
Select Tales. Charlottesville: 1833. V. 63; 66

MARTIN, JOSEPH G.
Martin's Boston Stock Market. Eighty-Five Years from Jan. 1798 to Jan. 1886...with Full Descriptive Notes Relating to the Different Securities. Boston: 1886. V. 62

MARTIN, LOUIS
L'Eschole De Salerne en Svite Le Poeme Macraroniqve. Paris: 1664. V. 66

MARTIN, MARIA
History of the Captivity and Sufferings of Maria Martin, Who Was Six Years a Slave in Algiers. New York: 1813. V. 64

MARTIN, MARIE B.
Within the Rock. New York: 1925. V. 67

MARTIN, P. J.
A Geological Memoir on a Part of Western Sussex; With Some Observations Upon Chalk-Basins, The Weald-Denudation and Outliers by Protrusion. London: 1828. V. 66

MARTIN, PAUL S.
Lowry Ruins in Southwestern Colorado. Chicago: 1936. V. 64

MARTIN, PETE
Will Acting Spoil Marilyn Monroe?. New York: 1956. V. 66

MARTIN, R. D.
Primate Origins and Evolution, a Phylogenetic Reconstruction. Princeton: 1990. V. 64

MARTIN, ROBERT BERNARD
Gerard Manley Hopkins - A Very Private Life. London: 1991. V. 64

MARTIN, ROBERT MONTGOMERY
History of the Colonies of the British Empire in the West Indies, South America, North America, Asia, Austral-Asia, Africa and Europe.... London: 1843. V. 64
The Political, Commercial and Financial Condition of the Anglo- Eastern Empire in 1832.... London: 1833. V. 63

MARTIN, SAMUEL
An Essay Upon Plantership, Humbly Inscribed to His Excellency George Thomas, Esq.... Antigua and London: 1765. V. 63

MARTIN, SAMUEL MC DONALD
New Zealand: In a Series of Letters.... London: 1845. V. 64

MARTIN, SARA
Gulf Coast Blues. New York: 1923. V. 66

MARTIN, SARAH CATHERINE
Old Mother Hubbard. Oxford. V. 64

MARTIN, T. C.
The Electric Motor and its Applications. New York: 1892. V. 62

MARTIN, T. MOWER
Canada Painted by.... London: 1907. V. 67

MARTIN, THOMAS
The Circle of the Mechanical Arts, Containing Practical Treatises on the Various Manual Arts, Trades and Manufactures. London: 1815. V. 63
The Nature and Improvement of the Christian Ministry: a Sermon Preached in the Methodist Chapel, Bath, June 30, 1812, Before the Preaches of the Bristol District. London: 1812. V. 64

MARTIN, THOMAS RICAUD
The Great Parliamentary Battle and Farewell Addresses of the Southern Senators on the Eve of the Civil War. New York & Washington: 1905. V. 63; 65

MARTIN, W. A. P.
A Cycle of Cathay or China, South and North. London: 1896. V. 62

MARTIN, WILLIAM
A New System of Natural Philosophy, on the Principle of Perpetual Motion.... Newcastle: 1821. V. 63

MARTIN, WILLIAM MAXWELL
Lyrics and Sketches. Nashville: 1861. V. 62

MARTINDALE, T.
Sport Indeed. Philadelphia: 1901. V. 67

MARTINDALE, THOMAS
Hunting in the Upper Yukon. Philadelphia: 1913. V. 64

MARTIN DU GARD, ROGER
Summer 1914. New York: 1941. V. 66

MARTINE, GEORGE
Essays & Observations on the Construction and Graduation of Thermometers and On the Heating and Cooling of Bodies. Edinburgh: 1780. V. 65

MARTINEAU, HARRIET
British Rule in India: an Historical Sketch. London: 1857. V. 65
A Complete Guide to the English Lakes. London: 1855. V. 65
A Complete Guide to the English Lakes. Windermere: 1858. V. 65
A Complete Guide to the English Lakes. London: 1866. V. 63
Deerbrook. London: 1839. V. 65; 67
Eastern Life, Present and Past. London: 1848. V. 64; 65
England and Her Soldiers. London: 1859. V. 65
English Lakes. Windermere: 1858. V. 66
The Factory Controversy: a Warning Against Meddling Legislation.... Manchester: 1855. V. 62
Feats on the Fiord. (with) *The Billow and the Rock.* London: 1846. V. 65
Guide to Windermere, with Tours to the Neighbouring Lakes and Other Interesting Places.... Windermere: 1854. V. 66
Harriet Martineau's Autobiography. London: 1877. V. 63; 64; 66
The History of England During the Thirty Years' Peace: 1816-1846. London: 1849-1850. V. 65
History of the Peace: Being a History of England from 1816 to 1854, With an Introduction 1800 to 1815. Boston: 1864. V. 66
Illustrations of Political Economy. London: 1832-1833. V. 66
Letters from Ireland. London: 1852. V. 63
Poor Laws and Paupers Illustrated. London: 1833-1834. V. 65
Retrospect of Western Travel. London: 1838. V. 65
The Sickness and Health of the People of Bleaburn. Boston: 1853. V. 63
Society in America. London: 1837. V. 65
Society in America. New York: 1837. V. 66

MARTINEAU, JAMES
Ireland and Her Famine: a Discourse. 1847. V. 63
Unitarianism Defended: a Series of Lectures by Three Protestant Dissenting Ministers of Liverpool. Liverpool: 1839. V. 66

MARTINEAU, L.
La Prostitution Clandestine. Paris: 1885. V. 66

MARTINEAU, R. A. S.
Rhodesian Wild Flowers. Cape Town: 1953. V. 67

MARTINEAU, VIOLET
John Martineau, the Pupil of Kinglsey. London: 1921. V. 67

MARTINELLI *Nuova Raccolta dei Costumi della Corte Ponteficia e Suoi Addetti Alle Cerimonie.* Rome: 1870. V. 64

MARTINELLI, AGOSTINO
Descrittione di Diversi Ponti Esistenti Sopra li Fiumi Nera, e Tevere con un Discorso Particolare della Navigatione da Perugia a Roma. Rome: 1676. V. 65

MARTINET, J. F.
The Catechism of Nature; for the Use of Children. London: 1797. V. 63
The Catechism of Nature, for the Use of Children. Trenton: 1812. V. 66

MARTINEZ, DIONOSIO
Bad Alchemy. New York: 1995. V. 67

MARTINEZ, TOMAS
Lugar Comun de la Muerte. Caracas: 1978. V. 67

MARTINSSON-WALLIN, HELENE
Ahu - the Ceremonial Stone Structures of Easter Island. Uppsala: 1994. V. 66

MARTINUS, EMMANUEL
Epistolarum Libri Duodecim. Amsterdam: 1738. V. 67

MARTON, FRANCESCA
Mrs. Betsy or Widowed and Wed. New York: 1955. V. 66

MARTYN, BENJAMIN
An Impartial Enquiry Into the State and Utility of the Province of Georgia. London: 1741. V. 63; 66
Timoleon. London: 1730. V. 66

MARTYN, C.
A Chronological Series of Engravers from the Invention of the Art to the Beginning of the Present Century. Cambridge: 1770. V. 67

MARTYN, THOMAS
Aranei, or a Natural History of Spiders.. 1793. V. 64
Guide du Voyageur en Italie. Lausanne: 1791. V. 64

MARTYN, WYNDHAM
Stones of Enchantment. London: 1948. V. 67

MARTZ, HENRY
Alaska-Yukon Pacific Exposition 1909. An International Fair June 1 to October 15 Showing the Products, Resources, Advantages and Scenic Beauty of the Alaska-Yukon Country. Seattle: 1908. V. 63

MARULLI, VINCENZO
L'Arte di Ordinare i Giardini. Naples: 1804. V. 64

MARVAL, JACQUELINE
Extrait de L'Art d'Aujourd'hui. Paris: 1932. V. 63

MARVELL, ANDREW
The Complete Works in Verse and Prose of Andrew Marvell. London: 1872-1875. V. 64
Miscellaneous Poems. London: 1923. V. 62
Poems and Letters. Oxford: 1971. V. 63

MARX, ENID
An A B C Of Birds and Beasts. London: 1985. V. 66

MARX, GROUCHO
Memoirs of a Mangy Lover. New York: 1963. V. 63

MARX, KARL
Lo Capital. Paris: 1875. V. 66; 67
Capital. London: 1901. V. 64
Capital. Chicago: 1919-1915-1909. V. 65
Capital. Chicago: 1932. V. 64

MARYE, GEORGE T.
From '49 to '83 In California and Nevada. Chapters from the Life of George Thomas Mayre, a Pioneer of '49. San Francisco: 1923. V. 63; 66

MARYLAND
The Report of and Testimony Taken Before the Joint Committee of the Senate and House of Delegates of Maryland To Which Was Referred the Memorials of John B. Morris, Reverdy Johnson and Others.... Annapolis: 1836. V. 63; 66

MARY'S *New Doll: Its Fortunes and Misfortunes.* London: 1866. V. 64

MARZIO, PETER C.
Democratic Art. Pictures for a 19th Century America. Boston and Ft. Worth: 1979. V. 62

MASCAGNI, PAOLO
Prodromo Della Grande Anatomia. Opera Postuma.... Milan: 1821. V. 65; 67
Vasorum Lymphaticorum Corporis Humani Historia et Ichnographia. Sienna: 1787. V. 65

MASCALL, EDWARD JAMES
A Digest of the Duties of Customs and Excise, Payable Upon All Foreign Articles Imported Into or Exported from Great Britain.... London: 1810. V. 62

MASCOU, JOHN JACOB
The History of the Ancient Germans, Including that of the Cimbri, Celtae, Teutones, Alemanni, Saxons and Other Ancient Northern Nations Who Overthrew the Roman Empire and Established that of the Germans and Most of the Kingdoms of Europe. London and Westminster: 1737-1738. V. 64

MASEFIELD, JOHN
The Coming of Christ. New York: 1928. V. 63
The Country Scene. London: 1937. V. 67
The Dream. London: 1922. V. 63
The Hawbucks. London: 1929. V. 64
John M. Synge: a Few Personal Recollections. Churchtown, Dundrum: 1915. V. 62; 64; 67
King Cole. 1921. V. 67
The Ledbury Scene as I Have Used It In My Verse. Oxford: 1951. V. 62
Martin Hyde - the Duke's Messenger. London: 1910. V. 64
Midsummer Night and Other Tales in Verse. London: 1928. V. 63
Odtaa - a Novel. London: 1926. V. 62; 64
Salt Water Ballads. 1913. V. 63
Sea Life in Nelson's Times. London: 1905. V. 62
Shopping in Oxford (a Poem). London: 1941. V. 62; 65
Some Memories of W. B. Yeats. Dublin: 1940. V. 62; 65
The Wanderer of Liverpool. London: 1930. V. 64

MASEFIELD, ROBERT BLACHFORD
The Log of the Water Lily Being Three Cruises on the Rhine, Neckar, Main, Moselle, Danube, Saone, and the Rhone. London: 1873. V. 67

MASEN, JAKOB
Sarcotis Carmen. Coloniae Agrippinae, et veni: 1757. V. 64; 66

MASI, GIROLAMO
Teoria e Pratica di Archittettura Civile. Rome: 1788. V. 64

MASINI, L. V.
Art Nouveau. Secaucus: 1984. V. 65

MASINI, NICOLO
De Gelidi Potus Abusu Libri Tres. Caesenae: 1587. V. 64

THE MASK. Florence: 1927. V. 66

MASKELL, ALFRED
Wood Sculpture. London: 1911. V. 64

MASKELL, WILLIAM
Holy Baptism. London: 1848. V. 66

MASKELYNE, JOHN NEVIL
Sharps and Flats. London: 1894. V. 66

MASKELYNE, NEVIL
An Account of the Going of Mr. John Harrison's Watch, at the Royal Observatory, from May 6th 1766 to March 4th 1767.... London: 1767. V. 65

MASON, A. E. W.
At the Villa Rosa. New York: 1910. V. 67
The Broken Road. New York: 1906. V. 64
The Life of Francis Drake. London: 1941. V. 62
The Royal Exchange - a Note on the Bicentenary of the Royal Exchange Assurance. London: 1920. V. 62
The Sapphire. London: 1933. V. 65
The Three Gentlemen. Garden City: 1932. V. 65

MASON, A. J.
What Became of the Bones of St. Thomas?. Cambridge: 1920. V. 67

MASON, ARTHUR
The Wee Men of Ballywooden. Garden City: 1930. V. 64

MASON, BERNARD
Clock and Watchmaking in Colchester England. London: 1969. V. 65

MASON, BOBBIE ANN
The Girl Sleuths. 1975. V. 65
In Country. New York: 1985. V. 67
Nabokov's Garden: a Guide to Ada. Ann Arbor: 1974. V. 63
Shiloh and Other Stories. New York: 1982. V. 62; 63; 66; 67
With Jazz. Monterey: 1994. V. 62; 64

MASON, CHARLES WELSH
The Chest of Opium. London: 1898. V. 63
The Chinese Confessions of Charles Welsh Mason. London: 1924. V. 67

MASON, EDWARD T.
Songs of Fairy Land. New York: 1886. V. 65

MASON, FRANCIS
Vindiciae Ecclesiae Anglicanae.... London: 1625. V. 63

MASON, GEORGE
An Essay on Design in Gardening. London: 1768. V. 64

MASON, GEORGE FINCH
Flowers of the Hunt. London: 1889. V. 67
Sporting Recollections of Hunting, Shooting, Steeplechasing, Racing, Cricket &c. London: 1886. V. 67

MASON, GEORGE HENRY
The Punishments of China. London: 1808. V. 65

MASON, HENRY J. M.
Primitive Christianity in Ireland: a Letter to Thomas Moore. London: 1836. V. 66

MASON, JAMES
Before I Forget - an Autobiography of Drawings. London: 1981. V. 62
The Old Nursery Rhymes or the Merrie Heart. London: 1874. V. 63

MASON, JOANNIS
C. Plinii Secundi Junioris Vita Ordine Chronologico sic Digesta. Amsterdam: 1709. V. 65

MASON, JOHN
An Essay on Elocution or, Pronunciation. London: 1751. V. 62; 65
Memoir of the Case of St. John Mason, Esq. Barrister at Law, Who Was Confined, as a State-Prisoner in Kilmainham (Prison, Co. Meath), for More than 2 Years.... Dublin: 1807. V. 63
Paper Making as an Artistic Craft. London: 1959. V. 65
Paper Making as an Artistic Craft. Leicester: 1963. V. 62
Paper Making as an Artistic Craft. London: 1963. V. 67

MASON, KENNETH
Abode of Snow. 1955. V. 63; 65
Abode of Snow. London: 1955. V. 63; 64

MASON, OTIS TUFTON
Aboriginal American Basketry: Studies in a Textile Art Without Machinery. Washington: 1904. V. 63; 64
Women's Share in Primitive Culture. New York: 1894. V. 65

MASON, RICHARD
Angling Experiences and Reminiscences. 1900. V. 67
The Gentleman's New Pocket Farrier.... Richmond: 1828. V. 64

MASON, ROBERT LINDSAY
The Lure of the Great Smokies. Boston: 1927. V. 63; 66

MASON, STUART
Art and Morality. London: 1908. V. 66
Bibliography of Oscar Wilde. London: 1914. V. 62; 67
Oscar Wilde. Oxford: 1905. V. 63

MASON, THOMAS H.
The Islands of Ireland. 1938. V. 67

MASON, VAN WYCK
The Rio Casino Intrigue. New York: 1941. V. 66
The Shanghai Bund Murders. Garden City: 1933. V. 66
Spider House. New York: 1932. V. 67

MASON, WILLIAM
Caractacus. A Dramatic Poem. York: 1777. V. 65
The English Garden. London: 1772. V. 62
The English Garden. York: 1777-1781. V. 66
The English Garden. York: 1783. V. 62; 66
An Heroic Epistle to Sir William Chambers. London: 1773. V. 66
An Heroic Epistle to Sir William Chambers. 1773-1774. V. 66
Isis an Elegy. London: 1749. V. 62; 65
Musaeus: a Monody to the Memory of Mr. Pope. London: 1747. V. 63
Musaeus: a Monody to the Memory of Mr. Pope. London: 1748. V. 62
Ode to Mr. Pinchbeck, Upon His Newly Invented Patent Candle Snuffers by Malcolm McGreggor. London: 1776. V. 62
Odes. Cambridge: 1756. V. 63; 64; 65
Odes. London: 1756. V. 66
Poems. London: 1764. V. 62
Poems. York: 1771. V. 62
Poems. York: 1779. V. 62
Poems. York: 1796. V. 66
Poems. York: 1796-1797. V. 62

MASON, WILLIAM MONCK
Suggestions Relative to the Project of a Survey and Valuation of Ireland.... Dublin: 1825. V. 65

MASPERO, G.
The Dawn of Civilization: Egypt and Chaldea. London: 1894. V. 62
The Passing of the Empires 850 B.C. to 330 B.C. New York: 1900. V. 67
The Struggle of the Nations, Egypt, Syria and Assyria.... London: 1896. V. 62

MASQUES IV. Baltimore: 1991. V. 66

MASSACHUSETTS
Record of the Massachusetts Volunteers 1861-1865. Boston: 1968. V. 65

MASSACHUSETTS. CONSTITUTION - 1780
An Address for the Convention for Framing a New Constitution of Government, for the State of Massachusetts Bay, to Their Constituents. Boston: 1780. V. 63

MASSACHUSETTS. CONSTITUTION - 1853
Official Report of the Debates and Proceedings of the State Convention, Assembled May 4th, 1853 to Revise and Amend the Constitution of...Massachusetts. Boston: 1853. V. 64

MASSACHUSETTS. LAWS, STATUTES, ETC. - 1793
Acts and Laws Passed by the General Court of Massachusetts...An Act for Regulating and Governing the Militia of the Commonwealth of Massachusetts. Boston: 1793. V. 64

MASSACHUSETTS. LAWS, STATUTES, ETC. - 1836
The Revised Statutes of...Passed November 4, 1835; to Which are Sub-joined an Act in Amendment...Passed in Febrarury 1836.... Boston: 1836. V. 65

MASSACHUSETTS BAY COLONY. LAWS, STATUTES, ETC. - 1774
An Act, Passed by the Great and General Court or Assembly of the Province of the Massachuseets Bay in New England. Boston: 1774. V. 64

MASSACHUSETTS GENERAL HOSPTIAL
Memorial and Historical Volume. (with) Proceedings of the Centennial of the Opening of the Hospital. Boston: 1921. V. 64

MASSACHUSETTS HORTICULTURAL SOCIETY
Catalogue of the Library of the Massachusetts Horticultural Society. Mansfield: 1994. V. 67

MASSACHUSETTS MEDICAL SOCIETY
The Acts of Incorporation, Together with the By-Laws and Orders of the Massachusetts Medical Society. Salem: 1806. V. 66
Address to the Community, on the Necessity of Legalizing the Study of Anantomy. Boston: 1829. V. 66
Medical Communications of the Massachusetts Medical Society. Second Series. Volume I parts 1 and 2. Boston: 1830-1831. V. 64; 66
Medical Papers, Communicated to the Massachusetts Medical Society. Boston: 1790. V. 63; 66
Medical Papers Communicated to the Massachusetts Medical Society.... Salem: 1806-1810. V. 64

MASSACHUSETTS SANITARY COMMISSION
Report of the Sanitary Commission of Massachusetts 1850. Cambridge: 1948. V. 65

THE MASSACRE of Lieutenant Grattan and His Command by Indians. Glendale: 1983. V. 65

MASSE, GERTRUDE
A Bibliography of First Editions of Books Illustrated by Walter Crane. London: 1923. V. 62; 67

MASSETT, STEPHEN C.
Drifting About or What Jeems Pipes of Pipesville Saw and Did. New York: 1863. V. 63; 65; 66

MASSEY, WILLIAM
A History of England During the Reign of George the Third. London: 1855-1863. V. 66

MASSIE, JOSEPH
Facts Which Shew the Necessity of Establishing a Regular Method for the Punctual, Frequent and Certain Payment of Seamen Employed in the Royal Navy. London: 1758. V. 62; 66

MASSIE, WILLIAM
Sydenham; or, Memoirs of a Man of the World. London: 1830. V. 65

MASSINGER, PHILIP
The Dramatic Works. London: 1851. V. 67
The Dramatick Works. London: 1779. V. 63
The Plays. London: 1813. V. 62
The Plays. London: 1830. V. 62

MASSINGHAM, H. J.
Country Relics. Cambridge: 1939. V. 63

MASSON, ANDRE
Nocturnal Notebook. New York: 1944. V. 62; 63; 64

MASSON, CHARLES
Narrative of Various Journeys in Balochinstan, Afghanistan, and the Panjab...(with) Narrative of a Journey to Kalat.... London: 1842-1843. V. 62; 66

MASSUET, PIERRE
Recherches Interessantes sur l'Origine, la Formation, le Development, la Structure &c.... Amsterdam: 1733. V. 64

MASSY, RICHARD TUTHILL
Analytical Ethnology; the Mixed Tribes in Great Britain and Ireland Examined, and the Political, Physical and Metaphysical Blunderings on the Celt and Saxon Exposed. (with) Mild Medicine in Contradistinction to Severe Medicine. London: 1855. V. 67

THE MASTER of Mysteries. 1912. V. 63

MASTERMAN, WALTER S.
The Wrong Letter. London: 1926. V. 65

MASTERPIECES of American Eloquence. New York: 1900. V. 63

MASTERS, E. L.
Psychedelic Art. New York: 1968. V. 66

MASTERS, EDGAR LEE
Across Spoon River, an Autobiography. New York: 1936. V. 63
Children of the Marketplace. New York: 1922. V. 62
Domesday Book. New York: 1920. V. 62
Godbey: a Dramatic Poem. New York: 1931. V. 66
The Great Valley. New York: 1916. V. 62
Maximillian: a Play in Five Acts. Boston: 1902. V. 62
The Serpent in the Wilderness. New York: 1932. V. 62
Spoon River Anthology. New York: 1915. V. 63; 65
Spoon River Anthology. London: 1917. V. 62
Spoon River Anthology. New York: 1942. V. 65

MASTERS, JOHN
The Deceivers. London: 1952. V. 63

MASTERS, JOSEPH G.
Shadows Across the Little Big Horn. Laramie: 1951. V. 65; 67

MASTERS, M. T.
Vegetable Teratology, an Account of the Principal Deviations from the Usual Construction of Plants. London: 1869. V. 62; 63

MASTERS, MARTIN KEDGWIN
Progress of Love. Boston: 1808. V. 62; 67

MASTERS, PRISCILLA
And None Shall Sleep. London: 1997. V. 67
Catch the Fallen Sparrow. London: 1996. V. 65; 67
Winding Up the Serpent. London: 1995. V. 65; 67
A Wreath for My Sister. London: 1997. V. 65; 67

MASUCCIO
The Novellino of Masuccio. London: 1895. V. 62; 64

MASUDA, H.
Coastal Fishes of Southern Japan. Tokyo: 1975. V. 62; 65
The Fishes of the Japanese Archipelago. Tokyo: 1984. V. 65

MASUI, MITSUZO
A Bibliography of Finance. New York: 1969. V. 62

MATHER, COTTON
Psalterium Americanum. The Book of Pslams, in a Translation Exactly Conformed Unto the Original; But All in Blank Verse.... Boston: 1718. V. 63
Ratio Disciplinae Fratrum Nov-Anglorum. A Faithful Account of the Discipline Professed and Practised; in the Churches of New England. Boston: 1726. V. 63; 66

MATHER, GEORGE MARSHALL
Neptune's Care, a Masque. Edinburgh: 1840. V. 64

MATHER, INCREASE
Brief History of the War with the Indians in New England from June 24, 1675.... London: 1676. V. 63; 66

MATHER, SAMUEL
An Apology for the Liberties of the Churches in New England. Boston: 1738. V. 66
The Life of the Very Reverend and Learned Cotton Mather. Boston: 1729. V. 65; 67

MATHER, WILLIAM
The Young Man's Companion; or Arithmetick Made Easy. London: 1755. V. 63

MATHERS, E. POWYS
A Circle of Seasons. Waltham St. Lawrence: 1929. V. 65
Love Night: a Laotian Gallantry. Waltham St. Lawrence: 1936. V. 62
Maxims and Considerations of Chamfort. Waltham St. Lawrence: 1926. V. 64
Procreant Hymn. Waltham St. Lawrence: 1926. V. 62
Red Wise. Waltham St. Lawrence: 1926. V. 62; 63; 65; 66

MATHERS, HELEN
A Man of To-Day. London: 1894. V. 65
My Lady Green Sleeves. London: 1879. V. 65

MATHES, J. HARVEY
Old Guard in Gray...Sketches of Memphis Veterans Who Upheld Her Standard in the War, and of Other Confederate Worthies. Memphis: 1897. V. 62; 63

MATHESON, ELIZABETH
Blithe Air: Photographs from England, Wales and Ireland. Winston Salem: 1995. V. 63

MATHESON, EWING
Works in Iron. Bridge and Roof Structures. London: 1873. V. 62

MATHESON, JAMES
The Present Position and Prospects of the British Trade with China. London: 1836. V. 64

MATHESON, JOHN
The Needle in the Haystack. New York: 1930. V. 66

MATHESON, RICHARD
Collected Stories. Los Angeles: 1989. V. 66
The Gun Fight. New York: 1993. V. 67
Hell House. New York: 1971. V. 62; 63
I Am Legend. New York: 1970. V. 62; 63
Journal of the Gun Years. New York: 1991. V. 67
Noir: Three Novels of Suspense. Delavan: 1997. V. 66
7 Steps to Midnight. New York: 1993. V. 67

MATHEW, JOHN
Certain Material and Useful Considerations About the Laws Positive, and Laws of Necessity, Relating to the Unhappy Distractions of the Present Times. London: 1680. V. 66

MATHEWS, ALFRED E.
Pencil Sketches of Colorado: Its Cities, Principal Towns and Mountain Scenery. Denver: 1961. V. 64

MATHEWS, ANNE
Memoirs of Charles Mathews, Comedian. London: 1839. V. 63

MATHEWS, CHARLES
The London Mathews.... London: 1825. V. 63
Sketches of Mr. Mathews' Celebrated Lecture on Character, Manners and Peculiarities, Entitled the Home Circuit.... London: 1827. V. 67

MATHEWS, CHARLES EDWARD
The Annals of Mont Blanc. London: 1898. V. 62; 63; 64; 66

MATHEWS, EDWARD B.
Report on the Location of the Boundary Line Among the Potomac River Between Virginia & Maryland. Baltimore: 1928. V. 63

MATHEWS, ELKIN
A Catalogue of Books Including a Fine and Important Collection of Scarce Works in Belles Lettres from the Private Library of Elkin Mathews. London: 1923. V. 64

MATHEWS, G. M.
Checklist to the Mathews Ornithological Collection. Canberra: 1966. V. 62
Systema Avium Australasianarm. 1927. V. 62; 63; 64; 66

MATHEWS, GEORGE
Account of the Extraordinary and Shocking Case of George Mathews, Who Was Capitally Convicted at the Old Bailey in February 1818, on a False Charge of Robbing His Master Colonel Whaley.... London: 1818. V. 63

MATHEWS, HARRY
The Conversions. New York: 1962. V. 67
Selected Declarations of Dependence. Calais: 1977. V. 66
Singular Pleasures. New York: 1988. V. 62; 64; 67
Tlooth. Garden City: 1966. V. 66
The Way Home. New York: 1988. V. 64

MATHEWS, J.
A Collection of Anthems and Choruses, Used in the Cathedral Church of Lichfield. Lichfield: 1821. V. 65

MATHEWS, SHAILER
The Woman Citizen's Library: a Systematic Course of Reading in Preparation for the Larger Citizenship. Volume III: Woman and the Law. Chicago: 1913. V. 65
The Woman Citizen's Library...Volume XI: Woman and the Larger Citizenship. Chicago: 1914. V. 65

MATHIAS, PETER
The Brewing Industry in England 1700-1830. Cambridge: 1959. V. 66

MATHIAS, THOMAS
The Pursuits of Literature.... London: 1797. V. 65

MATHIAS, THOMAS JAMES
An Essay on the Evidence, External and Internal, Relating to the Poems Attributed to Thomas Rowley and Others in the Fifteenth century. London: 1784. V. 64
The Grove. London: 1797. V. 63
Odes, English and Latin. 1798. V. 64
The Pursuits of Literature. London: 1798. V. 66

MATLOCK, J. EUGENE
Gone Beyond the Law. Dallas: 1940. V. 65

MATON, WILLIAM GEORGE
Observations Relative Chiefly to the Natural History, Picturesque Scenery and Antiquities of the Western Counties of England Made in the Years 1794 and 1796. Salisbury: 1797. V. 64

THE MATRIMONIAL Preceptor; a Collection of Examples and Precepts Relating to the Married State, from the Most Celebrated Writers Ancient and Modern. London: 1755. V. 63

MATRIX.. Andoversford: 1982-2000. V. 67

MATRIX 2. Andoversford: 1986. V. 64
MATRIX 2. 1993. V. 65

MATRIX 3. Winter 1983. Andoversford: 1963. V. 62

MATRIX 6. Andoversford: 1986. V. 64

MATRIX 7. Andoversford: 1987. V. 62; 64
MATRIX 7. Gloucestershire: 1987. V. 64

MATRIX 8. Andoversford: 1988. V. 62; 64

MATRIX 9. Andoversford: 1989. V. 62
MATRIX 9. Gloucestershire: 1989. V. 64

MATRIX 10. N.P: 1990. V. 64
MATRIX 10. Andoversford: 1991. V. 64

MATIRX 11. Gloucestershire: 1990. V. 64

MATRIX 11. Andoversford: 1991. V. 64

MATRIX 12. N.P: 1992. V. 64

MATRIX 13. Leonminster: 1993. V. 64

MATRIX 14. 1994. V. 65
MATRIX 14. Leonminster: 1994. V. 64

MATRIX 15. N.P: 1995. V. 64

MATRIX 16. N.P: 1996. V. 64

MATRIX 17. N.P: 1997. V. 64

MATRIX 18. N.P: 1998. V. 62; 64

MATRIX 19. 1999. V. 65

MATSON, DONALD
Thr Treatment of Acute Compound Injuries of the Spinal Cord Due to Missiles. Springfield: 1948. V. 67

MATSON, WALTER J.
Salmon and Trout Fishing in Ireland. 1910. V. 63

MATSUURA, K.
Catalog of the Freshwater Fish Collection in the National Museum (Natural History Institute). Tokyo: 1992-1995. V. 65

MATTHEW, GEORGE KING
The English Lakes, Peaks and Passes, from Kendal to Keswick. Kendal: 1866. V. 64

MATTHEW, PATRICK
On Naval Timber and Arboriculture; with Critical Notes on Authors who Have Recently Treated the Subject of Painting. London: 1831. V. 62

MATTHEW, W. D.
Climate and Evolution. New York: 1939. V. 62; 63

MATTHEWS, ADRIAN
Vienna Blood. London: 1999. V. 65

MATTHEWS, BRANDER
Tales of Fantasy and Fact. New York: 1896. V. 64; 66

MATTHEWS, C. C.
Twixt Here and Sun Down. St. Louis: 1957. V. 64; 67

MATTHEWS, ELIZA KIRKHAM
What Has Been. A Novel. Alexandria: 1803. V. 62

MATTHEWS, FREDERICK C.
American Merchant Ships 1850-1900. Salem: 1930-1931. V. 62; 65

MATTHEWS, HENRY
The Diary of an Invalid Being the Journal of a Tour in Pursuit of Health in Portugal, Italy, Switzerland and France in the Years 1817, 1818 and 1819. London: 1822. V. 67

MATTHEWS, I. J.
South African Proteaceae in New Zealand. Manakau via Levin: 1983. V. 64

MATTHEWS, JAMES M.
A Guide to Commissioners in Chancery, with Practical Forms for the Discharge of Their Duties, Adapted to the Statute Law of Virginia. Richmond: 1871. V. 66

MATTHEWS, JOHN
A Voyage to the River Sierra-Leone, on the Coast of Africa.... London: 1788. V. 66

MATTHEWS, JOSEPH M.
A Treatise on Diseases of the Rectum, Anus and Sigmoid Flexure. New York: 1895. V. 66; 67

MATTHEWS, L. HARRISON
The Humpback Whale, Megaptera Nodosa. 1937. V. 67

MATTHEWS, LEONARD
A Long Life in Review. St. Louis: 1927. V. 66

MATTHEWS, RICHARD
A Digest of the Law Relating to Offences Punishable by Endictment and By Information in the Crown Office. London: 1833. V. 67

MATTHEWS, SALLIE R.
Interwoven, a Pioneer Chronicle. El Paso: 1958. V. 63; 67

MATTHEWS, THOMAS
Advice to Whist Players. New York: 1813. V. 66

MATTHEWS, WASHINGTON
Ethnography and Philology of the Hidatsa Indians. Washington: 1877. V. 67
Navaho Legends. Boston: 1897. V. 65
The Night Chant, a Navajo Ceremony. New York: 1902. V. 66

MATTHEWS, WILLIAM
A Collection of Affidavits and Certificates, Relative to the Wonderful Cure of Mrs. Ann Mattingly, Which Took Place in the City of Washington, D.C. on the Tenth of March 1824. City of Washington: 1824. V. 64
Running the New Road. New York: 1970. V. 64

MATTHEY, ANDRE
Nouvelles Recherches sur les Maladies de l'Esprit Precedes de Considerations sur les Difficultes de l'Art de Guerir. Paris/Geneve: 1816. V. 65

MATTHIAS, LEE
Sherlock Holmes and Harry Houdini in the Aventure of the Pandora Plague. Noeshkoro: 1984. V. 63

MATTHIESSEN, PETER
At Play in the Fields of the Lord. New York: 1965. V. 62; 63; 64; 65; 67
At Play in the Fields of the Lord. London: 1966. V. 62; 65
The Cloud Forest. New York: 1961. V. 62; 66
In the Spirit of Crazy Horse. New York: 1983. V. 62; 63; 64; 65; 66; 67
Indian Country. New York: 1984. V. 62; 64; 65; 67
Killing Mister Watson. New York: 1990. V. 62
Lost Man's River. New York: 1997. V. 67
Midnight Turning Gray. Bristol: 1984. V. 65
On the River Styx. New York: 1989. V. 67
Oomingmak, the Expedition to the Musk Ox Island in the Bering Sea. Hastings: 1967. V. 63
Oomingmak. The Expedition to the Musk Ox Island in the Bering Sea. New York: 1967. V. 63; 65; 66
Partisans. New York: 1955. V. 62; 64; 66
Profile: Cesar Chavez. Los Angeles: 1969. V. 63
Race Rock. New York: 1954. V. 62; 63
Raditzer. New York: 1961. V. 62
Sal Si Puedes. New York: 1969. V. 64

MATTHIESSEN, PETER continued
Sand Rivers. New York: 1981. V. 62; 64; 67
The Shorebirds of North Ameica. New York: 1967. V. 62; 63; 64; 65; 67
The Snow Leopard. Franklin Center: 1978. V. 62; 64; 65; 67
The Snow Leopard. New York: 1978. V. 62; 67
The Tree Where Man Was Born. New York: 1972. V. 62
The Tree Where Man Was Born. New York: 1992. V. 64; 67
Under the Mountain Wall. New York: 1962. V. 62; 66; 67
Wildlife in America. New York: 1959. V. 62; 64
The Wind Birds. New York: 1973. V. 62

MATTHISSON, FRIEDRICH VON
Letters Written from Various Parts of the Continent, Between the Years 1785 and 1794.... London: 1799. V. 62

MATTIOLI, PIETRO ANDREA
Kreutterbuch. Frankfurt am Main: 1600. V. 66

MATTISON, HIRAM
The Rappers; or, the Mysteries, Fallacies and Absurdities of Spirit-Rapping, Table-Tipping and Entrancement. New York: 1854. V. 63

MATTOCKS, BREWER
Minnesota as a Home for Invalids. Philadelphia and St. Paul: 1871. V. 65

MATURIN, CHARLES R.
Melmoth, the Wanderer. 1892. V. 62
Women; or, Pour et Contre. Edinburgh: 1818. V. 65

MAUD, CONSTANCE
Wagner's Heroes. (and) Wagner's Heroines. London: 1900. V. 63

MAUDE, THOMAS
A Legend of Ravenswood; and Other Poems. London: 1823. V. 63

MAUDSLEY, ATHOL
Highways and Horses. London: 1888. V. 62

MAUDSLEY, HENRY
Body and Mind: an Inquiry into Their Connection and Mutual Influence, Specially in Reference to Mental Disorders. London: 1873. V. 64; 65
Body and Will: Being an Essay Concerning Will In Its Metaphysical, Physiological and Pathological Respects. New York: 1884. V. 65
The Pathology of Mind. A Study of Its Distempers, Deformities and Disorders. London: 1895. V. 65
The Physiology and Pathology of the Mind. London: 1868. V. 65
The Physiology of Mind. London: 1876. V. 65
Responsibility in Mental Disease. New York: 1874. V. 65
Responsibility in Mental Disease. New York: 1897. V. 67

MAUDUIT, ANTOINE RENE
A New and Complete Treatise of Spherical Trigonometry.... London: 1768. V. 65

MAUGHAM, R. C. F.
Africa As I Have Known It. London: 1929. V. 63
Zambezia. London: 1910. V. 62

MAUGHAM, WILLIAM SOMERSET
Ah King. London: 1933. V. 63
Ashenden. London: 1928. V. 64; 66
Cakes and Ale. London: 1930. V. 65; 66
Catalina - a Romance. London: 1948. V. 65
Catalogue of the Collection of Impressionist and Modern Pictures Formed by W. Somerset Maugham Over the Last Fifty Years. London: 1962. V. 64
Christmas Holiday. London. V. 63
Christmas Holiday. London: 1939. V. 64
Creatures of Circumstance. London: 1947. V. 64
Don Fernando or Variations on Some Spanish Themes. London: 1935. V. 64
First Person Singular. London: 1931. V. 64
The Gentleman in the Parlour. London: 1930. V. 64
Liza of Lambeth. London: 1897. V. 64
Liza of Lambeth. London: 1947. V. 62, 63
The Making of a Saint. Boston: 1898. V. 67
The Making of a Saint. London: 1898. V. 62; 64
A Man of Honour: a Tragedy. London: 1912. V. 66
The Merry-Go-Round. London: 1905. V. 62
Mr. Ashenden Agent Secret. Paris: 1930. V. 63
The Mixture as Before. London: 1940. V. 62
The Narrow Corner. Garden City: 1932. V. 66
Of Human Bondage. Garden City: 1936. V. 64; 67
Of Human Bondage. New York: 1938. V. 64
The Painted Veil. London: 1925. V. 64
La Passe Dangereuse. (The Painted Veil). Paris: 1926. V. 62
The Razor's Edge. Garden City: 1944. V. 62; 65
The Sacred Flame - a Play in Three Acts. London: 1928. V. 65
The Summing Up. Garden City: 1954. V. 66
The Vagrant Mood. London: 1952. V. 64
The Vagrant Mood. Melbourne: 1952. V. 63
A Writer's Notebook. London: 1949. V. 62; 64

MAUGHAN, ROBIN
Testament, Cairo 1898. London: 1972. V. 63

MAULDIN, BILL
Mud, Mules and Mountains. 1944. V. 64

MAULE, HARRY
The Man from Main Street. New York: 1953. V. 65

MAUND, BENJAMIN
The Botanic Garden.... London: 1825-1832. V. 63

MAUNDRELL, HENRY
A Journey from Aleppo to Jerusalem at Easter, A.D. 1697. Oxford: 1749. V. 66

MAUNSELL, G. W.
The Fisherman's Vade Mecum. 1933. V. 67

MAUNZIO, PAOLO
Apophthegmatvm Ex Optimis Vtrivsqve. Lingvae Scriptoribvs Libri LLX. Venetiis: 1604. V. 67

MAUPERTUIS, PIERRE LOUIS MOREAU DE
La Figure de la Terre, Determinee Par Les Observations de Messieurs de Maupertuis, Clairaut, Camus, Le Monnier, de l'Academie Royale des Sciences.... Amsterdam: 1738. V. 64
The Figure of the Earth, Determined from Observations Made by Order of the French King. London: 1738. V. 63
Oeuvres. Lyon: 1756. V. 65

MAURER, EVAN M.
The Native American Heritage: a Survey of North American Indian Art. Chicago: 1977. V. 67

MAURIAC, FRANCOIS
L'Enfant Charge de Chaines. Paris: 1913. V. 67

MAURIBER, SAUL
The Photography of Carl Van Vechten. Indianapolis/New York: 1978. V. 63

MAURICE, ALFRED
Bouwkundig Teekenen. Initiation a l'Architecture. Gent: 1937. V. 67

MAURICE, FREDERICK DENISON
Administrative Reform and Its Connexion and Working Men's Colleges. An Address.... Cambridge: 1855. V. 64
The Concluding Essay and Preface to the Second Edition of Mr. Maurice's Theological Essays. London: 1854. V. 65
The Epistle to the Hebrews.... London: 1846. V. 65
The Life of Frederick Denison Maurice, Chiefly Told in His Own Letters. London: 1884. V. 65
On the Reformation of Society, and How All Classes May Contribute To It. Southampton: 1851. V. 64
Reasons for Co-operation: a Lecture Delivered at the Office for Promoting Working Men's Associaton, 76, Charlotte Street, Fitzroy Square on Wednesday December 11th 1850. London: 1851. V. 64

MAURICE, JEAN BAPTISTE
Le Blason des Armoiries de Tous les Chevaliers de l'Ordre de la Toson d'or Depuis la Preimiere Institution Jusques a Present. La Haye: 1667. V. 66

MAURICE, SENDAK
Very Far Away. Kingswood, Surrey: 1959. V. 65

MAURICE, THOMAS
Select Poems.... London: 1803. V. 63

MAURICE, WILLIAM
Mercy Triumphant: a Discourse Delivered at Fetter-Lane meeting, London June 15, 1800; Occasioned by the Death of John Osborn Dawson, Who Was Executed for Forgery, at Newgate June 5, 1800. London: 1800. V. 63

MAURICEAU, A. M.
The Married Woman's Private Medical Companion. New York: 1847. V. 64; 66
The Married Woman's Private Medical Companion. New York: 1848. V. 65
The Married Woman's Private Medical Companion. New York: 1851. V. 64
The Married Woman's Private Medical Companion. New York: 1854. V. 63; 66
The Married Woman's Private Medical Companion. New York: 1855. V. 65

MAURICEAU, FRANCOIS
Traite des Maladies des Femmes Grosses, et de Celles Qui Sont Accouchees. (with) Observations sur la Grossesse e l'Accouchement des Femmes, et sur Lesurs Maladies.... Paris: 1740-1738. V. 62

MAUROIS, ANDRE
Ariel ou La Vie de Shelley. Paris: 1923. V. 64
A Civil War Album of Paintings by Prince de Joinville. New York: 1964. V. 67
Par la Faute de M. Balzac. Paris: 1923. V. 66
Les Souffrances du Jeuen Werther. Paris: 1926. V. 66

MAURUS, TERENTIANUS
De Litteris Syllabis Pedibvs et Metris. Utrecht & London: 1825. V. 64

MAURY, DABNEY HERNDON
Recollections of a Virginian in the Mexican, Indian and Civil Wars. New York: 1894. V. 62; 66; 67

MAURY, MATTHEW FONTAINE
Literary Societies of the University of Virginia. Richmond: 1855. V. 63
Physical Geography of the Sea. New York.
The Physical Geography of the Sea. New York: 1855. V. 63; 65; 66
The Physical Geography of the Sea. New York: 1856. V. 63; 64; 67
The Physical Geography of the Sea. London: 1857. V. 62
The Physical Geography of the Sea. London: 1860. V. 65

MAURY, RICHARD L.
The Battle of Williamsburg and the Charge of the 24th Virginia, of Early's Brigade. Richmond: 1880. V. 62; 63
A Brief Sketch of the Work of Matthew Fontaine Maury During the War 1861-1865. Richmond: 1915. V. 62

MAUTZ, CARL
Biographies of Western Photographers: a Reference Guide to Photographers Working in the 19th Century American West. Nevada City: 1997. V. 65

MAUVILLON, ELEAZAR
Histoire de Pierre I, Surnomme Le Grand, Empereur de Toutes les Russies, Roi de Siberie, de Casan, d'Astracan, Grand Duc de Moscovie &c.... A Amsterdam et a Leipzig: 1742. V. 66

MAVOR, W.
New Description of Blenheim: a Picturesque Tour of the Gardens and Park.... 1800. V. 66

MAVROGORDATO, J. G.
A Falcon in the Field. 1966. V. 64

MAVROGORDATO, JOHN
Letters from Greece - Concerning the War of the Balkan Allies 1912- 1913. London: 1914. V. 62

MAW, S., SON & THOMPSON
The Nurses' Handbook and Catalogue of Nursing Requisites. 1898. V. 65

MAWE, JOHN
Familiar Lessons on Mineralogy and Geology.... London: 1820. V. 62; 64
Familiar Lessons on Mineralogy and Geology.... London: 1823. V. 66
Familiar Lessons on Mineralogy and Geology.... London: 1825. V. 64
The Linnaean System of Conchology. 1823. V. 66
The Mineralogy of Derbyshire. 1802. V. 64
The Mineralogy of Derbyshire. London: 1802. V. 62
A Treatise on Diamonds and Precious Stones, Including their History.... London: 1813. V. 62; 65

MAWE, THOMAS
The Complete Gardener, or Gardener's Calendar. London: 1836. V. 67
Every Man His Own Gardener. London: 1791. V. 64
Every Man His Own Gardener. London: 1818. V. 62; 66
Every Man His Own Gardener. London: 1822. V. 64

MAWMAN, JOSEPH
An Excursion to the Highlands of Scotland and the English Lakes.... London: 1805. V. 66
A Picturesque Tour through France, Switzerland, on the Banks of the Rhine and through Part of the Netherlands. London: 1817. V. 66

MAWSON, DOUGLAS
The Home of the Blizzard. London: 1915. V. 62

MAWSON, THOMAS H.
Amounderness. London: 1937. V. 62; 64
The Art and Craft of Garden Making. 1900. V. 63
The Art and Craft of Garden Making. London: 1900. V. 62
The Art and Craft of Garden Making. London: 1926. V. 64; 65; 67

MAX Ernst: Beyond Painting. New York: 1948. V. 67

MAXCY, EATON
The Ladies Museum. Providence: 1825-1826. V. 65

MAXCY, VIRGIL
The Maryland Resolutions and the Objections to Them Considered. Baltimore: 1822. V. 63

MAXIMILIANUS, R. D.
Manuale Exorcismorum: Continens Instructiones & Exorcismos ad Eiiciendos e Corporibus Obsessis Spiritus Malignos & ad Quaeuis Maleficia Depellenda & Ad Quascumque.... Antuerpiae: 1635. V. 66

MAXIMS and Precepts of the Saviour. London: 1848. V. 65

MAXIMUS OF TYRE
Philosophici Platonici, Scriptoris Amoenissimi.... Lugduni: 1630. V. 65

MAXWELL, ANNA
Hampstead: Its Historic Houses: its Literary and Artistic Associations. Boston: 1912. V. 63

MAXWELL, C. N.
Malayan Fishes. Singapore: 1921. V. 66

MAXWELL, CECIL
The Story of Three Sisters. London: 1874. V. 66

MAXWELL, CONSTANTIA
Country and Town in Ireland Under the Georges. 1949. V. 67
Dublin Under the Georges, 1714-1830. 1937. V. 67
The Stranger in Ireland from the Reign of Elizabeth to the Great Famine. 1954. V. 67

MAXWELL, H.
History of Tucker County, West Virginia. Kingwood: 1884. V. 66

MAXWELL, HERBERT
British Fresh Water Fish. 1904. V. 67
British Fresh Water Fishes. London: 1904. V. 63
Chronicles of the Houghton Fishing Club. 1822-1908. 1908. V. 63; 65; 67
Life and Times of the Right Honourable William Henry Smith, M.P. Edinburgh: 1893. V. 64
The Lowland Scots Regiments. Glasgow: 1918. V. 62
Passages in the Life of Sir Lucian Elphin of Castle Weary. London: 1889. V. 66

MAXWELL, MARIUS
Stalking Big Game With a Camera in Equatorial Africa. London: 1925. V. 67

MAXWELL, MARY ELIZABETH BRADDON
Belgravia Annual. (1869). My Wife's Promise. A Tale. London: 1869. V. 67
Belgravia Annual (1876). Sir Luke's Return. 1876. V. 67

MAXWELL, ROBERT
The Practical Husbandman: Being a Collection of Miscellaneous Papers on Husbandry. Edinburgh: 1757. V. 63

MAXWELL, WILLIAM
The Folded Leaf. New York: 1945. V. 65; 66

MAXWELL, WILLIAM A.
Crossing the Plains. Days of '57. San Francisco: 1915. V. 65

MAXWELL, WILLIAM H.
The Field Book; or, Sports and Pastimes of the British Islands. London: 1833. V. 65
The Field Book or Sports and Pastimes of the United Kingdom. 1836. V. 62
The Fortunes of Hector O'Halloran, and His Man Mark Anthony O'Toole. London: 1853. V. 65
Wanderings in the Highlands and Islands. 1844. V. 63; 64
Wild Sports of the West. London: 1843. V. 64

MAY, J. B.
The Hawks of North America, Their Field Identification and Feeding Habits. New York: 1935. V. 67

MAY, JOHANN CARL
Versuch in Handlungs-Briefen und Grossen Kauffmannischen Aufsatze Nach den GeleIrtschen Regeln. Lubeck: 1789. V. 65

MAY, JOSEPH
Joseph Priestley, LL.D., F.R.S.: a Discourse Delivered in the First Unitarian Church of Philadelphia on Sunday March 18, 1888. Philadelphia: 1888. V. 67

MAY, PHIL
Gutter-Snipes. London: 1896. V. 67
The Phil May Album. London: 1900. V. 64

MAY, ROBERT L.
Rudolph, the Red Nosed Reindeer. 1939. V. 64; 65; 67

MAY, ROLLO
The Art of Counseling. New York: 1939. V. 67

MAY, ROSE E.
Baby Mary and Her Little Friends. London: 1890. V. 62

MAY, THOMAS
The History of the Parliament of England, Which Began November the Third, MDCXL.... London: 1812. V. 63
The Reigne of King Henry the Second. London: 1633. V. 64
The Victorious Reigne of King Edward the Third. London: 1638. V. 64

MAY, TRACEY
The Tabb-fur Family. London: 1948. V. 66

MAY, WILLIAM
Sermons on Various Subjects, Preached to Young People on New Year's Days. London: 1753. V. 63; 67

MAYAKOVSKY, VLADIMIR
Ya! (I). N.P: 1913. V. 65; 67

MAYBRICK, FLORENCE ELIZABETH
Mrs. Maybrick's Own Story: My Fifteen Lost Years. New York: 1905. V. 63

MAYDON, H. C.
Big Game Shooting in Africa. London: 1932. V. 62; 66; 67
Big Game Shooting in Africa. 1951. V. 63
Big Game Shooting in Africa. Philadelphia: 1951. V. 64

MAYER, ALFRED M.
Sport with Gun and Rod in American Woods and Waters. New York: 1883. V. 66; 67

MAYER, BILL
Golf-O-Rama, the Whacky Nine-Hole Pop-Up Mini-Golf Book. New York: 1994. V. 67

MAYER, BRANTZ
Captain Canot; or, Twenty Years of an African Slaver. New York: 1854. V. 63
Mexico As It Was and As It Is. New York London & Paris: 1844. V. 67

MAYER, JOHANN C. A.
Anatomisch-Physiologische Abhandlung vom Gehirn Ruckmark und Ursprung der Nerven. Berlin and Leipzig: 1779. V. 62

MAYER, JOHN
The Southern Chant Book of the Protestant Episcopal Church Arranged for the Use of Choirs. Columbia: 1861. V. 63; 65

MAYER, LUIGI
Interesting Views in Turkey. London: 1819. V. 64
Views in the Ottoman Empire, Chiefly in Caramania, a Part of Asia Hitherto Unexplored.... London: 1803. V. 62

MAYER, TOM
The Weary Falcon. Boston: 1971. V. 66

MAYES, FRANCES
The Book of Summer. Woodside: 1995. V. 64

MAYFIELD, JOHN S.
Mark Twain vs. The Street Railway. N.P: 1926. V. 63

MAYFIELD, ROBINSON
A Final Letter. Robinson Mayfield in Essex, North Carolina to Hutchins Mayfield in Oxford, England, June 15 to November 27, 1955. Los Angeles: 1980. V. 62

MAYHALL, JOHN
The Annals of Yorkshire, from the Earliest Period to the Present Time. Leeds: 1862. V. 63; 65

MAYHEW, AUGUSTUS
Faces for Fortunes. London: 1865. V. 66
Paved with Gold or the Romance and Reality of the London Streets. London: 1858. V. 62

MAYHEW, HENRY
The Greatest Plague of Life; or the Adventures of a Lady in Search of a Good Servant.... London: 1847. V. 67
London Labour and the London Poor. London: 1851. V. 64
London Labour and the London Poor. London: 1861-1865. V. 64
London Labour and the London Poor. London: 1865. V. 62
Lost Wages, Their Causes and Consequences. London: 1851. V. 64
The Mormons, or, Latter-Day Saints: a Contemporary History. London: 1852. V. 63
The Upper Rhine: the Scenery of Its Banks and the Manners of Its People. London: 1858. V. 62; 66

MAYHEW, JONATHAN
A Discourse on Rev. XV 3d, 4th. Occasioned by the Earthquakes in November 1755. Boston: 1755. V. 63
God's Hand and Providence to Be Religiously Acknowledged In Public Calamities. A Sermon Occasioned by the Great Fire in Boston, New England, Thursday, March 20, 1760. Boston: 1760. V. 63

MAYHEW, THE BROTHERS
The Good Genius that Turned Everything Into Gold, or the Queen Bee and the Magic Dress. London: 1847. V. 63
The Greatest Plague of Life; or the Adventures of a Lady in Search of a Good Servant. London: 1847. V. 62
The Image of His Father; or, One Boy is More Trouble than a Dozen Girls.... London: 1848. V. 62; 65

MAYNARD, CHARLES J.
The Birds of Eastern North America.... Newtonville: 1881. V. 64; 67
The Birds of Eastern North America.... Newtonville: 1896. V. 67
Butterflies of New England. Boston;: 1886. V. 62
Eggs of North American Birds. Boston: 1890. V. 62; 63; 64; 66; 67
A Field Ornithology of the Birds of Eastern North America. West Newton: 1016. V. 67
Handbook of the Sparrows, Finches, etc. of New England. Newtonville: 1896. V. 63
Manual of North American Butterflies. Boston: 1891. V. 64
The Naturalist's Guide in Collecting and Preserving Objects of Natural History.... Boston: 1870. V. 65

MAYNARD, HENRY N.
Handbook to the Crumlin Viaduct Monmouthshire.... Crumlin: 1862. V. 62; 66

MAYNARD, JOYCE
Baby Love. New York: 1981. V. 63
Looking Back: a Chronicle of Growing Up Old in the Sixties. Garden City. 1973. V. 63

MAYNE, LEGER D., PSEUD.
What Shall We Do Tonight?. New York: 1873. V. 65

MAYNE, R. G.
An Expository Lexicon of the Terms, Ancient and Modern, in Medical and General Science.... London: 1860. V. 66

MAYNE, RICHARD
Four Years in British Columbia and Vancouver Island. London: 1862. V. 66

MAYNEVILLE, PSEUD.
Chronique du Temps Qui Fut La Jacquerie. Paris: 1903. V. 62

MAYNWARING, ARTHUR
The Life and Posthumous Works.... London: 1715. V. 63

MAYO, HERBERT
The Philosophy of Living. London: 1837. V. 66
The Philosophy of Living. London: 1838. V. 65

MAYO, JOSEPH
Guide to Magistrates: with Practical Forms for the Discharge of their Duties Out of Court. Richmond: 1850. V. 64; 67

MAYO, ROBERT
The Affidavit of Andrew Jackson, Taken by the Defendants in the Suit of Robert Mayo vs. Blair and Rives for Libel, Analyzed and Refuted. Washington: 1480. V. 66
Political Sketches of Eight Years in Washington, in Four Parts.... Baltimore: 1839. V. 63

MAYO, THOMAS
Elements of the Pathology of the Human Mind. London: 1838. V. 65

MAYOR, ARCHER
Borderlines. New York: 1990. V. 65; 66
Open Season. New York: 1988. V. 66

MAYOR, F. M.
The Third Miss Symons. London: 1913. V. 64

MAYOR, MATTHIAS LOUIS
La Medecine et la Chirurgie Populaires, en Rapport Avec l'Etat Actuel de ces Sciences et de la Civilisation. Lausanne: 1845. V. 65

MAYS, WILLIE
Say Hey: the Autobiography of Willie Mays. New York: 1988. V. 63

MAYUYAMA & CO., LTD.
Mayuyama, Seventy Years. Tokyo: 1976. V. 62; 63; 64; 66

MAZEL, MADAME
Narrative of the Barbarous Murder of Madame Mazel, a French Lady of Distinction. London: 1825. V. 63

MAZENOD, LUCIEN
Les Femmes Celebres. Paris: 1960-1961. V. 63; 67

MAZRO, SOPHIA
Turkish Barbarity. Providence: 1828. V. 64

MAZUCHELLI, NINA
The Indian Alps and How We Crossed Them. London: 1876. V. 66

MAZZANOVICH, ANTON
Trailing Geronimo. Hollywood. V. 65
Trailing Geronimo. Hollywood: 1931. V. 67

MAZZEI, FILIPPO
Recherches Historiques et Politiques sur les Etats-Unis de l'Amerique Septentrionale, ou l'on Traite des Etablissments des Treize Colonies, de Leurs Rapports & De Leurs Dissentions Avec la Grande-Bretagne.... Colle & Paris: 1788. V. 64; 67

MAZZINI, GIUSEPPE
The Duties of Man. London: 1862. V. 64

M'BAIN, J.
The Merrick and the Neighbouring Hills. Ayr. V. 62

M'BURNIE, JAMES
A Catechism for Romanists and Protestants, Respectfully Presented to the Citizens of Wheeling and Its Vicinity. Wheeling: 1848. V. 63

MC ALPINE'S Halifax City Directory 1908-1909. Volume XI. Halifax: 1908. V. 65

MC GILL UNIVERSITY
The Lawrence Lande Collection of Canadiana in the Redpath Library of McGill University: a Bibliography.... Montreal: 1965. V. 62

MC LOUGHLIN BROTHERS
Prints of McLoughlin Brothers Wood Blocks: Part One and Two. Los Angeles: 1980. V. 64

M'CABE, JOHN COLLINS
Scraps. Richmond: 1835. V. 62

MC ADIE, MARY R. B.
Alexander Mc Adie, Scientist and Writer.... Charlottesville: 1949. V. 67

MC ALAVY, DON
High Plains History of East Central New Mexico. N.P: 1980. V. 67

M'CALL, H. B.
The Early History of Bedale in the North Riding of Yorkshire. London: 1907. V. 62; 65

MC ALLISTER, JAMES GRAY
Sketch of Captain Thompson McAllister. Petersburg: 1896. V. 62

MC ALLISTER, LAURA KIRLEY
Gumbo Trails. N.P: 1957. V. 64

M'CALLUM, P. F.
Le Livre Rouge; or a New and Extraordinary Red Book. London: 1810. V. 64; 65

MC ALMON, ROBERT
A Hasty Bunch. Dijon: 1922. V. 64
A Hasty Bunch. Paris: 1922. V. 62; 65
Post-Adolescence. Paris: 1923. V. 66

MC ALPINE, ARTHUR
Man in a Metal Cage. Easthampton: 1977. V. 65

MC ARTHUR, LEWIS A.
Oregon Geographic Names. Portland: 1928. V. 66

MC ATEE, JOHN
Brief for the Cherokee Strip Live Stock Association. Bryan: 1999. V. 64

MC AULIFFE, EUGENE
History of Union Pacific Coal Mines 1868-1940. Omaha: 1940. V. 64

MC BAIN, ED
And All through the House. New York: 1994. V. 67
Ax. New York: 1964. V. 65; 67
The 87th Precinct. 1959. V. 64; 66
The 87th Precinct. New York: 1959. V. 62
The 87th Squad. 1960. V. 64; 66
Ice. New York: 1983. V. 67
Jigsaw. 1970. V. 64; 66
Lady Killer. New York: 1958. V. 67
Like Love. 1962. V. 64; 66
Ten Plus One. 1963. V. 63; 64; 66
Ten Plus One. New York: 1963. V. 66

MC BAIN, ED continued
'Til Death. 1959. V. 64; 66
Where There's Smoke. New York: 1975. V. 67

MC BURNIE, DAVID
Mental Exercises of a Working Man. London: 1854. V. 62

MC CABE, JAMES D.
The Grayjackets: and How They Lived, Fought and Died for Dixie. Richmond: 1867. V. 62; 65
Life and Campaigns of General Robert E. Lee. Atlanta: 1866. V. 62
Life and Campaigns of General Robert E. Lee. St. Louis: 1866. V. 63

MC CABE, JOSEPH
Life and Letters of George Jacob Holyoake. London: 1908. V. 64

MC CABE, W. GORDON
Brief Sketch of Andrew Reid Venable Jr. Richmond: 1909. V. 63

MC CAIN, CHARLES W.
History of the Hudson's Bay Comapny's S.S. Beaver - Being a Graphic and Vivid Sketch of This Noted Pioneer Steamer and Her Romantic Cruise for Over Half a Century on the Placid Island Dotted Waters of the North Pacific. Vancouver: 1894. V. 62; 64

MC CALEB, WALTER F.
The Aaron Burr Conspiracy. New York: 1936. V. 63; 67

MC CALL, G. A.
Letters from the Frontier - Written During a Period of Thirty Years Service in the Army of the United States. Philadelphia: 1868. V. 64; 67

MC CALL, H. B.
Richmondshire Churches. London: 1910. V. 65

MC CAMMON, ROBERT R.
Swan Song. Arlington: 1989. V. 66
They Thirst. London: 1990. V. 62

MC CANDLESS, BARBARA
New York to Hollywood: The Photography of Karl Struss. Fort Worth: 1995. V. 63

MC CANN, COLUM
This Side of Brightness. London: 1998. V. 67

MC CANN, IRVING GOFF
With the National Guard on the Border. St. Louis: 1917. V. 67

MC CARRY, CHARLES
The Miernik Dossier. New York: 1973. V. 67
The Miernik Dossier. London: 1974. V. 62
The Tears of Autumn. London: 1975. V. 62

MC CARTHY, ALBERT
The PL Yearbook of Jazz 1946. London: 1946. V. 66

MC CARTHY, CARLTON
Contributions to a History of the Richmond Howitzer Battalion. Richmond: 1883-1886. V. 62; 63
Detailed Minutiae of Soldier Life in the Army of Northern Virginia 1861-1865. Richmond: 1882. V. 62; 63; 65
Detailed Minutiae of Soldier Life in the Army of Northern Virginia 1861-1865. Richmond: 1884. V. 63; 66

MC CARTHY, CORMAC
All the Pretty Horses. London: 1992. V. 62; 63
All the Pretty Horses. New York: 1992. V. 62; 63; 64; 65; 66; 67
Blood Meridian. New York: 1985. V. 62; 64; 65; 66; 67
Blood Meridian. London: 1990. V. 63; 66
Child of God. New York: 1973. V. 62; 64; 65; 67
Child of God. London: 1975. V. 62
Cities of the Plain. New Orleans: 1998. V. 66; 67
Cities of the Plain. New York: 1998. V. 66
The Crossing. London: 1994. V. 62; 64; 66; 67
The Gardener's Son. Hopewell: 1996. V. 66
The Orchard Keeper. New York: 1965. V. 63; 67
The Orchard Keeper. London: 1966. V. 65; 67
Outer Dark. New York: 1968. V. 64; 65; 66; 67
Outer Dark. London: 1970. V. 64; 66
The Stonemason. Hopewell: 1994. V. 62; 63; 64; 66; 67
Suttree. New York: 1979. V. 64; 67

MC CARTHY, DESMOND
Portraits I. London: 1931. V. 65

MC CARTHY, JOHN G.
Irish Land Questions Plainly Stated and Answered. 1870. V. 67

MC CARTHY, JUSTIN
The Flower of France. A Novel. London: 1906. V. 66
A History of Our Own Times, from the Accession of Queen Victoria to the General Election of 1880 (to the Diamond Jubilee). London: 1900-1901. V. 64
A History of the Four Georges (and of William IV). London: 1884-1901. V. 64
Irish Literature. New York: 1904. V. 67
The Reign of Queen Anne. New York and London: 1902. V. 66

MC CARTHY, MARY
Birds of America. New York: 1971. V. 66
Cast a Cold Eye. New York: 1950. V. 64
Fighting Fitzgerald and Other Papers. 1930. V. 67
Une Jeune Fille Sage. (Memories of a Catholic Girlhood). Paris: 1959. V. 63
Medina. New York: 1972. V. 62
Vietnam. New York: 1967. V. 62
Winter Visitors. New York: 1970. V. 66

MC CARTHY, SAMUEL T.
The Mac Carthys of Munster. 1922. V. 67
The Mac Carthys of Munster. Arkansas: 1997. V. 63

MC CARTNEY, PAUL
Paul Mc Cartney Composer/Artist. London: 1981. V. 66

MC CAULEY, JAMES E.
A Stove Up Cowboy's Story. Austin: 1941. V. 67
A Stove Up Cowboy's Story. Austin: 1942. V. 64

MC CLAREN, L. L.
High Living. San Francisco;: 1904. V. 66

MC CLATCHY, J. D.
Kilim. New York: 1987. V. 66

MC CLELLAN, EDWIN N.
United States Marine Corps in the World War. Washington: 1920. V. 67

MC CLELLAN, GEORGE B.
Manual of Bayonet Exercise Prepared for the Army of the United States. Philadelphia: 1862. V. 67
Report of the Secretary of War, Communicating the Report of Captain George B. McClellan...Sent to the Seat of War in Europe in 1855 and 1856. Washington: 1857. V. 67

MC CLELLAN, HENRY BRAINARD
Life and Campaigns of Major General J.E.B. Stuart. Boston and New York: 1885. V. 62; 65
Life and Campaigns of Major General J.E.B. Stuart. Bloomington: 1958. V. 63

MC CLELLAND
The Trout Fly Dresser's Cabinet of Device of How to Tie Flies for Trout and Grayling Fishing. London: 1931. V. 67
The Trout Fly Dresser's Cabinet of Device or How to Tie Flies for Trout and Grayling Fishing. London: 1949. V. 67

MC CLENDON, LISE
The Bluejay Shaman. New York: 1994. V. 63

MC CLINTOCK, F. L.
The Voyage of the Fox in the Arctic Seas. London: 1859. V. 62

MC CLINTOCK, JAMES H.
Arizona - Prehistoric - Aboriginal - Pioneer- Modern. The Nation's Youngest Common Wealth Within a Land of Ancient Culture. Chciago: 1916. V. 63
Mormon Settlement in Arizona. A Record of Peaceful Conquest on the Desert. Phoenix: 1921. V. 63; 66

MC CLINTOCK, WALTER
Old Indian Trails. Boston: 1923. V. 67
The Old North Trail or Life, Legends and Religion of the Blackfeet Indians. London: 1910. V. 62; 66; 67

MC CLUNG, JOHN A.
Sketches of Western Adventure.... Philadelphia: 1832. V. 66

MC CLURE, A. K.
Three Thousand Miles through the Rocky Mountains. Philadelphia: 1869. V. 66

MC CLURE, EDMUND
Historical Church Atlas. London: 1897. V. 66

MC CLURE, F. A.
The Bamboos, a Fresh Perspective. 1966. V. 66
Chinese Handmade Paper. Newtown: 1986. V. 64

MC CLURE, JAMES
The Caterpillar Cop. London: 1972. V. 66
Four and Twenty Virgins. London: 1973. V. 66

MC CLURE, MEADE
Major Andrew Drumm. Missouri: 1919. V. 64

MC CLURE, MICHAEL
The Cherub. Los Angeles: 1970. V. 62
Little Odes. Jan-March 1961. New York: 1968. V. 66

MC CLYMONT, JAMES ROXBURGH
Pedraluarez Cabral.... London: 1914. V. 67

MC COMAS, E. S.
A Journal of Travel. Champoeg: 1954. V. 67

MC CONATHY, DALE
Hollywood Costume. New York: 1976. V. 62; 63; 64; 66

MC CONKEY, HARRIET E. BISHOP
Dakota War Whoop. St. Paul: 1864. V. 63

MC CONKEY, JAMES
Chekhov and Our Age: Responses to Chekhov by American Writers and Scholars. Ithaca: 1984. V. 66
Rowan's Progress. New York: 1992. V. 67
Stories from My Life with Other Animals. Boston: 1993. V. 67

MC CONNELL, JOSEPH C.
The West Texas Frontier. Jacksboro: 1933. V. 67

MC CONNELL, W. J.
Early History of Idaho. Caldwell: 1913. V. 65

MC CONNELL, WILLIAM M.
Five Years a Cavalryman; of Sketches of Regular Army Life on the Texas Frontier, Twenty Odd Years Ago. Jackboro: 1889. V. 62; 65; 67

MC CONNOCHIE, A. I.
The Deer and Deer Forests of Scotland. London: 1923. V. 67
Deer Forest Life. 1932. V. 62; 63
Deer Stalking in Scotland. 1924. V. 62
The Rivers Oykell and Cassley in Sutherland and Ross. 1924. V. 67

MC CORKLE, JILL
The Cheer Leader. Chapel Hill: 1984. V. 63; 64; 66; 67
Crash Diet. Chapel Hill: 1992. V. 67
July 7th. Chapel Hill: 1984. V. 62; 66; 67
Tending to Virginia. Chapel Hill: 1987. V. 67

MC CORKLE, JOHN
Three Years with Quantrell (sic)...told by His Scout. Armstrong: 1914. V. 62

MC CORKLE, SAMUEL
Incident on the Bark Columbia. Being Letters Received and Sent by Captain McCorkle and the Crew of His Whaler 1860-1862. Cummington: 1941. V. 62; 64; 67

MC CORMICK, HENRY
Across the Continent in 1865 as told in the Diary of the Late Colonel Henry McCormick. Harrisburg: 1944. V. 62; 65

MC CORMICK, RICHARD C.
Arizona: Its Resources and Prospects, a Letter to the Editor of the New York Tribune. New York: 1865. V. 62; 65

MC COURT, FRANK
Angela's Ashes. London. 1996. V. 65
Angela's Ashes. New York: 1996. V. 62; 65; 66; 67
'Tis. New York: 1999. V. 65; 66; 67

MC COY, ESTHER
Five California Architects: Maybeck, Irving, Gill, Charles and Henry Greene, R. M. Schindler. New York: 1960. V. 62; 65
The Second Generation. Salt Lake City: 1984. V. 65

MC COY, GARNETT
Printing, Printers and Presses in Early Detroit. Grosse Point: 1962. V. 63

MC COY, HORACE
Kiss Tomorrow Good-bye. New York: 1948. V. 63
No Pockets in a Shroud. New York: 1948. V. 67
Scalpel. New York: 1952. V. 65
They Shoot Horses, Don't They?. London: 1935. V. 65

MC COY, JOSEPH G.
Historic Sketches of the Cattle Trade of the West and Southwest. Washington: 1932. V. 65

MC COY, L.
William Mc Coy and His Descendants. Battle Creek: 1904. V. 63

MC COY, TRUDA W.
The McCoys: Their Story as Told to the Author by Eye Witnesses and Descendants. Pikeville: 1976. V. 64

MC CRACKEN, ELIZABETH
The Giant's House. New York: 1996. V. 67
Here's Your Hat What's Your Hurry. New York: 1993. V. 62; 64; 65; 66; 67

MC CRACKEN, HAROLD
The American Cowboy. Garden City: 1973. V. 65
The Beast That Walks Like Man. 1957. V. 67
The Charles M. Russell Book: The Life and Work of the Cowboy Artist. Garden City: 1957. V. 64; 66
The Frank Tenney Johnson Book. Garden City: 1974. V. 64; 65
Frederic Remington - Artist of the Old West. New York: 1947. V. 64; 67
Frederic Remington: Artist of the Old West. Philadelphia: 1947. V. 67
The Frederic Remington Book. Garden City: 1966. V. 66
George Catlin and the Old Frontier. New York: 1959. V. 62; 63; 64; 66
Nicolai Fechin. New York: 1961. V. 66
Portraits of the Old West with a Bibliographical Check List of Western Artists. New York: 1952. V. 64; 67

MC CRADY, EDWARD
An Historic Church. Charleston: 1901. V. 67
The History of South Carolina 1670-1783. New York: 1897-1902. V. 63

MC CRARY, GEORGE W.
A Treatise on the American Law of Elections. Keokuk: 1875. V. 65

MC CREADY, T. L.
Mr. Stubbs. New York: 1956. V. 65
Pekin White. New York: 1955. V. 65

MC CREIGHT, M. I.
Buffalo Bone Days - Authentic Story of the Buffalo. Du Bois: 1950. V. 62
Chief Flying Hawk's Tales. The True Story of Custer's Last Fight. New York: 1936. V. 65; 67
Firewater and Forked Tongues - a Sioux Chief Interprets U.S. History. Pasadena: 1947. V. 65

MC CRUMB, SHARYN
If I'd Killed Him When I Met Him. New York: 1995. V. 67
The Windsor Knot. New York: 1990. V. 67

MC CUAIG, RONALD
Vaudeville. Sydney: 1938. V. 65

MC CUBBIN, C.
Australian Butterflies. Melbourne: 1971. V. 62; 63

MC CULLAGH, W. TORRENS
Memoirs of the Right Honourable Richard Lalor Sheil. London: 1855. V. 64
On the Use and Study of History. Dublin: 1842. V. 67

MC CULLERS, CARSON
The Ballad of the Sad Cafe. Boston: 1951. V. 62
The Ballad of the Sad Cafe. London: 1952. V. 62; 66
Clock Without Hands. Boston: 1961. V. 64
The Heart is a Lonely Hunter. Boston: 1940. V. 63; 65
The Heart is a Lonely Hunter. Kyoto: 1980. V. 62
The Member of the Wedding. New York: 1951. V. 66
Reflections in a Golden Eye. Cambridge: 1941. V. 66
The Square Root of Wonderful. Boston: 1958. V. 66
The Square Root of Wonderful. London: 1958. V. 63

MC CULLIN, DON
Hearts of Darkness. London: 1980. V. 66

MC CULLOCH, A. R.
A Check-List of the Fishes Recorded from Australia. Sydney: 1929-1930. V. 65
The Fishes and Fish-Like Animals of New South Wales. Sydney: 1927. V. 63; 65

MC CULLOCH, JOHN RAMSAY
A Dictionary, Practical, Theoretical and Historical of Commerce and Commercial Navigation. London. 1834. V. 64; 67
A Dictionary Practical, Theoretical and Historical of Commerce and Commercial Navigation.... London: 1869-1880. V. 62
London in 1850-1851. London: 1851. V. 62
On Fluctuations in the Supply and Value of Money, and the Banking System of England. Edinburgh;: 1826. V. 63
The Principles of Political Economy.... Edinburgh: 1843. V. 63; 64
The Principles of Political Economy.... Edinburgh: 1849. V. 64
Statements Illustrative of the Policy and Deep Ploughing. 1841. V. 62
A Statistical Account of the British Empire; Exhibiting Its Extent, Physical, Capacities, Population, Industry and Civil and Religious Institutions.... London: 1839. V. 62

MC CULLOH, RICHARD S.
Memorial to the Congress of the United States, Requesting an Investigation and Legislation in Relation to the New Method for Refining Gold.... Princeton: 1851. V. 66

MC CULLOUGH, COLLEEN
Morgan's Run. New York: 2000. V. 67
The Thorn Birds. New York: 1977. V. 65

MC CULLOUGH, ROSE G.
Yesterday When It Is Past. Richmond: 1957. V. 66

MC CULLY, EMILY ANROLD
Mirette on the High Wire. New York: 1992. V. 65

MC CUNE, EVELYN
The Arts of Korea. Rutland: 1962. V. 62; 63; 64; 66

MC CURDY, R.
Life of the Greatest Guide. 1981. V. 67

MC CURRACH, J. C.
Palms of the World. New York: 1960. V. 67

MC CUTCHEON, GEORGE BARR
The Daughter of Andrew Crow. New York: 1907. V. 67
Graustark. The Story of a Love Behind a Throne. Chicago: 1901. V. 64; 67

MC CUTCHEON, JOHN T.
In Africa. Hunting Adventures in the Big Game Country. Indianapolis: 1910. V. 62

MC DADE, M.
The Annals of Murder - a Bibliography of Books and Pamphlets On Ameariican Murders from Colonial Times to 1900. Norman: 1961. V. 63; 66

MC DERMID, VAL
The Wire in the Blood. Blakeney: 1997. V. 65

MC DERMOTT, ALICE
At Weddings and Wakes. New York: 1992. V. 67
A Bigamist's Daughter. New York: 1982. V. 63; 65; 66
Charming Billy. New York: 1998. V. 62; 66; 67
That Night. New York: 1987. V. 65; 66; 67

MC DERMOTT, EDITH SWAN
The Pioneer History of Greeley County Nebraska. Greeley: 1939. V. 66

MC DERMOTT, GERALD
Arrow to the Sun - A Pueblo Indian Tale. New York: 1974. V. 65
Daughter of Earth-A-Roman Myth. New York: 1984. V. 65

MC DERMOTT, JOHN FRANCIS
Tixier's Travels on the Osage Prairies. Norman: 1940. V. 63

MC DERMOTT-STEVENSON, MYRA E.
Lariat Letters. N.P: 1907. V. 62

MC DONALD, A.
A Complete Dictionary of Practical Gardening.... 1807. V. 65

MC DONALD, A. JAMES
The Llano Co-operative Colony and What It Taught. Leesville: 1950. V. 64

MC DONALD, ARCHIE P.
Make Me a Map of the Valley. Dallas: 1973. V. 65

MC DONALD, CORNELIA
Diary With Reminiscences of the War and Refugee Life in the Shenandoah Valley. Nashville: 1935. V. 62; 63; 65

MC DONALD, D.
Agricultural Writers, from Sir Walter of Henley to Arthur Young 1200-1800. London: 1908. V. 63

MC DONALD, DONALD
A History of Plantinum from the Earliest Times to the Eighteen-Eighties. London: 1960. V. 62

MC DONALD, EDWARD D.
A Bibliography of the Writings of D. H. Lawrence. Philadelphia: 1925. V. 64
A Bibliography of the Writings of Norman Douglas. Philadelphia: 1927. V. 66

MC DONALD, GREGORY
Fletch. 1974. V. 66
Love Among the Mashed Potatoes. 1978. V. 66
Running Scared. 1964. V. 66

MC DONALD, WILLIAM N.
A History of the Laurel Brigade. Balimore: 1907. V. 62; 63; 65
A History of the Laurel Brigade. Baltimore: 1969. V. 67

MC DONNELL, JOSEPH
Five Hundred Years of the Art of the Book in Ireland. 1500 to the Present Day. 1997. V. 62
Gold-Tooled Bookbindings Commissioned by Trinity College Dublin in the Eighteenth Century. London: 1987. V. 67

MC DOUGALL, JOHN
On Western Trails in the Early Seventies, Frontier Pioneer Life in the Canadian Northwest. Toronto: 1911. V. 62

MC DOUGALL, WILLIAM
Body and Mind. A History and a Defense of Animism. London: 1913. V. 66

MC DOWALL, WILLIAM
History of the Burgh of Dumfries. Edinburgh: 1867. V. 62
History of the Burgh of Dumfries.... Edinburgh: 1873. V. 62

MC DOWELL, JAMES
Speech of James McDowell on the Formation of Governments for New Mexico and California. Washington: 1849. V. 65

MC DOWELL, S. B.
The Systematic Position of Lanthanotus and the Affinities of the Anguinomorphan Lizards. New York: 1954. V. 63

MC ELDOWNEY, JOHN C.
History of Wetzel County, West Virginia. N.P: 1901. V. 62

MC ELHENNEY, JOHN
Recollections of the Rev. John Mc Elhenney, D.D. Richmond: 1893. V. 66
Semi-Centenary Sermon. Lewisburg: 1858. V. 64
A Sermon Delivered at the First Meeting of the Greenbrier Presbytery, at Lewisburg. Charleston: 1838. V. 64

MC ELROY, C. J.
Mc Elroy Hunts Asia. 1989. V. 67

MC ELROY, JOSEPH
A Smuggler's Bible. New York: 1966. V. 65; 67

MC ELROY, ROBERT MC NUTT
The Winning of the Far West. New York: 1914. V. 63; 66

MC EWAN, IAN
Amsterdam. London: 1998. V. 62
Black Dogs. London: 1992. V. 63; 67
The Cement Garden. New York: 1978. V. 62; 66
The Child in Time. London: 1987. V. 62; 63
The Child in Time. London: 1989. V. 64
The Comfort of Strangers. London: 1981. V. 62
First Love, Last Rites. London: 1975. V. 62; 65
First Love, Last Rites. New York: 1975. V. 62
The Imitation Game.... London: 1981. V. 64
In Between the Sheets. London: 1978. V. 62; 65
In Between the Sheets. New York: 1979. V. 66

MC FALL, FRANCES ELIZABETH CLARK
The Beth Book. New York: 1897. V. 65

MC FARLAND, LOUIS BURCHETTE
Memoirs and Addresses of L. B. McFarland. Memphis?: 1922. V. 62; 65

MC FARLAND, RON
James Welch. Lewiston: 1986. V. 67

MC FARLAND, ROSS A.
Human Factors in Air Transportation: Occupational Health and Safety. New York: 1953. V. 63
The Psychological Effects of Oxygen Deprivation (Anoxemia) on Human Behavior. New York: 1932. V. 66

MC FARLAND, W. I.
Salmon of the Atlantic. New York: 1925. V. 65

MC FARLING, LLOYD
Exploring the Northern Plains. Caldwell: 1955. V. 67

MC FEE, WILLIAM
The Harbourmaster. Garden City: 1931. V. 62
Sailors of Fortune. Garden City: 1929. V. 62

MC GAHERN, JOHN
The Barracks. London: 1963. V. 63
The Collected Stories. London: 1992. V. 62
The Dark. London: 1965. V. 62
The Leavetaking. London: 1974. V. 62; 66
Nightlines. London: 1970. V. 63
The Photographer. London: 1979. V. 62
The Pornographer. London: 1979. V. 62

MC GARRELL, ANN
Flora. Poems. Mt. Horeb: 1990. V. 64

MC GARRITY, MICHAEL
Tularosa. New York: 1996. V. 67

MC GEE, THOMAS D.
The Poems of Thomas D. McGee. New York: 1869. V. 63

MC GEE, TOM G.
Who Killed Pat Hennessey. Oklahoma: 1941. V. 65

MC GILL, WILLIAM M.
Caverns of Virginia. Richmond: 1933. V. 66

MC GILLYCUDDY, JULIA B.
Mc Gillycuddy Agent. Stanford: 1941. V. 65; 67

MC GINNIES, W. G.
Deserts of the World an Appraisal of Research into Their Physical and Biological Environments. 1968. V. 63

MC GINNIS, EDITH B.
The Promised Land, a Narrative Featuring the Life History and Adventures of Frank J. Brown, Pioneer, Buffalo Hunter, Indian Fighter. Grand Rapids: 1947. V. 67

MC GIVERN, ED
Ed McGivern's Book On Fast and Fancy Revolver Shooting. Springfield: 1938. V. 63; 66

MC GLASHAN, C. F.
History of the Donner Party - a Tragedy of the Sierras. Truckee: 1879. V. 66

MC GOVERN, WILLIAM MONTGOMERY
To Lhasa in Disguise: a Secret Expedition through Mysterious Tibet. New York and London: 1924. V. 65

MC GOWAN, EDWARD
California Vigilantes. Oakland: 1946. V. 64; 67

MC GOWAN, HELEN
Motor City Madam. New York: 1964. V. 65

MC GRATH, HAROLD P.
The Harold P. McGrath Collection of the Prints of Leonard Baskin. West Hatfield: 1987. V. 65

MC GRATH, P. T.
Newfoundland in 1911, Being the Coronation Year of King George V and the Opening of the Second Decade of the Twentieth Century. London: 1911. V. 64

MC GRATH, PATRICK
Blood and Water and Other Tales. New York: 1988. V. 63

MC GRAW, ELOISE
The Moorchild. New York: 1996. V. 65

MC GREEVY, THOMAS
Poems. London: 1934. V. 65

MC GREGOR, DUNCAN
A Narrative of the Loss of the Kent East Indiaman, by Fire, in the Bay of Biscay, on the 1st of March, 1825. Edinburgh: 1825. V. 66

MC GREGOR, JAMES H.
The Wounded Knee Massacre from Viewpoint of the Sioux. Minneapolis: 1950. V. 65

MC GREGOR, R. C.
A Manual of Philippine Birds. Manila: 1909. V. 63; 67

MC GREW, CHARLES B.
Italian Doorways: Measured Drawings and Photographs. Cleveland: 1929. V. 62; 63; 66

MC GUANE, THOMAS
The Bushwacked Piano. New York: 1971. V. 64

MC GUANE, THOMAS continued
Keep the Change. Boston: 1989. V. 62; 66
Live Water. Far Hills: 1996. V. 64; 67
92 in the Shade. New York: 1973. V. 64
92 in the Shade. London: 1974. V. 65
Nothing but Blue Skies. Boston: 1992. V. 63; 64; 66
Panama. New York: 1978. V. 62
Some Horses. New York: 1999. V. 67
The Sporting Club. New York: 1968. V. 62; 63; 66; 67
The Sporting Club. New York: 1969. V. 62
The Sporting Life. London: 1969. V. 66

MC GUCKEN, WILLIAM
Nineteenth Century Spectroscopy; Development of the Understanding of Spectra 1802-1897. Baltimore: 1969. V. 67

MC GUIRE, HUNTER
The Confederate Cause and Conduct in the War Between the States...and Other Confederate Papers. Richmond: 1907. V. 63; 65

MC GUIRE, J. A.
In the Alaska-Yukon Gamelands. Cincinnati: 1921. V. 62; 63; 64; 66; 67

MC GUIRE, JOSEPH D.
Pipes of Smoking Customs of the American Indian Aborigines. Washington: 1899. V. 65

MC HANEY, PEARL AMELIA
Writers' Reflections Upon First Reading Welty. Athens: 1999. V. 63

MC HARG, I. L.
Design with Nature. New York: 1969. V. 65

MC HATTON-RIPLEY, ELIZA
From Flag to Flag. New York: 1889. V. 63; 65

MC HENRY, LAWRENCE
Garrison's History of Neurology. Springfield: 1969. V. 64; 66

MC ILHANY, EDWARD WASHINGTON
Recollections of a '49er. Kansas City: 1908. V. 63; 66

MC ILHENNY, E. A.
Befo' De War Spirituals. Boston;: 1930. V. 63

MC ILVAINE, EILEEN
P. G. Wodehouse, a Comprehensive Bibliography and Checklist. London: 1990. V. 63

MC ILVANNEY, WILLIAM
Docherty. London: 1975. V. 63

MC ILVIANE, WILLIAM
Sketches of Scenery and Notes of Personal Adventure in California and Mexico. San Francisco: 1951. V. 65

MC ILWAINE, RICHARD
Memories of Three Score Years and Ten. New York: 1908. V. 62; 63

MC INERNEY, JAY
Bright Lights, Big City. New York: 1984. V. 63; 64
Bright Lights, Big City. London: 1985. V. 65

MC INNES, ALEX P.
Chronicles of the Cariboo Number One, Being a True Story of the First Discovery of Gold in the Cariboo District on the Horsefly River by Peter C. Dunlevey (sic). Lillooet: 1938. V. 64

MC INTOSH, C.
The Flower Garden. 1838. V. 63

MC INTOSH, JOHN
The Origin of the North American Indians.... New York: 1843. V. 65

MC INTOSH, LACHLAN
Class Despotism, as Exemplified During the Four Years' Struggle for Freedom in the United States of America.... London: 1867. V. 64

MC INTOSH, MICHAEL
Classics of American Sporting Fiction. Clinton: 1984. V. 65

MC IVOR, W. G.
Notes of the Propagation and Cultivation of the Medicinal Cinchonas, or Peruvian Bark Trees. Madras: 1867. V. 63; 64; 65; 66

MC KAY, BARRY
Marbling Methods and Receipts from Four Centuries; with Other Instructions Useful to Bookbinders. Kidlington/New Castle: 1990. V. 62; 64
Patterns and Pigments in English Marbled Papers: an Account of the Origins, Sources and Documentary Literature in 1881. N.P: 1988. V. 64

MC KAY, CLAUDE
Spring in New Hampshire and Other Poems. London: 1920. V. 62

MC KAY, DONALD
Daring Donald McKay; or the Last War Trail of the Modocs. Erie: 1885. V. 65; 67

MC KAY, JAMES
Pendle Hill in History and Literature. London: 1888. V. 65; 66

MC KAY, MALCOLM S.
Cow Range and Hunting Trail. New York: 1925. V. 63; 66

MC KAY, R. H.
Little Pills, an Army Story. Pittsburgh: 1918. V. 62; 63; 64; 65; 67

MC KAY, SETH SHEPARD
Debates in the Texas Constitutional Convention of 1875. Austin;: 1930. V. 65

MC KEAN, G. B.
Making Good - a Story of Northwest Canada. New York: 1920. V. 63

MC KECHINE, SUE
British Silhouette Artists and Their Work 1760-1860. London: 1978. V. 63

MC KEE, BARBARA
Havasupai Baskets and their Makers. 1930-1940. Flagstaff: 1975. V. 67

MC KEE, BILL
Trail of Iron: the CPR and the Bird of the West 1880-1930. Vancouver: 1983. V. 63

MC KEE, E. D.
The Environment and History of the Toroweap and Kailab Formations of Northern Arizona and Southern Utah. Washington: 1938. V. 65

MC KEE, IRVING
Alonzo Delano's California Correspondence. Sacramento: 1952. V. 65

MC KEE, JAMES COOPER
Narrative of the Surrender of a Command of U.S. Forces at Fort Fillmore, N.M. New York: 1881. V. 63

MC KEE, ROBERT E.
The Zia Company in Los Alamos, a History. El Paso: 1950. V. 67

MC KEE, RUTH K.
Mary Richardson Walker: White Woman to Cross the Rockies. Caldwell: 1945. V. 65

MC KELVEY, S. D.
Botanical Exploration of the Trans-Mississippi West 1790-1850. Jamaica Plain: 1955. V. 63
The Lilac, a Monograph. New York: 1928. V. 64

MC KENNA, JAMES
A Black Range Tales Chronicling Sixty Years of Life and Adventure in the Southwest. New York: 1936. V. 62; 66

MC KENNA, M. C.
Classification of Mammals Above the Species Level. New York: 1997. V. 62

MC KENNA, RICHARD
The Sand Pebbles. New York and Evanston: 1962. V. 63; 67

MC KENNA, TERENCE
Synesthesia. New York: 1992. V. 64

MC KENNEY, THOMAS LORRAINE
Sketches of a Tour to the Lakes. Barre: 1972. V. 67
To the Public. N.P: 1828. V. 63

MC KENNY, MARGARET
Little White Pig. Portland: 1945. V. 63

MC KERNAN, H.
An Experienced Colour-Maker and Dyer. London: 1829. V. 64

MC KERROW, RONALD BRUNLEES
Printer's and Publisher's Devices in England and Scotland 1485-1640. 1949. V. 67

MC KERROW, W. S.
The Ecology of Fossils. 1978. V. 67

MC KIE, JAMES
The Ayrshire Wreath MDCCCXLV.... Kilmarnock: 1844. V. 62

MC KIM, RANDOLPH HARRISON
The Gettysburg Campaign. Richmond: 1915. V. 63; 65
In Memoriam. A Sermon Preached on the Occasion of the Death of Gen. Robert E. Lee. Baltimore: 1870. V. 62
The Numerical Strength of the Confederate Army. New York: 1912. V. 62; 63; 65
A Soldier's Recollections. New York: 1910. V. 63
A Soldier's Recollections. New York: 1911. V. 62; 63; 65
The Soul of Lee. London: 1918. V. 62; 63

MC KINLEY, ANDREW
The Trial of Andrew McKinley Before the High Court...at Edinburgh, on the 19th Day of July 1817.... Edinburgh: 1818. V. 63

MC KINLEY, RICHARD
The Surnames of Lancashire. London: 1981. V. 65

MC KINLEY, ROBIN
The Blue Sword. New York: 1982. V. 65
The Hero and the Crown. New York: 1985. V. 65

MC KINLEY, WILLIAM
Speeches and Addresses of William McKinley from March 1, 1897 to May 30, 1900. New York: 1900. V. 63

MC KINNEY, E. P.
Life in Tent and Field. Boston: 1922. V. 65; 67

MC KINNEY, SAM
Bligh: A True Account of Mutiny Aboard His Majesty's Ship Bounty. Camden: 1989. V. 63; 64

MC KINNEY, WILLIAM M.
A Treatise on the Law of Fellow Servants. Long Island: 1890. V. 65

MC KISSACK, PATRICIA
The Dark-Thirty: Southern Tales of the Supernatural. New York: 1992. V. 65

MC KITTERICK, DAVID
A History of Cambridge University Press. Volume 1. Cambridge: 1992. V. 62
A New Specimen Book of Curwen Pattern Papers. Gloucestershire: 1987. V. 64
A New Specimen Book of Curwen Pattern Papers. London: 1987. V. 65
Stanley Morison & D. B. Updike: Selected Correspondence. New York: 1979. V. 64
Wallpapers by Edward Bawden. Andoversford: 1989. V. 64

MC KOY, HENRY BACON
The Story of the Reedy River. Greenville: 1969. V. 67

MC LAREN, ALEXANDER
The Trial of Alexander McLaren and Thomas Baird...at Edinburgh on the 5th and 7th March 1817 for Sedition. Edinburgh: 1817. V. 63

MC LAREN, DUNCAN
In Ruins; the Once Great Houses of Ireland. 1980. V. 67

MC LAREN, JACK
A Diver Went Down. London: 1929. V. 65; 66

MC LAUGHLIN, DANIEL
Sketch of a Trip from Omaha to Salmon River. Chicago: 1954. V. 63; 66

MC LAUGHLIN, JAMES
My Friend the Indian. Boston: 1926. V. 67

MC LEAN, BRUCE
Retrospective King For a Day and 999 Other Pieces/Works/Things Etc. London: 1972. V. 63

MC LEAN, C. H.
Prominent People of New Brunswick in the Religious, Educational, Political, Professional, Commercial and Social Activities of the Province. N.P: 1937. V. 67

MC LEAN, COLIN
At Dawn and Dusk. London: 1954. V. 67

MC LEAN, J. G.
The Growth of Integrated Oil Companies. Boston: 1954. V. 65

MC LEAN, RUARI
Benjamin Fawcett. London: 1988. V. 64
Motif. 1958-1964. V. 64
Victorian Book Design and Colour Printing. London: 1963. V. 67
Victorian Book Design and Colour Printing. London: 1972. V. 66
Victorian Publishers' Book-Bindings in Cloth and Leather. Berkeley and Los Angeles: 1973. V. 63

MC LEARY, A. C.
Humorous Incidents of the Civil War. N.P: 1903. V. 62; 63; 65

MC LENNAN, J. S.
Louisbourg from Its Foundation to Its Fall 1713-1758. London: 1918. V. 66

MC LEOD, ALEXANDER
Pigtails and Gold Dust. Caldwell: 1947. V. 63

MC LEOD, DONALD
History of Wiskonsan, From Its First Discovery to the Present Period. Buffalo: 1846. V. 62; 66

MC LEOD, ROBERT RANDALL
Markland or Nova Scotia: Its History, Natural Resources and Native Beauties. N.P: 1903. V. 67

M'CLINTOCK, FRANCIS LEOPOLD
In the Arctic Seas. Philadelphia. V. 65
The Voyage of the Fox in the Arctic Seas. Boston: 1860. V. 63

MC LOUGHLIN, MAURICE E.
Tennis As I Play It. New York: 1915. V. 63; 65

MC LUHAN, HERBERT MARSHALL
The Mechanical Bridge. New York: 1951. V. 63

MC LUHAN, T. C.
Dream Tracks: The Railroad and American Indian 1890-1930. New York: 1985. V. 63; 64

M'CLUNE, ROBERT LE M.
The Discovery of the Northwest Passage by H.M.S. "Investigator" Capt. R. M'Clure 1850, 1851, 1852, 1853, 1854. Rutland/Tokyo: 1969. V. 64

M'CLUNG, JOHN
Sketches of Western Adventure.... Maysville: 1832. V. 62

M'CLURE, ROBERT
The Discovery of the North-West Passage by H.M.S. Investigator.... London: 1856. V. 62
The Discovery of the North-West Passage by H.M.S. Investigator.... Rutland/Tokyo: 1969. V. 62

MC MAHAN, VALRIE
Fan and Fannie: The Baseball Twins. New York: 1928. V. 64

MC MAHON, JO
Dennie Folks and Friends of Theirs. Joliet: 1925. V. 62

MC MANUS, GEORGE
Bringing Up Father. New York: 1919-1926. V. 66
Jiggs is Back. 1986. V. 67
The Newlyweds and Their Baby's Comic Pictures for Painting and Crayoning. Akron; New York: 1917. V. 66

MC MASTER, FITZ HUGH
History of the First Presbyterian Church and Its Churchyard. Columbia. V. 67

MC MECHEN, EDGAR CARLISLE
Life of Governor Evans - Second Territorial Governor of Colorado. Denver: 1924. V. 66

MC MILLAN, GEORGE
The Old Breed: a History of the First Marine Division in World War II. Washington: 1949. V. 67

MC MILLAN, NORA F.
British Shells. London: 1968. V. 62

MC MILLAN, TERRY
Disappearing Acts. New York: 1989. V. 67
Mama. Boston: 1987. V. 63; 64; 66
Waiting to Exhale. New York: 1992. V. 64

MC MILLAN, WILLIAM
The Story of the Scottish Flag. Glasgow: 1925. V. 62

MC MORRIES, EDWARD YOUNG
History of the First Regiment, Alabama Volunteer Infantry, C.S.A. Montgomery: 1904. V. 62; 63

MC MULLEN, R. T.
An Experimental Cruise, Single-Handed in the Procyon, 7 Ton Lugger. London: 1880. V. 62
Orion, or How I Came to Sail Alone a 19 Ton Yacht. London: 1878. V. 65

MC MURRAY, WILLIAM J.
History of the Twentieth Tennessee Regiment Volunteer Infantry, C.S.A. Nashville: 1904. V. 62; 63; 65

MC MURRICH, J. PLAYFAIR
Leonardo Da Vinci. The Anatomist (1452-1519). Baltimore: 1930. V. 64

MC MURTRIE, DOUGLAS
Early Printing in Colorado. Denver: 1935. V. 64; 66
Early Printing in New Orleans 1764-1810, with Bibliography of the Issues of the Louisiana Press. New Orleans: 1929. V. 66
Early Printing in Tennessee, with a Bibliography of the Issues of the Tennessee Press 1793-1830. Chicago: 1933. V. 63; 64; 66
Early Printing in Wisconsin. Seattle: 1931. V. 62; 66
Eighteenth Century North Carolina Imprints 1749-1800. Chapel Hill: 1938. V. 67
The First Printing In New Mexico. (with) *Cuaderno de Ortografia.* Chicago: 1929. V. 63; 65
A History of Printing in the United States. New York: 1936. V. 63
Jean Gutenberg, Inventor of Printing.... New York: 1926. V. 66
The Mining Laws of the Third District of Idaho. Evanston: 1944. V. 65
Oregon Imprints 1847-1870. Eugene: 1950. V. 66

MC MURTRY, LARRY
All My Friends Are Going to Be Strangers. New York: 1972. V. 62; 66
Anything for Billy. New York: 1988. V. 66; 67
Cadillac Jack. New York: 1982. V. 67
Crazy Horse. N.P: 1999. V. 62
Desert Rose. New York: 1983. V. 62; 65; 67
Duane's Depressed. New York: 1999. V. 62
Horseman Pass By. New York: 1961. V. 64; 67
In a Narrow Grave - Essays on Texas. Austin: 1968. V. 67
It's Always We Rambled. An Essay on Rodeo. New York: 1974. V. 66
The Last Picture Show. New York: 1966. V. 62; 65; 67
Leaving Cheyenne. New York: 1963. V. 62
Lonesome Dove. New York: 1985. V. 62; 63; 64; 65; 66; 67
Moving On. New York: 1970. V. 62; 65; 66
Moving On. New York: 1989. V. 67
Pretty Boy Floyd. New York: 1994. V. 67
Somebody's Darling. New York: 1978. V. 62; 63; 66
Terms of Endearment. New York: 1975. V. 62
Texasville. New York: 1987. V. 67

MC NABB, VINCENT
Geoffrey Chaucer - a Study in Genius and Ethics. Ditchling: 1934. V. 62

MC NAGNY, BOB
Noah's Nightmare. Indianapolis: 1926. V. 63

MC NAIR, JAMES B.
Citrus Products. Chicago: 1926. V. 62; 63

MC NALLY, DENNIS
Desolate Angel - a Biography - Jack Kerouac.... New York: 1979. V. 65

MC NAMARA, JOHN J.
In Perils by Mine Own Countrymen: Three Years on the Kansas Border. New York: 1856. V. 66

MC NAMEE, EOIN
The Last of Deeds. Dublin: 1989. V. 65
Resurrection Man. London: 1994. V. 64

MC NAUGHTON, DANIEL
Report of the Trial of Daniel Mcnaughton at the Central Criminal Court (Friday, the 3rd and Saturday the 4th of March 1843) for the Wilful Murder of Edward Drummond Esq. London: 1843. V. 63

MC NAUGHTON, MARGARET
Overland to Cariboo, an Eventful Journey of Canadian Pioneers to the Gold Fields of British Columbia in 1862. Toronto: 1896. V. 62; 65

MC NEAL, T. A.
When Kansas Was Young. Topeka: 1934. V. 67

MC NEER, MAY
War Chief of the Seminoles. New York: 1954. V. 63

MC NEIL, MARION L.
The Blue Elephant and the Pink Pig. Akron: 1931. V. 65

MC NEIL, MORRIS
Hokum. Wellesley Hills: 1978. V. 64

MC NEILE, H. C.
Bulldog Drummond Strikes Back. Garden City: 1933. V. 66

MC NEMAR, RICHARD
A Selection of Hymns and Poems.... Watevliet (i.e. Watervliet): 1833. V. 63

MC NEMEE, A. J.
Brother Mack The Frontier Preachers - a Brief Record of the Difficulties and Hardships of a Pioneer Itinerant. Portland: 1924. V. 67

MC NITT, FRANK
The Indian Traders. Norman: 1962. V. 63
Navajo Wars - Military Campaigns Slave Raids and Reprisals. Norman: 1972. V. 67
Richard Wetherill Anasazi. Albuquerque: 1957. V. 63

MC NULTY, JOHN
A Man Gets Around. Boston: 1951. V. 67

M'COMBIE, WILLIAM
Memoirs of Alexander Bethune, Embracing Selections from His Correspondence and Literary Remains.... Aberdeen: 1845. V. 63

MC PALMER, JOHN
History of the 22nd United States Infantry. N.P: 1972. V. 67

MC PHAIL, JAMES
A Treatise on the Culture of the Cucumber.... London: 1795. V. 64

MC PHAIL, RODGER
Fishing Season. An Artist's Fishing Year. 1990. V. 63; 65; 67
Open Season. London: 1986. V. 67

MC PHARLIN, PAUL
Puppetry. A Yearbook of Puppets and Marionettes. Volume One-Volume Sixteen. Detroit and New York: 1930-1947. V. 65
Puppets in America 1739 to Today. Birmingham: 1936. V. 64
A Repertory of Marionette Plays Chose and Translated with Notes, Bibliography and Lists of Marionette Play Producers in England and America. New York: 1929. V. 64

MC PHEE, JOHN
Alaska. Images of the Country. San Francisco: 1981. V. 62; 64
Annals of the Former World. New York: 1981-1983. V. 64
Annals of the Former World. New York: 1983. V. 62; 64; 66; 67
The Control of Nature. New York: 1989. V. 66
The Crofter and the Laird. New York: 1970. V. 62
The Headmaster. New York: 1966. V. 62; 64; 67
In Suspect Terrain. New York: 1983. V. 64; 66
Level of the Game. New York: 1969. V. 64; 65
Oranges. New York: 1967. V. 62
The Pine Barrens. New York: 1968. V. 64; 67
La Place De La Concorde Suisse. New York: 1984. V. 62; 65
A Roomful of Hovings and Other Profiles. New York: 1968. V. 62; 64; 67
A Sense of Where You Are. New York: 1965. V. 62
A Sense of Where You Are. New York: 1966. V. 63
Table of Contents. New York: 1985. V. 62
Wimbledon, a Celebration. New York: 1972. V. 67

MC PHERREN, IDA
Imprints on Pioneer Trails. Boston: 1950. V. 63
Trails End. Casper: 1938. V. 63; 66

MC PHERSON, AIMEE SEMPLE
Divine Sermons. Los Angeles: 1920. V. 65
Give Me My Own God. New York: 1936. V. 66
The Holy Spirit. Los Angeles: 1931. V. 65
Tabernacle Revivalist. Echo Park: 1925. V. 63
This is That: Personal Experiences, Sermons and Writings. Los Angeles: 1921. V. 65

MC PHERSON, EDWARD
A Handbook of Politics for 1876 Being a Record of Important Political Action, National and State.... Washington: 1876. V. 67

MC PHERSON, JAMES ALAN
Hue and Cry. Boston and Toronto: 1969. V. 63; 65
Railroad. New York: 1976. V. 62

MC PHERSON, SANDRA
Beauty in Use. Vermont: 1997. V. 62
Elegies for the Hot Season. Bloomington & London: 1970. V. 67
Responsibility for Blue. Denton: 1985. V. 66

MC PHERSON, WILLIAM
From San Diego to the Colorado in 1849.... Los Angeles: 1932. V. 66
Testing the Current. London: 1985. V. 62

MC QUADE, JAMES
The Cruise of the Montauk, to Bermuda, the West Indies and Florida. New York: 1885. V. 65

MC QUEEN, A. S.
History of Okefenokee Swamp. Clinton: 1926. V. 66

MC QUILLAN, KARIN
Deadly Safari. 1990. V. 64; 66
Deadly Safari. New York: 1990. V. 63; 65

MC REYNOLDS, ROBERT
Thirty Years on the Frontier. Colorado Springs: 1906. V. 63; 66

MC RILL, ALBERT
And Satan Came Also an Inside Tory of a City's Social and Political History. Oklahoma City: 1955. V. 66

MC TAGGART, M. F.
Mount and the Man. London: 1927. V. 67

MC VEY, J. P.
CRC Handbook of Mariculture. Boca Raton: 1990. V. 65

MC WHORTER, L. V.
Hear Me My Chiefs. Nez Perce History and Legend. Princeton: 1919. V. 66
Hear Me My Chiefs, Nez Perce History and Legend. Caldwell: 1952. V. 63
Tragedy of the Wahk-Shum. Prelude to the Yakima Indian War, 1855-1856. The Killing of Major Andrew J. Bolon. Eyewitness Account by Su-el-Lil Locating the Place of Bolon's Death. Yakima: 1937. V. 63
Yellow Wolf: His Own Story. Caldwell: 1948. V. 64

MC WILLIAMS, JOHN
Recollections of...His Youth Experience in California and the Civil War. Princeton: 1919. V. 63

M'DERMOT, M.
The Beauties of Modern Literature in Verse and Prose. 1824. V. 67

M'DONNELL, R.
Observations on the Functions of the Liver. Dublin: 1865. V. 67

M'DOWALL, WILLIAM
Memorials of St. Michael's. Edinburgh: 1876. V. 62; 66

MEACHAM, A. B.
Wi-Ne-Ma (The Woman-Chief) and Her People. Hartford: 1876. V. 63
Wigwam and Warpath or the Royal Chief in Chains. Boston: 1875. V. 64; 65; 67

MEAD, ELWOOD
Report of Irrigation Investigations in Utah. Washington: 1903. V. 67

MEAD, HERMAN RALPH
Incunabula in the Huntington Library. San Marino: 1937. V. 62

MEAD, MARGARET
Kinship in the Admirality Islands. New York: 1934. V. 63
The Maoris and Their Arts. New York: 1928. V. 67

MEAD, PETER B.
An Elementary Treatise on Grape Culture and Wine Making. New York: 1867. V. 66

MEAD, RICHARD
De Imperio Solis ac Lunae in Corpora Humana, et Morbis Inde Oriundis. Londini: 1704. V. 65
A Discourse Concerning the Action of the Sun and Moon on Animal Bodies and the Influence Which This May Have in Many Diseases. London: 1708. V. 65
A Discourse on the Plague.... London: 1744. V. 66; 67
A Discourse on the Small Pox and Measles. London: 1748. V. 62
A Mechanical Account of Poisons in Several Essays. London: 1708. V. 62; 66
Medical Precepts and Cautions. London: 1755. V. 64; 66
The Medical Works. London: 1762. V. 64; 66
The Medical Works. Edinburgh: 1775. V. 66
Monita et Praecepta Medica. Londini: 1751. V. 65

MEAD, STELLA
Hopping Timothy. London: 1945. V. 65

MEAD, WILLIAM EDWARD
The English Medieval Feast. Boston and New York: 1931. V. 63
The Grand Tour in the Eighteenth Century. 1914. V. 67

MEADE, GEORGE
The Life and Letters of George Gordon Meade, Major General U.S. Army. New York: 1913. V. 64

MEADE, GLENN
Brandenburg. London: 1994. V. 66
The Sands of Sakkara. London: 1999. V. 66
Snow Wolf. London: 1995. V. 66

MEADE, L. T.
The Home of Silence. London: 1907. V. 66
Stories from the Diary of a Doctor. Philadelphia: 1895. V. 63

MEADE, RICHARD H.
A History of Thoracic Surgery. Springfield: 1961. V. 64
An Introduction to the History of General Surgery. Philadelphia: 1968. V. 64

MEADE, ROBERT D.
Patrick Henry: Patriot in the Making. (with) Patrick Henry: Practical Revolutionary. Philadelphia & New York: 1957-1969. V. 65

MEADE KING, ERIC
The Silent Horn. London: 1938. V. 67

MEADLEY, GEORGE WILSON
Memoirs of William Paley. Sunderland: 1809. V. 66

MEADOWS, DON
Orange County Under Spain, Mexico and the United States. Los Angeles: 1966. V. 62

MEADOWS, KENNY
Heads of the People; or Portraits of the English Drawn by Kenny Meadows.... London: 1840-1841. V. 62

MEADOWS, PHILIP
Observations concerning the Dominion and Sovereignty of the Seas.... In the Savoy: 1689. V. 63

MEADOWS, T.
Thespian Gleanings.... Ulverston: 1805. V. 62

MEADOWS, THOMAS TAYLOR
Desultory Notes on the Government and People of China, and on the Chinese Language.... London: 1847. V. 62

MEANS, EDGAR ALEXANDER
Mammals of the Mexican Boundary of the United States. Washington: 1907. V. 63; 64

MEANS, JAMES
Manflight. Boston: 1891. V. 62

MEANS, ROBERT
Considerations Respecting the Genuineness of the Pentateuch, with Special Reference to a Pamphlet Entitled the Connexion Between Geology and the Pentateuch. Columbia: 1834. V. 66; 67

MEANY, E. S.
Diary of Wilkes in the Northwest. Seattle: 1926. V. 66
A New Vancouver Journal on the Discovery of Puget Sound by a Member of the Chatham's Crew. Seattle: 1915. V. 66

MEARES, EDWIN HARTLEY
On British Colonization: Particulary in Reference to South Australia. London: 1839. V. 64

MEARES, JOHN
Voyages Made in the Years 1788 and 1789, from China to the Northwest Coast of America.... London: 1790. V. 66
Voyages Made in the Years 1788 and 1789, from China to the N.W. Coast of America. London: 1791. V. 63

MEARS, JAMES EWING
Practical Surgery: Including Surgical Dressings, Bandaging, Ligations and Amputations. Philadelphia: 1878. V. 63; 65

MEASE, JAMES
An Inaugural Dissertation on the Disease Produced by the Bite of a Mad Dog, or Other Rabid Animal.... Philadelphia. V. 66; 67
An Inaugural Dissertation on the Disease Produced by the Bite of a Mad Dog, or Other Rabid Animal.... Philadelphia: 1792. V. 63

MEATH, REGINALD BRABAZON, EARL OF
Prosperity or Pauperism?. London: 1888. V. 64

MEATYARD, RALPH EUGENE
The Family Album of Lucybelle Crater. North Carolina: 1974. V. 63

MECHEL, CHRISTIAN VON
Verzeichniss der Gemalde Kaiserlich Koniglichen Bilder Gallerie in Wien.... Wien: 1783. V. 64

MECKEL, JOHANN FRIEDRICH
Dissertatio Inauguralis medica Anatomico, Physiologica de Quinto Pare Nervorom Cerebri.... Tottingae: 1748. V. 62; 66

MECKLENBURG, A. F., DUKE OF
From the Congo to the Niger and the Nile. Philadelphia: 1914. V. 62
In the Heart of Africa. 1910. V. 62; 63; 64

MECKLIN, JOHN MOFFATT
The Ku Klux Klan. New York: 1924. V. 67

THE MEDALLION - *The Ancient Civilization of Southern Arizona.* 1929-1935. V. 63

MEDEM, RICARDO
En La Cruz del Anteojo. Madrid: 1974. V. 64; 66; 67

MEDHURST, G.
Calculations and Remarks, Tending to Prove the Practicability, Effects and Advantages of a Plan for the Rapid Conveyance of Goods and Passengers Upon an Iron Road Through a Tube of 30 Feet in Area by the Power and Velocity of Air. London: 1812. V. 63

MEDHURST, W. H.
China: Its State and Prospects. London: 1838. V. 67

MEDICAE Artis Principes, Post Hippocratem & Galenum. Geneva: 1567. V. 64

MEDICAL and Surgical Reports of the Episcopal Hospital. Philadelphia: 1913-1930. V. 67

MEDICAL Leaves 1942. Chicago. V. 65

MEDICAL SOCIETY OF NEW JERSEY
The Law Incorporating Medical Societies and the By-Laws, Rules and Regulations with the Table of Fees and Rates for Chargeing of the Medical Society of New Jersey.... New Brunswick: 1830. V. 63; 66

MEDICAL SOCIETY OF THE DISTRICT OF COLUMBIA
Constitution of the Medical Society of the District of Columbia; to Which is Prefixed the Act of Incorporation. Washington: 1820. V. 63

MEDICAL SOCIETY OF THE STATE OF WASHINGTON
Constitution and By-Laws of the Medical Society of the State of Washington. Adopted at Tacoma, October 22, 1889. Olympia: 1889. V. 63

MEDINA POMAR, DUKE DE
Who Is She? A Mystery of Mayfair. London: 1878. V. 66

MEDWAY, L.
The Birds of Malay Peninsula Volume V. London: 1976. V. 67

MEDWIN, THOMAS
Conversations of Lord Byron: Noted During a Residence with His Lordship at Pisa, in the Years 1821 and 1822. London: 1824. V. 63; 64; 65
Journal of the Conversations of Lord Byron, Noted During a Residence with His Lordship at Pisa, in the Years 1821 and 1822. London: 1824. V. 63
Journal of the Conversations of Lord Byron, Noted During a Residence with His Lordship at Pisa in the Years 1821 and 1822. New York: 1824. V. 65

MEE, HUAN, PSEUD.
Solving the Unsolvable. London: 1980. V. 65

MEE, JOHN L.
The Three Little Frogs. Joliet: 1924. V. 63

MEEHAN, T.
The Native Flowers and Ferns of the United States, in Their Botanical, Horticultural and Popular Aspects. Boston: 1878. V. 64

MEEK, A. S.
A Naturalist in Cannibal Land. London & Leipsic: 1913. V. 65; 67

MEEK, C. K.
The Northern Tribes of Nigeria. London: 1925. V. 62; 66
A Sudanese Kingdom, An Ehtnographical Study of the Jukun-Speaking Peoples of Nigeria. London: 1931. V. 62

MEEK, M. R. D.
Hang the Consequences. London: 1984. V. 65
The Sitting Ducks. London: 1984. V. 65

MEEK, S. E.
The Marine Fishes of Panama. Chicago: 1923-1928. V. 65

MEEK, STEPHEN
The Autobiography of a Mountain Man 1805-1889. Pasadena: 1948. V. 65

MEEKER, CLAUDE
The Home of the Brontes. 1916. V. 66

MEEKER, EZRA
The Busy Life of Eighty-Five Years. Seattle: 1916. V. 65
Pioneer Reminiscences of Puget Sound - the Tragedy of Lesch. Seattle: 1905. V. 66
Ventures and Adventures of Ezra Meeker or Sixty Years of Frontier Life - the Oregon Trail. Seattle: 1908. V. 66

MEEKER, N. C.
Life in the West, or Stories of the Mississippi Valley. New York: 1868. V. 63; 66

MEEKEREN, JOB JANSZOON VAN
Observationes Medico-Chirurgicae, ex Belgico in latinum.... Amstelodami: 1682. V. 66

MEGAW, E.
Wild Flowers of Cyprus. 1973. V. 63

MEGGENDORFER, LOTHAR
Allerlei Tiere (All Kinds of Animals). Munchen: 1888. V. 64
Always Jolly. London: 1886. V. 64
Die Brave Berta und Die Bose Lina. (The Good Bertha and the Bad Lina). Munchen: 1882. V. 64
Im Sommer (In the Summer). Munchen: 1883. V. 65
Lustig! (Always Jolly). Munchen: 1886. V. 63
Lustige Drehbilder. (Humorous Rotating Pictures). Esslingen: 1892. V. 63
Neue Thierbilde. Munchen: 1890. V. 62
Princess Rose Petal and Her Adventures. London: 1890. V. 64
Schau Mich An! (Look at Me!). Esslingen: 1884. V. 63
Voyages et Aventures Extraordinaires de Mr. Rapahel de Rubensmouche L'Illustre Ariste! et de Nicodeme Pitenbraise son fidele rapin. (Lord Thumb and His Man Damian). Paris: 1900. V. 63

MEGGOTT, RICHARD
Sermon Preached at St. Martins in the Fields at the Funeral of the Rev. Dr. Hardy, Dean of Rochester, June 9th, 1670. London: 1670. V. 67

MEGLINGER, KASPAR
Der Todtentanz Gemalde auf der Muhlenbrucke in Lucern.... Lucern: 1867. V. 64; 67

MEGSON, EDMUND V.
Old Rhymes in a New Setting. First Series. N.P: 1900. V. 67

MEHRA, JAGDISH
The Historical Development of Quantum Theory. New York: 1982. V. 63

MEIGE, HENRY
Tics and Their Treatment. Birmingham: 1990. V. 65

MEIGHN, MOIRA
Charmers and Catiffs Sometimes Called Catiffs of the Deville, Being a Miscellanie of Secret, Strange and Curious Pieces.... London: 1832. V. 64

MEIGS, CHARLES DELUCENA
A Treatise on Acute and Chronic Diseases of the Neck of the Uterus. Philadelphia: 1854. V. 63

MEIGS, J. FORSYTH
A History of the First Quarter of the Second Century of the Pennslyvania Hospital.... Philadelphia: 1877. V. 66; 67
A Practical Treatise on the Diseases of Children. Philadelphia: 1848. V. 65

MEIGS, JOHN
The Cowboy in American Prints. Chicago: 1972. V. 66

MEIGS, WILLIAM M.
The Life of John Caldwell Calhoun. New York: 1917. V. 64

MEIKL, R. S.
After Big Game. 1915. V. 64

MEIKLE, D.
Wild Flowers of Cyprus. London and Chichester: 1973. V. 65

MEIKLE, JAMES
An Analysis of the Profits of Life Assurance, Being Four Papers Read Before the Acturial Society, Edinburgh, Inquiring Into the Sources of the Profits of Life Assurance, with a View to Their Equitable Distribution. London: 1865. V. 66

MEIKLE, R. S.
After Big Game. The Story of an African Holiday. 1915. V. 63

MEIKLEHAM, ROBERT STUART
A Dictionary of Architecture.... London: 1830. V. 64

MEIKLEJOHN, J. M. D.
Life and Letters of William Ballantyne Hodgson, LL.D., Late Professor of Economic Service in the University of Edinburgh. Edinburgh: 1883. V. 62

MEILAN, MARK ANTHONY
Sermons for Children; Being a Course of Fifty-Two Subjects Suited to Their Tender Age and in a Style Adapted to the Understanding of The Rising Generation. London: 1789. V. 62

MEINE *Lieben, Lieben Teddys.* Leipzig: 1920. V. 66

MEINERTZHAGEN, RICHARD
Birds of Arabia. Edinburgh: 1954. V. 62; 67
Diary of a Black Sheep. London: 1964. V. 62
The Life of a Boy - Daniel Meinertzhagen, 1925-1944. 1947. V. 62
Middle East Diary. 1960. V. 67
Nicoll's Birds of Egypt. London: 1930. V. 62
Pirates and Predators, The Piratical and Predatory Habits of Bird. London: 1959. V. 64

MEINHOLD, WILLIAM
Sidonia the Sorceress - The Supposed Destroyer of the Whole Reigning Ducal House of Pomerania - Mary Schweidler - the Amber Witch. London: 1894. V. 62

MEISS, MILLARD
The Great Age of Fresco: Discoveries, Recoveries and Survivals. New York: 1970. V. 64; 66

MEIXNER, HANS K.
Aschenbrodel. Munchen: 1936. V. 64

A MELANCHOLY *Event Improved.* Newcastle: 1823. V. 62

MELEAGER
The Songs of Meleager. London: 1937. V. 62; 64; 65; 66; 67

MELFORD, CHARLOTTE
Twin Sisters; or, Two Girls of Nineteen...To Which is Added, The Orphan of the Castle: a Gothic Tale. Philadelphia: 1827. V. 62; 63; 64

MELINE, JAMES F.
Two Thousand Miles on Horseback - Santa Fe and Back - Summer Tour through Kansas, Nebraska, Colorado and New Mexico in the Year 1866. New York: 1867. V. 67

MELISH, JOHN
A Geographical Description of the United States, with the Contiguous British and Spanish Possessions, Intended as an Accompaniment to Melish's Map of These Countries.... Philadelphia: 1816. V. 62
A Geographical Description of the United States, with the Contiguous Countries, Including Mexico and the West Indies.... Philadelphia: 1822. V. 62
Information and Advice to Emigrants to the United States.... Philadelphia: 1819. V. 62

MELISSELOGIA. (Greek type) *Or, the Female Monarchy.* London: 1744. V. 65

MELL, PATRICK HUES
Baptism in Its Mode and Subjects. Charleston: 1853. V. 67

MELLARD, LOUIS
Nottinghamshire and Derbyshire Past and Present. Nottingham: 1926. V. 65

MELLICK, ANDREW D.
The Story of an Old Farm, or, Life in New Jersey in the Eighteenth Century. Somerville: 1889. V. 63; 66

MELLIFONT, ARTHUR VICTOR
Malenfant Families. 1983. V. 67

MELLISS, J. C.
St. Helena: a Physical, Historical and Topographical Description of the Island, Including Its Geology, Fauna, Flora and Meteorology. 1875. V. 65

MELLO FRANCO, FRANCISCO DE
Reino da Estupidez, Poema. Paris: 1818. V. 62

MELLON, ANDREW W.
Taxation: the People's Business. New York: 1924. V. 67

MELLQUIST, JEROME
Paul Rosenfeld. Voyager in the Arts. New York: 1948. V. 64; 67

MELMOTH, WILLIAM
The Letters of Sir Thomas Fitzosborne on Several Subjects. London: 1784. V. 63; 66
Of Active and Retired Life, An Epistle. London: 1735. V. 66

MELMOTH, WILLIAM HENRY
The Universal Story Teller, or a Modern Picture of Human Life.... London: 1799. V. 62

MELO, FRANCISCO MANUEL DE
The Government of a Wife; or Wholsom(e) and Pleasant Advice for Married Men. London: 1697. V. 67

THE MELODIES of Stephen C. Foster. Pittsburgh: 1909. V. 67

MELTZER, DAVID
The Process. Berkeley: 1965. V. 62; 66
Yesod. London: 1969. V. 64

MELVILLE, GEORGE
Use of Liquid Fuel for Purposes of Navigation. Brussels: 1905. V. 67

MELVILLE, GEORGE JOHN WHYTE
General Bounce or the Lady and the Locusts. London: 1855. V. 63; 65

MELVILLE, GEORGE W.
In the Lena Delta; a Narrative of the Search for Lieut. Commander DeLong and His Companions Followed by an Account of the Greely Relief Expedition and a Proposed Method of Reaching the North Pole. Boston: 1885. V. 65

MELVILLE, HENRY DUNDAS, 1ST VISCOUNT
A Letter from Lord Viscount Melville to the Right Hon. Spencer Perceval, on the Subject of Naval Timber. London: 1810. V. 65
The Trial by Impeachment of Henry Lord Viscount Melville, for High Crimes and Misdemeanors Before the House of Peers in Westminster Hall.... Edinburgh: 1806. V. 63
The Trial of Henry Lord Viscount Melville, Before the Right Honorable the House of Peers, in Westminster Hall, in Full Parliament, for High Crimes and Misdemeanors, Upon an Impeachment by the Knights, Citizens and Burgesses in Parliament Assembled.... London: 1806. V. 63

MELVILLE, HERMAN
Battle Pieces and Aspects of the War. New York: 1866. V. 62; 66
Benito Cereno. London: 1926. V. 62; 63; 64; 65; 66
Clarel. A Pome and Pilgrimage in the Holy Land.... New York: 1876. V. 65
Israel Potter: His Fifty Years of Exile. New York: 1855. V. 62; 63; 64; 67
Journal of a Visit to London and the Continent. Cambridge: 1948. V. 63; 64
Mardi; and a Voyage Thither. New York: 1849. V. 62; 64; 67
Moby-Dick, or, The Whale. New York: 1851. V. 62; 64; 65
Moby-Dick or, the Whale. Chicago: 1930. V. 64
Moby-Dick, or, the Whale. New York: 1975. V. 66; 67
Narrative of a Four Months' Residence Among the Natives of a Valley of the Marquesas Islands.... London: 1846. V. 63; 64; 67
Omoo. London: 1847. V. 67
Omoo. New York: 1847. V. 62; 64; 65; 67
Omoo. Oxford: 1961. V. 62
Omoo. (with) Typee. London: 1850. V. 67
On the Slain Collegians. New York: 1971. V. 62; 64; 67
Pierre; or, the Ambiguities. New York: 1852. V. 62; 63; 64; 67
Pierre, or the Ambiguities. New York: 1929. V. 67
Redburn: His First Voyage. New York: 1849. V. 62; 64; 65
Redburn: His First Voyage. New York: 1850. V. 64
The Refugee. Philadelphia: 1865. V. 67
Rock Rodondo. Bremen and New York: 1981. V. 62
Typee. New York: 1846. V. 67
Typee. New York: 1847. V. 63
Typee. London: 1850. V. 67
White Jacket; or, the World in a Man-of-War. New York: 1850. V. 62; 64; 67
White Jacket; or, the World in a Man-of-War. London: 1853. V. 67
The Works. Boston: 1900-1905. V. 65

MELVILLE, JAMES
The Chrysanthemum Chain. London: 1980. V. 65
The Wages of Zen. London: 1979. V. 65

MELVILLE, LEWIS
The Beaux of Regency. London: 1908. V. 63

MELVILLE, LEWIS continued
The Life and Letters of Tobias Smollet. Boston and New York: 1927. V. 64

MEMIS, JOHN SMYTHE, MRS.
Precipitance: a Highland Tale. Edinburgh: 1823. V. 65

A MEMOIR of Mary Ann. New York: 1961. V. 65

MEMOIR of the Military Career of the Marquis De Lafayette During the Revolutionary War, Down to the Present Time, Including His Reception in New York, Boston and the Principal Towns in New England. Boston: 1824. V. 64

MEMOIRES de Frederic Henri Prince d'Orange. A Amsterdam: 1733. V. 66

Memoirs for the History of Madame de Maintenon and the Last Age. London: 1757. V. 62

MEMOIRS of an Oxford Scholar. London: 1756. V. 62; 65

MEMOIRS OF Elizabeth Farnesio, the Present Queen Dowager of Spain. London: 1746. V. 66

MEMOIRS of Jeremy Didler the Younger. London: 1887. V. 66

MEMOIRS of Lady Hamilton with Illustrative Anecdotes of Many of Her Most Particular Friends and Distinguished Contemporaries. London: 1815. V. 65; 66

THE MEMOIRS of the Harcourt Family: a Tale for Young Ladies. London: 1816. V. 62

MEMOIRS Of the Life of Robert Wilks, Esq. London: 1732. V. 66

MEMOIRS of the Literary and Philosophical Society of Manchester. Volume I-III. Warrington: 1785-1790. V. 67

MEMOIRS of the Little Man and the Little Maid So Wonderfully Contrived As to Be Either Sung or Said.... Philadelphia: 1824. V. 64

MEMOIRS of the Lord Viscount Dundee, the Highland Clans and the Massacre of Glenco (sic).... London: 1714. V. 63

MEMOIRS of the Voluptuous Conduct of the Capuchins in Regard to the Fair Sex: Represented in a Variety of Curious Scenes, Exhibited to Public View by a Brother of the Order. London: 1755. V. 65

THE MEMOIRS of Two Things, Called Trials. One Entitled, Too- Barefaced; or, Counsellor Dumb. The Other, The Diversions; or, the Frolicks of Ideson and His Tools.... London: 1799. V. 62

MEMORIAL Addresses on the Life and Character of Leland Stanford. Washington: 1894. V. 63

MEMORIAL of Henrietta Maria Peel, Crag Cottage, Windhill. Bradford: 1864. V. 64

MEMORIAL of the 121st and of the 122nd Anniversary of the Settlement of Truro by the British Natal Day, Sep. 13, 1882. Truro: 1894. V. 64

MEMORIAL R G S. Cambridge: 1864. V. 66

MEMORIALS of Acadia College and Horton Academy for the Half Century 1828-1878. Montreal: 1881. V. 65

MEMORIALS of Edward Burne-Jones. New York: 1904. V. 64

MEMORIALS of James Henderson, M.D., Medical Missionary to China. London: 1868. V. 63

MEMORIALS of the Church of SS. Peter and Wilfrid, Ripon. London: 1882-1908. V. 66

MENABONI, ATHOS
Menaboni's Birds. New York: 1950. V. 64; 66

MENAKER, DANIEL
The Old Left. New York: 1987. V. 62

MENAPACE, JOHN
Letter in a Klein Bottle. Highlands: 1984. V. 63

MENCKEN, HENRY L.
The American Language. Supplement II. New York: 1947. V. 63
The American Language: Supplement Two. New York: 1948. V. 62
A Book of Prefaces. New York: 1917. V. 65
George Bernard Shaw, His Plays. Boston: 1905. V. 63
The Gist of Nietzsche. Boston: 1910. V. 66
Happy Days: 1880-1892. New York: 1940. V. 62
Heliogabalus: a Buffoonery in Three Acts. New York: 1920. V. 65
In Defense of Women. New York: 1918. V. 65
Letters of H. L. Mencken. New York: 1961. V. 65
Newspaper Days 1899-1906. New York: 1941. V. 62
The Philosophy of Friedrich Nietzsche. London: 1908. V. 66
Prejudices Fifth Series. New York: 1926. V. 67
Prejudices Fourth Series. New York: 1924. V. 62
Prejudices Sixth Series. New York: 1927. V. 67
A Treatise on the Gods. New York: 1930. V. 63

MENDELEEV, DIMITIRI IVANOVICH
Osnovyi Khimii (Principles of Chemistry). St. Petersburg: 1869-1871. V. 66

MENDELSOHN, ERIC
Eric Mendelsohn 1887-1953. San Francisco: 1955. V. 63

MENDELSOHN, JANE
I Was Amelia Earhart. New York: 1996. V. 62; 66; 67

MENDELSSOHN, MOSES
Jerusalem Oder Uber Religiose Macht Und Judentum. Berlin: 1783. V. 64

MENDES, PETER
Clandestine Erotic Fiction in English 1800-1930. London: 1993. V. 67

MENDES PINTO, FERNAO
The Voyages and Adventures of Fernand Mendez Pinto.... London: 1653. V. 62

MENGARINI, S. J.
Recollections of the Flathead Mission.... Glendale: 1977. V. 67

MENGHI, GIROLAMO
Compendio dell'Arte Essorcistica, et Possibilita Delle Mirabili & Stupende Operationi delli Demoni.... Venice: 1605. V. 64; 66
Flagellum Daemonum, Exorcismos Terribiles, Potentissimos et Efficaces. Venice: 1599. V. 62

MENGS, ANTONIO RAFFAELLO
Opere.... Bassano: 1783. V. 64

MENHER DE KEMPTEN, VALENTIN
Arithmetique Seconde. Colophon: 1556. V. 66

MENINSKI, FRANCISCI A MESGNIEN
Linguarum Orientalium Turcicae, Arbicae, Persicae Institutiones seu Grammatica Turcica, in Qua Orthographia, Etymologia, Syntaxis, Prosodia & Reliqua.... Vienna: 1680. V. 65

MENKE, L.
Das Hermanns-Denkmal und der Teutoburger Wald, Nach der Natur Aufgenommen.... 1875. V. 62
Das Hermanns-Denkmal und der Teutoburger Wald, nach der Natur Aufgenommen.... Detmold: 1875. V. 67

MENKEN, ADAH ISAACS
Infelicia. London: 1868. V. 63
Infelicia. Second Issue. London: 1869. V. 62

MENNIE, DOUGLAS
The Pageant of Peking Comprising Sixty-six Vandyck Photogravures of Peking and Environs from Photographs.... Shanghai: 1920. V. 62

MENNINGER, E. A.
Flowering Vines of the World.... New York: 1970. V. 67

MENNINGER, KARL
Sparks. New York: 1973. V. 65

MENNINGER, WILLIAM
Juvenile Paresis. Baltimore: 1936. V. 66

MENOCHIUS, JACOBUS
De Praesumptionibus, Coniecturis, Signis, & Indicis in Sex Distincta Libros.... Coloniae: 1595. V. 67

MENPES, DOROTHY
Paris. London: 1909. V. 64; 66
Venice. London: 1904. V. 65

MENPES, FLORA
India. 1905. V. 67

MENPES, MORTIMER
Japan, a Record in Colour, Transcribed by Dorothy Menpes.... London: 1905. V. 63; 65
Whistler as I Knew Him. London: 1904. V. 63; 64

MENSAERT, G. P.
Le Peintre Amateur et Curieux, ou Description General des Tableaux des Plus Habiles Maitres qui Font l'Ornement des Eglises, Couvents, Abbayes, Prieures and Cabinets Particuliers dans l'Etendue des Pays-Bas Autrichiens. Brussels: 1763. V. 64

MENTORIANA; or, Letter...to the Duke of York, Relative to Corruption, Oppression, Cowardly Revenge, Agency-Monopoly, Meretricious Influence, and Other Subjects Connected with the Army. London: 1807. V. 66

MENZIES, ARCHIBALD
Menzies' Journal of Vancouver's Voyage April to October 1792. Victoria: 1923. V. 63

MENZIES, W.
The Salmon. Its Life Story. 1931. V. 67

MERA, H. P.
Ceramic Clues to the Prehistory of North Central New Mexico. Santa Fe: 1935. V. 62
Navajo Textile Arts. Sante Fe: 1940. V. 63
Pueblo Indian Embroidery. Santa Fe: 1943. V. 62; 63; 64; 65
The Rain Bird a Study in Pueblo Design. Santa Fe: 1937. V. 64; 66
The Rain Bird a Study in Pueblo Design. Santa Fe: 1938. V. 63; 64
Style Trends of Pueblo Pottery in the Rio Grande and Little Colorado Cultural Areas from the Sixteenth to the Nineteenth Centuries. Santa Fe: 1939. V. 64

MERCATOR, GERARD
The Treatise of Gerard Mercator. Literarum Latinarum, Quas Italicas, Cusoriasque Vocant, Scribendarum Ratio (Antwerp 1540). Verona: 1930. V. 65

MERCER, A. H. H.
The Late Captain Henry Mercer, of the Royal Artillery, Who Was Killed by Undue and Useless Exposure at the Battle of Rangiriri, New Zealand. Nov. 1863.... Toronto: 1865. V. 63

MERCER, A. S.
Washington Territory. Seattle: 1939. V. 64

MERCER, ASA J.
The Banditti Of the Plains or the Cattleman's Invasion of Wyoming in 1892. San Francisco: 1936. V. 62

MERCER, DAVID
The Monster of Karlovy Vary and Then and Now. London: 1979. V. 62

MERCER, PHILIP
The Life of the Gallant Pelham. Macon: 1929. V. 66

MERCER, THOMAS
A Vocabulary, Latin and English, On a New Plan.... London: 1817. V. 62

MERCHANTS & MANUFACTURERS CO. OF NEW YORK
The Prize Depository of the Merchants & Manufacturers of New York, No.s 542 & 544 Broadway, Is Now Open for the Exhibition and Distribution of Valuable and Magnificent Goods, Contributed by the Company, to be Disposed of by Ballot to Purchasers of Shares. New York: 1866. V. 63

MERCIER, LOUIS SEBASTIEN
Memoirs of the Year Two Thousand Five Hundred. Philadelphia: 1795. V. 64; 66

MERCIER, S. A. B.
The Tell El-Amarna Tablets. Toronto: 1939-1951. V. 62; 66

MERCIER, VIVIAN
1000 Years of Irish Prose. New York: 1953. V. 63; 66

MERCURY Project Summary, Including Results of the Fourth Manned Orbital Flight, May 15 and 16, 1963. Washington: 1963. V. 67

MERCY for Methodists Prov'd to Be the Law and the Prophets, the Gospel and the Reformation. Occasion'd by the Late Cruel Treatment of a Widow at F(rom)e In S(o)m(er)s(et)shire. London: 1752. V. 64

MEREDITH, CHARLES, MRS.
Notes and Sketches of New South Wales, During a Residence in that Colony from 1839 to 1844. (with) Letters from the Shores of the Baltic. London: 1846. V. 67

MEREDITH, DE WITT
Voyages of the Velero III. Los Angeles: 1939. V. 65

MEREDITH, GEORGE
The Amazing Marriage. London: 1895. V. 66; 67
Ballads and Poems of Tragic Life. London: 1887. V. 62
Beauchamp's Career. London: 1876. V. 66
The Egoist. London: 1879. V. 62
Jump to Glory Jane. London: 1892. V. 64
Letters of George Meredith. London: 1912. V. 64
The Letters of George Meredith to Alice Meynell with Annotations Thereto. London: 1923. V. 62; 63; 65
Lord Ormont and His Aminta. London: 1894. V. 62
Modern Love and Poems of the English Roadside with Poems and Ballads. London: 1862. V. 64
One of Our Conquerors. London: 1891. V. 65; 66
The Ordeal of Richard Feveral. London: 1859. V. 66
The Shaving of Shagpat. London: 1856. V. 66
The Tale of Chloe - The House on the Beach - The Case of General Ople and Lady Camper. London: 1894. V. 67
The Tale of Chloe - the House on the Beach - The Case of General Ople and Lady Camper. London: 1894-1895. V. 64
Three Poems. London: 1999. V. 67
The Tragic Comedians. London: 1881. V. 66

MEREDITH, GRACE E.
Girl Captives of the Cheyenne - A True Story of the Capture and Rescue of Pioneer Girls. Los Angeles: 1927. V. 65

MEREDITH, LOUISA ANNE TWAMLEY
My Home in Tasmania, During a Residence of Nine Years. London: 1852. V. 65
Notes and Sketches of New South Wales, Being a Residence In that Colony from 1839 to 1844. London: 1844. V. 63
Our Wild Flowers Familiarly Described and Illustrated. London: 1843. V. 62; 66
The Romance of Nature; or, the Flower Series. London: 1836. V. 62

MEREDITH, ROY
The Face of Robert E. Lee in Life and Legend. New York: 1947. V. 65

MEREDITH, WILLIAM
Hazard, the Painter. New York: 1975. V. 64
Ships and Other Figures. Princeton: 1948. V. 64

MERENESS, NEWTON D.
Maryland as a Proprietory Province. New York: 1901. V. 63

MERIGOT, J.
Promenades ou Itineraire des Jardins de Chantilly.... Paris: 1791. V. 64

MERIMEE, PROSPER
Carmen. London: 1916. V. 64
Carmen. 1941. V. 62; 65
Letters Libres a Stendhal. Paris: 1927. V. 64

MERITON, GEORGE
The Praise of York-shire Ale Wherein is Enumerated Several Sorts of Drink.... York: 1697. V. 63

MERIVALE, HERMAN
Lectures on Colonization and Colonies Delivered Before the University of Oxford in 1839, 1840 and 1841. London: 1861. V. 63

MERIVALE, JOHN HERMAN
Poems Original and Translated. London: 1838. V. 62; 67

MERIWETHER, ELIZABETH A.
A Chapter in the History of Vivum-Ovo. Memphis: 1882. V. 65

MERIWETHER, LOUISE
Daddy was a Number Runner. Englewood Cliffs: 1970. V. 67

MERIWETHER, ROBERT L.
The Expansion of South Carolina 1729-1765. Kingsport: 1940. V. 63

MERK, FREDERICK
Manifest Destiny and Mission in American History - a Reinterpretation. New York: 1963. V. 67

MERKELY, CHRISTOPHER
Biography of.... Salt Lake City: 1887. V. 62; 65

MERLE, ROBERT
Week-End at Auydcoote. London: 1950. V. 65

MERLE, WILLIAM HENRY
Odds and Ends. London: 1831. V. 65

MERLEAU PONTY, MAURICE
La Structure du Comportement. Paris: 1942. V. 67

MERLETTE, GERMAINE MARIE
La Vie et l'Oeuvre d'Elizabeth Barrett Browning. Paris: 1905. V. 63

MERNAGH, LAURENCE R.
Enamels. Their Manufacture and Application to Iron & Steel Ware. London and Philadelphia: 1928. V. 67

MERRIAM, ALAN P.
A Bibliography of Jazz. New York: 1954. V. 63; 64

MERRIAM, C. HART
The Dawn of the World, Myths and Weird Tales Told by the Mewan Indians of California. Cloveland: 1910. V. 63; 65

MERRIAM, JOHN C.
The Felidae of Rancho Le Brea. Washington: 1932. V. 66

MERRICK, GEORGE BYRON
Old Times on the Upper Mississippi - The Recollections of a Steam Boat Pilot from 1854 to 1863. Cleveland: 1909. V. 67

MERRICK, RICE
A Book of Glamorganshire's Antiquities.... 1825. V. 64

MERRIL, JUDITH
Shadow of the Hearth. London: 1953. V. 65

MERRILL, E. D.
Additions to Our Knowledge of the Hainan Flora II. Canton: 1935. V. 67
A Bibliography of Eastern Asiatic Botany. 1938. V. 63
A Bibliography of Eastern Asiatic Botany. Jamaica Plain: 1938. V. 67
Merrileana. Waltham: 1946. V. 63
Plantae Elmerianae Borneenses. Berkeley: 1929. V. 63

MERRILL, JAMES
Braving the Elements. New York: 1972. V. 62; 64
Bronze. New York: 1984. V. 66
The Changing Light at Sandover. New York: 1982. V. 66
The Country of a Thousand Years of Peace and Other Poems. New York: 1959. V. 62; 64; 66
David Jackson: Scenes from His Life. New York: 1994. V. 67
A Different Person: a Memoir. New York: 1993. V. 67
The Firescreen. New York: 1969. V. 64
From the First Nine. Poems 1946-1976. New York: 1982. V. 64; 66
Hellen's Book. New York: 1991. V. 62; 64; 67
Ideas, Etc. New York: 1980. V. 66
The Image Maker. A Play In One Act. N.P. 1986. V. 62; 67
The Inner Room. New York: 1988. V. 64; 67
Japan: Prose of Departure. New York: 1987. V. 66; 67
Japan. Prose of Departure. New York: 1988. V. 62; 64
Last Poems. New York: 1998. V. 62; 64; 67
Marbled Paper. Salem: 1982. V. 66
Metamorphosis of 741. Pawlet: 1977. V. 62; 63
Mirabell: Books of Number. New York: 1978. V. 62; 64; 67
Nights and Days. New York: 1966. V. 62; 64; 67
Nine Lives. New York & Kripplebush: 1993. V. 62; 64; 66; 67
Occasions and Inscriptions. New York: 1984. V. 62; 64; 67
Overdue Pilgrimage to Nova Scotia. New York: 1990. V. 62; 64; 66
Peter. Old Deerfield: 1982. V. 67
Plays of Light. Ann Arbor: 1984. V. 64; 67
Samos. Los Angeles: 1980. V. 66
Santorini: Stopping the Leak. Worcester: 1982. V. 67
Scripts for the Pageant. New York: 1980. V. 62; 67
Selected Poems. London: 1961. V. 62
Self-Portrait in Tyvek Windbreaker and Other Poems. Dublin: 1995. V. 66
The Seraglio. New York: 1957. V. 62
Short Stories. Pawlet: 1954. V. 64; 67
Souvenirs. Nadja: 1984. V. 64

MERRILL, JAMES continued
Souvenirs. New York: 1984. V. 66
Three Poems. Dorset: 1988. V. 62
Two Poems. London: 1972. V. 67
Unframed Originals: Recollections. New York: 1982. V. 67
Voices from Sandover. N.P: 1982. V. 66
Volcanic Holidays. New York: 1992. V. 64
Water Street. New York: 1962. V. 62; 64; 66
Yannina. New York: 1973. V. 62; 64; 67

MERRILL, MARION
The Animated Three Little Kittens. New York: 1946. V. 66

MERRILL, SELAH
East of the Jordan: a Record of Travel and Observation in the Countries of Moab Gilhead and Bashan During the Years 1875-1877. New York: 1881. V. 65

MERRIN, J.
The Lepidopterist's Calendar. 1875. V. 67

MERRITT, A.
The Black Wheel. New York: 1947. V. 67
Burn Witch Burn!. London: 1935. V. 66
The Fox Woman/The Blue Pagoda. New York: 1946. V. 63
Seven Footprints to Satan. 1928. V. 67
The Ship of Ishtar. Los Angeles: 1949. V. 67

MERRITT, EDWARD PERCIVAL
Horace Walpole, Printer: a Paper Read by Edward Percival Merritt at a Meeting of the Club of Odd Volumes, 17 April, 1907. Boston: 1907. V. 64

MERRITT, H. HOUSTON
The Cerebrospinal Fluid. Philadelphia: 1938. V. 66

MERRITT, HENRY
Dirt and Pictures Separated in the Works of the Old Masters. London: 1854. V. 67

THE MERRY Alphabet A to Z. New York: 1888. V. 64

MERRY Christmas ABC. New York: 1900. V. 65

MERRY, ELEANOR C.
The Flaming Door: a Preliminary Study of the Mission of the Celtic Folk Soul by Means of Legends and Myths. 1936. V. 65

MERRYMAN, JOHN
The Proceedings in the Case of John Merryman, of Baltimore County, Maryland, Before the Hon. Roger Brooke Taney, Chief Justice of the Supreme Court of the United States. Baltimore: 1861. V. 62

MERRYMAN, MILDRED PLEW
Bonbon and Bonbonette. Chicago: 1924. V. 65; 67
Mister Wubble's Bubbles. Minneapolis: 1927. V. 62

MERRYWEATHER, FREDERICK SOMNER
Lives and Anecdotes of Misers; or the Passion of Avarice Displayed; in the Parsimonious Habits, Unaccountable Lives and Remarkable Deaths of the Most Notorious Misers of All Ages, with Few Words on Frugality and Saving. London: 1850. V. 66

MERRYWEATHER, JAMES COMPTON
The Fire Brigade Handbook.... London: 1888. V. 64

MERRYWHISTLER, MARMADUKE, PSEUD.
Isn't It Odd?. London: 1822. V. 67

MERSHON, GRACE L. O.
My Folks. Story of the Forefathers of Oliver Francis Mershon, M.D. N.P: 1946. V. 63; 66

MERSHON, W. B.
The Passenger Pigeon. New York: 1907. V. 64; 65

MERTON, THOMAS
Boris Pasternak/Thomas Merton. Six Letters. Lexington: 1973. V. 62
Early Poems/1940-1942. Lexington: 1971. V. 64
The Seven Storey Mountain. New York: 1948. V. 66

MERULA, PAULUS
Opera Varia Posthuma, De Sacrificiis, Sacerdotibus, Legibus, Comitiis, Praemiis &c Romanorum. Lugd. Batavorum: 1684. V. 66

MERWIN, ELIAS
The Principles of Equity and Equity Pleading. Indianapolis: 1895. V. 64

MERWIN, W. S.
The Dancing Bears. New Haven: 1954. V. 62; 64
Fox Sleep. New York: 1996. V. 62; 64
KOA. New York: 1988. V. 66
The Moving Target. Poems. New York: 1963. V. 66
A New Right Arm. Oshkosh. V. 65
Opening the Hand. New York: 1983. V. 62
The Real World of Manuel Cordova. Sherman Oaks: 1995. V. 62; 64
Signs. Iowa City: 1971. V. 62; 67
The Sun at Midnight. New York: 1985. V. 66
Three Poems. New York: 1968. V. 62; 64; 67

MERYON, EDWARD
On the Functions of the Sympathetic System of Nerves, as a Physiolgoical Basis for a Rational System of Therapeutics. London: 1872. V. 64

MERZBACHER, GOTTFRIED
Aus Den Hochregionen des Kaukasus. Wanderungen, ERlebnisse, Beobachtungen. Leipzig: 1901. V. 62

MESDAMES Les Femmes par un Medecin. Paris: 1840. V. 66

MESENS, E. L. T.
Third Front and Detached Pieces. London: 1944. V. 66
Troisieme Front - Poems de Guerre, Suivi de Pieces Detachees. London: 1944. V. 64

MESERVE, FREDERICK HILL
The Photographs of Araham Lincoln. New York: 1944. V. 63

MESKER AND BRO.
Mesker and Bro. Manufacturers of Complete House Fronts. Trade Catalogue. St. Louis: 1904. V. 62

MESMERIC Phenomena; Their Reality and Importance, Attested by Dr. Maitland. London: 1851. V. 67

MESONERO ROMANOS, D. RAMON DE
Manuel Historico-Topografico y Administrativo y Artistic de Madrid. Madrid: 1844. V. 67

MESSAGES from the Governors of Maryland and Pennsylvania, Transmitting the Reports of the Joint Commissioners and of Lieut. Col. Graham...in Relation to the Intersection of the Boundary Lines of the States of Maryland, Pennsylvania and Delaware, Being a. Chicago: 1862. V. 63

MESSEL, L.
A Garden Flora, Trees and Flowers Grown in the Gardens at Nymans 1890-1915. 1918. V. 63

MESSLER, ABRAHAM
Centennial History of Somerset County. Somerville: 1878. V. 63; 66
First Things in Old Somerset. Somerville: 1899. V. 63; 66

MESSNER, R.
The Challenge. 1977. V. 65
Solo Nanga Parbat. 1980. V. 65

MESTACH, J. W.
Songye Studies. Form and Symbolism, an Analytical Essay. Munich: 1985. V. 62

METASTASIO, PIETRO DOMENICO BUONAVENTURA
Alessandro nell' Indie, Dramma per Musica la Rappresentarsi nel Gran Teatro Nouveamente Eretto alla Rea Corte di Lisbona.... Lisbon: 1755. V. 62

METCALF, D. M.
Metallurgy in Numismatics. London: 1980-1993. V. 66

METCALF, ELEANOR MELVILLE
Herman Melville: Cycle and Epicycle. Cambridge: 1953. V. 63

METCALF, JOHN
What Is Canadian Literature?. Guelph: 1988. V. 64

METCALF, PAUL
Firebird. Minneapolis: 1987. V. 62; 64; 67
Land, Skin and Blindness. Laurinburg: 1977. V. 62

METCALF, PAUL C.
Both. N.P: 1976. V. 63
Genoa: A Telling of Wonders. Highlands: 1965. V. 63
The Middle Passage (A Triptych of Commodities). Highlands: 1976. V. 63
Patagoni. Penland: 1971. V. 63
Will West. Asheville: 1956. V. 63; 67

METCALF, SAMUEL L.
A Collection of Some of the Most Interesting Narratives of Indian Warfare in the West.... Lexington: 1821. V. 66

METCALFE, C. R.
Anatomy of the Dicotyledons.... Oxford: 1950. V. 63
Anatomy of the Monocotyledons. VII. Helobiae. Oxford: 1982. V. 65; 66

METCALFE, JOHN
The Feasting Dead. 1954. V. 66
The Feasting Dead. Sauk City: 1954. V. 63; 64

METCALFE, SAMUEL L.
Caloric: Its Mechanical Chemical and Vital Agencies in the Phenomena of Nature. London: 1843. V. 65

METCHNIKOFF, IL IA IL'ICH
Lectures on the Comparative Pathology of Inflammation. London: 1893. V. 66

METEYARD, ELIZA
The Life of Josiah Wedgwood from His Private Correspondence and Family Papers. London: 1865. V. 63
The Life of Josiah Wedgwood from His Private Correspondence and Family Papers. London: 1865-1866. V. 67

METHODIST EPISCOPAL CHURCH. NEW JERSEY ANNUAL CONFERENCE
Minutes of the Seventeenth (-Twenty Third) Annual Conference...1853 (-1859). 1853-1859. V. 66

METHODIST EPISCOPAL CHURCH. NEWARK CONFERENCE
Minutes of the Thirty-Ninth (-Sixty Fifth) Session...1896-(1922). 1896-1922. V. 66

METHODIST MISSIONARY SOCIETY
Letter from the Methodist Missionary Society to the Superintendent General of Indian Affairs Respecting British Columbia Troubles.... Toronto: 1889. V. 64

METHOLD, KEN
Sherlock Holmes in Australia: the Adventure of the Kidnapped Kanakas. Sydney: 1991. V. 66

METHUEN, HENRY H.
Life in the Wilderness, or Wanderings in South Africa. 1846. V. 62

METHVIN, J. J.
In the Limelight or History of Anadarko (Caddo County) and Vicinity from the Earliest Days. Oklahoma City. V. 66

METIUS, ADRIAEN
Arithmeticae et Geometricae Practica. Franeker: 1611. V. 66
Arithmeticae Libri Duo et Geometriae Libri VI. Huic Adiungitur Trigonometriae Planorum Methodus Succincta Altera Vero Praeter Alia, Nova Regulae Proportionalis Inventa Proponit.... Leiden: 1626. V. 66

METLAKE, GEORGE
The Life and Writings of St. Columban, 542?-615. Philadelphia: 1914. V. 63; 66

A METRICAL Description of a Fancy Ball given at Washington, 9th April 1858. Washington: 1858. V. 62

METROPOLITAN MUSEUM OF ART, NEW YORK
The Painterly Print: Monotypes from the 17th to the 20th Century. 1981. V. 62; 65

METTA, VICTORIA FULLER
Fresh Leaves from Western Woods. Buffalo: 1853. V. 66

METTENIUS, C.
Alexander Braun's Leben, Nach Seinem Handschriftlichen Nachlass. Berlin: 1882. V. 66

METTLER, CECILIA C.
History of Medicine. Birmingham: 1986. V. 66

METTLER, FREDERICK ALBERT
Selective Partial Ablation of the Frontal Cortex: a Correlative Study of Its Effects on Human Psychotic Subjects. New York: 1949. V. 65

MEURSIUS, JOANNES
Atticarum Lectionum. (with) Regnum Atticum. Lugduni Batavorum: 1617. V. 66
Regnum Atticum sive, De Regibus Atheniensium, Eorumque Rebus Gestis, Libri III. Amstelodami: 1633. V. 66

MEUZE, M.
African Art. Cleveland: 1968. V. 62

MEWBURN, FRANCIS
Memoir of Fra: Mewburn, Chief Bailiff of Darlington, and First Railway Solicitor, by His Son. August 1867. 1867. V. 62

M'EWEN, WILLIAM
Grace and Truth; or the Glory and Fulness of the Redeemer Displayed. Edinburgh: 1763. V. 66

MEWETT, ALFRED
A Brief History of Troop A 107th Regiment of Cavalry Ohio National Guard, the Black Horse Troop. Cleveland: 1923. V. 64

THE MEXICAN War. Review of the Annual Message of the President of the United States to Congress, December 7, 1847. Washington: 1848. V. 65

MEYDER DE SCHAUENSEE, R.
A Guide to the Birds of Venezuela. Princeton. 1978. V. 63

MEYER, ADOLF
The Collected Papers of Adolph Meyer. Baltimore: 1950-1952. V. 63
The Commonsense Psychiatry of Dr. Adolf Meyer: Fifty Two Selected Papers. New York: 1948. V. 65
Psychobiology: a Science of Man. Springfield: 1957. V. 65

MEYER, AGNES E.
Chinese Painting as Reflected in the Thought and Art of Li Lung-Mien 1070-1106. New York: 1923. V. 62; 63; 64

MEYER, CARL
Nach Dem Sacramento. Germany: 1855. V. 65

MEYER, CHARLES A.
Whaling and the Art of Scrimshaw. New York: 1976. V. 63; 64

MEYER, DUTCH
from what i know: Dutch Meyer. Seattle: 1998. V. 64

MEYER, F. W.
The Best Hardy Perennials. Liverpool: 1901. V. 62

MEYER, FRANZ
Marc Chagall. New York: 1957. V. 62; 65; 67

MEYER, GEORG HERMANN VON
Procrustes Ante Portas. Why the Shoe Pinches. Edinburgh: 1863. V. 66

MEYER, H. L.
Coloured Illustrations of British Birds and Their Eggs. London: 1842-1850. V. 65; 67
Illustrations of British Birds. London: 1835-1844. V. 64

MEYER, J.
Vues Pittoresques des Palais et Jardins Imperiaux aux Environs de St. Petersburg, Dessinees d'Apres Nature pa I. Meyer et Lithographiees par C. Schultz. St. Petersburg: 1850. V. 64

MEYER, NICHOLAS
Target Practice. New York: 1974. V. 62

MEYER, THOMAS
May. Champaign: 1983. V. 63
Monotypes and Tracings. German Romantics. London: 1994. V. 62; 64
Sappho's Raft. Highlands: 1982. V. 63
Sonnets and Tableaux. London: 1987. V. 64
Staves Calends Legends. Highlands: 1979. V. 63
The Umbrella of Aesculapius. Poems. Highlands: 1975. V. 63

MEYER DE SCHAUENSEE, R.
The Birds of Columbia and Adjacent Areas of South and Central America. Narberth: 1964. V. 63; 67
The Birds of the Republic of Colombia. Bogota: 1949-1952. V. 62; 67
A Guide to the Birds of Venezuela. Princeton: 1978. V. 67
The Species of Birds of South America and Their Distribution. Narberth: 1966. V. 67

MEYERHOF, O.
Chemical Dynamics of Life Phaenmena. Philadelphia: 1924. V. 67

MEYEROWITZ, JOEL
Joel Meyerowitz Photographs of Wild Flowers. Boston: 1983. V. 63; 65

MEYERS, DWIGHT
In Celebration of the Book: Literary New Mexico. Albuquerque and Santa Fe: 1982. V. 64

MEYERS, JOHN BERNARD
The Poets of the New York School. Philadelphia: 1969. V. 62

MEYERS, WALTER DEAN
The Golden Serpent. New York: 1980. V. 65

MEYERS, WILLIAM H.
Journal of a Cruise to California and the Sandwich Island in the United States Sloop-of-War Cyane...1841-1844. San Francisco: 1955. V. 66
Naval Sketches of the War on California. San Francisco: 1939. V. 63; 66

MEYERSTEIN, E. H. W.
A Boy of Clare. London: 1937. V. 67
Division. Oxford: 1946. V. 66
Sonnets, in Exitu Israel, Peace: an Ode. London: 1939. V. 66

MEYNELL, ALICE
The Children. London: 1897. V. 63
Collected Poems of.... London: 1913. V. 65
Hearts of Controversy. London: 1917. V. 65
A Keepsake for the A.I.G.A. from Francis Meynell. London: 1930. V. 62
Mary, the Mother of Jesus. London: 1912. V. 62
Poems. London: 1893. V. 65
The Poems of Alice Meynell - Complete Edition. London: 1923. V. 63
Preludes. London: 1875. V. 62
The Rhythm of Life and Other Essays. London: 1893. V. 65; 66; 67

MEYNELL, VIOLA
Alice Meynell: A Memoir. London: 1929. V. 65

MEYNERT, THEODOR HERMANN
Psychiatry: a Clinical Treatise on Diseases of the Fore-Brain Based Upon a Study of Its Structure, Functions and Nutrition. New York and London: 1885. V. 65

MEYRINK, GUSTAV
The Golem. London: 1928. V. 66

MEZERAY, FRANCOIS EUDES DE
A General Chronological History of France, Beginning Before the Reign of King Pharamond, and Ending with the Reign of King Henry the Fourth.... London: 1683. V. 62

MEZZROW, MILTON
Really the Blues. New York: 1946. V. 65

M'FADDEN, JAMES
The Present and the Past of the Agrarian Struggle in Gweedore. Londonderry: 1889. V. 65

M'GEE, THOMAS
Popular History of Ireland. New York: 1863. V. 67

M'GREGOR, J. J.
New Picture of Dublin. 1821. V. 63

MIALL, ANDREW D.
Principles of Sedimentary Basin Analysis. New York: 1990. V. 67

MIALL, JAMES G.
Congregationalism in Yorkshire. London: 1868. V. 64; 65

MICANZIO, FULGENZIO
The Life of the Most Learned Father Paul, of the Order of the Servie. London: 1651. V. 62

MICHAEL, A. C.
An Artist in Spain. London. V. 64

MICHAEL, A. D.
British Tyroglyphidae. London: 1901-1903. V. 63; 66

MICHAEL, C. D.
The Slave and His Champions. London. V. 64; 66

MICHAEL Servetus. Baltimore: 1909. V. 66

MICHAELIS, CATHERINE
How Seeds Travels. Vashon Island: 1995. V. 63

MICHAELIS, H. VON
Birds of the Gauntlet. 1952. V. 62; 66
Birds of the Gauntlet. London: 1952. V. 64

MICHAEL-PODMORE, S.
Rambles and Adventures in Australasia, Canada, India, etc. 1909. V. 64

MICHAELS, BARBARA
The Grey Beginning. New York: 1984. V. 67

MICHAELSEN, W.
Die Fauna Sudwest-Australiens. Jena: 1907-1930. V. 62

MICHALOWSKI, KAZIMIERZ
Art of Ancient Egypt. New York: 1968. V. 66

MICHALS, DUANE
Sequences. Garden City: 1970. V. 63

MICHAUX, FRANCIS ANDRE
The North American Sylva. Paris: 1817-1819. V. 62
North American Sylva. Philadelphia: 1865-1859. V. 62

MICHAUX, FRANCOIS ANDRE
The North American Sylva. Philadelphia: 1853. V. 64; 65
Travels to the Westward of the Allegany Mountains, in the States of Ohio, Kentucky and Tennessee.... London: 1805. V. 63; 66
A Voyage a l'Ouest des Monts Alleghanys.... Paris: 1804. V. 64
Voyage a L'Ouwest des Monts Alleghanys.... Paris: 1808. V. 66

MICHAUX, HENRI
Light through Darkness - Explorations Among Drugs. London: 1964. V. 63
The Major Ordeals of the Mind and the Countles Minor Ones. London: 1974. V. 64
Les Reves et la Jambe. Anvers: 1923. V. 67

MICHAUX, RICHARD RANDOLPH
Sketches of Life in North Carolina. Culler: 1894. V. 66; 67

MICHEAUX, OSCAR
The Conquest.... Lincoln: 1913. V. 63

MICHEL, A.
Reports of...On the Gold Region of Canada. Ottawa: 1866. V. 64

MICHEL, HENRI
Instruments des Sciences dans l'Artet l'Histoire. Paris: 1966. V. 67

MICHELHAM, LORD
The Collection of the Late Lord Michelham at 20 Arlington St., London, S.W. (Sale Catalogue). London: 1926. V. 67

MICHELINI, FAMINAO
Trattato della Direzione de'Fiumi Nel Quale si Dimostrano da' Suoi Veri Principi i Modi Piu Sicuri, e Meno Dispendiosi di Riparare a'Danni, Che Sogliono Farsi dall'Acque. Firenze: 1664. V. 62

MICHELL, E. B.
The Art and Practice of Hawking. London: 1900. V. 62

MICHELL, THOMAS
Russian Pictures Drawn with Pen and Pencil. London: 1889. V. 62

MICHELS, NICHOLAS
Blood Supply and Anatomy of the Upper Abdominal Organs with Descriptive Atlas. Philadelphia: 1955. V. 67

MICHELSON, A. A.
Light Waves and Their Uses. Chicago: 1903. V. 66
On the Application of Interference Methods to Spectroscopic Measurements. Washington: 1892. V. 64

MICHENER, C. D.
A Classification of the Bees of the Australian and South Pacific Regions. 1965. V. 63
A Classification of the Bees of the Australian and South Pacific Regions. London: 1965. V. 62

MICHENER, JAMES ALBERT
Alaska. New York: 1988. V. 62
The Bridges at Tokyo-Ri. New York: 1953. V. 66
Caribbean. New York: 1989. V. 62
A Century of Sonnets. Austin: 1997. V. 62; 64; 67
Chesapeake. New York: 1978. V. 62
Collectors, Forgers - and a Writer: a Memoir. New York: 1983. V. 64; 65
The Drifters. New York: 1971. V. 65; 67
The Drifters. New York: 1974. V. 67
The Eagle and the Raven. Austin: 1990. V. 63; 64; 67
Facing East. New York: 1970. V. 62; 66
The Floating World. New York: 1954. V. 66
The Hokusai Sketchbooks. Rutland: 1975. V. 66
Iberia: Spanish Travels and Reflections. New York: 1968. V. 62; 67
Japanese Prints: from the Early Masters to the Modern. Rutland and Tokyo: 1959. V. 64; 67
Kent State: What Happened and Why. New York: 1971. V. 65
Legacy. New York: 1987. V. 62
Literary Reflections. Austin: 1993. V. 63; 64; 65; 66; 67
Mexico. New York: 1992. V. 62; 64; 65; 66
Miracle in Seville. New York: 1995. V. 62; 64; 66
My Lost Mexico. Austin: 1992. V. 63; 66; 67
Poland. New York: 1983. V. 62
The Quality of Life. Philadelphia: 1970. V. 66
Recessional. New York: 1994. V. 64; 66
Return to Paradise. New York: 1951. V. 65
Sayonara. New York: 1954. V. 63
South Pacific. San Diego: 1992. V. 66
Space. New York: 1982. V. 62
Tales of the South Pacific. London: 1947. V. 65
Tales of the South Pacific. New York: 1947. V. 63
Tales of the South Pacific. New York: 1950. V. 63
Texas. New York: 1985. V. 62
Ventures in Editing. Huntington Beach: 1995. V. 62; 66
The Watermen. New York: 1979. V. 66

MICHIE, THOMAS J.
A Treatise on the Law of Banks and Banking. Charlottesville: 1913. V. 65
The Virginia Scrivener. Staunton: 1833. V. 66

MICHIELE, PIETRO
Il Dispaccio di Venere. Epistole Heroiche & Amorose. Riposte di Diversi. Al Epistole Heroiche del Michiele. Epistole Amorose. Venice: 1640. V. 66

MICHIGAN
Botanist. 1962-1997. V. 66

MICHIGAN. CONSTITUTION - 1907
Manual of the Constitutional Convention of Michigan 1907. Lansing: 1907. V. 67
Proceedings and Debates of the Constitutional Convention of the State of Michigan Convened in the City of Lansing, Tuesday, Oct. 22, 1907. Lansing: 1907. V. 66

MICHLER, N.
Routes from the Western Boundary of Arkansas to Santa Fe and the Valley of the Rio Grande.... Washington: 1850. V. 63; 66

MICKLE, ISAAC
Reminiscences of Old Gloucester; or Incidents in the History of the Counties of Gloucester, Atlantic and Camden, New Jersey. Philadelphia: 1845. V. 63; 66

MICKLE, WILLIAM JULIUS
General Paralysis of the Insane. London: 1880. V. 65

MICKLER, ERNEST MATTHEW
White Trash Cooking. Highlands: 1986. V. 63

MICKLETON FRIENDLY SOCIETY
Rules and Regulations of the Mickleton Friendly Society. Instituted April 28th 1834. Stratford-upon-Avon: 1850. V. 67

MICQUELLUS, JOHANNES LODOICUS
Aureliae Vrbis Memorabilis Ab Anglis Obsidio anno 1428. Paris: 1560. V. 65

MICROCOSM
of Oxford. London: 1840-1850. V. 62

MIDDLEBROOK, ELIJAH
Middlebrook's Almanack for the Years 1818, 1827, 1829, 1831, 1832, 1833, 1834 (2 copies), 1835, 1837, 1840, 1844, 1845, 1847, 1856, 1862, 1882. Bridgeport. V. 65

MIDDLEBROOK, LOUIS F.
Maritime Connecticut During the American Revolution 1775-1783. Salem: 1925. V. 66

MIDDLESEX
County Directory. 1896. New Brunswick: 1896. V. 63; 66

MIDDLETON, ARTHUR P.
Tobacco Coast a Maritime History of Chesapeake Bay in the Colonial Era. Newport News: 1953. V. 63

MIDDLETON, BERNARD C.
A History of English Craft Bookbinding Technique. New York and London: 1963. V. 63
Recollections: My Life in Bookbinding. Newtown: 1995. V. 64

MIDDLETON, CHARLES
Designs for Gates and Rails Suitable to Parks, Pleasure Grounds, Balconys, &c., also Some Designs for Trellis Work. London: 1810. V. 64
Picturesque and Architectural Views for Cottages Farm Houses and Country Villas.... London: 1795. V. 64

MIDDLETON, CONYERS
A Free Enquiry into the Miraculous Powers, Which are Supposed to Have Subsisted in the Christian Church. London: 1749. V. 67
The History of the Life of Marcus Tullius Cicero. London: 1741. V. 66; 67
A Letter from Rome, Showing an Exact Conformity Between Popery and Paganism... (with) A Free Inquiry Into the Miraculous Powers, Which are supposed to Have Subsisted in the Christian Church from the Earliest Ages Through Several Successive Centuries. London: 1729. V. 66
Miscellaneous Tracts...Never Before Published.... London: 1752. V. 67
The Origin of Printing: In Two Essays: I. The Substance of Dr. Middleton's Dissertation on the Origin of Printing in England. II. Mr. Meerman's Account of the First Invention of Art. London: 1774. V. 65

MIDDLETON, E. E.
The Cruise of The Kate. London: 1953. V. 65

MIDDLETON, ERASMUS
The New Complete Dictionary of Arts and Sciences.... London: 1778. V. 64

MIDDLETON, HARRY
The Bright Country. New York: 1993. V. 67
The Earth is Enough. New York: 1989. V. 67
Rivers of Memory. Boulder: 1993. V. 67

MIDDLETON, J. HENRY
The Engraved Gems of Classical Times with a Catalogue of the Gems in the Fitzwilliam Museum. Cambridge: 1891. V. 63

MIDDLETON, JAMES
Oldham Past and Present. Rochdale: 1903. V. 63

MIDDLETON, JOHN
View of the Agriculture of Middlesex; with Observations on the Means if Its Improvement and Several Essays on Agriculture in General. London: 1807. V. 63

MIDDLETON, PETER
A Medical Discourse, or an Historical Inquiry into the Ancient and Present State of Medicine.... New York: 1769. V. 62

MIDDLETON, RICHARD
The Day Before Yesterday. London: 1912. V. 65

MIDDLETON, STANLEY
Distractions. London: 1975. V. 62
Holiday. London: 1974. V. 62; 65

THE MIDNIGHT
Ambulator; or, the Nocturanl Rambles, and Hair-Breadth Escapes, &c.... London: 1802. V. 63

MIDOLLE, J.
Recueil ou Alphabet de Lettres, Initiales Historiques Avec Bordures et Fleurons d'Apres le 14 et 15 Siecles. Ghent: 1846. V. 64

THE MIDSHIPMAN
in China: or, Recollections of the Chinese. London: 1845. V. 64

MIEGE, GUY
The Great French Dictionary. London: 1688. V. 64
The Present State of Great Britain and Ireland in 3 parts... (with) The Present State of H. M. Dominions in Germany. 1723-1722. V. 62; 65
A Relation of Three Embassies from His Sacred Majestie Charles II to the Great Duke of Muscovie, the King of Sweden and The King of Denmark. London: 1669. V. 63
The Short French Dictionary, in Two Parts. London: 1690. V. 64
The Short French Dictionary in Two Parts. Hague: 1697. V. 67

MIERS, JOHN
Contributions to Botany.... London: 1851-1871. V. 66
Illustrations of South American Plants. London: 1849-1857. V. 66
On the Apocynaceae of South America. London: 1878. V. 66
Travels in Chile and La Plata.... London: 1826. V. 65

MIGAHID, A. M.
Flora of Saudi Arabia. 1970. V. 66

MIGEOD, FREDERICK WILLIAM HUGH
Across Equatorial Africa. London: 1923. V. 65

MIGNAN, ROBERT
Travels in Chaldaea, Including a Journey from Bussorah to Bagdad, Hillah & Bablyon. London: 1829. V. 65

MIHALAS, DIMITRI
Galactic Astronomy; Structure and Kinematics. New York: 1981. V. 67

MILBANK, JEREMIAH
Turkey Hill Plantation. Ridgeland?: 1966. V. 67

MILES, ALFRED H.
The Poets and the Poetry of the Century. Robert Bridges and Contemporary Poets. London: 1893. V. 64

MILES, ANN PETTE
Monmouth Families. N.P: 1980-1981. V. 63; 66

MILES, EMMA R
The Spirit of the Mountains. New York: 1905. V. 65

MILES, HENRY DOWNES
Pugilistica: the History of British Boxing. Edinburgh: 1906. V. 65

MILES, KEITH
Bullet Hole. London: 1986. V. 66; 67
Flagstick. London: 1991. V. 66

MILES, NELSON A.
Personal Recollections and Observations of General Nelson A. Miles. Chicago: 1896. V. 64; 65; 67
Serving the Republic. New York: 1911. V. 67

MILES, T. J.
A History of Withernsea, with Notices of Other Parishes In South Holderness. Hull. 1911. V. 63

MILES, W. H.
Early History of Frontier County, Nebraska. Maywood. V. 67

MILES, WILLIAM
Journal of the Sufferings and Hardships of Capt. Parker H. French's Overland Expedition to California, Which Left New York City May 13, 1850 and Arrived at San Francisco Dec. 14th. New York: 1916. V. 63

MILES, WILLIAM J.
Modern Practical Farriery. London. V. 66
Modern Practical Farriery. London: 1874. V. 64
Modern Practical Farriery. 1880. V. 62; 64

MILHAUSER, STEVEN
Portrait of a Romantic. New York: 1977. V. 66

MILHOUS, KATHERINE
The Egg Tree. New York: 1950. V. 65

THE Military Execution of American Citizens by Order of the President.
Washington: 1857. V. 67

MILITARY HISTORICAL SOCIETY
Bulletin. Nottingham: 1973-1985. V. 66

MILITARY
History of Kentucky, Chronologically Arranged. Frankfort: 1939. V. 65

THE MILITARY Mentor.
London: 1804. V. 64

MILIZIA, FRANCESCO
Dell'Arte di Vedere Nelle Belle Arti del Disegno Secondo i Principii di Sulzer e di Mengs.... Venezia: 1792. V. 64

MILL, HUGH ROBERT
The English Lakes. London: 1895. V. 65

MILL, JAMES
Analysis of the Phenomena of the Human Mind. London: 1829. V. 64
Analysis of the Phenomena of the Human Mind. London: 1878. V. 64
Elements of Political Economy. London: 1824. V. 64; 67
Elements of Political Economy. London: 1844. V. 64

MILL, JOHN STUART
Auguste Comte and Positivism. London: 1865. V. 64
Auguste Comte and Positivism. London: 1866. V. 62
Autobiography. London: 1873. V. 62; 64
Autobiography. London: 1874. V. 64
Autobiography. (with) *Three Essays on Religion.* London: 1873-1874. V. 66
Chapters and Speeches on the Irish Land Question. London: 1870. V. 62; 66
Considerations on Representative Government. London: 1861. V. 64
Dissertations and Discussions. London: 1859-1867. V. 64
Essays on Some Unsettled Questions of Political Economy. London: 1844. V. 62; 65
The Evidence of John Stuart Mill, Taken Before the Royal Commission of 1870, on the Administration and Operation of the Contagious Diseases Acts of 1866 and 1869. London: 1871. V. 65
An Examination of Sir William Hamilton's Philosophy and of the Principal Philosophical Questions Discussed in His Writings. London: 1865. V. 63; 64; 67
The Letters. London: 1910. V. 64
Nature, the Utility of Religion and Theism. London: 1874. V. 64
On Liberty. London: 1859. V. 62; 63; 64; 65; 66; 67
On Liberty. London: 1864. V. 64
On Liberty. London: 1874. V. 64
Principles of Political Economy. London: 1848. V. 62
Principles of Political Economy. London: 1849. V. 64
Principles of Political Economy. London: 1857. V. 64
Principles of Political Economy. London: 1865. V. 64
Principles of Political Economy. London: 1871. V. 64
Speech on the Admission of Women to the Electoral Franchise. Spoken in the House of Commons May 20 1867. London: 1867. V. 63
The Subjection of Women. London: 1869. V. 64; 65; 66
The Subjection of Women. New York. 1869. V. 64
The Subjection of Women. London: 1870. V. 64
The Subjection of Women. London: 1878. V. 64
A System of Logic. London: 1846. V. 64
A System of Logic. New York: 1848. V. 63
A System of Logic. London: 1856. V. 64
A System of Logic. London: 1865. V. 64; 65
A System of Logic. London: 1868. V. 62
A System of Logic. London: 1872. V. 65
A System of Logic. London: 1875. V. 64
Thoughts on Parliamentary Reform.... London: 1859. V. 63
Utilitarianism. London: 1863. V. 64
Utilitarianism. London: 1864. V. 64
Utilitarianism. London: 1888. V. 64

MILLAIS, JOHN EVERETT
A Collection of Drawings on Wood. London: 1866. V. 64
Life and Letters of J. E. Millais. London: 1902. V. 63
Millais's Illustrations. London: 1866. V. 64

MILLAIS, JOHN GUILLE
A Breath from the Veldt. London: 1895. V. 62
A Breath from the Veldt. 1974. V. 62; 63; 64
British Deer and Their Horns. London: 1897. V. 65
British Diving Ducks. London: 1913. V. 65; 67
Far Away Up the Nile. 1924. V. 62; 63; 64; 66
Far Away Up the Nile. London: 1924. V. 64; 66
Game Birds and Shooting Sketches. London: 1892. V. 65; 66; 67
Game Birds and Shooting Sketches. London: 1894. V. 62
The Life and Letters of Sir John Everett Millais. London: 1878. V. 64
Life of Frederick Courtenay Selous. 1918. V. 62; 63; 67
Magnolias. 1972. V. 66
The Mammals of Great Britain and Ireland. London: 1904. V. 67
The Natural History of British Game Birds. London: 1909. V. 62; 67
The Natural History of the British Surface Feeding Ducks. London: 1902. V. 62

MILLAIS, JOHN GUILLE continued
The Natural History of the British Surface Feeding Ducks. London: 1909. V. 67
Newfoundland and Its Untrodden Ways. 1907. V. 63; 64
Newfoundland and Its Untrodden Ways. London: 1907. V. 67
Wanderings and Memories. London: 1919. V. 67
The Wildfowler in Scotland. London: 1901. V. 62

MILLANT, ROGER
J. B. Vuillaue, Sa Vie et Son Oeuvre. London: 1972. V. 65

MILLAR, C.
The Battle for the Bundu. 1974. V. 67

MILLAR, H. R.
The Silver Fairy Book. London: 1898. V. 65

MILLAR, JOHN
An Historical View of the English Government, From the Settlement of the Saxons in Britain to the Revolution in 1688. London: 1812. V. 62; 63
A History of the Witches of Renfrewshire. Paisley: 1877. V. 62
The Origin of the Distinction of Ranks; or, an Inquiry into the Circumstances Which Give Rise to Influence and Authority.... London: 1779. V. 63
The Origin of the Distinction of Ranks, or an Inquiry Into the Circumstances Which give Rise to Influence and Authority.... Basle: 1793. V. 63

MILLAR, KENNETH
Blue City. New York: 1947. V. 62; 64; 65

MILLAR, MARGARET
Beast in View. New York: 1955. V. 63
Vanish in an Instant. New York: 1952. V. 66

MILLARD, CHARLES
Charles Sheeler: American Photographer. Culpeper: 1967. V. 63

MILLARD, CHRISTOPHER
The Printed Work of Claud Lovat Fraser. London: 1923. V. 62

MILLAY, EDNA ST. VINCENT
Aria Da Capo. New York: 1921. V. 62
The Ballad of the Harp-Weaver. New York: 1922. V. 63
Collected Sonnets. New York: 1941. V. 65
Conversation at Midnight. New York: 1937. V. 65
Fear. New York: 1927. V. 63
The Harp Weaver and Other Poems. New York: 1923. V. 65
The King's Henchmen. New York: 1927. V. 62; 63
The Lamp and The Bell. New York: 1921. V. 62
Make Bright the Arrows: 1940 Notebook. New York and London: 1940. V. 66
Renascence and Other Poems. New York: 1917. V. 62; 63; 64
Sonnets. New York and London: 1931. V. 62
Two Slatterns and a King. A Moral Interlude. Cincinnati: 1921. V. 62; 63

MILLER, A. P.
Tom's Experience in Dakota. Minneapolis: 1883. V. 65

MILLER, A. V.
Hegel's Philosophy of Nature.... London: 1970. V. 66

MILLER, AGNES
The Colfax Book-Plate. New York: 1926. V. 65

MILLER, ALBERT E.
The Immortal Pioneers - Founders of St George, Utah. N.P: 1996. V. 65

MILLER, ANNA RIGGS
Letters from Italy. London: 1776. V. 63
Letters from Italy. London: 1777. V. 66

MILLER, ANNE
Out of the Blue. Southampton: 1988. V. 65

MILLER, ARTHUR
After the Fall. New York: 1964. V. 66
All My Sons. New York: 1947. V. 67
Chinese Encounters. New York: 1979. V. 67
The Creation of the World and Other Business. New York: 1973. V. 62; 65; 66
The Crucible. New York: 1953. V. 66
Death of a Salesman. New York: 1949. V. 63; 67
Death of a Salesman. New York: 1984. V. 65
Enemy of the People. New York: 1951. V. 67
Focus. New York: 1945. V. 67
Homely Girl, a Life. New York: 1992. V. 62; 63; 64; 66; 67
Homely Girl, a Life and Other Stories. New York: 1995. V. 66
Jane's Blanket. New York: 1963. V. 67
The Misfits. New York: 1961. V. 62; 64; 65; 67
Playing for Time. Illinois: 1985. V. 66
The Portable Arthur Miller. New York: 1971. V. 66
Salesman in Beijing. New York: 1984. V. 67
Situation Normal. New York: 1944. V. 62; 63; 65; 67
Timebends. New York: 1987. V. 67
A View from the Bridge - Two One Act Plays. New York: 1955. V. 65

MILLER, CHARLES
(Verses) To Lady Horatia Waldegrave, on the Death of the Duke of Ancaster. Strawberry Hill: 1780. V. 67

MILLER, DAVID
Practical Horse Farrier.... Hamilton: 1830. V. 63

MILLER, DAVID E.
Hole-in-the Rock- and Epic in the Colonization of the Great American West. Salt Lake City: 1959. V. 65

MILLER, DAVID H.
Custer's Fall - the Indians Side of the Story. New York: 1957. V. 67

MILLER, DAVID PRINCE
The Life of a Showman. London: 1853. V. 65
Life of a Showman. London: 1886?. V. 67

MILLER, E. D.
Fifty Years of Sport. London: 1920. V. 67

MILLER, EDGAR G.
American Antique Furniture. Baltimore: 1937. V. 63

MILLER, EDWARD W.
The Book of Trades. Philadelphia: 1847. V. 62

MILLER, EMILY VAN DORN
A Soldier's Honor. New York: 1902. V. 65

MILLER, ERNEST
John Wilkes Booth - Oilman. New York: 1947. V. 63

MILLER, FLOYD R.
The Michael Miller and Susana Bechtol Family Record. Bridgewater: 1993. V. 66

MILLER, FRANCIS TREVELYAN
The Photographic History of the Civil War. New York: 1911. V. 64
The Photographic History of the Civil War. New York: 1911-1912. V. 66

MILLER, G. S.
Catalogue of the Mammals of Western Europe. London: 1912. V. 63; 64; 66; 67

MILLER, GEORGE
Latter Struggles in the Journey of Life; or the Afternoon of My Days.... Edinburgh: 1833. V. 64; 65

MILLER, GEORGE C.
Blackburn: the Evolution of a Cotton Town. Blackburn: 1951. V. 66
Hoghton Tower in History and Romance. Preston: 1954. V. 65

MILLER, GLENN
Glen Miller's Method for Orchestral Arranging. New York: 1943. V. 66

MILLER, H.
The Testimony of the Rocks. Edinburgh: 1857. V. 63; 66

MILLER, HENRY
Black Spring. (with) Tropic of Cancer. (with) Tropic of Capricorn. New York: 1963-1961-1961. V. 65
The Colossus of Maroussi. San Francisco: 1941. V. 62; 65
The Cosmological Eye. Norfolk: 1939. V. 62
Echolalia. Berkeley: 1945. V. 64; 67
Echolalia. London: 1945. V. 63
Henry Miller: Between Heaven and Hell. Big Sur: 1961. V. 63; 64; 66
Into the Night Life. Berkeley: 1947. V. 62
Love Between the Sexes. New York: 1978. V. 62
Max and the White Phagocytes. Paris: 1938. V. 62; 67
Money and How It Gets That Way. Paris: 1938. V. 62
Mother, China and the World Beyond. Santa Barbara: 1977. V. 62; 67
On Turning Eighty. Journey to an Antique Land. Santa Barbara: 1972. V. 62; 67
Quiet Days in Clichy. Paris: 1956. V. 62
The Red Notebook. Highlands: 1958. V. 63
The Rosy Crucifixion. Paris: 1953. V. 62
Stand Still Like the Hummingbird!. Norfolk: 1962. V. 62
Sunday After the War. Norfolk: 1944. V. 63
Tropic of Cancer. Paris: 1934. V. 62
Tropic of Cancer. New York: 1940. V. 67
Tropic of Cancer. (and) Tropic of Capricorn. New York: 1961. V. 64
The World of Lawrence. Santa Barbara: 1980. V. 64

MILLER, HUNTER
Northwest Water Boundary. Report of the Experts Summoned by the German Emperor as Arbitrator. Seattle: 1942. V. 66
San Juan Archipelago. Study of the Joint Occupation of San Juan Island. Bellows Falls: 1943. V. 63

MILLER, J. S.
A Natural History of the Cinoidea, or Lily-Shaped Animals.... Bristol: 1821. V. 64; 65

MILLER, JAMES
The Humours of Oxford. London: 1730. V. 65
Of Politeness. An Epistle to...William Stanhope, Lord Harrington. London: 1738. V. 66

MILLER, JAMES H.
History of Summers County: from the Earlist Settlement to the Present Time. Hinton: 1908. V. 66

MILLER, JOAQUIN
'49 the Gold-Seeker of the Sierras. New York: 1884. V. 67
True Bear Stories. Covelo: 1985. V. 66
Unwritten History: Life Amongst the Modocs. Hartford: 1874. V. 63

MILLER, JOE
Joe Miller's Jests; or the Wits Vade Mecum Being a Collection of the Most Brilliant Jests.... London: 1739. V. 62

MILLER, JOHN
The Country Gentleman's Architect, in a Great Variety of New Designs.... London: 1789. V. 64
Memoirs of General Miller, in the Service of the Republic of Peru. London: 1828. V. 67
On the Present Unsettled Condition of the Law and Its Administration. London: 1839. V. 63

MILLER, KELLY
Kelly Miller's History of the World War for Human Rights.... N.P: 1919. V. 62

MILLER, LEE
Wrens in Camera. London: 1945. V. 65

MILLER, LEWIS B.
A Crooked Trail. Boston: 1911. V. 63; 67

MILLER, LIAM
The Dolmen Press Yeats Centenary Papers MCMLXV. Dublin: 1968. V. 66

MILLER, M. A.
Birds. A Guide to the Literature. New York: 1986. V. 62

MILLER, MARY BRITTON
Menagerie. New York: 1928. V. 63

MILLER, NYLE
Why the West Was Wild, a Contemporary Look at Some Highly Publicized Kansas County Personalities. Topeka: 1963. V. 64; 66; 67

MILLER, O. T.
The First Book of Birds. Boston: 1900. V. 67

MILLER, PATRICK
Ana the Runner. Waltham St. Lawrence: 1937. V. 64; 66
The Green Ship. Waltham St. Lawrence: 1936. V. 67

MILLER, PHILIP
The Gardener's and Botanist's Dictionary. 1807. V. 63; 65; 66
The Gardener's Dictionary. London: 1731. V. 63
The Gardeners Dictionary. London: 1759. V. 64; 67
The Gardener's Dictionary. 1768. V. 66
The Gardener's Kalendar. London: 1762. V. 64; 66

MILLER, RICHARD GORDON
A History and Atlas of the Fishes of the Antarctic Ocean. Carson City: 1993. V. 64

MILLER, S. H.
The Fenland, Past and Present. London: 1878. V. 64

MILLER, S. N.
The Roman Fort at Balmuildy (Summerston, Near Glasgow) on the Antoine Wall. Glasgow: 1922. V. 66

MILLER, SAMUEL
A Brief Retrospect of the Eighteenth Century.... New York: 1803. V. 63; 66
An Inquiry into the Cause of Motion; or, a General Theory of Physics, Grounded Upon the Primary Qualities of Matter. London: 1781. V. 64
Letters on Clerical Manners and Habits: Addressed to a Student in the Theological Seminary, at Princeton, N.J. New York: 1827. V. 63; 66
A Sermon Delivered January 19, 1812, at the Request of a Number of Young Gentleman of the City of New York, who Had Accembled to Express Their Condolence and the Inhabitants of Richmond, on the Late Mournful Dispensation of Providence in that City. 1812. V. 63

MILLER, SAMUEL M.
Notes of Hospital Practice, Parts I and II. Philadlephia: 1880. V. 67

MILLER, STEVE
Hurricane Lake. Madison: 1979. V. 64; 66

MILLER, SUE
The Good Mother. New York: 1986. V. 63

MILLER, T. L.
History of Hereford Cattle.... Chillicothe: 1903. V. 65

MILLER, THOMAS
Common Wayside Flowers. 1873. V. 63
Common Wayside Flowers. London: 1873. V. 62
Gideon Giles the Roper. London: 1841. V. 66
Turner and Girtin's Picturesque Views, Sixty Years Since. London: 1854. V. 62; 63

MILLER, VAL
Standard Recipes for Ice Cream Makers. Chicago: 1909. V. 67

MILLER, WADE
Calamity Fair. New York: 1950. V. 67

MILLER, WALTER M.
A Canticle for Leibowitz. Philadelphia/New York: 1960. V. 63; 67

MILLER, WILLIAM
The Costume of the Russian Empire. London: 1803. V. 65

MILLERAN, RENE
Nouvelles Lettres Familiers et Autres sur Toutes Sortes de Sujets.... Bruxeles: 1736. V. 64

MILLER PARKER, AGNES
Wood Engravings from the Fables of Esope. (with) Wood Engravings from XXI Welsh Gypsy Folk-Tales. London: 1996-1997. V. 67

MILLER'S Planters' and Merchants' Almanac, for the Year of Our Lord 1849. Charleston: 1848. V. 66

THE MILLER'S Wife (No. 2). Greenfield: 1844. V. 64

MILLES DE SOUVIGNY, JEAN
Praxis Ciminis Perseqvendi Elegantibvs Aliqvot Figvris Illvstrata. Parisiis: 1541. V. 64

MILLGATE, MICHAEL
The Achievement of William Faulkner. London: 1965-1966. V. 64

MILLHAUSER, STEVEN
Edwin Mullhouse. New York: 1972. V. 63; 66; 67
From the Realm of Morpheus. New York: 1986. V. 66
In the Penny Arcade Stories. New York: 1986. V. 66
Martin Dressler. New York: 1996. V. 66
Martin Dressler. Norwalk: 1997. V. 65
Portrait of a Romantic. New York: 1977. V. 66

MILLICAN, PERCY
The Register of the Freemen of Norwich 1548-1713. Norwich: 1934. V. 63

MILLIER, ARTHUR
Millard Sheets. Los Angeles: 1935. V. 62
Millard Sheets. Los Angeles: 1995. V. 63

MILLIGAN, SPIKE
Puckoon. 1956. V. 67

MILLIKAN, ROBERT ANDREWS
The Autobiography of Robert A. Millikan. New York: 1950. V. 63

MILLIKIN, ROBERT
Historico Masonic Tracts, Being a Concise History of Freemasonry. Cork: 1848. V. 63; 66

MILLIN, AUBIN LOUIS
Monumens Francois, Tels que Tombeaux, Inscriptions, Statues Vitraux, Mosaiques, Fresques, etc., Tires des Abbayes, Monasteres, Chateaux et Autres Lieux. Paris: 1802. V. 64

MILLINGEN, J. G.
Aphorisms on the Treatment and Management of the Insane: with Considerations on Public and Private Lunatic Asylums, Pointing Out Errors in the Present System. Philadelphia: 1842. V. 65
Mind and Matter, Illustrated by Considerations on Hereditary Insanity and the Influence of Temperament in the Development of the Passions. London: 1847. V. 64

MILLINGEN, JAMES
Ancient Unedited Monuments. Series I (II); Painted Greek Vases, Statues, Busts, Bas-Reliefs from Collections in Various Countries, Principally Great Britain. London: 1822-1826. V. 62; 67

MILLOT, CLAUDE FRANCOIS XAVIER
Elements of the History of France.... Dublin: 1772. V. 62

MILLS, ANSON
My Story. Washington: 1918. V. 63; 65; 67

MILLS, ARTHUR
Colonial Constitutions: an Outline of the Constitutional History and Exisiting Government of the British Dependencies.... London: 1856. V. 64
Shroud of Snow. London: 1950. V. 67

MILLS, BILL
25 Years Behind Prison Bars. N.P. V. 64; 67

MILLS, CHARLES
American Clydesdale Stud Book. Volume I. Springfield: 1882. V. 66
American Clydesdale Stud Book. Volume II. Springfield: 1883. V. 66
The History of Chivalry or Knighthood and Its Times. London: 1826. V. 64
The History of the Crusades, for the Recovery and Possession of the Holy Land. London: 1820. V. 66
The Travels of Theodore Ducas in Various Countries in Europe at the Revival of Letters and Art. London: 1822. V. 67
Tumors of the Cerebellum. New York: 1905. V. 66
Tumors of the Cerebrum. New York: 1905. V. 66

MILLS, CHARLES K.
Harvest of Barre Regrets, The Army Career of Frederick William Benteen. Glendale: 1985. V. 65; 67

MILLS, CHARLES KARSNER
The Nervous System and Its Diseases: a Practical Treatise on Neurology for the Use of Physicians and Students. Philadelphia: 1898. V. 65

MILLS, F. W.
An Index to the Genera and Species of the Diatomaceae and Their Synonyms (1816-1932). 1933-1935. V. 63
An Index to the Genera and Species of the Diatomaceae and Their Synonyms (1816-1932). London: 1933-1935. V. 62

MILLS, FREDERICK J.
The Life of John Carter. New York: 1868. V. 66

MILLS, JAMES W.
The Labyrinth and Other Poems. London: 1930. V. 63

MILLS, JOHN
D'Horsay; or, the Follies of the Day. London: 1844. V. 62; 63
An Essay on the Weather; with Remarks on the Shepherd of Bunbury's Rules for Judging of Its Changes; and Directions for Preserving Lives and Buildings of the Fatal Effects of Lightening. London: 1770. V. 64
The Flyers of the Hunt. London: 1859. V. 62; 64; 65
The Old English Gentleman, or, the Fields and the Woods. London: 1841. V. 67
The Sportsman's Library. 1845. V. 66; 67
Too Fast to Last. London: 1881. V. 67

MILLS, JOYCE
Stories of the Dreamwalkers. Santa Fe: 1989. V. 63

MILLS, LESTER
A Sagebrush Saga. Springville: 1956. V. 65

MILLS, MAGNUS
The Restraint of Beasts. London: 1998. V. 63

MILLS, W. H.
Forty Years at El Paso 1858-1898. 1901. V. 65; 67
Forty Years at El Paso 1858-1898. El Paso: 1962. V. 64; 65; 67

MILLSPAUGH, CHARLES F.
Flora of Santa Catalina Island (California). Chicago: 1923. V. 62; 63

MILMAN, HENRY HART
History of Latin Christianity; Including That of the Popes to the Pontificate of Nicholas V. London: 1883. V. 62; 66
The History of the Jews. London: 1829. V. 66

MILNE, ALAN ALEXANDER
Four Days Wonder. London: 1933. V. 67
A Gallery of Children. 1925. V. 62; 67
A Gallery of Children. London: 1925. V. 65
A Gallery of Children. Philadelphia: 1925. V. 62
The House at Pooh Corner. London: 1928. V. 62; 63; 64; 65; 66
The Hums of Pooh. London: 1929. V. 65
The King's Breakfast. Berkeley: 1996. V. 64
Michael and Mary. London: 1930. V. 63
Now We Are Six. London: 1927. V. 62; 63; 64; 65
Now We Are Six. New York: 1927. V. 63
The Secret and Other Stories. New York: 1929. V. 62; 64; 67
Three Plays. London: 1923. V. 64
Toad of Toad Hall. London: 1929. V. 62; 63; 64
When We Were Very Young. London: 1925. V. 65
Winnie the Pooh. London: 1926. V. 62; 63; 64; 65
Winnie the Pooh and Eeyore's Tale. New York: 1952. V. 64
Winnie the Pooh and the Bees. New York: 1952. V. 64

MILNE, COLIN
A Botanical Dictionary; or Elements of Systematic Botany. London: 1778. V. 64

MILNE, EWART
Diamond Cut Diamond: Selected Poems. London: 1950. V. 65
Elegy for a Lost Submarine. Burnham-on-Crouch, Essex: 1951. V. 65
Galion: a Poem. Dublin: 1953. V. 65
Life Arboreal: Poems. Tunbride Wells: 1953. V. 65

MILNE, JOHN
The End of Religious Controversy, in a Friendly Correspondence Between a Religious Society of Protestants, and a Roman Catholic Divine. London: 1819. V. 62

MILNER, DUNCAN C.
Lincoln and Liquor. New York: 1920. V. 62; 63; 65

MILNER, HARRY
Until Bengal - Poems in War. Calcutta: 1945. V. 64

MILNER, J.
An Inquiry into Certain Vulgar Opinions Concerning the Catholic Inhabitants and Antiquites of Ireland. 1808. V. 65

MILNER, JOE E.
California Joe, Noted Scout and Indian Fighter With an Authentic Account of Custer's Last Fight by Col. W. O. Bowen. Caldwell: 1935. V. 65; 67

MILNER, JOHN
The End of Religious Controversy, in a Friendly Correspondence Between a Religious Society of Protestants, and a Roman Catholic Divine. London: 1819. V. 65

MILNER, JOSEPH
Gibbon's Account of Christianity Considered; Together with Some Strictures on Hume's Dialogues Concerning Natural Religion. York: 1781. V. 65
The History of the Church of Christ. London: 1824. V. 66

MILNER-GIBSON-CULLUM, GERY
Pedigree of Wittenwronge of Ghent in Flanders, Stanton Barry (Bucks) and Rothamstead House (Herts), together with those of their Descendants Lawes, Capper, Brooke, Gery, Le Heup and Cullum. London: 1905. V. 67

MILNES, JAMES
Sectionum Conicarum Elementa Nova Methodo Demonstrata. Oxford: 1702. V. 65

MILNES, W. H.
Etchings in and About Wakefield. Wakefield: 1886. V. 63

MILNES, W. J.
Modern Practical Farriery. 1880. V. 62

MILNOR, WILLIAM
Memoirs of the Gloucester Fox Hunting Club Near Philadelphia. New York: 1927. V. 66

MILOSZ, CZESLAW
Bells in Winter. New York: 1978. V. 67
The Captive Mind. London: 1953. V. 63
The Captive Mind. New York: 1983. V. 62; 63; 64; 66
Czeslaw Milosz: a Selection of Poems. New York: 1996. V. 62
The Issa Valley. New York: 1981. V. 62

MILTON, JOHN
L'Allegro and Il Penseroso.... 1848. V. 63
Areopagitica. London: 1644. V. 65
Areopagitica.... Hammersmith: 1907. V. 62; 67
Areopagitica.... Cambridge: 1973. V. 64; 65
A Brief History of Moscovia and Of Other Less-Known Countries Lying Eastward of Russia as Far as Cathay. 1929. V. 65
Comus. New Rochelle: 1902. V. 65
Comus, a Masque. London: 1906. V. 62; 63; 65; 67
A Defence of the People of England. N.P: 1692. V. 67
Four Poems L'Allegro. Il Penseroso. Arcades. Lycidas. Newtown: 1933. V. 65
Literae Pseudo-Senatus Anglicani, Cromwellii, Reliquorumque Perduellium.... London: 1676. V. 63; 64
The Mask of Comus. London: 1937. V. 66
The Masque of Comus. Cambridge: 1954. V. 63; 64; 66
The Minor Poems of John Milton. London: 1898. V. 64
On the Morning of Christ's Nativity. 1933. V. 62; 65
On the Morning of Christ's Nativity. 1981. V. 67
Paradise Lost. London: 1668. V. 64; 65
Paradise Lost. London: 1730. V. 62
Paradise Lost. London: 1746. V. 62
Paradise Lost. London: 1749. V. 66; 67
Paradise Lost. London: 1750. V. 66
Paradise Lost. Birmingham: 1760. V. 63; 66
Paradise Lost. Dublin: 1765. V. 62
Paradise Lost. Glasgow: 1771-1772. V. 63
Paradise Lost. London: 1790. V. 62
Paradise Lost. London: 1794. V. 62; 67
Paradise Lost. London: 1825. V. 63; 65
Paradise Lost. London: 1834. V. 67
Paradise Lost. London: 1882. V. 67
Paradise Lost. Liverpool: 1906. V. 62
Paradise Lost. Waltham St. Lawrence: 1937. V. 65
Paradise Lost. (and) Paradise Regain'd. Hammersmith: 1902-1905. V. 62; 67
Paradise Lost. (with) Paradise Regained. London: 1931. V. 66
Paradise Lost...(and) Paradise Regain'd. Birmingham: 1760. V. 62; 66
Le Paradise Perdu, Poeme de Milton. Paris: 1779. V. 62
Paradise Regain'd. London: 1671. V. 66; 67
Paradise Regain'd. London: 1753. V. 62
Paradise Regained. London: 1795. V. 66
Paradise Regained, Samson Agonistes, Comus, Arcades, Lycidas, etc, etc. Chiswick: 1823. V. 63
Paradise Regained. London: 1924. V. 65
The Poems. New York: 1925. V. 65
Poems in English. London: 1926. V. 62; 65
The Poetical Works. London: 1794. V. 66
The Poetical Works. London: 1794-1797. V. 64
Poetical Works. London: 1809. V. 67
The Poetical Works. London: 1826. V. 62; 63; 64; 67
Poetical Works. London: 1835. V. 62; 66
The Poetical Works. London: 1852. V. 62; 65
The Poetical Works. London: 1859. V. 67
The Poetical Works. Boston: 1908. V. 64
The Practical Beekeeper; or Concise and Plain Instructions for the Management of Bees and Hives. London: 1851. V. 62
Samson Agonistes - a Dramatic Poem. Norwich: 1979. V. 65
Three Poems. 1896. V. 67
The Works. London: 1753. V. 65
The Works. London: 1851. V. 63
The Works. London: 1863. V. 62

MILTON, THOMAS
The Seats and Demesnes of the Nobility and Gentry of Ireland. London: 1783. V. 62

MILTOUN, FRANCIS
Italian Highways and Byways from a Motor Car. Boston: 1909. V. 67

MILVAINE, WILLIAM
Sketches of Scenery and Notes of Personal Adventure in California and Mexico. San Francisco: 1951. V. 62

MILWARD-OLIVER, EDWARD
Len Deighton: an Annotated Bibliography 1954-1985. N.P: 1985. V. 62; 65
Len Deighton, an Annotated Bibliography 1954-1985. London: 1985. V. 62

MILWAUKEE, LAKE SHORE AND WESTERN RAILROAD CO.
By-Laws Milwaukee, Lake Shore and Western Rail Road Co. Newark: 1875. V. 63

MINAMOTO, H.
An Illustrated History of Japanese Art. Kyoto: 1935. V. 62; 63

MINARIK, ELSE HOLMELUND
Father Bear Comes Home. New York: 1959. V. 64
A Kiss for Little Bear. New York: 1968. V. 64
Little Bear. New York: 1957. V. 64
Little Bear's Visit. 1962. V. 67

MINCHIN, H.
The Legion Book. London: 1929. V. 63

MINCOFF, ELIZABETH
Pillow Lace. A Practical Handbook. London: 1907. V. 62; 66

MIND, GOTTFRIED
Katzengruppen Nebst Kurzer Nachricht von dessen Leben. Leipzig: 1827. V. 63

MINER, FREDERICK R.
The Outdoor Southland of California. Los Angeles: 1923. V. 67

MINER, H. S.
Orchids, the Royal Family of Plants. Boston: 1885. V. 63
Orchids, the Royal Family of Plants. London: 1885. V. 62

MINERAL COUNTY HERITAGE SOCIETY
Mineral Co., West Virginia, Family Traits, Tracks and Trails, 1980. Mineral Co: 1980. V. 66

MINERALS and Metals; their Natural History and Uses in the Arts, with Indicental Accounts of Mines and Mining. London: 1837. V. 65

MINETT, JONATHAN
Double Suicide!!! A Full Report of the Coroner's Inquests Upon the Bodies of Eliz. Varney and Hannah Smith, Who Drowned Themselves at the Same Time in the River Leam, June 30, 1840, to Which is added an Account of the Interment of the Bodies, and Address. Royal Leamington Office: 1840. V. 66

MINGAY, G. E.
The Victorian Countryside. London: 1981. V. 63; 66

MINGHELLA, ANTHONY
The English Patient: a Screenplay. New York: 1996. V. 62

MINICK, ROGER
Delta West: the Land and People of the Sacramento-San Joaquin Delta. Berkeley: 1969. V. 63

MINKOFF, GEORGE ROBERT
A Bibliography of the Black Sun Press,. Great Neck;: 1970. V. 62

MINNESOTA in the Civil and Indian War. 1891. V. 65

MINNESOTA in the Civil and Indian Wars 1861-1865. St. Paul: 1893. V. 65

MINNEY, RUBEIGH JAMES
A Woman of France. London: 1945. V. 66

MINNICH, J. W.
Inside of Rock Island Prison, from December 1863 to June 1865. Nashville: 1908. V. 62; 63; 65

MINNIGERODE, MEADE
Some Personal Letters of Herman Melville and a Bibliography. New York: 1922. V. 67

MINNIGH, LUTHER
Gettysburg: What They Did Here. Gettysburg: 1900. V. 62; 63; 65

MINOGUE, ANNA C.
Loretto - Annals of the Century. New York: 1912. V. 64; 67

MINOR, LOUISA H. A.
The Meriwethers and Their Connections. Albany: 1892. V. 63

MINOR, LUCIAN
Reasons for Abolishing the Liquor Traffic. Richmond: 1853. V. 66

MINOR, MARIA W.
The Walkers of Woodberry Forest 1720-1973. 1973. V. 64

MINOT, C. S.
The Problem of Age Growth and Death.... New York: 1907. V. 67

MINOT, SUSAN
Monkeys. New York: 1986. V. 66

MINSHULL, JOHN
A Comic Opera, Entitled Rural Felicity; with the Humour of Patrick and Marriage of Shelty. New York: 1801. V. 63; 66

MINSTEL, M.
List of French Doctoral Dissertations on Africa, 1884-1961. Boston: 1966. V. 62

THE MINSTREL; or, Anecdotes of Distinguished Personages in the Fifteenth Century. Philadelphia: 1802. V. 66

MINTO, EMMA ELEANOR KYNYNMOUND, COUNTESS OF
A Memoir of the Right Honourable Hugh Elliot. Edinburgh: 1868. V. 65

MINTO, GILBERT ELLIOT, 1ST EARL OF
Life and Letters...from 1751 to 1806, When His Public Life in Europe Was Closed to His Appointment to the Vice-Royalty of India. London: 1874. V. 64

MINTO, JOHN
Rhymes on Life in Oregon. Salem: 19--. V. 66

Speculations on the Contemporary Painter - a Lecture Delivered at the City of Birmingham College of Arts and Crafts on 25 June 1952. Birmingham: 1952. V. 63

MINTON, S. A.
Venomous Reptiles. New York: 1969. V. 67

MINTORN, JOHN
The Hand-Book for Modelling Wax Flowers. London: 1853. V. 62

M'INTOSH, C.
The Book of the Garden. 1853-1855. V. 66
The New and Improved Practical Gardener and Modern Horticulturist. 1839. V. 63; 66

M'INTOSH, W. C.
The Marine Invertebrates and Fishes of St. Andrews. Edinburgh and London: 1875. V. 62
On the Development and Life Histories of the Teleostean Food - and Other Fishes. Edinburgh: 1890. V. 65

MINTZ, LANNON W.
The Trail - a Bibliography of the Travelers on the Overland Trail to California, Oregon, Salt Lake City and Montana 1841-1869. Albuquerque: 1987. V. 67

A MINUTE and Circumstantial Narrative of the Loss of the Steam-Packet Pulaski, Which Burst Her Boiler, and Sunk on the Coast of North Carolina, June 14, 1838. Providence: 1839. V. 66

A MINUTE Detail of the Attempt to Assassinate His Royal Highness the Duke of Cumberland and of the Facts, Circumstances and Testimonies of Numerous Persons.... London: 1810. V. 63

MIQUEL, FRIEDRICH ANTON WILHELM
Systema Piperacearum. Rotterdam: 1848. V. 64

MIRABEAU, HONORE GABRIEL RIQUETTI, COMTE DE
Letters, During His Residence in England. London: 1832. V. 66

MIRABEAU, OCTAVE HENRI MARIE
Fortune Garden. New York: 1949. V. 63

THE MIRACLES of Our Lord. London: 1848. V. 63

THE MIRACULOUS Power of Clothes and Dignity of the Taylors; Being an Essay on the Words, Clothes Make Men. Philadelphia: 1772. V. 64

MIRANDA, FRANCISCO DE
The Diary of Francisco de Miranda. Tour of the United States 1783- 1784. New York: 1928. V. 67
The History of Don Francisco De Miranda's Attempt to Effect a Revolution in South America in a Series of Letters by a Gentleman Who was an Officer Under that General to His Friend int he United States. Boston: 1810. V. 62; 63

MIRANDA, or the Discovery. Norwich: 1800. V. 62

MIRANDULA, OTTAVIANUS
Viridarium Illustrium Poeta(rum) cum Ipso(rum) Concordantiis in Alphabetica Tabula Accuratissime Conte(n)tis. Venice: 1507. V. 62

MIRO, JOAN
Joan Miro. London: 1966. V. 62; 64

MISCELLANEOUS and Fugitive Pieces. London: 1774. V. 64

MISCELLANEOUS Poems and Translations. By Several Hands Particularly The First Book of Statius (etc.) by Mr. Pope. London: 1714. V. 63

MISCELLANEOUS Poems Selected from the United States Literary Gazette. Boston: 1826. V. 62

MISCELLANY of the Scottish Burgh Records Society. Edinburgh: 1881. V. 62

MISCELLANY Sermons, Preached by Sundry Divines in Two Parts. Edinburgh: 1744. V. 65

MISES, RICHARD VON
Elemente der Technischen Hydromechanik. Leipzig: 1914. V. 67

MISHIMA, YUKIO
Confessions of a Mask. Norfolk: 1958. V. 66
Death in Midsummer and Other Stories. London: 1966. V. 62
Five Modern No Plays. New York: 1957. V. 65
The Temple of the Golden Pavilion. New York: 1959. V. 66
Thirst for Love. New York: 1969. V. 64

MISRACH, RICHARD
Desert Cantos. Albuquerque: 1987. V. 65
Richard Misrach 1979. San Francisco: 1979. V. 65

MISSAE in Agenda Defunctorum.. Venice: 1736. V. 65

MISSION Furniture, How to Make It. Chicago: 1909-1910. V. 66

MISSION DE VALBOURG, HENRI
Memoires et Observations Faites par un Voyageur en Angleterre.... Amsterdam: 1698. V. 62

MISSIRINI, MELCHIOR
Del Tempio Eretto in Possagno da Antonio Canova Esposizione. Venice: 1833. V. 67

MISSISSIPPI. LAWS, STATUTES, ETC. - 1861
Journal of the State Convention and Ordinances & Resolutions Adopted in January, 1861. Jackson: 1861. V. 63

MISSISSIPPI. LAWS, STATUTES, ETC. - 1865
Laws of the State of Mississippi, Passed at a Called Session of the Mississippi Legislature, Held in Columbus, Feb. and March, 1865. Meridan: 1865. V. 63

MISSISSIPPI VALLEY SANITARY FAIR, SAINT LOUIS
Catalogue of the Art Gallery of the Mississippi Valley Santiary Fair Saint Louis. 1864. St. Louis: 1864. V. 64

MISSON, FRANCOIS MAXIMILIEN
Nouveau Voyage d'Italie, Avec un Memoire Contenant des Avis Utiles a Ceuxqui Voudront Faire le Mesme Voyage. La Haye: 1702. V. 67

MISSON, HENRI SIEUR DE VALBOURG
M. Misson's Memoirs and Observations in His Travels Over England. London: 1719. V. 64

MISSOURI. STATE CONVENTION - 1861
Journal and Proceedings of the Missouri State Convention, Held at Jefferson City and St. Louis, March, 1861. St. Louis: 1861. V. 65

MISSY, JEAN ROUSSET DE
The History of Cardinal Alberoni: Chief Favourite of their Catholick Majesties and Universal Minister of the Spanish Monarchy; from His Birth to the Year 1719. London: 1719. V. 67

MR. FRANK, the Underground Mail-Agent. Philadelphia: 1853. V. 64; 66

MISTER, MARY
Mungo: or the Little Traveller. Dublin: 1822. V. 64

MISTRAL, GABRIELA
Desolacion. New York: 1922. V. 67

MITCHARD, JACQUELYN
The Deep End of the Ocean. New York: 1996. V. 62; 63; 64; 65; 66; 67

MITCHEL, JOHN
Jail Journal. Dublin: 1913. V. 63

MITCHEL, O. W.
The Planetary and Stellar Worlds; a Popular Exposition.... New York: 1848. V. 64

MITCHELL & HINMAN
An Accompaniment to Mitchell's Reference & Distance Map of the U.S. Philadelphia: 1835. V. 64

MITCHELL, ADRIAN
Out Loud. London: 1968. V. 62
Oxford Poetry - 1955. Swinford, Eynsham: 1956. V. 64
Who Killed Dylan Thomas?. Swansea: 1998. V. 62

MITCHELL, ANNIE R.
King of the Tulares and Other Tales from the San Joaquin Valley 1772-1852. Visalia: 1941. V. 63; 64

MITCHELL, ARTHUR
Labour in Irish Politics 1890-1930. 1974. V. 67

MITCHELL, AUGUSTUS
An Accompaniment to Mitchell's Map of the World, on Mercator's Projection. Philadelphia: 1839. V. 65

MITCHELL, C. H.
The Illustrated Books of the Nanga, Maruyama, Shijo and Other Related Schools of Japan: a Bibliography. Los Angeles: 1972. V. 64

MITCHELL, DONALD GRANT
American Lands and Letters. New York: 1897-1899. V. 62
American Lands and Letters. New York: 1901. V. 62
Bound Together: a Sheaf of Papers. New York: 1884. V. 64

MITCHELL, DUGALD
A Popular History of the Highlands and Gaelic Scotland from the Earliest Times Till the Close of the 'Forty-Five. Paisley: 1900. V. 62; 66

MITCHELL, F. S.
The Birds of Lancashire. London: 1885. V. 62; 65; 67

MITCHELL, FLORA H.
Vanishing Dublin. 1966. V. 62; 65

MITCHELL, GEORGE
A Catalogue of the Library of George Mitchell Esquire. London: 1869. V. 66

MITCHELL, GLADYS
Churchyard Salad. London: 1969. V. 67
Here Comes a Chopper. London: 1946. V. 65; 67
Here Lies Gloria Mundy. London: 1982. V. 65
Mingled with Venom. London: 1978. V. 67
The Rising of the Moon. London: 1945. V. 67
Uncoffin'd Clay. London: 1980. V. 65
Watson's Choice - a Detective Story. London: 1955. V. 62

MITCHELL, ISAAC
A Short Account of the Courtship of Alonzo and Melissa. Plattsburgh: 1811. V. 62; 64

MITCHELL, J. A.
The Silent War. New York: 1906. V. 64

MITCHELL, J. W. S.
The History of Free-Masonry: From the Building of the House of the Lord.... Philadelphia: 1900. V. 67

MITCHELL, JOHN
The Art of Conversation by Captain Orlando Sabrtash. London: 1850. V. 64
Manual of Agricultural Analysis. London: 1845. V. 62
Manual of Practical Assaying, Intended for the Use of Metallurgists, Captains of Mines and Assayers in General. London: 1854. V. 64; 66
Treatise on the Falsifcation of Food, and the Chemical Means Employed to Detect Them. London: 1848. V. 65; 66

MITCHELL, JOHN D.
Lost Mines of the Great Southwest, Including Stories of Hidden Treasures. Phoenix: 1933. V. 67

MITCHELL, JOHN EDWARD
Records of the Royal Horse Artillery, From Formation to the Present Time. London: 1888. V. 62; 66

MITCHELL, JOSEPH
The Bottom of the Harbor. Boston: 1959. V. 62; 64; 67
The Bottom of the Harbor. New York: 1991. V. 64
Chosen Poems: a Selection from My Books of Verse. New York: 1935. V. 62
Old Mr. Flood. New York: 1948. V. 62; 64; 67
Up in the Old Hotel and Other Stories. New York: 1992. V. 62

MITCHELL, K. W. S.
Tales from Some Eastern Jungles. 1928. V. 67

MITCHELL, MARGARET
Gone with the Wind. New York: 1936. V. 63; 64; 66
Gone with the Wind. New York: 1968. V. 63

MITCHELL, MARTIN
History of the County of Fond Du Lac, Wis. Fon Du Lac: 1854. V. 63

MITCHELL, MURIEL MOSCRIP
The Adventures of Nip and Tuck. Joliet: 1927. V. 64

MITCHELL, ROBERT
Plans and Views in Perspective, With Descriptions of Buildings Erected in England and Scotland, and Also an Essay to Elucidate the Grecian, Roman and Gothic Architecture.... London: 1801. V. 62; 64

MITCHELL, RUTH COMFORT
Army with Banners. New York: 1928. V. 65

MITCHELL, SAMUEL AUGUSTUS
An Accompaniment to Mitchell's Reference and Distance Map of the United States.... Philadelphia: 1834. V. 64
A General View of the United States. Philadelphia: 1846. V. 65

MITCHELL, SILAS WEIR
Clinical Lesions on Nervous Diseases. Philadelphia: 1897. V. 64
A Contribution to the Study of the Effect the Venom of Crotalus Adamanteus Upon the Blood of Man and Animals. Washington: 1898. V. 65
Doctor and Patient. Philadelphia: 1888. V. 65
Fair in the Forest. Philadelphia: 1889. V. 67
Fat and Blood: and How to Make Them. Philadelphia and London: 1879. V. 65; 66
Injuries of Nerves and Their Consequences. Philadelphia: 1872. V. 67
Lectures on Diseases of the Nervous System, Especially in Women. Philadelphia: 1881. V. 65
Lectures on Diseases of the Nervous System, Especially in Women. Philadelphia: 1885. V. 65
A Masque and Other Poems. Boston: 1887. V. 65
Mr. Kris Kringle. A Christmas Tale.... Philadelphia: 1904. V. 66
New Samaria and the Summer of St. Martin. Philadelphia: 1904. V. 64; 66; 67
The Physician. Boston: 1900. V. 64
Researches Upon the Venoms of Poisonous Serpents. Washington: 1886. V. 65
Researches Upon the Venoms of Poisonous Serpents. 1890. V. 66
The Tendon-Jerk and Muscle-Jerk in Disease Especially in Posterior Sclerosis. 1886. V. 66

MITCHELL, SUSAN
Secret Springs of Dublin Song. 1918. V. 67

MITCHELL, THOMAS LIVINGSTONE
Journal of an Expedition into the Interior of Tropical Australia, in Search of a Route from Sydney to the Gulf of Carpentaria. London: 1848. V. 62

MITCHELL HENRY, L.
Tunny Fishing at Home and Abroad. 1934. V. 67

MITCHELL'S Traveller's Guide through the United States. Philadelphia: 1836. V. 63; 64

MITCHENER, C. H.
Ohio Annals: Historic Events in the Tuscarawas & Muskingum Valleys & In Other Portions of the State of Ohio. Dayton: 1876. V. 67

MITCHILL, S. L.
Fishes of New York. New York: 1815. V. 66

MITCHILL, SAMUEL LATHAM
The Case of Manufacturers of Soap and Candles, in the City of New York, Stated and Examined. New York: 1797. V. 62

MITCHISON, NAOMI
The Big House. London: 1950. V. 67

MITELLI, GIUSEPPE MARIA
L'Arti per via Disegnate, Intagliate et Offerte al Grande et Alto Nettuno Gigante Sig. della Piazza di Bologna. Bologna: 1660. V. 64

MITFORD, EARDLEY
The Law of Wills, Codicils and Revocations, with Plain and Familiar Instructions for Executors, Administrators, Devisees and Legatees.... London: 1812. V. 65

MITFORD, JOHN
The Adventures of Johnny Newcome in the Navy. London: 1819. V. 62; 67
The Adventures of Johnny Newcome in the Navy. London: 1823. V. 66
The Important Trial of John Mitford on the Prosecution of Lady Viscountess Perceval, for Perjury, at Guildhall, on Thursday, Feb. 24, 1814.... London: 1814. V. 63

MITFORD, MARY RUSSELL
Atherton and Other Tales. London: 1854. V. 65
Belford Regis; or, Sketches of a Country Town. London: 1846. V. 65
Country Stories. London: 1837. V. 65
Foscari; a Tragedy. London: 1826. V. 65
The Life of.... New York: 1870. V. 63
Our Village. London: 1824. V. 66
Our Village. London: 1824-1832. V. 65
Our Village. London: 1893. V. 65; 67
Our Village. London: 1910. V. 66
Recollections of a Literary Life; or, Books, Places and People. London: 1853. V. 65; 67

MITFORD, NANCY
The Sun King. London: 1969. V. 65

MITFORD, WILLIAM
The History of Greece. London: 1838. V. 66

MITRA, S. K.
Postharvest Physiology and Storage of Tropical and Subtropical Fruits. Wallingford: 1997. V. 63

MITSCH, E.
The Art of Egon Schiele. 1975. V. 65

MITSUDA, HISATOSHI
Clinical Genetics in Psychiatry: Problems in Nosological Classification. Tokyo: 1967. V. 65

MITSUI MINING DEPARTMENT
The Mining Enterprise of the Mitsui Firm. Tokyo: 1910. V. 67

MIVART, G.
Lessons from Nature, as Manifested in Mind and Matter. London: 1876. V. 66

MIVART, ST. G.
The Cat. 1881. V. 66
The Cat. London: 1881. V. 64
Contemporary Evolution. An Essay on Some Recent Social Changes. London: 1876. V. 62
Henry Standon; or, Love's Debt to Duty. London: 1894. V. 65
A Monograph of the Lories or Brush-Tongued Parrots.... London: 1896. V. 67

MIXSON, FRANK M.
Reminiscences of a Private. Columbia: 1910. V. 63; 65

MIYABE, K.
Flora of Saghalin. N.P: 1915. V. 67

MIZAULD, ANTOINE
De Hortensium Arborum Insitione Opusculum.... Paris: 1560. V. 62
Ephemerides Aeris Perpetuae: seu Popularis & Rustica Tempestatum Astrologia, Ubique Terrarum et Vra & Certa. Antwerp: 1555. V. 62

M'KAY, ARCHIBALD
The History of Kilmarnock. Kilmarnock: 1858. V. 62

M'KEAN, JOHN
Address by the Manager of the Scottish Widows' Fund, and Life Assurance Society, Instituted January 2, 1815.... Edinburgh: 1829. V. 63
Exposition of the Objects and Principles of the Scottish Widows' Fund, and Life Assurance Society. Edinburgh: 1819. V. 63
Exposition of the Objects and Principles of the Scottish Widows' Fund, and Life Assurance Society.... Edinburgh: 1823. V. 63

M'KEEVOR, THOMAS A.
A Voyage to Hudson's Bay During the Summer of 1812.... London: 1819. V. 66

M'KIE, JAMES
Bibliotheca Burnsiana. Life and Works of Burns.... Kilmarnock: 1866. V. 67

M'LACHLAN, ALEXANDER
The Emigrant, and Other Poems. Toronto: 1861. V. 66

M'LEOD, ALEXANDER
Trial of Alexander M'Leod, for the Murder of Amos Durfee; and as an Accomplice in the Burning of the Steamer Caroline, in the Niagara River, During the Canadian Rebellion in 1837-1838. New York: 1841. V. 62; 66

M'LEOD, JOHN
Voyage of His Majesty's Ship Alceste, Along the Coast of Corea, to the Island of Lewchew, with an Account of Her Subsequent Shipwreck. London: 1818. V. 65
Voyage of His Majesty's Ship Alceste, to China, Corea and the Island of Lewchew.... London: 1819. V. 62

M'MURTRIE, H.
Sketches of Louisville and Its Environs: Including, Among a Great Variety of Miscellaneous Matter, a Florula Louisvillensis.... Louisville: 1819. V. 67

M'NAIR, JAMES
A Guide from Glasgow, to Some of the Most Remarkable Scenes in the Highlands of Scotland, and to the Falls of the Clyde. Glasgow: 1797. V. 62; 66

MO, TIMOTHY
An Insular Possession. London: 1986. V. 65
The Monkey King. London: 1978. V. 62; 65
The Monkey King. Garden City: 1980. V. 66
Sour Sweet. London: 1982. V. 64; 65

MOBERLY, HENRY JOHN
When Fur Was King. London: 1929. V. 66

MOBIUS, AUGUST FERDINAND
Der Barycentrische Calcul. Ein Neues Hulfsmittel zur Analytischen Behandlung der Geometrie.... Leipzig: 1827. V. 64; 66

MOCENIGO, GIOVANNI
Fenomeni Singolari D'Interferenza fra i Movimenti Molecolari delle Correnti Termo-Elettriche d'un Circuito Chiuso e Quelli Promossi Meccanicamente sul Legno ed Altri Corpi Elastici. Bassano: 1875. V. 64

MOCHI, UGO
Hoofed Mammals of the World. New York: 1953. V. 66

MODELSKI, ANDREW
Railroad Maps of North America; the First Hundred Years. Washington: 1984. V. 63

MODERN American Poetry. Buenos Aires: 1954. V. 62

MODERN Beauties in Prose and Verse, Selected from the Most Eminent Authors.... Darlington: 1793. V. 65

MODERN Belles. London: 1818. V. 62

MODERN Ethicks and Mental Philosophy; in a Series of Letters to a Friend. Halifax: 1843. V. 64

THE MODERN London Catalogue of Books, With Their Sizes, Prices and Publishers. London: 1818. V. 65

MODERN Observational Techniques for Comets; Proceedings of a Workshop Held at Goddard Space Flight Center...October 22-24, 1980. Pasadena: 1981. V. 67

MODJESKA, HELENA
Memories and Impressions of Helena Modjeska. New York: 1910. V. 65

MODJESKI, WEBSTER & DALL
Report to the Delaware River Bridge Joint Commission of the States of Pennsylvania and New Jersey on the Bridge over the Delaware River Connecting Philadelphia, Pa. & Camden N.J. 1921. V. 65

MODY, N. H. N.
A Collection of Nagasaki Colour Prints and Paintings Showing the Influence of Chinese and European Art on that of Japan. Rutland: 1969. V. 62; 63; 64; 66

MOE, LOUIS
Peter Kroak the Largest Green Frog in the Pond. Chicago: 1932. V. 65
Tommy-Tatters and the Four Bears. New York: 1929. V. 62

MOEHSEN, JOHANN CARL WILHELM
Verzeichnis einer Samlung von Bildnissen, Grostentheils Beruhmter Aertze.... Berlin: 1771. V. 63

MOELIONO, B. M.
Cauline or Carpellary Placentation Among Dicotyledons. Assen: 1970. V. 63

MOENS, JEAN BAPTISTE PHILLIPPE CONSTANT
On the Falsification of Postage Stamps or, a General Nomenclature of All the Imitations and Forgeries as Well as the Various Essay Stamps of All Countries. Falmouth: 1862. V. 64

MOENS, WILLIAM JOHN CHARLES
The Walloons and Their Church at Norwich 1565-1832. Lymington: 1888. V. 63

MOERMAN, D. E.
Native American Ethnobotany. Portland: 1999. V. 65; 66

MOFFAT, ALFRED
Little Songs of Long Ago. London: 1912. V. 64

MOFFAT, R. BURNHAM
The Barclays of New York: Who They Are and Who They Are Not.... New York: 1904. V. 63; 66

MOFFAT, ROBERT
Missionary Labours and Scenes in Southern Africa. New York: 1843. V. 65

MOFFETT, CLEVELAND
The Mysterious Card. Boston: 1912. V. 65
True Detective Stories, from the Archives of the Pinkertons. New York: 1898. V. 62; 65

MOFFITT, MARY ANNA
The Juvenile Tourist; or, the Poetical Geography of Europe. Philadelphia: 1858. V. 66

MOGGRIDGE, J. T.
Harvesting Ants and Trap-Door Spiders, with Supplement. 1873-1874. V. 66

MOGRIDGE, GEORGE
Loiterings Among the Lakes of Cumberland and Westmoreland. London: 1849. V. 64; 65; 66
Loiterings Among the Lakes of Cumberland and Westmoreland. London: 1850. V. 66
Sarah Martin, the Prison-visitor of Great Yarmouth. London: 1872. V. 65
Sergeant Bell and His Raree-Show. London: 1839. V. 62; 63; 64; 66

MOHAN LAL
Travels in the Panjab, Afghanistan and Turkistan in Balk, Bokhara and Heart.... Punjab: 1971. V. 63

MOHOLY, LUCIA
A Hundred Years of Photography: 1839-1939. Hammondsworth: 1939. V. 63

MOHOLY-NAGY, L.
Painting, Photography, Film. Cambridge: 1969. V. 63
Vision in Motion. Chicago: 1947. V. 62; 63; 64

MOHOLY-NAGY, S.
Carlos Raul Villanueva and the Architecture of Venezuela. New York: 1964. V. 62; 65
Moholy-Nagy: Experiment in Totality. New York: 1950. V. 65
Moholy-Nagy: Experiment in Totality. Cambridge and London: 1969. V. 63
Native Genius in Anonymous Architecture. New York: 1957. V. 65

MOHR, EDWARD
To the Victoria Falls of the Zambesi. London: 1876. V. 62

MOINAUX, GEORGE
Three Stories. Bromrigg/Dollar: 1978. V. 62

MOIR, DAVID MAC BETH
The Life of Mansie Wauch, Tailor in Dalkeith. Edinbrugh: 1839. V. 62; 65

MOIR, JOHN
Preventive Policy; or the Worth of Each, the Safety of All.... London: 1796. V. 62

MOISEEV, P. A.
Soviet Fisheries Investigations in the Northeast Pacific. Jerusalem: 1968. V. 65

MOISY, ALEXANDRE
Les Fontaines de Paris, Anciennes et Nouvelles. Paris: 1813. V. 67

MOIVRE, ABRAHAM DE
Annuities on Lives. London: 1750. V. 65
Annuities Upon Lives; or, the Valuation of Annuities Upon any Number of Lives.... London: 1725. V. 66

MOKLER, ALFRED JAMES
Fort Caspar (Platte Bridge Station). Casper: 1939. V. 65
History of Natrona County, Wyoming 1888-1922. Chicago: 1923. V. 64; 67
Transitions of the West. Chicago: 1927. V. 65; 67

MOKO and Koko in the Jungle. London: 1961. V. 63

MOLBECH, CHRISTIAN
Leben und Kunst des Schwedischen Malers Peter Horberg. Copenhagen: 1819. V. 64

MOLD, F. E.
Presenting the Fly to the Trout. 1967. V. 67

MOLDENKE, CHARLES E.
The New York Obelisk: Cleopatra's Needle. New York: 1891. V. 65

MOLESWORTH, MRS.
The Children of the Castle. London: 1890. V. 64
A Christmas Posy. London: 1888. V. 64
The Cuckoo Clock. Philadelphia: 1914. V. 63
Nurse Heatherdale's Story. London: 1891. V. 64

MOLEVILLE, BERTRAND DE
The Costume of the Hereditary States of the House of Austria.... London: 1804. V. 64; 65

MOLIERE, JEAN BAPTISTE POQUELIN DE
The Misanthrope. New York: 1955. V. 65
Les Oeuvres de Moliere. Paris: 1880. V. 67

MOLINA, J. I.
The Geographical, Natural and Civil History of Chili. 1808. V. 62

MOLINARI, RICARDO
Imaginero. Buenos Aires: 1927. V. 67

MOLINO, FRANCOIS
Grande Methode Complete Pour Guitare ou Lyre Dediee a S. A. R. Madae la Duchesse de Berry et Composee par Francois Molino Professeur de Violon et de Guitare Attache a la Chapelle de S. M. le Roi de Sardaigne. Paris: 1818. V. 64

MOLINOS, L.
Traite Theorique et Pratique de la Construction des Ponts Metalliques. Paris: 1857. V. 65

MOLL, HERMAN
A Set of Fifty New and Correct Maps of England and Wales, &c. 1724. V. 67
A Set of Fifty New and Correct Maps of England and Wales, &c. London: 1724. V. 66

MOLLIEN, GASPAR
Travels in the Interior of Africa, to the Sources of the Senegal and Gambia, Performed by Command of the French Government in the Year 1818. London: 1820. V. 65
Voyages dans l'Interieur de l'Afrique, Aux Sources du Senegal et de la Gambie. Paris: 1820. V. 62

MOLLO, JOHN
Uniforms of the Royal Navy During the Napoleonic Wars. London: 1965. V. 64

MOLLOY, BRIAN ARTHUR
Analysis of the Report and Evidence of the Select Committee of the House of Commons on the Operation of the Laws of Mortmain and the Restrictions of the Power of Making Deeds and Wills. Dublin: 1845. V. 65

MOLLOY, CHARLES
De Jure Maritimo et Navali; or, a Treatise of Affairs Maritime and of Commerce. London: 1744. V. 62

MOLLOY, FITZGERALD
The Life and Adventures of Edmund Kean, Tragedian. London: 1888. V. 65

MOLLOY, J. FITZGERALD
Court Life Below Stairs or London Under the First Georges 1714-1760. (and) London Under the Last Georges 1760-1830. London: 1882-1883. V. 66

MOLNAR, ANDREW R.
Undergrounds in Insurgent, Revolutionary and Resistance Warfare. Washington: 1963. V. 64

MOMADAY, N. SCOTT
House Made of Dawn. New York: 1968. V. 63; 66
House Made of Dawn. London: 1969. V. 63
In the Presence of the Sun. New York: 1992. V. 65
In the Presence of the Sun. Santa Fe: 1992. V. 63; 64
Owl in the Cedar Tree. N.P: 1965. V. 63
The Way to Rainy Mountain. Albuquerque: 1969. V. 64; 67

MOMMENS, NORMAN
Zoz a Story of Glory. London: 1959. V. 67

MOMMSEN, THEODORE
The Provinces of the Roman Empire from Caesar to Diocletian. London: 1886. V. 65

MOMOTARO.. Tokyo: 1900. V. 66

MOMOTARO or Little Peachling. Tokyo. V. 63

MONACO, DOMENICO
Specimens from the Naples Museum. London: 1884. V. 62; 66

MONAGHAN, JAY
Custer - the Life of George Armstrong Custer. Boston: 1959. V. 67
Last of the Bad Men. The Legend of Thom Horn. Indianapolis: 1946. V. 64
Lincoln Bibliography 1839-1939. Springfield: 1943. V. 64

THE MONARCHY of Bees, a Poem: Illustrated with Notes Exhibiting some of the Most Remarkable Circumstances in the History of that Little Insect. London: 1821. V. 66

MONCRIEFF, A. R. HOPE
Bonnie Scotland. London: 1904. V. 65

MONCRIEFF, JOHN
Camillus. A Dialogue on the Navy. London: 1748. V. 62

MONCRIEFF, W. T.
The Pickwickians; or, the Peregrinations of Sam Weller. London: 1872?. V. 62
Sam Weller, or, The Pickwickians. London: 1837. V. 62
The Spectre Bridegroom; or a Ghost in Spite of Himself. New York: 1821. V. 67

MONCRIF, FRANCOIS AUGUSTIN PARADIS DE
Cats. Le Chats. Waltham St. Lawrence: 1961. V. 62; 65; 66

MONDON, JEAN
Oeuvre. Paris: 1736. V. 67

MONELL, S. H.
High Frequency, Electric Currents in Medicine and Denistry. New York: 1910. V. 62

MONETTE, JOHN W.
History of Discovery and Settlement of the Valley of the Mississippi by the Three Great European Powers, Spain, France and Great Britain and the Subsequent Occupation, Settlement and Extension of Civil Government by the United States Until the Year 1846. New York: 1846. V. 67

MONETTE, PAUL
Borrowed Time. London: 1988. V. 67
The Carpenter at the Asylum. Boston: 1975. V. 64; 67

MONEY: Its Nature, History, Uses and Responsibilities. London: 1850. V. 63

MONEY, WILLIAM
A Vade Mecum of Morbid Anatomy, Medical and Chirurgical.... London: 1843. V. 66

MONGELLAZ, FANNIE BURNIER
De l'Influence des Femmes sur Les Moeurs et les Destinees des Nations, sur Leurs Familles et la Societe, et de l'Influence des Moeurs sur le Bonheur de la Vie. Paris: 1831. V. 65

MONGREDIEN, A.
Trees and Shrubs for English Plantations. London: 1870. V. 67

MONIER, PIERRE
The History of Painting, Sculpture, Architecture, Graving and of Those Who Have Excelled in Them. London: 1699. V. 67

MONIZ, EGAS
Egas Moniz Centenary Scientific Reports. Lisbon: 1977. V. 67

MONK, CHARLES JAMES
The Golden Horn: and Sketches in Asia Minor, Egypt, Syria and the Hauraan. London: 1851. V. 62

MONK, EDWIN
Small Boat Building. New York: 1934. V. 67

MONK, MARIA
Awful Disclosures, by Maria Monk, of the Hotel Dieu Nunnery of Montreal. New York: 1836. V. 63

MONK, MARY MOLESWORTH
Marinda. Poems and Translations Upon Several Occasions. London: 1716. V. 66

MONK, SAMUEL
The Sublime. A Study of Critical Theories in XVIIIth Century England. New York: 1935. V. 65

MONK, THYMOL
An Altar of Earth. London: 1894. V. 64

MONNIER, ADRIENNE
Fableaux. Paris: 1932. V. 65

MONNIER, HENRY
Moeurs Administratives, Dessinees d'Apres Nature. Paris: 1828. V. 67

MONOTYPE CORPORATION LTD., LONDON
Pastonchi. 1928. V. 65
Pastonchi. Verona: 1928. V. 62; 64; 66

MONRO, A. M.
The Beautiful Lady Chichester. London: 1886. V. 67

MONRO, ALEXANDER
The Anatomy of the Human Bones and Nerves.... Edinburgh: 1828. V. 66; 67
Observations on the Structure and Functions of the Nervous System. Edinburgh: 1783. V. 62; 66
The Structure and Physiology of Fishes Explained.... Edinburgh: 1785. V. 62; 63; 65; 66
A System of Anatomy and Physiology, with the Comparative Anatomy of Animals. Edinburgh: 1795. V. 66
Traite d'Anatomie Comparee.... Paris: 1786. V. 65

MONRO, DONALD
Praelectiones Medicae Ex Cronii Instituto Annis 1774 et 1775 et Oratio Anniversaria ex Harveii Instituto die Octobris 18...anni 1775. London: 1776. V. 66; 67

MONRO, HAROLD
The Collected Poems of Harold Monro. London: 1933. V. 65
Elm Angel. London: 1930. V. 63
Real Property. London: 1922. V. 64
Trooc. London: 1016. V. 62; 65

MONRO, HECTOR
The Sonneteer's History of Philosophy. Victoria: 1981. V. 62

MONRO, HENRY
Remarks on Insanity. Its Nature and Treatment. London: 1851. V. 62; 66

MONROE, ARTHUR
San Juan Silver. Grand Junction: 1940. V. 65

MONROE, B. L.
A Distributional Survey of the Birds of Honduras. 1968. V. 67

MONROE, DEBRA
The Source of Trouble. Athens: 1990. V. 63

MONROE, HARRIET
Chosen Poems: a Selection from My Books of Verse. New York: 1935. V. 66
The Difference and Other Poems. Chicago: 1924. V. 67
A Poet's Life - Seventy Years in a Changing World. New York: 1938. V. 65
You and I. New York: 1914. V. 62

MONROE, HORACE
Foulis Castle and the Monroes of Lower Iveagh. 1929. V. 63; 66

MONROE, JAMES
A Narrative of a Tour of Observation, Made During the Summer of 1817...through the North-Eastern and North-Western Departments of the Union.... Philadelphia: 1818. V. 67

MONSARRAT, NICHOLAS
Richer than All His Tribe. London: 1968. V. 65

MONSELL, J. R.
Polichinelle - Old Nursery Songs of France. London: 1928. V. 65

MONSON, WILLIAM
Naval Tracts, In Six Books. London: 1902-1914. V. 62
Sir William Monson's Naval Tracts: in Six Books. London: 1703. V. 65

THE MONSTER Book for Children. London: 1930. V. 65

MONTAGNE, PROSPER
Larousse Gastronomique. Paris: 1938. V. 63; 66

MONTAGU, BASIL
The Opinions of Different Authors Upon the Punishment. London: 1809. V. 62; 67
The Private Tutor; or Thoughts Upon the Love of Excelling and the Love of Excellence. London: 1820. V. 64

MONTAGU, CHARLES
Works and Life of the Right Honourable Charles, Late Earl of Halifax, Including the History of His Lordship's Times. London: 1715. V. 64

MONTAGU, ELIZABETH ROBINSON
An Essay on the Writings and Genius of Shakespeare. London: 1772. V. 62; 66
An Essay on the Writings and Genius of Shakespeare. Dublin: 1778. V. 63

MONTAGU, FREDERIC
Gleanings in Craven: in a Tour from Bolton-Abbey to Ambleside. London: 1838. V. 66

MONTAGU, G.
Testacea Britannica, or Natural History of British Shells. London: 1803. V. 62

MONTAGU, J. A.
A Guide to the Study of Heraldry. London: 1840. V. 62; 65; 67

MONTAGU, M. F. ASHLEY
Adolescent Sterility. Springfield: 1946. V. 64
Studies and Essays in the History of Science and Learning Offered in Homage to George Sarton on the Occasion of His Sixtieth Birthday, 31 August 1944. New York: 1946. V. 64

MONTAGU, MARY PIERREPONE WORTLEY, LADY
Essays and Poems and Simplicity. Oxford: 1977. V. 63
The Letters and Works. Paris: 1837. V. 65
Letters and Works. London: 1861. V. 62
The Letters and Works. London: 1886. V. 64
The Letters and Works. London: 1887. V. 65
Letters of the Right Honourable Lady.... London: 1763. V. 64; 66
Letters of the Right Honourable Lady.... London: 1778. V. 67
Letters of the Right Honourable...Written During Her Travels in Europe, Asia and Africa.... London: 1790. V. 62
The Poetical Works. London: 1768. V. 64
The Poetical Works. London: 1784. V. 63
The Poetical Works. London: 1785. V. 66
Verses Address'd to the Imitator of the First Satire of the Second Book of Horace. London: 1733. V. 62
The Works. London: 1803. V. 62
The Works. London: 1817. V. 65

MONTAGUE, CHARLES EDWARD
Dramatic Values. London: 1911. V. 64
The Manchester Stage 1880-1900. London: 1900. V. 64
Right Off the Map. London: 1927. V. 64

MONTAGUE, FRANCIS C.
The Limits of Individual Liberty. An Essay. London: 1885. V. 63

MONTAGUE, J.
Wild Bill, a Westerner's Story. New York: 1926. V. 62; 65

MONTAGUE, JOHN
Home Again. Belfast: 1966. V. 63
Home Again. Belfast: 1967. V. 63
The Rough Field. Dublin: 1972. V. 63
Tides. Dublin: 1970. V. 62; 64

MONTAGUE, W. K.
The Golf of Our Fathers. Duluth: 1953. V. 63

MONTAGUE, WILLIAM L.
The Richmond Directory and Business Advertiser for 1852. Richmond: 1852. V. 62

MONTAIGNE, MICHEL DE
The Diary of Montaigne's Journey to Italy by Way of Switzerland and Germany in 1580 and 1581. London: 1929. V. 65
Essays. London: 1685. V. 67
Essays. London: 1700. V. 62
The Essays. London: 1759. V. 67
The Essays. Dublin: 1760. V. 66
Essays. Boston an New York: 1902. V. 62
Essays. London: 1931. V. 62; 63; 65; 67

MONTALBANO, WILLIAM D.
A Death in China. 1984. V. 64; 66
A Death in China. New York: 1984. V. 67

MONTALE, EUGENIO
Mottetti: the Motets of Eugenio Montale in Italian. San Francisco: 1973. V. 64
Mottetti/Motets. Iowa City: 1981. V. 62; 66

MONTANA. CONSTITUTION - 1889
Constitution of the State of Montana. Helena: 1889. V. 67

MONTANA. A State Guide Book. New York: 1939. V. 65; 67

MONTANA - Echoes from the Prairies - a History of North Toole County. Shelby: 1976. V. 63

MONTANA HISTORICAL SOCIETY
Collections of the Historical Society of Montana. Boston: 1966. V. 66
Contributions to the Historical Society of Montana Volume Ten 1940. Helena: 1940. V. 66
Contributions to the Historical Society of Montana With Its Transactions, Act of Incorporation, Constitution, Ordinances, Officers and Members. Volume I. Helena: 1902. V. 66

MONTANA TERRITORY. LAWS, STATUTES, ETC. - 1866
Council Journal of the First Legislative Assembly of Montana. Virginia City: 1866. V. 62

MONTANA TERRITORY. LAWS, STATUTES, ETC. - 1870
Laws, Memorials and Resolutions of the Territory of Montana, Passed at the Sixth Session of the Legislative Assembly, Begun at Virginia City, Monday, Dec. 6, 1869 and Concluded Jan. 7, 1870.... Helena: 1870. V. 64

MONTANA TERRITORY. LAWS, STATUTES, ETC. - 1877
Laws, Memories and Resolutions of the Territory of Montana Passed at the Tenth Regular Session of the Legislative Assembly Held at the Town of Helena, the Capital of the Said Territory, Commencing Jan. 8. A.D. 1877 and Ending Feb. A.D. 1877. Helena: 1877. V. 63; 66

MONTANA TERRITORY. LEGISLATURE - 1866
Council Journal of the First Legislative Assembly of Montana Territory, Convened at Bannack, December 12, 1864. Virginia City: 1866. V. 63

MONTANA TERRITORY. LEGISLATURE - 1877
Council Journal of the 10th Session of the Legislature Assembly of the Territory of Montana, Begun at Helena, the Capital of Said Territory on the Eighth Day of January A.D. 1877 and Concluded on the Sixteenth Day of February A.D. 1877. Helena: 1877. V. 63; 66

MONTANUS, ARNOLDUS
De Nieuwe en Onbekende Weereld of Beschryving van America en 't Zuid-Land.... Amsterdam: 1671. V. 67

MONTE, GUIDOBALDO
Planisphaeriorum Universalium Theorica. Pesaro: 1579. V. 66

MONTEATH, ROBERT
The Forester's Guide and Profitable Planter. Edinburgh: 1824. V. 62; 66
The Forester's Guide and Profitable Planter. 1836. V. 63; 66

MONTECINO, MARCEL
The Crosskiller. New York: 1988. V. 62

MONTEFIORE, LEONARD ABRAHAM
Essays and Letters Contributed to Various Periodicals Between September 1877 and August 1879. Together With some Unpublished Fragments. London: 1881. V. 67

MONTEIRO, ARISTIDES
War Reminiscences by the Surgeon of Mosby's Command. Richmond: 1800. V. 63

MONTEITH, ROBERT
An Theater of Mortality; or, the Illustrious Inscriptions Extant Upon the Several Monuments Over the Dead Bodies...(with) An Theater of Mortality; or, a Further Collection of Funeral Inscriptions Over Scotland.... Edinburgh: 1704. V. 66
An Theater of Mortality... (and) An Theater of Mortality; or, a Further Collection of Funeral Inscriptions over Scotland.... Edinburgh: 1704-1713. V. 62

MONTENARI, GIOVANNI
Del Teatro Olimpico di Andrea Palladio in Vicenza.... Padua: 1749. V. 67

MONTES DE OCA, RAFAEL
Ensayo Ornitologico de los Troquilideos O'Colibries de Mexico. Mexico: 1875. V. 66

MONTESQUIEU, CHARLES LOUIS DE SECONDAT, BARON DE LA BREDE
Considerations sur les Causes de la Grandeur des Romains et de Leur Decadence. Amsterdam: 1734. V. 67
Considerations sur les Causes de la Grandeur des Romains, et de Leur Decadence. Lausanne: 1749. V. 67
De l'Esprit des Loix. Copenhague et a Geneve: 1759. V. 67
De L'Esprit Des Loix. Geneva: 1748. V. 63; 67
Lettres Persanes de Charles de Secondat, Baron de la Brede et de Montesquieu. Paris: 1926. V. 64
Persian Letters. Glasgow: 1751. V. 63
Persian Letters. London: 1899. V. 64
The Spirit of the Laws. Dublin: 1751. V. 65

MONTEZ, LOLA
Lectures of Lola Montez (Countess of Landsfeld). New York: 1858. V. 64

MONTFAUCON, BERNARD DE
The Antiquities of Italy...Being the Travels from Paris through Italy in the Years 1698 and 1689.... London: 1725. V. 62
Antiquity Explained, and Represented in Sculptures by the Learned Father Montfaucon. London: 1721-1722. V. 66
Antiquity Explained, and Represented in Sculptures. (with) Supplement. London: 1721-1725. V. 64
Antiquity Explained, and Represented in Sculptures... (with) Supplement to Antiquity Explained.... London: 1725. V. 62

MONTFERRAND, A. RICARD DE
Plans et Details du Monument Consacre a la Memoire de l'Empereur Alexandre. Paris: 1836. V. 65

MONTGOMERIE, H. S.
William Bligh of the Bounty in Fact and Fable. London: 1937. V. 65

MONTGOMERY, BERNARD L.
El Alamein to the River Sangro. 1946. V. 65

MONTGOMERY, ELIZABETH
Guidebook for the Health and Personal Development Primer Happy Days with Our Friends. Chicago: 1948. V. 62
Happy Days with Our Friends. Chicago: 1954. V. 66

MONTGOMERY, FANNY CHARLOTTE
On the Wing: a Southern Flight. London: 1875. V. 65

MONTGOMERY, FRANCES TREGO
Christmas with Santa Claus. Akron: 1905. V. 65

MONTGOMERY, JAMES
Greenland, and Other Poems. London: 1819. V. 67
Montgomery's Christmas Annual 1950: Art in the Blood and What Is This Thing Called Music?. Philadelphia: 1950. V. 66
Montgomery's Christmas Annual 1951: Sidelights on Sherlock. Philadelphia: 1951. V. 66
Montgomery's Christmas Annual 1952: Three Trifling Monographs. Philadelphia: 1952. V. 66
Montgomery's Christmas Annual 1953: Shots from the Canon. Philadelphia: 1953. V. 66
Montgomery's Christmas Annual 1954: a Study in Pictures. Philadelphia: 1954. V. 63; 66
Montgomery's Christmas Annual 1955: a Case of Identity. Philadelphia: 1955. V. 63; 66

Poems on the Abolition of the Slave Trade.... London: 1810. V. 67
The Wanderer in Switzerland, and Other Poems. Edinburgh: 1813. V. 64; 66
The World Before the Flood. London: 1815. V. 64; 66

MONTGOMERY, L. M.
Mistress Pat. 1935. V. 67

MONTGOMERY, MORTON L.
History of Berks County, Pennsylvania in the Revolution from 1774 to 1783. Reading: 1894. V. 65

MONTGOMERY, ROBERT
Oxford. A Poem. Oxford: 1831. V. 62; 65; 66

MONTGOMERY, ROSS G.
Franciscan Awatovi, the Excavation and Conjectural Reconstruction of a 17th Century Spanish Mission Establishment at a Hopi Indian Town in Northeastern Arizona. Cambridge: 1949. V. 63; 66

MONTGOMERY, RUTHERFORD G.
High Country. New York: 1938. V. 64

MONTGOMERY, SOPHIA FLORENCE
Thrown Together: a Story. London: 1872. V. 65
Thwarted or Ducks' Eggs in a Hen's Nest: a Village Story. London: 1874. V. 65
The Town-Crier, to Which is Added The Children with the Indian-Rubber Ball: a Christmas Story Book for Young Children. London: 1874. V. 65

MONTGOMERY, WALTER A.
Appomattox and the Return Home. Raleigh: 1938. V. 62; 63

MONTGOMERY-MASSINGBERD, HUGH
Burke's and Savills Guide to Country Houses. London: 1978-1981. V. 64; 66

MONTGOMERY OF ALAMEIN, BERNARD LAW MONTGOMERY, 1ST VISCOUNT
The Path to Leadership. London: 1961. V. 62
Ten Chapters 1942 to 1945. 1945. V. 64

A MONTH at Gastein; or, Footfalls in the Tyrol. London: 1873. V. 67

MONTHAN, DORIS
R. C. Gorman: The Lithographs. Flagstaff: 1978. V. 62; 64; 65; 66

MONTHAN, GUY
Art and Indian Individualists. Flagstaff: 1975. V. 63; 66

MONTHLY Chronicle of North-Country Lore and Legend. Newcastle-upon-tyne: 1887-1891. V. 66

MONTI, VINCENZO
Tragedie. Florence: 1818. V. 65

MONTJOSIEU, LOUIS DE
Ludovici Demontiosii Gallus Romae Hospes. Rome: 1585. V. 67

MONTMORT, PIERRE REMOND DE
Essai d'Analyse sur les Jeux de Hazards. Paris: 1714. V. 66

MONTOLIEU, JEANNE ISABELLE PAULINE POLIER DE BOTTENS
Anecdotes Sentimentales. Londres: 1811. V. 67

MONTON, BERNARDO
Secretos de Artes Liberales y Mecanicas. Barcelona: 1761. V. 64

MONTORGUEIL, GEORGES
Louis XI. Paris: 1905. V. 62; 64
Paris Dansant. Paris: 1898. V. 62

MONTOYA, JUAN DE
New Mexico in 1602, Juan De Montoya's Relation of the Discovery of New Mexico. Albuquerque: 1938. V. 63

MONYPENNY, WILLIAM F.
The Life of Benjamin Disraeli. London: 1910-1920. V. 62; 64
The Life of Benjamin Disraeli, Earl of Beaconsfield. New York: 1913. V. 65

MONZ, L.
Ein Buch fur Die Judische Ghefrau. Zurich: 1946. V. 67

MOODIE, SUSANNA
Life in the Clearings. London: 1853. V. 65
Roughing It In the Bush, or Life in Canada. New York: 1852. V. 62

MOODY, BILL
The Jazz Exiles. Reno: 1992. V. 66

MOODY, RICK
The Ice Storm. Boston: 1994. V. 67
The Ring of Brightest Angels Around Heaven. Boston: 1995. V. 67

MOODY, T. W.
A New History of Ireland. Volume III. 1976. V. 67
Queen's, Belfast 1845-1949. The History of a University. 1959. V. 63; 66

MOON, ANNA MARIA
In Memoriam. The Rev. W. Leeves, Author of the Air of "Auld Robin Gray". Brighton: 1873-1881. V. 65

MOON, CARL
The Flaming Arrow. New York: 1927. V. 64

MOON, GRACE
Wongo and the Wise Old Crow. Chicago: 1923. V. 63

MOON, WILLIAM
Light for the Blind: a History of the Origin and Success of Moon's Society for Embossing and Circulating the Bible and Other Books in Moon's Type for the Blind. Brighton, Sussex: 1884. V. 66
Soldiers of Lucknow; in Type for the Blind. Brighton: 1857. V. 64

MOON, WILLIAM LEAST HEAT
Blue Highways: a Journey into America. Boston: 1983. V. 63

MOONEY, CHARLES W.
Doctor in Belle Starr Country. Oklahoma City: 1975. V. 67

MOONEY, H. A.
Disturbance and Ecosystems, Components of Response. Berlin: 1983. V. 63

MOONEY, TED
Easy Travel to Other Planets. New York: 1981. V. 63

MOOR, ANN
An Account of the Extraordinary Abstinence of Ann Moor, of Tutbury, Staffordshire, Who Has, For More than Two Years, Lived Entirely Without Food.... Philadelphia: 1810. V. 62

MOOR, BARTHOLOMAEI DE
Cogitationum De Instauratione Medicinae, ad Sanitatis Tutelam, Morbos Profligandos.... Amsterdam: 1695. V. 64; 66

MOOR, EDWARD
Bealings Bells. Woodbridge: 1841. V. 62

MOOR, J. F.
The Birth-Place, Home, Churches and Other Places Connected with the Author of The Christian Year.... Winchester: 1866. V. 64

MOORCOCK, MICHAEL
Stormbringer. London: 1965. V. 64

MOORDAFF, ARTHUR
Records of Otter Hunting, &c. 1885. V. 62; 64

MOORE, ADOLPHUS WARBURTON
The Alps in 1864. 1902. V. 63; 65
The Alps in 1864. Oxford: 1939. V. 62; 63; 64

MOORE, BEN
Butterfield - Seven Years with the Wild Indians. O'Donnel: 1945. V. 67

MOORE, BILL
Bastrop County 1691-1900. San Angelo: 1973. V. 67

MOORE, BRIAN
An Answer to Limbo. Boston: 1962. V. 65
The Feast of Lupercal. Boston: 1957. V. 65
Intent to Kill. London: 1956. V. 64
Judith Hearne. London: 1955. V. 65
No Other Life. London: 1993. V. 62
Tema Onn. Toronto: 1965. V. 67
Two Stories. 1970. V. 64

MOORE, C. C.
Observations Upon Certain Passages in Mr. Jefferson's Notes on Virginia, Which Appear to Have a Tendency to Subvert Religion and Establish a False Philosophy. New York: 1804. V. 63; 66

MOORE, C. L.
Shambleau and Others. New York: 1953. V. 63; 64

MOORE, CHARLES FOREST
Judge Moore's Fireside Filosophy. Lewisburg: 1929. V. 67

MOORE, CLEMENT
A Plain Statement, Addressed to the Proprietors of Real Estate, in the City and County of New York. New York: 1818. V. 66

MOORE, CLEMENT CLARKE
Denslow's Night Before Christmas. Chicago: 1913. V. 66
The Night Before Christmas. Newark: 1910. V. 65
The Night Before Christmas. London: 1931. V. 66
The Night Before Christmas. New York: 1935. V. 62; 66
The Night Before Christmas. Racine: 1935. V. 62
The Night Before Christmas. Philadelphia: 1942. V. 63
The Night Before Christmas. New York: 1947. V. 64
The Night Before Christmas. New York: 1948. V. 64
The Night Before Christmas. Chicago: 1949. V. 66
The Night Before Christmas. Worcester: 1962. V. 63
The Night Before Christmas. New York: 1981. V. 66

MOORE, D. M.
Flora of Tierra del Fuego. Oswestry: 1983. V. 63

MOORE, DORIS LANGLEY
E. Nesibt, a Biography. London: 1933. V. 67

MOORE, EDWARD
Fables for the Female Sex. London: 1744. V. 63; 66
Fables for the Female Sex. London: 1771. V. 63

MOORE, EDWARD A.
The Story of a Cannoneer Under Stonewall Jackson. New York and Washington: 1907. V. 63
The Story of a Cannoneer Under Stonewall Jackson. Lynchburg: 1910. V. 63; 65; 66

MOORE, F. FRANKFORT
The Truth About Ulster. 1914. V. 67

MOORE, FRANCIS
Cases Collect (sic) and Report Per Sir Francis Moore. London: 1663. V. 63

MOORE, FRANK
Lyrics of Loyalty. New York: 1864. V. 66

MOORE, GEOFFREY
Poetry from Cambridge in Wartime. London: 1944. V. 62

MOORE, GEORGE
Aphrodite in Aulis. 1930. V. 65
Aphrodite in Aulis. London: 1930. V. 64
The Apostle. 1923. V. 67
Avowals. London: 1919. V. 62
The Brook Kerith. London: 1929. V. 62; 64; 66
The Coming of Gabrielle. 1920. V. 67
A Communication to My Friends. London: 1933. V. 65; 67
Confessions of a Young Man. 1904. V. 64; 67
Elizabeth Cooper. Dublin and London: 1913. V. 66
Esther Waters. 1894. V. 65
A Flood. New York: 1930. V. 63; 64; 66; 67
Flowers of Passion. London: 1878. V. 63
Hail and Farewell. 1911-1914. V. 62; 65
Hail and Farewell. 1925. V. 62; 65
Hail and Farewell. London: 1925. V. 62; 64; 66
Hail and Farewell. 1947. V. 67
Heloise and Abelard. 1921. V. 63; 66
Heloise and Abelard. London: 1921. V. 64
Heloise and Abelard. New York: 1921. V. 65
Heloise and Abelard. (with) Fragments from Heloise. 1921. V. 65; 67
In Single Strictness. London: 1922. V. 64
Letters from George Moore to Ed. Dujardin 1886-1922. New York: 1929. V. 62; 63; 66
The Making of an Immortal. New York: 1927. V. 62
Memoirs of My Dead Life of Galanteries, Meditations and Remembrances, Soliloquies or Advice to Lovers.... London: 1921. V. 64
Peronnik the Fool. London: 1926. V. 64
Peronnik the Fool. London: 1933. V. 63; 64
The Power of the Soul Over the Body, Considered in Relation to Health and Morals. London: 1845. V. 64
Sister Teresa. London: 1901. V. 66; 67
Ulick and Soracha. London: 1926. V. 62; 65
Works. New York: 1922. V. 63

MOORE, GEORGE H.
The Treason of Charles Lee, Major General. New York: 1860. V. 67

MOORE, HENRY
Picturesque Excursions from Derby to Matlock Bath.... Derby: 1818. V. 66

MOORE, HENRY SPENCER
Carvings and Bronzes 1961-1970. New York: 1970. V. 63
Henry Moore on Sculpture - a Collection of the Sculptor's Writings and Spoken Words. London: 1966. V. 63
Sculpture and Drawings 1921-1964. London: 1957-1965. V. 63
Shelter Sketch Book. London: 1945. V. 66

MOORE, J. E. S.
The Tanganyika Problem.... 1903. V. 66

MOORE, J. HAMILTON
The Young Gentleman and Lady's Monitor, and English Teacher's Assistant.... London: 1791. V. 64

MOORE, JAMES
Kilpatrick and Our Cavalry.... New York: 1865. V. 63; 66
Two Letters to Dr. Jones on the Composition of the Eau Medicinale d'Husson. London: 1811. V. 64

MOORE, JAMES CARRICK
A Narrative of the Campaign of the British Army in Spain, Commanded by His Excellency Lieut. General Sir John Moore. London: 1809. V. 62; 64

MOORE, JOEL R.
The History of the American Expedition Fighting the Bolsheviki. Detroit: 1920. V. 65

MOORE, JOHN
Among the Quiet Folks. Philadelphia: 1967. V. 67
Edward: Various Views of Human Nature Taken from Life and Manners, Chiefly in England. London: 1796. V. 66
A Journal During a Residence in France, from the Beginning of August to the Middle of December 1792. London: 1793. V. 63
A Journal During a Residence in France, from the Beginning of August to the Middle of December 1792. London: 1793-1794. V. 66
The Life and Letters of Edward Thomas. London: 1939. V. 64
Medical Sketches: in Two Parts. London: 1786. V. 65; 66
A Treatise on Domestic Pigeons.... London: 1765. V. 64

MOORE, JOHN continued
A View of Society and Manners in France, Switzerland, and Germany.... London: 1793. V. 66
A View of Society and Manners in Italy. London: 1781. V. 62; 67
A View of Society and Manners in Italy. London: 1790. V. 66
A View of Society and Manners in Italy. London: 1792. V. 62
A View of the Causes and Progress of the French Revolution. Dublin: 1795. V. 62
A View of the Causes and Progress of the French Revolution. London: 1795. V. 66
A View of the Society and Manners in Switzerland, and Germany. London: 1779. V. 67
The Waters Under the Earth. London: 1965. V. 67
The Year of the Pigeons. London: 1963. V. 67
You English Words. London: 1961. V. 67
Zeluco, Various Views of Human Nature, Taken from Life and Manners, Foreign and Domestic. London: 1789. V. 62
Zeluco: Various Views of Human Nature, Taken from Life and Manners, Foreign and Domestic. London: 1790. V. 66

MOORE, JOHN B.
History and Digest of the International Arbitrations to Which the United States Has Been a Party. (Volume VI, only). Washington: 1898. V. 63

MOORE, JOHN BAYLY
A Digested Index to the Reports of All the Cases Argued and Determined in the House of Lords, from 1813 to 1819, in the Court of King's Bench, from Michaelmas Term, 1819 to Michaelmas Term, 1821; In the Court of Exchequer, from Hilary Term, 1818 to Hilar. London: 1822. V. 65

MOORE, JOHN M.
The West. Wichita Falls: 1935. V. 63

MOORE, JOHN T.
The Old Cotton Gin. Philadelphia: 1910. V. 64

MOORE, L. B.
The Oxford Book of New Zealand Plants. Wellington: 1978. V. 66

MOORE, LORRIE
Anagrams. New York: 1986. V. 62; 64; 65; 66
Like Life. New York: 1990. V. 65; 67
Self Help. New York: 1985. V. 63; 67

MOORE, MARGARET
Certainly, Carrie, You Can Cut the Cake. Poems from A to Z. Indianapolis: 1971. V. 62

MOORE, MARIANNE
The Absentee: a Comedy in Four Acts. New York: 1962. V. 64
Alyse Gregory Remembered. Loughton: 1968. V. 62
Collected Poems. London: 1951. V. 62; 65
The Complete Poems of Marianne Moore. New York: 1967. V. 65
The Complete Poems of Marianne Moore. New York: 1981. V. 65
Dress and Kindred Subjects. New York: 1965. V. 62; 66
Eight Poems. New York: 1962. V. 64
Like a Bulwark. New York: 1956. V. 62; 64; 66
A Marianne Moore Reader. New York: 1961. V. 65
O To Be A Dragon. New York: 1959. V. 62; 64
Observations. New York: 1924. V. 62
Occasionem Cognosce. Lunenburg: 1963. V. 67
The Pangolin and Other Verse. London: 1936. V. 64; 65
Poems. London: 1921. V. 64
Poetry and Criticism. Cambridge: 1965. V. 62
Predilections. New York: 1955. V. 62; 64; 65; 67
Predilections. London: 1956. V. 62; 66
Selected Poems. London: 1935. V. 63
Selected Poems. New York: 1935. V. 64
Silence. Boston: 1965. V. 62
Tell Me, Tell Me. New York: 1966. V. 62; 64
Tipoo's Tiger. New York: 1967. V. 62

MOORE, MARINDA B.
The First Dixie Reader: Designed to Follow the Dixie Primer. Raleigh: 1863. V. 62

MOORE, MERRILL
Case Record From a Sonnetorium. New York: 1951. V. 64
The Noise that Time Makes. New York: 1929. V. 62
Sonnets from the Fugitive (1922-1926). Boston: 1937. V. 62

MOORE, MILCAH MARTHA HILL
Miscellanies, Moral and Instructive, in Prose and Verse.... Burlington: 1796. V. 63; 66

MOORE, NICHOLAS
The Glass Tower. London: 1944. V. 66

MOORE, NORMAN
The History of St. Bartholomew's Hospital. London: 1918. V. 62; 65
The History of the Study of Medicine in the British Isles, the Fitz-Patrick Lectures for 1905-1906. Oxford: 1908. V. 62

MOORE, SAMUEL
An Accurate System of Surveying.... Litchfield: 1796. V. 64; 66

MOORE, T.
Every Man His Own Gardner. 1822. V. 63
Illustrations of Orchidaceous Plants.... 1857. V. 62

MOORE, TEX
The West. Wichita Falls: 1935. V. 65; 67

MOORE, THOMAS
British Wild Flowers. London: 1867. V. 62
The Epicurean, a Tale. Paris: 1827. V. 63
The Epicurean, a Tale. London: 1839. V. 63; 66
Fables for the Holly Alliance, Rhymes on the Road &c. London: 1823. V. 65
The History of Ireland. 1835-1846. V. 63
Irish Melodies. Dublin: 1820. V. 62
Irish Melodies. London: 1846. V. 63; 64
Irish Melodies. London: 1853. V. 65
Irish Melodies and a Monologue Upon National Music. 1820. V. 65
Irish Melodies, Lala Rookh, National Airs, Legendary Ballads, Songs &c. with a Memoir by J. F. Waller. London. V. 64
Lalla Rookh. 1846. V. 67
Lalla Rookh. London: 1868. V. 66
Lalla Rookh. Boston: 1887. V. 63
Letters and Journals of Lord Byron; with Notices of His Life.... London: 1833. V. 67
The Loves of the Angels, a Poem. London: 1823. V. 65
M.P. or the Blue Stocking, a Comic Opera in Three Acts. London: 1811. V. 63
Memoirs of the Life of Richard Brinsley Sheridan. 1827. V. 65
Moore's Irish Melodies. London: 1866. V. 67
Nature Printed British Ferns. London: 1863. V. 65
Odes Upon Cash, Corn, Catholics and Other Matters. London: 1828. V. 65
Paradise and the Peri. London: 1860. V. 67
The Parson's Horn-Book. Dublin: 1831. V. 67
The Poetical Works. London: 1853. V. 62; 64
The Poetical Works. London: 1868-1869. V. 65
The Poetical Works. London: 1869. V. 67
The Poetical Works. 1880. V. 67

MOORE, THOMAS STURGE
Armour for Aphrodite. 1929. V. 65
Armour for Aphrodite. London: 1929. V. 63
The Centaur's Booty. The Route of the Amazons. The Gazelles and Other Poems. Pan's Prophecy. To Leda and Other Odes. Theseus, Medea and Lyrics. London: 1903-1904. V. 64
Danae, a Poem. London: 1903. V. 65
Hark to These Three: Talk About Style. London: 1915. V. 64
The Passionate Pilgrim and the Songs of Shakepeare's Plays. London: 1896. V. 64
The Vinedresser and Other Poems. London: 1899. V. 64; 66

MOORE, VIRGINIA
The Life and Eager Death of Emily Bronte. 1936. V. 63

MOORE, WILLIAM
The Addresses for Blood and Devastation and the Addressers Exposed.... London: 1776. V. 66

MOOREHEAD, WARREN K.
The American Indian in the United States Period 1850-1914. Andover: 1914. V. 65; 66
Hematite Implements of the United States - Together with Chemical Analysis of Various Hematites. Andover: 1912. V. 66
Tonda. A Story of the Sioux. Cincinnati: 1904. V. 63

MOORHEAD, MAX L.
New Mexico's Royal Road, Trade and Travel on the Chihuahua Trail. Norman: 1958. V. 67

MOORMAN, JOHN J.
Mineral Springs of North America, How to Reach and How to Use Them. Philadelphia: 1873. V. 65
The Virginia Springs. Philadelphia: 1847. V. 64
The Virginia Springs. Richmond: 1855. V. 64

MOORMAN, MADISON B.
The Journal of...1850-1851. San Francisco: 1948. V. 63; 65; 66

MOORMAN, MARY
William Wordsworth - a Biography. The Early Years 1770-1803. London: 1957. V. 65
William Wordsworth - a Biography. The Early Years 1770-1803. Oxford: 1957. V. 63
William Wordsworth - a Biography. The Early Years 1770-1803. The Later Years 1803-1850. Oxford: 1957-1965. V. 65
William Wordsworth - a Biography. The Later Years 1803-1850. Oxford: 1965. V. 63

MOOSO, JOSIAH
The Life and Travels of...A Life on the Frontier Among the Indians and Spaniards.... Winfield: 1888. V. 64; 67

MOOTZ, HERMAN E.
Pawnee Bill A Romance of Oklahoma. Los Angeles: 1928. V. 67

MORA, GILLES
Walker Evans: The Hungry Eye. New York: 1993. V. 63

MORA, JO
Trail Dust and Saddle Leather. New York: 1946. V. 64; 67

MORAES, DOM
Green Is the Grass. Bombay and Calcutta: 1951. V. 64

THE MORAL Legacy; or, Simple Narratives. London: 1808. V. 64

MORAN, EUGENE F.
Tugboat, the Moran Story. New York: 1956. V. 67

MORAN, JAMES
The Double Crown Club a History of Fifty Years. 1974. V. 65
The Double Crown Club: a History of Fifty Years. London: 1974. V. 62; 63; 64

MORAN, PATRICK F.
The Analecta of David Rothe, Bishop of Ossory. 1884. V. 66
Essays on the Origin, Doctrines and Discipline of the Early Irish Church. 1864. V. 67

MORANCE, ALBERT
L'Architecture au XXe Siecle. Choix des Meilleures, Constructions Nouvelles, Hotels, Maisons de Rapport, Villas, etc. Paris: 1920. V. 65
Transports en Commun. Paris: Sep. 1930. V. 65

MORAND, PAUL
Closed All Night. London: 1924. V. 67

MORAND, RENE
La Porte Lourde. Paris: 1929. V. 64

MORAND, S. F.
Opuscule de Chirurgie. Paris: 1768-1772. V. 64

MORANDI, GIAMBATTISTA
Historia Botanica Practica.... Milan: 1744. V. 64

MORANT, GEORGE FRANCIS
Game Preservers and Bird Preservers. London: 1875. V. 64

MORATH, INGE
Portraits. New York: 1963. V. 67

MORAVIA, ALBERTO
L'Amore Coniugale e Altri Racconti. Milan and Rome: 1949. V. 66

MORAVIAN MUSIC FOUNDATION
Publications. Winston Salem: 1956-1974. V. 64

MORAY BROWN, J.
Stray Sport. 1893. V. 62; 63; 64; 66

MORDAUNT, ELINOR
Shoe and Stocking Stories. London: 1926. V. 67

MORDECAI, SAMUEL
Richmond in By-Gone Days: Being Reminiscences of an Old Citizen. Richmond: 1856. V. 64
Richmond in Bygone Days. Richmond: 1946. V. 64
Virginia, Especially Richmond, in By-Gone Days. Richmond: 1860. V. 62

MORDEN, WILLIAM J.
Across Asia's Snows and Deserts. New York: 1927. V. 66

MORE, ADELYNE, PSEUD.
Fecundity Versus Civilisation.... London: 1916. V. 65

MORE Adventures of Rupert (1953). London. V. 65

MORE, ALEXANDER
Fides Publica, Contra Calumnias Ionnis Miltoni. Hagae-Comitum: 1654. V. 65

MORE, ALEXANDER G.
Contributions Towards a Cybele Hibernica, Being Outlines of the Geographical Distribution of Plants in Ireland. 1898. V. 63; 66

MORE, CHARLES ALBERT
A French Volunteer of the War of Independence. New York: 1897. V. 66
A French Volunteer of the War of Independence. Paris: 1898. V. 66; 67

MORE, HANNAH
Christian Morals. London: 1813. V. 65
Coelebs in Search of a Wife. London: 1809. V. 65
Essays on Various Subjects, Principally Designed for Young Ladies. London: 1785. V. 62
Florio; a Tale for Fine Gentlemen and Fine Ladies; and the Bas Bleu; or, Conservation: Two Poems. London: 1786. V. 64
Florio. Sir Eldred of the Bower and the Bleeding Rock. Ode to Dragon. London: 1787. V. 66
Hints Towards Forming the Character of a Young Princess. London: 1805. V. 64; 65
Memoirs of the Life and Correspondence of Mrs. Hannah More. London: 1835. V. 66; 67
The Miscellaneous Works. London: 1840. V. 65
Moral Sketches of Prevailing Opinions and Manners, Foreign and Domestic. London: 1819. V. 65
Moral Sketches of Prevailing Opinions and Manners, Foreign and Domestic.... London: 1821. V. 64; 65
Remarks on the Speech of M. Dupont, Made in the National Convention of France, on the Subjects of Religion and Public Education. London: 1793. V. 62; 65
Stories for the Middle Ranks of Society and Tales for the Common People. London: 1818. V. 65
Strictures on the Modern System of Female Education. London: 1799. V. 62; 65; 66
Strictures on the Modern System of Female Education. London: 1826. V. 65
Thoughts on the Importance of the Manners of the Great to General Society. London: 1788. V. 66
Thoughts on the Importance of the Manners of the Great to General Society. London: 1818. V. 62; 64; 65; 66
Tragedies. London: 1818. V. 65

MORE, HENRY
Divine Dialogues, Containing Sundry Disquisitions and Instructions Concerning the Atttributes and Providence of God. London: 1668. V. 65
An Exposition of the Seven Epistles to the Seven Churches.... London: 1669. V. 63
A Modest Enquiry into the Mystery of Iniquity.... London: 1664. V. 64

MORE, JAMES F.
The History of Queens County N.S. Halifax: 1873. V. 66

MORE, THOMAS
A Frutefull Pleasant and Wittie Worke, of the Beste State of a Publique Weale, and of the New Yule, Called Utopia.... London: 1556. V. 64
Utopia. London: 1685. V. 64
Utopia. 1906. V. 67
The Workes. London: 1557. V. 67
The Workes. London: 1978. V. 63

MOREAU, EMILE
Histoire Naturelle des Poissons de la France. Paris: 1881-1891. V. 65

MOREAU, F. J.
A Practical Treatise on Midwifery, Exhibitig the Present Advanced State of the Science. Philadelphia: 1844. V. 64

MOREAU, JACOB NICOLAS
The Mystery Reveal'd; or, Truth Brought to Light, Being a Discovery of Some Facts, In Relation to the Conduct of the Late M----y.... London: 1759. V. 67

MOREAU, R. E.
The Bird Faunas of Africa and Its Islands. London: 1966. V. 67

MOREAU-MARMONT, J.
Memoire sur la Therapeutique des Anomalies de l'Appareil Dentaire. Paris: 1878. V. 65

MORECAMP, ARTHUR
Live Boys in the Black Hills: or, the Young Texas Gold Hunters - a Narrative of Adventure During a Second Trip Over the Great Texas Cattle Trail: Life Among the Miners and Experiences with the Indians. Boston: 1880. V. 63; 66
Live Boys, or Charley and Nasho in Texas - a Narrative. Boston: 1879. V. 63

MOREL, C.
Le Cerveau Sa Topographie Anatomique. Paris: 1880. V. 64

MORELAND *Vale; or the Fair Fugitive.* New York: 1801. V. 62; 64

MORELL, DAVID
First Blood. New York: 1972. V. 67

MORELL, JOHN REYNELL
Algeria: the Topography and History, Political, Social and Natural of French Africa. London: 1854. V. 65

MORELLA, JOE
The It Girl. New York: 1976. V. 66

MORENHOUT, JACQUES ANTOINE
The Inside Story of the Gold Rush. San Francisco: 1935. V. 65

MORERI, LOUIS
The Great Historical, Geographical and Poetical Dictionary.... London: 1694. V. 62

MORES, EDWARD ROWE
A Dissertation Upon English Typographical Founders and Founderies. New York: 1924. V. 62

MORETON, C. OSCAR
The Auricula, Its History and Character. London: 1963. V. 64
The Auricula, Its History and Character. London: 1964. V. 62

MOREWOOD, SAMUEL
An Essay on the Inventions and Customs of...Inebriating Liquors.... London: 1824. V. 64

MOREY, P.
Charpente de la Cathedrale de Messine.... Paris: 1841. V. 64

MORFI, JUAN AGUSTIN
History of Texas 1673-1779. Albuquerque: 1935. V. 65

MORFORD, HENRY
John Jasper's Secret: Being a Narrative of Certain Events Following and Explaining The Mystery of Edwin Drood. London: 1871-1872. V. 62
The Spur of Monmouth; or, Washington in Arms. Philadelphia: 1876. V. 63

MORGAGNI, GIOVANNI BATTISTA
Adversaria Anatomica Omnia. Lugduni Batavorum: 1723. V. 64; 65
Epistolae Anatomicae Duae Novas Observationes, et Animadversiones Complectentes.... Venetiis: 1762. V. 64
Opuscula Miscellanea Quorum Non Pauca Nunc Primum Prodeunt, Tres in Partes Divisa. Neapoli: 1763. V. 64; 66
The Seats and Causes of Diseases Investigated by Anatomy; in Five Books.... New York: 1983. V. 65

MORGAIN, W. H.
Personal Reminiscences of the War of 1861-1865. Lynchburg: 1911. V. 64

MORGAN, ALBERT T.
Yazoo: or, the Picket Line of Freedom in the South. Washington: 1884. V. 67

MORGAN, BARBARA
Martha Graham: Sixteen Dances in Photographs. New York: 1941. V. 63
Photomontage. Dobbs Ferry: 1980. V. 63; 65
Summer's Children. Scarsdale: 1951. V. 63

MORGAN, CHARLES
The Gunroom. London: 1919. V. 64; 65

MORGAN, DALE
California as I Saw It. Los Gatos: 1960. V. 63; 66

MORGAN, DALE continued
In Pursuit of the Golden Dreams. Stoughton: 1970. V. 64
Jedediah Smith and the Opening of the West. Indianapolis: 1953. V. 63; 64; 66
Overland in 1846 - Diaries and Letters of the California-Oregon Trail. Georgetown: 1963. V. 63
The Rocky Mountain Journals of William Marshall Anderson. The West in 1834. San Morino: 1960. V. 66
Santa Fe and the Far West. Los Angeles: 1949. V. 65
The West of William H. Ashley.... Denver: 1964. V. 62; 65

MORGAN, EDWIN
Siesta of a Hungarian Snake. N.P: 1971. V. 63

MORGAN, GEORGE DILLON
Poems. San Angelo: 1951. V. 62

MORGAN, GWENDA
The Wood Engravings of Gwenda Morgan. London: 1985. V. 65

MORGAN, HENRY J.
Sketches of Celebrated Canadians, and Persons Connected with Canada, from the Earlist Period in the History of the Province Down to the Present Time. Montreal: 1865. V. 63

MORGAN, HILARY
Burne-Jones, The Pre-Raphaelites and Their Century. 1989. V. 64

MORGAN, HUGH
A Sermon, Preached at St. Mary's Church in Oxford, Before the Governors of the Radcliffe Infimary, 1794. Oxford: 1794. V. 62

MORGAN, J.
A Compleat History of the Present Seat of War in Africa, Between the Spaniards and Algerines.... London: 1732. V. 66

MORGAN, JAMES M.
Recollections of a Rebel Reefer. Boston and New York: 1917. V. 64

MORGAN, JOHN
Four Dissertations on the Reciprocal Advantages of a Perpetual Union Between Great Britain and Her American Colonies.... Philadelphia: 1766. V. 66; 67

MORGAN, JOHN HILL
The Life Portraits of Washington and Their Replicas. Philadelphia: 1931. V. 62

MORGAN, JOHN MINTER
The Revolt of the Bees. London: 1839. V. 64

MORGAN, JONNIE
History of Wichita Falls. Wichita Falls: 1931. V. 62; 65

MORGAN, LEWIS H.
The American Beaver and His Works. Philadelphia: 1868. V. 66
Houses and House-Life of the American Aborigines. Washington: 1881. V. 63
League of The So-De-No-Sau-Nee or Iroquis. New York: 1922. V. 63; 66

MORGAN, LEWIS K.
The Indian Journals 1859-1863. 1959. V. 67

MORGAN, MARSHALL
The Battle of Franklin. Franklin: 1931. V. 62; 63; 65

MORGAN, MURRAY
Dixie Raider. New York: 1948. V. 63

MORGAN, RICHARD WILLIAM
Raymond de Monthault, the Lord Marcher: a Legend of Welch Borders. London: 1853. V. 66

MORGAN, SETH
Homeboy. New York: 1990. V. 65; 67

MORGAN, SYDNEY OWENSON
The Book of the Boudoir. Paris: 1829. V. 65
Dramatic Scenes from Real Life. London: 1833. V. 65
Florence Macarthy. London: 1819. V. 65
France. London: 1818. V. 66
France in 1829-1830. London: 1830. V. 62; 63; 66
Italy. London: 1821. V. 62; 65; 67
The Novice of Saint Dominick. London: 1806. V. 65
The O'Briens and the O'Flahertys. London: 1827. V. 65
O'Donnel. London: 1814. V. 64; 65; 66
O'Donnel. London: 1835. V. 65
Passages from My Autobiography. London: 1859. V. 65
The Princess; or the Beguine. London: 1835. V. 65
The Wild Irish Girl: a National Tale. London: 1807. V. 65
The Wild Irish Girl: a National Tale. Philadelphia: 1807. V. 65
Woman: or, Ida of Athens. London: 1809. V. 64

MORGAN, THOMAS
Romano-British Mosaic Pavements: a History of Their Discovery and a Record and Interpretation of Their Designs. London: 1886. V. 63; 66; 67

MORGAN, THOMAS HUNT
The Development of the Frog's Egg. New York: 1897. V. 63
Evolution and Genetics. Princeton: 1932. V. 66
The Formation of Fish Embryo. Boston: 1895. V. 63
The Genetic and the Operative Evidence Relating to Secondary Sexual Characters. Washington: 1919. V. 63
The Physical Basis of Heredity. Philadelphia and London: 1919. V. 67

MORGAN, W. SCOTT
History of the Wheel and Alliance and the Impending Revolution. Fort Scott: 1889. V. 64

MORGAN, W. W.
An Atlas of Stellar Spectra, with an Outline of Spectral Classification. Chicago: 1943. V. 67

MORGAN, WILLIAM
The Deed of Settlement of the Society for Equitable Assurances on Lives and Survivorships, as the Same is Inrolled in His Majesty's Court of King's Bench at Westminster. London: 1811. V. 63
Illustrations of Masonry. Chicago: 1872. V. 67
Narrative of the Facts and Circumstances Relating to the Kidnapping and Presumed Murder of William Morgan, and of the Attempt to Carry Off David C. Miller and to Burn or Destroy the Printing Office of the Latter.... Batavia: 1827. V. 64; 66
The Principles and Doctrine of Assurances, Annuities on Lives and Contingent Reversions.... London: 1821. V. 64

MORGAN, WILLIAM H.
Personal Reminiscences of the War of 1861-1865. Lynchburg: 1911. V. 62; 63; 65

MORGENSTEIN, GARY
Take Me Out to the Ball Game. New York: 1980. V. 67

MORICE, A. G.
First Collection of Minor Essays Mostly Anthropological. 1902. V. 63
Le Petit Cathechisme a l'Usage des Sauvages Porteurs. Mission du Lac Stuart: 1891. V. 64

MORIER, JAMES
A Journey through Persia, Armenia and Asia Minor to Constantinople, in the Years 1808 and 1809. London: 1812. V. 64
An Oriental Tale. Brighton: 1839. V. 67

MORIER, JAMES JUSTINIAN
The Adventures of Jahhi Baba, of Ispahan, in England. New York: 1828. V. 62

MORIS, GIUSEPPE GIACINTO
Flora Sardoa seu Historia Plantarum in Sardinia et Adjacentibus Insulis vel Sponte.... Torino: 1837-1859. V. 67

MORISON, DOUGLAS
Views of Haddon Hall. London: 1842. V. 62

MORISON, SAMUEL ELIOT
History of U.S. Naval Operations in World War II. Boston: 1947-1960. V. 63

MORISON, STANLEY
The Art of the Printer. 250 Title and Text Pages Selcted from the Books Composed in the Roman Letter Printed from 1500 to 1900. London: 1925. V. 64
Edward Topham 1751-1820 Eton and Trinity College, Cambridge. Cambridge: 1933. V. 65
The English Newspaper, Some Account of the Physical Development of Journals Printed in London Between 1622 and the Present Day. Cambridge: 1932. V. 62
Eustachio Celebrino Da Udene. Paris: 1929. V. 64
The Fleuron: a Journal of Typography, VII. Cambridge/Garden City: 1930. V. 64
Four Centuries of Fine Printing. London: 1924. V. 62
German Incunabula in the British Museum. London: 1928. V. 62
Handbuch Der Druckerkunst: 250 Beispiele Mustergultiger Antiquadrucke aus den Jahren 1500-1900. Berlin: 1925. V. 66
Ichabod Dawks and His News-Letter. Cambridge: 1931. V. 64; 65
John Bell 1745-1831. Bookseller, Printer, Publisher, Typefounder, Journalist &c. Cambridge: 1930. V. 62; 65
John Fell the University Press and the Fell Types.... Oxford: 1967. V. 62; 64; 65; 66; 67
On Type Faces: Examples of the Use of Type for the Printing of Books. London/Westminster: 1923. V. 64
The Portraiture of Thomas More by Hans Holbein and After. Cambridge: 1958. V. 65
Talbot Baines Reed. Author, Bibliographer, Typefounder. Cambridge: 1960. V. 62
The Times and the Post Office: a Paper Presented to the Postal History Society. London: 1946. V. 65
The Typographic Book 1450-1935. London: 1963. V. 64; 65
The Typographical Book 1450-1935, a Study of Fine Typography through Five Centuries. Chicago: 1963. V. 62

MORITZ, KARL PHILIPP
Anton Reiser. Ein Psychologischer Roman. Berlin: 1785-1790. V. 67

MORITZI, ALEXANDER
Die Pflanzen Graubundens. Ein Verzeichniss der Bisher in Graubunden Gefundenen Pflanzen, mit Besonderer Berucksichtigung Ihres Vorkommens.... Neuchatel: 1839. V. 65

MORKILL, JOHN WILLIAM
The Parish of Kirkby Malhamdale in the West Riding of Yorkshire. Gloucester: 1933. V. 66

MORLAND, GEORGE
A Collection of Nine Selected Sketches of Villagers, Favourite Animals &c &c. London: 1806. V. 66

MORLAND, SAMUEL
Elevation des Eaux par Toute Sorte de Machines Reduite a la Mesure, au Poids.... Paris: 1685. V. 63

MORLEY, CHRISTOPHER DARLINGTON
Mandarin in Manhattan. Garden City: 1933. V. 62
Parnassus on Wheels. Garden City: 1917. V. 62
Sherlock Holmes and Dr. Watson. 1944. V. 62; 66; 67
Sherlock Holmes and Dr. Watson. New York: 1944. V. 65
Thunder on the Left. Garden City: 1925. V. 62
Where the Blue Begins. London and New York: 1925. V. 64; 67

MORLEY, FRANCES, COUNTESS OF
The Flying Burgermaster, a Legend of the Black Forest. 1832. V. 67

MORLEY, HENRY
The Chicken Market and Other Fairy Tales. London: 1860. V. 64
A Defence of Ignorance. London: 1851. V. 64
Oberon's Horn-A Book of Fairy Tales. London: 1861. V. 64
Obseron's Horn-A Book of Fairy Tales. London: 1881. V. 64

MORLEY, JOHN
The Life of William Ewart Gladstone. London: 1903. V. 64
Machiavelli. The Romanes Lecture Delivered in the Sheldonian Theatre, June 2, 1897. London: 1898. V. 62

MORLEY, MARGARET WARNER
The Carolina Mountains. Boston: 1913. V. 67

MORLEY, S. G.
The Covered Bridges of California. Berkeley: 1938. V. 62; 63

MORLEY, SUSAN
Throstlethwaite. London: 1875. V. 65

MORLEY, SYLVANUS GRISWOLD
An Introduction to the Study of the Maya Hieroglyphs. Washington: 1915. V. 62

MORLINI, HIERONYMOUS
Opus Morlini, Complectens Novellas, Fabulas et Comoediam. Parisiis: 1799. V. 64

MORNAY
A Picture of St. Petersburgh, Represented in a Collection of Twenty Interesting Views of the City, the Sledges and the People. London: 1815. V. 65

MORNER, KAREL GUSTAV HJALMAR, GRAF VON
Miscelleaneous Sketches of Contracts Drawn by Hjalmor Morner. London: 1831. V. 64

MORNER, NILS AXEL
Earth Rehology, Isostasy and Eustasy. 1980. V. 67

MORNEY, PHILIPPE DE
The Mysterie of Iniquitie.... London: 1612. V. 62

MORPHOLOGY of the Giant Panda. Beijing: 1986. V. 66

MORRELL, DAVID
First Blood. London: 1972. V. 66
First Blood. New York: 1972. V. 63; 64; 65; 67
Rambo III. London: 1988. V. 66

MORRELL, JOHN REYNELL
Algeria: The Topography and History, Political, Social and Natural of French Africa. London: 1854. V. 64

MORRELL, W. WILBERFORCE
The History and Antiquities of Selby. London: 1867. V. 62
The History and Antiquities of Selby, in the West Riding of the County of York.... Selby: 1867. V. 63; 64; 65; 66; 67

MORRILL, CLAIRE
A Taos Mosaic: Portrait of a New Mexico Village. Albuquerque: 1973. V. 63; 64; 66

MORRIS, ALEXANDER
The Treaties of Canada with the Indians of Manitoba and the North-West Territories, Including the Negotiations on Which They Were Based, and Other Information Relating Thereto. Toronto: 1880. V. 65

MORRIS, BEVERLEY R.
British Game Birds and Wildfowl. London: 1891. V. 63
British Game Birds and Wildfowl. London: 1895. V. 65; 67

MORRIS, CHARLES
Finding the North Pole. N.P: 1909. V. 64

MORRIS, CLIFF H.
From Indian Country to Wall Street. A Personal Autobiography. N.P: 1959. V. 66

MORRIS, E. P.
The Fore-and-Aft Rig in America. New Haven/London: 1927. V. 66

MORRIS, EARL H.
Basket Maker Two: Sites Near Durango, Colorado. Washington: 1954. V. 64

MORRIS, EASTIN
The Tennessee Gazetteer, or Topographical Dictionary.... Nashville: 1834. V. 63; 66

MORRIS, FRANCIS ORPEN
A History of British Birds. 1851-1857. V. 62
A History of British Birds. London: 1860-1864. V. 63
A History of British Birds. London: 1870. V. 67
A History of British Birds. London: 1888. V. 63
A History of British Birds. 1903. V. 65
A History of British Birds. London: 1903. V. 66
History of British Butterflies. London: 1895. V. 62
A Natural History of British Moths. 1891. V. 66
A Series of Picturesque Views of Seats of the Noblemen and Gentlemen of Great Britain and Ireland. London. V. 66

MORRIS, FRANCIS W. JARRETT
Elva's Revenge: a Legendary Poem, in Five Cantos. London: 1834. V. 64

MORRIS, GEORGE P.
The Deserted Bride and Other Poems. New York: 1838. V. 63
The Little Frenchman and His Water Lots, with Other Sketches of the Times. Philadelphia: 1839. V. 64

MORRIS, GOUVERNEUR
Advantages of the Proposed Canal from Lake Erie to the Hudson's River, Fully Illustrated in a Correspondence. New York: 1814. V. 63

MORRIS, HENRY
Bird and Bull Pepper Pot. North Hills: 1977. V. 64
The Bird and Bull Press Commemorative 100 Coronas. Newtown: 1988. V. 64
Dard Hunter and Son. Newtown: 1998. V. 62
Omnibus: Instructions for Amateur Papermakers with Notes and Observations on Private Presses.... N.P: 1967. V. 64
The Private Press-Man's Tale. Newtown. V. 64
A Visit to Hayle Mill: Written from Notes Made During a Visit to J. Barcham Green, Limited. North Hills: 1970. V. 64

MORRIS, HERBERT W.
The Celestial Symbol Interpreted; or the Natural Wonders and Spiritual Teachings of the Sun, As Revealed by the Triumphs of Modern Science. Philadelphia: 1889. V. 66

MORRIS, IVAN
The Tale of the Genji Scroll. Tokyo: 1971. V. 62

MORRIS, J.
A Catalogue of British Fossils.... London: 1843. V. 64
Mollusca from the Great Oolite, Chiefly from Minchinhampton and the Coast of Yorkshire. 1850-1853. V. 67

MORRIS, J. B.
Catalogue of the Described Lepidoptera of North America. Washington: 1860-1862. V. 62; 63

MORRIS, J. P.
The North Lonsdale Magazine and Lake District Miscellany. Ulverston: 1866-1867. V. 64

MORRIS, JAMES
The Hashemite Kings. London: 1959. V. 62; 65; 66

MORRIS, JAN
A Machynlleth Triad. 1993. V. 65

MORRIS, JOHN
From the Third Programme: a Ten Years' Anthology. London: 1956. V. 65
Living with Pechas. London: 1938. V. 62

MORRIS, JOHN PAYNE
Coronation Gem; or, a Panoramic View of the Pedigree of Her Most Gracious Majesty Queen Victoria, from Egbert.... London: 1838. V. 65

MORRIS, LEWIS
The Papers of Lewis Morris, Governor of the Province of New Jersey from 1738 to 1746. New York: 1852. V. 63; 64
Plans of Harbours, Bars, Bays and Roads in St. George's Channel, Lately Survey'd Under the Direction of the Lords of the Admiralty.... London: 1748. V. 67

MORRIS, M. C. F.
Francis Orpen Morris, a Memoir by His Son. 1897. V. 63

MORRIS, MAURICE O'CONNOR
Rambles in the Rocky Mountains with a Visit to the Gold Fields of Colorado. London: 1864. V. 64

MORRIS, PAUL C.
American Sailing Coasters of the North Atlantic. Chardon: 1973. V. 64; 65; 66

MORRIS, RICHARD
Essays on Landscape Gardening, and on Uniting Picturesque Effect with Rural Scenery, Containing Directions for Laying Out and Improving the Grounds Connected with a Country Residence. London: 1825. V. 64; 66

MORRIS, ROBERT
Coins of the Grand Masters of the Order of Malta; or Knights Hospitallers of St. John of Jerusalem. Boston: 1884. V. 67
Lectures on Architecture. London: 1734. V. 64

MORRIS, W. MEREDITH
British Violin Makers, a Biographical Dictionary of British Makers of Stringed Instruments and Bows and a Critical Description of Their Work. London: 1920. V. 67

MORRIS, WILLIAM
An Address Delivered at the Distribution of Prizes to Students of the Birmingham Municipal School of Art on Feb. 21, 1894. London: 1898. V. 65; 66; 67
Art and the Beauty of the Earth. London: 1898. V. 65; 67
Art and the Beauty of the Earth. London: 1899. V. 65
Atalanta's Race and Other Tales from the Earthly Paradise. Boston and New York: 1888. V. 63
Chants for Socialists. London: 1885. V. 66
Child Christopher and Goldilind the Fair. 1895. V. 62
The Collected Works. London: 1901-1902. V. 62
Collected Works. London: 1910. V. 62; 65; 67
The Collected Works. London: 1910-1913. V. 64
The Decorative Arts: Their Relation to Modern Life and Progress: an Address Delivered Before the Trades' Guide of Learning. London: 1878. V. 64
The Defence of Guenevere and Other Poems. London: 1858. V. 63; 64
The Defence of Guenevere and Other Poems. London: 1904. V. 62
The Defense of Guenevere and Other Poems. Hammersmith: 1892. V. 64
The Earthly Paradise. London: 1905. V. 63
Glass: Artifact and Art. Seattle and London: 1989. V. 62
Gothic Architecture: a Lecture for the Arts and Crafts Exhibition Society. 1893. V. 62; 64; 65
The History of Pattern Designing: the Lesser Arts of Life. London: 1882. V. 64

MORRIS, WILLIAM *continued*
Hopes and Fears for Art. Five Lectures Delivered in Birmingham, London and Nottingham 1878-1881. London: 1882. V. 67
The Life and Death of Jason. London. V. 62
The Life and Death of Jason. London: 1867. V. 64
News from Nowhere. London: 1891. V. 64; 67
News from Nowhere. Hammersmith: 1892. V. 63
A Note by William Morris on His Aims in Founding the Kelmscott Press. Hammersmith: 1898. V. 67
A Note by William Morris on His Aims in Founding the Kelmscott Press.... London: 1898. V. 65
Old French Romances Done into English.... London: 1896. V. 62; 65
Poems by the Way. 1891. V. 62
Poems by the Way. London: 1891. V. 64
Printing: an Essay by William Morris and Emery Walker.... Park Ridge: 1903. V. 66
The Roots of the Mountains Wherein is Told Somewhat of the Lives of the Men of Burgdale Their Friends Their Neighbours their Foemen and Their Fellows in Arms. London: 1890. V. 64; 66
A Short Account of the Commune in Paris. London: 1886. V. 66
Socialist Diary. Iowa City: 1981. V. 66
Some Hints on Pattern Designing. London: 1899. V. 62; 63
The Story of Amis and Amile. Portland: 1899. V. 64
The Story of Sigurd the Volsung and the Fall of the Niblings. London: 1876. V. 62
The Story of Sigurd the Volsung and the Fall of the Niblungs. London: 1887. V. 65
The Story of the Glittering Plain. 1891. V. 62
The Story of the Glittering Plain.... London: 1891. V. 64
The Sundering Flood. 1897. V. 63
A Tale of the House of the Wolfings and All the Kindreds of the Mark Written in Prose and Verse. London: 1889. V. 64
Under an Elm-Tree. Aberdeen: 1891. V. 62; 63; 66
The Water of the Wondrous Isles. London: 1897. V. 66; 67
The Well at the World's End, a Tale. London: 1896. V. 62
The Wood Beyond the World. Hammersmith: 1894. V. 63
The Wood Beyond the World. London: 1895. V. 65
The World of Romance - Being Contributions to the Oxford and Cambridge Magazine, 1856. London: 1906. V. 64

MORRIS, WILLIE
My Dog Skip. New York: 1995. V. 66
A Prayer for the Opening of the Little League Season. New York: 1995. V. 64
A Southern Album: Recollections of Some People and Places and Times Gone By. Birmingham: 1975. V. 62

MORRIS, WRIGHT
About Fiction. New York: 1975. V. 62
The Inhabitants. New York and London: 1946. V. 63
The Man Who Was There. New York: 1945. V. 66
My Uncle Dudley. New York: 1942. V. 62
The Origin of Sadness. Alabama: 1984. V. 67
War Games. Los Angeles: 1972. V. 63; 64; 66

MORRISON, ALEX J.
Better Golf Without Practice. New York: 1940. V. 66

MORRISON, ARTHUR
A Child of Jago. London: 1896. V. 65
Cunning Murrell. London: 1900. V. 66
The Hole in the Wall. London: 1902. V. 66
Tales of Mean Streets. London: 1894. V. 65
To London Town. London: 1899. V. 65

MORRISON, C.
A Complete System of Practical Book-keeping; Applicable to All Kinds of Business.... Glasgow: 1822. V. 66
An Essay on the Relations Between Labour and Capital. London: 1854. V. 62; 64

MORRISON, H. S.
Modern Ulster: Its Character, Customs, Politics and Industries. 1920. V. 67

MORRISON, INGRAM & CO.
Illustrated Catalogue and Price List of Sanitary Appliances. Manchester: 1890. V. 64

MORRISON, J. S. F.
Around Golf. London: 1939. V. 66

MORRISON, JAMES
The Influence of English Railway Legislation on Trade and Industry. London: 1848. V. 66
The Journal of James Morrison, Boatswain's Mate of the Bounty.... Waltham St. Lawrence: 1935. V. 64; 66

MORRISON, JIM
The Lords and the New Creatures. New York: 1970. V. 63

MORRISON, JOHN
Medicine No Mystery; Being a Brief Outline of the Principles of Medical Science.... London: 1830. V. 65

MORRISON, PEGGY
Our Bunty's ABC. London: 1926. V. 65

MORRISON, TONI
Beloved. London: 1987. V. 62; 65
Beloved. New York: 1987. V. 65; 66; 67
Beloved. New York: 1998. V. 67
Birth of a Nation'Hood. New York: 1997. V. 67
The Dancing Mind. New York: 1996. V. 67
Jazz. Franklin Center: 1992. V. 62; 65; 67
Jazz. London: 1992. V. 62
Jazz. New York: 1992. V. 65; 67
Paradise. New York: 1998. V. 67
Playing in the Dark. Cambridge: 1992. V. 62; 64; 66
Song of Solomon. New York: 1977. V. 64; 65; 67
Sula. New York: 1974. V. 62; 64; 65
Tar Baby. Franklin Center: 1981. V. 64; 67
Tar Baby. New York: 1981. V. 67

MORRISON, WILLIAM
Morrison's Strangers' Guide to the City of Washington and Its Vicinity. Washington: 1844. V. 66
Morrison's Stranger's Guide to the City of Washington and Its Vicinity. Washington: 1852. V. 64
The Second Series of Border Sketches. No publisher: 1840. V. 64

THE MORRISTOWN Ghost. Newark: 1896. V. 63

MORROW, BRADFORD
The Almanac Branch. New York: 1991. V. 67
A Bestiary. New York: 1990. V. 64
A Bibliography of the Black Sparrow Press. Santa Barbara: 1981. V. 65
Come Sunday. New York: 1985. V. 67
Conjunctions: 1-14. New York: 1981-1989. V. 62
Danae's Progress. N.P.: 1982. V. 62

MORROW, ELIZABETH
Beast, Bird and Fish, an Animal Alphabet. New York: 1933. V. 62; 63

MORROW, JAMES
Towing Jehovah. New York: 1994. V. 67
The Wine of Violence. New York: 1981. V. 65

MORROW, MABLE
Indian Rawhide, an American Folk Art. Norman: 1975. V. 63; 66

MORROW, PRINCE
Atlas of Skin and Venereal Diseases. New York: 1889. V. 66

MORROW, PRINCE A.
A System of Genito-Urinary Diseases, Syphilology and Dermatology by Various Authors. Volume III Dermatology. New York: 1895. V. 66; 67

MORROW, R. A. H.
Story of the Springhill Disaster.... St. John: 1891. V. 66

MORSCH, LUCILLE
Check List of New Jersey Imprints 1784-1800. Baltimore: 1939. V. 63; 66

MORSE, E. S.
Observations on Living Brachiopoda. Boston: 1902. V. 63; 65

MORSE, EDWARD
First Book of Zoology. New York: 1875. V. 65

MORSE, JEDEDIAH
The American Geography; or, A View of the Present Situtation of the United States of America. Elizabeth Town: 1789. V. 64; 66

MORSE, JEDIDIAH
The American Geography; or, a View of the Present Situation of the United States of America.... London: 1792. V. 67
The American Geography; or, a View of the Present Situation of the United States of America.... London: 1794. V. 64; 65
A New and Correct Edition of the American Geography. Edinburgh;: 1795. V. 63
A Report to the Secretary of War of the United States on Indian Affairs, Comprising a Narrative of a Tour Performed in the Summer of 1820... for the Purpose of Ascertaining...the Actual State of the Indian Tribes in Our Country. New Haven: 1822. V. 63
The Traveller's Guide; or Pocket Gazetteer of the United States. New Haven: 1823. V. 62

MORSE, SAMUEL
His Letters and Journals.... Boston and New York: 1914. V. 62
The Present Attempt to Dissolve the American Union, a British Aristocratic Plot. New York: 1862. V. 62; 66
Time of Year - a First Book of Poems. Cummington: 1943. V. 62

MORSE, SAMUEL FRENCH
Wallace Stevens - a Preliminary Checklist of His Published Writings 1898-1954. New Haven: 1954. V. 64

MORSE, SIDNEY
The Cerographic Missionary Atlas. New York: 1848. V. 62
A Geographical, Statistical and Ethical View of the American Slaveholders' Rebellion. New York: 1863. V. 64
System of Geography, for the Use of Schools. New York: 1844-1845. V. 64

MORSE, WILLIAM INGLIS
Acadiensia Nova. London: 1935. V. 63; 67
Catalogue of the William Inglis Morse Collection of Books, Pictures, Maps, Manuscripts, Etc. at Dalhousie University Library Halifax, Nova Scotia. Plaistow: 1938. V. 63
Gravestones of Acadie and Other Essays on Local History, Genealogy and Parish Records of Annapolis County, Nova Scotia. London: 1929. V. 63
The Land of the New Adventure (The Georgian Era in Nova Scotia). London: 1932. V. 63
Pierre Du Gua Sieur de Monts Records: Colonial and "Saintongeois". London: 1939. V. 63

MORTENSEN, H. C. C.
Studies in Bird Migration, Being the Collected Papers of.. Copenhagen: 1950. V. 67

MORTENSEN, WILLIAM
Monsters and Madonnas. San Francisco: 1946. V. 63

MORTIER, CHARLES
Les Delices de la France ou Description des Provinces & Villes Capitales d'icelle Depuis la Paix de Ryswyk. Amsterdam: 1699. V. 67

MORTIMER, GEOFFREY
Chapters on Human Love. Watford, London: 1900. V. 64

MORTIMER, J. R.
Forty Years' Researches in British and Saxon Burial Mounds of East Yorkshire. London: 1905. V. 62; 66

MORTIMER, JOHN
Charade. London: 1947. V. 62
Collaborators. London: 1973. V. 65
Cotton from Field to Factory, Including a Description of the Manchester Ship Canal. Manchester: 1894. V. 64
Samples from the Note Books of an Uncommercial Traveller. Manchester: 1898. V. 65
Three Plays - the Dock Brief: I Spy; What Shall We Tell Caroline. London: 1958. V. 63

MORTIMER, ROGER
The Jockey Club. London: 1958. V. 67

MORTIMER, THOMAS
The British Plutarch, Containing the Lives of the Most Eminent Statesmen, Patriots, Divines, Warriors, Philosophers, Poets and Artists of Great Britain and Ireland, from the Accession of Henry VIII to the Present Time. London: 1791. V. 66
Every Man His Own Broker; or a Guide to Exchange-Alley. London: 1761. V. 64
Every Man His Own Broker; or a Guide to Exchange-Alley.... London: 1769. V. 62
The Student's Pocket Dictionary; or, Compendium of Universal History, Chronology, and Biography. London: 1789. V. 64

MORTIMER, W. GOLDEN
Peru. History of Coca. The Divine Plant of the Incas. New York. 1901. V. 67

MORTIMER, WILLIAM WILLIAMS
The History of the Hundred of Wirral, with a Sketch of the City and County of Chester. London: 1848. V. 62; 65; 66

MORTON, DESMOND
Telegrams of the North-West Campaign 1885. Toronto: 1972. V. 62; 63

MORTON, DUDLY J.
The Grampas' Toyshop. Milford: 1922. V. 66

MORTON, H.
Views Illustrative of Hastings and its Vicinity. London: 1817. V. 62; 67

MORTON, J. B.
By the Way. London: 1931. V. 64
The Death of the Dragon - New Fairy Tales. London: 1934. V. 65

MORTON, JELLY ROLL
Original Jelly Roll Blues. Chicago. V. 67

MORTON, JOHN
On the Nature and Property of Soils. London: 1840. V. 65

MORTON, JOHN WATSON
The Artillery of Nathan Bedford Forrest's Cavalry. Nashville. 1909. V. 62

MORTON, JOSEPH W.
Sparks from the Camp Fires or Tales of the Old Veterans. Philadelphia: 1890. V. 65; 67

MORTON, LESLIE T.
Garrison and Morton's Medical Bibliography. London: 1954. V. 66; 67

MORTON, NATHANIEL
New England's Memorial; or, a Brief Relation of...the Planters of New England in America.... Newport: 1772. V. 62; 64

MORTON, OREN F.
A History of Monroe County, West Virginia. Staunton: 1916. V. 64

MORTON, RICHARD
Opera Medica.... Lyons: 1707. V. 64; 67

MORTON, SAMUEL G.
Crania Americana; or, a Comparative View of the Skulls of Various Aboriginal Nations of North and South America.... Philadelphia: 1839. V. 62
Illustrations of Pulmonary Consumption, Its Anatomical Characters, Causes, Symptoms and Treatment. Philadelphia: 1834. V. 63
Letter to the Rev. John Bachman, D.D., on the Question of Hybridity in Animals, Considered in Reference to the Unity of the Human Species. Charleston: 1850. V. 62

MORTON, SARAH E.
John Morton of Trinidad. Toronto: 1916. V. 63

MORTON, THOMAS
The Children in the Wood. Boston: 1795. V. 66
Engravings Illustrating the Surgical Anatomy of the Head and Neck, Axilla, Bend of the Elbow and Wrist, with Descriptions. London: 1845. V. 65

MORTON, THOMAS GEORGE
The History of the Pennsylvania Hospital. Philadelphia: 1897. V. 65

MORTON, WILLIAM T. G.
Statements Supported by Evidence, of Wm. T. G. Morton, M.D. On his Claim to the Discovery of the Anaesthetic Properties of Ether.... Washington: 1853. V. 66

MOSBY, HENRY S.
The Wild Turkey in Virginia: Its Status, Life History and Management. Richmond: 1943. V. 63; 66

MOSBY, JOHN S.
The Memoirs of Colonel John S. Mosby. Boston: 1917. V. 65
Mosby's War Reminiscences and Stuart's Cavalry Campaigns. Boston: 1887. V. 62; 63; 65
Stuart's Cavalry in the Gettysburg Campaign. New York: 1908. V. 63; 65

MOSCARDO, LODOVICO
Note Overo Memorie del Museo di Lodovico Moscardo.... Verona: 1672. V. 62

MOSEL, ARLENE
The Funny Little Woman. New York: 1972. V. 65

MOSELEY, BENJAMIN
Commentaries on the Lues Bovilla; or Cow Pox.... London: 1806. V. 64; 67
A Treatise on Sugar, with Miscellaneous Medical Observations. London: 1800. V. 64

MOSELEY, EPHRAIM
Teeth, Their Natural History; with the Physiology of the Human Mouth, in Regard to Artificial Teeth. London: 1862. V. 67

MOSELEY, H. F.
Textbook of Surgery. St. Louis: 1952. V. 64; 67

MOSELEY, H. N.
Challenger Voyage. Zoology. Part 7. Hydroid, Alcyonarian and Madreporarian Corals. 1881. V. 66
On the Inhabitants of the Admiralty Islands. 1877. V. 67

MOSELEY, MARGARET
Bonita Faye. 1996. V. 64; 66
Bonita Faye. Dallas: 1996. V. 62

MOSELEY, WALTER MICHAEL
An Essay on Archery, Describing the Practice of that Art, in all Ages and Nations. Worcester: 1792. V. 62

MOSELY, MARTIN E.
The British Caddis Flies (Trichoptera). London: 1939. V. 62
Insect Life and Management of a Trout Fishery. 1926. V. 67

MOSER, BARRY
Adventures of Huckleberry Finn. West Hatfield: 1985. V. 65
Fifty Wood Engravings. Northampton: 1978. V. 62; 64
The Wonderful Wizard of Oz. West Hatfield: 1985. V. 62

MOSER, JOSEPH
The Adventures of Timothy Twigg, Esq. in a Series of Poetical Epistles. London: 1794. V. 63; 67

MOSER, JUSTUS
Harlequin; or a Defence of Grotesque Comic Performances. London: 1766. V. 65

MOSER, WILHELM GOTTFRID
Grundsaze der Forst-Oeconomie. Frankfort and Leipzig: 1757. V. 64

MOSES, HENRY
The Gallery of Pictures Painted by Benjamin West, Esq. London: 1811-1816. V. 62

MOSES, MYER
Oration Delivered at Tammany-Hall on the Twelfth May, 1831. New York: 1831. V. 62

MOSES BEN MAIMON
More Nevuchim: Doctor Perplexorum. Basil: 1629. V. 63
Moses Maimonides on the Causes of Symptoms. Berkeley: 1974. V. 63

MOSGROVE, GEORGE DALLAS
Kentucky Cavaliers in Dixie. Jackson: 1957. V. 62; 63

MOSHEIM, JOHANN LORENZ VON
A Concise Ecclesiastical History, from the Birth of Christ, to the Beginning of the Present Century. London: 1781. V. 64

MOSLEY, JAMES
Journal of the Printing Historical Society: Parts I-II. N.P: 1972. V. 64

MOSLEY, NICHOLAS
Catastrophe Practice. London: 1979. V. 62

MOSLEY, WALTER
Black Betty. New York and London: 1994. V. 67
Devil in a Blue Dress. New York and London: 1990. V. 63; 64; 65; 66; 67
Gone Fishin'. Baltimore: 1997. V. 67
A Little Yellow Dog. New York: 1996. V. 67
My Discovery of America. Toronto: 1985. V. 64
RL's Dream. New York: 1995. V. 67
A Red Death. New York: 1991. V. 63; 64; 65; 66; 67
White Butterfly. 1990. V. 66
White Butterfly. New York: 1992. V. 62; 64; 65; 66; 67

MOSS, A. M.
On the Sphingidae of Peru. 1912. V. 63; 64

MOSS, ARTHUR B.
The Workman's Foe. (and) Paul the Rebel. London: 1895. V. 63

MOSS, FLETCHER
Pilgrimages to Old Homes, Mostly on the Welsh Border. Didsbury: 1903. V. 65

MOSS, FRANK
Persecution of Negroes by Roughs and Policemen in the City of New York, August 1900. New York: 1900. V. 66

MOSS, GEORGE H.
Double Exposure. Early Stereographic Views of Historic Monmouth County, New Jersey.... Sea Bright: 1971. V. 63; 66

MOSS, HOWARD
Instant Lives. New York: 1974. V. 64

MOSS, WILLIAM
An Essay on the Management, Nursing and Diseases of Children, from the Birth.... Egham: 1794. V. 62

MOSS, WILLIAM P.
Rough and Tumble. The Autobiography of a Texas Judge. New York: 1954. V. 63; 66

MOSSER, MARJORIE
Good Maine Food. New York: 1939. V. 62; 64

MOSSMAN, ISAAC VAN DORSEY
A Pony's Express Man's Recollection. Portland: 1955. V. 65

MOSSO, ANGELO
The Palaces of Crete and Their Builders. London: 1907. V. 65

MOTHER GOOSE
The Children's Mother Goose. Chicago;: 1921. V. 62
The Cozy Book of Mother Goose. Racine: 1926. V. 62
The Jolly Jump-Ups Mother Goose Book. Springfield: 1946. V. 65
Jolly Mother Goose Annual. London: 1914. V. 67
The Little Mother Goose. New York: 1918. V. 65
Mother Goose. London: 1881. V. 65
Mother Goose. Philadelphia: 1903. V. 64
Mother Goose. New York: 1913. V. 63
Mother Goose. London: 1920. V. 65
Mother Goose. New York: 1925. V. 62
Mother Goose. Boston: 1940. V. 64
Mother Goose. New York: 1940. V. 65
Mother Goose. New York: 1942. V. 64
Mother Goose. New York: 1944. V. 63
Mother Goose ABC. Akron: 1916. V. 65
Mother Goose Finger Plays. Philadelphia: 1915. V. 62
Mother Goose Her Own Book. Chicago: 1932. V. 63; 64
Mother Goose Melodies. New York: 1869. V. 62
Mother Goose Nursery Tales. Philadelphia: 1904. V. 63
Mother Goose of '93.... Boston: 1893. V. 63
Mother Goose, or, Harlequin and the Golden Egg. London: 1880. V. 66
Mother Goose Rhymes. New York: 1940. V. 64
Mother Goose Rhymes and Other Stories. New York: 1916. V. 63
Mother Goose's ABC. London: 1890. V. 65
Mother Goose's Fairy Rhymes. New York: 1886. V. 65
Mother Goose's Melodies. Philadelphia: 1850. V. 62
Mother Goose's Nursery Rhymes. London: 1895. V. 62
Mother Goose's Nursery Rhymes. Boston: 1899. V. 63
Mother Goose's Nursery Tales. London: 1923. V. 65
Mother Goose's Rag Book. London: 1910. V. 65
Old Mother Goose's Rhymes and Tales. London: 1889. V. 65
The Tall Book of Mother Goose. New York: 1942. V. 65
Willy Pogany's Mother Goose. New York: 1928. V. 65

MOTHER Hubbard. Philadelphia: 1850. V. 62

MOTHER Shipton Part I and II. London: 1771. V. 63

MOTHERBY, GEORGE
A New Medical Dictionary.... London: 1775. V. 62

MOTHER'S Little Rhyme Book. London: 1913. V. 65

THE MOTHER'S Picture Alphabet. London: 1862. V. 67

MOTHERWELL, ROBERT
The Dada Painters and Poets: an Anthology. New York: 1951. V. 62

THE MOTHS of America North of Mexico. Fasc. 13.2A & 13.2B. Pyraloidea: Pyralidae Comprising the Subfamily Evergestinae. London: 1976. V. 65

THE MOTHS of North Of Mexico. Fasc. 20, Pts. 2A and 2B. Bombycoidea, Saturniidae. London: 1971-1972. V. 65

MOTION, ANDREW
Independence. Edinburgh: 1981. V. 64
Inland. Burford: 1976. V. 66
The Poetry of Edward Thomas. London: 1980. V. 62
Two Poems. Childe Okeford: 1988. V. 63

MOTIONS Adresses a l'Assemblee Nationale en Faveur du Sexe. N.P: 1789. V. 63

MOTLEY, JOHN LOTHROP
History of the United Netherlands: from the Death of William the Silent to the Twelve Years Truce 1609. London: 1860-1867. V. 64
History of the United Netherlands from the Death of William the Silent to...1609. London: 1875. V. 62
The Rise of the Dutch Republic. (with) The United Netherlands. (with) Life and Death of John of Barneveld.... London: 1904. V. 62

THE MOTOR Boat Manual. London: 1909. V. 64

THE MOTORING Annual and Motorist's Year Book for 1903, Including World's Motor Records....* London: 1903. V. 62

MOTORISTS' Route Guide from Clapham. Clapham: 1910. V. 65

MOTT, D. W.
Legends and Love of Long Ago. Los Angeles: 1929. V. 67

MOTT, ED
The Black Homer of Jimtown. New York: 1900. V. 63; 66

MOTT, F. W.
The Bi-Polar Cells of the Spinal Cord. 1890. V. 67

MOTTE, STANDISH
Outline of a System of Legislation, for Securing Protection to the Aboriginal Inhabitants of all Countries Colonized by Great Britain. London: 1840. V. 62

MOTTELAY, PAUL FLEURY
Bibliographical History of Electricity and Magnetism.... New York: 1992. V. 65; 67

MOTTEVILLE, FRANCOIS DE
Memoirs for the History of Anne of Austria, Wife to Lewis XIII of France. London: 1726-1725. V. 67

MOTTEVILLE, MADAME DE
Memoires Pour Servir a l'Histoire d'Anne D'Autriche, Epouse de Louis XIII, Roi de France. Amsterdam: 1770. V. 65

MOTTLEY, JOHN
The History of the Life and Reign of the Empress Catherine: Containing a Short History of the Russian Empire.... London: 1744. V. 64
The History of the Life and Reign of the Empress Catherine; Containing a Short History of the Russian Empire.... London: 1754. V. 67
The History of the Life of Peter I, Emperor of Russia. London: 1739. V. 64
The Life of Peter I, Emperor of Russia. London: 1739. V. 67

MOTTRAM, RALPH HALE
The Spanish Farm. London: 1924. V. 64
Three Personal Records of the War. London: 1929. V. 64

MOTTRAM, WILLIAM
The True Story of George Eliot in Relation to "Adam Bede" Giving the Real Life History of the More Prominent Characters. London: 1905. V. 63

MOUAT, JAMES
The Rise of the Australian Wool Kings. London: 1892. V. 64; 65

MOUHOT, HENRI
Travels in the Central Parts of Indo-China (Siam), Cambodia and Laos, During the Years 1858, 1859 and 1860. London: 1864. V. 62

MOULIN, ETIENNE
Catheterisme Rectiligne, ou Nouvelle Maniere de Pratiquer Cette Operation Chez l'Homme.... Paris: 1828. V. 65

MOULTON, GARY E.
Atlas of the Lewis and Clark Expedition - the Journals of Lewis the Lewis Clark Expedition, Volume I. Lincoln: 1999. V. 66

MOULTON, H. FLETCHER
The Girl He Left Behind. London: 1927. V. 65

MOULTON, LOUIS CHANDLER
Juno Clifford. A Tale. New York: 1856. V. 64

MOULTRIE, WILLIAM
Memoirs of the American Revolution, So Far As It Is Related to the States of North and South Carolina, and Georgia.... New York: 1802. V. 63; 66

MOUNT, H.
Mr. Crabtree's Guide to Good Fishing Tackle. 1969. V. 67

MOUNT LUCAS ORPHAN AND GUARDIAN INSTITUTE
First Annual Report of the Incorporated Trusees (sic) of the Mount Lucas Orphan and Guardian Institute. Princeton: 1845. V. 66

MOUNTAIN View Farm Morgan Horses 1912. East Burke: 1912. V. 66

MOUNTBATTEN, LOUIS MOUNTBATTEN, EARL OF
An Introduction to Polo. London: 1931. V. 67

MOUNTENEY-JEPHSON, A. J.
Emin Pasha and the Rebellion at the Equator. New York: 1890. V. 62; 64

MOUNTFORD, C. H.
The Tiwi. Their Art, Myth and Ceremony. London: 1958. V. 62

MOUNTFORT, WILLIAM
Six Plays. London: 1720. V. 62; 65

MOUNTMORRES, HERVEY REDMOND, 2ND VISCOUNT
The Crisis. London: 1794. V. 62

MOURANT, A. E.
The Genetics of the Jews. Oxford: 1978. V. 63

MOURE, NANCY D. W.
California Art: 450 Years of Painting and Other Media. Los Angeles: 1998. V. 63
Publications in Southern California Art 1, 2 and 3. Glendale: 1984. V. 63

MOURELLE, DON FRANCISCO ANTONIO
Voyage of the Sonora in the Second Bucareli Expedition to Explore the Northwest Coast, Survey the Port of San Francisco and Found Franciscan Missions and a Presidio and Pueblo at that Port.... San Francisco: 1920. V. 64; 66

MOURLOT, FERNAND
The Lithographs of Chagall. Monte Carlo and Boston: 1960. V. 66
Picasso Lithographs. Boston: 1970. V. 62

MOUTAINE, WILLIAM
The Seaman's Vade Mecum. London: 1782. V. 63

MOVIUS, HALLAM L.
The Irish Stone Age: Its Chronology, Development and Relationships. Cambridge: 1942. V. 63; 66

MOWAT, FARLEY
My Discovery of America. Toronto: 1985. V. 67
A Whale for the Killing. Toronto: 1972. V. 67

MOWBRAY, ALAN
A Bang and Two Echoes. Portland: 1938. V. 66

MOWRIS, J. A.
A History of the 117th Regiment, N.Y. Volunteers (4th Oneida). Hartford: 1866. V. 63

MOXON, JOSEPH
Mechanick Exercises on the Whole Art of Printing (1683-1684). London: 1962. V. 67
Mechanick-Powers, or the Mystery of Nature and Art Unvail'd. London: 1696. V. 66
A Tutor to Astronomie and Geographie. Or an Easie and Speedy Way to Know the Use of Both the Globes.... London: 1670. V. 64

MOYER, JOHN W.
Trophy Heads. 1962. V. 67

MOYES, PATRICIA
To Kill a Coconut. London: 1977. V. 65; 67
Who is Simon Warwick?. London: 1978. V. 66

MOYES, PHILIP J. R.
Bomber Squadrons of the R.A.F. and Their Aircraft. London: 1964. V. 67

MOYLE, WALTER
The Works of Walter Moyle, Esq. London: 1726. V. 63

MOYLLUS, DAMIANUS
A Newly Discovered Treatise on Classic Letter Design Printed at Parma by Damianus Moyllus ca. 1480. Paris: 1927. V. 66

MOYNAHAM, J. M.
The Ace Powell Book. Kalispell: 1974. V. 64; 67

MOYNE, LORD
Walkabout: a Journey in Lands Between the Pacific Oceans.... 1936. V. 67

MOYNIHAN, B. G. A.
Duodenal Ulcer. Philadelphia: 1910. V. 67

MOYNIHAN, BERKELEY
The Spleen and Some of Its Diseases. Philadelphia: 1921. V. 66

MOZART, WOLFGANG AMADEUS
Il Dissoluto Punito Osia Don Giovanni. Leipzig: 1801. V. 62

MOZELIUS, GABRIEL E.
Elephas Breviter Delineatus, Quem Consensu Amplissimi Collegii Philosophici in Regia Academia Upsaliensi.... Upsala: 1693. V. 63

MOZINO SUAREZ DE FIGUEROA, JOSEPH MARIANO
Noticias De Nutka. Diccionario De La Lengua De Los Nutkeses y Descripcion Del Volcan De Tuxtla. Mexico City: 1913. V. 66

MOZLEY, CHARLES
Concerning Ulysses and the Bodley Head. London: 1961. V. 62; 66

MOZLEY, JAMES BOWLING
Letters.... London: 1885. V. 65

MOZLEY, THOMAS
Reminiscences Chiefly of Oriel College and the Oxford Movement. London: 1882. V. 65

MPHAHLELE, EZEKIEL
The Wanderers. New York: 1971. V. 63; 64

M'QUEEN, JAMES
A Geographical and Commercial View of Northern Central Africa.... Edinburgh: 1821. V. 62

MRABET, MOHAMMED
The Boy Who Set the Fire and Other Stories. Los Angeles: 1974. V. 64; 66
Love with a Few Hairs. London: 1967. V. 67

MRACEK, FRANZ
Atlas of Diseases of the Skin Including an Epitome of Pathology and Treatment. Philadelphia: 1900. V. 65

MRS. Lovechild's Golden Present, For All Good Little Boys and Girls. London: 1820. V. 66

MRS. Lovechild's Golden Present for All Good Little Boys. York: 1820. V. 66

MRS. Pleasant's Story Book, Composed for the Amusement of Her Little Family.... Philadelphia: 1802. V. 66

MUDFORD, WILLIAM
Historical Account of the Campaign in the Netherlands in 1815 Under the Duke of Wellington. London: 1817. V. 62; 67

MUDGE, ISADORE G.
A George Eliot Dictionary. London: 1924. V. 63

MUDGE, THOMAS
A Description, with Plates of the Time-Keeper, Invented by the Late Thomas Mudge. London: 1799. V. 66

MUDGE, W.
An Account of the Operations Carried on for Accomplishing a Trigonometical Survey of England and Wales.... 1799-1804. V. 62

MUDIE, ROBERT
The British Naturalist. London: 1835. V. 65; 67
The Complete Governess. London: 1826. V. 63; 64; 65
The Feathered Tribes of the British Islands. London: 1835. V. 63; 65; 66
The Feathered Tribes of the British Islands. London: 1853. V. 67
The Picture of Australia: Exhibiting New Holland, Van Diemen's Land, and All the Settlements from the First at Sydney to the Last at the Swan River. London: 1829. V. 63

MUELLER, JOHANN GOTTHILF
Species Plantarum.... Berlin: 1757. V. 62

MUELLER, JOHANNES REGIOMONTANUS
Epytoma in Almagestum Ptolomei. Venice: 1496. V. 65

MUELLER, LISEL
Dependencies. Chapel Hill: 1965. V. 62; 64; 67

MUELLER, RALPH
Report After Action, the Story of the 103rd Infantry Division. Innsbruck;: 1945. V. 65

MUELLER, SAMUEL
Vade Mecum Botanicum, Oder Beytragliches Krauter-Buchlein, Darinnen der Vornehmsten und in Der Artzney-Kunst.... Frankfurt und Leipzig: 1694. V. 64

MUELLER-DOMBOIS, D.
Aims and Methods of Vegetation Ecology. New York: 1974. V. 63

MUENSTER, SEBASTIAN
Cosmographie Universdalis Lib. Vi. in Quibus Iuxta Certioris Fidei Scriptorum Traditionem Describuntur.... Basel: 1559. V. 62

MUENTZ, J. H.
Encaustic; or, Count Caylus's Method of Painting in the Manner of the Ancients. London: 1760. V. 67

MUGGERIDGE, MALCOLM
Autumnal Face. London: 1931. V. 62

MUGGLETON, LODOWICK
The Answer to William Penn, His Book Entitled the New Witnesses Proved Old Hereticks.... London: 1753. V. 63

MUHLBACH, L.
Joseph II and His Court. Mobile: 1864. V. 63

MUIR, EDWIN
First Poems. London: 1925. V. 63, 65
Journeys and Places: Poems. London: 1937. V. 65
One Foot in Eden. London: 1956. V. 65
Scott and Scotland - the Predicament of the Scottish Writer. London: 1936. V. 65
The Three Brothers. London: 1931. V. 65
Transition - Essays on Contemporary Literature. London: 1926. V. 63; 64
Variations on a Time Theme. London: 1934. V. 65
We Moderns: Enigmas and Guesses. London: 1918. V. 64

MUIR, JOHN
The Cruise of the Corwin. Boston and New York: 1917. V. 62; 63; 64
My First Summer in the Sierra. Boston: 1911. V. 62; 67
My First Summer in the Sierra. Covelo: 1988. V. 64
Our National Parks. Boston: 1901. V. 63
Steep Trails. Boston and New York: 1918. V. 63; 65
A Thousand Mile Walk to the Gulf. Boston and New York: 1916. V. 63; 64
Yosemite and the Sierra Nevada. Boston: 1948. V. 63

MUIR, PERCY H.
A. J. A. Symons 1900-1941. N.P: 1941. V. 67
The Antiquarian Bookseller and His Client. London: 1956. V. 64
Catnachery. San Francisco: 1955. V. 64
English Children's Books 1600 to 1900. London: 1954. V. 64
The Good Housekeeping Book of Fairy Stories. London: 1946. V. 64
Hambros Bank Ltd. London 1839-1939. London: 1939. V. 64
Minding My Own Business. An Autobiography. London: 1956. V. 67
Points: 1874-1930: Being Extracts from a Bibliographer's Note-Book. London/New York: 1931. V. 64; 65
Points 1874-1930, Being Extracts from a Bibliographer's Note-Book. (with) Points: Second Series 1866-1934. London: 1931-1934. V. 62

MUIR, PERCY H. continued
Points: Second Series 1866-1934. London: 1934. V. 64; 66
Private Presses: an Address. Amsterdam: 1966. V. 64
Talks on Book Collecting - Delivered Under the Authority of the Antiquarian Association. London: 1952. V. 63
Victorian Illustrated Books. London: 1971. V. 63; 64
Victorian Illustrated Books. New York, Washington: 1971. V. 62

MUIR, THOMAS
An Account of the Trial of Thomas Muir, Esq., Younger of Huntershill...at Edinburgh. Edinburgh: 1793. V. 63
Contributions to the History of Determinants 1900-1920. London: 1930. V. 62
The Theory of Determinants in the Historical Order of Its Development. London: 1906. V. 62
The Trial of Thomas Muir, Younger, of Huntershill, Before the High Court of Justiciary, at Edinburgh, on the 30th and 31st Days of August. London: 1793. V. 63

MUIR, WILLA
Songs from the Auvergnat. Done Into Modern Scots. Warlingham, Surrey: 1931. V. 66

MUIRHEAD, ARNOLD
Grace Revere Osler. A Brief Memoir. London: 1931. V. 64; 66

MUIRHEAD, GEORGE
The Birds of Berwickshire. 1889. V. 67
The Birds of Berwickshire. Edinburgh: 1889. V. 62

MUIRHEAD, JAMES PATRICK
The Life of James Watt.... London: 1858. V. 64
The Origin and Progress of the Mechanical Inventions of James Watt.... London: 1854. V. 62

MUIRHEAD, THORBURN
Strange to Relate. 1937. V. 66; 67

MUKHOPADHYAYA, GIRANDRANATH
History of Indian Medicine. New Delhi: 1974. V. 66

MULDER, CAROL JUNE WOODBRIDGE
Imported Foundation Stock of North American Arabian Horses. Alhambra: 1969. V. 66
Imported Foundation Stock of North American Arabian Horses. Alhambra: 1972. V. 66
Imported Foundation Stock of North American Arabian Horses. N.P: 1991. V. 66

MULDOON, PAUL
Meeting the British. London: 1987. V. 63; 64
Names and Addresses: Poems. Belfast: 1978. V. 62
The O-O's Party, New Year's Eve. Dublin: 1980. V. 62
Out of Siberia. Dublin and Old Deerfield: 1982. V. 63

MULFORD, A. F.
Fighting in the 7th United States Cavalry, Custer's Favorite Regiment. N.P: 1930. V. 67

MULFORD, ISAAC S.
A Civil and Political History of New Jersey.... Philadelphia: 1851. V. 63

MULFORD, PRENTICE
Prentice Mulford's Story - Life by Land and Sea, a Personal Narrative. New York: 1889. V. 62; 65

MULFORD, WILLIAM C.
Historical Tales of Cumberland County, New Jersey. Bridgeton: 1941. V. 63; 66

MULGRAVE, CONSTANTINE JOHN PHIPPS, 2ND BARON
A Voyage Towards the North Pole Undertaken by His Majesty's Command 1773. London: 1774. V. 66

MULHALL, MICHAEL G.
The Dictionary of Statistics. London: 1892. V. 64

MULHERN, D. S.
Donald Stephenson's Reminiscences: a True Story. Pittsburgh: 1891. V. 67

MULLAN, J.
Report on the Construction of a Military Road from Walla Walla to Fort Benton. Washington: 1863. V. 64

MULLER, CHRISTIAN HEINRICH
Vollstandiges und Systematisch Geordnetes Sach -und Namen-Register zu den 76 Banden der Vom Prof. Dr. Ludwig Wilhelm gilbert vom Jahre 1799 bis 1824.... Leipzig: 1826. V. 64

MULLER, F. MAX
Biographies of Words and The Home of the Aryas. London: 1888. V. 64
The Languages of the Seat of the War in the East. London: 1855. V. 64
Lectures on the Science of Languages Delivered at the Royal Institution of Great Britain in April May & June, 1861. (with) Second Series. London: 1861-1864. V. 64

MULLER, HERMANN
The Fertilisation of Flowers. London: 1883. V. 63; 64

MULLER, JOHANNES
Beschreibung der Insel Java.... Berlin: 1860. V. 67
On Certain Variations in the Vocal Orangs of the Passeres.... Oxford: 1878. V. 67

MULLER, JOSEPH
The Star Spangled Banner. New York: 1935. V. 65

MULLER, KARL
Geographi Graeci Minores, E Codicibus Recognovit Prolegomenis Annotatione Indicibus.... 1965. V. 65

MULLER, MARCIA
Ask the Cards a Question. New York: 1982. V. 62; 65
Beyond the Grave. New York: 1986. V. 63
The Cheshire Cat's Eye. New York: 1983. V. 62; 65
Deceptions. Eugene: 1991. V. 65
Edwin of the Iron Shoes. New York: 1977. V. 62; 65
Games to Keep the Dark Away. New York: 1984. V. 62; 65
Leave A Message for Willie. New York: 1984. V. 62; 65
The Legend of the Slain Soldiers. New York: 1985. V. 67
There's Nothing to be Afraid Of. New York: 1984. V. 65

MULLER, MAX
A History of Ancient Sanskrit Literature So Far As It Illustrates the Primitive Religion of the Brahmans. London: 1860. V. 65

MULLER, W. E. G.
Use of Aquatic Invertebrates as Tools for Monitoring of Environmental Hazards. Stuttgart: 1994. V. 64

MULLER, WILLIAM
Topographical and Military Description of Germany and the Surrounding Country. London: 1813. V. 63
Topographical and Military Description of Germany and the Surrounding Country. London: 1826. V. 63

MULLGARDT, L. C.
The Architecture and Landscape Gardening of the Exposition; a Pictorial Survey.... San Francisco: 1915. V. 65

MULLINGER, JAMES BASS
The University of Cambridge from the Earliest Times to the Decline of the Platonist Movement.... London: 1873-1911. V. 63

MULSON, THOMAS
Callistus; or, the Man of Fashion. London: 1768. V. 62

MUMEY, NOLIE
Alexander Taylor Rankin (1803-1885): His Diary and Letters. Boulder: 1966. V. 63; 66
Amos Stack (1822-1908) Forty Niner: His Overland Diary to California.... Denver: 1981. V. 63; 64; 66
Barker's Diary 1822-1895 - Pioneer Guilder and Early Settler of America. Denver: 1959. V. 66
The Black Ram of Dinwoody Creek, a Story of Rocky Mountain Sheep. Denver: 1951. V. 65
Bloody Trails Along the Rio Grande. Denver: 1958. V. 62, 63, 64, 65, 66
Calamity Jane 1852-1903: a History of Her Life and Adventures in the West. Denver: 1950. V. 64; 67
Cap, Pin and Diploma - a History of the Colorado Training School the Oldest in the State for Nurses. Boulder: 1968. V. 65
Charles Preuss Maps of 1846. Denver: 1952. V. 65
Clark Gruber and Company (1860-1865): A Pioneer Denver Mint. Denver: 1950. V. 63
Creede - The Hisory of a Colorado Silver Mining Town. Denver: 1949. V. 64; 67
Edward Dunsha Steele 1829-1865, Pioneer, Schoolteacher, Cabinetmaker and Musician.... Boulder: 1960. V. 63; 66
History of the Early Settlements of Denver 1599-1860. Glendale: 1972. V. 65
History of Tin Cup, Colorado (Virginia City) - An Alpie Mining Camp Which Refused to Become a Ghost Town. Boulder: 1963. V. 63; 66
Hoofs to Wings, the Pony Express, Dramatic Story of a Mail Service from East to West Which Exisited One Hundred Years Ago. Boulder: 1960. V. 67
James Pierson Beckwourth 1856-1866 - an Enigmatic Figure of the West. Denver: 1957. V. 63
John Williams Gunnison (1812-1853) The Last of the Western Explorers. Denver: 1955. V. 65; 67
The Life of Jim Baker. New York: 1972. V. 66
March of the Dragoons to the Rocky Mountains in 1836.... Denver: 1952. V. 65
Old Forts and Trading Posts of the West.... Denver: 1956. V. 63; 64; 65
Pioneer Denver: Including Scenes fo Central City, Colorado City and Nevada City. Denver: 1948. V. 63; 64; 65; 66
Poker Alice - Alice Ivers, Duffield, Tibbs Huckert (1851-1930), History of a Woman Gambler in the West. Denver: 1951. V. 63; 65; 67
Quartercentenary of the Publcation of Scientific Anatomy (1543-1943).... Denver: 1944. V. 62; 63; 64; 66
A Reproduction of Alfred E. Mathews Pencil Sketches of Colorado with a Facsimile of Mathews' Civil War Account and a Biography of Mathews by Dr. Mumey. Denver: 1961. V. 65
Rocky Mountain Dick (Richard W. Rock) Stories of His Adventures in Capturing Wild Animals. Denver: 1953. V. 63; 64; 66
The Saga of Auntie Stone and Her Cabin: Elizabeth Hickok Robbins Stone, (1801-1895).... Boulder: 1964. V. 63; 64
The Teton Mountains Their History and Traditions. Denver: 1947. V. 64
The Ute War. A History of the White River Massacre. Boulder: 1964. V. 65

MUMEY, NORMA L.
Nolie Mumey, M.D. 1891-1894: Surgeon, Aviator, Author, Philosopher, and Humanitarian. Boulder: 1987. V. 63; 64; 66

MUMFORD, GEORGE SALTONSTALL
Twenty Harvard Crews. Cambridge: 1923. V. 66

MUMFORD, JOHN KIMBERLEY
Oriental Rugs. New York: 1900. V. 65
Oriental Rugs. London: 1901. V. 62
Oriental Rugs. Toronto: 1901. V. 66

MUMFORD, KENNETH
John Ledyard an American Marco Polo. Portland: 1939. V. 64

MUMFORD, LEWIS
The Brown Decades - a Study of the Arts in America. New York: 1931. V. 62

MUMMERY, A. F.
My Climbs in the Alps and Caucasus. 1895. V. 63; 65
My Climbs in the Alps and Caucasus. London: 1895. V. 62; 63; 64

MUMMERY, J. H.
The Microscopic and General Anatomy of the Teeth. Human and Comparative. Oxford: 1924. V. 67

MUN, THOMAS
A Discourse of Trade from England Unto the East Indies, Answering to Diverse Objections Which are Usually Made Against the Same. London: 1621?. V. 66
England's Benefit and Advantage by Forraign Trade. Stockholm: 1732. V. 63
England's Treasure by Forraign Trade. London: 1669. V. 64
The Petition and Remonstrance of the Governour and Company of Merchants of London Trading to the East Indies.... London: 1641. V. 63

MUNARI, BRUNO
Animals for Sale. New York: 1957. V. 64

MUNBY, A. N. L.
Phillipps Studies no. 1. Cambridge: 1951. V. 63
Phillipps Studios Nos. 1-5. Cambridge: 1951-1960. V. 62; 63
Sale Catalogues of Libraries of Eminent Persons. London: 1971-1975. V. 63
Some Caricatures of Book Collectors - an Essay. London: 1948. V. 62; 63

MUNCHAUSEN
The Travels and Surprising Adventures of Baron Munchausen. London: 1877. V. 66

MUNDEN, THOMAS S.
Memoirs of Joseph Shepherd Munden, Comedian. London: 1844. V. 65; 66

MUNDT, C.
Henry VIII and His Court, or, Catherine Parr. Mobile: 1864. V. 62

MUNDY, GODFREY CHARLES
Our Antipodes: or, Residence and Rambles In the Australasian Colonies with a Glimpse of the Gold Fields. London: 1852. V. 66

MUNDY, RODNEY
Narrative of Events in Borneo and Celebres, Down to the Occupation of Labuan.... London: 1848. V. 62

MUNDY, TALBOT
Rung Ho!. New York: 1914. V. 64; 66
The Thunder Dragon Gate. New York and London: 1937. V. 66

MUNGER, THOMAS LAURENCE
Detroit Today. Detroit: 1921. V. 66

MUNK, JOSEPH AMASA
Activities of a Lifetime. Los Angeles: 1924. V. 64
Arizona Sketches. New York: 1905. V. 66
Southwest Sketches. New York: 1920. V. 64

MUNKACSI, MARTIN
Style in Motion. New York: 1979. V. 67

MUNN, H. WARNER
Tales of the Werewolf Clan. Volume I. 1979. V. 64
Tales of the Werewolf Clan. Volume II. 1980. V. 64

MUNN, HENRY TOKE
Tales of the Eskimo. London Philadelphia. V. 66

MUNN, PAUL SANDBY
Landscape Figures, Sketched from Nature Intended for the Use of Amateurs and Young Students in Landscapes. London: 1816. V. 67

MUNN, RICHARD
The Loyal Subject, or Monarchy Defended, and Republican Principles Exploded by the Word of God. London: 1793. V. 62

MUNNINGS, A. J.
Pictures of Horses and English Life. 1939. V. 62; 64
Pictures of Horses and English Life. London: 1939. V. 64
The Tale of Anthony Bell: a Hunting Ballad. N.P: 1921. V. 63

MUNNINGS, ALFRED
The Autobiography of.... London: 1950-1952. V. 62; 65

MUNRO, A. D.
Reproductive Seasonality in Teleosts: Environmental Influences. Boca Raton: 1990. V. 65

MUNRO, ALICE
The Beggar Maid. Stories of Flo and Rose. New York: 1979. V. 67
Friend of My Youth. New York: 1990. V. 66
The Love of a Good Woman. New York: 1998. V. 62
The Progress of Love. Toronto: 1986. V. 67
Selected Stories. New York: 1996. V. 67

MUNRO, HECTOR HUGH
Beasts and Superbeasts. London & New York: 1914. V. 62; 66; 67
The Chronicles of Clovis. London: 1912. V. 67
Reginald. London: 1904. V. 67
Reginald in Russia and Other Sketches. London: 1911. V. 67
The Short Stories... The Novels. London: 1930-1933. V. 62

The Square Egg and Other Sketches. London: 1924. V. 62; 64; 67
The Unbearable Bassington. London: 1912. V. 67
The Westminster Alice. London: 1902. V. 63
When William Came. London and New York: 1914. V. 67

MUNRO, I. S. R.
The Fishes of New Guinea. Port Moresby: 1967. V. 65
The Fishes of the New Guinea Region. London: 1958. V. 62
The Marine and Fresh Water Fishes of Ceylon. Camberra: 1955. V. 63; 65

MUNRO, J. N.
The Rasp. Kansas: 1914. V. 66

MUNRO, NEIL
The Clyde. London: 1907. V. 66; 67

MUNRO, ROBERT
Palaeolithic Man and Terramara Settlements in Europe, Being the Munro Lectures in Anthropology. New York: 1912. V. 67
Prehistoric Scotland and Its Place In European Civilisation. London: 1899. V. 62

MUNSELL, M. E.
Flying Sparks as Told by a Pullman Conductor. Kansas City: 1914. V. 62; 65

MUNSON, JOHN WILLIAM
Reminiscences of a Mosby Guerrilla. New York: 1906. V. 62; 63; 64; 65; 66; 67

MUNTER, FREDERIK
Den Stromaegtigste Konges Kong Frederick den Siettes...og den Stormaegtigste Dronnings, Dronning Marie Sophie Frederikes.... Copenhagen: 1818. V. 62

MUNTER, ROBERT
A Dictionary of the Irish Print Trade 1550-1775. New York: 1988. V. 64

MURAKAMI, KASUKE
Select Flower Arrangements of Moribana and Heikwa. New York: 1936. V. 66

MURALT, BEAT LOUIS DE
Letters Describing the Character and Customs of the English and French Nations. London: 1726. V. 63; 67

MURASAKI, SHIKIBU
The Tale of the Genji: a Novel in Six Parts. London: 1935. V. 64

MURATORI, LODOVICO ANTONIO
A Relation of the Missions of Paraguay. London: 1759. V. 63

MURBARAK, SCOTT J.
Compartment Syndromes and Volkmann's Contracture. Philadelphia: 1981. V. 67

MURCHISON, CHARLES
Clinical Lectures on Diseases of the Liver, Jaundice and Abdominal Dropsy. London: 1885. V. 62; 66
A Treatise on the Continued Fevers of Great Britain. London: 1884. V. 62; 66

MURCHISON, RODERICK IMPEY
On the Distribution of Flint Drift of the South-East of England to the South and North of the Weald. 1851. V. 64
Outline of the Geology of the Neighbourhood of Cheltenham. Cheltenham: 1834. V. 62
Siluria. London. 1854. V. 63, 64
Siluria. London: 1859. V. 62
Siluria. London: 1872. V. 64
The Silurian System.... London: 1839. V. 62

MURDOCH, IRIS
An Accidental Man. London: 1971. V. 66
The Bell. London: 1958. V. 62
The Book and the Brotherhood. London: 1987. V. 65; 66
The Book and the Brotherhood. Franklin Center: 1988. V. 62
Dans le Filet. Paris: 1957. V. 64
The Existentialist Political Myth. West Midlands: 1989. V. 66
A Fairly Honourable Defeat. London: 1970. V. 66
The Fire and the Sun - Why Plato Banished the Artists - Based Upon the Romanes Lecture for 1976. London: 1977. V. 64
The Fire and the Sun: Why Plato Banished the Artists. Based Upon the Romanes Lecture 1976. Oxford: 1977. V. 66
The Flight from the Enchanter. London: 1956. V. 62; 66
The Good Apprentice. London: 1985. V. 62; 63
The Italian Girl. London: 1964. V. 66
The Italian Girl. 1986. V. 62
Joanna Joanna. 1994. V. 62
Joanna Joanna. London: 1994. V. 64
The Message of the Planet. London: 1898. V. 65
The Nice and the Good. London: 1968. V. 66
Reynolds Stone - an Address Given by Iris Murdoch in St. James's Church, Piccadilly on 20 July 1979. London: 1981. V. 65; 66
The Sacred and Profane Love Machine. London: 1974. V. 66
The Sandcastle. 1957. V. 62
Sartre. 1953. V. 62
Sartre. London: 1953. V. 63
The Sea, The Sea. London: 1978. V. 66
The Servants (Opera). 1980. V. 62
A Severed Head. London: 1961. V. 62; 66
Something Special - Four Poems and a Story. Helsinki: 1990. V. 62

MURDOCH, IRIS continued
The Sovereignty of Good Over Other Concepts. The Leslie Stephen Lecture 1967. Cambridge: 1967. V. 66
The Time of the Angels. London: 1966. V. 66
Under the Net. 1954. V. 62
The Unicorn. London: 1963. V. 64; 66
An Unoffical Rose. London: 1962. V. 66
A Year of Birds. 1978. V. 62
A Year of Birds. Tisbury: 1978. V. 66

MURDOCH, PATRICK
Mercator's Sailing, Applied to the True Figure of the Earth. London: 1741. V. 62; 66

MURDOCK, CHARLES
A Backward Glance at Eighty. San Francisco: 1921. V. 66

MURDOCK, HAROLD
Percy Dines Abroad. Boston: 1924. V. 65

MURE, WILLIAM
A Critical History of the Language and Literature of Antient (Sic) Greece.... London: 1850. V. 65
Selections from the Family Papers Preserved at Caldwell. Glasgow: 1854. V. 62; 66

MURFIN, JAMES V.
The Gleam of Bayonets. The Battle of Antietam and the Maryland Campaign of 1862. New York and London: 1965. V. 62; 63; 65

MURFREE, MARY N.
The Champion. Boston and New York: 1902. V. 62
The Phantoms of the Foot-Bridge and Other Stories. New York: 1895. V. 62

MURGER, HENRY
Vie de Boheme. London: 1949. V. 64

MURIE, JAMES
On the Organization of the Caaing Whale, Globiocephalus Melas. 1867. V. 67

MURIE, JAMES R.
Ceremonies of the Pawnee: Part 1 the Skiri and Part 2 The South Bands. Washington: 1981. V. 63

MURPHY, ARTHUR
The Gray's-Inn Journal. London: 1756. V. 62
The Life of David Garrick. London: 1801. V. 63
The Way to Keep Him. London: 1785. V. 64
The Works.... London: 1786. V. 62

MURPHY, CLIVE
Freedom for Mr. Mildew and Nigel Someone. London: 1975. V. 67

MURPHY, D. F.
The Jeff Davis Piracy Cases. Full Report of the Trial of William Smith for Piracy as One of the Crew of the Confederate Privateer, the Jeff Davis. Philadelphia: 1861. V. 62; 63

MURPHY, DENIS
Triumphalia Chronologica Monasterii Sanctae Crucis in Hibernia. 1891. V. 64

MURPHY, IGNATIUS
The Diocese of Killaloe (1700-1850). 1991-1992. V. 67

MURPHY, JAMES
The Inside Passenger. 1913. V. 67
Lays and Legends of Ireland. Dublin: 1911. V. 67

MURPHY, JAMES CAVANAH
The Arabian Antiquities of Spain. London: 1813-1815. V. 64

MURPHY, JOHN BENJAMIN
Resection of Arteries and Veins Injured in Continuity...End-to-End Suture. New York: 1987. V. 64; 67
Stereo-Clinic - Hysterectomy for Pelvic Inflammatory Disease. (with) Arthoplasty for Ankylosis of the Knee. Baltimore: 1910. V. 67

MURPHY, JOHN NICHOLAS
Ireland; Industrial, Political and Social. 1870. V. 62; 65; 67
Terra Incognita or Convents of the United Kingdom. London: 1873. V. 62; 66

MURPHY, MARTIN
Report on the Subsidized Railways and Other Public Works in the Province of Nova Scotia, for the Year 1890. Halifax: 1891. V. 64

MURPHY, RICHARD
Niches. Old Deerfield: 1978. V. 66
Sailing to an Island. London: 1963. V. 63; 64
The Woman of the House - an Elegy. Dublin: 1959. V. 62

MURPHY, ROBERT
Murder in Waiting. New York: 1938. V. 67

MURPHY, ROBERT CUSHMAN
Bird Islands of Peru. New York: 1925. V. 62; 63; 64; 66; 67
Oceanic Birds of Sotuh America. New York: 1936. V. 62; 63; 64; 65; 66; 67
Oceanic Birds of South America. New York: 1948. V. 62

MURPHY, STANLEY
Martha's Vineyard Decoys. Boston: 1978. V. 65

MURPHY, THOMAS D.
Oregon, the Picturesque; a Book of Rambles in the Oregon Country and in the Wilds of Northern California. Boston: 1917. V. 62

MURPHY, WILLIAM
A Comprehensive Classical Atlas, with a Memoir n Ancient Geography, Drawn and Engraved from the Best Authorities. Edinburgh: 1832. V. 63; 65
The Forgotten Battalion. Spokane: 1937. V. 65

MURRAY, A. H. H.
The High-Road of Empire. 1905. V. 66

MURRAY, A. J.
Cattle and Their Diseases. Chicago: 1887. V. 62

MURRAY, A. S.
White Athenian Vases in the British Museum. London: 1896. V. 64

MURRAY, ALBERT
The Hero and the Blues. 1973. V. 63
The Hero and the Blues. Columbia: 1973. V. 64; 66
The Omni-Americans. New York: 1970. V. 63
The Spyglass Tree. New York: 1991. V. 67
Stomping the Blues. New York: 1976. V. 63; 64; 67
Train Whistle Guitar. New York: 1974. V. 66

MURRAY, ALEXANDER
Geological Survey of Newfoundland. London: 1881. V. 64
Journal Du Yukon. 1847-1848. Ottawa: 1910. V. 64

MURRAY, AMELIA
Letters from the United States, Cuba and Canada. New York: 1856. V. 65
Remarks on Education. London: 1845?. V. 64; 65

MURRAY, ANDREW
The Geographical Distribution of Mammals. 1866. V. 63; 66
The Geographical Distribution of Mammals. London: 1866. V. 62

MURRAY, CHARLES AUGUSTUS
Travels in North America, During the Years 1834, 1835 and 1836. London: 1839. V. 63; 66
Travels in North America...A Summer Residence with the Pawnee Tribe of Indians.... London: 1854. V. 62; 65

MURRAY, DAVID
Early Burgh Organisation in Scotland. Glasgow: 1924. V. 63
Museums, Their History and Their Use. New York: 1999. V. 63
Museums, Their History and Their Use. Staten Island: 2000. V. 66
Robert and Andrew Foulis and the Glasgow Press with Some Account of the Glasgow Academy of the Fine Arts. Glasgow: 1913. V. 64

MURRAY, DAVID CHRISTIE
In His Grip. London: 1907. V. 66
One Traveller Returns. London: 1887. V. 65

MURRAY, GILBERT
The Airplane Spider. London: 1921. V. 65

MURRAY, HUGH
Historical Account of Discoveries and Travels in North America.... London: 1829. V. 62; 65; 66

MURRAY, J. A.
The Avifauna of British India and Its Dependencies.... London: 1887-1890. V. 67

MURRAY, J. H. P.
Papua or British New Guinea. New York: 1912. V. 65

MURRAY, J. OGDEN
Three Stories in One. The Statesman. The Confederate Soldier, the Ideal Soldier of the World. The South's Peerless Women of the World. N.P: 1915. V. 62

MURRAY, J. W.
Atlas of Invertebrate Macrofossils. London: 1985. V. 67

MURRAY, JAMES
A Dissertation on the Influence of Heat and Humidity, with Practical Observations on the Inhalation of Iodine and Various Vapours in Consumption, Catarrh, Croup, Asthma and Other Diseases. London: 1829. V. 65
Runs with the Lanarkshire and Renfrewshire Fox-Hounds, and Other Sporting Incidents. Glasgow: 1874. V. 62

MURRAY, JOHN
Bathymetrical Survey of the Scottish Fresh-Water Lochs During the Years 1897 to 1909. Edinburgh: 1910. V. 62
Handbook for Travellers in Constantinople, Brusa and the Troad. London: 1893. V. 65
A Handbook for Travellers in India, Burma and Ceylon, Including All British India, the Portugese and French Posessions and the Indian States. London: 1938. V. 65
A Handbook for Visitors to Paris.... London: 1874. V. 64
Handbook of London Past and Presetn. London: 1850. V. 65
The History of the Presbyterian Church in Cape Breton. Truro: 1921. V. 64
A Manual of Experiments Illustrative of Chemical Science.... London: 1833. V. 64
A Memoir on the Diamond. London: 1831. V. 64
Murray's Handbook for Travellers in France.... London: 1854. V. 67
Murray's Handbook for Travellers in Switzerland. Part I. London: 1892. V. 62
Remarks on the Disease Called Hydrophobia: Prophylactic and Curative. London: 1830. V. 67

MURRAY, JOHN OGDEN
The Immortal Six Hundred.... Winchester: 1905. V. 63; 65

MURRAY, JOHN OGDEN continued
The Immortal Six Hundred.... Roanoke: 1911. V. 63
Three Stories in One. The Statesman. The Confederate Solider, The Ideal Soldier of the World. The South's Peerless Women of the World. N.P: 1915. V. 63

MURRAY, JUDITH SARGENT STEVENS
The Gleaner; a Miscellaneous Production. Boston: 1798. V. 62

MURRAY, KENNETH M.
Wings Over Poland. New York: 1932. V. 67

MURRAY, LOIS L., MRS.
Incidents of Frontier Life. Goshen: 1880. V. 63

MURRAY, MARISCHAL
Union Castle Chronicle 1853-1953. London: 1953. V. 66

MURRAY, NICHOLAS
Notes, Historical and Biographical, Concerning Elizabeth-Town, Its Eminent Men, Churches and Ministers. Elizabeth Town: 1844. V. 63; 66

MURRAY, PATRICK
The Irish Annual Miscellany. 1850-1853. V. 65

MURRAY, ROBERT
An Account of the Constitution and Security of the General Bank of Credit. London: 1683. V. 62; 66

MURRAY, ROBERT A.
Fort Laramie Visions of a Grand Old Past. Fort Collins: 1974. V. 67
Military Posts in the Power River Country of Wyoming 1865-1894. Lincoln: 1968. V. 67
Military Posts of Wyoming. Fort Collins: 1974. V. 64

MURRAY, ROBERT F.
His Poems. London: 1894. V. 64

MURRAY, THOMAS BOYLES
Pitcairn: the Island, the People and the Pastor. London: 1855. V. 63
Pitcairn: the Island, the People and the Pastor. 1856. V. 67
Pitcairn: the Island, the People and the Pastor. London: 1857. V. 63
Pitcairn: The Island, The People and the Pastor. London: 1858. V. 65
Pitcairn: the Island, the People and the Pastor. London: 1860. V. 63; 65

MURRAY, W. H. H.
Daylight Land. Boston: 1888. V. 64; 67

MURRAY, WILLIAM
The Hard Knocker's Lock. New York: 1985. V. 65
Tip on a Dead Crab. New York: 1984. V. 65
A Treatise on Emotional Disorders of the Sympathetic System of Nerves. New York: 1872. V. 65

MURRAY'S Berkshire Architectural Guide. London: 1949. V. 62

MURRAY'S Buckinghamshire Architectural Guide. London: 1949. V. 62

MURTON, R. K.
The Wood Pigeon. London: 1965. V. 62

MUSA Proterva: Love Poems of the Restoration. London and Bungay: 1902. V. 62; 67

MUSAEUS
Hero and Leander - the Divine Poem of Musaeus. Shaftesbury: 1936. V. 63
Musaei, Moschi & Bionis, Quae Extant Omnia: Quibus Accessere Quaedam Selectiora Thoooriti Eidyllia. 1655. V. 66

MUSAUS, JOHANN CARL AUGUST
The Three Sons-in-Law. Edinburgh and New York: 1861. V. 67

MUSCATINE, CHARLES
The Book of Geoffrey Chaucer. An Account of the Publication of Geoffrey Chaucer's Works from the Fifteenth Century to Modern Times. 1963. V. 65

MUSCULUS
Loci Communes Sacri, Ex Patribus Orthodoxis Ecclesiae.... Francfordiae ad Oderam: 1590. V. 66

MUSCUT, JAMES
Sermons on Several Subjects. Cambridge: 1760. V. 67

LE MUSEE de Versailles, Ses Principaux Tableaux et Statues, Graves par Revell. Vues du Parc et du Chateau, Dessinees et Gravees par Leonce l'Huillier. Paris: 1837. V. 66

MUSEO REALE BORBONICO
Raccolta Delle Piu Interessante Dipintura e de' Piu Belli...Musaici Rinvenuti Negli Scavi di Ercolano, di Pompei e di Stabia,Che Emmiransi Nel Museo Reale Borbonico. Naples: 183-?. V. 64

LES MUSES en Belle Humour ou Chansons et Autres Poesies Joyeuses. Ville Franche: 1760. V. 65

MUSGRAVE, PERCY
Notes on the Ancient Family of Musgrave of Musgrave, Westmorland and Its Various Branches in Cumberland, Yorkshire, Northumberland, Somerset &c. Leeds: 1911. V. 65

MUSGRAVE, SAMUEL
Two Dissertations. I. On the Graecian Mythology. II. An Examination of Sir Isaac Newton's Objections of the Chronology of the Olympiads. London: 1782. V. 62

MUSGRAVE, T. B. C.
Historical and Descriptive Sketch of the Colony of St. Vincent. 1891. V. 62

MUSGRAVE, WILLIAM
Antiquitates Britanno-Belgicae, Pracipue Romanae, Figuris Illustratae, Tribus Voll. Comprehensae.... Exeter: 1719. V. 63; 67
Belgium Britannicum in Quo Illius Limites, Fluvii, Urbes, Viae Militares, Populus, Lingua.... Bishop: 1719. V. 65
De Aquilitate Anomala, Sive Interna, Dissertatio. Exeter: 1707. V. 65
Regiae Societatis Utriusque Socii Geta Britannicus. Exeter: 1715. V. 65

MUSHET, ROBERT
An Attempt to Explain from Facts the Effect of the Issues of the Bank of England Upon Its Own Interests, Public Credit and Country Banks. London: 1826. V. 64
An Enquiry Into the Effects Produced ont he National Currency and Rates of Exchange, by the Bank Restriction Bill.... London: 1810. V. 64

MUSICAL Travels through England. London: 1758. V. 63

THE MUSICIAN. A Monthly Publication Devoted to the Educational Interests of Music. Philadelphia: 1896. V. 65

MUSICK, JOHN R.
Stories of Missouri. New York: 1897. V. 64; 67

MUSIL, ROBERT
Prosa, Dramen, Spate Briefe. Hamburg: 1957. V. 64
Tonka and Other Stories. London: 1965. V. 67
Die Verwirrungen des Zoglings Torless. (The Man Without Qaulities). Vienna: 1906. V. 67
Young Torless. London: 1955. V. 64

LES MUSIQUES de la Guerre. Hymnes Allies. Paris: 1915. V. 65

MUSKOGEE NATION
Constitution and Laws of the Muskogee Nation. Muskogee, Indian Territory: 1890. V. 62

MUSPRATT, JAMES SHERIDAN
Chemistry Theoretical, Practical and Analytical as Applied and Relating to the Arts and Manufactures. Glasgow: 1853-1861. V. 64
Chemistry, Theoretical, Practical and Analytical, as Applied and Relating to the Arts and Manufactures. Glasgow Edinburgh London: 1857-1860. V. 64

MUSSCHENBROEK, PETRUS VONA
Introductio ad Philophiam Naturalem. Leiden: 1762. V. 62

MUSSEAU, J. C. L.
Manuel des Amateurs d'Estampes. Paris: 1821. V. 64

MUSSELWHITE, A.
Behind the Lens in Tigerland. 1933. V. 66

MUSSET, ALFRED DE
La Confession d'un Enfant du Siecle. Paris: 1891. V. 67
The Confession of a Child of the Century. London: 1901. V. 62
Fantasio. 1929. V. 65
Lorenzaccio. Drame. Verona: 1974. V. 65
Oeuvres Posthumes. Paris: 1876. V. 66

MUSSET, PAUL DE
The Last Abbe. Paris. V. 62
Mr. Wind and Madam Rain. London: 1864. V. 65

MUSSETT, NIGEL J.
Cadets at Giggleswick 1910 1980. Giggleswick: 1980. V. 65

MUSSI, ANTONIO
Disegno di Lezioni di Ricerche sulla Lingua Ebraica. 1792. V. 67

MUSTERS, JOHN CHADWORTH
Hunting Songs and Poems. Nottingham. V. 62

MUTER, GLADYS NELSON
About Bunnies. Chicago: 1924. V. 63

MUTIS, ALVARO
Diario de Lecumberri. Xalapa: 1960. V. 67
Los Elementos del Desastre. Buenos Aires: 1953. V. 67

MUTUAL Criticism Oneida. Oneida: 1876. V. 63

MUYBRIDGE, EADWEARD
The Human Figure in Motion, an Electro-Photographic Investigation of Consecutive Phases of Muscular Actions. London: 1919. V. 66

MUYS, JOHANNES
Praxis Chirurgica Rationalis Seu Observationes Chirurgicae Secundum Solida Verge Philosophiae Fundamenta Resolutae, Quinque Decades. Leiden: 1685. V. 66

MUZEL, HEINRICH WILHELM
Verzeichniss Einer Sammlung Hauptsachlich zu des Alterthumern der Historie den Schonen Kunsten.... Berlin: 1783. V. 64

MY Baby's Rhymes. New York: 1889. V. 65

MY Brother - a Poem. New York: 1830. V. 63

MY Dollie's ABC. London: 1920. V. 62

MY First Book: the Experiences of Walter Besant, James Payn, W. Clark Russell, Grant Allen, Hall Caine, George R. Sims, Rudyard Kipling, A. Conan Doyle, M. E. Braddon, F. W. Robinson, H. Rider Haggard...Robert Louis Stevenson. London: 1894. V. 67

MY Little Song Book By My Friend. Concord: 1843. V. 64

MY Mother: a Poem for a Good Little Girl. New Haven: 1835. V. 64

MY Poetry Book. Philadelphia: 1934. V. 62

MY Story Book. London. V. 65

MYER, JESSE S.
Life and Letters of Dr. William Beaumont Including Hitherto Unpublished Data Concerning the Case of Alexis St. Martin. St. Louis: 1912. V. 66

MYER, REGINALD
Chats on Old English Tobacco Jars. Philadelphia: Sep. 1930. V. 62

MYERS & CO.
Novelty Rose Memento of the English Lakes. London: 1860. V. 66

MYERS, B. S.
The German Expressionists: a Generation in Revolt. New York: 1957. V. 62

MYERS, FRANK M.
The Comanches - A History of White's Battalion, Virginia, Cavalry Laurel Brigade, Hampton Div. A.N.V. Gaithersburg: 1987. V. 67

MYERS, GRACE WHITING
History of the Massachusetts General Hospital June 1872 to December 1900. Boston: 1929. V. 67

MYERS, JOHN M.
Doc Holiday. Boston and Toronto: 1955. V. 65

MYERS, R. L.
Ecosystems of Florida. Orlando: 1990. V. 63

MYERS, SYLVESTER
Myers' History of West Virginia. New Martinsville: 1915. V. 66

MYERS, WILLIAM H.
Naval Sketches of the War in California. New York: 1939. V. 64

MYERS, WILLIAM STARR
The Story of New Jersey. New York: 1945. V. 63; 66

MYERSON, JOEL
Studies in the American Renaissance. Charlottesville c: 1983-1996. V. 62

MYLAR, ISAAC L.
Early Days at the Mission, San Juan Bautista, a Narrative of Incidents Connected With the Days When California Was Young. Watsonville: 1929. V. 62

MYNTER, HERMAN
Appendicitis and Its Surgical Treatment. Philadelphia: 1897. V. 67

MYRICK, DAVID F.
Railroads of Arizona. Berkeley/Glendale: 1975-1998. V. 63
Railroads of Arizona. Volume I. The Southern Roads. San Diego: 1975. V. 67

MYRICK, HERBERT
Cache La Poudre: the Romance of a Tenderfoot in the Days of Custer. New York: 1905. V. 67

MYRON, MAY
The Little Wee Bear and Gold Hair. London: 1910. V. 66
The Peek-A-Boos in Camp. London: 1915. V. 64

MYRTLE, ANDREW SCOTT
Practical Observations on the Harrogate Mineral Waters. 1874. V. 65
Practical Observations on the Harrogate Mineral Waters. Harrogate: 1893. V. 64; 65; 66

THE MYSTERIES of Matrimony, with Sundry Revelations. Papermill Village: 1846. V. 64

MYSTERIES of the Unknown. Alexandria: 1992. V. 67

THE MYSTERY Scene Reader. Cedar Rapids: 1987. V. 63; 65

MYTHOGRAPHI Latini. Amstelodami: 1681. V. 64

MYZK, WILLIAM
The History and Origins of the Virginia Gold Cup since 1922. Warrenton: 1987. V. 64

N

N., F.
A Method for Executing the Powers, Relating to the Militia and Trained-Bands, According to the Acts of Parliament Since the Happy Restauration of Our Gracious Sovereign K. Charles II. London: 1684. V. 66

N., J.
Select Lessons in Prose and Verse, from Various Authors.... Bristol: 1774. V. 62; 64

N., N.
The Scarlet Gown, or the History of the Present Cardinals of Rome. London: 1653. V. 63

NABOKOV, VALDIMIR
Bend Sinister. New York: 1947. V. 63; 64; 65

NABOKOV, VLADIMIR
Chambre Obscure. (Camera Obscura). Paris: 1934. V. 63
Conclusive Evidence. New York: 1951. V. 62; 65; 66
La Course de Fou. (The Defence). Paris: 1934. V. 65
Despair. London: 1937. V. 66
Despair. 1966. V. 65
Despair. New York: 1966. V. 62
Despair. 1986. V. 62
Le Don. (The Gift). Paris: 1967. V. 64
The Eye. New York: 1965. V. 67
Feu Pale. (Pale Fire). Paris: 1965. V. 63
The Gift. 1963. V. 62
Invitation au Supplice. Paris: 1960. V. 63
Invitation to a Beheading. New York: 1959. V. 63
Kamera Obskura. Paris: 1933. V. 65
Laughter in the Dark. New York: 1950. V. 65
Lolita. Paris: 1955. V. 62
Lolita. London: 1959. V. 62; 64; 66
(title in Russian) Lolita. New York: 1967. V. 62
Nabokov's Quartet. New York: 1966. V. 63; 64; 67
Nikolai Gogol. Norfolk: 1944. V. 62; 64; 66
Otcharnie. (Despair). Petrolopis/Berlin: 1936. V. 65
The Pale Fire. London: 1962. V. 66
Pale Fire. New York: 1962. V. 62
The Real Life of Sebastian Knight. Norfolk: 1941. V. 66
The Real Life of Sebastian Knight. London: 1945. V. 62
(Collected Works in Russian). Moscow: 1990. V. 62

NACHTWEY, JAMES
Deeds of War. New York: 1989. V. 66

NACK, CARL
Reichstift Neresheim. Eine kurze Geschichte Dieser Benediktinerabtey in Schwaben, und Beschreibung inrer im Jahre 1792 Eingeweihten Neuen Kirche. Gedrukt und im Verlage: 1792. V. 67

NACLERIO, EMIL
Bronchopulmonary Diseases Basic Aspects, Diagnosis and Treatment. New York: 1959. V. 67

NADAILLAC, MARQUIS DE
Pre-Historic America. New York: 1884. V. 64
Pre-Historic America. London: 1885. V. 67

NADAL, GERONIMO
Adnotationes et Meditationes in Evangelia Quae in Sacrosancto Missae Sacrificio Toto ann Leguntur.... Antwerp: 1595. V. 62

NADAU, MAURICE
Les Lettres Nouvelles - Nouvelle Serie: No. 1. Paris: 1959. V. 65

NADEAU, REMI A.
The Water Seekers. Santa Barbara,Salt Lake City: 1974. V. 63

NADEN, CORINNE J.
The Haymarket Affair, Chicago 1886. New York: 1968. V. 67

NAEF, WESTON J.
The Collection of Alfred Stieglitz: Fifty Pioneers of Modern Photography. New York: 1978. V. 63
Era of Exploration: the Rise of Landscape Photography in the American West 1860-1885. Boston;: 1975. V. 64

NAEGELE, FRANZ CARL
The Obliquely Contracted Pelvis, Containing Also an Appendix of the Most Important Defects of the Female Pelvis. New York: 1939. V. 65

NAEGELI, OTTO
Differential Diagnosis in Internal Medicine.... Chicago: 1940. V. 66

NAIL, LESLIE
Resurrection Ball. Tuscaloosa: 1982. V. 66

NAIPAUL, SHIVA
The Chip-Chip Gatherers. London: 1957. V. 64
The Chip-Chip Gatherers. London: 1973. V. 62; 64; 66
Fireflies. London: 1970. V. 66
Fireflies. New York: 1971. V. 63; 64

NAIPAUL, VIDIADHAR SURAJPRSAD
A Flag on the Island. London: 1967. V. 62
India. A Million Mutinies Now. London: 1990. V. 63; 66; 67
India: a Wounded Civilization. London: 1977. V. 62
Mr. Stone and the Knights Companion. New York: 1964. V. 66
The Mystic Masseur. New York: 1959. V. 63; 64; 66; 67
The Overcrowded Barracoon. London: 1972. V. 62
The Overcrowded Barracoon. New York: 1973. V. 65
A Turn in the South. Franklin Center: 1989. V. 67
A Way in the World. New York: 1994. V. 66

NAIRN, A. E. M.
The Ocean Basins and Margins. New York: 1973-1975. V. 65

NAIRN, KATHARINE
The Trial of Katharine Nairn and Patrick Ogilvie, for the Crimes of Incest and Murder. Edinburgh: 1765. V. 65

NAIRN, PHILIP SIDNEY
Poems, Letters and Memoiries. London: 1916. V. 64

NAIRN, THOMAS
A Letter from South Carolina: Giving an Account of the Soil, Air, Product, Trade, Government, Laws, Religion.... London: 1718. V. 63; 66

NAISMYTH, JOHN
Observations on the Different Breeds of Sheep, and the State of Sheep Farming in the Southern Districts of Scotland.... Edinburgh: 1795. V. 63

NAKAMURA, TATSUYUKI
Nude. Tokyo: 1955. V. 63

NAKED Came the Manatee. New York: 1996. V. 63; 65; 66; 67

NALL, G. H.
The Life of the Sea Trout. 1930. V. 63; 65; 67

NALSON, JOHN
A Letter from a Jesuit at Paris, to His Correspondent in London: Shewing the Most Effectual Way to Ruine the Government and Protestant Religion. Dublin: 1679. V. 62
A Letter from a Jesuit in Paris, to His Correspondent in London: Shewing the Most Effectual Way to Ruine the Government and Protestant Religion. London: 1679. V. 66

NANCE, R. MORTON
Sailing Ship Models. London: 1924. V. 64; 66; 67

NANCREDE, P. J. G. DE
L'Abeille Francois, or Nouveau Recueil de Morceaux Brillans des Auteurs Francois les Plus-Celebres. Boston: 1792. V. 63; 64

NANI, BATTISTA
The History of the Affairs of Europe in This Present Age, but More Particularly of the Republic of Venice. London: 1673. V. 63

NANKIEVELL, JOHN H.
History of the Military Organization of the State of Colorado 1860-1935. Denver: 1935. V. 64

NANSEN, FRIDTJOF
Fame Over Polhavet. Kristiana: 1897. V. 64
Farthest North. London: 1897. V. 66
Farthest North. New York: 1897. V. 62; 63
Farthest North. Westminster: 1897. V. 63; 65
Farthest North. London: 1898. V. 62; 64
The First Crossing of Greenland. London: 1890. V. 62
Fram over Polhavet den Norshe Polarfaerd 1893-1896. Oslo: 1897. V. 67
The Norwegian Polar Expedition 1893-1896, Scientific Results. New York: 1969. V. 63
Sporting Days in Wild Norway. London: 1925. V. 66
Through Siberia - the Land of the Future. New York and London: 1914. V. 65

NAOGEORGUS, THOMAS
Reprint of the Popish Kingdome or Reigne of Antichrist Written in Latin Verse by.... London: 1880. V. 65

NAPIER, CHARLES
The Navy: Its Past and Present State. London: 1851. V. 62

NAPIER Hibben's Guide to the Cities of Vancouver Island. Victoria: 1912. V. 63

NAPIER, JOHN
Logarithmorum Canonis Descriptio Seu Arithmeticarum Supputationum Mirabilis Abbreviatio. Lugduni: 1620. V. 66
Habdologiae, seu Numerationis per Virgulas Libri Duo; Cum Appendice de Expeditissimo Multiplicationis Promptuario. Edinburgh: 1617. V. 63; 67

NAPIER, P. H.
Catalogue of Primates in the British Museum (Natural History). 1976-1990. V. 66

NAPIER, ROBERT
Catalogue of the Works of Art Forming the Collection of Robert Napier of West Shandon, Dumbartonshire. London: 1865. V. 66
John Thomson of Duddington, Landscape Painter. His Life and Work, with Some Remarks on the Practice, Purpose and Philosophy of Art. Edinburgh & London: 1919. V. 64

NAPIER, WILLIAM FRANCIS PATRICK
English Battles and Sieges in the Peninsula. London: 1861. V. 64
History of the War in the Peninsula and in the South of France, from the Year 1807 to the Year 1814. London: 1828-1840. V. 62; 67

NAPLETON, JOHN
Considerations on the Public Exercises for the First and Second Degrees in the University of Oxford. N.P: 1773. V. 66

NAPOLEON I, EMPEROR OF THE FRENCH
The Officer's Manual. Napoleon's Maxims of War. Richmond: 1862. V. 62

NAPTON, WILLIAM B.
Over the Santa Fe Trail 1857. Santa Fe. 1964. V. 62

NAQVI, N. H.
Blood Pressure Measurement. An Illustrated History. New York: 1998. V. 64; 67

NARAYAN, R. K.
An Astrologer's Day and Other Stories. London: 1947. V. 63
The Financial Expert. London: 1952. V. 62
The Man-Eater of Malgudi. London: 1962. V. 64
Mr. Sampath. London: 1949. V. 63

NARBROUGH, JOHN
An Account of Several Late Voyages and Discoveries. London: 1711. V. 67

NARBROUGH, JOHN M.
An Account of Several Late Voyages and Discoveries. Amsterdam/New York: 1970. V. 66

NARDELLI, F.
The Rhinoceros, a Monograph. 1988. V. 63
The Rhinoceros, a Monograph. London: 1988. V. 62

NARDI, JACOPO
Le Historie della Citta di Fiorenza.... Lione: 1582. V. 67

NARDINI, LEONARDO
Novelle Scelte Degli Autori Piu Celebri Italiani Raccolte e di Note Gramaticali Illustrate.... Londra: 1818. V. 63

NARES, ROBERT
A Glossary of Words, Phrases, Names and Allusions in the Works of English Authors, Particuarly of Shakespeare and His Contemporaries. London: 1905. V. 64
A Glossary: or, Collection of Words, Phrases, Names and Allusions to Customs, Provebs, &c. Which Have Been Thought to Require Illustration in the Works of English Authors.... London: 1822. V. 65

NARKISS, BEZALEL
Hebrew Illuminated Manuscripts. Jerusalem: 1974. V. 62

NARODNY, IVAN
The Art of Robert Winthrop Chanler. New York: 1922. V. 65

NARRATIVE of an Ill Favoured Attempt to Pervert the Duke of Gloucester, Extracted Out of Divers Letters from France. London: 1654. V. 65

NARRATIVE of Facts in the Case of Passmore Williamson. Philadelphia: 1855. V. 62; 66

NARRATIVE of Sojourner Truth: a Bondswoman of Olden Time. Boston: 1873. V. 66

NARRATIVE of Some Things of New Spain and of the Great City of Temestitan, Moxico. New York: 1917. V. 64

NARRATIVE of the Loss of Halsewell East-Indiaman, Capt. Rich. Pierce...off Seacombe...Dorsetshire Jan. 6, 1786. London: 1803. V. 66

NARRATIVE of the Loss of the Centaur Man of War...in the...Atlantic Ocean, September 23, 1782.... London: 1803?. V. 66

NARRATIVE of the Loss of the Comet, Steam Packet, On Her Passage from Inverness to Glasgow on Friday, the 21st October 1825.... Edinburgh: 1825. V. 62

NARRATIVE of the Loss of the Winterton East Indiaman...Off.. Madagascar, August 20th, 1792. London: 1800?. V. 66

A NARRATIVE of the Proceedings of Admiral B---g and of His Conduct off Mahon, on the 20th of May. London: 1756. V. 66

NARRATIVE of the Surveying Voyages of His Majesty's Ships Adventure and Beagle Between the Years 1826 and 1836. London: 1839. V. 67

A NARRATIVE of Voyages, Undertaken by Order of Prince Henry, Including Those of Gongales, Zarco, Vaz Texiera, Gillianes, Baldaya, Nuno, Tristan, Lancerota &c. to Africa.... London: 1790. V. 62; 64

NARRIEN, JOHN
An Historical Account of the Origin and Progress of Astronomy. London: 1833. V. 65

NASATIR, ABRAHAM
Before Lewis and Clark Documents Illustrating the History of the Missouri 1765-1805. St. Louis: 1952. V. 64
French Activities in California an Archival Calendar - Guide. New York: 1945. V. 63; 66
A French Journalist in the California Gold Rush. Georgetown: 1964. V. 63; 66

NASH, C. W.
Vertebrates of Ontario. Toronto: 1908. V. 63

NASH, CHARLES EDWARD
Biographical Sketches of Gen. Pat Cleburne and Gen. T. C. Hindman. Little Rock: 1898. V. 62; 63; 65

NASH, FREDERICK
A Series of Views, Interior and Exterior of the Collegiate Chapel of St. George, at Windsor. London: 1805. V. 64

NASH, JOHN
The Artist Plantsman. London: 1976. V. 62
Bucks - Shell Guide. London: 1936. V. 62
English Garden Flowers. 1948. V. 67
The Wood Engravings of John Nash. Liverpool: 1987. V. 62; 64; 65; 67

NASH, JORGEN
Salvi Dylvo. Copenhagen: 1945. V. 62

NASH, JOSEPH
The Mansions of England in the Olden Time.... London: 1869. V. 65
A Practical Treatise on British Song Birds.... London: 1824. V. 62; 66
A Series of Views Illustrative of Pugin's Examples of Gothic Architecture.... London: 1830. V. 62

NASH, N. RICHARD
The Rainmaker. New York: 1955. V. 66

NASH, OGDEN
Four Prominent So and Sos. New York: 1934. V. 62; 66

NASH, OGDEN continued
Hard Lines and Others. London: 1932. V. 64
The Private Dining Room and Other New Verses. Boston: 1953. V. 62
You Can't Get There From Here. Boston;: 1984. V. 64

NASH, PAUL
Dear Mercia: Paul Nash Letters to Mercia Oakley. Denby Dale: 1991. V. 65
Dear Mercia: Paul Nash Letters to Mercia Oakley. London: 1991. V. 64
Monster Field: a Discovery Recorded by Paul Nash. Oxford: 1946. V. 66
A Private World. London: 1978. V. 62
Room and Book. London: 1932. V. 66
The Wood Engravings. Woodbridge: 1997. V. 62; 65; 67

NASH, RAY
Durer's 1511 Drawing of a Press and Printer. Cambridge: 1947. V. 62; 63; 64; 66

NASHE, THOMAS
Works.... Oxford: 1966. V. 62; 63; 65

NASMITH, JOSEPH
Modern Cotton Spinning Machinery, its Principles and Construction. Manchester: 1890. V. 63

NASMYTH, JAMES
James Nasmyth, Engineer: an Autobiography. London: 1883. V. 64

NASR, SEYYED HOSSEIN
Islamic Science; an Illustrated Study. United Kingdom: 1976. V. 66

NASSAU, W. SENIOR
Journals, Conversations and Essays Relating to Ireland. 1868. V. 62

NASTI, MAURO
Schmied. Schio: 1991. V. 64

NATALIBUS, PETRUS DE
Catalogus Sanctorum et Gestorum Eorum. Vicenza: 1493. V. 64
Catalogus Sanctorum et Gestorum Eorum. Strasbourg: 1513. V. 64

NATES, J. C.
Bath, Illustrated by a Series of Views.... London: 1806. V. 64

NATHAN, GEORGE JEAN
The Theatre Book of the Year. A Record and an Interpretation. New York: 1943-1951. V. 63; 64

NATHAN, LEONARD
The Matchmaker's Lament and Other Astonishments. Northampton: 1967. V. 65

NATHAN, ROBERT
Autumn. New York: 1921. V. 62
A Cedar Box and Other Poems. Indianapolis: 1929. V. 62

NATION, CARRY A.
The Use and Need of the Life of Carry A. Nation. Topeka: 1909. V. 63

NATIONAL AMERICAN KENNEL CLUB
Stud Book. Volume I. 1878. St. Louis: 1879. V. 67

NATIONAL BOOK LEAGUE
The Book Nos. 1-6 (complete). Cambridge: 1955. V. 62

NATIONAL CONFERENCE OF CHARITIES AND CORRECTIONS
Proceedings of the National Conference of Charities and Corrections. Boston and London: 1901. V. 66

NATIONAL COUNCIL OF JEWISH WOMEN
Proceedings of the First Convention, Held at New York, November 15, 16, 17, 18 and 19, 1896. Philadelphia: 1897. V. 65

NATIONAL GALLERY OF ART
Early Italian Engravings from the National Gallery of Art. Washington: 1973. V. 62
Jacques Callot, Prints and Related Drawings. Washington: 1975. V. 62

THE NATIONAL Gallery of Pictures by the Great Masters, Presented by Individuals or Purchased by Grant of Parliament. London: 1840?. V. 62

NATIONAL LIVESTOCK ASSOCIATION
Proceedings of the Fourth Annual Convention of the National Livestock Association, Salt Lake City, January 15, 16, 17 and 18, 1901. Denver: 1901. V. 67
Proceedings of the Second Annual Convention of the National Livestock Association, Denver, Colorado, January 24, 25, 26 and 27. Denver: 1899. V. 67
Proceedings of the Third Annual Convention of the National Livestock Association, Fort Worth, Texas, Jan. 16, 17, 18 and 19. With an Appendix on the Great Resources of Denver and Colorado. Denver: 1900. V. 66

NATIONAL LOCK CO.
Furniture Trimmings Catalog #192. Rockford: 1950. V. 64

NATIONAL MARITIME MUSEUM
Catalogue of the Library, Volume I. Voyages and Travel. London: 1968. V. 65

THE NATIONAL Orange and Protestant Minstrel: Being a Collection of Constitutional and Protestant Songs, Hymns, Toasts, Sentiments and Recitations, Original and Select. Bradford: 1852. V. 66

NATIONAL Park Seminary (Inc.), a Junior College for Young Women 1934-1935. Forest Glen: 1935. V. 65

NATIONAL PHYSICAL LABORATORY
Collected Researches. London: 1905-1935. V. 63

NATIONAL RADIO INSTITUTE
N.R.I. Service Manual. Washington: 1946. V. 63

NATIONAL RAILROAD CONVENTION
Proceedings of the National Railroad Convention...in Regard to the Construction of the Texas and Pacific Railway as a Southern Trans-Continental Line from the Mississippi Valley to the Pacific Ocean. St. Louis: 1875. V. 65

NATIONAL STOCK GROWERS CONVENTION
Proceedings of the First.... Denver: 1898. V. 67

NATIONAL UNION OF WOMEN WORKERS OF GREAT BRITAIN AND IRELAND
Women Workers. The Official Report of the Conference Held at Croydon on October 26th, 27th, 28th and 29th 1897. Croydon: 1897. V. 65

NATKIN, MARCEL
Photography and the Art of Seeing. London: 1935. V. 65
Photography and the Art of Seeing. London: 1948. V. 63

NATTES, JOHN CLAUDE
Bath Illustrated by a Series of Views. Bristol: 1806. V. 67
Bath Illustrated by a Series of Views. London: 1806. V. 66

NATUERLYKE Historie van de Couchenille, Beweezen Met Authentique Documenten. Amsterdam: 1729. V. 67

NATURAL History for Children.... London: 1819. V. 64

THE NATURAL History of Birds.... London: 1791. V. 67

THE NATURAL History of Quadrupeds and Cetaceous Animals.... Bungay: 1811. V. 62

NATURAL HISTORY SOCIETY OF GLASGOW
The Glasgow Naturalist. Glasgow: 1909-1926. V. 66
Proceedings and Transactions of the Natural History Society of Glasgow. New Series Volumes 1-8. Glasgow: 1887-1911. V. 63

NATURAL Obelisk in Thunder Mountain. Chicago: 1903. V. 63

THE NATURE and Making of Papyrus. Arkston, Ash, Yorks: 1973. V. 63

NATZLER, GERTRUDE
Cermaics. Los Angeles: 1968. V. 64

NATZLER, OTTO
Gertrud and Otto Natzler Ceramics. Catalog of the Collection of Mrs. Leonard M. Sperry and a Monograph by Otto Natzler. Los Angeles: 1968. V. 65

NAUBERT, CHRISTIANE BENEDIETE EUGENIE
Herman of Unna: a Series of Adventures of the Fifteenth Century, In Which the Proceedings of the Secret Tribunal Under the Emperors Winceslaus and Sigismond, Are Delineated.... London: 1794. V. 65

NAUDE, GABRIEL
Instructions Concerning Erecting of a Library; presented to My Lord the President De Mesme. Cambridge: 1903. V. 66

NAUGERIUS, ANDREAS
Oratoris et Poetae Clarissimi Opera Omnia.... Patavii: 1718. V. 67

NAUGHTON, BILL
Pony Boy. London: 1946. V. 64

NAUMANN, EMIL
The History of Music. London: 1882-1886. V. 65

NAUMBURG, MARGARET
Schizophrenic Art: Its Meaning in Psychotherapy. London: 1950. V. 65
Schizophrenic Art: Its Meaning in Psychotherapy. New York: 1950. V. 65

NAUNTON, ROBERT
The Court of Queen Elizabeth.... London: 1814. V. 67

NAVA, MICHAEL
Goldenboy. Boston: 1988. V. 66
The Little Death. Boston: 1986. V. 66
The Little Death. Boston: 1988. V. 63

NAVAL Anecdotes Illustrating the Character of British Seamen. London: 1806. V. 64

NAVAL OBSERVATORY LIBRARY
Catalog of the Naval Observatory Library, Washington, D.C. Boston: 1976. V. 63

NAVIER, L. M. H.
Rapport a Monsieur Becquey, Conseiller d'Etat, Directeur General des Ponts et Chaussees et des Mines; et memoire sur les Ponts Suspendus.... Paris: 1830. V. 65

NAVY Nonsense: A Companion to Khaki Komedy. Chicago: 1918. V. 65

NAXAGORAS, E.
Ausfuhrliche Beschreibung der un Weit Zwickau in Meissen zu Niederhohendorff und Anderer Umliegenden Orten Gefundene Goldishen Sande. 1696. V. 62
Chymischer Oder Alchymistischer Particular, das ist Treuer Unterricht vom Gold-und Silber-Machen. Rostock: 1706. V. 63

NAYLER, GEORGE
A Collection of Coats of Arms Borne by The Nobilitity of the Country of Glocester. London: 1792. V. 66
The Coronation of His Most Sacred Majesty King George the Fourth. London: 1824. V. 67
The Coronation of His Most Sacred Majesty King George the Fourth.... London: 1839. V. 62

NAYLOR, GLORIA
Linden Hills. New York: 1985. V. 66
Mama Day. New York: 1988. V. 66
The Women of Brewster Place. New York: 1982. V. 62; 64; 66; 67

NAYLOR, LEONARD E.
Dachshunds. London: 1945. V. 67

NAYLOR, PHYLLIS REYNOLDS
Shiloh. New York: 1991. V. 65

NAYLOR, W.
Trades Waste: Its Treatment and Utilisation. London: 1902. V. 63

NEAD, PETER
Primitive Christianity, or a Vindication of the Word of God. Staunton: 1834. V. 66

NEAL, AVON
Pigs and Eagles. North Brookfield: 1978. V. 66

NEAL, BASIL LLEWELIN
A Son of the American Revolution. Washington: 1914. V. 62

NEAL, BILL
The Last Frontier - the Story of Hardeman Country. N.P: 1966. V. 67

NEAL, DANIEL
The History of the Puritans or Protestant Non-Conformists from the Reformation to the...Act of Toleration in the Reign of King William and Queen Mary in the Year 1688.... Bath: 1793-1797. V. 62

NEAL, DOROTHY JENSEN
Captive Mountain Waters. El Paso: 1961. V. 65
The Cloud-Climbing Railroad. Alamogordo: 1966. V. 66

NEAL, JOHN
Battle of Niagara, a Poem Without Notes, and Goldau, or the Maniac Harper. Baltimore: 1818. V. 63
Charcoal Sketches; or, Scenes in a Metropolis. Philadelphia: 1838. V. 62

NEAL, JOSEPH C.
In Town and About or Pencillings and Pennings. Philadelphia: 1843. V. 66

NEAL, L. W.
Pressed Glass Slat Dishes of the Lacy Period 1825-1850. Philadelphia: 1962. V. 63

NEAL, W. KEITH
Forsyth and Co., Patent Gunmakers. London: 1969. V. 62; 67

NEALE, EDWARD VANSITTART
Labour and Capital. A Lecture Delivered by Request of the Society for Promoting Working-Men's Associations, at the Marylebone Literary and Scientific Institution, on the 29th of March. London: 1852. V. 64

NEALE, ERSKINE
The Living and the Dead. London: 1827. V. 67
Whychcotte of St. John's. Or, the Court, the Camp, the Quarter-Deck, and the Cloister. London: 1833. V. 67

NEALE, HANNAH
Amusement Hall; or, an Easy Introduction to the Attainment of Useful Knowledge. London: 1794. V. 64

NEALE, JAMES
The Abbey Church of Saint Alban: Hertfordshire. London: 1878. V. 66

NEALE, JOHN MASON
Good King Wenceslas. Birmingham: 1895. V. 63; 64; 66

NEALE, JOHN PRESTON
The History and Antiquities of the Abbey Church of St. Peter, Westminster.... London: 1818-1823. V. 67
Views of the Most Interesting Collegiate and Parochial Churches in Great Britain.... London: 1824. V. 64

NEALE, WALTER
The Betrayal: a Novel. New York: 1910. V. 65
The Sovereignty of the States.... New York: 1910. V. 63

NEALE, WILLIAM JONSON
Gentleman Jack. London: 1837. V. 67

NEBENZAHL, KENNETH
Maps of the Holy Land: Images of Terra Sancta through Two Millennia. New York: 1986. V. 65

NEBRASKA: a Guide to the Cornhusker State. New York: 1939. V. 65

THE NECESSITY of Some of the Positive Institutions of Ch---ty Consider'd. London: 1731. V. 66

NECKER, CLAIRE
Four Centuries of Books, a Bibliography 1570-1970. Metuchen: 1972. V. 63

NECKER, JACQUES
De l'Administration des Finances de la France. N.P: 1785. V. 63
State of the Finances of France, Laid Before the King, by Mr. Necker, Director-General of the Finances, in the Month of January 1781. London: 1781. V. 62
Sur le Compte Rendu au Roi en 1781. Paris: 1788. V. 62
A Treatise on the Administration of the Finances of France. London: 1785. V. 62

NECKER DE SAUSSURE, ALBERTINE ADRIENNE, MME DE.
L'Education Progressive ou Etude du Cours de la Vie. Paris: 1828-1838. V. 67

NEEDHAM, H.
Croquet with Illustrations by the author, with the Revised Laws of 1902. London: 1902. V. 62

NEEDHAM, J. G.
A Handbook of the Dragonflies of North America. Springfield: 1929. V. 66

NEEDHAM, JOSEPH
Biochemistry and Morphogenesis. Cambridge: 1942. V. 65
Clerks and Craftsmen in China and the West. Lectures and Addresses on the History of Science and Technology. Cambridge: 1970. V. 65
Science and Civilisation in China. Cambridge: 1965-1971. V. 62
Science and Civilisation in China. Volume 4. Physics and Physical Technology. Part II. Mechanical Engineering. Cambridge: 1965. V. 62

NEEDHAM, P.
Twelve Centuries of Bookbindings 400-1600. New York: 1979. V. 62

NEEDHAM, RAYMOND
Somerset House Past and Present. London: 1905. V. 66

NEEL, JANET
Death of a Partner. London: 1991. V. 66
Death on Site. London: 1989. V. 66
Death's Bright Angel. London: 1988. V. 66

NEELY, BARBARA
Blanche on the Lam. New York: 1992. V. 62; 65

NEELY, F. TENNYSON
Greater American - Heroes, Battles, Camps - Dewey Islands, Cuba and Puerto Rico. New York: 1898. V. 66

NEESE, GEORGE M.
Three Years in the Confederate Horse Artillery. New York: 1911. V. 62

NEESEN, VICTOR
Dr. Neesen's Book on Wheeling. New York: 1899. V. 65

NEFF, IVAN C.
Dictionary of Oriental Rugs with a Monograph on Indentification by Weave. New York: 1977. V. 63

NEFF, ROBERT
Blues. Boston: 1975. V. 66

NEHRLING, HENRY
Our Native Birds of Song and Beauty.... Milwaukee: 1893-1896. V. 62; 66
Tho Plant World in Florida. New York: 1933. V. 66

NEIGHBOUR, ALFRED
The Apiary; or, Bees, Bee-Hives and Bee Culture.... London: 1865. V. 65
The Apiary; or, Bees, Beehives and Bee Culture. London: 1878. V. 62

NEIHARDT, JOHN C.
Black Elk Speaks, Being the Life Story of a Holy Man of the Ogalala Sioux Retold To.... New York: 1932. V. 65; 67

NEIL, SAMUEL
The Home Teacher. London: 1886-1888. V. 64

NEILL, EDWARD
Dahkotah Land and Dahkotah Life with the History of the Fur Trade of the Extreme Northwest During the French and British Dominions. Philadelphia: 1859. V. 62
History of Rice County Including Explorers and Pioneeers of Minnesota...Also Sioux Massacre of 1862. Minneapolis: 1882. V. 67
History of Washington County and the St. Croix Valley, Including the Explorers and Pioneers of Minnesota. Minnesota: 1881. V. 62

NEILL, JOHN
Outlines of the Arteries With Short Description. Philadelphia: 1945. V. 66; 67

NEILL, JOHN R.
Lucky Bucky in Oz. Chicago: 1942. V. 63

NEILSON, HARRY B.
The Puppy Dogs' Dance. London: 1910. V. 63
The Pussy-Cat Hunt. London: 1910. V. 63
Uncle Jumbo's Party. London: 1910. V. 63

NEISON, FRANCIS G. P.
Observations on the Efficient Valuation of Friendly Societies. London: 1885. V. 66

NELIGAN, J. MOORE
Atlas of Cutaneous Diseases. Philadelphia: 1859. V. 65
Atlas of Cutaneous Diseases. Philadelphia: 1867. V. 65

NELIGAN, WILLIAM C.
An Account of Ancient Glass Beads and Cylinders, Found on the Strand of Dunworley Bay, Co. Cork. London: 1858. V. 65

NELSON, B.
Galapagos Island of Birds. New York: 1968. V. 67
The Sulidae. Gannets and Boobies. London: 1978. V. 67

NELSON, E. C.
An Irish Flower Garden Replanted. 1998. V. 63
An Irish Flower Garden Replanted. London: 1998. V. 62

NELSON, E. T.
Herbarium and Plant Description. Boston: 1889. V. 63

NELSON, EDNA CHAMBERLAIN
The Magnificent Percheron. Los Angeles: 1963. V. 66

NELSON, EDWARD
The Eskimo About Bering Strait. New York: 1971. V. 62

NELSON, EDWARD W.
Report Upon Natural History Collections Made in Alaska Between the Years 1877 and 1881. Washington: 1887. V. 62; 64; 65

NELSON, GEORGE
George Nelson on Design. New York: 1979. V. 62

NELSON, HARRY B.
An Animal ABC. London: 1901. V. 65

NELSON, HENRY LOOMIS
Uniforms of the United States Army. New York: 1959. V. 63

NELSON, J. B.
Sulidae: Gannets and Boobies. Oxford: 1978. V. 63; 64; 67

NELSON, JOHN
Memoirs of the Late Mr. John Nelson, of Bristol, One of the First Methodist Preachers in Connection with the Late Mr. John Wesley. Birmingham: 1807. V. 64

NELSON, MARY CARROLL
The Legendary Artists of Taos. New York: 1980. V. 63; 64

NELSON, O. N.
History of the Scandinavians and Successful Scandinavians in the United States. Minneapolis: 1900. V. 64

NELSON, PAUL
Cargo. Iowa City: 1972. V. 66

NELSON, ROBERT
An Address to Persons of Quality and Estate. London: 1715. V. 62
An Address to Persons of Quality and Estate. Dublin: 1752. V. 67
The Life of Dr. George Bull, Lae Lord Bishop of St. David's. London: 1714. V. 63

NELSON, T.
The English Lakes. London: 1859. V. 65

NELSON, T. H.
The Birds of Yorkshire. 1907. V. 66; 67

NELSON, W.
Fishing in Eden. 1922. V. 67

NELSON, WILLIAM
Fifty Years of Historical Work in New Jersey. Paterson: 1898. V. 63; 66
History of Paterson and Its Environs. New York: 1920. V. 63; 66
Illustrated Catalogue of New Jersey Memorabilia and Rare and Valuable Books and Documents Comprising the Extensive Library of the Late William Nelson of New Jersey, to be Sold.... New York: 1915. V. 63; 66
The Laws Concerning Game. Of Hunting, Hawking, Fishing and Fowling, &c.... London: 1753. V. 62; 63
The Laws of England Concerning the Game of Hunting, Hawking, Fishing and Fowling &c. London: 1736. V. 64
Lex Maneriorum; or, the Law and Customs of England, Relating to Manors and Lords of Manors, Their Stewards, Deputies, Tenants and Others, viz. Of the Lords Right to Deodands, Felons, Goods...Of their Privileges of Their Tenants.... London: 1733. V. 65
The New Jersey Coast in Three Centuries. New York: 1902. V. 66
The Office and Authority of a Justice of Peace.... London: 1736. V. 63
Records of the Paterson Fire Association 1821-1854. Paterson: 1894. V. 63; 66

NEMEROV, HOWARD
The Melodramatists. New York: 1949. V. 65
Poets on Poetry. London: 1966. V. 65
Stories, Fables and Other Diversions. Boston: 1971. V. 62

NEMESIUS, BISHOP
The Nature of Man. London: 1636. V. 62; 66

NEMIROVITCH-DANTCHENKO, VLADIMIR
My Life in the Russian Theatre. London: 1937. V. 64

NEPOS, CORNELIUS
Corneli Nepotis Vitae Excelentium Imperatorum.... 1667. V. 65
Cornelius Nepos De Excelentibus Viris.... Amstelaedami: 1746. V. 65
Vitae Excellentium Imperatorum. Lugduni Batavorum: 1658. V. 64; 66

NERI, ANTONIO
Art de la Verrerie, de Neri, Merret et Kunckel, Auquel on a Ajoute Le Sol Sine Veste D'Orschall: L'Helioscopium Viendi Sine Veste solem Chymicum.... Paris: 1759. V. 65

NERNST, WALTER
Theoretical Chemistry from the Standpoint of Avogadro's Rule and Thermodynamics. London: 1923. V. 63

NERSESSIAN, SIRARPIE DER
Armenian Manuscripts in the Freer Gallery of Art. Washington: 1963. V. 62; 63

NERUDA, PABLO
Bestiary/Bestiario. New York: 1965. V. 65
Selected Poems. London: 1970. V. 62
Tercera Residencia. Buenos Aires: 1947. V. 62
We Are Many. London: 1967. V. 64

NESBIT, EDITH
The Book of Dragons. London: 1901. V. 63
The Enchanted Castle. London: 1907. V. 66
Hardings' Luck. London: 1909. V. 65
The House of Arden. London: 1908. V. 62
The Lark. London: 1922. V. 64
The Magic World. London: 1912. V. 62
The New Treasure Seekers. London: 1904. V. 63; 66
Nine Unlikely Tales for Children. London: 1901. V. 65
A Pomander of Verse. London: 1895. V. 64
The Railway Children. London: 1906. V. 64
The Story of the Amulet. London: 1906. V. 65
The Story of the Treasure Seekers - Being the Adventures of Bastable Children in Search of a Fortune. London: 1899. V. 64
Wings and the Child or the Building of Magic Cities. London: 1913. V. 63
The Wonderful Garden or the Three C's. London: 1911. V. 65

NESS, ELIOT
The Untouchables. New York: 1957. V. 65

NESS, EVALINE
Sam, Bangs and Moonshine. New York: 1966. V. 65

NETHERSOLE-THOMPSON, DESMOND
The Dotterel. London: 1973. V. 62
The Greenshank. London: 1951. V. 62

NETTER, FRANK H.
The Ciba Collection of Medical Illustrations. Summit: 1970-1979. V. 63

NETTLEFOLD, FREDERICK JOHN
Catalogue of the Pictures and Drawings in the Collection of Frederick John Nettlefold. London: 1933-1938. V. 67

NETTLEFOLD, J. S.
Practical Housing. Letchworth: 1908. V. 64

NETTLEINGHAME, F. T.
Polperro Proverbs and Others. Polperro: 1927. V. 65

NETTLETON, THOMAS
A Treatise on Virtue and Happiness. London: 1736. V. 63
A Treatise on Virtue and Happiness. London: 1751. V. 62; 67

NEUBERG, FREDERIC
Glass in Antiquity. London: 1949. V. 62

NEUBURG, VICTOR B.
A Green Garland. Bedford: 1908. V. 66

NEUBURGRE, MAX
Die Medizin im Flavius Josephus. Bad Reichenhall: 1919. V. 63

NEUER, R.
Ukiyo-E; 250 Years of Japanese Art. New York: 1979. V. 62; 65

NEUHAUS, E.
William Keith: the Man and the Artist. Berkeley: 1938. V. 62; 65

NEUMANN, A. H.
Elephant Hunting in East Equatorial Africa. 1898. V. 63; 64

NEUMANN, E.
Bauhaus and Bauhaus People: Personal Opinions and Recollections of Former Bauhaus Members and Their Contemporaries. New York: 1970. V. 65

NEUMANN, GEORGE C.
The History of Weapons of the American Revolution. London: 1967. V. 67

NEUMANN, N.
Avifauna Africana. Johannesburg: 1965. V. 65

NEUMEYER, PETER F.
Donald and the.... Reading: 1969. V. 63; 66

NEVADA Historical Papers 1913-1916. Carson City: 1917. V. 64; 67

NEVADA HISTORICAL SOCIETY
First Biennial Report of the Nevada Historical Society 1907-1908. Carson City: 1909. V. 64

NEVADA NED
Mexican Bill, The Cowboy Detective a Daring Horse Thief. Chicago: 1889. V. 66

NEVE, A.
The Tourist's Guide to Kashimir, Ladakh, Khardo &c. 1918. V. 66

NEVE, ERNEST F.
Beyond the Pir Panjal. 1912. V. 66; 67

NEVE, PHILIP
Cursory Remarks on Some of the Ancient Poets, Particularly Milton. London: 1789. V. 62

NEVE, RICHARD
The City and County Purchaser's and Builder's Dictionary.... London: 1736. V. 64

NEVILL, RALPH
Floreat Etons - Anecdotes and Memories of Eton College. London: 1911. V. 63
Old English Sporting Prints and Their History. London: 1923. V. 63
Old Sporting Prints. London: 1970. V. 67
Piccadilly to Pall Mall. London: 1908. V. 62

NEVILLE, A. W.
The History of Lamar County (Texas). Paris: 1937. V. 63
The Red River Then and Now. Paris: 1948. V. 63; 66

NEVILLE, GEORGE
Horses and Riding. London: 1877. V. 62

NEVILLE, HENRY
The Isle of Pines. Katoomba: 1991. V. 62; 64

NEVILLE, RICHARD
Playpower. London: 1970. V. 62

NEVILLE, RICHARD CORNWALLIS
Antiqua Explorata: Being the Result of Excavations Made...In and About the Roman Station at Chesterford, and Other Spots in the Vicinity of Audley End. Saffron Waldon: 1847. V. 63

NEVINS, ALLAN
Ford. New York: 1957-1963. V. 65
Fremont: the West's Greatest Adventurer.... New York and London: 1928. V. 62; 63; 67

NEVINS, FRANCIS M.
First You Dream Then You Die. New York: 1988. V. 67
Nightwebs. New York: 1971. V. 63

NEVINS, IRIS
Varieties of Spanish Marbling: a Handbook of Practical Instruction with Twelve Original Marbled Samples. N.P: 1991. V. 64

NEVINSON, C.
History of Stamford. Stamford: 1879. V. 66

NEVINSON, C. R. W.
Exodus A. D. - a Warning to Civilians. London: 1934. V. 62
Paint and Prejudice. London: 1937. V. 62

NEVINSON, HENRY WOOD
The Plea of Pan. New York: 1901. V. 67

NEVIZANUS, GIOVANNI
Sylvae Nuptiales, Ercelsum Iuriscoful.... Lyon: 1540. V. 65

A **NEW** Academy of Compliments; or, the Lover's Secretary.... London: 1760?. V. 66

THE **NEW** American Clerk's Magazine and Complete Practical Conveyancer. Hagers-town: 1806. V. 65

A **NEW** and Accurate Description of the Present Great Roads and the Principal Cross Roads of England and Wales. London: 1756. V. 66; 67

THE **NEW** and Complete Newgate Calendar; or, Malefactor's Universal Register. London: 1818. V. 63

NEW and General Biographical Dictionary.... London: 1784. V. 64

A **NEW** and Improved History and Description of the Tower of London.... London: 1827. V. 66

THE **NEW** Art of Memory, Founded Upon the Principles Taught by Gregor Von Feinagle.... London: 1812. V. 67

THE **NEW** Bedford Directory, Containing the City Register, a General Directory of the Citizens, and Special Directory of Trades, Professions, &c. New Bedford;: 1849. V. 62

A **NEW** Book of Natural History of Various British Birds; for the Amusement of Good Children. Chelmsford: 1820. V. 62

THE **NEW** Brunswick City and Business Directory. 1888. York: 1888. V. 63; 66

NEW Brunswick City Directory 1886-1887. New Brunswick: 1886. V. 63; 66

NEW Brunswick City Directory. 1893. New Brunswick: 1893. V. 66

NEW Brunswick City Directory 1897. New Brunswick: 1897. V. 63; 66

NEW Brunswick Directory for 1880-1881. New Brunswick: 1880. V. 63; 66

NEW Brunswick Directory for 1883-1884. New Brunswick: 1883. V. 63; 66

NEW BRUNSWICK
Population and Other Statistics of the Province of New Brunswick for the Year 1851, Printed by Order of the House of Assembly, Dated 3rd April 1852. Fredericton: 1852. V. 64

THE **NEW** Cabinet of Entertainment and Instruction. London: 1835. V. 66

NEW Campus Writing No. 2. New York: 1957. V. 63

NEW ENGLAND ANTI-IMPERIALIST LEAGUE
Liberty Poems: Inspired by the Crisis of 1898-1900. Boston: 1900. V. 65

NEW England Book of Fruits. Salem: 1847. V. 66

NEW ENGLAND SOCIETY OF NEW YORK
Seventy-First Anniversary Celebration of the New England Society of New York at Delmonico's Dec. 22 1876. New York: 1877. V. 65

NEW English Dramatists. Harmondsworth: 1959-1970. V. 66

NEW English Dramatists 14. Harmondsworth: 1970. V. 66

THE **NEW** Family Receipt Book.... London: 1824. V. 63

THE **NEW** Fiction. Urbana: 1974. V. 62

THE **NEW** Forget-Me-Not - a Calendar. London: 1929. V. 63; 65

A **NEW** Friendship's Garland. N.P: 1899. V. 64

THE **NEW** Gothic. New York: 1991. V. 65

NEW HAMPSHIRE. CONSTITUTION - 1792
Articles in Addition to an Amendment of the Constitution of the State of New Hampshire, Agreed to by the Convention of Said State and Submitted to the People Thereof for Their Approbation. Dover: 1792. V. 66

THE **NEW** Harrogate Guide; Being a Concise Description and History of What is Most Remarkable in that Neighbourhood, for Antiquity, Elegance or Rural Beauty.... Knaresborough: 1837. V. 67

THE **NEW** Harrogate Guide.... Harrogate. V. 65

NEW Hints, by an Old Professor, on the Art of Miniature Painting. London: 1837. V. 67

THE **NEW** Jamaica Almanack and Registr..for the Year...1788. Kingston: 1787. V. 62

NEW JERSEY
Index of Wills, Inventories, etc. in the Office of the Secretary of State Prior to 1901. Trenton: 1912-1913. V. 63
Index of Wills, Inventories, etc. in the Office of the Secretary of State Prior to 1901. Baltimore: 1969. V. 63
Index of Wills, Office of the Secretary of State, State of New Jersey 1750 to 1804 (1804 to 1830). Trenton: 1901. V. 63

NEW JERSEY. ARCHIVES
Archives of the State of New Jersey. Subset: Extracts from American Newspapers Relating to New Jersey 1704-1782. 1894-1923. V. 66
Archives of the State of New Jersey. Subset: Journal of the Governor and Council 1682-1775. Trenton: 1890-1893. V. 63; 66

NEW JERSEY. CHANCERY COURT
The Joint and Several Answers of Edwin A. Stevens, James Neilson and John R. Thomson, Defendants to the Bill of Complaint of John D. Hager, Complainant. N.P: 1847. V. 66

NEW JERSEY. CONSTITUTIONAL CONVENTION - 1844
Journal of the Proceedings of the Convention to Form a Constitution for the Government of the State of New Jersey.... Trenton: 1844. V. 66

NEW JERSEY. GENERAL ASSEMBLY - 1865
Debates in the Eighty-Ninth General Assembly of the State of New Jersey on the Bill to Ratify an Amendment to the Constitution of the United States. Trenton: 1865. V. 66

NEW JERSEY. GEOLOGICAL SURVEY - 1855
First Annual Report of the Geological Survey of the State of New Jersey for the Year 1854. Trenton: 1855. V. 66

NEW JERSEY. GEOLOGICAL SURVEY - 1878
Report on the Clay Deposits of Woodbridge, South Amboy and Other Places In New Jersey, Together with their Uses for Fire Brick, Pottery &c. Trenton: 1878. V. 66

NEW JERSEY. LAWS, STATUTES, ETC. - 1752
The Acts of the General Assembly of the Province of New Jersey, from the Time of the Surrender of the Government...to this Present Time...(with) The Acts of the General Assembly of the Province of New Jersey, from 1753.... Philadelphia: 1752. V. 63; 64

NEW JERSEY. LAWS, STATUTES, ETC. - 1758
The Grants, Concessions and Original Constitutions of the Province of New Jersey. The Acts Passed During the Proprietary Governments, and Other Material Transactions.... Philadelphia: 1758. V. 63; 64

NEW JERSEY. LAWS, STATUTES, ETC. - 1776
Acts of the General Assembly of the Province of New Jersey, from the Surrender of the Government to Queen Anne on the 17th Day of April in the Year of Our Lord 1702, to the 14th Day of Jan. 1776. Burlington: 1776. V. 63; 64; 66

NEW JERSEY. LAWS, STATUTES, ETC. - 1784
Acts of the Council and General Assembly of te State of New Jersey, from the Establishment of the Present Government and Declaration of Independence, to the End of...December 1783.... Trenton: 1784. V. 63; 66

NEW JERSEY. LAWS, STATUTES, ETC. - 1800
Laws of the State of New Jersey. Newark: 1800. V. 63; 66
Laws of the State of New Jersey, Revised.... New Brunswick: 1800. V. 63; 64; 66

NEW JERSEY. LAWS, STATUTES, ETC. - 1811
Laws of the State of New Jersey. Trenton: 1811. V. 63; 66

NEW JERSEY. LAWS, STATUTES, ETC. - 1832
Acts Relative to the Delaware and Raritan Canal Company and Camden and Amboy Rail Road and Transportation Company. Passed by the Legislature of the State of New Jersey. N.P: 1832. V. 63; 66

NEW JERSEY. LAWS, STATUTES, ETC. - 1840
Acts Relative to the Delaware and Raritan Canal Company and Camden and Amboy, Rail Road and Transportation Company, Passed by the Legislature of New Jersey. Princeton: 1840. V. 63; 66

NEW JERSEY. LAWS, STATUTES, ETC. - 1847
Statutes of the State of New Jersey. Trenton: 1847. V. 63; 66

NEW JERSEY. LAWS, STATUTES, ETC. - 1901-1950
Acts of the One Hundred and Twenty-Fifth-(One Hundred Seventy-Third) Legislature of the State of New Jersey. Trenton: 1901-1950. V. 63; 66

NEW JERSEY. LAWS, STATUTES, ETC. - 1911
Compiled Statutes of New Jersey. Newark: 1911. V. 66

NEW JERSEY. LEGISLATURE - 1865
Debates in the Eighty-Ninth General Assembly of the State of New Jersey, on the Bill to Ratify an Amendment to the Constitution of the United States. Trenton: 1865. V. 63

NEW JERSEY. LEGISLATURE - 1873
Manual of the Legislature. State of New Jersey. Ninety-Seventh Session...1873. Morristown: 1873. V. 63; 66

NEW JERSEY. LEGISLATURE - 1879
Manual of the One Hundred and Fourth Session of the Legislature of New Jersey 1880. Trenton: 1879. V. 66

NEW JERSEY. SECRETARY OF STATE - 1901
Index of Wills, Office of Secretary of State, State of New Jersey, 1705 to 1804 (1804-1830). Trenton: 1901. V. 66

NEW JERSEY. SECRETARY OF STATE - 1912-1913
Index of Wills, Inventories, Etc. in the Office of the Secretary of State Prior to 1901. Trenton: 1912-1913. V. 66

NEW JERSEY. STATE GEOLOGIST - 1888
Final Report of the State Geologist...Topography, Magnetism, Climate. Trenton: 1888. V. 66

NEW JERSEY. STATE GEOLOGIST - 1889
Final Report of the State Geologist: Mineralogy, Botany, Zoology. Trenton: 1889. V. 63; 66

NEW JERSEY. STATE GEOLOGIST - 1894
Report on Water-Supply, Water-Power, the Flow of Streams and Attendant Phenomena. Trenton: 1894. V. 66

THE NEW Jersey Freeman. Boonton: 1844-. V. 66

NEW JERSEY GEOLOGICAL SURVEY
First Annual Report of the Geological Survey of the State of New Jersey for the Year 1854. Trenton: 1855. V. 63
Report on the Clay Deposits of Woodbridge, South Amboy and Other Places in New Jersey, Together with their Uses for Fire Brick, Pottery &c. Trenton: 1878. V. 63

NEW JERSEY HISTORICAL SOCIETY
Proceedings of the New Jersey Historical Society. Newark: 1845-. V. 66
Proceedings of the New Jersey Historical Society. Newark: 1845-1950. V. 63
Proceedings of the New Jersey Historical Society. Newark: 1845-1986. V. 63
Proceedings of the New Jersey Historical Society. Newark: 1916-. V. 66
Proceedings of the New Jersey Historical Society. Volume III 1848-1849-(Volume X 1865-1866). Newark: 1849-1867. V. 66

THE NEW Jersey Preacher; or, Sermons on Plains and Practical Subjects. Trenton: 1813. V. 63; 66

NEW JERSEY RAILROAD & TRANSPORTATION CO.
Report of the Directors of the...to the Stockholders. With the Proceedings of the Annual Meeting June 4, 1857. Newark: 1857. V. 63

NEW Jersey Register, for the Year Eighteen Hundred and Thirty- Seven.... Trenton: 1837. V. 63; 66

THE NEW Jerusalem Church Repository for the Years 1817 and 1818. Volume I. Philadelphia: 1818. V. 63

NEW Jolly Jester, or Wit's Pocket Companion.... London: 1800. V. 62; 66

THE NEW Keepsake - a Christmas, New Year and Birthday Present for Persons of Both Sexes. London: 1931. V. 63

THE NEW Loyal and Patriotic Jester, or Complete Library of Fun.... London: 1800. V. 62; 66

A NEW Manual of Devotions. In Three Parts. 1802. V. 65

NEW Manual of Private Devotions: in Three Parts. Charleston: 1810. V. 64

NEW Market Day at V. M. I. N.P: 1903. V. 63

NEW MEXICO. CATTLE SANITARY BOARD - 1915
Brand Book of the State of New Mexico. Albuquerque: 1915. V. 64

NEW MEXICO. GOVERNOR - 1903
Report of the Governor of New Mexico for the Year Ending June 30, 1903. Washington: 1903. V. 63

NEW MEXICO. LAWS, STATUTES, ETC. - 1852
New Mexico. Letter from the Secretary of the Territory of New Mexico (Wm. S. Allen), Transmitting Copies of the Acts, Resolutions &c. of that Territory. Washington: 1852. V. 64

NEW MEXICO. LEGISLATURE - 1889
Acts of the Legislative Assembly of the Territory of New Mexico. Santa Fe: 1889. V. 62

NEW MEXICO. SURVEYOR-GENERAL - 1884
Report of the Surveyor-General of New Mexico on the Private Land Claim of the Town of Albuquerque. Washington: 1884. V. 64

NEW MEXICO. (TERRITORY) - 1863
Register of Volunteer Officers Head Quarters, Department of New Mexico General Orders 21. Santa Fe: 1863. V. 67

NEW MEXICO. (TERRITORY) - 1884
Official Reports of the Territory of New Mexico for the Years 1882 and 1883. Santa Fe: 1884. V. 66

NEW Mexico, a Guide to the Colorful State. New York: 1940. V. 67

NEW Mexico Brand Book 1915. Albuquerque: 1915. V. 63

NEW Mexico Statutes Annotated. Denver: 1915. V. 66

NEW Mexico - The Land of Opportunity - Offical Data on the Resources and Industries of New Mexico - The Sunshine State. Albuquerque: 1915. V. 63

A NEW Natural History: Intended as a Present for Good Boys and Girls. Otley: 1830. V. 62; 65

THE NEW Newgate Calendar, Containing the Remarkable Lives and Trials of Notorious Criminals, Past and Present. London: 1863-1865. V. 63

THE NEW Our Big Book. Chicago: 1951. V. 65

THE NEW Peerage, or Ancient and Present State of the Nobility of England, Scotland and Ireland.... London: 1778. V. 63

THE NEW Picture of Edinburgh. Edinburgh. V. 67

THE NEW Reading Made Easy; Being One of the Best Books Extant for Teaching the First Rudiments of Reading and Spelling. Lincoln: 1803. V. 64

NEW Readings of Old Authors. London: 1830-1835. V. 67

A NEW Riddle Book, or a Whetstone for Dull Wits. Derby: 1760-1790?. V. 64

NEW Road 1944 - New Directions in European Art and Letters. London: 1944. V. 65

THE NEW Robinson Crusoe. Cooperstown: 1838. V. 62

THE NEW Rupert Book (Annual for 1938). V. 67

NEW Scenes of Monkey Life. London: 1880. V. 65

THE NEW Seaman's Guide and Coaster's Companion. London: 1815. V. 65

THE NEW South Wales Calendar and General Post Office Directory 1833. Sydney: 1833. V. 66

NEW Stories. Oxford: 1935. V. 65

A NEW System of Agriculture, or, a Plain, Easy and Demonstrative Method of Speedily Growing Rich.... London: 1755. V. 63

THE NEW Universal Mould Book Containing Latest Styles of Mouldings... Rails, Balusters and Newel Posts.... Chicago: 1886. V. 66

THE NEW Universal Parish Officer. London: 1774. V. 62

A NEW Valentine Writer for Ladies and Gentlemen.... Newcastle. V. 62

THE NEW Vocal Enchantress. London: 1788. V. 62

NEW YORK. (CITY)
Manual of the Corporation of the City of New York. New York: 1865. V. 65
Manual of the Corporation of the City of New York. New York: 1866. V. 65
Regulations for the Day and Night Police of the City of New York, with Instructions as to the Legal Powers and Duties of Policemen. New York: 1845. V. 64
Report and Proceedings of the Senate Committee Appointed to Investigate the Police Department of the City of New York. Albany: 1895. V. 65

NEW YORK. (STATE)
Annual Report of the Canal Commissioners of the State of New York 1875. Albany: 1875. V. 65
Names of Persons for Whom Marriage Licences Were Issued by the Secretary of the Province of New York, Previous to 1784. Albany: 1860. V. 65

NEW YORK. (STATE). CONSTITUTION - 1822
Constitution of the State of New York, Adopted in Convention, November 10th, 1821. New York: 1822. V. 62

NEW YORK ACADEMY OF MEDICINE
Catalogue of an Exhibition of Early and Later Medical Americana. New York: 1926. V. 67

THE NEW York Book of Poetry. New York: 1837. V. 62

THE NEW York Book of Prices for Manufacturing Cabinet and Chair Work. (with) Additional Revised Prices. New York: 1834. V. 64

NEW YORK CITY HUMANE SOCIETY
A Report of a Committee...Appointed to Inquire Into the Number of Tavern Licenses; the Manner of Granting Them.... New York: 1810. V. 64

THE NEW York Cries. New York: 1835. V. 64

NEW YORK FIRE DEPARTMENT BENEVOLENT ASSOCIATION
Official Year Book, New York Fire Department Benovolent Association, City of New York. New York: 1915. V. 63

NEW YORK HISTORICAL SOCIETY
Report of the Committee of the New York Historical Society, on a National Name March 31, 1845. New York: 1845. V. 62

NEW YORK ODONTOLOGICAL SOCIETY
Transactions of.... Philadelphia: 1899. V. 66

A NEW York Portfolio: 14 Poets, 1 Artist. Highlands: 1958. V. 63

NEW YORK PUBLIC LIBRARY
The Arents Collection of Books in Parts and Associated Literature, a Complete Check-List. New York: 1957. V. 63
Calendar of the Emmet Collection of Manuscripts, Etc. Relating to American History. New York: 1900. V. 66

NEW YORK SOCIETY LIBRARY
The Charter, Bye-Laws and Names of the Members of the New York Society Library; with a Catalogue of the Books Belonging to the Said Library. New York: 1793. V. 62

NEW YORK YACHT CLUB
Constitution for the Government of the New York Yacht Club. New York: 1861. V. 64

NEWALL, D. J. F.
The Highlands of Central India. 1887. V. 63; 64; 66; 67

NEWALL, J. T.
Hog-Hunting in the East and Other Sports. London: 1867. V. 67

NEWALL, R. S., & SON
Wire Ropes. Washington: 1897. V. 66

NEWARK
Proceedings Commemorative of the Settlement of Newark, New Jersey, On Its Two Hundredth Anniversary. Newark: 1866. V. 66

THE NEWARK Anniversary Poems. New York: 1917. V. 63; 66

NEWARK INDUSTRIAL EXHIBITION
Report and Catalogue of the First Exhibition of Newark Industries, Exclusively 1872. Newark: 1882. V. 66

NEWBERRY, CLARE TURLAY
April's Kittens. New York: 1940. V. 63
Babette. New York: 1937. V. 63
Herbert the Lion. New York: 1939. V. 64
The Kittens' ABC. New York: 1946. V. 64
Mittens. New York: 1936. V. 62
Pandora. New York: 1944. V. 64; 65
Smudge. New York: 1948. V. 64

NEWBERRY, JOHN
Arithmetic Made Familiar and Easy to Younge Gentlemen and Ladies. London: 1788. V. 62

NEWBERRY, JOHN S.
Fossil Fishes and Fossil Plants of the Triassic Rocks of New Jersey and the Connecticut Valley. 1888. V. 65; 66

NEWBERRY LIBRARY
A Keepsake for the Exhibition Giovanni Mardersteig's Officina Bodoni. Chicago: 1981. V. 62

NEWBERY, JOHN
The Art of Poetry on a New Plan.... London: 1762. V. 62
Newbery's Spelling Dictionary of the English Language on a New Plan for the Use of Young Gentlemen, Ladies and Foreigners. London: 1806. V. 64
The Newtonian System of Philosophy Explained by Familiar Objects.... Philadelphia: 1808. V. 66
Rhetoric Made Familiar and Easy to Young Gentlemen and Ladies.... London: 1769. V. 62

NEWBOLT, HENRY
Drake's Drum and Other Songs of the Sea. London: 1914. V. 67
The Story of the Oxfordshire and Buckinghamshire Light Infantry. London: 1915. V. 66

NEWBROUGH, JOHN B.
Oahspe: a New Bible in the Words of Jehovih and His Angel Ambassadors. New York: 1882. V. 66

NEWBY, ERIC
The Last Grain Race. London: 1956. V. 63

NEWBY, P. H.
A Step to Silence. London: 1952. V. 67

NEWCASTLE, THOMAS PELHAM HOLLES, DUKE OF
The Duke of Newcastle's Letter, by His Majesty's Order, to Monsieur Michell, the King of Prussia's Secretary of the Embassy in Answer to the Memorial and Other Papers, Deliver'd by Monsieur Michell, to Duke of Newcastle on the 23rd of November.... London: 1753. V. 65; 66

NEWCASTLE, WILLIAM CAVENDISH, MARQUIS OF
The Phanseys...Addressed to Margaret Lucas, and Her Letters in Reply. London: 1956. V. 67

NEWCOMB, F. JOHNSON
Navajo Omens and Taboos. Santa Fe. 1940. V. 64

NEWCOMB, RAYMOND LEE
Our Lost Explorers: the Narrative of the Jeannette Arctic Expedition, as Related by the Survivors...Last Records.... Hartford: 1888. V. 62

NEWCOMB, REXFORD
Mediterranean Domestic Architecture in the United States. Cleveland: 1928. V. 62; 67

NEWCOMB, W. W.
Indian Tribes of Texas. Waco: 1971. V. 66

NEWCOMBE, C. F.
The First Circumnavigation of Vancouver Island. Victoria: 1914. V. 67

NEWCOMBE, SAMUEL PROUT
Little Henry's Holiday at the Great Exhibition. London: 1851. V. 63

A NEWE Book of Copies 1574. London: 1959. V. 63

NEWELL, GORDON
The H. W. Mc Curdy Marine History of the Pacific Northwest. 1966- 1976. Seattle: 1977. V. 64; 66

NEWELL, HOMER E.
High Altitude Rocket Research. New York: 1953. V. 67

NEWELL, PETER
The Hole Book. New York: 1908. V. 63; 65; 67
Pictures and Rhymes. New York: 1899. V. 66
The Slant Book. New York: 1910. V. 63
Topsys and Turveys. New York: 1893. V. 64; 65; 66
Topsys and Turvys - Number 2. New York: 1894. V. 64

NEWELL, ROBERT
Robert Newell's Memoranda: Travels in the Territorie of Missourie.... Portland: 1959. V. 63; 64; 66

NEWENHAM, THOMAS
View of the Natural, Political and Commercial Circumstances of Ireland. 1809. V. 62; 65

THE NEWEST Keepsake for 1840. Norwch (sic): 1840. V. 64

NEWFOUNDLAND.. Sep. 1960. V. 64

NEWFOUNDLAND
Report Upon the Inspection of Protestant Schools in Newfoundland for the Year 1861. St. John's: 1862. V. 64

THE NEWGATE Calendar, Containing the Lives and Characters of the Most Notorious House-Breakers, Highwaymen, Thieves, Robbers, Murderers, Pirates, &c. Derby: 1845. V. 63

NEWHALL, BEAUMONT
The History of Photography from 1839 to the Present Day. New York: 1949. V. 63
William H. Jackson. Fort Worth: 1974. V. 67

NEWHALL, NANCY
Ansel Adams, Photographs 1923-1963. Washington: 1963. V. 66

NEWHAM, WILLIAM
Essay on Superstition: Being an Inquiry into the Effects of Physical Influence on the Mind, in the Production of Dreams, Vision, Ghosts.... London: 1830. V. 65

NEWHOUSE, A.
The Trapper's Guide.... Wallingford: 1867. V. 66

NEWHOUSE, S.
The Trapper's Guide. 1869. V. 67

NEWHOUSE, V.
Wallace K. Harrison, Architect. New York: 1989. V. 65

NEWKIRK, ROLAND W.
Skylab: a Chronology. Washington: 1978. V. 66

NEWLAND, HENRY
The Erne, Its Legends and Its Fly-Fishing. London: 1851. V. 62

NEWLAND, JANE
A Short Account of the Life and Death of Jane Newland, of Dublin, Who Departed This Life, October 22, 1789. London: 1790. V. 64

NEWLANDS, JAMES
The Carpenter and Joiner's Assistant: Being a Comprehensive Treatise on the Selection, Preparation, and Strength of Materials and the Mechanical Principles of Framing.... London: 1887-1880. V. 66

NEWLANDS, JOHN A. R.
On the Discovery of the Periodic Law and on Relations Among the Atomic Weights. London: 1884. V. 65

NEWMAN, BERNARD
The Cavalry Went Through. London: 1930. V. 64

NEWMAN, CHARLES
The Art of Sylvia Plath - a Symposium. London: 1970. V. 65

NEWMAN, CHARLES L. NORRIS
Matabeleland and How We Got It. London: 1895. V. 62

NEWMAN, DORA LEE
Marion Co. in the Making. Fairmont: 1917. V. 63

NEWMAN, FRANCES
The Short Story's Mutations. New York: 1924. V. 62

NEWMAN, FRANCIS WILLIAM
Anglo-Saxon Abolition of Negro Slavery. London: 1889. V. 64; 67
An Appeal to the Middle Classes on the Urgent Necessity of Numerous Radical Reforms, Financial and Organic. London: 1848. V. 66
Europe of the Near Future. London: 1871. V. 67

NEWMAN, J. A.
The Auobiography of an Old Fashioned Boy. Oklahoma City: 1923. V. 62; 65

NEWMAN, J. S.
Southern Gardener's Practical Manual. 1906. V. 64

NEWMAN, JACQUELINE M.
Chinese Cookbooks. New York: 1987. V. 64

NEWMAN, JEREMIAH WHITTAKER
The Lounger's Common-Place Book, or, Miscellaneous Anecdotes. London: 1796-1799. V. 64

NEWMAN, JOHN HENRY, CARDINAL
Apologia Pro Vita Sua.... London: 1864. V. 62; 63; 65; 66
Apologia Pro Vita Sua.... Oxford: 1967. V. 65
Christ Upon the Waters. Birmingham: 1850. V. 63
Discourses Addressed to Mixed Congregations. London: 1849. V. 65
Discourses on the Scope and Nature of University Education. Dublin: 1851. V. 65
The Dream of Gerontius. London: 1908. V. 67
An Essay on the Development of Christian Doctrine. London: 1845. V. 63
The Idea of a University Defined and Illustrated. Oxford: 1976. V. 65
Lectures on Catholicism in England. Birmingham: 1851. V. 66

NEWMAN, JOHN HENRY, CARDINAL continued
Lectures on Justification. London: 1838. V. 65
Letters and Correspondence of John Henry Newman During His Life in the English Church. London: 1891. V. 65
Letters of John Henry Newman - a Selection. London: 1957. V. 65
Orate pro Anima Jacobi Roberti Hope Scott. London: 1873. V. 63
Sermons Chiefly on the Theory of Religious Belief, Preached Before the University of Oxford. London: 1844. V. 65
Verses on Religious Subjects. Dublin: 1853. V. 62
Verses on Various Occasions. London: 1868. V. 66

NEWMAN, JOHN P.
The Thrones and Palaces of Bablyon and Nineveh from Sea to Sea, a Thousand Miles on Horseback. New York: 1876. V. 65

NEWMAN, KIM
Anno-Dracula. London: 1991. V. 66
Anno-Dracula. London: 1992. V. 65

NEWMAN, RALPH GEOFFREY
Great and Good Books, a Bibliographical Catalogue of the Limited Editions Club 1929-1985. Chicago: 1989. V. 62

NEWMARK, HARRIS
Sixty Years in Southern California 1853-1913. New York: 1916. V. 63

NEWNAN, JOHN
The Tennessee Administration Advocate. Nashville: 1828. V. 64

NEWNES' Pictorial Knowledge. London: 1930. V. 67

NEWNHAM, WILLIAM
Essay on Superstition: Being an Inquiry into the Effects of Physical Influence on the Mind.... London: 1830. V. 65

NEW ORLEANS CHESS, CHECKERS AND WHIST CLUB
Charter and By-Laws of the New Orleans Chess, Checkers and Whist Club. New Orleans: 1884. V. 63

NEWPORT, MAURICE
Sereniss. Principi Carolo Secundo Mag. Brit. Fran. et Hib. Regi Votum Candidum Vivat Rex. London: 1669. V. 66

THE NEWS-READERS Pocket Book: or, a Military Dictionary. London: 1759. V. 65

NEWSOM, S.
A Thousand Years of Japanese Gardens. Tokyo: 1957. V. 65

NEWSON, J. A.
The Life and Practice of the Wild and Modern Indians. Oklahoma City: 1923. V. 63; 66

NEWSPAPER CARTOONISTS ASSOCIATION OF BRITISH COLUMBIA
British Columbians As We See'Em. 1910. and 1911. Vancouver: 1911?. V. 66

NEWSTEAD, R.
Monograph of the Coccidae of the British Isles. London: 1901-1903. V. 64; 65; 66; 67

NEWTE, JOHN
The Lawfulness and Use of Organs in the Christian Church. Asserted in a Sermon Preached at Tiverton in the County of Devon Upon the 13th of September 1696. London: 1696. V. 64

NEWTON, ADDISON
The Saloon Keeper's Companion and Book of Reference. Worcester: 1875. V. 62; 64

NEWTON, ALFRED EDWARD
The A. Edward Newton Collection. New York: 1941. V. 63
The Amenities of Book Collecting. Boston: 1918. V. 66
The Amenities of Book-Collecting and Kindred Affections. London: 1920. V. 63
The Greatest Book in the World and Other Papers. Boston: 1925. V. 63
Rare Books, Original Drawings, Autograph Letters and Manuscripts Collected by the Late A. Edward Newton. New York: 1941. V. 62
This Book Collecting Game. Boston: 1928. V. 64
A Tourist in Spite of Himself. Boston: 1930. V. 62; 63; 64; 66

NEWTON, E. T.
The Vertebrata of the Forest Bed Series of Norfolk and Suffolk. 1882. V. 66

NEWTON, ERIC
Christopher Wood. 1901-1930. London: 1938. V. 63

NEWTON, G. W.
A Treatise on the Growth and Future Management of Timber Trees and On Other Rural Subjects. London: 1859. V. 67

NEWTON, HELMUT
47 Nudes. London: 1982. V. 66

NEWTON, ISAAC
Arithmetica Universalis; sive De Compositione et Resolutione Arithmetica Liber. Londini: 1722. V. 65
A Catalogue of the Portsmouth Collection of Books and Papers Belonging to Sir Isaac Newton...Presented by the Earl of Portsmouth to the University of Cambridge.... Cambridge: 1888. V. 62
The Correspondence. Cambridge: 1959-1977. V. 62
The Mathematical Principles of Natural Philosophy. London: 1729. V. 63; 64
The Mathematical Principles of Natural Philosophy. London: 1968. V. 63
Optice: sive de Reflexionibus, Refractionibus, Inflexionibus et Coloribus Lucis.... Londini: 1706. V. 63
Opticks; or a Treatise of the Reflections, Refractions, Inflections and Colours of Light. London: 1730. V. 65
Opuscula Mathematica, Philosophica et Philologica. Lausannae and Genevae: 1744. V. 62; 66
Philosophiae Naturalis Principia Mathematica. London: 1687. V. 67
Philosophiae Naturalis Principia Mathematica. London: 1726. V. 63; 64; 65; 66; 67
Philosophiae Naturalis Principia Mathematica. Cambridge: 1972. V. 62
Sir Isaac Newton's Principia Reprinted for Sir William Thomson...and Hugh Blackburn.... Glasgow: 1871. V. 62

NEWTON, JOHN
*An Authentic Narrative of Some Remarkable and Interesting Particulars in the Life of ******.* London: 1786. V. 62
Letters to a Wife, by the Author of Cardiphonia. London: 1793. V. 62

NEWTON, R. H.
Town and Davis, Architects: Pioneers in American Revivalist Architecture 1812-1870. 1942. V. 65
Town and Davis, Architects: Pioneers in American Revivalist Architecture 1812-1870. Columbia: 1942. V. 62

NEWTON, RICHARD
The King's Highway; or, Illustrations of the Commandments. London: 1863. V. 65
Pluralities Indefensible. London: 1745. V. 67

NEWTON THEOLOGICAL INSTITUTION
Catalogue of the Books Belonging to the Library of the Newton Theological Institution August 1, 1833. Boston: 1833. V. 63

NEWTON, VIRGINIUS
The Confederate States Ram Merrimac or Virginia. Richmond: 1907. V. 62; 63; 65

NEWTON, WILLIAM
The History and Antiquities of Maidstone. London: 1741. V. 65

THE NEWTONIANS System of Philosophy, Explained by Familiar Objects in an Entertaining Manner, for the Use of Young Persons.... London: 1806. V. 65

NEXO, MARTIN ANDERSEN
Days in the Sun. London: 1929. V. 67

NH'AT HANH, THICH
Tho Viet Nam. Santa Barbara: 1967. V. 63

THE NIAGARA Book. Buffalo: 1893. V. 63
THE NIAGARA Book. New York: 1901. V. 63

NIALL, IAN
English Country Traditions. London: 1988. V. 65
Trout from the Hills. 1961. V. 67

NICASTRO, GIOVANNI DI
Descrizione dle Celebre Arco Eretto in Benvento a Marco Ulpio Trajano, XIV Imperadore dal Senato e Popolo di Roma.... Benevento: 1723. V. 67

NICE, M. M.
The Watcher at the Nest. New York: 1939. V. 64; 67; 67

NICELY, WILSON S.
The Great Southwest. St. Louis: 1867. V. 66

NICERON, JEAN FRANCOIS
La Perspective Curieuse.... Paris: 1652-1651. V. 67

NICHOL, JOHN PRINGLE
The Planet Neptune: an Exposition and History. Edinburgh and London: 1848. V. 65

NICHOLAS, NICHOLAS HARRIS
A History of the Royal Navy from the Earliest Times to the Wars of the French Revolution. London: 1847. V. 62
Memoir of Augustine Vincent, Windsor Herald. London: 1827. V. 66

NICHOLAS, SAMUEL SMITH
Letters on the Presidency, by a Kentucky Democrat. Louisville: 1840. V. 66
A Review of the Argument of President Lincoln and Attorney General Bates, in Favor of Presidential Power to Suspend the Privilege of the Writ of Habeas Corpus. Louisville: 1861. V. 62

NICHOLAS, THOMAS
The History and Antiquities of Glamorganshire and the Families. London: 1874. V. 66

NICHOLLS, GEORGE
A History of the Irish Poor Laws. New York: 1967. V. 67
A History of the Scotch Poor Law, in Connexion with the Condition of the People. London: 1856. V. 67
Poor Laws-Ireland. Three Reports. 1838. V. 66

NICHOLLS, W.
The History and Traditions of Mallerstang Forest and Pendragon Castle. Manchester: 1883. V. 64; 65; 66
History and Traditions of Prestwich. Manchester: 1905. V. 66
The History and Traditions of Ravenstonedale. Manchester: 1877. V. 64; 65
The History and Traditions of Ravenstonedale, Westmorland. Volume II. Manchester: 1910. V. 62; 63; 65

NICHOLS, EDWARD J.
Toward Gettysburg. A Biography of General John F. Reynolds. 1958. V. 62; 63

NICHOLS, GEORGE WASHINGTON
A Soldier's Story of His Regiment (61st Georgia) and Incidentally of the Lawton-Gordon-Evans Brigade, Army Northern Virginia. Jessup: 1898. V. 62; 63; 65

NICHOLS, J. B.
Account of the Royal Hospital and Collegiate Church of St. Katharine, Near the Tower of London. London: 1824. V. 62; 67
The History of the Royal Hospital and Collegiate Church of St. Katharine, near the Tower of London. London: 1782. V. 62

NICHOLS, J. C. M.
Birds of Marsh and Mere and How to Shoot Them. London: 1928. V. 67

NICHOLS, J. P.
Alaska. A History of Its Administration, Exploitation and Industrial Development During Its First Half Century Under the Rule of the United States. Cleveland: 1924. V. 66

NICHOLS, J. T.
The Fishes of Porto Rico and the Virgin Islands. New York: 1929-1930. V. 65
Fresh-Water Fishes of China. New York: 1941. V. 64
The Fresh-Water Fishes of China. New York: 1943. V. 62; 63; 65; 66

NICHOLS, JAMES WILSON
Now You Hear My Horn. Austin: 1967. V. 62

NICHOLS, JOHN
Anecdotes, Biographical and Literary, of the Late Mr. William Bowyer, Printer. London: 1778. V. 62; 64; 65
Biographical Anecdotes of William Hogarth.... London: 1782. V. 62
The Milagro Beanfield War. New York: 1974. V. 62; 63; 65
The Milagro Beanfield War. New York: 1994. V. 67
The Nirvana Blues. New York: 1981. V. 67
On the Mesa. Salt Lake City: 1986. V. 67
The Sterile Cuckoo. New York: 1965. V. 62; 63; 65

NICHOLS, JOHN GOUGH
The Armorial Windows of Woodhouse Chapel. London: 1860. V. 64

NICHOLS, LAURA
Gemini. Boston: 1878. V. 63

NICHOLS, LEIGH
Shadowfires. New York: 1987. V. 62

NICHOLS, MARY S. GOVE
Nichols' Health Manual.... London: 1886. V. 65

NICHOLS, R. S.
Italian Pleasure Gardens. 1929. V. 63
Spanish and Portuguese Gardens. 1924. V. 63
Spanish and Portuguese Gardens. Boston: 1924. V. 64

NICHOLS, ROBERT
Aurelia and Other Poems. London: 1920. V. 66
Invocation: War Poems and Others. London: 1915. V. 64
The Smile of the Sphinx. London: 1920. V. 64

NICHOLS, ROSS
The Cosmic Shape. 1946. V. 67

NICHOLSON, ASENATH
Nature's Own Book. New York: 1835. V. 63

NICHOLSON, BEN
Ben Nicholson: Drawings, Paintings & Reliefs 1911-1968. New York and London: 1969. V. 62; 65

NICHOLSON, CORNELIUS
The Annals of Kendal.... London: 1861. V. 65
A Descriptive Account of the Roman Villa Near Brading, Isle of Wright. London: 1880. V. 62

NICHOLSON, FRANCIS
Six Views of Fountains Abbey in Yorkshire.... London: 1825. V. 62; 67

NICHOLSON, GEORGE
The Advocate and Friend of Woman. Stourport: 1810. V. 63
The Illustrated Dictionary of Gardening. 1884-1901. V. 66
The Illustrated Dictionary of Gardening. London: 1885-1888. V. 64
The Illustrated Dictionary of Gardening. London: 1885-1889. V. 65
The Illustrated Dictionary of Gardening. 1885-1890. V. 67
The Illustrated Dictionary of Gardening. London: 1890-1901. V. 64

NICHOLSON, H. A.
A Manual of Palaeontology. 1879. V. 63
A Manual of Palaeontology. London: 1879. V. 62

NICHOLSON, H. B.
Origins of Religious Art and Iconography in Pre-Classic Mesoamerica. Los Angeles. 1970. V. 62

NICHOLSON, HAROLD
Journey to Java. London: 1957. V. 67

NICHOLSON, HUBERT
Date. Bristol: 1935. V. 63

NICHOLSON, JAMES B.
A Manual of the Art of Bookbinding. Philadelphia: 1871. V. 67
A Manual of the Art of Bookbinding. Philadelphia: 1887. V. 67
A Manual of the Art of Bookbinding. Philadelphia: 1902. V. 64; 66
A Manual of the Art of Bookbinding. Sussex: 1986. V. 62

NICHOLSON, JOHN
Airedale in Ancient Times. London: 1825. V. 64; 65
The Farmer's Assistant. Albany: 1814. V. 62; 64

NICHOLSON, JOHN PAGE
Catalogue of Library of Brevet Lieutenant-Colonel John Page Nicholson...Relating to the War of the Rebellion 1861-1866. Philadelphia: 1914. V. 62

NICHOLSON, JOSIAH WALKER
Crosby Garrett, Westmorland. Kirkby Stephen: 1914. V. 62; 65

NICHOLSON, NORMAN
Birth by Drowning. London: 1960. V. 62
A Match for the Devil. London: 1955. V. 62; 65; 66
Prophesy to the Wind. London: 1950. V. 62; 65; 66
Rock Face. London: 1948. V. 62; 65; 66
Wednesday Early Closing. London: 1975. V. 63; 64; 65
William Cowper. London: 1951. V. 62; 64; 65

NICHOLSON, PETER
An Architectural Dictionary, Containing a Correct Nomenclature and Derivation of the Terms Employed by Architects, Builders and Workmen.... London: 1819. V. 64
The Carpenter and Joiner's Assistant.... London: 1810. V. 62
The Carpenter's New Guide. London: 1808. V. 66
The Carpenter's New Guide. London: 1819. V. 64
The Carpenter's New Guide. Philadelphia: 1830. V. 64
The Carpenter's New Guide. Philadelphia: 1854. V. 64
The Mechanic's Companion.... Philadelphia: 1850. V. 62
The New and Improved Practical Builder, and Workman's Companion.... London: 1845-1846. V. 66
The Student's Instructor in Drawing and Working the Five orders of Architecture.... London: 1810. V. 64

NICHOLSON, RENTON
Dombey and Daughter: a Moral Fiction. London: 1847. V. 62

NICHOLSON, WILLIAM
An Almanac of Twelve Sports. London: 1897. V. 67
An Almanac of Twelve Sports. London: 1898. V. 66; 67
An Alphabet. Andoversford: 1978. V. 64
The Book of Blokes. London: 1929. V. 66
Clever Bill. New York: 1926. V. 64; 65
(Greek Title) or an Exposition of the Apostles Creed, Delivered in Several Sermons. London: 1661. V. 67
The First Principles of Chemistry. London: 1790. V. 64
The First Principles of Chemistry.... 1796. V. 62
The Great Duty of Thanksgiving. A Sermon Preach'd At Christ's-Church, Dublin on August 1st 1719. Dublin;: 1719. V. 65
London Types. London: 1898. V. 66
London Types.... New York: 1898. V. 67
The Petition of Sir William Nicholson of Glenbervy, Baronet...(with) Information for Sir William Nicholson...Against Margaret, Marchioness of Lothian. N.P.;: 1729. V. 62
Smoke Abatement. London: 1905. V. 63

NICKLIN, PHILIP H.
Letters Descriptive of the Virginia Springs.... Philadelphia: 1835. V. 63

NICKOLLS, JOHN
Original Letters and Papers of State, Addressed to Oliver Cromwell.... London: 1743. V. 65

NICKSON, GEOFFREY
A Portrait of Salmon Fishing. 1976. V. 65; 67
A Portrait of Salmon Fishing. London: 1976. V. 67

NICODEMUS and the Goose. New York: 1945. V. 62

NICOL, W.
The Forcing, Fruit and Kitchen Gardener. Edinburgh: 1809. V. 62
The Practical Planter or a Treatise on Forest Planting. 1803. V. 63
The Villa Garden Directory.... Edinburgh: 1809. V. 64

NICOLAI, GIAMBATTISTA
Nova Analyseos Elementa. Padua: 1786-1793. V. 67

NICOLAS, NICHOLAS HARRIS
The Dispatches and Letters of Vice Admiral Lord Viscount Nelson, with Notes.... London: 1845. V. 67
Memoirs and Remains of Lady Jane Grey.... London: 1831. V. 63
The Statutes of the Order of the Guelphs. London: 1828. V. 63

NICOLAUS DE AUSMO
Supplementum Summae Pisanellae. Nuremberg: 1488. V. 64; 66

NICOLAY, CHARLES G.
The Oregon Territory: a Geographical and Physical Account of that Country and Its Inhabitants.... London: 1846. V. 62

NICOLAY, JOHN G.
Abraham Lincoln: a History. New York: 1890. V. 63

NICOLL, ALLARDYCE
The World of Harlequin - a Critical Study of the Commedia dell'Arte. Cambridge: 1963. V. 62

NICOLL, M. J.
Nicoll's Birds of Egypt. London: 1930. V. 67

NICOLL, W. ROBERTSON
Literary Anecdotes of the Nineteenth Century: Contributions Towards a Literary History of the Period. London: 1895-1896. V. 63; 64

NICOLLET, JOSEPH N.
Report Intended to Illustrate a Map of the Hydrographical Basin of the Mississippi River.... Washington: 1843. V. 64

NICOLS, THOMAS
A Lapidary; or, the History of Pretious (sic) Stones.... Cambridge: 1652. V. 62

NICOLSON, BENEDICT
Joseph Wright of Derby. Painter of Light. London: 1968. V. 63

NICOLSON, HAROLD
Diplomacy. London: 1939. V. 63

NICOLSON, J.
The History and Antiquities of the Counties of Westmorland and Cumberland. London: 1777. V. 62; 65; 66

NICOLSON, MARJORIE HOPE
Newton Demands the Muse. Newton's Optics and the Eighteenth Century Poets. Princeton: 1946. V. 63

NICOLSON, WILLIAM
Leges Marchiarum, or Border-Laws.... London: 1705. V. 62; 66
Miscellany Accounts of the Diocese of Carlisle, with the Terriers Delivered In to Me at My Primary Visitation. London: 1877. V. 65

NIEBUHR, BARTHOLD GEORGE
The Life and Letters of.... London: 1852. V. 62; 65

NIEBUHR, CARSTEN
Beschreibung von Arabien Aus Eigenen Beobachtungen und im Lande Selbst Gesammelten Nachrichten. Kopenhagen: 1772. V. 62
Description de l'Arabie d'Apres les Observations et Recherches Faites dans le Pays Meme. Copenhagen: 1773. V. 62; 65

NIEDECK, PAUL
With a Rifle in Five Continents. 1908. V. 64

NIEDECKER, LORINE
From This Condensery: The Complete Writing of Lorine Niedecker. Highlands: 1985. V. 63; 64; 67
My Life by Water. Collected Poems 1936-168. London: 1970. V. 64
North Central. London: 1968. V. 62; 64
T & G. Collected Poems (1936-1966). Penland: 1968. V. 63

NIELSEN, CHRISTIAN
Wooden Boat Designs. New York: 1980. V. 64; 65

NIELSEN, J. M.
A Textbook of Clinical Neurology. New York: 1941. V. 67

NIELSEN, KAY
The Bookman Portfolio for Christmas 1925. London: 1925. V. 62

NIELSON & CO.
Locomotive Engine Made at the Hydepark Locomotive Works, Glasgow. Glasgow: 1863. V. 65

NIEMI, T. M.
The Dead Sea, the Lake and Its Setting. New York: 1997. V. 65

NIENHUIS, P. H.
The Oosterschelde Estuary (the Netherlands).... Dordrecht: 1994. V. 65

NIEREMBERG, JUAN EUSEBIO
Historia Naturae, Maxime Peregrinae, Libris XVI. Distincta. Antwerp: 1635. V. 67

NIETZSCHE, FRIEDRICH
Also Sprach Zarathustra. Chemnitz: 1883-1884. V. 62; 66
Also Sprach Zarathustra. Chemnitz: 1883-1891. V. 65
Also Sprach Zarathustra. Leipzig: 1891. V. 63
Also Sprach Zarathustra. Leipzig: 1908. V. 64
The Antichrist of Nietzsche. London: 1934. V. 62
Jenseits Von Gut Und Bose. (Beyond Good and Evil). Leipzig: 1886. V. 63; 64

NIEUPOORT, G. H.
Rituum, Qui Olim Apud Romanos Obtinuerunt, Succincta Explicatio; Ad Intelligentiam Veterum Auctorum Facile Methodo Conscripta a G. H. Nieupoort. Trajecti ad Rhenum: 1723. V. 66

NIGER, DOMINICUS MARIUS
Geographiae Commentariorum Libri XI, Nunc Primum in Lucem Magno Studio Editi, Quibus Non Solum Orbis Totius Habitabilis Loca.... Basel: 1557. V. 65

THE NIGHT Before Christmas. Akron: 1905. V. 66

THE NIGHT Before Christmas. London: 1910. V. 65
THE NIGHT Before Christmas. Akron: 1941. V. 62
THE NIGHT Before Christmas. Racine: 1943. V. 66
THE NIGHT Before Christmas. Akron: 1945. V. 62

THE NIGHT Watch; or, Tales of the Sea. London: 1828. V. 65

NIGHTINGALE, ANNA ELIZABETH
Gleanings From the South, East and West. London: 1843. V. 62

NIGHTINGALE, B.
The Ejected of 1662 in Cumberland and Westmorland. Manchester: 1911. V. 65
History of the Old Independent Chapel, Tockholes, Near Blackburn, Lancashire. London: 1886. V. 66
The Story of the Lancashire Congregational Union 1806-1906. Manchester: 1906. V. 66

NIGHTINGALE, FLORENCE
Cassandra. N.P: 1935?. V. 63
Notes on Hospitals: Being Two Papers Read Before the National Association for the Promotion of Social Science at Liverpool in October 1858. London: 1859. V. 65
Notes on Nursing: What It Is and What It Is Not. Boston: 1860. V. 66
Notes on Nursing; What It Is, and What It Is Not. London: 1860. V. 65; 65; 66
Notes on Nursing: What It Is and What It is Not. New York: 1860. V. 64; 65
Notes on Nursing: What It Is and What It Is Not. New York: 1860. V. 64
Scutari and Its Hospitals. London: 1855. V. 66

NIGHTINGALE, J. E.
The Church Plate of the County of Wilts. Salisbury: 1891. V. 67
The History and Antiquities of the Parochial Church of St. Saviour, Southwark.... London: 1818. V. 62; 67

NIGHTINGALE, JOSEPH
The Bazaar, Its Origin, Nature and Objects Explained and Recommended As a Important Branch Of Political Economy. London: 1816. V. 64
A Portraiture of Methodism; Being an Impartial View of the Rise, Progress, Doctrines, Discipline, and Manners of the Wesleyan Methodists. London: 1807. V. 64

NIHELL, JACOBO
Novae Rareque Observationes Circa Variarum Crisium Praedictionem ex Pulsu Nullo Habito Respectu ad Signa Critica Antiquorum.... Venetiis: 1748. V. 64

NIKELSBURGER, JACOB
Koul Jacob in Defence of the Jewish Religion.... New York: 1816. V. 66

NIKITIN, ALEXANDER
Popular Dietetics; or Directions on How to Maintain Good Health. St. Petersburg: 1852. V. 62

NIKOLSKY, G. V.
The Ecology of Fishes. New York: 1963. V. 65

NILSON, ARVID
The Timber Trees of New South Wales. Sydney: 1884. V. 66

NILSSON, S.
Illuminerade Figurer til Skandinaviens Fauna. Lund: 1829-1840. V. 63

NIMITZ, CHESTER W.
The Great Sea War: the Story of Naval Action in World War II. Englewood Cliffs: 1960. V. 63

NIMMO, JOSEPH
Commerce Between the United States and Mexico. Washington: 1884. V. 65
Range and Cattle Traffic - Letter from the Secretary of State...48th Congress 2nd Session Ex Doc. 267. Washington: 1885. V. 67
Uncle Sam's Farm - the Reclamation of the Arid Region of the United States by Means of Irrigation. Washington: 1890. V. 65

NIMMO, WILLIAM
History of Stirlingshire. London: 1817. V. 62; 66

NIMS, FRANKLIN A.
The Photographer and the River 1889-1890: The Colorado Canon Diary of Franklin A. Nims with the Brown-Stanton Railroad Survey Expedition. Santa Fe: 1967. V. 66

NIMS, JOHN FREDERICK
The Six Cornered Snowflake. New York: 1991. V. 66

NIN, ANAIS
Children of the Albatross. New York: 1947. V. 62; 65
The House of Incest. Paris: 1936. V. 65
Winter of Artifice. New York. V. 64
The Winter of Artifice. Paris: 1938. V. 62

NINE O'Clock Stories by Fourteen Authors. London: 1934. V. 62; 63

NINNINGER, H. H.
A Comet Strikes the Earth. El Centro: 1942. V. 67

NISARD, CHARLES
Histoire des Livres Populaires ou de la Litterature du Colportage.... Paris: 1864. V. 67

NISBET, ALEXANDER
A System of Heraldry Speculative and Practical; with the True Art of Blazon.... Edinburgh: 1722-1742. V. 63; 65

NISBET, CHARLES
An Address to the Students of Dickinson College, Carlisle. Edinburgh: 1786. V. 65

NISBET, HUME
The Great Secret. A Tale of Tomorrow. London: 1895. V. 63
Where Art Begins. London: 1892. V. 67

NISBET, JAMES COOPER
4 Years on the Firing Line. Jackson: 1963. V. 63

NISBET, JOHN
The Forester, A Practical Treatise on British Forestry and Aboriculture for Landowners, Land Agents and Foresters. Edinburgh: 1905. V. 62

NISHIKAWA, Y.
Average Distribution of Larvae of Oceanic Species of Scombroid Fishes 1956-1981. 1985. V. 65

NISTICO, G.
Progress in Non-mammalian Brain Research. Boca Raton: 1983. V. 62

NITECKI, M. H.
Neutral Models in Biology. New York: 1987. V. 67

NIVEN, LARRY
N-Space. New York: 1990. V. 62
Neutron Star. London: 1969. V. 64

NIX, EVETT DUMAS
Oklahombres: Particularly the Wilder Ones. St. Louis: 1929. V. 64; 66; 67

NIX, JON W.
The Tale of Two Schools and Springtown-Parker County. Fort Worth: 1945. V. 63; 66

NIX, NELLEKE
Remembered: Translated and Retold from My Diary. Seattle: 1991. V. 62

NIXON, FRANCIS H.
Population; or, a Plea for Victoria. Melbourne: 1862. V. 67

NIXON, HERMAN
Forty Acres and Steel Mules. Chapel Hill: 1938. V. 65

NIXON, HOWARD M.
Five Centuries of English Bookbinding. London: 1978. V. 67
Sixteenth Century Gold Tooled Bookbindings in the Pierpont Morgan Library. New York: 1971. V. 63

NIXON, MARY F. ROULET
Lasca, and Other Stories. St. Louis: 1898. V. 63

NIXON, PAT IRELAND
The Early Nixons of Texas. El Paso: 1956. V. 64

NIXON, RICHARD MILHOUS
The Challenge We Face. New York: 1960. V. 63
Leaders. New York: 1982. V. 64
The Memoirs of.... New York: 1978. V. 65
No More Viet Nams. New York: 1985. V. 65
Real Peace. New York: 1983. V. 66
The Real War. New York: 1980. V. 63; 64; 66
Six Crises. Garden City: 1962. V. 63

NIZAMI
The Poems of Nizami. London: 1928. V. 62
The Poems of Nizami Described by Laurence Binyon. London: 1938. V. 64

NIZAN, PAUL
Aden Arabie. Paris: 1931. V. 67

NOAH'S Ark. Enkhuizen. V. 63

THE NOAH'S Ark. London: 1900. V. 64

NOAH'S Ark ABC. New York: 1910. V. 62

THE NOAH'S Ark Annual for 1937. London: 1937. V. 64

NOAILLES, MARQUIS DE
What is Poland?. London: 1863. V. 66

NOAKES, V.
Edward Lear 1812-1888. New York: 1986. V. 63

NOBBS, PERCY E.
Salmon Tactics. London: 1924. V. 67
Salmon Tactics. 1934. V. 67

NOBILE, UMBERTO
With the Italia to the North Pole. New York: 1931. V. 65

NOBILI, RICCARDO
The Gentle Art of Faking, a History of the Methods of Producing Imitations and Spurious Works of Art From the Earliest Times Up to the Present Day. London: 1922. V. 67

NOBLE, ALGERNON
Siberian Days, An Engineer's Record of Travel and Adventure in the Wilds of Siberia. London: 1928. V. 67

THE NOBLE and Renowned History of Guy Earl of Warwick. Chiswick: 1821. V. 64

NOBLE, G. K.
The Biology of the Amphibia. New York: 1931. V. 64; 66

NOBLE, JAMES
An Arabic Vocabulary and Index for Richardson's Arabic Grammar, in Which the Words are Explained According to the Parts of Speech.... Edinburgh: 1820. V. 63
The Orientalist; or, Letters of a Rabbi. Edinburgh;: 1831. V. 63

NOBLE, JOHN
Our Imports and Exports; with Some Remarks Upon the Balance of Trade. London: 1870. V. 63

NOBLE, MARK
Memoirs of the Protectoral-House of Cromwell; Deduced from an Early Period and Continued Down to the Present Time; and also the Families Allied to, or Descended from Them.... Birmingham: 1787. V. 65; 67
Two Dissertations Upon the Mint and Coins of the Episcopal Palatines of Durham. Birmingham: 1780. V. 63; 66

NOBLE, MARY E.
Register of Births, Deaths and Marriages of the Parish of Bampton, in the County of Westmorland from 1637 to 1812. Kendal: 1897. V. 65; 66
The Register of the Parish of Askham in the County of Westmorland from 1566 to 1812. London: 1904. V. 66
The Registers Of the Parish of Shap in the County of Westmorland. Kendal: 1912. V. 65

NOBLE, PETER
The Negro in Films. London: 1949. V. 62

NOBLE, SAMUEL H.
Life and Adventures of Buckskin Sam. 1900. V. 65
Life and Adventures of Buckskin Sam. Rumford: 1900. V. 67

NOBLE-IVES, SARAH
The Story of Teddy the Bear. Springfield: 1923. V. 62; 66

NOBODY Knows. London: 1910. V. 64

NOCETI, CARLO
De Iride et Aurora Boreali Carmina...cum Notis Josephi Rogerii Boscovich. Rome: 1747. V. 62

NOCK, ARTHUR DARBY
Essays on Religion and the Ancient World. Oxford: 1986. V. 65

NODAL, J. H.
Country Notes: a Journal of Natural History and Out-door Observations. Manchester: 1882-1883. V. 65

NODIER, CHARLES
The Luck of the Bean-Rows a Fairy Tale. London: 1921. V. 64

NOE, AMEDEE CHARLES HENRY DE, COUNT
Turlupinades Contrarietes et Autres Amusemens Negatifs, par Cham. Paris: 1860. V. 65

NOE, BIACHI
Viaggio da Venezia Al S. Sepolcro e Al Monte Sinae.... Bassano: 1742. V. 66

NOEL, E. B.
A History of Tennis. London: 1924. V. 62

NOEL, LUCIE
James Joyce and Paul L. Leon - the Story of a Friendship. New York: 1950. V. 62

NOEL, THEOPHILUS
Autobiography and Reminiscences Of.... Chicago: 1904. V. 62; 63; 65; 66
A Campaign from Santa Fe to Mississippi, Being a History of the Old Sibley Brigade. Houston: 1961. V. 63; 65
A Campaign from Sante Fe to the Mississippi. Raleigh: 1961. V. 63

NOEL-BERTIER, OLYMPE
Ou Va la Raison???. Constantinople: 1873. V. 63

NOEL-FEARN, HENRY
The Money Market: What It Is, What It Does, and How It Is Managed. London: 1867. V. 64

NOGAROLA
Ludovici Nogarolae Comitis Dialogus Qui Inscribatur Timotheus Sive De Nilo. 1626. V. 66

NOICE, HAROLD
With Stefansson In the Arctic. New York. V. 66

NOKES, WILLIAM
The Nature, Title and Evidence of Eternal Life Given in Jesus Christ by the Gospel Briefly Stated. London: 1709. V. 63

NOLAN, EDWARD HENRY
The History of the War Against Russia. London: 1856. V. 65
Illustrated History of the War Against Russia. London: 1855-1857. V. 63; 66

NOLAN, FREDERICK
The Life and Death of John Henry Tunstall. Albuquerque: 1965. V. 67
The Lincoln County War, A Documentary History. Norman: 1992. V. 67

NOLAN, MICHAEL
A Treatise of the Laws for the Relief and Settlement of the Poor. London: 1808. V. 67

NOLAN, OREN W.
Galloping Down the Texas Trail, Sketches of Texas Cowboys, Rangers, Sheriffs, Cattle, Horses, Guns and Game. Oden: 1947. V. 63; 66

NOLAN, WILLIAM
Fassadinin: Land, Settlement and Society in the South End of East Ireland 1600-1850. 1979. V. 67

NOLAN, WILLIAM F.
Dashiell Hammett: a Casebook. Santa Barbara: 1969. V. 65; 67

NOLEN, JOHN
San Diego. A Comprehensive Plan for Its Improvement. Boston: 1908. V. 63

NOLL, ARTHUR HOWARD
Doctor Quintard. Swanee: 1905. V. 62; 63
General Kirby-Smith. Sewanee: 1907. V. 62; 63; 65

NOLLET, JEAN ANTOINE, ABBE
Lettres sur l'Electricite. Paris: 1753. V. 64

THE NONESUCH Century - an Appraisal, a Personal and a Bibliography of the First Hundred Books Issued by the Press 1923-1934. London: 1936. V. 63

NONNE, MAX
Syphilis and the Nervous System: for Practioners, Neurologists and Syphilogists. Philadelphia: 1916. V. 65

NONNUS PANOPOLITUS
Dionysiaca. Petri Cvnaei Animadversionvm Liber. Hanoviae: 1610. V. 64
(Greek title, then): Dionysiaca. Antverpiae: 1569. V. 64
(Greek title, then): Dionysiaca. Hanoviae: 1605. V. 64

NONSENSE Rhymes. London, Paris, Berlin. V. 62

NOODT, GERARDUS
The Power of the Sovereign and the Right of Liberty of Conscience, in Two Discourses, Pronounc'd by Mr. Noodt. London: 1721. V. 62

NOON, JEFF
Automated Alice. London: 1996. V. 64; 66
Vurt. London: 1993. V. 66
Vurt. New York: 1995. V. 67

NOONAN, JOHN T.
Contraception. A History of Its Treatment by the Catholic Theologians and Canonists. Cambridge: 1966. V. 65

NOORTHOUCK, JOHN
An Historical and Classical Dictionary...Lives and Characters of.... London: 1778. V. 66

NORDAN, LEWIS
Growing Up White in the South. Chapel Hill: 1993. V. 67
Music of the Swamp. Chapel Hill: 1991. V. 63; 65; 67
Wolf Whistle. Chapel Hill: 1993. V. 67

NORDAU, MAX
How Women Love and Other Tales (Soul and Analysis). New York: 1896. V. 67

NORDEN, JOHN
England an Intended Guyde, for English Travailers. London: 1625. V. 66

NORDENSKIOLD, A. E.
The Voyage of the Vega Round Asia and Europe, with a Historical Review of Previous Journeys Along the North Coast of the Old World. New York: 1882. V. 65

NORDENSKIOLD, E.
An Historical and Ethnological Survey of the Cuna Indians. Goteborg: 1938. V. 62

NORDENSKIOLD, GUSTAV E. A.
Ruiner af Klippboningar I Mesa Verde's Canons. Stockholm: 1893. V. 65

NORDHEIMER, ISAAC A.
Grammatical Anaylsis of Selections from the Hebrew Scriptures, with an Exercise in Hebrew Composition. New York: 1838. V. 62

NORDHOFF, CHARLES
California; for Health, Pleasure, and Residence. New York: 1873. V. 65
California for Health, Pleasure and Residence. Franklin Square: 1874. V. 62; 63
California: for Health, Pleasure and Residence. New York: 1874. V. 67
The Communistic Societies of the United States. New York: 1875. V. 64
Mutiny!. London: 1933. V. 62
Northern California, Oregon, and the Sandwich Islands. New York: 1874. V. 65

NORDNESS, LEE
Art USA Now. Lucerne: 1962. V. 62; 65

NORDYKE, LEWIS T.
The Angels Sing. Oxford: 1964. V. 63; 66

NORELLI, M. R.
American Wildlife Painting. New York: 1975. V. 67

NORFLEET, J. FRANK
Norfleet: the Actual Experiences of a Texas Rancher's 30,000 Mile Transcontinental Chase After Five Confidence Men. Sugar Land: 1924. V. 67

NORFOLK, LAWRENCE
Lempriere's Dictionary. London: 1991. V. 64; 67
The Pope's Rhinoceros. London: 1996. V. 67

NORIE, J. W.
The Naval Gazetteer, Biographer and Chronologist.... London: 1842. V. 64

NORIS, MATTEO
In Greco in Troia, Festa Teatrale.... Florence: 1688. V. 65

NORMAN, AARON
The Great Air War. New York: 1968. V. 64

NORMAN, DON CLEVELAND
The 500th Anniversary Pictorial Census of the Gutenberg Bible. Chicago: 1961. V. 62; 66; 67

NORMAN, FRANCIS MARTIN
Martello Tower in China and the Pacific in H.M.S. Tribune 1856-1860. London: 1902. V. 63

NORMAN, FRANK
Bang to Rights. London: 1958. V. 66

NORMAN, GEORGE W.
Letter to Charles Wood, Esq., M.P. on Money and the Means of Economizing the Use of It. London: 1841. V. 64
Papers on Various Subjects. London: 1869. V. 62

NORMAN, GURNEY
Divine Right's Trip. New York: 1972. V. 62

NORMAN, HASKELL F.
The Haskell F. Norman Library of Science and Medicine. New York: 1998. V. 62
One Hundred Books Famous in Medicine. New York: 1995. V. 63; 66

NORMAN, HOWARD
The Bird Artist. New York: 1994. V. 64; 65; 66
Kiss in the Hotel Joseph Conrad and Other Stories. New York: 1989. V. 63; 64; 66; 67
The Northern Lights. New York: 1987. V. 63; 65; 67

NORMAN, J. R.
A Draft Snyopsis of the Orders, Families and Genera of Recent Fishes and Fish-Like Vertebrates.... London: 1957. V. 65
A Draft Synopsis of the Orders, Families and Genera of Recent Fishes and Fish-Like Vertebrates. London: 1966. V. 62
Giant Fishes, Whales and Dolphins. New York: 1938. V. 65
Oceanic Fishes and Flatfishes Collected in 1925-1927. London: 1930-1938. V. 65

NORMAN, JEREMY M.
Morton's Medical Bibliography. 1991. V. 64
Morton's Medical Bibliography. Aldershot: 1991. V. 66

NORMAN, JOHANNES MUSAEUS
Quelques Observations de Morphologie Vegetale Faites au Jardin Botanique de Christiania et Publiees avec l'Autorisation du Senat Academique. Christiania: 1857. V. 65

NORMAN, JOHN C.
Medicine in the Ghetto. New York: 1969. V. 65

NORMAN, M. W.
A Popular Guide to the Geology of the Isle of Wight with a Note On its Relation to that of the Isle of Purbeck. 1887. V. 62; 63

NORMAN, WILLIAM M.
A Portion of My Life. Winston-Salem: 1959. V. 63

NORMANBY, CONSTANTINE HENRY PHIPPS, MARQUIS OF
The English in Italy. London: 1825. V. 62
Matilda; a Tale of the Day. London: 1825. V. 67
A Year of Revolution, from a Journal Kept in Paris in 1848. London: 1857. V. 65
Yes and No: a Tale of the Day. London: 1828. V. 67

NORMAN-NERUDA, I.
The Climbs of Norman-Neruda. 1899. V. 63; 65

NORMENT, MARY C.
The Lowrie History as Acted in Part by Henry Berry Lowrie, the Great North Carolina Bandit with Biographical Sketch of His Associates. Lumberton: 1909. V. 67

NORONA, D.
West Virginia Imprints 1790-1863. Moundsville: 1958. V. 64

NORRIS, B. F., & CO.
Designs for Jewelers and Engravers. Chicago: 1876. V. 66

NORRIS, CHARLES G.
Pig Iron. New York: 1926. V. 65

NORRIS, FRANK
Frank Norris: Collected Letters. San Francisco: 1986. V. 64
The Pit. New York: 1903. V. 62
The Responsibilities of the Novelist and Other Literary Essays. New York: 1903. V. 62
Vandover and the Brute. Garden City: 1914. V. 65

NORRIS, J. E.
History of the Lower Shenandoah Valley Counties of Frederick, Berkeley. Berryville: 1972. V. 64

NORRIS, JOHN
A Collection of Miscellanies: Consisting of Poems, Essays, Discourses and Letters.... London: 1692. V. 63
A Practical Treatise Concerning Humility. London: 1707. V. 65

NORRIS, K. S.
Whales, Dolphins and Porpoises. Berkeley: 1966. V. 64

NORRIS, KATHLEEN
Dakota. New York: 1993. V. 67

NORRIS, LESLIE
Vernon Watkins 1906-1997. London: 1970. V. 65

NORRIS, SAMUEL
Manx Memories and Movements. Douglas: 1938. V. 66

NORRIS, T.
American Fish Culture, Embracing All the Details of Artificial Breeding and Rearing of Trout, the Culture of Salmon, Shad and Other Fishes. Philadelphia: 1868. V. 62

NORRIS, THOMAS
A Short Essay on the Singular Virtues of an Highly Exalted Preparation of Antimony. London: 1775?. V. 65

NORRIS, WILLIAM EDWARD
Adrian Vidal. London: 1885. V. 63; 67
My Friend Jim. London: 1886. V. 67

NORSTOG, K. J.
The Biology of the Cycads. Ithaca: 1997. V. 64

NORTH, A. J.
Nests and Eggs of Birds Found Breeding in Australia and Tasmania. Sydney: 1901-1914. V. 67

NORTH American Big Game, A Book of the Boone and Crockett Club. New York: 1939. V. 66

NORTH, ANTHONY
The Book of Guns and Gunsmiths. London: 1977. V. 67

NORTH, ARTHUR W.
Camp and Camino in Lower California. 1910. V. 62

NORTH, C. N. MC INTYRE
Leabhar Comunn Nam Fior Ghael: The Book of the Club of the True Highlanders. 1881. V. 65

NORTH CAROLINA. LAWS, STATUTES, ETC. - 1862
Ordinances and Resolutions Passed by the State Convention of North Carolina, First Session in May and June 1861. Raleigh: 1862. V. 63; 65

NORTH Dakota, a Guide to the Northern Prairie State. Fargo: 1938. V. 64

NORTH Dakota Brand Book 1944. San Diego: 1969. V. 67

NORTH, DANBY
The Mildmayes or the Clergyman's Secret; a Story of Twenty Years Ago. London: 1856. V. 67

THE NORTH East, and Western Midlands of England and Wales. 1910. V. 64

NORTH, ERIC
The Ant Men. Philadelphia and Toronto: 1955. V. 64

NORTH, ESCOTT
The Saga of the Cowboy, All About the Cattleman, and the Part He Has Played in the Great Drama of the West. London. V. 65

NORTH, F. K.
Petroleum Geology. Boston: 1990. V. 67

NORTH, JOHN
Sherlock Holmes and the Arabian Princess. Romford, Essex: 1990. V. 67

NORTH, JOHN S.
The Last Great Adventure, the Daily Log Kept by John S. North Aboard the Yacht Idle Hour, December 27, 1939 to June 24, 1940. New York: 1941. V. 64

NORTH, JOSEPH
Men in the Ranks: the Story of 12 Americans in Spain. New York: 1939. V. 65

NORTH, MARIANNE
Recollections of a Happy Life. London: 1892. V. 64

NORTH, OLIVER
Rambles After Sport, or Travels and Adventures in the Americans at Home. London: 1874. V. 62

NORTH, or Cherokee Georgia. Its Advantages to Emigrants and Families with Small Capital. Rome: 1876. V. 63

NORTH, ROGER
A Discourse of Fish and Fish Ponds. London: 1773. V. 62

NORTH, THOMAS
The Church Bells of Northamptonshire: Their Inscriptions, Traditions and Peculiar Uses, with Chapters on Bells and Northrants Bell Founders. Leicester: 1878. V. 63
The Church Bells of Rutland: Their Inscriptions, Traditions and Peculiar Uses, with Chapters on Bells and Bell Founders. Leicester: 1880. V. 63

NORTHAMPTON, MARGARET COMPTON CLEPHANE, MARCHIONESS OF
Irene, a Poem, in Six Cantos. Miscellaneous Poems. London: 1833. V. 63

NORTHAMPTONSHIRE Notes and Queries: a Quarterly Journal Devoted to the Antiquaries, Family, History, Traditions, Parochial Records, Folk-lore, Quaint Customs &c. of the County. Northampton: 1886-1888-. V. 66

NORTHCLIFFE, LORD
At the War. London: 1916. V. 64

NORTHCOTE, JAMES
Fables, Original and Selected. Second Series. London: 1833. V. 63
One Hundred Fables, Embellished with Two Hundred and Eighty Engravings.... London: 1828-1833. V. 62; 64; 66

NORTHCOTE, ROSALIND
Devon. Its Moorlands, Streams and Coasts. London: 1908. V. 62

NORTHCOTT, W. HENRY
A Treatise on Lathes and Turning, Simple, Mechanical and Ornamental. London: 1868. V. 66

NORTHERN Numbers: Selections from Scottish Poets. Edinburgh: 1920. V. 62

NORTHERN ELECTRIC & MANUFACTURING CO.
How to Build Rural Telephone Lines. Toronto: 1910. V. 64

THE NORTHERN Heroine. London: 1727. V. 65

THE NORTHERN Imposter: Being a Faithful Narrative of the Adventures, and Deceptions of James George Semple, Commonly Called Major Semple, Alias Major Harrold, Major Maxwell, Major Grant, Major Cunningham, Major Winter &c. London: 1786. V. 65

THE NORTHERN Iris. Aberdeen: 1816. V. 67

NORTHERN PACIFIC RAILROAD
Sectional Land Map of Western Washington Containing a Detailed Account Of Its Cities, Counties, Mines...in the Puget Sound Country, Pacific Coast Region. St. Paul: 1891. V. 64

THE NORTHERN Tourist. London: 1835-1836. V. 62

NORTHEY, W. BROOK
The Gurkhas. London: 1928. V. 66

NORTHROP, CLAUDIA BIRD
Southern Odes, by the Outcast, a Gentleman of South Carolina. Charleston: 1861. V. 63; 65

NORTHROP, HENRY D.
The College of Life or Practical Self-Educator.... Richmond: 1897. V. 64

NORTHUP, CLARK SUTHERLAND
A Bibliography of Thomas Gray. New Haven: 1917. V. 64

NORTHWEST TERRITORY. CENSUS - 1886
Census of the Three Provisional Districts of the North-West Territories. 1884-1885. Ottawa: 1886. V. 64

NORTHWOOD, J. D'A.
Familiar Hawaiian Birds. Honolulu: 1940. V. 67

NORTON, ANDRE
Breed to Come. New York: 1972. V. 64; 66
Judgment on Janus. 1963. V. 64
Victory of Janus. 1966. V. 64

NORTON, ARTHUR P.
A Star Atlas and Reference Handbook. London: 1927. V. 66

NORTON, CAROLINE
Letters to the Mob. London: 1848. V. 65
Lost and Saved. London: 1864. V. 65
The Undying One and Other Poems. London: 1830. V. 63; 65; 67

NORTON, CHARLES B.
Report On the Munitions of War. Washington: 1868. V. 64

NORTON, DOREEN M.
The Palomino Horse. Los Angeles: 1949. V. 62

NORTON, E.
The Fight For Everest: 1924. 1925. V. 63; 65

NORTON, HERMAN
Record of Facts Concerning the Persectuions at Madeira in 1843 and 1846: The Flight of a Thousand Converts to the West India Islands.... New York: 1849. V. 62; 63; 65; 66

NORTON, JAMES
New Jersey in 1793, an Abstract and Index to the 1793 Militia Census of the State of New Jersey. Salt Lake City: 1973. V. 66

NORTON, L. A.
Life and Adventures Of.... Oakland: 1887. V. 64; 67

NORTON, MARY
The Borrowers Aloft. London: 1961. V. 62
The Magic Bed-Knob. New York: 1943. V. 63; 64

NORTON, THOMAS
The Ordinall of Alchimy of Bristoll. Being a Facsimile Reproduction from Theatrum Chemicum Britannicum.... London: 1920. V. 63

NORTON, WILLIAM A.
An Elementary Treatise on Astronomy; in Four Parts. New York: 1845. V. 67

NORVELL, SANDERS
Forty Years of Hardware. New York: 1924. V. 64; 67

THE NORWICH Magazine 1835. Norwich: 1835. V. 67

NORWICH, OSCAR I.
Norwich's Maps of Africa.... Norwich: 1997. V. 65

NORWOOD, RICHARD
Trigonometrie. London: 1631. V. 66

NOSNHOJ, R. S.
A Novel Railroad Strike, One Hundred Thirty-Nine. Aurora: 1877. V. 62; 67

NOSPHITZ, JOSEPH D.
Basic Handbook of Child Psychiatry. New York: 1979-1987. V. 65

NOSSACK, HANS ERICH
Gedichte. Kurger: 1947. V. 67

NOSTRUMS and Quackery. Chicago: 1912. V. 63

NOT A Station but a Place. San Francisco: 1979. V. 66

NOTT, CARGILL GILSTON
Napier Tercentenary Memorial Volume,. London: 1915. V. 62

NOTT, J. P.
In Sun and Shower. Bristol: 1912. V. 67

NOTT, STANLEY CHARLES
Chinese Jade through the Ages. Rutland and Tokyo: 1962. V. 67

NOTTER, FLORENCE
Santa Claus Toy Book. Chicago: 1913. V. 64

THE NOTTINGHAM and Derby Railway Companion. London: 1839. V. 63

NOTTINGHAM, HENEAGE FINCH, 1ST EARL OF
An Exact and Most Impartial Accompt of the Indictment Arraignment, Trial and Judgement (according to Law) of Twenty Nine Regicides, the Murtherers of His Late Sacred Majesty.... London: 1660. V. 62

NOTTINGHAM NATURALISTS' SOCIETY
Annual Reports and Transactions. Thirty Seventh to Sixtieth Reports. Nottingham: 1889-1912. V. 65

NOURSE, ALAN E.
Trouble of Titan. Philadelphia and Toronto: 1954. V. 64

NOUVEAU Dictionnaire d'Historie Naturelle, Appliquee Aux Arts Principalement a l'Agriculture et a l'Economie Rurale et Domestique. Paris: 1803-1804. V. 62

NOUVEAU Dictionnaire de Poche.... Leipzig: 1809. V. 66

NOVA, CRAIG
Turkey Hash. New York: 1972. V. 66

NOVA SCOTIA
The Report and Statistical Tables of the Superintendent of Education and Principal of the Normal School for 1857. Halifax: 1857. V. 64

NOVA SCOTIA. LAWS, STATUTES, ETC. - 1805
The Statutes at Large, Passed in the Several General Assembiles Held in His Majesty's Province of Nova Scotia; from the First Assembly, which Met in Halifax the Second Day of October in the Thirty-Second Year of His Late Majesty Geo. II.... Halifax: 1805. V. 67

NOVA SCOTIA. LAWS, STATUTES, ETC. - 1816
The Statutes at Large, Passed in the Several General Assembiles Held in His Majesty's Province of Nova Scotia; from the Sixth Session of the Eighth General Assemjbly, which Met at Halifax, the Twenty-Eighth Day of Nov.... 1816. V. 67

NOVA SCOTIA. LAWS, STATUTES, ETC. - 1827
The Statutes at Large, Passed in the Several General Assembiles Held in His Majesties Province of Nova-Scotia from the Year 1817 to the Year 1826, Inclusive.... Halifax: 1827. V. 67

NOVA SCOTIA. LAWS, STATUTES, ETC. - 1835
The Statutes of the Province of Nova Scotia. Volume the Fourth from the A.D. 1827-1828; George IV to A.D. 1835; 5 William IV. Both Inclusive. Halifax: 1835. V. 67

NOVA Scotia's Industrial Centre New Glasgow, Stellarton, Westville, Trenton. The Birthplace of Steel in Canada. New Glasgow: 1916. V. 63

NOVERRE, JEAN GEORGES
Lettres sur la Danse e sur les Ballets. Stuttgart and Lyo: 1760. V. 67

NOVICE, GEORGE WILLIAM
Lights in Art, a Review of Ancient and Modern Pictures. Edinburgh: 1874. V. 67

NOWELL-SMITH, SIMON
Sadleir Sadleirized: a Book Review. London: 1949. V. 64

NOYE, WILLIAM
A Treatise of the Principall Grounds and Maximes of the Lawes of this Kingdome. London: 1641. V. 63

NOYES, ALFRED
Mystery Ships (Trapping the U-Boat). London: 1916. V. 64

NOYES, ALVA J.
In the Land of Chinook, or the Story of Blaine County. N.P: 1917. V. 65; 67
In the Land of the Chinook, or the Story of Blaine County. Helena: 1917. V. 62
The Story of Ajax - Life in the Big Hole Basin. New York: 1966. V. 65

NOYES, ARTHUR PERCY
Modern Clinical Psychiatry. Philadelphia and London: 1934. V. 65

NOYES, DAVID
The History of Norway.... Norway, Maine: 1852. V. 62

NOYES, ETHEL J. R.
The Women of the Mayflower and Women of Plymouth Colony. Plymouth: 1921/. V. 66

NOYES, JOHN H.
The Berean; a Manual for the Help of Those who Seek the Faith of the Primitive Church. Putney: 1847. V. 67

NOYES, JOHN HUMPHREY
Male Continence. Oneida: 1877. V. 62; 65

NOZEMAN, C.
Nederlandsche Vogelen. Amsterdam: 1770-1829. V. 62

NUCKEL, O.
Destiny. New York: 1930. V. 64; 66

NUEVO Concinero Americano en Forma de Diccionario. Paris: 1888. V. 67

NUGENT, GEORGE
A Letter to the Electors of Aylesbury, on the Catholick Question. Aylesbury: 1820. V. 62
Memorials of John Hampden, His Party and His Times. London: 1832. V. 62

NUGENT, GEORGE GRENVILLE, BARON
Legends of the Library at Lilies, by the Lord and Lady There. London: 1832. V. 65

NUGENT, ROBERT CRAGGS NUGENT, EARL OF
Considerations Upon a Reduction of the Land Tax. London: 1749. V. 67

NUGENT, THOMAS
The New Pocket Dictionary of the French and English Languages. London: 1793. V. 64
Travels through Germany. London: 1768. V. 65

NULL, ALBERT
Revolt for Democracy; a Plan of Physical Revolution. New York: 1959. V. 67

NUNEZ CABECA DE VACA, ALVAR
Alvar Nunez Cabeza de Vaca. The Journey and Route of the First European to Cross the Continent of North America 1534-1536. Glendale: 1940. V. 66
The Narrative of Alvar Nunez Cabeza De Vaca. Barre: 1972. V. 63; 66
Relation that Alvar Nunez Cabeca de Vaca Gave of What Befel the Armament in the Indias Whither Panphilo de Narvaez went for Governor (from the years 1527 to 1537).... San Francisco;: 1929. V. 64

NUNIS, DOYCE B.
Andrew Sublette - Rocky Mountain Price 1813-1853. Los Angeles: 1960. V. 64; 67
The Hudson's Bay Company's First Fur Brigade to Sacramento Valley: Alexander McLeod's 1829 Hunt. Sacramento: 1968. V. 65
The San Francisco Vigilance Committee of 1856 - Three Views.... Los Angeles: 1971. V. 67
Women in the Life of Southern California. Los Angeles: 1996. V. 62

NUNN, W. C.
Escape from Reconstruction. Fort Worth: 1956. V. 63
Ten Texans in Gray. Hillsboro: 1968. V. 63; 65

NURSERY Nonsense. London: 1950. V. 63

NURSERY Numbers - A New Book of Old Rhymes. London: 1880. V. 64

NURSERY Rhymes. London: 1919. V. 66

NURSERY Rhymes and New Stories Bookano Models Series No. 2. London: 1934. V. 63

NURSERY Rhymes and Proverbs. London. V. 66

THE NURSERY Zoo. New York: 1920. V. 62

NURSEY, PERRY
Evening, with Other Poems. Norwich: 1829. V. 67

NUSBAUM, AILEEN
The Seven Cities of Cibola. New York: 1926. V. 67

NUTALAYA, P.
Geology and Mineral Resources of Southeast Asia. Bangkok: 1978. V. 67

NUTAPHAND, W.
The Turtles of Thailand. Bangkok: 1979. V. 65

NUTT, DAVID
A Catalogue of Theological Books in Foreign Languages, Including the Sacred Writings.... London: 1857. V. 64; 65

NUTT, FREDERIC
The Complete Confectioner; or the Whole Art of Confectionary Made Easy. New York: 1807. V. 63

NUTT, THOMAS
Humanity to Honey Bees; Or, Practical Directions for the Management of Honey Bees Upon an Improved and Humane Plan.... Wisbech: 1834. V. 65

NUTTALL, JEFF
Bomb Culture. London: 1968. V. 64

NUTTALL, THOMAS
A Journal of Travels into the Arkansas Territory, During the Year 1819.... Philadelphia: 1821. V. 63; 66
A Manual of the Ornithology of the United States and of Canada. Cambridge: 1832. V. 63

NUTTALL, ZELIA
New Light on Drake, a Collection of Documents Relating to His Voyage of Circum-Navigation 1577-1580. London: 1914. V. 63

NUTTING, C. C.
American Hydroids. Washington: 1900-1915. V. 62
American Hydroids. Part II. The Sertularidae. Washington: 1904. V. 63
Fiji-New Zealand Expedition.... Iowa City: 1924. V. 62; 63
Narrative and Preliminary Report of Bahama Expedition. Iowa City: 1895. V. 63

NUTTING, J. H.
An Essay on Some of the Principles of Medical Delusion. Boston: 1853. V. 63

NUTTING, WALLACE
Wallace Nutting's Biography. Framingham: 1936. V. 63

NYBERG, BJORN
The Return of Conan. 1957. V. 66

NYBLOM, HELENA
Jolly Calle & Other Swedish Fairy Tales. London: 1913. V. 65

NYE, ROBERT
Doubtfire. London: 1967. V. 67

NYE, WILBUR S.
Bad Medicine and Good - Tales of the Iowas. Norman: 1962. V. 67
Carbine and Lance. Norman: 1937. V. 65
Plains Indian Raiders - the Final Phases of Warfare from the Arkansas to the Red River. Norman: 1968. V. 67

NYMAN, CARL FREDRIK
Sylloge Florae Europaeae Seu Plantarum Vascularium Europae Indigenarum Enumeratio Adjectis Synonymis Gravioribus et Indicata Singularum Distributione Geographica. Oerebroae: 1854-1865. V. 64

NYSCHENS, IAN
Months in the Sun. 1997. V. 62; 63; 64; 66

O

OAKES, CLIFFORD
The Birds of Lancashire. London: 1953. V. 65

OAKES, WILLIAM
Scenery of the White Mountains. Boston: 1848. V. 62
Scenery of the White Mountains. Somersworth: 1970. V. 67
Views of the Profile Mountain and the Profile Rock, or the Old Man of the Mountain at Franconia, New Hampshire. Boston: 1847. V. 62

OAKESHOTT, W.
Classical Inspiration in Medieval Art: Rhind Lectures for 1956. London: 1959. V. 65

OAKLEY, GILES
The Devil's Music. A History of the Blues. New York: 1970. V. 63

OAKLY, OBADIAH
Expedition to Oregon. New York: 1914. V. 63

OAKS, GEORGE WASHINGTON
Man of the West, Reminiscences of 1840-1917 Recorded by Ben Jaastad, Editor, and Annotated by Arthur Woodward. Tucson: 1956. V. 67

OASIS: The Middle East Anthology of Poetry From the Forces. Cairo;: 1943. V. 65

OASTLER, RICHARD
The Fleet Papers: Being Letters to Thomas Thornhill, Esq. of Riddlesworth in the County of Norfolk from Richard Oastler, His Prisoner in the Fleet.* London: 1841-. V. 67

OATES, FRANK
Matabele Land and the Victoria Falls. London: 1889. V. 64

OATES, J. C. T
Cambridge University Library: a History. I. From the Beginnings to the Copyright Act of Queen Anne. II. The Eighteenth and Nineteenth Centuries. Cambridge: 1986. V. 62

OATES, JOYCE CAROL
The Assassins. New York: 1975. V. 67
By the North Gate. New York: 1963. V. 67
Cupid and Psyche. New York: 1970. V. 62
The Edge of Impossibility. New York: 1972. V. 62
Foxfire: Confessions of a Girl Gang. 1993. V. 65
Foxfire: Confessions of a Girl Gang. New York: 1993. V. 67
Funland. Concord: 1983. V. 62
The Girl. Cambridge: 1974. V. 62
The Hostile Sun: The Poetry of D. H. Lawrence. Los Angeles: 1973. V. 66
Invisible Woman. Princeton;: 1982. V. 62
A Middle-Class Education. New York: 1980. V. 62
Mysteries of Winterhurn. Franklin Center: 1984. V. 63; 64; 66; 67
On Boxing. Garden City: 1987. V. 62
Son of the Morning. New York: 1978. V. 65
Them. New York: 1969. V. 64; 67
Unholy Loves. New York: 1979. V. 66
What I Lived For. New York: 1994. V. 67
The Wheel of Love and Other Stories. London: 1971. V. 62
With Shuddering Fall. New York: 1964. V. 67
Women in Love and Other Poems. New York: 1968. V. 62
You Must Remember This. Franklin Center: 1987. V. 67
You Must Remember This. New York: 1987. V. 67

OATES, STEPHEN B.
Confederate Cavalry West of the River. Austin: 1861. V. 64
Confederate Cavalry West of the River. Austin: 1961. V. 67

OATES, TITUS
(Greek title) or, the Picture of the Late King James Drawn from the Life. London: 1696. V. 65

OATTS, L. B.
Proud Heritage, the Story of the Highland Light Infantry. London and Glasgow: 1959. V. 66

OBAN, Staffa and Iona. London: 1859. V. 62

OBEDIENCE Due to the Present King, Notwithstanding Our Oaths to the Former. London: 1689. V. 62

O'BEIRNE, THOMAS LEWIS
A Candid and Impartial Narrative of the Transactions of the Fleet, Under the Command of Lord Howe.... London: 1778. V. 64

OBER, FREDERICK A.
Travels in Mexico, and Life Among the Mexicans. Boston: 1884. V. 65

OBERHOLSER, H. C.
The Bird Life of Texas. Austin: 1974. V. 67

OBERNDORFFER, JOHANN
Apologia Chymico-Medica Practica Johan. Amberg?: 1610. V. 65

OBITUARY Addresses Delivered on the Occasion of the Death of Zachary Taylor, President of the United States, in the Senate and House of Representatives, July 10, 1850.... Washington;: 1850. V. 66

OBJECTIONS To the Ballot, Answered from the Writings and Speeches of Mill, Grote, &c. London: 1837. V. 67

O'BRENNAN, MARTIN A.
Antiquities and a School History of Ireland. 1858. V. 67

O'BRIAN, PATRICK
Clarissa Oakes. 1992. V. 64
Clarissa Oakes. London: 1992. V. 63; 66
Desolation Island. London: 1978. V. 62; 63; 64
The Far Side of the World. London: 1984. V. 62; 63; 64
The Fortune of War. London: 1979. V. 62; 63; 64
The Ionian Mission. London: 1981. V. 66
Master and Commander. Philadelphia: 1969. V. 64
Master and Commander. London: 1970. V. 64
The Mauritius Command. New York: 1978. V. 66
Men-of-War. London: 1974. V. 63; 64
Nutmeg of Consolation. London: 1991. V. 62; 65
Pablo Ruiz Picasso - a Biography. London: 1976. V. 62
Post Captain. London: 1972. V. 62
Reverse of the Medal. London: 1986. V. 62
Surgeon's Mate. London: 1980. V. 65
The Thirteen Gun Salute. London: 1989. V. 66
Treason's Harbour. London: 1983. V. 63

O'BRIEN, CHARLES
A Treatise on Calico Printing, Theoretical and Practical; Including the Latest Philosohpical Discoveries, any Way Applicable.... London: 1792. V. 67

O'BRIEN, CHARLOTTE
Wild Flowers of the Undercliffe, Isle of Wight. 18881. V. 62

O'BRIEN, EDNA
August is a Wicked Month. London: 1965. V. 66
James and Nora - Portrait of Joyce's Marraige. Northridge: 1981. V. 65
The Lonely Girl. London: 1962. V. 62
A Pagan Place - a Play. London: 1973. V. 63

O'BRIEN, FLANN
At Swim-Two Birds. London: 1939. V. 66
At Swim-Two Birds. 1951. V. 62; 65
Cruiskeen Lawn. Dublin: 1943. V. 65
The Dalkey Archive. London: 1964. V. 63; 66
Faustus Kelly - a Play in Three Acts. Dublin: 1943. V. 64
The Hard Life. London: 1961. V. 66
The Hard Life. New York: 1962. V. 64
The Poor Mouth. (an Beal Bocht). London: 1973. V. 62

O'BRIEN, GEOFFREY
Hardboiled America: The Lurid Years of Paperbacks. New York: 1981. V. 65

O'BRIEN, GEORGE
The Economic History of Ireland in the 17th Century. 1919. V. 63; 66

O'BRIEN, IVAR
O'Brien of Thomond. The O'Briens in Irish History 1500-1865. 1886. V. 67

O'BRIEN, JOHN
Leaving Las Vegas. Kansas: 1990. V. 64
A Treatise on American Military Laws and the Pracitce of Courts Martial. Philadelphia: 1846. V. 66

O'BRIEN, MICHAEL J.
A Hidden Phase of American History; Ireland' Part in America's Struggle for Liberty. New York: 1921. V. 66
The Mc Carthys in Early American History. 1921. V. 62; 65

O'BRIEN, PAUL
A Practical Grammar of the Irish Language. Dublin: 1809. V. 64

O'BRIEN, ROBERT C.
Mrs. Frisby and the Rats of NIMH. New York: 1971. V. 65

O'BRIEN, TIM
Going After Cacciato. Lawrence: 1978. V. 64
Going After Cacciato. London: 1978. V. 65
Going After Cacciato. New York: 1978. V. 62; 65; 66; 67
If I Die in a Combat Zone. N.P: 1973. V. 62
If I Die in a Combat Zone. New York: 1973. V. 63; 65
In the Lake of the Woods. Boston: 1994. V. 64; 65; 66
Northern Lights. New York: 1975. V. 62; 66; 67
The Nuclear Age. Portland: 1981. V. 62; 66
The Nuclear Age. New York: 1985. V. 62; 66
Speaking of Courage. Santa Barbara: 1980. V. 62; 67
The Things They Carried. Boston: 1990. V. 62; 64; 65; 66; 67

O'BRIEN, TIM continued
The Things They Carried. Franklin Center: 1990. V. 62
The Things They Carried. Toronto: 1990. V. 63; 67
Tomcat in Love. Franklin Center: 1998. V. 67
Tomcat in Love. New York: 1998. V. 64; 67

O'BRIEN, W. P.
The Great Famine in Ireland and a Retrospect of the Fifty Years 1845-1895. 1896. V. 63; 66

O'BRIEN, WILLIAM
Golden Memories: the Love Letters and Prison Letters of William O'Brien. 1929. V. 67

OBSERVATIONS on Mr. Gladstone's Denunciation of Certain Millowners of Lancashire, Contained in a Speech Delivered by Him at Newcastle, on the 7th of October 1862. London: 1862. V. 63

OBSERVATIONS on the Conduct of Great Britain, with Regard to the Negociations and Other Transactions Abroad. Edinburgh: 1729. V. 67

OBSERVATIONS On the Conduct of Great Britain, with Regard to the Negociations and Other Transactions Abroad. London: 1729. V. 63

OBSESSION.. Rockville: 1994. V. 64; 67

OBST, F. J.
The Completely Illustrated Atlas of Reptiles and Amphibians for the Terrarium. Neptune City: 1988. V. 66

O'BYRNE, DANIEL
The History of the Queen's County...Containing an Historical and Traditional Account of Its Foundries. Dublin: 1856. V. 63

O'BYRNE, WILLIAM R.
A Naval Biographical Dictionary.... London: 1849. V. 64

O'CALLAGHAN, ANDREW
Thoughts on the Tendency of Bible Societies as Affecting the Established Church and Christianity Itself.... London: 1817. V. 67

O'CALLAGHAN, JOHN C.
History of the British Brigades in the Service of France. Glasgow. V. 64
History of the Irish Brigades in the Service of France. 1969. V. 67

OCAMPO, VICTORIA
338171 T.E. Buenos Aires: 1942. V. 65

O'CASEY. SEAN
Autobiographies.... London: 1981. V. 62

O'CASEY, SEAN
Collected Plays. 1949-1951. V. 63
I Knock at the Door. Pictures in the Hallway. Drums Under the Windows. Inishfallen Fare Thee Well. Rose and Crown. Sunset and Evening Star. 1939-1954. V. 63; 66
The Story of the Irish Citizen. Dublin and London: 1919. V. 67
Two Plays. Juno and Paycock. The Shadow of a Gunman. London: 1925. V. 66

OCCOM, SAMSON
A Sermon Preached at the Execution of Moses Paul, an Indian; Who Was Executed at New Haven on the Second of September 1772 for the Murder of Mr. Moses Cook, later of Waterbury, on the 7th of December 1771. New Haven: 1772. V. 62

THE OCEAN; a Description of Wonders and Important Products of the Sea. London: 1833. V. 67

OCEAN Liners of the Past. The Cunard White Star Quadruple-Screw Liner Queen Mary. London: 1972. V. 66

O'CIANAIN, TADHG
The Flight of the Earls. 1916. V. 66

OCLAND, CHRISTOPHER
Anglorum Praelia ab Anno Domini 1327-1558. 1582. V. 65

O'CLUNY, THOMAS
The Merry Multifleet and the Mount Multicorps. London: 1904. V. 67

O'CONNELL, CAROL
Killing Critics. Blakeney, Gloucestershire: 1995. V. 63; 66
Mallory' Oracle. London: 1994. V. 62; 64; 65; 66; 67
Mallory's Oracle. New York: 1994. V. 67
The Man Who Cast Two Shadows. New York: 1995. V. 67
The Man Who Lied to Women. London: 1995. V. 65; 66; 67
The Same River Twice. New York: 1993. V. 67

O'CONNELL, D. J. K.
The Green Flash, and Other Low Sun Phenomena. Amsterdam: 1958. V. 66

O'CONNELL, DANIEL
Correspondence of Daniel Cornell the Liberator. London: 1888. V. 64

O'CONNELL, J. J.
Catholicity in the Carolinas and Georgia: Leaves of Its History. New York: 1879. V. 67

O'CONNELL, JOHN
An Argument for Ireland. Dublin: 1844. V. 67
The Commercial Injustices. Dublin: 1843. V. 65
The Taxation Injustice. Dublin: 1843. V. 65

O'CONNELL, M. J., MRS.
The Last Colonel of the Irish Brigade. 1892. V. 63; 64; 67

O'CONNELL, MAURICE R.
Irish Politics and Social Conflict in the Age of the American Revolution. Philadelphia: 1965. V. 67

O'CONNOR, ANNE
From the Stone Age to the 'Forty-Five. Edinburgh: 1983. V. 67

O'CONNOR, ARTHUR
The Trial of James O'Coigly, Otherwise Called James Quigley, Otherwise Called James John Fivey, Arthur O'Connor, Esq.... London: 1798. V. 63

O'CONNOR, FLANNERY
The Artificial Nigger and Other Tales. London: 1957. V. 67
The Complete Stories. New York: 1971. V. 62
Everything that Rises Must Converge. New York: 1965. V. 62; 63
A Good Man is Hard to Find. New York: 1955. V. 62; 63
The Habit of Being. New York: 1979. V. 63; 64; 65; 67
Mystery and Manners. New York: 1969. V. 62
Wise Blood. New York: 1952. V. 65; 67
Wise Blood. London: 1955. V. 62

O'CONNOR, FRANK
Guests of the Nation. 1931. V. 64; 67
Guests of the Nation. London: 1931. V. 63; 66
Little Monasteries. 1963. V. 64; 67
The Saint and Mary Kate. London: 1932. V. 66
Three Old Brothers and Other Poems. 1936. V. 67
W. B. Yeats: a Reminiscence. Edinburgh: 1982. V. 64
The Wild Bird's Nest. Dublin: 1922. V. 63
The Wild Bird's Nest. Dublin: 1932. V. 62

O'CONNOR, JACK
The Art of Hunting Big Game in North America. New York: 1967. V. 62; 67
Game in the Desert. 1993. V. 67
The Hunting Rifle. New York: 1970. V. 67

O'CONNOR, JEANNIE
The Wood Engravings of John O'Connor. London: 1989. V. 65

O'CONNOR, JOHN
Knipton: a Leicestershire Village. London: 1996. V. 65

O'CONNOR, P. F.
Shark!. 1954. V. 67

O'CONNOR, R.
An Introduction to the Field Sports of France. 1846. V. 67

O'CONNOR, RICHARD
Sheridan the Inevitable. Indianapolis & New York: 1953. V. 62

O'CONNOR, ROBERT
Buffalo Soldiers. New York: 1993. V. 62; 64; 67

O'CONNOR, V. C. SCOTT
The Charm of Kashmir. London: 1920. V. 65
Mandalay and Other Cities of the Past in Burma. London: 1907. V. 65
The Silken East. London: 1904. V. 62
The Silken East. London: 1928. V. 65

O'CONOR, NORREYS J.
Changing Ireland: Literary Backgrounds of the Irish Free State 1889-1922. Cambridge: 1924. V. 67

O'CROULEY, PEDRO ALONSO
A Description of the Kingdom of New Spain. N.P: 1972. V. 66

OCTAVIUS
M. Minucii Octavius...Ex Recensione Jacobi Gronvii.... Lugduni Batavorum: 1709. V. 65

O'DAY, EDWARD F.
Bel-Air Bay. A Country Place by the Sea. Los Angeles: 1927. V. 62

AN ODD Bestiary; or a Compendium of Instructive and Entertaining Descriptions of Animals.... 1982. V. 62

THE ODD Volume. London: 1908. V. 65

ODELL, GEORGE C. D.
Annals of the New York Stage. 1927-1949. V. 63

ODELL, ROBIN
Jack the Ripper in Fact and Fiction. London: 1965. V. 64

O'DELL, THOMAS E.
Matopaha - the Story of Bear Butte. Spearfish: 1942. V. 65

ODEN, BILL
Early Days on the Texas-New Mexico Plains. Canyon: 1965. V. 63; 65

ODETS, CLIFFORD
Golden Boy. New York: 1937. V. 62

ODIER, LOUIS
Instruction sur les Moyens de Purifier l'Air et d'Arreterles Progres de la Contagion, a l'Aide des Fumigations de Gaz Nitrique.... Geneva: 1801. V. 65
Manuel de Medecine-Pratique ou Sommaire d'un Cours Gratuit Donne en 1800, 1801, et 1804, Aux Officiers de Sante du Dept. du Leman.... Geneva: 1821. V. 65
Registres Mortuaires de Geneve. N.P: 1814. V. 65

ODIORNE, THOMAS
The Progress of Reinfement, a Poem, in Three Books. Boston: 1792. V. 63

ODLING, WILLIAM
A Course of Practical Chemistry. London: 1854. V. 65

O'DOHERTY, BRIAN
American Masters: The Voice and the Myth. New York: 1973. V. 63; 64

O'DONNELL, FRANK HUGH
A History of the Irish Parliamentary Party. 1910. V. 63; 66; 67
A History of the Irish Parliamentary Party. London: 1910. V. 66

O'DONNELL, LILLIAN
Death Schuss. New York: 1963. V. 67

O'DONNELL, PETER
Cobra Trap. London: 1996. V. 66
Dead Man's Handle. London: 1985. V. 66
Dragon's Claw. London: 1978. V. 66
Dragon's Claw. 1985. V. 67
Golden Urchin. London: 1986. V. 66
I, Lucifer. London: 1967. V. 66
The Impossible Virgin. London: 1971. V. 66
Last Day in Limbo. London: 1973. V. 66
Last Day in Limbo. London: 1976. V. 67
Modesty Blaise. London: 1963. V. 65
Modesty Blaise. London: 1965. V. 66; 67
Modesty Blaise: a Taste for Death. 1969. V. 63
Modesty Blaise: Last Day in Limbo. 1970. V. 63
Modesty Blaise: The Impossible Virgin. 1971. V. 63
Modesty Blaise: The Silver Mistress. 1973. V. 63
The Night of Morningstar. London: 1982. V. 66
Sabre-Tooth. London: 1966. V. 66; 67
The Silver Mistress. London: 1973. V. 66; 67
The Silver Mistress. 1981. V. 67
A Taste of Death. London: 1969. V. 66
The Xanadu Talisman. London: 1981. V. 66
The Xanadu Talisman. 1984. V. 67

O'DONOGHUE, DAVID J.
The Humour of Ireland. 1894. V. 67

O'DONOGHUE, JOHN
Historical Memoirs of the O'Briens. 1860. V. 62
Historical Memoirs of the O'Briens. Dublin: 1860. V. 67

O'DONOVAN, JEREMIAH
A Brief Account of the Author's Interview with His Countrymen, and of the Parts of the Emerald Isle Whence They Emigrated Together With a Direct Reference to Their Present Location. Pittsburgh: 1864. V. 65
A History of Ireland.... Pittsburgh: 1854. V. 63
Irish Immigration in the United States. New York: 1969. V. 65

O'DONOVAN, JOHN
The Economic History of Live Stock in Ireland. 1940. V. 65

O'DONOVAN, MARY JANE
Irish Lyrical Poems. New York: 1868. V. 65

O'DOODLE, PHELIM, PSEUD.
The Subaltern's Check-Book; or, Exercises and Evolutions for the Preservation of Cash and Character. London: 1848. V. 62

O'DRISCOLL, ROBERT
The Untold Story. The Irish in Canada. 1988. V. 67

O'DRISCOLL, W. JUSTIN
A Memoir of Daniel Maclise, R.A. 1871. V. 65

ODUM, HOWARD W.
The Negro and His Songs. Chapel Hill: 1925. V. 63; 65; 67
Negro Workaday Songs. Chapel Hill: 1926. V. 63; 65; 66; 67
Wings on My Feet. Indianapolis: 1929. V. 62

OEDER, GEORGE CHRISTIAN
(Flora Danica) Icones Planaturm Sponte Nascentium in Regnis Daniae et Norvegiae. Hafniae: 1761-. V. 67

OEHLER, GOTTLIEB F.
Description of a Journey and Visit to the Pawnee Indians April 22-May 18, 1851 and a Description of the Manners and Customs of the Pawnee Indians. New York: 1914. V. 64; 65
Description of a Journey and Visit to the Pawnee Indians...Platte River...1851. 1914. V. 67

OENSLAGER, D.
Stage Design: Four Centuries of Scenic Invention. New York: 1975. V. 65

OERSTED, H. C.
The Discovery of Electromagnetism Made in the Year 1820. Copenahgen: 1920. V. 62

OESCHGER, JOHANNES
Thirty Letters to and From Basle 1504-1940. Basle: 1960. V. 66; 67

OESTERREICH, MATHIAS
Des Hernn Daniel Stenglin in Hamburg Sammlung von Italienischen, Hollandischen und Deutschen Gemahlden. Berlin: 1763. V. 64

O'FAOLAIN, JULIA
Man in the Cellar: Stories. London: 1974. V. 66

O'FAOLAIN, SEAN
Bird Alone. 1936. V. 63; 66
The Born Genius. Detroit: 1936. V. 62; 65
The Collected Stories of.... 1980-1982. V. 65
The Finest Stories of Sean O'Faolain. Boston: 1957. V. 67
King of the Beggars: A Life of Daniel O'Connell. New York: 1938. V. 63; 66
Midsummer Night Madness and Other Stories. London: 1932. V. 65

O'FERRALL, CHARLES T.
Forty Years of Active Service. New York and Washington: 1904. V. 62; 63; 65

OFF for the Holidays. London: 1890. V. 63

OFFENBACH, JACQUES
America and the Americans. London: 1876. V. 64

OFFICIAL Book of the State of South Dakota. Pierre: 1937. V. 66

OFFICIAL Brand Book of the State of South Dakota. Pierre: 1937. V. 63

THE OFFICIAL Confessions of William Burke, Executed at Edinburgh for Murder, on Wednesay, the 295h January 1829. Together with an Authenticated Confession, Containing Minute Details of All the Murders Committed by Him.... Glasgow: 1829. V. 63

OFFICIAL Records of the Union and Confederate Navies in the War of the Rebellion. Washington: 1894. V. 65

OFFICIAL Register and Directory of Physicians and Surgeons in the State of California. San Francisco. 1903. V. 63

OFFICIAL Report of the Battle of Chickamauga. Richmond: 1864. V. 62; 63

THE OFFICINA Bodoni. Paris/New York: 1929. V. 64
THE OFFICINA Bodoni. Verona: 1980. V. 66

OFFICINA BODONI
The Officina. Verona: 1929. V. 66

OFFUTT, CHRIS
Kentucky Straight. New York: 1992. V. 64; 66; 67
Out of the Woods. New York: 1999. V. 66
The Same River Twice. New York: 1993. V. 63; 65; 67
Tar Pit Love Lettered. Castle Rock: 2000. V. 67
Two-Eleven All Around. Santa Monica: 1998. V. 62; 66

O'FLAHERTY, DANIEL
General Jo Shelby. Undefeated Rebel. Chapel Hill: 1954. V. 63; 64; 67

O'FLAHERTY, JOSEPH H.
The South Coast and Los Angeles. Los Angeles: 1992. V. 62

O'FLAHERTY, LIAM
The Assassin. 1928. V. 67
The Assassin. London: 1928. V. 65; 66
The Black Soul. 1924. V. 64; 67
The Black Soul. 1929. V. 65
The Ecstasy of Angus. London: 1931. V. 66
The Fairy Goose and Two Other Stories. New York: 1927. V. 66
Famine. London: 1937. V. 65
Hollywood Cemetery. 1935. V. 65
The House of Gold. 1929. V. 62
The House of Gold. London: 1929. V. 65; 66
Land. New York: 1946. V. 66
The Martyr. 1933. V. 62; 65; 67
Mr. Gilhooley. London: 1926. V. 66
The Mountain Tavern and Other Stories. London: 1929. V. 65
The Puritan. 1932. V. 62
The Puritan. London: 1932. V. 65
Red Barbara, and Other Stories. New York: 1928. V. 63
Return of the Brute. 1929. V. 67
Return of the Brute. London: 1929. V. 63; 64; 66
Shame the Devil. 1934. V. 65; 67
Shame the Devil. London: 1934. V. 66
Skerrett. 1932. V. 67
Skerrett. London: 1932. V. 66
Skerrett. New York: 1932. V. 64
Spring Sowing. 1924. V. 67
Spring Sowing. London: 1924. V. 66
The Tent. London: 1926. V. 65; 66
Thy Neighbours Wife. 1923. V. 67
Thy Neighbour's Wife. London: 1923. V. 66
A Tourist's Guide to Ireland. London. V. 65
A Tourist's Guide to Ireland. 1929. V. 65; 67
Two Lovely Beasts and Other Stories. 1948. V. 67
The Wild Swan and Other Stories. London: 1932. V. 66

OGDEN, ADELE
The California Sea Otter: Trade 1784-1848. Berkeley: 1941. V. 63

OGDEN, GEORGE W.
Letters from the West.... New Bedford: 1823. V. 66

OGDEN, J.
Yorkshire's River Derwent. 1974. V. 67

OGDEN, PETER SKENE
Snake Country Journals 1824-1826, 1826-1827, 1827-1828, 1828-1829. London: 1950. V. 67
Traits of American Indian Life By a Fur Trader. San Francisco: 1933. V. 66

OGG, DAVID
England in the Reign of Charles II. Oxford: 1955. V. 67

OGG, FREDERIC A.
The Opening of the Mississippi. A Struggle for Supremacy in the American Interior. New York: 1904. V. 67

OGG, OSCAR
Three Classics of Italian Calligraphy. New York: 1953. V. 67

OGILBY and Morgan's Pocket-Book of the Roads, with Their Computed and Measured Distances and the Distinction of Market and Post-Towns. London: 1732. V. 67

OGILBY, J. D.
Edible Fishes and Crustaceans of New South Wales. Sydney: 1893. V. 65

OGILBY, JOHN
The Traveller's Pocket-Book; or Ogilby and Morgan's Book of the Roads. London: 1765. V. 66; 67
The Traveller's Pocket-Book; or Ogilby and Morgan's Book of the Roads Improved and Amended. London: 1775. V. 62

OGILBY, W.
Observations on the History and Classification of the Marsupial Quadrupeds of New Holland. London: 1839. V. 67

OGILBY'S and Morgan's Pocket-Book of the Roads, with Their Computed and Measured Distances and the Distinction of Market and Post Towns. London: 1732. V. 66

OGILVIE, JOHN
The Comprehensive English Dictionary.... London: 1870. V. 64
The Imperial Dictionary, English, Technological and Scientific.... London: 1850. V. 66
The Imperial Dictionary, English, Technological and Scientific.... London: 1876. V. 64
The Imperial Dictionary of the English Language.... London: 1896-1898. V. 64
The Student's English Dictionary.... London: 1866. V. 64

OGILVIE, WILL H.
A Handful of Leather. London: 1928. V. 67

OGILVIE-GRANT, W. R.
British Ornithologists' Union Expedition and the Wollaston Expedition in Dutch New Guinea, 1910-1913. Reports on the Collections. 1916. V. 65; 66
British Ornithologists' Union Expedition and the Wollaston Expedition in Dutch New Guinea, 1910-1913. Reports on the Collections. London: 1916. V. 64
The Gun at Home and Abroad. British Game Birds and Wildfowl. London: 1912. V. 62; 67
A Hand-Book to the Game Birds. London: 1895-1897. V. 67
A Hand-Book to the Game Birds. 1896-1897. V. 63
A Hand-Book to the Game Birds. London: 1896-1897. V. 62; 64; 65

OGLE, THOMAS
Our English Lakes, Mountains and Waterfalls. London: 1864. V. 62

OGLESBY, RICHARD
Manuel Lisa and the Opening of the Missouri Fur Trade. Norman: 1963. V. 67

OGNEV, S. I.
Mammals of U.S.S.R. and Adjacent Countries. Volume IV-VII. Rodents. Jerusalem: 1963-1966. V. 62

O'GRADA, CORMAC
Ireland, a New Economic History 1780-1939. 1994. V. 67

O'GRADY, STANDISH HAYES
Toruigheacht Dhiarmuda Agus Ghrainne; or the Pursuit After Diarmuid O'Duibhne and Grainne. 1857. V. 62
Caithreim Thoirdhealbhaigh. 1929. V. 65

THE OGRES Of Oyeyama. Tokyo: 1890. V. 65

O'HAGEN, THOMAS
Intimacies in Canadian Life and Letters. (with) The Tide of Love. Ottawa: 1927. V. 63

O'HANLON, JAMES
Murder at 300 to 1. New York: 1938. V. 65

O'HANLON, JOHN C.
Life and Scenery in Missouri, Reminiscences of a Missouri Priest. Dublin: 1890. V. 64; 67

O'HANLON, REDMOND
Into the Heart of Borneo. Edinburgh: 1984. V. 64; 65; 67
Into the Heart of Borneo. London: 1984. V. 66
Joseph Conrad and Charles Darwin. The Influence of Scientific Thought on Conrad's Fiction. Edinburgh: 1984. V. 67

O'HARA, CLEOPHAS C.
The Badland Formations of the Black Hills Region in South Dakota School of Mines. Rapid City: 1910. V. 67

O'HARA, FRANK
A City in Winter and Other Poems. New York: 1951. V. 64; 66; 67
In Memory of My Feelings. New York: 1967. V. 66
Lunch Poems. San Francisco;: 1964. V. 62; 64
Meditations In an Emergency. New York: 1957. V. 64
Nature and New Painting. New York: 1967. V. 62
Second Avenue. New York: 1960. V. 62

O'HARA, JOHN
Appointment in Samarra. New York: 1934. V. 67
The Instrument. New York: 1967. V. 62; 67
The Lockwood Concern. New York: 1965. V. 62; 66; 67
Pal Joey. New York: 1952. V. 66
Sermons and Soda Water. London: 1961. V. 64; 67
Ten North Frederick. New York: 1955. V. 65
Waiting for Winter. New York: 1966. V. 62; 67

O'HARE, KATE RICHARDS
In Prison, being a Report by...to the President of the United States as to the Conditions Under which Women Federal Prisoners are Confined in the Missouri State Penitentiary.... St. Louis: 1920. V. 63; 65

O'HART, JOHN
The Irish and Anglo-Irish Landed Gentry. When Cromwell Came to Ireland.... 1892. V. 65
Irish Pedigrees; or, the Origin and Stem of the Irish Nation. New York: 1923. V. 66
Irish Pedigrees; or the Origin and Stem of the Irish Nation. 1989. V. 67

O'HEGARTY, P. S.
A History of Ireland Under the Union, 1801-1922. 1952. V. 67

OHIO STATE MEDICAL SOCIETY
Transactions of the Forty-Fourth Annual Meeting of the Ohio State Medical Society Held at Youngstown May 22, 23 and 24, 1889. Cleveland: 1889. V. 67

OINOPHILUS, BONIFACE, PSEUD.
Ebrietatis Encomium. New York: 1910. V. 64

OJALA, AATOS
Aestheticism and Oscar Wilde. Helsinki: 1954. V. 66

OKADA, Y.
Studies on the Freshwater Fishes of Japan. 1959-1960. V. 65
Studies on the Freshwater Fishes of Japan. Tokyo: 1959-1960. V. 62
The Tailless Batrachians of the Japanese Empire (Includes Taiwan and Korea). Tokyo: 1931. V. 67

OKE, GEORGE C.
The Law of Turnpike Roads. London: 1854. V. 66
The Magisterial Synopsis: Comprising Summary Convictions, the Offences, Penalties &c. and the Stages of Procedure.... London: 1849. V. 63

OKE, WILLIAM SAMWAYS
Practical Examinations on the Immediate Treatment of the Principal Emergencies that Occur in Surgery and Midwifery.... London: 1831-1835. V. 62

OKEDEN, FITZMAURICE, MRS.
Felicia's Dowry. London: 1866. V. 65

O'KEEFE, ADELAIDE
Zenobia, Queen of Palmyra: a Narrative, Founded on History. London: 1814. V. 65

O'KEEFE, GEORGIA
Georgia O'Keefe. New York: 1976. V. 62; 63; 64

O'KEEFE, JOHN
The Agreeable Surprise. Dublin: 1784. V. 65
The Castle of Andalusia, a Comic Opera in Three Acts. Dublin: 1790. V. 65
Fontainbleu, or, Our Way in France. A Comic Opera in Three Acts. As Performed at the Theatres Royal in Covent Garden and Smock-Alley. Dublin: 1790. V. 65
The Poor Soldier. A Comic Opera. Dublin: 1786. V. 65
Recollections of the Life of John O'Keefe,. Philadelphia: 1827. V. 67
The Son-in-Law, a Comic Opera, As It is Acted at the Theatre-Royal, Smoke Alley. Dublin: 1788. V. 65

O'KEEFE, R.
Cowboy Life. San Antonio: 1936. V. 62; 65

O'KELLY, J. J.
Ireland: Elements of Her Early Story from the Coming of Ceasair to the Anglo-Norman Invasion. 1921. V. 67

OKEN, L.
Elements of Physio-Philosophy.... London: 1847. V. 67

OKIGBO, CHRISTOPHER
Heavensgate. Ibadan Mbari Publications: 1962. V. 63

OKLADNIKOV, A. P.
Yakutia, Before Its Incoporation into the Russian State. 1970. V. 62

OKRI, BEN
Astonishing the Gods. London: 1995. V. 63; 65
Incidents at the Shrine. London: 1986. V. 65

O'LAVERTY, JAMES
An Historical Account of the Dioceses of Down and Connor: Anicent and Modern. 1878-1895. V. 64

OLCOTT, FRANCES JENKINS
Good Stories for Great Holidays. Boston: 1914. V. 63

OLCOTT, H. S.
Sorgho and Imphee,the Chinese and African Sugar Cases.... New York: 1857. V. 67

THE OLD and the New: or Discourses and Proceedings at the Dedication of the Re-modelled Unitarian Church in Charleston, S.C. on Sunday April 2, 1854. Charleston: 1854. V. 67

THE OLD Ballad of the Babes in the Woods. London: 1972. V. 62

OLD Ballads, Historical and Narrative, with Some of Modern Date. London: 1784. V. 62

THE OLD Brewery, and the New Mission House at the Five Points. New York: 1854. V. 65

OLD Dutch Nursery Rhymes. London: 1917. V. 62; 66

OLD Edinburgh Beaux and Belles Faithfully Presented. Edinburgh: 1886. V. 67

OLD Fairy Tales. London: 1920. V. 65

OLD French Nursery Songs. London: 1920. V. 62; 66

OLD Mother Bantry. New York: 1870. V. 62

OLD Mother Hubbard and Her Dog. Philadelphia: 1867. V. 62

OLD Nursery Rhymes. 1911. V. 63

THE OLD Nursery Stories and Rhymes. London. V. 63

THE OLD Oak Chest. New York: 1890. V. 63

OLD Plays; Being a Continuation of Dodsley's Collection, with Notes Critical and Explanatory. London: 1816. V. 67

OLD Princeton's Neighbours. N.P: 1939. V. 66

OLD Settlers' History of York County and Individual Biographies. N.P: 1913. V. 66

OLD Woman and Her Silver Penny. London: 1858. V. 67

OLD-Time Ships of Salem. Salem: 1922. V. 63

OLDEN, SARAH E.
Little Slants at Western Life - a Notebook of Travel and Reflection. New York: 1927. V. 67

OLDENBURG, CLAES
Drawings and Prints. London/New York: 1969. V. 64
Notes in Hand. 1971. V. 63
Store Days. New York: 1967. V. 63; 64; 66

OLDENBURG, HENRY
The Correspondence of Henry Oldenburg. Madison: 1965-1973. V. 63
The Correspondence of Henry Oldenburg. 1965-1986. V. 62
The Correspondence of Henry Oldenburg: Volume I 1641-1662. Madison: 1965. V. 67

OLDENDORP, CHRISTIAN GEORG ANDREAS
Oldendorp's Geschichte der Evangelischen Bruder auf den Caraibischen Inseln S. Thomas, S. Croix und S. Jan. Barby: 1777. V. 63

OLDFIELD, JOSIAH
The Evils of Butchery. London: 1895. V. 62
The Penalty of Death or the Problem of Capital Punishment. London: 1901. V. 62

OLDFIELD, OTIA
A Pictorial Journal of a Voyage Aboard the Three Masted Schooner Louise. San Francisco: 1969. V. 63

OLDFIELD, THOMAS HENRY BURLEY
History of the Original Constitution of Parliaments, from the Time of the Britons to the Present Day.... London: 1797. V. 62; 67

OLDHAM, J. BASIL
English Blind-Stamped Bindings. Cambridge: 1952. V. 64; 65; 66
English Blind-Stamped Bindings and Blind Panels of English Binders. Cambridge: 1952-1958. V. 62
Shrewsbury School Library Bindings. Catalogue Raisonne. Oxford: 1943. V. 62

OLDHAM, JOHN
Works. Together with His Remains. London: 1722. V. 62

OLDHAM, R. D.
A Manual of the Geology of India. Stratigraphical and Structural Geology. Calcutta: 1893. V. 65

OLDMIXON, JOHN
The Critical History of England, Ecclesiastical and Civil.... London: 1724. V. 65
The History of England, During the Reigns of the Royal House of Stuart, Wherein the Errors of Late Histories are Discover'd and Corrected.... London: 1729. V. 66
A Letter to the Seven Lords of the Committee Appointed to Examine Gregg. London: 1711. V. 66

OLDROYD, IDA SHEPARD
The Marine Shells of the West Coast of North America. Stanford: 1924-1927. V. 62; 63; 65; 66
Marine Shells of the West Coast of North America. Stanford: 1975-1978. V. 66
The Marine Shells of the West Coast of North America. Stanford: 1978. V. 65

OLDS, IRVING S.
Bits and Pieces of American History as Told by a Collection of American Naval and Other Historical Prints and Paintings.... New York: 1951. V. 63

OLDS, SHARON
The Gold Cell. Poems. New York: 1987. V. 64

OLDYS, WILLIAM
The British Librarian: Exhibiting a Compendious Review or Abstract of Our Most Scarce, Useful and Valuable Books in all Sciences. London: 1738. V. 63; 66

O'LEAHY, O.
Trylongs and Perisites. New York: 1939. V. 65

O'LEARY, ARTHUR
Miscellaneous Tracts on Several Interesting Subjects. 1791. V. 63; 66
Miscellaneous Tracts.... Dublin: 1781. V. 63
Rev. Arthur O'Leary's Address to the Lords Spiritual and Temporal of the Parliament of Great Britain.... London: 1800. V. 66

O'LEARY, BRIAN
Mars 1999; Exclusive Preview of the U.S. Soviet Manned Mission. Harrisburg: 1987. V. 67

OLFERS, SIBYLLE VON
Etwas von den Wurzelkindern. Esslingen und Munchen: 1906. V. 64

OLIPHANT, J. ORIN
On the Cattle Rangers of the Oregon County. Seattle: 1968. V. 63; 66

OLIPHANT, LAURENCE
Altoiora Peto. Edinburgh: 1883. V. 65
Haifa or Life in Modern Palestine. Edinburgh and London: 1887. V. 64
A Journey to Katmandu (The Capital of Nepaul) with the Camp of Jung Bahadoor.... London: 1852. V. 65
The Land of Gilead with Excursions in the Lebanon. Edinburgh: 1880. V. 62
Minnesota and the Far West. Edinburgh/London: 1855. V. 63; 66
Narrative of the Earl of Elgin's Mission to China and Japan in the Years 1857, 1858, 1859. Edinburgh. 1859. V. 65
Piccadilly. London: 1928. V. 64
The Russian Shores of the Black Sea in the Autumn of 1852, with a Voyage Down the Volga and a Tour through the Country of the Don Cossacks. Edinburgh and London: 1853. V. 65; 66
The Russian Shores of the Black Sea in the Autumn of 1852 with a Voyage Down the Volga and a Tour through the Country of the Don Cossacks. Edinburgh and London: 1854. V. 63
Sympneumata or Evolutionary Forces Now Active in Man. Edinburgh: 1885. V. 65

OLIPHANT, MARGARET
Annals of a Publishing House. Edinburgh and London: 1897. V. 64
The Autobiography and Letters. Edinburgh;: 1899. V. 63
Carita. Leipzig: 1877. V. 65
The Curate In Charge. London: 1885. V. 65
Harry Muir. London: 1853. V. 65
He That Will Not When He May. London: 1880. V. 65
Kirsteen: the Story of a Scotch Family Seventy Years Ago. Leipzig: 1891. V. 65
Lady Car: the Sequel of a Life. London: 1889. V. 65
Madam. London: 1885. V. 65
The Makers of Florence, Dante, Giotto, Savonarola and Their City. London: 1891. V. 65
Memoir of Count de Montalembert, Peer of France, Deputcy for the Department of Doubs.... Edinburgh: 1872. V. 65
Memoir of the Life of Laurence Oliphant and of Alice Oliphant, His Wife. Edinburgh: 1891. V. 65
Mrs. Arthur. London: 1877. V. 65
The Second Son. London: 1888. V. 65
Sir Robert's Fortune: the Story of a Scotch Moor. Leipzig: 1890. V. 65
A Son of the Soil. London: 1883. V. 65
That Little Cutty, Dr. Barrere, Isabel Dysart. London: 1898. V. 65
Whiteladies. New York: 1892. V. 65

OLIPHANT, MARGARET OLIPHANT WILSON
Jerusalem. Its History and Hope. London: 1891. V. 62
John Drayton: Being a History of the Early Life and Development of a Liverpool Engineer. London: 1851. V. 66
The Sisters Bronte. London. 1897. V. 66
William Blackwood and His Sons, Their Magazine and Friends. Edinburgh and London: 1897-1898. V. 62

OLIVER, CHAD
Mists of Dawn. 1952. V. 65
The Winds of Time. 1957. V. 66
The Winds of Time. New York: 1957. V. 64

OLIVER, D.
The Botany of the Speke and Grant Expedition.... 1873-1875. V. 62
Illustrations of the Principal Natural Orders of the Vegetable Kingdom. London: 1874. V. 62

OLIVER, DANIEL
An Address, Delivered Before the New Hampshire Medical Society at Concord, June 4, 1833. Concord. 1833. V. 62

OLIVER, E. H.
The Canadian North West. Ottawa: 1914. V. 64

OLIVER, GEORGE
The History of Exter. (with) Historic Collections,. Exeter: 1821. V. 66
The Monumental Antiquities of Great Grimsby. 1825. V. 65

OLIVER, HARRY
Desert Rough Cuts - a Haywire History of the Borego Desert. Los Angeles: 1938. V. 67

OLIVER, J. RUTHERFORD
Upper Teviotdale and the Scots of Buccleuch, a Local and Family History. Hawick: 1887. V. 67

OLIVER, J. W.
The Life of William Beckford. London: 1932. V. 64

OLIVER, MARY
No Voyage and Other Poems. Boston: 1965. V. 62; 63
The River Styx, Ohio and Other Poems. New York: 1972. V. 62

OLIVER, N. W., MRS.
Sephora; a Hebrew Tale, Descriptive of the Country of Palestine.... London: 1826. V. 65

OLIVER, PAUL
Screening the Blues. London: 1968. V. 63; 65

OLIVER, PETER
The Scripture Lexicon, or Dictionary of Above Three Thousand Proper Names of Persons and Places, Mentioned in the Bible.... Birmingham: 1784. V. 62; 66

OLIVER, THOMAS
Maladies Caused by the Air We Breathe Inside and Outside the Home.... London: 1906. V. 63

OLIVER, W. R. B.
The Moas of New Zealand and Australia. Wellington: 1949. V. 62; 63
New Zealand Birds. Wellington: 1930. V. 63; 67

OLIVER, WILLIAM
A Practical Dissertation on Bath Waters. London: 1707. V. 62
A Practical Dissertation on Bath Waters. London: 1764. V. 62

OLIVIER, EDITH
The Love Child. London: 1927. V. 64

OLIVIER, GUILLAUME ANTOINE
Atlas to Illustrate the Travels in the Ottoman Empire, Egypt, and Persia, Undertaken by Order of the Government of France. London: 1802. V. 62

OLIVIERI, BERNARDINO
Vedute Degli Avanzi Monumenti Antichi Delle Due Sicilie. Rome: 1794. V. 64

OLLIER, CHARLES
Ferrers. London: 1842. V. 67

OLLIER, LOUIS XAVIER EDOUARD LEOPOLD
Traite Experimental et Clinque de la Regeneration des Os et de la Production Artificielle du Tissu Osseux. Paris: 1867. V. 66

OLLIVIER, C. P.
Traite De La Moelle Epiniere et de Ses Maladies, l'Historie, Anatomique, Physiologique et Pathologique de Ce Centre Nerveux Chex L'Homme. Paris: 1827. V. 64

OLMSTED, CHARLES H.
Reminiscences of Service with the First Volunteer Regiment of Georgia, Charleston Harbor in 1863. Savannah: 1879. V. 62

OLMSTED, FREDERICK LAW
Frederick Law Olmsted Architect 1822-1903. New York: 1928. V. 67
A Journey in the Seaboard Slave States, with Remarks on Their Economy. New York: 1856. V. 62
A Journey through Texas or a Saddle Trip on the Southwestern Frontier with a Statistical Appendix. New York: 1957. V. 63

OLMSTED, T.
The Musical Olio. New London: 1811. V. 64

OLSEN, D. B.
Cats Don't Smile. Garden City: 1945. V. 66

OLSEN, TILLIE
Tell Me a Riddle. New York: 1978. V. 63
Yonnondio from the Thirites. N.P: 1974. V. 62

OLSHAUSEN, THEODOR
Geschichte der Mormonen oder Jungsten = Tages = Heisigne in Nordamerika. Gottingen: 1856. V. 64

OLSON, CHARLES
Apollonius of Tyana. Black Mountain: 1951. V. 64
Archaeologist of Morning. London: 1970. V. 62
Call Me Ishmael. New York: 1958. V. 64
Charles Olson and Robert Creeley: the Complete Correspondence. Santa Barbara: 1980-1987. V. 64
Charles Olson and Robert Creeley: The Complete Correspondence. Santa Barbara & Santa Rosa: 1980-1996. V. 64
Charles Olson in Connecticut: Last Lectures. Iowa City: 1974. V. 66
Human Universe and Other Essays. San Francisco: 1965. V. 64
In Cold Hell, In Thicket. 1953. V. 66
The Maximus Poems. New York: 1960. V. 62
The Maximus Poems 1-10. The Maximus Poems 11-22. Stuttgart: 1953-1956. V. 64; 65
Maximus Poems IV, V, VI. London: 1968. V. 65
Mayan Letters. 1953. V. 63
Mayan Letters. Palma de Mallorca: 1953. V. 64; 66
O'Ryan 1 2 3 4 5 6 7 8 9 10. San Francisco: 1965. V. 64; 66
Projective Verse. New York: 1959. V. 64
Some Early Poems. Iowa City: 1978. V. 62; 66
The Special View of History. Berkeley: 1970. V. 62
Stocking Cap. N.P: 1966. V. 62; 64
West. London: 1966. V. 63; 64; 65

OLSON, R. K.
The Response of Western Forests to Air Pollution. New York: 1992. V. 65; 67

OLSON, RONALD
The Quinault Indians. Seattle: 1936. V. 66

OLSON, TOBY
Maps. Mt. Horeb: 1969. V. 66
The Pool, from the Novel Dorit in Lesbos. Mt. Horeb: 1991. V. 64

OLTON, DAVID S.
Memory Dysfunctions: an Integration of Animal and Human Research. New York: 1985. V. 65

OLYMPIA,
London September-October 1919. London: 1919. V. 67

OLYMPIC GAMES, 1936
Report of the American Olympic Committee. Games of the XIth Olympiad, Berlin, Germany, August 1 - 16, 1936. IVth Olympic Winter Games, Garmisch Partenkirchen, Germany, Feb. 6 to 16, 1936. New York: 1937. V. 67

O'MALLEY, BRIAN
The Animals of Saint Gregory. Rhandirmyn: 1981. V. 63

O'MALLEY, C. D.
Leonardo da Vinci on the Human Body. New York: 1952. V. 67

OMAN, JOHN CAMPBELL
The Brahmans, Theists and Muslins of India. London: 1907. V. 66

OMAR KHAYYAM
The Quatrains.... London: 1898. V. 63
The Quatrains.... Worcester: 1906. V. 64
The Rubaiyat. New York. V. 67
Rubaiyat. Singapore. V. 65
Rubaiyat. London: 1872. V. 65
Rubaiyat. Boston: 1890. V. 67
Rubaiyat. London: 1891. V. 65
The Rubaiyat. London: 1898. V. 63
Rubaiyat. London: 1899. V. 67
Rubaiyat. London: 1900. V. 63
Rubaiyat. New York: 1900. V. 66
The Rubaiyat. 1903. V. 64
Rubaiyat. 1909. V. 67
Rubaiyat. London: 1909. V. 62; 64
Rubaiyat. 1910. V. 62
The Rubaiyat. New York: 1911. V. 63
Rubaiyat. London: 1913. V. 67
Rubaiyat. 1920. V. 67
Rubaiyat. 1922. V. 67
The Rubaiyat. London: 1924. V. 63
The Rubaiyat. London: 1928. V. 62
Rubaiyat. 1930. V. 67
Rubaiyat. New York: 1930. V. 62; 63
Rubaiyat. New York: 1932. V. 67
Rubaiyat. London: 1940. V. 62; 64
Rubaiyat. Leigh-on-Sea: 1944. V. 62

OMMANNEY, F. D.
South Latitutde. 1938. V. 67

OMOHUNDRO, MALVERN H.
The Omohundro Genealogical Record: the Omohundros and Allied Familes in America. Goochland: 1951. V. 64

OMOND, GEORGE W. T.
Belgium. London: 1908. V. 64

O'MULLALLY, DENNIS P.
History of O'Mullally and Lally Clan. Chicago: 1941. V. 67

ON Equal Terms.
Tuscaloosa: 1984. V. 62

ON Heather Hills.
Paisley: 1891. V. 67

ON Land Concentration and Irresponsibility of Political Power as Causing the Anomaly of a Widespread State of Want by the Side of the Vast Supplies of Nature.
London: 1886. V. 67

ON the Causes of the Progressive Depreciaton of the Price of Grain Prior to the Late Scarcity, with Observations on the Madras Ryotwar System.
Madras: 1834. V. 67

ON the Deteriorated Condition of Our Saddle-Horses: the Causes and the Remedy.
London: 1853. V. 65

ON the Distressed State of the Country.
London: 1830. V. 67

ON the Importance of the Study of Anatomy.
Boston: 1825. V. 64

ON the Plains - the Companion Library.
Boston: 1897. V. 66

ON the Poverty of Student Life.
New York: 1967. V. 63

O'NAN, STEWART
In the Walled City. Pittsburgh: 1993. V. 63; 64; 65; 66; 67
A Prayer for the Dying. New York: 1999. V. 67
Snow Angels. New York: 1994. V. 62; 63; 64; 65; 67

ONDAATJE, MICHAEL
Aardvark (for the memory of emma peel). Toronto. V. 63
Anil's Ghost. Toronto: 2000. V. 66; 67
Coming through the Slaughter. 1976. V. 62
The Dainty Monsters. Toronto: 1967. V. 63
The English Patient. London: 1992. V. 62; 63; 64; 66; 67
The English Patient. New York: 1992. V. 67
The English Patient. Toronto: 1992. V. 62; 66; 67
Handwriting. Toronto: 1998. V. 62; 67
In the Skin of a Lion. New York: 1987. V. 62
In the Skin of a Lion. Toronto: 1987. V. 62; 65; 67
Leonard Cohen. Toronto: 1970. V. 62
The Man with Seven Toes. Toronto: 1969. V. 65
Running in the Family. Toronto: 1982. V. 62
Running in the Family. Toronto: 1983. V. 62
Secular Love. Toronto: 1984. V. 62
Secular Love. New York: 1985. V. 62
Tin Roof. Lantzville: 1982. V. 62

ONE and Twenty. Duke Narrative Verse 1924-1945. Durham: 1945. V. 63

ONE Hundred Years Of Mountmellick School. Dublin: 1886. V. 63

1001 Notable Nativities. London. V. 62

ONE Two Three Four. New York: 1894?. V. 65

ONE Two, Buckle My Shoe, or Good Boys and Girls Don't You Think We Shall Do. London: 1820. V. 64

O'NEAL, BILL
The Arizona Rangers. Austin: 1987. V. 63; 65; 67

O'NEAL, WILLIAM
The Work of William Lawrence Bottomley in Richmond. Charlottesville: 1989. V. 62

O'NEIL, A.
A Dictionary of Spanish Painters. London: 1833. V. 65

O'NEIL, HENRY
Lectures on Painting Delivered at the Royal Academy with Additional Notes and Appendix. 1866. V. 63
Lectures on Painting Delivered at the Royal Academy with Additional Notes and Appendix. London: 1866. V. 66

O'NEIL, JAMES B.
They Die But Once. New York: 1925. V. 67
They Die But Once. New York: 1935. V. 67

O'NEILL, CHARLES
The Practice and Principles of Calico Printing, Bleaching, Dyeing, Etc. Manchester: 1878. V. 63
Wild Train. The Story of the Andrews Raiders. New York: 1956. V. 62; 63

O'NEILL, EUGENE GLADSTONE
Ah, Wilderness!. New York: 1933. V. 66; 67
Beyond the Horizon, a Play in Three Acts. New York: 1920. V. 63
The Complete Works. New York: 1924. V. 62; 64; 67
Desire Under the Elms. New York: 1925. V. 66
Dynamo. New York: 1929. V. 62; 64
Gold. New York: 1920. V. 64
The Hairy Ape, Anna Christie, The First Man. New York: 1922. V. 63
The Iceman Cometh. New York: 1946. V. 66
The Iceman Cometh. New York: 1982. V. 62; 63; 64; 66
Long Day's Journey Into Night. New Haven: 1956. V. 66
Marco Millions. New York: 1927. V. 62; 64; 67
Mourning Becomes Electra. 1931. V. 67
Mourning Becomes Electra. New York: 1931. V. 62
The Plays of Eugene O'Neill. New York: 1934. V. 62; 64
Strange Interlude. New York: 1928. V. 62; 63; 64; 67
Thirst. Boston: 1913. V. 62
Thirst. Boston: 1914. V. 62; 63; 66; 67

O'NEILL, J. W.
The Aboriginal Races of North America. Philadelphia: 1859. V. 64

O'NEILL, PHIL
Twenty Years of the G.A.A. 1910-1930. Kilkenny: 1931. V. 67

O'NEILL, ROSE
The Kewpies and Dotty Darling. London: 1913. V. 65
The Kewpies Their Book. New York: 1913. V. 65

ONETTI, JUAN CARLOS
El Pozo. N.P: 1939. V. 67

ONIONS, OLIVER
The Debit Account. London: 1913. V. 65

ONIONS, R. T.
Shakespeare's England, an Account of the Life and Manners of His Age. Oxford: 1950. V. 63

ONO, TAKETOSHI
Brain Mechanisms of Perception and Memory: from Neuron to Behavior. New York: 1993. V. 65

ONSLOW-FORD, GORDON
Painting in the Instant. London: 1964. V. 65
Painting in the Instant. New York: 1964. V. 62

ONTARIO AND ST. LAWRENCE STEAMBOAT CO.
Handbook for Travelers to Niagara Falls, Montreal and Quebec, and through Lake Champlain to Saratoga Springs. Buffalo: 1852. V. 64; 65

ONWHYN, THOMAS
Etiquette Illustrated, or, Hints.... London: 1849. V. 62
Mr. Tiddlely Winks. 1835. V. 62; 67
Mrs. Caudle in Crinoline. London: 1858. V. 67
300 a Year, or Single and Married Life, Dedicated to All Young Bachelors. London: 1859. V. 67
Twelve Illustrations to the Pickwick Club by T. Onwhyn. London: 1894. V. 67

OOI, K.
English Japanese Conversations of Those Who Learn the English Language. Tokio: 1886. V. 64

THE OOJAH Annual (for 1923). London: 1922. V. 65

OPDYKE, GEORGE
A Treatise on Political Economy. New York: 1851. V. 65

OPIE, AMELIA
Adeline Mowbray, or the Mother and Daughter, a Tale. London: 1805. V. 65
Detraction Displayed. London: 1828. V. 63; 65
Illustrations of Lying, In All Its Branches. London: 1825. V. 65
New Tales. London: 1818. V. 65
Tales of Real Life. London: 1813. V. 64; 65
Valentine's Eve. London: 1816. V. 63

OPIE, IONA
I Saw Esau - the Schoolchild's Pocket Book. London: 1992. V. 62; 65

THE OPIUM Trade in China, by an Eyewitness. London: 1858. V. 66

OPLER, MORRIS E.
An Apache Life-Way. The Economic Social, Religious Institution of the Chiricahua Indians. Chicago: 1941. V. 62
Myths and Tales of the Jicarilla Apache Indians. New York: 1938. V. 62
Myths and Legends of the Lipan Apache Indians. New York: 1940. V. 64
Myths and Tales of the Chiricahua Apache Indians. New York: 1942. V. 64

OPPE, A. P.
Thomas Rowlandson: His Drawings and Water-Colours. London: 1923. V. 64

OPPEN, GEORGE
Alpine. Mt. Horeb: 1969. V. 64; 66
Discrete Series. New York: 1934. V. 67

OPPENHEIM, E. C.
New Climbs in Norway. London: 1898. V. 63; 64

OPPENHEIM, E. PHILLIPS
Crooks in the Sunshine. London: 1932. V. 66
The Peer and the Woman. London: 1895. V. 66

OPPENHEIMER, AMY V.
Us Kids. New York: 1932. V. 66

OPPENHEIMER, JOEL
The Dutiful Son. Highlands: 1956. V. 64
New Hampshire Journal. Perry Township: 1994. V. 64; 67

OPPENHEIMER, LEHMANN J.
The Heart of Lakeland. Manchester: 1908. V. 63; 64

OPPENORD, GILLES-MARIE
Oeuvre.... Paris: 1745. V. 64

OPPIAN
Oppiani Poetae Cilicis...De Venatione...De Piscatu...Cum Interpretatione Latina, Commentariis & Indice Rerum...Confectis Studio & Opera Conradi Rittershusii.... Lugduni Batavorum: 1597. V. 66

ORAGE, A. R.
Essays and Aphorisms. London: 1954. V. 63

ORAM, WILLIAM
Precepts and Observations on the Art of Colouring in Landscape Painting. London: 1810. V. 66; 67

ORANGE, JAMES
Narrative of the Late George Vason of Nottingham. Derby: 1840. V. 65

ORANGES and Lemons. London: 1892. V. 64

ORAZIONI, CRISTIANE
Ovvero. Venice: 1766. V. 66

ORBELIANI, SULKAN-SABI
Six Tales Being of the Book of Lies and Wisdom. 1982. V. 63

ORCUTT, C. R.
Southern and Lower California, Flora. Oquawka: 1883. V. 62

ORCUTT, SAMUEL
The Indians of the Housatonic and Naugatuck Valleys. Hartford: 1882. V. 63

ORCUTT, WILLIAM DANA
The Book in Italy During the Fifteenth and Sixteenth Centuries Shown in Facsimile Reproductions from the Most Famous Printed Volumes. London: 1928. V. 65
In Quest of the Perfect Book. Boston: 1926. V. 67
Master Makers of the Book: Being a Consecutive Story of the Book from a Century Before the Invention of Printing through the Era of the Doves Press,. Boston: 1929. V. 62

ORCZY, BARONESS
The Man in the Corner. 1909. V. 66
The Man in the Corner. New York: 1909. V. 64

ORD, RICHARD
The Sedgefield Country in the Seventies and Eighties.... Darlington: 1904. V. 64; 65; 67

ORD-HULME, ARTHUR W. J. G.
Clockwork Music. London: 1973. V. 62
The Musical Box. 1995. V. 64

ORDRONAUX, JOHN
Manual of Instructions for Military Surgeons on the Examination of Recruits and Discharge of Soldiers.... New York: 1863. V. 66

O'REGAN, WILLIAM
Memoirs of the Legal, Literary and Political Life of the Late Rt. Hon. John Philpot Curran, Once Master of the Rolls in Ireland.... 1817. V. 63
Memoirs of the Legal, Literary and Political Life of the Late Rt. Hon. John Philpot Curran, Once Master of the Rolls in Ireland.... London: 1817. V. 66

THE OREGON Trail, the Missouri to the Pacific Ocean. New York: 1939. V. 66

O'REILLY, BERNARD
Greenland, the Adjacent Seas and the North-West Passage to the Pacific Ocean.... London: 1818. V. 66

O'REILLY, EDWARD
Sanas Gaoidhilge-Sagsbhearla. An Irish-English Dictionary.... Dublin: 1817. V. 64

O'REILLY, JOHN BOYLE
Athletics and Manly Sport. Boston: 1890. V. 65

ORFILA, MATTHIEU JOPEPH BONAVENTURE
Appendix to the General System of Toxicology; or a Treatise on Mineral, Vegetable and Animal Poisons. London: 1821. V. 65

ORFORD, ROBERT WALPOLE, EARL OF
A Further Report from the Committee of Secresy, Appointed to Enquire Into the Conduct of Robert, Earl of Orford, During the Last Ten Years of His Being First Commissioner of the Treasury.... London: 1742. V. 66

ORGANIC Chemistry. New York: 1953. V. 65

ORGEL, DORIS
Sarah's Room. London: 1972. V. 65

ORIAS, OSCAR
The Heart-Sounds in Normal and Pathological Conditions. London: 1939. V. 63

ORIBASIUS
Oribasii Sardiani Synopseos Ad Evstathium Filivm Libri Novem: Qvibus Tota Medicina in Compendium Redacta Continetvr.... Venetiis: 1554. V. 64; 65

THE ORIENTAL Annual, or Scenes in India. London: 1834. V. 62

ORIENTAL CARPET MANUFACTURERS, LTD.
Oriental Carpets. Smyrna: 1909. V. 62

THE ORIGIN of Printing: in Two Essays. London: 1774. V. 64; 66

THE ORIGIN, Progress and Present State of the Thames Tunnel and the Advantages Likely to Accrue From It, Both to the Proprietors and to the Public. London: 1827. V. 63

THE ORIGINAL Bath Guide, Containing an Essay on the Bath Waters, with a Description of the City, and a Variety of Useful Information. Bath: 1837. V. 65

THE ORIGINAL Design, Progress and Present State of the Scots Corporation at London, of the Foundation of K. Charles II. To Which is Added a List of the Masters and Treasurers.... London: 1718. V. 67

AN ORIGINAL Letter from a Gentleman to His friend, Giving a Short Account of a Work Intitled Pia et Catholica Institutio.... London: 1802. V. 65

ORIGINAL Papers Relating to the Expedition to Carthagena. London: 1744. V. 64

ORIGO, IRIS
A Need to Testify - Portraits of Lauro de Bosis, Ruth Draper, Gaetano Salvemini, Ignazio Silone and an Essay on Biography. London: 1984. V. 65

ORIOLI, GIOVANNI
Adventures of a Bookseller. Florence: 1937. V. 63

ORIOLI, PINO
Some Letters of Pino Orioli to Mrs. Gordon Crotch. Edinburgh: 1974. V. 64

ORISINI, FULVIA
Carmina Novem Illustrium Feminarvm: Sapphus Mytidis, Praxillae, Erinnae, Corinnae, Nossidis, Myrus, Telesillae, Anytae Et Lyricorum Alcanis, Ibyi, Stesichori & Mimmermi. Antwerp: 1568. V. 65

ORLANDO, PELLIGRINO ANTONIO
Repertorium Sculptile-Typicum; or a Complete Collection and Explanation of the Several Marks and Cyphers.... London: 1730. V. 64

ORLEAN, SUSAN
The Orchid Thief. New York: 1998. V. 67

ORLEANS, CHARLES, DUC DE
Poesies. Leipzig: 1914. V. 67

ORLEANS, DUC D'
Croisiere Oceanographique Accomplie a Bord De La Belgica Dan La Mer Du Gronland, 1905. Bruxelles: 1907. V. 66

ORLEANS, LOUIS PHILIPPE D'
The Trades' Unions of England. London: 1869. V. 67

ORLOV, YU
Fundamentals of Paleontology. Volume 9. Boston: 1875-1876. V. 66

ORLOVSKY, PETER
Lepers Cry. New York: 1972. V. 62

ORMATHWAITE, LORD
Astronomy and Geology Compared. London: 1871. V. 63

ORMEROD, A.
Don Whillans. Portrait of a Mountaineer. 1971. V. 63

ORMEROD, T.
Calderdale. Burnley: 1906. V. 65; 66

ORMISTON & GLASS
English Lakes. Edinburgh. V. 65

ORNEMENS Dedies a S.A.R. Princess Marie. Paris: 1836. V. 66

ORNITHOLOGIA Nova; or, a New History of Birds, Extracted from the Best Authorities in Various Languages.... 1745. V. 64

ORNSTEIN, MARTHA
The Role of the Scientific Societies in the Seventeenth Century. New York: 1913. V. 67

O'RORKE, T.
The History of Sligo: Town and Country. 1890. V. 65

OROSIUS, PAULUS
Les Histoires. Paris: 1491. V. 62
Historia Adversus Paganos. Augsburg: 1471. V. 65

O'ROURKE, JOHN
The History of the Great Irish Famine of 1847, with Notices of Earlier Irish Famines. Dublin: 1902. V. 67

ORPEN, GODDARD H.
Ireland Under the Normans. 1911-1920. V. 63

ORPEN, WILLIAM
Stories of Old Ireland and Myself. 1924. V. 65

ORPHAN Annie Goofy Circus. Chicago?: 1939. V. 62

THE ORPHANS, a Tale in Verse for Children. Philadelphia. V. 65

ORPHAN'S Advocate and Social Monitor. Boston: 1849-1854. V. 67

ORR, GREGORY
Burning the Empty Nests. New York: 1973. V. 63

ORR, H. WINNETT
A List of Books and Pamphlets on the History of Surgery and Orthopedic Surgery. The Collection of Dr. H. Winnett Orr, M.D. Lincoln: 1943. V. 66

ORR, HECTOR
A History of Free Masonry; and the Duties Incumbent on the Craft.... Boston: 1798. V. 63
The Native American: a Gift for the People. Philadelphia: 1845. V. 65

ORR, THOMAS
Life History of....Pioneer Stories of California and Utah. Placerville: 1930. V. 63; 66

ORTA, GARCIA DE
Dell'Historia de i Semplici Aromati, et Altre Cose; Che Vengono Portate dall'Indie Orientalis Pertinenti all'vso Della Medicina. Venice: 1589. V. 64; 66

ORTEGA Y GASSET, JOSE
Meditaciones del Quijote. Madrid: 1914. V. 67
Meditaciones del Quijote. Madrid: 1921. V. 67

THE ORTHODOX Communicant, by Way of Meditation On the Order for the Administration of the Lord's Supper or Holy Communion.... London: 1721. V. 66

ORTIZ, SIMON
After and Before the Lightning. Tucson: 1994. V. 66; 67

ORTMANN, A. E.
A Monograph of the Naiades of Pennsylvania. Part III. Pittsburgh: 1919. V. 64; 65
South American Naiades.... Pittsburgh: 1921. V. 65

ORTON, HAROLD
The Linguistic Atlas of England. London: 1978. V. 66
Survey of English Dialects. Leeds: 1962-1969. V. 66

ORTON, JAMES
Amazon and the Andes; or Across the Continent of South America. New York: 1870. V. 64

ORTON, JOE
Crimes of Passion: The Ruffian on the Star - the Erpingham Camp. London: 1967. V. 65
Entertaining Mr. Sloane. London: 1964. V. 66
Head to Toe. London: 1971. V. 62
The Orton Diaries .... London: 1986. V. 65

ORVIN, MAXWELL CLAYTON
In South Carolina Waters 1861-1865. Charleston: 1961. V. 63

ORVIS, CHARLES F.
Fishing With the Fly. Boston & New York: 1892. V. 64

ORWELL, GEORGE
Animal Farm, a Fairy Story. London: 1945. V. 66
The Collected Essays, Journalism and Letters of George Orwell. London: 1968. V. 65
Coming Up for Air. London: 1939. V. 64
Coming Up for Air. London: 1948. V. 65
Critical Essays. London: 1945. V. 66
Down and Out in Paris and London. London: 1933. V. 62; 64; 66
England Your England: Essays. London: 1953. V. 66
The English People. London: 1947. V. 62; 64; 65; 66
Homage to Catalonia. London: 1938. V. 62; 64
Inside the Whale. London: 1940. V. 64
James Brunham and the Managerial Revolution. London: 1946. V. 62
Kolhosp Tuarin. (Animal Farm). Munich: 1947. V. 63
Nineteen Eighty-Four. London: 1949. V. 62; 63; 65; 66
Nineteen Eighty-Four. New York: 1949. V. 62; 63; 64
Nineteen Eighty-Four. London: 1970. V. 67
Nineteen Eighty-Four - the Facsimile of the Extant Manuscript. London and Weston: 1984. V. 62
Politics and the English Language. Evansville: 1947. V. 62; 64
The Road to Wigan Pier. London: 1937. V. 64
The Road to Wigan Pier. 1957. V. 63
Shooting the Elephant and Other Essays. London: 1950. V. 63
The Works. London: 1996. V. 66; 67

OSBECK, PETER
A Voyage to China and the East Indies...Together with a Voyage to Suratte...and an Account of the Chinese Husbandry. London: 1771. V. 64

OSBORN, BENJAMIN
Truth Displayed: in a Series of Elementary Principles.... Rutland: 1816. V. 63; 66

OSBORN, H. F.
Are Acquired Variatons Inherited?. Boston: 1891. V. 67
A Complete Mosasa Skeleton, Osseous and Cartilaginous; and a Skeleton of Diplodocus. 1899. V. 67
A Contribution to the Internal Structure of the Amphibian Brain. Boston: 1888. V. 67
Craniometry of the Equidae. New York: 1912. V. 64; 67
A Memoir Upon Loxolophodon and Uintatherium...Accompanied by a Stratigraphical Report on the Bridger Beds. Princeton: 1881. V. 67
The Structure and Classification of the Mesozoic Mammalia. Philadelphia: 1887. V. 67
The Titanotheres of Ancient Wyoming, Dakota and Nebraska. Washington: 1929. V. 63

OSBORN, HENRY
Plants of the Holy Land with Their Fruits and Flowers. Philadelphia: 1865. V. 66

OSBORN, LAUGHTON
Handbook of Young Artists and Amateurs in Oil Painting.... New York: 1845. V. 66; 67

OSBORN, PAUL
On Borrowed Time. New York: 1938. V. 62

OSBORN, SELLECK
Poems Moral, Sentimental and Satirical. Boston: 1823. V. 62; 67

OSBORN, SHERARD
A Cruise in Japanese Waters. London: 1859. V. 62
Stray Leaves from an Arctic Journal. London: 1852. V. 64

OSBORNE, CHARLES
Swansong - Poems. London: 1968. V. 63

OSBORNE, DUFFIELD
Engraved Gems: Signets, Talismans and Ornamental Intaglious, Ancient and Modern. New York: 1912. V. 63

OSBORNE, EDWARD CORNELIUS
Osborne's London and Birmingham Railway Guide. Birmingham: 1840. V. 65

OSBORNE, EGBERT H.
Lectures. Memphis: 1869. V. 63

OSBORNE, FRANCIS
Advice to a Son; or Directions for Your Better Conduct, Through the Various and Most Important Encounters of This Life.... Oxford: 1656. V. 64
Advice to a Son. Or Directions for Your Better Conduct... (with) Advice to a Son. The Second Part. (with) Politicall Reflections Upon the Government of the Turks. Oxford: 1658-1662. V. 64
Political Reflections Upon the Government of the Turks. Nicolas Machiavel. The King of Sweden's Descent into Germany. The Conspiracy of Piso and Vindex Against Nero. the Greatness and Corruption of the Court of Rome. The Election of Pope Leo the XI. The. London: 1656. V. 62

OSBORNE, JOHN
Almost a Gentleman - an Autobiography - Volume II 1955-1960. London: 1991. V. 62
The Entertainer. London: 1957. V. 62; 66
Look Back in Anger. 1956. V. 65
Look Back in Anger. London: 1957. V. 62; 66
A Patriot for Me. London: 1966. V. 62
A Place Calling Itself Rome. Helsinki: 1989. V. 63
Time Present/The Hotel in Amsterdam. London: 1968. V. 62
Tom Jones. A Film Script. London: 1964. V. 62
The World of Paul Slickey - a Comedy of Manners with Music. London: 1959. V. 63; 66

OSBORNE, S. GODOLPHIN
Gleanings in the West of Ireland. London: 1850. V. 67

OSBORNE, THOMAS
A Catalogue of the Libraries of the Honourable Sir Luke Schaub, Bart. London: 1759. V. 65
A Collection of Some Memorable and Weighty Transactions in Parliament, in the Year 1678 and Afterwards; In Relation to the Impeachment of Thomas, Earl of Danby. London: 1695. V. 65

OSBOURN, JAMES
North Carolina Sonnets, or a Selection of Choice Hymns, for the Use of Old School Baptists.... Baltimore: 1844. V. 66

OSBURN, WILLIAM
The Monumental History of Egypt. London: 1854. V. 66

OSCAR Wilde and the Grave of Shelley. Edinburgh: 1992. V. 64

OSGOOD, CORNELIUS
Contributions to the Ethnography of the Kutchin. New Haven: 1936. V. 65

OSGOOD, ERNEST STAPLES
The Day of the Cattleman. Minnesota: 1929. V. 64; 67
The Field Notes of Captain William Clark 1803-1805. New Haven: 1964. V. 65

O'SHEA, ELENA ZAMORA
El Mesquite, a Story of the Early Spanish Settlements Between the Nueces and the Rio Grande.... Dallas: 1935. V. 66

OSLER, WILLIAM
Aequanimitas. With Other Addresses. Philadelphia: 1905. V. 65
Aequanimitas. With Other Addresses.... Philadelphia: 1910. V. 65
Bibliotheca Osleriana. London: 1929. V. 64
Bibliotheca Osleriana. Oxford: 1929. V. 66
Bibliotheca Osleriana. Oxford: 1929. V. 65; 66; 67
Bibliotheca Osleriana. Montreal: 1967. V. 64; 66; 67
Bibliotheca Osleriana. London: 2000. V. 67
The Collected Essays. Birmingham: 1985. V. 63
Elisha Bartlett. A Rhode Island Philosopher. Providence: 1900. V. 67
The Evolution of Modern Medicine. Birmingham: 1982. V. 63
Incunabula Medica. A Study of the Earliest Printed Medical Books 1467-1480. London: 1923. V. 64; 66; 67
Internal Medicine as a Vocation. New York: 1897. V. 67
Michael Servetus. Baltimore: 1909. V. 64
Modern Medicine. New York: 1907-1910. V. 62
On the Etiology and Diagnosis of Cerebro Spinal Fever. London: 1899. V. 64; 66; 67
Over-Strain of the Heart, as Illustrated by a Case of Hypertrophy, Dilation and Fatty Degeneration of the Heart.... Montreal: 1878. V. 64
The Principles and Practice of Medicine. New York: 1892. V. 62; 66
The Principles and Practice of Medicine. New York: 1893. V. 64; 66; 67
The Principles and Practice of Medicine. Edinburgh: 1895. V. 64; 66; 67
The Principles and Practice of Medicine. New York: 1897. V. 63; 66
The Principles and Practice of Medicine. Edinburgh: 1898. V. 64; 66; 67
The Principles and Practice of Medicine. Edinburgh: 1901. V. 66
The Principles and Practice of Medicine. New York: 1930. V. 67
The Principles and Practice of Medicine. New York: 1938. V. 67
The Principles and Practice of Medicine. New York: 1944. V. 67
Science and Immortality. Boston: 1904. V. 63
Sir Kenelm Diby's Powder of Sympathy. Los Angeles: 1972. V. 64
The Treatment of Disease...Address in Medicine Before Ontario Medical Association. London: 1909. V. 67
William Osler's Collected Papers on Cardiovascular System. Birmingham: 1988. V. 63

OSLEY, A. S.
Calligraphy and Palaeography: Essays presented to Alfred Fairbank on His 70th Birthday. New York: 1966. V. 63
Luminario, an Introduction to the Italian Writing-Books of the Sixteenth Centuries. Nieuwkoop: 1973. V. 62

OSORIO, JEROME
The History of the Portuguese, During the Reign of Emmanuel.... London: 1752. V. 67

OSSAT, CARDINAL D'
Lettres de l'Illustrissime et Hevendissime Cardinal D'Ossat Euesque de Baieux, Au Roy Henri Le Grand, et a Monsieur de Villeroy. Paris: 1624. V. 67

OSSMAN, DAVID
The Sullen Art - Interviews with Modern American Poets. New York: 1963. V. 65

OSSOLI, SARAH MARGARET FULLER, MARCHESA D'
Memoirs of.... Boston: 1852. V. 65
Memoirs of.... London: 1852. V. 65
Summer on the Lakes in 1843. Boston: 1844. V. 66

OSTENFELD, C. H.
The Flora of Iceland and the Faeroes. Copenhagen: 1934. V. 67

OSTEN SACKEN, C. R.
Prodrome of a Monograph of the Tabanidae of the United States. Part I. Part II. Boston: 1875-1876. V. 64

OSTER, HARRY
Living Country Blues. Detroit: 1969. V. 67

OSTERBROCK, DONALD
Eye on the Sky; Lick Observatory's First Century. Berkeley: 1988. V. 67
Pauper and Prince; Ritchey, Hale and Big American Telescopes. Tucson: 1993. V. 67

OSTRANDER, ALSON
After Sixty Years. Seattle: 1925. V. 67
An Army Boy of the Sixties. A Story of the Plains. New York: 1924. V. 63; 66
The Bozeman Trail Forts, Under General Philip St. George Cooke in 1866. Seattle: 1932. V. 65; 67

OSTRANDER, ISABEL
The Mathematics of Guilt. New York: 1926. V. 65

OSTRANDER, TOBIAS
The Planetarium and Astronomical Calculator.... Lyons: 1832. V. 63; 65

OSTROGA, YVONNE
De Bonnes Histories. Paris: 1924. V. 64

OSTROM, J. H.
Marsh's Dinosaurs: the Collection from Como Bluff. New Haven: 1966. V. 64

O'SULLIVAN, FLORENCE
The History of Kinsale. 1916. V. 67

O'SULLIVAN, PHILIP
Historiae Catholicae Iberniae Compendium. Dublin: 1850. V. 66

O'SULLIVAN, SEAMUS
Facetiae Et Curiosa: Being a Selection from the Notebook of the Late J. H. Orwell. 1937. V. 66
Personal Talk, a Book of Verses. 1936. V. 66
Poems 1930-1938. 1938. V. 66

O'SULLIVAN, THOMAS F.
Romantic Hidden Kerry. 1931. V. 65

O'SULLIVAN, VINCENT
Master of Fallen Years. Edinburgh: 1990. V. 66
Opinions. 1959. V. 63

OSWALD, E. J.
By Fell and Fjord or Scenes and Studies in Iceland. London: 1882. V. 66

OSWALD, EUGEN
Der Wolf und Die sieben Jungen Geislein. Wiesbaden: 1910. V. 65

OSWALD, FELIX
Index of Potters' Stamps on Terra Sigillata "Samian Ware" with a Supplement.... 1931. V. 62

OSWALD, JOHN
Poems; to Which is Added, the Humours of John Bull, an Operatical Farce, in Two Acts. London: 1789. V. 63

OSWALD, JOHN CLYDE
Printing in the Americas. New York: 1937. V. 62; 63; 64; 65

OSWALDO-CRUZ, E.
The Brain of the Opposum (Didelphis Marsupialis): a Cytoarchitectonic Atlas in Sterotaxic Coordiantes. Rio de Janiero: 1968. V. 65; 67

OSWELL, WILLIAM EDWARD
William Cotton Oswell, Hunter and Explorer. London: 1900. V. 62

OTERO, MIGUEL ANTONIO
My Life on the Frontier 1864-1882. New York: 1935. V. 63; 67
My Nine Years as Governor of the Territory of New Mexico. Albuquerque: 1940. V. 63
The Real Billy the Kid - With New Light on the Lincoln County War. New York: 1936. V. 62; 65
The Report of the Governor of New Mexico. Washington: 1901. V. 65

OTIS, ELWEK S.
The Indian Question. New York: 1878. V. 67

OTIS, F. N.
Illustrated History of the Panama Railroad; Together with a Traveler's Guide and Businessman's Handbook for the Panama Railroad and Its Connections. New York: 1861. V. 64

OTIS, FESSENDEN
Stricture of the Male Urethra Its Radical Cure. London: 1885. V. 66

OTIS, GEORGE
A Report on Amputations at the Hip-Joint in Military Surgery. Washington: 1867. V. 62
A Report on Excisions of the Head of the Femur for Gunshot Injury. Washington: 1869. V. 62
Reports on the Extent and Nature of the Materials Available for the Preparation of a Medical and Surgical History of the Rebellion. Philadelphia: 1866. V. 62

OTLEY, JONATHAN
A Concise Description of the English Lakes.... Kirkby Lonsdale: 1823. V. 66
A Concise Description of the English Lakes.... London: 1823. V. 63

OTT, I.
New Irish Jokes and Monologues. Baltimore: 1907. V. 67

OTT, SUSANNA CLAYTON
A Masque - the Story of the Nativity for the Commonwealth of Los Angeles. Los Angeles: 1915. V. 62

OTTENBERG, SIMON
Masked Rituals of Alikpo: the Context of African Art. 1975. V. 62; 65

OTTER, WILLIAM
The Life and Remains of the Rev. Edward Daniel Clarke. London: 1824. V. 62

OTTLEY, WILLIAM YOUNG
A Collection of Facsimiles of Scarce and Curious Prints, Illustrative of the History of Engraving. London: 1828. V. 63; 67

OTTO, JACOB AUGUSTUS
A Treatise on the Structure and Preservation of the Violin and All Other Bow Instruments. London. V. 67

OTTO, WHITNEY
How to Make an American Quilt. New York: 1991. V. 63; 64; 66; 67

OTTO YOUNG & CO.
Illustrated Wholesale Catalogue of Cameras, Camera Supplies, Graphophones, Graphopone Records and Olympia Music Boxes 1900 and 1901. Chicago: 1900. V. 66

OTTOSEN, P. H.
Trench Artillery A.E.F. The Personal Experiences of Lieutenants and Captains of Artillery Who Served With Trench Mortars. Boston: 1931. V. 65

OTWAY, THOMAS
The History and Fall of Caius Marius. London: 1680. V. 62
Works. London: 1712. V. 62

OUCHTERLONY, JOHN
Mineralogical Report Upon a Portion of the Districts of Nellore, Cuddapah and Guntoor. Mardas: 1841. V. 62

OUDEMANS, C. A.
Enumeratio Systematica Fungorum. The Hague: 1919-1924. V. 65

OUGHTRED, WILLIAM
Clavis Mathematicae Denuo Limata, Sive Potius Fabricata. Oxoniae: 1693. V. 62; 66

OULD, E. A.
Old Cottages, Farm Houses and Other Half Timber Buildings in Shropshire, Herefordshire and Cheshire Illustrated on One Hundred Plates.... London: 1904. V. 62; 63

OUR Big Book. Chicago: Sep. 1930. V. 64

OUR Children's Times, or Sketches of the Past and Present; from the French Revolution of 1848 to the Fall of Sebastopol 1885.... London: 1856. V. 67

OUR Darlings. London. V. 67

OUR Exagmination Round His Factification for Incamination of Work in Progress. Paris: 1929. V. 62; 64; 65

OUR Famous Women. Hartford: 1883. V. 65

OUR Favourite Dish - The Theatre Recipe Book - 250 Recipes Contributed by Members of the British Theatrical Profession. London: 1952. V. 64

OUR Living Painters; Their Lives and Works. London: 1859. V. 67

OUR National Cathedrals.. London: 1887-1889. V. 66

OUR Northern Domain: Alaska; Picturesque, Historic and Commercial. Boston: 1910. V. 65

OUR Old Nursery Rhymes. 1911. V. 64

OUR Women in the War. The Lives They Lived; the Deaths they Died. Charleston: 1887. V. 63; 65

OURSLER, WILL
Folio on Florence White. New York: 1942. V. 67

OUSELEY, WILLIAM GORE
Notes on the Slave-Trade, With Remarks on the Measures Adopted for Its Suppression. London: 1850. V. 67
Remarks on the Statistics and Political Institution of the United States, With Some Observations on the Ecclesiastical System of America.... London: 1812. V. 67

OUT of the West. Northridge: 1979. V. 63; 64; 66

THE OUTCAST Poets. New York: 1947. V. 65

OUTHWAITE, GRENBRY
The Enchanted Forest. London: 1921. V. 63; 64

OUTHWAITE, IDA RENTOUL
A Bunch of Wild Flowers. Sydney: 1933. V. 64
The Little Green Road to Fairyland. London: 1922. V. 63

OVENDEN, G.
Alphonse Mucha: Photographs. New York and London: 1974. V. 65
A Victorian Album. Julia Margaret Cameron and Her Circle. London: 1975. V. 64

OVER the Sierra. San Francisco: 1890. V. 63

OVERBECK, ALICE O'READDON
Sven the Wise and Svea the Kind and Other Stories of Lappland. New York: 1932. V. 63

OVERBURY, THOMAS
His Wife. London: 1632. V. 64

OVERFIELD, DONALD
Famous Flies and Their Originators. 1972. V. 67

OVERFIELD, LOYD
The Little Big Horn 1876 - the Official Communications, Documents and Reports. Glendale: 1971. V. 65; 67

OVERS, JOHN
Evenings of a Working Man. London: 1844. V. 62

OVERTON, CHARLES
The History of Cottingham. Hull: 1861. V. 63

OVERTON, GRANT
American Nights Entertainment. New York: 1923. V. 64; 65

OVERTON, RICHARD
A New Bull-Bayting; or a Match Play'd at the Town Bull of Ely. Nod-Nol: 1649. V. 62

OVERTON, ROBERT
A Chase Around the World. London: 1900. V. 65

OVIDIUS NASO, PUBLIUS
Amores. Verona: 1932. V. 65
Amores. Waltham St. Lawrence: 1932. V. 64; 65
L'Art d'aimer. Chamonix: 1946. V. 67
The Art of Love. New York: 1971. V. 62
The Fasti, Tristia, Pontic Epistles, Ibis ad Halieuticon of Ovid. London: 1851. V. 63
Heroides, in Iterarum Studiosae Iuventutis Usum, cum Variorum et Suis Adnotationibus J. Terpstra Edidit.... Lugduni Batavorum Leiden: 1829. V. 66
Heroidum Epistolae. colophon: 1502. V. 66
Metamorphose. Amsterdam: 1650. V. 64
Metamorphoseon Libri XV. Lugduni: 1541. V. 65
Metamorphoses. Waltham St. Lawrence: 1958. V. 62; 65
Les Metamorphoses D'Ovide, en Latin et Francois Divisees en XV. Amsterdam: 1702. V. 64
Metamorphoses in 15 Books. London: 1717. V. 63; 66
Metamorphoses, in 15 Books. London: 1727. V. 66
Metamorphoses in Latin and English. Amsterdam: 1732. V. 62
Metamorphoses, Oder Wunder-Wurdige Gestalts-Veranderungen der Menschen.... Salzburg: 1705. V. 62
Opera. Lvgd(uni) Batavorvm: 1629. V. 63
Opera Omnia. Amsterdam: 1683-1702. V. 66
Opera Omnia, in Tres Tomos Divisa, Cum Integris Nicolai Heinsii, D. F. Amstelodami: 1683. V. 64
Opera Quae Extant. Londini: 1745. V. 64
Operum.... Amsterdam: 1661. V. 64; 67
Ovid's Epistles; with His Amours. London: 1725-1724. V. 62
Ovid's Metamorphoses. Philadelphia: 1790. V. 66
Ovid's Metamorphoses. New York: 1958. V. 64
Ovid's Metamorphosis Englished by G.S. London: 1626. V. 66
Ovyde Hys Booke of Methamorphose. Books X-XV. Boston and New York: 1924. V. 65, 67
Ovyde, Hys Booke of Methamorphose, Books X XV. Oxford: 1924. V. 62
Las Transformaciones de Ovidio en Lengua Espanola.... Antwerp: 1595. V. 62
A Translation of the First Book of Ovid's Tristia. New York: 1821. V. 66
Tristium Libri V. Argumentis, et Notis Hispanicis Illustrata. Barcinone: 1720?. V. 66

OVIEDO Y VALDES, GONZALO FERNANDEZ DE
The Conquest and Settlement of the Island of Boriquen or Puerto Rico. Avon: 1975. V. 64

OVINGTON, RAY
A Sportsman-Artist's Game Bag. Clinton: 1989. V. 65

OWEN, CHARLES
An Essay Towards the Natural History of Serpents. London: 1742. V. 62; 66

OWEN, CHARLES H.
The Justice of the Mexican War. New York: 1908. V. 63; 65

OWEN, DAVID DALE
Report of a Geological Exploration of Part of Iowa, Wisconsin and Illinois. Washington: 1840. V. 63
Report of a Geological Reconnoisance of the State of Indiana: Made in the Year 1837. Indianapolis: 1839. V. 63; 66

OWEN, EDMUND
Traite Pratique De Chirurgie Infantile. Paris: 1891. V. 64

OWEN, H. F.
A Complete Mosasa Skeleton, Oseous and Cartilaginous; and a Skeleton of Diplodocus. 1899. V. 65

OWEN, HAROLD
Aftermath. London: 1970. V. 65
Journey from Obscurity - Memoirs of the Owen Family: Wilfred Owen 1893-1918. London: 1963. V. 63
Journey from Obscurity: Wilfred Owen 1893-1918. London: 1963-1970. V. 67
Journey from Obscurity: Wilfred Owen 1893-1918. London: 1972-1964-1965. V. 62
The Staffordshire Potter...With a Chapter on the Dangerous Processes in the Potting Industry by the Duchess of Sutherland. London: 1901. V. 64

OWEN, HENRY
The Intent and Propriety of the Scripture Miracles Considered and Explained, in a Series of Sermons.... London: 1773. V. 62

OWEN, HUGH
A History of Shrewsbury. London: 1825. V. 66
Some Account of the Ancient and Present State of Shrewsbury. Shrewsbury: 1808. V. 62

OWEN, I.
Trout Fisherman's Saga. 1959. V. 67

OWEN, JOANNES
Epigrammatium Joan Owen Cambro-Britanni Oxoniensis. Amsterdam: 1647. V. 66

OWEN, JOHN
A Complete Collection of the Sermons...Formerly Published.... London: 1721. V. 64
The Journals and Letters of Major John Owen, Pioneer of the Northwest 1850-1871.... New York: 1927. V. 66
Travels into Different Parts of Europe, in the Years 1791 and 1792. London: 1796. V. 62

OWEN, M.
Wildfowl of Europe. 1977. V. 67

OWEN, MARY ALICIA
Old Rabbit, the Voodoo and other Sorcerers. London: 1898. V. 62; 64; 67
Voodoo Tales as Told Among the Negroes of the Southwest. New York: 1893. V. 62

OWEN, RICHARD
Description of the Cavern of Bruniquel (France) and Its Organic Contents.... 1864. V. 67
Essays on the Conrio-Hypophysial Tract and Aspects of the Body in the Vertebrate and Invertebrate Animals. London: 1883. V. 67
Evidence of a Carnivorous Reptile.... 1876. V. 67
A History of British Fossil Mammals and Birds. 1846. V. 62
A History of British Fossil Mammals and Birds. London: 1846. V. 64
A History of British Fossil Reptiles. London: 1849-1884. V. 67
The Life of Richard Owen, by His Grandson the Rev. Richard Owen. London: 1894. V. 63
Odontography; or, a Treatise on the Comparative Anatomy of the Teeth. London: 1840-1845. V. 62; 63
On the Anatomy of Vertebrates. London: 1866-1868. V. 64
On the Classification and Geographical Distribution of the Mammalia.... London: 1859. V. 62
On the Extinct Animals of the Colonies of Great Britain...Read at the Seventh Ordinary General Meeting of the Royal Colonial Institute. 1879. V. 62
On the Osteology of the Dodo. 1866. V. 67
On the Skull and Dentition of a Triassic Mammal; on the Crocodilian and Verteral Characters of the Crocodilian Genus.... 1884. V. 67
Palaeontology. London: 1860. V. 64
Palaeontology. Edinburgh: 1861. V. 64
The Zoology of Captain Beechy's Voyage. 1839. V. 62

OWEN, ROBERT
Debate on Evidences of Christianity.... Cincinnati: 1829. V. 64
Debate on the Evidences of Christianity. London: 1839. V. 67
A Development of the Principles and Plans on Which to Establish Self-Supporting Home Colonies.... London: 1841. V. 63
Essays on the Formation of Human Character. Manchester: 1837. V. 63
Essays on the Principle of the Formation of the Human Character. Manchester: 1837. V. 65
Letters to the Human Race on the Coming Universal Revolution. London: 1850. V. 64
A New View of Society; or, Essays on the Formation of the Human Character Preparatory to the Development of a Plan for Gradually Ameliorating the Condition of Mankind. London: 1817. V. 64
Public Discussion Between John Brindley and Robert Owen, on the Questions What is Socialism: and What Would Be Its Practical Effects Upon Society?. Birmingham: 1841. V. 66
The Revolution in the Mind and Practice of the Human Race; or The Coming Change from Traditionally to Rationality. London: 1849. V. 64

OWEN, ROBERT DALE
Beyond the Breakers. Philadelphia: 1870. V. 62
The Debatable Land Between This World and the Next. New York: 1872. V. 64
Footfalls on the Boundary of Another World. Philadelphia: 1860. V. 62
Hints on Public Architecture, Containing Among Other Illustrations, Views and Plans of the Smithsonian Institution.... New York: 1849. V. 62; 63; 66
Pocahontas: a Historical Drama. New York: 1837. V. 66
Tracts on Republican Government and National Education. London: 1851. V. 64

OWEN, ROSAMOND DALE
I. Robert Owen: Co-operation Versus Communism: a Play in Four Acts. II. Arcadia: the Bridal Mystery. Worthing: 1924. V. 64

OWEN, SAMUEL
Views on the Thames, from the Source to the Sea. London: 1811. V. 62

OWEN, WILFRED
Collected Letters. London: 1967. V. 63
The Collected Poems. London: 1963. V. 63
The Collected Poems. New York: 1964. V. 62
The Complete Poems and Fragments. London: 1983. V. 63
Poems. London: 1921. V. 63
The Poems. London: 1931. V. 66
Thirteen Poems. Northampton: 1956. V. 65

OWEN, WILLIAM
Owen's New Book of Roads; or, a Description of the Roads of Great Britain.... London: 1782. V. 66; 67

OWEN, WILLIAM MILLER
In Camp and Battle with the Washington Light Artillery of New Orleans. Boston: 1885. V. 63; 65

OWENS, JESSE
I Have Changed. New York: 1972. V. 63

OWENS, JOHN
The Journals and Letters of Major John Owens. New York: 1927. V. 66
Plain Papers Relating to the Excise of the Inland Revenue Department from 1621 to 1878.... Linlithgow;: 1879. V. 64

OWENS-ADAIR, B. A.
Dr. Owens-Adair. Some of Her Life Experiences. Portland: 1905. V. 63

THE OWLET of Owlstone Edge. London: 1856. V. 64

OWSLEY, FRANK LAWRENCE
C.S.S. Florida: Her Building and Operation. Philadelphia: 1965. V. 63

OXBERRY, WILLIAM
The Actor's Budget of Wit and Merriment, Consisting of Monologues, Prologues, Epilogues, Tales, Comic Songs, Rare and Genuine Theatrical Anecdotes and Jests. London: 1820. V. 62; 66; 67

OXENBURY, HELEN
The Helen Oxenbury Nursery Story Book. London: 1985. V. 67

OXENHAM, E. J.
A Divided Patrol. 1992. V. 67

OXFORD English Dictionary. Oxford: 1884-1933. V. 64

THE OXFORD English Dictionary. Oxford: 1961. V. 64; 65

OXFORD English Dictionary. New York: 1971. V. 64
OXFORD English Dictionary. London: 1979. V. 65; 66

OXFORD Poetry 1923. 1923. V. 62
OXFORD Poetry 1923. London: 1923. V. 63
OXFORD Poetry 1923. Oxford: 1923. V. 66

OXFORD Poetry 1924. Oxford: 1924. V. 62; 63; 66

OXFORD Poetry 1927. Oxford: 1927. V. 62

OXFORD Poetry 1928. Oxford: 1928. V. 62

OXFORD Poetry 1953. Swinford, Wynsham: 1953. V. 65

OXFORD Prize Poems.... Oxford: 1810. V. 62

OXFORD, ROBERT HARLEY, 1ST EARL OF
Catalogus Bibliothecae Harleianae. London: 1743-1745. V. 62
The Tryal of Robert Earl of Oxford and Earl Mortimer, Upon the Impeachment of that House of Commons, Exhibited against Him for High Treason and Other High Crimes and Misdeameanours.... London: 1717. V. 66

OXFORD UNIVERSITY
Academiae Francofurtanae ad Viadrum Encaenia Secularia Oxonii in Theatro Sheldoniano Apr. 26 Anno Fundat 201 Annoque Dom. 1706. Oxonii: 1706. V. 66
Academiae Oxoniensis Gratulatio Pro Exoptato Serenissimi Regis Guilelmi Ex Hibernia Reditu. Oxoniae: 1690. V. 66
Parecbolae Sive Excerpta e Corpore Stautorum Universitatis Oxoniensis.... Oxford: 1794. V. 66

THE OXFORD University and City Guide, On a New Plan.... Oxford: 1819?. V. 66

THE OXFORD University and City Guide, on a New Plan.... Oxford: 1823. V. 62

OXFORD UNIVERSITY PRESS
General Catalogue. London: 1916-1954. V. 64

OYLER, THOMAS H.
The Parish Churches of the Diocese of Canterbury with Descriptive Notes. London: 1910. V. 66

OZ, TAHSIN
Turkish Cermaics. N.P: Sep. 1950. V. 65

OZANAM, JACQUES
Dictionaire Mathematique, ou Idee Generale des Mathematiques. Amsterdam: 1691. V. 65
Recreations in Mathematics and Natural Philosophy.... London: 1803. V. 62; 66
L'Usage du Compas de Proportion, Explique et Demonstre d'une Maniere Courte & Facile, & Augmente d'un Traite de la Division des Champs. Paris: 1688. V. 67

OZEKI, RUTH
My Year of Meats. New York: 1998. V. 67

OZICK, CYNTHIA
Bloodshed and Three Novellas. New York: 1976. V. 66

P

P., C.
The Three Establishments concerning the Pay of the Sea-Officers. London: 1705. V. 62

P., P.
Studley Royal; or the New Guide Book. Knaresborough: 1847. V. 64

PAASCH, H.
From Keel to Truck. Marine Dictionary. London: 1894. V. 62

PABOR, WILLIAM E.
Colorado as an Agricultural State, Its Farms, Fields and Garden Lands. New York: 1883. V. 65

PACCARD, A.
Traditional Islamic Craft in Moroccan Architecture. France: 1980. V. 65

PACHECO, JOSE EMILIO
Tree Between Two Walls. Los Angeles: 1969. V. 62; 64

PACHO, JEAN RAIMOND
Relation d'un Voyage dans la Marmarique, la Cyrenaique et les Oasis d'Audjeleh et de Maradeh.... Paris: 1827. V. 64

THE PACIFIC Northwest. Facts Relating to the History, Topography...of Oregon and Washington Territory with a Map and Illustrations. New York: 1882. V. 63

THE PACIFIC Northwest. Information for Settlers and Others. Oregon and Washington Territory. New York: 1883. V. 63

THE PACIFIC Tourist. New York: 1879. V. 67

PACIOLI, LUCA
De Divina Proportione Di Luca Pacioli. Verona: 1956. V. 65

PACKARD, A. S.
Bombycine Moths of America North of Mexico. Washington?: 1895. V. 67
The Cave Fauna of North America, with Remarks on the Anatomy of the Brain and Origin of the Blind Species. Washington: 1888. V. 62
Monograph of the Bombycine Moths of No. America. Washington: 1895-1914. V. 66
Monograph of the Geometrid Moths of the U.S. Washington: 1876. V. 66

PACKARD, E. L.
Mollusca Fauna from San Francisco Bay. Berkeley: 1914-1918. V. 63; 65

PACKARD, FRANCIS R.
The History of Medicine in the United States. Philadelphia: 1901. V. 64
Life and Times of Ambroise Pare (1510-1590).... New York: 1921. V. 65

PACKARD, FRANK L.
Jimmie Dale and the Blue Envelope Murder. Garden City: 1930. V. 67

PACKARD, G.
Southwest 1880 with Ben Whittick - Pioneer Photographer of Indian and Frontier Life. Santa Fe: 1970. V. 67

PACKER, J. G.
Flora of the Russian Arctic.... Alberta: 1995-1996. V. 65; 67

THE PACK'S Address: to Which is Added the Loss of the Pack. N.P: 1840. V. 65

PACKWOOD, GEORGE
Packwood's Whim. The Goldfinch's Nest; or, the Way to Get Money and Be Happy. London: 1796. V. 62; 66

PACY, JOSEPH
The Reminiscences of a Gauger. Imperial Taxation, Past and Present Compared. Newark: 1873. V. 62

PADDOCK, A. G., MRS.
The Fate of Madame La Tour: a Tale of Great Salt Lake. New York: 1881. V. 66

PADDOCK, B. B.
History of Texas Fort Worth and the Texas Northwest. Chicago: 1922. V. 62; 65

PADEN, IRENE
The Big Oak Flat Road - an Account of Freighting from Stockton to Yosemite Valley. San Francisco;: 1955. V. 65

PADGETT, ABIGAIL
Child of Silence. 1993. V. 64
Child of Silence. New York: 1993. V. 62; 65; 67
Strawgirl. New York: 1994. V. 65

PADGETT, EARL CALVIN
Skin Grafting from a Personal and Experimental Viewpoint. Springfield: 1942. V. 66

PADGETT, LEWIS
Mutant. 1953. V. 64; 65; 66
Mutant. New York: 1953. V. 66
Tomorrow and Tomorrow and the Fairy Chessmen. 1951. V. 64; 66

PADGETT, LORENZO
Castleford and District in the Olden Time. London: 1904. V. 65

PADGETT, RON
New and Selected Poems. Boston: 1995. V. 67

PADILLA, HERBERTO
Sent Off the Field. London: 1972. V. 67

PADLEY, JAMES SANDBY
Selections from the Antient Monastic, Ecclesiastical and Domestic Edifices of Lincolnshire. Lincoln: 1851. V. 66

PADMORE, GEORGE
The Gold Coast Revolution - the Struggle of an African People from Slavery to Freedom. London: 1953. V. 63
How Russia Transformed Her Colonial Empire - a Challenge to the Imperialist Powers. London: 1946. V. 63
Pan-Africanism or Communism?. London: 1956. V. 63

PADOVANI, GIOVANNI
Viridarium Mathematicorum.... Venice: 1563. V. 63

PADRE Kino: Memorable Events in the Life and Times of the Southwest Depicted in Drawings by De Grazia. Los Angeles: 1962. V. 64

PAE, DAVID
The Coming Struggle Among the Nations of the Earth; or, the Political Events of the Next Fifteen Years Described in Accordance with Prophecies in Ezekiel, Daniel and the Apocalypse. London: 1853. V. 67

PAEZ, DON R.
Wild Scenes in South America; or, Life in the Llanos of Venezuela. New York: 1862. V. 64

PAGE, FREDERICK
A Letter to a Friend, Containing Observations on the Comparative Merits of Canals and Railways, Occasioned by the Reports of the Committe of the Liverpool and Manchester Railway. London: 1832. V. 63

PAGE, HUBBARD FULTON
Lyrics and Legends of the Cape Fear Country. Durham: 1932. V. 67

PAGE, J. L. W.
An Exploration of Exmoor and the Highlands of West Somerset. 1890. V. 62; 64

PAGE, JAKE
The Stolen Gods. New York: 1993. V. 66

PAGE, JAMES MADISON
The True Story of Andersonville Prison. New York: 1908. V. 62; 63; 65

PAGE, JAMES R.
A Descriptive Catalogue of the Book of Common Prayer and Related Material in the Collection of James R. Page. N.P: 1955. V. 64
A Descriptive Catalogue of the Book of Common Prayer and Related Material in the Collection of James R. Page. Los Angeles: 1955. V. 63

PAGE, JOHN
Receipts for Preparing and Compounding the Principal Meidines Made Use of by the Late Mr. Ward. Together with an Introduction. London: 1763. V. 65

PAGE, THOMAS
The Art of Painting in its Rudiment, Progress and Perfection: Delivered Exactly as It Is Put in Practice, So that the Ingenious May Easily Understand His Nature to Perform It. Norwich: 1720. V. 67

PAGE, THOMAS NELSON
In Ole Virginia; or, Marse Chan and Other Stories. New York: 1887. V. 67
John Marvel Assistant. New York: 1909. V. 62
Robert E. Lee. Man and Soldier. New York: 1911. V. 62; 63
The Shepherd Who Watched by Night. New York: 1916. V. 64
Washington and Its Romance. New York: 1923. V. 63

PAGE, W. G. B.
The Hull and East Riding Portfolio. Volume I No. I - VI (February 1887-December 1887). Hull: 1887. V. 63

PAGE, WILLIAM
The Victoria History of the County of Nottingham. London: 1906-1910. V. 65

PAGEL, J.
Biographisches Lexikon Hervorragender Arzte des Neunzehnten Jahrhunderts. Mansfield Centre. V. 65

PAGET, FRANCIS EDWARD
Tales of the Village. London: 1868. V. 67

PAGET, GEORGE
The Light Cavalry Brigade in the Crimea - Extracts from the Letters and Journal of the Late General Lord George Paget.... London: 1881. V. 66

PAGET, GUY
The Melton Mowbray of John Ferneley 1782 to 1860. 1931. V. 64

PAGET, J. OTHO
The Art of Beagling. London: 1938. V. 67

PAGET, JOHN
The New Examen or an Inquiry into the Evidence Relating to Certain Passages in Lord Macaulay's History.,.. Edinburgh: 1861. V. 67

PAGET, VIOLET
Ariadne in Mantua, a Romance in Five Acts. Oxford: 1903. V. 63
Belcaro, Being Essays on Sundry Aesthetical Questions. London: 1887. V. 65
Euphorion: Being Studies of the Antique and the Medieval in the Renaissance. London: 1884. V. 65
For Maurice: Five Unlikely Stories. London: 1927. V. 65
The Golden Keys and Other Essays on the Genius Loci. London: 1925. V. 65
Gospels of Anarchy and Other Contemporary Studies. London: 1908. V. 65
Hauntings: Fantastic Stories. London: 1906. V. 65
Juvenilia: Being a Second Series. London: 1887. V. 62
Music and its Lovers - an Empirical Study of Emotion and Imaginative Responses to Music. London: 1932. V. 63; 65
The Sentimental Traveller.... London: 1908. V. 65
Studies of the Eighteenth Century. London: 1907. V. 66
Studies of the Eighteenth Century in Italy. London: 1880. V. 65
Vanitas: Polite Stories. London: 1892. V. 65

PAHER, STANLEY W.
Nevada: an Annotated Bibliography. Las Vegas: 1980. V. 63
A Preliminary Nevada Bibliography. Las Vegas: 1974. V. 63; 66

PAIGE, LEROY
Maybe I'll Pitch Forever. Garden City: 1962. V. 66

PAIN, BARRY
Stories in Grey. London: 1911. V. 66
Wilhelmina in London. London: 1906. V. 67

PAIN, C. EARNEST
Fifty Years on the Test. 1934. V. 67

PAIN, EVA
Stories Barry Told Me. London: 1927. V. 62

PAIN, WILLIAM
The Builder's Companion and Workman's General Assistant.... London: 1758. V. 62
Pain's British Palladio; or, the Builder's General Assistant. London: 1790. V. 66
The Practical Builder, or Workman's Assistant.... Boston: 1792. V. 62
The Practical House Carpenter; or, Youth's Instructor.... London: 1805. V. 64

PAINE, ALBERT BIGELOW
Captain Bill McDonald Texas Ranger. A Story of Frontier Reform. New York: 1909. V. 65
Hollow Tree Stories. New York. V. 63
Mark Twain a Biography. New York: 1912. V. 63

PAINE, BAYARD H.
Pioneers, Indians and Buffaloes. 1935. V. 65
Pioneers, Indians and Buffaloes. Curtis: 1935. V. 67

PAINE, THOMAS
Agrarian Justice, Opposed to Agrarian Law, and to Agrarian Monopoly.... London: 179-. V. 62
Agrarian Justice, Opposed to Agrarian Law, and to Agrarian Monopoly.... London: 1797. V. 62
The American Crisis and a Letter to Sir Guy Carleton, on the Murder of Captain Huddy and the Intended Retaliation on Captain Asgill of the Guards. London: 1795. V. 62
The Complete Writings.... New York: 1945. V. 63
The Decline and Fall of the English System of Finance. Paris: 1796. V. 62
Dissertacao Obre os Principios Fundamentaes do Governo, Traduzida da Lingua Ingleza por Zid Es Oan.... Philadelphia: 1822. V. 62
Dissertation on First Principles of Government. London: 1795. V. 62
Dissertations on Government, the Affairs of the Bank and Paper Money. Philadelphia: 1786. V. 64
Droits de l'Homme, en Reponse a l'Attaque de M. Burke sur la Revolution Francoise.... Paris: 1791. V. 64; 66
A Letter Addressed to the Abbe Raynal on the Affairs of North America. London: 1792. V. 62
Letter Addressed to the Addressers on the Late Proclamation. London: 1792. V. 62
Letters by the Author of Common Sense. First, to the Earl of Shelburne,..on the Subject of American Indepdendence. Second, to Sir Guy Carleton...on the Murder of Captain Huddy. Albany: 1792. V. 63
The Life and Work of Thomas Paine. New Rochelle: 1925. V. 66
Life and Writings of Thomas Paine. New York: 1908. V. 66
Miscellaneous Articles....Consisting of a Letter to the Marquis of Lansdowne. A Letter to the Authors of the Republican. A Letter to the Abbe Syeyes. Thoughts on the Peace. London: 1792. V. 62
Die Rechte des Menschen. Kopenhagen: 1793. V. 64; 66
Rights of Man: Part the Second. London: 1792. V. 62
Rights of Man.... London: 1819. V. 62
Le Sens Commun. Paris: 1791. V. 64; 66
Thoughts on the Peace, and the Probable Advantages Thereof to the United States of America. London: 1791. V. 62
The Whole Proceedings of the Trial of an Information...Against Thomas Paine for a Libel Upon the Revolution and Settlement of the Crown.... Dublin: 1793. V. 63
The Whole Proceedings of the Trial of an Information...Against Thomas Paine for a Libel Upon the Revolution and Settlement of the Crown.... London: 1793. V. 63

PAINTER, J. W.
American Indian Artifacts. The John Painter Collection. Cincinnati: 1992. V. 62

PAINTER, WILLIAM
The Palace of Pleasure. 1929. V. 62
The Palace of Pleasure. London: 1929. V. 64

PAKENHAM, THOMAS
The Year of Liberty; the Story of the Great Irish Rebellion of 1798. 1969. V. 67

PAKULA, MARVIN
Centennial Album of the Civil War. New York: 1960. V. 67

PAL, PRATAPADITYA
Buddhist Book Illuminations.... Hong Kong: 1988. V. 62

PALADIN, VIVIAN
E. E. Heikka Sculptor of the American West. Great Falls/Seattle: 1990. V. 63

PALAHNIUK, CHUCK
Fight Club. New York and London: 1996. V. 64; 65

PALARDY, JEAN
The Early Oak Furniture of French Canada. Toronto: 1963. V. 64; 66

PALATINO, GIOVANNI BATTISTA
Libro nel Qual S'Insegna a Scriver Ogni Sorte Lettera. In Roma: 1553. V. 64; 66

PALEOTTO, ALFONSO
Esplicatione del Sacro Lenzuolo ove fu Involto il Signore et delle Piaghe in Esso Impresse col Suo Pretiosos Sangue Confrontate con la Scrittura Sacra, Profeti, e Pardi con Pie Meditationi de 'Dolori Della Beata Verg(i)ne. Bologna: 1599. V. 62

PALERMO, EVANGELISTA
A Grammar of the Italian Language. London: 1755. V. 62; 64

PALEY, GRACE
The Collected Stories. New York: 1994. V. 67
The Little Disturbances of Man. Garden City: 1959. V. 63

PALEY, WILLIAM
Caution Recommended in the Use and Application of Scripture Language. Cambridge: 1777. V. 65

PALEY, WILLIAM continued
Natural Theology or Evidences of the Existence and Attributes of the Deity, Collected from the Appearances of Nature. Boston: 1839. V. 64
The Principles of Moral and Political Philosophy. London: 1787. V. 62
The Principles of Moral and Political Philosophy. Boston: 1801. V. 62
The Works.... London: 1825. V. 63

PALGRAVE, FRANCIS
Corporate Reform. Observations on the Principles to be Adopted in the Establishment of New Municipalities.... London: 1833. V. 67

PALGRAVE, FRANCIS TURNER
Amenophis and Other Poems Sacred and Secular. London: 1892. V. 67
A Golden Treasury of Songs and Lyrics. New York: 1911. V. 63; 67
The Golden Treasury of Songs and Lyrics. New York: 1919. V. 63
The Golden Treasury of the Best Songs and Lyrical Poems in the English Language. Cambridge: 1861. V. 65
The Treasury of Sacred Song Selected from the English Lyrical Poetry of Four Centuries with Notes Explanatory and Biographical. Oxford: 1889. V. 62; 63

PALGRAVE, WILLIAM GIFFORD
Narrative of a Year's Journey through Central and Eastern Arabia (1862-1863). London: 1865. V. 62

PALINURIUS, PSEUD.
The Paper Boat. London: 1897. V. 67

PALLADINO, L. B.
Indian and White in the Northwest or a History of Catholicity in Montana 1831-1891. Baltimore: 1891. V. 67
Indian and White in the Northwest or a History of Catholicity in Montana, 1831-1891. Baltimore: 1894. V. 65
Indian and White in the Northwest or a History of Catholicity in Montana 1831-1891. 1922. V. 67
Indian and White in the Northwest or a History of Catholicity in Montana 1831-1891. Lancaster: 1922. V. 65; 66

PALLADIO, ANDREA
The Four Books of Andrea Palladio's Architecture.... London: 1738. V. 66

PALLAS, EMMANUEL
De l'Influence de l'Electricite Atmospherique et Terresttre sur l'Organisme, et de l'Effet de l'Isolement Electrique Considere Comme Myen Curatif et Preservatif d'un Grand Nombre de Maladies. Paris: 1847. V. 65

PALLAS, PETER SIMON
Miscellanea Zoologica.... Hagae Comitum: 1766. V. 67

PALLIS, MARCO
Peaks and Lamas. London: 1939. V. 63

PALLISER, FANNY MARRYAT
A Descriptive Catalogue of the Collection of Lace in the South Kensington Museum. London: 1881. V. 62
History of Lace. London: 1865. V. 65

PALLISER, GEORGE
Palliser's American Cottage Homes. Bridgeport: 1878. V. 64; 67

PALLISER, HUGH
The Trial of Sir Hugh Palliser...for Neglect and Disobedience Orders.... London: 1779. V. 66

PALLISER, JAMES H.
Rawdon and Its History. Rawdon: 1914. V. 65

PALLISER, JOHN
Solitary Rambles and Adventures of a Hunter in the Prairies. London: 1853. V. 63

PALLISER'S Model Homes. Bridgeport: 1878. V. 67

PALMER, A. H.
The Life of Joseph Wolf. Animal Painter. London: 1895. V. 65; 66

PALMER, ALBERT W.
The Mountain Trail and Its Message. Boston: 1911. V. 65

PALMER, BENJAMIN M.
A Discourse Before the General Assembly of South Carolina, On December 10, 1863, Appointed by the Legislature as a Day of Fasting, Humiliation and Prayer. Richmond: 1863. V. 63
The Oath of Allegiance to the United States, Discussed in Its Moral and Political Bearings. Richmond: 1863. V. 65

PALMER, C. H.
The Salmon Rivers of Newfoundland. Boston: 1928. V. 67

PALMER, CHARLES
A Collection of Select Aphorisms and Maxims. London: 1748. V. 63

PALMER, EDWARD HENRY
The Desert of the Exodus. Cambridge: 1871. V. 62

PALMER, EVE
Trees of Southern Africa. Cape Town: 1972-1973. V. 66

PALMER, FRIEND
Early Days in Detroit.... Detroit: 1906. V. 63

PALMER, H.
Mountaineering and Exploration in the Selkirks. 1914. V. 63; 65

PALMER, H. MARION
Donald Duck Sees South America. Boston: 1945. V. 65
The Three Caballeros. New York: 1944. V. 64

PALMER, HARRY CLAY
Athletic Sports in America, England and Australia.... Philadelphia: 1889. V. 66

PALMER, HENRY SPENCER
British Columbia. Williams Lake and Cariboo Districts, and on the Fraser River from Fort Alexander to Fort George. New Westmisnter: 1863. V. 63

PALMER, HERBERT E.
Jonah Comes to Nineveh: a Ballad. Stanford Dingley: 1930. V. 65

PALMER, J. W.
The New and the Old, or, California and India in Romantic Aspects. New York and London: 1859. V. 63; 65; 66

PALMER, JOEL
Journal of Travel Over the Rocky Mountains to the Mouth of the Columbia River, Made During the Years 1845 and 1846. Cincinnati: 1847. V. 66

PALMER, JOHN
Papers Relative to the Agreement Made by the Government with Mr. Palmer, for the Reform of the Posts. London: 1797. V. 65

PALMER, JOHN HORSLEY
The Causes and Consequences of the Pressure Upon the Money-Market: with a Statement of the Action of the Bank of England from 1st October 1833 to 27th December 1836. London: 1837. V. 64

PALMER, RALPH S.
Handbook of North American Birds. New Haven: 1962-1988. V. 63; 64; 67
Handbook of North American Birds. New Haven: 1976-1988. V. 67

PALMER, RICHARD
The Bible Atlas, or Sacred Geography Delineated in a Complete Series of Scriptural Maps. Boston: 1836. V. 66

PALMER, ROBIN
Mickey Never Fails. Boston: 1939. V. 65

PALMER, SAMUEL
The Letters of Samuel Palmer. London: 1974. V. 65
The Life and Letters of Samuel Palmer. London: 1892. V. 66
Moral Essays on Some of the Most Curious and Significant English, Scotch and Foreign Proverbs. London: 1710. V. 62; 66

PALMER, STUART
The Adventure of the Marked Man and One Other. Boulder: 1973. V. 67
The Monkey Murder and Other Hildegarde Withers Stories. New York: 1950. V. 67
The Riddles of Hildegarde Withers. New York: 1947. V. 67

PALMER, T. S.
Index Generum Mammalium.... 1968. V. 62

PALMER, THOMAS FYSHE
An Account of the Trial of Thomas Fyshe Palmer, Unitarian Minister, Dundee, Before the Circuit-Court...at Perth, on the 12th and 13th Days of September 1793. Perth: 1793. V. 63

PALMER, W. T.
The Complete Hill Walker Rock Climber and Cave Explorer. London: 1934. V. 63; 64
The English Lakes. London: 1908. V. 62; 65
The Lakes. London: 1966. V. 62
The Tarns of Lakeland. London: 1960. V. 62

PALMER, WILLIAM
Illustrated and Unabridged Edition of the Times Report of the Trial of William Palmer, for Poisoning John Parsons Cook, at Rugeley. London: 1856. V. 63
The Queen v. Palmer: Verbatim Report of the Trial of William Palmer. London: 1856. V. 64

PALMERSTON, HENRY JOHN TEMPLE, 3RD VISCOUNT
The Fudger Fudged; or, the Devil and T***y M***e. MDCCCLXXXVIII. London: 1819. V. 67

PALMQUIST, PETER E.
Carleton E. Watkins: Photographer of the American West. Albuquerque: 1983. V. 63
Lawrence and Houseworth/Thomas Houseworth and Co.: a Unique View of the West, 1860-1886. Ohio: 1980. V. 63
Redwood and Lumbering in California Forests. San Francisco: 1983. V. 63

PALOU, FRANCISCO
Historical Memoirs of New California. Berkeley: 1926. V. 62

PALTOCK, ROBERT
The Life and Adventures of Peter Wilkins.... Boston: 1835. V. 63

PAMMEL, L. H.
Ecology. Ames: 1903. V. 64

PANAS, FOTINOS
Lecons sur le Strabisme, les Paralysies Oculaires, Le Nystagmus, Le Blepharospasme &c. Paris: 1873. V. 64

PANASSIE, HUGUES
Le Jazz Hot. Paris: 1934. V. 66

PANCAKE, BREECE D'J.
The Stories of Breece D'J Pancake. Boston: 1983. V. 62

PANCIROLI, GUIDO
Rerum Memorabilium Sive Deperditarum. Frankfurt: 1646. V. 64

PANCIROLI, GUIDO continued
Rerum Memorabilium Sive Deperditarum. Frankfurt: 1660. V. 64

PANCOAST, JOSEPH
A Treatise on Operative Surgery.... Philadelphia: 1846. V. 64; 66

PANGBORN, EDGAR
West of the Sun. New York: 1953. V. 67

THE PANIZZI Lectures. Nos. 1-6. London: 1986-1991. V. 63

PANKEY, GEORGE E.
John Pankey of Manakin Town, Virginia and His Descendants. Ruston: 1969. V. 63

PANKHURST, EMMELINE
My Own Story. London: 1914. V. 65

PANKHURST, ESTELLE SYLVIA
The Suffragette Movement: an Intimate Account of Persons and Ideals. London: 1931. V. 65
The Suffragette; the History of the Women's Militant Suffrage Movement 1905-1910. London: 1911. V. 65

PANOFSKY, E.
Albrecht Durer. Princeton: 1948. V. 62; 65

PANORAMA. By an Artist. London: 1934. V. 67

THE PANORAMA; or, Traveller's Instructive Guide; through England and Wales. London: 1812. V. 67

THE PANORAMIC Automobile Map and Tourist Guide Book of Sothern California. Los Angeles: 1915. V. 62

PANSAERS, CLEMENT
Le Pan-Pan au Cul du Nu Negre. Brussels: 1920. V. 67

PANTIN, WILLIAM ABEL
Documents Illustrating the Activities of the General and Provincial Chapters of the English Black Monks 1215-1540. London: 1931-1937. V. 67

PANUM, HORTENSE
The Stringed Instruments of the Middle Ages, Their Evolution and Development.... London: 1971. V. 67

PANVINIO, ONOFRIO
Antiquitatum Veronensium Libri Octo Nunc Primum In Lucem Editi. Verona: 1647. V. 62; 67
Romanorum Principum...Libri III Eiusdem De Comitiis Imperatoriis Liber.... Basileae: 1558. V. 66

PAOLI, PAOLO ANTONIO
Antichita di Pozzuoli. Puteolanae Antiquitates. Naples: 1768. V. 62
Rovine Della Citta di Pesto, Detta Ancova Posidonia. Rome: 1784. V. 67

PAPADOPOULO, ALEXANDRE
Islam and Muslim Art. London: 1980. V. 62

PAPADOPOULOS, S. A.
The Greek Merchant Marine (1453-1850). Athens: 1972. V. 66

PAPAILIOU, D. D.
Frontiers in Propulsion Research: Laser, Matter-Antimatter, Excited Helium, Energy Exchange, Thermonuclear Fusion. Pasadena: 1975. V. 66

PAPANIN, I.
The Soviet Wintering Station on the Drifting Ice. Moscow: 1939. V. 64

THE PAPER Hanger, Painter, Grainer and Decorator's Assistant: Containing Full Infomration As to the Best Methods practised in Paper Hanging, Panelling, Room Decoration, Distempering, Graining, Marbling, Sign Writing.... London: 1879. V. 62; 66

THE PAPER War, Carried on at the Nottingham Election, 1803, Containing the Whole of the Addresses, Songs, Squibs &c.... Nottingham: 1803. V. 67

PAPERS Relative to the Mission of Hon. T. Butler King, to Europe. Milledgeville: 1863. V. 63

PAPILLON, JEAN BAPTISTE MICHEL
Traite Historique et Pratique de la Gravure en Bois. Paris: 1766. V. 62; 65

PAPP, C. S.
An Illustrated Catalog of the Cryptorhynchinae of the New World.... Sacramento: 1979. V. 66

PAPPE, L.
Synopsis of the Edible Fishes at the Cape of Good Hope. Cape Town: 1853. V. 65

PAPWORTH, JOHN
Essay on the Causes of the Dry Rot In Buildings.... London: 1803. V. 67

PAPWORTH, JOHN BUONAROTTI
Essay on the Causes of Dry Rot in Buildings, Contained in a Series of Letters Addressed to George Ernest James Wright, Esq.... London: 1803. V. 65
Hints on Ornamental Gardening.... London: 1823. V. 64; 66
Rural Residences, Consisting of a Series of Designs for Cottages, Decorated Cottages, Small Villas and Other Ornamental Buildings.... London: 1818. V. 64
Select Views of London: with Historical and Descriptive Sketches of Some of the Most Interesting of Its Public Buildings. London: 1816. V. 66

The Parables from the Gospels. London: 1903. V. 63

PARABLES of Our Lord. London: 1847. V. 64; 65
PARABLES of Our Lord. New York: 1848. V. 64
PARABLES of Our Lord. London: 1870. V. 66

PARACELSUS
Die Paracelsus Trilogie. Die Rindheit des Paracelsus. Das Gestirn des Paracelsus. Das Dritte Reich des Paracelsus. Munich: 1935. V. 64

PARADIN, CLAUDE
Symbola Heroica. Antverpiae: 1583. V. 66

PARAMORE, EDWARD E.
The Ballad of Yukon Jake. New York: 1928. V. 64; 67
The Ballad of Yukon Jake. Los Angeles: 1934. V. 63

PARCHER, MARIE L.
Dry Ditches. Bishop: 1934. V. 63

PARDIES, IGNACE GASTON
Opera Mathematica, Continentia Elementa Geometriae Discursum de Motu Locali Staticam and Duas Machinas, ad Conficienda Horologia solaria Habiles. Jena: 1694. V. 62

PARDOE, JULIA
Beauties of the Bosphorus. London: 1839. V. 65
The City of the Magyar, or Hungary and Her Institutions in 1839-1840. London: 1840. V. 62
The Romance of the Harem. London: 1839. V. 65

PARDON, GEORGE FREDERICK
The Faces in the Fire. London: 1844. V. 63
The Faces in the Fire. London: 1849?. V. 62
Whist, Its History and Practice. London: 1843. V. 67

PARE, AMBROISE
The Workes of the Famous Chirurgion Ambrose Pare.... Pound Ridge: 1968. V. 63; 65

PARENT-DUCHATELET, ALEXANDRE JEAN BAPTISTE
Recherches sur l'Inflammation de l'Arachnoide Cerebrale et Spinale, ou Histoire Theorique et Pratique de l'Arachnitis.... Paris: 1825. V. 65

THE PARENT'S Cabinet of Amusement and Instruction. London: 1837. V. 64

PARET, J. PARMLY
Psychology and Advanced Play of Lawn Tennis. New York: 1927. V. 67

PARETSKY, SARA
Bitter Medicine. New York: 1987. V. 63; 65; 66
Deadlock. Garden City: 1984. V. 63
Deadlock. London: 1984. V. 64
Guardian Angel. Bristol: 1992. V. 65
Indemnity Only. New York: 1982. V. 63
Killing Orders. New York: 1985. V. 63; 64; 66
Toxic Shock. London: 1988. V. 66
Tunnel Vision. New York: 1994. V. 67
V. I. for Short. London: 1995. V. 66

PARGETER, EDITH
Hortensius. Friend of Nero. London: 1936. V. 65
A Means of Grace. London: 1956. V. 67

PARHAM, LOUIS L.
Chattanooga, Tennessee County, and Lookout Mountain. Chattanooga: 1876. V. 63

PARIJANINE, MAURICE
The Krassin. New York: 1929. V. 64

PARINI, JAY
The Norton Book of American Auto-Biography. New York: 1999. V. 67

PARIS, ABBE
The Elements of Astronomy and Geography Explained on the Cards, Beautifully Engraved and Coloured by the Abbe Paris. London: 1795. V. 66

PARIS, JOHN AYRTON
The Elements of Medical Chemistry.... London: 1825. V. 65
The Life of Sir Humphrey Davy, Bart.... London: 1831. V. 63; 65
Pharmacologia. London: 1822. V. 65
Pharmacologia. New York: 1828. V. 64

PARIS, LOUIS, PHILIPPE ALBERT D'ORLEANS, COMTE DE
Battle of Gettysburg. Philadelphia: 1886. V. 62

PARIS, LOUIS PHILIPPE ALBERT D'ORLEANS, COMTE DE
Histoire de la Guerre Civile en Amerique. Volume 1 only. Paris: 1874. V. 65
History of the Civil War in America. Philadelphia: 1876. V. 64

PARIS, MATTHEW
Matthaei Paris Monachi Albanensis Angli, Historia Major; Juxta Exemplar Londinense, 1571.... Paris: 1644. V. 63

PARISH, W. D.
A Dictionary of the Sussex Dialect and Collection of Provincialisms in Use in the County of Sussex. Lewes: 1875. V. 64

PARIVAL, J.
The History of This Iron Age: Wherein is Set Down the True State of Europe As It Was in the Year 1500. Also, The Original, and Causes of All the Warres and Commotions, That Have Happened. London: 1656. V. 66

PARK, EDGAR
The Merry Adventures of Robin Hood and Santa Claus. Boston: 1922. V. 64

PARK, JAMES
The Cyanide Process of Gold Extraction: a Textbook for the Use of Mining Students, Metallurgists and Cyanide Operators. London: 1904. V. 62

PARK, MAUD WOOD
Front Door Lobby. Boston: 1960. V. 65

PARK, MUNGO
Travels in the Interior of Africa, in the Years 1795 1796 and 1797. London: 1799. V. 62

PARK, ROBERT
History of Oklahoma State Penitentiary Located at McAlester, Oklahoma. MacAlester: 1914. V. 66

PARK, ROBERT EMORY
Sketch of the Twelfth Alabama Infantry. Richmond: 1906. V. 62

PARK, ROSWELL
Selected Papers Surgical and Scientific. Buffalo: 1914. V. 66
A Treatise on Surgery by American Authors. Philadelphia: 1896. V. 64; 66; 67

PARK, THOMAS
Heliconia. London: 1815. V. 62; 64
Sonnets and Other Small Poems. London: 1797. V. 66

PARKE, ADELIA
Memoirs of an Old Timer. Weiser: 1955. V. 67

PARKE, H. W.
The Delphic Oracle. Oxford: 1956. V. 65

PARKE, THEODORE
The Trial of Theodore Parker, for the Misdemeanor of a Speech in Faneuil Hall Against Kidnapping, Before the Circuit Court of the United States, at Boston, April 3, 1855. Boston: 1855. V. 62

PARKE, URIAH
The Farmers' and Mechanics' Practical Arithmetic. Winchester: 1822. V. 66

PARKER, A. C.
Iroquois Uses of Maize and Other Food Plants. 1910. V. 62

PARKER, ALFRED BROWNING
You and Architecture: a Pratical Guide to the Best Building. New York: 1965. V. 65

PARKER, B.
The A's and the K's or Twice Three is Six. London: 1920. V. 62
Frolic Farm. London: 1910. V. 64

PARKER, BENJAMIN
Philosophical Meditations, with Divine Inferences....(with) Philosophical Dissertations, with Proper Reflections... (with) A Journey thro' the World.... Birmingham: 1738. V. 65

PARKER, C. A.
The Gosforth District: Its Antiquities and Places of Interest. Kendal: 1904. V. 65
The Story of Shelagh, Olaf Curan's Daughter. Kendal: 1909. V. 65

PARKER, DOROTHY
Enough Rope. New York: 1926. V. 63
Not So Deep as a Well: the Collected Poems of Dorothy Parker. New York: 1936. V. 62; 66

PARKER, ELINOR
I Was Just Thinking - a Book of Essays. New York: 1959. V. 64

PARKER, ERIC
Elements of Shooting. London: 1924. V. 67
Fine Angling for Coarse Fish. London: 1930. V. 67
The Lonsdale Anthology of Sporting Prose and Verse. London: 1932. V. 67
The Lonsdale Keeper's Book. London: 1929. V. 67
Shooting by Moor, Field and Shore. 1929. V. 67

PARKER, EVELYN FRANCES
Valley of Chiomonte. London: 1883. V. 63

PARKER, F. H. M.
The Pipe Rolls of Cumberland and Westmorland 1222-1260. Kendal: 1905. V. 64; 65

PARKER, FOXHALL A.
The Fleets of the World. The Galley Period. New York: 1876. V. 64

PARKER, GEORGE
The Elementary Nervous System. Philadelphia: 1919. V. 66
Humoral Agents in Nervous Activity. Cambridge: 1932. V. 66
Iowa Pioneeer Foundations. Iowa City: 1940. V. 63

PARKER, GEORGE HOWARD
What Evolution Is. Cambridge: 1925. V. 65

PARKER, GRANVILLE
The Formation of the State of West Virginia, and Other Incidents of the Late Civil War. Wellsburg: 1875. V. 64

PARKER, J.
Aluminum in Modern Architecture. Louisville: 1956. V. 62

PARKER, J. M.
An Aged Wanderer, a Life Sketch of J. M. Parker. A Cowboy On the Western Plains in the Early Days, San Angelo, Texas, Headquarters, Elkorn Wagon Yard. N.P. V. 65

PARKER, JAMES
The Old Army Memories. Philadelphia: 1929. V. 65; 67

PARKER, JOEL
Habeas Corpus and Martial Law. Cambridge: 1861. V. 63

PARKER, L. A.
This Fishing, or Angling Arts and Artifices. Salisbury: 1948. V. 67

PARKER, LUCRETIA
Piratical Barbarity or the Female Captive. New York: 1826. V. 66

PARKER, MATTHEW
De Antiquitate Britannicae Ecclesiae et Privlegiis Ecclesiae Cantuariensis cum Archiepiscopis Eiusdem LXX.. London: 1729. V. 63

PARKER, NATHAN H.
The Minnesota Handbook for 1856-1857. Boston: 1857. V. 64

PARKER, O. K.
A Strenuous Trip into the Grand Canyon of Arizona. Syracuse: 1912. V. 67

PARKER, ROBERT B.
A Catskill Eagle. New York: 1985. V. 62
Ceremony. New York: 1982. V. 67
Crimson Joy. 1988. V. 67
Crimson Joy. New York: 1988. V. 66
Double Deuce. New York: 1992. V. 66
Early Autumn. New York: 1981. V. 67
God Save the Child. 1974. V. 66
Introduction to Raymond Chandler's Unknown Thriller: The Screenplay of Playback. New York: 1985. V. 65; 67
The Judas Goat. 1978. V. 64
The Judas Goat. Boston: 1978. V. 67
Looking for Rachel Wallace. New York: 1980. V. 67
Mortal Stakes. Boston: 1975. V. 67
Pastime. New York: 1991. V. 66
Playmates. New York: 1989. V. 66
Promised Land. 1976. V. 64; 66
Promised Land. Boston: 1976. V. 66
Surrogate. Northridge: 1982. V. 65; 66; 67
Three Weeks in Spring. Boston: 1978. V. 67
Valediction. New York: 1984. V. 66
The Widening Gyre. New York: 1983. V. 67
Wilderness. 1979. V. 64; 66
Wilderness. New York: 1979. V. 65; 66; 67
Wilderness. New York: 1987. V. 66

PARKER, S. P.
Synopsis and Classification of Living Organisms. New York: 1982. V. 67

PARKER, SAMUEL
Journal of an Expedition Tour Beyond the Rocky Mountains. Ithaca: 1842. V. 66
Journal of an Exploring Tour Beyond the Rocky Mountains. Ithaca: 1838. V. 63
Journal of an Exploring Tour Beyond the Rocky Mountains. Ithaca: 1840. V. 63; 67
A Journey Beyond the Rocky Mountains in 1835, 1836 and 1837.... Edinburgh: 1841. V. 63

PARKER, T. JEFFERSON
Easy Street. Royal Oaks: 2000. V. 67

PARKER, T. JEFFERY
William Kitchen Parker, F.R.S.... London: 1893. V. 67

PARKER, THEODORE
Sermon on the Public Function of Woman. Boston: 1853. V. 67
Two Sermons Preached Before the Twenty-Eighth Congregational Society in Boston...on Leaving Their Old an Entering a New Place of Worship. Boston: 1853. V. 63

PARKER, THOMAS N.
An Essay on the Construction, Hanging and Fastening of Gates. London: 1804. V. 64
An Essay, or Practical Enquiry Concerning the Hanging and Fastening of Gates and Wickets.... London: 1801. V. 63

PARKER, W. K.
Challenger Voyage. Zoology. Part 5. Development of the Green Turtle. 1880. V. 66

PARKER, W. THORNTON
Personal Experiences Among Our North American Indians from 1867 to 1885. Northampton: 1913. V. 67

PARKER, WILLIAM FREDERICK
Daniel McNeill Parker, M.D. His Ancestry and a Memoir of His Life - Daniel Mc Neill and His Descendants. Toronto: 1910. V. 64

PARKER, WILLIAM HARWAR
Recollections of a Naval Officer 1841-1865. New York: 1883. V. 62; 63; 65
Recollections of a Naval Officer 1841-1865. New York: 1885. V. 63; 65

PARKER-HALE
Everything for Shooting. Birmingham: 1956. V. 67
Service Section Catalogue. Birmingham: 1939. V. 67

PARKES, BESSIE RAYNER
Summer Sketches and Other Poems. London: 1854. V. 62

PARKES, EDMUND ALEXANDER
A Manual of Practical Hygiene Prepared Especially for Use in the Medical Service of the Army. London: 1864. V. 65; 66

PARKES, M. B.
The Medieval Manuscripts of Keble College, Oxford, a Descriptive Catalogue with Summary Descriptions of the Greek and Oriental Manuscripts. London: 1979. V. 62; 67

PARKES, S.
The Chemical Catechism.... London: 1814. V. 62
The Chemical Catechism.... 1822. V. 62

PARKES, SAMUEL
Chemical Essays. London: 1823. V. 64

PARKES, WILLIAM, MRS.
Domestic Duties; or, Instructions to Young Married Ladies. London: 1828. V. 64; 65
Domestic Duties; or, Instructions to Young Married Ladies.... New York: 1830. V. 64

PARKIN, M.
Louis Wain's Cats. London: 1983. V. 67

PARKINS, JOHN
The Book of Miracles; or, Celestial Museum, Being an Entertaining Instructive Treatise on Love, Law, Trade and Physic with the Bank of Heaven.... London: 1817. V. 65
Ecce Homoe! Critical Remarks on the Infamous Publications of John Parkins, of Little Gonerby, Near Grantham, Better Known as Doctor Parkins.... Grantham: 1819. V. 66

PARKINSON, J. C.
The Ocean Telegraph to India. London: 1852. V. 65
The Ocean Telegraph to India. Edinburgh and London: 1870. V. 62

PARKINSON, JAMES
Medical Admonitions to Families, Respecting the Preservation of Health, and the Treatment of the Sick. Portsmouth: 1803. V. 65
Organic Remains of a Former World. London: 1811-1820. V. 65; 67
Outlines of Oryctology. 1833. V. 62
The Soldier's Tale. London: 1793?. V. 62
The Village Association or the Politics of Edley. London: 1793?. V. 62

PARKINSON, JOHN
The Dinosaur in East Africa. London: 1930. V. 62
Paradisi in Sole Paradisus Terrestris. London: 1629. V. 63; 66
Paradisi in Sole Paradisus Terrestris. 1904. V. 67
Paradisi in Sole Paradisus Terrestris. London: 1904. V. 63

PARKINSON, RICHARD
The Experienced Farmer, Enlarged and Improved; or Complete Practice of Agriculture According to the Latest Improvements.... London: 1807. V. 66

PARKINSON, SYDNEY
A Journal of a Voyage to the South Seas, in His Majesty's Ship the Endeavor. London: 1784. V. 63
A Journal of a Voyage to the South Seas, in His Majesty's Ship, the Endeavor. Adelaide: 1972. V. 63

PARKINSON, THOMAS
Hart Crane and Yvor Winters - Their Literary Correspondence. Berkeley Los Angeles and Lon: 1978. V. 64

PARKMAN, FRANCIS
The Book of Roses. Boston: 1866. V. 64
The Journals of Francis Parkman. New York and London: 1947. V. 64
The Oregon Trail. Garden City: 1945. V. 65

PARKS, FANNY
Wanderings of a Pilgrim, in Search of the Picturesque, During Four and Twenty-Four Years in the East; with Revelations of Life in the Zenana. London: 1850. V. 66

PARKS, GEORGE BRUNER
Richard Hakluyt and the English Voyages. New York: 1828. V. 67
Richard Hakluyt and the English Voyages. New York: 1928. V. 63; 64; 66

PARKS, JOSEPH H.
General Edmund Kirby Smith, C.S.A. Baton Rouge: 1954. V. 62; 63; 65

PARKS, ROSA
Dear Mrs. Parks. A Dialogue with Today's Youth. New York: 1996. V. 63

PARKS, STEPHEN
R. C. Gorman: a Portrait. Boston: 1983. V. 64

PARKYNS, MANSFIELD
Life in Abyssinia: Being Notes Collected During Three Years' Residence and Travels in that Country. New York: 1854. V. 65

THE PARLIAMENTARY or Constitutional History of England....
London: 1751-1761. V. 67

PARLOA, M.
Camp Cookery. Boston: 1878. V. 64

THE PARLOR Magician, or 100 Tricks for Drawing Room. New York: 1875. V. 67

PARLOUR Magic: a Manual of Amusing Experiments, Transmutations, Sleights and Subtleties, Legerdemain, &c. London: 1861. V. 66

THE PARLOUR Spelling Book. Philadelphia: 1806. V. 63; 66

PARMELIN, HELENE
Picasso: Women. Cannes and Mougins 1954-1963. Paris and Amsterdam. V. 63

LA PARNASSE des Dames. Paris: 1819. V. 66

PARNELL, HENRY
A History of the Penal Laws Against the Irish Catholics from the Treaty of Limerick to the Union. Dublin: 1808. V. 67
On Financial Reform. London: 1830. V. 64

PARNELL, THOMAS
Poems by Thomas Parnell. Dublin: 1927. V. 67
Poems on Several Occasions. London: 1726. V. 66
Poems on Several Occasions. London: 1747. V. 63
The Poetical Works. Glasgow: 1786. V. 65

PARNELL, WILLIAM
Maurice and Berghetta; or the Priest of Rahery. London: 1817. V. 67

THE PARNELLITE Split; or, the Disruption of the Irish Parliamentary Party. From the Times.... 1891. V. 65

PARNY, EVARISTE DESIRE DE FORGES, VICOMTE DE
Chansons Madecasses. London: 1787. V. 63
La Guerre des Dieux. Poeme en Dix Chants.... London: 1796. V. 63

PARR, CAPTAIN
Catalogue of the Valuable and Interesting Library of a Collector.... London: 1867. V. 62

PARR, HARRIET
Legends from Fairyland. Philadelphia: 1907. V. 65
Loving and Serving. London: 1883. V. 65
Mrs. Denys of Cote. London: 1880. V. 65
A Poor Squire. London: 1882. V. 65
Straightforward. London: 1878. V. 65

PARR, LOUISA
Robin. London: 1882. V. 65

PARR, MARGARET
Legends from Fairyland Narrating the History of Princess Glee and Princess Trill, the Cruel Persecutions.... London: 1908. V. 67

PARR, RICHARD
The Life of the Most Reverend Father in God, James Usher, Late Lord Arch-Bishop of Armagh.... London: 1686. V. 63

PARR, SAMUEL
Characters of the Late Charles James Fox. London: 1809. V. 63
A Sequel to the Printed Paper Lately Circulated in Warwickshire by the Rev. Charles Curtis, Brother of Alderman Curtis, a Birmingham Rector &c. London: 1792. V. 67

PARR, WILLIAM
The Visitor's Hand Book and Guide to Knaresborough.... Knaresborough: 1875. V. 65

PARRA, NICANOR
Cancionero Sin Nombre. Santiago de Chile: 1937. V. 67

PARRIS, O. A.
Christian Soldier. Jasper: 1945. V. 65

PARRISH, ANNE
The Story of Appleby Gapple. New York: 1950. V. 64

PARRISH, JOSEPH
An Inaugural Dissertation on the Influence of the Passions Upon the Body, in the Production and Cure of Diseases.... Philadelphia: 1805. V. 64

PARRISH, LYDIA
Slave Songs of the Georgia Sea Islands. New York: 1942. V. 63; 67

PARRISH, M. L.
Victorian Lady Novelists. London: 1933. V. 63

PARRISH, T. MICHAEL
Confederate Imprints. A Bibliography of Southern Publications from Secession to Surrender. Austin: 1987. V. 62; 63

PARROT, ANDRE
Sumer. London: 1960. V. 66

THE PARROT-Keeper's Guide. London: 1854. V. 65

PARRY, D. A. D.
Fibrous Proteins: Scientific, Industrial and Medical Aspects. London: 1979-1980. V. 66

PARRY, EDWARD ABBOTT
Butterscotia; or a Cheap Trip to Fairyland. London: 1896. V. 63

PARRY, J. D.
An Historical and Descriptive Account of the Coast of Sussex. Brighton: 1833. V. 62; 67
History and Description of Woburn and Its Abbey. London: 1831. V. 64

PARRY, JOHN S.
Extra-Uterine Pregnancy: Its Causes, Species, Pathological Anatomy, Clinical History, Diagnosis, Prognosis and Treatment. Philadelphia: 1876. V. 66

PARRY, JUDGE
Don Quixote of the Mancha. New York: 1900. V. 64

PARRY, MRS.
Olive Hastings. London: 1856. V. 65

PARRY, WILLIAM
The Last Days of Lord Byron. London: 1825. V. 66

PARRY, WILLIAM EDWARD
Journal of a Second Voyage for the Discovery of a North-West Passage from the Atlantic to the Pacific. London: 1824. V. 67
Journal of a Voyage for the Discovery of a North West Passage from the Atlantic to the Pacific Performed in the Years 1819-1820, in His Majesty's Ships Hecla and Griper, Under the Orders of William Edward Parry.... London: 1821. V. 65

PARRY, WILLIAM EDWARD continued
Journal of a Voyage for the Discovery of a North-West Passage from the Atlantic to the Pacific.... London: 1821-1824. V. 64; 66

A Supplement to the Appendix of Captain Parry's Voyage.... London: 1824. V. 62

PARSEY, ARTHUR
The Art of Miniature Painting On Ivory. London: 1831. V. 66

PARSHALL, H. F.
Armature Windings of Electric Machines. New York and London: 1895. V. 62

PARSON, THEOPHILIUS
A Treatise on the Law of Partnership. Boston: 1867. V. 63

PARSON, WILLIAM
History, Directory and Gazetteer of the Counties of Cumberland and Westmorland.... Leeds: 1829. V. 66

History, Directory and Gazetteer of the Counties of Cumberland and Westmorland.... Beckermet: 1976. V. 63

PARSONS, ARTHUR JEFFREY
Catalog of the Gardiner Greene Hubbard Collection of Engravings Presented to the Library of Congress by Mrs. Hubbard. Washington: 1905. V. 64

PARSONS, BENJAMIN
The Mental and Moral Dignity of Woman. London: 1856. V. 65

PARSONS, C. S. M.
China Mending and Restoration. London: 1963. V. 66

PARSONS, CHUCK
James Madison Brown; Texas Sheriff, Texas Turfman. Wolfe City: 1993. V. 67

PARSONS, CLERE
Oxford Poetry 1928. Oxford: 1928,. V. 66

PARSONS, ELSIE CLEWS
American Indian Life: by Several of Its Students. New York: 1922. V. 63; 64; 66

Folk-Lore of the Sea Islands, South Carolina. Cambridge and New York: 1923. V. 66

Folk-Lore of the Sea Islands, South Carolina. Cambridge and New York: 1924. V. 63

Hopi and Zuni Ceremonialism. Menasha: 1933. V. 67

Pueblo Indian Religion. Chicago: 1939. V. 66

The Pueblo of Jemez. New Haven: 1925. V. 63

The Social Organization of the Tewa of New Mexico. 1929. V. 62

Tewa Tales. New York: 1926. V. 66

PARSONS, FRANK
The City for the People, or the Muncipalization of the City Government and of Local Franchises. Philadelphia: 1898. V. 65

PARSONS, GEORGE W.
The Private Journal of George W. Parsons Adventure in the American West - Tombstone In Its Troubled Days. Tombstone: 1972. V. 63; 66

PARSONS, HORATIO A.
The Book of Niagara Falls. Buffalo: 1836. V. 62

Steele's Book of Niagara Falls. Buffalo: 1838. V. 64

Steele's Book of Niagara Falls. Buffalo: 1840. V. 62

PARSONS, JAMES
Philosophical Observations on the Analogy Between the Propagation of Animals and that of Vegetables. 1752. V. 62

Philosophical Observations on the Analogy Between the Propagation of Animals and that of Vegetables. London: 1752. V. 63; 67

PARSONS, JOHN E.
The Peacemaker and Its Rivals - an Account of the Single Action Colt. New York: 1950. V. 67

PARSONS, M.
The Butterflies of Papua New Guinea. 1998. V. 63

PARSONS, R. H.
The Developments of the Parsons Steam Turbine. London: 1936. V. 64

PARSONS, ROBERT
A Conference About the Next Succession to the Crown of England.... London: 1681. V. 67

Elizabethae Reginae Angliae Edictum Promulgatum Londini 29 Novemb. Anni MDXCI. 1593. V. 65

A Treatise of Three Conversions of England. (with) A Relation of the Triall...Between the Bishop of Evereux and L. Plessis Mornay. (and) A Review of Ten Publike Disputations...Under K. Edward & Qu. Mary, Concerning Some Principall Points in Religion. St. Omer: 1603-1604. V. 67

PARSONS, THOMAS, & SONS
A Tint of Historical Colours Suitable for Decorative Work. Mitcham: 1961. V. 66

PARSONS, TYLER
Mormon Fanaticism Exposed. Boston: 1841. V. 66

PARSONS, WILLIAM
The Tent of Darius Explain'd; or the Queens of Persia at the Feet of Alexander. London: 1703. V. 62; 67

PARTINGTON, CHARLES F.
The British Cyclopaedia of Arts and Sciences, Manufactures, Commerce, Literature, History, Politics, Biography, Natural History, Biblical Criticism and Theology. London: 1833-1838. V. 66

The British Cyclopaedia of Biography.... London: 1837. V. 62

PARTINGTON, J. R.
A History of Chemistry. London: 1961-1970. V. 63

A History of Chemistry. New York: 1996. V. 62

PARTINGTON, WILFRED
Thomas J. Wise in the Original Cloth, the Life and Record of the Forger of the Nineteenth Century Pamphlets. London: 1946. V. 62; 63; 64

PARTON, JAMES
Noted Women of Europe and America.... Hartford: 1883. V. 67

PARTON, JOHN
Some Account of the Hospital and Parish of St. Giles, in the Fields, Middlesex. London: 1822. V. 62

PARTRIDGE, ALDEN
Journal of a Tour of a Detachment of Cadets, from the A.L.S. and M. Academy, Middletown, to the City of Washington, in December 1826. Middletown: 1827. V. 64

PARTRIDGE, D. C.
The Most Remarkable Echo in the World. Hastings-on-Hudson: 1933. V. 66

PARTRIDGE, ELIZABETH
Dorothea Lange: A Visual Life. Washington and London: 1994. V. 63

PARTRIDGE, ERIC
A Dictionary of the Underworld, British and American.... London: 1950. V. 64

An Original Issue of The Spectator Together With the Story of the Famous English Periodical and Of Its Founders, Joseph Addison and Richard Steele. San Francisco: 1939. V. 64

PARTRIDGE, FRANCES
Everything to Lose: Diaries 1945-1960. London: 1985. V. 66

Julia, a Portrait of Julia Strachey.... London: 1983. V. 66

A Pacifist's War. London: 1978. V. 66

PARTRIDGE, WILLIAM
A Practical Treatise on Dying of Woolen, Cotton and Skein Silk. New York: 1823. V. 64; 66

PARTS of the Pacific by a Peripatetic Parson. London: 1896. V. 67

PARTSCH, HERMAN
The Ills of Indigestion. Their Causes and Their Cures, in Three Essays. North Berkeley: 1896. V. 63

PAS, JAN
Mathematische of Wiskundige Behandeling der Schryfkonst, Behelzende Een Manier om Alle de Gemeene Letteren van het Regt- en Schuin Romeins.... Amsterdam: 1737. V. 63; 67

PASCAL, BLAISE
Oeuvres. The Hague: 1779. V. 64

Les Pensees. London: 1971. V. 67

Les Provinciales, or the Mystery of Jesuitisme. Discovered in Certain Letters, Written Upon Occasion of the Present Differences at Sorbonne.... London: 1658. V. 67

Thoughts on Religion and Other Important Subjects. London: 1802. V. 65

Traitez de l'Equilibre des Liqueurs, et de la Pesanteur de la Masse de l'Air. Paris: 1663. V. 64; 66

PASCHAL, GEORGE W.
History of North Carolina Baptists. Raleigh: 1930. V. 63

A History of Printing in North Carolina. Raleigh: 1946. V. 67

PASCHOUD, M.
Historico-Politcal Geography; or, a Particular Description of the Several Countries in the World. London: 1726. V. 62; 65

PASCOLI, LIONE
Vite de' Pittori, Scultori ed Architetti Perugini.... Rome: 1732. V. 67

PASHLEY, ROBERT
Pauperism and Poor Laws. London: 1852. V. 64

PASOLINI, PIER PAOLO
Poesie a Casarsa. Bologna: 1942. V. 67

A Violent Life. London: 1968. V. 65

PASQUIER, R. F.
Masterpieces of Bird Art. New York: 1991. V. 65

PASSERON, R.
Impressionist Prints. New York: 1974. V. 62; 65

PASSINGHAM, ROBERT
The Whole Trial of Col. Rob. Passingham and John Edwards, for a Conspiracy Against George Townshend Forrester.... London: 1805. V. 63

PASSY, HIPPOLYTE PHILIBERT
On Large and Small Farms, and Their Influence on the Social Economy...(with) Aristocracy Considered in Its Relations with the Progress of Civilization.... London: 1848. V. 67

PAST Days in India. 1874. V. 66

PASTA, ANDREA
Le Pitture Notabile di Bergamo.... Bergamo: 1775. V. 64

PASTERNAK, BORIS
Bliznets v Tuchakh. (Twins in the Stormclouds). Moscow: 1914. V. 65; 67

Doctor Zhivago. Milan: 1958. V. 62

Doktor Zhivago. Ann Arbor: 1959. V. 65

PASTEUR, LOUIS
Etudes sur la Maladie des Vers a Soie, Moyen Pratique Assure de la Combattre et d'en Prevenir Le Retour. Paris: 1870. V. 63; 64
Les Microbes Organises Leur Role dans la Fermentation, la Putrefaction et al Contagion. Paris: 1878. V. 63
Oeuvres. Paris: 1922-1939. V. 66
Studies on Fermentation: the Diseases of Beer, Their Causes and the Means of Preventing Them.... London: 1879. V. 64
Sur les Corpuscles Organises qui Existent dans l'Atmosphere. Paris: 1861. V. 63

PASTON, JOHN
Original Letters, Written During the Reigns of Henry VI, Edward IV and Richard III. London: 1787-1789. V. 62

THE PASTON Letters 1422-1509 A.D. Westminster: 1900-1901. V. 63

THE PASTOR Chief; or, the Escape of the Vaudois. London: 1843. V. 65

PASTORET, CLAUDE EMMANUEL JOSEPH PIERRE, MARQUIS DE
Zorastre, Confucius et Mahomet, Compares Comme Sectaires, Legislateurs, et Moralistes.... Paris: 1787. V. 66

PASTORINI, BENEDICT
A New Book of Designs for Girandoles and Glass Frames in the Present Taste. London: 1775. V. 67

PATCH, JOSEPH DORST
The Battle of Ball's Bluff. Leesburg: 1958. V. 63

PATCH, RICHARD
Springsguth's Enlarged Edition of the Trial of Richard Patch for the Wilful Murder of Mr. Isaac Blight, Late Ship-Breaker of Deptford.... London: 1806. V. 63
The Trial of Richard Patch for the Wilful Murder of Isaac Blight.... London: 1806. V. 63

PATCHEN, KENNETH
Before the Brave. New York: 1936. V. 63
Fables and Other Little Tales. Karlsruhe/Baden: 1953. V. 63; 65
Hurrah for Anything. Highlands: 1957. V. 63; 64
Outlaw of the Lowest Planet. London: 1946. V. 62
Poem-Scapes. Highlands: 1958. V. 63
When We Were Here Together. New York: 1957. V. 66

PATCHETT, ANN
The Patron Saint of Liars. Boston: 1992. V. 64; 66

PATCHING, TALLCUT
A Religious Convincement and Plea for the Baptism and Communion of the Spirit.... Buffalo: 1822. V. 62

PATE, H. CLAY
The American Vade Mecum; or the Companion of Youth and Guide to College. Cincinnati: 1852. V. 65

PATENCIO, FRANCISCO
Stories and Legends of the Palm Springs Indians. Los Angeles: 1943. V. 63; 64

PATENT Artificial Slate Manufactory, Woodford Bridge, Essex, for Covering Roofs, Fronts of Houses and Ricks; also Water Pipes, and Gutters. London: 1786?. V. 66

PATER, WALTER
The Chant of the Celestial Sailors - an Unpublished Poem. London: 1928. V. 62
Marius the Epicurean. London: 1913. V. 63
The Renaissance: Studies in Art and Poetry. Verona: 1976. V. 62; 63; 64; 66
Sebastian Van Storck. London: 1927. V. 67

PATERCULUS
C. Velleii Paterculi Quae Supersunt Tex Historiae Romanae Voluminibus Duobus.... Roterdam: 1756. V. 65
(Historiae Romanae). Amstelodami: 1664. V. 65

PATERNOSTER Review. London: 1890-1891. V. 64

PATERNOSTER, SIDNEY
The Hand of the Spoiler. London: 1908. V. 66

PATERSON, ARTHUR
The Better Man. London: 1890. V. 67
The Homes of Tennyson. London: 1905. V. 62

PATERSON, CAROLINE
Three Fairy Princesses. London: 1885. V. 64

PATERSON, DANIEL
A New and Accurate Description of All the Direct and Principal Cross Roads in England and Wales. London: 1784. V. 63
A New and Accurate Description of All the Direct and Principal Cross Roads in England and Wales. London: 1789. V. 65
A New and Accurate Description of all the Direct and Principal Cross Roads in England and Wales.... London: 1796. V. 62
A New and Accurate Description of all the Direct and Principal Cross Roads in England and Wales.... London: 1803. V. 64; 66
A New and Accurate Description of all the Direct and Principal Cross Roads in Great Britain.... London: 1776. V. 62
A Travelling Dictionary. London: 1787. V. 62
A Travelling Dictionary. London: 1797. V. 63

PATERSON, EDNA B.
Nevada's Northeast Frontier. Sparks: 1969. V. 67

PATERSON, J. H.
Gastric Surgery; Being the Hunterian Lectures. 1906. V. 67

PATERSON, JAMES
A Compelete Commentary, with Etymological Explanatory, Critical and Classical Notes. London: 1744. V. 65
Pietas Londinensis; or, the Present Ecclesiastical State of London.... London: 1714. V. 62

PATERSON, THOMAS
The Man Paterson. God Versus Paterson. London: 1843. V. 63

PATERSON, WILLIAM
An Enquiry into the State of the Union of Great Britain, and the Past and Present State of the Trade and Publick Revenues thereof. London: 1717. V. 65
An Inquiry Into the Reasonableness and Consequences of an Union with Scotland. London: 1706. V. 67

PATMORE, COVENTRY
The Angel in the House. London: 1863. V. 65
The Angel in the House. Book I - The Betrothal. Book II - the Espousals. London: 1858. V. 65
The Angel in the House. Book II. The Espousals. London: 1856. V. 65
The Angel in the House: the Betrothal. London: 1854. V. 62; 65
Faithful for Ever. London: 1860. V. 65
Hastings, Lewes, Rye and the Sussex Marshes. London: 1887. V. 65
How I Managed and Improved My Estate. London: 1886. V. 65
Poems. London: 1844. V. 65
Poems. London: 1886. V. 65
The Unknown Eros and Other Odes. Odes I-XXXI. London: 1877. V. 65
The Unknown Eros. I-XLVI. London: 1878. V. 65

PATMORE, D.
Colour Schemes for the Modern Home. London: 1936. V. 65

PATON, ALAN
Cry, the Beloved Country. London: 1948. V. 63; 64; 67
Debbie Go Home and Other Stories. Helsinki: 1985. V. 62
The Land and People of South Africa. Philadelphia: 1955. V. 62; 67
The Negro in America Today. New York: 1954. V. 62

PATON, E. RICHMOND
The Birds of Ayrshire. 1929. V. 62; 65

PATON, J. NOEL
Specimen of Twenty Illustrations of the Anicent Mariner by Samuel Taylor Coleridge. London: 1863. V. 64

PATON, JAMES
British History and Papal Claims from the Norman Conquest to the Present Day. London: 1893. V. 63
Scottish History and Life. Glasgow: 1902. V. 62

PATON, LUCY A.
Selected Bindings from the Gennadius Library. Cambridge: 1924. V. 62

PATRICK, CHANN
The House of Retrogression. New York: 1932. V. 65; 66

PATRICK, JOHN
The Teahouse of the August Moon. New York: 1952. V. 66

PATRICK, Q.
File on Fenton and Farr. New York: 1937. V. 66

PATRICK, REMBERT W.
Jefferson Davis and His Cabient. Baton Rouge: 1944. V. 67

PATRICK, SYMON
Advice to a Friend. London: 1673. V. 65
The Parable of the Pilgrim. London: 1673. V. 66

PARTRIDGE'S Children's Annual. London: 1915. V. 65

PATRIOTIC Competition Against Self-Interested Combination Recommended; by a Union Between the Nobility, the Landed and Independent Interest, the Clergy and Consumer.... London: 1800. V. 67

PATRIX PALAW, EMMANUEL G.
Traite sur le Cancer de la Matrice et sur les Maladies des Voies Uterines. Paris: 1820. V. 66

PATTEE, FRED LEWIS
The Poems of Philip Freneau. Poet of the American Revolution. Princeton;: 1902-1907. V. 64

PATTEN, C. J.
The Aquatic Birds of Great Britain and Ireland. 1906. V. 63; 66

PATTEN, WILLIAM
Christianity the True Theology and Only Perfect Moral System.... Warren: 1795. V. 64

PATTERSON, A. W.
The Code Duello with Special Reference to the State of Virginia. Richmond: 1927. V. 63

PATTERSON, ARTHUR H.
Through Broadland in a Breydon Punt. 1920. V. 63
Wild Life on a Norfolk Estuary. 1907. V. 67
Wildfowlers and Poachers. 1929. V. 67

PATTERSON, C.
The Braincase of Pholidophorid and Leptolepid Fishes.... London: 1975. V. 65

PATTERSON, EDNA B.
Nevada's Northeast Frontier. Sparks: 1969. V. 64

PATTERSON, GEORGE
A Few Remains of the Rev. James MacGregor, D.D. Philadlephia: 1859. V. 66
Memoir of the Rev. James MacGregor, D.D. Philadelphia: 1859. V. 66
Missionary Life Among the Cannibals: Being the Life of the Rev. John Geddie, D.D.... Toronto: 1882. V. 65

PATTERSON, J. B.
Autobiography of Ma-Ka-Tai-Me-She-Kia-Kiak or Black Hawk. Oquawka: 1882. V. 65
Life of Ma-Ka-Tai-Me-She-Kia-Kiak or Black Hawk. Boston: 1834. V. 63

PATTERSON, J. H.
In the Grip of the Nyika; Further Adventures in British East Africa. London: 1909. V. 65

PATTERSON, JAMES
The Jericho Commandment. New York: 1979. V. 67
Virgin. New York: 1980. V. 65

PATTERSON, R. F.
Mein Rant. London: 1940. V. 65

PATTERSON, ROBERT
Narrative of the Campaign in the Valley of the Shenandoah in 1861. Philadelphia: 1865. V. 62; 63; 65
On the Study of Natural History as a Branch of General Education. Belfast: 1840. V. 67

PATTERSON, ROBERT LLOYD
The Birds, Fishes and Cetacea of Belfast Lough. 1881. V. 63; 66

PATTERSON, SAMUEL W.
Horatio Gates. Defender of Liberty. New York: 1941. V. 67

PATTIE, JAMES O.
The Personal Narrative of James O. Pattie of Kentucky During an Expedition from St. Louis, through the Vast Regions Between that Place and the Pacific Ocean.... Cleveland: 1905. V. 64

PATTILO, T. R.
Moose-Hunting, Salmon-Fishing and Other Sketches of Sport. London: 1902. V. 67

PATTISON, MARK
The Estiennes, a Biographical Essay. San Francisco: 1949. V. 62

PATTISON, WILLIAM
The Poetical Works of Mr. William Pattison, Late of Sidney College, Cambridge. London: 1728. V. 66

PATTON, SADIE
Sketches of Polk County History. Asheville: 1950. V. 63; 67
The Story of Henderson County. Asheville: 1947. V. 66

PATTON, SADIE SMATHERS
Sketches of Polk County History. Asheville: 1950. V. 63; 67

PATTON, W. S.
Insects, Ticks, Mites and Venimous Animals of Medical and Veterinary Importance. 1929-1931. V. 67

PAUCKER, PAULINE
New Borders. The Working Life of Elizabeth Friedlander. London: 1998. V. 62; 67
New Borders; the Working Life of Elizabeth Friedlander. Oldham: 1998. V. 62

PAUCTON, ALEXIS JEAN PIERRE
Theorie des Lois de La Nature, ou la Science des Causes et des Effets Suivie d'une Dissertation sur les Pyramides d'Egypte. Paris: 1781. V. 64; 67

PAUL A.
Bennett 1897-1966: a Memorial Keepsake. New York: 1966. V. 64

PAUL, ELLIOT
The Death of Lord Haw Haw. No. I. Personality of World War No. 2; Being an Account of the Last Days of the Foremost Nazi Spy and News Commentator, the Mysterious English Traitor. New York: 1940. V. 66
Low Run Tide. (and) Lava Rock. New York: 1929. V. 67
The Stars and Stripes Forever. New York: 1939. V. 66

PAUL, GEORGE ONESIPHOROUS
An Address Delivered at a General Meeting of the Nobility, Gentry, Clergy and Others Assessed to the County Rate for the County of Gloucester, Convened by the High Sheriff, for the Purpose of Receiving a Statement of the Proceedings of the Committee Appo. Gloucester: 1792?. V. 65
Considerations on the Defects of Prisons, and Their Present System of Regulation.... London: 1784. V. 65
General Regulations for Inspection and Control of All Prisons, Together with the Rules, Orders and Bye Laws for the Government of the Gaol and Penitentiary House for the County of Gloucester.... Glocester: 1790. V. 65
Proceedings of the Grand Juries, Magistrates, and Other Noblemen and Gentlemen of the County of Gloucester, on Designing and Executing a General Reform in the Construction and Regulation of the Prisons for the Said County. (with) Call of a General Meetin. Glocester: 1808. V. 65

PAUL, HENRY N.
Joseph Paull of Ilminster, Somerset, England and Some of His Descendants Who Have Resided in Philadelphia. N.P: 1933. V. 63; 66

PAUL, NATHANIEL
An Address Delivered on the Celebration of the Abolition of Slavery, in the State of New York, July 5, 1827. Albany: 1827. V. 63

PAUL, RODMAN W.
The California Gold Discovery. Sources, Documents, Accounts and Memoirs Relating to the Discovery of Gold at Sutter's Mill. Georgetown: 1966. V. 65

PAULDEN, THOMAS
An Account of the Taking and Surrendering of Pontefact Castle, and of the Suprisal of General Rainsborough in His Quarters at Doncaster, Anno 1648. Oxford: 1747. V. 66

PAULDING, J. K.
John Bull in America; or, the New Munchausen. New York: 1825. V. 64
The Merry Tales of the Three Wise Men of Gotham. New York: 1826. V. 64; 66

PAULHAN, JEAN
La Patrie Se Fait Tous Les Jours - Textes Francais 1939-1945. Paris: 1947. V. 64

PAULIN, TOM
Theoretical Locations. Belfast: 1975. V. 63

PAULINE
and the Matches and Other Stories. New York: 1890. V. 63

PAULING, LINUS
No More War!. New York: 1958. V. 63

PAULLIN, CHARLES O.
Atlas of the Historical Geography of the United States. New York: 1932. V. 66

PAULLINUS A SANCTO BARTHOLOMAEO, JOHANNES PHILIPPUS WERDIN
Systema Brahmanicum Liturgicum Mythologicum Civile ex Monumentis Indicis Musei Borgiani Velitris Dissertationibus Historico-Criticis Illustravit. Rome: 1791. V. 67

PAUL OF AEGINATA
The Seven Books of Paulus Aeginata. London: 1844-1847. V. 64; 66

PAULSON, L. L.
Hand-Book and Directory of Alameda County. San Francisco: 1876. V. 63

PAULSSON, T.
Scandinavian Architecture: Guildings and Society in Denmark, Finland, Norway and Sweden.... London: 1958. V. 65

PAULUS, CAROLUS
Some Forgotten Facts in the History of Sheffield and District.... Sheffield: 1907. V. 63; 65
Unpublished Pages Relating to the Manor and Parish of Eccleshall.... Sheffield: 1927. V. 65

PAULY, ALPHONSE
Bibliogrpahie des Sciences Medicales. Bibliographie. Histoire. Epidemies. Endemies Histoire des Ecoles et des Hopituax. Litterature medicale. Histoire Professionelle. London: 1954. V. 63

PAUSANIAS
The Description of Greece, by Pausanias. London: 1794. V. 67

PAUSANIUS
Graeciae Descriptio Accurata...Cum Latina Romuli Amasaei Interpretatione. Lipsiae: 1696. V. 65

PAUSE, WALTER
Salute the Mountains. London: 1962. V. 63; 64

PAVLOV, IVAN PETROVICH
An Address on the Investigation of the Higher Nervous Functions.... 1913. V. 64
Die Arbeit der Verdauungsdrusen. Wiesbaden: 1898. V. 62; 66
Conditioned Reflexes. London: 1940. V. 67
Lectures on Conditioned Reflexes. New York: 1928. V. 64; 66; 67
Lectures on Conditioned Reflexes. London: 1941. V. 67
Le Travail des Glandes Digestives Lecons.... Paris: 1901. V. 66
The Work of the Digestive Glands. London: 1902. V. 66
The Work of the Digestive Glands. London: 1910. V. 65

PAVLOVSKY, B. V.
Decorative Arts of Industrial Urals. Moscow: 1975. V. 65

PAWSEY, J. L.
Radio Astronomy. Oxford: 1955. V. 67

PAXTON, MARY W.
Where Tempests Blow. London: 1885. V. 66

PAXTON, PETER
Specimen Physico-Medicum de Corpote Humano & Ejus Morbis. London: 1711. V. 63

PAYEN, ANSELME
Precis de Chimie Industrielle.... Paris: 1855. V. 64

PAYER, JULIUS
New Lands Within the Arctic Circle. New York: 1877. V. 64; 67

PAYN, JAMES
The Backwater of Life, or Essays of a Literary Veteran. London: 1899. V. 67
The Burnt Million. London: 1891. V. 67
A Description of Furness Abbey and Its Neighbourhood. London: 1864. V. 66
The Heir of the Ages. London: 1886. V. 67
High Spirits Being Certain Stories Written in Them. (with) Second Series. Leipzig: 1879-1880. V. 67
The Lakes in Sunshine. Windermere: 1868. V. 62
Leaves from Lakeland. London: 1858. V. 67
A Modern Dick Whittington; or a Patron of Letters. London: 1893. V. 67
The Mystery of Mirbridge. Leipzig: 1888. V. 67
A Perfect Treasure. London: 1869. V. 67
Some Literary Recollections. Leipzig: 1884. V. 67

PAYN, JAMES continued
Some Private Views.... London: 1881. V. 67
Some Private Views.... Leipzig: 1882. V. 67
The Youth and Middle Age of Charles Dickens.... London: 1883. V. 62

PAYNE, A. A.
A Handbook of British and Foreign Orders, War Medals and Decorations Awarded to the Army and Navy. Sheffield: 1911. V. 66

PAYNE, ALFRED C.
Dutton's Holiday Annual for 1905. London: 1905. V. 65

PAYNE, BROOKE
The Paynes of Virginia. Richmond: 1937. V. 67

PAYNE, BUCKER H.
The Negro: What Is His Ethnological Status?. Cincinnati: 1872. V. 66

PAYNE, C. H.
The Florist's Bibliography. 1908-1924. V. 64
The Stars of High Luminosity. New York: 1930. V. 66

PAYNE, EDWARD F.
The Charity of Charles Dickens - His Interest in the Home for Fallen Women and the Strange Case of Caroline Maynard Thompson. Boston: 1929. V. 64
Dickens Days in Boston. Boston and New York: 1927. V. 64
The Romance of Charles Dickens and Maria Beadnell Winter. Boston: 1929. V. 62

PAYNE, H. A.
Past and Present - the Magazine of Brighton Grammar School: E. J. Marshall Memorial Number. 1900. V. 62

PAYNE, HUMFRY
Archaic Marble Sculpture from the Acropolis. London. V. 64

PAYNE, JOHN
Twelve Designs of Country Houses, of Two, Three and Four Rooms on a Floor, Proper for Glebes and Small Estates.... Dublin: 1757. V. 64

PAYNE, JOHN HOWARD
Home! Sweet Home!. Philadelphia: 1823-1824. V. 64
Memoirs of John Howard Payne, the American Roscius.... London: 1815. V. 62

PAYNE, N. F.
Technique for Wildlife Habitat Management of Wetlands. New York: 1992. V. 63; 65

PAYNE, WILLIAM
Maxims for Playing the Game of Whist; with All Necessary Calculations and Laws of the Game. Winton: 1783. V. 67
A Practical Discourse of Repentance, Rectifying the Mistakes About It, Especially Such as Lead Either to Despair, or Presumption.... London: 1693. V. 67

PAYNE, WYNDHAM
Town and Country, a Collection of Designs and Decorations by Wyndham Payne. London: 1925. V. 62; 63

PAYNE GALLWEY, RALPH
The Crossbow Mediaeval and Modern, Military and Sporting. 1964. V. 67
The Fowler in Ireland or Notes on the Haunts and Habits of Wildfowl and Seafowl.... London: 1882. V. 66; 67
The Fowler in Ireland or Notes on the Haunts and Habits of Wildfowl and Seafowl.... Southampton: 1983. V. 67
Letters to Young Shooters. London: 1890. V. 64
Letters to Young Shooters - Second Series. 1892. V. 67

PAYSON, GEORGE
Golden Dreams and Leaden Realities. New York: 1853. V. 64; 67

PAYTIAMO, JAMES
Flaming Arrow's People by an Acoma Indian. New York: 1932. V. 67

PAYTON, CHARLES A.
Days of a Knight. London: 1924. V. 67

PAYTON, WILLIAM
The Last Man Over the Trail. N.P: 1939. V. 65

PAZ, OCTAVIO
Air Bor/Hijos del Aire. Mexico City: 1979. V. 62
Alternating Current. New York: 1973. V. 62
Cuatro Chopos. The Four Poplars. Purchase: 1985. V. 64
Marcel Duchamp: Appearance Stripped Bare. New York: 1978. V. 66
An Octave - for Octavio Paz. London: 1972. V. 65
Raiz del Hombre. Mexico: 1937. V. 67
Selected Poems of Octavio Paz. Bloomington: 1963. V. 62
Solo a dos Voces. Barcelona: 1973. V. 67
Stanzas for an Imaginary Garden. Tuscaloosa: 1990. V. 64
Sun Stone. New York: 1963. V. 62
Tres Poemas/Three Poems. 1987. V. 62
Tres Poemas/Three Poems. New York: 1987. V. 64
Vrindaban. Geneve: 1966. V. 64

PAZZINI, ADALBERTO
Storia Della Medicina. Milano: 1947. V. 64

PEABODY, ELIZABETH P.
Holiness; or the Legend of St. George: a Tale from Spencer's Faerie Queene, by a Mother. Boston: 1836. V. 64
Record of a School: Exemplifying the General Principles of Spiritual Culture. Boston and New York: 1836. V. 63; 64

PEABODY, OLIVER
An Essay to Revive and Encourage Military Exercises, Skill and Valour Among the Sons of God's People in New England. Boston: 1732. V. 64

PEACH, B. N.
Chapters on the Geology of Scotland. Oxford: 1930. V. 65
The Geological Structure of the North-West Highlands. 1907. V. 67
The Silurian Rocks of Britain. Edinburgh: 1899. V. 62
The Silurian Rocks of Britain. Volume I. Scotland. 1899. V. 67

PEACH, L. DU GARDE
The Company of Cutlers in Hallamshire in the County of York 1901- 1956. Sheffield: 1960. V. 62; 65

PEACH, WILLIAM
Cwm Dhu; or, the Black Dingle: Windermere: The Curse of Earth; and Other Poems. London: 1853. V. 62

PEACHAM, HENRY
The Compleat Gentleman Fashioning Him Absolute in the Most Necessary and Commendable Qualities.... London: 1622. V. 66
The Compleat Gentleman. (with) The Gentleman's Exercise. London: 1634. V. 63
The Valley of Varietie; or Discourse Fitting for the Times Containing Very Learned and Rare Passages of Antiquity, Philosophy and History.... London: 1638. V. 64

PEACHEY, EMMA
The Royal Guide to Wax Flower Modelling. London: 1851. V. 62; 66

PEACOCK, DOUG
Daja!. Booton: 1001. V. 67
Grizzly Years. New York: 1990. V. 67

PEACOCK, E. H.
A Game Book for Burma and Adjoining Territories. London: 1933. V. 62

PEACOCK, EDWARD
The Army Lists of the Roundheads and Cavaliers, Containing the Names of the Officers in the Royal and Parliamentary Armies of 1642. London: 1874. V. 63

PEACOCK, FERDINAND MANSEL
A Military Crime. (bound with) From Reveille to Lights Out (or, Lionel Tregarthen, Lieutenant) (and) A Soldier and a Maid: a Romance of the War in Burmah. 1891. V. 66

PEACOCK, GEORGE
A Collection of Examples of the Applications of the Differential and Integral Calculus. Cambridge: 1820. V. 65; 66
Notes on the Isthmus of Panama and Darien. Exter: 1879. V. 65

PEACOCK, JAMES
Oikidia, or Nutshells.... 1785. V. 67

PEACOCK, LUCY
The Adventures of the Six Princesses of Babylon, in Their Travels to the Temple of Virtue: an Allegory. London: 1785. V. 65
Ambrose and Eleanor; or The Adventures of Two Children Deserted on an Uninhabited Island. London: 1807. V. 65
The Little Emigrant, a Tale: Interspersed with Moral Anecdotes and Instructive Conversations. London: 1802. V. 65

PEACOCK, ROBERT BACKHOUSE
A Glossary of the Dialect of the Hundred of Lonsdale, North and South of the Sands, in the County of Lancaster.... 1869. V. 62
A Glossary of the Dialect of the Hundred of Lonsdale, North and South of the Sands, in the County of Lancaster.... London: 1869. V. 64, 65

PEACOCK, THOMAS LOVE
Collected Novels. Headlong Hall. Nightmare Abbey. Maid Marian. Crotchet Castle. London: 1837. V. 66
Crotchet Castle. London: 1831. V. 62; 66
Letters to Edward Hookham and Percy B. Shelley with Fragments of Unpublished Manuscripts. Boston: 1910. V. 64
The Misfortunes of Elphin. London: 1829. V. 62; 65
Palmyra and Other Poems. London: 1806. V. 67
The Works.... London: 1875. V. 63

PEAKE, HAROLD
The Bronze Age and the Celtic World. Bronze: 1922. V. 65

PEAKE, JAMES
A Concise Method of Calculating the Displacement of Ships and Floating Bodies With Reference to the Present Law for Tonnage Registration. London: 1856. V. 62
Rudiments of Naval Architecture; with Practice of Ship Building. London: 1867. V. 62

PEAKE, MERVYN
Captain Slaughterboard Drops Anchor. London: 1945. V. 62; 64; 65; 67
The Glassblowers. London: 1950. V. 62
Letters from a Lost Uncle. London: 1948. V. 64; 67
Mr. Pye. Melbourne: 1953. V. 62
A Reverie of Bone and Other Poems. London: 1967. V. 62; 65
Ride a Cock-Horse and Other Nursery Rhymes. London: 1940. V. 63
Selected Poems. London: 1972. V. 65
Shapes and Sounds. London: 1941. V. 62
Titus Alone. London: 1959. V. 62
Titus Groan. 1946. V. 64; 66
Titus Groan. London: 1946. V. 63
Twelve Poems - 1939-1960. Hayes, Middlesex: 1975. V. 62; 66

PEAKE, ORA BROOKS
The Colorado Range Cattle Industry. Glendale: 1937. V. 65

PEAKE, RICHARD BRINSLEY
The Characteristic Costume of France, from Drawings Made on the Spot.... London: 1819-1822. V. 64

PEALE, REMBRANDT
Account of the Skeleton of the Mammoth, a Non-Descript Carnivorous Animal of Immense Size, Found in America. London: 1802. V. 66

PEARCE, DONN
Cool Hand Luke. New York: 1965. V. 63; 66
Pier Head Jump. Indianapolis: 1972. V. 65; 67

PEARCE, JOSEPH P.
Romantic Tales of Old Lancashire. Ormskirk: 1931. V. 66

PEARCE, MICHAEL
The Mamur Zapt and the Camel of Destruction. London: 1993. V. 66
The Snake-Catcher's Daughter. London: 1994. V. 66

PEARCE, THOMAS
The Dog; with Simple Directions for His Treatment, and Notices of the Best Dogs of the Day and Their Breeders or Exhibitors. London. V. 67

PEARCE, W. M.
The Matador Land and Cattle Company. Norman: 1964. V. 65

PEARCE, WILLIAM
General View of the Agriculture in Berkshire.... London: 1794. V. 63; 65

PEARCH, GEORGE
A Collection of Poems in Four Volumes. London: 1770. V. 65
A Collection of Poems in Four Volumes by Several Hands. London: 1783. V. 62

PEARD, FRANCES MARY
A Madrigal and Other Stories. London: 1876. V. 67
The Rose Garden. London: 1872. V. 67
Schloss and Town. London: 1882. V. 65
Thorpe Regis. London: 1874. V. 65; 67

PEARL, CYRIL
Remarks on African Colonization and the Abolition of Slavery. Windsor: 1833. V. 64
Youth's Booth on the Mind, Embracing the OUtlines of the Intellect, the Sensibilities and the Will. Portland: 1847. V. 64

PEARL, RAYMOND
Alcohol and Longevity. New York: 1926. V. 66
The Ancestry of the Long Lived. Baltimore: 1934. V. 65

PEARS, IAIN
An Instance of the Fingerpost. London: 1997. V. 67
The Titian Committee. London: 1991. V. 63; 66

PEARS, J. WAYNE
The Wild Turkey Book, an Anthology. Clinton: 1981. V. 65

PEARSALL, DORA W.
The Story of Four Little Sabots. London: 1906. V. 64

PEARSALL SMITH, LOGAN
Saved from the Salvage. Edinburgh. V. 67

PEARSE & CO.
Sample Book of Corset Laces. Nottingham: 1900. V. 62

PEARSE, A.
Homoiothermism; the Origin of Warm Blood Vertebrates. New York: 1928. V. 67

PEARSE, JAMES
A Narrative of the Life.... Rutland: 1825. V. 66

PEARSE, PADRAIC H.
The King (An Ri), a Morality. New York: 1916. V. 65

PEARSON, ABEL
An Analysis of the Principles of the Divine Government in a Series of Conversations...The Rise and Fall of the Beast. Athens: 1833. V. 63

PEARSON, ALEXANDER
Annals of Kirkby Lonsdale and Lunesdale in Bygone Days. 1930. V. 63; 65
Annals of Kirkby Lonsdale and Lunesdale in Bygone Days. Kendal: 1930. V. 62; 64; 65; 66

PEARSON, ANTHONY
The Great Case of Tithes Truly Stated, Clearly Open'd and Full Resolv'd. London: 1754. V. 64

PEARSON, C. C.
Overland in 1849 - from Missouri to California by the Paltee River and the Salt Lake Trail - an Account from the Letters of G. C. Pearson. Los Angeles: 1961. V. 63; 66

PEARSON, CHARLES
The Substance of an Address Delivered by Charles Pearson, Esq. at a Public Meeting on the 11th, 12th and 18th of December, 1843, the Late John Travers, Esq., in the Chair, Containing a Brief History of the Corporation of London as Asylum of English Freed. London: 1844. V. 67

PEARSON, GEORGE
Evenings by Eden-Side, or Essays and Poems. Kendal: 1832. V. 64; 65

PEARSON, H. H. W.
Gnetales. Cambridge: 1929. V. 63; 66

PEARSON, J., & CO.
First Editions of One Hundred Famous Books from Homer to Tennyson. London: 1900. V. 62

PEARSON, JOHN
An Exposition of the Creed by John, Lord Bishop of Chester. London: 1683. V. 66
The Life of William Hey, Esq. London: 1822. V. 65
Practical Observations on Cancerous Complaints.... London: 1793. V. 63

PEARSON, KARL
The Grammar of Science. London: 1892-1911. V. 65
Karl Pearson's Early Statistical Papers. Cambridge: 1956. V. 63

PEARSON, L.
Diseases and Enemies of Poultry. Harrisburg: 1897. V. 62

PEARSON, P. D.
Alvar Aalto an the International Style. 1978. V. 65

PEARSON, PHILLIPA M.
Acrostic Dictionary Containing More than Thirty Thousand Words with their Initials and Finals Alphabetically Arranged. London: 1884. V. 64

PEARSON, RIDLEY
Probable Cause. New York: 1990. V. 67

PEARSON, T. F.
A Short History of a Small Place. New York: 1985. V. 66

PEARSON, T. GILBERT
Birds of America. New York: 1917. V. 63; 67
Birds of North Carolina. Raleigh: 1942. V. 63; 64

PEARY, J. D.
My Arctic Journal. A Year Among Ice-Fields and Eskimos. New York and Philadelphia: 1893. V. 64
The Snow Baby. A True Story with True Pictures. New York: 1901. V. 63
The Snow Baby and Her Mother. Children of the Arctic. New York: 1903. V. 63

PEARY, ROBERT E.
Die Entdeckung des Nordpols. Berlin: 1910. V. 64
Nearest the Pole: a Narrative of the Polar Expedition of the Peary Arctic Club in the S.S. Roosevelt 1905-1906. London: 1907. V. 65
Nearest the Pole: A Narrative of the Polar Expedition of the Peary Arctic Club in the S.S. Roosevelt 1905-1906. New York: 1907. V. 65
The North Pole. London: 1910. V. 63; 65; 66
Northward Over the Great Ice. London: 1898. V. 62
Northward Over the Great Ice. New York: 1898. V. 62; 63; 64; 67

PEASE, A. E.
Half a Century of Sport. 1932. V. 67

PEASE, MARY BALL JOHNSON
Mahlon Johnson Family of Littleton, New Jersey. Ancestors and Descendants. Morristown: 1931. V. 63; 66

PEATTIE, DONALD CULROSS
The Bright Lexicon. New York: 1934. V. 62; 67
Forward the Nation. New York: 1942. V. 67
Immortal Village. Chicago: 1945. V. 64
A Natural History of Pearson's Falls and Some of Its Human Associations. Tryon: 1932. V. 67

PECHELL, JOHN
The History of the University of Oxford, from the Death of William the Conqueror, to the Demise of Queen Elizabeth. London: 1773. V. 62

PECK, ANDREW JAY
The Date Being-? A Compendium of Chronological Data. 1970. V. 66

PECK, EPAPHRODITUS
The Property Rights of Husband and Wife Under the Law of Connecticut. Hartford: 1904. V. 67

PECK, FRANCIS
Desiderata Curiosa. London: 1732. V. 63
Desiderata Curiosa. London: 1732-1735. V. 65
Desiderata Curiosa. London: 1779. V. 64
Memoirs of the Life and Actions of Oliver Cromwell; as Delivered in Three Panegyrics of Him.... London: 1740. V. 63
New Memoirs of the Life and Poetical Works of Mr. John Milton.... London: 1740. V. 62

PECK, GEORGE W.
Peck's Bad Boy and His Chums. Chicago: 1907-1908. V. 65

PECK, GEORGE WASHINGTON
Aurifodina; or, Adventures in the Gold Region. New York: 1849. V. 64

PECK, HERBERT WATSON
The Book of Pecks. 1954. V. 63

PECK, J. M.
A Guide for Emigrants Containing Sketches of Illinois, Missouri and the Adjaent Parts. Boston: 1831. V. 64
A New Guide for Emigrants in the West, Containing Sketches of Michigan, Ohio, Indiana, Illinois, Missouri, Arkansas, with the Territory of Wisconsin and the Adjacent Parts. Boston: 1837. V. 67

PECK, M. E.
A Manual of the Higher Plants of Oregon. Portland: 1941. V. 63

PECK, MARY G.
Carrie Chapman Catt, a Biography. New York: 1944. V. 67

PECK, R. D.
Fly-fishing for Duffers. London: 1934. V. 64

PECK, RICHARD
A Long Way from Chicago - a Novel in Stories. New York: 1998. V. 65

PECK, WILLIAM
A Topographical Account of the Isle of Axholme, Being the West Division of the Wapentake of Manley, in the County of Lincoln. Volume I. Doncaster: 1815. V. 63

PECK, WILLIAM D.
Catalogue of Books to be Sold at Auction.... Cambridge: 1823. V. 62

PECK, WILLIAM DANDRIDGE
Natural History of the Slug Worm. Boston: 1799. V. 62

PECKET & SONS, LTD.
Some Views in the Workshops and a Few Examples of the Locomotives Built Therein by Pecket & Sons Ltd., Atlas Locomotive Works, St. George, Bristol. London: 1920. V. 63

PECKHAM, HENRY
The Tour of Holland, Dutch Brabant, the Austrian Netherlands and Part of France.... London: 1772. V. 64

PECOCK, REGINALD
The Repressor of Over Much Blaming of the Clergy. London: 1860. V. 67

PEDLEY, CHARLES
The History of Newfoundland from the Earliest Times to the Year 1860. London: 1863. V. 63

PEDRAZAS, ALLAN
The Harry Chronicles. New York: 1995. V. 67

PEDRETTI, C.
Leonardo Da Vinci on Painting: a Lost Book.... Berkeley: 1964. V. 65

PEEBLES, J. M.
Vaccination a Curse and a Menace to Personal Liberty, with Statistics Showing Its Dangers and Cimrinality. N.P: 1910. V. 62

PEEBLES, WILLIAM
Poems: Consiting Chiefly of Odes and Elegies. Glasgow: 1810. V. 66

PEEDIE, JEAN MURDOCH
Donald in Numberland. New York: 1927. V. 64

PEEK, CLIFFORD H.
Five Years--Five Centuries--Five Campaigns. Munich: 1945. V. 63

THE PEEK-A-BOOS and Mr. Plopper. London: 1917. V. 63

PEEL, C. V. A.
Wild Sport in the Outer Hebrides. 1901. V. 63

PEEL, DOROTHY CONSTANCE
How We Lived Then 1914-1918: a Sketch of Social and Domestic Life in England During the War. London: 1929. V. 65

PEEL, FRANK
The Risings of the Luddites, Chartists and Plugdrawers. Heckmondwyke: 1888. V. 63; 64; 66
The Risings of the Luddites, Chartists and Plugdrawers. Brighouse: 1895. V. 64

PEEL, HELEN
Polar Gleams. An Account of a Voyage on the Yacht Blencathra. Chicago: 1894. V. 64

PEEL, ROBERT
Sir Robert Peel's Address on the Establishment of a Library and Reading-Room at Tarnworth. On the 19th of January 1841. London: 1841. V. 67
Speeches by the Right Honourable Sir Robert Peel, Bart, M.P. During his Administration; also His Address to the Electors of the Borough of Tarnworth and Speech at the Grand Entertainment in Honor of Him.... 1835. V. 67

PEELE, GEORGE
The Works. London: 1888. V. 62

PEERY, JANET
Alligator Dance. Dallas: 1993. V. 64; 67
The River Beyond the World. New York: 1966. V. 65

PEETERS, FLOR
The Organ and Its Music in the Netherlands 1500-1800. Antwerp: 1971. V. 63

PEGGE, SAMUEL
Anecdotes of the English Language: Chiefly Rearding the Local Dialect of London and Its Environs. London: 1803. V. 67
Anonymiana; or, Ten Centuries of Observations on Various Authors and Subjects. London: 1809. V. 67
Fitz-Stephen's Description of the City of London. London: 1772. V. 63
Sketch of the History of Bolsover and Peak Castles in the County of Derby. London: 1785. V. 62

PEGGY and Her Playmates. London: 1915. V. 66

PEGUES, ALBERT W.
Our Baptist Minsters and Schools. Springfield: 1892. V. 63

PEHNT, W.
German Architecture 1960-1970. New York: 1970. V. 65

PEICH, MICHAEL
The Red Ozier: a Literary Fine Press. History and Bibliography 1976-1987. Council Bluffs: 1993. V. 64

PEIRCE, BENJAMIN
Physical and Celestial Mechanics. Boston: 1855. V. 65

PEIRCE, JAMES
A Vindication of the Dissenters: in Answer to Dr. William Nichols's Defence of the Doctrine and Discipline of the Church of England.... London: 1718. V. 62

PEIRCE, JEREMIAH
(Caption title): An Account of a Very Extraordinary Tumour in the Knee of a Person, Whose Leg Was Taken Off by Mr. Jer. Peirce, Surgeon at Bath.... Bath?: 1737. V. 65

PEIRCE, JOHN
The New American Spelling Book. Philadelphia: 1808. V. 63

PEIRCE, WILLIAM
Full Report of the Great Gold Robbery.... London: 1855. V. 63

PELECANOS, GEORGE P.
The Big Blowdown. New York: 1996. V. 65; 66; 67
Down by the River Where the Dead Men Go. New York: 1995. V. 64; 65; 66; 67
A Firing Offense. New York: 1992. V. 65; 66; 67
Nick's Trip. 1993. V. 62
Shame on the Devil. Tucson: 1999. V. 66; 67
Shoedog. New York: 1994. V. 62; 65; 66
The Sweet Forever. Boston: 1998. V. 65; 66
Sweet Forever. New York: 1998. V. 67
The Sweet Forever. Tucson: 1998. V. 65; 66; 67

PELETIER, JACQUES
De Occulta Parte Numerorum, quam Algebram Vocant, Libri Duo. Paris: 1560. V. 66

PELHAM, CAMDEN, PSEUD.
The Chronicles of Crime; or, the New Newgate Calendar. London: 1887. V. 63

PELHAM, HERBERT GREVILLE
Walter Hurst; or Early Struggles at the Bar. London: 1854. V. 67

PELL, DEREK
Not Guilty, Number One. New York: 1975. V. 64

PELL, WILLIAM J.
Treatise on the Games of Dominoes. New York: 1844. V. 66

PELLET, MARCELLIN
Etude Historique et Biographique sur Theroigne de Mericourt. Paris: 1886. V. 63

PELLETIER, DAVID
The Graphic Alphabet. New York: 1996. V. 65

PELLEW, CLAUGHTON
Claughton Pellew: Five Wood Engravings Printed from the Original Blocks.... Denby Dale: 1987. V. 65

PELLEW, GEORGE
The Life and Correspondence of Henry Addington, First Viscount Sidmouth. London: 1847. V. 64

PELTIER, JEAN GABRIEL
The Trial of John Peltier, Esq. for a Libel Against Napoleon Buonaparte.... London: 1803. V. 63

PELTIER, LESLIE C.
Starlight Nights: the Adventures of a Star-Gazer. New York: 1965. V. 67

PELTON, JOHN COTTER
Life's Sunbeams and Shadows - Poems and Prose. San Francisco: 1893. V. 66

PELZER, LOUIS
The Cattleman's Frontier. A Record of the Trans-Mississippi Cattle Industry.... Glendale: 1936. V. 64; 66
Marches of the Dragoons in the Mississippi Valley. Iowa City: 1917. V. 65; 67

PEMBER, PHOEBE YATES
A Southern Woman's Story. New York: 1879. V. 65
A Southern Woman's Story. Jackson: 1959. V. 63

PEMBERTON, EBENEZER
Divine Original and Dignity of Government Asserted; and an Advantageous Prospect of the Rulers Mortality Recommended. A Sermon Preached Before His Excellency the Governour.... Boston: 1710. V. 63; 66
A Funeral Sermon on the Death of that Learned and Excellent Divine the Reverend Mr. Samuel Willard, Pastor of a Church of Christ in Boston, and Vice President of Harvard College. Boston: 1707. V. 63; 66

PEMBERTON, HENRY
The Dispensatory of the Royal College of Physicians, London. London: 1746. V. 64
The Dispensatory of the Royal College of Physicians, London. London: 1751. V. 63
A View of Sir Isaac Newton's Philosophy. London: 1728. V. 63; 64

PEMBERTON, JOHN C.
Pemberton, Defender of Vicksburg. Chapel Hill: 1945. V. 63; 65

PEMBERTON, MAX
The Garden of Swords. 1899. V. 64; 66

PEMBERTON, MAX continued
The Gold Wolf. London: 1903. V. 64; 66
Iron Pirate. 1897. V. 64; 66
The Phantom Army. 1898. V. 64; 66

PEMBERTON, T. EDGAR
The Life of Bret Harte. London: 1903. V. 67

PEMBERTON, THOMAS
A Letter to Lord Langdale on the Recent Proceedings in the House of Commons on the Subject of Privilege. London: 1837. V. 67

PEMBROKE, HENRY HERBERT, 10TH EARL OF
Military Equitation; or a Method of Breaking Horses and Teaching Soldiers to Ride. Sarum: 1778. V. 62; 66

PEMBROKE, THOMAS HERBERT, EARL OF
Nummi Anglici et Scotici cum Aliquot Numismatibus Recentioribus.... N.P: 1746. V. 62

PEN-LENS Views of the Galena-Empire Mining Camp. N.P: 1899. V. 65

PENCHANT, PHILIP
The Mysteries of Fitchburg. Fitchburg: 1844. V. 62

PENDELTON, JOHN
Our Railways. London: 1896. V. 63

PENDER, WILLIAM DORSEY
The General to His Lady. The Civil War Letters of William Dorsey Pender to Fanny Pender. Chapel Hill: 1965. V. 63; 65

PENDLETON, EDMUND
An Address to the American Citizens on the Present State of Our Country. Boston: 1799. V. 63

PENDLETON, WILLIAM C.
History of Tazewell County and Southwest Virginia 1748-1920. Richmond: 1920. V. 64

PENDRAY, G. EDWARD
The Coming Age of Rocket Power. New York: 1945. V. 66

PENE DU BOIS, WILLIAM
The 21 Balloons. New York: 1947. V. 65

PENFIELD, EDWARD
Posters in Miniature. London: 1896. V. 64
Posters in Miniature. New York and London: 1897. V. 63

PENFIELD, WILDER
Canadian Army Manual of Military Neurosurgery. Ottawa: 1941. V. 66
The Cerebral Cortex of Man. New York: 1930. V. 66
Cytology and Cellular Pathology of the Nervous System. New York: 1932. V. 66
Cytology and Cellular Pathology of the Nervous System. New York: 1965. V. 66
Epilepsy and Cerebral Localization. Springfield: 1941. V. 66
Epilepsy and the Functional Anatomy of the Human Brain. Boston: 1954. V. 66
Epileptic Seizure Patterns. A Study of the Localizing Value of Initial Phenomena in Focal Cortical Seizures. Springfield: 1957. V. 64; 66
The Excitable Cortex in Conscious Man. Liverpool: 1958. V. 66
The Second Career with Other Essays and Addresses. Boston: 1963. V. 66
Speech and Brain Mechanisms. Princeton: 1959. V. 64; 65; 66

PENFOLD, JOHN B.
The Clockmakers of Cumberland. London: 1977. V. 66

PENGELLY, HESTER
A Memoir of William Pengelly, of Torquay. London: 1897. V. 62; 66

THE PENGUIN Film Review. 1946-1949. V. 63

PENINGTON, ISAAC
The Works of the Long Mournful and Sorely Distressed Whom the Lord... Relieved by the Ministry of This Despised People Called Quakers. 1761. V. 67
The Works of the Long Mournful and Sorely Distressed Whom the Lord... Relieved by the Ministry of This Despised People Called Quakers.... London: 1761. V. 62

PENLEY, AARON
Sketching from Nature in Water Colours. London: 1875. V. 62; 67
Sketching from Nature in Water Colours. London: 1880. V. 67

PENMAN, SHARON KAY
Here Be Dragons. New York: 1985. V. 66

PENN, GRANVILLE
Remarks Preparatory to the Issue of the Renewed Negociaton for Peace. London: 1797. V. 65

PENN, I. GARLAND
The Afro-American Press and Its Editors. Springfield: 1891. V. 64

PENN, IRVING
Issey Miyake. Boston: 1988. V. 66; 67
Moments Preserved. New York: 1960. V. 63; 65
Passage. A Work Record. New York: 1991. V. 65
Worlds in a Small Room. New York: 1974. V. 62

PENN, JAMES
Under-Grammar Master, Christ's Hospital. London: 1762. V. 63

PENN, R.
Maxim's and Hints for an Angler: and Miseries of Fishing to Which are Added Maxims and Hints for a Chess Player.... 1839. V. 67

PENN, WILLIAM
A Brief Account of the Rise and Progress of the People Called Quakers. Philadelphia: 1816. V. 67
A Collection of the Works of William Penn. London: 1726. V. 63; 66
Letter from William Penn to His Wife and Children. Salem: 1837. V. 63; 66
No Cross, No Crown. London: 1694. V. 62
Some Fruits of Solitude, in Reflections and Maxims. London: 1718. V. 62
Some Fruits of Solitude, in Reflections and Maxims. London: 1735?. V. 62; 64
Some Fruits of Solitude, in Reflections and Maxims. London: 1901. V. 62

PENNAC, DANIEL
The Fairy Gunmother. London: 1997. V. 67

PENNANT, THOMAS
Arctic Zoology. London: 1784-1787. V. 62; 67
British Zoology. 1812. V. 65
British Zoology. London: 1812. V. 66; 67
History of Quadrupeds. London: 1781. V. 62; 64
The History of the Parishes of Whiteford and Holywell. London: 1796. V. 62; 66
Indian Zoology. London: 1790. V. 62
The Literary Life of the Late...by Himself. London: 1793. V. 62; 63
Some Account of London. London: 1793. V. 62
A Tour from Downing to Alston-Moor. 1801. V. 65
A Tour in Scotland. Chester: 1771. V. 66
A Tour in Scotland. London: 1772. V. 62
A Tour in Scotland, and A Voyage to the Hebrides. Warrington: 1774. V. 66
A Tour in Scotland, and A Voyage to the Hebrides. London: 1776. V. 62
A Tour in Wales MDCCLXX. London: 1778. V. 66
Tours in Wales. London: 1810. V. 64; 66
The View of Indosstan. London: 1798. V. 65

PENNANT, WILLIAM
A Tour in Scotland, and Voyage to the Hebrides MDCCLXIX (and) MDCCLXXII. Warrington: 1774. V. 65

PENNELL, ELIZABETH ROBINS
The Life of James McNeil Whistler. Philadelphia: 1908. V. 64

PENNELL, JOSEPH
The Adventures of an Illustrator.... Boston: 1925. V. 64
Lithography & Lithographers. New York: 1898. V. 64
Pen Drawing and Pen Draughtsmen Their Work and Their Methods. London: 1894. V. 62
Pen Drawing and Pen Draughtsmen, Their Work and Their Methods. London: 1897. V. 64
Two Pilgrims' Progress. Boston and London: 1886. V. 64

PENNELL-ELMHIRST, CAPTAIN
The Best Season on Record. London: 1885. V. 64

PENNETHORNE, JOHN
The Geometry and Optics of Ancient Architecture.... London and Edinburgh: 1878. V. 64

PENNEY, NORMAN
The Household Account Book of Sarah Fell of Swarthmore Hall. 1920. V. 62

PENNINGTON, JOHN H.
A System of Aerostation, or Steam Aerial Navigation. Washington City: 1842. V. 63

PENNINGTON, L. E.
The Purchas Handbook. London: 1997. V. 63

PENNINGTON, LADY
Letters on Different Subjects...Amongst Which are Interspers'd the Adventures of Alphonse, After the Destruction of Lisbon. London: 1766-1767. V. 67
A Mother's Advice to Her Absent Daughters; with an Additional Letter on the Management and Education of Infant Children. London: 1817. V. 66
An Unfortunate Mother's Advice to Her Absent Daughters, in a Letter to Miss Pennington. London: 1761. V. 62
An Unfortunate Mother's Advice to Her Absent Daughters, in a Letter to Miss Pennington. London: 1773. V. 64

PENNINGTON, MONTAGU
Memoirs of the Life of Mrs. Elizabeth Carter. London: 1808. V. 65

PENNINK, FRANK
Homes of Sport - Golf. London: 1952. V. 63

THE PENNSYLVANIA Magazine. Philadelphia: 1775. V. 63

PENNSYLVANIA SOCIETY FOR PROMOTING THE ABOLITION OF SLAVERY
The Constitution of the Pennsylvania Society, for Promoting the Abolition of Slavery and the Relief of Free Negroes, Unlawfully Held in Bondage.... Philadelphia: 1787. V. 63; 64

PENNSYLVANIA SOCIETY FOR THE PROMOTION OF POLITICAL ECONOMY
Report of the Library Committee...Concerning a Summary of the Information Communicated by Sundry Citizens, in a Reply to the Circular Letter of the Committee of Superintendence of Feb. 21, 1817. Philadelphia: 1817. V. 63

PENNSYLVANIA STEEL CO.
Rails, Splice Bars and Accessory Rolled Sections for Tracks. Philadelphia: 1912. V. 67

PENNY, ANNE
Cardington Crescent. New York: 1987. V. 67

PENNY, F. E.
Southern India - Painted by Lady Lawley. London: 1914. V. 63; 64

PENNY, JOHN
The Trial at Large of John Penny, William Penny, Thomas Collins...for the Wilful Murder of W. Ingram.... Gloucester: 1816. V. 63

THE PENNY Magazine of the Society for the Diffusion of Useful Knowledge. London: 1836. V. 66

PENRHYN, W. COUSSENS
A Child's Book of Stories. New York: 1915. V. 63

PENROSE, CHARLES B.
The Rustler Business. Douglas: 1959. V. 63; 66

PENROSE, MATT R.
Pots 'O Gold. Reno: 1935. V. 62; 65

PENROSE, ROLAND
The Road is Wider than Long, an Image Diary from the Balkans July- August 1938. London: 1980. V. 67

PENROSE'S Pictorial Annual. London: 1905. V. 64

PENRUDDOCK, a Tale. London: 1835. V. 65

PENTON, STEPHEN
The Guardian's Instruction; or the Gentleman's Romance. (with) New Instructions to the Guardian.... London: 1688-1694. V. 64

PENZER, N. M.
The Most Noble and Famous Travels of Marco Polo Together with the Travels of Nicolo De Conti. London: 1929. V. 64

PENZER, NORMAN
An Annotated Bibliography of Sir Richard Francis Burton. New York: 1970. V. 67
An Annotated Bibliography of Sir Richard Francis Burton. 1994. V. 65
Selected Papers on Anthropology, Travel and Exploration. London: 1924. V. 67

PENZLER, OTTO
Murder for Love. New York: 1996. V. 66

PEOPLE of the Old World. Concord: 1850. V. 64

PEPLER, HILARY DOUGLAS CLARK
The Devil's Devices, or Control Verses Service. London: 1931. V. 65
The Hand Press. Ditchling, Sussex: 1934. V. 65
The Hand Press. An Essay. Ditchling: 1952. V. 67

PEPLER, HILDARY DOUGLAS CLARK
Saint Dominic. Scenes from the Life of the Saint in the Form of a Play. Ditchling: 1929. V. 66

PEPLOW, EDWARD H.
History of Arizona. New York: 1958. V. 63; 66

PEPPER, ADELINE
The Glass Gaffers of New Jersey and Their Creations from 1739 to the Present. New York: 1971. V. 63; 66

PEPPER, GEORGE H.
Pueblo Bonito. New York: 1920. V. 63; 64

PEPPER, JOHN HENRY
The Playbook of Metals.... London: 1862. V. 62; 66

PEPPER, WILLIAM
A Text-Book of the Theory and Practice of Medicine. Philadelphia: 1894. V. 64; 67

PEPYS, SAMUEL
The Diary of Samuel Pepys. London: 1893. V. 66
The Diary of Samuel Pepys. London: 1893-1899. V. 63; 67
Diary of Samuel Pepys. London: 1900-1902. V. 63
The Diary of Samuel Pepys. London: 1920. V. 63
The Diary of Samuel Pepys. New York: 1942. V. 64
The Diary of Samuel Pepys. London: 1949. V. 62
The Diary of Samuel Pepys. London: 1970-1983. V. 62; 63; 67
Everybody's Pepys. The Diary of Samuel Pepys 1660-1669. London: 1926. V. 62; 66
Memoirs Relating to the State of the Royal Navy of England, for Ten Years, Determin'd December 1688. London: 1690. V. 64
Private Correspondence and Miscellaneous Papers of Samuel Pepys 1679-1703 in the Possession of J. Pepys Cockerell. London: 1926. V. 66

PERAGALLO, H.
Diatomees Marines de France et des Districts Maritimes Voisins. Grez-sur-Loing: 1897-1908. V. 65; 66

PERCE, ELBERT
Gulliver Joi: His Three Voyages.... New York: 1851. V. 64

PERCEVAL
Syr Perecyvelle of Gales. 1895. V. 67

PERCEVAL, DON
Bucking Horse Portfolio. Los Angeles: 1962. V. 64
Maynard Dixon Sketchbook. Flagstaff: 1967. V. 67
A Navajo Sketchbook. Flagstaff: 1962. V. 63; 64; 66

PERCIVAL, A. B.
A Game Ranger's Note Book. London: 1924. V. 67
A Game Ranger's Note Book. 1927. V. 67

PERCIVAL, THOMAS
Essays Medical and Experimental (...Philosophical, Medical and Experimental Essays). London: 1772-1776. V. 63
Moral and Literary Dissertations, on the Following Subjects: 1. On Truth and Faithfulness. 2. On Habit and Association. 3. On Inconsistency of Expectation in Literary Pursuits. 4. On a Taste for the General Beauties of Nature. 5. On a Taste for the Fine. Warrington: 1784. V. 65; 67

PERCY, ALFRED
Old Place Names. Madison Heights: 1950. V. 63

PERCY, HENRY ALGERNON GEORGE, EARL OF
Highlands of Asiatic Turkey. London: 1901. V. 62

PERCY, JOHN
Metallurgy. London: 1861-1880. V. 64; 66
Metallurgy. London: 1875. V. 64

PERCY, STEPHEN
Robin Hood and His Merry Foresters. New York: 1844. V. 65

PERCY, THOMAS, BP. OF DROMORE
Ancient Songs Chiefly on Morrish Subjects. Oxford: 1932. V. 67
Five Pieces of Runic Poetry. London: 1763. V. 63; 64
The Hermit of Warkworth. Alnwick: 1806. V. 66; 67
Reliques of Ancient English Poetry. London: 1767. V. 62
Reliques of Ancient English Poetry. London: 1839. V. 63; 66
Reliques of Ancient English Poetry. 1847. V. 67
Reliques of Ancient English Poetry. London: 1876. V. 66

PERCY, WALKER
Bourbon. Winston-Salem: 1979. V. 64
Lancelot. New York: 1977. V. 66; 67
The Last Gentleman. New York: 1966. V. 62; 63; 64; 65; 66
The Last Gentleman. London: 1967. V. 64; 67
Lost in the Cosmos: the Last Self-Help Book. New York: 1983. V. 66
Love in the Ruins. New York: 1971. V. 62; 64; 66; 67
The Message in the Bottle. New York: 1975. V. 63; 65
The Moviegoer. New York: 1961. V. 62
The Moviegoer. London: 1963. V. 62
The Moviegoer. Franklin Center: 1980. V. 65; 66
Questions They Never Asked Me. Northridge: 1979. V. 64; 67
The Second Coming. New York: 1980. V. 62; 63; 64; 65; 66; 67
The State of the Novel: Dying Art or New Science?. New Orleans: 1987. V. 66
Symbol as Hermeneutic in Existentialism. N.P: 1956. V. 64
The Thanatos Syndrome. Franklin Center: 1987. V. 67
The Thanatos Syndrome. New York: 1987. V. 66

PERCY, WILLIAM ALEXANDER
Sewanee. New York: 1982. V. 66

PERDUE, VIRGINIA
The Case of the Foster Father. Garden City: 1942. V. 67

PEREC, GEORGES
Les Choses. Paris: 1965. V. 67

PEREIRA DA SILVA, MATHIAS
A Fenix Renascida, ou Obras Poeticas dos Melhores Engenhos Portuguezes.... Lisbon: 1746. V. 62

PEREIRA DE BERREDO, BERNARDO
Annaes Historicos do Estado do Maranhao. Lisbon: 1749. V. 62

PERES, SHIMON
From These Men, Seven Founders of the State of Israel. New York: 1979. V. 65

PERET, BENJAMIN
Remove Your Hat - Twenty Poems. London: 1936. V. 64

PEREZ, NISSAN
Focus East: Early Photograph in the Near East 1839-1885. New York: 1988. V. 63

PEREZ-GUERRA, ANNE
Poppy or the Adventures of a Fairy. Chicago: 1934. V. 63

PEREZ REVERTE, ARTURO
The Club Dumas. New York: 1996. V. 65; 67
The Dumas Club. London: 1996. V. 65; 66; 67
The Fencing Master. London: 1999. V. 65; 66; 67
The Flanders Panel. New York: 1994. V. 65; 67
The Seville Communion. London: 1998. V. 65; 66; 67

PERIAM, J.
The Groundswell, a History of the Origin, Aims and Progress of the Farmers' Movement.... Cincinnati and Chicago: 1874. V. 63

PERICLES
The Funeral Oration of Pericles. London: 1948. V. 67

PERIER, ALESSANDRO
Disinganno de' Peccatori...Utilissimo a Missionarii ed a Tutti i Predicatori.... Rome: 1726. V. 65

PERIER, JACQUES CONSTANTIN
Sur Les Machines...Vapeur. Paris: 1810. V. 66

PERILLO, GREGORY
Perillo: Artist of the American West. New York: 1981. V. 62; 63

PERING, RICHARD
A Brief Enquiry into the Causes of Premature Decay, in Our Wooden Bulwarks.... Plymouth-Dock: 1812. V. 65
On the Preservation of the British Navy, When in a State of Ordinary. Plymouth Dock: 1813. V. 65
A Reply to Some Strictures in the Quarterly Review (No. XIX) on Indian-Built Ships.... Plymouth Dock: 1814. V. 65

PERINI, LODOVICO
Geometria Pratica in Cui Oltre i Principi de Essa vi sono Molti Insegnamenti Intorno alle Varie Misure de Terre, Acque, Fieni, Pietre, Grani, Fabbrice, ed Altro Secondo l'uso di Verona, e di Tutte l'Altre Citta d'Italia. Bassano: 1781. V. 67

PERI ROSSI, CRISTINA
Ship of Fools. London: 1989. V. 67

PERKINS, CHARLES ELLIOTT
Family Letters 1861-1869. Boston: 1949. V. 67
The Phantom Bull. New York: 1932. V. 63
The Pinto Horse. Santa Barbara: 1937. V. 63; 66

PERKINS, E. E.
A Treatise on Haberdashery and Hosiery.... London: 1836. V. 63

PERKINS, E. E., MRS.
The Elements of Botany, With Illustrations. 1837. V. 67

PERKINS, E. J.
The Biology of Estuaries and Coastal Waters. London: 1974. V. 65

PERKINS, ELISHA DOUGLAS
Gold Rush Diary. Being the Journal of.... Lexington: 1967. V. 67
Gold Rush Diary, Being the Journal of.... Lexington: 1968. V. 65

PERKINS, F. O.
Pathology in Marine Science. San Diego: 1990. V. 65

PERKINS, GEORGE
The Diagnosis, Treatment and End Results of Tuberculosis Disease of the Hip Joint. London: 1926. V. 65

PERKINS, JOHN B.
History of Hyde County South Dakota from Its Organizaton to the Present Time. N.P: 1908. V. 62

PERKINS, KENNETH
Voodoo'd. New York: 1931. V. 67

PERKINS, MARGARET
Echoes of Pawnee Rock. Wichita: 1908. V. 63; 66

PERKINS, MARY E.
Old Houses of the Antient Town of Norwich 1660-1800. Norwich: 1895. V. 67

PERKINS, SIMEON
The Diary of Simeon Perkins 1766-1812. Toronto: 1948-1978. V. 62; 63; 64; 66
The Diary of Simeon Perkins 1804-1812. Toronto: 1978. V. 62; 63; 66

PERL, JED
Trevor Winkfield's Pageant. West Stockbridge: 1997. V. 62

PERLES, ALFRED
Art and Outrage: a Correspondence About Henry Miller. London: 1959. V. 65
Delta - Number 2. Paris: 1938. V. 63
My Friend Henry Miller. London: 1955. V. 62
Round Trip. London: 1946. V. 64
Scenes from a Floating Life. London: 1968. V. 62

PERLEY, MOSES HENRY
Reports on the Sea and River Fishers of New Brunswick. Fredericton: 1852. V. 64

PERLMAN, BARBARA H.
Allan Houser. Boston: 1987. V. 63
Allan Houser (Ha-O-Zous). Japan: 1987. V. 67

PERNETTI, JACQUES
Philosophical Letters Upon Physiognomies. London: 1751. V. 63

PERNHOPF, EDUARD
Topographische Anatomie des Menschen. Lehrbuch und Atlas der Regionar-Stratigraphischen Praparation.... Wien: 1952-1957. V. 64

PEROWNE, BARRY
Raffles of the M. C. C. London: 1979. V. 67

PERRAULT, CHARLES
La Belle Au Bois Dormant & Le Petit Chaperon Rouge Deux Contes de Ma Mere L'Oye. 1899. V. 62
Cinderella. Albany: 1816. V. 66
Cinderella. New York: 1886?. V. 64
The Fairy Tales. London: 1922. V. 66
The Fairy Tales. New York: 1922. V. 62; 65
Histoire de Peau D'ane. Hammersmith: 1902. V. 62
Old-Time Stories. New York: 1921. V. 67
Puss in Boots. New York: 1990. V. 65

PERRAULT, CLAUDE
A Treatise of the Five Orders of Columns in Architecture.... London: 1708. V. 67

PERRET, FRANK ALVORD
The Volcano-Seismic Crisis at Montserrat, 1933-1937. Washington: 1939. V. 63
Volcanological Observations. Washington: 1950. V. 63

PERREVE, VICTOR
Traite des Retrecissements Organiques d l'Uretre. Emploi methodique des Dilatateurs Mecaniques dans le Traitement de ces Maladies. Paris: 1847. V. 65

PERRIE, GEORGE W.
Buckskin Mose; or, Life from the Lakes to the Pacific, as Actor, Circus-Rider, Detective, Ranger, Gold-Digger, Indian Scout and Guide. New York: 1890. V. 67
Buckskin Mose; or, Life from the Lakes to the Pacific, as Ranger, Gold-Digger, Indian Scout and Guide. New York: 1873. V. 64; 67

PERRIER, FRANCOIS DES
Segmenta Nobilium Signorum et Statuaru(m) Quae...Vrbis Aeternae Ruinis Erepta.... Rome: 1638. V. 62

PERRIN, H.
British Flowering Plants. 1914. V. 63

PERRIN, IDA SOUTHWELL ROBINS
British Flowering Plants. London: 1914. V. 66

PERRIN, JEAN
Atoms. London: 1923. V. 67

PERRIN, JEAN BAPTISTE
The Elements of English Conversation.... Bordeaux: 1808. V. 64
Entertaining and Instructive Exercises with the Rule of the French Syntax. London: 1787,. V. 64

PERRIN, W. H.
Kentucky: History of the State. Louisville & Chicago: 1888. V. 66

PERRINCHIEF, RICHARD
The Life and Death of King Charles the First..together with Eikon Basiliki.... London: 1697. V. 64
The Royal Martyr; or the Life and Death of King Charles I. London: 1676. V. 64
The Sicilian Tyrant; or, the Life of Agathocles. London: 1676. V. 65

PERRINE, CHARLES D.
Determination of the Solar Parallax, from Photographs of Eros Made With the Crossley Reflector of the Lick Observatory, University of California. Washington: 1910. V. 66

PERRINE, FRED S.
Military Escorts on Santa Fe Trail. 1927-1928. V. 65; 67

PERRING, F. H.
Atlas of the British Flora. 1962. V. 67

PERRINS, C. W. DYSON
The Dyson Perrins Collection. London: 1958-. V. 62

PERRONET, JEAN RODOLPHE
Description des Projets et de la Consturction des Ponts de Neuilly, de mantes d'Orleans & Autres....(with) Supplement. Paris: 1782-1789. V. 65

PERRONET, VINCENT
Some Strictures on a Few Places of the Late Reverend Mr. Hervey's Letters to the Reverend Mr. John Wesley. London: 1766. V. 64

PERROT, ADOLPHE
Recherches sur l'Action Chimique de l'Etincelle d'Induction de l'Appareil Ruhmkorff. Paris: 1861. V. 65

PERROT, GEORGES
History of Art in Sardinia, Judaea, Syria and Asia Minor. London: 1890. V. 66

PERROTT, JOHN
An Authentic Narrative of the Proceedings Under a Commission of Bankrupcy Against John Perrott, Late of Ludgate Hill, Laceman, who was Executed at Smithfield, on Wednesday Nov. 11, 1761.... London: 1761. V. 63

PERRY, ANNE
Bethelhem Road. New York: 1990. V. 65; 67
Cardington Crescent. New York: 1987. V. 65
A Dangerous Mourning. New York: 1991. V. 67

PERRY, ARTHUR LATHAM
Williamstown and Williams College. New York: 1899. V. 64

PERRY, BELA C.
A Treatise on Human Hair. Bedford: 1859. V. 66

PERRY, BLISS
Park Street Papers. Boston: 1908. V. 62

PERRY, CHARLOTTE BRONTE
The History of the Coloured Canadian in Windsor, Ontario 1867-1967. Windsor: 1969. V. 66

PERRY, G.
Conchology. London: 1811. V. 62

PERRY, GEORGE
The Book of the Great Western. London: 1970. V. 62; 66

PERRY, JAMES
The Electric Eeel; or Gymnotus Electricus. London: 1777. V. 67

PERRY, MATTHEW CALBRAITH
Narrative of the Expedition of an American Squadron to the China Seas and Japan, Performed in the Years 1852, 1853 and 1854.... Washington: 1856. V. 62; 63

PERRY NURSERY CO.
The Perry Hand Book of Choice Fruits, Ornamentals, Roses, Shrubs, Hardy Perennials, Bulbs Etc. Rochester. V. 67

PERRY, THOMAS
Big Fish. New York: 1985. V. 67
The Butcher's Boy. 1982. V. 66
The Butcher's Boy. New York: 1982. V. 64
Experiments with Windmills. Washington: 1899. V. 63
Metzger's Dog. New York: 1983. V. 65; 66
Vanishing Act. New York: 1995. V. 67

PERRY, WILLIAM STEVENS
Historical Collections Relating to the American Colonial Church. Hartford: 1878-1880. V. 64

PERSEPOLIS Illustrata: Or the Ancient and Royal Palace of Persepolis in Persia, Destroyed by Alexander the Great, About Two Thousand Years Ago.... London: 1739. V. 64

PERSHING, JOHN J.
My Experiences in the World War. New York: 1931. V. 63; 66

PERSIUS
The Satires of Persius. 1827. V. 62; 65

PERSON, DAVID
Varities, or, a Surveigh of Rare and Excellent Matters, Necessary and Delectable for All Sorts of Persons. London: 1635. V. 63; 65; 66

PERSOON, C. H.
Synopsis Plantarum, seu Enchiridium botanicum.... Paris: 1805-1807. V. 66

PERTELOTE, a Sequel to Chanticleer: Being a Bibliography of the Golden Cockerel Press, October 1936-1943 April. Waltham St. Lawrence: 1943. V. 64

PERVIGILIUM VENERIS
Pervigilium Veneris. Hammersmith: 1911. V. 62; 67
Pervigilium Veneris. London: 1924. V. 62
The Vigil of Venus. Waltham St. Lawrence: 1939. V. 64; 66
The Vigil of Venus. Cummington: 1943. V. 63

PESNER, NIKOLAUS
High Victorian Design - a Study of the Exhibits of 1851. London: 1951. V. 63

PESSOA, FERNANDO
English Poems. Lisbon: 1921. V. 65

PETAU, PAUL
Explication de Plusieurs Antiquites, Recuellies par Paul Petau, Conseiller au Parlement de Paris.... Amsterdam: 1757. V. 67

PETER Parley's Universal History on the Basis of Geography. London: 1839. V. 65
PETER Parley's Universal History on the Basis of Geography. New York: 1840. V. 65
PETER Parley's Universal History on the Basis of Geography. New York: 1850. V. 62

PETER Rabbit. Springfield: 1931. V. 64

PETER Rabbit and Jimmy Chipmunk. Chicago: 1918. V. 64

PETER Rabbit and Sammy Squirrel. Akron: 1918. V. 64

THE PETER Habbit Story Book. New York: 1935. V. 64

PETER, ROBERT
The History of the Medical Department of Transylvania University. Louisville: 1905. V. 67

PETER Thompson of Needwood Forest; or, Industry Rewarded. Wellington: 1824. V. 65

PETER I, CZAR OR RUSSIA
Journal de Pierre le Grand Depuis l'Annee 1698 Jusqu'a la Conclusion de la Paix de Nouotadt (1721). A Berlin: 1773. V. 66

PETERKIN, ALEXANDER
Letter to the Landholders, Clergy and Other Gentlemen, of Orkney and Zetland, with Relative Documents and Correspondence Betwixt J. A. Maconochie, Esq. Sheriff-Depute and Alex. Peterkin. Edinburgh: 1823. V. 64

PETERKIN, JULIA
Black April. Indianapolis: 1927. V. 64; 67
Roll, Jordan, Roll. London: 1934. V. 62; 64; 67

PETERS, ALAN
Who Killed the Doctors?. New York: 1934. V. 65

PETERS, C. H. F.
Ptolemy's Catalogue of Stars.... Washington: 1915. V. 64

PETERS, DE WITT
Kit Carson's Wild West. New York: 1880. V. 66
The Life of Kit Carson: the Nestor of the Rocky Mountains. New York: 1858. V. 64

PETERS, ELIZABETH
The Deeds of the Disturber. 1988. V. 67
The Jackal's Head. 1968. V. 64; 66; 67
The Murders of Richard III. New York: 1974. V. 65
Street of the Five Moons. New York: 1978. V. 65
Summer of the Dragon. 1979. V. 66

PETERS, ELLIS
Black is the Colour of My True Love's Heart. London: 1967. V. 63; 66
By Firelight. London: 1948. V. 65
The Cadfael Companion. New York: 1995. V. 67
City of Gold and Shadows. London: 1973. V. 66
Death Mask. Garden City: 1960. V. 66
Death to the Landlords!. London: 1972. V. 66
The Devil's Novice. London: 1983. V. 65; 66; 67
An Excellent Mystery. London: 1985. V. 62; 65; 66
Flight of a Witch. London: 1964. V. 63; 64; 66
The Horn of Roland. London: 1974. V. 66
The Knocker on Death's Door. London: 1970. V. 64
The Marriage of Meggotta. London: 1979. V. 67
Monk's-Hood. London: 1980. V. 62; 64; 65; 66
Monk's-Hood. 1981. V. 67
A Morbid Taste for Bones. London: 1977. V. 66; 67
Mourning Raga. London: 1969. V. 66
Never Pick Up Hitch-Hikers. London: 1976. V. 66
One Corpse Too Many. 1979. V. 64; 66
One Corpse Too Many. London: 1979. V. 65; 66; 67
One Corpse Too Many. London: 1980. V. 64; 65; 66
The Piper on the Mountain. London: 1966. V. 63; 64; 66
Rainbow's End. 1979. V. 65; 66
The Raven in the Foregate; the Twelfth Chronicle of Brother Cadfael. London: 1986. V. 66; 67
Saint Peter's Fair. London: 1981. V. 67
Saint Peter's Fair. New York: 1981. V. 67
The Sanctuary Sparrow. London: 1983. V. 62

PETERS, H. S.
The Birds of Newfoundland. Boston: 1951. V. 62; 64; 67

PETERS, J. T.
History of Fayette Co., W. V. Parsons: 1972. V. 65

PETERS, MATTHEW
The Rational Farmer; or a Treatise on Agriculture and Tillage.... London: 1771. V. 63

PETERS, ROBERT L.
Design of Liquid, Solid and Hybrid Rockets. New York: 1965. V. 66

PETERSBURG, VIRGINIA. LIBRARY
Catalogue of the Library of Petersburg, Virginia. New York: 1854. V. 64

PETERSEN, KAREN D.
Howling Wolf, A Cheyenne Warrior's Graphic Interpretation of His People. Palo Alto: 1968. V. 67

PETERSEN, R. H.
Evolution in the Higher Basidiomycetes, an International Symposium. Knoxville: 1971. V. 63

PETERSEN, WILLIAM F.
Hippocratic Wisdom For Him who Wishes to Pursue Properly the Science of Medicine. London: 1734. V. 66
Hippocratic Wisdom for Him Who Wishes to Pursue Properly the Science of Medicine. Springfield: 1946. V. 66

PETERSEN, WILLIAM J.
Steamboating on the Upper Mississippi: the Water Way to Iowa. Iowa City: 1937. V. 67
Towboating on the Mississippi. South Brunswick: 1979. V. 65

PETERSHAM, MAUD
The Rooster Crows, A Book of American Rhymes and Jingles. New York: 1945. V. 63

PETERSON, ALLAN
Stars on a Wire. University of Alabama: 1989. V. 64

PETERSON, DANIEL H.
The Looking-Glass: Being a True Report and Narrative of the Life, Travels and Labors of a Colored Clergyman. New York: 1854. V. 66

PETERSON, FREDERICK
Mental Diseases. Philadelphia: 1903. V. 65

PETERSON, HAROLD L.
The Book of the Gun. London: 1966. V. 67

PETERSON, KAREN DANIELS
Plains Indian Art from Fort Marion. Norman: 1971. V. 63

PETERSON, O. A.
The American Diceratheres. Pittsburgh: 1920. V. 66
A Revision of the Entelodontidae. Pittsburgh: 1909. V. 66

PETERSON, ROGER TORY
A Field Guide to the Birds. Boston and New York: 1934. V. 62; 63; 64; 66
Field Guide to the Birds. Boston: 1980. V. 63
Roger Tory Peterson Field Guides. Norwalk: 1984-1997. V. 67

PETERSON, SUSAN
The Living Tradition of Maria Martinez. Tokyo, New York, and S.F: 1977. V. 62; 63; 64
The Living Tradition of Maria Martinez. New York: 1978. V. 62

PETERSON, WILLIAM S.
The Kelmscott Press, a History of William Morris's Typographical Adventure. Oxford: 1991. V. 62

PETIEVICH, GERALD
Money Men and One Shot Deal. New York: 1981. V. 65

PETIS DE LA CROIX, FRANCOIS
The Persian and Turkish Tales.... London: 1714. V. 63

PETIT, ANTOINE FRANCOIS
Catalogue Des Livres De la Bibliotheqie De Feu Le Citoyen Antoine- Francois Petit.... Paris: 1796. V. 64; 66

PETIT, JEAN LOUIS
Traite des Maladies Chirurgicales et des Operations qui leur Conviennent. Paris: 1774-1776. V. 65
Traite Des Maladies De Os, Dans Lequel on a Represente les Appareils & Les Machines Qui Conviennent a Leur Guerison. Paris: 1758. V. 64
Traite Des Maladies De Os, Dans Lequel on a Represente les Appareils & Les Machines qui Conviennent a Leur Guerison.... Paris: 1741. V. 66

PETIT Paroissien de la Jeunesse. Paris: 1840. V. 67

PETIT, VICTOR
Habitations Champetres, Recueil de Maisons, Villas, Chalets, Pavillons, Kiosques, Parcs, et Jardins. Paris: 1855. V. 64

THE PETITION for the Prelates Briefly Examined. London: 1641. V. 66

PETITOT, E.
Monographie des Dene-Dindjie. Paris: 1876. V. 64

PETITOT, JEAN
Les Emaux de Peitot du Musee Imperial Du Louvre, Portraits de Personnages Historiques et de Femmes Celebre du Siecle de Louis XIV.... Paris: 1862-1864. V. 66

PETKO, EDWARD
At Seventy: Richard Hoffman. Los Angeles: 1982. V. 64

PETO, SAMUEL MORTON
Resources and Prospects of America, Ascertained During a Visit to the States in the Autumn of 1865. London and New York: 1866. V. 64; 67
Taxation: Its Levy and Expenditure, Past and Future.... London: 1863. V. 67

PETRACONE, ENZO
La Commedia Dell'Arte. Storia. Technica. Scenari. Napoli: 1927. V. 65

PETRAKIS, HARRY MARK
Chapter Seven from The Hour of the Bell, a Novel Concerning the Greek War of Independence. Mt. Horeb: 1976. V. 64

PETRARCA, FRANCESCO
(Rime) Il Petrarca Con Nuoue, E Breui Dichiarationi. Lyone: 1551. V. 64
The Triumphs of Francesco Petrarch. Boston: 1906. V. 66

PETRARCA, FRANCESO
Chronica de la Vite de Pontefici et Imperadori Romanis.... Colophon: 1534. V. 63

PETRIE, GEORGE
Christian Inscriptions in the Irish Language. 1870-1877. V. 62; 65

PETRI VON ARTENFELS, GEORG CHRISTOPH
Elephantographia Curiosa, Seu Elephanti Descriptio, Juxta Methodum et Leges Imperialis Academiae Leopoldino Carolinae Naturae Curiosorum Adornata.... Erfurt: 1715. V. 62; 65

PETRONIO, ALESSANDRO TRAJANO
Del Viver Delli Romani, et di Conservar La Sanita. In Roma: 1592. V. 64

PETRONIUS
Complete Works. 1927. V. 62
Petronii Arbitri Satyricon.... Lutetiae Parisiorum: 1601. V. 65
Satyricon. Amstelodami: 1669. V. 64
Satyricon. Amstelaedami: 1743. V. 64; 66
Satyricon Quae Supersunt. (bound with) Commenta...et Indices. Utrecht: 1709. V. 66
Satyricon Quae Supersunt Cum Integris Doctorum Virorum Commentariis & Notis Nicolai Heinsii.... Lugduni Batavorum: 1743. V. 65

PETRUNKEVITCH, A.
A Study of Palaeozoic Arachnida. New Haven: 1949. V. 66

PETRUS DE PALUDE
Sermones Thesauri Novi de Tempore et de Sanctis. Nuremberg: 1487. V. 66

PETTAS, WILLIAM A.
The Giunti of Florence, Merchant Publishers of the Sixteenth Century. San Francisco: 1980. V. 62

PETTEE, JAMES H.
A Chapter of Mission History in Modern Japan. Tokyo: 1895. V. 63; 67

PETTER, NICOLAES
Klare Onderrichtige der Voortreffelijcke Worstel-Konst. Amsterdam: 1674. V. 67

PETTES, HELEN
Make Believe Gift Box. New York: 1917. V. 62

PETTIGREW, J. B.
Anatomical Preparation-Making as Devised and Practised at the University of Edinburgh. 1901. V. 67
On the Mechanical Appliances by Which Flight is Attained in the Animal Kingdom.... 1868. V. 67
On the Physiology of Wings. Edinburgh: 1871. V. 67

PETTIGREW, JAMES JOHNSTON
Notes on Spain and the Spainards, in the Summer of 1859, with a Glance at Sardinia. Charleston: 1861. V. 62; 63; 65; 66

PETTIGREW, THOMAS JOSEPH
Medical Portrait Gallery. London: 1838-1840. V. 65
Memoirs of the Life of Lord Viscount Nelson, K.B. London: 1849. V. 65
On Supersititions Connected With the History and Practice of Medicine and Surgery. London: 1844. V. 65

PETTINGILL, O. S.
Living Birds. Ithaca: 1962-1970. V. 64

PETTMAN, WILLIAM
A Letter Addressed to the Freeman of the Town and Port of Sandwich, Respecting the Proceedings...of the Ramsgate Committee...at Their Town-Hall, Oct. 28, 1806. London: 1807. V. 66
A Letter to Arthur Young, Esq. Secretary to the Board of Agriculture, on the Situation of the Growers of Corn in Great Britain. Canterbury: 1815. V. 64

PETTUS, JOHN
Fleta Minor. The Laws of Art and Nature in Knowing, Judging, Assaying, Fining, Refining...The Bodies of Confin'd Metals. London: 1683. V. 62; 64
The Laws of Art and Nature in Knowing, Judging, Fining, Refining and Inlarging the Bodies of Confin'd Metals. London: 1683. V. 65

PETTY, JOHN
The History of the Primitive Methodist Connexion from Its Origin to the Conference of 1859. London: 1860. V. 62
The History of the Primitive Methodist Connexion, From Its Origin to the Conference of 1860.... London: 1880. V. 66

PETTY, WILLIAM
Sir William Petty's Political Survey of Ireland, with the Establishment of that Kingdom.... London: 1719. V. 62

PETVIN, JOHN
Letters Concerning the Mind. To Which is added, A Sketch of Universal Arithmetic.... London: 1750. V. 65

PETYT, WILLIAM
The Antient Right of the Common of England Asserted; or, a Discourse Proving by Records and the Best Historians, That the Commons of England Were Ever an Essential Part of Parliament. London: 1680. V. 64; 67
Britannia Languens, or a Discourse of Trade. London: 1680. V. 66
Catalogue of the Petyt Library at Skipton, Yorkshire. Gargrave: 1964. V. 67
Miscellanea Parliamentaria.... London: 1680. V. 63

PEVSNER, N.
An Enquiry Into Industrial Art in England. New York: 1937. V. 65

PEYROT, J.
Petite Encyclopedie Mathematique, a l'Usage des Deux Sexes.... Paris: 1829-1831. V. 63

PEYTON, J. LEWIS
The Adventures of My Grandfather. Charlottesville: 1963. V. 67
History of Augusta County, Virginia. Staunton: 1882. V. 62
History of Augusta County, Virginia. Bridgewater: 1953. V. 64

PEYTON, JOHN ROWZEE
3 Letters from St. Louis. Denver: 1958. V. 63; 64; 66

PEZZI, LAURENTIUS
Vinea Domini. Cum Brevi Descriptione Sacramentorum et Paradisi Limbi Purgatorij, Atque Inferni, a Catechismo Catholicisque Patribus Excerpta. Venice: 1588. V. 65

PFAFF, CHRISTIAN
Der Elektro Magnetismus, eine Historisch-Kritische Darstellung der Bisherigen Entdeckungen auf dem Gebiete Desselben.... Hamburg: 1824. V. 65

PFEFFER, P. E.
Nuclear Magnetic Resonance in Agriculture. Boca Raton: 1989. V. 63

PFEFFERKORN, IGNAZ
Pfefferkorn's Description of Sonora. Albuquerque: 1949. V. 63

PFEIFFER, EMILY
Flying Leaves from East and West. London: 1885. V. 65

PFEIFFER, LEE
The Essential Bond. London: 1998. V. 67

PFEIFFER, RUDOLF
Callimachus. Oxonii: 1965. V. 65

PFLUG, F. A.
Wagons fur den Eisenbahn-Train der Kaiserl. Berlin: 1864. V. 65

PFLUGER, EDOUARD FRIEDRICH WILHELM
Ueber die Eierstocke der Saugethiere und des Menshcen. Leipzig: 1863. V. 65
Untersuchungen aus dem Physiologischen Laboratorium zu Bonn. Berlin: 1865. V. 65
Untersuchungen Uber die Physiologie des Electrotonus. Berlin: 1859. V. 65

PHAEDRUS
Fabularum Aesopiarum Libri V. Amstelaedami;: 1701. V. 66
Phaedri Aug. Liberati Fabularum Aesopiarum Libri V. Notis Illustravit in Usum Serenissimi Principis Nassavii.... Amstelodami: 1701. V. 66
Phaedri Aug. Liberti Fabularum Aesopiarum Libri V. Lugduni Batavorum: 1778. V. 65; 66

PHALARIS
The Epistles of Phalaris. London: 1749. V. 62
The Epistles of Phalaris. London: 1759. V. 63

PHALLIC Miscellanies. Facts and Phases of Ancient and Modern Sex Worship. 1891. V. 67

PHALLIC Objects, Monuments and Remains. London: 1889. V. 67

PHARIS, R. P.
Plant Growth Substances 1988. Berlin: 1990. V. 64

PHELPS, ALMIRA HART LINCOLN
The Female Student; or Lectures to Young Ladies on Female Education. London: 1841. V. 65

PHELPS, CHARLES
Traumatic Injuries of the Brain and Its Membranes. New York: 1897. V. 64

PHELPS, HUMPHREY
Phelp's Travellers' Guide through the United States. New York: 1849. V. 66

PHELPS, T. T.
Fishing Dreams. London: 1949. V. 67

PHELPS, WILLIAM LYON
A Dash at the Pole. Boston: 1910. V. 63

PHIBBS, GEOFFREY
It Was Not Jones: Poems. London: 1928. V. 66

PHIFER, CHARLES H.
Genealogy and History of the Phifer Family. Charlotte: 1910. V. 67

PHILADELPHIA Judiciary 1874-1895. Philadelphia: 1895. V. 66

PHILALETHA, EIRAENEUS
Erklarung der Hermetisch Poetischen Werke.... Hamburg: 1741. V. 64

PHILANDER, JOACHIM, PSEUD.
Vitulus Aureus: the Golden Calf. London: 1749. V. 65

PHILANTHROPIC SOCIETY
First Report of the Philanthropic Society. Instituted in London, September 1788, for the Prevention of Crimes. London: 1789. V. 63

PHILBRICK, NATHANIEL
In the Heart of the Sea. New York: 2000. V. 67

PHILBY, H. ST. JOHN BRIDGER
A Pilgrim in Arabia. Waltham St. Lawrence: 1943. V. 64; 65; 66

PHILIDOR, FRANCOIS ANDRE DANICAN
Analysis of the Game of Chess...to Which is Added, Several Parties, Played by the author Blindfold, Against Three Adversaries. London: 1790. V. 65

PHILIP, ALEXANDER WILSON
An Experimental Essay on the Manner in Which Opium Acts on the Living Body. Edinburgh;: 1795. V. 63

PHILIPPI, DONALD
This Wine of Peace, This Wine of Laughter: A Complete Anthology of Japan's Earliest Songs. New York: 1968. V. 63; 64

PHILIPPOTEAUX, PAUL
Cyclorama of the Battle of Gettysburg. Boston: 1825. V. 67

PHILIPPS, FABIAN
The Pretended Perspective-Glass; or, Some Reasons of Many More Which Might be Offered, Against the Proposed Registering Reformation. London: 1669. V. 66

PHILIPS, CASPER JACOBSZ
Verzaameling van alle de Huizen en Prachtige Gebouwen Langs de Keizers en Heere-Grachten der Stadt Amsterdam.... Amsterdam: 1768-1771. V. 67

PHILIPS, CATHERINE C.
Jesse Benton Fremont - A Woman Who Made History. San Francisco: 1935. V. 64; 67

PHILIPS, ERASMUS
Miscellaneous Works, Consisting of Essays Political and Moral. London: 1752. V. 62

PHILIPS, FRANCIS CHARLES
The Dean and His Daughter. London: 1887. V. 66
The Strange Adventures of Lucy Smith. London: 1887. V. 66

PHILIPS, JOHN
Poems on Several Occasions. London: 1720. V. 65
Poems on Several Occasions. London: 1728. V. 63

PHILIPS, JUDSON P.
Red War. New York: 1936. V. 67

PHILIPS, KATHERINE
Poems by the Most Deservedly Admired Mrs. Katherine Philips, the Matchless Orinda. London: 1678. V. 65

PHILIPS, N. G.
Views of the Old Halls of Lancashire and Cheshire. London: 1893. V. 66

PHILIPS BIRT, DOUGLAS H. C.
Motor Yacht and Boat Design. New York: 1953. V. 67

PHILIPSON, JOHN
Harness: As It Has Been, As It Is and As It Should Be. Newcastle-upon-Tyne: 1882. V. 62; 67

PHILLEO, CALVIN WHEELER
Twice Married: a Story of Connecticut Life. New York: 1855. V. 64; 66

PHILLIMORE, JOSEPH
A Letter Addressed to a Member of the House of Commons, on the Subject of the Notice Given by Mr. Brougham, for a Motion Respecting the Orders in Council and Licence Trade.... London: 1812. V. 67

PHILLIMORE, W. P. W.
County Pedigrees. Nottinghamshire. Volume I (all published). London: 1910. V. 65
The Index Library. A Calendar of Wills Relating to the Counties of Northampton and Rutland, Proved in the Court of the Archdeacon of Northampton 1510 to 1652. London: 1888. V. 66
Northamptonshire Parish Registers. Marriages. London: 1908. V. 66

PHILLIPPS, E. M.
The Gardens of Italy With Historical and Descriptive Notes. 1919. V. 63; 66

PHILLIPPS, S. MARCH
A Treatise on the Law of Evidence:. New York: 1849. V. 67

PHILLIPPS-WOLLEY, C.
Big Game Shooting. 1894. V. 62; 63; 64; 66; 67
Big Game Shooting. 1895-1894. V. 63; 64
Big Game Shooting. 1901. V. 62; 63; 64; 66; 67
Big Game Shooting. 1902-1903. V. 64

PHILLIPPS-WOOLEY, C.
Big Game Shooting. Volume I. London: 1894. V. 67

PHILLIPS, A.
The Birds of Arizona. Tucson: 1964. V. 65; 67

PHILLIPS, A. V.
The Lott Family in America, Including the Allied Families: Cassell, Davis, Graybeal, Haring, Hegeman, Hogg, Kerley, Phillips, Thompson, Walter and Others. Trenton: 1942. V. 63; 66

PHILLIPS, C. E. L.
The Rothschild Rhododendrons, a Record of the Gardens at Exbury. New York: 1967. V. 67

PHILLIPS, CATHERINE
Reasons Why the People Called Quakers Cannot so Fully Unite With the Methodists, in Their Missions to the Negroes in the West India Islands and Africa.... London: 1792. V. 63

PHILLIPS, CATHERINE COFFIN
Cornelius Cole - California Pioneer and United States Senator.... San Francisco: 1929. V. 66
Coulterville Chronicle - the Annals of a Mother Lode Mining Town. San Francisco: 1942. V. 62; 65
Jesse Benton Fremont: a Woman who Made History. San Francisco: 1935. V. 63; 64; 67
Portsmouth Plaza: the Cradle of San Francisco. San Francisco: 1932. V. 63

PHILLIPS, CHARLES
Curran and His Contemporaries. Edinburgh: 1851. V. 63
The Speeches, Delivered at the Bar, and on Various Public Occasions, in Ireland and England. London: 1822. V. 63
Vacation Thoughts on Capital Punishments. Brighton: 1856. V. 63

PHILLIPS, FREDERIC NELSON
Phillips' Old - Fashioned Type Book. New York: 1945. V. 62

PHILLIPS, G. F.
A Practical Treatise on Drawing, and On Painting in Water Colours.... London: 1839. V. 62; 63; 66
Principles of Effect and Colour, as Applicable to Landscape Painting. London: 1839. V. 66; 67

PHILLIPS, GEORGE SEARLE
Lincolnshire, A Pastoral.... London: 1850. V. 62

PHILLIPS, HARLAN B.
Felix Frankfurter Reminiscences. New York: 1960. V. 63

PHILLIPS, HENRY
Floral Emblems. London: 1825. V. 67
Sylva Florifera: The Shrubbery Historically and Botanically Treated.... London: 1823. V. 64
The True Enjoyment of Angling. 1843. V. 63; 65; 67

PHILLIPS, HUGH
Mid-Georgian London. A Topographical and Social Survey. London: 1964. V. 67

PHILLIPS, J. A.
The Mining and Metallurgy of Gold and River. London: 1867. V. 64

PHILLIPS, J. B.
St. Luke's Life of Christ. London: 1956. V. 64

PHILLIPS, J. S.
Explorers', Miners', and Metallurgists' Companion. San Francisco: 1879. V. 63

PHILLIPS, JAYNE ANNE
Black Tickets. New York: 1979. V. 66
The Secret Country. Winston-Salem: 1982. V. 62
Sweethearts. Carrboro: 1976. V. 62

PHILLIPS, JOHN
Figures and Descriptions of the Palaeozoic Fossils of Cornwall, Devon and West Somerset. 1841. V. 65
Geology of Oxford and the Valley of the Thames. Oxford: 1871. V. 62; 63; 64; 65; 66
Geology of Oxford and the Valley of the Thames. London: 1971. V. 65
Illustrations of the Geology of Yorkshire; or, a Description of the Strata and Organic Remains. York: 1829. V. 62; 67
Illustrations of the Geology of Yorkshire; or a Description of the Strata and Organic Remains. London: 1835-1836. V. 65
Maronides or Virgil Travesty, Being a Paraphrase Upon the Sixth Book of Virgils Aeneids in Burlesque Verse. London: 1673. V. 62
The Rivers, Mountains and Sea-Coast of Yorkshire. 1853. V. 67

PHILLIPS, JOHN continued
The Rivers, Mountains and Sea-Coast of Yorkshire. London: 1853. V. 64; 65
The Rivers, Mountains and Sea-Coast of Yorkshire. London: 1855. V. 66
A Treatise on Geology. 1837-1839. V. 65
A Treatise on Geology. London: 1837-1839. V. 64
Vesuvius. Oxford: 1869. V. 62; 66

PHILLIPS, JOHN C.
A Natural History of the Ducks. Boston and New York: 1922-1926. V. 63; 64; 67
Quick-Water and Smooth. Brattleboro: 1935. V. 64

PHILLIPS, JONAS
Tales for Leisure Hours. Philadelphia: 1827. V. 62

PHILLIPS, JONATHAN
Messages of the Presidents of the United States from the Formation of the General Government, Down to the Close of the Administration of President Van Buren.... Columbus: 1841. V. 65

PHILLIPS, JOSEPH
The Trial of Joseph Phillips, for a Libel on the Duke of Cumberland, and the Proceedings Thereto Arising Out of the Suicide of Sellis, in 1810.... London: 1833. V. 63

PHILLIPS, LANCE
Folks I Knowed and Horses They Rode. Ashland: 1975. V. 64

PHILLIPS, LE ROY
A Bibliography of the Writings of Henry James. Boston and New York: 1906. V. 64; 65

PHILLIPS, MARY PALMER
The Family Record of David Lehman Booher and His Wife Elizabeth Nutts. Pinnacle: 1956. V. 67

PHILLIPS, MORRIS
Abroad and At Home, Practical Hints from Tourists. New York: 1891. V. 63

PHILLIPS, MR.
Speech of Mr. Phillips, Delivered in the Court of Common-Pleas, Dublin, in the Case of Guthrie Versus Sterne. London: 1815. V. 65

PHILLIPS, P.
Pre-Columbian Steel Engravings from the Craig Mound at Spiro, Oklahoma. Cambridge: 1982. V. 62

PHILLIPS, PAUL C.
The Fur Trade. Norman: 1961. V. 64; 67
Medicine in the Making of Montana. Missoula: 1962. V. 63

PHILLIPS, PHILIP A. S.
Paul de Lamerie Citizen and Goldsmith of London. London: 1935. V. 63

PHILLIPS, PHILIP LEE
A List of Geographical Atlases in the Library of Congress. 1996. V. 65
A List of Maps of America in the Library of Congress. 1967. V. 65

PHILLIPS, RICHARD
Four Dialogues Between an Oxford Tutor and a Disciple of the Common-Sense Philosophy, Relative to the Proximate Causes of Material Phenomena. London: 1824. V. 62; 65
A Letter to the Schoolmasters and Governesses of England and Wales, on the New Theories of Education, and On the Plans Under Legislative Consideration, for Reforming or Altering the Systems of Public Schools. London: 1835. V. 64
A Million of Facts, and Correct Data, in the Entire Circle of the Sciences, and On All Subjects of Speculation and Practice.... London: 1833?. V. 67
The Natural and Artificial Wonders of the United Kingdom.... London: 1825. V. 66

PHILLIPS, SAMPSON AND CO.
Catalogue of the Publications...with Indexes. Boston: 1856. V. 64

PHILLIPS, SANDRA
Helen Levitt. N.P: 1991. V. 63; 65

PHILLIPS, STEPHEN
Armageddon - a Modern Epic Drama in a Prologue Series of Scenes and an Epilogue Written Partly in Prose and Partly in Verse. London: 1915. V. 65
Christ in Hades. London: 1917. V. 62
The New Inferno. London: 1911. V. 66

PHILLIPS, T.
Lectures on the History and Principles of Painting. London: 1833. V. 66; 67

PHILLIPS, THOMAS
Wales; the Language, Social Condition, Moral Character, and Religious Opinions of the People, Considered in their Relation to Education.... London: 1849. V. 67

PHILLIPS, TOM
Lesbia Waltz. London: 1971. V. 66
The Sketches of Tom Phillips. Kansas City. V. 63; 66
Works Texts to 1974. Stuttgart: 1974. V. 63

PHILLIPS, W.
An Elementary Introduction to Mineralogy...Description of Minerals... and Especially Localities of British Minerals. London: 1819. V. 64
An Elementary Introduction to the Knowledge of Mineralogy. 1823. V. 62; 65; 66
An Elementary Treatise on Mineralogy: Containing the Latest Discoveries in American and Foreign Mineralogy. Boston: 1844. V. 65

PHILLIPS, W. S.
Indian Tales for Little Folks. New York: 1928. V. 67
Totem Tales. Indian Stories Indian Told. Gathered in the Pacific Northwest. Chicago: 1896. V. 66

PHILLIPS, W. W. A.
Manual of the Mammals of Ceylon. Colombo: 1933. V. 66
Manual of the Mammals of Ceylon. Colombo: 1935. V. 64; 66

PHILLIPS, WILLARD
The Inventor's Guide. Boston and New York: 1837. V. 63

PHILLIPS, WILLIAM
Eight Lectures on Astronomy, Intended as an Introduction to the Science, for the Use of Young Persons. London: 1820. V. 63

PHILLIPS, WILLIAM SANDFORD
Considerations on the Increase and Progress of Crime, Accompanied by Documentary Evidence as to the Propriety and Necessity of a Revision and Amendment of the Existing Penal Statutes. Liverpool: 1839. V. 66

PHILLPOTTS, EDEN
Brunel's Tower. New York: 1915. V. 66

PHIL MUSICO, PSEUD.
The Song Singer's Amusing Companion. Boston: 1818. V. 62

PHILO JUDAEUS
Lucubrationes Omnes Quotquot Haberi Potuerunt, Latinae ex Graecis Factae, per sigismundum Gelenium. Basiliae: 1561. V. 66
Lucubrationes Omnes Quotquot Haberi Potuerunt, Nunc Primum Latinae ex Graecis Factae.... Lyons: 1555. V. 64
Opera Quae Reperiri Potuerunt Omnia...Universa Notis and Observationibus Illustravit Thomas Mangey.... London: 1742. V. 65

THE PHILOSOPHIC Mirrour; or, General View of Human Oeconomy.... Dublin: 1759. V. 63

PHILOSOPHICAL SOCIETY OF MANCHESTER
Memoirs of the Literary and Philosophical Society of Manchester. Warrington: 1785-1790. V. 63

PHILOSTRATUS
The First Two Books, of Philostratus, Concerning the Life of Apollonius Tyaneus.... London: 1680. V. 66

PHIN, J.
Open Air Grape Culture. New York: 1862. V. 63; 64
Open Air Grape Culture. New York: 1876. V. 63

PHINNEY, MARY A.
Allen-Isham Genealogy, Jirah Isham Allen, Montana Pioneer, Government Scout, Guide, Interpreter and Famous Hunter During Four Years of Indian Warfare in Montana and Dakota. Rutland. V. 63

PHIPPS, E.
The Ferguson's; or Woman's Love and the World's Favor. London: 1839. V. 64

PHIPPS, HOWARD
Further Interiors: Wood Engravings by Howard Phipps. London: 1992. V. 65

PHIPSON, CECIL BALFOUR
The Redemption of Labour; or Free Labour Upon Freed Land. London: 1888-1892. V. 64

PHIPSON, E.
The Animal-Lore of Shakespeare's Time.... London: 1883. V. 62

PHISALIX, M.
Animaux Venimeux et Venins. Paris: 1922. V. 66

THE PHOENIX Bookshop: a Nest of Memories. Candia, New Haven: 1997. V. 65

PHOENIX BRIDGE CO.
Album of Designs of the Phoenix Bridge Company, Successors to Clarke, Reeves and Co. Phoenixville Bridge Works. Philadelphia: 1888. V. 65

PHOTOGRAMS of the Year 1903. London: 1903. V. 63

PHOTOGRAMS of the Year 1930. London: 1931. V. 63

PHOTOGRAMS of the Year 1934-1935. London: 1935. V. 63

THE PHOTOGRAPHER: From a Motion Picture about Edward Weston. Monterey: 1946. V. 63; 65

PHOTOGRAPHIC Handbook of the Antiquities of Worksop and Its Neighbourhood. Worksop: 1860. V. 65

PHRASE Book; or Idiomatic Exercises in English and Tamil. Jaffna: 1841. V. 63

THE PHYSICAL and Moral Condition of the Children and Young Persons Employed in Mines and Manufactures.... London: 1843. V. 64

PHYSICK, J. F.
Catalogue of the Engraved Work of Eric Gill. London: 1963. V. 65

PIAGET, E.
Les Pediculines. Leiden: 1880-1885. V. 65; 66

PIAGET, HENRY F.
The Watch; Its Construction, its Merits and Defects. New York: 1860. V. 64

PIAGET, JEAN
Recherche. Lausanne: 1918. V. 67

PIALLOUX, GEORGE
Maurice Ravel, Le Basque. 1994. V. 62

PIANKOFF, ALEXANDRE
The Shrines of Tut-Ankh-Amon. New York: 1955. V. 62

PIASSETSKY, PAVEL IAKOVLEVICH
Russian Travellers in Mongolia and China. London: 1884. V. 62

PIAZZETTA, GIOVANNI BATTISTA
Etudes de Peinture.... Venice: 1764. V. 64

PIC, JEAN
The Dream of Alcibiades. London: 1749. V. 66

PICABIA, FRANCIS
La Sainte-Vierge. Antwerp: 1993. V. 64; 65; 66

PICART, BERNARD
Ceremonies et Coutumes Religieuses de Tous les Peuples du Monde. Amsterdam: 1723-1743. V. 67
A New Drawing Book of Modes. London: 1733. V. 64
Les Peintures de Charles Le Brun et d'Eustache Le Sueur Qui sont Dans l'Hotel du Chastelet, cy Devant la Maison du President Lambert. Paris: 1740. V. 64

PICASSO, PABLO
The Blue and Rose Periods. A Ctalogue Raisonne of the Paintings 1900-1906. Greenwich: 1967. V. 64
Picasso Lithographe: Notices et Catalogue Etablis par Fernand Mourlot. I-IV. Monte Carlo: 1949-1964. V. 64

PICCOLOMINI, ALESSANDRO
Notable Discors en Forme De Dialogue Touchant La Vraye et Prafaicte Amitie Duquel Toutes Personnes & Principalement les Dames.... Lyon: 1577. V. 65

PICCOLPASSO, CIPRIANO
The Three Books of the Potter's Art. London: 1980. V. 67

PICHARD, M. E.
The Midwest Pioneer His Ills, Cures and Doctors. New York: 1946. V. 67

PICHON, JEROME, BARON
The Life of Count Hoym, Ambassador from Saxony-Poland to France and Eminent French Bibliophile 1694-1736. New York: 1899. V. 62

PICHON, THOMAS
Genuine Letters and Memoirs, Relating to the Natural, Civil and Commercial History of the Islands of Cape Breton and Saint John. London: 1760. V. 67

PICHOT, M. AMEDEE
Les Mormons. Paris: 1854. V. 67

PICKARD, MADGE E.
The Midwest Pioneer: His Ills, Cures and Doctors. New York: 1946. V. 63

PICKARD, TOM
High on the Walls. London: 1967. V. 63

PICKEN, ANDREW
The Dominie's Legacy: Consisting of a Series of Tales.... London: 1831. V. 67

PICKENELL, ANNIE
Pioneer Women in Texas. Austin: 1929. V. 66

PICKERING, CHARLES
Chronological History of Plants: Man's Record of His Own Existence Illustrated Through Their Names, Uses and Companionship. Boston: 1879. V. 65

PICKERING, H. G.
Angling or the Test of True Love Under Stress: Being a Diurnal Postulation of Problems of Connubial Infelicity Which Will Bring No Comfort to Any Married Male Angler. New York: 1936. V. 62; 63; 64; 66

PICKERING, HENRY
The Ruins of Paestum; and Other Compositions in Verse. (with) *Athens; and Other Poems.* Salem. 1822-1824. V. 62; 64

PICKERING, TIMOTHY
Instructions to the Envoys Extraordinary and Ministers Plenipotentiary from the United States.... Philadelphia: 1798. V. 63

PICKERING, WILLIAM
Catalogue of Biblical Classical and Historical Manuscripts and of Rare and Curious Books Including Spceimens of Caxton Pynson Wynkyn De Worde Fust and Schoiffer (sic) Aldus Jenson... English Chronicles.... London: 1834. V. 62; 64; 67

PICKET, A.
Picket's Juvenile Spelling Book or Analogical Pronouncer of the English Language. Wheeling: 1825. V. 63; 66

PICKETT, GEORGE E.
The Heart of a Soldier, as Revealed in the Intimate Letters of George E. Pickett. New York: 1913. V. 62; 63

PICKETT, LA SALLE CORBELL
Bugles of Gettysburg. Chicago: 1913. V. 65
What Happened to Me. New York: 1917. V. 63; 65

PICKTHALL, MARMADUKE
Brendle. London: 1905. V. 67
Knights of Araby. A Story of the Yaman in the Fifth Islamic Century. London: 1917. V. 66
Larkmeadow. A Novel of the Country Districts. London: 1912. V. 66
The Valley of the Kings. London: 1909. V. 66

PICKWICK'S Schooldays. London: 1890. V. 62

PICON, GAETAN
Surrealism 1919-1939. London: 1977. V. 62; 63; 64
Surrealists and Surrealism 1919-1939. New York: 1977. V. 62; 63; 64; 66

PICOT, GEORGES
Un Devoir Social et les Longements d'Ouvriers. Paris: 1885. V. 64

PICTON, THOMAS
Evidence Taken at Port of Spain, Island of Trinidad, in the Case of Luisa Calderon, under a Mandamus Issued by the Court of the King's Bench.... London: 1806. V. 65

PICTORIAL A B C for Good Children. New York: 1850. V. 62

THE PICTORIAL Handbook of London Comprising Its Antiquities, Architecture, Arts, Manufacture, Trade.... London: 1854. V. 65

PICTORIAL History of the County of Lancaster.... London: 1844. V. 65

PICTORIAL History of the Great Eastern Steam-ship. London: 1859. V. 64

THE PICTORIAL Museum of Animated Nature. London: 1860. V. 62

PICTORIAL Records of the English in Egypt.... London. V. 63

THE PICTURE Book, or Familiar Objects Described. 1840. V. 65

THE PICTURE Gallery Explored; or, an Account of Various Ancient Customs and Manners. London: 1824. V. 63

THE PICTURE Show: a Novel Picture Book for Children. London: 1895. V. 66

PICTURE Treasures for the Little Folks. London: 1895. V. 62

PICTURES and Biographies of Brigham Young and His Wives. Salt Lake City: 1896?. V. 66

PICTURES and Stories from Uncle Tom's Cabin. Boston: 1853. V. 64

PICTURES for Our Pets. London: 1872. V. 66

PICTURESQUE Excursions from Bridlington-Quay, Being a Descriptive Guide to the Most Interesting Scenery in that Neighbourhood. Bridlington: 1836. V. 64; 65; 66

PICTURESQUE Views of the Principal Seats of the Nobility and Gentry in England and Wales. London: 1786-1788. V. 64

PICUS DE MIRANDULA, JOHANNES
(Aureae Epistolae). Paris: 1500. V. 64

PIDGEON, WILLIAM
Traditions of Dee-Coo-Dah and Antiquarian Researches.... New York: 1853. V. 63

PIDGIN, CHARLES FELTON
The Chronicles of Quincy Adams Sawyer, Detective. 1912. V. 64; 66
The Chronicles of Quincy Adams Sawyer, Detective. Boston: 1912. V. 65

PIEPER, JOSEPH
The End of Time, a Meditation on the Philosophy of History.... London: 1954-1963. V. 66

PIERCE, B. K.
Audubon's Adventures or Life in the Woods. New York: 1889. V. 65

PIERCE, D. H.
Histories of Game Strains. N.P: 1927. V. 63; 67

PIERCE, EDWARD L.
A Treatise on the Law of Railroads. Boston: 1881. V. 65

PIERCE, F.
The Genitalia of the British Rhopalocera, and the Larger Moths. 1941. V. 62
The Genitalia of the Tineid Families of the Lepidoptera of the British Islands. 1935. V. 62

PIERCE, FRANK CUSHMAN
A Brief History of the Lower Rio Grande Valley. Menasha: 1917. V. 65

PIERCE, GEORGE WINSLOW
The Life Romance of an Algebraist. Boston: 1891. V. 66

PIERCE, GERALD S.
Texas Under Arms. Austin: 1969. V. 62; 67

PIERCE, HENRY H.
Report of an Expedition from Fort Colville to Puget Sound. Washington: 1883. V. 63

PIERCE, NEWTON B.
California Vine Disease. A Preliminary Report of Investigations. Washington: 1892. V. 66

PIERCE, PARKER I.
Antelope Bill. 1962. V. 67

PIERCE, RICHARD A.
H. M. S. Sulphur at California 1837 and 1839. San Francisco: 1969. V. 66

PIERCE the Ploughman's Crede. London: 1814. V. 67

PIERCE, WILLIAM HENRY
From Potlatch to Pulpit. Vancouver: 1933. V. 63

PIERCY, JOHN
The History of Retford, in the County of Nottingham. Retford: 1828. V. 65

PIERCY, MARGE
Breaking Camp. Poems. Middletown: 1968. V. 67

PIERS, HARRY
Master Goldsmiths and Silversmiths of Nova Scotia and Their Marks. Halifax: 1948. V. 63

PIERSON, B. T.
Directory of the City of Newark for 1841-1842, with a Historical Sketch. Newark: 1841. V. 63; 66

PIERSON, B. T. continued
Directory of the City of Newark for 1844-1845. Newark: 1844. V. 63; 66
Directory of the City of Newark for 1849-1850. Newark: 1849. V. 63; 66
Directory of the City of Newark for 1857-58. Newark: 1857. V. 63; 66
Directory of the City of Newark for 1858-1859. Newark: 1858. V. 66

PIERSON, DAVID LAWRENCE
History of the Oranges to 1921. New York: 1922. V. 63; 66

PIERSON, HAMILTON W.
In the Brush; or, Old-Time Social, Political and Religious Life in the Southwest. New York: 1881. V. 63

PIESSE, GEORGE WILLIAM SEPTIMUS
The Art of Perfumery. London: 1855. V. 62

PIGAFETTA, ANTONIO
Magellan's Voyage Around the World. Cleveland: 1906. V. 66
Magellan's Voyage. A Narrative Account of the First Circumnavigation. New Haven: 1969. V. 62
The Voyage of Magellan. The Journal of Antonio Pigafetta. Englewood Cliff: 1969. V. 66

PIGAL, EDME JEAN
Recueil de Scenes de Societe. Paris: 1822. V. 62; 67

PIGAULT-LEBRUN, CHARLES ANTOINE GUILLAUME PIGAULT DE L'EPNOY
My Uncle Thomas. A Romance. New York: 1810. V. 64

PIGGOTT, GEORGE WEST ROYSTON
On the Harrogate Spas, and Change of Air.... Churchill and Harrogate: 1856. V. 65
On the Harrogate Spas and Change of Air.... London: 1856. V. 64

PIGOT, R.
Twenty-Five Years Big Game Hunting. 1928. V. 63; 64; 66; 67
Twenty-Five Years Big Game Hunting. 1928. V. 63

PIGOTT, CHARLES
The Female Jockey Club, or a Sketch of the Manners of the Age. (with) The Female Jockey Club.... New York: 1794. V. 63
The Jockey Club; or a Sketch of the Manners of the Age. New York: 1793. V. 63

PIGOU, A. C.
The Economy and Finance of the War. London: 1916. V. 65
Industrial Fluctuations. London: 1927. V. 62
The Problem of Theism and Other Essays. London: 1908. V. 62

PIIS, AUGUSTIN
Chansons Nouvelles. Paris: 1785. V. 64

PIKE, ALBERT
Hymns to the Gods and Other Poems. Washington: 1872. V. 64; 67
Hymns to the Gods and Other Poems. Little Rock: 1916. V. 66
Lyrics and Love Songs. Little Rock: 1916. V. 66

PIKE, GUSTAVUS D.
Singing Campaign for Ten Thousand Pounds or the Jubilee Campaign for Ten Thousand Pounds or the Jubilee Singers in Great Britain. London: 1874. V. 64

PIKE, NICOLAS
The New Complete System of Arithmetic. Boston: 1802. V. 67

PIKE, SAMUEL
In an Evangelical Manner, at the Casuistical Lecture in Little St. Helen's Bishopgate Street...The Spiritual Companion, or the Professing Christian.... Savannah: 1826. V. 67

PIKE, W.
The Barren Ground of Northern Canada. 1892. V. 67
The Barren Ground of Northern Canada. New York: 1917. V. 66

PIKE, ZEBULON MONTGOMERY
An Account of Expeditions to the Sources of the Mississippi and through the Western Parts of Louisiana. San Francisco: 1947. V. 63
The Expeditions of Zebulon Montgomery Pike, To Headwaters of the Mississippi River, through Louisiana Territoy, and in New Spain, During the Years 1805-1806-1807. New York: 1895. V. 66; 67
Exploratory Travels - Pike's Explorations by the Order of the U. S. Government - to the Source of the Mississippi in 1805 through the Territory of Louisiana and Provinces of New Spain in 1806-1807. Denver: 1889. V. 65
The Journals of Zebulon Montgomery Pike. Norman: 1966. V. 63
Journals. With Letters and Related Documents. Norman: 1966. V. 64
The Southwestern Expedition of Zebulon M. Pike. Chicago: 1925. V. 65

PILCHER, LEWIS A.
A List of Books by Some of the Old Masers of Medicine and Surgery. Brooklyn: 1918. V. 64; 66

PILCHER, VELONA
The Searcher - a War Play. London: 1929. V. 63

PILES, ROGER DE
The Art of Painting, with Lives and Characters of ABove 300 of the Most Eminent Painters.... London: 1750?. V. 63; 67
Nouveau Traite D'Anatomie Accomodee Aux Arts de Peinture et de Sculpture.... Paris: 1799. V. 64

THE PILGRIM Fathers; a Journal of Their Coming in the Mayflower to New England and Their Life and Adventures There. Waltham St. Lawrence: 1939. V. 66

PILGRIM, G. E.
Catalogue of the Pontian Bovidae of Europe in the Department of Geology. London: 1928. V. 62

PILGRIM, THOMAS
Live Boys; or, Charley and Nasho in Texas. Boston: 1879. V. 66

PILKINGTON, JAMES
The Burnynge of Paules Church in London in the Yeare of Our Lord 1561 and the iiii day of June by Lyghtnynge, at Three of the Clocke, at After Noone.... London: 1563. V. 67

PILKINGTON, JOHN
The History of the Lancashire Family of Pilkington and its Branches from 1066 to 1600. Liverpool: 1894. V. 62

PILKINGTON, MARY
Tales of the Hermitage. London: 1798. V. 66
Tales of the Hermitage: in English and Italian. London: 1809. V. 65

PILKINGTON, MATTHEW
A Rational Concordance or an Index to the Bible. Nottingham: 1749. V. 66

PILKINGTON, MRS.
A Mirror for the Female Sex. London: 1798. V. 67

PILKINGTON, W.
A Natural and Chymical Treatise on Agriculture, by the Late Gustavus Gyllenorg. 1822. V. 65

A PILL to Purge State Melancholy, or a Collection of Excellent New Ballads. London: 1715. V. 63; 67

PILLET, R. L.
Warshawsky: les Impressions De Paris. Paris: 1948. V. 65

PILLET, RENE MARTIN
L'Angleterre Vue a Londres et dans ses Provinces, Pendant un Sejour de Dix Annees, Dont Six Somme Prisonnier de Guerre. Paris: 1815. V. 66

PILLET, ROGER
Les Oraisons Amoureuses de Jeanne Aurelie Grivolin Lyonnaise un Pauvre Amour. Paris: 1922. V. 64

PILLING, JAMES CONSTANTINE
Bibliography of the Algonquian Languages. Washington: 1891. V. 62

PILLSBURY, PARKER
Acts of Anti-Slavery Apostles. Concord: 1883. V. 65

PILSBRY, H. A.
The Aquatic Mollusks of the Belgian Congo. 1927. V. 62; 66
The Aquatic Mollusks of the Belgian Congo. New York: 1927. V. 65
Land Mollusca of North America. North of Mexico. Philadelphia: 1939-1948. V. 66
Review of Land Mollusca of the Belgian Congo. New York: 1919. V. 62; 63; 65

PIM, JONATHAN
The Condition and Prospects of Ireland and the Evils Arising from the Present Distribution of Landed Property.... Dublin: 1848. V. 65

PIMBLETT, W. MELVILLE
Story of the Soudan War. London: 1885. V. 63

PINART, ALPHONSE
Journey to Arizona in 1876. Los Angeles: 1962. V. 67

PINAULT, M.
The Painter as Naturalist, from Durer to Redoute. Paris: 1991. V. 63; 65

PINCHARD, ELIZABETH
The Blind Child, or Anecdotes of the Wyndham Family. London: 1791. V. 62

PINCHARD, MRS.
The Blind Child, or Anecdotes of the Wyndham Family. London: 1791. V. 66

PINCHBECK, IVY
Women Workers and the Industrial Revolution 1750-1850. London: 1930. V. 65

PINCHOT, GIFFORD
A Primer for Forestry. Washington: 1900. V. 63

PINCKARD, GEORGE
Notes on the West Indies: Written During the Expedition Under the Command of the Late General Sir Ralph Abercromby.... London: 1806. V. 67

PINCKNEY, CHARLES
Three Letters, Written and Originally Published Under the Signature of a South Carolina Planter. Philadelphia: 1799. V. 63

PINCKNEY, HENRY L.
Address to the Electors of Charleston District, South Carolina, on the Subject of Slavery. Washington: 1836. V. 64

PINCKNEY, JOSEPHINE
Sea-Drinking Cities. Poems. New York and London: 1927. V. 64; 67

PINDARUS
Carmina et Fragmenta. Oxonii: 1807. V. 65
The Pythian, Nemean and Isthmian Odes of Pindar. London: 1778. V. 66
Pythian Odes. London: 1927. V. 64
Pythian Odes. London: 1928. V. 63; 64

PINEDA, PEDRO
A Short and Compendious Method for the Learning to Speak, Read and Write the Spanish Language.... London: 1726. V. 62

PINEL, PHILLIPE
Traite Medico-Philosophique sur 'Alienation Mentale, ou la Manie. Paris: 1801. V. 65
Traite Medico-Philosophique sur l'Alienation Mentale. Paris: 1809. V. 65
A Treatise on Insanity, In Which are Contained the Principles of a New and More Practical Nosology of Maniacal Disorders Than Has Yet Been Offered to te Public.... Sheffield: 1806. V. 65

PINEL, SCIPION
Traite de Pathologie Cerebrale ou des Maladies du Cerveau.... Paris: 1844. V. 65

PINERA, VIRGILIO
Las Furias. Havana: 1941. V. 67

PINERO, ARTHUR WING
Iris - a Drama in Five Acts. London: 1902. V. 63
The Second Mrs. Tanqueray. London: 1895. V. 62; 66

PINETTE, J.
Theorie de l'escrime a La Baionette. Paris: 1848. V. 67

PINGET, ROGER
La Mainvelle - Piece Radiophonique. Paris: 1960. V. 65

PINGREE, E. M.
A Debate on the Doctrine of Universal Salvation: Held in Cincinnati, Ohio from March 24 to April 1, 1845. Cincinnati: 1848. V. 64

PINHEY, F. C. G.
Butterflies of Rhodesia, with a Short Introduction to the Insect World. Salisbury: 1949. V. 65

PINKERTON, A. FRANK
Saved at the Scaffold or Nic Brown the Chicago Detective. Chicago: 1888. V. 63

PINKERTON, ALLAN
Claude Melnotte as a Detective. 1875. V. 64; 66
The Expressman and the Detective. Chicago: 1874. V. 64
Thirty Years a Detective. 1886. V. 64; 66
Thirty Years a Detective, a Thorough and Comprehensive Expose of Criminal Practices of all Grades and Classes.... New York: 1886. V. 65

PINKERTON, JOHN
A Dissertation on the Origin and Progress of the Scythians or Goths. London: 1797. V. 62
The Medallic History of England. London: 1802. V. 62

PINKERTON, ROBERT
Russia; or, Miscellaneous Observations on the Past and Present State of that Country and Its Inhabitants. London: 1833. V. 64

PINKHAM, LYDIA
Lydia E. Pinkham's Private Text-Book. Lynn. V. 67

PINKS, WILLIAM
The History of Clerkenwell. London: 1880. V. 62

PINNER, ROBERT
Turkoman Studies I: Aspects of the Weaving and Decorative Arts of Central Asia. London: 1980. V. 65

PINNEY, JOEL
An Exposure of the Causes of the Present Deteriorated Condition of Health and Diminished Duration of Human Life.... London: 1830. V. 62

PINSENT, ROBERT JOHN
Newfoundland Our Oldest Colony. London: 1884. V. 64

PINSKY, ROBERT
An Explanation of America. Princeton: 1979. V. 62; 66
The Rhyme of Reb Nachman. Winnetka: 1998. V. 62; 66

PINTER, HAROLD
Betrayal. London: 1978. V. 62; 66
The Birthday Party. 1959. V. 65
The Birthday Party. London: 1959. V. 63; 66; 67
The Birthday Party and Other Plays. London: 1960. V. 66
The Caretaker. London: 1960. V. 62; 67
The Dwarfs. London: 1990. V. 62
Family Voices. London: 1981. V. 67
The French Lieutenant's Woman. A Screenplay. Boston & Toronto: 1981. V. 62; 67
The French Lieutenant's Woman. A Screenplay. London: 1981. V. 66
Monologue. London: 1973. V. 62
Plays: Four. Old Times, No Man's Land, Betrayal, Monologue, Family Voices. London: 1981. V. 67
Poems. London: 1968. V. 64; 66; 67
Poems. London: 1972. V. 67
The Room and the Dumbwaiter. London: 1970. V. 67

PINTO, EDWARD
Tunbridge and Scottish Souvenir Woodware. London: 1970. V. 64

PINTO DE AZEREDO, JOSE
Ensaios Sobre Algumas Enfermedades d'Angola. Lisbon: 1799. V. 62

PIONEER Trails and Trials, Madison County, Montana, 1863-1920. Great Falls: 1976. V. 62; 65

PIOZZI, HESTER LYNCH SALUSBURY THRALE
Anecdotes of the Late Samuel Johnson, LL.D. London: 1786. V. 62; 63
Autobiography, Letters and Literary Remains. London: 1861. V. 65; 67
British Synonymy; or, an Attempt at Regulating the Choice of Words in Familiar Conversation. London: 1794. V. 66
A Compleat Introduction to the Art of Writing Letters, Universally Adapted to All Classes and Conditions of Life.... London: 1758. V. 62
Dr. Johnson and Mrs. Thrale. Including Mrs. Thrale's Unpublished Journal of the Welsh Tour Made in 1774.... London and New York: 1910. V. 63
Johnsonia, a Collection of Miscellaneous Anecotes and Sayings. London: 1845. V. 62
Letters to and From the Late Samuel Johnson, LL.D. London: 1788. V. 66
Observations and Reflections Made In...a Journey through France, Italy and Germany. London: 1789. V. 66
Retrospection; or a Review of the Most Striking and Important Events, Characters, Situations and Their Consequences.... London: 1801. V. 63; 65; 67

PIP and Squeak Annual 1939. V. 67

PIPER, H. BEAM
Murder in the Gunroom. New York: 1953. V. 63

PIPER, JOHN
Brighton Aquatints. London: 1939. V. 62; 67
British Romantic Artists. London: 1942. V. 63
Catalogue of an Exhibition of Works by John Piper - at the Tate Gallery from 30th November 1983 - 22nd January 1984. London: 1983. V. 63
80th Anniversary Portfolio. 1983. V. 67
The Gaudy Saint, and Other Poems. Bristol: 1924. V. 62; 67
Grongar Hill. Hackney: 1982. V. 62; 67
Indian Love Poems. London: 1977. V. 62
The Jesse Tree. London: 1972. V. 62; 67
John Piper's Stowe. London: 1983. V. 62; 67
The Mountains. New York: 1968. V. 62; 67
Paintings, Drawings and Theatre Designs 1932-1954. London: 1955. V. 63

PIPER, MYFANWY
Reynolds Stone. London: 1951. V. 62

PIPPENGER, WESLEY E.
John Alexander, A Northern Neck Proprietor: His Family, Friends and Kin. Baltimore: 1990. V. 67

PIRANDELLO, LUIGI
A Character in Distress. London: 1938. V. 62

PIRANESI, GIOVANNI BATTISTA
Magnificenz Di Roma. Milano: 1961. V. 65

PIRKIS, CATHERINE LOUISA
In a World of His Own. London: 1878. V. 66

PIROVANO, GABRIELE
Defensio Astronomiae. Colophon Milan: 1507. V. 66

PIRSIG, ROBERT M.
Zen and the Art of Motorcycle Maintenance. New York: 1974. V. 62; 63; 65

PISO, WILLEM
De Indiae Utriusque re Naturali et Medica. Leyden: 1658. V. 62

PISSARRO, LUCIEN
Notes on the Eragny Press and a Letter to J. B. Manson. Cambridge: 1957. V. 67

PISTOFILO, BONAVENTURA
Opolmachia...Nella Quale Con Dottrina Morale, Politica, e Militare, e cöl Mezzo delle Figure si Tratta per Via di Teorica e di Practica del maneggio, e dell'vso delle Armi. Siena: 1621. V. 62

THE PISTOL As a Weapon of Defence in the House and on the Road. New York: 1875. V. 64; 66

PITCAIRN, ARCHIBALD
The Assembly; or, Scotch Reformation: a Comedy. Edinburgh: 1766. V. 62
The Whole Works. London: 1727. V. 62; 66

PITCAIRN, ROBERT
Uppingham School. London: 1870. V. 64

PITISCUS, BARTOLOMEO
Trigonometriae, sive de Dimensione Triangulorum Libri Quinque. Frankfurt: 1612. V. 66

PITKIN, TIMOTHY
A Statistical View of the Commerce of the United States of America.... Hartford: 1816. V. 67
A Statistical View of the Commerce of the United States of America.... Hartford: 1817. V. 65

PITMAN, BENN
The Assassination of President Lincoln and the Trial of the Conspirators. New York: 1865. V. 64

PITMAN, C. R. S.
A Game Warden Takes Stock. 1945. V. 67
A Guide to the Snakes of Uganda. Kampala: 1938. V. 66
A Guide to the Snakes of Uganda. 1974. V. 65

PITMAN, ISAAC
The Fonografic Correspondent for the Year 1850. London: 1850. V. 66
Phonography, or Writing by Sound. London: 1840. V. 63; 65
The Reporter; or, Phonography Adapted to Verbatim Reporting. Bath and London: 1846. V. 63

PITMAN, JOSEPH S.
Report of the Trial of Thomas Wilson Dorr, for Treason.... Providence: 1844. V. 62

PITRONE, JEAN MADDERN
The Dodges, the Auto Family Fortune and Misforutne. South Bend: 1981. V. 66

PITROU, ROBERT
Recueil de Differentes Projets d'Architecture de Charpente et Autres Concernant la Construction des Ponts. Paris: 1756. V. 65

PITT, JAMES
Instructions in Etiquette, Intended for the Use of Schools and Young Persons. London: 1840?. V. 64

PITT, JOHN
How to Brew Good Beer. London: 1859. V. 63

PITT, WILLIAM
Correspondence of William Pitt When Secretary of State with Colonial Governors and Military and Naval Commissioners in America. New York: 1906. V. 67
Letters Written by the Late Earl of Chatham to His Nephew Thomas Pitts.... Cambridge: 1805. V. 63
The Speech of the Right Hon. William Pitt, in the British House of Commons on Thursday Jan. 31, 1799. Dublin: 1799. V. 66

PITT, WILLIAM MORTON
A Plan for the Extension and Regulation of Sunday Schools.... London: 1789... V. 64

PITTENDRIGH, COLIN S.
Biology and the Exploration of Mars. Washington: 1966. V. 67

PITTER, RUTH
Collected Poems. Petersfield: 1990. V. 65
A Trophy of Arms: Poems 1926-1935. London: 1936. V. 62

PITTILOCH, ROBERT
Oppression Under the Colour of the Law.... Edinburgh: 1827. V. 62; 66

PITTIS, WILLIAM
Dr. Radcliffe's Life and Letters. London: 1716. V. 65
Dr. Radcliffe's Life and Letters. London: 1736. V. 64

PITTMAN, EDWARD F.
The Mineral Resources of New South Wales. 1901. V. 62

PITTMAN, PHILIP
The Present State of the European Settlements on the Mississippi. Cleveland: 1906. V. 65

PITT-RIVERS, A. H. L.
On the Development and Distribution of Primitive Locks and Keys. London: 1883. V. 62

PITT-RIVERS, GEORGE HENRY LANE FOX
The Clash of Culture and the Contact of Races. London: 1927. V. 63

PITTS, CHARLES F.
Chaplains in Gray. Nashville: 1957. V. 65

PIUS XI, POPE
Climbs on Alpine Peaks. 1923. V. 65

PIZZEY, G.
A Field Guide to the Birds of Australia. Princeton: 1980. V. 64

PLAN for a General Enclosure Bill, for Commons of a Limited Extent, In Which the Practicability and Advantages of Such a Bill Are Fully and Clearly Explained, and Some Further Improvements.... London: 1816. V. 65

A PLAN for the Establishment of a General System of Secular Education in the County of Lancaster. London: 1847. V. 66

PLANCHE, FREDERICK D'ARROS
Evening Amusements for Every One. Philadelphia: 1873?. V. 66

PLANCHE, JAMES ROBINSON
Beauty and the Beast: a Grand, Comic, Romantic, Operatic, Melodramatic Fairy Extravaganza. London: 1841. V. 65
Descent of the Danube from Ratisbon to Vienna, During the Autumn of 1827. London: 1828. V. 64
An Old Fairy Tale Told Anew. London: 1865. V. 64
Rudolph the Wolf; or Columbine Red Riding Hood: a Comic-Melodramatic Pantomime.... London: 1819. V. 65

PLANCHON, J. E.
Memoire sur la Famille des Guttiferes. Paris: 1862. V. 66

PLANCK, MAX
Das Princip der Erhaltung der Energie. Leipzig: 1887. V. 64
The Universe in th Light of Modern Physics. London: 1937. V. 65
Vorlesungen uber Thermodynamik.... Leipzig: 1897. V. 65

PLANS of Flower Gardens, Bed, Borders, Roseries and Aquariums, Accompanied by Rules and Directions for Their Formation, Descriptions of the Suitable Plants, Their Arrangement and Culture. London: 1868. V. 66

PLANT, ROBERT
History of Cheadle, in Staffordshire and Neighbouring Places, With Chapters on Croxden Abbey by Charles Lynam and the Cheadle Coal-Field.... Leek: 1881. V. 65

PLANTATION Wages Table, for Twenty-Six Working Days. New Orleans: 1869. V. 63

PLATEA, FRANCISCUS DE
Opus Restitutionum Usuratum Excommunicationum. Venice: 1474. V. 67

PLATH, IONA
The Decorative Arts of Sweden. 1948. V. 63

PLATH, SYLVIA
Ariel. London: 1965. V. 64; 65
The Bell Jar. London: 1963. V. 67
The Bell Jar. London: 1966. V. 65
Child. Exeter: 1971. V. 65
The Colossus. London: 1960. V. 62; 63; 64; 67
The Colossus and Other Poems. New York: 1962. V. 62; 64
Dialogue Over a Ouija Board - a View Dialogue. London: 1981. V. 63
Johnny Panic and the Bible of Dreams: Short Stories, Prose and Diary Extracts. New York: 1983. V. 65
Letters Home by Sylvia Plath. New York: 1975. V. 62
The Magic Mirror, a Study of the Double in Dostoevsky. 1989. V. 64
Two Poems. Knotting, Bedfordshire: 1980. V. 62
Uncollected Poems. London: 1965. V. 62
Winter Trees. London: 1971. V. 66

PLATINA, BARTOLOMEO
Historia.... 1626. V. 66
Hystoria de Vitis Pontificum Periucunda (and other works). Venetiis: 1504. V. 64
The Lives of the Popes from the Time of Our Saviour Jesus Christ to the Reign of Sixtus IV. London: 1685. V. 67

PLATO
The Apology of Socrates. London: 1929. V. 65
Crito: a Socratic Dialouge by Plato. Paris: 1926. V. 63; 64; 66
Dialogue. Oxford: 1771. V. 67
The Dialogues of Plato. Oxford: 1875. V. 65
Opera Quae Feruntur Omnia. Turici: 1839. V. 66
The Phaedo. Waltham St. Lawrence: 1930. V. 62; 66
Platonis Opera Mnia Quae Extant. Francofurti: 1602. V. 65
Plato's Symposium or Supper. London: 1925. V. 64
The Republic of Plato. London: 1898. V. 62
La Republica.... Venice: 1554. V. 63
The Trial and Death of Socrates. Verona: 1962. V. 63; 64; 66

PLATT, CHARLES
An Inquiry into the Efficacy of Oxygene, in the Cure of Syphilis.... London: 1802. V. 64

PLATT, P. L.
Traveler's Guide Across the Plains Upon the Overland Route to California. San Francisco: 1963. V. 63; 65; 66

PLATTER, FELIX
De Corporis Humani Structura et Usu. Basel: 1583. V. 64
Observationum, in Hominis Affectibus Plerisque, Corpori et Animo, Functionum Laesione, Dolore, Aliave Molestia & Vitio Incommodantibus, Libri Tres. Basel: 1614. V. 62; 64; 66

PLATTS, W. CARTER
Grayling Fishing. 1939. V. 63; 65
Modern Trout Fishing. London: 1938. V. 67

PLAUT, J. S.
Oskar Kokoschka. Boston: 1948. V. 62; 66
Steuben Glass: a Monograph. New York: 1948. V. 62; 65

PLAUTUS, TITUS MACCIUS
Comedies of Plautus.... London: 1769-1774. V. 66
Comoediae. Londini: 1847. V. 65
M. Acci Plauti Comoediae Superstites XX. Amstelodami: 1652. V. 66

PLAW, JOHN
Rural Architecture or Designs from the Simple Cottage to the Decorated Villa.... London: 1794. V. 64

THE PLAY Room; or, In-Door Games for Boys and Girls. New York: 1866. V. 65

PLAYFAIR, JOHN
Biographical Account of the Late Dr. James Hutton, F.R.S. Edinburgh: 1805. V. 65
The Works of John Playfair. Edinburgh: 1822. V. 65

PLAYFAIR, R. LAMBERT
A Bibliography of Algeria from the Expedition of Charles V in 1541 to 1887. 1999. V. 65
Handbook for Travellers in Algeria and Tunis. London: 1890. V. 62
Travels in the Footsteps of Bruce in Algeria and Tunis. London: 1877. V. 62

PLAYFAIR, WILLIAM
British Family Antiquity Illustrative of the Origin and Progress of the Rank, Honours and Personal Merit of the Nobility of the United Kingdom. 1809-1811. V. 64; 67
A Letter on Our Agricultural Distresses, Their Causes and Remedies. London: 1821. V. 67
A Treatise on the Science and Practice of Midwifery. London: 1876. V. 65

PLAYFORD, JOHN
Vade Mecum; or, the Necessary Companion. London: 1692. V. 66

PLAYFUL Pussy. London: 1917. V. 64

PLAYING The Harpsicord (sic), Spinnet or Piano Forte, Made Easy by New Instructions Wherein the Italian Manner of Fingering is Shewn by Variety of Examples.... London: 1775. V. 65

PLAYNE, ARTHUR TWISDEN
A History of the Parishes of Minchinhampton and Avening. Gloucester: 1915. V. 63

PLAYTHINGS ABC. London: 1910. V. 65

THE PLEADER'S Assistant; Containing a Select Collection of Precedents of Modern Pleadings, in the Courts of the King's Bench and Common Pleas, &c. 1795. V. 63

PLEASANTON, A. J.
The Influence of the Blue Ray of the Sunlight and of the Blue Colour of the Sky in Developing Animal and Vegetable Life, in Arresting Disease. Philadelphia: 1876. V. 65

PLEASANTS, W. J.
Twice Across the Plains 1849/1856. San Francisco: 1906. V. 66

PLEASE Tell Me Another Tale. 1890. V. 67

THE PLEASING Art of Money-Catching, and the Way to Thrive, by Turning a Penny to Advantage.... Falkirk: 1840. V. 62

PLENCK, JOSEPH JAKOB VON
Tratado de la Enfermedaes de los Ojois.... Cadiz: 1797. V. 66

PLESCH, A.
Botanical Library of Stiftung fur Botanik. London: 1975-1976. V. 63
The Magnificent Botanical Library of the Stiftung for Botanik. 1975-1976. V. 64; 66; 67

PLESCH, ARPAD
The Magnificent Botanical Library of the Stiftung Fur Botanik Collected by Arpad Plesch, Vaduz, Liechtenstein.... 1975. V. 62

PLETSCH, OSCAR
Schnick Schnack: Trifles for the Little Ones. London: 1867. V. 67

PLIMPTON, GEORGE
The Education of Shakespeare. New York: 1933. V. 64

PLIMPTON, SARAH
Single Skies. New York: 1976. V. 63

PLIMSOLL, SAMUEL
Our Seamen. An Appeal. London: 1873. V. 62

PLINIUS CAECILIUS SECUNDUS, C.
C. Plini Caecilii Secundi Epistolae et Panygyricus.... London: 1767. V. 65; 66
C. Plinii Caecilii Secundi Novocomensis Epistolarum Libri Decem.... Lugduni: 1547. V. 65
C. Plinni Caecilii Secundi, Novocomens. Epistolarum Lib X. Paris: 1533. V. 65
Epistolae et Panegyricus. Parisiis: 1788. V. 64; 66
Epistolarum Libri Decem (and other works). Basilea: 1521. V. 64; 66
Epistolarum Libri X. London: 1790. V. 66
The Letters of Pliny the Consul.... London: 1747. V. 65; 67
The Letters of Pliny the Younger: with Observations on Each Letter; and an Essay on Pliny's Life. London: 1751. V. 66; 67

PLINIUS SECUNDUS, C.
Des Wytheroemden Booch. Arnheim: 1610. V. 63; 66
Histoire de la Peinture Ancienne, Extraite de l'Histoire Naturelle de Pline Liv. XXXV. London: 1725. V. 65; 66
Historiae Mundi Libri XXXVII.... Basiliae: 1554. V. 66
The Historie of the World. 1634. V. 66
The Historie of the World. Commonlie Called the Natural History. London: 1601. V. 62
The Historie of the World Commonly Called the Natural Historie of C. Plinius Secundus. London: 1635-1634. V. 64
The Letters of Pliny the Counsul; with Occasional Remarks.... London: 1747. V. 64
Natura Historiarum Libri XXXVII, e Castigationibus Hermolae Barbari Quam Emendatissime Editi.... Hageneau: 1518. V. 62
Naturalis Historie Libri XXXVI. Paris: 1516. V. 62; 64; 66

PLOKKER, J. H.
Artistic Self-Expression in Mental Disease. 1964. V. 66
The Artistic Self-Expression in Mental Disease: The Shattered World of Schizophrenics. London: 1964. V. 65

PLOMER, HENRY RAUP
Wynkyn de Worde and His Contemporaries from the Death of Caxton to 1535. London: 1925. V. 62; 64

PLOMER, WILLIAM
Address Given at the Memorial Service for Ian Fleming. London: 1964. V. 65
Cecil Rhodes. London: 1933. V. 65
A Choice of Ballads. London: 1960. V. 67
Collected Poems. London: 1960. V. 62
Conversation with My Younger Self. Ewelme: 1963. V. 62
The Fivefold Screen. London: 1932. V. 64
Museum Pieces. London: 1952. V. 63
They Never Come Back. New York: 1932. V. 66
Turbott Wolfe. London: 1925. V. 64

PLOOS VAN AMSTEL, CORNELIA
Aanleiding Tot de Kennis der Anatomie, in Tekenkunst, Betreklyk Tot Het Menschbeeld. Amsterdam: 1783. V. 64

PLOT, ROBERT
The Natural History of Oxfordshire. Oxford: 1677. V. 66
The Natural History of Oxfordshire. Oxford: 1705. V. 62; 65
The Natural History of Stafford-shire. Oxford: 1686. V. 63
The Natural History of Stafford-Shire. 1973. V. 65

PLOUCQUET, HERRMAN
The Comical Creatures of Wurtemburg, Including the Story of Reynard the Fox. London: 1851. V. 63

PLOUGHMAN, WILLIAM
Brewer at Romsey. Romsey: 1800. V. 62

PLOUGHSHARE, JAN, PSEUD.
The Royal Progress to Maidstone. Rochester: 1800. V. 62

PLOWDEN, EDMOND
An Exact Abridgment of the Commentaries, or Reports of the Learned and Famous Lawyer Edmond Plowden, an Apprentice of the Common Law. London: 1659. V. 65

PLOWMAN, GEORGE T.
Etching and Other Graphic Arts: an Illustrated Treatise. New York: 1922. V. 65

PLUCHE, NOEL ANTOINE
The History of the Heavens, Considered According to the Notions of the Poets and Philosophers.... London: 1740. V. 64
Spectacle de la Nature; or Nature Display'd. London: 1737. V. 64

PLUES, MARGARET
Rambles: In Search of Flowerless Plants. London: 1864. V. 64
Rambles in Search of Flowerless Plants. London: 1865. V. 67

PLUMIER, CHARLES
L'Art de Tourner, ou de Faire en Perfection Toutes Sortes d'Ouvrages au Tour. Paris: 1706. V. 65
L'Art de Tourner, ou de Faire en Perfection Toutes Sortes d'Ouvrages au Tour. Leipzig: 1776. V. 62; 66

PLUMMER, CAROLUS
Vitae Sanctorum Hiberniae. 1910. V. 63

PLUMMER, CHARLES
Bethada Naem Nerenn: Lives of the Irish Saints. 1968. V. 66
Vitae Santicorum Hiberniae. 1910. V. 66

PLUMMER, J.
The Last Flowering. French Painting in Manuscripts 1420-1530. New York and London: 1982. V. 62

PLUNKETT, JOSEPH MARY
The Poems. London: 1916. V. 66

PLUNKETT GREENE, H.
Where the Bright Waters Meet. 1924. V. 62; 63; 65; 67

PLUTARCHUS
Alcuni Opusculetti de la Cose Morali del Divino Plutarco. Ventia: 1559. V. 63
Alcuni Opusculi de le Cose Morali del Divino Plutarco.... Venetia: 1567. V. 67
Apothegmato. London: 1741. V. 65
De Placitis Philosophorum Libri V. Latine Reddidit Recensuit... Edvardus Corsinus.... Florentia: 1750. V. 66
The Lives of the Noble Grecians and Romaines.... London: 1612. V. 62
The Lives of the Noble Grecians and Romanes. Oxford: 1928. V. 64
The Lives of the Noble Grecians and Romanes. London: 1929. V. 62; 64; 66
The Lives of the Noble Grecians and Romanes. London: 1929-1930. V. 62
The Lives of the Noble Grecians and Romanes.... London: 1933. V. 63
(Greek title) Moralia Opuscula, Multis Mendarum Milibus Expurgata. Basle: 1542. V. 62; 65
Les Oeuvres Morales de Plutarque.... Paris: 1606. V. 65
Plutarch's Lives. Boston: 1859. V. 66
Plutarch's Morals. London: 1704. V. 64
Plutarch's Morals. London: 1718. V. 67
Vitae Comparatae Illustrium Viriorum Graecorum & Romanorum. Lvgdvni: 1566. V. 63

PLYMLEY, JOSEPH
General View of the Agriculture of the County of Shropshire; with Observations. London: 1803. V. 63

THE PLYMOUTH County Directory, and Historical Register of the Old Colony.... Middleboro: 1867. V. 64

PLYMOUTH INSTITUTION
Summary of the Proceedings of the Plymouth Institution, with a List of the Lectures from the Commencement to the Present Time. Plymouth: 1833. V. 63

PLYMPTON, A. G.
The Glad Year Round for Boys and Girls. Boston: 1882. V. 64

POAGUE, WILLIAM THOMAS
Gunner with Stonewall. Jackson: 1957. V. 62; 63

THE POCKET Companion; or, Every Man His Own Lawyer. Philadelphia: 1819. V. 62

THE POCKET Navigator, Consisting of a Collection of the Most Select Voyages. London: 1808. V. 65

POCOCK, LEWIS
A Catalogue of the Unique Collection of Johnsoniana, Formed with Great Care and Indefatigable Zeal by Lewis Pocock, F.S.A. London: 1875. V. 62

POCOCK, NICHOLAS
Records of the Reformation. The Divorce 1527-1533. Oxford: 1870. V. 63; 67

POCOCK, ROGER
Following the Frontier. New York: 1903. V. 65

POCOCK, W. F.
Architectural Designs for Rustic Cottages, Picturesque Dwellings, Villas &c.... London: 1823. V. 67

PODMORE, FRANK
Robert Owen: a Biography. London: 1923. V. 64

POE, EDGAR ALLAN
Arthur Gordon Pym. London: 1898. V. 64; 66
The Complete Works of Edgar Allan Poe. New York: 1902. V. 62
The Conchologist's First Book; or a System of Testaceous Malacology.... Philadelphia: 1839. V. 62; 64
Edgar Allan Poe Letters Till Now Unpublished. Philadelphia: 1925. V. 62; 64
Erstaunliche Geschichte und Unheimliche Begebenheiten. (Tales). Stuggart: 1859. V. 63; 64
Eureka: a Prose Poem, an Essay on the Material and Spiritual Universe. San Francisco: 1991. V. 62
The Fall of the House of Usher. Paris: 1928. V. 64
The Fall of the House of Usher. N.P: 1985. V. 62; 63; 64; 66
Histoires Extraordinaires. Paris: 1856. V. 65
The Journal of Julius Rodman. San Francisco: 1947. V. 66
The Murders in the Rue Morgue. 1895. V. 64
The Murders in the Rue Morgue. Antibes: 1958. V. 62
The Narrative of Arthur Gordon Pym. 1838. V. 63
The Narrative of Arthur Gordon Pym. London: 1838. V. 64
The Narrative of Arthur Gordon Pym. New York: 1838. V. 64; 67
Poems. New York: 1872. V. 64
Poems d'Edgar Poe. Bruxelles: 1888. V. 62; 63; 64
The Poetical Works. London: 1859. V. 65
The Poetical Works. London: 1860. V. 62; 64
The Poetical Works. New York: 1912. V. 64
The Poets and Poetry of America. 1887. V. 64
Prose Tales of Mystery and Imagination. New York: 1903. V. 65
The Raven. New York: 1845. V. 62
The Raven. Louisville: 1871. V. 66
The Raven and the Pit and the Pendulum. London: 1899. V. 63; 64; 67
The Raven: Together with the Philosophy of Composition. New York: 1930. V. 67
Selections from Marginalia. Pittsburgh: 1930. V. 66
Tales. New York: 1845. V. 63; 64
The Tales and Poems. London: 1884. V. 63; 64
The Tales and Poems of.... Philadelphia: 1895-1905. V. 62
Tales and Sketches. London: 1852. V. 62
Tales of Mystery and Imagination. London: 1919. V. 62; 65; 67
Tales of Mystery and Imagination. New York: 1923. V. 64
Tales of Mystery and Imagination. London: 1928. V. 64
Tales of Mystery, Imagination and Humour and Poems. London: 1852. V. 67
Tamerlane and Other Poems. London: 1884. V. 62
Tamerlane and Other Poems. San Francisco: 1923. V. 62; 63; 64; 66
The Works. New York: 1850-1856. V. 64
The Works. London: 1896. V. 65

POE, JOHN W.
Billy the Kid - Notorious New Mexico Outlaw. Los Angeles: 1923. V. 63; 66
The Death of Billy the Kid. Boston: 1933. V. 64; 67

POE, SOPHIE A.
Buckboard Days. Caldwell: 1936. V. 66

A POEM Inscribed to a Friend: To Which is Added an Ode. London: 1769. V. 63

POEMS.. Berkeley: 1969. V. 62; 64

POEMS by Wotton, Raleigh and Others. London: 1857. V. 62

POEMS, Chiefly Lyrical from Romances and Prose-Tracts of the Elizabethan Age.... London: 1890. V. 67

POEMS Fit for a Bishop; Which Two Bishops Will Read. London: 1780. V. 65

POEMS for Roy Fuller on His Seventieth Birthday. Oxford: 1982. V. 67

POEMS for Alan Hancox. Andoversford: 1993. V. 64; 65
POEMS for Alan Hancox. Lower Marston: 1993. V. 63

POEMS from the Virginia Quarterly Review 1925-1967. Charlottesville: 1969. V. 62

POEMS of Death. London: 1945. V. 65

POEMS on Affairs of the State: from the Time of Oliver Cromwell, to the Abdication of K. James the Second. London: 1697. V. 63

POEMS Selected and Printed by a Small Party of English, Who Made This Amusement a Substitute for Society.... Strasburg: 1792. V. 62

THE POETICAL Magazine; or, Temple of the Muses...Chiefly of Original Poems. London: 1804. V. 66

POETRY from Oxford in Wartime. London: 1945. V. 62

POETRY of the Anti-Jaocbin. London: 1801. V. 62

THE POETRY Quartos. New York: 1929. V. 62

POETS of Today VII: Presenting James Dickey, Paris Leary and Jon Swain. New York: 1960. V. 64

POET'S CLUB
The Second Book of the Poet's Club. London: 1911. V. 63

POETS of Tomorrow - Third Selection. London: 1942. V. 62

THE POET'S Pack of George Washington High School by Members of the Poetry Club and the Poetry Class 1927-1931. New York: 1932. V. 63

POEY, F.
Ictiologia Cubana. Havana: 1962. V. 65

POGANY, WILLY
Willy Pogany's Oil Painting Lessons. New York: 1954. V. 62

POGGI, MAURO
Alfabeto Di Lettere Iniziali...Incise Dall' Abate Lorenzo Lorenzi. Florence: 1730. V. 62

POHANKA, BRIAN C.
Nelson A. Miles, a Documentary Biography of His Military Career 1861-1903. Glendale: 1985. V. 67

POHARNOK, ZOLTAN
A Real Balaton Story. N.P: 193-. V. 64

POHL, FREDERIK
Drunkard's Walk. 1960. V. 64; 66
The Feast of All Saints. 1979. V. 64
Gateway. Norwalk: 1988. V. 63; 64
Man Plus. 1976. V. 64; 66
Rogue Star. London: 1972. V. 62; 66
Search the Sky. 1954. V. 66
The Space Merchants. 1953. V. 64; 66
The Space Merchants. London: 1955. V. 64
Star Science Fiction Stories. No. 2. 1953. V. 62
Undersea City. New York: 1958. V. 66

POINSETT, JOEL R.
Defence of the Western Frontier. Washington: 1840. V. 64

POINSINET, ANTOINE ALEXANDER
Tom Jones, Comedie Lyrique.... Paris: 1778. V. 65

POINSTO, LOUIS
Theorie Nouvelle de la Rotation des Corps. Paris: 1852. V. 67

POINTER, JOHN
Miscellanea in Usum Juventis Academicae.... Oxford: 1718. V. 64
Miscellanea in usum Juventiutis Academicae.... London: 1718. V. 66

POINTS of Humour. London: 1823-1824. V. 66

POKAGAON, SIMON
O'gi-Maw-Kwe Mit-I-Gwa-Ki (Queen of the Woods). Hatford: 1901. V. 65

POL, B. VAN DER
Operrational Calculus Based on the Two-Sided LaPlace Integral. Cambridge: 1950. V. 67

POLAND, J.
Traumatic Separation of the Epiphyses. London: 1898. V. 67

POLE, REGINALD
De Summo Pontifice Christi in Terris Vicario, Eiusque Officio & Potestate.... Louanii: 1569. V. 62

POLE, WILLIAM
The Life of Sir William Siemens, F.R.S. London: 1888. V. 62

POLEHAMPTON, ARTHUR
Kangaroo Land. London: 1862. V. 67

POLEJAEFF, N.
Challenger Voyage. Zoology. Part 24. Calcarea. 1883. V. 66
Challenger Voyage. Zoology. Part 31. Keratosa. 1884. V. 66

POLEMON
Physionomia e Graeco in Latinum Versa per Carolum Montecuccolum.... Mutinae: 1612. V. 65

POLENI, GIOVANNI
Memorie Istoriche Della Gran Cupola del Tempio Vaticano, e de' Danni Di Essa, e De' Ristoramenti Loro, Divise in Libri Cinque. Padua: 1748. V. 64; 65

POLICHINELLE Prenant ses Vacances. Paris: 1845?. V. 63

POLIDORI, FRANCESCO
Il Losario. Poema Eroico. romanzesco di Ser Francesco Polidori. Firenze: 1851. V. 63

POLIGNAC, MELCHIORIS DE, CARDINAL
Anti-Lucretius, Sive de Deo et Natura...Opus Posthulum.... Paris: 1747. V. 64

POLITI, LEO
Little Pancho. New York: 1938. V. 63
Piccolo's Prank. New York: 1965. V. 63
Song of the Swallows. New York: 1949. V. 65

POLITICAL and Moral Justice or, the Principles of a Free Government, Supported by the Highest Authorities. Boston?: 1808. V. 64; 67

A POLITICAL Dialogue Between a Whig and an Intelligent Radical Reformer. Leeds: 1822. V. 63

POLITICAL Dialogues Between the Celebrated Statues of Pasquin and Masorio at Rome. London: 1736. V. 63

POLITICAL Dictionary; Forming a Work of Universal Reference, Both Constitutional and Legal.... London: 1845-1846. V. 64

POLITICAL Essays; the Result of Occaional Reflections on the Times. By a Patriotic Observer. London: 1808. V. 67

THE POLITICAL History of Europe or a Faithful and Exact Relation of the Present State of the Church and Religion, Public Affairs, the War, Maritime Affairs and Learning.... London: 1697. V. 67

THE POLITICS of 1837, by an Old Reformer, Respectfully Addressed to Viscount Melbourne. London: 1837. V. 67

POLIZIANO, ANGELO
Stanze di Messer Angelo Politiano Cominciate per la Giostra del Magnifico Giuliano di Piero de Medici. Venice: 1541. V. 65

POLLARD, ALFRED W.
Shakespeare's Fight with the Pirates and the Problems of the Transmission of His Text. London: 1917. V. 63

POLLARD, EDWARD A.
La Cause Perdue, Histoire de la Guerre des Confederes. New Orleans: 1867. V. 67
The First Year of the War. Richmond: 1862. V. 62; 63; 65
The Lost Cause: a New Southern History of the War of the Confederates. New York: 1866. V. 64; 67
The Lost Cause Regained. New York: 1868. V. 63
Observations in the North: Eight Months in Prison and On Parole. Richmond: 1865. V. 62; 63; 65

POLLARD, H. B. C.
Automatic Pistols. 1920. V. 62; 63; 66; 67
Book of the Pistol and Revolver. 1917. V. 62; 63; 64; 66; 67
British and American Game Birds. 1945. V. 66; 67
British and American Game Birds. London: 1945. V. 62
Game Birds, Rearing, Preservation and Shooting. London: 1929. V. 64; 67
Game Birds and Game Bird Shooting. Boston: 1936. V. 67
The Gun Room Guide. 1930. V. 62; 63; 67
Wildfowl and Waders. London: 1928. V. 67

POLLARD, JOHN G.
Code of Virginia as Amended to Adjournment of General Assembly 1904. St. Paul: 1904. V. 66

POLLARD, JOSEPH
The Land of the Monuments. London: 1898. V. 64

POLLARD, PERCIVAL
Masks and Minstrels of New Germany. Boston: 1911. V. 67

POLLEN, THOMAS
The Fatal Consequences of Adultery, to Monarchies as Well as to Private Families.... London: 1772. V. 63

POLLEY, JOSEPH BENJAMIN
A Soldier's Letters to Chamring Nellie. New York: 1908. V. 62; 63; 65

POLLNITZ, KARL LUDWIG, BARON
Les Amusemens de Spaw; or, the Gallentries of the Spaw in Germany... Virtues of Every Spring.... London: 1745. V. 66

POLLOCK, A. J. O.
Sporting Days in Southern India. 1894. V. 66; 67

POLLOCK, FREDERICK
The History of English Law: Before the Time of Edward. Cambridge: 1895. V. 67

POLLOCK, JOHN
The Grass Beneath the Wire. London: 1966. V. 63

POLLOCK, SIMON O.
The Russian Bastille. Chicago: 1908. V. 64

POLLOCK'S The Battle of Waterloo. London: 1920. V. 62

POLLOK, ROBERT
The Course of Time, a Poem. New York: 1833. V. 66

POLLUX, JULIUS
Iulii Pollucis Onomasticon, Decem Libris Constans...Adiecta Interpretatio Latina Rodolphi Gualthori...(Studio Atque Opera Wolfgangi Seberi) Frankfurt: 1608. V. 66
Vocabularium (in Greek...). Venice: 1502. V. 62; 63

POLO, MARCO
The Book of Ser Marco Polo, the Venetian.... London: 1903. V. 63
The Most Noble and Famous Travels...Together with the Travels of Nicolo de' Conti. 1929. V. 65

POLUNIN, O.
Flowers of Europe, a Field Guide. London: 1969. V. 67

POLWHELE, RICHARD
Poems, Chiefly by Gentlemen of Devonshire and Cornwall. Bath: 1792. V. 65

POLYAK, S.
The Vertebrate Visual System.... Chicago: 1957. V. 63

POLYBIUS
The General History of Polybius in Five Books. London: 1756. V. 67
The History of Polybius the Megalopolitan. London: 1634. V. 62
Polybii Megalopitani Historiarum Libri Priores Quinque, Nicolae Perotto Episcopo Sipontino.... Basiliae: 1549. V. 65

POMEROY, LAURENCE
The Grand Prix Car 1906-1939. London: 1949. V. 66

POMEROY, MARK M.
Life and Public Services of Benjamin F. Butler, Major-General in the Army and Leader of the Republican Party. New York: 1868. V. 62

POMET, PIERRE
A Compleat History of Drugs. London: 1712. V. 65
A Compleat History of Drugs. London: 1725. V. 66
A Compleat History of Drugs. 1748. V. 66
A Compleat History of Drugs. London: 1748. V. 65

POMFRET, JOHN
Miscellany Poems on Several Occasions. London: 1702. V. 65

POMFRET, JOHN E.
Province of West New Jersey 1609-1702. Princeton: 1956. V. 67

POMME, PIERRE
Traite des Affections Vaporeuses des Deux Sexes.... Lyon: 1763. V. 65

POMONA
The Proposed Long Term General Plan for the City of Pomona. Pomona: 1956. V. 65

POMONA Fire Department Souvenir. Los Angeles: 1903. V. 65

POMPADOUR, JEANNE ANTOINETTE POISSON, MARQUISE DE
Catalogue des Livres de la Bibliotheque de Feue Madame la Marquise de Pompadour, Dame du Palais de la Reine. Paris: 1765. V. 62
Memoires de Mme. La Marquise de Pompadour. (with) Lettres de Madame La Marquise de Pomadour, Depuis 1746 jusqu'a 1752.... Liege: 1768. V. 67
Memoirs of the Marchioness of Pompadour. London: 1766. V. 63

POMPDORO, GIOVANNI
La Geometria Prattica...Cauata da gl'Elementi d'Euclide.... Moneta: 1667. V. 63

POND, FRED E.
The Life and Adventures of Ned Buntline with Ned Buntline's Anecdotes of Frank Forester and Chapter of Angline Sketches. New York: 1919. V. 66

POND, JAMES B.
Eccentricites of Genius. New York: 1900. V. 63; 64; 66
Eccentricities of Genius. London: 1901. V. 63

POND, JOHN
The Sporting Kalendar. London: 1753. V. 67

PONENTE, NELLO
The Structures of the Modern World 1850-1900. Geneva: 1965. V. 63

PONIATOWSKA, ELENA
Lilus Kikus. Mexico City: 1954. V. 67

PONICSAN, DARRYL
The Last Detail. New York: 1970. V. 63

PONSONBY, EMILY
Katherine and Her Sisters. London: 1861. V. 65

PONSONBY, FREDERICK
The Grenadier Guards in the Great War of 1914-1918. London: 1920. V. 62

PONSONBY, GEORGE
The Speech...on the Question Relative to the Privileges of the House of Commons, as Connected with the Commital of Sir Francis Burdett, and Gale Jones. London: 1810. V. 63

PONSONBY, JOHN
The Ponsonby Family. 1929. V. 62

PONSOT, MARIE
True Minds. San Francisco: 1956. V. 67

PONTEY, WILLIAM
The Forest Pruner, or Timber Owner's Assistant. Huddersfield: 1805. V. 62; 63; 66
The Forest Pruner; or, Timber Owner's Assistant: a Treatise on... British Forest Trees.... London: 1808. V. 62; 64
The Profitable Planter. Huddersfield: 1808. V. 64

PONTING, HERBERT G.
The Great White South or With Scott in the Antarctic. London: 1932. V. 62
In Lotus-Land Japan. London New York: 1922. V. 63; 65; 66

PONTING, TOM CANDY
Life of Tom Candy Ponting an Autobiography. Evanston: 1952. V. 63; 64; 66

PONTIO, PIETRO
Dialogo...ove si Tratta della Theorica e Prattica di Musica. Parma: 1595. V. 62; 65

PONTIS, LOUIS DE
Memoirs of the Sieur de Pontis.... London: 1694. V. 67

PONTOPPIDAN, ERICH
The Natural History of Norway. London: 1755. V. 62; 63; 64; 65; 66

POOL, J. LAWRENCE
Acoustic Nerve Tumors. Early Diagnosis and Treatment. Springfield: 1970. V. 66; 67
The Early Diagnosis and Treatment of Acoustic Nerve Tumors. Springfield: 1957. V. 67
Izaak Walton. The Compleat Angler and His Turbulent Times. London: 1976. V. 67
The Neurological Institute of New York 1909-1974. 1975. V. 64; 66
The Neurosurgical Treatment of Traumatic Paraplegia. Springfield: 1951. V. 64; 66; 67

POOLE, BRAITHWAITE
The Commerce of Liverpool. London: 1854. V. 64

POOLE, ERNEST
His Family. New York: 1917. V. 62

POOLE, GEORGE
Churches of Yorkshire. Leeds: 1854. V. 64; 65; 66

POOLE, JOHN H.
American Cavalcade: a Memoir on the Life and Family of DeWitt Clinton Poole. Pasadena: 1939. V. 67

POOLE, MATTHEW
Annotations Upon the Holy Bible. London: 1696. V. 67
A Dialogue Between a Popish Priest and an English Protestant. London: 1676. V. 67
Synopsis Criticorum Aliorumque S. Scripturae Interpretum. London: 1669-1676. V. 67

POOLE, MONICA
The Wood Engravings of John Farleigh. London: 1985. V. 62

POOR, HENRY VARNUM
Money and its Laws: Embracing a History of Monetary Theories, and a History of the Currencies of the United States. New York: 1877. V. 66

POOR, M. C.
Denver South Park and Pacific, a History of the Denver South Park and Pacific Railroad and Allied Narrow Gauge Lines of the Colorado and Southern Railway Company. Denver: 1949. V. 66

POORE, GEORGE VIVIAN
Essays on Rural Hygiene. London: 1893. V. 67

POORTENAAR, JAN
De Papierwereld. Naarden: 1951. V. 64

THE POP-UP Pinocchio. New York: 1932. V. 64

POPA, VASKO
Kora. Belgrade: 1953. V. 67
The Little Box. Washington;: 1970. V. 65

POPE, ALEXANDER
The Dunciad. London: 1729. V. 62; 65
An Epistle...to Dr. Arbuthnot. London: 1734. V. 63
An Essay on Man. London: 1748. V. 62
An Essay on Man To Which are Added the Universal Prayer and Other Valuable Pieces.... New York: 1825. V. 63
A Key to the Lock. London: 1715. V. 62
Letters of Mr. Alexander Pope, and Several of His Friends. London: 1737. V. 67
Letters of Mr. Pope. And Several Eminent Persons, from 1705-1711. and From the Year 1711.... London: 1735. V. 63
Miscellaneous Poems and Translations. By Several Hands. London: 1714. V. 66
Of the Characters of Women: an Epistle to a Lady. London: 1735. V. 62; 65
Poetical Miscellanies: the Sixth Part. London: 1709. V. 64
The Poetical Works. Glasgow: 1785. V. 62; 65
Pope's Own Miscellany. London: 1935. V. 63; 67
The Rape of the Lock. London: 1714. V. 62
A Select Collection of Poems, viz. An Essay on Man An Essay on Criticism, The Messiah &c. Together with an Account of the Life of the Author. New London: 1796. V. 66
The Universal Prayer. London: 1738. V. 62; 65
The Works. London: 1737-1741. V. 66
The Works. London: 1752. V. 65
The Works. London: 1754. V. 62
The Works. London: 1766. V. 64
Works. London: 1788. V. 65
Works. London: 1822. V. 64
The Works. London: 1847. V. 63
The Works. London: 1860. V. 62

POPE, ARTHUR UPHAM
A Survey of Persian Art. Sopa: 1981. V. 62

POPE, C. H.
The Reptile World, a Natural History of the Snakes, Lizards, Turtles and Crocodilians. New York: 1955. V. 67

POPE, CLIFFORD H.
The Reptiles of China, Turtles, Crocodilians, Snakes, Lizards. New York: 1935. V. 62; 65; 66

POPE, DUDLEY
Buccaneer. London: 1981. V. 64
The Great Gamble. London: 1972. V. 62
Ramage - a Novel. London: 1965. V. 65
Ramage and the Drum Beart - a Novel. London: 1967. V. 65

POPE, FRANKLIN LEONARD
Evolution of the Electric Incandescent Lamp. Elizabeth: 1889. V. 62

POPE, JESSIE
Bobbity Flop. London: 1920. V. 67
Chuckles. A Picture Book with Verses by Jessie Pope. V. 67
Jessie Pope's War Poems. London: 1915. V. 64
Punch and Judy. London and Melbourne: 1930. V. 65
The Teddy Bear Scouts. London: 1910. V. 63

POPE, JOSEPH
The Tour of Their Royal Highnesses, The Duke and Duchess of Cornwall and York through the Dominion of Canada in the Year 1901. Ottawa: 1903. V. 65

POPE, SAXTON T.
The Medical History of Ishi. Berkeley: 1920. V. 62

POPE, SIMEON
A Letter to the Right Hon. William Curtis, Lord Mayor of the City of London, on the National Debt and Resources of Great Britain.... London: 1796. V. 65

POPE, WALTER
The Wish. London: 1710. V. 65

POPE, WILLIAM F.
Early Days in Arkansas - Being for the Most Part the Personal Recollections of an Old Settler. Little Rock: 1895. V. 65

POPE-HENNESSY, UNA
Charles Dickens 1812-1817. London: 1945. V. 62

POPENOE, P.
The Date Palm. Coconut Grove: 1973. V. 64; 66

POPEYE.. New York: 1937. V. 64

POPEYE and the Pirates. New York: 1945. V. 63

POPEYE: The Fighting Sailor Man. Racine: 1937. V. 65

POPEYE'S Cruise. London. V. 65

POPHAM, ARTHUR
Stalking Game from Desert to Tundra. Clinton: 1985. V. 65

POPOFICH, JOHN A.
The Voice of the Curlew. J. K. Ralston's Story of His Life. N.P: 1986. V. 64

POPOVICH, P.
Orbits of Peace and Progress. Moscow: 1988. V. 67

POPPE, CARL
Sammlung von Ornamenten und Fragmenten Antiker Architectur, Sculptur Mosaik und Toreutik.... Berlin: 1845. V. 62

POPPE, J. H. M.
Neuer Wunder-Schauplatz der Kunste Und Interessantesten Erscheinungen.... Stuttgart: 1839. V. 64

POPPER, KARL
Conjectures and Refutations: the Growth of Scientific Knowledge. New York: 1962. V. 64
The Open Society and Its Enemies. London: 1966. V. 63

POPPING, J. F.
Orbis Illustratus seu Nova Historico-Politico-Geographica, Imperiorum Rerumque Publicarum per Totum Terrarum Orbem, Descriptio.... Razeburg: 1668. V. 66

POPPLE, WILLIAM
The Lady's Revenge. London: 1734. V. 65

POPULAR Encyclopaedia or Conversations Lexicon. London: 1877. V. 63; 66

PORCACCHI, TOMASSO
Fvnerali Antichi di Diuersi Popoli, et Nationi. Venice: 1574. V. 64

PORCACCHI, TOMMASO
Funerali Antichi di Diversi Popoli, et Nationi: Forma, Ordine, et Pompa di Sepolture, di Essequie, di Consecrationi Antiche et d'Altro.... Venice: 1591. V. 63

PORCHER, FRANCIS PEYRE
Resources of the Southern Fields and Forests, Medical, Economical and Agricultural. Charleston: 1863. V. 63; 65
Resources of the Southern Fields and Forests, Medical, Economical and Agricultural.... Charleston: 1869. V. 63

PORCHIA, ANTONIO
Voices. Cosigny: 1977. V. 64

PORCHIER, JEAN
Medieval French Miniatures. New York: 1955. V. 62

PORPHYRIUS
Philosophi Pythagorici de Abstinentia ab Animalibus Necandis. Libri Quatuor. Cambridge: 1655. V. 65

PORPHYRY
Select Works of Porphyry. London: 1823. V. 63; 64

PORSON, RICHARD
Adversaria. Cantabrigiae: 1812. V. 62

PORTA, GIOVANNI BATTISTA DELLA
Magiae Naturalis sive de Miraculis Rerum Naturalium Libri IIII. Lyon: 1561. V. 64
Natural Magick.... London: 1669. V. 63

PORTAL, ABRAHAM
Nuptial Elegies. London: 1774. V. 66

PORTAL, ANTOINE
Historie de L'Anatomie et De la Chirurgie, Contenant L'Origine & Les Progres des Principales Decouvertes, & un Catalogue des Ouvrages d'Anatomie & de Chirurgie, des Memories Academiques.... Paris: 1770-1773. V. 64

PORTAL, GERALD HERBERT
My Mission to Abyssinia. London: 1892. V. 62

PORTER, ALEXANDER
A Check to Methodism, in Reply to James E. Glenn, Elder of the Methodist Church. Augusta: 1814. V. 64

PORTER, ANNA MARIA
Don Sebastian; or, the House of Braganza. London: 1809. V. 65
The Fast of St. Magdalen, a Romance. London: 1818. V. 64
The Fast of St. Magdalen, a Romance. London: 1819. V. 65
Honor O'Hara. London: 1826. V. 65
The Knight of St. John, a Romance. London: 1818. V. 65
The Lake of Killarney, a Novel. London: 1804. V. 65
The Recluse of Norway. London: 1814. V. 65
Roche-Blanche; or, the Hunters of the Pyrenees. London: 1822. V. 65

PORTER, BURTON B.
One of the People, His Own Story. N.P: 1907. V. 62; 65

PORTER, CLYDE
Matt Field on the Santa Fe Trail. Norman: 1960. V. 63; 64; 66

PORTER, COLE
Red Hot and Blue. A Musical Comedy. New York: 1936. V. 63

PORTER, DAVID
An Exposition of the Facts and Circumstances Which Justified the Expedition to Foxardo, and the Consequences Thereof. Washington: 1825. V. 62
Journal of a Cruise Made to the Pacific Ocean...in the United States Frigate Essex in the Years 1812, 1813 and 1814. Philadelphia: 1815. V. 64

PORTER, EDWIN H.
The Fall River Tragedy. Fall River: 1893. V. 65

PORTER, ELIOT
American Places. New York: 1981. V. 63; 64; 66
Antarctica. New York: 1978. V. 64
Birds of North America. New York: 1972. V. 67
Forever Wild: the Adirondacks. New York: 1966. V. 67
Galapagos. The Flow of Wilderness. San Francisco: 1968. V. 63
In the Wildness is the Preservation of the World. San Francisco: 1962. V. 62
The Place No One Knew. N.P: 1966. V. 62

PORTER, EUGENE O.
San Elizario: a History. Austin: 1973. V. 63

PORTER, FRANK THORPE
Gleanings and Reminiscences. Dublin: 1875. V. 67

PORTER, GENE STRATTON
Birds of the Bible. Cincinnati: 1909. V. 67
Let Us Highly Resolve. Garden City: 1927. V. 65
Michael O'Halloran. Garden City: 1915. V. 62; 64; 67
Music of the Wild. Cincinnati: 1910. V. 63
Music of the Wild. Garden City: 1911. V. 65

PORTER, GEORGE RICHARDSON
The Cabinet Cyclopaedia (General Title). A Treatise on the Origin, Progressive Improvement and Present State of the Silk Manufacture. Philadelphia: 1832. V. 64
The Progress of the Nation, In Its Various Social and Economical Relations from the Beginning of the 19th Century. 1847. V. 62; 67
The Progress of the Nation, In Its Various Social and Economical Relations, from the Beginning of the Nineteenth Century. London: 1851. V. 64
A Treatise on the Origin, Progressive and Present State of the Silk Manufacture. Philadelphia: 1832. V. 63
A Treatise on the Origin, Progressive, Improvement and Present State of the Manufacture of Porcelain and Glass. London: 1832. V. 62; 66
A Treatise on the Origin, Progressive Improvement and Present State of the Silk Manufacture. London: 1831. V. 63; 66

PORTER, JANE
Coming Out; and the Field of the Forty Footsteps. London: 1828. V. 65
Duke Christian of Luneburg; or, Tradition from the Hartz. London: 1824. V. 65
The Pastor's Fire-side, a Novel. London: 1817. V. 65
The Pastor's Fire-Side, a Novel. London: 1849. V. 63
The Scottish Chiefs. London: 1811. V. 62; 65
The Scottish Chiefs. London: 1820. V. 65
The Scottish Chiefs. Exeter: 1834. V. 63
The Scottish Chiefs. New York: 1921. V. 63; 64
Thaddeus of Warsaw. London: 1803. V. 64
Thaddeus of Warsaw. London: 1804. V. 65
Thaddeus of Warsaw. Boston: 1809. V. 63

PORTER, JOHN W. H.
Record of Events in Norfolk County, Virginia, from April 19th 1861 to May 10th 1862. Portsmouth: 1892. V. 62; 63

PORTER, KATHERINE ANNE
A Christmas Story. New York: 1967. V. 62; 64
The Collected Essays and Occasional Writings.... New York: 1970. V. 63; 64; 66
The Days Before. New York: 1952. V. 64
Flowering Judas. New York: 1930. V. 67
Flowering Judas. New York: 1936. V. 63; 64; 66
Hacienda. New York: 1934. V. 62; 64
Katherine Anne Porter's French Song-Book. Paris: 1933. V. 62; 64
The Leaning Tower and Other Stories. New York: 1944. V. 62; 67
Pale Horse, Pale Rider. New York: 1939. V. 62; 64; 67

Ship of Fools. Boston and Toronto: 1962. V. 63; 66

PORTER, KENNETH W.
John Jacob Astor: Business Man. Cambridge: 1931. V. 67

PORTER, LUTHER H.
Wheels and Wheeling. Boston: 1892. V. 64

PORTER, MILLIE JONES
Memory Cups of Panhandle Pioneers. Clarendon: 1945. V. 66

PORTER, NOAH
Commending the Gospel to the Conscience, a Sermon, Delivered at the Ordination of Noah Porter, Jun. to the Pastoral Care of the First Church of Christ in New Milford, April 27, 1836. New Haven: 1836. V. 65
The Human Intellect: with an Introduction Upon Psychology and the Soul. New York: 1868. V. 62; 64

PORTER, ROBERT KER
A Narrative of the Campaign in Russia During the Year 1812. Hartford: 1814. V. 62
A Narrative of the Campaign in Russia During the Year 1812. Hartford: 1815. V. 63
Travelling Sketches in Russia and Sweden During the Years 1805, 1806, 1807, 1808. Philadelphia: 1809. V. 65
Travelling Sketches in Russia and Sweden During the Years 1805, 1806, 1807, 1808. London: 1813. V. 64

PORTER, ROBERT P.
Report of Indians Taxed and Not Taxed in the United States. Washington: 1894. V. 63; 66

PORTER, VALERIE
Cattle, a Handbook to the Breeds of the World. 1991. V. 67

PORTER, WILLIAM D.
State Sovereignty and the Doctrine of Coercion...Together with a Letter from Hon. J(ames) K(irke) Paulding.... Charleston: 1860. V. 62
Washington Light Infantry of Charleston, S.C. Charleston: 1873. V. 62

PORTER, WILLIAM H.
Billy Porter's Clown Songster. Lancaster: 1871. V. 65

PORTER, WILLIAM SYDNEY
Cabbages and Kings. New York: 1904. V. 63; 67
The Gift of the Magi. London: 1939. V. 62; 64
Waifs and Strays. Garden City: 1917. V. 67
Whirligigs. New York: 1910. V. 62

PORTER, WILLIAM WARREN
Engravings from Drawings of.... London: 1806. V. 67

PORTER, WILLIS
Flight Identification of European Raptors. 1974. V. 67

PORTERFIELD, WILLIAM
A Treatise on the Eye. Edinburgh: 1759. V. 67
A Treatise on the Eye, the Manner and Phaeonomena of Vision. Birmingham: 1987. V. 63

PORTEUS, BEILBY
Sermons on Several Subjects. London: 1784. V. 66

PORTLAND, DUKE OF
Fifty Years and More of Sport in Scotland, Deerstalking, Salmon Fishing, Grouse Shooting and Other Pleasant Memories 1880-1932. London: 1933. V. 64
The Red Deer of Langwell and Braemore. 1935. V. 63; 64

PORTLOCK, J. E.
Report on the Geology of the County of Londonderry, and Parts of Tyrone and Fermanagh. Dublin: 1843. V. 62; 64; 65; 66

PORTLOCK, NATHANIEL
A Voyage Round the World, but More Particularly to the North-West Coast of America. London: 1789. V. 64; 67
A Voyage Round the World; but More Particularly to the North-West Coast of America. New York: 1968. V. 66

PORTRAIT and Biographical Album of Barry and Eaton Counties, Michigan. Chicago: 1891. V. 67

PORTRAIT and Biographical Album of Gratiot County, Michigan. Chicago: 1884. V. 67

PORTRAIT and Biographical Album of Ingham and Livingston Counties. Chicago: 1891. V. 67

PORTRAIT and Biographical Record of Denver and Vicinity Colorado. Chicago: 1898. V. 66

PORTRAIT and Biographical Record of Hunterdon and Warren Counties, New Jersey. New York: 1898. V. 66

PORTRAIT and Biographical Record of Leavenworth, Douglas and Franklin Counties, Kansas. Chicago: 1899. V. 65

PORTRAIT Biographical Album of Ionia and Montcalm Counties, Michigan. Chicago: 1891. V. 63

PORTRAITS and Lives of Remarkable and Eccentric Characters. London: 1819. V. 65

PORTRAITS of Principal Reformers of the Sixteenth Century. New York: 1836. V. 66

PORTRAITS of the Presses of Fleece, Gregynog, I. M. Imprimit, Old Stile, Rampant Lions, Rocket, Tern, Whittington & CTD. Herefordshire: 1997. V. 64

PORVENSEN, ALICE
My Little Hen. New York: 1973. V. 65

PORZIO, SIMONE
Se L'Hvomo Diventa Bvono o Cattivo Volontariamente. Florence: 1551. V. 62

POSNER, DAVID
A Rake's Progress - a Poem in Five Sections. London: 1967. V. 64; 66

POSSELIUS, JOANNES
Calligraphia Oratoria Linguae Graecae, ad Propietatem, Elegantiam, et Copiam Graeci Sermonis Parandam Utilissima.... Hanoviae: 1609. V. 66

POST, C. C.
Driven from Sea to Sea; or Just a Campin'. Philadelphia: 1889. V. 65
Ten Years a Cowboy. Chicago: 1898. V. 65

POST, CHANDLER R.
A History of Spanish Painting. Cambridge: 1930-1938. V. 64

POST, EMILY
Etiquette: The Blue Book of Social Usage.... New York: 1937. V. 63

POST, G. E.
Flora of Syria, Palestine and Sinai. Beirut: 1896. V. 62
Flora of Syria, Palestine and Sinai. Beirut: 1932-1933. V. 62

POST, ISAAC
Voices from the Spirit World, Being Communications from Many Spirits. Rochester: 1852. V. 63

POST, MARK
My Little Coon Book. London: 1910. V. 62

POST, MELVILLE DAVISSON
Monsieur Jonquelle. New York: 1923. V. 66
The Revolt of the Birds. New York: 1927. V. 67
The Silent Witness. 1930. V. 64; 66
The Strange Schemes of Randolph Mason. New York: 1896. V. 67
Walker of the Secret Service. 1924. V. 66

THE POST Office Directory of Lincolnshire. 1876. London: 1876. V. 63

THE POST Office Directory of North and East Ridings of Yorkshire and the City of York. London: 1872. V. 63

THE POST Office Directory of the Counties of Cambridge, Norfolk and Suffolk. London: 1879. V. 66

POST Roads of Europe. London: 1820. V. 63

POSTERITY: Its Verdicts and Methods, or Democracy A.D. 2100. London: 1897. V. 63

POSTERS in Miniature. New York: 1896. V. 63

POSTGATE, RAYMOND
The Good Food Guide 1951-1952. London: 1951. V. 63

POSTL, KARL
Life in the New World; or Sketches of American Society. New York: 1844. V. 65
Nathan, der Squatter-Regulator, Oder der Erste Amerkaner in Texas. Stuttgart: 1843. V. 66

POSTLETHWAITE, JOHN
The Geology of the English Lake District With Notes on the Minerals. Keswick: 1897. V. 64
The Geology of the English Lake District with Notes on the Minerals. Carlisle: 1906. V. 64; 65
Mines and Mining in the (English) Lake District. Whitehaven: 1913. V. 65; 66

POSTLETHWAITE, T. N.
Some Notes on Urswick Church and Parish. Ulverston: 1906. V. 66

POSTLETHWAYT, MALACHY
The Universal Dictionary of Trade and Commerce. London: 1751-1755. V. 64

POSTON, CHARLES D.
Apache Land. San Francisco: 1878. V. 67

POTE, JOSEPH
The History and Antiquities of Windsor Castle, and the Royal College, and Chapel of St. George with the Institution, Laws and Ceremonies of the Most Noble Order of the Garter, Including Several Foundations in the Castle, from their First Establishment to. Eton: 1749. V. 66

POTOCKI, JOSEPH
Sport in Somaliland. 1988. V. 67

POTOK, CHAIM
The Chosen. New York: 1967. V. 62; 65; 67

THE POTOMAC Muse, by a Lady, a Native of Virginia. Richmond: 1825. V. 62; 67

POTT, PERCIVAL
The Chirurgical Works. London: 1779. V. 64; 66
Further Remarks on the Useless State of the Lower Limbs in Consequence of a Curvature of the Spine.... London: 1782. V. 65
Some Few General Remarks on Fractures and Dislocations. London: 1769. V. 66; 67
A Treatise on Ruptures. London: 1756. V. 62; 66

POTTER, ALONZO
The School and the Schoolmaster. New York: 1842. V. 66

POTTER, BEATRIX
Appley Dapply's Nursery Rhymes. London: 1917. V. 62
The Complete Tales of Beatrix Potter. London: 1989. V. 64; 67
Fairy Caravan. New York: 1951. V. 64
The Journal of Beatrix Potter from 1881 to 1897. London: 1966. V. 64; 65; 66
Peter Rabbit. Cleveland: 1920. V. 65
Peter Rabbit. Cleveland: 1930. V. 63
Peter Rabbit. Racine: 1947. V. 65
The Peter Rabbit Gift Box. New York: 1921. V. 63
Peter Rabbit's Almanac for 1929. London: 1928. V. 63
The Pie and The Patty-Pan. London: 1905. V. 62; 63
The Story of a Fierce Bad Rabbit. London: 1906. V. 62; 64
The Story of Miss Moppet. London: 1906. V. 63; 64
The Story of Peter Rabbit. Racine: 1922. V. 65
The Tailor of Gloucester. London: 1902. V. 63
The Tailor of Gloucester. London: 1903. V. 62
The Tailor of Gloucester. London: 1968. V. 64
The Tale of Benjamin Bunny. New York: 1904. V. 65
The Tale of Jemima Puddle-Duck. London: 1908. V. 63; 65; 67
The Tale of Johnny Town-Mouse. London: 1919. V. 67
The Tale of Little Pig Robinson. London: 1930. V. 63
The Tale of Little Pig Robinson. London: 1940. V. 63
The Tale of Mr. Tod. London: 1912. V. 63; 65
The Tale of Mrs. Tittlemouse. London: 1910. V. 63; 64
The Tale of Mrs. Tittlemouse. New York: 1910. V. 63; 65
The Tale of Peter Rabbit. London: 1902. V. 65
The Tale of Peter Rabbit. London: 1904. V. 66
The Tale of Peter Rabbit. Philadelphia: 1907. V. 63
The Tale of Peter Rabbit. Akron: 1916. V. 64
The Tale of Peter Rabbit. New York: 1927. V. 63
The Tale of Peter Rabbit. New York: 1928. V. 65
The Tale of Peter Rabbit. Akron: 1942. V. 63
The Tale of Peter Rabbit. New York: 1995. V. 64
The Tale of Pigling Bland. London: 1913. V. 63; 64
The Tale of Squirrel Nutkin. London: 1903. V. 63; 65
The Tale of Timmy Tiptoes. London: 1911. V. 62; 63; 64; 65; 66
The Tale of Tom Kitten. London: 1907. V. 62; 63; 67
Wag-by-Wall. Boston: 1944. V. 64

POTTER, DAVID M.
Trail to California, The Overland Journal of Vincent Geiger and Wakeman Bryarly. New Haven: 1945. V. 67

POTTER, DENNIS
Son of Man - a Play. London: 1970. V. 65

POTTER, ELAM
The Author's Account of His Conversion and Call to the Gospel Ministry: Being an Apology for His Itinerant Preaching. Boston: 1772. V. 66

POTTER, FRANCIS
An Interpretation of the Number 666. Oxford: 1642. V. 63; 65; 66; 67

POTTER, JACK
Cattle Trails of the Old West. Clayton: 1925. V. 63
Cattle Trails of the Old West. Clayton: 1939. V. 62; 64; 65; 66; 67

POTTER, JOHN
Archaeologia Graeca, or The Antiquities of Greece. Edinburgh: 1820. V. 65

POTTER, MARY KNIGHT
The Art of the Venice Academy. Boston: 1906. V. 63

POTTER, MAUD
The Willises of Virginia. Mars Hill: 1968. V. 67

POTTER, SIDNEY PELL
A History of Wymeswold (Leicestershire). London: 1915. V. 66

POTTER, STEPHEN
Pedigree: Words from Nature, Essays on Etymology of Words from Nature. London: 1973. V. 62; 64

POTTER, THOMAS
Concrete: Its Use in Building and the Construction of Concrete Walls, Floors, Etc. London: 1894. V. 62

POTTER, W. R., MRS.
History of Montague County. Austin: 1912. V. 64; 67

POTTER, W. W.
History of Barry County. Grand Rapids: 1912. V. 66

POTTER, WOODBURNE
The War in Florida.... Baltimore: 1836. V. 63

POTTINGER, HENRY
Travels in Beloochistan and Sinde.... London: 1816. V. 62

POTTS, CHARLES SOWER
Nervous and Mental Diseases: a Manual for Students and Practioners. Philadelphia: 1900. V. 65

POU-ROU: an Historical and Critical Enquiry into the Physiology and Pathology of Parliaments. Dublin: 1787. V. 67

POUCHER, W. A.
Lakeland Scrapbook. 1950. V. 63
The Magic of Skye. London: 1949. V. 62
The Magic of the Dolomites. London: 1951. V. 63

POUCHET, FELIX ARCHIMEDE
Recherches et Experiences sur les Animaux Ressuscitants. Paris: 1859. V. 65

POUILLY, LOUIS JEAN LEVESQUE DE
The Theory of Agreeable Sensations; in Which the Laws Observed by Nature in the Distribution of Pleasure are Investigated.... London: 1774. V. 66

POULAIN DE NOGENT, MADEMOISELLE
Lettres de Madame la Comtesse de la Riviere a Madame la Baronne de Neufpont, son Amie.... Paris: 1776. V. 66

POULLAIN DE LA BARRE, FRANCOIS
De L'Egalite des Deux Sexes Discours Physique et Moral ou l'on Voit l'Importance de se Defaire des Prejugez. Paris: 1673. V. 66
De L'Egalite des Deux Sexes, Discourses Physique et Moral. (with) De L'Excellence Des Hommes.... Paris: 1679. V. 65

POULSON, GEORGE
The History and Antiquities of the Seigniory of Holderness, in the County of York.... London: 1840-1841. V. 62

POULTNEY, EVAN
An Appeal to the Creditors of the Bank of Maryland, and the Public Generally. Baltimore: 1835. V. 64

POULTON, EDWARD B.
The Colours of Animals. New York: 1890. V. 63

POUNCY, JOHN
Dorsetshire Photographically Illustrated. London: 1857. V. 64

POUND, ARTHUR
The Turning Wheel, The Story of General Motors through Twenty-Five Years 1908-1933. Garden City: 1934. V. 63

POUND, EZRA LOOMIS
ABC of Reading. London: 1934. V. 62
Antheil and the Treatise on Harmony. Paris: 1924. V. 62; 64; 65
Antheil and the Treatise on Harmony. Chicago: 1927. V. 64
An Autobiographical Outline. New York: 1980. V. 67
Canto CX. Paris: 1967. V. 63
The Cantos (1-95). New York: 1956. V. 64
Cantos LII-LXXI. London: 1940. V. 65
Cantos LXXII & LXXIII. Milano: 1983. V. 64; 67
The Cantos of Ezra Pound. London: 1954. V. 63
The Cantos of Ezra Pound. London: 1964. V. 63
Canzoni. London: 1911. V. 64; 67
Cathay. London: 1915. V. 62; 64; 65
Cavalcanti Poems. 1966. V. 65
Certain Noble Plays of Japan: from the Manuscripts of Ernest Fenollosa.... Dundrum: 1916. V. 64
The Classic Anthology Defined by Confucius. Cambridge: 1954. V. 62
Confucius: the Unwobbling Pivot and the Great Digest. N.P: 1947. V. 63; 64; 66
De Moribus Brachmanorum: Liber Santo Ambrosio Falso Adscriptus. Milan: 1956. V. 66
Des Imagistes. An Anthology. New York: 1914. V. 64
Diptych Rome-London. Homage to Sextus Propertius & Hugh Selwyn Mauberley. London: 1957. V. 62; 64; 65; 67
A Draft of Cantos XXXI-XLI. London: 1935. V. 65
A Draft of XXX Cantos. Paris: 1930. V. 64
A Draft of XXX Cantos. London: 1933. V. 63; 65; 67
A Draft of XXX Cantos. New York: 1933. V. 64
Drafts & Fragments of Cantos CX-CXVII. New York: 1968. V. 62; 64; 66; 67
Drafts and Fragments of Cantos CX-CXVII. London and Iowa City: 1968-1969. V. 65
Drafts and Fragments of Cantos CX-CXVII. 1969. V. 62
Drafts and Fragments of Cantos CX-CXVII. New York: 1969. V. 65
Eleven New Cantos XXXI-XLI. New York: 1934. V. 67
Etre Citoyen Romain Etait un Privilege. Etre Citoyen Moderne est une Calamite. Liege: 1965. V. 66
Exultations. London: 1909. V. 64
Ezra Pound in Italy, from the Pisan Cantos: Spots and Dots. Venice: 1970. V. 66
The Fifth Decad of Cantos. 1937. V. 62
Forked Branches. Iowa City: 1985. V. 64; 67
Gaudier-Brzeska. London: 1916. V. 67
Guide to Kulchur. London: 1952. V. 62
Homage to Sextus Propertius: a Poem. London: 1934. V. 62; 64; 65; 67
Hugh Selwyn Mauberley by E. P. London: 1920. V. 63; 64
Imaginary Letters. Paris: 1930. V. 62; 63; 64; 65; 67
Indiscretions; or, Une Revue De Deux Mondes. Paris: 1923. V. 64
Instigations of Ezra Pound. Together with An Essay on the Chinese Written Character by Ernest Fenollosa. New York: 1920. V. 64
The Letters of Ezra Pound 1907-1941. London: 1941. V. 62; 66
The Letters of Ezra Pound 1907-1941. London: 1951. V. 64
Literary Essays of Ezra Pound. New York: 1954. V. 62
Lustra. London: 1916. V. 62; 64; 65; 67
Lustra of Ezra Pound with Earlier Poems. New York: 1917. V. 64
Make It New: Essays. London: 1934. V. 64
Noh or Accomplishment: a Study of the Classical Stage of Japan. London: 1916. V. 64; 67
Pavannes and Divisions. New York: 1918. V. 64; 65
Personae. London: 1909. V. 62; 64; 67
Personae. New York: 1926. V. 62; 64
Personae. London: 1952. V. 66
The Pisan Cantos. London: 1949. V. 64; 67
Poems 1918-1921. New York: 1921. V. 62; 64
Provenca. Boston: 1910. V. 62; 64
Quia Pauper Amavi. London: 1919. V. 62; 64; 67
Ripostes of Ezra Pound. Boston: 1913. V. 64
Ripostes. Whereto are appended the Complete Poetical Works of T. E. Hulme. London: 1915. V. 62; 65
Section: Rock Drill 85-95 de los Cantares. Milan: 1955. V. 62; 65
Selected Poems. London: 1928. V. 64; 66
A Selection of Poems. London: 1940. V. 66
Seventy Cantos. London: 1950. V. 62; 66
The Sonnets and Ballate of Guido Cavalcanti. Boston: 1912. V. 67
The Spirit of Romance: an Attempt to Define Somewhat the Charm of the Pre-Renaisance Literature of Latin Europe. London: 1910. V. 62; 64; 67
Ta Hio. The Great Learning. Seattle: 1928. V. 62; 64
Ta Hio: the Great Learning. London: 1936. V. 67
The Translations of Ezra Pound. London: 1953. V. 66
Umbra. The Early Poems of Ezra Pound. London: 1920. V. 62; 64; 65; 66; 67
What is Money For?. London: 1939. V. 64

POUND, WILLIAM
Remarks Upon the Best Mode of Carrying Out a National Education. London, Oxford & Cambridge: 1868. V. 63

POURADE, RICHARD F.
Anza Conquers the Desert: the Anza Expeditions from Mexico to California and the Founding of San Francisco, 1874 to 1876. San Diego: 1971. V. 64

POURRET, JESS G.
The Ferrari Legend. Scarsdale: 1977. V. 65

POUSSART, A.
Dictionnaire des Termes de Marine a Voiles et a Vapeur. Paris: 1860. V. 65

POUTEAU, CLAUDE
Melanges de Chirurgie. Lyon: 1760. V. 65

POUTLON, E. B.
Hope Reports. Oxford: 1897-1958. V. 66

POVERMAN, C. E.
The Black Velvet Girl. Iowa City: 1978. V. 66

POWE, JOHN HARRINGTON
Reminiscences and Sketches of Confederate Times. Columbia: 1909. V. 63; 65

POWELL, A. M.
Trailing and Camping in Alaska. 1909. V. 67
Trailing and Camping in Alaska. New York: 1909. V. 63; 64

POWELL, A. W. B.
The Paryphantidae of New Zealand. 1930-1946. V. 64

POWELL, ANTHONY
The Acceptance World. London: 1955. V. 62; 64; 65
Afternoon Men. 1931. V. 63
At Lady Molly's. London: 1957. V. 62; 63; 64; 65; 66
Books Do Furnish a Room. London: 1971. V. 64; 66
A Buyer's Market. London: 1952. V. 62; 67
Caledonia. 1934. V. 62
Casanova's Chinese Restaurant. London: 1960. V. 63; 64
A Dance to the Music of Time. London: 1951-1975. V. 62; 66
The Fisher King. London: 1986. V. 64
Hearing Secret Harmonies. London: 1975. V. 63; 64
John Aubrey and His Friends. London: 1948. V. 62
The Kindly Ones. London: 1962. V. 64
The Military Philosophers. London: 1968. V. 62; 63; 64; 66
A Question of Upbringing. London: 1951. V. 66; 67
A Reference for Mellors. London: 1966. V. 66
A Reference for Mellors. London: 1994. V. 64
The Soldier's Art. London: 1966. V. 62; 64; 66
Temporary Kings. 1973. V. 67
Temporary Kings. London: 1973. V. 63; 64
The Valley of Bones. London: 1964. V. 62; 66
Venusberg. (and) Agents and Patients: Two Novels. New York: 1952. V. 66

POWELL, BADEN
Essays on the Spirit of the Inductive Philosophy, the Unity of Worlds and the Philosophy of Creation. London: 1855. V. 64
A General and Elementary View of the Undulatory Theory as Applied to the Dispersion of Light, and Other Subjects. London: 1841. V. 66
An Historical View of the Progress of the Physical and Mathematical Sciences. London: 1834. V. 67

POWELL, CUTHBERT
Twenty Years of Kansas City's Livestock Trade and Traders. Kansas City: 1893. V. 67

POWELL, DAWN
The Bride's House. New York: 1929. V. 63; 64; 66

POWELL, E. ALEXANDER
Slanting Lines of Steel. New York: 1933. V. 64

POWELL, ENOCH
Dancer's End/The Wedding Gift. London: 1951. V. 65; 66; 67
First Poems. Fifty Short Lyrics. Oxford: 1937. V. 64

POWELL, GABRIEL
A Consideration of the Papists Reasons of State and Religion, for Toleration of Poperie in England.... Oxford: 1604. V. 66

POWELL, GEORGE T.
Foundations and Foundation Walls for All Classes of Buildings, Pile Driving, Building Stones & Bricks.... New York: 1879. V. 63

POWELL, H. M. T.
The Santa Fe Trail to California. San Francisco: 1931. V. 65
The Santa Fe Trail to California. New York: 1981. V. 62; 63; 65

POWELL, J. W.
Down the Colorado. New York: 1969. V. 62
Exploration of the Colorado River of the West and Its Tributaries Explored in 1869-70-71 and 72. Washington: 1875. V. 64
Outlines of the Philosophy of the North American Indians. New York: 1877. V. 63
Report on the Lands of the Arid Region of the United States with a More Detailed Account of the Lands of Utah. Washington: 1879. V. 66

POWELL, JOHN
Essay Upon the Law of Contracts and Agreements. London: 1790. V. 65

POWELL, LAWRENCE CLARK
From the Heartland. Flagstaff: 1976. V. 65
Heart of the Southwest: a Selective Bibliography of Novels, Stories and Tales Laid in Arizona and New Mexico and Adjacent Lands. Los Angeles: 1955. V. 64
Land of Fact: A Companion to Land of Fiction. Los Angeles: 1992. V. 64
Landscape and Literature. Dallas: 1990. V. 65
The Little Package: Pages on Life, Literature and Landscape from a Traveling Bookman's Baggage. Cleveland & New York: 1964. V. 65
Madeleine. Pasadena: 1990. V. 64
My New Mexico Literary Friends. Santa Fe: 1986. V. 66
Philosopher Pickett. Berkeley: 1942. V. 65
Photographs of the Southwest. Boston: 1976. V. 62
The River Between. Santa Barbara: 1979. V. 63; 64
Robinson Jeffers: The Man and His Work. Pasadena: 1940. V. 64
Southwestern Books - a Reader's Guide to the Heartland of New Mexico and Arizona. Albuquerque: 1963. V. 67
A Southwestern Century: a Bibliography of One Hundred Books of Non- Fiction About the Southwest. Van Nuys: 1958. V. 64
The Three H's. Los Angeles: 1971. V. 65
Where Water Flows: the Rivers of Arizona. Flagstaff: 1980. V. 63; 64

POWELL, PADGETT
Edisto. New York: 1984. V. 63; 65

POWELL, PETER J.
People of the Sacred Mountain. San Francisco: 1979. V. 67
People of the Sacred Mountain. San Francisco: 1981. V. 63
Sweet Medicine, the Continuous Role of the Sacred Arrows, the Sun Dance, and the Sacred Buffalo Hat in Northern Cheyenne. Volumes I-II. Norman: 1969. V. 67

POWELL, RICHARD
Proceedings of a General Court Martial Held at the Horse Guards on the 24th and 27th of March, 1792, for the Trial of Capt. Richard Powell, Lieut. Christopher Seton, and Lieut. John Hall.... London: 1809. V. 63

POWELL, WILLIAM H.
Officers of the Army and Navy (Volunteer) Who Served in the Civil War. Philadelphia: 1893. V. 66

POWELL, WILLIAM SAMUEL
Discourses on Various Subjects.... London: 1776. V. 67

POWELSON, B. F.
History of Co. K. of the 140th Regiment, Pennsylvania Volunteers (1862-1865). Steubenville: 1906. V. 62

POWER, BERTHA K.
William Henry Knight: California Pioneer. N.P: 1932. V. 63

POWER, D'ARCY
Sir D'Arcy Power, Selected Writings, 1877-1930. Oxford: 1931. V. 63

POWER, J. H.
Anatomy of the Arteries of the Human Body.... Dublin and London: 1881. V. 67

POWER, JOHN CARROLL
History of an Attempt to Steal the Body of Abraham Lincoln. Springfield: 1890. V. 62

POWER, KEVIN
Work in Progress. London: 1977. V. 67

POWER, PATRICK
Crichad an Chaoilli. 1932. V. 67

POWER, SUSAN
The Grass Dancer. New York: 1994. V. 65

POWER, WILLIAM TYRONE
Sketches in New Zealand.... London: 1849. V. 62

A POWERFULL
Pititfull, Citi-Full Cry, of Plentifull Children and Their Admirable, Lamentable Complaint. London: 1643. V. 65

POWERS, CALEB
Great Speech of Caleb Powers. Georgetown: 1903. V. 65

POWERS, GRANT
Historical Sketches of the Discovery, Settlement and Progress of Events in the Coos Country and Vicinity, Principally Included Between the Years 1754 and 1785. Haverhill: 1841. V. 66

POWERS, H. P.
Female Education. An Address Delivered in Trinity Church, Newark, N. J. on the Anniversary of the Newark Inst. for Young Ladies, July 21, 1826. Newark: 1826. V. 63

POWERS, J. F.
The Prince of Darkness and Other Stories. Garden City: 1947. V. 62; 67

POWERS, LAURA BRIDE
Old Monterey. California's Adobe Capital. San Francisco: 1934. V. 67

POWERS, MABEL
The Indian as Peacemaker. New York: 1932. V. 67

POWERS, PERRY F.
A History of Northern Michigan and Its People. Chicago: 1912. V. 66

POWERS, RICHARD
The Gold Bug Variations. New York: 1991. V. 62; 63; 64; 65; 66; 67
Prisoner's Dilemma. New York: 1988. V. 63; 64; 67
Three Farmers on Their Way to a Dance. New York: 1985. V. 63; 65; 67

POWERS, STEPHEN
Afoot and Alone - a Walk from Sea to Sea. Austin: 1995. V. 66

POWERS, TIM
On Stranger Tides. New York: 1987. V. 65
The Skies Discrowned. 1993. V. 64; 66

POWNALL, HENRY
Some Particulars Relating to the History of Epsom. Epsom: 1825. V. 63

POWYS, JOHN COWPER
Atlantis. London: 1954. V. 65; 66
Confessions of Two Brothers. Rochester: 1916. V. 66
Confessions of Two Brothers. London: 1982. V. 64
Dorothy M. Richardson. London: 1931. V. 66
Ducdame. London: 1925. V. 66
In Defence of Sensuality. London: 1930. V. 65
Lucifer. A Poem. London: 1956. V. 66
The Meaning of Culture. London: 1930. V. 64
The Meaning of Culture. London: 1932. V. 66
Morwyn; or the Vengenance of God. London: 1937. V. 64
One Hundred Best Books. New York: 1922. V. 66
Poems. London: 1899. V. 66
Rodmoor. New York: 1916. V. 64
Samphire: Poems. New York: 1922. V. 66
The Secret of Self-Development. Girard: 1926. V. 66
Visions and Revisions - a Book of Literary Devotions. New York and London: 1915. V. 64; 66
Wolf Solent. London: 1929. V. 66
Wolf Solent. New York: 1929. V. 64
Wood and Stone. New York: 1915. V. 66

POWYS, LAURENCE
At the Harlot's Burial. London: 1930. V. 63

POWYS, LLEWELYN
A Baker's Dozen. Herrin: 1939. V. 66
The Book of Days. Waltham St. Lawrence: 1937. V. 64
Ebony and Ivory. New York: 1923. V. 66
The Twelve Months. London: 1936. V. 65
The Verdict of Bridlegoose. London: 1927. V. 64

POWYS, THEODORE FRANCIS
Black Byrony. London: 1923. V. 66
Christ in the Cupboard. London: 1930. V. 66
The Dewpond. London: 1928. V. 65; 66
Fables. London: 1929. V. 63; 65; 66
Goat Green. Waltham St. Lawrence: 1937. V. 64
The House With the Echo. Twenty-Six Stories. London: 1928. V. 65; 66
Innocent Birds. London: 1926. V. 65
The Key of the Field. London: 1930. V. 67
Kindness in a Corner. London: 1930. V. 62; 65
The Left Leg - containing the Left Leg, Hester Dominy (and) Men. London: 1923. V. 65
Mark Only. London: 1924. V. 65; 66
Mr. Tasker's Gods. London: 1925. V. 63; 66
Mr. Weston's Good Wine. London: 1927. V. 63; 65
The Only Penitent. London: 1931. V. 66
Soliloquies of a Hermit. London: 1918. V. 64; 66
The Soliloquy of a Hermit. New York: 1916. V. 66
The Two Thieves. London: 1932. V. 62; 65; 66
Uncle Dottery, a Christmas Story. Cleverdon, Bristol: 1931. V. 66
The White Paternoster and Other Stories. London: 1930. V. 66

POYNTER, F. N. L.
A Bibliography of Gervase Markham. 1962. V. 67
Chemistry in the Service of Medicine. Philadelphia and Montreal: 1963. V. 64

POYRICK, DAVID F.
Railroads of Nevada and Eastern California. Berkeley: 1962-1963. V. 63

POZZI, ANTONIA
Poems. London: 1955. V. 67

PRACTICAL Economy; or, the Application of Modern Discoveries to the Purposes of Domestic Life. London: 1821. V. 63

THE PRACTICK Part of the Law: Shewing the Office of an Attorney and a Guide for Solicitors in All the Courts of Westminster.... In the Savoy: 1711. V. 62

PRAED, ROSA CAROLINE MURRAY-PRIOR
The Ladies' Gallery. London: 1890. V. 65
Mrs. Tregaskiss: a Novel of Anglo-Australian Life. New York: 1895. V. 65
My Australian Girlhood: Sketches and Impressions of Bush Life. London: 1902. V. 65

PRAED, W. MACKWORTH
The Poems. London. V. 65
Poems. Boston and New York: 1909. V. 62

PRAEGER, ROBERT LLOYD
Irish Topographical Botany. 1901. V. 63
The Natural History of Ireland. 1950. V. 66; 67
Official Guide to County Down and the Mourne Mountains. 1898. V. 67
Official Guide to County Down and the Mourne Mountains. 1900. V. 67
The Way That I Went. Dublin. 1937. V. 62
The Way That I Went, an Irishman in Ireland. 1937. V. 62; 64; 65

PRAEGER, S. ROSAMUND
How They Came Home from School. London: 1911. V. 67

PRATCHETT, TERRY
Feet of Clay. London: 1996. V. 67
Strata. Gerrards Cross: 1981. V. 65

PRATT, A.
Our Native Songsters. London: 1857. V. 65; 67

PRATT, A. T. CAMDEN
People of the Period, Being a Collection of the Biographies of Upwards of 6000 Living Celebrities. London: 1897. V. 64

PRATT, ALICE DAY
The Homesteaders Portfolio. New York: 1922. V. 67

PRATT, ANNE
The Flowering Plants and Ferns of Great Britain. London. V. 66
The Flowering Plants, Grasses, Sedges and Ferns of Great Britain. London: 1873. V. 64
The Flowering Plants, Grasses, Sedges and Ferns of Great Britain. London: 1899. V. 62
The Flowering Plants, Grasses, Sedges and Ferns of Great Britain. London: 1899-1900. V. 62
The Flowering Plants, Grasses, Sedges and Ferns of Great Britain. 1899-1905. V. 63
The Grasses, Sedges and Ferns of Great Britain and Their Allies the Club Moses, Pepperworts and Horsetails. London and New York: 1889. V. 64
Poisonous, Noxious and Suspected Plants of Our Fields and Woods. 1857. V. 66
Poisonous, Noxious and Suspected Plants of Our Fields and Woods. London: 1857. V. 63; 64
Wild Flowers. London: 1860. V. 63

PRATT, BENJAMIN
A Sermon Preached Before the Honourable House of Commons, at St. Andrew's Church, Dublin, May XXIX, 1709. Dublin: 1709. V. 65

PRATT, FLETCHER
The Marines' War: an Account of the Struggle for the Pacific from Both American and Japanese Sources. New York: 1948. V. 67

PRATT, GEORGE W.
An Account of the British Expedition Above the Highlands of the Hudson River, and of the Events Connected With the Burning of Kingston in 1777. Albany: 1861. V. 64

PRATT, H. D.
A Field Guide to the Birds of Hawaii and the Tropical Pacific. Princeton: 1987. V. 64

PRATT, JOHN
The Law Relating to Friendly Societies and Benefit Building Societies.... London: 1838. V. 67

PRATT, JULIUS HOWARD
Reminiscences, Personal and Otherwise. N.P: 1910. V. 63; 66

PRATT, PARLEY PARKER
Key to the Science of Theology; Designed as an Introduction to the First Principles of Spiritual Philosophy. Liverpool: 1855. V. 62

PRATT, R. T. C.
The Genetics of Neurological Disorders. London: 1967. V. 67

PRATT, SAMUEL JACKSON
Emma Corbett or the Miseries of Civil War. London: 1781?. V. 62
Pity's Gift: A Collection of Interesting Tales, to Excite the Compassion of Youth for the Animal Creation. London: 1801. V. 65
Pity's Gift: a Collection of Interesting Tales, to Excite the Compassion of Youth for the Animal Creation. London: 1816. V. 67

PRAZ, MARIO
The Hero in Eclipse in Victorian Fiction. Cumberlege: 1956. V. 66
The Romantic Agony. London: 1933. V. 62; 66

PREBBLE, J.
The Highland Clearances. 1963. V. 67

PREBLE, E. A.
A Biological Investigation of the Athabaska-Mackenzie Region. Washington: 1908. V. 63

PREBLE, GEORGE HENRY
History of the Flag of the United States and of the Naval and Yacht Club Signals, Seals and Arms and Principal National Songs of the United States. Boston: 1880. V. 63; 64
History of the United States Navy Yard, Portsmouth. Washington: 1892. V. 65

PRECIADO DELLA VEGA, FRANCISCO
Arcadia Pictorica en Sueno, Alegoria o Poema Prosaico Sobre le Teorica practica de la Pintura, Escrita por Parrasio Tebano.... Madrid: 1789. V. 64

PRECIS Historique de la Vie De Mad. La Comtesse Du Barry. Paris: 1774. V. 65

PRECISO dos Sucessos, Que Tiverao Lugar em Pernambuco, Desde a Faustissima e Gloriozissima Revolucao Operada Felismente na Praca do Recife aos Seis do Corrente Mez de Marco.... Pernambuco: 1817. V. 62

PREJEVALSKY, NIKOLAI M.
From Kulja, Across the Tian Shan to Lob-Nor. London: 1879. V. 62

PRENDERGAST, MABEL
The Little Yellow Duckling. Leeds: 1907. V. 66

PRENTICE, ARCHIBALD
History of the Anti-Corn-Law League. London: 1853. V. 64

PRENTICE, GEORGE D.
Biography of Henry Clay. Hartford: 1831. V. 64

PRENTIS, NOBLE L.
Kansas Miscellanies. Topeka: 1889. V. 64

PRESBYTERIAN CHURCH. PRESBYTERY OF NEW BRUNSWICK
Rules Established by the Presbytery of New Brunswick, for Their Own Government and Recommended...to the Observations of Their Churches. Together with a Pastoral Letter, Addressed to all the Churches.... New Brunswick: 1800. V. 66

PRESBYTERIAN CHURCH IN THE CONFEDERATE STATES OF AMERICA
Address of the General Assembly of the Presbyterian Church in the Confederate States of America to all the Churches of Jesus Christ Throughout the Earth. Augusta: 1861. V. 63

PRESCOT, KENRICK
Letters Concerning Homer, the Sleeper in Horace; with Additional Classic Amusements. Cambridge: 1773. V. 64; 66

PRESCOTT, G. W.
A Synopsis of North American Desmids. Part II. Lincoln: 1975-1977. V. 65

PRESCOTT, H. F. M.
The Man on a Donkey. London: 1952. V. 67

PRESCOTT, J. E.
The Register of the Priory of Wetheral. London: 1897. V. 66

PRESCOTT, WILLIAM
The Prescott Memorial. Boston: 1870. V. 65

PRESCOTT, WILLIAM HICKLING
Biographical and Critical Miscellanies. London: 1845. V. 64
The Conquest of Mexico. London: 1922. V. 62; 66
History of Ferdinand and Isabella. Boston: 1838. V. 64
History of the Conquest of Mexico. New York: 1843. V. 64
History of the Conquest of Mexico. London: 1880. V. 64
History of the Conquest of Peru. London: 1847. V. 65
History of the Conquest of Peru. New York: 1847. V. 67
History of the Reign of Ferdinand and Isabella. New York: 1967. V. 62; 63; 64; 66
History of the Reign of Philip the Second, King of Spain. Boston: 1855. V. 63
History of the Reign of Philip the Second, King of Spain. Boston: 1855-1858. V. 64
History of the Reign of Philip the Second, King of Spain. London: 1855-1859. V. 64

THE PRESENT State of New England, with Respect to the Indian War. London: 1675. V. 63

PRESGRAVES, JAMES C.
Wythe Co. Chapters. Pulaski: 1972. V. 65

PRESLAR, CHARLES J.
A History of Catawaba County. Salisbury: 1954. V. 63; 67

PRESSLY, WILLIAM L.
The Life and Art of William Barry. New Haven: 1981. V. 67

PREST, THOMAS PECKETT
Nicholas Nickelbery. London: 1840. V. 62
Pickwick in America. N.P: 1838-1839. V. 62

PRESTELE, J.
Drawn from Nature, the Botanical Art of Joseph Prestele and His Sons. Washington: 1984. V. 63

PRESTET, JEAN
Elemens de Mathematiques ou Principes Generaux de Toutes les Sciences qui ont les Grandeurs Pour Objet.... Paris: 1675. V. 66

PRESTON
The Royal Charters of Preston 1179-1974. Preston: 1979. V. 64

PRESTON, CHLOE
The Chunkies' Adventures. London: 1921. V. 67
Somebody's Darlings. London: Sep. 1920. V. 63

PRESTON, GEORGE R.
Thomas Wolfe: a Bibliography. New York: 1943. V. 64

PRESTON, HAYTER
Windmills. London: 1923. V. 65

PRESTON, JOHN
Life Eternall or a Treatise of the Knowledge of the Divine Essence and Attribvtes Delivered in XVIII Sermons. London: 1633. V. 66

PRESTON, THOMAS L.
Historical Sketches and Reminiscences of an Octogenarian. Richmond: 1900. V. 63

PRESTON, WILLIAM
The Poetical Works. Dublin: 1793. V. 62

PRESTRUD, EARL
Bishop's Wildfowl. St. Paul: 1948. V. 64; 66

PRESTWICH, JOSEPH
Address Delivered at the Anniversary Meeting of the Geological Society of London, on the 16th of February, 1872, also that for 1871. (with) The Past and Future of Geology...Parts 1, 2, 7, 3. 1854-1875. V. 65
Geology: Chemical, Physical and Straigraphical. Oxford: 1886-1888. V. 65; 67

PRETTY *Name ABC.* New York: 1901. V. 62

PRETTY *Rhyme Alphabet for Good Children.* London: 1870. V. 62

PRETTYMAN, HERBERT EDWARD
Journal of Herbert Edward Prettyman, Lieutenant Grenadier Guards. 1892. V. 62

PREUSS, CHARLES
Exploring with Fremont, The Private Diaries of Charles Preuss, Cartographer for John C. Fremont.... Norman: 1958. V. 63

PREUSS, JULIUS
Biblical and Talmudic Medicine. New York: 1978. V. 62
Biblisch-Talmudische Medizin. Beitrage zur Geschichte der Heilkunde und der Kultur Uberhaupt. Berlin: 1911. V. 63

PREVOST, ANTOINE FRANCOIS, CALLED PREVOST D'EXILES
The Life and Entertaining Adventures of Mr. Cleveland, Natural Son of Oliver Cromwell. London: 1734-1735. V. 63

PREVOST, FLORENT
Histoire Naturelle d'Oiseaux d'Europe (Passereaux). Paris: 1864. V. 67

PREVOST, ISAAC BENEDICT
Mouvements Produits par le Contact Mutuel de Diverses Substances, et Explication de ces Mouvements. Geneva: 1826. V. 67

PREVOST, JEAN LOUIS
Medicina Pauperum: Mira Serie Continens Remedia ad Aegrotos Cuiuscunqe.... Leyden: 1660. V. 64

PREVOST, PIERRE
De Quelques Apparences Visuelles sans Object Exterieur. Geneva: 1832. V. 67
Du Calorique Rayonnant. Paris: 1809. V. 67
Exposition Elementaire des Principes qui Servent de Base a la Theorie de la Chaleur Rayonnante, Faisant Suite a l'Ouvrage Intitule du Calorique Rayonnant. Geneva: 1832. V. 67
Memoire sur la Constitution Mecanique des Fluides Elastiques. Geneva: 1828. V. 67
Memoire sur une Apparence Douteuse de Mirage. Geneva: 1834. V. 67
Recherches Physico-Mecaniques sur la Chaleur. Geneva: 1792. V. 67

PRICE, A. C.
A History of Leeds Grammar School from Its Foundations to the End of 1918. Leeds: 1919. V. 65

PRICE, ANTHONY
Colonel Butler's Wolf. London: 1972. V. 66
The Hour of the Donkey. London: 1980. V. 67
A New Kind of War - a Novel. London: 1987. V. 63
Tomorrow's Ghost. London: 1979. V. 65; 67

PRICE, B. BYRON
Crafting a Southwestern Masterpiece: J. Evetts Haley and Charles Goodnight: Cowman and Plainsman. Midland: 1986. V. 66

PRICE, BONAMY
Oxford Reform. Oxford and London: 1875. V. 67

PRICE, C.
Memories of Old Montana. Hollywood: 1945. V. 64; 67
Trails I Rode. Memories of Old Cowboy Days and Charlie Russell. Pasadena: 1947. V. 64; 67

PRICE, DAVID
Chronological Retrospect or Memoirs of the Principal Events of Mahommedan History from the Death of the Arabian Legislator to the Accession of the Emperor Akbar and the Establishment of the Moghul Empire in Hundustaun.... London: 1811-1820. V. 62

PRICE, DEREK
The Equatorie of the Planets. Cambridge: 1955. V. 66

PRICE, DOUGHBELLY
Short Stirrups. The Saga of.... Los Angeles: 1960. V. 65

PRICE, ELIZABETH
The True Countess of Banbury's Case, Relating to Her Marriage. London: 1696. V. 62

PRICE, F. G. H.
The Signs of Old Lombard Street. London: 1890. V. 66

PRICE, FRANCIS
The British Carpenter. London: 1735. V. 64
The British Carpenter. London: 1785. V. 62
A Series of Particular and Useful Observations Made with Great Diligence and Care, Upon the Admirable Structure, the Cathedral Church of Salisbury, Calculated for the Use and Amusement of Gentlemen and Other Curious Persons.... London: 1753. V. 64
A Treatise on Carpentry. London: 1733. V. 63; 64

PRICE, G. F. HILTON
The Signs of Old Lombard Street. London: 1902. V. 63

PRICE, GEORGE F.
Across the Continent with the Fifth Cavalry. New York: 1883. V. 67
Across the Continent with the Fifth Cavalry. 1959. V. 67
Across the Continent with the Fifth Cavalry. New York: 1959. V. 65

PRICE, HARRY
Confessions of a Ghost Hunter. London: 1936. V. 66
Leaves from a Psychist's Case Book. London: 1933. V. 66

PRICE, HUMPHREY
Reasons in Support of an Extension of the Elective Franchise to the Working Classes, Submitted to the Serious Consideration of the King and His Ministers. London: 1836. V. 64

PRICE, J.
The Buyer's Manual and Business Guide. San Francisco: 1872. V. 63

PRICE, J. E.
A Description of the Remains of Roman Buildings at Morton, Near Brading, Isle of Wight. London: 1881. V. 62
A Description of the Roman Tessellated Pavement Found in Buckelbury... (with another work On a Bastion of London Wall). Westminster: 1870-1880. V. 67
A Description of the Roman Tessellated Pavement Found in Bucklesbury.... Westminster: 1870. V. 67
A Descriptive Account of the Guildhall of the City of London, Its History and Associations. London: 1886. V. 62
Roman Antiquities Illustrated by Remains Recently Discovered on the Site of the National Safe Deposit Company's Premises. London: 1873. V. 67

PRICE, J. H.
The Shore Environment. Volume 2 (of 2). London: 1980. V. 65

PRICE, JOHN
An Historical Account of the City of Hereford. Hereford: 1796. V. 62

PRICE, JONATHAN
Poems. Swinford, Eynsham: 1954. V. 64

PRICE, LEE & CO.
Metal Trades Directory, for New England and New York City, Containing Alphabetical and Classified Lists of Hardware, Manufacturers and Dealers, Machinists and Machinery Manufacturers, Engine Builders, Boiler Makers, Iron and Brass Founders and Manufactur. New Haven: 1887. V. 66

PRICE, LUCY M. S.
The Sydney Smith & Clagett Price Genealogy. Strasburg: 1927. V. 65

PRICE, M. PHILIPS
America After Sixty Years - The Travel Diaries of Two Generations of English Men. London: 1936. V. 63

PRICE, PATTIE
The Afrikaner Little Boy. London: 1935. V. 65

PRICE, R. K.
Astbury, Wheldon and Ralph Wood Figures and Toby Jugs, Collected by Captain R. K. Price. 1922. V. 67

PRICE, REYNOLDS
The Annual Heron. New York: 1980. V. 62
Back Before Day. 1989. V. 62
Back Before Day. Rocky Mount: 1989. V. 63; 64; 67
Blue Calhoun. New York: 1992. V. 64
Christ Child's Song at the End of the Night. New York: 1978. V. 64
A Common Room. Essays 1954-1957. New York: 1987. V. 64
The Forseeable Future. New York: 1991. V. 67
A Generous Man. New York: 1966. V. 63; 64
Good Hearts. New York: 1988. V. 64; 67
The Good News According to Mark. N.P: 1976. V. 63
The Honest Account of a Memorable Life. 1994. V. 62
Kate Vaiden. New York: 1986. V. 64
Late Warning. New York: 1968. V. 62; 64; 67
Lessons Learned. Seven Poems. New York: 1977. V. 62; 64; 67
A Long and Happy Life. New York: 1962. V. 63; 66
The Names and Faces of Heroes. New York: 1963. V. 66
Oracles. Six Versions from the Bible. Durham: 1977. V. 62; 64
Private Contentment. New York: 1984. V. 62; 64; 67
Question and Answer. Chattanooga: 1979. V. 62

PRICE, REYNOLDS continued
The Surface of Earth. New York: 1975. V. 63; 64; 66
The Tongues of Angels. New York: 1990. V. 67
Torso of an Archaic Apollo. New York: 1969. V. 62; 64

PRICE, RICHARD
Additional Observations on the Nature and Value of Civil Liberty, and the War with America.... London: 1777. V. 62
Bloodbrothers. Boston: 1976. V. 66
A Discourse Addressed to a Congregation at Hackney, on February 21, 1781. London: 1781. V. 65
A Discourse on the Love of Our Country, Delivered on Nov. 4, 1789, at the Meeting-House in the Old Jewry, to the Society for Commemorating the Revolution in Great Britain. London: 1789. V. 62
A Discourse on the Love of Our Country, Delivered on Nov. 4, 1789... to the Society for Commemorating the Revolution in Great Britian. London: 1790. V. 62
Four Dissertations. I. On Providence. II. On Prayer. III. On the Reason for Expecting that Virtuous Men Shall Meet After Death in a State of Happiness. IV. On the Importance of Christianity, the Nature of Historical Evidence and Miracles. London: 1772. V. 62
Observations on Reversionary Payments: on Schemes for Providing Annuities for Widows.... London: 1812. V. 66
Observations on the Nature of Civil Liberty, the Principles of Government, and the Justice and Policy of the War with America. London: 1776. V. 62
A Review of the Principal Questions and Difficulties in Morals. London: 1769. V. 65
The Wanderers. Boston: 1974. V. 63; 64; 67

PRICE, ROSE LAMBERT
The Two Americas: an Account of Sport and Travel. Philadelphia: 1877. V. 67

PRICE, TAFF
Lures for Game, Coarse and Sea Fishing. 1972. V. 67

PRICE, THEOPHILUS
Interest Tables, Calculated from Two and a Half to Eight Per Cent.... London: 1803. V. 64

PRICE, THOMAS
The Literary Remains. Llandovery: 1854-1855. V. 65

PRICE, UVEDALE
An Essay on the Picturesque, as Compared with the Sublime and Beautiful.... London: 1794. V. 63; 65
Essays on the Picturesque, as Compared with the Sublime and Beautiful.... London: 1810. V. 63; 66

PRICE, VINCENT
I Like What I Know. Garden City: 1959. V. 67

PRICE, WILLIAM T.
Historical Sketches of Pocahontas Co., West Virginia. Marinton: 1901. V. 66
On to Grafton. An Account of One of the First Campaigns of the Civil War, May 1861. Marlinton: 1901. V. 62

PRICHARD, ARTHUR C.
An Appalachian Legacy: Mannington Life and Spirit. Parsons: 1983. V. 67

PRICHARD, HESKETH
Sport in Wildest Britain. 1921. V. 67

PRICHARD, JAMES A.
The Overland Diary of James A. Prichard from Kentucky to California in 1849. Denver: 1959. V. 63; 64; 66

PRICHARD, JAMES COWLEY
Researches into the Physical History of Mankind. London: 1836-1837. V. 65

PRICHARD, REES
The Welchman's Candle; or the Divine Poems of Mr. Rees Prichard, Sometime Vicar of Landovery, in Carmarthenshire. Carmarthen: 1771. V. 63; 67

PRIDE, W. F.
The History of Forty Riley. N.P: 1926. V. 67

PRIDEAUX, HUMPHREY
Directions to Church-Wardens for the Faithful Discharge at Their Office. London: 1730. V. 62; 66
The Old and New Testament Connected in the History of the Jews and Neighbouring Nations, from the Delcensions of the Kingdoms of Israel and Judah to the Time of Christ. London: 1718. V. 67
The True Nature of Imposture Fully Display'd in the Life of Mahomet. (with) A Discourse Vindicating of Christianity from the Charge of Imposture. London: 1698. V. 64

PRIDEAUX, MATTHIAS
An Easy and Compendious Introduction for Reading All Sorts of Histories.... Oxford: 1664. V. 66

PRIDEAUX, SARA T.
A Catalogue of Books Bound by S. T. Prideaux Between MDCCCXC and MDCCCC with Twenty-Six Illustrations. London: 1900. V. 62
Modern Bookbindings. Their Design and Decoration. London: 1906. V. 64

PRIDEAUX, WILLIAM F.
A Bibliography of the Works of Robert Louis Stevenson. London: 1917. V. 67
Notes for a Bibliography of Edward FitzGerald. London: 1901. V. 67

PRIDGEN, T.
Courage, the Story of Modern Cockfighting. Boston: 1938. V. 66

PRIEST, JOSIAH
American Antiquities and Discoveries in the West. Albany: 1833. V. 64; 66
American Antiquities and Discoveries in the West. Albany: 1834. V. 65
Slavery, As It Relates to the Negro or African Race, Examined in the Light of Circumstances, History and Holy Scriptures.... Albany: 1843. V. 64; 66

PRIESTLEY, HERBERT INGRAM
Tristan de Luna - Conquistador of the Old South - a Study of Spanish Imperial Strategy. Glendale: 1936. V. 64; 66; 67

PRIESTLEY, JOHN BOYNTON
Angel Pavement. London: 1930. V. 62
Brief Diversions, Being Tales Travesties and Epigrams. Cambridge: 1922. V. 66
Farthing Hall. London: 1929. V. 63

PRIESTLEY, JOSEPH
An Address to Protestant Dissenters of All Denominations on the Approaching Election of Members of Parliament.... London: 1774. V. 62
An Appeal to the Public, On the Subject of the Riots in Birmingham. London: 1791. V. 67
An Appeal to the Public, on the Subject of the Riots in Birmingham. Birmingham: 1792. V. 62
The Conduct to be Observed by Dissenters in Order to Procure and Repeal of the Corporation and Test Acts, Recommended in a Sermon Preached Before the Congregations of the Old and New Meetings, at Birmingham Nov. 5, 1789. Birmingham: 1789. V. 63; 67
Copies of Original Letters Recently Written by Persons in Paris to Dr. Priestley in America. London: 1798. V. 67
Defences of Unitarianism for the Year 1786, (1787 and 1788 and 1789). Birmingham: 1788-1790. V. 64
A Description of a System of Biography.... Philadelphia: 1803. V. 63
A Discourse on Occasion of the Death of Dr. Price; Delivered at Hackney on Sunday, May 1, 1791. London: 1791. V. 62
Disquisitions Relating to Matter and Spirit. (with), The Doctrine of Philosophical Necessity Illustrated.... London: 1777. V. 67
Dr. Priestley's Letter to the Inhabitants of Birmingham: Mr. Keir's Vindication of the Revolution Dinner; and Mr. Russell's Account of the Proceedings Relating to It with the Toasts &c. London: 1791. V. 67
An Essay on the First Principles of Government, and on the Nature of Political, Civil and Religious Liberty, Including Remarks on Dr. Brown's Code of Education, and on Dr. Balguy's Sermon on Church Authority. London: 1771. V. 64
An Examination of Dr. Reid's Inquiry Into the Human Mind on the Principles of Common Sense, Dr. Beattie's Essay on the Nature and the Immutability of Truth.... London: 1774. V. 65
Experiments and Observations on Different Kinds of Air (...Volume II; ...Volume III) (and) Experiments and Observations Relating to Various Branches of Natural Philosophy (...Volume II). London: 1781-1776, 1777. V. 63
Experiments and Observations Relating to Various Branches of Natural Philosophy. London: 1779. V. 64
A Familiar Introduction to the Study of Electricity. London: 1777. V. 64
A Free Discussion of the Doctrines of Materialism, and Philosophical Necessity in a Correspondence Between Dr. Price and Dr. Priestley. London: 1778. V. 66
The History and Present State of Discoveries Relating to Vision, Light, and Colours. London: 1772. V. 65; 67
The History and Present State of Electricity, with Original Experiments. London: 1767. V. 62; 66
Institutes of Natural and Revealed Religion. London: 1772-. V. 67
Lectures on History and General Policy; to which is Prefixed, an Essay on a Course of Liberal Education for Civil and Active Life. Birmingham: 1788. V. 64
Letters to a Philosophical Unbeliever. Part I. (with) Part II. Birmingham: 1787. V. 65
Letters to Jews; Inviting Them to an Amicable Discussion of the Evidences of Christianity. (with) Part II. Birmingham: 1786-1787. V. 65
Letters to the Inhabitants of Northumberland. 1799. V. 62; 65
Letters to the Inhabitants of Northumberland. Northumberland: 1799. V. 63
Letters to the Philosophers and Politicians of France, on the Subject of Religion. London: 1793. V. 62
Letters to the Right Honourable Edmund Burke, Occasioned by His Reflections on the Revolution in France &c. Birmingham: 1791. V. 62; 64; 67
Memoirs of Dr. Joseph Preistley, to the Year 1795, Written by Himself.... London: 1806. V. 65
Memoirs of Dr. Joseph Priestley. London: 1806-1807. V. 62
An Outline of the Evidences of Revealed Religion. Philadelphia: 1797. V. 66
Socrates and Jesus Compared. London: 1803. V. 62; 66
The Use of Christianity, Especially in Difficult Times: a Sermon Delivered...March 30, 1794. London: 1794. V. 62

PRIESTLEY, RAYMOND E.
Antarctic Adventure: Scott's Northern Party. London: 1914. V. 65

PRIETO, GUILLERMO
San Francisco in the Seventies: the City As Viewed by a Mexican Political Exile. San Francisco: 1938. V. 62

PRIJS, JOSEPH
Die Basler Hebraischen Drucke (1492-1866). N.P: 1964. V. 64; 66

PRIME, ALFRED COXE
Arts and Crafts in Philadelphia, Maryland and South Carolina 1786- 1800. 1932. V. 66

PRIME, WILLIAM C.
Pottery and Porcelain. New York: 1878. V. 64; 65

PRIMEIRA Parte de las Sentencias Que Hasta Nuestros Tiemps, Para Edificaion de Buenos Costumbres, Estan por Diuersos Autores Escritas.... Coimbra: 1555. V. 62

THE PRIMER, Set Foorth by the Kynges Majestie and His Clergie.... London: 1545. V. 62

PRIMITIVE Painting, an Anthology of the World's Native Painters. Zagreb: 1981. V. 63

PRIN, ALICE
The Education of a French Model...Kiki's Memoirs. New York: 1950. V. 65

PRIN, ALICE continued
Kiki's Memoirs. Paris: 1930. V. 63; 64

PRINA, GIROLAMO ANTONIO
Il Trionfo di S. Gaudenzo, Primo Vescovo e Protettore dell' Inclita Citta di Novara, nel Solennissimo Glorioso Trasporto del Sacro Adorabile suo Corpo. Milan: 1711. V. 67

PRINCE EDWARD ISLAND
Abstract of the Census of the Population and Other Statistical Returns of Prince Edward Island Taken in the Year 1855, by Virute of an Act of the General Assembly. Charlottetown: 1856. V. 64
Extracts of the Report of the Visitor of Schools, as Submitted to the Legislature, and Ordered to be Published for General Information. Charlottetown: 1855. V. 64

PRINCE, F. T.
Collected Poems. London: 1979. V. 64
Memoirs in Oxford. London: 1970. V. 63; 66

PRINCE, L. BRADFORD
A Concise History of New Mexico. Cedar Rapids: 1914. V. 63; 66
New Mexico's Struggle for Statehood. Santa Fe: 1910. V. 63
Spanish Mission Churches of New Mexico. Cedar Rapids: 1915. V. 66

PRINCE, NANCY
A Narrative of the Life and Travels. Boston: 1850. V. 64; 67

PRINCE, THOMAS
The Vade Mecum for America.... Boston: 1732. V. 63

PRINCE William: The Story of Its People and Places. Manassas: 1961. V. 64

PRINCE, WILLIAM ROBERT
The Pomological Manual; or a Treatise on Fruits.... New York: 1831. V. 62; 63
The Pomological Manual; or a Treatise on Fruits.... New York: 1832. V. 64

PRINCETON UNIVERSITY
Catalogue of the Officers and Students of Nassau-Hall, December 1823. N.P: 1823. V. 66
Catalogus Collegi Neo-Caesariensis...Anno XLVI. Tridenti: 1821. V. 66

PRINCETONIANS...A Biographical Dictionary. Princeton: 1976-1991. V. 66

PRINCETON'S Fire Fighters 1788-1938. Princeton: 1938. V. 66

THE PRINCIPAL Charters Which Have Been Granted to the Corporation of Ipswich in Suffolk. London: 1754. V. 65

PRINDLE, CHARLES
Prindle's Almanac for the Year of Our Lord 1825, 1848 and 1851. Bridgeport: 1825-1848. V. 65

PRINGLE, ANDREW
Practical Photo-Micrography. London: 1893. V. 67

PRINGLE, E. L. L.
Pennington's Butterflies of Southern Africa. Cape Town: 1994. V. 63

PRINGLE, EDWARD J.
Slavery in the Southern States. Cambridge: 1852. V. 63; 65

PRINGLE, ELIZABETH
A Woman Rice-Planter. New York: 1913. V. 63

PRINGLE, JOHN
A Discourse on the Theory of Gunnery. London: 1778. V. 64
Medulla Medicinae Universae; or, a New Compendious Dispensatory. London: 1752. V. 63
Observations on the Diseases of the Army.... Philadelphia: 1812. V. 64; 66

PRINGLE, ROGER
Poems for Shakespeare. London: 1977. V. 62

PRINGLE, THOMAS
African Sketches. London: 1834. V. 62

PRINGSHEIM, ERNST GEORG
Selected Papers of Georg Pringsheim. Rutgers: 1963. V. 67

PRINSEP, HENRY THOBY
Tibet, Tartary and Mongolia: their Social and Political Condition and the Religion of Boodh, as There Existing.... London: 1852. V. 62

PRINSEP, JOHN
Bengal Sugar. An Account of the Method and Expence of Cultivating the Sugar Cane in Bengal. London: 1794. V. 63

PRINTERS' Choice. Catalogue of an Exhibition Held at the Grolier Club, New York, December 19, 1978 - February 3, 1979. Austin: 1983. V. 62

A PRINTER'S Dozen: Eleven Spreads from Unrealized Books.... 1993. V. 62

PRINTZ, H.
The Vegetation of the Siberian-Mongolian Frontiers. Trondhjem: 1921. V. 64

PRINTZ, HANS
Schiller. Vienna: 1920. V. 67

PRINZHORN, HANS
Artistry of the Mentally Ill: a Contribution to the Psychology and Psychopathology of Configuration. New York: 1972. V. 65

PRIOR, JAMES
The Life of Oliver Goldsmith, M.B. from a Variety of Original Sources. London: 1837. V. 67
Memoir of the Life and Character of the Right Hon. Edmund Burke.... London: 1824. V. 64

PRIOR, MATTHEW
Miscellaneous Works. London: 1740. V. 62; 64
An Ode Humbly Inscrib'd to the Queen. London: 1706. V. 62
Poems on Several Occasions. London: 1709. V. 63; 65
Poems on Several Occasions. London: 1709-1708. V. 62
The Poetical Works. London: 1779. V. 64; 65; 66
Selected Poems. London: 1889. V. 65

PRIOR, THOMAS
A List of the Absentees of Ireland, and the Yearly Value of Their Estates and Incomes Spent Abroad. London: 1730. V. 62

PRIOR, WILLIAM MATTHEW
The King's Vesture: Evidence from Scripture and History. Boston: 1862. V. 66

PRISCIANUS
Prisciani Grammataici Caesariensis Libri Omnes. Venetiis: 1527. V. 66

PRITCHARD, A.
A History of Infusoria, Including the Desmidiaceae and Diatomaceae, British and Foreign. London: 1861. V. 67
A History of Infusorial Animalcules, Living and Fossil. 1852. V. 66
A History of Infusorial Animalcules, Living and Fossil. London: 1852. V. 64

PRITCHARD, EDWARD WILLIAM
A Complete Report of the Trial of Dr. E. W. Pritchard for the Alleged Poisoning of His Wife and Mother-in-Law. Edinburgh: 1865. V. 63
Observations on Filey as a Watering Place; or, a Guide for Visitors. Leeds: 1856. V. 65

PRITCHARD, H. HESKETH
Hunting Camps in Wood and Wilderness. London: 1910. V. 67

PRITCHETT, V. S.
Balzac. London: 1973. V. 66
Blind Love and Other Stories. London: 1969. V. 66
Books in General. London: 1953. V. 63
Build the Ships. London: 1946. V. 66
A Cab at the Door: an Autobiography: Early Years. London: 1968. V. 66
A Cab at the Door; an Autobiography: Early Years. London: 1969. V. 66
The Camberwell Beauty. London: 1974. V. 62
Collected Stories. London: 1956. V. 66
Collected Stories. London: 1982. V. 66
Complete Collected Stories. New York: 1990. V. 66
Dead Man Leading. 1984. V. 66
Dublin: a Portrait. London: 1967. V. 66
In My Good Books. London: 1942. V. 66
It May Never Happen and Other Stories. London: 1945. V. 66
The Living Novel and Later Appreciation. New York: 1964. V. 66
London Perceived. London: 1962. V. 66
London Perceived. New York: 1962. V. 66
A Man of Letters: Selected Essays. London: 1985. V. 66
Marching Spain. London: 1933. V. 66
Midnight Oil. New York: 1972. V. 66
Mr. Beluncle. London: 1951. V. 66
The Myth Makers: Essays on European Russian and South American Novelists. London: 1979. V. 66
On the Edge of the Cliff and Other Stories. London: 1980. V. 66
Shirley Sanz. London: 1932. V. 16
The Tale Bearers: Essays on English, American and Other Writers. London: 1980. V. 66
The Turn of the Years. Wilton: 1982. V. 66
When My Girl Comes Home. London: 1961. V. 66
You Make Your Own Life - Fourteen Short Stories. London: 1938. V. 65

PRITT, T. E.
An Angler's Basket Filled in Sunshine and Shade through the Space of Forty Years.... Manchester: 1896. V. 67
Around Settle. Settle: 1888. V. 65
The Book of the Grayling.... Leeds: 1888. V. 67

PRITZEL, G. A.
Thesaurus Literaturae Botanicae: Omnium Gentium; Inde a Rerum Botanicarum Initiis Ad Nostra Usque Tempora.... 1995. V. 65

PRIVATE Letters Now First Printed from the Original MSS. 1694-1732. Edinburgh: 1829. V. 67

PRIVATE Libraries in Renaissance England. A Collection and Catalogue of Tudor and Early Stuart Book-Lists. Binghamton: 1992-1995. V. 62

THE PRIVILEGES and Practice of Parliaments in England.... London: 1680. V. 66

PRIZE Stories of 1942. New York: 1942. V. 67

PRIZE Stories of 1943. New York: 1943. V. 67

PRIZE Stories of 1947. Garden City: 1947. V. 63

PROBY, W. C.
Man Hunters of the North. Tacoma: 1928. V. 66

PROCEEDINGS at the Reception and Dinner in Honor of George Peabody... by the Citizens of Danvers.... Boston: 1856. V. 64

PROCEEDINGS Commemorative of the Settlement of Newark, New Jersey On Its Two Hundredth Anniversary. Newark: 1866. V. 63

PROCEEDINGS Of a Convention of Delegates, from the Different Counties in the State of New York, Opposed to Free-Masonry, Held in the Capitol in the City of Albany on the 19th, 20th and 21st Days of February 1829. Rochester: 1829. V. 64

PROCEEDINGS Of a Convention of Delegates Opposed to Free Masonry, Which Met at Le Roy, Genesee Co., New York, March 6, 1828. Rochester: 1828. V. 64

PROCEEDINGS of the Anti-Slavery Convention of American Women, Held in Philadelphia May 15-18, 1838. Philadelphia: 1838. V. 64

PROCEEDINGS of the Dinner Given by the Medical Profession of...New York April 12, 1883 to O. W. Holmes.... New York: 1883. V. 64

THE PROCEEDINGS Upon the Bill of Divorce Between His Grace the Duke of Norfolke (1655-1701) and the Lady Mary Mordant (Later Mary Germain 1655-1701).... London: 1700. V. 65

PROCHNOW, OSKAR
Formenkunst Der Natur. Berlin: 1934. V. 65

PROCLUS
The Philosophical and Mathematical Commentaries of Proclus.... London: 1788-1789. V. 63

PROCOPIUS
De Bello Gottorum. Rome: 1506. V. 62

PROCTER, ADELAIDE ANNE
The Complete Works. London: 1905. V. 63
Legends and Lyrics. London: 1866. V. 62; 64
Legends and Lyrics, A Book of Verses. (and) Legends and Lyrics. Second Volume. London: 1861-1863. V. 62; 67
The Victoria Regia. London: 1861. V. 64; 65

PROCTER, BEN
Not Without Honor: the Life of John H. Reagan. Austin: 1962. V. 63

PROCTER, BRYAN WALLER
Marcia Colonna an Italian Tale with Three Dramatic Scenes and Other Poems. London: 1820. V. 63

PROCTER, RICHARD WRIGHT
Memorials of Bygone Manchester, with Glimpses of the Environs. Manchester: 1880. V. 65

PROCTER, W.
Biological Survey of the Mount Desert Region (Maine). Philadelphia: 1927-1938. V. 63; 65
Biological Survey of the Mount Desert Region (Maine). Part VII. The Insect Fauna.... Philadelphia: 1946. V. 67

PROCTOR, E. H.
The Rabbits' Day in Town. London: 1908. V. 66

PROCTOR, MAURICE
The Devil Was Handsome. London: 1961. V. 67
The Spearhead Death. London: 1960. V. 67

PROCTOR, RICHARD A.
The Expanse of Heaven: a Series of Essays on the Wonders of the Firmament. London: 1876. V. 67
The Moon. Her Motions, Aspect, Scenery and Physical Condition. New York: 1878. V. 63
Other Worlds than Ours: the Plurality of Worlds Studied Under the Light of Recent Scientific Researches. New York: 1895. V. 63
Watched by the Dead: a Loving Study of Dickens' Half Told Tale. London: 1887. V. 62

PROCTOR, RICHARD WRIGHT
Memorials of Manchester Streets. Manchester: 1874. V. 65

PROCTOR, ROBERT
Narrative of a Journey Across the Cordillera of the Andes and Of a Residence in Lima and Other Parts of Peru, in the Years 1823 and 1824. London: 1825. V. 67
The Printing of Greek in the Fifteenth Century. Oxford: 1900. V. 62

PROEHL, CARL W.
The Fourth Marine Division in World War II. Washington: 1946. V. 63

PROFUSION of Paper Money, Not Deficiency in Harvests; Taxation not Speculation, the Principal Causes of the Sufferings of the People.... London: 1802. V. 62

THE PROGRESS of Nations or the Principles of National Development in Their Relation to Statesmanship. A Study in Analytical History. London: 1861. V. 67

PROGRESS of Saskatchewan. Saskatoon: 1932. V. 63

PROGRESSIVE Men of the State of Montana. Chicago: 1902. V. 63; 66

PROGULSKE, DONALD R.
Yellow Ore, Yellow Hair, Yellow Pine. Brookings: 1974. V. 67

PROKOSCH, FREDERIC
The Carnival: Poems. London: 1938. V. 65
Death at Sea. New York: 1940. V. 62

PROLOGUES and Epilogues, Celebrated for Their Poetical Merit. Oxford: 1789. V. 65

PROLUSIONES Academicae; or Exercises which Having Obtained a Prize in the University of Cambridge Were Recited in the Senate House 10 June 1902. Cambridge: 1902. V. 64

PRONZINI, BILL
Blowback. New York: 1977. V. 67
Blue Lonesome. New York: 1995. V. 67
Games. New York: 1976. V. 67
A Killing in Xanadu. Richmond: 1980. V. 62; 65; 67
Masques. New York: 1981. V. 67
1001 Midnights: the Aficionado's Guide to Mystery and Detective Fiction. New York: 1986. V. 65
Scattershot. New York: 1982. V. 67
Starvation Camp. Garden City: 1984. V. 67

PROPERT, J. L.
A History of Miniature Art. London and New York: 1887. V. 62; 65

PROPERT, W. A.
The Russian Ballet in Western Europe 1909-1920. New York: 1921. V. 66

PROPERTIUS
Sex. Aurelii Propertii Elegiarum...Cum Commentario Perpetuo Petri Burmanni Secundi et Multis Doctorum Notis Ineditis. Utrecht: 1780. V. 65

PROPOSALS at Large, for the Easy and Effectual Amendment of the Roads, by Some Further Necessary Laws and Regulations, Concerning the Wheels of All Carriages, and the Methods or Rules of Travelling.... London: 1753. V. 63

PROSCH, THOMAS
David S. Maynard and Catherine T. Maynard. Biographies of Two of the Oregon Immigrants of 1850. Seattle: 1906. V. 66
McCarver and Tacoma. Seattle: 1906. V. 63; 66

PROSE, e Versi per Onorare la Memoria di Liviv Doria Caraffa...di Alcuni Rinomati Autori. Parma: 1784. V. 64; 66

PROSPER OF AQUITAINE, SAINT
Poeme de S. Prosper Contre Les Ingrats.... Paris: 1650. V. 66

PROTESTANT EPISCOPAL CHURCH
The Book of Common Prayer and Administration of the Sacraments, and other Rites and Ceremonies as Revised and Proposed to the Use of the Protestant Episcopal Church, at a Convention...Held in Philadelphia...1785. Philadelphia: 1786. V. 64

PROTHERO, DONALD R.
The Evolution of Perissodactyls. New York: 1989. V. 67
The Terrestrial Eocene-Oligocene Transition in North America. Cambridge: 1996. V. 64

PROUDHON, P. J.
What is Property. An Inquiry Into the Principle of Right and of Government. New York: 189-?. V. 64; 66

PROULX, E. ANNIE
Accordion Crimes. New York: 1996. V. 62; 66; 67
Close Range: Wyoming Stories. New York: 1999. V. 66; 67
The Complete Dairy Foods Cookbook. Emmaus: 1982. V. 62; 63; 67
Heart Songs. New York: 1988. V. 62; 64; 65; 66; 67
Heart Songs. London: 1995. V. 62; 64; 67
Postcards. New York: 1992. V. 62; 64; 66; 67
The Shipping News. New York: 1993. V. 62; 65; 66; 67

PROUST, MARCEL
A La Recherche du Temps Peru. Paris: 1913. V. 65
L'Indifferent. New York: 1991. V. 66
Jean Santeuil. Paris: 1952. V. 62
Les Plaisirs et les Jours. Paris: 1896. V. 67
A Vision of Paris. New York: 1963. V. 63

PROUT, SAMUEL
Facsimiles of Sketches Made in Flanders and Germany and Drawn on Stone by Samuel Prout. London: 1833. V. 62
Hints on Light and Shadow, Composition, Etc., as Applicable to Landscape Painting. London: 1876. V. 62; 66
Studies of Boats and Coast Scenery, for Landscape and Marine Painters, Drawn and Etched in Imitation of Chalk. London: 1816. V. 67

PROUT, W.
Chemistry, Meteorology and the Function of Digestion, Considered with Reference to Natural Theology.... 1845. V. 62
An Inquiry Into the Nature and Treatment of Diabetes, Clavulus and Other Affections of the Urinary Organs.... 1825. V. 62

PROVENSEN, ALICE
The Egg. New York: 1970. V. 65
The Glorious Flight. New York: 1983. V. 65
A Horse and a Hound a Goat and a Gander. New York: 1980. V. 65
The Provensen Book of Fairy Tales. London: 1972. V. 67

PROVERBS And Pictures. London: 1859. V. 65

PROVERBS; or, the Manual of Wisdom.... London: 1804. V. 64

PROVOST, ANDREW J.
Biographical and Genealogical Notes of the Provost Family from 1545 to 1895. New York: 1895. V. 63; 66

PROWELL, GEORGE R.
The History of Camden County, New Jersey. Philadelphia: 1886. V. 63; 66

PROWELL, SANDRA WEST
By Evil Means. New York: 1992. V. 66
By Evil Means. 1993. V. 64; 66
By Evil Means. New York: 1993. V. 62; 65; 66; 67

PROZIO, LUCA ANTONIO
The Soldier's Vide Mecum; or, the Method of Curing the Diseases and Preserving the Health of Soldiers. London: 1747. V. 65

PRUDENTIUS, AURELIUS CLEMENS
Aurelii Prudentii Clementis Quae Extant. Halae Magdeburgicae: 1703. V. 66
Opera. Paris: 1687. V. 66
(Opera) Aurelius Prudentius Clemens Theodori Pulmanni Cranenburgii, et Victoris Giselini Opera...Commentarius. Antverpiae: 1564. V. 66
Quae Exstant (Opera). Amstelodami: 1667. V. 63; 66

PRUDHOMME, LOUIS MARIE
Les Crimes des Reines de France, Depuis le Commencement de la Monarchie Jusqu'a Marie-Antoinette. Paris: 1791. V. 65

PRUFER, H.
Die Wollen und Halbwollen Stuckfarberei in Ihrem Ganzen Umfange. Leipzig: 1878. V. 67

PRUNETTI, MICHEL ANGELO
Descrizione Storico-Critico-Mitologica delle Celebri Pitture Esistenti nei reali Palazzi Farnese e Farnesina in Roma.... Rome: 1816. V. 67
Regras da Arte de Pintura, com Breves Reflexoes Criticas Sobre os Caracteres Distinctivos de suas Escolas, Vidas, e Quadros de seus Mais Celebres Professores. Lisbon: 1815. V. 67

PRYCE, WILLIAM
Archaeologia Cornu-Britannica; or, an Essay to Preserve the Ancient Cornish Language. Sherborne: 1790. V. 64; 67
Mineralogia Cornubensis; a Treatise on Minerals, Mines and Mining. 1778. V. 63; 65; 66
Mineralogia Cornubensis: a Treatise on Minerals, Mines and Mining. London: 1778. V. 62

PRYCE TANNATT, T. E.
How to Dress Salmon Flies. 1914. V. 67
How to Dress Salmon Flies. London: 1948. V. 67
How to Dress Salmon Flies. 1977. V. 65; 67

PRYME, GEORGE
Ode to Trinity College, Cambridge. London: 1812. V. 64
A Syllabus of a Course of Lectures on the Principles of Political Economy.... Cambridge: 1819. V. 63

PRYNN, WILLIAM
The Substance of a Speech made in the House of Commons...on Munday the Fourth of December 1648. London: 1649. V. 67

PRYNNE, J. H.
Aristeas. London: 1968. V. 65
Day Light Songs. Pampisford and Cheltenham: 1968. V. 65
Down Where Changed. 1979. V. 62
Fire Lizard. Barnet: 1970. V. 65
Into the Day. Cambridge: 1972. V. 64
Kitchen Poems. London: 1968. V. 65
News of Warring Clans. London: 1977. V. 64
The White Stones. London: 1969. V. 65

PRYNNE, WILLIAM
The Antipathie of the English Lordly Prelacie, Both to Regall Monarchy, and Civil Unity.... London: 1641. V. 63
God, No Impostor, Nor Deluder. London: 1630. V. 64
The History of King John, King Henry III. And the Most Illustrious King Edward the I, Wherein the Ancient Sovereign Dominion of the Kings of England, Scotland, France and Ireland, Over All Persons in All Causes.... London: 1670. V. 63
An Humble Remonstrance to His Majesty Against the Tax of Ship-money Imposed, Laying Open the Illegalitie, Abuse and Inconvenience Thereof. London: 1641. V. 62
A Plea for the Lords: or, a Short Yet Full and Necesary Vindication of the Judiciary and Legislative Power of the House of Peeres. London: 1648. V. 64
Romes Master-Peece; or, the Grand Conspiracy of the Pope and His Jesuited Instruments, to Extripate the Protestant Religion.... London: 1644. V. 66
A Soveraign Antidote to Prevent, Appease, and Determine Our Unnaturall and Destructive Civill Warres and Dissentions. London: 1642. V. 62

PRYOR, A. R.
A Flora of Hertfordshire. 1887. V. 66

PRYOR, ROGER A.
Reminiscences of Peace and War. New York: 1904. V. 65

PRYOR, SARA
My Day. Reminiscences of a Long Life. New York: 1909. V. 62; 63; 65
Reminiscences of Peace and War. New York: 1904. V. 63

PSALMANAZAR, GEORGE
An Historical and Geographical Description of Formosa. London: 1705. V. 63
An Historical and Geograpical Description of Formosa. London: 1704. V. 67
An Historical and Geographical Description of Formosa. London: 1926. V. 62

PSALMS, Hymns and Anthems: Sung in the Chapel of the Hospital, for the Maintenance and Education of Exposed and Deserted Children. London: 1795. V. 63; 67

PSYCHIATRY Journal of the Biology and the Pathology of Interpersonal Relations. Baltimore: 1938. V. 65

PTOLEMAEUS, CLAUDIUS
Centum Ptolemaei Sententiae Eiusdem Pontani Libri XIIII. Venice: 1519. V. 65
Geographicae Enarrationis Libri Octo. Lyon: 1535. V. 62
Geographicae Enarrationis Libri Octo. Lyons: 1541. V. 62; 63; 65
Hoc in Libro Nunquam Ante Typis Aeneis in Lucem Edita Haec Insunt. Tetrabiblos...Karpos (graece). Libri Quatuor Compositi Syro Fratri. Nuremberg: 1535. V. 62
Libri Viii. de Geographia e Graeco Denuo Traducti. Nominibus Graecis e Regione Appositis, Atque in Indicem Quam Locupletissimum Recactis Nunquam Antea Uisa Commoditate Simili.... Cologne: 1540. V. 67
Theatri Geographiae Veteris Tomus Prior in Quo Cl. Ptol. Alexandrini Geographiae Libri VIII.... Amsterdam: 1619. V. 66

THE PUBLIC Domain: Its History, with Statistics. Washington: 1880. V. 66

THE PUBLIC Edifices of the British Metropolis. London: 1825. V. 62

PUBLIC School Verse. London: 1919-1926. V. 63

PUCKETT, J. L.
History of Oklahoma and Indian Territory and Homeseekers Guide. Vinita: 1906. V. 65; 67

PUCKETT, NEWBELL N.
Folk Beliefs of the Southern Negro. Chapel Hill: 1926. V. 63; 66

PUCKLE, JAMES
The Club: in a Dialogue Between Father and Son. London: 1817. V. 62; 67
England's Path to Wealth and Honour, in a Dialogue Between and Englishman and a Dutchman. London: 1750. V. 65

PUCKLER-MUSKAU, HERMANN LOUIS HENRI, PRINCE DE
Semilasso in Africa. London: 1837. V. 62

PUECH, ALBERT
Une Ville au Temps Jadis ou Nimes a la Fin du XVIe Siecle.... Nimes: 1884. V. 67

PUFFENDORF, SAMUEL, FREIHERR VON
The Compleat History of Sweden, From Its Origin to this Time.... London: 1702. V. 67
The Divine Feudal Law; or Covenants with Mankind Represented. Together with Means for the Uniting of Protestants. London: 1703. V. 64
An Introduction to the History of the Principal Kingdoms and States of Europe.... London: 1699. V. 67
An Introduction to the History of the Principal States of Europe. London: 1764. V. 65

PUGET Sound Co-Operative Colony. Milwaukee: 1886. V. 63

PUGET SOUND MARINE STATION
Publications. Volumes 1-7. Seattle: 1915-1931. V. 65

PUGET DE LA SERRE, JEAN
Histoire de l'Entree de la Reyne Mere du Roy Tres-Chrestien, dans la Grande Bretagne. London: 1639. V. 62

PUGGIE'S Stories. London: 1900. V. 64

PUGH, DAVID
Walks through London.... London: 1817. V. 62

PUGH, EDWARD
Cambria Depicta: a Tour through North Wales. London: 1816. V. 62; 67

PUGH, EDWIN W.
A Street in Suburbia. London: 1895. V. 64

PUGH, JOHN
A Treatise on the Science of Muscular Action. 1970. V. 66; 67

PUGHE, DAVID WILLIAM
Illustrated History of Caernarvon Castle. Caernarvon: 1853. V. 67

PUGIN, AUGUSTUS WELBY NORTHMORE
An Apology for the Revival of Christian Architecture in England. London: 1843. V. 64
The Present State of Ecclesiastical Architecture in England. London: 1843. V. 67
Pugin's Gothic Furniture. London: 1840. V. 67
Select Views in Islington, Pentonville Highbury, Canonbury, etc. on Thirty-One Coper Plates. London: 1810-1819. V. 62
The True Principles of Pointed or Christian Architecture Set Forth in Two Lectures.... London: 1853. V. 67

PUIG, MANUEL
Betrayed by Rita Hayworth. New York: 1971. V. 62; 66; 67
Blood of Requited Love. New York: 1984. V. 67
Buenos Aires Affair. New York: 1976. V. 67
Eternal Curse on the Reader of These Pages. New York: 1982. V. 67
Heartbreak Tango. New York: 1973. V. 67
Kiss of the Spider Woman. New York: 1979. V. 64; 67

PUISIEUX, MADELEINE D'ARSANT, MME. DE.
Les Caracteres. Londres: 1750. V. 67

PUISIEUX, MADELEINE D'ARSANT, MME. DE
Memoires d'un Homme de Bien. Paris: 1768. V. 67

PULCI, ANTONIA
The Story of Santa Guglielma. Northampton: 1984. V. 62

PULLEN, H. F.
The Pullen Expedition in Search of Sir John Franklin. Toronto: 1979. V. 62

PULLEN, HARRIET S.
Soapy Smith Bandit of the Skagway, How He Lived and Died. Juneau. V. 63; 64

PULLEN, JOHN J.
Twentieth Maine. A Volunteer Regiment in the Civil War. Philadelphia and New York: 1957. V. 62

PULLEN, P. H.
Pestalozzi's System of Practical Geography, Sacred - Ancient & Modern.... London: 1822. V. 67

PULLEN, WILLIAM HENRY
The Fight at Dame Europa's School: Showing How the German Boy Thrashed the French Boy.... New York: 1871. V. 67

PULLER, TIMOTHY
The Moderation of the Church of England, considered as Useful for Allaying the Present Distempers.... London: 1679. V. 66

PULLEYNE, EDWARD, MRS.
Out of Society. London: 1875. V. 65

PULLIAS, C. M.
Spiritual Songs. Nashville: 1932. V. 66

PULMAN, G. P. R.
The Vade Mecum of Fly-Fishing for Trout.... 1851. V. 67

PULSIFER, HAROLD TROWBRIDGE
Rowen a Collection of Verse. Boston: 1937. V. 67

PULSIFER, WILLIAM H.
Notes for a History of Lead and an Inquiry into the Development of the Manufacture of White Lead and Lead Oxides. New York: 1888. V. 62

PULTENEY, RICHARD
Historical and Biographical Sketches of the Progress in Botany, From Its Origin to the Introduction of the Linnaean System. London: 1790. V. 65

PULTENEY, WILLIAM
Considerations on the Present State of Public Affairs and Means of Raising the Necessary Supplies. London: 1779. V. 64; 66
An Enquiry into the Conduct of Our Domestick Affairs from the Year 1721 to the Present Time. London: 1734. V. 63
The Politicks on Both Sides With Regard to Foreign Affairs, Stated from Their Own Writings.... London: 1734. V. 63
A Proper Reply to a Late Scurrilous Libel: Intitled Sedition and Defamation Display'd. London: 1731. V. 63

PULTON, FERDINANDO
A Collection of Sundrie Statutes, Frequent in Use.... London: 1632. V. 62
De Pace Regis...A Treatise Declaring Which be the Great and Generall Offences of the Relame, and the Chiefe Impediments of the Peace of the King and the Kingdome, as Menaces, Assaults, Batteries, Treasons, Homicides and Felonies.... London: 1609. V. 65

PULU, TUPOU L.
Whaling: A Way of Life. Anchorage. V. 66

PUMPELLY, RAPHAEL
Geology of the Green Mountains of Massachusetts. Washington: 1894. V. 67
My Reminiscences. New York: 1918. V. 62

PUNCH
and Judy. London: 1855. V. 63
PUNCH and Judy. London: 1870. V. 67
PUNCH and Judy. London: 1875. V. 65

PUNCH'S
Guide to the Chinese Collection. London: 1844. V. 62

PUNCH'S
Pocket Book for 1845. London: 1845. V. 62

PUNCH'S
Pocket Book for 1877. London: 1877. V. 62

PUNCH'S
Pocket Book/ A.D. 1880. London: 1880. V. 62

PUNKIN, JONATHAN, PSEUD.
Downfall of Freemasonry, Being and Authentic History of the Rise, Progress and Triumph of Antimasonry.... Harrisburg: 1838. V. 63

PUNKY
Dunk. The Funniest Cat Ever. Chicago: 1912. V. 62

PUNNET, R. C.
Mimicry in Butterflies. Cambridge: 1915. V. 64

PURCELL, HENRY
Orpehus Britannicus. (with) Orpheus Britannicus...The Second Book. London: 1706-1702. V. 64

PURCHAS, SAMUEL
The Purchas Handbook. Studies of the Life, Times and Writings of Samuel Purchas, 1577-1626. London: 1997. V. 63; 67

PURCHON, R. D.
The Biology of the Mollusca. 1968. V. 66

PURDEY, T. D. S.
The Shot Gun. 1936. V. 67

PURDY, JAMES
Children Is All. New York: 1961. V. 62
Color of Darkness. New York: 1957. V. 63
Don't Call Me by My Right Name and Other Stories. New York: 1956. V. 62; 63; 64; 67
Eustace Chisholm and the Works. New York: 1967. V. 62
Lessons and Complaints. New York: 1978. V. 62
Malcolm. New York: 1959. V. 62
Mr. Evening: A Story and Nine Poems. Los Angeles: 1968. V. 62
On the Rebound: A Story and Nine Poems. Los Angeles: 1970. V. 63; 64; 66
An Oyster is a Wealthy Beast. San Francisco: 1967. V. 62
63: Dream Palace. New York: 1956. V. 62; 64
Sleep Tight. New York: 1979. V. 66

PUREFOY, GEORGE W.
A History of the Sandy Creek Baptist Association, From Its Organization in A.D. 1758 to A.D. 1858.... New York: 1859. V. 66; 67

PUREY-CUST, A. P.
The Heraldry of York, Minster.... Leeds: 1890-1896. V. 66
Walks Round York, Minster. Leeds: 1907. V. 65

PURNELL, IDELLA
Bambi. Boston: 1944. V. 65

PURPLE, EDWIN R.
In Memoriam Edwin R. Purple. New York: 1881. V. 66

PURSH, F.
Journal of a Botanical Excursion in the Northeastern Parts of the States of Pennsylvania and New York, During the Year 1807. Philadelphia: 1896. V. 66

PURTON, T.
A Botanical Description of British Plants in the Midland Counties. London: 1821. V. 62

PURVES STEWART, JAMES
Intracranial Tumours. London: 1927. V. 67

PURVIS, ROBERT
Appeal of Forty Thousand Citizens, Threatened With Disfranchisement to the People of Pennsylvania. Philadelphia: 1838. V. 62; 64

PUSCHMANN, THEODOR
Handbuch der Geschichte der Medizin. Herausgegeben von Max Neuberger und Julius Pagel. Jena: 1902-1905. V. 64
A History of Medical Education. New York: 1966. V. 63

PUSEY, EDWARD BOUVERIE
Collegiate and Professional Teaching and Discipline. Oxford and London: 1854. V. 65

PUSEY, WILLIAM ALLEN
The History of Dermatology. Springfield: 1933. V. 63

THE PUSHCART
Prize XIV. Wainscott: 1989. V. 62

PUSHKIN, ALEKSANDR SERGEEVICH
The Bakchesarian Fountain. An Other Poems. Philadelphia: 1849. V. 63
Boris Godunov. St. Petersburg: 1831. V. 63
The Captain's Daughter. New York: 1971. V. 64; 66
Eugene Onegin. N.P: 1943. V. 64; 66
Eugene Onegin. London: 1964. V. 66
Eugene Onegin. New York: 1964. V. 63; 65
Eugene Onegin. N.P: 1971. V. 63
The Golden Cockerel. New York: 1949. V. 64
The Golden Cockerel. New York: 1950. V. 62; 64
The Letters of Alexander Pushkin. Bloomington and Philadelphia: 1963. V. 66
Skazka o Tsare Saltane (The Tale of Tsar Saltan). St. Petersburg: 1905. V. 64
The Tale of the Golden Cockerel. 1907. V. 62; 65
Volbga. Petrograd: 1904. V. 62; 66

PUSS
in Boots. New York: 1888. V. 65
PUSS in Boots. New York: 1895. V. 62
PUSS in Boots. Akron: 1910. V. 66
PUSS in Boots. London: 1920. V. 65
PUSS in Boots. New York: 1934. V. 65

PUSSIES
Party. New York: 1871. V. 62

PUSSIKINS..
London: 1910. V. 64

PUSSY
Cat Circus Picture Book. London. V. 64

THE PUSSY-C
at Hunt Pictures and Verses for Little Folk. London: 1910. V. 64

PUTMAN, GEORGE HAVEN
Some Memories of the Civil War. New York: 1928. V. 67

PUTNAM, ALLEN
Mesmerism, Spiritualism, Witchcraft and Miracle.... Boston: 1881. V. 64

PUTNAM, DANIEL
Twenty-Five Years with the Insane. Detroit: 1885. V. 65

PUTNAM, ELIZABETH
Mrs. Putnam's Receipt Book; and Young Housekeeper's Assistant. Boston;: 1850. V. 62

PUTNAM, GEORGE GRANVILLE
Salem Vessels and Their Voyages. Salem: 1924-1930. V. 66

PUTNAM, GEORGE HAVEN
Books and Their Makers During the Middle Ages. New York: 1896. V. 64

PUTNAM, GEORGE PALMER
American Facts. London: 1845. V. 62

PUTNAM, J. PICKERING
The Open Fireplace in All Ages. Boston: 1882. V. 62

PUTNAM, JAMES JACKSON
Studies in Neurological Diagnosis. Boston: 1902. V. 65

PUTNAM, MARY TRAILL SPENCE LOWELL
Fifteen Days, an Extract from Edward Colvil's Journal. Boston: 1866. V. 65

PUTNAM, RUTH
Life and Letters of Mary Putnam Jacobi. New York: 1925. V. 65

PUTZEL, LEOPOLD
A Treatise on Common Forms of Functional Nervous Diseases. New York: 1880. V. 65

PUYDT, EMILE DE
Les Orchidees, Histoire Iconographique Organographie Classification Geographie Collectiosn Commerce.... Paris: 1880. V. 66

PUYVELDE, LEO VAN
Hubert and Jan Van Eyck. New York: 1956. V. 62

PUZO, MARIO
The Dark Arena. New York: 1955. V. 62; 64; 66
The Godfather. London: 1969. V. 65
The Godfather. New York: 1969. V. 62; 64; 66

THE PUZZLING Cap; a Choice Collection of Riddles, in Familiar Verse with a Curious Cut to Each. Boston: 1789-1791. V. 63

PYCROFT, JAMES
The Cricket-Field or the History and Science of the Game of Cricket. London: 1862. V. 67

PYE, CHARLES
A New Dictionary of Antient Geography, Exhibiting the Modern in Addition to the Ancient Names of Places. London: 1803. V. 63

PYE, DAVID RANDALL
George Leigh Mallory. A Memoir. London: 1927. V. 62; 63

PYE, H. J.
The Sportsman's Dictionary; or Gentleman's Companion for Town and Country.... 1785. V. 66

PYE, VIRGINIA
Red-Letter Holiday. London: 1940. V. 63

PYE, WILLIAM HENRY
The Twenty Ninth of May: Rare Doings at the Restoration.. London: 1825. V. 63

PYLE, HOWARD
The Merry Adventures of Robinhood. New York: 1888. V. 67
Pepper and Salt, or Seasoning for Young Folks. New York: 1886. V. 63
The Story of the Grail and the Passing of Arthur. New York: 1910. V. 63

PYM, BARBARA
Excellent Women. London: 1952. V. 65
Less than Angels. London: 1955. V. 63; 66
Less than Angels. New York: 1957. V. 67
No Fond Return of Love. London: 1961. V. 64
Quartet in Autumn. London: 1977. V. 62; 63
Quartet in Autumn. Few Green Leaves. An Unsuitable Attachment. Crampton Hodnet. Civil to Strangers. London: 1977-1987. V. 63

PYM, HORACE N.
Chats in the Book-Room, with Portrait by Molly Evans, with Two Photogravures of the Book Room. London: 1896. V. 65

PYNCHON, THOMAS
The Crying of Lot 49. Philadelphia and New York: 1965. V. 62; 64; 66
The Crying of Lot 49. Philadelphia: 1966. V. 62; 65; 67
Gravity's Rainbow. London: 1973. V. 62
Gravity's Rainbow. New York: 1973. V. 62; 65; 67
Low-Lands. London: 1978. V. 62
Mason and Dixon. New York: 1997. V. 62; 63; 64; 66
Slow Learner. Boston: 1984. V. 62
V. London: 1963. V. 62; 63; 65
V. Philadelphia & New York: 1963. V. 67
Vineland. Boston: 1990. V. 62

PYNE, HENRY R.
The History of Camden County, New Jersey. Trenton: 1871. V. 66
The History of the First New Jersey Cavalry (Sixteenth Regiment, New Jersey Volunteers). Trenton: 1871. V. 63

PYNE, J. B.
Lake Scenery of England. London: 1859. V. 62; 65; 66

PYNE, W. B.
Lancashire Illustrated in a Series of Views, Towns, Public Buildings, Streets, Docks, Churches, Antiquities, Abbeys, Castles, Seats of the Nobility &c. London: 1831. V. 66

PYNE, WILLIAM
The History of the Royal Residences. London: 1819. V. 67

PYNE, WILLIAM HENRY
The Costume of Great Britain. London: 1808. V. 64
On Rustic Figures in Imitation of Chalk. London: 1813. V. 64
On Rustic Figures in Imitation of Chalk. London: 1817. V. 67

PYPER, GEORGE
The Romance of an Old Playhouse. Salt Lake City: 1928. V. 62; 65

PYROTECHNICA Loyolana, Ignatian Fireworks, or, the Fiery Jesuits Temper and Behaviour. London: 1667. V. 65

Q

QUACKENBOS, JOHN DUNCAN
Hypnotism in Mental and Moral Culture. New York: 1900. V. 66

QUAD, M.
Brother Gardner's Lime Kiln Club: Being the Regular Proceedings of the Regular Club for the Last Three Years.... Chicago: 1882. V. 63; 64

QUADRI, ANTONIO
Il Canal Grande Di Venezia Descritto Da Antonio Quadri... E Rappresentato In XXXXVUIII Tavole. Venezia: 1838. V. 65

QUAGLIO, JOHANN MARIA VON
Praktische Anleitung zur Perspektiv mit Anwendungen auf die Baukunst.... Munich: 1811. V. 67

QUAIFE, M. M.
Yellowstone Kelly - the Memoirs of Luther S. Kelly. New Haven: 1926. V. 65; 67

QUAIN, JONES
The Bones and Ligaments of the Human Body: in a Series of Plates.... London: 1842. V. 65
Elements of Anatomy. London: 1837. V. 62
The Nerves of the Human Body.... London: 1839. V. 63

QUAIN, RICHARD
A Dictionary of Medicine Including General Pathology, General Therapeutics, Hygiene and the Dieases of Women and Children. London: 1894. V. 63

THE QUAKER Queries: New England Queries in Past and Present. Boston: 1969. V. 63

QUAMMEN, DAVID
Natural Acts. New York: 1985. V. 63; 64
To Walk the Line. New York: 1970. V. 63; 64; 67

QUANTI, Q.
Qudrille Elucidated, being a Historical, Critical and Practical Treatise on that Admirable Game. Cheltenham: 1822. V. 63

QUARENGHI, GIACOMO
Fabbriche e Disegni.... Milan: 1821. V. 64

QUARITCH, BERNARD
A Catalogue of Books and Manuscripts Issued to Commemorate the One Hundredth Anniversary of the Firm of Bernard Quaritch 1847-1947. London: 1947. V. 63; 65
A Catalogue of Books and Manuscripts Issued to Commemorate the One Hundredth Anniversary of the Firm of Bernard Quaritch 1847-1947.... London: 1947. V. 63
A Catalogue of Illuminated and Other Manuscripts Together with Some Works on Palaeography. London: 1931. V. 62
A General Catalogue of Books, Arranged in Classes, Offered for Sale by Bernard Quaritch. London: 1868. V. 66
A General Catalogue of Books Offered to the Public at Affixed Prices. London: 1880. V. 64
A General Catalogue of Books, Offered to the Public at the Affixed Prices by Bernard Quaritch. The Supplement 1875-1877. London: 1877. V. 64
Monuments of Typography and Xylography: Books of the First Half Century of the Art of Printing. London: 1897. V. 62

QUARLES, BENJAMIN
The Negro and the American Revolution. Chapel Hill: 1961. V. 64; 66

QUARLES, FRANCIS
Argalus and Parthenia.... London: 1647. V. 64
Boanerges and Barnabas. Judgment and Mercy; or Wine and Oyle for Wounded and Afflicted Souls.... London: 1651. V. 64

QUARRIE, GEORGE
Within a Jersey Circle. Tales of the Past Grave and Gay, As Picked Up From Old Jerseyites. Somerville: 1910. V. 63; 66

QUARTERMAIN, L. B.
New Zealand and the Antarctic. Wellington: 1971. V. 64

THE QUARTO. London: 1896-1898. V. 64; 66

QUATRE Contes Russes. Paris: 1923. V. 64

QUATREFAGES DE BREAU, ARMAND DE
The Pygmies. London: 1895. V. 63
The Rambles of a Naturalist on the Coasts of France, Spain and Sicily. 1857. V. 66
The Rambles of a Naturalist on the Coasts of France, Spain and Sicily. London: 1957. V. 62; 64

QUAYLE, ERIC
The Collector's Book of Detective Fiction. London: 1972. V. 65; 66; 67

QUE Meyo Se Podera Tomar Pera Extinguir o Iudaismo de Portugal. N.P: 1630-1640. V. 62

QUEEN, ELLERY, PSEUD.
The Adventures of Ellery Queen. 1934. V. 66; 67
The American Gun Mystery. 1933. V. 66
Cat of Many Tails. Boston: 1949. V. 62
The Chinese Orange Mystery. 1934. V. 66
The Detective Short Story, a Bibliography. Boston: 1942. V. 67
The Door Between. 1937. V. 64
The Dragon's Teeth. 1939. V. 64; 66; 67

QUEEN, ELLERY, PSEUD. continued
The Egyptian Cross Mystery. 1932. V. 64
The Female of the Species: The Great Women Detectives and Criminals. Boston: 1943. V. 67
The Four of Hearts. 1938. V. 64; 66
The Four of Hearts. New York: 1938. V. 67
The French Powder Mystery. New York: 1930. V. 63
The Golden Eagle Mystery. 1942. V. 67
The Greek Coffin Mystery. 1932. V. 64; 66
Halfway House. 1936. V. 66
The Misadventures of Sherlock Holmes. 1944. V. 62
The Misadventures of Sherlock Holmes. Boston: 1944. V. 66; 67
Murder by Experts. 1947. V. 67
Murder by Experts. Chicago: 1947. V. 65
The Murderer is a Fox. 1945. V. 63

QUEEN, ELLERY, PSEUD
The New Adventures of Ellery Queen. 1940. V. 67

QUEEN, ELLERY, PSEUD.
Queen's Quorum. Boston: 1951. V. 65; 66; 67
Queen's Quorum. New York: 1969. V. 66; 67
The Roman Hat Mystery. 1979. V. 64; 66
The Spanish Cape Mystery. 1935. V. 64; 66
The Spanish Cape Mystery. New York: 1935. V. 67
Ten Days Wonder. Boston: 1948. V. 67
There Was An Old Woman. Boston: 1943. V. 66

THE QUEEN'S Book of the Red Cross. London: 1939. V. 63

THE QUEEN'S Budget Opened, or Correspondence Extraordinary Relative to the Defence of Her Maejsty, etc. London: 1820. V. 66

THE QUEEN'S Closet Opened. London: 1710. V. 64

QUEENS of the Circulating Library. Selections from Victorian Lady Novelists, 1850-1900. London: 1950. V. 63

THE QUEEN'S Story Book. New York: 1898. V. 62

QUEENY, EDGAR M.
Cheechako. 1941. V. 64

QUEIROZ, ECA DE
The City and the Mountains. London: 1955. V. 64
The Sweet Miracle. London: 1905. V. 64

QUEKETT, JOHN
Lectures on Histology, Delivered at the Royal College of Surgeons of England in the Session 1850-1851. London: 1852. V. 65
A Practical Treatise on the Use of the Microscope. Lincolnwood: 1987. V. 67

QUELCH, J. J.
Challenger Voyage. Zoology. Part 46. Reef Corals. 1886. V. 66

QUENEAU, RAYMOND
La Vol D'Icare. Paris: 1968. V. 66

QUENNELL, PETER
A Letter to Mrs. Virginia Woolf. London: 1932. V. 63
Masques & Poems. Berkshire: 1922. V. 67
Poems. London: 1926. V. 62

QUENTIN, GEORGE AUGUSTUS
The Trial of Colonel Quentin, of the Tenth, or, Prince of Wales's Own Regiment of Hussars, by a General Court Martial, Held at Whitehall on Monday, the 17th of October 1814. London: 1814. V. 63

QUENTIN, HARRIET
Mrs. Q-----and Windsor Castle.... London: 1906. V. 65

QUENTIN, PATRICK
Cottage Sinister. 1931. V. 64; 66
Puzzle for Players. New York: 1938. V. 65

QUERO, J. C.
Clofeta I-III, Check List of the Fishes of the Eastern Tropical Atlantic. Lisbon: 1990. V. 65

QUERRY, RON
The Death of Bernadette Lefthand. Santa Fe: 1963. V. 62; 65; 66
Growing Old at Willie Nelson's Picnic. College Station: 1983. V. 67
I See By My Get-Up. Albuquerque: 1987. V. 66; 67

QUERRY, RONALD J.
Growing Old at Willie Nelson's Picnic. College Station: 1983. V. 64

QUESNEY, FRANCOIS
Essai sur l'Administration des Terres. Paris: 1759. V. 67

QUETELET, LAMBERT ADOLPHE JACQUES
Anthropometrie ou Mesure des Differentes Facultes de l'Homme. Brussels, Leipzig & Ghent: 1871. V. 65
Sur l'Homme et le Developement de Ses Facules ou Essai de Physique Sociale. Paris: 1835. V. 62; 65; 66

QUEVEDO Y VILLEGAS, FRANCISCO GOMEZ DE
Les Oeuvres.... Brusselles: 1699. V. 67
The Visions. London: 1702. V. 64

QUIGGIN, A. H.
A Survey of Primitive Money, the Beginnings of Currency. London: 1949. V. 62

QUIGGIN, E. C.
Essays and Studies Presented to William Ridgeway On His Sixteith Birthday 6th August 1913. Cambridge: 1913. V. 66

QUILLER-COUCH, ARTHUR THOMAS
The Astonishing History of Troy Town. London: 1888. V. 62
In Powder and Crinoline. N.P: 1912. V. 63
In Powder and Crinoline. London: 1913. V. 64
The Oxford Book of English Verse 1250-1918. Oxford. V. 67
The Oxford Book of Victorian Verse. Oxford: 1913. V. 65
The Sleeping Beauty and Other Fairy Tales. London: 1910. V. 63; 67
The Splendid Spur: Being Memoirs of the Adventures of Mr. John Marvel, a Servant of His Late Majesty King Charles I, in the Years 1642-43. London: 1889. V. 67
Twelve Dancing Princesses and Other Fairy Tales. New York. V. 65
The Twelve Dancing Princesses and Other Fairy Tales. New York: 1920. V. 64

QUILLER-COUCH, MABEL
The Treasure Book of Children's Verse. New York: 1911. V. 63
The Treasure Book of Children's Verse. New York: 1925. V. 63

QUILLET, CLAUDE
Callipaediae: or, An Art How to Have Handsome Children. London: 1710. V. 62; 64; 65

QUILLIET, FREDERIC
La Arte Italiane in Ispagna. Rome: 1825. V. 64

QUILLINAN, DORA WORDSWORTH
Journal of a Few Month's Residence in Portugal and Glimpses of the South of Spain. London: 1858. V. 66

QUILLINAN, EDWARD
Woodcuts and Verses (Used at the Lee Priory Press). Ickham, Kent: 1820. V. 62; 67

QUIN, FREDERICK
Homooopathic Society - Men of the Day. 1872. V. 66

QUIN, TARELLA
Gum Tree Brownie and Other Faerie Folk of the Never Never. Melbourne, Sydney, Adelaide: 1912. V. 66

QUINAULT, PHILIPPE
La Mere Coquette ou Les Amants Brouilles. Paris: 1666. V. 66

QUINBY, G. W.
The Gallows, the Prison and the Poor-House. Cincinnati: 1856. V. 63

QUINCY, JOHN
Lexicon Physico-Medicum; or a New Medicinal Dictionary.... London: 1726. V. 62

QUINCY, JOSIAH
Remarks on Some of the Provisions of the Laws of Massachusetts Affecting Poverty, Vice and Crime. Cambridge: 1822. V. 63

QUINDLEN, ANNA
Black and Blue. New York: 1998. V. 67
Object Lessons. New York: 1991. V. 67
One True Thing. New York: 1994. V. 67

QUINE, W. V. O.
A System of Logistic. Cambridge: 1934. V. 67

QUINLAN, JAMES E.
Tom Quick, the Indian Slayer; and the Pioneers of Minisink and Wawarsink. Monticello: 1851. V. 63; 66

QUINN, DAVID B.
The Hakluyt Handbook. London: 1974. V. 66
A Particular Discourse Concerninge the Greate Necessite and Manifolde Commodyties that are Like to Growe to This Realme of Englande by the Westerne Discoueries Lately Attempted.... London: 1993. V. 66

QUINN, ELISABETH V.
The Kewpie Primer. New York: 1916. V. 65

QUINN, JOHN
Complete Catalogue of the Library of John Quinn.... New York. V. 65

QUINN, SEABURY
The Phantom Fighter. 1966. V. 66

QUINT, ALONZO H.
The Potomac and the Rapidan, Army Notes from the Failure at Winchester to the Reinforcement of Hosencrans, 1861-1863. Boston: 1864. V. 63

QUINTANILLA, LUIS
All the Brave: Drawings of the Spanish War. New York: 1939. V. 65; 66

QUINTARD, C. T.
Confederate Soldier's Pocket Manual of Devotions. Charleston: 1863. V. 62

QUINTILLIANUS, MARCUS FABIUS
Declamationes, Quae ex CCCLXXXXVIII. Paris: 1580. V. 62; 65
The Declamations...Being and Exercitation or Praxis Upon His XII Books, Concerning the Institution of Oratory.... London: 1686. V. 67
M. Fabii Quintilliani, ut Ferunt Declamationes XIX Majores...Et Calpurnii Flacii Delcmationes... (with) De Institutione Oratoria. Lugduni Batavorum: 1720. V. 66

QUINTON, JOHN ALLAN
Working Men's Essays on the Sabbath. London: 1849. V. 67

QUINTUS SMYRNAEUS
Paralippomeni D'Omero. Modena: 1815. V. 65
Quinti Calabri...Praetermissorum ab Homero Libri Quatuordecim.... Basiliae: 1569. V. 65; 66

QUIRKE, W. M.
Recollections of a Violinist. 1914. V. 63

QUIZEM, CALEB
Annals of Sporting. London: 1809. V. 62; 65; 66

R

R., E.
Geography and History. Southampton: 1794. V. 65

R., T.
An Honest Letter to a Doubtfull Friend, About the Rising of the Twentieth Part of His Estate. London: 1642. V. 66

RABAN, JONATHAN
Granta 29 (New World). London: 1989. V. 67

RABELAIS, FRANCOIS
Five Books of the Lives, Heroic Deeds and Sayings of Gargantua and His Son Pantagruel. London: 1892. V. 62
The Works of.... London: 1874. V. 62
The Works of.... London: 1921. V. 63

RACCONTO Delle Sontuose Esequie Fatta Alla Serenissima Isabella Reina di Spagna Nella Chiesa Maggiore della Citta di Milano il Giorno XXII. Milan: 1645. V. 65

RACINE, JEAN
Phaedra. San Francisco: 1958. V. 64

RACINET, A. C. A.
L'Ornement Polychrome Cent Planches en Couleurs or et Argent Contenant Environ 2000 Motifs de Tous les Styles. Art Ancien et Asiatique Moyen Age Renaissance, XVIIe et XVIIIe Siecle. Recueil Historique et Pratique. (Premiere Serie...; Deuxieme Serie). Paris: 1869-1887. V. 64

RACK, JOHN
French Wine and Liquor Manufacturer. New York: 1875. V. 67

RACKHAM, ARTHUR
The Arthur Rackham Fairy Book: A Book of Old Favourites with new Illustrations. London: 1933. V. 63; 64

RACKHAM, BERNARD
A Book of Porcelain, Fine Examples in the Victoria and Albert Museum. London: 1910. V. 65

RACZ, ISTVAN
Art Treasures of Medieval Finland. London: 1962. V. 64

RADBILL, SAMUEL X.
Bibliography of Medical Ex Libris Literature. Los Angeles: 1951. V. 64; 66; 67

RADCLIFFE, ALEXANDER
The Ramble an Anti-Heroick Poem. Together with Some Terrestrial Hymns and Carnal Ejaculations. London: 1682. V. 66

RADCLIFFE, ANN
The Castles of Athlin and Dunbayne. A Highland Story. London: 1793. V. 62
The Castles of Athlin and Dunbayne. A Highland Story. London: 1811. V. 67
The Castles of Athlin and Dunbayne. A Highland Story. London: 1823. V. 65
Gaston de Blondeville. London: 1826. V. 65
The Italian, or the Confessional of the Black Penitents. London: 1797. V. 62; 65
The Ladies Elegant Jester, or Fun for the Female Sex.... London: 1800. V. 62; 66
The Mysteries of Udolpho. Dublin: 1794. V. 64
The Mysteries of Udolpho. London: 1794. V. 62; 64
The Mysteries of Udolpho. London: 1806. V. 65
The Mysteries of Udolpho. Paris: 1808. V. 65
The Mysteries of Udolpho. London: 1816. V. 67
The Mysteries of Udolpho. London: 1824. V. 65
The Mysteries of Udolpho. London: 1826. V. 66
The Romance of the Forest. London: 1726. V. 62
The Romance of the Forest. London: 1792. V. 62; 65
The Romance of the Forest. London: 1816. V. 67
The Romance of the Forest. London: 1825. V. 65

RADCLIFFE, CHARLES BLAND
On Diseases of the Spine and of the Nerves. Philadelphia: 1871. V. 65

RADCLIFFE, E. DELME
Falconry. London: 1971. V. 67

RADCLIFFE, F. P. DELME
The Noble Science. London: 1839. V. 63
The Noble Science. 1893. V. 62; 64
The Noble Science. 1911. V. 62

RADCLIFFE, J.
Bibliotheca Chethamensis sive Bibliothecae Publicae Mancuniensis.... Manchester: 1791-1826. V. 65; 66

RADCLIFFE, W.
Fishing from the Earliest Times. 1921. V. 67

RADCLIFFE-BROWN, A. R.
The Andaman Islanders. Cambridge: 1933. V. 62

RADCLYFFE, C. W.
The Palace of Blenheim. Oxford: 1842. V. 67

RADDALL, THOMAS H.
The Markland Sagas. Liverpool: 1934. V. 64

RADDIN, GEORGE GATES
Hocquet Caritat and the Early New York Literary Scene. Dover: 1953. V. 62; 62; 67

RADER, JESSE L.
South of Forty, from the Mississippi to the Rio Grande: a Bibliography. Norman: 1947. V. 64

RADFORD, GEORGE
Yorkshire by the Sea. Leeds: 1891. V. 64; 65; 66

RADICE, WILLIAM
Eight Sections. London: 1974. V. 65

RADIN, PAUL
The Italians of San Francisco their Adjustment and Acculturation. N.P: 1935. V. 64

RADIO Fun 1945. V. 67

RADIO Fun Annual 1942. V. 65

RADL, E.
The History of Biological Theories. Oxford: 1930. V. 64

RADLEY, SHEILA
The Chief Inspector's Daughter. London: 1981. V. 63
Death and the Maiden. London: 1978. V. 63; 66

RADNOR, H. M., COUNTESS OF
Catalogue of the Pictures in the Collection of the Earl of Radnor. London: 1909. V. 64

RAE, JOHN
Granny Goose. Joliet: 1926. V. 63
Life of Adam Smith. London: 1895. V. 65
Rae's Arctic Correspondence 1844-1855. London: 1953. V. 64; 65

RAE-BROWN, COLIN
Edith Dewar; or, Glimpses of Scottish Life and Manners in the Nineteenth Century. London: 1875. V. 66

RAFFALD, ELIZABETH
The Experienced English Housekeeper. London: 1780. V. 64
Experienced English Housekeeper. London: 1794. V. 64; 67
Experienced English Housekeeper. London: 1806. V. 67

RAFFALOVICH, ARTHUR
La Misere en Angleterre: la Condition du Pauvre a Bristol. Paris: 1885. V. 67

RAFFALOVICH, GEORGE
The History of a Soul: an Attempt at Psychology. London: 1910. V. 64

RAFFALOVICH, MARK
A Willing Exile. London: 1890. V. 66

RAFFLES, THOMAS
Letters During a Tour through Some Parts of France, Savoy, Switzerland, Germany and the Netherlands, in the Summer of 1817. Liverpool: 1818. V. 65

RAFINESQUE, C. S.
Annals of Nature or Annual Synopsis of New Genera and Species of Animals, Plants, &c. Lexington: 1820. V. 62
Florula Ludoviciana: or a Flora of the State of Louisiana. New York: 1817. V. 63; 66
A Monograph on the Fluviatile Bivalve Shells of the River Ohio Containing Twelve Genera and Sixty-Eight Species. Philadelphia: 1832. V. 62
Principes Fondamentaux de Somiologie ou les Loix de la Nomenclature et de la Classification de l'Empire Oraganique ou des Animaux et des Vegetaux Contenant les Regles Essentielles de l'Art de Eur Imposer des Noms Immuables.... Palermo: 1814. V. 62

RAFTER, MICHAEL
Savindroog; or the Queen of the Jungle. London: 1848. V. 65

RAGATZ, LOWELL JOSEPH
A Guide for the Study of British Caribbean History 1763-1834 Including the Abolition and Emancipation Movements. 2000. V. 65

RAGGE, D. R.
Grasshoppers, Crickets and Cockroaches of the British Isles. London: 1965. V. 62; 65; 66; 67

RAGGUAGLIO Delle Nozze Della Maesta di Filippo Quinto e di Elisabetta Farnese...Celebrate in Parma l'Anno 1714.... Parma: 1717. V. 65

RAGHAVAN, V.
Experimental Embryogenesis in Vascular Plants. London: 1976. V. 66

RAGLAND, J. FARLEY
A Little Slice of Living. Richmond: 1953. V. 62
Rhymes of the Times. New York: 1946. V. 62

RAHMAS, SIGRID
A Day in Fairyland. 1940. V. 64

RAHT, CARLYSLE G.
The Romance Old Davis Mountains and Big Bend Country - a History. El Paso: 1919. V. 64

RAIKES, RICHARD
Considerations on the Alliance Between Christianity & Commerce Applied to the Present State of This Country. London: 1806. V. 67

RAIKES, THOMAS
A Portion of the Journal...from 1831 to 1847. London: 1856-1857. V. 62; 65

RAILROAD Picture Book. New York: 1903. V. 63

THE RAIL-ROADS, History and Commerce of Chicago. Chicago: 1854. V. 67

THE RAILWAY Train. London: 1910. V. 63

RAIMOND, C. E.
George Mandeville's Husband. London: 1894. V. 64

THE RAINBOW Annual 1937. V. 67

RAINE, ANGELO
Mediaeval York, a Topographical Survey Based on Original Sources. London: 1955. V. 63

RAINE, CRAIG
The Electrification of the Soviet Union. London: 1986. V. 62
Rich. London: 1983. V. 64

RAINE, JAMES
Saint Cuthbert; with an Account of the State in Which His Remains Were Found Upon the Opening of His Tomb in Durham Cathedral in the Year MDCCCXXVII. Durham: 1828. V. 65

RAINE, JOHN
The History and Antiquities of the Parish of Blyth, in the Counties of Nottingham and York. Westminster: 1860. V. 63

RAINE, KATHLEEN
Autobiography. London: 1973-1977. V. 65
Blake and Tradition. Princeton: 1968. V. 64
Ninfa Revisited. London: 1968. V. 65
The Pythoness and Other Poems. London: 1949. V. 63; 65
Selected Poems. New York: 1952. V. 65
Six Dreams and Other Poems. London: 1968. V. 62
What is Man?. Ipswich: 1980. V. 65; 67
The Written Word. London: 1963. V. 65
The Written Word. London: 1967. V. 62
The Year One - Poems. London: 1952. V. 65
Yeats the Initiate: Essays on Certain Themes in the Work of W. B. Yeats. Dublin: 1986. V. 65

RAINE, W.
Bird Nesting in North-West Canada. Toronto: 1892. V. 67

RAINE, WILLIAM MAC LEOD
The Sheriff's Son. Boston: 1918. V. 66
Wyoming. New York: 1908. V. 63

RAINES, C. W.
A Bibliography of Texas. Austin: 1934. V. 64

RAINES, REV. CANON
The Vicars of Rochdale. Manchester: 1883. V. 65

RAINEY, GEORGE
No Man's Land, the Historic Story of a Landed Orphan. Enid: 1937. V. 65; 67

RAINEY, R. C.
Migration and Meteorology.... Oxford: 1989. V. 62

RAINEY, T. C.
Along the Old Trail. Pioneer Sketches of Arrow Rock and Vicinity. Marshall: 1914. V. 66

RAINEY, THOMAS
Ocean Steam Navigation and the Ocean Post. New York/London: 1858. V. 64; 65

RAINY, ALEXANDER
On the Transfer of Property by Public Auction and Private Contract.... London: 1678. V. 65

RAISSON, HORACE NAPOLEON
Code de la Toilette, Manual Complete d'Elegance et d'Hygiene, Contenant les Lois, Regles Applications et Examples de l'Art de Soigner sa Personne, et de s'habiller avec Gout et Methode.... Bruxelles: 1828. V. 66

RAISTRICK, ARTHUR
The Hatchett Diary. Truro: 1967. V. 64
A History of Lead Mining in the Pennines. London: 1965. V. 65
The Lead Industry of Wensleydale and Swaledale. Volume I. The Mines. Volume II. The Smelting Mills. Buxton: 1975. V. 64; 66
Lead Mining in the Mid-Pennines. Truro: 1973. V. 65
Malham and Malham Moor. Clapham: 1947. V. 65
Mines and Miners of Swaledale. Clapham: 1955. V. 65
Two Centuries of Industrial Welfare. London: 1938. V. 65

RAIT, ROBERT
The Story of an Irish Property. 1908. V. 67

RAJAN, B.
The Yeats Companion. London: 1952. V. 62

RAK, MARY KIDDER
Border Patrol. Cambridge: 1938. V. 67

RAKOCY, WILLIAM
...For Art Anything. N.P: 1972. V. 63; 64; 66
Ghosts of Kingston and Hillsboro New Mexico: a Pictorial Documentary of the Great Black Range Country. N.P: 1983. V. 63; 64; 66

RALEIGH & GASTON RAILROAD
Proceedings of the Fourteenth Annual Meeting of the Stockholders of the Raleigh and Gaston Railroad Co.... Raleigh: 1864. V. 62

RALEIGH, WALTER
An Abrigement of Sir Walter Raleigh's History of the World in Five Books.... London: 1698. V. 63
The Discoverie of the Large, Rich and Bewtiful Empyre of Guiana, with a Relation of the Great and Golden Citie of Manoa.... London: 1596. V. 64
Die Funffte Kurtze Wunderbare Beschreibung ...Goldreichen Konigreichs Guianae in America Oder Neuen Welt. Noribergae: 1603. V. 64
The History of the World. London: 1665. V. 63
The History of the World. London: 1687. V. 64
The Last Fight of the Revenge. 1908. V. 67
The Letters of Sir Walter Raleigh (1879-1922). New York: 1926. V. 62
Poems. London: 1845. V. 67
Remains...Maxims of State. Advice to His Son.... London: 1702. V. 64
Remains...Maxims of State. Advice to His Son.... London: 1726. V. 63
A Report of the Truth Concerning the Last Sea-Fight of the Revenge. Boston: 1902. V. 63
The Works of Sir Walter Ralegh...Together with His Letters an Poems, The Whole Never Before Collected.... London: 1751. V. 63

RALFE, JAMES
The Naval Chronology of Great Britain; or an Historical Account of Naval and Maritime Events, from the Commencement of the War in 1803, to the End of the Year 1816.... London: 1820. V. 67

RALFE, P. G.
The Birds of the Isle of Man. Edinburgh: 1905. V. 62

RALFS, J.
The British Desmidieae. London: 1848. V. 65

RALPH, JAMES
A Critical Review of the Public Buildings, Statues and Ornaments in and About London and Westminster. London: 1734. V. 62
The Fasionable Lady; or, Harlequin's Opera. London: 1730. V. 63
The History of England During the Reigns of K. William, Q. Anne and K. George I. London: 1744-1746. V. 67
Of the Use and Abuse of Parliaments. London: 1744. V. 65
The Other Side of the Question; or, an Attempt to Rescue the Characters of the Two Royal Sisters Q. Mary and Q. Anne.... London: 1742. V. 62; 63
The Touch-stone; or Historical, Critical, Political, Philosophical and Theological Essays on the Reigning Diversions of the Towns. London: 1729. V. 62

RALPH, JULIAN
On Canada's Frontier. New York: 1892. V. 65

RALPH Walker, Architect of Voorhees Gmelin; Walker Voorhees Walker Foley; Smith Voorhees Walker Smith & Smith. New York: 1957. V. 65

RALSTON, J. K.
Rhymes of a Cowboy. Billings: 1969. V. 63, 64, 66, 67

RAM, JAMES
A Treatise on Facts as Subjects of Inquiry by a Jury. New York: 1873. V. 65

RAMADGE, FRANCIS HOPKINS
Consumption Curable; and the Manner in Which Nature as Well as Remedial Art Operates in Effecting a Healing Process in the Cases of Consumption. London: 1836. V. 63

RAMASWAMY, CAVELLY VENKATA
A Digest of the Different Castes of India. Madras: 1837. V. 67

RAMAZZINI, BERNARD
Opera Omnia Medica et Physiologica. London: 1739. V. 65

A RAMBLE through Newburgh Park and the York and Ainsty Hunt. York: 1871. V. 67

RAMBLES in Teesdale by the Authors of Holiday Rambles on the Yorkshire Moors. London: 1877. V. 65

RAMBLES Round Guildford.... Guildford: 1840. V. 62

RAMEL, JEAN PIERRE
Narrative of the Deportation to Cayenne, of Barthelemy, Pichegru, Willot, Marbois, La Rue, Ramel &c., &c. in Consequence of the Revolution of the 18th Fructidor (September 4, 1797).... London: 1799. V. 65

RAMELLI, AGOSTINO
Schatzkammer, Mechanischer Kunste...Darinnen Viel Unterschiedene Wunderbahre.. Leipzig: 1620. V. 62; 63

RAMIE, GEORGES
Ceramics of Picasso. Barcelona: 1985. V. 63; 64

RAMON Y CAJAL, SANTIAGO
Degeneration and Regeneration of the Nervous System. London: 1928. V. 66
Histology. Baltimore: 1933. V. 66
Structure and Connections of Neurons. 1952. V. 65

RAMOS, MANUEL
The Ballad of Rocky Ruiz. New York: 1993. V. 64; 66

RAMOS, MEL
The Girls of Mel Ramos. London and Chicago: 1975. V. 65

RAMPANT LIONS PRESS
Miscellany 2. Cambridge: 1998. V. 62

RAMPLING, CHARLOTTE
With Compliments. London and New York: 1987. V. 66

RAMSAY, A. C.
The Geology of North Wales. 1866. V. 62
The Geology of North Wales. 1881. V. 65
The Old Glaciers of Switzerland and North Wales. London: 1860. V. 63; 64

RAMSAY, A. MAITLAND
Atlas of External Diseases of the Eye. Glasgow: 1898. V. 65

RAMSAY, ALEXANDER
A Series of Plates of the Heart, Cranium and Brain, an Imitation of Dissections. Edinburgh: 1813. V. 63

RAMSAY, ALLAN
A Dialogue on Taste. London: 1762. V. 64
The Ever Green, Being a Collection of Scots Poems. Edinburgh: 1724. V. 64
The Ever Green, Being a Collection of Scots Poems. Edinburgh: 1761. V. 62
The Gentle Shepherd, a Pastoral Comedy. Glasgow: 1788. V. 62; 64
The Poems. London: 1800. V. 67
The Tea-Table Miscellany. Glasgow: 1871. V. 65

RAMSAY, ANDREW MICHAEL
The Travels of Cyrus. London: 1730. V. 62
The Travels of Cyrus. London: 1739. V. 62
The Travels of Cyrus. Glasgow: 1763. V. 62

RAMSAY, DAVID
An Eulogium Upon Benjamin Rush, M.D. Professor of the Institutes and Practice of Medicine and Clinical Practice in the University of Pennsylvania.... Philadelphia: 1813. V. 64
The History of South Carolina, from Its Settlement in 1670 to the Year 1808. Charleston: 1809. V. 63
The History of the American Revolution. Dublin: 1793. V. 65
The History of the Revolution in South Carolina, from a British Province to an Independent State. Trenton: 1785. V. 63; 66
The Life of George Washington. London: 1807. V. 62

RAMSAY, EDWARD BANNERMAN
Two Lectures on Some Changes in Social Life and Habits. Edinburgh: 1857. V. 67

RAMSAY, GEORGE
A New Dictionary of Anecdotes, Illustrative of Character and Events, from Genuine Sources. London: 1822. V. 63

RAMSAY, JAMES
Examination of the Rev. Mr. Harris's Scriptural Researches on the Licitness of the Slave Trade. London: 1788. V. 65
Objections to the Abolition of the Slave Trade, With Answers to Which are Prefixed, Strictures on a Late Publication.... London: 1788. V. 65

RAMSAY, W. M.
Studies in the History and Art of the Eastern Provinces of the Roman Empire.... Aberdeen: 1906. V. 62

RAMSBOTTOM, FRANCIS H.
The Principles and Practice of Obstetric Medicine and Surgery, in Reference to the Process of Parturition. London: 1845. V. 63; 67

RAMSBOTTOM, JOHN
Mushrooms and Toadstools. London: 1953. V. 62

RAMSDEN, A. R.
Assam Planter. 1945. V. 67

RAMSDEN, CHARLES
French Bookbinders. 1789-1848. London: 1989. V. 64

RAMSEY, ALF
Talking Football. London: 1952. V. 63; 64

RAMSEY, JAMES
The Annals of Tennessee. Charleston: 1853. V. 63
The Annals of Tennessee. Philadelphia: 1860. V. 63

RAMSEY, MERLE
Pioneer Days of Laguna Beach. Laguna Beach: 1967. V. 62

RAMUS, PETRUS
Hoc est, Septem Artes Liberales, in Regia Cathedra, Per Ipsum Parisiis Apodictio Docendi Denere Propositae. Basel: 1576. V. 65

RANCHER
Forrard-On!. London: 1930. V. 67

RANCHIN, GUILLAUME
A Review of the Councell of Trent, Wherein are Contained the Several Nullities Of It.... Oxford: 1638. V. 62

RAND, A. L.
Handbook of New Guinea Birds. 1967. V. 63; 66
Handbook of New Guinea Birds. Garden City: 1968. V. 63; 67

RAND, AYN
Atlas Shrugged. New York: 1957. V. 62; 64
Capitalism: the Unknown Ideal. New York: 1966. V. 63
Philosophy: Who Needs It. Indianapolis: 1982. V. 66
The Romantic Manifesto. Cleveland: 1969. V. 67

RAND, EDWARD SPRAGUE
Bulbs: a Treatise on Hardy and Tender Bulbs and Tubers. Boston: 1866. V. 63; 64
The Rhododendron and American Plants a Treatise on the Culture, Propagation, and Species of the Rhododendron.... Boston: 1871. V. 63

RAND, HARRY
The Clouds. Washington: 1996. V. 62; 64

RAND, ISAAC
Observations on Phthisis Pulmonalis, and the Use of the Digitalis Purpurea in the Treatment of that Disease.... Boston: 1804. V. 67

RAND, McNally & Co.'s Indexed County and Railroad Pocket Map and Shipper's Guide of North Carolina. Chicago & New York: 1890. V. 63

RAND, SILAS TERTIUS
Dictionary of the Language of Micmac Indians, Who Reside in Nova Scotia, New Brunswick, Prince Edward Island, Cape Breton and Newfoundland. Halifax: 1888. V. 63
A Dictionary of the MicMac Language from Phonographic Word Lists. Charlottetown: 1902. V. 66

RANDALL, C. B.
The Romance of Books through the Ages. New Castle: 1925. V. 62

RANDALL, DAVID A.
Dukedom Large Enough. New York: 1969. V. 64

RANDALL, HENRY S.
The Life of Thomas Jefferson. New York: 1858. V. 64
The Practical Shepherd: A Complete Treatise on the Breeding and Management and Diseases of Sheep. New York: 1871. V. 67
Sheep Husbandry: Being a Treatise on the Acclimation of Sheep in the Southern States and an Account of the Different Breeds. New York: 1851. V. 64

RANDALL, J.
The New Book of Knowledge; or, Young Man's Best Instructor in the Arts and Sciences. London: 1787. V. 67

RANDALL, J. E.
Sharks of Arabia. London: 1986. V. 65

RANDALL, JOHN
Our Coal and Iron Industries and the Men Who Have Wrought in Connection With Them - The Wilkinsons.... Barrow-in-Furness: 1917. V. 64

RANDALL, L. M. C.
Medieval and Renaissance Manuscripts in the Walters Art Gallery. Volume II: France 1420-1540. Parts I and II. Baltimore and London: 1992. V. 62
Medieval and Renaissance Manuscripts in the Walters Art Gallery. Volumes I, II and III. Baltimore/London: 1989-1997. V. 63

RANDALL MAC IVER, DAVIS
Villanovans and Early Etruscans. Oxford: 1924. V. 67

RANDERS-PHERSON, JUSTINE
The Surgeon's Glove. Springfield: 1960. V. 64

RANDISI, ROBERT J.
An Eye for Justice: the Private Eye Writers of America Anthology. New York: 1988. V. 63; 66
The Eyes Have It. New York: 1984. V. 63
Justice for Hire: Fourth Private Eye Writers of America Anthology. New York: 1990. V. 62; 66
Mean Streets: the Second Private Eye Writers of America Anthology. New York: 1986. V. 63; 66

RANDLE, E. H.
Characteristics of the Southern Negro. New York: 1910. V. 63

RANDOL, ALANSON M.
Last Days of the Rebellion. San Francisco: 1883. V. 64

RANDOLPH, BUCKNER M.
Ten Years Old and Under: The Recollections of a Childhood Spent on a Farm Which Lay in the Battle Ground of the War Between the States...1873- 1880. Boston: 1935. V. 67

RANDOLPH, CLARE
The Adventures of Jack and Jill. Chicago: 1948. V. 62

RANDOLPH, CORLISS F.
A History of Seventh Day Baptists in West Virginia. Plainfield: 1905. V. 62

RANDOLPH, EDMUND
A Vindication of Mr. Randolph's Resignation. Philadelphia: 1795. V. 63; 66

RANDOLPH, JANE
The Circus in Peter's Closet. New York: 1955. V. 66

RANDOLPH, JOHN
Letters of John Randolph, to a Young Relative: Embracing a Series of Years from Early Youth, to Mature Manhood. Philadelphia: 1834. V. 65
Marsman in Burma. Houston: 1946. V. 67

RANDOLPH, MARY
Virginia Housewife or Methodical Cook. Washington: 1831. V. 67
Virginia Housewife or Methodical Cook. Baltimore: 1836. V. 67
The Virginia Housewife; or, Methodical Cook. Philadelphia: 1846. V. 67

RANDOLPH, SARAH N.
The Domestic Life of Thomas Jefferson. New York: 1871. V. 64

RANDOLPH, THOMAS
Poems. London: 1652. V. 62

RANDS, WILLIAM BRIGHTY
Tangled Talk; an Essayist's Holiday. London: 1864. V. 67

RANGER VII Photographs of the Moon: Part II: Camera "B" Series. Washington: 1965. V. 66

RANHOFER, CHARLES
Epicurean. New York: 1984. V. 67

RANJITSINHJI, K. S.
The Jubilee Book of Cricket. Edinburgh and London: 1897. V. 62; 66

RANKE, LEOPOLD VON
A History of England Principally in the Seventeenth Century. Oxford: 1875. V. 66
The Popes of Rome. London: 1866. V. 67
Zur Kritik Neuerer Geschichtschreiber. Leipzig and Berlin: 1824. V. 67

RANKIN, ALEXANDER TAYLOR
Alexander Taylor Rankin (1803-1885): His Diary and Letters. Boulder: 1966. V. 64

RANKIN, D. J.
A History of the County of Antigonish Nova Scotia. Toronto: 1929. V. 64

RANKIN, IAN
The Black Book. London: 1993. V. 65
Dead Souls. London: 1999. V. 67
The Flood. Edinburgh: 1986. V. 63
A Good Hanging and Other Stories. London: 1992. V. 65
The Hanging Garden. Blakeney: 1998. V. 65
The Hanging Garden. London: 1998. V. 67
Hide and Seek. London: 1991. V. 65; 67
Mortal Causes. London: 1994. V. 66
Rebus: The Early Years. London: 1999. V. 65; 66; 67
Set in Darkness. London: 2000. V. 67
Strip Jack. London: 1992. V. 67
Watchman. London: 1988. V. 66
Watchman. New York: 1991. V. 65; 66

RANKIN, M. WILSON
Reminiscences of Frontier Days - Including an authentic Account of the Thornburg and Meeker Massacres. Denver: 1938. V. 66; 67

RANKINE, DAVID
A Popular Exposition of the Effect of Forces Applied to Draught. Glasgow: 1828. V. 62

RANKINE, W.
Shipbuilding, Theoretical and Practical. London: 1866. V. 64

RANKINE, W. J. MAC QUORN
The Cyclopaedia of the Machine and Hand Tools.... London: 1869. V. 65
A Manual of Machinery and Millwork. London: 1869. V. 62

RANKING, JOHN
Historical Researches on the Conquest of Peru, Mexico, Bogota, Natchez and Talomeco, in the Thirteenth Century, by the Mongolds, Accompanied with Elephants.... London: 1827. V. 67

RANN, JOHN
The Life of Jack Rann, Otherwise Sixteen-String Jack, the Noted Highwayman, who Was Executed at Tyburn, November 30, 1774. Durham: 1838. V. 63

RANNEY, AMBROSE L.
Applied Anatomy of the Nervous System, Being a Study of the Portion of the Human Body from a Standpoint to Its General Interest and Practical Utility.... New York: 1881. V. 65
Eye-Strain in Health and Disease. Philadelphia: 1897. V. 64; 66; 67
Lectures on Nervous Diseases from the Standpoint of Cerebral and Spinal Localization and the Later Methods Employed in the Diagnosis and Treatment of These Affections. Philadelphia: 1888. V. 65

RANSOM, HARRY HUNTT
The Conscience of the University and Other Essays. Austin: 1982. V. 63

RANSOM, J. H.
Who's Who and Where in Horsedom. Lexington: 1955. V. 66

RANSOM, JAMES M.
Vanishing Ironworks of the Ramapos. New Brunswick: 1966. V. 63

RANSOM, JOHN CROWE
Chills and Fevers. New York: 1924. V. 64
Grace After Meat. London: 1924. V. 62
The Kenyon Critics: Studies in Modern Literature from the Kenyon Review. Cleveland and New York: 1951. V. 62; 64
The New Criticism - an Examination of the Critical Theories of I. A. Richards, T. S. Eliot, Yvor Winters, William Empson. Norfolk: 1941. V. 62
Poems About God. New York: 1919. V. 64; 67
Selected Poems. New York: 1945. V. 64; 66
Selected Poems. New York: 1963. V. 62
Two Gentlemen in Bonds. New York: 1927. V. 64

RANSOM, WILL
The First Days of the Village Press - Extracts from the Diary.... New York: 1937. V. 65
Kelmscott, Doves and Ashendene: the Private Press Credoes. London: 1952. V. 62
Kelmscott, Doves and Ashendene: the Private Press Credos. Los Angeles: 1952. V. 64; 66
Private Presses and Their Books. New York: 1929. V. 64

RANSOME, ARTHUR
Aladdin and His Wonderful Lamp. London: 1919. V. 66
Aladdin and His Wonderful Lamp. New York: 1920. V. 63
Aladdin in Rhyme. London: 1919. V. 63
Highways and Byways in Fairyland. London: 1906. V. 63
A History of Story-Telling. London: 1909. V. 64
Mainly About Fishing. 1959. V. 62; 63; 65
Mainly About Fishing. London: 1959. V. 67
Missie Lee, the Swallows and Amazons Have Fabulous Adventure in the Chinas Seas. London: 1941. V. 65
Old Peter's Russian Tales. London: 1927. V. 62
On the Measurement of the Movement of the Chest. Manchester: 1869. V. 67
The Picts and the Martyrs; or Not Welcome at All. London: 1943. V. 62
Racundra's First Cruise. London: 1923. V. 62
Swallows and Amazons. Philadelphia: 1931. V. 65

RANSOMES & RAPIER
Ransomes & Rapier, Engineers and Railway Materials Manufacturers, 5, Westminster Chambers, London; and Waterside Iron-works, Ipswich. London: 1885. V. 65

RANSON, JOHN L
Andersonville Diary, Escape and List of the Dead, with Name, Co., Regiment, Date Death and No. of Grave in Cemetery. Auburn: 1881. V. 63

RAPALJE, STEWART
A Digest or Railway Decisions. Long Island: 1895. V. 65

RAPER, ARTHUR
The Tragedy of Lynching. Chapel Hill: 1933. V. 63

RAPER, K. B.
A Manual of the Penicillia. Baltimore: 1949. V. 62

RAPHAEL, FREDERIC
After the War. London: 1988. V. 67
The Earlsdon Way. London: 1958. V. 64
Like Men Betrayed. London: 1970. V. 67
Richard's Things. London: 1973. V. 67
Who Were You with Last Night?. London: 1971. V. 67

RAPHAEL'S LTD.
Raphael's Ltd., Hatton Garden, Catalogue. London: 1911. V. 63; 67

RAPHAEL SANZIO D'URBINO
Leonis X, Admiranda Virtutis Imagines. (with) Picturae Omniumque Bonarum Artium Cultori Eximio. Rome: 1640. V. 62

RAPHALL, M. J.
Bible View of Slavery. New York: 1861. V. 62

RAPHSON, JOSEPH
Analysis Aequationum Universalis, Seu a Aequationes Algebraicas Resolvendas methodus Generalis & Expedita.... London: 1702. V. 66

RAPIN, RENE
Of Gardens. London: 1673. V. 62
Of Gardens. 1718. V. 63
Reflections Upon the Eloquence of These Times.... London: 1672. V. 62

RAPIN THOYRAS, PAUL DE
Acta Regia: Being the Account Which Mr. Rapin de Thoyras Published.... London: 1732. V. 62
Acta Regia; or, an Account of the Treaties, Letters and Instruments Between the Monarchs of England and Foreign Powers.... London: 1726-1727. V. 62
The History of England. London: 1732,. V. 67

RAPP, GEORGE
Thoughts on the Destiny of Man, Particulary with Reference to the Present Times. New Harmony: 1824. V. 63

RAPSAET, J. J.
Les Droits du Seigneur. Recherches sur l'Origine et la Nature des Droits Connus Anciennement Sous Les Noms de Droits des Premieres Nuits, de Markette, d'Afforage, etc. Rouen: 1879. V. 63

RASHID, MAULAY, SULTAN OF MOROCCO
Histoire de Muley Arxid Roy de Tafilete, Fez, Maroc, and Tarudent. Paris: 1670. V. 62

RASHLEIGH, PHILIP
Specimens of British Minerals. 1797-1802. V. 66
Specimens of British Minerals. London: 1797-1802. V. 63

RASKIN, ELLEN
The Westing Game. New York: 1978. V. 64

RASMUSSEN, KNUD
Across Arctic America. Narrative of the Fifth Thule Expedition. New York, London: 1927. V. 65
Report of the Fifth Thule Expedition 1921-1924. Botany. Vasular Plants, Mosses and Lichens, Mammals, Zoology II. Birds, Fishes, Insects, Crustacea. Copenhagen: 1937. V. 66

RASMUSSEN, W. D.
Agriculture in the United States, A Documentary History. New York: 1975. V. 63

RASPE, RUDOLPH ERICH
The Adventures of Baron Munchausen. London: 1880. V. 62
Complete Original Edition of the Surprising Travels and Adventures of Baron Munchausen, in Russia, the Caspian Sea, Iceland, Turkey, Egypt, Gibraltar, up the Mediterranean, on the Atlantic Ocean, and through the Centre of Mount Etna, into the South Sea. London: 1819. V. 65
A Critical Essay on Oil Painting, Proving that the Art of Painting in Oil, Was Known Before the Pretended Discovery of John and Hubert Van Eyck.... London: 1781. V. 62
Original Travels and Surprising Adventures of Baron Munchausen. Boston: 1889. V. 64
Surprising Adventures of Baron Munchausen...Also, an Account of a Voyage into the Moon and Dog Star.... London: 1819. V. 63
Surprising Adventures of the Renowned Baron Munchausen.... London: 1809. V. 62
The Travels and Surprising Adventures of Baron Munchausen. London: 1859. V. 65; 67
The Travels and Surprising Adventures of Baron Munchausen. London: 1877. V. 63

RASTALL, B. M.
The Cripple Creek of 1893. Colorado Sprints: 1905. V. 65

RASTALL, W. DICKINSON
A History of the Antiquities of the Town and Church of Southwell, in the County of Nottingham. London: 1787. V. 65; 66

RASWAN, CARL
The Raswan Index and Handbook for Arabian Breeders. Santa Barbara: 1990. V. 66

RATCHFORD, FANNIE E.
The Brontes Web of Childhood. New York: 1949. V. 63
Letters of Thomas J. Wise to John Henry Wrenn. A Further Inqiury into the Guilt of Certain Nineteenth-Century Forgers. New York: 1944. V. 67

RATCHFORD, J. W.
Some Reminiscences of Person and Incidents of the Civil War. Austin: 1971. V. 63

RATCLIFF, CARTER
Gilbert and George: the Singing Sculpture. London: 1993. V. 66

RATCLIFFE, DOROTHY UNA
Dale Dramas. London: 1923. V. 64; 65
The Gone Away. London: 1930. V. 65; 67
Hoops of Steel. London: 1935. V. 64; 65
Nightlights. London: 1929. V. 64; 65

RATCLIFFE, HENRY
Observations on the Rate of Mortality and Sickness Existing Amongst Friendly Societies.... Manchester: 1850. V. 64

RATH, VIRGINIA
Ferryman, Take Him Across!. Garden City: 1936. V. 66

RATHBONE, HANNAH MARY
So Much of the Diary of Lady Willoughby as Relates to Her Domestic History.... London: 1873. V. 65

RATHBUN, JOHN B.
Motorcycle Operation, Adjustment and Repair. Chicago: 1920. V. 64

RATHBUN, M. J.
The Cancroid Crabs of America. Washington: 1930. V. 64
The Grapsoid Crabs of America. Washington: 1918. V. 64
The Spider Crabs of America. Washington: 1925. V. 64; 66

RATHMAN, PEGGY
Officer Buckle and Gloria. New York: 1995. V. 65

RATHMELL, WILLIAM
Life of the Marlows, as Related by Themselves. Ouray. V. 65

RATTAN, S. S.
The Resupinate Aphyllophorales of the North Western Himalayas. Vaduz: 1977. V. 64

RATTI, ACHILLE
Climbs on Alpine Peaks. 1923. V. 63

RATTIGAN, TERENCE
Separate Tables. New York: 1955. V. 66
The Winslow Boy. London: 1946. V. 62

RATTIGAN, TERRENCE
The Winslow Boy. London: 1948. V. 65

RATTRAY, JOHN
Forestry and Forest Products. Edinburgh: 1885. V. 67
A Revision of the Genus Coscinodiscus and Some Allied Genera. Edinburgh: 1889. V. 67

RATTRAY, R. S.
Ashanti. London: 1923. V. 62
The Leopard Priestess. London: 1934. V. 66

RATTRAY, W. J.
The Scot in British North America. Toronto: 1880. V. 67

RATTY, JOHN
A Spiritual Diary, and Soliloquies. 1796. V. 64

RAU, CHARLES
Prehistoric Fishing in Europe and North America. Washington City: 1884. V. 64

RAUCHER, HERMAN
Summer of '42. New York: 1971. V. 63

RAUCOURT DE CHARLEVILLE, ANTOINE
A Manual of Lithography, or Memoir of Lithography or Memoir on the Lithographical Experiments Made in Paris.... London: 1820. V. 67
Memoire sur les Experiences Lithographiques (sic) Faites a l'Ecole Royale des Ponts et Chaussees de France ou Manuel Theorique et Pratique du Dessinateur et de l'Imprimeur Lithographes. Toulon: 1819. V. 67

RAUH, WERNER
Bromeliads for Home, Garden and Greenhouse. 1979. V. 66

RAUM, JOHN O.
The History of New Jersey, From Its Earliest Settlement to the Present Time. Philadelphia: 1877. V. 63; 66

RAUTHMEL, RICHARD
The Roman Antiquities of Overborough. London: 1746. V. 64; 65
The Roman Antiquities of Overborough. Kirkby Lonsdale: 1824. V. 64; 65

RAVEL, JEROME
Raoul, or the Magic Star. New York: 1849. V. 62

RAVEN, C. E.
English Naturalists from Neckam to Ray.... Cambridge: 1947. V. 62; 64; 66
John Ray, Naturalist. Cambridge: 1942. V. 62
John Ray-Naturalist, His Life and Works. Cambridge: 1950. V. 62

RAVEN Introductions 4. Dublin: 1986. V. 65

RAVEN, J. J.
The Church Bells of Cambridgeshire. Cambridge: 1881. V. 65

RAVEN, JOHN
Mountain Flowers. London: 1956. V. 63

RAVEN, RALPH
Golden Dreams and Leaden Realities. New York: 1853. V. 67

RAVENSHAW, THOMAS F.
Antiente Epitaphes (From A.D. 1250 to A.D. 1800). London: 1878. V. 66

RAVENSWAAY, C. VAN
Drawn from Nature, the Botanical Art of Joseph Prestele and His Sons. Washington: 1984. V. 62; 66

RAVERAT, GWEN
Gwen Raverat: Wood Engraver. 1996. V. 65
The Wood Engravings of Gwen Raverat. London: 1959. V. 63

RAVILIOUS, ERIC
The Wood Engravings of Eric Ravilious. London: 1972. V. 65

RAVISIUS, TEXTOR
De Memorabilibus et Claris Mulieribus Aliquot Diversorum Scriptorum Opera. Parisiis: 1521. V. 65

RAWLE, E. J.
Annals of the Ancient Royal Forest of Exmoor. Taunton: 1893. V. 62; 64

RAWLET, JOHN
A Dialogue Betwixt Two Protestants, (n Answer to a Popish Catechism, Called a Short Catechism Against all Sectaries).... London: 1685. V. 66

RAWLING, C. J.
A History of the First Regiment Virginia Infantry. Philadelphia: 1887. V. 63; 65

RAWLING, L. B.
Landmarks and Surface Markings of the Human Body. London: 1904. V. 67

RAWLINGS, MARJORIE KINNAN
Cross Creek Cookery. New York: 1942. V. 64
The Marjorie Rawlings Reader. New York: 1956. V. 64
The Secret River. New York: 1955. V. 64
The Sojourner. New York: 1953. V. 62; 64
South Moon Under. New York: 1933. V. 67
The Yearling. New York: 1938. V. 62; 64
The Yearling. New York: 1940. V. 65

RAWLINSON, GEORGE
Ancient Egypt. London: 1895. V. 64
History of Ancient Egypt. London: 1881. V. 66

RAWLINSON, RICHARD
History of...Sir John Perrott...Lord Lieutenant of Ireland. 1728. V. 65

RAWNSLEY, H. D.
A Book of Bristol Sonnets. Hamilton: 1877. V. 66
A Book of Bristol Sonnets. London: 1877. V. 62
Five Addresses on the Lives and Work of St. Kentigern and St. Herbert, Delivered in St. Kentigern's Church, Crosthwaite. Carlisle: 1888. V. 64

RAWNSLEY, H. D. continued
Poems at Home and Abroad. Glasgow: 1909. V. 62
The Resurrection of Oldest Egypt. Laleham: 1904. V. 62
Sonnets Round the Coast. London: 1887. V. 62

RAWNSLEY, JOHN E.
Antique Maps of Yorkshire and Their Makers. London: 1970. V. 63

RAWORTH, TOM
The Big Green Day. London: 1968. V. 62; 65

RAWSON, CLAYTON
The Great Merlini. Boston: 1979. V. 65; 67
The Headless Lady. New York: 1940. V. 65
No Coffin for the Corpse. Boston: 1942. V. 67

RAWSON, EDWARD KIRK
Twenty Famous Naval Battles, Salamis to Santiago. London: 1900. V. 62

RAWSON, GEOFFREY
Nelson's Letters from the Leeward Islands and Other Original Documents in the Public Record Office and the British Museum. Waltham St. Lawrence: 1953. V. 65

RAWSON, SAMUEL
The Producer and Consumer. Birmingham: 1887. V. 67

RAWSTORNE, LAWRENCE
Gamonia, or the Art of Preserving Game. 1929. V. 63
Gamonia; or the Art of Preserving Game. London: 1929. V. 66; 67

RAY, ANTHONY
English Delftware Pottery in the Robert Hall Warren Collection, Ashmolean Museum, Oxford. Boston: 1968. V. 67

RAY, DOROTHY JEAN
Aleut and Eskimo Art: Tradition and Innovation in Southern Alaska. Seattle: 1980-1981. V. 62
Eskimo Art, Tradition and Innovation in North Alaska. Seattle: 1977. V. 64

RAY, G. B.
Murder at the Corners. San Antonio: 1957. V. 67

RAY, G. N.
The Illustrator and the Book in England 1790-1914. New York: 1976. V. 62

RAY, GORDON
Nineteenth Century English Books: Some Problems in Bibliography. Urbana: 1952. V. 64

RAY, ISAAC
Contributions to Mental Pathology. Boston: 1873. V. 65
Conversations on the Animal Economy: Designed for the Instruction of Youth and the Persual of General Readers. Portland: 1829. V. 65
Mental Hygiene. Boston: 1863. V. 65
A Treatise on the Medical Jurisprudence of Insanity. Boston: 1838. V. 65
Treatise on the Medical Jurisprudence of Insanity. Boston: 1853. V. 63

RAY, JAMES
A Compleat History of the Rebellion, from Its First Rise in 1745 to Its Total Suppression at the Glorious Battle of Culloden in April 1746. Manchester: 1747?. V. 65
A Compleat History of the Rebellion, from Its First Rise, in 1745, to Its Total Suppression at the Glorious Battle of Culloden in April 1746. London: 1757. V. 63; 66
A Compleat History of the Rebellion, From Its First Rise in 1745 to Its Total Suppression at the Glorious Battle of Culloden in April 1746. London: 1758. V. 62

RAY, JOHN
Catalogus Plantarum Angliae, et Insularum Adjacentium. London: 1670. V. 63; 64; 66
A Collection of Curious Travels and Voyages. London: 1693. V. 64
A Collection of English Proverbs Digested into a Convenient Method for the Speedy Finding Any One Upon Occasion.... Cambridge: 1678. V. 64
A Compleat Collection of English Proverbs. London: 1742. V. 62; 64
A Compleat Collection of English Proverbs. 1768. V. 63
A Complete Collection of English Proverbs. London: 1817. V. 64
The Correspondence of.... 1848. V. 64
Further Correspondence. London: 1928. V. 62; 63; 64
Historia Pantarum Species Hactenus Editas Aliasque Insuper Multas Noviter Inventas & Descriptas. London: 1686-1688. V. 62
Methodus Plantarum Emendata et Aucta.... 1703. V. 63
Observations Topographical, Moral and Physiological Made in a Journey through Part of the Low Countries, Germany, Italy and France.... London: 1673. V. 64
Philosophical Letters Between the Late Learned Mr. Ray and Several of His Ingenious Correspondents.... London: 1718. V. 64; 65; 66; 67
Synopsis Methodica Animalium Quadrupedum et Serperntini Generis. London: 1693. V. 63
Synopsis Methodica Avium & Piscium: Opus Posthumum, Quod Vivus Recensuit & Perfecit.... Londini: 1713. V. 63; 67
Synopsis Methodica Stirpium Britannicarum. London: 1696. V. 65
Synopsis Methodica Stirpium Britannicarum. Londini: 1724. V. 64
Travels through the Low-Countries, Germany, Italy and France... (with) A Collection of Curious Travels and Voyages.... London: 1738. V. 67
The Wisdom of God Manifested in the Works of the Creation. London: 1709. V. 62
The Wisdom of God Manifested in the Works of the Creation. 1714. V. 63
The Wisdom of God Manifested in the Works of the Creation. London: 1844-1846. V. 65

RAY, MAN
Alphabet Pour Adultes. Paris: 1970. V. 65
Self Portrait. Boston: 1963. V. 65

RAY, OPHELIA
Daughter of the Tejas. 1965. V. 66

RAY, PATRICK HENRY
Report of the International Polar Expedition to Point Barrow, Alaska. Washington: 1885. V. 62; 63; 65; 66

RAY, V. F.
The Sanpoil and Nespelem: Salishan Peoples of Northeastern Washington. 1932. V. 62

RAY, WILLIAM
Horrors of Slavery; or the American Tars in Tripoli. New York: 1808. V. 64

RAY, WORTH S.
Down in the Cross Timbers. Austin: 1947. V. 67

RAYBOLD, GEORGE A.
Reminiscences of Methodism in West Jersey. New York: 1849. V. 66

RAY JONES, TONY
A Day Off. An English Journal. London: 1974. V. 66

RAYLEIGH, JOHN WILLIAM STRUTT, BARON
The Theory of Sound. London: 1877-1878. V. 66
The Theory of Sound. London and New York: 1894. V. 62

RAYLEIGH, ROBERT STRUTT
Argon, a New Constituent of the Atmosphere. Washington: 1896. V. 62

RAYMER, ROBERT GEORGE
Montana: The Land and the People. Chicago: 1930. V. 63; 64; 67

RAYMOND, ALEX
Flash Gordon on the Planet Mongo. Racine: 1934. V. 63; 64; 66

RAYMOND, ANTONIN
Antonin Raymond, Architectural Details. Tokyo: 1938. V. 65
Architectural Details. Tokyo: 1938. V. 67

RAYMOND, DEREK
The Devil's Home on Leave. London: 1985. V. 65

RAYMOND, DORA N.
Captain Lee Hall of Texas. Norman: 1940. V. 62; 65

RAYMOND, GEORGE
Memoirs of Robert William Elliston, Comedian. London: 1846. V. 66

RAYMOND, JEAN PAUL
Oscar Wilde. London: 1932. V. 62; 64
Recollections of Oscar Wilde. London: 1932. V. 65

RAYMOND, R. W.
The Man in the Moon and Other People. 1875. V. 64

RAYMOND, ROSSITER W.
Camp and Cabin: Sketches of Life and Travel in the West. New York: 1880. V. 67
Statistics of Mines and Mining in the States and Territories West of the Rocky Mountains. Washington: 1875. V. 63; 66

RAYMOND, W. O.
Winslow Papers A.D. 1776-1826. St. John: 1901. V. 67

RAYMOND, WALTER
Gentleman Upcott's Daughter. London: 1892. V. 67
Young Sam and Sabina. London: 1894. V. 67

RAYNAL, GUILLAUME THOMAS FRANCOIS
Histoire du Stadhouderat Depuis son Origine Jusqua a Present. Amsterdam?: 1760. V. 66
Histoire Philosophique et Politique des Establissemens et du Commerce des Europeens dans les Deux Indes. Geneve: 1781. V. 66
A Philosophical and Political History of the Settlements and Trade of the Europeans in the East and West Indies. London: 1777. V. 67
A Philosophical and Political History of the Settlements and Trade of the Europeans in the East and West Indies. London: 1788. V. 63
Revolution de l'Amerique. London: 1781. V. 66

RAYNAL, MAURICE
Matisse, Munch, Rouault: Fauvism Expressionism. Geneva: 1950. V. 66
Peinture Moderne. Geneve: 1953. V. 63; 64

RAYNARD, A. C.
Observations Made During Total Solar Eclipses.... London: 1879. V. 66

RAYNE, M. L.
What Can a Woman Do or Her Position in the Business and Literary World. Detroit: 1884. V. 64; 67

RAYNER, B. L.
Sketches of the Life, Writings and Opinions of Thomas Jefferson.... New York: 1832. V. 63

RAYNER, D. H.
The Geology and Mineral Resources of Yorkshire. 1974. V. 62; 65; 67
The Geology and Mineral Resources of Yorkshire. Yorkshire: 1974. V. 66

RAYNOLDS, W. F.
Reports on the Exploration of the Yellowstone. Washington: 1868. V. 66

REA, CALEB
The Journal of Dr. Caleb Rea.... Salem: 1881. V. 63

REACH, ANGUS B.
The Natural History of Humbugs. London: 1847. V. 64

READ, BENJAMIN M.
Guerra Mexico-Americana. Santa Fe: 1910. V. 63; 64; 66

READ, C. H.
Antiquities from the City of Benin and from Other Parts of West Africa in the British Museum. London: 1899. V. 62

READ, C. RUDSTON
What I Heard, Saw and Did at the Australian Gold Fields. London: 1853. V. 66

READ, GEORGIA W.
Gold Rush, Journals, Drawings and Other Papers of J. Goldborough Bruff April 2 1949-July 20, 1851. New York. V. 65

READ, H. H.
The Geology of Central Sutherland. Sheets 108 and 109. 1931. V. 65
The Geology of Central Sutherland. Sheets 108 and 109. London: 1931. V. 66

READ, HERBERT
Art and Society. London: 1937. V. 62
Collected Essays in Literary Criticism. London: 1938. V. 63
The End of a War. London: 1933. V. 64
English Prose Style. London: 1928. V. 66
Henry Moore - a Study of His Life and Work. London: 1965. V. 62
Jan Le Witt. New York: 1971. V. 63; 64
The Knapsack - A Pocket-Book of Verse and Prose. London: 1939. V. 64
Naked Warriors. London: 1919. V. 63; 66
Pursuits and Verdicts. Edinburgh: 1983. V. 63
Pursuits and Verdicts. London: 1983. V. 63
The Tenth Muse - Essays in Criticism. London: 1957. V. 65
A World Within a War. London: 1944. V. 65

READ, J. MARION
A History of the California Academy of Medicine 1870 to 1930. (with) History of the California Academy Medicine 1930-1960. San Francisco: 1930. V. 63

READ, JOHN
Humour and Humanism in Chemistry. London: 1947. V. 67

READ, JOHN M.
Speech of Hon. John M. Read, at the Regular Quarterley Meeting of the Joint Board of Directors of the United Delaware and Raritan Canal Co., Camden and Amboy Railroad and Transportation Co. April 20, 1871. Philadelphia: 1871. V. 63

READ, JOHN MEREDITH
A Historical Inquiry Concerning Henry Hudson, His Friends, Relatives and Early Life.... Albany: 1866. V. 64

READ, MISS
Storm in the Village. Boston: 1959. V. 67

READ, THOMAS BUCHANAN
A Summer Story, Sheridan's Ride and Other Poems. Philadelphia: 1865. V. 67

READ, W. W.
Annals of Cricket, a Record of the Game Compiled from Authentic Sources.... London: 1896. V. 66

READE, B.
Aubrey Beardsley. New York: 1967. V. 65

READE, CHARLES
Christie Johnstone. London: 1853. V. 67
Christie Johnstone: a Novel. London: 1884. V. 67
The Cloister and the Hearth. London: 1861. V. 66
The Cloister and the Hearth. London: 1868. V. 67
The Course of True Love Never Did Run Smooth. London: 1857. V. 63; 67
The Eighth Commandment. London: 1860. V. 66
Good Stories of Man and Other Animals. London: 1884. V. 67
Griffith Gaunt; or Jealousy. London: 1867. V. 66
Hard Cash. London: 1864. V. 66
Hard Cash. London: 1882. V. 67
It Is Never Too Late to Mend. London: 1882. V. 67
Put Yourself in His Place. London: 1870. V. 67
Put Yourself in His Place. London: 1884. V. 67
A Simpleton: a Story of the Day. London: 1873. V. 67
The Wandering Heir: a Matter-of-Fact Romance. Leipzig: 1875. V. 67
The Wandering Heir: a Matter-of-Fact Romance. London: 1884. V. 67
White Lies. London: 1857. V. 67

READE, COMPTON
The Smith Family: Being a Popular Account of Most Branches of the Name, However Spelt from the 14th Century Downwards. 1904. V. 63; 66

READE, JOHN EDMUND
The Light of Other Days. London: 1858. V. 65

READER, SIMON
Thirteen Sermons on the Parable of the Virgins. With Three Others on Personal and Family Religion. London: 1765. V. 64

READING, JOSEPH
The Ogowe Band: a Narrative of African Travels. Philadelphia: 1890. V. 65

READING, NATHANIEL
The Tryal of Nathaniel Reading Esq; for Attempting to Stifle the Kings Evidence as to the Horrid Plot. London: 1679. V. 63

READING No Preaching; or the Fashionable Mode of Delivering Sermons Considered, as Opposite to Scripture, the Practice of the Primitive Church, Reason and Common Sense of Mankind, in a Letter to a Clergyman of the Church of England. London: 1788. V. 65

READING, PETER
Water and Waste. Walton-on-Thames: 1970. V. 64

READWIN, THOMAS ALLISON
The Gold Discoveries in Merionetshire and a Mode for Its Economic Extraction. Manchester: 1860. V. 62

REAGAN, JOHN H.
Memoirs. With Special Reference to Secession and the Civil War. New York and Washington: 1906. V. 63; 65

REAGAN, RONALD
Speaking My Mind: Selected Speeches. New York: 1989. V. 62; 63
Where's the Rest of Me?. New York: 1965. V. 65

REAL, ANTONY
The Story of the Stick in All Ages and Lands. New York: 1875. V. 64

REASONS Against Government Interference in Education: Shewing the Dangerous Consequences of Entrusting a Central Government with the Education of Its Subjects and Explaining the Advantages of Leaving It to Be Regulated by Individual Family;.... London: 1843. V. 64

REASONS for a Registry; shewing Briefly the Great Benefits and Advantages that May Accrue to this Nation Thereby. London: 1797. V. 65

REAUMUR, RENE ANTOINE FERCHAULT DE
L'Art de Convertir le Fer Forge en Acier, et l'Art d'Adoucir le Fer Fondu, ou de Faire des Ouvrages de fr Fondu Aussi Finis Que de Fer Forge. Paris: 1722. V. 65
Art de Faire Eclorre et D'Elever en Toite Saison des Oiseau Domestiques de Toute Especes.... Paris: 1751. V. 64
Memoires Pour Servir a l'Histoire des Insectes. Paris: 1734-1742. V. 63

REAVEY, GEORGE
The Colours of Memory. New York: 1955. V. 62

REAVIS, L. U.
The Life and Military Services of General William Selby Harney. St. Louis: 1878. V. 65

THE REBEL Songster. Richmond: 1864. V. 63

REBELLO, STEPHEN
The Art of Hercules: the Chaos of Creation. 1977. V. 66

REBIERE, A.
Les Femmes dans la Science. Paris: 1894. V. 67

REBUFFAT, G.
Starlight and Storm. 1956. V. 65

RECENT Scenes and Occurences in Ireland; or Animadversions on a Pamphlet Entitled One Year of the Administration of the Marquess Wellesley. 1823. V. 63; 66

RECHINGER, K. H.
Flora of Lowland Iraq. 1964. V. 66

RECOLLECTIONS of a Detective Police Officer. London: 1972. V. 64

RECOLLECTIONS of the Early Days of the Vine Hunt and Its Founder, William John Chute, Esq., M.P. of the Vine.... London: 1865. V. 67

THE RECONCILER. A Kingdom Divided Against Itself, Is Brought to Desolation. London: 1716. V. 65

RECORDE, ROBERT
The Grovnd of Artes, Teaching the Perfect Worke and Practice of Arithmeticke.... London: 1596. V. 64

RECORDS of the Borough of Nottingham. Nottingham: 1882-1956. V. 66

THE RECORDS of the Swedish Lutheran Churches at Raccoon and Penns Neck 1713-1786. N.P: 1938. V. 66

RECREATIONS in Rhyme; or, Leisure Moments Beguiled. (with)....Second Series. Doncaster: 1840. V. 66

RECTOR, MARGARET
Cowboy Life on the Texas Plains - the Photographs of Ray Rector. College Station: 1982. V. 62; 65

RECUEIL D'Estampes Representant les Differents Evenemens de la Guerre qui a Procure l'Independence aux Etats Unis de l'Amerique. Paris: 1784?. V. 62; 66

RECUEIL D'Observations D'Anatomie et De Chirurgie, Pour Servir de Base a la Theorie des Lesions de la Tete.... Paris: 1766. V. 64

RED Cartoons of 1927 from the Daily Worker. Chicago: 1927. V. 67

RED Riding Hood. Boston: 1863. V. 63

RED Riding Hood and the Letters. London: 1945. V. 66

REDDALL, HENRY F.
Scissors or the Funny Side of Politics. Boston: 1888. V. 62

REDDING, CYRUS
History and Description of Modern Wines. London: 1851. V. 67
Memoirs of William Beckford of Fonthill.... London: 1859. V. 64

REDDING, M. WOLCOTT
Antiquities of the Orient Unveiled. New York: 1873. V. 63

REDDINGTON, WILLIAM
A Practical Treatise on Brewing; Containing Various Instructions and Precautions, Useful and Necesary in the Exercise of the Art. London: 1780. V. 66

REDE, LEMAN THOMAS
York Castle in the Nineteenth Century; Being an Account of all The Principal Offences Committed in Yorkshire, from the Year 1800 to the Present Period.... Leeds: 1831. V. 63

REDE, WILLIAM LEMAN
Peregrinations of Pickwick.... New York and Philadelphia: 1837. V. 62

REDESDALE, ALGERNON BERTRAM FREEMAN-MITFORD, 1ST BARON
The Bamboo Garden. London: 1896. V. 64

REDFERN, PERCY
The Story of the C.W.S. The Jubilee History of the Co-operative Wholesale Society Ltd. 1863-1913. London: 1913. V. 63

REDFERN, RON
Corridors of the Time: 1,700,000,000 Years of Earth at Grand Canyon. New York: 1980. V. 67

REDFIELD, ISAAC F.
The Law of Railways. Boston: 1869. V. 67

REDFIELD, W. C.
Letter...on the History and Causes of Steamboat Explosions and the Means of Prevention.... New York: 1839. V. 62
Observations on the Hurricanes and Storms of the West Indies and the Coast of the United States: the New Brunswick Tornad. New Haven: 1822. V. 62

REDFORD, GEORGE
The History of the Ancient Town and Borough of Uxbridge, and an Appendix. Uxbridge: 1818. V. 63

REDFORD, THOMAS
Thomas Redford, Plaintiff; and Hugh Hornby Birley, Alexander Oliver, Richard Worthington, and Edward Meagler, Defendants. For an Assault on 16th of August, 1819.. Manchester: 1822. V. 63

REDGRAVE, MICHAEL
The Aspern Papers: a Comody of Letters Adapted for the Theatre from Henry James' Story by Michael Redgrave. London: 1959. V. 62; 64

REDGRAVE, RICHARD
A Century of Painters of the English School; With Critical Notices of Their Works, and An Account of the Progress of Art in England. London: 1866. V. 67

REDGROVE, PETER
Love's Journeys. Bow, Crediton: 1971. V. 65

REDI, FRANCESCO
Bacco in Toscana. Ditirambo...con le Annotazioni. Florence: 1685. V. 64; 66
Esperienze Intorno alla Generazione degl'Insetti...e da lui Scritte in Una Lettera all'Illustrissimo Signor Carlo Dati. Florence: 1668. V. 63
Opere.... Venice: 1762. V. 63
Opusculorum Pars Prior (only), Sive Experimenta Circa Gnerationem Insectorum. Amstelaedami: 1686. V. 64
Osservazioni Alle Vipere. 1664. V. 64
Osservazioni...Intorno Agli Animali Viventi che si Trovano Negli Animali Viventi. Florence: 1684. V. 62

REDMAYNE, J. S.
Fruit Farming on the Dry Belt of British Columbia the Why and Wherefore. London: 1912. V. 63

REDMOND, PATRICK
The Wishing Game. London: 1999. V. 65; 66

REDOUTE, P. J.
Album de Redoute. 1954. V. 66
Facsimile Prints...from the Collection of the Hunt Institute. Regensburg and Pittsburgh: 1972. V. 63
A Redoute Treasury. Regensburg and Pittsburgh: 1972. V. 62
Roses. London: 1954. V. 64
Roses 2. London: 1956. V. 64

REDPATH, JAMES
The Roving Editor or Talks with Slaves in the Southern States. New York: 1859. V. 67

REDSTROM, ERNEST L.
Bugles, Banners and War Bonnets. Caldwell: 1977. V. 65

REECE, RICHARD
A Practical Dictionary of Domestic Medicine.... London: 1808. V. 62

REED, A. W.
Treasury of Maori Folklore. Wellington: 1967. V. 65

REED, BRIAN
Crewe to Carlisle. London: 1969. V. 63; 65

REED, C. A.
North American Birds Eggs. New York: 1904. V. 67

REED, E. J.
Our Iron-Clad Ships: Their Qualities, Performances and Cost. London: 1869. V. 64

REED, ELIOT
Skytip. 1950. V. 64; 66

REED, F. R. COOPER
The Geological History of the Rivers of East Yorkshire. 1901. V. 63

REED, HELEN LEAH
Brenda's Summer at Rockley. Boston: 1910. V. 63

REED, HENRY
A Map of Verona. London: 1946. V. 66

REED, HENRY M.
The A. B. Frost Book. Rutland: 1967. V. 65

REED, I.
Bibliotheca Reediana. A Catalogue of the Curios and Extensive Library of the Late Isaac Reed, Esq. of Staple Inn.... London: 1807. V. 62

REED, ISHMAEL
The Free-Lance Pallbearers. Garden City: 1967. V. 67

REED, JEREMY
The Lipstick Boys - a Novel. London: 1984. V. 63
Lorca's Death. Jersey: 1990. V. 62
Sky Writing. Jersey: 1990. V. 62
Wilde and the Night. N.P: 1994. V. 67

REED, JOHN
Ten Days That Shook the World. New York: 1919. V. 65
Ten Days That Shook the World. London: 1926. V. 63

REED, MYRTLE
Myrtle Reed Cook Book. New York: 1916. V. 67

REED, NATHANIEL
Life of Texas Jack. Tulsa: 1936. V. 63; 66

REED, RONALD
The Nature and Making of Parchment. Leeds: 1975. V. 62
Specimens of Parchment. Los Angeles: 1976. V. 64

REED, WALT
Harold Von Schmidt - Draws and Paints the Old West. Flagstaff: 1972. V. 66
John Clymer, an Artist's Rendezvous with the Frontier West. Flagstaff: 1976. V. 63; 64; 67

REED, WILLIAM
Olaf Wieghorst. Flagstaff: 1969. V. 63; 66

REEDSTROM, ERNEST L.
Bugles, Banners and War Bonnets. Caldwell: 1977. V. 65; 67

REEES, JAMES J.
History of the Twenty-Fourth Regiment, New Jersey Volunteers. Camden: 1889. V. 66

THE REEFCOMBER. 1980-1984. V. 66

REEMELIN, CHARLES
The Vine-Dresser's Manual, an Illustrated Treatise on Vineyards and Wine Making. New York: 1856. V. 63

REES, J. D.
H. H. H. The Duke of Clarence and Avondale in Southern India. 1801. V. 63; 64; 66; 67

REES, THOMAS
A New System of Stenography or Short Hand. Philadelphia: 1800. V. 62; 63

REESE, A. M.
The Alligator and Its Allies. New York: 1915. V. 64

REESE, DAVID MEREDITH
Humbugs of New York: Being a Remontrance Against Popular Delusion Whether in Science, Philosophy or Religion. New York: 1838. V. 63
Phrenology Known By Its Fruits.... New York: 1836. V. 64; 66; 67

REEVE, ARTHUR B.
The Golden Age of Crime. New York: 1931. V. 67

REEVE, CLARA
The Old English Baron: A Gothic Story. London: 1780. V. 62; 65
The Old English Baron. A Gothic Story. London: 1789. V. 63
The Old English Baron: A Gothic Story. London: 1797. V. 62; 64; 65

REEVE, FRANK D.
History of New Mexico. New York: 1961. V. 67

REEVE, JOHN
A Divine Looking Glass; or, the Third and Last Testament of Lord Jesus Christ.... London: 1661. V. 63
Verae Fidei Gloria Est Corona Vitae. N.P: 1755. V. 66

REEVE, L.
Conchologia Iconica, a Collection of 11 Monographs. 1845-1850. V. 66
Conchologia Systematica.... London: 1841-1842. V. 66
Elements of Conchology.... London: 1860. V. 62
The Land and the Freshwater Mollusks Indigenous to, or Naturalised in the British Isles. London: 1863. V. 64; 66

REEVE, TAPPING
The Law of Baron and Femme. New Haven: 1816. V. 65

REEVES, CHARLES E.
Directory of the City of Spokane Falls for the Year 1888. Spokane: 1888. V. 63

REEVES, DIANNE L.
From Fiber to Paper. Houston: 1991. V. 64

REEVES, GEORGE
A New History of London, from Its Foundation to the Present Year.... London: 1764. V. 62

REEVES, H. A.
Human Morphology.... London: 1882. V. 67

REEVES, JAMES
Arcadian Ballads. Andoversford: 1977. V. 64
Arcadian Ballads. London: 1977. V. 65
The Natural Need. Deya and London: 1935. V. 65; 67
The Secret Shoemakers and Other Stories. London: 1966. V. 62

REEVES, JAMES J.
History of the Twenty-Fourth Regiment, New Jersey Volunteers. Camden: 1889. V. 63

REEVES, MARTHA
Dancing in the Street, Confessions of a Motown Diva. New York: 1994. V. 67

REEVES, ROLEYNE
Colburn's Kalendar of Amusements in Town and Country for 1840. London: 1840. V. 66; 67

REEVES, WILLIAM
Acts of Archbishop Colton in His Metropolitan Visitation of the Diocese of Derry. 1850. V. 64

REEVES, WILLIAM P.
The Long White Cloud (Ao Tea Roa). London: 1924. V. 65
New Zealand. London: 1908. V. 65

REFLECTIONS on Communities of Women and Monastic Institutions, by a Friend of Religious and Civil Liberty. Taunton: 1815. V. 62; 65

REFLECTIONS on the Pernicious Custom of Recruiting by Crimps and Other Modes Now Practised in the British Army. London: 1795. V. 63; 67

REGAN, C. TATE
The Antarctic Fishes of the Scottish National Antarctic Expedition. Edinburgh: 1913. V. 63
Biologia Centrali-Americana: Pisces. London: 1906-1908. V. 62; 65
Biologia Centrali-Americana: Pisces. 1909-1916. V. 63
Deep-Sea Angler Fishes (Ceratiodiea). Copenhagen: 1932. V. 63
Fishes. London: 1914. V. 65
The Fishes of the Families Stomiatidae and Malacosteidae. Copenhagen: 1930. V. 65

REGAN, JOHN
The Emigrant's Guide to the Western States of America; or, Backwoods and Prairies. Edinburgh: 1852. V. 63

REGAN, MICHAEL
Stars, Moguls, Magnates: the Mansions of Beverly Hills. Los Angeles: 1966. V. 65

REGARDIE, ISRAEL
Roll Away the Stone, an Introduction to Aleister Crowley's Essays on the Psychology of Hashish. St. Paul: 1968. V. 67

REGEMORTES, LOUIS DE
Description du Nouveau Pont de Pierre, Construit sur la Riviere d'Allier a Moulins.... Paris: 1771. V. 64

REGIMEN Sanitatis Salernitanum. Oxford: 1830. V. 67

REGIMEN SANITATIS SALERNITANUM
De Conservanda Bona Valetudine. Francoforti: 1557. V. 64

REGISTER of Officers and Agents, Civil, Military and Naval in the Service of the U.S. on the 30th of Sept. 1829. Washington City: 1830. V. 63

THE REGISTERS of St. Bees, Cumberland. Newcastle-Upon-Tyne: 1968. V. 66

REGISTERS of the Commissioned Officers and Privates of the New Jersey Volunteers, in the Service of the United States. Jersey City: 1863. V. 66

REGNAULT, NICOLAS FRANCOIS
Les Ecarts de la Nature. Ou Recueil des principales Monstruosties. Paris: 1775. V. 63

REGO, PAULA
The Children's Crusade. London: 1999. V. 64

REGRA & Statutos da Hordem Adujs. Colophon: 1516. V. 62

REGTEREN ALTENA, C. O. VAN
The Marine Mollusca of Suriname. Leiden: 1969-1975. V. 66

REHBERG, FREDERICK
Drawings Faithfully Copied from Nature at Naples...(with) Outlines of Figures and Drapery, Collected with great Care for Ancient Statues (etc.).... 1794. V. 64

REHN, J. A. G.
The Grasshoppers and Locusts (Acridoidea) of Australia. Melbourne: 1952-1957. V. 64

REICH, WILHELM
Cosmic Superimposition: Man's Orgonotic Roots in Nature. Rangeley: 1951. V. 65
The Function of the Orgasm: Sex-Economic Problems of Biological Energy. New York: 1942. V. 65
Massenpsychologie des Faschismus: zur Sexualokonomie der Politischen Reaktion und zur Proletarischen Sexualpolitik. Kopenhagen: 9133. V. 65
Orgone Energy Accumulator: Its Scientific and Medical Use. Orgonon, Rangeley, Maine: 1951. V. 65
People in Trouble. Orgonon, Rangeley, Maine: 1953. V. 65
Psychischer Kontakt und Vegetative STromung. Kopenhagen: 1935. V. 65
The Sexual Revolution. New York: 1945. V. 65
The Sexual Revolution. London: 1951. V. 64

REICHARD, GLADYS A.
Dezba: Woman of the Desert. New York: 1939. V. 66
Navaho Religion - a Study of Symbolism. New York: 1950. V. 63; 66
Navaho Religion - A Study of Symbolism. 1963. V. 66
Navaho Religion - a Study of Symbolism. New York: 1963. V. 63
Navajo Shepherd and Weaver. New York: 1936. V. 62; 67
Social Life of the Navaho Indians - with Some Attention to Minor Ceremonies. New York: 1928. V. 66
Spider Woman, a Story of Navajo Weavers and Chanters. New York: 1934. V. 62

REICHARDT, J.
Cybernetics, Art and Ideas. 1971. V. 65

REICHENBACH KLINKE, H.
The Principal Diseases of Lower Vertebrates. 1965. V. 66

REICHER, OTTO
Tauernreise. N.P: 1938. V. 64

REICHERT, E. T.
A Biochemic Basis for the Study of Problems of Taxonomy, Heredity, Evolution, etc.... Washington: 1919. V. 63; 66; 67
The Differentiation and Specificity of Corresponding Proteins and Other Vital Substances in Relation to Biological Classification and Organic Evolution.... Washington: 1909. V. 62; 67
The Differentiation and Specificity of Starches in Relation to Genera, Species, Etc.... Washington: 1913. V. 67

REID, AGNES JUST
Letters of Long Ago. Caldwell: 1923. V. 65

REID, ANTHONY
Laughter in the Sun. London: 1952. V. 67

REID, DAVID BOSWELL
Illustrations of the Theory and Practice of Ventilation, with Remarks on Warming.... London: 1844. V. 64

REID, ELIZABETH
Mayne Reid. A Memoir of His Life. London: 1890. V. 67

REID, FORREST
Pirates of the Spring (and a Garden by the Sea). Dublin: Sep. 1920. V. 64
Walter De La Mare: a Critical Study. 1929. V. 67
Walter de la Mare: a Critical Study. London: 1929. V. 66

REID, HIRAM A.
History of Pasadena. Pasadena: 1895. V. 65

REID, HUGO
The Indians of Los Angeles County. Los Angeles: 1926. V. 62

REID, JESSE WALTON
History of the Fourth Regiment of S.C. Volunteers, from the Commencement of the War Until Lee's Surrender.... Greenville: 1892. V. 62; 63; 65

REID, JOHN
Essays on Hypochrondriasis and Other Nervous Affections. London: 1823. V. 64
Physiological, Anatomical and Pathological Researches. Edinburgh: 1848. V. 67

REID, JOHN C.
Reid's Tramp or a Journal of the Incidents of Ten Months Travel through Texas, New Mexico, Arizona, Sonora and California. Austin: 1935. V. 67

REID, JOSEPH V.
You Can Make a Stadivarius Violin. Chicago: 1950. V. 67

REID, MAX W.
Lake George and Lake Champlain, the War Trail of the Mohawk and the Battleground of France and England in Their Contest for Control of North America. New York: 1910. V. 63

REID, MAYNE
The Bush-Boys, or The History and Adventures of a Cape Farmer and His Family in the Wild Karvos of Southern Africa. London: 1856. V. 66
The Death Shot. London: 1887. V. 67
Gwen Wynn: a Romance of the Wye. London: 1877. V. 67
The Hunter's Feast; or Conversations Around the Camp-Fire. London: 1875. V. 67
Lost Lenore; or the Adventures of a Rolling Sone. London: 1875. V. 67
The Quadroon; or, a Lover's Adventures in Louisiana. London: 1856. V. 66

REID, SAMUEL C.
Scouting Expeditions of McCulloch's Texas Rangers. Philadlephia: 1859. V. 62

REID, THOMAS
Essays on the Active Powers of Man. London: 1788. V. 65
Essays on the Active Powers of Man. Dublin: 1790. V. 63
Essays on the Intellectual Powers of Man. Dublin;: 1786. V. 66
Essays on the Intellectual Powers of Man...(with) Essays on the Active Powers of Man.... Edinburgh: 1785-1788. V. 64
An Inquiry into the Human Mind, on the Principles of Common Sense. New York: 1824. V. 63

REID, THOMAS continued
Treatise on Clock and Watch Making, Theoretical and Practical. Philadelphia: 1832. V. 62; 64

REID, W.
An Attempt to Develop the Law of Storms by Means of Facts, Arranged According to Place and Time.... London: 1838. V. 63

REID, WEMYSS
Charlotte Bronte. London: 1877. V. 65
Charlotte Bronte. New York: 1877. V. 63
The Life, Letters and Friendships of Richard Monckton Milnes, 1st Lord Houghton. London: 1891. V. 64
Life of the Right Honourable William Edward Forster. London: 1888. V. 64
William Black, Novelist, a Biography. New York: 1902. V. 67

REID, WHITELAW
Ohio in the War. Cincinnati: 1868. V. 65
Ohio in the War, Her Statemen, Her Generals and Soldiers. New York: 1868. V. 65
Ohio in the War: Her Statesmen, Generals and Soldiers. Columbus: 1893. V. 63

REID, WILLIAM
Reid's Leith and London Smack Directory, Containing a Correct Chart and Table.... Leight: 1819. V. 63

REIDE, THOMAS
A Treatise on the Duty of Infantry Officers and the Present System of Military Discipline. London: 1795. V. 66

REIGARD, JOHN FRANKLIN
The Life of Robert Fulton. Philadelphia: 1856. V. 62; 64

REIGER, GEORGE
Profiles in Saltwater Angling. 1973. V. 67

REIL, JOHANN CHRISTIAN
Rhapsodien Uber die Anwendung der Psychischen Kurmethode auf Geisteszerruttungen. Halle: 1803. V. 65

REILLY, CATHERINE W.
English Poetry of the First World War - a Bibliography. London: 1978. V. 62; 65

REILLY, HELEN
All Concerned Notified. Garden City: 1939. V. 66
Death Demands and Audience. Garden City: 1940. V. 66

REINAGLE, PHILIP
Drawings from Original Pictures of Philip Reinagle. N.P: 1826. V. 67

REINHARDT, DJANGO
Album Souvenir. Paris: 1953. V. 67

REINHARDT, JOHANN CHRISTIAN
A Collection of Swiss Costumes in Miniature. London: 1822. V. 67

REINHARDT, KARL HEINRICH LEOPOLD
*Lettres sur Dresde a Madame *** Contenant une Esquisse, de ce Que Celle Ville Offre de Plus Remarquable Aux Etrangers.* Berlin: 1800. V. 64

REINZER, FRANZ
Meteorologia Philosophico-Politica. Augsburg: 1709. V. 64; 66

REISNER, ROBERT GEORGE
Bird. The Legend of Charlie Parker. New York: 1962. V. 64; 66

REITLINGER, GERALD
The Economics of Taste. New York: 1961. V. 63
The Economics of Taste: The Rise an Fall of Picture Prices 1760-1960, The Rise and Fall of Objets d'Art.. London: 1961-1970. V. 63

REITMAN, BEN
The Second Oldest Profession. New York: 1931. V. 63; 65

REITTER, E.
Beetles. New York: 1961. V. 64

REITTER, EDMUND
Fauna Germanica. Stuttgart: 1908-1916. V. 66

THE REJECTED Addresses; Together with the Prize Addresses, Presented for the Prize Medal, Offered for the Best Address on the Opening of the New Park Theatre. New York: 1821. V. 67

RELANDER, CLICK
Drummers and Dreamers: The Story of Snowhala the Prophet and His Nephew, Puck Hyat Toot. Caldwell: 1956. V. 64; 65

RELATION Veridique Qui a l'Air d'un Songe. A La Haye: 1782. V. 63

RELHAN, R.
Flora Cantabrigensis, Exhibens Plantas Agro Cantabrigensis Indegenas. 1785. V. 65; 67
Flora Cantabrigiensis.... Cambridge: 1785. V. 63; 64; 65; 66

RELLA, ETTORE
A History of Burlesque. San Francisco: 1940. V. 65

RELPH, JOSIAH
A Miscellany of Poems, Consisting of Original Poems, Translations, Pastorals in the Cumberland Dialect.... Glasgow: 1747. V. 62; 66
Poems.... Carlisle: 1798. V. 66

REMAINS of St. Mary's Abbey Dublin, Their Explorations and Researches 1886. 1887. V. 67

REMAK, ROBERT
Untersuchungen Uber die Entwickelung der Wirbelthiere. Berlin: 1850-1855. V. 62

REMARKABLE Convictions. Edinburgh: 1865. V. 63

A REMARKABLE Dialogue, Which Lately Happened in the Gardens of Luxembourg at Paris, Between an Old Impartial English Whig and a Nonjuror of the Church of England.... Edinburgh: 1749-1750. V. 62

THE REMARKABLE Life of John Elwes, Esq. London: 1797. V. 63

REMARKABLE Shipwrecks; or, a Collection of Interesting Accounts of Naval Disasters. Hartford: 1813. V. 63; 66

REMARKS On a Voyage to the Hebrides, in a Letter to Samuel Johnson, LL.D. London: 1775. V. 64

REMARKS on Fog's Journal, of February 10, 1732-1733. London: 1733. V. 66

REMARKS on the Consumption of Public Wealth by the Clergy of Every Christian Nation, and Particularly by the Established Church in England and Wales and in Ireland. London: 1822. V. 64

REMARKS On the Trial of John Peter Zenger, Printer of the New York Weekly Journal. London: 1738. V. 64

REMARKS Upon Mr. Webber's Scheme and the Draper's Pamphlet. London: 1741. V. 65; 66

REMARKS Upon the Emigration of Hill Coolies. Colophon: 1840. V. 65

REMARQUE, ERICH MARIA
All Quiet on the Western Front. Boston: 1929. V. 63
All Quiet on the Western Front. London: 1929. V. 67
All Quiet on the Western Front. N.P: 1969. V. 63
The Road Back. Boston: 1931. V. 63; 65
Spark of Life. New York: 1952. V. 64

REMBERT, W. R.
The Georgia Bequest. Manolia; or the Vale of Tallulah. Augusta: 1854. V. 62

REMEMBERING Ray. Santa Barbara: 1993. V. 62

REMEMBRANCES of the Great Exhibition. London: 1851. V. 66

REMILINUS, JOHANN
A Survey of the Microcosme; or, the Anatomy of the Bodies of Man and Woman. London: 1702. V. 62

REMINGTON, FREDERIC
Crooked Trails. New York: 1898. V. 63; 66
Done in the Open. New York: 1902. V. 62; 64; 66
Drawings. New York: 1897. V. 64; 67
Pony Tracks. New York: 1895. V. 63
Pony Tracks. Columbus: 1951. V. 67
Remington's Frontier Sketches. Chicago: 1898. V. 63; 66
The 2nd Bronze World of Frederic Remington. Tulsa: 1976. V. 64
Stories of Peace and War. New York: 1899. V. 65

REMINISCENCES Of Chicago During the Civil War. Chicago: 1914. V. 66

REMISE, JAC
The Golden Age of Toys. Lausanne: 1967. V. 66

REMSBURG, JOHN
Charles Reynolds, Soldier, Hunter, Scout and Guide. Kansas City: 1931. V. 65; 67

REMY, JULES
A Journey to Great Salt Lake City. London: 1861. V. 63; 64; 65
Voyage au Pays des Mormons: Relation, Geograpie, Histoire Naturelle, Histoire, Theologie, Moeurs et Costumes. Paris: 1860. V. 63; 65

RENAN, M. E.
An Essay on the Age and Antiquity of the Book of Nabathaean Agriculture. To which is Added an Inaugural Lecture on the Position of Shemitic Nations in the History of Civilization. London: 1862. V. 63

RENARD, L.
Fishes, Crayfishes and Crabs. Baltimore: 1995. V. 65

RENAUD, F.
A Short History of the Rise and Progress of the Manchester Royal Infirmary from the Year 1752 to 1877. Manchester: 1898. V. 66

RENAUDOT, THEOPHRASTE
A General Collection of Discourses of the Virtuosi of France, Upon Questions of All Sorts of Philosophy.... London: 1664. V. 62; 64

RENAULT, MARY
Funeral Games. New York: 1981. V. 63

RENDEL, J. M.
To the Rev. Canon Rogers. Report on the Practicability of Forming a Harbour, at the Mouth of the Loe Pool, in Mount's Bay, Near Helston, in the County of Cornwall. Plymouth: 1837. V. 62; 63

RENDELL, RUTH
Asta's Book. Bristol: 1993. V. 63; 65
The Best to Die. Garden City: 1970. V. 67
The Bridesmaid. London: 1989. V. 64
The Crocodile. London: 1993. V. 65
A Dark Adapted Eye. London: 1986. V. 65; 67
A Demon in My View. London: 1976. V. 62; 66

RENDELL, RUTH continued
The Face of Trespass. Garden City: 1974. V. 67
The Face of Trespass. London: 1974. V. 62; 63; 65; 66; 67
The Fallen Curtain and Other Stories. London: 1976. V. 64
From Doon with Death. London: 1964. V. 66
A Guilty Thing Surprised. London: 1970. V. 66
A Judgement in Stone. London: 1977. V. 64
A Judgment in Stone. Garden City: 1978. V. 67
Kissing the Gunner's Daughter. London: 1992. V. 67
Make Death Love Me. London: 1979. V. 63; 65
Matters of Suspense. Helsinki: 1986. V. 63; 66
Means of Evil and Other Stories. London: 1979. V. 65
Murder Being Once Done. London: 1972. V. 66
Murder Being Once Done. New York: 1972. V. 64
A New Lease of Death. London: 1967. V. 66
One Across, Two Down. London: 1971. V. 62; 63; 65; 66; 67
Put On by Cunning. London: 1981. V. 66
Road Rage. Blakeney: 1997. V. 65; 66
The Secret House of Death. London: 1968. V. 66
Shake Hands for Ever. London: 1975. V. 62; 63; 66
A Sight for Sore Eyes. Blakeney: 1998. V. 66
A Sleeping Life. London: 1978. V. 66
Some Lie and Some Die. London: 1973. V. 62; 66
The Speaker of Mandrian. London: 1983. V. 63
Three Cases for Inspector Wexford. Helsinki: 1991. V. 62
To Fear a Painted Devil. Garden City: 1965. V. 67
An Unkindness of Ravens. London: 1985. V. 66
Vanity Dies Hard. London: 1966. V. 65
Wolf to the Slaughter. London: 1967. V. 66

RENDER, WILHELM
A Tour through Germany; Particularly Along the Banks of the Rhine, Mayne, &c.... London: 1801. V. 64

RENDLE, WILLIAM
Old Southwark and Its People. London: 1878. V. 63

RENEHAN, ALOIS
Songs from the Black Mesa. Santa Fe: 1900. V. 63

RENEHAN, LAURENCE F.
History of Music. 1858. V. 67

RENIER, G. J.
Oscar Wilde. London: 1933. V. 66

RENIERS, P.
The Springs of Virginia, Life, Love and Death at the Waters 1775-1900. Chapel Hill: 1941. V. 65

RENN, LUDWIG
War. London: 1929. V. 64

RENNELL, JAMES
Memoir of a Map of Hindoostan; or the Mogul Empire.... London: 1792. V. 63

RENNER, F. G.
A Selected Bibliography on Management of Western Ranges, Livestock and Wildlife. Washington: 1938. V. 67

RENNER, FREDERIC G.
Charles M. Russell: Paintings, Drawings and Sculpture in the Amon G. Carter Collection, a Descriptive Catalog. Fort Worth: 1966. V. 65
Paper Talk, Illustrated Letters of Charles M. Russell. Fort Worth: 1962. V. 62; 65

RENNEVILLE, CONSTANTIN DE
The French Inquisition; or, the History of the Bastille in Paris, The State-Prison in France.... London: 1715. V. 66

RENNIE, JAMES
Alphabet of Angling. 1849. V. 65; 67

RENNISON, WILLIAM H.
Succession List of the Bishops, Cathedral and Parochial Clergy of the Dioceses of Waterford and Lismore. 1920. V. 62

THE RENO Court of Inquiry. Fort Collins: 1983. V. 67

RENOUARD, ANTOINE AUGUSTINE
Annales de l'Imprimerie des Alde, ou Histoire des Trois Manuce et de Leurs Editions. Paris: 1834. V. 65

RENOUARD, P. V.
History of Medicine...to the Nineteenth Century. Cincinnati: 1856. V. 66

RENSHAW, C. A.
England's Boys. London: 1916. V. 65

RENTOL, ANNIE
Fairyland. New York: 1929. V. 65

RENTON, EDWARD
Intaglio Engraving: Past and Present. London: 1896. V. 63

RENTON, WILLIAM
Bishopspool: a Romance of the Last Generation. London: 1883. V. 67

RENTOUL, ANNIE R.
Fairyland. New York: 1929. V. 63

RENWICK, ARTHUR
Report of the Executive Commissioner for New South Wales to the World's Columbian Exposition, Chicago, 1893. Sydney: 1894. V. 64

RENWICK, JOYCE
John Gardner: an Interview. N.P: 1980. V. 66

RENWICK, W. G.
Marble and Marble Working: Handbook for Architects, Sculptors.... New York and London: 1909. V. 62

A REPLY of a Member of Parliament to the Mayor of His Corporation. London: 1733. V. 65

A REPLY to a Nameless Pamphlet, Intitutled, an Answer to a Speech Without Doors, Etc. or a defence of Master Chaloner's Speech. London: 1646. V. 65

A REPLY to Dr. Huddesford's Observations Relating to the Delegates of the Press. Oxford: 1756. V. 62; 65

A REPLY to Lucius Junius Brutus's Examination of the President's Answer to the New Haven Remonstrance.... New York: 1801. V. 63

THE REPOSITORY of Useful Arts and Sciences, or Ingenious Man's Companion.... London: 1843. V. 64

A REPRESENTATION, of the Present State of Religion, with Regard to the Late Excessive Growth of Infidelity, Heresy and Profaneness: Drawn Up by the Upper House of Convocation, of the Province of Canterbury.... London: 1711. V. 65

REPRESENTATIONS of the Embossed, Chased and Engraved Subjects and Descriptions Which Decorate the Tobacco Box and Cases Belonging to the Past Overseers Society of the Parishes of St. Margaret and St. John the Evangelist in the City of Westminster. London: 1824. V. 62; 67

REPRESENTATIVE British Freemasons. A Series of Biographies and Portraits of Early Twentieth Century Freemasons. London: 1915. V. 62; 65

REPRESENTATIVE Men of Colorado in the Nineteenth Century. New York: 1902. V. 66

REPS, JOHN
Cities on Stone: Nineteenth Century Lithograph Images of the Urban West. Fort Worth: 1976. V. 63; 66

REPTON, HUMPHREY
The Art of Landscape Gardening. Boston and New York: 1907. V. 63; 64
The Landscape Gardening and Landscape Architecture of the Late Humphry Repton. London: 1840. V. 64
Observations on the Theory and Practice of Landscape Gardening. 1803. V. 67
Observations on the Theory and Practice of Landscape Gardening. London: 1805. V. 64
The Red Books. London: 1976. V. 67
Variety; or a Collection of Essays Written in the Year, 1787. London: 1788. V. 67

REPUBLIC of Cluny Annual Register and Miscellany 1909-1913. Shanghai: 1909-1913. V. 66

REQUA, RICHARD S.
Architectural Details: Spain and the Mediterranean. Cleveland: 1927. V. 65

REQUENO, VINCENZO
Saggi sul Ristabilimento dell'Antica Arte de Greci e Romani Pittori.... Parma: 1787. V. 63

RERESBY, JOHN
The Memoirs of Sir John Reresby of Thrybergh, Bart. M.P. for York &c. 1634-1689. London: 1875. V. 66
The Memoirs of...Containing Several Private and Remarkable Transactions, from the Restoration to the Revolution Inclusively. London: 1734. V. 66

RESEARCH DEFENCE SOCIETY
Experiments on Animals. Pamphlets Issued by the Research Defence Society, February-August 1908. London: 1908. V. 62

RESEARCH STUDY CLUB OF LOS ANGELES
Studies of the VIII Nerve. St. Louis: 1937. V. 63

THE RESIDENTS. Freakshow. N.P: 1992. V. 64

RESIST Much, Obey Little. Salt Lake City: 1985. V. 67

RESPUBLICA Romana. Leiden: 1629. V. 64

RESTON, JAMES
The Artillery of the Press. New York: 1967. V. 67
Sketches in the Sand. New York: 1967. V. 67

RETFORD, WILLIAM C.
Bows and Bow Makers. London: 1964. V. 67

RETI, L.
The Unknown Leonardo. New York: 1974. V. 65

RETROGRESSION. Boston: 1839. V. 62

A RETROSPECT of Andrew Jackson's Administration. N.P: 1832. V. 64

THE RETROSPECT of Practical Medicine and Surgery. New York: 1840-1873. V. 66

RETTELBUSCH, ERNST
Stilhandbuch: Ornamentik, Mobel, Innenausbau Von Den Altesten Zeiten Bis Zum Biedermeier. Stuttgart: 1937. V. 65

RETURN Relative to Fire Brigades and Fires in England and Wales, for the Year 1903. London: 1906. V. 64

RETZIUS, GUSTAF
Das Gehororgan der Wirbelthiere. Stockholm: 1881-1884. V. 62

RETZSCH, MORITZ
Fantasien. Umrisse zum Erstenmal Von Den Original-Platten Abgedruckt, Gezeichnet von Moritz Retzsch.... London: 1834. V. 64

REUBEN, SHELLY
Julian Solo. New York: 1988. V. 66

REUCHLIN, JOHANNES
Etsi Thalmud and Rab Alphes Impressione Praepeditus Nedu Hinc ad Septum Menses Mesperatam Tuis Posse.... 1522. V. 65

REUGER, HENRY
Reuger's Plat Atlas of Business Portion of Los Angeles City. Los Angeles: 1903. V. 65

REUMAUX, P.
Atlas des Cortinaires. 1990-1995. V. 64

REUSNER, NICOLAUS
Emblemata. Frankfurt: 1581. V. 64; 66

REUTER, JOHANN
Neo-Confessarius Practice Instructus.... Lovanii: 1772. V. 64

REUTER, ODO MORANNAL
Finlands Fiskar/The Fishes of Finaldn. Helsinki: 1883-1893. V. 64

REUTHER, WALTER P.
Selected Papers. New York: 1961. V. 64

REUTTER, K. J.
Tectonics of the Southern Central Andes. Structure and Evolution of an Active Continental Margin. Berlin: 1994. V. 67

REVE, GERARD
Parents Worry. London: 1990. V. 67

REVEL, ALPHONSE
De la Cause de l'Insensibilitie Produite par l'Inspiration des Vapeurs Etherees. Chambery: 1848. V. 65

REVELATIONS of Life in Nottingham by the English Asmodeus. Nottingham: 1861. V. 65

REVERDY, PIERRE
Selected Poems. New York: 1969. V. 62

REVERE, JOSEPH WARREN
Keel and Saddle: a Retrospect of Forty Years of Military and Naval Service. Boston: 1872. V. 62; 67

REVIEW.. Charlottesville: 1979-1998. V. 63

A REVIEW of Mrs. Crawford and Mrs. Siddons, in the Character of Belvidera: in a Letter to a Gentleman at Bath. London: 1782. V. 65

A REVIEW of Some of the Arguments Which are Commonly Advanced Against Parliamentary Interference on Behalf of the Negro Slaves. Manchester: 1824. V. 66

A REVIEW of the Department of Police, Trenton, New Jersey. Trenton: 1899. V. 66

A REVIEW of the History of the North of England an the Borders, Volumes VI-XIX. Leeds University: 1971-1983. V. 65

A REVIEW of the Late Engagement at Sea, Being a Collelction of Private Letters Never Before printed.... London: 1706. V. 62

A REVIEW of the Lectures on the Relative Strength of Catholicity and Protestantism. St. Louis: 1854. V. 62

REVILLE, ALBERT
Lectures on the Origin and Growth of Religion as Illustrated by the Native Religions of Mexico and Peru. London: 1895. V. 65

REVOLUTIONARY Radicalism: Its History, Purpose and Tactics. Albany: 1920. V. 67

REXROTH, KENNETH
Between Two Wars. Athens & San Francisco: 1982. V. 64
In What Hour. New York: 1940. V. 64
The New British Poets. Verona: 1948. V. 62; 64; 67
One Hundred Poems from the French. Cambridge: 1972. V. 66
One Hundred Poems from the Japanese. N.P: 1955. V. 66
The Phoenix and The Tortoise. Norfolk: 1944. V. 63; 66

REY, G.
The Matterhorn. 1907. V. 63; 65
The Matterhorn. London: 1907. V. 64
The Matterhorn. 1913. V. 65
Peaks and Precipices. Scrambles in the Dolomites and Savoy. 1914. V. 65

REY, H. A.
Cecily G. and the 9 Monkeys. Boston: 1942. V. 64
Raffy and the 9 Monkeys. London: 1939. V. 66

REYBAUD, LOUIS
Jerome Paturot a la Recherche d'une Position Sociale. Paris: 1846. V. 62; 66

REYBAUD, MARIE LOUIS
Etudes sur les Reformateurs Contemporains, ou Socialistes Modernes, Saint Simon, Ch. Fourier, Robert Owen.... Paris: 1842. V. 67

REYNARD, FRANK H.
Hunting Notes from Holderness. Squire Draper, Tom Hodgson, James Hall and Others 1726-1914. 1914,. V. 63

REYNARD THE FOX
Opus Poeticum. De Admirabili Fallacia et Astutia Vulpeculae Reinikes Libros IV nunc Primum ex Idiomate Germanico Latinitate Donatos, Adiectis.... Frankfurt: 1567. V. 62

REYNAUD, ADELINE
Voyage Extraordinaire de Mr. Tramontane. Paris: 1910. V. 65

REYNAUD, JEAN JOSEPH
Observation sur une Fistule Aerienne, avec Occlusion Complete de la Partie Inferieure du Larynx.... Paris: 1830. V. 65

REYNOLDS, BAILLE, MRS.
Accessory After the Fact. London: 1928. V. 66
The Affair at the Chateau. Garden City: 1929. V. 67
The Affair at the Chateau. London: 1929. V. 66
Black Light. London: 1937. V. 66

REYNOLDS, CATHERINE A.
Cowboy Artists of America. E. Paso: 1988. V. 63; 67

REYNOLDS, CHARLES R.
American Indian Portraits: from the Wanamaker Expedition of 1913. Brattleboro: 1971. V. 63; 65

REYNOLDS, FREDERICK
The Life and Times of Frederick Reynolds. London: 1826. V. 64

REYNOLDS, FREDERICK MANSEL
The Coquette: a Novel. Philadelphia: 1834?. V. 65
The Keepsake for MDCCCXXIX. London: 1829. V. 64
Miserrimus. London: 1933. V. 65

REYNOLDS, G. W.
The Aloes of South Africa. Johannesburg: 1950. V. 64
The Aloes of South Africa. Cape Town: 1969. V. 64
The Aloes of Tropical Africa and Madagascar. Mbabanae: 1966. V. 64

REYNOLDS, GEORGE
An Historical Essay Upon the Government of the Church of England, from the Earliest to the Present Time. London: 1743. V. 65

REYNOLDS, GEORGE W. M.
Master Timothy's Book-Case; or the Magic-Lanthorn of the World. London: 1844. V. 62
The Mysteries of London. London: 1847-1850. V. 63
Pickwick Abroad; or the Tour in France. London: 1839. V. 62
Pickwick Abroad; or, the Tour in France. London: 1846?. V. 62

REYNOLDS, GRAHAM
The Early Paintings and Drawings of John Constable. New Haven: 1996. V. 63

REYNOLDS HISTORICAL LIBRARY
Rare Books and Collections of the Reynolds Historical Library. A Bibliography. Birmingham: 1968. V. 66
Rare Books and Collections of the Reynolds Historical Library. A Bibliography. Volume 2. Birmingham: 1994. V. 66

REYNOLDS, HORACE
A Providence Episode in the Irish Literary Renaissance. 1929. V. 63

REYNOLDS, J.
Andrea Palladio and the Winged Device: a Panorama...ARchitect of Vicenza, Italy 1518-1580. New York: 1948. V. 62; 65

REYNOLDS, JAMES
The Confessions of a Pencil Case.... London: 1847. V. 67

REYNOLDS, JOHN HAMILTON
The Fancy. London: 1905. V. 64

REYNOLDS, JOHN N.
A Kansas Hell - or - Life in the Kansas Penitentiary. Atchison: 1889. V. 66

REYNOLDS, JOHN S
Reconstruction in South Carolina 1865-1877. Columbia: 1905. V. 63; 65; 66

REYNOLDS, JOSHUA
Delle Arti del Disegno Discorsi.... Florence: 1788. V. 65
Johnson and Garrick. London: 1816. V. 65
The Literary Works of Sir Joshua Reynolds.... London: 1819. V. 62
Notes and Observations on Pictures, Chiefly of the Venetian School, Being Extracts from His Italian Sketch Books.... London: 1859. V. 64
Portraits - Character Sketches of Oliver Goldsmith, Samuel Johnson and David Garrick.... London: 1952. V. 65
The Works of Sir Joshua Reynolds.... London: 1797. V. 67
The Works of Sir Joshua Reynolds.... London: 1809. V. 65; 66; 67

REYNOLDS, REVELL A.
A Morning of Childhood. London: 1905. V. 65

REYNOLDS, SHERI
Bitterroot Landing. New York: 1994. V. 63; 67

REYNOLDS, W. F. R.
Fly and Minnow. London: 1930. V. 67

REY ROSA, RODRIGO
The Path Doubles Back. New York: 1982. V. 66
The Pelcari Project. Tiburon: 1997. V. 62

REZANOV, NIKOLAI PETROVICH
Rezanov Reconnoiters California, 1806. San Francisco: 1972. V. 64; 65

REZEK, ANTOINE IVAN
History of the Diocese of Sault Ste. Marie and Marquette. Houghton: 1906-1907. V. 67

REZNIKOFF, CHARLES
Five Groups of Verse. New York: 1927. V. 62
In Memoriam: 1933. New York: 1934. V. 64
The Jews of Charleston. New York: 1950. V. 67
Nine Plays. New York: 1927. V. 64
Rhythms. Brooklyn: 1918. V. 65; 67
Separate Way. New York: 1936. V. 62; 64
Testimony. New York: 1934. V. 62

RHEAD, G. WOOLISCROFT
Staffordshire Pots and Potters. 1906. V. 67

RHEAD, LOUIS
A Collection of Book Plate Designs. Boston: 1907. V. 62

RHEINHEIMER, G.
Aquatic Microbiology. Chichester: 1992. V. 64

RHEMREV, PSEUD.
Big Game Hunt in Java. Leiden: 1884. V. 66

RHIND, WILLIAM
A History of the Vegetable Kingdom. 1857. V. 63
A History of the Vegetable Kingdom. London: 1877. V. 66

RHINEHART, LUKE
The Diceman. New York: 1971. V. 65

RHOAD, ALBERT O.
Santa Gertrudis Breeders International Recorded Herds. Kingsville: 1953-1966. V. 64

RHODE ISLAND. (COLONY). LAWS, STATUTES, ETC. - 1752
Acts and Laws of Majesty's Colony of Rhode-Island and Providence Plantations, in New England in America. From Anno 1745 to Anno 1752. Newport: 1752. V. 64

RHODE, JOHN
Death at the Helm. New York: 1941. V. 66
Death Invades the Meeting. London: 1944. V. 67
Dr. Priestly Investigates. New York: 1930. V. 67
The House on Tollard Bridge. London: 1929. V. 65
The Murders in Praed Street. 1928. V. 66
The Murders in Praed Street. New York: 1928. V. 64
The Robthorne Mystery. Toronto: 1934. V. 67
The Telephone Call. London: 1948. V. 66
The Tower of Evil. New York: 1938. V. 67
Tragedy at the Unicorn. 1928. V. 66
Tragedy at the Unicorn. New York: 1928. V. 64
The Venner Crime. London: 1933. V. 65; 67

RHODENIZER, VERNON BLAIR
Canadian Literature in English. (with) Index. Montreal: 1965. V. 67

RHODES, CHARLES D.
History of the Cavalry of the Army of the Potomac, Including that of the Army of Virginia (Pope's) and Also the History of the Operations of the Federal Cavalry in West Virginia During the War. Kansas City: 1900. V. 63

RHODES, CHARLES PARKER
The French Maritime-Commercial Directory. Havre: 1861. V. 67

RHODES, DENNIS E.
Bookbindings and Other Bibliophily: Essays in Honour of Anthony Hobson. Verona: 1994. V. 63
Essays in Honour of Victor Scholderer. Mainz: 1970. V. 63

RHODES, EUGENE MANLOVE
Beyond the Desert. Boston: 1934. V. 64
Good Men and True. New York: 1910. V. 62
The Little World Waddies. Chico: 1946. V. 64; 67
The Little World Waddies. El Paso: 1946. V. 66
Penalosa. Santa Fe: 1934. V. 62; 64; 66; 67
The Trusty Knaves. Boston: 1933. V. 64; 67

RHODES, JOHN W.
Melini, or the Victim of Guilt. Boston: 1844. V. 63; 66

RHODES, THOMAS
Poetical Miscellanies. Coventry: 1810. V. 63

RHODES, WILLIAM
Recollections of Dakota Territory. Fort Pierre: 1931. V. 63

RHODES-JAMES, MONTAGUE
The Sculptured Bosses in the Roof of the Bauchun Chapel of Our Lady of Pity in Norwich Cathedral. Norwich: 1908. V. 62

RHODIUS, JOHANNES
De Acia Dissertatio ad Cornelii Celsi Mentem Qua Simul Universa Fibulae Ratio Explicatur. Copenhagen;: 1672. V. 63

RHYMERS' CLUB, LONDON
The Book of the Rhymers' Club. London: 1892. V. 64; 65
The Second Book fo the Rhymers' Club. London: 1894. V. 62; 64

RHYMES of Old Times. London: 1925. V. 63

RHYS, ERNEST
Letters from Limbo. London: 1936. V. 63
A London Rose and Other Rhymes. London: 1894. V. 64
Sir Frederic Leighton. London: 1895. V. 64

RHYS, GRACE
In Wheel About and Cockalone. 1918. V. 65

RHYS, JEAN
After Leaving Mr. Mackenzie. New York: 1931. V. 66
Good Morning Midnight. London: 1939. V. 65
My Day - 3 Pieces. New York: 1975. V. 64; 65
Postures. London: 1928. V. 65
Sleep It Off Lady - Stories. London: 1976. V. 62
Tigers Are Better Looking.... London: 1968. V. 65
Voyage in the Dark. London: 1934. V. 66
Voyage in the Dark. London: 1967. V. 64
Wide Sargasso Sea. London: 1966. V. 66

RHYS, KEIDRICH
Poems from the Forces - a Collection of Verses by Serving Members of the Navy, Army and Air Force. London: 1941. V. 65

RIBALOW, HAROLD U.
Arnold Wesker. New York: 1965. V. 66

RIBELIN, W. E.
The Pathology of Fishes. Madison: 1975. V. 63; 66

RICARDO, DAVID
Des Principes de l'Economie Politique, et de l'Impot. Paris: 1819. V. 64
Letters...to Hutches Trower and Others 1811-1823. Oxford: 1899. V. 63
On Protection to Agriculture.... London: 1822. V. 63
On the Principles of Political Economy and Taxation. London: 1817. V. 64; 65; 67
On the Principles of Political Economy and Taxation. London: 1821. V. 63; 64
The Works. London: 1871. V. 64

RICARDO, JOHN LEWIS
The Anatomy of the Navigation Laws. London: 1847. V. 64

RICCARDI, A. C.
The Cretaceous System of Southern South America. 1988. V. 67

RICCATI, VINCENZO
Institutiones Analyticae. Bologna: 1765-1767. V. 64; 67

RICCI, BARTOLOMEO
Apparatvs Latinae Locvtionis. Argentorati: 1535. V. 64; 66
De Imitatione Libri Tres. Venetiis: 1545. V. 63; 66

RICCI, JAMES V.
The Genealogy of Gynaecology. Philadelphia: 1943. V. 66
One Hundred Years of Gynaecology 1800-1900. Mansfield Centre: 1999. V. 65

RICCI, MARCO
Francisco Comiti Algarotto.... 1792-1793. V. 64

RICCI, SEYMOUR DE
English Collectors of Books and Manuscripts (1530-1930) and Their Marks of Ownership. Cambridge: 1930. V. 64
English Collectors of Books and Manuscripts (1530-1930) and Their Marks of Ownership. New York: 1930. V. 62
Louis XVI Furniture. London: 1913. V. 65

RICCIOLI, GIAMBATTISTA
Geographicae Crucis Fabrica et Usus ad Repraesentandam Mira Facilitate, Omnem Dierum Noctiumque Ortuum Solis & Occasium, Horarumque Omnium Vareitatem.... Bologna: 1643. V. 63

RICCIUTI, I. W.
New Orleans and Its Environs: the Domestic Architecture 1727-1870. New York: 1938. V. 62; 65

RICCOBONI, LUIGI
Histoire du Theatre Italien.... Paris: 1728. V. 66
An Historical and Critical Account of the Theatres of Europe, viz. The Italian, Spanish, Frnech, English, Dutch, Flemish and German.... London: 1741. V. 64; 66

RICCOBONI, MARIE JEANNE LABORAS DE MEZIERES
Les Amours de Roger et de Gertrude. Paris: 1780. V. 63
Letters from Juliet Lady Catesby, to Her Friend Lady Henrietta Campley. London: 1780. V. 67
Lettres de Milady Juliette Catesby, a Milady Henriette Campley, Son Amie. Amsterdam: 1759. V. 65
Lettres de Mistress Fanni Buterld, a Milord Charles Alfred, duc de Caitombridge, Ecrites en 1735. Paris: 1759. V. 67
Lettres de Mistriss Fanni Butlerd a Milord Charles Alfred de Caitombridge, Comte de Plisinte, Duc de Raslingth. (with) Lettres de Milady Juliette Catesby, a Milday Henriette Campley, Son Amie. Amsterdam: 1759. V. 63

RICCOBONI, MARIE JEANNE LABORAS DE MEZIERES continued
Recueil de Pieces Detachees. Paris: 1772. V. 67

RICE, ALICE HEGAN
Our Ernie. New York and London: 1939. V. 64

RICE, ALLEN THORNDIKE
The Diary of a Public Man. Chicago: 1945. V. 63

RICE, ANNE
Beauty's Release. 1985. V. 64
Belinda. New York: 1986. V. 66; 67
Cry to Heaven. New York: 1982. V. 62; 66
Exit to Eden. 1985. V. 64; 66
Exit to Eden. New York: 1985. V. 65; 66
The Feast of All Saints. New York: 1979. V. 62; 63; 64; 66
Interview with the Vampire. London: 1976. V. 62; 64; 65; 66
Interview with the Vampire. New York: 1996. V. 62; 63
Lasher. New York: 1993. V. 67
Memnoch the Devil. New York: 1995. V. 63; 66
The Mummy or Ramses the Damned. London: 1989. V. 66
Queen of the Damned. New York: 1988. V. 66
The Tale of the Body Thief. New York: 1992. V. 66
The Vampire Armand. London: 1998. V. 63
The Vampire Lestat. New York: 1985. V. 64; 65; 66
Vittorio the Vampire. Franklin Center: 1999. V. 65; 67
Vittorio, the Vampire. New York: 1999. V. 62

RICE, CRAIG
The April Robin Murders. New York: 1958. V. 67
The Big Midget Murders. New York: 1942. V. 65
Innocent Bystander. New York: 1949. V. 67

RICE, ELMER
Seven Plays. New York: 1950. V. 62

RICE, GEORGE WHARTON
The Shipping Days of Old Boothbay. From the Revolution to the World War with Mention of Adjacent Towns. Boothbay Harbor: 1938. V. 64

RICE, HERBERT
The Theory and Practice of Interpolation; Including Mechanical Quadrature & Other Important Problems Concerned with the Tabular Values of Functions. Lynn: 1899. V. 67

RICE, HOWARD C.
The American Campaigns of Rochambeau's Army 1780, 1781, 1782, 1783. Princeton: 1972. V. 62
The Rittenhouse Orrery; Princeton's Eighteenth Century Planetarium 1767-1954.... Princeton: 1954. V. 67

RICE, LEE M.
They Saddled the West. Cambridge: 1975. V. 63

RICE, WILLIAM
Indian Game, from Quail to Tiger. 1884. V. 62

RICH, ADRIENNE
A Change of World. New Haven: 1951. V. 63; 65
Leaflets: Poems 1965-1968. New York: 1966. V. 66
Leaflets: Poems 1965-1968. New York: 1969. V. 66
The Meaning of Our Love for Women Is What We Have Constantly to Expand. New York: 1977. V. 64
Necessities of Life. Poems 1962-1965. New York: 1966. V. 66

RICH, ANTHONY
A Dictionary of Roman and Greek Antiquities. London: 1901. V. 65

RICH, HENRY
What Is To Be Done?. London: 1844. V. 66

RICH, P. V.
The Fossil Vertebrate Record of Australasia. Clayton: 1982. V. 62

RICHA, GIUSEPPE
Notizie Istoriche delle Chiese Fiorentine. Florence: 1754-1762. V. 64

RICHARD, ACHILLE
Botanique Medicale, ou Histoire Naturelle et Medicale des Medicamens, des Poisons et des Alimens Tires du Regne Vegetal. Paris: 1823. V. 65
Nouveaux Elemens de Botanique, Appliquee a la Medecine, a l'Usage des Eleves qui Suivent les Cors de la Faculte de Medecine et du Jardin du Roi. Paris: 1819. V. 66

RICHARD Dunston Limited, Shipbuilders. London: 1953. V. 66

RICHARD, HENRY
Letters on the Social and Political Condition of the Principality of Wales. London: 1866. V. 64; 67
Memoirs of Joseph Sturge. London: 1864. V. 64

RICHARD, MARK
Fishboy. New York: 1993. V. 64; 67
The Ice at the Bottom of the World. New York: 1989. V. 64; 67

RICHARD, PETER
Charles Augustus Milverton on Stage, Screen and Radio. London: 1960. V. 63

RICHARDS, CLARICE E.
A Tenderfoot Bride. New York: 1920. V. 67

RICHARDS, COOMBE
Informative Fishing. London: 1951. V. 67

RICHARDS, E. F., MRS.
My Mother's Cook Book. Saint Louis: 1875. V. 62; 64

RICHARDS, FRANK
Big Chief Bunter. London: 1963. V. 63
Bill Bunter's Beanfest. London: 1952. V. 63; 65
Bunter Comes for Christmas. London: 1959. V. 67
Bunter Keeps It Dark. London: 1960. V. 63
Bunter Out of Boards. London: 1959. V. 63
Bunter the Stowaway. London: 1964. V. 63
Bunter the Ventriloquist. London: 1961. V. 63
The Greyfriars Holiday Annual for Boys and Girls 1933. London: 1933. V. 63
Old Soldier Sahib. London: 1936. V. 62

RICHARDS, GEORGE
Modern France: a Poem. Oxford: 1793. V. 64

RICHARDS, GRANT
Author Hunting. Memories of Years Spent Mainly in Publishing. London: 1960. V. 67

RICHARDS, J. M.
The Castles on the Ground. (with) The Castles on the Ground - the Anatomy of Suburbia. London: 1946-1973. V. 63
High Street. London: 1938. V. 64; 65

RICHARDS, LAURA E.
Captain January. Boston: 1924. V. 63

RICHARDS, P. W.
The Tropical Rain Forest, an Ecological Study. Cambridge: 1952. V. 63

RICHARDS, RAYMOND
Old Cheshire Churches. London: 1947. V. 62; 66

RICHARDS, T. ADDISON
Tallulah and Jocasee; or, Romances of Southern Landscape & Other Tales. Charleston: 1852. V. 66

RICHARDS, WALTER
Her Majesty's Army. London: 1889-1890. V. 62; 67

RICHARDSON, ALBERT
Beyond the Mississippi: from the Great River to the Great Ocean - Life and Adventures on the Prairies, Mountains and Pacific Coast. Hartford: 1867. V. 64; 66
Garnered Sheaves - From the Writing of Albert P. Richardson. Hartford: 1871. V. 63; 66

RICHARDSON, BENJAMIN WARD
The Health of Nations. A Review of the Works of Edwin Chadwick. London: 1887. V. 62

RICHARDSON, C. J.
Picturesque Designs for Mansions, Villas, Lodges, &. with Decorations, Internal and External, Suitable to Each Style. London: 1870. V. 66

RICHARDSON, CHARLES
The Chancellorsville Campaign. Fredericksburg to Salem Church. New York: 1907. V. 62; 63
A New Dictionary of the English Language.... London: 1856. V. 64
A New Dictionary of the English Language.... London: 1858. V. 64
The Severn Tunnel. Bristol: 1887. V. 62

RICHARDSON, DAVID
Richardson's Virginia and North Carolina Almanac for the Year for Our Lord 1861 (through 1879). Richmond: 1860-1878. V. 63; 65
Richardson's Virginia and North Carolina Almanac, for the Year of Our Lord 1862.... Richmond: 1861. V. 65
Southern Almanac for 1864. Lynchburg: 1863. V. 63; 65

RICHARDSON, DOROTHY M.
John Austen and the Inseparables. London: 1930. V. 66
Pilgrimage. London: 1938. V. 62
The Trap. London: 1925. V. 66

RICHARDSON, ERIC
Pennine Lead-Miner. London: 1979. V. 64

RICHARDSON, FRANK
From Sunrise to Sunset: Reminiscence. Bristol: 1910. V. 67

RICHARDSON, GEORGE
Aedes Pembrochianae; a New Account and Description of the Statues, Bustos, Relievos, Paintings, Medals and Other Curiosities in Wilton-House.... Salisbury: 1795. V. 62
A Collection of Ornaments in the Antique Style Comprised in XXXVII Plates.... London: 1816. V. 62; 66
The New Vitruvius Britannicus.... London: 1810-1808. V. 67

RICHARDSON, GEORGE W.
Speech of George W. Richardson, of Hanover, In Committee of the Whole, on the Report of the Committee on Federal Relations in the Convention of Virginia April 4, 1861. Richmond: 1862. V. 63; 65

RICHARDSON, H.
Monograph on the Isopods of North America. Washington: 1905. V. 64; 66

RICHARDSON, H. G.
The Irish Parliament in the Middle Ages. Philadelphia: 1952. V. 63

RICHARDSON, HAROLD
The Poet and Other Animals. London: 1909. V. 64

RICHARDSON, HENRY HANDEL, PSEUD.
The End of a Childhood and Other Stories. London: 1934. V. 63
The Fortunes of Richard Mahony. London: 1930. V. 63
Two Studies. London: 1931. V. 63; 64

RICHARDSON, J.
An Account of Some of the Statues, Bas-Reliefs, Drawings and Pictures in Italy &c with Remarks. London: 1754. V. 66
Furness Past and Present: Its History and Antiquities. Barrow-in-Furness: 1880. V. 64

RICHARDSON, JAMES D.
A Compilation of the Messages and Papers of the Confederacy. Nashville: 1906. V. 62; 63

RICHARDSON, JOHN
An Account of the Life of That Ancient Servant of Jesus Christ, Giving a Relation of Many of His Trials and Exercises...in England, Ireland, America, etc. London: 1774. V. 63
Arctic Ordeal. The Journal of John Richardson. Kingston and Montreal: 1985. V. 64
Arctic Searching Expedition: a Journal of a Boat-Voyage through Rupert's Land and the Arctic Sea.... New York: 1969. V. 63
A Catalogue of the Whole of the Travelling Theatres, Which for Excellence and Incompleteness, Stand Unrivaled. London: 1836. V. 65
Fauna Boreali-Americana.... London: 1831. V. 67
Furness Past and Present: Its History and Antiquities. Barrow-in-Furness: 1870-1880. V. 66
John Austen and the Inseparables. London: 1930. V. 64
Lakes, Peaks and Passes. Barrow-in-Furness: 1870. V. 66
The Museum of Natural History. Glasgow: 1859-1862. V. 66
The Museum of Natural History. London: 1859-1862. V. 62; 66
The Museum of Natural History. Glasgow: 1868. V. 66
Observations on the Proposed Railway from Newcastle upon Tyne to North Shields and Tynemouth. Newcastle: 1831. V. 62
The Philosophical Principles of the Science of Brewing. London: 1805. V. 66
Report on the Ichthyology of the Seas of China and Japan. London: 1846. V. 63
Statical Estimates of the Materials of Brewing; or, A Treatise on the Application and Use of the Saccharometer.... London: 1784. V. 66

RICHARDSON, JOHN F.
The Kill. 1989. V. 62

RICHARDSON, JONATHAN
Explanatory Remarks upon Milton's Paradise Lost. With a Life of the Author and a Discourse on the Poem. London: 1734. V. 62; 66
The Works. London: 1773. V. 66; 67
The Works. 1792. V. 64
The Works. London: 1792. V. 66
The Works. Twickenham: 1792. V. 65

RICHARDSON, JOSIAH
The New England Farrier and Family Physician. Exeter: 1828. V. 62

RICHARDSON, M. A.
The Local Historian's Table Book, of Remarkable Occurrences, Historical Facts, Traditions, Legendary and Descriptive Ballads &c.... Newcastle-upon-Tyne: 1841. V. 66

RICHARDSON, MARY E.
The Life of a Great Sportsman (John Maunsell Richardson). London: 1919. V. 63

RICHARDSON, R. H.
Wickedness in High Places. Chicago: 1854. V. 64

RICHARDSON, ROBERT
Bellringer Street. London: 1988. V. 63
The Law of Testaments and Last Wills.... London: 1769. V. 62
Story of the Niger: a Record of Travel and Adventure from the Days of Mungo Park to the Present Time. London: 1888. V. 65

RICHARDSON, RUPERT N.
The Commanche Barrier to Southern Plains Settlement. Abilene: 1991. V. 66
The Frontier of Northwest Texas 1846 to 1876.... Glendale: 1963. V. 66
The Great Southwest. Glendale: 1934. V. 62; 64; 65

RICHARDSON, SAMUEL
Anti-Pamela; or Feigned Innocence Detected.... London: 1741. V. 62
A Collection of the Moral and Instructive Sentiments, Maxims, Cautions and Reflexions, Contained in the Histories of Pamela, Clarissa and Sir Charles Grandison. London: 1755. V. 62
The Correspondence.... London: 1804. V. 63
The History of Sir Charles Grandison. London: 1753-1754. V. 64; 66
The History of Sir Charles Grandison. London: 1754. V. 64; 65
The History of Sir Charles Grandison. London: 1770. V. 64
A New System of Short-Hand, by Which More May Be Written In One Hour, Than in an Hour and a Half by Any Other System Hitherto Published.... London: 1810. V. 67
Pamela, or Virtue Rewarded. London: 1785. V. 62; 63
The Paths of Virtue Delineated; or, the History in Miniature of the Celebrated Pamela, Clarissa, Harlowe and Sir Charles Grandison. London: 1773. V. 62

RICHARDSON, W. A.
Reprints of Rare Tracts and Imprints of Antient Manuscripts, &c.... Newcastle-upon-Tyne: 1847-1849. V. 62

RICHARDSON, WILLIAM
Chemical Principles of the Metallic Arts Designed Chiefly for the Use of Manufactures. Birmingham: 1790. V. 65
The Monastic Ruins of Yorkshire, from Drawings by William Richardson, With Historical Descriptions by the Rev. Edward Churton. London: 1843. V. 66
A Philosophical Analysis and Illustration of Some of Shakespeare's Remarkable Characters. London: 1775. V. 65
Poems Chiefly Rural. Glasgow: 1776. V. 62

RICHARDSON, WILLIAM H.
A Manual of Infantry and Rifle Tactics, with Honors Paid by the Troops, Inspections, Reviews, &c. Richmond: 1861. V. 62

RICHARDSON'S Virginia and North Carolina Almanac for the Year of Our Lord 1863. Richmond: 1862. V. 62; 63; 65

RICHARDT, F.
Prospecter af Danske Herregaarde. Copenhagen: 1844-1870. V. 67

RICHDALE, L. E.
A Population Study of Penguins. Oxford: 1957. V. 67

RICHELET, PIERRE
Dictionnaire Portratif de La Langue Francoise.... Lyons: 1761. V. 64

RICHELIEU, ARMAND JEAN DU PLESSIS, CARDINAL
The Compleat Statesman; or, the Political Will and Testament, of that Great Minister of State Cardinald Duke de Richilieu. London: 1695. V. 67

RICHERAND, A.
Elements of Physiology.... London: 1812. V. 64; 66; 67

RICHEY, J. E.
The Geology of Aradnamurchan, North-West Mull and Coll. London: 1930. V. 65

RICHEY, MATTHEW
Sermons Delivered on Various Occasions. Toronto: 1840. V. 65

RICHIE, DONALD
The Masters Book of Ikebana, Background and Principles of Japanese Flower Arrangement. Tokyo: 1966. V. 63; 64

RICHLER, MORDECAI
The Acrobats. London: 1954. V. 63
The Apprenticeship of Duddy Kravitz. Boston and Toronto: 1959. V. 63; 67
Hunting Tigers Under Glass - Essays and Reports. Toronto: 1968. V. 64
Hunting Tigers Under Glass - Essays and Reports. London: 1969. V. 63
Joshua Then and Now. New York: 1980. V. 64
Shovelling Trouble. Toronto: 1972. V. 64
Son of a Smaller Hero. London: 1955. V. 63
The Street. Toronto/Montreal: 1969. V. 64

RICHMOND, A.
Native Daughter, the Story of Anita Whitney. San Francisco: 1942. V. 65

RICHMOND, Capital of Virginia. Approaches to Its History. Richmond: 1938. V. 63

RICHMOND, HERBERT
The Navy in India 1763-1783. London: 1931. V. 62

RICHMOND, MARY E.
Marriage and the State, Based Upon Field Studies of the Present Day Adminstration of the Marriage Laws in the United States. New York: 1929. V. 65

RICHMOND'S Directory of Perth Amboy, Woodbridge, Carteret, Chrome, Sewaren, Port Reading, Fords and Keasbey. Yonkers: 1913. V. 63; 66
RICHMOND'S Directory of Perth Amboy, Woodbridge, Carteret, Chrome, Sewaren, Port Reading, Fords and Keasbey. Yonkers: 1914. V. 63; 66
RICHMOND'S Directory of Perth Amboy, Woodbridge, Carteret, Chrome, Sewaren, Port Reading, Fords and Keasbey. Yonkers: 1915. V. 63

RICHTER, AUGUST GOTTLIEB
Chirurgische Bibliothek. Gottingen und Gotha: 1771-1796. V. 65

RICHTER, CARL FRIEDRICH
Anfang von Einer Neuen Methode Unter Wasser zu Bauen Ohne Fangedamme zu Machen und das Wasser Auszupumpen von Einer Tiefe bis 30 Fuss Unter Wasser bey Ebbe und Fluth. Berlin und Leipzig: 1765. V. 65

RICHTER, CONRAD
Brothers of No Kin. New York: 1924. V. 67
The Grandfathers. New York: 1964. V. 62
The Light in the Forest. New York: 1961. V. 62
The Town. New York: 1950. V. 62; 65

RICHTER, HANS
Hans Richter. London: 1971. V. 65

RICHTER, JEAN PAUL FRIEDRICH
Levana; or, the Doctrine of Education. London: 1848. V. 67

RICHTON, MICHAEL
Sphere. New York: 1987. V. 65

RICKARD, T. A.
Journeys of Observation. San Francisco: 1907. V. 65
Through the Yukon and Alaska. San Francisco: 1909. V. 66

RICKARDS, C. G.
The Ruins of Mexico. London: 1910. V. 62

RICKENBACKER, EDWARD
Fighting the Flying Circus. New York: 1919. V. 63; 64; 66
Rickenbacker. Englewood Cliffs: 1967. V. 63; 67

RICKETS, CHARLES
De la Typographie et de l'Harmonie de la Page Imprimee. 1898. V. 67

RICKETSON, SHADRACH
Means of Preserving Health and Preventing Diseases.... New York: 1806. V. 62

RICKETT, HAROLD WILLIAM
Wild Flowers of the United States. New York: 1966. V. 62; 64; 65; 66; 67
Wild Flowers of the United States. New York: 1966-1973. V. 62; 66
Wild Flowers of the United States. Volume 2. The Southeastern States. New York: 1967. V. 64; 66
Wild Flowers of the United States. Volume 3. Texas. New York: 1969. V. 66
Wild Flowers of the United States. Volume 4. Southwestern States. New York: 1970. V. 66
Wild Flowers of the United States. Volume 5. Northwestern States. New York: 1971. V. 66
Wild Flowers of the United States. Volume 6. Central Mountains and Plains. New York: 1973. V. 66

RICKETTS, CHARLES
Beyond the Threshold. 1929. V. 62
Charles Ricketts R.A. - Sixty Five Illustrations. London: 1933. V. 63
A Defence of the Revival of Printing. London: 1899. V. 64
Oscar Wilde: Recollections.... London: 1932. V. 62; 65
Unrecorded Histories. London: 1933. V. 64

RICKETTS, W. P.
50 Years in the Saddle. Sheridan: 1942. V. 66

RICKEY, DON
Forty Miles on Beans and Hay. Norman: 1963. V. 67
History of Custer Battlefield. Montana: 1967. V. 67

RICKLIN, FRANZ
Wish Fulfillment and Symbolism in Fairy Tales. New York: 1915. V. 67

RICKMAN, PHILIP
A Bird Painter's Sketch Book. 1931. V. 67
A Bird Painter's Sketch Book. 1935. V. 66; 67

RICKMAN, THOMAS
An Attempt to Discriminate the Styles of Architecture in England, from the Conquest to the Reformation.... 1825. V. 67
An Attempt to Discriminate the Styles of English Architecture. Liverpool: 1819. V. 66; 67

RICKOVER, HYMAN G.
How the Battleship Maine was Destroyed. Washington: 1976. V. 63

RICKS, MELVIN
Alaska Bibliography. Portland: 1970. V. 67

RICKWORD, EDGELL
Scrutinies by Various Writers. London: 1928. V. 62

RICORD, FREDERICK W.
History of Union County, New Jersey. Newark: 1897. V. 63; 66

RIDDELL, CHARLES JAMES BUCHANAN
Magnetical Instruction for the Use of Portable Instruments Adapted for Magnetical Surveys and Portable Observatories (with) Supplement.... London: 1844-1846. V. 65

RIDDELL, CHARLOTTE
The Earl's Promise. London: 1873. V. 65
Far Above Rubies; and Otbher Stories. London: 1874. V. 65
A Life's Assize. London: 1871. V. 65
Maxwell Drewitt. London: 1866. V. 65

RIDDELL, R.
A Manual of Gardening for Western India. Madras: 1845. V. 63

RIDDELL, ROBERT
The Elements of Hand Railing. Philadelphia: 1860. V. 62

RIDDLE, KENYON
Records and Maps of the Old Santa Fe Trail. Raton: 1949. V. 64

RIDEING, WILLIAM
A Saddle in the Wild West. London: 1879. V. 64
A Saddle in the Wild West. New York: 1879. V. 66; 67

RIDER, CARDANUS
British Merlin: for the Year of Our Lord God 1773. London: 1773. V. 64

RIDER, SARAH
The Misplaced Corpse. Boston: 1940. V. 66

RIDER, WILLIAM
A New History of England, from the Descent of the Romans to the Demise of His Late Majesty, George III.... London: 1761-1764. V. 64
Views of Cottages, Lodges and Abbey of Stoneleigh.Views. Leamington: 1825. V. 62

RIDES To Town. 1914. V. 65

RIDGE, LOLA
Firehead. New York: 1929. V. 64; 66

RIDGEWAY, WILLIAM
A Report of the Trial of John Killen and John McCann for High Treason. 1803. V. 64
A Report of the Trial of Walter Clare - High Treason. 1803. V. 64; 67

RIDGWAY, R.
The Birds of North and Middle America, a Descriptive Catalogue.... Washington: 1901-1911. V. 67
The Birds of North and Middle America.... Washington: 1901-1950. V. 63; 67
A Manual of North American Birds. Philadelphia: 1896. V. 64
The Ornithology of Illinois. Bloomington: 1913. V. 65

RIDGWAY, S. H.
Handbook of Marine Mammals. London: 1981. V. 62

RIDING, LAURA
Collected Poems. London: 1938. V. 65
Contemporaries and Snobs. London: 1928. V. 64
Description of Life. New York: 1980. V. 62
Laura and Francisca. Deya, Majorca: 1931. V. 62; 64
The Life of the Dead. London. V. 62; 64
Love as Love, Death as Death. Hammersmith/London: 1928. V. 62; 64; 65
Though Gently. Deya, Majorca: 1930. V. 62; 64
A Trojan Ending. Deya: 1937. V. 64

RIDINGS, P. SAM
The Chisholm Trail a History of the World's Greatest Cattle. Guthrie: 1936. V. 66

RIDLER, ANNE
The Jesse Tree. London: 1972. V. 63; 66
The Shadow Factory. London: 1946. V. 62; 65
Working for T. S. Eliot: a Personal Reminiscence. London: 2000. V. 66

RIDLER, WILLIAM
British Modern Press Books - a Descriptive Check List of Unrecorded Items. London: 1971. V. 63

RIDLEY, BROMFIELD L.
Battles and Sketches of the Army of Tennessee. Mexico: 1906. V. 63; 65

RIDLEY, CALEB A.
The Southern Mountaineer. Atlanta: 1925. V. 63; 67

RIDLEY, GLOCESTER
The Life of Dr. Nicholas Ridley, Sometime Bishop of London.... London: 1763. V. 62; 63

RIDLEY, H. N.
The Dispersal of Plants throughout the World. London: 1930. V. 62; 64
On the Flora of the Eastern Coast of the Malay Peninsula. 1893. V. 62
Species. London: 1912. V. 64

RIDLEY, HENRY ALSOP
An Atlas of the Basal Ganglia, Brain Stem and Spinal Cord Based on Myelinstained Material. Baltimore: 1943. V. 64

RIDLEY, JAMES
Selected Tales of the Genii. London: 1861. V. 67
The Tales of the Genii. London: 1764. V. 63
The Tales of the Genii. London: 1805. V. 67
The Tales of the Genii. London: 1820. V. 67

RIDLEY, S. O.
Challenger Voyage. Zoology. Part 59. Monaxonida. 1887. V. 66

RIDPATH, GEORGE
The Massacre of Glenco, Being a True Narrative. Edinburgh: 1818. V. 66

RIEFENSTAHL, LENI
The Last of the Nuba. New York: 1973. V. 62
The Last of the Nuba. 1977. V. 67
Leni Riefenstahl's Africa. London: 1982. V. 65
Schonheit im Olympischen Kampf. Berlin: 1937. V. 67

RIEMANN, GEORG FRIEDRICH BERNHARD
Bernhard Reimmann's Gessamelte Mathematische Werke und Wissenschaftlicher Nachlass. Leipzig: 1876. V. 65

RIETHMULLER, CHRISTOPHER JAMES
Aldersleigh. London: 1868. V. 66

RIGAUD, STEPHEN PETER
Defence of the Resolution for Omitting Mr. Panizzi's Bibliographical Notes from the Catalogue of the Royal Society. London: 1838. V. 65

RIGAUT, JACQUES
Papiers Posthumes. Paris: 1934. V. 67

RIGBY, CUTHBERT
From Midsummer to Martinmas. A West Cumberland Idyl. London: 1891. V. 66

RIGBY, EDWARD
Framingham, Its Agriculture &c. Including the Economy of a Small Farm. Norwich;: 1820. V. 63
Holkham, Its Agriculture &c.... Norwich: 1817. V. 63

RIGBY, REGINALD
Alfred the Elephant. London: 1903. V. 64
A Book of Rhymes for Odd Times. London. V. 64

RIGBY, WALLIS
The 7-Foot Model Train Book. New York: 1950. V. 65

RIGBYE, R. G. K.
Time-Honoured Lancaster. Lancaster: 1891. V. 63; 65

RIGG, A. N.
The Industrial History of the Parish of Egton with Newland Up to the Nineteenth Century. Ulverston: 1966. V. 65

RIGG, ARTHUR
A Practical Treatise on the Steam Engine. London: 1894. V. 64

RIGG, J. LINTON
The Alluring Antilles. London: 1963. V. 62

RIGG, JAMES HARRISON
The Present Position of Methodism in Regard to National Education and the Denominational System. London: 1869. V. 63

RIGGE, HENRY FLETCHER
Cartmel Priory Church, North Lancashire. Cartmel: 1879. V. 65
Cartmel Priory Church, North Lancashire. Cartmel: 1885. V. 65

RIGGS, ELIAS
A Manual of the Chaldee Language: Containing a Chaldee Grammar. New York: 1842. V. 62

RIGGS-MILLER, ANNE
Letters from Italy, Describing the Manners, Customs, Antiquities, Paintings &c.... London: 1776. V. 62

RIGHTS, DOUGLAS L.
The American Indian in North Carolina. Durham: 1947. V. 63; 67
The American Indian in North Carolina. Winston Salem: 1957. V. 67

THE RIGHTS of the Publick to the Valuable Library at St. Nicholas' Church, Newcastle, Duly Considered. Newcastle: 1820. V. 65

RIGHYNI, R. V.
Advanced Salmon Fishing. London: 1980. V. 67
Peches Completes du Saumon. 1984. V. 67
Salmon Taking Times. 1965. V. 63; 65; 67
Salmon Taking Times. London: 1965. V. 63; 66; 67

RIGNANO, EUGENIO
Upon the Inheritance of Acquired Characters. Chicago: 1911. V. 66

RIHA, V.
Berona. Prague: 1921. V. 64
Liliana. Prague: 1920. V. 64
Maruiska. Prague: 1918. V. 64

RIIS, JACOB A.
The Battle with the Slum. New York: 1902. V. 67
Out of Mulberry Street: Stories of Tenement Life in New York City. New York: 1898. V. 63

RIKER, JAMES
The Annals of Newtown, in Queens County, New York.... New York: 1852. V. 63

RIKHOFF, JIM
Fair Chase. Clinton: 1984. V. 65
Mixed Bag. Clinton: 1979. V. 65

RIKS, JOEL E.
The History of a Valley - Cache Valley, Utah-Idaho. Logan: 1956. V. 65

RILEY, C. V.
Insect Life, Devoted to the Economy and Life-Habits of Insects, Especially in Their Relations to Agriculture. Washington: 1888-1890. V. 63

RILEY, FRANKLIN L.
General Robert E. Lee After Appomattox. New York: 1922. V. 64

RILEY, FREDERIC
The Ribble from Its Source to the Sea. Settle: 1914. V. 63; 65
The Settle District and North-West Yorkshire Dales. Settle: 1923. V. 65

RILEY, HENRY ALSOP
An Atlas of the Basal Ganglia. Brain Spine and Spinal Cord Based on Myelinstained Material. Baltimore: 1943. V. 66

RILEY, HENRY THOMAS
Chronica Monasterii S. Albani. Gesta Abbatum Monasterii Sancti Albani. London: 1867-1869. V. 63
Liber Albus: The White Book of the City of London. London: 1861. V. 62; 63

RILEY, J. RAMSDEN
History of the Royal Yorkshire Lodge No. 265, Keighley.... Keighley: 1889. V. 65

RILEY, JAMES
An Authentic Narrative of the Loss of the American Brig Commerce, Wrecked on the Western Coast of Africa, in the Month of August 1815, with an Account of the Sufferings of the Surviving Officers and Crew.... Hartford: 1846. V. 65
An Authentic Narrative of the Loss of the American Brig Commerce, Wrecked on the Western Coast of Africa...August 1815. Hartford: 1850. V. 63

RILEY, JAMES WHITCOMB
Afterwhiles. Indianapolis: 1888. V. 65
All the Year Round. Indianapolis: 1912. V. 66
Armazindy. Indianapolis: 1894. V. 65
The Book of Joyous Children. New York: 1902. V. 65
A Child-World. Indianapolis and Kansas City: 1897. V. 62; 64; 65; 67
A Defective Santa Claus. Indianapolis: 1904. V. 63
The Flying Islands of the Night. Indianapolis: 1892. V. 65
The Flying Islands of the Night. Indianapolis: 1913. V. 62
Green Fields and Running Brooks. Indianapolis: 1893. V. 65
His Pa's Romance. Indianapolis: 1903. V. 65
Home-Folks. Indianapolis: 1900. V. 65
Morning. Indianapolis: 1907. V. 67
The Old Swimming-Hole and 'Leven More Poems. Indianapolis: 1891. V. 65
Poems Here and There. New York: 1893. V. 65
Rhymes of Childhood. Indianapolis: 1891. V. 65
Riley Child Verse. Indianapolis: 1906. V. 62
Riley Farm-Rhymes. Indianapolis: 1901. V. 65
Rubaiyat of Doc Sifers. New York: 1897. V. 65
Sketches in Prose. Indianapolis: 1891. V. 65
While the Heart Beats Young. Indianapolis: 1906. V. 67

RILEY, L. W.
Aristotle Texts and Commentary to 1700 in the University of Pennsylvania Library, a Catalogue. Philadelphia: 1961. V. 66; 67

RILEY, PATRICIA
Growing Up Native American. New York: 1993. V. 62

RILEY, WILLIAM
Psalms and Hymns for the Use of the Chapel of the Asylum, or House of Refuge for Female Orphans. London. V. 66; 67

RILING, RAY
Guns and Shooting: a Selected Chronological Bibliography. Philadelphia: 1982. V. 63
The Powder Flask Book. New Hope: 1953. V. 66

RILKE, RAINER MARIA
Duineser Elegien, Elegies from the Castle of Duino. Leipzig: 1931. V. 65
Last Poems. Oakland: 1989. V. 64
The Lay of the Love and Death of Cornet Christoph Rilke. San Francisco: 1983. V. 64
Leben und Lieder, Bilder und Tagebuchblatter. Strassburg & Leipzig: 1894. V. 67
Die Sonette an Orpheus. Leipzig: 1923. V. 64

RIMBAUD, ARTHUR
Le Bateau Ivre. New York: 1992. V. 64
Une Saison en Enfer. Bruxelles: 1873. V. 65
A Season in Hell. New York: 1986. V. 67
10 Poems. New York: 1982. V. 64

RIMBAUD, ISABELLE
Reliques. Paris: 1921. V. 67

RIMMER, WILLIAM
Elements of Design. Book First. For the Use of Parents and Teachers. Boston: 1864. V. 62

RINDER, FRANK
Old World Japan. Legends of the Land of the Gods. London: 1895. V. 64; 67

RINEHART, F. A.
Rinehart's Indians. Omaha: 1899. V. 64

RINEHART, MARY ROBERTS
The Circular Staircase. 1908. V. 67
The Circular Staircase. Indianapolis: 1908. V. 65

RING, BETTY
Needleworth, an Historical Survey. New York: 1975. V. 63

RINGHIERI, INNOCENTIO
Cento Givochi Liberali, et d'Ingegno. Bologna: 1551. V. 64

RINGLING, ALFRED T.
Life Story of the Ringling Brothers Illustrated. Chicago: 1900. V. 63

RINHART, FLOYD
American Daguerreian Art. New York: 1967. V. 65

RINK, HEINRICH JOHANNES
Tales and Traditions of the Eskimo with a Sketch of Their Habits, Religion, Language and Other Peculiarties. Edinburgh and London: 1875. V. 65; 66

RINTOUL, A. N.
Transparent Painting on Glass for the Magic Lantern in Water, Oil and Varnish Colours.... 1876. V. 67

RIORDAN, E. J.
Modern Irish Trade and Industry. 1920. V. 67

RIOU, STEPHEN
The Grecian Orders of Architecture Delineated and Explained from the Antiquities of Athens.... London: 1768. V. 67
Short Principles for the Architecture of Stone Bridges. London: 1760. V. 62

RIPLEY, GEORGE
A Letter Addressed to the Congregational Church in Purchase Street Street. Boston: 1840. V. 64

RIPLEY, HENRY
Hand-Clasp of the East and West: a Story of Pioneer Life on the Western Slope of Colorado. Denver: 1914. V. 65

RIPLEY, MARY CHURCHILL
The Oriental Rug Book. New York: 1904. V. 64

RIPLEY, ROBERT
Everlast Boxing Record 125. New York: 1925. V. 66

RIPLEY, S. DILLON
Ornithological Books in the Yale University Library, Including the Library of William Robertson Coe. New Haven: 1961. V. 63
Rails of the World. Boston: 1977. V. 64; 67
Rails of the World. London: 1977. V. 64

RIPLEY, SHERMAN
The Raggedy Animal Book. Chicago: 1928. V. 65

RIPLEY, WILLIAM Y. W.
Vermont Rifleman in the War for the Union, 1861 to 1865. A History of Co. F, First United States Sharp Shooters. Rutland: 1883. V. 62

RIPON Millenary. *A Record of the Festival. Also a History of the City.* Ripon: 1892. V. 62; 66

RISBECK, JOHANN KASPAR
Travels through Germany. Dublin: 1787. V. 62

RISCHBEITER, HENNING
Art and the Stage in the 20th Century. Painters and Sculptors Work for the Theatre. Greenwich: 1970. V. 66

RISEING, WILLIAM H.
The Overland Express. Ashland: 1970. V. 67

RISK, EVALD
Technical Americana: a Checklist of Technical Publications Printed Before 1831. Millwood: 1981. V. 62

RISK, ROBERT K.
Songs of the Links. London: 1919. V. 66

RISSIK, ANDREW
The James Bond Man - the Films of Sean Connery. London: 1983. V. 65; 67

RISTER, CARL COKE
Border Captives - the Traffic in Prisoners by Southern Plains Indians 1835-1875. Norman: 1940. V. 67
Border Command, General Phil Sheridan in the West. Norman: 1944. V. 67
Comanche Bondage...Beagle's Settlement...Sarah Ann Horn's Narrative of Her Captivity Among the Comanches. Glendale: 1955. V. 62
Robert E. Lee in Texas. Norman: 1946. V. 67
Southern Plainsmen. Norman: 1938. V. 67
The Southwestern Frontier 1865-1881. Cleveland: 1928. V. 65; 67

RITCH, W. G.
Illustrated New Mexico. Santa Fe: 1885. V. 62; 65
Inaugural Address of...Historical Society of New Mexico Delivered Before the Society Feb. 21, 1881. at the Palace Santa Fe, New Mexico. Santa Fe: 1881. V. 62; 63; 65

RITCHIE, ANNA CORA
Reviewers Reviewed: a Satire. New York: 1837. V. 64

RITCHIE, ANNE ISABELLA THACKERAY
A Book of Sibyls. London: 1883. V. 62; 63; 65; 66
To Esther and Other Sketches. London: 1869. V. 66

RITCHIE, G. W. H.
Ten Etchings. New York: 1886. V. 63

RITCHIE, J.
The Influence of Man on Animal Life in Scotland.... Cambridge: 1920. V. 62; 63; 64

RITCHIE, JAMES EWING
Here and There in London. London: 1859. V. 67
The Life and Discoveries of David Livingstone. London. V. 63
The Life and Times of the Right Honble. William Ewart Gladstone.... London: 1882. V. 64
The Life and Times of Viscount Palmerston.... London: 1866-1867. V. 64
The Night Side of London. London: 1858. V. 64

RITCHIE, JOHN
Ward Gutenberg - a Fanciful Story of the Fifteenth Century. Los Angeles: 1940. V. 62

RITCHIE, LEITCH
The Game of Life. London: 1851. V. 67
Heath's Picturesque Annual for 1836. London: 1836. V. 62
Heath's Picturesque Annual, Ireland Picturesque and Romantic. 1837. V. 62; 65
Heath's Picturesque Annual, Ireland Picturesque and Romantic. 1838. V. 62; 65
The Magician. Belfast: 1846. V. 67
Scott and Scotland. London: 1835. V. 62
Travelling Sketches in the North of Italy, and on the Rhine. London: 1832. V. 62
Travelling Sketches on the Sea-Coasts of France. London: 1834. V. 62
Wanderings by the Loire. London: 1833. V. 63
Wanderings by the Seine, from Rouen to the Source.... London: 1835. V. 62

RITCHIE, NEIL
Harold Acton, a Bibliography. Florence: 1984. V. 62

RITCHIE, THOMAS EDWARD
An Account of the Life and Writings of David Hume. London: 1807. V. 63

RITCHIE, WARD
Art Deco: the Books of Francois-Louis Schmied, Artist/Engraver/Printer. San Francisco: 1987. V. 64
Of Bookmen and Printers: a Gathering of Memories. Los Angeles: 1989. V. 64
Variations and Quotations. N.P: 1990. V. 64

I RITI *Nuziali Degli Antichi Romani per le Nozze di S. E. Don Giovanni Lambertini con S. E. Donna Lucrezia Savorgnan.* Bologna: 1762. V. 65

RITNER, JOSEPH
Vindication of General Washington from the Stigma of Adherence to Secret Socieites...Together with a Letter to Daniel Webster and His Reply. Boston: 1841. V. 63

RITNER, WILLIAM D.
Juan, the White Slave; and the Rebel Planter's Daughter. Philadelphia: 1865. V. 66

RITSON, JOSEPH
Ancient English Metrical Romances. Edinburgh: 1884. V. 62; 65
The Caledonian Muse: a Chronological Selection of Scottish Poetry from the Earliest Time. London: 1821. V. 63
The English Anthology. London: 1793-1794. V. 64
Northern Garlands. London: 1810. V. 67
Pieces of Ancient Popular Poetry: From Authentic Manuscripts and Old Printed Copies. London: 1791. V. 63; 66
Robin Hood; a Collection of All the Ancient Poems, Songs and Ballads, Now Extant, Relative to that Celebrated English Outlaw. London: 1795. V. 67
Robin Hood: a Collection of All the Ancient Poems, Songs and Ballads, Now Extant, Relative to that Celebrated English Outlaw. London: 1820. V. 63
The Spartan Manual, or Tablet of Morality. Glasgow: 1873. V. 63

RITTENHOUSE, JACK D.
Cabezon: a New Mexico Ghost Town. Santa Fe: 1965. V. 64
Carriage Hundred: a Bibliography on Horse-Drawn Transporation. Houston: 1961. V. 64
Diary of an Excursion to the Ruins of Abo, Quarra and Gran Quivira in New Mexico in 1953 Under the Command of Major James Henry Carleton. Santa Fe: 1965. V. 67
The Man Who Owned Too Much - Maxwell Land Grant. Houston: 1958. V. 63; 64; 65; 66
New Mexico Civil War Bibliography, 1861-1865. Houston: 1961. V. 64
The Santa Fe Trail: a Historical Bibliography. Albuquerque: 1971. V. 65; 67
Wendish Language Printing in Texas. Los Angeles: 1962. V. 62; 64

RITTER, FRANZ
Astrolabium, Das Ist: Gruendlliche Beschreibung und Unterricht, Wie, Solches Heerliche, und Hochnuezliche Astronomische Instrument.... Nuremberg: 1613. V. 66

RITTER, M. B.
More than Gold in California 1849-1933. Berkeley: 1933. V. 64; 67

RITTICH, W.
Architektur und Bauplastik der Gegenwart. Berlin: 1938. V. 65

RITZENTHALER, ROBERT E.
The Miller Collection. Milwaukee: 1961. V. 65; 67

RIVAZ, C. A. G.
Indian Small Game Shooting for Novices. 1912. V. 67

RIVERA, DIEGO
Portrait of America. London: 1935. V. 65

RIVERA, IGNACIO CHAVEZ
Coma, Sincope y Shock. Mexico: 1966. V. 67

RIVERA, JOSE EUSTASIO
La Voragine. Bogota: 1924. V. 62

RIVERO, MARIANO EDWARD
Peruvian Antiquities. New York: 1854. V. 62

RIVERS, HENRY J.
The Tale of Two Cities: a Drama in Three Acts. London: 1862. V. 62

RIVERS, LARRY
Larry Rivers. New York: 1965. V. 62; 64
What Did I Do?. New York: 1992. V. 64

THE RIVERS of Great Britain - Rivers of the East Coast. 1889. V. 67

RIVERS, R. H.
Elements of Mental Philosophy. Nashville: 1862. V. 62

RIVERS, THOMAS
The Miniature Fruit Garden or the Culture of Pyramidal and Bush Fruit Trees. New York: 1877?. V. 64
The Miniature Fruit Garden or the Culture of Pyramidal and Bush Fruit Trees with Instructions for Root Pruning. London: 1877. V. 64
The Rose Amateur's Guide.... London: 1846. V. 65

RIVERS, WILLIAM JAMES
A Sketch of the History of South Carolina to the Close of the Proprietary Government by the Revolution of 1719. Charleston: 1856. V. 63; 66; 67

RIVES, GEORGE L.
The United States and Mexico 1821-1848. New York: 1913. V. 67

RIVIERE, B. B.
A History of the Birds of Norfolk. London: 1930. V. 63; 67

RIVIERE, CHARLES
Vues de Londres, Dessinees d'Apres Nature et Lithographiees. Paris: 1862. V. 67

RIVIERE, GEORGES
Renoir et Ses Amis. Paris: 1921. V. 65

RIVIERE, LAZARE
The Compleat Practice of Physick.... London: 1655. V. 66
Opera Medica Universa Quibus Continentur Continentur.... Coloniae Allobrogum Geneva: 1665. V. 66

RIVIERE, LAZARE continued
The Practice of Physick.... London: 1672. V. 63

RIVINGTON, WALTER
The Medical Profession: Being the Essay...Awarded First Carmichael Prize...Royal College of Surgeons, Ireland, 1879. 1879. V. 63; 66

RIVIUS, GREGORIUS
Puritani Monastica Historia.... Leipzig: 1737. V. 66

RIVOIRA, G. T.
Lombardic Architecture - Its Origin, Development and Derivatives. Oxford: 1933. V. 66
Le Origini Della Architettura Lombarda & Delle Sue Principali Derivazioni Nei Passi D'Oltr'alpe. Roma: 1907. V. 64
Roman Architecture and Its Principles of Construction Under the Empire. Oxford: 1925. V. 66

RIVOIRE, ANTOINE
Nouveaux Principes de Perspective Lineaire.... Amsterdam: 1757. V. 64

RIX, M.
The Art of the Plant World, the Great Botanical Illustrators and Their Work. Woodstock: 1981. V. 63; 67

RIZK, A. F. M.
Poisonous Plant Contamination of Edible Plants. Boca Raton: 1991. V. 63

ROA BASTOS, AUGUSTO
Hijo de Hombre. Buenos Aires: 1960. V. 67
Son of Man. London: 1965. V. 67

ROACH SMITH, CHARLES
Catalogue of the Museum of London Antiquities, Collected By, and Property of Charles Roach Smith. London: 1844. V. 62

THE ROADS and Railroads, Vehicles and Modes of Travelling, of Ancient and Modern Countries.... London: 1839. V. 63; 67

ROATCAP, ADELA SPINDLER
Raymond Duncan: Printer...Expatriate...Eccentric Artist. N.P: 1991. V. 62; 63

ROBB, DAVID M.
The Art of the Illuminated Manuscript. South Brunswick and New York: 1973. V. 62

ROBB, JAMES B.
A Collection of Patent Cases, Decided in the United States. Boston: 1854. V. 67

ROBBE-GRILLET, ALAIN
Les Gommes. Paris: 1953. V. 67

ROBBIN, ARCHIBALD
A Journal Comprising an Account of the Loss of the Brig Commerce of Hartford, Connecticut, James Riley, Master Upon the Western Coast of Africa, August 28th, 1815.... Hartford: 1829. V. 64

ROBBINS, HAROLD
The Dream Merchants. New York: 1949. V. 62
A Stone for Danny Fisher. New York: 1952. V. 63

ROBBINS, LIONEL
An Essay on the Nature and Significance of Economic Science. London: 1932. V. 64

ROBBINS, MILLS
Gleanings of the Robins, or Robbins Family of England. Devizes: 1908. V. 62

ROBBINS, TOM
Another Roadside Attraction. Garden City: 1971. V. 62; 64; 66; 67
Another Roadside Attraction. London: 1973. V. 62
Even Cowgirls Get the Blues. Boston: 1976. V. 66; 67
Fierce Invalids Home from Hot Climates. New York: 2000. V. 67
Guy Anderson. Seattle: 1977. V. 62
Jitterbug Perfume. New York: 1984. V. 64; 65; 66; 67
Skinny Legs and All. New York: 1990. V. 66; 67
Still Life with Woodpecker. New York: 1980. V. 67
Still Life with Woodpecker. Los Angeles: 1982. V. 67

ROBE, JANE
The Fatal Legacy. London: 1723. V. 66

ROBENS, J. P.
The Old Flag, First Published by Union Prisoners at Camp Ford, Tyler, Texas. New York: 1864. V. 64

ROBERT, ANTONIUS
Clavis Homerica, Sive Lexicon Vocabulorum Omnium, Quae Continentur in Homeri Iliade et Potissima Parte Odyssaeae. Londini: 1741. V. 66

ROBERT, N.
Variae ac Multiformes Florum species; Diverses Fleurs. London: 1975. V. 64

ROBERT HOUDIN, JEAN F.
Memoirs of Robert-Houdin, Ambassador, Author and Conjuror. Written by Himself. London: 1859. V. 66

ROBERTI, ANTONIUS
Clavis Homerica, Sive Lexicon Vocabulorum Omnium, Quae Continentur in Homeri Iliade et Potissima Parte Odyssaeae. Londini: 1741. V. 62

ROBERT LA DIABLE
Robert the Devil. Iowa City: 1981. V. 62; 64; 67
Roberte the Deuyll. London: 1798. V. 62; 64; 67

ROBERTS, AL
Enduring Friendships. Maine: 1970. V. 62

ROBERTS, AUSTIN
The Mammals of South Africa. Cape Town: 1951. V. 62
The Mammals of South Africa. Cape Town: 1954. V. 62

ROBERTS, B. H.
The Mormon Battalion: Its History and Achievements. Salt Lake City: 1919. V. 64; 66

ROBERTS, BARIE
Sherlock Holmes and the Devil's Grail. London: 1995. V. 67

ROBERTS, BARRIE
Sherlock Holmes and the Railway Maniac. London: 1994. V. 66

ROBERTS, C. E. B.
The Trial of William Joyce. 1946. V. 67

ROBERTS, CAROLINE ALICE
Marchcroft Manor. London: 1882. V. 66

ROBERTS, CHARLES
The Complete Billiard Player. London: 1911. V. 66
The Detection of Colour-Blindness and Imperfect Eyesight. London: 1884. V. 64
The Private Library of the Late Charles Roberts of Philadelphia. 1918. V. 63

ROBERTS, DAN W.
Rangers and Sovereignty. San Antonio: 1914. V. 63

ROBERTS, DANIEL
Some Memoirs of the Life of John Roberts. London: 1796. V. 62

ROBERTS, DAVID
Fantasy for Flute. Oxford: 1940. V. 64
Holy Land, Syria, Idumea, Arabia, Egypt, Nubia. London: 1855. V. 67
The Town of Cambridge As It Ought to Be Reformed. The Plan of Nicholas Hawksmoor Interepted in an Essay by David Roberts. Cambridge: 1955. V. 62

ROBERTS, EDWARD
With the Invaders, Glimpses of the Southwest. San Francisco: 1885. V. 62; 65

ROBERTS, ELIZABETH MADOX
Black is My Truelove's Hair. New York: 1938. V. 64
Not by Strange Gods. New York: 1941. V. 64; 67
The Time of Man. New York: 1945. V. 65

ROBERTS, GEORGE
A Guide, Descriptive of the Beauties of Lyme-Regis.... Lyme: 1830. V. 67
Parish Memorials Relating to Norton Disney in the Diocese an County of Lincoln. Newark: 1893. V. 65

ROBERTS, GILLIAN
Caught Dead in Philadelphia. New York: 1987. V. 64; 65; 66

ROBERTS, HENRY
The Dwellings of the Labouring Classes, Their Arrangement and Construction. London: 1850. V. 64

ROBERTS, ISAAC
A Selection of Photographs of Stars, Star-Clusters and Nebulae.... London: 1894-1900. V. 64

ROBERTS, JACK
The Wonderful Adventures of Ludo the Little Green Duck. Paris: 1924. V. 64

ROBERTS, JAMES A.
New York in the Revolution as Colony and State. Albany: 1898. V. 63; 66

ROBERTS, JOHN K.
History of Union Presbyterian Church. Carthage: 1910. V. 67

ROBERTS, JOSEPH
The Hand Book of Artillery. Richmond: 1861. V. 62

ROBERTS, KEITH
The Furies. London: 1966. V. 65
Machines and Men - Science Fiction Stories. London: 1973. V. 63

ROBERTS, KENNETH
Boon Island. Garden City: 1956. V. 65
Cowpens: the Great Morale Builder. N.P: 1957. V. 66; 67
I Wanted to Write. Garden City: 1949. V. 67
Northwest Passage. Garden City: 1937. V. 66
Oliver Wiswell. New York: 1940. V. 64
Trending Into Maine. Boston: 1938. V. 64; 65
Why Europe Leaves Home. N.P: 1922. V. 63

ROBERTS, LEWIS
The Merchants Map of Commerce.... London: 1700. V. 63; 65

ROBERTS, LYNETTE
Gods with Stainless Ears - a Heroic Poem. London: 1951. V. 62

ROBERTS, MARGARET
A Child of the Revolution. London: 1886. V. 65
In the Olden Time. London: 1883. V. 65
Lilian and Lili. London: 1891. V. 65
Mademoiselle Mori: a Tale of Modern Rome. London: 1886. V. 65
On the Edge of the Storm. London: 1869. V. 65

ROBERTS, MARGARET continued
Sydonie's Dowry. London: 1865. V. 65

ROBERTS, MARY
The Conchologist's Companion. London: 1834. V. 65
Ruins and Old Trees Associated With Remarkable Events in English History. London: 1843. V. 64; 65
The Wonders of the Vegetable Kingdom Displayed. In a Series of Letters. London: 1822. V. 63

ROBERTS, MICHAEL
New Country. Prose and Poetry by the Authors of New Signatures. London: 1933. V. 62
New Signatures - Poems by Several Hands. London: 1932. V. 65

ROBERTS, MICHELE
The Wild Girl. London: 1984. V. 65

ROBERTS, MORLEY
Lord Linlithgow: a Novel. London: 1900. V. 67
Painted Rock Tales and Narrative of Painted Rock, South Panhandle Texas. Philadelphia: 1907. V. 66
Strong Men and True. London: 1897. V. 67
The Western Avernus, or Toil and Travel in Further North America. Westminster: 1896. V. 62; 63; 66

ROBERTS, R.
The River Side, or The Trout and Grayling and How to Take Them. 1866. V. 67

ROBERTS, ROBERT
The House Servant's Directory, or a Monitor for Private Families.... Boston: 1828. V. 62; 64

ROBERTS, S. C.
The Strange Case of the Megatherium Thefts. Cambridge: 1945. V. 66

ROBERTS, SAMUEL
The Blind Man and His Son: a Tale for Young People. London: 1816. V. 63

ROBERTS, T. S.
Birds of Minnesota. 1932. V. 64
The Birds of Minnesota. Minneapolis: 1932. V. 62; 66

ROBERTS, VERNE L.
Bibliotheca Mechanica. New York: 1991. V. 67

ROBERTS, W.
The Book-Hunter in London, Historical and Other Studies of Collectors and Collecting. Chicago: 1895. V. 66

ROBERTS, W. MILNOR
Report...to the President and Managers of the Erie Canal Company of Pennsylvania. Erie: 1868. V. 64
Special Report of a Reconnaissance of the Route for the Northern Pacific Railroad Between lake Superior and Puget Sound, Via the Columbia River, Made in 1869. Philadelphia: 1867-1870. V. 63

ROBERTS, WILLIAM
Memoirs of the Life and Correspondence of Mrs. Hannah More. London: 1834. V. 62; 64
Memorials of Christie's: a Record of Art Sales from 1766 to 1896. London: 1897. V. 63; 65
A Treatise on the Construction of the Statues: 13 Eliz. C. 5, & 27 Eliz. C. 4, Relating to Voluntary & Fraudulent Conveyances.... Burlington: 1845. V. 65

ROBERTS, WILLIAM HAYWARD
Poems. London: 1774. V. 62

ROBERTSON, ALAN W.
Post Roads, Post Towns, Postal Rates 1635-1839. Pinner. Middlesex: 1961. V. 67

ROBERTSON, ANDREW
Letters and Papers of Andrew Robertson (1777-1845), Miniature Power to His Late Royal Highness the Duke of Sussex.... London: 1895. V. 67

ROBERTSON, COLIN
Colin Robertson's Correspondence Book, September 1817 to September 1822. 1939. V. 62

ROBERTSON, DAVID
Reports of the Trials of Colonel Aaron Burr...for Treason and for a Misdemeanor in Preparing the Means of a Military Expedition Against Mexico.... Philadelphia: 1808. V. 63; 66
The Trial of Aaron Burr for Treason. New York: 1875. V. 65

ROBERTSON, DON
The Ideal, Genuine Man. Bangor: 1987. V. 66

ROBERTSON, EDNA
Artists of the Canyons and Caminos. N.P: 1976. V. 63

ROBERTSON, F. K.
The Book of Health, or Thomsonian Theory and Practice of Medicine, Including the Latest Views of Physiology, Pathology, and Therapeutics.... Bennington: 1843. V. 64

ROBERTSON, FLORENCE H.
Shadow Land: Stories of the South. Boston: 1906. V. 64

ROBERTSON, FREDERICK W.
An Address Delivered to the Members of the Working Man's Institute, at the Town Hall, Brighton...April 18, 1850, on the Question of the Introduction of Sceptical Publications into the Lbrary. Brighton: 1850. V. 65
Lectures and Addresses on Literary and Social Topics. London: 1858. V. 67
Two Lectures on the Influence of Poetry on the Working Classes, Delivered Before the Members of the Mechanics' Inst. February 1852. Brighton: 1852. V. 62

Two Lectures on the Influence of Poetry on the Working Classes, Delivered Before the Members of the Mechanics' Institution Feb. 1852. Brighton: 1853. V. 64

ROBERTSON, GEORGE F.
A Small Boy's Recollections of the Civil War. Clover: 1932. V. 63

ROBERTSON, GEORGE SCOTT
The Kafirs of the Hindu-Kush. London: 1896. V. 63; 66

ROBERTSON, H. M.
Aspects of the Rise of Economic Individualism. Cambridge: 1933. V. 63

ROBERTSON, JAMES
History of the Mission of the Secession Church to Nova Scotia and Prince Edward Island from Its Commencement in 1765. Edinburgh: 1847. V. 66

ROBERTSON, JAMES A.
Concise Historical Proofs Respecting the Gael of Alban; or Highlanders of Scotland.... Edinburgh and London: 1866. V. 63

ROBERTSON, JAMES ALEXANDER
Louisiana Under the Rule of Spain, France and the United States 1785-1807. Cleveland: 1911. V. 67

ROBERTSON, JOHN
A Complete Treatise on Mensuration. London: 1739. V. 64
A General Treatise of Mensuration. London: 1779. V. 64
The Hand-Book of Angling for Scotland and the Border Counties Embracing the Practical Experience of Thirty Years' Fishing. London: 1861. V. 62
Michigan in the War. Lansing: 1882. V. 65
Walt Whitman, Poet and Democrat. Edinburgh: 1884. V. 62

ROBERTSON, JOHN W.
Francis Drake and Other Early Explorers Along the Pacific Coast. San Francisco: 1927. V. 62; 63

ROBERTSON, JOSEPH
A Sermon Preached in the Parish Church of Whitby, Before the Friendly Society at the Anniversary Meeting on Whit-Monday, May 24, 1779 and Published by Request. York: 1779. V. 67

ROBERTSON, KEVIN
The Perfect Shot. 2000. V. 67

ROBERTSON, MARGARET MURRAY
The Bairns; or Janet's Love and Service. London: 1870. V. 65

ROBERTSON, MORGAN
The Wreck of the Titan. N.P: 1912. V. 65

ROBERTSON, R. MAC DONALD
Wade the River, Drift the Loch. 1948. V. 67

ROBERTSON, ROBERT S.
From the Wilderness to Spotsylvania. Cincinnati: 1884. V. 67

ROBERTSON, W.
Forest Sketches. 1865. V. 62; 63

ROBERTSON, W. GRAHAM
The Blake Collection of W. Graham Robertson. London: 1952. V. 66
Carol Pictures by the Guild of Country Players. A Memory. N.P: 1918. V. 67

ROBERTSON, WILLIAM
Collection de Differentes Especes de Serres Chaudes, Pour Forcer des Ananas, des Arbres Fruitiers, et Pour Preserver des Plantes Exotiques Delicates.... London: 1798. V. 67
An Historical Disquisition Concerning the Knowledge Which the Ancients Had of India; and the Progress with that Country Prior to the Discovery of the Passage To It by the Cape of Good Hope. London: 1791. V. 67
The History of America. London: 1788. V. 67
The History of America. London: 1820. V. 63
The History of America. Books IX and X. Philadelphia: 1799. V. 67
The History of Scotland During the Reigns of Queen Mary and King James VI. London: 1759. V. 67
The History of Scotland During the Reigns of Queen Mary and of King James VI, Till His Accession to the Crown of England.... London: 1781. V. 66
The Life and Times of the Right Hon. John Bright. Rochdale: 1877. V. 64
Life and Times of the Right Honourable John Bright, M.P. London: 1883. V. 64
The Works of William Robertson. Edinburgh: 1829. V. 64

ROBERTSON, WILLIAM H. P.
The History of the Thoroughbred Racing in America. 1965. V. 66

ROBERTUS MONACHUS
Bellum Christianorum Principum, Praecipue Gallorum, Contra Saracenos. Basel: 1533. V. 64

ROBES of Splendor - Native American Painted Buffalo Hides. New York: 1993. V. 67

ROBESON, PAUL
Here I Stand. London: 1958. V. 66

ROBIANO, COMTE DE
Collection des Desseins des Figures & Des Croupes Qui Ont ete Faits de Neige.... Antwerp: 1773. V. 64

ROBICSEK, FRANCIS
The Smoking Gods. Tobacco in Maya Art, History and Religion. 1978. V. 66

ROBIDOUX, ORRAL M.
Memorial to the Robidoux Brothers Who Blazed the Western Trails for Civilization. Kansas City: 1924. V. 64

ROBIN HOOD
A Lytell Geste of Robyn Hode and His Meiny.... San Francisco: 1932. V. 62
Robin Hood. Philadelphia: 1917. V. 63
Robin Hood. London: 1920. V. 63
Robin Hood and the Curtall Fryer. Leeds: 1900. V. 66

ROBIN Red-breast (Number 10). Greenfield: 1845. V. 64

ROBIN Tanner and the Old Style Press: the Imprinted Examples of 20 Original Patterned Paper Designs.... 1994. V. 62

THE ROBINS at Home. London: Sep. 1890. V. 64

ROBINS, EDWARD COOKWORTHY
Technical School and College Building, Being a Treatise on the Design and Construction of Applied Science and Art Buildings.... London: 1887. V. 62; 66; 67

ROBINS, SANDERSON
An Argument for the Royal Supremacy. London: 1851. V. 65

ROBINSON, ALAN JAMES
An Odd Bestiary. 1982. V. 63

ROBINSON, ALBERT G.
Cuba and the Intervention. London: 1905. V. 66

ROBINSON, ALVIN
The Massachusetts Collection of Martial Musick.... Exeter: 1820. V. 66

ROBINSON & McCallister's Minstrel Songster. Troy: 1883. V. 67

ROBINSON, BENJAMIN COULSON
The Law of Warrants of Attorney, Cognovits and Consents to Judges' Orders for Judgement. London: 1844. V. 63

ROBINSON, BERT
The Basket Weavers of Arizona. Albuquerque: 1954. V. 66

ROBINSON, BRUCE
The Peculiar Memories of Thomas Penman. London: 1998. V. 67

ROBINSON, BRYAN
A Treatise of the Animal Oeconomy. Dublin: 1734. V. 64

ROBINSON, C.
Skyscraper Style: Art Deco New York. New York: 1975. V. 65

ROBINSON, C. E.
A Royal Warren, or Picturesque Rambles in the Isle of Purbeck. London: 1882. V. 66

ROBINSON, CHANDLER A.
J. Evetts Haley: Cow-Historian. El Paso: 1967. V. 63

ROBINSON, CHARLES
Absurdities-A Book of Collected Drawings. London: 1934. V. 63
The Achievements of Our Seamen. The Honours of Our Ships. London: 1901. V. 65
Black Doggies. London: 1907. V. 65
Britannia's Bulwarks. London: 1901. V. 62; 64
Celebrities of the Army. London: 1900. V. 62
My Life of Life. London: 1938. V. 63
Old Naval Prints Their Artists and Engravers. London: 1924. V. 64

ROBINSON, CONWAY
Abstract of the Proceedings of the Virginia Company of London 1619- 1624.... Richmond: 1888. V. 63
An Account of Discoveries in the West Until 1519, and of Voyages to and Along the Atlantic Coast of North America, from 1520-1573. Richmond: 1848. V. 67
Practice in the Courts of Law and Equity in Virginia. Richmond: 1823-1839. V. 67

ROBINSON, CORINNE ROOSEVELT
My Brother Theodore Roosevelt. New York: 1923. V. 65

ROBINSON Crusoe. Boston: 1863. V. 62

ROBINSON, DOANE
History of South Dakota. Chicago: 1930. V. 67
A History of the Dakota or Sioux Indians. 1956. V. 65
South Dakota Historical Collections. Volume IX. Pierre: 1918. V. 63

ROBINSON, DUNCAN
William Morris, Edward Burne-Jones and the Kelmscott Chaucer. London: 1982. V. 62

ROBINSON, EDWIN ARLINGTON
Amaranth. New York: 1934. V. 62
Avon's Harvest. New York: 1921. V. 62
Cavender's House. New York: 1929. V. 62
The Children of the Night. Boston: 1897. V. 63
Collected Poems. New York: 1922. V. 65
Collected Poems. New York: 1930. V. 62
Fortunatus. Reno: 1928. V. 65
The Glory of the Nightingales. New York: 1930. V. 62
The Man Who Died Twice. New York: 1924. V. 62
Roman Bartholow. New York: 1923. V. 62; 65
Sonnets 1889-1927. New York: 1928. V. 63; 64
Talifer. New York: 1933. V. 62
The Torrent and the Night Before. New York: 1928. V. 62
Tristram. New York: 1927. V. 62

ROBINSON, EMMA
The Merry Wives of Stamboul; an Eastern Tale.... London: 1846. V. 62; 66
Whitefriars; or, the Days of Charles the Second. London: 1844. V. 65

ROBINSON, FRANCIS KILDALE
A Glossary of Yorkshire Words and Phrases, Collected in Whitby and Neighbourhood. London: 1835. V. 65
A Glossary of Yorkshire Words and Phrases, Collected in Whitby.... London: 1855. V. 64; 66

ROBINSON, FREDERICK WILLIAM
The House of Elmore. London: 1856. V. 67
Poor Zeph and Other Tales. London: 1880. V. 66
Prison Characters Drawn from Life. London: 1866. V. 63
Wildflower. London: 1857. V. 65

ROBINSON, H. C.
The Birds of the Malay Peninsula.... London: 1927-1928. V. 63; 67

ROBINSON, H. M.
The Great Fur Land or Sketches of Life in Hudson's Bay Territory. New York: 1879. V. 63
The Remarkable Activities of the Gentlemen Adventurers of the Great Huon's Bay Company During the Years 1670-1879. Ashland: 1977. V. 63

ROBINSON, H. WHEELER
The Baptists of Yorkshire. London: 1912. V. 64

ROBINSON, HELEN M.
Fun Wherever We Are. Chicago: 1962. V. 62
Fun With Our Family. Chicago: 1962. V. 62
Fun with Our Family and Fun Wherever We Are. Chicago: 1962. V. 62
The New Guess Who. Chicago: 1962. V. 62; 65

ROBINSON, HENRY CRABB
Diary Reminiscences and Correspondence. London: 1869. V. 62

ROBINSON, J. C.
Catalogue of the Soulages Collection...Exhibited at the Museum of Ornamental Art, Marlborough House. London: 1856. V. 64
South Kensington Museum. Italian Sculpture of the Middle Ages and Period of the Revival of Art.... London: 1862. V. 62; 64

ROBINSON, J. H.
The Lone Star: or, the Texan Bravo. Boston: 1852. V. 62

ROBINSON, JANCIS
The Oxford Companion to Wine. 1999. V. 67

ROBINSON, JOAN
The Economics of Imperfect Competition. London: 1933. V. 62

ROBINSON, JOHN
Letter to Sir John Sinclair, Bart, from John Robinson, Esq., Surveyor-General of Woods and Forests (on Inclosing and Improving Waste Lands and Commons) 5th April, 1794. London: 1794. V. 63
The Savage, by Piomingo, a Headman and Warrior of the Muscogulee Nation. Philadelphia: 1810. V. 62
A Theological, Biblical and Ecclesiastical Dictionary.... London: 1815. V. 64

ROBINSON, JOHN CHARLES
Descriptive Catalogue of the Drawings by the Old Masters, Forming the Collection of John Malcolm of Poltalloch, Esq. London: 1869. V. 67
The Treasury of Ornamental Art. London: 1857. V. 67

ROBINSON, JOHN ROBERT
Old Q. A Memoir of William Douglas, Fourth Duke of Queensberry, Kt. London: 1895. V. 63; 64

ROBINSON, KIM STANLEY
Green Mars. London: 1993. V. 66
Red Mars. 1993. V. 66
The Wild Shore. London: 1986. V. 64; 66

ROBINSON, LEIGH
The South Before and at the Battle of the Wilderness. Richmond: 1878. V. 62; 63; 65

ROBINSON, LENNOX
Crabbed Youth and Age. 1924. V. 65
The Irish Theatre. 1939. V. 65
Three Homes. 1938. V. 67
Two Plays: Harvest; The Clancy Name. 1911. V. 67

ROBINSON, LYNDA S.
Murder at the God's Gate. New York: 1995. V. 62
Murder in the Place of Anubis. 1994. V. 64; 66
Murder in the Place of Anubis. New York: 1994. V. 62; 65; 66

ROBINSON, M. S.
The Mac Pherson Collection of Maritime Prints and Drawings in National Maritime Museum Greenwich. New York: 1950. V. 62

ROBINSON, MARIA ELIZABETH
The Wild Wreath. London: 1804. V. 65

ROBINSON, MARILYNNE
Housekeeping. New York: 1980. V. 66; 67
Housekeeping. New York: 1981. V. 62

ROBINSON, MARY
Poems. London: 1791. V. 65

ROBINSON, MONCURE
Report...Upon the Plan of the New York and Eire Rail Road. New York: 1835. V. 62

ROBINSON, P. F.
Designs for Ornamental Villas. London: 1836. V. 64
Rural Architecture, or a Series of Designs for Ornamental Cottages. London: 1823. V. 64
Rural Architecture; or a Series of Designs for Ornamental Cottages. London: 1836. V. 66; 67
Vitruvius Britannicus. London: 1847. V. 64

ROBINSON, P. R.
Catalogue of Dated and Datable Manuscripts c. 737-1600. Cambridge: 1988. V. 62

ROBINSON, PETER
Gallows View. 1990. V. 66
Gallows View. New York: 1990. V. 64
Gallows View. 1992. V. 64; 66
A Necessary End. 1989. V. 64; 66

ROBINSON, ROBERT
The Nature and Necessity of Early Piety. Cambridge: 1772. V. 62
Political Catechism. London: 1782. V. 64

ROBINSON, SOLON
Facts for Farmers; also for the Family Circle. New York: 1873. V. 64

ROBINSON, THOMAS
The Anatomie of the English Nunnery at Lisbon in Portugall.... London: 1623. V. 66
The Anatomy of the Earth. London: 1694. V. 63
An Essay Towards a Natural History of Westmorland and Cumberland. London: 1709. V. 63; 65; 66

ROBINSON, W.
The English Flower Garden and Home Grounds. London: 1902. V. 66
Proportioned Architecture, or the Five Orders Regulated by Equal Parts. London: 1736. V. 64

ROBINSON, W. W.
Land in California: The Story of Mission Lands, Ranchos, Squatters, Mining Claims, Railroad Grants, Land Scrip, Homesteads. Los Angeles: 1948. V. 63
The Malibu - Southern California Famous Rancho - Its Romantic History and Present Charm. Los Angeles: 1958. V. 63

ROBINSON, WILL H.
The Story of Arizona. Phoenix: 1919. V. 63; 66

ROBINSON, WILLARD B.
American Forts: Architectural Form and Function. Forth Worth: 1977. V. 65

ROBINSON, WILLIAM
Friends of Half a Century: Fifty Memorial Portraits of Members of the Society of Friends. 1892. V. 64; 67
The Garden Beautiful. Home Woods and Home Landscape. London: 1907. V. 64
The Virgin's Bower. London: 1912. V. 62
The Wild Garden. London: 1870. V. 64
The Wild Garden. London: 1903. V. 62

ROBINSON, WILLIAM H.
Catalogue 81. A Selection of Precious Manuscripts, Historic Documents and Rare Books, the Majority from the Renowned Collection of Sir Thomas Phillipps, Bt. London: 1950. V. 62; 65

ROBINSON, WILLIAM HEATH
The Adventures of Uncle Lubin. New York: 1902. V. 62
Bill the Minder. London: 1912. V. 62; 63
Bill the Minder. 1930. V. 65
Bo-Peep. London: 1907. V. 65
Cement Roofing as Seen By.... Trafford Park, Manchester. V. 65
Heath Robinson's Book of Goblins. London: 1934. V. 65
Heath Robinson's Ideal Home. The Gadgets. At the Daily Mail Ideal Home Exhibition, 1934. 1934. V. 64
How To Live in a Flat. London: 1936. V. 65
How to Make a Garden Grow. London: 1938. V. 62

ROBINSON, WILLIAM M.
The Confederate Privateers. New Haven: 1928. V. 62; 63; 65

ROBINSON, WIRT
A Flying Trip to the Tropics, a Record of an Ornithological Visit tohe United States of Colombia, South America and to the Island of Curacao West Indies in the Year 1892. Cambridge: 1895. V. 67

ROBISON, MARY
Days. New York: 1979. V. 63; 67

ROBSON, G. C.
Monograph of Recent Cephalopoda.... 1929-1932. V. 63

ROBSON, JOHN S.
How A One-Legged Rebel Lives. Charlottesville: 1888. V. 62

ROBSON, THOMAS CHARLES
A Treatise on Marine Surveying. London: 1834. V. 66

ROBSON, W. J.
Silsden Primitive Methodism. Silsden: 1910. V. 65

ROBSON, WILLIAM
John Railton; or, Read and Think. London: 1862. V. 67
The Old Play-Goer. London: 1854. V. 63

ROBY, J.
Traditions of Lancashire. London: 1829-1831. V. 66
Traditions of Lancashire. London: 1843. V. 62
Traditions of Lancashire. London: 1928-1930. V. 65

ROCA, PAUL M.
Paths of the Padres through Sonora - an Illustrated History and Guide to Its Spanish Churches. Tucson: 1967. V. 63

ROCCHIETTI, JOSEPH
Lorenzo and Oonalaska from Casal. Winchester: 1835. V. 66

ROCCUS, FRANCESCO ROCCI
A Manual of Maritime Law. Philadelphia: 1809. V. 67

ROCH, ERNST
Arts of the Eskimo: Prints. Barre: 1975. V. 63

ROCHAMBEAU, JEAN B. D. DE VIMEUR, COMTE DE
Memoires Militaires, Historiques.... Paris: 1809. V. 63

ROCHA PITTA, SEBASTIAO DA
Historia da America Portugueza Desde o Anno de Mil e Quinhentos. Lisboa: 1730. V. 62

ROCHDALE FIELD NATURALISTS
Journal. Rochdale: 1886. V. 65

ROCHE, REGINA MARIA
The Children of the Abbey. 1845. V. 66

ROCHE, THOMAS MAXWELL
A Report of the Trial of Thomas Maxwell Roche, Upon an Indictment for High Treason. Dublin: 1803. V. 63

ROCHE, W. J.
The Yukon Territory; Its History and Resources. Ottawa: 1916. V. 65

ROCHEFORT, CHARLES DE
Histoire Naturelle et Morale des Iles Antilles de l'Amerique.... Rotterdam: 1665. V. 63

ROCHESTER, JOHN WILMOT, EARL OF
Perfect and Imperfect Enjoyments: Poems by John Wilmot Earl of Rochester. London: 1992. V. 66
The Poetical Works. Halifax: 1933. V. 65
Sodom or the Quintessence of Debauchery. Paris: 1957. V. 67

ROCHOUX, J. A.
Recherches sur l'Apoplexie et sur Pleurieurs Autres Maladies de L'Appareil Nerveux Cerebro-Spinal. Paris: 1833. V. 64

ROCK, J. F.
A Monographic Study of the Hawaiian Species of the Tribe Lobeliodieae Family Campanulaceae. Honolulu: 1919. V. 65

ROCKBRIDGE HISTORICAL SOCIETY
Proceedings. Volumes 1-3, 6-8. 1941-1974. V. 63

ROCKEFELLER, DAVID
Creative Management in Banking. New York: 1964. V. 63

ROCKEFELLER, JOHN D.
Addresses by John D. Rockefeller, Jr. Denver: 1915. V. 64
Random Reminiscences of Men and Events. New York: 1909. V. 63

ROCKEFELLER, MICHAEL CLARK
The Asmat of New Guinea. The Journal of Michael Clark Rockefeller. 1966. V. 62

ROCKFELLOW, J. A.
Log of an Arizona Trail Blazer. 1933. V. 67
Log of an Arizona Trail Blazer. Tucson: 1955. V. 67

ROCKNE, KNUTE
Autobiography. South Bend: 1931. V. 67

ROCKWELL, A. D.
Rambling Recollections. New York: 1920. V. 65

ROCKWELL, NORMAN
The Norman Rockwell Album. Garden City: 1961. V. 66

ROCKWOOD, HARRY
Nat Foster the Boston Detective. 1883. V. 65

ROCQ, MARGARET MILLER
California Local History: a Bibliography and Union List of Library Holdings. Palo Alto: 1970. V. 63; 65

ROCQUE, JOHN
An Alphabetical Index of the Streets, Squares, Lanes, Alleys &c., Contained in the Plan of the Cities of London and Westminster.... London: 1747. V. 62
A Plan of the Cities of London. Lymphne Castle: 1971. V. 62; 67

RODD, E. H.
The Birds of Cornwall and the Scilly Islands. London: 1880. V. 62

RODDIS, LOUIS
A Short History of Nautical Medicine. New York: 1941. V. 64

RODDIS, LOUIS H.
The Indian Wars of Minnesota. Cedar Rapids: 1956. V. 63; 66

RODEN, CLAUDIA
A Book of Middle Eastern Food. London: 1968. V. 62

RODENBAUGH, THEODORE F.
The Bravest Five Hundred of Their Noble Deeds Described by Themselves, Together With an Account of Some Gallant Exploits of Our Soldiers in Indian Warfare - How the Medal of Honor Wars Were Won. New York: 1891. V. 67
From Everglade to Canon with the Second Dragoons...an Authentic Account of Service in Florida, Mexico, Virginia and the Indian Country... 1836-1875. New York: 1875. V. 67

RODENHURST, T.
A Description of Hawkstone, the Seat of Sir Richard Hill. Shrewsbury: 1784. V. 66

RODGER, ALEXANDER
Poems and Songs, Humorous and Satirical. Glasgow: 1838. V. 67

RODGER, ELLA HILL BURTON
Aberdeen Doctors at Home and Abroad. The Narrative of a Medical School. Edinburgh: 1893. V. 65

RODGERS, CAROLYN
The Heart as Ever Green. Garden City: 1978. V. 63; 64

RODGERS, RICHARD
Oklahoma. New York: 1943. V. 63
Pipe Dream. New York: 1956. V. 65
South Pacific. New York: 1949. V. 63

RODIN, AUGUST
Cathedrals of France. London: 1965. V. 67

RODING, JOHANN HINRICH
Allgemeines Worterbuch Der Marine in Allen Europaeischen Seesprachen Nebst Vollstaendigen Erklaerungen. Hamburg: 1794-1798. V. 66

RODITI, EDOUARD
The Delights of Turkey - Twenty Tales. New York: 1977. V. 63
Orphic Love. New York: 1986. V. 66

RODKER, JOHN
Dartmoor. Paris: 1926. V. 66
Hymns. London: 1920. V. 65

RODMAN, SELDEN
Horace Pippin. A Negro Painter in America. New York: 1947. V. 66

RODOCANACHI, C. P.
Forever Ulysses. New York: 1938. V. 63

RODOREDA, MERCE
Two Tales. New York: 1983. V. 66

RODRIGUES, EUGENE
Lettres sur la Religion et la Politique 1829; Suivies de l'Education du Genre Humain.... Paris: 1831. V. 66

RODRIGUES, JOSE CARLOS
Bibliotheca Brasiliense, Catalogo Annotado Dos Livros Sobre O Brasil. 1999. V. 65

RODRIGUEZ, CHRISTOVAL
Bibliotheca Universal de la Polygraphia Espanola.... Madrid: 1738. V. 62

RODRIGUEZ, MANUEL MORENO
Tipos Espanoles. Madrid: 1890. V. 67

RODRIGUEZ DE CASTRO, JOSE
Biblioteca Espanola. Madrid: 1781-1786. V. 62

RODWELL, GEORGE HERBERT BUONAPARTE
Woman's Love; a Romance of Smiles and Tears!. London: 1857. V. 66

ROE, ALFRED S.
The Fifth Regiment Massachusetts Volunteer Infantry. Boston: 1911. V. 65; 67

ROE, CHARLES F.
Custer's Last Battle. New York: 1927. V. 65

ROE, FRANCIS M. A.
Army Letters from an Officer's Wife 1871-1888. New York: 1909. V. 66; 67

ROE, FRANK GILBERT
The North American Buffalo - a Critical Study of the Species in Its Wild State. Toronto: 1951. V. 64

ROEBLING, JOHANN AUGUST
Diary of My Journey from Muehlhausen in Thuringia via Bremen to the United States of North America in the Year 1831. Trenton: 1931. V. 63

ROEBLING, JOHN A.
Long and Short Span Railway Bridges. New York: 1869. V. 65
Report and Plan for a Wire Suspension Bridge, Proposed to be Erected Over the Ohio River at Cincinnati. Cincinnati: 1846. V. 62

ROEBUCK, JOHN ARTHUR
The Colonies of England: a Plan for the Government of some Portion of Our Colonial Possessions. London: 1849. V. 63
History of the Whig Ministry of 1830, to the Passing of the Reform Bill. London: 1852. V. 67

ROEBUCK, KENNETH C.
Where Spaniels Spring. N.P: 1993. V. 65

ROEDER, CHARLES
Prehistoric and Subsequent Mining at Alderley Edge, with a Sketch of the Archaeological Features of the Neighbourhood. Manchester: 1902. V. 64; 65

ROEDIGER, VIRGINIA MORE
Ceremonial Costumes of the Pueblo Indians: Their Evolution, Fabrication and Significance in the Prayer Drama. Berkeley: 1941. V. 63; 64

ROEMER, J. J.
Genera Insectorum Linnaei et Fabricii Iconibus Illustrata. Winterthur: 1789. V. 65; 66

ROENIGK, ADOLPH
Pioneer History of Kansas. N.P: 1933. V. 64; 66
Pioneer History of Kansas. Lincoln: 1933. V. 63; 67

ROENTGEN, WILHELM
Eine Neue Art Von Strahlen. Wurzburg: 1896. V. 64; 66

ROERICH, NICHOLAS
Himalaya, a Monograph. (and) Banners of the East. New York: 1926. V. 62; 65

ROESLIN, EUCHARIUS
De Partu Hominis, et Qua Circa Ipsum Accidunt. Libellvs De. Evcha rii Rhodionis Medici. Venice: 1536. V. 62
De Partu Hominis, et Quae Curca Ipsum Accidunt, Aedeoque de Parturientum & Infantium Morbis Atqu.... Franc: 1551. V. 65

ROESSEL, ROBERT A.
Pictorial History of the Navajo from 1860 to 1910. Rough Rock: 1980. V. 64

ROETHEL, H. K.
Benjamin Kandinsky: Catalogue Raisonne of the Oil Paintings. Volume I. 1900-1915. London: 1982. V. 65
Kandinsky: Catalogue Raisonne of the Oil Paintings, 1900-1915. London: 1981. V. 62

ROETHKE, THEODORE
Collected Poems. New York: 1966. V. 62
Dirty Dinky and Other Creatures. Garden City: 1973. V. 66
The Lost Son and Other Poems. Garden City: 1948. V. 64
The Lost Son and Other Poems. London: 1949. V. 62
Memory. New York: 1961. V. 64; 67
Open House. New York: 1941. V. 63; 64; 67
Sequence Sometimes Metaphysical. Poems. Iowa City: 1963. V. 62; 64
The Waking. New York: 1961. V. 64; 67

ROETHLISBERGER, M.
Claude Lorrain, the Drawings. Berkeley: 1968. V. 62; 65

ROEWER, C. F.
Katalog der Araneae von 1758 bis 1940. Bremen & Brussels: 1942-1954. V. 66

ROGERS, ARTEMAS
Trial of Daniel Davis Farmer, for the Murder of the Widow Anna Ayer, at Goffstown, on the 4th of April 1821. Concord: 1821. V. 63

ROGERS, BRUCE
The Centaur Types. Chicago: 1949. V. 64
Paragraphs on Printing Elicited from Bruce Rogers in Talks with James Hendrickson on the Fuctions of the Book Designer. New York: 1943. V. 63; 64; 66
Report on the Typography of the Cambridge University Press. Cambridge: 1950. V. 62; 65
Report on the Typography of the Cambridge University Press. London: 1950. V. 67
Typographical Partnership: Ten Letters Between Bruce Rogers and Emery Walker 1907-1931. Cambridge: 1971. V. 63

ROGERS, CAMERON
Full and By. Garden City: 1925. V. 64

ROGERS, ELIZA
Poems. London: 1857. V. 64; 65

ROGERS, FRED BLACKBURN
Bear Flag Lieutenant - the Life of Henry L. Ford 1822-1860. San Francisco: 1951. V. 63; 65; 67
Montgomery and the Portsmouth. San Francisco: 1958. V. 64; 66
Soldiers of the Overland, Being Some Account of the Services of General Patrick Edward Conner and His Volunteers in the Old West. San Francisco: 1938. V. 66

ROGERS, HENRY D.
Report on the Geological Survey of the State of New Jersey. Philadelphia: 1836. V. 63

ROGERS, HORATIO
Private Libraries of Providence. Providence: 1878. V. 63

ROGERS, J.
Sport in Vancouver and Newfoundland. 1912. V. 62; 63; 64; 66; 67

ROGERS, J. A.
Africa's Gift to America. Detroit: 1959. V. 65; 67

ROGERS, JAMES EDWARD
Ridicula Rediviva or a Book of Old Nursery Rhymes. London: 1869. V. 63

ROGERS, JAMES EDWIN THOROLD
Cobden and Modern Political Opinion. Essays on Certain Political Topics. London: 1873. V. 67
Six Centuries of Work and Wages. The History of English Labour. London: 1884. V. 64

ROGERS, JANE
Separate Tracks. London: 1983. V. 63

ROGERS, JASPER W.
Letter to the Landlords and Ratepayers of Ireland, Detaling Mean for the Permanent and Profitable Employment of the Peasantry Without Ultimate Cost to the Land or the Nation.... London: 1846. V. 67

ROGERS, JOHN
Groups of Statuary by John Rogers. New York: 1871. V. 64
The Summe of Christianitie, Reduced Unto Eight Propositions, Briefly and Plainly Confirmed Out of the Holy Worde of God. London: 1679. V. 64

ROGERS, JOHN C.
English Furniture. London: 1950. V. 64

ROGERS, JOHN W.
Finding Literature On the Texas Plains. Dallas: 1931. V. 65

ROGERS, JUSTUS H.
Colusa County: Its History Traced from a State of Nature through the Early Period of Settlement and Development to the Present Day. Orland: 1891. V. 62; 63

ROGERS, NEHEMIAH
The True Convert. London: 1620. V. 62

ROGERS, ROBERT
Journals of Major Robert Rogers.... London: 1765. V. 64

ROGERS, SAMUEL
Human Life, a Poem. London: 1819. V. 62
Italy, a Poem. London: 1830. V. 62; 65
Italy, a Poem. (with) Poems. London: 1838. V. 63
The Pleasures of Memory, and Other Poems...and the Pains of Memory.... New York: 1808. V. 66; 67
Poems. London: 1834. V. 62; 64

ROGERS, T. B.
A Century of Progress 1831-1931. Cadbury, Bournville. 1931. V. 67

ROGERS, W. A.
A World Worthwile, a Record of Old Acquaintance. New York: 1922. V. 67

ROGERS, WALTER THOMAS
A Manual of Bibliography Being an Introduction to the Knowledge of Books, Library Management and the Art of Cataloguing. New York: 1891. V. 64

ROGERS, WILLIAM B.
A Reprint of Annual Reports and Other Papers, on the Geology of the Virginias. New York: 1884. V. 63

ROGERSON, IAN
Moods and Tenses: The Portraits and Characters of Peter Reddick. 1999. V. 65
Moods and Tenses: The Portraits and Characters of Peter Reddick. London: 1999. V. 64

ROGERSON, SIDNEY
Both Sides of the Road. London: 1949. V. 63; 65

ROGERSON, SYDNEY
Our Bird Book. London: 1947. V. 64

ROGET, JOHN LEWIS
A History of the Old Water-Colour Society Now the Royal Society of Painters in Water Colours, with Biographical Notices of Its Older and of All Deceased Members and Associates. London: 1891. V. 62

ROGET, PETER MARK
Animal and Vegetable Physiology. 1834. V. 62
Animal and Vegetable Physiology. London: 1834. V. 66
Thesaurus of English Words and Phrases.... London: 1852. V. 64

ROH, FRANZ
German Art in the 20th Century. 1968. V. 62; 65
Photo-Eye 76 Photos of the Period. Stuttgart: 1929. V. 66

ROHAN, THOMAS
In Search of the Antique. 1927. V. 67

ROHAULT, JACQUES
Rohault's System of Natural Philosophy.... London: 1723. V. 65

ROHDE, ELEANOR SINCLAIR
A Garden of Herbs. London: 1920. V. 67
Garden-Craft in the Bible and Other Essays. London: 1927. V. 62; 63
Gardens of Delight. 1934. V. 67
The Old English Gardening Books. 1924. V. 66
The Old English Gardening Books. London: 1924. V. 63; 64
Old English Herbals. London: 1922. V. 64; 67
Shakespeare's Wild Flowers. London: 1935. V. 62

ROHLFS, GERARD
Adventures in Morroco and Journeys through the Oases of Draa and Tafilet.... London: 1874. V. 62

ROHMANN, ERIC
Time Flies. New York: 1994. V. 65

ROHMER, SAX
Bat-Wing. London: 1921. V. 63
Bimbashi Baruk of Egypt. New York: 1944. V. 66
The Day the World Ended. New York: 1930. V. 66; 67
The Emperor of America. Garden City: 1929. V. 67
Fu Manchu's Bride. Garden City: 1933. V. 66; 67
The Golden Scorpion. New York: 1920. V. 63; 64
The Island of Fu Manchu. New York: 1941. V. 63
(Little Tich). Little Tich. London: 1911. V. 63
The Mask of Fu Manchu. 1932. V. 66
President Fu Manchu. Garden City: 1936. V. 66
The Return of Dr. Fu Manchu. 1916. V. 66
The Return of Dr. Fu Manchu. 1920. V. 64
Sinister Madonna. London: 1956. V. 66
The Trail of Fu Manchu. 1934. V. 67
The Yellow Claw. New York: 1915. V. 63; 64

ROHNER, J.
Der Economicshe Kunstler, Oder Sammlung Von Kunsten und Vortheilen der Haus-Und Landwirche, Kunstler Und Professionisten. St. Gallen: 1813. V. 65

ROHR, RENE
Sundials: History, Theory and Practice. Paris: 1965. V. 66

ROJAS, ARNOLD R.
These Were the Vaqueros. N.P: 1975. V. 65
The Vaquero. Santa Barbara: 1964. V. 62; 66

ROLAND, CHARLES P.
Albert Sidney Johnston, Soldier of The Republic. Austin: 1964. V. 67

ROLAND, MANON JEANNE PHILPON
Souvenir de la Revolution. Madamde Roland. Sa Detention a l'Abbaye et a Sainte-Pelagie, 1793. Paris: 1886. V. 66

ROLAND, MME. DE
Memoires de Madame de Roland. Paris: 1884. V. 63

ROLFE, FREDERICK WILLIAM
Amico di Sandro - a Fragment of a Novel. N.P: 1951. V. 65
The Armed Hands and Other Stories and Pieces. London: 1974. V. 65
The Cardinal Perfect of Propaganda and Other Stories. London: 1957. V. 66
A Catalogue of Letters, Manuscript Papers and Books of Frederick Rolfe. London. V. 64
Chronicles of the House of Borgia. London: 1901. V. 63
Collected Poems. London: 1974. V. 63
The Desire and Pursuit of the Whole: a Romance of Modern Venice. New York: 1953. V. 66
Don Renato. An Ideal Content. London: 1963. V. 63
Don Tarquinio: a Kataleptic Phantasmic Romance. London: 1905. V. 67
Hubert's Arthur.... London: 1935. V. 62; 63
In His Own Imago. London: 1901. V. 67
A Letter from Baron Corvo to John Lane Relating to the Titlepage Design for In His Own Images with a Suggested Colophon Here Printed for the First Time. N.P. (Hurst, England): 1958. V. 67
Letters to Grant Richards. Hurst, Berkshire: 1952. V. 67
Letters to Harry Bainbridge. 1977. V. 62; 65; 66
Letters to Harry Bainbridge. London: 1977. V. 65; 67
Letters to Leonard Moore. London: 1960. V. 66
Three Tales of Venice. N.P: 1850. V. 65
Without Prejudice. One Hunded Letters (hitherto unpublished) to John Lane. London: 1963. V. 63; 64

ROLFE, JOHANN HEINRICH
Unweisung dem Weinstocke den Hochsten Nussen Abzugewinnen. Erfurt: 1828. V. 62

ROLFSON, JARL BURHEWEN
The Battles of Stamford Bridge and Hastings. Simla: 1910?. V. 63

ROLLAND, ROMAIN
Jean Christophe. Paris: 1904-. V. 64

ROLLE, ANDREW
An American in California. The Biography of William Heath Davis 1822-1909. San Marino: 1956. V. 66

ROLLENHAGEN, GABRIEL
Nvclevs Emblematvm Selectissimorvm. (with) Selectorum Emblematum Centuria Secunda. Coloniae: 1611. V. 64
Nvclevs Emblematvm Selectissimorvm. (with) Selectorum Emblematum Centuria Secunda. Coloniae: 1611-1613. V. 66

ROLLESTON, G.
The Modifications of the External Aspects of Organic Nature Produced by Man's Interference...a Lecture. London: 1880. V. 67
Scientific Papers and Addresses.... Oxford: 1884. V. 62

ROLLESTON, HUMPHRY DAVY
The William Sydney Thayer and Susan Read Thayer Lectures in Clinical Medicine. Lecture I. The Hereditary Factor in Some Diseases of the Haemopoietic System. Lecture II. Some Diseases in the Jewish Race. Baltimore: 1928. V. 63

ROLLESTON, T. W.
The Tale of Lohengrin after the Drama of Richard Wanger. London: 1913. V. 64; 65
Tannhauser, a Dramatic Poem. London: 1911. V. 65; 67

ROLLIN, CHARLES
The Ancient History of the Egyptians, Carthaginians, Assyrians, Medes and Persians, Macedonians and Grecians. Dublin: 1736. V. 66

ROLLIN, M.
The Ancient History of the Egyptians, Assyrians, Babylonians, Medes and Persians, Grecians and Macedonians. London: 1851. V. 63
The Ancient History of the Egyptians, Carthaginians, Assyrians, Babylonians, Medes and Persians, Grecians and Macedonians. London: 1857. V. 64; 66

ROLLINGS, PHILIP A.
The Discovery of the Oregon Trail, Robert Stuart's Narrative of His Overland Trip East from Asteria in 1812-1813. New York: 1935. V. 63

ROLLINS, CHARLEMAE
Christmas Gif'. Chicago: 1963. V. 63

ROLLINS, PHILIP A.
The Cowboy. New York: 1922. V. 65

ROLLINSON, JOHN K.
Pony Trails in Wyoming - Hoof Prints of a Cowboy and a U.S. Ranger. Caldwell: 1941. V. 64; 67
Wyoming Cattle Trails - History of the Migration of Oregon Raised Herds to Midwestern Markets. Caldwell: 1948. V. 63; 66; 67

ROLPH, C. H.
The Trial of Lady Chatterley: Regina v. Penguin Books Ltd. London: 1961. V. 64

ROLPH, GEORGE M.
Something About Sugar. San Francisco: 1917. V. 66

ROLT, L. T. C.
Green and Silver. 1949. V. 67

ROLT-WHEELER, ETHEL
Ireland's Veils and Other Poems. 1913. V. 67

ROLVAAG, OE
Giants in the Earth. 1927. V. 65

ROMAINE, BENJAMIN
State Sovereignty and Certain Dissoulution of the Union. New York: 1832. V. 62

ROMAINE, LAWRENCE B.
A Guide to American Trade Catalogs, 1744-1900. New York: 1960. V. 62

ROMAINS, JULES
Men of Good Will, Book VIII. Provincial Interlude. London: 1935. V. 67

ROMAN, ALFRED
The Military Operations of General Beauregard in the War Between the States 1861 to 1865. New York: 1884. V. 62; 63

THE ROMANCE of King Arthur and His Knights of the Round Table. New York: 1917. V. 63

THE ROMANCE of Oklahoma. Oklahoma City: 1920. V. 63; 66; 67

ROMANES, E.
The Life and Letters of George John Romanes. London: 1896. V. 64; 66

ROMANES, GEORGE
Mental Evolution in Animals. London: 1883. V. 62

ROMANS, BERNARD
Annals of the Troubles in the Netherlands. Hartford: 1778. V. 66

ROMBAUER, IRMA S.
Joy of Cooking. Indianapolis: 1946. V. 67

ROMBERG, MORITZ HEINRICH
A Manual of the Nervous Diseases of Man. London: 1853. V. 65

ROMER, A. S.
Osteology of the Reptiles. Chicago: 1956. V. 67

ROMER, F.
Makers of History - a Story of the Development of the History of Our Country and the Part Played In It by Colt. Hartford: 1926. V. 63

ROMERO, GEORGE
Martin. New York: 1977. V. 67

ROMERO, MATIAS
Coffee and India-Rubber Culture in Mexico. New York and London: 1898. V. 66

ROMIEU, MARIE SINCERE
La Femme au XIXe Siecle. Paris: 1858. V. 63

ROMILLY, SAMUEL
The Life of Sir Samuel Romilly, Written by Himself. London: 1842. V. 64

ROMM, MICHAEL
The Ascent of Mount Stalin. 1936. V. 65
The Ascent of Mount Stalin. London: 1936. V. 63; 64

ROMNEY, HENRY SIDNEY, EARL OF
Diary of the Times of Charles the Second.... London: 1843. V. 62

ROMTVEDT, DAVID
Moon. Saint Paul: 1984. V. 63; 64; 66

RONALDS, ALFRED
The Fly-Fisher's Entomology. London: 1849. V. 62
The Fly-Fisher's Entomology. London: 1862. V. 62; 67
The Fly-Fisher's Entomology. London: 1868. V. 66; 67
The Fly-Fisher's Entomology. 1883. V. 65; 67
The Fly-Fisher's Entomology. London: 1921. V. 62; 67

RONALDS, FRANCIS
Catalogue of Books and Papers to Electricity, Magnetism, the Electric Telegraph etc. Including the Ronalds Library. Mansfield: 1995. V. 65

RONDTHALER, EDWARD
Life of John Heckewelder. Philadelphia: 1847. V. 66; 67
The Memorabilia of Fifty Years 1877-1927. (with) Appendix.... Raleigh: 1928. V. 67

RONQUILLO, ESTANISLAO N.
Collection de Leyes del Territorio de Nuevo Mexico. Las Vegas: 1881. V. 66

ROOK, CLARENCE
Switzerland: The Country and Its People. New York: 1907. V. 65

ROOKE, HAYMAN
Descriptions and Sketches of Some Remarkable Oaks in the Park at Welbeck.... 1790. V. 62
A Narrative of What Passed at the Revolution House at Whittington, County of Derby, in...1688. Nottingham: 1788. V. 63

ROOKES, RICHARD
A New and Accurate System of Natural History.... London: 1763. V. 66

ROOKS, CONRAD
Chappaqua. Paris?: 1966. V. 66

ROOPER, G.
Thames and Tweed. 1870. V. 67

ROOSE, ROBSON
Nerve Prostration and Other Functional Disorders of Daily Life. New York: 1888. V. 65

ROOSEBOOM, MARIA
Microscopium. Leiden: 1956. V. 62

ROOSEVELT, ELEANOR
It's Up to the Women. New York: 1933. V. 63
On My Own: The Years Since the White House. New York: 1958. V. 62; 63
This I Remember. New York: 1949. V. 63; 65; 67
This Is My Story. New York: 1937. V. 62
When You Grow Up to Vote. New York: 1932. V. 63

ROOSEVELT, FRANKLIN DELANO
Our Realization of Tomorrow. Chicago: 1945. V. 67
The Public Papers and Addresses of Franklin D. Roosevelt. New York: 1938. V. 65

ROOSEVELT, KERMIT
The Happy Hunting Grounds. New York: 1920. V. 67

ROOSEVELT, ROBERT
Game Fish of the Northern States of America, and British Provinces. New York: 1862. V. 66
The Game Fish of the Northern States of America and British Provinces. New York: 1869. V. 66
Superior Fishing; or, the Striped Bass, Trout and Black Bass of the Northern States. New York: 1865. V. 63

ROOSEVELT, THEODORE
African Game Trails. 1910. V. 62; 63; 64
African Game Trails. New York: 1910. V. 66
Big Game Hunting in the Rockies and on the Great Plains. New York: 1899. V. 65; 67
The Deer Family. New York: 1902. V. 67
East of the Sun and West of the Moon. 1926. V. 62; 63; 64; 66; 67
Fear God and Take Your Own Part. New York: 1916. V. 63
Fear God and Take Your Own Part. New York: 1916. V. 63
Good Hunting in Pursuit of Big Game in the West. 1907. V. 67
Hunting Trips of a Ranchman. New York: 1885. V. 67
Life Histories of African Game Animals. New York: 1914. V. 62
Outdoor Pastimes of an American Hunter. New York: 1905. V. 63; 65
Ranch Life and the Hunting Trail. New York: 1888. V. 62; 65
The Summer Birds in Franklin County, New York.... New York: 1925. V. 66
Through the Brazilian Wilderness. New York: 1914. V. 66
Through the Brazilian Wilderness. London: 1929. V. 62
The Works of Theodore Roosevelt. New York: 1926. V. 65

ROOT, FRANK A.
The Overland Stage to California. Topeka: 1901. V. 62; 65

ROOT, HENRY
Henry Root - Surveyor, Engineer and Inventor - Personal History and Reminiscences. San Francisco: 1921. V. 63; 66

ROOT, J. W.
The British West Indies and the Sugar Industry. Liverpool: 1899. V. 63

ROOT, SIDNEY
Primary Bible Questions for Young Children. Atlanta: 1864. V. 62; 64; 66

ROOT, WILLIAM PITT
A Journey South. A Poem. Port Towsend: 1977. V. 63

ROOTS, GEORGE
The Charters of the Town of Kingston Upon Thames. London: 1797. V. 62

ROPER, MOSES
A Narrative of the Adventures and Escape of Moses Roper, from American Slavery.... London: 1838. V. 64

ROPER, R. S. DONNISON
A Treatise on the Revocation and Republication of Wills and Testaments; Together with Tracts Upon the Law Concerning Baton and Feme. London: 1800. V. 62

ROPES, H. A., MRS.
Six Months in Kansas. Boston: 1856. V. 64

ROPES, JOHN C.
Story of the Civil War; a Concise Account of the War in America. New York: 1894-1913. V. 62

ROQUES, J.
Phytographie Medicale, Histoire des Substances Heroiques et des Poisons Tires du Regne Vegetale. Paris: 1835. V. 64; 65

ROREM, NED
Paul's Blues. New York: 1984. V. 64; 67

RORER, DAVID
A Treatise on the Law of Railways. Chicago: 1884. V. 67

ROS, AMANDA MC KITTRICK
Irene Iddesleigh. Belfast: 1897. V. 65
Irene Iddesleigh. Bloomsbury: 1926. V. 65

ROSA, JOSEPH C.
They Called Him Wild Bill. The Life and Adventures of James Butler Hicock. Norman: 1964. V. 64; 67

ROSA, SALVATOR
Serie di LXXXV Disegni in Varie Grandezze Composte dal Celebre Pittore Salvator Rosa.... Roma: 1780. V. 62; 67

ROSALES, VICENTE PEREZ
California Adventure. San Francisco: 1947. V. 63

ROSCHER, W. H.
Ausfuhrliches Lexikon der Griechischen und Romicchon Mytholgie.... Hildesheim: 1965. V. 65

ROSCOE, E. S.
Rambles with a Fishing Rod. 1883. V. 67

ROSCOE, HENRY
A Digest of the Law of Evidence on the Trial of Actions at Nisi Prius. London: 1844. V. 63

ROSCOE, MARGARET
Floral Illustrations of the Seasons, Consisting of Representations Drawn from Nature of Some of the Most Beautiful, Hardy and Rare Herbaceous Plants.... London: 1829. V. 62

ROSCOE, THOMAS
The Italian Novelists. London: 1836. V. 66
Rambles in France and Switzerland. London: V. 62
The Tourist in Switzerland and Italy. London: 1830. V. 66
The Tourist in France. London: 1834. V. 62
The Tourist in Italy. London: 1831. V. 62
Tourist in Spain and Alusia. London: 1836. V. 62
Wanderings and Excursions in North Wales. London: 1836. V. 65
Wanderings and Excursions in North Wales. (with) Wanderings and Excursions in South Wales.... London: 1836-1837. V. 62; 66

ROSCOE, WILLIAM
(Sale) Catalogue of the Genuine and Entire Collection of Drawings and Pictures.... Liverpool: 1816. V. 64

ROSCOE, WILLIAM CALDWELL
Violenzia: a Tragedy. London: 1851. V. 64; 65

ROSCOE, WILLIAM STANLEY
Poems. London: 1834. V. 62

ROSCOMMON, WENTWORTH DILLON, EARL OF
An Essay on Translated Verse. 1709. V. 65
Poems. London: 1717. V. 63; 65
The Works. Glasgow: 1752. V. 66
The Works. Glasgow: 1753. V. 66

ROSE, A. H.
The Yeasts. Volume I. London: 1987. V. 64

THE ROSE Book for Girls. London. V. 62

THE ROSE Book of the Fairies. London: 1926. V. 62

ROSE, DAN
The Ancient Mines of Ajo. Tucson: 1936. V. 65

ROSE, GEORGE
Observations on the Historical Work of the Late Right Honourable Charles James Fox...with a Narrative of the Events Which Occurred in the Enterprise of the Earl of Argyle in 1685.... London: 1809. V. 62; 63

ROSE, JOHN
The United States' Arithmetician; or the Science of Arithmetic Simplified. Bridgeton: 1830. V. 63

ROSE, JOSHUA
Modern Machine-Shop Practice. New York: 1892. V. 63

ROSE Petals from Georgia. Decatur: 1920. V. 65

ROSE, VICTOR M.
The Life and Services of General Ben McCulloch. Austin: 1958. V. 65
Roses' Texas Brigade: Being a Narrative of Events Connected with its Service in the Late War Between the States. Louisville: 1881. V. 62; 63; 65
Ross' Texas Brigade. Kennesaw: 1960. V. 67

ROSE, WILLIAM G.
The Radium Book. Cleveland: 1905. V. 64

ROSE, WILLIAM S.
The Court and Parliament of Beasts Freely Translated.... London: 1819. V. 65
Letters from the North of Italy. Addressed to Henry Hallam Esq. London: 1819. V. 63

ROSEN, GEORGE
The Reception of William Beaumont's Discovery in Europe. New York: 1942. V. 63

ROSEN, KENNETH
The Man to Send Rain Clouds. New York: 1974. V. 64
Voices of the Rainbow. New York: 1975. V. 64

ROSEN, PETER
Pa-Ha-Sap-Pa - the Black Hills of South Dakota. St. Louis: 1895. V. 67

ROSEN, R. D.
Srike Three You're Dead. New York: 1984. V. 67

ROSENAU, H.
Boullee and Visionary Architecture. London: 1976. V. 62; 65

ROSENBACH, ABRAHAM SIMON WOLF
A Book Hunter's Holiday: Adventures with Books and Manuscripts. New York: 1936. V. 63
Books and Bidders. Boston: 1927. V. 62
Books and Bidders. London: 1928. V. 67
The Libraries of the Presidents of the United States. Worcester: 1935. V. 64
The Unpublishable Memoirs. London: 1924. V. 62

ROSENBERG, CHARLES G.
The Roman Soprano; or, the Captain of the Swiss Guard. New York: 185-. V. 66

ROSENBERG, F.
Big Game Shooting in British Columbia and Norway. 1928. V. 62; 63; 64; 66; 67

ROSENBERG, ISAAC
The Collected Poems. London: 1949. V. 63; 65
Moses. London: 1916. V. 64
Moses. London: 1990. V. 63
Poems. London: 1922. V. 62; 67
Youth. London: 1915. V. 64; 65

ROSENBLATT, JULIA CARLSON
Dining with Sherlock Holmes. 1976. V. 66

ROSENBLITH, W. A.
Sensory Communication, Contributions to the Symposium on Principles of Sensory Communication. Cambridge and New York: 1961. V. 66

ROSENBLUM, R.
Cubism and 20th Century Art. New York: 1976. V. 65

ROSENE, W.
The Bobwhite Quail, Its Life and Management. New Brunswick: 1969. V. 63; 67

ROSENMAN, SAMUEL I.
The Public Papers and Addresses of Franklin Delano Roosevelt. New York: 1938. V. 64

ROSENTHAL, MORITZ
A Clinical Treatise on the Diseases of the Nervous System. New York: 1879. V. 65; 67

ROSEN VON ROSENSTEIN, NILS
Underrattelser om Barn-Sjukdomar och Deras Bote-Medel: Tilforene Styckewis Utgifne Uti de Sma Almanachorna.... Stockholm: 1764. V. 62

ROSENWALD, LESSING J.
The Fortsas Catalogue, a Facimile. North Hills: 1970. V. 62
Vision of a Collector: the Lessing J. Rosenwald Collection in the Library of Congress. Washington: 1991. V. 62

ROSENZWEIG, FRANZ
Hegel und der Staat. Munich and Berlin: 1920. V. 67

ROSES of Sharon. Waltham St. Lawrence: 1937. V. 64

ROSE-TROUP, FRANCES
The Western Rebellion of 1549. London: 1913. V. 63

ROSETTA STONE INSCRIPTION
Report of the Committee Appointed by the Philomathean Society of the University of Pennsylvania to Translate the Inscription of the Rosetta Stone. Philadelphia: 1859. V. 63

ROSEVEAR, D. R.
The Bats of West Africa. London: 1965. V. 62
The Rodents of West Africa. London: 1969. V. 62

ROSINUS, JOANNE
Antiquitatum Romanarum. Lugduni: 1609. V. 66
Antiquitatum Romanarum. Lugduni Batavaorum: 1663. V. 66

ROSKELL, ARTHUR
Six Years of a Tramp's Life in South Africa. Capetown. V. 67

ROSKILL, S. W.
The War at Sea. London: 1954-1961. V. 65

ROSLIN WILLIAMS, MARY
The Dual Purpose Labrador. 1969. V. 67

ROSNEK, CARL
Skystone and Silver - the Collector's Book of Southwest Indian Jewelry. Englewood Cliffs: 1976. V. 63; 66

ROSNER, CHARLES
The Growth of the Book-Jacket. Cambridge: 1954. V. 62

ROSS, AL
The Destroyer Escort England. London: 1985. V. 67
The Escort Carrier Gambier Bay. London: 1993. V. 67

ROSS, ALAN
The Bandit on the Billiard Table - a Journey through Sardinia. London: 1954. V. 62
Time Was Away - a Notebook of Corsica. London: 1948. V. 62

ROSS, ALEXANDER
Adventures of the First Settlers on the Oregon or Columbia Rivers.... London: 1849. V. 66
Arcana Mirocosmi; or, the Hid Secrets of Man's Body Discovered.... London: 1652. V. 66
Mystagogus Poeticus, or the Muses Interpreter.... London: 1672. V. 64
Pansebeia, or, a View of all Religions in the World, from the Creation to These Times.... London: 1653. V. 66

ROSS, BERNARD
Welcum Hinges. New York: 1942. V. 65

ROSS, CHARLES H.
High Tide at Any Hour. 1879. V. 66
Ye Comical Rhymes of Ancient Times Dug Up Into Jokes for Small Folks. Sep. 1860. V. 65

ROSS, CLYDE P.
Water-Supply Paper: the Lower Gila Region, Arizona. Washington: 1923. V. 63

ROSS, EDWARD ALSWORTH
The Russian Bolshevik Revolution. New York: 1921. V. 66

ROSS, FITZGERALD
Cities and Camps of the Confederate States. Urbana: 1958. V. 63
A Visit to the Cities and Camps of the Confederate States. Edinburgh & London: 1865. V. 63

ROSS, FRANK ALEXANDER
A Bibliography of Negro Migration. New York: 1934. V. 65

ROSS, FREDERICK
The Ruined Abbeys of Britain. 1882. V. 64
The Ruined Abbeys of Britain. London: 1882. V. 66

ROSS, J. BURY
On Peripheral Neuritis: a Treatise. London: 1893. V. 67

ROSS, JAMES CLARK
A New Edition of Capt. Ross's Voyage to the North Pole. London: 1835. V. 62; 65

ROSS, JOHN
The Book of the Red Deer and Empire Big Game. 1925. V. 62; 63; 64; 66; 67
The Book of the Red Deer and Empire Big Game. London: 1925. V. 62; 67
Narrative of a Second Voyage in Search of a North-West Passage and of a Residence in the Arctic Regions During the Years 1829-1833.... London: 1835. V. 65
A New Edition of Captain Ross's Voyage to the North Pole: Giving an Account of the Captain's Early Appointments and Services in the Navy.... Newcastle: 1834?. V. 66
On Communication to India, in Large Steam-ships, by the Cape of Good Hope.... London: 1838. V. 62; 63
Relation du Second Voyage fait a la Recherche d'un Passage au Nord-Ouest.... Bruxelles: 1835. V. 63
A Treatise on Navigation by Steam.... London: 1828. V. 62
A Voyage of Discovery Made Under the Orders of Admiralty, in His Majesty's Ships Isabella and Alexander, for the Purpose of Exploring Baffin's Bay and Inquiring into the Probability of a North-West Passage. London: 1819. V. 64

ROSS, JOHN D.
Scottish Poets in America.... New York: 1889. V. 62

ROSS, MALCOLM
A Climber in New Zealand. London: 1914. V. 64; 66
Machine Age in the Hills. New York: 1933. V. 65

ROSS, MARVIN C.
George Catlin, Episodes from Life Among the Indians and Last Rambles.... Norman: 1959. V. 67

ROSS, MRS.
The Balance of Comfort; or The Old Maid and Married Woman. London: 1817. V. 63; 65
The Balance of Comfort; or the Old Maid and Married Woman. London: 1818. V. 65

ROSS, RONALD
Memoirs. London: 1923. V. 62

ROSS, THOMAS
The Money Harvest. New York: 1975. V. 67

ROSS, VICTOR
A History of the Canadian Book of Commerce with an Account of the Other Banks.... Toronto: 1920-1934. V. 63

ROSS, WILLIAM STEWART
Woman: Her Glory, Her Shame and Her God. London: 1894. V. 63

ROSS-CRAIG, S.
Drawings of British Plants. London: 1948-1973. V. 62

ROSSE, HERMAN
Designs and Impressions. Chicago: 1920. V. 65

ROSSER, ARCHIBALD
A Letter to the...Speaker of the House of Commons; Containing a Narrative of the Circumstances Connected With the Proceedings of that Honorable House Against Christopher Bolton, Esq. of Hull, and Four Others, for a Brief of Privilege.... London: 1821. V. 63

ROSSETTI, CHRISTINA
Commonplace and Other Short Stories. London: 1870. V. 65
Goblin Market. London: 1862. V. 62
Goblin Market. London: 1879. V. 64
Goblin Market. London: 1893. V. 64; 65
Goblin Market. London: 1933. V. 62; 66
Goblin Market. Philadelphia: 1933. V. 67
Goblin Market. London: 1939. V. 63; 66
Maude. A Story for Girls. London: 1897. V. 62
New Poems. London: 1896. V. 65; 67
New Poems. London: 1900. V. 65
A Pageant and Other Poems. Boston: 1881. V. 66
A Pageant and Other Poems. London: 1881. V. 63; 64; 65
Poems. Boston: 1910. V. 67
Poems. (with) New Poems. London: 1896. V. 65
The Prince's Progress and Other Poems. London: 1866. V. 62; 66
Selected Poems. London: 1907. V. 65
Sing-Song. London: 1872. V. 65
Sing-Song. London: 1893. V. 64
Speaking Likenesses. London: 1874. V. 62; 65
Verses. London: 1893. V. 63

ROSSETTI, DANTE GABRIEL
Ballads and Narrative Poems. London: 1894. V. 64; 66
Ballads and Sonnets. London: 1881. V. 62; 67
The Collected Works of Dante Gabriel Rossetti. London: 1897. V. 66
Hand and Soul. Upper Mall, Hammersmith: 1895. V. 62; 64; 67
Hand and Soul. London: 1899. V. 67
Henry the Leper. Boston: 1905. V. 62; 65
His Family Letters with a Memoir by William Michael Rossetti. London: 1895. V. 66
Letters to His Publisher F. S. Ellis. London: 1928. V. 64
Poems. 1870. V. 64
Poems. London: 1870. V. 62; 63
Poems. Leipzig: 1873. V. 62
Poems. London: 1881. V. 65
Poems. New York: 1884?. V. 64
The Poems. Troy: 1903. V. 64
A Rossetti Cabinet. Boston: 1898. V. 64
Sonnets and Lyrical Poems. 1894. V. 64
Sonnets Written in Youth. New York: 1992. V. 64
Two Poems Written In Youth. New York: 1994. V. 64

ROSSETTI, MARIA FRANCESCA
Exercises in Idiomatic Italian through Literal Translation from the English. London and Edinburgh: 1867. V. 66
A Shadow of Dante. London Oxford and Cambridge: 1872. V. 63

ROSSETTI, WILLIAM MICHAEL
Bibliography of the Works of Dante Gabriel Rossetti. London: 1905. V. 64
The Germ. London: 1901. V. 66
Swinburne's Poems and Ballads. London: 1866. V. 64; 65

ROSSI, GIOVANNI GHERARDO DE
Scherzi Poetici e Pittorici. Parma: 1795. V. 67

ROSSI, MARIO M.
Pilgrimage in the West. Dublin: 1933. V. 62; 64; 67
Swift or The Egoist. 1934. V. 67

ROSSI, PAOLO
Francis Bacon; from Magic to Science. Chicago: 1968. V. 67

ROSSKAM, EDWIN
Washington Nerve Center. New York: 1939. V. 63

ROST, LEONHARD
Atlas Portatilis Coelestis, Der Compendiose Vorstellung des Gantzen Welt-Gebaudes, in den Anfangs'Grunden Astronomie.... Nuremerg: 1723. V. 62

ROSTAND, EDMOND
Cyrano de Bergerac Comedie Heroique en Cinq Actes en Vers. Paris: 1898. V. 62; 65

ROSTEN, LEO
Captain Newman, M.D. New York: 1962. V. 67

ROSTOVTZEF, M.
The Social and Economic History of the Roman Empire. London: 1998. V. 65

ROSTREVOR, GEORGE
Bergson and Future Philosophy: an Essay on the Scope of Intelligence. London: 1921. V. 67

ROSWEYDUS
Vitae Patrum. De Vita Et Verbis Seniorum Sive Historiae Ermeticae Libri X...Opera et Studio Heriberti Rosweydi.... Antwerpiae: 1628. V. 66

ROT, DITER
246 Little Clouds. New York: 1968. V. 66

ROTERS, E.
Painters of the Bauhaus. New York: 1969. V. 65

ROTH, C.
Plastisch-Anatomischer Atlas Zum Studium des Modells und Der Antike. Entworfen und Gezeichnet von Prof. Ch. Roth.... Stuttgart: 1892. V. 64

ROTH, D. LUTHER
Acadie and the Acadians. Philadelphia: 1890. V. 64

ROTH, DAVID
Sacred Honor. A Biography of Colin Powell. Grand Rapids: 1993. V. 62

ROTH, GEORGES
La Geste De Cuchulain, Le Heros de l'Ulster d'Apres Les Aniens Textes Irlandais. 1927. V. 65

ROTH, H. L.
The Aborigines of Tasmania. Halifax: 1899. V. 62
The Aborigines of Tasmania. Hobart: 1960. V. 62
Oriental Silverwork. Malay and Chinese. A Handbook.. London: 1910. V. 62; 66

ROTH, HENRY
Nature's First Green. New York: 1979. V. 66

ROTH, L. M.
The Biotic Associations of Cockroaches. Washington: 1960. V. 62; 63; 66
The Medical and Veterinary Importance of Cockroaches. and The Biotic Association of Cockroaches. Washington: 1957-1960. V. 67

ROTH, PHILIP
American Pastoral. Boston: 1997. V. 62; 67
American Pastoral. Franklin Center: 1997. V. 62; 65; 66
The Anatomy Lesson. New York: 1983. V. 66
The Breast. New York: 1972. V. 66
The Facts. New York: 1988. V. 66
The Ghost Writer. New York: 1979. V. 66; 67
Goodbye, Columbus. Boston: 1959. V. 62; 63
Goodbye, Columbus. London: 1959. V. 63
Goodbye, Columbus. Franklin Center: 1978. V. 62; 63; 66
I Married a Communist. Franklin Center: 1998. V. 62
Letting Go. New York: 1962. V. 65; 66
Looking at Kafka. Helsinki: 1990. V. 63
Portnoy's Complaint. New York: 1969. V. 62; 65; 66
When She Was Good. London: 1967. V. 65
When She Was Good. New York: 1967. V. 66; 67
Zuckerman Bound. New York: 1985. V. 62
Zuckerman Bound. The Ghost Writer. Zuckerman Unbound. The Anatomy Lesson. Epilogue: the Prague Orgy. New York: 1985. V. 66
Zuckerman Unbound. New York: 1981. V. 66

ROTHA, PAUL
The Film Till Now - a Survey of the Cinema. London: 1930. V. 65

ROTHE, DAVID
The Analecta. 1884. V. 63

ROTHENBERG, JEROME
Improvisations. N.P: 1991. V. 64
Letters and Numbers. Madison: 1979. V. 66
The 17 Horse Songs of Frank Mitchell Nos. X-XIII. London: 1969. V. 65

ROTHENSTEIN, IDA
An Introduction to English Painting. London: 1933. V. 63

ROTHENSTEIN, J.
Turner. London: 1965. V. 65

ROTHENSTEIN, WILLIAM
Contemporaries: Portrait Drawings. London: 1937. V. 63
Since Fifty - Men and Memories 1922-1938: Recollections. London: 1939. V. 64
Twenty-Four Portraits. London: 1923. V. 63

ROTHERAY, LISTER
Flora of Skipton and District. Skipton: 1900. V. 64

ROTHERT, OTTO A.
The Outlaws of Cave-in Rock, Historical Accounts of the Famous Highwaymen and River Pirates in Pioneer Days Upon the Ohio and Mississippi Rivers and Over the Old Natchez Trace. Cleveland: 1927. V. 62; 65

ROTHERY, G. A.
A Diary of the Wreck of His Majesty's Ship Challenger, on the Western Coast of South America. London: 1836. V. 62

ROTHFELD, OTTO
With Pen and Rifle in Kishtwar. 1918. V. 66

ROTHROCK, MARY U.
The French Broad Holston Country, a History of Knox County, Tennessee. Knoxville: 1946. V. 63; 66; 67

ROTHSCHILD, CLEMENTINA DE
Letters to a Christian Friend on the Fundamental Truths of Judaism. London: 1869. V. 63

ROTHSCHILD, L. W.
Dear Lord Rothschild, Birds, Butterflies and History. 1983. V. 63

ROTHSCHILD, LORD
The Genus Dedrolagus (Tree Kangaroos). 1936. V. 62

ROTHSCHILD, MIRIAM
Fleas, Flukes and Cuckoos. 1952. V. 67
Fleas Flukes and Cuckoos. London: 1952. V. 62

ROTHSCHILD, NATHANIEL MAYER VICTOR, BARON
The Rothschild Library: a Catalogue of the Collection of Eighteenth Century Printed Books and Manuscripts. Cambridge: 1954. V. 64

ROTHSHUH, KARL E.
History of Physiology. Huntington: 1973. V. 67

ROTHSTEIN, S. I.
Parasitic Birds and Their Hosts.... New York: 1998. V. 65

ROUAULT, GEORGES
Miserere. London: 1950. V. 63

ROUCHER, JEAN ANTOINE
Collection Universelle des Memoires Particuliers Relatifs a l'Histoire de France. Londres: 1785-1791. V. 64; 66

ROUILLE, GUILLAUME
Prima (Secunda) Pars Promptvarii Iconvm Insigniorvm a Secvlo Hominum. Lvgdvni: 1553. V. 64; (66)

ROUNDELL, CHARLES, MRS.
Ham House Its History and Art Treasures. London: 1904. V. 65

ROUNTREE, HARRY
Rountree's Ridiculous Rabbits. No. 2. Fun in the Furlimbunnie Ingenook. London: 1916. V. 63

ROUPPE, LUDOVICUS
De Morbis Navigantium. Leiden: 1764. V. 67

ROUQUETTE, FRANCOIS DOMINIQUE
Fleurs d'Amerique Poesies Nouvelles. Nouvelle Orleans: 1856. V. 64

ROURKE, C.
Charles Scheeler: Artist in the American Tradition. New York: 1938. V. 62; 65

ROURKE, CONSTANCE
Troupers of the Gold Coast or the Rise of Lotta Crabtree. New York: 1928. V. 67

ROURKE, J.
The Proteas of Southen Africa. Cape Town: 1980. V. 64

ROUS, FRANCIS
Archaeologiae Atticae Libri Septem. Oxford: 1649. V. 64

ROUSE, HUNTER
History of Hydraulics. N.P: 1957. V. 67

ROUSE, JAMES
The Beauties and Antiquities of the County of Sussex. London: 1825. V. 67
Scraps of Sussex. London: 1825. V. 67

ROUSE, JOHN F.
World Cattle. Norman: 1970. V. 66

ROUSMANIERE, JOHN
The Golden Pastime, a New History of Yachting. New York: 1986. V. 65
A Picture History of the America's Cup. Atlanta: 1989. V. 65

ROUSSEAU, A.
Treatise on Therapeutics. New York: 1880. V. 67

ROUSSEAU, JEAN BAPTISTE
Pieces Interesantes et Peu Connues, Pour Servir a l'Histoire. Brussels: 1781. V. 65

ROUSSEAU, JEAN-JACQUES
La Botanique. Paris: 1805. V. 65; 66
Collection Complete des Oeuvres. Kehl: 1783-1789. V. 64; 66
Les Confessions. Geneva: 1782. V. 64
The Confessions. New York: 1856. V. 66
The Confessions. London: 1897. V. 67
The Confessions. London: 1938. V. 63; 65
Discours sur l'Origine et Les Fondemens de L'Inegalite Parmi Les Hommes. Amsterdam: 1755. V. 64; 66
A Discourse Upon the Origin and Foundation of the Inequality Among Mankind. London: 1761. V. 62
Du Contract Social; Ou Principes du Droit Politique. Amsterdam: 1762. V. 64; 66
Emile, ou de l'Education. Amsterdam: 1762. V. 67
Julia; or the Eloisa. Edinburgh;: 1773. V. 63
Original Letters, to M. de Malesherbes, M. D'Alembert, Madame la M. de Luxembourg &c. London: 1799. V. 62
Principes du Droit Politique (Du Contract Social). Amsterdam: 1762. V. 62
Suite of Plates for Les Oeuvres. Paris: 1793-1800. V. 62
A Treatise on the Social Compact; or Principles of Politic Law. London: 1764. V. 64

ROUSSEL, GEORGE A.
Traite Theorique et Pratique des Couronnes Artificielles et Du Bridge Work. Paris: 1906. V. 65

ROUSSEL, J.
Transfusion of Human Blood by the Method of J. Roussel.... London: 1877. V. 65

ROUSSEL, NAPOLEON
Mon Voyage en Algerie, Raconte a mes Enfans. Paris: 1840. V. 66

ROUSSEL, RAYMOND
La Doublure. Paris: 1897. V. 67

ROUSSELET, R. P.
Historie et Description de l'Eglise Royale de Brou Elevee a bourg en Bresse, Sous Les Ordres de Marguerite d'Autriche.... Paris: 1767. V. 64

ROUSSET, FRANCOIS
Usterotomotokias. (id est) Caesarei Partus Assertio Historiologica. Paris: 1590. V. 65

ROUSSET, JEAN
Exposition des Motifs Apparens et Reels Qui sont Cause & Perpetue La Guerre Presente. Amsterdam: 1746. V. 67

ROUSSET DE MISSY, JEAN
Histoire Du Cardinal Alberoni, et de Son Ministere. Londona Haye: 1720. V. 66

ROUTH, EDWARD JOHN
A Treatise on Dynamics of a Particle. Cambridge: 1898. V. 65

ROUTH, J.
Rambles in Swaledale, and Neighbourhood. (with) A Railway Ride through Wensleydale.... Hawes: 1880. V. 65
Rambles in Wensleydale and Swaledale...(with) Rambles in Swaledale and Neighbourhood. Hawes: 1879-1880. V. 65

ROUTLEDGE, JAMES
Chapters in the History of Popular Progress, Chiefly in Relation to the Freedom of the Press and Trial by Jury. 1660-1820. London: 1876. V. 65

ROUTLEDGE, WILLIAM
The Children's Musical Cinderella. London: 1879. V. 62

ROUTLEDGE'S Coloured Picture Book. London: 1890. V. 64

ROUTLEDGE'S Etiquette for Ladies. London: 1864. V. 64

ROUTLEDGE'S Nursery Picture Book. London: 1862. V. 67

ROUX, ROBERT J.
L'Epopee Matra Sports 1964-1974. Paris: 1977. V. 66

ROVIROSA, JOSE N.
Pteridografia del Sur de Mexico.... Mexico: 1910. V. 65

ROWAN, ARCHIBALD HAMILTON
A Full Report of the Trial at Bar, in the Court of King's Bench...for Having Published a Seditious Libel, January 29, 1794. Dublin: 1794. V. 63
Report of the Trial of Archibald Hamilton Rowan, Esq. on an Information...for the Distribution of a Libel.... Dublin: 1794. V. 63

ROWAN, PETER
Historical Sketch of the Flathead Indian Nation from the Year 1813- 1890. Helena: 1890. V. 62; 65

ROWAN, THOMAS
Coal: Spontaneous Combustion and Explosions Occurring in Coal Cargoes: the Treatment and Prevention. London: 1882. V. 67

ROWAN-HAMILTON, NORAH
Both Sides of the Jordan: a Woman's Adventures in the Near East. London: 1928. V. 65

ROWE, ELIZABETH
Friendship in Death: in Twenty Letters. London: 1745. V. 63
Friendship in Death: In Twenty Letters. N.P. 1750. V. 64
The Miscellaneous Works in Prose and Verse of.... London: 1739. V. 62; 65

ROWE, GEORGE
Picturesque Scenery of Hastings, and Its Vicinity, Sketched from Nature and Drawn on Stone. Hastings: 1823-1825. V. 62; 67

ROWE, GEORGE S.
A Flower from Freejee. A Memoir of Mary Calvert. London: 1857. V. 65

ROWE, JEREMY
Photographers in Arizona 1850-1920: a History and Directory. Nevada City: 1997. V. 63

ROWE, MIKE
Chicago Breakdown. London: 1973. V. 65

ROWE, NATHANIEL
The Tragedy of Jane Shore. London: 1714. V. 66

ROWE, NICHOLAS
Tamerlane. London: 1703. V. 62

ROWE, WALTER WHEAT
The History of the Baptists of Greensboro, N.C. with Particular Reference to the Work and Growth of the First Baptist Church 1850-1926. Greensboro: 1926. V. 67

ROWELL, GALEN
Alaska: Images of the Country. San Francisco: 1981. V. 63
The Vertical World of Yosemite: a Collection of Writings and Photographs on Rock Climbing in Yosemite. Berkeley: 1974. V. 63

ROWFANT CLUB
Bibliographical Notes on a Collection of Editions of the Book Known as Puckle's Club; from the Library of a Member of the Rowfant Club, as Shown at the Club House, March 1896. Cleveland: 1899. V. 63

ROWLAND Ward's Records of Big Game. London: 1969. V. 67
ROWLAND Ward's Records of Big Game. London: 1971. V. 67

ROWLAND, AMY F.
The Thyroid Clinics of George W. Crile and Associates. Philadelphia: 1922. V. 63
The Thyroid Gland. Clinics of George W. Crile and Associates. Philadelphia: 1922. V. 63; 65

ROWLAND, BENJAMIN
The Wall Paintings of India, Central Asia and Ceylon, a Comparative Study. Boston: 1938. V. 67

ROWLAND, DUNBAR
History of Mississippi. Heart of the South. Volumes 1 and 2. Chicago: 1925. V. 64
The Official and Statistical Register of the State of Mississippi 1908. Nashville: 1908. V. 64

ROWLAND, ERON
Andrew Jackson's Campaign Against the British or the Mississippi Territory in the War of 1812. New York: 1926. V. 63; 67

ROWLAND, HENRY
Physical Papers. Baltimore: 1902. V. 65

ROWLANDS, HENRY
Mona Antiqua Restaurata. An Archaeological Discourse on the Antiquities, Natural and Historical, of the Isle of Anglesey.... London: 1766. V. 64

ROWLANDS, WILLIAM
Cambrian Bibliography Containing an Account of the Books Printed in the Welsh Language or Relating to Wales.... 1869. V. 62

ROWLANDSON, THOMAS
The Amorous Illustrations of Thomas Rowlandson. London: 1969. V. 62
The Beauties of Tom Brown, Consisting of Humorous Pieces in Prose and Verse.... London: 1808. V. 63; 67
Dr. Syntax in Paris, or a Tour in Search of the Grotesque. London: 1820. V. 67
Hungarian and Highland Broad Sword. London: 1799. V. 62; 65
Loyal Volunteers of London and Environs. London: 1798-1799. V. 62
Medical Caricatures. New York: 1971. V. 66; 67
Miseries of Human Life. London: 1808. V. 63; 67
The Rhedarium For the Sale of All Sorts of Carriages, by Gregory Gigg. A New Book of Horses and Carraiges. London: 1784. V. 65
The Tour of Doctor Prosody in Search of the Antique and Picturesque through Scotland, the Hebrides, the Orkney and Shetland Isles. London: 1821. V. 67
Twelfth Night Characters. London: 1811. V. 62

ROWLEY, HUGH
Sage Stuffing for Goslingsor, Saws for the Goose and Saws for the Gander. London: 1872. V. 62

ROWLEY, RICHARD
The City of Refuge and Other Poems. London: 1917. V. 67
The Old Gods and Other Poems. 1925. V. 67
Selected Poems. 1931. V. 67

ROWLEY, WILLIAM
An Essay on the Cure of Ulcerated Legs, Without Rest, Exemplified by a Variety of Cases, in Which Laborious Exercise Was Used During the Cures. London: 1770. V. 65
An Essay on the Ophthalmia or Inflammation of the Eyes, and the Diseases of the Transparent Corena.... London: 1771. V. 65

ROWLING, J. K.
Harry Potter and the Chamber of Secrets. Bloomsbury: 1998. V. 65
Harry Potter and the Chamber of Secrets. 1999. V. 66
Harry Potter and the Goblet of Fire. New York: 2000. V. 66
Harry Potter and the Prisoner of Azkaban. London: 1999. V. 65
Harry Potter and the Prisoner of Azkaban. New York: 1999. V. 64; 67
Harry Potter and the Prisoner of Azkaban. Toronto: 1999. V. 64; 66; 67

ROWNTREE, ARTHUR
The History of Scarborough. London: 1931. V. 65

ROWS, JOHN
This Rol Was Laburd and Finishid by Master John Rows of Warrewyk. London: 1859. V. 65

ROWTON, FREDERIC
The Female Poets of Great Britain. London: 1848. V. 67

ROY, ARUNDHATI
The God of Small Things. London: 1997. V. 63; 64; 66
The God of Small Things. Toronto: 1997. V. 62; 67

ROY, BERNARD
Les Trois Papillons Roses. Paris: 1947. V. 67

ROY, BRANDON
Guy Mervyn; a Novel. London: 1891. V. 67

ROY, C. S.
On the Regulation of the Blood Supply of the Brain. 1890. V. 67

ROY, OLIVIA FITZ
The Hill War. London: 1950. V. 67
The House in the Hills. London: 1946. V. 67
The Island of Birds. London: 1954. V. 67
Steer by the Stars. London: 1944. V. 67

ROYAERD, JEAN
Homiliae in Evangelia et Epistolas Feriales Qvadragesimae. Lvgdvni: 1573. V. 63; 66

ROYAL ACADEMY OF ARTS
Exhibition of British Primitive Paintings from the Twelfth to the Early Sixteenth Century. Oxford: 1924. V. 64

ROYAL AGRICULTURAL SOCIETY
Journal. London: 1840-1845. V. 64; 66

ROYAL ASTRONOMICAL SOCIETY
Memoirs of the Royal Astronomical Society: Volume IX. London: 1836. V. 67
Memoirs. Volume XLII. 1873-1875. London: 1875. V. 67
Memoirs Volume XLVI. 1880-1881. London: 1881. V. 67
Memoirs. Volume XLVII 1882-1883. London: 1883. V. 67
Memoirs. Volume XXXI. 1863. London: 1863. V. 67

THE ROYAL Book of Sports. London: 1850. V. 66

THE ROYAL Cabinet Atlas and Compendious Universal Gazeteer of All Places in the Known World. London: 1832. V. 66

THE ROYAL Charters of Preston 1179-1974. Preston: 1979. V. 65

ROYAL COLLEGE OF PHYSICIANS
The Statutes of the Colledge (sic) of Physicians London.... London: 1693. V. 64

ROYAL GEOLOGICAL SOCIETY OF CORNWALL
Transactions. 1818. V. 62; 65

ROYAL HISTORICAL SOCIETY
Writings on British History, 1901-1933. London: 1968-1970. V. 63; 64

ROYAL HORTICULTURAL SOCIETY
Dictionary of Gardening. 1951-1959. V. 66
Dictionary of Gardening. London: 1951-1959. V. 64
Dictionary of Gardening. 1956. V. 65
Dictionary of Gardening. London: 1956. V. 62
Dictionary of Gardening.... Oxford: 1956. V. 64
The Fruit Year Book. 1947-1958. V. 64
The Fruit Year Book. London: 1947-1958. V. 67
Report of the Third International Conference, 1906 on Genetics.... London: 1907. V. 63

THE ROYAL Illuminated Book of Legends. Edinburgh: 1880. V. 62

ROYAL INSTITUTION OF GREAT BRITAIN
The Archives in Facsimile: Minutes of Managers' Meetings 1799-1903. London: 1971-1976. V. 62
A Catalogue of the Library of the Royal Institution of Great Britain. London: 1809. V. 65
The Charter. Act of Parliament and Bye Laws of the Royal Institution of Great Britain.... London: 1823. V. 66
The Prospectus, Charter, Ordinances and Bye-Laws.... London: 1800. V. 62

ROYAL IRISH ACADEMY
Transactions. Dublin: 1787. V. 65

ROYAL IRISH ART UNION
Fine Arts in Ireland. (First) Report of the Committee of Selections of the Royal Irish Art Union; or the Society for the Encouragement of the Fine Arts in Ireland, by the Purchase and Diffusion of the Works of Living Artists, for the Year 1839-1840. Dublin: 1840. V. 62

THE ROYAL Letter-Bag, Containing Epistles from Royal Personages... Relative to the Queen. London: 1820. V. 66

ROYAL Prosecutions...Impartial Considerations on the Various Prosecutions Commenced by the Attorney General, for Libels on His Majesty and the Dukes of York and Sussex, More Particularly Those Contained in Cobbett's Register, The Times, and Examiner, the. London: 1809. V. 63

ROYAL SOCIETY FOR THE PREVENTION OF CRUELTY TO ANIMALS
Cruelty to Animals. Acts of Parliament and Suggestions. London: 1880. V. 63

ROYAL SOCIETY OF ARTS
Essays on the Street Re-alignment, Reconstruction and Sanitation of Central London and on the Re-housing of the Poorer Classes. London: 1886. V. 64

ROYAL SOCIETY OF CANADA
Proceedings and Transactions of the Royal Society of Canada for the Years 1882 and 1883, Volume I - Volume XII for the Year 1894. 1883-1895. V. 65

ROYAL SOCIETY OF EDINBURGH
Transactions. London: 1832. V. 62

ROYAL SOCIETY OF LONDON
The Philosophical Transactions Abridged.... London: 1734-1756. V. 63
Philosophical Transactions of the Royal Society of London. Volume 17, 1731-1732. New York: 1963. V. 66

ROYALL, ANNIE
The Black Book; or a Continuation of Travels in the United States. Washington City: 1828. V. 63

ROYALL, WILLIAM L.
Some Reminiscences. New York: 1909. V. 62; 63; 65

ROYCE, C. C.
John Bidwell: Pioneer, Statesman, Philantropist. Chico: 1906. V. 67

ROYCE, JOSIAH
California from the Conquest in 1846 to the Second Vigilance Committee in San Francisco. Boston: 1886. V. 62; 63; 65

ROYCE, SARAH
A Frontier Lady - Recollections of the Gold Rush and Early California. New Haven: 1932. V. 65

ROY'S
Wife of Aldivalloch. To Which is Added, The Highland Plaid, Neil Gow's Farewell, John Anderson, My Jo, Maris. London: 1823. V. 65

ROYSE, JOHN
The Geology and Prehistoric Man of Castleton in the High Peak. London. V. 64; 65

ROYSTON, P.
History of Rudston: A Sketch of Its History and Antiquities.... Bridlington-Quay: 1873. V. 65

ROZAN, S. J.
China Trade. 1994. V. 65; 66
China Trade. New York: 1994. V. 66; 67
Concourse. New York: 1995. V. 67

ROZIER, FIRMIN A.
Rozier's History of the Early Settlement of the Mississippi Valley. St. Louis: 1890. V. 65

ROZIER, FRANCOIS
Introduction aux Observations sur la Physique, sur l'Histoire Naturelle et sur les Arts. (with) Observations sur la Physique, sur l'Histoire Naturelle et sur les Arts.... Paris: 1777. V. 67

ROZWADOWSKI, ZDZISLAW
50 Years of Breeding Pure Blood Arabian Horses in Poland in Their Genealogical Charts 19198-1968. Warsaw: 1972. V. 64

RUARK, ROBERT
Grenadine Etching: Her Life and Loves. Garden City: 1947. V. 67
The Horn of the Hunter. 1953. V. 63; 64
The Horn of the Hunter. 1954. V. 66; 67
I Didn't Know It Was Loaded. Garden City: 1948. V. 67
The Old Man and the Boy. New York: 1957. V. 61; 66; 67
The Old Man's Boy Grows Older. New York: 1961. V. 64; 67
One for the Road. Garden City: 1949. V. 67
Something of Value. London: 1955. V. 63
Use Enough Gun. New York: 1966. V. 64; 67
Women. New York: 1967. V. 63; 64; 66

RUARK, ROBERTS
Grenadine's Spawn. Garden City: 1952. V. 62

RUBENS, BERNICE
Madame Sousatzka. London: 1962. V. 62
Set on Edge. London: 1960. V. 63

RUBENS, PETER PAUL
Book Illustrations and Titlepages by Peter Paul Rubens. London: 1978. V. 66
La Gallerie du Palais du Luxembourg, Peinte par Rubens.... Paris: 1710. V. 64
Palazzi di Genova. Antwerp: 1622. V. 67
Selected Drawings. London and New York: 1959. V. 64

RUBENSTEIN, HELENA
Food for Beauty. New York: 1938. V. 66

RUBENSTEIN, PASACH N.
Trial of...for the Murder of Sarah Alexander, in the Town of New Lots (near Brooklyn Bridge), on the 12th day of December, 1875. New York: 1876. V. 65

RUBEUS, THEODOSIUS
Discursus Circa Literas Apostolicas in Forma Brevis S.D.M. Urbani Papae VIII. Rome: 1639. V. 65

RUBIN, JERRY
We Are Everywhere. New York: 1971. V. 67

RUBIN, LOUIS D.
Southern Renascence. The Literature of the Modern South. Baltimore: 1953. V. 62; 64

RUBINO, JANE
Death of a DJ. Aurora. 1995. V. 62

RUBINSTEIN, CHARLOTTE STREIFER
American Women Sculptors. Boston: 1990. V. 65

RUBLOWSKY, J.
Pop Art. New York: 1965. V. 62

RUBOVITS, NORMA
Marbled Vignettes. Los Angeles: 1992. V. 64

RUCKER, MAUDE A.
The Oregon Trail an Some Of It's Makers. New York: 1930. V. 66

RUCKERT, ERNST FERDINAND
Traitement Homoeopathique des maladies de la Peau.... Paris and London: 1838. V. 65

RUDD, MARY AMELIA
Records of the Rudd Family. Bristol: 1920. V. 62; 65

RUDDER, SAMUEL
The History and Antiquities of Gloucester.... Cirencester: 1781. V. 66

RUDDIMAN, THOMAS
Grammatical Exercises, on the Moods, Tenses and Syntax of the Latin Language.... Charleston: 1823. V. 66

RUDDIMAN, WALTER
A Collection of Scarce Curious and Valuable Pieces. Edinburgh: 1773. V. 66

RUDGE, ANN
Memoir. 1840. V. 64

RUDGE, BRADFORD
Views of Burghley House, Northamptonshire. Under the Patronage of, and Dedicated by Permission to, the Most Hon. the Marquis of Exeter, K.G.... London: 1842-1845. V. 62

RUDGE, M. M.
Madam Pussy Purr. London: 1910. V. 62

RUDIMENTA Grammaticae Hebraeae: ad Usum Seminarii Patavini. Vennetiis: 1681. V. 66

RUDING, WALT
An Evil Motherhood. London: 1896. V. 63

RUDISILL, RICHARD
Mirror Image: the Influence of the Daguerreotype On American Society. Albuquerque: 1971. V. 63; 65; 66

RUDOLPH, JOSEPH
Early Life and Civil War Reminiscences of Captain Joseph Rudolph. Hiram: 1941. V. 65

RUDY, W. H.
Racing in America 1960-1979. New York: 1980. V. 62

RUEHLMANN, WILLIAM
Saint With a Gun: the Unlawful American Private Eye. New York: 1974. V. 63

RUELLE, JEAN DE LA
De Natura Stirpium Libri Tres. Basel: 1537. V. 64

RUFF, SIEGFRID
Compendium of Aviation Medicine. Washington: 1942. V. 63; 65

RUFFIA, CAROLO BISCARETTI DI
Auto 1955. New York: 1954. V. 65

RUFFIN, EDMUND
Agricultural, Geological and Descriptive Sketches of Lower North Carolina. Raleigh: 1861. V. 62; 63; 65; 66
American Colonization Unveiled. Washington: 1860. V. 62
An Essay on Calcareous Manures. Shellbanks: 1835. V. 66
Report of the Commencement and Progress of the Agricultural Survey of South Carolina for 1843. Columbia: 1843. V. 63

RUFFNER, W. H.
A Report on Washington Territory. New York: 1889. V. 66

RUFINUS
The Herbal of Rufinus. Chicago: 1946. V. 66

RUFUS or the Red King. A Romance. London: 1838. V. 66

RUGGLES, ROWENA GODDING
The One Rose, Mother of the Immortal Kewpies. Albany: 1972. V. 65

RUHEMANN, HELMUT
The Cleaning of Paintings: Problems and Potentialities. London: 1968. V. 62; 65

RUHMER, ERNST
Konstruktion, Bau und Betrieb von Funkeninduktoren und Deren Anwendung, Mit Besonderer Beruckschtigung der Rontgenstrahlen-Technik.... Leipzig: 1904. V. 64

RUHRAH, JOHN
Pediatrics of the Past. New York: 1925. V. 64

RUIZ LOPEZ, HIPOLITO
Florae Peruvianae, et Chilensis Prodromus Sive Novorum Generum Plantarum Peruvianarum.... Romae: 1796. V. 65

RUKEYSER, MURIEL
A Turning Wind - Poems. New York: 1939. V. 62

RULAND, MARTIN
Synonyma Copia Graecorum Verborum Omnium Absolutiss(ima).... Augustae Vindelicorum: 1571. V. 66

RULES for the Management and Cleaning of the Rifle Musket, Model 1863 for the Use of Soldiers. Washington: 1863. V. 63

RULES of the Cheddleton Association for the Prosecution of Felons. Leek: 1859. V. 64

RULFO, JUAN
El Elano en Llamas. Mexico City: 1953. V. 67
Pedro Paramo. New York: 1959. V. 67

RUMI, JALALUDDIN MOHAMMAD
Moses and the Shepherd. New York: 1987. V. 64

RUMMONDS, RICHARD GABRIEL
Printing on the Iron Handpress. 1998. V. 62
Printing on the Iron Handpress. London: 1998. V. 67

RUMP. Or an Exact Collection of the Choycest Poems and Songs Relating to the Late Times. 1874. V. 62; 66

RUMPF, G. E.
Theasurus Imaginum Piscium Testaceorum. Leyden: 1741. V. 62

RUMPLE, JETHRO
History of Rowan County, North Carolina. Salisbury: 1881. V. 63; 66

RUMSEY, JAMES
A Short Treatise on the Application of Steam Whereby is Clearly Shewn, from Actual Experiments, that Steam May be Applied to Propel Boats or Vessels of any Burthen Against Rapid Currents with Great Velocity. Philadelphia: 1788. V. 64

RUNCIMAN, STEVEN
Byzantine Civilisation. London: 1933. V. 65
A History of the Crusades. Cambridge: 1957. V. 64

RUNDALL, L. B.
The Ibex of Sha-Ping and Other Himalayan Studies. 1915. V. 62; 63; 64; 66; 67
The Ibex of Sha-Ping and Other Himalayan Studies. London: 1915. V. 62; 67

RUNDELL, MARIA ELIZA KETELBY
American Domestic Cookery. New York: 1823. V. 66; 67
The New Family Receipt Book.... London: 1824. V. 63
A New System of Domestic Cookery. Boston: 1807. V. 63
A New System of Domestic Cookery. Philadelphia: 1810. V. 63
A New System of Domestic Cookery. London: 1816. V. 62
A New System of Domestic Cookery. London: 1823. V. 67
A New System of Domestic Cookery. London: 1824. V. 63
New System of Domestic Cookery. London: 1829. V. 64
A New System of Domestic Cookery. London: 1830. V. 62
A New System of Domestic Cookery. London: 1840. V. 62
A New System of Domestic Cookery. Halifax: 1854. V. 66
A New System of Domestic Cookery. London: 1860. V. 67
New System of Domestic Cookery. London: 1865. V. 64; 67

RUNDLE, THOMAS
A Sermon Preached at St. George Church, Hanover Square, on Sunday, February 17, 1734. London: 1734. V. 63

RUNDQVIST, D. V.
Precambrian Geology of the U.S.S.R. Amsterdam: 1993. V. 67

RUNYON, DAMON
All Horse Players Die Broke. N.P: 1946. V. 63
Guys and Dolls. New York: 1931. V. 63
In Our Town. New York: 1946. V. 65
My Old Man. New York: 1939. V. 66
Runyon from First to Last. London: 1954. V. 63; 64

RUPERT, CHARLES G.
Apostle Spoons. London: 1929. V. 66

RUPORT, ARCH
The Art of Cockfighting. New York: 1949. V. 63; 64

RUPP, I. DANIEL
A Collection of Upwards of Thirty Thousand Names of German, Swiss, Dutch, French and Other Immigrants in Pennsylvania from 1727 to 1776. Philadelphia: 1880. V. 65
He Pasa Ekklesia. An Original History of the Religious Denominations at Present Existing in the United States. Philadelphia: 1844. V. 63

RUPRECHT, J. B. BALAZS
Catalogue of Star Clusters and Associatons: Supplement 1, Parts B1 and B2. Budapest: 1981. V. 66

RUSCA, LUIGI
Raccolta dei Disegni...Recueil des Dessins de Differens Batimens Construits a Saint Petersbourg, et dans l'Interieur de l'Empire de Russie. St. Petersburg: 1810. V. 67

RUSCHA, EDWARD
Colored People. Hollywood: 1972. V. 65
Crackers. Hollywood: 1969. V. 63; 65
Every Building on the Sunset Strip. Los Angeles: 1966. V. 66
A Few Palm Trees. Hollywood: 1971. V. 65
Hard Light. Hollywood: 1978. V. 65
I Don't Want No Retro Spective: The Works of Edward Ruscha. New York and San Francisco: 1982. V. 66
Nine Swimming Pools and a Broken Glass. N.P: 1968. V. 65; 66; 67
Royal Road Test. Los Angeles: 1967. V. 65
Some Los Angeles Apartments. Los Angeles: 1970. V. 65
Thirtyfour Parking Lots in Los Angeles. Los Angeles: 1974. V. 66
Twenty-six Gasoline Stations. Alhambra: 1969. V. 65; 66
Various Small Fires and Milk. 1964. V. 66; 67
Various Small Fires and Milk. Los Angeles: 1970. V. 65

RUSCHENBERGER, W. S. W.
Three Years in the Pacific: Including Brazil, Bolivia and Chile. Philadelphia: 1834. V. 66

RUSCONI, GIOVANNI ANTONIO
I Dieci Libri d'Architettura...Secondo i Precetti di Vetruvio.... Venice: 1660. V. 62

RUSCONI, M.
Amours des Salamandres Aquatiques. Milan: 1821. V. 62

RUSH, BENJAMIN
Benjamin Rush's Lectures on the Mind. Philadelphia: 1981. V. 65
Medical Inquiries and Observations. Philadelphia: 1809. V. 62
Medical Inquiries and Observations. Philadelphia: 1827. V. 62
Medical Inquiries and Observations Upon the Diseases of the Mind. Philadelphia: 1812. V. 65
Medical Inquiries and Observations Upon the Diseases of the Mind. Philadelphia: 1830. V. 66

RUSH, BENJAMIN continued
Medical Inquiries and Observations Upon the Diseases of the Mind. Philadelphia: 1835. V. 65

RUSH, CAROLINE
The North and South, or Slavery and Its Contrasts. Philadelphia: 1852. V. 67

RUSH, JAMES
Hamlet; a Dramtic Prelude; in Five Acts. Philadelphia: 1834. V. 66
The Philosophy of the Human Voice; Embracing Its Physiological History; Together With a System of Principles.... Philadelphia: 1833. V. 62; 64

RUSH, JOHN
The Hand-Book to Veterinary Homeopathy; or, the Homoeopathic Tratment of the Horse, the Ox, the Sheep, the Dog and the Swine. Philadelphia: 1858. V. 66

RUSH, NORMAN
Mating. New York: 1991. V. 64; 67
Whites. London: 1986. V. 63
Whites. New York: 1986. V. 64; 65; 67

RUSH, OSCAR B.
The Open Range and Bunk House Philosophy. Colorado: 1930. V. 64; 67

RUSH, RICHARD
Collection of Letters on Freemasonry, in Chronological Order. Boston: 1849. V. 64
A Residence at the Court of London. London: 1833. V. 65

RUSHDIE, SALMAN
East, West. London: 1994. V. 62; 63; 66; 67
Good Advice is Rarer than Rubies. New York: 1995. V. 67
Grimus. London: 1975. V. 62
Grimus. Woodstock: 1979. V. 67
The Ground Beneath Her Feet. London: 1999. V. 67
Haroun and the Sea of Stories. London: 1990. V. 62; 64
Imaginary Homelands. London: 1991. V. 62; 63
Midnight's Children. New York: 1980. V. 67
Midnight's Children. London: 1981. V. 62; 63; 65
Midnight's Children. New York: 1981. V. 66
The Moor's Last Sigh. London: 1995. V. 62; 63; 64; 67
The Moor's Last Sigh. New York: 1995. V. 65
The Moor's Last Sigh. New York: 1996. V. 62
The Satanic Verses. London: 1988. V. 62; 63; 64; 66
The Satanic Verses. New York: 1988. V. 62; 63; 64; 66; 67
The Satanic Verses. New York: 1989. V. 62; 64; 66; 67
Shame. London: 1983. V. 62; 66; 67
Two Stories. London: 1989. V. 64; 67

RUSHTON, EDWARD
Poems and Other Writings. London: 1824. V. 62; 65

RUSHWORTH, JOHN
Historical Collection of Private Passages of State. London: 1659. V. 67
Historical Collection of Private Passages of State. London: 1721. V. 62; 67
The Tryal of Thomas Earl of Strafford...Upon an Impeachment of High Treason by the Commons Then Assembled in Parliament. London: 1680. V. 65
The Tryal of Thomas Earl of Strafford...Upon an Impeachment of High Treason by the Commons then Assembled in Parliament.... London: 1700. V. 63

RUSK, RALPH LESLIE
The Literature of the Middle Western Frontier. New York: 1925. V. 65

RUSKIN, JOHN
Ariadne Florentina. Six Lectures on Wood and Metal Engraving. London: 1876. V. 66
Cambridge School of Art. Mr. Ruskin's Inaugural Address. Delivered at Cambridge, Oct. 29, 1858. Cambridge: 1858. V. 63
The Elements of Drawing; in Three Letters to Beginners. London: 1857. V. 62; 63; 67
The Elements of Perspective Arranged for the Use of Schools and Intended to be Read in Connection with the first three Books of Euclid. London: 1859. V. 67
The Ethics of the Dust: Ten Lectures to Little Housewives on the Elements of Crystallisation. London: 1866. V. 67
Fors Clavigera. Letters to the Workmen and Labourers of Great Britain. London: 1872-1895. V. 65
Fors Clavigera.... London: 1899-1907-1896. V. 65
General Statement Explaining the Nature and Purposes of St. George's Guild. Sunnyside, Orpington, Kent: 1882. V. 62
Hortus Inclusus. Messages from the Wood to the Garden, Sent in Happy Days to the Sister Ladies of the Thwaite, Coniston, by Their Thankful Friend. Orpington: 1887. V. 65
The King of the Golden River. London: 1932. V. 62; 63
The King of the Golden River. Philadelphia: 1932. V. 63
The King of the Golden River. London: 1939. V. 66; 67
Lectures on Architecture and Painting. New York: 1854. V. 64
Letters from John Ruskin to Ernest Chesneau. London: 1894. V. 64; 65
Letters from John Ruskin to Rev. F. A. Malleson. London: 1896. V. 63
Letters on Art and Literature. London: 1894. V. 63; 64
Letters to M.G. and H.G. London: 1903. V. 65
Modern Painters. London: 1844. V. 65
Modern Painters. London: 1873. V. 63
Modern Painters. London: 1888. V. 64
Munera Pulveris, Essays on Political Economy. London: 1871. V. 66
The Nature of Gothic. Hammersmith: 1892. V. 67
Notes by Mr. Ruskin on His Collection of Drawings by the Late J. W. M. Turner. London: 1878. V. 63
Notes on the General Principles of Employment for the Destitute and Criminal Classes. N.P: 1868. V. 62
On the Nature of Gothic Architecture; and Herein of the True Functions of the Workman in Art. London: 1854. V. 64
Praeterita. Outlines of Scenes and Thoughts Perhaps Worthy of Memory in My Past Life. Orpington: 1886-1889. V. 63
Pre-Raphaelitism. London: 1851. V. 62; 65
St. Mark's Rest. The History of Venice. 1877. V. 67
Salsette and Elephanta. Oxford: 1839. V. 62; 64
Sesame and Lilies. London: 1865. V. 63
The Seven Lamps of Architecture. London: 1855. V. 66
The Stones of Venice. London: 1851-1853. V. 62
The Stones of Venice. London: 1874-1886. V. 65
The Stones of Venice. London: 1898. V. 66
Stray Letters...to a London Bibliophile. London: 1892. V. 64
Studies in Both Arts: Being Ten Subjects Drawn and Described. Orpington & London: 1895. V. 62; 63; 64
Three Letters and an Essay on Literature. London: 1893. V. 64; 65
Unto This Last. London: 1862. V. 64; 65
Unto This Last. London: 1902. V. 62; 65
Unto This Last. Hammersmith: 1907. V. 65
Verona and Other Lectures. Orpington: 1894. V. 65
War. A Lecture Delivered at the Royal Military Academy, Woolwich. London: 1866. V. 65
The Works. London: 1879-1895. V. 67

RUSS, CAROLYN H.
The Log of a Forty-Niner. Boston: 1923. V. 63; 66

RUSS, K.
The Speaking Parrots; a Scientific Manual. London: 1895. V. 63; 67

RUSSEL, CHARLES E. B.
Working Lads' Clubs. London: 1908. V. 63

RUSSELL, A.
The Salmon. 1864. V. 67

RUSSELL, ADDISON PEALE
Sub-Coelum: a Sky-Built Human World. Boston and New York: 1893. V. 62

RUSSELL, ALAN
No Sign of Murder. New York: 1990. V. 66

RUSSELL, ANDY
Horns in the High Country. 1973. V. 67

RUSSELL, ARCHIBALD G. B.
The Engravings of William Blake. Boston: 1912. V. 66

RUSSELL, BERTRAND
The Analysis of Matter. London: 1927. V. 64
The Autobiography. London: 1967-1969. V. 63; 64; 66
History of the World in Epitome. London: 1962. V. 64
Introduction to Mathematical Philosophy. London. V. 67
Mysticism and Logic. 1929. V. 66
Philosophical Essays. London: 1910. V. 62
The Policy of the Entente 1904-1914. London. V. 64
Principia Mathematica. Cambridge: 1910-1927. V. 66
Scientific Method in Philosophy; the Herbert Spencer Lecture Delivered at the Museum 18 November 1914. Oxford: 1914. V. 63

RUSSELL, C. E. M.
Bullet and Shot in Indian Forest, Plain and Hill. 1900. V. 67

RUSSELL, CARL P.
Firearms, Traps and Tools of the Mountain Men. New York: 1967. V. 64; 67
Guns on the Early Frontiers. Berkeley: 1957. V. 63; 66

RUSSELL, CHARLES E.
The Greatest Trust in the World. New York: 1905. V. 63

RUSSELL, CHARLES MARION
Back Trailing On the Old Frontier. Great Falls: 1922. V. 64; 67
Good Medicine - The Illustrated Letter Of.... Garden City: 1930. V. 64; 65
More Rawhides. Great Falls: 1925. V. 62; 65
More Rawhides. Pasadena: 1946. V. 66
Paper Talk: Illustrated Letters of Charles M. Russell. Fort Worth: 1962. V. 65
Pen and Ink Drawings Book 1 and 2. Pasadena: 1946. V. 64; 67
Rawhide Rawlins Rides Again Or, Behind Swinging Doors. Pasadena: 1948. V. 64; 67
Rawhide Rawlins Stories. Pasadena: 1946. V. 65; 66
Studies of Western Life. Spokane: 1909. V. 63
Trails Plowed Under. Garden City: 1927. V. 64
Trails Plowed Under. New York: 1927. V. 62; 65

RUSSELL, DAVID H.
Our Big Red Story Book. Boston: 1957. V. 62

RUSSELL, DON
One Hundred and Three Fights and Skirmishes - the Story of General Reuben F. Bernard. Washington: 1936. V. 64; 67

RUSSELL, DORA
Beneath the Wave: a Novel. London: 1878. V. 65

RUSSELL, E. S.
The Interpretation of Development and Heredity. Oxford: 1930. V. 67

RUSSELL, ERIC FRANK
Deep Space. Reading: 1954. V. 63

RUSSELL, F.
Explorations in the Far North. Ames: 1898. V. 66

RUSSELL, F. STANLEY
Letters of F. Stanley Russell. Baltimore: 1963. V. 63

RUSSELL, FRANK
Nouveau Architecture. New York: 1979. V. 62; 65

RUSSELL, FREDERICK S.
The Seas. London: 1975. V. 62

RUSSELL, GEORGE WILLIAM
By Still Waters, Lyrical Poems Old and New. Dundrum, Dublin: 1906. V. 64
Dark Weeping. London: 1929. V. 62; 65; 67
The Divine Vision and Other Poems. 1903. V. 65
The Divine Vision and Other Poems. New York: 1904. V. 63; 66
Enchantment and Other Poems. New York: 1930. V. 62; 65; 66
A Gold Standard for Literature. Norton: 1939. V. 67
Letters from A.E. 1961. V. 67
Midsummer Eve. New York: 1928. V. 62; 67
Some Passages from the Letters of A. E. to W. B. Yeats. Dublin: 1936. V. 62; 64; 65
Thoughts for a Convention. 1917. V. 67
Thoughts for a Convention. Dublin and Ireland: 1917. V. 64

RUSSELL, HAROLD
Chalkstream and Moorland. London: 1911. V. 67

RUSSELL, HENRY R.
An Illustrated History of Our War with Spain: Its Causes, Incidents and Results. Hartford: 1898. V. 67

RUSSELL, ISRAEL C.
Volcanoes of North America, A Reading Lesson for Students of Geography and Geology. New York: 1904. V. 62

RUSSELL, J. H.
Cattle on the Conejo. New York: 1957. V. 67

RUSSELL, JOHN
Adventures in the Moon, and Other Worlds. London: 1836. V. 65
Alfred Barton; the Absent. London: 1858. V. 67
Don Carlos; or Persecution. London: 1822. V. 67
Instructions for the Drill and the Method of Performing the Eighteen Manoeuvres. Philadelphia: 1814. V. 66
The Life of William Lord Russell, with Some Account of the Times in Which He Lived. London: 1820. V. 67
Max Ernst: Life and Work. New York: 1967. V. 62; 63; 64; 65; 66
Seurat. London: 1965. V. 63
A Tour in Germany and Some of the Southern Provinces of the Austrian Empire. Edinburgh: 1825. V. 63

RUSSELL, L. B.
Granddad's Autobiography. Comanche: 1927-1930. V. 64; 67

RUSSELL, LEONARD
The Saturday Book. London: 1944. V. 67

RUSSELL, M.
Polynesia: or an Historical Account of the Principal Islands in the South Sea Including New Zealand. Edinburgh: 1842?. V. 63

RUSSELL, OSBOURNE
Journal of a Trapper 1834-1943. Boise: 1921. V. 63; 66
Journal of a Trapper 1834-1943. Portland: 1955. V. 64

RUSSELL, PETER
Picnic to the Moon - Poems. London: 1944. V. 64

RUSSELL, R. B.
The Tribes and Castes of the Central Provinces of India. Oosterhout: 1969. V. 62

RUSSELL, R. V.
Central Provinces District Gazetteers, Sangor District. Allahabad: 1907. V. 63

RUSSELL, RACHEL WRIOTHESLEY VAUGHAN, LADY
Letters.... London: 1801. V. 67
Some Account of the Life...Followed by a Series of Letters...to Her Husband, William Lord Russell.... London: 1819. V. 63

RUSSELL, RICHARD
A Dissertation on the Use of Sea-Water in the Diseases of Glands, Particularly The Scurvy, Jaundice, Kings-Evil, Leprosy and the Glandular Consumption.... London: 1752. V. 62; 65
The Oeconomy of Nature in the Acute Diseases of the Glands. London: 1755. V. 62; 66

RUSSELL, ROSS
Bird Lives! The High Life and Hard Times of Charlie (Yardbird) Parker. New York: 1973. V. 63; 64; 65

RUSSELL, W. H.
A Memorial of the Marriage of HRH Albert Edward Prince of Wales and HRH Alexandra Princess of Denmark. London: 1863. V. 66
The War from the Death of Lord Raglan to the Evacuation of the Crimea. London: 1856. V. 66
The Wedding at Windsor. A Memorial of the Marriage of H.R.H. Albert Edward Prince of Wales and H.R.H. Alexandra Princess of Denmark. London: 1864. V. 62

RUSSELL, W. RITCHIE
Traumatic Aphasia: a Study of Aphasia in War Wounds of the Brain. London: 1961. V. 65

RUSSELL, WILLIAM
Address on Infant Schools: Delivered at the Request of the Managers of the Infant School Society. Boston: 1829. V. 66
The History of Modern Europe, with an Account of the Decline and Fall of the Roman Empire.... London: 1805-1810. V. 67

RUSSELL, WILLIAM CLARK
The Emigrant Ship. London: 1894?. V. 66
A Marriage at Sea. London: 1891. V. 66
Master Rockafellar's Voyage. London: 1891. V. 66
Memoirs of Mrs. Laetitia Boothby. London: 1872. V. 66
An Ocean Free-Lance. From a Privateersman's Log, 1812. London: 1882. V. 67
What Cheer!. London: 1896. V. 66

RUSSELL, WILLIAM HOWARD
My Diary North and South. Boston: 1863. V. 62

RUSSELL, WILLIAM O.
A Treatise on Crimes and Misdemeanors. Philadelphia: 1845. V. 66

RUSSO, RICHARD
Mohawk. New York: 1986. V. 63; 66
Nobody's Fool. New York: 1993. V. 67
The Risk Pool. New York: 1988. V. 66

RUSSOM, J.
A Word to the Working Classes on Their Improvement (With Other Pieces). London: 1850. V. 67

RUST, BRIAN
The Complete Entertainment Discography. New Rochelle: 1973. V. 67
Jazz Records 1897-1942. New Rochelle: 1978. V. 63

RUTGERS, A.
Encyclopaedia of Aviculture. London and Poole: 1970-1977. V. 64; 65; 66

RUTHERFORD, A. W.
Hints from Holland; or, Gold Buillion as Dear in Dutch Currency as in Bank-Notes... (and) Hints from Holland, Part the Second; or the Influences of the Continental Ratios of the Coinage of England. London: 1811. V. 65

RUTHERFORD, ERNEST
Radiations from Radioactive Substances. Cambridge: 1930. V. 64
Radio-Activity. Cambridge: 1904. V. 62
Radioactive Substances and Their Radiations. Cambridge: 1913. V. 62; 64; 65; 66

RUTHERFORD, JOHN
Rutherford's Border Hand Book.... Kelso: 1849. V. 62

RUTHERFORTH, THOMAS
A System of Natural Philosophy, Being the Lectures in Mechanics, Optics, Hydrostatics, and Astronomy.... Cambridge: 1748. V. 65

RUTKOW, I. M.
The History of Surgery In the United States 1775-1900. San Francisco: 1988. V. 64; 66

RUTLAND, JOHN HENRY, DUKE OF
Correspondence Between....William Pitt and Charles, Duke of Rutland, Lord Lieutenant of Ireland. 1781-1787. 1890. V. 65
A Tour through Part of Belgium and the Rhenish Provinces. London: 1822. V. 62

RUTLEDGE, ARCHIBALD
The Beauty of the Night. New York: 1967. V. 64
Collected Poems. Charleston: 1925. V. 67
Deep River. Columbia: 1960. V. 63
The Everlasting Light and Other Poems. Athens: 1949. V. 64; 67
Fireworks in the Peafield Corner. Clinton: 1986. V. 65
God's Children. Indianapolis & New York: 1947. V. 65
The Hearts of the Citadel and Other Poems. Richmond: 1953. V. 64
Home by the River. Indianapolis and New York: 1941. V. 64; 67
Hunter's Choice. West Hartford: 1946. V. 63
Old Plantation Days. New York: 1921. V. 64
Peace in the Heart. New York: 1930. V. 64; 67
Plantation Game Trails. Boston & New York: 1921. V. 64; 65
Poems in Honor of South Carolina Tricentennial. Columbia: 1970. V. 67
The World Around Hampton. New York: 1960. V. 64

RUTLEDGE, MARYSE
The Silver Peril. New York: 1931. V. 67

RUTTEN, M. G.
The Geology of Western Europe. Amsterdam: 1969. V. 63; 66

RUTTENBER, E. M.
History of Orange County, New York, With Illustrations and Biographical Sketches of Many of Its Pioneers and Prominent Men. Philadelphia: 1881. V. 64
History of the Town of New Windsor, Orange County, New York. Newburgh: 1911. V. 65

RUTTER, JOAN
Here's Flowers: an Anthology of Flower Poems. Waltham St. Lawrence: 1937. V. 65

RUTTER, JOHN
Delineations of Fonthill and Its Abbey. Shaftesbury: 1823. V. 62; 67
Delineations of the North West Division of Somerset. Shaftesbury: 1829. V. 62; 67

RUTTER, OWEN
The Monster of Mu. London: 1932. V. 65
Tiadatha. London. V. 67
We Happy Few. Waltham St. Lawrence: 1946. V. 62; 63; 66

RUTTLEDGE, HUGH
Everest 1933. London: 1934. V. 63; 65; 66
Everest: The Unfinished Adventure. 1937. V. 63; 65
Everest: the Unfinished Adventure. London: 1937. V. 63; 64

RUTTLEDGE, R. F.
Ireland's Birds. 1966. V. 67
Ireland's Birds: Their Distribution and Migrations. 1967. V. 65

RUTTY, JOHN
A Spiritual Diary, and Soliloquies. 1796. V. 62; 65

RUXTON, GEORGE FREDERICK
Adventures in Mexico and the Rocky Mountains. New York: 1848. V. 63; 64
Life in the Far West. Edinburgh: 1849. V. 63; 64
Ruxton of the Rockies. Norman: 1950. V. 67

RUYSCH, FREDERIK
Adversariorum Anatomico-Medico-Chirurgicorum Decas Prima (-Tertia).... Amsterdam: 1715-1720. V. 62

RYALL, E. CANNY
Operative Cystoscopy. London: 1925. V. 65

RYAN, ABRAM J.
Father Ryan's Poems. Mobile: 1879. V. 64

RYAN, ANDREW
News from Fort Craig, New Mexico, 1863: Civil War Letters of Andrew Ryan, with the California Column. Santa Fe: 1966. V. 64

RYAN, CORNELIUS
Conquest of the Moon. New York: 1953. V. 66

RYAN, DESMOND
The Invisible Army: A Story of Michael Collins. London: 1932. V. 63; 66
Remembering Sion. 1934. V. 67

RYAN, G. S.
The Cancellations of Hungarin Post Offices on the First Issue of Hungary 1867-1871. 1988. V. 67

RYAN, JOHN
Irish Monasticism, Origins and Early Development. 1931. V. 65

RYAN, MICHAEL
The Philosophy of Marriage, in Its Social, Moral and Physical Relations. London: 1839. V. 64
The Philosophy of Marriage, in Its Social, Moral and Physical Relations. Paris: 1839. V. 65
Threats Instead of Trees. New Haven & London: 1974. V. 62

RYAN, NOLAN
Nolan Ryan's Pitcher's Bible. New York: 1991. V. 66; 67

RYAN, THOMAS F.
The London Company of Virginia: a Brief Account of Its Transactions in Colonizing Virginia. New York & London: 1908. V. 65

RYAN, WILLIAM P.
Literary London, Its Lights and Comedies. London: 1898. V. 67

RYAN, WILLIAM REDMOND
Personal Adventures in Upper and Lower California in 1848-1849. London: 1850. V. 65; 67

RYCE, JOHN
The Rector of Amcoty. London: 1891. V. 65

RYDEN, S.
Andean Excavations. 1957. V. 62

RYDER, H. P.
Cycling and Shooting Knickerbocker Stockings. London: 1902. V. 63

RYDER, JOHN
Six on the Black Art. London. V. 62

RYDER, JONATHAN
Trevayne. New York: 1973. V. 66

RYE, ANTHONY
Gilbert White and His Selborne. London: 1970. V. 62

RYE, E. C.
British Beetles: an Introduction to the Study of Our Indigenous Coleoptera. London: 1866. V. 62

RYE, EDGAR
The Quirt and the Spur, Vanishing Shadows of the Texas Frontier. Chicago: 1909. V. 62

RYE, GEORGE
A Treatise Against the Nonconforming Nonjurors. London: 1719. V. 66

RYE, GRAHAM
The James Bond Girls. London: 1995. V. 67

RYERSON, EGERTON
The Loyalists of America and Their Times: from 1620 to 1816. Toronto: 1880. V. 67

RYERSON, LOUIS JOHNES
The Genealogy of the Ryerson Family in America. 1646-1902. New York: 1902. V. 66

RYLAND, ELIZABETH H.
King William Co., Virginia, From Old Newspapers and Files. Richmond: 1955. V. 63; 67

RYLANDS, GEORGE
A Distraction of Wits Nutured in Elizabethan Cambridge.... Cambridge: 1958. V. 62

RYLANDS, JOHN PAUL
The Visitation of Cheshire in the Year 1580, Made by Robert Glover, Somerset Herald, for William Flower.... 1882. V. 63

RYLE, GILBERT
The Concept of Mind. London: 1949. V. 67

RYMES of the Minstrels. Shaftesbury: 1927. V. 67

RYNNE, ETIENNE
North Munster Studies: Essays in Commemoration of Monsignor Michael Molony. 1967. V. 64

RYUS, WILLIAM HENRY
The Second William Penn: a True Account of Incidents that Happened Along the Old Santa Fe Trail in the Sixties. Kansas City: 1913. V. 64; 67

RYVES, BRUNO
Anglia Ruina; or, England's Ruine, Represented in the Barbarous and Sacrilegious Outrages of the Sectaries of the Kingdome.... 1647. V. 64; 67
Anglia Ruina; or, Englands Ruine, Represented in the Barbarous and Sacrilegious Outrages of the Sectaries of This Kingdome.... London: 1647. V. 65
Mercurius Rusticus; or, the Countries Complaint of the Barbarous Out-Rages Committed by the Sectaries of this Late Flourishing Kingdome.... London: 1646. V. 64
Mercurius Rusticus; or, the Countries Complaint of the Barbarous Outrages Commited by the Sectaries of this Late Flourishing Kingdom. London: 1685. V. 64

S

S., A.
The Last Dying Speech and Confession, Birth, Parentage and Education, Life, Character and Behaviour, of Mr. Alderman S-; Together With a Copy of a Very Pentient Letter That He Sent to His Late Masters This Morning. N.P: 1780. V. 65

S., E.
The Godmother's Tales. London: 1808. V. 63

S., T.
A Faithful Account of the Sickness, Death and Burial of Capt. William Bedlow, who Dyed August 20th and was Buried August the 22d 1680. London: 1680. V. 65

SAABYE, SVEND
Lysttisker Liv. 1981. V. 67

SABARTES, JAIME
Picasso Toreros. New York: 1961. V. 65

SABATIER, WILLIAM
Letter to Robert Peel, Esq. MP. London?: 1796. V. 63

SABATO, ERNESTO
On Heroes and Tombs. Boston: 1981. V. 67
Uno y el Universo. Buenos Aires: 1945. V. 67

SABATTINI, GIAMBATTISTA
Tavola Anatomiche per li Pittori e Gli Scultori. Bologna: 1814. V. 65

SABBAG, ROBERT
Snowblind. Indianapolis and New York: 1976. V. 65
Snowblind. Edinburgh: 1998. V. 66

SABELLICO, MARCANTONIO
Croniche che Tractano de la Origine de Veneti, e del Principio da la Cita. Milan: 1510?. V. 62

SABIN, EDWARD
Kit Carson Days. Chicago: 1914. V. 64

SABIN, EDWIN L.
Kit Carson Days, Adventures in the Path of Empire. New York: 1935. V. 66
Wild Men of the Wild West. New York: 1929. V. 67

SABIN, ELIJAH R.
The Life of Reflections of Charles Observator: In Which is Displayed the Real Characters of Human Life. Boston: 1816. V. 66

SABIN, JOSEPH
Dictionary of Books Relating to America From Its Discovery to the Present Time. 1998. V. 65

SABINE, LORENZO
Biographical Sketches of Loyalists of the American Revolution, with an Historical Essay. Boston: 1864. V. 67

SACCO, LUIGI
Trattao Di Vaccinzaione con Osservazioni sul Giavardo e Vajuolo Pecorino. Milano: 1809. V. 66

SACHAR, LOUIS
Holes. New York: 1998. V. 65

SACHS, BERNARD
Nervous & Mental Disorders from Birth through Adolescence. New York: 1926. V. 65

SACHS, ERNEST
The Care of the Neurosurgical Patient, Before, During and After Operation. St. Louis: 1945. V. 65
The History and Development of Neurological Surgery. New York: 1952. V. 64; 67

SACHS, J. VON
History of Botany (1530-1860). Oxford: 1906. V. 65

SACKEN, C. R. OSTEN
Catalogue of the Described Diptera of North America. Wasington: 1868. V. 65

SACKHEIM, ERIC
The Silent Zero, in Search of Sound.... New York: 1968. V. 63; 64; 66

SACKS, B.
Be It Enacted: the Creation and the Territory of Arizona. Phoenix: 1964. V. 67

SACKS, JEN
Nice. New York: 1998. V. 67

SACKS, OLIVER
Seeing Voices. Berkeley: 1989. V. 67

SACKVILLE, GEORGE
The Trial of...Lord George Sackville, at a Court-Martial, Held at Horse Guards, Feb. 29, 1760, for an Enquiry into His Conduct, Being Charged with Disobedience of Orders, While he Commanded the British Horse in Germany, Together with His Defence.... London: 1760. V. 66

SACKVILLE-WEST, EDWARD
The Rescue - a Melodrama for Broadcasting Based on Homer's Odyssey. London: 1945. V. 64

SACKVILLE-WEST, REGINALD WINDSOR
Historical Notices of the Parish of Withyham in the County of Sussex.... London: 1857. V. 64

SACKVILLE-WEST, VICTORIA MARY
All Passion Spent. London: 1931. V. 67
Aphra Ben. London: 1927. V. 67
Berkeley Castle - an Illustrated Survey of the Gloucestershire Home of Captain R. G. Berkeley. London: 1950?. V. 63
Country Notes. 1939. V. 67
The Dark Island. London: 1934. V. 63; 65

SACKVILLE WEST, VICTORIA MARY
Daughter of France - the Life of Anne Marie Louise d'Orleans Duchesse de Montpensier 1627-1693. London: 1959. V. 65

SACKVILLE-WEST, VICTORIA MARY
The Dragon in Shallow Waters. London: 1921. V. 65
The Eagle and the Dove--a Study in Contrasts--St.Teresa of Avila--St. Therese of Lisieux. London: 1943. V. 65
Faces. Profiles of Dogs. London: 1961. V. 64
Family History. London: 1932. V. 63
The Garden. London: 1946. V. 63
Grey Wethers - a Romantic Novel. London: 1923. V. 64; 67
Heritage. London: 1919. V. 62
Knole and the Sackvilles. London: 1922. V. 62; 64; 66
The Land. London: 1926. V. 63
The Letters of Vita Sackville-West to Virginia Woolf. London: 1984. V. 63
The Marie Curie Hospital. London: 1946. V. 63
More for Your Garden. London: 1955. V. 62
No Signposts in the Sea. London: 1961. V. 64
Orchard and Vineyard. London: 1921. V. 64; 65
Passenger to Teheran. London: 1926. V. 63
Poems of West and East. London: 1917. V. 65
Solitude - a Poem. London: 1938. V. 62; 66
Twelve Days - An Account of a Journey Across the Bakhtiari Mountains in South-Western Persia. London: 1928. V. 63; 64
The Women's Land Army. London: 1944. V. 64

SACROBOSCO, JOHANNES DE
Sphaera...Emendata Eliae Vineti...Scholia. Venice: 1569. V. 62

SADDLEBAGS, JEREMIAH
Journey to the Gold Diggins. 1950. V. 66

SADE, DONATIEN ALPHONSE FRANCOIS, COMTE, CALLED MARQUIS DE
Les 120 Journees de Sodome. Paris (Berlin): 1904. V. 64

SA DE MIRANDA, FRANCISCO DE
As Obras...Agora de Nuouo Impressas Com a relacaeo de Sua Calidade, e Vida. Lisbon: 1614. V. 62

SA'DI
Tales from the Gulistan. London: 1928. V. 65

SADLEIR, MICHAEL
The Anchor: a Love Story. New York: 1920. V. 63
Anthony Trollope and His Publishers. London: 1924. V. 63
Archdeacon Francis Wrangham 1769-1842. London: 1937. V. 63; 65
Bagatelles (These Foolish Things). Paris: 1949. V. 63
Bentley's Standard Novel Series: Its History and Achievement. Colophon: 1932. V. 65
Bibliography of the First Editions of the Prose Works of Herman Melville. London: 1923. V. 65
Blessington D'Orsay: a Masquerade. London: 1933. V. 63
Books and the Public. London: 1927. V. 64
Catalogue of First Editions in English Literature, Private Press Books and Bibliography, the Property of Late Michael Sadleir, Esq. London: 1958. V. 64
Daumier: the Man and the Artist. London: 1924. V. 63
Desolate Splendour. London: 1923. V. 63
Desolate Splendour. London: 1948. V. 64
Dublin University Magazine: Its History, Contents and Bibliography: a Paper Read Before the Bibliographical Society of Ireland, 26th April 1937. Dublin: 1938. V. 63
The Evolution of Publisher's Binding Styles 1770-1900. London: 1930. V. 62
Excursions in Victorian Bibliography. 1922. V. 64
Excursions in Victorian Bibliography. London: 1922. V. 62; 63; 67
Fanny by Gaslight. London: 1940. V. 63
Fanny by Gaslight. London: 1956. V. 63
Forlorn Sunset. Toronto: 1946. V. 63
Forlorn Sunset. London: 1947. V. 63; 64
Hyssop. London: 1915. V. 63
In Memoriam Dorothy Wynne Willson 1900-1932. London: 1932. V. 63
Lappalien Poems. M.T.H.S. to E.G. 1907. V. 63
Michael Ernest Sadleir (Sir Michael Sadleir K.C.S.I) 1861-1943: a Memoir. London: 1949. V. 64
Minerva Press Publicity. London: 1940. V. 63
Mr. Michael Sadleir's Collection of XIXth Century Fiction. London: 1945. V. 63
More Wrangham: A Supplement to the Paper: Archdeacon Francis Wrangham 1769-1842, Printed in Oxford in 1937. London: 1939. V. 63; 65
XIX Century Fiction. Cambridge: 1951. V. 62
XIX Century Fiction: a Bibliographical Record Based On His Own Collection. London: 1951. V. 64
XIX Century Fiction: a Bibliographical Record Based on His Own Collection. New York: 1969. V. 62
The Noblest Frailty. London: 1925. V. 63; 64
The Northanger Novels - A Footnote to Jane Austen. London: 1927. V. 64
The Political Career of Richard Brinsley Sheridan. Oxford: 1912. V. 63
Privilege: a Novel of the Transition. London: 1921. V. 63
Privilege: a Novel of the Transition. New York: 1921. V. 63
Publishers' Advertising: Being the Reactions of a Practising Publisher-Advertiser to the Exhortations of Non-Publisher Theorists, Based on Articles First Published in Constable's Monthly List. 1930. London: 1930. V. 63
Servants of Books: a Lecture Delivered to the London Branch of the Associated Booksellers at Stationers' Hall 24th Sept. 1924. London: 1925. V. 63
Thackeray's Letters: a Review. London: 1947. V. 64
These Foolish Things. London: 1937. V. 63; 64
Things Past. London: 1944. V. 63; 64
Tommy. Oxford: 1943. V. 63; 64
Trollope - a Bibliography.... London: 1928. V. 63; 65
Trollope: a Commentary. London: 1927. V. 63

SADLEIR, MICHAEL THOMAS
The Law of Population.... London: 1830. V. 64

SADLEIR, THOMAS
Edwin Wilkins Field: a Memorial Sketch. London: 1872. V. 64

SADLER, JAMES
Balloon an Authentic Narrative of the Aerial Voyage of Mr. Sadler, Across the Irish Channel, from Belvedere House.... Dublin: 1812. V. 64

SADLER, MICHAEL ERNEST
K. A Breviate of the Life and Work of Eva Margaret Gilpin 1869-1940. London: 1944. V. 64

SADLER, MICHAEL T.
Ireland: Its Evils and Their Remedies.... London: 1829. V. 67

SADLER, PERCY
Paris in July and August 1830; an Historical Narration of the Revolution of the 27th, 28th, and 29th of July 1830.... Paris: 1830. V. 67

SADLER, RALPH
Letters and Negotiations of Sir Ralph Sadler, Ambassador of King Henry VIII of England to Scotland. Edinburgh: 1720. V. 63
The State Papers and Letters of Sir Ralph Sadler.... Edinburgh: 1809. V. 62

SAENZ, BENJAMIN ALIRE
Carry Me Like Water. New York: 1995. V. 67

SAFFELL, W. T. R.
Records of the Revolutionary War. Balitmore: 1894. V. 67

SAFFORD, W. E.
The Useful Plants of the Island of Guam. Washington: 1905. V. 67

THE SAGA of Gisli Son of Sor. New York: 1936. V. 66

SAGA of Inyo County. Covina: 1977. V. 63

SAGE, JOHN
The Principles of the Cyprianic Age, with Regard to Episcopal Power and Jurisdiction.... In the Savoy: 1695. V. 65

SAGE, RUFUS B.
Rufus B. Sage - His Letters and Papers 1836-1847.... Glendale: 1956. V. 63; 66

SAGGIO de Caratteri Della Fonderia Reale di Torino. Turin: 1830. V. 63

THE SAGHALIAN Convict and Other Stories. London: 1892. V. 64

SAGRA, RAMON DE LA
Histoire Physique, Politique et Naturelle de l'Ile de Cuba. Paris: 1839. V. 67

SAHAGUN, BERNARDINO DE
Florentine Codex: General History of the Things of New Spain. Santa Fe: 1950-1969. V. 65
Historia General de Las Cosas de Nueva Espana. Mexico: 1938. V. 65

SAHAI, BALDEO
India Shipping: a Historical Survey. New Delhi: 1996. V. 67

SAHAK, JUDY HARVEY
Dorothy Drake and the Scripps College Press. Claremont: 1992. V. 64

SAHULA, ISAAC BEN SOLOMON
Mashal Haqadmoni. (Fables of the Ancients). Woodmere: 1987. V. 64

SAILING Into the Past. Roskilde: 1986. V. 64; 66

SAINSBURY, W. NOEL
Calendar of State Papers, Colonial Series. America and West Indies, 1669-1676, also Addenda 1574-1674. London: 1888. V. 66

THE ST. Albans Raid. Investigation of the Police Committee, of the City Council of Montreal into the Charges Perferred by Councillor B. Develin, Against Guillaume Lamothe, Esq., Chief of Police.... Montreal: 1864. V. 62

THE ST. James's Hall Christy Minstrels' Christmas Annual. London: 1868. V. 64

SAINT John New Brunswick Canada The Tourist's and Sportsman's Paradise. Battle Creek & Montreal: 191?. V. 63

SAINT JOHN RELIEF AND AID SOCIETY
Report of The Saint John Relief and Aid Society. Disbursements of Contributions for the Sufferers by the Fire in Saint John of 20th June, 1877. Saint John: 1879. V. 63

SAINT CLAIR, HARRIETT
Dainty Dishes. Edinburgh: 1866. V. 65

SAINT CLAIR, PHILIP R.
Frederic Remington - the American West. Kent: 1978. V. 63; 66

SAINT DENNIS, MADELON
The Death Kiss. New York: 1932. V. 67

SAINTE BEUVE, CHARLES AUGUSTIN
Volupte. Paris: 1834. V. 65

SAINT-ETIENNE, M. RABAUT DE
The History of the Revolution of France. Dublin: 1792. V. 62; 63

SAINT EVREMOND, CHARLES DE SAINT DENIS
The Works.... London: 1714. V. 67

SAINT-EXUPERY, ANTOINE DE
Flight to Arras. New York: 1942. V. 62; 65
The Little Prince. New York: 1943. V. 62; 64; 65
Night Flight. New York: 1932. V. 63
Wind, Sand and Stars. New York: 1939. V. 65

SAINT GEORGE, ELEANOR
The Dolls of Yesterday. London: 1948. V. 67

SAINT GERMAN, CHRISTOPHER
Two Dialogues in English, Between a Doctour of Divinity and a Student in the Laws of England.... London: 1673. V. 63

SAINTHILL, RICHARD
The Old Countess of Desmond: an Inquiry. 1861-1863. V. 63; 66
The Old Countess of Desmond: an Inquiry. 1863. V. 62

SAINT JOHN, CHARLES
Natural History and Sport in Moray. 1863. V. 62; 63; 64; 66
Natural History and Sport in Moray. 1882. V. 64; 67
Natural History and Sport in Moray. Edinburgh: 1882. V. 65
Short Sketches of the Wild Sports and Natural History of the Highlands. 1846. V. 62; 63
Short Sketches of the Wild Sports and Natural History of the Highlands. London: 1872. V. 67
Sketches of the Wild Sports and Natural History of the Highlands. London: 1878. V. 62; 65; 67
A Tour in Sutherlandshire. 1849. V. 62
Wild Sports and Natural History of the Highlands. 1878. V. 63; 64
Wild Sports and Natural History of the Highlands. 1919. V. 63; 66
Wild Sports and Natural History of the Highlands. London: 1919. V. 67
Wild Sports and Natural History of the Highlands. London: 1924. V. 67
Wild Sports and Natural History of the Highlands. Edinburgh: 1927. V. 62
Wild Sports and Natural History of the Highlands. London: 1948. V. 67

SAINT JOHN, CHRISTOPHER
Ellen Terry and Bernard Shaw, a Correspondence. New York: 1931. V. 66

SAINT JOHN, DAVID
The Figure You. New York: 1998. V. 64; 67
For Lerida. Poems. Lisbon: 1973. V. 64; 67
Hush. Boston: 1976. V. 67
No Heaven. Boston: 1985. V. 67
The Shore. Boston: 1980. V. 67
Terraces of Rain: an Italian Sketchbook. Poems. Santa Fe: 1991. V. 67

SAINT JOHN, JAMES AUGUSTUS
Egypt and Nubia. London: 1845. V. 62
Egypt and Nubia, their Scenery and Their People. London: 1867. V. 63; 66
There and Back Again in Search of Beauty. London: 1853. V. 66

SAINT JOHN, PERCY BOLINGBROKE
A Hunter's Experiences in the Southern States of America. London: 1866. V. 66

SAINT JOHN WEBB, MARION
Mr. Papingay's Flying Shop. London. V. 62

SAINT LOUIS, KANSAS CITY & NORTHERN RAILWAY
Centennial Excursion Routes Round-Trip Tickets from Missouri River Points to Philadelphia and New York:. St. Louis: 1876. V. 63

SAINT MARIE, ETIENNE
Eloge Historique de M. Jean Emmanuel Gilibert, Medecin a Lyon. Lyon: 1814. V. 65

SAINT MAUR, ALGERNON, MRS.
Impression of a Tenderfoot During a Journey in Search of Sport in the Far West. London: 1890. V. 63

SAINT MERY, MOREAU DE
Mordeau de St. Mery's American Journey (1793-1798). Garden City: 1947. V. 67

SAINT PAUL, HENRY
Our Home and Foreign Policy. Mobile: 1863. V. 63; 65

SAINT PIERRE, JACQUES HENRI BERNARDIN DE
Harmonies of Nature, Being a Sequel to His "Studies of Nature". London: 1815. V. 62
Paul and Mary, an Indian Story. London: 1789. V. 62
Paul and Virginia. London: 1795. V. 64
Paul and Virginia. 1802. V. 63
Paul et Virginie (& La Chaumiere Indienne). Paris: 1838. V. 67
Studies of Nature. London: 1798. V. 62

SAINT QUINTIN, G.
The History of Glenalmond. Edinburgh: 1956. V. 67

SAINTSBURY, GEORGE
Minor Poets of the Caroline Period. Oxford: 1968. V. 65

SAINT VENANT, MME. DE
Emilie de Choin. Paris: 1811. V. 63

SAINZ, GUSTAVO
Gazapo. Mexico City: 1965. V. 67

SAITO, M.
Geology and Mineral Resources of Japan. 1962. V. 67

SAKAGUTI, KAZUYA
A Monograph of the Siphonaptera of Japan. Tokyo: 1962. V. 63; 66

SAKAI, T.
Crabs of Japan and Adjacent Seas. Tokyo: 1976. V. 66
The Crabs of Sagami Bay. Tokyo: 1965. V. 66
Studies on the Crabs of Japan. Tokyo: 1936-1939. V. 64
Studies on the Crabs of Japan. IV Brachgnatha. Tokyo: 1939. V. 66

SAKAMOTO, KAZUYA
Japanese Toys: Play with History. Tokyo: 1965. V. 63; 64; 66

SAKEL, MANFRED JOSHUA
The Pharmacological Shock Treatment of Schizophrenia. New York Washington: 1938. V. 65

SALA, ANGELO
Ternarius Ternariorum Hemeticorum Bezoardicorum Laudanorum.... Erfurt: 1630. V. 64

SALA, GEORGE AUGUSTUS
After Breakfast: or Pictures Done with a Quill. London: 1864. V. 66
Charles Dickens. London: 1870. V. 62

SALADIN, CHARLES
l'Angleterre en 1800. Cologne & Paris: 1801. V. 63

SALAMAN, M. C.
Fine Prints of the Year, An Annual Review of Contemporary Etching and Engraving. London: 1926. V. 63
Old English Mezzotints. London: 1910. V. 65

SALAMANCA, J. R.
Lilith. New York: 1961. V. 63; 67
A Sea Change. New York: 1969. V. 67

SALAMON, G.
Radiologic Anatomy of the Brain. 1976. V. 67

SALE, EDITH TUNIS
Historic Gardens of Virginia. Richmond: 1930. V. 67

SALEMAKIS, ABBE, PSEUD.
Letters of Abbe Salemakis to a Friend in Ireland. Philadelphia: 1810. V. 63

SALIMAH AGA KHAN, PRINCESS
Jewels from the Personal Collection.... Geneva: 1995. V. 65

SALINGER, JEROME DAVID
The Catcher in the Rye. Boston: 1951. V. 64; 65; 66; 67
The Complete Uncollected Short Stories. 1974. V. 64; 65
Franny and Zooey. Boston and Toronto: 1961. V. 62; 64; 66
Franny and Zooey. London Melbourne Toronto: 1962. V. 64
Raise High the Roof Beam, Carpenters and Seymour, an Introduction. New York: 1959. V. 62

SALISBURY, EDWARD
Downs and Dunes. London: 1952. V. 62

THE SALISBURY Guide; or, an Account, Historical and Descriptive of the Objects of Interest in Salisbury and Its neighbourhood by J.B. Salisbury: 1848. V. 62

SALIVET, LOUIS GEORGES ISAAC
Manuel du Tourneur. A Paris: 1792-1796. V. 64; 66

SALK, JONAS
Man Unfolding. New York: 1972. V. 63

SALLEY, ALEXANDER SAMUEL
The Happy Hunting Ground. Columbia: 1926. V. 63
Tentative Roster of the Third Regiment, South Carolina Volunteers, Confederate States Provisional Army. Columbia: 1908. V. 62; 63

SALLIS, JAMES
Black Hornet. New York: 1994. V. 67
Eye of the Cricket. Blakeney: 1997. V. 65
A Few Last Words. New York: 1970. V. 65
The Guitar Players. New York: 1982. V. 65; 67
The Long-Legged Fly. New York: 1992. V. 65; 66; 67
Moth. New York: 1993. V. 65
Renderings. Seattle: 1996. V. 66

SALLUSTIUS CRISPUS, C.
C. Crispii Sallustii Opera Omnia Quae Extant.... Amstelodami: 1690. V. 65; 66
C. Sallustii Crispi De Coniuratione Catilinae, Et De Bello Iugurthio Historiae.... Venice: 1556. V. 65
Caii Crispi Sallustii Opera Omnia Excussa Ad Editionem Cortii Cum Editionibus.... London: 1789. V. 65
Caius Crispus Sallustius the Historian. London: 1715. V. 67
...De Coniuratione Catalinae Historia. Paris: 1544. V. 62; 65
Cum Veterum Historicorum Fragmentis. Amsterdam: 1658. V. 66
Cum Veterum Historicorum Fragmentis. Amsterdam: 1671. V. 62
(Opera). Amstelodami: 1651. V. 65
(Opera). Amstelodami: 1658. V. 65
Opera Omnia Excusa Ad Editionem Cortii Cum.... 1789. V. 66
Opera Quae Supersunt, Omnia.... Glasgow: 1777. V. 65
Opera Sallustiana.... Colophon: 1517. V. 65
(Opera) Quae Extant. 1697. V. 65
Quae Exstant Opera. Parisiis: 1761. V. 64
Quae Extant Ex Recensione J. F. Gronovii cum Variorum Observationibus ab Ant. Thysio Collectis. Lugd. Batavorum et Roterodam: 1665. V. 66
(Extant Works). Amstelodami: 1641. V. 64
The Works. London: 1744. V. 67

SALMAGUNDI: a Miscellaneous Combination of Original Poetry.... London: 1791. V. 62

SALMAN, MARK
The Laughing Sutra. New York: 1991. V. 67

SALMAN, ROBERT
Fleurons, Vignettes, Frises, Bandeaux, Culs de Lampe.... Paris: 1966. V. 67

SALMASIUS, C. L.
Cl. Salmasii De Re Militarii Romanorum Liber. Opus Pothumum. Lugd. Batavorum: 1657. V. 65
Claudii Salmasii De Hellenistica Commentarius, Controversiam De Lingua Hellnistica Decidens and Plenissime Petractans Originem & Dialectos. (with) Funus Linguae Hellenisticae Sive Confutatio Exercitationis de Helenistis Et Linguae Hellenistica.... Lugd. Batav: 1644. V. 66
Defensio Regia Pro Carolo I. Ad Serenissimum Magnae Britannia Regem Carolum II.... Amsterdam: 1652. V. 62; 65

SALM DYCK, CONSTANCE
Poesies. Paris: 1817. V. 67

SALMI, MARIO
Italian Miniatures. New York: 1954. V. 62

SALMON, D. E.
Special Report on the History and Present Condition of the Sheep Industry of the United States. Washington: 1892. V. 65

SALMON, THOMAS
The Chronological Historian. London: 1733. V. 62
A Critical Essay Concerning Marriage. London: 1724. V. 65
An Impartial Examination of Bishop Burnet's hIstory of His Own Times. London: 1724. V. 63
Salmon's Geographical and Astronomical Grammar Including the Ancient and Present State of the World.... London: 1785. V. 64; 67

SALMON, WILLIAM
Doron Medicum; or, a Supplement to the New London Dispensatory. London: 1688. V. 65
The Family Dictionary; or Household Companion.... London: 1695. V. 64; 65
Horae Mathematicae seu Urania. The Soul of Astrology: Containing that Art in all Its Parts.... London: 1679. V. 65
The London and Country Builder's Vade Mecum; or, the Compleat and Universal Architect's Assistant. London: 1748. V. 62
The London and Country Builder's Vade Mecum; or the Complete and Universal Estimator. London: 1773. V. 66

SALOMONSEN, FINN
Gronlands Fugle. The Birds of Greenland. Copenhagen: 1950-1951. V. 67

SALPOINTE, J. B.
Soldiers of the Cross - Notes on the Ecclesiastical History of New Mexico, Arizona and Colorado. Banning: 1898. V. 64

SALSMAN, LILLIAN V.
Homeland: Country Harbour, Nova Scotia 1783-1983. Hantsport and Marbledhead: 1984. V. 65

SALT, HENRY S.
The Life of Henry David Thoreau. London: 1896. V. 66

SALT, SAMUEL
Statistics and Calculations Essentailly Necessary to Persons Connected with Railways or Canals.... London: 1846. V. 66

SALTEN, FELIX
Bambi: a Life in the Woods. New York: 1928. V. 62

SALTER, EDWIN
History of Monmouth and Ocean Counties, Embracing a Genealogical Record of Earliest Settlers in Monmouth.... Bayonne: 1890. V. 63; 66
A History of Monmouth and Ocean Counties.... Toms River. V. 63; 66
Old Times in Old Monmouth. Baltimore: 1980. V. 63; 66

SALTER, GEORGE
Am Wegesrand.... Frankfurt: 1961. V. 64

SALTER, JAMES
The Arm of Flesh. New York: 1961. V. 66; 67
Dusk and Other Stories. 1988. V. 67
Dusk and Other Stories. San Francisco: 1988. V. 63; 64; 65; 66; 67
Forgotten Kings. New York: 1998. V. 64
In Memory of Sheridan Lord 1926-1994. New York: 1995. V. 66; 67

SALTER, ROBERT BRUCE
Textbook of Disorders and Injuries of the Musculoskeletal. Baltimore: 1970. V. 67
Textbook of Disorders and Injuries of the Musculoskeletal System. Balitmore: 1983. V. 64; 66; 67

SALTER, T. F.
The Angler's Guide.... London: 1825. V. 67

SALTZMANN, ANN B.
Commedia Dell'Arte: a Celebration.... Los Angeles: 1993. V. 67

SALUS, PETER H.
For W. H. Auden - February 21, 1972. New York: 1972. V. 64

SALVADORI, MATTEO
Del Morbo Tisico Libri Tre. Torino: 1789. V. 65

SALVAGE, JEAN GALBERT
Anatomie du Gladiateur Combattant, Applicable aux Beaux Arts.... Paris: 1812. V. 65; 66

SALVATOR, LUDWIG LOUIS
Eine Blume aus dem Goldenen Lande, Oder Los Angeles. Prag: 1878. V. 65

SALVIN, FRANCIS HENRY
Falconry in the British Isles. London: 1855. V. 62
Falconry in the British Isles. London: 1873. V. 63
Falconry in the British Isles. Maidenhead: 1971. V. 67

SALWEY, REGINALD E.
Ventured in Vain. London: 1894. V. 67

SALZMAN, MARK
Iron and Silk. New York: 1986. V. 66
The Laughing Sutra. New York: 1991. V. 67

SALZMAN, MAURICE
Plagiarism, the Art of Stealing Literary Material. Los Angeles: 1931. V. 66

SALZMANN, CHRISTIAN G.
Elements of Morality, for the Use of Children.... London: 1791. V. 67

SAMEWELL, DAVID
Captain Cook and Hawaii. San Francisco: 1957. V. 63

SAMLUNG Augspurgischer Kleider Trachten.... Augsburg. V. 67

SAMOUELLE, G.
The Entomological Cabinet; Being a Natural History of British Insects. 1833-1834. V. 66
The Entomologist's Useful Compendium. 1824. V. 66

SAMPSON, LOW & CO.
The American Catalogue of Books; or, English Guide to American Literature, Giving the Full Title of Original Works Published in the United States Since the Year 1800. London: 1856. V. 62

SAMPSON, WILLIAM
Memoirs of William Sampson: Including Particulars of His Adventures in Various Parts of Europe.... Leesburg: 1817. V. 67
Memoirs of...an Irish Exile, Including Particulars of His Adventures in Various Parts of Europe.... London: 1832. V. 64

SAMS, CONWAY WHITTLE
The Conquest of Virginia, The First Attempt. Norfolk: 1924. V. 63
The Conquest of Virginia, the Forest Primeval. New York: 1916. V. 63

SAMS, S.
A Complete and Universal System of Stenography, or Short-Hand, Rendered Easy and Familiar to the Meanest Capacity on a Plan Entirely New. London: 1812. V. 63

SAMSON, GEORGE WHITEFIELD
To Daimonion or the Spiritual Medium. Boston: 1852. V. 62

SAMUEL, HORACE B.
Unholy Memories of the Holy Land. London: 1930. V. 65

SAMUEL, JOHN
Letters on Welsh History. Philadelphia: 1852. V. 64

SAMUEL, MARK
The Amateur Aquarist, How to Equip and Maintain a Self-Sustaining Aquarium. New York: 1904. V. 67

SAMUELS, E. A.
The Birds of New England and Adjacent States.... Boston: 1872. V. 67
The Birds of New England and Adjacent States.... Boston: 1883. V. 67
A Descriptive Catalogue of the Birds of Massachusetts. Boston: 1864. V. 66
Ornithology and Oology of New England.... Boston: 1868. V. 65
Ornithology and Oology of New England.... Boston: 1869. V. 65
Our Northern and Eastern Birds. New York: 1883. V. 67

SAMUELSON, ROBERT E.
Architecture: Columbus. Columbus: 1976. V. 65

SAMWAYS, G. R.
Ballads of the Flying Corps. London: 1917. V. 67

SAMWELL, DAVID
Captain Cook and Hawaii. San Francisco: 1957. V. 62

SAN FRANCISCO CHAMBER OF COMMERCE
Law and Order in San Francisco, a Beginning. San Francisco: 1916. V. 64

THE SAN Francisco Directory for the Year Commencing September 1862. San Francisco: 1862. V. 65

THE SAN Francisco Directory for the Year Commencing December 1869. San Francisco: 1869. V. 65

SAN Luis Obispo County City and Telephone Directory. San Francisco: 1939. V. 63

SANBORN, F. B.
The Romance of Mary W. Shelley, John Howard Payne, and Washington Irving. Boston: 1907. V. 62

SANBORN, MARGARET
Robert E. Lee. Philadelphia and New York: 1966. V. 65; 67
Robert E. Lee. A Portrait: 1807-1861. (with) *Robert E. Lee. The Complete Man: 1861-1970.* Philadelphia: 1966-1967. V. 63

SANCHEZ, FRANCISCO
Brocensis....Minerva, Seu de Causis Linguae Latinae Commentarius... (Cum Animadversionibis) Jac. Perizonii. Amstelaedami: 1733. V. 66

SANCHEZ DE LA BROZAS, FRANCISCO
Franc. Sanctii...Minerva, Seu de Causis Linguae Latinae Commentarius.... Amsterdam: 1754. V. 62

SANCTUM Provinciale Concilium Mexici Celebratum Anno Domini Millessimo Quingentessimo Octuagessimo Quinto.... Mexico: 1622. V. 62

SAND, GEORGE, PSEUD. OF MME. DUDEVANT
Album Sand. Paris: 1973. V. 67
Correspondence, 1812-1876. Paris: 1882. V. 62
Francis the Waif. London: 1889. V. 63
Handsome Lawrence. Boston: 1871. V. 67
Histoire du Veritable Gribouille. 1881. V. 64; 65
Indiana. Paris: 1847. V. 63
Indiana. Paris: 1856. V. 63
Letters of George Sand. London: 1886. V. 63
La Mare au Diable. Paris: 1846. V. 63
Moliere. Paris: 1851. V. 63
Valentine Cora. Paris: 1853. V. 67

SAND, RUDOLF
Those Were the Days. 1992. V. 62; 63

SANDBERG, WALT
The Turn in the Trail, Northwoods Tales of the Upper Great Lakes. Clinton: 1980. V. 65

SANDBURG, CARL
Abraham Lincoln. The Prairie Years. New York: 1926. V. 64; 65; 66; 67
Abraham Lincoln. The War Years. New York: 1939. V. 62; 63; 64; 65; 66; 67
Always the Young Strangers. New York: 1953. V. 64
Chicago Poems. New York: 1916. V. 65
The Chicago Race Riots, July 1919. New York: 1919. V. 62
Cornhuskers. New York: 1918. V. 62
Lincoln Collector. The Story of Oliver R. Barrett's Great Private Collection. New York: 1949. V. 62; 63; 64; 65
The People, Yes. New York: 1936. V. 66
Potato Face. New York: 1930. V. 67
Prairie-Town Boy. New York: 1955. V. 67
Remebrance Rock. New York: 1948. V. 62; 64; 67
The Sandburg Range. New York: 1940. V. 65
Smoke and Steel. New York: 1920. V. 62
Steichen the Photographer. New York: 1929. V. 62; 63

SANDBY, WILLIAM
The History of the Royal Academy of Arts From Its Foundation in 1768 to the Present Time. London: 1862. V. 66

SANDEMAN, CHRISTOPHER
Thyme and Bergamot. London: 1947. V. 62; 66

SANDEMAN, FRASER
By Hook and By Crook. London: 1892. V. 67

SANDERS, ALVIN HOWARD
The Cattle of the World - Their Places in the Human Scheme - Wild Types and Modern Breeds in Many Lands. Washington: 1926. V. 63
The History of the Percheron Horse Including Hitherto Unpublished Data. Chicago: 1917. V. 64
Red White and Roan. Chicago: 1936. V. 67
Short-Horn Cattle a Series of Sketches, Memoirs and Records of the Breed, Etc. Chicago: 1918. V. 64

SANDERS, BRUCE
Secret Dragnet. London: 1956. V. 67

SANDERS, CYRUS
Early Iowa: The Iowa City Republican Leaflet #1-8. Iowa City: 1880. V. 65

SANDERS, DANIEL C.
A History of the Indian Wars with the First Settlers of the United States, Particularly in England.... Montpelier: 1812. V. 66

SANDERS, DORI
Clover. Chapel Hill: 1990. V. 64
Clover. New York: 1993. V. 62; 64; 66; 67

SANDERS, ED
Bugger: an Anthology. New York: 1964. V. 63

SANDERS, F. C. S.
California as a Health Resort. San Francisco: 1916. V. 63

SANDERS, FRANCIS WILLIAM
Surrenders of Copyhold Property Considered, With Reference to Future and Springing Uses. London: 1819. V. 63

SANDERS, G. D.
Elizabeth Gaskell, with a Bibliography.... 1929. V. 63
Elizabeth Gaskell, with a Bibliography.... New Haven: 1929. V. 66

SANDERS, GORDON E.
Oscar E. Berninghaus, Taos, New Mexico - Master Painter of American Indians and the Frontier West. Albuquerque: 1985. V. 66

SANDERS, HELEN S.
Trails through the Western Woods. New York: 1910. V. 64; 67

SANDERS, LAWRENCE
The Anderson Tapes. New York: 1970. V. 62

SANDERS, LOUISE
The Knave of Hearts. New York: 1925. V. 63

SANDERS, WILLIAM P.
Days that Are Done. Los Angeles: 1915. V. 66

SANDERSON, G. P.
Thirteen Years Among the Wild Beasts of India. 1912. V. 67

SANDERSON, GORDON
Architectural Features of the Settle District. London: 1911. V. 64

SANDERSON, JAMES M.
The Langham Hotel Guide to London. London: 1867. V. 66

SANDERSON, PATRICK
The Antiquities of the Abbey or Cathedral Church of Durham. Newcastle-upon-tyne: 1767. V. 64; 65

SANDERSON, ROBERT
Episcopacy...Not Prejudicial to Regal Power. London: 1673. V. 63
Reasons of the Present Judgement of the University of Oxford, Concerning the Solemn League and Covenant. London: 1647. V. 62
Reasons of the Present Judgment of the University of Oxford, Concerning the Solemn League and Covenant.... London: 1660. V. 65

SANDERSON, ROBERT continued
Twelve Sermons Preached. London: 1632. V. 64

SANDERSON, THOMAS
A Companion to the Lakes of Lancashire, Westmoreland and Cumberland. Carlisle: 1807. V. 65

SANDERSON, WILLIAM
Aulicus Coquinariae, or a Vindication in Answer to a Pamphlet Entituled The Court and Character of King James. London: 1650. V. 62
A Compleat History of the Life and Raigne of King Charles from His Cradle to His Grave. London: 1658. V. 66
A Compleat History of the Lives and Reigns of Mary Queen of Scotland, and of Her Son and Successor, James the Sixth, King of Scotland.... London: 1656. V. 67

SANDES, FLORA
The Autobiography of a Woman Soldier: a Brief Record of Adventure With the Serbian Army 1916-1919. New York: 1922. V. 65

SANDFORD, CHRISTOPHER
Clervis and Belamie. Heathercombe: 1932. V. 63

SANDFORD, E.
A Manual of Exotic Ferns and Selaginella Comprising Descriptions of Over One Thousand Species and Varities.. London: 1882. V. 67

SANDFORD, ELIZABETH
Female Improvement. London: 1836. V. 63
Woman, in Her Social and Domestic Character. London: 1839. V. 67

SANDFORD, FRANCIS
A Genealogical History of the Kings and Queens of England and Monarchs of Great Britain &c. From the Conquest Anno 1066 to the Year 1707.... London: 1707. V. 67
The History of the Coronation of the Most High, Most Mighty, and Most Excellent Monarch, James II. London: 1687. V. 63; 64

SANDFORD, JOHN
Eyes of Prey. New York: 1991. V. 67
Mind Prey. New York: 1995. V. 67
Rules of Prey. New York: 1969. V. 66
Rules of Prey. New York: 1989. V. 64; 65
Shadow Prey. New York: 1990. V. 65

SANDHAM, ELIZABETH
The History of William Selwyn. London: 1815. V. 65
The School-Fellows, a Moral Tale. London: 1818. V. 65

SANDHURST, PHILLIP T.
The Great Centennial Exhibition. Philadelphia: 1876. V. 66

SANDLIN, TIM
Sex and Sunsets. London: 1987. V. 67
Sex and Sunsets. New York: 1987. V. 63; 64; 67

SANDOR, BORTNYIK
Tatters and Scraps, Two Paper Dolls in Toy Land. Chicago: 1933. V. 63

SANDOVAL, JUDITH H.
Historic Ranches of Wyoming. Casper: 1984. V. 63; 66

SANDOZ, MARI
The Beaver Men - Spearheads of Empire. New York: 1964. V. 66
Crazy Horse - the Strange Man of the Ogalalas - a Biography. New York: 1942. V. 65; 66; 67
Love Song to the Plains. New York: 1961. V. 62
Son of the Gamblin' Man. New York: 1960. V. 62

SANDRART, JOACHIM VON
Iconologia Deorum, Oder Abbildung der Botter.... Nurnemberg: 1680. V. 64

SANDS, ALEXANDER H.
History of a Suit in Equity, as Prosecuted and Defended in the Virginia State Courts and in the United States Circuit Courts. Richmond: 1882. V. 65

SANDS, BENJAMIN
Metamorphosis; or, a Transformation of Pictures, with Poetical Explanations for the Amusement of Young Persons. New York: 1819. V. 64

SANDS, FRANK
A Pastoral Prince, the History and Reminiscences of J. W. Cooper. Santa Barbara: 1893. V. 67

SANDWEISS, MARTHA
Eyewitness to War - Prints and Daguerreotypes of the Mexican War. Fort Worth: 1989. V. 62
Laura Gilpin: an Enduring Grace. Forth Worth: 1986. V. 65; 66

SANDWITH, F. M.
Egypt as a Winter Resort. London: 1889. V. 64

SANDY, STEPHEN
End of the Picaro. Pawlet: 1977. V. 63; 66

SANDYS, FREDERICK
Reproductions of Woodcuts 1860-1866. 1910. V. 64

SANDYS, GEORGE
A Paraphrase Upon the Psalmes of David and Upon the Hymnes Dispersed Throughout the Old and New Testaments. London: 1636. V. 66
A Relation of a Journey Begun in An: Dom: 1610. London: 1615. V. 65

SANDYS, WILLIAM
Specimens of Macaronic Poetry. London: 1831. V. 63

SANDZEN, BIRGER
In the Mountains: Reproductions of Photographs and Wood Cuts of the Colorado Rockies. McPherson: 1925. V. 65

SANFORD, EZEKIEL
A History of the United States Before the Revolution; with Some Account of the Aborigines. Phiadelphia: 1819. V. 63

SANFORD, JOHN
The Land that Touches Mines. Garden City: 1953. V. 62
The Old Man's Place. New York: 1935. V. 62
Seventy Times Seven. New York: 1939. V. 62

SANFORD, JOHN B.
The Old Man's Place. New York: 1935. V. 63

SANGER, DONALD B.
James Longstreet. I. Soldier II. Politician, Officeholder and Writer. Baton Rouge: 1952. V. 62

SANGER, EUGENE F.
Report of Malpractice. A Paper Read Before the Maine Medical Association, June 12, 1878. Portland: 1878. V. 63

SANGER, MARGARET
Margaret Sanger: an Autobiography. New York: 1938. V. 63
The Practice of Contraception: an International Symposium and Survey. Baltimore: 1931. V. 63

SANGER, WILLIAM
The History of Prostitution, Its Extent, Causes and Effects throughout the World. New York: 1858. V. 65

SANGSTER, JOHN
The Rights and Duties of Property; with a Plan for Paying the National Debt. London: 1851. V. 64

SANGSTER, MARGARET E.
The Art of Home-Making in City and Country - In Mansion and Cottage. New York: 1898. V. 64

SANGSTER, WILLIAM
Umbrellas and Their History. London: 1855. V. 64
Umbrellas and Their History. London: 1861. V. 62

SANGSTON, LAURENCE
The Bastiles of the North. Baltimore: 1863. V. 65

SANNES, SANNE
The Face of Love. South Brunswick/New York: 1972. V. 63

SANSOM, CLIVE
In the Midst of Death. London: 1940. V. 62

SANSOM, GEORGE S.
Climbing at Wasdale Before the First World War. Somerset: 1982. V. 63; 64; 65

SANSONE, ANTONIO
The Printing of Cotton Fabrics, Composing Calico Bleaching, Printing and Dyeing. Manchester: 1887. V. 63

SAN SOUCI, ROBERT D.
The Faithful Friend. New York: 1995. V. 65

SANSOVINO, FRANCESCO
Del Secretartio. Libri VII.... Venice: 1584. V. 64

SANTA Claus and the Little Lost Kitten. USA: 1952. V. 67

THE SANTA Claus Picture Book. New York: 1901. V. 62

SANTA Claus (Twas the Night Before Christmas). London: 1910. V. 65

SANTA MARIA, FATHER
The First Spanish Entry Into San Francisco Bay, 1775. San Francisco: 1971. V. 63

SANTANGELO, ANTONIO
The Development of Italian Textile Design from the 12th to the 18th Century. 1964. V. 67

SANTE, GERRET VAN
Naamlyste Gesteld Naar't Alphabeth van Alle de Commandeurs, die Sedert den Jaare 1700. Op Groenland en Sedert den Jaare 1719. op de Straad Davids, voor Holland Hebben Gevaren.... Zaandam: 1753. V. 64

SANTEE, ROSS
Cowboy. New York: 1928. V. 63; 66
Horses and Men. New York: 1926. V. 65

SANTORIO, SANTORIO
De Statica Medicina et de Responsione ad Stationmasticem.... Hague-Comitis: 1657. V. 66
Medica Statica: Being the Aphorisms of Sanctorius.... London: 1728. V. 66; 67
Science de La Transpiration Ou Medecine Statique, c'est a Dire Maniere Ingenieuse de se Peser Pour Conserver & Retablir.... Lyon: 1695. V. 64

SANZ, CARLOS
Bibliotheca Americana Vetustissima. Madrid: 1960. V. 63

SAORSTAT Eireann: Irish Free State Official Handbook. Dublin: 1932. V. 67

SAPPHIRE
American Dreams. New York: 1996. V. 67

SAPPHO
Fragmenta Nova. Berkeley and Brookstone: 1981. V. 62; 64; 67
Poems and Fragments. Ann Arbor: 1965. V. 62; 64; 67
The Poems of Sappho, Poems, Epigrams, and Fragments.... London: 1909. V. 66
The Songs. New York: 1925. V. 65

SARABIEWSKI, MACIEJ KAZIMIERZ
Wood-Notes: the Silviludia Poetica.... Newcastle-upon-Tyne: 1848. V. 64; 65

THE SARAH-AD: Or, a Flight for Fame. London: 1742. V. 66

SARAYNA, TORELLO
De Origine et Amplitudine Civitatis Veronae.... Verona: 1540. V. 67

SARDA, MICHEL
Marion Pike the Art and the Artist. Phoenix: 1990. V. 62; 63; 64

SARDINHA MIMOSO, P. JOAO
Relacion de la Real Graticomedia con Que Los Padres de la Compania de Jesus en su Colegio de S. Antom de Lisboa Recibieron a la Magestad Catolica de Felipe II de Portugal.... Lisbon: 1620. V. 62

SARDUY, SEVERO
Gestos. Barcelona: 1962. V. 67

SARG, TONY
Tony Sarg's Alphabet. New York: 1945. V. 64
Who's Who in Tony Sarg's Zoo. Springfield: 1937. V. 65

SARGANT, WILLIAM LUCAS
Recent Political Economy. London: 1867. V. 67
The Science of Social Opulence. London: 1856. V. 67
Social Innovators and Their Schemes. London: 1858. V. 67

SARGEAUNT, B. E.
The Isle of Man and the Great War. Douglas: 1920. V. 66

SARGENT, CHARLES SPRAGUE
Forest Flora of Japan. Notes on the Forest Flora of Japan. Boston: 1894. V. 65; 67
Plantae Wilsonianae. An Enumeration of the Woody Plants Collected in Western China for the Arnold Arboretum of Harvard University During the Years 1907, 1908 and 1910. Portland: 1988. V. 64; 66

SARGENT, F. L.
Corn Plants, Their Uses and Ways of Life. Boston: 1899. V. 63

SARGENT, J. L., MRS.
Amador County History. Jackson: 1927. V. 64; 67

SARGENT, JOHN
The Mine: a Dramatic Poems. London: 1785. V. 62; 66

SARLANDIERE, CHEVALIER J.
Systematized Anatomy, or Human Organography, in Synoptic Tables, with Numerous Plates. London: 1835. V. 66

SARO-WIWA, KEN
Prisoners of Jeb. Port Harcourt, Nigeria: 1988. V. 65

SAROYAN, WILLIAM
The Adventures of Wesley Jackson. New York: 1946. V. 62
The Daring Young Man on the Flying Trapeze. New York: 1934. V. 62; 63
The Daring Young Man on the Flying Trapeze. N.P: 1984. V. 64
The Gay and Melancholy Flux. London: 1937. V. 62
Get Away Old Man. New York: 1944. V. 64
I Used to Believe I Had Forever Now I'm Not So Sure. N.P: 1968. V. 63, 64
Inhale and Exhale. London: 1936. V. 62
My Name is Aram. New York: 1940. V. 62
A Native American. San Francisco: 1938. V. 62; 63
Peace, It's Wonderful. New York: 1939. V. 62
Peace It's Wonderful. London: 1940. V. 63

SARPI, PAOLO
The Historie of the Council of Trent. London: 1620. V. 64
The History of the Council of Trent. London: 1676. V. 67
The Letters of the Renowned Father Paul, Counsellor of State.... London: 1693. V. 62
The Maxims of the Government of Venice. London: 1707. V. 62; 63

SARRAUTE, NATHALIE
Portrait of a Man Unknown. New York: 1958. V. 63; 64
Tropismes. Paris: 1939. V. 67

SARRAZ DU FRANQUESNAY, JACQUES DE LA
Le Minstre Public Dans les Cours Etrangeres, ses Fonctions et ses Prerogatives. Paris: 1731. V. 63

SARS, G. O.
An Account of the Crustacea of Norway.... Bergen: 1895-1928. V. 64
An Account of the Crustacea of Norway.... 1960. V. 63
Challenger Voyage. Zoology. Part 37, 55 & 56. Schizopoda, Cumacea and Phyllocaridaby. 1885-1887. V. 66
On Some Remarkable Forms of Animal Life from the Great Deeps of the Norwegian Coast. Christiania: 1872-1875. V. 62

SARTON, GEORGE
A History of Science: Hellenistic Science and Culture in the Last Three Centuries B.C. Cambridge: 1959. V. 64
Introduction to the History of Science. Baltimore: 1927-1948. V. 64; 66; 67
Introduction to the History of Science. Volume II. From Rabbi Ben Ezra to Roger Bacon. Baltimore: 1931. V. 66; 67

SARTON, MAY
A Durable Fire - New Poems. New York: 1972. V. 62
Encounter in April. Boston: 1937. V. 67
The Fur Person. New York: 1957. V. 64
The House by the Sea. New York: 1977. V. 67
I Knew a Phoenix - Sketches for an Autobiography. New York: 1959. V. 65
Journal of a Solitude. New York: 1973. V. 64; 67
The Land of Silence. New York: 1953. V. 62
Mrs. Stevens Hears the Mermaids Singing. New York: 1965. V. 64; 67
Plant Dreaming Deep. New York: 1968. V. 67
Recovering; a Journal. New York: 1980. V. 66
A World of Light. New York: 1976. V. 64; 67

SARTORIS, ADELAIDE
A Week in a French Country-House. London: 1867. V. 65

SARTRE, JEAN-PAUL
Explication de l'Etranger. Paris: 1946. V. 64
Five Plays. Franklin Center: 1978. V. 62; 64; 67
L'Imagination. Paris: 1936. V. 67
Iron in the Soul. London: 1950. V. 62
La Nausee. Paris: 1938. V. 65
The Roads to Freedom Trilogy. London: 1947-1950. V. 62

SARYTSCHEW, GAWRILA
Account of a Voyage of Discovery to the North-East of Siberia, the Frozen Ocean and the North Sea. Amsterdam/New York: 1969. V. 64; 65

SASA, M.
Chironomidae (Diptera) of Japan. Tokyo: 1995. V. 65

SASEK, MIROSLAV
This is Edinburgh. New York: 1961. V. 65
This Is London. New York: 1959. V. 65
This is New York. New York: 1960. V. 65
This is Paris. New York: 1959. V. 65
This Is Rome. New York: 1960. V. 65
This is San Francisco. New York: 1962. V. 65
This is Venice. New York: 1961. V. 65

SASOWSKI, N.
The Prints of Reginald Marsh.... New York: 1976. V. 62; 65

SASSOON, SIEGFRIED LORRAINE
Collected Poems. London: 1947. V. 65; 67
The Complete Memoirs of George Sherston. London: 1937. V. 62
The Daffodil Murderer. London: 1913. V. 62; 65
Four Poems. Cambridge: 1918. V. 66
The Heart's Journey. New York: 1927. V. 64; 67
Lenten Illuminations - Slight Sufficient. London: 1958. V. 62
Letters to a Critic. London: 1976. V. 67
Lingual Exercises for Advanced Vocabularians. Cambridge: 1925. V. 67
Memoirs of a Fox Hunting Man. London: 1929. V. 64; 65
Memoirs of a Fox Hunting Man. New York: 1929. V. 66
Memoirs of a Fox Hunting Man. London: 1977. V. 62; 63; 64
Memoirs of an Infantry Officer. London: 1930. V. 64; 67
Memoirs of an Infantry Officer. London: 1931. V. 62; 64; 65; 67
Memoirs of an Infantry Officer. New York: 1981. V. 63; 66
Meredith. London: 1948. V. 67
An Octave. 1966. V. 62
An Ode for Music. London: 1912. V. 64
The Old Century and Seven More Years. London: 1938. V. 64; 67
The Old Huntsman and Other Poems. London: 1917. V. 62; 67
On Chatterton: a Sonnet. Winchester: 1930. V. 64; 65
The Path to Peace: Selected Poems by.... Worcester: 1960. V. 62
Picture Show. Cambridge: 1919. V. 62; 67
Poems by Pinchbeck Lyre. London: 1931. V. 64
Poems Newly Selected 1916-1935. London: 1940. V. 67
Rhymed Ruminations. London: 1940. V. 67
Satirical Poems. London: 1926. V. 67
Selected Poems. London: 1925. V. 67
Sequences. London: 1956. V. 64
Sherston's Progress. London: 1936. V. 66
Siegfried's Journey 1916-1920. London: 1945. V. 67
Something About Myself. 1966. V. 62
Something About Myself. London: 1966. V. 67
Something About Myself. Worcester: 1966. V. 62; 65
The Tasking. Cambridge: 1954. V. 67
To My Mother. London: 1928. V. 62; 67
To the Red Rose. London. V. 67
The War Poems. London: 1919. V. 62; 63; 66; 67

THE SATIRIST, or Monthly Meteor. London: 1808. V. 67

SATO, SHOZO
The Art of Arranging Flowers. New York: 1965. V. 62; 63; 64; 66
The Art of Arranging Flowers. New York: 1966. V. 67

SATORRE, E. H.
Wheat, Ecology and Physiology of Yield Determination. New York: 1999. V. 66

SATTERTHWAIT, WALTER
At Ease with the Dead. New York: 1990. V. 62; 65; 66; 67
The Gold of Mayani, the African Stories of.... Gallup: 1995. V. 64; 66
The Hanged Man. New York: 1993. V. 67
Miss Lizzie. New York: 1989. V. 62; 65; 66; 67
Wall of Glass. New York: 1987. V. 62; 64; 65
Wall of Glass. New York: 1988. V. 66
Wilde West. New York: 1991. V. 67

SATTERTHWAYT, JOHN
A True and Perfect Narrative of the Tryal and Acquitment of Mr. John Satterthwayt, at the Assizes Held at Kingston, March 13, Being Accused for Firing the House of Mr. Peter Delanoy, Dyer in Southwark. London: 1679-1680. V. 65

SAUER, CARL ORTWIN
The Early Spanish Main. Berkeley: 1966. V. 63; 64

SAUER, G.
John Gould, the Bird Man, A Chronology and Bibliography. Melbourne: 1982. V. 63; 66

SAUNDERS, ALFRED
Our Domestic Birds, A Practical Poultry Book for England and New Zealand. 1883. V. 63

SAUNDERS, CHARLES F.
The Southern Sierras of California. New York: 1924. V. 65

SAUNDERS, E.
The Hymenoptera Aculeata of the British Islands. 1896. V. 66

SAUNDERS, EMILY
Spiritualism and Other Signs. London: 1865. V. 66

SAUNDERS, GEORGE
A Treatise on Theatres. London: 1790. V. 64

SAUNDERS, HOWARD
An Illustrated Manual of British Birds. London: 1889. V. 62

SAUNDERS, J. B.
Andreas Vesalius Bruxellensis: The Bloodletting Letter of 1539. New York: 1951. V. 64

SAUNDERS, JOHN
The History of the County of Lincoln, from the Earliest Period to the Present Time. London: 1833-1834. V. 66

SAUNDERS, JOHN CUNNINGHAM
A Treatise on Some Practical Points Relating to the Diseases of the Eye.... London: 1811. V. 65
Treatise on Some Practical Points Relating to the Diseases of the Eye.... Philadelphia: 1821. V. 62

SAUNDERS, KATHERINE
The High Mills. London: 1875. V. 65

SAUNDERS, LOUISE
The Knave of Hearts. New York: 1925. V. 63; 65
The Knave of Hearts. Racine: 1925. V. 63; 67

SAUNDERS, RICHARD
Angelographia Sive Pneumata Leiturgia Pneumatalogia.... London: 1701. V. 66

SAUNDERS, SARAH
The Fountain of Knowledge; or, Complete Family Guide, Containing Upwards of Five Hundred Other Curious Particulars of the Utmost Service to Families in General. London: 1781. V. 67

SAUNDERS, W. W.
Insecta Saundersiana; or Characters of Undescribed Insects in the Collection of W. W. Saunders. 1850-1869. V. 66
Insecta Saundersiana; or Characters of Undescribed Insects in the Collection of W. W. Saunders. London: 1850-1869. V. 62

SAUNDERS, WILLIAM
Observations on the Superior Efficacy of the Red Peruvian Bark, in the Cure of Agues and Other Fevers. London: 1782. V. 65

SAUNDERS, WILLIAM L.
Lessons from Our North Carolina Records. 1889. V. 65

SAUNDERSON, HENRY
The Saundersons of Castle Saunderson. 1936. V. 63
The Saundersons of Castle Saunderson. 1956. V. 66

SAUNDERSON, NICHOLAS
The Elements of Algebra, in Ten Books.... Cambridge: 1740-1741. V. 65

SAURAT, DENIS
Angels and Beasts. 1946. V. 62

SAUSMAREZ, MAURICE DE
Bridget Riley. London: 1970. V. 65

SAUSSURE, HENRI
Catalogue des Especes de l'Ancien Genre Scolia (sensu Latiori), Contenant les Diagnoses, les Descriptions et la Synonymie des Especes, Avec des Remarques Explicatives et Critiques. Geneva: 1864. V. 65
Observations sur les Moeurs de Divrs Oiseaux du Mexique. Geneva: 1858. V. 64

SAUSSURE, HORACE BENEDICT DE
Kurze Anzeige von dem Ruzen der Strahlableiter.... Zurich: 1772. V. 65

SAUTER, R. H.
Songs in Captivity. London: 1922. V. 65

SAVAGE, CHRISTOPHER
The Mandarin Duck. 1952. V. 67

THE SAVAGE Club Papers. 1897. V. 67

SAVAGE, EDWIN E.
A Record of All the Works Connected with Hexham Abbey since Jan. 1899, and Now in Progress. Hexham: 1907. V. 65

SAVAGE, HENRY
Reasons Shewing That There is No Need to Such a Reformation of the Publique. London: 1660. V. 63

SAVAGE, JAMES
Dorchester and Its Environs, During the British, Roman, Saxon and Norman Periods.... Dorchester: 1832. V. 62
Memorabilia; or Recollections, Historical, Biographical and Antiquarian. Taunton: 1820. V. 62; 65

SAVAGE, JOHN
A Select Collection of Letters of the Antients. London: 1703. V. 66

SAVAGE, MARMION W.
The Bachelor of the Albany. London: 1848. V. 67

SAVAGE, RICHARD
The Works of Richard Savage, Esq. London: 1777. V. 62

SAVAGE, S.
Catalogue of the Printed Books and Pamphlets in the Library of the Linnean Society of London. London: 1925. V. 67

SAVAGE, WILLIAM
A Dictionary of the Art of Printing. London: 1841. V. 62; 67

SAVARY, CLAUDE ETIENNE
Letters on Greece.... London: 1788. V. 62

SAVERIEN, ALEXANDRE
Dictionnaire Universel de Mathematique et de Physique, ou l'on Traite de l'Origine, du Progres de ces deux Sciences & des Arts qui en Dependent & des Diverses revolutions qui leur Sont Arrivees jusqu'a notre tems.... Paris: 1753. V. 67
Histoire des Progres de l'Esprit Humain dans les Sciences et dans les Arts qui en Dependent. Paris: 1776-1778. V. 65

SAVIGNY, FRIEDRICH CARL VON
Of the Vocation of Our Age for Legislation and Jurisprudence. London: 1831. V. 64

SAVILLE, MALCOLM
Christmas at Nettleford. London: 1953. V. 67
Dark Danger. London: 1965. V. 65
Lone Pine Five. 1949. V. 67
Not Scarlet but Gold. London: 1962. V. 65
The Secret of the Gorge. London: 1958. V. 65
Seven White Gates. London: 1944. V. 67
Susan, Bill and the Dark Stranger. London: 1956. V. 67
Where's My Girl?. 1972. V. 67
Wonder Why Book of Exploring the Seashore. 1979. V. 65

SAVONAROLA, DON JEREMY
Facts and Figures from Italy. London: 1847. V. 63

SAVONAROLA, JEROME
Fratis Hieronymi de Ferraria Triumphus Crucis de Veritate Fidei.... 1508. V. 66

SAVORY, A. B., & SONS, GOLDSMITHS
(Trade Catalogue). London: 1850. V. 67

SAVORY, ISABEL
A Sportswoman in India. 1900. V. 67
A Sportswoman in India. London: 1900. V. 66

THE SAVOY. London: 1896. V. 64

SAWER, J. C.
Odorographia, a Natural History of Raw Materials and Drugs Used in the Perfume Industry.... 1892-1894. V. 63; 66
Odorographia, a Natural History of Raw Materials and Drugs Used in the Perfume Industry.... London: 1892-1894. V. 64

SAWYER, CHARLES J.
Dickens v. Barabbas - Forster Intervening - a Study Based Upon Some Hietherto Unpublished Letters. London: 1930. V. 62
English Books 1475-1900. London: 1927. V. 62; 67
English Books 1475-1900. Westminster: 1927. V. 64

SAWYER, EDMUND
Memorials of Affairs of State in the Reigns of Q. Elizabeth and K. James I.... London: 1725. V. 67

SAWYER, EUGENE T.
The Life and Career of Tiburcio Vasquez, the California Bandit and Murderer. San Jose: 1875. V. 63; 66
The Life and Career of Tiburcio Vasquez the California Stage Robber. Oakland: 1944. V. 62; 63; 64; 66; 67

SAWYER, FRANK
Nymphs and Trout. 1958. V. 67

SAWYER, FREDERIC W.
The Merchant's and Shipmaster's Guide in Relation to Their Rights, Duties and Liabilities Under the Existing Commercial Regulations of the United States.... Boston: 1847. V. 62

SAWYER, H. C.
Nerve Waste: Practical Information Concerning Nervous Impairment in Modern Life, Its Causes, Phases and Remedies.... San Francisco: 1889. V. 65

SAWYER, LORENZO
Way Sketches - Containing Incidents of Travel Across the Plains from St. Joseph to California. New York: 1926. V. 63

SAWYER, RUTH
Roller Skates. New York: 1936. V. 62

SAXBY, HENRY L.
The Birds of Shetland with Observations on Their Habits, Migration and Occasional Appearance. Edinburgh: 1874. V. 62

SAXBY, JESSIE M. E.
Joseph Bell...An Appreciation by an Old Friend. Edinburgh: 1913. V. 65

SAXE, MAURICE, COMTE DE
The History. London: 1753. V. 64
Mes Reveries, Ouvrage Posthume de Maurice Comte De Saxe. A Amsterdam et A Leipzig: 1757. V. 66
Reveries, or Memoirs Upon the Art of War. London: 1757. V. 64; 66

SAY, ALLEN
Grandfather's Journey. Boston: 1993. V. 65

SAY, JEAN BAPTISTE
Historical Essay on the Rise, Progress and Probable Results of the British Dominion in India. London: 1824. V. 64
Letters to Mr. Malthus, on Several Subjects of Political Economy.... London: 1821. V. 67
Lettres a M. Malthus, sur Differens Sujets d'Economie Politique.... Paris: 1820. V. 64
A Treatise on Political Economy. London: 1821. V. 64
A Treatise on Political Economy. Philadelphia: 1853. V. 65

SAY, THOMAS
The Complete Writings of Thomas Say on the Entomology of North America. Philadelphia: 1891. V. 62; 64

SAYE, JAMES HODGE
Memoirs of Major Joseph McJunkin. Greenwood: 1925. V. 63; 66

SAYER, W.
History of Westmorland Containing the Substance of all the Remarkable Events Recorded by Burn & Nicolson.... London: 1847. V. 64

SAYER, W. F.
Spare Moments. Hackney: 1853. V. 62

SAYERS, DOROTHY L.
Busman's Honeymoon. New York: 1937. V. 63; 66
Catholic Tales. Oxford: 1918. V. 62
Creed or Chaos and Other Essay in Popular Theology. London: 1947. V. 65
Gaudy Night. 1935. V. 67
Gaudy Night. 1936. V. 64
In the Teeth of Evidence. London: 1939. V. 63; 65; 67
Lord Peter Views the Body. London: 1928. V. 63
Murder Must Advertise. New York: 1933. V. 66
The Mysterious English. London: 1941. V. 62
Suspicious Characters. New York: 1931. V. 66
Talboys. New York: 1972. V. 65
Wilkie Collins: a Critical and Biographical Study. Toledo: 1977. V. 67

SAYLE, CHARLES
Cambridge Fragments. Cambridge: 1913. V. 63

SAYLES, E. B.
An Archaeological Survey of Texas. Globe: 1935. V. 63; 66
The San Simon Branch Excavations at Cave Creek and in the San Simon Valley.... Globe: 1945. V. 63

SAYLES, JOHN
The Pride of the Bimbos. Boston: 1974. V. 67
Pride of the Bimbos. Boston: 1975. V. 66
Union Dues. Boston: 1977. V. 67

SAYLOR, H. H.
Architectural Styles for Country Houses. New York: 1912. V. 62

SAYLOR, STEVEN
Arms of Nemesis. New York: 1992. V. 67
The Venus Throw. New York: 1995. V. 67

SAYRE, LEWIS A.
A Practical Manual of the Treatment of Club-foot. New York: 1869. V. 62

SAYWELL, J. L.
The Parochial History of Ackworth, Yorks.... London: 1894. V. 65

SCAFE, JOHN
Court News; or, the Peers of King Coal.... London: 1820. V. 62

SCAIFE, H. LEWIS
Catawba Indians of South Carolina. Washington: 1930. V. 67

THE SCALWAGONS of Oz. Chicago: 1941. V. 65

SCALES, ALFRED M.
The Battle of Fredericksburg. Washington: 1884. V. 62

SCAMMON, CHARLES M.
The Marine Mammals of the North-Western Coast of North America and the American Whale Fishery. Riverside: 1969. V. 64; 67

SCAMOZZI, VINCENT
Oeuvres d'Architecture.... Hague: 1736. V. 62

SCANION, CHARLES M.
Indian Massacre and the Captivity of the Hall Girls. Milwaukee: 1915. V. 67

SCARFE, GERALD
Scarfe, by Scarfe. London: 1986. V. 67

SCARGILL, WILLIAM PITT
Blue Stocking Hall. London: 1829. V. 66
Truckleborough Hall: a Novel. London: 1827. V. 67

SCARNE, JOHN
The Odds Against Me: an Autobiography. New York: 1966. V. 63

SCARPA, ANTONIO
Additions au Traite de l'Aneurysme.... Paris: 1822. V. 63
Practical Observations on the Principal Diseases of the Eyes. Birmingham: 1984. V. 63

SCARRON, PAUL
Les Oeuvres de Monsieur Scarron, Revues, Corrigees & Augmentees de Nouveau. Amsterdam: 1695. V. 66
The Whole Comical Works. London: 1703. V. 65
The Whole Comical Works. London: 1759. V. 62; 67

SCATCHERD, NORRISON
Memoirs of the Celebrated Eugene Aram.... London: 1838. V. 64

SCENES Feeriques Legendes Merveilleuses Illustrees de Paysages Animes et Transparents. Pari: 1870. V. 64

SCENES in Florida. Chicago: 1894. V. 66

SCEVE, MAURIE
Delie, Object de Plus Haute Vertu. Poesies Amoureuses. Lyon: 1862. V. 62

SCHAACK, MICHAEL J.
Anarchy and Anarchists. A History of the Red Terror and the Social Revolution in America and Europe. Chicago: 1889. V. 62

SCHAAF, GREGORY
Hopi-Tewa Pottery. Santa Fe: 1998. V. 64

SCHAAFSMA, POLLY
Indian Rock Art of the Southwest. Santa Fe: 1980. V. 65

SCHAD, GEORGIA
Mary F. Hatfield La Follette, My Pioneer Mother. Weiser: 1954. V. 67

SCHAD, JOHANN ADAM XAVER
Effigies Ducum et Regum Hungariae. In Applausu Oblatae.... N.P: 1687. V. 64

SCHADOW, JOHANN GOTTFRIED
Wittenbergs Denkmaler. Wittenberg: 1825. V. 62; 67

SCHAEDLER, K. F.
Weaving in Africa. South of the Sahara. Munich: 1987. V. 62

SCHAEFER, JACK
Shane. Boston: 1949. V. 66

SCHAEFFER, CASPER
Memoirs and Reminiscences Together with Sketches of the Early History of Sussex County, New Jersey. Hackensack: 1907. V. 63; 66

SCHAEFFER, OSKAR
Atlas and Epitome of Labor and Operative Obstetrics. Philadelphia: 1901. V. 65

SCHAFER, OTTO
Katalog der Bibliothek Otto Schafer Schweinfurt.... Stuttgart: 1984. V. 63

SCHAFF, MORRIS
The Sunset of the Confederacy. Boston: 1912. V. 62; 63; 65

SCHAFFER, L. M.
Sketches of Travels in South America, Mexico and California. New York: 1860. V. 64

SCHALDACH, WILLIAM J.
Carl Rungius, Big Game Painter. West Hartford: 1945. V. 64
Coverts and Casts. New York: 1946. V. 67

SCHANILEC, GAYLORD
My Colorful Career. Newtown: 1996. V. 64

SCHAPERA, I.
The Bantu-Speaking Tribes of South Africa. London: 1937. V. 62

SCHAPIRO, MEYER
The Romanesque Sculpture of Moissac. New York: 1931. V. 67

SCHARF, ALFRED
A Catalogue of Pictures and Drawings from the Collection of Sir Thomas Merton.... London: 1960. V. 64

SCHARF, GEORGE
A Descriptive and Historical Catalogue of the Collection of Pictures at Woburn Abbey. London: 1890. V. 67

SCHARF, JOHN THOMAS
History of the Confederate States Navy, from Its Organization to the Surrender of Its Last Vessel. New York: 1887. V. 63

SCHATZ, AUGUST H.
Longhorns Bring Culture. Boston: 1961. V. 65
Opening a Country, a History of the Pioneer Struggle in Conquering the Prairies South of Black Hills. Ann Arbor: 1939. V. 67

SCHECKLEY, ROBERT
Untouched by Human Hands. London: 1955. V. 64

SCHEDEL, HARTMANN
Liber Chronicarum. Nuremberg: 1493. V. 62

SCHEEL, J. J.
Atlas of Killifishes of the Old World. Neptune City: 1990. V. 64

SCHEER, FREDERICK
The Letters of Diogenes to Sir Robert Peel, Bart. London: 1841. V. 62

SCHEINER, CHRISTOPH
Oculus, hoc est: Fundamentum Opticum, in Quo ex Accurata Oculi Anatome, Abstrarusarum Experientiarum Sedula per Vesitigatione.... Innsbruck: 1619. V. 63

SCHELL, JAMES P.
In the Ojibway Country - a Story of Early Missions on the Minnesota Frontier. Walhalla: 1911. V. 63

SCHELLING, FELIX E.
English Literature During the Lifetime of Shakespeare. New York: 1910. V. 66

SCHELTER & GIESECKE
Funfundsiebzig Jahre des Hauses J. G. Schelter & Giesecke in Leipzig. Leipzig: 1894. V. 65

SCHENCK, DAVID
North Carolina. 1780-1781. Raleigh: 1889. V. 62; 63; 66

SCHENCK, ELIZABETH HUBBELL
The Story of Fairfield, Fairfield County, Connecticut, from the Settlement of the Town in 1639 to 1818. New York: 1889. V. 64

SCHENK, PETER
Effigies Praecipuorum Aedificorum Publicorum Urbis Hamburgi Quae Aere Repraesentata.... Amsterdam: 1700. V. 64

SCHENK DE REGNIERS, BEATRICE
The Giant Story. New York: 1953. V. 65
Red Riding Hood. New York: 1972. V. 66

SCHER, STEPHEN K.
The Currency of Fame. Portrait Medals of the Renaissance. London: 1994. V. 63; 64

SCHERER, J. C.
Indians - the Great Photographs that Reveal North American Indian Life 1847-1929.... New York: 1973. V. 65

SCHERL, AUGUST
Ein Neues Schnellbahn-System. Vorschlage zur Verbesserung des Personen-Verkehrs. Berlin: 1909. V. 65

SCHERMERHORN, J. W.
School Material. New York: 1871. V. 63

SCHERMERHORN, WILLIAM E.
The History of Burlington, New Jersey, from the Early European Arrivals in the Delaware to the Quarter Millennial Anniversary...of the Settlement by English Quakers in 1677. Burlington: 1927. V. 63; 66

SCHERZER, KARL
Narrative of the Circumnavigation of the Globe.... London: 1861. V. 66

SCHEUBEL, JOHANN
Algebrae Compendiosa Facili'sque Descriptio, qua Depromuntur Magna Arithemtices Miracula. Paris: 1551. V. 62

SCHEUZER, JOHANN JAKOB
Herbarium Diluvianum Collectum.... Zurich: 1709. V. 62

SCHEVILL, MARGARET ERWIN
Beautiful on the Earth. Santa Fe: 1947. V. 65

SCHILLER, ELLY
First Photographs of the Holy Land. (and) The First Photographs of Jerusalem the Old City. Jerusalem: 1978. V. 66

SCHILLER, JOHANN CHRISTOPH FRIEDRICH VON
Early Dramas and Romances. The Robbers: Fiesco: Love and Intrigue: Demetrius: The Ghost-Seer. Sport of Destiny. London: 1849. V. 63
Historical Dramas - Don Carlos: Mary Stuart: Maid of Orleans: the Bride of Messina. London: 1847. V. 63
History of the Thirty Years' War. History of the Revolt in the Netherlands: Wallenstein: Wilhelm Tell. London: 1847. V. 63

SCHILLINGS, C. G.
In Wildest Africa. 1907. V. 62; 63; 64
In Wildest Africa. London: 1907. V. 62
With Flashlight and Rifle. 1906. V. 62; 64
With Flashlight and Rifle. London: 1906. V. 62; 67

SCHIMMELL, JILIE
The Art and Life of W. Herbert Dunton 1878-1936. Austin: 1984. V. 67

SCHIMPER, A. F. W.
Plant Geography Upon a Physiological Basis. Oxford: 1903. V. 64

SCHIMPER, W.
Monographie des Plantes Fossiles du Gres Bigarre de la Chaine des Vosges. Leipzig: 1844. V. 62

SCHINDLER, SOLOMON
Dissolving Views in the History of Judaism. Boston: 1888. V. 63

SCHINE, CATHLEEN
Alice in Bed. New York: 1983. V. 62; 67

SCHIRMACHER, KAETHE
Le Feminisme aux Etats-Unis, en France, dans la Grande-Bretagne, en Suede et en Russie. Paris: 1898. V. 63
The Modern Woman's Rights Movement: A Historical Survey. New York: 1912. V. 65

SCHJELDAHL, JAMES
Dreams. New York: 1973. V. 64

SCHLEGEL, AUGUSTUS WILLIAM
A Course of Lectures on Dramatic Art and Literature. London: 1815. V. 63

SCHLEGEL, HERMANN
De Vogels van Nederlandsch Indie/Les Oiseaux des Neerlandaises. Leiden: 1863-1866. V. 67
De Vogels Van Nederlandsch Indie/Les Oiseaux Indies Neerlandaises. Haarlem: 1863-1866. V. 65

SCHLEGEL, JOHAN FRIEDRICH WILHELM
Neutral Rights; or, an Impartial Examination of the Right of Search of Neutral Vessels Under Convoy.... Philadelphia: 1801. V. 67

SCHLESINGER, ARTHUR M.
Running for President. The Candidates and Their Images 1789-1992. New York: 1994. V. 64

SCHLEY, FRANK
Frank Schley's American Partridge and Pheasant Shooting. Frederick: 1877. V. 64

SCHLICH, W.
A Manual of Forestry. London: 1896-. V. 65

SCHLIEMANN, HEINRICH
Ilios. London: 1880. V. 64
Ilios, City and Country of the Trojans. 1881. V. 66
Ilios, City and Country of the Trojans. New York: 1881. V. 65
Ilios. Stadt und Land der Trojaner. Forschungen und Entdeckungen. Leipzig: 1881. V. 67
Tiryns. The Prehistoric Palace of the Kings of Tiryns. The Results of the Latest Excavations. London: 1886. V. 62; 66
Troy and Its Remains. London: 1875. V. 64; 66

SCHLOSS, DAVID FREDERICK
Methods of Industrial Renumeration. London: 1892. V. 67

SCHMALENBACH, W.
Kurt Schwitters. New York: 1967. V. 65
Kurt Schwitters. New York: 1969. V. 62

SCHMEISSER, G.
Syllabus of Lectures on Mineralogy. London: 1794. V. 65

SCHMEISSER, KARL
Ueber Vorkommen und Gewinnung der Nutzbaren Mineralien in der Sudafrikanischen Republik (Transvaal) Unter Besonderer Berucksichtigung des Goldbergbaues. Berlin: 1894. V. 66

SCHMID, HERMAN
The Bavarian Highlands and The Salzkammergut. London: 1874. V. 65

SCHMID, JOHANN CHRISTOPH VON
The Basket of Flowers; or, Piety and Truth Triumphant. London: 1868. V. 67
L'Enfant Perdu. Paris: 1832. V. 66

SCHMIDA, G.
The Cold Blooded Australians.... Sydney: 1985. V. 67

SCHMIDT, ARNO
Leviathan. Hamburg: 1949. V. 67

SCHMIDT KOENIG, K.
Animal Migration, Navigation and Homing, Symposium Held at the University of Tubingen, August 17-20, 1977. Berlin: 1978. V. 67

SCHMIED-DUPERREX, ANTOINETTE
The Lausanne Pipe Museum. 1980. V. 62

SCHMITT, MARTIN F.
The Cattle Drives of David Shirk. Portland: 1956. V. 63; 64; 66
Fighting Indians of the West. New York: 1947. V. 67
Fighting Indians of the West. New York: 1948. V. 66
General George Crook - His Autobiography. Norman: 1960. V. 67

SCHMITZ, E. ROBERT
The Capture of Inspiration. New York: 1935. V. 62; 63; 64

SCHMITZ, H.
Encyclopedia of Furniture: An Outline History in Egypt, Assyria, Persia, Greece, Rome, Russia, Near and Far East Up to the Middle of the 19th Century. New York: 1963. V. 65

SCHMOLLER, HANS
Chinese Decorated Papers. Newtown: 1987. V. 64
Mr. Gladstone's Washi: a Survey of Reports on the Manufacture of Paper in Japan; The Parkes Report of 1871. Newtown: 1984. V. 64; 65

SCHMOLLER, TANYA
Remondini and Rizzi: a Chapter in Italian Decorated Paper History. New Castle: 1990. V. 64

SCHMUTZLER, ROBERT
Art Nouveau. New York: 1964. V. 62; 63; 64

SCHNEEMAN, GEORGE
Homage to Allen G. New York: 1997. V. 64

SCHNEIR, JACQUES
Sculpture in Modern America. Berkeley: 1948. V. 62; 65

SCHNITZLER, ARTHUR
Uber Funktionelle Aphonie und Deren Behandlung Durch Hypnoser und Suggestion. Vienna: 1889. V. 67

SCHOBERL, FREDERIC
Picturesque Tour from Geneva to Milan by Way of the Simplon. London: 1820. V. 62; 64; 67

SCHOENBERG, ARNOLD
Harmonielehre. Leipzig & Vienna: 1911. V. 65; 67

SCHOENER, ALLON
Harlem on My Mind. Cultural Capital of Black America 1900-1968. New York: 1968. V. 63

SCHOEPFLIN, JOHANN DANIEL
Vindiciae Typographicae. Argentorati: 1760. V. 65; 66

SCHOETTLE, EDWIN J.
Sailing Craft Mostly Descriptive of Smaller Pleasure Sail Boats of the Day. New York: 1928. V. 62; 63; 66

SCHOFIELD, FRED
Humber Keels and Keelmen. Lavenham: 1988. V. 67

SCHOFIELD, JAMES
An Historical and Descriptive Guide to Scarborough and Its Environs. York: 1787. V. 64; 65

SCHOFIELD, JOHN M.
Forty-Six Years in the Army. New York: 1897. V. 67

SCHOFIELD, LILY
The Hippotamus Book. London: 1905. V. 65

SCHOLDER, FRITZ
Fritz Scholder - Paintings and Monotypes. Altadena: 1988. V. 66

SCHOLDERER, VICTOR
Greek Printing Types 1465-1927: Facsimiles from an Exhibition of Books Illustrating the Development of Greek printing Shown in the British Museum 1927. London: 1927. V. 63

SCHOLES, PERCY A.
God Save the Queen! - the History and Romance of the World's First National Anthem. London: 1954. V. 62

SCHOLLE, P. A.
Sandstone Depositional Environments. Tulsa: 1982. V. 67

SCHOMBER, ISAAC
Naval Chronology; or, an Historical Summary of Naval and Maritime Events, from the Time of the Romans, to the Treaty of Peace 1802. London: 1802. V. 62

SCHOMBERG, R.
Unknown Karakoram. 1936. V. 63; 65

SCHONERUS, JOHANNES
Algorithmus Demonstratus. Nuremberg: 1534. V. 66

THE SCHOOL Bag. 1997. V. 64

THE SCHOOL of Arts Improv'd; or Companion for the Ingenious. Gainsborough: 1776. V. 66

SCHOOLCRAFT, HENRY ROWE
Archives of Aboriginal Knowledge.... Philadelphia: 1860. V. 66; 67
Historical and Statistical Information Respecting the History, Condition and Prospects of the Indian Tribes of the United States...Part II. Philadelphia: 1851. V. 62
Historical Information Respecting the...Indian Tribes. Philadelphia: 1851-1857. V. 66
Information Respecting the History, Condition and Prospects of the Indian Tribes of the United States...Part II. Philadelphia: 1852. V. 62
Myth of Hiawatha and Other Oral Legends, Mythologic and Allegoric, of the North American Indians. Philadelphia: 1856. V. 62
Narrative Journal of Travels through the Northwestern Regions of the United States, Extending from Detroit through the Great Chain of American Lakes to the Sources of the Mississippi River. Albany: 1821. V. 67
Narrative of an Expedition through the Upper Mississippi to Itasca Lake, The Actual Source of This River.... New York: 1834. V. 65
Notes on Iroquois; or Contributions to American History, Antiquities and General Ethnology. Albany: 1847. V. 64

A View of the Lead Mines of Missouri: Including Some Observations on the Mineralogy, Geology, Geography, Antiquities, Soil, Climate, Population, and Productions of Missouri and Arkansaw and Other Sections of the Western Country. New York: 1819. V. 67

THE SCHOOLMASTER: Essays on Practical Education, Selected from the Works of Ascham, Milton, Locke and Butler, from the Quarterly Journal of Education and from Lectures Delivered Before the American Institute of Instruction. London: 1836. V. 65

SCHOONHOVIUS, FLORENTIUS
Emblemata Florentiae Schoonhoviae I. C. Goudani, Partim Moralia Partim Etiam Civilia. Leyden: 1626. V. 62

SCHOONOVER, J. J.
The Life and Times - General John A. Sutter. Sacramento: 1895. V. 66

SCHOPENHAUER, ARTHUR
Uber die Vierfache Wurzel des Satzes vom Zureichenden Grunde. Rudolstadt: 1813. V. 67

SCHORER, MARK
A House Too Old. New York: 1935. V. 67

SCHORGER, A. W.
The Passenger Pigeon: Its Natural History and Extinction. Norman: 1973. V. 67
Wild Turkey, Its History and Domestication. Norman: 1966. V. 64

SCHOTT, GASPAR
Cursus Mathematicus Sive Absoluta Omnium Mathematicarum Disciplinarum Encyclopaedia, in Libros XXVIII. Wurtzburg: 1661. V. 63

SCHOTTUS, FRANCISCUS
Itinerari Italiae Rerumque Romanorum. Antwerp: 1600. V. 64

SCHOULER, JAMES
A Treatise on the Law of Personal Property. Boston: 1884. V. 66

SCHRABISCH, MAX
Archaeology of Delaware River Valley, Between Hancock and Dingman's Ferry in Wayne and Pike Counties. Harrisburg: 1930. V. 66

SCHRADER, O.
Prehistoric Antiquities of the Aryan Peoples: a Manual of Comparative Philology and the Earlier Culture. New York: 1890. V. 67

SCHRAM, F. R.
Crustacea. New York: 1986. V. 67

SCHRAMKE, T.
Description of the New York Croton Aqueduct in English, German and French. New York and Berlin: 1846. V. 65

SCHRAMM, CARL CHRISTIAN
Abhandlung der Porte-Chaises. Nurnberg: 1737. V. 67

SCHRANTZ, WARD L.
Jasper County, Missouri, in the Civil War. Carthage: 1923. V. 65

SCHREBER, DANIEL GOTTLOB MORITZ
Medical Indoor Gymnastics or a System of Hygenic Exercises for Home Use to be Practised Anywhere Without Apparatus.... London, Edinburgh, Oxford: 1899. V. 65

SCHREBER, DANIEL PAUL
Denkwurdigkeiten Eines Nervenranken Nebst Nachtragen und Einem Anhang uber die Frage.... Leipzig: 1903. V. 62; 65

SCHREIBER, FRED
The Estiennes, an Annotated Catalogue of 300 Outstanding Books from their 16th and 17th Century Publishing Houses. Chapel Hill: 1982. V. 66

SCHREIBER, M. H.
Last of a Breed - Portraits of Working Cowboys. Austin: 1982. V. 67

SCHNEIDER, T.
Atlas of Classical Antiquities. London: 1895. V. 64; 66

SCHREINER, OLIVE
Dream Life and Real Life, a Little African Story. London: 1893. V. 64; 66
Dreams. London: 1891. V. 64; 65
An English-South African's View of the Situation, Words in Season. London: 1899. V. 65
Trooper Peter Halket of Mashonaland. Boston: 1897. V. 67
Trooper Peter Halket of Mashonaland. London: 1897. V. 64
Woman and Labour. London: 1911. V. 65

SCHRENK VON NOTZING, JACOB
Der Aller Durchluechigsten...Kayser...Koinigen und Ertzhertzogen... und Anderer Treflincher Berumbter Kriegshelden.... Innsbruck: 1603. V. 65

SCHREUDERS, PIET
Paperbacks, U.S.A. San Diego: 1981. V. 67

SCHREVEL, CORNELIUS
Lexicon Manuale Graeco Latinum et Latino Graecum.... Patavii: 1687. V. 66

SCHRODER, F. J. W.
Neue Alchymistische Bibliothek fur den Naturkundiger Unsers Jahrhunderts.... Frankfurt & Leipzig: 1771-1774. V. 64

SCHRODER, JOHN
Catalogue of Books and Manuscripts by Rupert Brooke, Edward Marsh and Christopher Hassall. Cambridge: 1970. V. 62

SCHRODER, JOHN F.
Himalaya to the Sea. Geology, Geomorphology and the Quarternary. 1993. V. 67

SCHROEDER, DANIEL J.
Astronomical Optics. San Diego: 1987. V. 67

SCHROEDER, JOHN FREDERICK
Memoir of the Life and Character of Mrs. Mary Anna Boardman.... New Haven: 1849. V. 65

SCHROEDER VAN DER KOLK, JACOB L. C.
On the Minute Structure and Functions of the Spinal Cord and Medulla Oblongata and on the Proximate Cause and Rational Treatment of Epilepsy. London. V. 64; 67
On the Minute Structure and Functions of the Spinal Cord and Medulla Oblongata, and on the Proximate Cause and Rational Treatment of Epilepsy. London: 1859. V. 65
Over het Fijnere Zamenstel en de Werking van het Verlengde Ruggemerg en Over de Naaste Oorzaak van Epilepsie en Hare Rationelle Behandeling. Amsterdam: 1858. V. 65

SCHROGER, A. W.
The T. B. Walker Collection of Indian Portraits. Madison: 1948. V. 65

SCHUBERT, GOTTHILF HEINRICH
Bilder Aus dem Heiligen Lande. Stuttgart: 1839. V. 62
Naturgeschichte der Saugetiere...zum Anschauungs Unterricht fur Jugend in Schulen und Familien. 1886. V. 65
Naturgeschichte der Vogel.... 1886. V. 65
Palastina. New Album of the Holy Land. Stuttgart: 1868. V. 63; 65; 67

SCHUBERT, H.
Modern Theatres: Architecture, Stage Design, Lighting. New York: 1971. V. 65

SCHUCHHARDT, C.
Schliemann's Excavations; an Archaeological and Historical Study. London: 1891. V. 65

SCHUCKARD, W. E.
Essay on the Indigenous Fossorial Hymenoptera. 1837. V. 66

SCHULBERG, BUDD
The Disenchanted. New York: 1950. V. 67
What Makes Sammy Run. New York: 1941. V. 66; 67
What Makes Sammy Run. New York: 1965. V. 66

SCHULIAN, D. M.
A Catalogue of Incunabula and Manuscripts in the Army Medical Library. New York: 1948. V. 66; 67

SCHULTES, HENRY
Flowers of Fancy, Exhibited in a Collection of Similes Taken from Various Authors.... London: 1829. V. 64

SCHULTES, R. E.
Plants of Gods.... 1979. V. 66

SCHULTZ, JACKSON
The Leather Manufacture in the United States.... New York: 1876. V. 62

SCHULTZ, JAMES WILLARD
Bird Woman (Sacajawea) - the Guide of Lewis and Clark. Boston: 1918. V. 62; 65
Blackfeet Tales of Glacier National Park. Boston: 1916. V. 66
Friends and Foes in the Rockies. Boston: 1933. V. 62
Friends of My Life as an Indian. Boston: 1923. V. 64; 66
An Indian Winter or with the Indians in the Rockies. Boston: 1913. V. 62; 65
The Quest of the Fish-Dog Skin. New York: 1913. V. 64
William Jackson - Indian Scout. Boston: 1926. V. 65
With the Indians in the Rockies. Boston: 1912. V. 63

SCHULTZ, JOY
The West Still Lives - A Book Based on the Paintings and Sculpture of Joe Ruiz Grandee. Dallas: 1970. V. 62; 65

SCHULTZ, L. P.
Fishes of the Marshall and Marianas Islands. Washington: 1953-1956. V. 62

SCHULTZE, FRITZ
Fetichism, Contribution to Anthropology and the History of Religion. New York: 1901. V. 65

SCHULZ, CHARLES M.
Charlie Brown's All-Stars. Cleveland and New York: 1966. V. 65
Here's Your Dog, Charlie Brown!. Cleveland and New York: 1968. V. 65
It Was a Short Summer, Charlie Brown. Cleveland and New York: 1970. V. 65

SCHULZ, H. C.
French Illuminated Manuscripts. San Francisco: 1958. V. 66

SCHULZ, J.
Venetian Painted Ceilings of the Renaissance. Berkeley: 1968. V. 65

SCHULZ, PETER H.
Moon Morphology: Interpretations Based on Lunar Orbiter Photography. Austin: 1976. V. 66

SCHULZE, F. E.
Challenger Voyage. Zoology. Part 53. Hexactinellida. 1887. V. 66

SCHUMANN *Album of Children's Pieces for Piano.* London: 1913. V. 66
SCHUMANN *Album of Children's Pieces for Piano.* London: 1915. V. 67

SCHURMAN, ANNA MARIA VAN
Dissertatio de Ingenii Muliebris ad Doctrinam & Meliores Litteras Aptitudine. Leiden: 1641. V. 64

SCHUSTER, CLAUD
Peaks and Pleasant Pastures. Oxford: 1911. V. 63; 64

SCHUSTER, M. LINCOLN
Eyes on the World. New York: 1935. V. 63

SCHUSTER, R. M.
Hepaticae and Anthocerotae of North America. New York: 1969-1974. V. 62

SCHUTZ, JOHN A.
Thomas Pownall British Defender of American Liberty.... Glendale: 1951. V. 64; 66

SCHUYLER, HAMILTON
The Roeblings. Princeton: 1931. V. 63

SCHUYLER, HARTLEY & GRAHAM
Illustrated Catalogue of Arms and Military Goods.... Greenwich: 1961. V. 66

SCHUYLER, JAMES
Collabs. New York: 1980. V. 62; 64
The Crystal Lithium. New York: 1972. V. 62; 64
Early in '71. Berkeley: 1982. V. 62
Freely Espousing. Poems. Garden City: 1969. V. 62; 64; 66
The Home Book: Prose and Poems 1951-1970. Calais. V. 64
Hymn to Life. New York: 1974. V. 62; 64
The Morning of the Poem. New York: 1980. V. 62
Shopping and Waiting - a Dramatic Pause. New York: 1953. V. 62; 65
Song. New York: 1976. V. 62; 64
A Sun Cab. New York: 1972. V. 62
What's for Dinner?. Santa Barbara: 1978. V. 62; 64

SCHWABACHER, E. K.
Arshille Gorky. New York: 1957. V. 62; 65

SCHWABE, WILLMAR
Pharmacopoea Homoeopathica Polyglotta.... Leipzig: 1879. V. 65

SCHWACHIUS, JOHANN
Discorsi Sopra l'Artigliarie Moderne. Von Der Artigliaria das ist von des Geschutzes der Stucke, Morseln, Fewerwecke, Petarden, und aller Darzugehorigen Kunste Erster Invention. Dresden: 1624. V. 62

SCHWANN, THEODOR
Microscopical Researches into the Accordance in the Structure and Growth of Animals and Plants. London: 1847. V. 64
Mikroskopische Untersuchungen Uber die Ubereinstimmung in der Struktur und dem Wachsthum der thiere und Pflanzen. Berlin: 1839. V. 62; 64

SCHWANTES, G.
Flowering Stones and Mid-Day Flowers.... London: 1957. V. 64

SCHWARTZ, A.
Amphibians and Reptiles of the West Indies.... Gainesville: 1991. V. 64

SCHWARTZ, C. W.
The Prairie Chicken in Missouri. 1944. V. 64; 66

SCHWARTZ, DELMORE
Genesis. Book One. New York: 1943. V. 62
I Am Cherry Alive, The Little Girl Sang. New York: 1979. V. 64
In Dreams Begin Responsibilities. Norfolk: 1938. V. 64
Shenandoah. Norfolk: 1941. V. 67
Vaudeville for a Princess and Other Poems. New York: 1950. V. 62
The World is a Wedding. Norfolk: 1948. V. 64
The World Is a Wedding. London: 1949. V. 62; 65

SCHWARTZ, MORRIE
Letting Go: Morrie's Reflections on Living While Dying. New York: 1996. V. 65

SCHWARTZ, SEYMOUR I.
The Mapping of America. New York: 1980. V. 63

SCHWARTZOTT, CAROL
A Brief History of the Basket. Niagara Falls: 1998. V. 64

SCHWARZ, GEORG
Almost Forgotten Germany. Deya, Majorca: 1936. V. 62
Almost Forgotten Germany. London: 1936. V. 63

SCHWARZ, HEINRICH
David Octavius Hill: Master of Photography. New York: 1931. V. 63

SCHWATKA, FREDERICK
The Children of the Cold. Boston: 1899. V. 62
Report of a Military Reconnaissance in Alaska, made in 1883. Washington: 1885. V. 65
Wonderland: Or Alaska and the Inland Passage, with Description of the Country Traversed by the Northern Pacific Raildroad. Chicago: 1886. V. 65

SCHWECHTEN, F. W.
Der Dom zu Meissen.... Berlin: 1823-1826. V. 67

SCHWEINITZ, EDMUND DE
Moravian Manual: Containing an Account of the Moravian Church or Unitas Fratrum. Bethlehem: 1869. V. 63; 66; 67

SCHWEITZER, ALBERT
Das Christentum Und Die Weltreligionem. Munich: 1947. V. 64
La Probleme de l'Ethique dans l'Evolution de la Pensee Humaine. Paris: 1952. V. 64

SCHWEIZER *Archiv fur Neurologie und Psychiatrie. Volume 1-43.* Zurich: 1917-1939. V. 65

SCHWEIZERISCHE Obstsorten: Herausgegeben Vom Schweizerischen Landwirthschaftlichen Verein. St. Gallen: 1863-1872. V. 65

SCHWENTER, DANIEL
Geometriae Practicae Novae. Nuremberg: 1617-1618. V. 62; 67

SCHWERKE, IRVING
Kings Jazz and David (Jazz et Davis Rois). Paris: 1927. V. 66

SCHWERNER, ARMAND
Bacchae Sonnets. Omaha: 1974. V. 63

SCHWETTMANN, MARTIN W.
Santa Rita. The University of Texas Oil Discovery. Austin: 1943. V. 62; 64

SCHWIND, MORITZ VON
Bilder fur die Jugend. Vokstrachten. Vienna: 1825. V. 67

SCIASCIA, LEONARDO
The Council of Egypt. London: 1966. V. 62

SCIDMORE, E. RUHAMAH
Alaska: its Southern Coast and the Sitkan Archipelago. Boston: 1885. V. 65

LA SCIENCE Curieuse, ou Traite de La Chyromance; Recueilly des plus Graves Autheurs Qui ont Traite de Cette Matiere & Plus Exactement Rerercche qu'il n'a este cy-devant par Aucun Autre. Paris: 1665. V. 62

SCIENCE and Public Policy. Washington: 1947. V. 65

SCIENTIFIC American. New York: 1846-1859. V. 63

SCIESZKA, JON
The Stinky Cheese Man and Other Fairly Stupid Tales. New York: 1992. V. 65

SCIGHTE.. New York: 1987. V. 64

SCLATER, PHILIP LUTLEY
Argentine Ornithology.... London: 1888-1889. V. 67
Catalogue of a Collection of American Birds. London: 1862. V. 67
Challenger Voyage. Zoology. Part 8. Report on the Birds. 1881. V. 66
A Field Guide to Australian Birds. Adelaide: 1970-1974. V. 67
A Monograph of the Jacamars and Puff-Birds, or, Families Galbulidae and Buccondiae. London: 1879-1882. V. 66; 67
On the Birds Collected by the Late Mr. T. K. Salmon in the State of Antioquin, United States of Colombia. London: 1879. V. 65
On the Struthious Birds Living in the Society's Menagerie. 1860. V. 67

SCLATER, WILLIAM L.
The Mammals of South Africa. London: 1900-1901. V. 62; 64; 66

SCOBELL, HENRY
A Collection of Acts and Ordinances of General Use, Made in the Parliament Begun and Held at Westminster the Third Day of November, Anno 1640...the 17th of September Anno 1656.... London: 1658. V. 62

SCORESBY, WILLIAM
An Account of the Arctic Regions, with a History and Description of the Northern Whale Fishery. Newton: 1969. V. 62
A Journal of a Voyage to the Northern Whale-Fishery.... Edinburgh: 1823. V. 62; 63

A SCOURGE for the Dissenters; or, Non-Conformity Unmasked.... London: 1790. V. 66

SCORZA, MANUEL
Redouble por Rancas. Barcelona: 1970. V. 67

THE SCOTCH Hut, a Poem, Addressed to Euphorbus, or, The Earl of the Grove. London: 1779. V. 65

SCOTLAND For Ever, a Gift-Book of the Scottish Regiments. London. V. 67

SCOTLAND. LAWS, STATUTES, ETC. - 1744
The Statutes at Large Concerning Elections of Members of Parliament for Scotland. Edinburgh: 1744. V. 63

THE SCOTS March from Barwick to Newcastle. Newcastle: 1827. V. 67

SCOTT, ALEXANDER MALCOLM
The Battle of Langside. Glasgow: 1885. V. 62

SCOTT, ALICE
Teddy Bear. London: 1905. V. 66

SCOTT, ANDREW
Report of a Trial in the Jury Court, Edinburgh, on the 25th June, 1821, for an Alleged Libel, in the Case of Rev. Andrew Scott.... Glasgow: 1821. V. 63

SCOTT, ANNA M.
A Year with Fairies. Chicago: 1914. V. 63

SCOTT, BENJAMIN
A Statistical Vindication of the City of London, or, Fallacies Exploded and Figures Explained. London: 1867. V. 67

SCOTT, CAROLINE LUCY
A Marriage in High Life. London: 1828. V. 65

SCOTT, CHARLES A.
My Unknown Friend. London: 1883. V. 62

SCOTT, CHARLES KENNEDY
The Chelsea Song Book. London: 1930. V. 63

SCOTT, CLEMENT
The Green Room: Stories by Those Who Frequent It. London: 1880. V. 64
Stories of the Stage. London: 1881. V. 64

SCOTT, CLEMENT WILLIAM
Round About the Islands; or, Sunny Spots Near Home. London: 1874. V. 63

SCOTT, COLONEL
A Journal of a Residence in the Esmailla of Abd-El-Kader and of Travels in Morocco and Algiers. London: 1842. V. 64

SCOTT, DAVID
Grass of Parnassus from the Bents O'Buchan. Peterhead: 1997. V. 62

SCOTT, EDWIN J.
Random Recollections of a Long Life, 1806 to 1876. Columbia: 1884. V. 63; 65

SCOTT, FLORENCE E.
Kindergarten Limericks. New York: 1915. V. 62

SCOTT, FRANK J.
The Art of Beautifying Suburban Home Grounds.... New York: 1870. V. 62; 65

SCOTT, G.
The Labrador Dog, It's Home and History. 1990. V. 63

SCOTT, GENIO C.
Fishing in American Waters. New York: 1875. V. 65

SCOTT, GEOFFREY
A Box of Paints. London: 1923. V. 62

SCOTT, GEORGE RYLEY
The History of Cockfighting. London: 1955. V. 63; 64
The History of Cockfighting. London: 1975. V. 67

SCOTT, GEORGE W.
The Black Hill Story. Fort Collins: 1953. V. 67

SCOTT, HUGH L.
Some Memories of a Soldier. New York: 1928. V. 65; 67

SCOTT, HUGH STOWELL
From One Generation to Another. London: 1892. V. 66
The Grey Lady. London: 1899. V. 63
The Grey Lady. London: 1902. V. 65
The Money-Spinner and Other Character Notes. London: 1896. V. 63
With Edged Tools. London: 1894. V. 66
The Works. London: 1909-1925. V. 63

SCOTT, J.
Piranesi. London: 1975. V. 65

SCOTT, JAMES
Commentaries on the Use and Necessity of Lavements in the Correction of Habitual Constipation and in the Treatment of Those Diseases Which are Occasioned or Aggravated in Intestinal Accumulation and Irritation.... London: 1829. V. 63

SCOTT, JOANNA
Fading, My Parmachene Belle. New York: 1987. V. 67

SCOTT, JOB
Journal of the Life, Travels and Gospel Labours of that Faithful Servant and Minister of Christ, Job. Scott. New York: 1797. V. 67

SCOTT, JOCK
Lake Fishing for Salmon, Trout and Pike. London: 1932. V. 67
Spinning Up to Date. London: 1939. V. 67

SCOTT, JOHN
The House of Mourning, a Poem: with Some Smaller Pieces. London: 1817. V. 63; 65
The Lost Principle or the Sectional Equilibrium. Richmond: 1860. V. 63
Paris Revisited in 1815, by Way of Brussels.... London: 1816. V. 67
Partisan Life with Col. John S. Mosby. New York: 1867. V. 62; 63; 64; 65
War Inconsistent with the Doctrine and Example of Jesus Christ. London: 1796. V. 62

SCOTT, JONATHAN
Tales, Anecdotes and Letters. Shrewsbury: 1800. V. 63

SCOTT, JOSEPH
The Art of Preserving the Loss of the Teeth, Familiarly Explained.... London: 1833. V. 63; 64; 66
A Geographical Description of Pennsylvania, also of the Counties Respectively in the Order in Which They were Established by the Legislature. Philadelphia: 1806. V. 62
The United States Gazetteer; Containing an Authentic Description of the Several States. Philadelphia: 1795. V. 62; 64

SCOTT, K. L.
Later Gothic Manuscripts 1390-1490. London: 1996. V. 62

SCOTT, KELLY W.
Lariats and Chevrons or Corporal Jack Wilson, US LA RR. Guthrie: 1905. V. 62; 65

SCOTT, LEADER
Echoes of Old Florence, Her Palaces and Those Who Have Lived in Them. Florence: 1901. V. 63

SCOTT, MARION D.
Montpelier: the Recollections of Marion Dupont Scott. N.P: 1976. V. 64

SCOTT, MARY H.
The Oregon Trail through Wyoming. Aurora: 1958. V. 64; 67

SCOTT, PAUL
After the Funeral. 1979. V. 62
After the Funeral. London: 1979. V. 67
The Bender - Pictures from an Exhibition of Middle Class Portraits. London: 1963. V. 64
Johnny Sahib. London: 1952. V. 63
A Male Child. London: 1956. V. 64
Staying On. London: 1977. V. 63; 65

SCOTT, PETER
Morning Flight. London: 1942. V. 64
Wild Chorus. 1938. V. 62; 63; 66
Wild Chorus. London: 1942. V. 64
Wild Chorus. London: 1949. V. 62; 66
Wildfowl of the British Isles. London: 1957. V. 67

SCOTT, R.
Scott's Practical Cotton Spinner and Manufacturer.... London: 1867. V. 63

SCOTT, R. W.
The Alpine Flora of the Rocky Mountains. Volume I. The Middle Rockies. Salt Lake City: 1995. V. 65

SCOTT, RALPH
A Soldier's Diary. London: 1923. V. 64

SCOTT, RANDALL W.
Management and Control of Growth. Washington: 1975. V. 67

SCOTT, REGINALD
The Discoverie of Witchcraft, Wherein the Lewde Dealing of Witches and Witchmongers is Notablie Detected.. London: 1584. V. 63

SCOTT, ROBERT FALCON
The Diaries of Captain Robert Scott. Tylers Green: 1968. V. 65
Scott's Last Expedition. London: 1913. V. 63; 65; 66
Scott's Last Expedition. New York: 1913. V. 62
Scott's Last Expedition. London: 1914. V. 62
The Voyage of the Discovery. New York/London: 1905. V. 64
The Voyage of the Discovery. New York/London: 1907. V. 63

SCOTT, S. H.
A Westmorland Village. London: 1904. V. 65

SCOTT, SARAH E.
Every-Day Cookery for Every Family. Philadelphia: 1880. V. 67

SCOTT, SIBBALD DAVID
To Jamaica and Back. London: 1876. V. 65

SCOTT, TEMPLE
The Silver Age and Other Dramatic Memories. New York: 1919. V. 66

SCOTT, THOMAS
The British Parasitic Copepoda. Copepoda Parasitic on Fish. London: 1913. V. 64; 65; 67
Robert Earle of Essex, His Ghost Sent From Elizian: to the Nobility, Gentry and Communaltie of England. (and) A Postscript, or, a Second Part of Robert Earle of Essex His Ghost. printed in Paradise: 1624. V. 66

SCOTT, TOM
The Golfers' Year. London: 1950. V. 63

SCOTT, W. B.
The Mammalia of the Uinta Formation. Philadelphia: 1889. V. 67

SCOTT, W. R.
The Deaf and Dumb, Their Position in Society and the Principles of Their Education, Considered. London: 1844. V. 65

SCOTT, W. W.
A History of Orange County, Virginia. Richmond: 1907. V. 65

SCOTT, WALTER
The Abbot. Edinburgh: 1820. V. 62; 63; 65; 66; 67
Anne of Geierstein; or, the Maiden of the Mist. Edinburgh: 1829. V. 63; 65
Border Antiquities of England and Scotland. London: 1889. V. 65
Chronicles of the Canongate by the Author of Waverley. London: 1827. V. 62
Demonology and Witchcraft. New York: 1830. V. 66
The Fortunes of Nigel. Edinburgh: 1822. V. 65; 66
Guy Mannering, the Astrologer, or the Prophecy of Meg Merrilies, the Gipsey. London: 1816. V. 62
The History of Scotland. London: 1831. V. 67
Ivanhoe. Edinburgh: 1820. V. 64
Ivanhoe. Philadelphia: 1823. V. 64
Kenilworth: a Romance. Edinburgh: 1821. V. 63; 65
The Lay of the Last Minstrel. London: 1808. V. 63
The Lay of the Last Minstrel. London: 1810. V. 62
The Lay of the Last Minstrel. Edinburgh: 1854. V. 62
Letters on Demonology and Witchcraft. New York: 1833. V. 65
The Life of Napoleon Buonaparte, Emperor of the French.... Exeter: 1828. V. 64
The Lord of the Isles, a Poem. Philadelphia: 1815. V. 65
Memoirs of John Dryden. Paris: 1826. V. 67
The Monastery. Edinburgh: 1820. V. 62; 67
Paul's Letters to His Kinsfolk. Edinburgh: 1816. V. 62
Peveril of the Peak. Edinburgh: 1822. V. 62; 65; 66; 67
The Pirate. Edinburgh: 1822. V. 62; 66
The Poetical Works. Edinburgh: 1833-1834. V. 63
The Poetical Works. Edinburgh: 1843. V. 67
The Poetical Works. Boston: 1866. V. 62; 64
The Poetical Works. London: 1913. V. 62
Quentin Durward. Edinburgh: 1823. V. 64; 66; 67
Redgauntlet. Edinburgh: 1824. V. 66
Rokeby. Edinburgh: 1815. V. 62
Tales of a Grandfather. Edinburgh: 1829. V. 62
Tales of a Grandfather. Paris: 1831. V. 62
Tales of a Grandfather. Edinburgh: 1842. V. 62
The Vision of Don Roderick and Other Poems. Edinburgh: 1811. V. 67
Waverley. Edinburgh: 1814. V. 63
Waverley Novels. Edinburgh: 1829-1833. V. 63
Waverley Novels. Exeter: 1831. V. 64
Waverley Novels. Edinburgh: 1842. V. 62; 63
Waverley Novels. Edinburgh: 1852-1853. V. 62; 67
Waverley Novels. Edinburgh: 1886-1887. V. 62
The Waverley Novels. London: 1892-1894. V. 62
The Waverley Novels. Edinburgh: 1901-1902. V. 62
Woodstock, or the Cavalier. Edinburgh: 1826. V. 62; 65; 66

SCOTT, WALTER SIDNEY
The Athenians. Waltham St. Lawrence: 1943. V. 64
Harriet and Mary Being the Relations Between Percy Bysshe Shelley, Harriet Shelley, Mary Shelley and Thomas Jefferson Hogg.... Waltham St. Lawrence: 1944. V. 64; 65
Letters of Maria Edgeworth and Anna Letitia Barbauld, Selected from the Lushington Papers. Waltham St. Lawrence: 1953. V. 65
Shelley at Oxford. Waltham St. Lawrence: 1944. V. 64

SCOTT, WILLIAM
An Essay of Drapery or the Complete Citizen. London: 1635. V. 64
Picturesque Scenery in the County of Sussex, Sketched from Nature, Drawn on Stone.... London: 1821. V. 62; 67
The Riviera. London: 1907. V. 66

SCOTT, WILLIAM BELL
Antiquarian Gleanings in the North of England.... London. V. 67
Autobiographical Notes of the Life of.... New York: 1892. V. 64
Chorea Sancti Viti; or Steps in the Journey of Prince Legion. London: 1851. V. 64
William Blake. London: 1878. V. 64

SCOTT, WILLIAM HENRY
British Field Sports. Shooting, Hunting, Coursing, Racing, Cocking, Fishing. 1818. V. 62

SCOTT, WILLIAM ROBERT
The Constitution and Finance of English, Scottish and Irish Joint Stock Companies to 1720. 1912-1910-1911. V. 65

SCOTT-GATTY, ALFRED
Domestic Ditties. Book I. London: 1901. V. 63

SCOTT-HUGHES, JOHN
Famous Yachts. London: 1928. V. 62; 66

THE SCOTTISH Celtic Review. 1885. V. 67

SCOTTISH Tourist. Edinburgh: 1852. V. 67

THE SCOTTISH Zoo and Variety Circus. Glasgow: 1901. V. 67

SCOUGAL, HENRY
The Life of God in the Soul of Man; or the Nature and Excellency of the Christian Religion. London: 1756. V. 64

SCOUTETTEN, RAOUL HENRI JOSEPH
La Methode Ovalaire, ou Nouvelle Methode Pour Amputer dans les Articulations. Paris: 1827. V. 66

SCOUTETTEN, ROBERT JOSEPH HENRI
L'Ozone, ou Recherches Chimiques, Meteorologiques, Physiologiques et Medicales sur l'Oxygene Electrise. Paris: 1856. V. 65

SCOUTING and the Jewish 'Boy. New York: 1929. V. 63

SCRATCHLEY, J.
The London Dissector; or System of Dissection Practised in the Hosptials and Lecture Rooms of the Metropolis.... London: 1816. V. 62

SCRIPPS, JAMES E.
Five Months Abroad, or, the Observations and Experiences of an Editor in Europe. Detroit: 1882. V. 62; 63; 64; 66

SCRIPPS, JOHN LOCKE
Life of Abraham Lincoln. New York: 1860. V. 64

SCRIPTORES Rei Rusticae Veteres Latini Cato, Varro, Columella, Palladius Quibus Ninc Accedit Vegetius De Mulo-Medicina et Gargilii Martialis Fragmentum.... Lipsiae: 1735. V. 65

SCRIPTORES Rei Rusticae...Veteres Latini Cato, Varro, Columella Palladius Quibus Nunc Accedit Vegetius de Mulo-Medicina et Gargilii Martialis Gramentum.... Lipsiae: 1785. V. 66

SCRIPTURE Histories Selected from the Old Testament and Explained... in the Way of Question and Answer. Manchester: 1817-1820. V. 62

SCRIVEN, A.
The Dartmoor Shepherd. 50 Years in Prison. Oswestry: 1930. V. 62; 66

SCRIVENOR, J. B.
The Geology of Malaya. London: 1931. V. 67

SCROGGINS, D.
20,000 Spanish American Pseudonyms. Lanham & London: 1997. V. 62

SCROGGS, WILLIAM
The Practice of Courts-Lett, and Courts-Baron. London: 1701. V. 65

SCROPE, GEORGE JULIUS POULETT
Considerations on Volcanos, the Probable Causes of their Phenomena, the Laws Which Determine Their March, the Disposition of Their Products and Their Connexion with the Present State and Past History of the Globe.... London: 1825. V. 65; 66
The Geology and Extinct Volcanos of Central France. 1858. V. 63; 66
The Geology of the Extinct Volcanos of Central France. London: 1858. V. 64; 65; 67
The Rights of Industry, or the Social Problem of the Day.... London: 1848. V. 63
Volcanos. The Character of Their Phenomena, Their Share in the Structure and Composition of the Surface of the Globe and Their Relation to Its Internal Forces. London: 1862. V. 64; 65
Volcanos. The Character of Their Phenomena.... London: 1872. V. 62

SCROPE, RICHARD
A Letter to ... ..., Esq. Occasioned by a Late Misrepresentation of the Circumstances of a Prosecution Commenced A.D. 1763.... Salisbury: 1773. V. 62; 65

SCROPE, W.
Days and Nights Salmon Fishing In the Tweed. 1921. V. 67

SCROPE, WILLIAM
The Art of Deer Stalking. London: 1897. V. 62
Days of Deer Stalking in the Scottish Highlands Including an Account of the Nature and Habits of the Red Deer.... London: 1883. V. 65
Days of Deer-Stalking in the Scottish Highlands. London: 1894. V. 62

SCRUTON, WILLIAM
Thornton and the Brontes. Bradford: 1898. V. 66

SCUDAMORE, CHARLES
Cases Illustrating and Confirming the Remedial Power of the Inhalation of Iodine and Conium in Tubercular Phthisis and Various Disordered States of the Lungs and Air Passages. London: 1834. V. 62
A Treatise on the Nature and Cure of Gout and Rheumatism. London: 1819. V. 65

SCUDDER, ANTOINETTE
The Grey Studio. Boston: 1934. V. 67

SCUDDER, CHARLES LOCKE
The Treatment of Fractures with notes Upon a Few Common Dislocations. Philadelphia: 1911. V. 65

SCUDDER, S. H.
The Tertiary Insects of North America. Washington: 1890. V. 65

SCUDERY, MADELEINE DE
Artamenes; or, the Grand Cyrus, That Excellent Romance. London: 1690-1691. V. 64

SCULL, E. MARSHALL
Hunting in the Arctic and Alaska. Philadelphia: 1914. V. 65; 66

SCULLY, JULIA
Disfarmer. The Heber Springs Portraits. 1939-1946. Danbury: 1976. V. 67

SCULLY, VINCENT
Pueblo: Mountain, Village, Dance. New York: 1975. V. 65

SCULPTURA Historico-Technica: or, The History and the Art of Engraving. London: 1770. V. 62

SCULPTURA-Historico-Technica: or the History and the Art of Engraving. London: 1747. V. 66

SCULPTURE in Ceramics by Miro and Artigas. New York: 1956. V. 64

SCUPHAM, PETER
The Gift. Love Poems. Surrey: 1973. V. 66
The Small Containers. Cheshire: 1972. V. 67
Under the Barrage. Bonholt: 1988. V. 64

SCURFIELD, GEORGE
A Stickful of Nonpareil. Cambridge: 1956. V. 62

SCURLOCK, DAVID
Thoughts on the Influence of Religion in Civil Government and Its Tendency to Promote and Preserve the Social Liberty and Rights of Man. London: 1792. V. 63

SCURRY, JAMES
The Captivity, Sufferings and Escape of James Scurry Who Was a Prisoner During Ten Years in the Dominion of Hyder Ali and Tipoo Saib, Written by Himself. London: 1824. V. 63

SEABORG, GLENN T.
Nuclear Milestones: a Collection of Speeches...Volume One: Builders and Discoverers. 1971. V. 63

SEALSFIELD, CHARLES
The Americans as They Are.... London: 1828. V. 66

SEALY, HENRY NICHOLAS
A Treatise on Coins, Currency, and Banking. London: 1858. V. 67

SEALY, J. R.
A Revision of the Genus Camellia. London: 1958. V. 64

SEAMAN, M.
Popular Psalmody, Being a Selection of Congregational Psalm and Hymn Tunes.... London: 1836. V. 66

SEARLE, JANUARY, PSEUD.
The Life, Character, and Genius of Ebenezer Elliott the Corn Law Rhymer. London: 1850. V. 64
Memoirs of Ebenezer Elliott, the Corn Law Rhymer.... London: 1852. V. 64

SEARLE, MARK
Turn-Pikes and Toll-Bars. London: 1930. V. 67

SEARLE, ROBERT
Slightly Foxed But Still Desirable. 1989. V. 66

SEARLE, RONALD
Haven't We Met Before Somewhere?. London: 1966. V. 64
Looking at London and People Worth Meeting. London: 1953. V. 63
To the Kwai - and Back. London: 1986. V. 63
To the Kwai and Back. 1986. V. 67

SEARS, J. H.
The Physical Geography, Geology, Mineralogy and Palaeontology of Essex County, Massachusetts. Salem: 1905. V. 63; 64; 66

SEARS, LOUIS MARTIN
John Slidell. Durham: 1925. V. 63

SEARS, M.
Oceanography, Invited Lectures Presented at the International Oceanographic Congress Held in New York. Washington: 1961. V. 67

SEARS, ROEBUCK & CO.
Color Perfect Wallpaper. Philadelphia: 1940. V. 62; 65

A SEASONAL Speech Made by Alderman Atkins in the Rump-Parliament. London: 1660. V. 62

THE SEASONS. New York. V. 62

THE SEASONS (Number 3). Greenfield: 1848. V. 64

SEATON, BENJAMIN M.
The Bugle Softly Blows - The Confederate Diary of Benjamin M. Seaton. Waco: 1965. V. 62; 63; 64; 67

THE SEATS of the Nobility and Gentry, in England and Scotland. London: 1770-1786. V. 64

SEAVER, EDWIN
Cross Section. A Collection of New American Writing. New York: 1944. V. 65

SEAVER, GEORGE
Birdie Bowers of the Antarctic. London: 1938. V. 63

SEAVER, ROBERT
Ye Butcher, Ye Baker, Ye Candelstick Maker. Boston: 1908. V. 65

SEAWARD, JOHN
Observations on the Advantages and Possibility of Successfully Employing Steam Power in Navigating Ships Between This Country and the East Indies. London: 1834. V. 62; 63

SEAWARD, SAMUEL
Specification of the Patent Granted to Samuel Seaward, of the Parish of All Saints, Poplar, in the County of Middlesex, Engineer for Certain Improvements in the Construction of Steam-Engines. Sealed October 17, 1834. London: 1835. V. 64

SEAWELL, MARY WRIGHT
Our Father's Care. A Ballad. Richmond: 1864. V. 63; 65

SEBALD, W. G.
The Emigrants. London: 1996. V. 63; 65

SEBASTIAN, IZZARD
One Hundred Masterpieces from the Collection of Dr. Walter A. Compton. London: 1992. V. 66

SEBASTIANI, LEOPOLDO
Descrizione del Palazzo di Caprarola. Rome: 1791. V. 64

SEBOEK, T. A.
Native Languages of the Americas. New York: 1976-1977. V. 62

SEBRIGHT, JOHN
Observations Upon Hawking. London: 1828. V. 62

SECCHI, PIETRO ANGELO
Le Soleil. Paris: 1875-1877. V. 64; 67
L'Unite des Forces Physiques. Essai de Philosophie Naturelle.... Paris: 1874. V. 64

SECCOMBE, JOSEPH
A Discourse Utter'd in Part at Ammauskeeg-Falls in the Fishing-Season 1739. Barre: 1971. V. 62
Some Occasional Thoughts on the Influence of the Spirit. Boston: 1742. V. 63; 66

SECCOMBE, T. S.
The Story of Prince Hildebrand and the Princess Ida. London: 1880. V. 62

SECHENOV, IVAN MIKHAILOVIC
Neue Versuche am Hirn und Ruckenmark des Frosches. Berlin: 1865. V. 63

SECHENOV, IVAN MIKHAILOVIC continued
Physiologische Studien Uber die Hemmungsmechanisem fur die Reflexthatigkeit des Ruckenmarks im Gehirne des Frosches. Berlin: 1863. V. 63

THE SECOND Book of the Poets' Club. London: 1911. V. 65

THE SECOND Chapter of a New Book Lo! in the Chair of the Great City, Sits a Worthy Prototype of the Saint, Who Uses His Active Energies to Procure Food for the Hungery Tygers that Year for Proofs of Treason.... London: 1820?. V. 67

THE SECOND War of Revolution; or the Great Principles Involved in the Present Controversy Between Parties. Washington: 1839. V. 65

THE SECRET History of the Most Renown'd Q. Elizabeth and Earl of Essex. Cologne: 1767. V. 64; 66

SECRETAN, E.
Catalogue of the Celebrated Collection of Paintings by Modern and Old Masters and of Water-Colours and Drawings Formed by Mr. E. Secretan, Which Will Be sold by Auction...on Monday, First of July 1889.... Paris: 1889. V. 66

SECRETS Concernans les Arts et Metiers. Avignon: 1738. V. 64

SECUNDUS, JOANNES NICOLAUS
Kisses. London: 1775. V. 65
Kisses. London: 1778. V. 62
Kisses. London: 1927. V. 66

SEDGEWICK, MISS
Letters from Abroad to Kindred at Home. New York: 1841. V. 63

SEDGFIELD, W. J.
The Place Names of Cumberland and Westmorland. Manchester: 1915. V. 65

SEDGWICK, ADAM
A Discourse on the Studies of the University of Cambridge. London: 1850. V. 65
A Memorial by the Trustees of Cowgill Chapel.... Cambridge: 1868. V. 66
On the Classification and Nomenclature of the Lower Palaeozoic Rocks of England and Wales.... 1852. V. 62
On the Physical Structure of Those Formations Which are Immediately Associated with the Primitive Ridge of Devonshire and Cornwall. (with) On the Physical Structure of the Lizard District in the County of Cornwall. Cambridge: 1820-1835. V. 65
Preface to the Catalogue of the Cambrian and Silurian Fossils in the Geologial Museum of the University of Cambridge. Cambridge: 1872. V. 62

SEDGWICK, C. M.
A New England Tale; or Sketches of New England Character and Manners. New York: 1822. V. 66

SEDGWICK, JAMES
Remarks, Critical and Miscellaneous, on the Commentaries of Sir William Blackstone. London: 1800. V. 62

SEDGWICK, JANE MINOT
Songs from the Greek. London: 1896. V. 64

SEDGWICK, JOHN
The Wonder-Working God, to Bee Seene In the Desolation of Wicked Enemies: In Giving Peace Unto His Churches; with an Application of the Same to the Present Times. London: 1641. V. 65

SEDGWICK, NOEL
The Gun on Saltings and Stubble. London: 1949. V. 67
A Shooting Man's Year. London: 1947. V. 67

SEDGWICK, THEODORE
A Memoir of the Life of William Livingston, Member of Congress in 1774, 1775 and 1776; Delegate to the Federal Convention in 1787 and Governor of the State of New Jersey from 1776 to 1790. New York: 1833. V. 63; 66

SEDLEY, CHARLES
Bellamira, or the Mistress, a Comedy: As It Is Acted by Their Majesties Servants. London: 1687. V. 65
The Miscellaneous Works of the Honourable Charles Sedley. London: 1702. V. 64

SEDULIUS, C.
From the Opus Paschale. Lexington: 1955. V. 66

SEE, LISA
Flower Net. 1997. V. 64; 66

SEEBHOM, HENRY
The Birds of Siberia. 1901. V. 64

SEEBOHM, HENRY
The Geographical Distribution of the Family Charadriidae. London. V. 62; 66
The Geographical Distribution of the Family Charadriidae. London: 1887-1888. V. 67
A History of British Birds. 1883-1925. V. 67
A History of British Birds with Notes on Their Classification and Geographical Distribution. London: 1896. V. 65; 67
A Monograph of the Turdidae, or Family of Thrushes. London: 1898-1902. V. 67
Notes on the Birds of the Lower Petchora. London: 1876. V. 62

SEEGER, ALAN
Alan Seeger, Le Poete De La Legion Etrange. Ses Lettres et Poemes Ecrits Durant la Guerre Reunis par son Pere et Traduits par Odette Raimondi- Matheron. Paris: 1918. V. 64

SEEGER, PETE
Carry It On!: A History in Song and Picture of the Working Men and Women of America. New York: 1985. V. 63

SEELEY, HOWARD
A Lone Star Bo-Peep and Other Tales of Texas Ranch. New York: 1885. V. 63; 66

SEELEY, J.
Stowe. A Description of the House and Gardens.... Buckingham: 1817. V. 64

SEELEY, J. R.
The Expansion of England. Two Courses of Lectures. London: 1883. V. 67

SEELEY, JOHN
Ecce Home, a Survey of the Life and Works of Jesus Christ. London: 1866. V. 66

SEELEY, MABEL
Eleven Came Back. Garden City: 1943. V. 66
The Whispering Cup. Garden City: 1940. V. 66

SEELEY, ROBERT BENTON
Memoirs of the Life and Writings of Michael Thomas Sadler. London: 1842. V. 64

SEELY, H. G.
Phillips' Manual of Geology, Theoretical and Practical. 1885. V. 65; 66

SEELY, JOHN B.
The Wonders of Elora; or, the Narrative of a Journey to the Temples and Dwellings Excavated Out of a Mountain of Granite.... London: 1824. V. 66

SEELY, L., MRS.
Mrs. Seeley's Cook Book. New York: 1908. V. 67

SEEMANN, BERTHOLD
Viti: an Account of a Government Mission to the Vitian or Fijian Islands in the Years 1860-1861. Cambridge: 1862. V. 65

SEEMES, RAPHAEL
The Cruise of the Alabama and the Sumter. London: 1864. V. 65

SEFERIS, GEORGE
The King of Asine and Other Poems. London: 1948. V. 66

SEGALAS D'ETCHEPARE, PIERRE SALOMON
Essai sur la Gravelle et la Pierre, Consideree Sous le Rapport de Leurs Causes, de Leurs Effets, et de Leurs Divers Modes de Traitement. Paris: 1839. V. 63

SEGALE, BLANDINA
At the End of the Santa Fe Trail. Columbus: 1932. V. 63; 66

SEGAR, WILLIAM
Original Institutions of the Princely Orders of Collars. Edinburgh: 1823. V. 62; 67

SEGARD, ACHILLE
Mary Cassatt. Un Peintre des Enfants et des Meres. Paris: 1913. V. 63

SEGER, JOHN H.
Tradition of the Cheyenne Indians. 1905. V. 66

SEGOE, LADISLAS
Local Planing Administration. Chicago: 1941. V. 65

SEGRAVE, CHARLES W.
The Segrave Family 1066-1935. 1936. V. 64

SEGUIN, LISBETH GOOCH
The Children's Pastime: Pictures and Stories. London: 1884. V. 65
Rural England: Loiterings Along the Lanes, the Common-Sides and the Meadow-Paths, With Peeps into Halls, Farms and Cottages. London: 1884. V. 67

SEGUR, ADRIENNE
Les Aventurs de Cotonnet. Paris: 1930. V. 65

SEGUR, COMTESSE DE
Histoire de Blondine de Bonne-Biche et de Beau-Minon. (Story of the Pretty Young Blond Girl and the Pretty Pussycat). Montronge: 1945. V. 62; 67

SEGUR, MARQUIS DE
Le Royaume de la rue Saint-Honore, Madame Geoffrin et sa Fille. Paris: 1909. V. 63

SEGUR, PHILIPPE PAUL DE, COUNT
Histoire de Russie et de Pierre-le-Grand. Paris: 1829. V. 66
History of the Expedition to Russia, Undertaken by the Emperor Napoleon, in the Year 1812. London: 1825. V. 65

SEGUR, SOPHIE ROSTOPCHINE, COMTESSE DE
Old French Fairy Tales. Philadelphia: 1920. V. 64

SEGUY, E. A.
Bouquets et Frondaisons 60 Motifs en Couleur. Paris: 1925. V. 64
Papillons, Vingt Planches en Phototypie Coloriees a Patron Donnant 81 Papillons et Compositions Decoratives. Paris: 1925. V. 64

SEIA, HUGO
Mundjamba. The Life Story of an African Hunter. 1995. V. 62; 63; 64

SEIDEL, M.
Bruegel. New York: 1971. V. 62

SEIDLER, T.
The Dulcimer Boy. London: 1981. V. 63

SEIDMANN-FREUD, TOM
Buch Erfullten Wunsche. Potsdam: 1929. V. 64
Die Fischreise. Berlin: 1925. V. 64
Peregrin and the Goldfish. New York: 1929. V. 63

SEIFERT, HOWARD S.
Space Technology. New York: 1959. V. 63

SEIGNE, J. W.
A Bird Watcher's Note Book: Studies of Woodcock, Snipe and Other Birds. 1930. V. 67
Irish Bogs. 1928. V. 67
Woodcock and Snipe. 1936. V. 67

SEIGNOBOSC, FRANCOISE
Chouchou. New York: 1958. V. 62
Fanchette and Jeannot. New York: 1937. V. 62

SEITZ, A.
Macrolepidoptera of the World. Volume I. Suppl. to Palaearctic Butterflies. Stuttgart: 1932. V. 62
Macrolepidoptera of the World. Palearctic Fauna. Volume 2. Bombyces and Sphinges. Stuttgart: 1913. V. 62; 63; 64; 65; 66
The Macrolepidoptera of the World. Volume 5. The American Butterflies. Stuttgart: 1924. V. 62
Macrolepidoptera of the World. Volume 9. Rhopalocera of Indo Australica. Stuttgart: 1927. V. 62

SEITZ, DON C.
Braxton Bragg, General of the Confederacy. Columbia: 1924. V. 62; 63; 65; 67
Writings by and About James Abbott Mc Neill Whistler, a Bibliography. Edinburgh: 1910. V. 62; 64

SEITZ, JOHANN CHRISTIAN
Annua Tortiuc Saecularis Inventae Artis Typographicae. Harlemi: 1741. V. 65; 66

SEIXAS, JAMES
Manual Hebrew Grammar for the Use of Beginners. Andover: 1833. V. 62

SELBORNE, JOANNA
British Wood-Engraved Book Illustration 1904-1940. Oxford: 1998. V. 62; 64; 65
Gwen Raverat, Wood Engraver. Denby Dale: 1996. V. 62; 64; 65

SELBY, ANGELICA
In the Sunlight. London: 1890. V. 65

SELBY, CHARLES
Barnaby Rudge. A Domestic Drama in Three Acts. London: 1841. V. 62

SELBY, HUBERT
Last Exit to Brooklyn. New York: 1964. V. 62; 63; 65; 66

SELBY, JOHN
Sam. New York: 1939. V. 62

SELBY, PRIDEAUX JOHN
A History of British Forest-Trees, Indigenous and Introduced. London: 1842. V. 63
Illustrations of British Ornithology. Edinburgh: 1833. V. 62
The Natural History of Parrots. Edinburgh: 1836. V. 66
Ornithology. Volume V. Gallinaceous Birds, Part III. Pigeons. Edinburgh: 1835. V. 66
Ornithology. Volume VI. Parrots. Edinburgh: 1836. V. 66

SELBY, W. F.
An Inaugural Dissertation, on the Analogy Between Plants and Animals. Philadelphia: 1806. V. 65; 67

SELDEN, JOHN
A Brief Discourse Touching the Office of the Lord Chancellor of England...Together with a True Catalogue of Lord Chancellors and Keepers of the Great Seal.... London: 1677. V. 64
De Dis Syris Syntagmata. II. Adversarai Nempe de Numinibus Commentitiis in Veteri.... Amsterdam: 1680. V. 63
Table Talk: being the Discourses...or His Sense of Various Matters of Weight and High Consequence Relating Especially to Religion and State. London: 1689. V. 66
Titles of Honor. London: 1614. V. 62
Titles of Honor. London: 1672. V. 62; 63; 66

SELECT Documents Illustrating the Four Voyages of Columbus.... London: 1930-1933. V. 64

SELECT Essays, from the Batchelor, or Speculations of Jeoffrey Wagstaffe, Esq. Dublin: 1772. V. 63

SELECT Lives of Foreigners, Eminent in Piety. Dublin: 1796. V. 67

SELECT Portions of Psalms and Hymns, for the Use of Berkeley Chapel, John Street, Berkeley Square. London: 179-. V. 64

A SELECTION of Drawings from the Worker 1924-1960. New York: 1960?. V. 67

A SELECTION of Fac-Similes of Water-colour Drawings from the Works of the Most Distinguished British Artists. London: 1825. V. 64

A SELECTION of Psalms and Hymns, for the Use of the Parish Church of Skipton. Skipton: 1833. V. 64; 65

A SELECTION of Views in the County of Lincoln. London: 1805. V. 62

SELETZ, E.
Surgery of the Peripheral Nerves. Springfield: 1951. V. 64

SELF-CONSCIOUSNESS of Noted Persons. Cambridge: 1882. V. 66

THE SELF Instructor, or Young Man's Best Companions.... Liverpool: 1807. V. 63

SELF, MARGARET C.
A World of Horses: an Anthology. 1961. V. 67

SELF, WILL
Cock and Bull. London: 1992. V. 63; 66
The Quantity Theory of Insanity. Together with Five Supporting Propositions. London: 1991. V. 65; 66
The Sweet Smell of Psychosis - a Story. London: 1996. V. 63

SELFRIDGE, THOMAS O.
Trial of Thomas O. Selfridge, Attorney at Law, Before the Hon. Isaac Parker, Esquire, for Killing Charles Austin, on the Public Exchange, in Boston, August 4th, 1806. Boston: 1807. V. 67

SELIGMAN, G. SAVILLE
Domestic Needlework. London: 1926. V. 62; 66

SELKIRK, EARL OF
Statement Respecting the Earl of Selkirk's Settlement Upon the Red River, In North America.... Toronto: 1969. V. 65

SELKIRK, THOMAS DOUGLAS, 5TH EARL OF
Observations on the Present State of the Highlands of Scotland, with a View of the Causes and Consequences of Emigration. Edinburgh: 1805. V. 62
Observations on the Present State of the Highlands of Scotland, with a View of the Causes and Consequences of Emigration. London: 1805. V. 63; 66

SELL, COLLEEN
Biblio. Eugene: 1996-. V. 66

SELLER, ALVIN V.
Classics of the Bar, Stories of the World's Great Legal Trials.... Baxley: 1917. V. 62

SELLERS, TERENCE
The Correct Sadist. New York: 1983. V. 66

SELLEY, HARRY GOVIER
The Ornithosauria; an Elementary Study of the Bones of Pterodactyles, Made from the Remains Found in the Cambridge Upper Greensand, an Arranged in the Woodwardian Museum of the University of Cambridge. Cambridge: 1870. V. 62

SELLS, A. LYTTON
The Paradise of Travellers. London: 1964. V. 67

SELL'S Brother's Regal Roman Hippodrome. Buffalo: 1891. V. 65

SELOUS, EDMUND
The Bird Watcher in the Shetlands. 1905. V. 63
The Bird Watcher in the Shetlands. London: 1905. V. 62

SELOUS, FREDERICK COURTENEY
African Nature Notes and Reminiscences. London: 1908. V. 64
A Hunter's Wanderings in Africa. 1890. V. 62; 63
Recent Hunting Trips in British North America. 1907. V. 66; 67
Recent Hunting Trips in British North America. London: 1907. V. 65
Sport and Travel East and West. 1900. V. 62; 63; 64; 66; 67
Travel and Adventure in South East Africa. 1893. V. 63; 64

SELPH, CARL
In the Galloping Wind. Fayetteville: 1953. V. 67

SELPH, FANNIE EOLINE
The South in American Life and History. Nashville: 1928. V. 67

SELVES, J. B.
Explication de l'Origine et du Secret du Vrai Jury, et Comparaison avec le Jury Anglais et le Jury Francais.... Paris: 1811. V. 66

SELWYN, ALFRED F. C.
Geolgoical and Natural History Survey of Canada, Report of Progress for 1880-1882. Montreal: 1883. V. 62

SELWYN-BROWN, ARTHUR
The Physician Throughout the Ages. New York: 1928. V. 63
The Physician Throughout the Ages. New York: 1938. V. 64

SELYE, HANS
The Physiology and Pathology of Exposure to Stress. Montreal: 1950. V. 63

SEMMES, JOHN E.
John H. B. Latrobe and His Times 1803-1891. Baltimore: 1917. V. 65

SEMMES, RAPHAEL
The Cruise of the Alabama and the Sumter. London: 1864. V. 62; 63; 65
The Cruise of the Alabama and the Sumter. New York: 1864. V. 64; 65
The Cruise of the Alabama and the Sumter. New York: 1867. V. 62
My Adventures Afloat. London: 1869. V. 66

SEMPILL, HUGH
A Short Address to the Public, on the Practice of Cashiering Military Officers Without a Trial; and a Vindication of the Conduct and Political Opinions of the author. London: 1793. V. 65

SEMPLE, ELLEN CHURCHILL
American History and Its Geographic Conditions. New York: 1904. V. 63

SEMPLE, GEORGE
A Treatise on Building in Water. Dublin: 1776. V. 64

SEMPLE, JAMES ALEXANDER
Representative Women of Colorado. Denver: 1911. V. 65
Representative Women of Colorado. Denver: 1914. V. 66

SEMPLE, JAMES GEORGE
Memoirs of the Northern Imposter, or Prince of Swindlers. London: 1786. V. 63

SEMPLE, ROBERT B.
History of the Rise and Progress of the Baptists in Virginia. Richmond: 1810. V. 64; 65

SENATOR, HERMANN
Health and Disease in Relation to Marriage and the Married State. New York: 1904. V. 65

SENDAK, MAURICE
Caldecott and Co. Notes on Books and Pictures. New York: 1988. V. 65
Hector Protector and As I Went Over the Water - Two Nursery Rhymes with Pictures. London: 1967. V. 63
Higglety Pigglety Pop! or There Must Be More to Life. New York: 1979. V. 64
In the Night Kitchen. New York: 1970. V. 65
The Juniper Tree and Other Tales from Grimm. New York: 1973. V. 62; 63
The Nutshell Library. London: 1964. V. 65
Outside Over There. New York: 1981. V. 65
Pictures. New York: 1971. V. 65
Questions to an Artist Who Is Also an Author: a Conversation Between Maurice Sendak and Virginia Haviland. Washington: 1972. V. 62; 67
The Sign on Rosie's Door. London: 1969. V. 65
Where the Wild Things Are. New York: 1969. V. 64

SENECA, LUCIUS ANNAEUS
L. Aennaei Senecae Et Aliorum Tragoediae. Amserodami: 1568. V. 66
L. Annaei Senecae Philosophi Et M. Annaei Senecae Rheoris Quae Extant Opera. 1609. V. 66
L. Annaei Senecae Philosophi Opera Ad Optimas Editiones Collata Praemittitur Notitia Literaria Studiis Societatis Bipontinae.... Biponti: 1782. V. 66
Morals of a Happy Life; of Anger and Clemency. London: 1678. V. 66
A New Translation of the Morals of Seneca.... London: 1745. V. 63
Opera Quae Exstant Omnia. Antverpiae: 1652. V. 65
Philosophia Opera Quae Extant Omnia. Antwerpiae: 1652. V. 66
Philosophi Opera, Quae Exstant Omnia. Antwerp: 1605. V. 62
Seneca De' Benefizii, Tradotto In Volgar Fiorentino Da M. Benedetto Varchi.... In Venigia: 1565. V. 65
Seneca's Morals by Way of Abstract. London: 1682. V. 64
Seneca's Morals by Way of Abstract. London: 1756. V. 67
Sittliche Zuchtbucher, des Hochtberumpten Philosophi ind Leres Lucii Annei Senece.... Strasbourg: 1536. V. 65; 67
The Tragedies.... London: 1702. V. 63
Tragiodiae. 1634. V. 66
Tragoediae cum Notis Integris Johannis Frederici Gronovii.... Delft: 1728. V. 65
The Workes of...Both Morral and Naturall. London: 1614. V. 66

SENEFELDER, ALOIS
The Invention of Lithography. New York: 1911. V. 62; 63; 64; 66

SENGUERDIUS, WOLFERDUS
Tractatus Physicus de Tarantula.... Lugdvni Bat: 1668. V. 64

SENICH, P. R.
The German Assault Rifle 1935-1945. 1987. V. 67

SENIOR, JAMES
Patrick Bronte. Boston: 1921. V. 63

SENIOR, NASSAU WILLIAM
Biographical Sketches. London: 1863. V. 67
Conversations with M. Thiers, M. Guizot and Other Distinguished Persons, During the Second Empire. London: 1878. V. 62
Essays on Fiction. London: 1864. V. 66
From the Report of the Commissioners on Hand-Loom Weaving. On the Improvement of Designs and Patterns and Extension of Copyright. London: 1841. V. 65
Historical and Philosophical Essays. London: 1865. V. 63
Journals, Conversations and Essays Relating to Ireland. 1868. V. 65
Statement of the Provision for the Poor and of the Labouring Classes, in a Considerable Portion of America and Europe.... London: 1835. V. 63

SENIOR, W.
Waterside Sketches. 1885. V. 67

SENN, EDWARD L.
Deadwood Dick and Calamity Jane. Deadwood: 1939. V. 65
Wild Bill Hickok - Prince of Pistoleers - a Tale of Facts and Not Fiction and Romance. Deadwood: 1939. V. 65

SENN, NICHOLAS
Intestinal Surgery. Chicago: 1889. V. 63
Principles of Surgery. Philadelphia: 1890. V. 64; 66; 67

SENNERT, DANIEL
Practicae Medicinae Liber Primus (Secundus) Daniele Sennerto.... 1654. V. 64; 66

SENNETT, A. R.
Garden Cities in Theory and Practice. London: 1905. V. 62; 64; 66

SENTER, ISAAC
The Journal of Physician and Surgeon to the Troops Detached from the American Army Encamped at Cambridge, Mass., on a Secret Expedition Against Quebec.... Philadelphia: 1846. V. 67

SEPTCHENES, LE CLERC DE
The Religion of the Ancient Greeks Illustrated by an Explanation of Their Mythology. London: 1788. V. 63

SEPTEM Illustrium Virorum Poemata.... Amstelodami: 1672. V. 63

SERA, Y.
Old Imari, Blue and White Porcelain. Kyoto: 1959. V. 62

SERANELLA, BARBARA
No Human Involved. New York: 1997. V. 62; 64; 65; 66; 67

SEREDY, KATE
The White Stag. New York: 1937. V. 64; 65

SERGEANT, JOHN
A Vindication of the Doctrine Contained in Pope Benedict XII, His Bull, and in the General Council of Florence.... Paris: 1659. V. 66

SERGEANT, THOMAS
Constitutional Law: Being a View of the Practice and Jurisdiction of the Courts of the United States and of Constitutional Points Decided. Philadelphia: 1830. V. 66

SERGIUS, J.
Messieurs les Anglais.... Paris: 1900. V. 67

A SERIES of Interesting Delineations of Remarkable Views and of the Most Celebrated Remains of Antiquity.... London: 1825. V. 63

A SERIES of Plates Representing the Most Extraordinary and Interesting Basaltic Mountains, Caverns and Causeways in the Known World. London: 1825. V. 63

A SERIES of Portraits of the Founders of the Colleges in Both Universities. London: 1815-1816. V. 65

SERIMAN, ZACCARIA
Viaggi di Enrico Wanton alle Terre Incognit Australi, Ed ai Regni Delle Scimie.... Naples: 1756-1765. V. 62; 65

THE SERIO-Comic Drama of Punch and Judy. London: 1835. V. 64

A SERIOUS Address to the Inhabitants of Bristol, on the Subject of the Multiplicity of Religious Distinctions, Which Prevail in that City.... Bristol: 1820. V. 67

SERLE, AMBROSE
The American Journal of Ambrose Serle: Secretary to Lord Howe 1776- 1778. San Marino: 1940. V. 63; 64; 66

SERLE, JOHN
A Plan of Mr. Pope's Garden, As It Was Left at His Death.... London: 1745. V. 64

SERMONS by Artists. Waltham St. Lawrence: 1934. V. 62; 65

SERRE, MICHEL
Traite sur l'Art de Restaurer les Difformites de la Face, Selon la Methode par Deplacement, ou Methode Francaise. Montpellier: 1842. V. 65

SERRES, DOMINICK
Liber Nauticus and Instructor in the Art of Marine Drawing. London: 1979. V. 64; 67

SERRES, MARCEL DE
L'Autriche, ou Moeurs Usages et Costumes des Habitans de cet Empire.... Paris: 1821. V. 64

SERRES, OLIVIA WILMOT
Letters of the Late Right Hon. Earl of Brooke and Warwick to Mrs. Wilmot Serres, Illustrated with Poems and Memoirs of His Lordship. London: 1819. V. 63

SERVANT'S Guide and Family Manual with New and Improved Receipts.... London: 1830. V. 62; 67

SERVEN, JAMES
Colt Firearms (from 1836). 1981. V. 62; 63; 64; 66; 67
Conquering the Frontiers. La Habra: 1974. V. 67

SERVENTY, D. L.
A Wild Heritage, Watercolours of Birds and Wildflowers of Western Australia by B. Fremlin. Perth: 1983. V. 67

SERVICE, ROBERT WILLIAM
Ballads of Cheechako. Toronto: 1909. V. 66
Rhymes of a Red Cross Man. New York: 1916. V. 67
The Spell of the Yukon and Other Verses. New York: 1907. V. 67

SESTIER, AMI-DAMIEL FELIX
De La Foudre de ses Formes et de ses Effets sur l'Homme, les Animaux, les Vegetaux et les Corps Bruts des Moyens de s'en Preserver et des Paratonnerres.... Paris: 1866. V. 65

SETH, VIKRAM
An Equal Music. Leicester: 1999. V. 63
The Golden Gate. London: 1986. V. 62; 63
The Golden Gate. New York: 1986. V. 65; 67
Mappings. Saratoga: 1980. V. 63
A Suitable Boy. New York: 1992. V. 64
A Suitable Boy. London: 1993. V. 62; 64; 65; 66
A Suitable Boy. New Delhi: 1993. V. 62; 64
Three Chinese Poets. London: 1992. V. 62; 66

SETH SMITH, DAVID
Parrakeets. A Handbook to the Imported Species. 1903. V. 67

SETON, BRUCE
The Pipes of War. Glasgow: 1920. V. 62

SETON, ERNEST THOMPSON
The Arctic Prairies.... New York: 1911. V. 62
Great Historic Animals, Mainly About Wolves. New York: 1937. V. 64
Life Histories of Northern Animals. New York: 1909. V. 62

SETON, ERNEST THOMPSON continued
Life Histories of Northern Animals. London: 1910. V. 62
Lives of the Game Animals. New York: 1929. V. 63
Lives of the Game Animals. New York: 1929-1953. V. 66
Lives of the Game Animals.... New York: 1937. V. 64
Lives of the Hunted.... New York: 1901. V. 64
Two Little Savages, Being the Adventures of Two Boys Who Lived as Indians and What They Learned. New York: 1903. V. 64

SETON, JULIA M.
The Pulse of the Pueblo, Personal Glimpses of Indian Life. Santa Fe: 1939. V. 63

SETON-KARR, H. W.
Bear-Hunting in the White Mountains or Alaska and British Columbia Revisited. 1891. V. 62; 63
Bear-Hunting in the White Mountains or Alaska and British Columbia Revisited. London: 1891. V. 67
My Sporting Holidays. 1904. V. 62; 63; 66

SETOUN, GABRIEL
The Child World. London: 1896. V. 62

SETTLE, ELKANAH
The Empress of Morocco. London: 1673. V. 62
A Narrative. London: 1683. V. 64

SETTLE, MARY LEE
The Killing Ground. New York: 1982. V. 62
The Kiss of Kin. Now York: 1955. V. 66
Know Nothing. New York: 1960. V. 64; 67
The Love Eaters. New York: 1954. V. 66
O Beulah Land. New York: 1956. V. 66

SETTLE, RAY
The March of the Mounted Riflemen. Glendale: 1940. V. 64; 67

SEUPHOR, M.
Piet Mondrian: Life and Work. New York. V. 62

SEURAT, CLAUDE
An Account of the Most Extraordinary and Interesting Phenomenon, Claude Seurat Called the Living Skeleton.... London: 1825. V. 62

SEURRE, E.
New Practical Cookery Guide. London: 1913. V. 67

SEUSS, EDUARD
Das Antlitz der Erde. Wien: 1888-1909. V. 65
The Face of the Earth. Oxford: 1904-1908. V. 64; 65

SEUTONIUS
Duodecim Caesars, cum Philippi Beroaldi Bononiensis, Marcique item Antonii Sabellici Commentariis & Bapt. Aegnatii.... Lugduni: 1548. V. 66
XII Caesaribus Libri VIII.... Parisiis: 1610. V. 66

SEVEN SAGES
The Sayings of the Seven Sages of Greece. Verona: 1976. V. 65

THE SEVEN Sermons Preached at the Consecration and Re-Opening of the Parish Church of Leeds.... Leeds: 1841. V. 66

SEVERIM DE FARIA, MANOEL
Discursos Varios Politicos. Evora: 1624. V. 62

SEVERIN, MARK
Engraved Bookplates - European Ex Libris 1950-1970. London: 1972. V. 64

SEVIGNE, MARIE DE RABUTIN CHANTAL, MARQUISE DE
Lettres Choisies de Madame de Sevigne. Lille: 1900. V. 63
Lettres de Madame de Sevigne. Paris: 1843. V. 63
Lettres de Madame de Sevigne.... Paris: 1853. V. 66
Recueil Des Lettres de Madame de Sevigne. Paris: 1801. V. 67

SEVILLE, WILLIAM P.
Narrative of the March of Company A. Engineers from Fort Leavenworth, Kansas to Fort Bridger, Utah and Return May 6 to October 3, 1858. Washington: 1912. V. 65

SEWALL, MAY WRIGHT
Neither Dead Nor Sleeping. Indianapolis: 1920. V. 65
The World's Congress of Representative Women. Chicago and New York: 1894. V. 63

SEWALL, RICHARD B.
The Life of Emily Dickinson. London: 1976. V. 63

SEWALL, THOMAS
An Examination of Phrenology in Two Lectures Delivered to the Students of the Columbian College. Boston: 1839. V. 64; 65; 66
An Examination of Phrenology, in Two Lectures, Delivered to the Students of the Columbian College, District of Columbia, Feb. 1837. Boston: 1893. V. 65

SEWARD, A. C.
Fossil Plants for Students of Botany and Geology. New York: 1963. V. 64

SEWARD, A. D.
Darwin and Modern Science. Cambridge: 1909. V. 67

SEWARD, ANNA
The Beauties of Anna Seward.... London: 1813. V. 65
Letters...Written Between the Years 1784 and 1807. Edinburgh: 1811. V. 63
Llangollen Vale, with Other Poems. London: 1796. V. 64
Memoirs of the Life of Dr. Darwin, Chiefly During His Residence at Lichfield.... London: 1804. V. 66
Original Sonnets on Various Subjects; and Odes Paraphrased from Horace. London: 1799. V. 66

SEWARD, WILLIAM
Anecdotes of Distinguished Persons, Chiefly of the Last and Two Preceding Centuries. London: 1804. V. 66
Anecdotes of Distinguished Persons, Chiefly of the Present and Preceding Two Centuries. London: 1798. V. 62; 66
Speech of Mr. Seward, at Sitka, August 12th, 1869. Victoria: 1869. V. 63

SEWEL, WILLIAM
The History of the Rise, Increase and Progress of the Christian People Called Quakers. London: 1722. V. 62; 66
The History of the Rise, Increase and Progress of the Christian People Called Quakers. London: 1725. V. 66

SEWELL, ANNA
Black Beauty. London: 1880. V. 65
Black Beauty. London: 1885. V. 65
Black Beauty. Boston: 1890. V. 63; 64

SEWELL, BROCARD
Three Private Presses - Saint Dominic's Press, the Press of Edward Walters (and) Saint Albert's Press. London: 1979. V. 62
Three Private Presses: Saint Dominic's Press, The Press of Edward Walters, Saint Albert's Press. Wellingborough: 1979. V. 63

SEWELL, ELIZABETH MISSING
Cleve Hall. London: 1855. V. 65
The Earl's Daughter. London: 1850. V. 66
The Earl's Daughter. London: 1851. V. 66
Gertrude. London: 1847. V. 66
A Glimpse of the World. London: 1863. V. 65
Impressions of Rome, Florence and Turin. London: 1862. V. 63
Ivors. London: 1857. V. 66
Katharine Ashton. London: 1854. V. 64; 65
Margaret Percival. London: 1847. V. 66

SEWELL, GEORGE
The (sic) Resigners Vindicated. Part 11. and Last. London: 1718. V. 65

SEWELL, HELEN
ABC for Everyday. New York: 1930. V. 64

SEWELL, HENRY
A Letter to Lord Worsley, on the Burthens Affecting Real Property Arising from the Present State of the Law.... London: 1846. V. 67

SEWELL, MARY
Patience Hart's First Experience in Service. London: 1862. V. 65

SEWELL, WILLIAM
Hawkstone: a Tale of and for England in 184-. London: 1846. V. 66

SEWTER, A. CHARLES
The Stained Glass of William Morris and His Circle. New Haven;: 1974-1975. V. 64

SEXTON, ANNE
The Book of Folly. Boston: 1972. V. 62
Live or Die. Boston: 1966. V. 62
Live or Die. London: 1967. V. 62
Love Poems. Boston: 1969. V. 62
Selected Poems. London: 1964. V. 64; 66
To Bedlam and Part Way Back. Boston: 1960. V. 62; 64
To Bedlam and Part Way Back. Cambridge: 1960. V. 67
Transformations. Boston: 1971. V. 62; 64

SEXTON, GROVER F.
The Arizona Sheriff. N.P: 1925. V. 63; 67

SEXTUS AURELIUS, VICTOR
Historia Romana...Curante Joanne Arntezenio.... Amstelodami: 1733. V. 66

SEYBERT, ADAM
Statistical Annals: Embracing Views of the Population, Commerce, Navigation, Fisheries, Public Lands, Post Office Establishment, Revenues, Mint, Military and Naval Establishments, Expenditures, Public Debt and Sinking Fund of the United States of America. Philadelphia: 1818. V. 62; 64

SEYBOLD, DAVID
Fathers and Sons. New York: 1992. V. 64; 66

SEYD, ERNEST
California and Its Resources. London: 1858. V. 63; 66

SEYFFERT, O.
Spielzeug. Berlin: 1922. V. 65

SEYMER, JOHN GUNNING
The Romance of Ancient Egypt: Second Series of the Romance of Ancient History. London: 1835. V. 67

SEYMOUR, A. B.
Host Index of the Fungi of North America. Cambridge: 1929. V. 62; 63

SEYMOUR, H. D.
Russia on the Black Sea and Sea of Azof; Being a Narrative of Travels in the Crimea and Bordering Provinces; with Notices of the Naval, Military and Commercial Resources of Those Countries. London: 1855. V. 66

SEYMOUR, R.
Humorous Sketches. 1878. V. 62; 63; 66; 67
Humorous Sketches. 1888. V. 62

SEYMOUR, RALPH
Across the Gulf: a Narration of a Short Journey through Parts of Yucatan with a brief Account of the Ancient Maya Civilization. Chicago: 1928. V. 66

SEYMOUR, ROBERT
The Heiress. London: 1830. V. 62; 67

SHAARA, JEFF
Gods and Generals. New York: 1996. V. 62; 66

SHAARA, MICHAEL
The Broken Place. New York: 1968. V. 63
The Killer Angels. New York: 1974. V. 62

SHABERMAN, RAPHAEL B.
George MacDonald a Bibliographical Study. 1990. V. 67

SHACKLETON, EDWARD A.
Arctic Journeys. The Story of the Oxford University Ellesmere Land Expedition 1934-1935. London: 1937. V. 63

SHACKLETON, ERNEST HENRY
South, the Story of Shackleton's 1914-1917 Expedition. London: 1925. V. 66
South. The Story of Shackleton's Last Expedition 1914-1917. Turnhout: 1982. V. 63

SHACOCHIS, BOB
Easy In the Islands. New York: 1985. V. 63
The Next New World. New York: 1989. V. 67
Swimming in the Volcano. New York: 1993. V. 67

SHADWELL, JOHN LANCELOT
A System of Political Economy. London: 1877. V. 62

SHADWELL, LIONEL LANCELOT
Enactments in Parliament Specially Concerning the University of Oxford and Cambridge the Colleges and Halls Therein and the Colledges of Winchester, Eton and Westminster. Oxford: 1912. V. 62

SHADWELL, THOMAS
The Complete Works. London: 1927. V. 62; 63; 64
The History of Timon of Athens, the Man-Hater. London: 1688. V. 62; 65
Some Reflections Upon the Pretended Parallel in the Play Called The Duke of Guise, in a Letter to a Friend. London: 1685. V. 67

SHAFFER, ANTHONY
Sleuth. New York: 1970. V. 65; 66
The Woman in the Wardrobe. London: 1951. V. 65

SHAFFER, PETER
Amadeus. London: 1980. V. 62; 63; 66
Equus - A Play. London: 1973. V. 64
Five Finger Exercise - a Play in Two Acts and Four Scenes. London: 1958. V. 64

SHAFTESBURY, ANTHONY ASHLEY COOPER, 1ST EARL OF
Some Memoirs; or, a Sober Essay for a Just Vindication of the Right Honourable the Earl of Shaftesbury. London: 1681. V. 67

SHAFTESBURY, ANTHONY ASHLEY COOPER, 3RD EARL OF
Characteristicks of Men, Manners, Opinions, Times. Birmingham: 1773. V. 62; 65; 67
Characteristics.... London: 1744-1745. V. 62
A Letter Concerning Enthusiasm, to My Lord.... London: 1708. V. 62
A Notion of the Historical Draught or Tablature of the Judgement of Hercules, According to Prodicus.... London: 1713. V. 62
Two Speeches. I. The Earl of Shaftesbury's...20th of October 1675. II. The D. of Buckingham...16th of Nov. 1675...Together with the Protection, and Reasons...for the Dissolution of this Parliament. Amsterdam: 1675. V. 62

SHAFTESBURY, ANTHONY ASHLEY COOPER, 7TH EARL OF
Report of the Metropolitan Commissioners in Lunacy, to the Lord Chancellor. London: 1844. V. 65

SHAFTOE, FRANCES
Mrs. Frances Shaftoe's Narrative. London: 1707. V. 62

SHAHN, BEN
An Alphabet of Creation. New York: 1954. V. 62; 65

SHAILER, MATHEW
The Woman Citizen's Library...Volume VII: Woman Suffrage. Chicago: 1914. V. 65

SHAKESEPAR, JOHN
A Grammar of the Hindustani Language. London: 1818. V. 66

THE SHAKESPEARE Head Press Booklets. No. I (VI). Stratford-upon-Avon: 1906. V. 66

SHAKESPEARE, WILLIAM
Antony and Cleopatra. London: 1979. V. 64
As You Like It. London: 1909. V. 62; 65
As You Like It. London: 1930. V. 63; 65; 67
The Beauties of Shakespear. London: 1752. V. 67
Bell's Edition of Shakespeare's Plays, a They Are Now Performed at the Theatres Royal in London. London: 1774. V. 62
A Collection of Poems, viz. I. Venus and Adonis. II. The Rape of Lucrece. III. The Passionate Pilgrim. IV. Sonnets to Sundry Notes of Musick. London: 1709. V. 65
The Comedies, Histories and Tragedies. 1939-1940. V. 62
Comedy of the Tempest. London: 1908. V. 62
The Complete Sonnets of William Shakespeare. 1955. V. 65
The Complete Works. New York: 1855. V. 66
The Complete Works. London: 1912. V. 67
Complete Works. London: 1953. V. 62; 64
Coriolanus. Hammersmith: 1914. V. 62; 64; 65
The Dramatic Works. Boston: 1802-1804. V. 62
The Dramatic Works. London: 1820. V. 63
The Dramatic Works. London: 1899. V. 65; 67
The Dramatick Works. London: 1823. V. 62
Facsimile of the First Folio of Shakespeare. London: 1876. V. 66
The First Folio of Shakespeare. The Norton Facsimile. London: 1968. V. 64
Hamlet: Prince of Denmark. 1922. V. 63
Hamlet, Prinz af Denmark. Copenhagen: 1777. V. 65
The Tragedy of Hamlet. London: 1703. V. 66; 67
Tragedy of Hamlet. London: 1920. V. 64
Henry the Fourth - Part I. New York: 1939. V. 65
Henry the Fourth - Part II. New York: 1939. V. 65
Julius Caesar. London: 1688. V. 65; 66; 67
Julius Caesar - the First Folio Text. New York: 1939. V. 65
King John - the First Folio Text. New York: 1940. V. 65
Lucrece. Hammersmith: 1915. V. 62; 65; 67
A Midsommer Nights Dreame. 1924. V. 65
A Midsummer Night's Dream. London: 1816. V. 66
A Midsummer Night's Dream. New York: 1908. V. 64
A Midsummer Night's Dream. London: 1914. V. 63
A Midsummer Night's Dream. London: 1977. V. 66
Miscellaneous Papers and Legal Instruments Under the Hand and Seal of William Shakespeare: Including the Tragedy of King Lear and a Small Fragment of Hamlet. London: 1796. V. 62
New Readings of Old Authors.... London: 1830-1835. V. 67
The Norton Facsimile, The First Folio of Shakespeare. New York: 1968. V. 64
The Old Spelling Shakespeare.... New York and London: 1907-1909. V. 64
Othello, the Moor of Venice. London: 1705. V. 66
The Passionate Pilgrim. 1896. V. 65
The Plays. London: 1825. V. 66
Plays and Poems. New York: 1939-1941. V. 67
The Plays and Poems of Shakespeare, with a Life. London: 1832-1834. V. 62
The Plays and Poems, with the Corrections and Illustrations of Various Commentators.... London: 1821. V. 63
The Plays.... London: 1765. V. 62
The Plays.... London: 1773. V. 63
The Plays.... London: 1805. V. 65
The Plays.... London: 1813. V. 67
Poems. London: 1775. V. 62
The Poems. London: 1825. V. 63
Poems. London: 1893. V. 65
The Poems. London: 1898. V. 66
The Poems. New York: 1941. V. 65
The Poems and Sonnets. Waltham St. Lawrence: 1960. V. 62
Richard the Second - the First Folio Text. New York: 1940. V. 65
Romeo and Juliet. London. V. 62; 64
Romeo et Juliette. Paris: 1929. V. 63
Scenes from Winter's Tale. London: 1866. V. 65
Shakespeare's Comedies, Histories and Tragedies.... Oxford: 1902. V. 66
The Songs and Sonnets of Shakespeare. London. V. 65
The Songs and Sonnets of William Shakespeare. London: 1915. V. 62
Songs from Shakespeare's Plays. 1974. V. 67
Songs from Shakespeare's Plays. Verona: 1974. V. 65
Songs of William Shakespeare. London: 1865. V. 65
Shake-speare's Sonnets. Hammersmith: 1909. V. 62
Shake-Speares Sonnets. Lexington: 1956. V. 64
Shakespeare's Sonnets. 1956. V. 65
Shakespeare's Sonnets. 1974. V. 65
Shakespeare's Sonnets. London: 1982. V. 65
The Sonnets. London: 1913. V. 65
The Sonnets. London: 1975. V. 65
The Sonnets, with, an Explanatory Introduction to Thorpe's Edition of Shakespeare's Sonnets, 1609. Aldington, Kent: 1950. V. 65
The Taming of the Shrew - the First Folio Text. New York: 1940. V. 65
The Tempest. London: 1695. V. 62
The Tempest. London: 1901. V. 64
The Tempest. London: 1908. V. 63; 64
The Tempest. Montagnola: 1924. V. 65
The Tragedie of Anthony and Cleopatra. Hammersmith: 1912. V. 63; 65
The Tragedie of Julius Caesar. Hammersmith: 1913. V. 62; 66
The Tragedie of King Lear. 1924. V. 65
The Tragedie of King Lear. Bangor/Newark: 1986. V. 62; 64
The Tragedie of Othello. San Francisco: 1956. V. 62
The Tragedy of Coriolanus. Hammersmith: 1914. V. 67

SHAKESPEARE, WILLIAM continued
The Tragedy of Hamlet. London: 1919. V. 66
The Tragedy of MacBeth. London: 1951. V. 65
The Tragicall Historie of Hamlet Prince of Denmarke. Hammersmith: 1909. V. 62
Der Tragische Geschichte von Hamlet Prinzen von Daenemark.... 1929. V. 65
Twelfth-Night. London: 1908. V. 62; 65
Twenty-Five Sonnets of Shakespeare. Stratford-upon-Avon: 1922. V. 63; 66
Venus and Adonis. Hammersmith: 1912. V. 62
Venus and Adonis. Paris: 1930. V. 63
The Winter's Tale. New York: 1922. V. 64
The Winter's Tale - the First Folio Text. New York: 1940. V. 65
(The Works). London: 1787. V. 64
The Works. London: 1733. V. 62
The Works. London: 1745. V. 64
The Works. London: 1859. V. 62
The Works. London: 1895. V. 66
The Works. London: 1897. V. 62
The Works. London: 1899. V. 67
The Works. London: 1904. V. 62
The Works. London: 1929. V. 64; 66
Works. London: 1929-1933. V. 62
The Works...in Six Volumes. (with) The Works...Volume the Seventh. Containing, Venus and Adonis, Tarquin & Lucrece and His Miscellany Poems. With Critical Remarks on His Plays, &c.... London: 1709-1710. V. 64

SHAKESPEAREANA. *Catalogue of All the Books, Pamphlets, etc., Relating to Shakespeare.* London: 1827. V. 62

SHAKESPEARE'S *England. An Account of the Life and Manners of His Age.* Oxford: 1962. V. 65; 66

SHALER, WILLIAM
Journal of a Voyage Between China and the Northwest Coast of America, Made in 1804. Claremont: 1935. V. 64; 65; 66

SHALLOR, BARBARA
Portrait of a Philadelphia Collector, William McIntire Elkins 1882-1947. Philadelphia: 1956. V. 62

SHAMES, LAURENCE
The Big Time. New York: 1986. V. 65; 66; 67
Florida Straits. New York: 1992. V. 67

THE SHANACHIE. Dublin: 1906. V. 64

SHAND, P. MORTON
A Book of French Wines. London: 1963. V. 66

SHANGE, NTOZAKE
For Colored Girls Who Have Considered Suicide/When the Rainbow is Enuf. New York: 1977. V. 62
From Okra to Greens. St. Paul: 1984. V. 67

SHANKLE, RALPH O.
The Twins of Space; the Story of Project Gemini. Philadelphia: 1964. V. 67

SHANKS, EDWARD
The Dogs of War. London: 1948. V. 67

SHANNON, C. HAZELWOOD
The Pageant 1807 1807. London: 1896. V. 64

SHANNON, DAVID
No, David!. New York: 1998. V. 65

SHANNON, FRED ALBERT
The Organization and Administration of the Union Army. Cleveland: 1928. V. 62

SHANNON, MICHAEL OWEN
Modern Ireland, a Bibliography on Politics, Planning, Research and Development. 1981. V. 67

SHAPIRO, KARL
American Poetry. New York: 1960. V. 62
Auden (1907-1973). Davis: 1974. V. 62
Essay on Rime. New York: 1945. V. 62
Poems. Baltimore: 1935. V. 64; 66
16 Poems. 1962. V. 66

SHAPLEY, HARLOW
Star Clusters. New York: 1930. V. 67

SHARE, F. A. C.
The Registers of the Parish Church of Linton-in-Craven, Co. York. 1562-1812. 1900-1903. V. 66

SHARP, ARCHIBALD
Bicycles and Tricycles: an Elementary Treatise on Their Design and Construction With Examples and Tables. London: 1896. V. 65

SHARP, GRANVILLE
A Declaration of the People's Natural Right to a Share in the Legislature.... London: 1774. V. 62; 63; 64; 67
A Declaration of the People's Natural Right to a Share in the Legislature.... London: 1775. V. 64
The Legal Means of Political Reformation, Proposed in Two Small Tracts. London: 1780. V. 62

Remarks Concerning the Encroachments on the River Thames Near Durham-Yard. London: 1771. V. 66
A Short Treatise on the English Tongue. London: 1767. V. 62

SHARP, HENRY
The Gun Afield and Afloat. 1904. V. 67
The Gun: Afield and Afloat. London: 1904. V. 63
Practical Wildfowling. 1895. V. 62; 63

SHARP, JOHN
Life and Letters of James David Forbes. London: 1873. V. 65

SHARP, MARGERY
The Rescuers. Boston: 1959. V. 62
The Rescuers. London: 1959. V. 65

SHARP, MARY
A Record of the Parish of Padworth and Its Inhabitants. Reading: 1911. V. 66

SHARP, PAUL F.
Whoop-Up Country: The Canadian American West 1865-1885. Minneapolis: 1955. V. 63; 64

SHARP, RICHARD
Epistles in Verse. London: 1828. V. 62; 63

SHARP, S. Z.
The Educational History of the Church of the Brethren. Elgin: 1923. V. 63; 66

SHARP, SAMUEL
A Critical Enquiry Into the Present State of Surgery. London: 1761. V. 65
A Treatise on the Operations of Surgery, with a Description and Representation of the Instruments Used in Performing Them.... London: 1769. V. 64; 66; 67

SHARP, STEWART & CO.
Locomotives for Broad Gauge Railways, Manufactured by Sharp, Stewart and Co., Limited, Atlas Works, Manchester, England. Manchester: 1886. V. 65

SHARP, WILLIAM
Dante Gabriel Rossetti. 1882. V. 64
The Distant Country, and Other Prose Poems. Portland: 1907. V. 63
The Gypsy Christ and Other Tales. Chicago: 1895. V. 64
The Immortal Hour. London: 1939. V. 64
The Laughter of Peterkin. London: 1897. V. 64

SHARPE, CHARLES KIRKPATRICK
A Ballad Book by MDCCCXXIII.... Edinburgh and London: 1880. V. 62

SHARPE, GREGORY
Two Dissertations: I. Upon the Origin, Construction, Division and Relation of Languages. II. Upon the Original Power of Letters.... London: 1751. V. 62; 65

SHARPE, P. B.
Complete Guide to Handloading. 1942. V. 63; 64; 66; 67

SHARPE, R. B.
An Analytical Index to the Works of the Late John Gould, F.R.S.... London: 1893. V. 67
A Hand-Book to the Birds of Great Britain. London: 1896-1897. V. 64; 67
A Hand-List of the Genera and Species of Birds. London: 1899-1912. V. 64
Sketch-Book of British Birds. London: 1898. V. 65; 67

SHARPE, REGINALD R.
Calendar of Letters from the Mayor and Corporation of the City of London, Circa A.D. 1350-1370. London: 1885. V. 67
London and the Kingdom, a History Derived Mainly from the Archives at Guildhall.... London: 1894-1895. V. 63

SHARPE, RICHARD SCRAFTON
Dame Wiggins of Lee and Her Seven Wonderful Cats. Orpington: 1885. V. 62

SHARPE, SAMUEL
The History of Egypt from the Earliest Times Till the Conquest by the Arabs A.D. 640. London: 1852. V. 64
The New Testament. London: 1856. V. 64

SHARPE, TOM
Blott on the Landscape. London: 1975. V. 65
Indecent Exposure. London: 1973. V. 63; 64

SHARPEY SCHAEFER, A. E.
Some Teachings of Development Being the Substance of the Last two Series of Twelve Lectures on Animal Development Delivered at the Royal Institution. London: 1880. V. 67

SHARROCK, J. T. R.
Rare Birds in Britain and Ireland. 1976. V. 67

SHARROCK, R.
The History of the Propagation and Improvement of Vegetables by the Concurrence of Art and Nature. Oxford: 1660. V. 66

SHATTUCK, GEORGE CHEYNE
Three Dissertations on Boylston Prize Questions for the Years 1806 and 1807. Boston: 1808. V. 64; 67

SHATTUCK, LEMUEL
Letter to the Secretary of State on the Registration of Births, Marriages and Deaths in Massachusetts. Boston: 1845. V. 62

SHAVER, LEWELLYN A.
A History of the Sixtieth Alabama Regiment, Gracie's Alabama Brigade. Montgomery: 1867. V. 62; 63; 65

SHAVER, LONA
Chuch Wagon Windies. San Antonio: 1934. V. 67

SHAW, ALBERT
A Cartoon History of Roosevelt's Career. New York: 1910. V. 65

SHAW, C. JAMES
North from Texas - Incidents in the Early Life of a Range Cowman in Texas, Dakota, Wyoming 1852-1883. Evanston: 1952. V. 63; 66

SHAW, CHARLES
Heaven Knows Mr. Allison. New York: 1952. V. 65

SHAW, D. A.
Eldorado, or, California as Seen by a Pioneer 1850-1900. Los Angeles: 1900. V. 63

SHAW, EDWARD
Civil Architecture.... Boston: 1834. V. 64

SHAW, EYRE
Records of the London Fire Engine Establishment. London: 1870. V. 62

SHAW, F. G.
The Science of Dry Fly Fishing. London: 1906. V. 64
The Science of Fly Fishing for Trout. 1925. V. 67

SHAW, FREDERICK B.
One Hundred and Forty Years of Service in Peace and War - History of the Second Infantry United States Army. Detroit: 1930. V. 65; 67

SHAW, G. C.
John Chavis 1763-1838. Binghamton: 1931. V. 63

SHAW, GEORGE
John Wyndham; or the Gospel Among the Fishermen. London: 1878. V. 64

SHAW, GEORGE BERNARD
Androcles and the Lion, Overruled, and Pygmallion. London: 1916. V. 65
The Apple Cart: A Political Extravaganza. London: 1930. V. 63; 64; 65
Back to Methusaleh.... London: 1922. V. 62
Bernard Shaw: Collected Letters 1874-1910, 1965-1972. V. 66
Buoyant Billions. London: 1949. V. 66
Cashel Byron's Profession. London: 1886. V. 64; 66
Collected Letters 1874-1910. 1965-1972. V. 63
The Collected Works. New York: 1930. V. 64
The Complete Works of.... 1930-1932. V. 65
The Doctor's Dilemma, Getting Married, and The Shewing Up of Blanco Posnet. London: 1911. V. 64
Dramatic Opinions and Essays. New York: 1907. V. 65
Fabian Essays in Socialism. London. V. 66
Flyleaves. Austin: 1977. V. 62
Geneva: a Fancied Page of History in Three Acts. 1939. V. 62
Geneva: a Fancied Page of History in Three Acts. London: 1939. V. 65
Heartbreak (and Five Other Minor Plays). London: 1919. V. 66
How to Settle the Irish Question. Dublin and London: 1917. V. 64; 65
The Intelligent Woman's Guide to Socialism and Capitalism. London: 1928. V. 62; 66
London Music in 1888-1889.... London: 1937. V. 65
Misalliance, the Dark Lady of the Sonnets, and Fanny's First Play. London: 1914. V. 65
On Going to Church. East Aurora: 1896. V. 62; 67
On the Rocks: a Compendium of Contemporary Politics. 1933. V. 62
Our Theatres in the Nineties. 1954. V. 67
A Plan of Campaign for Labor. London: 1894. V. 65
The Plays of George Bernard Shaw. London: 1927. V. 67
Pygmalion: a Romance in Five Acts. New York: 1942. V. 63
Pygmalion and Candida. Avon: 1974. V. 62; 64
The Quintessence of Ibsenism. London: 1891. V. 64; 65
The Quintessence of Ibsenism. London: 1913. V. 64
Ruskin's Politics. London: 1921. V. 66
Saint Joan: a Chronicle Play in Six Scenes and an Epilogue. London: 1924. V. 64; 66
Shaw Gives Himself Away: an Autobiographical Miscellany. Newtown: 1939. V. 67
Too True to Be Good, Village Wooing and on the Rocks. London: 1934. V. 62
Two Plays for Puritans. London: 1966. V. 63
Widower's Houses.... London: 1893. V. 64
The Works of Bernard Shaw. London: 1930-1938. V. 65

SHAW, GEORGE C.
The Chinook Jargon and How to Use It. Seattle: 1909. V. 63

SHAW, GEORGE, REVEREND
Old Grimsby. Grimsby: 1897. V. 63

SHAW, GEORGE RUSSELL
The Genus Pinus. Cambridge: 1914. V. 64

SHAW, GEORGE T.
History of the Athenaeum, Liverpool 1798-1898. Liverpool: 1898. V. 63; 65

SHAW, H. BATTY
Hyperpiesia and Hyperpiesis (Hypertension). London: 1922. V. 63

SHAW, HENRY
Booke of Sundry Draughtes, Principaly Serving for Glaisiers, and Not Impertinent for Plasterers and Gardeners.... London: 1848. V. 62; 66
Details of Elizabethan Architecture. London: 1839. V. 62; 64
Dresses and Decorations of the Middle Ages. London: 1843. V. 62
Dresses and Decorations of the Middle Ages. London: 1858. V. 62; 67

SHAW, IRWIN
Bread Upon the Waters. New York: 1981. V. 62
Mixed Company. New York: 1950. V. 64
Rich Man, Poor Man. New York: 1970. V. 65
Sailor Off the Bremen. New York: 1939. V. 63
Welcome to the City and Other Stories. New York: 1942. V. 62
Whispers in Bedlam. London: 1972. V. 65
The Young Lions. New York: 1948. V. 65

SHAW, JAMES
The Parochial Lawyer, or, Churchwarden and Overseer's Guide and Assistant.... London: 1833. V. 67

SHAW, JOHN
Poems by the Late Doctor John Shaw. Philadelphia and Baltimore: 1810. V. 66

SHAW, JOSEPH
Parish Law; or, a Guide to Justices of the Peace, Ministers, Church-Wardens, Overseers of the Poor, Constables, Surveyors of the Highways.... In the Savoy: 1736. V. 65

SHAW, JOSEPH T.
The Hard-Boiled Omnibus. New York: 1946. V. 67

SHAW, LUELLA
True History of Some of the Pioneers of Colorado. Hotchkiss: 1909. V. 65

SHAW, NAPIER
The Smoke Problem of Great Cities. London: 1925. V. 63

SHAW, P.
A New Practice of Physic.... London: 1728. V. 62

SHAW, R. C.
Across the Plains in Forty-Nine. N.P: 1896. V. 66

SHAW, RALPH R.
American Bibliography. 1802-1810, 1814-1819. 1828, 1831-1839. New York: 1958-1988. V. 63

SHAW, ROBERT
The Sun Doctor - a Novel. London: 1961. V. 62

SHAW, S.
A Tour to the West of England in 1788. London: 1789. V. 65

SHAW, T.
Igbo-Ukwu: an Account of Archaeological Discoveries in Eastern Nigeria. London: 1970. V. 62

SHAW, THOMAS
Recent Poems, on Rural and Other Miscellaneous Subjects.... Huddersfield: 1824. V. 63
Travels, or Observations Relating to Several Parts of Barbary and the Levant. Oxford: 1738. V. 67

SHAW, WILLIAM H.
History of Essex and Hudson Counties, New Jersey. Philadelphia: 1884. V. 63; 66

SHAW'S Tourist's Picturesque Guide to the Western Highlands (Connemara). 1877. V. 63

SHAY, JOHN C.
Twenty Years in the Backwoods of California. Boston: 1923. V. 63

SHEA, JOHN GILMARY
Discovery and Exploration of the Mississipi Valley, with Original Narratives of Marquette, Allouez, Membre, Hennepin and Anastase Douay. New York: 1852. V. 67
A History of the Catholic Church within the United States. New York: 1886-1892. V. 64
Perils of the Ocean and Wilderness, or Narratives of Shipwreck and Indian Captivity.... Boston: 1886. V. 63; 65; 66

SHEAHAN, JAMES JOSEPH
History and Description of the Town and Port of Kingston-upon-Hull. London: 1864. V. 62

SHEARAR, JAMES
Prinkle and His Friends. London: 1877. V. 67

SHEARER, FREDERICK E.
The Pacific Tourist: Adam's and Bishop's Illustrated Trans-Continental Guide of Travel from the Atlantic to the Pacific Ocean. New York: 1886. V. 62; 63

SHEARMAN, MONTAGUE
Football (and Rugby Union). London: 1901. V. 67

SHEARN, W. B.
The Practical Fruiterer and Florist. London. V. 62

SHEARS, PHILIP J.
The Story of the Border Regiment 1939-1945. London: 1948. V. 63; 65

SHECKLEY, ROBERT
Untouched by Human Hands. London: 1955. V. 66

SHECUT, JOHN L. E. W.
Flora Carolinaeenis: or, a Historical, Medical and Economic Display of the Vegetable Kingdom.... Charleston: 1806. V. 66
Shecut's Medical and Philosophical Essays. Charleston: 1819. V. 63

SHEE, MARTIN ARCHER
Elements of Art, a Poem: in Six Cantos.... London: 1809. V. 66; 67

SHEERAN, JAMES B.
Confederate Chaplain. A War Journal. Milwaukee: 1960. V. 63

SHEERES, HENRY
An Essay on the Certainty and Causes of the Earths Motion On Its Axis, Etc. London: 1698. V. 65

SHEETS, HENRY
A History of the Liberty Baptist Association From Its Organization in 1832 to 1906, Containing Much History Incidentally Connected with this Body. Raleigh: 1907. V. 67

SHEFFIELD and Neighbourhood.... Sheffield: 1899. V. 63

SHEFFIELD, F.
How I Killed the Tiger. 1902. V. 67

SHEFFIELD, JOHN BAKER HOLROYD, 1ST EARL OF
Observations on the Commerce of the American States.... London: 1784. V. 63
Observations on the Impolicy, Abuses and False Interpretation of the Poor Laws and on the Reports of the Two Houses of Parliament. London: 1818. V. 63
Observations on the Manufactures, Trade and Present State of Ireland. London: 1785. V. 67
Observations sur le Commerce des Etats Americains. Rouen: 1789. V. 63; 64

SHEFFIELD UNIVERSITY GEOLOGICAL SOCIETY
Journal. Sheffield. V. 65

SHEFFY, L. F.
The Francklyn Land and Cattle Company. A Panhandle Enterprise 1882- 1957. San Antonio: 1963. V. 66
The Life and Times of Timothy Dwight Hobart. Canyon: 1950. V. 64; 66

SHEIL, RICHARD LALOR
The Speeches of the Right Honourable Richard Lalor Shiel, M.P. London: 1847. V. 67

SHELDON, ADDISON ERWIN
Poems and Sketches of Nebraska. Lincoln: 1908. V. 64; 66

SHELDON, CHARLES
The Wilderness of the North Pacific Coast Islands. 1912. V. 62; 63; 64; 66
The Wilderness of the Upper Yukon: a Hunter's Explorations for Wild Sheep in Sub-Arctic Mountains. New York: 1911. V. 64; 66

SHELDON, HAROLD P.
Tranquility Tales of Sport with the Gun. New York: 1936. V. 64; 65; 66
Tranquility, Tranquility Regained (and) Tranquility Revisited. Oshkosh: 1986. V. 65

SHELDON, SIDNEY
The Naked Face. 1970. V. 64; 65

SHELDON, WILLIAM
Mormonism Examined: or Was Joseph Smith a Divinely Inspired Prophet?. Bordhead: 1876?. V. 63

SHELDON-WILLIAMS, RALF FREDERIC LARDY
The Canadian Front in France an Flanders. London: 1920. V. 65

SHELFORD, LEONARD
The Law of Railways, Including Three General Consolidation Acts, 1845.... London: 1846. V. 63
A Practical Treatise on the Law Concerning Lunatics, Idiots and Persons of Unsound Mind. London: 1834. V. 67

SHELFORD, R. W. C.
A Naturalist in Borneo. 1916. V. 66

SHELLER, JOHN
Cetus the Whale. Pacific Palisades: 1996. V. 62; 64

SHELLEY, DONALD A.
The Fraktur-Writings or Illuminated Manuscripts of the Pennsylvania Germans. Allentown: 1961. V. 66

SHELLEY, G. E.
A Handbook to the Birds of Egypt. 1872. V. 62

SHELLEY, GEORGE
Sentences and Maxims Divine, Moral and Historical, in Prose and Verse. London: 1730. V. 66

SHELLEY, MARY WOLLSTONECRAFT GODWIN
The Choice. London: 1876. V. 62
Frankenstein; or the Modern Prometheus. West Hatfield. 1818. V. 62
Frankenstein; or the Modern Prometheus. London: 1823. V. 65
Frankenstein, or the Modern Prometheus. London: 1831. V. 63
Frankenstein, or the Modern Prometheus. Philadelphia: 1833. V. 67
Frankenstein; or the Modern Prometheus. Halifax: 1865. V. 63; 67
Frankenstein; or, the Modern Prometheus. West Hatfield: 1983. V. 62
History of Six Week's Tour through a Part of France, Switzerland, Germany and Holland. London: 1817. V. 65
The Last Man. London: 1826. V. 65
Letters of.... Boston: 1918. V. 65

SHELLEY, PERCY BYSSHE
Adonais. London: 1886. V. 65
Adonais. London: 1900. V. 63
Adonais. London: 1935. V. 62; 63; 64; 65; 66
The Cenci. Livorno: 1819. V. 65
The Cenci. Rome: 1819. V. 67
The Cenci. London: 1821. V. 66
The Complete Works. London: 1926-1930. V. 67
Epipsychidio. Montagnola: 1923. V. 64
Harriet and Mary. Waltham St. Lawrence: 1944. V. 62
Note-Books of Percy Bysshe Shelley. Boston: 1911. V. 65
The Poems. London: 1901. V. 66
The Poems. London: 1901-1902. V. 63; 64
Poems. Hammersmith: 1914. V. 65
The Poems. Cambridge: 1971. V. 62; 63; 64; 66
Posthumous Poems. London: 1824. V. 63
Poetical Works. London: 1839. V. 63
Poetical Works. London: 1870. V. 62
The Poetical Works. London: 1892. V. 65
The Poetical Works. London: 1902. V. 62
Poetical Works. Prose Works. From the Original Editions. London: 1888. V. 67
Posthumous Poems. London: 1824. V. 62; 64; 65; 67
Prometheus Unbound. London: 1820. V. 62; 64; 67
Queen Mab. London: 1821. V. 67
Queen Mab. New York: 1821. V. 66
Queen Mab; with Notes. New York: 1831. V. 67
The Revolt of Islam: a Poem. London: 1818. V. 64
Rosalind and Helen...with Other Poems. London: 1819. V. 62; 64; 65; 67
The Senstive Plant. London: 1911. V. 63
Shelley. Hammersmith: 1914. V. 62
Zastrozzi. Waltham St. Lawrence: 1955. V. 62; 66; 67

SHELLSHEAR, J.
The Brain of the Aboriginal Australian. 1937. V. 67
A Comparative Study of the Endocranial Cast of Sinanthropus. 1934. V. 67

SHELLY, GEORGE F.
Early History of American Fork with Some History of a Latter Day. American Fork City: 1945. V. 65

SHELTON, CHARLES E.
Photo Album of Yesterday's Southwest. Palm Desert: 1961. V. 67

SHELTON, LOLA
Charles Marion Russell: Cowboy, Artist, Friend. New York: 1962. V. 66

SHELTON, MAURICE
An Historical and Critical Essay on the True Rise of Nobility, Political and Civil; from the First Ages of the World, Thro the Jewish, Grecian, Roman Commonwealths &c. Down to this Present Time. London: 1718. V. 65

SHELVOCKE, GEORGE
A Voyage Round the World by Way of the Great South Sea Peform'd in the Years 1719, 1720, 1721, 1722. London: 1726. V. 67

SHENANDOAH Valley Railway Co. Corporate History. Philadelphia: 1891. V. 63

SHENSTONE, WILLIAM
Men and Manners. Waltham St. Lawrence: 1927. V. 65; 66
The Works in Verse and Prose. London: 1764-1769. V. 66
The Works in Verse and Prose. Edinburgh: 1768. V. 66
The Works in Verse and Prose. Dublin: 1777. V. 64
The Works, in Verse and Prose. London: 1777. V. 64

SHEPARD, ERNEST H.
Drawn from Life. London: 1961. V. 64
Drawn from Memory. London: 1957. V. 63; 64; 66
Fun and Fantasy, A Book of Drawings.... London: 1927. V. 66

SHEPARD, JIM
Flights. New York: 1983. V. 66

SHEPARD, LUCIUS
The Jaguar Hunter. Sauk City: 1987. V. 64; 66

SHEPARD, SAM
A Lie of the Mind. New York: 1984. V. 66
A Lie of the Mind. San Francisco: 1993. V. 66

SHEPHERD, DAVID
The Man Who Loves Giants. 1975. V. 67

SHEPHERD, HENRY ELLIOT
The Life of Robert Edward Lee. New York and Washington: 1906. V. 62; 63; 65; 67
Narrative of Prison Life at Baltimore and Johnson's Island, Ohio. Baltimore: 1917. V. 62; 63; 65

SHEPHERD, J. C.
Italian Gardens of the Renaissance. New York: 1925. V. 64

SHEPHERD, JEAN
Wanda Hickey's Night of Golden Memories and Other Disasters. New York: 1971. V. 65

SHEPHERD, R. H.
Tennysoniana. London: 1879. V. 67

SHEPHERD, RICHARD
An Essay on Education in a Letter to Sir William Jones, Esq. London: 1782. V. 65

SHEPHERD, SAMUEL
The Statutes at Large of Virginia. Richmond: 1835. V. 62

SHEPHERD, THOMAS H.
London and Its Environs in the Nineteenth Century. London: 1829. V. 62

SHEPHERD, W.
Prairie Experiences in Handling Cattle and Sheep. New York: 1885. V. 66
Systematic Education; or, Elementary Instruction in Various Departments of Literature and Science.... London: 1817. V. 64

SHEPHERD, W. R.
The Benedictines of Caldey Island.... 1907. V. 66

SHEPHERD, WILLIAM
Prairie Experiences in Handing Cattle and Sheep. New York: 1885. V. 64; 67

SHEPHERD, WILLIAM R.
Guide to the Materials for the History of the United States in Spanish Archives. Washington: 1907. V. 67

THE SHEPHERD'S
Kalendar, or, the Citizen's and Country Man's Daily Companion.... London: 1706. V. 62

SHEPPARD, ERIC W.
Bedford Forrest: The Confederacy's Greatest Cavalryman. New York: 1930. V. 64

SHEPPARD, SAM
Endure and Conquer. Cleveland: 1966. V. 66

SHEPPARD, THOMAS
Evolution of the Drama in Hull and District. Hull: 1927. V. 63
Geological Rambles in East Yorkshire. London. V. 65
The Lost Towns of the Yorkshire Coast. Hull: 1912. V. 63

SHEPPARD, WILLIAM
The Touchstone of Common Assurances; or a Plain and Familiar Treatise, Opening the Learning of the Common Assurances, or Conveyances of the Kingdom. New York: 1808. V. 67

SHEPPERD, TAD
Pack and Paddock. New York: 1938. V. 67

SHEPPERSON, WILLIAM G.
War Songs of the South. Richmond: 1862. V. 62

SHERARD, ROBERT HARBOROUGH
Emile Zola: a Biographical and Critical Study. London: 1893. V. 66

SHERBOURNE, LORD
A Calendar of the Charters, Rolls and Other Documents...at Sherbourne House in Gloucester Belonging to...Lord Sherbourne. 1900. V. 63

SHERER, MOYLE
Recollections of the Peninsula. London: 1825. V. 67
Sketches of India, Written by an Officer for Fire-Side Travellers at Home. London: 1821. V. 66

SHERIDAN, LOUISA HENRIETTA
The Comic Offering.... London: 1834. V. 66
The History of the Fairchild Family; or, the Child's Manual. London: 1819. V. 65

SHERIDAN, LYDIA
The Trial of Mrs. Lydia Sheridan, Wife of Major Henry Sheridan, for Adultery with Francis Newman, Esq.... London: 1787. V. 65

SHERIDAN, PHILIP H.
Outline Descriptions of the Posts in the Military Division of the Missouri Accompanied by Tabular List of Indian Superintendencies, Agencies and Fort Reservations and a Summary of Certain Indian Tribes. Fort Collins: 1972. V. 67
Personal Memoirs of P. H. Sheridan. New York: 1888. V. 62; 64; 65; 67
Records of Engagements with Hostile Indians. Washington: 1882. V. 65
Report of the Lieutenant General of the Army. Washington: 1885. V. 64
Reports of Inspection Made in the Summer of 1877 by.... Washington: 1878. V. 62; 65

SHERIDAN, RICHARD BRINSLEY BUTLER
The Critic; or a Tragedy Rehearsed. London: 1781. V. 66
The Duenna. Dublin: 1787. V. 65
The Duenna. 1925. V. 67
Plays and Poems. Oxford: 1928. V. 63; 65
The Plays of Richard Brinsley Sheridan. 1883. V. 67
The Rivals. London: 1775. V. 64; 66
The School for Scandal. Dublin: 1782. V. 67
The School for Scandal. Dublin: 1793. V. 67
The School for Scandal. London: 1911. V. 66
The Speech of R. B. Sheridan, Esq. Member for Stafford, on Wednesday, the 7th of February 1787, in Bringing Forward the Fourth Charge Against Warren Hastings, Esq. Relative to the Begums of Oude. London: 1787. V. 63
Verses to the Memory of David Garrick. London: 1779. V. 66
The Works.... London: 1821. V. 66

SHERIDAN, THOMAS
A Complete Dictionary of the English Language.... London: 1789. V. 62; 64
A Complete Dictionary of the English Language.... London: 1797. V. 64
A Course of Lectures on Elocution. London: 1796. V. 62; 64
A Course of Lectures on Elocution; Together with Two Dissertations on Language. London: 1798. V. 67
A General Dictionary of the English Language. London: 1780. V. 62
The Life of the Rev. Dr. Jonathan Swift, Dean of St. Patrick's Dublin. London: 1734. V. 66

SHERIDAN, W. C. F. G.
A Topographical and Historical Guide to the Isle of Wight.... London: 1833. V. 65

SHERINGHAM, H. T.
The Book of the Fly Rod. 1931. V. 67

SHERLOCK, P. T.
The Case of Ireland Stated Historically from the Earliest Times to the Present; Together with a Gazetteer. Chicago: 1880. V. 67

SHERLOCK, THOMAS
A Letter from the Lord Bishop of London, to the Clergy and People of London and Westminster; on Occasion of the Late Earthquakes. London: 1750. V. 62
The Use and Intent of Prophecy (along with other works). (bound with) A Vindication of the Corporation and Test Acts. London: 1728-1718. V. 63; 66

SHERLOCK, WILLIAM
A Practical Discourse Concerning Death. Glasgow: 1775. V. 63
A Practical Discourse Concerning Death. Edinburgh: 1806. V. 63
A Vindication of the Doctrine of the Holy and Ever Blessed Trinity and the Incarnation of the Son of God. London: 1691. V. 67

SHERMAN, ANDREW M.
Historic Morristown, New Jersey: The Story of Its First Century. Morristown: 1905. V. 66

SHERMAN, ELEAZER
The Narrative of Eleazer Sherman, Giving an Account of His Life, Experience, Call to the Ministry of the Gospel and Travels.... Providence: 1828. V. 63; 64

SHERMAN, FREDERICK BARREDA
From the Guadalquivir to the Golden Gate by Way of Lima, Baltimore, New York, Newport, Washington, London, Paris and Cuajiniquilapa.... Mill Valley: 1977. V. 63; 64; 66

SHERMAN, ROGER
An Astronomical Diary; or, Almanack for the Year of Our Lord Christ, 1760.... Boston: 1760. V. 67

SHERMAN, W. T.
Memoirs of General.... New York: 1892. V. 65

SHERNINGHAM, H. T.
The Book of the Fly Rod. 1936. V. 67

SHERRARD J. KNOX
Philip Alwyne. London: 1888. V. 67

SHERRIFF, R. C.
Journey's End: a Play in Three Acts. London: 1929. V. 63; 64

SHERRILL, MILES O.
A Soldier's Story: Prison Life and Other Incidents in the War of 1861-1865. Raleigh: 1904. V. 62; 63; 65

SHERRINGTON, C. S.
Notes on the Arrangment of Some Motor Fibres in the Lumbo-Sacral Plexus. London: 1892. V. 67

SHERRINGTON, CHARLES
The Endeavour of Jean Fernel. Cambridge: 1946. V. 64; 65; 66; 67
The Integrative Action of the Nervous System. London: 1906. V. 64; 66
The Integrative Action of the Nervous System. London: 1911. V. 67
The Integrative Action of the Nervous System. New Haven: 1918. V. 66; 67
The Integrative Action of the Nervous System. New Haven: 1920. V. 67

SHERRINGTON, CHARLES SCOTT
The Endeavour of Jean Fernel. Cambridge: 1946. V. 65

SHERRY, JANE
Venus Unbound. New York: 1993. V. 64

SHERRY, LAURA
Old Prairie du Chien. Paris: 1931. V. 65

SHERWELL, SAMUEL
Old Recollections of an Old Boy. New York: 1923. V. 63; 66

SHERWOOD, ADIEL
A Gazetteer of the State of Georgia. Philadelphia: 1829. V. 62

SHERWOOD, MARY MARTHA BUTT
The History of George Desmond, Founded on Facts Which Occurred in the East Indies.... Boston: 1822. V. 66
The History of Henry Milner, a Little Boy, Who Was No Brought Up According to the Fashions. London: 1835-1831. V. 65
The History of the Fairchild Family, or, The Child's Manual. London: 1853. V. 66
The Lady of the Manor. London: 1841-1846. V. 65
The Re-Captured Negro. (with) The History of Fidelity and Profession. Wellington, Salop: 1821-1819. V. 65
Roxobel. London: 1831. V. 65

SHERWOOD, MIDGE
Days of Vintage, Years of Vision. San Marino: 1982-1987. V. 63

SHERWOOD, W. E.
Oxford Rowing. A History of Boat-Racing at Oxford from the Earliest Times.... London: 1900. V. 67

SHERZER, WILLIAM H.
Glaciers of the Canadian Rockies and Selkirks. Washington: 1907. V. 65

SHEW, JOEL
The Water-Cure Manual.... New York: 1848. V. 64

SHIEL, M. P.
The Evil Men Do. London: 1904. V. 63
Isle of Lies. London: 1909. V. 63
The Lord of the Sea. London: 1901. V. 66

SHIEL, M. P. continued
Prince Zaleski. 1895. V. 63
Prince Zaleski. London: 1895. V. 63; 64
Say Au R'Voir, but not Goodbye. London: 1933. V. 65
This Above All. New York: 1933. V. 63
This Knot of Life. London: 1909. V. 63
The Young Men Are Coming. New York: 1937. V. 66

SHIEL, ROGER R.
Early to Bed and Early to Rise. Twenty Years in Hell With the Beef Trust. Facts Not Fiction. Indianapolis: 1909. V. 62; 65

SHIELDS, CAROL
The Box Garden. Toronto: 1977. V. 62; 63
Flatties: Their Various Forms and Uses. Toronto: 1997. V. 67
Happenstance. Toronto: 1980. V. 63; 64; 66; 67
Larry's Party. N.P: 1997. V. 63; 67
Mary Swann. London: 1990. V. 67
The Orange Fish. Toronto: 1989. V. 63; 65; 66; 67
The Republic of Love. Toronto: 1992. V. 64; 66; 67
Small Ceremonies. Toronto: 1976. V. 67
The Stone Diaries. New York: 1993. V. 65; 66
The Stone Diaries. Toronto: 1993. V. 65; 67
The Stone Diaries. New York: 1994. V. 62; 66; 67
The Stone Diaries. Toronto: 1994. V. 66; 67
Swann. New York: 1987. V. 67
Various Miracles. London: 1994. V. 67

SHIELDS, F. W.
The Strains on Structures of Ironwork; with Practical Remarks on Iron Construction. London: 1861. V. 62

SHIELDS, G. O.
The Battle of the Big Hole. Chicago: 1889. V. 65; 67
The Big Game of North America. 1890. V. 62; 63; 64; 66; 67
The Big Game of North America, Its Habits, Habitat, Haunts and Characteristics.... Chicago and New York: 1890. V. 64; 66
The Blanket Indian of the Northwest. New York: 1921. V. 65; 67

SHIELDS, JAMES
Monozygotic Twins Brought Up Apart and Brought Up Together. London: 1962. V. 65

SHIELDS, JAMES T.
Clinch-Dale Farm Short Horn and Jersey Herd Book. Bean Station?: 1877. V. 64
Letter of Judge James T. Shields. Morristown; 1881. V. 64

SHIELDS, WILMER, MRS.
Plantation Life Since Sins Dis Time. New Orleans: 1887. V. 64

SHIELLS, WILLIAM
An Account of the Atholl System of Planting and Rearing Larch, as Practised by the Late Duke of Atholl, at Dunkeld. Edinburgh: 1831. V. 67

SHIELS, ARCHIE
Little Journeys Into the History of Russian America and the Purchase of Alaska. Bellingham: 1949. V. 64

SHIERCLIFFE, EDWARD
The Bristol and Hotwell Guide; or Useful Entertaining Pocket Companion for All Persons Residing At, or Resorting to Bristol, the Hotwell, or their Vicinities.... Bristol: 1789. V. 63

SHIFREEN, LAWRENCE J.
Henry Miller: a Bibliography of Primary Sources. Ann Arbor: 1993. V. 62

SHIICHI, TAJIMA
Toyo Bijutsu Taikan 6. Tokyo: 1909. V. 66

SHIIKAMA, T.
Selected Shells of the World. Tokyo: 1963-1964. V. 62

SHILLABER, BENJAMIN P.
Life and Sayings of Mrs. Partington. New York and Boston: 1854. V. 63
Mrs. Partington's Carpet-Bag of Fun. New York: 1854. V. 63

SHILLITOE, CHARLES
The Country Book Club, a Poem. 1964. V. 62

SHILTON, RICHARD PHILLIPS
The History of Southwell, in the County of Nottingham, Its Hamlets and Vicinage.... London: 1818. V. 63
The History of Southwell, in the County of Nottingham, Its Hamlets and Vicinage.... Newark: 1818. V. 65
The History of the Town of Newark Upon Trent, in the County of Nottingham, Comprising an Account of Its Antiquities, Edifices, Public Institutions, Charities, Charters, etc. Newark: 1820. V. 65

SHILTS, RANDY
And the Band Played On: Politics, People and the AIDS Epidemic. New York: 1987. V. 63

SHIMAI, K.
The Skin Especially on the Sweat Glands; a Collection of Themes in Commemoration of Dr. Torqatoshi Taniguchi's 25th Anniversary of His Professorship. Tokyo: 1961. V. 67

SHIMEALL, R. C.
The Second Coming of Christ, or the Impending Approach of the Restitution of All Things.... New York: 1873. V. 64

SHINN, CHARLES H.
Mining Camps: a Study in American Frontier Government. New York: 1885. V. 67

The Story of the Mine as Illustrated by the Great Comstock Lode of Nevada. New York: 1896. V. 63; 66

SHIP and Shore; or Leaves from the Journal of a Cruise to the Levant. New York: 1835. V. 63

SHIPLEY, THORNE
Classics in Psychology. New York: 1961. V. 63

SHIPMAN, O. L., MRS.
Letters Past and Present to My Nephews and Nieces. N.P. V. 65

SHIPP, HORACE
Edward Seago. London: 1952. V. 65

SHIPP, JOHN
Memoirs of the Extraordinary Military Career of John Shipp, Later a Lieut. in His Majesty's 87th Regiment. London: 1894. V. 64

SHIPPEN, WILLIAM
Three Speeches Against Continuing the Army &c. As They Were Spoken in the House of Commons the Last Session of Parliament. London: 1718. V. 62

SHIPS of the Great Lakes, a Pictorial History. Detroit: 1976. V. 67

SHIPTON, E.
Mountains of Tartary. 1951. V. 65

SHIPTON, ERIC
Nanda Devi. London: 1936. V. 63; 64

SHIRAHATA, S.
Les Alps. 1980. V. 65

SHIRAKAWA, Y.
Himalayas. 1986. V. 63; 65

SHIRAS, GEORGE
Hunting Wild Life with Camera and Flashlight. 1936. V. 67

SHIRK, DAVID
The Cattle Drives of David Shirk. Portland: 1956. V. 64

SHIRLEY, JAMES
The Doubtful Heir: a Tragi-Comedie, as It Was Acted at the Private House in Blackfriars. London: 1952. V. 66
Dramatic Works and Poems.... London: 1833. V. 63

SHIRLEY, THOMAS
The Angler's Museum; or, the Whole Art of Float and Fly Fishing. London: 1784. V. 63; 64

SHIRREFF, JAMES HALES
Disputatio Medica Inauguralis de Diabete Mellito...Pro gradu Doctoris.... Edinburgh: 1804. V. 62

SHIRREFS, ANDREW
Poems, Chiefly in the Scottish Dialect. Edinburgh: 1790. V. 64; 65

SHIVERS, LOUISE
Here to Get My Baby Out of Jail. New York: 1983. V. 66

SHOBERL, FREDERIC
Persia; Containing a Description of the Country, with an Account of Its Government, Laws and Religion.... Philadelphia: 1834. V. 62
Tales of Woman. London: 1828. V. 67

SHOCKLETON, JANE
Facts and Fancies in Prose and Verse. London: 1864. V. 64; 65

SHOEMAKER, F. C.
Missouri Day by Day. Jefferson: 1943. V. 64; 67

SHOEMAKER, HENRY W.
Extinct Pennsylvania Animals. Altoona: 1917-1919. V. 62
Indian Folk-Songs of Pennsylvania. Ardmore: 1927. V. 66

SHOEMAKER, MICHAEL MEYERS
Quaint Corners of Ancient Empires: Southern India, Burma and Manila. New York: 1899. V. 63

SHOOTER, JOSEPH
The Kafirs of Natal and Zulu Country. London: 1857. V. 62

SHOOTING Notes and Comments. A Book Containing Matters of Interest to Sportsmen. Birmingham: 1910. V. 63

SHORE, FREDERICK JOHN
Notes on Indian Affairs. London: 1837. V. 62

A SHORT Account of the Educational Society of Japan. Tokyo: 1892. V. 64

A SHORT Account of the Plague, Which Prevailed in the City of London in the Year 1665. London: 1793. V. 67

A SHORT History of the Bible. Harrisburg: 1838. V. 63

SHORT, IAN
Medieval French Textual Studies in Memory of T. B. W. Reid. 1984. V. 67

A SHORT Inquiry Into the Antiquity and Pretensions of Free Masonry.... New York: 1826. V. 64; 66

A SHORT Introduction of Grammar.... London: 1789. V. 62

SHORT, L. L.
Woodpeckers of the World. Greenville: 1982. V. 63; 67

A SHORT State of the War and the Peace. London: 1715. V. 62

SHORT, THOMAS
A Comparative History of the Increase and Decrease of Mankind in England, and Several Countries Abroad.... London: 1767. V. 63
Discourses on Tea, Sugar, Mil, Made-wines, Spirits, Punch, Tobacco &c.... London: 1750. V. 66

SHORT, THOMAS VOWLER
A Letter Addressed to the Very Reverend the Dean of Christ Church, on the State of the Public Examinations in the University of Oxford. Oxford: 1822. V. 64

A SHORT View of the Dispute Between the Merchants of London, Bristol and Liverpool, and the Advocates of a New Joint Stock Company Concerning the Regulation of the African Trade. London: 1750. V. 62

A SHORT Way to Know the World, or the Rudiments of Geography.... London: 1712. V. 65

A SHORT-HAND Dictionary, To Which is Prefixed all the Rules or Principles of that Useful and Pleasing Art.... London: 1777?. V. 64

SHORTCUT, DAISY
Our Show: a Humorous Account of the International Exposition in Honor of the Centennial Anniversary of American Independence. Philadelphia: 1876. V. 67

SHORTEN, MONICA
Squirrels. London: 1954. V. 62

SHORTER, ALFRED H.
Paper Mills and Paper Makers in England 1495-1800. Hilversum: 1957. V. 66

SHORTER, CLEMENT K.
The Brontes Life and Letters. London: 1908. V. 64; 66
Charlotte Bronte and Her Circle. New York: 1896. V. 63; 64

THE SHORTER Oxford English Dictionary, on Historical Principles. Oxford: 1933. V. 66

SHORTHOUSE, J. D.
Biology of Insect Induced Galls. New York: 1992. V. 66

SHORTHOUSE, JOSEPH HENRY
Blanche, Lady Falaise; a Tale. London: 1891. V. 66; 67
Ellie. Birmingham: 1883. V. 62

SHORTRIDGE, G. C.
The Mammals of South-West Africa. London: 1934. V. 62; 66

THE SHOTOVER Papers, or, Echoes from Oxford...1874-1875. Oxford: 1875. V. 64

SHOTWELL, WALTER G.
The Civil War in America. London and New York: 1923. V. 62

SHOURDS, THOMAS
History and Genealogy of Fenwick's Colony. Bridgeton: 1876. V. 63; 66

SHREFFLER, PHILIP A.
The Noble Bachelors' Red Covered Volume. St. Louis: 1974. V. 66

SHREVE, ANITA
The Pilot's Wife. Boston: 1998. V. 67

SHREVE, F.
Vegetation and Flora of the Sonoran Desert. Stanford: 1964. V. 64

SHREWSBURY, CHARLES JOHN CHETWYND TALBOT, 19TH EARL OF
Meliora; or, Better Times to Come. London: 1852. V. 67

SHRINER, CHARLES A.
Paterson, New Jersey. Paterson: 1890. V. 63; 66

THE SHROPSHIRE Gazetteer, with an Appendix, Including a Survey of the County, and Valuable Miscellaneous Information. London: 1824. V. 63

SHROPSHIRE COUNTY GAOL
General Rules, Orders, Regulations and Bye-Laws, for the Inspection and Government of the Gaol and House of Correction for the County of Salop. Shrewsbury: 1797. V. 65

SHTERENBERG, DAVID
Moi Igrushki (My Toys). Moscow and Leningrad: 1930. V. 63; 64

SHUCKARD, W. E.
British Bees. London: 1866. V. 64
Essay on the Indigenous Fossorial Hymenoptera. London: 1837. V. 64

SHUDAKOV, GRIGORY
Pioneers of Soviet Photography. New York: 1983. V. 63

SHUFELDT, R. W.
Osteology of Birds. New York: 1909. V. 64
Remarks upon Extinct Mammals of the United States. Chicago and New York: 1889. V. 67

SHULBE, ERNEST
Cake Decoration. London. V. 67

SHULDHAM, EDWARD
Pictures from Birdland, With Rhymes.... London: 1899. V. 63; 65

SHULEVITS, URI
Snow. New York: 1998. V. 65

SHULMAN, NEIL
Finally... I'm a Doctor. New York: 1976. V. 62; 65
What? Dead...Again. Baton Rouge: 1979. V. 62

SCHUMANN Album of Children's Pieces for Piano. Philadelphia: 1915. V. 62

SHUMWAY, HARRY
I Go South: an Unprejudiced Visit to a Group of Cotton Mills. Boston: 1930. V. 67

SHURCLIFF, S. N.
Jungle Islands. New York: 1930. V. 62; 63; 64; 66

SHURTLEFF, NATHANIEL B.
A Decimal System for the Arrangement and Administration of Libraries. Boston: 1856. V. 66

SHUTE, DANIEL A.
A Sermon Preached.... Boston: 1768. V. 65

SHUTE, NEVIL
On the Beach. Melbourne, London, Toronto: 1957. V. 62; 64; 65
Vinland the Good. N.P.: 1946. V. 64

SHUTTLE, PENELOPE
Delicious Babies. London: 1996. V. 62

SHUTTLEWORTH, J.
Guide Book to Ilkley and Vicinity. Ilkley: 1863. V. 65

SHVIDKOVSKY, O. A.
Building in the U.S.S.R. 1917-1932. London: 1971. V. 65

SIBBES, RICHARD
A Miracle of Miracles; or, Christ In Our Nature. London: 1656. V. 66
The Soul's Conflict and Victory Over Itself by Faith. (with) The Bruised Reed and Smoking Flax. A Fountain Sealed. A Description of Christ. London: 1837-1838. V. 62; 65

SIBELLI, CASPAR
In Historiarm Sanati Lvnatii Conciones Saccrae. Amsterdam: 1634. V. 66

SIBLEY, C. G.
Distribution and Taxonomy of Birds of the World. New Haven: 1990. V. 63
Distribution and Taxonomy of Birds of the World and Supplement. New Haven: 1990-1993. V. 63; 67
Phylogeny and Classification of Birds, a Study in Molecular Evolution. New Haven: 1991. V. 62; 67

SIBLEY, GRETA D.
Tea Time in Korea. Easthampton: 1994. V. 62

SIBLEY, HENRY C.
Iron Face, the Adventures of Jack Frazer, Frontier Warrior, Scout and Hunter. Chicago: 1950. V. 65; 67

SIBLEY, HENRY HASTINGS
Sibley. Autobiography and Letters. 1932. V. 67

SIBLEY, W.
Notes on the University of Strasburg (Its Medical Teaching and Facilities). London: 1890. V. 67

SIBORNE, W.
History of the War in France and Belgium in 1815.... Philadelphia: 1845. V. 65

SIBREE, J.
Madagascar and Its People, Notes of a Four Years' Residence. London: 1870. V. 63
A Naturalist in Madagascar. 1915. V. 67
A Naturalist in Madagascar. London: 1915. V. 66

SIBTHORP, JOHN
Florae Graecae Prodromus.... London: 1806-1816. V. 67

SICK, H.
Birds in Brazil. Princeton: 1993. V. 62; 63; 66; 67

SICKLER, JOSEPH S.
The History of Salem County, New Jersey. Salem: 1937. V. 63; 66
The Old Houses of Salem County. Salem: 1949. V. 63; 66

SICKLES, DAN
New York at Gettysburg. Albany: 1900. V. 65; 67

SIDDONS, A. R.
The House Next Door. Atlanta: 1993. V. 67
John Chancellor Makes Me Cry. Garden City: 1975. V. 65

SIDDONS, HENRY
Practical Illustrations of Rhetorical Gesture and Action, Adapted to the English Drama.... London: 1807. V. 66

SIDDONS, SARAH KEMBLE
The Reminiscences of Sarah Kemble Siddons, 1773-1785. Cambridge: 1942. V. 67

SIDES, DOROTHY SMITH
Decorative Art of the Southwestern Indians. Santa Ana: 1936. V. 63; 64

SIDGWICK, HENRY
The Methods of Ethics. London: 1877. V. 67

SIDJANSKI, DIMITRI
Cherrywood Cannon. New York: 1978. V. 63

SIDNEY, ALGERNON
The Arraignment, Tryal and Condemnation of Algernon Sidney, Esq. for High Treason, for Conspiring the Death of the King.... London: 1684. V. 62
Discourses Concerning Government. 1698. V. 63

SIDNEY, ALGERNON continued
Discourses Concerning Government. London: 1763. V. 65
Letters of the Honourable Algernon Sydney, to the Honourable Henry Savile, Ambassador in France. In the Year 1679. London: 1742. V. 66

SIDNEY, EDWIN
The Philosophy of Food and Nutrition in Plants and Animals. London: 1849. V. 67

SIDNEY, MARGARET
Five Little Peppers and How They Grew. Boston: 1880. V. 64

SIDNEY, PHILIP
Astrophel and Stella. London: 1931. V. 65
Certain Sonnets from the Countess of Pembroke's Arcadia. Cleveland: 1890. V. 65
The Correspondence of Sir Philip Sidney and Hubert Languet. London: 1845. V. 67
The Countess of Pembrokes Arcadia. London: 1590. V. 67
The Countess of Pembroke's Arcadia. 1638. V. 63
The Countess of Pembroke's Arcadia. London: 1674. V. 63
The Defense of Poetry. London: 1810. V. 65
The Prose Works. 1963. V. 64

SIDNEY, S.
The Book of the Horse. London: 1893. V. 67

SIDNEY, SAMUEL
The Three Colonies of Australia. London: 1852. V. 63
The Three Colonies of Australia. Auburn: 1854. V. 62

SIEBECK, RUDOLF
Guide Pratique du Jardinier Paysagiste. Paris: 1863. V. 67

SIEBER, R.
African Textiles and Decorative Arts. New York: 1972. V. 62

SIEBERT, FRANK T.
The Frank T. Siebert Library of the North American Indian and American Frontier. New York: 1999. V. 65

SIEBOLD, PHILIPP FRANZ VON
Philipp Franz Von Siebold's Ukiyo-E Collection. Tokyo: 1978. V. 62

SIEFF, ISRAEL
Memoirs. London: 1970. V. 67

SIEGEL, C.
Structure and Form in Modern Architecture. New York: 1962. V. 62; 65

SIEGEL, RUDOLPH E.
Galen's System of Physiology and Medicine. An Analysis of His Doctrines and Observations on Bloodflow, Respiration, Humors and Internal Diseases. Basel: 1968. V. 65

SIEMENS, C. WILLIAM
On the Conservation of Solar Energy. London: 1883. V. 62; 63; 67

SIENKIEWICZ, HENRYK
Quo Vadis. Verona: 1959. V. 62; 66

SIERRA CLUB
The Sierra Club Bulletin. San Francisco: 1950. V. 63

SIERRA LEONE COMPANY
Substance of the Report Delivered by the Court of Directors of the Sierra Leone Company to the General Court of Proprietors...1794 (bound with) Substance of the Report...1795. Philadelphia: 1795. V. 64; 66

SIEVEKING, L. DE GIBERNE
Dressing Gowns and Glue. London: 1914. V. 62
Stampede. 1924. V. 64; 65

SIEVERS, HARRY J.
Benjamin Harrison: Hoosier Warrior. New York: 1959. V. 65

SIGAUD DE LA FOND, JOSEPH AIGNAN
Elemens de Physique Theorique et Experimentale, Pour Servir de Suite a la Description & l'Usage d'Un Cabinet de Physique Experimentale. Paris: 1787. V. 64

SIGERIST, HENRY
The Great Doctors. New York: 1950. V. 64; 66; 67

SIGERSON, DORA
The Fairy Changeling, and Other Poems. London: 1898. V. 64
Madge Linsey and Other Poems. Dublin and London: 1913. V. 64
New Poems. Dublin and London: 1912. V. 64

SIGONIUS, CAROLUS
Historiarum de Occidentali Imperio Libri XX. Ad Illustriss et Excellentiss. Bononiae: 1578. V. 66

SIGOURNEY, LYDIA
Border Beagles: a Tale of Mississippi. Philadelphia: 1840. V. 62
Pocahontas and Other Poems. New York: 1841. V. 63
Selections from Various Sources. Worcester: 1863. V. 67

SIGSBEE, C. D.
Description of the Sounding-Machine, Water-Bottle and Detacher Used on Board the Blake. Cambridge: 1880. V. 67
The Maine. An Account of Her Destruction in Havana Harbour. London: 1899. V. 65

SIGSBY, WILLIAM
Life and Adventures of Timothy Murphy, the Benefactor of Schoharie. Schoharie: 1839. V. 63

SIKES, S. K.
The Natural History of the African Elephant. London: 1971. V. 64

SIKES, WILLIAM WIRT
British Goblins: Welsh Folk-Lore, Fairy Mythology, Legends and Traditions. Boston: 1881. V. 63

SILBERRAD, U.
Dutch Bulbs and Gardens. 1909. V. 63

SILER, JENNY
Easy Money. New York: 1998. V. 67

SILIUS ITALICUS
Del Bello Punico Libri Septemdecim. Paris: 1531. V. 65
Punicorum Libri Septemdecim...Curante Arnoldo Drakenborch. Trajecti Ad Rhenum: 1717. V. 66
Punica. London: 1792. V. 63

SILKIN, JON
The Peaceable Kingdom. London: 1954. V. 63
The Two Freedoms. London: 1958. V. 62

SILKO, LESLIE MARMON
Almanac of the Dead. New York: 1991. V. 67
Ceremony. New York: 1977. V. 62; 64; 67
Rain. New York: 1996. V. 64; 67
Storyteller. New York: 1981. V. 62; 67

SILLAR, DAVID
Poems.... Kilmarnock: 1789. V. 64

SILLAR, FREDERICK CAMERON
The Symbolic Pig. London: 1961. V. 62

SILLIMAN, BENJAMIN
A Journal of Travels in England, Holland and Scotland and of Two Passages Over the Atlantic in the Years 1805 and 1806. New York: 1810. V. 63

SILLITOE, ALAN
The Ragman's Daughter. London: 1976. V. 63
Saturday Night and Sunday Morning. New York: 1959. V. 67

SILLS, DAVID L.
International Encyclopedia of the Social Sciences. London: 1968. V. 66

THE SILLY Jelly-Fish. Tokyo: 1890. V. 65

SILURIENSIS, LEOLINUS
The Anatomy of Tobacco; or Smoking Methodised, Divided and Considered After a New Fashion. London: 1884. V. 63

SILVA, DANIEL
The Unlikely Spy. London: 1996. V. 67

SILVA, ERCOLE
Dell'Arte dei Giardini Inglesi. Milan: 1801. V. 64

SILVA, P. C.
Catalogue of the Benthic Marine Algae of the Indian Ocean. Berkeley: 1996. V. 65

SILVA, TONY
A Monograph of Macaws and Conures. London: 1993. V. 67

SILVA COUTHINHO, JOAO MARTINS DA
Relatorio. Manaos: 1861. V. 62

THE SILVER Fairy Book. London: 1898. V. 66

SILVER, ARTHUR P.
Farm Cottage, Camp and Canoe in Canada of the Call of Nova Scotia to the Emigrant and Sportsman. London: 1907. V. 66; 67

THE SILVER Book of English Sonnets: a Selection of Less-Known Sonnets. Haarlem: 1927. V. 62

SILVER, GEORGE
A Practical Treatise on the Prevention and Cure of Smoky Chimneys. Glasgow: 1836. V. 64

SILVER, KIT
Three London Cats. 1999. V. 65

SILVER, LEON T.
Geologic Implications of Impacts of Large Asteroids and Comets of the Earth. Boulder: 1982. V. 66

SILVERBERG, ROBERT
Time of the Great Freeze. 1964. V. 65; 66

SILVERMAN, JONATHAN
For the World to See: the Life of Margaret Bourke-White. New York: 1983. V. 63

SILVERSTEIN, ARTHUR M.
A History of Immunology. San Diego: 1989. V. 66

SILVERSTEIN, SHEL
Take Ten. Tokyo: 1955. V. 63
Uncle Shelby's Zoo, Don't Bump the Grump!. New York: 1964. V. 66

SILVEUS, W. A.
Texas Grasses. San Antonio: 1933. V. 63

SIM, G.
The Vertebrate Fauna of Dee... the Ichthyological Portion Includes the Fishes of the East Coast from Wick to the Firth of Forth. Aberdeen: 1903. V. 62

SIMAK, CLIFFORD D.
Time and Again. London: 1956. V. 64; 66

SIMCOE, JOHN GRAVES
Simcoe's Military Journal. New York: 1844. V. 66

SIMENON, GEORGES
Across the Street. London: 1954. V. 67
Act of Passion - a Novel. New York: 1952. V. 64
Affairs of Destiny. 1945. V. 64
African Trio. New York: 1979. V. 63; 66
Escape in Vain. London: 1943. V. 64
Inspector Maigret and the Burglar's Wife. Garden City: 1956. V. 67
Inspector Maigret and the Strangled Stripper. Garden City: 1954. V. 66
Maigret and Monsieur Charles. London: 1973. V. 67
Maigret and the Burglar's Wife. London: 1955. V. 65; 67
Maigret and the Flea. London: 1972. V. 67
Maigret and the Gangsters. London: 1974. V. 67
Maigret and the Millionaires. London: 1974. V. 67
Maigret Goes to School. London: 1957. V. 66; 67
Maigret Hesitates. London: 1970. V. 67
Maigret in Society. London: 1962. V. 65
Maigret Loses His Temper. London: 1965. V. 66
Maigret's Failure. London: 1962. V. 67
The Negro. London: 1959. V. 62; 67
The Novel of a Man. New York: 1964. V. 67
The Shadow Falls. London: 1945. V. 66
The Son. London: 1958. V. 65; 67
The Strangers in the House. London: 1951. V. 66
The Window Over the Way. London: 1951. V. 65

SIMES, THOMAS
The Regulator; or Instructions to Form the Officer and Complete the Soldier, Upon Fixed Principles.... London: 1780. V. 65

SIMIC, CHARLES
The Chicken Without a Head. Portland: 1983. V. 62
Dismantling the Silence. London: 1971. V. 62; 63
Displaced Person. New York: 1995. V. 64; 67
Nine Poems. A Childhood Story. Cambridge: 1989. V. 62; 64
On the Music of the Spheres. New York: 1996. V. 62; 64; 67
The Pieces of the Clock Lie Scattered. Poem. Syracuse: 1997. V. 62; 64; 65
Return to a Place Lit by a Glass of Milk. New York: 1974. V. 67
School for Dark Thoughts. Pawlet: 1978. V. 62
Selected Poems 1963-1983. New York: 1985. V. 66
They Forage at Night. N.P: 1980. V. 62
Three Poems. Syracuse: 1998. V. 62; 64; 65
Wendy's Pinball. Poems. East Hampton: 1996. V. 62; 64; 66; 67
What the Grass Says. San Francisco: 1967. V. 63

SIMINGTON, ROBERT C.
The Civil Survey A.D. 1654-1656 County of Limerick. 1938. V. 64; 67
The Civil Survey AD 1654-1656 Co. of Tipperary. 1931-1934. V. 64; 67

SIMKINS, CLEVELAND S.
Functional Human Anatomy. Dubuque: 1949. V. 67

SIMKINS, FRANCIS BUTLER
South Carolina During Reconstruction. Chapel Hill: 1932. V. 63
The Tillman Movement in South Carolina. Durham: 1926. V. 63; 67
The Women of the Confederacy. Richmond and New York: 1936. V. 62; 63; 65

SIMMONDS, A. J.
On the Big Range. A Centennial History at Cornish and Trenton, Cache County, Utah 1870-1970. N.P: 1970. V. 64; 67

SIMMONDS, P. L.
Waste Products and Undeveloped Substances; or Hints for Enterprise in Neglected Fields. London: 1862. V. 65

SIMMONDS, W. H.
The Practical Grocer. 1909. V. 67
The Practical Grocer; a Manual and Guide for the Grocer, the Provision Merchant and Allied Trades.... London: 1909. V. 64

SIMMONS, AMELIA
American Cookery, or, the Art of Dressing Viands, Fish, Poultry and Vegetables and The Best Mode of Making Puff-Pastes, Pies, Tarts, Puddings, Custards and Preserves. Poughkeepsie: 1815. V. 64; 66

SIMMONS, CHARLES
Powdered Eggs. New York: 1964. V. 66; 67

SIMMONS, DAN
Carrion Comfort. Arlington Heights: 1989. V. 65
Song of Kali. New York: 1985. V. 62; 64; 65
Summer Sketches. Northridge: 1992. V. 67

SIMMONS, HERBERT
Corner Boy. Boston: 1957. V. 65

SIMMONS, JAMES
Ballad of a Marriage. Belfast: 1966. V. 63
In the Wilderness and Other Poems. London: 1969. V. 63
Judy Garland and the Cold War. Belfast: 1976. V. 63
No Land Is Waste, Dr. Eliot. Richmond: 1972. V. 63
Ten Poems. Belfast: 1967. V. 63

SIMMONS, JOHN
An Account of a Simple, Easy and Effectual Method for Preserving His Majesty's Navy.... 1774. V. 65

SIMMONS, LEO W.
Sun Chief. The Autobiography of Hopi Indian. New Haven: 1942. V. 66

SIMMONS, MARC
Albuquerque. Albuquerque: 1982. V. 63; 66
Along the Santa Fe Trail. Albuquerque: 1986. V. 63; 66
Border Comanches - Seven Spanish Colonial Documents 1785-1819. Santa Fe: 1967. V. 66

SIMMONS, MARK
The Sena Family: Blacksmiths of Santa Fe. Santa Fe: 1981. V. 63; 64; 66

SIMMONS, NOAH
Heroes and Heroines of the Fort Dearborn Massacre. Lawrence: 1896. V. 63

SIMMS, FREDERICK WALTER
Practical Tunnelling. Explaining in Detail, the Setting Out of the Works: Shaft Sinking, and Healing Driving; Ranging the Lines and Levelling Under Ground.... London: 1844. V. 65

SIMMS, J. R.
The American Spy, or Freedom's Early Sacrifice: a Tale of the Revolution. Albany: 1846. V. 64
The American Spy, or Freedom's Early Sacrifice: a Tale of the Revolution. New York: 1846. V. 62

SIMMS, WILLIAM GILMORE
The Book of My Lady. Philadelphia: 1833. V. 63; 64
The Damsel of Darien. Philadelphia: 1839. V. 62; 64; 67
Eutaw, a Sequel to the Forayers, or the Raid of the Dog Days, a Tale of the Revolution. New York: 1856. V. 64; 67
The Forayers or the Raid of the Dog-Days. New York: 1855. V. 62
The History of South Carolina from its First European Discovery to Its Erection into a Republic with a Supplementary Book. New York: 1860. V. 63
The Kinsmen; or the Black Rider's of the Congaree.... Philadelphia: 1841. V. 62
The Life of Francis Marion. New York: 1844. V. 63
Mellichampe. New York: 1836. V. 67
Pelayo. New York: 1838. V. 62
Sack and Destruction of the City of Columbia. To Which is added a List of Property Destroyed. Columbia: 1865. V. 63; 65
Vasconselos. New York: 1853. V. 62; 64
War Lyrics and Songs of the South. London: 1866. V. 63; 65
War Poetry of the South. New York: 1866. V. 63
War Poetry of the South. New York: 1867. V. 63; 65

SIMON, ANDRE L.
Bibliotheca Gastronomica, a Catalogue of Books and Documents on Gastronomy. London: 1953. V. 63
Bibliotheca Vinaria. A Bibliography of Books and Pamphlets Dealing with Viticulture, Wine-Making, Distillation, the Management, Sale, Taxation, Use and Abuse of Wines and Spirits. 1979. V. 67
Bottlescrew Days. Boston: 1927. V. 66
By Request - an Autobiography. London: 1957. V. 64
A Concise Encyclopaedia of Gastronomy. London: 1952. V. 67
What About Wine?. London: 1953. V. 66
The Wines of the World Pocket Library. 1951. V. 67

SIMON, C. F.
Der Industriose Geschaftsmann Ober 375 Unweifungen. Qedlinburg und Leipzig: 1845. V. 65

SIMON, JOHN
English Sanitary Institutions, Reviewed in Their Course of Development and In Some of Their Political and Social Relations. London: 1890. V. 64

SIMON, NEIL
Last of the Red-Hot Lovers. New York: 1970. V. 66
Lost in Yonkers. New York: 1991. V. 66
The Odd Couple. New York: 1966. V. 67
Promises, Promises. New York: 1969. V. 66
The Star Spangled Girl. New York: 1967. V. 64

SIMON, OLIVER
The Curwen Press Miscellany. 1931. V. 62; 65
The Double Crown Club. Cambridge: 1949. V. 64
Printer and Playground - an Autobiography. London: 1956. V. 62

SIMON, RICHARD
A Critical History of the Old Testmaent..(and) a Critical History of the text of the New Testament...(and) The Critical History of the Versions of the New Testament. London: 1682. V. 67

SIMOND, LOUIS
Journal of a Tour and Residence in Great Britain, During the Years 1810 and 1811. Edinburgh: 1815. V. 65; 66
Journal of a Tour and Residence in Great Britain, During the Years 1810 and 1811. Edinburgh: 1817. V. 64
Switzerland; or a Journal of a Tour and Residence in that Country in the Years 1817, 1818 and 1819.... London: 1823. V. 67
A Tour In Italy and Sicily. London: 1828. V. 65

SIMONDE DE SISMONDI, JEAN CHARLES EDWARD
Political Economy and the Philosophy of Government. London: 1847. V. 67

SIMONIN, JEAN BAPTISTE
Le Merite des Femmes. Travesti, Poeme Burlesque. Paris: 1825. V. 63

SIMONS, ALBERT
The Octagon Library of Early American Architecture, Volume I. New York: 1927. V. 63; 66; 67

SIMONS CANDEILLE, AMELIE JULIE
Souvenirs de Brighton, de Londres et de Paris: et Quelques Fragmens de Litterature Legere. Paris: 1818. V. 67

SIMPER, PAUL
The Saint from Big Screen to Small Screen and Back. London: 1997. V. 67

SIMPER, ROBERT
Beach Boats of Britain. Woodbridge: 1959. V. 67

SIMPKINS, CUTHBERT ORMOND
Coltrane. A Biography. New York: 1975. V. 65; 67

SIMPKINSON, JOHN NASSAU
The Washingtons. A Tale of a Country Parish in the 17th Century. London: 1860. V. 64

SIMPLE, NED, PSEUD.
New Rules and Orders of the Hen Peck'd Husband's Society, Reformation Act, &c. Bingley: 183-. V. 63

SIMPSON, A. L.
Pioneers: Biographical Sketches of Leaders in Various Paths. London: 1861. V. 64

SIMPSON, ANNA PRATT
Problems Women Solved. San Francisco: 1915. V. 64

SIMPSON, C.
Trencher and Kennel. 1927. V. 62

SIMPSON, C. T.
A Descriptive Catalogue of the Naiades or Pearly Fresh-Water Mussels. Detroit: 1914. V. 64
Synopsis of the Naiades, or Pearly Freshwater Mussels. Washington: 1900. V. 63; 64; 66

SIMPSON, CHARLES
El Rodeo. London: 1925. V. 67
The Harboro' Country. 1927. V. 64
Manners and Mannerisms. London: 1929. V. 67
Trencher and Kennel. London: 1927. V. 64; 65; 67

SIMPSON, DAVID
A Discourse on Dreams and Night Visions; with Numerous Examples Ancient and Modern. Macclesfield: 1791. V. 65

SIMPSON, DOROTHY
Puppet for a Corpse. London: 1983. V. 63

SIMPSON, G. G.
The Principles of Classification and a Classification of Mammals. New York: 1945. V. 62

SIMPSON, GEORGE
Fur Trade and Empire, George Simpson's Journal. Cambridge: 1931. V. 63

SIMPSON, GEORGE C.
British Antarctic Expedition 1910-1913. Calcutta/London: 1919-1923. V. 64

SIMPSON, HAROLD B.
Frontier Forts of Texas. Waco: 1966. V. 67
Gaines' Mill to Appomattox. Waco and McLennan County in Hood's Texas Brigade. Waco: 1963. V. 62; 63; 65
Texas in the War 1861-1865. Texas: 1964. V. 65

SIMPSON, HENRY I.
The Emigrant's Guide to the Gold Mines - Three Weeks in the Gold Mines or Adventures with Gold Diggers of California in August 1848. Haverford: 1978. V. 63

SIMPSON, J.
The Wild Rabbit in a New Aspect, or Rabbit Warrens that Pay. 1895. V. 67

SIMPSON, J. PALGRAVE
For Ever and Never. London: 1884. V. 67

SIMPSON, J. Y.
Archaic Sculpturings of Cups, Circles, Etc. Upon Stones and Rocks in Scotland, England and Other Countries. Edinburgh: 1867. V. 64

SIMPSON, JAMES
The Philosophy of Education.... Edinburgh: 1836. V. 64

SIMPSON, JAMES H.
Navaho Expedition. Norman: 1964. V. 67

SIMPSON, JAMES L.
Report of the Secretary of War, Communicating...Captain Simpson's Report and Map of Wagon Road Routes in Utah Territory. Washington: 1859. V. 62

SIMPSON, JAMES Y.
Anaesthesia, Hospitalism, Hermaphroditism and a Proposal to stamp Out Smallpox and Other Contagious Diseases. Edinburgh: 1871. V. 65
Homoeopathy: Its Tenets and Tendencies, Theoretical, Theological and Therapeutical. Philadelphia: 1854. V. 63

SIMPSON, JOHN
Complete System of Cookery. London: 1816. V. 62; 66

SIMPSON, JUSTIN
Obituary and Records of the Counties of Lincoln, Rutland and Northampton, From the Commencement of the Present Century to the End of 1859. Stanford: 1861. V. 66

SIMPSON, LEONARD FRANCIS
The Handbook of Dining; or, How to Dine Theoretically, Philosophically and Historically Considered. London: 1859. V. 64

SIMPSON, LLOYD
Notes on Thomas Jefferson. Philadelphia: 1885. V. 65

SIMPSON, LOUIS
Armidale. Brockport: 1979. V. 62; 64
The Arrivistes. Poems 1940-1949. New York: 1949. V. 63

SIMPSON, MONA
Anywhere but Here. New York: 1987. V. 62; 63; 65; 67

SIMPSON, R. C.
Fish and Find Out. London: 1937. V. 67

SIMPSON, THOMAS
Select Exercises for Young Proficients in the Mathematicks. London: 1752. V. 65; 66

SIMPSON, W. DOUGLAS
The Celtic Church in Scotland. Aberdeen: 1935. V. 62

SIMPSON, W. G.
The History and Antiquities of Freemasonry in Saintfield. 1924. V. 67

SIMPSON, WILLIAM
The Seat of War in the East. London: 1855-1856. V. 65

SIMPSON, WILLIAM WOOLLEY
Observations in Reference to the Present Mode of Effecting Sales of Landed Estates, and Other Property.... London: 1838. V. 62

SIMS, AMY
Buffs and Boy or the Isles of Innocence. London. V. 66

SIMS, GEORGE
Coat of Arms. London: 1984. V. 67
A Darkened Being. N.P: 1991. V. 67
Deadhand. London: 1971. V. 67
The Despain Papers. Philadelphia: 1992. V. 67
The End of the Web. London: 1976. V. 67
For Bibliophiles. N.P: 1961. V. 67
Hunter's Point. London: 1973. V. 67
The Immanent Goddess. London: 1947. V. 67
The Keys of Death. London: 1982. V. 67
The Keys to Death. Bath: 1982. V. 67
The Last Best Friend. London: 1967. V. 67
The Last Best Friend. New York: 1968. V. 67
The Last Best Friend. London: 1986. V. 67
Last of the Rare Book Game. Philadelphia: 1990. V. 67
A Life in Catalogues and Other Essays. Philadelphia: 1994. V. 67
Likes and Dislikes. Edinburgh: 1981. V. 67
More of the Rare Book Game. Philadelphia: 1988. V. 67
Poems. London: 1944. V. 67
The Rare Book Game. Phiadelphia: 1985. V. 67
Rex Mundi. London: 1978. V. 67
Rex Mundi. Bath: 1989. V. 67
The Sand Dollar. London: 1969. V. 67
Saudades: Poems. N.P: 1952. V. 67
Sixteen Poems Written 1942-1943. Edinburgh: 1966. V. 67
Sleep No More. London: 1965. V. 67
Sleep No More. London: 1966. V. 67
Sleep No More. Bath: 1992. V. 67
Some Cadences. Poems Written in 1945. N.P: 1960. V. 67
The Swallow Lovers. N.P: 1941. V. 67
The Terrible Door. London: 1964. V. 67
Who is Cato?. London: 1981. V. 67
Who is Cato?. Bath: 1984. V. 67

SIMS, J. MARION
The Story of My Life. New York: 1898. V. 65

SIMS, JOHN
Dissertatio Medica Inauguralis, Quadam de Cerebri Concussione Malisque inde Orlundis. Edinburgh: 1818. V. 64

SIMS, ORLAND L.
Cowpokes, Nesters and So Forth. Austin: 1970. V. 63; 64; 65

SIMSON, FRANK B.
Letters on Sport in Eastern Bengal. London: 1886. V. 65

SIMSON, ROBERT
Elements of the Conic Sections...The First Three Books. Edinburgh: 1775. V. 66
Opera Quaedam Reliqua. Glasgow: 1776. V. 66; 67
Sectionum Concarum Libri V. Edinburgi: 1787. V. 63

SIMSON, THOMAS
De Remedica Diffeartationes Quatuor Thomae Simsoni, Medicinae & Anatomices, In Acaemia Scotorum ad Fanum Andrea, Professoris Candossensis. Edinburgh: 1726. V. 65

SIMSON, WALTER
A History of Gipsies.... New York: 1866. V. 62

SINCLAIR, ARTHUR
Two Years on the Alabama. Boston: 1895. V. 65
Two Years on the Alabama. London: 1896. V. 62

SINCLAIR, BERTRAND
The Land of Frozen Suns. New York: 1910. V. 62

SINCLAIR, CATHERINE
A Kaleidoscope of Anecdotes and Aphorisms. London: 1851. V. 65
Lord and Lady Harcourt; or, Country Hospitalities. London: 1850. V. 65
Modern Accomplishments, or the March of Intellect. Edinburgh: 1836. V. 65
Scotland and the Scotch; or the Western Circuit. Edinburgh: 1840. V. 65
Scotland and the Scotch; or the Western Circuit. Edinburgh: 1849. V. 65

SINCLAIR, GEORGE
Hortus Gramineus Woburnensis.... London: 1825. V. 62; 63; 66
Satan's Invisible World Discovered, Etc. Edinburgh: 1780. V. 64

SINCLAIR, IAIN
White Chappell: Scarlet Tracings. Uppingham: 1987. V. 63; 65

SINCLAIR, JOHN
An Account of the Systems of Husbandry Adopted in the More Improved Districts of Scotland.... Edinburgh: 1812. V. 62
Address to the Society for the Improvement of British Wool.... London: 1791. V. 62; 63
Appendix to the History of the Public Revenue of the British Empire. London: 1789. V. 65
The Code of Agriculture.... Hartford: 1818. V. 64; 66
The Code of Agriculture.... London: 1832. V. 67
The Night the Bear Came Off the Mountain. Santa Fe: 1991. V. 63; 64
Observations on the Scottish Dialect. London: 1782. V. 64

SINCLAIR, ROBERT
Catalogue of Books Belonging to Robert Sinclair. Rome: 1887. V. 62

SINCLAIR, UPTON
The Goose-Step, A Study of American Education. Pasadena: 1923. V. 67
The Jungle. New York: 1906. V. 62; 63; 64
The Jungle. Baltimore: 1965. V. 63; 64
The Jungle. New York: 1965. V. 64
Mental Radio. Pasadena: 1930. V. 66
Mountain City - A Novel. London: 1930. V. 65

SINCLAIR, W. B.
The Grapefruit.... Berkeley: 1972. V. 66

SINGER, CHARLES
The Earliest Chemical Industry. London: 1948. V. 64
The Evolution of Anatomy. London: 1925. V. 67
The Evolution of Anatomy. New York: 1925. V. 64; 66
A History of Technology. New York: 1954. V. 65
A History of Technology. New York and London: 1954-1955. V. 62
A History of Technology. New York: 1954-1958. V. 64; 67
A History of Technology. Oxford: 1954-1958. V. 62
Science, Medicine and History, Essays on the Evolution of Scientific Thought and Medical Practice.... London: 1953. V. 62
Studies in the History and Method of Science. Oxford: 1917-1921. V. 64; 66
Vesalius on the Human Brain. London: 1952. V. 64; 66; 67

SINGER, GEORGE JOHN
Elemens d'Electricite et de Galvanisme.... Paris: 1817. V. 64
Elements of Electricity and Elector-Chemistry. London: 1814. V. 64

SINGER, I. J.
The River Breaks Up. New York: 1938. V. 65

SINGER, ISAAC BASHEVIS
Alone in the Wild Forest. New York: 1971. V. 62; 67
The Death of Methuselah and Other Stories. Franklin Center: 1988. V. 65; 67
The Death of Methuselah and Other Stories. New York: 1988. V. 66
Di Familie Mushkat. New York: 1950. V. 67
Elijah the Slave. A Hebrew Legend Retold. New York: 1970. V. 66
Enemies, a Love Story. New York: 1972. V. 62
The Estate. New York: 1969. V. 66
The Gentleman from Cracow. The Mirror. New York: 1979. V. 66
The Golem. New York: 1982. V. 65
The Image and Other Stories. New York: 1985. V. 62; 67
Joseph and the Koza or the Sacrifice to the Vistula. New York: 1970. V. 62; 67
The King of the Fields. New York: 1988. V. 67
The King of the Fields. London: 1989. V. 65
The Magician from Lublin. New York: 1984. V. 65
On Literature and Life. Tucson: 1979. V. 66
One Day of Happiness. New York: 1982. V. 64; 67
Reaches of Heaven. New York: 1980. V. 64; 67
Satan in Goray. New York: 1981. V. 64
A Young Man in Search of Love. Garden City: 1978. V. 62; 64; 67
Zlateh the Goat and Other Stories. New York: 1966. V. 63; 65; 67

SINGER, JOHN
The Holiday Book. Glasgow: 1946. V. 63

SINGER, MARCUS
The Human Brain in Sagittal Section. Springfield: 1954. V. 64; 66; 67
The Human Brain in Sagittal Section. Springfield: 1964. V. 67

SINGER, R.
Agaricales in Modern Taxonomy. Weineheim: 1962. V. 66

SINGER, SAMUEL WELLER
Some Account of the Book, Printed at Oxford in MCCCCLXVIII, Under the Title of Exposicio Sancti Jeronimi in simbolo Apostolorum. London: 1812. V. 62

SINGH, KHUSHWANT
The Mark of Vishnu and Other Stories. London: 1950. V. 67

SINGH, M.
Himalayan Art: Wall-Painting and Sculpture in Ladakh, Lahaul and Spiti, the Siwalik Ranges, Nepal, Sikkim and Bhutan. 1968. V. 62; 65

SINGH, N. K.
Jim Corbett: Portrait of an Artist. 1991. V. 67

SINGLETON-GATES, G. R.
Bolos and Barishynas. Aldershot: 1920. V. 66

SINGLETON-GATES, PETER
The Black Diaries. London: 1959. V. 65
The Black Diaries. New York: 1959. V. 65

SINHA, A. K.
Contemporary Geoscientific Research in Himalaya. Dehra Dun: 1981-1983. V. 67
Geology of the Higher Central Himalaya. Chichester: 1989. V. 67

SINIGAGLIA, L.
Climbing Reminiscences of the Dolomites. 1896. V. 63; 65

SINISE, JERRY
George Washington Arrington: Civil War Spy, Texas Ranger, Sheriff and Rancher. Burnet: 1979. V. 67

SINNOTT, MARY ELIZABETH
Annals of the Sinnott, Rogers, Coffin, Corlies, Reeves, Bodine and Allied Families. Philadelphia: 1905. V. 66

SIODMAK, KURT
F.P.I. Does Not Reply. Boston: 1933. V. 64; 66

SIONS *Groans for Her Distressed, or Sober Endeavours to Prevent Innocent Blood, and to Establish the Nation in the Best of Settlements.* London: 1661. V. 66

SIORDET, I. M.
A Letter to the Right Hon. Sir John Sinclair, Bart, M.P. Supporting His Arguments in Refutation of Those Advanced by Mr. Huskisson.... London: 1811. V. 67

SIOUX *Indian Painting.* Nice: 1938. V. 66

SIPE, C. HALS
The Indian Chiefs of Pennsylvania - or a Story of the Paw Hayes by the American Indians in the History of Pennsylvania. Butler: 1927. V. 66

SIRAT BANI HILAL
The Celebrated Romance of the Stealing of the Mare. London: 1892. V. 63

Sire *Degrevaunt.* 1896. V. 62

SIREN, OSVALD
China and Gardens of Europe of the Eighteenth Century. New York: 1950. V. 64
Gardens of China. New York: 1949. V. 62; 63; 64
A History of Later Chinese Painting. New York: 1978. V. 62

SIREUL, M. DE
(Sale) Catalogue des Tableaux et Dessins Precieux. Paris: 1781. V. 64

SIRIANNI, J. E.
Growth and Development of the Pigtailed Macaque. Boca Raton: 1985. V. 62

SIRINGO, CHARLES ANGELO
A Cowboy Detective. Chicago: 1912. V. 62; 64
A Cowboy Detective. New York: 1912. V. 65
A Lone Star Cowboy. Santa Fe: 1919. V. 62; 63; 64; 65
Riata and Spurs. Boston: 1927. V. 64; 66; 67
Riata and Spurs. Boston: 1931. V. 64; 67
A Texas Cowboy or Fifteen Years on the Hurricane Deck of a Spanish Pony. Chicago: 1912. V. 63; 66
Texas Cowboy or Fifteen Years on the Hurricane Deck of a Spanish Pony. New York: 1950. V. 66
Two Evilisms - Pinkerton and Anarchism. Austin: 1967. V. 64; 66

SIS, PETER
Tibet through the Red Box. New York: 1998. V. 65

SISSON, C. H.
Versions and Perversions of Heine. 1955. V. 62

SISSON, JAMES E.
Jack London First Editions. Oakland: 1979. V. 63

SISTER Alionushka and Little Brother Ivanushka. Moscow: 1903. V. 66

SISTER Susie and the Twins. London: 1915. V. 65

SITGREAVES, L.
Report of an Expedition Down the Zuni and Colorado Rivers. Washington: 1854. V. 66
Report of an Expedition Down the Zuni and Colorado Rivers. Chicago: 1962. V. 63

SITTERSON, JOSEPH CARLYLE
The Secession Movement in North Carolina. Chapel Hill: 1939. V. 67

SITWELL, EDITH
Alexander Pope. London: 1930. V. 64
Clowns' Houses. Oxford: 1918. V. 63; 66
The Collected Poems of Edith Sitwell. London: 1930. V. 67
The English Eccentrics. Boston and New York: 1933. V. 66
The English Eccentrics. London: 1933. V. 64; 67
Epithalamium. London: 1931. V. 66
Facade, an Entertainment. London: 1972. V. 62; 67
The Outcasts: Poems. London: 1962. V. 66
Popular Song. London: 1928. V. 66
Troy Park. London: 1925. V. 62
Twentieth Century Harlequinade and Other Poems. Oxford: 1916. V. 66
Victoria of England. London: 1936. V. 62
Wheels 1916. Oxford: 1916. V. 64
Wheels 1917. A Second Cycle. Oxford: 1916. V. 64
Wheels 1918. A Third Cycle. Oxford: 1917. V. 64
Wheels 1920. Fifth Cycle. London: 1928. V. 64

SITWELL, GEORGE
The Barons of Pulford in the Eleventh and Twelfth Centuries and Their Descendants. 1889. V. 66
The Barons of Pulford in the Eleventh and Twelfth Centuries and Their Descendants. Scarborough: 1889. V. 66
The Hurts of Haldworth and Their Descendents at Savile Hall, the Ickles and Hesley Hall. Oxford: 1930. V. 64
On the Making of Gardens. London: 1909. V. 64
On the Making of Gardens. London: 1949. V. 62; 64

SITWELL, H. D.
The Crown Jewels and Other Regalia in the Tower of London. London: 1953. V. 64; 66

SITWELL, OSBERT
Argonaut and Juggernaut. London: 1919. V. 64
At the House of Mrs. Kinfoot: Four Satires. London: 1921. V. 62; 66
England Reclaimed - A Book of Eclogues. London: 1927. V. 64
Four Songs of the Italian Earth. New York: 1948. V. 63
Four Songs of the Italian Earth. Pawlet: 1948. V. 62
Left Hand, Right Hand! An Autobiography. London: 1945-1950. V. 64; 67
Miracle on Sinai. London: 1933. V. 66
On the Continent. London: 1958. V. 67
Sing High! Sing Low!: a Book of Essays. London: 1944. V. 66
Three Quarter Length Portrait of Michael Arlen. London: 1931. V. 66
Who Killed Cock Robin?. London: 1921. V. 64

SITWELL, SACHEVERELL
All Summer in a Day - an Autobiographical Fantasia. London: 1926. V. 64
A Book of Towers and Other Buildings of Southern Europe - a Series of Dry-Points Engraved by Richard Wyndham.... London: 1928. V. 62
Canons of Giant Art - Twenty Torsos in Heroic Landscapes. London: 1933. V. 62
Conversation Pieces - a Survey of English Domestic Portraits and Their Painters. London: 1936. V. 62
The Cyder Feast and Other Poems. London and New York: 1927. V. 64; 66
Doctor Donne and Gargantua - The First Six Cantos. London: 1930. V. 62; 63
Doctor Donne and Gargantua First Canto. London: 1921. V. 62
Exalt the Eglantine and Other Poems. London: 1926. V. 63
Far From My Home: Stories, Long and Short. London: 1931. V. 66
Fine Bird Books 1700-1900. London and New York: 1953. V. 64; 66; 67
The Gothick North: a Study in Mediaeval Life, Art and Thought. London: 1929-1930. V. 66
The Gothick North: a Study of Mediaeval Life, Art and Thought. Boston and New York: 1929. V. 62; 67
Great Flower Books 1700-1900. London: 1956. V. 64
Great Flower Books 1700-1900. London: 1963. V. 63
The Hunters and the Hunted. London: 1947. V. 64
Narrative Pictures - a Survey of English Genre and Its Painters. London: 1937. V. 65
Old Fashioned Flowers. London: 1939. V. 67
Old Garden Roses. London: 1955-1957. V. 62; 64
The People's Palace. Oxford: 1918. V. 62
Poltergists: an Introduction and Examination Followed by Chosen Instances. London: 1940. V. 67
To Henry Woodward. London: 1972. V. 64
Valse Des Fleurs: a Day in St. Petersburg and a Ball at the Winter Palace in 1868. York: 1980. V. 64; 67

SITWELL, WILLIAM
Stones of Northumberland and Other Lands. Newcastle-upon-Tyne: 1930. V. 64; 65

SIX Letters from a Very High Personage; the First Four on the Nature of His Character and Government; and the Last Two Addressed to Miss Martineau and Dr. Malthus on the Subject of the New Poor Laws. London: 1834. V. 66

SIX Months in West Indies. London: 1826. V. 64

SIX Scenes in the Life of James Green Esqre a Special Constable, Sketched by a Special. London: 1848. V. 63

SIZER, NELSON
Forty Years in Phrenology: Embracing Recollections of History. New York: 1892. V. 64; 66; 67
Heads and Faces and How to Study Them: a Manual of Phrenology and Physiognomy for the People. New York: 1890. V. 63

SJOQVIST, OLOF
Studies on Pain Conduction in the Trigeminal Nerve. Helsingfors: 1938. V. 66

SJOWALL, MAJ
The Laughing Policeman. New York: 1970. V. 65; 66
The Man on the Balcony. New York: 1968. V. 66

SKAGGS, WILLIAM H.
The Southern Oligarchy. New York: 1924. V. 67

SKARGON, YVONNE
The Importance of Being Oscar and Lily and Hodge and Dr. Johnson. 1997. V. 65

SKARR, GRACE
All About Dogs. New York: 1947. V. 62

SKARSTEN, M. O.
George Drouillard - Hunter and Interpreter for Lewis and Clark and Fur Trade 1807-1810. Glendale: 1964. V. 67

SKEAN, MARION H.
Circle Left! Folk-Play of the Kentucky Mountains. Ary: 1939. V. 65

SKEAT, WALTER W.
An Etymological Dictionary of the English Language. Oxford: 1882. V. 64

SKEAVINGTON, GEORGE
The Modern System of Farriery, Comprehending the Present Entire Improved Mode of Practice. London: 1860. V. 66

SKEET, FRANCIS JOHN ANGUS
Stuart Papers, Pictures, Relics, Medals and Books in the Collection of Miss Maria Widdrington. Leeds: 1930. V. 62

SKELDING, SUSIE BARSTOW
Flowers from Sunlight and Shade. (with) *Flowers Here and There.* New York: 1885. V. 67

SKELTON, JOHN
The Harmony of Birds. 1928. V. 67
The Tunning of Elynour Rumming. London: 1928. V. 64

SKELTON, JOSEPH
Engraved Illustrations of the Principal Antiquities of Oxfordshire.... Oxford: 1823. V. 62; 63; 64; 65
Oxonia Antiqua Restorata.... Oxford: 1823. V. 66

SKELTON, R. A.
A Description of Maps and Architectural Drawings in the Collection Made by William Cecil, First Baron Burghley Now at Hatfield House. Oxford: 1971. V. 62
Explorer's Maps, Chapters in the Cartographic Record of Geographical Discovery. London: 1958. V. 66

SKELTON, ROBIN
Herbert Read - a Memorial Symposium. London: 1970. V. 65

SKELTON, W. C.
Reminiscences of Joe Bowman and the Ullswater Foxhounds. Kendal: 1921. V. 66; 67
Reminiscences of Joe Bowman and the Ullswater Foxhounds. Kendal: 1923. V. 67

SKENE, ALEXANDER J. C.
Medical Gyncoology. New York: 1896. V. 67

SKENE, HARRIET
The Diary of Martha Bethune Baliol from 1753 to 1754. London: 1853. V. 65

SKENE, JOHN
De Verborum Significatione, The Exposition of the Termes and Difficill Wordes Conteined in the Foure Buikes of Regiam Majestatem. Edinburgh: 1820. V. 65

SKENE, PHILIP ORKNEY
The History of Little Jack in French and English.... London: 1828. V. 63

A SKETCH of Grundy County; Its Cities and Towns and Official Directory. Trenton: 1882. V. 66

A SKETCH of Modern France. In a Series of Letters to a Lady of Fashion. London: 1798. V. 66

A SKETCH Of the Present State of France. London: 1805. V. 65

SKETCH of the Rise and Progress of the Royal Society Club. London: 1860. V. 62

A SKETCH of Worthing As It Was - and Now Is and the Places Adjacent.... Worthing: 1817. V. 66

SKETCHES from Real Life. Edinburgh: 1843. V. 67

SKETCHES of Grange and the Neighbourhood. Kendal: 1850. V. 66; 67

SKETCHES of Men of Mark. New York: 1871. V. 64

SKETCHES of Persia. From the Journals of a Traveller in the East. 1827. V. 66

SKETCHES of the Domestic Manners and Institutions of the Romans. London: 1826. V. 63

SKETCHES of the Institutions, and Domestic Manners of the Romans. London: 1826. V. 62

SKETCHES of the Inter-Mountain Staines - Utah, Idaho, Nevada, 1847- 1909. Salt Lake City: 1909. V. 62; 65

SKETCHES of War History 1861-1865 - Papers Read Before the Ohio Commandery of the Military Order of the Loyal Legion of the United States. Cincinnati: 1888. V. 67

SKETCHLEY, W.
The Cocker; Containing Every Information to the Breeders and Amateurs of that Noble Bird, the Game Cock. London: 1814. V. 66

SKEWES, JOSEPH HENRY
A Complete and Popular Digest of the Polity of Methodism, Each Subject Alphabetically Arranged. London: 1869. V. 63

SKIDMORE, HUBERT
Hill Lawyer. Garden City: 1942. V. 65

SKIDMORE, OWINGS AND MERRILL
Architecture and Urbanism 1973-1983. New York and Stuttgart: 1983. V. 62; 65

SKIDMORE, THOMAS
The Rights of Man to Property!. New York: 1829. V. 64; 66

SKILLING, THOMAS
The Science and Practice of Agriculture. Dublin: 1846. V. 63; 66

SKINKER, THOMAS K.
Samuel Skinker and His Descendants: an Account of the Skinker Family and All Their Kindred Who Have the Blood of Samuel Skinker in Their Veins. St. Louis: 1923. V. 65

SKINNE, ADA M.
A Very Little Child's Book of Stories. New York: 1924. V. 66

SKINNER, B. F.
The Behavior of Organisms. An Experimental Analysis. New York: 1938. V. 67

SKINNER, EMORY F.
Reminiscences. Chicago: 1908. V. 62

SKINNER, JOHN
A Letter to Norman Sievwright M.A. in Vindication of the Episcopal Clergy of Scotland from His Charge of Innovations in Politics and Religion. Aberdeen: 1767. V. 62

SKINNER, ROBERT
2 Guns from Harlem. New York: 1997. V. 66

SKINNER, ROBERT P.
Abyssinia of To-Day. London: 1906. V. 62

SKINNER, STEPHEN
Etymologicon Linguae Anglicanae, seu Explicatio Vocum Anglicarum Etymologica ex Propriis Fontibus.... London: 1671. V. 62; 66

SKINNER, THOMAS
The Life of General Monk. London: 1723. V. 62
The Life of General Monk. London: 1724. V. 67

THE SKINNERS' Company versus the Honourable the Irish Society and Others. 1836. V. 63

SKIPP, JOHN
Book of the Dead. Willimantic: 1989. V. 66

SKIPWIRTH, P.
The Great Bird Illustrators and Their Art 1730-1930. New York: 1979. V. 62; 63; 66

SKIRVING, WILLIAM
The Trial of William Skirving, Secretary to the British Convention, Before the High Court...on the 6th and 7th of January 1794 for Sedition.... Edinburgh: 1794. V. 63

SKRIMSHIRE, FENWICK
A Series of Essays Introductory to the Study of Natural History. London: 1805. V. 62

SKRINE, HENRY
A General Account of the Rivers of Note in Great Britain.... London: 1801. V. 62

SKRYABIN, K. I.
Key to Parasitic Nematodes. New Delhi: 1984. V. 66

SKUES, G. E. M.
The Angling Letters of G.E.M. Skues. London: 1975. V. 67
The Chalk-Stream Angler. Sidelights, Sidelines and Reflections. 1976. V. 67
Minor Tactics of the Chalk Stream and Kindred Studies. 1910. V. 67
Minor Tactics of the Trout Stream. 1924. V. 67
Silk, Fur and Feather. 1950. V. 67
The Way of a Trout with a Fly. 1921. V. 67
The Way of a Trout With a Fly. 1928. V. 67
The Way of a Trout With a Fly. 1973. V. 63; 65; 67
The Way of a Trout with a Fly and Some Further Studies in Minor Tactics. London: 1955. V. 67

SKULSKI, JANUSZ
The Battleship FUSO. London: 1998. V. 67
The Battleship Yamato. London: 1968. V. 67

SKUTCH, A. F.
Life Histories of Central American Birds. Berkeley: 1954-1969. V. 65
A Naturalist in Costa Rica. Gainesville: 1971. V. 63

SKUTSCH, OTTO
The Annals of Q. Ennius. Oxford: 1986. V. 65

SKVORECKY, JOSEF
The Bass Saxophone - Two Novellas. New York: 1979. V. 64

SLADE, GURNEY
Led by Lawrence. London: 1934. V. 62

SLADE, WILLIAM
A Memorial to the Legislature of Vermont, for the Repeal of Acts Incorporating the Grand Lodge and Grand Chapter of Vermont Presented Oct. 23, 1830. Monpelier?: 1830. V. 64
Slade and Roebuck's Directory of the Borough and Neighbourhood of Leeds. Leeds: 1851. V. 66

SLADEK, JOHN
The Best Seller - a Synopsis. London: 1966. V. 65
Black Aura. London: 1974. V. 65; 66
The Lunatics of Terra. London: 1984. V. 64
Red Noise. New Castle: 1982. V. 63
The Reproductive System. London: 1968. V. 64; 65
Roderick or the Education of a Young Machine. London: 1980. V. 64

SLADEN, DOUGLAS
London and Its Leaders. London: 1908. V. 62

SLADEN, F. L. W.
The Humble Bee.... 1912. V. 63

SLADEN, W. P.
Challenger Voyage. Zoology. Part 51. Asteroidea. 1889. V. 66

SLANGE, NIELS
Den Stormaegtigste Konges Christian Den Fierdes, Konges Til Danmark Og Norge...Histoire. Kjobenhavn: 1749. V. 63

SLATER, ELIZA
Little Princes. London: 1845. V. 62

SLATER, H.
Manual of the Birds of Iceland. Edinburgh: 1901. V. 62

SLATER, ISAAC
Slater's Royal National Commercial Directory of the Counties of Cumberland and Westmoreland and the Cleveland District, with Historical Sketches of the Counties and of Each Town and Village. Manchester: 1876-1877. V. 66

SLATER, J. H.
Early Editions. 1894. V. 67

SLATER, JOHN
El Morro - Inscription Rock New Mexico. Los Angeles: 1961. V. 64; 65

SLATER, JOHN C.
Electromagnetism. New York and London: 1947. V. 63

SLATER, JOHN ROTHWELL
Printing and the Renaissance: a Paper Read Before the Fortnightly Club of Rochester New York. New York: 1921. V. 62

SLATIN, RUDOLPH CARL, FREIHERR VON
Fire and Sword in the Sudan, a Personal Narrative of Fighting and Serving the Dervishes 1879-1895. V. 67

SLATTER, JOHN
El Morro - Inscription Rock New Mexico. Los Angeles: 1961. V. 62

SLATTER, W.
Views of All the Colleges, Halls and Public Buildings in the University and City of Oxford, with Descriptions.... Oxford: 1824. V. 62; 67
Views of All the Colleges, Halls and Public Buildings in the University and City of Oxford; with Descriptions.... Oxford: 1825. V. 67

SLAUGHTER, PHILIP
A History of Bristol Parish, Virginia. Richmond: 1879. V. 63; 64
A Sketch of the Life of Randolph Fairfax. Richmond: 1864. V. 62; 63; 65
A Sketch of the Life of Randolph Fairfax. Baltimore: 1878. V. 62; 63

SLAUSON, ALLAN B.
A History of the City of Washington: Its Men and Institutions. Washington: 1903. V. 67

SLAVERY. A Treatise, Showing that Slavery Is Neither a Moral, Political, Nor Social Evil. Penfield: 1844. V. 63; 66

SLAVERY and Marriage. Oneida: 1850. V. 63

SLAVERY. From the Hull Rockingham of January 31, 1824. Liverpool: 1824. V. 67

SLAVIK, J.
Fluorescence Microscopy and Fluorescent Probes. Volume 2. New York: 1998. V. 67

SLEEMAN, JAMES L.
From Rifle to Camera. London: 1947. V. 67

SLEEMAN, JAMES L. continued
Tales of a Shikari. 1919. V. 67

SLEEN, W. G. N. VAN DER
Four Months' Camping in the Himalayas. London: 1929. V. 62

SLEIDAN, JOHN
De Quatuor Monarchiis Libri Tres. Cambridge: 1686. V. 66
De Quatuor Summis Imperiis Libri Tres. Amsterdam: 1678. V. 66
The General History of the Reformation of the Church, from the Errors and Corruptions of the Church of Rome, Begun in Germany by Martin Luther.... London: 1689. V. 62

SLEIGH, ADDERLEY W.
Nautical Re-Organization and Increase of the Trading Marine.. London: 1840. V. 62; 63

SLEIGH, BERNARD
A Faerie Pageant. Birmingham: 1924. V. 65

SLICK, SAM
Yankee Notions; or the American Joe Miller. London: 1839. V. 62; 67

SLIJPER, E. J.
Whales. New York: 1962. V. 64

SLINGSBY, HENRY
The Diary of Sir Henry Slingsby, of Scriven Now First Published Entire from the MS. London: 1836. V. 63
The Severall Tryals of Sir Henry Slingsby Kt. John Hewet D.D. and John Mordant, Esq. for Hight Treason..2 of June 1658.... London: 1658. V. 62

SLIPHER, EARL C.
The Photographic Story of Mars. Cambridge: 1962. V. 66

SLOAN, ALFRED P.
Adventures of a White-Collar Man. New York: 1941. V. 63; 65

SLOAN, JOHN ALEXANDER
North Carolina in the War Between the States. Washington: 1883. V. 62; 63; 65
Reminiscences of the Guilford Grays, Co. B, 27th N.C. Regiment. Washington: 1883. V. 62; 63; 65

SLOAN, SAMUEL
Sloan's Constructive Architecture: a Guide to the Practical Builder and Mechanic.... Philadelphia: 1866. V. 64; 66
Sloan's Homestead Architecture, Containing Forty Designs for Villas, Cottages and Farm Houses with Essays on Style, Construction, Landscape Gardening, Furniture, etc. Philadelphia: 1861. V. 63; 66

SLOANE, HANS
A Voyage to the Islands Madera, Barbados, Nieves, S. Christophers and Jamaica.... London: 1707-1725. V. 63

SLOCUM, JOSHUA
Sailing Alone Around the World. New York: 1900. V. 64

SLOTKIN, RICHARD
The Fatal Environment - the Myth of the Frontier in the Age of Industrialization 1800-1890. New York: 1985. V. 65; 67

THE SLOVENLY Boy. Cincinnati: 1882. V. 63

SLUD, P.
The Birds of Costa Rica, Distribution and Ecology. New York: 1964. V. 67

SLUGG, J. T.
Reminiscences of Manchester Fifty Years Ago. Manchester: 1881. V. 63

SMAIL, DAVID CAMERON
Prestwick Golf Club. Prestwick: 1989. V. 62

SMALL, ANDREW
Interesting Roman Antiquities Recently Discovered in Fife.... Edinburgh: 1823. V. 64

SMALL, GEORGE G.
Odd-Fellowship Exposed. New York: 1872. V. 62; 64

SMALL, GEORGE W.
Fred Douglass and His Mule; a Story of the War. New York: 1873. V. 64; 65

SMALL, HERBERT
Handbook of the New Library of Congress. Boston: 1897. V. 63

SMALL, J.
An Inquiry into the Nature and Character of Ancient and Modern Slavery. Portland: 1836. V. 63

SMALL, J. K.
Flora of the Southeastern United States. New York: 1913. V. 67
Manual of the Southeastern Flora.... New York: 1933. V. 63; 66

SMALL, JAMES
A Treatise on Ploughs and Wheel Carriages. Edinburgh: 1784. V. 63; 67

SMALL, ROBERT
A Statistical Account of the Parish and Town of Dundee, in the Year MDCCXCII. Dundee: 1793. V. 64

SMALL, T.
Houses of Wren and Early Georgian Periods. London: 1928. V. 62; 65

SMALL, WILLIAM
To Kill a Messenger. New York: 1970. V. 67

SMALLEY, GEORGE W.
Anglo-American Memories. (with) Second Series. London: 1910-1912. V. 67

SMALLEY, JOHN
Eternal Salvation on No Account a Matter of Just Debt; or, Full Redemption.. Hartford: 1785. V. 66

SMALLWOOD, J. R.
The Book of Newfoundland. St. John's: 1937-1967. V. 67

SMART, ALASTAIR
Allan Ramsay, Painter, Essayist and Man of the Enlightenment. New Haven & London. V. 67

SMART, B. C.
The Dialect of the English Gypsies. London: 1875. V. 64

SMART, B. H.
The Practice of Elocution, or a Course of Exercises for Acquiring the Several Requisites of a Good Delivery. London: 1832. V. 64

SMART, CHRISTOPHER
The Nonpareil; or, the Quintessence of Wit and Humour. London: 1757. V. 62
On the Eternity of the Supreme Being. (with) On the Immensity of the Supreme Being. (with) On the Power of the Supreme Being. (with) On the Omniscence of the Supreme Being. (with) On the Goodness of the Supreme Being. Cambridge: 1750-1756. V. 65
Out of Bedlam. Dublin: 1956. V. 62
Poems. Princeton: 1950. V. 63
Poems on Several Ocassions. London: 1752. V. 65; 66
The Poems...(and) An Account of His Life and Writings.... Reading: 1791. V. 66
Rejoice In the Lamb - A Song from Bedlam. London: 1939. V. 64
A Song to David. London: 1924. V. 62; 64
A Song to David. Cambridge: 1960. V. 67

SMART, HAWLEY
False Cards. London: 1876. V. 67
The Outsider. London: 1886. V. 66
Sunshine and Snow. London: 1879. V. 67

SMART, JOHN
Tables of Interest &c. Abridged for the Use of Schools, In Order to Instruct Young Gentlemen in Decimal Fractions.. London: 1735. V. 67
Tables of Interest, Discount, and Annuities &c. London: 1726. V. 65; 66
Tables of Simple Interest, at 3, 4, 5, 6, 7, 8, 9 and 10 per cent.... London: 1719. V. 65

SMART, THOMAS BURNETT
The Bibliography of Matthew Arnold. London: 1892. V. 65

SMART, WILLIAM
Economic Annals of the Nineteenth Century, 1801-1820, 1821-1830. London: 1910-1917. V. 64; 65

SMEAD, W.
Land of the Flatheads. St. Paul: 1905. V. 62; 65

SMEATON, G. A.
The Builder's Pocket Manual, or, Rules and Instructions in the Art of Carpentry, Masonry, and Bricklaying.... London: 1825. V. 64

SMEATON, JOHN
Eddystone Lighthouse. A Narrative of the Building and a Description of the Construction of the Eddystone Lighthouse with Stone.... London: 1813. V. 66
Experimental Inquiry Concerning the Natural Powers of Wind and Water to Turn Mills and Other Machines Depending on a Circular Motion. London: 1796. V. 64; 66
A Narrative of the Building and a Description of the Construction of the Edystone Lighthouse with Stone.... London: 1791. V. 65

SMEATON, OLIPHANT
A Mystery of the Pacific. London: 1899. V. 66

SMEDES, SUSAN D.
Memorials of a Southern Planter. Baltimore: 1888. V. 62

SMEDES, W. C.
A Digest of the Cases Decided and Reported in the High Court of Errors and Appeals and the Superior Court of Chancery of the State of Mississippi. Boston: 1847. V. 63

SMEDLEY, CONSTANCE
Crusaders - the Reminiscences. London: 1929. V. 62

SMEDLEY, FRANK E.
The Fortunes of the Colville Family; or, A Cloud and Its Silver Lining. London: 1853. V. 66
Frank Fairleigh, or Scenes from the Life of a Private Pupil. London. V. 67
Harry Coverdale's Courtship and All that Came Of It. London. V. 67
Lewis Arundel.... London: 1860. V. 67

SMEDLEY, MENELLA BUTE
Poems Written for a Child. London: 1868. V. 65

SMEDLEY, WILLIAM
Across the Plains in '62. Denver: 1916. V. 63
Across the Plains in '62. Denver: 1962. V. 66

SMEE, ALFRED
Elements of Electro-Metallurgy. London: 1843. V. 64; 66
Elements of Electro-Metallurgy. London: 1851. V. 62
Instinct and Reason: Deduced from Electro-Biology. London: 1850. V. 65
My Garden Its Plan and Culture, Together with a General Description of Its Geology, Botany and Natural History. London: 1872. V. 64

SMEE, ALFRED continued
Nouveau Manuel d'Electricite Medicale ou Elements d'Electro Biologie Suivi d'un Traite sur la Vision.... Paris: 1850. V. 65
The Potatoe Plant, Its Use and Properties: Together with the Cause of the Present Malady. London: 1846. V. 65

SMEETON, GEORGE
Biographia Curiosa; or Memoirs of Remarkable Characters of the Reign of George the Third. London: 1822. V. 66

SMEETS, W. J. A. J.
Phylogeny and Development of Catecholamine Systems in the CNS of Vertebrates. Cambridge: 1994. V. 64; 66

SMELLIE, WILLIAM
An Abridgement of the Practice of Midwifery and a Set of Anatomical Tables with Explanations. Boston: 1786. V. 64
Philosophy of Natural History. Philadelphia: 1791. V. 64
A Set of Anatomical Tables, with Explanations and An Abridgement of the Practice of Midwifery.... Worcester: 1793. V. 62; 64
A Sett of Anatomical Tables with Explanations and an Abridgment of the Practice of Midwifery, with a View to Illustrate a Treatise on that Subject and Collection of Cases. 1971. V. 65

SMET, PIERRE JEAN DE
Letters and Sketches with a Narrative of a Year's Residence Among the Indian Tribes of the Rocky Mountains. Philadelphia: 1843. V. 63; 64
New Indian Sketches. New York: 1865. V. 63
Western Missions and Missionaries: a Series of Letters. New York: 1881. V. 66

SMIBERT, THOMAS
Rhyming Dictionary for the Use of Young Poets.... Edinburgh: 1856. V. 66

SMIDT, D. P.
Pacific Material Culture. Essays in Honor of Dr. Simon Kooijman on the Occasion of His 80th Birthday. Leiden: 1995. V. 62

SMILES for All Seasons: or, Mirth for Midsummer, Merriment for Michaelmas.... London: 1825. V. 65

SMILES, SAMUEL
Duty: with Illustrations of Courage, Patience and Endurance. London: 1880. V. 67
History of Ireland and the Irish People Under the Government of England. London: 1844. V. 64
Industrial Biography: Iron Workers and Tool Makers. London: 1863. V. 62; 64
James Nasmyth, Engineer. London: 1883. V. 62
Josiah Wedgwood F.R.S.: His Personal History. London: 1894. V. 64
The Life of George Stephenson, Railway Engineer. London: 1857. V. 64
Lives of the Engineers. London: 1861-1862. V. 64
Lives of the Engineers. London: 1862-1865. V. 62
Lives of the Engineers. London: 1874. V. 66
Men of Invention and Industry. London: 1884. V. 64
Self-Help. London: 1873. V. 64
Self-Help. London: 1895. V. 64
Thrift. London: 1875. V. 63; 67

SMILEY, F. J.
A Report Upon the Boreal Flora of the Sierra Nevada of California. Berkeley: 1921. V. 62

SMILEY, F. T.
History of Plainfield and North Plainfield. Plainfield: 1901. V. 63; 66

SMILEY, JANE
The Age of Grief. New York: 1987. V. 67
At Paradise Gate. New York: 1981. V. 62
Barn Blind. New York: 1980. V. 67
Duplicate Keys. London: 1984. V. 65
Duplicate Keys. New York: 1984. V. 64; 66; 67
Duplicate Keys. New York: 1991. V. 65
The Greenlanders. New York: 1988. V. 67
The Life of the Body. A Story. Minneapolis: 1990. V. 66
Moo. New York: 1995. V. 67
Ordinary Love and Good Will. New York: 1989. V. 66; 67
A Thousand Acres. New York: 1991. V. 62; 63; 64; 65; 66; 67

SMILEY, JEROME C.
Semi-Centennial History of the State of Colorado. Chicago: 1913. V. 64

SMITH, A. H.
English Place Name Elements. London: 1956. V. 67
A Monograph on the Genus Galerina Earle. New York: 1964. V. 62
The Place Names of the West Riding of Yorkshire. 1961. V. 65
The Place-Names of the West Riding of Yorkshire. 1961-1963. V. 66
The Place-Names of Westmorland. Volumes 42 and 43. London: 1967. V. 62

SMITH, A. M.
Sport and Adventure in the Indian Jungle. 1904. V. 67

SMITH, A. R.
Catalogue of Books Relating to America. London: 1871. V. 64

SMITH, AARON
The Atrocities of the Pirates.... Waltham St. Lawrence: 1929. V. 62

SMITH, ADAM
A Catalogue of the Library of Adam Smith. London: 1894. V. 66
Essays on Philosophical Subjects. Dublin: 1795. V. 67
Essays on Philosophical Subjects. London: 1795. V. 64
An Enquiry Into the Nature and Causes of the Wealth of Nations. London: 1776. V. 67
An Inquiry into the Nature and Causes of the Wealth of Nations. London: 1778. V. 64; 67
An Inquiry into the Nature and Causes of the Wealth of Nations. London: 1784. V. 67
An Inquiry into the Nature and Causes of the Wealth of Nations. London: 1786. V. 62; 63; 64
An Inquiry Into the Nature and Causes of the Wealth of Nations. London: 1796. V. 63
An Inquiry into the Nature and Causes of the Wealth of Nations. London: 1799. V. 66
An Inquiry into the Nature and Causes of the Wealth of Nations. Dublin: 1805. V. 66
An Inquiry into the Nature and Causes of the Wealth of Nations. Glasgow: 1805. V. 65
An Inquiry into the Nature and Causes of the Wealth of Nations. London: 1805. V. 63
An Inquiry into the Nature and Causes of the Wealth of Nations. Edinburgh: 1809. V. 63
Inquiry into the Nature and Causes of the Wealth of Nations. Hartford: 1811. V. 66
An Inquiry into the Nature and Causes of the Wealth of Nations. London: 1811. V. 64; 65
An Inquiry into the Nature and Causes of the Wealth of Nations. Edinburgh: 1817. V. 64
An Inquiry into the Nature and Causes of the Wealth of Nations. London: 1826. V. 64
An Inquiry into the Nature and Causes of the Wealth of Nations. Edinburgh: 1828. V. 62; 66
An Inquiry into the Nature and Causes of the Wealth of Nations. Edinburgh: 1846. V. 65
An Inquiry into the Nature and Causes of the Wealth of Nations. London: 1904. V. 66
The Theory of Moral Sentiments. London: 1749. V. 65
The Theory of Moral Sentiments. London: 1761. V. 66
The Theory of Moral Sentiments. London: 1797. V. 65
The Theory of Moral Sentiments. Edinburgh: 1808. V. 64
The Theory of Moral Sentiments. New York: 1822. V. 64
The Works of Adam Smith, LL.D. London: 1812-1812-1811-. V. 62

SMITH, ALBERT
Mont Blanc. London: 1860. V. 63
A Pottle of Strawberries, to Beguile a Short Journey, or a Long Half Hour. London: 1848. V. 67
The Pottleton Legacy, a Story of Town and Country. London: 1849. V. 62; 66; 67
The Social Parliament.... London: 1848. V. 67
The Story of Mont Blanc. London: 1854. V. 62; 63; 64; 66
The Struggles and Adventures of Christopher Tadpole at Home and Abroad. London: 1838. V. 67
To China and Back: Being a Diary Kept, Out and Home. London: 1859. V. 62
Wild Oats and Dead Leaves. London: 1860. V. 62; 67

SMITH, ALEXANDER
Alfred Hagart's Household. London: 1866. V. 66
Dreamthorp. London: 1863. V. 62
Dreamthorp. Portland: 1913. V. 63
A General History of the Lives and Adventures of the Most Famous Highwaymen, Murderers, Street Robbers &c. London: 1734. V. 64

SMITH, ALFRED
The Harrogate Medical Guide.... London: 1842. V. 64; 65; 66

SMITH, ALFRED RUSSELL
A Catalogue of Rare, Curious and Valuable Books on Sale. London: 1882. V. 65

SMITH, ALISON
John Petts and the Caseg Press. 2000. V. 67

SMITH, ANDREW
Illustrations of the Zoology of South Africa. London: 1849. V. 62

SMITH, ARTHUR
The Bubble of the Age; or the Fallacies of Railway Investments, Railway Accounts and Railway Dividends. London: 1848. V. 66

SMITH, ARTHUR DONALDSON
Through Unknown African Countries. London: 1897. V. 62

SMITH, ASHBEL
The Cholera Spasmodica, as Observed in Paris in 1832.... New York: 1832. V. 62
An Oration Pronounced Before the Phi Beta Kappa Society of Yale College. New Haven: 1849. V. 65

SMITH, BENJAMIN
A Fugitive from Hell - Fifteen Years and Outlaw. Joplin: 1935. V. 64; 67

SMITH, BERNARD
European Vision and the South Pacific 1768-1850. Oxford: 1960. V. 63; 64; 66

SMITH, BLANCHE LUCAS
North Carolina's Confederate Monuments and Memorials. Raleigh: 1941. V. 63

SMITH, BRADLEY
Mexico: a History in Art. Garden City: 1968. V. 63; 64
Spain: a History in Art. New York: 1966. V. 63

SMITH, C. FOX
Here and There in England with the Painter Brangwyn. Leigh-on-Sea: 1945. V. 66

SMITH, C. H.
The Natural History of Dogs.... Edinburgh: 1839-1840. V. 62; 63; 66
The Natural History of the Human Species. Edinburgh: 1848. V. 62

SMITH, C. HENRY
The Mennonite Immigration to Pennsylvania in the Eighteenth Century. Norristown: 1929. V. 64

SMITH, C. L.
Estuarine Research in the 1980's.... Albany: 1992. V. 65; 67

SMITH, C. W.
Thin Men of Haddam. New York: 1973. V. 62; 65

SMITH, CALEB
The Description, Use and Excellency of a New Instrument, or of a New Sea Quadrant.... London: 1740. V. 67

SMITH, CALEB B.
Fort Ridgely and South Pass Wagon Road. Washington: 1862. V. 67

SMITH, CAROLINE ESTES
The Philharmonic Orchestra of Los Angeles: "The First Decade" 1919- 1929. Los Angeles: 1930. V. 65

SMITH, CECIL HARCOURT
A Catalogue of the Principal Works of Art at Chequers. London: 1923. V. 63

SMITH, CHARLES
The American War, from 1775 to 1783.... New York: 1797. V. 64
The Old Manor House. London: 1793. V. 65
Report of a Conference on Secondary Education. Cambridge: 1896. V. 67
Smith's New Pocket Companion to the Roads of England and Wales and Part of Scotland. London: 1826. V. 66
Three Tracts on the Corn-Trade and Corn-Laws: Viz. 1. A Short Essay on the Corn-trade, and the Corn-laws, Containing, a General Relation of the Present Method of Carying on the Cord-trade.... London: 1766. V. 66; 67
The Voyages, Travels and Adventures of Charles Smith, who After Repeated Insults, Defeats and Crafty Wiles of his Mother-in-Law. 1801. V. 67

SMITH, CHARLES A.
A Comprehensive History of Minnehaha County, South Dakota. Mitchell: 1949. V. 66

SMITH, CHARLES HAMILTON
Selections of the Ancient Costume of Great Britain and Ireland from the Seventh to the Sixteenth Century. London: 1814. V. 63; 64

SMITH, CHARLES HENRY
Stephen Decatur and the Suppression of Piracy in the Mediterranean. An Address...April 19. A.D. 1900. N.P: 1900. V. 67

SMITH, CHARLES MANBY
The Working-Man's Way in the World.... London: 1853. V. 65

SMITH, CHARLES MANLEY
A Treatise on the Law of Master and Servant.... London: 1860. V. 64

SMITH, CHARLES P.
Upper Atmosphere Research Report No. XXI. Washington: 1954. V. 65

SMITH, CHARLES R.
Marines in the Revolution: A History of the Continental Marines in the American Revolution 1775-1783. Washington: 1975. V. 67

SMITH, CHARLES W.
Journal of a Trip to California Across the Continent from Weston, Mo. to Weber Creek, California in the Summer of 1850. New York: 1920. V. 63; 66

SMITH, CHARLIE
Canaan. New York: 1984. V. 63; 65; 67

SMITH, CHARLOTTE
The Banished Man. London: 1794. V. 62
Celestina. London: 1791. V. 65
Desmond. Dublin: 1792. V. 65
Elegiac Sonnets. London: 1792. V. 65
Elegiac Sonnets. (with) Elegiac Sonnets and Other Poems. London: 1795 1797. V. 66
Emmeline, the Orphan of the Castle. London: 1789. V. 62
Ethelinde, or the Recluse of the Lake. London: 1789. V. 62; 65
Marchmont: a Novel. London: 1796. V. 62
Minor Morals, Interspersed with Sketches of Natural History, Historical Anecdotes and Original Stories. London: 1799. V. 66
The Old Manor House. London: 1793. V. 62; 65
The Young Philosopher: a Novel. London: 1798. V. 62

SMITH, CLARE SYDNEY
The Golden Reign. The Story of My Friendship with "Lawrence of Arabia". London: 1978. V. 67

SMITH, CLARK ASHTON
The Abominations of Yondo. Sauk City: 1960. V. 63
The Dark Chateau. Sauk City: 1951. V. 64
From the Crypts of Memory. 1973. V. 66
Genius Loci and Other Tales. Sauk City: 1948. V. 62; 63; 64; 66
Lost Worlds. Sauk City: 1944. V. 64
Other Dimensions. Sauk City: 1970. V. 62; 63; 65; 66
Tales of Science and Sorcery. Sauk City: 1964. V. 63

SMITH, CONSTANCE
The Repentance of Paul Wentworth. London: 1889. V. 65

SMITH, DANIEL P.
Company K. First Alabama Regiment, or Three Years in the Confederate Service. Prattville: 1885. V. 62; 63; 65

SMITH, DAVE
The Fisherman's Whore. Athens: 1974. V. 63

SMITH, DAVID EUGENE
Rara Arithmetica. A Catalogue of the Arithmetics Written Before the Year MDCI with a Description of Those in the Library of George Arthur Plimpton of New York. Mansfield Centre: 1996. V. 65; 67
The Sumario Compendioso of Brother Juan Diez. The Earliest Mathematical Work of the New World. Boston: 1921. V. 67

SMITH, DAVID J.
Inequality in Northern Ireland. London: 1991. V. 67

SMITH, DAVID R.
Conrad's Manifesto. Preface to a Career. The History of the Preface to The Nigger of the Narcissus. Philadelphia: 1966. V. 65

SMITH, DE COST
Martyrs of the Oblong and Little Nine. Caldwell: 1948. V. 63
Red Indian Experiences. Caldwell: 1943. V. 65

SMITH, DWIGHT L.
The Photographer and the River 1889-1890 - Franklin A Nims' Colorado Canyon Diary. Santa Fe: 1967. V. 65

SMITH, E. BOYD
The Country Book. New York: 1924. V. 65
Fun in the Radio World. New York: 1923. V. 62
The Story of Noah's Ark. Boston: 1905. V. 63

SMITH, E. E.
The Vortex Blaster. 1960. V. 63

SMITH, E. F.
Bacteria in Relation to Plant Diseases. Washington: 1905-1914. V. 63

SMITH, E. H.
A Discourse, Delivered April 11, 1798 at the Request and Before the New York Society for Promoting the Manumission of Slaves and Protecting Such of Them as Have Been or May be Liberated. New York: 1798. V. 64

SMITH, EDGAR NEWBOLD
American Naval Broadsides. New York: 1974. V. 63
American Naval Broadsides. Philadelphia: 1974. V. 64

SMITH, EDGAR W.
Appointment in Baker Street: a Repertory of the Characters, One and All, Who Walked and Talked with Sherlock Holmes. New York: 1938. V. 65
Baker Street and Beyond. 1940. V. 62; 67
The Napoleon of Crime: Prolegomena to a Memoir of Professor James Moriarty. Summit: 1953. V. 63; 66
Profile by Gaslight. New York: 1944. V. 65; 67

SMITH, EDGARD C.
A Short History of Naval and Marine Engineering. London: 1937. V. 66

SMITH, EDMUND
Phaedra and Hippolitus. London: 1707. V. 62

SMITH, EDMUND WARE
A Tomato Can Chronicle and Other Stories of Fishing and Shooting. New York: 1937. V. 64

SMITH, EDWARD
A Sermon Preached Before their Excellencies the Lords Justices at Christ-Church Dublin, on the 3d of Dec. 1702. Dublin: 1703. V. 65
Smith's Trial. A Full and Authentic Report of the Trial of Ensign Edward Smith, for a Rape Alleged to Have Been Committed on the Body of Miss Sarah Rawson.... Dublin: 1800. V. 63

SMITH, EDWARD E.
Children of the Lens. 1954. V. 64; 66
Galactic Patrol. 1950. V. 64; 66
Skylark of Valeron. 1949. V. 64; 66
Skylark of Valeron. Reading: 1949. V. 64
Triplanetary. 1948. V. 64; 66
The Vortex Blaster. 1960. V. 64; 66

SMITH, EDWIN W.
The Ila-Speaking peoples of Northern Rhodesia. London: 1920. V. 62

SMITH, ELIAS
An Essay on the Fall of Angels and Men; with Remarks on Dr. Edward's Notion of the Freedom of the Will, and the System of University. Boston: 1812. V. 64

SMITH, ELIHU HUBBARD
The Diary of.... Philadelphia: 1973. V. 65

SMITH, ELIZA
The Compleat Housewife; or, Accomplish'd Gentlewoman's Companion. London: 1750. V. 62; 65
The Compleat Housewife; or, Accomplish'd Gentlewoman's Companion.... London: 1753. V. 62; 65

SMITH, ELIZABETH
Fragments in Prose and Verse. Bath: 1808. V. 65
Fragments in Prose and Verse. Bath: 1809. V. 62
Fragments in Prose and Verse. London: 1809. V. 62
The Irish Journals of Elizabeth Smith 1840-1850. 1980. V. 67

SMITH, ELIZABETH OAKES
Bertha and Lily; or, the Parsonage of Beech Glen, a Romance. New York: 1854. V. 63; 65
Shadow Land; or the Seer. New York: 1851. V. 65

SMITH, ERNEST BRAMAH
The Bravo of London. London: 1934. V. 65
The Celestial Omnibus - Some Kai Lung Stories of Ernest Bramah. London: 1963. V. 62
English Farming and Why I Turned It Up. 1894. V. 62; 64; 66
English Farming and Why I Turned It Up. London: 1894. V. 62; 65
Kai Lung Unrolls His Mat. Garden City: 1928. V. 64
Kai Lung Unrolls His Mat. New York: 1928. V. 64
Kai Lung's Golden Hours. London: 1922. V. 66
The Transmutation of Ling. London: 1911. V. 63
The Wallet of Kai Lung. London: 1900. V. 66
The Wallet of Kai Lung. London: 1923. V. 64; 66

SMITH, ESTER RUTH
The History of Del Norte County California - Including the Story of Its Pioneers with Many of Their Personal Narratives. Oakland: 1953. V. 66

SMITH, EUGENE W.
Minamata: Life Sacred and Profane. N.P: 1973. V. 63; 65

SMITH, F.
The Canary: Its Varieties, Management and Breeding. London: 1868. V. 65; 67

SMITH, FLORENCE M.
Mary Astell. New York: 1916. V. 63

SMITH, FRANCIS
The Canary, Its Varieties, Management and Breeding with Portaits of the Author's Own Birds. London: 1870. V. 63

SMITH, FRANCIS H.
The Armchair at the Inn. New York: 1912. V. 62
Colonel Carters of Cartersville. Boston and New York: 1891. V. 63
The Virginia Military Institute, Its Building and Rebuilding. Lynchburg: 1912. V. 62; 63; 65

SMITH, FRANCIS WILLIAM
The Natural Waters of Harrogate. London: 1899. V. 65

SMITH, FRANK
The Life and Work of Sir James Kay-Shuttleworth. London: 1913. V. 62

SMITH, FRANK MERIWEATHER
San Francisco Vigilance Committee of '56 with Some Interesting Sketches of Events Succeeding 1846. San Francisco: 1883. V. 63

SMITH, G.
A Collection of Ornamental Designs After the Manner of the Antique, Composed for the Use of Architects, Ornamental Painters, Statuaries, Carvers.... London: 1812. V. 64

SMITH, G. M.
Cryptogamic Botany. New York: 1955. V. 64; 67

SMITH, G. M., MRS.
George Smith. A Memoir with Some Pages of Autobiography. London: 1902. V. 66

SMITH, GEORGE
Alden of Aldenholme. London: 1873. V. 67
Assyrian Discoveries: an Account of Explorations and Discoveries on the Site of Nineveh, During 1873 and 1874. New York: 1875. V. 65
Assyrian Discovery, an Account of Explorations and Discoveries on the Site of Nineveh, During 1873 and 1874. London: 1875. V. 67
A Compleat Body of Distilling. London: 1725. V. 64
A Compleat Body of Distilling. London: 1731. V. 62
A Compleat Body of Distilling. London: 1749. V. 63; 65
A Full Account of the Extraordinary Elopment of a Young Lady with Her Groom. London: 1865. V. 63
A Narrative of an Exploratory Visit to Each of the Consular Cities of China and to the Islands of Hong Kong and Chusan in Behalf of the Church Missionary Society in the Years 1844, 1845, 1846. New York: 1847. V. 65

SMITH, GEORGE A.
Lovebirds and Related Parrots. 1979. V. 67

SMITH, GEORGE BARNETT
Illustrated British Ballads, Old and New. London: 1881. V. 64
The Life of the Right Honourable William Ewart Gladstone. London: 1880-1882. V. 64

SMITH, GEORGE G.
The Life and Times of George Foster Pierce. Nashville: 1888. V. 67

SMITH, GEORGE L.
Ireland: Historical and Statistical. 1844-1849. V. 63

SMITH, GEORGE O.
Highways in Hiding. 1955. V. 64

SMITH, GEORGE WINSTON
Chronicles of the Gringos. Albuquerque: 1968. V. 67

SMITH, GERARD
The Ferns of Derbyshire. London: 1877. V. 62

SMITH, GERRIT
Report from the County of Madison. Peterboro: 1843. V. 62
Speech of Gerrit Smith, Made in the National Liberty Party Convention at Buffalo, Sept. 17th 1851. Buffalo: 1851. V. 63

SMITH, GERTRUDE
Viewed from a Valley. Nellysford: 1965. V. 66

SMITH, GODFREY
Literary Memoirs of Germany and the North, Being a Choice Collection.... London: 1759. V. 64

SMITH, GOLDWIN
The Foundation of the American Colonies. A Lecture Delivered Before the University of Oxford, June 12, 1860. Oxford and London: 1861. V. 67
An Inaugural Lecture. Oxford and London: 1859. V. 63
A Letter to a Whig Member of the Southern Independence Association. London: 1864. V. 67
The Study of History. Two Lectures. Oxford and London: 1861. V. 63

SMITH, GREGOR IAN
The Cruise of the Marjery Daw. Leicester: 1940. V. 64

SMITH, GUSTAVUS WOODSON
The Battle of Seven Pines. New York: 1891. V. 62; 63; 65
Confederate War Papers. Fairfax Court House, New Orleans, Seven Pines, Richmond and North Carolina. New York: 1884. V. 62; 63; 65
Generals J. E. Johnston and G. T. Beauregard at the Battle of Manassas, July 1861. New York: 1892. V. 62; 63

SMITH, GYLES, PSEUD.
Serious Reflections on the Dangerous Tendency of the Common Practice of Card-Laying.... London: 1754. V. 62

SMITH, H.
Retreivers and How to Break Them. 1898. V. 67

SMITH, H. J. CROWTHER
A Croquet Nonsense Book. London: 1929. V. 62

SMITH, H. LLEWELLYN
The Story of the Dockers' Strike, Told by Two East Londoners. London: 1889. V. 64

SMITH, H. M.
The Fresh-Water Fishes of Siam, or Thailand. London: 1945. V. 62
Handbook of Lizards. Ithaca: 1946. V. 63; 66
Synopsis of the Herpetofauna of Mexico. Augusta and North Bennington: 1971-1993. V. 66

SMITH, HAMPDEN HARRISON
Stonewall Jackson: a Character Sketch. Blackstone. V. 65
Stonewall Jackson. A Character Sketch. Richmond: 1924-1925. V. 63

SMITH, HAROLD F.
American Travellers Abroad: a Bibliography of Accounts published Before 1900. Lanham et al: 1999. V. 65

SMITH, HARVEY H.
Lincoln and the Lincolns. New York: 1931. V. 67

SMITH, HELEN ZENNA
Not So Quiet... Stepdaughters of War. London: 1930. V. 62

SMITH, HENRY
Spinoza and His Environment. Cincinnati: 1886. V. 67

SMITH, HENRY ECROYD
Annals of Smith of Cantley, Balby and Doncaster, County York.... London: 1878. V. 63

SMITH, HENRY H.
Anatomical Atlas Illustrative of the Structure of the Human Body. Philadelphia: 1854. V. 66; 67

SMITH, HOMER
The Physiology of the Kidney. New York: 1937. V. 67

SMITH, HORACE
Brambletye House; or Cavaliers and Roundheads. Boston: 1826. V. 67
Brambletye House; or, Cavaliers and Roundheads. London: 1826. V. 65
Gaities and Gravities.... London: 1825. V. 67

SMITH, HORATIO
Festivals Games and Amusements. London: 1831. V. 67
Festivals, Games and Amusements. New York: 1831. V. 63
Horace in London: Consisting of Imitations of the First Two Books of the Odes of Horace. Boston: 1813. V. 66

SMITH, HUGH M.
Japanese Goldfish: Their Varieties and Cultivation. A Practical Guide to the Japanese Methods of Goldfish Culture for Amateurs and Professionals. Washington: 1909. V. 64

SMITH, IAIN CRICHTON
Deer on the High Hills. Edinburgh: 1962. V. 63

SMITH, J. E.
A History of Pittsfield. Springfield: 1876. V. 63; 64

SMITH, J. F.
White Pillars: Early Life and Architecture of the Lower Mississippi Valley County. Helburn: 1941. V. 65

SMITH, J. GREGORY, MRS.
Notes of Travel in New Mexico and California. St. Albans: 1886. V. 62; 65

SMITH, J. JAY
American Historical and Literary Curiosities.. Philadelphia: 1847. V. 66

SMITH, J. L. B.
The Fishes of the Seychelles. Grahamstown: 1969. V. 66
Ichthyological Papers, 1931-1943. Grahamstown: 1969. V. 64
The Sea Fishes of Southern Africa. Cape Town: 1961. V. 63; 66

SMITH, J. P.
Paper on Dunald Mill Hole Read Before the Barrow Naturalists' Field Club on Monday November 11, 1889. Barrow-in-Furness: 1890. V. 64; 65

SMITH, JAMES
Comic Miscellanies in Prose and Verse. London: 1841. V. 66
Domestic Encyclopaedia or Household Guide. Lewes: 1889. V. 64
The Mechanic; or, Compendium of Practical Inventions.... London: 1825. V. 66
The Panorama of Science and Art; Embracing the Sciences of Aerostation, Agriculture and Gardening, Architecture, Astronomy, Chemistry, Electricity, Galvanism.... Liverpool: 1816. V. 64
The Panorama of Science and Art.... London: 1835. V. 66
Rejected Addresses; or, the New Theatrum Poetarum. London: 1833. V. 67

SMITH, JAMES EDWARD
The English Flora. London: 1828. V. 66
Filamentous Fungi. New York: 1975-1978. V. 62
Flora Britannica. 1800-1804. V. 67
An Introduction to Physiological and Systematical Botany. London: 1827. V. 62

SMITH, JESSIE WILCOX
A Child's Stamp Book of Old Verses. New York: 1915. V. 65

SMITH, JOHN
The Art of Painting in Oil. London: 1759. V. 62
The Art of Painting in Oyl. 1723. V. 67
The Art of Painting in Oyl. London: 1723. V. 66
Choir Guard; the Grand Orrery of the Ancient Druids, Commonly Called Stonehenge, on Salisbury Plain.... Salisbury: 1771. V. 62
The Curiosities of Common Water; or the Advantages Thereof, in Preventing and Curing Many Distempers. London: 1724. V. 64
Galic Antiquities; Consisting of a History of the Druids, Particularly Those of Caledonia.... Edinburgh: 1780. V. 64
Hand-book of Dental Anatomy and Surgery for the Use of Students and Practioners. London: 1871. V. 65
The Pourtract of Old Age. London: 1666. V. 65; 66
Remarks on Rural Scenery. London: 1797. V. 64
The Sea-Mans Grammar and Dictionary, Explaining All the Difficult Terms in Navigation and the Practical Navigator and Gunner.... London: 1691. V. 64
Select Views in Italy. London: 1792-1799. V. 64
Select Views in Italy. London: 1796-1817. V. 67
Travels and Works of Captain John Smith, President of Virginia and Admiral of New England, 1580-1631. Edinburgh: 1910. V. 63; 66
The True Travels, Adventures and Observations of Captaine John Smith, in Europe, Asia, Africke and America. New York: 1930. V. 63; 64
Works, 1608-1631. Birmingham: 1884. V. 65

SMITH, JOHN JAY
Recollections of John Jay Smith. Philadelphia: 1892. V. 63; 66

SMITH, JOHN L.
Antietam to Appomattox with 118th Pennsylvania Volunteers, Corn Exchange Regiment. Philadelphia: 1892. V. 65

SMITH, JOHN THOMAS
Antiquities of Westminster. London: 1807-1809. V. 67
A Book for a Rainy Day; or Recollections of the Events of the Last Sixty-Six Years. London: 1845. V. 62
The Cries of London: Exhibiting Several of the Intinerant Trades of Ancient and Modern Times. London: 1839. V. 62
Nollekens and His Times. London: 1829. V. 63
Observations on the Duties and Responsibilities Involved in the Management of Mints.... Madras: 1848. V. 65

SMITH, JONATHAN
The Married Women's Statutes and Their Results Upon Divorce and Society. An Essay Read Before the Social Science Club at Clinton, Feb. 19, 1884. Clinton: 1884. V. 63

SMITH, JOSEPH
A Catalogue of Books Adverse to the Society of Friends. London: 1873. V. 63
An Examination of Mr. Paine's Decline and Fall of the English System of Finance, in a Letter to a Friend. London: 1796. V. 62

SMITH, JOSEPH JENCKS
Civil and Military List of Rhode Island 1800-1850. (with) New Index to the Civil and Military Lists of Rhode Island. Providence: 1901-1907. V. 67

SMITH, JOSEPH MATHER
A Discourse on the Epidemic Cholera Morbus of Europe and Asia, Delivered as an Introductory Lecture at the College of Physicians and Surgeons in the City of New York, Nov. 9, 1831. New York: 1831. V. 62

SMITH, JOSEPH W.
Gleanings from the Sea; Showing the Pleasures, Pains and Penalties of Life Afloat, with Contingencies Ashore. Andover: 1887. V. 66

SMITH, JOSHUA TOULMIN
The Parish. Its Obligations and Powers: Its Officers and Their Duties. London: 1854. V. 62
The Parish. Its Powers and Obligations at Law, as Regards the Welfare of Every Neighbourhood and in Relation to the State, Its Officers and Committees and the Responsibility of Every Parishioner. London: 1857. V. 63

SMITH, JOSIAH WILLIAM
A Compendium of the Law of Real and Personal Property, Connected with Conveyancing. London: 1855. V. 63
A Manual of Equity Jurisprudence Founded on the Works of Story, Spence and Other Writers.... London: 1866. V. 63

SMITH, JULIA E.
Abby Smith and Her Cows. Hartford: 1877. V. 63

SMITH, JULIE
Death Turns a Trick. New York: 1982. V. 63
New Orleans Mourning. 1990. V. 66
New Orleans Mourning. New York: 1990. V. 65
The Sourdough Wars: a Rebecca Schwartz Mystery. New York: 1984. V. 63; 64; 66
True-Life Adventure. New York: 1985. V. 63; 66

SMITH, KEN
Burned Books. Newcastle-upon-Tyne: 1981. V. 65

SMITH, L. B.
Studies in the Bromeliaceae. Parts I to XVII. 1977. V. 63; 66

SMITH, L. C.
North American Indian Arts: an Index of Prices and Auctions 1985- 1986-1987. Albuquerque: 1988. V. 62

SMITH, LEE
Bob, a Dog. Chapel Hill: 1988. V. 62; 64
Cakewalk. New York: 1981. V. 66
Family Linen. New York: 1985. V. 67
Oral History. New York: 1983. V. 67
Something in the Wind. New York: 1971. V. 63; 67

SMITH, LOGAN
Cousin Crowe. London: 1961. V. 63

SMITH, LOGAN PEARSALL
A Portrait of Logan Pearsall Smith Drawn from His Letters and Diaries. London: 1950. V. 67
Trivia. London: 1918. V. 64
The Youth of Parnassus and Other Stories. London: 1895. V. 66

SMITH, M.
The History of Daniel, the Prophet, the Son of Josiah, King of Judah. Charleston: 1822. V. 62

SMITH, M. A.
The British Amphibians and Reptiles. London: 1951. V. 63
Fauna of British India: Reptilia and Amphibia. 1931. V. 66
Fauna of British India: Reptilia and Amphibia. 1931-1961. V. 63

SMITH, MARTIN CRUZ
The Analog Bullet. New York: 1977. V. 66
Canto for a Gypsy. 1972. V. 64
Nightwing. New York: 1977. V. 66

SMITH, MARY ELIZABAETH
Picture Writing from Ancient Southern Mexico. Norman: 1973. V. 63

SMITH, MARY STUART
Virginia Cookery-Book. New York: 1912. V. 67

SMITH, MEREDITH J.
Marsupials of Australia. Melbourne: 1980. V. 62

SMITH, MICHAEL
A Geographical View of the British Possessions in North America.... Balitmore: 1814. V. 62
A Geographical View of the British Possessions in North America.... Baltimore: 1815. V. 63
A Geographical View of the British Possessions in North America.... Richmond: 1815. V. 66

SMITH, MOSES
History of the Adventures and Sufferings of Moses Smith. Brooklyn: 1812. V. 67
History of the Adventures and Sufferings of Moses Smith. Albany: 1814. V. 63

SMITH, N. G. ROYDE
The Second Problems Book: Prizes and Proximes from the Westminster Gazette 1908 1919. London: 1909. V. 65
The Westminster Problems Book: Prose and Verse. 1908. V. 65

SMITH, NATHAN
Medical and Surgical Memoirs...Late Professor of Surgery and of the Theory and Practice of Physick in Yale College. Baltimore: 1831. V. 64, 66

SMITH, NATHAN R.
Legends of the South. Baltimore: 1869. V. 63

SMITH, NILA BANTON
Our First Book. New York: 1945. V. 62

SMITH, NORA ARCHIBALD
Boys and Girls of Bookland. New York: 1923. V. 62; 67

SMITH, PAMELA COLMAN
Annancy Stories. New York: 1899. V. 63

SMITH, PETER C.
The Design and Construction of Stables and Ancillary Buildings. London: 1967. V. 67

SMITH, PHILIP
New Directions in Bookbinding. London: 1974. V. 62
New Directions in Bookbinding. New York: 1974. V. 63; 64; 66

SMITH, PHILIP CHADWICK FOSTER
The Frigate Essex Papers: Building the Salem Frigate 1798-1799. Salem: 1974. V. 63
More Marine Paintings and Drawings in the Peabody Museum. Salem: 1979. V. 67

SMITH, PHILIP H.
Acadia. A Lost Chapter in American History. Pawling: 1884. V. 63

SMITH, R. DIXON
Jeremy Brett and David Burke: an Adventure in Canonical Fidelity. Minneapolis: 1986. V. 65

SMITH, R. H.
Twigs for Nests, or Notes on Nursery. London: 1866. V. 62

SMITH, R. MORRIS
The Burlington Smiths, a Family History. Philadelphia: 1877. V. 65

SMITH, RICHARD BRYAN
Notes Made During a Tour in Denmark, Holstein, Mecklenburg-Schwerin, Pomerania, the Isle of Rugen, Prussia, Poland, Sacony, Brunswick, Hannover, the Hanseatic Territories.... London: 1827. V. 67

SMITH, RICHARD GORDON
Ancient Tales and Folklore of Japan. London: 1908. V. 65

SMITH, RICHARD MC ALLISTER
The Confederate First Reader.... Richmond: 1864. V. 63; 65

SMITH, ROBERT
A Compleat System of Opticks in Four Books. Cambridge: 1738. V. 63; 64
Harmonics, or the Philosophy of Musical Sounds. London: 1759. V. 67

SMITH, ROBERT ANGUS
Memoir of John Dalton, and History of the Atomic Theory Up to His Time. London: 1856. V. 66

SMITH, ROBERT HARVEY
An Aberdeenshire Village Propaganda Forty Years Ago. Edinburgh;: 1889. V. 64

SMITH, ROSS
Reminiscences of an Old Timer. N.P: 1930. V. 67

SMITH, ROSWELL CHAMBERLAIN
Louisiana English Grammar. Shreveport: 1865. V. 62; 63; 65

SMITH, S. COMPTON
Chile Con Carne or the Camp and the Field. New York: 1887. V. 62; 65

SMITH, SAMUEL
The History of the Colony of Nova Caesaria, or New Jersey.... Burlington: 1765. V. 63; 64; 66
Social Reform. London: 1884. V. 63

SMITH, SAMUEL J.
Miscellaneous Writings of the Late Samuel J. Smith of Burlington, N. J. Philadelphia: 1836. V. 63; 66

SMITH, SAMUEL STANHOPE
Discourse on the Nature and Reasonableness of Fasting, and on the Existing Causes that Call Us to that Duty. Philadelphia: 1795. V. 63; 66
The Divine Goodness to the United States of America. London: 1795. V. 63; 66
An Essay on the Causes of the Variety of Complexion and Figure in the Human Species. Edinburgh: 1788. V. 62
An Essay on the Causes of the Variety of Complexion and Figure in the Human Species.... New Brunswick: 1810. V. 63; 66
An Oration, Upon the Death of General George Washington, Delivered in the State House at Trenton, on the 14th of Jan. 1800.... Trenton: 1800. V. 63; 66

SMITH, SARAH
The Vanished Child. New York: 1992. V. 66

SMITH, SARAH WINTHROP
Suffrage a Right of Citizenship. Washington: 1893. V. 63

SMITH, SETH LEWIS, MRS.
North Carolina's Confederate Monuments and Memorials. Raleigh: 1941. V. 62

SMITH, SIDNEY
The Mother Country; or, the Spade, the Wastes and the Eldest Son. London: 1849. V. 64
The Principles of Phrenology. London: 1849. V. 64

SMITH, SOLOMON
Theatrical Management in the West and South for Thirty Years. New York: 1868. V. 62; 66; 67

SMITH, STEPHEN
Fruitless Experiment. An Examination and Critical Analysis of the Claims Advanced on Behalf of Vivisection. London: 1904. V. 66

SMITH, STEVIE
The Frog Prince and Other Poems. London: 1966. V. 64
A Good Time Was Had by All. London: 1937. V. 65
Mother, What Is Man?. London: 1942. V. 62
Over the Frontier. London: 1938. V. 64
Some are More Human than Others. London: 1958. V. 65

SMITH, SYDNEY
Bon Mots. London: 1893. V. 63
Elementary Sketches of Moral Philosophy, Delivered at the Royal Institution in the Years 1804, 1805 and 1806. London: 1850. V. 63
The Works. London: 1848. V. 65

SMITH, THEONE
A B C Block-Building Book. New York: 1917. V. 65

SMITH, THEOPHILUS
Sheffield and Its Neighbourhood Photographically Illustrated. London: 1865. V. 62

SMITH, THOMAS
The Commonwealth of England and the Manner of the Government Thereof. London: 1609. V. 65
De Republica Anglorum.. Lug. Batavorum: 1625. V. 66
De Republica Anglorum, Libri Tres. Leyden: 1641. V. 66
De Republica et Administratione Anglorum.... Londini: 1610. V. 66
Scott's 900 Eleventh New York United States Volunteer Cavalry Associ ation. N.P: 1906. V. 65
A Topographical and Historical Account of the Parish of St. Mary-Le-Bone. London: 1833. V. 67

SMITH, THOMAS B.
Backward Glances. Halifax: 1898. V. 66
Little Mayflower Land. Halifax: 1900. V. 66
Nova Scotia: Trial and Relief. Windsor: 1929. V. 66

SMITH, THOMAS SOUTHWOOD
A Treatise on Fever. London: 1830. V. 63

SMITH, THORNE
Biltmore Oswald - the Diary of a Hapless Recruit. London: 1918. V. 64
Biltmore Oswald: the Diary of a Hapless Recruit. New York: 1918. V. 63
Lazy Bear Lane. Garden City: 1931. V. 63; 64
Out O' Luck. New York: 1919. V. 64

SMITH, TOM
A History of Longridge and District. Preston: 1888. V. 62; 65
History of the Parish of Chipping, in the County of Lancaster.... Preston: 1894. V. 62

SMITH, TUNSTALL
James McHenry Howard. A Memoir. Balitmore: 1916. V. 62; 63

SMITH, V. E.
Middleburg and Nearby. N.P: 1986. V. 64

SMITH, W.
A Synopsis of the British Diatomaceae. 1853-1856. V. 63; 66
A Synopsis of the British Diatomaceae. London: 1853-1856. V. 64

SMITH, W. A.
The Anson Guards: Company C, Fourteenth Regiment, North Carolina Volunteers 1861-1865. Charlotte: 1914. V. 62; 63; 65

SMITH, W. H. B.
The Book of Rifles. Harrisburg: 1965. V. 67
Walther Pistols and Rifles. 1962. V. 67

SMITH, W. M'COMBIE
The Romance of Poaching in the Highlands. 1904. V. 62
The Romance of Poaching in the Highlands of Scotland as Illustrated by the Lives of John Farquharson and Alexander Davidson. Stirling: 1904. V. 67

SMITH, W. W.
The Genus Primula. 1977. V. 63; 66

SMITH, WALKER C.
The Everett Massacre. Chicago: 1919?. V. 67

SMITH, WALTER E.
The Bronte Sisters, a Bibliographical Catalogue of First an Early Editions 1846-1860.... Los Angeles: 1991. V. 62
Charles Dickens in the Original Cloth. Los Angeles: 1982. V. 62; 67
Charles Dickens in the Original Cloth: a Bibliographical Catalogue. Los Angeles: 1982-1983. V. 62

SMITH, WHITE MOUNTAIN, MRS.
Indian Tribes of the Southwest. Stanford: 1933. V. 67

SMITH, WILBUR
When the Lion Feeds. London: 1964. V. 63

SMITH, WILLIAM
Annual Statement of the Trade and Commerce of Cincinnati.... Cincinnati: 1855. V. 66
A Dictionary of Greek and Roman Geography. London: 1966. V. 66
A Dissertation on the Nerves: Containing An Account, 1. Of the Nature of Man. 2. Of the Nature of Brutes. 3. Of the Nature and Connection of Soul and Body. 4. Of the Threefold Life of Man. 5. Of the Symptoms, Causes and Cure of all Nervous Diseases. London: 1768. V. 64; 66; 67
The History of the Post Office in British North America 1639-1870. 1920. V. 64
The History of the Post Office in British North America 1639-1870. Cambridge: 1920. V. 63
History of the Province of New York, from Its Discovery to the Appointment of Governor Colden in 1762. New York: 1829. V. 63
Morley, Ancient and Modern. London: 1886. V. 66
Old Yorkshire with an Introduction by Rev. Robert Collyer. London: 1881-1884. V. 66
The Progress of Civil and Mechanical Engineering and Shipbuilding (Illustrated), Being a Series of Selected Examples of Construction in Marine, Locomotive and Stationery Engines.... London: 1877. V. 65
Relation Historique de l'Expedition Contre les Indiens de l'Ohio en MDCCLXIV. Amsterdam: 1769. V. 66

SMITH, WILLIAM CUZACK
The Maze: a Poem. London: 1815. V. 62

SMITH, WILLIAM HAWKES
Kenilworth Castle in the 16th, 18th and 19th Centuries, Displayed in Thirteen Lithographic Plates. Birmingham: 1821. V. 62; 67

SMITH, WILLIAM JAY
Poems. New York: 1947. V. 63

SMITH, Z. F.
The Battle of New Orleans. Louisville: 1904. V. 67
The History of Kentucky. Louisville: 1886. V. 63

SMITH, ZADIE
White Teeth. New York: 2000. V. 67

SMITHERS, R. H. N.
A Check List of the Birds of Southern Rhodesia. 1957. V. 67

SMITHSONIAN INSTITUTION
Annual Report of the Board of Regents of the Smithsonian Institution, Showing the Operations, Expenditures and condition of the Institution for the Year ending June 30, 1902. Washington: 1904. V. 64
Annual Report of the Board of Regents of the Smithsonian Institution, Showing the Operations, Expenditures and Condition of the Institution to July 1885; Part II. Washington: 1886. V. 64
Annual Report of the U. S. National Museum, for the Years Ending June 30, 1905-1943. 1905-1943. V. 62
Report of the Secretary of the Smithsonian Institution (on the) Astrophysical Observatory; Appropriations Expended, Results Reached, and Present Condition of the Work. Washington: 1902. V. 67

SMITHURST, DENJAMIN
Britain's Glory, and England's Bravery. London: 1000. V. 66

SMOLLETT, TOBIAS GEORGE
The Adventures of Ferdinand Count Fathom. London: 1753. V. 62
The Adventures of Ferdinand Count Fathom. London: 1771. V. 62
The Adventures of Peregrine Pickle. London: 1751. V. 62; 65; 66
The Adventures of Peregrine Pickle. Edinburgh: 1779. V. 62
The Adventures of Peregrine Pickle. London: 1706. V. 66
The Adventures of Peregrine Pickle. Harrisburgh: 1807. V. 62; 64
The Adventures of Peregrine Pickle. London: 1831. V. 65
The Adventures of Peregrine Pickle. Oxford: 1936. V. 62; 63; 64
The Adventures of Roderick Random. London: 1748. V. 62
The Adventures of Roderick Random. London: 1766. V. 62
The Adventures of Roderick Random. London: 1770. V. 62
The Adventures of Roderick Random. Edinburgh: 1784. V. 62
The Adventures of Roderick Random. Philadelphia: 1809. V. 62
The Adventures of Sir Launcelot Greaves. London: 1762. V. 62
The Adventures of Sir Launcelot Greaves. Edinburgh: 1783. V. 62
The Expedition of Humphry Clinker. London: 1771. V. 62
The Expedition of Humphry Clinker. London: 1795. V. 62
The History and Adventures of an Atom. London: 1769. V. 62
The History and Adventures of an Atom. London: 1795. V. 64
The History of England from the Revolution to the Death of George the Second. London: 1793. V. 65
The Miscellaneous Works. Edinburgh: 1806-1811. V. 66
The Miscellaneous Works. Edinburgh: 1811. V. 62; 66
The Miscellaneous Works. Edinburgh: 1820. V. 66
The Novels. Boston: 1926. V. 66
Select Essays on Commerce, Agriculture, Mines, Fisheries and Other Useful Subjects. London: 1754. V. 63
Travels through France and Italy. Dublin: 1766. V. 66
Travels through France and Italy. London: 1766. V. 66; 67
Travels through France and Italy. London: 1778. V. 66
The World. New York: 1902. V. 65

SMUTS, M. M. S.
Anatomy of the Dromedary. Oxford: 1987. V. 62

SMYTH, A. L.
John Dalton, 1766-1844. A Bibliography of Works by and About Him. Manchester: 1966. V. 62; 65

SMYTH, AMELIA GILLESPIE
Olympia Morata: Her Times, Life and Writings. London: 1837. V. 63

SMYTH, C. PIAZZI
Madeira Meteorologic. Edinburgh: 1882. V. 65
Our Inheritance in the Great Pyramid. London: 1864. V. 66
Teneriffe, an Astonomer's Experiment: Or, Specialities of a Residence Above the Clouds. London: 1858. V. 65
The Visual (Grating and Glass Lens) Solar Spectrum in 1884. Edinburgh: 1886. V. 64

SMYTH, ELAINE
Plain Wrapper Press 1966-1988. Austin: 1993. V. 64

SMYTH, FRASER
The Diaries of Mrs. John H. Watson nee Morstan. Tetbury: 1995. V. 66

SMYTH, GEORGE LEWIS
The Monuments and Genii of St. Paul's and Westminster Abbey. London: 1826. V. 66

SMYTH, HENRY DE WOLF
A General Account of the Development of Methods of Using Atomic Energy for Military Purposes Under the Auspices of the United States Government 1940-1945. Washington: 1945. V. 64

SMYTH, JAMES CARMICHAEL
A Description of the Jail Distemper, as It Appeared Amongst the Spanish Prisoners, at Winchester, in the Year 1780.... London: 1795. V. 64

SMYTH, R. BROUGH
The Gold Fields and Mineral Districts of Victoria, With Notes on the Modes of Occurence of Gold and Other Metals and Minerals. Melbourne: 1869. V. 66

SMYTH, WARINGTON W.
A Year with the Turks or Sketches of Travel in the European and Asiatic Dominions of the Sultan. Redfield: 1854. V. 66

SMYTH, WILLIAM
Lectures on Modern History, from the Irruption of the Northern Nations to the Close of the American Revolution. London: 1840. V. 66

SMYTH, WILLIAM HENRY
The Cycle of Celestial Objects, Continued at the Hartwell Observatory to 1859.... London: 1860. V. 66
A Cycle of Celestial Objects, for the Use of Naval, Military and Private Astronomers. London: 1844. V. 65; 66
The Sailor's Word Book. 1867. V. 67
The Sailor's Word Book. London: 1867. V. 64

SMYTHE, F.
An Alpine Journey. 1934. V. 63
Camp Six. 1937. V. 63; 65
Kamet Conquered. 1932. V. 63; 65
The Kangchenjunga Adventure. London: 1930. V. 63; 64
The Valley of Flowers. 1938. V. 63; 65

SMYTHE, P. M.
The Diary of an All-Round Angler. 1956. V. 67

SMYTHE, WILLIAM E.
The Conquest of Arid America. New York: 1905. V. 64; 67

SMYTHE, WILLIAM JAMES, MRS.
Ten Months in the Fiji Islands. Oxford and London: 1864. V. 65

SMYTHIES, B. E.
The Birds of Borneo. Edinburgh: 1960. V. 62
The Birds of Borneo. Edinburgh: 1968. V. 64
Birds of Burma. Rangoon: 1940. V. 62; 67
The Birds of Burma. Edinburgh: 1953. V. 63; 67
The Birds of Burma. London: 1953. V. 62

SMYTHIES, E. A.
Big Game Shooting of Nepal. Calcutta: 1942. V. 63; 66

SMYTHIES, HARRIETTE MARIA
Married for Love. London: 1857. V. 65

SMYTHIES, R. H. RAYMOND
Records of the Smythies Family. London: 1912. V. 63

SNAGG, THOMAS
Recollections of Occurrences. The Memoirs of Thomas Snagg.... London: 1951. V. 64

SNAITH, STANLEY
April Morning. London: 1926. V. 62
A Flying Scroll. London: 1928. V. 62

SNARE, JOHN
The Velasquez Cause. Jury Court, Edinburgh, Saturday 26th and Monday 28th July 1851. Edinburgh: 1851. V. 63

SNART, JOHN
Thesaurus of Horror; or, the Charnal-House Explored!. London: 1817. V. 67

SNEED, JOHN L. T.
Lawyers and the Law. Nashville: 1876. V. 64

SNEIDER, VERN J.
The Teahouse of the August Moon. London: 1952. V. 63

SNELGRAVE, WILLIAM
A New Account of Some Parts of Guinea and the Slave Trade. London: 1734. V. 62; 65

SNELL, BRUNO
Tragicorum Graecorum Fragmenta. 1977-1986. V. 65

SNELL, HENRY JAMES
Practical Instructions in Enamel Painting on Glass, China, Tiles, etc. London: 1890. V. 66

SNELL, JAMES P.
History of Sussex and Warren Counties, New Jersey. Philadelphia: 1881. V. 63; 66
History of Sussex and Warren Counties, New Jersey. Sussex: 1971. V. 66

SNELL, W. H.
Boleti of Northeastern North America. Lehre: 1970. V. 66

SNELLING, THOMAS
Seventy-One Plates of Gold and Silver Coin, with Their Weight, Fineness and Value. London: 1760. V. 62; 65

SNELLING, W. J.
The Polar Region of the Western Continent Explored. Boston: 1831. V. 65

SNIDER, C. H. J.
Under the Red Jack. Privateers of the Maritime Provinces of Canada in the War of 1812. Toronto. V. 66

SNIDOW, GORDON
Gordon Snidow: Chronicler of the Contemporary West. Flagstaff. V. 66

SNIFFEN, M. K.
The Indians of the Yukon and Tanana Valleys, Alaska. Philadelphia: 1914. V. 63

SNODGRASS, O. T.
Realistic Art and Times of the Mibres Indians. El Paso: 1977. V. 63; 66

SNODGRASS, R. E.
Shore Fishes of the Revillagigedo, Clipperton, Cocos and Galapagos Islands. Washington: 1905. V. 67

SNODGRASS, W. D.
Autumn Variations. New York: 1990. V. 67
Heart's Needle. New York: 1959. V. 63; 64; 67
Heart's Needle. London: 1960. V. 63
If Birds Build with Your Hair. New York: 1979. V. 67
The Kinder Capers. Poems. New York: 1986. V. 66; 67
Magda Goebbels. N.P: 1983. V. 65
Six Troubadour Songs. Providence: 1977. V. 65
Spring Suite. New York: 1994. V. 67
To Shape a Song. New York: 1988. V. 67

SNOW, C. H.
A Geography of Boston, County of Suffolk and the Adjacent Towns. Boston: 1830. V. 66

SNOW, C. P.
The Affair. London: 1960. V. 62
A Coat of Varnish. London: 1979. V. 64
The Masters. London: 1951. V. 63
The New Men. London: 1954. V. 65

SNOW, CHESTER
The Hypergeometric and Legendre Functions with Applications to Integral equations of Poetential Theory. Washington: 1942. V. 67

SNOW, D. W.
An Atlas of Speciation in African Non-Passerine Birds. London: 1978. V. 64

SNOW, ERASTUS
One Year in Scandinavia: Results of the Gospel in Denmark and Sweden - Sketches and Observations of the Country and People.... Liverpool: 1851. V. 66

SNOW, JACK
The Shaggy Man of Oz. Chicago: 1949. V. 62

SNOW, ROBERT
Memorials of a Tour on the Continent. London: 1845. V. 63

SNOWDEN, KEIGHLEY
The Master Spinner. A Life of Sir Swire Smith. London: 1930. V. 64; 65

SNOWDON, LORD
Israel - a First View. London: 1986. V. 62

SNOWMAN, A. KENNETH
The Art of Carl Faberge. London: 1953. V. 64

SNYDER, GARY
The Back Country. London: 1967. V. 62; 63; 64; 67
The Blue Sky. New York: 1969. V. 62; 64
Earth House Hold. London. V. 62
Earth House Hold. New York: 1969. V. 62; 63
Good Wild Sacred. Madley: 1984. V. 62
Hands, Joining: a Calligraphic Anthology. Waldron Island: 1988. V. 62
Left Out in the Rain - New Poems 1947-1985. San Francisco: 1986. V. 62
Mountains and Rivers Without End. Washington: 1996. V. 62; 64; 66; 67
Myths and Texts. New York: 1960. V. 62; 64; 66; 67
A Range of Poems. London: 1966. V. 62; 64; 65
Regarding Wave. Iowa City: 1969. V. 64; 67
Regarding Wave. London: 1970. V. 64
Regarding Wave. New York: 1970. V. 62; 65
Riprap. Ashland: 1959. V. 62; 63
Six Selections from Mountains and Rivers Without End. San Francisco: 1965. V. 62; 65
Six Selections from Mountains and Rivers Without End. London: 1967. V. 62
Smokey the Bear Sutra. Oakland: 1993. V. 64
True Night. San Juan: 1980. V. 62; 65; 67
Turtle Island. New York: 1974. V. 62

SNYDER, JAMES U.
Cain and Other Poems. Mexico: 1908. V. 67

SOAME, JOHN
Hampstead-Wells; or, Directions for the Drinking of those Waters. London: 1734. V. 65

SOANE, GEORGE
New Curiosities of Literature: and Book of the Months. London: 1849. V. 64

SOANE, JOHN
Description of the Residence of John Soane, Architect, with Some General Remarks on the State of Architectue in England.... London: 1830. V. 62; 64
Sketches in Architecture: Containing Plans and Elevations of Cottages, Villas and Other Useful Buildings.... London: 1798. V. 64

SOAR, C. D.
The British Hydracarina. London: 1925-1929. V. 64; 66

SOBEL, DAVA
Longitude. New York: 1995. V. 64; 67

SOBIESKI, JOHN
Life Story and Personal Reminiscences of Col. John Sobieski. Shelbyville: 1900. V. 63; 65; 67

SOCIAL Architecture; or, Reasons and Means for the Demolition and Reconstruction of the Social Edifice. London: 1876. V. 64

SOCIAL Science: Being Selections from John Cassell's Prize Essays, by Working Men and Women. London: 1861. V. 66

THE SOCIAL Science of the Constitution of Society or the Cause and Cure of Its Present Evils. London: 1862. V. 62

SOCIALISM - What Is Its Tendency? No. II. Edinburgh: 1847?. V. 66

SOCIETE GEOLOGIQUE DE FRANCE
Memoires de la Societe Geologique de France. Series I. Paris: 1833-1837. V. 66

SOCIETE OECONOMIQUE DE BERNE
Essays on the Spirit of Legislation, in the Encouragement of Agriculture, Population, Manufactures and Commerce. London: 1772. V. 66

SOCIETE ROYALE ET CENTRALE D'AGRICULTURE
Instruction Concernant la Propagation la Culture en Grand, et la Conservation des Pommes de Terre, Ainsi que l'Emploi de Leurs Produits, Considerés Comme Ailimentaires et Comme Pouvant etre Utilement Appliques.... Paris: 1829. V. 66

SOCIETIES FOR REFORMATION OF MANNERS
Sermons Preached to the Societies at St. Mary-Le-Bow.... London: 1727-1736. V. 66

SOCIETY FOR CONSTITUTIONAL INFORMATION
An Address to the Public from the Society for Constutional Information. London?: 1780. V. 62

SOCIETY FOR ENCOURAGEMENT OF ARTS, MANUFACTURES AND COMMERCE
Premiums Offered by the Society Instituted at London, for the Encouragement of Arts, Manufactures and Commerce. London: 1772. V. 65
Transactions of the Society.... London: 1785. V. 66

SOCIETY FOR THE CONVERSION AND RELIGIOUS INSTRUCTION
The Charter of the Society for the Conversion and Religious Instruction and Education of the Negro Slaves in the British West India Islands; to Which is Prefixed, a Short Account of the Charitable Fund, for the Application and Management of Which the Sai. London: 1825. V. 63
Report of the Incorporated Society for the Conversion and Religious Instruction and Education of the Negro Slaves in the British West India Islands for the Year MDCCCXXV. London: 1826. V. 63
Report of the Incorporated Society for the Conversion and Religious Instruction and Education of the Negro Slaves in the British West India Islands for the Year MDCCCXXX. London: 1831. V. 63
Report of the Incorporated Society for the Conversion...of the Negro Slaves in the British West India Islands from July to December, MDCCCXXIII. London: 1824. V. 63

SOCIETY FOR THE EXTINCTION OF THE SLAVE TRADE
Prospectus of the Society...Instituted June 1839. London: 1840?. V. 66

SOCIETY FOR THE IMPROVEMENT OF PRISON DISCIPLINE
Remarks on the Form and Construction of Prisons; With Appropriate Designs. London: 1826. V. 62; 66
Rules for the Government of Gaols, Houses of Correction and Penitentiaries. London: 1821. V. 63

SOCIETY FOR THE PROMOTION OF AGRICULTURE, ARTS & MANUFACTURE
Transactions of the Society for the Promotion of Agriculture, Arts and Manufactures...in...New York. Albany: 1801. V. 66

SOCIETY OF ANTIQUARIES
A List of the Society of Antiquaries of London, from the Revival in 1717 to June 19, 1796. London: 1796. V. 64

SOCIETY OF BERNE
Essays on the Spirit of Legislation, in the Encouragement of Agriculture, Population, Manufactures, and Commerce. London: 1772. V. 63

SOCIETY OF CALIFORNIA PIONEERS
Transactions of....Jan. 1st to May 7th 1863, Part I. Volume II. San Francisco: 1863. V. 67

SOCIETY OF DILETTANTI
Historical Notices of the Society of Dillettanti. London: 1855. V. 62
The Unedited Antiquities of Attica, Comprising the Architectural Remains of Eleusis, Rhamnus, Sunium. London: 1817. V. 64

SOCIETY OF DYERS AND COLOURISTS
Journal. London: 1885-1886. V. 64

SOCIETY OF FRIENDS
Transactions of the Central Relief Committee of the Society of Friends During the Famine in Ireland in 1846 and 1847. Dublin: 1852. V. 66

SOCIETY OF GENTLEMEN
The Complete Farmer; or, a General Dictionary of Husbandry.... London: 1777. V. 64

SOCIETY OF INDEPENDENT ARTISTS
Catalogue of the 9th Annual Exhibition...Waldorf Astoria. New York: 1925. V. 62

SOCIETY OF NAVAL ARCHITECTS AND MARINE ENGINEERS
Transactions. New York: 1893. V. 64

SOCIETY OF VOYAGES ROUND THE WORLD
Round the World in Three Hundred and Twenty Days. London: 1877. V. 66

THE SOCK Stories. New York: 1863. V. 66

SMITH, WILLIAM JAY
Poems. New York: 1947. V. 63

SMITH, Z. F.
The Battle of New Orleans. Louisville: 1904. V. 67
The History of Kentucky. Louisville: 1886. V. 63

SMITH, ZADIE
White Teeth. New York: 2000. V. 67

SMITHERS, R. H. N.
A Check List of the Birds of Southern Rhodesia. 1957. V. 67

SMITHSONIAN INSTITUTION
Annual Report of the Board of Regents of the Smithsonian Institution, Showing the Operations, Expenditures and condition of the Institution for the Year ending June 30, 1902. Washington: 1904. V. 64
Annual Report of the Board of Regents of the Smithsonian Institution, Showing the Operations, Expenditures and Condition of the Institution to July 1885; Part II. Washington: 1886. V. 64
Annual Report of the U. S. National Museum, for the Years Ending June 30, 1905-1943. 1905-1943. V. 62
Report of the Secretary of the Smithsonian Institution (on the) Astrophysical Observatory; Appropriations Expended, Results Reached, and Present Condition of the Work. Washington: 1902. V. 67

SMITHURST, BENJAMIN
Britain's Glory, and England's Bravery. London: 1689. V. 66

SMOLLETT, TOBIAS GEORGE
The Adventures of Ferdinand Count Fathom. London: 1753. V. 62
The Adventures of Ferdinand Count Fathom. London: 1771. V. 62
The Adventures of Peregrine Pickle. London: 1751. V. 62; 65; 66
The Adventures of Peregrine Pickle. Edinburgh: 1779. V. 62
The Adventures of Peregrine Pickle. London: 1795. V. 66
The Adventures of Peregrine Pickle. Harrisburgh: 1807. V. 62; 64
The Adventures of Peregrine Pickle. London: 1831. V. 65
The Adventures of Peregrine Pickle. Oxford: 1936. V. 62; 63; 64
The Adventures of Roderick Random. London: 1748. V. 62
The Adventures of Roderick Random. London: 1766. V. 62
The Adventures of Roderick Random. London: 1770. V. 62
The Adventures of Roderick Random. Edinburgh: 1784. V. 62
The Adventures of Roderick Random. Philadelphia: 1809. V. 62
The Adventures of Sir Launcelot Greaves. London: 1762. V. 62
The Adventures of Sir Launcelot Greaves. Edinburgh: 1783. V. 62
The Expedition of Humphry Clinker. London: 1771. V. 62
The Expedition of Humphry Clinker. London: 1795. V. 62
The History and Adventures of an Atom. London: 1769. V. 62
The History and Adventures of an Atom. London: 1795. V. 64
The History of England from the Revolution to the Death of George the Second. London: 1793. V. 65
The Miscellaneous Works. Edinburgh: 1806-1811. V. 66
The Miscellaneous Works. Edinburgh: 1811. V. 62; 66
The Miscellaneous Works. Edinburgh: 1820. V. 66
The Novels. Boston: 1926. V. 66
Select Essays on Commerce, Agriculture, Mines, Fisheries and Other Useful Subjects. London: 1754. V. 63
Travels through France and Italy. Dublin: 1766. V. 66
Travels through France and Italy. London: 1766. V. 66; 67
Travels through France and Italy. London: 1778. V. 66
The Works. New York: 1902. V. 65

SMUTS, M. M. S.
Anatomy of the Dromedary. Oxford: 1987. V. 62

SMYTH, A. L.
John Dalton, 1766-1844. A Bibliography of Works by and About Him. Manchester: 1966. V. 62; 65

SMYTH, AMELIA GILLESPIE
Olympia Morata: Her Times, Life and Writings. London: 1837. V. 63

SMYTH, C. PIAZZI
Madeira Meteorologic. Edinburgh: 1882. V. 65
Our Inheritance in the Great Pyramid. London: 1864. V. 66
Teneriffe, an Astronomer's Experiment: Or, Specialities of a Residence Above the Clouds. London: 1858. V. 65
The Visual (Grating and Glass Lens) Solar Spectrum in 1884. Edinburgh: 1886. V. 64

SMYTH, ELAINE
Plain Wrapper Press 1966-1988. Austin: 1993. V. 64

SMYTH, FRASER
The Diaries of Mrs. John H. Watson nee Morstan. Tetbury: 1995. V. 66

SMYTH, GEORGE LEWIS
The Monuments and Genii of St. Paul's and Westminster Abbey. London: 1826. V. 66

SMYTH, HENRY DE WOLF
A General Account of the Development of Methods of Using Atomic Energy for Military Purposes Under the Auspices of the United States Government 1940-1945. Washington: 1945. V. 64

SMYTH, JAMES CARMICHAEL
A Description of the Jail Distemper, as It Appeared Amongst the Spanish Prisoners, at Winchester, in the Year 1780.... London: 1795. V. 64

SMYTH, R. BROUGH
The Gold Fields and Mineral Districts of Victoria, With Notes on the Modes of Occurence of Gold and Other Metals and Minerals. Melbourne: 1869. V. 66

SMYTH, WARINGTON W.
A Year with the Turks or Sketches of Travel in the European and Asiatic Dominions of the Sultan. Redfield: 1854. V. 66

SMYTH, WILLIAM
Lectures on Modern History, from the Irruption of the Northern Nations to the Close of the American Revolution. London: 1840. V. 66

SMYTH, WILLIAM HENRY
The Cycle of Celestial Objects, Continued at the Hartwell Observatory to 1859.... London: 1860. V. 66
A Cycle of Celestial Objects, for the Use of Naval, Military and Private Astronomers. London: 1844. V. 65; 66
The Sailor's Word Book. 1867. V. 67
The Sailor's Word Book. London: 1867. V. 64

SMYTHE, F.
An Alpine Journey. 1934. V. 63
Camp Six. 1937. V. 63; 65
Kamet Conquered. 1932. V. 63; 65
The Kangchenjunga Adventure. London: 1930. V. 63; 64
The Valley of Flowers. 1938. V. 63; 65

SMYTHE, P. M.
The Diary of an All-Round Angler. 1956. V. 67

SMYTHE, WILLIAM E.
The Conquest of Arid America. New York: 1905. V. 64, 67

SMYTHE, WILLIAM JAMES, MRS.
Ten Months in the Fiji Islands. Oxford and London: 1864. V. 65

SMYTHIES, B. E.
The Birds of Borneo. Edinburgh: 1960. V. 62
The Birds of Borneo. Edinburgh: 1960. V. 64
Birds of Burma. Rangoon: 1940. V. 62; 67
The Birds of Burma. Edinburgh: 1953. V. 63; 67
The Birds of Burma. London: 1953. V. 62

SMYTHIES, E. A.
Big Game Shooting of Nepal. Calcutta: 1942. V. 63; 66

SMYTHIES, HARRIETTE MARIA
Married for Love. London: 1857. V. 65

SMYTHIES, R. H. RAYMOND
Records of the Smythies Family. London: 1912. V. 63

SNAGG, THOMAS
Recollections of Occurrences. The Memoirs of Thomas Snagg.... London: 1951. V. 64

SNAITH, STANLEY
April Morning. London: 1926. V. 62
A Flying Scroll. London: 1928. V. 62

SNARE, JOHN
The Velasquez Cause. Jury Court, Edinburgh, Saturday 26th and Monday 28th July 1851. Edinburgh: 1851. V. 63

SNART, JOHN
Thesaurus of Horror, or, the Charnal-House Explored!. London: 1817. V. 67

SNEED, JOHN L. T.
Lawyers and the Law. Nashville: 1876. V. 64

SNEIDER, VERN J.
The Teahouse of the August Moon. London: 1952. V. 63

SNELGRAVE, WILLIAM
A New Account of Some Parts of Guinea and the Slave Trade. London: 1734. V. 62; 65

SNELL, BRUNO
Tragicorum Graecorum Fragmenta. 1977-1986. V. 65

SNELL, HENRY JAMES
Practical Instructions in Enamel Painting on Glass, China, Titles, etc. London: 1890. V. 66

SNELL, JAMES P.
History of Sussex and Warren Counties, New Jersey. Philadelphia: 1881. V. 63; 66
History of Sussex and Warren Counties, New Jersey. Sussex: 1971. V. 66

SNELL, W. H.
Boleti of Northeastern North America. Lehre: 1970. V. 66

SNELLING, THOMAS
Seventy-One Plates of Gold and Silver Coin, with Their Weight, Fineness and Value. London: 1760. V. 62; 65

SNELLING, W. J.
The Polar Region of the Western Continent Explored. Boston: 1831. V. 65

SNIDER, C. H. J.
Under the Red Jack. Privateers of the Maritime Provinces of Canada in the War of 1812. Toronto. V. 66

SNIDOW, GORDON
Gordon Snidow: Chronicler of the Contemporary West. Flagstaff. V. 66

SNIFFEN, M. K.
The Indians of the Yukon and Tanana Valleys, Alaska. Philadelphia: 1914. V. 63

SNODGRASS, O. T.
Realistic Art and Times of the Mibres Indians. El Paso: 1977. V. 63; 66

SNODGRASS, R. E.
Shore Fishes of the Revillagigedo, Clipperton, Cocos and Galapagos Islands. Washington: 1905. V. 67

SNODGRASS, W. D.
Autumn Variations. New York: 1990. V. 67
Heart's Needle. New York: 1959. V. 63; 64; 67
Heart's Needle. London: 1960. V. 63
If Birds Build with Your Hair. New York: 1979. V. 67
The Kinder Capers. Poems. New York: 1986. V. 66; 67
Magda Goebbels. N.P: 1983. V. 65
Six Troubadour Songs. Providence: 1977. V. 65
Spring Suite. New York: 1994. V. 67
To Shape a Song. New York: 1988. V. 67

SNOW, C. H.
A Geography of Boston, County of Suffolk and the Adjacent Towns. Boston: 1830. V. 66

SNOW, C. P.
The Affair. London: 1960. V. 62
A Coat of Varnish. London: 1979. V. 64
The Masters. London: 1951. V. 63
The New Men. London: 1954. V. 65

SNOW, CHESTER
The Hypergeometric and Legendre Functions with Applications to Integral equations of Poetential Theory. Washington: 1942. V. 67

SNOW, D. W.
An Atlas of Speciation in African Non-Passerine Birds. London: 1978. V. 64

SNOW, ERASTUS
One Year in Scandinavia: Results of the Gospel in Denmark and Sweden - Sketches and Observations of the Country and People.... Liverpool: 1851. V. 66

SNOW, JACK
The Shaggy Man of Oz. Chicago: 1949. V. 62

SNOW, ROBERT
Memorials of a Tour on the Continent. London: 1845. V. 63

SNOWDEN, KEIGHLEY
The Master Spinner. A Life of Sir Swire Smith. London: 1930. V. 64; 65

SNOWDON, LORD
Israel - a First View. London: 1986. V. 62

SNOWMAN, A. KENNETH
The Art of Carl Faberge. London: 1953. V. 64

SNYDER, GARY
The Back Country. London: 1967. V. 62; 63; 64; 67
The Blue Sky. New York: 1969. V. 62; 64
Earth House Hold. London. V. 62
Earth House Hold. New York: 1969. V. 62; 63
Good Wild Sacred. Madley: 1984. V. 62
Hands, Joining: a Calligraphic Anthology. Waldron Island: 1988. V. 62
Left Out in the Rain - New Poems 1947-1985. San Francisco: 1986. V. 62
Mountains and Rivers Without End. Washington: 1996. V. 62; 64; 66; 67
Myths and Texts. New York: 1960. V. 62; 64; 66; 67
A Range of Poems. London: 1966. V. 62; 64; 65
Regarding Wave. Iowa City: 1969. V. 64; 67
Regarding Wave. London: 1970. V. 64
Regarding Wave. New York: 1970. V. 62; 65
Riprap. Ashland: 1959. V. 62; 63
Six Selections from Mountains and Rivers Without End. San Francisco: 1965. V. 62; 65
Six Selections from Mountains and Rivers Without End. London: 1967. V. 62
Smokey the Bear Sutra. Oakland: 1993. V. 64
True Night. San Juan: 1980. V. 62; 65; 67
Turtle Island. New York: 1974. V. 62

SNYDER, JAMES U.
Cain and Other Poems. Mexico: 1908. V. 67

SOAME, JOHN
Hampstead-Wells; or, Directions for the Drinking of those Waters. London: 1734. V. 65

SOANE, GEORGE
New Curiosities of Literature: and Book of the Months. London: 1849. V. 64

SOANE, JOHN
Description of the Residence of John Soane, Architect, with Some General Remarks on the State of Architectue in England.... London: 1830. V. 62; 64
Sketches in Architecture: Containing Plans and Elevations of Cottages, Villas and Other Useful Buildings.... London: 1798. V. 67

SOAR, C. D.
The British Hydracarina. London: 1925-1929. V. 64; 66

SOBEL, DAVA
Longitude. New York: 1995. V. 64; 67

SOBIESKI, JOHN
Life Story and Personal Reminiscences of Col. John Sobieski. Shelbyville: 1900. V. 63; 65; 67

SOCIAL Architecture; or, Reasons and Means for the Demolition and Reconstruction of the Social Edifice. London: 1876. V. 64

SOCIAL Science: Being Selections from John Cassell's Prize Essays, by Working Men and Women. London: 1861. V. 66

THE SOCIAL Science of the Constitution of Society or the Cause and Cure of Its Present Evils. London: 1862. V. 62

SOCIALISM - What Is Its Tendency? No. II. Edinburgh: 1847?. V. 66

SOCIETE GEOLOGIQUE DE FRANCE
Memoires de la Societe Geologique de France. Series I. Paris: 1833-1837. V. 66

SOCIETE OECONOMIQUE DE BERNE
Essays on the Spirit of Legislation, in the Encouragement of Agriculture, Population, Manufactures and Commerce. London: 1772. V. 66

SOCIETE ROYALE ET CENTRALE D'AGRICULTURE
Instruction Concernant la Propagation la Culture en Grand, et la Conservation des Pommes de Terre, Ainsi que l'Emploi de Leurs Produits, Consideres Comme Ailimentaires et Comme Pouvant etre Utilement Appliques.... Paris: 1829. V. 66

SOCIETIES FOR REFORMATION OF MANNERS
Sermons Preached to the Societies at St. Mary-Le-Bow.... London: 1727-1736. V. 66

SOCIETY FOR CONSTITUTIONAL INFORMATION
An Address to the Public from the Society for Constutional Information. London?: 1780. V. 62

SOCIETY FOR ENCOURAGEMENT OF ARTS, MANUFACTURES AND COMMERCE
Premiums Offered by the Society Instituted at London, for the Encouragement of Arts, Manufactures and Commerce. London: 1772. V. 65
Transactions of the Society.... London: 1785. V. 66

SOCIETY FOR THE CONVERSION AND RELIGIOUS INSTRUCTION
The Charter of the Society for the Conversion and Religious Instruction and Education of the Negro Slaves in the British West India Islands; to Which is Prefixed, a Short Account of the Charitable Fund, for the Application and Management of Which the Sai. London: 1825. V. 63
Report of the Incorporated Society for the Conversion and Religious Instruction and Education of the Negro Slaves in the British West India Islands for the Year MDCCCXXV. London: 1826. V. 63
Report of the Incorporated Society for the Conversion and Religious Instruction and Education of the Negro Slaves in the British West India Islands for the Year MDCCCXXX. London: 1831. V. 63
Report of the Incorporated Society for the Conversion...of the Negro Slaves in the British West India Islands from July to December, MDCCCXXIII. London: 1824. V. 63

SOCIETY FOR THE EXTINCTION OF THE SLAVE TRADE
Prospectus of the Society...Instituted June 1839. London: 1840?. V. 66

SOCIETY FOR THE IMPROVEMENT OF PRISON DISCIPLINE
Remarks on the Form and Construction of Prisons; With Appropriate Designs. London: 1826. V. 62; 66
Rules for the Government of Gaols, Houses of Correction and Penitentiaries. London: 1821. V. 63

SOCIETY FOR THE PROMOTION OF AGRICULTURE, ARTS & MANUFACTURE
Transactions of the Society for the Promotion of Agriculture, Arts and Manufactures...in...New York. Albany: 1801. V. 66

SOCIETY OF ANTIQUARIES
A List of the Society of Antiquaries of London, from the Revival in 1717 to June 19, 1796. London: 1796. V. 64

SOCIETY OF BERNE
Essays on the Spirit of Legislation, in the Encouragement of Agriculture, Population, Manufactures, and Commerce. London: 1772. V. 63

SOCIETY OF CALIFORNIA PIONEERS
Transactions of...Jan. 1st to May 7th 1863, Part I. Volume II. San Francisco: 1863. V. 67

SOCIETY OF DILETTANTI
Historical Notices of the Society of Dillettanti. London: 1855. V. 62
The Unedited Antiquities of Attica, Comprising the Architectural Remains of Eleusis, Rhamnus, Sunium. London: 1817. V. 64

SOCIETY OF DYERS AND COLOURISTS
Journal. London: 1885-1886. V. 64

SOCIETY OF FRIENDS
Transactions of the Central Relief Committee of the Society of Friends During the Famine in Ireland in 1846 and 1847. Dublin: 1852. V. 66

SOCIETY OF GENTLEMEN
The Complete Farmer; or, a General Dictionary of Husbandry.... London: 1777. V. 64

SOCIETY OF INDEPENDENT ARTISTS
Catalogue of the 9th Annual Exhibition...Waldorf Astoria. New York: 1925. V. 62

SOCIETY OF NAVAL ARCHITECTS AND MARINE ENGINEERS
Transactions. New York: 1893. V. 64

SOCIETY OF VOYAGES ROUND THE WORLD
Round the World in Three Hundred and Twenty Days. London: 1877. V. 66

THE SOCK Stories. New York: 1863. V. 66

SODDY, FREDERICK
The Interpretation of Radium. London: 1909. V. 62

SODERSTROM, J.
A. Sparrman's Ethnographical Collection from James Cook's 2nd Expedition (1772-1775). 1939. V. 67

SOEMMERRING, SAMUEL THOMAS VON
Abbildungen und Beschreibungen Einiger Misgeturten Die Sich Ehemals auf Dem Anatomischen Theater zu Cassell Befanden.... Mainz: 1791. V. 64
De Basi Encephali et Originibus Nervorum Cranio Egredientium. Gottingen: 1778. V. 62; 64
De Corporis Humani Fabrica. Trajecti ad Moenum: 1794-1801. V. 65
Icones Embryonum Humanorum. Frankfurt: 1799. V. 63
Uber das Organ der Seele. Konigsberg: 1796. V. 62; 63; 64; 66
Uber Den Saft, Welcher aus den Nerven Wieder Eingesaught wird Im Gesunden Und Kranken Zustande des Menschlichen Korpers.... Landshut: 1811. V. 66

SOHO Centenary. London: 1944. V. 62

SOILLEUX, JOHN
An Easy Method to Acquire the Italian Language, by the Help of the French and English.... London: 1793. V. 62

SOLARI, BROGLIO, MARCHIONESS
Letters...Containing a Sketch of Her Life and Recollections of Celebrated Characters. London: 1845. V. 64

SOLBRIG, O. T.
Topics in Plant Population Biology. New York: 1979. V. 66

A SOLDIER'S Album. London: 1826. V. 62

SOLDO, MAURO
Descrizione Degl Instrumenti, Delle Macchine, e Delle Soppelletili. Faenza: 1766. V. 66

SOLE, WILLIAM
Menthae Britannicae Being a New Botanical Arrangement of All the British Mints Hitherto Discovered. Bath: 1798. V. 65; 66

SOLEM, A.
Endodontoid Land Snails from Pacific Islands. Chicago: 1976-1986. V. 66

SOLIS Y RIBADENEYRA, ANTONIO DE
Historia de la Conquista de Mexico, Poblacion, y Progressos de la America Septentrional.... Madrid: 1684. V. 62
The History of the Conquest of Mexico by the Spaniards. London: 1724. V. 66

SOLLAS, W. J.
Challenger Voyage. Zoology. Part 63. Tetractinellida. 1888. V. 66

SOLLID, ROBERT B.
Calamnity Jane - a Study in Historical Criticism. Helena: 1958. V. 67

SOLLOWAY, JOHN
The Alien Benedictines of York. Leeds: 1910. V. 63; 65

SOLLY, HENRY
The Life of Henry Morley, Professor of the English Language and Literature at University College, London. London: 1898. V. 67
These Eighty Years, or, the Story of an Unfinished Life. London: 1893. V. 64
Working Men's Social Clubs and Educational Institutes.... London: 1904. V. 64

SOLLY, N. Neal
Memoir of the Life of David Cox.... London: 1873. V. 62

SOLLY, SAMUEL
The Human Brain: Its Structure, Physiology and Disases, with a Description of the Typical Forms of Brain in the Animal Kingdom. Philadelphia: 1848. V. 64; 67

SOLOGUEREN, JAVIER
Dedalo Dormido. Mexico City: 1944. V. 67

SOLON, M. L.
A Brief History of Old English Porcelain and Its Manufactories.... London: 1903. V. 62
Ceramic Literature: an Analytical Index to the Works.... London: 1910. V. 62

SOLOVYEVA, M.
Matreshki. Moscow: 1930. V. 64

SOLZHENITSYN, ALEXANDER
August 1914. The Red Wheel/Knot 1. New York: 1989. V. 62; 64
Dria Polizy Dela. Chicago: 1963. V. 67
Odin den' Ivana Denisovicha. Moscow: 1963. V. 67
Odin den'Ivana Denisovicha. (One Day in the Life of Ivan Denisovich). London. V. 67
One Day in the Life of Ivan Denisovich. London: 1963. V. 64; 67

SOMASEGARAN, P.
Handbook for Rhizobia, Methods in Legume-Rhizobium Technology. New York: 1994. V. 67

SOMBART, WERNER
The Jews and Modern Capitalism.... London: 1913. V. 63

SOME Account of the Conduct of the Religious Society of Friends Towards the Indian Tribes in the Settlement of the Colonies of East and West Jersey and Pennsylvania.... London: 1844. V. 62; 63; 66

SOME Account of the Orang Outang, Collected from the Best Authorities. Boston: 1844. V. 62

SOME Brief Memoirs of the Life of David Hall; with an Account of the Life of His Father, John Hall.... London: 1799. V. 67

SOME British Ballads. New York: 1920. V. 65

SOME Further Particulars in Relation to the Case of Admiral Byng. London: 1756. V. 65

SOME Historical Memoires of the Life and Actions of His Royal Highness, the Renowned and Most Illustrious Prince James Duke of York and Albany, &c...from His Birth, Anno 1633...1682. London: 1683. V. 62

SOME Imagist Poets, 1915. Boston: 1915. V. 62

SOME Observations on the Bill, Intitled "An Act for Granting to His Majesty an Excise Upon Wines, and Spirits Distilled, sold by Retail or Consumed Within this Province...". Boston: 1754. V. 66

SOME Particular Matter of Fact, Relating to the Administration of Affairs in Scotland Under the Duke of Lauderdale. London: 1679. V. 62; 65

SOME Queries on the Minutes of the Council of War Held at Gibraltar the Fourth of May Last, from Which Good Reasons May be Drawn, for a Noble Colonel's Having Taken so Large a Part in the Defence of Admiral B---g. London: 1757. V. 65

SOME Remarks on a Pamphlet Intituled, Reflections on the Expediency of Opening the Trade with Turkey. London: 1753. V. 65

SOME Southwestern Pottery Types. Series I-V: Together With a Method for the Designation of Southwestern Pottery Types. Gila Pueblo: 1930-1936. V. 63; 66

SOMEREN, V. D. VAN
A Bird Watcher in Kenya. 1958. V. 67

SOMERS, JOHN SOMERS
The Security of Englishmen's Lives, or the Trust, Power and Duty of the Grand Juries of England. Tewksbury: 1798. V. 65; 66

SOMERSET, EDWARD ADOLPHUS SEYMOUR, 11TH DUKE OF
Alternate Circles and their Connexion with the Ellipse. London: 1850. V. 66
A Treatise in Which the Elementary Properties of the Ellipse are Deduced from the Properties of the Cricle and Geometrically Demonstrated. London: 1843. V. 66

SOMERSFT, H.
Our Village Life. 1884. V. 65
Our Village Life. London: 1884. V. 64

SOMERSET, HENRY
Songs of Adieu. London: 1889. V. 63

SOMERVELL, JOHN
Isaac and Rachel Wilson, Quakers of Kendal 1714-1785. London: 1924. V. 63
Isaac and Rachel Wilson, Quakers of Kendal 1714-1785. London: 1925. V. 65
Water-Power Mills of South Westmorland on the Kent Bela and Gilpin and Their Tributaries. London: 1909. V. 62
Water-Power Mills of South Westmorland on the Kent, Bela and Gilpin and Their Tributaries. Kendal: 1930. V. 64

SOMERVELL, T. HOWARD
After Everest. London: 1936. V. 63

SOMERVILLE, A.
At Midnight Comes the Killer. 1962. V. 63

SOMERVILLE, ALEXANDER
The Autobiography of a Working Man, by One Who Was Whistled at the Plough. London: 1848. V. 67
Conservative Science of Nations, (Preliminary Instalment) being the First Complete Narrative of Somerville's Diligent Life in the Service of Public Safety in Britain. Montreal: 1860. V. 67
The Whistler at the Plough.... Manchester: 1852-1853. V. 67

SOMERVILLE, BOYLE T.
Ocean Passages for the World. London: 1950. V. 62; 66

SOMERVILLE, EDITH OENONE
All on the Irish Shore - Irish Sketches. London: 1903. V. 64
Beggars on Horseback: a Riding Tour in North Wales. Edinburgh: 1895. V. 65
Dan Russel the Fox.... London: 1911. V. 65
French Leave. 1928. V. 65
Further Experiences of an Irish R.M. London: 1908. V. 64
Happy Days!. London: 1946. V. 65
In Mr. Knox's Country. London: 1915. V. 64
In the Vine Country. London: 1893. V. 65
An Incorruptible Irishman. 1932. V. 67
An Incorruptible Irishman, Being an Account of the Chief Justice Charles Kendal Bushe and of His Wife, Nancy Crampton and Their Times 1767- 1843. London: 1932. V. 65
An Irish Cousin. London: 1889. V. 65; 66
Irish Memories. London: 1917. V. 65
Maria and Some Other Dogs. London: 1949. V. 65
Mount Music. London: 1919. V. 64
Naboth's Vineyard: a Novel. London: 1891. V. 65
Notions in Garrison. London: 1941. V. 65
A Patrick's Day Hunt. London. V. 64; 66; 67
A Patrick's Day Hunt. Westminster: 1902. V. 65
The Real Charlotte. London: 1894. V. 65
Sarah's Youth. London: 1938. V. 65
The Silver Fox. London: 1898. V. 65
Slipper's ABC of Fox Hunting. 1903. V. 62; 64
Slipper's ABC of Fox Hunting. London: 1903. V. 65
Some Experiences of an Irish R.M. London: 1899. V. 65

SOMERVILLE, EDITH OENONE continued
Somerville and Ross - a Biography. London: 1968. V. 64
The Sporting Works. New York: 1927. V. 64; 65
The States through Irish Eyes. Boston and New York: 1930. V. 65
The States through Irish Eyes. 1931. V. 62; 64
The Story of the Discontented Little Elephant. London: 1912. V. 65
Stray-Aways. London: 1920. V. 65
The Sweet Cry of Hounds. London: 1936. V. 62
Through Connemara in a Governess Cart. London: 1893. V. 65
Wheel-Tracks.... London: 1923. V. 65

SOMERVILLE, JOHN SOUTHEY
Facts and Observations Relative to Sheep, Wool, Ploughs and Oxen, in Which the Importance of Improving the Short-Wooled Breeds of Sheep, by a Mixture of the Merino Blood.... London: 1809. V. 63

SOMERVILLE, MARTHA
Personal Recollections, from Early Life to Old Age, of Mary Somerville; with Selections from Her Correspondence. Boston: 1874. V. 67

SOMERVILLE, MARY
On Molecular and Microscopic Science. London: 1869. V. 65
Personal Recollections, from Early Life to Old Age, of Mary Somerville. London: 1873. V. 64

SOMERVILLE, WILLIAM
The Chace. London: 1735. V. 66
The Chace. Dublin: 1799. V. 62
The Chace. New York: 1929. V. 67
The Chase. London: 1802. V. 67
Field-Sports. A Poem. Humbly Address'd to His Royal Highness the Prince. London: 1742. V. 66
Occasional Poems, Translations, Fables, Tales &c. London: 1727. V. 66

SOMERVILLE LARGE, PETER
The Coast of West Cork. 1972. V. 67

SOMES, JOSEPH H. V.
Old Vincennes, the History of a Famous Old Town and Its Glorious Past. New York: 1962. V. 62

SOMMER, ANNIE VAN
Daylight in the Harem, a New Era for Moslem Women. Edinburgh and London: 1911. V. 65

SOMMERVILLE, FRANKFORT
The Spirt of Paris. London: 1913. V. 65

SOMNER, WILLIAM
A Treatise on the Roman Ports and Forts in Kent. Oxford: 1693. V. 66

SONDHEIM, STEPHEN
Anyone Can Whistle. New York: 1964. V. 66
Company. New York: 1970. V. 66
Do I Hear a Waltz?. New York: 1966. V. 66
Follies. New York: 1971. V. 66
A Funny Thing Happened on the Way to the Forum. New York: 1962. V. 66
Pacific Overtures. New York: 1977. V. 66
Sunday in the Park with George. New York: 1986. V. 63; 64; 66
Sweeney Todd. New York: 1979. V. 66
West Side Story. New York: 1957. V. 66

SONDLEY, FOSTER ALEXANDER
A History of Buncombe County, North Carolina. Asheville: 1930. V. 66

SONENSHINE, D. E.
Ecological Dynamics of Tick-Borne Zoonoses. New York: 1994. V. 65

THE SONG-Singer's Amusing Companion. Boston: 1818. V. 63

THE SONG of Roland. London: 1937. V. 64

SONGS and Stories. Charlestown: 1857. V. 65

SONGS, Duets, Trios and Choruses in the New Vaudeville Called She Would In She Could. London: 1828. V. 63

SONGS, Madrigals and Sonnets. London: 1849. V. 67

SONGS of Our Fathers - Re-set in Guinness Time. Dublin: 1936. V. 62

SONGS of Our Grand Fathers: Reset In Guinness Time. Dublin: 1936. V. 66

SONGS of the Chace...Hunting, Shooting, Racing, Coursing, Angling, Hawking.... 1811. V. 64

SONGS of the Edinburgh Angling Club. Edinburgh: 1879. V. 66

SONGS of the North. London: Sep. 1920. V. 62

SONGS of the South. Richmond: 1862. V. 63

THE SONGSTER'S Jewel. Durham: 1838. V. 62; 65
THE SONGSTER'S Jewel. London: 1840. V. 62; 65

SONMEZ, NEDIM
From Ebru to Marbled Paper: on the History of Marbled Paper in the Orient and Its Way to Europe. Tubingen: 1995. V. 64
A History of Marbled Flowers. Tubingen: 1991. V. 64
Turkisch Papir/Ebru/Turkish Marbled Paper. Tubingen: 1987. V. 64

SONN, HAROLD A.
A History of Colonel Joseph Beavers (2nd Regt. N. J. Militia) (1728-1 816) of Hunterdon County, New Jersey. Short Hills: 1948. V. 63; 66

SONNENSCHEIN, WILLIAM SWAN
The Best Books. A Reader's Guide to the Choice of the Best Available Books (about 100,000) in Every Department of Science, Art and Literature, with the Dates of the First and Last Editions.... New York: 1910. V. 66

SONNICHSEN, C. L.
Alias Billy the Kid. Albuquerque: 1955. V. 64; 66
The Mescalero Apaches. Norman: 1958. V. 67
Pass of the North. El Paso: 1968. V. 63
The State National Since 1881: the Pioneer Bank of El Paso. El Paso: 1971. V. 65
Ten Texas Feuds. Albuquerque: 1957. V. 63; 64; 66

SONNINI, CHARLES NICOLAS
Travels in Upper and Lower Egypt. London: 1799. V. 65; 66

SONTAG, J.
Hints for Non-Commissioned Officers on Actual Service. London: 1804. V. 66

SONTAG, SUSAN
Against Interpretation and Other Essays. New York: 1966. V. 66
Dancers on a Plane. Cage, Cunningham, Johns. London: 1989. V. 64
Death Kit. New York: 1967. V. 65
I, Etcetera. New York: 1978. V. 64
Illness as Metaphor. New York: 1978. V. 63
The Way We Live Now. London: 1991. V. 64

SOOS, TROY
Murder at Fenway Park. New York: 1994. V. 66; 67

SOPATER, OF BEREA
Letter Addressed to the Right Rev. Father in God, Ricardus, D.D. by Divine Permission Bishop of the Diocese of Virginia. America: 1819. V. 66

SOPER, EILEEN
Happy Rabbit. London: 1947. V. 65

SOPER, JACK
The Black Cliff. The History of Rock Climbing on Clogwyn du'r Arddu. London: 1971. V. 64

SOPHIAN, ABRAHAM
Epidemic Cerebrospinal Meningitis. St. Louis: 1912. V. 67

SOPHOCLES
Antigone. Haarlem: 1975. V. 62; 63; 64; 66
Antigone. Greenbrae: 1978. V. 62
Sophoclis Quae Extant Omnia Cum Veterum Grammaticorum Scholiis.... Londini: 1824. V. 65
Sophoclis Tragoediae Septum. Geneva: 1568. V. 64
Tragaediae cum Commentariis (in Greek). Venice: 1502. V. 63; 66

SOPPE, JOAN
Awkward Peeping. Cedar Rapids: 1995. V. 64
Trespasses. Cedar Rapids: 1993. V. 64

SOPWITH, THOMAS
An Account of the Mining Districts of Alston Moor, Weardale and Teesdale in Cumberland and Durham.... Alnwick: 1833. V. 64; 65; 66

SORBELLONE, FRANCESCO
Informatione a Regi, e Gran Prencipi d'un Padiglione da Letto in Forma Quadra a Sua Proportione, Ben Composto Pretioso & Superbissimo. Milan: 1625. V. 67

SORBIERE, SAMUEL DE
A Voyage to England, Containing Many Things Relating to the State of Learning, Religion and Other Curiosities of that Kingdom. London: 1709. V. 62

SORDO, E.
Moorish Spain: Cordoba, Seville, Granada. New York: 1963. V. 65

SOREDD, CURTIUS
One Hundred and Thirty Quatrains. Pasadena: 1928. V. 64

SORENSON, ALFRED
Early History of Omaha: Walks and Talks Among the Old Settlers: a Series of Sketches in the Shape of a Connected Narrative of the Events and Incidents of Early Times in Omaha, Together with a Brief Mention of the Most Important Events of Later Years. Omaha: 1876. V. 65

SORET, JACQUES LOUIS
Sur la Loi des Equivalents Electro-Chimiques. Geneva: 1855. V. 64

SORREL, G. MOXLEY
Recollections of a Confederate Officer. Jackson: 1958. V. 63
Recollections of a Confederate Staff Officer. New York and Washington: 1905. V. 63

SORRENTINO, GILBERT
A Beehive Arranged on Humane Principles. New York: 1986. V. 64
The Darkness Surrounds Us. Highlands: 1960. V. 63
The Sky Changes. New York: 1966. V. 67

SOSEKI, MUSO
Sun at Midnight. New York: 1985. V. 64

SOTHEBY & CO.
Catalogue of the Newton Papers...Which Will Be Sold by Auction by Sotheby & Co. London: 1936. V. 62

SOTHEBY & CO. continued
Catalogue of Valuable Printed Books from the Broxbourne Library Illustrating the Spread of Printing. London: 1977-1978. V. 62

SOTHEBY, WILLIAM
Constance de Castile. A Poem in Ten Cantos. London: 1810. V. 62; 67
Saul, A Poem, in Two Parts. London: 1807. V. 64
A Tour through Parts of Wales, Sonnets, Odes and Other Poems. London: 1794. V. 64; 66

SOTO, HERNANDO DE
Narratives of the Career of Hernando De Soto in the Conquest of Florida, As Told by a Knight of Elvas and In Relation by Luys Hernandez de Biedma, Factor of the Expedition. New York: 1922. V. 66

SOULE, FRANK
The Annals of San Francisco. New York: 1855. V. 62; 63

SOULE, H. H.
Canoe and Camp Cookery. New York: 1885. V. 67

SOULE, MAURICE
Le Grande Adventure - LePoPee Du Comte De Raousset - Boulbon Au Mexique (1850-1854). Paris: 1926. V. 64; 67

SOULSBY, B. H.
Catalogue of the Work of Linneaus.... London: 1933. V. 67

SOULT, NICOLAS, JEAN DE DIEU
Extracts from the Journal of Marshal Soult. Newburyport: 1817. V. 66

THE SOURCE of the Mechanical Opera. Cincinnati: 1995. V. 62

SOUTH and Southwest Texas - a Work for Newspaper and Library Reference. N.P: 1928. V. 64

SOUTH CAROLINA. CONVENTION - 1852
Journal of the State Convention of South Carolina; Together with the Resolution and Ordinance. Columbia: 1852. V. 63; 65; 66

SOUTH CAROLINA. LEGISLATURE - 1831
Debate in the South Carolina Legislature, in December 1830, on the Reports of the Committees of Both Houses in Favor of Convention &c. Columbia: 1831. V. 66

SOUTH CAROLINA. SECESSION - 1860
Declaration of the Immediate Causes Which Induce and Justify the Secession of South Carolina from the Federal Union; and the Ordnance of Secession. Charleston: 1860. V. 63; 66

SOUTH CAROLINA. SENATE - 1878
Report of the Joint Committee on Public Frauds and Election of Hon. J. J. Patterson to the United States Senate, Made by the General Assembly of South Carolina at the Regular Session 1877-1878. Columbia: 1878. V. 67

SOUTH Dakota. Pierre: 1938. V. 65; 67

SOUTH DAKOTA
Constitutional Debates 1885. Volume I. Huron: 1907. V. 63; 66
Constitutional Debates 1889. Volume II. Huron. V. 63; 66

SOUTH Dakota Brand Book 1898-1899. Fort Pierre: 1899. V. 62

SOUTH Dakota Historical Collections. Volume I. Aberdeen: 1902. V. 65

SOUTH Dakota Historical Collections. Volume VI. Sioux Falls: 1912. V. 65

SOUTH in the Building of the Nation. Richmond: 1909. V. 62

SOUTH KENSINGTON EDUCATIONAL MUSEUM
Catalogue of the Educational Division of the South Kensington Educational Museum. London: 1862. V. 66; 67

SOUTH, R.
The Moths of the British Isles. London: 1907-1909. V. 62

SOUTH, ROBERT
Animadversions Upon Dr. Sherlock's Book Entituled a Vindication of the Holy and Ever Blessed Trinity.... London: 1693. V. 67

SOUTH Wales Association for the Improvement of Roads. 1792. V. 66

SOUTHAM, B. C.
Jane Austen: The Critical Heritage. London: 1969-1987. V. 63

SOUTHARD, ELMER ERNEST
The Kingdom of Evils: Psychiatric Social Work Presented in 100 Case Histories Together with a Classification of Social Divisions in Evil. New York: 1922. V. 65
Neurosyphilis: Modern Systematic Diagnosis and Treatment Presented Hundred and Thirty-Seven Case Histories. Boston: 1917. V. 65

SOUTHCOTT, JOANNA
Answer to Five Charges in the Leeds Mercury, Four of Which are Absolutely False.... London: 1805. V. 65
Letters on Various Subjects from Mrs. Joanna Southcott to Miss Townley. London: 1804. V. 65

SOUTHERN Chivalry. The Adventures of G. Whillikens, C.S.A., Knight of the Golden Circle and of Guinea Pete, His Negro Squire. Philadelphia: 1861. V. 62; 63

THE SOUTHERN Christian Leadership Conference Story in Words and Pictures. Atlanta: 1964. V. 67

THE SOUTHERN Harmony Songbook. New York: 1939. V. 65

THE SOUTHERN Literary Messenger. Richmond: 1839-1844. V. 67

SOUTHERN Oregon. Stockton: 1961. V. 63

SOUTHERN PACIFIC CO.
Southwest Louisiana on the Line of the Southern Pacific Co. Chicago: 1892. V. 65

SOUTHERN Scenes and Scenery. Charleston: 1856. V. 63; 66

SOUTHERN, TERRY
Blue Movie. London: 1973. V. 62
Candy. New York: 1964. V. 64
The Magic Christian. New York: 1960. V. 64
Red Dirt Marijuana and Other Tastes. New York: 1967. V. 66

SOUTHERNE, THOMAS
The Fate of Capua. London: 1700. V. 64
The Spartan Dame. London: 1719. V. 66
The Works. Volume the First (The Second). London: 1721. V. 62

SOUTHERN EXPOSITION, LOUISVILLE
Illustrated Catalogue of the Art Gallery of the Southern Exposition Louisville, Ky. August 16-October 25, 1884. Louisville: 1884. V. 64

SOUTHESK, EARL OF
Origins of Pictish Symbolism, with Notes on the Sun Boar.... Edinburgh: 1893. V. 63

SOUTHEY, CHARLES CUTHBERT
The Life and Correspondence of the Late Robert Southey. London: 1849-1850. V. 64

SOUTHEY, ROBERT
All for Love and the Pilgrim to Compostella. London: 1829. V. 65
The Doctor &c. London: 1834-1847. V. 65
The Life of Nelson. London: 1884. V. 67
Lives of Uneducated Poets, to Which are Added Attempts in Verse, by John Jones, an Old Servant. London: 1836. V. 66
Madoc. London: 1805. V. 66
Omnia, or Horae Otiosores. London: 1812. V. 62; 65
Poems. (with) Poems. Second Volume. Bristol: 1797. V. 62
Poems. (with) Poems. Second Volume. Bristol: 1797-1800. V. 65
The Poetical Works. London: 1853. V. 62; 66
The Poet's Pilgrimage to Waterloo. London: 1816. V. 65
Roderick, the Last of the Goths. London: 1815. V. 62

SOUTHGATE, RICHARD
Museum Southgatianum, Being a Catalogue of the Valuable Collection of Books, Coins, Medals and Natural History.... London: 1795. V. 65

SOUTHWART, ELIZABETH
Bronte Moors and Villages. London: 1923. V. 63

SOUTHWELL, HENRY
The New Book of Martyrs; or Complete Christian Martyrology. London: 1765?. V. 63

SOUTHWELL, ROBERT
The Complete Poems. 1872. V. 63

SOUTHWELL, T.
Fauna of British India. Cestoda. 1930. V. 63
Fauna of British India. Cestoda. London: 1930. V. 62; 66
The Seals and Whales of the British Seas. London: 1881. V. 62

SOUTHWOOD, MARION
Tit for Tat. New York: 1856. V. 63

SOUTHWOOD, MARY
Beauty and Booty The Watchword of New Orleans. New York: 1867. V. 62

SOUTHWOOD, T. R. E.
Land and Water Bugs of the British Isles. London: 1959. V. 62

SOUVENIR of Scotland. Edinburgh: 1895. V. 67

SOUVENIR Of Scotland, Its Cities, Lakes and Mountains. London: 1897. V. 62

SOUVENIR of the West Highlands and the Caledonian Canal. London: 1892. V. 62

SOUVENIR Of Yarmouth Nova Scotia. Yarmouth: 1902?. V. 63

SOUVENIR to the West Highlands Tourist's Guide to the West Highlands, from Stirling to Oban, Staffa, and Iona.... London. V. 62; 63

SOUVESTRE, EMILE
Translations from the French of Emile Souvestre. By Elizabeth Strachey. N.P: 1856. V. 66

SOUVESTRE, PIERRE
The Long Arm of Fantomas. New York: 1924. V. 67

SOUZA, ADELAIDE MARIE EMILIE
Adele De Senage, ou Lettres de Lord Syndenham. Geneve & Paris: 1798. V. 65
Adele de Senange, ou Lettres de Lord Sydenham. Londres: 1794. V. 67
Eugene de Rothelin. Paris: 1810. V. 63
Mademoiselle de Tournon. Paris: 1820. V. 63; 67
Oevures. Paris: 1865. V. 63

SOUZA-ARAUJO, HERACLIDES CESAR DE
Historia da Lepra no Brasil. Rio de Janeiro: 1946-1948. V. 65

THE SOVERAIGNTY Of Kings; or an Absolute Answer and Confutation of the Groundlesse Vindication of Psalme 105.15. London: 1642. V. 67

THE SOVIET Arctic. Moscow/Leningrad: 1939. V. 66

SOWERBY, A. DE C.
Nature in Chinese Art. New York: 1940. V. 62

SOWERBY, G. B.
Companion to Mr. Kingsley's Glaucus. Cambridge: 1858. V. 65
A Conchological Manual. London: 1842. V. 62
A Conchological Manual. London: 1852. V. 64
Illustrated Index of British Shells. 1887. V. 63
Illustrated Index of British Shells.... London: 1887. V. 62
Thesaurus Conchyliorum, or Monographs.... London: 1847-1887. V. 66

SOWERBY, GITHA
Childhood. London: 1907. V. 64
The Happy Book. London. V. 64
The Wise Book. London: 1906. V. 64

SOWERBY, HENRY
Popular Mineralogy. London: 1850. V. 63

SOWERBY, J.
The Genera of Recent and Fossil Shells. 1820-1834. V. 66

SOWERBY, J. DE C.
Tortoises, Terrapins and Turtles. Ithaca: 1970. V. 66

SOWERBY, J. G.
Rooks and their Neighbours. London: 1895. V. 67

SOWERBY, JAMES
A Botanical Drawing Book, or an an Easy Introduction to Drawing Flowers According to Nature. London: 1807. V. 66
English Botany. 1790-1814. V. 65
English Botany. London: 1790-1834. V. 65
English Botany. London: 1847-1854. V. 62
English Botany. London: 1863-1886. V. 62
English Botany.... London: 1902. V. 64

SOWERBY, JOHN EDWARD
British Wild Flowers. London: 1894. V. 62
British Wild Flowers. London: 1914. V. 62

SOYER, ALEXIS
The Gastronomic Regenerator; a Simplified and Entirely New System of Cookery with Nearly Two Thousand Practical Receipts. London: 1846. V. 62

SPACE Technology. Los Angeles: 1958. V. 66

SPAENDONCK, G. VAN
Flowers Drawn from Nature.... 1957. V. 66

SPAIN. CONSTITUTION - 1812
Constitucion Politica de la Monarquia Espanola. Cadiz: 1812. V. 62

SPALDING, V. M.
The White Pine. Washington: 1899. V. 63

SPALLANZANI, LAZZARO
Dissertations Relative to the Natural History of Animals and Vegetables. London: 1789. V. 67
Experiences sur la Digestion de l'Homme et de Differentes Especes d'Animaux. Geneva: 1783. V. 65
Opuscules de Physique, Animale et Vegetale. Padua & Paris: 1787. V. 67

SPALTEHOLZ, WERNER
Hand Atlas of Human Anatomy. Philadelphia. V. 67

SPANISH American Folk Songs of New Mexico. N.P: 1936-1937. V. 63

SPARE, AUSTIN OSMAN
Axiomata. The Witches Sabbath. 1992. V. 66

SPARGO, JOHN
The Potters and Potteries of Bennington (Vermont). Boston: 1926. V. 66

SPARK, MURIEL
The Bachelors. London: 1960. V. 62
Child of Light: a Reassessment of Mary Wollstonecraft Shelley. Hadleigh, Essex: 1951. V. 63; 65
Doctors of Philosophy - a Play. London: 1963. V. 65
The Driver's Seat. London: 1970. V. 65
The Fanfarlo and Other Verse. Aldington: 1952. V. 62
John Masefield. London: 1953. V. 65
Not to Disturb. London: 1971. V. 63
The Portobello Road and Other Stories. Helsinki: 1990. V. 63; 65
The Very Fine Clock. London: 1969. V. 65

SPARKE, ARCHIBALD
A Bibliography of the Dialect Literature of Cumberland, Westmorland and Lancashire North-of-the-Sands. Kendal: 1907. V. 64

SPARKMAN, ROBERT S.
The Texas Surgical Society: The First Fifty Years. Dallas: 1965. V. 64

SPARKS, JARED
Correspondence of the American Revolution: Being Letters of Eminent Men to George Washington from the Time of His Taking Command of the Army to End of His Presidency. Boston: 1853. V. 65
Travels and Adventures of John Ledyard.... London: 1834. V. 64

SPARKS, WILLIAM
The Apache Kid, a Bear Fight and Other True Stories of the Old West. Los Angeles: 1926. V. 65

SPARLING, HENRY HALLIDAY
The Kelmscott Press and William Morris Master-Craftsman. London: 1924. V. 62; 63

SPARRMAN, ANDERS
A Voyage Round the World with Captain James Cook in HMS Resolution. Waltham St. Lawrence: 1944. V. 66
A Voyage to the Cape of Good Hope, Towards the Antarctic Polar Circle and Round the World.... London: 1785. V. 64

SPARROW 1-12. Los Angeles: 1973. V. 65

SPARROW, JOHN
Line Upon Line an Epigraphical Anthology. Cambridge: 1967. V. 64; 67
Poems in Latin Together with a Few Inscriptions. London: 1941. V. 67
Visible Words - a Study of Inscriptions in and As Books and Works of Art. Cambridge: 1969. V. 62

SPARROW, WALTER SHAW
Angling in British Art Through Five Centuries: Prints, Pictures, Books. London: 1923. V. 64
British Sporting Artists from Barlow to Herring. London: 1922. V. 66; 67
The English House. London: 1908. V. 63
Henry Alken. London and New York: 1927. V. 62

SPATER, GEORGE
A Marriage of Two Minds - an Intimate Portrait of Leonard and Virginia Woolf. London: 1977. V. 65

SPAULDING, E. G.
Resource of War...the Credit of the Government Made Immediately Available. Buffalo: 1869. V. 62

SPAULDING, EDWARD S.
Adobe Days Along the Channel. N.P: 1957. V. 63; 66
Adobe Days Along the Channel. Santa Barbara: 1957. V. 62
Ed Borein's West. Santa Barbara: 1952. V. 66

SPAULDING, THOMAS M.
Early Military Books in the University of Michigan Libraries. Ann Arbor: 1941. V. 63

THE SPEAKING Picture Book. N.P: 1890. V. 64; 65

SPEAKING Picture-Book for the Amusement of Children by Image, Verse and Sound. Sonneberg: 1880. V. 65

SPEAR, DAVID M.
The Neugents. Close to Home. Winston-Salem: 1993. V. 63

SPEAR, ELSA
Bozeman Trail Scrapbook. Sheridan: 1967. V. 65
Fort Phil Kearny Dakota Territory 1866-1868. Sheridan: 1939. V. 65; 67

SPEARS, JOHN R.
Captain Nathaniel Brown Palmer. New York: 1922. V. 62
The Gold Diggings of Cape Horn: a Study of Life in Tierra Del Fuego and Patagonia. New York: 1895. V. 65
A History of the Mississippi Valley From Its Discovery to the End of Foreign Domination. New York: 1903. V. 67
Illustrated Sketches of Death Valley and Other Borax Deserts of the Pacific Coast. Chicago: 1892. V. 63; 66

SPEARS, VERA SMITH
The Fairforest Story. Charlotte: 1974. V. 67

SPECHT, R. L.
Records of the American - Australian Scientific Expedition to Arnhem Land. 4. Zoology. Parkville: 1964. V. 63

SPECIAL Services Held at St. Philip's Church, Charleston, S.C. on the 12th and 13th of May, 1875, in Commemoration of the Planting of the Church of England in the Province of Carolina. With the Sermon Preached.... Charleston;: 1876. V. 67

SPECIMENS of American Poetry. Boston: 1829. V. 67

SPECK, FRANK G.
Naskapi - the Savage Hunters of the Labrador Peninsular. Norman: 1935. V. 63

THE SPECTATOR. London: 1808. V. 64; 65

SPECTATOR'S Gallery. London: 1933. V. 63

SPEDDING, JAMES
Publishers and Authors. London: 1867. V. 65

SPEDON, ANDREW LEARMONT
Rambles Among the Blue-Noses; or, Reminiscences of a Tour through New Brunswick and Nova Scotia During the Summer of 1862. Montreal: 1861. V. 64

SPEECE, CONRAD
The Mountaineer. Harrisonburg: 1818. V. 66

THE SPEECH that Was Intended to Have Been Spoken by the Terrae- Filius, in the Theatre at O----d, July 13, 1713. London: 1713. V. 62

A SPEECH Without Doors Concerning Exportation of Wool. Edinburgh?: 1704. V. 63

SPEECHLY, WILLIAM
A Treatise on the Culture of the Pineapple and the Management of the Hot-House. Together with a Description of Every Species of Insect that Infest Hot-Houses.... York: 1779. V. 64

SPEECHLY, WILLIAM continued
A Treatise on the Culture of the Vine; with New Hints on the Formation of Vineyards in England...A Treatise on the Culture of the Pine Apple.... London: 1821. V. 63

SPEED, JOHN
The History of Great Britaine Under the Conquests of Ye Romans, Saxons, Danes and Normans. Their Orchids, Manners, Warres, Coines and Seales.... London: 1611. V. 65

SPEEDY, TOM
Craigmillar and Its Environs. Selkirk: 1892. V. 62
The Natural History of Sport in Scotland with Rod and Gun. 1920. V. 66
The Natural History of Sport in Scotland with Rod and Gun. London: 1920. V. 62; 65
Sport in the Highlands and Lowlands of Scotland with Rod and Run. London: 1886. V. 67

SPEER, EMORY
Lincoln, Lee, Grant and Other Biographical Addresses. New York: 1909. V. 62; 63; 65

SPEER, JOHN
Life of General James H. Lane - the Liberator of Kansas. Garden City: 1896. V. 64; 67

SPEER, MARION A.
Western Trails. Huntington Beach: 1931. V. 64; 67

SPEICH, JOHN
Notes on Blood Meridian. Louisville: 1993. V. 67

SPEIDELL, JOHN
A Geometricall Extraction, or a Compendious Collection of the Chiefe and Choyse Problems, Collected Out of the Best, and Latest, Writers. London: 1617. V. 65

SPEIGHT, HARRY
Chronicles and Stories of Old Bingley. London: 1898. V. 65
The Craven and North-West Yorkshire Highlands. London: 1892. V. 64; 65; 66
The Craven and North-West Yorkshire Highlands. Otley: 1989. V. 65
Kirkby Overblow and District. London: 1903. V. 64; 65
Lower Wharfedale. London: 1902. V. 62; 65
Nidderdale and the Garden of the Nidd: a Yorkshire Rhineland. London: 1894. V. 65
Nidderdale from Nun Monkton to Whernside. London: 1906. V. 65
Romantic Richmondshire. London: 1897. V. 65
Tadcaster and Environs. London. V. 65
Tramps and Drives Round Skipton, Grassington, and Malham. Bradford: 1903. V. 65
Upper Nidderdale, with Forest of Knaresborough. London: 1906. V. 65; 66
Upper Wharfedale. London: 1900. V. 65

SPEIGHT, THOMAS WILKINSON
A Barren Title. London: 1886. V. 67
The Doom of Siva. London: 1899. V. 67
The Grey Monk. London: 1895. V. 67

SPEISER, W.
Oriental Architecture in Colour. London: 1965. V. 62; 65

SPEKE, JOHN HANNING
Journal of the Discovery of the Source of the Nile. 1863. V. 65

SPELMAN, HENRY
De non Temerandis Ecclesiis, Churches Not to be Violated. Oxford: 1646. V. 63
Glossarium Archaeiologicum: Continens Latino-Barbara. London: 1687. V. 63
Glossarium Archaiologicum: Continens Latino-Barbara. Londini: 1664. V. 65
Tithes Too Hot to Be Touched. London: 1646. V. 63

SPELMAN, JOHN
Aelfredi Magni Anglorum Regis Invictissimi Vita Tribus Libris Comprehensa.... Oxford: 1678. V. 62; 65; 66

SPELTA, ANTONIO MARIA
Historia...De'fatti Notabili Occorsi Nell'Universo & in Particolare del Regno de'Gothi, de Longobardi, de i Duchi di Milano & d'Altre Segnalate Persone, dall'anno di Nostra Salute VL sino al MDIIIC.... Pavia: 1602-1603. V. 62

SPENCE, GEORGE
An Address to the Public and More Especially to the Members of the House of Commons, on the Present Unsatisfactory State of the Court of Chancery.... London: 1839. V. 63

SPENCE, JOSEPH
An Essay on Mr. Pope's Odyssey. London: 1747. V. 67
Observations, Anecdotes and Characters of Books and Men. London: 1820. V. 62; 66
Observations, Anecdotes and Characters of Books and Men Collected from Conversation. Oxford: 1966. V. 65
A Parallel: in the Manner of Plutarch. London: 1759. V. 62
A Parallel; in the Manner of Plutarch.... 1758. V. 62; 63; 66
Polymetis; or, an Enquiry Concerning the Agreement Between the Works of the Roman Poets and the Remains of the Ancient Artists. London: 1747. V. 67

SPENCE, ROBERT
A Nazi Story Book by Doktor Schrecklichkeit. London: 1941. V. 65

SPENCE, THOMAS
Manitoba and the North West of the Dominion, Its Resources and Advantages to the Emigrant and Capitalist.... Toronto: 1871. V. 63

SPENCE, WILLIAM
Britain Independent of Commerce. London: 1807. V. 67
Britain Independent of Commerce. London: 1808. V. 64
Tracts on Political Economy. London: 1822. V. 67

SPENCER, A. M.
Generation, Accumulation and Production of Europe's Hydrocarbons. Oxford: 1991. V. 67

SPENCER, B.
The Arunta. A Study of a Stone Age People. London: 1927. V. 62

SPENCER, BALDWIN
Wanderings in Wild Australia. London: 1928. V. 66

SPENCER, BERNARD
Aegean Islands and Other Poems. London: 1946. V. 64
The Twist in the Plotting - Tewnty Five Poems. Reading: 1960. V. 65

SPENCER, BRIAN A.
Prairie School Tradition; the Prairie Archives of the Milwaukee Art Center. New York: 1979. V. 62; 65

SPENCER, C.
A Bibliography of the Navajo Indians. New York: 1940. V. 62

SPENCER, CHARLES
The Bicycle: Its Use and Action. London: 1870. V. 65

SPENCER, CLAIRE
Gallows Orchard. New York: 1930. V. 65

SPENCER, CLARISSA YOUNG
One Who Was Valiant. Caldwell: 1940. V. 67

SPENCER, CORNELIA PHILLIPS
The Last Ninety Days of the War in North Carolina. New York: 1866. V. 63; 65

SPENCER, EDMUND
Turkey, Russia and the Black Sea, and Circassia. London: 1855. V. 64; 65

SPENCER, ELIZABETH
The Voice at the Back Door. New York: 1956. V. 62

SPENCER, HERBERT
An Autobiography. London: 1904. V. 64
Education: Intellectual, Moral and Physical. London: 1861. V. 66
An Epitome of the Synthetic Philosophy.... London: 1889. V. 64
Essays: Scientific, Political and Speculative. London: 1858. V. 63; 65
Essays: Scientific, Political and Speculative. London: 1868-1878. V. 64
First Principles. London: 1862. V. 63; 66
First Principles. London: 1870. V. 66
The Inadequacy of Natural Selection. 1893. V. 67
The Man Versus the State.... London and Edinburgh: 1884. V. 63; 64; 65
The Principles of Biology. London: 1898. V. 64
The Principles of Ethics. London: 1893-1897. V. 64
The Principles of Psychology. London: 1855. V. 64
The Principles of Psychology. London: 1870-1872. V. 64; 66
A Rejoinder to Professor Weismann. New York: 1894. V. 65
Works. New York: 1897. V. 63

SPENCER, ISOBEL
Walter Crane. New York: 1975. V. 62

SPENCER, J. W. W.
The Falls of Niagara, Their Evolution and Varying Relations to the Great Lakes.... Ottawa: 1907. V. 67

SPENCER, JOHN
De Legibus Hebraeorum Ritualibus et Earum Rationibus Libri IV.... Cantabrigiae: 1727. V. 67

SPENCER, LLOYD
A History of the State of Washington. New York: 1937. V. 62; 65

SPENCER, MARIANNE
Almack's. A Novel. London: 1826. V. 63

SPENCER, PLATT ROGERS
Spencerian or Semi-Angular Exercise Principle in Penmanship. New York: 1857. V. 62

SPENCER, RAINE
The Spencers on Spas. London: 1983. V. 65

SPENCER, STANLEY
Scrapbook Drawings.... London: 1964. V. 62

SPENCER, THOMAS
Spencer's Illustrated Guide to Richmond, It's Castle and Neighbourhood; Easby Abbey, Reeth, Rokeby and Wensleydale. Richmond: 1890. V. 65

SPENDER, HAROLD
The Man Who Went. London: 1919. V. 62

SPENDER, STEPHEN
China Diary. London: 1982. V. 62
Collected Poems 1928-1953. London: 1955. V. 66
Collected Poems 1928-1985. London: 1985. V. 64
The Destructive Element. a Study of Modern Writers and Beliefs. London: 1935. V. 66
The Edge of Being. London: 1949. V. 62
The Generous Days. New York: 1971. V. 62
Henry Moore. O.M.: A Memorial Address Delivered in Westminster Abbey on 18th November 1986. London: 1987. V. 62
Hockney's Alphabet: Drawings by David Hockney. London: 1991. V. 63
Journals 1939-1983. Franklin Center: 1985. V. 62; 67
Journals 1939-1983. London: 1985. V. 62; 66
A Memorial Address Delivered at Christ Church Cathedral. Oxford: 1973. V. 62

SPENDER, STEPHEN continued
Poems. London: 1933. V. 62; 65; 66
Poems. London: 1934. V. 62; 67
Poems. London: 1953. V. 65
Poems of Dedication. London: 1947. V. 62
Poems of Dedication. New York: 1947. V. 62; 64; 67
Recent Poems. London: 1978. V. 64; 65
Returning to Vienna 1947. Pawlet: 1947. V. 62; 64
Ruins and Visions - Poems. London: 1942. V. 62; 64; 66
The Still Centre. London: 1939. V. 62; 63; 65; 66
Trial of a Judge - a Tragedy. London: 1937. V. 65
Trial of a Judge: a Tragedy. London: 1938. V. 62; 66
Twenty Poems. Oxford: 1930. V. 62
Vienna. London: 1934. V. 62; 64; 65
W. H. Auden. 1973. V. 65
W. H. Auden - a Memorial Address - Delivered at Christ Church Cathedral, Oxford on 27 Oct. 1973.... London: 1973. V. 62
World Within World: The Autobiography. London: 1951. V. 67

SPENSER, EDMUND
Amoretti and Epithalamion. London: 1927. V. 65; 66
Epithalamion and Amoretti. London: 1903. V. 66
The Faerie Queen. London: 1611. V. 64
The Faerie Queen. 1611-1613. V. 64
The Faerie Queen. New York: 1953. V. 63
The Faerie Queene. London: 1751. V. 62
The Faerie Queene. Chelsea: 1923. V. 64
The Faerie Queene. 1953. V. 62; 65
The Faerie Queene. Oxford: 1953. V. 66
The Faerie Qveen. London: 1611-1613. V. 65; 66
Minor Poems. 1925. V. 67
Of the Brood of Angels. 1939. V. 65
Poems of Spenser. Edinburgh: 1906. V. 62; 64; 67
The Poetical Works. London: 1839. V. 64; 65; 66
Prothalamion: Epithalamion. Boston and New York: 1902. V. 66
The Wedding Songs of Edmund Spenser.... Waltham St. Lawrence: 1923. V. 64
The Works. Oxford: 1930. V. 64
Works. Oxford: 1930-1932. V. 62

SPERONI DEGLI ALVAROTTI, SPERONE
Dialoghi Di M. Speron Speroni, Nuovamente Ristampi, & con Molta Diligenza Riueduti, & Corretti. In Vinegia: 1552. V. 66

SPERRY, ARMSTRONG
Call It Courage. New York: 1940. V. 65

SPERRY GYROSCOPE CO.
The Sperry Gyro-Compass & Navigation Equipment. New York: 1912. V. 63

SPHYROERAS, VASILIS
Maps and Map-Makers of the Aegean. Athens: 1985. V. 65

SPICER, BART
Blues for the Prince. 1950. V. 66

SPICER, JACK
After Lorca. San Francisco: 1957. V. 62; 64; 65; 67
Billy the Kid. Stinson Beach: 1959. V. 63; 64; 66
Billy the Kid. London: 1969. V. 64
Lament for the Makers. Po: Jack Spicer. III: Graham Mackintosh. Oakland: 1962. V. 65
A Lost Poem by Jack Spicer. Verona: 1974. V. 62

SPICER, JOHN
Correlation Methods of Comparing Idiolects in a Transition Area. N.P: 1952. V. 64

SPIEGEL, ADRIAAN VAN DE
Isagoges in Rem Herbarium Libri Duo. Leyden: 1633. V. 64
Opera Quae Extant Omnia.... Amsterdam: 1645. V. 62

SPIEGELMAN, ART
Maus: a Survivor's Tale. New York: 1986. V. 62; 63

SPIELMAN, JEAN E.
The Stool Pigeon and the Open Shop Movement. Minneapolis: 1923. V. 64

SPIELMANN, M. H.
Adventures in Wizard Land. London: 1905. V. 64
Father Christmas at Home. London: 1906. V. 64
Harry and Herodotus. London: 1902. V. 64
The History of Punch. New York: 1895. V. 65
Hugh Thomson, His Art, His Letters, His Humour and His Charm. London: 1931. V. 62; 63
Kate Greenaway. London: 1905. V. 62; 63
The Rainbow Book. London: 1909. V. 62
The Rainbow Book. London: 1913. V. 64
The Title-Page of the First Folio of Shakespeare's Plays, a Comparative Study of the Doreshout Portrait and the Stratford Bookment.... London: 1924. V. 64

SPIER, LESLIE
Yuman Tribes of the Gila River. Chicago: 1933. V. 63

SPIER, PETER
Dreams. New York: 1986. V. 65

SPIERS, ANN
The Herodotus Poems. Waldron Island: 1989. V. 63

SPIERS, R. PHENE
The Orders of Architecture, Greek, Roman and Italian. London: 1890. V. 66

SPIES, WERNER
Albers. New York. V. 66

SPIKES, NELLIE W.
Through the Years - a History of Crosby County, Texas. San Antonio: 1952. V. 62

SPILLANE, MICKEY
Kiss Me, Deadly. 1952. V. 66
Kiss Me, Deadly. New York: 1952. V. 64; 65
The Last Cop Out. London: 1973. V. 67

SPILLER, B. L.
Drummer in the Woods. 1962. V. 67

SPILLER, BURTON L.
Firelight. New York: 1937. V. 64; 66
Fishin' Around. New York: 1974. V. 65
More Grouse Feathers. New York: 1938. V. 64; 66

SPILLER, ROBERT E.
The Philobiblon Club of Philadelphia, the First Eighty Years 1893- 1973. Philadelphia: 1973. V. 62

SPILSBURY, WILLIAM HOLDEN
Lincoln's Inn Its Ancient and Modern Buildings. London: 1850. V. 63

SPINELLI, JERRY
Maniac Magee. Boston: 1990. V. 65
Wringer. New York: 1997. V. 65

SPINETO, MARQUIS
Lectures on the Elements of Hieroglyphics and Egyptian Antiquities. London: 1829. V. 65

SPINNER, ALICE, PSEUD.
A Study in Colour. London: 1894. V. 65

SPINOZA, BARUCH
Opera Posthuma. Amsterdam: 1677. V. 64; 66

THE SPIRIT of the Fair. New York: 1864-1865. V. 65

THE SPIRIT of the Nation. Ballads and Songs by Writers of "The Nation". 1846. V. 63

SPIRITUAL Communications and the Comfort They Bring; by the Disembodied Spirit of Charles Dickens, through a Melbourne Medium. Melbourne: 1873. V. 62

SPITTA, EDMUND J.
Photo Microscopy. London: 1899. V. 66

SPITTA, HEINRICH
Die Schlaf und Traumzustande der menschlichen Seele Mit Besonderer Berucksichtigung Ihres Verhaltnisses zu den Psychischen Alienationen. Tubingen: 1878. V. 65

SPITZKA, EDWARD
Insanity: Its Classification, Diagnosis and Treatment. New York: 1883. V. 65
A Study of the Brains of Six Eminent Scientists and Scholars Belonging to the American Anthropometric Society, Together with a Description of the Skull of Professor E. D. Cope. Philadelphia: 1907. V. 66; 67

SPIVAK, JOHN L.
The Devil's Brigade: the Story of the Hatfield McCoy Feud. New York: 1930. V. 62; 63; 64; 65

SPIVEY, RICHARD L.
Maria. Flagstaff: 1979. V. 63; 66

SPLAN, JOHN
Life with The Trotters. Chicago: 1889. V. 66

SPLICEM, SAM, PSEUD.
Joke Upon Joke. New Haven: 1818. V. 64

SPOERRI, DANIEL
Topographie Anecdotee du Hasard. Paris: 1961. V. 67

SPOFFORD, HARRIET ELIZABETH PRESCOTT
Ballads and Authors. Boston: 1887. V. 63; 64; 66
In Titian's Garden and Other Poems. Boston: 1903. V. 63

SPOKES, Spurs and Cockle Burs. Fort Benton: 1976. V. 67

SPOLLEN, JAMES
Trial of James Spollen for the Murder of Mr. George Samuel Little, at the Broadstone Terminus of the Midland Great Western Railway, Ireland, August 7th-11th, 1857. Dublin: 1857. V. 63

SPON, ERNEST
Workshop Receipts for Manufacturers, Mechanics and Scientific Amateurs. London: 1909. V. 64
Workshop Receipts for the Use of Manufacturers, Mechanics and Scienti fic Amateurs. London: 1890-1892. V. 62

SPON, JACOB
De l'Usage du Caphe, du The et du Chocolate. Lyon: 1671. V. 63
Traitez, Nouveaux et Curieux du Cafe, du The et du Chcolate.... Lyon: 1685. V. 63

SPONETONE, CIRO
Hercole Difensore d'Homero. Verona: 1595. V. 64

SPOONER, HENRY J.
Wealth from Waste. Elimination of Waste: a World Problem. London: 1918. V. 63

SPOONER, LYSANDER
Considerations for Bankers; and Holders of United States Bonds. Boston: 1864. V. 62
A Defence for Fugitive Slaves, Against the Acts of Congress of Feb. 12, 1793 and September 18, 1850. Boston: 1850. V. 64
The Unconstitutionality of Slavery. Boston: 1845. V. 67

SPOONER, S.
Anecdotes of Painters, Engravers, Sculptors and Architects and Curiosities of Art. New York: 1880. V. 67

THE SPORTING Repository. London: 1822. V. 67

THE SPORTING Repository. London: 1904. V. 67

THE SPORTSMAN In Ireland. London: 1897. V. 67

SPORTSMAN of the Past. London. V. 62

THE SPORTSMAN'S Dictionary; or, the Country Gentleman's Companion, in all Rural Recreations.... London: 1735. V. 62; 64; 66; 67

SPORTSMAN'S Dictionary, or the Gentleman's Companion for Town and Country.... London: 1792. V. 63

THE SPORTSMAN'S Vade Mecum for the Himalayas. 1891. V. 67

SPOTORNO, GIOVANNI BATTISTA
Codice Diplomatico Colombo-Americano Ossis Raccolta di Documenti Originali et Inediti, Spettanti a Cristofor Colombo.... Genoa: 1823. V. 65

SPOTTISWOOD, JOHN
The History of the Church and State of Scotland, Beginning in the Year of Our Lord 203 and Continued to the End of the Reign of King James the VI. London: 1677. V. 63

SPOTTS, DAVID L.
Campaigning With Custer. Los Angeles: 1928. V. 65; 67

SPRAGUE, FRANK J.
Report on the Exhibits at the Palace Electrical Exhibition, 1882. Washington: 1883. V. 62

SPRAGUE, J. T.
The Treachery in Texas, the Secession of Texas and the Arrest of the United States Officers and Soldiers Serving in Texas. New York: 1862. V. 63; 65

SPRAGUE, KURTH
The Promise Kept. Austin: 1975. V. 65

SPRAGUE, P. E.
The Drawings...a Catalogue of the Frank Lloyd Wright Collection at the Avery Architectural Library. Princeton: 1979. V. 62; 65

SPRAKE, LESLIE
A Shooting Man's Calendar Concerning the Preservation and Pursuit of Pheasants, Partridges and Ground Game. London: 1927. V. 67

SPRAT, THOMAS
History of the Royal Society of London, for the Improving of Natural Knowledge. London: 1667. V. 65
The History of the Royal Society of London, for the Improving of Natural Knowledge. London: 1734. V. 64

SPRATT, GEORGE
Obstetric Tables. London: 1835. V. 65
Obstetric Tables. Philadelphia: 1847. V. 64; 67
Obstetric Tables. Philadelphia: 1848. V. 67

SPRENGEL, M. C.
Allgemeines Historisches Taschenbuch Oder Abrisz der Merkwudigsten Neuen Welt-Begebenheiten Enthaltend fur 1784 Die Geschichte der Revolution von Nord-America. Berlin: 1784. V. 63; 66

SPRENGER, JACOBUS
Malleus Maleficarum. Nuremberg: 1494. V. 65

SPRIGGE, JOSHUA
Anglia Rediviva; Englands Recovery: Being the History of the Motions, Actions and Successes of the Army Under the Immediate Conduct of His Excellancy, Sr. Thomas Fairfax.... London: 1647. V. 64

SPRIGGE, S. SQUIRE
The Methods of Publishing. London: 1890. V. 65

SPRING, AGNES WRIGHT
Caspar Collins, the Life and Exploits of Indian Fighter of the Sixties. New York: 1927. V. 63; 66
The Cheyenne and Black Hills Stage and Express Routes. Glendale: 1949. V. 65; 67
70 Years Cow Country, Seventy Years a Panoramic History of the Wyoming Stockgrowers Association Interwoven...Cattle Industry in Wyoming. Gillette: 1942. V. 64; 67
William Chapin Deming of Wyoming Pioneer Publisher, and State and Federal Officer - a Biography. Glendale: 1944. V. 62; 65

SPRINGFIELD, LINCOLN
A Galaxy Girl and Other Stories. London: 1898. V. 67

SPRINGS, KATHERINE WOOTEN
The Squires of Springfield. Charlotte: 1965. V. 63

SPROAT, G. M.
Scenes and Studies of Savage Life. London: 1868. V. 64

SPROAT, IAIN
Wodehouse at War. New Haven and New York: 1981. V. 64

SPRUNGER, S.
Orchids from the Botanical Register. Basel: 1990. V. 64

SPRUNT, ALEXANDER
Carolina Low Contry Impressions. New York: 1964. V. 67
Florida Bird Life. New York: 1954. V. 67
South Carolina Bird Life. Columbia: 1949. V. 67

SPRUNT, JAMES
Derelicts. Wilmington: 1920. V. 62; 63
Tales and Traditions of the Lower Cape Fear 1661-1896. Wilmington: 1896. V. 62; 63; 65
Tales of the Cape Fear Blockade. Wilmington: 1960. V. 63

SPRY, W. J. J.
The Cruise of Her Majesty's Ship Challenger.... Toronto: 1877. V. 66

SPUDE, ROBERT
Central Arizona Ghost Towns. Las Vegas: 1978. V. 63; 66

SPURLING, J.
Sail. The Romance of the Clipper Ships. New York: 1972. V. 62; 66

SPURLING, R. GLEN
Lesions of the Cervical Intervertebral Disc. Springfield: 1956. V. 67
Medical Department United States Army. Surgery in World War II. Neurosurgery. Washington: 1958. V. 67

SPURR, JOSIAH EDWARD
Economic Geology of the Georgetown Quadrangle (Together with the Empire District) Colorado. Washington: 1908. V. 66
Geology of the Aspen Mining District, Colorado. Washington: 1898. V. 67

SPURZHEIM, GEORGE
A Sketch of the Natural Laws of Man. London: 1825. V. 65
A View of the Elementary Principles of Education.... 1828. V. 64
A View of the Elementary Principles of Education.... Boston: 1836. V. 64; 66; 67

SPURZHEIM, JOHANN GASPAR
The Anatomy of the Brain. London: 1826. V. 65; 67
The Anatomy of the Brain. Boston: 1836. V. 64; 65; 66; 67
Observations on the Deranged Manifestations of the Mind; or, Insanity. Boston: 1836. V. 65
Phrenology, in Connection with the Study of Physiognomy. London: 1826. V. 64; 66
Phrenology in Connexion with the Study of Physiognomy. 1826. V. 62
Phrenology, or the Doctrine of the Mental Phenomena. Boston: 1833. V. 64
Phrenology, or the Doctrine of the Mind and the Relations Between Its Manifestations and the Body. London: 1825. V. 63; 67
The Physiognomical System of Drs. Gall and Spurzheim.... London: 1815. V. 62; 66

SPYRI, JOHANNA
Heidi. Philadelphia: 1919. V. 65; 66
Heidi. Philadelphia: 1922. V. 62

SQUIER, EPHRAIM GEORGE
Honduras: Descriptive, Historical and Statistical. London: 1870. V. 65
Notes on Central America; Particularly the States of Honduras and San Salvador...and the Proposed Honduras Inter-Oceanic Railway. New York: 1855. V. 65
Peru: Incidents of Travel and Exploration in the Land of the Incas. New York: 1877. V. 65; 67

SQUIRE, J. C.
The Gold Tree. London: 1917. V. 62
The Grub Street Nights Entertainments. London: 1924. V. 65
Poems and Baudelaire Flowers. London: 1909. V. 65

SQUIRE, JANE
A Proposal to Determine Our Longitude. London: 1743. V. 63; 67

SQUIRES, W. H. T.
The Days of Yester-Year in Colony and Commonwealth: a Sketch Book of Virginia. Portsmouth: 1928. V. 65; 67
Virginia Historical Quartette. Portsmouth: 1928. V. 63

SRIDHARAN, K.
A Maritime History of India. New Delhi: 1982. V. 67

STAAL DE LAUNAY, MARGUERITE JEANNE CORDIER
Memoires de Madame de Staal.... Amsterdam et a Leipzig: 1756. V. 67

STAATS, H. PHILIP
Californian Architecture in Santa Barbara. New York: 1929. V. 67

STABLES, GORDON
Our Friend, the Dog, a Complete Guide. London: 1883. V. 63

STACK, AMOS
Amos Stack (1822-1908) Forty Niner: His Overland Diary to California.... Denver: 1981. V. 64

STACKHOUSE, THOMAS
Two Lectures on the Remains of Ancient Pagan Britain.... London: 1833. V. 63

STACPOOLE, H. DE VERE
The Blue Lagoon - a Romance. London: 1908. V. 65

STAEHLIN VON STORCKSBURG, JAKOB
Originalanekdoten von Peter dem Grossen. Leipzig: 1785. V. 66

STAEL HOLSTEIN, ANNE LOUISE GERMAINE NECKER, BARONNE DE
Corinne on L'Italie. Paris: 1809. V. 65
De La Litterature Consideree dans ses Rapports avec les Institutions Sociales.... Paris and London: 1812. V. 65
De l'Allemagne. Paris: 1813. V. 64; 65
De l'Influence des Passions sur le Bonheur des Individus et des Nations. Lausanne: 1796. V. 66; 67
Germany. London: 1814. V. 65
The Influence of the Passions Upon the Happiness of Individuals and of Nations. London: 1813. V. 66
Madame de Stael and the Grand-Duchess Louise. A Selection from the Unpublished Correspondence of Madame de Stael and the Grand Duchess Louise of Saxe-Weimar, from 1800 to 1817.... London: 1862. V. 67
Memoirs of the Private Life of My Father. London: 1818. V. 65; 66

STAFFORD, JEAN
Boston Adventure. New York: 1944. V. 63
The Interior Castle. New York: 1953. V. 67
The Lion and the Carpenter and Other Tales from The Arabian Nights. New York: 1962. V. 66

STAFFORD, KIM
Apple Bough Soliloquy. Eugene: 1925. V. 63
Apple Bough Soliloquy. Eugene: 1995. V. 64

STAFFORD, MALLIE
The March of Empire through Three Decades Embracing Sketches of California History. San Francisco: 1884. V. 65

STAFFORD, THOMAS
Pacata Hibernia. 1633. V. 63

STAFFORD, WILLIAM
Absolution. Knotting, Bedfordshire: 1980. V. 62
All About Light. Athens: 1978. V. 62
Allegiances. New York: 1970. V. 62
A Compendious or Briefe Examination of Certayne Ordinary Complaints of Divers of Our Country Men in These of Our Days.... London: 1587. V. 66
The Design on the Oriole. N.P: 1977. V. 62
Going Places. Poems. Reno: 1974. V. 62
In the Clock of Reason. Victoria: 1973. V. 62; 65
Smoke's Way. Port Townsend: 1978. V. 62; 64; 67
Stories and Storms and Strangers. Resburg: 1984. V. 62
Stories That Could be True. New York: 1977. V. 66
Traveling Through the Dark. New York and Evanston: 1962. V. 64; 67
Tuned in Late One Night. Northampton: 1978. V. 62
Words in the Cold Air. Salt Lake City: 1993. V. 62
Wyoming Circuit. N.P: 1980. V. 62; 67

STAFFORD, WILLIAM, VISCOUNT
The Tryal of William Viscount Stafford for High Treason. London: 1680-1681. V. 62

STAGG, JOHN
The Cambrian Minstrel; Being a Poetical Miscellany of Legendary, Gothic and Romantic Tales.... Manchester: 1821. V. 62
The Minstrel of the North; or Cumbrian Legends. London: 1810. V. 62; 66

STAHL, F. A.
Rolling Stones. Glendale: 1928. V. 65

STAHL, GEORG ERNEST
De Motus Haemorrhoidalis, et Fluxus Haemorrhodium Diversitate, bene Distinguenda.... Veneunt Parisiis: 1730. V. 67

STAHL, P. J.
La Journee de Mademoiselle Lili. Paris. V. 65

STAINTON, H. T.
British Butterflies and Moths. London: 1867. V. 62; 63

STALKER, JOHN
A Treatise of Japanning and Varnishing 1688. 1960. V. 67

STALLWORTHY, JON
The Astronomy of Love. London: 1961. V. 63
Wilfred Owen - a Biography. London: 1974. V. 62

STALNAKER, ELDER C.
A History of the Mt. Pisgah Baptist Association, Through Its One Hundred Annual Sessions from 1854-1957. Charleston?: 1957. V. 63

STAMP, J. C.
British Incomes and Property. London: 1916. V. 65

STAMP, WILLIAM W.
Historical Notices of Wesleyan Methodism, in Bradford and Its Vicinity. Bradford: 1841. V. 65

STAMPART, FRANZ
Prodromus Oder Vor-Licht des Eroffineten Schau- und Wunder- Prachtes.... Vienna: 1735. V. 62; 67

STANDARD Atlas of Kit Carson County Colorado. Chicago: 1922. V. 63

STANDARD MANUFACTURING CO.
The Bathroom, a New Interior. N.P: 1931. V. 63

STANDISH, FRANK HALL
The Life of Voltaire.... London: 1821. V. 67

STANDS IN TIMBER
Cheyenne Memories. New Haven: 1967. V. 65; 67

STANESBY, SAMUEL
The Bridal Souvenir. London: 1866. V. 66
The Floral Gift. London: 1860. V. 62; 66

STANFORD, CHARLES V.
The Complete Collection of Irish Music. 1902-1905. V. 62; 65

STANFORD, J. K.
A Keeper's Country. London: 1968. V. 67

STANHOPE, CHARLES MAHON, VISCOUNT
Considerations on the Means of Preventing Fraudulent Practices on the Gold Coin. London: 1775. V. 66

STANHOPE, GEORGE
A Paraphrase and Comment Upon the Epistles and Gospels. London: 1715. V. 67

STANHOPE, HORACE
The Rebel: a Tale. London: 1826. V. 65

STANHOPE, MARIANNE SPENCER
Almack's a Novel. London: 1826. V. 65

STANISLAVSKY, CONSTANTIN
An Actor Prepares. New York: 1946. V. 63
Moia Zhizn' V Iskusstve. (My Life in Art). 1925. V. 67
My Life in Art. Boston: 1933. V. 66

STANKIEWICZ, W. J.
A Guide to Democratic Jargon. 1976. V. 62

STANKOVIC, S.
The Balkan Lake Orchid and Its Living World. The Hague: 1960. V. 64

STANLEY, ARTHUR PENRHYN
England and India. A Sermon Preached in Westminster Abbey Oct. 11, 1875.... London: 1875. V. 67
Sermon Preached by Arthur Penrhyn Stanley, D.D. Dean of Westminster in Westminster Abbey June 19, 1870.... London: 1870. V. 62
Sinai and Palestine in Connection with Their History. London: 1866. V. 65

STANLEY, COLONEL
Bibliotheca Stanleiana. London: 1813. V. 62

STANLEY, D. J.
Geological Evolution of te Mediterranean Basin. New York: 1985. V. 67

STANLEY, DONALD
Holmes Meets 007. San Francisco: 1967. V. 63; 65; 67

STANLEY, E. J.
Life of Rev. L. B. Stateler - a Story of Life on the Old Frontier. Richmond: 1916. V. 64; 67

STANLEY, EDWARD
Heads for the Arrangement of Local Information in Every Department of Parochial and Rural Interest. London: 1848. V. 63
Report to the House of Representatives...Vindicating the Rights of Charles T. Jackson to the Discovery of the Anaesthetic Effects of Ether Vapor and Disproving the Claims of W. T. G. Morton to that Discovery. Washington: 1852. V. 64

STANLEY, F.
The Apaches of New Mexico 1540-1940. Pampa: 1962. V. 64; 65; 67
The Civil War in New Mexico. N.P: 1960. V. 66
The Civil War in New Mexico. Denver: 1960. V. 65; 67
Clay Allison. Denver: 1956. V. 64
Desperadoes of New Mexico. Denver: 1953. V. 64; 65; 67
E. V. Summer, Major General U.S. Army 1797-1863. 1969. V. 63
E. V. Summer, Major General U.S. Army 1797-1863. Borger: 1969. V. 67
Fort Bascom Comanche Kiowa Barrier. Pampa: 1961. V. 67
Fort Craig. Pampa: 1963. V. 67
Fort Union, New Mexico. N.P: 1953. V. 62; 63; 64; 66; 67
The Grant that Maxwell Bought. Denver: 1952. V. 64
The Jicarilla Apaches of New Mexico, 1540-1967. Pampa: 1967. V. 63; 64; 67
The Last Vegas Story. Denver: 1951. V. 63
New Mexico Pamphlets. 1960-1973. V. 66
No Tears for Black Jack Ketchem. Denver: 1958. V. 65
One Half Mile from Heaven, or, the Cimarron Story. Denver: 1949. V. 63; 66
Raton Chronicle. Denver: 1949. V. 64
Satanta and the Kiowas. Borger: 1968. V. 65; 67
Socorro, the Oasis. Denver: 1950. V. 62; 65
Story of the Texas Panhandle Railroads. Borger: 1976. V. 64

STANLEY, HENRY MORTON
The Congo and the Founding of Its Free State: a Story of Work and Exploration. London: 1885. V. 65
In Darkest Africa or the Quest, Rescue and Retreat of Emin Governor of Equatoria. London: 1890. V. 62; 64; 66
In Darkest Africa; or the Quiet, Rescue and Retreat of Emin, Governor of Equatoria. New York: 1890. V. 66
My Early Experiences in America and Asia. New York: 1895. V. 67
My Early Experiences in America and Asia. New York: 1905. V. 65
My Early Travels and Adventures in America and Asia. London: 1895. V. 62
My Early Travels and Adventures in America and Asia. New York: 1895. V. 63
Through the Dark Continent. New York: 1878. V. 66

STANLEY, HENRY MORTON continued
Through the Dark Continent. London: 1899. V. 62

STANLEY, J. L.
The Arts of Africa. An Annotated Bibliography. 1986-1989. V. 62

STANLEY, JACOB
Essays and Fragments on Various Subjects. Dudley: 1829. V. 66

STANLEY, THOMAS
The History of Philosophy.... London: 1701. V. 64

STANLEY, WILLIAM FORD
Notes on the Nebular Theory, in Relation to Stellar, Solar, Planetary, Cometary and Geological Phenomena. London: 1895. V. 66

STANNARD, HENRIETTA
Lumley the Painter. London: 1891. V. 65

STANNARD, MARTIN
Evelyn Waugh - The Critical Heritage. London: 1984. V. 65

STANNUS, GRAYDON, MRS.
Old Irish Glass. London: 1921. V. 67

STANSBERRY, DOMENIC
The Last Days of Il Duce. 1998. V. 62; 64; 66

STANSBERY, LON R.
The Passing of the 3D Ranch. Tulsa: 1930. V. 63

STANSBURY, ELIJAH
Life and Times of Hon. Elijah Stansbury, an "Old Defender" and Ex- Mayor of Baltimore; Together with Early Reminiscences.... Baltimore: 1874. V. 67

STANSBURY, HOWARD
Exploration and Survey of the Valley of the Great Salt Lake of Utah.... Philadelphia: 1852. V. 63

STANSFIELD, JAMES
Repeal of the Contagious Diseases Acts Relating to Women Speech... Delivered in Birmingham, November 1883. London: 1884. V. 65

STANTON, DANIEL
A Journal of the Life, Travels and Gospel Labours, of a Faithful Minister of Jesus Christ, Daniel Stanton.... Philadelphia: 1772. V. 65

STANTON, ELIZABETH CADY
Free Speech: at the Fourth Annual N.Y. State Anti-Slavery Convention at Association Hall, Albany, New York, February 4th and 5th, 1861. Albany: 1861. V. 63
History of Woman Suffrage. Rochester: 1881-1902. V. 65

STANTON, IRVING
Sixty Years in Colorado - Reminiscences, and Recollections of a Pioneer 1860. Denver: 1922. V. 63; 66

STANTON, J. E.
By Middle Seas: Photographic Studies Reflecting the Architectural... Mediterranean. Los Angeles: 1927. V. 62; 65

STANTON, KATE E.
Old Southern Songs of the Confederacy: The Dixie Trophy Collection. New York: 1926. V. 62

STANTON, LOUISA
The Extraordinary and Unprecedented Trial of Louisa Stanton, Late Bradley, of No. 4, Upper George Street, Portman Square, for Wilful and Corrupt Perjury Against Her Husband...10th January 1815. London: 1815. V. 63

STANTON, MARGARET
The Trial of Margaret Stanton, for Cutting and Maiming Her Husband with a Razor.... London: 1820?. V. 65

STANTON, PHOEBE
The Gothic Revival and American Church Architecture: an Episode in Taste 1840-1856. Baltimore: 1968. V. 66

STANTON, THEODORE
Elizabeth Cady Stanton as Revealed in Her Letters, Diary and Reminiscences. New York: 1922. V. 67

STANWOOD, AVIS A. BURNHAM
Fostina Woodman. The Wonderful Adventurer. Boston: 1854. V. 65

STANYAN, TEMPLE
The Grecian History. London: 1751. V. 67

STAPF, O.
On the Flora of Mount Kinabalu in North Borneo. London: 1894. V. 67

STAPLEDON, W. OLAF
Last Men in London. London: 1932. V. 62

STAPLES, THOMAS S.
Reconstruction in Arkansas 1862-1874. New York: 1923. V. 62

STAPLETON, HENRY
Memorials of Calverley Parish Church and Its Forty-One Vicars. Leeds: 1912. V. 64; 65

STAPLETON, THOMAS
Angli...Promptuarium Catholicum, Ad Instructionem concionatorum Contra Haereticos Nostri Temporis. Coloniae: 1592-1595. V. 66
Magni Rotuli Scaccarii Normanniae Sub Regibus Angliae. London: 1840. V. 62
Promptarium Morale Super Evangelia Domincilia Totius Anni.... Antverpiae: 1593. V. 66
Tres Thomae Sev De S. Thomae Apostoli Rebus Gestis. De S. Thoma Archiepiscopo Cantuariensi & Martyre. D. Thomae Mori Angliae Quondam Cancellarij Vita. Dvaci: 1588. V. 65

STARBUCK, ALEXANDER
History of the American Whale Fishery from Its Earliest Inception to the Year 1876. Washington: 1878. V. 62; 66
History of the American Whale Fishery from Its Earliest Inception to the Year 1876. New York: 1964. V. 62; 66

STARHORN, CARRIE A.
Fifteen Thousand Miles by Stage - A Woman's Unique Experience During Thirty Years of Path Finding and Pioneering from the Missouri to the Pacific and from Alaska to Mexico. New York: 1911. V. 66

STARK, A. W.
Instruction for Field Artillery.... Richmond: 1864. V. 62; 63; 65

STARK, FREYA
Baghdad Sketches. Baghdad: 1932. V. 64; 65; 66
Baghdad Sketches. London: 1937. V. 64
Beyond Euphrates. London: 1951. V. 64
The Coast of Incense. London: 1953. V. 64
Dust in the Lion's Paw. London: 1961. V. 64
Letters 1914-1980.. London: 1977-1982. V. 64
The Minaret of Djam. London: 1970. V. 64
Rivers of Time. 1982. V. 67
Roads Round Asolo.... 1965. V. 65
Rome on the Euphrates the Story of a Frontier. London: 1966. V. 64
Seen in the Hadhramaut. London: 1938. V. 64; 66
The Southern Gates of Arabia. 1936. V. 67
The Southern Gates of Arabia. London: 1936. V. 64
Space, Time and Movement in Landscape. London: 1969. V. 64; 66
Traveller's Prelude. London: 1950. V. 64
The Valley of the Assassins and Other Persian Travels. London: 1934. V. 64
A Winter in Arabia. London: 1940. V. 64

STARK, JAMES H.
The Loyalists of Massachusetts and the Other Side of the American Revolution. Salem: 1910. V. 63

STARK, RICHARD
The Blackbird. New York: 1969. V. 67

STARK, ROBERT M.
A Popular History of British Mosses.... London: 1860. V. 63

STARK, SHARON
The Dealers' Yard. New York: 1985. V. 63

STARKE, MARIANA
Travels in Europe, for the Use of Travellers on the Continent and Likewise in the Island of Sicily. Paris: 1836. V. 65
Travels in Europe, for the Use of Travellers on the Continent and Likewise in the Island of Sicily.... Paris: 1839. V. 63
Travels on the Continent, Written for the Use and Particular Information of Travellers. London: 1820. V. 67

STARKEY, DIGBY
Ireland. The Political Tracts of Menenius. 1848. Dublin: 1849. V. 65

STARKEY, JAMES
Twenty-five Lyrics. Flansham: 1933. V. 62

STARKEY, MARION L.
The Cherokee Nation. New York: 1946. V. 67

STARKIE, ENID
Baudelaire. London: 1957. V. 65
From Gautier to Eliot - the Influence of France on English Literature 1851-1939. London: 1960. V. 62
Petrus Borel - the Lycanthrope - His Life and Times. London: 1954. V. 62

STARKIE, JAMES
Facetiae et Curiosa. 1937. V. 63
Personal Talk, A Book of Verses. 1936. V. 63
Poems 1930-1938. 1938. V. 63
This is the House and Other Verses. 1942. V. 63

STARKIE, THOMAS
A Practical Treatise of the Law of Evidence. Philadelphia: 1869. V. 65

STARKWEATHER, CARLTON L.
A Brief Genealogical History of Robert Starkweather of Roxbury and Ipswich, Massachusetts. Occoquan: 1904. V. 67

STARLING, ERNEST H.
Mercers' Company Lectures on Recent Advances in the Physiology of Digestion. Chicago: 1907. V. 63

STARR, BELLA
Bella Starr, the Bandit Queen, or the Female Jesse James: a Full and Authentic History of the Dashing Female Highwayman.... Austin: 1960. V. 63; 64

STARR, EMMET
History of the Cherokee Indian and Their Legend and Folklore. Oklahoma City: 1921. V. 64; 67

STARR, F. RATCHFORD
Farm Echoes. New York: 1881. V. 64

STARR, FREDERICK
Congo Natives. Chicago: 1912. V. 64

STARR, JIMMY
Three Short Biers. Hollywood: 1945. V. 65

STARR, MOSES ALLEN
Familiar Forms of Nervous Disease.... New York: 1890. V. 65
Organic Nervous Diseases. New York: 1903. V. 65

STARR, STEPHEN Z.
The Union Cavalry in the Civil War. Baton Rouge: 1979. V. 65

STARR, WALTER A.
Guide to the John Muir Trail and High Sierra Region. San Francisco: 1934. V. 62
My Adventures in the Klondike and Alaska, 1898-1900. San Francisco: 1960. V. 64

STARRAT, M.
The Picture of Dublin, or Visiter's (sic) Guide through the Irish Metropolis. 1835. V. 62; 65

STARRETT, AGNES
The Darlington Memorial Library: University of Pittsburgh. Pittsburgh: 1938. V. 66

STARRETT, HELEN EKIN
The Future of Educated Women and Men, Women and Money. Chicago: 1885. V. 67

STARRETT, VINCENT
Buried Caesars. 1923. V. 62
Oriental Encounters: Two Essays in Bad Taste. Chicago: 1938. V. 62; 64; 65; 67
Penny Wise and Book Foolish. New York: 1929. V. 66
Persons from Porlock. Chicago: 1923. V. 67
The Private Life of Sherlock Holmes. New York: 1933. V. 62
The Private Life of Sherlock Holmes. Chicago: 1960. V. 67
The Quick and the Dead. Sauk City: 1965. V. 65
Stephen Crane. A Bilbiography. Philadelphia: 1923. V. 67
221B: Studies in Sherlock Holmes. New York: 1940. V. 66

STASHOWER, DANIEL
The Adventure of the Ectoplasmic Man. New York: 1985. V. 67

THE STATE of Representation of England and Wales, Delivered to the Society, the Friends of the People, Associated for the Purpose of Obtaining a Parliamentary Reform, On Saturday the 9th of Feb. 1793. London: 1793. V. 66

THE STATE of the Palatines for Fifty Years Past to This Present Time. London: 1710. V. 65

STATE Papers and Publick Documents of the United States...1797. Boston: 1815. V. 67

STATEMENT of the Conditions and Resources of the Kansas Central Railway (Narrow Gauge) from Leavenworth, Kansas, to Denver, Colorado. Leavenworth: 1871. V. 66

A STATEMENT of the Grounds Upon Which the Trustees of the Liverpool Docks Propose Applying to Parliament, Next Session for Authority to Provide Additional Dock Space. Liverpool: 1810. V. 64

STATEMENT Respecting the Earl of Selkirk's Settlement of Kildonan, Upon the Red River, in North America.... London: 1817. V. 63

STATHAM, H. HEATHCOTE
A Short Critical History of Architecture. London: 1927. V. 63

STATISTICAL Account of the Shetland Isles. London: 1841. V. 62

STATISTICAL History of John Ridgway's Vertical Revolving Battery. Boston: 1865. V. 62

A STATISTICAL Inquiry Into the Condition of the People of Colour, of the City and Districts of Philadelphia. Philadelphia: 1849. V. 64

STATIUS
Sylvarum Libri V. Cantabrigiae: 1651. V. 66
The Thebaid of Statius. London: 1773. V. 66

STATON, FRANCES M.
A Bibliography of Canadiana Being Items in the Public Library of Toronto, Canada, Relating to the Early History and Development of Canada. Toronto: 1934. V. 67
Bibliography of Canadiana: Being Items in the Public Library of Toronto, Canada, Relating to the Early History and Development of Canada. Volume 2. First Supplement. Toronto: 1934-1939. V. 65

STATON, KATE E.
Old Southern Songs of the Confederacy: the Dixie Trophy Collection. New York: 1926. V. 63; 65

STATTON, ROBERT BURCHER
The Heroes in Gray. Lynchburg: 1894. V. 62

STAUNTON, GEORGE
An Authentic Account of an Embassy from the King of Great Britain to the Emperor of China.... London: 1798. V. 64

STAVELEY, E. F.
British Spiders: an Introduction to the Study of the Araneidae of Great Britain and Ireland. London: 1866. V. 63

STAVELEY, THOMAS
The Romish Horseleech; or, an Impartial Account of the Intolerable Charge of Popery to this Nation. London: 1767. V. 66

STAWELL, MAUD MARGARET
The Fairy of Old Spain. London: 1912. V. 64
My Days With the Fairies. London: 1913. V. 67

STAWELL, RODOLPH, MRS.
Fairies I Have Met. London: 1907. V. 65

STEAD, CHRISTINA
Letty Fox: Her Luck. London: 1947. V. 65
The Salzburg Tales. New York: 1934. V. 63; 64; 66; 67

STEAD, WILLIAM THOMAS
The Despised Sex: the Letters of Callicrates to Dione, Queen of the Xanthians Concerning England and the English. London: 1903. V. 65

STEADMAN, RALPH
Dog Bodies. London: 1970. V. 66
The Grapes of Ralph - Wine According to Ralph Steadman. London: 1992. V. 62; 64
The Grey Penitents. N.P. V. 67
I, Leonardo. London: 1983. V. 62
I, Leonardo. New York: 1983. V. 66
Sigmund Freud. New York: 1979. V. 66
Who? Me? No! Why?. London: 1986. V. 66

THE STEAM-BOAT Companion from London to Gravesend, Southend, Margate and Ramsgate.... Margate: 1835. V. 62

STEAMERS v. Stages; or, Andrew and His Spouse. London: 1830. V. 67

STEARNE, JOHN
The Death and Burial of John Asgill, Esq. and some Other Verses Occasion'd by His Books. Dublin: 1702. V. 64; 66

STEARNS, FLORENCE DICKINSON
Strange Dimension. New York: 1938. V. 67

STEARNS, SAMUEL
An Account of the Terrible Effects of the Pestilential Infection in the City of Philadelphia. Providence: 1793. V. 64

STEARNS, W. A.
New England Bird Life, Being a Manual of New England Ornithology.... Boston: 1881-1883. V. 63; 67

STEBBING, E. P.
The Diary of a Sportsman Naturalist in India. London: 1920. V. 64; 67
The Forests of India. 1922-1926. V. 66
Jungle By-Ways in India. London: 1911. V. 67
A Manual of Elementary Forest Zoology for India. Calcutta: 1908. V. 62
Stalks in the Himalaya. 1912. V. 62; 63; 64

STEBBING, HENRY
A Fragment. London: 1751?. V. 64
Remains; or Fragments of Poems. London: 1825. V. 66

STEBBING, R. R.
Challenger Voyage. Zoology. Part 67. Amphipoda. 1888. V. 66

STEBBING, W.
Analysis of Mr. Mill's System of Logic. London: 1864. V. 64

STEBBINS, C.
Harvard Lyrics. Boston: 1899. V. 63

STEBBINS, H. M.
Pistols: a Modern Encyclopedia. 1961. V. 67

STECK, FRANCIS BORGIA
The Jolliet Marquette Expedition 1673. Glendale: 1928. V. 67

STEDMAN, CHARLES
The History of the Origin, Progress and Termination of the American War. London: 1794. V. 63

STEDMAN, CHARLES M.
Memorial Address Delivered May 10th, 1890.... Wilmington: 1890. V. 63

STEDMAN, EDMUND CLARENCE
Catalogue of the Library of Association and Autograph Collection of Edmund Clarence Stedman. New York: 1911. V. 66
The Poems of Edmund Clarence Stedman. Boston and New York: 1908. V. 62
Poets of America. Cambridge: 1885. V. 64

STEDMAN, JOHN GABRIEL
Narrative of a Five Years' Expedition, Against the Negroes of Surinam, in Guiana, on the Wild Coast of South America.... London: 1806-1813. V. 62; 63; 67
Narrative of a Five Years' Expedition Against the Revolted Negroes of Surinam in Guiana on the Wild Coast of South America. Barre: 1971. V. 66
Narrative of a Five Year's Expedition, Against the Revolted Negroes of Surinam.... London: 1806. V. 63; 64
Viaggio al Surinam e nell' Interno Della Guiana Ossia Relazione di Cinque Anni di Corse e di Osservazioni Fatte in Questo Interessante e Poco Conosciuto Paese. Milan: 1818. V. 62

STEEDMAN, AMY
Legends and Stories of Italy for Children. London: 1909. V. 64

STEEDMAN, CHARLES J.
Bucking the Sagebrush or the Oregon Trail in the Seventies. New York: 1904. V. 63; 66

STEEL, A. G.
Cricket. London: 1888. V. 67

STEEL, DAVID
Elements and Practice of Rigging and Seamanship. London: 1794. V. 62
Naval Chronologist of the Late War from Its Commencement in February 1793 to Its Conclusion in 1801. London: 1803. V. 65
The Shipwright's Vade-Mecum. London: 1822. V. 62

STEEL, FLORA ANNIE
English Fairy Tales. London: 1918. V. 64; 66
English Fairy Tales. 1927. V. 65
India. London: 1905. V. 63
India. London: 1912. V. 65
Tales of the Punjab. London: 1894. V. 65

STEEL, JOHN
Across the Plains in 1850. Chicago: 1930. V. 65

STEEL, JOHN H.
An Analysis of the Mineral Waters of Saratoga and Ballston.... Saratoga Springs: 1825. V. 64
An Analysis of the Mineral Waters of Saratoga and Ballston.... Saratoga Springs: 1838. V. 62

STEELE, ANNE
Miscellaneous Pieces in Verse and Prose by Theodosia. Bristol. 1780. V. 67

STEELE, D. A.
One Hundred Years with the Baptists of Amherst, N.S. 1810-1910. Amherst: 1911. V. 63

STEELE, EDWARD DUNSHA
Edward Dunsha Steele, 1829-1865. Pioneer Schoolteacher, Cabinetmaker and Musician, A Diary of His Journey from Lodi Wisconsin Across the Plains to Boulder, Colorado in the Year 1849. Boulder: 1960. V. 63; 64

STEELE, H. THOMAS
The Hawaiian Shirt. Its Art and History. New York: 1984. V. 65

STEELE, ISOBEL K. C.
The Enchanted Capital of Scotland. Edinburgh: 1945. V. 62

STEELE, J. W.
New Guide to the Pacific Coast, Santa Fe Route, California, Arizona, New Mexico, Colorado and Kansas. Chicago: 1893. V. 62; 65
The Sons of the Border Sketches of the Life and People of the Far Frontier. Topeka: 1873. V. 67

STEELE, JOHN
In Camp and Cabin...Mining Adventures in California During 1850 and Later. Lodi: 1901. V. 62

STEELE, MATTHEW F.
American Campaigns. Washington: 1909. V. 63; 66

STEELE, RICHARD
An Account of the State of the Roman-Catholick Religion Throughout the World. London: 1715. V. 62; 66
The Christian Hero: an Argument Proving That No Principles But Those of Religion are Sufficient to Make a Great Man. London: 1710. V. 64
The Conscious Lovers. Gli Amanti Interni Commedia Inglese. London: 1724. V. 64
The Crisis: or a Discourse Representing The Most Authentic Record, the Just Causes of the Late Happy Revolution.... London: 1714. V. 63; 65
The Englishman: Being the Close of the Paper So Called. (with) Mr. Steele's Apology for Himself and His Writings.... London: 1714. V. 64
The Epistolary Correspondence.... London: 1809. V. 62; 67
The Guardian. London: 1789. V. 62
The Guardian. London: 1797. V. 65
A Letter to the Earl of O----d Concerning the Bill of Peerage. London: 1719. V. 63
The Lover, to which is added The Reader. London: 1715. V. 63
The Plebeians. London: 1719. V. 67
Poetical Miscellanies, Consisting of Original Poems and Translations. London: 1714. V. 66
The Political Writings. London: 1715. V. 64
The Romish Ecclesiastical History of Late Years. London: 1714. V. 66
The State of the Case Between the Lord Chamberlain of His Majesty's Household and the Governor of the Royal Company of Comedians. London: 1720. V. 63; 66
The Tender Husband; or, the Accomplish'd Fools. London: 1705. V. 65

STEELE, ROBERT
Renaud of Montauban. London: 1897. V. 63
The Revival of Printing, a Bibliographical Catalogue of Works Issued by the Chief Modern English Presses. London: 1912. V. 62; 63; 65
The Story of Alexander. London: 1894. V. 63

STEELE, S. B.
Forty Years in Canada - Reminiscences of the Great Northwest. Toronto/London: 1915. V. 67

STEELE, SILAS S.
Song, On the Death of President Lincoln. Tune---Annie Laurie. Philadelphia: 1865. V. 64

STEELE, T. S.
Paddle and Portage, from Moosehead Lake to the Aroostook River, Maine. Boston: 1882. V. 63

STEELE, WILLIAM
A Summary of the Powers and Duties of Juries in Criminal Trials in Scotland. Edinburgh: 1833. V. 63

STEELMAN, ABSALOM
Autobiography of Rev. Absalom Seelman, of Succasunna. Dover: 1875. V. 63; 66

STEEN, MARGUERITE
The Tavern. London: 1935. V. 66

STEENIS, C. G. G. J. VAN
Pacific Plant Areas. Manila and Leiden: 1963-1975. V. 66

STEER, JOHN
Parish Law: Being a Digest of the Law Relating to Parishes.... London: 1830. V. 63

STEERS, J. A.
Scolt Head Island, the Story of Its Origin: The Plant and Animal Life of the Dunes and Marshes. Cambridge: 1934. V. 67

STEEVENS, G. W.
Monologues of the Dead. London: 1896. V. 64

STEEVENS, GEORGE
Bibliotheca Steevensiana. A Catalogue of the Valuable Library of George Stevens, Esq. Comprehending an Extraordinary Fine Collection of Books.... London: 1800. V. 63

STEEVES, SARAH HUNT
Book of Remembrance of Marion County, Oregon, Pioneers 1840-1860. Portland: 1927. V. 66

STEFANSSON, VILHJALMUR
The Friendly Arctic. New York: 1921. V. 62
Hunters of the Great North. New York: 1922. V. 65
My Life with the Eskimo. New York: 1913. V. 62
My Life with the Eskimo. New York: 1921. V. 62; 66
Ultima Thule. New York: 1940. V. 64

STEFFAN, ENNO
Spies in Ireland. 1963. V. 67

STEFFEN, RANDY
The Horse Soldier 1776-1943. Norman: 1977. V. 64; 67
The Horse Soldier 1776-1943. Norman: 1977-1979. V. 62; 63
The Horse Soldier: The United States Cavalryman: His Uniforms, Arms, Accoutrements and Equipments. Volume II. Norman: 1978. V. 66

STEFFENS, LINCOLN
The Shame of the Cities. New York: 1904. V. 63

STEFFY, J. W.
The Valley Harmonist, Containing a Collection of Tunes from the Most Approved Authors. New Market: 1845. V. 62

STEGGALL, JOHN
Elements of Botany.... London: 1831. V. 64

STEGNER, PAGE
Catching the Light: Remembering Wallace Stegner. N.P: 1996. V. 66

STEGNER, WALLACE
All the Little Live Things. New York: 1967. V. 62; 66; 67
The American Novel from James Fenimore Cooper to William Faulkner. New York: 1965. V. 67
Angle of Repose. Taiwan: 1971. V. 67
Beyond the Hundredth Meridian. Boston: 1954. V. 65
Beyond the Hundredth Meridian. Lincoln: 1982. V. 62
The Big Rock Candy Mountain. New York: 1943. V. 62
The Big Rock Candy Mountain. Franklin Center: 1978. V. 67
The City of the Living and Other Stories. Boston: 1956. V. 66
Collected Stories. New York: 1990. V. 67
Conversations with Wallace Stegner on Western History and Literature. Salt Lake City: 1983. V. 67
Crossing to Safety. Franklin Center: 1987. V. 62; 66
Crossing to Safety. New York: 1987. V. 66; 67
Discovery!. Beirut: 1971. V. 67
The Gathering of Zion. New York Toronto London: 1964. V. 66
The Preacher and the Slave. Boston: 1950. V. 67
Recapitulation. Franklin Center: 1979. V. 64; 67
Recapitulation. Garden City: 1979. V. 66
Recapitulation. New York: 1979. V. 67
Remembering Laughter. Boston: 1937. V. 65
Second Growth. Boston. 1947. V. 62
A Shooting Star. New York: 1961. V. 66
The Spectator Bird. Franklin Center: 1976. V. 63; 64; 67
The Spectator Bird. New York: 1976. V. 67
Stanford Short Stories 1964. Stanford: 1964. V. 63; 64
Two Rivers. Covelo: 1990. V. 66
The Uneasy Chair. Garden City: 1974. V. 67
Where the Bluebird Sings to the Lemonade Springs. New York: 1992. V. 66
Wildlands in Our Civilization. San Francisco: 1964. V. 65
Wolf Willow: a History, a Story and a Memory of the Last Plains Frontier. New York: 1962. V. 66

STEHR, F. W.
Immature Insects. Dubuque: 1987. V. 64

STEICHEN, EDWARD
The Family of Man. New York: 1955. V. 63
The First Picture Book. New York: 1991. V. 64; 67
A Life in Photography. New York: 1963. V. 67
U.S. Navy War Photographs. New York: 1946. V. 64

STEIG, WILLIAM
The Agony in the Kindergarten. New York: 1950. V. 62
Ariel's Island. New York: 1976. V. 65
Dreams of Glory. New York: 1953. V. 62
Male/Female. New York: 1971. V. 62
The Rejected Lovers. New York: 1951. V. 62
The Steig Album. New York: 1953. V. 62
Sylvester and the Magic Pebble. New York: 1969. V. 65
Till Death Do Us Part. New York: 1947. V. 62

STEIN, AUREL
On Alexander's Track to the Indus: Personal Narrative of Explorations on the North-West Frontier of India Carried Out Under the Orders of H. M. Indian Government. London: 1929. V. 65
Sand Buried Ruins of Khotan, Personal Narrative of a Journey of Archaeology and Geographical Exploration in Chinese Turkestan. London: 1903. V. 67

STEIN, ELIZABETH P.
David Garrick, Dramatist. New York: 1938. V. 64

STEIN, FRIEDRICH
Der Organismus der Infusionsthiere Nach Eigenen Forschungen.... Leipzig: 1859-1883. V. 63

STEIN, GERTRUDE
Blood on the Dining Room Floor. 1948. V. 62
Brewsie and Willie. New York: 1946. V. 62; 66; 67
Dix Portraits. Paris: 1930. V. 62
An Elucidation: printed in Transition April 1927. Paris: 1927. V. 62
Everybody's Autobiography. London: 1938. V. 63
Four in America. New Haven: 1947. V. 63; 64
Four Saints in Three Acts. New York: 1934. V. 64
The Geographical History of America or the Relation of Human Nature to the Human Mind. New York: 1936. V. 62
Geography and Plays. Boston: 1922. V. 62; 64; 66; 67
The Gertrude Stein First Reader and Three Plays. Boston: 1948. V. 65
Have They Attacked Mary He Giggled. N.P: 1917. V. 62
How to Write. Paris: 1931. V. 65
Last Operas and Plays. New York: 1949. V. 63; 64
Lectures in America. New York: 1935. V. 63; 64
Lucretia Borgia: a Play. New York: 1968. V. 66
The Making of Americans: the Hersland Family. New York: 1934. V. 66
Narration - Four Lectures. Chicago: 1935. V. 63; 66
Operas and Plays. Paris: 1932. V. 62; 63; 64; 66
Paris France. London: 1940. V. 63
Selected Writings. New York: 1946. V. 63; 64; 66
Tender Buttons. Objects, Food, Rooms. New York: 1914. V. 65
Things As They Are. Pawlet: 1950. V. 62
Two (Hitherto Unpublished) Poems. New York: 1948. V. 62; 64; 67
Useful Knowledge. London. V. 63; 64
Wars I Have Seen. London: 1945. V. 63
What Are Masterpieces?. Los Angeles: 1940. V. 67

STEIN, MARC AUREL
On Alexander's Track to the Indus. London: 1929. V. 66
On Ancient Central-Asian Tracks. London: 1933. V. 66

STEINBACH, HENRY
The Punjaub. London: 1846. V. 65

STEINBECK, JOHN ERNST
America and Americans. London: 1966. V. 65
Un Americain a New York et a Paris. Paris: 1956. V. 62
Burning Bright. New York: 1950. V. 62; 64; 67
Cannery Row. New York: 1945. V. 64; 65
Cup of Gold. New York: 1929. V. 62; 63; 65
Cup of Gold. New York: 1936. V. 63
Des Souris et des Hommes (Of Mice and Men). Paris: 1939. V. 63
East of Eden. New York: 1952. V. 62; 63; 64; 65; 67
The Forgotten Village. New York: 1941. V. 67
The Grapes of Wrath. London: 1939. V. 62; 64; 65; 66; 67
The Grapes of Wrath. London: 1940. V. 65
The Grapes of Wrath. New York: 1940. V. 64
His Language. Aptos: 1970. V. 62; 64; 67
In Dubious Battle. London: 1936. V. 63
Journal of a Novel. New York: 1969. V. 63; 67
The Log from the Sea of Cortez.... London: 1958. V. 64
The Moon is Down. New York: 1942. V. 62; 63; 65
Of Mice and Men. New York: 1937. V. 62; 64; 66; 67
The Portable Steinbeck. New York: 1946. V. 64
Positano. Salerno: 1955. V. 62
The Red Pony. New York: 1937. V. 62; 66
A Russian Journal. New York: 1948. V. 65
Saint Katy the Virgin. Mount Vernon: 1936. V. 64
Sea of Cortez. New York: 1941. V. 62; 65
The Short Reign of Pippin IV. New York: 1957. V. 66
Sweet Thursday. New York: 1953. V. 62; 64
De Vliegenvanger. (The Moon is Down). Utrecht: 1944. V. 66
The Wayward Bus. New York: 1947. V. 66
The Winter of Our Discontent. New York: 1961. V. 62; 63; 64; 66; 67

STEINBECK, JOHN S.
Fabulous Redmen: the Carlisle Indians and Their Famous Football Teams. Harrisburg: 1951. V. 63

STEINBERG, LOIS
Voices Round the River. San Francisco: 1977. V. 62

STEINBRUNNER, CHRIS
Detectionary. Lock Haven: 1972. V. 65

STEINER, CHARLOTTE
Lulu. New York: 1939. V. 63

STEINER, F. GEORGE
Malice. Oxford: 1952. V. 67

STEINER, GEORGE
Tolstoy or Dostoevsky. An Essay in the Old Criticism. New York: 1959. V. 67

STEINER, RUDOLF
Goethe the Scientist. New York: 1950. V. 65
The Story of My Life. London: 1928. V. 65

STEINGRUBER, JOHANN DAVID
Practische Burgerliche Baukunst Mit den Haupt-und Specialrissen und Gesimslehren.... Nuremberg: 1773. V. 64

STEINHAUS, E. A.
Insect Pathology. An Advanced Treatise. New York: 1963. V. 67

STEINMETZ, CHARLES PROTEUS
Elementary Lectures on Electric Discharges, Waves and Impulses and Other Transients. New York and London: 1911. V. 63

STEINSCHNEIDER, MORITZ
Die Hebraischen Uebersetzungen des Mittelalters und die Juden als Dolmetscher. Berlin: 1893. V. 63

STEJNEGER, L.
Results of Ornithological Explorations in the Commander Islands and in Kamtschatka. Washington: 1885. V. 62; 64

STELL, I.
The Hastings Guide.... Hastings: 1815. V. 66
The Hastings Guide.... 1830. V. 66

STELLA, FRANK
Working Space. Cambridge: 1986. V. 63

STENBOCK, ERIC, COUNT
The True Story of a Vampire. Edinburgh: 1989. V. 67

STENGEL, E.
Attempted Suicide. London: 1958. V. 66

STENGEL, HANSGEORG
So ein Struwwelpeter. Berlin: 1970. V. 66

STENHOUSE, T. B. H., MRS.
Expose of Polygamy in Utah. A Lady's Life Among the Mormons. New York: 1872. V. 67
Tell It All: The Story of a Life' Experience in Mormonism - an Autobiography. Harford: 1875. V. 64; 67

STENNETT, SAMUEL
Discourses on Domestick Duties. London: 1783. V. 62

STENO, NICOLAUS
Steno in Six Languages. Denmark: 1986. V. 63

STENT, HENRY
Conjugal Infidelity; or, the Fatal Elopment; a Warning to Matrons.... London: 1819. V. 63

STEP, EDWARD
Bees, Wasps, Ants and Allied Insects of the British Isles. 1932. V. 67
Wayside and Woodland Blossoms. London: 1963. V. 62
Wayside and Woodland Trees. London: 1904. V. 62

STEPHANIDES, THEODORE
Climax in Crete. London: 1946. V. 67

STEPHANINI, J.
The Narrative of J. Stephanini, a Native of Arta, in Greece. Charleston: 1829. V. 66

STEPHANUS, CAROLUS
Dictionarium Historicum, Geographicum, Poeticum...Gentium, Hominum, Deorum (etc). Geneva: 1650. V. 67

STEPHEN, ADRIAN
The Dreadnought Hoax. London: 1936. V. 62

STEPHEN, ALEXANDER
Hopi Journal. New York: 1936. V. 63; 65
Hopi Journal. Mansfield Centre: 1998. V. 67

STEPHEN, GEORGE
Adventures of an Attorney in Search of Practice. London: 1839. V. 66
Antislavery Recollections: in a Series of Letters.... London: 1854. V. 65
The Royal Pardon Vindicated in Reference to the Claims of Mr. W. H. Barber on the Justice of the Country. London: 1852. V. 63

STEPHEN, GEORGE MILNER
Report of the Argus Libel Case; the Queen on the Prosecution of George Milner Stephen Versus Wilson and MacKinnon, Proprietors of the "Argus". Feb. 20th-March 2nd, 1857. Melbourne: 1857. V. 63

STEPHEN, J. K.
Lapsus Calami. Cambridge: 1891. V. 64

STEPHEN, JAMES
War in Disguise. London: 1805. V. 63
War in Disguise. London: 1807. V. 66

STEPHEN, JAMES FITZJAMES
A History of the Criminal Law of England. London: 1883. V. 63
Liberty, Equality, Fraternity. London: 1873. V. 64

STEPHEN, LESLIE
English Utilitarians. London: 1912. V. 64
History of English Thought in the Eighteenth Century. New York: 1876. V. 64
Hours in a Library. London: 1909. V. 65
Life of Henry Fawcett. London: 1885. V. 66
The Science of English Ethics. London: 1907. V. 64
Sketches from Cambridge. London: 1865. V. 64

STEPHENS, ABEDNEGO
Address to the Alumni Society of Nashville University on the Influence of Institutions for High Letters on the Mental and Moral Character of the Nation.... Nashville: 1838. V. 66

STEPHENS, ALEXANDER
Memoirs of John Horne Tooke, Interspersed with Original Documents. London: 1813. V. 63; 66

STEPHENS, ALEXANDER HAMILTON
A Constitutional View of the Late War Between the States: Its Causes, Character, Conduct and Results. Philadelphia: 1868. V. 63
Constitutional View of the Late War Between the States: Its Causes, Character, Conduct and Results. Philadelphia: 1868-1870. V. 62; 63; 65
A Constitutional View of the Late War Between the States: Its Causes, Character, Conduct and Results. Philadelphia: 1870. V. 62

STEPHENS, ARCHIBALD J.
The Law of Nisi Prius, Evidence in Civil Actions and Arbitration and Awards. Philadelphia: 1844. V. 67

STEPHENS, CHARLES H.
The Origin and History of the Hopi-Navajo Boundary Dispute in Northern Arizona. Provo: 1961. V. 63

STEPHENS, DAN V.
Peter Stephens and Some of His Descendants. Fremont: 1936. V. 62

STEPHENS, EDGAR
The Clerks of the Counties 1360-1960. (With) Supplement 1960-1974. London: 1961. V. 66

STEPHENS, EDWARD
Reflections Upon the Occurrences of the Last Year. From 5 Nov. 1688 to 5 Nov. 1689. London: 1689. V. 64

STEPHENS, F. G.
Notes on a Collection of Drawings and Woodcuts by Thomas Bewick Exhibited at the Fine Art Society's Rooms 1880. London: 1881. V. 63

STEPHENS, HENRY
The Book of the Farm (Detailing the Labors of the Farmer, Steward, Plowman, Hedger, Cattle-Man, Shepherd, Field-Wonder, and Dairymaid). New York: 1851. V. 64

STEPHENS, HENRY L.
Mother Goose's Melodies for Children, or Songs for the Nursery. New York: 1872. V. 64

STEPHENS, J. F.
Illustrations of British Entomology, Haustellata Only.. 1020-1034. V. 65; 66
Illustrations of British Entomology; or, a Synopsis of Indigenous Insects. London: 1827-1846. V. 62

STEPHENS, JAMES
Collected Poems. 1926. V. 62; 64; 65; 67
Collected Poems. London: 1926. V. 63
The Crock of Gold. 1912. V. 67
Crock of Gold. London: 1912. V. 62
The Crock of Gold. 1922. V. 67
The Crock of Gold. New York: 1922. V. 63
The Hill of Vision. 1912. V. 63
Hunger. Dublin: 1918. V. 62
Insurrections. Dublin: 1909. V. 63
Irish Fairy Tales. London: 1920. V. 63
Julia Elizabeth. New York: 1929. V. 62; 65; 67
Little Things. 1924. V. 67
Theme and Variations. New York: 1930. V. 67

STEPHENS, JEREMIAH
An Apology for the Ancient Right and Power of the Bishops to Sit and Vote in Parliaments: as the First and Principal of the Three Estates of the Kingdome, as Lord Coke sheweth.... London: 1660. V. 63

STEPHENS, JOHN
An Historical Discourse, Briefly Setting Forth the Nature of Procurations, and How They Were Antiently Paid.... London: 1661. V. 65

STEPHENS, JOHN LLOYD
Incidents of Travel in Central America, Chiapas, and Yucatan. London: 1841. V. 62; 65
Incidents of Travel in Central America, Chiapas and Yucatan. New York: 1841. V. 62; 67
Incidents of Travel in Central America, Chiapas and Yucatan. London: 1842. V. 64
Incidents of Travel in Central America, Chiapas and Yucatan. London: 1844. V. 67
Incidents of Travel in Central America, Chiapas and Yucatan. 1852. V. 62
Incidents of Travel in Egypt, Arabian, Petreaea and the Holy Land. New York: 1838. V. 65
Incidents of Travel in Greece, Turkey, Russia and Poland. New York: 1838. V. 65
Incidents of Travel in Yucatan. New York: 1847. V. 67

STEPHENS, LOUISE G.
Letters from an Oregon Ranch. Chicago: 1905. V. 63; 64

STEPHENS, PHILIP
Catalogus Horti Botanici Oxoniensis... (with) Second Part. Oxford: 1638. V. 64

STEPHENS, ROBERT W.
Walter Durbin, Texas Ranger and Sheriff. 1970. V. 63

STEPHENS, STEPHEN DE WITT
The Mavericks. American Engravers. New Brunswick: 1950. V. 63; 66

STEPHENS, WALTER
Notes on the Mineralogy of Part of the Vicinity of Dublin. 1812. V. 65

STEPHENSON, GEORGE
A Report on the Practicability and Utility of the Limerick and Waterford Railway, or of Such Parts Thereof as Ought to be Completed Immediately. London: 1831. V. 62

STEPHENSON, J.
Medical Zoology and Mineralogy or Illustrations and Descriptions of the Animals and Minerals Employed in Medicine. 1832. V. 65; 66
The Oligochaeta. Oxford: 1930. V. 63

STEPHENSON, NEAL
The Dig U. New York: 1004. V. 67
The Diamond Age. New York: 1995. V. 67
Snow Crash. 1992. V. 63

STEPHENSON, P. R.
Sydney Sails. Sydney: 1962. V. 62

STEPHENSON, ROBERT
The Triumph of Science. Carnarvon: 1849. V. 62

STEPHENSON, T. A.
The British Sea Anemones. London: 1928-1935. V. 66

STEPHENSON, TERRY E.
Caminos Viejos - Tales Found in the History of California of Especial Interest to Those who Love the Valleys, the Hills and the Canyons of Orange County, Its Traditions and Its Landmarks. Santa Ana: 1930. V. 63; 66
The Shadows of Saddleback. Santa Ana: 1948. V. 64; 67

STERLAND, W. J.
The Birds of Sherwood Forest, With Notes on Their Habits, Nesting, Migrations, &c. London: 1869. V. 67

STERLING, ADALINE W.
The Book of Englewood. Englewood: 1922. V. 63; 66

STERLING, ALEXANDER WILLIAM, EARL OF
Recreations with the Muses. London: 1637. V. 62

STERLING, BRUCE
The Artificial Kid. New York: 1980. V. 63; 67

STERLING, GEORGE
Rosamund - a Dramtic Poem. San Francisco: 1920. V. 64

STERLING, RICHARD
Our Own Second Reader: for the Use of Schools and Familes. Greensboro: 1862. V. 62; 63; 65

STERLING, WILLIAM
Annals of the Artists of Spain. London: 1848. V. 63; 65

STERN, F. C.
Snowdrops and Snowflakes, a Study of the Genera Galanthus and Lecojum. London: 1956. V. 64
A Study of the Genus Paeonia. London: 1946. V. 64

STERN, GERALD
The Naming of Beasts and Other Poems. Omaha: 1973. V. 64
Paradise Poems. New York: 1984. V. 67

STERN, HENRY A.
Wanderings Among the Falashas in Abyssinia.... London: 1862. V. 62

STERN, JAMES
The Hidden Damage. New York: 1947. V. 63; 66
The Man Who Was Loved. New York: 1951. V. 63
The Stories of James Stern. London: 1968. V. 66

STERN, JO LANE
Roster Commissioned Officers Virginia Volunteers 1871-1920. Richmond: 1921. V. 64

STERN, M. E.
Andachtsbuch Deutsche Gebete...(und) Israeliten.... Wien: 1899. V. 67

STERN, PHILIP VAN DOREN
An End to Valor. The Last Days of the Civil War. Boston: 1958. V. 62
Secret Missions of the Civil War. Chicago: 1959. V. 63

STERN, RICHARD MARTIN
The Tower. New York: 1973. V. 65

STERN, RUDI
Let There Be Neon. New York: 1979. V. 62; 65

STERNBERG, MARTHA L.
George Miller Sternberg - a Biography. Chicago: 1920. V. 64

STERNDALE, MARY
The Panorama of Youth. London: 1807. V. 65
Vignettes of Derbyshire. London: 1824. V. 64

STERNDALE, ROBERT ARMITAGE
The Afghan Knife. London: 1879. V. 66
Denizens of the Jungles: A Series of Sketches in Pen and Pencil. Calcutta: 1881. V. 62
Natural History of the Mammals of India and Ceylon. 1884. V. 63

STERNE, ASHLEY
Problems of a Structural Engineer. Bolton, Lancashire: 1930. V. 65

STERNE, LAURENCE
The Beauties of Sterne.... London: 1782. V. 65
Letters from Yorick to Eliza. London: 1775. V. 64
Original Letters...Never Before Published. London: 1788. V. 62
Sterne's Letters to His Friends on Various Occasions. (with) Letters from Yorick to Eliza. London: 1775. V. 62
The Life and Letters of Laurence Sterne. London. V. 64
The Life and Opinion of Tristram Shandy, Gentleman. London: 1926. V. 62
The Life and Opinions of Tristram Shandy, Gentleman. London: 1760-1767. V. 62; 64; 65; 67
The Life and Opinions of Tristram Shandy, Gentleman. London: 1781. V. 62
The Life and Opinions of Tristram Shandy, Gentleman. London: 1794. V. 62
The Novels of.... London: 1920. V. 64
Oeuvres Completes de Sterne.... Paris: 1818. V. 66
Original Letters...Never Before Published. London: 1788. V. 66
A Sentimental Journey through France and Italy. London: 1768. V. 62; 63; 64; 65; 66; 67
A Sentimental Journey through France and Italy. London: 1769. V. 63
A Sentimental Journey through France and Italy. London: 1792. V. 66
A Sentimental Journey through France and Italy. New York: 1884. V. 67
A Sentimental Journey through France and Italy. London: 1897. V. 67
A Sentimental Journey through France and Italy. London: 1910. V. 62; 66
A Sentimental Journey through France and Italy. New York: 1910. V. 64
A Sentimental Journey through France and Italy. Reading: 1928. V. 65
A Sentimental Journey through France and Italy. Waltham St. Lawrence: 1928. V. 65; 67
A Sentimental Journey through France and Italy. High Wycombe: 1936. V. 62; 63; 64; 65
A Sentimental Journey...and the Continuation Thereof by Eugenius. London: 1784. V. 62
The Sermons of Mr. Yorick. London: 1761. V. 62
Tristram Schandis. Hamburg: 1774. V. 66; 67
Tristram Schandis Leben und Meynungen. Frankfurt und Leipzig: 1776-1777. V. 67
La Vie et les Opinions de Tristram Shandy. Londres: 1784-1785. V. 66
La Vie et les Opinions de Tristram Shandy. Paris: 1785. V. 62
Voyage Sentimental en France. Paris: 1792. V. 62
Voyage Sentimental en France et en Italie. Paris: 1884. V. 65; 67
The Works. London: 1783. V. 62
The Works. London: 1788. V. 63
The Works. London: 1795. V. 64
The Works. London: 1823. V. 62

STERNE, SIMON
On Representative Government and Personal Representation. Philadelphia: 1871. V. 66

STERNFELD, JOEL
Campagna. New York: 1992. V. 65

STERRY, CONSIDER
The American Youth: Being a New and Complete Course of Introductory Mathematics.... Providence: 1790. V. 63; 66

STERRY, J. ASHBY
The Shuttlecock Papers. London: 1873. V. 65

STEUART, HENRY
The Planter's Guide. Edinburgh: 1828. V. 63; 66
The Planter's Guide. London: 1828. V. 67
The Planter's Guide. New York: 1832. V. 63; 66
The Planter's Guide. 1848. V. 63
The Planter's Guide. Edinburgh: 1848. V. 66

STEUART, JAMES
An Inquiry Into the Principles of Political Oeconomy.... London: 1767. V. 64

STEUART, JOHN A.
Letters to Living Authors. London: 1890. V. 67
Robert Louis Sevenson: Man and Writer: A Critcal Biography. London: 1924. V. 67

STEUBEN, FRIEDRICH WILHELM VON
Regulations for the Order and Discipline of the Troops of the United States. Worcester: 1788. V. 64
Regulations for the Order and Discipline of the Troops of the United States. New York: 1794. V. 63; 66

STEVEN, EDWARD MILLAR
Medical Supervision in Schools Being an Account of the Systems at Work in Great Britain, Canada, the United States, Germany and Switzerland. London: 1910. V. 64

STEVEN, ROBERT
Remarks on the Present State of Ireland: with Hints for Ameliorating the Condition and Promoting the Education and Moral Improvement, of the Peasantry of that Country. London: 1822. V. 64

STEVENS, ABEL
The Centenary of American Methodism: a Sketch of Its History, Theology, Practical System & Success. New York: 1865. V. 67
History of the Life and Times of John Wesley, Embracing the History of Methodism.... London: 1864. V. 63

STEVENS, C. E.
Comparative Physiology of the Vertebrate Digestive System. Cambridge: 1988. V. 64; 66

STEVENS, EDWARD P.
The American Hospital of the Twentieth Century. New York: 1918. V. 67

STEVENS, EZRA A.
Geographical Keys, Containing a Brief Explanation of the Terms Used in Geography.... Portsmouth: 1819. V. 62

STEVENS, F. L.
Through Merrie England. London: 1928. V. 62

STEVENS, FLORA ELLICE
Shores of Nothing. Waco: 1942. V. 64

STEVENS, FREDERIC H.
Santo Tomas Interment Camp...1942-1945. N.P: 1946. V. 66

STEVENS, GEORGE ALEXANDER
A Lecture on Heads. London: 1808. V. 67
A Lecture on Heads. London: 1812. V. 64
Songs, Comic and Satyrical. London: 1801. V. 64; 65

STEVENS, GEORGE T.
Functional Nervous Diseases - Their Causes and Their Treatment. New York: 1887. V. 66; 67

STEVENS, HENRY
An Account of the Proceedings at the Dinner Given by Mr. George Peabody to the Americans Connected with the Great Exhibition at the London Coffee House Ludgate Hill on the 27th October 1851. London: 1851. V. 66
Benjamin Franklin's Life and Writings, a Bibliographical Essay on the Stevens' Collection of Books and Manuscripts Relating to Dr. Franklin. London: 1881. V. 63
Bibliotheca Historica.... Boston: 1870. V. 66
Recollections of Mr. James Lenox of New York and the Formation of His Library. London: 1886. V. 63
Who Spoils Our New English Books Asked and Answered. London: 1884. V. 62; 65

STEVENS, HOLLY
Souvenirs and Prohecies: the Young Wallace Stevens. New York: 1977. V. 67

STEVENS, I.
Avian Biochemistry and Molecular Biology. Cambridge: 1996. V. 67

STEVENS, J. K.
Three Dimensional Confoal Microscopy. (Volume Investigation of Biological Specimens). London: 1994. V. 66

STEVENS, JOHN
An Historical Account of all Taxes, Under What Denomination Soever.... London: 1733. V. 62
A New Spanish Grammar.... London: 1739. V. 62
The Royal Treasury of England; or an Historical Account of All Taxed, Under What Denomination Soever, From the Conquest to the Present Year. London: 1725. V. 65; 66
The Spanish Libertines.... London: 1709. V. 63; 65

STEVENS, JOHN W.
Leather Manufacture, a Treatise on the Practical Workings of the Leather Manufacture Including Oil Shoe Grain, Imitation Goat and Calf, Bright Oil, English and American Boot Grain.... London: 1891. V. 64

STEVENS, L.
Avian Biochemistry and Molecular Biology. Cambridge: 1996. V. 65

STEVENS, LEWIS TOWNSEND
The History of Cape May County, New Jersey.... Cape May City: 1897. V. 63; 66

STEVENS, LOUIS
Here Comes Pancho Villa - the Anecdotal History of a Genial Killer. New York: 1930. V. 67

STEVENS-NELSON PAPER CORPORATION
Specimens: a Stevens-Nelson Paper Catalogue. New York: 1954. V. 62

STEVENS, SHANE
Go Down Dead. 1966. V. 67
Way Uptown in Another World. New York: 1971. V. 67

STEVENS, THOMAS
Around the World on a Bicycle from Teheran to Yokohama. London: 1888. V. 65

STEVENS, WALLACE
The Auroras of Autumn. New York: 1950. V. 62; 64; 65; 67
The Collected Poems. New York: 1954. V. 65
Description Without Place. Sewanee: 1945. V. 62
Esthetique du Mal. Cummington: 1945. V. 62; 64
Harmonium. New York: 1923. V. 63; 66; 67
Harmonium. New York: 1931. V. 63; 67
Ideas of Order. New York: 1935. V. 62; 64; 65
Ideas of Order. New York: 1936. V. 62; 64
Letters of Wallace Stevens. New York: 1966. V. 62; 67
Letters of Wallace Stevens. London: 1967. V. 63
The Man With the Blue Guitar and Other Poems. New York: 1937. V. 64
The Man With the Blue Guitar and Other Poems. New York: 1945. V. 64
The Man With the Blue Guitar Including Ideas of Order. New York: 1952. V. 62; 64; 67
Mattino Domenicale Ed Altre Poesie. Torino: 1954. V. 62; 64; 67
The Necessary Angel. New York: 1951. V. 62; 64; 67
Notes Toward a Supreme Fiction. Cummington: 1942. V. 64; 67
Notes Toward a Supreme Fiction. Cummington: 1943. V. 64
Opus Posthumous. New York: 1957. V. 65; 66
The Palm at the End of the Mind. New York: 1971. V. 64; 66; 67
Parts of a World. New York: 1942. V. 62
A Primitive Like an Orb. New York: 1948. V. 62; 64; 67
Raoul Dufy. New York: 1953. V. 64; 67
The Relations Between Poetry and Painting. New York: 1951. V. 64
Selected Poems. London: 1952. V. 62; 64
Three Academic Pieces. The Realm of Resemblance, Someone Puts a Pineapple Together, Of Ideal Time and Choice. Cummington: 1947. V. 64
Transport to Summer. New York: 1947. V. 64; 66; 67

STEVENS, WALTER B.
The Brown-Reynolds Duel. St. Louis: 1911. V. 62

STEVENS, WILLIAM
A System for the Discipline of the Artillery of the United States of America, or, the Young Artillerist's Pocket Companion. New York: 1797. V. 64; 66

STEVENS, WILLIAM BACON
A History of Georgia from Its First Discovery by Europeans to the Adoption of the Present Constitution in MDCCXCVIII. New York: 1847. V. 64

STEVENSON, ANNE
Living in America. Poems. Ann Arbor: 1965. V. 64
Selected Poems 1956-1986. Oxford: 1987. V. 66

STEVENSON, DAVID
Life of Robert Stevenson. Edinburgh: 1878. V. 62

STEVENSON, EDWARD LUTHER
Terrestrial and Celestial Globes: Their History and Construction, Including a Consideration of Their Value as Aids in the Study of Geography and Astronomy. 1998. V. 65

STEVENSON, H. M.
The Birdlife of Florida. Gainesville: 1994. V. 64

STEVENSON, IAN
Cases of the Reincarnation Type. Chicago: 1975. V. 62

STEVENSON, J. B.
The Species of Rhododendron. 1930. V. 63; 66
The Species of Rhododendron. London: 1930. V. 62
The Species of Rhododendron. 1947. V. 62; 63; 66

STEVENSON, JOHN
Cataract; a Familiar Description of Its Nature, Symptoms, and Ordinary Modes of Treatment.... London: 1834. V. 63
On the Morbid Sensibility of the Eye, Commonly Called Weakness of Sight. Hartford: 1815. V. 62
The Principles of Murathee Grammar. Bombay: 1868. V. 63

STEVENSON, JOHN HALL
Makarony Fables; with the New Fable of the Bees. London: 1768. V. 62

STEVENSON, JOHN R.
Thomas Stevenson of London, England, and His Descendants. Flemington: 1902. V. 63; 66

STEVENSON, JOSEPH
Documents Illustrative of the History of Scotland from the Death of King Alexander the Third to the Accession of Robert Bruce MCCLXXDXVI-MCCCVI. Edinburgh: 1870. V. 62

STEVENSON, LLOYD G.
Nobel Prize Winners in Medicine and Physiology 1901-1950. New York: 1953. V. 66

STEVENSON, MERRITT
Marine Atlas of the Pacific Coastal Waters of South America. Berkeley/Los Angeles: 1970. V. 64

STEVENSON, R. RANDOLPH
The Southern Side: or, Andersonville Prison. Baltimore: 1876. V. 62; 63; 65

STEVENSON, ROBERT LOUIS BALFOUR
Across the Plains. London: 1892. V. 63
The Amateur Emigrant. Chicago: 1895. V. 62; 67
Ballads. London: 1890. V. 62; 64; 67
The Black Arrow; a Tale of the Two Roses. London: 1888. V. 63; 67
The Black Arrow (A Tale of the Two Roses). New York: 1888. V. 63
Catriona.... London: 1893. V. 63; 67
A Child's Garden of Verses. London: 1896. V. 64; 65
A Child's Garden of Verses. New York: 1900. V. 63
A Child's Garden of Verses. New York: 1905. V. 62; 63
A Child's Garden of Verses. London: 1908. V. 64
A Child's Garden of Verses. New York: 1909. V. 63
A Child's Garden of Verses. Philadelphia: 1926. V. 65
A Child's Garden of Verses. New York: 1927. V. 65
A Child's Garden of Verses. London: 1931. V. 65
A Child's Garden of Verses. New York: 1932. V. 62
A Child's Garden of Verses. Akron: 1940. V. 64
A Child's Garden of Verses. New York: 1942. V. 66
A Child's Garden of Verses. New York: 1944. V. 63; 64
A Child's Garden of Verses. Kenosha: 1947. V. 65
A Child's Garden of Verses. San Francisco: 1978. V. 64
Diogenes at the Savile Club. Chicago: 1921. V. 62
The Dynamiter. London: 1885. V. 67
The Ebb Tide. Chicago and Cambridge: 1894. V. 62; 67
The Ebb Tide. London: 1894. V. 64; 67
Edinburgh: Picturesque Notes. London: 1879. V. 62; 64
Edinburgh: Picturesque Notes. London: 1954. V. 63; 65
The Essay on Walt Whitman, With a Little Journey to the Home of Whitman by Elbert Hubbard. East Aurora: 1900. V. 67
Fables. New York: 1896. V. 63
Fables. London: 1914. V. 66
Father Damien. London: 1890. V. 62
In the South Seas, Being an Account of Experiences and Observations in the Marquesas, Paumotus and Gilbert Islands in the Course of Two Cruises on the Yacht Casco (1888) and the Schooner Equator (1889). London: 1900. V. 67
Island Night's Entertainment. London: 1893. V. 62; 63; 66; 67
The Jolly Jump-Ups: a Child's Garden of Verses. Springfield: 1946. V. 63
Kidnapped. London: 1886. V. 63; 66
Kidnapped. New York: 1913. V. 64
The Letters: Robert Louis Stevenson to His Family and Friends. New York: 1899. V. 63; 64
The Letters to His Family and Friends. London: 1900. V. 62
A Lodging for the Night: Being a Tale Concerning One of Life's Lesser Hardships - Commonly Called Trouble. East Aurora: 1902. V. 63
Macaire. Chicago: 1895. V. 63
Macaire. London: 1897. V. 63
The Master of Ballantrae. London: 1889. V. 64; 66
The Master of Ballantrae. London: 1965. V. 63
The Merry Men and Other Tales and Fables. London: 1887. V. 62
New Arabian Nights. London: 1882. V. 65
New Arabian Nights. New York: 1882. V. 66
New Arabian Nights. London: 1889. V. 64
The New Arabian Nights. Avon: 1976. V. 63; 64
On the Thermal Influence of Forests. Edinburgh: 1883-1895. V. 62; 65
Poems. London: 1913. V. 62
La Porte de Maletroit. Cagnes-sur-Mer/San Francisco: 1952. V. 64
Prayers Written at Vailima. 1999. V. 65
Prince Otto. London: 1885. V. 64
Prince Otto. Boston: 1886. V. 62; 65
Records of a Family of Engineers. London: 1912. V. 66
St. Ives - Being the Adventures of a French Prisoner in England. London: 1898. V. 63; 67
The Silverado Squatters. San Francisco: 1952. V. 63; 66
Songs with Music from A Child's Garden of Verses. London: 1918. V. 62
Strange Case of Dr. Jekyll and Mr. Hyde. London: 1886. V. 62; 66; 67
The Strange Case of Dr. Jekyll and Mr. Hyde. London: 1896. V. 67
Strange Case of Dr. Jekyll and Mr. Hyde. New York: 1929. V. 62
The Strange Case of Dr. Jekyll and Mr. Hyde. London: 1930. V. 66
The Strange Case of Dr. Jekyll and Mr. Hyde. New York: 1930. V. 64
The Strange Case of Dr. Jekyll and Mr. Hyde. New York: 1941?. V. 67
The Strange Case of Dr. Jekyll and Mr. Hyde. London: 1948. V. 65
Strange Case of Dr. Jekyll and Mr. Hyde. New York: 1952. V. 65
The Suicide Club and the Rajah's Diamond. London: 1894. V. 66
Tales and Fantasies. Leipzig: 1905. V. 67
Three Short Poems. Chicago: 1902. V. 62; 64
Ticonderoga. Edinburgh: 1887. V. 62; 64
Treasure Island. London: 1883. V. 64
Treasure Island. New York: 1911. V. 64
Treasure Island. New York: 1941. V. 65
Treasure Island. London: 1949. V. 63
Underwoods. London: 1887. V. 67
Virginibus Puerisque and Other Papers. London: 1910. V. 65
Weir of Hermiston; an Unfinished Romance. London: 1896. V. 62; 67
Works. London: 1924. V. 67
Works. London: 1924-1925. V. 67
The Wrecker. London: 1892. V. 62
The Wrong Box. London: 1889. V. 67

STEVENSON, ROBERT LOUIS, MRS.
The Cruise of the Janet Nichol Among the South Sea Islands. New York: 1914. V. 62

STEVENSON, WILLIAM
Historical Sketch of the Progress of Discovery, Navigation and Commerce, from the Earliest Records to the Beginning of the Nineteenth Century. Edinburgh: 1824. V. 67
Some Account of the Religious Institutions of Old Nottingham (First, Second and Third) Series. Nottingham: 1895-1899. V. 65

STEVENSON, WILLIAM G.
Thirteen Months in the Rebel Army; Being a Narrative of Personal Adventures in the Infantry Ordnance, Cavalry, Courier and Hospital Services. New York: 1863. V. 65

STEVENSON-HAMILTON, J.
Animal Life in Africa. London: 1912. V. 62; 67
The Low-Veld: Its Wild Life and Its People. London: 1929. V. 63

STEWARD, DONALD O.
A Parody Outline of History. New York: 1921. V. 63

STEWARD, RICHARD
An Answer to a Letter Written at Oxford, and Superscribed to Dr. Samuel Turner, Concerning the Church and the Revenues Thereof. London: 1647. V. 63

STEWARD, SAMUEL
$tud. Washington: 1966. V. 64

STEWARD, WILLIAM
Gouldtown, a Very Remarkable Settlement of Ancient Date.... Philadelphia: 1913. V. 66

STEWART, A. E.
Round the World with Rod and Rifle. 1936. V. 67
Tiger and Other Game. 1927. V. 64; 66

STEWART, A. F.
Paintings, Drawings and Prints in the Collection.... London: 1920. V. 64

STEWART, AGNES M.
Stories of Richard Coeur de Lion, for the Instruction and Amusement of Young People. Dublin: 1847. V. 67

STEWART, ALVAN
A Legal Argument Before the Supreme Court of the State of New Jersey at the May Term, 1845, at Trenton, for the Deliverance of Four Thousand Persons from Bondage. New York: 1845. V. 66

STEWART, ANNA BIRD
The Gentlest Giant (and Other Pleasant Persons). New York: 1913. V. 64
The Gentlest Giant (and Other Pleasant Persons). New York: 1915. V. 62; 66

STEWART, ARCHIBALD
The Trial of Archibald Stewart, Esq.; Late Lord Provost of Edinburgh, Before the High Court of Justiciary in Scotland for Neglect of Duty and Misbehaviour in the Execution of His Office.... Edinburgh: 1747. V. 63

STEWART, CECIL
Topiary. Waltham St. Lawrence: 1954. V. 62

STEWART, CHARLES
The Killin Collection of Gaelic Songs, with Music and Translations. Edinburgh: 1884. V. 62

STEWART, CHARLES E.
Through Persia in Disguise. London: 1911. V. 66

STEWART, DOROTHY N.
Adobe Notes. Taos: 1930. V. 62

STEWART, DUGALD
Elements of the Philosophy of the Human Mind. London: 1792. V. 62; 64; 65; 67
Elements of the Philosophy of the Human Mind. Albany: 1822. V. 67
Philosophical Essays. Edinburgh: 1810. V. 64
Philosophical Essays. Philadelphia: 1811. V. 63
Philosophical Essays. Edinburgh: 1816. V. 66
Philosophical Essays. London: 1816. V. 66

STEWART, EDGAR I.
Custer's Luck. Norman: 1955. V. 65; 67

STEWART, EDGAR T.
Washington Northwest Frontier. New York: 1957. V. 64

STEWART, FRANK
Cross Country with Hounds. 1936. V. 62
Hark to Hounds. 1937. V. 62
Hunting Countries. 1935. V. 62

STEWART, FRANK H.
Notes on Old Gloucester County, New Jersey. Woodbury: 1917-1964. V. 63; 66

STEWART, GEORGE R.
Take Your Bible in One Hand: the Life of William Henry Thomas.... San Francisco: 1939. V. 64; 67

STEWART, GORDON T.
Documents Relating to the Great Awakening in Nova Scotia 1760-1791. Toronto: 1982. V. 63

STEWART, HAROLD
Orpheus and Other Poems. Sydney: 1956. V. 63; 66
Phoenix Wings. Poems 1940-1946. Sydney: 1948. V. 63

STEWART, HENRY
The Culture of Farm Crops. Millington: 1887. V. 64

STEWART, HUGH
Provincial Russia. London: 1913. V. 65

STEWART, J. I. M.
Appleby and the Ospreys. London: 1986. V. 63
The Aylwins. London: 1966. V. 62

Conspiracy. London: 1984. V. 63
Eight Modern Writers. 1963. V. 62
Eight Modern Writers. Oxford: 1963. V. 63
Honeybath's Haven. London: 1977. V. 63
Mungo's Dream - a Novel. London: 1973. V. 63
The Naylors - a Novel. London: 1985. V. 63
An Open Prison - a Novel. London: 1984. V. 63
Our England is a Garden and Other Stories. London: 1979. V. 64
A Use of Riches. London: 1957. V. 62

STEWART, JAMES
Index of Abridgement of the Acts of Parliament and Convention from the Reign of King James the First. Edinburgh: 1702. V. 62

STEWART, JIMMY
Jimmy Stewart and His Poems. New York: 1989. V. 65

STEWART, JOHN
Antarctica: an Encyclopedia. Jefferson: 1990. V. 64; 65

STEWART, KENSEY
A Geography for Beginners. Richmond: 1864. V. 63; 65

STEWART, LUCY SHELTON
The Reward of Patriotism. New York: 1930. V. 62

STEWART, MARY
The Way to Wonderland. London: 1914. V. 66
The Way to Wonderland. London: 1918. V. 63

STEWART, MATTHEW
An Examination of the Principles and Tendency of the Ministerial Plan of Reform. Edinburgh: 1831. V. 66
Tracts, Physical and Mathematical. Edinburgh: 1761. V. 66

STEWART, P. M.
Round the World with Rod and Rifle. London: 1925. V. 67

STEWART, PHILEMON
A Holy Sacred and Divine Roll and Book; from the Lord God of Heaven to the Inhabitants of the Earth. Canterbury: 1843. V. 63

STEWART, RICK
Charles M. Russell, Sculptor. Ft. Worth: 1994. V. 64; 66

STEWART, THOMAS GRAINGER
An Introduction to the Study of the Diseases of the Nervous System.... Edinburgh: 1884. V. 64; 66; 67

STEWART, W. C.
The Practical Angler. 1857. V. 65; 67

STEWART, WILL
Seetee Ship. 1951. V. 63

STEWART, WILLIAM H.
A Pair of Blankets. New York: 1911. V. 62; 63; 65
The Spirit of the South. New York and Washington: 1908. V. 62; 63

STEWART-BROWN, R.
The Tower of Liverpool, with Some Notes on the Clayton Family of Crooke, Fulwood, Adlington and Liverpool. Liverpool: 1910. V. 62; 65

STEWART-MURPHY, CHARLOTTE A.
A History of British Circulating Libraries: The Book Labels and Ephemera of the Papantonio Collection. Newtown: 1992. V. 64

STIBITZ, GEORGE R.
Mathematics and Computers. New York: 1957. V. 67

STICKLEY, GUSTAV
Craftsman Homes. New York: 1909. V. 65
More Craftsman Homes. New York: 1912. V. 65

STIEGLITZ, ALFRED
America and Alfred Stieglitz: a Collective Portrait. Garden City: 1934. V. 63
Camera Work: an Ilusrated Quarterly Magazine Devoted to Photography and to the Activities of the Photo-Secession. New York: 1912. V. 66
Camera Work: an Illustrated Quarterly Magazine Devoted to Photography and to the Activities of the Photo Secession. New York: 1913. V. 66
Exhibition of Photographs by Alfred Steiglitz. Washington: 1958. V. 63
Georgia O'Keefe a Portrait. New York: 1978. V. 65; 66

STIEHL, HENRY
The Life of a Frontier Builder - Autobiography of.... Salt Lake City: 1941. V. 65

STIELER Hand Atlas. Gotha: 1875. V. 65

STIERIUS, JOANNIUS
Praecepta Doctrinae Logicae, Ethicae, Physicase, Metaphysicae, Sphericae.... London: 1652. V. 66

STIGAND, C. H.
The Game of British East Africa. 1909. V. 62; 63
The Game of British East Africa. London: 1913. V. 62
The Land of Zinj. 1913. V. 66

STILES, JOSEPH CLAY
Capt. Thomas E. King; or a Word to the Army and the Country. Charleston: 1864. V. 62

STILES, JOSEPH CLAY continued
Modern Reform Examined: or, the Union of North and South on the Subject of Slavery. Philadelphia: 1858. V. 65
National Rectitude, the Only True Basis of National Prosperity; an Appeal to the Confederate States. Petersburg: 1863. V. 62; 63

STILGEBAUER, EDWARD
The Ship of Death: a Novel of the War. London: 1918. V. 64

STILKE, HERMINE
The Year Its Leaves and Blossoms. London: 1868. V. 64

STILL, GEORGE F.
The History of Pediatrics. The Progress of the Study of Diseases of Children Up to the End of the VIIIth Century. 1931. V. 64

STILLINGFLEET, BENJAMIN
An Essay on Conversation. London: 1737. V. 66
Miscellaneous Tracts Relating to Natural History, Husbandry and Physick. 1762. V. 63
Miscellaneous Tracts Relating to Natural History, Husbandry and Physick. London: 1762. V. 65
Miscellaneous Tracts Relating to Natural History, Husbandry and Physick. London: 1775. V. 65; 66
Miscellaneous Tracts Relating to Natural History, Husbandry and Physick. 1791. V. 63

STILLINGFLEET, EDWARD
The Bishop of Worcester's Answer to Mr. Locke's Second Letter.... London: 1698. V. 63; 67
The Case of an Oath of Abjuration Considered and the Vote of the Honorable House of Commons Vindicated. London: 1693. V. 62
The Council of Trent, Examin'd and Disprov'd by Catholic Tradition.... London: 1688. V. 62; 66
A Discourse Concerning Bonds of Resignation of Benefices, in Point of Law and Conscience. London: 1695. V. 67
The Jesus Loyalty.... London: 1677. V. 62
Sermons Preached on Several Occasions. London: 1673. V. 67
A Vindication to the Answer to Some Late Papers Concerning the Unity and Authority of the Catholick Church, and the Reformation of the Church of England. London: 1687. V. 62

STILLMAN, CHAUNCEY DEVEREUX
Charles Stillman 1810-1875. New York: 1956. V. 66

STILLMAN, SAMUEL
A Sermon Preached Before the Honourable Council and the House of Representatives of the State of Massachusetts-Bay in New England, at Boston May 26, 1779.... Boston: 1779. V. 66

STILLWELL, CHARLES H.
The Executor's Administrator's and Guardian's Guide.... Columbus: 1845. V. 66

STILLWELL, MARGARET BINGHAM
The Annmary Brown Memorial. A Descriptive Essay. Providence: 1925. V. 64
Incunabula and America 1450-1800. New York: 1931. V. 64
Incunabula in American Libraries. New York: 1940. V. 64

STIMMEL, SMITH
Personal Reminiscences of Abraham Lincoln. Minneapolis: 1928. V. 66

STIMPSON, WILLIAM
Synopsis of the Marine Invertebrata of Grand Manan, or the Region about the Mouth of the Bay of Fundy, New Brunswick. Washington: 1853. V. 64

STIRLING, EDWARD
The Battle of Life, a Drama in Three Acts. London: 1860?. V. 62
The Fortunes of Smike; or a Sequel to Nicholas Nickleby.... London: 1940. V. 62
Martin Chuzzlewit! A Drama in Three Acts. London: 1844. V. 62
Mrs. Harris! A Farce in One Act. London: 1846?. V. 62
Nicholas Nickleby. London: 1838. V. 62
Nicholas Nickleby. (with) The Fortunes of Smike, or a Sequel to Nicholas Nickleby. London: 1838-1840. V. 62
The Pickwick Club; or, the Age We Live In!. London: 1837?. V. 62

STIRLING, JAMES
Naphtali, or the Wrestlings of the Church of Scotland for the Kingdom of Christ. London: 1680. V. 62; 63

STIRLING, JAMES HUTCHISON
As Regards Protoplasm in Relation to Professor Huxley's Essay. Edinburgh & London: 1869. V. 67
Sir William Hamilton: Being the Philosophy of Perception. London: 1865. V. 66
Text-Book to Kant. Edinburgh: 1881. V. 64

STIRLING, JOHN
A System of Rhetorick, in a Method Entirely New. Dublin: 1786. V. 64

STIRLING, PATRICK JAMES
The Philosophy of Trade: or, Outlines of a Theory of Profits and Prices, Including an Examination of the Principles Which Determine the Relative Value of Corn, Labour and Currency. Edinburgh: 1846. V. 66

STIRLING, T. S.
The Cruise of the Dry Dock. Chicago: 1917. V. 63

STIRLING, WILLIAM
Some Apostles of Physiology. 1902. V. 67
Some Apostles of Physiology. London: 1902. V. 66

STIRLING, WILLIAM ALEXANDER, EARL OF
Recreations with the Muses. London: 1637. V. 64; 66

STIRLING-MAXWELL, WILLIAM
Don John of Austria or Passages from the History of the Sixteenth Century 1547-1578. London: 1883. V. 63

STOBAEUS, JOANNES
Loci Communes Sacri et Profani Sententiarvm Omnis Generis Ex Authoribvs Graecis Plvs Qvam Trecentis Congestarvm. (with) Eclogarvm Libri Dvo...Interprete Gulielmo Cantero. Francofvrti: 1581. V. 64; 65

STOCK, A.
International Sport, Horseshowing. London: 1930. V. 67

STOCK, CHRISTIAN
Clavis Linguae Veteris (& Novi) Testamenti Vocabularum Significationes tum Generales tum Speciales Ordine Concinno Exhibens tam Tironum Quam.... Leipzig: 1752-1753. V. 66

STOCK, DENNIS
Jazz Street. Garden City: 1960. V. 66
Jazz Street. New York: 1960. V. 66

STOCKARD, S. W.
The History of Alamance. Raleigh: 1909. V. 67

STOCKDALE, FREDERICK WILLIAM LITCHFIELD
Etchings...and Antiquities in the County of Kent. London: 1810. V. 62; 67

STOCKDALE, JAMES
Annales Caermoelenses; or Annals of Cartmel. Ulverston: 1872. V. 66

STOCKDALE, JOHN
The Whole Proceedings on the Trial of an Information Ex Officio, by the King's Attorney General, Against John Stockdale, for a Libel on the House of Commons, Tried in the Court of King's Bench Westminster, on Wednesday, the Ninth of December 1789.... London: 1790. V. 63

STOCKDALE, JOHN JOSEPH
The History of the Inquisitions; Including the Secret Transactions of Those Horrific Tribunals. London: 1810. V. 66
Sketches, Civil and Military of the Island of Java. London: 1812. V. 62

STOCKDALE, MARY R.
The Mirror of the Mind. Poems. London: 1810. V. 63

STOCKER, HARRY EMILIUS
A History of the Moravian Mission Among the Indians on the White River in Indiana. Bethlehem: 1917. V. 65

STOCKER, RICHARD D.
Physiognomy: Ancient and Modern or Phreno-Metoposcopy. London: 1900. V. 65

STOCKGROWERS'
Directory of Marks and Brands for the State of Montana 1872-1900...Also a Complete Classified Directory of Sheep and Wool Growers. Helena: 1974. V. 63

STOCKLEY, C. H.
Big Game Hunting in the Indian Empire. 1928. V. 67
Shikar. 1928. V. 64
Stalking in the Himalayas and Northern India. 1936. V. 62; 63; 64; 66; 67

STOCKLEY, G. M.
Report on the Geology of the Zanzibar Protectorate; together with Report on the Palaeontology of the Zanzibar Protectorate. Zanzibar: 1927-1928. V. 65; 67

STOCKLEY, V. M.
Big Game Shooting in India, Burma and Somaliland. 1913. V. 66

STOCKLEY, W. F. P.
Essays in Irish Biography. 1933. V. 67

STOCKTON, FRANK RICHARD
The Bee-Man of Orn. London: 1967. V. 65
The Griffin and the Minor Canon. New York: 1963. V. 62; 64
The Griffin and the Minor Canon. London: 1968. V. 63
The Lady or the Tiger?. New York: 1884. V. 62; 63; 64; 66
Ting a Ling. New York: 1882. V. 67

STOCKTON, LUCIUS HORATIO
An Address Delivered Before the Convention of the Friends of Peace of the State of New Jersey, July 14, 1814. N.P: 1814. V. 66

STODART, JOHN RIDDLE
Manhood Suffrage Combined with Relative Equality in Representation: a Contribution Towards Parliamentary Reform. London: 1857. V. 66

STODART, M. A.
Every-Day Duties; in Letters to a Young Lady. London: 1841. V. 64
Hints on Reading: Addressed to a Young Lady. London: 1839. V. 67
Principles of Education Practically Considered: with an Especial Reference to the Present State of Female Education in England. London: 1844. V. 65; 66

STODDARD, AMOS
Sketches, Historical and Descriptive of Louisiana. Philadelphia: 1812. V. 66; 67

STODDARD, C. W.
Exits and Entrances, a Book of Essays and Sketches. Boston: 1903. V. 63

STODDARD, H. L.
The Bobwhite Quail, Its Habits, Preservation and Increase. New York: 1931. V. 62; 63

STODDARD, W. S.
Adventure in Architecture: Building the New Saint John's.... New York: 1958. V. 65

STODDART, D. R.
Coral Reefs: Research Methods. 1978. V. 63

STODDART, JOHN
Remarks on Local Scenery and Manners in Scotland During the Years 1799 and 1800. London: 1801. V. 66

STODDART, THOMAS TOD
The Angler's Companion. 1853. V. 67
The Angler's Companion. London: 1892. V. 67
The Angler's Companion. London: 1923. V. 67
Angling Reminiscences. 1837. V. 65; 67
Angling Songs. London: 1889. V. 62; 67

STODDART, W. H. B.
Mind and Its Disorders. London: 1908. V. 65

STOERCK, ANTON VON
An Essay on the Medicinal Nature of Hemlock. Edinburgh: 1762. V. 62

STOHL, WILLIAM C.
New Method for Plectrum Banjo. 1920. V. 63

STOHLMANN, FREDERICH
Die Lebendigbegrabenen, und wi Schientodte Nebst Andern Verungluckten zu Behande Sind. New York: 1851. V. 66

STOKE, WILL E.
Episodes of Early Days in Central and Western Kansas. Great Bend: 1926. V. 67

STOKER, BRAM
Dracula. London: 1897. V. 62
Dracula. 1927. V. 67
The Jewel of the Seven Stars. 1904. V. 66
The Jewel of the Seven Stars. New York: 1904. V. 64
Lady Athlyne. London: 1908. V. 63
The Lady of the Shroud. London: 1909. V. 63
The Man. London: 1905. V. 63
The Mystery of the Sea. New York: 1902. V. 64
Personal Reminiscences of Henry Irving. London: 1906. V. 63
The Watter's Mou'. Westminster: 1895. V. 64

STOKES, ANSON PHELPS
Memorials of Eminent Yale Men. New Haven: 1914. V. 64

STOKES, ARTHUR H.
Lead and Lead Mining in Derbyshire. Matlock: 1964. V. 65

STOKES, J.
The Cabinet-Maker and Upholsterer's Companion. Philadelphia: 1852. V. 64

STOKES, T.
Birds of the Atlantic Ocean. Feltham: 1968. V. 67

STOKES, WILLIAM
An Introduction to the Use of the Stethoscope; with Its Application to the Diagnosis in Disease of the Thoracic Viscera.... Edinburgh: 1825. V. 65
A Treatise on the Diagnosis and Treatment of Diseases of the Chest. Philadelphia: 1837. V. 63; 64; 67
A Treatise on the Diagnosis and Treatment of Diseases of the Chest. Philadelphia and New Orleans: 1839. V. 64
A Treatise on the Diagnosis and Treatment of Diseases of the Chest, Dieases of the Lung, Windpipe. Philadelphia: 1844. V. 67
William Stokes: His Life and Work, 1804-1878. 1898. V. 63; 66

STOKOKE, W. J.
The Caterpillars of the British Moths. London: 1958. V. 62

STOLL, MAXIMILLIAN
Medecine Pratique de Maximilien Stoll.... Bordeaux: 1778. V. 66

STOLL, WILLIAM T.
Silver Strike, The True Story of Silver Mining in the Coeur d'Alenes. Boston: 1932. V. 63; 66

STOLPER, J. R.
Stephen Crane. A List of His Writings and Articles About Him. NewarK;: 1930. V. 67

STONE, A.
American Pep. New York: 1918. V. 66

STONE, ARTHUR L.
Following Old Trails. Missoula: 1913. V. 64

STONE, BENJAMIN
Pictures. Records of National Life and History Reproduced from the Collection of Photographs Made by Sir Benjamin Stone. London: 1905-1906. V. 62; 67

STONE, ELIZABETH A.
Unita County: Its Place in History. Laramie: 1924. V. 63; 66

STONE, FRANCIS
Picturesque Views of All the Bridges Belonging to the County of Norfolk, in a Series of Eighty Four Prints in Lithography. London: 1830-1832. V. 67

A STONE *Garden in Japan: Theme and Variatons.* Rutland/Tokyo: 1959. V. 62

STONE, GEORGE CAMERON
A Glossary of the Construction, Decoration and Use of Arms and Armor in All Countries and in All Times. New York: 1961. V. 62

STONE, HEBERT L.
Millions for Defense, a Pictorial History of the Races for the America's Cup. New York: 1934. V. 66; 67

STONE, JOAN
Alba. Madison: 1976. V. 62

STONE, JOHN A.
Put's Golden Songster - Containing the Largest and Most Popular Collections of California Songs Ever Published. San Francisco: 1858. V. 65

STONE, JULIUS F.
Canyon Country: the Romance of a Drop of Water and a Grain of Sand. New York: 1932. V. 63

STONE, L.
Domesticated Trout. 1896. V. 67

STONE, MARY
Children's Stories that Never Grow Old. Chicago. V. 65

STONE, PETER
A Guide to Coarse Fishing. 1964. V. 67

STONE, REYNOLDS
Engravings. London: 1977. V. 67
Reynolds Stone Engravings. London: 1977. V. 63
Wood Engravings by Thomas Bewick. London: 1953. V. 67

STONE, ROBERT
Dog Soldiers. Boston: 1974. V. 62; 63; 64; 65; 66; 67
Dog Soldiers. Boston: 1978. V. 67
A Flag for Sunrise. New York: 1981. V. 66; 67
Hall of Mirrors. Boston: 1967. V. 67
A Hall of Mirrors. London: 1968. V. 62
Outerbridge Reach. 1992. V. 67

STONE, SIDNEY
Railway Carriages and Wagons: Their Design and Construction. Part I. Chapters I to VII. London: 1905. V. 65

STONE, WILLIAM L.
The Campaign of Lieut. Gen. John Burgoyne, and the Expedition of Lieut. Col. Barry St. Leger. Albany: 1877. V. 67
Narrative of the Festivities Observed in Honor the Completion of the Grand Erie Canal.... New York: 1825. V. 63

STONE, WITMER
Bird Studies at Old Cape May. Philadelphia: 1937. V. 62; 63; 66; 67

STONEBACK, H. R.
Cartographers of the Deus Loci: the Mill House. North Hills: 1982. V. 62

STONEHAM, C. T.
Big Stuff. The Lure of Big Game. African Big Game and It's Hunters. 1954. V. 67

STONEHENGE, J. H. WALSH
The Dog in Health and Disease. 1859. V. 64
The Shot Gun and Sporting Rifle. 1862. V. 63

STONEHOUSE, J. H.
Catalogue of the Library of Charles Dickens from Gadshill...Catalogue of His Pictures and Objects of Art...Catalogue of the Library of W. M. Thackeray...and Relics from His Library. London: 1935. V. 65

STONER, FRANK
Chelsea, Bow and Derby Porcelain Figures, Their Distinguishing Characteristics. Newport: 1955. V. 67

STONER, ROBERT D.
A Seed-Bed of the Republic. A Study of the Pioneers in the Upper (Southern) Valley of Virginia. Kingsport: 1962. V. 64
A Seed-Bed of the Republic: a Study of the Pioneers in the Upper (Southern) Valley of Virginia. Roanoke: 1962. V. 66

STONEX, ELMA
The Golden Retriever. London: 1953. V. 67

STONEY, BARBARA
Enid Blyton - a Biography. London: 1974. V. 67

STONEY, SAMUEL GAILLARD
Charleston: Azaleas and Old Bricks. Boston: 1937. V. 63; 66
The Dulles Family in South Carolina. Columbia: 1955. V. 67
Plantations of the Carolina Low Country. Charleston: 1938. V. 65; 66; 67
Plantations of the Carolina Low Country. Charleston: 1955. V. 63

STONG, PHIL
State Fair. New York: 1932. V. 67

STONIER, G. W.
The Memoirs of a Ghost. London: 1947. V. 66
My Dear Bunny. London: 1946. V. 66

STOOKEY, BYRON
Surgical and Mechanical Treatment of Peripheral Nerves. Philadelphia: 1922. V. 66
Trigeminal Neuralgia. Its History and Treatment. Springfield: 1959. V. 66

STOPES, MARIE CARMICHAEL
Contraception (Birth Control) Its Theory, History and Practice. London: 1923. V. 65
A Journal from Japan. A Daily Record of Life.... London: 1910. V. 62

STOPES, MARIE CARMICHAEL continued
Kings and Heroes. London: 1937. V. 63
Love Songs for Young Lovers. London: 1939. V. 63
Married Love. London: 1932. V. 63
Plays of Old Japan - The No. London: 1913. V. 64

STOPFORD, EDWARD
A Brief Review of the...Acts and Bills Relating to Compositions for Tithes in Ireland. 1836. V. 67

STOPPARD, TOM
Albert's Bridge and Other Plays. New York: 1977. V. 66
Dalliance and Undiscovered Country. London: 1983. V. 66
Enter a Free Man. London: 1968. V. 62
Every Good Boy Deserves Favor and Professional Foul. New York: 1978. V. 66
In the Native State. London: 1991. V. 66
Indian Ink. London: 1995. V. 66
Jumpers. London: 1986. V. 66
Lord Malquist and Mr. Moon. London: 1966. V. 63; 64; 66
Night and Day. New York: 1979. V. 66
The Real Inspector Hound. London: 1968. V. 62
The Real Thing. London and Boston: 1983. V. 66
Rosencrantz and Guildenstern are Dead. London: 1967. V. 62; 64; 65; 66; 67

STORCK, ANTHONY
An Essay on the Medicinal Nature of Hemlock. London: 1760. V. 63
An Essay on the Medicinal Nature of Hemlock. 1762. V. 63
An Essay on the Medicinal Nature of Hemlock. Edinburgh: 1762. V. 65
A Second Essay on the Medicinal Virtues of Hemlcok. London: 1761. V. 64

STORER, D. H.
A Report on the Fishes, Reptiles and Birds of Massachusetts. Boston: 1839. V. 62; 63; 64; 66
A Synopsis of the Fishes of North America. Cambridge: 1846. V. 62; 63; 66

STORER, JAMES
Antiquarian and Topographical Cabinet, Containing a Series of Elegant Views of the Most Interesting Objects of Curiosity in Great Britain. London: 1807-1811. V. 62; 67
Delineations, Graphical and Descriptive Fountains Abbey, in the West Riding of the County of York.... Ripon: 1820. V. 62
Select Views of London and Its Environs.... London: 1804. V. 67
Views in Edinburgh and Its Vicinity.... Edinburgh: 1820. V. 62

STORER, JOHN
The Wild White Cattle of Great Britain. London: 1873. V. 63

STORER, T. I.
A Synopsis of the Amphibia of California. Berkeley: 1925. V. 63

STOREY, DAVID
Flight Into Camden. London: 1960. V. 66
Pasmore. London: 1972. V. 64
Saville. London: 1976. V. 63
This Sporting Life. London: 1960. V. 66

STOREY, H.
Hunting and Shooting in Ceylon. 1907. V. 62; 67

STORIES by a Mother, for the Use of Her Own Children. London: 1818. V. 63

STORIES for Little Girls: an Amusing Book for the Moral Improvement of Children. Guben: 1870. V. 62

THE STORIES of Ben Sailorman. London: 1899. V. 62; 64

STORIES Selected from the History of Scotland for Children Intended as A Companion to the Stories Selected from the History of England. London: 1820. V. 63

STORK, WILLIAM
An Account of East Florida, with a Journal Kept by John Bartram of Philadelphia, Botanist to His Majesty for the Floridas.... London: 1766. V. 62; 66
A Description of East Florida, With a Journal Kept by John Bartram.... London: 1769. V. 63; 66

STORM, COLTON
A Catalogue of the Everett D. Graff Collection of Western Americana. Chicago: 1968. V. 65

STORR, JOHN S.
Published Correspondence on Commissions, Mercantile and Professional. London: 1877. V. 67

A STORY of a Cock and a Bull. Northampton: 1720. V. 62

STORY and Paint Book: Some of America's Famous Men. Wilkes-Barre: 1935. V. 63

STORY, ISAAC
A Parnassian Shop, Opened in the Pindaric Stile. Boston: 1801. V. 62

STORY, JOSEPH
Commentaries on Equity Jurisprudence, as Administered in England and America. Boston and London: 1846. V. 67
Commentaries on Equity Jurisprudence as Administered in England and America. Boston: 1849. V. 63
Commentaries on the Constitution of the United States.... Boston: 1833. V. 62
Commentaries on the Law of Agency, as a Branch of Commercial and Maritime Jurisprudence.... Boston: 1839. V. 64
Commentaries on the Law of Bailments, with Illustrations from the Civil and the Foreign Law. Boston and London: 1846. V. 65
Commentaries on the Law of Bills of Exhange, Foreign and Inland, As Administered in England and America. Boston and London: 1843. V. 63
Discourse Pronounced Before the Phi Beta Kappa Society at the Anniversary Celebration on the Thirty-First Day of August 1826. Boston: 1826. V. 64
A Discourse Pronounced Upon the Inauguration of the Author, as Dane Professor of Law in Harvard University. Boston: 1829. V. 66
Life and Letters of Joseph Story.... Boston: 1851. V. 64

THE STORY of Arthur and Guinevere.... London: 1870. V. 62

THE STORY of Bluenose. Lunenburg: 1933. V. 63

THE STORY of Jack and the Giants. London: 1858. V. 66

THE STORY of Simple Samuel. New York: 1927. V. 64

THE STORY of Simple Simon. London: 1918. V. 64

THE STORY of the Fifty-Fifth Regiment Illinois Volunteer Infantry in the Civil War. Clinton: 1887. V. 62; 67

THE STORY of the Frog Who Would A-Wooing Go. London: 1911. V. 64

THE STORY of the Good Ship Bounty and Her Mutineers and Mutinies in Highland and Regiments. Edinburgh: 1896. V. 63

THE Story of the Two Bulls. New York: 1856. V. 65

STORY, THOMAS
A Journal of the Life of Thomas Story. Newcastle-upon-Tyne: 1747. V. 62; 63; 66

STORY, WILLIAM W.
Life and Letters of Joseph Story. Boston: 1851. V. 64

STOTHARD, THOMAS
Album with Seventeen Proof Impressions by Thomas Stothard for The Pilgrim's Progress. London: 1839. V. 66

STOURTON, WILLIAM JOSEPH
Two Letters to the Right Honourable the Earl of Liverpool, First Lord of the Treasury, on the Distresses of Agriculture and Their Influence on the Manufactures, Trade and Commerce.... London: 1821. V. 66

STOUT, BENJAMIN
Narrative of the Loss of the Ship Hercules, Comanded by Captain Benjamin Stout, on the Coast of Caffaria...also Travels...Africa. New York: 1797. V. 67

STOUT, H. B.
The Registers of St. Bees, Cumberland. Newcastle Upon Tyne: 1968. V. 65
The Registers of St. James's Whitehaven. 1964. V. 65

STOUT, L. H.
Reminiscences of General Braxton Bragg. Hattiesburg: 1942. V. 62; 63; 65

STOUT, REX
Alphabet Hicks. 1941. V. 64; 66
And Be a Villain. New York: 1948. V. 67
Before Midnight. New York: 1955. V. 65; 66; 67
Champagne for One. 1958. V. 66
Champagne for One. New York: 1958. V. 65
Death of a Doxy. New York: 1966. V. 65; 66; 67
Death of a Dude. New York: 1969. V. 64; 65; 66; 67
The Doorbell Rang. New York: 1965. V. 64; 66
Double for Death. New York: 1939. V. 67
The Father Hunt. New York: 1968. V. 64; 65; 66; 67
The Final Deduction. New York: 1961. V. 64; 65; 66
Forest Fire. London: 1934. V. 65; 66
The Golden Spiders. New York: 1953. V. 65
How Like a God. 1929. V. 64; 66
How Like a God. London: 1931. V. 62
In the Best Families. New York: 1950. V. 66
Might as Well Be Dead. New York: 1956. V. 67
The Mother Hunt. New York: 1963. V. 64; 66; 67
The Nero Wolfe Cook Book. New York: 1973. V. 65; 66
Please Pass the Guilt. New York: 1973. V. 67
Plot It Yourself. New York: 1959. V. 67
Prisoner's Base. 1952. V. 66
Prisoner's Base. New York: 1952. V. 64; 67
The Second Confession. New York: 1949. V. 65
The Silent Speaker. 1946. V. 66
The Silent Speaker. New York: 1946. V. 64; 65
Three Aces. New York: 1971. V. 67
Three at Wolfe's Door. New York: 1960. V. 64
Three for the Chair. New York: 1957. V. 63
Too Many Crooks. 1938. V. 64
Too Many Crooks. New York: 1938. V. 67
Too Many Women. New York: 1947. V. 65
Triple Zeck. New York: 1974. V. 67
Trouble in Triplicate. New York: 1949. V. 64

STOUT, TOM
Montana: Its Story and Biography - a History of Aboriginal and Territorial Montana and Three Decades of Statehood. Chicago: 1921. V. 67

STOUT, WAYNE
Hosea Stout Utah's Pioneer Statesman. Salt Lake City: 1953. V. 64

STOUT, WAYNE continued
Hosea Stout Utah's Pioneer Statesman. Salt Lake City: 1963. V. 65

STOUT, WILLIAM
Autobiography of William Stout of Lancaster.... London: 1851. V. 63; 65; 66
The Autobiography of William Stout of Lancaster.... Manchester: 1967. V. 62; 66

STOVER, ELIZABETH M.
Son-of-a-Gun Stew. Dallas: 1945. V. 67

STOW, ADA
More Baby Lays. London: 1898. V. 64; 66

STOW, JOHN
Annales, or, a Generall Chronicle of England, Begun First by Maister John Stow.... London: 1615. V. 62
A Survay (sic) of London. London: 1598. V. 62
The Survay (sic) of London.... London: 1618. V. 62
The Survey of London.... London: 1633. V. 62
A Survey of the Cities of London and Westminster.... London: 1720. V. 62
A Survey of the Cities of London. London: 1754-1755. V. 62

STOW, RANDOLPH
Tourmaline. London: 1963. V. 67

STOWE, CHARLES EDWARD
Harriet Beecher Stowe...by Her Son and Her Grandson. London: 1911. V. 65

STOWE, HARRIET ELIZABETH BEECHER
Caba F'ewyrth Twm. (Uncle Tom's Cabin). London: 1853. V. 65
La Cabane de l'Oncle Tom Ou Les Noirs en Amerique. Paris: 1853. V. 65
La Case de l'Oncle Tom. Paris: 1853. V. 65
Dred, a Tale of the Dismal Swamp. Boston: 1856. V. 62; 63; 64; 65; 67
Little Foxes; or The Insignificant Little Habits Which Mar Domestic Happiness. London: 1866. V. 65
Little Pussy Willow. London: 1871. V. 65
Old Stories Told Anew. Uncle Tom's Cabin. 1819. V. 66
Oldtown Fireside Stories. Boston: 1872. V. 66
Sunny Memories of Foreign Lands. London: 1854. V. 66
Uncle Tom's Cabin. Boston: 1852. V. 62; 63; 66
Uncle Tom's Cabin. Cleveland: 1852. V. 63
Uncle Tom's Cabin. London: 1852. V. 62; 65
Uncle Tom's Cabin. Edinburgh: 1853. V. 65
Uncle Tom's Cabin. 1938. V. 64
Uncle Tom's Cabin. New York: 1938. V. 66

STOWERS, JAMES HERBERT
Two Lectures on Lupus. London: 1876?. V. 67

STOYE, J. W.
English Travellers Abroad, 1604-1667. London: 1952. V. 67

STRABO
De Situ Orbis Grece & Latine...olim..ut Putater, a Guarino Veronensi & Gregorio Trifernate in Latinum Conversi.... Basiliae: 1549. V. 66
Straboni Rerum Geographicarum.... 1620. V. 65
Strabonis Rerum Geographicarum.... Amstelaedami: 1707. V. 65

STRACEY, P. D.
Reade, Elephant Hunter. 1967. V. 67

STRACHAN, ALEXANDER
The Life of the Rev. Samuel Leigh, Missionary to the Settlers and Savages of Australia and New Zealand.... London: 1863. V. 66

STRACHEY, JULIA
The Man on the Pier. London: 1951. V. 66

STRACHEY, LYTTON
Characters and Commentaries. London: 1933. V. 62
Elizabeth and Essex. London: 1928. V. 64
Elizabeth and Essex. New York: 1928. V. 67
Ermyntrude and Esmeralda. London: 1969. V. 62; 63; 66
Euphrosyne. A Collection of Verse. Cambridge: 1905. V. 66
Portraits in Miniature and Other Essays. London: 1931. V. 62; 64
Queen Victoria. London: 1921. V. 64

STRACHEY, RAY
The Cause: a Short History of the Women's Movement in Great Britain. London: 1928. V. 65
Women's Suffrage and Women's Service. London: 1927. V. 65

STRADA, FAMIANUS
Prolusiones Academicas...Oratoriam, Poeticam, Historiamque Spectantes.... Amstelodami: 1658. V. 65; 66

STRADA, JACOPO
Imperatorum Romanorum Omnium Orientalium et Occidentalium Verissimae Imagines.... Zurich: 1549. V. 64

STRAHAN, KAY CLEAVER
Footprints. Garden City: 1929. V. 66

STRAHAN, R.
The Australian Museum Complete Book of Australian Mammals.... London: 1984. V. 63
Finches, Bowerbirds and Other Passeriaes of Australia. Sydney: 1996. V. 63; 67

STRAHORN, CARRIE A.
Fifteen Thousand Miles by Stage - a Woman's Unique Experience During Thirty Years of Path Finding and Pioneering from the Missouri to the Pacific and From Alaska to Mexico. New York: 1911. V. 63

STRAIGHT, SUSAN
Aquaboogie. Minneapolis: 1990. V. 67
I Been in Sorrow's Kitchen and Licked Out All the Pots. New York: 1992. V. 67

STRAINS from a Dulcimore. Atlanta: 1930. V. 65

STRALEY, JOHN
The Woman Who Married a Bear. New York: 1992. V. 63; 67

STRALEY, W.
Pioneer Sketches Nebraska and Texas. Hico: 1915. V. 65

THE STRAND Fairy Book. London: 1905. V. 66

STRAND, MARK
The Continuous Life. Iowa City: 1990. V. 62; 64; 67
Dark Harbor. New York: 1993. V. 67
Darker. New York: 1970. V. 67
18 Poems from the Quechua. Cambridge: 1971. V. 67
89 Clouds. New York: 1999. V. 67
Hopper. New York: 1994. V. 67
The Late Hour. New York: 1978. V. 62; 66; 67
The Monument. New York: 1978. V. 62; 66; 67
The Planet of Lost Things. New York: 1982. V. 67
Prose - Four Poems. Portland: 1987. V. 64; 67
Prose, Four Poems. Sweden: 1987. V. 62
Reasons for Moving. New York: 1968. V. 67
The Sargeantville Notebook. Providence: 1973. V. 67
Selected Poems. New York: 1980. V. 67
Sleeping With One Eye Open. Iowa City: 1964. V. 62; 63; 64; 67
The Story of Our Lives. New York: 1973. V. 67
Strand: a Profile. Iowa City: 1979. V. 66
A Suite of Appearances. Portland: 1993. V. 62
A Suite of Appearances. Portland: 1996. V. 67

STRAND, PAUL
Living Egypt. New York: 1969. V. 63
Time in New England. New York: 1950. V. 63
Tir A'Mhurain: Outer Hebrides. New York: 1968. V. 65

STRANG, E. B.
General Stoneman's Raid; or, the Amusing Side of Army Life. Philadelphia: 1911. V. 67

STRANG, HERBERT
The Red Book for Boys. London. V. 64

STRANG, JOHN
The Cruise, with Other Poems. London: 1812. V. 62

STRANG, WILLIAM
Death and the Ploughman's Wife: a Ballad.... London: 1894. V. 64
The Earth Fiend: a Ballad. London: 1892. V. 64

STRANGE, E. F.
The Colour-Prints of Hiroshige. London: 1925. V. 62; 65

STRANGE, JOHN STEPHEN
The Man Who Killed Fortescue. Garden City: 1928. V. 67

STRANGE, ROBERT
An Enquiry Into the Rise and Establishment of the Royal Academy of Arats, to Which is Prefixed a Letter to the Earl of Bute. London: 1775. V. 63

THE STRANGER in Liverpool; or, an Historical and Descriptive View of the Town of Liverpool and Its Environs. Liverpool: 1816. V. 62; 66

THE STRANGER'S Companion in Chester. Chester: 1830. V. 66

THE STRANGER'S Guide and Official Directory for the City of Richmond. Richmond: 1863. V. 63; 65

THE STRANGER'S Guide through Lincoln Cathedral, with an Historical Summary, Plan &c. Lincoln: 1848. V. 66

THE STRANGER'S Guide through the City of York, and Its Cathedral. York: 1837. V. 67

THE STRANGER'S Guide through the Town of Nottingham, Being a Description of the Principal Buildings and Objects of Curiosity in that Ancient Town. Nottingham: 1827. V. 65

STRANGER'S Guide to the Garden City. Chicago: 1883. V. 64

STRANSKY, M. PAULO
Respublica Bojema. Leiden: 1643. V. 64

STRAPAROLA, GIOVANNI FRANCESCO
The Nights of Straparola. London: 1894. V. 62

STRATFORD-UPON-AVON & MIDLAND JUNCTION RAILWAY
Rules and Regulations for the Guidance of the Officers and Men in the Service of the...Company. London: 1919. V. 62

STRATTON, CHARLES
The American General Tom Thumb. New York: 1850. V. 64
The Life of General Tom Thumb. Troy: 1856. V. 67

STRATTON, MARY CHASE
Ceramic Processes. N.P: 1941. V. 65

STRATTON, R. B.
Among the Indians or the Captivity of the Oatmen Girls Among the Apache and Mohave Indians. San Francisco: 1935. V. 64
Captivity of the Oatman Girls.... San Francisco: 1857. V. 67

STRAUB, PETER
If You Could See Me Now. New York: 1977. V. 67
Ishmael. London: 1972. V. 62
Julia. London: 1977. V. 65

STRAUCH, AEGIDIUS
Breviarium Chronologicum. Or a Treatise Describing the Terms and Most Celebrated Characters, Periods and Epocha's Used in Chronology. London: 1704. V. 62

STRAUS, RALPH
John Baskerville. A Memoir. Cambridge: 1907. V. 62; 64

STRAUSBAUGH, P. D.
Flora of West Virginia. Morgantown: 1952-1977. V. 64

STRAUSS, DARIN
Chang and Eng. New York: 2000. V. 67

STRAUSS, DAVID FRIEDRICH
The Life of Jesus. London: 1846. V. 65
The Life of Jesus. London: 1892. V. 65

STRAUSS, E.
Irish Nationalism and British Democracy. 1951. V. 67
Sir William Petty: Portrait of a Genius. Illinois: 1954. V. 65

STRAUSS, WALTER L.
Chiaroscuro. New York: 1973. V. 66

STRAVINSKY, IGOR
Selected Correspondence. London: 1982-1985. V. 65

STREATFIELD, NOEL
The Theater Cat. Chicago: 1951. V. 66

STREDDER, E.
Lost in the Wilds of Canada. London: 1893. V. 66

STREET, B.
Historical Notes on Grantham and Grantham Church. Grantham: 1857. V. 65

STREET, Business and General Directory of Collingswood and General Information of the Town.... Collingswood: 1921. V. 63; 66

STREET, C. J. C.
The Administration of Ireland, 1920. 1921. V. 67
Ireland in 1921. 1922. V. 67

STREET, G. S.
The Autobiography of a Boy.... London: 1894. V. 64

STREET, GEORGE EDMUND
Some Account of Gothic Architecture in Spain. London: 1914. V. 62; 65

STREETER, EDWIN W.
The Great Diamonds of the World. Their History and Romance.... London: 1882. V. 64
Precious Stones and Gems, Their History, Sources and Characteristics. London: 1892. V. 63

STREETER, N. R.
Gems from an Old Drummer's Grip. Groton: 1889. V. 66

STREETER, RUSSELL
Mirror of Calvinistic Fantaticism, or Jedediah Burchard and Co. During a Protracted Meeting of Twenty-Six Days in Woodstock. Woodstock: 1835. V. 66

STREETER, THOMAS WINTHROP
The Celebrated Collection of Americana.... New York: 1966. V. 63
The Celebrated Collection of Americana.... New York: 1966-1970. V. 63
The Celebrated Collection of Americana...Volume II. New York: 1967. V. 63
The Celebrated Collection of Americana...Volume III. New York: 1967. V. 63
The Celebrated Collection of Americana...Volume IV. New York: 1969. V. 63

STREHL, DAN
The Spanish Cook: a Selection of Recipes from Encarnacion Pinedo's el Cocinero Espanol. Pasadena: 1992. V. 64

STRETSER, THOMAS
Arbor Vitae; or, the Natural History of the Tree of Life. 1742. V. 65

STRETTELL, G. W.
The Ficus Elastica in Burma Proper.... Rangoon: 1876. V. 63

STRETTON, HESBA
Carola. London: 1884. V. 65

STRETTON, JULIA DE WINTON
The Queen of the County. London: 1865. V. 65

STRETTON, WILLIAM
The Stretton Manuscripts: Being Notes on the History of Nottinghamshire. Nottingham: 1910. V. 65

STRETZER, THOMAS
Merryland Displayed; or Plagiarism, Ignorance and Impudence Detected. Bath: 1741. V. 62
A New Description of Merryland. Bath: 1741. V. 62

STREVELL, CHARLES N.
As I Recall Them. N.P: 1943. V. 64; 67

STREWEL-Peter: a Picture Book for Boys and Girls. New York: 1898. V. 63

STRIBLING, ROBERT M.
Gettysbury Campaign and Campaigns of 1864 and 1865 in Virginia. Petersburg: 1905. V. 62

STRIBLING, T. S.
Clues of the Caribees. 1929. V. 66
Clues of the Caribees. New York: 1929. V. 64

STRICKER, CHRISTIAN
Descrizione ed Uso delle Macchine Accensibili.... Milan: 1823. V. 64

STRICKLAND, AGNES
Floral Sketches, Fables and Other Poems. London: 1836. V. 67
Letters of Mary, Queen of Scots and Documents Connected with Her Personal History. London: 1842. V. 65
Lives of the Queens of England. London: 1857. V. 65
Patriotic Songs. London: 1830. V. 65
The Rival Crusoes, or, the Shipwreck. Also a Voyage to Norway; and the Fisherman's Cottage. London: 1826. V. 63

STRICKLAND, JANE
Life of Agnes Strickland. Edinburgh: 1887. V. 66
Rome, Regal and Republican. London: 1854. V. 65

STRICKLAND, REX W.
El Paso in 1854. El Paso: 1969. V. 65

STRICKLAND, SAMUEL
Twenty Seven Years in Canada West; or, the Experience of an Early Settler. London: 1854. V. 63

STRICKLAND, W. P.
Sketches of Western Methodism: Biographical, Historical & Miscellaneous.... Cincinnati & New York: 1880. V. 67

STRICKLAND, WILLIAM
Reports, Specifications and Estimates of Public Works in the United States of America. London: 1841. V. 62

STRICKLER, HARRY M.
Old Homes of Massanutten Block Printed As of 1776-1800. N.P: 1910. V. 64
A Short History of Page County, Virginia. Richmond: 1952. V. 64

STRICTURES on the Prince of Wales's Letter to Mr. Pitt in a Letter Addressed to His Royal Highness, by Candour. London: 1789. V. 66

STRID, A.
Flora Hellenica. Volume I. Gymnospermae to Carophyllaceae. 1997. V. 63

STRIEBER, WHITLEY
Black Magic. New York: 1982. V. 67
The Hunger. New York: 1981. V. 66
The Wolfen. New York: 1978. V. 66

STRIGELIUS, VICTORINUS
Statuti et Constitutioni del Ordine di Santo Stefano. fondato, et Dotato dal Illustrissimo, et Eccellentissimo Signore Cosimo de Medici.... Florence: 1565. V. 62

STRIKER, FRAN
The Telltale Scar. New York: 1947. V. 66

STRINDBERG, AUGUST
Paria, Simoon - Two Plays. London: 1914. V. 63

STRINGER, ARTHUR
The House of Intrigue. 1918. V. 63; 64; 66
The Lamp in the Valley. Indianapolis: 1938. V. 66
Phantom Wires. Boston: 1907. V. 65
The Shadow. New York: 1913. V. 65
The Wire Tappers. Boston: 1906. V. 65

STRINGER, GEORGE ALFRED
Leisure Moments in Gough Square, or the Beauties and Quaint Conceits of Johnson's Dictionary. Buffalo: 1886. V. 62

THE STRIPTEASER; The Teaser, Pure and Simple. Paris: 1953-1954. V. 64

STRIXNER, JOHANN NEPOMUK
Albrecht Durers Christlich-Mythologische Handzeichnungen. Munich: 1808. V. 62

STRONG, A. B.
Illustrated Natural History of the Three Kingdoms.... New York: 1848. V. 66

STRONG, ARTURO
Corrido de Cocaine. Tucson: 1990. V. 67

STRONG, D. E.
Catalogue of the Carved Amber in the Department of Greek and Roman Antiquities. London: 1966. V. 62

STRONG, ISABEL
Memories of Vailima. Westminster: 1903. V. 67

STRONG, LEONARD ALFRED GEORGE
The Garden. London: 1931. V. 65
The Hansom Cab and the Pigeons.... Waltham St. Lawrence: 1935. V. 62; 63; 64; 65; 66
Sea Wall. London: 1935. V. 65

STRONG, NEHEMIAH
Astronomy Improved; or, a New Theory of the Harmonious Regularity Observable in the Mechanism or Movements of the Planetary System, in Three Lectures...in New Haven, Begun Feb. 17, 1781. New Haven: 1784. V. 66

STRONG, R. M.
A Bibliography of Birds. Chicago: 1939-1959. V. 63

STRONG, RICHARD P.
Harvard School of Tropical Medicine. Report of First Expediton to South America, 1913. Cambridge: 1915. V. 65; 67

STRONG, ROY
The Destruction of the Country House 1875-1975. London: 1974. V. 64
The English Icon: Elizabethan and Jacobean Portraiture. London: 1969. V. 63

STRONG, S. ARTHUR
The Masterpieces in the Duke of Devonshire's Collection of Pictures. London: 1901. V. 64

STROTHER, D. H.
Illustrated Life of General Winfield Scott, Command-in-Chief of the Army in Mexico. New York: 1847. V. 67

STROTHER, EDWARD
Criticon Febrium; or, a Critical Essay on Fevers.... London: 1716. V. 64
An Essay on Sickness and Health. London: 1725. V. 65; 66
Pharmacopoeia Practica.... London: 1719. V. 64

STROUD, DOROTHY
Capability Brown. London: 1957. V. 62

STROUD, R.
Stroud's Digest on the Diseases of Birds.... Minneapolis: 1943. V. 67

STROUSE, NORMAN
The Passionate Pirate. North Hills: 1964. V. 62
The Silverado Episode. St. Helena: 1966. V. 67

STROYER, JACOB
My Life in the South. Salem: 1898. V. 66

STRUMPELL, ADOLF
A Text Book of Medicine for Students and Practitioners. New York: 1896. V. 67

STRUTHERS, J.
On the Bones, Articulations and Muscles of the Rudimentary Hind-Limb of the Greenland Right-Whale. London: 1881. V. 67

STRUTHERS, JOHN
How to Improve the Teaching in the Scottish Universities. Edinburgh: 1859. V. 63

STRUTT, ELIZABETH
Six Weeks on the Loire with a Peep Into La Vendee. London: 1833. V. 66
A Spinster's Tour in France, the States of Genoa &c. During the Year 1827. London: 1828. V. 64

STRUTT, JOSEPH
The Bumpkin's Disaster; or the Journey to London....(with) The Test of Guilt; or Traits of Antient Supertition. London: 1808. V. 66
The Sports and Pastimes of the People of England.... London: 1876. V. 67

STRUVE, CHRISTIAN AUGUSTUS
A Practical Essay on the Art of Recovering Suspended Animation, Together with a Review of the Most Proper and Effectual means to be Adopted in Cases of Imminent Danger. Albany: 1803. V. 62; 63; 65

STRYKER, M. WOOLSEY
In Memoriam - Funeral Oration of Obsequies of Major General Henry W. Lawton, U.S. Volunteers. Washington: 1900. V. 67

STRYKER, WILLIAM S.
The Battle of Monmouth. Princeton: 1927. V. 63; 66
The Battles of Trenton and Princeton. Boston: 1898. V. 63; 66
Official Register of the Officers and Men of New Jersey in the Revolutionary War. Trenton: 1872. V. 63; 66
Record of Officers and Men of New Jersey in the Civil War 1861-1865. Trenton: 1976. V. 63; 66

STRYPE, JOHN
Annals of the Reformation and Establishment of Reglion and Other Various Occurrences in the Church of England During Queen Elizabeth's Happy Reign.... New York: 1965. V. 63
Ecclesiastical Memorials; Relating Chiefly to Religion and the Reformation Of It.... London: 1721. V. 64; 67
Ecclesiastical Memorials: Relating Chiefly to Religion and the Reformation Of it.... London: 1816. V. 62
Historical Collections of the Life and Acts of the Reverend Father in God, John Aylmer, Lord Bishop of London in the Reign of Queen Elizabeth. London: 1701. V. 67
The History of the Life and Acts of the Most Reverend Father in God, Edmund Grindal, The First Bishop of London and the Second Archbishop of York and Canterbury Successively in the Reign of Queen Elizabeth. London: 1710. V. 63; 67
The Life and Acts of Matthew Parker, the First Archbishop of Canterbury, in the Reign of Queen Elizabeth. Oxford: 1821. V. 63
Life and Acts of Matthew Parker, The First Archbishop of Canterbury, in the Reign of Queen Elizabeth.... London: 1711. V. 63
The Life and Acts of Matthew Parker...(with) The History of the Life and Acts of the Most Reverend Father in God, Edmund Grindal.... London: 1711-1710. V. 65
The Life and Acts of the Most Reverend Father in God, John Whitgift, D.D. London: 1718. V. 66; 67
The Life of the Learned Sir John Cheke, Kt. London: 1705. V. 67
Life of the Learned Sir Thomas Smith... Life of the Learned Sir John Cheke...Historical Collections of the Life and Acts of the Right Reverend... John Aylmer.... Oxford: 1820-1821. V. 65
Memorials of the Most Reverend Father in God, Thomas Cranmer. London: 1694. V. 63

STUART, ALEX H. H.
A Narrative of the Leading Incidents of the First Organization of the First Popular Movement in Virginia in 1865 to Re-establish Peaceful Relations Between the Northern and Southern States and of the Subsequent Efforts of the Committee of Nine in 1869. Richmond: 1888. V. 65

STUART, ANDREW
Considerations on the Present State of East-India Affairs and Examination of Mr. Fox's Bill, Suggesting Certain Material Alterations for Adverting Dangers and Preserving the Benefits of the Bill. London: 1784. V. 66
Letters to the Rt. Hon. Lord Mansfield. London: 1773. V. 66

STUART, C. M. VILLIERS
Gardens of the Great Mughals. London: 1913. V. 67

STUART, CHARLES
A Letter to General Richard Smith, in Reply to the Charges Introduced into the Ninth Report of the Select Committe, Affecting the Character of Mr. Stuart. London: 1783. V. 66

STUART, DOROTHY MARGARET
Christina Rossetti. London: 1930. V. 63

STUART, ERSKINE
The Bronte Country. London: 1888. V. 63; 64

STUART, FRANCIS
Glory. London: 1933. V. 64
Good Friday's Daughter. London: 1952. V. 65

STUART, GILBERT
Observations Concerning the Public Law, and Constitutional History of Scotland.... Edinburgh: 1779. V. 65
Tableau des progres de la Societe en Europe, Traduit de l'Anglois. Paris: 1789. V. 66

STUART, GLORIA
Writing a Poem About Flying a Kite: Which is Printed With Hand Set Type on Handmade paper and on a Hand Press in Four Versions. Los Angeles: 1987. V. 64

STUART, GRANVILLE
Diary and Sketchbook of a Journey to America in 1866 and Return Trip Up the Missouri River to Fort Benton. Los Angeles: 1963. V. 65
Forty Years on the Old Frontier as Seen by.... Cleveland: 1925. V. 67

STUART, HAMISH
Lochs and Loch Fishing. London: 1899. V. 62

STUART, HENRY
The Planter's Guide.... Edinburgh and London: 1828. V. 64

STUART, JAMES
Correspondence Between James Stuart, Esq., Youngr of Dunearn and Lord Advocate. No. 1 - Letter from Mr. Stuart to the Lord Advocate. (with) Correspondence Between James Stuart, Esq. and the Printer of the Beacon. Edinburgh: 1821. V. 65
Poems on Various Subjects. Belfast: 1811. V. 64
Three Years in North America. Edinburgh: 1833. V. 66; 67
The Trial of James Stuart, Esq. Younger of Dunearn, Before the High Court of Justiciary, at Edinburgh on Monday June 10, 1822. Edinburgh: 1822. V. 63

STUART, JESSE
Beyond Dark Hills. New York: 1938. V. 65
Come Back to the Farm. New York: 1971. V. 66
God's Oddling. The Story of Mick Stuart, My Father. New York: 1960. V. 64; 67
The Good Spirit of Laurel Ridge. New York: 1953. V. 63
Kentucky is My Land. N.P: 1952. V. 67

STUART, JOHN
Extracts from the Council Register of the Burgh of Aberdeen 1398-1570 and 1570-1625. Aberdeen: 1844-1848. V. 62
Vestiarium Scoticum: from the Manuscript Formerly in the Library of the Scots College at Douay. Edinburgh: 1842. V. 65

STUART, MOSES
A Grammar of the Hebrew Language. Andover: 1831. V. 62
A Grammar of the Hebrew Language. Andover: 1838. V. 62
A Hebrew Chrestomathy. Andover: 1832. V. 62

STUART, REGINALD R.
Calvin B. West of the Umpqua - an Obscure Chapter in the History of Southern Orgeon. San Francisco: 1961. V. 67
Calvin B. West of the Umpqua. An Obscure Chapter in the History of Southern Oregon. Stockton: 1961. V. 64; 65

STUART, ROBERT
The Discovery of the Oregon Trail, Robert Stuart's Narrative of His Overland Trip East from Asteria in 1812-183. New York: 1935. V. 66

STUART, W. J.
Forbidden Planet. 1956. V. 64

STUBBE, HENRY
A Caveat for the Protestant Clergy. London: 1678. V. 62

STUBBE, HENRY continued
The Miraculous Conformist; or an Account of Several Marvailous Cures Performed by the Stroaking of the Hands of Mr. Valentine Greatarick.... Oxford: 1666. V. 62; 66

STUBBES, PHILIP
The Anatomie of Abuses. Edinburgh: 1836. V. 62
The Anatomie of Abuses. London: 1836. V. 67

STUBBS, CHARLES WILLIAM
Village Politics: Addresses and Sermons on the Labour Question. London: 1878. V. 66

STUCK, HUDSON
The Alaskan Missions of the Episcopal Church. New York: 1920. V. 67
The Ascent of Denali (Mount McKinley). New York: 1914. V. 63
Ten Thousand Miles with a Dog Sled. New York: 1914. V. 62

STUCKEY, RONALD
The Lithographs of Stow Wengenroth 1931-1972. Boston: 1974. V. 62; 63; 65; 66

STUDDY, G. E.
Bonzo and Us. London: 1931. V. 63
Bonzo Book. London: 1925. V. 65
Bonzo: the Great Big Midget Book. London: 1934. V. 63
The Bonzooloo Book. London: 1929. V. 63; 65
Bonzo's Annual. London: 1947. V. 64
Bonzo's Annual. London: 1951. V. 65
Playful Animals. England: 1950. V. 63

STUDER, J. H.
Popular Ornithology. The Birds of North America. New York and Columbus: 1882. V. 62
Studer's Popular Ornithology. Birds of North America... (with) Ornithology; or the Science of Birds. Columbus: 1878. V. 65
Studer's Popular Ornithology. The Birds of North America. New York: 1977. V. 67

THE STUDIO Year-Book of Decorative Art 1906. London: 1906. V. 67

STUKELEY, WILLIAM
Some Account of Croyland Abbey, Linconshire. Ashby-de-la-Zouch: 1856. V. 66

THE STUPID Boy. London: 1850. V. 64

STURDEE, ALFRED B.
The Twin-Stern Steamer, with a Protected Propeller.... London: 1851. V. 63

STURGE, JOSEPH
A Visit to the United States In 1841. London: 1842. V. 64

STURGEON, MARY
Michael Field. London: 1922. V. 65

STURGEON, THEODORE
Sturgeon's West. Garden City: 1973. V. 62; 65
Thunder and Roses. London: 1957. V. 64; 66
A Touch of Strange. 1958. V. 66
A Touch of Strange. New York: 1958. V. 64
Without Sorcery. 1948. V. 64

STURGES, LILLIAN BAKER
The Toys of Nuremberg. Chicago: 1915. V. 65

STURLESON, S.
The Himskringla; or Chronicle of the Kings of Norway. London: 1844. V. 65

STURM, C. C.
Reflections on the Works of God.... Bungay: 1803. V. 66
Reflections on the Works of God.... London: 1817. V. 63

STURM, JOHANN CHRISTOPH
Collegium Experimentale, sive Curiosum in Quo Primaria Huius Seculi Inventa and Experimenta Physico-Mathematica. (with) Ad Virum Celeberrinum Henricum Morum Cantabrigiensem Epistola qua de Ipsius Principio Hylarchio seu Spiritu Naturae & Familiari Modern. Nuremberg: 1701-1715. V. 62
Mathesis Enucleata; or the Elements of the Mathematicks. London: 1724. V. 63
Physicae Conciliatricis per Generalem Pariter ac Specialem Partem.... Nuremburg: 1687. V. 64

STYLE, D. C. W.
Songs of the Fell Packs. Cockermouth. V. 67

STYLES, JOHN
Memoirs of the Life of the Right Honourable George Canning. London: 1828. V. 64

STYRON, WILLIAM
A Chance in a Million. N.P: 1993. V. 62
The Confessions of Nat Turner. New York: 1967. V. 62; 64; 66; 67
The Confessions of Nat Turner. Franklin Center: 1979. V. 67
Grateful Words About F. Scott Fitzgerald. Rockville: 1997. V. 62; 64; 67
Lie Down in Darkness. Indianapolis and New York: 1951. V. 62; 62; 63; 64; 67
Lie Down in Darkness. London: 1952. V. 62
Set This House on Fire. New York: 1960. V. 64; 65; 66; 67
Sophie's Choice. New York: 1979. V. 62
This Quiet Dust. New York: 1967. V. 63; 64; 67
A Tidewater Morning. Helsinki: 1990. V. 63
A Tidewater Morning. New York: 1993. V. 62

SUAREZ DE ALARCON, JUAN
La Iffanta Coronada, por El Rey Don Pedro, Dona Ines de Castro. Lisbon: 1606. V. 62

SUBIRA, ORIOL VALLSI
A Lively Look at Papermaking. North Hills: 1980. V. 62; 64

SUBLETTE COUNTY ARTISTS GUILD
Tales of the Seeds-Ke-Dee. Denver: 1963. V. 63

SUBMISSION Exemplified; or the Amiable Stranger. London: 1818. V. 67

SUBRAMANIAN, LAKSHMI
Medieval Seafarers. New Delhi: 1999. V. 67

SUB ROSA, PSEUD.
Drifting, or the Romance of an Octopus. Chicago: 1904. V. 63

SUBSTANCE of the Speeches Made in the House of Commons, on Wednesday, the 15th of December, 1779. On Mr. Burke's Giving Notice of His Intention to Bring in a Bill.... London: 1779. V. 62

SUCKLING, JOHN
A Ballad Upon a Wedding. Waltham St. Lawrence: 1927. V. 62; 64; 66
The Poems of Sir John Suckling. London: 1896. V. 63
Selections from the Works...(with) a Life of the Author.... London: 1836. V. 63
The Works. London: 1709. V. 65
The Works. Dublin: 1766. V. 65
The Works. London: 1770. V. 63

SUCKOW, RUTH
The Folks. New York: 1934. V. 67

SUDDABY, DONALD
Prisoners of Saturn - an Interplanetary Adventure. London: 1957. V. 65

SUDHOFF, KARL
Essays in the History of Medicine. New York: 1926. V. 64; 66

SUDRE, ALFRED
Histoire du Communisme ou Refutation Historique es Utopies Socialistes. Paris: 1849. V. 66

SUE, EUGENE
The Wandering Jew. London: 1844-1845. V. 67

SUE Sew-and-Sew. New York: 1931. V. 65

SUESS, E.
The Face of the Earth. Oxford: 1904-1908. V. 67

SUETONIUS TRANQUILLUS, GAIUS
C. Suetonii Tranquilli XII Caesares. Antverpiae: 1592. V. 65
C. Suetonius Tranquillus, Ex Recensione Georgii Graevii...Ut & Commentario Integro Laevinii Torrentii, Et Isaaci Casauboni.... Utrecht: 1672. V. 65
Cum Animadversionibus Io. Augusti Ernesti.... Lipsize: 1748. V. 66
Et in Eum Commentarius, Exhibente Joanne Schidio. Lugduni Batavorum: 1662. V. 66
In Hoc Volumine Haec Continentur. XII Caesares. Venice: 1516. V. 65
The Lives of the Twelve Caesars. 1963. V. 65
Suetonii Tranquilli Duodecim Caesares. Lugduni: 1548. V. 65
XII Caesaribus Libros VIII. Hagae-Comitum: 1727. V. 66
(Opera) ex recensione Joannis Georgii Graevii.... Trajecti ad Rhenum: 1672. V. 66
(Opera Omnia).... Amsterdam: 1736. V. 67

SUFFOLK, EDWARD HOWARD, 8TH EARL OF
Miscellanies in Prose and Verse, by a Person of Quality. London: 1725. V. 63

THE SUFFOLK Garland; or, a Collection of Poems, Songs, Tales, Ballads, Sonnets and Elegies, Legendary and Romantic.... Ipswich: 1818. V. 62; 65

SUFFOLK Trust and Investment Co. Boston: 1887. V. 65

SUFFOLK & BERKSHIRE, EARL OF
The Encyclopaedia of Sport. 1897. V. 63; 64; 66

SUFLING, ERNEST R.
English Church Brasses from the 13th to the 17th Century. London: 1910. V. 62

SUGDEN, ALAN VICTOR
A History of English Wallpaper 1509-1914. London: 1925. V. 65

SUGDEN, EDWARD BURTENSHAW
A Practical Treatise...of the Law of Vendors and Purchasers of Estates. London: 1805. V. 63

SUKENICK, RONALD
The Death of the Novel and Other Stories. New York: 1969. V. 62
Out. Chicago: 1973. V. 62
Up. New York: 1968. V. 62

SULGHER-FANTASTICI, FORTUNATA ELISABETTA
Componimenti Poetici di Fortunata Sulgher Fantastici, fra gli Arcadi Temira Parraside Accademica Fiorentina &c. Firenze: 1785. V. 63

SULLINS, D.
Recollections of an Old Man: Seventy Years in Dixie 1827-1897. Bristol: 1910. V. 63; 64

SULLIVAN, ARABELLA JANE
Recollections of a Chaperon. London: 1833. V. 65
Recollections of a Chaperon. London: 1849. V. 67
Tales of the Peerage and the Peasantry. London: 1835. V. 65

SULLIVAN, EDWARD
Protection to Native Industry. London: 1870. V. 63

SULLIVAN, ELEANOR
Whodunit: a Biblio-Bio-Anecdotal Memoir of Frederick Dannay. New York: 1984. V. 65

SULLIVAN, FRANK S.
A History of Meade County, Kansas. Topeka: 1916. V. 64; 67

SULLIVAN, HARRY STACK
Schizophrenia: Its Conservative and Malignant Features. Baltimore: 1924. V. 67

SULLIVAN, JOHN
Letters and Papers of, Continental Army. Concord: 1930-1939. V. 63

SULLIVAN, JOHN L.
Report on the Origin and Increase of the Paterson Manufactories, and the Intended Diversion of Their Waters by the Morris Canal Company.... Paterson: 1828. V. 66

SULLIVAN, JOHN T.
Report of Historical and Technical Information Relating to the Problem of Inter-Oceanic Communication by the Way of the American Isthmus. Washington: 1883. V. 63

SULLIVAN, LOUIS H.
A System of Architectural Ornament, According with a Philosophy of Man's Powers. Chicago: 1964. V. 62; 65

SULLIVAN, M. F.
Ireland of To-Day; the Causes and Aims of Irish Agitation. Philadelphia: 1881. V. 67

SULLIVAN, MAURICE S.
Jedediah Smith, Trader and Trailbreaker. New York: 1936. V. 62; 65
The Travels of Jedediah Smith.... Santa Ana: 1934. V. 62; 63; 64; 67

SULLIVAN, MAY KELLOGG
A Woman Who Went to Alaska. Boston;: 1903. V. 65

SULLIVAN, MICHAEL
The Cave Temples of Maichishan. London: 1959. V. 66

SULLIVAN, PAT
The Felix Annual: Pictures Stories of the Film Cat. London: 1926. V. 62
The Felix Annual. Pictures Stories of the Film Cat. London: 1928. V. 65

SULLIVAN, RICHARD JOSEPH
A View of Nature, in Letters to a Traveller Among the Alps. London: 1794. V. 63

SULLIVAN, T. D.
Bantry, Berehaven and the O'Sullivan Sept. 1908. V. 63
Green Leaves. A Volume of Irish Verses. 1885. V. 65

SULLIVANT, WILLIAM S.
Icones Muscorum...(with) Supplement. Cambridge: 1864-1874. V. 63; 66
The Musci and Hepaticae of the United States East of the Mississippi River. New York: 1856. V. 63; 66

SULLY, MAXIMILIEN DE BETHUNE, DUC DE
Memoirs.... London: 1778. V. 63
Memoires ou Oeconomies Royales D'Estat, Domestiques, Politiques et Militaires de Henry Le Grand. Paris: 1664. V. 67

SULPICIUS
Sulpicii Severi Presbyteri Opera Omnia Cum Lectissimus Accurate Georgio Hornio. Lugduni Batavor: 1647. V. 65; 66

SULTAN, LARRY
Evidence. Greenbrae/Santa Cruz: 1977. V. 63

SULTZBERGER, HARTMANN HENRY
All About Opium. London: 1884. V. 64

SULZER, ELMER G.
Twenty-Five Kentucky Folk Ballads. Lexington: 1936. V. 65

SUMMER Haunts, Hotels and Boarding Houses in the White Mountains and Other Popular Resorts. Bethlehem. V. 63

SUMMER Saunterings by the B. & L. Boston: 1886. V. 64

SUMMER Songs with Music from Flower Fairies of the Summer. London: 1926. V. 62

SUMMERHAYES, MARTHA
Vanished Arizona. Philadelphia: 1908. V. 64; 66; 67
Vanished Arizona. Salem: 1911. V. 66

SUMMERHAYES, V. A.
Wild Orchids. London: 1951. V. 62

SUMMERING in Colorado. Denver: 1874. V. 63; 65

SUMMERS, FESTUS P.
The Baltimore and Ohio in the Civil War. New York: 1939. V. 64

SUMMERS, GEORGE W.
First Celebration by the Old Dominion Society, of the City of New York...Settlement at Jamestown, Va. New York: 1860. V. 63

SUMMERS, JAMES
The Rudiments of the Chinese Language with Dialogues, Exercises and a Vocabulary. London: 1864. V. 64; 66

SUMMERS, LEWIS P.
Annals of Southwest Virginia. Abingdon: 1929. V. 63
Annals of Southwest Virginia, 1769-1800. Johnson City: 1992. V. 66

History of Southwest, Virginia 1746-1786. Washington County, 1777-1870. Richmond: 1903. V. 63; 64

SUMMERS, MONTAGUE
A Gothic Bibliography. New York: 1964. V. 67
The History of Witchcraft and Demonology. London: 1926. V. 66
A Popular History of Witchcraft. London: 1937. V. 64
The Vampire: His Kith and Kin. London: 1928. V. 63
The Vampire, His Kith and Kin. New York: 1929. V. 66
The Vampire in Europe. London: 1929. V. 62; 63; 66
The Werewolf. London: 1933. V. 63; 66

SUMMERS, SUSAN
A Crown of Flowers. Market Drayton, Shropshire: 1997. V. 64

SUMNER, JOHN BIRD
A Series of Sermons on the Christian Faith and Character. London: 1826. V. 62
A Treatise on the Records of the Creation and on the Moral Attributes of the Creator. London: 1825. V. 62

SUMNER, L.
Birds and Mammals of the Sierra with Records from Sequoia and Kings Canyon National Parks. Berkeley: 1953. V. 62

SUN INSURANCE OFFICE
Instructions for the Agents of the Sun Fire-Office. London: 1834. V. 63

SUNDAY Reading for Good Children. London: 1865. V. 65

SUNDER, JOHN E.
The Fur Trade on the Upper Missouri 1840-1865. Norman: 1965. V. 67

SUNDERLAND, CHARLES SPENCER, 3RD EARL OF
Bibliotheca Sunderlandiana. London: 1881-1883. V. 62

SUNNY Days and Children's Ways. London: 1868. V. 62
SUNNY Days and Children's Ways. 1880. V. 67

SUPERVIELLE, JULES
Selected Writings. New York: 1967. V. 65

SUPPRESSION of the Taiping Rebellion in the Departments around Shanghai. Shanghai: 1871. V. 64

THE SUPTA-SARI, or Chundi-Pat.... Calcutta: 1823. V. 64

SURETTE, DICK
Trout and Salmon Fly Index. 1974. V. 67

THE SURPRISING, Unheard of and Never-to-be-Surpassed Adventures of Young Munchausen. London: 1865. V. 65

SURTEES, ROBERT
The History of the County Palatine of Durham. Sunderland: 1908. V. 63
The History of the County Palatine of Durham. Sunderland: 1909. V. 63
The History of the County Palatine of Durham. Sunderland: 1910. V. 63

SURTEES, ROBERT SMITH
The Analysis of the Hunting Field. 1846. V. 64
The Analysis of the Hunting Field. London: 1846. V. 67
Ask Mamma; or the Richest Commoner in England. London: 1858. V. 64; 67
Bridle and Brush. London: 1937. V. 67
Handley Cross. London: 1854. V. 62; 65; 67
Handley Cross; Hawbuck Grange; Plain or Ringlets? Mr. Sponge's Sporting Tour; Ask Mama. London: 1890. V. 63
Handley Cross or Mr. Jorrock's Hunt. London: 1902. V. 62
Hawbuck Grange or the Sporting Adventures of Thomas Scott. London: 1902. V. 62
Hillingdon Hall or the Cockney Squire; a Tale of Country Life. New York: 1935. V. 67
Hunts with Jorrocks. London: 1908. V. 67
Jorrocks's Jaunts and Jollities. London: 1843. V. 62
Mr. Fancy Romford's Hounds. London: 1865. V. 65; 67
Mr. Jorrock's Lectors, from Handley Cross. London: 1910. V. 62; 66; 67
Mr. Romford's Hounds.... London: 1902. V. 62
Mr. Sponge. Hawbuck Grange. Facey Romford. Plain or Ringlets. Handley Cross. Ask Mama. 1926. V. 62
Mr. Sponge's Sporting Tour. London. V. 67
Mr. Sponge's Sporting Tour. London: 1853. V. 64; 65
Mr. Sponge's Sporting Tour. London: 1860. V. 62; 64
Plain or Ringlets?. London: 1860. V. 64; 66; 67
Plain or Ringlets?. London: 1892. V. 66
The Sporting Novels. London: 1899. V. 67

SUSANN, JACQUELINE
Valley of the Dolls. New York: 1966. V. 66

SUSKIND, PATRICK
Perfume. New York: 1986. V. 65

SUSSEX ARCHAEOLOGICAL SOCIETY
Sussex Archaeological Collections, Illustrating the History and Antiquities of the County. Volume I - Volume XXXII, plus General Index to Volumes I-XXV. Sussex: 1848-1882. V. 63

SUSSEX Parish Churches &c. Specimens of Church Architecture Including Doorways, Windows, Fonts, Effigies &c.... Brighton: 1874. V. 67

SUTCLIFF, ROBERT
Travels in Some Parts of North America. Philadelphia: 1812. V. 64

SUTCLIFF, ROSEMARY
The Chronicles of Robin Hood. London: 1950. V. 67
Knight's Fee. London: 1960. V. 67
The Mark of the Horse Lord. London: 1965. V. 67
Song for a Dark Queen. 1978. V. 67

SUTCLIFFE, HALLIWELL
The Striding Dales. London: 1929. V. 65

SUTCLIFFE, THOMAS
An Exposition of Facts Relating to the Rise and Progress of the Woollen, Linen and Cotton Manufactures of Great Britain. Manchester: 1843. V. 63; 65

SUTER, H.
Manual of the New Zealand Mollusca. 1913-1915. V. 66

SUTHERLAND, ALEXANDER
A Medical Essay, with Observations, Towards Ascertaining a New, Safe and Easy Method for Promoting the Eruption and Completing the Maturation in the Small Pox. London: 1750. V. 65

SUTHERLAND, DAVID
A Tour Up the Straits, from Gibraltar to Constantinople. London: 1790. V. 64

SUTHERLAND, JAMES
The Adventures of an Armenian Boy. Ann Arbor: 1964. V. 65
The Adventures of an Elephant Hunter. London: 1912. V. 65

SUTHERLAND, L. W.
Aces and Kings. Sydney: 1935. V. 63; 67

SUTHERLAND, MARY A.
The Story of Corpus Christi. Corpus Christi: 1916. V. 67

SUTHERLAND, THOMAS JEFFERSON
A Letter to Her Majesty the British Queen, with Letters to Lord Durham, Lord Glenelg and Sir George ARthur. Albany: 1841. V. 63

SUTHERLIN, W. T.
Danville Riot, November 3, 1883 Report of the Committee of Forty With Sworn Testimony of Thirty Seven Witnesses &c. Richmond: 1883. V. 66

SUTNAR, LADISLAV
Packaage Design: the Force of Visual Selling. New York: 1953. V. 65

SUTRO, ADOLPH
Closing Argument of Adolph Sutro on the Bill Before Congress to Aid the Sutro Tunnel, Delivered Before the Committe on Mines and Mining of the House or Representatives of the United States of America, Monday April 22, 1872. Washington: 1873. V. 64

SUTRO, ALFRED
The Batheaston Parnassus Fairs, a Manuscript Identified. San Francisco: 1936. V. 63

SUTTER, JOHANN AUGUST
The Diary of Johann August Sutter. San Francisco: 1932. V. 63; 66
New Helvetia Diary. A Record of Events Kept by John A. Sutter and His Clerks at New Helvetia, California from Sept 9. 1845 to May 25, 1848. San Francisco: 1939. V. 62; 63; 66
Pioneers of the Sacramento. San Francisco: 1953. V. 66

SUTTON, ADAH
Mr. Bunny, His Book. Springfield: 1900. V. 65
Mushroom Fairies. Akron: 1910. V. 67
Teddy Bears. Akron: 1907. V. 65

SUTTON, B.
A Century of Mycology. Cambridge: 1996. V. 64

SUTTON, ERNEST V.
A Life Worth Living - Early Days in Ohio - Dakota - Minnesota - California. Pasadena: 1948. V. 66

SUTTON, G. M.
Birds in the Wilderness.... New York: 1936. V. 67
The Birds of Southampton Island. Pittsburgh: 1932. V. 66
Eskimo Year. A Naturalist's Adventures in the Far North. New York: 1934. V. 66
Mexican Birds.... Norman: 1951. V. 67

SUTTON, JOHN
An Important Discovery for the Destruction of the Turnip Fly. Salisbury: 1824. V. 62; 65; 66

SUTTON, JOHN FROST
The Date-Book of Remarkable and Memorable Event Connected with Nottingham and Its Neighbourhood. Nottingham: 1884. V. 65

SUTTON, MARTIN A. F.
Golf Courses. Reading: 1905. V. 66

SUTTON, R.
The Methodist Church Property Case. New York: 1851. V. 63

SUTTON, R. L.
An African Holiday. 1924. V. 62; 63
An Arctic Safari with Camera and Rifle in the Land of the Midnight Sun. St. Louis: 1932. V. 65
The Long Trek. 1930. V. 67
Tiger Trails in Southern Asia. 1926. V. 67
The Trails in Southern Asia. St. Louis: 1926. V. 62

SUTTON, ROBERT
A Complete Guide to Landlords, Tenants and Lodgers, Being a Methodical Arrangement of the Whole Law.... London: 1812. V. 65

SUTTON, ROYAL
The Face of Courage: the Indian Photographs of Frank A. Rinehart. Fort Collins: 1972. V. 63; 64; 66

SUVATTI, C.
Fauna of Thailand. Bangkok: 1950. V. 62; 64; 66
Index to the Fishes of Siam. Bangkok: 1936. V. 62

SUZANNE, P. H.
De la Maniere D'Etudier les Mathematiques, Ouvrage Destine a Servir de Guide Aux Jeaunes Gens, a Ceux Sur-Tout qui Veulent Approfondir cette Science.... Paris: 1806-1809. V. 65

SVEND WOHLERT INC.
Danish Furniture. San Francisco: 1962. V. 65

SVENSSON, G. S. O.
Fresh Water Fishes from the Gambia River.... Stockholm: 1933. V. 67

SVETLOV, VALERIAN
Le Ballet Contemporain. Paris: 1912. V. 66
Thamar Karsavina. London: 1922. V. 66

SVEVO, ITALO
As a Man Grows Older. London and New York: 1932. V. 64
James Joyce. A Lecture Delivered in Milan in 1927 by His Friend Italo Svevo. Milan: 1950. V. 67

SVININ, PAUL
Picturesque United States of America 1811, 1812, 1813. New York: 1930. V. 63

SWAAN, W.
The Gothic Cathedral. London: 1969. V. 65

SWAIM, JAMES
The Mural Diagraph or the Art of Conversing Through a Wall. Philadelphia: 1829. V. 64

SWAIM, WILLIAM
Some Remarks Upon a Publication by the Philadelphia Medical Society Concerning Swaim's Panacea. Philadelphia: 1828. V. 66

SWAIN, CHARLES
Metrical Essays, on Subjects of History and Imagination. London: 1828. V. 65

SWAIN, JOSEPH
Redemption, a Poem in Five Books. Charleston: 1819. V. 63; 66

SWAINSON, C.
A Handbook of Weather Folk-Lore Being a Collection of Proverbial Sayings in Various Languages Relating to the Weather.... London: 1873. V. 66

SWAINSON, WILLIAM
The Elements of Modern Conchology.... London: 1835. V. 62
Flycatchers. Edinburgh: 1838. V. 62
The Naturalist's Guide for Collecting and Preserving All Subjects of Natural History and Botany. London: 1835?. V. 62
A Treatise on the Geography and Classification of Animals. 1835. V. 63
A Treatise on the Geography and Classification of Animals. London: 1835. V. 62; 64
Zoological Illustrations, or Original Figures and Descriptions of New, Rare, or Interesting Animals... (and) Second Series.... London: 1820-1833. V. 65

SWALLOW, G. C.
Geological Report of the Country Along the Line of the South-Western Branch of the Pacific Railroad. State of Missouri. St. Louis: 1859. V. 65

SWAMMERDAM, JEAN
Histoire General des Insectes. Utrecht: 1685. V. 63

SWAN, ABRAHAM
The British Architect, or the Builder's Treasury of Stair-Cases. London: 1745. V. 67

SWAN, ANNIE S.
We Travel Home. London: 1935. V. 63

SWAN, JOHN
A Trio to the Gold Mines of California in 1882. San Francisco: 1960. V. 62; 65

SWAN, JOSEPH
Delineations of the Brain in Relation to Voluntary Motion. London: 1864. V. 64
A Demonstration of the Nerves of the Human Body. London: 1834. V. 62; 65

SWAN, MYRA
Shallows. London: 1801. V. 65

SWANBERG, W. A.
First Blood. The Story of Fort Sumter. New York: 1957. V. 62; 63

SWANBOROUGH, F. G.
United States Military Aircraft Since 1909. London: 1963. V. 65

SWANEPOEL, D. A.
Butterflies of South Africa, Where, When and How They Fly. Cape Town: 1953. V. 65; 66

SWAN LAND & CATTLE COMPANY, LTD.
Prospectus - The Stuart Land and Cattle Company. Edinburgh: 1883. V. 66

SWANN, HOWARD KIRKE
A Monograph of the Birds of Prey. London: 1924-1925. V. 62

SWANN, HOWARD KIRKE continued
A Synopsis of the Accipitres.... London: 1921-1922. V. 63

SWANN, WIM
The Gothic Cathedral. Garden City: 1969. V. 64; 66

SWAN'S Views of the Lakes of Scotland: a Series of Views...with Historical and Descriptive Illustrations.... Glasgow: 1836. V. 64

SWANSON, E. B.
A Century of Oil and Gas in Books. New York: 1960. V. 62; 64

SWANTON, E. W.
The Mollusca of Somerset, Land, Freshwater, Estuarine and Marine. Taunton: 1912. V. 66

SWANTON, JOHN R.
Early History of the Creek Indians and Their Neighbors. Washington: 1922. V. 62
Tlingit Myths and Texts. Washington: 1909. V. 63

SWANWICK, MICHAEL
Stations of the Tide. 1991. V. 66

SWARTZ, O.
Flora Indiae Occidentalis Aucta Atque Illustrata sive Descriptiones Plantarum inProdromo Recensitarum. Erlangae: 1797. V. 66

SWARZENSKI, GEORG
Europaisches Amerika. Frankfurter: 1927. V. 65

SWAYNE, H. G. C.
Through the Highlands of Siberia. London: 1904. V. 62

SWAYSLAND, W.
Familiar Wild Birds. 1883-1888. V. 62
Familiar Wild Birds. London: 1903. V. 62

SWEDENBORG, EMANUEL
De Coelo et Ejus Mirabilibus, et de Inferno, ex Auditis & Visis. Londini: 1758. V. 67
De Nova Hierosolyma et Ejus Doctrina Coelsti; ex Auditis e Coelo. Londini: 1758. V. 67
The Principia; or, the First Principles of Natural Things.... London: 1845-1846. V. 63; 65
A Treatise on the Nature of Influx, or, of the Intercourse Between Soul and Body. Boston: 1794. V. 65; 66

SWEENEY, JAMES JOHNSON
Joan Miro. New York: 1970. V. 66

SWEENEY, R. C. H
Snakes of Nyasaland. Zomba: 1961. V. 66

SWEENEY, W. ALLISON
History of the American Negro in the Great World War. 1919. V. 63; 66

SWEENY, LENORA H.
Amherst County, in the Revolution Including Extracts from the Lost Order Book 1773-1782. Lynchburg: 1951. V. 64

SWEERT, E.
Florilegium, Tractans de Variis Floribus et Aliis Indicis Plantis.... Frankfurt: 1615-1614. V. 63

SWEET, ALEX
On a Mexican Mustang. London: 1905. V. 64
On a Mexican Mustang. Hartford: 1883. V. 65
Sketches from Texas Siftings. New York: 1882. V. 64

SWEET, HOMER D. L.
Twilight Hours in the Adirondacks; the Daily Doings and Several Sayings of Seven Sober, Social, Scientific Students in the Wilderness of Northern New York. Syracuse: 1870. V. 67

SWEET, R.
The British Flower Garden. London: 1823-1838. V. 65
The British Flower Garden. 1850. V. 66
The Ornamental Flower Garden and Shrubbery.... 1854. V. 65

SWEETMAN, LUKE D.
Back Trailing on the Open Range. Caldwell: 1951. V. 65

SWEETSER, WILLIAM
Mental Hygiene; or, an Examination of the Intellect and Passions Designed to Show How They Affect and Are Affected by the Bodily Functions, and Their Influence on Health and Longevity. New York: 1850. V. 65

SWEM, E. G.
Brothers of the Spade, Correspondence of Peter Collinson of London and John Custis of Williamsburg. Worcester: 1949. V. 64
Jamestown 350th Anniversary Historical Booklets...No. 1-23. 1957. V. 64

SWEM, EARL G.
A Bibliography of Virginia Part II. Richmond: 1917. V. 63
Maps Relating to Virginia in the Virginia State Library and Other Departments of the Commonwealth with the 17th and 18th Century Atlas Maps in the Library of Congress. Richmond: 1914. V. 62

SWENDSEN, HAAGEN
The Tryals of Haagen Swendsen, Sarah Baynton, John Hartwell and John Spurr. London: 1703. V. 63

SWETT, CHARLES
A Trip to British Honduras and to San Pedro, Republic of Honduras. New Orleans: 1868. V. 62

SWETT, MORRIS
Fort Sill - a History. Fort Sill: 1921. V. 66

SWEZEY, KENNETH M.
Science Magic. New York: 1952. V. 67

SWIETEN, GERALD VON
Commentaria in Hermanni Boerhaave Aphorismos De Cognoscendis et Curandis Morbis.... Venice: 1759-1764. V. 64; 67

SWIFT, DEANE
An Essay Upon the Life, Writings and Character of Dr. Jonathan Swift. London: 1755. V. 67

SWIFT, GRAHAM
Ever After. London: 1992. V. 67
Last Orders. London: 1996. V. 67
Last Orders. New York: 1996. V. 63; 67
Learning to Swim. London: 1982. V. 67
Out of This World. London: 1988. V. 67
Out of This World. New York: 1988. V. 64; 65
Shuttlecock. London: 1981. V. 67
The Sweet Shop Owner. London: 1980. V. 63; 64; 67
Waterland. London: 1983. V. 62; 63
Waterland. New York: 1984. V. 67

SWIFT, HELEN
My Father and My Mother. Chicago: 1937. V. 66

SWIFT, HILDEGARDE HOYT
North Star Shining. A Pictorial History of the American Negro. New York: 1943. V. 63

SWIFT, JONATHAN
Baucis and Philemon: a Poem.... London: 1709. V. 66
Des Capitain Lemuel Gullivers Reise in das Land Derer Houyhnhnms. Berlin: 1919. V. 66
A Complete Collection of Genteel and Ingenious Conversation According to the Most Polite Mode and Method Now Used at Court.... London: 1738. V. 62; 63; 64; 67
The Conduct of the Allies, and of that late Ministry, in Beginning and Carrying on the Present War. London: 1711. V. 62
Directions to Servants. Waltham St. Lawrence: 1925. V. 62
Directions to Servants in General; and in Particular to the Butler, Cook, Footman, Coachman.... London: 1745. V. 62
A Discourse of the Contents and Dissensions Between the Nobles and the Commons in Athens and Rome, with the Consequences they Had Upon Both those States. London: 1701. V. 64; 65; 66
An Essay Upon the Life, Writings and Characters of Dr. Jonathan Swift.... London: 1755. V. 62
Gulliver's Travels. London: 1909. V. 62
Gulliver's Travels. Philadelphia: 1918. V. 63
Gulliver's Travels. London: 1930. V. 65
Gulliver's Travels. 1939. V. 67
Gulliver's Travels. New York: 1940. V. 66
Gulliver's Travels. New York: 1947. V. 66
Her Majesties Most Gracious Speech to Both Houses of Parliament. On Thursday the Ninth Day of April, 1713. (and) The Humble Address of the... Lords Spiritual and Temporal...Presented to Her Majesty on Saturday the Eleventh Day of April 1713. London: 1713. V. 66
Hibernian Patriot.... London: 1730. V. 63
The History of the Four Last Years of the Queen.... London: 1758. V. 62; 65
Letters Written by the Late Jonathan Swift, D.D. Dean of St. Patrick's, Dublin.... London: 1766-1768. V. 63; 67
The Life and Genuine Character of Doctor Swift. London: 1733. V. 66
Miscellaneous Poems. Waltham St. Lawrence: 1928. V. 62
Miscellanies in Prose and Verse. London: 1711. V. 62
Miscellanies in Prose and Verse. London: 1713. V. 63; 65
Miscellanies.... London: 1722. V. 62
Poems. Oxford: 1966. V. 63
Poetical Works. London: 1967. V. 67
The Publick Spirit of the Whigs: set Forth in Their Generous Encouragement of the Author of the Crisis. London: 1714. V. 62
The Right of Precedence Between Physicians and Civilians Enquir'd Into. London: 1720. V. 62; 65
The Select Works. London: 1823. V. 67
Selected Essays. Waltham St. Lawrence: 1925. V. 62
A Tale of a Tub. 1704. V. 66
A Tale of a Tub. London: 1704. V. 62; 63; 64
A Tale of a Tub. Dublin: 1705. V. 62
A Tale of a Tub. London: 1705. V. 62; 66
A Tale of a Tub.... London: 1710. V. 65
A Tale of a Tub.... London: 1711. V. 66
Travels into Several Remote Nations of the World. London: 1726. V. 62
Travels Into Several Remote Nations of the World. London: 1727. V. 65; 66
Travels into Several Remote Nations of the World. Montrose: 1819. V. 62; 65
Travels into Several Remote Nations of the World. Waltham St. Lawrence: 1925. V. 62; 62; 64
Travels...by Lemuel Gulliver.... 1840. V. 65
A Vindication of His Excellency the Lord C----t, from the Charge of Favouring None but Tories, High-Churchmen and Jacobites. London: 1730. V. 64
Voyages de Gulliver. Paris: 1762. V. 65
The Wonderful Wonder of Wonders. London: 1722. V. 62
The Works. 1754-1775. V. 62; 65
The Works. Edinburgh and Glasgow: 1756. V. 62
Works. London: 1760. V. 62
The Works. London: 1808. V. 62
The Works. 1864. V. 64; 67

SWIFT, JONATHAN continued
Works. (with) Letters. London: 1768. V. 62

SWIFT, JOSEPH GARDNER
Memoirs of the First Graduate of the United States Military Academy at West Point, Chief Engineer of the U.S. Army from 1812-1818, 1800 to 1865, to which is added a Genealogy of the Family of Thomas Swift of Dorchester, Mass., 1634. Boston: 1890. V. 63
Memoirs of the First Graduate of the U.S. Military Academy, West Point, Chief Engineer, U.S. Army 1812-1818, 1800-1865. N.P: 1890. V. 64

SWIFT, L. H.
Botanical Bibliographies, a Guide to Bibliographic Materials Applicable to Botany. Minneapolis: 1970. V. 64

SWIFT, THEOPHILUS
The Monster at Large; or, the Innocence of Rhynwick Williams Vindicated in a Letter to Sir Francis Buller, Bart. London: 1790. V. 63

SWIGGETT, S. A.
The Bright Side of Prison Life. Baltimore: 1897. V. 62; 65

SWINBORNE, FREDERICK
Gustavus Adolphus: an Historical Poem and Romance of the Thirty Years War. 1884. V. 67

SWINBURNE, ALGERNON CHARLES
Atalanta in Calydon. London: 1865. V. 63
Auguste Vacquerie. Paris: 1875. V. 62
A Channel Passage and Other Poems. London: 1904. V. 62; 67
Grace Darling. London: 1893. V. 62
Hide and Seek. London: 1975. V. 65
Hymn to Proserpine. Waltham St. Lawrence: 1944. V. 64
Laus Veneris. New York: 1866. V. 66
Laus Veneris. Waltham St. Lawrence: 1948. V. 62; 64; 65
Letters to Victor Hugo. London: 1917. V. 63
Locrine a Tragedy.... London: 1887. V. 62
Lucretia Borgia. London: 1942. V. 64; 66
Lucretia Borgia. Waltham St. Lawrence: 1942. V. 64; 65; 66
Note of an English Republican on the Muscovite Crusade. London: 1876. V. 63; 64; 65
A Note on Charlotte Bronte. London: 1877. V. 64
Notes on Poems and Reviews. London: 1866. V. 63
Ode on the Proclamation of the French Republic. 1870. V. 64
Pasiphae. London: 1950. V. 63; 64
Pasiphae. Waltham St. Lawrence: 1950. V. 62; 66
Poems and Ballads. London: 1866. V. 62; 66
The Poetical Works. London: 1904. V. 62
Posthumous Poems. London: 1917. V. 64
Selected Poems. New York: 1928. V. 67
The Sisters; a Tragedy. London: 1892. V. 67
Songs Before Sunrise. London: 1909. V. 62
Songs of Two Nations. London: 1875. V. 66
The Springtide of Life. London: 1918. V. 62; 66
The Springtide of Life. Philadelphia: 1918. V. 63
The Springtide of Life. London: 1919. V. 66
The Tragedies. London: 1905-1906. V. 62; 67
A Year's Letters. Portland: 1901. V. 63

SWINDLER, D. R.
Comparative Primate Biology. New York: 1986. V. 62

SWINDLER, MARY HAMILTON
Ancient Painting from the Earliest Times to the Period of Christian Art. New Haven: 1931. V. 64

SWINFORD, T. A.
Custeriana - a Field Guide to Custer Literature. 1999. V. 67

SWINNERTON, EMILY
George Eliot, Her Early Home. London: 1880. V. 63

SWINSTEAD-SMITH, K.
The Marchesa and Other Stories. London: 1936. V. 64

SWINTON, G.
Sculpture of the Eskimo. London: 1972. V. 62; 65

SWINTON, JOHN
Considerations Concerning a Proposal for Dividing the Court of Session into Classes or Chambers, and for Limiting Litigation in Small Causes.... Edinburgh: 1789. V. 62

SWIRE, HERBERT
The Voyage of the Challenger. London: 1938. V. 66
The Voyage of the Challenger. Waltham St. Lawrence: 1938. V. 62; 65; 66

SWISHER, CARL BRENT
Stephen J. Field, Craftsman of the Law. Washington: 1930. V. 63

SWISHER, JAMES
How I Know or Sixteen Years' Eventful Experiences - an Authentic Narrative. Cincinnati: 1881. V. 65; 67

SWISS Gateaux Designs and Decorations. London: 1905. V. 66

SWITZER, STEPHEN
An Introduction to a General System of Hydrostaticks and Hydraulicks, Philosophical and Practical. London: 1729. V. 65

SWITZERLAND a Hundred Years Ago. London. V. 66

SWOPE, JOHN
Camera Over Hollywood. New York: 1939. V. 63

SWORD, WILEY
Shiloh: Bloody April. New York: 1974. V. 63

SYDENHAM, THOMAS
Dissertatio Epistolaris ad Speclatissimum Dochissimumq; Virum Gulielmum Cole, M.D. London: 1682. V. 64; 67
Dr. Sydenham's Compleat Method of Curing Almost All Diseases.... London: 1695. V. 64; 66
The Entire Works of .... London: 1763. V. 64; 66
Opera Medica. Venetiis: 1735. V. 66; 67
Opera Medica. Genevae: 1767. V. 66; 67
The Works of Thomas Sydenham, M.D. London: 1848. V. 65

SYDNEY HARBOUR BRIDGE
Contract for the Construction of a Cantilever Bridge Across Sydney Harbour from Dawes Point to Milson's Point, Sydney, New South Wales, Australia. Specification. Sydney: 1921. V. 62

SYDNEY HARBOUR BRIDGE ADVISORY BOARD
Report on Designs and Tenders Submitted in Connection with the Proposed Bridge Over Sydney Harbour to Connect Sydney with North Sydney. New South Wales: 1903. V. 62

SYKES, BRIGADIER-GENERAL
The Right Honourable Sir Mortimer Durand, a Biography. London: 1926. V. 63

SYKES, CHRISTOPHER
Character & Situation: Six Short Stories. London: 1949. V. 67
Four Studies in Loyalty. London: 1946. V. 65

SYKES, D. F. E.
The History of Huddersfield and Its Vicinity. Huddersfield: 1898. V. 62; 63

SYKES, JOHN
Local Records; or Historical Register of Remarkable Events, Which Have Occurred Exclusively in Northumberland and Durham, Newcastle Upon Tyne, and Berwick Upon Tweed.... Newcastle: 1865-1866. V. 63; 65

SYKES, MARK MASTERMAN
Catalogue of the Splendid, Curious and Extensive Library of the Late Sir Mark Masterman Sykes, Bart. London: 1824. V. 62
Dar-Ul-Islam a Record of a Journey through Ten of the Asiatic Provinces of Turkey. London: 1904. V. 62

SYKES, W. J.
The Principles and Practice of Brewing. London: 1897. V. 63

SYLVA-TAROUCA, VON E.
Kein Heger, Kein Jager!. 1899. V. 66; 67

SYLVESTER, CHARLES
The Philosophy of Domestic Economy.... Nottingham: 1819. V. 63

SYLVESTER, HERBERT MILTON
Indian Wars of New England. Boston: 1910. V. 66

SYMANSKI, RICHARD
Wild Horses and Sacred Cows. Flagstaff: 1985. V. 64

SYME, JAMES
Contributions to the Pathology and Practice of Surgery. Edinburgh: 1848. V. 64
Excision with the Scapula. Edinburgh: 1864. V. 64
Observations on Clinical Surgery. Edinburgh: 1861. V. 64
On Diseases of the Rectum. Edinburgh: 1846. V. 64
On Stricture of the Urethra and Fistula in Perineo. Edinburgh: 1849. V. 64

SYME, JOHN
Fighting Officialdom: a Three Years' Battle Against Police and Home Office Persecution.... Westminster: 1913. V. 63

SYME, PATRICK
A Treatise on British Song Birds. Edinburgh: 1823. V. 62
Werner's Nomenclature of Colours.... Edinburgh: 1821. V. 66

SYMES, MICHAEL
An Account of an Embassy to the Kingdom of Ava, Sent by the Governor-General of India, in the Year 1795. London: 1800. V. 62

SYMINGTON, ANDREW JAMES
Pen and Pencil Sketches of Faroe and Iceland.... London: 1862. V. 66; 67
Samuel Lover; a Biographical Sketch.... London: 1880. V. 67

SYMINGTON, J.
In a Bengal Jungle. 1935. V. 67
The Topographical Anatomy of the Child. Edinburgh: 1887. V. 67

SYMINGTON, J. ALEXANDER
The Brotherton Library. A Catalogue of Ancient Manuscripts and Early Printed Books, Collected by Edward Allen Barton Brotherton of Wakefield. Leeds: 1931. V. 66
Catalogue of the Museum and Library, the Bronte Society. Haworth: 1927. V. 65
Some Unpublished Letters of Walter Scott.... Oxford: 1932. V. 62

SYMINGTON, N.
The Night Climbers of Cambridge. 1937. V. 63

SYMMES, FRANK R.
History of the Old Tennent Church. Cranbury: 1904. V. 63; 66

SYMMONS, EDWARD
A Vindication of King Charles, or a Loyal Subjects Duty. London: 1648. V. 67

SYMONDS, A. J. A.
The Quest for Corvo - an Experiment in Biography. London: 1934. V. 62

SYMONDS, B.
A Treatise on Field Diversions.... 1824. V. 66

SYMONDS, EMILY MORSE
Little Memoirs of the Eighteenth Century. New York: 1901. V. 63

SYMONDS, H. D.
Catalogue of New Books Printed for H. D. Symonds, No. 20, Paternoster Row, London, 1805. London: 1805. V. 62

SYMONDS, J. A.
A Problem in Greek Ethics. London: 1901. V. 62
Walt Whitman, a Study. London: 1893. V. 62

SYMONDS, JOHN
Elfrida and the Pig. London: 1959. V. 65
Remarks Upon an Essay, Intituled, the History of the Colonization of the Free States of Antiquity, Applied to the Present Contest Between Great Britain and Her American Colonies. London: 1778. V. 64; 66

SYMONDS, JOHN ADDINGTON
Animi Figura. London: 1882. V. 65
In the Key of Blue, and Other Prose Essays. London: 1893. V. 64; 66
Letters and Papers of.... London: 1923. V. 65
New and Old - a Volume of Verse. London: 1880. V. 64
On the English Family of Symonds. London: 1894. V. 64
Our Life in the Swiss Highlands. London: 1892. V. 63; 64
A Problem in Greek Ethics; Being a Enquiry into the Phenomenon of Sexual Inversion. London: 1901. V. 64; 65; 67
A Problem in Modern Ethics: Being an Enquiry into the Phenomenon of Sexual Inversion. London: 1896. V. 64
Sleep and Dreams: Two Lectures Delivered at the Bristol Literary and Philosophical Institution. London: 1851. V. 67
Waste: a Lecture Delivered at the Bristol Institution for the Advancement of Science, Literature and Arts on Tuesday, February the 10th, 1863. London: 1863. V. 63
Wine, Women and Songs. London: 1884. V. 65

SYMONDS, W. S.
Old Stones: Notes and Lectures on the Plutonic, Silurian and Devonian Rocks in the Neighbourhood of Malvern. Malvern: 1855. V. 67

SYMONDS, WILLIAM
Naval Costume. 1840. V. 62

SYMONS, A. J. A.
An Anthology of Nineties Verse. 1928. V. 63; 66
A Bibliographical Catalogue of the First Loan Exhibition of Books and Manuscripts. London: 1922. V. 64; 64
Books of the Nineties. London. V. 67
Emin, the Governor of Equatoria. London: 1928. V. 64
An Episode in the Life of the Queen of Sheba Discovered by A.J.A. Symons. London: 1929. V. 64
Inaugural Address of His Oddshippe Bro. A. J. A. Symons (Speculator). Delivered to the Sette of Odd Volumes at Its 525th meeting Held at the Savoy Hotel on October 18, 1938. N.P: 1938. V. 67
Inaugural Address of His Oddshippe Bro. A. J. A. Symons (Speculator). Delivered to the Sette of Odd Volumes In Its 525th Meeting Held at the Savoy Hotel on October 18, 1938. London: 1938. V. 66
The Quest for Corvo. London: 1934. V. 64; 67
The Quest for Corvo. London: 1952. V. 63
The Quest for Corvo. East Lansing: 1955. V. 67
Stanley. London: 1935. V. 64

SYMONS, ARTHUR
Confessions - a Study of Pathology. New York: 1930. V. 64
An Introduction to the Study of Browning. London: 1886. V. 66
An Introduction to the Study of Browning. London: 1906. V. 64
Love's Cruelty. London: 1923. V. 64
Plays, Acting and Music - a Book of Theory. London: 1909. V. 63
Romantic Movement in English Poetry. London: 1909. V. 64
Silhouettes. London: 1892. V. 64
Studies in Seven Arts. London: 1906. V. 65
Studies in Strange Souls. London: 1929. V. 65
Wanderings. London: 1931. V. 64

SYMONS, JULIAN
A. J. A. Symons Brother Speculator. N.P: 1995. V. 67
The Belting Inheritance. London: 1965. V. 67
The Blackheath Poisonings. London: 1978. V. 64; 67
Bland Beginning. New York: 1949. V. 67
Bland Beginning. London: 1955. V. 67
Bogue's Fortune. New York: 1956. V. 67
The Broken Penny. London: 1953. V. 67
The Broken Penny. New York: 1953. V. 67
The Colour of Murder. London: 1957. V. 67
Confusions About X. London: 1939. V. 62; 67
The Criminal Comedy of the Contented Couple. London: 1985. V. 67
Critical Observations. New Haven and New York: 1981. V. 67
Death's Darkest Face. London: 1990. V. 67
The Detective Story in Britain. London: 1962. V. 67
The Detling Murders. London: 1982. V. 67
The End of Solomon Grundy. London: 1964. V. 67
The Gigantic Shadow. London: 1958. V. 67
Horatio Bottomley. London: 1955. V. 67
The Hundred Best Crime Stories. London: 1959. V. 67
The Immaterial Murder Case. London: 1948. V. 67
The Immaterial Murder Case. London: 1954. V. 67
The Kentish Manor Murders. London: 1988. V. 67
The Man Who Killed Himself. London: 1967. V. 67
The Man Who Lost His Wife. London: 1970. V. 67
The Man Whose Dreams Came True. New York: 1968. V. 67
The Modern Crime Story. Edinburgh: 1980. V. 67
The Mystique of the Detective Story. N.P: 1982. V. 67
The Name of Anabel Lee. London: 1983. V. 67
The Name of Anabel Lee. New York: 1983. V. 67
The Narrowing Circle. London: 1954. V. 67
1948 and 1984. Edinburgh: 1984. V. 67
Notes from Another Country. London: 1972. V. 67
The Object of an Affair and Other Poems. Edinburgh: 1974. V. 67
Orwell's Prophecies. N.P: 1984. V. 67
Oscar Wilde: a Problem in Biography. Council Bluffs: 1988. V. 67
The Paper Chase. London: 1956. V. 67
The Penguin Classic Crime Omnibus. London: 1984. V. 67
The Plain Man. New York: 1962. V. 67
The Plain Man. New York: 1963. V. 67
The Players and the Game. London: 1972. V. 67
Playing Happy Families. London: 1994. V. 67
The Plot Against Roger Rider. London: 1973. V. 67
Portrait of an Artist. Conan Doyle. London: 1979. V. 67
The Progress of a Crime. London: 1960. V. 67
The Second Man. London: 1943. V. 67
Something Like a Love Affair. London: 1992. V. 67
Sweet Adelaide. London: 1980. V. 67
The Thirties. A Dream Revolved. London: 1960. V. 67
The Thirties. A Dream Revolved. London: 1975. V. 67
The 31st of February. New York: 1950. V. 67
A Three Pipe Problem. London: 1975. V. 67
The Tigers of Subtopia and Other Stories. London: 1982. V. 67
Two Brothers: Fragments of a Correspondence. Edinburgh: 1985. V. 65; 67

SYMONS, R.
A Geographical Dictionary or Gazetteer of the County of Cornwall. 1884. V. 62

SYMONS, THOMAS W.
Report of an Examination of the Upper Columbia River and the Territory in Its Vicinity. Washington: 1882. V. 62; 67

SYMSON, PATRICK
The Historie of the Church, Since the Dayes of Our Saviour Jesus Christ, Until This Present Age.... London: 1634. V. 62; 64

SYNGE, EDWARD
An Account of the Erection, Government and Number of Charity Schools in Ireland. Dublin: 1717. V. 65
The Reward of Converting Sinners from the Error of Their Ways. Dublin: 1719. V. 65

SYNGE, JOHN MILLINGTON
The Aran Islands. Dublin: 1907. V. 63
The Aran Islands. Boston: 1928. V. 66
The Autobiography of J. M. Synge. Dublin: 1965. V. 62
A Few Personal Recollections.... Churchtown, Dundrum: 1915. V. 62; 65
The Playboy of the Western World. Dublin: 1907. V. 62; 64; 65; 66
The Playboy of the Western World. Boston: 1911. V. 65
The Playboy of the Western World. Barre: 1970. V. 63
Poems and Translations. New York: 1909. V. 62; 64
Poems and Translations. 1911. V. 63
Queens. Mountrath, County Laois: 1986. V. 67
Riders to the Sea. 1969. V. 64
Riders to the Sea. New York: 1969. V. 67

SYNGE, MILLINGTON HENRY
Canada in 1848. London: 1848. V. 64

SYZ, PATRICK
Japanese Sword Fittings. Masterpieces from the Randolph B. Caldwell Collection. London: 1994. V. 63

SZABAD, EMERIC
The State Policy of Modern Europe, From the Beginning of the Sixteenth Century to the Present Time. London: 1857. V. 64

SZALAY, M.
African Art, from the Han Coray Collection 1916-1928. Munich and New York: 1998. V. 62

SZARKOWSKI, JOHN
The Idea of Louis Sullivan. Minneapolis: 1956. V. 63; 65
Irving Penn. New York: 1984. V. 63

SZATHMARY, LOUIS
Cookery Americana. New York: 1973. V. 63

SZERELMEY, N. C.
On the Encaustic and Sopissa Processes, as Applied by the Ancients for Indurating and Preserving Stone, Cements, Brick Timber, Sculpture and Paintings.... London: 1850. V. 66

SZOBEL, GEZA
Civilisation - Drawings in Colour and Black and White. London: 1942. V. 63

SZUKALSKI, STANISLAW
Projects in Design. Chicago: 1929. V. 62; 65

T

T., G.
The Practick Part of the Law; Shewing the Office Of an Attorney, and a Guide for Solicitors In all the Courts of Westminster.... London: 1711. V. 65

T., H. F.
Observations sur les Ombres Colorees.... Paris: 1782. V. 64

TABACK, SIMMS
There Was an Old Lady Who Swallowed a Fly. New York: 1997. V. 65

TABER, GLADYS BAGG
Lyonnesse. Atlanta: 1929. V. 63

TABLE Talk, or, the Modern Scrap Book. London: 1829. V. 65

TABLES of the Emperour, Kings, Electoral and All the Other Sovereign Princes, That Are Now, or Have Lately Been Alive in Europe. London: 1701. V. 67

TABOR, ELIZA
The Blue Ribbon. London: 1873. V. 65
Eglantine. London: 1875. V. 65
Nature's Noblemman. London: 1869. V. 65

TABOR, SILVER
Star of Blood. Denver: 1909. V. 65

TABULAR View of Characteristic British Fossils, Strategically Arranged. London: 1853. V. 65

TACITUS, CORNELIUS
The Annales of Cornelius Tacitus. London: 1612. V. 63; 67
C. Cornel. Tacitus et in em M. Z. Boxhornii, et H. Grotii Observationes. (Works with commentary). Venice: 1683. V. 64
C. Cornelii Taciti Opera Exstant, Ex Iusti Lipsi Editione Ultima.... Antverpiae: 1585. V. 66
C. Cornelii Tacti Opera Exstant: Iustus Lipsius Postremum Recensuit.... Antverpiae: 1600. V. 66
De Vita et Moribus Juli Agricolae Liber. Hammersmith: 1900. V. 65; 67
Jaarboeken En Historien, Ook Zyn Germanie, En't Leeven Van J. Agricola.... Amsterdam: 1684. V. 65
(Opera). Lvgdvni Batavorvm: 1640. V. 63; 66
Opera. Parisiis: 1771. V. 62
Opera Omnia.... 1792. V. 66
Opera Quae Exstant. Amstelodami: 1672. V. 63; 66
Opera Quae Extant, A Iusto Lipsio Postremum Recensita.... Antwerpiae: 1658. V. 65; 66
Quae Exstant Opera. Parisiis: 1760. V. 65; 66
The Works. London: 1728. V. 67
The Works. London: 1805. V. 63

TACOMA CHAMBER OF COMMERCE AND COMMERCIAL CLUB
Tacoma Columbian Fair Souvenir. Tacoma: 1893. V. 66

TACQUET, ANDREAS
Arithmeticae Theoria et Praxis. Amsterdam: 1704. V. 65
Cylindricorum et Annularium Libri IV. Item De Circulorum Volutione per Planum Dissertatio Physiomath. Antwerp: 1651. V. 63

TAFT, C. M.
Artists and Illustrators of the Old West 1850-1900. New York: 1953. V. 67

TAFT, L.
The History of American Sculpture. New York: 1930. V. 65

TAFT, ROBERT
Artist and Illustrators of the Old West, 1859-1900. New York and London: 1953. V. 64
Photography and the American Scene. A Social History 1839-1889. New York: 1938. V. 63; 64

TAFT, WILLIAM HOWARD
Political Issues and Outlooks. New York: 1909. V. 63

TAGLIACOZZI, GASPARE
Cheirurgia Nova...De Narium, Aurium, Labiorumque(m), Perinsitionem Cutis ex Humero Arte, Hactenus Omnibus Ignora, Farciendo. Frankfurt: 1598. V. 62

TAGORE, RABINDRANATH
Hungry Stones and Other Stories. London: 1916. V. 62

TAI, F. L.
A List of Fungi Hitherto Known from China. Peping: 1937. V. 63

The TAIN - from the Irish Tain Bo Cualinge. Dublin: 1969. V. 63

TAINE, H. A.
The History of English Literature. Edinburgh;: 1873-1874. V. 64

TAINE, HIPPOLYTE
English Positivism. London: 1870. V. 64
A Tour Through the Pyrenees. New York: 1875. V. 65

TAINE, JOHN
The Forbidden Garden. 1947. V. 67
Seeds of Life. 1951. V. 64; 66; 67

TAIT, JOHN HUNTER
A Treatise on the Law of Scotland as Applied to the Game Laws and Trout and Salmon Fishing. Edinburgh: 1928. V. 67

TAIT, PETER GUTHRIE
Life and Scientific Work of Peter Guthrie Tait, Supplement the Two Volues of Scientific Papers Published in 1898 and 1900.... Cambridge: 1911. V. 64; 67

TAIT, R. LAWSON
One Hundred and Ten Consecutive Cases of Abdominal Section Performed Since the 1st of November 1880. London: 1881. V. 67

TAIT, WILLIAM
Magdalenism. An Inquiry Into the Extent, Causes and Consequences of Prostitution in Edinburgh. Edinburgh: 1840. V. 65

TAKAHASHI, K. T.
The Anti-Japanese Petition. Appeal in Protest Against a Threatened Persecution. Montreal: 1897. V. 63

TAKA TSUKASA, NOBUSUKE
The Birds of Nippon. Tokyo: 1967. V. 67

TAKHTAJAN, A.
Diversity and Classification of Flowering Plants. New York: 1997. V. 63; 66

TALDOT, CATHERINE
The Works.... London: 1809. V. 63

TALBOT, D. AMAURY
The People of Southern Nigeria. A Sketch of Their History, Ethnology and Languages.... 1926. V. 65
Woman's Mysteries of a Primitive People. The Ibibios of Southern Nigeria. London: 1915. V. 63

TALBOT, EDWARD STUART
Slavery as Affected by Christianity. London: 1869. V. 66

TALBOT, ELEANOR W.
My Lady's Casket. Boston: 1885. V. 67

TALBOT, HAKE
Rim of the Pit. New York: 1944. V. 65

TALBOT, THOMAS
The Granvilles. An Irish Tale. London: 1882. V. 67

TALBOT, WILLIAM
The Rev. Mr. Talbot's Narrative of the Whole of His Proceedings Relative to Jonathan Britain. Bristol: 1772. V. 65

TALBOT-BOOTH, E. C.
Dumpy Books. London. V. 64
Merchant Ships 1949-1950. London: 1949. V. 66

TALCOTT, DUDLEY VAILL
North of North Cape. London: 1936. V. 64

TALCOTT, T. M. R.
General Lee's Strategy at the Battle of Chancellorsville. Richmond: 1906. V. 62; 63; 65

THE TALE of Igor. London: 1918. V. 65

THE TALE of Peter Rabbit Animated. New York: 1943. V. 63

THE TALE of the Emperor Coustans and Of Over the Sea. 1894. V. 62

A TALE of the Olden Time. London: 1821. V. 63

A TALE of the West, or, Life with a Sister. Providence: 1846. V. 66

TALES and Talks About Animals. London: 1907. V. 64

TALES and Talks for Nursery Land. London: 1910. V. 67

TALES of My Aunt Martha: Containing I. The Larid, a Scottish Tale; II. The Sisters, an English Tale, III. The Chateau in La Vendee, a French Tale. London: 1821. V. 65

TALES of the Classics: a New Delineation of the Most Popular Fables, Legends and Allegories Commemorated in the Works of Poets, Painters and Sculptors. London: 1830. V. 64

TALES to Tell - Six Traditional Tales. London: 1984. V. 65

TALES Told in the Twilight. London: 1915. V. 66

TALFOURD, THOMAS NOON
Final Memorials of Charles Lamb.... London: 1848. V. 65

TALIAFERRO, HARDEN E.
Fisher's River (North Carolina) Scenes and Characters. New York: 1859. V. 62; 64

TALLACK, WILLIAM
The California Overland Express, The Longest Stage-Ride in the World. Los Angeles: 1935. V. 64

TALLENT, A. E.
Black Hills or Last Hunting Grounds of the Dakotahs. St. Louis: 1899. V. 65

TALLENT, ANNIE D.
The Black Hills; or, the Last Hunting Grounds of the Dakotahs. St. Louis: 1899. V. 67
Black Hills or Last Hunting Grounds of the Dakotahs. St. Louis: 1974. V. 67

TALLEY, THOMAS W.
Negro Folk Rhymes, Wise and Otherwise. New York: 1922. V. 66

TALLIS, JOHN
London Street Views, 1838-1840, together with the Revised and Enlarged Views of 1847.... London: 1969. V. 67

TALLIS'S History of England for the Young. London: 1855. V. 65

TALLIS'S Illustrated Atlas and Modern History of the world. London: 1851. V. 62

TALLMADGE, THOMAS E.
The Story of Architecture in America. New York: 1927. V. 67

TALLON, DANIEL
Distress in the West and South of Ireland. 1898. V. 62

TALMUD
The Living Talmud. New York: 1960. V. 64

TAMBIMUTTU, M. J.
Out of this War. London: 1941. V. 66

TAMPLIN, J. M. A.
The Lambeth and Southwark Volunteers. London: 1965. V. 62

TAMURA, T.
Art of Landscape Garden in Japan. Tokyo: 1936. V. 64

TAN, AMY
The Chinese Siamese Cat. New York: 1994. V. 67
The Hundred Secret Senses. Franklin Center: 1995. V. 65; 67
The Hundred Secret Senses. New York: 1995. V. 64; 66; 67
The Joy Luck Club. New York: 1989. V. 62; 63; 64; 65; 66; 67
The Kitchen God's Wife. Franklin Center: 1991. V. 66; 67
The Kitchen God's Wife. New York: 1991. V. 67
The Moon Lady. New York: 1992. V. 62; 64; 65; 67

TANGYE, H. LINCOLN
In the Torrid Sudan. Boston: 1910. V. 67

TANGYE, RICHARD
The Two Protectors: Oliver and Richard Cromwell. London: 1899. V. 62

TANNER, CLARA LEE
Southwest Indian Painting. Tucson: 1957. V. 63
Southwest Indian Painting. 1973. V. 65
Southwest Indian Painting. Tucson: 1973. V. 67

TANNER, HENRY S.
An Atlas of Ancient Geography. Philadelphia: 1826. V. 62
A Description of the Canal and Rail Roads of the United States, Comprehending Notices of All the Works of Internal Improvement throughout the Several States. New York: 1840. V. 67
A New Picture of Philadelphia; or the Stranger's Guide to the City and Adjoining Districts.... New York: 1844. V. 62

TANNER, J. M.
A Biographical Sketch of James Jenson. Salt Lake City: 1911. V. 63; 66

TANNER, THOMAS
Notitia Monastica; or an Account of All the Abbies, Priories and Houses of Friers, Heretofore in England and Wales.... London: 1744. V. 63

TANNER, WILLIAM
The Book of Bond or Everyone His Own 007. London: 1965. V. 67

TANNER, WILLIAM R.
Reminiscences of the War Between the States. Cowpens: 1931. V. 62; 63; 65

TANNER, Z. L.
Report on the Construction and Outfit of the U.S. Fish Commission Steamer Albatross. Washington: 1885. V. 62

TANSELLE, G. THOMAS
Guide to the Study of United States Imprints. Cambridge: 1971. V. 66

TANSILLO, LUIGI
The Nurse, a Poem. Liverpool: 1798. V. 67
The Nurse, a Poem. Liverpool: 1800. V. 66

TANSLEY, A. G.
The British Isles and Their Vegetation. 1939. V. 62

TANS'UR, WILLIAM
The American Harmony, or Royal Medlody Complete. Newburyport: 1770?. V. 63
A Musical Grammar, and Dictionary; or a General Introduction to the Whole Art of Music. Stokesley: 1823. V. 66

TANTY, FRANCOIS
Cuisine Francaise. Chicago: 1893. V. 64

TAPLIN, WILLIAM
The Sportsman's Cabinet; or, a Correct Delineation of the Various Dogs Used in the Spots of the Field.... London: 1803-1804. V. 67

TAPPAN, DAVID
Lectures on Jewish Antiquities: Delivered at Harvard University in Cambridge, A.D. 1802 and 1803. Boston: 1807. V. 62

TAPPAN, H.
Paleobiology of Plant Protists. San Francisco: 1980. V. 64

TAPPING, THOMAS
A Treatise on the Derbyshire Mining Customs and Mineral Court Act, 1852.... London: 1854. V. 66

TAPPLY, WILLIAM G.
Death at Charity's Point. 1984. V. 66
Death at Charity's Point. New York: 1984. V. 64; 65
The Dutch Blue Error. New York: 1984. V. 64; 66

TARAKHOVSKII, E.
Zheleznaya Doroga. Moscow: 1928. V. 64

TARBELL, IDA M.
All in the Day's Work: an Autobiography. New York: 1939. V. 63
The History of the Standard Oil Company. New York: 1904. V. 62

TARBOTON, W.
Birds of Southern Africa. Cape Town: 1994. V. 64; 66

TARBOTTON, M. O.
History of the Old Trent Bridge, with a Descriptive Account of the New Bridge, Nottingham. Nottingham: 1871. V. 65

TARBOX, I. N.
Memoirs of James H. Schneider & Edward Schneider. Boston: 1867. V. 65

TARBUCK, EDWARD LANCE
The Builder's Practical Director or Buildings for All Classes, Containing Plans, Sections and Elevations for the Erection of Cottages, Villas, Farm Buildings.... Leipzig & Dresden: 1855-1858. V. 66; 67
The Encyclopaedia of Practical Carpentry and Joinery. London: 1860. V. 66

TARENTUM, ETIENNE MAC DONALD, DUKE OF
Recollections of Marshal MacDonald, Duke of Tarentum. London: 1892. V. 66

TARG, WILLIAM
The Making of the Bruce Rogers World Bible. Cleveland: 1949. V. 62; 63; 64

TARIN, PIERRE
Osteo-Graphie, Ou Description Des Os De L'Adulte, du Foetus, &...Des Parties Solides Du Corps Humain. Paris: 1753. V. 66

TARKINGTON, BOOTH
Claire Ambler. Garden City: 1928. V. 67
Claire Ambler. New York: 1928. V. 62; 63; 65
The Fascinating Stranger and Other Stories. Garden City: 1923. V. 62; 64; 67
The Gentleman from Indiana. New York: 1899. V. 62; 64; 66; 67
Rumbin Galleries. Garden City: 1937. V. 67
Some Old Portraits. A Book About Art and Human Beings. New York: 1939. V. 62
The Two Vanrevels. New York: 1902. V. 62

TARLETON, BANASTRE
History of the Campaigns of 1780 and 1781, in the Southern Provinces of North America. Dublin: 1787. V. 63
A History of the Campaigns of 1780 and 1781, in the Southern Provinces of North America. London: 1787. V. 63; 66

TARN, NATASHA
Multitude of One. New York: 1994. V. 64

TARRANT, MARGARET
The Margaret Tarrant Christmas Book. Boston: 1940. V. 67
The Margaret Tarrant Nursery Rhyme Book. New York: 1940. V. 62

TARRANT, MARGARET W.
The Margaret Tarrant Nursery Rhyme Book. New York: 1944. V. 66

TARTAROTTI, GIROLAMO
Raziocinio Critico Teologica su L'Apologia del Congresso Notturno Delleammie per Opera del.... Venezia: 1754. V. 66

TARTT, DONNA
The Secret History. New York: 1992. V. 63; 67

TASCH, P.
Paleobiology of the Invertebrates. Data Retrival from the Fossil Record. New York: 1973. V. 67

TASHJIAN, VIRGINIA
Once There Was and Was Not - Armenian Tales Retold. Boston and Toronto: 1966. V. 64

TASSO, TORQUATO
Aminta. In Leida: 1656. V. 63; 66
Aminta. In Parigi: 1745. V. 65
Aminta. Crisopoli: 1796. V. 66
Aminta. Londra: 1809. V. 65
Aminta. Verona: 1939. V. 65
L'Aminte du Tasse. La Haye: 1679. V. 67
La Gerusalemme Liberata. Parigi: 1771. V. 63; 66

TASSO, TORQUATO continued
La Gerusalemme Liberata. Parigi: 1785. V. 66
La Gerusalemme Liberta. London: 1822. V. 64
Godfrey of Boulogne; or the Recoverie of Jerusalem. London: 1624. V. 65
Godfrey of Bulloigne: or the Recovery of Jerusalem. London: 1687. V. 64; 65; 66
Jerusalem Delivered: an Heroic Poem. London: 1807. V. 65

TASSONI, ALESSANDRO
La Secchia Rapita; or, the Rape of the Bucket; an Heroi-Comical Poem, in Twelve Cantos. London: 1827. V. 65

TATE, ALLEN
Christ and the Unicorn. West Branch: 1966. V. 67
Collected Essays. Denver: 1959. V. 62; 65
Essays of Four Decades. Chicago: 1968. V. 66
The Fathers. New York: 1938. V. 62; 64
The Forlorn Demon. Chicago: 1953. V. 62; 67
The Golden Mean and Other Poems. Nashville: 1923. V. 62; 64; 65; 67
The Hovering Fly and Other Essays. Cummington: 1949. V. 62; 64
The Mediterranean and Other Poems. New York: 1936. V. 64; 65; 67
Mr. Pope and Other Poems. New York: 1928. V. 62; 64; 65; 67
Ode to the Confederate Dead. New York: 1930. V. 64
Poems. New York: 1960. V. 62
Poems 1922-1947. New York: 1948. V. 62; 67
Poems: 1928-1931. New York: 1932. V. 62; 65
Princeton Verse Between Two Wars. Princeton: 1942. V. 65
Selected Poems. New York: 1937. V. 66
Stonewall Jackson. The Good Soldier. New York: 1928. V. 62; 63; 65
T. S. Eliot - the Man and His Work. London: 1966. V. 64
(Three Poems). Ode to the Confederate Dead...to Which are Added Message from Abroad, and The Cross. New York: 1930. V. 65
Two Conceits for the Eye to Sing, If Possible. Cummington: 1950. V. 62; 67

TATE, BENJAMIN
An Analytical Digested Index of the Reported Cases of the Court of Appeals and General Court of Virginia. Richmond: 1847. V. 62; 65

TATE, C. M.
Our Indian Missions in British Columbia. Toronto: 1901?. V. 63

TATE, CHARLES SPENCER
Pickway - a True Narrative. N.P: 1905. V. 63; 66

TATE, JAMES
Apology for Eating Geoffrey Movius' Hyacinth. Santa Barbara: 1972. V. 65
Bewitched. Llangynog: 1989. V. 62; 64; 66; 67
Cages. Poems. Iowa City: 1966. V. 62; 65; 67
Constant Defender: Poems. New York: 1983. V. 67
Deaf Girl Playing. Cambridge: 1970. V. 65
The Destination. Cambridge: 1967. V. 62; 64; 67
Hints to Prelims. Cambridge: 1971. V. 64
Hottentot Ossuary. Cambridge: 1974. V. 64; 65
If It Would All Please Hurry. Amherst: 1980. V. 62; 64
Just Shades. Tuscaloosa: 1985. V. 62; 64; 65
Land of Little Sticks. Worcester: 1981. V. 62; 67
The Lost Pilot. New Haven: 1967. V. 63
Notes of Woe. Poems. Iowa City: 1968. V. 64
The Oblivion Ha-Ha - Sixty Poems. Boston and Toronto: 1970. V. 65
Riven Doggeries. New York: 1979. V. 67
Shepherds of the Mist. Los Angeles: 1969. V. 62; 66; 67
The Torches. Santa Barbara: 1968. V. 64; 67
Viper Jazz. Middletown: 1976. V. 67
Worshipful Company of Fletchers. Poems. Hopewell: 1994. V. 67

TATE, JOSEPH
A Digest of the Laws of Virginia...by Judicial Decisions...(with) Index of the Names of the Cases. Richmond: 1823. V. 63

TATE, N.
The History of King Lear, Acted at the Queen's Theatre. London: 1689. V. 65

TATE, NAHUM
Dido and Aeneas. Bangor/Newark: 1989. V. 62

TATE, R.
A Plain and Easy Account of the Land and Fresh Water Mollusks of Great Britain. London: 1866. V. 62

TATE, THOMAS
Drawing for Schools; Containing Expositions of the Method of Teaching Drawing in Schools.... London: 1854. V. 67

TATE, WILLIAM
The Modern Cambist, Forming a Manual of Foreign Exchanges in the Different Occupations of Bills of Exchange and Bullion.... London: 1842. V. 66

TATHAM, GEORGE
An Exposition of the Character and Management of the New Jersey Joint Monopolies, the Camden and Amboy Railroad and Transportation Company.... Philadelphia: 1852. V. 63

TATHAM, H. F. W.
The Footprints in the Snow and Other Tales. London: 1910. V. 66

TATHAM, WILLIAM
National Irrigation, or the Various Methods of Watering Meadows; Affording Means to Increase the Populations, Wealth and Revenue of the Kingdom, by an Agricultural, Commercial and General Economy in the Use of Water. London: 1801. V. 64

THE TATLER. London: 1789. V. 66

TATON, RENE
History of Science. The Beginnings of Modern Science. New York: 1964. V. 65

TATTERSALL, GEORGE
Tablets of an Intinerant. London: 1836. V. 65

TATTERSFIELD, NIGEL
Bookplates by Beilby and Bewick. A Biographical Dictionary of Bookplates from the Workshop of Ralph Beilby, Thomas Bewick and Robert Bewick 1760-1849. London: 1998. V. 64

TATUM, GEORGE B.
Penn's Great Town: 250 Years of Philadelphia Architecture. 1961. V. 65

TATUM, GEORGIA LEE
Disloyalty in the Confederacy. Chapel Hill: 1934. V. 63; 65

TATUM, LAWRIE
Our Red Brothers and the Peace Policy of President Ulysses S. Grant. Philadelphia: 1899. V. 67

TAUBERT, SIGFRED
Bibliopola. Pictures and Texts About the Book Trade. Hamburg: 1966. V. 65; 66

TAUBES, FREDERIC
Paintings and Essays on Art. New York: 1950. V. 65

TAUNT, HENRY WILLIAM EDWARD
Goring, Streatley and the Neighbourhood, Including Aldworth, Ashampstead, Basildon, Nobes's Tomb, Goring Heath, Hart's Wood, Checkendon, Collin's End, Ipsden, South Stoke.... Oxford: 1894. V. 65
A New Map of the River Thames, from Thames Head to London, from Entirely New Surveys Finished During the Summer of 1878. Oxford: 1879. V. 62

TAUNTON, T. H.
Portraits of Celebrated Racehorses of the Past and Present Centuries.... London: 1887-1888. V. 66; 67

TAUTOPHEUS, JEMIMA MONTGOMERY, BARONESS VON
Cyrilla. London: 1853. V. 65

TAVANNES, JACQUES DE SAULX, COMTE DE
Memoires de Messire Jacques de Saulx, Comte de Tavannes, Lieutenant General Des Arme'es Du Roy. Paris: 1691. V. 65; 66

TAVERNER, ERIC
Salmon Fishing. 1945. V. 67
Trout Fishing from All Angles. 1946. V. 67
Trout Fishing from All Angles. London: 1969. V. 67

TAVERNER, J.
Certaine Experiments Concerning Fish and Fruite, 1600.... Manchester: 1928. V. 63

TAVERNER, JAMES
An Essay Upon the Witham Spa. Or, a Brief Enquiry into the Nature, Virtues and Uses of a Mineral Chalybeate Water at Witham in Essex. London: 1737. V. 65

TAVISTOCK, MARQUESS
Biographical Catalogue of the Pictures at Woburn Abbey. London: 1890. V. 62; 66
Parrots and Parrot-Like Birds in Aviculture. 1929. V. 67

TAYLER, CHARLES BENJAMIN
Edward; or Almost an Owenite. London: 1840. V. 66
Facts in a Clergyman's Life. London: 1859. V. 67
May You Like It. London: 1823. V. 67
May You Like It. London: 1823-1824. V. 65

TAYLER, JAMES
A Practical Treatise on Fly Fishing. 1888. V. 65; 67

TAYLER, THOMAS
A Law Glossary of the Latin, Greek, Norman, French and Other Languages.... London: 1819. V. 64

TAYLOR, ALBERT PIERCE
Under Hawaiian Skies. Honolulu: 1922. V. 67

TAYLOR, ALFRED SWAINE
On Poisons in Relation to Medical Jurisprudence and Medicine. Philadelphia: 1859. V. 64
The Principles and Practice of Medical Jurisprudence. London: 1883. V. 65

TAYLOR and His Campaigns. A Biography of Major-General Zachary Taylor, with a Full Account of His Military Services. Philadelphia: 1848. V. 64

TAYLOR, ANDREW
The Mortal Sickness. Blakeney, Gloucestershire: 1995. V. 63
Waiting for the End of the World. London: 1984. V. 65

TAYLOR, ANN
Practical Hints to Young Females, on the Duties of a Wife, a Mother and a Mistress of a Family. London: 1815. V. 65

TAYLOR, ARNOLD
Four Great Castles: Caernarfon, Conway, Harlech, Beaumaris. 1983. V. 65

TAYLOR, BAYARD
Colorado: a Summer Trip. New York: 1867. V. 65
Eldorado, or Adventures in the Path of Empire. New York: 1850. V. 62; 63
The National Ode. July 4, 1876. Boston: 1876. V. 64

TAYLOR, BENJAMIN F.
Attractions of Language. Hamilton: 1843. V. 65
Short Ravelings from a Long Yarn, or Camp March Sketches of the Santa Fe Trail. Santa Ana: 1936. V. 62

TAYLOR, BROOK
Contemplation Philosophica: A Posthumous Work, of the Last Brook Taylor, LL.D.... London: 1793. V. 65

TAYLOR, C. J.
England. New York: 1899. V. 67

TAYLOR, CHARLES
A Familiar Treatise on Perspective, in Four Essays. London: 1816. V. 64
The General Genteel Preceptor by Francis Fitzgerald Esq., Being a Summary Introduction to Polite Learning. London: 1797. V. 64
Surveys of Nature, Historical, Moral and Entertaining, Exhibiting the Principles of Natural Science in Various Branches. London: 1787. V. 65

TAYLOR, CHARLES B.
Is This Religion? Or, a Page from the Book of the World. Georgetown: 1827. V. 66

TAYLOR, DEEMS
Fantasia. New York: 1940. V. 65
Writer Classificaiton and Its Probelms. New York: 1944. V. 63

TAYLOR, E. G. R.
The Mathematical Practioners of Hanoverian England 1714-1840. Cambridge: 1966. V. 65
The Mathematical Practioners of Hanoverian England 1714-1840. Cambridge: 1989. V. 65
The Mathematical Practioners of Tudor and Stuart England. Cambridge: 1954. V. 62; 65; 66
The Mathematical Practioners of Tudor and Stuart England. Cambridge: 1970. V. 65

TAYLOR, E. H.
Contributions to the Herpetology of Thailand. 1958. V. 64
A Taxonomic Study of the Cosmopolitan Scincoid Lizards of the Genus Eumeces.... Lawrence: 1935. V. 63; 64

TAYLOR, EDWARD
Cursory Remarks on Tragedy, on Shakespeare and on Certain French and Italian Poets. London: 1774. V. 62

TAYLOR, ELIZABETH
Authentic Memoirs of Mrs. Clarke, In Which is Portrayed the Secret History and Intrigues of Many Characters in the First Circles of Fashion and High Life.... London: 1809. V. 65
A Dedicated Man and Other Stories. London: 1965. V. 65

TAYLOR, ELLEN M.
Madeira: Its Scenery and How to See It, with Letters of a Year's Residence and Lists of Trees, Flowers, Ferns and Seaweeds. London: 1889. V. 65

TAYLOR, F.
Angling in Earnest. 1969. V. 67

TAYLOR, FRANCES MAGDALEN
Religious Orders; or, Sketches of Some of the Orders and Congregations of Women. London: 1862. V. 62; 66

TAYLOR, FRED
Reflections of a Countryman. 1982. V. 67

TAYLOR, FREDERICK W.
The Principles of Scientific Management. New York and London: 1911. V. 63; 64

TAYLOR, G.
An Account of the Genus Meconopsis. 1934. V. 63
An Account of the Genus Meconopsis. London: 1934. V. 66

TAYLOR, GEOFFREY
The Absurd World of Charles Bragg. New York: 1980. V. 62; 63; 64

TAYLOR, GEORGE B.
Virginia Baptist Minister. Lynchburg: 1935. V. 63

TAYLOR, HENRY
The Statesman. London: 1836. V. 64; 66

TAYLOR, HENRY OSBORN
The Mediaeval Mind. A History of the Development of Thought and Emotion in the Middle Ages. London: 1911. V. 67

TAYLOR, I. T.
The Cavalcade of Jackson County. San Antonio: 1938. V. 63

TAYLOR, ISAAC
Fanaticism. London: 1833. V. 64; 66
History of the Transmission of Ancient Books to Modern Times. London: 1827. V. 64
Home Education. London: 1838. V. 64
Scenes in Europe, for Amusement and Instruction of Little Tarry-at- Home Travelelrs. Philadelphia: 1824. V. 62
Specimens of Gothic Ornaments Selected from the Paris Church of Lavenham in Suffolk in Forty Plates. London: 1796. V. 65
Specimens of Gothic Ornaments Selected from the Parish Church of Lavenham in Suffolk. London: 1837. V. 67

TAYLOR, J.
Arator, Being a Series of Agricultural Essays, Practical and Political.... Petersburg: 1818. V. 63
Big Game and Big Game Rifles. 1948. V. 62; 63
Bristol and Its Environs, Historical, Descriptive and Scientific. London: 1875. V. 62
Decorations for Parks and Gardens, Designs for Gates, Garden Seats, Alcoves, Temples Baths, Entrance Gates, Lodges, Facades, Prospect Towers, Cattle Shields, Ruins, Bridges, Greenhouses.... London: 1810. V. 64
Pondoro, the Last of the Ivory Hunters. 1955. V. 63

TAYLOR, J. H.
Taylor on Golf. Impressions, Comments and Hints. London: 1905. V. 67

TAYLOR, JAMES
The Age We Live In: a History of the 19th Century. London: 1885. V. 64

TAYLOR, JANE
Little Ann and Other Poems. London: 1883. V. 65
Memoirs and Political Remains of the Late.... London: 1826. V. 63
Rural Scenes, or a Peep into the Country for Children. London: 1826. V. 62

TAYLOR, JEREMY
(Greek title) or, a Collection of Polemicall Discourses, Wherein the Church of England...is Defended..Together with Some Additional Pieces. London: 1674. V. 63
Epiautos (Graece). A Course of Sermons for All the Sundaies of the Year. London: 1653. V. 63
The Golden Grove. London: 1735. V. 62
The Golden Grove - Select Passages from the Sermons and Writings of Jeremy Taylor. London: 1930. V. 65
The Great Exemplar.... London: 1849. V. 67
A Selection of Writings. Waltham St. Lawrence: 1923. V. 62; 65
XXV Sermons Preached at Golden Grove: Being for the Winter Half-Year, Beginning on Advent Sunday. London: 1653. V. 64
XXVIII Sermons Preached at Golden Grove. (with) A Discourse of the Divine Institution. 1651. V. 62
XXVIII Sermons Preached at Golden Grove...Together with a Discourse of the Divine Institution, Necessity, Sacredness and Separation of the Office Ministeriall. London: 1651. V. 63; 67
The Whole Works of.... 1839. V. 63

TAYLOR, JOE F.
The Indian Campaign on the Staked Plains 1874-1875. Canyon: 1962. V. 63

TAYLOR, JOHN
African Rifles and Cartridges. New Jersey: 1977. V. 67
All the Workes of Iohn Taylor the Water Poet. London: 1630. V. 65
Arator, Being a Series of Agricultural Essays. Petersburg: 1818. V. 63
A Dog of War. 1927. V. 65
A Dog of War. London: 1927. V. 63
Essays on Gothic Architecture. London: 1800. V. 63
Geological Essays, and Sketch of the Geology of Manchester and the Neighbourhood. London: 1864. V. 62
The History of the Travels and Adventures of the Chevalier John Taylor Ophthalmiater.... Birmingham: 1990. V. 63
The Illustrated Guide to Sheffield and the Surrounding District, Comprising Accounts of the Early History and Progress of the Town, Its Public and Religious Bodies, Edifices and Institutions.... Sheffield: 1879. V. 63
An Inquiry into the Principles and Policy of the Government of the United States. Fredericksburg: 1814. V. 67
The Lady's Monitor: Selected from the Writings of Lady Jane Grey, Queen Catharine Parr, Lady Elizabeth Brooke, Elizabeth Smith, Sir Thomas More, Sir John Cheeke and William Penn. London: 1828. V. 67
Marmor Sandvicense cum Commentario et Notis. Cantabrigiae: 1743. V. 62; 66
New Views of the Constitution of the U.S. Washington: 1823. V. 62
Oratio Habita Corum Academia Cantabrigiensi in Templo Beate Mariae, Die Solenni Martyrii Caroli Primi Regis, A.D. MDCCXXX. Londoni: 1730. V. 65
Pondoro, Last of the Ivory Hunters. New York: 1955. V. 66
The Proposed Reformation of Parliament, Considered, as Delivered, in Part, at the County Meeting Held at York, Jan. 1st, 1784. London: 1785. V. 62
Records of Mining. Part I (all published). London: 18289. V. 64

TAYLOR, JOHN BROUGH
The Legend of St. Cuthbert, with the Antiquities of the Church of Durham. Sunderland: 1816. V. 62

TAYLOR, JOHN RUSSELL
The Art Nouveau Book in Britain. London: 1966. V. 62

TAYLOR, JOSEPH
The Danger of Premature Interment, Proved from Many Instances of People Who Have Recovered after Being Laid Out for Dead and of Others Entombed Alive.... London: 1816. V. 67
The Wonders of Nature and Art. London: 1832. V. 63

TAYLOR, JOSEPH H.
Frontier and Indian Life and Kaleidoscopic Lives. Valley City: 1932. V. 65
Sketches of Frontier and Indian Life on the Upper Missouri and Great Plains, Embracing the Author's Personal Recollections of Noted Frontier Characters. Pottstown: 1889. V. 67

TAYLOR, KATHERINE AMES
Lights and Shadows of Yosemite. Being a Collection of Favorite Yosemite Views. San Francisco: 1926. V. 63; 66

TAYLOR, LONN
The American Cowboy. Washington: 1983. V. 63

TAYLOR, LUCY
Close to the Bone. Woodinville: 1993. V. 66
The Flesh Artist. Woodinville: 1994. V. 66

TAYLOR, MARY L.
The Tiger's Claw. 1956. V. 62; 63; 64; 66; 67

TAYLOR, MAURICE
Bulletin in Bold Characters. Santa Fe: 1990. V. 67

TAYLOR, MICHAEL
A Bibliography of St. Dominic's Press 1916-1937. 1995. V. 65
Tables of Logarithms of All Numbers, from 1 to 101000; and of the Sines and Tangents to Every Second of the Quadrant.... London: 1792. V. 62; 65

TAYLOR, MICHAEL WAISTELL
The Old Manorial Halls of Westmorland and Cumberland. Kendal: 1892. V. 62

TAYLOR, MILDRED D.
Roll of Thunder, Hear My Cry. New York: 1976. V. 65

TAYLOR, MORRIS F.
O. P. McMains and the Maxwell Land Grant Conflict. Tucson: 1979. V. 65
A Sketch of Early Days on the Purgatory. Trinidad: 1959. V. 64

TAYLOR, N.
Flora of the Vicinity of New York, a Contribution to Plant Geography. 1915. V. 64

TAYLOR, NATHANIEL W.
Life on a Whaler or Antarctic Adventures in the Isle of Desolation. New London: 1929. V. 62

TAYLOR, NORA PITT
The Adventure Book: The Adventures of Junkie. London: 1910. V. 66

TAYLOR, PETER
The Collected Stories of Peter Taylor. New York: 1969. V. 62; 64; 66; 67
Happy Families Are All Alike. A Collection of Stories. New York: 1959. V. 64; 66; 67
In the Miro District and Other Stories. New York: 1977. V. 62; 66; 67
In the Tennessee Country. New York: 1994. V. 66
Literature, Sewanee and the World. Sewanee: 1972. V. 62; 64; 67
A Long Fourth and Other Stories. New York: 1948. V. 64; 67
Miss Leonora When Last Seen and 15 Other Stories. New York: 1963. V. 64; 66; 67
The Old Forest and Other Stories. Garden City: 1985. V. 64; 66
The Oracle at Stoneleigh Court. Stories. New York: 1993. V. 64; 66
Presences: Seven Dramatic Pieces. Boston: 1973. V. 66
A Stand in the Mountains. New York: 1985. V. 67
A Summons to Memphis. New York: 1986. V. 62; 64; 66; 67
Tennessee Day In St. Louis. New York: 1957. V. 62; 66; 67
The Widows of Thornton. New York: 1954. V. 62; 64; 65
A Woman of Means. New York: 1950. V. 66

TAYLOR, PETER ALFRED
Some Account of the Taylor Family (Originally Taylard). London: 1873. V. 66

TAYLOR, PHILIP MEADOWS
Confessions of a Thug. London: 1840. V. 65
The Story of My Life. Edinburgh: 1877. V. 67

TAYLOR, PHOEBE ATWOOD
The Crimson Patch. New York: 1936. V. 65
Punch with Care. 1946. V. 66

TAYLOR, REX
Michael Collins. London: 1958. V. 62

TAYLOR, RICHARD
Destruction and Reconstruction: Personal Experiences of the Late War. Edinburgh and London: 1879. V. 63
Destruction and Reconstruction: Personal Experiences of the Late War. New York: 1879. V. 62; 63; 64; 67
Index Monasticus; or the Abbeys and Other Monasteries, Alien Priories, Friaries.... London: 1821. V. 63

TAYLOR, ROBERT
Fiddle and Bow. Chapel Hill: 1985. V. 64; 67
Syntagma of the Evidence of the Christian Religion. London: 1828. V. 63
Trial of the Rev. Robert Taylor Upon A Charge of Blasphemy, with His Defence, as Delivered by Himself Before the Lord Chief Justice...Wednesday October 24, 1827.... London: 1827. V. 63

TAYLOR, ROBERT LEWIS
The Travels of Jaimie McPheeters. Garden City: 1958. V. 64; 65

TAYLOR, ROBERT W.
A Clinical Atlas of Venereal and Skin Diseases, Including Diagnosis, Prognosis and Treatment. Philadelphia: 1889. V. 62; 66; 67

TAYLOR, S.
The History and Antiquities of Harwich and Dovercourt, in the County of Essex.... 1732. V. 66

TAYLOR, SAMUEL
An Essay Intended to Establish a Standard for an Universal System of Stenography, or Short Hand Writing. London: 1786. V. 62; 65
Sabrina Fair. New York: 1954. V. 66

TAYLOR, T. U.
The Chisholm Trail and Other Routes. San Antonio: 1936. V. 64

Jesse Chisolm. Bandera: 1939. V. 62

TAYLOR, THEODORE
Thackeray the Humourist and the Man of Letters. London: 1864. V. 66

TAYLOR, THOMAS
A Memoir of Mr. Joseph Harbottle, Baptist Minister, Accrington. London: 1866. V. 63

TAYLOR, THOMAS JOHN
An Inquiry Into the Operation of Running Streams and Tidal Waters.... London: 1851. V. 62; 66

TAYLOR, TOM
Leicester Square: Its Associations and Its Worthies. London: 1874. V. 63
A Tale of Two Cities. A Drama, in Two Acts and a Prologue.... London: 1860. V. 62

TAYLOR, TORY
Hunting on Big Game Trails. Clinton: 1988. V. 65

TAYLOR, UNA
Nets for the Wind. London: 1896. V. 64

TAYLOR, W. B. SARSFIELD
A Manual of Fresco and Encaustic Painting Containing Ample Instructions for Executing Works of These Descriptions. London: 1843. V. 66; 67
The Origin, Progress and Present Condition of the Fine Arts in Great Britain and Ireland. London: 1841. V. 66; 67

TAYLOR, W. C.
The Natural History of Society in the Barbarous and Civilized State. 1840. V. 67
The Revolutions, Insurrections and Conspiracies of Europe. London: 1843. V. 66

TAYLOR, W. P.
The Deer of North America. 1956. V. 66

TAYLOR, W. THOMAS
Twenty-One Years of Bird and Bull: a Bibliography, 1958-1979. Newtown: 1980. V. 64

TAYLOR, WALTER HERRON
Four Years with General Lee. New York: 1877. V. 63; 65
General Lee. His Campaigns in Virginia 1861-1865, with Personal Reminiscences. Norfolk: 1906. V. 62; 63; 65

TAYLOR, WILLIAM
California Life Illustrated. New York: 1858. V. 63; 66
A Complete System of Practical Arithmetic. Birmingham: 1800. V. 62; 65

TAYLOR, WILLIAM COOKE
Life and Times of Sir Robert Peel. London: 1846-1851. V. 64

TAYLOR HALL, MARY ANN
Come and Go, Molly Snow. New York: 1995. V. 67

TCHANG, T. L.
The Study of Chinese Cyprinvid Fishes. 1933. V. 62

TEAGUE, W. D.
Design This Day: the Technique of Order in the Machine Age. London: 1946. V. 65

TEALE, THOMAS PRIDGIN
Dangers to Health: a Pictorial Guide to Domestic Sanitary Defects. London: 1883. V. 64
A Treatise on Neuralgic Diseases, Dependent Upon Irritation of the Spinal Marrow and Ganglia of The Sympatheic Nerve. Philadelphia: 1830. V. 62; 65

TEALL, J. J. H.
British Petrography. 1888. V. 62; 66; 67
British Petrography. London: 1888. V. 62; 64

TEASDALE, SARA
Dark of the Moon. New York: 1926. V. 62
Rivers to the Sea. New York: 1915. V. 64

TEASDALE BUCKELL, G. T.
Experts on Guns and Shooting. London: 1900. V. 66; 67
Experts on Guns and Shooting. 1986. V. 66

TEBB, BARRY
Five Quiet Shouters - an Anthology of Assertive Verse. London: 1966. V. 63

TEDDY and Sambo Picture and Story Book. London: 1915. V. 62

TEDDY Bear Bread. New York: 1908. V. 63

TEENY-Weeny's Box of Books. London: 1931. V. 63

THE TEEPEE Book - the Custer Battle, June, 1925. V. 65

THE TEEPEE Book - The Custer Battle June 1926. V. 67

TEERINK, H.
The History of John Bull for the First Time Faithfully Re-issued from the Original Pamphlets, 1712, Together with an Investigation Into Its Composition.... Amsterdam: 1925. V. 65; 66

TEFERTILLER, CASEY
Wyatt Earp - the Life Behind the Legend. New York: 1997. V. 63; 65

TEGETMEIER, W. B.
The New Game Bird, Palla's Sand Grouse. 1888. V. 62
Pheasants their Natural History and Practical Management. London: 1897. V. 67
Pheasants, Their Natural History and Practical Management. London: 1911. V. 67

TEGG, THOMAS
Chronology, or the Historian's Companion.... London: 1811. V. 63

TEGG, WILLIAM
Meetings and Greetings. The Salutations, Obeisances and Courtesies of Nations.... London: 1877. V. 64

TEGNER, ESAIAS
Frithiof's Saga; a Scandinavian Legend of Royal Love. Woodbridge: 1833. V. 65

TEGNER, HENRY
A Border County. London: 1955. V. 67
Game for the Sporting Rifle. London: 1963. V. 67

TEICHMANN, LUDWIG
Das Saugadersystem vom Anatomischen Standpunkte. Leipzig: 1861. V. 65

TEIGNMOUTH, LORD
Memoirs of the Life, Writings and Correspondence of Sir William Jones. London: 1806. V. 67
The Smugglers. Picturesque Chapters in the History of Contraband. New York: 1924. V. 63

TEILHET, DARWIN
The Crimson Hair Murders. Garden City: 1936. V. 65
Skwee-Gee. New York: 1940. V. 62

TEISER, RUTH
Catherine Haroun. San Francisco: 1970. V. 66
Lawton Kennedy, Printer. N.P: 1988. V. 62; 63
Lawton Kennedy, Printer. Los Angeles: 1988. V. 65
Lawton Kennedy Printer. San Francisco: 1988. V. 64; 66
Printing as a Performing Art. San Francisco: 1970. V. 64

TEIVE, DIOGO DE
Commentarius de Rebus in India apud Dium Gestis Anno Salutis Nostrae MDXLVI. Coimbra: 1548. V. 62
Epodon Siue Labicorum Carminum Libri Tres.... Lisbon: 1565. V. 62

TEIXEIRA FEO, BENTO
Relacao do Naufragio Que Fizeram as Naos.... Lisbon: 1650. V. 62

TEIXIDOR, JOAN
Antoni Tapies. Barcelona: 1965. V. 62

TELESIO, BERNARDINO
Der Rerum Natura Iuxta Propria Principia, Liber Primus et Secundus, Denuo Editi. (with) De His, Quae in Aere Siunt & de Terrae-Motibus, Liber Unicus. (with) De Colorum Generatione Opusculum. (with) De Mari, Liber Unicus. Naples: 1570. V. 62

TELFORD, THOMAS
Life of Thomas Telford, Civil Engineer, Written by Himself.... London: 1838. V. 65

TELLER, EDWARD
The Legacy of Hiroshima. New York: 1962. V. 63

TELLES, BALTHAZAR
Chronica da Companhia de Iesu, na Provincia de Portugal.... Lisbon: 1645-1647. V. 62; 65

TELLIER, JULES
Abd-er-Rhaman in Paradise. Waltham St. Lawrence: 1928. V. 62; 65

TELLMAN, JOHN
Practical Hotel Steward. Chicago: 1900. V. 67

TEM, STEVE RASNIC
High Fantastic. Denver: 1995. V. 65

TEMPEL, E.
New Finnish Architecture. New York: 1968. V. 65

TEMPERANCE Cook Book....
Philadelphia: 1841. V. 63

TEMPLE, J. H.
History of North Brookfield, Massachusetts. North Brookfield: 1887. V. 66

TEMPLE, JAMES GRAHAM
The Scotch Forcing Gardener.... Edinburgh: 1828. V. 64

TEMPLE, NEVILLE
Tannhauser; or, the Battle of the Bards a Poem. Mobile: 1863. V. 63

TEMPLE, OLIVER P.
East Tennessee and the Civil War. Cincinnati: 1899. V. 65

TEMPLE, RICHARD
Journals Kept in Hyderabad, Kashmir, Sikkim and Nepal. London: 1887. V. 65
Palestine Illustrated. London: 1888. V. 62

TEMPLE, WILLIAM
Memoirs of What Passed in Christendom, from the War Begun 1672 to the Peace Concluded 1679. London: 1709. V. 63
Miscellanea (in 3 Parts). Memoirs the 3rd Part. London: 1720. V. 66
Miscellanea. The Third Part. London: 1701. V. 66
Miscellanea. (with) Miscellanea. The Second Part. London: 1681. V. 66
Miscellanies. I. A Survey of the Constitutions and Interests of the Empire...II. An Essay Upon the Original and Nature of Government. III. An Essay Upon the Advancement of Trade in Ireland. IV. Upon the Conjuncture of Affairs in Octob. 1673. V. Upon the. London: 1680. V. 66
Observations Upon the United Provinces of the Netherlands. London: 1673. V. 65
Observations Upon the United Provinces of the Netherlands. London: 1693. V. 62; 67
The Works. London: 1720. V. 62; 63
Works. London: 1757. V. 64

TEMPLEMAN, JAMES
Gilbert; or, the Young Carrier. London: 1808. V. 62

TEMPLEMAN, THOMAS
A New Survey of the Globe: Or, an Accurate Mensuration of All the Empires, Kingdoms, Countries, States, Principal Provinces, Counties & Islands in the World.... London: 1729?. V. 64

TEMPLEMOYLE AGRICULTURAL SEMINARY
Report of the Agricultural Seminary at Templemoyle, County of Londonderry, Established May 1827. Londonderry: 1836. V. 67

TEN Little Colored Boys. New York: 1942. V. 62

TEN Little Nigger Boys. Buffalo: 1910. V. 65
TEN Little Nigger Boys. London: 1920. V. 65
TEN Little Nigger Boys. London: 1926. V. 65

TEN Little Niggers. England: 1910. V. 65

THE TEN Little Niggers. New York: 1915. V. 62

TEN Singers - An Anthology. London: 1925. V. 64

TEN Tales. Huntington Beach: 1994. V. 63; 65

TEN Years ARTEF. New York: 1937. V. 63

TENCIN, CLAUDINE ALEXANDRINE GUERIN
Anecdotes de la Cour et du Regne d'Edouard III, Roi d'Angleterre. Paris: 1776. V. 67

TENFOLD: Poems for Frances Horovitz. N.P: 1983. V. 62

TENNANT GALLERY
Catalogue of Pictures in the Tennant Gallery, 34 Queen Anne's Gate, S.W. London: 1912. V. 62; 64

TENNANT, WILLIAM
Anster Fair, a Poem. Edinburgh: 1812. V. 66

TENNENT, GILBERT
The Necessity of Holding Fast the Truth Represented in Three Sermons on Rev. III 3. Boston: 1743. V. 63; 66

TENNENT, J. E.
Belgium. London: 1841. V. 63
Ceylon, an Account of the Island, Physical, Historical and Topographical. 1860. V. 62

TENNENT, MADGE
Autobiography of an Unarrived Artist. New York: 1949. V. 62

TENNESSEE
Report of the Bureau of Agriculture, Statistics and Mines for 1876. Nashville: 1877. V. 67
Report of the Bureau of Agriculture, Statistics and Mines for the State of Tennessee 1877 and 1878. Nashville: 1878. V. 67

TENNESSEE. LAWS, STATUTES, ETC. - 1861
Public Acts of the State of Tennessee, Passed at the Extra Session of the Thirty-Third General Assembly, April 1861. Nashville: 1861. V. 63

TENNESSEE. SUPREME COURT - 1838
Reports of Cases Argued and Determined in the Supreme Court of Tennessee. Volume I-X. Nashville: 1832-1838. V. 64

TENNEY, E. P.
Colorado and Homes in the New West. Boston: 1880. V. 62

TENNISON, HARRY
An African Affair. 1988. V. 64

TENNYSON, ALFRED TENNYSON, 1ST BARON
Ballads and Other Poems. London: 1880. V. 64
Demeter and Other Poems. London: 1889. V. 62
Elaine. London: 1868. V. 65
Enoch Arden. Berlin: 1876. V. 64
Guinivere. New Rochelle: 1902. V. 64
The Holy Grail and Other Poems. London: 1870. V. 67
Idylls of the Hearth. London: 1864. V. 62
Idylls of the King. London: 1892. V. 62
(Idylls of the King: comprising): Enid; Elaine; Vivienne; Guinevere. London: 1868. V. 62
In Memoriam. London: 1850. V. 62; 65
In Memoriam. London: 1933. V. 63; 64; 65; 66
The Lady of Shalott. New York: 1981. V. 62
The Life and Works. London: 1898-1899. V. 62; 65
The Lover's Tale. London: 1879. V. 67
Maud. London: 1855. V. 62; 64; 67
Maud. 1893. V. 62; 67
Maud. London: 1905. V. 67
Maud. London: 1922. V. 63
The May Queen. London: 1870. V. 65
The May Queen. London: 1872. V. 65
The Morte D'Arthur. London: 1903. V. 65
Poems. London: 1827. V. 62
Poems. London: 1833. V. 62; 64
Poems. London: 1842. V. 64; 67
Poems. London: 1857. V. 64
Poems. London: 1862. V. 64; 65; 66
Poems. London: 1863. V. 62
Poems. London: 1864. V. 65

TENNYSON, ALFRED TENNYSON, 1ST BARON continued
Poems. London: 1866. V. 67
Poems. 1974. V. 62
The Poems. Cambridge: 1974. V. 62; 63
Poems Chiefly Lyrical. London: 1830. V. 62; 63
The Princess. London: 1854. V. 63
The Princess. London: 1856. V. 62; 65; 67
The Princess. 1911. V. 63
Seven Poems and Two Translations. Hammersmith: 1902. V. 62; 65; 66
The Story of Elaine. London: 1871. V. 63
Tennyson's Suppressed Poems. New York and London: 1903. V. 62; 67
Tiresias and Other Poems. London: 1885. V. 62
Vivien. London: 1867. V. 65
A Welcome. London: 1863. V. 65
The Works. London: 1884. V. 67

TENNYSON, FREDERICK
Days and Hours. London: 1854. V. 63

TENNYSON, JULIAN
Rough Shooting for the Owner Keeper Month by Month. London: 1938. V. 67

TENREIRO, FRANCISCO JOSE
Ilha de Nome Santo. Coimbra: 1942. V. 67

TERAMOTO, KAIYU
Nanban Torai Kibun. Tokyo: 1980. V. 62; 63; 64

TERAN, BOSTON
God is a Bullet. New York: 1999. V. 67

TERAN, LISA ST. AUBIN DE
The High Place. London: 1985. V. 64

TERCERO Cathecismo y Exposicion de la Doctrina Christina, por Sermones....
Los Reyes: 1505. V. 62

TERENTIUS AFER, PUBLIUS
Andria, a Comedy. Verona: 1971. V. 62; 65
Andria Oder Das madchen Von Andros. 1971. V. 65
The Comedies of Terence. London: 1768. V. 67
Comoediae. Amsterdam: 1700. V. 64; 66
Comoediae. Birminghame: 1772. V. 62; 63; 64; 65; 66
Comoediae Sex. Parisiis: 1536. V. 65; 66
Comoediae Sex. Amstelaedami: 1669. V. 65
Comoediae Sex. Hagae Comitum: 1732. V. 63; 66
Habes Hic Amice Lector P. Terentii Comedias una Cum Scholiis ex Donati, Asperi & Cornuti Commentariis Decepti, Multo Quam Antehac Unquam Prodierunt Emendatiores.... Basel: 1532. V. 65

TERENZ, S.
The Prints of F. Robert Motherwell...A Catalogue Raisonne 1943-1984. New York: 1984. V. 65

TERENZIO, S.
The Prints...A Catalogue Raisonne 1943-1984. New York: 1984. V. 62

TERESA, SAINT
The Flaming Hart.... Antwerp: 1642. V. 62

TERICK, W. GUY
Obituraries from Newspapers of Northern West Virginia. Clarksburg: 1933. V. 64

TERKEL, STUDS
American Dreams: Lost and Found. New York: 1980. V. 64; 66
Talking to Myself. New York: 1977. V. 64; 66

TERMIER, HENRI
Etude Geologique sur la Maroc Central et le Moyen Atlas Septentrional. Rabat: 1936. V. 65

TERNAN, TREVOR
The Story of the Tyneside Scottish. Newcastle-upon-Tyne: 1920. V. 62

TERRAY, L.
Conquistadors of the Useless. From the Alps to Annapurna. 1963. V. 63; 65

TERRAY, LIONEL
Conquistadors of the Useless, from the Alps to Annapurna. London: 1963. V. 66

TERRELL, ISAAC L.
Old Houses in Rockingham, County, 1750 to 1850. Verona: 1975. V. 64

TERRELL, JOHN U.
War for the Colorado River. Glendale: 1965. V. 64

TERRINGTON, WILLIAM
Cooling Cups and Dainty Drinks. London: 1869. V. 67

THE TERRITORY of Wyoming - Its History, Soil, Climate, Resources, Etc. Laramie City: 1874. V. 66
THE TERRITORY of Wyoming - Its History, Soil, Climate, Resources, Etc. Cheyenne: 1889. V. 63

TERRY, DANIEL
British Theatrical Gallery. London: 1825. V. 67

TERRY, ELLEN
The Story of My Life. London: 1908. V. 62; 64; 65

TERRY, MARIAN DICKINSON
Old Inns of Connecticut. Hartford: 1937. V. 65

TERRY, T. PHILIP
Terry's Guide to Cuba. Boston: 1929. V. 63

TERRY, WALLACE
Bloods. New York: 1984. V. 66

TERTULLIAN, QUINTUS
Liber De Pallio. Claudius Salamasis Ante Mortem Recensuit.... Lugduni Batavorum: 1656. V. 66
Scripta & Plura Quam Ante & Diligentius per Industriam Bene Literatorum Aliquot. Basle: 1550. V. 66
...Operum. Paris: 1566. V. 63
Opera ad Vetustissimorum Exemplarium Fiden Sedulo Emendata Dligentia.. Paris: 1675. V. 65

TESKE, EDMUND
Images from Within: The Photographs of Edmund Teske. Carmel: 1980. V. 63

TESNOHLIDEK, RUDOLF
The Cunning Little Vixen. New York: 1985. V. 62; 64; 65

TESSIER, THOMAS
In Sight of Chaos. London: 1971. V. 65

TEVIS, WALTER
The Hustler. New York: 1959. V. 66
The Hustler. London: 1960. V. 65

TEW, DAVID
The Oakham Canal. Wymondham: 1968. V. 62

TEWARI, D. N.
Tropical Forest Produce. Dehra Dun: 1994. V. 63

TEXAS
First Annual Report of the Agricultural Bureau of the Department of Agriculture, Insurance, Statistics and History. Austin: 1889. V. 64
Second Annual Report of the Superintendent of the Bureau of Immigration of the State of Texas. (with) *Third Annual Report....* Austin: 1873-1874. V. 64

TEY, JOSEPHINE
The Daughter of Time. London: 1951. V. 66
The Franchise Affair. New York: 1949. V. 67
Richard of Bordeaux: a Play in Two Parts. London: 1935. V. 67
The Singing Sands. London: 1952. V. 63; 65; 66
Three by Tey. New York: 1954. V. 65
To Love and Be Wise. London: 1950. V. 65; 66

THAARUP, FRED
Manuel des Beaux Arts et des Curiosites a Copenhague. Copenhagen: 1828. V. 67

THACHER, GEORGE A.
Why Some Men Kill or Murder Mysteries Revealed. N.P: 1919. V. 64

THACHER, JAMES
American Medical Biography. Boston: 1828. V. 66; 67
American Modern Practice; or, a Simple Method of Prevention and Cure of Disease.... Boston: 1817. V. 64
An American New Dispensatory.... Boston: 1810. V. 62
A Military Journal During the American Revolutionary War.... Boston: 1823. V. 62
Military Journal During the American Revolutionary War.... Boston: 1827. V. 63
Observations on Hydrophobia, Produced by the Bite of a Mad Dog, or Other Rabid Animal. Plymouth: 1812. V. 64; 67

THACKER, R. E.
The Four-in-Hand Illustrated Book of Saddlery. Walsall: 1905. V. 62

THACKERAY, WILLIAM MAKEPEACE
The Adventures of Philip on His Way through the World.... London: 1862. V. 62; 66; 67
Christmas Books. Mrs. Perkins's Ball. Our Street. Dr. Birch. London: 1857. V. 65
Comic Tales and Sketches. London: 1841. V. 66
Donic Duval. London: 1867. V. 64
Doctor Birch and His Young Friends. London: 1849. V. 64
The English Humorists of the Eighteenth Century. London: 1853. V. 62; 65; 66
An Essay on the Genius of George Cruikshank. 1840. V. 62
The Four Georges: Sketches of Manners, Morals, Court and Town Life. London: 1861. V. 66
The History of Henry Esmond, Esq. London: 1852. V. 62; 63; 66; 67
The History of Henry Esmond, Esq. London: 1853. V. 66
The History of Pendennis. London: 1848-1850. V. 67
The History of Pendennis. London: 1849. V. 66
The History of Pendennis. London: 1849-1850. V. 62; 67
The History of Samuel Titmarsh and the Great Hoggarty Diamond. London: 1849. V. 67
The Irish Sketch-Book. London: 1845. V. 65
Letters and Private Papers. London: 1945. V. 62; 63; 65
Lovel the Widower. London: 1866. V. 66
The Loving Ballad of Lord Bateman. London: 1839. V. 62
The Loving Ballad of Lord Bateman. London: 1851. V. 62
The Memoirs of Barry Lyndon, Esq. of the Kingdom of Ireland. London: 1856. V. 65
Mrs. Perkin's Ball. London: 1847. V. 64
The Newcomes. London: 1853-1855. V. 62; 67
The Newcomes. London: 1854. V. 65

THACKERAY, WILLIAM MAKEPEACE continued
The Newcomes. London: 1854-1855. V. 62; 67
The Newcomes. London: 1855. V. 62; 65
The Newcomes.... New York: 1954. V. 62; 63
Notes of a Journey from Cornhill to Grand Cairo, by Way of Lisbon, Athens, Constantinople and Jerusalem. London: 1846. V. 66
The Orphan of Pimlico, and Other Sketches, Fragments and Drawings. London: 1876. V. 63
The Paris Sketch Book. London: 1840. V. 66
Reading a Poem. New York: 1911. V. 63; 64; 66
Rebecca and Rowena. London: 1850. V. 62
The Rose and the Ring; or, the History of Prince Giglio and Prince Bulbo. London: 1855. V. 65
Roundabout Papers. London: 1863. V. 66
The Snob: a Literary and Scientific Journal. Volume I. Nos. 3, 4, 5 and 6. Cambridge: 1829. V. 66
Vanity Fair. London: 1848. V. 62; 63; 65; 66; 67
Vanity Fair. London: 1910. V. 62; 64; 66
Vanity Fair. London: 1913. V. 66
The Virginians. London: 1858. V. 64; 65
The Virginians. London: 1858-1859. V. 62; 64; 67
The Works. London: 1879. V. 62; 66
The Works. London: 1883. V. 62; 65; 67
The Works. London: 1899-1913. V. 67
The Works. London: 1900-1904. V. 66
The Works. London: 1901. V. 62
The Works. London: 1902-1903. V. 62; 67
The Works. London: 1911. V. 67

THACKRAH, C. TURNER
The Effects of the Principal Arts, Trades and Professions and Civic States and Habits of Living on Health and Longevity.... Philadelphia: 1831. V. 62; 64

THADEN, LOUIE
High, Wide and Frightened. New York: 1938. V. 67

THATCHER, MARGARET
The Downing Street Years. New York: 1993. V. 65

THAYER, ELI
A History of the Kansas Crusade - Its Friends and Its Foes. New York: 1889. V. 65

THAYER, EMMA HOMAN
Wild Flowers of Colorado: From Original Water Color Sketches Drawn from Nature. New York: 1885. V. 64

THAYER, GERALD H.
Concealing Coloration in the Animal Kingdom. New York: 1909. V. 62; 63; 64
Concealing Colouration in the Animal Kingdom, an Exposition of the Laws of Disguise.... New York: 1918. V. 63; 64; 66

THAYER, STEVE
St. Mudd. New York: 1992. V. 66; 67

THAYER, T. H.
Concealing Colouration in the Animal Kingdom.... New York: 1909. V. 62

THAYER, WILLIAM S.
Osler and Other Papers. Baltimore: 1931. V. 64; 66; 67

THEAKSTON, MICHAEL
British Angling Flies. 1888. V. 67
A List of Natural Flies that are Taken by Trout, Grayling and Smelt in the Streams of Ripon. 1853. V. 67

THEAKSTON, SOLOMON WILKINSON
Handbook for Visitors in Scarborough. Scarborough: 1859. V. 65
Theakston's Guide to Scarborough.... Scarborough: 1860. V. 65

THEARLE, SAMUEL J. P.
Naval Architecture: a Treatise on Laying Off and Building Wood, Iron and Composite Ships. Volume II Only. New York. V. 67

THE THEATRE of the Present War in the Netherlands and Upon the Rhine.... London: 1745. V. 67

THEBES, A. DE
L'Enigme de la Main. Paris: 1900. V. 67

THEEL, H.
Challenger Voyage Zoology. Parts 13 and 39 Holothurioidea. 1881-1885. V. 66

THELWALL, JOHN
The Rights of Nature, Against the Usurpations of Establishments. London: 1796. V. 62
The Speech of John Thelwall, at the General Meeting of the Friends of Parliamentary Reform, Called by the London Corresponding Society, and Held in the Neighbourhood of Copenhagen-House, on Monday October 26, 1795. London: 1795. V. 62

THEMERSON, STEFAN
Kurt Schwitters in England. London: 1958. V. 63; 65

THEOBALD, F. V.
A Monograph of the Culicidae or Mosquitoes.... London: 1901-1910. V. 64

THEOBALD, LEWIS
The Grove; or a Collection of Original Poems, Translations &c. London: 1721. V. 62
Shakespeare Restored; or, a Specimen of the Many Errors, as Well Committed, as Unamended, by Mr. Pope in His Late Edition of This Poet. London: 1726. V. 65; 66

Vocal Parts of an Entertainment, Called Apollo and Daphne; or the Burgo-Master Trucked. London: 1726. V. 65

THEOBALD, W.
Descriptive Catalogue of the Reptiles of British India. Calcutta: 1876. V. 62
Observations on Some Indian and Burmese Species of Trionyx (Reptilia)...Observations on Some Indian and Burmese Species of Trionyx with a Rectification. Calcutta: 1874-1875. V. 67

THEOCRITUS
The Complete Poems. London: 1929. V. 63; 64; 66
The Complete Poems. Waltham St. Lawrence: 1930. V. 64; 66
Poetae Clarissimi Idyllia Trigintasex, Recens e Graeco in Latinum, ad Verbum.... Venetiis: 1539. V. 66
Sixe Idilia. Oxford: 1883. V. 64
Sixe Idyllia. New York: 1971. V. 62; 66

THEODOSIUS
Sphaericorum Libri Tres. Oxford: 1707. V. 67

THEOPHILUS
D. Justiniani Sacratissimi Principis Institutionum, Sive Elementorum Libri Quatuor Quibus Subjugitur Theophili Pharaphraseos Vesrio Latina.... 1733. V. 66

THEOPHRASTUS
De Historia et Causis Plantarum Libri IX. Treviso: 1483. V. 64
De Historia Plantarum Libri Decem. Amsterdam: 1644. V. 64
De Suffructicibus Herbisque Ac Frugibus. Strassburg: 1528. V. 64
Opera Quae Quidem a Tot Saeculis Adhuc Restant Omnia.... Basiliae: 1541. V. 65

THE THEORY of Effect, Embracing the Contrast of Light and Shade of Colour and Harmony. Philadelphia: 1851. V. 67

THERESE D'AVILA
Les Oeuvres de Sainte Therese. Paris: 1687. V. 67

THEROIGNE et Populus, ou Le Triomphe de la Demoratie, Drame National, en Vers Civique. (with) L'Ami des Lois. London: 1790. V. 66

THEROUX, ALEXANDER
History is Made at Night and Other Poems. West Chester: 1992. V. 63
Three Wogs. Boston: 1972. V. 67

THEROUX, PAUL
The Consul's File. Boston: 1977. V. 63; 66
The Family Arsenal. London: 1976. V. 64; 67
Girls at Play. Boston: 1969. V. 66
The Happy Isles of Oceania. Paddling the Pacific. London: 1992. V. 67
Jungle Lovers. Boston: 1971. V. 62
Kowloon Tong. Franklin Center: 1997. V. 67
Kowloon Tong. Franklin Center: 1998. V. 65
The Mosquito Coast. Boston: 1982. V. 64
O-Zone. Franklin Center: 1986. V. 67
The Old Patagonian Express by Train through the Americas. Boston;: 1979. V. 66; 67
Picture Palace. London: 1978. V. 67
The Pillars of Hercules: a Grand Tour of the Mediterranean. London: 1995. V. 67
Sailing through China. London: 1983. V. 62
Sailing through China. Wilton, Salisbury: 1983. V. 66
Saint Jack. Boston: 1973. V. 62; 63; 64
The Shortest Day of the Year: A Christmas Fantasy. Leamington Spa: 1986. V. 67
Sinning with Annie and Other Stories. Boston: 1972. V. 64
Sinning with Annie and Other Stories. 1975. V. 65
Sir Vidia's Shadow. Boston: 1998. V. 62
Waldo. Boston: 1967. V. 63

THE THESPIAN Dictionary; or Dramatic Biography of the Present Age.... London: 1805. V. 62; 65

THE THESPIAN Preceptor, or, a Full Display of the Scenic Art.... Boston: 1810. V. 64; 66

THICKNESSE, PHILIP
Pere Pascal, a Monk of Montserrat, Vindicated in a Charge Brought Against Him by a Noble Earl of Great Britain. London: 1803. V. 62
Useful Hints to Those Who made the Tour of France, in a Series of Letters. London: 1770. V. 65
A Year's Journey through France and Part of Spain. London: 1778. V. 66
A Year's Journey through the Pais Bas; or, Austrian Netherlands. London: 1786. V. 65

THIELEN, BETH
Why the Revolving Door: the Neighborhood, the Prisons. California: 1993. V. 64

THIEMMEDH, J.
Fishes of Thailand; Their English, Scientific and Thai Names. Bangkok: 1966. V. 67

THIENEMANN, FRIEDRICH A. L.
Systematische Darstellung der Fortpflanzung der Vogel Europa's Mit Abbildung der Eier. Leipzig: 1925-1938. V. 67

THIERS, LOUIS ADOLPHE
De La Properiete. Paris: 1848. V. 66

THILLAYE, M.
Essai sur l'Emploi Medical de l'Electricite. Paris: 1803. V. 64

THIMM, CARL A.
Complete Bibliography of the Art of the Fence. London: 1890. V. 62

THIMM, FRANZ
Thimm's London Fur 1859; Ein Praktischer Fuhrer Durch England's Hauptstadt und Deren Umgebung. London und Leipzig: 1859. V. 67

THINGS by Their Right Names: a Novel. Boston: 1812. V. 66

THIOLLET, FRANCOIS
Nouveau Recuel de Menuiserie et de Decorations Interieures et Exterieures.... Paris: 1837. V. 64

THIOLLIERE, V.
Description des Poissons Fossiles Provenant des Giements Corallines du Jura dans Le Bugey.... Paris Lyons & Strasburg: 1854-1873. V. 62

THIRKELL, ANGELA
County Chronicle. New York: 1950. V. 65

THIROUX D'ARCONVILLE, MARIE GENEVIEVE CHARLOTTE DARLUS
De l'Amitie. Amsterdam: 1761. V. 67
De L'Amitie. Amsterdam: 1764. V. 63

32 Counties - Photographs of Ireland.... London: 1989. V. 64

THIS is the House That Jack Built. London: 1880. V. 65

THIS is Tomorrow. London: 1956. V. 67

THIS Way for Fun. London: 1920. V. 67

THISELTON-DYER, T. F.
Folk-Lore of Women as Illustrated by Legendary and Traditionary Tales, Folk-Rhymes, Proverbial Sayings, Suprstitions &c. London: 1905. V. 65
Folk-Lore of Women, as Illustrated by Legendary and Tradtionary Tales.... Chicago: 1906. V. 64

THISTLEWOOD, ARTHUR
The Trials of Arthur Thistlewood, James Ings, John Thomas Brunt, Richard Tidd, William Davidson, and Others for High Treason...April 1820.... London: 1820. V. 63

THOBURN, JOSEPH
Oklahoma - A History of the State and Its People. New York: 1929. V. 64; 67

THOBY-MARCELIN, PHILIPPE
Canape-Vert. New York: 1944. V. 63

THOM, ADAM
The Claims to the Oregon Territory Considered. London: 1844. V. 64

THOM, WALTER
Pedestrianism; or, an Account of the Performances of Celebrated Pedestrians During the Last and Present Century.... Aberdeen: 1813. V. 66

THOM, WILLIAM
Donaldsoniad. J----n D----n Detected; or an Account How the Authentic Address of the --- Was Discovered. Glasgow: 1763. V. 66
Rhymes and Recollections of a Hand-Loom Weaver. 1844. V. 62

THOMAS, ALAN
Great Books and Book Collectors. 1975. V. 67
Great Books and Book Collectors. London: 1975. V. 62

THOMAS, ALFRED BARNABY
Forgotten Frontiers. A Study of the Spanish Indian Policy of Don Juan Buatiste de Anza, Governor of New Mexico. Norman: 1932. V. 63; 66
The Plains Indians and New Mexico 1751-1778. Albuquerque: 1940. V. 66
Teodoro De Croix and the Northern Frontier of New Spain 1776-1783. Norman: 1941. V. 63; 66

THOMAS, ANTOINE LEONARD
Essai sur le Caractere, Les Moeurs et l'Espirit des Femmes dans les Differens Siecles. Amsterdam: 1772. V. 65
Essai sur le Caractere, les Moeurs et l'Esprit des Femmes Dans Les Differens Siecles. Paris: 1772. V. 63
Essay on the Character, Manners and Genius of Women in Different Ages. London: 1773. V. 65

THOMAS, CHARLES
Adventures and Observations on the West Coast of Africa and Its Islands. New York: 1860. V. 64

THOMAS, CLARENCE
General Turner Ashby, the Centaur of the South. Winchester: 1907. V. 62; 63; 65

THOMAS, CRAIG
Rat Trap. London: 1976. V. 67
Wolfshane. London: 1978. V. 67

THOMAS, D. A.
The Growth and Direction of Our Foreign Trade in Coal During the Last Half Century. London: 1903. V. 63

THOMAS, D. B.
The Book of Vagabonds and Beggars.... London: 1932. V. 65

THOMAS, D. M.
Personal and Possessive. London: 1964. V. 62
The White Hotel. London: 1981. V. 62
The White Hotel. New York: 1981. V. 66

THOMAS, D. O.
A Bibliography of the Works of Richard Price. Aldershot: 1993. V. 62

THOMAS, DAVID
Travels through the Western Country in the Summer of 1816.... Auburn: 1819. V. 63; 64

THOMAS, DAVIS
People of the First Man. Life Among the Plains Indians in Their Final Days of Glory. New York: 1976. V. 63; 66

THOMAS, DONALD
Cracksman on Velvet. London: 1974. V. 65

THOMAS, DYLAN MARLAIS
Adventures in the Skin Trade. London: 1955. V. 62
Adventures in the Skin Trade and Other Stories. Norfolk and New York: 1955. V. 62; 64
A Child's Christmas in Wales. Norfolk: 1955. V. 65
A Child's Christmas in Wales. London: 1978. V. 62; 66
Collected Poems 1934-1952. London: 1952. V. 62; 66
Collected Poems 1934-1952. London: 1967. V. 62
Conversations About Christmas. New York: 1954. V. 62; 64
Deaths and Entrances. London: 1946. V. 63; 64; 65
The Doctor and the Devils. London: 1953. V. 62
The Doctor and the Devils. Norfolk: 1953. V. 62
Early One Morning. Norfolk: 1954. V. 62
18 Poems. London: 1934. V. 65
18 Poems. London: 1942. V. 65
In Country Sleep. New York: 1952. V. 62; 63; 65
The Map of Love: Verse and Prose. London: 1939. V. 63
New Poems. Norfolk: 1943. V. 64
Poemas. Madrid: 1955. V. 66
Poet in the Making: the Notebooks of Dylan Thomas. London: 1968. V. 63; 64; 66
Portrait de l'Artiste en Jeune Chien. (Portrait of the Artist as a Young Dog). Paris: 1947. V. 64
Portrait of the Artist as a Young Dog. Norfolk: 1940. V. 62
A Prospect of the Sea. London: 1955. V. 62
Quite Early One Morning. London: 1954. V. 63
Quite Early One Morning. New York: 1954. V. 64
Selected Writings. New York: 1946. V. 64
Twenty Years A-Growing. London: 1964. V. 63
Twenty-Five Poems. London: 1936. V. 62; 65; 66
Twenty-Six Poems. Norfolk: 1949. V. 63
Under Milk Wood.... London: 1954. V. 62; 63; 65
Under Milkwood. London: 1958. V. 66

THOMAS, EDITH M.
Babes of the Year. New York: 1888. V. 66

THOMAS, EDWARD
Beautiful Wales.... London: 1905. V. 62
British Country Life. London: 1907. V. 64
The Chessplayer and Other Essays. Andoversford: 1981. V. 65
The Chessplayer and Other Essays. London: 1981. V. 63
The Childhood of Edward Thomas - a Fragment of Autobiography. London: 1937. V. 64
Chosen Essays. 1926. V. 64
Chosen Essays. Newtown: 1926. V. 63
Cloud Castle and Other Papers. London: 1922. V. 64
Collected Poems. London: 1920. V. 62
The Collected Poems. Oxford: 1978. V. 62
George Borrow. The Man and His Books. 1912. V. 67
Horae Solitariae. London: 1902. V. 67
The Icknield Way. London: 1913. V. 64
The Last Sheaf. London: 1928. V. 67
A Literary Pilgrim in England. 1916. V. 64
Norse Tales. London: 1912. V. 64
Oxford. 1903. V. 64
Poems. London: 1917. V. 64
Rose Acre Papers, Including Essays from Horae Solitariae. London: 1910. V. 64
Selected Poems. Newtown: 1927. V. 62; 63; 65
The Tenth Muse. London: 1917. V. 67

THOMAS, EUGENE
Yellow Magic. New York: 1934. V. 67

THOMAS, EVAN J.
Now at Eve and Other Poems. 1937. V. 65

THOMAS, FRANK
Sherlock Holmes and the Masquerade Murders. Los Angeles: 1986. V. 66

THOMAS, FREDERICK WILLIAM
The Emigrant, or Reflections Whilte Descending the Ohio. Cincinnati: 1833. V. 63; 66

THOMAS, GABRIEL
An Historical and Geographical Account of the Province and Country of Pensilvania; and of West New Jersey in America. New York: 1848. V. 63; 66

THOMAS, GORDON
Enola Gay. New York: 1977. V. 63

THOMAS, HELEN
A Memory of W. H. Hudson. Wakefield: 1984. V. 62
World Without End. London: 1931. V. 67

THOMAS, HERBERT
Classical Contributions to Obstetrics and Gynecology. Springfield: 1935. V. 64; 66; 67

THOMAS, ISAIAH
The History of Printing in America. Worcester: 1810. V. 62; 63
The History of Printing in America. Barre: 1970. V. 63; 64

THOMAS, J. H.
Systematic Arrangement of Lord Coke's First Institute of the Laws of England. Philadelphia: 1836. V. 63

THOMAS, J. J.
The American Fruit Culturist.... Auburn: 1849. V. 63

THOMAS, JAMES
Selections from Original Contributions. Liverpool: 1889. V. 63

THOMAS, JAMES A.
Emancipation in the West Indies. New York: 1838. V. 63
A Pioneer Tobacco Merchant in the Orient. Durham: 1928. V. 67

THOMAS, JEAN
Devil's Ditties. Chicago: 1931. V. 67

THOMAS, JENNIE
Biography and Early Life Sketch of the Late Abram Sortore Including His Trip to California and Back. Alexandria: 1909. V. 66

THOMAS, JOHN
Dry Martini: a Gentleman Turns to Love. London: 1926. V. 67

THOMAS, JOHN P.
Career and Character of General Micah Jenkins, C.S.A. Columbia: 1903. V. 63; 65

THOMAS, JOSEPH B.
Hounds and Hunting through the Ages. New York: 1928. V. 63

THOMAS, LAURENCE
The Death of Laurence Vining. London: 1928. V. 65

THOMAS, LESLIE
Midnight Clear. London: 1978. V. 63

THOMAS, LEWIS
Could I Ask You Something?. New York: 1984. V. 64

THOMAS, LORD ARCHBISHOP OF YORK
A Sermon Preach'd at the Cathedral Church of York, September 22nd, 1745. London: 1745. V. 67

THOMAS, LOWELL
With Lawrence in Arabia. New York: 1924. V. 64

THOMAS, MYFANWY
Women Must Love. London: 1937. V. 67

THOMAS, OLDFIELD
Account of a Collection of Human Skulls from Torres Straits. London: 1885. V. 67
Catalogue of the Marsupialia and Monotremata in the Collection of the British Museum. 1888. V. 66
Catalogue of the Marsupialia and Monotremata in the Collection of the British Museum. London: 1888. V. 63
The Duke of Bedford's Zoological Exploration in Eastern Asia. 1906-1907. V. 62
On the Homologies and Succession of the Teeth in the Dasyuridae with an Attempt to Trace the History of the Evolution of Mammalian Teeth. 1887. V. 67

THOMAS, PETER
Bikupan: The Story of a Trip to Visit a Hand Paper Mill in Sweden.... Santa Cruz: 1992. V. 64
A Collection of Paper Samples from Hand Papermills in the United States of America. Santa Cruz: 1993. V. 64
Papermaking in Seventeenth Century England. Santa Cruz: 1990. V. 64

THOMAS, PIRI
Down These Mean Streets. New York: 1967. V. 67

THOMAS, R. S.
An Acre of Land. Newtown: 1952. V. 62
The Bread of Truth. London: 1963. V. 62
Collected Poems 1945-1990. London: 1993. V. 62; 65
Destinations. Shipston-on-Stour: 1985. V. 62
Frequencies. London: 1978. V. 62; 63
Frieze. Schondorf am Ammersee: 1992. V. 62; 64
H'm - Poems. London: 1972. V. 62; 63; 65
Ingrowing Thoughts. Bridgend: 1985. V. 62
Laboratories of the Spirit. London: 1975. V. 62
Later Poems - a Selection 1972-1982. London: 1983. V. 63
The Minister. Newtown: 1953. V. 62
The Mountains. New York: 1968. V. 64
Not That He Brought Flowers. London: 1968. V. 62; 63; 65
Pieta. London: 1966. V. 62
Poetry for Supper. London: 1958. V. 62; 63
Poet's Meeting. Stratford-upon-Avon: 1983. V. 62
Selected Poems - 1946-1968. London: 1973. V. 62; 63
Six Poems. Shipston-on-Stour: 1997. V. 62; 65
Song at the Year's Turning. London: 9155. V. 62
The Stones of the Field. Carmarthen: 1946. V. 62; 63
Tares. London: 1961. V. 62

Three Poems. Child Okeford: 1988. V. 62; 66
The Way Of It - Poems. Sunderland: 1977. V. 62; 63
What is a Welshman?. Llandybie: 1974. V. 63
Words and the Poet - the W. D. Thomas Memorial Lecture Delivered at the University College of Sansea on November 19, 1963. Cardiff: 1964. V. 62
Young and Old. London: 1972. V. 62; 63

THOMAS, RALPH
Swimming, with Lists of Books Published in English, German, French and Other European Languages and Critical Remarks on the Theory and Practice of Swimming and Resuscitation.... London: 1904. V. 62

THOMAS, RICHARD
Report on a Survey of the Mining District of Cornwall from Chasewater to Camborne. 1819. V. 62

THOMAS, ROBERT
The Modern Practice of Physic. New York: 1811. V. 65
The Modern Practice of Physic. New York: 1813. V. 63
The Modern Practice of Physic. New York: 1815. V. 66
The Modern Practice of Physic. London: 1821. V. 65

THOMAS, ROSS
The Backup Men. New York: 1971. V. 65; 66
The Brass Go-Between. New York: 1970. V. 66
Briarpatch. New York: 1984. V. 67
Cast a Yellow Shadow. New York: 1967. V. 62; 63; 64; 65; 66; 67
Chinaman's Chance. 1967. V. 64
Chinaman's Chance. 1978. V. 64; 66
Chinaman's Chance. New York: 1978. V. 65; 67
The Eighth Dwarf. New York: 1979. V. 67
The Fools in Town Are on Our Side. New York: 1971. V. 65
The Fourth Durango. London: 1989. V. 67
The Highbinders. London: 1974. V. 67
The Highbinders. New York: 1974. V. 65; 66; 67
If You Can't Be Good. New York: 1973. V. 62
Missionary Stew. New York: 1983. V. 65
Missionary Stew. London: 1984. V. 67
The Money Harvest. New York: 1975. V. 65; 67
The Mordida Man. New York: 1981. V. 67
Out on the Rim. New York: 1987. V. 67
The Porkchoppers. New York: 1972. V. 63; 64; 65; 66; 67
The Seersucker Whipsaw. New York: 1967. V. 62; 65; 67
The Singapore Wink. 1969. V. 67
Spies, Thumbsuckers, etc. Northridge: 1980. V. 67
Spies, Thumbsuckers, etc. Northridge: 1989. V. 65
Twilight at Mac's Place. New York: 1990. V. 66; 67
Voodoo, Ltd. New York: 1992. V. 67
Yellow-Dog Contract. New York: 1977. V. 62; 65; 67
Yellow-Dog Contract. New York: 1980. V. 65
Yellow-Dog Contract. New York: 1985. V. 66

THOMAS, S.
The Banker's Sure Guide; or Monies Man's Assistant in Three Parts.... London: 1803. V. 63; 66

THOMAS, SHIRLEY
Men of Space: Profiles of the Leaders in Space Research, Development and Exploration. Philadelphia: 1960-1968. V. 66

THOMAS, T.
Excursion of the Cardiff Naturalists' Society to the Steep Holm... with a Flora of the Island. Cardiff: 1884. V. 67

THOMAS, TERRY
Casting. A Textbook of Fishing Casts. London: 1960. V. 67

THOMAS, THOMAS E.
Anti-Slavery Conflict. (with) Letters 1829-1874. Oxford: 1909-1913. V. 67

THOMAS, WILLIAM CAVE
The Science of Moderation; or, the Quantitative Theory of the Good and the Beautiful. Formative Ethics. London: 1867. V. 65

THOMAS, WILLIAM H.
On Land and Sea or California in the Years 1843, '44 and '45. Boston: 1884. V. 65

THOMAS, WILLIAM S.
Trails and Tramps in Alaska and Newfoundland. New York/London: 1913. V. 63

THOMAS A KEMPIS, SAINT
The Christian's Pattern; or, a Treatise of the Imitation of Christ. London: 1735. V. 64

THOMAS AQUINAS, SAINT
Basic Writings of Saint Thomas Aquinas. New York: 1944. V. 66
Selected Writings of Saint Thomas Aquinas. Chatham: 1969. V. 62
Sermones Valde pii et Docti Pro Dominicis et Festivis Diebus ex Bibliotheca Vaticana Nunc Primum in Lucem Editi.... Rome: 1570. V. 67
Sermones Valde Pii et Docti Pro Dominicis et Festivis Diebus ex Bibliotheca Vaticana Nunc Primum in Lucem Editi.... Rome: 1571-1570. V. 66
Summa Totius Theologiae D. Thomae De Aquino. Venetiis: 1596. V. 66
Summa Totius Theologiae. (with) Indices Omnes in D. Thomae Summam. Lugduni: 1663. V. 67
Summae Theologicae. Paris: 1514. V. 65

THOMAS AQUINAS, SAINT continued
Thomae Aquinatis Summa Theologica; In Qua Ecclesiae Catholicae Doctrina Universa.... 1614. V. 65

THOMASSIN, SIMON
Recueil des Figures, Groupes, Thermes, Fontaines, Vases, STatues et Autres Ornemens de Versailles.... Amsterdam: 1695-1701. V. 64

Recueil des Statues, Groupes, Fontaines, Termes, Vases, et Autres Magnifiques Ornamens du Chateau & Parc de Versailles. The Hague: 1724. V. 62

THOME, JAMES
Emancipation in the West Indies, a Six Month's Tour in Antigua, Barbadoes and Jamaica in the Year 1837. New York: 1838. V. 67

THOMLINSON, M. H.
The Garrison of Fort Bliss 1849-1916. El Paso: 1945. V. 63; 66

THOMPSON, A. B.
Petroleum Mining and Oil-Field Development. A Guide to the Exploration of Petroleum Lands and a Study of the Engineering Problems Connected With the Winning of Petroleum Including Statistical Data of Important Oil-Fields, Notes on the Origin and Distribu. London: 1910. V. 65

THOMPSON, A. HAMILTON
Military Architecture in England During the Middle Ages. London: 1912. V. 62; 66

Visitations in the Diocese of Lincoln 1517-1531. Volume II. Visitations of Rural Deaneries by John Longland, Bishop of Lincoln, and of Religious Houses by Bishops Atwater and Longland and by His and Their Commissaries 1517-1531. Lincoln: 1944. V. 63

THOMPSON, ALBERT W.
The Story of Early Clayton, New Mexico. Clayton: 1933. V. 65
They Were Open Range Days. Denver: 1946. V. 63; 66

THOMPSON, ALFRED
The Mask: a Humourous and Fantastic Review of the Month. London: 1868. V. 63

THOMPSON, CHARLES
Rules for Bad Horsemen. London: 1765. V. 62

THOMPSON, D. P.
Lucy Hosmer, or the Guardian and Ghost; a Tale of Avarice and Crime Defeated. Burlington: 1848. V. 66
May Martin; or the Money Diggers. A Green Mountain Tale. Montpelier: 1835. V. 64

THOMPSON, D'ARCY W.
Fun and Earnest; or Rhymes with Reason. London: 1865. V. 67
North Sea Fisheries Investigation Committee, Second Report (Northern Area) on Fishery and Hydrographical Investigations in the North Sea and Adjacent Waters, Conducted for the Fishery Board for Scotland.... London: 1906-1908. V. 64

THOMPSON, DUNSTAN
The Phoenix in the Desert - a Book of Travels. London: 1951. V. 64
The Third Murderer. London: 1944. V. 64

THOMPSON, E. P.
The Note-Book of a Naturalist. London: 1845. V. 67
William Morris. Romantic to Revolutionary. New York: 1961. V. 66

THOMPSON, EDWARD
Sailor's Letters. London: 1766. V. 62
Sailor's Letters. London: 1767. V. 62
These Men Thy Friends. New York: 1926. V. 64

THOMPSON, EDWARD J.
The Knight Mystic and Other Verses. London: 1907. V. 62

THOMPSON, EDWIN PORTER
History of the First Kentucky Brigade. Cincinnati: 1868. V. 62

THOMPSON, ELIZABETH
Kindergarten Homes. New York: 1882. V. 63

THOMPSON, ERA BELL
American Daughter. Chicago: 1946. V. 65

THOMPSON, FLORA
Bog-Myrtle and Peat. London: 1922. V. 65
Candelford Green. London: 1943. V. 63; 64
Lark Rise to Candelford. London: 1945. V. 63; 64

THOMPSON, FRANCIS
The Collected Poetry. London: 1913. V. 64
The Hound of Heaven - Ten Drawings for the Poem of Francis Thompson. London: 1914. V. 64
New Poems. Boston: 1897. V. 66
New Poems. Westminster: 1897. V. 67
Sister-Songs: an Offering to Two Sisters. London: 1895. V. 66; 67

THOMPSON, G. H.
The Noah's Ark. London: 1900. V. 63

THOMPSON, GEORGE
Letters and Addresses by George Thompson, During His Mission in the United States. Boston: 1837. V. 67
The Prison Bard; or Poems on Various Subjects. Hartford: 1848. V. 63
Prison Life and Reflections. Hartford: 1830. V. 67
Prison Life and Reflections; or a Narrative of the Arrest, Trial, Conviction, Imprisonment, Treatment, Observations, Reflections and Deliverance of Work, Burr and Thompson.... Oberlin: 1847. V. 66

Thompson in Africa, or an Account of the Missionary Labors, Sufferings, Travels, Observations &c.... Cleveland: 1852. V. 62; 63

THOMPSON, GEORGE CHARLES
A View of the Holy Land: Its Present Inhabitants, Their Manners and Customs, Polity and Religion. Wheeling: 1850. V. 65

THOMPSON, GEORGE D.
Bat Masterson: the Dodge City Years.... Topeka: 1943. V. 64

THOMPSON, H. S.
Ireland in 1839 and 1869. 1870. V. 64; 67
Sub-Alpine Plants of the Swiss Woods and Meadows. 1912. V. 67

THOMPSON, HARRY, MRS.
Clayton: The Friendly Town in Union County, New Mexico. Denver: 1962. V. 63; 66
History of Clayton and Union County, New Mexico. Denver: 1962. V. 65

THOMPSON, HENRY YATES
A Descriptive Catalogue of the Second Series of Fifty Manuscripts (Nos. 51-100) in the Collection of Henry Yates Thompson.... Cambridge: 1902. V. 63

THOMPSON, HUNTER S.
The Curse of Lono. Toronto New York London: 1983. V. 62; 67
Fear and Loathing in Las Vegas. New York: 1971. V. 62; 64; 65; 66
Fear and Loathing in Las Vegas. New York: 1998. V. 66
Fear and Loathing on the Campaign Trail '72. San Francisco: 1973. V. 66
Generation of Swine. The Gonzo Papers. Volume 2. Tales of Shame and Degradation in the '80s. New York: 1988. V. 66
Girls in the Grass. New York: 1991. V. 67
The Great Shark Hunt. New York: 1979. V. 64
Hell's Angels. New York: 1967. V. 63; 65; 66; 67
Hell's Angels. New York: 2000. V. 66
Proud Highway. The Fear and Loathing Letters, Volume I. Saga of a Desparate Southern Gentleman. New York: 1997. V. 66; 67
The Rum Diary. New York: 1998. V. 62; 63
Screwjack. Santa Barbara. 1991. V. 00

THOMPSON, I. OWEN
Adventures and Day Dreams. Long Beach: 1913. V. 63; 66

THOMPSON, ILSE
Your Vigor for Life Appalls Me. Seattle: 1998. V. 63

THOMPSON, J. ERIC S.
Maya Hieroglyphic Writing. Norman: 1960. V. 63

THOMPSON, J. J.
History of the Feud Between the Hill and Evans Parties of Garrard County, Kentucky. Cincinnati: 1854. V. 66

THOMPSON, J. V.
A Catalogue of Plants Growing in the Vicinity of Bewick Upon Tweed. 1807. V. 67

THOMPSON, JAMES
Historical Sketches of Bridlington. Bridlington: 1821. V. 67
Poems in the Scottish Dialect. Edinburgh: 1801. V. 62

THOMPSON, JAMES WESTFALL
The Medieval Library. Chicago: 1939. V. 63
The Medieval Library. New York: 1957. V. 67

THOMPSON, JERRY
Sabres on the Rio Grande. Austin: 1974. V. 67

THOMPSON, JIM
The Alcoholics. New York: 1953. V. 66
Bad Boy. New York: 1953. V. 67
Child of Rage. Los Angeles. 1991. V. 65; 66; 67
Fireworks: the Last Writings of Jim Thompson. New York: 1988. V. 65
The Getaway. New York: 1959. V. 66
The Grifters. Evanston: 1963. V. 65
Heed the Thunder. New York: 1946. V. 62; 67
A Hell of a Woman. New York: 1954. V. 66
The Killer Inside Me. New York: 1952. V. 64; 65; 67
The Killer Inside Me. Los Angeles: 1989. V. 67
Now and On Earth. Belen: 1986. V. 65; 67
Texas by the Tail. Greenwich: 1965. V. 66
The Trangressors. New York: 1961. V. 63

THOMPSON, JOHN
The Life of John Thompson, a Fugitive Slave. Worcester: 1856. V. 63; 65; 66
The Pleasure Tours in Ireland. Edinburgh: 1825. V. 63
The Universal Calculator; or the Merchant's Tradesman's and Family's Assistant. Edinburgh: 1793. V. 63

THOMPSON, KAY
Eloise. New York: 1955. V. 63
Eloise at Christmastime. New York: 1958. V. 63; 65
Eloise at Christmastime. London: 1959. V. 63; 67
Eloise in Moscow. New York: 1959. V. 63; 66
Eloise in Paris. New York: 1957. V. 62; 66

THOMPSON, LAWRENCE S.
The New Sabin: Books Described by Joseph Sabin and His Successors, Now Described Again on the Basis of Examination of Originals and Fully Indexed by Title.... Troy: 1974-1986. V. 62; 63

THOMPSON, PETER
Peter Thompson's Narrative of the Little Big Horn Campaign 1876. Glendale: 1974. V. 65

THOMPSON, PISHEY
The History and Antiquities of Boston and the Villages of Skirbeck, Fishtoft, Freiston, Butterwick, Benington, Leverton, Leake and Wrangle.... Boston: 1856. V. 62

THOMPSON, R.
The Young Ladies and Gentlemens Amo(u)rous Amusement. London: 1748. V. 63

THOMPSON, R. H.
Tokens of the British Isles 1575-1750. London: 1984-1996. V. 66

THOMPSON, ROBERT
The Gardener's Assistant.... London: 1859. V. 64
The Gardener's Assistant.... London: 1878. V. 63; 64
The Gardener's Assistant.... London: 1892. V. 62; 65
The Gardener's Assistant.... London: 1905. V. 62

THOMPSON, ROBERT ELLIS
Social Science and National Economy. Philadelphia: 1875. V. 62

THOMPSON, RUTH PLUMLY
Captain Salt in Oz. Chicago: 1936. V. 63; 65
The Cowardly Lion of Oz. Chicago: 1923. V. 66
The Curious Cruise of Captain Santa. Chicago: 1926. V. 62
The Gnome King of Oz. Chicago: 1927. V. 62
The Hungry Tiger of Oz. Chicago: 1926. V. 65
King Kojo. Philadelphia: 1938. V. 62
The Perhappsy Chaps. Chicago: 1918. V. 64
Piggy at the Fair. New York: 1920. V. 63
Pirates in Oz. Chicago: 1931. V. 62; 63
The Princess of Cozytown. Chicago: 1922. V. 65
Speedy in Oz. Chicago: 1934. V. 63
The Wishing Horse of Oz. Chicago: 1935. V. 63
The Yellow Knight of Oz. Chicago: 1930. V. 63

THOMPSON, S. P.
Notes on the De Magnete of Dr. William Gilbert. London: 1901. V. 64

THOMPSON, SEYMOUR D.
The Law of Carriers of Passengers. Illustrated by Leading Cases and Notes. St. Louis: 1880. V. 66

THOMPSON, SILVANUS P.
Dynamo-Electric Machinery: a Manual for Students of Electrotechnics. New York: 1893. V. 63
Light: Visible and Invisible. New York: 1897. V. 66

THOMPSON, SLASON
Eugene Field, a Study In Heredity and Contradictions. New York: 1901. V. 63

THOMPSON, STANBURY
The Story of Jenny Diver, a Memoir of a Famous Female Criminal. 1940. V. 67

THOMPSON, STEPHEN
Old English Homes. London: 1876. V. 62

THOMPSON, STITH
Motif-Index of Folk Literature: a Classification of Narrative Elements in Folktales, Myths, Fables, Mediaeval Romances.... Copenhagen: 1955-1958. V. 65

THOMPSON, SUSAN OTIS
American Book Design and William Morris. New York: 1977. V. 62

THOMPSON, THEOPHILUS
On the Improvement of Medicine. The Oration Delivered Before the Medical Society of London, at Their Sixty-Fifth Anniversary, March 8th, 1838. London: 1838. V. 66

THOMPSON, THOMAS
Ocellum Promentorium; or, Short Observations on the Ancient State of Holderness. Hull: 1821. V. 63

THOMPSON, THOMAS PERRONET
The Article on Free Trade, from the Westminster Review, No. XXIII for Janury 1830. London: 1830.. V. 66
The Article on the Six Acts, Especially Taxes on Literature.... London: 1830. V. 67
Slavery in the West Indies. London: 1830. V. 67

THOMPSON, W.
Recollections of Mexico. New York and London: 1846. V. 64

THOMPSON, W. R.
The Tachinids (Diptera) of Trinidad. 1961-1968. V. 66

THOMPSON, WADDY
Recollections of Mexico. New York and London: 1846. V. 63; 65; 67

THOMPSON, WILLIAM
Appeal of One Half of the Human Race, Women Against the Pretensions of the Other Half, Men to Retain them in Political and Thence in Civil and Domestic Slavery.... London: 1825. V. 63
An Illustrated Guide to Sedbergh, Garsdale and Dent.... Leeds: 1894. V. 64; 65
An Inquiry into the Principles of the Doistribution of Wealth Most Conductive to Human Happiness, applied to the Newly Proposed System of Voluntary Equality of Wealth. London: 1824. V. 63
Reminiscences of a Pioneer. San Francisco: 1912. V. 65; 67
Sedbergh Garsdale and Dent. Leeds: 1892. V. 62; 63; 64; 65; 66
Sedbergh Garsdale and Dent. Leeds: 1910. V. 65
Sedbergh Garsdale and Dent. Leeds: 1925. V. 65

THOMPSON, WILLIAM TAPPAN
Major Jones' Courtship or Adventures of a Christmas Eve. Savannah: 1850. V. 62

THOMSON, A. L.
Britain's Birds and Their Nests. London: 1910. V. 67
A New Dictionary of Birds. New York: 1964. V. 67

THOMSON, ALEX
An Enquiry into the Nature, Causes and Method of Cure, of Nervous Disorders. London: 1782. V. 65

THOMSON, ALEXANDER
Letters of a Traveller, in the Various Countries of Europe, Asia and Africa.... London: 1798. V. 63

THOMSON, ANDREW
The Hendersonian Testimony, Being Five Essays by Working Men of Glasgow on the Advantages of the Sabbath to the Working Classes. Edinburgh: 1849. V. 66

THOMSON, ANTHONY T.
A Conspectus of the Pharmacopaeias of the London, Edinburgh & Dublin Colleges of Physicians and of the U.S. Pharmacopaeia. New York: 1849. V. 66

THOMSON, CHARLES WYVILLE
The Depths of the Sea, an Account of the General Results of the Dredging Cruises of H.M.S.S. Porcupine and Lightning 1868-1870. London: 1874. V. 64
On the Echinoidea of the Porcupine Deep-Sea Dredging Expeditions. 1874. V. 67
The Voyage of the Challenger. London: 1877. V. 63
The Voyage of the Challenger. New York: 1878. V. 62; 65; 66

THOMSON, D.
Handy Book of Fruit Culture Under Glass. Edinburgh and London: 1873. V. 63

THOMSON, DAVID
Directions for Acquiring a Knowledge of the Principal Fixed Stars with Tables. London: 1824. V. 66

THOMSON, DAVID CROAL
The Water-Colour Drawings of Thomas Bewick. Chipping Campden: 1930. V. 63

THOMSON, EDWARD
The Adventures of a Carpet Bag. London: 1853. V. 65

THOMSON, HARRIET DIANA
The Witch of Melton Hill; a Tale. London: 1855. V. 67

THOMSON, J. ANSTRUTHER
Eighty Years' Reminiscences. London: 1904. V. 67

THOMSON, J. C.
Bibliography of the Writings of Alfred, Lord Tennyson. Wimbledon: 1905. V. 62

THOMSON, J. J.
Applications of Dynamics to Physics and Chemistry. London: 1888. V. 63; 67
Conduction of Electricity through Gases. Cambridge: 1903. V. 67
Conduction of Electricity through Gases. London: 1903. V. 64
Discharge of Electricity through Gases. New York: 1898. V. 63

THOMSON, JAMES
Biographical and Critical Studies. London: 1896. V. 67
The Castle of Indolence. London: 1748. V. 66
The City of Dreadful Night and Other Poems. London: 1880. V. 63
Coriolanus, a Tragedy. London: 1749. V. 63
Poems in the Scottish Dialect. Edinburgh: 1801. V. 64
The Poetical Works. London: 1768. V. 67
The Poetical Works. Glasgow: 1784. V. 63; 67
The Poetical Works. Edinburgh: 1869. V. 65
The Seasons. London: 1752. V. 62
The Seasons. Edinburgh: 1774. V. 62
The Seasons. Leipzig: 1781. V. 63
The Seasons. Glasgow: 1792. V. 63
The Seasons. London: 1793. V. 64
The Seasons. London: 1802. V. 63; 65
The Seasons. London: 1805. V. 62; 65
The Seasons. Edinburgh: 1809. V. 62
The Seasons. London: 1927. V. 62; 65
The Works. London: 1744-1738. V. 66
The Works. London: 1750. V. 63; 67

THOMSON, JOHN
An Account of the Varioloid Epidemic Which Has Lately Prevailed in Edinburgh and Other Parts of Scotland.... 1820. V. 62
Etymons of English Words. Edinburgh: 1826. V. 64
The Letters of Curtius.... Richmond: 1804. V. 63; 66

THOMSON, JOHN MAITLAND
The Register of the Great Seal of Scotland 1424-1633. Edinburgh: 1890. V. 66

THOMSON, JOHN W.
Jeb Stuart. New York and London: 1930. V. 67

THOMSON, JOSEPH
Through Masai Land.... London: 1887. V. 62
Travels in the Atlas and Southern Morocco. London: 1889. V. 62

THOMSON, JUNE
The Secret Files of Sherlock Holmes. London: 1990. V. 63; 66

THOMSON, P.
The Cabinet-Maker's Sketch Book, a Series of Original Details for Modern Furniture. Glasgow and Edinburgh: 1852-1853. V. 67

THOMSON, RICHARD
Chronicles of London Bridge, by an Antiquary. London: 1827. V. 62
An Historical Essay on the Magna Charta of King John to Which are Added the Great Charta in Latin and English. London: 1829. V. 64
Historical Notes and Other Literary Materials Now First Collected Towards the Formation of a Systematic Bibliographical Description of Medieval Illuminated Manuscripts.... London: 1858. V. 63

THOMSON, ROBERT
Divine Authority of the Bible, or, Revelation and Reason, Opposed to Sophistry and Ridicule.... Boston: 1807. V. 63
A Treatise on the Law of Bills of Exhange, Promissory-Notes, Bank- Notes, Bankers' Notes and Checks on Bankers in Scotland.... Edinburgh;: 1836. V. 66
Treatise on the Progress of Literature, and Its Effects on Society.... Edinburgh: 1834. V. 67

THOMSON, ROBERT DUNDAS
Experimental Researches on the Food of Animals, and the Fattening of Cattle. London: 1846. V. 67

THOMSON, RON
The Wildlife Game. 1992. V. 67

THOMSON, SAMUEL
A Narrative of the Life and Medical Discoveries of Samuel Thomson.... Boston: 1822. V. 62
New Guide to Health; or Botanic Family Physician. Boston: 1822. V. 64
New Guide to Health; or Botanic Family Physician. Boston: 1825. V. 64
New Guide to Health; or Botanic Family Physician. Boston: 1835. V. 66; 67

THOMSON, SPENCER
Health Resorts of Britain; and How to Profit by Them. London: 1860. V. 64

THOMSON, THOMAS
History of the Royal Society, from Its Institution to the End of the Eighteenth Century. London: 1812. V. 67
A System of Chemistry. Edinburgh: 1802. V. 62
A System of Chemistry. 1817. V. 62
Western Himalaya and Tibet. London: 1852. V. 62

THOMSON, VIRGIL
Portraits for Piano Solo - Album 2. New York: 1949. V. 65

THOMSON, W.
Treatise on Natural Philosophy. 1879-1883. V. 67

THOMSON, W. G.
Tapestry Weaving in England From the Earliest Times to the End of the XVIIIth Century. London: 1914. V. 62; 63; 64

THOMSON, WILLIAM
Atlantic Telegraph Cable. Address of Professor William Thomson, LL. D., F.R.S., Delivered Before the Royal Society of Edinburgh, Dec. 18th, 1865. London: 1866. V. 65
Mathematical and Physical Papers: Volume II: Articles LXIV-XCI. Cambridge: 1884. V. 66

THOMSON, WILLIAM T.
Notes on the Pecuniary Interests of Heirs of Entail with Calculations Regarding Such Interests in Reference to the Acts of Parliament Affecting Entails and Tables Showing the Values of Different Interests. Edinburgh: 1849. V. 65

THOMSON-GREGG, W.
A Desperate Character: a Tale of the Gold Fever. London: 1873. V. 66

THON, MELANIE RAE
Meteors in August. New York: 1990. V. 64

THORBURN, ARCHIBALD
British Birds. London: 1915-1918. V. 64; 66; 67
British Birds. 1917-1918. V. 62
British Birds. 1925. V. 67
British Birds. London: 1925-1926. V. 62; 64; 66
British Birds. London: 1926. V. 62
British Mammals. 1920-1921. V. 67
The Complete Illustrated Thorburn's Birds. New York: 1989. V. 67
Game Birds and Wild-Fowl of Great Britain and Ireland. 1923. V. 62
Game Birds and Wild-Fowl of Great Britain and Ireland. London: 1923. V. 64; 67
A Naturalist's Sketch Book. London: 1919. V. 64; 67

THOREAU, HENRY DAVID
Cape Cod. Boston: 1865. V. 64; 66; 67
Cape Cod. Boston and New York: 1893. V. 66
Collected Poems. Chicago: 1943. V. 62
Excursions. Boston: 1863. V. 64; 66
The First and Last Journeys of Thoreau. Boston: 1905. V. 64
The Heart of Thoreau's Journals. Boston and New York: 1927. V. 64; 67
Huckleberries. Iowa City: 1970. V. 66
The Journal of Henry David Thoreau. New York: 1962. V. 67
Letters to Various Persons. Boston: 1865. V. 62; 64; 66; 67
The Maine Woods. Boston: 1864. V. 63; 66
Night and Moonlight. New York: 1921. V. 67
Of Friendship. Cambridge: 1901. V. 66
Some Unpublished Letters of Henry D. and Sophia E. Thoreau. Jamaica, Queensborough: 1899. V. 66
Transmigration of the Seven Brahmans. New York: 1931. V. 62
Transmigration of the Seven Brahmans. New York: 1932. V. 62
Walden. Boston: 1854. V. 67
Walden. Boston: 1865. V. 66
Walden. London: 1886. V. 66
Walden. Boston: 1909. V. 62; 64; 66
Walden. Boston: 1936. V. 65
Walden. New York: 1936. V. 62; 65
Walden (in German). Munich: 1897. V. 64
A Week on the Concord and Merrimack Rivers. Boston and Cambridge: 1849. V. 67
A Week on the Concord and Merrimack Rivers. Boston: 1862. V. 62; 64; 65
A Week on the Concord and Merrimack Rivers. Boston: 1868. V. 65
Where I Lived and What I Lived For. Waltham St. Lawrence: 1924. V. 67
Winter. Boston and New York: 1888. V. 62
The Writings. Boston and New York: 1906. V. 62; 67
A Yankee in Canada. Boston: 1866. V. 62; 65; 66

THOREK, M.
The Human Testis. Philadelphia and London: 1924. V. 67

THOREK, PHILIP
Anatomy in Surgery. Philadelphia: 1951. V. 67

THORELL, T.
Descriptive Catalogue of the Spiders of Burma Based Upon the Collection Made by E. W. Oates. London: 1895. V. 62; 63; 66

THORER, ALBAN
De Re Medica. Basileae: 1528. V. 65; 66

THORESBY, RALPH
The Diary of Ralph Thoresby, F.R.S.... London: 1830. V. 64
Loidis and Elmete; or, an Attempt to Illustrate the Districts Described in Those Words by Bede and Supposed to Embrace the Lower Portions of Aredale and Wharfdale.... London: 1816. V. 66

THORGERSON, S.
Album Cover Album. New York: 1977. V. 65

THORIUS, RAPHAEL
Hymnus Tabaci; a Poem in Honour of Tabaco. London: 1651. V. 64; 66

THORN, ISMAY
Ins and Outs. London: 1885. V. 65

THORNBER, WILLIAM
Penny Stone; or, a Tradition of the Spanish Armanda. Preston: 1886. V. 66

THORNBURG, NEWTON
Knockover. Greenwich: 1968. V. 67

THORNBURY, GEORGE WALTER
Every Man His Own Trumpeter. London: 1858. V. 66

THORNBURY, WALTER
Haunted London. London: 1880. V. 67
The Life of J. M. W. Turner. London: 1862. V. 64; 66
Old and New London. London: 1875?. V. 62

THORNDIKE, LYNN
A History of Magic and Experimental Science. New York and London: 1923-1958. V. 62
Science and Thought in the Fifteenth Century. Studies in the History of Medicine and Surgery, Natural and Mathematical Science, Philosophy and Politics. New York: 1929. V. 64

THORNDIKE, RUSSELL
Doctor Syn Returns. London: 1935. V. 66
The Further Adventures of Doctor Syn. London: 1936. V. 66

THORNE, E.
Decorative Draperies and Upholstery. Garden City: 1937. V. 62; 65

THORNE, GUY
The Secret Service Submarine. London: 1915. V. 65

THORNE, JAMES
Rambles by Rivers. 1844-1885. V. 67

THORNE, SABINA
Of Gravity and Grace. Newark: 1982. V. 63

THORNHILL, J. B.
Adventures in Africa Under the British, Belgian and Portugese Flags. London: 1915. V. 63; 64

THORNTON, ABRAHAM
Horrible Rape and Murder!!! The Affecting Case of Mary Ashford, a Beautiful Young Virgin, Who Was Diabolically Ravished, Murdered and Thrown Into a Pit... Trial of Abraham Thornton, for the Wilful Murder...8th of August 1817. London: 1817. V. 63
Thornton's Trial!!! The Trial of Abraham Thornton, at the Warwick Summer Assize, on Friday the 8th Day of August 1817, for the Murder of Mary Ashford.... Warwick: 1817. V. 63

THORNTON, BONNELL
Plain English; in Answer to City Latin; or Critical and Political Remarks on the Latin Inscription on Laying the First Stone of the Intended New Bridge.... London: 1761. V. 62

THORNTON, CATHERINE
The Fothergills of Ravenstonedale: The Lives and Letters. London: 1905. V. 64; 65; 66

THORNTON, EDWARD
India, Its State and Prospects. London: 1835. V. 66
India, Its State and Prospects. Parbury: 1835. V. 63

THORNTON, ERNEST
Leaves from an Afghan Scrapbook. London: 1910. V. 62

THORNTON, J. P.
The Sectional System of Gentlemen's Garment Cutting, Comprising Coates, Vests, Breeches, Trousers &c. London: 1894. V. 64; 65

THORNTON, RICHARD
Recognition of Robert Frost. New York: 1937. V. 65

THORNTON, ROBERT JOHN
Elements of Botany. Part I. Classification. Part II. Terms of Science. London: 1812. V. 65; 67
A New Family Herbal, or Popular Account of the Nature and Properties of the Various Plants Used in Medicine, Diet and the Arts. London: 1810. V. 62
The Philosophy of Medicine; Or, Medical Extracts on Nature of Health and Disease.... London: 1799-1800. V. 63; 67
Temple of Flora. London: 1812. V. 62
Thornton's Temple of Flora. 1951. V. 66

THORNTON, T.
A Sporting Tour through the Northern Parts of England and a Great part of the Highlands of Scotland. London: 1804. V. 62

THORNTON, THOMAS C.
Theological Colloquies; or a Compendium of Christian Divinity.... Baltimore: 1837. V. 65

THORNTON, WILLIAM
The New, Complete and Universal History, Description and Survey of the Cities of London and Westminster.... London: 1784. V. 67

THORNTON, WILLIAM THOMAS
A Plea for Pleasant Proprietors: with the Outlines of a Plan for Their Establishment in Ireland. London: 1848. V. 66

THORNWELL, JAMES H.
Hear the South! The State of the Country. New York: 1861. V. 65
The Rights and the Duties of Masters. Charleston: 1850. V. 66
The State of the Country: an Article Republished from the Southern Presbyterian Review. Columbia: 1861. V. 63; 65

THOROTON, ROBERT
Thoroton's History of Nottinghamshire.... London: 1797. V. 63

THOROTON SOCIETY
Transactions of the Thoroton Society, an Antiquarian Society for Nottingham and Nottinghamshire. Nottingham: 1898-1981. V. 65

THOROWGOOD, THOMAS
Iewes in America, or, Probabilities that the Americans Are of that Race. London: 1650. V. 64

THORP, JACK
Pardner of the Wind. Caldwell: 1944. V. 66

THORP, JOSEPH
Early Days in the West Along the Missouri One Hundred Years Ago. Liberty: 1924. V. 62; 64; 65
Eric Gill. London: 1929. V. 67

THORP, RAYMOND W.
Doc W. F. Carver: Spirit Gun of the West. Glendale: 1957. V. 62
Indian Killer- the Sage of Liver-Eating Johnson. Indiana: 1959. V. 67

THORP, RODERICK
Nothing Lasts Forever. New York: 1979. V. 67

THORP, W. H.
John N. Rhodes, A Yorkshire Painter 1809-1842. Leeds: 1904. V. 64

THORPE, ADAM
Ulverton. London: 1992. V. 62; 65

THORPE, C.
British Marine Conchology. London: 1844. V. 62; 63

THORPE, FRANCIS NEWTON
William Pepper M.D., LL.D. (1843-1898).... Philadelphia: 1904. V. 67

THORPE, JOHN
The Tourist's Guide to the Beauties of Netherdale, and Its Adjacent Mountain Scenery.... Harrogate: 1866. V. 67

THORPE, JOHN HOUSTON
Roster of Nash County (North Carolina) Confederate Soldiers, and Copy of Edgecombe County Register. Raleigh: 1925. V. 62; 63; 65

THORPE, JOSEPH
A New Treatise of Arithmetic; Wherein the Vulgar and Decimal Fractions (Especially the latter) are Apply'd to Practice In all Its Parts, and all the Mose Useful Rules Demonstrated in the Most Easy and Concise Manner.... Exon: 1754. V. 63; 67

THORPE, MARION
Peter Pears - a Tribute on His 75th Birthday. London: 1985. V. 65

THORPE, R. S.
Andesites: Orogenic Andesites and Related Rocks. 1984. V. 67

THORPE, ROSA HARTWICK
Curfew Must Not Ring To-Night. Boston: 1883. V. 62

THORPE, T. A.
In Vitro Embryogenesis in Plants. Dordrecht: 1995. V. 66

THORPE, THOMAS B.
The Hive of The Bee Hunter. 1854. V. 64
The Master's House. A Tale of Southern Life. New York: 1854. V. 64

THORPE, THOMAS EDWARD
A Dictionary of Applied Chemistry. London: 1912-1913. V. 63

THORSON, G.
Reproduction and Larval Devleopment of Danish Marine Bottom Invertebrates. Copenhagen: 1946. V. 64

THORTON, COLONEL
A Sporting Tour Through Various Parts of France in the Year 1802.... N.P: 1805-1806. V. 64

THORY, C.
Monographie ou Histoire Naturelle du Genre Groseillier.... Paris: 1829. V. 63
Rosa Redoutea, Seu Descriptio Novae Speciaei Generis Rosae Dedicata Petro Josepho Redoute. Paris: 1817. V. 62

THOU, JACQUES AUGUSTE DE
A True Narration of the Horrible Conspiracy Against King James and the Whole Parliament of England, Commonly Called the Gun Powder Treasons.... Edinburgh: 1885. V. 66

THOUGHTS and Suggestions On Our Relations with Ireland. London: 1847. V. 66

THOUGHTS on Libels; and an Impartial Inquiry Into the Present State of the British Army; With a Few Words, In Answer to Cobbett's Critique on the Book Before It Was Published!!. London: 1809. V. 65

THOUGHTS on the Importance of the Manners of the Great to General Society. Philadelphia: 1788. V. 64

THOUGHTS on the Present Proceedings of the House of Commons. London: 1788. V. 66

THOURET, MICHEL AUGUSTIN
Rapport sur les Exhumations du Cimetiere et de l'Eglise des Saints Innocents; Lu dans le Seance de la Societe Royale de Medecine, Tenue au Louvre le 3 Mars 1789. Paris: 1789. V. 63

THRALL, HOMERS
A Pictorial History of Texas from the Earliest Visits of European Adventures to A.D. 1879. St. Louis: 1879. V. 66

THRAPP, DAN L.
Al Sieber; Chief of Scouts. Norman: 1964. V. 64; 66; 67
The Conquest of Apacheria. Norman: 1967. V. 63; 64; 67
Encyclopedia of Frontier Biography. Glendale: 1988. V. 64
General Crook and the Sierra Madre Adventure. Norman: 1972. V. 64
Victoria and the Mimbres Apaches. Norman: 1974. V. 63; 66

THRASHER, H.
The Hunter and Trapper. New York: 1868. V. 66; 67

THE THREE Bears. London: 1915. V. 63
THE THREE Bears. Portland: 1983. V. 64

THE THREE Bears Picture Book. London: 1876. V. 66

THE THREE Blind Mice. New York: 1860. V. 62

THE THREE Chances. London: 1858. V. 66

THREE Dialogues Between a Minister and One of His Hearers. Staunton: 1812. V. 65

THREE Erfurt Tales 1497-1498. N.P: 1962. V. 64

THREE Famous New Songs Called Effects of Whisky. The Valley Below. Larry O'Gaff. Paisley: 1820. V. 62; 65

THE THREE Kittens. Racine: 1935. V. 62

THREE Little Kittens. London: 1880. V. 64
THREE Little Kittens. Akron: 1910. V. 64
THREE Little Kittens. Chicago: 1943. V. 62

THE THREE Little Pigs and Goldilocks and The Three Bears. London: 1965. V. 63

THREE Painters - Basil Rakoczi, Kenneth Hall, Patrick Scott. Dublin: 1945?. V. 65

THREE Years in Central Africa Being a History of the Oxford, Cambridge, Dublin and Durham Mission. London: 1863. V. 66

THRIEPLAND, STEWART
Letters Respecting the Performances at the Theatre Royal, Edinburgh.... Edinburgh: 1800. V. 62

THRIFT, MINTO
Memoir of the Rev. Jesse Lee, with Extracts from His Journals. New York: 1823. V. 65

THROSBY, JOHN
The History and Antiquities of the Ancient Town of Leicester. Leicester: 1791. V. 63
Letter to the Earl of Leicester, on the Recent Discovery of the Roman Cloaca, or Sewer, at Leicester with Some Thoughts on Jewry Wall. Leicester: 1793. V. 66

THROWER, NORMAN J. W.
The Three Voyages of Edmond Halley in the Paramore 1698-1701. London: 1981. V. 64

THRUM, THOMAS G.
Hawaiian Folk Tales. A Collection of Native Legends. Chicago: 1907. V. 65

THUBRON, COLIN
Behind the Wall: a Journey through China. London: 1987. V. 67
A Cruel Madness. London: 1984. V. 67
Emperor. London: 1978. V. 67
The Hills of Adonis. London: 1968. V. 65
Journey into Cyprus. London: 1975. V. 63
Mirror to Damascus. London: 1967. V. 63; 65

THUCYDIDES
De Bello Peloponesiaco Libri Octo.... Oxonii: 1811. V. 66
The History of the Grecian War. London: 1676. V. 63
The History of the Grecian War. London: 1723. V. 62
The History of the Peloponnesian War. London: 1753. V. 67
History of the Peloponnesian War. Chelsea: 1930. V. 65
Thucydidis De Bello Peloponesiaco Libri Octo.... Oxonii: 1811. V. 65
Thucydidis Olori Filii, De Bello Peleponesiaco.... Frankfurt: 1594. V. 65

THUDICHUM, J. L. W.
Spirit of Cookery. London: 1895. V. 67
A Treatise on the Origin, Nature and Varieties of Wine. London: 1872. V. 64

THUNBERG, C. P.
Flora Capensis, sistens Plantas Promontorii Bonae Spei Atrices, Secundum Systema Sexuale Emendatum Redactas ad Classes.... Stuttgart: 1823. V. 63
Travels in Europe, Africa and Asia. London: 1795. V. 62
Voyage en Afrique et en Asie, Principalement au Japon.... Paris: 1794. V. 63; 65; 66

THURBER, F. B.
Coffee: from Plantation to Cup, a Brief History of Coffee Production and Consumption. New York: 1883. V. 63

THURBER, JAMES GROVER
Alarms and Diversions. New York: 1957. V. 65
The Beast in Me and Other Animals. New York: 1948. V. 64; 65; 67
Fables for Our Time and Famous Poems Illustrated. New York: 1940. V. 62
The Great Quillow. New York: 1944. V. 65
Many Moons. New York: 1943. V. 65
Many Moons. Saint Joseph: 1958. V. 63
The Middle-Aged Man on the Flying Trapeze. New York: 1935. V. 62
The 13 Clocks. New York: 1950. V. 65
The 13 Clocks. 1951. V. 67
Thurber's Men, Women and Dogs: a Book of Drawings. New York: 1943. V. 64; 65
The Wonderful O. New York: 1957. V. 65

THURLOW, EDWARD HOVEL, 2ND BARON
Select Poems. Chiswick: 1821. V. 63

THURMAN, HOWARD
Deep River. An Interpretation of Negro Spirituals. Oakland: 1945. V. 63; 64

THURMAN, WALLACE
The Blacker the Berry. New York: 1929. V. 62
Negro Life in New York's Harlem. Girard: 1928. V. 62

THURN, EVERARD F.
Among the Indians of Guiana: Being Chiefly Anthropologic Fromt he Interior of British Guiana. London: 1883. V. 65

THURNAM, JOHN
Observations and Essays on the Statistics of Insanity, and on Establishments for the Insane; to Which are Added the Statistics of The Retreat Near York. London: 1851?. V. 62

THURNEISSER ZUM THURN, LEONHARD
Zehen Bucher von Kalten, Warmen, Minerischen und Mettalischen Wassern.... Strassburg: 1612. V. 62

THURSFIELD, JAMES R.
Nelson and Other Naval Studies. New York: 1909. V. 67

THURSTON, JOSEPH
The Toilette. London: 1730. V. 63

THURSTON'S Pasadena City Directory 1937; Including Altadena, Lamanda Park and San Marino. Los Angeles: 1937. V. 62; 65

THURTELL, JOHN
The Fatal Effects of Gambling Exemplified in the Murder of Wm. Ware, and the Trial and Fate of John Thurtell, the Murderer and His Accomplices.... London: 1824. V. 63
Narrative of the Murder of Mr. Weare, at Gill's Hill, Near Aldenham, Hertfordshire, on the Evening of Friday, October 24 (1823). London: 1823. V. 63
Pierce Egan's Account of the Trial of John Hurtell and Joseph Hunt. London: 1824. V. 63

THWAITE, ANTHONY
Essays on Contemporary English Poetry - Hopkins to the Present Day. Tokyo: 1957. V. 65
Larkin at Sixty. London: 1982. V. 63

THWAITES, REUBEN GOLD
Early Western Travels 1748-1846 - Account of an Expedition from Pittsburgh to the Rocky Mountains. Cleveland: 1905. V. 66
Early Western Travels 1748-1846. Volume II. Cleveland: 1904. V. 62; 66
Early Western Travels 1748-1846. Volume III. Cleveland: 1904. V. 66
Early Western Travels 1748-1846. Volume IX. Cleveland: 1904. V. 66
Early Western Travels 1748-1846. Volumes XI and XII. Cleveland: 1905. V. 66
Early Western Travels 1748-1846. Volume XVIII. Cleveland: 1905. V. 66
Early Western Travels 1748-1846. Volume XIX. Clveland: 1905. V. 62
Early Western Travels 1748-1846. Volume XX. Cleveland: 1905. V. 62
Early Western Travels 1748-1846. Volume XXI. Cleveland: 1905. V. 66

TIBBLE, J. W.
John Clare, a Life. 1972. V. 63
The Letters of John Clare. London: 1951. V. 63

TIBBLES, T. H.
The Ponca Chiefs - an Indians Attempt to Appeal from the Tomahawk to the Courts. Boston: 1887. V. 66

TIBULLUS, ALBIUS
Elegies de Tibulle. Paris: 1798. V. 62
(Opera). Patavii: 1749. V. 65; 66

TICE, CHARLES
Disputatio Medica Inauguralis, Quaedam de Dysenteria Complectens.... Edinburgh: 1802. V. 65

TICE, HENRY ALLEN
Early Railroad Days in New Mexico. Santa Fe: 1965. V. 64

TICE, J. H.
Over the Plains and on the Mountains or, Kansas and Colorado Agriculturally, Mineralogically and Aesthetically Described. St. Louis: 1872. V. 67

TICEHURST, CLAUD B.
A History of the Birds of Suffolk. 1932. V. 67
A History of the Birds of Suffolk. London: 1932. V. 63

TICHBORNE, ROGER
The Tichborne Romance: a Full and Accurate Report of the Proceedings in the Extraordinary and Interesting Trial of Tichborne v. Lushington...for Forty Days from Wednesday May 10 to Friday July 7, 1871. Manchester: 1871. V. 63
The Tichborne Trial: The Summing Up by the Lord Chief Justice of England. London: 1874. V. 63
The Trial of Sir Roger C. D. Tichborne, Bart. in the Court of Queen's Bench at Westminster...for Perjury, Commencing Wednesday April 23, 1873.... London: 1875-1877. V. 63

TICK Tick. London: 1910. V. 65

TICKELL, JOHN
The History of the Town and Country of Kingston Upon Hull, From Its Foundation in the Reign of Edward the First to the Present Day. Hull: 1796. V. 64

TICKELL, RICHARD
An English Green Box; or, the Green Box of the R-t H-e E-d L-d Churllow, Given by the Celebrated Mrs. Harvey to Roger O'Tickle.... London: 1779. V. 62
Probationary Odes for the Laureateship; with a Preliminary Discourse, by Sir John Hawkins, Knt. London: 1785. V. 62
The Project. A Poem. London: 1778. V. 65

TICKELL, THOMAS
Oxford. A Poem. London: 1707. V. 62

TICKNOR, GEORGE
Life of William Hickling Prescott. London: 1864. V. 67

TIDCOMBE, MARIANNE
The Bookbindings of T. J. Cobden-Sanderson. A Study of His Work 1884-1893.... London: 1984. V. 62; 63; 66
The Doves Bindery. London: 1991. V. 62; 63; 64

TIDESLEY, MIRIAM L.
Sir Thomas Browne: His Skull, Portraits and Ancestry. 1923. V. 64

TIDYMAN, ERNEST
Shaft. New York: 1970. V. 64

TIEDEMAN, FREDERIC
The Anatomy of the Foetal Brain.... Edinburgh: 1826. V. 66; 67
Das Hirn des Negers mit dem des Europaers und Orang Outangs Verglichen. Heidelberg: 1837. V. 63
Tabulae Arteriarum Corporis Humani (with) Erklaruugen Seiner Abbildungen der Pulsadern des Menschlichen Korpers. Karlsruhe: 1822. V. 62

TIERNEY, GEORGE
The Real Situation of the East-India Company Considered, with Respect to Their Rights and Privileges, Under the Operation of the Late Acts of Parliament.... London: 1787. V. 65
Two Letters Addressed to the Right Hon. Henry Dundas, and the Hon. Henry Hobart.... London: 1791. V. 63

TIETZE, HANS
Titian: The Paintings and Drawings. New York: 1950. V. 63; 64

TIFFANY, ALEXANDER R.
A Treatise on the Powers and Duties of Justices of the Peace in the State of Michigan. Adrian: 1886. V. 67

TIFFANY, HERBERT T.
The Law of Real Property and Other Interests in Land. Saint Paul: 1903. V. 64

TIFFIN, TOM
John Peel. London: 1936. V. 67

TIGER Tim's Annual 1923. V. 67

TIGER Tim's Annual 1930. V. 67

TIGER Tim's Annual 1937. V. 67

TIGER Tim's Annual 1941. V. 65

TILDEN, FREEMAN
Following the Frontier with F. Jay Haynes, Pioneer Photographer of the Old West. New York: 1964. V. 63; 66

TILDESLEY, MIRIAM L.
Sir Thomas Browne: His Skull, Portraits and Ancestry. 1922. V. 64
Sir Thomas Browne: His Skull, Portraits and Ancestry. 1923. V. 66

TILGHMAN, CHRISTOPHER
In a Father's Place. New York: 1990. V. 63
Mason's Retreat. New York: 1996. V. 67

TILGHMAN, ZOE A.
Marshal of the Last Frontier - Life and Services of William Matthew (Bill) Tilghman, for 50 Years One of the Greatest Peace Officers of the West. Glendale: 1949. V. 62; 64; 66
Marshal of the Last Frontier - Life and Services of William Matthew (Bill) Tilghman, For Fifty Years One of the Greatest Peace Officers of the West. Glendale: 1964. V. 65
Quanah, the Eagle of the Comanches. Oklahoma City: 1938. V. 63

TILLESTON, MARY WILDER
Tender and True. Poems of Love. Boston: 1892. V. 67

TILLICH, PAUL
The Religious Situation. New York: 1932. V. 67

TILLINGHAST, OTIS H.
Mr. President and the Gentlemen of the Court. N.P: 1859. V. 67

TILLMAN, LYNNE
Haunted Houses. New York: 1987. V. 65

TILLMANNS, HERMANN
The Principles of Surgery and Surgical Pathology General Rules Governing Operations and the Application of Dressings. New York: 1897. V. 67

TILLOTSON, F. H.
How to Be a Detective. Kansas City: 1909. V. 64

TILLOTSON, JOHN
Lives of Illustrious Women of England. London: 1853. V. 63
Lives of Illustrious Women of England. London: 1855. V. 65
A Sermon Preached at the Funeral of the Reverend Mr. Thomas Gouge, the 4th of November 1681. London: 1682. V. 64

TILLOTT, P. M.
A History of Yorkshire: The City of York. London: 1961. V. 63
A History of Yorkshire: The City of York. London: 1982. V. 63

TILLYARD, AELFRIDA
Cambridge Poets 1900-1913. An Anthology. Cambridge: 1913. V. 65

TILMAN, H. W.
The Ascent of Nanda Devi. 1937. V. 63; 65
China to Chitral. 1951. V. 63; 65
China to Chitral. Cambridge: 1951. V. 62; 63; 64; 66
Mischief Among the Penguins. 1961. V. 63; 65
Mischief in Patagonia. Cambridge: 1957. V. 62
Mount Everest 1938. 1948. V. 63; 64; 65
Nepal Himalaya. 1952. V. 63; 65
Snow on the Equator. 1937. V. 63; 65
Two Mountains and a River. 1949. V. 65
Two Mountains and a River. Cambridge: 1949. V. 62
When Men and Mountains Meet. 1946. V. 63; 65
When Men and Mountains Meet. Cambridge: 1946. V. 67

TILNEY, FREDERICK
The Brain from Ape to Man: A Contribution to the Study of the Evolution and Development of the Human Brain. New York: 1928. V. 65
Form and Functions of the Central Nervous System. New York: 1938. V. 67
The Master of Destiny: a Biography of the Brain. New York: 1930. V. 65

TILSLEY, HUGH
A Treatise on the Stamp Laws in Great Britain and Ireland.... London: 1847. V. 63

TILSON, MERCER V.
The Tilson Genealogy from Edmond Wilson at Plymouth, N.E. 1638-1911. Plymouth: 1911. V. 65

TILTON, CECIL G.
William Chapman Ralston; Courageous Builder. Boston: 1935. V. 63

TILTON, FRANCIS THEODORE
History of the Tilton Family in America. Clifton: 1927-1930. V. 63; 66

TILTON, THEODORE
The Sin of Sins. New York: 1871. V. 65

TIMBS, J.
A Picturesque Promenade Round Dorking, in Surrey. London: 1822. V. 63

TIMBS, JOHN
Ancestral Stories and Traditions of Great Families, Illustrative of English History. London: 1869. V. 65
Anecdote Biography. William Hogarth, Sir Joshua Reynolds, Thomas Gainsborough, Henry Fuseli, Sir Thomas Lawrence and J. M. W. Turner. London: 1860. V. 65
Something for Everybody. London: 1861. V. 65

TIMBURY, JANE
The Male-Coquette; or the History of the Hon. Edward Astell. London: 1770. V. 62

TIMEPIECES Collected by Quing Emperors in the Palace of the Forbidden City, Beijin. Hong Kong: 1995. V. 67

TIMERMAN, JACOBO
Prisoner Without a Name, a Cell Without a Number. New York: 1981. V. 67

TIMLIN, WILLIAM M.
The Ship That Sailed to Mars. London: 1923. V. 64; 65

TIMMONS, WILBERT H.
Morelos of Mexico: Priest, Soldier, Statesman. El Paso: 1963. V. 64

TIMOSHENKO, STEPHEN P.
History of Strength of Materials. New York: 1953. V. 62; 63

TIMPERLEY, C. H.
A Dictionary of Printers and Printing. London: 1839. V. 66
Encyclopedia of Literary and Typographical Anecdote.... London: 1842. V. 63; 64

TINBERGEN, NIKO
The Herring Gull's World. London: 1953. V. 62

TINDALE, THOMAS KEITH
Handmade Papers of Japan. Rutland: 1952. V. 64; 66

TINDALL, JOHN
Tindall's Yorkshire Farriery, Being a Treatise on the Diseases of Horses.... Huddersfield: 1814. V. 62

TINDALL, JOHN N.
Makers of Oklahoma. Guthrie: 1905. V. 63; 66

TINEL, J.
Nerve Wounds Symptomatology of Peripheral Nerve Lesions Caused by War Wounds. London: 1918. V. 66

TING, WALASSE
1(cent) Life. Bern: 1964. V. 66

TINGLEY, ELBERT R.
Poco Loco. Blair: 1900. V. 66

TINKER, CHAUNCEY BREWSTER
Addresses Commemorating the One Hundredth Anniversary of the Birth of William Morris Delivered Before the Yale Library Associates in the Sterling Memorial Library, XXIX October MCMXXXIV. N.P: 1935. V. 66

TINKER, EDWARD LAROCQUE
The Horsemen of the Americas. Austin: 1967. V. 64; 66
The Horsemen of the Americas. Austin: 1968. V. 67

TINKERBELL Tales. London: 1905. V. 62

TINKLE, LON
An American Original: the Life of J. Frank Dobie. Boston: 1978. V. 67
J. Frank Dobie: the Makings of an Ample Mind. Austin: 1968. V. 64; 67

TINSLEY, WILLIAM
Random Recollections of an Old Publisher. Bournemouth: 1900. V. 65

TIPHAIGNE DE LA ROCHE, CHARLES FRANCOIS
Giphantia; or, a View of What Has Passed, What is Now Passing, and, During the Present Century.... London: 1761. V. 62; 63

TIPPING, H. AVRAY
English Homes - Period IV - Volume I Late Stuart 1649-1714. London: 1929. V. 62

TIPPINS, L. R.
Modern Rifle Shooting in Peace, War and Sport. 1900. V. 62; 63; 66

TIRELLI, VITIGE
Schizofrenie: Bolletino Trimestrale del Primo Centro Provinciale di Studio della Demenze Precoce. Racconigi: 1931-1939. V. 65

TISA, JOHN
The Palette and the Flame. New York: 1979. V. 67

TISSANDIER, GASTON
Popular Scientific Recreations in Natural Philosophy, Astronomy, Geology, Chemistry, etc. London. V. 66

TISSOT, J. JAMES
The Life of Our Lord Jesus Christ. London: 1897. V. 62; 66

TISSOT, SAMUEL AUGUSTE ANDRE DAVID
An Essay on Diseases Incident to Literary and Sedentary Persons with Proper Rules for Preventing Their Fatal Consequences, and Instructions for Their Cure. London: 1769. V. 65
Onanism or a Treatise Upon the Disorder of Masturbation. London: 1776. V. 65
Traite Des Nerfs et de Leurs Maladies. Lausanne: 1784. V. 66; 67
A Treatise on the Diseases Produced by Onanism. New York: 1832. V. 63

TISSOT, SIMON ANDRE
Advice to People in General with Respect to Their Health. Dublin: 1774. V. 65
Advice to the People in General, with Regard to Their Health.... London: 1771. V. 65

TISSOT, SIMON ANDRE *continued*
Onanism; or, a Treatise Upon the Disorders Produced by Mastrubation.... London: 1767. V. 62

TITELMANN, FRANZ
Naturalis Philosphiae Compendium sive De Consideratione Rerum Naturalium Libri XII. Antverpiae: 1570. V. 62

TITI, FILIPPO
Descrizione Delle Pitture, Sculture e Architeture. Roma: 1763. V. 66

TITIEV, MISCHA
The Hopi Indians of Old Oraibi: Change and Continuity. Ann Arbor: 1972. V. 64
Old Oraibi: a Study of the Hopi Indians of Third Mesa. Cambridge: 1944. V. 64; 66

TITON, JEFF TODD
Early Downhome Blues. A Musical and Cultural Analysis. Urbana: 1977. V. 62; 67

TITOV, GHERMAN
Goluyaye Moye Planeta. (My Blue Planet). Moscow: 1973. V. 67

TITTSWORTH, W. G.
Outskirt Episodes. Avoca: 1927. V. 64

TITUS, EVE
Anatole and the Cat. New York: 1957. V. 64

TIZAC, H. D'ARDENNE DE
Animals in Chinese Art. London: 1923. V. 66

TIZARD, T. H.
Explorations of the Faroe Channel...in HM's hired ship "Knight Errant". Edinburgh: 1882. V. 67

TJADER, RICHARD
The Big Game of Africa. 1910. V. 63; 64

TO Doctor R. Essays Here Collected and Published in Honor of the Seventieth Birthday of Dr. A. S. W. Rosenbach, July 22, 1946. Philadelphia: 1946. V. 63

TO Mark Van Doren, May 22, Poet Scholar Teacher Master of Learning and of Life in Many Forms. New York: 1945. V. 64

TO Remember Gregg Anderson: Tributes by Members of the Columbiad, the Rounce and Coffin Club, the Roxburghe Club and the Zamorano Club. N.P: 1949. V. 64

TO Remember Ray Frederick Coyle: Six Reproductions of His Work. San Francisco: 1926. V. 64

TO RIOTERS and Incediaries. A Letter Containing the Last Advice of a Rioter to Two of His Former Associates. London: 1830. V. 66

TOBIE, EDWARD P.
First Maine Cavalry 1861-1865. Boston: 1887. V. 65

TOBLER, DOUGLAS F.
The History of the Mormons in Photographs and Text: 1830 to the Present. New York: 1987. V. 67

TOBLER, JOHN
The South Carolina and Georgia Almanac for the Year of Our Lord 1789. Charleston: 1788. V. 63

TOCKER, MARY ANN
Trial of Mary Ann Tocker, for an Alledged Libel on Mr. R. Gurney. London: 1818. V. 63; 65

TOCQUEVILLE, ALEXIS CHARLES HENRI MAURICE CLEREL DE
Correspondence and Conversations of Alexis de Tocqueville with Nassau William Senior from 1834 to 1859. London: 1872. V. 64
De La Democratie en Amerique.... Bruxelles: 1840. V. 62
Democracy in America. London: 1862. V. 65

TODA, KENJI
Japanese Scroll Painting. Chicago: 1935. V. 62; 64

TODD, CHARLES
A Test of Wills. New York: 1996. V. 63; 64; 65; 66; 67

TODD, CHARLES W.
Woodville; or, the Anchoret Reclaimed. Knoxville: 1832. V. 64; 66

TODD, F. S.
Natural History of the Waterfowl. Vista and San Diego: 1996. V. 67
Waterfowl: Ducks, Geese and Swans of the World. San Diego: 1979. V. 64

TODD, HENRY J.
Illustrations of the Lives and Writings of Gower and Chaucer, Collected from Authentick Documents. London: 1810. V. 64

TODD, J. E.
A Preliminary Report on the Geology of South Dakota. Sioux Falls: 1894. V. 65

TODD, JAMES HENTHORN
Descriptive Remarks on Illuminations in Certain Ancient Irish Manuscripts. 1869. V. 63; 66
Descriptive Remarks on Illuminations in Certain Ancient Irish Manuscripts. London: 1869. V. 62

TODD, MABEL LOOMIS
A Cycle of Sunsets. Boston: 1910. V. 64

TODD, MARGARET
The Life of Sophia Jex-Blake. London: 1918. V. 66

TODD, RUTHVEN
Over the Mountain. London: 1939. V. 65
The Planet in My Hand. Twelve Poems. London: 1944. V. 62; 66
Ten Poems. Edinburgh: 1940. V. 62; 64

TODD, W. B.
A Directory of Printers and Others in Allied Trades London and Vicinity 1800-1840. London: 1972. V. 63
Tauchnitz International Editions in English 1841-1955. A Bibliographical History. New York: 1988. V. 62

TODD, W. E. C.
Birds of the Labrador Peninsula and Adjacent Areas.... Tokyo: 1936. V. 63
Birds of Western Pennsylvania. Pittsburgh: 1940. V. 64; 67

TODHUNTER, ISAAC
A History of the Progress of the Calculus of Variations During the Nineteenth Century. Cambridge and London: 1861. V. 65; 66
A History of the Theory of Elasticity and of the Strength of Materials, from Galilei to the Present Time. Cambridge: 1886-1893. V. 62
William Whewell, D.D. Master of Trinity College, Cambridge. London: 1876. V. 65

TODHUNTER, JOHN
An Essay in Search of a Subject. 1904. V. 63; 66
Life of Patrick Sarsfield, Earl of Lucan. 1895. V. 67
Ye Minutes of Ye CLXXVIIth Meeting of Ye Sette of Odd Volumes, Extracted from Ye Diary of Samuel Pepys. 1896. V. 62; 67

TOIBIN, COLM
New Writing from Ireland. Winchester: 1994. V. 63

THE TOKEN. Boston: 1828. V. 64

TOKLAS, ALICE B.
Eight Models for Pierre Balmain. Paris: 1946. V. 66
What is Remembered. New York, Chicago, S.F: 1963. V. 65

TOKUNAGA, S.
Natural Science Research of the First Scientific Expedition to Manchoukuo. Tokyo: 1936. V. 63

TOLAND, JOHN
The Life of John Milton.... London: 1761. V. 62; 63

TOLD, SILAS
An Account of the Life and Dealings of God with Silas Told, late Preacher of the Gospel. Salford: 1805. V. 64

TOLEDANO, HENRY
Goreyography: a Divers Compendium of and Price Guide to the Works of Edward Gorey. San Francisco: 1996. V. 64

TOLFREY, F.
Jones' Guide to Norway. 1994. V. 67

TOLKIEN, JOHN RONALD REUEL
The Adventures of Tom Bombadil and Other Verses from the Red Book. London: 1962. V. 63; 64; 66
The Devil's Coach Horses. London: 1925. V. 62; 67
Farmer Giles of Ham. London: 1949. V. 63
The Father Christmas Letters. London: 1976. V. 67
The Fellowship of the Ring, Being the First Part of the Lord of the Rings. London: 1953. V. 64
The Hobbit. New York: 1977. V. 66
The Letters of J. R. R. Tolkien. London: 1981. V. 64
The Lord of the Rings. London: 1966. V. 65
Middle English Losenger. Paris: 1953. V. 62; 67
The Road Goes Ever On. London: 1968. V. 66
The Silmarillion. London: 1977. V. 64
Tree and Leaf. Boston: 1965. V. 64
The Two Towers. Boston: 1955. V. 63

TOLLEMACHE, EMMA
In the Light - Poems. London: 1948. V. 63

TOLLER, ERNST
Brokenbow. London: 1925. V. 64
Pastor Hall: a Play. London: 1939. V. 66
Die Wandlung. Potsdam: 1919. V. 67

TOLLER, SAMUEL
A Treatise of the Law of Tithes.... London: 1808. V. 65

TOLSTOI, LEV NIKOLAEVICH
Anna Karenina. Moscow: 1878. V. 63
Anna Karenina. New York: 1886. V. 64; 65
Anna Karenina. Cambridge: 1951. V. 65
Anna Karenina. New York: 1951. V. 63; 64
Resurrection. London: 1900. V. 62; 66
Voina i Mir. Moscow: 1868-1869. V. 63
War and Peace. Glasgow: 1938. V. 64
War and Peace. New York: 1938. V. 62

TOM Thumb. London: 1880. V. 65
TOM Thumb. New York: 1880. V. 64

TOM Thumb's Exhibition, Being an Account of Many Valuable and Surprising Curiosities which He Has Collected in the Course of His Travels; for the Instruction and Amusement of the British Youth. London: 1815. V. 63

TOM Thumb's Folio; or, a New Penny Play-thing for Little Giants.... 1825. V. 66

TOMASCHEK, WENZEL JOHANN
Sechs Gesaenge aus C. E. Eberts Bohmilchnationalem Epos Wlasta mit Begleitung des Piano-Forte. 1820. V. 65

TOMBAUGH, CLYDE
Out of the Darkness: the Planet Pluto. Harrisburg: 1981. V. 67

TOMBLESON, THOMAS
Thombleson's Thames. London: 1835. V. 62

TOMBLESON, WILLIAM
Tombleson's Views of the Rhine. 1832. V. 66; 67

TOMITA, KOJIRO
Portfolio of Chinese Paintings in the Museum (of Fine Arts, Boston) (Han to Sung Periods). Cambridge: 1933. V. 62

TOMKINS, CALVIN
Paul Strand: Sixty Years of Photographs. Millerton: 1979. V. 63

TOMKINS, THOMAS
Poems on Various Subjects, Selected to Enforce the Practice of Virtue. London: 1780. V. 66

TOMKINSON, G. S.
A Select Bibliography of the Principal Modern Presses Public and Private in Great Britain and Ireland. London: 1928. V. 62

TOMKINSON, WILLIAM H.
Caroline, or the Happy Marriage.... London: 1795. V. 62

TOMLINS, THOMAS EDLYNE
A Familiar Explanation of the Law of Wills and Condicils, and the Law of Executors and Administrators.... London: 1796. V. 62

TOMLINSON, CHARLES
Cyclopaedia of Useful Arts, Mechanical and Chemical, Manufactures, Mining and Engineering. London: 1854. V. 62; 65
The Necklace. Eynsham: 1955. V. 62
Relations and Contraries. Aldington, Kent: 1951. V. 62; 67

TOMLINSON, DAVID
African Wildlife in Art. 1991. V. 62; 63; 64; 66; 67

TOMLINSON, HENRY MAJOR
All Our Yesterdays. London: 1930. V. 64; 65; 67
A Brown Owl. 1928. V. 67
Gallion's Reach - a Romance. London: 1927. V. 65
Illusion: 1915. London: 1929. V. 64
London River. New York: 1921. V. 64
Norman Douglas. London: 1931. V. 64
Out of Soundings. London: 1931. V. 64
The Sea and the Jungle. London: 1930. V. 62; 64; 67
The Snows of Helicon. London: 1933. V. 64
Thomas Hardy. New York: 1929. V. 62; 63; 64; 66

TOMLINSON, JOHN
The Etymology of Our District (Doncaster) with Historical Paraphrases. London: 1875. V. 64
The Level of Hatfield Chace and Parts Adjacent. Doncaster: 1882. V. 63
Some Interesting Yorkshire Scenes. London: 1865. V. 63

TOMLINSON, W.
Bookcloth 1823-1980. A Study of Early Use and the Rise of Manufacture, Winterbottom's Dominance of the Trade in Britain and America.... Stockport, Cheshire: 1996. V. 62

TOMPKINS, D. A.
Cotton and Cotton Oil. Charlotte: 1901. V. 63; 64; 67

TOMPKINS, EDMUND P.
Rockbridge County, Virginia: an Informal History. Richmond: 1952. V. 64

TOMPKINS, FRANK
Chasing Villa. Harrisburg: 1934. V. 65

TOMPKINS, HAMILTON BULLOCK
Burr Bibliography. A List of Books Relating to Aaron Burr. Brooklyn: 1892. V. 67

TOMS, W.
Thirty-Six New and Practical Designs for Chairs Adapted for the Drawing and Dining Room, Parlour and Hall.... Bath: 1830. V. 64

TONER, J. M.
Address Before the Rocky Mountain Medical Associaton June 6, 1877. Washington: 1877. V. 67

TONEY, MARCUS B.
The Privations of a Private. Nashville: 1905. V. 62; 65
The Privations of a Private. Nashville and Dalls: 1907. V. 65

TONGUE, CORNELIUS
Records of the Chase and Memoirs of Celebrated Sportsmen.... London: 1854. V. 63

TONGUE, MARGARET
A Book of Kinds. Iowa City: 1958. V. 67

TONNA, CHARLOTTE ELIZABETH
Derry, a Tale of the Revolution. London: 1833. V. 63
The Glory of Israel; or, Letters to Jewish Children on the Early History of Their Nation. Philadelphia: 1843. V. 64
Personal Recollections. London: 1841. V. 65
The Rockite; an Irish Story. London: 1846. V. 66

TOOGOOD, CORA CASSARD
A Child's Prayer. Philadelphia: 1928. V. 63

TOOKE, JOHN HORNE
A Letter to a Friend, on the Reported Marriage of His Royal Highness the Prince of Wales. London: 1787. V. 62; 63; 66
A Letter to John Dunning, Esq. London: 1778. V. 62
A Letter to Lord Ashburton for Mr. Horne, Occasioned by Last Tuesday's Debate in the House of Commons, on Mr. Pitt's Motion. London: 1782. V. 63
Two Pair of Portraits, Presented to all Unbiassed (sic) Electors of Great Britain and Especially to the Electors of Westminster. London: 1788. V. 63

TOOKE, THOMAS
A Letter to Lord Grenville, On the Effects Ascribed to the Resumption of Cash Payments on the Value of the Currency. London: 1829. V. 64
On the Currency in Connexion with the Corn Trade; and On the Corn Laws. London: 1829. V. 64

TOOKE, WILLIAM
View of the Russian Empire, During the Reign of Catharine the Second, and to the Close of the Eighteenth Century.... London: 1800. V. 62; 66

TOOLE, JOHN KENNEDY
A Confederacy of Dunces. Baton Rouge: 1980. V. 65

TOOLE-STOTT, RAYMOND
A Bibliography of English Conjuring 1569-1876. Derby: 1976. V. 62
Circus and Allied Arts. A World Bibliography 1500-1982. Derby & Chippenham: 1958-1992. V. 65

TOOLEY, MICHAEL J.
Gertrude Jekyll, Artist, Gardener, Craftswoman. Witton-le-Wear: 1984. V. 64

TOOLEY, R. V.
Dictionary of Map Makers. Tring: 1978. V. 62
English Books with Coloured Plates 1790 to 1860.... London: 1973. V. 63

TOOMBS, SAMUEL
New Jersey Troops in the Gettysburg Campaign from June to to July 31, 1863. Orange: 1888. V. 63; 66

TOOMER, JEAN
Essentials. Definitions and Aphorisms. Chicago: 1931. V. 62; 64
The Flavor of Man. Philadelphia: 1949. V. 64; 65

TOONE, WILLIAM
A Glossary and Etymological Dictionary of Obsolete and Uncommon Words, Antiquated Phrases.... London: 1834. V. 64
The Magistrate's Manual or a Summary of the Duties and Power of a Justice of the Peace.... London: 1813. V. 65
The Magistrate's Manual; or a Summary of the Duties and Powers of Justice of the Peace.... London: 1817. V. 63

TOPFFER, RUDOLPHE
The Adventures of Mr. Obadiah Oldbuck.... London: 1846. V. 67

TOPHAM, CAPTAIN
The Remarkable Life of John Elwes, Esq. London: 1845. V. 63

TOPHAM, EDWARD
The Life of Mr. Elwes, the Celebrated Miser. London: 1796. V. 62

TOPHAM, JOHN
An Epitome of Chemistry.... London: 1822. V. 65

TOPHAM, W. F.
The Lakes of England. London: 1869. V. 62; 66; 67

TOPOLSKI, FELIKS
Portrait of G. B. S. London: 1946. V. 66

TOPONCE, ALEXANDER
Reminiscences of Alexander Toponce, Pioneer 1839-1923. Ogden: 1923. V. 62; 65

TOPP, CHESTER W.
Victorian Yellowbacks and Paperbacks 1849-1905. Volume I: George Routledge. Denver: 1993. V. 66
Victorian Yellowbacks and Paperbacks 1849-1905. Volume I: George Routledge. Volume II: Ward & Lock. Denver: 1993-1995. V. 62
Victorian Yellowbacks and Paperbacks 1849-1905. Volume II. Ward and Lock. Denver: 1995. V. 66
Victorian Yellowbacks and Paperbacks. 1849-1905. Volume III. Hotten, Chatto, & Windus. Denver: 1997. V. 62; 63; 64; 66
Victorian Yellowbacks and Paperbacks, 1849-1905. Volume IV. Frederick Warne and Co. and Sampson Low and Co. Denver: 1999. V. 64; 66

TOPSELL, EDWARD
The Fowles of Heaven or History of Birdes. Austin: 1972. V. 64
The Historie of Fore-Footed Beastes. 1607. V. 65
The Historie of Foure-Footed Beastes. London: 1607. V. 66
The History of Four-Footed Beasts and Serpents.... London: 1658. V. 66

TORCH - Summer 1970. 1970. V. 63

TORCHIANA, H. A.
California Gringos. San Francisco: 1930. V. 62; 65

TORCZYNER, HARRY
Magritte: Ideas and Images. New York: 1977. V. 62; 63; 64

TORKILDSEN, ARNE
Ventriculocisternostomy. A Palliative Operation in Different Types of Non-Communicating Hydrocephalus. Oslo: 1947. V. 66

TORKINGTON, RICHARD
Ye Oldest Diarie of Englysshe Travell: Being the Hitherto Unpubished Narrative of the Pilgrimage of Sir Richard Torkington to Jerusalem in 1517. London: 1883. V. 67

TORNER, JOHANNES
Dissertationem Publicarum De Pyrobolica Festiva.... Upsala: 1738. V. 62

TORNIELLO, FRANCESCO
L'Alfabeto Di Francesco Torniello Da Novara (1517). Verona: 1970. V. 65

TORQUEMADA, JUAN DE, CARDINAL
Monarquia Indiana. Mexico: 1969. V. 63
Sume de Ecclesia Domini Joannis de Turrecremata; Cardinalis Sancti Sixti Vulgo Nuncapati Repertosiu seu Tabula Alphabetica. Colophon: 1496. V. 66

TORR, JAMES
The Antiquities of York City, and the Civil Government Thereof.... York: 1719. V. 67

TORRANCE, JARED SIDNEY
The Descendants of Lewis Hart and Anne Elliott. Los Angeles: 1923. V. 63; 65

TORRE, VINCENT
Forty Four Woodcuts of the Nude. New York: 1978. V. 64
Rhymes and Fables. New York: 1996. V. 64
Sixty-Two Limericks. New York: 1994. V. 64
Songs and Fables. New York: 1990. V. 64
Tales and Fables. New York: 1987. V. 64
Verse and Fables. New York: 1993. V. 64

TORRE FARFAN, FERNANDO DE LA
Fiestas de la S. Iglesia Metropolitana y Patriarcal de Sevilla, al Nuevo Culto del Senor Rey S. Fernando el Tercero de Castilla y de Leon. Seville: 1671. V. 62

TORRENCE, BRUCE
Hollywood: the First 100 Years. Hollywood: 1979. V. 65

TORRENCE, CLAYTON
Winston of Virginia and Allied Families. Richmond: 1927. V. 64

TORRENCE, RIDGELY
Granny Maumee. The Rider of Dreams. Simon the Cyrenian. Plays for a Negro Theatre. New York: 1917. V. 63

TORRENS, HENRY
By His Majesty's Command. Field Exercise and Evolutions of the Army. London: 1824. V. 65

TORRENS, W. M.
History of Cabinets from the Union with Scotland to the Acquisition of Canada and Bengal. 1894. V. 67
Twenty Years in Parliament. London: 1893. V. 64

TORRES BOLLO, DIEGO DE
Relatione Breve del P. Diego de Torres...Procuratore della Prouincia del Peru.... Rome: 1603. V. 62

TORREY, CHARLES T.
Home! Or the Pilgrims Faith Revived. Salem: 1845. V. 63

TORREY, J.
Flora of the State of New York.... Albany: 1843. V. 64

TORREY, JESSE
Portraiture of Domestic Slavery in the United States.... Ballston Spa: 1818. V. 63; 66

TORRIANO, GIO
The Italian Tutor or a New and Most Compleat Italian Grammer (sic).... London: 1640. V. 64

TORROJA, EDUARDO
The Structures...an Autobiography of Engineering Accomplishment. New York: 1958. V. 62; 65

TORTI, FRANCESCO
Ad Criticam Dissertationem de Abusu Chinae Chinae Mutienensibus medicis Perperam Objecto a...Bernardino Ramazzino.... Modena: 1715. V. 62

TORY, GEOFFROY
Champ Fleury. New York: 1927. V. 62; 63

TOTH, KARL
Woman and Rococo in France. Philadelphia: 1931. V. 63

TOTTEL'S Miscellany (1557-1587). Cambridge: 1928-1929. V. 63

TOTTI, POMPILIO
Ritratto di Roma Antica. Rome: 1627. V. 67

A TOUCH of the Times, a New Ballad. London: 1740. V. 66

TOUCH and Go: A Book of Changing Pictures. London: 1895. V. 65

TOUHY, FRANK
Yeats. 1976. V. 66

TOULMIN, CAMILLA
Landmarks of a Literary Life 1820-1892. London: 1893. V. 67
Lays and Legends Illustrative of English Life. London: 1845. V. 65

TOULMIN, HARRY
A Description of Kentucky, in North America.... London: 1792. V. 63; 66

TOUR In Holland in the Year 1819. London: 1823. V. 64

THE TOUR of Doctor Prosody, in Search of the Antique and Picturesque, through Scotland, the Hebrides, the Orkney and Shetland Islands. London and Edinburgh: 1821. V. 62; 64

THE TOURIST'S Guide, Being a Concise History and Description of Ripon, Studley Royal, Fountains, Markenfield Hall, Brimham Rocks, Hackfall, Swinton, masham, Tanfield, Norton Conyers, Newby Hal, Boroughbridge, Aldborough, Ripley, Harrogate.... Ripon: 1838. V. 65

TOURIST'S Guide to Scarborough and Its Neighbourhood. London: 1880. V. 62

TOURNEFORT, JOSEPH PITTON DE
A Voyage into the Levant.... London: 1718. V. 67

TOURNIER, MICHEL
Gemini. London: 1981. V. 64

TOURNON, CARLO TOMMASO MAILLARD DE
Relazione del Viaggio dell'Isola di Tenarif Nelle Canarie Fino a Pondiceri Nella Costa di Coromandel. Rome: 1704. V. 67

TOURTEL, MARY
The Monster Rupert. London: 1949. V. 67
Rupert Stories, Verse and Drawings.... London. V. 67

TOUSEY, THOMAS G.
Military History of Carlisle and Carlisle Barracks. Richmond: 1939. V. 67

TOUSSAINT, FRANCOIS V.
Manners. London: 1749. V. 63
Manners. London: 1752. V. 65

TOUSSAINT, FRANZ
The Garden of Caresses. Waltham St. Lawrence: 1934. V. 64

TOUSSANINT-SAMAT, JEAN
Shoes That Had Walked Twice. Philadelphia: 1933. V. 65

TOVEY, DUNCAN C.
Gray and His Friends - Letters and Relics.... Cambridge: 1890. V. 64

TOWER, CHARLEMAGNE
Tower Genealogy. Cambridge: 1891. V. 63

TOWER, DONALD B.
The Nervous System. New York: 1975. V. 65

TOWER, F. B.
Illustrations of the Croton Aqueduct. New York and London: 1843. V. 65

THE TOWER of Babel. West Burke: 1975. V. 64

TOWERS, ALTON
Bunny's Tale of Adventure by Land and Sea. London: 1907. V. 65

TOWERS, JOSEPH
A Letter to the Rev. John Wesley: In Answer to His Late Pamphlet, Entitled "Free Thoughts on the Present State of Public Affairs". London: 1771. V. 64

TOWLE, CHARLES L.
Railroad Postmarks of the United States 1861 to 1886. 1968. V. 66

THE TOWN and Country Magazine, or Universal Repository of Knowledge, Instruction & Entertainment. London: 1773. V. 67

TOWNE, ARTHUR E.
Old Prairie Days. Otsego: 1941. V. 62; 65

TOWNE, ROBERT D.
Little Johnny and the Teddy Bears. Chicago: 1907. V. 62; 65
The Teddy Bears in Fun and Frolic. Chicago: 1908. V. 65

TOWNE, THOMAS
The Automatical Camera-Obscura: Exhibiting Scenes from Nature, Delineated by an Unerring Pencil, and Preserved in Ancient Port Folio.... London: 1821-1823. V. 66; 67

TOWNES, H.
Ichneumon-Flies of America North of Mexico. Washington: 1959-1962. V. 64

TOWNSEND, C. W.
The Birds of Essex County, Massachusetts. Cambridge: 1905. V. 67
In Audubon's Labrador. Boston and New York: 1918. V. 63
A Labrador Spring. Boston: 1910. V. 64

TOWNSEND, CHARLES
Winchester, and a Few Other Compositions. Winchester: 1835. V. 67

TOWNSEND, CHARLES E.
Essays on Mind, Matter, Forces, Theology, Etc. (and Sequel). New York: 1876-1878. V. 67

TOWNSEND, F.
Flora of Hampshire, Including the Isle of Wight. 1883. V. 62

TOWNSEND, F. TRENCH
Ten Thousand Miles of Travel, Sport and Adventure. London: 1869. V. 64; 67

TOWNSEND, FORBES
Transatlantic and Coastwise Steamship Funnel Marks, House-Flags and Night Signals.... New York: 1874. V. 62

TOWNSEND, GEORGE ALFRED
Campaigns of the Non-Combatant and His Romaunt Abroad During the War. New York: 1866. V. 65

TOWNSEND, GEORGE FLYER
The Town and Borough of Leonminster.... Leonminster: 1865. V. 63

TOWNSEND, JOHN
Memoirs of the Rev. John Townsend, Founder of the Asylum for the Deaf and Dumb and of the Congregational School. Boston: 1831. V. 62

TOWNSEND, LUTHER T.
History of the Sixteenth Regiment, New Hampshire Volunteers. Washington: 1897. V. 63

TOWNSEND, W.
The Biography of Pope Pius XI. 1930. V. 63

TOWNSEND, WILLIAM C.
The Lives of Twelve Eminent Judges of the Last and of the Present Century. London: 1846. V. 63; 64
Modern State Trials. London: 1850. V. 63

TOWNSEND, WILLIAM H.
Lincoln and the Bluegrass. Slavery and Civil War in Kentucky. Lexington: 1955. V. 63; 65

TOWNSEND, WILLIAM THOMPSON
The Cricket on the Hearth. London: 1860. V. 62

TOWNSHEND, CHAUNCEY HARE
Facts in Mesmerism, or Animal Magnetism with Reasons for a Dispassionate Inquiry Into It.... Boston: 1841. V. 66

TOWNSHEND, FRANK
Earth. London: 1929. V. 67

TOWNSHEND, R. B.
Last Memories of a Tenderfoot. London: 1926. V. 67
A Tenderfoot in Colorado. London: 1923. V. 64
The Tenderfoot in New Mexico. London: 1923. V. 63; 64
The Tenderfoot in New Mexico. London & New York: 1924. V. 67

THE TOWNSHIP of Sandwich (Past and Present). Windsor: 1909. V. 65

THE TOY Maker: How a Tree Became A Toy Village. New York: 1935. V. 62

TOYE, NINA
The Twice Murdered Man. London: 1935. V. 67

TOYE, STANLEY
Cyanide. London: 1940. V. 65

TOYNBEE, ARNOLD
The Destruction of Poland: a Study in German Efficiency. London: 1916. V. 64
Lectures on the Industrial Revolution in England.... London: 1884. V. 63; 64
Progress and Poverty, a Criticism of Mr. Henry George. London: 1883. V. 63

TOZER, KATHARINE
Mumfie's Uncle Samuel. London: 1939. V. 63

TRACTENBERG, MARVIN
Architecture: from Prehistory to Post-Modernism/The Western Tradition. Englewood Cliffs & New York: 1986. V. 65
The Campanile of Florence Cathedral Giotto's Tower. New York: 1971. V. 65

TRACTS And Miscellanies Relating to Lincoln Cathedral, the City, Castle, Palace Ruins, etc., with Some Original Letters and Curious Documents Hitherto.... Lincoln: 1864. V. 65

TRACTS (Chiefly Rare and Curious Reprints) Relating to Northamptonshire. Northampton: 1870-1876-. V. 66

TRACTS for the Times. London: 1834-1868. V. 65

TRACTS for the Times. No. 90. London: 1841. V. 65

TRACTS Relating to Ireland. 1841. V. 65
TRACTS Relating to Ireland. 1841-1843. V. 65

TRACY, JOSHUA L.
Tracy's Guide to Missouri and St. Louis. St. Louis: 1871. V. 62

TRACY, LOUIS
The Albert Gate Mystery. New York: 1904. V. 67
The Manning-Burke Murder. New York: 1930. V. 67

TRACY, RICHARD
A Brief Short Declaracyon Made, Wherebye Everye Chrysten Man Maye Knowe, What is a Sacrament. London: 1548. V. 63

TRACY, RUSSEL
Some Experiences of Russel Lord Tracy. N.P: 1941. V. 64; 67

TRACY, T. H.
The Book of the Poodle. London: 1951. V. 67

THE TRADER'S Ready Assistant; or, Accomptant's Sure Guide, in Buying and Selling All Sorts of Commodities. Birmingham: 1792. V. 65

TRADITION and Experiment in Present-Day Literature: Addresses Delivered at the City Literary Institute. London: 1929. V. 65

TRAFZER, CLIFFORD
Earth Song, Sky Spirit: Short Stories of the Contemporary Native American Experience. New York: 1993. V. 62

TRAGER, FRANK N.
Burma: A Selected and Annotated Bibliography. New Haven: 1973. V. 65

TRAHERNE, MAJOR
The Habits of the Salmon. 1889. V. 67

TRAHERNE, THOMAS
Poetical Works. (with) *Centuries of Meditations.* London: 1903. V. 62

TRAIL, WILLIAM
Account of the Life and Writings of Robert Simson, M.D. Late Professor of Mathematics in the University of Glasgow. London: 1812. V. 65
Elements of Algebra. Edinburgh: 1789. V. 65
Elements of Algebra for the Use of Students in Universities.... Edinburgh: 1796. V. 66

TRAILL, GEORGE WILLIAM
An Elementary Treatise on Quartz and Opal, Including Their Varieties.... Edinburgh: 1870. V. 64

TRAILL, H. D.
The Barbarous Britishers: a Tip-Top Novel. London: 1896. V. 64

TRAITTE de la Peinture de Leonardo de Vinci, Donne au Public et Traduit en Francais. Paris: 1651. V. 64

TRAKL, GEORG
Gedichte. Leipzig: 1913. V. 65; 67

TRALBAUT, MARC EDO
Vincent Van Gogh. New York: 1969. V. 62; 63; 64; 66

TRALL, R. T.
The New Hydropathic Cookbook.... New York: 1854. V. 63

TRANSFORMATION Pictures and Comical Fixtures. London: 1893. V. 63

TRANSTROMER, TOMAS
Twenty Poems. Madison: 1970. V. 65

TRANSYLVANIA UNIVERSITY
A Catalogue of the Officers and Students of Transylvania University, Lexington, Kentucky, Jan. 1831. Lexington: 1831. V. 63; 66

TRAPHAM, THOMAS
A Discourse of the State of Health in the Island of Jamaica. London: 1679. V. 64

TRAPIDO, BARBARA
Brother of the More Famous Jack. London: 1982. V. 63; 65

TRAPP, JOSEPH
Praelectiones Poeticae. In Schola Naturalis Philosophiae Oxon. Habitae. Oxford: 1711-1715. V. 62; 65

THE TRAPPER'S Bride: or Spirit Of Adventure. Cincinnati: 1850. V. 65

TRAQUAIR, R. H.
The History of Scottish Fossil Ichthyology; on the Genus Dipterus; on the Structure of Amphicentum Granulosum. Edinburgh: 1880. V. 67
On Some Fossil Fishes from the Neighbourhood of Edinburgh. 1875. V. 67
On the Structure and Affinites of the Platysomidae (Fossil Fish). Edinburgh: 1879. V. 67

TRASK, JOHN B.
Report on the Geology of Northern and Southern California. N.P: 1856. V. 64

TRASK, LEONARD
A Brief Historical Sketch of the Life and Sufferings of Leonard Trask, the Wonderful Invalid. Portland: 1858. V. 66

TRATTINNICK, LEOPOLD
Fungi Austriaci, Cum Descriptionibus ac Historia Naturali Completa.... Wien: 1804-1805. V. 65; 67

TRAUBEL, HORACE
Camden's Compliment to Walt Whitman May 31, 1889. Notes, Addresses, Letters, Telegrams. Philadelphia: 1889. V. 64
In Re Walt Whitman. Philadelphia: 1893. V. 64; 66

THE TRAVELER: an Illustrated Monthly Journal of Travel and Recreation. San Francisco: 1893. V. 65

THE TRAVELLER; or, an Entertaining Journey Round the Habitable Globe.... London: 1825. V. 63

THE TRAVELLER'S Companion in a Pedestrian Excursion from Chester through North Wales, Including a Description of the Suspension Bridge at Bangor. Chester: 1825. V. 63

THE TRAVELLER'S Guide to Paris: Exhibiting the Roads.... London: 1814. V. 63

TRAVELS in South Eastern Asia, Compiled from the Most Authentic and Recent Sources. Dublin: 1823. V. 64

THE TRAVELS of Capts. Lewis & Clarke (sic) from St. Louis, by Way of the Missouri and Columbia Rivers, to the Pacific Ocean, Performed in the Years 1804, 1805 and 1806.... London: 1809. V. 63; 66; 67

TRAVELS through Denmark and Some Parts of Germany; by Way of Journal in the Retinue of the English Envoy in 1702.. London: 1707. V. 67

TRAVELS to the Source of the Missouri River and Across the American Continent to the Pacific Ocean. London: 1814. V. 67

TRAVEN, B.
The Death Ship. New York: 1934. V. 66
The Death Ship. London: 1940. V. 63
Der Marsch in Reich Caoba. Zurich: 1933. V. 66
Die Rebellion der Gehenkten. Zurich: 1936. V. 66
The Rebellion of the Hanged. London: 1952. V. 63
The Rebellion of the Hanged. New York: 1952. V. 62; 64; 67
The Treasure of the Sierra Madre. New York: 1935. V. 67
Die Troza. Zurich: 1936. V. 66

TRAVER, JOHN CHARLES
Muggleton College, Its Rise and Fall. Westminster: 1894. V. 67

TRAVER, ROBERT
Anatomy of a Fisherman. Santa Barbara and Salt Lake: 1978. V. 67
Anatomy of a Murder. New York: 1958. V. 67
Danny and the Boys. Cleveland: 1951. V. 67
The Jealous Mistress. Boston: 1967. V. 67
Small Town D. A. New York: 1954. V. 66

TRAVERS, BENJAMIN
An Inquiry Concerning that Disturbed State of the Vital Functions Usually Denominated Constitutional Irritation. New York: 1826. V. 66
An Inquiry Concerning that Disturbed State of the Vital Functions Usually Denominated Constitutional Irritation. London: 1827. V. 65

TRAVERS, HENRY
Miscellaneous Poems and Translations. London: 1731. V. 66

TRAVERS, JOHN
A Sermon Preach'd at Christ Church in Dublin Before His Grace, James Duke of Ormonde, on Monday the fifth of Nov. 1711. Dublin: 1711. V. 65

TRAVERS, MORRIS W.
A Life of Sir William Ramsay. London: 1956. V. 66

TRAVERS, P. L.
Johnny Delaney. New York: 1944. V. 66
Mary Poppins and the House Next Door. London: 1988. V. 63
Mary Poppins Comes Back. New York: 1935. V. 67
Mary Poppins from A-Z. New York: 1962. V. 66
Mary Poppins in the Park. New York: 1952. V. 63

TRAVERS, R.
Essay on Personal Identity. Dublin: 1872. V. 67

TREADWELL, FREDERICK PEARSON
Analytical Chemistry. London: 1908-1909. V. 63

TREASURES of Disney Animation Art. New York: 1982. V. 65

TREAT, PAYSON J.
The National Land System 1785-1820. New York: 1910. V. 67

A TREATISE Against the Abating of Interest. London: 1641. V. 62

A TREATISE Paraentical...Wherein is Shewed...the Right Way and True Meanes to Resist the Violence of the Castilian King..and to Ruinate His Puissance.... London: 1598. V. 62

TREATT, C. C.
Out of the Beaten Track. 1931. V. 67

TREBOR. As It May Happen; a Story of American Life and Character. Philadelphia: 1879. V. 65

TREDGOLD, THOMAS
Elementary Principles of Carpentry.... London: 1828. V. 65
Elementary Principles of Carpentry.... London: 1853. V. 62
The Principles of Warming and Ventilating Public Buildings, Dwelling Houses, Manufactories, Hospitals, Hot-Houses, Conservatories, &c.... London: 1836. V. 63
The Steam Engine; Its Invention and Progressive Improvement. London: 1838. V. 65

TREDREY, F. D.
The House of Blackwood 1804-1954: the History of a Publishing Firm. Edinburgh: 1954. V. 65

TREE, IRIS
The Marsh Picnic. Cambridge: 1966. V. 63

TREE, ISABELLA
The Ruling Passions of John Gould. A Biography of a Bird Man. London: 1991. V. 67

TREECE, HENRY
Dylan Thomas - Dog Among the Fairies. London: 1949. V. 62

TREFUSIS, VIOLET
Pirates at Play. London: 1950. V. 62

TREGAR, MARY
Arts of China. Tokyo and Palo Alto: 1972. V. 65

TREHERNE, GEORGE G. T.
Record of the University Boat Race Commemoration Dinner, 1881. Oxford: 1883. V. 62

TREMAIN, HENRY EDWIN
The Closing Days About Richmond; or the Last Days of Sheridan's Cavalry. New York: 1873. V. 62
Last Hours of Sheridan's Cavalry. New York: 1904. V. 62

TREMAIN, ROSE
Restoration. London: 1989. V. 67

TREMAINE, MARIE
A Bibliography of Canadian Imprints 1751-1800. Toronto: 1952. V. 67

TREMAYNE, SYDNEY
Tatlings. Epigrams. London: 1922. V. 67

TREMBLEY, ABRAHAM
Instructions D'Un Pere a Ses Enfans sur la Nature et Sur la Religion. Neuchatel: 1779. V. 64

TRENCH, RICHARD CHENEVIX
On Some Deficiencies in Our English Dictionaries. London: 1857. V. 63
The Remains of the Late Mrs. Richard Trench.... London: 1862. V. 65

TRENCH, W. STEUART
Realities of Irish Life. London: 1868. V. 64

TRENCHARD, HENRY
The Private Soldier's and Milita Man's Friend. London: 1786. V. 65

TRENCHARD, JOHN
An Argument, Shewing that a Standing Army is Inconsistent with a Free Government and Absolutely Destructive to the...English Monarchy. London: 1697. V. 63
A Letter from the Author of the Argument Against a Standing Army, to the Author (Somers) of the Ballancing Letter. London: 1697. V. 63
A Short History of Standing Armies in England. London: 1698. V. 63

TRENCHFIELD, CALEB
A Cap of Gray Hairs for a Green Head, or the Fathers Counsel to His Son, an Apprentice in London. London: 1710. V. 62

TRENHAILE, JOHN
Kyril. London: 1981. V. 67
Nocturne for the General. London: 1985. V. 67

TRENHOLM, VIRGINIA
The Arapahoes Our People. Norman: 1970. V. 67
Footprints on the Frontier Saga of the La Ramie Region of Wyoming. Douglas: 1945. V. 67

TRENT, COUNCIL OF, 1545-1563
Sacrosancti et Oecumenici Concilii Tridentini Paulo III. Ijlio III & Pio IIII. Pont. Maximo Celebrati, Canones et Decreta. Lyon: 1580. V. 62

TRESEDER, N. G.
The Book of Magnolias. 1981. V. 66
The Book of Magnolias. London: 1981. V. 64

TRESSALL, ROBERT
The Ragged Trousered Philanthropists. London: 1914. V. 64

TRESSELT, ALVIN
Sun Up. New York: 1949. V. 66

TREULEIN, THEODORE E.
Pfefferkorn's Description of Sonora. Albuquerque: 1949. V. 66

TREUX, RAYMOND
Detailed Atlas of the Head and Neck. New York: 1948. V. 64

TREVANIAN
The Eiger Sanction. New York: 1972. V. 65

TREVELYAN, CHARLES
The Irish Crisis. N.P: 1848. V. 64

TREVELYAN, R. C.
Aftermath. London: 1941. V. 64
Polyphemus and Other Poems. London: 1901. V. 63, 66

TREVES, FREDERICK
The Elephant Man and Other Reminiscences. London: 1923. V. 64
Made in the Trenches.... London: 1916. V. 63
A Manual of Operative Surgery. Philadelphia and New York: 1903. V. 66

TREVIGAR, A. M.
Sectionum Conicarum Elementa Methodo Facillima Demonstrata. Cambridge: 1731. V. 65

TREVOR, ROY
En Route. London: 1908. V. 64

TREVOR, WILLIAM
The Ballroom of Romance and Other Stories. New York: 1972. V. 66
The Ballroom of Romance and Other Stories. London: 1970. V. 66
Beyond the Pale and Other Stories. London: 1981. V. 65; 66
Collected Stories. London: 1993. V. 64; 67
Death of a Professor. London: 1997. V. 65
Dreaming. London: 1973. V. 62; 64; 67
Elizabeth Alone. London: 1973. V. 65
Excursions in the Real World. London: 1993. V. 62; 63; 67
The Love Department. London: 1966. V. 63; 65
Lovers of Their Time: an Extract. London: 1978. V. 63; 66
Lovers of Their Time and Other Stories. New York: 1979. V. 66
Miss Gomez and the Brethren. London: 1971. V. 65
Mrs. Eckdorf in O'Neill's Hotel. London: 1969. V. 65
The Piano Turner's Wives. Alton, Hampshire: 1998. V. 63

TREVOR-BATTYE, AUBYN
Ice-Bound on Kolguev. London: 1895. V. 66
Ice-Bound on Kolguev. Westminster: 1895. V. 65

TREW, CECIL G.
The Accoutrements of the Riding Horse. London. V. 67

THE TRI-QUARTERLY Anthology of Contemporary Latin American Literature. New York: 1969. V. 66

TRIAL of John Jasper...for the Murder of Edwin Drood, Engineer. London: 1914. V. 62

TRIAL of the Assassins and Conspirators at Washington, D.C., May and June, 1865, for the Murder of President Abraham Lincoln. Philadelphia: 1865. V. 62

TRIAL of the Officers and Crew of the Privateer Savannah, on the Charge of Piracy.... New York: 1862. V. 67

THE TRIALS of George Robert Fitzgerald, Esq., Timothy Brecknock, John Fulton and Others for the Murder of Patrick Randal MacDonnell, and Charles Hipson...Also the Trial of John Gallagher and Others.... London: 1786. V. 65

THE TRIALS Of Matrimony, or, Simple Smoothly, and Her False Accusations and Base Procedings Against Her Husband.... Nottingham?: 1794. V. 63

TRIANA, JOSE MARIA MARTIN
Suite Lirica: En Homenaje A Wallace Stevens. Verona: 1982. V. 64

A TRIBUTE Offered by the University of Aberdeen to the Memory of William Kelly, LL.D. A.R.S.A. Aberdeen: 1949. V. 67

A TRIBUTE to Austin Clarke on His Seventieth Birthday 9 May, 1966. 1966. V. 67

TRIBUTE to Walter de la Mare on His Seventy-Fifth Birthday. London: 1948. V. 63; 64; 65

TRIBUTES to Edward Johnston, Calligrapher. Kent: 1948. V. 62

TRIBUTES to Graham Greene. 1992. V. 63

TRIBUTES to Graham Greene, OM, CH 1904-1991, at the Memorial Requiem Mass at Westminster Cathedral. London: 1992. V. 64

TRIBUTES to Graham Greene, OM, CH 1904-1991, at the Memorial Requiem Mass at Westminster Cathedral. Rugby: 1992. V. 65

TRICKLER, W.
The Water Garden.... New York: 1897. V. 64

TRIENENS, ROGER J.
Pioneer Imprints from Fifty States. Washington: 1973. V. 66

TRIER, WALTER
10 Little Negroes - A New Version. London: 1944. V. 65

TRIFLES from Harrogate. London: 1797. V. 65

TRIGG, R.
Haworth Idyll. 1946. V. 66
Haworth Idyll. London: 1946. V. 63

TRIGGS, HARRY INIGO
Garden Craft in Europe. London: 1913. V. 66; 67

TRIGGS, J. H.
History and Directory of Laramie City Wyoming Territory and a History of Cheyenne and Northern Wyoming Embracing the Gold Fields of the Black Hills. Laramie: 1955. V. 65

TRIMBLE, MARSHALL
Co Bar, Bill Owen Depicts the Historic Babbitt Ranch. Flagstaff: 1982. V. 63; 66

TRIMBLE, WILLIAM J.
The Mining Advance Into the Inland Empire, A Comparative Study of the Beginnings of the Mining Industry in Idaho and Montana, Eastern Washington, and Oregon and the Southern Interior of British Columbia. Madison: 1914. V. 65

TRIMMER, SARAH
A Description of a Set of Prints of English History; Contained in a Set of Easy Lessons. London: 1792. V. 64
A Description of a Set of Prints of Scripture History...(with) A Series of Prints of Scripture History.... London: 1786. V. 62
Fabulous Histories. London: 1788. V. 65
Fabulous Histories. Dublin: 1800. V. 62
Fabulous Histories. London: 1811. V. 64; 65
Fabulous Histories. London: 1818. V. 62
Fabulous Histories. London: 1821. V. 67
The Robins. London. V. 67
Sacred History, Selected from the Scriptures.... London: 1801. V. 65
A Series of Prints of Ancient History...Part I (Part II). (with) A Description of a Set of Prints of Ancient History; Contained in a Set of Easy Lessons. London: 1788. V. 63
A Series of Prints of Roman History.... London: 1789. V. 63
The Two Farmers, an Exemplary Tale.... London: 1819. V. 63

TRINKA, ZENA IRMA
Out Where the West Begins. St. Paul: 1920. V. 62; 63; 64

TRINKLER, EMIL
The Stormswept Roof. 1931. V. 67

TRIP Trap. Haiku Along the Road from San Francisco to New York, 1959. 1973. V. 63

A TRIP through London: Containing Observations on Men and Things. London: 1728. V. 63

TRIPLES from Harrogate. London: 1797. V. 64

TRIPLETT, FRANK
The Life, Times and Treacherous Death of Jesse James. New York: 1970. V. 66

TRIPP, C. E.
Ace High the 'Frisco Detective. San Francisco: 1948. V. 65

TRIPP, F. E.
British Moses, Their Homes, Aspects, Structure and Uses. London: 1874. V. 62; 64; 66

TRIPPLETT, FRANK
Conquering the Wildnerness. 1883. V. 64

TRISSEL, JAMES
Color for the Letterpress. 1987. V. 64
Daedalus. 1993. V. 64
LETTERpressworkBOOK. 1997. V. 64

TRISSINO, GIOVANNI GIORGIO
La Italia Liberata da Gotthi. Rome: 1547. V. 65; 67

TRISTAN
The Romance of Tristan and Iseult. New York: 1960. V. 62
The Romance of Tristram of Lyones and La Beale Isoude. St. Albans: 1920. V. 66
The Story of Tristan & Iseult. London: 1907. V. 62

TRISTRAM, H. B.
The Great Sahara: Wanderings South of the Atlas Mountains. London: 1860. V. 62
The Land of Israel: a Journal of Travels in Palestine.... London: 1865. V. 66

TRISTRAM, JOHN
The Ill State of Physick in Great Britain: Truly Represented...and an Apology for the Regular Physicians. London: 1727. V. 66

TRISTRAM, W. OUTRAM
Coaching Days and Coaching Ways. London and New York: 1893. V. 67

TRITHEMIUS, JOHANNES
In Praise of Scribes. (De Laude Scriptorum). Vancouver: 1977. V. 63

TRITTON, JOSEPH
Baptist Missionary Society, Rise and Progress of the Work on the Congo River. London: 1884. V. 62
...Rise and Progress of the Work on the Congo River. London: 1884. V. 62

THE TRIUMPH of Goodnature, Exhibited in the History of the Master Harry Fariborn and Master Trueworth Interspersed with Tales and Fables.... London: 1801. V. 67

THE TRIUMPH of Goodnature (sic) Exhibited in the History of Master Harry Fariborn and Master Trueworth. Interspersed with Tale and Fables. London: 1810. V. 62; 67

TROBRIAND, PHILLIPPE REGIS DE
Military Life in Dakota, the Journal of Phillippe Regis De Trobriand. St. Paul: 1951. V. 67

TROCCHI, ALEXANDER
Cain's Book. New York: 1960. V. 64
Young Adam. London: 1961. V. 63; 65

TROCHECK, KATHY HOGAN
Every Crooked Nanny. New York: 1992. V. 62; 64; 65; 66

TROILI, GIULIO
Paradossi per Pratticare la Prospettiva Senza Aperla, Fiori, per Facilitare, l'Intelligenza, Frutti.... Bologna: 1683. V. 62; 63

TROLLOPE, ANTHONY
The American Senator. London: 1877. V. 62; 66; 67
An Autobiography. Edinburgh and London: 1883. V. 66; 67
Ayala's Angels. London: 1881. V. 67
Barchester Novels. London: 1878. V. 67
Barchester Towers. Garden City: 1945. V. 65
The Belton Estate. London: 1866. V. 65
The Belton Estate. Philadelphia: 1866. V. 67
British Sports and Pastimes. London: 1868. V. 65
Can You Forgive Her?. London: 1864. V. 63; 67
Can You Forgive Her?. New York: 1865. V. 67
Can You Forgive Her?. London: 1948. V. 63
Castle Richmond. Leipzig: 1860. V. 62; 65
Castle Richmond. London: 1860. V. 67
Christmas Day at Kirkby Cottage. London: 1947. V. 63
The Chronicles of Barsetshire. London: 1878-1885. V. 62
Cousin Henry. London: 1879. V. 65; 67
Dr. Wortle's School. London: 1881. V. 66; 67
The Duke's Children. London: 1880. V. 65; 66
An Editor's Tales. London: 1876. V. 67
The Eustace Diamonds. London: 1950. V. 63
The Fixed Period. Leipzig: 1882. V. 65
The Fixed Period. London: 1882. V. 67
Framley Parsonage. London: 1861. V. 65; 67
He Knew He Was Right. London: 1869. V. 62; 65; 67
How the Mastiff Went to Iceland. London: 1878. V. 67

TROLLOPE, ANTHONY continued
Hunting Sketches. London: 1865. V. 65
John Caldigate. London: 1879. V. 65; 66; 67
The Kellys and the O'Kellys. London: 1848. V. 62
The Kellys and the O'Kellys. London: 1880. V. 65
Lady Anna. London: 1874. V. 67
The Landleaguers. London: 1883. V. 67
The Last Chronicle of Barset. London: 1867. V. 62; 63
The Last Chronicle of Barset. New York: 1867. V. 67
The Last Chronicle of Barset. London: 1872. V. 65
The Letters. Stanford: 1983. V. 66
The Life of Cicero. London: 1880. V. 67
London Tradesmen. London: 1927. V. 64
The Macdermots of Ballycloran. London: 1866. V. 65
Marion Fay. London: 1882. V. 67
Miss Mackenzie. London: 1865. V. 67
Miss Mackenzie. London: 1866. V. 65
Mr. Scarborough's Family. London: 1883. V. 67
North America. New York: 1862. V. 65; 66
An Old Man's Love. London: 1884. V. 67
Orley Farm. London: 1862. V. 63; 65
Phineas Redux. London: 1874. V. 67
The Prime Minister. London: 1876. V. 62
Rachel Ray. London: 1863. V. 65; 66
Rachel Ray. London: 1868. V. 65
Ralph the Heir. London: 1871. V. 62; 65; 67
Sir Harry Hotspur. London: 1871. V. 67
The Small House at Allington. New York: 1864. V. 63; 65; 67
South Australia and Western Australia. London: 1874. V. 62
Tales of All Countries. London: 1861. V. 67
Tales of All Countries. Second Series. London: 1863. V. 65
Thackeray. London: 1879. V. 67
The Three Clerks. London: 1858. V. 67
The Three Clerks. London: 1865. V. 63
La Vendee. London: 1883?. V. 65
The Vicar of Bullhampton. London: 1870. V. 62; 65; 67
The Way We Live Now. London: 1875. V. 66
The Way We Live Now. London: 1877. V. 65
The West Indies and the Spanish Main. New York: 1860. V. 63
Why Frau Frohmann Raised Her Prices. London: 1882. V. 67
William Makpeace Thackeray. London: 1879. V. 66
Works. New York: 1900. V. 64

TROLLOPE, FRANCES MILTON
The Attractive Man. London: 1860. V. 65
The Barnabys in America, or Adventures of the Widow Wedded. Paris: 1843. V. 65
The Blue Bells of England. Paris: 1842. V. 65
Charles Chesterfield; or the Adventures of a Youth of Genius. London: 1841. V. 65
Domestic Manners of Americans. London: 1832. V. 66
Domestic Manners of Americans. New York: 1832. V. 65; 66
Domestic Manners of the Americans. London: 1927. V. 64
Jessie Phillips. London: 1843. V. 65
Life and Adventures of Michael Armstrong, the Factory Boy. London: 1840. V. 65
Moeurs Domestiques des Americains. (Domestic Manners of the Americans). Paris: 1833. V. 67
Vienna and the Austrians; with Some Account of a Journey through Swabia, Bavaria, the Tyrol and the Salzbourg. London: 1838. V. 66
A Visit to Italy. London: 1842. V. 62
The Ward of Thorpe-Combe. London: 1842. V. 63
The Widow Barnaby. Paris: 1840. V. 65

TROLLOPE, THOMAS ADOLPHUS
A Decade of Italian Women. London: 1859. V. 63

TROLLOPE, WILLIAM
A History of the Royal Foundation of Christ's Hospital with an Account of the Plan of Education. London: 1834. V. 62; 66

TRONCHIN, THEODORE
De Colica Pictonum. Genevae: 1757. V. 67

TRONCON, JEAN
L'Entree Triomphante de Leurs Maiestez Louis XIV, Roy de France et de Navarre, et Marie Therese d'Austriche, son Espouse dans la ville de Paris.... Paris: 1662. V. 65

TROTSKY, LEON
The Defence of Terrorism (Terrorism and Communism) - a Reply to Karl Kautsky. London: 1921. V. 64

TROTTER, COUTTS
The Principles of Currency and Exchanges Applied to the Report from the Select Committee of the House of Commons, Appointed to Inquire Into the High Price of Gold Bullion &c.... London: 1810. V. 64

TROTTER, THOMAS
Sea Weeds: Poems, Written on Various Occasions.... Newcastle: 1829. V. 62
A View of the Nervous Temperament. 1807. V. 63
A View of the Nervous Temperament. Troy: 1808. V. 66; 67

TROTTMAN, NELSON
History of the Union Pacific - a Financial and Economic Survey. New York: 1923. V. 63; 66

THE TROUBLES of a Good Husband. Northampton: 1818. V. 64

TROUP, R. S.
The Silviculture of Indian Trees. Oxford: 1921. V. 63

TROVILLART, PIERRE
Memoires des Comtes de Maine. Le Mans: 1643. V. 65

TROW, GEORGE W. S.
Within the Context of No Context. Chicago: 1992. V. 62

TROW, M. J.
The Adventures of Inspector Lestrade. London: 1985. V. 65
Brigade: Further Adventures of Inspector Lestrade. London: 1986. V. 63
Lestrade and the Ripper. London: 1988. V. 63; 66

TROWBRIDGE, MARY E. DAY
Pioneer Days: the Life Story of Gershoma and Elizabeth Day.... Philadelphia: 1895. V. 64; 67

TRUAX, CHARLES
The Mechanics of Surgery. Chicago: 1899. V. 62

A TRUE Account of the Most Considerable Occurences that Have Hapned in the Warre Between the English and the Indians in New England, from the Fifth of May, 1676 to the Fourth of August Last.... London: 1676. V. 63

TRUE and Exact Relation of the Kings Entertainment in the City of Chester. London: 1642. V. 65

TRUE, F. W.
An Account of the Beaked Whales of the Family Ziphiidae in the Collection of the United States national Museum, with Remarks on Some Specimens in Other American Museums,. Washington: 1910. V. 65
The Whalebone Whales of the Western North Atlantic.... Washington: 1904. V. 62; 67

A TRUE Life and Interesting History of Che-Mah the Celebrated Chinese Dwarf. New York: 1882. V. 63

THE TRUE Manor and Forme of the Proceeding to the Funerall of the Right Honourable Robert Earle of Essex and Ewe...Late Lord Generall of the Forces Raised and Employed by the Parliament of England.... London: 1646. V. 66

TRUE News from Oxford Being a Relation of the Magnificent Valour of the Scholars in Number 500.... London: 1642. V. 62

A TRUE Relation of the Faction Begun at Wisbich, by Fa. Edmonds, Alias Weston, a Iesuite, 1595.... London: 1601. V. 66

THE TRUE State of England. London: 1729. V. 63

TRUE Stories; or Interesting Anecdotes of Children.... York: 1810. V. 62

THE TRUE Story Book. London: 1893. V. 62

TRUEITT, VELMA S.
On the Hoof in Nevada. Los Angeles: 1950. V. 63

TRUELOVE, EDWARD
In the High Court of Justice. Queen's Bench Division, February 8, 1878. The Queen v. Edward Truelove, for publishing the Hon. Robert Dale Owen's Moral Physiology.... London: 1878. V. 63

TRUELOVE'S Tales. 1837. V. 65

TRUEX, RAYMOND C.
Detailed Atlas of the Head and Neck. New York: 1948. V. 67

TRUMAN, BEN C.
Occidental Sketches. San Francisco: 1881. V. 65

TRUMAN, C.
History of the World's Fair. New York: 1893. V. 63

TRUMAN, HARRY
Memoirs. Garden City: 1955-1956. V. 63
Year of Decisions. Garden City: 1955. V. 62

TRUMBO, DALTON
Johnny Got His Gun. New York, Philadelphia: 1939. V. 67

TRUMBULL, COLONEL
Catalogue of Paintings by Colonel Trumbull, Including Eight Subjects of the American Revolution With Near 250 Portraits.... New Haven: 1840. V. 67

TRUMBULL, HENRY
History of the Discovery of America.... Boston: 1836. V. 62
Life and Adventures of Robert, the Hermit of Massachusetts, Who Has Lived 14 Years in a Cave.... Providence: 1829. V. 66

TRUMBULL, L. R.
A History of Industrial Paterson: Being a Compendium of the Establishment, Growth, and Present Status in Paterson, N.J. of the Silk, Cotton, Flax, Locomotive, Iron and Miscellaneous Industries. Paterson: 1882. V. 63; 66

TRUMELET, CORNEILLE
Etudes sur les Regions Sahariennes. Histoire de l'Insurrection dans le Sud de la Province d'Alger in 1864 (-1869). Alger: 1879-1884. V. 64

TRUSLER, JOHN
The Honours of the Table, or Rules for Behaviour During meals.... Dublin: 1791. V. 62
Life; or, the Adventures of William Ramble, Esq. London: 1793. V. 65
Poetic Endings; or a Dictionary of Rhymes, Single and Double.... London: 1783. V. 64
Practical Husbandry; or the Art of Farming, with a Certainty of Gain.... London: 1780. V. 66
A System of Etiquette.... Bath: 1805?. V. 64

TRUSLER, JOHN *continued*
The Works of William Hogarth.... London: 1833. V. 64

TRUSS, SELDON
Turmoil at Brede. New York: 1931. V. 66; 67

TRUTH Against Craft; or Sophistry and Falsehood Detected in Answer to a Pamphlet Intitled the Case Fairly Stated.... Dublin;: 1754. V. 65

TRUTH, SOJOURNER
Narrative of Sojourner Truth: a Bondswoman of Olden Time.. Boston: 1875. V. 65

TRUTHS Illustrated by Great Authors, A Dictionary of Nearly Four Thousand Aids to Reflection, Quotations of Maxims, Metaphors, Counsels, Cautions, Aphorisms, Proverbs.... London: 1853. V. 63

TRYCKARE, T.
The Lore of Sportfishing. New York: 1983. V. 67

TRYON, G. W.
Manual of Conchology; Structural and Systematic, with Illustrations of the Species. Philadelphia: 1879-1898. V. 66
Structural and Systematic Conchology.... Philadelphia: 1882-1884. V. 62; 63; 65; 66

TRYON, THOMAS
Harvest Home. New York: 1973. V. 66
The Other. New York: 1971. V. 65; 66
The Way to Health, Long Life and Happiness.... London: 1697. V. 65

TRYPHIODORUS
(Title Greek, then) Excidium Troiae. Florentiae: 1765. V. 65

TSCHICHOLD, JAN
Chinese Color Prints from the Manual of the Mustard-Seed Garden. London/Basel: 1952. V. 64
Chinese Color Prints of Today. Basle: 1946. V. 64
Chinesische Farbendrucke der Gegenwart. Basel: 1945. V. 64
Hu Cheng-yen: A Chinese Wood-Engraver and Picture Printer. Basle: 1946. V. 64

TSCHIRNAUS, EHRENFRIED WALTER VON
Medicina Mentis, Sive Artis Inveniendi Praecepta Generalia Editio Nova...(with) Medicina Corporis seu Cogitationes Admodum Probabiles De Conservanda Sanitate. Lipsiae: 1695. V. 64

TSCHNIK, CAJETAN
The Victim of Magical Delusion; or the Mystery of the Revolution of Portugal. Dublin: 1795. V. 64

TSCHUDI, F. VON
Das Thierleben der Alpenwelt. Naturansichten und Thierzeichnungen aus dem Schweizerlischen Gebirge. Leipzig: 1860. V. 65
Nature in the Alps. 1856. V. 63; 64; 66; 67

TSCHUDI, J. J. VON
Travels in Peru, During the Years 1838-1842, on the Coast, in the Sierra.... New York: 1849. V. 65

TSENG, YU-HO ECKE
Chinese Calligraphy. Philadelphia: 1971. V. 67

TSUBOI, ISUKE
Illustrations of the Japanese Species of Bamboo. Tokyo: 1916. V. 62

TSVETAEVA, MARINA
Vechernii al'bom. (Evening Album). Moscow: 1910. V. 65; 67

TUBBEE, LAAH CEIL MANATOI ELAAH
Sketch of the Life of Okah Tubbee, Alias William Chubbee, Son of the Head Chief, Mosholeh Tubbee, of the Choctaw Nation of Indians. Springfield: 1848. V. 63

TUBERVILLE, A. S.
Johnson's England. An Account of the Life and Manners of His Age. Oxford: 1933. V. 67

TUCHMAN, BARBARA
The Lost British Policy. Britain and Spain Since 1700. London: 1938. V. 63; 66

TUCK, D.
The New Complete English Setter. 1964. V. 67

TUCKER, ANNA B.
Simple Songs for Little Singers. Honolulu: 1931. V. 63

TUCKER, ANNE WILKES
Robert Frank: New York to Nova Scotia. Houston: 1986. V. 63

TUCKER, BENJAMIN
Benj. R. Tucker's Unique Catalogue of Advanced Literature. New York: 1906-1907. V. 66
Sacred and Profane History Epitomized.... Philadelphia: 1806. V. 63

TUCKER, BENJAMIN R.
Instead of a Book by a Man Too Busy to Write One. A Fragmentary Exposition of Philosophical Anarchism. New York: 1897. V. 62

TUCKER, CHARLOTTE MARIA
A L(ady) O(f) E(ngland)'s Sunday Picture Book.... London: 1871. V. 67

TUCKER, E. M.
Catalogue of the Library of Arnold Arboretum of Harvard University. 1999. V. 66

TUCKER, ELIZABETH S.
Little Rosebuds. New York: 1898. V. 64

TUCKER, EPHRAIM W.
Five Months in Labrador and Labrador and Newfoundland During the Summer of 1838. Concord: 1839. V. 63

TUCKER, GEORGE
The Life of Thomas Jefferson. London: 1837. V. 62
The Life of Thomas Jefferson. Philadelphia: 1837. V. 63

TUCKER, GLENN
High Tide At Gettysburg: the Campaign in Pennsylvania. Indianapolis and New York: 1958. V. 67

TUCKER, HENRY S. G.
Commentaries on the Laws of Virginia, Comprising the Substance of a Course of Lectures Delivered to the Winchester Law School. Winchester: 1837. V. 65

TUCKER, JANE E.
Beverley Tucker, A Memoir by His Wife. Richmond: 1890. V. 63

TUCKER, JOHN RANDOLPH
The Old and the New South. Columbia: 1887. V. 63

TUCKER, MARWOOD
Michael Tressider. A Cornish Tale. London: 1872. V. 62; 65

TUCKER, NATHANIEL
Burmudian: a Poem. (with) The Anchoret: a Poem. Hull: 1808-1776. V. 63

TUCKER, NATHANIEL B.
The Partisan Leader: a Novel.... Richmond: 1862. V. 62

TUCKER, PATRICK T.
Riding the High Country. Caldwell: 1933. V. 64; 67

TUCKER, POMEROY
Origin, Rise and Progress of Mormonism Biography Of Its Founders and History of the Church. New York: 1867. V. 64

TUCKER, SARAH
Abbeokuta: or Sunrise within the Tropics.... London: 1856. V. 62

TUCKER, SOPHIE
What Every Woman Needs. Newcastle: 1996. V. 62

TUCKER, ST. GEORGE
A Dissertation on Slavery: With a Proposal for the Gradual Abolition of It in the State of Virginia. Philadelphia: 1796. V. 62; 63
Hansford: a Tale of Bacon's Rebellion. Richmond: 1857. V. 64

TUCKER, WILLIAM
The Family Dyer and Scourer: being a Complete Treatise on the Arts of Dyeing and Cleaning Every Article of Dress, Bed and Window Furniture, Silks, Bonnets, Feathers &c. Philadelphia: 1831. V. 66

TUCKER, WILLIAM W.
His Imperial Highness, the Grand Duke Alexis in the United States of American During the Winter of 1871-1872.... Cambridge: 1872. V. 67

TUCKER, WILSON
The Long Loud Silence. 1952. V. 64

TUCKERMAN, EDWARD
Collected Lichenological Papers of Edward Tuckerman. Weineheim: 1964. V. 62

TUCKERMAN, HENRY THEODORE
Leaves from the Diary of a Dreamer. London: 1853. V. 64

TUCKETT, ELIZABETH
How We Spent the Summer or a Voyage en Zigzag in Switzerland and Tyrol.... London: 1866. V. 65

TUCKETT, HARVEY
The Indian Revenue System As It Is. A Letter Addressed to the President, Vice President and Members of the Manchester Chamber of Commerce and Manufactures....for the East India Cotton Company. London: 1840. V. 66

TUCKEY, C. LLOYD
Treatment by Hypnotism and Suggestive; or Psycho-Therapeutics. New York: 1901. V. 66

TUCKEY, JAMES KINGSTON
Narrative of an Expedition to Explore the River Zaire.... London: 1818. V. 62; 65

TUDOR, EMMA
October Dawn. Cambridge: 1926. V. 63; 64

TUDOR, JOHN R.
The Orkneys and Shetland. London: 1883. V. 62

TUDOR, TASHA
A is for Anna Belle. New York: 1954. V. 64
The County Fair. New York: 1940. V. 63; 65
The Dolls' Christmas. New York: 1950. V. 64
Dorcas Porkus. New York: 1942. V. 62
Edgar Allan Crow. New York: 1953. V. 64
The Creat Corgiville Kidnapping. Boston: 1997. V. 63
Linsey Woolsey. New York: 1946. V. 63; 64; 65
Pumpkin Moonshine. New York: 1938. V. 63
Snow Before Christmas. New York: 1941. V. 64
A Tale for Easter. New York: 1941. V. 64
Thistly B. New York: 1949. V. 63
The White Goose. New York: 1943. V. 63; 65

TUDOR-CRAIG, ALGERNON TUDOR
The Romance of Melusine and de Lusignan. Together with Genealogical Notes and Pedigrees of Lovekyn of London, Lovekyn of Lovekynsmede ad of Luckyn of Little Waltham and Lukyn of Mashbery, All in the County of Essex and of Lukin of Felbrigg, Co. Norfolk. 1932. V. 65

TUDOT, EDMOND
Vues du Chateau de Veauce. Moulins: 1850. V. 62; 67

TUER, ANDREW WHITE
The Book of Delightful and Strange Designs Being One Hundred Facsimile Illustrations of the Art of the Japanese Stencil Cutter.... 1925. V. 65
History of the Horn-Book. London: 1896. V. 64; 67
London Cries.... London: 1883. V. 64
Old London Street Cries and the Cries of Today. London: 1885. V. 64; 65
Old London Street Cries and the Cries of Today. London: 1890. V. 67
Pages and Pictures From Forgotten Children's Books.... London: 1898-1899. V. 62; 65; 67

TUFTS, MARSHALL
Shores of Vespucci; or Romance Without Fiction. Lexington: 1833. V. 62; 64

TUIT, J. E.
The Tower Bridge, Its History and Construction from the Date of the Earliest Projects to the Present Time. London: 1894. V. 62

TUKE, DANIEL HACK
Chapters in the History of the Insane in the British Isles. London: 1882. V. 65
A Dictionary of Psychological Medicine. London: 1892. V. 65
Illustrations of the Influence of the Mind Upon the Body in Health and Disease. Philadelphia: 1884. V. 65
Prichard and Symonds In Especial Relation to Mental Science. London: 1891. V. 65

TUKE, JAMES HACK
Achill and West of Ireland. Report of the Distribution of the Seed Potato Fund in the Spring of 1886. 1886. V. 65
Irish Distress and Its Remedies. The Land Question. London: 1880. V. 65

TUKE, JOHN
General View of the Agriculture of the North Riding of Yorkshire. London: 1800. V. 66; 67

TUKE, JOHN BATTY
The Insanity of Over-Exertion of the Brain. Edinburgh: 1894. V. 65

TUKE, SAMUEL
Description of the Retreat, an Institution Near York for Insane Persons of the Society of Friends. York: 1813. V. 65

TUKER, M. A. R.
Rome. London: 1905. V. 65

TULASNE, L. R.
Selecta Funogorum Carpologia. Oxford: 1931. V. 62

TULK, A.
Anatomical Manipulation...Use of the Microscope. London: 1844. V. 67

TULL, JETHRO
The Horse-Hoeing Husbandry. London: 1733-1740. V. 67
Horse-Hoeing Husbandry. London: 1751. V. 63
The Horse-Hoeing Husbandry. 1829. V. 65
The Horse-Hoeing Husbandry. London: 1829. V. 63; 64
Horse-Hoeing Husbandry. London: 1851. V. 63

TULLEY, SAMUEL
Report of the Trial of Samuel Tulley and John Dalton on an Indictment of Piracy. Boston: 1812. V. 67

TULLY *Filmus.* Cleveland: 1963. V. 65

TULLY, RICHARD
Narrative of a Ten Years' Residence at Tripoli in Africa. London: 1817. V. 64

THE TUNBRIDGE AND Bath Miscellany for the Year 1714. London: 1714. V. 65

THE TUNBRIDGE Wells Guide; or an Account of the Ancient and Present State of that Place, to Which is Added a Particular Description of the Towns and Villages, Gentlemens Seats, Remains of Antiquity, Founderies, &c. &c. Tunbridge Wells: 1786. V. 63; 67

TUNBRIDGE, WILLIAM
A Report of the Proceedings in the Mock Trial of an Information... Against William Tunbridge, for the Publication of a Book Called Palmer's Principles of Nature as an Alledged Blasphemous Libel Upon the Christian Religion and the Holy Scriptures.... London: 1823. V. 63

TUNNARD, WILLIAM H.
A Southern Record. The History of the Third Regiment Louisiana Infantry. Baton Rouge: 1866. V. 62; 63; 65

TUNNICLIFFE, C. F.
The Peregrine Sketchbook. 1996. V. 67
Shorelands Summer Diary. 1952. V. 63; 67
Shorelands Summer Diary. London: 1952. V. 63; 64; 65; 66

TUNNICLIFFE, CHARLES
Mereside Chronicle, with a Short Interlude on Lochs and Lochans. London: 1948. V. 63
My Country Book. London: 1942. V. 63

TUNSTALL, CUTHBERT
De Arte Supputandi Libri Quqtuor. Paris: 1538. V. 66

TUPINIER, M.
Observations on the Dimensions of the Ships of the Line and Frigates in the French Navy. London: 1830. V. 67

TUPPER, JAMES PERCHARD
An Essay on the Probability of Sensation in Vegetables.... London: 1811. V. 64; 67

TUPPER, MARTIN FARQUHAR
Proverbial Philosophy.... London: 1838. V. 65
Proverbial Philosophy.... New York: 1847. V. 65
A Third Series of Proverbial Philosophy. London: 1867. V. 65
Stephan Langton. London: 1858. V. 65

TURBERVILLE, A. S.
Johnson's England. An Account of the Life and Manners of His Age. Oxford: 1933. V. 64

TURENNE, LOUIS DE LA TOUR D'AUVERGNE, PRINCE OF
Theses Ex Universa Philosophia. 1679. V. 64; 66

TURGENEV, IVAN SERGEEVICH
Dvoryanksoe Gnyezdo (A Nest of Gentlefolk, a Novel). Moscow: 1859. V. 63
Mumu and the Diary of a Superfluous Man. London: 1884. V. 63; 67
Spring Floods...a Lear of the Steppe. New York: 1874. V. 62; 65
The Torrents of Spring. Westport: 1976. V. 63; 64
Virgin Soil. London: 1878. V. 64
Zapiski Okhotnika. Moscow: 1852. V. 67

TURGEON, ONESIPHORE
Un Tribut a la Race Acadienne Memoires 1871-1927. Montreal: 1928. V. 67

TURILLAZZI, C.
Natural History and Evolution of Paper-Wasps. Oxford: 1996. V. 63

TURNBULL & CO.
Sportsman's and Tourist's Handbook to Iceland. 1901. V. 67

TURNBULL, ALEXANDER
An Investigation into the Remarkable Medicinal Effects Resulting from the External Application of Veratria. Edinburgh: 1834. V. 62

TURNBULL, ANDREW
Thomas Wolfe. New York: 1967. V. 64

TURNBULL, ARCHIBALD DOUGLAS
Commodore David Porter 1780-1843. New York: 1929. V. 64; 65

TURNBULL, ROBERT J.
A Visit to the Philadelphia Prison.... London: 1797. V. 64; 65; 66

TURNBULL, WILLIAM
The Chronometer's Companion; or a Compendium of Nautical Astronomy.... London: 1856. V. 65
Reports on the Construction of the Piers of the Aqueduct of the Alexandria Canal Across the Potomac River at Georgetown, District of Columbia. Washington: 1873. V. 65

TURNBULL, WILLIAM P.
The Birds of East Lothian, and a Portion of the Adjoining Counties. Glasgow: 1867. V. 65
The Birds of East Pennsylvania and New Jersey. Glasgow: 1869. V. 63; 66

TURNEAURE, FREDERICK E.
Cyclopedia of Civil Engineering: A General Reference Work. Chicago: 1908. V. 67

TURNELL, G. M.
Refuge of Fire. 1932. V. 67

TURNER, A. LOGAN
Diseases of the Nose, Throat and Ear.... New York: 1927. V. 64
Joseph, Baron Lister Centenary Volume 1827-1927. Edinburgh: 1927. V. 65
The Skiagraphy of the Accessory Nasal Sinuses. New York: 1912. V. 67

TURNER, AVERY, MRS.
These High Plains. 1941. V. 67

TURNER, BENJAMIN BANNISTER
Chronicles of the Bank of England. London: 1897. V. 64

TURNER, CARLTON
Cocaine, an Annotated Bibliography. Jackson: 1988. V. 63

TURNER, DECHERD
The Rhemes New Testament: Being a Full and Particular Account of the Origins, Printing and Subsequent Influences of the First Roman Catholic New Testament in English, with the Divers Controversies Occasioned by Its Publication Diligently Explounded.... San Francisco: 1990. V. 64

TURNER, E.
Elements of Chemistry.... Edinburgh: 1827. V. 62
Elements of Chemistry.... Edinburgh: 1834. V. 62

TURNER, EDWARD RAYMOND
The New Market Campaign, May 1864. Richmond: 1912. V. 63

TURNER, ELIZABETH
The Daisy.... London. V. 62

TURNER, FRANCIS
Animadversions Upon a Late Pamphlet Entituled the Naked Truth; or the True State of the Primitive Church. London: 1676. V. 65

TURNER, FREDERICK J.
The Character and Influence of the Indian Trade in Wisconsin. Baltimore: 1891. V. 62; 66

TURNER, FREDERICK J. continued
The Frontier in American History. New York: 1920. V. 64; 67
The Significance of the Frontier in American History. Madison: 1894. V. 64

TURNER, G. L'E.
The Great Age of the Microscope. The Collection of the Royal Microscopical Society through 150 Years. Bristol;: 1989. V. 67

TURNER, GEORGE
Narrow Gauge Nostalgia. Harbor City: 1965. V. 67
Nineteen Years in Polynesia: Missionary Life, Travels and Researches in the Islands of the Pacific. London: 1861. V. 64

TURNER, J. HORSFALL
Ancient Bingley; or, Bingley, Its History and Scenery. Bingley: 1897. V. 65
Haworth Past and Present, a History of Haworth, Stanbury and Oxenhope. Brighouse: 1879. V. 63; 66
History of Brighouse Rastrick and Hipperholme: With Manorial Notes on Coley, Lightcliffe, Northowram, Shelf, Fixby, Clifton and Kirklees. Bingley: 1893. V. 65

TURNER, JIM
Lost Days. Poems. Andoversford: 1981. V. 62; 63

TURNER, JOHN
A Vindication of the Rights and Privileges of the Christian Church. London: 1707. V. 67

TURNER, JOHN P.
The Northwest Mounted Police. Ottawa: 1930. V. 65; 67

TURNER, JOSEPH MALLORD WILLIAM
An Antiquarian and Picturesque Tour Round the Southern Coast of England.... London: 1849. V. 62
The Turner Gallery. London: 1880. V. 64; 66

TURNER, L. M.
Contributions to the Natural History of Alaska. Washington: 1886. V. 62

TURNER, LUCY MAE
'But Cullud Folkses. New York: 1938. V. 67

TURNER, MEGAN WHALEN
The Thief. New York: 1996. V. 65

TURNER, REGINALD
Cynthia's Damages: a Story of the Stage. London: 1901. V. 64

TURNER, ROBERT
Ars Notaria; the Notary Art of Solomon, Shewing the Cabbalistic Key of Magical Operations, the Liberal Sciences, Divine Revelation.... London: 1657. V. 65

TURNER, SAMUEL
Costs in the Court of Chancery.... London: 1791. V. 65
My Climbing Adventures in Four Continents. 1911. V. 63; 65
My Climbing Adventures in Four Continents. London: 1913. V. 63; 64
Siberia: a Record of Travel Climbing and Exploration. London: 1905. V. 63; 64; 66
Siberia, A Record of Travel, Climbing and Exploration. 1911. V. 66

TURNER, SHARON
The History of England During the Middle Ages. London: 1823. V. 65

TURNER, THOMAS
Narrative of a Journey, Associated with a Fly, From Gloucester to Aberystwith and from Aberystwith through North Wales, July 31st to September 8th 1837. London: 1840. V. 62; 66

TURNER, W.
Challenger Voyage. Zoology. Part 68 Seals. 1888. V. 66
Challenger Voyage. Zoology. Parts 30, 50 and 79, Polyzoa. 1884-1889. V. 66
Lectures on Comparative Anatomy of the Placenta. First Series. Edinburgh: 1876. V. 67
A New Herbal. London: 1996. V. 62
On the Placentation of Lemurs. Edinburgh: 1876. V. 67
On the Placentation of the Sloths (Choloepus Hoffmanni). Edinburgh: 1873. V. 67

TURNER, W. J.
The Man Who Ate the Popomack - a Tragi-Comedy of Love in Four Acts. Oxford: 1922. V. 62
Marigold - an Idyll of the Sea. London: 1926. V. 62

TURNER, W. R.
Old Homes and Familes in Nootoway (Virginia). Blackstone: 1932. V. 65

TURNER, WHITELEY
A Spring-Time Saunter: Round and About Bronte Land. Halifax: 1913. V. 65

TURNER, WILLIAM
The Ceramics of Swansea and Nantgarw: a History of the Factories. London: 1897. V. 66
Sound Anatomiz'd in a Philosophical Essay on Musick. London: 1724. V. 62
Sunday Schools Recommended in a Sermon, Preached Before the Associated Dissenting Ministers in the Northern Counties, at Their Annual Meeting at Morpeth, June XIII MDCCLXXXVI and Published at Their Request. Newcastle: 1786. V. 66
Turner on Birds. 1903. V. 66

TURNER DE LOND, WILLIAM
Six Views on the New Line of Road Communicating Between Stirling and Carlisle.... Edinburgh: 1825. V. 62

TURNER-TURNER, J.
The Giant Fish of Florida. 1902. V. 62

TURNEY-HIGH, HARRY HOLBERT
Ethnography of the Kutenai. Menasha: 1941. V. 63

TURNILL, REGINALD
Jane's Spaceflight Directory. London: 1984. V. 66

TURNOR, CHRISTOPHER HATTON
Astra Castra Experiments and Adventures in the Air. London: 1865. V. 67

TURNOR, EDMUND
Collections for the History of the Town and Soke of Grantham. London: 1806. V. 63; 65
A Short View of the Proceedings of the Several Committees and Meetings Held in the Consequence of the Intended Petition to Parliament, for the County of Lincoln.... London: 1782. V. 62

TURNOR, THOMAS
The Case of the Bankers and Their Creditors. London: 1675. V. 66

TUROW, SCOTT
The Burden of Proof. Franklin Center: 1990. V. 66
One L. 1977. V. 66

TURPIN, RICHARD
The Life and Trial of Richard Turpin, a Notorious Highwayman.... London: 1820. V. 65
The Life of Richard Turpin, a Most Notorious Highwayman; Giving an Account of His Daring Robberies and Burglaries.... Derby: 1840?. V. 63

TURRELL, G.
Raman Microscopy. Development and Applications. London: 1996. V. 66

TURRILL, W. B.
The Plant Life of the Balkan Peninsula.... Oxford: 1929. V. 64

TURTON, W.
A Conchological Dictionary of the British Islands. 1819. V. 66
A Conchological Dictionary of the British Islands. London: 1819. V. 62; 64
Conchylia Insularum Britannicarum. London and Leicester: 1830. V. 66
A Manual of the Land and Fresh Water Shells of British Islands. 1840. V. 64; 65
A Manual of the Land and Fresh Water Shells of the British Islands. 1857. V. 63; 66

TURYN, ALEXANDER
Dated Greek Manuscripts of the Thirteenth and Fourteenth Centuries in the Libraries of Italy. Urbana, Chicago, London: 1972. V. 62

TUSKA, JON
The Detective in Hollywood. Garden City: 1978. V. 63

TUSON, EDWARD WILLIAM
The Dissector's Guide; or Student's Companion. Boston: 1844. V. 67

TUSSER, THOMAS
Five Hundred Points of Good Husbandry. London: 1610. V. 62
Five Hundredth Pointes of Good Husbandrie (in Verse), as Well for the Champion or Open Countrie, as Also for the Woodland or Severall, Mixed in Everie Month with Huswiferie, Over and Besides the Booke of Huswiferie.... London: 1585. V. 63

TUTCHIN, JOHN
The Whiskers Whisk'd: or a Farewel Sermon Prepared to be Prepach'd at Turners-Hall in Phillpot Lane. London: 1703. V. 65

TUTEN, FREDERIC
The Adventures of Mao on the Long March. New York: 1971. V. 63
Tin Tin in the New World: a Romance. New York: 1993. V. 63; 67

TUTHILL, FRANKLIN
The History of California. San Francisco: 1866. V. 62; 63

TUTHILL, L. C., MRS.
I Will Be a Sailor. Boston: 1864. V. 64

TUTTLE, CHARLES
Japan: Theme and Variations, a Collection of Poems by Americans. Rutland: 1959. V. 66

TUTTLE, DANIEL S.
Reminiscences of a Missionary Bishop. New York: 1906. V. 63; 66

TUTTLE, SARAH
Conversations on the Choctaw Mission.... Boston: 1830. V. 65

TUTTLE, WILLIAM PARKHURST
Bottle Hill and Madison. Glimpses and Reminiscences from Its Earliest Settlement to the Civil War. N.P: 1917. V. 66

TWAMLEY, LOUISA ANNE MEREDITH
Our Wild Flowers Familiarly Described and Illustrated. London: 1843. V. 62

'TWAS the Night Before Christmas. Chicago: 1939. V. 62
'TWAS the Night Before Christmas. Racine: 1939. V. 62

TWEED, JOHN
The Redeemer. A Poem. Bocking: 1798?. V. 62

TWEEDALE, CHARLES L.
Reflecting Telescope Making: Also Extraordinary Cosmetic Experiences, the Great Daylight Comet of 1910, the Total Solar Eclipse of 1929. London: 1943. V. 66

TWELVE Parables of Our Lord. London: 1870. V. 67

TWELVE SOUTHERNERS
I'll Take My Stand: the South and the Agrarian Tradition. New York and London: 1930. V. 67

TWENEY, GEORGE
The Washington 89. Morongo Valley: 1989. V. 66

A TWENTIETH Century History of Southwest Texas. Chicago: 1907. V. 67

THE TWENTIETH Century Peerless Atlas and Pictorial Gazetteer of All Lands. Springfield: 1902. V. 66

TWENTIETH Century Poetry in English. Washington: 1949. V. 66

THE 29TH of May; or, The Restoration: Being a Short View of the Many Calamities Brought Upon These Nations, by the Tyrannical Usurpers During the Grand Rebellion. London: 1718. V. 65

TWINING, E. W.
Model Aeroplanes: How to Build and Fly Them. London: 1909. V. 64

TWINING, HENRY
On the Philosophy of Painting: a Theoretical and Practical Treatise.... London: 1849. V. 63

TWISLETON, TOM
Poems in the Craven Dialect. Settle: 1886. V. 64; 65

TWISS, TRAVERS
The Black Book of the Admirality, with an Appendix. London: 1871. V. 64
The Law of Nations Considered as Independent Political Communities. London: 1861-1863. V. 64
View of the Progress of Political Economy in Europe Since the Sixteenth Century. London: 1847. V. 63

TWITCHELL, GEORGE S.
Trial and Conviction of George S. Twitchell, Jr. for the Murder of Mrs. Mary E. Hill, His Mother-in-Law. Philadelphia: 1869. V. 66

TWITCHELL, RALPH EMERSON
Historical Sketch of Governor William Carr Lane - Together With Diary of His Journey from St. Louis, Missouri to Santa Fe. Albuquerque: 1917. V. 62
The History of the Military Occupation of New Mexico from 1846 to 1851. Denver: 1909. V. 65; 67
The Leading Facts of New Mexican History. Cedar Rapids: 1911. V. 64; 66
The Leading Facts of New Mexico History. Albuquerque: 1963. V. 62; 65
The Military Occupation of New Mexico 1846-1851. Denver: 1909. V. 64
Old Santa Fe – The Story of New Mexico's Ancient Capital. Sante Fe: 1925. V. 64
The Spanish Archives of New Mexico. Cedar Rapids: 1914. V. 62; 64

TWO Addresses to the Inhabitants of the Several Parishes in the Deanries of Louth-Esk and Ludburgh, Calcewaith, Horncastle, Gartree.... London: 1800?. V. 62

TWO Epistles on Happiness. to a Young Lady. 1754. V. 66

TWO Men: Walter Lewis and Stanley Morison at Cambridge. Cambridge: 1968. V. 62

TWO Years of Harriman, Tennessee. Established by the East Tennessee Land Company, February 26, 1890. New York: 1892. V. 67

TWOPENY, WILLIAM
English Metal Work: Ninety-Three Drawings. London: 1904. V. 62

TWYMAN, MICHAEL
Early Lithographed Books, a Study of the Design and Production of Improper Books in the Age of the Hand Press. London: 1990. V. 63
Lithography 1800-1850.... London: 1970. V. 63

TYACKE, R. H.
In Quest of Game. Calcutta: 1927. V. 66
The Sportsman's Manual in Quest of Game in Kulu, Lahoul and Ladak to the Tso Morari Lake. Calcutta: 1907. V. 62

TYAS, I.
Favourite Field Flowers. Series 2. 1850. V. 63

THE TYBURN Chronicle; or, Villainy Display'd in All Its Branches. London: 1768. V. 65

TYERS, THOMAS
Political Conferences Between Several Great Men in the Last and Present Century.... London: 1781. V. 62; 65

TYLER, ANNE
The Accidental Tourist. New York: 1985. V. 62; 66; 67
Breathing Lessons. Franklin Center: 1988. V. 65; 66; 67
Breathing Lessons. New York: 1988. V. 66
Celestial Navigation. New York: 1974. V. 64; 65; 67
The Clock Winder. New York: 1972. V. 66
Dinner at the Homesick Restaurant. New York: 1982. V. 65; 66
Earthly Possessions. New York: 1977. V. 64; 65; 66
If Morning Ever Comes. New York: 1964. V. 62; 67
Ladder of Years. Franklin Center: 1995. V. 65
Ladder of Years. New York: 1995. V. 65
Morgan's Passing. New York: 1980. V. 63; 64; 65; 66
Saint Maybe. Franklin Center: 1991. V. 65
Saint Maybe. New York: 1991. V. 65; 67
Searching for Caleb. New York: 1976. V. 62; 64; 65; 67
A Slipping Down Life. New York: 1970. V. 65; 66
The Tin Can Tree. New York: 1965. V. 67
Tumble Tower. New York: 1993. V. 64; 65; 67

TYLER, JAMES
The Shooter's Manual, or the Art of Shooting.... London: 1837. V. 64

TYLER, JOHN
An Address Delivered Before the Two Literary Societies of Randolph Macon College. Richmond: 1838. V. 67

TYLER, JOSIAH
Livingstone Lost and Found, or Africa and Its Explorers. Hartford: 1873. V. 63

TYLER, LYON GARDINER
The Cradle of the Republic: Jamestwown and James River. Richmond: 1900. V. 66
Narratives of Early Virginia 1606-1625. New York: 1907. V. 66

TYLER, RON
Alfred Jacob Miller: Artist on the Oregon Trail. Fort Worth: 1982. V. 64; 67
Audubon's Great National Work. Austin: 1993. V. 64

TYLER, ROYALL
The Algerine Captive; or, the Life and Adventures of Doctor Updike Underhill, Six Years a Prisoner Among the Algerines. Hartford: 1816. V. 62

TYLER, SAMUEL
A Discourse of the Baconian Philosophy. Frederick City: 1846. V. 65

TYLOR, A.
Colouration in Animals and Plants. London: 1886. V. 63

TYMMS, W. R.
The Art of Illuminating as Practiced in Europe from the Earliest Times. London: 1865. V. 65

TYNAN, KATHARINE
Irish Love-Songs. London: 1892. V. 64
A Little Book of XXIV Carols. Portland: 1907. V. 62; 65
Miracle Plays: Our Lord's Coming and Childhood. London: 1895. V. 64
Twilight Songs. Oxford: 1927. V. 62

TYNAN, PATRICK J. P.
The Irish National Invincibles and Their Times. 1896. V. 63; 66; 67

TYNDALE, WALTER
An Artist in Italy. London: 1913. V. 64
Below the Cataracts. London: 1907. V. 66

TYNDALL, JOHN
Essays on the Floating-Matter of the Air in Relation to Putrefaction and Infection. London: 1881. V. 64
The Glaciers of the Alps. London: 1896. V. 63; 64
Lectures on Light. Delivered in the United States in 1872-1873. New York: 1873. V. 65
Mountaineering in 1861. A Vacation Tour. 1862. V. 63; 65
The Optical Deportment of the Atmosphere in the Relation to the Phenomena of Putrefaction and Infection. (with) Further Researches on the Department and Vital Persistence of Putrefactive and Infective Organisms from a Physical Point of View. London: 1876-1877. V. 66
Sound, A Course of Eight Lectures Delivered at the Royal Institution of Great Britain. London: 1867. V. 63

A TYPOGRAPHICAL Masterpiece: an Account by John Dreyfus of Eric Gill's Collaboration with Robert Gibbings in Producing the Golden Cockerel Press Edition of The Four Gospels. San Francisco: 1990. V. 64

TYRRELL, DUKE
A Sermon Preach'd at St. Andrew's Dublin, October 23d 1719, Being the Anniversary Thanksgiving-day for the Deliverance from the Horrid Rebellion Which Broke Out the 23d of October 1641. Dublin: 1719. V. 65

TYRRELL, HENRY
The Doubtful Plays of Shakespeare.... London. V. 66

TYRRELL, JAMES W.
Across the Sub-Arctics of Canada: a Journey of 3200 Miles by Canoe and Snowshoe Through the Hudson Bay Region. Toronto: 1908. V. 64

TYSON, EDWARD
Orang-Outang, sive Homo Sylvestris; or, the Anatomy of a Pygmie Compared with that of a Monkey, an Ape and a Man. London: 1699. V. 66
A Philological Essay Concerning the Pygmies...of the Ancients. London: 1894. V. 63

TYSON, IAN
The Life and Times of Baby Woojams. 1980. V. 66
Transliniations. 1979. V. 66

TYSSEN, SAMUEL
Catalogue of the Entire Museum, of the Late Samuel Tyssen, Esq. F.A. S. of Narborough-Hall, in the County of Norfolk.... London: 1802. V. 65

TYSSOT DE PATOT, SIMON
Voyages et Avantures de Jaques Masse. Bordeaux, i.e. Le Hague: 1710. V. 67

TYTLER, ALEXANDER FRASER
Elements of General History, Ancient and Modern. Edinburgh: 1812. V. 67
An Essay on Military Law and the Practice of Court Martial.... London: 1814. V. 63
Essay on the Principles of Translation. Edinburgh: 1813. V. 64

TYTLER, PATRICK FRASER
England Under the Reigns of Edward VI and Mary.... London: 1839. V. 63
Historical View of the Progress of Discovery on the More Northern Coasts of America.... Edinburgh: 1832. V. 63
Lives of Scottish Worthies. London: 1831. V. 64
The Northern Coasts of America and the Hudson's Bay Territories. London: 1853. V. 65

TYTLER, SARAH
Jane Austen and Her Works. London: 1884. V. 63

TYTLER, WILLIAM
An Historical and Critical Enquiry into the Evidence Produced by the Earls of Murray and Morton, Against Mary Queen of Scots. Edinburgh: 1760. V. 66
An Inquiry, Historical and Critical Into the Evidence Against Mary Queen of Scots and an Examination of the Histories of Dr. Robertson and Mr Hume, with Respect to that Evidence. Edinburgh: 1767. V. 65

TZARA, TRISTAN
The First Celestical Adventure of Mister Benzedrine. 1996. V. 64
Midis Gagnes. Paris: 1939. V. 65

U

UCHIDA, S.
Photographs of Bird-Life in Japan. Tokyo & Osaka: 1930-1931. V. 62

UDALL, NICHOLAS
Ralph Roister Doister, a Comedy. London: 1847. V. 67

UDELL, JOHN
Incidents of Travel to California, Across the Great Plains. Jefferson: 1856. V. 66

UDRY, JANICE MAY
The Moon Jumpers. London: 1979. V. 65

UFANO, DIEGO
Tratado de la Artilleria y Uso Della.... Brussels: 1612?. V. 62

UKERS, WILLIAM H.
All About Tea. New York: 1935. V. 66

ULITIUS, JANUS
Autores Rei Venatice Antiqui cum Commentarys; ad Christianam Augustam. 1653. V. 62
Venatio Novantiqua Celsissimo Arausionis Principa Guilhelmo Dicata. 1645. V. 62

ULLMAN, JAMES RAMSEY
Americans on Everest. London: 1965. V. 64

ULLOA, DON ANTONIA DE
A Voyage to South America. London: 1760. V. 64
A Voyage to South America. London: 1772-1807. V. 62
A Voyage to South America. London: 1806. V. 65

ULLYETT, HENRY
Rambles of a Naturlist Round Folkestone, with Occasional Papers on the Fauna and Flora of the District.... Folkestone: 1880. V. 66

ULMANN, ALEC
The Sebring Story. Philadelphia: 1969. V. 67

ULMANN, DORIS
The Appalachian Photographs of Doris Ulmann. Penland: 1971. V. 63

ULMER, ULRICUS
Fraternitas Cleri. Ulm: 1480. V. 67

ULMUS, MARCUS ANTONIUS
Uterus Muliebris hoc est de Indiciis Cognoscendi Temperamenta Uteri uel Partium Genitalium Ipsius Mulieris. Bononiae: 1601. V. 65

ULVERSTON & District Industrial and Fine Art Exhibition Catalogue 1873. Barrow-in-Furness: 1873. V. 65

ULYSSES, CHARLES
Travels through Various Provinces of the Kingdom of Naples in 1789. London: 1795. V. 62

UMFREVILLE, EDWARD
The Present State of Hudson's Bay. London: 1790. V. 64; 66
The Present State of Hudson's Bay. Toronto: 1954. V. 66

UMGROVE, J. H. F.
Structural History of the East Indies. 1949. V. 67

UMLAUFT, F.
The Alps. 1889. V. 65

UNCLE Ben Jay's Wonder Book-The Book that Comes Alive. New York: 1944. V. 63

UNCLE Ben's New Jersey Almanac for 1844. Princeton: 1843. V. 63; 66

UNCLE Buncle's Stories of Little Peter's Visit to the Farm. London: 1845. V. 65

UNDER Dixie Sun - a History of Washington County by Those Who Loved Their Forebears. Panguitch: 1950. V. 67

UNDER Twenty-Five. Brisbane: 1966-1967. V. 62

UNDERHILL, E. A.
Patchwork. 1932. V. 66

UNDERHILL, EDWARD BEAN
Dr. Underhill's Letter. A Letter Addressed to the Right Honourable E. Cardwell.... London: 1865. V. 66

UNDERHILL, FRANCIS T.
Driving for Pleasure or, the Harness Stable and Its Appointments. New York: 1897. V. 64

UNDERHILL, HAROLD A.
Masting and Rigging, the Clipper Ship and Ocean Carrier. Glasgow: 1946. V. 67
Plank-on-Frame Models. Glasgow: 1981. V. 67

UNDERRENTNING om Det Tit Gamle Soldaters...Fader-og Moderlose Soldater Borns. Copenhagen;: 1765-1772. V. 64

UNDERWOOD, CLARENCE F.
Some Pretty Girls. London: 1901. V. 63

UNDERWOOD, GEORGE C.
History of the Twenty-Sixth Regiment of the Carolina Troops, in the Great War 1861-1865. Goldsboro: 1901. V. 62

UNDERWOOD, LAMAR
The Bobwhite Quail Book. Clinton: 1980. V. 65
The Deer Book. Clinton: 1980. V. 65

UNDERWOOD, THOMAS
Poems, &c. Bath: 1768. V. 62

UNDERWOOD, TIM
Fear Itself: the Horror Fiction of Stephen King. 1982. V. 62
Fear Itself: the Horror Fiction of Stephen King. San Francisco/Columbia: 1982. V. 66
Kingdom of Fear: the World of Stephen King. San Francisco and Columbia: 1986. V. 66

UNGAR, I. A.
Ecophysiology of Fascular Halophytes. Boca Raton: 1991. V. 66

UNGER, DOUGLAS
Leaves the Land. New York: 1984. V. 63

UNION OF AMERICAN HEBREW CONGREGATIONS
Proceedings of Union of American Hebrew Congregations at Its Second Annual Session (& Its 3rd). Cincinnati: 1875-1876. V. 65

UNION SOCIETY OF POLITICAL PROTESTANTS OF BILLINGHAM
Declaration and Rules of the Political Protestants. Newcastle upon Tyne: 1820. V. 66

UNION STEAMSHIP CO.
Our Coastal Trips. Vancouver: 1923. V. 64

UNITED Cattle and Horse Grower's Association of Idaho 1916. 1916. V. 65

THE UNITED Service Journal and Naval and Military Magazine. London: 1831-1832. V. 67

UNITED STATES. AGRICULTURE DEPARTMENT - 1887
Third Annual Report of Animal Industry for the Year 1886. Washington: 1887. V. 65

UNITED STATES. AGRICULTURE DEPARTMENT - 1936
The Western Range. Letter from the Secretary of Agriculture. Washington: 1936. V. 63; 66

UNITED STATES. ARMY - 1857
Reports Upon the Purchase, Importation and Use of Camels and Dromedaries, to be Employed for Military Purposes. Washington: 1857. V. 65

UNITED STATES. ARMY - 1864
A Bound Volume Containing General Orders Nos. 1-133. Washington: 1864. V. 64

UNITED STATES. ARMY - 1882
Specifications for Means of Transportation, Paulins, Stoves and Ranges, and Lamps and Fixtures for the Use in the United States Army. Washington: 1882. V. 65

UNITED STATES. BUREAU OF AMERICAN ETHNOLOGY - 1919
Thirty-third Annual Report of the Bureau of American Ethnology 1911-1912. Washington: 1919. V. 65

UNITED STATES. BUREAU OF AMERICAN ETHNOLOGY - 1932
Forty-Seventh Annual Report. Washington: 1932. V. 63

UNITED STATES. BUREAU OF INDIAN AFFAIRS - 1876
Annual Report of the Commissioner of Indian Affairs. Washington: 1876. V. 62

UNITED STATES. BUREAU OF INDIAN AFFARIS - 1879
Annual Report of the Commissioner of Indian Affairs...for the Year 1879. Washington: 1879. V. 63

UNITED STATES. CENSUS - 1865
Manufactures of the United States in 1860; Compiled from the Original Returns of the 8th Census.... Washington: 1865. V. 64

UNITED STATES. COAST & GEODETIC SURVEY - 1853
Report of the Superintendent, 1853. Washington: 1854. V. 65

UNITED STATES. COAST & GEODETIC SURVEY - 1898
Report of the Superintendent, Year Ending with June 1897. Washington: 1898. V. 65

UNITED STATES. COMMISSION OF AGRICULTURE - 1863
Report of the Commissioner of Agriculture for the Year 1862. Washington;: 1863. V. 64

UNITED STATES. COMMISSION OF FISH & FISHERIES - 1884
Part XII. Report of the Commissioner for 1884. Washington: 1886. V. 63

UNITED STATES. COMMISSIONER ON EDUCATION - 1871
Special Report of the Commissioner of Education on the Condition and Improvement of Public Schools in the District of Columbia. Washington: 1871. V. 63

UNITED STATES. CONGRESS - 1855
Reports of Explorations and Surveys to Ascertain the Most Practicable and Economical Route for a Railroad from the Mississippi River to the Pacific Ocean, Made Under the Direction of the Secretary of War in 1853-1854.... Washington: 1855. V. 64

UNITED STATES. CONGRESS - 1858
Reports of Explorations and Surveys, to Ascertain the Most Practicable and Economical Route for a Railroad from the Mississippi River to the Pacific Ocean, Made Under the Direction of the Secretary of War in 1853-1856.... Washington: 1858. V. 64

UNITED STATES. CONGRESS - 1860
Difficulties on Southwestern Frontier. 36th Congress, 1st Session Ex. Doc. 52. Washington: 1860. V. 63

UNITED STATES. CONGRESS - 1864
Returned Prisoners. Washington: 1864. V. 63

UNITED STATES. CONGRESS - 1866
Joint Committe on the Conduct of the War. Supplemental Report, 39th Congress. Washington: 1866. V. 65

UNITED STATES. CONGRESS - 1869
Report on the Treatment of Prisoners of War, by the Rebel Authorities During the War of the Rebellion.... Washington: 1869. V. 67

UNITED STATES. CONGRESS - 1959
Space Handbook: Astronautics and Its Applications. Washington: 1959. V. 65

UNITED STATES. CONGRESS. HOUSE OF REPRESENTATIVES - 1821
Executive Papers House of Representatives, Volume 8 1820-1821. Washington: 1821. V. 66

UNITED STATES. CONGRESS. HOUSE OF REPRESENTATIVES - 1825
Report of the Committee of Foreign Relations of the House of Representatives on Piracy and Outrages on American Commerce by Spanish Privateers. Washington: 1825. V. 67

UNITED STATES. CONGRESS. HOUSE OF REPRESENTATIVES - 1836
Road Portsmouth (Ohio) to Linville, N.C. Washington: 1836. V. 63

UNITED STATES. CONGRESS. HOUSE OF REPRESENTATIVES - 1857
Reports of Explorations, Surveys, to Ascertain the Most Practicable...Route for a Railroad from the Mississippi River... Volume VII. Washington: 1857. V. 62

UNITED STATES. CONGRESS. HOUSE OF REPRESENTATIVES - 1859
Reports of Explorations, Surveys, to Ascertain the Most Practicable...Route for a Railroad from Mississippi River... Volume X. London: 1913. V. 62

UNITED STATES. CONGRESS. HOUSE OF REPRESENTATIVES - 1866
39th Congress, 1st Session, Report #6. Transfer of Counties to West Virginia. Washington. 1866. V. 63

UNITED STATES. CONGRESS. HOUSE OF REPRESENTATIVES - 1873
Report of the Select Committee of the House of Representatives, Appointed Under the Resolution of Jan. 6, 1873. Washington: 1873. V. 65

UNITED STATES. CONGRESS. HOUSE OF REPRESENTATIVES - 1889
Investigation of the Fur-Seal and Other Fisheries of Alaska. Washington: 1889. V. 62
Protection of the Frontier of Texas - 35th Congress 2nd Session House of Reprensentatives Ex Doc. No. 27 - Jan. 6, 1859. Washington: 1889. V. 67

UNITED STATES. CONGRESS. HOUSE OF REPRESENTATIVES - 1904
Committee on Territories. Washington: 1904. V. 63

UNITED STATES. CONGRESS. SENATE - 1802
Debates in the Senate of the United States on the Judiciary, During the First Session of the Seventh Congress; Also, the Several Motions, Resolutions and Votes, Taken Upon That Momentous Subject.... Philadelphia: 1802. V. 66

UNITED STATES. CONGRESS. SENATE - 1855
Reports of Explorations, Surveys, from the Mississippi River to the Pacific Ocean... 1853-1856. Volume XI. Washington: 1855. V. 62

UNITED STATES. CONGRESS. SENATE - 1856
Reports of Explorations, Surveys to Ascertain the Most Practicable... Route for a Railroad from Mississippi River...Volume III. Washington: 1856. V. 62

UNITED STATES. CONGRESS. SENATE - 1862
Rules of the Senate of the United States, Consisting of Special Rules of the Senate, the Joint Rules of the Two Houses. Washington. 1862. V. 64

UNITED STATES. CONGRESS. SENATE - 1882
Report of the Board of Heavy Ordnance and Projectiles Appointed in Conformity with the Act of Congress Approved March 3, 1881. Washington: 1882. V. 66

UNITED STATES. CONGRESS. SENATE - 1896
Calendar #1144 Report (and Transcript of Hearings) on SB 1552 for the Further Prevention of Cruelty to Animals in the District of Columbia. Washington: 1896. V. 63

UNITED STATES. CONGRESS. SENATE - 1975
The Weather Underground. Senate Report. Washington: 1975. V. 63

UNITED STATES. CONSTITUTION - 1837
Constitution of the United States of America.... Washington: 1837. V. 64

UNITED STATES. CONSTITUTION - 1972
The Constitution of the United States of America. Washington: 1972. V. 63

UNITED STATES. CONTINENTAL CONGRESS - 1774
Extracts from the Votes and Proceedings of the American Continental Congress, held at Philadelphia on the 5th of September, 1774. Philadelphia, Printed: 1774. V. 62

UNITED STATES. CONTINENTAL CONGRESS - 1775
A Declaration by the Representatives of the United Colonies of North America, Now Met in General Congress, at Philadelphia.... Newport: 1775. V. 62

UNITED STATES. CONTINENTAL CONGRESS - 1776
Journal of the Proceedings of the Congress, held at Philadelphia, May 10, 1775. Published by Order of the Congress. London: 1776. V. 62

UNITED STATES. CONTINENTAL CONGRESS - 1904
Journals of the Continental Congress - 1776-1782. Washington: 1904. V. 66

UNITED STATES. GEOGRAPHICAL SURVEYS - 1875
Report Upon Geographical and Geological Explorations and Surveys West of the One Hundredth Meridian. Volume V. Zoology. Chapter III. Report Upon the Ornithological Collections.... Washington: 1875. V. 66

UNITED STATES. GEOGRAPHICAL SURVEYS - 1877
Annual Report Upon the Geographical Surveys of the One-Hundredth Meridian in the States and Territories of California, Oregon, Nevada, Texas, Arizona, Colorado, Idhao, Montana, New Mexico and Wyoming.... Washington: 1877. V. 63; 64

UNITED STATES. GEOGRAPHICAL SURVEYS - 1889
Report Upon United States Geographical Surveys West of the One Hundredth Meridian. Washington: 1889-1879. V. 63; 66

UNITED STATES. GEOLOGICAL SOCIETY - 1891
Eleventh Annual Report of the United States Geological Survey to the Secretary of the Interior 1889-1890. Washington: 1891. V. 64

UNITED STATES. GEOLOGICAL SURVEY - 1885
Fifth Annual Report 1883-1884. Washington: 1885. V. 63; 64

UNITED STATES. GEOLOGICAL SURVEY - 1888
Seventh Annual Report of the United States Geological Survey. Washington: 1888. V. 64

UNITED STATES. GEOLOGICAL SURVEY - 1889
Eighth Annual Report of the United States Geological Survey. Washington: 1889. V. 64

UNITED STATES. GEOLOGICAL SURVEY - 1901
Twenty-first Annual Report of the United States Geological Survey to the Secretary of the Interior 1899-1900...Part VII - Texas. Washington: 1901. V. 66

UNITED STATES. INTERIOR DEPARTMENT - 1871
Report of the Secretary of the Interior 1871. Washington: 1871. V. 63

UNITED STATES. INTERIOR DEPARTMENT - 1900
Annual Reports of the Department of the Interior for the Fiscal Year Ended June 30, 1900. Washington: 1900. V. 64

UNITED STATES. INTERIOR DEPARTMENT - 1902
Eighth Annual Report of the Commission to the Five Civilized Tribes to the Secretary of the Interior for the Fiscal Year ended June 30, 1901. Washington: 1902. V. 63

UNITED STATES. INTERIOR DEPARTMENT - 1906
Annual Reports. Washington: 1906. V. 64

UNITED STATES. INTERIOR DEPARTMENT - 1936
Report of the Feasibility of Gila Valley Project Arizona. N.P: 1936. V. 64

UNITED STATES. LABOR DEPARTMENT - 1888
Third Annual Report...Commissoner of Labor 1887 Strikes and Lockouts. Washington: 1888. V. 63

UNITED STATES. LAWS, STATUTES, ETC. - 1790
An Act for Giving Effect to the Several Acts Therein Mentioned in Respect to the State of North Carolina.... New York: 1790. V. 63

UNITED STATES. LAWS, STATUTES, ETC. - 1808
Acts Passed at the First Session of the Tenth Congress. Washington: 1808. V. 64

UNITED STATES. LAWS, STATUTES, ETC. - 1817
Acts Passed at the Second Session of the Fourteenth Congress. Washington: 1817. V. 64

UNITED STATES. LAWS, STATUTES, ETC. - 1818
Acts Passed at the First Session of the Fifteenth Congress. Washington: 1818. V. 64

UNITED STATES. LAWS, STATUTES, ETC. - 1819
Acts Passed at the Second Session of the Fifteenth Congress. Washington: 1819. V. 64

UNITED STATES. LAWS, STATUTES, ETC. - 1821
Acts Passed at the Second Session of the Sixteenth Congress. Washington: 1821. V. 64

UNITED STATES. LAWS, STATUTES, ETC. - 1822
Acts Passed at the First Session of the Seventeenth Congress. Washington: 1822. V. 64

UNITED STATES. LAWS, STATUTES, ETC. - 1823
Acts Passed at the Second Session of the Seventeenth Congress. Washington: 1823. V. 64

UNITED STATES. LAWS, STATUTES, ETC. - 1832
Acts Passed at the First Session of the Twenty-Second Congress. Washington: 1832. V. 64

UNITED STATES. LAWS, STATUTES, ETC. - 1833
Acts Passed at the Second Session of the Twenty Second Congress. Washington: 1833. V. 64

UNITED STATES. LAWS, STATUTES, ETC. - 1837
Acts Passed at the Second Session of the Twenty Fifth Congress. Washington: 1837. V. 64

UNITED STATES. LAWS, STATUTES, ETC. - 1843
Acts Passed at the Third Session of the Twenty Seventh Congress. Washington: 1843. V. 64

UNITED STATES. MARITIME COMMISSION - 1944
Vessel Construction Report no. 32.... Terminal Island: 1944. V. 63

UNITED STATES. NAVY - 1882
Report of Officers of the Navy on Ventilating and Cooling the Executive Mansion During the Illness of President Garfield. Washington: 1882. V. 64

UNITED STATES. NAVY - 1943
Diving Manual. 1943. Washington: 1943. V. 66

UNITED STATES. PATENT OFFICE - 1857
Report of the Commissioner of Patents for the Year 1856: Agriculture. Washington: 1857. V. 67

UNITED STATES. PATENT OFFICE - 1858
Report of the Commissioner of Patents for the Year 1857: Agriculture. Washington: 1858. V. 67

UNITED STATES. PRESIDENT - 1801
Message and Communication from the President...to the Senate and House of Representatives.... Washington: 1801. V. 67

UNITED STATES. PRESIDENT - 1805
Message from the President of the United States, Supplementary to His Message on the Sixth Instant, Communicating Documents Respecting Louisiana. Washington: 1805. V. 63; 66

UNITED STATES. PRESIDENT - 1849
Message from the President of the United States to the Two Houses of Congress at the Commencement of the First Session of the Thirty-First Congress. Dec. 24, 1849. Washington: 1849. V. 63; 66

UNITED STATES. PRESIDENT - 1850
California and New Mexico: Message from the President of the United States. Washington: 1850. V. 62

Message from the President (Millard Filmore)...Dec. 2 1850...Printed for the Senate. Washington: 1850. V. 67

UNITED STATES. PRESIDENT - 1856
Message from the President of the U.S. to the Two Houses of Congress at the Commencement of the First Session of the 34th Congress. Washignton: 1856. V. 64

UNITED STATES. PRESIDENT - 1863
By the President of the United States, a Proclamation. General Orders No. 1. Washington: 1863. V. 63

UNITED STATES. PRESIDENT - 1869
Message from the President of the United States to the Two Houses of Congress at the Commencement of the 3rd Session of the 40th Congress.... Washington: 1869. V. 67

UNITED STATES. REVENUE CUTTER SERVICE - 1899
Report of the Cruise of the U. S. Revenue Cutter Bear and the Overland Expedition for the Relief of the Whalers in the Arctic Ocean, from November 27, 1897 to September 13, 1898. Washington: 1899. V. 63; 65; 66

UNITED STATES. SANITARY COMMISSION - 1862
Soldiers' Aid Society of Northern Ohio, First Annual Report...to the U.S. Sanitary Commission. Cleveland: 1862. V. 65

UNITED STATES. STATE DEPARTMENT - 1887
Reports from the Consuls of the United States on Cattle and Dairy Farming. Washington: 1887. V. 63

UNITED STATES. STATE DEPARTMENT - 1903
State Papers and Correspondence Bearing Upon the Purchase of the Territory of Louisiana. Washington: 1903. V. 65

UNITED STATES. SUPREME COURT - 1849
The Dred Scott Decision: Opinion of Chief Justice Taney. New York: 1849. V. 67

UNITED STATES. SUPREME COURT - 1857
Report of the Decisions of the Supreme Court of the United States, and the Opinion of the Judges Thereof, in the Case of Dred Scott, versus John F.A. Sanford. New York: 1857. V. 62; 64

UNITED STATES. TREASURY DEPARTMENT - 1879
Eleventh Annual List of Merchant Vessls of the United States. Washington: 1879. V. 62

UNITED STATES. TREASURY DEPARTMENT - 1885
Report on the Internal Commerce of the United States. Washington: 1885. V. 66

UNITED STATES. WAR DEPARTMENT - 1830
Abstract of Infantry Tactics: Including Exercises and Maneuvers of Light Infantry and Rifleman.... Boston: 1830. V. 65; 66

UNITED STATES. WAR DEPARTMENT - 1850
Reports of the Secretary of War, with Reconnaissances of Routes from San Antonio to El Paso. Washington: 1850. V. 66

UNITED STATES. WAR DEPARTMENT - 1853
Reports of Explorations and Surveys...Volume V. Washington: 1853. V. 67

UNITED STATES. WAR DEPARTMENT - 1855
Pacific Railroad Survey. Volume II. Washington: 1855. V. 65

UNITED STATES. WAR DEPARTMENT - 1856
Pacific Railroad Survey. Volume III. Washington: 1856. V. 65

UNITED STATES. WAR DEPARTMENT - 1857
Pacific Railroad Survey. Volume VII. Washington: 1857. V. 67
Regulations for the Army of the U.S., 1857. New York: 1857. V. 64

UNITED STATES. WAR DEPARTMENT - 1859
Pacific Railroad Survey. Washington: 1859. V. 67

UNITED STATES. WAR DEPARTMENT - 1860
Pacific Railroad Survey. Volume XII. Book I. Washington: 1860. V. 65

UNITED STATES. WAR DEPARTMENT - 1861
Instructions for Officers on Outpost and Patrol Duty. Washington: 1861. V. 64

UNITED STATES. WAR DEPARTMENT - 1866
General Orders No. 92 - War Department, Adjutant General's Office Washington, November 23, 1866. Washington: 1866. V. 67

UNITED STATES. WAR DEPARTMENT - 1876
Report of the Secretary of War: Being Part of the Message and Documents Communicated to the Two Houses of Congress at the Beginning of the Second Session of the Forty-Fourth Congress. Volume I. Washington: 1876. V. 66

UNITED STATES. WAR DEPARTMENT - 1878
Annual Report of the Secretary of War 1878. Washington: 1878. V. 67

UNITED STATES. WAR DEPARTMENT - 1882
Annual Report of the General of the Army to the Secretary of the War for the Year 1882. Washington: 1882. V. 63

UNITED STATES. WAR DEPARTMENT - 1888
Report of the Tests of Metals and Other Materials. Washington: 1888. V. 66

UNITED STATES. WAR DEPARTMENT - 1892
Annual Report of the Secretary of War for 1891. Washington: 1892. V. 67

UNITED STATES. WAR DEPARTMENT - 1918
Manual of Medical Research Laboratory...Air Service Division of Military Aeronautics. Washington: 1918. V. 63

UNITED STATES. WAR DEPARTMENT - 1919
Air Service Medical. Washington: 1919. V. 63; 65
Manual of Neuro-Surgery Authorized by the Secretary of War. Washington: 1919. V. 66

UNITED States Artillery Firing. Nancy: 1918. V. 64

UNITED STATES CARTRIDGE CO.
Where to Hunt American Game. Lowell: 1898. V. 66

UNITED States Magazine. Philadelphia: 1779. V. 63

UNITED STATES MILITARY ACADEMY, WEST POINT
Catalogue of the Library of the U.S. Military Academy at West-Point, May 1830. New York: 1830. V. 62

UNITED STATES MOTOR COMPANY
Salesman's Manual, Stoddard-Dayton Division. N.P: 1912. V. 66

THE UNITED States Naval Astronomical Expedition to the Southern Hemisphere During the Years 1849-50-51-52. Washington: 1855. V. 63

UNITED STATES PACIFIC RAILROAD SURVEY
Reports of Explorations and Surveys, to Ascertain the Most Practicable and Economical Route for a Railroad from the Mississippi River to the Pacific Ocean 1853-1855. Volume XII. Book II. Washington: 1860. V. 64

THE UNIVERSAL Conjuror, or, The Whole Art of Legerdemain, As Practiced by the Famous Breslaw, Katterfelto, Jonas, Flockton, Comas, and by the Greatest Adepts in London and Paris.... London: 1829. V. 66

UNIVERSAL EXPOSITION, ST. LOUIS
Official Catalogue of Exhibitors, Universal Exposition, St. Louis, U. S.A., 1904. St. Louis: 1904. V. 64

THE UNIVERSAL Gazetteer; or a Description.... Dublin: 1759. V. 66

THE UNIVERSAL Officer of Justice. London: 1731. V. 62; 66

THE UNIVERSITY Geological Survey of Kansas. Topeka: 1896-1900. V. 63

UNIVERSITY OF CALIFORNIA
Publications in Botany. Berkeley: 1912-1930. V. 63
Publications in Botany. Berkeley: 1916-1922. V. 63
Publications in Botany. Berkeley: 1922-1924. V. 63
Publications in Zoology. Berkeley: 1910-1912. V. 63
Publications in Zoology. Berkeley: 1914-1916. V. 63

UNMUZZLED Oz (Volume One Number Four). New York: 1972. V. 66

THE UNNATURAL Mother and Ungrateful Wife, a Narrative. London: 1750. V. 66

UNRAU, JOHN D.
The Plains Across the Overland - Emigrants and the Trans-Mississippi West 1840-1860. Urbana: 1979. V. 67

UNSWORTH, BARRY
The Stone Virgin. Boston: 1986. V. 67

UNTERKIRCHER, F.
European Illuminated Manuscripts in the Austrian National Library. London: 1967. V. 62

UNTO the Right Honourable the Lords of Council and Session, the Petition of Mr. James Catanach, L.L.D. Advocate in Aberdeen and of Mr. Alexander Burnet, Sub-Principal, Dr. James Gregory, Professor of Medicine, Mr. Alexander Raitt.... N.P: 1744. V. 63

UPASAKA, SHIKI
Peonies Kana: Haiku by the Upasaka Shiki. New York: 1972. V. 64

UP DE GRAFF, F. W.
Head-Hunters of the Amazon, Seven Years of Exploration and Adventure. London: 1923. V. 64

UPDIKE, DANIEL BERKELEY
Printing Types, their History, Forms and Use. Cambridge: 1937. V. 62
Printing Types Their History, Forms and Use. London: 1937. V. 64
Printing Types, Their History, Forms, and Use. Cambridge: 1962. V. 63

UPDIKE, JOHN
The Afterlife. Leamington Spa: 1987. V. 66; 67
The Afterlife. New York: 1994. V. 67
Assorted Prose. New York: 1965. V. 62; 64
Baby's First Step. Huntington Beach: 1993. V. 67
Bech: a Book. New York: 1970. V. 67
Bech at Bay. New York: 1998. V. 62
Bech is Back. New York: 1982. V. 67
Brazil. Franklin Center: 1994. V. 65; 67
Brazil. New York: 1994. V. 67
Buchanan Dying. New York: 1974. V. 67
The Carpentered Hen and Other Tame Creatures. New York: 1958. V. 62; 64; 67
The Centaurs. New York: 1963. V. 63; 65
The Chaste Plant. Worcester: 1980. V. 67
The Coup. New York: 1978. V. 66; 67
Couples: a Short Story. Cambridge: 1976. V. 62; 67
Cunts. New York: 1974. V. 62
Ego and Art in Walt Whitman. New York: 1980. V. 66; 67
Emersonianism. Cleveland: 1984. V. 67
Getting Older. Helsinki: 1986. V. 62
Getting the Words Out. Northridge: 1988. V. 65
Going Abroad. Helsinki: 1987. V. 62
Going Abroad. Helsinki: 1988. V. 65
A Good Place: Being a Personal Account of Ipswich, Massachusetts, Written on the Occassion of Its Seventeenth-Century Day, 1972, by a Resident. N.P: 1973. V. 62
Hawthorne's Creed. New York: 1981. V. 67
Hoping for a Hoopoe. London: 1959. V. 62; 65
Hub Fans Bid Kid Adieu. Northridge: 1977. V. 65
Hugging the Shore: Essays and Criticism. New York: 1983. V. 66; 67
In Memoriam Felis Felis. Leamington Spa: 1990. V. 64; 67
In the Beauty of the Lilies. Franklin Center: 1996. V. 67
In the Beauty of the Lilies. New York: 1996. V. 67
In the Cemetery High Above Shillington. Concord: 1995. V. 62; 64; 66; 67
Just Looking. Essays on Art. New York: 1989. V. 66; 67
Memories of the Ford Administration. New York: 1992. V. 62; 65; 67
Midpoint and Other Poems. New York: 1969. V. 66; 67
A Month of Sundays. New York: 1975. V. 66
More Matter: Essays and Criticism. New York: 1999. V. 66; 67
More Stately Mansions. Jackson: 1987. V. 67
Museums and Women and Other Stories. New York: 1972. V. 67
The Music School: Short Stories. New York: 1966. V. 64
The Music School: Short Stories. London: 1967. V. 62
Odd Jobs. Essays and Criticism. New York: 1991. V. 66; 67
Of the Farm. New York: 1965. V. 62; 64; 65; 67
People One Knows, Interview with Insufficiently Famous Americans. Northridge: 1980. V. 66; 67
Picked-Up Pieces. New York: 1975. V. 62; 65; 67
Pigeon Feathers and Other Stories. London: 1962. V. 62
The Poorhouse Fair. New York: 1959. V. 63
Problems. New York: 1979. V. 67
Problems. Queensland: 1980. V. 62
Query. New York: 1974. V. 66; 67
Rabbit Angstrom: the Four Novels. New York: 1995. V. 62
Rabbit at Rest. Franklin Center: 1990. V. 65
Rabbit at Rest. New York: 1990. V. 62; 64; 67
Rabbit is Rich. New York: 1981. V. 62; 64; 67
Rabbit Redux. New York: 1971. V. 64; 66
Rabbit, Run. New York: 1960. V. 67
Rabbit, Run. Harmondsworth: 1964. V. 62
Rabbit Run. Franklin Center: 1977. V. 67
Roger's Version. Franklin Center: 1986. V. 67
Roger's Version. New York: 1986. V. 66; 67
S. London: 1988. V. 67
The Same Door - Short Stories. London: 1962. V. 62
Self-Consciousness. Memoirs. New York: 1989. V. 67
Six Poems. N.P: 1973. V. 62; 64; 67
Sixteen Sonnets. Cambridge: 1979. V. 62; 67
Talk from the Fifties. Northridge: 1979. V. 67
Thanatopses. Cleveland: 1991. V. 66
Three Illuminations in the Life of an American Author. New York: 1979. V. 64; 67
Too Far to Go: the Maples Stories. New York: 1979. V. 67
Toward the End of Time. Franklin Center: 1997. V. 62; 65; 67
Trust Me. New York: 1987. V. 66; 67
The Twelve Terrors of Christmas. New York: 1994. V. 62; 64; 67
Warm Wine. New York: 1973. V. 66; 67
The Witches of Eastwick. Franklin Center: 1984. V. 67
The Witches of Eastwick. New York: 1984. V. 62; 64; 66; 67
The Witches of Eastwick. Franklin Center: 1986. V. 66

UPFIELD, ARTHUR
The Battling Prophet. London: 1956. V. 67
Bony and the Kelly Gang. London: 1960. V. 65; 66
Death of Swagman. London: 1946. V. 66
Madman's Bend. London: 1963. V. 65
The Mystery of Swordfish Reef. 1943. V. 64; 66
The New Show. Garden City: 1951. V. 65; 66
Valley of Smugglers. Garden City: 1960. V. 67
The Will of the Tribe. Garden City: 1960. V. 67

UPHAM, CHARLES W.
Salem Witchcraft; with an Account of Salem Village and A History of Opinions on Witchcraft and Kindred Subjects. Boston: 1867. V. 62

UPHAM, ELIZABETH
Little Brown Bear. New York: 1942. V. 62

UPHAM, J. C.
Life Explorations and Public Services of John Charles Fremont. Boston: 1856. V. 64

UPHAM, THOMAS C.
Elements of Mental Philosophy, in Two Volumes. Boston: 1831. V. 64
Outlines of Imperfect and Disordered Mental Action. New York: 1840. V. 64; 65

UPSON, WILLIAM HAZLETT
Alexander Botts. New York: 1929. V. 66
Botts in War, Botts in Peace. New York: 1944. V. 66
Earthworms in Europe. New York: 1931. V. 66
Keep 'Em Crawling. New York: 1943. V. 66

UPTON, BERTHA
The Adventures of Two Dutch Dolls and a "Golliwogg". Boston: 1895. V. 63
The Golliwogg's Bicycle Club. London: 1896. V. 62; 64; 67
The Golliwogg's Christmas. London: 1907. V. 63
The Golliwogg's Desert Island. London: 1906. V. 63
The Golliwogg's Polar Adventures. London. V. 62
The Vegemen's Revenge. London: 1897. V. 65

UPTON, CHARLES E.
Pioneers of El Dorado. Placerville: 1906. V. 62; 65

UPTON, EMORY
The Military Policy of the United States. Washington: 1904. V. 67

UPTON, JOHN
Critical Observations on Shakespeare. London: 1746. V. 66
Critical Observations on Shakespeare. London: 1748. V. 62

UPTON, ROBERT
Dead on the Stick. New York: 1986. V. 67

UPTON, ROGER
O for a Falconer's Voice. London: 1987. V. 67

UPTON, WILLIAM
The School Girl. London: 1820. V. 62

UPWARD, ALLEN
A Bride's Madness. London: 1897. V. 64; 66
The Queen Against Owens. London: 1894. V. 64; 66

UPWARD, EDWARD
Christopher Isherwood: Notes in Remembrance of a Friendship. London: 1996. V. 66
In the Thirties. London: 1962. V. 67
The Night Walk and Other Stories. London: 1987. V. 66
The Railway Accident - and Other Stories. London: 1969. V. 62
Remembering the Earlier Auden. London: 1998. V. 66
The Rotten Elements - a Novel of Fact. London: 1969. V. 65

URBAN, JOSEPH
Theatres. New York: 1929. V. 67

URBINO, L. B.
Art Recreations. Boston: 1861. V. 64

URE, ANDREW
The Cotton Manufacture of Great Britain Systematically Investigated and Illustrated.... London: 1836. V. 63
A Dictionary of Arts, Manufactures and Mines. 1839. V. 62
Dictionary of Arts, Manufactures and Mines Containing a Clear Exposition of Their Principles and Practice. London: 1867. V. 66
The Philosophy of Manufactures, or, an Exposition of the Scientific, Moral and Commercial Economy of the Factory System of Great Britain. London: 1835. V. 64
Ure's Dictionary of Arts, Manufactures and Mines. New York: 1866. V. 67
Ure's Dictionary of Arts, Manufactures and Mines Containing a Clear Exposition of Their Principles and Practice. London: 1878. V. 65; 66

URE, DAVID
The History of Rutherglen and East-Kilbride. Glasgow: 1793. V. 62

URIS, LEON
The Angry Hills. New York: 1955. V. 66
Battle Cry. 1953. V. 67
Battle Cry. New York: 1953. V. 64
Exodus. Franklin Center: 1977. V. 67
The Haj. Franklin Center: 1984. V. 66
Topaz. New York: 1967. V. 66

URLIN, ETHEL L.
Dancing Ancient and Modern. London: 1911. V. 63

URQUHART, A. R.
Auld Perth. Perth: 1906. V. 62

URQUHART, B. L.
The Camellia. 1956-1960. V. 66
The Camellia. Sharpthorne, Sussex: 1956-1960. V. 64
The Rhododendron. London: 1958-1962. V. 63

URQUHART, DAVID
The Spirit of the East, Illustrated in a Journal of Travels through Roumeli During an Eventful Period. London: 1838. V. 67
Wealth and Want; or Taxation, as Influencing Private Riches and Public Liberty. London: 1845. V. 64

URQUHART, WILLIAM POLLARD
Life and Times of Francesco Sforza, Duke of Milan. Edinburgh and London: 1852. V. 64

URREA, LUIS ALBERTO
Across the Wire. New York: 1990. V. 64; 67
The Fever of Being. New York: 1994. V. 65
Nobody's Son. Tucson: 1998. V. 67

URRETA, LUIS DE
Historia Eclesiastica, Politica, Natural y Moral de Los Grandes y Remotos Reynos de la Etiopia, Monarchia del Emperador.... Valencia: 1610. V. 62

URRUTIA, JOSE DE
Coleccion de Exercicios Facultativos Para la Uniforme Instruccion de la Tropa del Real Cuerpo de Artilleria. Filadelfia: 1827. V. 66

THE URSULINE Manual or a Collection of Prayers, Spiritual Exercises, Etc.... New York: 1840. V. 62

URWICK, THOMAS A.
Records of the Family of Urswyk, Urswick, or Urwick. St. Albans: 1893. V. 64; 65; 66

USHER, FRANK
A Strange Love. London: 1874. V. 67

USHER, JAMES
Clio, or a Discourse on Taste. London: 1803. V. 63

USHER, JAMES WARD
An Art Collector's Treasures. London: 1916. V. 66

USINGER, R. I.
Aquatic Insects of California with Keys to North American Genera and California Species. Berkeley: 1956. V. 64

USLAR PIETRI, ARTURO
Las Lanzas Coloradas. Madrid: 1931. V. 67

USSHER, JAMES
The Annals of the World. London: 1658. V. 67
A Body of Divinity or The Summe and Substance of Christian Religion. 1648. V. 62
A Body of Divinity, or the Summe and Substance of Christian Religion. London: 1648. V. 64

USSHER, PERCY
The Midnight Court and the Adventures of a Luckless Fellow. 1926. V. 64; 67

USSHER, RICHARD J.
The Birds of Ireland. 1900. V. 66

USSHER, W. A. E.
The Geology of the Country Around Torquay. 1933. V. 67
The Post-Tertiary (Recent) Geology of Cornwall. 1879. V. 62

USTINOV, PETER
The Love of Four Colonels. London: 1952. V. 66

UTAMARO, KITAGAWA
Twelve Wood-Block Prints of Kitagawa Utamaro. San Francisco: 1965. V. 64

UTILITY; or, Sketches of Domestic Education. London: 1815. V. 64

UTLEY, ROBERT M.
Custer and the Great Controversy. Los Angeles: 1962. V. 67
Frontier Regulars to United States Army and the Indian 1866-1890. New York: 1973. V. 67
Frontiermen in Blue - the United States Army and the Indian 1848- 1865. New York: 1967. V. 65; 67
The Reno Court of Inquiry. Fort Collins: 1983. V. 65

UTTLEY, ALISON
Adventures of Sam Pig. London: 1940. V. 65
Cuckoo Cherry-Tree. London: 1943. V. 67
Fuzzypeg Goes to School. London: 1938. V. 65
Fuzzypeg Goes to School. London: 1955. V. 67
Hare and Guy Fawkes. London: 1956. V. 67
Hare and the Rainbow. London: 1975. V. 67
High Meadows. London: 1938. V. 67
The Knot Squirrel Tied. London: 1937. V. 62
Little Grey Rabbit Goes to the North Pole. London: 1970. V. 67
Little Grey Rabbit's Christmas. London: 1939. V. 67
Little Grey Rabbit's Paint Box. London: 1958. V. 67
Squirrel Goes Skating. London: 1934. V. 67
The Stuff of Dreams. London: 1953. V. 65
The Washerwoman's Child - a Play on the Life and Stories of Hans Christian Andersen. London: 1945. V. 65
Wise Owl's Story. London: 1935. V. 65

UZANNE, OCTAVE
L'Art dans la Decoration Entreieure des Livres en France et a Letranger. Paris: 1898. V. 67
La Femme a Paris. Nos Contemporaines, Notes Successives sur Les Parisiennes de Ce Temps Dans Leurs Divers Millieux.... Paris: 1894. V. 62
The French Bookbinders of the Eighteenth Century. Chicago: 1904. V. 62; 63; 64; 66
The Frenchwoman of the Century. London: 1886. V. 63; 64; 66
Son Altesse, La Femme. Paris: 1885. V. 62

UZIELLI, MATTHEW
Catalogue of the Various Works of Art. London: 1861. V. 66

V

VACHE, JACQUES
Lettres de Guerre. Paris: 1919. V. 65; 67

VACHELL, HORACE
Life and Sport on the Pacific Slope. 1900. V. 67
Sport and Life on the Pacific Slope. London: 1908. V. 66

VACHER, FRANCIS
Engravers and Engraving. Manchester: 1887. V. 62; 66

VACHSS, ANDREW
Flood. New York: 1985. V. 66

THE VADE Mecum for America.... Boston: 1732. V. 66

VAIL, ISRAEL E.
Three Years on the Blockade. New York: 1902. V. 62; 63

VAIL, SHARON
Four Poems. 1942. V. 63

VAILLANT, SEBASTIEN
Botanicon Parisiense ou Denombrement par Ordre Alphabetique des Plantes.... Leiden and Amsterdam: 1727. V. 64

VAJDA, MIKLOS
Winged by Their Own Need - Poems by the Winners and Jurors of the Robert Graves Prize for Best Hungarian Poem of the Year 1970-1986. Mallorca;: 1988. V. 64

VALDEZ, RAUL
Wild Sheep and Sheep Hunters of the New World. 1988. V. 63; 64; 66
Wild Sheep and Wild Sheep Hunters of the Old World. 1983. V. 62; 63; 64; 66

VALE, G.
The Beacon. New York: 1838. V. 64

VALE, GILBERT
The Poetry of Thomas Paine. New York: 1850. V. 67

VALENCIENNES, P. H.
Elemens de Perspective Pratique, a l'Usage des Artistes, Suivis de Reflexions et Sonseil a un Eleve sur la Peinture, et Particulierement sur le Genre du Paysage. Paris: 1800. V. 67

VALENTI Angelo: Author, Illustrator, Printer. 1976. V. 67

VALENTINE, EDWARD PLEASANTS
The Edward Pleasants Valentine Papers, Abstracts of Records in Virginia. Richmond: 1929. V. 64

VALENTINO, RUDOLPH
Reflections. Chicago: 1923. V. 63

VALENZUELA, LUISA
Clara. New York: 1976. V. 67

VALERDE DE HAMUSCO, JUAN
Vivae Imagines Partium Corporis Humani, Aereis Formis Expressae. Antverpiae: 1579. V. 65

VALERIUS FLACCUS, CAIUS
Commentarii Pio Bononiesi Auctore: Cum Codicis Poetae Emendatione Ex Antiquo Exemplari Dacico Additis Libris Tribus.... 1519. V. 66
Setini Balbi Argonauticon Lib. VIII. Antverpiae: 1566. V. 66

VALERIUS MAXIMUS, GAIUS
Dictorum Facatorum Q(ue) Memorabilium Exempla.... 1550. V. 65
Dictorum, Factorumque Memorabilium Libri Novem.... Venetiis: 1581. V. 65
Exempla Quattuor and Viginti Nuper Inventa Ante Caput de Ominbus. (and) Plutarchi Cheronei Parellela Addita Propter Materiae Similitudinem. Florence: 1526. V. 65
Exempla Quatuor. Venetiis: 1514. V. 66
Fracatorum Dictorumque Memorabilium.... Leidae: 1726. V. 65; 66
Valerius Maximus cum Selectis Variorum Observat, et Nova Resensione a Thysii.... Lugd. Batavorum: 1660. V. 66

VALERY, PAUL
La Cimetiere Marin. Paris: 1920. V. 65
Dialogues. New York: 1956. V. 65
Eupalinos or the Architect. London: 1932. V. 65
The Graveyard by the Sea. Philadelphia: 1932. V. 63
The Graveyard by the Sea. London: 1946. V. 62; 65
Introduction to the Method of Leonardo Da Vinci. London: 1929. V. 62; 63; 64; 66

VALERY, PAUL continued
La Jeune Parque. Paris: 1917. V. 65
Lettre a Madame C.... Paris: 1928. V. 66
Moralities. Paris: 1932. V. 67
Le Serpent. London: 1924. V. 65

VALESI, FRANCESCO
Museum Cortonense in Quo Vetera Monumenta Complectuntur.... Rome: 1750. V. 67

VALIN, JONATHAN
Dead Letter. 1981. V. 66
Dead Letter. New York: 1981. V. 67
Final Notice. New York: 1980. V. 64; 65; 66; 67
Fire Lake. New York: 1987. V. 67
The Lime Pit. 1980. V. 62; 66
The Lime Pit. New York: 1980. V. 64; 67

VALLA, LORENZO
Laurentii Vallae de Linguae Latinae Elegantia Libri Sex, Una Cum Libello de Reciprocatione Sui and Suus, Cum Optimis Editionibus Summa Cura & Diligentia Recogniti and Colati. Cambrigae: 1688. V. 65

VALLANCE, AYMER
Greater English Church Screens. London: 1947. V. 64
Old Crosses and Lychgates. London: 1920. V. 62; 63

VALLANCEY, CHARLES
The Art of Tanning and Currying Leather.... London: 1780. V. 62

VALLAVINE, PETER
Observations on the Present Condition of the Current Coin of This Kingdom. London: 1742. V. 66

VALLEE, RUDY
Vagabond Dreams Come True. New York: 1930. V. 63; 67

VALLEJO, CESAR
Twenty Poems of Cesar Vallejo. Madison: 1962. V. 65

VALLENTIN, ELINOR FRANCES
Illustrations of the Flowering Plants and Ferns of the Falkland Islands. 1921. V. 65
Illustrations of the Flowering Plants and Ferns of the Falkland Islands. London: 1921. V. 67

VALLERY RADOT, RENE
The Life of Pasteur. London: 1919. V. 67
La Vie de Pasteur. 1900. V. 67
La Vie de Pasteur. Paris: 1919. V. 65

VALLIER, D.
Braque: L'Oeuvre Grave Catalogue Raisonne. Lausanne: 1982. V. 65

VALPURGIS; or the Devil's Festival. London: 1831. V. 62

VALSECCHI, MARCO
Landscape Painting of the 19th Century. Greenwich: 1971. V. 63; 64

VALUABLE Secrets Concerning Arts and Trades; or, Approved Directions, from the Best Artists. Norwich: 1795. V. 62; 64

VALUABLE Secrets Concerning Arts and Trades &c. New York: 1809. V. 64

VALUABLE Secrets in Arts, Trades, &c. New York: 1816. V. 62

VALVERDE DE HAMUSCO, JUAN
Vivae Imagines Partium Corporis Humani, Aereis Formis Expressae. Antverpiae: 1572. V. 67

VAN AMBURGH & CO.
Illustrated and Descriptive History of the Animals Contained in Van Ambrugh & Co.'s New Great Golden Menagerie Combination. New York: 1877. V. 65

VAN ALLSBURG, CHRIS
Bad Day at Riverbend. Boston: 1995. V. 62; 64; 65
Jumanji. Boston: 1981. V. 63; 65
Just a Dream. Boston: 1990. V. 62
The Polar Express. Boston: 1985. V. 63; 65; 66
The Stranger. Boston: 1986. V. 64
The Sweetest Fig. Boston: 1993. V. 64
Two Bad Ants. Boston: 1988. V. 63
The Widow's Broom. Boston: 1992. V. 62; 67
The Wreck of the Zephyr. Boston: 1983. V. 62
The Wretched Stone. Boston: 1991. V. 63; 64; 65
The Z was Zapped. Boston: 1987. V. 63

VAN ANTWERP, WILLIAM C.
A Collector's Comment on His First Editions of the Works of Sir Walter Scott. San Francisco: 1932. V. 62; 63; 64; 66

VAN AUKEN, WILBUR R.
Notes On a Half Century of U.S. Naval Ordnance 1880-1930. Washington: 1939. V. 65

VANBRUGH, JOHN
The Complete Works. Bloomsbury: 1924. V. 62

VAN BUREN, MARTIN
Considerations in Favour of the Appointment of Rufus King, to the Senate of the United States. New York: 1819. V. 66

VANCE, JACK
City of the Chasch. 1979. V. 64; 66
The Dying Earth. 1976. V. 64; 66
The Killing Machine. 1981. V. 64; 66
The Pnume. 1981. V. 64
Servants of the Wankh. 1980. V. 66
To Live Forever. 1956. V. 66
To Live Forever. London: 1956. V. 64

VANCE, JOEL M.
Confessions of an Outdoor Maladroit. Clinton: 1983. V. 65

VANCE, ZEBULON BAIRD
The Duties of Defeat. An Address Delivered Before the Two Literary Socieities of the University of North Carolina June 7th 1866. Raleigh: 1866. V. 63; 65

VAN COURT, DEWITT C.
The Making of Champions in California. Los Angeles: 1926. V. 62; 63

VANCOUVER, GEORGE
A Voyage of Discovery to the North Pacific Ocean, and Round the World.... Amsterdam/New York: 1967. V. 62
The Voyage of George Vancouver 1791-1795. 1984. V. 67
The Voyage of George Vancouver 1791-1795. London: 1984. V. 64; 65
A Voyage to Discovery...1791-1795. London: 1984. V. 63

VAN DAAME, W.
Sculpture from Africa and Oceania. Otterlo;: 1990. V. 62

VAN DEBURGH, J.
The Reptiles of Western North America. 1922. V. 62

VANDELEUR, SEYMOUR
Campaigning on the Upper Nile and Niger. London: 1898. V. 66

VANDEN, L. J.
On the Trail of the Pigmies, an Anthropological Exploration Under the Co-operaiton of the American Museum of Natural History and American Universities. New York: 1921. V. 62

VAN DEN BROECKE, MARCEL
Ortellus Atlas Maps: an Illustrated Guide. Netherland: 1996. V. 65

VANDERBILT, HAROLD S.
Enterprise. The Story of the Defense of the America's Cup in 1930. New York: 1931. V. 64; 65

VANDERBILT, WILLIAM K.
To Galapagos on the Ara, 1926, the Events of a Pleasure-Cruise to the Galapagos Islands and a Classification of a Few Rare Aquatic Findings.... London: 1927. V. 62; 63

VAN DER BURG, P.
School of Painting for the Imitation of Woods and Marbles. London: 1908. V. 64

VAN DER ELST, VIOLET
On the Gallows. London: 1937. V. 62

VANDERHAEGHE, GUY
Homesick. Toronto: 1989. V. 67
My Present Age. Toronto: 1984. V. 63; 65; 67
Things As They Are?. Toronto: 1992. V. 64; 67

VAN DERHOLM, CARL
Notices and Voyages of the Famed Queque Mission to the Pacific Northwest. Portland: 1956. V. 65

VAN DER HOOP
Indonesian Ornamental Design. Jakarta: 1949. V. 62

VAN DER STRAETEN, EDMUND
The History of the Violin; Its Ancestors and Collateral Instruments. London: 1933. V. 64

VANDERVELL, HARRY
A Shuttle of an Empire's Loom; or, Five Months Before the Mast On a Modern Steam Cargo-Boat. Edinburgh: 1898. V. 67

VANDERVELL, HENRY EUGENE
A System of Figure-Skating. London: 1869. V. 65

VAN DER ZEE, JAMES
James Van Der Zee. Dobbs Ferry: 1973. V. 63

VAN DE VYVER, A.
Les Premieres Traductions Latines (Xe-XIe Siecles) de Traites Arabes sur l'Astrolabe. Brussels: 1931. V. 65

VAN DE WATER, FREDERIC F.
Glory Hunter - a Life of General Custer. New York: 1934. V. 65; 67

VAN DE WETERING, JAN WILLEM
Mangrove Mama and Other Tropical Tales of Terror. Tucson: 1995. V. 63

VANDIVER, CLARENCE
The Fur Trade and Early Western Exploration. Cleveland: 1929. V. 63

VANDIVER, FRANK
Confederate Blockade Running through Bermuda 1861-1865: Letters and Cargo Manifests. Austin: 1947. V. 67
Mighty Stonewall. New York: 1957. V. 63
Ploughshares into Swords. Josiah Gorgas and Confederate Ordnance. Austin: 1952. V. 63; 65

VAN DONGEN, P. L. F.
Masterpieces from the National Museum of Ethnology. Leiden: 1987. V. 62

VAN DOREN, MARK
An Anthology of World Poetry. New York: 1936. V. 65

VAN DRUTEN, JOHN
Leave Her to Heaven: a Play in Three Acts. New York: 1941. V. 66

VAN DUSEN, W. W.
Blazing the Way or Pioneer Experiences in Idaho Washington and Oregon. New York: 1905. V. 66

VAN DYKE, H. B.
The Physiology and Pharmacology of the Pituitary Body. Chicago: 1936. V. 63; 67

VAN DYKE, JOHN C.
The Open Spaces - Incidents of Nights and Days Under the Blue Sky. New York: 1922. V. 63

VAN DYKE, T. S.
The City and County of San Diego: Illustrated and Containing Biographical Sketches of Prominent Men and Pioneers. San Diego: 1888. V. 62
Flirtation Camp, or The Rifle, Rod and Gun in California. 1881. V. 63
Millionaires of a Day: an Inside History of the Great Southern California Boom. New York: 1890. V. 62; 63

VANE, HENRY
The Tryal of Sir Henry Vane, Kt. June the 2d and 6th 1662.... London: 1662. V. 62

VANEIGEM, RAOUL
Traite de Savoir-Vivre a l'Usage des Jeunes Generations. Paris: 1967. V. 67

VAN GELDEREN, D. M.
Conifers, the Illustrated Encyclopedia. Portland: 1996. V. 67

VAN GIESON, JUDITH
North of the Border. 1988. V. 64; 66
North of the Border. New York: 1988. V. 63
Raptor. New York: 1990. V. 62; 63; 65; 67

VAN GOGH, VINCENT
Complete Letters. Greenwich: 1959. V. 62

VAN GULIK, R. B.
The Gibbon in China - an Essay in Chinese Animal Lore. Leiden: 1967. V. 64

VAN GULIK, ROBERT
The Chinese Bell Murders. London: 1958. V. 64; 66
The Chinese Gold Murders. New York: 1961. V. 63
The Chinese Lake Murders. London: 1960. V. 63; 65; 67
The Chinese Lake Murders. New York: 1962. V. 67
The Chinese Maze Murders. The Hague and Bandung: 1956. V. 63
The Chinese Nail Murders. New York: 1961. V. 66
The Chinese Nail Murders. New York and Evanston: 1962. V. 63; 67
The Emperor's Pearl. London: 1963. V. 65
The Emperor's Pearl. New York: 1964. V. 63
The Given Day. San Antonio: 1984. V. 65; 66; 67
The Haunted Monastery. Kuala Lumpur: 1961. V. 62
The Haunted Monastery. London: 1963. V. 65
Judge Dee at Work. London: 1967. V. 65
The Lacquer Screen. London: 1962. V. 65; 66
The Lacquer Screen. New York: 1969. V. 67
The Lacquer Screen. New York: 1970. V. 63; 67
The Monkey and the Tiger. London: 1965. V. 64; 66
The Monkey and the Tiger. New York: 1966. V. 63; 67
Murder in Canton. London: 1966. V. 65
Murder in Canton. New York: 1967. V. 63
Necklace and Calabash. London: 1967. V. 66
Necklace and Calabash. New York: 1971. V. 67
New Year's Eve in Lan-Fang: a Judge Dee Story. Beirut: 1958. V. 62
The Phantom of the Temple. London: 1966. V. 65
The Phantom of the Temple. New York: 1966. V. 63
Poets and Murder. London: 1968. V. 64; 65; 66
Poets and Murder. New York: 1972. V. 67
The Red Pavilion. Kuala Lumpur: 1961. V. 65; 66; 67
The Red Pavilion. London: 1964. V. 65; 66
The Red Pavilion. New York: 1968. V. 63
Vier Vingers. (Four Fingers). Amsterdam: 1964. V. 67
The Willow Pattern. London: 1965. V. 65
The Willow Pattern. New York: 1965. V. 63; 67

VAN HAGEN, ERIC
The Sleeping Beauty (An Activity Book). Cincinnati: 1950. V. 65

VAN HEURCK, HENRI
The Microscope: Its Construction and Management.... London: 1893. V. 64

VAN HEUVEL, J. A.
El Dorado: Being a Narrative of the Circumstances Which Gave Rise to Reports, in the Sixteenth Century, of the Existence of a Rich and Splendid City in South America.... New York: 1844. V. 67

VAN HOLST, H.
The Constitutional and Political History of the United States. Chicago: 1877. V. 67

VAN MOE, EMILE A.
The Decorated Letter from the VIIIth to the XIIth Century. Paris: 1950. V. 62

VAN NOSTRAND, JEANNE
Edward Vischer's Drawings of the California Missions 1861-1878. San Francisco: 1982. V. 63
The First Hundred Years of Painting in California 1775-1875. San Francisco: 1980. V. 62; 66

VAN NOTEN, F.
The Archaeology of Central Africa. Graz: 1982. V. 62

VANNOZ, MME. DE
Epitres d'une Femme sur la Conversation; Suigives de Poesie Fugitives. Paris: 1812. V. 67

VAN OSDEL, A. L.
Historic Landmarks in the Great Northwest, Being a History of Early Explorers and Fur Traders with a Narrative of their Adventures in the Wilds of the Great Northwest Territory. N.P: 1951. V. 64; 67

VAN PATTEN, NATHAN
Preface to Arthur Machen's Bridles and Spurs. San Francisco: 1951. V. 63

VAN PEEBLES, MELVIN
Bear for the F. B. I. New York: 1968. V. 67

VAN PELT, GARRETT
Old Architecture of Southern Mexico. Cleveland: 1926. V. 62; 63

VAN REGENMORTER, BERTHE
Some Oriental Bindings in the Chester Beatty Library. Dublin: 1961. V. 62; 64

VAN RENSSELAER, J.
An Essay on Salt.... New York: 1823. V. 62
Lectures on Geology: Being Outlines of the Science, Delivered in the New York Athenaeum...1825. New York: 1825. V. 66

VAN SCHOOTEN, FRANS
Tabulae Sinuum Tangentium Secantium ad Radium 10000000; Avecq l'Usage d'Icelles es Triangles Plans. Amsterdam: 1627. V. 65

VAN SICHEM, GEORG
Der Todten-Tanz, Wie Derselbe in Der Weit-beruhmten Stadt Basel. Basel. V. 66

VANSICKEL, S. S.
A Story of Real Life on the Plains. Cedar Rapids: 1895. V. 64

VANSITTART, HENRY
A Letter to the Proprietors of East India Stock - Occasioned by a Late Anonymous Pamphlet and by the East-India Observer, No. VI. London: 1767. V. 66
A Narrative of the Transactions in Bengal, fromt he Yar 1760 to the Year 1764, During the Government of Mr. Henry Vanstittart. London: 1766. V. 62

VAN SOMEREN, V. D.
A Bird Watcher in Kenya. 1958. V. 62; 63; 64; 66

VAN THAL, HERBERT
The Prime Ministers. London: 1974. V. 66

VAN TRAMP, JOHN C.
Prairie and Rocky Mountain Adventures; or Life in the West.... Columbus: 1869. V. 63; 66

VAN URK, J. BLAN
The Horse, The Valley and The Chagrin Valley Hunt. New York: 1947. V. 62

VAN VECHTEN, CARL
The Blind Bow-Boy. New York: 1923. V. 65
Fragments from an Unwritten Autobiography. New Haven: 1955. V. 66
Music After the Great War and Other Studies. New York: 1915. V. 64
Spider Boy. New York: 1928. V. 62; 65
The Tattooed Countess. New York: 1924. V. 64; 65; 67

VANVITELLI, LUIGI
Dichiarazione dei Disegni del Reale Palazzo di Caserta.... Naples: 1756. V. 67

VAN VOGT, A. E.
The Book of Ptath. Reading: 1947. V. 63
Destination Universe!. New York: 1952. V. 64
Destination: Universe!. London: 1953. V. 65
Out of the Unknown. 1948. V. 66
The Weapon Shops of Isher. London: 1952. V. 64

VAN VOORHIES, WILLIAM
Oration Before the Society of California Pioneers at Their Celebration of the Anniversary of the Admission of the State of California into the Union. San Francisco: 1853. V. 62; 63
Oration Before the Society of California Pioneers at their Celebration of the Anniversary of the Admission of the State of California into the Union. San Francisco: 1982. V. 63

VAN VORST, BESSIE
The Woman Who Toils. New York: 1903. V. 67

VAN WATERS, GEORGE
The Poetical Geography. Milwaukee: 1848. V. 66
The Poetical Geography. Cincinnati: 1852. V. 67

VAN WATERSCHOOT, W. A. J. M.
Theory of Continental Drift. Tulsa: 1928. V. 67

VAN WINKLE, DANIEL
History of the Municipalities of Hudson County, New Jersey 1630-1923. New York: 1924. V. 63; 66

VAN WORMER, J.
The World of the Pronghorn. 1969. V. 67

VANZOLINI, P. E.
South American Anoles: The Geographic Differentiation and Evolution of the Anolis Chrysolepis Species Group (Sauria, Iguanidae). Sao Paulo: 1970. V. 63

VARCHI, BENEDETTO
Lezzioni...Raccolte Nuovamente e la Maggior Parte Non Piu Date in Luce.... Florence: 1590. V. 64
Orazione Funerale dim Ben3edetto Varchi Fatta, e Recitata da Lui Pubblicamente nell'Essequie di Michelagnolo Buonarroti in Firenze, nella Chiesa di San Lorenzo. Florence: 1564. V. 62

VARDON, BETH
The Little Zoo. N.P: 1940. V. 66

VARDON, HARRY
The Complete Golfer. London: 1924. V. 66

VARELA, MARIA ELENA CRUZ
My Century in Your Face. Silver Spring: 1998. V. 64

VARENIUS
Geographia Generalis. Amstelodami: 1650. V. 66
Geographia Generalis. Cantabrigiae: 1712. V. 66

VARET, ALEXANDRE LOUIS
The Nunns Complaint Against the Fryars. London: 1676. V. 66

VARGA, ALBERTO
Varga: the Esquire Years. 1987. V. 66

VARGAS LLOSA, MARIO
Captain Pantoja and the Special Service. New York: 1978. V. 66
The Cubs. New York: 1979. V. 66
The Cubs. Helsinki: 1989. V. 63
The Green House. New York: 1968. V. 65
In Praise of the Stepmother. New York: 1990. V. 66
Los Jefes. Barcelona: 1959. V. 67
The Perpetual Orgy. Flaubert and Madame Bovary. New York: 1986. V. 66
The Real Life of Alejandro Mayta. New York: 1986. V. 67
The Time of the Hero. New York: 1966. V. 62; 63; 67
The War of the End of the World. New York: 1984. V. 66
Who Killed Palomino Molero?. New York: 1987. V. 66

VARIAN, SUSEEN
Cuchulain. A Cycle of Irish Plays. 1910. V. 67

VARII Historiae Romanae Scriptores, Partim Graeci, Partim Latini....
Geneva: 1568. V. 65

VARILLAS, ANTOINE
The History of William de Croy, Surnamed the Wise, Governor to the Emperour Charles V. London: 1687. V. 67

VARLEY, HENRY
De Mistakes of Moses, Ha! Ha!!. San Francisco;: 1890. V. 63

VARLO, CHARLES
Nature Display'd, a New Work. London: 1793. V. 64
Reflections Upon Friction, with a Plan of the New Machine for Taking It Off In Wheel-Carriages, Windlasses of Ships, &c. London: 1772. V. 63

VARTHEMA, LUDOVICO DI
The Itinerary of (L.D.V.) of Bologna from 1502 to 1508.... London: 1928. V. 62

VASARELY, VICTOR
From the Fine Arts..to Plastic Unity. N.P: 1966. V. 63

VASARI, GIORGIO
Choice Observations Upon the Art of Painting. London: 1719. V. 64, 66, 67
Lives of the Most Eminent Painters. Verona: 1966. V. 65
Lives of the Most Eminent Painters, Sculptors and Architects. London: 1900. V. 67
Le Vite de' Piu Eccellenti Pittori, Scultori et Architettori... Di Nuovo dal Medesimo Riviste et Ampliate Con i Ritratti Loro et con l'Aggiunta delle Vite de'Vivi & de'Morti Dall'anno 1550. Florence: 1568. V. 63; 64

VASCONCELLOS, P. SIMAO DE
Chronica da Companhia de Jesu do Estado do Brasil.... Lisbon: 1663. V. 62
Vida do Veneravel Padre Joseph de Anchieta da Companhia de Iesu, Taumaturgo do Nouo Mundo, na Provincia do Brasil.... Lisbon: 1672. V. 62

VASE, GILLAN, PSEUD.
A Great Mystery Sold: Being a Sequel to The Mystery of Edwin Drood. London: 1878. V. 62
A Great Mystery Solved, Being a Continuation of and Conclusion to The Mystery of Edwin Drood. London: 1914. V. 62

VASI, MARIEN
Itineraire Instructif de Rome Ancienne et Moderne, ou Description Generale des Monumens.... Rome: 1820. V. 67

VASILIEV, M.
Puteshestviya v Kosmos. (Trips Into Space). Moscow: 1958. V. 65

VASILISA the Beautiful. (Title in Russian).
Moscow: 1902. V. 64

VASSAL, GABRIELLE M.
My Lfie in French Congo. London: 1925. V. 65

VASSALL, SPENCER THOMAS
Memoir of the Life of Lieutenant-Colonel Vassall. Bristol: 1819. V. 67

VASSE, LOYS
In Anatomen Corporis Humani Tabulae Quatuor.... Venice: 1549. V. 67

VASSILIKOS, VASSILIS
Z. London: 1969. V. 62

VASSOS, RUTH
Contempo. This American Tempo. New York: 1929. V. 65
Humanities. New York: 1935. V. 65
Ultimo. An Imaginative Narration of Life Under the Earth. New York: 1930. V. 65

VATSAYANA
The Kama Sutra of Vatsayana. Benares (London): 1883. V. 62

VATTEL, EMERICH DE
The Law of Nations, or, Principles of the Law of Nature. London: 1797. V. 62; 64

VAUCHER, C. A.
East African Wildlife. Lausanne: 1967. V. 67

VAUGHAN, ALFRED J.
Personal Record of the Thirteenth Regiment of Tennessee Infantry By Its Old Commander. Memphis: 1897. V. 62; 63

VAUGHAN, BENJAMIN
Letters, on the Subject of the Concert of Princes and Dismemberment of Poland and France. London: 1793. V. 66
The Rural Socrates; or an Account of a Celebrated Philosohical Farmer, Lately Living in Switzerland and Known by the Name of Kliyogg. Hallowell: 1800. V. 64

VAUGHAN, CHARLES JOHN
The Revised Code of the Committee of Council on Education Dispassionately Considered. Cambridge and London: 1861. V. 63

VAUGHAN, HAROLD S.
Congenital Cleft Lip Cleft Palate and Associated Nasal Deformaties. Philadelphia: 1940. V. 67

VAUGHAN, HENRY
Olor Iscanus. A Collection of Some Select Poems and Translations. London: 1651. V. 64
Poems. Newtown: 1924. V. 62; 64; 65
Poems..., an Essay..., Two Letters from MSS. in the Bodleian Library. London: 1924. V. 62
Silex Scintillans. Sacred Poems. London: 1847. V. 67
The Works. Oxford: 1914. V. 63

VAUGHAN, HENRY HALFORD
The Effects of a National Taste for General and Diffucive Reading: a Prize Essay Read in the Sheldonian Theatre, Oxford June 15 1836. N.P: 1836?. V. 66

VAUGHAN, JAMES D.
Crowning Praises: for Sunday Schools, Revivals, Conventions, etc. Lawrenceburg: 1911. V. 66
Voices for Jesus. Lawrenceburg: 1910. V. 66

VAUGHAN, KEITH
Journal and Drawings 1939-1965. London: 1966. V. 63

VAUGHAN, RICHARD
History of Valois Burgundy. London: 1962-1973. V. 63

VAUGHAN, ROBERT
The Age of Great Cities; or, Modern Society.... London: 1843. V. 64
Congratulations; or the Polity of Intepdendent Churches, Viewed in Relation to the State and Tendencies of Modern Society.... London: 1842. V. 62

VAUGHAN, T.
Love's Vagaries; or, the Whim of the Moment. (with) The Hotel; or, the Double Valet. London: 1791. V. 62

VAUGHAN, W. E.
Autobiographica, with a Gossip on the Art of Printing in Colours. London: 1900. V. 62; 67

VAUGHAN KIRBY, F.
In Haunts of Wild Game. 1896. V. 62; 63; 64

VAUGHN, J. W.
The Battle of Platte Bridge. Norman: 1963. V. 67
Indian Fights - New Facts on Seven Encounters. Norman: 1966. V. 67
The Reynolds Campaign on Power River. Norman: 1961. V. 67
With Crook at the Rosebud. Harrisburg: 1955. V. 65; 67

VAUGHN, ROBERT
Then and Now or Thirty-Six Years in the Rockies. 1900. V. 65
Then and Now; or, Thirty-Six Years in the Rockies. Minneapolis: 1900. V. 66; 67

VAURIE, C.
The Birds of the Palaearctic Fauna.... London: 1959-1965. V. 63; 67
The Birds of the Palearctic Fauna. Volume 2. Non-Passeriformes. London: 1965. V. 62; 66

VAUX, CALVERT
Villas and Cottages. New York: 1857. V. 64
Villas and Cottages. A Series of Designs.... London: 1864. V. 63
Villas and Cottages: A Series of Designs.... New York: 1869. V. 62; 65

VAUX, LUDOVIC DE, BARON
Les Hommes d'Epee. Paris: 1882. V. 65

VAUX, ROBERTS
Memoirs of the Life of Anthony Benezet. Philadelphia: 1817. V. 63

VAUX, W. S. W.
Nineveh and Persepolis: an Historical Sketch of Ancient Assyria and Persia.... London: 1850. V. 65

VAVASOUR, ANNE
My Last Tour and First Work; or, a Visit to the Baths of Wildbad and Rippoldsau. London: 1842. V. 63

VAZ COUTINHO, GONCALO
Historia do Successo Que na Ilha de S. Miguel Ovve Com Armada Ingresa Que Sobre a Ditta Ilha Foy, Sendo Gouernador della Goncalo Vaz Coutinho.... Lisbon: 1630. V. 62

VAZ DE ALMADA, FRANCISCO
Tratado do Successo Que Teve a Nao Sam Joam Baptista e Iornada Que fez a Gente, Que Della Escapou, Desde Trinta & Tres Graos no Cabo da Boa Esperanca, onde fez Naufragio, ate Zofala Indo Sempre Marchando Por Terra. Lisbon: 1625. V. 62

VEBLEN, THORSTEIN
Absentee Ownership and Business Enterprise in Recent Times. New York: 1923. V. 66; 67
The Higher Learning in America: a Memorandum on the Conduct of Universities by Business Men. New York: 1918. V. 66
The Theory of the Leisure Class. New York: 1899. V. 62; 67

VEDDER, ALAN C.
Furniture of Spanish New Mexico. Santa Fe: 1977. V. 63

VEDDER, ELIHU
The Digressions of V. Boston: 1910. V. 67

VEE, JAY
Wild Oats. Topeka: 1914. V. 66

VEESOMMAI, U.
Plant Materials in Thailand. Bangkok: 1998. V. 63

VEGA, LOPE DE
Isidro. Poema Castellano. Madrid: 1935. V. 67
The Star of Seville. Newtown: 1935. V. 62

VEGETIUS, RENATUS
Vier Bucher der Ritterschafft. Mit einem Zusatz von Buchsen Geschoss, Pulver, Fewrerck, Auff ain Newes Gemeeret unnd Gebessert. Augsburg: 1529. V. 62

VEHSE, E.
Memoirs of the Court, Aristocracy and Diplomacy of Austria. London: 1856. V. 66

VEITCH, J., & SONS
Manual of the Coniferae.... 1900. V. 63; 66

VEITCH, JAMES H.
Hortus Veitchii, a History of the Rise and Progress of the Nurseries of Messrs. James Veitch and Sons.... London: 1906. V. 63; 64
A Traveller's Notes, or (Horticultural) Notes of a Tour through India, Malaysia, Japan, Corea, the Australian Colonies and New Zealand During the Years 1891-1893. 1896. V. 63; 66

VEITCH, JOHN
The Feeling for Nature in Scottish Poetry. London: 1887. V. 62

VELA, ARQUELES
El Cafe de Nadie. Jalapa, Veracruz: 1926. V. 67

VELARDE, PABLITA
Old Father the Story Teller. Globe: 1960. V. 64; 67

VELAZQUEZ DE LA CADENA, MARIANO
A Pronouncing Dictionary of the Spanish and English Languages.... New York: 1860. V. 64

VELIKOVSKY, IMMANUEL
Worlds in Collision. New York: 1950. V. 65

VELLEIUS PATERCULUS, MARCUS
Historiae Romanae Quae Supersunt. Londini: 1725. V. 63
The Roman History.... London: 1724. V. 67

VELNET, MARY
An Affecting History of the Captivity and Suffering of Mrs.... Boston: 1804?. V. 65

VELPEAU, A.
Surgical Clinic of La Charite. Lessons Upon the Diagnosis Treatment of Surgical Disease.... Boston: 1866. V. 64; 67

VENABLE, MATTHEW W.
Eighty Years After or Grandpa's Story. Charleston: 1929. V. 63

VENABLE, W. H.
Beginnings of Literary Culture in the Ohio Valley Historical and Biographical Sketches. Cincinnati: 1891. V. 63

VENABLES, BERNARD
The Angler's Companion. 1958. V. 65
The Angler's Companion. 1959. V. 67

VENABLES, EDMUND
Chronicon Abbatie de Parco Lude. The Chronicle of Louth Park Abbey with Appendix of Documents. Horncastle: 1891. V. 62

VENABLES, L. S. V.
Birds and Mammals of Shetland. London: 1955. V. 62

VENABLES, R.
The Experienced Angler. 1827. V. 62; 63

VENABLES, ROBERT
The Experienced Angler or Angling Improved. London: 1825-1827. V. 67

VENEGAS, MIGUEL
Histoire Naturelle et Civile de la Californie, Contenant une Description Exacte de ce Pays.... Paris: 1767. V. 64; 66

VENERONI, GIOVANNI
The Italian Master; or, the Easiest and Best Method for Attaining the Language.... London: 1729. V. 62; 64; 66

VENETTE, NICOLAS
Tableau de l'Amour Considere Dans l'Estat du Marriage. Parme: 1689. V. 63; 65

VENN, JOHN
The Logic of Chance. London: 1876. V. 64
The Logic of Chance. London and New York: 1888. V. 63

VENNER, TOBIAS
Via Recta ad Vitam Longam. Or, a Ttreatise Wherein the Right Way and Best Manner of Living for Attaining to a Long and Healthful Life, is Clearly Demonstrated.... London: 1650. V. 62; 65

VENNING, M. A.
A Geographical Present; Being Descriptions of the Principal Countries of the World.... London: 1817. V. 63
Rudiments of Conchology.... 1837. V. 66

VENTOUILLAC, L. T.
The French Librarian or Literary Guide, Pointing Out the Best Works of the Principal Writers of France.... London: 1829. V. 65

VENTRIS, MICHAEL
Documents in Mycenaean Greek.... Cambridge: 1973. V. 65

THE VENTURE. *An Annual of Art and Literature.* London: 1905. V. 63; 65

VENTURE *and Valour.* New York: 1900. V. 67

VENTURI, LIONELLO
Italian Painting: the Creators of the Renaissance. Geneva: 1950. V. 64; 66

VENUTI, NICCOLO MARCELLO, MARCHESE
A Description of the First Discoveries of the Antient City of Heraclea, Found Near Portici.... London: 1750. V. 62

VENUTI, RIDOLFINO
Vetera Monumenta Quae in Hortis Caelimontanis et in Aedibus Matthaeiorum Adservantur Nunc primum in Unum Collecta.... Rome: 1776-1779. V. 62

VERAN, JULES
Les Poetesses Provencales du Moyen Age et de Nos Jours. Paris: 1946. V. 67

VER BECK, FRANK
Little Black Sambo and the Baby Elephant. Philadelphia: 1925. V. 66
Little Black Sambo and the Baby Elephant. New York: 1935. V. 63
Little Black Sambo and the Tiger Kitten. Philadelphia: 1926. V. 66

VERCAMMEN-GRANDJEAN, P. H.
The Chigger Mites of the World. Volume III. San Francisco: 1976. V. 63; 66

VERDELLE, A. J.
The Good Negress. Chapel Hill: 1995. V. 65; 66; 67

VERDOORN, F.
Manual of Bryology. The Hague: 1932. V. 63; 64; 66
Plants and Plant Science in Latin America. London: 1945. V. 62

VEREINIGTE MASCHINENFABRIK AUGSBURG UND MASCHINENBAU GESELLS
Brucken und Eisenhochbauten Ausgefuhrt von der Bruckenbauanstalt Gustavsburg B. Mainz. Mainz: 1900. V. 65

VERGA, GIOVANNI
Cavalleria Rusticana and Other Stories. New York: 1927. V. 62; 64
Cavalleria Rusticana and Other Stories. New York: 1928. V. 67
Cavalleria Rusticana and Other Tales of Sicilian Peasant Life. London: 1893. V. 64

VERGANI, ANGELO
The Beauties of English Poetry; or a Collection of Poems Extracts from the Best Authors. Paris: 1803. V. 66

VERGENNES, CHARLES GRAVIER, COMTE DE
Memoire Historique et Politique sur la Louisiane. Paris: 1802. V. 64; 66

VERGER, PIERRE
Mexico. Mexico City: 1938. V. 63

VERGILIUS, POLYDORUS
An Abridgement of the Notable Worke of Polidore Virgile.. London: 1560. V. 63
De Gli Inventori Delle Cose, Libri, Otto. In Fiorenza: 1587. V. 67
De Rerum Inventioribus Libri Octo.... Romae: 1585. V. 64

VERGILIUS MARO, PUBLIUS
The Aeneid. London: 1952. V. 62; 66
The Aeneid of Virgil. London: 1876. V. 66; 67
Appendix, Cum Spplemento Multorum Nunquam Excusorum Poematum Veterum Poetarum. Lvgdvni: 1573. V. 65; 67
Bucolica, Georgica, et Aeneis. Birminghamiae: 1757. V. 62; 65
Bucolica, Georgica, et Aeneis. Glasgow: 1778. V. 66
Bucolica Georgica et Aeneis. Strasbourg: 1789. V. 65

VERGILIUS MARO, PUBLIUS continued
Bucolica, Georgica et Aeneis ex Codice Mediceo Laurentino.... Romae: 1763-1765. V. 66; 67
Carmina Omnia. Parisiis: 1858. V. 62
The Eclogues of Vergil in the Original Latin with an English Prose Translation by J. H. Mason. Weimar: 1927. V. 66
The Eclogues of Virgil. 1927. V. 65
An English Version of the Eclogues of Virgil. London: 1884. V. 67
L'Eneide di Virgilio. In Parigi: 1760. V. 65
L'Eneide...Commendatore Annibal Caro.... Padoa: 1608. V. 64
Georgica/Les Georgiques. Paris: 1937-1950. V. 65
Georgicorum Libri Quator. The Georgicks of Virgil. London: 1741. V. 64
Opera. Leipzig: 1596. V. 63; 65
Opera. Lipsiae: 1767-1775. V. 65
Opera. London: 1809. V. 66
Opera. Lipisiae: 1842. V. 66
Opera, cum Integris Commentariis.... Leeuwarden: 1717. V. 63; 66
Opera, cum integris commentariis.... Venetiis: 1736. V. 66
Opera Interpretatione et Notis Illustrauit Carolus Ruaevs Soc. Jesus.... Paris: 1699. V. 67
Opera: Interpretatione et Notis Illustravit Carolus Ruaeus.... Parisiis: 1682. V. 66
Opera Omnia. Francofurti: 1616. V. 66
Opera Omnia. Lugd. Batav: 1666. V. 65
Opera, Pristino Nitori Restituta.... Parisiis: 1790. V. 65; 67
Opera Vergiliana Docte and Familiariter Exposita: Docte Quide(m) Bucolica: & Georgica a Seruio. Donato Manicello & Probo Nuper Addito.... Lyons: 1517. V. 62
The Pastorals of Virgil. London: 1821. V. 65
Publii Virgilii Maronio: Bucolica Georgica et Aeneis. Glasgow: 1778. V. 64
The XII Aenedis of Virgil.... London: 1632. V. 65; 67
Virgil's Aeneis. Edinburgh: 1710. V. 64
The Works of Virgil. London: 1748. V. 66
The Works of Virgil. Birmingham: 1766. V. 65

VERGNAUD, N.
L'Art de Creer les Jardins.... Paris: 1839. V. 64

VERHAEREN, EMILE
Belgium's Agony. London: 1915. V. 64

VERHEYEN, PHILIP
Corporis Humani Anatomiae Liber Primus In Quo Tam Veteru.... Brussels: 1710. V. 64

VERHOEFF, MARY
The Kentucky Mountains: Transportation and Commerce 1750 to 1911. Louisville: 1911. V. 65; 67

VERINO, UGOLINO
Vita di anta Chiara Vergine. 1921. V. 62; 67
Vita di Santa Chiara Vergine. London: 1921. V. 63; 64; 65

VERITY STEELE, QUEENIE
The Book on Pekingese. Leith: 1945. V. 67

VERKAUF, WILLY
Dada: a Monograph of a Movement. New York: 1957. V. 62

VERLOT, B.
Les Plantes Alpines.. Paris: 1873. V. 64

VERMONT
State of Vermont Annual Directory for the Use of the General Assembly. Montpelier: 1868. V. 62

VERMONT CONSTITUTIONAL CONVENTION
Journal of the Convention, Holden at Montpelier, on the fourth Day of January, 1843, Agreeable to the Ordinance of the Council of Censors...to Consider Certain Amendments Proposed to the Constitution of the State of Vermont. Montpelier: 1843. V. 63

VERNE, JULES
Caesar Cascabel. New York: 1890. V. 64; 66
The Chase of the Golden Meteor. London: 1909. V. 62
The Child of the Cavern; or Strange Doings Underground. London: 1877. V. 62
Claudius Bambarnac. London: 1894. V. 62
A Floating City and the Blockade Runners. Boston: 1882. V. 65
Meridiana: The Adventures of Three Englishmen and Three Russians, in South Africa. New York: 1874. V. 63
The Tour of the World in 80 Days. Boston: 1875. V. 65
A Trip to the Moon. New York: 1893. V. 63
Le Volcan D'Or. Paris: 1906. V. 62; 63
A Voyage Round the World, Australia. London and New York: 1877. V. 62

VERNER, COOLIE
The North Part of America. Toronto: 1979. V. 63; 66

VERNER, WILLOUGHBY
Sketches in the Soudan. London: 1886. V. 66

VERNEUR, JACQUES THOMAS
Singularites Anglaises, Ecossaises et Irlandaises, ou Recueil d'Anecdotes Curieuses, d'Actions Bizarres et de Traits Piquans Propres a Faire Connaitre l'Esprit, les Moeurs et la Caractere des Peuples de la Grande-Bretagne.... Paris: 1814. V. 66

VERNEY, FRANCES PARTHENHOPE
Memoirs of the Verney Family During the Civil War/Commonwealth/from the Restoration to the Revolution.... London: 1892-1899. V. 62

VERNON, C. W.
Bicentenary Sketches and Early Days of the Church in Nova Scotia. Halifax: 1910. V. 67
Cape Breton, Canada at the Beginning of the Twentieth Century. A Treatise of Natural Resources and Development. Toronto: 1903. V. 63

VERNON, EDWARD JOHNSTON
A Guide to the Anglo-Saxon Tongue: a Grammar.... London: 1846. V. 64

THE VERNON Gallery: Its Pictures and Their Painters. London: 1856. V. 64

VERNON, JOSEPH S.
Along the Old Trail a History of the Old and a Story of the New Santa Fe Trail. Cimarron: 1910. V. 65

VEROLA, PAUL
Rama. Poeme Dramatique En Trois Actes. Paris: 1898. V. 64

VERONESE, PAUL
Exhibition of Paintings in Fresco by Paul Veronese, Brought from the Soranza Palace.... London: 1825. V. 62; 64

VERPLANCK, JAMES DELANCEY
A Country of Shepherds. Boston: 1934. V. 63; 64

VERRENT, ANN
The Little Black Boys. London: 1950. V. 66

VERRILL, A. E.
Monograph of the Shallow-Water Starfishes of the North Pacific Coast from the Arctic Ocean to California. 1914. V. 63; 66

VERRIUS FLACCUS, MARCUS
M. Verrii Flacci Quae Extant et Se. Pompei Festi de Verborum Significatione.... Venice: 1559. V. 62

VERSCHOYLE, DEREK
The English Novelists - a Survey of the Novel by Twenty Contemporary Novelists. London: 1936. V. 62

VERSTEGAN, RICHARD
A Restitution of Decayed Intelligencer: in Antiquities, Concerning the Most Noble and Renowned English Nation.... 1605. V. 64

VERSTEGEN, RICHARD
Restitution of Decayed Intelligence, in Antiquities Concerning the Most Noble and Renowned English Nation. London: 1653. V. 65

VERTES, MARCEL
Variations. Greenwich: 1961. V. 64

VERTOT, RENE AUBERT DE
Histoire des Chevaliers Hospitaliers de S. Jean de Jerusalem.... Paris: 1761. V. 63
The Revolutions of Portugal. London: 1721. V. 66

VERVE.. Paris: 1938. V. 67

VERVLIET, H. D. L.
The Book Through 5000 Years, a Survey. New York: 1972. V. 63

VERY, JONES
Essays and Poems. Boston: 1839. V. 62; 64

VERY, LYDIA
Red Riding Hood. Boston: 1863. V. 63

VERZURE, MME. DE
Reflexions Hazardees d'une Femme Ignorante, qui ne Connoit les Defauts des Autres que par les Siens & le Monde, que Par Relation & Par Oui- Dire. Amsterdam & Paris: 1766. V. 67

VESALIUS, ANDREAS
Anatomische Erklarung der Original Figuren von Andreas Vesal, Samt Einer Anwendung der Winslowischen Zergliederungslehre in Sieben Buchem. Ingolstadt: 1783. V. 66
De Humani Corporis Fabrica. Libri Septem. Venetiis F. F. Senensem and: 1568. V. 62
Icones Anatomicae. New York and Munich: 1934. V. 62; 66
The Illustrations from Works of Andreas Vesalius of Brussels.... Cleveland: 1950. V. 66
Opera Omnia Anatomica & Chirurgica, Cura Hermanni Boerhaave & Bernardi Siegfried Albini. Leiden: 1725. V. 66

VESEY, ELIZABETH
Conversations, or the Bas Bleu. 1977. V. 65

VESEY FITZGERALD, BRIAN
The Book of the Dog. London: 1948. V. 62; 66; 67

VESPUCCI, AMERIGO
The First Four Voyages.... London: 1893. V. 62

VESTAL, STANLEY
Sitting Bull, Champion of the Sioux - a Biography. Boston: 1932. V. 65; 67
Warpath - the True Story of the Fighting Sioux Told in a Biography of Chief White Bull. Boston: 1934. V. 67

VETERANS OF THE FUR TRADE ASSOCIATION
Pamphlet Ordered to Be Printed by the Veterans of the Fur Trade Associaton Showing Their Ownership of 7,455,552 Acres of Land Being the One- Tenth of Lord Selkirk's Estate, in the Country, formerly Known as the District of Assiniboia. Prince Albert: 1906. V. 66

VETHAKE, HENRY
An Introductory Lecture on Political Economy, Delivered at Nassau Hall Jan. 31, 1831. Princeton: 1831. V. 66
Principles of Political Economy. Philadelphia: 1838. V. 66

VETSCH, EARNEST
Little Black Sambo. Racine: 1926. V. 64

VETTIER, JACQUES
Big Game Hunting in Asia, Africa and Elsewhere. 1993. V. 64

VETTORI, PIETRO
Trattato...Delle Lodi, e Della Cultivatione de gl Ulivi Di Nuovo Ristampato. Florence: 1574. V. 64

VEXIN, NOEL
Murder in Montmartre. New York: 1960. V. 62; 63

VEZIN, CHARLES
Suffer Little Children to Come Unto You: a Homily on Birth Control. New York: 1917. V. 65

VIAGGIO Pittoresco Alla Vallombrosa. Florence: 1819. V. 67

VIAN, BORIS
Les Fourmis. Paris: 1949. V. 65
J'irai Cracher sur vos Tombes. Paris: 1946. V. 67

VIATOR, PSEUD.
The Washington Sketch-Book. New York: 1864. V. 63

THE VICAR Of Bray. London: 1771. V. 63

VICAT, P. R.
Histoire des Plantes Veneneuses de la Suisse.... Yverdon: 1776. V. 65; 66

VICK, JAMES
Vick's Monthly Magazine. 1886. V. 64

VICKERS, C. L.
History of the Arkansas Valley, Colorado. Chicago: 1881. V. 66

VICKERS LTD.
The Protection of Merchant Ships Against Moored Mines. London: 1917. V. 66

VICKERS, ROY
The Department of Dead Ends. New York: 1947. V. 67
Murder Will Out. London: 1950. V. 67
Seven Chose Murder. London: 1959. V. 65; 66
The Whispering Death. London: 1932. V. 66

VICKERS, SONS AND CO. LTD.
The Works at Barrow in Furness of the Naval Construction and Armaments Company. London: 1896. V. 64

VICKERY, D. O.
Indian Massacre and Tales of the Red Skins.... 1890. V. 67
Indian Massacre and Tales of the Red Skins.... Augusta: 1895. V. 67

VICKERY, SUKEY
Emily Hamilton. Worcester: 1803. V. 63

VICKERY, W. F.
Advanced Gunsmithing. 1951. V. 67

VICO, ENEA
Augustarum Imagines Aereis Formis Expressae.... Vinegia: 1558. V. 65; 67

THE VICTIM in Five Letters to Adolphus. London: 1809. V. 65

VICTOR, BENJAMIN
The History of the Theatres of London and Dublin, from the Year 1730 to the Present Time. (with) The History of the Theatres of London from the Year 1760 to the Present Time. London: 1761-1771. V. 65
Memoirs of the Life of Barton Booth, Esq.... London: 1733. V. 65

VICTOR, FRANCES AURETTA FULLER
The New Penelope and Other Stories and Poems. San Francisco: 1877. V. 66
The River of the West, Life and Adventures in the Rocky Mountains and Oregon.... Columbia: 1950. V. 67

VICTORIA FIRE DEPARTMENT
Constitution, By-Laws, and Rules of Order of the Victoria Fire Department Victoria, Vancouver Island, B.C. Victoria: 1873. V. 66

VICTORIA, QUEEN OF GREAT BRITAIN
Leaves from the Journal of Our Life in the Highlands from 1848 to 1861. London: 1868. V. 62; 63; 65; 66
Leaves from the Journal of Our Life in the Highlands from 1848 to 1861. (with) More Leaves from the Journal of a Life in the Highlands. London: 1868-1884. V. 64; 66
Leaves from the Journal of Our Life in the Highlands. (with) More Leaves from the Journal of Our Life in the Highlands. 1868-1884. V. 62
The Letters of Queen Victoria.... London: 1907. V. 63; 65
More Leaves from the Journal of a Life in the Highlands, from 1862 to 1882. London: 1884. V. 65

VICZ D'AZYR, FELIX
Traite d'Anatomie et de Physiologie. Paris: 1786. V. 62

VIDA, MARCO GIROLAMO
Christiados Libri Sex. Cremonae: 1535. V. 65; 67
De Arte Peotica (and other Works). Lugduni: 1536. V. 65
Poeticarum Libri Tres. Oxoniae: 1701. V. 67
Vida's Art of Poetry. London: 1725. V. 62
Vida's Art of Poetry. London: 1742. V. 63

VIDAL, EMERIC ESSEX
Picturesque Illustrations of Buenos Ayres and Monte Video. London: 1820. V. 62

VIDAL, GORE
The Best Man - A Play About Politics. Boston: 1960. V. 65
Burr. Franklin Center: 1979. V. 67
Dark Green, Bright Red. New York: 1950. V. 62
Death Before Bedtime. New York: 1953. V. 67
Death Before Bedtime. 1990. V. 67
Death in the Fifth Position. New York: 1952. V. 64; 67
Death Likes it Hot. New York: 1953. V. 67
Empire. Franklin Center: 1987. V. 62; 67
In a Yellow Wood. New York: 1947. V. 66; 67
Myron. New York: 1974. V. 65
Rocking the Boat. Boston: 1962. V. 62
Romulus. New York: 1966. V. 62
A Search for the King: a 12th Century Legend. New York: 1950. V. 63; 66
The Smithsonian Institution. Franklin Center: 1998. V. 67
A Thirsty Evil. New York: 1956. V. 66; 67
Visit to a Small Planet and Other Television Plays. Boston: 1956. V. 66
Visit to a Small Planet. The Best Man. On a March to the Sea. London Melbourne Toronto: 1962. V. 63
Williwaw. New York: 1946. V. 67

VIDARI, GIOVANNI MARIA
Il Viaggio in Pratica o sia Istruzione Generale, e Ristretta per Tutte Quelle Persone, Che Volessero Viaggare per Tutte le Strade e Poste d'Europa. Venice: 1730. V. 67

VIDOCQ, FRANCOIS
Histoire de Vidocq, Chef De la Brigade De La Surete. Paris: 1830. V. 67
Memoires de Vidocq. Paris: 1828-1829. V. 64

VIDYASAGAR, ESHWAR CHANDRA
Marriage of Hindu Widows. Calcutta: 1856. V. 65

VIEILLOT, LOUIS JEAN PIERRE
Songbirds of the Torrid Zone. Kent: 1979. V. 65; 67

VIEIRA, ANTONIO
Historia do Futuro: Livro Anteprimeyr Prologomeno a Toda a Historia do Futuro.... Lisboa Occidental: 1718. V. 67

VIELE, EGBERT L.
Following the Drum. New York: 1858. V. 62; 67

VIELE, TERESA
Following the Drum: a Glimpse of Frontier Life. New York: 1858. V. 65

VIERECK, H. L.
The Hymenoptera, or Wasp-Like Insects of Connecticut. Hartford: 1916. V. 63

VIERECK, PETER
Terror and Decorum Poems 1940-1948. New York: 1949. V. 67

VIETE, FRANCOIS
Opera Mathematica, in Unum Volumen Congesta, Ac Recognita, Opera atque Studio Francisci a Schooten Leydensis, Matheseos Professoris. Leyden: 1646. V. 66

VIEUSSENS, RAYMOND
Neurographia Universalis. Frankfurt (und Ulm): 1690. V. 64

VIEUSSEUX, GASPARD
De La Saignee et de Son Usage dans la Plupart des Maladies. Paris & Geneva: 1815. V. 65

A VIEW of Old London, As It Appeared in 1560, Described by Numerous References and Historical Notices.... London: 1851. V. 66

A VIEW of the Causes of Our Late Prosperity and of Our Present Distress and of the Means Which Have Been Proposed for Our Relief. Exeter: 1816. V. 66

A VIEW Of the New-York State Prison in the City of New York. New York: 1815. V. 66

A VIEW of the Present Condition of the Three Kingdomes of England, Scotland and Ireland. London: 1642. V. 66

A VIEW of the Progress, in Political Character, of the People of England and of the Probable Consequences of Attempts to Resist that Progress. York: 1819. V. 66

VIEWS in the White Mountains. Portland: 1878. V. 63

VIEWS of Battle Abbey. Battle: 1840. V. 62; 67

VIEWS of the English Lakes. Windermere: 1860. V. 63

VIEWS of the English Lakes. Drawn and Engraved by Edward Banks. Edinburgh: 1860. V. 67

VIEYRA, ANTHONY
A Dictionary of the Portuguese and English Language.... London: 1773. V. 62

VIEYRA, D. I.
Fill 'Er Up: an Architectural History of America's Gas Stations. New York: 1979. V. 62; 65

VIGERUS, FRANCISCUS
De Praecipuis Graecae Dictionis Idiotismis.... Londini: 1647. V. 63

VIGNE, GODFREY THOMAS
Travels in Kashmir, Ladak, Iskardo.... London: 1842. V. 62
Travels in Kashmir, Ladak, Iskardo.... 1844. V. 66

VIGNOLAS, GIACOMO BAROZZI DA
Reigle des Cinq Ordres d'Architecture. Paris. V. 64

VIGO, JOHN
The Whole Worke of that Famous Chirurgion Maister John Vigo.... London: 1586. V. 62

VILLA, JOSE GARCIA
A Celebration of Edith Sitwell. Norfolk: 1948. V. 64

VILLA, LEO
The Record Breakers. Sir Malcolm and Donald Campbell, Land and Water Speed Kings of the 20th Century. London: 1979. V. 64; 65

VILLAGE Annals, Containing Austerus and Humanus. Philadelphia: 1814. V. 62; 65

THE VILLAGE Green or Sports of Youth. New Haven: 1825. V. 62

VILLAGE Incidents; or Religious Influence in Domestic Scenes. London: 1828. V. 65

VILLAGRA ALCALA, GASPAR PEREZ DE
History of New Mexico. Los Angeles: 1933. V. 66

VILLAGUTIERE SOTOMAYOR, JUAN DE
Historia de la Conquista de la Provincia de el Itza, Reduccion y Progressos de la de el Lacandon y Otras naciones de Indios Barbaros, de la Mediacion de el Reyno de Guatimala.... Madrid: 1701. V. 62

VILLAMIL, RICHARD DE
Newton: the Man. London: 1931. V. 63

VILLARD, HENRY
Memoirs of Henry Villard, Journalist and Financier 1835-1900. Boston and New York: 1904. V. 62; 63
The Past and Present of Pike's Peak Gold Regions. Princeton: 1932. V. 67

VILLARD, LEONIE
Jane Austen, Sa Vie Et Son Oeuvre 1775-1817. Lyon/Paris: 1915. V. 66

VILLARD, OSWALD G.
Segregation in Baltimore and Washington. Baltimore?: 1913. V. 63

VILLAURRUTIA, XAVIER
La Poesia de los Jovenes de Mexico. Mexico: 1924. V. 67

VILLEDIEU, MARIE CATHERINE HORTENSE DESJARDINS DE
Le Comte de Dunois. Paris: 1671. V. 63
The Husband Forc'd to be Jealous, or, the Good Fortune of Those Women that Have Jealous Husbands. London: 1668. V. 63
Oevures de Madame de Ville-Dieu. Paris: 1715-1721. V. 63

VILLER, FREDERICK
The Black Tortoise: Being the Strange Story of Old Frick's Diamond. London: 1901. V. 66

VILLIERS, ALAN
Sons of Sinbad, An Account of Sailing with the Arabs in Their Dhows, in the Red Sea. New York: 1940. V. 67

VILLIERS-STUART, C. M.
Spanish Gardens, their History, Types and Features. 1929. V. 63; 66
Spanish Gardens, Their History, Types and Features. New York: 1929. V. 64
Spanish Gardens, Their History, Types and Features. 1936. V. 63; 66

VILLON, FRANCOIS
Autres Poesies. 1901. V. 63; 65
The Complete Works of Francois Villon. New York: 1960. V. 65
The Lyrical Poems of Francois Villon. New York: 1979. V. 62; 63; 64; 66
The Poems of Master Francois Villon of Paris. Portland: 1900. V. 62; 63
The Works.... London: 1930. V. 65; 67

VIMAR, A.
En Automobile. N.P: 1890. V. 67

VINCE, SAMUEL
A Complete System of Astronomy. Cambridge: 1797-1808. V. 65
The Elements of Astronomy: Designed for the Use of Students in the University. Cambridge: 1801. V. 63
The Elements of the Conic Sections.... Cambridge: 1781. V. 65
The Elements of the Conic Sections.... Cambridge: 1800. V. 63

VINCENT, CLOVIS
J. Babinski (1857-1932). 1932. V. 64

VINCENT, JOHN
Fowling a Poem. London: 1808. V. 63

VINCENT, LEON H.
De Witt Miller, a Biographical Sketch. Cambridge: 1912. V. 62

VINCENT, STEPHEN
O California! Nineteenth and Early Twentieth Century California Landscapes and Observations. San Francisco: 1990. V. 63; 65

VINCENT, THOMAS
Christ's Sudden and Certain Appearance to Judgment. Wheeling: 1823. V. 66

VINCENT, WILLIAM
A Discourse Addressed to the People of Great Britain, May 13th, 1792. Canterbury: 1793. V. 62

VINCENTINO, LUDOVICO DEGLI ARRIGHI
The Calligraphic Models.... Paris: 1926. V. 66

VINDEX, PSEUD.
A Letter to the Burgesses of Nottingham. Nottingham: 1803. V. 65

VINDEX to Verax, or Remarks Upon a Letter to the Rev. Thomas Coke, LL.D. London: 1792. V. 65

A VINDICATION of Mr. Randolph's Resignation. Philadelphia: 1795. V. 63

VINES, RICHARD
The Hearse of the Renowned, the Right Honourable Robert Earl of Essex and Ewe, Viscount Hereford.... London: 1646. V. 66

VINES, SHERARD
Whips and Scorpions: Specimens of Modern Satiric Verse 1914-1931. London: 1932. V. 66

VINGE, JOAN D.
The Snowqueen. 1980. V. 64; 66

VINGE, VERNOR
A Fire Upon the Deep. 1992. V. 64; 66

VINNIKOV, Y. A.
The Organ of Corti. Its Historphysiology and Histochemistry. New York: 1964. V. 65

VINNIUS, ARNOLDUS
In Quatuor Libros Institutionum Imperialum Commentarius Acaemicus & Forensis. Lugduni Batavorum: 1726. V. 67

VINTAGE SPORTS-CAR CLUB
Golden Jubilee Book 1934-1984. Newbury: 1984. V. 64

VINTON, STALLO
John Colter, Discoverer of Yellowstone Park. New York: 1926. V. 64; 67

VINYCOMB, JOHN
Fictitous and Symbolic Creatures in Art.... 1906. V. 67

VIOLLET LE DUC, E.
Dictionnaire de l'Architecture. Paris: 1854-1868. V. 64
Le Massif du Mont Blanc. Paris: 1876. V. 65
Mont Blanc, A Treatise on Its Geodesical and Geological Constitution. 1877. V. 62

VIPONT, ELFRIDA
Bless This Day - A Book of Prayer for Children. London: 1958. V. 65

VIRCHOW, RUDOLF
Cellular Pathology. New York: 1860. V. 64
Cellular Pathology. Birmingham: 1978. V. 63

VIRDEN, KATHARINE
The Thing in the Night. Garden City: 1930. V. 67

VIREY, JULIEN JOSEPH
Traite de Pharmacie Theorique et Pratique.... Paris: 1823. V. 65

VIRGIL, E. H.
A Leaf of Express History. Albany: 1880. V. 64

VIRGINIA
The Articles of Confederation; The Declaration of Rights; the Constitution of this Commonwealth, and the Articles of the Definitive Treaty Between Great Britain and United States of America. Richmond: 1785. V. 63
Calendar of Virginia State Papers and Other Manuscript. Richmond: 1884. V. 64
Pay Rolls of Militia Entitled to Land Bounty Under the Act of Congress of Sept. 28, 1850. Richmond: 1851. V. 64

VIRGINIA. CONSTITUTION - 1864
Constitution of the State of Virginia, and the Ordinances Adopted by the Convention Which Assembled at Alexandria on the 13th Day of February, 1864. Alexandria: 1864. V. 62
Journal of the Constitutional Convention Which Convened at Alexandria on the 13th Day of February 1864. Alexandria: 1864. V. 62

VIRGINIA. HOUSE OF DELEGATES - 1863
Journal of the House of Delegates of the State of Virginia for the Called Session of 1862 (and) for the Adjourned Session, 1863. Richmond: 1862-1863. V. 63

VIRGINIA. LAWS, STATUTES, ETC.
General Assembly Acts 1862 Called Session; Acts 1863 Adjourned Session; & New Constitution 1860-1861 of the State of Virginia Passed in 1861-1862. Richmond. V. 65

VIRGINIA. LAWS, STATUTES, ETC. - 1785
A Collection of All Such Public Acts of the General Assembly and Ordinances of the Conventions of Virginia, Passed since the Year 1768 as Are Now in Force. Richmond: 1785. V. 66

VIRGINIA. LAWS, STATUTES, ETC. - 1816
A Collection of the Several Acts of Assembly, Relating to the Literary Fund and to the Appointment and Duties of Escheators. Richmond: 1816. V. 65

VIRGINIA. LAWS, STATUTES, ETC. - 1861
Acts of the General Assembly of the State of Virginia Passed in 1816, in the Eighty-Fifty Year of the Commonwealth. Richmond: 1861. V. 63

VIRGINIA. LAWS, STATUTES, ETC. - 1862
Acts of the General Assembly of the State of Virginia, Passed in 1861-1862.... Richmond: 1862. V. 62
Acts of the General Assembly Passed at the Regular Session, Held Dec. 2, 1861 at the City of Wheeling. Wheeling: 1862. V. 65

VIRGINIA. LAWS, STATUTES, ETC. - 1863
Acts of the General Assembly of the State of Virginia Passed at Session 1863.... Richmond: 1863. V. 62

VIRGINIA. LAWS, STATUTES, ETC. - 1864
Acts of the General Assembly of the State of Virginia, Passed at Called Session, 1863. (with)....Passed at Called Session, 1863-1864. Richmond: 1863-1864. V. 63

VIRGINIA. STATE CONVENTION - 1830
Proceedings and Debates of the Virgina State Convention of 1829- 1830.... Richmond: 1830. V. 62

VIRGINIA. STATE CONVENTION - 1975
Statutes of Virginia. Charlottesville: 1975. V. 63

VIRGINIA CRAFTSMEN, INC.
The Charm of Traditional Colonial Furniture Authentically Reproduced for Homes of Today. Harrisonburg: 1935. V. 64

VIRGINIA Historical Register. Richmond: 1848-1853. V. 63

VIRGINIA HISTORICAL SOCIETY
Description of Virginia House in Henrico Co., Near Richmond, Virginia. The Home of Alexander Wilbourne Weddell. Richmond: 1947. V. 63

VIRGINIA Land Records: From the Virginia Magazine of History and Biography, The William and Mary College Quarterly and Tyler's Quarterly. Baltimore: 1982. V. 64

VIRGINIA Military Records: from the Virginia Magazine of History and Biography, The William and Mary College Quarterly and Tyler's Quarterly. Baltimore: 1983. V. 64

THE VIRGINIA Primer. Richmond: 1864. V. 63; 65

VIRGINIA Revolutionary Claims - Bounty Land and Commutation Pay. Washington: 1840. V. 65

VIRGINIA Will Records: from the Virginia Magazine of History and Biography, The William and Mary College Quarterly and Tyler's Quarterly. Baltimore: 1982. V. 64

VIRKUS, FREDERICK A.
The Abridged Compendium of American Genealogy.... Chicago: 1925. V. 63

VIRTUE in a Cottage, or, a Mirror for Children in Humble Life. London: 1785. V. 67

VISCHER, GEORGE MATTHAEUS
Topographia Austriae Superioris Modernae, Das ist Contrafee und Abbildung Aller Statt Closter, Herrschafften und schlosser des Ertz- Hertzogthumbs Oesterreich ob der Enns. N.P: 1674. V. 62; 65

VISCONTI, P. Q.
A Series of Highly Finished Engravings Comprising a Few of the Principal Objects in a Collection of Eygtian Antiquities, the Property of Giovanni d'Athanasi.... London: 1837. V. 64

VISIAK, E. H.
The Battle Fiends. London: 1916. V. 66
Buccaneer Ballads. London: 1910. V. 63
Flints and Flashes. London: 1911. V. 67
The Phantom Ship and Other Poems. London: 1912. V. 67

VISIT to the Menagerie. New York: 1885. V. 63

A VISIT to Aunt Agnes. London: 1868. V. 63

THE VISITORS from Oz. Chicago: 1960. V. 64

VISSCHER, ROEMER
Zinne-Poppen: Alle Vericert met Rijmen, en Sommighe met Proze... (with) Brabbelingh.... Amsterdam. V. 65

VISSER, D. J. L.
Symposium on the Bushveld Igneous Complex and Other Layered Intrusions. Johannesburg: 1969. V. 67

VISSER, H. E. F.
The Exhibition of Chinese Art of the Society of Friends of Asiatic Art, Amsterdam 1925. The Hague: 1926. V. 62

VITALE, PIETRO
Le Simpatie dell' Allegrezza Tra Palermo...Relazione delle Massime Pompe Festive de' Palermitanti per la Vittoria Ottenuta Contro i Collegati su le Campagne di rhuega a 11 Decembre 1710.... Palermo: 1711. V. 62

VITRUVIUS POLLIO, MARCUS
The Architecture in Ten Books. London: 1826. V. 64
Della Architettvra Di Gio. Antonio Rvsconi, Con Centosessanta Figure Dissegnate Dal Medesmio.... In Venetia: 1590. V. 65

VITRY, JACQUES DE
The Exempla or Illustrative Stories from the Sermones Vulgares. London: 1890. V. 67

VITTADINI, C.
Descrizione dei Funghi Mangerecci Piu Communi d'Italia. Milan: 1835. V. 62

VITTORIA, VICENZO
Osservazioni Sopra il Libro Della Felsina Pittrice per Difesa Ode Raffaello da Urbino. Rome: 1703. V. 64

VITTORINI, ELIO
Piccola Borghesia. Milan: 1931. V. 67

VIVANTE, LEONE
English Poetry and Its Contribution to the Knowledge of Creative Experience. London: 1950. V. 63

VIVES, JUAN LUIS
De L'Ufficio del Marito, Como si Debba Portare Verso la Moglie. Venezia: 1546. V. 67

VIVIAN, H. HUSSEY
Notes of a Tour in America from August 7th to November 17th 1877. London: 1878. V. 62; 65

VIVIAN, MARTHA CAMPBELL
Down the Avenue of Ninety Years. N.P: 1924. V. 62

VIZETELLY, HENRY
A History of Champagne.... 1980. V. 66
Paris in Peril. London: 1882. V. 66

VOCAL Music or the Songsters Companion Containing a New and Choice Collection of the Greatest Variety of Songs, Cantatas &c.... London: 1771. V. 63

VODOPYANOV, M.
Moscow - North Pole - Vancouver, Washington. Moscow: 1939. V. 64

VOEGELIN, ERICH
Das Form des Amerikanischen Geistes. Tubingen: 1928. V. 67

VOEGELSLANG, ANDREAS
Musice Artive Micrologus. Leipzig: 1519. V. 67

VOELKE, W. M.
The Bernard H. Breslauer Collection of Manuscript Illuminations. New York: 1992. V. 62

VOGEL, GEERTUIDA
Spring Flowers. London. V. 67

VOGEL, S.
African Aesthetics, the Carlo Monzino Collection. 1986. V. 62

VOGEL, VIRGIL J.
American Indian Medicine. Norman: 1970. V. 63; 66

VOGELSANG, ANDREAS
Musice Artive Micrologus Andree Ornithoparchi Ostrofranci Meyningensis, Artius Magistri, Libris Quattuor Digestus. Leipzig: 1519. V. 63; 65

VOICES of the Garden, the Woods and the Fields; or, the Teachings of Nature as Seasons Change. London: 1859. V. 62

VOIGHT, CYNTHIA
Dicey's Song. New York: 1982. V. 65

VOITURE, VINCENT DE
Monsieur Voiture's Love-Letters. London: 1750?. V. 62

VOLCK, ADELBERT J.
Confederate War Etchings. Philadelphia: 1880-1890. V. 63; 65

VOLKHOVSKY, FELIX
A China Cup, and Other Stories for Children. London: 1892. V. 63

VOLLARD, AMBROISE
La Politique Coloniale du Pere Ubu. Paris and Zurich: 1919. V. 64

VOLLIER, GASTON
A History of Dancing from the Earliest Ages to Our Own Time, with a Sketch of Dancing in England by Joseph Grego. 1898. V. 67

VOLLMANN, WILLIAM T.
Butterfly Stories. New York: 1993. V. 63; 67
The Happy Girls. New York: 1990. V. 64
The Ice Shirt. New York: 1990. V. 62
(The Ice-Shirt). Seven Dreams. A Book of North American Landscapes. London: 1990. V. 66
The Rainbow Stories. New York: 1989. V. 62; 66
The Rifles. London: 1994. V. 64
Thirteen Stories and Thirteen Epitaphs. London: 1991. V. 65
Whores for Gloria. New York: 1991. V. 64
You Bright and Risen Angels. London: 1987. V. 62; 64; 65
You Bright and Risen Angels. New York: 1987. V. 62; 63; 64; 66

VOLLMER, AUGUST
The Police and Modern Society. Berkeley: 1936. V. 65

VOLLMER, CARL G. W.
Kalifornien Och Guld Febern. Stockholm: 1862. V. 65

VOLNEY, CONSTANTIN FRANCOIS
Tableau du Climat et du Sol des Etas-Unis D'Amerique.... Paris: 1803. V. 67
Travels through Egypt and Syria in the Years 1783, 1784 and 1785. New York: 1798. V. 63; 64
Travels through Syria and Egypt, in the Years 1783, 1784 and 1785. London: 1788. V. 65
A View of the Climate and Soil of the United States of America.... Philadelphia: 1804. V. 63; 66
Voyage en Syrie et en Egypte, Pendant Les Annees 1783, 1784 and 1785. Paris: 1787. V. 67

VOLNEY'S Ruins; or, Meditation on the Revolutions of Empires. New York: 1828. V. 66

VOLTAIRE, FRANCOIS MARIE AROUET DE
The Age of Lewis XIV. London: 1752. V. 63; 66
Babouc; or, the World As It Goes...To Which are Added, Letters Concerning His Disgrace at the Prussian Court.... London: 1754. V. 63; 66
Candide or Optimism. London: 1939. V. 64

VOLTAIRE, FRANCOIS MARIE AROUET DE continued
Candide or Optimism. New York: 1973. V. 62; 64
A Defence of My Uncle. London: 1768. V. 62
The Dramatic Works of.... London: 1761. V. 63
The Elements of Sir Isaac Newton's Philosophy. Birmingham: 1991. V. 64
La Henriade. Paris: 1770. V. 66
La Henriade, Poeme, Avec les Notes et Les Variantes; Suivi de l'Essai sur la Poesie Epique par Voltaire. Paris: 1805. V. 62
Histoire De La Guerre De Mil sept Cent Quarante et un. Londres: 1756. V. 67
Historical Memoirs of the Author of the Henriade. London: 1777. V. 66
The History of Charles XII, King of Sweden. London: 1732. V. 67
The History of Charles XII, King of Sweden. London: 1740. V. 62
The History of the Misfortunes of John Calas, a Victim of Fanaticism. Edinburgh: 1776. V. 62
The History of the Russian Empire Under Peter the Great. London: 1763. V. 66
L'Ingenu; or the Sincere Huron: a True History. London: 1768. V. 62
Letters Concerning the English Nation. London: 1733. V. 64
Letters Concerning the English Nation. London: 1741. V. 62; 64; 65
Letters Concerning the English Nation. London: 1776. V. 62
Lettres Ecrites de Londres sur les Anglois et Autres Sujets. Basle: 1734. V. 67
Memoirs of the Life of Voltaire. London: 1785. V. 62
Miscellanies...Containing His Memoirs; Young James; or the Sage and the Atheist. Tureau (sic) Blanc; or The White Bull. London: 1783. V. 62
Oeuvres Completes. Lyon: 1791-1792. V. 63
A Philosophical Dictionary.... London: 1843. V. 66
The Princess of Babylon. London: 1927. V. 63
La Pucelle d'Orleans. Londres: 1780. V. 66
La Pucelle D'Orleans. Paris: 1799. V. 65
La Pucelle d'Orleans, Poeme en vingt et Un Chants. Rouen: 1880. V. 62
Select Pieces. Viz Zadig; or Destiny. An Eastern History. Memmon. A Letter from a Turk. London: 1754. V. 62
Voltaire's Essay on Milton. Cambridge: 1954. V. 62; 64
Zadig and Other Romances. New York: 1929. V. 65

Voluspa: The Song of the Sybil. Iowa city: 1968. V. 62

VOLWILER, ALBERT T.
George Croghan and the Westward Movement. Cleveland: 1926. V. 65

VON BAYROS, MARQUIS
The Amorous Drawings. New York: 1968. V. 62; 65

VON BONIN, GERHARDT
Essay on the Cerebral Cortex. Springfield: 1950. V. 65

VON BONNINGHAUSEN
Therapeutic Pocket-Book for Homeopathic Physicians.... New York and London: 1847. V. 67

VON BRAUN, WERNHER
Das Marsprojekt. Frankfurt: 1952. V. 62

VON ERDBERG, E.
Chinese Influence on European Garden Structures. Cambridge: 1936. V. 64

VON FALKE, JACOB
Art in the House. Historical, Critical and Aesthetical Studies on the Decoration and Furnishing of the Dwelling. Boston: 1879. V. 63

VON GRAFF, L.
Challenger Voyage. Zoology. Parts 27 and 61 Myzostomida with Supplement. 1884-1887. V. 66

VON GRIMMELSHAUSEN, JOHANN
The Adventures of Simplicissimus. New York: 1981. V. 62

VON HAGEN, VICTOR WOLFGANG
The Aztec and Maya Papermakers. New York: 1944. V. 62; 63; 64; 66
Frederick Catherwood. New York: 1950. V. 66

VON HAMELN, GLUCKEL
Die Memoiren der Bluckel von Hameln. Wein: 1910. V. 63

VON HOLST, NIELS
Creators, Collectors, and Connoisseurs: the Anatomy of Artistic Taste from Antiquity to the Present Day. New York: 1967. V. 63

VON HUGEL, ANATOLE
Charles von Hugel, April 25, 1795 - June 2, 1870. Cambridge: 1903. V. 66

VON KOLLIKER, A.
Challenger Voyage. Zoology. Part 2. Pennatulida. 1880. V. 66

VON MOLTKE, J. W.
Dutch and Flemish Old Masters in the Collection of Dr. C. J. K. Van Aalst. Verona: 1939. V. 65

VONNEGUT, KURT
Bagombo Snuff Box. Uncollected Short Fiction. New York: 1999. V. 64
Bluebeard. Franklin Center: 1987. V. 65; 66; 67
Bluebeard. New York: 1987. V. 66; 67
Breakfast of Champions. New York: 1973. V. 62; 65; 66; 67
Deadeye Dick. New York: 1982. V. 66
Galapagos. Franklin Center: 1985. V. 62; 65; 66; 67
Galapagos. New York: 1985. V. 66
God Bless You, Mr. Rosewater or Pearls Before Swine. New York: 1965. V. 62; 64; 67
Hocus Pocus. Franklin Center: 1990. V. 66
Jailbird. Franklin Center: 1979. V. 66
Jailbird. New York: 1979. V. 66; 67
Nothing Is Lost Save Honor. Jackson: 1984. V. 66; 67
Palm Sunday. New York: 1981. V. 62; 64; 66
Player Piano. New York: 1952. V. 62; 63
Player Piano. New York: 1966. V. 62
The Sirens of Titan. New York: 1959. V. 62
Slapstick or Lonesome No More!. Franklin Center: 1976. V. 66
Slapstick or Lonesome No More!. New York: 1976. V. 66
Slaughterhouse Five. New York: 1969. V. 62; 62; 64; 67
Slaughterhouse Five. London: 1970. V. 62
Slaughterhouse Five. Franklin Center: 1978. V. 66
Slaughterhouse Five. Thorndike: 1998. V. 62
Timequake. New York: 1997. V. 66; 67
Wampeters, Foma and Granfalloons (Opinions). New York: 1974. V. 66
Welcome to the Monkey House. New York: 1968. V. 62
Welcome to the Monkey House. London: 1969. V. 62

VON NEUMAN, JOHN
The Computer and the Brain. New Haven: 1958. V. 66

VON RAUMER, J. F.
Pre-Mesozoic Geology in the Alps. Berlin: 1993. V. 64; 65; 67

VON ROSEN, B.
Game Animals of Ethiopia. 1953. V. 67

VON SCHMIDT-PHISELDBEK, C. F.
Europe and America, or, the Relative State of The Civilized World at a Future Period. Copenhagen: 1976. V. 65

VON SIEBOLD, PHILIPP FRANZ
Fauna Japonica. Tokyo: 1975. V. 62; 63; 64

VOORHEES, CHARLES S.
Speeches of Daniel W. Voorhees of Indiana. Cincinnati: 1875. V. 67

VOORHEES, D. W.
Speech of D. W. Voorhees Delivered at Greeneville, TN. June 23, 1885, in Defense of Capt. Edward T. Johnson.... Washington: 1885. V. 64

VOORHEES, LUKE
Personal Recollections of Pioneer Life. Cheyenne: 1920. V. 65

VOORHIS, HAROLD VAN BUREN
Negro Masonry in the United States. New York: 1940. V. 63

VOORHOEVE, A. G.
Liberian High Forest Trees.... 1965. V. 67

VOORN, HENK
Old Ream Wrappers: an Essay on Early Ream Wrappers of Antiquarian Interest. North Hills: 1969. V. 64

VOOUS, K. H.
Owls of the Northern Hemisphere. Cambridge: 1989. V. 67

VOSBURGH, W. S.
Cherry and Black. The Career of Mr. Pierre Lorillard on the Turf. New York: 1916. V. 64

VOSSIUS, GERARD JOANNES
De Historicis Latinis Libri III. Lugduni Batavorum: 1651. V. 67
De Veterum Poetarum Temporibus Libri Duo, qui Sunt de Poetis Graecis et Latinis. Amsterdam: 1662. V. 67
...De Logicae et Rhetoricae Natura et Constitutione Libri II. Haque: 1658. V. 62
Gerardi Ioanne Vossii De Arte Grammatica Libri Septem. Amsterdami: 1635. V. 66

VOSTELL, WOLF
Fantastic Architecture. 1967. V. 62; 65
Fantastic Architecture. N.P: 1969. V. 64

VOTES for Men. New York: 1913. V. 63

VOTH, HEINRICH R.
Oraibl Marau Ceremony. Chicago: 1912. V. 64
The Oraibi Oaqol Ceremony. Chicago: 1903. V. 66

VOYACHEK, W. F.
Fundamentals of Aviation Medicine.... Toronto: 1943. V. 63

LE VOYAGE de La Perouse sur les Cotes de L'Alaska et de la Californie. Baltimore: 1937. V. 64

THE VOYAGE of Commodore Anson Round the World. Dublin: 1825. V. 64

VOYAGE Philosophique d'Angleterre, Fait en 1783 et 1784. Londres: 1786. V. 65

A VOYAGE through the Islands of the Pacific Ocean.... London: 1831. V. 64

VOYAGES and Travels Mainly During the 16th and 17th Centuries. London: 1903. V. 66

VOYAGES through the Northern Pacific Ocean, Indian Ocean and Chinese Sea. Dublin: 1825. V. 64

VOYNICH, E. L.
The Gadfly. New York: 1897. V. 64; 66

VOZNESENSKY, ANDREI
Antiworlds and the Fifth Ace. London: 1968. V. 65

VREDENBURG, EDRIC
Children's Stories from Dickens. London and New York: 1900. V. 63
Curly Heads and Long Legs. London: 1914. V. 66
My Book of Favourite Fairy Tales. Philadelphia. V. 63; 65
My Book of Mother Goose Nursery Rhymes. Philadelphia: 1927. V. 65
Such Fun. London: 1925. V. 66

VRIES, HUGO DE
Die Mutationstheorie. Versuche und Beobachtungen Uber die Entstehung der Arten im Pflanzenreich. Leipzig: 1901-1903. V. 65
The Mutation Theory.... Chicago: 1909-1910. V. 66
Species and Varities, Their Origin by Mutation.... Chicago: 1905. V. 63
Species and Varities, Their Origin by Mutation.... Chicago: 1912. V. 63; 64

VUES des Palais, Batimens Celebres, Places, Mascarades, et Autres Beautes Singulierres de la Ville de Venise. Vues des Palais, Batimens Celebres, Places Mascarades, et Autres Beautes Singulieres de la Ville de Venise. Leiden: 1762. V. 67

VUILLIER, GASTON
A History of Dancing from the Earliest Ages to Our Own Time. New York: 1897. V. 64

VULLIER, GASTON
A History of Dancing from the Earliest Ages to Our Own Time. London: 1898. V. 62

VULPIUS, OSKAR
Treatment of Infantile Paralysis. New York: 1912. V. 65

VVEDENSKII, ALEKSANDR
Rybaki. Moscow and Leningrad: 1930. V. 64

VYNER, ROBERT
Notitia Venatica. A Treatise on Fox-Hunting. 1891. V. 62

VYSKOCIL, QVIDO MARIA
Rytirove, Parosi a Krasre Pastyrky. (The Knights, Pages and Beautiful Shepardesses). Olomouci: 1908. V. 64

VYVER, BERTHA
Memoirs of Marie Corelli. London: 1930. V. 67

W

WAAGEN, G. F.
Treasures of Art in Great Britain...(with) Galleries and Cabinets of Art in Great Britain.... London: 1854-1857. V. 67

WACHER, JOHN
Pleasures Without Change. London: 1947. V. 67

WACKETT, L. J.
Studies of an Angler. Melbourne: 1950. V. 65

WADD, WILLIAM
Maxims and Memoirs. London: 1827. V. 67

WADDELL, ALFRED MOORE
A Colonial Officer and His Times 1754-1773. Raleigh: 1890. V. 66; 67
A History of Hanover County and the Lower Cape Fear Region 1723-1800. Volume I. (all published). Wilmington: 1909. V. 66; 67

WADDELL, HELEN
The Abbe Prevost. London: 1933. V. 63
New York City. London: 1935. V. 64

WADDELL, JAMES D.
Biographical Sketch of Linton Stephens.... Atlanta: 1877. V. 62

WADDELL, L. A.
Buddha's Secret from a Sixth Century Pictorial Commentary and Tibetan Tradition. 1894. V. 67

WADDINGTON, RICHARD
Fly-Fishing for Salmon. London: 1951. V. 67

WADDINGTON, ROBERT
The Land Surveyor's Companion.... London: 1775. V. 63

WADE, BLANCHE ELIZABETH
Fairbanks' Juvenile History of the United States. Chicago: 1911. V. 64

WADE, E. B. H.
A Report on the Delimitation of the Turco-Egyptian Boundary. Cairo: 1908. V. 63

WADE, H. T.
With Boat and Gun in the Yangtze Valley. Shanghai: 1910. V. 63

WADE, HENRY
A Dying Fall. London: 1955. V. 66; 67

WADE, JOHN
The Black Book of England: Exhibiting the Existing State, Policy and Administration of the United Kingdom. London: 1847. V. 65; 65
The Black Book; or Corruption Unmasked. (with) New Parliament. An Appendix to the Black Book. London: 1820-1826. V. 64; 65
The Black Book; or Corruption Unmasked!. London: 1820. V. 66
The Book of Penalties; or, Summary of the Pecuniary Penalties Inflicted by the Laws of England, on the Commercial, Manufacturing, Trading and Professional Classes, in Their Several Occupations and Businesses. London: 1834. V. 63
The Extraordinary Black Book: an Exposition of the United Church of England and Ireland; Civil List and Crown Revenues, Incomes, Privileges.... London: 1831. V. 64; 65
The Extraordinary Black Book. (with) Appendix to the Black Book.... London: 1832. V. 64
The Extraordinary Black Book. (with) Appendix to the Black Book.... London: 1832-1835. V. 65
Women, Past and Present. London: 1865. V. 65

WADE GERY, H. T.
Terpsichore and Other Poems. Waltham St. Lawrence: 1921. V. 67

WADIA, RUTTONJEE ARDESHIR
The Bombay Dockyard and the Wadia Master Builders. Bombay: 1972. V. 62

WADSWORTH, NELSON
Through Camera Eyes. N.P: 1975. V. 63

WAEYEN, JOHANNES VANDER
De Betoverde Wereld Van D. Balthasar Bekker Ondersogt en Wbederlegt. Leeuwarden: 1693. V. 66

WAGENER, RICHARD
Zebra Noise with a Flatted Seventh. Berkeley: 1998. V. 62

WAGG, HENRY J.
A Chronological Survey of Work for the Blind. London: 1932. V. 67

WAGNER, ANTHONY
Heralds of England. London: 1967. V. 64; 66

WAGNER, ANTON
Los Angeles: Werden, Leben, und Gestalt: Der Zweimillionenstadt in Sudkalifornien. Leipzig: 1935. V. 65

WAGNER, ARTHUR L.
The United States Army and Navy: Their Histories, From the Era of the Revolution to the Close of the Spanish American War. Akron: 1899. V. 63

WAGNER, BETTY JANE
Limericks. Boston: 1973. V. 63

WAGNER, G.
Blankets and Moccasins. Caldwell: 1933. V. 65; 67
Old Neutriment. Boston: 1934. V. 65; 67

WAGNER, HENRY RAUP
Alphonse Pinart - Journey to Arizona in 1876. Los Angeles: 1962. V. 66
Apocryphal Voyages to the Northwest Coast of America. Worcester: 1931. V. 66
California Imprints. Berkeley: 1922. V. 62; 63
Cartography of the Northwest Coast of America to the Year 1800. Berkeley: 1937. V. 62
Cartography of the Northwest Coast of America to the Year 1800. 1998. V. 65
Juan Rodriguez Cabrillo: Discoverer of the Coast of California. San Francisco: 1941. V. 64
The Life and Writings of Bartolome de las Casas. Albuquerque: 1967. V. 66
Memorial and Proposals of Senor Done Jose Martin on the Californias. San Francisco: 1945. V. 64
Peter Pond, Fur Trader and Explorer. New Haven: 1955. V. 65
The Plains and the Rockies: a Bibliography of Original Narratives of Travel and Adventure 1800-1865. San Francisco: 1937. V. 62; 64
The Plains and The Rockies: a Critical Bibliography of Exploration, Adventure and Travel in the American West 1800-1865. San Francisco: 1982. V. 64; 65
Sir Francis Drake's Voyage Around the World. San Francisco: 1926. V. 65
Sir Francis Drake's Voyage Around the World. Amsterdam: 1969. V. 65
Sir Francis Drake's Voyage Around the World. San Francisco: 1976. V. 62; 64
Spanish Explorations in the Strait of Juan de Fuca. Santa Ana: 1933. V. 64
The Spanish Southwest 1542-1794. 1997. V. 65
Spanish Voyages to the Northwest Coast of America. San Francisco: 1929. V. 63; 64; 66

WAGNER, MORITZ
The Tricolor on the Atlas; or, Algeria and the French Conquest. London: 1854. V. 64; 65

WAGNER, RICHARD
The Flying Dutchman. London: 1938. V. 62
The Rhinegold and the Valkyrie. 1910. V. 65
The Rhinegold and the Valkyrie. London: 1910. V. 63; 64; 67
The Rhinegold and the Valkyrie. New York: 1912. V. 64
Siegfried and the Twilight of the Gods. London: 1911. V. 62

WAGNER, SALLIE R.
Yazz Navajo Painter. Flagstaff: 1983. V. 62; 65

WAGNER, W. F.
Adventures of Zenas Leonard, Fur Trapper and Trader 1831-1836. Cleveland: 1902. V. 65

WAGNER, WILHELM
Asgard and the Gods. Tales and Traditions of Our Northern Ancestors. London: 1882. V. 67

WAGSTAFFE, WILLIAM
A Comment Upon the History of Tom Thumb. London: 1711. V. 65
Miscellaneous Works of.... London: 1725. V. 66

WAHL, JAN
Hello Elephant. New York: 1964. V. 62
Pleasant Fieldmouse. New York: 1964. V. 64

WAHL, JAN *continued*
Pleasant Fieldmouse. London: 1969. V. 65

WAIN, JOHN
The Contenders. London: 1958. V. 62
Mixed Feelings - Nineteen Poems. Reading: 1951. V. 62

WAIN, LOUIS
Come to Catland. London: 1905. V. 65
Fun in Dogland Painting Book. London: 1907. V. 65
Merry Motorists Painting Book. London: 1917. V. 63
Music in Pussytown. London: 1920. V. 63
My Mascot: Postcard Painting. London: 1920. V. 65
Puss in Boots. London: 1904. V. 63
The Tale of the Naughty Kitty Cat. Dundee: 1920. V. 63

WAINEWRIGHT, JEREMIAH
A Mechanical Account of the Non-Naturals.... London: 1707. V. 65; 67

WAINEWRIGHT, LATHAM
The Literary and Scientific Pursuits Which are Encouraged and Enforced in the University of Cambridge, Briefly Described and Vindicated. London: 1815. V. 64

WAINWRIGHT, A.
A Bowland Sketchbook. Kendal: 1981. V. 65; 66
The Central Fells. Kentmere: 1958. V. 62; 63; 64; 65
The Central Highlands. Kendal: 1977. V. 62; 63; 64
A Dales Sketchbook. Kendal: 1976. V. 62; 63; 64; 65
The Eastern Fells. Kentmere: 1956. V. 64; 65
The Eastern Highlands. Kendal: 1978. V. 62; 63; 64
An Eden Sketchbook. Kendal: 1980. V. 64; 65
Ex-Fell Wanderer. Kendal: 1987. V. 63; 64; 65
The Far Eastern Fells. Kentmere: 1957. V. 62; 63; 64; 65
Fell Wanderer. Kendal: 1966. V. 62; 64; 65
A Fourth Lakeland Sketchbook. Kendal: 1972. V. 62; 65
A Furness Sketchbook. Kendal: 1978. V. 62; 65
Kendal in the Nineteenth Century. Kendal: 1977. V. 64; 65; 66
Lakeland Mountain Drawings. Kendal: 1983. V. 66
Lakeland Mountain Drawings. Volume Two. Kendal: 1981. V. 62; 63; 64; 66
The North-Western Highlands. Kendal: 1976. V. 62; 63; 64
The Northern Fells. Kentmere: 1962. V. 62; 63; 64; 65
The Northern Highlands. Kendal: 1974. V. 62; 63; 64
Old Roads of Eastern Lakeland. Kendal: 1985. V. 62; 64
The Outlying Fells. Kendal: 1974. V. 62; 63; 64; 65
A Peak District Sketchbook. Kendal: 1984. V. 64; 65
A Pennine Journey. London: 1986. V. 62; 64; 65
Pennine Way Companion. Kendal: 1968. V. 62; 63; 64; 65
A Ribble Sketchbook. Kendal: 1980. V. 64; 65; 66
A Second Dales Sketchbook. Kendal: 1978. V. 62; 64; 65
The Southern Fells. Kentmere: 1960. V. 64; 65
A Third Lakeland Sketchbook. Kendal: 1971. V. 62; 64; 65
Three Westmorland Rivers. The Kent, The Spring and the Mint. Kendal: 1979. V. 62
Wainwright in Lakeland. Kendal: 1983. V. 64
Wainwright in Lakeland. Kendal: 1985. V. 62; 63; 64; 65
Walks in Limestone Country. Kendal: 1970. V. 62; 63; 64; 65
Walks on the Howgill Fells and Adjoining Fells. Kendal: 1972. V. 63; 64; 65
Welsh Mountain Drawings. Kendal: 1976. V. 64
Welsh Mountain Drawings. Kendal: 1981. V. 64
The Western Fells. Kendal: 1966. V. 63
The Western Highlands. Kendal: 1976. V. 64
The Western Highlands. Kendal: 1977. V. 62
Westmorland Heritage. Kendal: 1975. V. 63; 64; 65
Westmorland Heritage. Kendal: 1988. V. 66
A Wyre Sketchbook. Kendal: 1982. V. 65; 66

WAINWRIGHT, CHARLES
A Diary of Battle. The Personal Journals of Colonel Charles S. Wainwright 1861-1865. New York: 1962. V. 67

WAINWRIGHT, JONATHAN M.
A Set of Chants Adapted to the Hymns in the Morning and Evening Prayer and to the Communion Service of the Protestant Episcopal Church in the United States of America. Boston: 1819. V. 63

WAINWRIGHT, NICHOLAS B.
Philadelphia in the Romantic Age of Lithography. Philadelphia: 1958. V. 65

WAIT, GEORGE W.
New Jersey's Money. Newark: 1976. V. 63; 66

WAIT, JOHN C.
The Car-Builder's Dictionary.... New York: 1895. V. 62

WAITE, ARTHUR EDWARD
The Question of the Golden Stairs - a Mystery of Kinghood in Faerie. London: 1927. V. 63
The Real History of the Rosicrucians Founded On Their Own Manifestoes and On Facts and Documents Collected from the Writings of Initiated Brethren. London: 1887. V. 64
Songs and Poems of Fairyland.... London: 1892. V. 65

WAITE, C. V., MRS.
The Mormon Prophet and His Harem, an Authentic History of Brigham Young, His Numerous Wives and Children. Cambridge: 1866. V. 65

WAITE, E. R.
Fishes. Adelaide: 1916. V. 63

WAITE, OTIS F. R.
New Hampshire in the Great Rebellion - Historical Sketches of the Several New Hampshire Regiments and Biographical Notices of Many of the Prominent Actors. Claremont: 1870. V. 67

WAKE, ISAAC
Rex Platonicus; Sive de Potentissimi Principis Iacobi Britanniarum Regis, ad Illustrissimam Academiiam Oxoniensem, Adventu Aug. 27, Anno. 1605. Oxford: 1607. V. 62

WAKEFIELD, GILBERT
Memoirs of the Life.... London: 1792. V. 63

WAKEFIELD, H. R.
The Clock Strikes Twelve. Sauk City: 1946. V. 64; 66

WAKEFIELD, PRISCILLA
Excursions in North America, Described in Letters from a Gentleman and His Young Companion, to Their Friends in England. London: 1806. V. 65
Instinct Displayed, in a Collection of Well Authenticated Facts, Exemplifying the Extraordinary Sagacity of Various Species of the Animal Creation. London: 1814. V. 64
An Introduction to Botany, in a Series of Familiar Letters, with Illustrative Engravings. London: 1796. V. 64
The Juvenile Travellers.... London: 1815. V. 62
Reflections on the Present Condition of the Female Sex; with Suggestions for Its Improvement. London: 1798. V. 63

WAKEFIELD, SAMUEL
The Christian's Harp.... Pittsburgh: 1832. V. 65; 66

WAKELY, ANDREW
The Mariner's Compass Rectified. London: 1755. V. 66

WAKEMAN, EDGAR
The Log of an Ancient Mariner. San Francisco: 1878. V. 63; 64; 65; 66

WAKEMAN, GEOFFREY
Functional Developments in Bookbinding. Oxford and New Castle: 1993. V. 62
Victorian Colour Printing. 1981. V. 64

WAKEMAN, GEORGE
Tryals of Sir George Wakeman Baronet, William Marshall, William Rumley and James Corker, Benedictine Monks, for High Treason. London: 1679. V. 63

WAKOSKI, DIANE
Coins and Coffins. New York: 1962. V. 62
Discrepancies and Apparitions. Garden City: 1966. V. 66
The Fable of the Lion and the Scorpion. Madison: 1975. V. 62
George Washington's Camp Cups. Madison: 1976. V. 66
Greed. Parts One and Two. Los Angeles: 1968. V. 66
The Managed World. New York: 1980. V. 66
Thanking My Mother for Piano Lessons. Mt. Horeb: 1969. V. 66

WAKOWSKI, DIANE
Saturn's Rings. New York: 1982. V. 63; 64

WALAM Olum, or Red Score. The Migration Legend of the Lenni Lenape or Delaware Indians.... Indianapolis: 1954. V. 63; 66

WALBRAN, F. M.
Grayling and How to Catch Them. 1895. V. 67

WALBRAN, J. R.
A Guide to Ripon, Studley, Fountains Abbey, Hackfall and Several Places of Interest in Their Vicinity. Ripon: 1858. V. 67

WALCHA, OTTO
Meissen Porcelain. New York: 1981. V. 63

WALCOT, THOMAS
The Tryals of Thomas Walcot, William Hone, William Lord Russell, John Rous and William Blagg, for High Treason, for Comprising the Death of the King, and Raising a Rebellion in This Kingdom. London: 1683. V. 63

WALCOTT, CHARLES D.
Forest Reserves. Washington: 1900. V. 62; 63; 65

WALCOTT, DEREK
The Antilles: Fragments of Epic Memory: the Nobel Lecture. New York: 1993. V. 67
The Bounty. New York: 1997. V. 67
The Castaway and Other Poems. London: 1965. V. 62
Dream on Monkey Mountain and Other Plays. New York: 1970. V. 66; 67
The Fortunate Traveller. New York: 1981. V. 66; 67
The Joker of Seville and O Babylon!. New York: 1978. V. 66; 67
Poems of the Caribbean. New York: 1983. V. 62
Sea Grapes. New York: 1976. V. 66
Selected Poems. New York: 1964. V. 62; 64; 67
The Star-Apple Kingdom. New York: 1979. V. 66
Tiepolo's Hound. London: 2000. V. 67

WALCOTT, MACKENZIE E. C.
Scot-Monasticon. The Ancient Church of Scotland. London: 1874. V. 62

WALD, PAUL
The Twelve Days Campaign of the Fifth Regiment Pa. State Militia, to Which were Attached the Four Allentown Companies. Allentown: 1862. V. 62; 63

WALDECK, T.
On Safarai. 1940. V. 67

WALDEMAR, GEORGE
Picasso Dessins. Paris: 1926. V. 62; 63; 64

WALDMAN, ANNE
Fast Speaking Woman and Other Chants. San Francisco: 1975. V. 66
Hotel Room. Boulder: 1976. V. 63; 64; 66

WALDMAN, DIANE
Anthony Caro. New York: 1982. V. 63
Roy Lichtenstein. New York: 1993. V. 65

WALDO, EDNA LA MOURE
Dakota - an Informal Study of Territorial Days Gleaned from Contemporary Newspapers. Bismarck: 1932. V. 65
Dakota - an Informal Study of Territorial Days, Gleaned from Contemporary Newspapers. Bismarck: 1936. V. 67

WALDOR, MELANIE
Poesies du Coeur. Paris: 1835. V. 67

WALDRON, ARTHUR JOHN
Should a Woman Tell?. London: 1914. V. 65

WALDRON, PHILIP
The Novels of James Joyce. Wellington: 1962. V. 63

WALDSTEIN, AGNES
Das Industrielbild, Vom Werden Einer Neuen Kunst. Berlin: 1930. V. 65

WALDSTEIN, CHARLES
Herculaneum Past, Present and Future. London: 1908. V. 64

WALES, GEORGE C.
Etchings and Lithographs of American Ships. Boston: 1927. V. 62; 65

WALES Illustrated in a Series of Views.... London: 1830. V. 62

WALEY, ARTHUR
The Books of Songs.... London: 1937. V. 65
More Translations from the Chinese. London: 1919. V. 63

WALFORD, CORNELIUS
The Insurance Guide and Hand Book.... London: 1857. V. 63

WALFORD, EDWARD
Greater London: a Narrative of Its History, Its People and Its Places. London: 1884. V. 63
Walford's County Families of the United Kingdom. London: 1900. V. 66
Walfords County Families of the United Kingdom. London: 1915. V. 63

WALGAMOTT, CHARLES S.
Six Decades Back. Caldwell: 1936. V. 66

WALKE, HENRY
Naval Scenes and Reminiscences of the Civil War in the United States, on the Southern and Western Waters During the Years 1861, 1862 and 1863. New York: 1877. V. 64

WALKEM, W. W.
Stories of Early British Columbia. Vancouver: 1914. V. 64

WALKER, A. E.
A Follow-Up Study of Head Wounds in World War II. Washington: 1961. V. 67
A History of Neurological Surgery. Baltimore: 1951. V. 64; 66
The Late Effects of Head Injury. Springfield: 1969. V. 66

WALKER, A. KATHARINE
An Introduction to the Study of English Fonts.... London: 1908. V. 63

WALKER, ALEXANDER
Beauty, Illustrated by an Analysis and Classification of Beauty in Woman, with a Critical View of te Hypothesis of Hume, Hogarth, Burke, Knight, Alison etc.... London: 1852. V. 65
Female Beauty, as Preserved and Improved by Regimen. London: 1837. V. 66
Intermarriage or the Mode in Which and the Cause Why. Philadelphia: 1866. V. 65
Woman Physiologically Considered, as to Mind, Morals, Marriage, Matrimonial Slavery, Infidelity and Divorce. London: 1840. V. 65
Woman Physiologically Considered as to Mind, Morals, Marriage, Matrimony, Slavery, Infidelity & Divorce. New York: 1840. V. 65

WALKER, ALICE
The Color Purple. New York: 1982. V. 67
The Complete Short Stories. London: 1994. V. 67
Good Night Willie Lee, I'll See You in the Morning. New York: 1979. V. 67
Horses Make a Landscape More Beautiful. New York: 1984. V. 67
In Search of Our Mothers' Gardens. San Diego: 1983. V. 66
Meridian. London: 1971. V. 67
Meridian. New York: 1976. V. 62; 64; 67
Possessing the Secret of Joy. New York: 1992. V. 62; 64; 67
The Same River Twice. New York: 1996. V. 62
The Temple of My Familiar. New York: 1989. V. 64
The Third Life of Grange Copeland. New York: 1970. V. 63; 66; 67
Warrior Marks. New York: 1993. V. 64; 67

WALKER, ARCHIBALD STODART
A Beggars Wallet - Containing Contributions in Prose, Verse and Pictorial Illusration, Gathered from Certain Workers in Art and Letters. Edinburgh: 1905. V. 63; 64

WALKER, ARTHUR EARL
The Primate Thalamus. Chicago: 1938. V. 63

WALKER, ARTHUR N.
The Holcombe Hunt. London: 1937. V. 67

WALKER, C. E.
Old Flies in New Dresses. 1898. V. 63; 65; 67

WALKER, C. F.
Angler's Odyssey. London: 1958. V. 67
Brown Trout and Dry Fly. 1955. V. 67
Lake Flies and Their Imitation. 1960. V. 67

WALKER, C. I.
The Life of Lieutenant General Richard Heron Anderson of the Confederate State Army. Charleston: 1917. V. 63; 65

WALKER, C. J.
Rolls and Historical Sketch of the Tenth Regiment, South Carolina Volunteers. Charleston: 1881. V. 62; 63; 65

WALKER, CHARLES D.
Biographical Sketches of the Graduates and Eleves of the Virginia Military Institute Who Fell During the War Between the States. Philadelphia: 1875. V. 62; 63; 64

WALKER, DALE L.
Death was the Black Horse. Austin: 1975. V. 67

WALKER, DONALD G.
The Genesis of the Rat Skeleton. Springfield: 1957. V. 65

WALKER, F.
Catalogue of the Specimens of Heteropterous Hempitera in the Collection of the British Museum. 1867-1873. V. 63; 66
Characters of Undescribed Lepidoptera Heterocera. 1869. V. 67

WALKER, FRANCIS A.
History of the Second Army Corps in the Army of te Potomac. New York: 1891. V. 67
The Wages Question. A Treatise on Wages and Wages Class. London: 1877. V. 65

WALKER, G.
Remarkable Cases of Hereditary Anchyloses..with Defects of the Little and Ring Fingers. Baltimore: 1901. V. 67

WALKER, G. GOOLD
The Honourable Artillery Company in the Great War 1914-1919. London: 1930. V. 62

WALKER, GEORGE
The Costume of Yorkshire. London: 1814. V. 62; 67
The Costume of Yorkshire in 1814. Leeds: 1885. V. 63; 65; 66
The Siege of Londonderry in 1689. 1893. V. 65
Theodore Cyphon; or, the Benevolent Jew. Dublin: 1819?. V. 65
Travels of Sylvester Tramper through the Interior of South of Africa.... London: 1813. V. 65

WALKER, H. WILFRID
Wanderings Among South Sea Savages and in Borneo and the Philippines. London: 1909. V. 62

WALKER, J.
Mountain Days in the Highlands and Alps. 1937. V. 63; 65

WALKER, J. A.
The History of Penrith, from the Earliest Period to the Present Time. Penrith: 1858. V. 65

WALKER, J. CRAMPTON
Irish Life and Landscape. 1926. V. 64

WALKER, J. W.
Wakefield. Its History and People. Wakefield: 1934. V. 65; 66

WALKER, JAN
The Singular Case of the Duplicate Homes. Romford, Essex: 1994. V. 67

WALKER, JOEL P.
A Pioneer of Pioneers - Narrative of Adventures thro' Alabama, Florida, New Mexico, Oregon, California. Los Angeles: 1953. V. 65

WALKER, JOHN
The Academic Speaker; or, a Selection of Parliamentary Debates, Orations, Odes, Scenes and Speeches.... London: 1803. V. 64
An Attempt Towards Recovering an Account of the Numbers and Sufferings of the Clergy of the Church of England.... London: 1714. V. 63
A Critical Pronouncing Dictionary.... New York: 1804. V. 63
A Critical Pronouncing Dictionary.... 1818. V. 64
A Dictionary of the English Language.... London: 1775. V. 64
Elements of Elocution; in Which the Principles of Reading and Speaking are Investigated.... London: 1799. V. 62; 65
Oxoniana. London: 1809. V. 62
A Rhyming Dictionary.... London: 1806. V. 64
Walker's Pronouncing Dictionary of the English Language. London: 1846. V. 64
Walker's Pronouncing Dictionary of the English Language. Halifax: 1864. V. 64

WALKER, JOHN W.
The History of the Old Parish Church of All Saints, Wakefield, Now the Cathedral Church of the Diocese of Wakefield. Wakefield: 1888. V. 63

WALKER, JOSEPH COOPER
Historical Memoir of Italian Tragedy, from the Earliest Period to the Present Time.... London: 1799. V. 66

WALKER, MARY WILLIS
The Red Scream. New York: 1994. V. 62; 63; 64; 65; 66; 67
Under the Bettle's Cellar. New York: 1995. V. 62
Zero at the Bone. New York: 1991. V. 63; 64; 65; 66; 67

WALKER, R.
The Flora of Oxfordshire and Its Contiguous Counties. Oxford: 1833. V. 64; 66
No Need to Lie. 1964. V. 67

WALKER, SAMUEL DUTTON
Nottinghamshire Villages and Churches: West Bridgford and its Approaches from Nottingham. Nottingham: 1863. V. 65

WALKER, TACETT B.
Stories of Early Days in Wyoming, Big Horn Basin. Casper: 1936. V. 64; 67

WALKER, THOMAS A.
The Severn Tunnel: Its Construction and Difficulties 1872-1887. London: 1888. V. 62

WALKER, THOMAS MERCHANT
The Whole Proceedings on the Trial of an Action Brought by Thomas Walker, Merchant, Against William Roberts, Barrister at Law, for a Libel. Manchester: 1791. V. 63

WALKER, WALTER JAMES
Chapters on the Early Registers of Halifax Parish Church. Halifax: 1885. V. 65

WALKER, WILLIAM
Christian Harmony. Philadelphia: 1873. V. 62
Idiomatologia Anglo-Latina, Sive Dictionarium Idiomaticum Anglo- Lantinum.... London: 1005. V. 66
The Southern Harmony and Musical Companion.... Spartanburg: 1835. V. 63; 66

WALKING the Twilight. Flagstaff: 1994. V. 66

WALKINGAME, FRANCIS
The Tutor's Assistant.... London: 1783. V. 64
The Tutor's Assistant.... York: 1818. V. 62; 66

WALKINGTON, THOMAS
The Optick Glasse of Humours or the Touchstone of a Golden Temperature.... London: 1664. V. 64

WALL, BERNHARDT
Abraham Lincoln, American. N.P: 1940. V. 64

WALL, GEORGE HENRY
The Emigrant's Lost Son or Life Alone in the Forest. London: 1875?. V. 67

WALL, JOHN P.
The Chronicles of New Brunswick, New Jersey 1667-1931. New Brunswick: 1931. V. 63; 66

WALL, MARTIN
Clinical Observations on the Use of Opium in Low Fevers and in the Synochus, Illustrated by Cases. Oxford: 1786. V. 62; 65

WALL, OSCAR G.
Recollections of the Sioux Massacre. Lake City: 1909. V. 65; 67

WALL, R.
This Side Up, Spatial Determination in the Early Development of Animals. Cambridge: 1990. V. 67

WALLACE, ALFRED RUSSEL
Contributions to the Theory of Natural Selection. London: 1870. V. 63
Island Life. London: 1880. V. 63; 66
Island Life. London: 1892. V. 64
The Malay Archipelago. 1869. V. 65
The Malay Archipelago. New York: 1869. V. 62; 63
A Narrative of Travels on the Amazon and Rio Negro.... London: 1889. V. 63
A Narrative of Travels on the Amazon and Rio Negro.... London: 1892. V. 63
On Miracles and Modern Spiritualism. Three Essays. London: 1875. V. 63

WALLACE, ANDREW
General August V. Kautz and the Southwestern Frontier. Tucson: 1967. V. 66

WALLACE, ANTHONY F. C.
King of the Delawares: Teedyuscung 1700-1763. Philadelphia: 1949. V. 67

WALLACE, CHANDOS LEIGH HUNT
366 Menus. London: 1855?. V. 67

WALLACE, D. MAC KENZIE
Russia. London: 1877. V. 63; 64

WALLACE, DAVID FOSTER
Broom of the System. New York: 1987. V. 62; 64; 65; 67
Girl with Curious Hair. New York: 1989. V. 63; 65; 67
Infinite Jest. Boston: 1996. V. 62; 63; 65; 66; 67

WALLACE, EDGAR
Bosambo of the River. London: 1914. V. 63; 64; 66
The Four Just Men. London: 1905. V. 63; 64; 65; 66; 67
The Green Ribbon. Garden City: 1930. V. 65; 67
Gunman's Bluff. Garden City: 1929. V. 65; 66; 67
The People of the River. London: 1912. V. 63; 64; 66
Sanders of the River. Garden City: 1930. V. 66
White Face. Garden City: 1931. V. 65; 66

WALLACE, ELIZABETH
Mark Twain and the Happy Island. Chicago: 1913. V. 63

WALLACE, ERNEST
Ranald S. MacKenzie On the Texas Frontier. Lubbock: 1964. V. 67
Ranald S. MacKenzie's Official Correspondence Relating to Texas 1871-1877 and 1873-1879. Lubbock: 1967-1968. V. 67

WALLACE, FREDERICK WILLIAM
Canadian Ports and Shipping Directory. Gardenvale: 1935. V. 66
Wooden Ships and Iron Men: The Story of the Square-Rigged Merchant Marine of British North America, the Ships, Their Builders and Owners, and the Men Who Sailed Them. Boston: 1937. V. 65

WALLACE, GEORGE S.
Cabell Co. Annals and Families. Richmond: 1935. V. 65

WALLACE, H. F.
The Big Game of Central and Western China. 1913. V. 62; 63; 64; 66
The Big Game of Central and Western China. 1992. V. 67
British Deer Heads. 1913. V. 62; 64
British Deer Heads. London: 1913. V. 62; 63
Stalks Abroad. 1908. V. 62; 63; 67

WALLACE, JAMES
Every Man His Own Letter-Writer; or the New and Complete Art of Letter Writing.... London: 1782?. V. 62

WALLACE, JOHN H.
The Horse of America. New York: 1897. V. 66

WALLACE, JOHN WILLIAM
An Old Philadelphian, Colonel William Bradford, the Patriot Printer of 1776. Philadelphia: 1884. V. 66

WALLACE, LEW
Ben Hur. New York: 1880. V. 63
Ben Hur. London: 1892. V. 63
Ben Hur. New York: 1960. V. 62
Lew Wallace: an Autobiography. New York: 1902. V. 64

WALLACE, PHILIP B.
Colonial Churches and Meeting Houses. New York: 1931. V. 67

WALLACE, ROBERT
Characteristics of the Present Political State of Great Britian. London: 1758. V. 62; 66
Various Prospects of Mankind, Nature and Providence. London: 1761. V. 65

WALLACE, THOMAS
Thoughts On the Elements of Civil Government, Tending to Prove as a Fundamental Principle, On the Authority of the Jurists...(with) Second Part of Thoughts on the Elements.... London: 1836. V. 64

WALLACE, W.
A Treatise on the Eye. New York: 1839. V. 62
A Treatise on the Veneral Disease. 1833. V. 62

WALLACE, WILLIAM S.
Antoine Robidoux, 1794-1866. Los Angeles. V. 64; 67

WALLACE-CRABBE, CHRIS
Timber. New York: 1998. V. 64

WALLACE-DUNLOP, M. A.
Glass in the Old World. London: 1882. V. 62
The Timely Retreat; or a Year in Bengal Before the Mutinies. London: 1858. V. 66

WALLAS, ADA
Clean Peter and the Children of Grubbylea. London: 1901. V. 62

WALLEN, WILLIAM
The History and Antiquities of the Round Church at Little Maplestead, Essex, Formerly to the Knights Hospitallers of Saint John of Jerusalem.... London: 1836. V. 66

WALLER, A. G.
The Proposed Bridge At Charing Cross. 1930. V. 65

WALLER, EDMUND
Poems &c. London: 1682. V. 64
Poems, &c... (with) The Second Part of Mr. Waller's Poems. London: 1693-1690. V. 62
The Works.. London: 1730. V. 62; 64; 66

WALLER, ERIK
Bibliotheca Walleriana. New York. V. 63
Bibliotheca Walleriana. Stockholm: 1955. V. 63; 64; 65

WALLER, HORACE
The Last Journals of David Livingstone in Central Africa, from 1865 to his Death. London: 1874. V. 64

WALLER, J. F.
The Imperial Dictionary of Universal Biography. London: 1857-1863. V. 63

WALLER, JOHN
The Confessions of Peter Pan. Oxford: 1941. V. 65
Middle East Anthology. London: 1946. V. 63

WALLER, ROBERT
Shadow of Authority. London: 1956. V. 67

WALLER, ROBERT JAMES
The Bridges of Madisn County. New York: 1992. V. 62; 64; 65; 66; 67

WALLER, WILLIAM
An Essay on the Value of the Mines, Late of Sir Carbery Price. London: 1698. V. 63

WALLICH, G. C.
The North Atlantic Sea Bed.... London: 1862. V. 62

WALLIHAN, A. G.
Camera Shots at Big Game. 1904. V. 62; 63; 64

WALLIS, A.
Examples of the Book-Binders' Art of the XVI and XVII Centuries, Selected Chiefly from Royal Continental Libraries. Exeter and London: 1890. V. 62

WALLIS, CEDRIC
Rondels. 1951. V. 65

WALLIS, EDGAR
The Law of the Three Just Men. Garden City: 1931. V. 66

WALLIS, GEORGE
The Art of Preventing Diseases and Restoring Health. New York: 1794. V. 67

WALLIS, HENRY
The Cloud Kingdom. London: 1905. V. 62
Egyptian Ceramic Art. London: 1898. V. 62

WALLIS, JOHN
Grammatica Lingaue Anglicanae.... London: 1765. V. 65

WALLIS, JONNIE LOCKHART
Sixty Years on the Brazos. Los Angeles: 1930. V. 65

WALLIS, N.
The Carpenter's Treasure, a Collection of Designs for Temples.... London: 1795. V. 64

WALLIS, THOMAS WILKINSON
Autobiography of Thomas Wilkinson Wallis, Sculptor in Wood, and Extracts from His Sixty Years' Journal. Lought: 1899. V. 62; 64

WALLIS-TAYLER, A. J.
Motor Cars or Power Carriages for Common Roads. London: 1897. V. 64

WALMSLEY, HUGH MULLENEUX
The Ruined Cities of Zulu Land. London: 1869. V. 62; 66

WALPOLE, FRED
Four Years in the Pacific in Her Majesty's Ship "Collingwood" from 1844 to 1848. London: 1849. V. 65; 66; 67

WALPOLE, HORACE
Anecdotes of Painting in England. (with) *A Catalogue of Engravers.* Strawberry Hill: 1762-1763. V. 63
Anecdotes of Painting in England. (with) *A Catalogue of Engravers.* Strawberry Hill: 1762-1771. V. 67
Il Castello di Otranto. 1795. V. 62
Il Castello di Otranto. London: 1795. V. 64
The Castle of Otranto. London: 1782. V. 65
The Castle of Otranto. London: 1786. V. 62
The Castle of Otranto. Parma: 1791. V. 64; 65
The Castle of Otranto. London: 1796. V. 64
Castle of Otranto. London: 1800. V. 62
The Castle of Otranto. 1975. V. 65
A Catalogue of Engravers, Who Have Been Born, or Resided in England; Digested by Mr. Horace Walpole from the MSS. of Mr. George Vertue.... Strawberry Hill: 1763. V. 66
A Catalogue of the Royal and Noble Authors.... Dublin: 1759. V. 62
A Catalogue of the Royal and Noble Authors.... London: 1806. V. 62; 67
Essay on Modern Gardening. Canton: 1904. V. 64
Hieroglyphic Tales. 1926. V. 65
Historic Doubts on the Life and Reign of King Richard the Third. London: 1768. V. 65
Horace Walpole's Marginal Notes. London: 1867. V. 63
Journal of the Printing-Office at Strawberry Hill. 1923. V. 66
Journal of the Reign of King George the Third, from the Year 1771 to 1783. London: 1859. V. 63
The Letters. London: 1840. V. 65
The Letters. Philadelphia: 1842. V. 65
The Letters. London: 1861-1866. V. 65; 67
Letters. London: 1877. V. 67
The Letters. London: 1880. V. 63; 65; 67
The Letters. Edinburgh: 1906. V. 67
Letters...to Sir Horace Mann, His Britannic Majesty's Resident at the Court of Florence from 1760 to 1785. London: 1843. V. 65
Memoirs of the Reign of King George the Third. London: 1894. V. 63
The Mysterious Mother. Dublin: 1791. V. 65
A Notebook of Horace Walpole. New York: 1927. V. 65
Private Correspondence of Horace Walpole, Earl of Orford. London: 1820. V. 67
The Works of Horace Walpole, the Earl of Orford. London: 1798. V. 62; 66

WALPOLE, HORATIO
The Complaints of the Manufacturers, Relating to the Abuses in Marking the Sheep and Winding the Wool.... London: 1752. V. 63

WALPOLE, HUGH
The Apple Trees: Four Reminiscences. Waltham St. Lawrence: 1932. V. 62
The Golden Scarecrow. London: 1915. V. 63; 65
Harmer John. An Unwordly Story. London: 1926. V. 65
Portrait of a Man with Red Hair. New York: 1925. V. 67
Seven Pillars of Wisdom: T. E. Lawrence in Life and Death. London: 1985. V. 66

WALPOLE, MICHAEL
A Briefe Admonition to All English Catholikes, Concerning a Late Proclamation Set Forth Against Them. St. Omer: 1610. V. 65; 67

WALPOLE, ROBERT
A Short History of the Parliament. London: 1713. V. 62; 65; 66
Some Considerations Concerning the Publick Funds, The Publick Revenues and the Annual Supplies.... London: 1735. V. 63; 64; 65; 66

WALPOLE-BOND, J.
A History of Sussex Birds. 1938. V. 63; 65; 66

WALSDORF, JOHN J.
Men of Printing: Anglo-American Profiles. N.P: 1976. V. 62

WALSER, MARTIN
Ehen in Philippsburg. Frankfurt: 1957. V. 67
Flugzeug Uber dem Haus und Andere Geschichten. Frankfurt: 1955. V. 67
Gadarene Club. London: 1960. V. 67
Marriage in Philippsburg. Norfolk: 1961. V. 67

WALSER, ROBERT
The Walk and Other Stories. London: 1957. V. 66

WALSH, CHRISTY
Intercollegiate Football, A Complete Pictorial and Statistical Review from 1869 to 1934. New York: 1934. V. 63

WALSH, E.
A Narrative of the Expedition to Holland, in the Autumn of the Year 799.... London: 1800. V. 62

WALSH, J. H.
British Rural Sports. 1871. V. 67
British Rural Sports. London: 1871. V. 62
The Shot Gun and Sporting Rifle. 1859. V. 66
The Shot Gun and Sproting Rifle. 1862. V. 62

WALSH, J. M.
Coffee, Its History, Classification and Description. Philadelphia: 1894. V. 64

WALSH, JAMES JOSEPH
Psychotherapy: Including the History of the Use of Mental Influence, Directly and Indirectly in Healing and the Principles for the Application of Energies Derived from the Mind to the Treatment of Disease. New York and London: 1912. V. 65

WALSH, JILL PATON
Knowledge of Angels. Cambridge: 1994. V. 62

WALSH, PAUL
Irish Men of Learning. 1947. V. 63

WALSH, RAY
The Mycroft Memoranda. London: 1984. V. 66

WALSH, ROBERT
Fingal and Its Churches: a Historical Sketch. 1888. V. 67
A Letter on the Genius and Dispositions of the French Government, Including a View of the Taxation of the French Empire. Baltimore: 1810. V. 66

WALSH, THEOBALD
George Sand. Paris: 1837. V. 67

WALSH, THOMAS
Journal of the Late Campaign in Egypt.... London: 1803. V. 64; 65; 67

WALSH, WILLIAM J.
The Irish University Question; Addresses. Dublin: 1890. V. 67

WALSHS LTD.
Catalogue of High-Class Dog Collars, Leads, Chains, Brushes, Combs, Dog Foods and all Canine Requisites. Blackburn: 1922. V. 67

WALSINGHAM, LORD
Fauna Hawaiiensis...Volume I, Part V, Microlepidoptera. Cambridge: 1907. V. 62
Shooting. Field and Covert. London: 1887. V. 67
Shooting. Moor and Marsh. London: 1893. V. 67

WALTER, COPELAND
The Black Cat Book. New York: 1905. V. 63

WALTER, EUGENE
The Shapes of the River. London: 1955. V. 65

WALTER, H.
Eleanora's Falcon, Adaptions to Prey and Habitat in a Social Raptor. Chicago: 1979. V. 63

WALTER, J.
Luger. The Encyclopedia of the Borchardt and the Borchardt-Luger Handguns 1885 to 1985. 1986. V. 67

WALTER, JAMES CONWAY
A History of Horncastle from the Earliest Period to the Present Time. Horncastle: 1908. V. 62

WALTER, JOHANN GOTTLIEB
Tabulae Nervorum Thoracis et Abdominis. Berlin: 1783. V. 64

WALTER, RICHARD
Anson's Voyage Round the World. London: 1928. V. 65
A Voyage Round the World, but More Particularly to the North West Coast of America. London: 1789. V. 65; 66
A Voyage Round the World in the Years 1740, 1741, 1742, 1743, 1744. London: 1828. V. 64; 66
A Voyage Round the World, in the Years MDCCXL, I, II, III, IV. London: 1748. V. 62; 66

WALTER, WILLIAM W.
The Great Understander. True Life Story of the Last of the Wells Fargo Express Messengers. Aurora: 1931. V. 63; 67

WALTERS ART GALLERY
The History of Bookbinding 525-1950 A.D., an Exhibition Held at the Baltimore Museum of Art November 12, 1957 to January 12, 1958. Baltimore: 1957. V. 63

WALTERS, E. W.
Heroines of the World-War. London: 1916. V. 63

WALTERS, H. B.
Catalogue of the Engraved Gems and Cameos, Greek, Etruscan and Roman, in the British Museum. London: 1926. V. 66
Catalogue of the Roman Pottery in the Departments of Antiquities, British Museum. London: 1908. V. 67
History of Ancient Pottery, Greek, Etruscan and Roman. London: 1905. V. 65
Marbles and Bronzes, Fifty-Two Plates from Selected Subjects in the Department of Greek and Roman Antiquities (in the British Museum). London: 1928. V. 64

WALTERS, HENRY
Incunabula Typographica; a Descriptive Catalogue of the Books Printed in the Fifteenth Century (1460-1500) in the Library of Henry Walters. Baltimore: 1906. V. 62

WALTERS, JOHN CUMING
In Tennyson Land Being a Brief Account of the Home and Early Surroundings of the Poet Laureate and an Attempt to Identify the Scenes and Trace the Influence of Lincolnshire in His Works. London: 1890. V. 62; 66

WALTERS, LETTICE D'OYLY
The Year's at the Spring. London: 1920. V. 63; 67
The Year's at the Spring. New York: 1920. V. 66

WALTERS, LORENZO D.
Tombstone's Yesterday. Tucson: 1928. V. 64; 67

WALTERS, MINETTE
The Dark Room. London: 1995. V. 66; 67
The Dark Room. New York: 1995. V. 67
The Dark Room. New York: 1996. V. 66
The Ice House. London: 1992. V. 62; 63; 64; 65; 66; 67
The Scold's Bridle. Bristol: 1994. V. 65; 66; 67
The Scold's Bridle. London: 1994. V. 66
The Scold's Bridle. New York: 1994. V. 67
The Sculptress. London: 1993. V. 63; 64; 65; 66; 67

WALTERS, S. M.
The European Garden Flora. 1986-1989. V. 62
The European Garden Flora. Cambridge: 1989. V. 64

WALTERSKIRCHEN, K. DE
Maurice de Vlaminck: Catalogue Raisonne de l'Oeuvre Grave. Paris: 1974. V. 65

WALTHALL, ERNEST T.
Hidden Things Brought to Light. Richmond: 1933. V. 67

WALTHAM, A. C.
Limestones and Caves of North-West England. London: 1974. V. 64, 65, 66

WALTHER, F. R.
Communication and Expression in Hoofed Mammals. 1984. V. 67

WALTHOE, J.
A Catalogue of the Common and Statute Law-Books of This Realm.... London: 1714. V. 62

WALTON, ELIJAH
English Lake Scenery. London: 1876. V. 62; 66; 67

WALTON, IZAAK
The Compleat Angler. London: 1826. V. 67
The Compleat Angler. 1901. V. 67
The Compleat Angler. London: 1925. V. 62
The Compleat Angler. London: 1929. V. 63; 65
The Compleat Angler. London: 1931. V. 62; 63; 64; 65; 67
The Compleat Angler. New York: 1948. V. 65
The Compleat Angler. 1976. V. 67
The Complete Angler. London: 1760. V. 64
The Complete Angler. London: 1808. V. 66; 67
The Complete Angler. 1824. V. 67
The Complete Angler. Edinburgh: 1833. V. 67
The Complete Angler. London: 1844. V. 67
The Complete Angler. New York: 1847. V. 64
The Complete Angler. New York: 1848. V. 62; 63; 66
The Complete Angler. New York: 1852. V. 62
The Complete Angler. 1853. V. 67
The Complete Angler. London: 1853. V. 62
The Complete Angler. London: 1856. V. 63; 64
The Complete Angler. London: 1876. V. 67
The Complete Angler. 1889. V. 63
The Complete Angler. 1889. V. 65
The Complete Angler. London: 1925. V. 67
The Life of Dr. Sanderson, Late Bishop of Lincoln. London: 1678. V. 62; 64; 67
The Lives. London: 1825. V. 65
The Lives of Dr. Donne, Sir Henry Wotton, Mr. Richard Hooker, Mr. George Herbert.... London: 1847. V. 63
The Lives of Dr. John Donne, Sir Henry Wotton, Mr. Richard Hooker, Mr. George Herbert.... London: 1670. V. 64
The Lives of Donne, Wotton, Hooker, Herbert and Sanderson. London: 1827. V. 63
The Universal Angler. London: 1971. V. 62

WALTON, PETER
Creamware and Other English Pottery at Temple Newsam House, Leeds. London: 1976. V. 64

WALTON, ROBERT
Random Recollections of the Midland Circuit (The First and Second Series). London: 1869-1873. V. 65

WALTON, THOMAS H.
Coal Mining: Described and Illustrated. Philadelphia and London: 1885. V. 64

WALTZBURG: A Tale of the Sixteenth Century.
London: 1833. V. 65

WAMBAUGH, JOSEPH
The Onion Field. New York: 1973. V. 67

WAMPEN, HENRY
Mathematical Instruction, in Constructing Models, for Draping the Human Figure. London: 1853. V. 63; 67

WANDELL, SAMUEL H.
Aaron Burr. A Biography. New York: 1925. V. 66

THE WAND'RING Jew's Chronicle (in Verse), or, A Brief History of Remarkable Passages from William the Conqueror to This Present Reign.
London: 1750. V. 63

THE WANDERINGS of Tom Starboard: or the Life of a Sailor, His Voyages and Travels, Perils and Adventures by Sea and Land.
London: 1830. V. 62

WANDREI, DONALD
The Eye and the Finger. 1944. V. 66
The Eye and the Finger. Sauk City: 1944. V. 64
Poems for Midnight. Sauk City: 1964. V. 62; 64
Strange Harvest. 1965. V. 66
Strange Harvest. Sauk City: 1965. V. 64
The Web of Easter Island. Sauk City: 1948. V. 64; 66

WANG, HUI-MING
Woodcut-Epoh Studio. Amherst: 1968. V. 62

WANG, K. F.
Study of the Teleost Fishes of Coastal Region of Shangtung. Nanking: 1933-1935. V. 63

WANGENSTEEN, OWEN H.
The Rise of Surgery from Empiric Craft to Scientific Discipline. Minnenapolis: 1978. V. 66

WANLEY, NATHANIEL
The Wonders of the Little World; or a General History of Man.... London: 1806. V. 67

WANSER, JARVIS
Vineland. Its Products, Soil, Manufacturing Industries and Commercial Interests.... Vineland: 1880. V. 63; 66

WANTRUP, JONATHAN
Australian Rare Books 1788-1900. Sydney: 1987. V. 65

WAP, DR.
De Koninklijke Bazar van den Heer De Boer aan de Scheveningsche Zeestraat. The Hague: 1854. V. 64

WAR Birds. Diary of an Unknown Aviator.
New York: 1927. V. 63

WARBURTON, A. B.
A History of Prince Edward Island from Its Discovery in 1534 Until the Departure of Lieutenant-Governor Ready in A.D. 1831. St. John: 1923. V. 64

WARBURTON, ELIOT
The Crescent and the Cross; or, Romance and Realities of Eastern Travel. London: 1845. V. 65
Darien; or a Merchant Prince. London: 1852. V. 62; 63; 66

WARBURTON, GEORGE D.
Hochelaga: England in the New World. London: 1851. V. 67

WARBURTON, JOHN
Vallum Romanum; or, The History and Antiquities of the Roman Wall.... London: 1753. V. 62; 66

WARBURTON, P. E.
Journey Across the Western Interior of Australia. London: 1875. V. 62

WARBURTON, R. E. E.
Hunting Songs. London: 1925. V. 62
Hunting Songs and Ballads. 1846. V. 64
Hunting Songs and Ballads. London: 1846. V. 62
Hunting Songs, Ballads, &c. Chester: 1834. V. 62

WARBURTON, WILLIAM
Letters from a Late Eminent Prelate to One of His Friends. New York: 1809. V. 64

WARD, A. W.
The Cambridge History of English Literature. Cambridge: 1909-1920. V. 66
Cambridge History of English Literature. Cambridge: 1932. V. 65

WARD, ARTEMAS
The Grocer's Encyclopedia. New York: 1911. V. 64

WARD, DALLAS T.
The Last Flag of Truck. Franklinton: 1915. V. 63

WARD, EDWARD
Hudibras Redivivus; or a Burlesque Poem on the Times. London: 1705-1707. V. 62
Nuptial Dialogues and Debates; or, an Useful Prospect of the Felicities and Discomforts of a Marry'd Life.... London: 1710. V. 63; 65
Female Policy Detected; or, the Arts of a Designing Woman Laid Open. Dublin: 1764. V. 64
The Republican Processions; or the Tumultuous Cavalcade. London: 1714. V. 64
The Secret History of the Calves-Head Clubb, or, the Republican Unmasqu'd Wherein Is Fully Shewn the Religion of the Calves Head Heroes.... London: 1703. V. 65
A Trip to Jamaica; with a True Character of the People and Island. Londod (sic): 1700. V. 65
A Walk to Islington: with a Description of New Tunbridge Wells and Sadler's Musick-House. London: 1701. V. 62

WARD, FAY E.
The Cowboy at Work. New York: 1958. V. 64

WARD, FRANCES
Fairies and Flowers. London: 1911. V. 66

WARD, H. A.
Catalogue of the Ward-Coonley Collection of Meteorites. Chicago: 1904. V. 63

WARD, H. B.
Fresh Water Biology. New York: 1959. V. 64

WARD, H. C.
Wild Flowers of Switzerland.... London: 1883. V. 64

WARD, H. G.
Mexico. London: 1829. V. 67

WARD, H. L. D.
Catalogue of Romances in the Department of Manuscripts in the British Museum. London: 1883-1961. V. 63

WARD, J.
Workmen and Wages at Home and Abroad or the Effects of Strikes, Combinations and Trades' Unions. London: 1868. V. 66

WARD, J. CLIFTON
The Geology of the Northern Part of the English Lake District. London: 1876. V. 64; 65; 66

WARD, JAMES
Fresco Painting, Its Art and Technique.... London: 1909. V. 62

WARD, JOHN
The Borough of Stoke-upon-Trent...also, the Manorial History of Newcastle-upon-Lyme, and Incidental Notices of Other Neighbouring Places and Objects. London: 1843. V. 66
A Compendium of Algebra.... London: 1724. V. 65
Letters, Epistles and Revelations of Jesus Christ, Addressed to the Believers in the Glorious Reign of Messiah. Birmingham: 1831. V. 64
The Lives of the Professors of Gresham College; to Which is Prefixed the Life of the Founder, Sir Thomas Gresham. London: 1740. V. 66
The Living Oracle; or, the Star Of Bethlehem.... Nottingham: 1830. V. 64
Master: My Name! My Nature! The Destroyer of Craft and Freedom's Planter.... Birmingham: 1840. V. 64
My Last: (No Man Hurt:) Man-Deity: or Creation by Christ Jesus, as Developed After the Manner of Man.... Birmingham: 1848. V. 64
Nelson, the Latest Settlement of the New Zealand Company. London: 1842. V. 64; 65
Skipton Castle: Including Sketches of Its Noble Owners, and Its Historical Associations. Skipton: 1866. V. 65
The Standard of Zion. Birmingham: 1831. V. 64
Wisdom Triumphant Over Vain Philosophy; or, What Is Truth!. Birmingham: 1835. V. 64
The Young Mathematician's Guide. London: 1719. V. 64; 65

WARD, LESLIE
Forty Years of Spy. New York: 1915. V. 63

WARD, LYND
God's Man. New York: 1929. V. 63; 64; 66
Madman's Drum. London: 1930. V. 63
Madman's Drum. New York: 1930. V. 65; 66
Prelude to a Million Years. New York: 1933. V. 65
The Silver Pony, a Story in Pictures. Boston: 1973. V. 63
Vertigo. New York: 1937. V. 65; 66
Wild Pilgrimage. New York: 1932. V. 65

WARD, MARCUS
A Practical Treatise on the Art of Illuminating With Examples, Chromographed in Fac-simile and in Outline.... London. V. 64

WARD, MARY AUGUSTA ARNOLD
Helbeck of Bannisdale. London: 1898. V. 66
The History of David Grieve. London: 1892. V. 66
Marcella. London: 1894. V. 65
The Microscope; or Descriptions of Various Objects of Especial Interest and Beauty. London: 1869. V. 67
The Microscope; or Descriptions of Various Objects of Especial Interest and Beauty. 1880. V. 67
Microscope Teachings: Descriptions of Various Objects of Especial Interest and Beauty. London: 1864. V. 65

WARD, MILTON
Poems. Plymouth: 1826. V. 66

WARD, N. L.
Orientals in British Columbia. Westminster: 1925. V. 64

WARD, NANDA
The Black Sombrero. New York: 1952. V. 62

WARD, PHILIP
Contemporary Designer Book-binders. London: 1995. V. 67

WARD, R.
The Buxton, Matlock and Castleton Guide. Wirksworth: 1818. V. 62; 67

WARD, R. GERALD
American Activities in the Central Pacific 1790-1870.... Ridgewood: 1966. V. 64; 65

WARD, RICHARD
The Life of the Learned and Pious Dr. Henry More.... London: 1710. V. 64

WARD, ROBERT
Anima'dversions of Warre. London: 1639. V. 67
Lectures from New Zealand, Addressed to Young Men. London: 1862. V. 66

WARD, ROBERT PLUMER
De Vere; or, the Man of Independence. London: 1827. V. 63; 65
Illustrations of Human Life. London: 1837. V. 64
Tremaine, or the Man of Refinement. London: 1825. V. 63; 65

WARD, ROWLAND
Records of Big Game. 1903. V. 62; 63; 64
Records of Big Game. 1907. V. 62; 63; 64; 67
Records of Big Game. 1914. V. 62; 63; 64; 67
Records of Big Game. London: 1914. V. 62
Records of Big Game. 1922. V. 62; 63; 64; 67
Records of Big Game. 1928. V. 62; 63; 64; 67
Records of Big Game. London: 1962-1964. V. 62
Records of Big Game (Africa). 1975. V. 63; 64
Records of Big Game and Measurements of Horns. 1896. V. 67
Rowland Ward's Records of Big Game. 1969. V. 62
The Sportsman's Handbook. 1891. V. 67
The Sportsman's Handbook. London: 1894. V. 67
The Sportsman's Handbook. 1906. V. 67
The Sportsman's Handbook. London: 1911. V. 67
The Sportsman's Handbook. 1923. V. 67

WARD, THOMAS
England's Reformation (from the Time of K. Henry VIII to the End of Oates's Plot). London: 1715. V. 64
Passaic, a Group of Poems Touching that River with Other Musings.... New York: 1842. V. 63; 66

WARD, W. G.
Capital and Labour: a Paper Read Before the Literary Section and General Members of the Nottingham County Liberal Club.... Nottingham: 1874. V. 66

WARD, W. H.
The Architecture of the Renaissance in France. London: 1926. V. 63

WARD, WILFRID
The Life of John Henry Cardinal Newman. London: 1913. V. 65

WARD, WILLIAM
Farewell Letters to a Few Friends in Britain and America on Returning to Bengal in 1821. Lexington: 1822. V. 62
James Boys of Old Missouri. Cleveland: 1907. V. 63; 67

WARDE, BEATRICE
Words in Their Hands. Cambridge: 1964. V. 64

WARDE, FREDERIC
Bruce Rogers. Designer of Books. Cambridge: 1925. V. 62; 67
Printers Ornaments Applied to the Composition of Decorative Borders, Panels and Patterns. London: 1928. V. 66

WARDELL, JAMES
An Historical Account of Kirkstall Abbey, Yorkshire. Leeds: 1857. V. 65

WARDELL, JOHN WILFORD
A History of Yarm. Sunderland: 1957. V. 63

WARDEN, JOHN
A Short Account of the Life of Daniel McNaughton, and Also a Correct Report of the Trial. Glasgow: 1843. V. 63

WARDEN, R. D.
C. M. Russell - Boyhood Sketchbook. 1972. V. 66
C. M. Russell - Boyhood Sketchbook. Bozeman: 1972. V. 63

WARDER, T. B.
Battle of Young's Branch; or, Manasas Plain, Fourth July 21, 1861. Richmond: 1862. V. 62; 63; 65

WARD-JACKSON, C. H.
Airman's Song Book - Being an Anthology of Squadron, Concert Party, Training and Camp Songs and Song Parodies.... London: 1945. V. 64

WARDLAW, C. W.
Banana Diseases Including Plantains and Abaca. London: 1961. V. 63

WARDLAW, RALPH
Lectures on Female Prostitution: Its Nature, Extent, Effects, Guilt, Causes and Remedy. Glasgow: 1842. V. 65

WARDLE, THOMAS
On Sewage Treatment and Disposal: for Cities, Towns, Villages, Private Dwellings and Public Institutions. Manchester: 1893. V. 63

WARDMAN, GEORGE
A Trip to Alaska: a Narrative of What Was Seen and Heard During a Summer Cruise in Alaskan Waters. San Francisco: 1884. V. 63; 65

WARDNER, JAMES F.
Jim Wardner of Wardner, Idaho. New York: 1900. V. 66

WARDROP, A. E.
Modern Pig Sticking. 1914. V. 62; 63
Modern Pig Sticking. 1930. V. 62

WARDROP, JAMES
Essays on the Morbid Anatomy of the Human Eye. Birmingham: 1984. V. 63
The Script of Humanism, Some Aspects of Humanistic Script 1460-1560. Oxford: 1963. V. 62; 66

WARE, EUGENE F.
The Indian War of 1864. Topeka: 1911. V. 63; 66

WARE, GEORGE F.
German & Austrian Porcelain. Germany: 1950. V. 67

WARE, J. REDDING
The Isle of Wight. London: 1870. V. 66

WARE, JAMES
Remarks on the Ophthalmy, Psorophthalmy and Purulent Eye. London: 1787. V. 63

WARE, THOMAS
Sketches of the Life and Travels of Rev. Thomas Ware. New York: 1839. V. 67
Wesley's. Salem: 1839. V. 63

WARFIELD, EDGAR
A Confederate Soldier's Memoirs. Richmond: 1936. V. 62; 63

WARFIELD, EDWARD
A Confederate Soldier's Memoirs. Richmond: 1936. V. 65

WARHOL, ANDY
A. New York: 1968. V. 66
Andy Warhol's Exposures. New York: 1979. V. 63
Eggs, Paintings, Polaroids and Desert Drawings. Cologne: 1997. V. 66
Exposures. New York: 1979. V. 62; 65
From A to B and Back Again - the Philosophy of Andy Warhol. London: 1975. V. 63
A Gold Book. N.P: 1957. V. 65
Photographs. New York: 1975. V. 66

WARING AND GILLOW
Italian Art. Furniture and Old Tapestries, Old Marble and Bronze Objects, Cathedral Lamps and Hangings, Old Vestments and Missals, Old Embroideries and Brocades, Red Lace and Old Silver, Pictures by Old Masters and Other Works of Art. London: 1906. V. 62
Modern Art in French and English Decoration and Furniture (Exhibiton Cataloque). London: 1928. V. 67

WARING, EDWARD JOHN
Bibliotheca Therapeutica, or Bibliography of Therapeutics.... London: 1878-1879. V. 62; 63; 67

WARING, GEORGE E.
Report on the Social Statistics of Cities. Washington: 1887. V. 64

WARING, J. B.
Examples of Metal-Work and Jewellery.... London: 1858. V. 63
Masterpieces of Industrial Art and Sculpture at the International Exhibition, 1862. London: 1863. V. 64

WARING, JOSEPH
St. James' Church, Goose Creek, S.C. A Sketch of the Parish from 1706 to 1896. Charleston: 1897. V. 67

WARING, SARAH
The Ministrelsy of the Woods; or, Sketches and Songs Connected with the Natural History of Some of the Most Interesting British and Foreign Birds. London: 1832. V. 62; 64

WARK, BJARNE
May This Hold Both Art and Science. 1997. V. 62

WARK, ROBERT R.
Drawings by Thomas Rowlandson in the Huntington Collection. San Marino: 1975. V. 63; 64

WARLOCK, PETER
Songs of the Gardens. London: 1925. V. 62; 67

WARMAN, CY
Snow on the Headlights. New York: 1899. V. 67
The Story of the Railroad. New York: 1898. V. 67

WARMOTH, H. C.
War, Politics and Reconstruction. Stormy Days in Louisiana. New York: 1930. V. 63

WARNE, JOSEPH
Phrenology in the Family. Philadelphia: 1839. V. 62

WARNER, ANNA B.
Gardening By Myself. New York: 1924. V. 67
Up and Down the House. New York: 1892. V. 63

WARNER BROS. CO.
Twentieth Century Models (Corsets & Chemises). Chicago: 1899. V. 67

WARNER, EZRA J.
Generals of the Civil War - Lives of the Union and Confederate Commanders. Baton Rouge: 1964-1965. V. 65; 67

WARNER, FERDINANDO
A Full and Plain Account of the Gout. London: 1768. V. 65

WARNER, FRANCIS
Physical Expression: Its Modes and Principles. New York: 1886. V. 65

WARNER, FRANK
The Silk Industry of the United Kingdom. Its Origin and Development. 1920. V. 63

WARNER, GEORGE F.
Illuminated Manuscripts in the British Museum. London: 1900-1904. V. 62

WARNER, HARRIOT W.
Autobiography of Charles Caldwell, M.D. Philadelphia: 1855. V. 63

WARNER, J. J.
An Historical Sketch of Los Angeles County California. Los Angeles: 1936. V. 66

WARNER, MATT
The Last of the Bandit Riders. Caldwell: 1940. V. 62

WARNER, OLIVER
An Introduction to British Marine Painting. London: 1948. V. 63

WARNER, OPIE L.
A Pardoned Lifer - Life of George Sontag, Forgotten Member of the Notorious Evans-Sontag Gang. San Bernardino: 1909. V. 64; 67

WARNER, REX
The Kite. Oxford: 1936. V. 65
The Loved One. London: 1948. V. 66
Men of Stones - a Melodrama. Philadelphia and New York: 1950. V. 65
The Professor. London: 1938. V. 62; 63
The Professor. London: 1944. V. 65
Return of the Traveller. Philadelphia and New York: 1944. V. 65
The Wild Goose Chase. London: 1937. V. 64; 65
The Wild Goose Chase. New York: 1938. V. 65

WARNER, RICHARD
Excursions from Bath. Bath: 1801. V. 64
A History of the Abbey of Glaston; and of the Town of Glastonbury. Bath: 1826. V. 67
An Illustration of the Roman Antiquities Discovered at Bath. Bath: 1797. V. 64
A Letter to David Garrick, Esq. Concerning a Glossary to the Plays of Shakespeare.... London: 1768. V. 66
A Second Walk through Wales...in August and September 1798. Bath: 1799. V. 65
A Tour through the Northern Counties of England, and the Borders of Scotland. Bath: 1802. V. 65; 66
A Walk through Some of the Western Counties of England. Bath: 1800. V. 66

WARNER, S. A.
Fair Play's a Jewel: a Narrative of Cirumstances Connected with My Mode of National Defence Against the Whole World. London: 1849. V. 62

WARNER, SAMUEL
Authentic and Impartial Narrative of the Tragical Scene Which was Witnessed in Southampton County (Virginia) on Monday the 22d of August Last, When Fifty-Five of Its Inhabitants.... New York: 1831. V. 62

WARNER, SUSAN BOGERT
The Old Helmet. New York: 1864. V. 63

WARNER, SYLVIA TOWNSEND
Boxwood. London: 1957. V. 65; 67
The Corner That Held Them. London: 1948. V. 63
Elinor Barley. London: 1930. V. 64
The Espalier. London: 1925. V. 62; 64
Letters. London: 1982. V. 64
Opus 7. London: 1931. V. 66
Tales from the Arab-Tribes - A Collection of the Stories.... London: 1949. V. 64
The True Heart. London: 1929. V. 64
Twenty-Eight Poems. Wells and London: 1957. V. 62; 64

WARNER, WILLIAM
Albions England. (with) A Continuance of Albions England. London: 1602-1606. V. 64

WARNES, JOHN
Flax Verses Cotton; or the Two-Edged Sword Against Pauperism and Slavery...No. 1. London: 1850. V. 63
On the Cultivation of Flax: the Fattening of Cattle with Native Produce: Box Feeding, and Summer Grazing. London: 1846. V. 63

WARNE'S Large Picture Toy Books. London: 1870. V. 65

WARRE, H.
Sketches in North America and the Oregon Territory. Barre: 1970. V. 63; 65; 66

WARREN, ALBERT H.
The Promises of Jesus Christ. London: 1866. V. 65

WARREN, ARTHUR
The Charles Whittinghams Printers. New York: 1896. V. 63

WARREN, B. H.
Report on the Birds of Pennsylvania.... Harrisburg: 1888. V. 65; 67
Report on the Birds of Pennsylvania.... Harrisburg: 1890. V. 62

WARREN, CHARLES
The Supreme Court in U.S. History. Boston: 1922. V. 63

WARREN, EARL
A Republic, If You Can Keep It. New York: 1972. V. 63

WARREN, EDWARD
The Life of John Collins Warren, M.D. Boston: 1860. V. 64

WARREN, ELIZA SPAULDING
Memories of the West. Portland: 1917. V. 62; 65

WARREN, ELIZABETH
Spiritual Thrift. or, Meditations Wherein Humble Christians (as in a Mirrour) May View the Verity of Their Saving Graces.... London: 1647. V. 63

WARREN, F. K.
California Illustrated: Including a Trip through Yellowstone Park. Boston: 1892. V. 62

WARREN, GEOFFREY C.
Elixir of Life (Uisge Beatha) Being a Slight Account Of the Romantic Rise to Fame of a Great House.... Dublin: 1925. V. 65

WARREN, HARRIS G.
The Sword Was Their Passport. Baton Rouge: 1943. V. 67

WARREN, HENRY
To and From. Philadlephia: 1908. V. 62; 65

WARREN, INA RUSSELLE
The Doctor's Window. Buffalo: 1898. V. 63

WARREN, J. LEICESTER
A Guide to the Study of Book-Plates. London: 1880. V. 63

WARREN, JOHN
The Matadors 1879-1951. N.P: 1952. V. 64

WARREN, JOHN C.
A Letter Addressed to a Republican Member of the House of Representatives of the State of Massachusetts on the Subject of a Petition for a New Incorporation to be entitled A College of Physicians. Boston: 1812. V. 67
A Letter to the Hon. Isaac Parker, Chief Justice of the Supreme Court of the State of Massachusetts.... Cambridge: 1826. V. 62
The Mastodon Giganteus of North America. Boston: 1852. V. 67

WARREN, JOHN COLLINS
A Comparative View of the Sensoral and Nervous System of Man and Animal. Boston: 1822. V. 66; 67
Surgical Observations on Tumours, with Cases and Operations. Boston: 1848. V. 63; 66

WARREN, JONATHAN MASON
Surgical Observations with Cases and Observations. Boston: 1867. V. 64; 66; 67

WARREN, JOSEPH
Revenge. New York: 1928. V. 65; 67

WARREN, K.
Explorations in the Dacota Country, in the Year 1855. Washington: 1856. V. 62

WARREN, LOUIS A.
Lincoln's Parentage and Childhood. New York: 1926. V. 63

WARREN, MAUDE RADFORD
Mother Goose and Her Friends Tommy Tucker's Stories. New York: 1925. V. 63
Tales Told by the Gander. New York: 1922. V. 63

WARREN, MERCY
Poems, Dramatic and Miscellaneous. Boston: 1790. V. 63

WARREN, ROBERT PENN
All the King's Men. London: 1948. V. 62
All the King's Men. Franklin Center: 1977. V. 67
All the King's Men. N.P: 1989. V. 62; 63; 64; 66
An Anthology of Stories from the Southern Review. Baton Rouge: 1953. V. 64
Audubon. A Vision. New York: 1969. V. 64; 66
Being Here. Poetry 1977-1980. New York: 1980. V. 64; 66
Blackberry Winter. Cummington: 1946. V. 62; 64
The Gods of Mount Olympus. New York: 1959. V. 64
Jefferson Davis Gets His Citzenship Back. Lexington: 1980. V. 64; 66
John Brown: the Making of a Martyr. New York: 1929. V. 67
New and Selected Poems. New York: 1985. V. 62; 64; 66; 67
Now and Then. Poems 1976-1978. New York: 1978. V. 62
A Plea in Mitigation: Modern Poetry and the End of an Era. Macon: 1966. V. 64
Promises. Poems 1954-1956. New York: 1957. V. 66
Rumor Verified. Poems. New York: 1981. V. 66
Selected Poems 1923-1975. Franklin Center: 1981. V. 67
Selected Poems: New and Old. 1923-1966. New York: 1966. V. 62
William Faulkner and His South. 1951. V. 64; 67

World Enough and Time. New York: 1950. V. 67

WARREN, SAMUEL
The Moral, Social and Professional Duties of Attornies and Solicitors. Edinburgh: 1848. V. 63
Now and then. Edinburgh: 1848. V. 67
Ten Thousand a year. Edinburgh and London: 1841. V. 66
Ten Thousand A-Year. Edinburgh: 1851. V. 67
The Works of.... Edinburgh: 1854-1855. V. 65

WARRINGTON, WILLIAM
The History of Wales, in Nine Books. London: 1786. V. 64

WARTENBERG, ROBERT
The Examination of Reflexes: a Simplification. Chicago: 1945. V. 65

WARTER, JOHN WOOD
Appendicia et Pertinentiae, or, Parochial Fragments, Relating to the Parish of West Tarring and the Figs He Introduced.... London: 1853. V. 66
The Last of the Old Squires.... London: 1861. V. 67

WARTON, JOSEPH
An Essay on the Genius and Writings of Pope. London: 1762. V. 64
Odes on Various Subjects. London: 1747. V. 66

WARTON, THOMAS
Anthologiae Graecae a Constantino Cephala Conditae Libri Tres. Oxford: 1766. V. 64
The History of English Poetry from the Close of the Eleventh Century to the Commencement of the Eighteenth Century. London: 1775-1781. V. 64; 65
The Lives of Those Eminent Antiquaries John Leland, Thomas Hearne and Anthony Wood.... Oxford: 1772. V. 63
Observations on the Faerie Queene of Spenser. London: 1754. V. 64
The Oxford Sausage: Being Select Poetical Pieces.... Cambridge: 1822. V. 64
The Pleasures of Melancholy. London: 1747. V. 66
Poems. London: 1777. V. 66
Poems on Various Subjects.... London: 1791. V. 64
The Union; or Select Scots and English Poems. Dublin: 1761. V. 63

WARWICK, PHILIP
Memoires of the Reigne of King Charles I. London: 1701. V. 62

WASHBURN, CEPHAS
Reminiscences of the Indians, With a Biography of the Author.... Richmond: 1869. V. 63; 64

WASHBURN, ROBERT COLLYER
The Jury of Death. Garden City: 1930. V. 67

WASHINGTON & MEXICAN MINING CO.
Washington & Mexican Mining Company of Inde, Durango, Mexico. Washington: 1882. V. 67

WASHINGTON Athletic Club, Seattle. Seattle: 1932. V. 64

WASHINGTON, BOOKER T.
Character Building. New York: 1902. V. 66
The Future of the American Negro. Boston: 1899. V. 62; 63; 67
The Life of Washington. Avon: 1974. V. 63
Putting the Most Into Life. New York: 1906. V. 62; 64; 67
Story of the Negro. The Rise and the Race from Slavery. New York: 1909. V. 67
Team Work. Tuskegee: 1915. V. 62; 63; 67
Up from Slavery. New York: 1901. V. 67
Up from Slavery. New York: 1970. V. 62

WASHINGTON, BUSHROD
Reports of Cases Argued and Determined in the Court of Appeals of Virginia. Philadelphia: 1823. V. 65

WASHINGTON, GEORGE
Official Letters to the Honorable American Congress, Written, During the War Between the United Colonies and Great Britain. London: 1795. V. 66
The Will of General George Washington.... Alexandria: 1800. V. 62

WASHINGTON, M. BUNCH
The Art of Romare Bearden: the Prevalence of Ritual. New York: 1972. V. 63

WASHINGTON NATIONAL GUARD
The Official History of the Washington National Guard. Camp Murray: Sep. 1960. V. 66

WASSAN, YOGI
Secrets of the Himalaya Mountain Masters and Ladder to Cosmic Consciousness. N.P: 1927. V. 66

WASSON, R. GORDON
The Hall Carbine Affair: an Essay in Historiography. Danbury: 1971. V. 64
Maria Sabina and Her Mazatec Mushroom Velada. New York and London: 1974. V. 66
Soma. Divine Mushroom of Immortality. New York. V. 65
Soma, Divine Mushroom of Immortality. N.P: 1968. V. 64
Soma, Divine Mushroom of Immortality. New York: 1971. V. 62
The Wondrous Mushroom.... New York: 1980. V. 65

WASSON, VALENTINA P.
Mushrooms, Russia and History. New York: 1957. V. 64

WATANABE, M.
Report on the Cloud Observations Made at the Mera Meteorological Observatory, Mera, Near Tokyo, April 1927 to March 1929. Tokyo: 1931. V. 65

THE WATER Cure. London: Sep. 1880. V. 63

WATERBURY, M.
Seven Years Among the Freedmen. Chicago: 1890. V. 66

WATERFIELD, R.
Dear David, Dear Graham, A Bibliophilic Correspondence. Oxford: 1989. V. 62

WATERHOUSE, BENJAMIN
A Prospect of Exterminating the Small Pox.... Boston: 1800,. V. 64
The Rise, Progress and Present State of Medicine. Boston: 1792. V. 62; 66

WATERHOUSE, KEITH
Billy Liar. London: 1960. V. 66

THE WATERLOO Medal Roll. London: 1992. V. 66

WATERMAN, C. H.
Flora's Lexicon.... Philadelphia: 1819. V. 64

WATERMAN, CHARLES F.
Ridge Runners and Swamp Rats. Clinton: 1983. V. 65

WATERMAN, T. H.
The Physiology of Crustacea. New York: 1960-1961. V. 63

WATERMAN, THOMAS TILESTON
The Early Architecture of North Carolina. Chapel Hill: 1947. V. 63; 64

WATERMAN, THOMAS W.
The American Chancery Digest. New York: 1851. V. 67

WATERS, A. T. H.
Researches on the Nature, Pathology and Treatment of Emphysema of the Lungs and Its Relation with Other Diseases of the Chest. London: 1862. V. 65

WATERS, C. E.
Ferns, a Manual for the Northeastern States with Analytical Keys. New York: 1903. V. 64

WATERS, DAVID W.
The Art of Navigation in England in elizabethan and Early Stuart Times. London: 1958. V. 63

WATERS, FRANK
Book of the Hopi. New York: 1963. V. 65
Brave are My People. Santa Fe: 1993. V. 64; 67
The Colorado. New York: 1946. V. 66
Leon Gaspard. Flagstaff: 1964. V. 65; 66
Leon Gaspard. Flagstaff: 1981. V. 62; 63; 64; 65
Masked Gods, Navaho and Pueblo Ceremonialism. Albuquerque: 1950. V. 63; 65
People of the Valley. New York: 1941. V. 62
The Yogi of Cockroach Court. New York: 1947. V. 63

WATERSTON, WILLIAM
A Cyclopaedia of Commerce, Mercantile Law, Finance, and Commercial Geography.... Edinburgh: 1843. V. 66

WATERTON, CHARLES
Wanderings in South America, the North-West of the United States and the Antilles. London: 1825. V. 64; 65; 67
Wanderings in South America. The North-West of the United States and the Antilles. London: 1828. V. 63; 64; 66; 67
Wanderings in South America, the North-West of the United States and the Antilles. London: 1866. V. 63

WATERWORTH, W.
Origin and Developments of Anglicanism; or a History of the Liturgies, Homilies, Articles, Bibles, Principles and Governmental System of the Church of England. London: 1854. V. 67

WATESON, GEORGE
The Cures of the Diseased in Forraine Attempts of the English Nation. Oxford: 1915. V. 67

WATHEN, CAPTAIN
Proceedings of the General Court Martial Upon the Trial of Captain Wathen, 15th King's Hussars (at Cork). 1834. V. 65

WATHEN, GEORGE H.
Arts, Antiquities and Chronology of Ancient Eygpt; from Observations in 1839. London: 1843. V. 65

WATHEN, JONATHAN
The Conductor and Containing Splints; or, a Description of Two Instruments, for the Safer Conveyance and Most Perfect Cure of Fractured Legs.... London: 1781. V. 63
A Dissertation on the Theory and Cure of the Cataract; In Which the Practice of Extraction is Supported.... London: 1785. V. 65

WATKIN, HUGH R.
The History of Totnes Priory and Medieval Town Devonshire Together with the Sister Priory of Tywardreath Cornwall.... Torquay: 1914-1917. V. 62

WATKIN, W. THOMPSON
Roman Lancashire; or a Description of Roman Remains in the County Palatine of Lancaster. Liverpool: 1883. V. 62

WATKINS, ALFRED
The Old Standing Crosses of Herefordshire. Hereford: 1930. V. 66

WATKINS, CARLETON
Carleton Watkins: Photographs of the Columbia River and Oregon. N.P: 1979. V. 63

WATKINS, CHARLES
An Essay Towards the Further Elucidation of the Laws of Descents.... London: 1819. V. 62
The Principles of Conveyancing, Designed for the Use of Students.... London: 1833. V. 63

WATKINS, J. ELFRETH
The Log of the Savannah. Washington: 1890. V. 66

WATKINS, JOHN
Memoirs of the Life and Writings of Lord Byron, with Anecdotes of Some of His Contemporaries. London: 1822. V. 67
Memoirs of the Public and Private Life of Richard Brinsley Sheridan. 1817. V. 65
An Universal Biographical and Historical Dictionary.... London: 1800. V. 62; 64

WATKINS, PAUL
Night Over Day Over Night. New York: 1988. V. 62; 63; 65; 66

WATKINS, SAM R.
Co. Aytch, Maury Grays, First Tennessee Regiment.... Nashville: 1882. V. 62; 63; 65
Co. Aytch, Maury Grays, First Tennessee Regiment.... Chattanooga: 1900. V. 62; 63; 65

WATKINS, THOMAS
Travels through Switzerland, Italy Sicily, the Greek Islands to Constantinople, through Part of Greece, Ragusa and the Dalmatian Isles; in a Series of Letters to Pennoyre Watkins...in the Years 1787, 1788, 1789. London: 1794. V. 62

WATKINS, VERNON
Ballad of the Mari Lwyd and Other Poems. London: 1941. V. 64
The Ballad of the Outer Dark and Other Poems. London: 1979. V. 67
The Lady with the Unicorn. London: 1948. V. 62

WATKINS PITCHFORD, D. J.
Tide's Ending. London: 1950. V. 66; 67

WATNEY, BERNARD
English Blue and White Porcelain of the Eighteenth Century. London: 1963. V. 64

WATROUS, GEORGE R.
The History of Winchester Firearms 1866-1975. Winchester: 1975. V. 65

WATSON, AARON
The Savage Club. London: 1907. V. 63

WATSON, ALFRED E. T.
The Badminton Magazine of Sports and Pastimes. Volume I. August to December 1895. London: 1895. V. 67
The Badminton Magazine of Sports and Pastimes. Volume VI. January to June 1898. London: 1898. V. 67
Fur, Feather, and Fin Series: The Hare.... London: 1896. V. 67
King Edward VII as a Sportsman. London: 1911. V. 67

WATSON, ARTHUR C.
The Long Harpoon. New Bedford: 1929. V. 64

WATSON, DONALD
Birds of Moor and Mountain. 1972. V. 67
One Pair of Eyes. 1994. V. 67

WATSON, DOUGLAS
Traits of American Indian Life A Fur Trader - Peter Skeene Ogden. San Francisco: 1933. V. 65

WATSON, DOUGLAS S.
West Wind. 1934. V. 63; 66
West Wind. Morongo Valley: 1984. V. 67

WATSON, FREDERICK
A Century of Gunmen - a Study in Lawlessness. London: 1931. V. 67
From a Northern Window. London: 1911. V. 67
Hunting Pie. New York: 1931. V. 62

WATSON, GEOFFREY G.
Early Man in the Halifax District. Halifax: 1952. V. 64; 65

WATSON, GEORGE
New Cambridge Bibliography of English Literature. Cambridge: 1969-1974. V. 66

WATSON, H. B. MARRIOTT
At the First Corner and Other Stories. London: 1895. V. 64

WATSON, IAN
Japan: a Cat's Eye View. N.P: 1969. V. 62
The Jonah Kit. London: 1975. V. 65

WATSON, J.
The Confessions of a Poacher. 1890. V. 66

WATSON, JAMES C.
A Popular Treatise on Comets. Philadelphia: 1861. V. 66

WATSON, JAMES D.
The Double Helix. London: 1968. V. 62
The Double Helix. New York: 1968. V. 64; 65

WATSON, JOHN
The Confessions of a Poacher. 1890. V. 63; 67
The English Lake District Fisheries. London: 1899. V. 63; 65; 67
The English Lake District Fisheries. London: 1925. V. 63; 67
Memoirs of the Ancient Earls of Warren and Surrey and Their Descendants to the Present Time. Warrington: 1782. V. 65

WATSON, JOHN B.
Behaviorism. New York: 1925. V. 63

WATSON, JOSEPH YARDLEY
A Compendium of British Mining.... 1843. V. 62

WATSON, LARRY
Montana 1948. Minneapolis: 1993. V. 64; 66; 67
Montana 1948. London: 1995. V. 67

WATSON, LAWRENCE
In a Dark Time. New York: 1980. V. 65

WATSON, M.
Challenger Voyage. Zoology. Part 18. Anatomy of the Spheniscidae (Penguins). 1883. V. 66
Observations in Human and Comparative Anatomy. Edinburgh: 1874. V. 67
On the Anatomy of the Female Organs of the Proboscidea. 1880. V. 67
Report on the Anatomy of the Spheniscidae (Penguins) Collected During the Voyage of H.M.S. Challenger. 1883. V. 67

WATSON, MISS
Rosamund, Countess of Clarenstein. London: 1812. V. 62; 65

WATSON, PETER WILLIAM
Dendrologia Britannica, or Trees and Shrubs that Will Live in the Open Air of Britain.... 1825. V. 65
Dendrologica Britannica, or Trees and Shrubs That Will Live in the Open Air of Britain Throughout the Year. London: 1825. V. 64

WATSON, R.
Christian Panoply. Shepherd's Town: 1797. V. 65

WATSON, RICHARD
Chemical Essays. Cambridge: 1781-1786. V. 64
A Letter to His Grace the Archbishop of Canterbury. London: 1783. V. 66
Poems and Songs of Teesdale. Darlington: 1930. V. 65

WATSON, SAMUEL J.
St. Albans Raid. Montreal: 1865. V. 63

WATSON, THOMAS
Lectures on the Principles and Practice of Physic: Delivered at King's College London. London: 1845. V. 63
Mineral Resources of Virginia. Lynchburg: 1907. V. 63

WATSON, VIRGINIA
With Cortes the Conqueror. Philadelphia: 1917. V. 63

WATSON, WILBUR J.
Bridge Architecture Containing Two Hundred Illustrations of the Most Notable Bridges of the World, Ancient and Modern.... New York: 1927. V. 62

WATSON, WILLIAM
Collected Poems. London: 1898. V. 66
Life in the Confederate Army, Being the Observations and Experiences of an Alien in the South During the American Civil War. New York: 1888. V. 63; 65
Orchids: Their Culture and Management. London: 1890. V. 64
Orchids: Their Culture and Management. London: 1892. V. 62

WATT, ALEXANDER
The Art of Paper Making. London: 1890. V. 65
Electro-Deposition. London: 1889. V. 63

WATT, GEORGE
An Essay on Dental Surgery for Popular Reading. Cincinnati: 1856. V. 66; 67

WATT, J. M.
The Medicinal and Poison Plants of Southern Africa. Edinburgh: 1932. V. 66

WATT, JAMES
Correspondence of the Late James Watt.... London: 1846. V. 62

WATT, JOHN J.
Anatomico-Chirurgical Views of the Nose, Mouth Larynx and Fauces. London: 1809. V. 67

WATT, ROBERT
Bibliotheca Britannica; or a General Index to British and Foreign Literature. Edinburgh: 1824. V. 66

WATTEL, J.
Geographical Differentiation in the Genus Accipiter. 1973. V. 67

WATTERS, REGINALD EYRE
A Checklist of Canadian Literature and Background Materials 1628- 1960. Toronto: 1972. V. 67

WATTERSTON, GEORGE
Letters from Washington, on the Constitution and Laws.... Washington: 1818. V. 63

WATTEVILLE, V. DE
Out in the Blue. 1927. V. 67
Out in the Blue. 1937. V. 67

WATTS, ALARIC A.
Liber Fluviorum; or, River Scenery of France. London: 1853. V. 66

WATTS, C. J.
Practical Yacht Construction. London: 1957. V. 67

WATTS, DIANA
The Renaissance of the Greek Ideal. London: 1914. V. 66

WATTS, ISAAC
The First Principles of Astronomy and Geography Explain'd by the Use of Globes and Maps. London: 1728. V. 65
An Humble Attempt Toward the Revival of Practical Religion Among Christians and Particularly the Protestant Dissenters. London: 1731. V. 65
The Knowledge of the Heavens and the Earth Made Easy.... London: 1728. V. 65
Logick; or the Right Use of Reason in the Enquiry After Truth. London: 1725. V. 63
Logick; or the Right Use of Reason in the Enquiry After Truth. London: 1793. V. 63
Philosophical Essay on Various Subjects.... London: 1768. V. 63
The Psalms of David, Imitated in the Language of the New Testament and Applied to Christian State and Worship. (with) *Hymns and Spiritual Songs.* London: 1787-1788. V. 67
The Redeemer and the Sanctifier; or the Sacrifice of Christ and the Operations of the Spirit Vindicated. (with) *The Holiness of Times, Places and People Under the Jewish and Christian Dispensations Consider'd and Compared...*(with) *Questions Proper for St.* London: 1737-1741. V. 62
Reliquiae Juveniles. Miscellaneous Thoughts in Prose and Verse on Natural, Moral and Divine Subjects.... London: 1789. V. 64
The Strength and Weakness of Human Reason; or, the Important Question about the Sufficiency of Reason to Conduct Mankind to Religion and Future Happiness, Argued.... London: 1737. V. 63
The World to Come; or Discourses on the Joys or Sorrows of Departed Souls at Death.... Oxford: 1823. V. 65

WATTS, JOHN
The Facts of the Cotton Famine. London: 1866. V. 64

WATTS, JOHN G.
Little Lays for Little Folks. London: 1867. V. 64

WATTS, MISS
Selections of Knitting, Netting and Crochet Work. London: 1843. V. 65

WATTS, ROGER
The Fine Art of Jujutsu. London: 1906. V. 62

WATTS, THOMAS
An Essay On the Proper Method for Forming the Man of Business.... London: 1716. V. 64

WATTS, WILLIAM
An Essay on Means and Expediency of Elevating the Profession of the Educator in the Estimation of the Public. Birmingham: 1840. V. 62; 67

WAUGH, ALEC
The Prisoners of Mainz. London: 1919. V. 62

WAUGH, ARTHUR
A Hundred Years of Publishing, Being the Story of Chapman & Hall Ltd. London: 1930. V. 62
The Square Book of Animals. London: 1900. V. 63; 65

WAUGH, EVELYN
Basil Seal Rides Again. Boston: 1963. V. 66
Basil Seal Rides Again. London: 1963. V. 63; 64; 66
Black Mischief. London: 1932. V. 62; 64
Brideshead Revisited.... London: 1945. V. 62
Edmund Campion. London: 1935. V. 62
The End of the Battle. Boston: 1961. V. 66
The Essays, Articles and Reviews of Evelyn Waugh. London: 1983. V. 63
Flere Flag. (Put Out More Flags). Copenhagen: 1946. V. 63
Helena. London: 1950. V. 63
The Holy Places. London: 1952. V. 63; 64
The Holy Places. London: 1953. V. 62
Labels: a Mediterranean Journal. London: 1930. V. 64
The Life of the Right Reverend Ronald Knox. London: 1959. V. 62; 63; 66
A Little Learning - the First Volume of an Autobiography. London: 1964. V. 63
Love Among the Ruins. London: 1953. V. 63; 64
The Loved One. London: 1948. V. 62; 64; 66
Men at Arms - a Novel. London: 1952. V. 63
Men at Arms. (with) *Officers and Gentlemen.* (with) *Unconditional Surrender.* London: 1952-1955. V. 67
Officers and Gentlemen. London: 1955. V. 63; 64; 65; 66; 67
The Ordeal of Gilbert Pinfold. London: 1957. V. 63; 64; 66
Put Out More Flags. London: 1942. V. 66
Remote People. London: 1931. V. 62
Scoop: a Novel About Journalists. London: 1938. V. 64
Suspended. 1948. V. 67
A Tourist in Africa. London: 1960. V. 63; 64
Unconditional Surrender. London: 1961. V. 63; 64; 66; 67
Waugh in Abyssinia. London: 1936. V. 62
Wine in Peace and War. London: 1947. V. 62; 64; 66; 67
Work Suspended and Other Stories.... London: 1948. V. 62

WAUGH, JOHN
Catalogue of the Library of John Waugh, C.E. of Stackhouse, Settle, Yorks. Bradford: 1901. V. 66

WAUGH, JOHN HUGH WHARRIE
Mathematical Essays, Doctrinal and Critical, Upon the Differential and Integral Calculus, Being in Vindication of the Newtonian Law of Indefinite Diminution. Edinburgh: 1854. V. 65; 66

WAUGH, LORENZO
Autobiography of.... Oakland: 1883. V. 63; 66

WAVLE, ARDRA
Here They Are. Boston: 1940. V. 65

THE WAY to Be Wise and Wealthy: Recommended to All: Apply'd, More Particularly and Accomodated To the Several Conditions and Circumstances of the Gentleman, the Scholar, the Soldier, the Tradesman, the Sailor.... London: 1755. V. 66

WAYLAND, FRANCIS
The Affairs of Rhode Island. A Discourse Delivered in the meeting- House of the First Baptist Church, Providence May 22, 1842. Boston: 1842. V. 66
The Affairs of Rhode Island. A Discourse Delivered in the Meeting- House of the First Baptist Church, Providence May 22, 1842. Providence: 1842. V. 62

WAYLAND, JOHN W.
Art Folio of the Shenandoah Valley. N.P: 1924. V. 64
Battle of New Market: Memorial Address, Sixty Second Anniversary of the Battle of New Market, Virginia, May 15, 1926. New Market: 1926. V. 64
Historic Homes of the Northern Virginia and the Eastern Panhandle of West Virginia. Staunton: 1937. V. 64
Historic Landmarks of the Shenandoah Valley.... Harrisonburg: 1924. V. 64
A History of Rockingham County, Virginia. Dayton: 1912. V. 64
A History of Shenandoah County, Virginia. Strasburg: 1969. V. 64; 66
A History of Shenandoah County, Virginia. Berryville: 1976. V. 67
The Pathfinder of the Seas. Richmond: 1930. V. 65
The Shenandoah Valley in History and Literature. Harrisonburg: 1915. V. 63
Twenty-Five Chapters on the Shenandoah Valley to Which is Appended a Concise History of the Civil War in the Valley. Strasburg: 1957. V. 64
The Valley Turnpike: Winchester to Staunton and Other Roads. Winchester: 1967. V. 64

WAYMAN, JOHN HUDSON
A Doctor on the California Trail: The Diary of Dr. John Hudson Wayman from Cambridge City, Indiana, to the Gold Fields in 1852. Denver: 1971. V. 64; 66

WAYNE, JANE ELLEN
Robert Taylor. New York: 1987. V. 66

WAYS and Means to Afford the People Cheap Provisions and Remunerative Employment. London: 1841. V. 62; 66

WAYTE, WILLIAM
A Dictionary of Greek and Roman Antiquities. London: 1914. V. 64

WE Asked Gwendolyn Brooks About the Creative Environment in Illinois. 1967. V. 67

WE Have All Been in the Wrong; or, Thoughts Upon the Dissolution of the Late, and Conduct of the Present Parliament and Upon Mr. Fox's East-India Bills. London: 1785. V. 65

WEALE, JOHN
Quarterly Papers on Architecture. London: 1843-1845. V. 67
Quarterly Papers on Architecture. London: 1844. V. 62

THE WEALTH of Great Britain in the Ocean; Being a Corret State of the British Fisheries.... London: 1749. V. 65

WEARIN, OTHA DONNER
Clarence Arthur Ellsworth. Shenandoah: 1967. V. 62

WEATHERFORD, MARK V.
Bannack-Piute War - the Campaign and Battles. Corvallis: 1957. V. 67

WEATHERLY, F. E.
Punch and Judy and Some of Their Friends. London: 1885. V. 63
Told in the Twilight. New York: 1883. V. 63
Told in the Twilight. New York: 1884. V. 62

WEAVER, C. H.
Palaeontology of the Jurassic and Cretaceous of West Central Argentina. Washington: 1931. V. 63; 66
Paleontology of the Jurassic and Cretaceous of West Central Argentina. Seattle: 1931. V. 64; 65; 67

WEAVER, C. S.
Living Volutes, a Monograph of the Recent Volutidae of the World. Greenville: 1970. V. 62; 66

WEAVER, LAWRENCE
Exhibitions and the Arts of Display. London: 1925. V. 62

WEAVER, R.
Monumenta Antiqua: or the Stone Monuments of Antiquity. 1840. V. 65

WEAVER, RAYMOND
Herman Melville, Mariner and Mystic. New York: 1921. V. 66

WEAVER, WILLIAM D.
Catalogue of the Wheeler Gift Books, Pamphlets and Periodicals in the Library of the American Institute of Electrical Engineers. Mansfield Centre. V. 67

WEBB, ANTHONY
Mr. Pendlebury's Hat Trick. London: 1938. V. 65
One Man Saw Them Die - a Mr. Pendlebury Story. London: 1940. V. 65

WEBB, BENJAMIN
The Complete Negociator.... London: 1767. V. 66

WEBB, BERESFORD
Scouting Achievements - a Record of Thirty Fortunate Years for the Youth of the World. London: 1937. V. 65

WEBB, CHARLES H.
Sea-Weed and What We Seed. New York: 1876. V. 63; 66

WEBB, DANIEL
An Inquiry Into the Beauties of Painting; and Into the Merits of the Most Celebrated Painters, Ancient and Modern. London: 1760. V. 66; 67
An Inquiry into the Beauties of Painting; and Into the Merits of the Most Celebrated Painters, Ancient and Modern. London: 1777. V. 66
Remarks on the Beauties of Poetry. London: 1762. V. 62

WEBB, E. A.
The Historical Directory of Sussex County, N.J. N.P: 1872. V. 66
A History of the Services of the 17th (The Leicestershire) Regiment.... London: 1911. V. 66
The Records of St. Bartholomew's Priory and of the Church and Parish of St. Bartholomew the Great, West Smithfield. Oxford: 1921. V. 66

WEBB, EDITH BUCKLAND
Indian Life at the Old Missions. Los Angeles: 1952. V. 62; 63

WEBB, EDWARD A.
The Historical Directory of Sussex County, N.J. N.P: 1872. V. 63

WEBB, GEORGE W.
Chronological Lists of Engagements Between the Regular Army Of the United States and Various Tribes of Hostile Indians Which Occurred During the Years 1790-1898. St. Joseph: 1939. V. 62; 65; 67

WEBB, J. J.
The Guilds of Dublin. 1929. V. 67
The Guilds of Dublin. London: 1929. V. 64

WEBB, JAMES
The Farmer's Guide; or a Treatise on the Management of Breeding-Mares and Cows.... Elgin: 1838. V. 62

WEBB, JAMES JOSIAH
Adventures in the Santa Fe Trade 1844-1847. Glendale: 1931. V. 64

WEBB, JOHN
A Catalogue of Seeds and Hardy Plants. London: 1760. V. 64
Haverhill, a Descriptive Poem, and Other Poems. London: 1810. V. 66
An Historical Essay Endeavoring a Probability that the Language of the Empire of Chine is the Primitive Language. London: 1669. V. 67

WEBB, M. I.
Michael Rysbrack Sculptor. London: 1954. V. 67

WEBB, MARION ST. JOHN
The Heath Fairies. London: 1927. V. 65
The House Fairies. London: 1925. V. 63
Mr. Paingay's Ship. London: 1925. V. 67
The Orchard Fairies. London: 1928. V. 64; 65
The Sea-Shore Fairies. London: 1925. V. 62
The Weather Fairies. London: 1927. V. 65

WEBB, MARY
Gone to Earth. London: 1917. V. 62; 63; 64; 66
Precious Bane. London: 1924. V. 62; 66

WEBB, PAUL
Bioastronautics Data Book. Washington: 1964. V. 63

WEBB, PHILA H.
The Katt's Kittens. Long Island City: 1935. V. 66

WEBB, RICHARD D.
The Life and Letters of Captain John Brown, Who Was Executed at Charlestown, Virginia Dec. 2, 1859, for an Armed Attack Upon American Slavery. London: 1861. V. 63

WEBB, ROBERT LLOYD
On the Northwest. Commercial Whaling in the Pacific Northwest. Vancouver: 1988. V. 63

WEBB, SIDNEY
English Poor Law History: Part II: The Last Hundred Years. London: 1929. V. 64
Soviet Communism. London: 1935. V. 65

WEBB, TODD
Georgia O'Keefe: the Artist's Landscape. Pasadena: 1984. V. 63; 65

WEBB, W. E.
Buffalo Land: an Account of the Discoveries, Adventures and Mishaps of a Scientific and Sporting Party in the Wild West. Cincinnati and Chicago: 1872. V. 63; 64

WEBB, W. H.
Standard Guide to Non-Poisonous Herbal Medicine. Southport: 1916. V. 64

WEBB, W. L.
Battles and Biographies of Missourians or the Civil War Period of Our State. Kansas City: 1900. V. 65

WEBB, WALTER PRESCOTT
The Great Plains. Boston: 1931. V. 63; 64
The Handbook of Texas. Austin: 1952. V. 66
The Texas Rangers. A Century of Frontier Defense. Boston: 1935. V. 66; 67

WEBB, WILLIAM
Dwellers at the Source: Southwestern Indian Photographs of A. C. Vroman 1895-1904. New York: 1973. V. 63; 66

WEBB, WILLIAM LARKIN
Battles and Biographies of Missourians or the Civil War Period of Our State. Kansas City: 1900. V. 63

WEBB, WILLIAM SEWARD
California and Alaska and Over the Canadian Pacific Railway. New York and London: 1890. V. 66
California and Alaska and Over the Canadian Pacific Railway. New York and London: 1891. V. 62

WEBBER, SAMUEL
Mathematics. Cambridge: 1808. V. 63
War, a Poem, in Three Parts. Cambridge: 1823. V. 63

WEBBR, SAMUEL GILBERT
Treatise on Nervous Diseases: Their Symptoms and Treatment, a Text- Book for Students and Practitioners. New York: 1885. V. 65

WEBER, BRUCE
O Rio de Janeiro. New York: 1986. V. 66

WEBER, CARL J.
Fore-Edge Painting. A Historical Survey of a Curious Art in Book Decoration. New York: 1966. V. 62
Thomas Hardy in Maine. Portland: 1942. V. 64
A Thousand and One Fore-edge Paintings. Waterville: 1949. V. 63

WEBER, DAVID J.
The Californios Versus Jedediah Smith, 1826-1827. A New Cache of Documents. Spokane: 1990. V. 67
The Extranjeros, Selected Documents from the Mexican Side of the Santa Fe Trail 1825-1828. Santa Fe: 1967. V. 64; 67
Richard H. Kern: Expeditionary Artist in the Far Southwest, 1848- 1853. Albuquerque: 1985. V. 65; 66
The Taos Trappers, the Fur Trade in the Far Southwest 1540-1846. Norman: 1968. V. 67

WEBER, DAVIE
Richard H. Kern Expedition Artists in the Far Southwst 1848-1853. Albuquerque: 1985. V. 63

WEBER, FRANCIS J.
A Bibliography of California Bibliographies. Los Angeles: 1968. V. 67

WEBER, FRIEDRICH AUGUST
Onomatologia Medico-Practica. Encyklopadicches Handbuch fur Ausubende Aerzte in Alphabetischer Ordnung.... Nuremberg: 1783-1786. V. 63

WEBER, FRIEDRICH CHRISTIAN
The Present State of Russia. London: 1723-1722. V. 67

WEBER, I. M. ERICH
Practical Cake and Confectionary Art Pra-Ca-Coa.... Dresden-Austria/Chicago: 1921. V. 62; 67

WEBER, J. C.
Die Alpen-Pflanzen Deutschlands und der Schweuz in Coloriten Addildungen nach der Natur und in Naturlichen Grosser Mit ein Erlauternden. Munchen. V. 66

WEBER, MAX
Cubist Poems. London: 1914. V. 64
Die Entwickelung des Solidarchaftprinzips und des Sondervermogens der Offenen Handelsgesellschaft aus den Haushafts und Gewerbegemeinschaften.... Stuttgart: 1889. V. 67

WEBER, W. E.
Mechanik der Menschlichen Gehwerkzeuge. Gottingen: 1836. V. 67

WEBER, WAYNE M.
Covered Bridges in Indiana. Midland: 1977. V. 65

WEBSTER, ALEXANDER
Calculations, with the Principles and Data on Which They are Instituted.... Edinburgh: 1748. V. 62

WEBSTER, BENJAMIN
Behind Time. A Farce. London: 1855. V. 66
Holly Tree Inn. London: 1907?. V. 62

WEBSTER, CHARLES A.
The Church Plate of the Diocese of Cork, Cloyne and Ross. 1909. V. 62
The Diocese of Cork. 1920. V. 64

WEBSTER, DANIEL
A Memorial to the Congress of the United States, on the Subject of Restraining the Increase of Slavery in the New States to be Admitted to the Union. Boston: 1819. V. 64
The Rhode Island Question. Washington: 1848. V. 63
Speech of Mr. Webster of Massachusetts, on the Subject of the Three Millions Appropriations...Delivered in the Senate of the United States, Jan. 14, 1836. Washington: 1836. V. 63; 66
The Writings and Speeches of.... Boston: 1905. V. 63

WEBSTER, FREDERICK
Philosophical Papers and Local Notes.... Nottingham: 1866. V. 65

WEBSTER, GEORGE G.
Around the Horn in '49. Hartford?: 1898. V. 63

WEBSTER, JEAN
Daddy-Long Legs. New York: 1912. V. 63

WEBSTER, JOHN
The Complete Works. London: 1927. V. 63
The Duchess of Malfey.... London: 1678. V. 65
The Duchess of Malfi. London: 1907. V. 65
Elements of Mechanical and Chemical Philosophy. Taunton: 1816. V. 65
Love's Graduate. Oxford: 1885. V. 63; 66
The Works.... London: 1830. V. 62; 65

WEBSTER, JOHN CLARENCE
The Forts of Chignecto. A Study of the Eighteenth Century Conflict Between France and Great Britain in Acadia. Shediac: 1930. V. 67
The Life of Thomas Pichon The Spy of Beausejour...An Account of His Career in Europe and America. Halifax: 1937. V. 67

WEBSTER, KIMBALL
The Gold Seekers of '49, a Personal Narrative of the Overland Trail and Adventures in California and Oregon from 1849 to 1854. Manchester: 1917. V. 63; 66

WEBSTER, M. M., MRS.
Pocahontas: a Legend. Philadelphia: 1849. V. 63; 64

WEBSTER, NOAH
An American Dictionary of the English Language. New York: 1828. V. 63
A Collection of Essays and Fugitive Writings. Boston: 1790. V. 62; 66
A Dictionary for Primary Schools. New York and New Haven: 1833. V. 62
A Dictionary of the English Language.... London: 1829. V. 64
Dissertations on the English Language; with Notes, Historical and Critical. Boston: 1789. V. 64
The Little Reader's Assistant.... Northampton: 1791. V. 66
The Prompter; Essays on Common Sayings and Common Subjects. London: 1818. V. 67
Webster's International Dictionary of the English Language. Springfield: 1903. V. 64

WEBSTER, PELATIAH
An Essay on Credit, In which the Doctrine of Banks Is Considered, and Some Remarks Are Made on the Present State of the Bank of North America. Philadelphia: 1786. V. 64

WECHSBERG, JOSEPH
The Glory of the Violin. New York: 1973. V. 67

WECKER, JOHANN JACOB
Practica Medicinae Generalis. Leyden: 1606. V. 64

WEDD, C. B.
The Geology of the Country Around Flint, Hawarden and Caergwerle. 1924. V. 67

WEDDELL, ALEXANDER W.
Virginia Historical Portraiture 1585-1830. Richmond: 1930. V. 64

WEDDLE, ROBERT S.
Plow Horse Cavalry. The Canery Creek Boys of Thirty-Fourth Texas. Austin: 1974. V. 63

WEDGWOOD, JOSIAH
An Address to the Young Inhabitants of the Pottery. 1783. V. 62

WEDL, CARL
Rudiments of Pathological Histology. London: 1855. V. 67

WEDMORE, FREDERICK
Dream of Provence (Orgeas and Miradou). London: 1905. V. 67
To Nancy. London: 1905. V. 67

WEEDEN, HOWARD
Bandanna Ballads Including Shadows on the Wall. New York: 1899. V. 64

WEEDEN, L. L.
Fairy Tales in Wonderland. London: 1900. V. 64
Moving Pictures. London: 1905. V. 64

WEEKES, REFIE
Poems, Religious and Historical Subjects. New York: 1820. V. 62

WEEKS, J. W.
Annual City Directory of Detroit for 1873-1874. Detroit: 1873. V. 67
Annual Directory of Detroit for 1876-1877. Detroit: 1876. V. 65
Detroit City Directory for 1878. Detroit: 1878. V. 67
Detroit City Directory for 1880. Detroit: 1880. V. 67
Detroit City Directory for 1881. Detroit: 1881. V. 67
Detroit City Directory for 1882. Detroit: 1882. V. 67
Detroit City Directory for 1883. Detroit: 1883. V. 67
Detroit City Directory for 1884. Detroit: 1884. V. 67
Detroit City Directory for 1885. Detroit: 1885. V. 67

WEEKS, LYMAN H.
A History of Paper Manufacturing in the U.S. 1690-1916. New York: 1916. V. 63

WEEMS, MASON LOCKE
The Drunkard's Looking-Glass. Philadelphia?: 1818. V. 63
God's Revenge Against Gambling.... Philadelphia: 1822. V. 63
God's Revenge Against Murder; or the Drown'd Wife, a Tragedy, Lately Performed...by Ned Findley, Esq. Philadelphia: 1808. V. 66
The Life of Washington. Avon: 1974. V. 64; 66
The Philanthropist; or, a Good Twenty-Five Cents Worth of Political Love Powder, for Honest Adamites and Jeffersonians. Dumfries: 1799. V. 66

WEGMAN, WILLIAM
A Showing of Weimaraner. New York: 1997. V. 64

WEGMANN, EDWARD
The Design and Construction of Masonry Dams; Giving the Method Employed in Determining the Profile of the Quaker Bridge Dam. New York: 1889. V. 64

WEHLE, ROBERT G.
Wing and Shot: Gun Dog Training. Scottsville: 1964. V. 64

WEHR, JULIAN
The Animated Picture Book of Alice in Wonderland. New York: 1945. V. 64

WEIBERT, DON L.
The 1874 Invasion of Montana - a Prelude to the Custer Disaster. Billings: 1993. V. 65

WEIBERT, HENRY
Sixty Six Years in Custer's Shadow. Billings: 1985. V. 65

WEIDENREICH, F.
The Skull of Sinanthropus Pekinensis.... Lancaster: 1943. V. 66

WEIDMAN, JEROME
Fiorello. New York: 1960. V. 66
I'll Never Go There Any More. New York: 1941. V. 67
The Lights Around the Shore. New York: 1943. V. 67
Too Early To Tell. New York: 1946. V. 67

WEIDNER, JOHANN LEONHARD
Hispanicae Dominationis Arcana. Lugd. Batavor: 1643. V. 65; 67

WEIGALL, ARTHUR E. P. B.
The Treasury of Ancient Egypt. Edinburgh and London: 1911. V. 62

WEIGEL, JOHN C.
Letter to Carl Sandburg After Reading His Autobiography.... New York: 1968. V. 62; 63; 64; 66

WEIGHTMAN, ALFRED E.
Heraldry in the Royal Navy Crests and Badges of H. M. Ships. Aldershot: 1957. V. 66

WEIGLE, MARTA
Hispanic Art and Ethnohistory. Santa Fe: 1983. V. 64

WEIL, ERNST
Catalogue of Books, Manuscripts, Photographs and Scientific Instruments Fully Described and Offered for Sale by Ernst Weil, 1943-1965.... Mansfield: 1995. V. 62; 65; 67

WEIL, JAMES L.
Another Last Poem. Verona: 1982. V. 66

WEIL, SIMONE
The Iliad or The Poem of Force. Iowa City: 1973. V. 64

WEIMANN, INGRID
Christopher Weimann (1946-1988): a Tribute. Tubingen: 1991. V. 64

WEIMER MACHINE WORKS CO.
How to Fill a Blast Furnace. Lebanon: 1882. V. 65

WEIMER, ROBERT J.
Guide to the Geology of Colorado. 1960. V. 67

WEINBAUM, STANLEY G.
The Black Flame. 1948. V. 64; 66
The Red Peri. 1952. V. 64
The Red Peri. Reading: 1952. V. 66

WEINSHANK, D. J.
A Concordance to Charles Darwin's Notebooks 1836-1844. Ithaca: 1990. V. 64

WEIR, GEORGE
Historical and Descriptive Sketches of the Town and Soke of Horncastle, in the County of Lincoln, and of Several Places Adjacent. London: 1820. V. 63

WEIR, ROBERT
The Badminton Library Riding, Polo. London: 1895. V. 66

WEISER, FREDERICK S.
The Pennsylvania German Fraktur of the Free Library of Philadelphia:. Breinigsville: 1976. V. 67

WEISHAMPEL, D. B.
The Dinosauria. Berkeley: 1990. V. 62

WEISKOPF, F. C.
The Firing Squad. New York: 1944. V. 65

WEISMANN, A.
Essays Upon Heredity and Kindred Biological Problems. Oxford: 1889-1892. V. 67
Studies in the Theory of Descent.... London: 1882. V. 67

WEISS, HARRY B.
Colonel Erkuries Beatty 1759-1823. Pennsylvania Revolutionary Soldier, New Jersey Judge, Senator, Farmer and Prominent Citizen of Princeton. Trenton: 1958. V. 63; 66
The Early Grist and Flouring Mills of New Jersey. Trenton: 1956. V. 63
The Early Lotteries of New Jersey. Trenton: 1966. V. 66
Early Sports and Pastimes in New Jersey. Trenton: 1960. V. 63; 66
The History of Applejack or Apple Brandy in New Jersey from Colonial Times to the Present. Trenton: 1954. V. 66
Something About Jumping Jacks and Jack-in-the-Box. Trenton: 1945. V. 66
They Took to the Waters. The Forgotten Mineral Spring Resorts of New Jersey and Nearby Pennsylvania and Delaware. Trenton: 1962. V. 63; 66
Thomas Say. Early American Naturalist. Springfield and Baltimore: 1931. V. 62; 63; 67
Trades and Tradesmen of Colonial New Jersey. Trenton: 1965. V. 63

WEISSL, AUGUST
The Mystery of the Green Car. London: 1913. V. 65

WEITBRECHT, J.
Syndesmologia; or a Description of the Ligaments of the Human Body. Dublin: 1829. V. 67

WEITZMANN, KURT
Illustrations in Roll and Codex, a Study of the Origin and method of Text Illustration. Princeton: 1970. V. 62

WELBY, T. EARLE
The Victorian Romantics 1850-1870. 1929. V. 64

WELCH, CHARLES
History of the Tower Bridge, and Of Other Bridges Over the Thames Built by the Corporation of London.... London: 1894. V. 62
Numismata Londinensia. Medals Struck by the Corporation of London to Commemorate Important Municipal Events 1831-1893. 1894. V. 67

WELCH, CHARLES A.
History of the Big Horn Basin. Salt Lake City: 1940. V. 62

WELCH, D'ALTE A.
Bibliography of American Children's Books Printed Prior to 1821. Worcester: 1963-1967. V. 62; 67

WELCH, DENTON
Brave and Cruel and Other Stories. London: 1948. V. 63
The Heartsong of Charging Elk. New York: 2000. V. 67
I Left My Grandfather's House. 1958. V. 65
I Left My Grandfather's House. London: 1958. V. 66
In Youth Is Pleasure. London: 1944. V. 64; 65; 66
The Indian Lawyer. New York: 1990. V. 67
A Last Sheaf. London: 1951. V. 65
A Lunch Appointment. 1993. V. 62; 67
A Lunch Appointment. New York: 1993. V. 64
A Lunch Appointment. North Pomfret: 1994. V. 62; 65
Maiden Voyage. London: 1943. V. 62; 65
A Voice through a Cloud. London: 1950. V. 62
Winter in the Blood. New York. 1974. V. 67

WELCH, EMILY S.
A Biographical Sketch - John Sedgewick, Major General. New York: 1899. V. 67

WELCH, F. G.
That Convention; or Five Days a Politician. New York and Chicago: 1872. V. 63

WELCH, J. J.
A Text Book of Naval Architecture for the Use of Officers of the Royal Navy. London: 1901. V. 67

WELCH, JAMES
The Death of Jim Loney. 1979. V. 66
The Death of Jim Loney. New York: 1979. V. 65
Fool's Crow. New York: 1986. V. 65; 67
The Indian Lawyer. New York: 1990. V. 64
Killing Custer. New York: 1994. V. 67
Riding the Earthboy 40. New York and Cleveland: 1971. V. 62; 63; 65; 66; 67
Riding the Earthboy 40. New York: 1976. V. 63
Winter in the Blood. New York: 1974. V. 62; 63; 64; 67

WELCH, JOSEPH
A List of Scholars of St. Peter's College, Westminster, as they Were Elected to Christ Church College, Oxford and Trinity College, Cambridge, from the Foundation by Queen Elizabeth, 1561, to the Present Time.... London: 1788. V. 63; 67

WELCH, LEWIS SHELDON
Yale. Her Campus, Class-Rooms and Athletics. Boston: 1899. V. 64

WELCH, MOSES C.
The Gospel to be Preached To All Men, Illustrated, In a Sermon, Delivered in Windham, (Conn.) at the Execution of Samuel Freeman, a Mulatto, Nov. 6, 1805 for the Murder of Hannah Simons. Windham: 1805. V. 63; 66

WELCH, SAUNDERS
A Proposal to Render Effectual a Plan to Remove the Nuisance of Common Prostitutes from the Streets of This metropolis.... London: 1758. V. 65

WELCH, SPENCER GLASGOW
A Confederate Surgeon's Letters to His Wife. New York and Washington: 1911. V. 62; 63; 65

WELCH, WILLIAM HENRY
Contributions to the Science of Medicine Dedicated by His Pupils on the Twenty-Fifth Anniversary of His Doctorate. Baltimore: 1900. V. 67

A WELCOME. *Original Contributions in Prose and Poetry.* London: 1863. V. 64

WELCOME, J.
Snaffles. The Work of Charlie Johnson Payne. 1987. V. 64

WELD, C. R.
Two Months in the Highlands. 1860. V. 64
A Vacation Tour in the United States and Canada. London: 1855. V. 66

WELD, EDWARD F.
The Ransomed Bride: a Tale of the Inquisition. New York: 1846. V. 62

WELD, ISAAC
Travels through the States of North America and the Provinces of Upper and Lower Canada During the Years 1795, 1796 and 1797. London: 1799. V. 63; 66

WELD, M. C.
The Percheron Horse in America/In France.... New York: 1886. V. 64

WELDON, FAY
Words of Advice. Brighton: 1974. V. 64

WELFORD, RICHARD GRIFFITHS
The Influences of the Game Laws.... London: 1846. V. 66

WELL Dressed Lines. Stripped from the Reels of Five New Englanders. New York: 1962. V. 64

WELLCOME LIBRARY
A Catalogue of Printed Books. I. New York: 1996. V. 62
A Catalogue of Printed Books in the Wellcome Historical Medical Library. London: 1976-1996. V. 63
A Catalogue of Printed Books in the Wellcome Historical Medical Library. I. Books Printed Before 1641. London: 1962. V. 64; 66
A Catalogue of Printed Books in the Wellcome Historical Medical Library II. Books Printed from 1641 to 1851. A-E. London: 1968. V. 64
Catalogue of Printed Books. Volumes I-IV. London: 1962-1995. V. 62

WELLES, ALBERT
History of the Welles Family in England and Normandy, with the Derviation from Their Progenitors of Some of the Descendants in the United States. New York: 1876. V. 63

WELLES, C. M.
Three Years' Wanderings of a Connecticut Yankee, in South America, Africa, Australia and California.... New York: 1860. V. 63

WELLES, EDWARD RANDOLPH
A History of Trinity Church, Woodbridge, New Jersey from 1698 to 1935. Southborough: 1935. V. 66

WELLES, ORSON
Mr. Arkadin. New York: 1956. V. 67

WELLESLEY, DOROTHY
The Annual - Being a Selection from Forget-Me-Nots, Keepsakes and Other Annuals of the Nineteenth Century. London: 1930. V. 62
Desert Wells. London: 1946. V. 64
Early Poems. London: 1913. V. 65
Jupiter and the Nun. London: 1932. V. 63
Lost Planet and Other Poems. London: 1942. V. 64
Matrix. London: 1928. V. 63
Rhymes for Middle Years. London: 1954. V. 64

WELLING, D. S.
Information for the People; or the Asylums of Ohio. Pittsburgh: 1851. V. 65

WELLINGTON, ARTHUR, DUKE OF
Civil Correspondence and Memoranda of Field Marshal Arthur, Duke of Wellington. 1860. V. 63
The Dispatches of Field Marshal the Duke of Wellington, During His Various Campaigns in India, Denmark, Portugal, Spain the Low Countries and France from 1799 to 1818. London: 1837-1871. V. 67

WELLINGTON, EVELYN
A Descriptive and Historical Catalogue of the Collection of Pictures and Sculpture at Apsley House, London. London: 1901. V. 65

WELLINGTON, GERALD WELLESLEY, 7TH DUKE OF
The Collected Works.... 1970. V. 67

WELLMAN, K. F.
A Survey of North American Indian Rock Art. Graz: 1979. V. 62

WELLMAN, MANLY WADE
Giant in Gray. New York: 1949. V. 62; 65
The Kingdom of Madison. Chapel Hill: 1973. V. 63; 67
Rebel Boast: First at Bethel - Last at Appomattox. New York: 1956. V. 63

WELLMAN, PAUL I.
The Callaghan Yesterday and Today. Encinal. V. 65
Death on the Prairie - the Thirty Years Struggle for the Western Plains. New York: 1934. V. 65; 67

WELLMAN, WILLIAM A.
Go, Get 'Em!. Boston: 1918. V. 65

WELLS, CAROLYN
The Jingle Book. New York: 1906. V. 65
Vicky Van. 1918. V. 66
Vicky Van. Philadelphia: 1918. V. 64

WELLS, CHARLES KNOX POLK
Life and Adventures of Polk Wells the Notorious Outlaw. N.P: 1907. V. 62; 63; 64; 66

WELLS, CHARLES WESLEY
Frontier Life, Sketches and Incidents of Homes in the West. Cincinnati: 1902. V. 66; 67

WELLS, EDMUND
Argonaut Tales - Stories of the Gold Seekers and the Indian Scouts of Early Arizona. New York: 1927. V. 65

WELLS, EDWARD
Elementa Arithmeticae Numerosae et Speciosae. Oxford: 1698. V. 66
A Treatise of Antient and Present Geography. Together with a Sett of Maps, Both Antient and Present Geography.... London: 1717. V. 67

WELLS, EDWARD L.
Hampton and His Cavalry in '64. Richmond: 1899. V. 62; 63; 65
Hampton and Reconstruction. Columbia: 1907. V. 63; 65
A Sketch of the Charleston Light Dragoons from the Earliest Formation of the Corps. Charleston: 1888. V. 65

WELLS, H. W.
A Treatise on the Law of Replevin as Administered in the Courts of the United States and England. Chicago: 1880. V. 66

WELLS, HENRY P.
City Boys in the Woods, or, a Trapping Venture in Maine. London: 1890. V. 67

WELLS, HENRY W.
Poet and Psychiatrist: Merrill Moore. Dublin: 1955. V. 62

WELLS, HERBERT GEORGE
The Anatomy of Frustration - a Modern Synthesis. London: 1936. V. 65
The Autocracy of Mr. Parham. London: 1930. V. 65
Babes in the Darkling Wood. 1940. V. 63; 64
Brynhild. London: 1937. V. 65
Certain Personal Matters. London: 1901. V. 67
Christina Alberta's Father. London: 1925. V. 62; 63; 66
The Country of the Blind. London: 1911. V. 64; 65
The Country of the Blind. Waltham St. Lawrence: 1939. V. 65
The Discovery of the Future; a Discourse Delivered to the Royal Institution on January 24, 1902. London: 1902. V. 67
An Englishman Looks at the World. London: 1914. V. 63
The First Men in the Moon. London: 1901. V. 67
The Food of the Gods. London: 1904. V. 67
God the Invisible King. London: 1917. V. 63
Great Thoughts from H. G. Wells. New York: 1912. V. 62
In the Days of the Comet. London: 1906. V. 62; 64; 66; 67
The Invisible Man. London: 1897. V. 62; 67
The Invisible Man. Leipzig: 1898. V. 67
The Island of Doctor Moreau. London: 1896. V. 67
The Island of Dr. Moreau. New York: 1896. V. 64; 66
Kipps: The Story of a Simple Soul. London: 1905. V. 62
Love and Mr. Lewisham. 1900. V. 67
Meanwhile. London: 1927. V. 63; 64
Meanwhile. New York: 1927. V. 65
Men Like Gods. London: 1923. V. 62; 64
Mr. Blettsworthy on Rampole Island. London: 1928. V. 65; 67
Mr. Britling Sees It Through. London: 1916. V. 63
A Modern Utopia. London: 1905. V. 65
The New America: The New World. London: 1935. V. 66
The Open Conspiracy. London: 1928. V. 64
The Outline of History. London: 1919-1920. V. 64
The Passionate Friends. London: 1913. V. 65
The Plattner Story. London: 1897. V. 64; 66
Russia in the Shadows. London: 1920. V. 62; 65; 66
The Salvaging of Civilization. London: 1921. V. 62
The Sea Lady. 1902. V. 66
The Sea Lady. New York: 1902. V. 64
The Secret Places of the Heart. London: 1922. V. 62; 64
Select Conversations with an Uncle (Now Extinct) and Other Reminiscences. London: 1895. V. 62; 63; 64
The Soul of a Bishop. London: 1917. V. 62; 67
Star Begotten - a Biological Fantasia. London: 1937. V. 65
Tales of Space and Time. Leipzig: 1900. V. 67
Tales of Space and Time. London: 1900. V. 64; 66
Text-Book of Biology. London: 1893-1894. V. 67
The Time Machine and The Island of Doctor Moreau. Leipzig: 1898. V. 67
Twelve Stories and a Dream. London: 1903. V. 64
Two Letters from H. G. Wells to Joseph Conrad. London: 1926. V. 64
The War in the Air. 1908. V. 66
The War in the Air. London: 1908. V. 62; 64; 65; 67
The War of the Worlds. London: 1898. V. 63
The War of the Worlds. New York: 1960. V. 62
The War of the Worlds. (with) The Time Machine. New York: 1964. V. 64
The War That Will End War. London: 1914. V. 64
The Way the World is Going. London: 1928. V. 65
What is Coming?. London: 1916. V. 64
When the Sleeper Wakes. 1899. V. 64; 66
The Wonderful Visit. London: 1895. V. 64; 66
The Work, Wealth and Happiness of Mankind. Garden City: 1931. V. 62
The World of William Clissold. London: 1926. V. 62; 64; 67

WELLS, J. M., MRS.
Darling Bright-Eyes Living Nursery Rhymes Newly Treated with Moving Pictures. London: 1873. V. 65

WELLS, J. R.
A New and Valuable Book, Entitled the Family Companion.... Boston: 1846. V. 63

WELLS, JAMES M.
With Touch of Elbow or Death Before Dishonor. Philadelphia: 1909. V. 63; 66

WELLS, LINTON
Around the World in Twenty Eight Days. 1926. V. 66

WELLS, NATHANIEL ARMSTRONG
The Picturesque Antiquities of Spain. London: 1846. V. 67

WELLS, POLK
Life and Adventures of Polk Wells, the Notorious Outlaw. N.P: 1907. V. 62; 65

WELLS, R. B. D.
A New Illustrated Hand-book of Phrenology...(with) A Delineation of the Character, Physiological Development and Present Condition. London: 1870. V. 64

WELLS, REBECCA
Divine Secrets of the Ya-Ya Sisterhood. New York: 1996. V. 67

WELLS, ROBERT
A Correspondence Between the Rev. Robert Wells, Chaplain to the Earl of Dunmore, and a Gentleman Under the Signature of Publicola (i.e. Sir Benjamin Hobhouse).... Bristol: 1791. V. 62

WELLS, ROLLA
Episodes of My Life. St. Louis: 1933. V. 63; 64; 66

WELLS, ROSEMARY
Forest of Dreams. New York: 1988. V. 64

WELLS, SAMUEL
A Letter to the Marquis of Tavistock, on the Best Means of Obtaining Pure and Less Expensive Elections, on the Dissolution of Parliament. London: 1825. V. 64

WELLS, SUSAN M.
Coral Reefs of the World. 1988. V. 67

WELLS, WALTER
The Water-Power of Maine. Augusta: 1869. V. 65; 66

WELLS, WILLIAM C.
Seventeenth Century Tokens of Northamptonshire (with an 8 page addenda at Corrigenda). London: 1914. V. 66

WELLS, WILLIAM CHARLES
Two Essays: One Upon Single Vision with Two Eyes; the Other on Dew. London: 1818. V. 62; 65

WELSCH, R. L.
An American Anthropologist in Melanesia. Honolulu: 1998. V. 62

WELSH, IRVINE
The Acid House. New York: 1995. V. 63
Ecstasy. London: 1996. V. 65; 67
Filth. London: 1998. V. 62; 64; 65
Marabou Stork Nightmares. New York: 1995. V. 66
Past Tense. South Queensferry: 1992. V. 62
Trainspotting. London: 1993. V. 64
Trainspotting. New York: 1996. V. 65

WELSH, WILLIAM
Report of a Visit to the Sioux and Ponca Indians of the Missouri River. Washington: 1872. V. 63; 65; 66; 67

WELTY, EUDORA
Acrobats in a Park. N.P: 1977. V. 64; 67
The Bride of Innisfallen and Other Stories. New York: 1955. V. 62; 64; 65; 67
The Collected Stories of Eudora Welty. New York and London: 1980. V. 64; 67
Country Churchyards. Jackson: 2000. V. 66
A Curtain of Green. Garden City: 1941. V. 64; 66
Delta Wedding. New York: 1946. V. 65
A Flock of Guinea Hens Seen from a Car. New York: 1970. V. 62
The Golden Apples. New York: 1949. V. 63; 64; 66
Henry Green: a Novelist of Imagination. Austin: 1961. V. 62; 64; 67
Ida M'Toy. Urbana: 1979. V. 65; 66
John Rood. Exhibition of Recent Sculpture. October 7-25. New York: 1958. V. 64; 67
The Little Store. Newton: 1985. V. 62
Losing Battles. New York: 1970. V. 63
Music from Spain. Greenville: 1948. V. 62
My Introduction to Katherine Anne Porter. 1990. V. 66
One Writer's Beginnings. Cambridge: 1984. V. 63; 64; 67
The Optimist's Daughter. New York: 1972. V. 64; 67
The Optimist's Daughter. London: 1973. V. 64
The Optimist's Daughter. Franklin Center: 1980. V. 67
A Pageant of Birds. New York: 1974. V. 62; 64; 66; 67
Photographs. 1989. V. 66
The Ponder Heart. London: 1954. V. 62; 64
The Robber Bridegroom. Garden City: 1942. V. 62
Short Stories. New York: 1949. V. 62
Some Notes on Time in Fiction. Jackson: 1973. V. 64; 67
Three Papers on Fiction. Northampton: 1962. V. 66; 67
White Fruitcake. New York: 1980. V. 65; 66
The Wide Net. New York: 1943. V. 65; 67

WELWOOD, JAMES
Memoirs of the Most Material Transactions in England, for the Last Hundred Years, Preceding the Revolution in 1688. London: 1702. V. 62
Memoirs of the Most Material Transactions in England, for the Last Hundred Years, Preceding the Revolution in 1688.... London: 1718. V. 63; 67

WEMMER, C. M.
Biology and Manangement of the Cervidae. 1987. V. 67

WENCKSTERN, FRIEDRICH VON
A Bibliography of the Japanese Empire; Being a Classified List of all Books, Essays and Maps in European Languages from 1859-1906. 1998. V. 65

WENDEBORN, F. A.
A View of England Towards the Close of the Eighteenth Century. London: 1791. V. 66

WENDELL Berry. Lewiston: 1991. V. 67

WENDORF, FRED
Archaeological Studies in the Petrified Forest National Monument. Flagstaff: 1953. V. 65
The Midland Discovery. Austin: 1955. V. 65

WENDOVER, ROGER DE
Chronica sive Flores Historianum, Nunc rimum Edidit Henricius O. Coxe. 1841-1844. V. 62

WENHAM, LESLIE P.
The Romano-British Cemetery at Trentholme Drive, York. London: 1968. V. 62

WENIGER, D.
Cacti of the Southwest, Texas, New Mexico, Oklahoma, Arkansas and Louisiana. Austin: 1970. V. 66

WENNERBERG, BRYNOLF
In Der Heimat, in Der Heimat.... Munchen: 1916. V. 65

WENTWORTH, ANNE ISABELLA BYRON, BARONESS
Remarks Occasioned by Mr Moore's Notices of Lord Byron's Life. London: 1830. V. 67

WENTWORTH, EDWARD N.
America's Sheep Trails, History, Personalities. Ames: 1948. V. 65
A Biographical Catalogue of the Portrait Gallery of the Saddle and Sirloin Club. Chicago: 1920. V. 64

WENTWORTH, FRANK L.
On the Road with Lizzie. Iowa City: 1930. V. 62

WENTWORTH, PATRICIA
A Marriage Under the Terror. London: 1910. V. 62
Silence in Court. Philadelphia: 1945. V. 65

WENZELL, A. B.
The Passing Show. New York: 1903. V. 65

WEPPNER, MARGARETHA
The North Star and Southern Cross; Being the Personal Experiences, Impressions and Observations of Margaretha Weppner, in a Two Years' Journey Round the World. London/Albany: 1882. V. 64

WERMUTH, H.
Schildkroten, Krokodile Bruckenechsen. Jena: 1961. V. 65

WERNER, CHARLES J.
Eric Mullica and His Descendants. New Gretna: 1930. V. 63; 66

WERNER, HERMAN
On the Western Frontier With the United States Cavalry...Fifty Years Ago. N.P: 1934. V. 64; 67

WERNER, J. R.
A Visit to Stanley's Rear-Guard at Major Barttelot's Camp on the Aruhwimi with an Account of River-Life on the Congo. Edinburgh: 1889. V. 62

WERNOE, T. B.
The Diagnostics of Pain. Copenhagen & London: 1936. V. 67

WERTH, LEON
Bonnard. Paris: 1930. V. 62; 63
Bonnard. Paris: 1981. V. 64

WERTHAM, FREDERIC
Seduction of the Innocent. New York: 1954. V. 63

WESCHER, H.
Collage. New York: 1968. V. 62; 65

WESCOTT, EDWARD NOYES
David Harum, a Story of American Life. New York: 1998. V. 63

WESCOTT, GLENWAY
Apartment in Athens. New York: 1945. V. 64
The Babe's Bed. Paris: 1930. V. 64
Natives of Rock: XX Poems: 1921-1922. New York: 1926. V. 62

WESKER, ARNOLD
The Wesker Trilogy - Chicken Soup with Barley, Roots, I'm Talking about Jerusalem. London: 1960. V. 62; 64

WESLEY, JOHN
A Calm Address to Our American Colonies. London: 1775. V. 66
A Collection of Hymns, for the Use of the People Called Methodists. London: 1797. V. 63
An Extract of the Christian's Pattern; or, a Treatise of the Imitation of Christ. Bristol: 1770. V. 64
An Extract of the Rev. John Wesley's Journal, from May 27, 1765 to May 18, 1768. XIV. London: 1771. V. 62
An Extract of the Rev. Mr. John Wesley's Journal from October 29, 1762 to May 25, 1765. XII. Bristol: 1768. V. 62
The Journal.... London: 1938. V. 63
The Letters of the Rev. John Wesley. London: 1931. V. 63
Primitive Physick; or, an Easy and Natural Method of Curing Most Diseases. Bristol: 1765. V. 64

WESLEY, JOHN continued
Primitive Physick; or, an Easy and Natural Method of Curing Most Diseases. London: 1772. V. 64; 66
A Sermon on the Death of the Rev. George Whitefield, Preached at the Chapel in Tottenham Court Road...on Sunday November 18th 1770.... London: 1770. V. 63
A Short English Grammar. London: 1778. V. 64
A Short Hebrew Grammar. London: 1769. V. 64
A Short Latin Grammar. London: 1813. V. 64

WESLEY, SAMUEL
A Letter from a Country Divine to His Friend in London. London: 1703. V. 65

WESSEL, JOHN
This No Further. New York: 1996. V. 67

WESSELHOEFT, LILY F.
The Fairy Folk of Blue Hill. Boston: 1895. V. 63

WESSON, MARIANNE
Render Up the Body. London: 1997. V. 65; 66

WEST, ALGERNON
Private Diaries of the Rt. Hon. Algernon West. New York: 1922. V. 67

WEST, ANTHONY
John Piper. London: 1979. V. 63

WEST, B.
Grover Cleveland on a Tramp. Chicago: 1895. V. 67

WEST, BENJAMIN
Christ Rejected, Catalogue of the Picture Representing the Above Subject.. London: 1814. V. 62
A Description of Mr. West's Picture of Death on the Pale Horse.... London: 1818. V. 65
Description of the Picture, Christ Healing the Sick in the Temple, Painted by Benjamin West, Esq. Philadelphia: 1817. V. 66
A Discourse Delivered to the Students of the Royal Academy, on the Distribution of the Prizes, December 10, 1792, by the President. London: 1793. V. 66
Select Groups, from the Picture of Christ Rejected, Painted by Benjamin Wst, Esq.... London: 1814. V. 62

WEST, CHARLES
On Some Disorders of the Nervous System in Childhood: Being the Lumleian Lectures Delivered at the Royal Collge of Physicians of London in March 1871. Philadelphia: 1871. V. 64; 67

THE WEST Coast Trade. Sixth Annual. New Year 1898. Tacoma: 1898. V. 63

WEST, D. C.
Forest Succession, Concepts and Application. New York: 1981. V. 65

WEST, DON
The Road is Rocky. New York: 1951. V. 67

WEST, E. S.
Garrett Co., Maryland, Health Resort, Summer Resort, Winter Resort. Oakland: 1910. V. 62

WEST, G. S.
A Treatise on British Freshwater Algae in Which are Included all the Pigmented and Protophyta Hitherto Found in British Freshwaters. 1927. V. 67

WEST, GILBERT
A Canto of the Fairy Queen. London: 1739. V. 65

WEST, HANS
Bidrag til Beskrivelse Over St. Croix Med en Kort Udsigt Over St. Thomas, St. Jean, Tortola, Spanishtown og Crabeneiland. Copenhagen;: 1793. V. 63

WEST, HERBERT FAULKNER
The Dreamer of Devon. An Essay on Henry Williamson. 1932. V. 62

WEST INDIA DOCK COMPANY
At a General Court of Proprietors of the West India Dock Company, Held at Their House in Billiter Square, on Friday the 6th January, 1809, Thomas Hughan, Esq. in the Chair, the Chairman Read to the Meeting a Report from a Committe of Directors on the Gen. London: 1809?. V. 66

WEST, JANE
The Loyalists, an Historical Novel. London: 1812. V. 62
A Tale of the Times. London: 1799. V. 62
A Tale of the Times. Alexandria: 1801. V. 66

WEST JERSEY SURVEYORS' ASSOCIATION
Proceedings, Constitution, By-Laws, List of Members &c.... Camden: 1880. V. 63; 66

WEST, JESSAMYN
The Woman Said Yes. Encounters with Life and Death. Memoirs. London: 1976. V. 63

WEST, JOHN
A Plea for the Education of the Children of the Gypsies. London: 1844. V. 64

WEST, JOHN C.
A Texan in Search of a Fight - the Diary and Letters of a Private Soldier in Hood's Texas Brigade. Waco: 1969. V. 67

WEST, LEONARD
The Natural Trout Fly and Its Imitation. London. V. 66
The Natural Trout Fly and Its Imitation. St. Helens: 1912. V. 67
The Natural Trout Fly and Its Imitation. Liverpool: 1921. V. 67

WEST, NATHANAEL
A Cool Million. New York: 1934. V. 62
A Cool Million. London: 1954. V. 67
The Day of the Locust. New York: 1939. V. 66
The Dream Life of Balso Snell. Paris: 1931. V. 67
Miss Lonelyhearts. London: 1949. V. 62

WEST, NATHANIEL
The Ancestry, Life and Times of Hon. Henry Hastings Sibley. St. Paul: 1889. V. 63

WEST Nebraska Grazing Country. N.P: 1895. V. 66

THE WEST of Buffalo Bill. New York. V. 63

WEST, PAUL
Alley Jaggers. New York: 1966. V. 67
Bela Lugosi's White Christmas. New York: 1972. V. 63; 64; 66; 67
Gala. New York: 1976. V. 67
I'm Expecting to Live Quite Soon. New York: 1970. V. 67
I'm Expecting to Live Quite Soon. London: 1971. V. 67
The Pearl and the Pumpkin. New York: 1904. V. 63; 65

WEST Port Murders; or an Authentic Account of the Atrocious Murders Committed by Burke and His Associates.... Edinburgh: 1829. V. 63

WEST, REBECCA
Black Lamb and Grey Falcon: the Record of a Journey through Yugoslavia in 1937. London: 1941. V. 62; 64
The Return of the Soldier. 1918. V. 66
The Return of the Soldier. London: 1918. V. 64
The Return of the Soldier. New York: 1918. V. 64
The Strange Necessity - Essays and Reviews. London: 1928. V. 64
The Thinking Reed - a Novel. London: 1936. V. 64

WEST, RICHARD
An Inquiry Into the Manner of Creating Peers. London: 1719. V. 66

WEST, RICHARD SAMUEL
Satire on Stone: the Political Cartoons of Joseph Keppler. Urbana and Chicago: 1988. V. 67

WEST, SAMUEL
Essays on Liberty and Necessity; in Which the True Nature of Liberty is Stated and Defended.... New Bedford: 1795. V. 66

WEST Shore. Portland: 1888. V. 64

WEST, THOMAS
The Antiquities of Furness. London: 1774. V. 64; 65; 66
The Antiquities of Furness. Ulverston: 1805. V. 66
The Antiquities of Furness. Beckermet: 1977. V. 64; 65
The Descriptive Part of Mr. West's Guide to the Lakes in Cumberland, Westmorland and Lancashire. Kendal: 1809. V. 66
A Guide to the Lakes: Dedicated to the Lovers of Landscape Studies.... London: 1778. V. 65; 66
A Guide to the Lakes, in Cumberland, Westmorland and Lancashire. London: 1780. V. 64; 65
A Guide to the Lakes, in Cumberland, Westmorland and Lancashire. Kendal: 1799. V. 65
A Guide to the Lakes, in Cumberland, Westmorland and Lancashire. Kendal: 1802. V. 63
A Guide to the Lakes in Cumberland, Westmorland and Lancashire. Kendal: 1821. V. 66

WEST VIRGINIA. LAWS, STATUTES, ETC. - 1863
Acts of the Legislature of West Virginia at Its First Session, Commencing June 20th, 1863. Wheeling: 1863. V. 63; 66

WEST VIRGINIA HISTORICAL & ANTIQUARIAN SOCIETY
The West Virginia Hsitorical Magazine Quarterly Volume 1 #1-Volume 4 #4. Charleston: 1900-1904. V. 65

THE WEST Virginia Lute. Designed for School, Revival, Sunday School and Miscellaneous Meetings. Parkersburg: 1870. V. 63

WEST, W.
A Monograph of the British Desmidiaceae. London: 1904-1923. V. 63

WEST, WILLIAM
Fifty Years' Recollections of an Old Bookseller.... Cork: 1836. V. 65
Fifty Years' Recollections of an Old Bookseller.... London: 1837. V. 65
The First (-Second) Part of Symboleographie; Which May Be Termed the Art of Description, of Instruments and Presidents. London: 1647-1641. V. 65

WESTAL, STANLEY
War Path and Council Fire. New York: 1948. V. 67

WESTALL, R.
Victories of the Duke of Wellington, from Drawings by R. Westall.. London: 1819. V. 62; 67

WESTALL, WILLIAM
Picturesque Tour of the River Thames. London: 1828. V. 62
Twelve Views of the Caves in Yorkshire. London: 1818. V. 64

WESTALL, WILLIAM BURY
Roy of Roy's Court. London: 1892. V. 66

WESTCOTT, GLENWAY
The Babe's Bed. Paris: 1930. V. 65
A Calendar of Saints for Unbelievers. Paris: 1932. V. 65

WESTELL, W. PERCIVAL
The Book of the Animal Kingdom - Mammals. London: 1910. V. 62

WESTERMAN, PERCY F.
Midst Arctic Perils. A Thrilling Story of Adventure in the Polar Regions. London: 1919. V. 64; 66
A Watch-Dog of the North Sea: a Naval Story of the Great War. London: 1916. V. 67

WESTERMARCK, EDWARD
The History of the Human Marriage. London: 1891. V. 63; 67

WESTERMEIER, CLIFFORD
Man, Beast, Dust: the Story of Rodeo. N.P: 1947. V. 63; 64
Trailing the Cowboy. Caldwell: 1955. V. 63; 64; 66

WESTERN CONFERENCE
The Rise of Methodism in the West - Being the Journal of the Western Conference 1800-1811. New York: 1920. V. 67

WESTERN Galaxy. Volume I. Salt Lake City: 1888. V. 65

WESTERN North Dakota Livestock Brand Record. N.P: 1937. V. 64

WESTERN SOUTH DAKOTA STOCK GROWERS ASSOCIATION
Brand Book of the Western South Dakota Stock Growers Association. Omaha: 1901. V. 62

THE WESTERN Tourist or Emigrant's Guide through the States of Ohio, Michigan, Indiana, Illinois and Missouri and the Territories of Wisconsin and Iowa. New York: 1846. V. 63; 64

WESTERNERS
The California Deserts - The Westerners' Brand Book Number 11. Los Angeles: 1964. V. 65
Chicago Westerners' Brand Book 1944. Chicago: 1946. V. 63; 65
Chicago Westerners' Brand Book 1945-1946. Chicago: 1947. V. 65
Westerners' Brand Book IV. Los Angeles: 1951. V. 65
The Westerners Brand Book.... Denver: 1952. V. 65

WESTERNERS. CHICAGO CORRAL
Brand Book 1944. Chicago: 1946. V. 67
Brand Book 1945-1946. Chicago: 1947. V. 67

WESTERNERS. DENVER POSSE
1946 Brand Book. Denver: 1947. V. 64
Brand Book, 1963. 19th Annual Edition. Denver: 1963. V. 63
Denver Westerners' Brand Book. Volume II. Denver: 1947. V. 63
Denver Westerners' Brand Book Volume III. Denver: 1948. V. 66
Denver Westerners' Brand Book. Volume IX. Denver: 1954. V. 66
Denver Westerners' Brand Book Volume V. Denver: 1949. V. 66
Denver Westerners' Brand Book Volume V. Denver: 1950. V. 66
Denver Westerners' Brand Book Volume VI. Denver: 1951. V. 63; 66
Denver Westerners' Brand Book Volume VII. Denver: 1952. V. 66
Denver Westerners' Brand Book Volume X. Denver: 1955. V. 66
Denver Westerners' Brand Book Volume XI. 1955. Denver: 1956. V. 66
Denver Westerners' Brand Book Volume XII. Denver: 1957. V. 63; 66
Denver Westerners' Brand Book. Volume XIII. Denver: 1958. V. 66
Denver Westerners' Brand Book Volume XIV. Denver: 1959. V. 63; 66
Denver Westerners' Brand Book Volume XVII. Boulder: 1962. V. 63; 66
Westerners' Brand Book for 1945. Denver: 1946. V. 63

WESTERNERS. LOS ANGELES CORRAL
Brand Book I. Los Angeles: 1947. V. 67
Brand Book II. Los Angeles: 1949. V. 67
Brand Book III. Los Angeles: 1949. V. 64; 67
Brand Book IV. Los Angeles: 1951. V. 67
Brand Book IX. Los Angeles: 1961. V. 64; 67
Brand Book VII. Los Angeles: 1957. V. 67
Brand Book X. Los Angeles: 1963. V. 64; 67
Westerners' Brand Book. Book V. Los Angeles: 1953. V. 64; 67
Westerners' Brand Book. Book VI. Los Angeles: 1956. V. 63; 64
Westerners' Brand Book. Book VII. Los Angeles: 1957. V. 64
The Westerners Brand Book, Los Angeles Corral: Volumes 1-18. Los Angeles: 1947. V. 64
The Westerners Brand Book. Number 11. Los Angeles: 1964. V. 62

WESTERNERS. NEW YORK
The Westerner's Brand Book. New York: 1954-1963. V. 64

WESTERNERS. SAN DIEGO CORRAL
Brand Book 2. San Diego: 1971. V. 67
Brand Book #3. San Diego: 1973. V. 67
Brand Book Number One: the San Diego Corral of the Westerners. San Diego: 1968. V. 64

WESTERNERS. TUCSON CORRAL
Tucson Corral of Westerners' Brand Books. Tucson: 1967-1984. V. 63

WESTERVELT, FRANCES A.
History of Bergen County, New Jersey 1630-1923. New York: 1923. V. 63; 66

WESTERVELT, W. D.
Hawaiian Legends of Volcanoes. Boston/London: 1916. V. 65

WESTGARTH, WILLIAM
Victoria and the Australian Gold Mines in 1857; with Ntoes on the Overland Route from Austrlia, Via Suez. London: 1857. V. 66

WESTLAKE, DONALD E.
The Curious Facts Preceding My Execution. New York: 1968. V. 64
Deadly Edge. New York: 1971. V. 64
Drowned Hopes. 1990. V. 64
I Gave at the Office. New York: 1971. V. 66
Killy. New York: 1963. V. 64
A Likely Story. 1984. V. 64; 66
Plunder Squad. New York: 1972. V. 66
Somebody Owes Me Money. New York: 1969. V. 67

WESTLAKE, N. H. J.
The Litany, Sketches from a Psalter Executed in England About 1320. 1858. V. 62

WESTMACOTT, CHARLES MOLLOY
The English Spy.... London: 1825-1826. V. 64

WESTON, COLE
Eighteen Photographs. Salt Lake City: 1981. V. 62

WESTON, EDWARD
The Cats of Wildcat Hill. New York: 1947. V. 63
The Daybooks of Edward Weston. Rochester: 1961. V. 63
The Daybooks of Edward Weston. 1961-1966. V. 63
Edward Weston. New York: 1932. V. 63
Edward Weston: Fifty Photographs. New York: 1947. V. 63; 66
My Camera on Point Lobos. Boston: 1950. V. 63; 65
Photography. Pasadena: 1934. V. 63; 65

WESTON, JAMES
Stenography Compleated or the Art of Short-Hand Brought to Perfection.... London: 1730. V. 64

WESTON, RICHARD
A Discours of Husbandrie Used in Brabant and Flanders.... London: 1652. V. 65

WESTON, STEPHEN
A Chinese Poem, Inscribed on Porcelain, in the Thirty-Third Year of the Cycle, A.D. 1776. London: 1816. V. 64; 65
Fan-hy-Cheu: a Tale, in Chinese and English. London: 1814. V. 64; 65
(Persian title) or, Persian Distichs, from Various Authors.... London: 1814. V. 64; 65

WESTPHAL, R.
Plein Art Painters of California: the North. Irvine. 1986. V. 62; 65

WESTRING, N.
Araneae Svecicae Descriptae. Gothenburg: 1861. V. 65

WESTWOOD, JOHN OBADIAH
The Butterflies of Great Britain With Their Transformations. 1860. V. 62
An Introduction to the Modern Classification of Insects. 1839-1840. V. 66
Palaeographia Sacra Pictoria.... London: 1843-1845. V. 62

WESTWOOD, T.
Bibliotheca Piscatoria. London: 1883. V. 65
Bibliotheca Piscatoria. New York: 1991. V. 62

WETMORE, A.
The Birds of Haiti and the Dominican Republic. Washington: 1931. V. 67
The Birds of the Republic of Panama. Washington: 1965-1984. V. 63
The Birds of the Republic of Panama. Washington: 1968-1984. V. 67

WETMORE, HELEN CODY
Last of the Great Scouts: The Life Story of Col. William F. Cody. Buffalo Bill. Chicago and Duluth: 1899. V. 63; 64; 67

WETZEL, CHARLES M.
American Fishing Books. Newark: 1950. V. 64; 66

WEYAND, LEONIE R.
An Early History of Fayette County. Lagrange: 1936. V. 66

WEYGAND, JAMES LAMAR
Elmer F. Gleason and Stratford Press. A History and Bibliography. Nappanee: 1965. V. 64

WEYGANDT, WILHELM
Atlas and Rundriss der Psychiatrie. Munich: 1902. V. 66

WEYMAN, STANLEY J.
A Gentleman of France. London: 1893. V. 66
The Red Cockade. London: 1895. V. 67

WEYMOUTH HISTORICAL SOCIETY
History of Weymouth, Massachusetts. Boston: 1923. V. 65

WHALE, GEORGE
British Airships, Past, Present and Future. London: 1919. V. 64

WHALEN, WILL W.
The Priest Who Vanished or Murderer at Large. Ozone Park: 1942. V. 65

WHALEY, C.
The Parish of Askrigg in the County of York, Including Low Abbotside and Bainbridge.... London: 1890. V. 64

WHALEY, NATHANIEL
A Preparatory Discourse of Death. Oxford: 1708. V. 62

WHALL, W. B.
Sea Songs and Shanties. Glasgow: 1927. V. 66

WHALLEY, JOYCE IRENE
The Art of Calligraphy, Wstern Europe and America. London: 1980. V. 62

WHARFDALE; Or, A Description of the Several Delightful Features of that Extensive, Splendid and Fascinating Valley.... Otley: 1813. V. 64

WHARTON, CLARENCE
History of Fort Bend County. San Antonio: 1939. V. 62
Satanta, the Great Chief of the Kiowas and His People. Dallas: 1935. V. 62; 65; 67

WHARTON, EDITH
The Age of Innocence. Avon: 1973. V. 62; 63; 64; 66
The Buccaneers. New York: 1938. V. 66
The Decoration of Houses. New York: 1897. V. 67
Ethan Frome. London: 1912. V. 64
Ethan Frome. New York: 1922. V. 62; 64; 67
French Ways and Their Meaning. New York: 1919. V. 64
The Gods Arrive. New York: 1932. V. 62
The House of Mirth. London: 1905. V. 64
The House of Mirth. New York: 1905. V. 62; 64
Italian Villas and Their Gardens. New York: 1904. V. 62
Madame De Treymes. New York: 1907. V. 63; 64
The Mother's Recompense. New York: 1925. V. 63; 65
A Motor-Flight Through France. New York: 1908. V. 62; 63
The Reef. New York: 1912. V. 62; 66
Sanctuary. New York: 1903. V. 62; 63
Tales of Men and Ghosts. New York: 1910. V. 62
The Writing of Fiction. New York: 1925. V. 62
Xingu and Other Stories. New York: 1916. V. 63

WHARTON, FRANCIS
A Digest of the International Law of the United States, Taken from Documents Issued by Presidents and Secretaries of State.... Washington: 1886. V. 65

WHARTON, GEORGE
The Works of the Late Most Excellent Philosopher and Astronomer Sir George Wharton. London: 1683. V. 63; 64; 66

WHARTON, HENRY
A Defence of Pluralites, or Holding Two Benefices with Cure of Souls, as Now Practised in the Church of England. London: 1692. V. 63

WHARTON, J. E.
History of the City of Denver from Its Settlement to the Present Time to Which is Added a Full and Complete Business Directory of the City. Denver: 1909. V. 65

WHARTON, JAMES B.
Squad. London: 1929. V. 64

WHARTON, PHILIP, DUKE OF
The Life and Writings. 1732. V. 64; 65
The Life and Writings. London: 1732. V. 63

WHARTON, RICHARD
Remarks on the Jacobinical Tendency of the Edinburgh Review, in a Letter to the Earl of Lonsdale. London: 1809. V. 63

WHARTON, THOMAS
Memoirs of the Life of the Most Noble Thomas, Late Marquess of Wharton...(with) A True Copy of the Last Will and Testament of the Most Honourable Thomas, Late Marquise of Wharton. London: 1715. V. 64; 65

WHARTON, W. J. L.
Hydrographical Surveying. London: 1882. V. 62; 66

WHARTON, WILLIAM
Birdy. London: 1979. V. 67
Birdy. New York: 1979. V. 63; 66
A Midnight Clear. New York: 1982. V. 63
Pride. London: 1986. V. 65

WHAT is Luxury? To Which is Added a Manipulus of Etymological and Other Nugae. London: 1829. V. 66

WHAT Is Matter? By an Inner Templar.... London: 1869. V. 65

WHAT the Children Like. London: 1897. V. 64

WHAT Will They Think of Next. A Guinness Inventory. 1954. V. 67

WHATELEY, ELIZABETH
English Life, Social and Domestic, in the Middle of the Nineteenth Century.... London: 1847. V. 64; 65

WHATELY, E. JANE
Life and Correspondence of Richard Wahtely, D.D. 1866. V. 62

WHATELY, RICHARD, ABP. OF DUBLIN
Introductory Lectures on Political Economy, Delivered at Oxford in Easter Term MDCCCXXXI. London: 1855. V. 66; 67
Irish Poor Laws. Dublin: 1838?. V. 66
Miscellaneous Lectures and Reviews. London: 1861. V. 66
Miscellaneous Remains from the Commonplace Book of Richard Whately, D.D.... London: 1864. V. 66
Remarks on Transportation and On a Recent Defence of the System, in a Second Letter to Early Grey. London: 1834. V. 66

WHATELY, THOMAS
Observations on Modern Gardening, Illustrated by Descriptions. London: 1770. V. 66
Observations on Modern Gardening, Illustrated by Descriptions. London: 1777. V. 65; 67

WHATMAN, SUSANNAH
Her Housekeeping Book. Cambridge: 1952. V. 64

WHEAT, CARL IRVING
Mapping the Trans Mississippi West. San Francisco: 1963. V. 66
Mapping the Trans-Mississippi West. San Francisco: 1957-1963. V. 62; 67
Mapping the Transmississippi West. San Francisco: 1959. V. 64
Mapping the Transmississippi West. 1995. V. 65; 67
The Maps of the California Gold Region 1848-1857. Storms-Mansfield: 1995. V. 65
Pioneer Visitors to Death Valley After the Forty-Niners. San Francisco: 1939. V. 63
Trailing the Forty-Niners through Death Valley. San Francisco: 1939. V. 63

WHEAT, MARVIN
Travels on the Western Slope of the Mexican Cordillera, in the Form of Fifty-One Letters. San Francisco: 1857. V. 64; 65

WHEATER, W.
A Guide to and History of Harrogate: Its Story, Grave and Gay, from and Before the Times When Plantaginet Kings and Queens Hunted and Sported On Its Stray and In Its Groves.... Leeds: 1890. V. 65
A Record of the Services of the Fifty-First (Second West York). The King's Own Light Infantry Regiment.... London: 1870. V. 63

WHEATLAND, DAVID P.
The Apparatus of Science at Harvard 1765-1800: Collection of Historical Scientific Instruments, Harvard University. Cambridge: 1968. V. 66

WHEATLEY, DENNIS
File on Bolitho Blane. 1930. V. 64
Murder Off Miami. London: 1936. V. 62; 65; 66

WHEATLEY, H. B.
Reliques of Old London. London: 1896-1909. V. 62
Remarkable Bindings in the British Museum, Selected for Their Beauty or Historic Interest. London and Paris: 1889. V. 62

WHEATLEY, PHILLIS
Poems on Various Subjects, Religious and Moral. London: 1773. V. 66; 67

WHEATLEY, RICHARD
Cathedrals and Abbeys in Great Britain and Ireland. New York: 1890. V. 63

WHEELER, A.
The Westmorland Dialect, with the Adjacency of Lancashire and Yorkshire, in Four Familiar Dialogues.... Kendal: 1821. V. 65

WHEELER, A. O.
The Selkirk Range. Ottawa: 1905. V. 65

WHEELER, ALFRED
Land Titles in San Francisco and the Laws Affecting the Same, with a Synopsis of All Grants and Sales of Land Within the Limits Claimed by the City. San Francisco: 1852. V. 62; 64

WHEELER, CHARLOTTE BICKERSTETH
Memorials of a Beloved Mother.... London: 1853. V. 67

WHEELER, DANIEL
Extracts from the Letters and Journal of Daniel Wheeler, While Engaged in a Religious Visit to the Inhabitants of Some of the Islands of the Pacific Ocean.... Philadelphia: 1840. V. 64

WHEELER, GEORGE M.
Preliminary Report Concerning Exploration and Surveys Principally in Nevada and Arizona. Washington: 1872. V. 63; 66
Report Upon United States Geographical and Geological Explorations and Surveys West of the One Hundredth Meridian. Volume V. Zoology. Washington: 1875. V. 62
Report Upon United States Geographical Surveys West of the One Hundredth Meridian. Washington: 1889-1879. V. 62

WHEELER, H. F. B.
The War in Wexford. 1910. V. 67

WHEELER, HOMER
The Frontier Trail; or From Cowboy to Colonel. Los Angeles: 1923. V. 65

WHEELER, J.
The Botanist's and Gardener's New Dictionary.... London: 1763. V. 63

WHEELER, J. TALBOYS
An Analysis and Summary of the Historical Geography of the Old and New Testaments. London: 1860. V. 63

WHEELER, JOHN H.
Historical Sketches of North Carolina. Philadelphia: 1851. V. 65
Historical Sketches of North Carolina from 1584 to 1851. New York: 1925. V. 67

WHEELER, JOSEPH
Revised System of Cavalry Tactics, for the Use of the Cavalry and Mounted Infantry, C.S.A. Mobile: 1863. V. 62; 63
The Santiago Campaign. New York: 1898. V. 63

WHEELER, KATE
Not Where I Started From. New York: 1993. V. 67

WHEELER, OLIN D.
Wonderland 1901. St. Paul: 1901. V. 67

WHEELER, POST
Albanian Wonder Tales. Garden City: 1936. V. 62

WHEELER, W. H.
A History of the Fens of South Lincolnshire, Being a Description of the Rivers Witham and Welland and Their Estuary, and an Account of Their Reclamation, Drainage and Enclosure of the Fens Adjacent Thereto. Boston: 1897. V. 65

WHEELER, W. M.
Ants, Their Structure, Development and Behaviour. New York: 1913. V. 63

WHEELER, WILLIAM OGDEN
Inscriptions on Tombstones and Monuments in the Burying Grounds of the First Presbyterian Church and St. Johns Church at Elizabeth, New Jersey 1664-1892. N.P: 1892. V. 63; 66

WHEELING, KENNETH EDWARD
Horse Drawn Vehicles at the Shelburne Museum. Shelburne: 1974. V. 64

WHEELOCK, ELEAZAR
A Continuation of the Narrative of the State, &c. of the Indian Charity School, at Lebanon, in Connecticut, from Nov. 27th, 1762 to Sept. 3rd, 1765. Boston: 1765. V. 63

WHEELOCK, IRENE G.
Birds of California. Chicago: 1904. V. 67

WHEELOCK, JOHN
Sketches of the History of Dartmouth College and Moors' Charity School, With a Particular Account of Some Late Remarkable Proceedings of the Board of Trustees, from the Year 1779 to the Year 1815. N.P: 1815. V. 64

WHEELWRIGHT, H.
Bush Wanderings of a Naturalist.... London: 1864. V. 62
Natural History Sketches. 1880. V. 62; 63; 64; 66; 67

WHEELWRIGHT, MARY C.
The Myth and Prayers of the Great Star Chant and the Myth of the Coyote Chant. Santa Fe: 1956. V. 64; 65

WHELEN, T.
Wilderness Hunting and Wildcraft. 1927. V. 62; 63; 64; 66; 67
Wilderness Hunting and Wildcraft. Marshallton: 1927. V. 66

WHELER, R. B.
History and Antiquities of Stratford-upon-Avon.... Stratford-upon-Avon: 1810. V. 66

WHELLAN, FRANCIS, & CO.
History, Topography and Directory of Northamptonshire.... London: 1874. V. 62

WHELLAN, WILLIAM
The History and Topography of the Counties of Cumberland and Westmoreland.... Pontefract;: 1860. V. 66
History, Gazetteer and Directory of Northamptonshire Comprising a General Survey of the County and a History of the Diocese of Peterborough.... London: 1849. V. 66

WHELLIER, ALEXANDER
The Complete English Lawyer; or, Every Man His Own Lawyer: Containing a Summary of the Constitution of England.... London: 1818. V. 63

WHELTON, PAUL
Death and the Devil. Philadelphia: 1944. V. 67

WHEN Mother Was a Little Girl.
London and New York. V. 63

WHEN the Circus Comes to Town.
Racine: 1930. V. 66

WHERRY, GEORGE
Alpine Notes and the Climbing Foot. Cambridge: 1896. V. 62; 63; 64

WHEWELL, WILLIAM
Architectural Notes on German Churches. Cambridge: 1830. V. 65
Architectural Notes on German Churches. Cambridge: 1835. V. 65
Astronomy and General Physics Considered with Heterece to Natural Theology. London. 1833. V. 66
Essay Towards a First Approximation to a Map of Cotidal Lines. 1833. V. 62
History of the Inductive Sciences, from the Earliest to the Present Time. London: 1847. V. 62
Lectures on Systematic Morality Delivered in Lent Term, 1846. London: 1846. V. 65
The Mechanics of Engineering Intended for Use in Universities and in Colleges of Engineers. Cambridge: 1841. V. 65
Of a Liberal Education in General, and with Particular Reference to the Leading Studies of the University of Cambridge. London: 1845. V. 65
On the Principles of English University Education. London: 1837. V. 64; 65
The Philosophy of the Inductive Sciences Founded Upon Their History. London: 1847. V. 62
The Platonic Dialogues for English Readers. Cambridge and London: 1859-1861. V. 65

WHIBLEY, CHARLES
Lord John Manners and His Friends. Edinburgh: 1925. V. 66

WHIFFEN, THOMAS
The North-West Amazons: Notes of Some Months Spent Among Cannibal Tribes. London: 1915. V. 65

WHILHELM, GOTTLIEB TOBIAS
Unterhaltungen Aus der Naturgeschichte: Der Saugethiere.... Vienna: 1808-1809. V. 64

WHINCOP, THOMAS
Scanderberg; or, Love and Liberty. London: 1747. V. 67

WHIPPLE, A. W.
Report of Explorations for a Railroad Route, Near the Thirty-Fifth Parallel of Latitude, from the Mississippi.... Washington: 1855. V. 62

WHIPPLE, EDWIN PERCY
Charles Dickens: the Man and His Work. Boston: 1912. V. 62

WHIPPLE, FRED L.
The Collected Contributions of Fred L. Whipple. Cambridge: 1972. V. 67

WHIPPLE, GEORGE C.
The Microscopy of Drinking Water. New York: 1933. V. 67
Typhoid Fever Its Causation, Transmission and Prevention. New York: 1908. V. 67

WHISHAW, FRED
The Diamond of Evil. London: 1902. V. 66

WHISTLE-Binkie or the Piper of the Party, Being a Collection of Songs for the Social Circle.
Glasgow: 1878. V. 67

WHISTLER, HUGH
A Popular Handbook of Indian Birds. London: 1928. V. 67
Popular Handbook of Indian Birds. 1949. V. 67
Popular Handbook of Indian Birds. 1963. V. 67

WHISTLER, JAMES MC NEILL
Eden Versus Whistler - the Baronet ad the Butterfly. Paris: 189. V. 65
The Gentle Art of Making Enemies. London: 1890. V. 67
The Gentle Art of Making Enemies. London: 1892. V. 65
Mr. Whistler's Ten O'Clock.... San Francisco: 1940. V. 63
Whistler Memorial Exhibition. London: 1905. V. 64

WHISTLER, LAURENCE
Armed October and Other Poems. London: 1932. V. 65
The Burning Glass. London: 1941. V. 66
Children of Hertha & Other Poems. Oxford: 1929. V. 67
The Konigsmark Drawings. London: 1952. V. 67
The Laughter and the Urn, the Life of Rex Whistler. London: 1985. V. 63
Oho!. London: 1946. V. 63; 66
The Work of Rex Whistler. London: 1960. V. 62

WHISTLER, REX
The Konigsmark Drawings. London: 1952. V. 62; 63
Scenes and Signs on Glass. 1985. V. 67

WHISTON, WILLIAM
Memoirs of the Life and Writings of (and) of Several of His Friends also. London: 1749. V. 60
Memoirs of the Life and Writings of Mr. William Whiston, Containing Memoirs of Several of His Friends Also. (with) Mr. Whiston's Account of the Exact Time when Miraculous Gifts Ceas'd in the Church. (with) A Sermon Preached.... London: 1749-1749-1746. V. 65
A New Theory of the Earth, from Its Original to the Consumation of All Things. 1737. V. 65
A New Theory of the Earth, from Its Original, to the Consummation of All Things. London: 1796. V. 62
A Vindication of the Sibylline Oracles. London: 1715. V. 64

WHITAKER, DANIEL K.
Sidney's Letters to William E. Channing, Occasioned by His Letter to Hon. Henry Clay, on the Annexation of Texas to the United States. Charleston: 1837. V. 66

WHITAKER, FESS
History of Corporal Fess Whitaker: Life in the Kentucky Mountains, Mexico and Texas. Louisville: 1918. V. 64

WHITAKER, HAROLD
A Descriptive List of Maps of Northumberland 1576-1900. London: 1949. V. 66

WHITAKER, J.
A Descriptive List of the Deer Parks and Paddocks of England. London: 1892. V. 62

WHITAKER, J. I. S.
The Birds of Tunisia, Being a History of the Birds Found in the Regency of Tunis. London: 1905. V. 67

WHITAKER, JOHN
The Ancient Cathedral of Cornwall Historically Surveyed. London: 1804. V. 63
The History of Manchester. London: 1771. V. 66
The History of Manchester. London: 1771-1775. V. 65
Mary Queen of Scots Vindicated. London: 1790. V. 66

WHITAKER, PETER
The New Wildfowler. London: 1961. V. 67

WHITAKER, RALPH
Song of the Outriggers. 1968. V. 67

WHITAKER, THOMAS DUNHAM
The History and Antiquities of the Deanery of Craven, in the County of York. London: 1805. V. 63; 65; 66
The History and Antiquities of the Deanery of Craven, in the County of York. London: 1878. V. 66
The History and Antiquities of the Deanery of Craven, in the County of York. Manchester: 1973. V. 64
An History of Richmondshire, in the North Riding of the County of York.... London: 1823. V. 64

WHITAKER, WALTER
A Centennial History of Almance County 1849-1949. Burlington: 1949. V. 67

WHITBREAD, S.
Southill. A Regency House. London: 1951. V. 64

WHITBY, DANIEL
Logos Ton Pieton (Graece) or An Endeavour to Evince the Certainty of the Christian Faith in Generall, and of the Resurrection of Christ in Particular.... Oxford: 1671. V. 63
A Paraphrase and Commentary on the New Testament.... London: 1718. V. 67

WHITCHURCH, SAMUEL
The Negro Convert, a Pome...(with) Hispaniola, a Poem.... Bath: 1785-1804. V. 62

WHITCOMB, SAMUEL
Two Lectures on the Advantages of a Republican Condition of Society, for the Promotion of the Arts, and the Cultivation of Science. Boston: 1833. V. 66

WHITE, A. E. H.
The Butterflies and Moths of Teneriffe. 1894. V. 63

WHITE, ALAIN R.
The Succulent Euphorbieae (Southern Africa). Pasadena: 1941. V. 63

WHITE, ANTONIA
Diaires. London: 1991-1992. V. 64
Frost in May. London: 1933. V. 64; 67
Living with Minka and Curdy - a Marmalade Cat and His Siamese Wife. London: 1970. V. 64
Minka and Curdy. London: 1957. V. 64

WHITE, BAILEY
Mama Makes Up Her Mind. New York: 1993. V. 64; 67

WHITE, CARLOS
Ece Femina: an Attempt to Solve the Woman Question. Hanover: 1870. V. 66

WHITE, CHARLES
An Account of the Regular Gradation in Man and Different Animals and Vegetables and for the Former to the Latter. London: 1799. V. 62; 66; 67
The Adventures of a King's Page. London: 1829. V. 67
Almack's Revisited. London: 1828. V. 63; 67
Cases in Surgery, with Remarks. London: 1770. V. 63
Images of Dignity: the Drawings.... 1967. V. 62; 65
Images of Dignity: the Drawings.... Los Angeles: 1967. V. 62
An Inquiry into the Nature and Cause of the Swelling, in One or Both of the Lower Extremities, Which Sometimes Happens to Lying-In Women. Warrington: 1784. V. 63

WHITE, CHARLES A.
Report on the Geological Survey of the State of Iowa. Des Moines: 1870. V. 62

WHITE, D.
Fossil Flora of the Lower Coal Measures of Missouri. Washington: 1899. V. 67

WHITE, DIANA
Preface to an Album of Poems from the Livre de Jade. 1948. V. 62

WHITE, E. E.
Service on the Indian Reservations. Little Rock: 1893. V. 66

WHITE, E. G., MRS.
Patriarchs and Prophets or the Great Conflict Between Good and Evil as Illustrated in the Lives of Holy Men of Old. Oakland: 1890. V. 62
Patriarchs and Prophets or the Great Conflict Between Good and Evil as Illustrated in the Lives of Holy Men of Old. Toronto: 1890. V. 63

WHITE, EDMUND
The Beautiful Room is Empty. New York: 1988. V. 67
Caracole. New York: 1985. V. 67
The Faber Book of Gay Short Fiction. Boston: 1991. V. 67
Forgetting Elena. New York: 1973. V. 64; 67
Genet. London: 1993. V. 67
Noctures for the King of Naples. New York: 1978. V. 67
States of Desire. New York: 1980. V. 67

WHITE, EDWARD LUCAS
Lukundoo and Other Stories. New York: 1927. V. 63

WHITE, ELIJAH VIERS
The First Iron-Clad Naval Engagement in the World...Monitor & Merrimac, 1862. New York: 1906. V. 65
History of the Battle of Bali's Bluff. Leesburg: 1902. V. 62; 63; 65

WHITE, ELWYN BROOKS
Charlotte's Web. New York: 1952. V. 62; 63; 64; 65
Here Is New York. New York: 1949. V. 64
Less than Nothing - or, the Life and Times of Sterling Finny. New York: 1927. V. 67
Letters of E. B. White. New York: 1976. V. 64; 66; 67
Stuart Little. New York and London: 1945. V. 62; 63; 65; 67
The Wild Flag. Boston: 1946. V. 66; 67

WHITE, EMMA SIGGINS
The Kinnears and Their Kin. Kansas City: 1916. V. 63

WHITE, ERIC W.
15 Poems for William Shakespeare. Stratford-upon-Avon: 1964. V. 63; 67
Images of H.D. London: 1976. V. 64

WHITE, ERIC WALTER
Walking Shadows - an Essay on Lotte Reininger's Silhouette Films. London: 1931. V. 65

WHITE, ETHELBERT
The Wood Engravings of.... 1992. V. 65

WHITE, EUGENE E.
Service on the Indians Reservations. Little Rock: 1893. V. 63

WHITE, F.
Forest Flora of Northern Rhodesia. London: 1962. V. 66

WHITE, F. B.
Challenger Voyage. Zoology. Part 19. Pelagic Hemiptera. 1883. V. 66

WHITE, FRANCIS BUCHANAN W.
The Flora of Perthshire. London: 1898. V. 62

WHITE, GEORGE
Combination and Arbitration Laws, Artizans and Machinery. London: 1824. V. 66

WHITE, GIFFORD
1840 Citizens of Texas. Austin: 1984. V. 62

WHITE, GILBERT
The Life and Letters of Gilbert White of Selborne. London: 1901. V. 62
The Natural History and Antiquities of Selborne. London: 1789. V. 62; 63
The Natural History and Antiquities of Selborne.... London: 1813. V. 62; 63; 65; 66; 67
The Natural History and Antiquities of Selborne.... London: 1833. V. 63
The Natural History and Antiquities of Selborne.... London: 1900. V. 63; 67
The Natural History and Antiquities of Selborne.... Philadelphia: 1900. V. 65; 66
The Natural History and Antiquities of Selborne.... London: 1901. V. 62
The Natural History and Antiquities of Selborne.... London: 1970. V. 62
The Natural History of Selborne. London: 1822. V. 63
The Natural History of Selborne. London: 1833. V. 63
The Natural History of Selborne. London: 1851. V. 62; 63
The Natural History of Selborne. London: 1854. V. 65; 66
The Natural History of Selborne. Ipswich: 1972. V. 62; 63; 64
The Natural History of Selborne. New York: 1972. V. 63
The Natural History of Selborne. London: 1973. V. 63
The Natural History of Selborne. London: 1977. V. 62
The Works in Natural History of the Late Rev. Gilbert White.... 1802. V. 65
Writings. London: 1938. V. 62; 63; 65

WHITE, GLEESON
Book-Song, an Anthology of Poems of Books and Bookmen from Modern Authors. London: 1893. V. 65

WHITE, HENNING
Memoriae Medicorum Nostri Seculi Clarissimorum Renovatate Decas Prima. Frankfurt am Main: 1676. V. 66

WHITE, HENRY
Geology, Oil Fields and Minerals of Canada West.... Toronto: 1865. V. 63

WHITE, HENRY KIRKE
The Poetical and Prose Works of.... Edinburgh and London: 1880. V. 66
The Remains.... London: 1819-1822. V. 65
The Remains.... London: 1821-1822. V. 63

WHITE, HERBERT M.
Old Ingleborough. London: 1904. V. 65

WHITE, J. J.
Cranberry Culture. New York: 1870. V. 63

WHITE, JACK
Minority Report: the Protestant Community in the Irish Republic. 1975. V. 67

WHITE, JAMES
The Adventures of King Richard Coeur-de-Lion. Dublin: 1791. V. 62
A Complete System of Farriery and Veterinary Medicine.... Pittsburgh: 1832. V. 66
The Great Depression 1932. Providence: 1996. V. 62
A Treatise on Veterinary Medicine, in Four Volumes. London: 1815. V. 64
The Village Poor-House. London: 1832. V. 66

WHITE, JAMES CLARKE
Dermatitis Venenata: an Account of the Action of External Irritants on the Skin. Boston: 1887. V. 65

WHITE, JAMES E.
A Genealogical History of the Descendants of Peter White, of New Jersey from 1670 and of William White and Deborah Tilton His Wife. St. John: 1906. V. 63; 64; 66

WHITE, JEFRREY R.
Products Liability, the First Twenty Five Years. Washington: 1983. V. 63

WHITE, JOHN
Art's Master-Piece, or a Companion for the Ingenious of Either Sex. London: 1720. V. 67
A Rich Cabinet, with Variety of Inventions, Unlock'd and Open'd for the Recreation of Ingenious Spirits.... London: 1689. V. 66
Some Account of the Proposed Improvements of the Western Part of London, by the Formation of the Regent's Park, the New Street...(with) Brief Remarks on the Proposed Regent's Canal. London: 1815. V. 62
Three Letters to a Gentleman Dissenting from the Church of England. London: 1748. V. 66

WHITE, JOHN CLAUDE
Sikhim and Bhutan. London: 1909. V. 62
Sikhum and Bhutan. New York: 1909. V. 67

WHITE, JOHN DUNCAN
The Trials of John Duncan White Alias Charles Marchant and Winslow Curtis Alias Sylvester Colson for the Murder of the High Seas of Edward Selfridge and Thomas P. Jenkins, Captain and Mate of the Schooner Fairy of Boston.. Boston: 1827. V. 67

WHITE, JOSEPH
Sermons Containing a View of Christianity and Mahometanism, in Their History, Their Evidence and Their Effects.... London: 1785. V. 66
Sermons, Preached Before the University of Oxford, in the Year 1784; at the Lecture. Boston: 1793. V. 64

WHITE, JOSEPH BLANCO
Letters from Spain by Don Leucadio Doblado. London: 1822. V. 67

WHITE, JOSEPH NELSON
Genealogy of Joseph Nelson White. Boston: 1902. V. 66

WHITE, JOSHUA
Memoirs of the Professional Life of the Latet Most Noble Lord Horatio Nelson... (bound with) Supplement...The Funeral. London: 1806. V. 63; 65

WHITE, KATHERINE KEOGH
King's Mountain Men. Dayton: 1924. V. 66; 67

WHITE, LESLIE A.
Pioneers in American Anthropology - The Bandelier - Morgan Letters 1873-1883. Albuquerque: 1940. V. 64; 66
The Pueblo of Santa Ana, New Mexico. Menasha: 1942. V. 65

WHITE, LONNIE J.
Hostiles and Horse Soldiers, Indian Battles and Campaigns in the West. Boulder: 1972. V. 67

WHITE, MARY LUCY
Our Nation. Bangor: 1860. V. 63; 64

WHITE, MICHAEL C.
A Brother's Blood. New York: 1996. V. 62; 63; 64; 65; 66; 67
A Brother's Blood. London: 1997. V. 65

WHITE, MUS
From the Mundane to the Magical (Ltd. Ed.): Photographically Illustrated Children's Books 1854-1945 and Beyond. Los Angeles: 1999. V. 65

WHITE, N. C.
Abbott H. Thayer, Painter and Naturalist. Connecticut: 1951. V. 64

WHITE, NANCY
Style in Motion: Munkacsi Photographs 20s, 30s, 40s. New York: 1977. V. 63

WHITE, NEWMAN I.
American Negro Folk-Songs. Cambridge: 1928. V. 63; 66; 67

WHITE, OWEN P.
The Autobiography of a Durable Sinner. New York: 1942. V. 64; 65
A Frontier Mother. New York: 1929. V. 66
Out of the Desert. The Historical Romance of El Paso. El Paso: 1923. V. 63

WHITE, PATRICK
The Aunt's Story. London: 1948. V. 62; 65; 66

WHITE, PAUL DUDLEY
Heart Disease. New York: 1949. V. 66

WHITE, PHILO
Philo White's Narrative of a Cruise in the Pacific to South America and California on the U.S. Sloop of War "Dale" 1841-1843. Denver: 1965. V. 64; 65; 66

WHITE, RANDY WAYNE
Batfishing in the Rainforest. New York: 1991. V. 64; 65; 66; 67
Captiva. New York: 1996. V. 67
The Heat Islands. New York: 1992. V. 62; 65; 66
The Man Who Invented Florida. New York: 1993. V. 62; 65
Sanibel Flats. New York: 1990. V. 62; 66
Tarpon Tales. Sanibel Island: 1990. V. 62; 63; 64; 66

WHITE, ROBERT
The Dukery Records, Being Notes and Memoranda Illustrative of Nottinghamshire Ancient History.... Nottingham: 1904. V. 65
The Tynemouth Nun, a Poem. Newcastle upon Tyne: 1829. V. 62

WHITE, RUTH
Belle Prater's Boy. New York: 1996. V. 65

WHITE, S. E.
African Camp Fires. 1914. V. 62; 63; 64; 66

WHITE, SAMUEL
History of the American Troops During the Late War, Under the Command of Colonels Fenton and Campbell.... Baltimore: 1829. V. 66

WHITE, SAMUEL S.
Catalogue of Dental Materials, Furniture, Instruments, etc.,...Jan. 1, 1867. Philadelphia: 1866. V. 62

THE WHITE Star Line of Mail Steamers, Official Guide.... London: 1877. V. 64

WHITE, STEPHEN
Higher Authority. New York: 1994. V. 67

WHITE, STEWART EDWARD
The Claim Jumpers. New York: 1901. V. 63
Gold. Garden City: 1913. V. 67
Gold. New York: 1913. V. 63

WHITE, T. P.
Archaeological Sketches in Scotland. Knapdale and Gigha; District of Kintyre. London: 1873. V. 62

WHITE, TERENCE
What Happened to Sherlock Holmes?. Los Angeles: 1984. V. 66

WHITE, TERENCE HANBURY
The Age of Scandal - An Excursion through a Minor Period. London: 1950. V. 64
The Book of Merlyn.... 1977. V. 67
England Have My Bones. London: 1936. V. 65; 66
First Lesson. London: 1932. V. 65
Gone to Ground - a Novel. London: 1935. V. 65
The Goshawk. London: 1951. V. 62; 66; 67
The Goshawk. 1953. V. 67
The Green Bay Tree or The Wicked Man Touches Wood. Cambridge: 1929. V. 64
The Ill-Made Knight. London: 1941. V. 63
Loved Helen, and Other Poems. London: 1929. V. 62; 63; 65; 66
The Sword in the Stone. London: 1938. V. 62; 63
The Winter Abroad. London: 1932. V. 65
The Witch in the Wood. London: 1940. V. 63; 64

WHITE, THOMAS
Naval Researches; or a Candid Inquiry into the Conduct of Admirals Byron, Graves, Hood and Rodney, in the Actions Off Grenada, Chesapeak, St. Christopher's and the Ninth and Twelfth of April 1782. London: 1830. V. 66

WHITE, W.
The Stapelieae. Pasadena: 1937. V. 64; 66

WHITE, W. HOLT
The Super-Spy. London: 1916. V. 64

WHITE, WALTER
A Month In Yorkshire. London: 1858. V. 65
Northumberland and the Border. London: 1859. V. 62

WHITE, WALTER GRAINGE
The Sea Gypsies of Malaya. London: 1922. V. 62

WHITE, WILLIAM
D. H. Lawrence, a Checklist 1931-1950. Detroit: 1950. V. 63
An Essay on the Diseases of the Bile, More Particularly Its Calculous Concretions Called Gall-Stones. York: 1771. V. 65
The History and Directory of the Towns and Principal Villages in the County of Lincoln.... Leeds: 1826. V. 65
History, Gazetteer and Directory of Lincolnshire, Including the City and Diocese of Lincoln.... Sheffield: 1856. V. 63
History, Gazetteer and Directory of Lincolnshire, Including the City and Diocese of Lincoln.... Sheffield: 1872. V. 62
History, Gazetteer and Directory of the East and North Ridings of Yorkshire. Sheffield: 1840. V. 63
Nathaniel West: a Comprehensive Bibliography. 1975. V. 65
The Story of a Great Delusion. London: 1885. V. 62
Wilfred Owen (1893-1918), a Bibliography. 1967. V. 62

WHITE, WILLIAM ALANSON
Medical Psychology: The Mental Factor in Disease. New York, Washington: 1931. V. 65

WHITE, WILLIAM ALLEN
The Court of Boyville. New York: 1899. V. 63

WHITE, WILLIAM F.
A Picture of Pioneer Times in California. San Francisco: 1881. V. 63; 66

WHITE, WILLIAM HALE
Catharine Furze. London: 1893. V. 66
Catharine Furze. London: 1894. V. 66
Miriam's Schooling and Other Papers. London: 1892. V. 66

WHITE, WILLIAM N.
Gardening for the South; or the Kitchen Fruit Garden.... New York: 1856. V. 63
Gardening for the South, or How to Grow Vegetables and Fruits. New York: 1868. V. 67

WHITE, WILLIAM S.
The Professional: Lyndon B. Johnson. Boston: 1964. V. 66

WHITEBROOK, ROBERT BALLARD
Coastal Exploration of Washington. Palo Alto: 1959. V. 64; 65; 66

WHITEFIELD, GEORGE
A Short Account of God's Dealing with the Reverend Mr. George Whitefield, A. B. Late of Pembroke College, Oxford.... London: 1740. V. 64

WHITEHEAD, ALFRED NORTH
Principia Mathematica. Cambridge: 1910. V. 62; 63; 64; 66

WHITEHEAD, CHARLES E.
The Camp Fires of the Everglades. 1891. V. 63; 64; 66
The Camp-Fires of the Everglades. Edinburgh: 1891. V. 62

WHITEHEAD, COLSON
The Intuitionist. New York: 1999. V. 67

WHITEHEAD, G. KENNETH
The Ancient White Cattle of Britain and Their Descendants. London: 1953. V. 62; 63
The Deer of Great Britain and Ireland. London: 1964. V. 64
Deer of the World. 1972. V. 64
Deer and Their Management in the Deer Parks of Great Britain and Ireland. London: 1950. V. 62; 66; 67
The Deer of Great Britain and Ireland. 1964. V. 62; 63; 66; 67
The Deer of Great Britain and Ireland. London: 1964. V. 62
Deer of the World. 1972. V. 62; 63; 64; 66; 67
Deer Stalking in Scotland. London: 1964. V. 67
The Deerstalking Grounds of Great Britain and Ireland. 1960. V. 63
The Deerstalking Grounds of Great Britain and Ireland. London: 1960. V. 62; 67
Hunting and Stalking Deer in Britain Throughout the Age. London: 1980. V. 67

WHITEHEAD, HENRY S.
Jumbee and Other Uncanny Tales. 1944. V. 66
Jumbee and Other Uncanny Tales. Sauk City: 1944. V. 64
West India Lights. Sauk City: 1946. V. 67

WHITEHEAD, JESSUP
American Pastry Cook (& Hotel Meat Cooking). Chicago: 1894. V. 65
Hotel Meat Cooking. Chicago: 1901. V. 67
Steward's Handbook and Dictionary. Chicago: 1903. V. 64; 67

WHITEHEAD, JOHN
The Judicial and Civil History of New Jersey. Boston?: 1897. V. 63; 66
The Passaic Valley, New Jersey, in Three Centuries. New York: 1901. V. 63; 66

WHITEHEAD, P. J. P.
Forty Drawings of Fishes made by the Artists Who Accompanied Captain James Cook on His Three Voyages to the Pacific. London: 1968. V. 63

WHITEHEAD, PAUL
The Case of the Honourable Alexander Murray, Esq.... London: 1751. V. 66
A Letter to a Member of Parliament in the Country, From His Friend in London, Relative to the Case of Admiral Byng, with Some Original Papers and Letters Which Passed During the Expedition. London: 1756. V. 65
Manners: a Satire. Islington: 1748. V. 62
The Poems and Miscellaneous Compositions.... London: 1787. V. 66

WHITEHEAD, RON
Beat Legacy, Connections, Influences: Allen Ginsberg. Louisville: 1994. V. 65

WHITEHEAD, T. H.
Geology of the Southern Part of South Staffordshire Coalfield (South of Bentley Faults). London: 1927. V. 62

WHITEHEAD, THOMAS
History of the Dales Congregational Churches. Bradford: 1930. V. 65
Original Anecdotes of the Late Duke of Kingston and Miss Chudleigh, Alias Mrs. Harvey, Alias Countess of Bristol, Alias Duchess of Kingston.... London: 1792. V. 62
Virginia: a Handbook. Richmond: 1893. V. 67

WHITEHEAD, W. B.
A Letter to the Right Honourable the Lord Viscount Sidmouth, His Majesty's Principal Secretary of State for the Home Department &c.... London: 1820. V. 66

WHITEHEAD, WILLIAM
Elegies. With an Ode to the Tiber. London: 1757. V. 63; 65
Poems on Several Occasions, with the Roman Father, a Tragedy. London: 1754. V. 66

WHITEHEAD, WILLIAM A.
Contributions to the Early History of Perth Amboy and Adjoining Country, with Sketches of Men and Events in New Jersey During the Provincial Era.... New York: 1856. V. 63; 66
East Jersey Under the Proprietary Governments: a Narrative of Events Connected with the Settlement and Progress of the Province, Until the Surrender of the Government to the Crown in 1703. Newark: 1875. V. 63; 66

WHITEHOUSE, MARY
Whatever Happened to Sex?. London: 1977. V. 64

WHITEHOUSE, P. B.
On the Narrow Guage. 1964. V. 67

WHITEHURST, JOHN
An Inquiry into the Origianl State and Formation of the Earth.... London: 1786. V. 62; 63
Observations on the Ventilation of Rooms; on the Construction of Chimneys.... London: 1794. V. 62

WHITEING, RICHARD
Mr. Sprouts His Opinions. London: 1868. V. 66

WHITELAW, G.
Raquel Forner. Buenos Aires: 1980. V. 65

WHITELAW, RALPH T.
Virginia's Eastern Shore. A History of Northampton and Accomack Counties. Richmond: 1951. V. 64

WHITELOCK, L. CLARKSON
A Mad Madonna and Other Stories. Boston: 1895. V. 62

WHITELOCKE, BULSTRODE
Memorials of the English Affairs; or, an Historical Account of What Passed from the Beginning of the Reign of King Charles the First.... London: 1682. V. 62
Three Speeches Made to the Lord-Maior, Aldermen and Common-Council of London, by the Lord Whitlok, Lord Fleetwood, Lord Disbrowe...November the 8th 1659. London: 1659. V. 62

WHITEMAN, JOHN
Sparks and Sounds from a Colonial Anvil. Melbourne: 1873. V. 65

WHITESIDE, JAMES
Italy in the Nineteenth Century. London: 1848. V. 62
Italy in the Nineteenth Century. London: 1851. V. 65

WHITFIELD, CHRISTOPHER
Mr. Chambers and Persephone. A Tale. Waltham St. Lawrence: 1937. V. 67
Together and Alone, Two Short Novels. Waltham St. Lawrence: 1945. V. 64

WHITFIELD, S.
Magritte. London: 1992. V. 65

WHITFORD, WILLIAM C.
Colorado Volunteers in the Civil War. Denver: 1907. V. 65
Colorado Volunteers in the Civil War, the New Mexico Campaign. Denver: 1906. V. 63; 66

WHITFORD, WILLIAM G.
Art Stories. Chicago: 1933. V. 62

WHITGIFT, JOHN
The Defense of the Aunswere to the Admonition Against the Replie of T. C. London: 1574. V. 66

WHITHARD, PHILIP
Illuminating and Missal Painting on Paper and Vellum. London: 1909. V. 66

WHITING, HELEN A.
Negro Folk Tales. & Negro Art, Music, Rhyme. Washington: 1938. V. 65

WHITING, LILIAN
After Her Death, the Story of a Summer. Boston: 1897. V. 65
Kate Field, a Record. Boston: 1899. V. 63

WHITING, THOMAS
Mathematical, Geometrical and Philsophical Delight.... London: 1792-1798. V. 63
The Poetical Delights. London: 1797. V. 63

WHITLEY, EDYTHE JOHNS RUCKER
Sam Davis Confederate Hero 1842-1863. Nashville: 1947. V. 65

WHITLEY, G. P.
The Fishes of Australia. Part I. The Sharks. Sydney: 1940. V. 67

WHITMAN, ROYAL
Clinical Lessons in Orthopaedic Surgery. New York: 1900. V. 66; 67

WHITMAN, WALT
American Bard Being the Preface to the First Edition of Leaves of Grass Now Restored To Its Native Verse Rhythms and Presented as a Living Poem. Santa Cruz: 1981. V. 64; 66
American Primer. Boston: 1904. V. 62; 64; 67
Calamus. A Series of Letters. Boston: 1897. V. 62; 67
Calamus: a Series of Letters Written...to Peter Doyle. Philadelphia: 1897. V. 64; 65
Complete Poems and Prose...Authenticated and Personal Book...(Handled by W.W.) ...Portraits from Life...Autographed. Camden: 1888. V. 66
Complete Poetry and Selected Prose and Letters. London: 1938. V. 66
Complete Prose Works. Philadelphia: 1892. V. 62; 64
Criticism. an Essay. Newark: 1913. V. 65
Dirge for Two Veterans...Set to Music. London: 1901. V. 64
Franklin Evans: or the Inebriate. New York: 1842. V. 62
Good-Bye My Fancy - 2nd Annex to Leaves of Grass. Philadelphia: 1891. V. 63
Leaves of Grass. New York and London. V. 62; 65
Leaves of Grass. Brooklyn: 1855. V. 64
Leaves of Grass. Boston: 1860. V. 62
Leaves of Grass. Washington: 1873. V. 66
Leaves of Grass. Boston: 1881-1882. V. 65; 66
Leaves of Grass. Phiadelphia: 1884. V. 63; 67
Leaves of Grass. Philadelphia: 1891-1892. V. 62; 65
Leaves of Grass. New York: 1930. V. 66
Leaves of Grass. New York: 1942. V. 63
New York Dissected: a Sheaf of Recently Discovered Newspaper Articles by the Author of Leaves of Grass. New York: 1936. V. 63; 64
November Boughs. Philadelphia: 1888. V. 62; 65
On the Beach at Night. 1992. V. 64
On the Beach at Night. Maine: 1992. V. 62
Poems. London: 1868. V. 65
Song of Myself. New York: 1992. V. 64
Song of the Open Road. New York: 1990. V. 65
Specimen Days and Collect. Philadelphia: 1882-1883. V. 62; 64
Two Rivulets. Camden: 1876. V. 62; 64; 67
The Wound Dresser. Boston: 1898. V. 64

WHITMIRE, BEVERLY T.
The Presence of the Past: Epitaphs of 18th & 19th Century Pioneers in Greenville Co., S.C. and Their Descendants. Baltimore: 1976. V. 67

WHITMORE, GEORGE
The Duty of Not Running in Debt: Considered in a Discourse, Preached Before the University of Cambridge, Jan. 1800. London: 1800?. V. 66

WHITMORE, WILLIAM H.
The Graveyards of Boston. Albany: 1878. V. 65

WHITNEY, ADELINE D. T.
Mother Goose for Grown Folks, a Christmas Reading. New York: 1860. V. 63
A Summer in Leslie Goldthwaite's Life. London: 1867. V. 65

WHITNEY, CASPAR
Jungle Trails and Jungle People. New York: 1905. V. 64
Musk-Ox, Bison, Sheep and Goat. New York: 1904. V. 62; 63; 64

WHITNEY, DANIEL H.
The Family Physician, an Guide to Health, in Three Parts. New York: 1833. V. 66

WHITNEY, HARRY
Hunting with the Eskimos. New York: 1910. V. 64; 66

WHITNEY, J. D.
The Climatic Changes of Later Geological Times.... Cambridge: 1882. V. 64
Geological Survey of California: Palaeontology. Volume I. 1864. V. 62

WHITNEY, J. D. continued
The Metallic Wealth of the United States, Described and Compared with that of Other Countries. Philadelphia: 1854. V. 62
The Yosemite Guide-Book: a Description of the Yosemite Valley and the Adjacent Region of the Sierra Nevada.... Sacramento: 1870. V. 62; 63

WHITNEY, J. PARKER
Reminiscences of a Sportsman. New York: 1906. V. 64; 67

WHITNEY, JAMES LYMAN
Catalogue of the Spanish Library and of the Portuguese Books Bequeathed by George Ticknor the the Boston Public Library. Together with the Collection of Spanish and Portuguese Literature in the General Library. Boston: 1879. V. 64

WHITNEY, JOSIAH D.
Names and Places. Studies in Geographical and Topographical Nomenclature. Cambridge: 1888. V. 64

WHITNEY, ORSON F.
The Poetical Writings...Poems and Poetic Verse. Salt Lake City: 1889. V. 64

WHITNEY, WILLIAM DWIGHT
The Century Dictionary and Cyclopediae with a New Atlas of the World. New York: 1911. V. 63

WHITSETT, WILLIAM H.
Life and Times of Judge Caleb Wallace, Some Time Justice of the Court of Appeals of the State of Kentucky. Louisville: 1888. V. 67

WHITSON, JOHN
Luther Burbank. His Methods and Discoveries and Their Practical Application. New York: 1914. V. 65
A Pious Meditation Composed in the Seventeenth Century. Bristol: 1829. V. 66

WHITTAKER, EDMUND T.
A History of the Theories of Aether and Electricity: Volume I. The Classical Theories. London: 1958. V. 67

WHITTAKER, FREDERICK
A Popular Life of General George A. Custer. New York: 1876. V. 65; 67

WHITTAKER, JOHN
Ceremonial of the Coronation of King George the Fourth.... Westminster: 1823. V. 67

WHITTAKER, MILO LEE
Pathbreakers and Pioneers of the Pueblo Region Comprising a History of Pueblo from the Earliest Times. N.P: 1917. V. 62; 64; 67

WHITTAKER, SOAME
The Law of Bankrupts, Their Creditors and Assignes; from the Issuing the Commission to the Allowance of the Certificate by the Lord Chancellor. London: 1812. V. 65

WHITTELL, H. M.
The Literature of Australian Birds: a History and a Bibliograhy of Australian Ornithology. Mansfield. V. 62

WHITTEN, LESLIE H.
Moon of the Wolf. Garden City: 1967. V. 66

WHITTEN, JAMES SALTER
The Silk Industry of Great Britain and Its Revival. London: 1882. V. 64

WHITTIER, JOHN GREENLEAF
The Literary Remains of John G. C. Brainard, with Sketch of His Life. Hartford: 1832. V. 62
Moll Pitcher, a Poem. Boston: 1832. V. 62; 64
Narrative of James Williams an American Slave, Who Was for Several Years a Driver on a Cotton Plantation in Alabama. New York: 1838. V. 62; 66
The Pennsylvania Pilgrim. Boston: 1872. V. 66
Poems. Boston: 1840. V. 62
Snow-Bound. Boston: 1866. V. 65
Snow-Bound. Boston: 1892. V. 62
Snow-Bound. New York: 1930. V. 64
The Tent on the Beach and Other Poems. Boston: 1867. V. 65

WHITTING, CLIFFORD
Crime in Whispers. London: 1964. V. 66

WHITTINGTON en Zijne Kat Eene Vertelling Van Vader Arthur Aan Zijne Kindere. (Whittington and His Cat - a Story by Father Arthur for His Children). Amsterdam: Sep. 1820. V. 64

WHITTINGTON, HARRY
The Devil Wears Wings. New York: 1960. V. 67
Man In the Shadow. New York: 1957. V. 66

WHITTINGTON PRESS
A Miscellany of Type. Andoversford: 1990. V. 64

WHITTLE, T.
The Plant Hunters, Being an Examination of Collecting with an Account of the Careers and the Methods of a Number of Those Who Have Searched the World for Wild Plants. Philadelphia: 1970. V. 67

WHITTLE, WILLIAM C.
Cruises of the Confederate States Steamers Shenandoah and Nashville. N.P: 1910. V. 62; 63; 65

WHITTLESEY, CHARLES
War Memoranda. Cheat River to the Tennessee 1861-1862. Cleveland: 1884. V. 62

WHITTOCK, NATHANIEL
The British Drawing Book; or, the Art of Drawing with Accuracy and Beauty.... London: 1850. V. 66
The Decorative Painters' and Glaziers' Guide.... London: 1827. V. 64; 66

WHITTON, B. A.
Ecology of European Rivers. Oxford: 1984. V. 64

WHITWORTH, CHARLES
An Account of Russia, as It Was in the Year 1710. 1758. V. 63
An Account of Russia As It Was in the Year 1710. Strawberry Hill: 1758. V. 65

WHITWORTH, R. H. DE WITT
Documentary and Historical Sketches of the Town of Mansfield. Mansfield: 1893. V. 65

WHO Burnt Columbia?. Charleston: 1873. V. 62; 63; 65; 66

WHO'S Who in Passaic County. Paterson: 1917. V. 66

WHO'S Who in Trenton. Trenton: 1908. V. 66

WHO'S Who in Yorkshire. Hereford: 1935. V. 62; 65

WHUR, CORNELIUS
Village Musings on Moral and Religious Subjects. Norwich: 1837. V. 65

WHY Do the Servants of the Nineteenth Century Dress as They Do?. Brighton;: 1859. V. 62

WHYMPER, C.
Egyptian Birds, for the Most Part Seen in the Nile Valley. London: 1909. V. 63

WHYMPER, EDWARD
The Ascent of the Matterhorn. 1880. V. 63; 65
A Guide to Chamonix and the Range of Mont Blanc. London: 1900. V. 63; 64
How to Use the Aneroid Barometer. 1891. V. 63; 65
Scrambles Amongst the Alps. 1871. V. 63; 65
Scrambles Amongst the Alps. London: 1871. V. 62; 63
Scrambles Amongst the Alps. 1890. V. 65
Scrambles Amongst the Alps. 1900. V. 63; 65
Scrambles Amongst the Alps. London: 1936. V. 63; 64
Travels Amongst the Great Andes of the Equator. London: 1891-1892. V. 62; 63; 64
Travels Amongst the Great Andes of the Equator. London: 1892. V. 63; 65
Travels Amongst the Great Andes of the Equator. New York: 1892. V. 65

WHYMPER, FREDERICK
Travel and Adventure in the Territory of Alaska. London: 1868. V. 62; 63; 67

WHYTE, ALEXANDER
Santa Teresa an Appreciation. Edinburgh: 1897. V. 67

WHYTE, CHRISTINA GOWANS
The Adventures of Merrywink. New York: 1906. V. 63

WHYTE, JON
Carl Rungius, Painter of the Western Wilderness. Salem: 1985. V. 67

WHYTE, SAMUEL
Miscellanea Nova. Dublin: 1800. V. 65

WHYTE, W. E.
O'er the Atlantic, or a Jouranl of a Voyage to and From Europe. New York: 1870. V. 66

WHYTE MELVILLE, GEORGE JOHN
Bones & I; or the Skeleton at Home. London: 1868. V. 67
Bones and I, or the Skeleton at Home. London: 1869. V. 67
Cerise: a Tale of the Last Century. London: 1866. V. 67
The Gladiators: a Tale of Rome and Judas. London: 1863. V. 67
The Queen's Maries; a Romance of Holyrood. London: 1862. V. 67
The Queen's Maries; a Romance of Holyrood. London: 1866. V. 67
Songs and Verses. London: 1924. V. 67
Tilbury Nogo; or, Passages in the Life of an Unsuccessful Man. London: 1854. V. 67

WHYTT, ROBERT
An Essay on the Vital and Other Involuntary Motions of Animals. Edinburgh: 1751. V. 64; 66
An Essay on the Vital and Other Involuntary Motions of Animals. Edinburgh: 1763. V. 64
Observations on the Nature, Causes and Cure of Those Disorders, Which Have Been Commonly Called Nervous, Hypochondriac or Hysteric to Which are Prefixed Some Remarks on the Sympathy of the Nerves. Edinburgh: 1765. V. 65

WICHMANN, JOHANN ERNST
Dissertation sur la Pollution Diurne Involontaire.... Lyon: 1817. V. 65

THE WICKEDNESS of a Disregard to Oaths; and the Pernicious Consequences of It to Religion and Government. London: 1723. V. 66

WICKERSHAM, JAMES
A Bibliography of Alaskan Literature 1724-1924. Cordova: 1927. V. 66
A Bibliography of Alaskan Literature 1724-1924. Fairbanks: 1927. V. 65

WICKES, STEPHEN
History of the Oranges in Essex County, N.J. from 1666 to 1806. Newark: 1892. V. 63; 66

WICKHAM, ANNA
The Man with a Hammer - Verses. London: 1916. V. 62

WICKS, JOHN HARRIS
The Merchants' and Artificers' Companion; and Practical Guide to Accounts.... London: 1811. V. 63

WICKSTEED, EDWARD
Books Printed For and Sold by Edward Wicksteed, at the Black Swan in Newgate Street, Near Warwick-Lane by Whom Country Booksellers May be Faithfully Supplied With Books in All Faculties, at the Very Lowest Prices. 1740. V. 65

WICKSTEED, JOSEPH H.
Blake's Innocence and Experience. London: 1928. V. 62

WIDDIFIELD, HANNAH
Widdifield's New Cook Book; or, Practical Receipts for the Housewife. Philadelphia. V. 67

WIDDRINGTON, THOMAS
Analecta Eboracensia: Some Remaynes of the Antient City of York. London: 1897. V. 62

WIDEMAN, JOHN EDGAR
A Glance Away. New York: 1967. V. 62; 64; 67

WIDENER, HARRY ELKINS
A Catalogue of Some of the More Important Books, Manuscripts and Drawings in the Library of Harry Elkins Widener. Philadelphia: 1910. V. 62

WIDMORE, RICHARD
An Enquiry into the Time of the First Foundation of Westminster Abbey.... London: 1743. V. 63
An History of the Abbey Church of St. Peter, Westminster, Commonly Called Westminster Abbey. London: 1751. V. 66

WIDNEY, R. M.
The Plan of Creation. Los Angeles: 1881. V. 62

WIECK, ROGER S.
Time Sanctified: the Book of Hours in Medieval Art and Life. New York: 1988. V. 63

WIEDEMANN, A.
Religion of the Ancient Egyptians. London: 1897. V. 66

WIEDEWELT, JOHANNES
Samling af Aegyptiske og Romerske Oldsager, I Deel. Copenhagen: 1786. V. 64

WIELAND, TERRY
Guy Coheleach. Camden: 1990. V. 65
Spiral-Horn Dreams. 1955. V. 62; 63; 64

WIELGORSKAYA, T.
Dictionary of Generic Names of Seed Plants. New York: 1995. V. 66

WIENER Kalender auf das Jahr 1790. Vienna: 1790. V. 65

WIENER, NORBERT
A Collection of His Writings 1948-1970. Cybernetics (1948). The Human Uses of Human Beings (1950). The Tempter (1959). Nonlinear Problems in Random Theory (1962). Gold and Golem, Inc. (1964). I Am a Mathematician: the Later Life of a Prodigy (1970). 1948-1970. V. 67
Cybernetics or Control and Communication in the Animal and the Machine. New York: 1948. V. 64
Ex-Prodigy: My Childhood and Youth. New York: 1953. V. 63
The Human Use of Human Beings. Cybernetics and Society. Boston: 1950. V. 65
Nonlinear Problems in Random Theory. New York: 1958. V. 67

WIENERS, JOHN
The Hotel Wentley Pems. San Francisco: 1958. V. 64
Nerves. London: 1970. V. 63; 66
Pressed Wafer. Buffalo: 1967. V. 66
Selected Poems 1958-1984. Santa Barbara: 1986. V. 62

WIERZBICKI, F. P.
California, As It Is and As It May Be, Of a Guide to the Gold Region. San Francisco: 1933. V. 62

WIESCHOFF, H. A.
Anthropologial Bibliography of Negro Africa. New Haven: 1948. V. 62

WIESE, KURT
You Can Write Chinese. New York: 1945. V. 62

WIESEL, ELIE
All Rivers Run to the Sea: Memoirs. New York: 1995. V. 62
One Generation After. London: 1971. V. 65

WIESELGREN, PETRUS
Deliciae Bibliothecae De La Gardianae in Loberod, Quas Leviter Adumbratas, Consent.... Lund: 1823. V. 64

WIFFEN, J. H.
Historical Memoirs of the House of Russell.... London: 1833. V. 62
Verses Written in the Portico of the Temple of Liberty, at Woburn Abbey, on Placing Before It the Statues, of Locke and Erskine, in the Summer of 1835. London: 1836. V. 67

WIGAN, ARTHUR LADBROKE
New View of Insanity. The Duality of Mind Proved by the Structure, Functions and Diseases of the Brain.... London: 1844. V. 65

WIGG, LORD
George Wigg. London: 1972. V. 65

WIGGIN, KATE DOUGLAS
The Birds' Christmas Carol. Boston: 1889. V. 63
Penelope's Experiences in England. (with) Penelope's Experiences in Scotland. Boston and New York: 1901. V. 63; 64
Penelope's Experiences in Ireland. Boston and New York: 1902. V. 64
Rebecca of Sunnybrook Farm. Boston and New York: 1903. V. 65
The Romance of a Christmas Card. Boston and New York: 1916. V. 64
Summer in a Canon, a California Story. Boston: 1889. V. 63

WIGGINS, IRA L.
Flora of the Galapagos Islands. Stanford: 1971. V. 63

WIGGINS, WALT
William Lumpkins Pioneer Abstract Expressionist. Ruidoso Downs: 1990. V. 66

WIGGLESWORTH, MICHAEL
The Day of Doom...with Other Poems. New York: 1929. V. 66; 67

WIGHT, ALEXANDER
A Treatise on the Laws Concerning the Election of the Different Representatives Sent from Scotland to the Parliament of Great Britain. Edinburgh: 1773. V. 64

WIGHT, JOHN
Mornings at Bow Street (and) More Mornings at Bow Street. London: 1824-1827. V. 62; 67

WIGHT, SAMUEL F.
Adventures in California and Nicaragua, in Rhyme. Boston: 1860. V. 63

WIGHT, THOMAS
A History of the Rise and Progress of the People alled Quakers in Ireland, from the Year 1653 to 1700. Dublin: 1751. V. 64; 66
A History of the...People Called Quakers in Ireland...1653-(1751). 1800. V. 64

WIGHTMAN, W. P. D.
Science and Renaissance. Edinburgh and: 1962. V. 63

WIGHTWICK, GEORGE
Hints to Young Architects. Together with a Model Specification. New York and London: 1847. V. 62

WIGLE, HAMILTON
History of the Wigle Family and Their Descendants. Kingsville: 1931. V. 65

WIGSTEAD, HENRY
An Excursion to Brightelmstone. London: 1790. V. 65
Remarks on a Tour to North and South Wales in the Year 1797. London: 1800. V. 62

WILBER, C. D.
The Great Valleys and Prairies of Nebraska and the Northwest. Omaha: 1881. V. 62; 63; 65; 66

WILBERFORCE, ROBERT ISAAC
The Life of William Wilberforce. London: 1838. V. 64

WILBERFORCE, SAMUEL
The Life of William Wilberforce. London: 1838. V. 67

WILBERFORCE, WILLIAM
A Letter on the Abolition of the Slave Trade.... London: 1807. V. 64

WILBRAHAM, RICHARD
Travels in the Trans-Caucasian Provinces of Russia, And Along the Southern Shore of the Lakes of Van and Urumiah, in the Autumn and Winter of 1837. London: 1839. V. 62

WILBRAHAM, ROGER
Three Letters Concerning the Surrender of Many Scotish (sic) Lords to the High Sheriffe of the County of Chester and the Condition of Duke Hamilton, Sir Marmaduke Langdale, Middleton and Others of Note. London: 1648. V. 62

WILBUR, JAMES BENJAMIN
Ira Allen, Founder of Vermont 1751-1814. Boston: 1928. V. 66

WILBUR, MARGUERITE EYER
The Indian Uprising in Lower California 1734-1737.... Los Angeles: 1931. V. 64; 67
A Pioneer of Sutter's Fort 1846-1850 - The Adventures of Heinrich Lienhard. Los Angeles: 1941. V. 66
Raveneau De Lussan - Buccaneer of the Spanish Main and Early French Filibuster of the Pacific. Cleveland: 1930. V. 64; 66
Raveneau de Lussan's Voyage to South Seas. Cleveland: 1930. V. 63; 64
Vancouver in California 1792-1794. Los Angeles: 1953-1954. V. 66

WILBUR, RICHARD
The Beautiful Changes and Other Poems. New York: 1947. V. 67
Ceremony and Other Poems. New York: 1950. V. 62; 65
Complaint. New York: 1968. V. 62; 67
Digging for China. Garden City: 1970. V. 65
A Late Aubade. N.P: 1964. V. 67
Loudmouse. New York: 1963. V. 62; 64
Lying and Other Poems. Omaha: 1987. V. 63
More Opposites. New York: 1991. V. 67
Poems 1943-1956. London: 1957. V. 62
Things of the World. New York: 1956. V. 62
A Walk in the Woods: Cummington. New York: 1989. V. 66

WILCOCK, JOHN
The Autobiography and Sex Life of Andy Warhol. New York: 1971. V. 66

WILCOX, ARTHUR
Moon Rocket. London: 1946. V. 67

WILCOX, DONALD E.
Damn Right I've Got the Blues. San Francisco: 1993. V. 67

WILCOX, ELLA WHEELER
Custer and Other Poems. Chicago: 1896. V. 67
Poems of Passion and Pleasure. London: 1919. V. 62

WILCOX, FRANK N.
Ohio Indian Trails. Cleveland: 1934. V. 66

WILCOX, JAMES
Modern Baptists. New York: 1983. V. 62

WILCOX, WALTER DWIGHT
Camping in the Canadian Rockies. 1896. V. 63; 65
The Rockies of Canada. 1900. V. 63; 65
The Rockies of Canada. New York: 1900. V. 63; 64

WILD, CHARLES
An Illustration of the Architecture and Sculpture of the Cathedral Church of Lincoln. London: 1819. V. 65
Select Examples of Architectural Grandeur in Belgium, Germany and France.... London: 1837. V. 66
Twelve Etched Outlines, Selected from the Architectural Sketches made in Belgium, Germany and France. (with) Twelve Etched Outlines...Second Series. London: 1833-1836. V. 64

WILDASH, PHILIP
Birds of South Vietnam. 1968. V. 67

WILDE, JANE FRANCESCA SPERANZA
Notes on Men, Women and Books. London: 1891. V. 65
Poems by Speranza. Glasgow: 1871. V. 65

WILDE, JOHN
44 Wilde 1944: Being a Selection of 44 Images from a Sketchbook Kept by John Wilde Mostly in 1944. Mt. Horeb: 1984. V. 66
The Story of Jane and Joan. Mt. Horeb: 1977. V. 64

WILDE, OSCAR
After Berneval. Letters of Oscar Wilde to Robert Ross. London: 1922. V. 64
After Berneval: Letters of Oscar Wilde to Robert Ross. Westminster: 1922. V. 64
After Reading. Letters of Oscar Wilde to Robert Ross. London: 1921. V. 64
After Reading: Letters of Oscar Wilde to Robert Ross. Westminster: 1921. V. 64
Album Wilde - Iconographie Choisie et Commentee par Jean Gattegno et Merlin Holland. Paris: 1996. V. 65
L'Anniversaire de l'Infante. Paris: 1928. V. 62
Art and Decoration, Being Extracts from Reviews and Miscellanies. London: 1936. V. 67
Art and Morality, a Defence of the Picture of Dorian Gray. London: 1908. V. 67
The Ballad of Reading Gaol. London: 1898. V. 64; 65; 67
The Ballad of Reading Gaol. East Aurora: 1905. V. 64; 67
The Ballad of Reading Gaol. London: 1924. V. 67
The Ballad of Reading Gaol. London: 1924-1925. V. 64
The Ballad of Reading Gaol. New York: 1928. V. 64
The Ballad of Reading Gaol. London: 1948. V. 65
Children in Prison and Other Cruelties of Prison Life. London: 1898. V. 62; 67
De Profundis. London: 1905. V. 62; 64
The Duchess of Padua. London: 1908. V. 65
Essays and Lectures. London: 1909. V. 67
The Fisherman and His Soul. San Francisco: 1939. V. 62; 63; 64; 66
For Love of the King. London: 1922. V. 62
The Happy Prince. London: 1888. V. 63; 64
The Happy Prince. London: 1913. V. 64; 65
The Happy Prince. New York: 1913. V. 65
The Happy Prince. Herrin: 1940. V. 67
The Happy Prince. New York: 1997. V. 62; 64
The Harlot's House and Other Poems. New York: 1929. V. 65
A House of Pomegranates. London: 1891. V. 62
A House of Pomegranates. London: 1915. V. 63
An Ideal Husband. London: 1899. V. 65
An Ideal Husband. London: 1909. V. 67
The Importance of Being Earnest. London: 1899. V. 64; 66
The Importance of Being Earnest. London: 1903. V. 67
The Importance of Being Earnest. London: 1910. V. 67
Impressions of America. Sunderland: 1906. V. 64
Intentions - the Decay of Lying, Pen, Pencil and Poison; the Critic as Artist: the Truth of Masks. 1891. V. 63
Intentions: The Decay of Lying, Pen Pencil and Poison, the Critic as Artist, the Truth of Masks. London: 1891. V. 64
Lady Windermere's Fan. London: 1893. V. 64; 65
Lady Windermere's Fan. London: 1894. V. 66
Lady Windermere's Fan. London: 1903. V. 67
A Letter from Oscar Wilde. Edinburgh: 1954. V. 64
The Letters of Oscar Wilde. London: 1962. V. 64; 66
Lord Arthur Savile's Crime. London: 1905. V. 67
The Picture of Dorian Gray. London: 1891. V. 64; 66
The Picture of Dorian Gray. Paris: 1908. V. 65
The Picture of Dorian Gray. Paris: 1908-1910. V. 64
The Picture of Dorian Gray. New York: 1930. V. 64
The Picture of Dorian Gray. London: 1968. V. 63
The Plays of Oscar Wilde. 1905-1907. V. 64
Poems. Boston: 1881. V. 63
Poems. London: 1881. V. 67
Poems. Together with His Lecture on the English Renaissance. Paris: 1903. V. 66
Poems with the Ballad of Reading Gaol. London: 1909. V. 67
Ravenna. Oxford: 1878. V. 64; 67
Rose-Leaf and Apple-Leaf: L'Envoi. London: 1904. V. 64; 67
Salome. Paris: 1893. V. 63
Salome. London: 1894. V. 64
Salome. London: 1912. V. 67
Salome. London: 1920. V. 65
Salome. Paris: 1922. V. 65
Salome. Paris: 1923. V. 66
Salome. New York: 1927. V. 66
Salome. New York: 1930. V. 63; 64
Salome. London: 1938. V. 62
Salome. 1939. V. 62
Sebastian Melmoth. London: 1911. V. 62
Selected Prose of Oscar Wilde. London: 1914. V. 67
Sixteen Letters from Oscar Wilde. London: 1930. V. 67
Some Letters from Oscar Wilde to Alfred Douglas 1892-1897. San Francisco: 1924. V. 64
The Sphinx. London: 1894. V. 62; 64; 65; 67
The Sphinx. London: 1920. V. 64
The Sphinx Without a Secret. 1904. V. 64
A Woman of No Importance. London: 1894. V. 62
A Woman of No Importance. Paris: 1903. V. 67
The Writings of Oscar Wilde. New York: 1925. V. 63

WILDE, W. R.
The Beauties of the Boyne and Its Tributary, the Blackwater. 1850. V. 64
The Beauties of the Boyne, Its Tributary, the Blackwater. 1949. V. 67
Narrative of a Voyage to Madeira, Teneriffe and Along the Shores of the Mediterranean. Dublin: 1840. V. 63

WILDENSTEIN, GEORGES
Fragonard - the Paintings. London: 1960. V. 66

WILDER, BURT G.
Intermembral Homologies. Boston: 1871. V. 67
Should Comparative Anatomy Be Included as a Medical Course?. New York: 1877. V. 67

WILDER, D. W.
The Annals of Kansas. Topeka: 1875. V. 62
The Annals of Kansas. Topeka: 1886. V. 64; 67

WILDER, F. W.
The Modern Packing House. Chicago: 1905. V. 63

WILDER, G. P.
Fruits of the Hawaiian Islands. Honolulu: 1911. V. 66

WILDER, L. B.
Colour in My Garden. Garden City: 1918. V. 64

WILDER, LAURA INGALLS
By the Shores of Silver Lake. New York: 1939. V. 62; 64
Farmer Boy. New York: 1933. V. 64
Little House in the Big Woods. New York: 1932. V. 65
The Long Winter. New York: 1953. V. 63
On the Banks of Plum Creek. New York: 1937. V. 63; 64
On the Banks of Plum Tree. New York: 1937. V. 66
These Happy Golden Years. New York: 1943. V. 64
These Happy Golden Years. New York: 1953. V. 63

WILDER, MARSHALL P.
The People I've Smiled With. New York: 1889. V. 63

WILDER, MITCHELL A.
Santos: the Religious Folk Art of New Mexico. Colorado Springs: 1943. V. 62

WILDER, THORNTON
The Angel that Troubled the Waters. New York: 1928. V. 65
The Bridge of San Luis Rey. New York: 1927. V. 63
The Bridge of San Luis Rey. New York: 1929. V. 62
The Bridge of San Luis Rey. New York: 1962. V. 66
The Cabala. New York: 1926. V. 63
The Eighth Day. New York: 1967. V. 62; 66
Heaven's My Destination. London: 1934. V. 62
The Ides of March. New York: 1948. V. 65
The Long Christmas Dinner and Other Plays in One Act. New York: 1931. V. 65
Our Town. New York: 1938. V. 66
The Merchant of Yonkers. New York: 1939. V. 63

WILDERSPIN, SAMUEL
A Manual for the Religious and Moral Instruction of Young Children in the Nursery and Infant School.... London: 1845. V. 62

WILDMAN, DANIEL
A Complete Guide for the Management of Bees Throughout the Year. London: 1801. V. 63; 65

WILDMAN, T.
A Treatise on the Management of Bees. 1768. V. 63

WILDMAN, W. B.
A Short History of Sherborne. Sherborne: 1930. V. 62

WILDSCHUT, WILLIAM
Crow Indian Beadwork - a Descriptive and Historical Study. New York: 1959. V. 65

WILEY, BELL I.
The Plain People of the Confederacy. Baton Rouge: 1943. V. 62

WILEY, BELL I. *continued*
They Who Fought Here. New York: 1959. V. 67

WILEY, SAMUEL T.
Biographical and Portrait Cyclopedia of the Third Congressional District of New Jersey, Comprising Middlesex, Monmouth and Somerset Counties.... Philadlephia: 1896. V. 63; 66
History of Monongalia County, West Virginia, From Its First Settlements to the Present Time. Kingwood: 1883. V. 67

WILEY, WILLIAM BELL
The Life of Billy Yank. Indianapolis: 1952. V. 63
The Life of Johnny Reb. Indianapolis: 1943. V. 63

THE WILFUL Girl and the Impatient Boy. New York: 1838. V. 65

WILHELM, CROWN PRINCE
From My Hunting Day-Book. 1912. V. 64

WILHELM, GOTTLIEB TOBIAS
Unterhaultungen aus der Naturgeschichte...Der Wurmer.... Viena: 1813. V. 67

WILKENS, W. H.
The Romance of Isabel Lady Burton.... New York: 1897. V. 63

WILKERSON, EVA E.
Index to Marriages of Old Rappahannock and Essex Counties Virginia 1655-1900. Richmond: 1953. V. 64

WILKES, CHARLES
Autobiography of Rear Admiral Charles Wilkes, U.S. Navy 1798-1877. Washington: 1978. V. 67
Narrative of the United States Exploring Expedition During the Years 1838, 1839, 1840, 1841, 1841. Philadelphia: 1845. V. 62; 63; 65; 66

WILKES, JOHN
The Correspondence of the Late John Wilkes, with His Friends.... London: 1805. V. 64
The History of England from the Revolution to the Accession of the Brunswick Line. London: 1768. V. 65
A Letter to His Grace the Duke of Grafton, First Commissioner of His Majesty's Treasury. London: 1767. V. 65
Letters from the Year 1774 to the Year 1796, Addressed to His Daughter.... London: 1805. V. 65
The Life and Political Writings of John Wilkes. Birmingham: 1769. V. 65
The North Briton. London: 1763. V. 64
The North Briton. London: 1772. V. 65

WILKESON, FRANK
Recollections of a Private Soldier in the Army of the Potomac. New York: 1887. V. 65; 67

WILKIE, FRANCES B.
A Sketch of Richard J. Oglesby. N.P: 1884. V. 65

WILKIE, GEORGE
Dissertatio Medica Inauguralis, de Rheumatisma.... Edinburgi: 1824. V. 67

WILKIE, WILLIAM
The Epigoniad. A Poem. London: 1759. V. 64
Fables. London: 1768. V. 62; 63

WILKIN, ANTHONY
Among the Berbers of Algeria. New York: 1900. V. 65

WILKIN, ELIZABETH
Dekho! The India that Was. 1958. V. 67

WILKIN, KAREN
Stuart Davis. New York: 1987. V. 63; 64

WILKINS, CHARLES
A Grammar of the Sankskrita Language. London: 1808. V. 66
The History of the Iron, Steel, Tinplate and Other Trades of Wales.... 1903. V. 62
History of the Literature of Wales from the Year 1300 to the Year 1650. Cardiff: 1884. V. 63; 64

WILKINS, G. H.
Undiscovered Australia. New York: 1929. V. 62; 63; 66

WILKINS, GEORGE
The Two Rectors. London: 1824. V. 62; 66

WILKINS, H. P.
Moon Maps.... New York: 1960. V. 66

WILKINS, JOHN
A Discovery of a New World, or, a Discourse Tending to Prove, That 'Tis Probable There May Be Another Habitable World in the Moon. London: 1684. V. 66
An Essay Towards a Real Character, and a Philosophical Language. (with) An Alphabetical Dictionary, Wherein all English Words...are Either Reffered To...Or Explained. London: 1668. V. 65; 67
The Mathematical and Philosophical Works.... London: 1707-1708. V. 64; 66
Mathematical Magick. London: 1648. V. 65; 66; 67
Mathematical Magick. London: 1691. V. 65
Mathematical Magic. London: 1680. V. 66

WILKINS, ROBERT H.
Neurosurgical Classics. New York: 1965. V. 63

WILKINS, ROY
Search and Destroy. 1973. V. 66

WILKINS, THURMAN
Thomas Moran - Artist of the Mountains. Norman: 1966. V. 63; 66

WILKINS, WILLIAM
Atheniensia or Remarks on the Topography and Buildings of Athens. London: 1816. V. 64

WILKINSON, A. M.
Wilfred of Ripon. Ripon: 1955. V. 65

WILKINSON, B.
Constitutional History of Medieval England 1216-1399 with Select Documents. London: 1948-. V. 67

WILKINSON, C. A.
Plain and Coloured - a Book of Wood-cuts. London: 1923. V. 63

WILKINSON, FREDERICK
Antique Firearms. London: 1977. V. 67

WILKINSON, G.
Experiments and Observations on the Cortex Salicis Latifoliae, or Broad-leaved Willow Bark.... Newcastle-upon-Tyne: 1803. V. 65

WILKINSON, GEORGE HUTTON
The Old Inmates of Harperley Park 1858. Cambridge: 1859. V. 63

WILKINSON, GEORGE THEODORE
An Authentic History of the Cato-Street Conspiracy; with the Trials at Large of the Conspirators for High Treason and Murder. London: 1820. V. 63

WILKINSON, HEYWOOD & CLARK LTD.
Varnishes, Japans and Colors. A Large and Most Elaborate Trade Catalogue for Wilkinson, Heywood & Clark Ltd. London: 1900. V. 66

WILKINSON, J. G.
On Color and the Necessity for a General Diffusion of Taste Among All Classes with Remarks on Laying Out Dressed or Geometrical Gardens. London: 1858. V. 63; 64

WILKINSON, J. GARDNER
Manners and Customs of the Ancient Egyptians. London: 1838. V. 65
The Manners and Customs of the Ancient Egyptians. New York: 1879. V. 64
The Manners and Customs of the Ancient Egytpians. London: 1878. V. 65

WILKINSON, JAMES
At a General Court Martial, of the Brigadier General Peter Gansevoort is President Covneted at Frederick-town in the State of Maryland, on the 2nd of September 1811, and Continued by Adjournments to the 25th of December Following.... Frederickstown: 1812. V. 63
Memoirs of General Wilkinson. Volume II. Burr's Conspiracy Exposed and General Wilkinson Vindicated Against the Slanders of His Enemies on that Important Occasion. Washington City: 1811. V. 67
Memoirs of My Own Times. New York. V. 65
Memoirs of My Own Times. Philadelphia: 1816. V. 67
Memoirs of My Own Times. New York: 1971. V. 63; 64

WILKINSON, JOHN
The Office and Authority of Coroners and Sheriffs. London: 1675. V. 63
A Treatise Collected Out of the Statutes of This Commonwealth, and According to Common Experience of the Lawes.... London: 1651. V. 65

WILKINSON, SIDNEY B.
Reminiscences of Sport in Ireland. 1932. V. 65

WILKINSON, SYLVIA
Moss on the North Side. Boston: 1966. V. 65

WILKINSON, TATE
Memoirs of His Own Life. York: 1790. V. 62; 64; 65

WILKINSON, THOMAS
Tours to the British Mountains with the Descriptive Poems of Lowther and Emont Vale. London: 1824. V. 62; 66

WILKOMIRSKI, BINJAMIN
Fragments - Memories of a Childhood 1939-1948. London: 1996. V. 65

WILKS, MARK
The Ban de la Roche, and Its Benefactor, M. Jean Frederic Oberlin, Lutheran Pastor at Waldbach, in the Department of the Vosges. London: 1820. V. 63

WILKS, ROBERT
Memoirs of the Life of...Containing His Reputation on the British Stage.... London: 1732. V. 66

WILKS, SAMUEL
Lectures on Diseases of the Nervous System. Philadelphia: 1883. V. 65

WILL, HEINRICH
Outlines of Chemical Analysis Prepared for the Chemical Laboratory at Giessen. Boston and Cambridge: 1855. V. 67

WILLAN, LEONARD
Astraea or, True Love's Myrrour A Pastoral. London: 1651. V. 63

WILLARD, EMMA
Ancient Atlas to Accompany the Universal Geography. Hartford: 1828. V. 63
Last Leaves of American History: Comprising Histories of the Mexican War and California. New York: 1849. V. 63; 66

WILLARD, FRANCES E.
How to Win. New York: 1900?. V. 65
A Woman of the Century: Fourteen Hundred-Seventy Biographical Sketches Accompanied by Portraits of Leading American Women in All Walks of Life. Detroit: 1967. V. 66

WILLARD, JAMES F.
The Trans-Mississippi West - Papers Read at a Conference Held at the University of Colorado June 18-June 21, 1929. Boulder: 1930. V. 63; 66

WILLARD, JOHN
Adventure Trails in Montana. Helena: 1964. V. 67
The C M R Book. Seattle: 1970. V. 63; 66

WILLARD, NANCY
Childhood of the Magician. New York: 1973. V. 65
Pish, Posh, Said Hieronomys Bosch. New York: 1991. V. 65
The Sorcerer's Apprentice. New York: 1993. V. 65
A Visit to William Blake's Inn. New York: 1981. V. 65

WILLARD, SIMON
The Columbian Union, Containing General and Particular Explanations of Government and the Columbian Constitution.... Albany: 1815. V. 62; 64

WILLARD, X. A.
Willard's Practical Butter Book.... New York: 1875. V. 63
Willard's Practical Dairy Husbandy.... New York: 1872. V. 64

WILLCOX, A. R.
The Rock Art of Africa. New York: 1984. V. 62

WILLEFORD, CHARLES
The Burnt Orange Heresy. 1971. V. 64; 66
The Burnt Orange Heresy. New York: 1971. V. 66; 67
Cockfighter. Chicago: 1962. V. 66; 67
Cockfighter. New York: 1972. V. 65, 66, 67
Cockfighter Journal. Santa Barbara: 1989. V. 65; 66; 67
A Guide for the Undehemorhoided. 1977. V. 63
High Priest of California. New York: 1953. V. 67
New Hope for the Dead. 1953. V. 64
New Hope for the Dead. 1985. V. 66
New Hope for the Dead. New York: 1985. V. 66; 67
The Outcast Poets. 1947. V. 64
The Outcast Poets. Yonkers: 1947. V. 66; 67
Sideswipe. New York: 1987. V. 67
The Way We Die Now. N.P: 1988. V. 66
Whip Hand. Greenwich: 1961. V. 67
The Woman Chaser. Chicago: 1960. V. 67

WILLEMENT, THOMAS
An Account of the Restorations of the Collegiate Chapel of St. George, Windsor. London: 1844. V. 62

WILLEMIN, NICOLAS XAVIER
Monumens Francais Inedits Pour Servir a l'Histoire des Arts Depuis le VIe Siecle Jusqu'au Commencement du XVIIe, Choix de Costumes Civils et Militaires, d'Armes, Armures, Instruments de Musique.... Paris: 1806-1839. V. 62; 67

WILLEMOES-SUHM, R. VON
On the Development of Lepas Fascicularis and the Archizoea of Cirripedia. 1875. V. 67

WILLERT, JAMES
Little Big Horn Diary Chronicle of the 1876 Indian War. La Mirada: 1977. V. 67
March of the Columns Chronicle of the 1876 Indian War, June 27 - September 16, 1876. El Segundo: 1994. V. 65; 67
The Terry Letters. Montclair: 1980. V. 67
To the Edge of Darkness - a Chronicle of the 1876 Indian War - General Gibbon's Montana Column and the Reno Scout - March 14 - June 20, 1876 - Custer Trails Series Volume 7. La Mirada: 1977. V. 65
To the Edge of Darkness - a Chronicle of the 1876 Indian War - General Gibbon's Montana Column and the Reno Scout March 14-June 20, 1876.... El Segundo: 1998. V. 67

WILLETT, C.
The History of Underclothes. London: 1951. V. 67

WILLETT, EDWARD
Letters Address to Mrs. Bellamy, Occasioned by her Apology. London: 1785. V. 65

WILLETT, ELBERT D.
History of Company B (Originally Pickens Planters) 40th Alabama Regiment. Anniston: 1902. V. 62; 63; 65

WILLETT, M.
The Strangers' Guide to the Banks of the Wye, Including Chepstow, Piercefield, Wyndcliff, Tintern Abbey, Raglan Castle and Other Parts of the Welsh Borders with Historical, Topographical and Antiquarian Remarks. Bristol: 1845. V. 66

WILLEY, A.
Amphioxus and the Ancestry of the Verterates. New York: 1894. V. 67

WILLIAM Faulkner. *An Exhibition of Manuscripts.* Austin: 1959. V. 62

WILLIAM, L. S.
Family Education and Government: A Discourse in the Choctaw Language. Boston: 1835. V. 63

WILLIAM, SAMUEL COLE
Early Travels in the Tennessee Country 1540-1800. Johnson City: 1928. V. 63

WILLIAM BEARDMORE & CO., LTD.
The Naval Construction Works of William Beardmore & Co. Ltd. London: 1913. V. 66

WILLIAM OF SWEDEN, PRINCE
Wild African Animals I Have Known. 1923. V. 63
Wild African Mammals I Have Known. London: 1923. V. 62; 67

WILLIAMS, A. B.
Game Trails in British Columbia. New York: 1925. V. 62; 63; 64; 66; 67
The Liberian Exodus. Charleston: 1878. V. 63

WILLIAMS, A. COURTNEY
A Dictionary of Trout Flies and of Flies for Sea-Trout and Grayling. London: 1965. V. 67
Fireside Fishing. London: 1928. V. 67

WILLIAMS, A. D.
Spanish Colonial Furniture. Milwaukee: 1941. V. 66

WILLIAMS, AARON
The Harmony Society, at Economy, Pennsylvania. Pittsburgh;: 1866. V. 66

WILLIAMS, ALFRED
Poems in Wiltshire. London: 1911. V. 62

WILLIAMS, ALPHEUS F.
The Genesis of the Diamond. London: 1932. V. 62; 64; 67

WILLIAMS, ARTHUR ANDERSON
The Registers of Colton Parish Church in Furness Fells. London: 1891. V. 66

WILLIAMS, B. J.
Bermudiana. Bermuda: 1936. V. 65

WILLIAMS, BENJAMIN SAMUEL
Choice Stove and Greenhouse Flowering Plants. London: 1870-1873. V. 64
Choice Stove and Greenhouse Flowering Plants. (with) Choice Stove and Greenhouse Ornamental Leaves Plants. London: 1883-1876. V. 64
Choice Stove and Greenhouse Ornamental Leaved plants. London: 1876. V. 64
The Orchid Grower's Manual. London: 1894. V. 62; 64

WILLIAMS, C. J.
Greenacre, or the Edgeware Road Murder. Derby: 1837. V. 63

WILLIAMS, C. K.
A Day for Anne Frank. Philadelphia: 1968. V. 64; 67
Flesh and Blood. New York: 1987. V. 67
I Am the Bitter Name. Boston: 1972. V. 67
Lies. Boston: 1969. V. 62; 64; 67
Misgivings: My Mother, My Father, Myself. New York: 2000. V. 66; 67
Poems 1963-1983. New York: 1988. V. 64
Tar. New York: 1983. V. 64
With Ignorance. Boston: 1977. V. 64; 67

WILLIAMS, C. R., MRS.
The Neutral French; or, the Exiles of Nova Scotia. Providence: 1841. V. 63

WILLIAMS, C. WYE
An Elementary Treatise on the Combustion of Coal and the Prevention of Smoke, Chemically and Practically Considered. London: 1858. V. 63

WILLIAMS, CARL M.
Silversmiths of New Jersey 1700-1825. Philadelphia: 1949. V. 63; 66

WILLIAMS, CHARLES
Descent into Hell. London: 1937. V. 62
Divorce. London: 1920. V. 62
Flecker of Dean Close. London and Edinburgh: 1946. V. 65
The Masque of Perusal...Set to Music by Hubert J. Foss. 1929. V. 66
Poems of Conformity. London: 1917. V. 62; 63; 65; 66
River Girl. New York: 1951. V. 66; 67
Rochester. London: 1935. V. 62
Seed of Adam and Other Plays. London: 1948. V. 62
Shadows of Ecstasy. London: 1933. V. 62
Taliessin through Logres: Poems. 1938. V. 66
Thomas Cranmer of Canterbury. London: 1936. V. 63
The Way of Exchange. 1941. V. 62
Windows of Night: Poems. London: 1924. V. 66
Witchcraft. London: 1941. V. 65

WILLIAMS, CHARLES H.
Sidelights on Negro Soldiers. Boston: 1923. V. 63; 64

WILLIAMS, CHARLES HANBURY
The Works of the Right Honourable Sir Charles Hanbury Williams, K.B. London: 1822. V. 65

WILLIAMS, CHARLES P.
The World Famous Williams Colored (Jubilee) Singers. Chicago: 1906. V. 63

WILLIAMS, CHAUNCEY PRATT
Lone Elk, the Life Story of Bill Williams, Trapper and Guide of the Far West. Denver: 1935-1936. V. 63; 66

WILLIAMS, CLARA ANDREWS
The Teddy Bears. New York: 1907. V. 62

WILLIAMS, D. E.
The Life and Correspondence of Sir Thomas Lawrence. London: 1831. V. 66

WILLIAMS, D. H.
A Geographical Report on the Damoodah Valley. London: 1850. V. 63

WILLIAMS, DAVID
The History of Monmouthshire. London: 1796. V. 66

WILLIAMS, DAVID continued
Lessons to a Young Prince, by an Old Statesman, on the Present Disposition in Europe to a General Revolution. (with) *Letters on Political Liberty and the Principles of the English and Irish Projects of Reform....* London: 1790. V. 66
Wedding Treasure. London: 1985. V. 66; 67

WILLIAMS, EDWARD
De Buckley, or Incidents of Australian Life. Birmingham: 1887. V. 64

WILLIAMS, EDWARD VAUGHAN
A Treatise on the Law of Executors and Administrators. London: 1832. V. 65

WILLIAMS, EDWIN
The Statesman's Manual. New York: 1853. V. 65

WILLIAMS, EMLYN
The Corn is Green. London: 1938. V. 64
Night Must Fall - a Play in Three Acts. London: 1935. V. 64

WILLIAMS, FREDERICK S.
Our Iron Roads: Their History, Construction and Administration. London: 1884. V. 64
Our Iron Roads; Their History, Construction and Social Influences. London: 1852. V. 62; 64; 66

WILLIAMS, G. F.
The Diamond Mines of South Africa. New York: 1906. V. 62

WILLIAMS, GOMER
Liverpool Privateers and Letters of Marque with an Account of the Liverpool Slave Trade. London: 1897. V. 66

WILLIAMS, GORDON R.
Fantasy in a Wood-Block or What Occurred When John James Audubon, the Naturalist, Visited with Thomas Bewick, the Engraver, in the Year 1827. Chicago: 1972. V. 63

WILLIAMS, GUS
Gus Williams' Autograph Songster. New York: 1874. V. 65

WILLIAMS, GUY ST. J.
The Irish Derby 1866-1979. 1980. V. 67

WILLIAMS, H. L.
Great Houses of America. New York: 1966. V. 65
The Sociable; or, One Thousand and One Home Amusements.... New York: 1866. V. 63

WILLIAMS, HAROLD
Book Clubs and Printing Societies of Great Britain and Ireland. London: 1929. V. 64

WILLIAMS, HARRY
Texas Trails, Legends of the Great Southwest. San Antonio: 1932. V. 62; 65

WILLIAMS, HELEN MARIA
Letters Containing a Sketch of the Politics of France, from the Thirty-First of May 1793, Till the Twenty-Eighth of July 1794, and of the Scenes Which Have Passed in the Prisons of Paris. London: 1795. V. 63
Letters from France.... London: 1792. V. 63
Letters Written in France in the Summer 1790, to a Friend in England.... London: 1794. V. 62
Letters Written in France, in the Summer 1790 to a Friend in England...(with) *Letters from France....* London: 1791. V. 65
A Narrative of the Events which have taken place in France, from the Landing of Napoleon Bonaparte, on the 1st of March, 1815, Till the Restoration of Louis XVIII. London: 1815. V. 63; 65
A Narrative of the Events Which Have Taken Place in France; with an Account of the Present State of Society and Public Opinion. London: 1816. V. 65
Poems. London: 1786. V. 63
Poems, Moral, Elegant and Pathetic.... London: 1796. V. 63
A Residence in France, During the Years 1792, 1793, 1794 and 1795.... Elizabeth-Town: 1798. V. 63; 65
Sketches of the State of Manners and Opinions in the French Republic, Towards the Close of the Eighteenth Century. London: 1801. V. 63
A Tour in Switzerland; or a View of the Present State of the Governments and Manners of Those Cantons.... London: 1798. V. 66

WILLIAMS, HENRY T.
Window Gardening, Devoted Specially to the Culture of Flowers and Ornamental Plants for Indoor Use. New York: 1877. V. 62

WILLIAMS, HENRY W.
A Practical Guide to the Study of the Diseases of the Eye.... Boston: 1862. V. 63; 67

WILLIAMS, HOWEL
The Geology of Crater Lake National Park, Oregon. Washington: 1942. V. 63

WILLIAMS, IOLO A.
Points in Eighteenth Century Verse: a Bibliographer's and Collector's Scrapbook. London: 1934. V. 62
Seven 18th Century Bibliographies. London: 1924. V. 64; 67

WILLIAMS, J. E.
Letter to A. B. J., Author of the Pamphlet Entitled The Union As It Was and The Constitution As It Is. New York: 1863. V. 63; 65

WILLIAMS, J. J.
The Isthmus of Tehuantepec: Being the Results of a Survey for a Railroad to Connect the Atlantic and Pacific Oceans. New York: 1852. V. 66

WILLIAMS, J. M.
The Dramatic Censor; or, Critical and Biographical Illustration of the British Stage for the Year 1811. London: 1812. V. 65

WILLIAMS, J. P.
Alaskan Adventure. 1955. V. 67

WILLIAMS, J. R.
Cowboys Out our Way - A Book of Cowboy Cartoons. New York: 1951. V. 66
Out Our Way. New York: 1943. V. 65; 66

WILLIAMS, JAMES
Seventy-Five Years on the Border. Kansas City: 1912. V. 67

WILLIAMS, JAMES J.
Mosby's Rangers: a Record of the Operations of the Forty-Third Battalion of Virginia Cavalry from Its Organization to the Surrender. New York: 1909. V. 65

WILLIAMS, JOHN
The Broken Landscape. Denver: 1949. V. 63; 64
Fairburn's Account of the Inhuman Murder of Mr. and Mrs. Williamson, and Their Woman Servant, at the King's Arms, New Gravel Lane.... London: 1811. V. 63
The History of the Powder Treason, with a Vindication of the Proceedings, and Matters Relating Thereunto...(with) *A Vindication of the History of the Gunpowder Treason....* London: 1681. V. 63
The Life of the Late Earl of Barrymore. London: 1793. V. 62
A Narrative of Missionary Enterprises in the South Sea Islands.... London: 1840. V. 63
New and Valuable Recipes for the Cure of Many Diseases. New York: 1828. V. 66
Night Song. London: 1962. V. 62
The Trial of John Williams, Francis Frederick, John P. Rog, Nils Peterson and Nathaniel White on Indictment for Murder on the High Seas. Boston: 1819. V. 67

WILLIAMS, JOHN AMBROSE
Trial...for a Libel on the Clergy, Contained in the Durham Chronicle of August 18, 1821. Durham: 1823. V. 63

WILLIAMS, JOHN G.
The Adventures of a Seventeen-Yer Old Lad and the Fortunes He Might Have Won. Boston: 1894. V. 65

WILLIAMS, JOHN S.
History of the Invasion and Capture of Washington. New York: 1857. V. 63

WILLIAMS, JONATHAN
Amen Huzza Selah. Highlands: 1960. V. 63; 66
Amen Huzza Selah. Karlsruhe-Durlach: 1960. V. 63
Aposiopeses (Odds and Ends).... Minneapolis: 1988. V. 66
Blues and Roots/Rue and Bluets: A Garland for the Appalachian. New York: 1971. V. 62; 66
A Celestial Centennial Reverie for Mr. Charles Ives. Highlands: 1975. V. 63
Elegies and Celebrations. Highlands: 1962. V. 63
Elite/Elate Poems. Selected Poems 1971-1975. 1979. V. 63
The Empire Finals at Verona. Poems. Highlands: 1959. V. 63
Epitaphs for Lorine. Penland: 1973. V. 63; 67
Four Stoppages/A Configuration. Stuttgart: 1953. V. 64
Get Hot or Get Out: a Selection of Poems 1957-1981. Metuchen and London: 1982. V. 67
Glees Swarthy Monotonies Rince Cochon and Chozzerai for Simon. Roswell: 1980. V. 63
Homage, Umbrage, Quibble and Chicane. Roswell: 1981. V. 63
Imaginary Postcards. London: 1972. V. 63
In the Azure Over the Squalor: Ransackings and Shorings. N.P: 1983. V. 64
In the Field at the Solstice. Seven Epitaphs for His Friends. Highlands: 1976. V. 64; 67
Letters to Mencken from the Land of Pink Lichen. New York: 1994. V. 66
Lines About Hills Above Lakes: Postals. Lauderdale: 1964. V. 67
The Loco Logodaedalist in Situ - Selected Poems 1968-1970. London: 1971. V. 63
The Lucidities, Sixteen in Visionary Company. London: 1967. V. 63
Lullabies Twisters Gibbers Drags.... Bloomington: 1967. V. 62; 64
The Macon County North Carolina Meshuga Sound Society.... Highlands: 1963. V. 63
Pairidaeza. Dentdale, Cumbria: 1975. V. 64; 67
The Plastic Hydrangea People Poems. Highpoint. V. 63
Portrait Photographs. Frankfort: 1979. V. 67
Sharp Tools for Catullan Gardens. Bloomington: 1968. V. 62; 64
62 Climerikews to Amuse Mr. Lear. Roswell/Denver: 1983. V. 63
Strung Out With Elgar on a Hill. Urbana: 1970. V. 64
Twelve Jargonelles from the Herbalist's Notebook 1965. Bloomington: 1965. V. 62; 64
La Vie Entre Les Gadarenes. Black Mountain: 1951. V. 62; 67
La Vie Entre Les Gadarenes. New York: 1951. V. 64

WILLIAMS, JOSEPH
Narrative of a Tour from the State of Indiana to the Oregon Territory in the Years 1841-1842. New York: 1921. V. 64

WILLIAMS, JOSEPH J.
Psychic Phenomena of Jamaica. New York: 1934. V. 64

WILLIAMS, JOSHUA
Principles of the Law of Real Property, Intended as a First Book for the Use of Students in Conveyancing. London: 1849. V. 63

WILLIAMS, JOY
State of Grace. Garden City: 1973. V. 62

WILLIAMS, L.
Forests of Southeast Asia, Puerto Rico and Texas. Washington: 1967. V. 67

WILLIAMS, MARY A. B.
Fifty Pioneer Mothers of McLean County, North Dakota. Washburn: 1932. V. 65

WILLIAMS, MARY FLOYD
History of the San Francisco Committee of Vigilance of 1851 - a Study of Social Control on the California Frontier in the Days of the Gold Rush. Berkeley: 1921. V. 66

WILLIAMS, MARY FLOYD continued
Papers of the San Francisco Committee of Vigilance of 1851. Berkeley: 1919. V. 62; 67

WILLIAMS, MEADE C.
Early Mackinac: The Fairy Island, A Sketch. St. Louis: 1898. V. 67

WILLIAMS, NIGEL
Jack be Nimble. London: 1980. V. 63

WILLIAMS, NOBLE CALHOUN
Echoes from the Battlefield; or, Southern Life During the War. Atlanta: 1902. V. 62

WILLIAMS, O. W.
A City of Refuge. N.P. V. 63

WILLIAMS, OSCAR
New Poems 1943. An Anthology of British and American Verse. N.P: 1943. V. 63

WILLIAMS, PHILIP
Report of the Proceedings in the Case of an Appeal Preferred by the Provost and Scholars of King's College, Cambridge, Against the Provost and Fellows of Eton College, to the Lord Bishop of Lincoln, the Visitor of Both Societies. London: 1816. V. 66

WILLIAMS, R. J.
Bermudiana. Bermuda: 1936. V. 62

WILLIAMS, ROSWELL
Madonna of the Damned. New York: 1935. V. 67

WILLIAMS, SAMUEL
Six Wood-Blocks to Illustrate McQuinn's Description of the Three-Hundred Animals. N.P: 1812. V. 67

WILLIAMS, SAMUEL COLE
Adair's History of the American Indians. Johnson City: 1930. V. 63
General John T. Wilder Commander of the Lighting Brigade. Bloomington: 1936. V. 62; 63; 66
History of the Lost State of Franklin. New York: 1933. V. 63; 66; 67
William Tatham-Watauga. Johnson City: 1947. V. 63; 66; 67

WILLIAMS, STEPHEN W.
American Medical Biography, or Memoirs Eminent Physicians, Embracing Principally Those Who Have Died Since the Publication of Dr. Thacher's Work.... Greenfield: 1845. V. 64; 66; 67
A Biographical Memoir of the Rev. John Williams. Greenfield: 1837. V. 63
The Cistercian Abbey of Strata Florida... London: 1889. V. 62

WILLIAMS, T. H.
A Walk on the Coast of Dorsetshire, from Lyme to Lulworth.... Exeter: 1828. V. 62; 67

WILLIAMS, T. HARRY
Beauregard, Napolean in Gray. Baton Rouge: 1954. V. 63
With Beauregard in Mexico. Baton Rouge: 1956. V. 63

WILLIAMS, TALIESIN
Cardiff Castle: a Poems. Merthyr-Tydfil: 1827. V. 65; 66; 67

WILLIAMS, TENNESSEE
Baby Doll. London: 1957. V. 62; 63; 64; 66
Camino Real. New York: 1953. V. 66
Cat on a Hot Tin Roof. New York: 1955. V. 66; 67
Cat on a Hot Tin Roof. London: 1956. V. 62
The Glass Menagerie. New York: 1945. V. 65, 66
The Gnadiges Fraulein. New York: 1967. V. 66
Grand. New York: 1964. V. 62
I Rise in Flame, Cried the Phoenix.... Norfolk: 1951. V. 64; 67
In the Winter of Cities. Norfolk: 1956. V. 63; 64; 66
The Kingdom of Earth with Hard Candy. A Book of Stories. N.P: 1954. V. 64
The Knightly Quest. New York: 1966. V. 66
Memoirs. Garden City: 1975. V. 65
The Milk Train Doesn't Stop Here Anymore. New York: 1964. V. 62; 64; 67
Moise and the World of Reason. New York: 1975. V. 66
The Night of The Iguana. New York: 1962. V. 66
One Arm. New York: 1949. V. 66
One Arm. New York: 1954. V. 66
The Remarkable Rooming House of Mme. Le Monde. New York: 1984. V. 66
The Roman Spring of Mrs. Stone. London: 1950. V. 62
The Roman Spring of Mrs. Stone. New York: 1950. V. 62; 66
The Rose Tattoo. London: 1954. V. 62
Something Cloudy, Something Clear. New York: 1996. V. 66
A Streetcar Named Desire. New York: 1947. V. 62; 66
A Streetcar Named Desire. London: 1949. V. 62
Summer and Smoke. London: 1952. V. 62
Tennessee Williams' Letters to Donald Windham 1940-1965. Verona: 1976. V. 64; 65
Un Tramway Nomme Desir. Paris: 1949. V. 64
27 Wagons Filled of Cotton. New York: 1945. V. 62
27 Wagons Full of Cotton and Other One Act Plays. London: 1949. V. 62
27 Wagons Full of Cotton and Other One Act Plays. Norfolk: 1953. V. 66
Where I Live. Selected Essays. New York: 1978. V. 66

WILLIAMS, TERRY TEMPEST
Leap. New York: 2000. V. 67
Pieces of White Shell. New York: 1984. V. 62; 64; 66; 67
Refuge. New York: 1991. V. 64; 67

WILLIAMS, THEO
Prophetic Mystery, or the Man Who Lives in Hell. Chicago: 1897. V. 62

WILLIAMS, THOMAS
The Trial of Thomas Williams, Esq. of Brynbras Castle, Caernarvonshire, Indicted with Ellen Evans and Ann Williams, Two of His Servants, for Forgery...On Monday April 9th, 1838.... London: 1838. V. 63

WILLIAMS, VALENTINE
The Clock Ticks On. London: 1933. V. 65
The Mysterious Miss Morrisot. Boston: 1930. V. 66
The Portcullis Room. Boston: 1934. V. 67

WILLIAMS, W.
New Mathematical Demonstrations of Euclid, Rendered Clear and Familiar to the Minds of Youth, with No Other Mathematical Instruments than the Triangular Piecs Commonly Called the Chinese Puzzle.... London: 1817. V. 64

WILLIAMS, W. MATTIEU
Through Norway with Ladies. London: 1877. V. 66
A Vindication of Phrenology. London: 1894. V. 65

WILLIAMS, WILLIAM CARLOS
At the Ballgame. Ferndale: 1981. V. 64
Autumn. Buffalo: 1998. V. 62; 64
A Beginning on the Short Story (Notes). Yonkers: 1950. V. 62
The Broken Span. 1941. V. 64
The Clouds, Aigeltinger, Russia, &c. 1948. V. 63; 64; 66; 67
The Clouds, Aigeltinger, Russia &c. Aurora: 1948. V. 64
The Collected Later Poems. Norfolk: 1950. V. 64
The Collected Later Poems. Norfolk: 1963. V. 66
The Collected Later Poems. London: 1965. V. 65
Collected Poems 1921-1931. New York: 1934. V. 64
The Complete Collected Poems of...1906-1938. Norfolk: 1938. V. 62
The Desert Music and Other Poems. New York: 1954. V. 62; 64; 65; 67
The Farmers' Daughters. The Collected Stories. Norfolk: 1940. V. 66
The Farmer's Daughters. The Collected Stories. Norfolk: 1961. V. 62
Flowers of August. Iowa City: 1983. V. 62
Go Go. New York: 1923. V. 62; 64
The Great American Novel. Paris: 1923. V. 64
Imaginations. New York: 1970. V. 66
In the American Grain. New York: 1925. V. 63; 64
Life Among the Passaic River. Norfolk: 1938. V. 63
Paterson. New York: 1949. V. 63
Paterson. (Book One-Book Five). New York: 1946-1958. V. 64; 66
Pictures from Brueghel and Other Poems. Norfolk: 1962. V. 67
Pictures from Brueghel and Other Poems. London: 1963. V. 65
Selected Essays of William Carlos Williams. New York: 1954. V. 63
The Selected Letters of William Carlos Williams. New York: 1957. V. 64; 67
Spring and All. Paris: 1923. V. 66
Two Poems. N.P: 1937. V. 62; 64; 67
A Voyage to Pagany. New York: 1928. V. 64; 65
The Wedge. Cummington: 1944. V. 62; 64
White Mule. Norfolk: 1937. V. 62

WILLIAMS, WIRT
History of Bolivar County, Mississippi. Jackson: 1948. V. 63

WILLIAMS-ELLIS, CLOUGH
In and Out of Doors. London: 1937. V. 65

WILLIAMSON, F. PHILLIPS
The Waterfowl Gunner's Book, an Anthology. Clinton: 1979. V. 65

WILLIAMSON, G.
Observations On the Human Crania Contained in the Museum of the Army Medical Department, Fort Pitt, Chatham. Dublin: 1857. V. 67

WILLIAMSON, GEORGE
Lady Anne Clifford, Countess of Dorset, Pembroke and Montgomery 1590-1676. Kendal: 1922. V. 62; 65
Memorials of the Lineage, Early Life, Education and Development of the Genius of James Watt. Edinburgh: 1856. V. 62; 67
Memorials of the Lineage, Early Life, Education and Development of the Genius of James Watt. London: 1856. V. 64

WILLIAMSON, HENRY
As the Sun Shines. London: 1947. V. 63
The Beautiful Years - a Tale of Childhood. London: 1921. V. 63
The Children of Shallowford. London: 1939. V. 62
A Clear Water Stream. 1958. V. 67
Dandelion Days. London: 1922. V. 63
Dandelion Days. London: 1930. V. 63
The Dark Lantern. London: 1951. V. 64
The Dream of Fair Women. London: 1931. V. 62
The Gale of the World. London: 1969. V. 63
The Golden Virgin. London: 1957. V. 64
The Innocent Moon. London: 1961. V. 62; 64
The Linhay on the Downs. London: 1929. V. 62; 65; 66
The Lone Swallows: Nature Essays. London: 1922. V. 66
On Foot in Devon, or Guidance and Gossip - Being a Monologue in Two Reels. London: 1933. V. 62
The Pathway. London: 1928. V. 62

WILLIAMSON, HENRY continued
The Peregrine's Saga and Other Stories of the Country Green. London: 1923. V. 63
The Star-Born. London: 1933. V. 62; 65
Tales of Moorland and Estuary. London: 1953. V. 62
Tarka the Otter. London: 1927. V. 63; 64; 66
Tarka the Otter. London: 1932. V. 62
A Test to Destruction. London: 1960. V. 64
The Village Book. London: 1930. V. 64
The Wet Flanders Plain. London: 1929. V. 65

WILLIAMSON, HUGH
The History of North Carolina. Philadelphia: 1812. V. 63; 66

WILLIAMSON, HUGH ROSS
Pavane for a Dead Infanta. London: 1972. V. 62; 67

WILLIAMSON, J. N.
Illustrious Client's Third Case-Book: Eighteen Sherlockian Essays, Four Quizzes, Three Tales in Verse, Three Poems, Two Limericks, Two Pastiches, a Parody. New York: 1984. V. 63

WILLIAMSON, JACK
Darker than You Think. Reading: 1948. V. 62

WILLIAMSON, JAMES J.
Mosby's Rangers: a Record of the Operation of the Forty-third Battalion of Virginia Cavalry from Its Organization to the Surrender. New York: 1909. V. 62
Mosby's Rangers; a Record of the Operations of the Forty Third Battalion of Virginia Cavalry from Its Organization to the Surrender. New York: 1896. V. 62; 63; 65
Prison Life in the Old Capitol and Reminiscences of the Civil War. West Orange: 1911. V. 62; 63

WILLIAMSON, JOHN
Advice to the Officers of the British Army. London: 1783. V. 65

WILLIAMSON, JOSEPH
A Bibliography of the State of Maine from the Earliest Period to 1891. Portland: 1896. V. 64

WILLIAMSON, R. T.
Diseases of the Spinal Cord. London: 1908. V. 65

WILLIAMSON, THOMAS
Foreign Field Sports, Fisheries, Sporting Anecdotes, &c. London: 1824. V. 62; 67
Foreign Field Sports, Fisheries, Sporting Anecdotes, &c. London: 1823. V. 67
Illustrations of Indian Field Sports. London: 1892. V. 67

WILLIAMSON, W. C.
The Morphology and Histology of Stigmaria Ficoides. 1887. V. 67
On the Recent Foraminifera of Great Britain. London: 1858. V. 66

WILLICH, A. F. M.
Lectures on Diet and Regimen.... London: 1799. V. 64; 65
Lectures on Diet and Regimen.... London: 1809. V. 64

WILLICH, CHARLES M.
Popular Tables Arranged in a New Form, Giving Information at Sight for Ascertaining, According to the Carlisle Table of Mortality, the Value of Lifehold, Leasehold and Church Property. London: 1853. V. 64

WILLIE, JOHN
Plusieurs Possibilities. Paris: 1985. V. 66

WILLINGHAM, CALDER
End as a Man. New York: 1947. V. 63
Natural Child. New York: 1952. V. 66
Reach to the Stars. New York: 1951. V. 66

WILLINS, EDWARD PRESTON
Quaint Old Norwich. 1884. V. 63

WILLIS, A.
The Eagles Nest in the Valley of Sixt.... 1860. V. 63

WILLIS, B.
Earthquake Conditions in Chile. Washington: 1929. V. 65
Index to the Stratigraphy of North America. Washington: 1912. V. 65; 67
Research in China. Washington: 1907. V. 64
Studies in Comparative Seismology. Washington: 1936. V. 67

WILLIS, BROWNE
The History and Antiquities of the Town, Hundred and Deanry of Buckingham.... London: 1755. V. 63
A Survey of the Cathedrals of York, Durham, Carlisle (and 24 others). London: 1742. V. 67

WILLIS, CONNIE
Doomsday Book. New York: 1992. V. 66
Fire Watch. New York: 1985. V. 66
Lincoln's Dreams. New York: 1987. V. 66

WILLIS, DEBORAH
Daguerrean and Studio Photographer. New York and London: 1993. V. 65

WILLIS, EDWARD J.
The Methods of Modern Navigation. The Line of Azimuth. Spherical Analytic Geometry. New York: 1925. V. 66

WILLIS, F. EARLE D'A.
A History of the Parish of Uffington with Casewick. London: 1914. V. 65

WILLIS, HENRY A.
The Fifty-Third Regiment Massachusetts Volunteers. Fitchburg: 1889. V. 66

WILLIS, JOHN
Mnemonica; or, the Art of Memory, Drained Out of the Pure Fountains of Art and Nature.... London: 1661. V. 67

WILLIS, NATHANIEL PARKER
American Scenery; or, Land, Lake and River. London: 1840. V. 65; 66
American Scenery; or Land, Lake and River Illustrations of Transatlantic Nature. (with) Canadian Scenery. London: 1840-1842. V. 62; 63; 66
Canadian Scenery. London: 1842. V. 65
The Winter Wreath. New York: 1853. V. 67

WILLIS, ROBERT
The Architectural History of the Conventual Buildings of the Monastery of Christ Church in Canterbury.... London: 1869. V. 66

WILLIS, THOMAS
The Anatomy of the Brain. New York: 1971. V. 64
The Anatomy of the Brain and Nerves. Montreal: 1965. V. 66
De Anima Brutorum Quae Hominis Vitalis ac Sensitiva est, Exercitationes Duae.... London: 1672. V. 64; 67
Diatribe Duae Medico-Philosophicae. Amstelodami: 1663. V. 64; 66; 67
Pharmaceutice Rationalis. Oxoniae: 1676-1678. V. 64
Opera Medica dn Physica, in Varios Tractatus Distributa: cummultis Figuris Aeneis. Lugduni: 1676. V. 66
Opera Omnia. Geneva: 1676. V. 64; 66
Opera Omnia Nitidius Quam Anquam Hactenus Edita, Plutimum Emendata.... Amsterdam: 1682. V. 64; 66; 67

WILLIS BUND, J. W.
Salmon Problems. London: 1885. V. 67

WILLITS, PHYLLIS L.
Scott County, Virginia Cemetery Records. Vancouver: 1970. V. 67

WILLKOMM, HEINRICH MORITZ
Bilder Atlas des Pflanzenreichs nach dem Naturlichen System. Stuttgart: 1895. V. 65

WILLMOTT, ROBERT
English Sacred Poetry, of the Sixteenth, Seventeenth, Eighteenth and Nineteenth Centuries. London: 1862. V. 62
Summer Time in the Country. London: 1858. V. 67

WILLOCKS, TIM
Bad City Blues. London: 1991. V. 65; 66
Green River Rising. London: 1994. V. 65; 67

WILLOUGHBY, HENRY POLLARD
The Apology of an English Landowner, Addressed to the Landed Proprietors of the County of Oxford. Oxford: 1827. V. 66

WILLOUGHBY, JOHN C.
East Africa and Its Big Game. London: 1889. V. 66; 67

WILLS, A.
The Eagles Nest in the Valley of Sixt.... 1860. V. 65

WILLS, JAMES
Lives of Illustrious and Distinguished Irishmen from the Earliest Times to the Present Period. 1843-1847. V. 67

WILLS, ROYAL BARRY
Houses for Homemakers. New York: 1945. V. 66

WILLS, W. H.
Poets' Wit and Humour. London: Sep. 1860. V. 63

WILLS, WILLIAM GORMAN
Life's Foreshadowings. London: 1859. V. 67

WILLS, WILLIAM HENRY
Old Leaves: Gathered from Household Words. London: 1860. V. 62

WILLSHIRE, WILLIAM HUGHES
An Introduction to the Study and Collection of Ancient Prints. 1874. V. 67

WILLSON, BECKLES
John Slidell and the Confderates in Paris (1862-1865). New York: 1932. V. 62; 63

WILLSON, DIXIE
Once Upon a Monday. Joliet: 1931. V. 63

WILLSON, E. B., MRS.
Cabin Days in Wyoming. Lusk: 1939. V. 67

WILLSON, H. BOWLBY
The Science of Ship-Building, Considered in Relation to the Laws of Nature. London: 1863. V. 64; 65

WILLSON, MEREDITH
The Music Man. New York: 1958. V. 66
The Unsinkable Molly Brown. New York: 1960. V. 66

WILLUGHBY, FRANCIS
De Historia Piscium Libri Quatuor.... London: 1686. V. 63
De Historia Piscium Libri Quatuor.... Oxford: 1743. V. 65; 66
The Ornithology of Francis Willughby. London: 1678. V. 65; 67
The Ornithology of Francis Willughby. London: 1972. V. 62; 66

WILLYAMS, COOPER
The History of Sudeley Castle in Gloucestershire. London: 1791. V. 64
A Voyage Up the Mediterranean in His Majesty's Ship the Swiftsure, One of the Squadron Under the Command of Rear Admiral Sir Horatio Nelson.... London: 1802. V. 63; 67

WILME, B. P.
A Manual of Writing and Printing Characters, Both Ancient and Modern.... London: 1845. V. 66

WILMER, BRADFORD
Observations on the Posionous Vegetables Which are Either Indigenous in Great Britain, or Cultivated for Ornament. London: 1781. V. 65

WILNER, ELEANOR
Precessional. Wallingford: 1998. V. 64

WILSON, A.
The Foresters: a Poem, Descriptive of a Pedestrian Journey to the Falls of Niagara.... West Chester: 1838. V. 63
Sport and Service in Assam and Elsewhere. 1924. V. 67

WILSON, A. PHILIPS
A Treatise on Febrile Diseases, Including Intermitting, Remitting and Continued Fevers.... Hartford: 1809. V. 66; 67

WILSON, ADRIAN
...The Highest Form of Flattery. Santa Cruz: 1982. V. 64
The Making of the Nuremberg Chronicle. Amsterdam: 1976. V. 62
The Making of the Nuremberg Chronicle. Amsterdam: 1978. V. 64
A Medieval Mirror: Speculum Humanae Salvationis 1324-1500. Berkeley/Los Angeles/London: 1984. V. 62, 64, 67

WILSON, ALBERT
The Flora of Westmorland. 1938. V. 62
The Flora of Westmorland. Arbroath: 1938. V. 65

WILSON, ALEXANDER
American Ornithology. Edinburgh: 1832. V. 66
American Ornithology; or the Natural History of the Birds of the United States. New York and Philadelphia: 1828-1829. V. 65; 67
American Ornithology; or the Natural History of the Birds of the United States. Edinburgh: 1831. V. 66
American Ornithology; or the Natural History of the Birds of the United States. London and Edinburgh: 1832. V. 67
American Ornithology; or, the Natural History of the Birds of the United States. London: 1876. V. 65
American Ornithology; or the Natural History of the Birds of the United States. Philadelphia: 1878. V. 65; 67
Wilson's American Ornithology. New York: 1853. V. 64

WILSON, ALEXANDER JOHNSTONE
The Resources of Modern Countries.... London: 1878. V. 64
The Rise and Progress of Sir Timothy Buncombe, Kt. and M.P.. Manchester: 1886. V. 67

WILSON, ANGUS
Anglo Saxon Attitudes. London: 1956. V. 62
A Bit off the Map and Other Stories. London: 1957. V. 62
The Middle Age of Mrs. Eliot - a Novel. London: 1958. V. 65
The Wrong Set and Other Stories. London: 1949. V. 64

WILSON, AUGUST
Seven Guitars. New York: 1996. V. 66

WILSON, B.
Australian Marine Shells. Kallaroo. V. 63; 66

WILSON, BARBARA
Ontario and the First World War. 1914-1918. A Collection of Documents. Toronto: 1977. V. 62

WILSON, BENJAMIN
Our Village. Bramley: 1860. V. 62; 65

WILSON, BOB
The Phoenix Book Shop. A Nest of Memories. Candia: 1997. V. 65

WILSON, CARROLL A.
Thirteen Author Collections of the Nineteenth Century and Five Centuries of Familiar Quotations. New York: 1950. V. 64

WILSON, CHARIS
California and the West. New York: 1940. V. 63
California and the West. Millerton: 1978. V. 63
Through Another Lens: My Years with Edward Weston. New York: 1998. V. 65

WILSON, CHARLES MORROW
Backwoods America. Chapel Hill: 1934. V. 67

WILSON, COLIN
Adrift in Soho. London: 1961. V. 65
Encyclopaedia of Murder. London: 1961. V. 66
The Mind Parasites. Sauk City: 1967. V. 64; 65
The Origins of the Sexual Impulse. New York: 1963. V. 67
The Outsider. London: 1956. V. 62; 64; 66
Ritual in the Dark. London: 1960. V. 66
Tree by Tolkien. Santa Barbara: 1974. V. 62

WILSON, COLONEL
Picturesque Palestine, Sinai and Egypt. New York: 1881-1883. V. 64

WILSON, D.
Henrietta Robinson. New York and Auburn: 1855. V. 65

WILSON, DANIEL
The Archaeology and Prehistoric Annals of Scotland. Edinburgh: 1851. V. 62; 66
Memorials of Edinburgh in the Olden Time. London: 1848. V. 64
Prehistoric Annals of Scotland. London and Cambridge: 1863. V. 62; 67

WILSON, DANIEL MUNRO
Where American Independence Began, Quincy, Its Famous Group of Patriots; Their Deeds, Homes and Descendants. Boston and New York: 1902. V. 67

WILSON, DAVID M.
The Bayeux Tapestry; the Complete Tapestry in Color. New York: 1985. V. 64

WILSON, E. H.
Aristocrats of the Garden. Boston: 1932. V. 64
The Lilies of Eastern Asia, a Monograph. Boston: 1929. V. 66
A Monograph of Azaleas, Rhododendron Subgenus Anthodendron. Cambridge: 1921. V. 62
More Aristocrats of the Garden. Boston: 1928. V. 63; 66
Plant Hunting. Boston: 1927. V. 63

WILSON, EDMUND
The Boys in the Back Room. San Francisco: 1941. V. 62
I Thought of Daisy. New York: 1929. V. 62; 63
Memoirs of Hecate County. Garden City: 1946. V. 63
The Shock of Recognition. Garden City: 1943. V. 67
To the Finland Station. A Study in the Writing and Acting of History. New York: 1940. V. 62; 64; 67
To the Finland Station: a Study in the Writing and Acting of History. London: 1941. V. 65
Travels in Two Democracies. New York: 1936. V. 62; 63
Undertaker's Garland. New York: 1922. V. 63
The Wound and the Bow. London: 1942. V. 62

WILSON, EDWARD
Diary of the Discovery Expedition. London: 1975. V. 65
Exciting Days of Early Arizona. Santa Fe: 1966. V. 64
An Unwritten History. A Record from the Exciting Days of Early Arizona. Santa Fe: 1966. V. 67

WILSON, EFFINGHAM
Wilson's Description of the New Royal Exchange Including an Historical Notice of the Former Edifices and a Brief Memoir of Sir Nicholas Gresham.... London: 1844. V. 62

WILSON, ELLEN
Lady Choughton. London: 1885. V. 66

WILSON, ERASMUS
A Three Weeks' Scamper throught he Spas of Germany and Belgium.... London: 1858. V. 64

WILSON, ERNEST H.
Ernest H. Wilson, Plant Hunter. Boston: 1931. V. 63
A Naturalist in Western China. London: 1913. V. 62

WILSON, FRANCIS
John Wilkes Booth. Fact and Fiction of Lincoln's Assisnation. Boston: 1929. V. 63

WILSON, FRANK I.
Sketches of Nassau. To Which is Added the Devil's Ball-Alley: an Indian Tradition. Raleigh: 1864. V. 62

WILSON, FREDERICK J.
The House that Jack Built, in Diversified Consideration.... London: 1888. V. 63

WILSON, G. V.
The Concealed Coalfield of Yorkshire and Nottinghamshire. 1926. V. 67

WILSON, GAHAN
Eddy Deco's Last Caper. New York: 1987. V. 67
Everybody's Favorite Duck. New York: 1988. V. 67

WILSON, GEORGE
Life of Dr. John Reid. Edinburgh: 1852. V. 67
A Practical Treatise of Fines and Recoveries.... London: 1753. V. 65
A Practical Treatise on Fines and Recoveries. London: 1793. V. 66

WILSON, GEORGE R.
Clinical Studies in Vice and Insanity. New York: 1899. V. 65

WILSON, GOODBRIDGE
Smyth County History and Traditions. Kingsport: 1932. V. 64, 67

WILSON, H. W.
With the Flag to Pretoria. London: 1901. V. 63
With the Flag to Pretoria. A History of the Boer War of 1899-1900. London: 1900-1901. V. 64

WILSON, HAROLD D.
Dry Law Facts Not Fiction. Newark: 1931. V. 65

WILSON, HARRIET E. ADAMS
Our Nig, or, Sketches from the Life of a Free Black.... Boston: 1859. V. 64

WILSON, HARRIETTE
Memoirs of.... London: 1825. V. 63; 65

WILSON, HENRY
Leybourn's Dialling Improved; or, the Whole Art Perform'd. London: 1721. V. 66; 67
Navigation Newly Modell'd; or a Treatise of Geometrical, Trigonometrical, Arithmetical, Instrumental and Practical Navigation. London: 1723. V. 65
Wilson's Wonderful Characters. Glasgow: 1845. V. 63

WILSON, HENRY L.
The Bungalow Book.... Chicago: 1910. V. 62

WILSON, HORACE HAYMAN
Select Specimens of the Theatre of the Hindus. London: 1835. V. 62

WILSON, IRIS H.
William Wolfskill, 1798-1866. Frontier Trapper to California Rancherco. Glendale: 1965. V. 65

WILSON, ISAIAH W.
A Geography and History of the County of Digby, Nova Scotia. Halifax: 1900. V. 64

WILSON, J.
A Synopsis of British Plants in Mr. Ray's Method. Newcastle-upon-Tyne: 1744. V. 64

WILSON, J. S.
Alexander Wilson, Poet Naturalist.... New York: 1906. V. 64

WILSON, J. T.
Observations Upon the Anatomy of the Muzzle of Ornithorhynchus. Sydney: 1895. V. 67

WILSON, JAMES
The Fire Eater. Edinburgh: 1823. V. 67
First Elements of the Theory of Series and Differences. London: 1822. V. 63
A Missionary Voyage to the Southern Pacific Ocean, Performed in the Years 1796, 1797, 1798 in the Ship Duff.... London: 1799. V. 63; 64
The Rod and the Gun. 1840. V. 62; 63; 66; 67
The Rod and the Gun. London: 1972. V. 67
A Treatise on Quadrupeds. Edinburgh: 1836. V. 62
The Trial of James Wilson for High Treason, With an Account of His Execution at Glasgow, September, 1820.... Glasgow: 1832. V. 63
The Victoria History of the County of Cumberland. London: 1901-1905. V. 66
A Voyage Round the Coasts of Scotland and the Isles. Edinburgh: 1842. V. 62; 65

WILSON, JAMES C.
A Treatise on the Continued Fevers. New York: 1881. V. 67

WILSON, JAMES G.
Appletons' Cyclopaedia of American Biography. New York: 1888. V. 65

WILSON, JAMES GRANT
Personal Recollections of the War of the Rebellion - Addresses Delivered Before the New York Commandery of the Loyal Legion of the United States 1883-1891. New York: 1891. V. 65; 67
Thackeray in the United States 1852-1853, 1855-1856. New York: 1904. V. 62; 67

WILSON, JAMES H.
Life and Service of William Farrar Smith. Wilmington: 1904. V. 67
Under the Old Flag Recollections of Military Operations in the War for the Union, the Spanish War, the Boxer Rebellion, etc. New York: 1912. V. 67

WILSON, JAMES HOLBERT
Temple Bar, The City Gologotha; a Narrative of the Historical Occurrences of a Criminal Character Associated with the Present Bar. London: 1853. V. 63

WILSON, JAMES P.
An Easy Introduction to the Knowledge of the Hebrew Language without the Points. Philadelphia: 1812. V. 66

WILSON, JOHN
A Memoir of Mrs. Margaret Wilson, of the Scottish Mission, Bombay.... Edinburgh: 1840. V. 65
The Royal Philatelic Collection. London: 1952. V. 66
A Synopsis of British Plant's in Mr. Ray's Method. Newcastle-upon-Tyne: 1744. V. 66
A Volume for All Libraries, Peculiarly Adapted to the Votaries of Correct Literature and Beneficial to Every Class of Learners.... Washington City: 1814. V. 63; 66
Wilson's Guide to Rothesay, and the Island of Bute.... Rothesay: 1848. V. 63

WILSON, JOHN A.
Reproduction of Thompson and West's History of Los Angeles County, California.... Berkeley: 1959. V. 66

WILSON, JOHN M.
The Rural Cyclopedia. Edinburgh: 1847. V. 64
The Rural Cyclopedia. Edinburgh: 1849. V. 64

WILSON, JOHN MAC KAY
Tales of the Borders and of Scotland. Gateshead-on-Tyne: 1870. V. 62

WILSON, JOSEPH
Memorabilia Cantabrigiae; or, An Account of the Different Colleges in Cambridge.... London: 1803. V. 64; 66

WILSON, JOYCE LANCASTER
The Swing, Poems and Illustrations. San Francisco: 1981. V. 62; 66

WILSON, KEN
Hard Rock. London: 1975. V. 63; 64

WILSON, LANFORD
The Hot L Baltimore. New York: 1973. V. 66

WILSON, LUZENA STANLEY
Luzena Stanley Wilson '49er. Memories Recalled Years Later for Her Daughter Correnah Wilson Wright. Oakland: 1937. V. 65

WILSON, MARGARET
One Came Out. New York: 1932. V. 67

WILSON, MONA
The Life of William Blake. London: 1927. V. 62; 63; 64

WILSON, O. S.
The Larvae of the British Lepidoptera and Their Food Plants. London: 1880. V. 64

WILSON, PROFESSOR
Noctes Ambrosianae. Edinburgh and London: 1856. V. 62

WILSON, R. G.
The Nature and Duty of Rejoicing in the Lord. A Sermon Preached in Chillicothe, February 8th, 1815, in Grateful Remembrance of the Victory Obtained by Major General Jackson over the British Forces at New Orleans on the 8th Ultimo. Chillicothe: 1815. V. 64

WILSON, R. L.
Colt, an American Legend. New York: 1985. V. 66
The Peacemakers - Arms and Adventures in the American West. New York: 1992. V. 65
Short Ravelings from a Long Yarn or Camp March Sketches of the Santa Fe Trail. Santa Ana: 1936. V. 65

WILSON, R. R.
History of Grant County Kansas. Wichita: 1950. V. 63

WILSON, RALPH
A Full and Impartial Account of All the Robberies Committed by John Hawkins, George Sympson, (Lately Executed for Robbing the Bristol Mails) and Their Companions. London: 1722?. V. 65

WILSON, RICHARD
Studies and Designs, by Richard Wilson, Done at Rome, in the Year 1752. Oxford: 1811. V. 67

WILSON, ROBERT
A Darkening Stain. London: 1998. V. 67
Observations on the Depreciation of Money and the State of Our Currency. Edinburgh: 1811. V. 64
Prostitution Suppressible and Resistance to the Contagious Diseases (Women's) Acts a Duty. London: 1871. V. 65
A Small Death in Lisbon. London: 1999. V. 67

WILSON, ROBERT A.
Ben K. Green; a Descriptive Bibliography of Writings by and About Him. Flagstaff: 1977. V. 67
Gertrude Stein a Bibliography. New York: 1974. V. 64; 66

WILSON, ROBERT THOMAS
A Full Report of the Trial of Major-General Sir Robert Thomas Wilson, Michael Bruce and Capt. John Hely Hutchinson, Before the Court of Assize at Paris, on the 22d of April 1816 and Two Following Days.... London: 1816. V. 63
History of the British Expedition to Egypt.... London: 1802. V. 66

WILSON, ROMER
Green Magic, a Collection of the World's Best Fairy Tales from All Countries. London: 1928. V. 63; 67

WILSON, SAMUEL ALEXANDER KINNIER
Aphasia. London. V. 64; 67
Neurology. Baltimore: 1940. V. 65
Neurology. Baltimore: 1955. V. 65

WILSON, SARAH
South African Memories. London: 1909. V. 66

WILSON, SCOTT BARCHARD
Aves Hawaiienses: the Birds of the Sandwich Islands. Honolulu: 1989. V. 67
The Birds of the Hawaiian Islands. London: 1899. V. 67

WILSON, T. BUTLER
Two Leeds Architects. Cuthbrt Brodrick and George Corson. Leeds: 1937. V. 64

WILSON, T. S.
The Early Diagnosis of Heart Failure. London: 1915. V. 67

WILSON, THOMAS
The Knowledge and Practice of Christianity Made Easy to the Meanest Capacities.... London: 1742. V. 63
Wilson's New Shepheards' Guide for Cumberland, Westmorland, and Lancashire. Lancaster: 1913. V. 62

WILSON, THOMAS C.
Pioneer Nevada. Reno: 1951-1956. V. 67

WILSON, W.
Bryologia Britannica.... London: 1855. V. 64

WILSON, WILLIAM
Gathered Together. Poems. London: 1860. V. 62
The System of Infants' Schools.... London: 1825. V. 63

WILSON, WILLIAM CARUS
The Friendly Visitor. Volume XXXII. Kirkby Lonsdale: 1850. V. 65

WILSON, WILLIAM H.
Rafnaland: the Strange Story of John Heath Howard. New York and London: 1900. V. 63

WILSON, WILLIAM JAMES ERASMUS
On Diseases of the Skin. London: 1847. V. 65

WILSON, WINIFRED
Playground and Indoor Games for Boys and Girls. London: 1895. V. 64

WILSON, WOODROW
A History of the American People. New York: 1902. V. 63

WILSON, YATES
More Alice. Capetown: 1959. V. 66

WILTON, THOMAS EGERTON, EARL OF
On the Sports and Pursuits of the English, As Bearing Upon Their National Character. London: 1868. V. 64

WILTSEE, ERNEST A.
Gold Rush Steamers of the Pacific. San Francisco: 1938. V. 63; 65; 66
The Pioneer Miner and the Pack Mule Express. San Francisco: 1931. V. 63; 64; 66
The Truth About Fremont, an Inquiry. San Francisco: 1936. V. 64; 65

WILTSHIRE, WILLIAM E.
Folk Pottery of the Shenandoah Valley. New York: 1975. V. 64

WINANS, WALTER
The Art of Revolver Shooting. 1901. V. 66

WINANT, LEWIS
Early Percussion Firearms. London: 1959. V. 67
Early Percussion Firearms. 1970. V. 67
Firearms Curiosa. New York: 1961. V. 67

WINBOLT, S. E.
Wealden Glass. The Survey-Sussex Glass Industry (A.D. 1226-1615). 1933. V. 67

WINBURNE, J. N.
Dictionary of Agricultural and Allied Terminology. East Lansing: 1962. V. 63

WINCH, FRANK
Thrilling Lives of Buffalo Bill and Pawnee Bill. New York: 1911. V. 67

WINCHELSEA, HENEAGE FINCH, 2ND EARL OF
A True and Exact Relation of the Late Prodigious Earthquake and Eruption of Mount Aetna, or, Monte Gibello.... London: 1669. V. 65

WINCHESTER, CLARENCE
Shipping Wonders of the World. London: 1937. V. 62; 66

WINCHESTER, ELHANAN
The Process and Empire of Christ; From His Birth to the End of the Mediatorial Kingdom: a Poem. Brattleboro: 1805. V. 64

THE WINCHESTER Guide; or a Description of the Curiosities and Antiquities of that Ancient City. Winton: 1780. V. 67

WINCHESTER, J. D.
Captain J. D. Winchester Experience on a Voyage...from Lynn Massachusetts to San Francisco California.... Salem: 1900. V. 66

WINCHILSEA, GEORGE FINCH, EARL OF
Letter from the Earl of Winchilsea to the President of the Board of Agriculture, on the Advantage of Cottagers Renting Land. London: 1796. V. 65

WINCKELMANN, JOHANN JOACHIM
Critical Account of the Situation and Destruction by the First Eruptions of Mount Vesuvius, of Herculaneum, Pompeii and Stabia.... London: 1771. V. 65
Geschichte der Kunst des Alterthums. Dresden: 1764. V. 62; 67
Histoire de l'Art chez les Anciens. Amsterdam: 1766. V. 67
Histoire de l'Art Chez les Anciens.... Paris: 1803. V. 64
Monuments Inedits De L'Antiquite, Statues, Peintures Antiques, Pierres Gravees, Bas-Reliefs De Marbre et De Terre Cuite.... Paris: 1808-1809. V. 65

WIND, EDGAR
Das Experiment und die Metaphysik. Tubingen: 1934. V. 67

WIND, HERBERT WARREN
The Story of American Golf. New York: 1948. V. 65

WINDELER, B. C.
Elimus: a Story. Paris: 1923. V. 63; 66

WINDHAM, WILLIAM
Speeches in Parliament, of the Right Honourable William Windham, to Which is Now Prefixed, Some Account of His Life.... London: 1812. V. 66

WINDISCH, CHARLES GOTTLIEB DE
Letters of..., on the Automaton Chess-Player of Mr. De Kempelen.... London: 1819. V. 65

WINDLE, BERTRAM C. A.
Remains of the Prehistoric Age in England. 1904. V. 67

WINDLE, MARY J.
Life in Washington, and Life Here and There. Philadelphia: 1859. V. 65

WINDSOR, DUCHESS OF
The Heart Has Its Reasons - the Memoirs of the Duchess of Windsor. London: 1956. V. 63

WINDSOR Ontario 1913 Canada.... Windsor: 1913. V. 63

WINDUS, JOHN
A Journey to Mequinez: the Residence of the Present Emperor of Fez and Morocco. London: 1725. V. 62; 65

WINE and Spirit Adulterators Unmasked in a Treatise, Setting Forth the Manner Employed and the Various Ingredients Which Constitute the Adulterations and Impositions Effected with the Different Wines and Spirits Offered to the Public.... London: 1828. V. 63

WINER, GEORGE B.
Grammar of the Chaldee Language, as Contained in the Bible and the Targums. Andover: 1845. V. 62

WINFIELD, CHARLES H.
Constitutional Amendment. Speech of Hon. C. H. Winfield, in the New Jersey Senate...Feb. 19, 1868 on the Resolutions to Withdraw the Assent of New Jersey to the Proposed Fourteenth Amendment.... Jersey City: 1868. V. 63
History of the County of Hudson, New Jersey from Its Earliest Settlement to the Present Time. New York: 1874. V. 63; 66

WINFREY, NORMAN H.
The Indian Papers of Texas and the Southwest 1825-1916. Austin: 1995. V. 67

WING, DONALD
Short-Title Catalogue of Books Printed in England, Scotland, Ireland, Wales and British America and of English Books printed in Other Countries 1641-1700. Volume I: A to England. New York: 1994. V. 62

WING, J. M.
The Tunnels and Water System of Chicago. Under the Lake and Under the River. Chicago: 1874. V. 65

WING, VINCENT
Geodaetes Practicus; or, the Art of Surveying. London: 1664. V. 65

WINGATE, W. J
A Preliminary List of Durham Diptera.... London: 1900. V. 63

WINGERT, P.
American Indian Sculpture, a Study of the Northwest Coast. New York: 1949. V. 62

WINGET, DON H.
Anecdotes of Buffalo Bill. Clinton: 1912. V. 62; 65
Anecdotes of Buffalo Bill. Chicago: 1927. V. 65

WINGFIELD, MARSHALL
A History of Caroline County Virginia. Richmond: 1924. V. 62
Pioneer Families of Franklin Co., Virginia. Berryville: 1964. V. 63

WINGFIELD, R. D.
Hard Frost. Blakeney: 1995. V. 63
Hard Frost. London: 1995. V. 65; 67
Night Frost. London: 1992. V. 65; 66; 67
Night Frost. London: 1995. V. 66
A Touch of Frost. London: 1990. V. 65
Winter Frost. London: 1999. V. 67

WINKLER, ANGELINA VIRGINIA
The Confederate Capital and Hood's Texas Brigade. Austin: 1894. V. 62; 63

WINKLER, ERNEST WILLIAM
Journal of the Secession Convention of Texas 1861. Austin: 1912. V. 65

WINN, GODFREY
Dreams Fade. London: 1928. V. 64

WINNALL, R. N.
Shore Shooting. London: 1948. V. 67

WINNECKE, CHARLES
Journal of the Horn Scientific Exploring Expedtion, 1894.... Adelaide: 1897. V. 62

WINNIE-the-Pooh Punch-Out. London: 1965. V. 65

WINNINGHAM, GEOFF
Going Texan: The Days of the Houston Livestock Show and Rodeo. Houston: 1972. V. 63

WINOGRAND, GARY
The Animals. New York: 1969. V. 63
Gary Winogrand. N.P: 1976. V. 63

WINSEMIUS, PIERIUS
Sirius. Franekerae: 1638. V. 65; 67

WINSHIP, GEORGE PARKER
The Coronado Expedition 1540-1542. Washington: 1896. V. 62
The Journey of Coronado 1540-1542. New York: 1904. V. 63; 66
The Journey of Coronado. 1540-1542. New York: 1922. V. 66
William Caxton. A Paper Read at the Meeting of the Club of Odd Volumes in Boston.... London: 1909. V. 66

WINSHROP, R. C.
Speech of the Hon. R. C. Winshrop, of Massachusetts, on the President's Message Transmitting the Constitution of California.... Washington: 1850. V. 62

WINSLOW, ANN
Trial Balances. New York: 1935. V. 65

WINSLOW, CARLETON MONROE
The Architecture and the Gardens of the San Diego Exposition: a Pictorial Survey of the Aesthetic Features of the Panama California International Exposition. San Francisco: 1916. V. 65

WINSLOW, DON
A Cool Breeze on the Underground. New York: 1991. V. 62; 65; 67
A Long Walk Up the Water Slide. New York: 1994. V. 64; 67

WINSLOW, DON continued
Way Down the High Lonely. New York: 1993. V. 65; 67

WINSLOW, FORBES BENIGNUS
The Anatomy of Suicide. London: 1840. V. 63; 67
Lettosmian Lectures on Insanity. London: 1854. V. 65
Obscure Diseases of the Brain and Mind. Philadelphia: 1866. V. 65
Physic and Physicians: a Medical Sketch Book.... London: 1839. V. 64

WINSLOW, MARJORIE
Mud Pies and Other Recipes. New York: 1961. V. 64

WINSLOW, W. H.
Cruising and Blockading. Pittsburgh: 1885. V. 62; 63

WINSLOW, WALKER
The Menninger Story. Garden City: 1956. V. 65

WINSOR, JUSTIN
Narrative and Critical History of America. Boston and New York: 1884. V. 63; 64

WINSTANLEY, JOHN
Poems Written Occasionally by.... Dublin: 1742. V. 64

WINSTANLEY, WILLIAM
England's Worthies. Select Lives of the Most Eminent Persons from Constantine the Great, to the Death of Oliver Cromwel Late Protector.... London: 1660. V. 64
Robert Robin's Intelligence Reviv'd; or a Narrative of the Late Dreadful Battels Between the Potent Prince de l'Or, and the Grand Duke of Penuria, alias Ragland. London: 1678. V. 62

WINSTON, JOHN G.
Modern Steam Practice, Engineering and Electricity. Philadelphia: 1883. V. 62

WINSTON, ROBERT W.
High Stakes and Hair Triggers. The Life of Jefferson Davis. New York: 1930. V. 62; 63; 65

WINSTONE, DAPHNE
Flame. London: 1945. V. 67

WINTER, A.
Coccolithophores. Cambridge: 1994. V. 64

WINTER, AMELIA
School Belles. New York: 1925. V. 64

WINTER, C. J. W.
Illustrations of the Rood-Screen at Randworth. Norwich: 1867. V. 62

WINTER, CHARLES E.
Grandson of Sierra. New York: 1907. V. 64

WINTER, DOUGLAS E.
Nightvisions 5. Arlington Heights: 1988. V. 66

WINTER, JOHN STRANGE
Cavalry Life or Sketches and Stories in Barracks and Out. London: 1881. V. 66

WINTER, MILO
Billy Popgun. Boston: 1912. V. 63; 65

WINTER, NEVIN O.
Chile and Her People of To-Day: an Account of the Customs, Characateristics, Amusements, History and Advancement of the Chileans, and the Devleopment and Resources of their Country. Boston: 1912. V. 65
Florida, the Land of Enchantment. Boston: 1919. V. 65

WINTER, ROBERT
The Arroyo Culture. Pasadena: 1999. V. 65

WINTER, WILLIAM
Life and Art of Edwin Booth. New York: 1893. V. 67

WINTER, WINTER
The Wallet of Time Containing Personal, Biographical and Critical Reminiscence of the American Theatre. New York: 1913. V. 65

WINTERICH, JOHN T.
Books and the Man. New York: 1929. V. 63

WINTERNITZ, E.
Leonardo Da Vinci As a Musician. New Haven: 1981. V. 65

WINTERNITZ, MILTON CHARLES
Collected Studies on the Pathology of War Gas Poisoning. New Haven: 1920. V. 66; 67

WINTERS, J. W.
True Veterans of Texas: an Authentic Account of the Battle of San JAcinto. N.P. V. 65

WINTERS, JOHN D.
The Civil War in Louisiana. Baton Rouge: 1963. V. 63

WINTER'S Tales 3. London: 1957. V. 63

WINTERS, YVOR
The Anatomy of Nonsense. Norfolk: 1943. V. 64
Collected Poems. London: 1963. V. 64
The Immobile Wind. Evanston: 1921. V. 64; 67

WINTERSON, JEANETTE
Art and Lies. London: 1994. V. 67
Art Objects: Essays on Ecstasy and Effrontery. London: 1995. V. 67
Fit for the Future - the Guide for Women Who Want to Live Well. London: 1986. V. 63; 64

Oranges Are Not the Only Fruit. London: 1985. V. 62; 64; 67
Oranges Are Not the Only Fruit. New York: 1987. V. 66
The Passion. London: 1987. V. 65
The Passion. New York: 1988. V. 66
Written on the Body. London: 1992. V. 62; 65; 67

WINTERTHUR MUSEUM
American Elegance, Classic and Contemporary Menus from Celebrated Hosts and Hostesses. New York: 1988. V. 65

WINTHER, OSCAR O.
The Old Oregon Country - a History of Frontier Trade, Transportation and Travel. Bloomington: 1950. V. 63; 66
The Story of San Jose 1777-1869. San Francisco: 1935. V. 62

WINTHROP, THEODORE
The Canoe and the Saddle or Klalam and Klickatat to Which are now First Added His Letters and Journals. Tacoma: 1913. V. 62; 65

WINTHROP, WILLIAM
Military Law and Precedents. Washington: 1920. V. 65

WINTHROP-BOWEN, CLARENCE
The History of the Centennial Celebration of the Inauguration of George Washington as First President of the United States. New York: 1892. V. 62

WINTLE, E.
The Birds of Montreal. Montreal: 1896. V. 62

WINTRINGHAM, CLIFTON
Commentarium Nosologicum, Morbus Epidemicos et Aeris Variationes in Urbe Eboracensi Locisque Vicinis, Per Fedecim Annos Graffantes Complectens. London: 1733. V. 65

WINWAR, FRANCES
Poor Splendid Wings: the Rossetti's and Their Circle. Boston: 1933. V. 64

WINWARD, WALTER
Rough Deal. London: 1977. V. 66

WIRE, H. C.
Marked Men. New York: 1934. V. 65

WIRT, ELIZABETH WASHINGTON
Flora's Dictionary. Baltimore: 1837. V. 64
Flora's Dictionary...Embellished by Miss Ann Smith. Baltimore. V. 67

WIRT, LOYAL LINCOLN
Alaskan Adventures. New York: 1957. V. 65

WIRT, WILLIAM
Sketches of the Life and Character of Patrick Henry. Philadelphia: 1817. V. 62
The Two Principal Arguments of William Wirt, Esquire, on the Trial of Aaron Burr, for High Treason, and on the Motion to Commit Aaron Burr and Others, for Trial in Kentucky. Richmond: 1808. V. 66

WISCHNITZER, R.
Architecture of the European Synagogue. Philadelphia: 1964. V. 62; 65

WISDEN, JOHN
Cricketers' Almanack for 1901. London: 1901. V. 67
Cricketers' Almanack for 1905. London: 1905. V. 67
Wisden Cricketers' Almanack 1940. London: 1940. V. 65

WISDOM in Miniature; or the Young Gentleman and Lady's Pleasing Instructor. Worcester: 1796. V. 64

WISDOM in Miniature; or the Young Gentleman and Lady's Pleasing Instructor; Being a Collection of Sentences, Divine, Moral and Historical.... Chester: 1797. V. 66

WISDOM in Miniature; or the Young Gentleman and Lady's Pleasing Instructor; Being A Collection of Sentences, Divine, Moral and Historical.... Coventry: 1797. V. 65

THE WISDOM of Crop the Conjurer. Wellington: 1820. V. 62

WISE, FRANCIS
A Letter to Dr. Mead Concerning Some Antiquities in Berkshire. Oxford: 1737. V. 64
A Letter to Dr. Mead, Concerning Some Antiquities in Berkshire, Particularly Shewing that the White Horse Which gives Name to the Vale... (with) Further Observations Upon the White Horse and Other Antiquities in Berkshire. Oxford: 1798-1742. V. 62

WISE, GEORGE
Campaigns and Battles of the Army of Northern Virginia. New York: 1916. V. 62; 63; 65

WISE, H. D.
Tigers of the Sea. New York: 1937. V. 63; 66

WISE, HENRY A.
Los Gringos. New York: 1849. V. 62; 63; 66
Los Gringos. New York: 1850. V. 63

WISE, JENNINGS C.
The Long Arm of Lee or the History of the Artillery of the Army of Northern Virginia with a Brief Account of the Confederate Bureau of Ordinance. Lynchburg: 1915. V. 62; 63; 64; 65; 67
The Military History of the Virginia Military Institute 1839 to 1865. Lynchburg: 1915. V. 62; 63

WISE, JOHN
The First of May: a Fairy Masque Presented in a Series of 52 Designs. Boston: 1881. V. 64

WISE, JOHN R.
The New Forest: Its History and Its Scenery. London: 1880. V. 64

WISE, JOHN S.
The End of an Era. Boston: 1899. V. 65
Memorial Address of Hon. John S. Wise Delivered at the Unveiling of a Monument to the Memory of the Southern Soldiers and V.M.I. Cadets. Roanoke: 1898. V. 63

WISE Sayings for Wee Folks. London: 1910. V. 65

WISE, THOMAS JAMES
The Ashley Library. A Catalogue of Printed Books. Volume IX. London: 1927. V. 66
The Ashley Library. A Catalogue of Printed Books. Volume XI. London: 1936. V. 66
The Ashley Library: a List of Books Printed for Private Circulation. London: 1897. V. 62
Between the Lines, Letters and Memoranda Interchanged by H. Buxton Forman and Thomas J. Wise. Austin: 1945. V. 66
A Bibliography of the Writings in Prose and Verse of Walter Savage Landor. London: 1919. V. 66
The Bronte Family: A Bibliography of the Writings in Prose and Verse. 1917. V. 63
The Bronte Family: a Bibliography of the Writings in Prose and Verse. London: 1972. V. 64
A Shelley Library; a Catalogue of Printed Books, Manuscripts and Autograph Letters by Percy Bysshe Shelley, Harriet Shelley and Mary Wollstonecraft Shelley, collected by Thomas James Wise. London: 1924. V. 62; 67

WISEMAN, NICHOLAS
Twelve Lectures on the Connexion Between Science and Revealed Religion. London: 1836. V. 65

WISEMAN, RICHARD
Eight Chirurgical Treatises on these Following Heads I. Of Tumours. II. Of Ulcers. III. Of Diseases of the Anus. IV. Of the King's Evil. V. Of Wounds. VI. Of Gun-Shot Wounds. VII. Of Fractures and Luxations. VIII. Of the Lues Venerea. London: 1719. V. 64

WISLIZENUS, F. A.
A Journey to the Rocky Mountains in the Year 1839. St. Louis: 1912. V. 63; 66

WISNER, F. D.
The Life of Harry Tracy. The Convict Outlaw. Medora: 1990. V. 64

WISNIEWSKI, DAVID
Golem. New York: 1996. V. 65

WISSHOFER, MATTHIAS
Entwurf Einer Elektrischen Flinte. Salzburg: 1780. V. 64

WISTAR, CASPAR
A System of Anatomy for the Use of Students of Medicine. Philadelphia: 1811 1814. V. 63

WISTER, OWEN
Lady Baltimore. New York: 1906. V. 62
Padre Ignacio or the Song of Temptation. New York: 1925. V. 66
The Pentecost of Calamity. New York: 1915. V. 66
Philosophy 4. A Story of Harvard University. New York: 1903. V. 66
The Virginian: a Horseman of the Plains. Los Angeles: 1951. V. 66

WIT, AUGUSTA DE
Facts and Fancies About Java. The Hague: 1900. V. 62

WITH, C.
The Danish Ingolf-Expedition. Volume III. 4. Copepoda I. Calanoida Amphascandria. Copenhagen: 1915. V. 63

WITHERBY, H. F.
The Handbook of British Birds. London: 1938-1941. V. 62; 63; 66
The Handbook of British Birds. Witherby: 1946-1947. V. 62
The Handbook of British Birds. 1948. V. 65
Handbook of British Birds. London: 1948. V. 64

WITHERING, WILLIAM
An Account of the Foxglove and Some of Its Medical Uses.... Birmingham: 1979. V. 63; 66
An Account of the Foxglove and Some of Its Medicinal Uses with Practical Remarks on Dropsy and Other Diseases. Birmingham: 1785. V. 62
An Account of the Scarlet Fever and Sore Throat, or Scarlatina Anginosa.... London: 1779. V. 65
An Account of the Scarlet Fever and Sore Throat, or Scarlatina Anginosa.... Birmingham: 1793. V. 63; 66; 67
An Arrangement of British Plants; According to the Latest Improvements of the Linnaean System. Birmingham: 1796. V. 66; 67

WITHEROW, THOMAS
The Boyne and Aghrim. 1879. V. 63

WITHERS, ALEXANDER SCOTT
Chronicles of Border Warfare. Parsons: 1970. V. 65
Chronicles of Border Warfare, or a History of the Settlement by the Whites of North Western Virginia. Clarksburg: 1831. V. 66
Chronicles of Border Warfare, or a History of the Settlement by the Whites of North Western Virginia. Cincinnati: 1895. V. 64
Chronicles of Border Warfare or a History of the Settlement by the Whites of North Western Virginia. Cincinnati: 1903. V. 64; 66

WITHERS, PAUL
British Coin-Weights. Llanfyllin (Powys): 1993. V. 66

WITHERS, T. H.
Catalogue of Fossil Cirripedia in the Department of Geology. London: 1928-1953. V. 63

WITHERSPOON, JOHN
Lectures on Moral Philosophy and Eloquence.... Philadelphia: 1810. V. 63; 66

A Serious Inquiry Into the Nature and Effects of the Stage; and a Letter Respecting Play Actors.... New York: 1812. V. 66
The Works of the Rev. John Witherspoon. Philadelphia: 1802. V. 66
The Works of the Rev. John Witherspoon. Philadelphia: 1802-1800-1801. V. 63

WITHROW, R. B.
Photoperiodism and Related Phenomena in Plants and Animals.... Washington: 1959. V. 66

WITKIN, JOEL PETER
The Bone House. Santa Fe: 1998. V. 67
The Bone House. Twin Palms: 1998. V. 67

WITLIFF, WILLIAM D.
William D. Wittliff and the Encino Press. Dallas: 1989. V. 67

THE WIT'S Magazine and Attic Miscellany. London: 1818. V. 65

WITT, CHARLES
An Effectual and Simple Remedy for Scarlet Fever and Measles.... London: 1865. V. 67

WITT, ROBERT
Catalogue of Painters and Draughtsmen Represented in the Library of Reproductions of Pictures and Drawings Formed by Robert and Mary Witt. London: 1920. V. 62

WITTE, HENNING
Memoriae Medicorum Nostri Seculi Clarissimorum Renovatate Decas Prima. Frankfurt am Main: 1676. V. 67

WITTE, J. DE
Description des Antiquites et Objets d'Art qui Composent le Cabinet. Paris: 1836. V. 66

WITTER, DEAN
Shikar. 1961. V. 64; 66; 67

WITTKOWER, R.
Art and Architecture in Italy 1600-1750. Baltimore: 1958. V. 65
Palladio and Palladianism. New York: 1974. V. 65

WITTON, P. H.
Views of the Ruins of the Principal Houses Destroyed During the Riots at Birmingham 1791. London: 1792. V. 62

THE WIZARD of Oz with Animations by Julian Wehr. Akron: 1944. V. 62; 65

WOART, JOHN
The Christian Soldier. Memorials of Lieutenant George W. Pyle, U.S.A. Third U.S. Cavalry. New York: 1870. V. 63

WODARCH, CHARLES
Introduction to the Study of Conchology. 1822. V. 64
Introduction to the Study of Conchology. London: 1825. V. 63

WODEHOUSE, PELHAM GRENVILLE
Aunts Aren't Gentlemen. London: 1974. V. 67
Bachelors Anonymous. London: 1973. V. 67
Bachelors Anonymous. New York: 1974. V. 64
Bertie Wooster Sees It Through. New York: 1955. V. 63
Big Money. New York: 1931. V. 62; 65
Bill the Conqueror. 1924. V. 65
Bill the Conqueror. New York: 1924. V. 63
Blandings Castle and Elsewhere. London: 1935-1936. V. 64
Bring On the Girls. 1953. V. 62; 65
Brinkley Manor: a Novel About Jeeves. Boston: 1934. V. 64
Carry On Jeeves. London: 1925. V. 64
The Clicking of Cuthbert. London: 1922. V. 64
Cocktail Time. London: 1958. V. 64; 67
The Code of the Woosters. New York: 1938. V. 62
Company for Henry. London: 1967. V. 64
A Damsel in Distress. New York: 1919. V. 63
Divots. New York: 1927. V. 63
Do Butlers Burgle Banks?. London: 1968. V. 64; 67
Doctor Sally. 1932. V. 67
Doctor Sally. London: 1932. V. 64
Eggs, Beans and Crumpets. London: 1940. V. 64
Eggs, Beans and Crumpets. New York: 1940. V. 66
A Few Quick Ones. London: 1959. V. 62
Fish Preferred. New York: 1929. V. 65
French Leave. London: 1956. V. 64
Frozen Assets. London: 1964. V. 64
Full Moon. Garden City: 1947. V. 62; 64; 67
Full Moon. London: 1947. V. 62; 64; 67
Galahad at Blandings. London: 1965. V. 67
The Girl in Blue. London: 1970. V. 67
The Globe by the Way Book. London: 1985. V. 63
The Gold Bat. London: 1904. V. 62; 66
The Gold Bat. London: 1923. V. 64
The Golf Omnibus. London: 1973. V. 64
The Golf Omnibus. New York: 1973. V. 63
Good Morning Bill. London: 1928. V. 64
The Great Sermon Handicap. New York: 1983. V. 64
The Head of Kay's. London: 1905. V. 64
Ice in the Bedroom. London: 1961. V. 66
If I Were You. London: 1931. V. 64
The Inimitable Jeeves. London: 1923. V. 62; 64; 67

WODEHOUSE, PELHAM GRENVILLE continued
The Intrusion of Jimmy. New York: 1910. V. 62; 64; 65
Jeeves and the Tie That Binds. New York: 1971. V. 62
Jeeves in the Offing. London: 1960. V. 62; 64; 67
Joy in the Morning. New York: 1946. V. 67
Laughing Gas. London: 1936. V. 65
The Little Nugget. New York: 1914. V. 62; 64
The Little Warrior. New York: 1920. V. 63
Lord Emsworth and Others. 1937. V. 67
Lord Emsworth and Others. London: 1937. V. 64
Love Among the Chickens. New York: 1909. V. 65
Love Among the Chickens. London: 1921. V. 64
The Luck of the Bodkins. London: 1935. V. 64
The Luck Stone. London: 1997. V. 64
The Mating Season. London: 1949. V. 64; 67
Mike. London: 1925. V. 64
Mike at Wrykyn. New York: 1953. V. 63
Mr. Mulliner Speaking. London: 1929. V. 64
Mr. Mulliner Speaking. Garden City: 1930. V. 63
Money for Nothing. London: 1928. V. 64
Money for Nothing. New York: 1928. V. 64
Much Obliged, Jeeves. London: 1971. V. 64
Mulliner Nights. London: 1930. V. 64
Mulliner Nights. London: 1933. V. 64
Mulliner Omnibus. London: 1935. V. 64
The Old Reliable. London: 1951. V. 64
Over Seventy: an Autobiography with Digressions. London: 1957. V. 63; 66
Pearls, Girls and Monty Bodkin. London: 1972. V. 64; 67
A Pelican at Blandings. London: 1969. V. 64
Performing Flea - a Self Portrait in Letters. London: 1953. V. 64
Pigs Have Wings. Garden City: 1952. V. 64
Pigs Have Wings. New York: 1952. V. 66
Plum Pie. New York: 1967. V. 62
Plum to Peter. Letters of P. G. Wodehouse to His Editor Peter S. New York: 1996. V. 64
The Pothunters. London: 1924. V. 64
A Prefect's Uncle. London: 1924. V. 64
The Prince and Betty. New York: 1912. V. 62; 63
Quick Service. London: 1940. V. 64
The Return of Jeeves. New York: 1954. V. 62; 64
Right Ho, Jeeves. London: 1934. V. 64
Sam in the Suburbs. New York: 1925. V. 63
Sam the Suddenn. London: 1925. V. 64
Service with a Smile. London: 1962. V. 64; 66; 67
The Small Bachelor. London: 1927. V. 64
Something Fishy. London: 1957. V. 64; 67
Spring Fever. Garden City: 1948. V. 67
Spring Fever. London: 1948. V. 64; 67
Stiff Upper Lip, Jeeves. London: 1960. V. 64
Stiff Upper Lip, Jeeves. London: 1963. V. 62; 64; 67
Stiff Upper Lip, Jeeves. New York: 1963. V. 64
Stiff Upper Lip, Jeeves. New York: 1965. V. 63
Summer Moonshine. London: 1938. V. 64
Sunset at Blandings. London: 1977. V. 64; 67
Sunset at Blandings. New York: 1978. V. 67
Tales of St. Austin's. London: 1926. V. 64
Thank You, Jeeves. London: 1934. V. 64
Ukridge. London: 1924. V. 64
Uncle Dynamite. London: 1948. V. 64; 66; 67
Uncle Fred in the Springtime. London: 1939. V. 64
Uncle Fred in the Springtime. New York: 1939. V. 62; 63; 64; 65
Uncle Fred in the Springtime. London: 1940. V. 64
Very Good, Jeeves. Garden City: 1930. V. 63
Very Good, Jeeves. London: 1930. V. 64
The White Feather. London: 1922. V. 64
William Tell Told Again. London: 1904. V. 63; 64; 65
Wodehouse on Golf. New York: 1940. V. 63
Young Men in Spats. London: 1936. V. 64

WODHULL, MICHAEL
Poems. London: 1804. V. 65

WODZICKI, K. A.
Introduced Mammals of New Zealand. 1950. V. 67

WOEIRIOT, PIERRE
Pinax Iconicus Antiquorum ac Variorum in Sepulturis Rituum ex Lilio Gregorio (Gyraldio) Excerpta. Lyon: 1556. V. 67

WOELFER, A. M.
Die Architectur Nebst Verzierungen aus dem Gebiete der Schonen Kunste Alterer und Neuerer Zeit.... Gotha: 1826. V. 67

WOIWODE, LARRY
What I'm Going to Do, I Think. New York: 1969. V. 63

WOJAHN, DAVID
Icehouse Lights. New Haven: 1982. V. 63

WOJCIECHOWSKA, MAIA
Shadow of a Bull. New York: 1964. V. 64

WOLCOT, JOHN
Bozzy and Piozzi, or the British Biographers; a Town Eclogue. Dublin: 1786. V. 66
Nil Admiriari; or, a Smile at a Bishop, Occasioned by an Hyperbolical Eulogy on Miss Hannah More, by Dr. Porteus.... London: 1799. V. 65
Odes of Importance. London: 1793. V. 66
Pindar's Odes.... London: 1790. V. 66
A Poetical, Serious and Possibly Imperinent Epistole to the Pope. London: 1793. V. 66
The Poetical Works of Peter Pindar, Esquire. Philadelphia: 1789. V. 67
The Rights of Kings; or Loyal Odes to Disloyal Academicians. London: 1791. V. 66
The Works. Dublin: 1792. V. 66
The Works. London: 1794. V. 66
The Works of Peter Pindar. London: 1794-1796. V. 66
The Works of Peter Pindar. London: 1794-1801. V. 62
The Works of Peter Pindar. London: 1812. V. 63

WOLCOTT, OLIVER
An Address, to the People of the United States, on the Subject of the Report of a Committee of the House of Representatives Appointed to Examine...Whether Monies Drawn from the Treasury.... Boston: 1802. V. 66

WOLCOTT, ROGER
Poetical Meditations, Being the Improvement of Some Vacant Hours.... New London: 1725. V. 62

WOLF, A.
A History of Science, Technology and Philosophy in the Eighteenth Century. New York: 1939. V. 67

WOLF, CHRISTA T.
Im Stein. (In the Stone). Gotha: 1998. V. 64
The Quest for Christa T. London: 1971. V. 64

WOLF, DANIEL
The American Space: Meaning in Nineteenth Century Landscape Photography. Middletown: 1983. V. 63; 64

WOLF, EDWIN
Rosenbach: a Biography. Cleveland and New York: 1960. V. 62; 64

WOLF, GARY K.
Who Censored Roger Rabbit?. New York: 1981. V. 65; 66

WOLF, H.
Rubber, a Story of Glory and Greed. New York: 1936. V. 62

WOLF, JOSEPH
The Life and Habits of Wild Animals. London: 1874. V. 62; 65
The Life and Habits of Wild Animals. New York: 1874. V. 62
Pheasant Drawings by Joseph Wolff.... Kingston Upon Hull: 1988. V. 67

WOLF, REINHART
New York in Photographs. New York: 1980. V. 66

WOLFE, BYRON B.
The Sketchbook of Byron B. Wolfe. Kansas City: 1972. V. 62; 63; 66

WOLFE, GENE
Plan(e)t Engineering. 1984. V. 64
Young Wolfe. 1992. V. 64; 66

WOLFE, HUMBERT
ABC of the Theatre. London: 1932. V. 65

WOLFE, JOSEPH
The Life and Habits of Wild Animals. London: 1874. V. 67

WOLFE, R. B.
English Prisoners in France, Containing Observations on Their Manners and Habits, principally with Reference to Their Religious State.... London: 1830. V. 66

WOLFE, RICHARD J.
Jacob Bigelow's American Medical Botany 1817-1821: an Examination of the Origin, Printing, Binding and Distribution of America's First Color Plate Book.... North Hills: 1979. V. 64
Louis Herman Kinder and Fine Bookbinding in America: a Chapter in the History of the Roycroft Shop. 1985. V. 62
Louis Herman Kinder and Fine Bookbinding in America: a Chapter in the History of the Roycroft Shop. Newtown: 1985. V. 64
Marbled Paper, Its History, Techniques and Patterns.... Philadelphia: 1990. V. 62
On Improvements in Marbling the Edges of Books and Paper. A Nineteenth Century Account. Newtown: 1983. V. 62
Secrets of Bookbinding: an Anonymous 19th Century Dutch Bookbinding Manual. N.P: 1991. V. 64
Secrets of Bookbinding (Geheimen der Boekbindeij).... Boston: 1991. V. 64
Three Early French Essays on Paper Marbling, 1642-1765. Newtown: 1987. V. 64

WOLFE, SUSAN
The Last Billable Hour. New York: 1989. V. 66

WOLFE, THOMAS CLAYTON
America. San Mateo: 1942. V. 64; 67
From Death to Morning. New York: 1935. V. 62; 64; 67
From Death to Morning. London: 1936. V. 63
Gentleman of the Press: a Play. Chicago: 1942. V. 64; 67
The Hills Beyond. New York: 1941. V. 63; 64; 66

WOLFE, THOMAS CLAYTON continued
The Hound of Darkness. N.P: 1986. V. 64
Look Homeward, Angel. New York: 1929. V. 65; 67
A Note on Experts: Dexter Vespasian Joyner. New York: 1939. V. 62; 64; 67
The Purple Decades. New York: 1982. V. 62
A Stone, a Leaf, a Door - Poems. New York: 1945. V. 62; 65; 67
The Story of a Novel. New York: 1936. V. 62; 64; 67
The Web and the Rock. London: 1947. V. 62; 64
...The Years Wandering in Many Lands and Cities. New York: 1949. V. 64

WOLFE, TOM
The Bonfire of the Vanities. Franklin Center: 1987. V. 65; 67
The Bonfire of the Vanities. New York: 1987. V. 63; 64
The Bonfire of the Vanities. London: 1988. V. 62; 65
The Electric Kool-Aid Acid Test. New York: 1968. V. 62; 66; 67
From Bauhaus to Our House. New York: 1981. V. 62; 64; 65
The Kandy Kolored Tangerine Flake Streamline Baby. New York: 1965. V. 62; 63; 64; 66; 67
A Man In Full. Franklin Center: 1998. V. 67
The New Journalism. New York: 1973. V. 62
The Purple Decades. New York: 1982. V. 62
Radical Chic and Mau-Mauing the Flak Catchers. London: 1971. V. 66
The Right Stuff. London: 1979. V. 65
The Right Stuff. New York: 1979. V. 65

WOLFE MURRAY, G.
The Tweedale Shooting Club. 1790-1940. V. 67

WOLFERT, IRA
Tucker's People. New York: 1943. V. 63

WOLFF, DICK
Parting Shots. Clinton: 1987. V. 65

WOLFF, HENRY W.
People's Banks. A Record of Social and Economic Success. London: 1896. V. 65

WOLFF, JEREMIAS
Dem Durchleuchtigsten Fursten und Herrn Ferdinand, Herzogen in Schlesien zu Jagar des Heyl.... Augsburg: 1700. V. 67

WOLFF, JULIAN
Practical Handbook of Sherlockian Heraldry, with a Visitation of Conanical Arms. New York: 1955-1956. V. 65

WOLFF, MAX
Explication of an Engraving Called the Origin of the Rites and Worship of the Hebrews.... New York: 1859-5619. V. 64

WOLFF, TOBIAS
Back in the World. Boston: 1985. V. 62; 65; 67
Hunters in the Snow. London: 1982. V. 62; 63
In the Garden of the North American Martyrs. New York: 1981. V. 65; 66; 67
The Other Miller. Derry & Ridgewood: 1989. V. 62
This Boy's Life. New York: 1989. V. 66; 67

WOLF HEIDEGGER, G.
Atlas of Systematic Human Anatomy. Volume II Splanchnologia.... Basel: 1962. V. 67

WOLHUTER, HARRY
Memories of a Game Ranger. Johannesburg: 1958. V. 67

WOLLASTON, T. V.
Catalogue of the Coleopterous Insects of the Canaries. London: 1864. V. 63; 64

WOLLASTON, WILLIAM
The Nature of Religion Delineated. London: 1724. V. 67
The Religion of Nature Delineated. London: 1731. V. 65

WOLLE, F.
Diatomaceae of North America. Bethlehem: 1890. V. 63; 66
Diatomaceae of North America. Bethlehem: 1894. V. 66

WOLLE, MURIEL SIBELL
Montana Pay Dirt; a Guide to the Mining Camps of the Treasure State. Denver: 1963. V. 64; 65; 66

WOLLSTONECRAFT, MARY
Letters to Imlay. London: 1879. V. 63; 65; 66
Letters Written During a Short Residence in Sweden, Norway and Denmark. London: 1796. V. 62; 65
Letters Written During a Short Residence in Sweden, Norway and Denmark. London: 1802. V. 63; 65
Original Stories from Real Life; with Conversations, Calculated to Regulate the Affections, and Form the Mind to Truth and Goodness. London: 1818?. V. 63
Posthumous Works of the Author of a Vindication of the Rights of Woman. London: 1798. V. 62
A Vindication of the Rights of Woman. London: 1792. V. 62; 63; 64; 65
A Vindication of the Rights of Woman. London: 1891. V. 65

WOLOSHUK, NICHOLAS
Edward Borein: Drawings and Painting of the Old West. Volume I: the Indians. Flagstaff: 1968. V. 63
Edward Borein Drawings and Paintings of the Old West - Volume II: the Cowboys. Santa Fe: 1974. V. 67

WOLOWSKI, LOUIS FRANCOIS MICHEL RAYMOND
La Question des Banques. Paris: 1864. V. 66

WOLPE, BERTHOLD
A Retrospective Survey. London: 1980. V. 63

WOLSELEY, CHARLES
Justification Evangelical; or a Plain Impartial Scriptural Account of God's Method of Justifying a Sinner. London: 1677. V. 63

WOLTMANN, ALFRED
History of Painting. London: 1880. V. 67

WOLZOGEN, ALFRED
Aus Schinkel's Nachlass. Reisetagebuchr, Briefe und Aphorismen.... Berlin: 1862-1864. V. 64

WOMACK, JACK
Ambient. London: 1988. V. 65
Heathern. London: 1990. V. 65
Terraplane. London: 1989. V. 65

THE WOMAN of Genius. London: 1821-1822. V. 65

WOMAN'S CHRISTIAN ASSOCIATION OF SIOUX CITY, IOWA
Cookery. Sioux City: 1883. V. 64; 66

THE WONDER City of Oz. Chicago: 1940. V. 65

THE WONDERFUL Life, and Surprising Adventures of that Renowned Hero Robinson Crusoe. London: 1794. V. 62

THE WONDERFUL Performing Dogs. New York: 1901. V. 62

WONDERFUL Visionary Enthusiasm: Containing a Sketch of the Wonderful Proceedings, of a Certain Wonderful Prophetess of Leeds.... London: 1804. V. 66

WONDERFUL Works of God. Irvington;: 1858. V. 66

THE WONDERS of a Toy Shop. New York: 1851-1865. V. 65

THE WONDERS of the Universe; or Curiosities of Nature and Art.... Philadelphia: 1846. V. 62

WONG QUINCEY, J.
Chinese Hunter. 1939. V. 62; 63; 64
Chinese Hunter. London: 1939. V. 67
Chinese Hunter. New York: 1939. V. 62; 63; 64; 67

WOOD, A. B.
Fifty Years of Yesterdays. Gering: 1945. V. 64

WOOD, ANTHONY
Athenae Oxonienses. London: 1691-1692. V. 63
Athenae Oxonienses. London: 1721. V. 62

WOOD, BENJAMIN FARMER
Verbatim Report of the Examination of Witnesses, Taken at the Cross Keys Inn, Darfield, January 15th 1875 Before Benjamin Bagshawe, Esq., Deputy Coroner, Touching the Death of Benjamin Wood, Farmer...who Died January 10th 1875. Sheffield: 1875. V. 63

WOOD, BUTLER
Charlotte Brontë 1816-1916. A Centenary Memorial Prepared by the Bronte Society. London: 1917. V. 63

WOOD, CASEY A.
The Fundus Oculi Of Birds Especially as Viewed by Ophthalmoscope. Chicago: 1917. V. 65; 67
An Introduction to the Literature of Vertebrate Zoology. Cambridge: 1992. V. 67
An Introduction to the Literature of Vertebrate Zoology. 1993. V. 65
A Physician's Anthology of English and American Poetry. London: 1920. V. 63

WOOD, CATHERINE M.
Palomar: from Tepee to Telescope. San Diego: 1937. V. 67

WOOD, CHRISTOPHER
James Bond and Moonraker. London: 1979. V. 65
James Bond, the Spy Who Loved Me. London: 1977. V. 65; 66

WOOD, DEAN EARL
The Old Santa Fe Trail from the Missouri River: Documentary Proof of the History and Route of the Old Santa Fe Trail. Kansas City: 1951. V. 64; 67

WOOD, EDWARD
A Complete Body of Conveyancing: in a Theory and Practice. London: 1790. V. 67

WOOD, EDWIN C.
Historic Mackinac. New York: 1918. V. 66

WOOD, ELLEN PRICE
East Lynne. Leipzig: 1861. V. 63
East Lynne. London: 1862. V. 65
Verner's Pride. Leipzig: 1863. V. 65

WOOD, EPHRAIM
Quakerism Unveiled: Truth Prevalent: in Two Letters, Addressed to the Members of the Society of Friends, Liverpool. Liverpool: 1815. V. 66

WOOD, ESTHER
Dante Rossetti and the Pre-Raphaelite Movement. London: 1894. V. 65

WOOD, FRED
Round About Sussex Downs. 1925. V. 67

WOOD, G. A. R.
Cocoa. London: 1985. V. 63

WOOD, G. J.
The Illustrated Naural History. London: 1865. V. 62

WOOD, GEORGE
The Arguments of the Counsel of Joseph Hendrickson, in a Cause Decided in the Court of Chancery of the State of New Jersey, Between Thomas L. Shotwell, Complainant and Joseph Hendrickson and Stacy Decow.... Philadelphia: 1833. V. 63
The Story of Morley. London. V. 65
The Subaltern Officer; a Narrative. London: 1826. V. 65

WOOD, GEORGE H.
Twenty Woodcuts. Manchester: 1927. V. 66

WOOD, H. C.
Contribution to the History of the Fresh Water Algae of North America. Washington: 1872. V. 62; 63
Nervous Diseases and Their Diagnosis: A Treatise Upon the Phenomena Produced by Diseases of the Nervous System.... Philadelphia: 1887. V. 66

WOOD, H. G.
A Treatise on the Law of Master and Servant. Albany: 1877. V. 65
A Treatise on the Law of Railroads. Boston: 1894. V. 67

WOOD, HARVEY
Personal Recollections of Harvey Wood. Pasadena: 1955. V. 65

WOOD, HENRY
Change for the American Notes: in Letters from London to New York. New York: 1843. V. 62; 67

WOOD, HORATIO C.
Brain-Work and Overwork. Philadelphia: 1880. V. 65
Nervous Diseases and Their Diagnosis: a Treatise Upon the Phenomena, Produced by Diseases of the Nervous System.... Philadelphia: 1887. V. 67

WOOD, J. G.
Animate Creation. New York: 1885. V. 62

WOOD, J. M.
A Handbook to the Flora of Natal. Durban: 1907. V. 66
A Handbook to the Flora of Natal. Durham: 1907. V. 65

WOOD, J. R.
The Welensky Papers: a History of the Federation of Rhodesia and Nyasaland. Durban: 1983. V. 66

WOOD, J. R. I.
A Handbook of the Yemen Flora. 1997. V. 63

WOOD, J. W.
Pasadena Historical and Personal. Pasadena: 1917. V. 63

WOOD, JOHN GEORGE
An Elementary Treatise on Sketching from Nature; with the Principles of Light and Shade, the Theory of Colours &c. London: 1850. V. 66; 67
Elements of Perspective; Containing the Nature of Light and Colours, and the Theory and Practice of Perspective, in Regard to Lines, Surfaces and Solids, with Its Application to Architecture.... London: 1799. V. 62
A Manual of Perspective...for the Use of Amateurs. Worcester: 1849. V. 66; 67
The Principal Rivers of Wales Illustrated.... London: 1813. V. 62; 63; 67
The Principles and Practice of Sketching Landscape Scenery from Nature, Systematically Arranged and Illustrated.... London: 1824-1825. V. 67

WOOD, LAWSON
Gran 'Pops' Annual. London: 1940. V. 64
Lawson Wood's Annual. London: 1951. V. 65
The Old Nursery Rhymes. London: 1933. V. 64

WOOD LEA PRESS
Omega Cuts. Woodbridge: 1998. V. 65

WOOD, M. E.
Laurence and Eleanor Hutton, Their Books of Association. New York: 1905. V. 66

WOOD, MAJOR
Nullification Speech of Major Wood, of M'Intosh County, on Chappell's Nullifying Resolutions, in the Senate of Georgia, November 26, 1833. Savannah: 1834. V. 63

WOOD, MARY ANNE EVERETT
Letters of Royal and Illustrious Ladies of Great Britain, from the Commencement of the Twelfth Century to the Close of the Reign of Queen Mary. London: 1846. V. 67

WOOD, NICHOLAS
A Practical Treatise on Rail-Roads and Interior Communication in General, Etc. Philadelphia: 1832. V. 64

WOOD, NORMAN B.
Lives of Famous Indian Chiefs. Aurora: 1906. V. 65

WOOD, R. E.
Life and Confessions of James Gilbert Jenkins: the Murderer of Eighteen Men. Napa City: 1864. V. 66

WOOD, RAYMOND F.
California's Aqua Fria. Fresno: 1954. V. 63

WOOD, RICHARD G.
Stephen Harriman Long 1784-1864. Glendale: 1966. V. 67

WOOD, ROBERT
Les Ruines de Palmyre, Autrement dite Tedmor au Desert. London: 1753. V. 67

WOOD, T. MARTIN
George du Maurier - The Satirist of the Victorians - a Review of His Art and Personality. London: 1913. V. 64; 67

WOOD, T. W.
Curiosities of Ornithology. London. V. 63
Curiosities of Ornithology. 1871. V. 67

WOOD, T. W., & SONS
Seeds and Bulbs for Fall Planting. Richmond: 1903. V. 64

WOOD, THOMAS
An Institute of the Laws of England. London: 1724. V. 65

WOOD, W. D.
A Partial Roster of the Officers and Men Raised in Leon County, Texas. Waco: 1963. V. 62; 63

WOOD, WALTER
The Northumberland Rusiliers. London: 1900. V. 62

WOOD, WILLIAM
Book-Keeping Familiarised; or, the Young Clerk's Manufacturer's and Shop-Keeper's Directory. Birmingham: 1784. V. 65
The History and Antiquities of Eyam; with a Full and Particular Account of the Great Plague, Which Desolated that Village A.D. 1666. London: 1842. V. 63
Index Entomologicus.... 1845. V. 66
Index Testaceologicus. 1818. V. 62
Index Testaceologicus. London: 1818. V. 62
Index Testaceologicus. 1856. V. 66
Index Testaceologicus. London: 1856. V. 62
Index Testacologicus. London: 1828. V. 62
A Survey of Trade. London: 1718. V. 64
A Survey of Trade. London: 1722. V. 66

WOOD, WILLIAM NATHANIEL
Reminiscences of Big I. Charlottesville: 1909. V. 62; 63; 65
Reminiscences of Big I. Jackson: 1956. V. 62; 63

WOODBRIDGE, SALLY B.
Bernard Maybeck, Visionary Architect. New York: 1992. V. 62; 65

WOODBRIDGE, WILLIAM C.
School Atlas to Accompany Woodbridge's Rudiments of Geography. Atlas on a New Plan, Exhibiting the Prevailing Religions.... Hartford: 1822. V. 64

WOODBURN, SAMUEL
The Lawrence Gallery, 9th and 10th Exhibitions Only. London: 1836. V. 62; 64

WOODBURY, AUGUSTUS
Major General Ambrose E. Burnside and the Ninth Army Corps. Providence: 1867. V. 65

WOODCOCK, A. W. W.
Golden Days. Salisbury: 1951. V. 67

WOODCOCK, GEORGE
Imagine the South. Pasadena: 1947. V. 65

WOODCROFT, B.
Patents for Inventions. Abridgments of Specifications Relating to Printing. London: 1859. V. 66

WOODFORD, A. F. A.
Kenning's Masonic Cyclopaedia and Handbook of Masonic Archaeology, History and Biography. London: 1878. V. 63

WOODFORDE, JAMES
Diary of a Country Parson; the Reverend James Woodforde. 1758-1781. London: 1926-1931. V. 63
Woodforde: Passages from the Five Volumes of the Diary of a Country Parson, 1758-1802. London: 1935. V. 62
Woodforde. Passages from the Five Volumes of the Diary of a Country Parson, 1758-1802. New York: 1935. V. 63

WOODHOUSE, A. S. P.
Puritanism and Liberty, Being the Army Debates (1647-49).... London: 1965. V. 64

WOODHOUSE, HENRY
Textbook Applied Aeronautic Engineering. New York: 1920. V. 63

WOODHOUSE, JAMES
Poems on Sundry Occasions. London: 1764. V. 62
Poems on Sundry Occasions. London: 1766. V. 63

WOODHOUSE, L. G. O.
Butterfly Fauna of Ceylon. Colombo: 1950. V. 62
The Butterfly Fauna of Ceylon. Colombo: 1951. V. 63

WOODHOUSE, ROBERT
A Treatise on Plane and Spherical Trigonometry. London: 1809. V. 65

WOODHOUSE, S. C.
Cats at School. London: 1913. V. 63

WOODHULL, VICTORIA C.
The Origin, Tendencies and Principles of Government.... New York: 1871. V. 62

WOODMAN, JOHN
The Rat-Catcher at Chelsea College. London: 1740. V. 62

WOODRELL, DANIEL
Muscle for the Wing. New York: 1988. V. 67
The Ones You Do. New York: 1992. V. 67
Under the Bright Lights. New York: 1986. V. 64; 65; 67
Woe to Live On. 1987. V. 66

WOODRING, W. P.
Geology of the Republic of Haiti. Port-au-Prince: 1924. V. 62

WOODROFFE, BENJAMIN
A Sermon Preach'd May 23 1700 At Feckenham in Leicester-Shire Before the Trustees Appointed by Thomas Cookes, Bart. Oxford: 1700. V. 67

WOODRUFF, ELIZABETH
Stories from a Magic World. Springfield: 1938. V. 63

WOODRUFF, FRANCIS E.
The Woodruffs of New Jersey, Who Came from Fordwich, Kent, England, by Way of Lynn, Massachusetts and Southampton, Long Island. New York: 1909. V. 63; 66

WOODRUFF, WILLIAM EDWARD
With the Light Guns in '61-65: Reminiscences of Eleven Arkansas, Missouri and Texas Light Batteries in the Civil War. Little Rock: 1903. V. 62; 63; 65

WOODRUFFE, ELIZABETH
Dickey Byrd. Springfield: 1928. V. 63

WOODS, ALVA
Intellectual and Moral Culture. Lexington: 1828. V. 64

WOODS, DANIEL B.
Sixteen Months at the Gold Diggins. New York: 1851. V. 62; 63; 65

WOODS, FREDERICK
A Bibliography of the Works of Sir Winston Churchill. London: 1963. V. 64

WOODS, GARY DOYLE
The Hicks Adams Bass Floyd Patillo and Collateral Lines 1840 1868. Salado: 1963. V. 64

WOODS, GEORGE
An Account of the Past and Present State of the Isle of Man.... London: 1811. V. 63

WOODS, JAMES
California Recollections - Recollections of Pioneer Work in California. San Francisco: 1878. V. 65
Recollections of Pioneer Work in California. San Francisco: 1878. V. 62; 65

WOODS, MARGARET LOUISA
Esther Vanhomrigh. London: 1891. V. 65

WOODS, SHIRLEY
Angling for Atlantic Salmon. Goshen: 1976. V. 63

WOODS, STUART
Chiefs. 1981. V. 64; 66
Chiefs. New York: 1981. V. 65; 66; 67
Grass Roots. New York: 1989. V. 67
Run Before the Wind. New York: 1983. V. 62; 65; 66

WOODSON, CARTER G.
The History of the Negro Church. Washington: 1945. V. 67

WOODVILLE, W.
Medical Botany.... 1810. V. 62

WOODWARD, A.
A Review of Uncle Tom's Cabin, or an Essay on Slavery. Cincinnati: 1853. V. 67

WOODWARD, A. S.
Catalogue of the Fossil Fishes in the British Museum. London: 1889-1901. V. 62
On the Palaeontology of Sturgeons. 1890. V. 67

WOODWARD, ASHBEL
Life of General Nathaniel Lyon. Hartford: 1862. V. 67

WOODWARD, B. B.
The History of Wales, from the Earliest Times, to Its Final Incorporation with the Kingdom of England.... London: 1853. V. 62; 66

WOODWARD, CHARLES L.
Bibliothica (sic)--Scallawagiana. Catalogue of a Matchless Collection of Books, Pamphlets, Autographs...Relating to Mormonism and the Mormons. New York: 1880. V. 63

WOODWARD, E. M.
History of Burlington and Mercer Counties, New Jersey with Biographical Sketches of Many of Their Pioneers and Prominent Men. Philadelphia: 1883. V. 63; 66

WOODWARD, GEORGE MOUTARD
Something Concerning Nobody. London: 1814. V. 63

WOODWARD, GRACE STEELE
The Cherokees. Norman: 1963. V. 66

WOODWARD, H. B.
The Geology of the Country Near Sidmouth and Lyme Regis. Sheets 326 and 340. 1906. V. 66
The Jurassic Rocks of Britain. Volumes III-IV. 1893-1894. V. 62
Stanford's Geological Atlas of Great Britain and Ireland with Plates of Characteristic Fossils. E. Stanford: 1913. V. 62

WOODWARD, HENRY
British Carboniferous Trilobites. London: 1883-1884. V. 67

WOODWARD, J. J.
The Medical and Surgical History of the War of the Rebellion 1861- 1865. Washington: 1870-1888. V. 64; 66

WOODWARD, JOHN
An Essay Towards a Natural History of the Earth and Terrestrial Bodies, Especially Minerals. London: 1695. V. 64
An Essay Towards a Natural History of the Earth and Terrestrial Bodies, Especially Minerals. London: 1723. V. 62
An Essay Towards a Natural History of the Earth and Terrestrial Bodyes.... London: 1723. V. 66
A Treatise on Ecclesiastical History. London: 1894. V. 63
A Treatise on Heraldry, British and Foreign, with English and French Glossaries. London: 1892. V. 63

WOODWARD, JOSEPH J.
Outlines of the Chief Camp Diseases of the United States Armies as Observed During the Present War. Philadelphia: 1863. V. 67

WOODWARD, JOSIAH
An Account of the Societies for Reformation of Manners in England and Ireland. (and) An Account of the Progress of the Formation of Manners, In England, Scotland, and Ireland and Other Parts of Europe and America. London: 1701-1706. V. 65
An Account of the Societies for Reformation of Manners, in London and Westminster and Other Parts of Kingdom. London: 1699. V. 64

WOODWARD, KATHLEEN
Jipping Street. Childhood in a London Slum. London: 1928. V. 66

WOODWARD, S. P.
A Manual of the Mollusca Being a Treatise on Recent and Fossil Shells. 1880. V. 67
A Manual of the Mullusca, Being a Treatise on Recent and Fossil Shells. London: 1890. V. 63

WOODWARD, SAMUEL
An Outline of the Geology of Norfolk. Norwich: 1833. V. 66

WOODWORTH, ROBERT B.
The Descendants of Robert and John Poage (Pioneer Settlers in Augusta County, Virginia). Staunton: 1954. V. 62

WOODY, CLARA T.
Globe, Arizona. Tucson: 1977. V. 64

WOOFTER, T. J.
Black Yeomanry: Life on St. Helena Island. New York: 1930. V. 63

WOOLDRIDGE, CLIFTON R.
Hands Up! In the World of Crime. Chicago: 1901. V. 65

WOOLDRIDGE, S. W.
The Weald. London: 1953. V. 63

WOOLER, JONATHAN
Every Man His Own Attorney. London: 1840?. V. 66

WOOLER, STEPHEN
Ebbing and Flowing. Accrington: 1935. V. 64; 65

WOOLER, THOMAS JONATHAN
A Verbatim Report of the Two Trials of T. J. Wooler, Editor of the Black Dwarf, for Alleged Libels.... London: 1917. V. 63

WOOLEY, L. H.
California 1849-1913, or the Rambling Sketches and Experiences of Sixty-Four Years' Residence in that State. Oakland: 1913. V. 63; 66

WOOLF, CECIL
Authors Take Sides on Vietnam - Two Questions on the War in Vietnam Answered by the Authors of Several Nations. London: 1967. V. 65; 66
A Bibliography of Frederick Rolfe, Baron Corvo. London: 1957. V. 67
A Bibliography of Norman Douglas. London: 1954. V. 67
New Quests for Corvo. London: 1965. V. 67

WOOLF, DOUGLAS
Spring of the Lamb, a Tale. N.P: 1972. V. 63

WOOLF, LEONARD
The Future of Constantinople. London: 1917. V. 65
The Journey Not the Arrival Matters: an Autobiography of the Years 1939-1969. London: 1969. V. 66

WOOLF, VIRGINIA
Between the Acts. London: 1941. V. 62; 65; 66
Between the Acts. New York: 1941. V. 62; 67
The Captain's Death Bed and Other Essays. London: 1950. V. 63; 66
The Captain's Death Bed and Other Essays. New York: 1950. V. 62; 66; 67
The Common Reader - Second Series. London: 1932. V. 65; 67
The Diaries of Virginia Woolf. London: 1977-1984. V. 63; 67
Flush - a Biography. London: 1933. V. 62; 65
Flush: a Biography. New York: 1933. V. 62
Granite and Rainbow. London: 1958. V. 65
A Haunted House and Other Stories. London: 1943. V. 62
Jacob's Room. New York: 1923. V. 63
Jacobs Run. Stockholm: 1927. V. 62
Journal d'un Ecrivain. (A Writer's Diary). Monaco: 1958. V. 67

WOOLF, VIRGINIA continued
A Letter to a Young Poet. London: 1932. V. 62
The Letters of Virginia Woolf. London: 1975-1980. V. 63; 65; 67
Mr. Bennett and Mrs. Brown. London: 1924. V. 62
The Moment and Other Essays. London: 1947. V. 62; 64; 65
Monday or Tuesday. London: 1921. V. 64
On Being Ill. N.P: 1930. V. 62
Orlando: a Biography. London: 1928. V. 66
Reviewing. London: 1939. V. 62; 67
A Room of One's Own. London: 1929. V. 64; 67
Street Haunting. San Francisco: 1930. V. 65; 66
Three Guineas. London: 1938. V. 62; 65; 67
To the Lighthouse. London: 1927. V. 67
To the Lighthouse. New York: 1927. V. 62; 67
Virginia Woolf and Lytton Strachey: Letters. London: 1956. V. 67
The Voyage Out. London: 1920. V. 65
Walter Sickert: a Conversation. London: 1934. V. 62
The Waves. London: 1931. V. 62; 62; 64; 67
A Writer's Diary. London: 1953. V. 62; 63; 66
The Years. London: 1937. V. 62; 63; 64

WOOLHOUSE, WESLEY STOKER BARKER
Essay on Musical Intervals, Harmonics and the Temperament of the Musical Scale &c. London: 1835. V. 65

WOOLLCOTT, ALEXANDER
Chateau Thierry - A Friendly Guide for American Pilgrims to the Shrines Between the Marine and the Vesle. Paris: 1919. V. 64
The Woolcott Reader: By Paths in the Realms of God (&) Second Reader. New York: 1935-1937. V. 65
The Woollcott Reader, Bypaths in the Realms of Gold. New York: 1935. V. 67

WOOLLEY, A.
The Fly-Fisher's Flies. 1938. V. 67

WOOLLEY, D. W.
A Study of Antimetabolites. New York: 1952. V. 63

WOOLLEY, LEONARD
A Report on the Work of the Archaeological Survey of India. London: 1939. V. 64

WOOLLEY, ROGER
Modern Trout Fly Dressing. 1932. V. 67
Modern Trout Fly Dressing. 1950. V. 67

WOOLMAN, JOHN
Serious Considerations on Various Subjects of Importance. London: 1773. V. 65
Serious Considerations on Various Subjects of Importance. New York: 1805. V. 66
The Works of John Woolman. Philadelphia: 1775. V. 63; 66

WOOLNER, THOMAS
My Beautiful Lady. London: 1863. V. 62

WOOLNOTH, THOMAS
The Study of the Human Face. London: 1865. V. 67

WOOLNOUGH, C. W.
A Pretty Mysterious Art. A Lecture to the Royal Society of Arts. London: 1996. V. 64

WOOLRICH, CORNELL
Angels of Darkness. New York: 1978. V. 63; 65; 66; 67
Beyond the Night. New York: 1959. V. 67
The Bride Wore Black. New York: 1940. V. 65
Darkness at Dawn. Carbondale: 1985. V. 66
Deadline at Dawn. London: 1947. V. 66
4 by Cornell Woolrich. London: 1983. V. 65; 66
Hotel Room. New York: 1958. V. 65; 66; 67
I Married a Dead Man. 1948. V. 66
If I Should Die Before I Wake. New York: 1945. V. 66
Night Has a Thousand Eyes. New York: 1945. V. 67
Nightwebs. New York: 1971. V. 65; 66
Phantom Lady. Philadelphia: 1942. V. 62
The Ten Faces of Cornell Woolrich. New York: 1965. V. 63

WOOLRYCH, HUMPHRY W.
The History and Results of the Present Capital Punishments in England.... London: 1832. V. 63

WOOLSEY, GAMEL
Death's Other Kingdom. London: 1939. V. 66

WOOLSEY, THEODORE D.
Communism and Socialism in Their History and Theory. New York: 1880. V. 66

WOOLSON, CONSTANCE FENIMORE
Horace Chase. A Novel. New York: 1894. V. 66
Rodman the Keeper: Southern Sketches. New York: 1880. V. 67

WOOSTER, DAVID
Alpine Plants. 1874. V. 63; 66; 67
Alpine Plants: Figures and Descriptions of Some of the Most Striking and Beautiful of the Alpine Flowers. (First and Second Series). London: 1874. V. 62; 66

WOOSTER, ROBERT
Recollections of Western Texas. Austin: 1995. V. 64

WOOTEN, MATTIE LLOYD
Women Tell the Story of the Southwest. San Anonio: 1940. V. 64; 67

WORCESTER, DEAN C.
The Philippines Past and Present. New York: 1930. V. 65

WORCESTER, EDWARD SOMERSET, MARQUIS OF
A Century of the Names and Scantlings of Such Inventions as At Present I Can Call to Mind to Have Tried and Perfected, Which (My Former Notes Being Lost) I Have, at the Instance of a Powerful Friend, Endeavoured Now in the Year 1655.... London: 1663. V. 65

WORCESTER, G. R. G.
The Junks and Sampans of the Yangtze. Annapolis: 1971. V. 64
Sail and Sweep in China. London: 1966. V. 62; 64; 67

WORCESTER, JOSEPH E.
Dictionary of the English Language. London: 1860. V. 62

WORDE, WYNKYN DE
A Short Account of the Life and Work of Wynkyn de Worde: with a Leaf from the Golden Legend Printed by Him at the Sign of the Sun in Fleet Street, London, the Year 1527. San Francisco: 1949. V. 64

WORDEN, FREDERIC GARFIELD
The Neurosciences: Paths of Discovery. Volume II. Boston Basel Berlin: 1992. V. 65

WORDSWORTH, CHRISTOPHER
Greece: Pictorial, Descriptive and Historical. London: 1853. V. 66
Greece: Pictorial, Descriptive and Historical. London: 1871. V. 65
Reasons for Declining to Become a Subscriber to the British and Foreign Bible Society, Stated in a Letter to the Clergyman of the Diocese of London. London: 1810. V. 65

WORDSWORTH, DOROTHY
Journals of Dorothy Wordsworth. London: 1941. V. 64; 65; 66
Journals of Dorothy Wordsworth. New York: 1941. V. 62
Recollections of a Tour Made in Scotland, A.D. 1803. Edinburgh: 1874. V. 62

WORDSWORTH, G. G.
Some Notes on the Wordsworths of Peniston and Their Aumbry. Ambleside: 1929. V. 66

WORDSWORTH, WILLIAM
A Decade of Years. Poems by William Wordsworth 1798-1807. Hammersmith: 1911. V. 65
A Description of the Scenery of the Lakes in the North of England. London: 1822. V. 66
A Description of the Scenery of the Lakes in the North of England. London: 1823. V. 66
Ecclesiastical Sketches. London: 1822. V. 67
The Excursion, Being a Portion of the Recluse, a Poem. London: 1814. V. 62; 67
A Guide through the District of the Lakes in the North of England, With a Description of the Scenery.... Kendal: 1835. V. 64; 66
Imitations of Immortality from Recollections of Early Childhood. 1991. V. 65
Lyrical Ballads. London: 1798-1800. V. 64
Lyrical Ballads, with a Few Other Poems. London: 1798. V. 62; 67
Lyrical Ballads, with Other Poems. London: 1800. V. 64; 67
Memorials of a Tour on the Continent, 1820. London: 1822. V. 62
The Miscellaneous Poems. London: 1820. V. 67
Ode on Intimations of Immortality. London: 1913. V. 66
Peter Bell, a Tale in Verse. London: 1819. V. 67
Poems. London: 1807. V. 62; 63; 67
The Poems. London: 1845. V. 62
Poems. 1902. V. 62; 67
The Poems. London: 1908. V. 64
Poems, in Two Volumes. London: 1807. V. 62; 64; 67
Poems: Including Lyrical Ballads and the Miscellaneous Pieces of the Author. London: 1815. V. 67
The Poetical Works. Paris: 1828. V. 62
The Poetical Works. London: 1832. V. 65
The Poetical Works. London: 1836. V. 62
Poetical Works. London: 1843. V. 64
The Poetical Works. London: 1849. V. 65
Poetical Works. London: 1892-1893. V. 67
The Prelude. London: 1850. V. 62; 63; 64; 67
The Prelude. London: 1926. V. 62
Selected Poems. 1987. V. 67
Selections from the Poems of William Wordsworth. London: 1834. V. 67
The Sonnets of.... London: 1838. V. 63
The Waggoner, a Poem. London: 1819. V. 67
Yarrow Revisited, and Other Poems. London: 1835. V. 62; 63; 65

WORK, JOHN
The Journal of John Work. Cleveland: 1923. V. 65; 67
The Journal of John Work, January to October 1835. Victoria: 1945. V. 63; 66

WORK, JOHN WESLEY
Folk Song of the American Negro. Nashville: 1915. V. 63; 66

WORK, MONROE
A Bibliography of the Negro in Africa and America. 1998. V. 65
Negro Year Book and Annual Encyclopedia of the Negro. Tuskegee Inst: 1913. V. 66

A WORKE for the Wisely Considerate. In Three Distinct Parts. London: 1641. V. 66

THE WORKINGTON Iron and Steel Company. 1914. V. 65

WORKMAN, FANNY BULLOCK
Ice Bound Heights of the Mustagh. 1908. V. 63; 65

WORKMAN, FANNY BULLOCK continued
In the Ice World of Himalaya. London: 1900. V. 63; 65
In the Ice World of Himalaya. New York: 1901. V. 65

WORKMAN, HERBERT B.
John Wyclif. A Study of the English Medieval Church. Hamden: 1966. V. 67

WORKMAN, WILLIAM HUNTER
The Call of the Snowy Hispar. London: 1910. V. 62

THE WORKS of the Most Celebrated Minor Poets...Never Before Collected and Publish'd Together. (with) A Supplement.... London: 1749-1750. V. 66

THE WORLD of Fashion and Continental Feuilletons.... London: 1835. V. 66

WORLD ORCHID CONFERENCE
Proceedings of the 10th World Orchid Conference. Johannesburg: 1982. V. 63
Proceedings of the 12th World Orchid Conference. Tokyo: 1987. V. 63
Proceedings of the 7th World Orchid Conference. Medellin: 1974. V. 63
Proceedings of the 9th World Orchid Conference. Bangkok: 1980. V. 63

THE WORLD Turned Upside Down, or No News and Strange News. York: 1820. V. 66

THE WORLD'S Great Detective Stories. New York. V. 65

WORLIDGE, JOHN
Dictionarium Rusticum, Urbanicum and Botanicum; or a Dictionary of Husbandry, Gardening, Trade, Commerece, and All Sorts of Country Affairs.... London: 1717. V. 62
Systema Agriculturae; the Mystery of Husbandry Discovered.... London: 1675. V. 66; 67
Systema Horti-culturae; or, the Art of Gardening. London: 1683. V. 64
Systema Horti-Culturae; or the Art of Gardening. In Three Books. London: 1688. V. 66

WORMALD, FRANCIS
The Winchester Psalter. London: 1973. V. 62

WORMLEY, THEODORE G.
Micro-Chemistry of Poisons, Including Their Physiological, Pathological and Legal Relations.... New York: 1867. V. 62

WORMS, HENRY
The Earth and Its Mechanism: Being an Account of the Various Proofs of the Rotation of the Earth. London: 1862. V. 65

WORRELL, JOHN
A Diamond in the Rough, Embracing Anecdote, Biography, Romance and History. Indianapolis. 1906. V. 63; 66

WORSAAE, J. J. A.
The Primeval Antiquities of Denmark. London: 1849. V. 64

WORSDELL, W. C.
Principles of Plant-Teratology. London: 1915-1916. V. 63

WORSFOLD, J. N.
History of Haddlesey: Its Past and Present. London: 1894. V. 65

WORSHAM, JOHN HENRY
One of Jackson's Foot Cavalry, His Experience and What He Saw During the War 1861-1865.... New York: 1912. V. 62; 63

WORSLEY, ISRAEL
Observations on the State and Changes in the Presbyterian Societies of England During the Last Half Century.... London: 1816. V. 63

WORSNOP, THOMAS
The Prehistoric Arts, Manufactures, Works, Weapons, Etc., of the Aborigines of Australia. South Australia: 1897. V. 64; 66

WORSTER, BENJAMIN
A Compendious and Methodical Account of the Principles of Natural Philosophy. London: 1730. V. 63; 65; 67

WORTH, BONNIE
Peter Cottontail's Surprise. Parsippany: 1985. V. 65

WORTH, MAURICE, PSEUD.
The Pagoda Mystery. London. 1928. V. 66

WORTH, PATIENCE
The Sorry Tale, a Story of the Time of Christ. New York: 1917. V. 65

THE WORTHINGTON Iron and Steel Company. London: 1914. V. 62

WORTHINGTON, THOMAS
Shiloh, or the Tennessee Campaign of 1862.... Washington City: 1872. V. 62

WORTHINGTON, W. H.
Portraits of the Sovereigns of England. London: 1824. V. 62

WORTHY PAPER COMPANY
A New Showing of Six Worthy Papers, Roxburgh, Aurelian, Georgian, Marlowe, Dacian, Hadrian. Massachusetts. V. 62

WOTTON, HENRY
A Parallel Between Robert Late Earle of Essex and George Late Duke of Buckingham.... London: 1641. V. 66
Poems. London: 1845. V. 67
Reliquiae Wottonianae.... London: 1651. V. 62
Reliquiae Wottonianae.... London: 1685. V. 65
The State of Christendom; or, a Most Exact and Curious Discovery of Many Secret Passages and Hidden Mysteries of the Times.... London: 1657. V. 63

WOTTON, WILLIAM
Cyfreithjeu Hywel Dda ac Eraill, seu Leges Wallicae Ecclesiasticae & Civiles Hoeli Boni et Aliorum Walliae Principum. London: 1730. V. 63
Reflections Upon Ancient and Modern Learning. London: 1697. V. 65

WOTY, WILLIAM
The Shrubs of Parnassus. London: 1760. V. 66

WOUK, HERMAN
The Caine Mutiny. Franklin Center: 1977. V. 67
The Caine Mutiny Court Martial - a Play. London: 1955. V. 65
Don't Stop the Carnival. Garden City: 1965. V. 62
Inside, Outside. Boston: 1985. V. 63; 64; 66
Marjorie Morningstar. Franklin Center: 1981. V. 67

WOULFE, STEPHEN
A Letter to a Protestant; or, the Balance of Evils.... Dublin: 1825. V. 66

WOUVERMAN, PHILIPPE
Oeuvres.... Paris: 1737. V. 64

WRATISLAW, A. H.
Sixty Folk-Tales from Exclusively Slavonic Sources. London: 1889. V. 64

WRATISLAW, THEODORE
Algernon Charles Swinburne: a Study. London: 1900. V. 64
Caprices. London: 1893. V. 66
Three Nineties Studies: W. B. Yeats, John Gray, Aubrey Beardsley. Edinburgh: 1980. V. 64

WRAXALL, NATHANIEL WILLIAM
Historical Memoirs of My Own Time. London: 1815. V. 64
The History of France, Under the Kings of the Race of Valois.... London: 1785. V. 67
Memoirs of the Courts of Berlin, Dresden, Warsaw and Vienna in the Years 1777, 1778 and 1779. London: 1800. V. 66
Posthumous Memoirs of His Own Time. London: 1836. V. 66

WRAY, MARY
The Ladies Library. London: 1714. V. 65

THE WRECK of the London. London: 1866. V. 64

WREN, CHRISTOPHER
Parentalia; or Memoirs of the Family of the Wrens. London: 1750. V. 64
Sir Christopher Wren A.D. 1632-1723. London: 1923. V. 62

WREN, PERCIVAL CHRISTOPHER
Mysterious Waye. New York: 1930. V. 65; 67

WRIFFORD, ALLISON
A New Plan of Writing Copies with Accompanying Explanations.... Boston: 1810. V. 64; 67
A New Plan of Writing Copies with Accompanying Explanations.... Boston: 1813. V. 67

WRIGHT, ALAN
Mrs. Bunnikins Busy Day. 1919. V. 65

WRIGHT, ALBERT HAZEN
Handbook of Snakes of the United States and Canada. Ithaca: 1957. V. 65
Handbook of Snakes of the United States and Canada. Ithaca: 1957-1961. V. 62

WRIGHT, ALMROTH E.
On the Nature of the Physiological Element in Emotion. 1895. V. 67
The Unexpurgated Case Against Woman Suffrage. New York: 1913. V. 63

WRIGHT, AUSTIN TAPPAN
Islandia. 1942. V. 67
Islandia. New York: 1942. V. 62; 63

WRIGHT, BARTON
The Hopi Photographs. Kate Cory 1905-1912. La Canada: 1986. V. 63
Kachinas: a Hopi Artist's Documentary. Flagstaff: 1973. V. 63
Kachinas of the Zuni. Flagstaff: 1985. V. 62; 66
Patterns and Sources of Zuni Kachinas. N.P: 1988. V. 64

WRIGHT, C.
Darwinism; Being an Examination of Mr. St. George Mivart's Genesis of Species.... London: 1871. V. 67
The History and Description of Arundel Castle, Sussex; the Seat of His Grace the Duke of Norfolk. London: 1818. V. 66
Poussin: Paintings: a Catalog Raisonne. New York: 1984. V. 65

WRIGHT, C. J.
Sir Robert Cotton as Collector. London: 1997. V. 62

WRIGHT, CECIL N.
Instrumental Music in Christian Workshop. Springfield: 1900. V. 65

WRIGHT, CHARLES
Bloodlines. Middletown: 1975. V. 62; 64
Colophons. Poems. Iowa City: 1977. V. 62; 64; 67
Dead Color. San Francisco: 1980. V. 62
Five Journals. New York: 1986. V. 64; 67
The Grave of the Right Hand. Middletown: 1970. V. 63; 66
Hard Freight. Middletown: 1973. V. 62
A Journal of the Year of the Ox. Iowa City: 1988. V. 64
The Messenger. New York: 1963. V. 65
Moments of the Italian Summer. Washington: 1976. V. 67
Private Madrigals. Madison: 1969. V. 62; 64; 67

WRIGHT, CHARLES continued
The Venice Notebook. Boston: 1971. V. 62; 64; 67
Xionia. Poems. Iowa City: 1990. V. 62; 64
Yard Journal. Poem. Richmond: 1986. V. 62; 64; 67

WRIGHT, DARE
The Doll and the Kitten. Garden City: 1960. V. 63
Edith and Little Bear Lend a Hand. New York: 1972. V. 63
Edith and Midnight. Garden City: 1978. V. 63
Edith and Mr. Bear. New York: 1964. V. 65
Edith and the Duckling. Garden City: 1981. V. 63
Holiday for Edith and the Bears. Garden City: 1958. V. 62; 64

WRIGHT, E. P.
Challenger Voyage. Zoology. Parts 64 and 81. Alcyonaria with Supplement. 1889. V. 66
Specilegia Biologica; or Papers on Zoological and Botanical Subjects...Part I.... 1870. V. 67

WRIGHT, E. W.
Lewis and Dryden's Marine History of the Pacific Northwest. New York: 1961. V. 66

WRIGHT, ED
Pardners. New York: 1958. V. 64; 67
The Representative Old Cowboy, Ed Wright. N.P: 1954. V. 67

WRIGHT, EDWARD
Some Observations Made in Travelling through France, Italy &c. in the Years 1720, 1721 and 1722. London: 1730. V. 67
Some Observations Made in Travelling through France, Italy &c. in the Years MDCCXX, MDCCXXI, and MDCCXXII.... London: 1764. V. 64

WRIGHT, EDWIN
Sketches in Bedlam; or Characteristic Traits of Insanity, as Displayed in the Cases of One Hundred and Forty Patients of Both Sexes.... London: 1823. V. 65

WRIGHT, ELIZABETH
Independence in All Things, Neutrality in Nothing - the Story of a Pioneer Journalist of the American West. San Francisco: 1973. V. 67
The Life of Joseph Wright. London: 1932. V. 64; 67

WRIGHT, ELIZABETH MARY
Rustic Speech and Folk-Lore. London: 1913. V. 64

WRIGHT, FRANCES
Views of Society and Manners in America.... New York: 1821. V. 65

WRIGHT, FRANCIS
Proceedings in the Court of King's Bench, on the Trial of an Action Brought by Francis Wright, Upholsterer, Against Colonel Wardle for the Furniture.... London: 1809. V. 63

WRIGHT, FRANK LLOYD
Architecture and Modern Life. New York: 1938. V. 66
An Autobiography. New York: 1938. V. 66
Autobiography. New York: 1943. V. 63
An Autobiography. London: 1945. V. 64
Drawings for a Living Architecture. New York: 1959. V. 62; 63; 64; 66
Frank Lloyd Wright on Architecture - Selected Writings 1894-1940. New York: 1941. V. 67
The Future of Architecture. New York: 1953. V. 64; 65; 67
Genius and the Mobocracy. New York: 1949. V. 67
The Life Work of the American Architect Frank Lloyd Wright. Santpoort: 1925. V. 64; 66
The Story of the Tower. New York: 1956. V. 62
Taliesin Drawings. Recent Architecture of Frank Lloyd Wright.... New York: 1952. V. 63
A Testament. New York: 1957. V. 66

WRIGHT, G. N.
A Guide to the County Wicklow. 1827. V. 62
An Historical Guide to Ancient and Modern Dublin. 1821. V. 65
The Rhine, Italy and Greece in a Series of Sketches from Nature. London and Paris: 1841. V. 62
Scenes in North Wales with Historical Illustrations, Legends and Biographical Notices. London: 1833. V. 64

WRIGHT, GEORGE
The Complete Bird-Fancyer; or Bird-Fancyer's Recreation.... London: 1765?. V. 62

WRIGHT, GEORGE N.
The Life and Reign of William the Fourth. London: 1837. V. 64
The Life and Reign of William the Fourth. London: 1840. V. 64

WRIGHT, HAROLD B.
Long Ago Told - Legends of the Pagago Indians. New York: 1929. V. 65
The Uncrowned King. Chicago: 1910. V. 65

WRIGHT, HELEN
Sweeper in the Sky; the Life of Maria Mitchell, First Woman Astronomer in America. New York: 1950. V. 66

WRIGHT, HENRY
Rehousing Urban America. New York: 1935. V. 67

WRIGHT, HENRY G.
Headaches Their Causes and Their Cure. Philadelphia: 1867. V. 67

WRIGHT, IRENE A.
Further English Voyages to Spanish America 1583-1594. London: 1951. V. 64

WRIGHT, J. M. F.
A Commentary on Newton's Principia with Supplementaray Volume Designed for the Use of Students at the Universities. London: 1833. V. 65

WRIGHT, JAMES
The Green Wall. New Haven: 1957. V. 62; 63; 64
Moments of the Italian Summer. Washington and San Francisco: 1976. V. 64
Saint Judas. Middletown: 1959. V. 64
Two Citizens. New York: 1973. V. 62

WRIGHT, JIM
History of Clear Creek County: Tailings, Tracks and Tommyknockers. Denver: 1956. V. 66

WRIGHT, JOHN H.
Compendium of the Confederacy. Wilmington: 1989. V. 63

WRIGHT, JOHN MICHAEL
An Account of His Excellence Roger Earl of Castlemaine's Embassy, from His Sacred majesty the IId, King of England, Scotland, France and Ireland.... London: 1688. V. 62

WRIGHT, JOSEPH
The English Dialect Dictionary. London: 1898. V. 64; 67
The English Dialect Dictionary. London: 1898-1905. V. 63

WRIGHT, JULIA MC NAIR
Complete Home. Philadelphia: 1879. V. 62; 66

WRIGHT, L. B.
The Arts in America: The Colonial Period. New York: 1966. V. 65

WRIGHT, L. R.
The Suspect. New York: 1985. V. 63

WRIGHT, LAURIE
Fats in Fact, with a Memoir from Ernie Anderson (and other Contributors). Chigwell: 1992. V. 65
King Oliver. Chigwell: 1987. V. 65
Mr. Jelly Lord. Chigwell: 1980. V. 62; 65; 67

WRIGHT, LEWIS
The Microscope. A Practical Handbook. London: 1927. V. 67

WRIGHT, LOUISE WIGFALL
A Southern Girl in '61. New York: 1905. V. 63

WRIGHT, M. W.
Svenska Faglar efter Naturen och pa Sten Ritade. Stockholm: 1924-1929. V. 67

WRIGHT, MARCUS
Texas in the Civil War 1861-1865. Waco: 1965. V. 62; 63

WRIGHT, PAUL
The New and Complete Life of Our Blessed Lord and Saviour Jesus Christ. Winchester: 1816. V. 63; 64
The New and Complete Life of Our Blessed Lord and Saviour Jesus Christ. Winchester: 1818. V. 67

WRIGHT, PETER
A Three Foot Stool. New York: 1909. V. 63

WRIGHT, R. G.
The Ducks of India: Their Habits, Breeding Grounds and Migrations.... London: 1925. V. 65

WRIGHT, RICHARD
Black Boy. New York: 1945. V. 62; 65
Black Power - A Record of Reactions in a Land of Pathos. New York: 1954. V. 65
A Catalogue of the Library of Richard Wright, M.D. Fellow of the Royal Society.... London: 1787. V. 65
Lawd Today. New York: 1963. V. 65
The Long Dream. Garden City: 1958. V. 63
Native Son. London: 1940. V. 66
Native Son. New York: 1940. V. 62; 63
The Outsider. New York: 1953. V. 67
12 Million Black Voices. New York: 1941. V. 62
12 Million Black Voices. New York: 1946. V. 63
12 Million Black Voices. London: 1947. V. 63; 67
Uncle Tom's Children - Four Novellas. New York: 1938. V. 64

WRIGHT, RICHARDSON
Hawkers and Walkers in Early America. Philadelphia: 1927. V. 62; 66

WRIGHT, ROBERT M.
Dodge City, the Cowboy Capital and the Great Southwest in the Days of the Wild Indian, The Buffalo, The Cowboy Dance Halls, Gambling Halls and Bad Men. Wichita: 1913. V. 62; 67

WRIGHT, SAMUEL
A Sermon Preach'd at Black-Fryars to a Society of Young Men, Jan. 1, 1712. London: 1712. V. 65
A Treatise on Being Born Again, Without Which No Man Can Be Saved. Washington: 1818. V. 62

WRIGHT, STEPHEN
Meditations in Green. New York: 1983. V. 63; 65

WRIGHT, T.
The Formation and Management of Floated Meadows.... Northampton: 1808. V. 63
Some Account of the Life of Richard Wilson, Esq. R.A. London: 1824. V. 63

WRIGHT, THOMAS
The Anglo-Latin Satirical Poets and Epigrammatists of the Twelfth Century. London: 1872. V. 63

WRIGHT, THOMAS continued
The Antiquities of the Town of Halifax in Yorkshire. Leeds: 1738. V. 63; 64; 65
Dictionary of Obsolete and Provincial English.... London: 1857. V. 64
Dictionary of Obsolete and Provincial English.... London: 1880. V. 64
Essays On Archaeological Subjects, and on Various Questions Connected with the History of Art, Science and Literature in the Middle Ages. London: 1861. V. 66
Essays on Subjects Connected With the Literature, Popular Superstitions and History of England in the Middle Ages. London: 1846. V. 65
Historical and Descriptive Account of the Caricatures of James Gillray. London: 1851. V. 67
Historical Cartoons. London: 1868. V. 64
The History of France. London: 1862?. V. 65
An Original Theory or New Hyptothesis of the Universe, Founded Upon the Laws of Nature.... London: 1750. V. 66
The Passions of the Minde in Generall. London: 1630. V. 62
The Tale of the Basyn and the Frere and the Boy. London: 1836. V. 62

WRIGHT, WILLARD
A History of the Comstock Mines - Mineral And Agricultural Resources of the Silver Land. Virginia: 1889. V. 65

WRIGHT, WILLARD HUNTINGTON
The Bishop Murder Case. 1929. V. 66
The Bishop Murder Case. New York: 1929. V. 67
The Canary Murder Case. New York: 1927. V. 65
The Casino Murder Case. New York: 1934. V. 65; 66
The Dragon Murder Case. New York: 1933. V. 64; 65; 66; 67
The Garden Murder Case. New York: 1935. V. 62; 65
The Gracie Allen Murder Case. 1938. V. 66
The Gracie Allen Murder Case. New York: 1938. V. 64; 67
The Greene Murder Case. New York: 1928. V. 64
The Greene Murder Case. 1938. V. 66
The Kennel Murder Case. New York: 1933. V. 62; 65
The Kidnap Murder Case. New York: 1936. V. 67
The Scarab Murder Case. 1930. V. 66
The Scarab Murder Case. New York: 1930. V. 64

WRIGHT, WILLIAM
The Brontes in Ireland, or Facts Stranger than Fiction. London: 1893. V. 64
The Brontes in Ireland; or Facts Stranger Than Fiction. London: 1894. V. 65
History of the Big Bonanza.... Hartford & San Francisco: 1876. V. 63
On the Varieties of Deafness and Diseases of the Ear.... London: 1829. V. 67

WRIGHTE, WILLIAM
Grotesque Architecture, or, Rural Amusements Consisting of Plans, Elevations and Sections for Huts, Retreats, Summer and Winter Hermitages.... London: 1790. V. 64

WRIGLEY, AMMON
Old Lancashire Words and Folk Sayings. Stalybridge: 1940. V. 63; 65
Old Saddleworth Days and Other Sketches. Oldham: 1920. V. 65
Saddleworth Chronological Notes from 1200 to 1900. Stalybridge: 1940. V. 63; 65

WRIGLEY, HENRY E.
Special Report on the Petroleum of Pennsylvania.... Harrisburg: 1875. V. 64

WRITERS in Revolt: an Anthology. New York: 1963. V. 62

WRITERS Take Sides - Letters About the War in Spain from 418 American Authors. New York: 1938. V. 62

WRIXON, HENRY
Jacob Shumate of the People's March: a Voice from the Ranks. London: 1903. V. 64

WRONG, GEORGE M.
Louisbourg in 1745. Toronto: 1897. V. 63

WROOT, HERBERT F
Sources of Charlotte Bronte's Novels - Persons and Places. Shipley: 1935. V. 63; 65

WROTH, LAWRENCE C.
The Early Cartography of the Pacific. 1998. V. 65
A History of Printing in Colonial Maryland 1686-1776. Baltimore: 1922. V. 64

WROTH, WARWICK
The London Pleasure Gardens of the Eighteenth Century. Hamden: 1979. V. 63; 66

WULFECK, DOROTHY F.
Marriages of Some Virginia Residents 1607-1800. Baltimore: 1986. V. 64

WULFF, L.
The Atlantic Salmon. 1958. V. 67

WUNDERLICH, O. A.
Geschichte der Medicin Vorlesungen Gehalten zu Leipig in Sommersemester 1858. Stuttgart: 1859. V. 64

WUORIO, EVA-LIS
The Island of Fish in the Trees. Cleveland: 1962. V. 66
The Island of Fish in the Trees. London: 1962. V. 63

WURFFBAIN, JOHANN PAUL
Salamandrologia.... Nuremberg: 1683. V. 67

WURM, TED
Hetch Hetchy and Its Dam Railroad. Berkeley: 1973. V. 67

WURTENBERGER, F.
Mannerism: the European Style of the 16th Century. New York: 1963. V. 62; 65

WURTZ, CHARLES ADOLPHE
Lecons Elementaires de Chimie Moderne. Paris: 1871. V. 64
Lecons Elementaires de Chimie Moderne. Paris: 1879. V. 64
La Theorie Atomique. Paris: 1879. V. 64

WYAT, GEORGE
Extracts from the Life of the Virtuous, Christian and Renowned Queen Anne Boleigne. London: 1817. V. 63

WYAT-EDGELL, E.
Heredity: Being a Village Dialogue on Some Causes of Degeneracy in Our Race. London: 1878. V. 66

WYATT, CLAUDE W.
British Brids.... London: 1899. V. 67

WYATT, HORACE
Malice in Kulturland. London: 1914. V. 64
Malice in Kulturland. London: 1915. V. 64

WYATT, LEO
A Suite of Little Alphabets. 1988. V. 64

WYATT, M. D.
The Art of Illuminating as Practicsed in Europe from the Earliest Times. London: 1866. V. 67

WYATT, T.
Manual of Conchology.... New York: 1838. V. 66

WYATT, THOMAS
Memoirs of the Generals, Commodores, and Other Commanders Who Distinguished Themselves in the American Army and Navy During the Wars of the Revolution and 1812. Philadelphia: 1848. V. 64; 67

WYCHERLEY, WILLIAM
Miscellany Poems: as Satyrs, Epistles, Love-Verses, Songs, Sonnets, &c. London: 1704. V. 62; 64

THE WYCKOFF Family in America. Rutland: 1934. V. 63

WYCKOFF, WILLIAM C.
The Silk Goods of America: A Brief Account of the Recent Improvements and Advances of Silk Manufacture in the United States. New York: 1879. V. 63

WYCLYFFE, JOHN
The Last Age of the Church. Dublin: 1840. V. 62; 65

WYDLER, H.
Essai Monographique sur le Genre Scrofularia. Geneva: 1828. V. 66

WYETH, B. J.
Christiana's World. Boston: 1982. V. 62; 65
Wyeth at Kuerners. (and) Christina's World: Paintings and Pre-Studies of Andrew Wyeth. Boston: 1976-1982. V. 64

WYETH, JOHN
Wyeth's Repository of Sacred Music. Part Second. Harrisburgh: 1813. V. 64

WYETH, JOHN ALLAN
Life of General Nathan Bedford Forrest. New York: 1899. V. 65
Life of Lieutenant-General Nathan Bedford Forrest. New York: 1908. V. 64
A Textbook on Surgery. New York: 1887. V. 63; 64; 66
A Textbook on Surgery. New York: 1888. V. 67
With Sabre and Scalpel. The Autobiography of a Soldier and Surgeon. New York and London: 1914. V. 62; 63; 64; 66

WYETH, JOHN B.
Oregon; or, a Short History of a Long Journey from the Atlantic Ocean to the Region of the Pacific by Land. Cleveland: 1905. V. 64

WYETH, NATHANIEL J.
The Correspondence and Journals of... 1831-1836. Eugene: 1899. V. 62; 65; 66

WYLD, HENRY CECIL
The Place Names of Lancashire. London: 1911. V. 62; 63; 65

WYLD, JAMES
Notes to Accompany Mr. Wyld's Model of the Earth, Leicester Square. 1851. V. 63

WYLDE, AUGUSTUS B.
Modern Abyssinia. London: 1901. V. 63

WYLDE, JAMES
The Circle of Sciences. London: Sep. 1860. V. 62

WYLIE, ALEXANDER
Labour, Leisure and Luxury. London: 1887. V. 66

WYLIE, DONOVAN
32 Counties - Photographs of Ireland.... London: 1989. V. 63; 67

WYLIE, ELINOR
Angels and Earthly Creatures. Henley-on-Thames: 1928. V. 62
Angels and Earthly Creatures. New York: 1929. V. 62
Black Armour. New York: 1923. V. 62
Collected Poems of Elinor Wylie. New York: 1932. V. 62; 67
Jennifer Lorn: a Sedate Extravaganza. New York: 1923. V. 62
Mr. Hodge and Mr. Hazard. New York: 1928. V. 62
Mortal Image. London: 1927. V. 62
Nets to Catch the Wind. New York: 1921. V. 62; 63; 66
The Orphan Angel. New York: 1926. V. 62

WYLIE, ELINOR continued
Rondeau. A Windy Day. N.P: 1935?. V. 62
Trivial Breath. New York: 1928. V. 62
The Venetian Glass Nephew. New York: 1925. V. 62

WYLIE, J. A.
The Papacy: its History, Dogmas, Genius and Prospects: Being the Evangelical Alliance First Prize Essay on Popery. Edinburgh: 1852. V. 65

WYLIE, PHILIP
Babes and Sucklings. New York and London: 1929. V. 66

WYLIE, WILLIAM HOWIE
The Nottingham Hand-Book and Guide to Places of Interest in the Environs. Nottingham: 1857. V. 65
A Popular History of Nottingham. Nottingham: 1893. V. 65

WYLLIE, W. L.
Marine Painting in Water-Colour. London: 1901. V. 67

WYMAN, LELAND C.
Beautyway - A Navajo Ceremonial Texts Recorder. New York: 1957. V. 63; 64; 67
Blessingway. Tucson: 1970. V. 64
Southwest Indian Drypainting. Santa Fe/Albuquerque: 1983. V. 63; 67

WYNDHAM, CHARLES
Sketches of Cockermouth Castle, in the County of Cumberland. Carlisle: 1845. V. 66

WYNDHAM, FRANCIS M.
Wild Life on the Fields of Norway. London: 1861. V. 66

WYNDHAM, HENRY PENRUDDOCKE
A Tour through Monmouthshire and Wales, Made in the Months of June and July 1774. London: 1781. V. 67
A Tour through Monmouthshire and Wales, Made in the Months of June, and July, 1774. London: 1794. V. 66

WYNDHAM, JOHN
Consider Her Ways and Others. London: 1961. V. 64
The Day of the Triffids. London: 1951. V. 62; 64
The Kraken Wakes. London: 1953. V. 62
The Midwich Cuckoos. London: 1957. V. 63

WYNDHAM, NEVILLE
Travels through Europe. London: 1790?. V. 66; 67

WYNEGAERDE, ANTON VAN DEN
Spanish Cities of the Golden Age. Berkeley. V. 66

WYNN, MARCIA R.
Pioneer Family of Whiskey Flat. 1945. V. 62

WYNNE, ANTHONY
The Fourth Finger. Philadelphia: 1929. V. 65; 67

WYNNE, DAVID
The Sculpture of David Wynne 1968-1974. London: 1974. V. 62

WYNNE, JAMES
Private Libraries of New York. New York: 1860. V. 67

WYNNE, JOHN
An Abridgment of Mr. Locke's Essay Concerning Humane Understanding. London: 1700. V. 63

WYNNE, JOHN HUDDLESTONE
Choice Emblems, Natural, Historical, Fabulous, Moral and Divine; for the Improvement and Pastime of Youth.... London: 1788. V. 67
Tales for Youth: in Thirty Poems.... London: 1794. V. 62; 66

WYNNE, MAY
Patient Pat. Philadelphia: 1929. V. 64

WYNNE, RICHARD
Essays on Education by Milton, Locke and the Authors of the Spectator &c. London: 1761. V. 62

WYNNE, WILLIAM
The Life of Sir Leoline Jenkins, Judge of the High-Court of Admiralty, and Prerogative Court of Canterbury, &c.... London: 1724. V. 62

WYNTER, HARRIET
Scientific Instruments. New York: 1975. V. 67

WYNTER, JOHN
Cyclus Metasyncriticus; or, an Essay on Chronical Diseases, the Methods of Cure; and Herein, More Fully, Of the Medicinal Waters of Bath and Bristol, Their Several Virtues and Differences. London and Bath: 1725. V. 65
Of Bathing in the Hot Baths, at Bathe.... London: 1728. V. 62

WYOMING
Wyoming Historical Collection with Second Biennial Report of the State Historian. Cheyenne: 1923. V. 63

WYOMING (TERRITORY). GOVERNOR - 1878
Report of the Governor of Wyoming Territory Made to the Secretary of the Interior for the Year 1878. Washington: 1878. V. 67

WYOMING (TERRITORY). GOVERNOR - 1886
Message of Francis E. Warren - Governor to the Legislature of Wyoming, Ninth Assembly and Records of Territorial Officers Jan. 1886. Laramie: 1886. V. 63; 64

WYOMING - A
Guide to It's History, Highways and People. New York: 1941. V. 62; 65

WYOMING
Brand Book - 1919. Laramie: 1919. V. 64

WYOMING STOCK GROWERS' ASSOCIATION
Brand Book for 1885. Cheyenne: 1885. V. 64

WYSE, THOMAS
An Excursion in the Peloponnesus in the Year 1858. London: 1865. V. 62

WYSS, JOHANN DAVID
The Swiss Family Robinson. London: 1845. V. 65
The Swiss Family Robinson. London: 1950. V. 65

WYTHE COUNTY HISTORICAL SOCIETY
Wythe County Historical Review. Wytheville: 1972-1996. V. 65

WYTTENBACH, JOHN HUGH
The Stranger's Guide to the Roman Antiquities of the City of Treves, from the German of Professor John Hugh Wyttenbach.... London: 1839. V. 62; 67

WYVILL, CHRISTOPHER
The Pretensions of the Triple Crown Examined: in Thrice Three Familiar Letters, Upon so Many Controverted Points.... London: 1672. V. 66

X

XANROF, L.
Bebe Qui Chante. Paris. V. 65

XENOPHON
Cyropaedia; or the Institutions of Cyrus. London: 1728. V. 62; 66
Cyropaedia: the Institution and Life of Cyrus.... Newtown: 1936. V. 65
De Cyri Expeditione Libri Septem.... Oxonii: 1735. V. 66
De Cyri Institutione. Oxonii: 1727. V. 65
De Cyri Institutione. Libri Octo. London: 1738. V. 65
The Ephesian Story. Waltham St. Lawrence: 1957. V. 62
History of the Affairs of Greece. 1770. V. 66
(Greek Title) or The Institution and Life of Cyrus the Great. London: 1685. V. 67
The Memorable Things of Socrates, Written by Xenophon. (and) The Life of Xenophon. London: 1712. V. 66
L'Opere Morali.... Venice: 1547. V. 65
Quae Exstant Opera. Lutetiae Parisiorum: 1625. V. 66
The Science of Good Husbandry; or, the Oeconomics of Xenophon. London: 1727. V. 66

Y

YABLON, G. A.
A Bronte Bibliography. London: 1978. V. 63

YADAMSUREN, U.
National Costumes of the M.P.R. Ulan Bator: 1967. V. 66

YALE TOWNE MANUFACTURING CO.
Yale Products Catalog #26. N.P: 1929. V. 64

YALE UNIVERSITY
Catalogue of Books in the Library of Yale College. New Haven: 1823. V. 67

YAMAGUCHI, H. S. K.
We Japanese. Volume II. Hakone: 1937. V. 66

YANAGI, SOETSU
The Unknown Craftsman. Tokyo: 1972. V. 64

YANCEY, BENJAMIN C.
Speech of Benjamin C. Yancey, Esq. of Edgefield, in Relation to the Bank of the State of South CArolina.... Hamburg: 1849. V. 66

YARRANTON, ANDREW
England's Improvement by Sea and Land. London: 1677. V. 65

YARRELL, WILLIAM
A History. London: 1836. V. 64; 66
A History of British Birds. London: 1837-1843. V. 64
A History of British Birds. 1843. V. 62; 66
A History of British Birds. 1845. V. 66
A History of British Birds. London: 1856. V. 65
A History of British Birds. London: 1871-1875. V. 63; 66
A History of British Birds. London: 1871-1875. V. 64
A History of British Birds. 1876-1885. V. 67
A History of British Fishes. 1836. V. 65

YARRELL, WILLIAM continued
A History of British Fishes. 1841. V. 67
A History of British Fishes. London: 1841. V. 62
A History of British Fishes. 1859. V. 63
A History of British Fishes. London: 1859. V. 64
On the Growth of the Salmon in Fresh Water. 1839. V. 62

YATES, CHRIS
A Passion for Angling. 1993. V. 67

YATES, DORNFORD
The House that Berry Built. London: 1945. V. 65
She Fell Among Thieves. London: 1935. V. 66; 67
She Painted Her Face. London: 1937. V. 66; 67

YATES, EDMUND
Edmund Yates: His Recollections and Experiences. London: 1884. V. 62
The Forlorn Hope. London: 1867. V. 65
Kissing the Rod. London: 1866. V. 65
Land at Last. London: 1866. V. 66
Nobody's Fortune. London: 1872. V. 65
A Waiting Race. London: 1872. V. 65

YATES, JAMES
Thoughts on the Advancement of Academical Education in England. London: 1826. V. 62; 66

YATES, RICHARD
Disturbing the Peace. New York: 1975. V. 62
Revolutionary Road. Boston: 1961. V. 63

YATES, W. W.
The Father of the Brontes. Leeds: 1897. V. 66

YATES, WILLIAM
A View of the Science of Life, on the Principles Established in the Elements of Medicine.... Philadelphia: 1797. V. 67

YAU, JOHN
Piccadilly or Paradise. Poems. Santa Rosa: 1995. V. 66

YAVNO, MAX
The Los Angeles Book. Boston: 1950. V. 63; 65

YCIAR, JUAN DE
A Facsimile of the 1550 Edition of Arte Subtilissima. London: 1958. V. 63

YEAGER, CHUCK
Press On!. New York: 1988. V. 67
Yeager. New York: 1985. V. 63

THE YEAR Book of the London School of Printing and Kindred Trades - Session 1925-1926. London: 1926. V. 64

THE YEARBOOK of Show Horses. New York: 1936. V. 64

THE YEAR'S Poetry - A Representative Selection. London: 1934. V. 65

YEARSLEY, JAMES
Deafness Practically Illustrated: Being an Exposition of Original Views as to the Causes and Treatment of Diseases of the Ear. (with) On a New Mode of Treating Deafness when Attended by Partial or Entire Loss of the Membrana Tympani.... London: 1848-1849. V. 62

YEATES, G. K.
The Land of the Loon, Being the Experiences of a Bird Watcher on Two Visits to Iceland. 1951. V. 67

YEATS, JACK BUTLER
Sailing, Sailing Swiftly. 1933. V. 67
The Scourge of the Gulph. London: 1903. V. 66

YEATS, JOHN BUTLER
Early Memories: Some Chapters of Autobiography. Churchtown, Dundrum: 1923. V. 62; 66
Early Memories: Some Chapters of Autobiography. Dublin: 1923. V. 65
Further Letters of John Butler Yeats. Dublin: 1920. V. 65

YEATS, WILLIAM BUTLER
Autobiographies; Reveries Over Childhood and Youth and Trembling of the Veil. 1926. V. 62; 65
Beltaine: Organ of the Irish Literary Theatre. 1899-1900. V. 63
A Book of Images. 1898. V. 62
A Book of Irish Verse. 1900. V. 64; 67
The Bounty of Sweden: a Meditation and a Lecture Delivered Before the Royal Swedish Academy and Certain Notes. Dublin: 1925. V. 62; 63; 64; 65
The Cat and the Moon. Dublin: 1924. V. 64
Cathleen ni Houlihan. London: 1906. V. 63
The Celtic Twilight. London: 1902. V. 62
The Celtic Twilight, Men and Women, Dhouls & Faeries. 1902. V. 64; 67
Die Chymische Rose. Hellerau: 1927. V. 64
The Countess Kathleen and Various Legends and Lyrics. Boston: 1892. V. 65
The Countess Kathleen, and Various Legends and Lyrics. London: 1892. V. 64
The Cutting of an Agate. New York: 1912. V. 62; 64
Dramatis Personae. 1936. V. 67
Dramatis Personae. New York: 1938. V. 66
Eight Poems. London: 1916. V. 63; 66
Estrangement: Being Some Fifty Thoughts from a Diary Kept...in the Year Nineteen Hundred and Nine. Dublin: 1926. V. 62
Fairy and Folk Tales of the Irish Peasantry. London: 1888. V. 64
Four Plays for Dancers. London: 1921. V. 66
Four Plays for Dancers. New York: 1921. V. 62; 64; 67
Four Years. Dublin: 1921. V. 65
The Herne's Egg. London: 1938. V. 62; 64
The Herne's Egg. New York: 1938. V. 65
Ideas Good and Evil. London: 1907. V. 64
Ideas of Good and Evil. 1914. V. 67
If I Were Four-and-Twenty. Dublin: 1940. V. 62; 64; 66
Irish Fairy and Folk Tales. 1907. V. 67
The King of the Great Clock Tower, Commentaries and Poems. Dublin: 1934. V. 67
The King's Threshold: and On Baile's Strand: Being Volume Three of Plays for an Irish Theatre. London: 1904. V. 64
Last Poems and Plays. London: 1940. V. 62
Last Poems and Plays. New York: 1940. V. 67
Last Poems and Two Plays. Dublin: 1939. V. 65
Letters on Poetry from W. B. Yeats to Dorothy Wellesley. London: 1940. V. 62
Michael Robartes and the Dancer. Churchtown: 1920. V. 64
October Blast. Dublin: 1927. V. 64
On the Boiler. Dublin: 1938. V. 66
On the Boiler. Dublin: 1939. V. 62; 64; 66
The Oxford Book of Modern Verse 1892-1935. London: 1936. V. 65
A Packet for Ezra Pound. Dublin: 1929. V. 63; 66
Per Amica Silentia Lunae. London: 1918. V. 62; 64
Plays and Controversies. New York: 1924. V. 62
Plays for an Irish Theatre. New York: 1903. V. 66
Poems. London: 1895. V. 65
Poems. London: 1899. V. 62
Poems. London: 1906. V. 62; 64
Poems. London: 1912. V. 66; 67
Poems. London: 1920. V. 63
Poems. London: 1929. V. 62
Poems of W. B. Yeats. San Francisco: 1990. V. 62; 64
The Poetical Works of William B. Yeats. New York: 1906. V. 66
Responsibilities. Dublin: 1914. V. 65
Responsibilities. New York: 1916. V. 62
A Selection from the Poetry of W. B. Yeats. Leipzig: 1913. V. 65
Some Letters from W. B. Yeats of John O'Leary and His Sister, from Originals in the Berg Collection. New York: 1953. V. 66
The Speckled Bird. Dublin: 1974. V. 65
Stories of Michael Robartes and His Friends: an Extract from a Record made by His Pupils; and a Play in Prose. Dublin: 1931. V. 62
Stories of Red Hanrahan. Dublin: 1904. V. 66
Stories of Red Hanrahan and the Secret Rose. London: 1927. V. 63; 67
Tables of the Law; and the Adoration of the Magi. Stratford-upon-Avon: 1914. V. 62
Three Things. London: 1929. V. 66
The Tower. London: 1928. V. 62; 64; 67
The Trees in Their Autumn Beauty. Dublin: V. 65
The Trembling of the Veil. London: 1922. V. 67
The Variorum Edition of the Poems of W. B. Yeats. New York: 1957. V. 62; 64; 66
A Vision. London: 1925. V. 67
A Vision. 1937. V. 65
A Vision. London: 1937. V. 67
The Wanderings of Oisin and Other Poems. London: 1889. V. 62; 64
Wheels and Butterflies. 1934. V. 64
Where There Is Nothing. Being Volume One of Plays for an Irish Theatre. London: 1903. V. 62
The Wind Among the Reeds. New York and London: 1899. V. 64; 67
The Winding Stair and Other Poems. 1933. V. 66
The Winding Stair and Other Poems. London: 1933. V. 62; 63
Words for Music Perhaps and Other Poems. Dublin: 1932. V. 65
The Words Upon the Window Pane; a Play in One Act.... Dublin: 1934. V. 62

THE YELLOW Book. London: 1894. V. 62

THE YELLOW Dwarf. London: 1875. V. 64

YELSEW, IFAN
Mountaineers: or, Bottled Sunshine for Blue Mondays. Nashville: 1902. V. 64

YELVERTON, THERESE
Zanita: a Tale of the Yo-semite. New York: 1872. V. 62

YENNE, BILL
One Foot on the Highway - Bob Dylan on tour. San Francisco: 1974. V. 64

YENSER, STEPHEN
Clos Camardon. New York: 1985. V. 64

YEOMAN, THOMAS
The Report...Concerning the Drainage of the North Level of the Fens, and the Outfal of the Wisbeach River. 1769. V. 66

YERKES, R. M.
The Great Apes, a Study of Anthropoid Life. New Haven: 1929. V. 64; 66
The Mind of a Gorilla. London: 1926. V. 62
Psychological Examining the United States Army. Washington: 1921. V. 62

YEVTUSHENKO, YEVGENY
Selected Poems. Helsinki: 1987. V. 65

YGLESIAS, RAFAEL
The Game Player. Garden City: 1978. V. 65

YING, T.
The Endemic Genera of Seed Plants of China. Beijing: 1993. V. 66

YO
! Yes?. New York: 1993. V. 65

YOLEN, JANE
Owl Moon. New York: 1987. V. 64

YONGE, CHARLOTTE MARY
The Armourer's Prentices. London: 1884. V. 66
Beechcroft at Rockstone. London: 1888. V. 65; 66
Bye-Words: a Collection of Tales New and Old. London: 1880. V. 65
The Chaplet of Pearls; or the White and Black Ribaumont. London: 1868. V. 65; 66
The Clever Woman of the Family. London: 1865. V. 64
The Daisy Chain; or, Aspirations. London: 1856. V. 66
The Daisy Chain; or, Aspirations. New York: 1856. V. 66
The Dove in the Eagle's Nest. London: 1866. V. 62; 65
Heartsease, or The Brother's Wife. London: 1854. V. 66
Heartsease or the Brother's Wife. Leipzig: 1855. V. 67
History of Christian Names. London: 1863. V. 64
The History of Sir Thomas Thumb. Edinburgh: 1855. V. 65
The History of Sir Thomas Thumb. London: 1855. V. 66
Hopes and Fears; or, Scenes from the Life of a Spinster. London: 1860. V. 66
Lady Hester, or Usula's Narrative. London: 1874. V. 65
The Lances of Lynwood. London: 1855. V. 65
Nuttie's Father. London: 1885. V. 65
The Rubies of St. Lo. London: 1894. V. 64
A Storehouse of Stories. London: 1870. V. 65
The Two Sides of the Shield. London: 1885. V. 66

YORINKS, ARTHUR
Bravo Minski. New York: 1988. V. 65
Hey, Al. New York: 1986. V. 65

YORK, FREDERICK, DUKE OF
Catalogue of the Extensive and Valuable Library of the Duke of York Deceased...Which...WIl be Sold by Auction by Mr. Sotheby...on Monday May 7, 1827. London: 1827. V. 65

YORK, JAMES, DUKE OF
Memoirs of the English Affairs, Chiefly Naval from the Year 1660 to 1673. London: 1729. V. 65

YORKSHIRE
Castles. Leeds. V. 64; 65; 66

YOSHINOBU, T.
The Tokugawa Collection, No Robes and Masks. New York: 1977. V. 62

YOST, KARL
A Bibliography of the Published Works of Charles M. Russell. Lincoln: 1971. V. 65
Charles M. Russell the Cowboy Artist: a Bibliography. Pasadena: 1948. V. 66

YOUATT, WILLIAM
The Horse; with a Treatise on Draught and a Copious Index. London: 1831. V. 66
The Obligation and Extent of Humanity to Brutes, Principally Considered with Reference to the Domesticated Animals. London: 1839. V. 66
Sheep: Their Breeds, Management and Diseases. London: 1837. V. 63
Sheep: Their Breeds, Management and Diseases. New York: 1865. V. 65

YOUDEN, W. W.
Computer Literature Bibliography 1946 to 1943. Washington: 1965. V. 62

YOULE, JOSEPH
An Inaugural Dissertation on Respiration: Being an Application of the Principles of New Chemistry to that Function.... New York: 1793. V. 66

YOUMANS, EDWARD LIVINGSTON
Chemical Atlas; or, the Chemistry of Familiar Objects.... New York: 1857. V. 65
The Hand-Book of Household Science. New York: 1857. V. 64

YOUNG
American Poets V. Norfolk: 1944. V. 67

YOUNG, AMNINIUS
A Methodist Missionary in Labrador. Toronto: 1916. V. 66

YOUNG, ANDREW
The Adversary. London: 1923. V. 62; 64
Boaz and Ruth and Other Poems. London: 1920. V. 62; 63; 64
Cecil Barclay Simpson: a Memorial by Two Friends. Edinburgh: 1918. V. 62
Collected Poems. London: 1936. V. 64
The Collected Poems. London: 1960. V. 62
Cyrstal and Flint: Selected Poems. 1991. V. 62
The Cuckoo Clock. London: 1928. V. 62
The New Shepherd. London: 1931. V. 64
A Prospect of Britain. London: 1956. V. 64
A Prospect of Flowers.... London: 1945. V. 62
Remembrance and Homage. Cranberry Isles: 1978. V. 62
Songs of Night. London: 1910. V. 64
Speak to the Earth. London: 1939. V. 64
Thirty-One Poems. London: 1922. V. 62; 64
The White Blackbird. London: 1935. V. 64
Winter Harvest. London: 1933. V. 64

YOUNG, ANN ELIZA
Wife Number Nineteen or the Story of a Life in Bondage. Hartford: 1876. V. 64

YOUNG, ANNA G.
Great Lakes' Saga, the Influence of One Family on the Development of Canadian Shipping on the Great Lakes 1816-1931. Toronto: 1965. V. 63

YOUNG, ARCHIBALD
An Historical Sketch of the French Bar from Its Origin to the Present Day.... Edinburgh: 1869. V. 63

YOUNG, ARTHUR
Axial-Polarity of Man's Word Embodied Ideas and Its Teachings. London: 1887. V. 64
The Example of France, a Warning to Britain. London: 1793. V. 62
The Farmer's Kalendar; or a Monthly Directory for All Sorts of Country Business.... London: 1771. V. 62; 64; 66
The Farmer's Letters to the People of England. (with) The Farmer's Letters to the Landlords of Great Britain. London: 1768-1771. V. 64
The Fractional Family.... London: 1864. V. 64
General View of the Agriculture of Lincolnshire. London: 1808. V. 63
General View of the Agriculture of the County of Suffolk.... London: 1797. V. 63
Nautical Dictionary Defining the Technical Language Relative to the Building and Equipment of Sailing Vessels and Steamers, Seamanship, Navigation, Nautical Astronomy, Naval Gunnery, Maritime Law and Commerce.... London: 1863. V. 64
Political Arithmetic. London: 1774. V. 65
Rural Oeconomy; or, Essays on the Practical Parts of Husbandry. London: 1770. V. 62
A Six Months Tour through the North of England. Dublin: 1770. V. 67
A Six Months Tour through the North of England. London: 1770. V. 65; 66
A Six Weeks Tour through the Southern Counties of England and Wales.... London: 1768. V. 65; 67
A Tour in Ireland in 1776 and 1779. 1892. V. 62
A Tour in Ireland: with General Observations on the Present State of that Kingdom Made in the Years 1776, 1777 and 1778 and Brought Down to the End of 1779. Dublin: 1780. V. 66

YOUNG, BENNETT H.
Confederate Wizards of the Saddle. Boston: 1914. V. 63; 65

YOUNG, C. B.
Overland Sketches. London: Sep. 1830. V. 62

YOUNG, CHARLES E.
Dangers of the Trail. Geneva: 1912. V. 65

YOUNG, DAVID
Lectures on the Science of Astronomy, Explanatory ad Demonstrative, Which Were First Delivered, at Various Places in New Jersey in the Years 1820.... Morris Town: 1821. V. 63
Observations Upon Fire. Edinburgh: 1784. V. 65; 66
The Wonderful History of the Morristown Ghost; Thoroughly and Carefully Revised. Newark: 1826. V. 63; 66

YOUNG, DOUGLAS
A Braird o Thristles: Scots Poems. Glasgow: 1947. V. 67

YOUNG, ED
Lon Po Po. (A Red Riding Hood Story from China). New York: 1989. V. 65

YOUNG, EDWARD
The Centaur Not Fabulous. London: 1755. V. 64
The Complaint. London: 1742-1744. V. 64
The Complaint. London: 1743-1745. V. 63
The Complaint. London: 1797. V. 63; 66
The Complaint. Hartford: 1833. V. 62
Labour in Europe and America: a Special Report on the Rates of Wages, the Cost of Subsistence and the Condition of the Working Classes in Great Britain, Germany, France, Belgium.... Washington: 1875. V. 66
Love of Fame, the Universal Passion. London: 1728. V. 65
Night Thoughts. London: 1802. V. 67
Le Notti Di Young. (Night Thoughts). Napoli: 1793. V. 66
Poetical Works. London: 1834. V. 65
Pre-Raffaelitism; or, a Popular Enquiry into Some Newly Asserted Principles.... London: 1857. V. 65
A Vindication of Providence; or a True Estimate of Human Life. Dublin;: 1728. V. 65
The Works of the Author of the Night-Thoughts. London: 1767. V. 66

YOUNG, EDWARD HUDSON
Our Young Family in America. Durham: 1947. V. 63

YOUNG, EGERTON RYERSON
By Canoe and Dog Train Among the Cree and Salteaux Indians. Toronto: 1890. V. 63

YOUNG, ELLA
Poems by Ella Young. Dublin: 1906. V. 67

YOUNG, FILSON
Titanic. London: 1912. V. 63
With the Battle Cruisers. London: 1921. V. 66

YOUNG, FRANCIS BRETT
The Christmas Box. London: 1938. V. 65
Five Degrees South. London: 1917. V. 64

YOUNG, FRANK C.
Across the Plains in '65 - a Youngster's Journal from "Gotham" to "Pikes Peak". Denver: 1905. V. 63
Echoes from Arcadia - the Story of Central City, as Told by One of "The Clan". Denver: 1903. V. 63; 66

YOUNG, G. W.
Collected Poems. 1936. V. 63; 65

YOUNG, GAVIN
An Inquiry into the Expediency of Applying the Principles of Colonial Policy to the Government of India; and of Effecting an Esstial Change in Its Landed Tenures.... London: 1822. V. 66
Worlds Apart - Travels in War and Peace. London: 1987. V. 62

YOUNG, GEORGE
Manitoba Memories: Leaves from My Life in the Prairie Province. Toronto: 1897. V. 65

YOUNG, GEORGE RENNY
On Colonial Literature, Science and Education.... Halifax: 1842. V. 64

YOUNG, HARRY
Hard Knocks - a Life Story of the Vanishing West. Chicago: 1915. V. 63; 66

YOUNG, J.
A Pattern of Wings and Other Wildfowling Tales. 1989. V. 67

YOUNG, JAMES C.
Marse Robert Knight of the Confederacy. New York: 1920. V. 63
Marse Robert Knight of the Confederacy. New York: 1929. V. 62

YOUNG, JAMES MARTIN
A Dog at My Heel. London: 1951. V. 67

YOUNG, JESSE BOWMAN
The Battle of Gettysburg. New York and London: 1913. V. 62; 65

YOUNG, JOHN
A Catalogue of the Pictures at Grosvenor House, London.... London: 1821. V. 64
A Catalogue of the Pictures at Leigh Court, Near Bristol, the Seat of Philip John Miles.... London: 1822. V. 67
A Criticism on the Elegy Written in a Country Chruch-Yard. Edinburgh: 1810. V. 64; 65
Essays on the Following Interesting Subjects: viz I. Government II. Revolutions. III. British Constitution. IV. Kingly Government. V. Parliamentary Representation and Reform. VI. Liberty and Equality. VII. Taxations. VIII. The Present War and the Stagnat. Edinburgh: 1794. V. 66
The Letters of Agricola on the Principles of Vegetation and Tillage, Written for Nova Scotia and Published First In the Acadian Recorder. Halifax: 1822. V. 64
A Series of Designs for Shop Fronts and Entrances to Buildings, Public and Private. London: 1835. V. 67

YOUNG, JOHN R.
Around the World with General Grant. New York: 1879. V. 65
Memoirs of John R. Young - Utah Pioneer 1847. Salt Lake City: 1920. V. 66

YOUNG Lady's Book: a Manual of Elegant Recreations, Exercises and Pursuits. London: 1829. V. 66

THE YOUNG Lady's Equestiran Manual, in Which the Principles and Practice of Horsemanship for Ladies are Thoroughly Explained. Philadelphia: 1854. V. 67

YOUNG Lady's Friend. Boston: 1837. V. 67

YOUNG, LAMBTON J. H.
Sea-Fishing as a Sport.... London: 1865. V. 64

YOUNG, LUCIEN
The Boston at Hawaii, or the Observations and Impressions of a Naval Officer During a Stay of Fourteen Months in Those Islands on a Man-of-War. Washington: 1898. V. 63

YOUNG, LYMAN
Tim Tyler in the Jungle. Chicago: 1935. V. 62

THE YOUNG Man and Maid's Delight; or, an Universal Book of Knowledge.... London: 1790. V. 65

THE YOUNG Man's Book of Amusement. Halifax: 1844. V. 64

THE YOUNG Man's Own Book. Halifax: 1837. V. 64

YOUNG, MARGUERITE
Prismatic Ground. New York: 1937. V. 67

YOUNG, MARIA
Memoirs of Mrs. Crouch. London: 1806. V. 65

YOUNG, OTIS E.
The First Military Escort on the Santa Fe Trail, 1829, from the Journal and Reports of Major Bennet Riley and Lieutenant St. George Cooke. Glendale: 1952. V. 64; 67
The West of Philip St. George Cooke 1809-1895. Glendale: 1955. V. 65; 67

YOUNG, PHILIP
The Hemingway Manuscripts: an Inventory. University Park and London: 1969. V. 63

YOUNG, RALPH W.
Grizzlies Don't Come Easy!. 1981. V. 67

YOUNG, ROBERT
An Essay on the Powers and Mechanism of Nature.... London: 1788. V. 62

YOUNG, S. GLENN, MRS.
Life and Exploits of S. Glenn Young - World Famous Law Enforcement Law Officer. Herrin: 1924. V. 63; 66; 67

YOUNG, S. GRANT
Retrospections of a Sheriff Soldier Horseman Also Ten Stories of His Immediate Ancestors Including Brigham Young and Orson Spencer. Salt Lake City: 1972. V. 63; 64

YOUNG, S. O.
A Thumb-Nail History of the City of Houston Texas. Houston: 1912. V. 65

YOUNG, S. P.
The Wolves of North America. Washington: 1944. V. 62; 66

THE YOUNG Surgeon's Dictionary; or, Pupils Instructor Wherein Their Terms are Explained from the Greek Authors and an Introduction to Anatomy, by Inserting the Definition of the Structure of Man. London: 1770. V. 65

YOUNG, THOMAS
A Course of Lectures on Natural Philosohy and the Mechanical Arts. London: 1807. V. 63; 65
A Syllabus of a Course of Lectures on Natural Experimental Philosophy. London: 1802. V. 65

YOUNG, THOMAS DANIEL
Critical Essays and A Bibliography. Baton Rouge: 1968. V. 65

YOUNG, WHITNEY
Beyond Racisim. New York: 1969. V. 67

YOUNG, WILLIAM
Fighters of Derry; Their Deeds and Descendants. 1932. V. 67

YOUNGBLOOD, BONNEY
An Economic Study of a Typical Ranching Area on the Edwards Plateau of Texas. College Station: 1922. V. 64

THE YOUNGER Choir. New York: 1910. V. 63

YOUNGER, COLE
The Story of Cole Younger by Himself. Houston: 1955. V. 64

YOUNGHUSBAND, F. E.
The Heart of a Continent. 1904. V. 67

YOUNGMAN, W. E.
Gleaning from Western Prairies. Cambridge: 1882. V. 63; 66

YUHASOVA, HELENE
A Lauriston Garden of Verses. 1946. V. 66

YULE Logs. London: 1898. V. 67

YULE, HENRY
A Glossary of Angl Indian Words and Phrases. London: 1903. V. 62

YULE Tide Yarns. 1901. V. 67

YURICK, SOL
The Warriors. New York: 1965. V. 65

Z

ZABOR, RAFI
The Bear Comes Home. New York and London: 1997. V. 62; 67

ZABRISKIE, GEORGE A.
Bon Vivant's Compaion. Ormond Beach: 1933. V. 66

ZACHARAKIS, CHRISTOS G.
Catalogue of Printed Maps of Greece 1477-1800. Nicosia: 1982. V. 65

ZACHARIE, ISSACHAR
Surgical and Practical Observations on the Diseases of the Human Foot, with Instructions for Their Treatment. London: 1876. V. 66

ZADOR, A.
Revival Architecture in Hungary Classicism and Romanticism. Budapest: 1985. V. 65

ZAEHNSDORF, JOSEPH W.
The Art of Bookbinding. London: 1880. V. 62; 63; 64; 67

ZAGOSKIN, LAVRENTII ALEXSEEVICH
Lieutenant Zagoskin's Travels in Russian America 1842-1844. Toronto: 1967. V. 63; 64; 65; 66

ZAHER, AMEEN
Arabian Horse Breeding and the Arabians of America. Cairo: 1961. V. 64

ZAHN, TIMOTHY
Star Wars: the Last Command. New York: 1993. V. 62

ZAHN, WILHELM
Ornamente aller Klassichen Kunst-Epochen nach den Originalien in Ihren Eigenthumlichen Farben. Berlin: 1849. V. 62

ZAKANI, OBAID-E
The Pious Cat. London: 1986. V. 66

ZALAMEA, JORGE
Le Grand Burundun-Burunda est Mort. Paris: 1954. V. 67

ZALESKI, BRONISLAS
La Vie des Steppes Kirghizes. Paris: 1865. V. 62; 67

ZAMBECCARI, FRANCESCO
Descrizione Della Macchina Aerostatica. Bologna: 1803. V. 64

ZAMORANO CLUB
Zamorano Club, 1929. Los Angeles: 1929. V. 62
The Zamorano 80. Los Angeles: 1945. V. 62; 63
The Zamorano Club: The First Half Century 1928-1978. Los Angeles: 1978. V. 63

ZAMYATIN, EVGENY
Uezdnoe. Petrograd: 1916. V. 67

ZANDER, C. G.
Photo-Trichromatic Printing in Theory and Practice. Leicester: 1896. V. 63; 65

ZANETTI, ANTONIO MARIA
Varie Pitture a Fresco de Principali Maestri Veneziani. Venice: 1760. V. 64

ZANGWILL, ISRAEL
The Forcing House or the Cockpit Continued.... London: 1922. V. 63
The Master. London: 1895. V. 67
Watchman, What of the Night?. New York: 1923. V. 63
The Works. 1925. V. 67
The Works. London: 1925. V. 66

ZAPATA, GIOVANNI BATTISTA
Li Maravigliosi Secreti di Medicina e Chirvrgia, Nvovamente Ritrovati per Guarire Ogni Sorte d'Infirmita. Venice: 1586. V. 62; 63

ZAPF, HERMANN
Pen and Graver. Alphabets and Pages of Calligraphy. New York: 1952. V. 64
Typographic Variations Designed by Hermann Zapf on Themes in Contemporary Book Design and Typography.... New York: 1964. V. 63
Zapf's Civilite Disclosed. 1994. V. 64
Zapf's Civilite Disclosed. Northampton: 1995. V. 66

ZATTA, ANTONIO
Catalogo di Libri Latini e Italiani che Trovansi Vendibili Nel Negozio...Nel Fine un Elenco dei Libri Francesi...Immagini e Stampe.... Venice: 1791-1790. V. 65

ZAWADIWSKY, CHRISTINE
The World at Large. Madison: 1978. V. 63; 64; 66

ZEIGLER, WILBUR G.
Heart of the Alleghanies or Western North Carolina Comprising Its Topography, History, Resources, People, Narratives, Incidents, and Pictures of Travel, Adventures in Hunting and Fishing and Legends of Its Wilderness. Raleigh: 1883. V. 63; 66

ZEILLER, MARTIN
Topographia Galliae. Frankfrut: 1655-1661. V. 66
Topographia Germaniae Inferioris. (with) Topographia Saxoniae Inferioris. Frankfurt: 1659. V. 64; 66

ZEIMANN, HUGO
White House Cook Book. Akron: 1904. V. 67

ZEISING, HENRICUS
Theatrum Machinarum. Altenburg: 1621-1614-1618. V. 64
Theatrum Machinarum, Anderer Theil (only) Part II. Altenburg: 1610. V. 64

ZELINSKY, PAUL O.
Rapunzel. New York: 1997. V. 63

ZELLMAN, MICHAEL DAVID
300 Years of American Art. Secaucus: 1987. V. 63

ZEMACH, MARGOT
Duffy and the Devil - a Cornish Tale. New York: 1973. V. 65

ZENDRINI, BERNARDINO
Trattato della Chinachina. Venice: 1715. V. 67

ZENTGRAF, JOHANNES MELCHIOR
Dissertatio Inauguralis Medica Sistens Morbos Aetatibus Speciatim Imminentes.... Strasbourg: 1716. V. 64; 65

ZERELLA Y YCOAGA, MANUEL DE
Tratado General y Matematico de Reloxeria, que Comprende el Modo de Hacer Reloxes de Todas Clases, y el de Saberlos Componer y Arreglar por Dificiles que Sean. Madrid: 1789. V. 62

ZETETIC *Astronomy: Earth Not a Globe. An Experimental Inquiry Into the True Figure of the Earth....* London: 1881. V. 66

ZETTLER, BERRIEN M.
War Stories and School-Day Incidents for Children. New York: 1912. V. 62; 63; 65

ZEYHER, J. M.
Beschreibung der Gartenanlagen zu Schwetzingen. Mannheim: 1825. V. 64

ZIEGLER, BENJAMIN M.
The International Law of John Marshall. Chapel Hill: 1939. V. 66

ZIEGLER, RICHARD
Judith the Widow of Bethulia: the Drawings and Script of Richard Ziegler. London: 1946. V. 66

ZIELEZINSKI, GEORGE
24 Drawings from the Concentration Camps in Germany. Munich: 1946. V. 62

ZIEMSSEN, HUGO WILHELM VON
Die Elektricitat in der medicin. Berlin: 1887. V. 65

ZIGROSSER, CARL
The Expressionists: a Survey of Their Graphic Art. New York: 1957. V. 62; 63; 64; 66

ZILBOORG, GREGORY
A History of Medical Psychology. New York: 1941. V. 67

ZIMARA, MARCO ANTONIO
Antrum Magico-Medicum, in Quo Arcanorum Magico-Physicorum, Sigillorum, Signaturarum & Imaginum Magicarum.... Frankfurt: 1625. V. 62

ZIMLER, RICHARD
The Last Kabbalist of Lisbon. Woodstock: 1996. V. 66
The Last Kabbalist of Lisbon. Woodstock and New York: 1998. V. 62

ZIMMER, HEINRICH
The Art of Indian Asia: its Mythology and Transformations. New York: 1960. V. 62; 63; 64
The Celtic Church in Britian and Ireland. 1902. V. 67

ZIMMER, J. T.
Catalogue of the Edward E. Ayer Ornithological Library. New York: 1974. V. 64
Catalogue of the Edward E. Ayer Ornithological Library. 1990. V. 63; 65
Studies of Peruvian Birds...Parts 2-15; 31-39 and 49. New York: 1931-1944. V. 63

ZIMMERMAN, J. G.
An Essay on National Pride. London: 1771. V. 66
An Essay on National Pride. 1805. V. 63
Solitude. London: 1799. V. 62
Solitude. London: 1800. V. 62

ZIMMERMANN, EBERHARDT AUGUST GUILLAUME
Zoologie Geographieque. N.P: 1784. V. 65

ZINCKE, F. BARHAM
Last Winter in the United States. London: 1868. V. 63

ZINZERLING, JUSTUS
Itinerarium Galliae...Cum Sppendice De Burdigala. Amsterlodami: 1649. V. 67
Jodoci Sinceri Itinerarium Galliae.... Amsterdam: 1655. V. 64

ZIPPERER, PAUL
The Manufacture of Chocolate and Other Cacao Preparations. London: 1902. V. 64

ZIRIN, HAROLD
The Solar Atmosphere. Waltham: 1966. V. 67

ZITTEL, KARL VON
History of Geology and Paleontology to the End of the Nineteenth Century. London: 1901. V. 64

ZOGBAUM, RUFUS F.
Horse, Foot and Dragoons, Sketches of Army Life at Home and Abroad. New York: 1888. V. 65; 67

ZOHARY, M.
Flora Palestina. Jerusalem: 1966-1986. V. 62
Geobotanical Foundation of the Middle East. Stuttgart: 1973. V. 62

ZOLA, EMILE
L'Assommoir. London: 1928. V. 65; 66
The Attack on the Mill. London: 1895. V. 64
Paris. London: 1898. V. 65
Les Quatre Evangiles: Travail. Paris: 1901. V. 62
Le Reve. Paris: 1892. V. 67
The Soil - a Realistic Novel. London: 1888. V. 64

ZOLLERS, GEORGE D.
Thrilling Incidents on Sea and Land: the Prodigal's Return. Mount Morris: 1892. V. 64

ZOLLIKOFER, GEORGE JOACHIM
Sermons on the Dignity of Man, and the Value of the Objects Principally Relating to Human Happiness. Worcester: 1807. V. 64

ZONCA, VITTORIO
Novo Teatro Di Machine et Edificii. In Padoua: 1656. V. 65; 66; 67

ZOOK, MARTIN L.
History of Camp Granville M. Dodge and the Accomplishments of Its Members. Nantes: 1919. V. 65

ZOOLOGICAL SOCIETY OF LONDON
List of the Vertebrated Animals Exhibited 1828-1927. 1929. V. 63
Proceedings. London: 1830-1918. V. 67
Transactions. London: 1869. V. 67

ZORN, JOHANNES
Dreyhundert Auserlesene Amerikanische Gewaechse. Nuremberg: 1785-1786. V. 63

ZOUCH, RICHARD
A Dissertation Concerning the Punishment of Ambassadors, Who Transgress the Laws of the Countries Where they Reside.... London: 1717. V. 62

ZOUCH, THOMAS
The Life of Isaac Walton; including Notices of His Contemporaries. London: 1823. V. 62

ZOUCHE, ROBERT CURZON, BARON
Visits to Monasteries in the Levant. London: 1849. V. 63
Visits to Monasteries in the Levant. Ithaca: 1955. V. 63

ZSCOKKE, HENRY
The History of the Invasion of Switzerland by the French and the Destruction of the Democratical Republics of Schwitz, Uri and Unterwalden. London: 1803. V. 67

ZSIGMONDY, E.
In the High Mountains. 1992. V. 65

ZUALLART, JEAN
Il Devotissimo Viaggio di Gierusalemme. Roma: 1595. V. 63

ZUCKERMAN, S.
The Ape in Myth and Art. London: 1998. V. 62; 63

ZUKOFSKY, LOUIS
A - 14. Kensington: 1967. V. 66
A - 14. London: 1967. V. 65
A 1-12.... Ashland: 1959. V. 62
After I's. Pittsburgh: 1964. V. 62; 65
All: the Collected Shorter Poems 1956-1964. New York: 1966. V. 62; 66
Arise, Arise. New York: 1973. V. 62; 66
Barely and Widely. New York: 1958. V. 65
Bottom: on Shakespeare. Austin: 1963. V. 63; 64; 65; 66
First Half of A-9. New York: 1940. V. 65
Found Objects: 1962-1926. Georgetown: 1964. V. 62; 64
Futura 5. Hamburg: 1966. V. 65
I's (pronounced eyes). New York: 1963. V. 62
It Was. Kyoto: 1961. V. 62; 64
Iyyob. London: 1965. V. 62; 64
Louis Zukofsky at the American Embassy, London, May 21, 1969. Newcastle-upon-Tyne: 1969. V. 62
Prepositions - the Collected Critical Essays. London: 1967. V. 62
Some Time. Stuttgart: 1956. V. 64
A Test of Poetry. New York: 1964. V. 64

ZULCH, KLAUS J.
Otfrid Foerster - Physician and Naturalist November 9, 1873 - June 15, 1941. Berlin: 1969. V. 64

ZULICK, C. MEYER
Report of the Governor of Arizona. Washington: 1886. V. 66

ZWEIFACH, BENJAMIN W.
Annotated Bibliography on Shock. Volume I (1950-1962). Volume II (1962-1964). Washington: 1963-1966. V. 63

ZWICKY, F.
Morphological Astronomy. Berlin: 1957. V. 66

ZWORYKIN, V. K.
Television: the Electronics of Image Transmission. New York: 1940. V. 64

ZYLBERZWEIG, ZALME
Album of Yiddish Theatre. New York: 1937. V. 64
Lexicon of the Yiddish Theatre. New York and Warsaw: 1931-1934. V. 64

ZYW, ALEKSANDER
Poles in Uniform - Sketches of the Polish Army, Navy and Air Force. London: 1943. V. 65

ISBN 0-7876-5308-X